COLLINS ENGLISH LEARNER'S DICTIONARY

SC EO

COLLINS ENGLISH LEARNER'S DICTIONARY

David J. Carver, Michael J. Wallace,
John Cameron

Collins
London and Glasgow

First Published 1974
Reprinted 1974
Latest reprint 1986

ISBN 0 00 433112 5

David J. Carver and Michael J. Wallace are lecturers at the
Scottish Centre for Education Overseas,
Moray House College of Education, Edinburgh.
John Cameron is lecturer at the University of London Institute of Education.

Note
Entered words which we have reason to believe constitute trademarks have been designated as such. However, neither the presence nor the absence of such designation should be regarded as affecting the legal status of any trademark.

Printed in Great Britain
at the Press of the Publishers, Glasgow

Contents

Preface

The editors would like to thank the many people who have given them advice and guidance during the writing of this dictionary, in particular Mrs. Margo Butt, Mrs. Terry Freedman and Mrs. Jean Petrie, who each read the complete text and made many useful suggestions. Our thanks are also due to the editorial staff of Collins who have throughout shown us the greatest helpfulness and understanding in our endeavours.

D. J. Carver
M. J. Wallace
J. Cameron

Collins Staff

Publishing Manager	William T. McLeod
Editor	Iseabail C. Macleod
Assistant Editor	Peter Terrell
Editorial Assistant	Carol Purdon
Designer	Alyson Blackadder

Introduction

This dictionary has been specially designed for people learning English. It is, therefore, particularly suitable for those learning English as a second or foreign language as well as for young people whose mother tongue is English. Those who will find this dictionary most useful will be beyond the elementary stage and they will want a dictionary which can, when necessary, be used outside a classroom situation. Great care has therefore been taken to make sure that definitions are *easy to understand* and *illustrations* have been used where helpful.

It is one of our aims that the reader should be able to use this dictionary not simply to understand new words, but also to make them part of his active vocabulary. For this reason plentiful use has been made of *example sentences and phrases.*

One of the great areas of difficulty for those past the elementary stages of learning English is the great wealth of *idioms* which is to be found in the language. We have devoted special attention to this, and if the reader will glance at such verbs as *get, go, put* he will see the amount of information that is given. To give the reader extra assistance compounds, phrasal verbs, idioms etc have been set out as sub-entries on separate lines, thus making them easier to find.

The emphasis throughout has been on *modern, up-to-date vocabulary* and archaisms have been excluded (except in very rare cases where they might be useful for reading). Where some words, though still current, seem to be going out of use, this has been indicated. Choice of vocabulary is of course one of the most difficult problems for a compiler as he must strike a balance between the huge, fast-growing vocabulary of English and the limitations of space. The editors have in mind a reader who reads modern novels, magazines and newspapers, and have tried to anticipate what puzzling words and expressions he might find in them. But we have also made space for more basic vocabulary which a non-native speaker writing or speaking the language might want advice on.

Similarly, we are aware that non-native users of English are often unsure of the *appropriateness of the vocabulary* they use. We have therefore given, as far as we could, information on such matters as whether a word is regularly formal or informal in its use, whether it is old-fashioned or restricted to a certain field, e.g. law, medicine.

In these ways, we hope that the dictionary will succeed in its general aim, which is to help the learner find his way through the enormous variety of modern idiomatic English.

What information can you get?

1 the meanings of about 25,000 useful modern English words.
2 a listing of thousands more words and phrases derived from or connected with these words, including idioms. Where the meaning of any of these words is not obvious, it is made clear by explanation or example.
3 example sentences and phrases to show how words and phrases are used.
4 pronunciation of the headwords and, where necessary, of derived forms.
5 parts of speech.

6 American spellings and meanings where these are significantly different from standard British English.

7 helpful notes on how to use certain words which, in the editors' experience, can cause difficulty to learners of English even at a fairly advanced stage.

8 information about whether a word is formal, informal or old-fashioned.

9 opposites – it is often difficult to decide whether an opposite should begin with, for example, *un-* or *in-*. Thus we have *unfaithful* but *inexperienced.*

10 plurals – normal rules for forming plurals are given, and those plurals which may give difficulty are indicated where they occur in the dictionary.

11 present participle, past participle, past tense of verbs – where these are irregularly formed or likely to be wrongly spelt, they are given in full – see also the list of irregular verbs in the appendix.

12 general information on differences between British and American English – see table of contents.

How to find the information you want

1. Order of Entries

The headwords are arranged in straightforward alphabetical order and are printed in **bold type.**

The headword is followed by its pronunciation and its part of speech with definition(s). Then come various related words and phrases printed in smaller bold type in this order:

(*a*) *grammatical forms related to the headword* e.g. plurals, past participle forms:

come . . . *past tense* **came.** *past part* **come.**

(*b*) *derivatives of the headword:*

hope[2] . . . **hopeful** *adj* . . . **hopefully** *adv.* **hopefulness** *nu.*

(*c*) *compound words which start with the headword:*

hair . . .	**horse . . .**	**news . . .**	**lead**[1] **. . .**
'hairbrush	**'horseback**	**'newsagent**	**'lead-line**
'haircut	**'horse box**	**'newsboy**	**'lead 'paint**
'hairdresser	**'horse 'chestnut**	**'newspaper**	**'lead 'pencil**

Note that these are arranged in alphabetical order according to the second element of the compound (i.e. *brush* comes before *cut* and *cut* comes before *dresser*).

(*d*) *compound words which end with the headword:*

card . . .	**march . . .**
'greetings card	**'dead march**
'playing card	**forced march**
'postcard	

Note that these are arranged in alphabetical order according to the first element of the compound (i.e. *greetings* comes before *playing* and *playing* comes before *post*).

(*e*) *phrasal verbs* (*for definition see p.* xi)*:*

get . . .
get about
get above oneself
get something across

Note that these are arranged in alphabetical order of the particle (i.e. *about* comes before *above* and *above* comes before *across*).

(*f*) *idioms:*

issue . . .
at issue
bring to a successful issue
face the issue
join/take issue with somebody

Note that these are arranged as far as possible in alphabetical order of the first important word.

2. Pronunciation

(For differences between British and American pronunciation, see the section on British and American English, p. xv)

English can be spoken in a huge variety of accents, many or perhaps most of them perfectly acceptable for every kind of use. In the small area of the British Isles alone, for example, it is usually fairly easy to distinguish English, Irish, Scottish and Welsh speakers, and within each of these countries there are also distinctive varieties of accent. Interesting though this variety may be, the foreign learner will want to study a type which has been (i) widely accepted wherever English is spoken, and (ii) authoritatively analysed and described. The accent of standard British English which best fulfils both of these requirements is known as *Received Pronunciation* or *RP*, and the pronunciation of words in this dictionary has been given this accent.

The system of indicating pronunciation used in this dictionary is a simple version of the International Phonetic Alphabet (IPA) which is already widely used in colleges, schools, English language textbooks etc.

Pronunciation Key

Vowels

symbol	*example*	*symbol*	*example*
[æ]	bat [bæt]	[ɔː]	board [bɔːd]
[ɑː]	farm [fɑːm]	[u]	full [ful]
[e]	set [set]	[uː]	root [ruːt]
[ə]	above [ə'bʌv]	[ʌ]	come [kʌm]
[əː]	fern [fəːn]	[ɔ̃]†	salon ['sælɔ̃]
[i]	pity ['piti]	[ɑ̃ː]†	carte blanche ['kɑːt'blɑ̃ːnʃ]
[iː]	green [griːn]		
[ɔ]	rot [rɔt]		

Diphthongs

symbol	*example*	*symbol*	*example*
[ai]	lie [lai]	[ɛə]	fair [fɛə*]
[au]	sow [sau]	[iə]	here [hiə*]
[ei]	fate [feit]	[ɔi]	toy [tɔi]
[ou]	ago [ə'gou]	[uə]	pure [pjuə*]

† used only in words taken from other languages.

Consonants

symbol	*example*	*symbol*	*example*
[b]	bet [bet]	[r]	rate [reit]
[d]	dime [daim]	[s]	sit [sit]
[f]	face [feis]	[t]	tell [tel]
[g]	go [gou]	[v]	vine [vain]
[h]	hit [hit]	[w]	wine [wain]
[j]	you [juː]	[z]	zero ['ziərou]
[k]	catch [kætʃ]	[ʒ]	leisure ['leʒə*]
[l]	lick [lik]	[ʃ]	shame [ʃeim]
[m]	roam [roum]	[θ]	thin [θin]
[n]	nut [nʌt]	[ð]	this [ðis]
[ŋ]	bank [bæŋk]	[x]	loch [lɔx]
[p]	pepper ['pepə*]	[tʃ]	church [tʃəːtʃ]
		[dʒ]	judge [dʒʌdʒ]

Points to be noted:

(i) the main stress of words is indicated by a small vertical line which appears *in front of* the syllable that is stressed. The word *insect*, for example, is written ['insekt] because the stress is on the first syllable, but the word *insist* is written [in'sist] because the stress is on the second syllable.

(ii) the stress of compounds is indicated where necessary – **'milkman, 'small talk.** Where no stress is marked give even stress to both words in the compound.

(iii) the sign * at the end of a pronunciation means that the letter *r* at the end of it is pronounced only if a vowel follows it. For example *better* not followed by a vowel is pronounced ['betə], but in a phrase like *a better idea*, the *r* would be pronounced.

(iv) the pronunciation of derivatives is given only where there is a change which is likely to cause difficulty. For example,

acid ['æsid] *adj* . . . **acidity** [ə'siditi] *nu.*

(v) in the main our guide has been the 13th edition of Daniel Jones's *English Pronouncing Dictionary* revised by A. C. Gimson (Dent, London, 1967). The principal exception is that in the pronunciation of the diphthong in words like 'go', we have followed the more conservative transcription of the 12th edition, i.e. [ou] instead of [əu]. We feel that the earlier transcription is still acceptable and this is also more likely to be familiar and more immediately comprehensible to our readers.

3. Grammatical Information

It is not enough to know what a word means; what is just as important is information on how to use it. We have tried to give this information in as simple a manner as possible.

This has been done, firstly, by giving helpful *examples* of the word in normal use e.g. under **testify** we find the following information:

> give evidence; state solemnly. *He testified in court that he was abroad at the time of the crime. I can testifiy to his honesty* i.e. that he is honest. *He will not testifiy against his own brother.*

In this extract the reader can see the use of *testify* with three different structures, and the corresponding shades of meaning with no preposition, followed by *to* and followed by *against*.

Secondly, we have given information about parts of speech. These can be divided into two main categories:

(*a*) lexical word classes: noun, verb, adjective, adverb. These are very large classes and are continually being added to. It is here that most of the growth in the language is taking place.

(*b*) structural word classes: auxiliary, conjunction, determiner, exclamation, intensifier, interjection, preposition, pronoun. These classes are fairly limited in the number of words they contain and this number of words is fairly stable. Although small in number, they are very important from the point of view of language function.

Some more detailed comments on these word classes follow. The abbreviation used in this dictionary is on the left-hand side.

nc and *nu* — *nc* means countable nouns like *chair, boy, desk.* These words can have a plural form.

nu refers to uncountable or mass nouns, e.g. *information, luggage* which are seldom, or never, used in the plural form. Some nouns are countable in some contexts and uncountable in others. The definitions and examples make clear which is which.

Please note that the distinction between *nc* and *nu* is not always clear-cut in English, so that the classification as *nc* and *nu* should be taken as a general guide only.

vi and *vt* — *vi* means intransitive verb, i.e. one which does not take an object noun or pronoun as, for example, in these sentences:

The boys are running.
He never comes here.
He is always reading.

vt means transitive verb, i.e. one which does take a noun or pronoun as an object. For example:

The boys were kicking a ball.
The waitress dropped some plates.
He is reading a book.

As you see, some verbs can be transitive in some sentences and intransitive in others.

Special Note on Phrasal Verbs

A phrasal verb consists of a verb combined with a particle (adverb or preposition) to form a new verb, e.g. *give* + *in, go* + *without.* Sometimes the verb may be combined with two particles, e.g. *put* + *up* + *with.*

Phrasal verbs can occur in different types of structures, and in this dictionary we distinguish three kinds. In addition, we note whether the object of the phrasal verb can be a person (*someone*), a thing (*something*) or both (*someone/something*).

1. No object (intransitive). *After much fighting, the enemy gave in.*
   Entered as: *give in.*
2. Object coming after the particle. *What do you make of his ideas?*
   Entered as: *make of someone/something.*
3. Object coming before or after the particle. *He picked up his hat/He picked his hat up.* *N.B.* if the object is a pronoun it always comes before the particle. *He picked it up.* If the object is a long phrase it normally comes after the particle. *He picked up the old green hat which his mother-in-law had given him.*
   Entered as: *pick something up.*

Some phrasal verbs do not always have to have an object and this is indicated by brackets e.g. *go without (something). He went without food for days. There is no food so you must go without.*

adj adjective. The word *good* is an adjective in the following sentences:
John is a good boy.
Exercise is good for you.
Mention is also made of two special types of adjective:

pred adj 1. predicative adjective. An example would be *alive* as in *The child is still alive.* We could never say *The alive child . . .*

attrib adj 2. attributive adjective. An example would be *utter* as in *It was an utter waste of time!* It would be unnatural to say *The waste of time was utter!*

adv adverb. Look at these sentences and note the adverbs (repeated in brackets).
He is doing well in his studies (well).
The time went quickly (quickly).
We shall have to leave now (now).
Nevertheless, I agree with you (nevertheless).
Mary will wait for you here (here).

Structural words:

aux auxiliary. The complete list (omitting past tense and changes according to person) is:
be, have, do, will, shall, can, may, must, ought, dare, need, used.

conj conjunction, i.e. words having a joining function e.g. *and, but, either . . . or, neither . . . nor, if, when, where* etc.
Peter and Mary were there (and).
Peter was there but Mary was not (but).
I shall come if you ask me to (if).

determiner Determiners are words which can occur in the same position as *the* in a sentence like: *The boys were present.*
Some determiners: *a/an, both, few, other, one, two, enough, this, these* etc.
Examples: *Have you enough sugar?* (enough)
Some scientists are very brilliant men (some).
Those boys have lost their bags (those *and* their).

intensifier Intensifiers are words which can occur in the same position as *very* in a sentence such as:
He plays football very well, but he is not very good at English.
Some intensifiers: *quite, rather, awfully, fairly, much* etc.
Examples: *John is quite clever* (quite).
Your neighbours are really nice (really).
My car can go much faster than yours (much).

interj Interjections are words like: *oh, well, really,* etc as in:
Oh, I must tell you something.
Well, here we are.
Really! What a rude man!

prep preposition. A fairly large structural class including such words as *above, across, against, among, beneath, beside, for, from, in, on, over, round, through, to, under, until, up, with* etc.

Examples: *across the street, over ten years, from London to Birmingham, until yesterday, with John and Mary.*

pron pronoun. Pronouns are very often used instead of repeating a noun. But this is not their only use, as you will see from the examples below. Some pronouns are *I, we, he, him, who, which, that, this, whoever* etc.

When I saw Mary standing there, I went over and spoke to her (I *and* her).
Anyone can learn English (anyone).
Who is that? (who *and* that).
He can speak twelve languages, which is most unusual (which).

4. Spelling

Both British and American spellings have been given in the dictionary. American spellings have been marked (*US*) where they differ from standard British English.

The following notes refer to spelling in British English. For the main points of difference in American English, the reader is referred to the section on British and American English on p. xv.

We do not intend here to give a comprehensive survey of the rules for spelling English words, because one of the purposes of the text of the dictionary is to help the learner in this respect. If he is not sure of the spelling of a word he should check it up in the dictionary.

The comments that follow are intended simply as a guide to the use of the dictionary. The comments are grouped under five headings: (i) plurals; (ii) verb forms; (iii) opposites; (iv) words ending in *-ise/-ize*; (v) the use of the hyphen.

N.B. Note that the consonant letters of English are *bcdfghjklmnpqrstvwxyz*. The vowel letters are *aeiou.*

(i) *Plurals*

Plural forms can be divided into two general classes:

(*a*) *Straightforward plurals*

The general rule in English is that plurals are formed by adding *-s* e.g. *boy – boys, desk – desks, field – fields, dog – dogs, house – houses, valley – valleys.*

BUT

1. if the word ends in *-s, -x, -z, -sh,* then we add *-es* e.g. *bus – buses, miss – misses, sex – sexes, bush – bushes* etc.

2. if the last two letters are *a consonant + y,* then the *-y* is replaced by *-ies* e.g. *city – cities, duty – duties* etc (compare these with *boys* and *valleys* when the last two letters are a vowel and *y*).

(*b*) *Difficult and irregular plurals*

We have recorded words which do not follow the rules in section (*a*), and also *all* words ending in *-o*, since learners often have difficulty with these. The reader will find spellings like these noted:

studio – studios, cargo – cargoes, crisis – crises, phenomenon – phenomena, scarf – scarves, salmon – salmon etc.

(ii) *Verb forms*

Three main forms are dealt with where necessary:

present participle (written *pres part*)
past tense (written *past tense*)
past participle (written *past part*)

Sometimes the past participle and the past tense are the same and this is indicated by *past*.

No special note is made in the dictionary in the following two cases.

(*a*) where it is simply a matter of adding
-ing to the *pres part*, and
-ed to the *past tense* and *past part* forms.

Example:

(headword)	talk
pres part	talking
past tense	talked
past part	talked

(*b*) where the verb ends in a 'silent' -e (e.g. close) and the -e is dropped.

Example:

(headword)	close
pres part	closing
past tense	closed
past part	closed

Special note has been made of those verb forms which may give rise to spelling problems e.g. *creep – crept, admit – admitted* etc. (See also the list of irregular verbs in the appendix.)

(iii) *Opposites*

A learner is sometimes puzzled when he has to find an opposite for a word such as 'ability'. Should it begin with *in-* or *un-*? In many cases, if he looks up the original form in the dictionary, he will find that its opposite is given.

(iv) *Verbs ending in ise/ize* (pronounced [aiz])

Where there is a choice in acceptable usage between *-ise* and *-ize* for the ending of certain verbs, we have followed the growing tendency to use *-ize* rather than *-ise* e.g. *civilize* rather than *civilise.*

This is also normal practice in American English, but certain differences remain (e.g. British *analyse*, American *analyze*).

(v) *Compounds and hyphens*

When should compounds be written as one word (e.g. *blackboard*), joined by a hyphen (e.g. *back-cloth*) or written as separate words (e.g. *garden party*)?

Unfortunately it is difficult to give a precise answer to this question. Indeed the learner may find the same compound printed in all three different ways in different books. Certain compounds have been used together as a unit for so long that there is no doubt or hesitation e.g. *blackbird.* Notice that this now means something different from *black bird.* There is also a difference in stress i.e. *'blackbird* but *'black 'bird.*

In modern usage there is a tendency not to use hyphens except in certain cases. For example, if a two-word compound comes before a noun it is normally hyphenated to avoid ambiguity. Thus: *a light-coloured box* but *a light, coloured box.*

Some expressions would look strange if written as one word (e.g. *steering wheel*). They are therefore written with a hyphen or as two separate words.

5. Appropriateness

Sometimes a word can have the correct 'meaning' but sound wrong because it is used in the wrong situation or at the wrong time. We have therefore pointed out *formal* and *informal* English. Formal language is used in government reports, on tax forms etc; it is not conversational English. Informal language is what people use in relaxed friendly situations but not in interviews, essays, business reports etc.

Similarly, when a word or one of the meanings of a word is restricted in use to a certain profession, subject, etc this has been indicated e.g. (law), (medicine).

Occasionally, words which are no longer commonly used have been included in the dictionary because the learner may come across them in his reading. Such words are marked (*o.f.*) i.e. old-fashioned and the learner is thus warned not to use them in modern English. In some cases an acceptable current equivalent is given.

6. Cross-References

Cross-reference is made when one word is related to another e.g.

fo'c'sle . . . see **forecastle.**

Where a phrase or idiom contains more than one significant word, the reader may find a cross reference e.g.

grief . . .
come to grief see **come.**
line[1] **. . .**
draw the line at see **draw**[1]**.**
horse . . .
flog a dead horse see **flog.**

7. Punctuation

In keeping with the modern style of the dictionary, the punctuation of abbreviations such as *nc, vt, pres part* etc has been simplified by omitting full stops. Note that such abbreviations are always printed in *italics*. Other abbreviations not in italics are punctuated in the normal way.

A few other points of style are worth noting:

(*a*) a semi-colon (;) is used between separate definitions with slight shifts of meaning, and between example phrases which are not sentences. In addition a semi-colon separates a sentence from a phrase example.

(*b*) an oblique stroke (/) is used to show choice or variation.

Examples:

vt/i means that a verb may be either transitive or intransitive.

someone/something means that a certain verb etc may be followed by either a person or a thing as its object.

rake through/over something means that there are two forms of this phrasal verb: rake through something and rake over something.

the reek of tobacco/smoke etc. means that reek is normally used with the word tobacco or smoke or certain words of similar meaning.

American English and British English

In areas where English is the native language, and in many places where it is a second language, certain characteristic forms of pronunciation, words and expressions are found. Accordingly we can speak of Indian English, Australian English, Malaysian English, West African English as well as British English and American English. However, the learner of English as a second language is most likely to base his own English on either the British or the American form, and quite often the learner has difficulties with the differences between these two forms.

It should be emphasized that the differences between British and American English form a very small part of the language which is actually used by both British and American people. The occasions when speakers of the two forms fail to understand each other are very few indeed. We list below a selection of the most outstanding differences. Note that in some cases we refer to Britain as a whole, in other cases to England, and in some cases to Received Pronunciation.

Pronunciation

1. /r/

at the end of a word or before a consonant.

Most Americans pronounce /r/ in these positions when there is a letter r in the spelling as do most Scots; most English people do not e.g.

	England	USA
far	/fɑː/	/fɑːr/
hard	/hɑːd/	/hɑːrd/

2. /æ/ and /ɑː/

Most Americans do not distinguish these two vowels; RP speakers do e.g.

	RP	USA
bath	/bɑːθ/	/bæθ/
hat	/hæt/	/hæt/

3. /ɔ/

Most Americans use a vowel like a short /ɑ/ where British people use /ɔ/ e.g.

	Britain	USA
hot	/hɔt/	/hɑt/
top	/tɔp/	/tɑp/

4. Individual words

In addition to the general differences in the pronunciation of individual sounds in the two forms of English, there are a few words in which there is a particular difference of pronunciation e.g.

	Britain	USA
lieutenant	/lef'tenənt/	/luː'tenənt/
missile	/'misail/	/'misl/

Spelling

1. -our and -or e.g.

Britain	USA
colour	color
honour	honor
labour	labor

2. -re and -er e.g.

Britain	USA
centre	center
theatre	theater

3. -ce and -se e.g.

	Britain	USA
	defence	defense
	offence	offense
BUT	licence (noun)	license
	license (verb)	license
	practice (noun)	practise
	practise (verb)	practise

4. -l and -ll e.g.

Britain	USA
travelled	traveled
traveller	traveler
levelled	leveled
skilful	skillful

6. Some individual words e.g.

Britain	USA
grey	gray
plough	plow

Vocabulary

There are many expressions which refer specifically to aspects of American life e.g. names of foodstuffs, features of the landscape, games etc which we will not discuss here. Similarly, we shall not discuss the many expressions which originated in America but which are now fully accepted in British English.

Then there are a fairly small number of cases in which British and American English have different expressions or sometimes different meanings for the same expressions e.g.

Britain	USA
aluminium	aluminum
flat	apartment
autumn	fall
tap	faucet
railway	railroad
windscreen	windshield

Abbreviations used in the dictionary

adj	adjective	*o.f.*	old-fashioned
adv	adverb	*opp*	opposite
art	article	*past*	past tense and past participle
attrib	attributive		
aux	auxiliary	*past part*	past participle
Brit	British	*pl*	plural
conj	conjunction	*pred adj*	predicative adjective
e.g.	for example	*prep*	preposition
esp.	especially	*pron*	pronoun
etc	etcetera	*pres*	present
fem	feminine	®	registered trademark
i.e.	that is	*Scot*	Scottish
interj	interjection	*sing*	singular
Ir	Irish	*US*	American
masc	masculine	usu.	usually
nc	countable noun	*vt*	transitive verb
nu	uncountable noun	*vi*	intransitive verb
nc/u	countable or uncountable noun	*vt/i*	transitive or intransitive verb

A

a[1] [ei, ə] *determiner* **1.** a particular one. *John has bought a new car* i.e. we are referring to one particular car. *pl: John has bought some/several/two new cars. James is a friend of mine/yours/his etc* i.e. James is one of my (your, his etc) friends. **2.** any one. *A new car costs a lot of money* i.e. any new car, not one in particular. *pl: New cars cost a lot of money.* **3.** one: *a gallon of petrol; a pound of butter. pl: two/three etc gallons of petrol etc.* **4.** for each one: *five pence a pound. pl: five pence for two/three etc pounds.* **5.** (with the name of a person) *an unknown person named . . . A Mr Smith is waiting to see you* i.e. a man named Mr Smith whom I (or you) don't know. (not usu. *pl*). **6.** (with the name of a person) somebody like. *There is always a danger of a Hitler becoming the ruler of a country.* (not usu. *pl*). **7.** (joined with other determiners) *A few spectators were there. Give him a little milk. There weren't a great many people there. He has a lot of money.*
Note: 1. a is used before words beginning with a consonant sound; *an* [æn, ən, n] is used before words beginning with a vowel sound. Notice that although the words *honour, hour, honourable, honest* etc begin with a consonant letter, the first sound in these words is a vowel so *an* is used. In the same way, although *union, united, useful, one* etc begin with a vowel letter, the first sound in these words is a consonant so *a* is used. Some people use *an* with *hotel, historian* and a few other words which usu. begin with a consonant sound; this is old-fashioned and not recommended. 2. The emphatic forms [ei] and [æn] are not often used; *one* is more common for emphasis (e.g. *I wanted 'one' book, not six* is more common than *I wanted 'a' book, not six*). *3. many a man, many a one*; these forms are rather old-fashioned; use *many men, many etc.*

a-[2] [ə] *prefix* as in **a-hunting** (*o.f.* – use **hunting** etc).

aardvark ['ɑːdvɑːk] *nc* large animal with long ears found in Africa. It comes out at night and eats insects.

aback [ə'bæk] *adv* only in **taken aback** i.e. surprised (esp. unpleasantly). *He was taken aback at/by the news.*

abandon [ə'bændən] *vt* leave, not intending to return; give up; have no more concern with. *We had to abandon the plan we first thought of. I don't think that John would abandon his friends if they were in trouble.* **abandonment** *nu.*
abandoned *adj* **1.** left, deserted. *We came to an old abandoned farmhouse.* **2.** uncontrolled (and often wicked). *He was living an abandoned life.*
abandon oneself allow oneself to be carried away by one's feelings (often unhappy or bad feelings). *She abandoned herself to a life of pleasure.*
with abandon in a wild and uncontrolled way.

abase [ə'beis] *vt* make somebody/something lower and less important (esp. in order to gain something).

abashed [ə'bæʃt] *adj* not sure what to do or say (usu. because of the behaviour or words of other people) (*opp* **unabashed**).

abate [ə'beit] *vt/i* (usu. of noise, pain, suffering, nuisance etc) become or make less.
abatement *nu.*

abattoir ['æbətwɑː*] *nc* place where animals are killed for food.

abbess ['æbis] *nc* woman in charge of a convent. (*masc* **abbot**).

abbey ['æbi] *nc* **1.** building(s) in which monks or nuns live. **2.** church which used to be part of an abbey (e.g. Westminster Abbey, London).

abbot ['æbət] *nc* man in charge of a monastery. (*fem* **abbess**).

abbreviate [ə'briːvieit] *vt* make shorter (usu. a word or phrase). *'United Kingdom' can be abbreviated to 'U.K.'*
abbreviation [əbriːvi'eiʃən] *nc/u* short form of a word or phrase. *'U.K.' is the abbreviation of/for 'United Kingdom'.*

abdicate ['æbdikeit] *vt/i* leave an important position (usu. that of king or queen). *He abdicated the throne in favour of his brother.*
abdication [æbdi'keiʃən] *nc/u.*

abdomen ['æbdəmən] *nc* **1.** part of the body containing the digestive organs. **2.** part of the body of an insect. **abdominal** [æb'dɔminl] *adj.*
Note: abdomen is best used as a medical or biological term; in ordinary use *stomach* would be better (e.g. *I have a pain in my stomach*). Medically, however, the word abdomen refers to all the digestive organs, while the stomach is only one of these organs. In medical use the word is pronounced [æb'doumən].

abduct [æb'dʌkt] *vt* carry somebody away against his will (usu. by force). **abduction** *nc/u.*

aberration [æbə'reiʃən] *nc/u* a going away from the right or usual course. **aberrant** [æ'berənt] *adj.*

abet [ə'bet] *vt/i* usu. in **to aid and abet somebody to do something** i.e. help somebody to do something wrong. (legal; for normal purposes use **help**).

abeyance [ə'beiəns] *nu* (usu. in **be in/fall into abeyance**) disuse or lack of use, possibly only temporary (of a custom, law, rule etc). *The custom has fallen into abeyance* i.e. the custom is no longer followed (but it might be brought back).

abhor [əb'hɔː*] *vt* hate very strongly. *Spitting in the street is a practice I abhor.* *past* **abhorred.**
abhorrence [əb'hɔrəns] *nu* feeling of strong hatred.

abide[1] [ə'baid] *vt* (usu. only with **can't** or **cannot**) like. *I can't abide that chap.* (*informal*).

abide² [ə'baid] *vi* live, dwell. *past* **abode** [ə'boud] (*o.f.* – use **live**).

abide by be faithful to, follow (a law, custom, agreement etc). *We must abide by the rules of the game.*

abiding [ə'baidiŋ] *adj* without end (o.f. – use **permanent** or **unending**).

ability [ə'biliti] *nc/u* power or cleverness to do something. (*opp* **inability**). see **able.**

abject ['æbdʒekt] *adj* contemptible; very miserable or unhappy (often without the courage or the ability to make oneself better). *He made an abject apology. The people lived in abject poverty.*

abjure [əb'dʒuə*] *vt* promise to stop believing in or following something. **abjuration** [æbdʒu'reiʃən] *nc/u.*

ablaze [ə'bleiz] *adv/pred adj* on fire; very bright; full of, overflowing with, an emotion (e.g. anger). *The house was ablaze with light. His followers were ablaze with enthusiasm.*

able ['eibl] *adj* **1.** having the power or cleverness or opportunity to do something. *Most children are able to walk at the age of 15 months* i.e. most children can walk at this age. *Are you able to help me? When will you be able to come?* (*opp* **unable**). **2.** (of people, speech, argument etc) doing what is intended or wanted in a very satisfactory or clever way. *He is an able administrator. The lawyer made a very able speech.* **3.** (of a person) not weak, although old. *The old woman was still quite able.* see **ability.**

'able-'bodied *adj* fit and strong.

'able-'bodied 'seaman fully-trained sailor.

ablution [ə'blu:ʃən] *nc/u* process of washing (esp. for ceremonial purposes).

abnormal [æb'nɔ:məl] *adj* not normal; strange. **abnormally** *adv.* **abnormality** [æbnɔ:'mæliti] *nc/u.*

aboard [ə'bɔ:d] *adv/prep* on a ship, train, aircraft etc.

all aboard call for passengers to enter a ship etc which is about to start.

abode¹ [ə'boud] *nc* place where one lives; home (o.f. – use **house** etc).

abode² [ə'boud] past of **abide².**

abolish [ə'bɔliʃ] *vt* stop something (esp. by law) so that it does not start again (e.g. slavery, poverty etc or a law, custom, practice etc). *Abraham Lincoln abolished slavery in the United States.* **abolition** [æbə'liʃən] *nu.*

abominable [ə'bɔminəbl] *adj* horrible, very unpleasant. **abominably** *adv.*

abominate [ə'bɔmineit] *vt* hate very strongly.

abomination [əbɔmi'neiʃən] *nc/u* **1.** something causing feelings of hate. **2.** feelings of hate.

aboriginal [æbə'ridʒənl] *adj* (usu. of inhabitants, animals, plants etc) living or existing in a country from the earliest times. **aborigine** [æbə'ridʒini:] *nc* (usu. *pl*) one of the first inhabitants of a country (esp. those living in Australia before it was colonized).

abortion [ə'bɔ:ʃən] *nc* **1.** intentional killing of an unborn child. **2.** birth of a child before the proper time so that the child dies (usu. legal or medical in sense **2.**).

Note: in ordinary use this accident is called a *miscarriage.*

3. anything not fully developed or misshapen.

abortive [ə'bɔ:tiv] *adj* (usu. of a plan, attempt, coup etc) ending in failure; stopped before fully developed.

abound [ə'baund] *vi* **1.** be present in great numbers. *Wild animals abound in Africa.* **2.** have plenty of (usu. some form of wealth or some good quality of character). *Saudi Arabia abounds in oil. He abounds in good intentions.*

about [ə'baut] *adv/prep* **1.** on the subject of etc: *a story about a little boy. He told me about his visit to France.* **2.** in; in different parts of. *He walked about the town for a long time.* **3.** on every side of. *There was a white fence about the house.* **4.** nearly or perhaps a little more. *The little boy is about six years old.* **5.** near. *Is John about?* i.e. is he here? (*informal*). **6.** in many directions; on all sides. *The little boy ran about looking for his mother.* **7.** in the other direction. *He turned about.*

about to just going to; on the point of. *The trial is about to begin* i.e. it will begin soon.

be up/out and about not have to stay indoors (e.g. after having recovered from an illness).

bring something about make something take place.

turn (and turn) about first one, then the other, and so on.

what about? what is your opinion of? *What about going home immediately?* i.e. what do you think of this suggestion?

above [ə'bʌv] *adv/prep* **1.** higher; over; on top. **2.** (in a book etc) before this point. **3.** in heaven.

above all see **all.**

a'bove'board *adv/pred adj* honest; being what it seems to be, without hiding anything from someone.

abrasion [ə'breiʒən] *nc/u* rubbing away of a surface: *an abrasion of the skin.*

abrasive [ə'breiziv] *adj* causing abrasion: *abrasive personality* i.e. annoying.

abreast [ə'brest] *adv* next to; by the side of.

two/three/four etc abreast with two/three/four etc people next to each other in a line.

keep/stay/be abreast of/with something know about new ideas and events: *abreast of the news; abreast of recent developments.*

abridge [ə'bridʒ] *vt* make shorter (often in order to make easier to read).

abridgement **1.** *nu* making shorter. **2.** *nc* something made shorter.

abridged *adj.* (*opp* **unabridged**).

abroad [ə'brɔ:d] *adv* **1.** in or to foreign countries. **2.** (esp. with reference to a rumour, news, story etc) over a wide area; everywhere.

abrogate ['æbrougeit] *vt* put an end to (usu. a law, custom etc). **abrogation** [æbrou'geiʃən] *nu.*

abrupt [ə'brʌpt] *adj* **1.** sudden and unexpected: *an abrupt change of direction; an abrupt decision.* **2.** rough and impolite.

abruptly *adv.* **abruptness** *nu.*

abscess ['æbsis] *nc* painful swelling in some part of the body, containing a thick liquid called pus or matter.

abscond [əb'skɔnd] *vi* go away secretly (esp. in order to avoid more punishment). *The boys absconded from school after breaking the window. The prisoners absconded from detention.* **absconder** *nc.*

absence ['æbsəns] *nc/u* **1.** failure to be at or in a place. *Your absence from the meeting was noticed by the chairman* i.e. the fact that you were not at the meeting was noticed. 2. lack of something. *Darkness is the absence of light* i.e. when there is no light somewhere, there is darkness.

absence of mind not noticing what is happening around one; forgetting many things (usu. because one is thinking about other things). see also **absent-minded.**

absent ['æbsənt] *adj* 1. not in or at a place. *John was absent from school today.* 2. not noticing what is happening around one. *He had an absent expression on his face.* Also [əb'sent] *vt* in **absent oneself** i.e. stay away from. *He absented himself from the meeting.*

absentee [æbsən'ti:] *nc* person who is absent: *absentee landlord* i.e. landowner who does not live on his land.

absently *adv* without noticing what is going on: *look at somebody absently.*

'absent-'minded *adj* not paying attention to one's surroundings (usu. because one is thinking of something else); forgetting many things. **absent-mindedly** *adv.* **absent-mindedness** *nu.*

absolute ['æbsəlu:t] *adj* 1. complete; very great: *absolute freedom/truth/stupidity.* 2. free from any control by the law. *The Queen of England is not an absolute ruler.*

absolutely [æbsə'lu:tli] *adv* 1. completely. 2. quite right!, certainly!, yes! (*informal*).

absolutism *nu* system of government in which the king etc is free from any control by the law.

absolution [æbsə'lu:ʃən] *nu* 1. freeing from guilt or blame for doing wrong (usu. with reference to the Roman Catholic religion). 2. freeing from the need to carry out a promise. see **absolve.**

absolve [əb'zɔlv] *vt* 1. state that someone is free from the guilt of having done wrong. *The priest absolved the man.* 2. set free from a promise or duty.

absorb [əb'zɔ:b] *vt* 1. take in (esp. a liquid). *A sponge absorbs water.* 2. study and learn very well. *The student absorbed everything he read.* 3. get full attention. *The lecture completely absorbed the attention of the students. The students were completely absorbed in their work.* **absorbent** *adj* (in sense 1.).

absorbed *adj* very interested in; giving all one's attention to something.

absorbing *adj* extremely interesting.

absorption [əb'zɔ:pʃən] *nu* 1. taking in. 2. very great interest in something.

abstain [əb'stein] *vi* stop using something; not use something (often for the sake of one's health): *abstain from alcohol.*

abstainer *nc* one who abstains (esp. from alcohol).

total abstainer one who does not take alcohol in any form.

abstemious [əb'sti:miəs] *adj* not taking too much food, drink etc. **abstemiously** *adv.* **abstemiousness** *nu.*

abstention [əb'stenʃən] *nc/u* act of abstaining.

abstinence ['æbstinəns] *nu* practice of not taking too much food/drink etc. **abstinent** *adj.*

total abstinence not taking alcohol in any form. see **abstain.**

abstract[1] ['æbstrækt] *adj* 1. concerned with the idea of a thing and not with actual examples (e.g. the idea of honesty rather than honest actions or honest people). 2. difficult to understand because of a concern with ideas rather than actual examples: *abstract ideas; an abstract argument.* 3. (with reference to some types of Western painting in the 20th century) not showing pictures of real things, but patterns, shapes and colours.

abstract noun noun such as *height, weight, whiteness, honesty* referring to an abstract idea.

abstract[2] ['æbstrækt] *nc* summary of a book, article, report etc.

abstract[3] [æb'strækt] *vt* 1. take out or take away (often dishonestly). 2. take information from.

abstracted [æb'stræktid] *adj* thinking very deeply so that one is not paying attention to other things. **abstractedly** *adv.*

abstraction [æb'strækʃən] 1. *nc* something thought of as an idea, and without verbal examples. see **abstract**[1]. 2. *nu* the taking out or away of something. see **abstract**[3]. 3. *nu* absent-mindedness. see **abstracted.**

abstruse [æb'stru:s] *adj* not easy to understand: *a very abstruse theory; abstruse ideas.*

absurd [əb'sə:d] *adj* foolish; not sensible; without a reason. **absurdly** *adv.*

absurdity *nc/u* (example of) foolishness, unreasonableness.

abundance [ə'bʌndəns] *nu* a large amount; very much. *He has an abundance of good stories.* **abundant** *adj.* **abundantly** *adv.* **in abundance** in great quantity.

abuse[1] [ə'bju:s] 1. *nu* bad and insulting language. 2. *nc* bad or dishonest action. *The commission of enquiry found a number of abuses in the granting of import licences.* 3. *nc* bad use of something.

abuse[2] [ə'bju:z] *vt* 1. use bad and insulting language. 2. use wrongly in a way not intended: *abuse somebody's trust in oneself* i.e. act wrongly after having been trusted not to; *abuse one's health* i.e. make oneself ill by working too hard or by not taking proper care of oneself.

abusive [ə'bju:siv] *adj* containing bad and insulting language: *an abusive letter; abusive language.* **abusively** *adv.*

abut [ə'bʌt] *vi* be joined to something at one side (usu. land or buildings). *My house abuts on to John's.* *past* **abutted. abutting** *adj.*

abysmal [ə'bizml] *adj* 1. very deep. 2. very much greater than is normal (in a bad sense): *abysmal ignorance.* **abysmally** *adv.*

abyss [ə'bis] *nc* 1. very deep hole (not very common – use **hole, pit** etc). 2. depths of something: *an abyss of misery.*

acacia [ə'keiʃə] *nc* shrub related to mimosa, often with sweet-smelling flowers, found in warm regions.

academic [ækə'demik] *adj* 1. referring to schools, colleges etc. 2. very theoretical, of little practical use: *an idea which is of academic interest only* i.e. not concerned with things as they really are. Also *nc* scholar; person who teaches in a university. **academically** *adv.*

academy [ə'kædəmi] *nc* 1. name for some secondary schools: *Accra Academy; Edinburgh Academy.* 2. school or college for the study of certain named subjects: *Academy of Music; Academy of Engineering; Military Academy.* 3. society of learned men and women, such as scientists, writers, painters etc who try to encourage science, art, literature etc.

accede [æk'si:d] *vi* 1. agree to; say yes to. *He acceded to any request.* 2. come into a position of authority after somebody else has left it. *He acceded to the throne* i.e. he became king. see **accession.**

accelerate [æk'seləreit] *vt/i* (usu. with reference to a car) (make something) go faster.
acceleration [æksələ'reiʃən] *nu* increase in speed.
accelerator [ək'seləreitə*] *nc* **1.** pedal in a car which the driver presses with his foot to control the speed of the car. **2.** anything which causes an increase in speed.

accent[1] ['æksent] *nc* **1.** way of speaking which is related to the place one comes from: *speak English with a London accent; speak French with an English accent.* **2.** marks written above some letters in certain languages (e.g. ´, `, ^ in French). **3.** special force or emphasis given to a word or syllable (e.g. in *many* the accent is on the first syllable).

accent[2] [æk'sent] *vt* say a word or syllable with special force or emphasis.

accentuate [æk'sentjueit] *vt* **1.** make something seem more important, more noticeable, bigger etc. *Some women paint their eyelids to accentuate the brightness of their eyes.* **2.** pronounce a word or syllable with special force or emphasis. **accentuation** [əksentju'eiʃən] *nu.*

accept [ək'sept] *vt* **1.** take something that is offered. *He accepted my offer. John accepted my suggestion.* **2.** believe in or take as satisfactory something that somebody says. *He accepted my excuse. The new theory became widely accepted* i.e. many people thought that the theory was true.
acceptable *adj* (usu. with reference to a gift, offer, invitation etc) pleasing, worth accepting. (*opp* **unacceptable**).
acceptance *nc/u* act of accepting what is offered. *We have sent out thirty invitations and so far we have had twenty acceptances* i.e. twenty people have agreed to come.

access ['ækses] *nu* **1.** way to or into a place. *Access to the town was across a narrow bridge.* **2.** opportunity or permission to use something, meet somebody etc. *Students have access to the library during the vacation. The prime minister had direct access to the king at any hour of the day or night.*
accessible [æk'sesibl] *adj* easy to reach. *Medicine should not be kept where it is accessible to children.* (*opp* **inaccessible**).
'access road road, sometimes roughly made, which makes a place easier to get to.

accessary, accessory [æk'sesəri] *nc* person who helps somebody to commit a crime.
accessary before/after the fact person who helps a criminal before or after the crime. (legal – use **partner** or **confederate**).

accession [æk'seʃən] **1.** *nu* arriving at a position (esp. that of a ruler): *accession to power.* see **accede. 2.** *nc/u* addition: *several new accessions to the library* i.e. some new books.

accessory [æk'sesəri] *nc* **1.** something which is added to the main thing (esp. parts of a motorcar such as lights, windscreen wipers, radio etc; or parts of a woman's costume such as shoes, hat, handbag etc). **2.** see **accessary.**

accident ['æksidənt] *nc* **1.** harmful and unexpected happening (usu. causing damage or injury). *Seventy-five people were killed in accidents at work last year.* **2.** something unexpected. *It was just an accident that I found the missing letter.*
accidental [æksi'dentl] *adj* not intentional. **accidentally** *adv.*
'accident-'prone more likely to have accidents than other people.
'road accident accident involving a car etc.
by accident without any intention or planning: *meet somebody by accident.*

acclaim [ə'kleim] *vt* shout a welcome; shout approval; congratulate somebody by shouting. *The crowd acclaimed the new king.*
acclamation [æklə'meiʃən] *nc/u* shouts of approval, welcome etc.
by acclamation (with reference to elections, making decisions etc) deciding by the shouts of the people present.

acclimatize [ə'klaimətaiz] *vt/i* (*Brit*) become or make somebody/something accustomed to a change of climate or surroundings. *John soon became acclimatized to the heat in India.* (*US* **acclimate** ['æklimeit]).

accolade ['ækəleid] *nc* **1.** official praise or reward. **2.** act by which a king or queen makes someone a knight: *receive the accolade of knighthood.*

accommodate [ə'kɔmədeit] *vt* **1.** have enough room for; accept people to live in. *This car accommodates six people quite comfortably.* **2.** change so as to please or help somebody else. *I can easily accommodate myself to your plans.* **3.** supply; give something which is needed (*o.f.*).
accommodating *adj* helpful; willing to make changes to help other people.
accommodation [əkɔmə'deiʃən] *nu* **1.** place to live in or sleep in (esp. for a short period only). *If you go to London for a holiday you will have no difficulty in finding accommodation.* **2.** adjustment (e.g. of the eye in order to see objects clearly at different distances).

accompany [ə'kʌmpəni] *vt* **1.** go with somebody. *The Prime Minister's wife accompanied him when he visited the northern region.* **2.** play music while someone sings or plays on a different instrument. *John accompanied his wife on the piano.* **3.** do something or happen, while something else is happening. *The lecturer accompanied his explanation with some tape recordings.* **4.** do something with somebody else. *Will you accompany me in a walk/in drinking a glass of wine?* (rather *o.f.* – use *will you go for a walk with me/have a drink with me* etc).
accompanied *adj.* (*opp* **unaccompanied**).
accompaniment [ə'kʌmpənimənt] *nc/u* **1.** something that goes with something else. *Disease is an accompaniment of poverty.* **2.** part of a piece of music which fits in with the main part of the music being sung or played on a different instrument or instruments. *Jane sang a song with a piano accompaniment by John Smith.*
accompanist *nc* musician who plays an accompaniment (in sense **2.**).

accomplice [ə'kʌmplis] *nc* person who helps somebody else to do something (esp. something wrong).

accomplish [ə'kʌmpliʃ] *vt* carry out successfully. *He accomplished a great deal during his first year.*
accomplished *adj* able to do something well (esp. able to play music, dance, hold interesting conversations etc). *Jane is a very accomplished dancer.*
accomplishment *nc* skill, ability of somebody who is accomplished.

accord[1] [ə'kɔ:d] *nu* friendly feelings (esp. between nations).

accord[2] [ə'kɔ:d] **1.** *vt* give with friendly feelings. *His friends accorded Tom their sincere thanks.* **2.** *vi* agree with; have the same meaning as. *Your story of what*

happened does not accord with what John has told us i.e. you and John say different things. **accordance** *nu.*
be in accord (with somebody) be in agreement (with somebody); have friendly feelings (for somebody).
of one's own accord willingly. *I did it of my own accord, not because anyone asked me to do it.*
in accordance with in agreement with; following. *In accordance with the law they had to pay a fine.*
according to somebody/something following what was said or written by somebody. *According to John, there will be a meeting next week* i.e. John says so (but he may be wrong). *According to the Bible the world was created in seven days.*

accordion [ə'kɔːdiən] *nc* type of musical instrument.

accost [ə'kɔst] *vt* go and speak to someone one does not know (esp. in a public place and in a troublesome or unpleasant way). *A stranger accosted me in the street yesterday and asked for money.*

account[1] [ə'kaunt] *vi* **1.** explain satisfactorily. *I can account for my strange behaviour last week; I was feeling ill and tired.* **2.** consider; think.

account[2] [ə'kaunt] *nc* **1.** story or explanation about something that has happened. *I read an account of the fire in the newspaper.* **2.** (often *pl*) written record of sums of money received and spent: *keep accounts/an account.* **3.** record of goods bought at a shop for which the customer pays some time after taking the goods away (usu. at the end of the month).
accountable *adj* responsible, expected or able to explain satisfactorily if asked to do so. *A child is not always accountable for its behaviour.*
accountancy *nu* work of keeping accounts i.e. making a record of sums of money received and spent.
accountant *nc* person whose work is accountancy.
of no account unimportant; useless.
on account 1. *buy something on account* i.e. to buy goods from a shop by taking the goods now and paying later (usu. at the end of the month). **2.** in part payment. *Here's five pounds on account* i.e. the rest of the money will be paid later.
on account of because of.
on no/not on any account for no reason. *On no account must you touch these books.*
on this account for this reason.
on one's own account for or by oneself.
take something into account consider; think about when making plans. *We must take all possibilities into account when planning for next year.*

accredit [ə'kredit] *vt* **1.** provide with documents etc to show official recognition. *An ambassador is the accredited representative of his country* i.e. he is officially recognized by his country. **2.** recognize as being due to. *He was accredited with having thought of the idea first.*

accrue [ə'kruː] *vi* increase in size or amount (esp. with reference to money). *A large sum should accrue to you by the end of the year.*

accumulate [ə'kjuːmjuleit] *vt/i* **1.** bring together, collect. *The old man had accumulated a lot of books/a great deal of experience during his lifetime.* **2.** increase; grow in number or amount. *If you don't clear away the rubbish regularly, it will just accumulate.*
accumulation [əkjuːmju'leiʃən] *nu.*
accumulator *nc* apparatus for storing electricity.

accurate ['ækjurit] *adj* **1.** completely right; correct. **2.** very careful; never making a mistake (esp. in one's work) (*opp* **inaccurate**). **accurately** *adv.*
accuracy *nu.* (*opp* **inaccuracy**).

accuse [ə'kjuːz] *vt* say that somebody has done wrong. *John accused his friend of stealing the money.*
accusation [ækjuː'zeiʃən] *nc*: *He made an accusation against her.*
the accused *n sing* or *pl* the person(s) accused of a crime in a court of law.

accusative [ə'kjuːzətiv] *adj* usu. in **the accusative (case)** i.e. grammatical form of nouns, pronouns and adjectives in Latin and some other languages, which shows that the noun or pronoun is a direct object.

accustom [ə'kʌstəm] *vt* usu. **accustom oneself** i.e. learn to accept trouble, difficulty etc without surprise or complaint. *You must learn to accustom yourself to hard work.*
accustomed *adj.* (*opp* **unaccustomed**).
be accustomed to be used to.

ace [eis] *nc* **1.** playing card with the value one. **2.** a person who is very good at something (e.g. a pilot).

ace (*def 1*)

be within an ace of something/doing something be very near to getting or not getting what one intended to get; very near success or failure.

acetic [ə'siːtik] *adj* (usu. in **acetic acid**) of or like vinegar.

acetylene [ə'setiliːn] *nu* type of gas.

ache [eik] *nc* pain which goes on for some time: *toothache*; *stomach ache*; *headache.* Also *vi*: *My foot aches.*
aches and pains aches in different parts of the body at the same time. (*informal*).

achieve [ə'tʃiːv] *vt* get by successfully doing something. *The runner achieved his ambition of running the mile in four minutes.*
achievable *adj.*
achievement *nc/u* something gained; act of successfully doing something one has tried to do.

acid ['æsid] *nc* **1.** chemical substance containing hydrogen, which turns litmus paper red. **2.** sour-tasting liquid (usu. also an acid in sense **1.**). Also *adj* **1.** acting like an acid. **2.** sour-tasting. **acidity** [ə'siditi] *nu.*
'acid 'test test which finally decides the value of something.

acknowledge [ək'nɔlidʒ] *vt* **1.** admit; say that one believes something to be true. *He acknowledged that he had done wrong.* **2.** generally agree about the position or value of. *John is acknowledged to be a good pianist* i.e. many people know that he is. **3.** say that one has received something (and usu.

that one thanks the person who has given it). *He acknowledged the gift from his aunt.*
acknowledg(e)ment *nc/u* statement that one has received something (usu. thanking the person who has given it).
acknowledged *adj* generally recognized. *He is an acknowledged expert on ancient history.*

acme ['ækmi] *nu* (with abstract nouns) highest point reached or able to be reached: *the acme of his career.*

acne ['ækni] *nu* spots or pimples (usu. on the face of boys or girls).

acolyte ['ækəlait] *nc* **1.** junior assistant in a church. **2.** any young person learning a profession or helping a more senior person. (*formal*).

acorn ['eikɔːn] *nc* nut or seed of an oak tree.

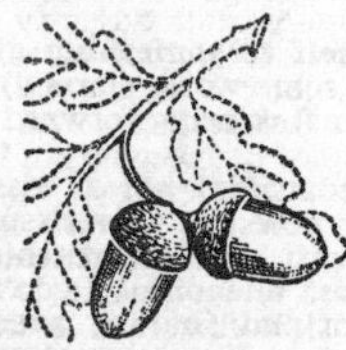

acorn

acoustic [ə'kuːstik] *adj* with reference to hearing or sound.
acoustics *npl* **1.** science of sound. **2.** things about a building etc which make music, speeches etc in it sound clear.

acquaint [ə'kweint] *vt* inform, make aware, tell: *acquaint oneself with the facts.*
acquaintance **1.** *nc* somebody one knows but not very well (contrasted with a friend). **2.** *nu* small amount of knowledge: *only a slight acquaintance with mathematics.*
be acquainted with know somebody/something, but not very well.
make the acquaintance of somebody meet or get to know somebody.

acquiesce [ækwi'es] *vi* accept or agree (although one is unwilling to do so) without protest or argument. *He acquiesced in the arrangements which I had made.* **acquiescent** *adj.* **acquiescence** *nu.*

acquire [ə'kwaiə*] *vt* get as one's own (usu. by one's own efforts): *acquire a knowledge of German.*
acquire a reputation for something/doing something become well-known for one's abilities or behaviour.
an acquired taste (a liking for) something which is not usu. liked at first.
acquisition [ækwi'ziʃən] *nc/u* something gained or acquired.
acquisitive [ə'kwizitiv] *adj* fond of getting new things (often from other people). **acquisitiveness** *nu.*

acquit [ə'kwit] *vt* **1.** decide by a trial or investigation that somebody is not guilty of some crime or wrongdoing. *He was acquitted of the robbery.* **2.** do one's duty satisfactorily. *He has acquitted himself very well in his new job. past* **acquitted.**
acquittal *nc* (usu. only in sense **1.**).

acre ['eikə*] *nc* area of 4840 square yards or approximately 4000 square metres.

acrid ['ækrid] *adj* (of smell or taste) bitter and stinging.

acrimonious [ækri'mouniəs] *adj* angry; showing personal hatred or dislike between the persons concerned: *an acrimonious argument.* **acrimoniously** *adv.*
acrimony ['ækriməni] *nu* feelings of anger and dislike in an argument etc.

acrobat ['ækrəbæt] *nc* person who is very clever at balancing, jumping, walking on his hands etc (esp. one who earns his living by entertaining people in this way).
acrobatic [ækrə'bætik] *adj.* **acrobatically** *adv.*
acrobatics [ækrə'bætiks] *npl* actions performed by an acrobat.

acropolis [ə'krɔpəlis] *nc* high fortified place inside an ancient Greek city.

across [ə'krɔs] *adv/prep* **1.** from one side to the other. *He walked across the bridge.* **2.** on the other side (of). *There is a shop across the road from my house.*
come across somebody/something find or meet by accident, without meaning to do so.

acrostic [ə'krɔstik] *nc* poem or piece of writing in which a word is made up when certain letters (often the first or last in each line) are read together.

act[1] [ækt] *nc* **1.** something done. **2.** division of a stage play. **3.** law: *act of Parliament.*
in the act while doing (usu. something wrong): *caught in the act of stealing the money.*
an act of God something which could not have been prevented by human beings (esp. earthquakes, floods, storms etc).
put on an act pretend to be what one is not. *John wasn't really angry, he was putting on an act.* (*informal*).

act[2] [ækt] *vi* **1.** do something. *We must act at once to stop this.* **2.** behave. *How did he act? He acted very strangely.* **3.** take part in a play. **4.** do some work or duty (often for somebody else). *John was asked to act as chairman of the meeting because Mr Brown was ill.* **5.** do what is advised, suggested etc. *I have decided to act on your advice.* **6.** have an effect on. *Acids act on most metals.*
acting *nu* art of being an actor. Also *adj* doing someone's work temporarily. *John was acting chairman at the meeting.*
act up behave badly. *My car has been acting up lately.* (*informal*).
act one's age behave as a person of one's age should (e.g. not like a small child). *His mother told him to act his age and stop crying.*
act the fool behave foolishly.

action ['ækʃən] **1.** *nc/u* something done. *We must have action not words.* **2.** *nu* effect: *the action of acid on metal.* **3.** *nu* fighting in war; a battle: *killed in action; go into action; in action.* **4.** *nc* (*legal*) usu. in **take/bring an action against somebody** i.e. ask for a decision to be made in a law court against somebody; ask a judge to decide by law that somebody has done wrong to oneself.
actionable *adj* enabling one to bring an action against someone. *Your remarks are actionable* i.e. what you have said is punishable by law.
take action do something in order to get what one wants or in order to stop something.

active ['æktiv] *adj* **1.** busy; able to move or work. *He is an active old man; an active volcano* i.e. one which is known to be able to send out fire and smoke etc. (*opp* **inactive**). **2.** real; practical. *I intend to play an active part in the society.* **3.** (grammar) form of the verb as in *he read the book; he helped his friend.* (*opp* **passive** in sense **3.**).
activity [æk'tiviti] **1.** *nu* state of being

active. 2. *nc* (usu. *pl*) things that one does. *He is fond of walking and other outdoor activities. The police were investigating the activities of a number of well-known criminals.*
activist ['æktivist] *nc* person who does a lot of work (esp. for a political party).
activate ['æktiveit] *vt* (usu. *passive*) cause to act or move.
in the active having the active form of the verb.
on active service involved in fighting during a war.
actor ['æktə*] *nc* man who acts in plays, films, on radio or television. (*fem* **actress**).
actual ['æktjuəl] *adj* real, not imaginary.
actually *adv* 1. really. 2. the truth is (often with the suggestion *although it seems strange or surprising* or *although you do not know it*).
actuate ['æktjueit] *vt* (usu. *passive*) cause to act or move.
acumen ['ækjumen] *nu* ability to think clearly and quickly and to make correct decisions. *He showed great business acumen* i.e. he conducted business matters successfully.
acute [ə'kju:t] *adj* 1. strongly felt: *acute pain; an acute illness.* 2. working better than or noticing more than other people: *an acute sense of hearing; very acute criticism; an acute remark.* **acutely** *adv.*
acute angle (geometry) angle of less than 90°.
adage ['ædidʒ] *nc* old and well-known wise saying; proverb.
adamant ['ædəmənt] *adj* determined; unwilling to change one's decision or opinion.
adamantly *adv.*
adapt [ə'dæpt] *vt* 1. change so as to make more suitable for or cause to fit in with certain conditions: *adapt oneself to the weather in England/to the new arrangements etc.* 2. change so as to make suitable for a new purpose or for new conditions. *My radio has been adapted for use in the tropics.*
adaptable *adj* able to adapt or be adapted. (*opp* **unadaptable**).
adaptation [ædæp'teiʃən] *nc/u* (esp. with reference to film, play etc made from a book) process of adapting; result of adapting. *An adaptation of David Copperfield was broadcast on the radio.*
add [æd] *vt/i* 1. join numbers or quantities together to make a larger number or quantity. *Add five to/and eighteen.* 2. put something with something else. *Add some more milk to your coffee.* 3. (usu. following direct speech) say in addition to something else. 4. increase. *The news of John's success added to our happiness.*
add (something) on add (something) to something else.
add (something) up add (something), put numbers together.
addendum [ə'dendəm] *nc* something to be added (esp. in a book). *pl* **addenda** [ə'dendə].
adder ['ædə*] *nc* name given to various types of snake; in Europe, a small poisonous snake with V-marking on the head. Also **viper**; in America, a small and harmless snake; in Africa, a large and poisonous snake.
addict ['ædikt] *nc* person who cannot stop himself from doing something or using something harmful: *drug addict.* **addiction** [ə'dikʃən] *nc/u.*
addicted [ə'diktid] *pred adj* unable to stop using some harmful substance or to stop doing something (usu. something wrong): *addicted to drugs; addicted to telling lies.*
addition [ə'diʃən] *nc/u* 1. adding together. see **add.** 2. sum of numbers to be added together; something added. **additional** *adj.*
additionally *adv.*
in addition (to something) besides; also; as well.
addled ['ædld] *adj* (only with reference to eggs) rotten and unfit for eating.
address [ə'dres] *nc* 1. details of street, town, district etc where a person lives. *What's your address?* i.e. where exactly do you live? 2. writing on letter or envelope showing where a letter is to be sent (and sometimes where it is from). 3. speech made to a meeting. (*formal* in sense 3.). Also *vt*: *address an envelope; address a public meeting.*
address oneself to something give careful attention to some work. (*formal*).
adduce [ə'dju:s] *vt* bring forward as a proof or reason.
adenoids ['ædənɔidz] *npl* 1. tissue at the back of the nose. 2. this tissue when it interferes with one's breathing: *suffer from adenoids.* **adenoidal** [ædə'nɔidl] *adj.*
adept ['ædept] *adj* having great skill in doing something. *He is very adept at playing games.* Also *nc* somebody who has such ability.
adequate ['ædikwit] *adj* enough; sufficient: *an adequate supply of food.* (*opp* **inadequate**). **adequately** *adv.*
adequacy *nu.* (*opp* **inadequacy**).
adhere [əd'hiə*) *vi* 1. (with reference to mud, paste, glue, oil etc) stick closely, firmly. 2. (with reference to custom, religion, political party etc) continue to follow or to be loyal. **adherence** *nu.*
adherent *nc* person who adheres to custom, religion etc.
adhesive [əd'hi:ziv] *adj* sticky; able to stick firmly. Also *nc/u.* **adhesion** [əd'hi:ʒən] *nu.*
adhesive tape 1. sticky material used for covering small cuts and for holding bandages in position. 2. sticky tape used for binding or repairing things.
ad hoc ['æd'hɔk] *adj* arranged for a special purpose, and not depending on a previous arrangement or theory: *an ad-hoc arrangement/committee* etc.
adieu [ə'dju:] *interj* goodbye (*o.f.* – use **goodbye**).
ad infinitum [ædinfi'naitəm] *adv* and so on for ever.
adjacent [ə'dʒeisənt] *adj* (usu. of land, rooms etc, not of numbers) next to in position.
adjective ['ædʒəktiv] *nc* (grammar) word like *black, clever, heavy, hot* which gives further information about a noun. **adjectival** [ædʒək'taivl] *adj.*
adjoin [ə'dʒɔin] *vt/i* be next to. *His fields adjoin mine.* **adjoining** *adj.*
adjourn [ə'dʒə:n] *vt/i* stop a meeting or discussion intending to start again at another time or place. *Shall we adjourn the meeting for a week?* **adjournment** *nc.*
adjudicate [ə'dʒu:dikeit] *vt/i* decide, judge (usu. who is the winner of a competition).
adjudication [ədʒu:di'keiʃən] *nc/u.* **adjudicator** *nc.*
adjunct ['ædʒʌnkt] *nc* something added or joined to something else more important.
adjust [ə'dʒʌst] *vt* change something so as to make it more satisfactory or comfortable: *adjust a seat to one's height.*

adjustable *adj* able to be adjusted.
adjustment *nc* **1.** act of adjusting. **2.** part in a machine by which something is adjusted.
adjutant ['ædʒətənt] *nc* army officer who does office work for a more senior officer.
administer [əd'ministə*] *vt* **1.** control, be in charge of. **2.** give to those who deserve or are in need, as one's work or duty: *administer medicine to the sick; administer justice.*
administration [ədminis'treiʃən] *nc/u* **1.** government of a country. **2.** control of a business or other organization. **3.** administering (in sense **2.**) of justice, medicine, an oath etc. **administrative** [əd'ministrətiv] *adj.*
administrator [əd'ministreitə*] *nc* somebody whose work is to control the organization of a business etc.
administer an oath (to somebody) make somebody promise to do something (usu. to tell the truth in a court of law, or to be loyal to the government).
admirable ['ædmərəbl] *adj* excellent; worthy of approval. **admirably** *adv.*
admiral ['ædmərəl] *nc* officer of very senior rank in the navy; officer in charge of a fleet.
admiralty *nc* (*Brit*) government department dealing with the navy.
admire [əd'maiə*] *vt* look at or consider somebody/something with pleasure and approval. **admiration** [ædmi'reiʃən] *nu.* see **admirable.**
admit [əd'mit] *vt/i* **1.** confess; agree that one has done something (usu. something wrong): *admit a crime.* **2.** allow someone inside: *admit somebody into a house. past* **admitted.**
admissible [əd'misibl] *adj* able to be considered or allowed: *admissible evidence.* (*opp* **inadmissible**).
admission [əd'miʃən] **1.** *nc* confession; saying that one has done something (usu. something wrong). **2.** *nu* allowing to come in: *no admission without tickets; gain admission to a house.*
admittance *nu* allowing to come in: *gain admittance.*
admixture ['ædmikstʃə*] *nc/u* **1.** substance added in mixing. **2.** mixture.
admonish [əd'mɔniʃ] *vt* **1.** explain to someone what he has done wrong; warn. **2.** give a slight punishment to somebody by talking to him and telling him not to do wrong again. **admonition** [ædmə'niʃən] *nc/u.* **admonishment** *nc/u.*
ado [ə'du:] *nu* disturbance; excitement; trouble (*o.f.*).
without more ado without any more delay, at once.
adolescent [ædə'lesnt] *nc* boy or girl between the ages of about 12 and 19. Also *adj.*
adolescence *nu* years during which one is changing from a child to an adult.
adopt [ə'dɔpt] *vt* **1.** make by law a child of other parents part of one's own family. **2.** accept and use a suggestion, habit etc of somebody else. **adoption** *nu.*
adore [ə'dɔ:*] *vt* **1.** worship; love very much. **2.** like. *I adore chocolate.* (*informal*). **adorable** *adj.* **adoration** [ædɔ'reiʃən] *nu.*
adorn [ə'dɔ:n] *vt* make more beautiful by decorating with flowers, jewels etc. **adornment** *nc/u.*
adrenalin [ə'drenəlin] *nu* substance produced by the body, which enables one to be active.
adrift [ə'drift] *adv/pred adj* (usu. with reference to ships and boats) moving without human control wherever taken by the winds and tides.
adroit [ə'drɔit] *adj* clever in using one's hands or one's mind. **adroitly** *adv.* **adroitness** *nu.*
adulation [ædju'leiʃən] *nc/u* too much praise, undeserved praise; praise which is not really deserved but is given to gain something.
adult ['ædʌlt] *nc* **1.** person who is fully grown (usu. over the age of 18). **2.** full-grown animal. Also *adj.*
adulterate [ə'dʌltəreit] *vt* make less pure or less good by adding something. **adulteration** [ədʌltə'reiʃən] *nc/u.*
adulterated *adj.* (*opp* **unadulterated**).
adultery [ə'dʌltəri] *nc/u* sexual relationship of a married person with somebody to whom he or she is not married. **adulterous** *adj.* **adulterer** *nc.* (*fem* **adulteress**).
advance [əd'vɑ:ns] *vt/i* **1.** go forward; cause to go forward; put forward. *He advanced twelve paces. The soldiers advanced towards the city. The general advanced his army. He had no chance to advance his opinion. The time of the meeting was advanced by an hour* i.e. the meeting was held earlier. *He advanced rapidly in his career* i.e. he became successful. **2.** pay or lend money before the proper time. *Can you advance me five pounds?* Also *nc* **1.** movement forward. **2.** money paid or lent before the proper time.
advanced *adj* forward; in front: *advanced ideas/theories etc* i.e. ideas/theories etc which are new and not yet accepted by most people; *advanced in years* i.e. old.
advancement *nu* development; progress: *the advancement of the country's economic growth; the advancement of learning.*
advance an opinion, suggestion etc give an opinion, make a suggestion etc.
make advances to somebody try to become the friend or lover of somebody (often against the wish of this person).
advantage [əd'vɑ:ntidʒ] *nc/u* anything which makes or is likely to make something/somebody better, luckier, happier etc than others. (*opp* **disadvantage**).
advantageous [ædvən'teidʒəs] *adj.* (*opp* **disadvantageous**). **advantageously** *adv.*
of advantage helpful; useful.
have an advantage over someone have a better opportunity of success.
take advantage of somebody/something make use of somebody/something to help oneself, sometimes unfairly or by a trick.
to (the best) advantage in the most useful way.
turn (something) to advantage make good use of (something); profit from (something).
advent ['ædvent] *nc* **1.** coming or arrival (*o.f.* – use **arrival**). **2.** **(Advent)** in the Christian Church, period of devotion before Christmas.
adventitious [ædven'tiʃəs] *adj* happening by chance; not planned.
adventure [əd'ventʃə*] *nc* unusual and exciting event (often involving danger).
adventurous *adj* liking or containing adventure. (*opp* **unadventurous**).
adventurer *nc* **1.** man who looks for adventures. **2.** man who lives (often in a dishonest way) by persuading other people to trust him.
adverb ['ædvə:b] *nc* (grammar) word like

quickly, always, there which gives information in a sentence about *how, when, where* etc. **adverbial** [əd'vəːbiəl] *adj*.

adversary ['ædvəsəri] *nc* enemy. (*formal* – use **enemy**).

adverse ['ædvəːs] *adj* unfavourable; making it difficult or impossible to do what one wants: *an adverse report; adverse winds; adverse circumstances.*

adversity [əd'vəːsiti] *nc/u* difficulty.

advertise ['ædvətaiz] *vt/i* **1.** make known through newspapers, public notices, radio, films etc what one has to sell or offer. **2.** make known in this way what one wants to buy, find, get back etc. *He advertised for a new housemaid. He advertised for his missing wallet.*

advertisement [əd'vəːtizmənt] *nc/u* something which advertises (esp. a public notice).

advice [əd'vais] *nu* something said by somebody about the best thing for somebody else to do: *give advice to somebody about his work. Let me give you some advice.* *Note:* 1. there is a *pl* form which is used in business, but this form is not in general use. For plural meaning, use *some advice*. 2. the *noun* is spelled with a c, but the verb *advise* is spelt with an *s*. Note also the difference of pronunciation.

advise [əd'vaiz] *vt* **1.** give advice to; say what one thinks is the best thing for somebody else to do. **2.** (commerce) inform (use **tell, inform** etc).

advisable *adj* for the best; to be advised. *It is not advisable to lend money to that man because he will not be able to repay it.* (*opp* **inadvisable**).

ill-/well-ad'vised acting in an unwise/wise way after receiving advice.

advocate[1] ['ædvəkit] *nc* person who speaks in defence of somebody/something (esp. in a court of law).

advocate[2] ['ædvəkeit] *vt* speak in support of something; recommend: *advocate a course of action; advocate going to see the doctor.*

advocacy *nu*.

aegis ['iːdʒis] *nc* protection, care or help coming from a stranger or from a more highly-placed person or organization: *be under the aegis of some organization.*

aerate ['ɛəreit] *vt* fill with air or gas: *aerated water.*

aerial ['ɛəriəl] *nc* wire used for receiving or sending radio waves. Also *adj* in or of the air: *aerial warfare.*

aerodrome ['ɛərədroum] *nc* (*Brit*) (usu. with reference to military planes) place where aeroplanes land and fly from. (*US* **airdrome**). see **airport.**

aeroplane ['ɛərəplein] *nc* (*Brit*) flying machine. (*US* **airplane**).

aeronautics [ɛərə'nɔːtiks] *nu* scientific study of aeroplanes and flying. **aeronautic** *adj*.

aesthetic, esthetic [is'θetik] *adj* **1.** referring to what is beautiful (esp. in art, literature and music). **2.** able to understand and like what is beautiful.

aesthetics, esthetics *nu* study of beauty.

afar [ə'fɑː*] *adv* far away (*o.f.* – use **distant** etc).

affable ['æfəbl] *adj* friendly; easy to talk to. **affably** *adv*. **affability** [æfə'biliti] *nu*.

affair [ə'fɛə*] *nc* **1.** something done or to be done; an event or incident (often a mysterious event). *We must try to get to the bottom of this affair* i.e. we must try to find out the truth. **2.** (in *pl*) business, duties etc: *many affairs to take charge of; Ministry of Foreign Affairs* i.e. Ministry which controls relations with other countries. *That's my affair* (*not yours*) i.e. I shall do that, I'm not going to give you any information about it etc. (rather *impolite*). **3.** love between a man and a woman (esp. love which lasts only for a short time) *have an affair with someone.*

affect [ə'fekt] *vt* **1.** have an effect on (often in a bad way). *His health was affected by the poor food he ate.* **2.** arouse feelings of pity, sorrow etc. *He was deeply affected by the news* i.e. he was made unhappy. **3.** pretend to be. **4.** like to have, like to use (often with the suggestion that some pretence is involved): *affect a carelessness in dress.*

affected *adj* **1.** influenced by. **2.** pretended, or not natural; put on to appear better or different from others: *an affected accent.* (*opp* **unaffected**).

affectation [æfek'teiʃən] *nc/u* behaviour which is affected.

Note: affect and *effect* are often confused. 1. both words are pronounced [ə'fekt]. 2. *affect* is usu. a verb; *effect* is usu. a noun and has the basic meaning *result of. effect* can also be a verb meaning *bring about. The members of the club effected a change in the rules.*

affection [ə'fekʃən] *nu* friendly or loving feelings: *show affection to somebody.*

affectionate [ə'fekʃənit] *adj* having friendly feelings. (*opp* **unaffectionate**). **affectionately** *adv*.

affidavit [æfi'deivit] *nc* (in a legal sense) written statement of the truth made to an officer of the law.

affiliate [ə'filieit] *vt/i* join together so as to make one. *The two societies decided to affiliate.*

affiliation [əfili'eiʃən] **1.** *nu* joining. **2.** *nc* club, society etc (usu. formed by joining together earlier associations).

affinity [ə'finiti] *nc/u* **1.** close connection between. *There is an affinity between the Bantu languages.* **2.** attraction or liking. *Salt has an affinity for water.*

affirm [ə'fəːm] *vt/i* say that something is true. (*opp* **deny**).

affirmation [æfə'meiʃən] *nc/u* saying, statement that something is true.

affirmative *adj* saying that something is true. see **negative.**

answer in the affirmative say 'yes'. (*formal* – use **say yes, agree, admit etc**).

affix[1] ['æfiks] *nc* prefix or suffix i.e. letter or group of letters put at the beginning or end of a word.

affix[2] [ə'fiks] *vt* fasten, stick. *He affixed a stamp to the letter.* (*formal* – use **stick, fasten** etc).

afflict [ə'flikt] *vt* cause pain, disease etc: *afflict somebody with extra work; afflicted with leprosy.*

affliction *nc/u* suffering, or something causing it.

affluent ['æfluənt] *adj* rich. **affluence** *nu*.

afford [ə'fɔːd] *vt* **1.** find the time or money for something. *We can afford a new car. We can afford the money for a new car.* **2.** give; provide. *Reading affords him a lot of pleasure.*

afforest [ə'fɔrist] *vt* plant a large number of trees in. **afforestation** [əfɔris'teiʃən] *nu*.

affray [ə'frei] *nc* fight in a public place. (chiefly legal – use **fight**).

affront [ə'frʌnt] *nc* word or act which

publicly and intentionally insults somebody. Also *vt*: *be affronted*.
afield [ə'fi:ld] *adv* at some distance from one's home: *go/wander far afield*.
afire [ə'faiə*] *adv/pred adj* burning (*o.f.* – use **on fire**).
aflame [ə'fleim] *adv/pred adj* burning.
afloat [ə'flout] *adv/pred adj* **1.** on the sea, river etc. **2.** spreading. *There's a rumour afloat that* . . . .
afoot [ə'fut] *adv/pred adj* going on; taking place. *Rumours/preparations were afoot*.
afore [ə'fɔ:*] *adv* (usu. in **aforementioned, aforesaid**) previously. (*formal* – use **previously**).
a fortiori ['eifɔ:ti'ɔ:ri:] for an even stronger or better reason.
afraid [ə'freid] *pred adj* feeling fear. *The travellers were afraid that they would be robbed. The small boy was afraid of the dark*.
be afraid (that) way of apologizing for saying something that is unpleasant for another person. *I'm afraid (that) I don't know. I'm afraid (that) I can't help you etc*.
afresh [ə'freʃ] *adv* again: *start afresh*.
after ['ɑ:ftə*] *adv/conj/prep* **1.** later in time: *after the meeting; after they had visited him; the day after tomorrow*. **2.** next in place; behind. *I was after him in the queue*. **3.** lower in rank: *a major comes after a general*. **4.** in pursuit of; in search of: *run after someone*.
'aftercare help or attention given to a patient after he has left hospital, to a prisoner after he has been released from prison etc.
'after-effect *nc* (usu. *pl*) effect which is experienced at a later time: *after-effects of an illness* i.e. the effects experienced after one has recovered from the illness.
'afterlife life after death.
after all see **all**.
after a fashion see **fashion**[2].
after you please go first (e.g. said when two people approach a door at the same time).
be named/called after someone see **name**[1].
one after another one following another, not all together.
take after someone see **take**.
aftermath ['ɑ:ftəmɑ:θ] *nu* what follows something: *the aftermath of war*.
afternoon ['ɑ:ftə'nu:n] *nc* period of the day between morning and evening (usu. between 12 or 1 p.m. and 4 or 5 p.m.).
afterwards ['ɑ:ftəwədz] *adv* later.
again [ə'gen] *adv* **1.** one more time. *Try again*. **2.** to the place or state in which one started etc. *Come home again. Get well again soon*. **3.** in addition; also; another point is.
twice/half as much again with an addition of twice/half the same amount.
against [ə'genst] *adv/prep* **1.** in opposition to: *act against somebody's wishes* i.e. do what somebody does not wish one to do. *That is against the law* i.e. the law says that must not be done; *be against war; protect against the cold*. **2.** touching or in contact with: *put something against the wall*. **3.** in contrast with something; with something as a background. *It is difficult to talk against this noise*. **4.** for, to prepare for. *They bought some warm clothes against the winter*.
age[1] [eidʒ] **1.** *nu* number of years somebody/something has lived or been in existence. *Children go to school in Britain at the age of five*. **2.** (*pl* in some phrases) period in history: *the Stone Age; the Middle Ages; the atomic age; in former ages*.
'age group people between certain ages thought of as a group.
be ages be slow; take a long time. *It's no use waiting for him, he'll be ages*. (*informal*).
come/be of age see **come**.
for ages for a long time. (*informal*).
take ages take a long time. *They took ages to mend the cooker*. (*informal*).
under age not old enough.
age[2] [eidʒ] *vi* show signs of growing old. *He is ageing rapidly*. *pres part* **ageing** or **aging**.
aged ['eidʒid] *adj* **1.** very old: *an aged man*. **2.** [eidʒd] of the age of: *a boy aged two*.
ageless *adj* old but appearing to be always young or new.
agenda [ə'dʒendə] *nc* (usu. *sing*) paper listing what is discussed at a meeting: *be on the agenda*.
agent ['eidʒənt] *nc* **1.** person whose work is to act for, or to manage the affairs of other people or companies. *He is an agent for Volkswagen* i.e. he is permitted to obtain goods from the Volkswagen company and sell them to the public. **2.** substance which produces an effect: *cleaning agents* i.e. things which clean, such as soap, water etc.
agency 1. *nc* business or office of somebody who acts for somebody else; permission to act for somebody else. *This company has the agency for Volkswagen*. see **agent**. **2.** *nu* action or effect: *the agency of acid on metal*. **3.** *nu* by means of. *He did it through the agency of his friends*.
agent-provocateur ['æʒɑ̃prɔvɔkæ'tə:*] *nc* person who works for the police or government, and who persuades criminals or enemies of the government to commit crimes so that they may be arrested.
aggrandizement [ə'grændizmənt] *nu* process of making oneself richer, stronger, more powerful etc (usu. by taking something from others).
aggravate ['ægrəveit] *vt* **1.** make worse. **2.** annoy. (*informal* and considered an incorrect use by some people; if in doubt use **annoy**). **aggravation** [ægrə'veiʃən] *nc/u*.
aggregate ['ægrigit] **1.** *nc* (often with reference to points or marks scored in a game, competition or examination) total. Also *adj*. Also ['ægrigeit] *vt*. **2.** *nu* mixture of sand, gravel and cement used in building.
aggression [ə'greʃən] *nc/u* attack; beginning of attack (often one made without good reason and often with reference to war made by one country against another): *commit an act of aggression against a neighbouring country*.
aggressive [ə'gresiv] *adj* fond of attacking others; attacking. **aggressively** *adv*. **aggressiveness** *nu*.
aggressor [ə'gresə*] *nc* country or person that commits aggression.
aggrieved [ə'gri:vd] *adj* angry and unhappy because somebody has done something wrong to one. *He was aggrieved at his friends' lack of interest in his success*.
aghast [ə'gɑ:st] *pred adj* having a strong feeling of shock, fear and dislike: *aghast at the suffering of war; aghast at the idea*.
agile ['ædʒail] *adj* moving easily; able to move easily and quickly. *She was still quite agile despite her age; an agile mind*. **agilely** *adv*. **agility** [ə'dʒiliti] *nu*.
agitate ['ædʒiteit] *vt/i* **1.** fill or become filled with feelings of fear and excitement. *He was agitated by the bad news*. **2.** move rapidly about; shake. **3.** ask very strongly that

something should be changed and made better. *The workers are agitating for higher wages and better conditions.*

agitation [ædʒi'teiʃən] *nu* **1.** feeling of fear and excitement. **2.** violent movement of sea or air. **3.** actions and speeches intended to cause trouble as a way of changing a situation (esp. a political situation).

agitator *nc* person who tries to bring about a political change by causing trouble (usu. an unfavourable word).

aglow [ə'glou] *adv/pred adj* **1.** shining with heat or light. *The house was aglow with lights.* **2.** bright, shining with excitement, after exercise, with health etc.

agnostic [æg'nɔstik] *nc* person who says that he does not know whether there is a God or not. Also *adj.* **agnosticism** [æg'nɔstisizəm] *nu.*

ago [ə'gou] *adv* in the past; before now: *three days ago; long ago. I left India a year ago.*

agog [ə'gɔg] *adv/pred adj* wishing very strongly to learn some news: *all agog to know what happened to John.*

agony ['ægəni] *nc/u* (often *pl*) great pain. *He suffered agonies in hospital.*

agonizing ['ægənaiziŋ] *adj* very painful. **agonizingly** *adv.*

in agony suffering great pain.

agrarian [ə'grεəriən] *adj* with reference to farming.

agree [ə'gri:] *vt/i* **1.** say or think the same as somebody else. *I agree with you.* **2.** allow somebody to do what he asks or suggests. *The headmaster agreed to the request for a half-term holiday.* **3.** say that one thinks something said by somebody else is true. *I agree we ought to try again.* **4.** come to the same idea after discussion. *We agreed on a date for the next meeting.* **5.** tell somebody else that one is willing to do something. *He agreed to help me.* **6.** be happy with; not quarrel with somebody. *John and his wife always agree.* **7.** have a good effect on one's health; not upset (one's stomach etc). *Pepper doesn't agree with me.* **8.** (grammar) go together in the same grammatical form. *The verb agrees with its subject in number and person.* (*opp* **disagree** except in senses **2.** and **8.**).

agreement *nc/u.* (*opp* **disagreement**).

agreeable *adj* **1.** pleasing and friendly. (*opp* **disagreeable**). **2.** willing to do something. *If you're agreeable we can start now.*

agreeably *adv.*

agriculture ['ægrikʌltʃə*] *nu* science or practice of farming. **agricultural** [ægri'kʌltʃərəl] *adj.* **agriculturalist** [ægri'kʌltʃərəlist] *nc.*

aground [ə'graund] *adv* (with reference to ships) at a place where the water has been too shallow for the ship to sail: *run aground.*

ahead [ə'hed] *adv* in front. *Walk ahead of me.*

ahoy [ə'hɔi] *interj* sound used by sailors to call somebody who is some distance away (esp. someone in another ship).

aid [eid] *nu* help (esp. help given by a rich country to a poorer one).

in aid of to help. *This money has been collected in aid of the dogs' home.*

aide-de-camp ['eiddə'kɑ̃] *nc* assistant to a senior army officer.

ail [eil] *vt* be wrong; trouble. *What ails him?* i.e. what is wrong with him?, what is causing him trouble? (*o.f.* – use **be wrong with, be the matter with**).

ailment ['eilmənt] *nc* illness (often a small and unimportant one).

aim[1] [eim] *vt/i* **1.** point or throw at somebody/something (usu. intending to hurt him or it): *aim a blow at somebody; aim a gun at the enemy; aim a camera* i.e. point a camera intending to take a photograph. **2.** intend; have in one's mind as the thing one wishes to do. *I aim to finish/at finishing this book by next week.*

aim[2] [eim] *nc* **1.** action of pointing a gun, throwing etc: *not a good aim* i.e. not hitting what was intended. **2.** intention; purpose; what one wishes to do. *His aim in life is to become rich.*

aimless *adj* without any plan or intention. **aimlessly** *adv.*

take aim prepare to throw, fire a gun etc.

ain't [eint] dialect pronunciation of **am not, is not, has not** or **have not.** see **be, have.**

air[1] [εə*] **1.** *nu* what we breathe; invisible, tasteless gases surrounding the earth. **2.** *nu* space above the earth: *fly in the air.* **3.** *nc* light wind. **4.** *nc* (music) tune. (rather *o.f.* – use **tune**). **5.** *nc* look, appearance. *He has a guilty air; to have an air of importance.*

'airborne *adj* (with reference to aeroplanes, bacteria etc) in the air.

'air conditioning method of making air in a building cooler, drier (or warmer and damper) than the air outside, so as to make the people in the building more comfortable.

'air-conditioned *adj* (with reference to a building, room etc) having machinery for changing the air in this way.

'aircraft *n sing* or *pl* aeroplane(s).

'aircraft carrier warship built so that aeroplanes can land on it and take off from it.

aircraft carrier

'airdrome see **aerodrome.**

'airdrop dropping of soldiers, materials and supplies from an aircraft in flight.

'airfield area of level ground where aeroplanes can land.

'airforce aeroplanes and men used for war and defence.

'airgun gun which fires a small metal object by using the pressure of air instead of gunpowder.

'airlift carrying of goods, men etc by air (at a time of need). Also *vt: airlift supplies.*

'airline company or state department whose business is to carry passengers and goods in aeroplanes.

'airliner *nc* large passenger aeroplane.

'airmail letters etc carried by aeroplane.

'airman member of an airforce.

'airplane see **aeroplane.**

'airport place where aeroplanes carrying passengers and goods start and land (esp. such a place near a large town or city e.g. *London Airport*).

'air raid attack from the air on a town or city.

'airsick *adj* feeling ill as a result of travelling in an aeroplane. **airsickness** *nu.*

'airspace sky above a country, which is considered by that country as part of its territory.
'airstrip small piece of land cleared of vegetation and flattened for aeroplanes to land on. (An **airstrip** is a much smaller place than an **airport**).
'airtight *adj* closed so that air cannot pass in or out.
'airworthy *adj* (of an aeroplane) in a safe condition for flying. **airworthiness** *nu*.
by air in an aeroplane: *send something to America by air.*
in the air **1.** (of a rumour, story, idea etc) being generally talked about. **2.** undecided. *Our plans to build a new house are still in the air at present.*
on the air sending out radio messages; broadcasting. *When the red light comes on, you're on the air.*
put on airs/give oneself airs act as though one were more important, better etc than one really is.
up in the air about very angry. (*informal*).
walk on air be very happy. (*informal*).

air² [ɛə*] *vt* leave something outside a house, near a window, uncovered etc, so that fresh air can get at it: *air clothes.*
aired *pred adj* **1.** (with reference to clothes) made ready for use (esp. after being washed) by being left in the fresh air or being dried in a warm place. **2.** (with reference to a bed) ready for use, having been left with the blankets pulled off the bed.
air one's views tell other people what one is thinking (often in order to find out what others are thinking).

airy ['ɛəri] *adj* **1.** with air moving about. **2.** not serious (and often quick and happy): *airy behaviour; an airy manner.* **airily** *adv.*

aisle [ail] *nc* way between blocks of seats in a church, classroom, theatre etc.
Note: the word *gangway* can also be used with this meaning, except for reference to a church, when *aisle* is generally the only word possible.

ajar [ə'dʒɑ:*] *adv* (with reference to a door) open a little way only.

akimbo [ə'kimbou] *adv* with arms as in the illustration: *stand with arms akimbo.*

akimbo

akin [ə'kin] *pred adj* **1.** similar. (*formal* – use **similar to**). **2.** members of the one family. (*formal* – use **related**).

à la carte [ælæ'kɑ:t] *adj/adv* chosen from a list of foods in a restaurant: *an à la carte meal.*

alacrity [ə'lækriti] *nu* quickness and willingness to do what is asked: *do something with alacrity.*

alarm [ə'lɑ:m] **1.** *nu* sudden fear caused by danger. **2.** *nc* warning of danger. *He gave the alarm when the thief appeared.* Also *vt* **1.** frighten. *I was alarmed when I heard the noise.* **2.** give warning to.
alarmist *nc* one who is always giving warnings of dangers which do not really exist.
a'larm clock clock which rings a bell at a time at which a person wishes to wake up.

alas [ə'læs] *interj* cry of unhappiness (*o.f.*).

albatross ['ælbətrɔs] *nc* very large bird living in the Pacific and South Atlantic.

albeit [ɔ:l'bi:it] *conj* although (*o.f.*).

albino [æl'bi:nou] *nc* **1.** person with a condition which causes very white skin and hair, and pink eyes. **2.** any animal or plant with a similar condition. *pl* **albinos.**

album ['ælbəm] *nc* book with blank pages to keep photographs or stamps in, or for people to write their signatures in.

albumen, albumin ['ælbjumin] *nu* **1.** the white part of an egg. **2.** one of a class of proteins found in the white of an egg, but also in many other animal and plant solids and fluids.

alchemy ['ælkimi] *nu* form of chemistry practised in the Middle Ages (esp. when concerned with attempts to turn other metals into gold).
alchemist *nc* person who studied this science.

alcohol ['ælkəhɔl] *nu* liquid contained in beer, wine, whisky etc, which causes these drinks to have an effect on people's minds and bodies; the drinks themselves.
alcoholic [ælkə'hɔlik] *adj.* Also *nc* person suffering from alcoholism. see below.
alcoholism *nu* illness caused by drinking too much alcohol.

alcove ['ælkouv] *nc* small room opening out of a bigger room, or a part of a big room divided from the main part in some way.

alderman ['ɔ:ldəmən] *nc* member of the local administration in England and America.

ale [eil] *nu* name given to various types of beer (*o.f.* – use **beer**).

alert [ə'lə:t] *adj* ready and waiting to act as soon as is necessary; quick to notice things. Also *nc* warning of some danger. Also *vt* give a warning of this kind. *The police have alerted all motorists to the need to drive carefully.*
on the alert watching and waiting for something to happen.

algebra ['ældʒibrə] *nu* branch of mathematics in which sums are worked out using letters for numbers which are unknown.
algebraic [ældʒi'breiik] *adj.*

alias ['eiliəs] *nc* name which is not one's own (often used for dishonest purposes). *John Smith alias Tom Brown* i.e. John Smith, who is also known as Tom Brown.

alibi ['ælibai] *nc* statement or fact that one was somewhere else when a crime was committed at a certain place: *have an alibi* i.e. be able to prove that one was somewhere else when a crime was committed.
Note: alibi is sometimes used to mean an excuse or reason. *His alibi for stealing the food was that he was hungry.* (This use is generally considered wrong – use *excuse* or *reason*).

alien ['eiliən] *nc* person living or working in a country which is not his own. (rather *formal* – use **foreigner**). Also *adj* **1.** foreign. **2.** very unlike; not what one would expect. *Kindness is quit alien to his nature* i.e. he is never kind.

alienate ['eiliəneit] *vt* **1.** make an enemy of

or lose the liking of by the way in which one behaves. *He alienated his sister by his unkindness. His sister was alienated from him by his unkindness.* 2. (legal) give away or take away goods, belongings.
alienation [eiliə'neiʃən] *nu* 1. losing somebody's liking. 2. giving or taking away goods, belongings.
alight[1] [ə'lait] *pred adj* burning.
alight[2] [ə'lait] *vi* get out of a vehicle, come down to the ground or to a resting place. *He alighted from the train. past* **alighted** or **alit** [ə'lit]. *Note: alit* is found in poetry.
align [ə'lain] *vt/i* come or bring into a straight line.
alignment 1. *nu* arrangement in a straight line. 2. *nc* friendship between countries: *the alignment between France and Germany.*
out of alignment not straight.
alike [ə'laik] *adv/pred adj* the same or not very different; in the same way. *They look alike* i.e. they have the same appearance.
alimony ['æliməni] *nu* regular supply of money paid under a court order by a man to a woman from whom he is divorced or separated.
alive [ə'laiv] *adv/pred adj* 1. not dead. 2. quick and active. 3. (with reference to ideas, influence, principles etc) still in use or having an effect etc.
look alive *interj* hurry up (*o.f.* – use **hurry up**).
be alive to know about; realize. *He was alive to the danger.*
alive with full of living things. *The kitchen was alive with ants.*
alkali ['ælkəlai] *nc* (chemistry) substance which forms salts when joined to an acid, and turns litmus paper blue. **alkaline** ['ælkəlain] *adj.*
all [ɔ:l] 1. *adj/determiner* every one of, the whole of: *all the pupils in the school; all the soup. All pupils must observe the rules.* 2. *pron* everything or everybody. *You'll find all you need in that box. All of them are going.* 3. *intensifier* completely: *all wrong; all finished.*
Note: 1. some people consider that it is incorrect to say *all of* with a noun: *all of the boys.* This usage is, however, very common. *all of* must be used before a pronoun: *all of us.* 2. *all* often comes after its noun (e.g. you can say either *All the boys wanted to* go or *The boys all wanted to* go).
all the better very much better. *I feel all the better for the rest.*
all but nearly: *all but empty.*
all at once suddenly.
all right 1. correctly; well. *Do you feel all right?* i.e. are you feeling well? 2. (used to show agreement) yes; certainly. *Will you do this? – All right, I'll do it.*
Note: the spelling *alright* is sometimes used, but it is considered wrong by some people.
all-'rounder man who is good at many sports, or at many parts of a particular sport.
all/just the same however; in spite of that. *He is rather boastful, but I like him all/just the same.*
all of a sudden without warning; unexpectedly.
all told including everything.
above all most importantly.
after all 1. (often to introduce an excuse or reason for not doing something) when everything is considered. *He doesn't work very hard, but after all, he is getting old.* 2. despite what was previously said. *I went to town after all* i.e. although I had earlier said that I would not.
at all (usu. in questions and negative sentences) even a little. *I don't remember him at all. He works seldom, if at all* i.e. perhaps he does no work.
be all ears be ready to listen to what someone has to say. (*informal*).
be all smiles/attention etc be full of smiles/attention etc.
be all up with somebody be finished (esp. having failed in some attempt). *It's all up with John; I don't think he will succeed now.* (*informal*).
go all out work, try etc with great effort and determination. (*informal*).
in all making a total of. *Six boys and two girls; that's eight in all.*
on all fours on one's hands and knees.
once and for all for the last time: *warn somebody once and for all.* (sometimes rather *impolite*; be careful about using this phrase).
not at all polite expression which one sometimes uses when someone thanks one. (It is not necessary to use this expression every time somebody thanks one).
allay [ə'lei] *vt* make less: *allay somebody's fear; allay the pain of a disease.*
allege [ə'ledʒ] *vt* give as a fact but without proof. **allegation** [æli'geiʃən] *nc.*
alleged *adj* said to have taken place: *the alleged crime.*
allegiance [ə'li:dʒəns] *nu* faithfulness and duty (esp. to a leader or an association that one is a member of).
allegory ['æligəri] *nc* story, intended to teach a lesson, in which either abstract ideas (such as hate, beauty, faithfulness) or animals, appear as though they were human beings. **allegorical** [æli'gɔrikl] *adj.*
allegorically *adv.*
alleluia [æli'lu:jə] *interj* see **hallelujah.**
allergy ['ælədʒi] *nc* condition in which one becomes ill or uncomfortable when brought into contact with something which usu. does not affect other people (in this way).
allergic [ə'lə:dʒik] *adj* 1. having an allergy. *He is allergic to fish* i.e. he becomes ill if he eats fish. 2. disliking intensely. (*informal* in sense 2.).
alleviate [ə'li:vieit] *vt* make less: *alleviate pain.* **alleviation** [əli:vi'eiʃən] *nu.*
alley ['æli] *nc* narrow street in a town (often dark and dirty).
alliance [ə'laiəns] *nc* joining together of countries or people in friendship.
allied ['ælaid] *adj* 1. joined together in agreement. 2. connected in some way. *Chemistry is allied to physics.* see **ally.**
in alliance joined in friendship or agreement.
alligator ['æligeitə*] *nc* large animal with long nose and sharp teeth which is found mostly in rivers in tropical America.
alliteration [əlitə'reiʃən] *nu* repeating the same sound at the beginning of a number of words (esp. in poetry e.g. *speak slowly and softly*). **alliterative** [ə'litərətiv] *adj.*
allocate ['æləkeit] *vt* give to someone for a purpose or as part of an arrangement. I *have allocated this room to you.* **allocation** [ælə'keiʃən] *nc/u.*
allot [ə'lɔt] *vt* give as a share. *past* **allotted.**
allotment *nc/u* used most often with reference to a piece of land. (For other purposes **allocation** is better).
allow [ə'lau] *vt/i* 1. say that somebody may

do what he wishes to do. *He allowed his children to go to the cinema.* **2.** give (esp. money). *He allowed his children fifteen pence a week.* **3.** keep or be prepared to use for a special purpose. *We must allow three days for travelling from London to Hong Kong.* **allowable** *adj.*
allowance *nc* amount of money given regularly to somebody for a special purpose. *He has an allowance from the government for travelling expenses.*
make allowances for remember somebody's difficulties or weakness when judging him for doing wrong, and so judge him less severely.
alloy ['ælɔi] *nc* substance made of two or more metals. Also *vt.*
allude [ə'lu:d] *vi* talk about something without mentioning it by name. *You mustn't even allude to his father's illness.*
allusion [ə'lu:ʒən] *nc/u.*
allusive [ə'lu:siv] *adj* making allusions; not direct. **allusively** *adv.*
allure [ə'ljuə*] *vt* make somebody do something (possibly something bad) by offering him something pleasant. Also *nu* attraction; charm. **alluring** *adj.*
allurement *nc* thing that tempts or attracts.
alluvial [ə'lu:viəl] *adj* (usu. with reference to soil, sand, gold etc) carried by running water.
alluvium *nu* mud, sand etc carried down by a river etc.
ally[1] ['ælai] *nc* person or country with whom one is joined in friendship, often in order to fight against somebody else or another country. see **alliance.**
ally[2] [ə'lai] *vt* join for a special purpose. *He allied himself to the other members of the society who supported his ideas.*
almanac ['ɔ:lmənæk] *nc* book with a list of the dates of (future) events during one year and often information about many other things as well.
almighty [ɔ:l'maiti] *adj* having the power to do anything.
The Almighty God.
almond ['ɑ:mənd] *nc* **1.** narrow, oval, light-brown nut. **2.** tree on which this nut grows.
almoner ['ɑ:mənə*] *nc* person who works in a hospital and who looks after the personal affairs of the patients.
almost ['ɔ:lmoust] *adv* nearly.
alms [ɑ:mz] *n sing* or *pl* money or goods given to help the poor (*o.f.* – use **charity**).
aloft [ə'lɔft] *adv/pred adj* above; a long way above the earth. (rather *o.f.*).
alone [ə'loun] *adv/pred adj* not with anybody or anything else: *work alone. He alone understands me; leave something alone* i.e. not touch or have anything to do with it.
let alone 1. (this expression is used with the general meaning that the thing already mentioned is enough in some way, and so the second idea introduced by **let alone** could not be attempted or considered) *I can't even read his writing, let alone understand his meaning* i.e. it is impossible to read his writing, and so I can't begin to try to understand his meaning. **2.** not bother. *Let me alone* i.e. don't bother me.
along [ə'lɔŋ] *adv/prep* onward or from end to end: *walk along the road.*
all along all the time. *He knew the answer all along, but he kept quiet.*
along with together with.
along'side by the side of (usu. a ship): *come alongside.*
aloof [ə'lu:f] *adv/pred adj* at some distance from other people (usu. in an unfriendly way): *stand/hold oneself aloof from somebody* i.e. not mix or talk very much with.
aloud [ə'laud] *adv.* so that one may be heard: *read aloud* i.e. speak the words one is reading. (*opp* **read to oneself** or **read silently**).
alpaca [æl'pækə] **1.** *nc* animal of Peru, which produces very soft wool. **2.** *nu* wool of this animal.
alpha ['ælfə] *nc* first letter in the Greek alphabet.
alpha and omega the first and last i.e. everything.
alphabet ['ælfəbet] *nc* letters used for writing a language.
alphabetical [ælfə'betikl] *adj* in the order of the alphabet, A first, B second, C third etc.
Note: the letters themselves (ABC etc) are referred to as *letters of the alphabet.* The plural *alphabets* can only be used to refer to the writing systems of various languages (e.g. *the alphabets of Russian and Greek*).
already [ɔ:l'redi] *adv* by or before a particular moment. *When we arrived, they were already there.*
alright ['ɔ:l'rait] *adv* all right. see **all.**
Note: this spelling is often thought incorrect.
Alsatian [æl'seiʃən] *nc* large intelligent dog, often trained for police work. Also (esp. *US*) **German Shepherd.**
also ['ɔ:lsou] *adv* in addition; besides; too. *John is also coming to the party.*
altar ['ɔ:ltə*] *nc* table, stone or other raised object which is the most important place in a building where a religious ceremony is held.
'altarpiece picture above an altar in a church.
lead a woman to the altar marry (*o.f.*).
alter ['ɔ:ltə*] *vt/i* change; become or make different.
alteration [ɔltə'reiʃən] *nc/u*: *make alterations* i.e. make changes.
alterable *adj* able to be altered. (*opp* **unalterable**).
altercation [ɔltə'keiʃən] *nc/u* noisy argument.
alternate[1] [ɔl'tə:nit] *adj* two things in turn, one thing and then the other and then the first and so on: *alternate stars and circles* i.e. *o*o*o etc; *on alternate days* i.e. Monday, Wednesday, Friday, Sunday etc. **alternately** *adv.*
alternate[2] ['ɔltə:neit] *vt/i* do a thing in turn (two people or two groups). *John and his sister alternate in coming to see me* i.e. John comes on one day, and his sister on the next etc. *John alternates hard work and/with laziness* i.e. he first shows hard work, then laziness, then hard work again etc. **alternation** [ɔltə:'neiʃən] *nc/u.*
alternating current electric current which flows first in one direction, then in the other at short, evenly timed intervals. (*opp* **direct current**).
alternative [ɔl'tə:nətiv] *adj* permitting a choice: *an alternative route.* Also *nc* one out of two or more choices. *The judge offered the criminal the alternative of a fine or six months in prison. You know the alternatives, now you must choose.* **alternatively** *adv.*
Note: some people use *alternative* only when there are two choices, not more, but many

people do not follow this rule.

although [ɔːl'ðou] *conj*: *Although the book is difficult to understand, it is interesting* i.e. the book is difficult to understand, but it is interesting.
Note: the difference between *although* and *though 1.* in the phrase *as though* we cannot use *although. 2. though,* but not *although,* is sometimes used after a clause, to mean that what was expected did not happen. *I went to town, I didn't see John though* i.e. I expected to see him but did not.

altimeter ['æltimiːtə*] *nc* instrument (e.g. in an aeroplane) which measures how high above sea level something is.

altitude ['æltitjuːd] *nc* (usu. with reference to aeroplanes or mountains) height above sea level. *Mt. Kenya has an altitude of over 17,000 feet.*

alto ['æltou] *nc* (music) **1.** highest adult male voice (above the tenor). **2.** lowest female voice. (Usu. **contralto**); person who sings with this type of voice. *pl* **altos.** Also *adj.*

altogether [ɔːltə'geðə*] *adv* **1.** completely; entirely. *The meeting was altogether a waste of time; an altogether stupid idea.* **2.** when all things are carefully considered. *Your plan would be very difficult and also dangerous, so altogether, I think it would be better to try something else.*
Note: most people would use *altogether* in the two senses given here, and *all together* with the meaning of with everybody or everything included. *He gathered his books all together. John and his friends were all together again.*

altruism ['æltruizəm] *nu* concern for what is best for other people rather than oneself. **altruist** *nc* person who concerns himself with the happiness of other people rather than himself. **altruistic** [æltru'istik] *adj.*

aluminium [ælju'miniəm] (*US* **aluminum** [ə'luːminəm]) *nu* light, silver-coloured metal, used for making parts of aeroplanes, saucepans etc.

always ['ɔːlweiz] *adv* at all times; on every occasion. *I will always remember her. George is always late for school.*

amalgam [ə'mælgəm] *nu* **1.** mixture of two substánces (esp. mercury and another metal). **2.** any mixture.
amalgamate [ə'mælgəmeit] *vt/i* (esp. with reference to two or more businesses or companies joining together) join together to form one thing. **amalgamated** *adj.* **amalgamation** [əmælgə'meiʃən] *nc/u.*

amass [ə'mæs] *vt* gather together a large amount of something (usu. wealth, information etc). *In his lifetime, he amassed a large fortune.*

amateur ['æmətəː*] *nc* **1.** (esp. with reference to playing football or other sports, playing music, painting pictures etc) person who does something because he enjoys doing it, and not for money or because it is his job. **2.** person who does something badly, because it is not his real job. Also *adj.* **amateurish** ['æmətəriʃ] *adj.*

amaze [ə'meiz] *vt* surprise very much. **amazement** *nu.*
amazing *adj* causing great surprise. **amazingly** *adv.*

ambassador [æm'bæsədə*] *nc* important government official whose work is to live in a foreign country and conduct business with the government of that country on behalf of his own government.
ambassadress [æm'bæsidris] *nc* **1.** female ambassador. **2.** wife of an ambassador.

amber ['æmbə*] *nu* **1.** type of hard orange or yellow substance used for making jewellery and other ornaments. **2.** (esp. with reference to traffic lights) colour of this substance. Also *adj.*

ambidextrous [æmbi'dekstrəs] *adj* using both hands equally well. **ambidextrously** *adv.*

ambience ['æmbiəns] *nu* surroundings. **ambient** *adj.*

ambiguous [æm'bigjuəs] *adj* **1.** having two or more different meanings. *The speaker gave an ambiguous reply.* **2.** doubtful; not clear. (*opp* **unambiguous**). **ambiguously** *adv.* **ambiguity** [æmbi'gjuiti] *nc/u.*

ambition [æm'biʃən] **1.** *nu* strong wish to do something (esp. to become rich, famous or successful). **2.** *nc* thing which one wishes to have. *My ambition is to be a rich man.*
ambitious *adj* **1.** having an ambition. **2.** needing a great deal of hard work if it is to succeed. *That is a very ambitious plan, but I hope it succeeds.* (*opp* **unambitious**). **ambitiously** *adv.*
achieve one's ambition get or become what one wants.

amble ['æmbl] *vi* **1.** (with reference to a horse) walk slowly, using the two legs on one side at the same time. **2.** (with reference to a person) walk without any hurry. *We ambled along the road together.*

ambrosia [æm'brouziə] *nu* **1.** food of the ancient Roman and Greek gods. **2.** anything that is pleasant to taste or smell.

ambulance ['æmbjuləns] *nc* vehicle for carrying the sick or injured to hospital.

ambush ['æmbuʃ] *vt* wait in hiding until one's enemies come past and then attack them by surprise. *The raiding party was ambushed in the forest.* Also *nc* **1.** attack made in this way. **2.** place where one hides to make an attack. **3.** people making such an attack.
lie in ambush for something wait in hiding and attack by surprise.

ameba [ə'miːbə] *nc* see **amoeba.**

ameliorate [ə'miːliəreit] *vt* make better or more pleasant: *ameliorate the conditions of the poor.* **amelioration** [əmiːliə'reiʃən] *nu.*

amen ['ɑː'men] *interj* word used at the end of a prayer, meaning 'May it be so' or 'May this prayer be granted'.
say amen to something approve of some hope or wish made by somebody.

amenable [ə'miːnəbl] *adj* **1.** willing to take advice, listen to the opinions of other people etc. *The young prince was amenable to the advice of his elders.* **2.** having to obey or follow a law etc. (*opp* **unamenable**).

amend [ə'mend] *vt/i* become or make better. *The new government amended the law.* **amendment** *nc/u* change (usu. in a law or rule).
make amends see **make**[1].

amenity [ə'miːniti] *nc* **1.** (usu. *pl*) something which helps to make life enjoyable (esp. in the place where one lives e.g. a cinema, a library, good roads etc). **2.** something pleasant and useful.

amiable ['eimiəbl] *adj* friendly and pleasant. *He is a very amiable person.* **amiably** *adv.* **amiability** [eimiə'biliti] *nu.*

amicable ['æmikəbl] *adj* friendly. **amicably** *adv.*

amid(st) [ə'mid(st)] *prep* in the middle of.

amiss [ə'mis] *adv/pred adj* wrong or wrongly: *something/not much amiss with it. As soon as I entered the house, I felt that there was something amiss* i.e. I felt that something was wrong.
take something amiss be angry or unhappy because of something said or done by somebody (usu. something which was not intended to have this effect).

amity ['æmiti] *nu* friendship (esp. between two or more countries).

ammeter ['æmitə*] *nc* instrument for measuring the strength of an electric current in amps (or amperes).

ammonia [ə'mouniə] *nu* **1.** strong-smelling gas. **2.** solution of this gas in water, used for cleaning clothes etc.

ammunition [æmju'niʃən] *nu* bullets, shells etc fired from a gun.
ammu'nition 'dump place where ammunition is stored by soldiers etc.

amnesia [æm'ni:ziə] *nu* illness in which a person cannot remember things.

amnesty ['æmnisti] *nc* pardon or forgiveness given by a government to people who have broken the law.

amoeba, ameba [ə'mi:bə] *nc* very small, simple type of animal life, of changing shape, living in water, unable to be seen without a microscope. *pl* **amoebas** or **amoebae** [ə'mi:bi:].
amoebic [ə'mi:bik] *adj* **1.** like an amoeba. **2.** (with reference to disease) caused by an amoeba: *amoebic dysentery*.

amok [ə'mɔk] see **amuck.**

among [ə'mʌŋ] *prep* surrounded by or with other things or people. *He lived among his own people for ten years.*
amongst [ə'mʌŋst] *prep* among.
Note: among usu. refers to more than two things or people; *between* can refer either to two or to more than two things or people.

amoral [æ'mɔrl] *adj* behaving or thinking in a way which does not recognize any difference between good and bad. see **immoral.**

amorous ['æmərəs] *adj* showing or having feelings of love; easily falling in love; concerned with love. **amorously** *adv.* **amorousness** *nu.*

amorphous [ə'mɔ:fəs] *adj* **1.** without definite shape, arrangement or order. **2.** (chemistry) in powder form. (*opp* **crystalline** in sense **2.**).

amount[1] [ə'maunt] *nc* (esp. of money) sum, quantity: *a small amount of money. A large amount of damage was done in a very short time.*

amount[2] [ə'maunt] *vi* **1.** (esp. of money) reach the total of, add up to. *The total cost of repairs amounted to sixty pounds.* **2.** be the same as; have the meaning of. *Keeping money which you find in the street amounts to stealing.*

amp [æmp], **ampere** ['æmpεə*] *nc* unit for measuring electric current (current that one volt can send through one ohm).

ampersand ['æmpəsænd] *nc* the sign '&' meaning 'and'.

amphibian [æm'fibiən] *nc* animal which can live on land and in water, such as a frog.
amphibious [æm'fibiəs] *adj* **1.** able to live on land and in water. **2.** by or for land and water: *amphibious attack; amphibious vehicle.*

amphitheatre ['æmfiθiətə*] *nc* **1.** round or oval building with seats all around an open unroofed area for sports, plays and other entertainments. **2.** part of a theatre in which the seats form a half circle.

ample ['æmpl] *adj* **1.** more than enough: *an ample supply of paper.* **2.** large; with plenty of space; big enough or more than big enough. *There is ample room for twelve desks here.* **amply** *adv.*

amplify ['æmplifai] *vt* make louder, fuller, greater etc, give more details etc. *The tunnel amplified the noise. Would you care to amplify that statement?* **amplification** [æmplifi'keiʃən] *nu.*
amplifier *nc* device for making sounds louder (esp. in a record player etc).

ampoule ['æmpu:l] *nc* glass container holding a quantity of a drug to be injected into a person.

amputate ['æmpjuteit] *vt* cut off part of the body for medical reasons. **amputation** [æmpju'teiʃən] *nc/u.*

amuck [ə'mʌk], **amok** [ə'mɔk] in **run amuck** i.e. be overcome by madness so that one runs about killing anyone one meets; act in a wild, uncontrolled way.

amulet ['æmjulit] *nc* something magical or religious which is worn on the body or carried about to protect one against harm.

amuse [ə'mju:z] *vt* make somebody laugh and be happy because of something funny. *The children were amused at/by the clown's jokes.*
amusement **1.** *nu* state of being amused. **2.** *nc* something which is amusing. **amusing** *adj.* **amusingly** *adv.*

an [æn, ən] *determiner* used before vowel sounds. see **a**[1].

anachronism [ə'nækrənizəm] *nc* use or mention of something in a story, play, film etc which could not have been mentioned or used at the time referred to by the story (e.g. it would be an anachronism if a story written today about Shakespeare spoke of him driving a car). **anachronistic** [ənækrə'nistik] *adj.*

anaconda [ænə'kɔndə] *nc* large South American snake which kills by crushing in its coils; any snake of this family.

anaemia [ə'ni:miə] (*US* **anemia**) *nu* illness in which a person does not have enough red corpuscles in the blood; this makes him very tired and weak. **anaemic** *adj.*

anaesthetic [ænis'θetik] (*US* **anesthetic**) *nc* liquid or gas which makes a person unable to feel pain, either by making him become unconscious, or by affecting one part of the body only, used by a doctor or dentist before operating on a person: *local anaesthetic* i.e. one which prevents pain being felt in one particular part of the body; *general anaesthetic.*
anaesthetics *npl* branch of medicine dealing with these substances.
anaesthesia [ænis'θi:ziə] *nu* lack of ability to feel pain etc.
anaesthetist [æ'ni:sθətist] *nc* person whose job it is to give an anaesthetic to a patient when a doctor is carrying out an operation.
anaesthetize [æ'ni:sθətaiz] *vt* cause to become unconscious by means of an anaesthetic.

anagram ['ænəgræm] *nc* word or phrase made by changing the order of letters in another word or phrase (e.g. *rat* is an anagram of *art*; *pain* is an anagram of *a pin*).

analgesic [ænæl'dʒi:sik] *nc* medicine which makes one feel less pain.

analogy [ə'nælədʒi] *nc/u* similarity or likeness; comparison between two things.

Shakespeare makes an analogy between the citizens of a country and the parts of a person's body. **analogous** [ə'næləgəs] *adj.*
argue by analogy argue by saying that because two things are similar or the same in one way, they must also be similar or the same in another way.

analyse ['ænəlaiz] (*US* **analyze**) *vt* examine something very carefully, and divide it into parts to see what it is made of, or what it actually is. *The food was carefully analysed to see if it contained anything harmful.*
analysis [ə'nælisis] *nc/u* careful examination in the manner described. *That newspaper has a very good analysis of the political situation.* *pl* **analyses** [ə'nælisi:z].
analyst ['ænəlist] *nc* **1.** person who analyses (esp. food, drugs, poisons, chemicals etc). **2.** see **psychoanalyst.**
in the last analysis when all the facts have been considered.

anapaest ['ænəpi:st] (*US* **anapest**) *nc* rhythm in poetry made up of two unstressed syllables followed by one stressed syllable (e.g. *with a 'leap and a 'bound*). **anapaestic** [ænə'pi:stik] *adj.*

anarchy ['ænəki] *nu* absence of law and government, so that each person does as he wishes (usu. causing harm to other people).
anarchism *nu* political belief that there should be no law or government in a country.
anarchist *nc* somebody who has this belief.

anathema [ə'næθimə] *nc/u* **1.** something which one dislikes very strongly. *Cigarette smoking is anathema to me.* **2.** solemn curse by one of the Christian churches, driving a person out of membership of the church.

anatomy [ə'nætəmi] *nu* **1.** science of the parts of the body. **2.** study of this science (usu. by medical students) by cutting up dead bodies of animals or human beings.
anatomical [ænə'tɔmikl] *adj.*
anatomist *nc* person who practises or knows this science.

ancestor ['ænsestə*] *nc* person's grandparents, great-grandparents, great-great-grandparents etc. (Not usu. with reference to a person's parents).
ancestral [æn'sestrl] *adj* coming from a person's ancestors. *They kept their ancestral customs.*
ancestry *nu* all the ancestors of a person.
trace one's ancestry (back to somebody) find out or know who one's ancestors were (to the earliest known ancestor, or to a famous ancestor).

anchor ['æŋkə*] *nc* heavy piece of iron attached to a rope or chain; it is lowered from a boat or ship to the bottom of the sea in order to prevent the ship from moving. Also *vt/i*: *The ship anchored in the harbour.*

anchor

anchorage *nc* place near the land where ships can anchor.
drop anchor see **drop**[2].
weigh anchor see **weigh.**
be/lie at anchor be unmoving, because the anchor has been lowered. *The ship was/lay at anchor all day.*
ride at anchor see **ride.**

anchovy ['æntʃəvi] *nc* type of small sea fish found in the Mediterranean.

ancient ['einʃənt] *adj* (esp. with reference to history) very old: *history of ancient Egypt; ancient monuments.*

ancillary [æn'siləri] *adj* helping something else which is more important: *ancillary services.*

and [ænd, ənd, ən] *conj* word which joins two or more words, phrases or clauses. *He likes books, films and plays. I like bread and butter* i.e. bread with butter on it. *He opened the door and looked round the room. Come and sit beside me. Come over here and I'll tell you a secret* i.e. if you come over here, I shall tell you a secret. *Wait and see* i.e. if you wait you will see.

anecdote ['ænikdout] *nc* short and often true story about some happening or person (usu. interesting or amusing).
anecdotal [ænek'doutl] *adj* full of or containing anecdotes.

anemone [ə'neməni] *nc* type of small, white wild flower found in woods; larger coloured kind often grown in gardens.
'sea anemone type of sea creature which looks a little like a flower.

aneroid ['ænərɔid] in **aneroid barometer** i.e. one which does not contain liquid.

anew [ə'nju:] *adv* again; in a new or different way (*o.f.* – use **again** etc).

angel ['eindʒəl] *nc* **1.** messenger of God (esp. in the Christian religion; usu. imagined as a beautiful person with wings). **2.** any very good person. (*informal* in sense **2.**).
angelic [æn'dʒelik] *adj* **1.** like or of an angel. **2.** (with reference to children) very well-behaved.

anger ['æŋgə*] *nu* feeling which makes one want to fight or quarrel with somebody who has done or said something wrong or hurtful. *He was filled with anger.* Also *vt* cause somebody to have this feeling by one's behaviour or words. *My explanation only angered him more.* see **angry.**

angle[1] ['æŋgl] *nc* size of the space made by two lines which meet at a point or by two surfaces which meet along one edge.

angle[2] ['æŋgl] *vi* **1.** try to catch fish with a rod and line. **2.** try to gain something without asking for it directly (usu. in a slightly deceitful or cunning way). *I think he was angling for a loan.*
angler *nc* person who tries to catch fish using a rod and line, for sport.
angling *nu* sport of catching fish in this way.

Anglican ['æŋglikən] *nc* member of, belonging to, the Church of England. Also *adj.*

anglicize ['æŋglisaiz] *vt* make English or make like English. *Many foreign town names are anglicized* (e.g. we say *Paris* not *Paree*).

Anglo- ['æŋglou] *prefix* English (e.g. *Anglo-French cooperation* i.e. cooperation between England and France).

angry ['æŋgri] *adj* **1.** having a feeling of anger. *Are you angry with him? What are you angry about?* **2.** (with reference to a wound, cut etc) red and painful-looking.
angrily *adv.* see **anger.**

anguish ['æŋgwiʃ] *nu* very great pain or unhappiness (esp. mental pain). **anguished** *adj.*

angular ['æŋgjulə*] *adj* **1.** with angles or

corners (esp. acute angles). **2.** (of a person) thin and with the bones showing under the skin.

animal ['æniml] *nc* **1.** living creature which is not a plant. **2.** living creature which is not a plant, a human, a bird, a fish, an insect or a reptile (e.g. a dog, a cat, a tiger). Also *adj*.

the 'animal 'kingdom all living creatures which are not plants.

'animal 'spirits natural happiness and playfulness such as children have (*o.f.*).

animate ['ænimeit] *vt* make alive; make active; make bright and lively. *When I showed the child a toy, curiosity animated his face.* Also ['ænimət] *adj* alive; living. (*opp* **inanimate**). **animation** [æni'meiʃən] *nu*.

animated *adj* full of ideas and arguments. *We had an animated discussion.* **animatedly** *adv*.

animated cartoon see **cartoon** (in sense **2.**).

animism ['ænimizəm] *nu* belief that there are spirits in trees, stones, plants etc.

animist *nc* person who has this belief.

animosity [æni'mɔsiti] *nu* strong hate or dislike. *I think that man feels great animosity towards you.*

aniseed ['ænisi:d] *nu* seed used for flavouring.

ankle ['æŋkl] *nc* part of the body between the foot and the leg.

anklet ['æŋklit] *nc* ring or band worn around the ankle for ornament, or by a prisoner.

annals ['ænəlz] *npl* history of what happened each year during a certain period.

annalist *nc* person who writes annals.

annex[1], annexe ['æneks] *nc* building near or joined to a bigger one, used because the bigger building is not big enough to hold all the people who want to use it: *build an annex to a school.*

annex[2] [ə'neks] *vt* take or join something to something else (often with reference to one country taking another country and ruling it).

annexation [ænek'seiʃən] **1.** *nu* act of annexing. **2.** *nc* something which has been annexed.

annihilate [ə'naiəleit] *vt* destroy something entirely, so that nothing is left. *The raiders annihilated the village.* **annihilation** [ənaiə'leiʃən] *nu*.

anniversary [æni'və:səri] *nc* date each year on which something happened in the past (e.g. if John and his wife got married on 15 February 1955, their wedding anniversary is 15 February every year).

annotate ['ænouteit] *vt* write or give written notes adding more information or explaining something hard to understand. *It is usually better to buy an annotated edition of a Shakespeare play.* **annotation** [ænou'teiʃən] *nc/u*.

announce [ə'nauns] *vt* say or make known something, so that everybody can hear or read it. *They have announced their wedding. The headmaster has announced that there will be a holiday tomorrow.* **announcement** *nc/u*.

announcer *nc* person who announces (esp. a person who reads the news and makes other announcements on the radio or television, or at a railway station etc).

annoy [ə'nɔi] *vt* do something which makes another person angry. *Children should not annoy their parents.* **annoyance** *nc/u*.

annoying *adj* causing somebody to be annoyed. **annoyingly** *adv*.

annual ['ænjuəl] *adj* taking place every year. **annually** *adv*.

annuity [ə'njuiti] *nc* fixed amount of money paid once a year to somebody.

annul [ə'nʌl] *vt* (usu. with reference to an agreement, law, rule etc) stop or end completely. *past* **annulled. annulment** *nc/u*.

anode ['ænoud] *nc* positive electrode in a battery etc. (*opp* **cathode**).

anoint [ə'nɔint] *vt* put oil on the head or body of somebody (esp. on the head of a king or queen who is being crowned).

anomalous [ə'nɔmələs] *adj* not following the usual or regular way; different from the others of a group.

anomaly *nc* something which does not follow the normal rule; something which is different. *A school with no books in it would be an anomaly these days.*

anonymous [ə'nɔniməs] *adj* written, made etc by a person whose name is not given or is not known. *He received an anonymous gift/letter/phone call etc. This poem is anonymous.* **anonymously** *adv*.

anonymity [ænə'nimiti] *nu* state of not giving one's name, or of one's name not being known.

anon short form of **anonymous,** written in books of poetry etc when the author of a poem is unknown.

anorak ['ænəræk] *nc* jacket with hood, which keeps out wind and rain.

another [ə'nʌðə*] *adj/pron* one more; a different one. *He ordered another drink. I don't like this shirt; show me another one.*

answer[1] ['ɑ:nsə*] *vt/i* **1.** say or write something in reply to what somebody else has said or written: *answer a question/a letter; answer somebody.* **2.** be satisfactory. *This plan will not answer our needs.*

answerable **1.** able to be answered. (*opp* **unanswerable**). **2.** in charge of; likely to be blamed or punished if something is found to be wrong.

answer back argue or be impolite when one is being told by somebody that one has done wrong.

answer for someone/something **1.** be responsible for someone/something or be blamed and punished. **2.** say that one believes that someone is honest, well-behaved etc. *I can answer for his honesty.*

answer the door/telephone open the door when somebody knocks or rings the bell/lift the telephone when it rings.

answer to a description/name look like the description given or have the name of (used esp. when looking for a pet animal that is missing). *Have you seen anyone answering to this description? The dog answers to the name Fido.*

answer[2] ['ɑ:nsə*] *nc* **1.** what is said, written etc when one answers somebody/something. **2.** correct result of a sum or calculation.

ant [ænt] *nc* small insect which can carry things heavier than itself.

'anteater one of the various types of animal which eats ants, particularly those found in tropical America.

'ant-hill **1.** heap of earth in which ants have their nest. **2.** any place in which there is a very large number of people and a lot of activity.

antagonism [æn'tægənizəm] *nu* feeling of hate or dislike for an enemy or person to whom one is opposed.

antagonist *nc* enemy or person with whom one is fighting, quarrelling.

antagonistic [æntægə'nistik] *adj* having feelings of hate or dislike towards an enemy.

antagonize *vt* make a person dislike one. *Do not antagonize that man, he is dangerous.*

Antarctic [ænt'ɑːktik] *adj* belonging to the region round the South Pole. Also *n*.

ante- ['ænti] *prefix* before (e.g. **antedate**). *Note:* do not confuse with *anti-* which means *against*.

antecedent [ænti'siːdnt] *nc* **1.** something which happened before something else. **2.** (grammar) noun or noun clause to which a pronoun refers. **3.** (usu. *pl*) past experience or history of a person/thing.

antedate [ænti'deit] *vt* **1.** have a date earlier than something else i.e. be older. **2.** put a date earlier than the correct one on a letter, cheque etc. (*opp* **postdate**).

antediluvian ['æntidi'luːviən] *adj* **1.** happening before Noah's Flood. **2.** happening a very long time ago. **3.** out-of-date.

antelope ['æntiloup] *nc* animal with horns, found in Africa and Asia, which can run very fast.

antenatal [ænti'neitl] *adj* before the birth of a baby: *antenatal clinic* i.e. a place where pregnant women are given medical care. (*opp* **postnatal**).

antenna [æn'tenə] *nc* **1.** one of the two feelers on the head of an insect. **2.** wire used in radio or television for sending or receiving radio waves; aerial. *pl* **antennae** [æn'teniː].

anteroom ['æntirum] *nc* small room leading into a bigger one.

anthem ['ænθəm] *nc* **1.** official song or piece of music of a country (usu. **national anthem**). **2.** any song of praise (esp. one sung in a Christian church with words from the Bible).

anthology [æn'θɔlədʒi] *nc* book of poems or prose passages written by more than one author.

anthologist *nc* person who makes an anthology.

anthracite ['ænθrəsait] *nu* hard type of coal, which burns very slowly, with little smoke or flame.

anthrax ['ænθræks] *nu* disease of sheep and cattle, which can also be caught by human beings.

anthropoid ['ænθrəpɔid] *adj* (usu. with reference to gorillas or chimpanzees etc) shaped like a man. Also *nc* large ape of this kind.

anthropology [ænθrə'pɔlədʒi] *nu* study of the beliefs, customs, and way of life of human beings. **anthropologist** *nc*. **anthropological** [ænθrəpə'lɔdʒikl] *adj*.

anthropomorphism [ænθrəpə'mɔːfizəm] *nu* process of regarding non-human things as being like humans in appearance or nature (e.g. regarding God as an old man with a beard). **anthropomorphic** *adj*.

anti- ['ænti] *prefix* against (e.g. **anti-aircraft; antisocial**). *Note:* do not confuse with *ante-* which means *before*.

anti-aircraft ['ænti'ɛəkrɑːft] *adj* for use in fighting against enemy aeroplanes: *anti-aircraft gun*.

antibiotic ['æntibai'ɔtik] *nc* drug or medicine which works by destroying the germs causing an illness. *Penicillin is an antibiotic.* Also *adj*.

antibody ['æntibɔdi] *nc* (often *pl*) substance in the body which attacks and destroys harmful germs and poisons.

antic ['æntik] *nc* (usu. *pl*) funny or foolish action (usu. made to cause laughter); amusing behaviour (esp. by an animal or a child). *The child's antics made us laugh.*

anticipate [æn'tisipeit] *vt* **1.** expect and think about something before it happens. *We did not anticipate any trouble.* **2.** do something before somebody else does it or asks for it. **3.** do something before the proper time. **anticipation** [æntisi'peiʃən] *nu*.

anticlimax ['ænti'klaimæks] *nc* occurrence of something foolish, unimportant, funny or unpleasant, when one had been expecting something of the opposite kind, something important, serious etc. *I thought the end of the story was an anticlimax.*

anti-colonialism ['æntikə'louniəlizəm] *nu* opposition to, or hatred of, colonialism.

antidote ['æntidout] *nc* **1.** medicine which stops the effect of a poison. **2.** anything which stops something bad or unpleasant. *Hard work is an antidote for unhappiness.*

antifreeze ['æntifriːz] *nu* substance added to the water in the radiator of a car to prevent freezing in cold weather.

antimissile ['ænti'misail] *nc* weapon designed to destroy an atomic missile.

antipathy [æn'tipəθi] *nu* strong and unchanging feelings of dislike.

antipodes [æn'tipədiːz] *npl* places at the opposite side of the world from where one lives (esp. Australia and New Zealand, which are the antipodes for people in Britain). **antipodean** [æntipə'diən] *adj*.

antiquarian [ænti'kwɛəriən] *nc* person who studies or collects objects made in ancient times. (Also **antiquary** ['æntikwəri]). Also *adj* concerned with old things.

antiquarianism *nu* interest in, or study of, objects made in ancient times.

antiquated ['æntikweitid] *adj* (usu. with reference to objects or ideas) of no use or interest, because very old.

antique [æn'tiːk] *adj* (usu. with reference to objects) very old. Also *nc* very old and valuable object.

Note: if we call something *antiquated* we mean that it is of no use or value; if we call it *antique* we mean that it is old and valuable.

antiquity [æn'tikwiti] **1.** *nu* the distant past (esp. the time of the Greeks and Romans). **2.** *nu* great age. *This house is of great antiquity* i.e. it is very old. **3.** (in *pl*) objects and buildings remaining from the past.

anti-Semitic ['æntisə'mitik] *adj* hating or disliking Jews. **anti-Semite** [ænti'siːmait] *nc*. **anti-Semitism** [ænti'semitizəm] *nu*.

antiseptic [ænti'septik] *adj* preventing the growth of germs and the spread of disease. Also *nc* substance which has this effect.

antisocial [ænti'souʃl] *adj* **1.** against the ideas of what is good which most people in society have agreed on (e.g. stealing, causing trouble to other people and murder are antisocial acts). **2.** unfriendly, not wanting any friends.

antithesis [æn'tiθisis] *nc* **1.** opposite of something. *Laughter is the antithesis of tears.* **2.** statement in which two ideas (usu. opposite in meaning) are presented in two sentences, phrases etc which are similar in form (e.g. *Many are called but few are chosen*). *pl* **antitheses** [æn'tiθisiːz].

antitoxin ['ænti'tɔksin] *nc* drug, medicine or substance in the body which stops a poison from doing any harm to a person.
antler ['æntlə*] *nc* (often *pl*) horn of a deer.

antlers

antonym ['æntənim] *nc* word which means the opposite of another word (e.g. *big* is the antonym of *small*) (*opp* **synonym**).
anus ['einəs] *nc* part of the body from which solid waste matter is sent out.
anvil ['ænvil] *nc* large block of iron or steel on which a blacksmith shapes metal.

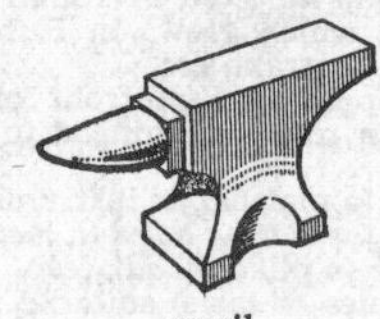
anvil

anxiety [æŋ'zaiəti] *nc/u* feeling of fear and uncertainty about what is going to happen.
anxious ['æŋkʃəs] *adj* **1.** filled with fear and uncertainty. *He is very anxious about the results of his test.* **2.** filled with a strong wish to do something. *The people here are very anxious to help you.* **anxiously** *adv*.
any ['eni] *determiner* **1.** one, it does not matter which. *Take any book you want to. Come any time you like. Any kind of box will do.* **2.** *determiner/pron/intensifier* (esp. in *negative* and *interrogative* sentences) some. *Have you got any children besides John? Do you want any of these? Can't this car go any faster? I don't want any more.*
'**anybody** *pron* any person.
'**anyhow** *adv* **1.** in any way. **2.** in a careless way. *He leaves his books about anyhow.* **3.** whatever happens. *The teacher will forbid it, but you must do it anyhow.* (*informal*).
'**anyone** *pron* any person.
'**anything** *pron* any thing.
'**anyway** *adv* whatever happens. *I know it is dangerous but you must go there anyway.*
'**anywhere** *adv* in or to any place.
apace [ə'peis] *adv* quickly (*o.f.*).
apart [ə'pɑːt] *adv* **1.** in or into separate pieces or parts: *take a watch apart.* **2.** away from; at a distance from other things or people: *stand apart from other people.*
apartheid [ə'pɑːtait] *nu* official policy of the South African government, of not allowing people of different races to work together, meet each other, have the same rights etc.
apartment [ə'pɑːtmənt] *nc* **1.** (*Brit*) separate room in a house. **2.** (*US*) set of rooms on a single floor of a building. *He lives in an apartment, not a house.* (*Brit* **flat**).
apathy ['æpəθi] *nu* lack of interest or feeling. *There is too much apathy about the need for further education.*
apathetic [æpə'θetik] *adj* having no interest or feeling.
ape[1] [eip] *nc* **1.** large monkey with no tail (esp. a gorilla, chimpanzee, orang-utan or gibbon). **2.** large clumsy person.
ape[2] [eip] *vt* copy somebody, do the same thing as somebody (as an ape copies the movements of human beings).
aperient [ə'piəriənt] *nc* medicine which helps one to get rid of waste matter in the bowels.
aperitif [ə'peritiv] *nc* drink (usu. alcoholic) which is taken before a meal to increase one's appetite.
aperture ['æpətjuə*] *nc* small hole (esp. one which lets light come in) (e.g. a camera has an aperture through which light passes to the film).
apex ['eipeks] *nc* top (esp. of a triangle); highest point.
aphasia [ə'feiziə] *nu* disease in which a person forgets all or part of his own language.
aphasic *adj*. Also *nc* person having this disease.
aphorism ['æfərizəm] *nc* short and clever or wise statement.
aphrodisiac [æfrou'diziæk] *nc* any substance which arouses or increases sexual feelings. Also *adj*.
apiece [ə'piːs] *adv* for each one.
aplomb [ə'plɔm] *nu* self-confidence; belief in one's own abilities: *do something with aplomb.*
apocalypse [ə'pɔkəlips] *nc* violent events destroying an established order (esp. the prophesied end of the world). **apocalyptic** [əpɔkə'liptik] *adj*.
apocrypha [ə'pɔkrifə] *nu* (usu. with reference to fourteen books, called the **Apocrypha**, which are included in the Roman Catholic bible but not in the Protestant bible) stories, ideas etc not accepted as genuine.
apocryphal *adj* probably untrue, although it is said to be true: *apocryphal story.*
apogee ['æpoudʒiː] *nc* **1.** point in the path of the moon or in the path of a planet round the sun when it is farthest from the earth. (*opp* **perigee**). **2.** highest point of something: *the apogee of his success.*
apology [ə'pɔlədʒi] *nc* statement that one is sorry.
apologize *vi* say that one is sorry for doing wrong. *He apologized for his mistake.*
apologetic [əpɔlə'dʒetik] *adj* excusing oneself. **apologetically** *adv*.
apoplexy ['æpəpleksi] *nu* illness in which one cannot move or think, caused when blood is stopped from reaching the brain. *Note: apoplexy* is rather *o.f.* people usually call the illness a *stroke*.
apoplectic [æpə'plektik] *adj* **1.** suffering from or causing apoplexy. **2.** very red in the face (and usu. very angry).
apostasy [ə'pɔstəsi] *nu* leaving one's religious faith.
apostate [ə'pɔstit] *nc* person who leaves his religion.
apostatize [ə'pɔstətaiz] *vi* leave one's own religion.
apostle [ə'pɔsl] *nc* **1.** one of the original twelve followers of Jesus Christ. **2.** any follower of a great man. **3.** leader of a new movement or belief.
apostolic [æpəs'tɔlik] *adj* **1.** of the twelve Apostles. **2.** of the Pope.
apostrophe [ə'pɔstrəfi] *nc* the mark ', as in *John's book* or *I've read that book.*
apothecary [ə'pɔθikəri] *nc* person who makes drugs and sells them in his shop (*o.f.* – use **chemist** or **pharmacist**).
apotheosis [əpɔθi'ousis] *nu* making a

human being into an object of worship.

appal [ə'pɔ:l] *vt* fill with a strong feeling of dislike and shock. *The number of people killed on the roads appals me. past* **appalled.** **appalling** *adj.* **appallingly** *adv.*

apparatus ['æpəreitəs] *nu* instruments, equipment, tools needed for a certain purpose.

apparel [ə'pærl] *nu* clothes (*o.f.* – use **clothes**). Also *vt* dress; put clothes on (*o.f.* – use **dress** or **clothe**). *past* **apparelled.** (*US* **appareled**).

apparent [ə'pærənt] *adj* **1.** easily seen or understood. *It's quite apparent that you do not understand me.* **2.** appearing or seeming to be true (although it may not in fact be true).

apparently *adv* it seems that . . . as far as one can judge etc. *Apparently he is a good player, although I have never seen him play myself.*

apparition [æpə'riʃən] *nc* appearance, or coming into sight of something (esp. a ghost or spirit).

appeal [ə'pi:l] *vi* **1.** ask very earnestly or seriously. *The teacher appealed to John to work harder.* **2.** ask for. *The injured man appealed for help. The prisoner appealed for one more chance.* **3.** interest. *This book does not appeal to children* i.e. is not interesting to them. **4.** ask somebody in a position of authority to change a decision made by somebody in a lower position. *Thousands of people appealed to the queen to pardon the condemned man.* Also *nc/u*: *make an appeal to somebody; have no appeal for somebody; make an appeal to a higher court.*

appealing *adj* pleasing or attractive in a touching way.

appear [ə'piə*] *vi* **1.** come into sight; be seen. *A face suddenly appeared at the window.* **2.** seem, look. *He appeared to be happy* i.e. he looked happy (but he may have been unhappy). *It appears that I am wrong* i.e. it seems, I am beginning to think that I am wrong. **3.** (with reference to an actor, singer, speaker etc) perform or be seen by an audience.

appearance *nc* **1.** coming into sight, being seen. (*opp* **disappearance**). **2.** what can be seen of somebody/something. *He has a friendly appearance* i.e. he looks friendly (but in fact he may not be). **3.** (with reference to an actor, singer etc) act of coming before an audience.

make an appearance appear; be seen.

judge by appearances decide whether something/somebody is good or bad etc by looking at what can be seen, and not considering what cannot be seen. *It is often a mistake to judge people by appearances.*

appease [ə'pi:z] *vt* make quiet, calm, friendly etc by giving what is wanted: *appease somebody* i.e. make somebody friendly by giving him what he wants; *appease somebody's curiosity* i.e. tell somebody what he wants to know. **appeasement** *nu.*

appellation [æpə'leiʃən] *nc* name or title (*o.f.*).

append [ə'pend] *vt* add or join something (esp. in writing).

appendage *nc* something added to a bigger thing.

appendicitis [əpendi'saitis] *nu* disease in which the appendix becomes very painful.

appendix [ə'pendiks] *nc* **1.** part of the inside of the body below the stomach. **2.** extra information found at the end of a book. *pl* **appendixes** or **appendices** [ə'pendisi:z].

appertain [æpə'tein] *vi* (with **to**) belong to; be a proper part of; be concerned with or related to.

appetite ['æpitait] *nc/u* strong wish (esp. for food).

appetizing *adj* making one want to eat. *Some very appetizing smells were coming from the kitchen.* (*opp* **unappetizing**). **appetizingly** *adv.*

have a good appetite be ready and able to eat one's food.

lose one's appetite stop wanting to eat (e.g. when one is ill).

applaud [ə'plɔ:d] *vt/i* show that one likes something/somebody (usu. by clapping the hands): *applaud an actor.*

applause [ə'plɔ:z] *nu* clapping of one's hands to show that one likes something/somebody.

apple ['æpl] *nc* type of round fruit with firm flesh which grows in Europe, North America, Australia etc.

Adam's apple part of front of throat, a hard lump more prominent in men than women.

appliance [ə'plaiəns] *nc* instrument or tool: *appliance for cutting holes in metal.*

applicable [ə'plikəbl] *adj* (esp. with reference to rules or laws) suitable to be used. *This rule is not applicable to government employees* i.e. government employees do not have to follow this rule. (*opp* **inapplicable**). **applicability** [əplikə'biliti] *nu.*

applicant ['æplikənt] *nc* person who asks for something (esp. for a post or job).

application [æpli'keiʃən] **1.** *nc* asking for something. *We have received twenty applications for this post.* **2.** *nc* putting something into use, way of using. *I don't understand the application of this word* i.e. how the word is to be used; *application of scientific knowledge to the development of agriculture.* **3.** *nu* act of putting something on something: *application of ointment to a wound; application of the brake.* **4.** *nu* hard work. *By application to his studies he succeeded in gaining a better job.*

on application to somebody by asking somebody. *Special permission may be received on application to the headmaster.*

apply [ə'plai] *vt/i* **1.** ask for. *Nobody applied for the reward.* **2.** put something on: *apply an ointment.* **3.** put something into use. *You must apply your intelligence if you hope to succeed. He applied the brake. We must apply our scientific knowledge to solving the problems of mankind.* **4.** be suitable to be used or considered. *This rule does not apply in Scotland* i.e. this rule is not followed in Scotland. *What I have just said does not apply to you* i.e. I was not referring to you; I did not mean you.

applied *adj* put to use: *applied mathematics; applied science.* (*opp* **pure mathematics/science** etc).

apply oneself work very hard. *John applied himself to his studies.*

appoint [ə'pɔint] *vt* **1.** give somebody a job or position. *They appointed Mr Jones headmaster.* **2.** decide on. *We must appoint a date for our next meeting.*

appointment *nc* **1.** job or position. **2.** arrangement or agreement to meet somebody. *John has an appointment with his housemaster today.*

break an appointment fail to come to meet

somebody after arranging to do so.
keep an appointment meet somebody as promised in a previous arrangement. *You can rely on him to keep an appointment.*
make an appointment arrange to meet somebody.

apportion [ə'pɔːʃən] *vt* share out; divide among a number of people/things by following some rule. *The food was apportioned equally to everyone.*

apposite ['æpəzit] *adj* well-chosen and very suitable. *That was a very apposite remark you made at the meeting.* **appositely** *adv.*

apposition [æpə'ziʃən] *nu* (grammar) way of putting an extra word or extra words into a sentence so as to give more information (e.g. in the sentence *Mr Jones, the new headmaster, is arriving today,* the words 'the new headmaster' are in apposition to 'Mr Jones').

appraise [ə'preiz] *vt* judge how good, valuable, useful etc something/somebody is. *An expert came to appraise the value of my antiques.*
appraisal [ə'preizl] *nc/u* suggestion, opinion or idea of how good, valuable, useful etc something/somebody is.

appreciable [ə'priːʃəbl] *adj* enough to be seen, felt, noticed (often in **to make an appreciable difference** i.e. to be different enough to be seen or felt or noticed etc).
appreciably *adv.*

appreciate [ə'priːʃieit] **1.** *vt* be thankful for something. *We appreciate everything that you have done for us.* **2.** *vt* understand and like something (e.g. poetry, music, art). *He appreciates good music.* **3.** *vi* become more valuable. *The value of this land has appreciated greatly recently.* **appreciation** [əpriːʃi'eiʃən] *nu.*
appreciative [ə'priːʃiətiv] *adj* **1.** showing thanks. **2.** showing understanding and liking. (*opp* **unappreciative**). **appreciatively** *adv.*

apprehend [æpri'hend] *vt* **1.** arrest, take and hold (a criminal). *The police apprehended three men yesterday.* **2.** fear or worry about what will happen. **3.** understand.
apprehension *nu.*
apprehensive *adj* frightened; full of fear; worried about what will happen. *That lady is very apprehensive about being attacked by thieves.* **apprehensively** *adv.*

apprentice [ə'prentis] *nc* person (usu. young) who works at some skilled trade or job for a number of years and receives very little money. (The apprentice is taught how to do the job properly during this time). Also *adj.* Also *vt* make somebody an apprentice. *Mr Smith apprenticed his son to an engineer.*
apprenticeship *nc* **1.** state of being an apprentice. **2.** time during which somebody is an apprentice.

apprise [ə'praiz] *vt* tell, inform: *apprise someone of something* (*o.f.*).

approach[1] [ə'proutʃ] *vt/i* **1.** move near. **2.** ask somebody for something or offer something to somebody. *He approached the headmaster with a request for some advice.*

approach[2] [ə'proutʃ] *nc/u* **1.** coming near. **2.** asking for something or suggesting something. **3.** road or path to a place. **4.** way of beginning to learn or do something. *There is no very easy approach to mathematics.*
approachable *adj* able to be approached. *The house is approachable by a path* i.e. one can reach it by a path. *The headmaster is approachable* i.e. he likes people to ask him for things, or to make suggestions to him. (*opp* **unapproachable**).

approbation [æprə'beiʃən] *nu* saying or thinking that somebody/something is good; approval.

appropriate[1] [ə'proupriət] *adj* proper; suitable; correct for a particular purpose. *What kind of badge would be appropriate for our new school?* (*opp* **inappropriate**).
appropriately *adv.*

appropriate[2] [ə'proupriet] *vt* **1.** keep for a certain purpose. *We have appropriated a small amount of money for office supplies.* **2.** take something belonging to somebody else; steal. **appropriation** [əproupri'eiʃən] *nc/u.*

approve [ə'pruːv] *vt/i* think or say that one is satisfied or pleased with something. *I must say I approve of that boy's fondness for hard work.* (*opp* **disapprove**).
approval *nu* **1.** feeling or showing satisfaction with something. (*opp* **disapproval**). **2.** permission for a plan etc.
approve a plan/scheme/project etc give permission to somebody to carry out the plan etc.
approved school special school for children who have committed various offences against the law.
have something on approval have goods from a shop or manufacturer with the agreement that one can return the goods if one wishes.

approximate[1] [ə'prɔksimət] *adj* not far from correct or exact; based on a guess or memory or without the need to be exactly right.
approximately *adv* roughly. *There were approximately 50 people there.*

approximate[2] [ə'prɔksimeit] *vt/i* come or be close to the correct answer, amount etc.
approximation [əprɔksi'meiʃən] *nc* something close to correct.

appurtenance [ə'pəːtinəns] *nc* anything added to a more important thing (esp. a small privilege attached to more important duties).

apricot ['eiprikɔt] *nc* **1.** small, sweet, yellow fruit with a stone in the middle, growing in cool regions. **2.** the tree on which this fruit grows.

April ['eiprl] *n* fourth month of the year.

apron ['eiprn] *nc* **1.** piece of cloth or other material worn over the front of the body to keep one's clothes clean while working. **2.** part of an airfield in front of hangars.

apron (*def 1*)

'apron 'stage (theatre) type of stage which projects out into the audience.
tied to someone's apron strings (with reference to a man) too much under the influence or control of a woman. (*informal*).

a propos [æprə'pou] *adv* (usu. with **of**) on the subject of.

apse [æps] *nc* rounded or many-sided area at the eastern end of a church.

apt [æpt] *adj* **1.** likely; inclined. *John is apt to be careless* i.e. he is often careless. **2.** suitable; fitting: *an apt remark* i.e. a remark which meant a lot at the time it was made. **3.** quick at learning: *a very apt pupil.*
aptitude ['æptitjuːd] *nu* **1.** ability to learn easily and quickly. *John has an aptitude for mathematics* i.e. he learns mathematics with very little effort. **2.** suitability; way in which something is suitable or fitting.

aqualung ['ækwəlʌŋ] *nc* apparatus which enables a swimmer to breathe under water.

aquarium [ə'kwɛəriəm] *nc* **1.** glass tank or bowl in which fish and other sea creatures are kept. **2.** building in a zoo etc in which fish can be seen. *pl* **aquariums** or **aquaria** [ə'kwɛəriə].

aquatic [ə'kwætik] *adj* living in or near, taking place in, water. *Seals are aquatic animals. He is fond of aquatic sports.*

aqueduct ['ækwidʌkt] *nc* canal or pipe for carrying water (esp. one built of stone etc carrying water on arches over a valley).

aqueous ['eikwiəs] *adj* full of water; containing water; formed by water.

aquiline ['ækwilain] *adj* long and thin (like the beak of an eagle): *aquiline nose.*

arabesque [ærə'besk] *nc* type of decoration in which there are many loops and curves.

arable ['ærəbl] *adj* used for growing crops on: *arable land; arable farming* i.e. growing crops, rather than breeding animals.

arbitrate ['ɑːbitreit] *vt/i* act as judge; decide what is right when people are quarrelling or disagreeing (usu. at the request of the people quarrelling).
arbitrator *nc* person who arbitrates.
arbitration [ɑːbi'treiʃən] *nu*: *The dispute between the workers and the employers went to arbitration* i.e. someone else decided between them.
arbiter ['ɑːbitə*] *nc* person given the power to judge between people who are quarrelling or disagreeing.
arbitrary ['ɑːbitrəri] *adj* based on somebody's wishes, feelings or opinions and not on what is just or lawful. *This is just an arbitrary decision.* **arbitrarily** *adv.*

arbour ['ɑːbə*] (*US* **arbour**) *nc* place in a garden under the shade of trees or bushes (and usu. with a seat).

arboreal [ɑː'bɔːriəl] *adj* with reference to trees; like trees; living in trees.

arc [ɑːk] *nc* **1.** part of a circle. **2.** electric current jumping across a gap between two conductors. Also *vi* (with reference to an electric current) jump across a gap in this way.
'arc light, 'arc lamp electric lamp in which the light is given by an electric arc.

arcade [ɑː'keid] *nc* passage or street covered by a roof (usu. with shops in the passage etc).

arch[1] [ɑːtʃ] *nc* **1.** part of a building or of a bridge, with curved shape as in the illustration. **2.** curved part underneath the foot.

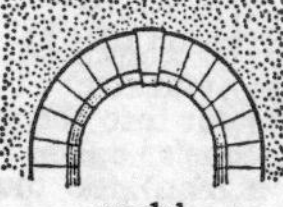

arch[1]

arch[2] [ɑːtʃ] *vt/i* **1.** curve or bend into the shape of an arch. *Cats arch their backs when they are angry.* **2.** build an arch to join two things together.
archway entrance, opening or path under an arch.

arch[3] [ɑːtʃ] *adj* playful or naughty (e.g. with reference to women and children).
archly *adv.* **archness** *nu.*

arch-[4] [ɑːtʃ] *prefix* chief, first, most important (e.g. **archbishop; archenemy**).

archaeology, archeology [ɑːki'ɔlədʒi] *nu* study of ancient buildings, materials, objects etc. **archaeological** [ɑːkiə'lɔdʒikəl] *adj.*
archaeologist *nc* person who studies archaeology.

archaic [ɑː'keiik] *adj* very old and no longer in use.
archaism *nc* word or expression which is very old and is no longer used.

archangel ['ɑːkeindʒl] *nc* chief angel.

archbishop ['ɑːtʃ'biʃəp] *nc* chief bishop.

arch-enemy ['ɑːtʃ'enimi] *nc* chief enemy (esp. the Devil or Satan).

archeology [ɑːki'ɔlədʒi] *nu* see **archaeology.**

archer ['ɑːtʃə*] *nc* person who shoots with a bow and arrow.
archery *nu* use of bows and arrows (esp. for sport or for war).

archetype ['ɑːkitaip] *nc* original model or form from which later copies and improvements are made.

archipelago [ɑːki'peligou] *nc* **1.** group of islands. **2.** sea with many islands in it. *pl* **archipelagoes.**

architect ['ɑːkitekt] *nc* person whose work is to make the plans for buildings, bridges etc.
architectural [ɑːki'tektʃərəl] *adj* with reference to architecture.
architecture *nu* **1.** science and art of making plans for buildings. **2.** buildings of a particular type: *Greek architecture* i.e. the buildings of the ancient Greeks.

archives ['ɑːkaivz] *npl* **1.** place in which government documents and other official or historical papers are kept. **2.** documents kept in such a place.
archivist ['ɑːkivist] *nc* person in charge of archives.

Arctic ['ɑːktik] *adj* **1.** of or near the North Pole. **2.** very cold. Also *n.*

ardent ['ɑːdnt] *adj* **1.** full of strong feelings (usu. of love, liking, support etc). *He was an ardent supporter of the school football team.* **2.** burning; hot. **ardently** *adv.*
ardour ['ɑːdə*] (*US* **ardor**) *nu* strong feelings (usu. of love, liking, support, eagerness etc).

arduous ['ɑːdjuəs] *adj* difficult and needing a lot of effort. *It must have been a very arduous task to build the pyramids.* **arduously** *adv.*

area ['ɛəriə] *nc* **1.** amount of surface, measurement of the surface of something (e.g. if a field is 30 metres long and 20 metres wide it has an area of $30 \times 20 = 600$ square metres). **2.** part of a country. **3.** part of anything: *area of knowledge.*

arena [ə'riːnə] *nc* **1.** central part of a Roman amphitheatre in which fights and other forms of entertainment took place. **2.** circular or oval place, surrounded by seats, for athletic competitions: *sports arena.* **3.** any place where people fight or compete against each other.

argue ['ɑːgjuː] *vt/i* **1.** talk with somebody, giving reasons for some plan or opinion, while the other person gives reasons against. *I argued with Peter all day about politics.* **2.** give one's opinion about some-

thing (when somebody else disagrees). *I argued that the earth must be round since all the other planets are.* **3.** be a sign of; be evidence for something. *The smoke coming from the chimney argues that there is somebody in the house.*
argument ['ɑːgjumənt] *nc/u* discussion or conversation between people who disagree about some idea or opinion.
argumentative [ɑːgju'mentətiv] *adj* fond of arguing; unwilling to agree with other people. **argumentatively** *adv.*
argue somebody into/out of something persuade somebody to do/not to do something, by arguing with him. *We argued him out of going on such a dangerous journey.*

aria ['ɑːriə] *nc* song for one singer in an opera.

arid ['ærid] *adj* **1.** dry; lacking water. *The soil was very arid.* **2.** dull and uninteresting. *The talk was too arid for the children to enjoy it.*

aright [ə'rait] *adv* in the right way (*o.f.* – use **in the right way, properly, well** etc).

arise [ə'raiz] *vi* **1.** come up; appear; start; be a result of. *A mist arose in the mountains. This discussion arises out of what we were saying last week.* **2.** get up; stand on one's feet (*o.f.* – use **get up, stand up** etc). *past* **arose** [ə'rouz]. *past part* **arisen** [ə'rizn].

aristocracy [æris'tɔkrəsi] *nu* **1.** small groups of people in some countries, who are considered to be more important in society than all the rest of the people (usu. owning land and having special titles such as *Duke*, *Earl*, *Lord* etc and often a lot of money). **2.** people who are better than the majority in some way (usu. those who are cleverer or richer). **3.** system of government in which members of the aristocracy are the rulers; country with this system of government.
aristocrat ['æristəkræt, (*US*) ə'ristəkræt] *nc* member of an aristocracy.
aristocratic [æristə'krætik] *adj* of or like an aristocrat; proud and noble in appearance or behaviour. **aristocratically** *adv.*

arithmetic [ə'riθmətik] *nu* science of numbers i.e. addition, subtraction, multiplication and division. **arithmetical** [æriθ'metikl] *adj.*

arm[1] [ɑːm] *nc* **1.** part of the body extending from the shoulder. **2.** sleeve of a coat, dress etc. **3.** (in *pl*) weapons, guns, swords etc. **4.** (in *pl*) official mark, sign or picture of a city, country, institution etc. **5.** division of military service (esp. *fleet air arm* i.e. aeroplanes (and the men who fly them) which fly from and land on aircraft carriers).
'armful *nc* as much as can be held in one arm or both arms.
'armchair chair with armrests.
'armhole opening in a coat, dress etc where the sleeve is put in.
'armpit hollow place under the top of the arm below the shoulder.
arm in arm with arms joined: *walking arm in arm.*
babe in arms child too young to walk.
hold someone/something at arm's length not allow someone to be too friendly; treat in an unfriendly and unwelcoming way.
welcome someone/something with open arms welcome very happily or enthusiastically.

arm[2] [ɑːm] *vt/i* **1.** get or supply weapons for fighting; prepare for war. (*opp* **disarm**). **2.** supply with things which will be useful. *John had armed himself with an excuse before he went to see the headmaster.*
the long arm of the law power or authority of the law.
coat of arms official sign of a country, city, family etc.

coat of arms

'firearm see **fire**[2].
present arms see **present**[2].

armada [ɑː'mɑːdə] *nc* fleet of warships (esp. Spanish fleet sent to invade England in 1588).

armadillo [ɑːmə'dilou] *nc* animal covered in hard plates, which comes out at night, found esp. in South America. *pl* **armadillos.**

armament ['ɑːməmənt] *nc* (usu. *pl*) guns and other weapons.

armistice ['ɑːmistis] *nc* agreement to stop fighting (usu. to discuss peace).

armour ['ɑːmə*] (*US* **armor**) *nu* **1.** metal covering for the body, formerly worn by men in battle. **2.** steel covering of a tank or ship. **3.** tanks.

armour (*def 1*)

armoured car car which is covered by steel plates to protect people inside from bullets.
'armour 'plate sheets or pieces of steel, used to protect ships, cars etc.

army ['ɑːmi] *nc* **1.** soldiers or fighting men of a country. **2.** any large organized body of people. *He had an army of assistants* i.e. very many assistants.

aroma [ə'roumə] *nc* pleasant smell (usu. of food or herbs).
aromatic [ærə'mætik] *adj* sweet-smelling.

arose [ə'rouz] past tense of **arise.**

around [ə'raund] *adv/prep* **1.** on all sides (of). *He looked around.* **2.** in different parts of. *We are going for a walk around the town.* **3.** in a circle about. *They sailed around the world.* **4.** surrounding; surrounding and closely placed to: *cut off an enemy town by placing troops around it; wear a scarf around one's shoulders.* **5.** approximately. *He earns around £4,000 a year.*

arouse [ə'rauz] *vt* make somebody/something be active. *The sleepy children were aroused by their father. Her anger was aroused by his rudeness.*

arraign [ə'rein] *vt* bring somebody before a court of law etc and accuse him of a crime; accuse somebody. **arraignment** *nc.*

arrange [ə'reindʒ] *vt/i* **1.** put in order;

make tidy. *The children had to arrange their books neatly on their desks.* (*opp* **disarrange**). **2.** plan something; agree to do something. *We will have to arrange another meeting. I must arrange to meet Peter. It was arranged that John should wait behind while Tom went on.*
arrangement *nc* **1.** way in which things are arranged or put in order. **2.** agreement. **3.** plan or preparation. *I hope there is no change in the arrangements.*

arrant ['ærənt] *adj* completely bad in some way: *an arrant fool* (*o.f.*).

array [ə'rei] *n sing* **1.** collection of things arranged in order. **2.** clothes (*o.f.* – use **clothes** etc). Also *vt* **1.** arrange in order. **2.** dress (*o.f.* – use **dress** etc).

arrears [ə'riəz] *npl* **1.** amounts of money which should have been paid, but were not. **2.** work which should have been done, but was not.
be in arrears be late in paying, doing work etc: *be in arrears with the rent.*

arrest [ə'rest] *vt* **1.** take to prison; bring before a judge; take to court etc. *The man was arrested and fined ten pounds.* **2.** stop a process: *arrest the growth of a tree/natural development etc.* **3.** cause to notice. *My attention was arrested by a box in the shop window* i.e. there was something about the box which caused me to notice it. Also *nc/u* act of taking to prison etc.
arresting *adj* catching the attention; making one take notice. **arrestingly** *adv.*
make an arrest take somebody to prison etc.
under arrest held by the police and charged.

arrive [ə'raiv] *vi* come to a place (esp. at the end of a journey); reach a time. *We arrived at our hotel at nine o'clock. The moment has arrived to serve coffee.*
arrival *nc/u* **1.** arriving. **2.** person arriving. *The new arrival entered the room.*
arrive at a decision decide what to do.
Note: notice the different constructions used with *arrive* and *reach. Arrive* has *at* before its object, *reach* does not. *We arrived at the village* but *We reached the village.*

arrogant ['ærəgənt] *adj* showing very great pride; acting as though one thought that other people were much less important than oneself. **arrogantly** *adv.* **arrogance** *nu.*

arrow ['ærou] *nc* **1.** stick shot from a bow. **2.** the sign → used to draw attention to something (e.g. in a map to show the direction of something etc).

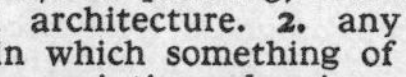

arrow (*def 1*)

arsenal ['ɑːsənl] *nc* building where guns and ammunition are stored or made (esp. for the army etc).

arsenic ['ɑːsnik] *nu* type of poison.

arson ['ɑːsn] *nu* crime of burning property (esp. buildings).

art[1] [ɑːt] *nc/u* **1.** painting, drawing, sculpture and architecture. **2.** any form of activity in which something of beauty is made (e.g. painting, drawing, sculpture, music, literature, dancing etc). **3.** activity which needs skill. *There's an art in driving this car* i.e. it is not easy to drive this car, one must have skill. **4.** (in *pl*) subjects such as languages, history, literature etc. **5.** cunning behaviour; tricks. see **artist.**
artful *adj* cunning; clever and dishonest. **artfully** *adv.* **artfulness** *nu.*
artless *adj* so honest as to be funny or foolish (like a child). **artlessly** *adv.* **artlessness** *nu.*
arty *adj* showing off one's interest in art. (*informal*).
fine arts painting, drawing, sculpture, architecture etc.
work of art something beautiful (esp. a painting, statue etc) made by a person who has special skill.

art[2] [ɑːt] pres tense of *be*, after *thou* (*o.f.*).

artefact ['ɑːtifækt] *nc* see **artifact.**

artery ['ɑːtəri] *nc* **1.** blood vessel which carries blood from the heart to the rest of the body. see **vein. 2.** main road; highway; important river or canal used by boats and ships.
arterial [ɑː'tiəriəl] *adj: arterial road.*

artesian [ɑː'tiːziən] *adj* in **artesian well** i.e. very deep well, in which the water is forced up to the surface, instead of staying at the bottom of the well.

arthritis [ɑː'θraitəs] *nu* disease which attacks the joints of the body. **arthritic** [ɑː'θritik] *adj.*

artichoke ['ɑːtitʃouk] *nc*: **globe artichoke** type of round vegetable with many overlapping leaves as in the illustration. **jerusalem artichoke** type of small root vegetable from a kind of sunflower.

globe artichoke

article ['ɑːtikl] *nc* **1.** particular thing or object. *There were various articles lying around the room.* **2.** complete piece of writing in a magazine or newspaper. **3.** (grammar) the words *a, an* and *the* and words in other languages which are used in the same way.
definite article (grammar) the.
indefinite article (grammar) a, an.
leading article see **lead**[2].

articulate[1] [ɑː'tikjuleit] *vt/i* **1.** speak clearly. **2.** connect by joining together: *articulated lorry* i.e. one in which the front and back parts are joined in a flexible way.
articulation [ɑːtikju'leiʃən] *nc/u* **1.** way of speaking. **2.** act of joining together.

articulate[2] [ɑː'tikjulət] *adj* **1.** clear, well-arranged, easy to understand. *He gave a very articulate account of what had happened.* **2.** (with reference to a person) able to speak well and clearly, able to explain one's ideas in speech. (*opp* **inarticulate**). **articulately** *adv.*

artifact, artefact ['ɑːtifækt] *nc* any object made by human skill.

artifice ['ɑːtifis] **1.** *nc* clever trick. **2.** *nu* cunning; skill which is a little dishonest.

artificial [ɑːti'fiʃl] *adj* **1.** not real, not natural, but appearing to be real: *artificial flowers.* **2.** made by man, not natural. *Electricity gives us artificial light.* **artificially** *adv.*
artificiality [ɑːtifiʃi'æliti] *nu* false behaviour or appearance; behaviour or appearance which seems to be what it is not.

artificial respiration process of helping a person who is nearly dead (often by drowning) to breathe more easily by pressing on his chest or by blowing air into his lungs.

artillery [ɑː'tiləri] *nu* **1.** big guns on wheels. **2.** part of an army which uses big guns.

artisan ['ɑːtizæn] *nc* man who has been trained to work with his hands (e.g. a carpenter, a mechanic).

artist ['ɑːtist] *nc* **1.** person who paints or draws pictures. **2.** person whose work is one of the arts (e.g. a musician, an architect, a dancer, a poet). **3.** person who does any skilled work extremely well. see **art**[1].

artistic [ɑː'tistik] *adj* **1.** done with great skill and a love of art. (*opp* **inartistic**). **2.** (with reference to a person) having a love and understanding of art. **artistically** *adv*.

artistry ['ɑːtistri] *nu* artistic skill.

as [æz] *adv/conj* **1.** since; because. *As he was drunk we would not let him into the house.* **2.** while; when. *As he pulled the rope, you could see his muscles quivering.* **3.** in the same way as. *Do as I say.*

as . . . as used to express a way in which two things or people are equal. *You are as strong as I (am).*

as good as nearly; almost. *It's as good as finished. He as good as told me that I was a fool* i.e. he didn't say this, but he showed that this was what he meant. (*informal*).

as it is in fact; really.

as it were one might say; it might be correct to say. *The English, the Scots and the Welsh are all, as it were, members of the same family.*

as long as if; on condition that. *As long as you understand, we shall say no more about it* i.e. if you understand, we shall not discuss it any more. (*informal* – use **if, since** etc).

as much so. *I thought as much* i.e. I thought so, and now I am sure (usu. with reference to something bad).

as one (man) together.

as a rule usually.

(just) as soon *I would just as soon not go* i.e. I don't mind whether I go or not (or, I prefer not to go).

as well too; also.

as yet (usu. *negative*). up to this time *Nothing unusual has happened as yet.*

asbestos [əs'bestəs] *nu* type of material which does not burn. It is often made into a kind of cloth which can be used for clothing, curtains etc and also for insulating.

ascend [ə'send] *vt/i* go up; climb up. **ascent** [ə'sent] *nc*.

ascension [ə'senʃən] *nc* act of ascending (usu. **the Ascension,** with reference to Jesus or Mary ascending to heaven; also with reference to other religious figures).

ascend the throne become king or queen.

ascendancy [ə'sendənsi] *nu* controlling power. **ascendant** *adj*.

gain the/an ascendancy over somebody get power or authority over somebody (usu. as the result of a struggle or contest).

have the ascendancy over somebody have power or authority over somebody.

ascertain [æsə'tein] *vt* find out; discover; make sure. *The detectives are trying to ascertain the truth. We could not ascertain how it happened.*

ascetic [ə'setik] *nc* person who does not allow himself any pleasures and comforts (usu. for religious reasons). Also *adj*.

ascetically *adv*. **asceticism** *nu*.

ascribe [əs'kraib] *vt* say or think that somebody/something is the cause, origin, author etc of something. *He ascribed his success to many years of hard work* i.e. he said the reason he was successful was that he had worked hard for many years.

ascription [əs'kripʃən] *nu*.

ash[1] [æʃ] *nc* type of tree.

ash[2] [æʃ] *nc/u* dust which is left after something has been burned.

'ashtray small dish for putting cigarette ash in.

ashamed [ə'ʃeimd] *pred adj* feeling unhappy because one has done something wrong or foolish, or because one is less clever, rich, strong etc than other people. *He was ashamed of his failure. He was ashamed of having failed. He was ashamed to tell anyone that he had failed.*

ashore [ə'ʃɔː*] *adv* (usu. with reference to ships and sailors) on or to the shore.

aside[1] [ə'said] *adv* on or to one side.

lay/put something aside see **lay**[1].

put/keep something aside see **lay**[1].

turn aside see **turn**[1].

aside[2] [ə'said] *nc* (esp. with reference to the theatre) words which are not addressed to everyone present, which are not supposed to be heard by everyone present.

ask [ɑːsk] *vt/i* say that one wants something or to know something. *I didn't understand, so I asked. I asked (him) his name. I asked how to mend the radio. I asked him to help me.*

for the asking for nothing. *It's yours for the asking.* (*informal*).

ask(ing) for trouble act(ing) in a dangerous or foolish way. (*informal*).

askance [əs'kɑːns] *adv* in **look askance at somebody** i.e. look at somebody as though he had done wrong or could not be trusted; disapprove of or distrust somebody.

askew [əs'kjuː] *adv/pred adj* not straight or level.

aslant [ə'slɑːnt] *adv/pred adj* in a slanting direction; at an angle to the horizontal or vertical.

asleep [ə'sliːp] *adv/pred adj* **1.** sleeping. **2.** not being able to feel properly because the blood has not been flowing freely; numb. *My foot is asleep, probably because I've been lying on it.*

asp [æsp] *nc* one of various types of poisonous snake found in North Africa.

asparagus [əs'pærəgəs] *nu* long, narrow pointed shoots of a plant, used as a vegetable.

aspect ['æspekt] *nc* **1.** appearance. **2.** direction in which a building faces. *His house has a southern aspect* i.e. it faces south. **3.** part of a problem, question, difficulty etc; way in which a problem etc can be studied or discussed. *I'm interested in all aspects of science. The most important aspect of this question is . . . .*

asperity [æs'periti] *nc/u* sharpness of manner; harshness; unkindness.

aspersion [əs'pəːʃən] *nc* untrue statement about somebody, saying that he has done something wrong.

cast aspersions make aspersions. *If he goes on casting aspersions on my good name, I'll complain to the headmaster.*

asphalt ['æsfælt] *nu* black substance used in making roads. Also *vt* cover with asphalt.

asphyxiate [əs'fiksieit] *vt* make someone die from lack of oxygen. **asphyxiation** [əsfiksi'eiʃən] *nu*.

asphyxia [əs'fiksiə] *nu* lack of air or oxygen (usu. causing death).
aspidistra [æspi'distrə] *nc* plant with large leaves, formerly very popular as a decoration in houses.
aspirate ['æspərit] *nc* sound like 'h' in *hate*. Also ['æspireit] *vt* make the sound 'h' (usu. at the beginning of a word).
aspire [əs'paiə*] *vi* in **aspire to** i.e. be eager to reach/win something.
aspiration [æspi'reiʃən] *nc/u* hope; ambition; wish etc.
aspirant ['æspirənt] *nc* person who aspires.
aspiring *adj*.
aspirin ['æsprin] **1.** *nu* medicine which lessens pain. **2.** *nc* tablet or pill containing aspirin.
ass [æs] *nc* **1.** animal, like a small horse, with long ears. **2.** foolish person. (*informal*).
assail [ə'seil] *vt* attack.
assailant *nc* attacker (*o.f.* or legal).
be assailed by doubts/regrets etc have sudden strong doubts/regrets.
assassinate [ə'sæsineit] *vt* murder somebody by a sudden attack (usu. for a political reason). **assassination** [əsæsi'neiʃən] *nc/u*.
assassin [ə'sæsin] *nc* person who assassinates.
assault [ə'sɔ:lt] *vt* attack. Also *nc* an attack. *There was an assault on the town before dawn*.
assault (and battery) *nu* crime of beating a person.
assay [ə'sei] *vt* test a metal (esp. gold or silver, an alloy etc) to find out how valuable or how pure it is. Also *nc*.
assemble [ə'sembl] **1.** *vt/i* gather together; bring together; collect in one place. *A large crowd assembled*. **2.** *vt* make by putting pieces together. *In that factory they can assemble a vehicle in less than a day*.
assembly [ə'sembli] **1.** *nc* number of people gathered together for a special purpose. **2.** *nc* collection of objects. **3.** *nc* something, such as an engine or a car, which is made of a number of parts put together. **4.** *nu* putting together of the parts of something.
'assembly line row of workers and machines in a factory. The product being manufactured by the factory passes along the assembly line and at each stage a new piece is added until the product is finished.
assent [ə'sent] *vi* agree to; say yes to. *The committee assented to our proposals*. Also *nu* agreement to something; permission.
assert [ə'sə:t] *vt* **1.** say very firmly. *He asserted his innocence. He asserted that he was innocent*. **2.** insist on and defend. *He asserted his right to a share in the money* i.e. he believed that he ought to have a share and he asked for it very firmly.
assertion *nc/u* firm statement: *make an assertion*.
assertive *adj* making firm statements, often asking other people to do what the speaker thinks they ought to do. *I think his behaviour is too assertive*. (*opp* **unassertive**).
assertively *adv*.
assert one's authority act in such a way as to make people do what one thinks they ought to do.
assess [ə'ses] *vt* decide how great some payment should be, or how valuable or useful something is. *His taxes were assessed at £200. They sent someone to assess the value of the house. It is difficult to assess the importance of the decision*. **assessment** *nc/u*.
assessor *nc* person whose job is to make assessments (esp. for the purpose of taxation or insurance).
asset ['æset] *nc* **1.** something valuable or useful which gives one an advantage. **2.** (in *pl*) property which one owns.
assiduous [ə'sidjuəs] *adj* working steadily and paying great attention to details. **assiduously** *adv*.
assiduity [æsi'djuiti] *nu* hard and careful work.
assign [ə'sain] *vt* **1.** give as a share or duty. *The teacher assigned the work to John*. **2.** tell somebody to do something as his duty. *The teacher assigned three boys to clean the room*. **assignment** *nc/u*.
assimilate [ə'simileit] *vt/i* take in and make a part of one's body or mind; take in and make like oneself. *It is difficult to assimilate a lot of information in a short time. Countries like Australia, which attract immigrants, try to assimilate them quickly*. **assimilation** [əsimi'leiʃən] *nu*.
assimilated *adj*. (*opp* **unassimilated**).
assist [ə'sist] *vt/i* help. *Scientists have assisted us in the stamping out of this disease*.
assistance *nu*.
assistant *nc* person who helps.
assizes [ə'saiziz] *npl* law court held in each area or county of England.
associate[1] [ə'souʃieit] **1.** *vt* think of something in connection with something else. *Christmas is usually associated with parties and giving presents*. **2.** *vi* join as a friend or partner. *I have always associated with many interesting people*.
associate[2] [ə'souʃiət] *nc* friend or partner in some activity, often in business. Also *adj*.
association [əsousi'eiʃən] *nc* **1.** partnership or friendship with somebody. **2.** connection between two or more ideas. *There is an association between Christmas and parties*. **3.** group of people who have joined together because of some interest or purpose which they share: *the Automobile Association*.
as'sociation 'football see **foot**.
assonance ['æsənəns] *nu* (with reference to words) condition of having the same or similar vowel sounds.
assortment [ə'sɔ:tmənt] *nc* a number of things not all of the same kind.
assorted [ə'sɔ:tid] *adj* of various kinds; mixed: *assorted chocolates* i.e. chocolates of different kinds.
'well-/'ill-a'ssorted mixing together well/badly: *ill-assorted collection of objects* i.e. objects which do not belong together and have no connection with each other.
assuage [ə'sweidʒ] *vt* (usu. with reference to pain, sorrow, suffering etc) make less. (*formal*).
assume [ə'sju:m] *vt* **1.** suppose; take to be true. *Let us assume that you are right* i.e. let us say that you are right (although we don't know whether you are or not). **2.** pretend to have something. *He assumed a look of surprise* i.e. he pretended to be surprised. **3.** take; begin to use. *The prince assumed power when he was only fifteen. He assumed authority over the other workers*.
assumption [ə'sʌmpʃən] *nc*.
assumed *adj* false. *He lived in France under an assumed name*.
assure [ə'ʃuə*] *vt* **1.** tell somebody something very firmly so that he feels safe or certain. *I assure you that I will do everything I can to help you. I assured him of my support for his application*. **2.** make certain.

The only way to assure success is to work hard. **3.** insure one's life. see **insure.**

assuredly [ə'ʃuəridli] *adv* certainly; without doubt. (rather *o.f.* – use **certainly**).

assurance **1.** *nc* firm statement which is meant to make somebody feel safe or certain. *The shopkeeper gave me many assurances about the radio.* **2.** *nu* feeling of strong belief. **3.** *nu* feeling that one is right, clever, successful etc. *He answered all my questions with complete assurance.* **4.** *nu* insurance of one's life. see **insure.**

asterisk ['æstərisk] *nc* the mark * (used to draw attention to a word in a piece of writing, and often to indicate that there is a note on the word).

astern [əs'tə:n] *adv* at or towards the back or stern of a ship.

asteroid ['æstərɔid] *nc* any one of a large number of small planets revolving round the sun between Mars and Jupiter.

asthma ['æsmə] *nu* disease which causes difficulty in breathing.

asthmatic [æs'mætik] *adj.* Also *nc* person having this disease. **asthmatically** *adv.*

astigmatism [æs'tigmətizəm] *nu* defect in the lens of the eye, causing poor vision.

astigmatic [æstig'mætik] *adj.*

astir [ə'stə:*] *adv/pred adj* moving about (esp. in an excited way).

astonish [əs'tɔniʃ] *vt* fill with sudden wonder. **astonishing** *adj.* **astonishingly** *adv.* **astonishment** *nu.*

astound [əs'taund] *vt* fill with very great surprise (usu. stronger than astonish).

astounding *adj.*

astray [əs'trei] *adv/pred adj* away from the correct path or away from the proper course of action.

lead astray see **lead**[1].

astride [əs'traid] *adv/prep* with one leg on each side: *sit astride a fence.*

astringent [əs'trindʒənt] *adj* **1.** (with reference to certain medicines and cosmetics) causing something to get smaller (often causing the blood vessels to get smaller so as to stop bleeding). **2.** sharp and bitter: *astringent humour* i.e. rather sharp or hurtful humour. **astringently** *adv.* **astringency** *nu.*

astrology [əs'trɔlədʒi] *nu* science which claims to be able to say how the stars influence the way people behave and the things which happen on earth. **astrological** [æstrə'lɔdʒikl] *adj.* **astrologer** *nc.*

Note: be careful to distinguish *astrology* from *astronomy.*

astronaut ['æstrənɔ:t] *nc* person who travels in a spaceship.

astronomy [əs'trɔnəmi] *nu* study of the sun, planets, stars and other objects in space.

astronomer *nc.*

astronomical [æstrə'nɔmikl] *adj* **1.** concerned with astronomy. **2.** so large that we cannot imagine it (like the distances and sizes studied by astronomers): *an astronomical distance; an astronomical amount.*

Note: be careful to distinguish *astronomy* from *astrology.* see above.

astute [əs'tju:t] *adj* quick in deciding what is best for oneself; clever. **astutely** *adv.* **astuteness** *nu.*

asunder [ə'sʌndə*] *adv* in or into pieces: *break something asunder* (*o.f.*).

asylum [ə'sailəm] *nc* **1.** hospital for insane people. (rather *o.f.* – use **mental hospital**). **2.** any place of safety.

asymmetrical [æsi'metrikl] *adj* opposite of symmetrical.

at [æt] *prep* **1.** in; on; by a place: *at my house; at school; at the door.* **2.** with reference to condition: *at peace; at war; at rest.* **3.** with reference to time: *at six o'clock; at Christmas time.* **4.** doing something: *at work; at play; at his books.* **5.** towards: *look at somebody; rush at somebody; throw a stone at somebody.* **6.** with reference to price. *He is selling them at four for £1.*

what is he etc at? what is he etc doing?

at once see **once.**

at that **1.** immediately after that. **2.** as well; also.

Note: we use *at* with a word referring to a place, if we think of the place as being one point rather than a large area. Such a place is often a small place, which we can think of as being one point (e.g. *he lives at a village called XY*); but if we think of *XY* as being a large area, we could say *he lives in a village called XY.* We normally think of large places as being areas rather than points, and so generally say *he lives in London; his house is in New York* etc. But if we think of the large place as a point, for instance a point in a journey, we could say *the plane didn't stop at New York.* We would not, however, use *at* with names of places bigger than a city.

atavism ['ætəvizəm] *nu* return in behaviour or belief to more primitive ways (esp. the ways of one's ancestors). **atavistic** [ætə'vistik] *adj.*

ate [et, eit] past tense of **eat.**

Note: (*Brit*) the pronunciation [et] is usual and [eit] is often thought to be wrong. (*US*) the normal pronunciation is [eit] and [et] is usu. considered wrong.

atheist ['eiθiist] *nc* person who believes that there is no God. see **agnostic.**

atheism ['eiθiizəm] *nu* belief that there is no God. **atheistic** [eiθi'istik] *adj.*

athlete ['æθli:t] *nc* person who is good at playing games which need strength and speed (esp. running and jumping). **athletic** [æθ'letik] *adj.* **athletically** *adv.*

athletics *n sing* or *pl* practising for or taking part in competitions in running and jumping etc.

atlas ['ætləs] *nc* book of maps.

atmosphere ['ætməsfiə*] *nc* **1.** the air surrounding the earth. **2.** the air in any place. **3.** the feelings and influence on the mind which one receives from a place or from particular conditions. *He grew up in an atmosphere of love and trust* i.e. he grew up in conditions of love and trust. *There was an atmosphere of excitement in the theatre* i.e. it was possible to notice that people in the theatre were excited.

atmospheric [ætməs'ferik] *adj* (usu. with reference to the air surrounding the earth).

atmospherics *npl/nu* noises heard on a radio and caused by electricity in the atmosphere, which prevent one hearing the radio clearly.

atoll ['ætɔl] *nc* ring-shaped island made of coral.

atom ['ætəm] *nc* **1.** smallest piece or part of any substance. **2.** very small piece or part.

atomic [ə'tɔmik] *adj.*

atomize *vt* **1.** divide something into separate atoms. **2.** make a liquid come out from a container in a fine spray.

atomizer *nc* something used to change a liquid into a spray.

'atom/a'tomic 'bomb bomb which

causes a very powerful explosion by splitting up atoms.
atomic pile apparatus for the production of atomic energy (usu. for industrial purposes).
atomic weight weight of any atom, compared with the weight of an atom of hydrogen, which is said to have an atomic weight of 1.

atone [ə'toun] *vi* do something which shows that one is sorry for having done something wrong: *atone for one's crimes.* **atonement** *nu.*

atrocious [ə'trouʃəs] *adj* very bad. **atrociously** *adv.*
atrocity [ə'trɔsiti] *nc* very cruel and wicked act (usu. causing pain or death to other people).

atrophy ['ætrəfi] *vt/i* (usu. with reference to parts of the body) become thin and useless. Also *nu* condition of becoming thin and useless.

attach [ə'tætʃ] *vt* **1.** fasten; join; stick to. *He attached a rope to his car. We attached a label to his suitcase.* **2.** consider something to have. *We didn't attach much importance to what he was saying* i.e. we didn't think that what he was saying was important. **3.** (usu. with reference to the army etc) send somebody on duty. *He was attached to headquarters for three months.*
attachment *nc* **1.** something attached (esp. something smaller attached to a larger and more important thing). *A sewing machine has various attachments for doing certain special stitches.* **2.** affection. *He has a strong attachment for his home.*

attaché [ə'tæʃei] *nc* person who does certain special jobs in an embassy (e.g. *a military attaché* is responsible for any work connected with the army etc; *a press attaché* is responsible for any work connected with the newspapers etc).
be attached to something/somebody be very fond of something/somebody; like very much. *He is very attached to his sister.*

attack [ə'tæk] *vt/i* go towards a person to fight him; do something to fight and hurt a person: *attack the enemy. The newspapers attacked the government* i.e. the newspapers wrote things in opposition to the government. *The team attacked their opponents' goal* i.e. they kicked the ball towards the other end of the field and tried to score a goal. Also *nc*: *an attack of malaria.*
'heart attack see **heart.**

attain [ə'tein] *vt* **1.** gain; get something by hard work. *He attained his ambition.* **2.** (usu. with reference to time or age) come to; arrive at. *He attained to a very great age* i.e. he became very old.
attainable *adj* able to be attained. (*opp* **unattainable**).
attainment *nc* skill or ability which has been attained; something which one does very well.

attempt [ə'tempt] *vt* try. *He attempted a very difficult piece of work. He attempted to find the old woman.* Also *nc*: *His attempt to become the first man to land on the moon will begin tomorrow* i.e. he will try to become the first man to land on the moon.
Note: attempt (noun) often refers to doing something brave or difficult.
make an attempt on somebody's life try to murder somebody.

attend [ə'tend] *vt/i* **1.** go to (esp. go to regularly): *attend school; attend church; attend a meeting.* **2.** (esp. with reference to doctors) give attention to; help. *I am being attended by Dr Brown* i.e. Dr Brown is treating me for my present illness. **3.** deal with; do something to; give attention to; listen to properly: *attend to one's work. You should attend to what your father tells you. I'm very busy, I can't attend to you now.* **4.** be at hand to obey the orders of somebody: *attend upon the king.*
attendance *nc/u* being present. *Attendance at school is compulsory* i.e. it is compulsory to go to school. *There was a large attendance at the meeting* i.e. many people were there.
attendant[1] *nc* person who attends upon somebody; servant; assistant or companion.
attendant[2] *adj* accompanying; going with: *the weakness which is attendant upon disease* i.e. the weakness which goes with or follows disease.
attention [ə'tenʃən] **1.** *nu* act of attending; noticing something; listening carefully etc: *give one's attention to something* i.e. take careful notice of it. **2.** *nc* (often *pl*) act of kindness or politeness. **3.** *nu* position in which somebody stands with his feet together, his arms by his sides, without moving (e.g. a soldier has to do this). 'Attention' is an order shouted by an officer etc to make somebody stand in this position.
attentive [ə'tentiv] *adj* giving attention; looking or listening carefully. (*opp* **inattentive**). **attentively** *adv.*
attract someone's attention make somebody notice.
come to attention/stand at attention stand in a position of attention (in sense **3.**).
pay attention to someone/something listen carefully; notice; look at carefully etc.

attenuate [ə'tenjueit] *vt/i* become or make thin or weak. **attenuation** [ətenju'eiʃən] *nu.*

attest [ə'test] **1.** *vt* say or show that something is true or real. *The students' hard work was attested by their good examination results.* **2.** *vi* say or show that one knows or believes something to be true, good, real etc (usu. in a court of law). *The witness attested to the good character of the prisoner* i.e. the witness told the judge that he believed the prisoner to be a good man.
attestation [ætes'teiʃən] *nc/u.*

attic ['ætik] *nc* small room under the roof of a house.

attire [ə'taiə*] *nu* dress; clothing (*o.f.* – use **clothing** etc). Also *vt* dress; clothe.

attitude ['ætitju:d] *nc* **1.** arrangement of the parts of the body. **2.** way of thinking or feeling: *not a very friendly attitude. My attitude would be to ignore him* i.e. I would think it best to ignore him.
adopt an attitude 1. put the body in a certain position. **2.** come to an opinion or state of feeling. *He adopted a very unfriendly attitude.*

attorney [ə'tə:ni] *nc* **1.** lawyer (*US* commoner than *Brit*). **2.** person given the power to act for somebody else in business or law.
A'ttorney 'General one of the chief law officers in the government of a country.
'letter of a'ttorney paper in which a person gives somebody the power to act for him in business or law.

attract [ə'trækt] *vt* **1.** make people notice. *The young man was very attracted by the girl* i.e. he noticed her and liked her. *Bright colours often attract young children.* **2.** draw towards. *A magnet attracts steel* i.e. pieces of steel move towards the magnet.

attractive *adj* pleasant and interesting; good-looking; causing attraction. (*opp* **unattractive**). **attractively** *adv*.

attraction 1. *nu* act of making people notice; act of making something move towards one. 2. *nc* something which attracts (usu. something pleasant). *There are many attractions in a big city* i.e. there are many pleasant or interesting things. *What is the attraction in collecting stamps?* i.e. why do people like collecting stamps?

attribute[1] ['ætribju:t] *nc* feeling, condition, object, sign, which is found in somebody /something. *Patience is an attribute of a good mother* i.e. a good mother is naturally patient. *Hard work is an attribute of a successful man* i.e. a man who is successful always works hard. *Language is an attribute of human beings* i.e. all human beings have a language.

attribute[2] [ə'tribju:t] *vt* 1. say that something is the cause of something else. *He attributed his success to good luck* i.e. he said that he was successful because of good luck. 2. say or think that somebody has a certain quality. *He attributed great cunning to his enemies* i.e. he said or thought that his enemies were very cunning. **attribution** [ætri'bju:ʃən] *nu*.

attributive [ə'tribjutiv] *adj* referring to a quality, condition, feeling etc possessed by something/somebody.

attributive adjective (grammar) in English, an attributive adjective usu. goes in front of a noun (e.g. in 'old man', 'old' is an attributive adjective).

attrition [ə'triʃən] *nu* action which gradually makes something smaller, weaker, less useful etc.

war of attrition war in which each side tries to win by killing as many men and damaging as much property of the other side as possible.

auburn ['ɔ:bən] *adj* (usu. with reference to hair) reddish brown.

auction ['ɔ:kʃən] *nc* public sale in which goods are sold to the person offering the highest price. *He sold it by auction.* Also *vt* sell goods in this way. *He auctioned all his old furniture.*

auctioneer [ɔ:kʃə'niə*] *nc* person who is in charge of an auction.

audacious [ɔ:'deiʃəs] *adj* 1. brave and ready to take a risk. 2. impudent and without any fear of authority. **audaciously** *adv*. **audacity** [ɔ:'dæsiti] *nc/u*.

audible ['ɔ:dibl] *adj* loud enough for somebody to hear. (*opp* **inaudible**). **audibly** *adv*. **audibility** [ɔ:di'biliti] *nu* condition of being audible.

audience ['ɔ:diəns] *nc* 1. the people watching a film or play, listening to a concert, listening to the radio, watching television etc. 2. formal meeting with a ruler of a country etc: *an audience with the Pope. The king granted John an audience* i.e. the king allowed John to come and meet him.

audit ['ɔ:dit] *vt* check in detail the record of money received and spent to see that the record is correct. Also *nc* examination of this kind.

auditor *nc* person whose work is to examine the accounts of business firms etc in this way.

audition [ɔ:'diʃən] *nc* test given to an actor etc before he is given a part in a play. Also *vt*.

auditorium [ɔ:di'tɔ:riəm] *nc* part of a theatre, concert hall etc in which the audience sits.

auditory ['ɔ:ditəri] *adj* referring to the sense of hearing: *auditory ability* i.e. ability to hear.

auger ['ɔ:gə*] *nc* tool for making holes in wood.

aught [ɔ:t] *pron* anything (*o.f.* – use **anything**).

augment [ɔ:g'ment] *vt/i* become or make larger by adding something. **augmentation** [ɔ:gmen'teiʃən] *nc/u*.

augur ['ɔ:gə*] *vt/i* 1. say what is going to happen in the future. 2. be a sign of what is going to happen in the future.

augury ['ɔ:gjuri] 1. *nu* science or art of knowing what will happen in the future. 2. *nc* sign showing what will happen in the future.

augur well/ill (for something) be a sign that something will/will not happen or succeed in the future.

August ['ɔ:gəst] *n* eighth month of the year.

august [ɔ:'gʌst] *adj* like a king; noble; impressive.

aunt [ɑ:nt] *nc* the sister of one's father or mother, or the wife of one's uncle.

au pair ['ou'peə*] *nc* 1. girl from another country who lives for a time with a family and does a little work for them, in order to improve her knowledge of the language or to have a holiday. *Have you met our au pair?* 2. arrangement by which a young person comes to another country and lives with a family (sometimes in exchange for a visit to their country by a member of that family). Also *adj*: *She is an au-pair girl.* Also *adv*: *She is staying with us au pair.*

aural ['ɔ:rəl] *adj* with reference to hearing.

auspices ['ɔ:spisiz] *npl* usu. in **under the auspices of something** i.e. with the help and encouragement of something. *The meeting was held under the auspices of the Ministry of Education.*

auspicious [ɔ:s'piʃəs] *adj* giving promise that something will succeed or be good in the future. (*opp* **inauspicious**). **auspiciously** *adv*.

austere [ɔs'tiə*] *adj* 1. strict and harsh; not offering much friendship and insisting that people should behave as well as possible. *His father was a very austere man who punished his children whenever they did the smallest thing wrong.* 2. simple; without any decoration: *an austere room, with only a table, a chair and a bed in it.* **austerely** *adv*.

austerity [ɔs'teriti] *nu* condition of being austere (often with reference to the economic conditions of a country when goods are expensive and difficult to find, and the government wants to prevent people from spending too much money).

authentic [ɔ:'θentik] *adj* true; not false; reliable: *authentic news* i.e. news which one can believe. **authentically** *adv*.

authenticate [ɔ:'θentikeit] *vt* show that something is true; find out that something is true. **authentication** [ɔ:θenti'keiʃən] *nu*.

authenticity [ɔ:θen'tisiti] *nu* condition of being true or genuine.

author ['ɔ:θə*] *nc* 1. person who writes plays, poems, novels, stories etc. 2. person who starts something: *the author of this idea/plan/scheme/proposal* i.e. the person who first thought of this idea etc.

authoress ['ɔ:θəris] *nc* woman author (*o.f.* –

use **author**).
authorship *nu* condition of being an author. *The authorship of this poem is unknown* i.e. nobody knows who wrote this poem.

authority [ɔː'θɔriti] **1.** *nu* power or right to order other people or to do something. *He was given authority over the other boys* i.e. he was given the power to give orders to them. *He had authority to buy more books for the library* i.e. he was allowed to do this. **2.** *nc* (often *pl*) person or persons who have the power or right to give orders. *The authorities have forbidden us to hold the meeting tomorrow.* **3.** *nc* person who is an expert on something. *He is an authority on the history of Russia.* **4.** *nc* book etc which can be trusted to give the truth.
authoritarian [ɔːθɔri'tɛəriən] *adj* having reference to orders; based on strong rule: *an authoritarian system of government* i.e. one in which the people are forced to obey the government even when they are very unwilling to do so.
authoritative *adj* **1.** true and to be believed in. *He gave an authoritative account of the recent events* i.e. he told a story which seems to be true and complete. **2.** giving orders or showing an ability to give orders. *He had a very authoritative manner.* **authoritatively** *adv.*
authorize ['ɔːθəraiz] *vt* give official permission to somebody (to do something). *I am authorized to buy more books for the library.*
authorization [ɔːθərai'zeiʃən] *nu* official permission to do something.
authorized *adj* allowed in this way. (*opp* **unauthorized**).

auto[1] ['ɔːtou] *nc* (*US*) car.

auto-[2] ['ɔːtou] *prefix* of or by oneself (e.g. **autosuggestion**).

autobiography [ɔːtoubai'ɔgrəfi] *nc/u* story of somebody's life written or told by himself. **autobiographical** [ɔːtəbaiə'græfikl] *adj.*

autocracy [ɔː'tɔkrəsi] *nc/u* system of government by a single person who can govern as he likes. **autocratic** [ɔːtə'krætik] *adj.* **autocratically** *adv.*
autocrat ['ɔːtəkræt] *nc* **1.** person who rules in this way. **2.** person who always tries to make other people do what he wants, without thinking about what they may want to do.

autograph ['ɔːtəgrɑːf] *nc* **1.** person's name written in his own handwriting. **2.** anything (e.g. manuscript) written by a person himself. Also *vt* write one's name in or on. *The famous composer autographed copies of his music.*

automatic [ɔːtə'mætik] *adj* **1.** working by itself; not needing a person to attend to it. **2.** done without thought or intention. *Breathing is an automatic action* i.e. we breathe without having to think about what we are doing. Also *nc* pistol or rifle in which the bullets automatically come into position for firing. **automatically** *adv.*
automation [ɔːtə'meiʃən] *nu* system of producing goods in a factory etc by the use of automatic machines, so that fewer workers are needed to produce the goods.
automaton [ɔː'tɔmətən] *nc* person who seems to behave/move/work etc like a machine. *pl* **automatons** or **automata** [ɔː'tɔmətə].

automobile ['ɔːtəməbiːl] *nc* (mainly *US*) motorcar. (*Brit* **car** or **motorcar**).

autonomy [ɔː'tɔnəmi] *nu* condition in which a country or part of a country governs itself, instead of being governed by another country or by the central government. **autonomous** [ɔː'tɔnəməs] *adj.* **autonomously** *adv.*

autopsy ['ɔːtɔpsi] *nc* examination of a dead person to find out why he died (usu. done by cutting open the body): *perform an autopsy on somebody* i.e. do an examination of this kind.

autosuggestion ['ɔːtousə'dʒestʃən] *nu* process of causing mental or physical changes in oneself by thinking.

autumn ['ɔːtəm] *nc* (*Brit*) season of the year when the leaves begin to fall from the trees and the crops are harvested; the months September, October and November. (*US* **fall**).

auxiliary [ɔːg'ziliəri] *adj* giving help: *an auxiliary nurse* i.e. a person who helps the nurses in a hospital; *auxiliary troops* i.e. soldiers sent to help other soldiers. Also *nc.*
auxiliary verb (grammar) verb which helps a main verb (e.g. 'am' in I am going; 'can' in I can see him).

avail[1] [ə'veil] *vt/i* use something for oneself; get an advantage from something. *He availed himself of the opportunity which he was offered.*

avail[2] [ə'veil] *nu* use; benefit; advantage.
of no avail useless.
to no avail uselessly; unsuccessfully.

available [ə'veiləbl] *adj* able to be used or obtained. *John is never available when I want to see him* i.e. he is never there; I can never find him when I want him. *This ticket is available until the end of the month* i.e. it can be used until the end of the month. (*opp* **unavailable**). **availability** [əveilə'biliti] *nu.*

avalanche ['ævəlɑːnʃ] *nc* **1.** mass of snow and ice which falls down a mountain. **2.** anything which falls on one like an avalanche: *an avalanche of questions.*

avant garde [ævɔŋ'gɑːd] *nu* the most advanced or most modern sort of literature, art, music etc. *He is a member of the avant garde.* Also *adj*: *avant-garde painting.*

avarice ['ævəris] *nu* strong wish to get and keep something. **avaricious** [ævə'riʃəs] *adj.* **avariciously** *adv.*

ave Maria ['ɑːveimə'riə] *nc* hail Mary (beginning of a prayer).

avenge [ə'vendʒ] *vt* do something to hurt or punish somebody in return for some wrong he has done to oneself: *avenge (the murder of) one's father; avenge an insult; avenge oneself on the murderer of one's father.*
Note: avenge and revenge *vt* are very similar in meaning. *Avenge* generally means to punish somebody for the harm he has done to oneself (with the idea that his punishment is a sort of unofficial justice); *revenge* generally means to hurt somebody for hurting oneself; there is not the same idea of justice in the use of this word. Do not use the person punished or hurt as the object of avenge or revenge (e.g. we cannot say *he avenged his enemy* to mean he punished his enemy; we must say *he avenged himself on his enemy* or *he avenged the murder done by his enemy*).

avenue ['ævənjuː] *nc* **1.** road (esp. one in a town, with trees on either side). **2.** wide street. **3.** way of getting something: *an avenue to success.*

aver [ə'vəː*] *vt* say very firmly that something is true. *past* **averred.**

average ['ævəridʒ] *nc* **1.** the result obtained when several numbers, quantities etc are added together and the total of this addition is divided by the number of quantities (e.g. the average of 7+8+3=(18÷3)=6). **2.** the usual kind or standard. Also *adj* **1.** found by calculating the average. **2.** normal; usual; most commonly found; neither very good nor very bad. Also *vt* **1.** calculate an average. **2.** produce work, or do something normally or usually. *He averages forty-five hours' work a week* i.e. sometimes he does more, sometimes less, but the total is usu. near forty-five.

below/above/up to (the) average below/above/at standard of the group, class, team etc.

on the average usually; normally.

averse [ə'vəːs] *adj* having a strong dislike for. *He is averse to hard work.*

aversion [ə'vəːʃən] *nu*: *He has an aversion to/for hard work.*

avert [ə'vəːt] *vt* **1.** (usu. with reference to eyes, gaze, face) turn away. *He averted his eyes from the dreadful sight* i.e. he turned away so as not to see it. **2.** prevent; stop from happening. *John's quick action averted a serious accident.*

aviary ['eiviəri] *nc* place where many birds are kept.

aviation [eivi'eiʃən] *nu* flying in an aeroplane; art or science of flying aeroplanes; the making or production of aircraft.

aviator ['eivieitə*] *nc* person who flies an aeroplane (*o.f.*).

avid ['ævid] *adj* with a strong wish to have: *avid for money/fame/success.* **avidly** *adv.* **avidity** [ə'viditi] *nu.*

avocado [ævə'kaːdou] *nc* type of pear-shaped green or black tropical fruit with soft pale flesh and a big stone. Also **avocado pear.** *pl* **avocados.**

avocation [ævə'keiʃən] *nc* **1.** something which one does in addition to one's normal work. **2.** one's normal work.

avoid [ə'vɔid] *vt* keep away from; move away from; act in such a way that something does not happen. *I tried to avoid meeting him. He has been avoiding me* i.e. he has been staying away from me so that he does not meet me; *avoid an accident* i.e. act in such a way that an accident does not happen. **avoidance** *nu.*

avoidable *adj* able to be avoided. (*opp* **unavoidable**). **avoidably** *adv.*

avoirdupois [ævədə'pɔiz] *nu* system of weights used in some English-speaking countries, in which 16 ounces = 1 pound.

avow [ə'vau] *vt* confess; state with strong belief. **avowed** *adj.* **avowal** *nc/u.*

await [ə'weit] *vt* wait for; be ready for.

awake[1] [ə'weik] *pred adj* not asleep; conscious and noticing what is happening around one.

awake[2] [ə'weik] *vt/i* stop sleeping or make somebody stop sleeping. *past tense* **awoke** [ə'wouk]. *past part* **awoken** or **awaked.**

Note: see also *wake*[1] which is more commonly used.

awaken [ə'weikən] *vt/i. past* **awakened.** see **wake**[1].

award [ə'wɔːd] *nc* something given to somebody who has done well in some way: *an award for gaining the highest marks in the class; an award in a competition.* Also *vt* give an award. *They awarded the first prize to John/They awarded John the first prize.*

aware [ə'wɛə*] *pred adj* knowing about; taking notice of; fully conscious of. *I am aware of the danger* i.e. I know about the danger. *I am aware that it is dangerous.* (*opp* **unaware**). **awareness** *nu.*

awash [ə'wɔʃ] *adv/pred adj* (esp. with reference to a ship or boat) covered by sea water.

away [ə'wei] *adv* **1.** at or to a distance from somebody/something: *go away; run away; away from home; three miles away: throw something away.* **2.** out of existence; until something is finished or made smaller. *The water has boiled away* i.e. it has boiled until there is no water left. *The noises died away* i.e. they became quieter until they could no longer be heard.

away with you/it/him etc! go away; take it/him away etc.

fall away (from somebody) leave somebody who is a leader. *The Prime Minister's supporters fell away from him.*

far and away the best/the easiest/the most interesting etc very much better/easier/more interesting etc than others.

give something away give to another person.

give oneself away do something which allows a person to discover a secret which one was trying to hide.

make/do away with oneself kill oneself.

pass away die (*o.f.* – use **die**).

right away immediately. (*informal*).

awe[1] [ɔː] *nu* feeling which one has for somebody/something very great and powerful. *The small boy felt a sense of awe when he entered the headmaster's room. The travellers felt a sense of awe when they saw the high mountains in the distance.*

stand/be in awe of somebody have a feeling of awe for somebody.

awe[2] [ɔː] *vt* (usu. *passive*) fill with awe. *The travellers were awed by the sight of the distant mountains.*

'awe-inspiring *adj* causing awe.

'awesome *adj* causing awe.

'awe-struck *adj* filled with awe.

'aweful, awful[1] *adj* causing awe.

'awful[2] *adj* very bad: *an awful pain; an awful lot of work.* (*informal*).

Note: since *aweful* meaning 'causing awe' is pronounced the same as the weaker word *awful* meaning 'very bad', aweful is not often used today; awesome or awe-inspiring are used instead.

awfully *adv/intensifier* very much or very badly: *thanks awfully. That's not awfully clear.* (*informal*).

awhile [ə'wail] *adv* for a short time. (rather *o.f.* – use **for a time; for a while; for a few minutes/hours/days** etc).

awkward ['ɔːkwəd] *adj* **1.** (with reference to a person or animal) not having much skill or ability in moving or doing something. *He's a very awkward boy, he's always knocking things over.* **2.** causing difficulty; difficult to use: *an awkward shape to paint* i.e. a shape which is difficult to paint properly. *It's very awkward to use this tool; an awkward part of the road* i.e. a part of the road where it is difficult to drive properly; *an awkward question* i.e. a question which is difficult to answer, or which causes one to feel uncomfortable or unhappy. *I can't meet you at six o'clock, it's a very awkward time for me.* **awkwardly** *adv.* **awkwardness** *nu.*

awl [ɔːl] *nc* tool for making small holes in wood or leather.

awning ['ɔːniŋ] *nc* piece of canvas or other strong cloth over or in front of a door, window etc to give protection from the sun or rain.

awoke [ə'wouk] past tense of **awake**[2].

awry [ə'rai] *adv/pred adj* not straight. *Her dress was all awry.*

go awry (usu. with reference to plans or schemes) go wrong; fail.

axe, ax [æks] *nc* tool for cutting down trees and cutting wood into pieces. Also *vt* suddenly end or stop.

Note: axe is more common than *ax*.

axe

axiom ['æksiəm] *nc* **1.** statement which is clearly true and which needs no proof. **2.** rule or action which one must follow if one wishes to succeed. **axiomatic** [æksiə'mætik] *adj*. **axiomatically** *adv*.

axis ['æksis] *nc* real or imaginary line through the middle of a turning object, around which the object turns. *pl* **axes** ['æksiːz].

axle ['æksl] *nc* piece of iron or other substance which joins together the centres of two wheels turning together.

ay(e) [ai] *interj* yes (*o.f.* or dialect – use **yes**).

the ayes the people who vote 'yes' for a particular idea, proposal etc (in a meeting) (*opp* **the noes**).

the ayes have it the people voting 'yes' are in the majority. (*opp* **the noes have it**).

azalea [ə'zeiliə] *nc* shrub with colourful flowers growing in cool northern areas.

azure ['eiʒə*] *nu* blue colour of the sky. Also *adj*.

B

baa [bɑː] *nc* noise made by a sheep. Also *vi* make this noise.
babble ['bæbl] *nu* **1.** foolish or childish talking. **2.** confused noise of many people talking at once. Also *vt/i* **1.** talk foolishly or childishly. **2.** tell something which one ought not to tell.
babe [beib] *nc* baby (*o.f.* – use **baby**).
babel ['beibl] *nu* (usu. of many people talking) loud confused sound.
baboon [bə'buːn] *nc* type of monkey which walks on all four legs on the ground and lives in Africa and Asia.
baby ['beibi] *nc* infant; youngest of a group. Also *adj* very small or young.
babyhood *nu* time when one is a baby; state of being a baby.
baby-sitter ['beibisitə*] *nc* person who stays in a house to look after children while their parents are out. **baby-sitting** *nu*. **baby-sit** *vi*.
bachelor ['bætʃlə*] *nc* **1.** unmarried man. (*fem* **spinster**). **2.** person who has taken a first degree at a university.
bacillus [bə'siləs] *nc* **1.** small creature living in the air, in water, in plants and animals. A bacillus is too small to be seen with the naked eye; some of them cause diseases. **2.** (more exactly) any of the rod-shaped bacteria. *pl* **bacilli** [bə'silai].
back[1] [bæk] *nc* **1.** part of the body of a person or animal. **2.** the bone in a person's or an animal's back. **3.** part of anything opposite the front; the upper part or more distant part of something: *at the back of the house; the back of one's hand. He sat in the back of the car* i.e. behind the driver; *the back of a chair* i.e. the part one's back rests against. **4.** (with reference to football and similar games) position of a player whose job it is to defend rather than attack.
'backbone the large bone in the back.
'back-cloth see **cloth**.
'back'door door at the back of a house. Also *adj*.
'back'fire *vi* **1.** (with reference to a car) make a sudden loud noise at the back caused by a fault in the engine. **2.** (with reference to plans, ideas, schemes etc) fail and cause harm to oneself. *He was punished when his evil plans backfired.* (*informal*).
backfiring *nu*: *I heard the backfiring of a car.*
'background **1.** part of a place or picture which is in the distance or at the back. **2.** (with reference to the colour of something) the main colour on which there are various patterns of other colours. **3.** information about where a person was born, who his parents were, where he has worked etc. **4.** things that have happened in the past in a story etc.
'backhand *nu* stroke in tennis made with the back of the hand facing the opponent. Also *adv*.
'backlash **1.** jarring or shaking of a piece of machinery which is not properly fitted. **2.** hostile or extreme reaction of some people to social or political changes which they do not like. *The government did not pass the act because of the possible backlash.*
'back 'number **1.** copy of a magazine or newspaper which is not the latest one on sale. **2.** person who was once important but is now forgotten or ignored. (*informal*).
'back 'pay payment which should have been given to somebody for the work he has done but which was in fact not given at the time.
'back'side part of the body on which one sits. (*informal*).
'backstroke *nu* method of swimming while lying on the back. Also *adv*: *swim backstroke.*
'backwash movement of water caused by a boat or ship moving along.
'backwater **1.** part of a river or stream where the water is cut off from the main stream. **2.** place or condition out of touch with new ideas. (*informal*).
behind somebody's back secretly; without the knowledge of somebody who ought to know.
get someone's back up make someone angry. (*informal*).
put one's back into something work very hard at something. (*informal*).
turn one's back on leave; go away from; abandon (often when one ought to stay).
with one's back to the wall in a difficult position, so that one has to fight or try hard. *This country has its back to the wall, so we must all work hard.* (*informal*).
back[2] [bæk] *adv* **1.** to or in an earlier position or place. *He ran back to the house* i.e. he had left the house and now he was returning to it. *He put the book back* i.e. the book had been taken away and now he was returning it. *I gave back the pencil which John had lent to me. He threw the ball to me and I threw it back.* **2.** to or at the back of something. *We sat a long way back at the theatre* i.e. we were not near the front. *Sit back in your chair* i.e. rest your back against the back of the chair. *Stand back!* i.e. keep away, do not interfere.
'backbite *vt/i* say bad things about somebody when the person is not present.
'backbiter *nc* person who does this. **backbiting** *nu*.
'backslide *vi* return to behaving wrongly or badly after one has stopped doing so for a time. *past tense* **backslid**. *past part* **backslidden**. **backslider** *nc*. **backsliding** *nu*.
back and forth first in one direction and then in the opposite direction.
go back on one's word fail to do what one has promised.
there and back to a place and away from it, returning to the starting place. *It's thirty miles there and back.*
back[3] [bæk] *vt/i* **1.** (esp. with reference to a car) go, cause to go, back. *Back the car carefully into the garage.* **2.** give support, help or encouragement to. *He decided to*

back the plan. 3. bet money that a horse will win in a race: *back a horse.*
backing *nu* 1. support or encouragement. *He had the backing of all his friends.* 2. material which covers the back of something. 3. musical accompaniment (esp. for popular music).
back away move back. *He backed away from the angry lion.*
back down change one's opinion or attitude (usu. because one is frightened of something). *At first John refused to do the work, but he soon backed down when he realized that he might be punished.*
back on to come near to at the back. *The garden backs on to the railway lines.*
back out (of something) (usu. an agreement, promise, arrangement etc) say that one will not do something, after agreeing, promising etc to do it. (*informal*).
back someone (up) give support, help, encouragement etc to.
backward ['bækwəd] *adj* 1. towards the back. *She went off without a backward glance.* 2. not as well-developed as others: *backward child* i.e. a child who is not as clever at learning as most children are. 3. (with reference to a person) slow in making friends or in doing something.
backwards *adv* towards the back: *walk backwards* i.e. walk in the direction in which one's back is facing.
backwards and forwards first in one direction and then in the opposite direction. *This train goes backwards and forwards between the two towns.*
bacon ['beikən] *nu* salted and smoked meat from the back and sides of a pig.
bacteria [bæk'tiəriə] *npl* creatures which are too small to be seen by the naked eye, which live in the air, in water, in animals and plants. Some bacteria cause disease. *Note:* the singular is *bacterium* [bæk'tiəriəm] but the word is generally used in the plural.
bacteriology [bæktiəri'ɔlədʒi] *nu* study of bacteria.
bacteriologist [bæktiəri'ɔlədʒist] *nc* person who studies this subject.
bad [bæd] *adj* not good; not what it should be; unwell; unpleasant etc: *a bad boy* i.e. a boy who does not do what he ought to. *This egg is bad* i.e. it is rotten; it is not fit to eat. *The light in this room is very bad* i.e. it is not easy to see well in this room; *a bad headache* i.e. a headache which is more painful than headaches usu. are; *a bad smell* i.e. an unpleasant smell. *comparative* **worse** [wə:s]. *superlative* **worst** [wə:st].
badly *adv*: 1. not well: *badly made.* 2. very much: *badly hurt. He badly needs a haircut.*
bad for harmful to one's health. *Reading in a dim light is bad for the eyes* i.e. it will cause damage to the eyes. *Running upstairs is bad for a weak heart.*
bad debt debt which will never be paid.
be bad at be unable to do well. *I'm bad at remembering names.*
in a bad temper angry (often about something unimportant).
go bad become rotten and unfit to eat.
go from bad to worse become worse.
not bad good. (*informal*).
bade [bæd] past of **bid**[2].
badge [bædʒ] *nc* something worn to show that a person is a member of a certain organization or has a certain post or occupation.
badger ['bædʒə*] *nc* type of small European animal with a white stripe on its nose, which lives in a hole in the ground and comes out at night.

badger

badinage ['bædinɑ:ʒ] *nu* friendly joking.
baffle ['bæfl] *vt* do something or be so difficult that somebody else cannot understand. *The thief was so clever that he completely baffled the police. Question No. 7 baffled all of us.* **bafflement** *nu.* **baffling** *adj.*
bag[1] [bæg] *nc* 1. something made of paper, cloth or leather for carrying things in: *a bag of apples.* 2. the animals killed by a hunter on any one occasion.
let the cat out of the bag let somebody know a secret without intending to do so. (*informal*).
bag[2] [bæg] *vt/i* 1. put in a bag. 2. capture or catch something. (*informal*). 3. kill an animal while hunting. *past* **bagged.**
baggy *adj* (with reference to clothes) larger than necessary and rather shapeless. **baggily** *adv.*
bagpipes ['bægpaips] *npl* musical wind instrument found in Scotland and some other countries.
baggage ['bægidʒ] *nu* cases, boxes etc which somebody takes with him on a journey.
bah [bɑ:] *interj* noise made to show that one thinks somebody/something is foolish, unimportant or annoying.
bail[1] [beil] *nu* sum of money which someone accused of a crime (or a friend or relative) gives to a court of law so that he can be free until it is time for him to be put on trial. If he comes back to the court when it is time for him to be tried, the money is given back.
be released on bail be allowed out of prison in this way.
bail someone out, stand/go bail for someone deposit, promise money in this way in order to let someone out of prison.
bail[2] [beil] *vt/i* in **bail out** i.e. throw out of a boat the water that has got into it (to prevent the boat sinking): *bail out the boat/the water.*
bail[3] [beil] *vi* in **bail out** i.e. jump from an aeroplane with a parachute. *When the aeroplane caught fire, the pilot bailed out.*
bailiff ['beilif] *nc* 1. officer of the law who assists a sheriff. 2. man who looks after the estate or property of someone else.
bait [beit] *nc* food or something which looks like food, used to catch a fish or an animal. Also *vt/i* put food somewhere in order to catch a fish or an animal.
bait a trap/hook put food in a trap/on a hook.
baize [beiz] *nu* thick, heavy, woollen cloth used for curtains, covering billiard tables etc.
bake [beik] *vt/i* 1. (esp. with reference to bread, biscuits and cakes) cook or be cooked in an oven. *He baked the bread. The bread is still baking.* 2. (esp. with reference to clay,

pottery, soil, bricks) make very hard by heating.
baker *nc* person who makes or sells bread, biscuits and cakes.
bakery *nc* place where a baker works.
'baking powder substance used in baking biscuits and cakes, which makes the biscuits and cakes swell or rise.

bakelite, Bakelite ['beikəlait] ® *nu* type of plastic material often used for insulating electrical equipment etc.

balaclava [bælə'klɑːvə] *nc* type of knitted hat which covers the ears, back of the head and chin (often worn by men and children).

balance[1] ['bæləns] **1.** *vt/i* put something in such a way that it does not fall down. *Because he never balances them very well, the books are always falling on the floor; balance on one's hands* i.e. stand on one's hands with one's legs up in the air. **2.** *vt* think about or weigh two things to decide which is more important or heavier. **3.** *vt* usu. in **balance the books, balance the accounts** i.e. find out how much money is earned and how much is spent, and what the difference between the two sums is.
balanced *adj* **1.** not falling down. **2.** thoughtful and mature; completely sane. (*opp* **unbalanced** esp. in sense **2.**).

balance[2] ['bæləns] **1.** *nu* state in which something does not fall down. *John lost his balance and fell from the ladder.* **2.** *nu* state in which two or more things are equal in power, strength, importance etc: *the balance of power in the world* i.e. condition in which no country is very much stronger or richer than any other country. **3.** *nu* condition in which the sums of money earned or paid in and sums of money spent are equal. **4.** *nc* apparatus for weighing things for scientific experiments. **5.** *nc* small wheel in a clock or watch which makes the clock or watch go at a certain speed. **6.** *nc/u* in **balance of accounts** i.e. amount of money remaining after certain sums have been paid out.
Note: if one buys something in a shop and gives the shopkeeper too much money, the money given back by the shopkeeper is called *the change*; it is not called *the balance*.
balanced diet all the various sorts of food which have to be eaten if one is to be healthy.
balance of payments money which is owed to a country or by a country, depending on its balance of trade. see below.
balance of trade the difference between the value of goods imported into a country and the value of goods exported from that country: *a favourable/unfavourable balance of trade*).
'balance wheel see **balance**[2] (in sense **5.**).
'credit balance the amount of money which one has in a bank.
(hang) in the balance (be) still undecided. *John's fate is hanging in the balance* i.e. it has not yet been decided what should be done about John, but the decision will soon be made.
keep one's balance be in such a state that one does not fall down. (*opp* **lose one's balance**).
on balance taking everything into consideration.
be thrown off balance be made to fall or nearly fall.

balcony ['bælkəni] *nc* **1.** ledge outside the window of the upper floor of a house surrounded by a wall or railing. **2.** part of a theatre or hall above the level of the floor.

bald [bɔːld] *adj* **1.** with very little or no hair on the head. **2.** containing only the facts, without any disguise or pretence: *a very bald account of the facts.* **baldly** *adv.* **baldness** *nu.*

balderdash ['bɔːldədæʃ] *nu* nonsense; foolish words. (*informal*).

bale [beil] *nc* quantity tied together to be carried by ship, lorry, aeroplane etc.

baleful ['beilful] *adj* full of evil or wickedness. **balefully** *adv.*

balk, baulk [bɔːlk] *vt/i* refuse or be unwilling to use something or do something. *John balked at having to do any more work.*

ball [bɔːl] *nc* **1.** any round object used in playing games: *football, cricket ball etc.* **2.** anything shaped like a ball: *a ball of string/wool.* **3.** large and very formal party with dancing.
Note: if the party or occasion is not formal the word *dance* is used.
'ball 'bearing 1. part of a machine which turns on small metal balls. **2.** one of the metal balls used for this purpose.
'ballpoint 'pen pen in which the ink comes round a small ball instead of through a metal point.
'ballroom room in which a ball or public dance is held.

ballad ['bæləd] *nc* type of poem or song which tells a story (usu. a traditional story).

ballast ['bæləst] *nu* heavy material which is carried in a ship to keep it steady. Also *vt: ballast a ship.*

ballerina [bælə'riːnə] *nc* woman ballet dancer who dances important parts.

ballet ['bælei] *nc/u* play or entertainment performed by dancers in a theatre (usu. with reference to a European entertainment of this type; the word *ballet* is not usu. applied to traditional dancing or folk dancing).

ballistics [bə'listiks] *npl* (followed by *sing* verb) science of guns and bombs. **ballistic** *adj.*

balloon [bə'luːn] *nc* bag made of rubber or other material, which swells when filled with air or other gas.

ballot ['bælət] *nc* process of voting in secret (usu. by marking a piece of paper and putting it into a box). Also *vi* vote in this way.
'ballot box box in which pieces of paper showing votes are put.

balm [bɑːm] *nu* **1.** sweet-smelling substance obtained from certain trees and used to lessen pain. **2.** anything which makes one feel less unhappy.
balmy *adj* **1.** sweet-smelling. **2.** (esp. with reference to winds) gentle and mild: *a balmy breeze.*

balsa ['bɔːlsə] *nu* type of very light wood. (Often **balsa wood**).

balustrade [bæləs'treid] *nc* type of open railing.

bamboo [bæm'buː] *nc/u* **1.** type of tall tropical or semi-tropical plant with a hollow stem. **2.** the wood obtained from this plant.
Note: this word is usu. uncountable; for the plural use *a lot of bamboo* (for the plant) and *pieces of bamboo* (for the wood).

bamboozle [bæm'buːzl] *vt* trick or deceive. (*informal*).

ban [bæn] *vt* say that something must not be done; forbid. *The police will soon ban the parking of cars in the High Street.* *past*

banned. Also *nc* order that something must not be done.
put a ban on something say that something must not be done.
banal [bə'nɑːl] *adj* very ordinary; in no way unusual or interesting: *a very banal remark.* **banality** [bə'næliti] *nu.*
banana [bə'nɑːnə] *nc* **1.** type of curved fruit, yellow or red in colour. **2.** tropical or semi-tropical plant which bears this fruit.
band[1] [bænd] *nc* **1.** group of musicians playing together.
Note: the word *band* is used if the musicians are playing popular music or dance music; if they are playing classical music or serious music the word *orchestra* is normally used. **2.** group of people joined together for some purpose (often a bad purpose): *a band of robbers.* **3.** strip of a different colour decorating something. **4.** thin piece of material for tying or fastening something. **5.** particular range of radio wave lengths.
band[2] [bænd] *vi* join in a group for a particular purpose. *The people banded together against the robbers.*
bandage ['bændidʒ] *nc* strip of cloth used for tying round a wound or injury. Also *vt* put a bandage on: *bandage a wound/a person.*

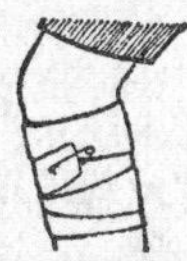

bandage

bandit ['bændit] *nc* robber who lives in mountains, forests or other wild places and who attacks travellers.
bandstand ['bændstænd] *nc* stage or platform in the open air on which musicians play to entertain people.
bandy[1] ['bændi] *adj* bent outwards: *bandy-legged* i.e. having the legs bent like this.
bandy[2] ['bændi] *vt* exchange words when arguing with somebody: *bandy insults.*
bandy somebody's name about speak about somebody in a disrespectful or insulting way so that many people hear of it.
bane [bein] *nu* cause of trouble or worry. *This work is the bane of my life* i.e. this work causes a great deal of worry and trouble to me.
baneful *adj* harmful; evil. **banefully** *adv.*
bang [bæŋ] *nc* **1.** sudden loud noise. *He heard a bang.* **2.** sudden blow: *a bang on the head.* Also *vt/i* make a bang: *bang the door; bang one's head on the wall.*
bangle ['bæŋgl] *nc* ring of metal or other substance worn round the wrist or arm as an ornament.
banish ['bæniʃ] *vt* **1.** make somebody go away (esp. to make somebody leave his own country as a punishment). **2.** put out of one's mind; stop thinking about. *He decided to banish the thought.* **banishment** *nu.*
banister ['bænistə*] *nc* (usu. *pl*) the rail and supports for the rail at the side of a staircase.
banjo ['bændʒou] *nc* type of stringed musical instrument. *pl* **banjoes** or **banjos.**
bank[1] [bæŋk] *nc* **1.** land along the side of a river, lake etc. **2.** earth which is heaped up in a field or garden. **3.** mass of snow, clouds, mud etc.
bank[2] [bæŋk] *vt/i* **1.** make into a pile or bank. *The clouds were banking up on the horizon* i.e. they were forming a pile or mass; *bank up a fire* i.e. put more coal or wood on to make it burn more slowly. **2.** lean sideways when turning. *The aeroplane banked sharply before coming down to land.*
bank[3] [bæŋk] *nc* place where money is kept and paid out, and in which business connected with money is carried on. Also *vt/i* **1.** put money into a bank: *bank one's money.* **2.** use as one's bank: *bank with Brown's Bank* i.e. keep one's money there.
banker *nc* person who is in charge of a bank or whose business is dealing in money.
banking *nu* the business of banks or bankers.
'bank 'holiday (in England) day on which the banks are closed and which is also a public holiday.
'banknote piece of paper money.
'bank rate official rate of interest on loans.
bank on something rely on; confidently expect. *We're banking on you to help us.* (*informal*).
bankrupt ['bæŋkrʌpt] *adj* **1.** officially declared by a court of law to be unable to pay one's debts. **2.** not having; lacking: *bankrupt of ideas; bankrupt of excuses.* Also *nc* person who is bankrupt. Also *vt* make bankrupt by causing somebody to spend all his money. **bankruptcy** *nu.*
go bankrupt be declared by a court of law as unable to pay one's debts.
banner ['bænə*] *nc* large piece of cloth, paper etc (usu. fastened to two sticks, having a sign or words on it and intended to be seen by many people).
banns [bænz] *npl* notice read out in a church that a certain man and woman are going to be married.
call the banns/have the banns called make, cause to make, this announcement.
banquet ['bæŋkwit] *nc* official meal, with a lot of food, at which speeches are made.
bantam ['bæntəm] *nc* small type of chicken.
banter ['bæntə*] *vt/i* make jokes, tease pleasantly.
baptism ['bæptizəm] *nu* ceremony or practice of most churches, in which drops of water are put on the head of a person, or in some cases, the person is put into the water, as a sign that the person has become a member of the church. **baptismal** [bæp'tizml] *adj.*
Baptist *nc* **1.** member of the Baptist Church which believes in practising baptism only when the person is an adult. Baptism in this church is carried out by putting the person in the water. **2.** person who baptizes (usu. only in the name of *John the Baptist*).
baptize [bæp'taiz] *vt* **1.** give baptism to a person. **2.** give a name to.
bar[1] [bɑː*] *nc* **1.** (usu. with reference to iron, gold, lead etc or chocolate or soap) piece of some solid material, longer than it is wide. **2.** long piece of metal or wood placed in front of a window or door. **3.** bank of sand under the water in a river, along a shore, at the entrance to a harbour. **4.** anything which prevents something moving forward or developing. *Lack of mineral resources was a bar to the economic development of the country.* **5.** room or building where alcoholic drinks and other refreshments are sold; the counter at which they are sold. **6.** the place in a court of law where the prisoner

stands. 7. the division of a piece of music into sections which are equal in time; the vertical line in written music which shows these equal divisions.

the Bar all the lawyers who appear in court.

'barmaid woman who serves drinks and other refreshments in a bar. (in sense 5.).

'barman man who does this.

'bartender (*US*) barman.

be called to the Bar (in England) become a barrister; become a lawyer. (*US* **be admitted to the Bar**).

behind bars in prison. (*informal*).

bar[2] [baː*] *vt* 1. make safe by putting in or fastening bars. *He barred all the doors and windows of his house.* 2. prevent somebody from going in a certain direction. *A high wall bars the way into his garden. past* **barred.**

barb [baːb] *nc* 1. sharp part of an arrow, fish hook, insect's sting, spear etc which points downwards or backwards. 2. piece of hurtful criticism. Also *vt* put a barb on something.

'barbed 'wire wire with barbs on it, used for fences etc.

barbarian [baː'bɛəriən] *nc* 1. (usu. with reference to uncivilized tribes in the times of the ancient Greeks and Romans) uncivilized person. 2. person who behaves in a rough and bad-mannered way, and who has no respect for art, literature, education etc. Also *adj.* **barbaric** [baː'bærik] *adj.* **barbarous** ['baːbərəs] *adj.*

Note: barbarian adj means 'like a barbarian' etc; *barbaric* is often used to refer to matters of culture (e.g. *barbaric art, barbaric splendour, barbaric ornaments*); *barbarous* is often used to refer to cruel behaviour (e.g. *barbarous torture, barbarous insults*).

barbarism ['baːbərizəm] 1. *nu* state of being a barbarian. 2. *nc* cruel act. **barbarity** [baː'bæriti] *nc/u.*

barbecue ['baːbikjuː] *nc* party or feast (usu. in the open air) at which the food (usu. meat) is cooked over an open fire. Also *vt* cook in this way: *barbecue the meat.*

barber ['baːbə*] *nc* person whose job is to cut men's hair.

Note: the word *hairdresser* is generally used for the person who cuts women's hair.

barbiturate [baː'bitjurət] *nc/u* type of strong drug, used for making one sleep etc.

bard [baːd] *nc* person who invents and sings poems and songs (usu. for a king or chief) (*o.f.* – use **poet** or **singer**). **bardic** *adj.*

bare [bɛə*] *adj* 1. not covered by clothes. 2. without decoration, furniture, vegetation etc. *The house looks rather bare; a bare hillside. The trees are bare in winter.* 3. just enough; very little. *He earns a bare living* i.e. he earns just enough, but he has no money to spare; *a bare possibility* i.e. a very small possibility. Also *vt* make bare (in senses 1. and 2.). **bareness** *nu.*

barely *adv* 1. in a bare way. 2. just enough and no more: *barely enough money.*

'bareback *adj/adv* (with reference to horse-riding) without a saddle.

'barefaced *adj* shameless: *barefaced liar.*

'barefoot, 'barefooted *adj* not wearing shoes, stockings etc on the feet.

bargain ['baːgin] *nc* 1. agreement with somebody to buy or sell something. 2. something bought or sold for less than its real value. Also *vt/i* buy something from, or sell something to, somebody by talking about the price and in the end coming to an agreement.

bargain for something 1. discuss the price of something in this way. 2. expect or hope for something: *more than I bargained for.* (*informal*).

drive a hard bargain make somebody come to an agreement which is favourable to oneself.

into the bargain as well; in addition. *That shopkeeper is a very rude man and a cheat into the bargain.* (*informal*).

make a bargain with somebody come to an agreement about the price of something or the amount of money etc to be paid.

barge[1] [baːdʒ] *nc* large flat-bottomed boat used for carrying goods on rivers.

bargee [baː'dʒiː] *nc* man who is in charge of a barge.

barge[2] [baːdʒ] *vt/i* push or enter roughly. *He barged into the room.* (*informal*).

baritone ['bæritoun] *adj* of a male voice between tenor and bass. Also *nc* singer with such a voice.

bark[1] [baːk] *nc* noise made by a dog. Also *vi* make this noise.

his bark is worse than his bite he becomes angry and shouts loudly, but he does not hurt people. (*informal*).

bark[2] [baːk] *nu* the hard outer covering of a tree. Also *vt* 1. take the bark off a tree. 2. take the skin off one's knuckles etc by hitting them accidentally.

barley ['baːli] *nu* type of plant whose seeds are used to make flour or bread and in the making of beer etc.

barn [baːn] *nc* building on a farm, used for storing crops or for sheltering animals.

barnacle ['baːnikl] *nc* small sea creature covered by a shell which attaches itself to rocks and the bottoms of ships.

barometer [bə'rɔmitə*] *nc* instrument which measures changes in air pressure and so can tell what changes there will be in the weather. **barometric** [bærə'metrik] *adj.*

baron ['bærn] *nc* title of nobility. (*fem* **baroness**). **baronial** [bə'rouniəl] *adj.*

baronet ['bærənet] *nc* (in Britain) title of nobility.

baroque [bə'rɔk] *adj* in the style of art, architecture etc found in Europe from about 1550 to 1750; having a great deal of ornament and many curved shapes. Also *nu* this style.

barracks ['bærəks] *npl* buildings where soldiers live.

barrage ['bæraːʒ] *nc* 1. heavy and continuous firing of big guns in battle. 2. large dam on a river (often a dam connected with other development projects).

barrel ['bærl] *nc* 1. large round container (usu. made of wood) wider in the middle than at the ends. (If the container is the same width along all its length, it is called a **drum**). 2. the long round part of a gun, along which the bullet or shell travels.

barrel (*def* 1)

barren ['bærn] *adj* **1.** not producing any crops, flowers, fruit etc. **2.** (with reference to a woman) unable to have a child. (rather *o.f.*). **3.** unable to think of anything new; dull, uninteresting. **barrenness** *nu*.

barricade [bæri'keid] *nc* anything put across a street in a hurry to prevent people moving along the street (often in times of riot or revolution). Also *vt* make a barricade: *barricade the main streets*.
Note: a *barricade* is hurriedly made and temporary. Something more permanent is called a *barrier*.

barrier ['bæriə*] *nc* **1.** wall, fence, gate etc which prevents people from going forward. **2.** anything which prevents people from going in a certain direction or which prevents progress.

barrister ['bæristə*] *nc* (in England) lawyer who speaks in a court of law.
Note: in England a lawyer who does not speak in a court of law is called a *solicitor*. In many countries all lawyers are allowed to speak in court.

barrow ['bærou] *nc* small vehicle with one or two wheels (usu. pushed by hand) used for carrying goods.

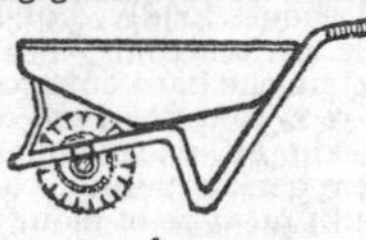

barrow

barter ['bɑːtə*] *vt/i* do business without using money by exchanging goods: *barter rice for cotton*. Also *nu* this system of doing business.

base[1] [beis] *nc* **1.** the lowest part of something, on which the upper parts rest. *The refrigerator is standing on a wooden base*. **2.** the place at which the stores and senior officers etc of a section of the army, navy etc are found (esp. in time of war). **3.** chemical compound which reacts with an acid to form a salt. **4.** (geometry) line at the bottom of a triangle etc. **5.** place to which the batter has to run in baseball. **6.** the most important or main part of anything.
Note: base (noun) usu. refers to some actual object; *basis* (noun) usu. refers to an idea, theory, opinion etc.

base[2] [beis] *vt* place on; build on; use as a base. *He based his argument on the fact that there have always been wars* i.e. this fact was his main point, from which he went on to make other points. *This book is based on a true story* i.e. the story told in the book really happened, but some changes have been made to the original story.
baseless *adj* without any cause or reason. **baselessly** *adv*.

base[3] [beis] *adj* **1.** selfish; bad; dishonest; cowardly etc. **2.** (with reference to metals) not valuable in comparison with silver and gold. **basely** *adv*. **baseness** *nu*.

baseball ['beisbɔːl] **1.** *nu* game played in America with a bat and ball on a field with four bases. see **base**[1] (in sense **5.**). **2.** *nc* the ball used in this game.

basement ['beismənt] *nc* part of a building partly or completely underground, in which people live or work.
Note: a part of a building partly or completely underground which is used for storing things is called a *cellar*.

bash [bæʃ] *vt* hit very hard. Also *nc* hard hit. (both *informal*).

bashful ['bæʃful] *adj* (usu. with reference to children or young people) shy; showing great discomfort and self-consciousness in the presence of other people; not knowing what to do or say in the presence of other people. **bashfully** *adv*. **bashfulness** *nu*.

basic ['beisik] *adj* most important; on which everything else depends. **basically** *adv*.

basilica [bə'zilikə] *nc* type of church, with a long hall and columns at the sides.

basin ['beisən] *nc* **1.** round bowl for containing liquid. **2.** (geography) land from which all rainwater drains to a river and its tributaries.

basis ['beisis] *nc* main or most important part, idea, facts etc. *pl* **bases** ['beisiːz]. see **base**[1] (in sense **6.**).

bask [bɑːsk] *vi* lie and take pleasure in warmth and light. *He was basking in the sun*.

basket ['bɑːskit] *nc* something made of strips of wood etc used for carrying things.
'basketball 1. *nu* game in which two teams try to toss a ball through a ring and into a net which is shaped like a basket. **2.** *nc* ball used in this game.

bass [beis] *adj* of the lowest male voice or the lowest notes in music. Also **1.** *nu* lowest male voice. **2.** *nc* singer with this voice.

bassoon [bə'suːn] *nc* (music) type of wind instrument.

bastard ['bɑːstəd] *nc* **1.** person whose mother and father were not married.
Note: many people consider this word impolite.
2. impolite way of referring to someone.

baste [beist] **1.** *vt* pour hot liquid over meat which is being roasted. **2.** *vt/i* attach pieces of cloth with long stitches.

bastion ['bæstiən] *nc* projecting part of a wall used for defence.

bat[1] [bæt] *nc* special piece of wood used for hitting a ball in a number of games. Also *vi* use a bat. *past* **batted. batter** *nc*.
Note: if the thing used to hit a ball has strings, as in the game of tennis, the word *racquet* is used instead of *bat*.

bat[2] [bæt] *nc* type of small flying animal which comes out at night and which can find its way by a kind of radar.
blind as a bat having very bad eyesight. (*informal*).

batch [bætʃ] *nc* amount or number of things/people dealt with together. *He received a batch of telegrams; a batch of loaves in the oven*.

bated ['beitid] *adj* usu. in **with bated breath** i.e. in great fear, interest, wonder, anxiety etc.

bath [bɑːθ] *nc* **1.** large container in which one can sit in order to wash the body. **2.** washing of the body in this way: *have a bath*. **3.** container for liquid in which something may be placed (e.g. a photographer uses a bath of developing fluid in his work). **4.** (usu. *pl*) public building in which people can have a bath, or in which they can swim. *pl* **baths** [bɑːðz]. Also *vt/i* take or give a bath.
Note: 1. the pronunciation of the plural. 2. see also *bathe*.
'bathroom room for a bath (in sense **1.**), washbasin, toilet etc.

bathe [beið] **1.** *vi* swim or dip oneself in the sea, a river, lake etc. see **bath. 2.** wash something (usu. a wound) carefully. **bather** *nc*. **bathing** *nu*.

bathos ['beiθɔs] *nu* sudden (usu. unintended) drop in writing or speech from something very important or serious to something ordinary and uninteresting (e.g. *The policy of this government is freedom of speech, peace, unity, and a reduction in the price of beef*).

baton ['bætn] *nc* **1.** stick used by the conductor of an orchestra to guide the players. **2.** stick used by certain people in authority (e.g. by the general of an army).

battalion [bə'tæliən] *nc* part of an army.

batten[1] ['bætn] *vi* in **batten down** i.e. fix securely (e.g. the hatches of a ship).

batten[2] ['bætn] *vi* in **batten on** i.e. eat greedily at someone else's expense.

batter[1] ['bætə*] *vt* hit very hard with many blows.

'battering ram large piece of wood etc formerly used to break down walls in war.

batter[2] ['bætə*] *nu* mixture of flour, milk, eggs etc used in cooking.

battery ['bætəri] **1.** *nc* device for producing an electric current. **2.** *nc* number of large guns used for war. **3.** *nc* number of things used together (esp. **a battery of tests**). **4.** *nu* (in a legal sense) crime of hitting a person.

battle ['bætl] *nc* **1.** fight between two or more groups of people (usu. between two armies, navies or groups of aeroplanes). **2.** any kind of fight or struggle. Also *vi* fight, struggle. *We must continue to battle against/with poverty and disease.*

'battle cry words shouted by soldiers in battle or by their leaders, to encourage them to fight.

'battlefield place where a battle is fought.

'battleship very large type of ship used for fighting.

battlement ['bætlmənt] *nc* (usu. *pl*) wall at the top of a tower etc with openings through which soldiers can shoot.

battlements

bauble ['bɔ:bl] *nc* something very bright and attractive which has no real value.

baulk [bɔ:lk] *vt/i* see **balk.**

bauxite ['bɔ:ksait] *nu* substance from which aluminium is obtained.

bawdy ['bɔ:di] *adj* having reference to jokes about obscene or sexual matters. Also *nu* jokes or talk of this kind. **bawdry** *nu.*

bawl [bɔ:l] *vt/i* shout or cry very loudly (usu. in an impolite or unpleasant way). *It is very bad manners to bawl at people in the street.*

bay[1] [bei] *nc* part of the land curved inwards at the edge of the sea or a lake.

bay[2] [bei] *nc* part of a wall or room divided off by pillars or other things.

'bay 'window type of window which projects out from a room.

bay[3] [bei] *nc* type of tree, the leaves of which are used to flavour meat etc.

bay[4] [bei] *vi* (with reference to the noise made by dogs when hunting) make a long deep noise. Also *nc.*

at bay in such a position that one has to turn and face one's enemies.

keep somebody at bay keep one's enemies from penetrating one's defences or coming too close to one.

bring somebody to bay make one's enemy turn and face one so as to defend himself.

bayonet ['beiənet] *nc* knife which can be fixed to the end of a gun. Also *vt* stick a bayonet into somebody.

bazaar [bə'zɑ:*] *nc* **1.** (with reference to countries in Asia) street/streets containing shops. **2.** (with reference to Britain or America) sale held for a special purpose.

bazooka [bə'zu:kə] *nc* type of gun used to attack tanks.

be [bi:] *v* infinitive form of **I am, you are, he is** etc; exist, happen etc used with other verbs to make compound tenses and passives.

be to do something must. *You are to come home at once* i.e. you must come home. *You are not to touch that* i.e. you must not.

have been to a place gone there and returned. *I have been to Africa* i.e. I went there and now I have returned.

beach [bi:tʃ] *nc* land at the edge of the sea or a lake (usu. consisting of sand or small stones). Also *vt/i* land on a beach from a boat; land a boat.

'beachcomber *nc* **1.** person who spends his time finding things of value on a beach. **2.** (in the Pacific Islands) person who has no regular work. **beachcombing** *nu.*

'beachhead the place where an invading army lands on the coast of an enemy country.

beacon ['bi:kən] *nc* light used to give warning of some danger (usu. to warn ships).

bead [bi:d] *nc* **1.** (usu. *pl*) small piece of glass, metal, wood etc with a hole through it, which can be put on a string and worn as an ornament. **2.** something like a bead: *bead of sweat* i.e. a drop of sweat.

Note: the word *bead* is not used to refer to precious stones or metal worn in this way.

beady *adj* (with reference to eyes) small and shining.

Note: to say that somebody has *beady eyes* suggests that he is greedy or cunning.

tell one's beads pray, using a rosary. see **rosary.**

beading ['bi:diŋ] *nu* long narrow piece of wood put on doors, pieces of furniture etc for decoration or for hiding joints.

beak [bi:k] *nc* **1.** the hard pointed part of a bird's mouth. **2.** magistrate. (*informal*). **3.** headmaster. (*informal*).

beaker ['bi:kə*] *nc* large cup or glass (esp. one used for chemical experiments).

beam [bi:m] *nc* **1.** long thick piece of wood used in a building. **2.** any long piece of wood or metal. **3.** ray or line of light. *A beam of sunlight was shining through a hole in the curtain.* **4.** radio, radar or television signal sent out in a particular direction. **5.** bright cheerful smile. Also *vi* smile very cheerfully. *The headmaster beamed with pleasure when he saw our good results.*

beaming *adj* very bright and cheerful.

bean [bi:n] *nc* the seed of certain plants, used as food.

bear[1] [bɛə*] *vt/i* **1.** carry, take the weight of, hold. *Will this beam bear the weight of the roof?* **2.** produce, have. *These trees bear fruit twice a year.* **3.** suffer or be able to suffer. *I didn't think I would be able to bear such pain.* **4.** behave in a good way (usu.

when suffering pain, danger, difficulty etc). *He bore himself like a soldier. past tense* **bore** [bɔ:*]. *past part* **borne** [bɔ:n].
Note: borne is the normal participle. However, when *bear* is used in the special phrase with the meaning of 'come into existence', *born* is used as the past participle. *She has borne twelve children* but *He was born in 1920.*
bearable *adj* that can be endured or suffered. (*opp* **unbearable**).
bearer *nc* **1.** person who carries something. **2.** (in Asia) house servant.
bearing **1.** *nu* connection (usu. in **have a/no bearing on something**). *That question has no bearing on the subject we are discussing.* **2.** *nc* part of a machine or engine on which a moving part rests. **3.** *nu* way of acting, walking, behaving.
bearings *npl* position (usu. in **take one's bearings** i.e. find one's position, find out exactly where one is) (*opp* **lose one's bearings**).
bear down on someone/something **1.** approach someone/something rapidly and with a look of wishing to say or do something important. **2.** press on, put pressure on.
bear on someone cause pain or difficulty to someone. *The new taxes bore heavily on the poor.*
bear on a subject/question/point etc have some connection with.
bear someone out/bear out what someone says agree with someone (and often, give further proof that what he says is true). *I can bear him out on that because I was there.*
bear up remain cheerful in pain, difficulty etc. (*informal*).
bear something up support, hold up something.
bear with somebody stay and listen to what somebody says although one may wish to go away (usu. in **if you will bear with me for a few more minutes, I will . . .**).
bear arms be a soldier (*o.f.*).
bear a grudge against someone/bear someone a grudge dislike someone because one thinks he has done something to harm oneself.
bear something in mind not forget something; remember something so as to make use of it at the proper time.
bear no resemblance to someone/something not look at all like someone/something.
bear right/left (used for telling somebody how to reach a place) turn right/left.
bear signs/marks/traces of something have, show signs of etc. *The house bore signs of having been recently occupied.*
doesn't bear thinking of is so bad, unpleasant, dangerous etc that one does not even want to think about it. (*informal*).
bear witness act as a witness. (rather *o.f.*).
bring one's intelligence/skill/attention to bear on something deal with something by using one's intelligence etc.
can't bear dislike very much. *I can't bear his singing. She can't bear to watch a boxing match.*

bear[2] [bɛə*] *nc* large, furry, meat-eating animal, many types of which sleep through the whole winter.

beard [biəd] *nc* hair on the cheeks and chin of a man.
Note: hair on the upper lip is called a *moustache.*
bearded *adj.* **beardless** *adj.*

beast [bi:st] *nc* **1.** animal (esp. an animal considered simply as an animal and not as a pet or an animal which works for man). **2.** cruel, unkind or unpleasant person.
beastly *adj* unpleasant, unkind etc.
beast of burden animal (e.g. a donkey or a camel) used for carrying loads.

beat[1] [bi:t] **1.** *vt/i* hit several times (usu. with a stick). **2.** *vt* defeat, gain a victory over, do something better than somebody. **3.** *vi* move regularly. *The bird's wings were beating. His heart stopped beating.* **4.** *vt/i* (cookery) stir vigorously. *past tense* **beat.** *past part* **beaten.**
Note: beat meaning 'hit' always has the sense of 'hit several times, hit repeatedly'. If only one or a few blows are involved, use *hit* instead of *beat*
beaten *adj* **1.** hit etc. **2.** defeated. (*opp* **unbeaten**). **3.** (usu. of a metal e.g. silver or gold) shaped by being hit with a hammer (e.g. by a silversmith or goldsmith).
beater *nc* **1.** piece of equipment used in a kitchen for mixing eggs etc. **2.** man who is employed to beat bushes etc in order to drive birds or animals towards a hunter.
beat down (with reference to the sun or rain) come down very heavily or strongly.
beat something down break (usu. in **beat down the door** i.e. enter a locked room by breaking the door).
beat someone up attack someone by hitting him, kicking him etc. (*informal*).
beat off an attack drive away those attacking.
beat out a tune etc tap one's fingers, hit something etc to make a tune.
beat out a fire put out a fire by hitting whatever is burning.
beat about the bush waste time by talking about something other than the most important point. (*informal*).
beat a retreat run away from danger.
beat time hit something, wave one's hands etc to show how fast a piece of music is to be played.

beat[2] [bi:t] *nc* **1.** sound or movement of something being hit or something moving regularly (usu. in **beat of a drum; heartbeat**). **2.** unit of time in music. **3.** area, path, street etc where somebody regularly travels. *The policeman was on his beat.*

beatify [bi'ætifai] *vt* **1.** (in the Roman Catholic Church) give officially the title 'Blessed' to someone who is dead. **beatification** [biætifi'keiʃən] *nu.*
beatific [biə'tifik] *adj*: *a beatific smile.*
beatitude [bi'ætitju:d] *nu* very great happiness.

beauty ['bju:ti] *nc/u* **1.** the quality which we find pleasing to look at, hear, smell, think about etc. *We were very impressed by the beauty of the scene.* **2.** fine example of something. *This apple's a beauty.*
beautify *vt* make beautiful.
beautiful *adj.* very attractive, pleasing to the senses or the mind: *a beautiful woman/view/idea. Beautiful, that's just what we need!*

beaver ['bi:və*] *nc* type of small animal which lives both in water and on land and is known for its ability to dam up streams by using mud, twigs etc.

becalm [bi'ka:m] *vt* (usu. *passive*) prevent a ship etc from moving through lack of wind.

became [bi'keim] past tense of **become.**

because [bi'kɔz] *conj* for the reason that.

Note: if we begin with an expression such as *The reason is . . .* we do not usu. follow this expression with *because*; *that* is used instead. *The reason I am late is that I missed the bus.*
because of owing to. *Our holiday was most enjoyable, mainly because of the good weather.*

beck [bek] *n* in **be at somebody's beck and call** i.e. be under somebody's command so that one has to do whatever he wants one to do.

beckon ['bekən] *vt/i* make a sign with a finger/the fingers. *He beckoned us to follow him. He beckoned us nearer, forward etc. He beckoned to us.*

become [bi'kʌm] *vt/i* change so as to be. *He becomes tired easily. He became a rich man. He became famous. past tense* **became** [bi'keim]. *past part* **become.**
become of happen to. *What became of John after he left school?*
become someone (usu. with reference to clothing etc or behaviour) be suitable for etc. *That colour becomes you* i.e. you look nice wearing something in that colour. *It does not become a senior pupil to cause all this trouble.*
becoming *adj* suitable; pretty. (*opp* **unbecoming**).

bed[1] [bed] *nc* **1.** piece of furniture on which one sleeps. **2.** any place where somebody sleeps. **3.** ground underneath the sea, a river, lake etc. **4.** piece of ground in a garden where flowers grow. **5.** material or substance on which something rests: *a bed of concrete.* **6.** layer of a particular type of substance in the earth: *a bed of clay.*
Note: a person is said to be *in bed/in his bed* if he is under the blankets; if he is on top of the blankets, he is said to be *on his bed.*
bedding *nu* sheets, blankets and pillows.
'bedbug small insect which lives in bedclothes and bites people while they are asleep.
'bedclothes sheets and blankets.
'bedridden *adj* unable to get out of bed because of illness or old age.
'bedrock the solid rock deep under the earth.
'bedroom room in which one sleeps.
'bedside the side of a bed. *The child's mother sat at his bedside until he recovered.*
'bed-'sitter, 'bed-'sitting room room which is both a bedroom and a sitting-room.
'bedstead the wooden or metal frame on which a mattress rests.
'bedtime time at which one goes to bed.
double bed bed for two people.
single bed bed for one person.
go to bed get into one's bed.
make a bed put sheets and blankets on a bed so as to make it ready for somebody to sleep in.

bed[2] [bed] *vt* **1.** put something on a base or foundations. *He bedded the plants in very good soil.* **2.** (with reference to an animal) put in a place where the animal can sleep. *He bedded down his horse. past* **bedded.**

bedeck [bi'dek] *vt* make beautiful etc by adding ornaments or decorations. *The altar was bedecked with flowers.*

bedevil [be'devl] *vt* (usu. *passive*) cause harm or trouble to on several occasions. *Our plans have been bedevilled by a series of misfortunes. past* **bedevilled.** (*US* **bedeviled**).

bedlam ['bedləm] *nu* place or state of noise and confusion. (*informal*).

bedraggled [bi'drægld] *adj* (usu. with reference to a person or clothes) untidy, dirty, wet etc.

bee [biː] *nc* flying insect which makes honey.
'beehive box or other place in which bees live.
'beeswax brown substance produced by bees which is used for making polish.
busy as a bee (esp. with reference to children) very busy. (*informal*).
make a beeline for something go by the shortest path to something. *When he saw that I was in the room he made a beeline for the door.* (*informal*).
have a bee in one's bonnet have strong ideas about something, be obsessed with something. (*informal*).

beech [biːtʃ] **1.** *nc/u* type of tree with smooth silvery bark. **2.** *nu* wood of this tree.

beef [biːf] *nu* meat of a cow, ox or bull.

been [biːn] past part of **be.**

beer [biə*] *nu* alcoholic drink made from barley.

beet [biːt] *nc/u* name of two types of plant; one has a red root which is eaten; the other has a white root which is made into sugar.

beetle ['biːtl] *nc* **1.** type of insect having two hard, shiny cases which cover the wings when folded. **2.** (popular use) any large black insect.

beetroot ['biːtruːt] *nc* red root of the beet, eaten in salads.

befall [bi'fɔːl] *vt/i* happen, happen to (*o.f.*). *past tense* **befell** [bi'fel]. *past part* **befallen.**

befit [bi'fit] *vt* be suitable for, be the proper behaviour for. *past* **befitted. befitting** *adj.*

before [bi'fɔː*] *conj/prep* **1.** at an earlier time than: *before six o'clock; before the end of the term. Haven't I met you somewhere before? He has never behaved like that before.* **2.** in front of: *before the king.*
Note: before in the sense of in front of is rather *o.f.* – use *in front of.*
beforehand *adv* before a certain time. *The meal was prepared beforehand.*

befriend [bi'frend] *vt* act as a friend; help.
Note: if the meaning is not merely to act as a friend but to become a friend, then *make friends (with somebody)* would be a better expression to use. *John soon made friends with several boys at his new school. The new boy soon made friends.*

befuddle [bi'fʌdl] *vt* make confused (as with alcohol etc).

beg [beg] *vt/i* **1.** ask (for) with great feeling. *He begged for forgiveness. He begged the judge to forgive him. I beg to apply for the post of junior clerk.* (In the last sense *wish* would be better). **2.** ask people for money (often those passing by). *past* **begged.** see **beggar.**
beg to differ (with somebody) politely disagree (with somebody).
beg pardon in **I beg your pardon 1.** I am sorry. **2.** please say that again.
beg the question talk as though the question which one is arguing about with somebody has already been agreed on.
go begging not wanted or taken by anybody. *Here's some food going begging.* (*informal*).

began [bi'gæn] past tense of **begin.**

beget [bi'get] *vt* **1.** be the father of (*o.f.*). **2.** cause. *Ignorance begets poverty and disease. past tense* **begot** [bi'gɔt]. *past part* **begot** or **begotten.** *old past tense* **begat** [bi'gæt].

beggar ['begə*] *nc* **1.** person who does not work to get money but asks people to give him money. **2.** person or creature. *Friendly little beggar, isn't he?* (*informal*). Also *vt* make somebody poor by causing him to spend or waste all his money.

beggarly *adj* very poor or mean. *His father gave him a beggarly allowance.*

beggary *nu* condition of being a beggar or having no money.

beggars can't be choosers those who ask for things must be content with whatever they get.

beggar (all) description be so good, bad etc that it is impossible to describe.

begin [bi'gin] *vt/i* start, do something for the first time. *My father began building a new house last week. The baby will soon begin to talk. The day began with rain. pres part* **beginning.** *past tense* **began** [bi'gæn]. *past part* **begun** [bi'gʌn]. **beginning** *nc/u.*

beginner *nc* one who is beginning or learning.

begone [bi'gɔn] *imperative* go away (*o.f.* – use **go away**).

begotten [bi'gɔtn] past tense of **beget.**

begrudge [bi'grʌdʒ] *vt* **1.** be unhappy because somebody else has been lucky in some way. **2.** be unhappy about giving somebody something. *The old man begrudged his workers their wages.*

beguile [bi'gail] *vt* **1.** make somebody do something by a trick or by telling lies; cheat somebody. *He beguiled the young man into lending him five hundred pounds.* **2.** make the time pass in a pleasant way: *beguile the time away.* **beguiling** *adj.* **beguilingly** *adv.*

behalf [bi'hɑːf] for somebody/something (in **on behalf of someone/something** i.e. for somebody; in order to help somebody). *They are collecting on behalf of charity. He spoke on behalf of all the members of the society.*

behave [bi'heiv] *vi* act in a certain way. (The verb by itself often means acting in a correct or good way). *They behaved very badly at the party. You must try to behave* i.e. you must try to act properly. *He behaved extremely well. How is your new car behaving?* i.e. is it running well or are you having trouble with it? **behaviour** [bi'heivjə*] *nu.* (*US* **behavior**).

behave yourself (usu. said to a child) act properly, be good.

be on one's best behaviour (usu. with reference to a child) behave very well, be very good.

behead [bi'hed] *vt* kill by cutting somebody's head off.

beheld [bi'held] past tense of **behold.**

behest [bi'hest] *nc* command, order (*o.f.*).

behind [bi'haind] *adv/prep* **1.** at/to the back of something. *He hid behind a tree. He looked behind but he couldn't see anyone coming.* **2.** in a lower position (usu. in school etc). *He was a long way behind the other boys in his class* i.e. they had done more work and knew more than he did. **3.** remaining (usu. after one's death). *He left a large family behind when he died.* Also *nc* part of the body on which one sits. (*informal*).

be'hindhand *pred adj* late, not having done something at the right time. *He is behindhand with his work.*

behind somebody's back secretly, without telling somebody who ought to know.

behind the times old-fashioned, not modern.

fall behind somebody fail to go as fast, work as hard etc as somebody else. *John could not run as fast as his two friends and he soon fell behind. He fell behind the others.*

behold [bi'hould] *vt* notice, look at, see (*o.f.* – use **see, notice** etc). *past* **beheld** [bi'held].

beholden [bi'houldn] *pred adj* owing thanks (usu. in **be beholden to somebody** i.e. owing thanks to somebody for what he has done) (*o.f.*).

beige [beiʒ] *nu* pale brownish-grey colour. Also *adj.*

being[1] ['biːiŋ] **1.** *nc* human (usu. in **human being**). **2.** *nu* life, existence.

being[2] ['biːiŋ] pres part of **be.**

belabour [bi'leibə*] (*US* **belabor**) *vt* hit very hard (*o.f.*).

belabour a point talk too much about it.

belated [bi'leitid] *adj* too late or very late; later than the usual time. *He received a belated invitation to the party* i.e. he received it after other people had received their invitations.

belch [beltʃ] **1.** *vi* send out wind from the stomach through the mouth. **2.** *vt* send out with great force. *A chimney belches (out) smoke. A volcano belches (out) flames.* Also *nc* the act or noise of sending wind from the stomach out through the mouth.

beleaguer [bi'liːgə*] *vt* besiege, attack on all sides in order to capture. **beleaguered** *adj.*

belfry ['belfri] *nc* tower or part of a tower in which bells are hung (esp. in a church).

belfry

belie [bi'lai] *vt* give a false idea of, fail to show the real thing. *His happy face belied his feeling of misery.*

belief [bi'liːf] **1.** *nu* feeling that something is true or that somebody is telling the truth. see **believe.** **2.** *nc* facts about a religion etc which somebody accepts as true. *The beliefs of the Christian Church.*

to the best of one's belief see **best.**

beyond belief so strange, unusual etc that it is difficult to believe. *His stupidity is beyond belief.*

believe [bi'liːv] *vt* having a feeling that somebody is telling the truth or that something is true. *I believe your story. I believe him to be a good man. I believe that you are telling the truth.* (*opp* **disbelieve**).

believable *adj* causing one to believe. (*opp* **unbelievable**).

believer *nc* one who believes (esp. in the existence of God) (*opp* **unbeliever**).

believe in someone/something **1.** have a strong feeling that someone/something exists. *I believe in God.* **2.** trust somebody. **3.** have a feeling that something is good. *I believe in helping other people.*

belittle [bi'litl] *vt* behave or talk, write etc as though something were small and unimportant. *We belittled the danger. Do not belittle what he has achieved.*

bell [bel] *nc* **1.** piece of metal which makes a noise when it is hit. **2.** sound made in this way.

sound as a bell perfectly strong and healthy.
ring a bell bring something back into one's mind. (*informal*).

belle [bel] *nc* beautiful girl or woman (*o.f.*).

bellicose ['belikous] *adj* fond of fighting.
bellicosity [beli'kɔsiti] *nu*.

belligerent [bi'lidʒərənt] *adj* fond of fighting or arguing. Also *nc* country which is fighting another. **belligerently** *adv*.
belligerence *nu* love of fighting or arguing; warlike or threatening behaviour.

bellow ['belou] *vi* make a deep roaring noise like a bull. *When the brick fell on the man's foot, he bellowed with pain.*

bellows ['belouz] *npl* instrument for blowing air (e.g. used to make a fire burn more brightly).

bellows

belly[1] ['beli] *nc* **1.** lower front part of the human body. **2.** soft underpart of an animal's body.
Note: *belly* is felt to be rather impolite (in sense **1.**) – use *stomach*.

belly[2] ['beli] *vi* (usu. with reference to sails) fill out when the wind blows. *The ship's sails bellied out in the wind.*

belong [bi'lɔŋ] *vi* **1.** be the property of. *That pen belongs to me* i.e. it is my pen. **2.** be a member of. *He belongs to the Labour Party* i.e. he is a member of that party. **3.** be in the proper place. *These shoes don't belong in this cupboard, take them out. Does this belong here?*
belongings *npl* things which belong to somebody.
Note: 1. *belongings* refers to personal possessions, not to houses, land, money etc. 2. *belongings* is *pl*. To refer to one personal possession we must say *one of somebody's belongings. Is this one of your belongings?*

beloved [bi'lʌvd] *adj* much loved. *The old man was beloved by/of everyone who knew him.* Also [bi'lʌvid] *n sing* person who is much loved. *He sighed for his beloved.*

below [bi'lou] *adv/prep* at or to a lower place; lower than something. *They looked out of the aeroplane window at the sea below. Miners work below the surface of the earth. The temperature is below freezing.*
see below (in a book etc) referred to later.
hit someone below the belt **1.** hit or attack someone in the lower part of the body. **2.** attack someone unfairly. (*informal*).

belt [belt] *nc* **1.** piece of cloth, leather etc, worn round the body. **2.** circular piece of leather, rubber etc used to connect wheels in a piece of machinery. **3.** any strip or band like a belt: *a belt of trees*.
con'veyor belt type of moving belt used in factories. (The article being manufactured is placed on the moving belt, which takes it to each worker so that he can do some work on it before it moves on to the next worker).
'green belt countryside around a city where building is not allowed.
hit someone below the belt see **below**.

bemoan [bi'moun] *vt* complain about something, show that one is unhappy because of some misfortune. *He bemoaned his bad luck. They bemoaned the fact that they had not been given another chance.*

bemuse [bi'mju:z] *vt* make confused or puzzled.

bench [bentʃ] *nc* **1.** long seat (usu. of wood and without a back). **2.** long table at which a carpenter, shoemaker etc works. **3.** place where a judge sits in a court.
the Bench the judges of a country.
raise somebody to the Bench appoint somebody to be a judge.

bend [bend] *vt/i* **1.** change the shape of something straight by using force. *I can't ride my bicycle because I've bent the wheel. He bent the knife out of shape.* **2.** become bent in this way. *He bent forward to look at the picture. He bent himself double.* **3.** turn in a new direction. *The road bends to the right when it leaves the town.* *past* **bent**. Also *nc*.
Note: when *bend* means 'turn in a new direction', it usu. refers to a road, path, river etc, not to a person who is travelling; we can say *The road bends to the right* but *The traveller/car turned to the right.*
bend over backwards make more effort than necessary to do something for someone.
be bent on something be determined to do something. *He is bent on becoming an engineer.*

beneath [bi'ni:θ] *adv/prep* below, lower than; in a lower place.
beneath contempt so bad, wicked, stupid etc that it is not worth taking notice of it.

benediction [beni'dikʃən] *nc* **1.** blessing (esp. one given by a priest in a church service). **2.** one of the services in the Roman Catholic Church.

benefactor ['benifæktə*] *nc* somebody who does a good or kind action to help another person/other people; somebody who gives money to an institution.
benefaction [beni'fækʃən] *nc/u* act of a benefactor.

benefice ['benifis] *nc* position and payment of a priest in the Church of England.

beneficence [bi'nefisəns] *nu* kindness, goodness.
beneficent *adj* kind, good.

beneficial [beni'fiʃl] *adj* helpful, having a helpful or good effect.
Note: a person is said to be *beneficent*; things such as fresh air, holidays, a rest, medicine etc are said to be *beneficial*.

beneficiary [beni'fiʃəri] *nc* person who receives something (often money or property).

benefit[1] ['benifit] *nc/u* help, good effect, advantage, profit. *I don't know what benefit this new arrangement will be* i.e. I don't know how the new arrangement will help anyone. *I feel the benefit of this medicine already* i.e. I can feel that the medicine is curing me.
'benefit match/performance football etc match or a performance of a play etc in which some of the money paid by the spectators or audience is given to one of the players or actors or to a charity.
give someone the benefit of the doubt believe that someone is probably right if it cannot be proved that he is wrong.

benefit[2] ['benifit] *vt/i* be of benefit, help etc; receive help. *This will not benefit you. You will not benefit by/from this.* *past* **benefited**.

benevolent [bə'nevələnt] *adj* kind, liking to help other people. **benevolently** *adv*.
benevolence *nu* kindness to other people.

benighted [bi'naitid] *adj* **1.** in great ignorance. *He is a poor benighted fool.* **2.** overtaken by night, still travelling when darkness falls. *The benighted travellers discovered that there was no hotel for five miles.*

benign [bi'nain] *adj* **1.** (usu. with reference to people) kind and friendly, not wishing to harm anyone. **2.** (with reference to climate) mild, pleasant, not too hot and not too cold. **3.** (with reference to certain diseases etc) not very harmful: *a benign tumour.*

bent[1] [bent] past of **bend.** Also *adj* dishonest. (*informal*).

bent[2] [bent] *nc* natural liking for or interest in. *He has a bent for engineering.*

benumb [bi'nʌm] *vt* make without feeling. *Note: numb* (verb) is more usual than *benumb.*

bequeath [bi'kwi:ð] *vt* leave to somebody (esp. after one dies). *He bequeathed a thousand pounds to his niece. He bequeathed a lot of trouble to his successor.*

bequest [bi'kwest] *nc* something which is bequeathed.

bereave [bi'ri:v] *vt* (usu. *passive*) take away from something/somebody (usu. by death). *He was bereaved of his wife and children* i.e. his wife and children died. *past* **bereaved** or **bereft** [bi'reft].

bereavement *nc/u* loss of someone through death.

bereft [bi'reft] past of **bereave.**

beret ['beri] *nc* type of hat.

beriberi ['beri'beri] *nu* type of tropical disease.

berry ['beri] *nc* small round fruit (usu. containing several seeds).

berserk [bə'zə:k] *adj/adv* so angry that one seems to be mad.

go berserk behave in this way. *The prisoner went berserk and wrecked the prison.*

berth [bə:θ] *nc* **1.** place on a ship or train where one sleeps. **2.** place where a ship anchors in a harbour etc. Also *vt* take a ship into a berth.

give someone/something a wide berth avoid, have no contact with someone/something. *That man is dangerous; if I were you, I would give him a wide berth.* (*informal*).

beseech [bi'si:tʃ] *vt* ask for with great feeling. *past* **besought** [bi'sɔ:t].

beset [bi'set] *vt* surround so as to cause difficulty or danger to somebody. *The expedition was beset with dangers. pres part* **besetting.** *past* **beset.**

besetting *adj* commonly causing difficulty (usu. in **besetting sin**). *His besetting sin is laziness.*

beside [bi'said] *prep* near, next to, at the side of. *You must sit beside this boy here. Put your book beside the window.*

beside oneself (with rage, anger etc) so angry etc that one has lost control of oneself. *When he saw his enemy escaping he was beside himself with rage.*

beside the point having no connection with the subject being discussed.

besides [bi'saidz] *adv/prep* in addition to, also, as well as. *That car is in a poor state of repair, and besides, it uses too much petrol. Have you any other books besides these?* i.e. have you any more books?

Note: do not confuse *beside* and *besides.* Study the meanings of these words and you will see that they are quite different.

besiege [bi'si:dʒ] *vt* **1.** surround an enemy town, city etc with soldiers in order to capture it. **2.** surround etc somebody/something for some purpose. *He was besieged with requests.*

besmirch [bi'smə:tʃ] *vt* make dirty or impure.

besought [bi'sɔ:t] past of **beseech.**

bespectacled [bi'spektikld] *adj* wearing glasses.

best [best] *adj/adv* superlative of **good, well.**

'best 'man man who helps the bridegroom at a wedding.

'best'seller book which sells a great many copies.

at best even in the most favourable circumstances. *At best we shall have only four good players in our team* i.e. this is the most we can hope for; we might have fewer than four.

to the best of one's ability as well as one can.

to the best of one's belief/knowledge as far as one can be sure (although one may be wrong).

the best part of something the largest part. *The thieves stole the best part of a thousand pounds.* (*informal*).

put one's best foot forward start off, keep going, intending to go as far as possible.

do one's best work etc as well as one can.

make the best of something (often **of a bad job**) accept something bad or unsatisfactory, and try to be cheerful about it.

with the best of them as well as anyone. *He can play cards with the best of them.*

bestial ['bestiəl] *adj* like an animal i.e. savage, stupid, unpleasant, dirty etc.

bestiality [besti'æliti] *nu.*

bestir [bi'stə:*] *vt* start to move quickly. *We must bestir ourselves, if we don't want to be late. past* **bestirred.**

bestow [bi'stou] *vt* give in an official way.

bestowal *nu.*

bestride [bi'straid] *vt* sit or stand with one leg on either side of something. *past tense* **bestrode** [bi'stroud]. *past part* **bestridden** [bi'stridn].

bet [bet] *vt/i* promise to give a certain sum of money to somebody if one is wrong about something; if one is right, one is given money by the other person. *He bet five pence. He bet me five pence. He bet me that he would win. He bet me five pence that he would win. pres part* **betting.** *past* **bet** or **betted.** Also *nc* agreement to pay money in this way.

betting *nu* putting of money on horses etc.

betide [bi'taid] *vt* happen to (*o.f.*).

woe betide somebody unhappiness, bad luck will come to somebody, somebody will be punished. *Woe betide any pupil who comes in late.* (rather *o.f.*).

betray [bi'trei] *vt* **1.** give information to an enemy, help the enemies of one's country or of one's friends. *He betrayed his friends to the enemy* i.e. he helped the enemy to capture or defeat his friends. **2.** show, be a sign of. *His face betrayed his fear* i.e. the expression on his face showed that he was afraid. **betrayer** *nc.*

betrayal *nc/u* act of betraying.

betroth [bi'trouð] *vt* make an arrangement for someone to marry a certain person. *He betrothed his daughter to a rich man. She is betrothed to a rich man* i.e. it has been arranged that she will marry him. **betrothal** *nc.* (both rather *o.f.*).

the betrothed person who has promised to marry someone. (rather *o.f.*).

better[1] ['betə*] *adj/adv* comparative of **good, well.**
better off richer, luckier, more fortunate etc. (*informal*).
get better improve; recover or begin to recover from an illness.
get the better of someone defeat, beat, overcome someone.
had better ought, should. *You had better finish what you're doing and go* i.e. you should do this.
have seen better days have been in a better condition at one time; be rather old and useless. *This suit has seen better days.* (*informal*).
know better than (to) do something have enough intelligence to avoid doing something. *You ought to know better than stay away from school.*
think better of something change one's mind, decide to do something other than what one first intended to do. *He was going to answer me back, but he thought better of it.*

better[2] ['betə*] *vt* improve, make better.
better oneself get a better job, better education etc.

between [bi'twiːn] *adv/prep* **1.** with something on either side. *3 comes between 2 and 4.* **2.** joining, connecting: *a connection between smoking and lung cancer; war between two countries; the journey between London and Edinburgh.* **3.** (with reference to time or distance) later or more than the first, but earlier or less than the second: *between four and six o'clock; between five and ten miles.* **4.** for two or more: *share something between several people.* see Note.
Note: some people consider that *between* should be used only when two people/things are involved and that *among* should be used when more than two are involved (e.g. *He divided his money between his two sons* but *He divided his money among his three sons*). However, many speakers of English do not follow this rule.
'go-between person who does something to bring two people together, or who carries messages between two people (often for a bad purpose).
between you and me (used to introduce a secret, or something which one does not want everyone to know) I will tell you, but I would not say this to everyone. (Also **between ourselves.**)
in between between; in the middle.

betwixt [bi'twikst] *adv/prep* between (*o.f.*).

bevel ['bevl] *nc* sloping edge. Also *vt* make a sloping edge. *past* **bevelled.** (*US* **beveled**).

beverage ['bevəridʒ] *nc* any kind of drink.

bevy ['bevi] *nc* group (esp. of young women).

bewail [bi'weil] *vt* show sorrow about something, cry or complain about something. *He bewailed the lack of opportunity in this town.*

beware [bi'wεə*] *vt/i* (used only in *imperative* or *infinitive*; does not form tenses). *Beware of falling rocks!* i.e. be careful in case a rock falls on you. *You must beware of losing your books* i.e. you must try not to lose them. *Beware how you do something.*

bewilder [bi'wildə*] *vt* make it difficult or impossible for somebody to understand something or to think clearly. *Most of the questions in the examination bewildered me. I was bewildered by the new rules.* **bewildering** *adj.* **bewilderment** *nu.*

bewitch [bi'witʃ] *vt* **1.** use magic on. **2.** attract; be so beautiful, attractive, charming etc that other people are very influenced. *The beautiful girl bewitched all the young men in the village.* **bewitching** *adj.* **bewitchingly** *adv.*

beyond [bi'jɔnd] *adv/prep* **1.** further (than), at a greater distance (than). *The house is beyond the village* i.e. you will come to the house after passing the village. **2.** past, later than: *beyond help* i.e. unable to be helped; *beyond belief* i.e. impossible to believe. *How he can tell such lies is beyond my understanding.*
beyond a joke too annoying to be funny. (*informal*).

bi- [bai] *prefix* twice; every two; having two of something (e.g. **biannual**).

biannual [bai'ænjuəl] *adj* occurring twice a year.
Note: do not confuse *biannual* and *biennial.*

bias[1] ['baiəs] *vt* make somebody come to a decision without allowing him to hear the full facts. *He was biassed against the plan from the beginning* i.e. he had decided that he was opposed to the plan before he had ever heard the arguments in favour of it. *The newspapers biassed their readers against the new government. He was biassed towards the plan* i.e. he was in favour of the plan before he had heard the full facts. *past* **biased** or **biassed.** Also *nc/u* leaning, prejudice.
biassed *adj.* (*opp* **unbiassed**).

bias[2] ['baiəs] *nc* in **cut something on the bias** i.e. cut something (e.g. a piece of cloth).

bib [bib] *nc* piece of cloth or plastic which is tied round a child's neck while he is eating.

Bible ['baibl] *nc* **1.** holy books of the Christian or Jewish religions bound in one volume. **2.** any book which one relies on for guidance and information. (often *informal* in sense **2.**). **biblical** ['biblikl] *adj.*

bibliography [bibli'ɔgrəfi] *nc* list of books and other writings about a particular subject or by a particular writer. **bibliographical** [bibliə'græfikl] *adj.*
bibliographer [bibli'ɔgrəfə*] *nc* person who compiles a bibliography.

bicarbonate [bai'kaːbənit] *nu* **1.** bicarbonate of soda i.e. substance used in cooking and for medical purposes. **2.** any salt of carbonic acid.

bicentenary [baisen'tiːnəri] *nc* celebration of something which happened 200 years ago.

biceps ['baiseps] *n sing* or *pl* (usu. *pl*) large muscle in the upper part of the arm.

bicker ['bikə*] *vi* quarrel about little things.
bickering *nu* quarrelling of this kind.

bicycle ['baisikl] *nc* vehicle with two wheels used for riding. *Everybody should learn how to ride a bicycle.* Also *vi* (not often used today; *cycle* is commoner as a verb).

bid[1] [bid] *vt* make an offer of money at an auction. *He bid five pounds for the chair* i.e. he offered to buy the chair for five pounds. *past* **bid.** Also *nc* an offer of this kind.
bidder *nc* person who makes a bid.
bidding *nu* all the bids made at an auction. *Was there much bidding?* i.e. did many people make bids?
make a bid for freedom etc try to get freedom etc.

bid[2] [bid] *vt* order, command (*o.f.* – use **order** etc). *past tense* **bade** [bæd]. *past part* **bidden.**
bidding *nu* command, order.
at somebody's bidding because somebody

has given an order. *I shan't do it at your bidding.*
do somebody's bidding do what somebody has ordered.
bid somebody goodbye, farewell, welcome etc say goodbye etc to somebody.
bidden ['bidn] past part of **bid**[2].
bide [baid] *vt* in **bide one's time** i.e. wait for the right moment or for the most favourable opportunity to do something.
biennial [bai'eniəl] *adj* occurring once every two years; continuing for two years.
Note: do not confuse *biennial* and *biannual.*
bier [biə*] *nc* movable stand or frame on which a dead body or a coffin is placed or carried at a funeral.
bifocal ['bai'foukl] *adj* having two focuses.
bifocals *npl* glasses in which each eyepiece has a lens divided into two parts.
big [big] *adj* large, not small etc. *comparative* **bigger.** *superlative* **biggest.**
'big 'game large animals such as lions, elephants, tigers, which are hunted for sport.
'big-'game 'hunter *nc* person who hunts big game. **big-game hunting** *nu.*
'big-'hearted *adj* kind, generous, willing to help other people.
bigamy ['bigəmi] *nu* act of being married by the official procedure of a country or in church when already married to another person; in many countries this is a crime and a sin. **bigamist** *nc.*
bigamous ['bigəməs] *adj*: *a bigamous marriage.* **bigamously** *adv.*
bigot ['bigət] *nc* person who has very strong beliefs (esp. religious beliefs) and who will not listen to other people's opinions. **bigoted** *adj.* **bigotry** *nu.*
bike [baik] *nc* informal form of **bicycle.**
bikini [bi'kiːni] *nc* very small swimming costume for women, consisting of two pieces.
bilateral [bai'lætərl] *adj* on both sides; made by two opposing groups; having two sides. *The two countries signed a bilateral agreement on trade.*
bile [bail] *nu* bitter liquid produced by the liver to help the digestion of food.
bilge [bildʒ] *nu* **1.** dirty water at the bottom of a ship. **2.** nonsense, foolish talk etc. (*informal* in sense **2.**).
bilingual [bai'liŋgwəl] *adj* **1.** speaking or knowing two languages. *Some children educated in foreign countries become bilingual.* **2.** written etc in two languages: *a bilingual text.* Also *nc* person who speaks two languages. **bilingualism** *nu.*
bilious ['biliəs] *adj* **1.** caused by too much bile: *a bilious attack* i.e. a slight illness caused by too much bile. **2.** bad-tempered. **3.** sickly: *a bilious colour.* **biliousness** *nu.*
bill[1] [bil] *nc* bird's beak.
bill[2] [bil] *nc* **1.** piece of paper which lists the amounts of money one owes for goods or service which one has received. **2.** law before it has been officially approved. (It is called an **act** when it has been officially approved by Parliament). **3.** notice or advertisement (esp. one stating what is to be seen at a theatre etc). **4.** piece of paper in which one promises to pay money on a certain date. **5.** (*US*) piece of paper money.
bill of lading list showing all the articles in a ship's cargo.
'billposter, 'billsticker person who sticks notices on walls etc.
billet ['bilit] *nc* private house where a soldier lives if he does not live in a barracks. Also *vt* send a soldier to live in somebody's private house. *Soldiers were billeted on all the villagers.*
billiards ['biliədz] *nu* game played on a big special table with ivory balls and long sticks.
billion ['biliən] *nc* **1.** (*Brit*) a million multiplied by a million (1,000,000,000,000). **2.** (*US*) a million multiplied by a thousand (1,000,000,000).
billow ['bilou] *nc* big wave of the sea. Also *vi* (usu. with reference to the sea) move in waves.
bin [bin] *nc* large container (usu. with a lid).
'dustbin (*Brit*) bin for putting rubbish in. (*US* **'trash can**).
binary ['bainəri] *adj* based on two, involving two of something.
bind [baind] *vt* **1.** use string, rope etc to tie or fasten things together. *He bound the sticks together.* **2.** fasten sheets of paper together to make a book. *After it had been printed the book was bound.* **3.** make somebody do something or promise to do something (usu. by law). *The contract binds us to complete the work within six months.* **4.** put an edge on something (e.g. a carpet or piece of material). **5.** make firmer. *When making a cake we can add an egg to bind the mixture.* *past* **bound** [baund].
binder *nc* **1.** man who binds books. **2.** something which fastens things together. **3.** machine which ties grain together after it has been cut.
binding[1] *nc* **1.** covering of a book; way in which the pages of a book are fastened together. **2.** something which covers the edge of a carpet or piece of material.
binding[2] *adj* forcing one to do something by law. *If you sign that agreement, it will be binding* i.e. you must do what it says.
bind someone over (to keep the peace) (with reference to a judge) make someone promise in a court of law not to cause any more trouble.
bind up a wound put a bandage on a wound.
bind oneself to do something promise to do something.
bingo ['biŋgou] *nu* type of gambling game.
binoculars [bi'nɔkjuləz] *npl* glasses which enable one to see things a long way away. (Often **a pair of binoculars**).

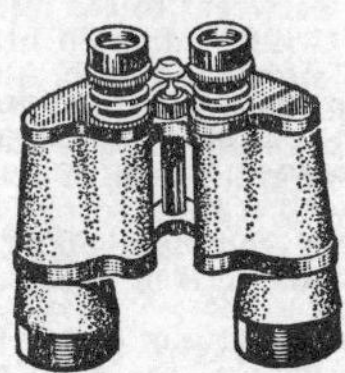

binoculars

binomial [bai'noumiəl] *adj* having two parts or terms (e.g. 6a + 3b is a binomial expression).
biochemistry ['baiou'kemistri] *nu* science of the chemistry of living things. **biochemical** *adj.* **biochemist** *nc.*
biography [bai'ɔgrəfi] *nc* story of somebody's life, written by another person. see **autobiography.** **biographical** [baiou'græfikl] *adj.* **biographer** *nc.*

biology [bai'ɔlədʒi] *nu* science of living things (e.g. plants and animals). **biological** [baiə'lɔdʒikl] *adj.* **biologist** *nc.*
biological warfare warfare in which germs carrying disease are used as weapons.
bipartisan [bai'pɑ:tizæn] *adj* concerned with, representing two parties (usu. political parties).
biped ['baiped] *adj* having two feet. Also *nc*: *A man or a bird is a biped.*
birch [bə:tʃ] **1.** *nc* type of tree having a smooth bark and thin branches. **2.** *nu* wood of this tree. **3.** *nc* bundle of birch twigs tied together, formerly used for beating schoolboys or criminals. Also *vt* beat somebody with this instrument.
bird [bə:d] *nc* **1.** type of creature having wings and a beak and usu. able to fly. **2.** girl, girlfriend. (*informal* in sense **2.**).
'bird bath small vessel filled with water (usu. on a pedestal) and placed in a garden to attract birds to visit the garden.
'bird's-'eye 'view view from above, covering a wide area.
'bird's nest shelter built by birds for their eggs and young.
bird of passage 1. bird which flies from one region to another as the seasons change. **2.** person who travels about a lot. (*informal* in sense **2.**).
bird of prey bird which kills and eats animals and other birds.
'bird sanctuary area where birds are protected and encouraged to stay.
'bird watcher *nc* someone who studies birds in their natural surroundings. **bird watching** *nu.*
birds of a feather (flock together) people of the same type (associate with each other, mix together).
a bird in the hand (is worth two in the bush) something which one has now is more useful than something larger, better which one might perhaps get later on.
kill two birds with one stone gain two things, carry out two jobs, by doing only one thing.
birth [bə:θ] *nc* **1.** act of being born: *the birth of a baby.* **2.** beginning of something: *the birth of a new political party.*
'birth control various methods of ensuring that babies are born only when parents wish to have them, so as to limit the size of the family.
'birthday date, returning each year, on which somebody was born. *My birthday is the 22nd of April.*
'birthmark mark on the skin which was there when somebody was born.
'birthplace town etc in which somebody was born.
'birth rate number of children born in one year in a country taken as a proportion of the total population.
'birthright something which belongs to a person because of the country or family into which he was born.
give birth have a baby. *She gave birth to a baby boy.*
at birth when first born. *He weighed seven pounds at birth.*
biscuit ['biskit] *nc* **1.** (*Brit*) type of hard, flat cake, often sweetened. **2.** (*US*) type of bread made into small buns.
bisect [bai'sekt] *vt* divide into two parts. **bisection** *nu.*
bishop ['biʃəp] *nc* clergyman of senior rank in many Christian churches.
bishopric ['biʃəprik] *nc* area ruled over by a bishop; position of a bishop.
bison ['baisn] *nc* type of wild ox with a large shaggy head, found in America. (Also **buffalo**).
bit[1] [bit] *nc* **1.** small piece. *Write it on a bit of paper. I'm going to sleep for a bit* i.e. for a short time. **2.** part of a drill which makes a hole. **3.** metal bar which is placed in a horse's mouth to control it.
bit by bit gradually, slowly.
not a bit not at all.
to bits into small pieces: *knocked to bits.*
bit[2] [bit] *adv* rather. *This job is a bit difficult* i.e. difficult but not as difficult as it could be. *He's a bit better* i.e. better but not completely recovered from his illness.
Note: not all *adjs* can have *a bit* in front of them.
bit[3] [bit] past tense of **bite.**
bitch [bitʃ] *nc* **1.** female dog or wolf. **2.** impolite way of referring to a woman (usu. one who is unpleasant) (*informal*).
bite [bait] *vt/i* **1.** use the teeth to cut or break something. *He bit the apple. The dog bit the man.* **2.** (usu. with reference to insects) sting. *I was bitten by a mosquito.* **3.** (with reference to acid) damage, make holes in. *The acid bit into the metal.* **4.** (with reference to frost) damage. *The frost has bitten all the flowers in my garden.* **5.** (with reference to fish) take food (called **bait**) off a hook. *Are the fish biting today? pres part* **biting.** *past tense* **bit** [bit]. *past part* **bitten.** Also *nc* **1.** act of biting. **2.** mark left by a bite or sting. **3.** mouthful of food. **4.** taking of food from the hook by a fish. *I was fishing for a long time before I had a bite.*
biting *adj* **1.** so cold as to cause pain: *a biting wind.* **2.** causing pain to somebody: *biting remarks.*
bitten ['bitn] past part of **bite.**
bitter ['bitə*] *adj* **1.** opposite of sweet; having a taste like beer or quinine. **2.** causing pain or unhappiness: *a bitter wind* i.e. a very cold wind. *His son's behaviour has been a bitter disappointment to him.* **3.** caused by or showing hate or great dislike. *Their friendship ended with a bitter quarrel.*
bitterly *adv.* **bitterness** *nu.*
bitumen ['bitjumən] *nu* name of a number of substances, including asphalt and petroleum.
bivouac ['bivuæk] *nc* soldiers' camp with no tents. Also *vt/i* stay or cause to stay in a bivouac.
bizarre [bi'zɑ:*] *adj* very strange, unnatural. **bizarrely** *adv.* **bizarreness** *nu.*
blab [blæb] *vt/i* talk too much (and esp. tell secrets in this way). *past* **blabbed.** (*informal*).
black [blæk] **1.** *nu* the colour of the print in this book. **2.** *nu* (with reference to people) the colour of the Africans south of the Sahara. **3.** *nc* African or person of African origin. Also *adj* dark, gloomy, dirty, threatening.
blacken *vt/i* become or make black in colour.
'blackbird 1. black songbird with a yellow beak related to the thrush. **2.** several types of bird the male of which has black feathers.
'blackboard large board (usu. black or dark in colour) in a classroom, on which the teacher writes with chalk.
'black 'eye dark-coloured bruise around the eye.
'blackhead small pimple on the skin, having a black head.
'blackleg person who works when other

people are on strike.
'blacklist *nc* list of people who have done wrong or who might do wrong. Also *vt* write someone's name on such a list.
'blackmail *nu* threat to tell somebody's secrets if he does not give one some money. Also *vt* make such a threat. **blackmailer** *nc*.
'black 'magic magic which causes harm to people; evil magic.
'black 'mark (against somebody) something which shows that somebody has failed to do something.
(the) 'black 'market see **market.**
'blackout *nc* **1.** loss of consciousness. **2.** turning out all the lights. Also *vi* lose consciousness, faint.
'black 'sheep (of the family) the person in a group or family who fails to do well or who behaves badly.
'blacksmith man whose work is to make things out of iron (esp. horseshoes).
be in somebody's black books be considered a dangerous or badly-behaved person by somebody. *John is in the teacher's black books; he was late for school every day last week.* (*informal*).
black and blue badly bruised. *After the fight he was black and blue.*
blacken somebody's character tell other people that somebody has done wrong or is a wicked person.
give somebody black looks/a black look look at somebody angrily.
in black and white in writing, in print.

bladder ['blædə*] *nc* **1.** bag inside the body which contains urine. **2.** rubber bag inside a football.

blade [bleid] *nc* **1.** part of a knife or sword which has a sharp edge or point. **2.** anything shaped like a knife blade: *a blade of grass.*

blame [bleim] *vt* say that somebody/something caused an accident or a failure of some kind. *He blamed his brother for breaking the window. He blamed the accident on his brother.* Also *nu*. **blamable** *adj*.
blameless *adj* not responsible, innocent.
blamelessly *adv*.
to blame responsible. *John is to blame for the accident* i.e. John caused the accident.
bear the blame be blamed, be made responsible. *You must bear the blame for this accident.*

blanch [blɑːntʃ] *vt/i* become or make white in colour (usu. with reference to 1. making certain foods white (e.g. celery). 2. in the case of people with light-coloured skins, becoming paler (through fear etc).

blancmange [blə'mɔnʒ] *nc/u* type of sweet food made from milk and cornflour.

bland [blænd] *adj* **1.** very gentle, too polite. **2.** (with reference to food) smooth and easily digested (and usu. without much taste).

blandishment ['blændiʃmənt] *nc* (usu. *pl*) gentle, polite words, which make somebody do something which he might not want to do. *After many blandishments, Mr Jones finally agreed to buy his daughter a new dress.*

blank[1] [blæŋk] *adj* lacking something, without something: *a blank piece of paper* i.e. one without any writing or drawing on it; *a blank wall* i.e. one without doors or windows; *a blank cartridge* i.e. one without a bullet in it. *There was a blank look on his face* i.e. his face showed no sign of thought or feeling.
'blank 'cheque one which is signed but on which the sum of money to be paid is not written.
'blank 'verse English poetry which has five stresses in each line and no rhyme.

blank[2] [blæŋk] *nc* **1.** space in which nothing is written. *Leave a blank if you don't know the answer.* **2.** blank cartridge. *The soldiers were firing blanks.* **3.** emptiness or absence of something. *His mind was a blank* i.e. he could not think of anything or remember anything. **blankly** *adv*. **blankness** *nu*.

blanket ['blæŋkit] *nc* **1.** warm cloth (usu. made of wool) used for covering someone/something (esp. someone sleeping in a bed). **2.** any thick covering: *a blanket of snow.* Also *vt* cover thickly. *A covering of snow blanketed the village.*

blare [blɛə*] *vt/i* make a loud noise like a trumpet. Also *nu*.
blaring *adj*: *The police car went by with its siren blaring.*

blasé ['blɑːzei] *adj* having experienced many pleasures etc and now interested in none.

blasphemy ['blæsfəmi] *nc/u* talking of God in a disrespectful or joking way. **blasphemous** *adj*. **blasphemously** *adv*.
blaspheme [blæs'fiːm] *vt/i* speak in this way. **blasphemer** *nc*.

blast[1] [blɑːst] *nc* **1.** sudden strong rush of air (esp. one caused by an explosion or by opening an oven or other place where air has been heated). *The blast from the explosion shattered hundreds of windows.* **2.** sound made by a trumpet or other wind instrument. **3.** explosion.
'blast furnace furnace in which a blast of hot air is used for raising the temperature, used for melting iron ore.

blast[2] [blɑːst] *vt* **1.** destroy by explosion. **2.** destroy by cold or heat or by lightning. *The frost blasted all the flowers in the garden.*
blasted *adj* **1.** destroyed by a blast of some kind. **2.** damned, cursed. (*informal* in sense **2.**).

blatant ['bleitənt] *adj* **1.** not trying to hide one's bad behaviour; shameless. *The student showed blatant disrespect for the rules of the college.* **2.** noisy and badly behaved.
blatantly *adv*.

blaze[1] [bleiz] *nc* (usu. only *sing*) **1.** bright flame: *the blaze of the fire.* **2.** bright light or bright colour. *There was a sudden blaze of light and then it became dark again.* **3.** fire which destroys a building etc. *The firemen fought the blaze for two hours before they put it out.*
a blaze of glory sudden popularity and success which does not last long.

blaze[2] [bleiz] *vi* **1.** burn fiercely or quickly. *The fire was blazing.* **2.** shine brightly. **3.** show strong feelings. *His eyes were blazing with anger.* **blazing** *adj*.
blaze away (at something) fire bullets very quickly and without stopping. (*informal*).
blaze up suddenly start to burn quickly.

blaze[3] [bleiz] *vt* mark a tree by cutting a piece of the bark (usu. to mark a path in a forest or to show which trees are to be cut down).
blaze a trail **1.** mark trees in this way to show the path in a forest. **2.** do something for the first time so that other people are encouraged to do it after one. *With his discoveries the famous scientist blazed a trail which many of his colleagues followed.*

blazer ['bleizə*] *nc* type of jacket, sometimes brightly coloured, worn by some schoolchildren in Britain, and by adults to show they are members of teams which play certain games (e.g. cricket, bowls etc).

blazon ['bleizn] *vt* make known as widely as possible. *John's success in the examination was soon blazoned abroad.*

bleach [bli:tʃ] *nu* chemical substance which takes the colour out of certain materials or which helps to make clothes clean. Also *vt/i* become or make something pale or clean by using bleach, or by exposure to sunlight. *The old curtains had been bleached by the sun.*

bleak [bli:k] *adj* **1.** exposed to cold winds. *The countryside here is very bleak in winter.* **2.** with very little hope of happiness. *Without money, the future looked bleak for John.* **3.** unhappy and unfriendly etc. *When we arrived, we got a rather bleak welcome.*
bleakly *adv.* **bleakness** *nu.*

bleary ['bliəri] *adj* unable to see clearly (usu. because of tiredness).

bleat [bli:t] *vi* make a noise like a sheep or goat. Also *nc* noise made by these animals.

bled [bled] past tense of **bleed.**

bleed [bli:d] *vi* lose blood. *The cut on his finger was bleeding. He was bleeding from the cut on his finger. past* **bled** [bled]. **bleeding** *nu.*

blemish ['blemiʃ] *nc* mark which makes something less beautiful or less perfect: *a blemish on one's reputation.* Also *vt* make something less beautiful or less perfect by adding a blemish.

blench [blentʃ] *vi* **1.** move away quickly because one is afraid etc. **2.** turn pale or white because one is afraid etc.

blend [blend] *vt/i* **1.** (esp. with reference to mixing different kinds of tea, coffee, whisky, tobacco) become, make mixed. **2.** (with reference to different colours) be suitable for putting together; change gradually from one colour into the other. *I like the way the colour of the carpet blends with the yellow curtains.* Also *nc* mixture (esp. of tea, coffee, whisky or tobacco).

bless [bles] *vt* **1.** ask God's help or protection for. *The priest blessed the people.* **2.** make holy. *past* **blessed** or **blest** both pronounced [blest].
blessed ['blesid] *adj* **1.** holy, given special help or protection by God. **2.** annoying, troublesome. (*informal* in sense **2.**).
blessing *nc* **1.** something given through the help or protection of God. **2.** prayer said by a priest which asks God to give help and protection to the people. **3.** anything which makes one happy and thankful. *Good health is a blessing.*
bless me, bless my soul, well I'm blessed etc expressions to show that one is surprised. (*informal* and rather *o.f.*).
bless you! an exclamation sometimes said by other people when somebody sneezes.
blessed with having or getting something which makes one happy and thankful. *He was blessed with good health.*
a blessing in disguise something which makes one happy, but which at first seemed unpleasant. *Not getting that job was actually a blessing in disguise, because I have now got a much better one.* (*informal*).
give someone/something one's blessing say that one is happy about someone's plans or intentions and that one hopes the plans will succeed.

blew [blu:] past tense of **blow¹.**

blight [blait] *nu* **1.** disease of plants. **2.** anything which spoils one's hopes, plans etc. Also *vt* spoil in this way. *The accident blighted his life.*

blind¹ [blaind] *adj* **1.** unable to see. *The old man with the white stick was blind.* **2.** unable to think or judge properly. *I just made a blind guess at the answer* i.e. I didn't think about it properly. *He killed the man in a blind fury* i.e. he was too angry to think about it properly. **3.** with no opening: *a blind alley* i.e. an alley with a wall at the end. Also *vt* make blind. **blindly** *adv.* **blindness** *nu.*
the blind blind people.
'blindfold *nc* piece of cloth tied over the eyes to prevent somebody from seeing. Also *vt* cover somebody's eyes in this way. Also *adj/adv* with the eyes covered in this way.
'blind spot **1.** small part of the eye which is not sensitive to light. **2.** prejudice against something.
be blind to something not see or not notice something. *He is blind to his own faults.*
blind as a bat see **bat².**
the blind leading the blind a person who needs help himself trying to give help to other people. (*informal*).

blind² [blaind] *nc* something (often cloth which can be rolled down and up) which covers a window to keep sunshine out or to stop people seeing in.

blink [bliŋk] *vt/i* **1.** shut the eyes and open them again quickly. **2.** (with reference to a light) shine unsteadily (usu. because the light is a long way away). **3.** turn a light on and off quickly (e.g. as a signal).

blinkers ['bliŋkəz] *npl* pieces of leather put at the side of a horse's eyes to make it look straight ahead.

bliss [blis] *nu* very great and peaceful happiness. **blissful** *adj.* **blissfully** *adv.*

blister ['blistə*] *nc* **1.** small swelling on the skin filled with a watery liquid (usu. caused by rubbing or burning). **2.** swelling on painted wood, caused by heat. Also *vt/i* get or cause blisters.

blithe [blaið] *adj* happy and cheerful (*o.f.*).
blithely *adv* happily, not showing any remorse, distress etc. *He blithely ignored me.*

blitz [blits] *nc* (only *sing*) **1.** (esp. with reference to attacks by German aeroplanes on London and other British cities during the Second World War) attack by aeroplanes dropping bombs on cities. **2.** any sudden and violent attack.
blitzed [blitst] *adj* (with reference to houses etc in a city) destroyed by bombing.

blizzard ['blizəd] *nc* snowstorm with a strong wind.

bloated ['bloutid] *adj* too fat, fat in an unhealthy way.

bloater ['bloutə*] *nc* herring which has been salted and smoked.

blob [blɔb] *nc* small round spot or object. *A blob of ice cream fell on her dress.*

bloc [blɔk] *nc* group of people or countries who act together in certain political activities. *There is an Afro-Asian bloc at the United Nations.*

block¹ [blɔk] *nc* **1.** large solid piece of wood or stone etc. **2.** (*Brit*) large tall building. *They are building a new block of offices near the school.* **3.** number of buildings surrounded by streets on four sides. *The place you're looking for is three blocks along the street.* **4.** number of seats that are together in a cinema or theatre. **5.** something which stops things moving (usu. **blockage,** or if reference is to traffic, **'traffic jam** is more usual). **6.** square piece of wood used as a child's toy. **7.** (in former times) piece of wood on which a person laid his head if he was to be executed by having his head cut off.

blockage *nc* something which prevents movement. *There is a blockage in the pipe, and so the water is not coming through.*

'blockhead stupid person.

'block 'letters LETTERS WRITTEN LIKE THIS.

block and tackle apparatus for lifting heavy loads.

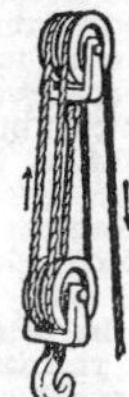

block and tackle

block² [blɔk] *vt* **1.** make movement impossible. *You can't leave the city, all the roads are blocked by snow. They will have to block up the entrance to the tunnel.* **2.** make it impossible for something to happen. *All our plans have been blocked by our opponents.* **3.** draw the outline of something without putting in the details. *The architect blocked in our house and garden on the drawing.*

blockade [blɔ'keid] *nc* surrounding a town, country etc to prevent people or supplies getting in or out. Also *vt* surround a town, country etc in this way.

run a blockade get in or out of a town or country which is being blockaded.

blonde [blɔnd] *nc* (esp. with reference to women) person having yellow or golden hair. Also *adj*.

blood [blʌd] *nu* red liquid in the body.

bloody *adj* **1.** covered with blood. **2.** cursed, annoying. (*informal* in sense **2.**). *Note:* the word in sense **2.** often has very little meaning. It is considered impolite except among friends. It can also be used as an *intensifier*: *bloody good.*

bloodless *adj* **1.** without any killing: *a bloodless revolution.* **2.** without blood. **3.** very pale.

'blood bank 1. place where blood is stored. (The blood is given to people who require blood transfusions because of an accident etc). **2.** blood which is stored in this way.

'bloodcurdling *adj* very frightening, horrifying: *bloodcurdling stories.*

'blood donor person who gives some of his blood for medical purposes.

'blood group type of blood. (Everybody's blood belongs to one of four main types).

'bloodhound large dog used for tracking people who have run away (e.g. criminals).

'blood money money given to a person as payment for killing somebody.

'blood poisoning disease of the blood. *If you don't clean that wound, you may get blood poisoning.*

'blood pressure pressure of the blood against the sides of the blood vessels.

'blood re'lation someone to whom one is directly related, not through marriage (e.g. a brother or sister).

'bloodshed killing. *The king defeated his enemies, but only after much bloodshed.*

'bloodshot *adj* (with reference to the eyes) red. *I think I must be reading too much because my eyes are rather bloodshot.*

'bloodthirsty *adj* having a liking for killing people or animals.

'blood transfusion (medicine) taking blood from one person's veins and putting it into another's.

'blood vessel tube inside the body through which blood flows.

bloody-minded *adj* behaving in a deliberately awkward way.

bad blood (between people) a quarrel or feeling of dislike which lasts a long time. *There has been bad blood between them for many years.* (*informal*).

in cold blood (usu. with reference to a cruel action done through love of cruelty and not out of anger) without showing any anger. *He shot down his enemy in cold blood.*

someone's blood is/was up somebody is/was very angry. *From the expression on his face, I could tell that his blood was up.* (*informal*).

one's own flesh and blood see flesh.

bloom [bluːm] **1.** *nc* flower. **2.** *nu* time when somebody/something is most perfect. *The girl was in the bloom of youth.* Also *vi* have flowers. *The trees are blooming.*

in bloom having flowers.

blossom ['blɔsəm] **1.** *nu* all the flowers on a fruit tree. **2.** *nc* one of these flowers. **3.** *nc* any flower. Also *vi* have flowers. *The trees are blossoming.*

in blossom with flowers.

blot [blɔt] *nc* **1.** stain of ink on a piece of paper. **2.** something which makes a person/thing less beautiful or less good: *a blot on somebody's character* i.e. a bad action or habit which spoils somebody's character. Also *vt* **1.** dry up ink with blotting paper etc. **2.** make a mark with ink. **3.** spoil something, make something less beautiful or less good. *past* **blotted.**

'blotting paper paper used for drying ink.

blot something out hide completely; cover up; destroy; make a blot which completely hides what has been written: *blot out a word.*

blotch [blɔtʃ] *nc* large roughly-shaped mark (esp. on somebody's face). Also *vt.* **blotchy** *adj.* **blotchiness** *nu.*

blouse [blauz] *nc* garment covering the upper part of the body (usu. worn by women).

blow¹ [blou] *vt/i* **1.** (with reference to wind, air etc) move or cause to move. *The wind was blowing. The wind blew my hat off.* **2.** be moved or carried away by air or wind. *All the papers blew off his desk; the wind blew them off.* **3.** (with reference to musical instruments) make, cause to make, a noise by the movement of air. *The trumpet was blowing. He blew the trumpet.* **4.** breathe hard. *The runners were blowing hard as they approached the tape. He blew his fingers to warm them.* **5.** (with reference to whales) send air mixed with water into the air from the breathing hole. **6.** (with reference to a fuse) melt. *If there is too much current in the circuit a fuse will blow. past tense* **blew** [bluː]. *past part* **blown** [bloun].

blower *nc* thing/person used for blowing air (e.g. a *glass-blower* is a man who shapes glass vessels by blowing hot glass at the end of a long tube).

blow out (with reference to a candle flame, burning match etc) stop burning, cause to stop burning, by the movement of air.
'blow-out 1. bursting of a tyre. 2. sudden escape of gas or steam. 3. large party. (*informal*).
blow up 1. explode, damage or destroy by an explosion. *The bomb blew up. He blew up the building.* 2. (with reference to a tyre, balloon etc) fill with air. 3. (with reference to a photograph) enlarge (usu. for scientific purposes).
blow one's brains out kill oneself by firing a bullet into the head. (*informal*).
blow hot and cold about/over something change several times from a favourable opinion to an unfavourable one. (*informal*).
blow one's nose breathe very hard through one's nose (usu. into a handkerchief) to clear the nose of dirt.

blow[2] [blou] *nc* 1. hard knock with the hand or a weapon: *hit/strike somebody a blow in the eye; give somebody a blow.* 2. disappointment, misfortune. *News of John's sudden death was a great blow to his friends.* 3. successful attack. *Our soldiers struck several hard blows at the enemy in the first week of the war.*
'blowpipe 1. tube used for blowing air into a flame to make it hotter. 2. tube through which a person blows darts, small stones, dried peas etc.
at a blow with one stroke. *He killed four of the enemy at a blow.*
come to blows start fighting.
exchange blows fight.
strike a blow for something fight for, support by fighting (usu. freedom, the cause, liberty etc).
without striking a blow without fighting.

blown [bloun] past part of **blow**[1].

blubber[1] ['blʌbə*] *nu* fat of whales and some other sea animals.

blubber[2] ['blʌbə*] *vi* cry in a noisy way. (*informal*).

bludgeon ['blʌdʒən] *nc* heavy stick used as a weapon. Also *vt* hit with a bludgeon.

blue [blu:] *nu* colour of the sky when the sun is shining, and other colours lighter and darker than this. Also *adj* 1. of this colour. 2. obscene.
blues *n sing* or *pl* type of jazz music (often rather slow and sad).
'blue 'blood 1. the aristocracy. 2. condition of being a nobleman. 3. supposed special characteristics of noblemen. (all *informal*).
'bluebottle type of large blue fly.
'blue 'pencil *nc* pencil which makes blue marks, used to edit or take out something which is unnecessary, offensive etc. Also *vt* **blue-pencil** censor.
'blueprint 1. photographic print of a plan for a building (usu. made of blue paper). 2. any plan or scheme for work to be done.
'blue 'ribbon, 'blue 'riband first prize, highest prize.
'bluestocking highly-educated woman. (*informal* and often rather *impolite*).
a bolt from the blue see **bolt**[2].
once in a blue moon see **moon.**
out of the blue unexpectedly. *The news came completely out of the blue.* (*informal*).

bluff[1] [blʌf] *vt/i* pretend to be cleverer, stronger etc than one really is in order to defeat one's enemy or to gain something. *The police were bluffing when they said that they knew who had committed the crime* i.e. the police said this although they did not really know who had committed the crime. Also *nc/u* pretence of this kind; action of bluffing.
call somebody's bluff challenge or tell somebody who is bluffing to do what he says he will do. (Since he is bluffing, he is not able to do what he says he will do).

bluff[2] [blʌf] *adj* rough and cheerful in behaviour.

blunder ['blʌndə*] *nc* a foolish (or careless) mistake. Also *vi* 1. make this kind of mistake. 2. move about without being able to see properly.

blunt[1] [blʌnt] *adj* (with reference to a knife etc) without a sharp edge or point. Also *vt* make blunt: *blunt a knife.*

blunt[2] [blʌnt] *adj* rough or direct in speech, saying what one thinks without trying to be polite or kind to other people. **bluntly** *adv.* **bluntness** *nu.*

blur [blə:*] *vt* make less clear or less easy to understand. *The rain has blurred the windows. Your writing is very blurred. Tears blurred her eyes.* *past* **blurred.** Also *nc* condition of being blurred; something which is not seen clearly.

blurb [blə:b] *nc* statement describing the contents of a book, packet, box etc as being good, interesting, exciting etc to encourage people to buy it.

blurt [blə:t] in **blurt something out** i.e. say something suddenly, often without thinking first: *blurt out a secret.*

blush [blʌʃ] *vi* become red in the face from shame or embarrassment. Also *nc* reddening of the skin in this way.

bluster ['blʌstə*] *vi* complain or threaten in a noisy and foolish way. Also *nu* complaints or threats of this kind.

blustery ['blʌstəri] *adj* (with reference to wind) noisy and violent.

boa ['bouə] *nc* 1. large type of snake which kills its prey by crushing it. 2. snake-shaped stole of feathers.

boar [bɔ:*] *nc* 1. male pig. 2. wild pig. (Also **wild boar** in sense 2.).

board[1] [bɔ:d] 1. *nc* thin piece of wood much longer than broad. 2. *nc* piece of wood or other material used for a special purpose (e.g. *chessboard* used for playing chess on; *noticeboard* used for pinning notices on; *blackboard* used for writing on with chalk). 3. *nc* group of officials: *board of governors* i.e. officials in charge of school or college. 4. *nu* supply of food (esp. in a lodging house).
board and lodging food and accommodation.
(all) above board (usu. with reference to business, administration etc) without any tricks or deception, completely honest.
go by the board (with reference to plans etc) be lost or abandoned. *The plan for a new swimming pool had to go by the board* i.e. it is not now planned to have a new swimming pool.
on board on a boat, ship or aeroplane.
sweep the board see **sweep**[1].

board[2] [bɔ:d] *vt/i* 1. get on a bus, train, ship, aeroplane etc: *board a bus etc.* 2. cover with boards: *board up the windows.* 3. give food to people who pay to live in one's house. 4. pay to live in somebody's house and be given food by this person. *He boards with an old lady. He boards at an old lady's house.*
boarder *nc* 1. somebody who pays to live in the house of another person and be

given food by that person. **2.** pupil in a school who lives at the school during the term and not at his parents' house.

'board room room in which the most important officials of a business or institution have meetings.

'boarding house 1. private house (not a hotel) where people can pay to live with the owner and be supplied with food. **2.** house in a boarding school in which pupils live.

'boarding school school at which some or all of the pupils live during the term.

boast [boust] *vt/i* **1.** speak too much in praise of oneself, one's country, family etc. *I don't like John, he is always boasting. He boasted that he was the strongest boy in the class.* **2.** be proud of having. *Our town boasts the largest secondary school in the country.* Also *nc* **1.** words used by somebody who is boasting. **2.** something which makes one proud or think very highly of oneself. *Until last week, it was our team's proud boast that they had not been beaten this year.* **boastful** *adj.* **boastfully** *adv.*

boat [bout] *nc* vessel used for travelling on water.

Note: in general, the difference between a *ship* and a *boat* is that small vessels are called *boats* and large ones are called *ships*. The following vessels are generally called *boats* – fishing boats; sailing boats; rowing boats; motorboats; ferryboats. The following vessels are generally called *ships* – the larger vessels of a country's navy (battleships, aircraft carriers etc); large ocean-going passenger liners. The following vessels can be called *boats* or *ships* – medium size of vessels which carry cargo and passengers.

boatswain, bosun ['bousn] senior member of the crew of a ship or boat (usu. in charge of the anchor, ropes etc).

be all in the same boat be all in the same position or condition (esp. an unpleasant or dangerous one) (*informal*).

burn one's boats see **burn.**

bob [bɔb] *vt/i* move quickly up and down. *The boats were bobbing on the water; bob one's head up and down. past* **bobbed.** Also *nc* a sudden movement of this kind.

bob up appear suddenly. (*informal*).

bobbin ['bɔbin] *nc* object for holding thread (e.g. in a sewing machine).

bode [boud] *vt/i* be a warning (usu. bad). *These changes bode ill for the future of the country* i.e. they are a bad sign.

bodice ['bɔdis] *nc* upper part of a woman's or child's dress or undergarment.

body ['bɔdi] *nc* **1.** the whole of a human being, animal etc considered as separate from the mind or soul. **2.** the main part of a human being, animal etc without the head, legs and arms. **3.** the main part of anything: *the body of the hall* i.e. the part where the audience sits; *the body of the work* i.e. the largest part of the work. **4.** dead person or animal: *bury the bodies after a battle.* **5.** group of people. *They went in a body to see the Prime Minister.* **6.** (science) physical mass: *falling body* i.e. an object which is falling; *heavenly body* i.e. a star, planet, comet etc. **7.** person. (*informal* in this sense except in compounds *anybody, nobody, somebody etc*). **bodily** *adj/adv.*

'bodyguard person/people whose job is to protect someone.

bog [bɔg] *nc* **1.** land which is wet and soft. **2.** lavatory. (*informal* in sense **2.**). **boggy** *adj.*

bogged down unable to move forward as though in a bog. *He was bogged down in a mass of details.*

bogus ['bougəs] *adj* false; untrue; pretending to be what it is not.

bohemian [bou'hiːmiən] *nc* person (often a writer, artist, musician etc) who lives a very free sort of life, not obeying the normal rules of society, but not being a criminal. Also *adj.*

boil[1] [bɔil] *vt/i* **1.** (with reference to liquid) become or be made so hot that the liquid begins to change into gas. *Water boils at 100° C. He boiled the water in a saucepan.* **2.** cook in this way in boiling water. *The potatoes are boiling. He boiled the potatoes.* **3.** be filled with a strong feeling of anger. *He was boiling with rage.*

boiler *nc* **1.** metal container for boiling water in a house. **2.** container for boiling water to make steam to drive the engines of a ship.

'boiling point temperature at which a liquid boils. *The boiling point of water is* 100° C.

boil over come over the side of the saucepan in cooking. *The potatoes have boiled over* i.e. the water in which the potatoes are being cooked has come over the side of the saucepan.

come/bring to the boil (cookery) become or make hot until the liquid boils.

boil[2] [bɔil] *nc* hard swelling on the body caused by infection.

boisterous ['bɔistərəs] *adj* (of people in their behaviour). noisy, cheerful and rough. **boisterously** *adv.* **boisterousness** *nu.*

bold [bould] *adj* **1.** without fear. *The bold young man attacked the robbers; a bold attempt.* **2.** without a proper feeling of shame or politeness. *This child is much too bold; he is always arguing with his parents.* **3.** easily seen; clear and well-marked. **4.** vigorous and imaginative: *a bold design; bold type* i.e. **type like this. boldly** *adv.* **boldness** *nu.*

bolster ['boulstə*] *nc* long pillow for a bed stretching from one side of a bed to the other.

bolster up give help and support to. *John's friends had to bolster up his courage.*

bolt[1] [boult] *nc* **1.** type of fastening for a door or window. **2.** piece of metal used to fasten two things together. **3.** part of a lock which is moved by a key. Also *vt* fasten or lock using a bolt (in any of the three senses given above). *He bolted the door. He bolted the two pieces of metal together.*

bolt[2] [boult] *vi* **1.** (usu. of horses) run away suddenly (usu. to escape) (*informal* if applied to people).

a bolt from the blue something sudden and unexpected. *The news was a bolt from the blue.* (*informal*).

make a bolt for it try to escape by running away suddenly. (*informal*).

bolt upright straight and stiff. *He was sitting bolt upright.*

bolt[3] [boult] *vt* eat food quickly.

bomb [bɔm] *nc* metal container filled with a substance which explodes. Also *vt* use bombs as weapons (usu. by dropping them from an aeroplane).

bomber *nc* aeroplane used for dropping bombs; person who uses bombs.

'bombshell great surprise (often an unpleasant one) (*informal*).

atomic bomb see **atom.**

bombard [bɔm'bɑːd] *vt* **1.** attack with fire from big guns. **2.** keep attacking. *The Members of Parliament bombarded the Prime Minister with questions.* **bombardment** *nc/u.*

bombardier [bɔmbə'diə*] *nc* **1.** member of an aeroplane crew who releases bombs. **2.** soldier in that part of an army which uses big guns.

bombastic [bɔm'bæstik] *adj* full of words which sound important but which mean very little. **bombastically** *adv.* **bombast** ['bɔmbæst] *nu.*

bona fide ['bounə'faidi] *adj* genuine; real. *He made a bona-fide enquiry* i.e. he really wanted to know.

bona fides *n sing* (but sometimes treated as *pl*) honest intention.

bond [bɔnd] *nc* **1.** written promise (usu. about money) which the law forces one to keep. **2.** piece of paper issued by a government or business saying that it has borrowed money which it will repay by a certain date. **3.** anything which joins or brings together. *The English language is a bond between Britain and America.* **4.** (in *pl*) chains; imprisonment.

bondage *nu* imprisonment.

bonded warehouse government storehouse in which certain goods are kept until tax is paid on them.

in bond (of goods) kept in a warehouse until tax is paid.

bone [boun] **1.** *nc* part of the hard inner framework of the body. **2.** *nu* the substance of which this framework is made. Also *vt* take the bones out of meat or fish before it is eaten.

bony *adj* **1.** very thin, so that the bones show through the skin. **2.** having a lot of bones (e.g. of a fish which one is eating).

'bone-'dry *adj* very dry. (*informal*).

bone of contention something which is a cause of argument.

as dry as a bone very dry. (*informal*).

have a bone to pick with somebody have cause to complain to somebody about something he has done wrong. (*informal*).

bonfire ['bɔnfaiə*] *nc* fire made in the open air.

bonnet ['bɔnit] *nc* **1.** hat tied under the chin (usu. worn by women or children). **2.** (*Brit*) front part of a car covering the engine or the boot. (*US* **hood**).

bonny ['bɔni] *adj* (usu. with reference to babies) big, healthy-looking and pretty.

bonus ['bounəs] *nc* something more than what was expected or agreed.

bon voyage [bɔ̃vwa'jaːʒ] good journey (said to someone about to travel).

boo [buː] *nc/interj* noise made to show dislike (usu. at a meeting). *pl* **boos.** Also *vt/i* make this noise. *The crowd booed the Prime Minister. past* **booed.**

booby ['buːbi] *nc* fool, stupid person. (*informal*).

'booby prize prize for person who comes last in a competition.

'booby trap **1.** a hidden bomb which is arranged to explode and kill somebody when he touches something or steps in a particular place. **2.** any hidden device which works in this way (usu. as a joke).

book[1] [buk] *nc* **1.** number of sheets of paper fastened together, either containing print or to be written on. **2.** division of the Bible and of certain long poems. **3.** something fastened together like a book: *a book of tickets; a book of stamps.* **4.** (in *pl*) accounts or record of money earned and spent in business.

bookish *adj* fond of books (and often with little experience of the world).

booklet *nc* thin book with soft outer pages.

'bookcase piece of furniture for keeping books in.

'book club club which regularly supplies books to its members at a lower price than is charged in shops.

'book-keeper *nc* person who keeps a record of money in a business etc. **book-keeping** *nu.*

'bookmaker person whose work is to take bets on sporting events (esp. on horse-racing).

'bookmark piece of paper, leather etc placed in a book to show how far one has read.

'bookworm **1.** any insect larva which eats the paper of books. **2.** person who is always reading. (*informal* in sense **2.**).

in somebody's good/bad books liked/disliked by somebody. (*informal*).

bring somebody to book ask somebody to explain why he has been behaving badly.

book[2] [buk] *vt/i* **1.** buy or arrange to have tickets for a film, play, journey etc before the actual occasion. **bookable** *adj.*

'booking clerk person who sells tickets (usu. at a railway station).

'booking office place where one buys tickets for a play, journey etc.

boom[1] [buːm] *nc* deep, hollow, roaring noise, such as that made by a gun or a supersonic aircraft. Also *vi* make this noise.

boom[2] [buːm] *nc* **1.** anything (esp. a chain or pieces of wood) stretched across the mouth of a harbour as a defence. **2.** pole at the bottom of a ship's sail for keeping it stretched out.

boom[3] [buːm] *nc* sudden increase in buying and selling in business.

boomerang ['buːməræŋ] *nc* **1.** curved stick, used by Australian aborigines, which can be thrown so that it will return to the thrower if it does not hit something. **2.** any idea, argument etc which harms the person who first thought of it. Also *vi* return to harm the originator.

boon [buːn] *nc* **1.** gift, favour or something that is a help (esp. given by an important person) (*o.f.*). **2.** advantage; help. *My new overcoat is a boon in this cold weather.*

boor [buə*] *nc* an ignorant, badly-behaved person. **boorish** *adj.* **boorishly** *adv.* **boorishness** *nu.*

boost [buːst] *vt* **1.** speak favourably of, advertise (esp. in order to persuade people to buy something). **2.** push forward or upwards. **3.** increase the power or speed of. Also *nc.*

boot [buːt] *nc* **1.** type of covering for the foot which also covers the ankle (and sometimes also part of the leg). **2.** (*Brit*) place in a car for luggage. (*US* **trunk**).

bootee [buː'tiː] *nc* soft boot for a baby; type of short boot for women.

bootless ['buːtlis] *adj* without any profit or advantage (*o.f.*).

to boot also (*o.f.*).

booth [buːð] *nc* **1.** small covered place where goods are sold at a market. **2.** place, separated off, in which one votes in an election or from which one can telephone. *pl* **booths.**

booty ['buːti] *nu* goods and money taken from the enemy in war or stolen by robbers.

booze [bu:z] *nu* alcoholic drink. Also *vi* drink alcoholic drinks. (both *informal*).

border ['bɔ:də*] *nc* edge or side of anything (esp. the land where two neighbouring countries meet). Also *vt* be on a border. *A thick forest borders the school grounds on the south side.*

'**borderline** line where two countries or districts join; division between two classes of things. *His marks in the examination were on the borderline between a pass and a fail.*

border on 1. be next to, have a border with. *Scotland borders on England.* **2.** be very near to. *His behaviour sometimes borders on madness.*

bore[1] [bɔ:*] *vt* make a round hole (esp. by using a tool which keeps turning round): *bore a hole in a piece of wood; bore a tunnel under the sea.* Also *nc* **1.** hole made in this way. **2.** diameter of a tube or gun barrel.

bore[2] [bɔ:*] *vt* make somebody tired and unhappy by talk, work, entertainment etc which is very uninteresting. *John always bores me when I meet him.* Also *nc* somebody/something that bores people. *John is a bore.*

boredom *nu* condition of being bored.

boring *adj* causing boredom. **boringly** *adv*.

bore[3] [bɔ:*] past tense of **bear**[1].

born [bɔ:n] past part of **bear**[1] only in **be born** i.e. come into the world. *He was born on 25th April 1939.* In other uses, past part of **bear**[1] is spelled **borne.** Also *adj* natural, by nature and not by training or education. *He is a born leader* i.e. he is naturally a leader, he did not have to learn how to lead other people.

borne [bɔ:n] past part of **bear**[1]. see **born** and *Note* on **bear**[1].

borough ['bʌrə] *nc* town or part of a large city which governs itself (and, in England, has its own Member of Parliament).

borrow ['bɔrou] *vt* get something from somebody with the promise that one will give it back. *May I borrow five pounds until Saturday? May I borrow your pen?*

Note: do not confuse *borrow* and *lend*. Compare *I borrowed John's dictionary* with *John lent me his dictionary.*

bosom ['buzəm] *nc* **1.** breasts of a woman. **2.** upper front part of the body. **3.** private or inner part: *in the bosom of one's family* i.e. within one's family. **4.** the heart or feelings. Also *adj* very close or dear: *a bosom friend.*

boss[1] [bɔs] *nc* chief; leader; most important person; owner of a business. (*informal*). Also *vt* act as a boss; tell other people what to do.

bossy *adj* liking to give orders to other people.

boss[2] [bɔs] *nc* raised part on a flat surface (esp. in the middle of a shield).

bosun ['bousn] *nc* see **boatswain.**

botany ['bɔtəni] *nu* study of plants.

botanical [bə'tænikl] *adj*.

botanist ['bɔtənist] *nc* person who studies plants.

botch [bɔtʃ] *vt* do work badly (esp. when repairing something). Also *nc* bad piece of work. (both *informal*).

both [bouθ] *determiner/adv/pron* the one and the other: *both men; both John and James; both of them. You can read both these books/both of these books. You can read them both. We both can go/We can both go. This machine can move both backwards and forwards.*

Note: both is only used when two things are involved, *all* when more than two things are involved. Do not say *all two of them*; the correct form is *both of them.*

bother ['bɔðə*] *vt/i* **1.** cause trouble or disturbance to. *Did the noise bother you last night?* **2.** take trouble to do something. *Don't bother to come with me, I shall be all right by myself.* Also *nc/u* cause of trouble or worry; state of worry. Also *interj* to express annoyance or slight anger. *Oh bother, I've forgotten my pen.* (*informal*).

bothersome *adj* causing bother.

bottle ['bɔtl] *nc* **1.** something for holding liquids (usu. made of glass or clear plastic and narrowing at the top): *a bottle of milk; a bottle of beer.* **2.** amount of liquid in a bottle. *He drank the whole bottle.* Also *vt* put into bottles.

'**bottleneck** place where progress is slowed down. *The narrow road through the town is a bottleneck for traffic.*

'**bottle party** party to which the guests bring their own drink.

bottle something up prevent one's feelings from being seen. *He bottled up his anger* i.e. he did not let anyone see that he was angry.

bottom ['bɔtəm] *nc* **1.** lowest part: *the bottom of the page; the bottom of the sea.* **2.** part of the body on which one sits. **3.** cause or origin. *We must get to the bottom of the trouble* i.e. we must find out the cause of the trouble. Also *adj* lowest: *the bottom shelf; the bottom rung of a ladder.*

bottomless *adj* very deep.

at bottom really; basically; when one knows all the facts. *He is a very kind man at bottom* i.e. he is really very kind, although he may appear to be unkind.

from the bottom of one's heart with one's truest and strongest feelings.

go to the bottom (of a ship or goods and people in a ship) sink.

knock the bottom out of an argument/idea etc show that an argument etc is quite untrue, unreasonable, impossible etc. (*informal*).

boudoir ['bu:dwa:*] *nc* lady's private room in a house (*o.f.*).

bough [bau] *nc* large branch of a tree (usu. growing out of the trunk).

bought [bɔ:t] past of **buy.**

boulder ['bouldə*] *nc* large rock smoothed by ice, water etc.

boulevard ['bu:ləva:d] *nc* wide street in a town or city.

bounce [bauns] *vt/i* **1.** come up quickly (esp. after hitting against something hard), cause to come up in this way. *The ball bounced in front of the goal. The boy was bouncing his ball against the wall.* **2.** move suddenly. *He bounced out of the room.*

bouncing *adj* **1.** moving in this way. **2.** (usu. only of babies) big and active: *a bouncing baby.*

bound[1] [baund] *vi* move in a number of jumps. Also *nc* jump.

by leaps and bounds see **leap.**

bound[2] [baund] *vt* be on the edge of, be a border or limit to. *The small country of Lesotho is bounded on all sides by South Africa. England is bounded in the south by the English Channel.* Also *nc* (usu. *pl*) limit. *We must keep our hopes within reasonable bounds* i.e. we must limit our hopes, we must not hope for too much.

boundless *adj* without limit: *boundless*

ambition.
out of bounds outside the area in which certain people (e.g. schoolchildren, soldiers) may go. *The two cinemas in the town are out of bounds to all junior pupils.*
in bounds within the permitted area.
bound[3] [baund] *adj* going to, about to go to (esp. of ships). *That ship is bound for Hong Kong.*
homeward bound (esp. of ships) going home.
outward bound (esp. of ships) going away from home.
bound[4] [baund] *pred adj* certain, sure. *He is bound to win* i.e. I am quite sure that he will win.
bound[5] [baund] past of **bind.**
bound up with having a close connection with. *Economic progress is closely bound up with educational development.*
boundary ['baundəri] *nc* (esp. of land) edge or limit: *the boundaries of the school playing fields; the boundary of the town.*
Note: boundary (when referring to land) is generally used to refer to divisions within a country; *border* is generally used to refer to the places where one country joins another.
bounden ['baundn] *adj* usu. only in **bounden duty** i.e. duty which one has to do because of the law or a promise one has made, one's feelings of what is right etc. (*formal*).
bounty ['baunti] **1.** *nu* willingness to give; generosity. **2.** *nc* something given (usu. by the government) as a reward to certain people (e.g. farmers). **3.** *nc* any generous gift or reward. **bounteous, bountiful** *adj.* **bountifully** *adv.*
bouquet [bu'kei] *nc* bunch of flowers for carrying in the hand (e.g. at a wedding).
bourgeois ['buəʒwɑː] *adj* of a member of the middle class of society (e.g. a businessman, shopkeeper, doctor, lawyer, teacher, government official etc) (Often used in a hostile way; **middle-class** *adj* is a more favourable term.) Also *nc.*
bourgeoisie [buəʒwɑː'ziː] *npl* people of the middle class.
bout [baut] *nc* **1.** contest or struggle (esp. a boxing match). **2.** period of work, exercise or illness. *I've just recovered from a bout of malaria.*
boutique [buː'tiːk] *nc* small shop selling fashionable clothes and other goods.
bovine ['bouvain] *adj* **1.** like a cow or ox. **2.** slow and stupid.
bow[1] [bau] *vt/i* **1.** bend the body forward as a sign of greeting, respect or worship. **2.** burden. *He was bowed down with troubles.* Also *nc* act of bending the body in a bow.
bow[2] [bou] *nc* **1.** piece of wood, bent by a cord fastened at each end, used for firing arrows. **2.** piece of wood with horsehair or other substance stretched along it, used for playing the violin and other stringed instruments. **3.** piece of ribbon, string etc tied as in the illustration. **4.** any curve or bend.

bows

'bow-'legged *adj* with legs bent outwards.
'bow 'tie tie as in the illustration.
bow[3] [bau] *nc* front part of a ship or boat.
bowel ['bauəl] *nc* (usu. *pl*) **1.** part of the body through which waste matter from the stomach passes out of the body. **2.** inner part of something (usu. in **the bowels of the earth** i.e. part of the earth deep below the surface).
bowl[1] [boul] *nc* **1.** deep round dish generally used for holding food or flowers. **2.** deep round part of something: *the bowl of a spoon.*
bowl[2] [boul] *vt/i* **1.** send a ball in certain games. **2.** (cricket) hit the batsman's wicket when bowling. *John bowled the captain of the other team with his first ball.* **3.** move along quickly in a vehicle. *He bowled along in his car.* Also *nc* heavy wooden ball used in certain games.
bowls *nu* game played with these balls.
bowler *nc* **1.** person who bowls. **2.** type of hard, round, black hat. (Also **bowler hat**).
box[1] [bɔks] *nc* **1.** container made of metal, wood, cardboard etc often rectangular in shape and with a lid. **2.** small compartment for a few members of the audience at a theatre. **3.** container in a post office or at a newspaper office, where the letters etc for a particular person are placed. Also *vt* put into boxes.
'box office place where tickets are sold in a theatre or cinema.
'Christmas box present given at Christmas time (esp. to tradesmen, postmen etc who call at one's house, or to people who work for one).
'sentry box small shelter in which a soldier stands when guarding a place.
'witness box place where a person stands to give evidence in a court of law.
box[2] [bɔks] *vt/i* fight by hitting with the fists (esp. when wearing padded gloves). Also *nc* blow with the hand (esp. on the ear or side of the head).
boxer *nc* **1.** man who fights with his fists, wearing padded gloves. **2.** type of dog.
boxing *nu* game or sport of fighting with the fists, wearing padded gloves.
'boxing gloves padded gloves used when boxing to avoid damage to hands and face.
boy [bɔi] *nc* **1.** male child, up to the age of about eighteen. **2.** male servant of any age in India, Africa and some other areas. (This use is now felt to be *impolite* and is becoming *o.f.* in most countries).
boyish *adj* like or of a boy.
boyhood *nu* time when somebody is a boy; state of being a boy.
'boyfriend usual male companion of a young woman.
boycott ['bɔikɔt] *vt* join with other people, nations etc in an agreement to have no contact, trade etc with a person, business, nation etc or to refuse to buy a particular product. *If they will not buy our goods, we will boycott theirs.* Also *nc* act of boycotting.
bra [brɑː] *nc* short form of **brassière.**
brace [breis] *nc* **1.** piece of metal, wood etc used to hold things together. **2.** (usu. in hunting) two animals or birds. Also *vt* give support or strength.
bracing *adj* involving some kind of effort, but nevertheless refreshing: *a bracing walk.*
brace oneself make oneself ready in order to

receive a blow, heavy weight, push etc.
bracelet ['breislit] *nc* ring or chain of metal or other material worn round the wrist or arm (usu. by women).
braces ['breisiz] *npl* (*Brit*) straps worn over the shoulders by men, used for holding up trousers. (*US* **suspenders**).
bracken ['brækən] *nu* type of coarse fern; a lot of ferns together.
bracket ['brækit] *nc* **1.** one of several signs ( ), [ ], { } etc used in writing and printing to separate something from the rest of the writing or print.
Note: these signs are used in pairs and the two e.g. ( ) are referred to as *a bracket* (*sing*) or *brackets* (*pl*).
2. bent or curved piece of metal used for supporting something such as a shelf, which is fastened to a wall. Also *vt* write or print inside brackets.
brackish ['brækiʃ] *adj* (with reference to water) tasting slightly of salt.
brag [bræg] *vt/i* speak too much in praise of oneself, one's family, country etc (often saying things that are untrue). *John said that he could fight anyone but we knew that he was only bragging. past* **bragged.** Also *nc/u* talk in praise of oneself etc.
braggart ['brægət] *nc* person who brags.
braid [breid] **1.** *nc* narrow piece of material made by twisting several strands or pieces together; pieces of hair twisted together. **2.** *nu* material of this type put along the edges of clothing or used as decoration on clothing. *His coat was covered with braid.* Also *vt* make into braid or put braid on.
braille [breil] *nu* system of reading and writing invented for use by the blind, in which the letters are represented by raised dots which can be read by feeling them with the fingers.
brain [brein] *nc* (sometimes *pl*) the matter in the head with which one thinks and feels. Also *vt* kill by hitting on the head.
brainless *adj* very foolish or stupid.
brainy *adj* very intelligent. (*informal* – use **intelligent**).
'brain-child somebody's invention or idea.
'brains trust group of experts or clever people who give advice and answer questions.
'brainwashing *nu* process by which a person is made to change his ideas (esp. political ideas) by the use of continual questioning and various types of ill-treatment. Also **brainwashed** *adj*.
blow one's brains out see **blow**[1].
braise [breiz] *vt* cook slowly in a container with a lid on, using very little water.
brake [breik] *nc* anything which makes a vehicle go more slowly or stop. Also *vt/i* slow down or stop by using a brake.
bramble ['bræmbl] *nc* type of small plant which has thorns (esp. a blackberry bush).
bran [bræn] *nu* the outer covering of grains of wheat, barley etc (usu. removed before the flour is made into bread).
branch [brɑːntʃ] *nc* **1.** part of a tree growing out from the main trunk. **2.** anything growing out of the main part, like a branch of a tree; part: *a branch line of a railway; a branch of a family; a branch of learning.* Also *vi* divide into branches or parts. *Keep straight on until the road branches.*
branch out take up new interests or activities (usu. keeping on the original interests etc). *John started by studying History, but then he decided to branch out into Economics* i.e. he now studies History and Economics.
brand [brænd] *nc* **1.** type or kind of manufactured product. *Smith and Co. sell three brands of tea.* **2.** mark made on the skin with a hot piece of iron (usu. done to cattle and horses to show who owns them). **3.** piece of burning wood. Also *vt* **1.** mark with a hot iron. **2.** leave a permanent mark on; condemn. *He was branded a traitor to his country.*
'brand-'new *adj* very new.
brandish ['brændiʃ] *vt* wave or shake (esp. in a threatening way). *The thief was brandishing a revolver.*
brandy ['brændi] *nu* type of strong alcoholic drink.
brash [bræʃ] *adj* self-confident and impolite. **brashly** *adv.* **brashness** *nu.*
brass [brɑːs] *nu* **1.** yellowish metal, an alloy of copper and zinc. **2.** money. (*informal*).
the brass brass instruments, or players of these instruments, in a band or orchestra.
get down to brass tacks discover the true facts; discuss seriously. (*informal*).
brassière ['bræsiə*] *nc* undergarment for supporting a woman's breasts. (Also **bra**).
brat [bræt] *nc* annoying or badly-behaved child. (rather *impolite*).
bravado [brə'vɑːdou] *nu* foolish courage or boldness; pretence of being brave without any real willingness to face danger or pain.
brave [breiv] *adj* without fear; willing to face something dangerous or painful. Also *vt* face danger or pain: *brave death* i.e. do something although one might be killed.
bravely *adv.* **braveness, bravery** *nu.*
bravo ['brɑː'vou] *nc/interj* shout meaning well done! excellent! very good! etc. *pl* **bravos** or **bravoes.**
brawl [brɔːl] *nc* noisy fight or quarrel, often in a public place. Also *vi* fight or quarrel in this way. **brawling** *nu.*
brawn [brɔːn] *nu* **1.** size and strength of a person (often *impolite*, suggesting that the person is unintelligent). **2.** pickled meat of a pig.
brawny *adj* big and strong.
bray [brei] *vi* make a sound like an ass or donkey. Also *nc* this sound.
brazen ['breizn] *adj* **1.** made of brass. **2.** without proper shame or respect for other people. *I saw the boy stealing the money, but he is so brazen that he tried to say that I had stolen it.*
brazen something out act as though one had not done something wrong even though everybody knows that one has. (*informal*).
brazier ['breiziə*] *nc* metal framework like a basket with legs for holding burning coal or charcoal.
breach [briːtʃ] *nc* **1.** act of breaking the law or failing to do what one has promised to do: *a breach of the peace* i.e. fighting or quarrelling in public; *a breach of contract* i.e. failure to do what one has agreed to do by signing a legal document. **2.** hole or opening made by breaking down part of a wall etc. Also *vt* make a breach in a wall etc.
breach of promise failure to marry somebody after promising to do so.
bread [bred] *nu* food made from flour, yeast and water, baked in an oven.
'breadboard wooden board on which bread is placed to be cut.
'breadwinner person in a family who works in order to get money to support the other members of the family.
bread-and-butter *nu* **1.** slices of bread

covered on one side with butter. **2.** food which is necessary for one to continue living. (*informal* in sense **2.**). Also *adj* ordinary and everyday, but necessary. (*informal*).

know which side one's bread is buttered on see **know**.

breadth [bretθ] *nc* **1.** distance from one side to the other. **2.** freedom of the mind; interest in or sympathy with a large number of different things and types of people (esp. in **breadth of mind**).

break [breik] *vt/i* **1.** become, cause to become, divided into several pieces. *He broke the window by throwing a stone through it. The cup broke when he dropped it.* **2.** become or make damaged. *He broke the chair when he jumped on it. My watch has broken.* **3.** (with reference to day or dawn) come suddenly or quickly. *Day was breaking when I woke up.* **4.** (with reference to arrangements) fail to do what is expected: *break a promise; break the law. past tense* **broke** [brouk]. *past part* **broken** ['broukən]. Also *nc* **1.** place where damage has occurred. **2.** interruption or pause: *a break in the conversation; a break for refreshments.* **3.** chance or opportunity: *give me a break.* (*informal* in sense **3.**).

broken *adj*. (*opp* **unbroken**).

breakable *adj* easily broken. (*opp* **unbreakable**).

breakage *nc/u* **1.** breaking; damage. **2.** loss caused by breaking. *All breakages must be paid for* i.e. one must pay for whatever is broken.

breaker *nc* large wave which breaks into foam.

'**breakneck** *adj* dangerously fast: *breakneck speed.*

'**breakwater** wall or barrier built out into the sea to lessen the force of the waves.

break down **1.** stop working because of some failure. *The car broke down on the road.* **2.** begin to weep.

'**breakdown** *nc* (usu. only *sing*) **1.** failure in health through mental strain: *a nervous breakdown.* **2.** failure of an engine etc. *We had a breakdown on the journey.* **3.** division into categories etc: *a breakdown of the figures.*

break something down **1.** destroy or overcome something by force: *break down a door; break down someone's resistance.* **2.** divide into categories.

break even carry out some business in which one neither loses nor gains. *He did not make a profit when he sold his house; he just broke even.*

break in (usu. with reference to a thief entering a house) enter by force.

break something in train an animal to work for one: *break in a horse.*

break something off stop suddenly: *break off a friendship; break off negotiations.*

break out begin suddenly. *A fire broke out.*

break through something overcome or pass by force: *break through a barrier.*

'**breakthrough** *nc* **1.** military attack which passes through the defence of the enemy. **2.** new and important discovery in science which enables further developments to take place.

break (something) up scatter; divide up. *The two friends broke up* i.e. they decided not to continue to be friends. *The headmaster broke up the fight* i.e. he stopped the children fighting.

break with someone stop being friendly with someone.

break one's/someone's heart be very unhappy; cause someone to be very unhappy. *She broke her heart when her boyfriend left her. The bad boy broke his mother's heart.* (*informal*).

break the news tell someone something unpleasant in a gentle way.

break a record (usu. with reference to sport) do something faster, better etc than anyone has done it previously: *break the record for the high jump.*

breakfast ['brekfəst] *nc/u* first meal of the day, eaten in the early morning. Also *vi* eat this meal.

breast [brest] *nc* **1.** one of the two parts of a woman's body at which a baby is fed with milk. **2.** the front part of the upper body. **3.** the feelings or emotions (thought of as being in the heart). Also *vt* face, come up to something: *breast a wave.*

'**breastfeed** *vt* feed with milk from the breasts (rather than with milk from a bottle). *Not all mothers are able to breastfeed their babies.*

'**breast'fed** *adj* fed in this way: *a breastfed baby.*

'**breastplate** piece of steel armour which covers the chest.

'**breast-'pocket** pocket over the chest in a coat or shirt.

'**breast-stroke** method of swimming in which the body is pushed forward by both arms moving through the water at the same time, followed by a strong movement with the legs.

make a clean breast of see **make[1]**.

breath [breθ] *nc/u* **1.** the air taken into the body and sent out again. **2.** a light wind or breeze. (Usu. **breath of air**).

breathless *adj* **1.** without enough air in the lungs (e.g. after running fast). *John was breathless after running for half a mile.* **2.** causing one to be unable to breathe freely: *breathless excitement.* **breathlessly** *adv*. **breathlessness** *nu*.

'**breathtaking** *adj* thrilling; causing great excitement. **breathtakingly** *adv*.

out of breath without enough air in the lungs (e.g. after running fast).

take one's breath away cause to be very much surprised. *The sight of the beautiful mountains took our breath away.*

under one's breath in a whisper. *He was speaking under his breath.*

with bated breath not breathing freely, through fear or excitement.

breathe [bri:ð] *vt/i* take air into the body and send it out again. *He was breathing noisily.* **breathing** *nu*.

breathe easy/easily feel that there is no longer any danger. *Half an hour after the robbers had left the house, the children felt that they could breathe easy/easily again.*

breathe in take air into the body.

breathe out send air out of the body.

breathe new life into somebody encourage somebody to feel that he can be successful; encourage somebody to try again etc.

not breathe a word remain silent; keep a secret. *Don't breathe a word about this* i.e. don't tell anyone about this. (*informal*).

bred [bred] past of **breed.**

'**well-'bred** *adj* (with reference to a person) well-behaved and from a good family. (*opp* **ill-bred**).

breech [bri:tʃ] *nc* part of a gun into which

the bullet or shell is put.
breeches ['britʃiz] *npl* old-fashioned type of garment, like trousers, but fastened just below the knee.
breed [bri:d] *vt/i* **1.** (with reference to animals) produce young. *Rats breed very quickly.* **2.** cause animals to produce young (usu. in order to earn money). *Many farmers breed cows and sheep.* **3.** cause. *This will breed trouble for all of us. past* **bred** [bred]. Also *nc* type of animal: *several different breeds of cattle; a good breed of sheep.*
breeder *nc* person who breeds animals.
breeding *nu* **1.** production of young animals. **2.** way in which one has been educated and trained to behave. *He has very good breeding* i.e. he behaves very politely. see **bred.**
breeze [bri:z] *nc* light wind.
breezy *adj* **1.** with light winds blowing: *a very breezy day.* **2.** (with reference to a person or his behaviour) light-hearted; cheerful; full of jokes. **breezily** *adv.* **breeziness** *nu.*
breeze block ['bri:z'blɔk] *nc (Brit)* concrete block used for building. (*US* **cinder block**).
brethren ['breðrən] *npl* brothers (*o.f.*).
breviary ['bri:viəri] *nc* book of prayers to be said every day by Roman Catholic priests.
brevity ['breviti] *nu* shortness; quality of not lasting for a long time. see **brief**[1].
brew [bru:] *vt/i* **1.** make beer. **2.** make a drink with hot water: *brew some tea.* **3.** plan; plot; cause to happen: *brew trouble; brew mischief.* **4.** become more likely: *some trouble is brewing.* Also *nc* drink or quality of drink made by brewing: *a brew of tea. The best brew of beer is made by XYZ.*
brewer *nc* person who makes beer.
brewery *nc* place where beer is made.
briar ['braiə*] **1.** *nu* type of hard wood found in Europe, used for making tobacco pipes. **2.** *nc* pipe made of this wood. **3.** *nc* see **brier.**
bribe [braib] *vt* offer money or other gifts to a person to persuade him to do something which he should not do. *He tried to bribe the policeman not to arrest him.* Also *nc* money or other gift offered in this way.
bribery *nu* giving and taking of bribes.
brick [brik] **1.** *nc* rectangular piece of baked clay (usu. red in colour) used in building. **2.** *nu* bricks considered as a building material. *His house is built of brick.* **3.** *nc* something shaped like a brick: *a brick of ice cream.*
'**brickbat** **1.** broken piece of brick used for throwing. **2.** piece of criticism. (*informal* in sense **2.**).
'**bricklayer** *nc* person whose work is to build with bricks. **bricklaying** *nu.*
'**brick 'red** *adj* brownish red, like a brick.
'**brickwork** wall or other part of a building which is made of bricks. *The brickwork in this house is not very good.*
bride [braid] *nc* woman who has just been married or who is just about to be married.
bridal *adj.*
'**bridegroom** man who has just been married or who is just about to be married.
'**bridesmaid** woman who helps a bride on the wedding day.
bridge[1] [bridʒ] *nc* **1.** road or path built over a river or railway line or above another road. **2.** place higher than the deck of a ship where the officer in command stands. **3.** the bony part of the nose. **4.** piece of wood over which the strings of a violin etc are stretched. Also *vt* build a bridge across: *bridge a river.*
bridge[2] [bridʒ] *nu* type of card game.
bridgehead ['bridʒhed] *nc* position captured by an invading army, from which further advances can be made.
bridle ['braidl] *nc* **1.** leather straps which fit over a horse's head, used for controlling the horse. **2.** anything which controls the movement of something/somebody. Also *vt/i* **1.** put a bridle on. *He bridled his horse.* **2.** control. *He learned to bridle his temper.* **3.** hold the head high or throw the head back, to show anger or pride. *She bridled at his rudeness.*
brief[1] [bri:f] *adj* lasting for a short time: *a brief period of happiness; a very brief visit.*
briefly *adv.* **briefness** *nu.* see **brevity.**
brief[2] [bri:f] *nc* **1.** summary of the main facts about a case, used by a lawyer when speaking in court. **2.** piece of work given to a lawyer or other person, in which some facts are to be discovered or something is to be decided. *Your brief is to find out who did this* i.e. I am giving you the job of finding out who did this. Also *vt* **1.** give a lawyer some work to do for oneself by giving him the information which he may need. **2.** prepare somebody for a piece of work by giving him the information he may need. *Before the soldiers advanced towards the enemy, they were briefed by their commanding officer.*
briefing *nc* information given to somebody before he begins a piece of work.
'**briefcase** flat case for carrying papers or books.
brier, briar ['braiə*] *nc* one of several types of bush, found in Europe, which have sharp thorns.
brigade [bri'geid] *nc* **1.** part of an army (usu. between 3,000 and 8,000 men). **2.** name given to certain organizations whose members wear uniform.
brigadier [brigə'diə*] *nc* officer in charge of a brigade.
brigand ['brigənd] *nc* robber (esp. one who lives in mountains or other wild places) (rather *o.f.* – use **bandit**).
bright [brait] *adj* **1.** shining; giving out much light: *a bright fire; a bright light.* **2.** with colours which are easily seen; not dark: *a bright-coloured dress.* **3.** intelligent; quick at learning: *a very bright pupil.*
brightly *adv.* **brightness** *nu.*
brighten *vt/i* become or make bright. *The weather is brightening* i.e. it is becoming sunny.
look on the bright side be cheerful, expect the best rather than the worst. (*informal*).
brilliant ['briliənt] *adj* **1.** shining very brightly; giving out a lot of light. **2.** very intelligent; very quick at learning: *a very brilliant pupil; a brilliant piece of work.*
brilliantly *adv.* **brilliance** *nu.*
brim [brim] *nc* **1.** the edge of a cup or bowl. **2.** the edge of a hat.
brimming *adj* full to the brim: a *brimming cup of tea.*
'**brim'ful** *pred adj* full to the brim; so full that no more can be added. *The cup was brimful.*
brimstone ['brimstoun] *nu* sulphur.
brindled ['brindld] *adj* (usu. with reference to animals) brown or grey, with spots or streaks of another colour.
brine [brain] *nu* salty water. **briny** *adj.*
bring [briŋ] *vt* carry or lead towards. *Bring*

me your book. He brought his dog to school. *past* **brought** [brɔːt].

bring about cause to happen. *He brought about a quarrel between his parents.*

bring something back cause to remember. *This brings back many memories for me.*

bring something down cause to become lower; cause to fall: *bring down prices.*

bring something forth produce (esp. produce a child) (*o.f.* – use **have a baby**).

bring something forward **1.** show. **2.** make earlier. *They decided to bring forward the date of the next meeting.*

bring something off succeed in: *bring off an important business deal.*

bring something on cause to happen: *bring on an attack of asthma.*

bring something out **1.** make to appear clearly. **2.** publish. *John is bringing out a new book next month.*

bring someone round **1.** persuade, cause somebody to change his mind. *At first he didn't want to go with us, but we soon brought him round.* **2.** cause to regain consciousness. *I was brought round by a policeman after I had been hit on the head by the thief.*

bring someone to cause to regain consciousness. *A doctor brought the injured man to.*

bring someone/something up **1.** (with reference to children) look after and train. **2.** vomit. *He was so ill that he brought up everything he ate.* **3.** mention as a topic of discussion. *John brought up the question of giving the school an extra week's holiday.*

bring upon oneself (usu. with reference to something unpleasant) cause to happen to oneself. *You've brought this punishment upon yourself.*

bring to an end cause to end.

bring home to someone cause to realize or fully understand. *The accident brought home to the children the importance of crossing the road carefully.*

bring to light find, allow people to see what had previously been hidden. *The investigation brought to light a number of interesting facts.*

bring into the open make known to everyone.

bring someone to his senses make someone stop acting or thinking in a foolish way.

bring up to date make modern.

brink [briŋk] *nc* **1.** edge of a cliff. **2.** edge of something dangerous or unpleasant. *He brought his country to the brink of war.*

on the brink of very near something dangerous or unpleasant.

brisk [brisk] *adj* quick and active in behaviour or speech. **briskly** *adv.* **briskness** *nu.*

bristle ['brisl] *nc* **1.** short stiff hair of an animal. **2.** hair used in a brush. Also *vi* make the hair stand up (e.g. when frightened or angry).

bristle with something have many of something (usu. something unpleasant). *The plan bristles with difficulties.*

brittle ['britl] *adj* hard and easily broken. **brittleness** *nu.*

broach [broutʃ] *vt* **1.** open something containing liquid (usu. a barrel). **2.** begin to talk about. *He broached the subject of the summer holiday.*

broad [brɔːd] *adj* **1.** wide; having reference to the size of something measured from one side to the other: *a broad river.* **2.** large; covering a large area: *the broad ocean; very broad experience.* **3.** (with reference to speech) easily noticeable; strongly marked: *a broad Irish accent.* **4.** general; main (usu. in **the broad outline** i.e. the main points).

broadly *adv.*

broaden *vt/i* become or make broad.

'**broad** '**bean** kind of bean of which the pod is not usu. eaten.

'**broad** '**daylight** complete daylight.

'**broad-'minded** *adj* not easily shocked or surprised by what others say or think.

broad-mindedness *nu.*

as broad as it is long the same one way as it is another. (*informal*).

broadcast ['brɔːdkɑːst] *vt/i* **1.** send out by radio or television. **2.** send out on all sides. Also *nc* programme sent out on radio or television.

broadcaster *nc* person who speaks on radio or television. **broadcasting** *nu.*

broadside ['brɔːdsaid] *nc* the firing of all the guns on one side of a ship. Also *adv* (usu. with reference to the side of a ship) with the side turned towards something.

brocade [brə'keid] *nu* cloth with woven designs which are raised above the surface of the cloth.

brochure ['brouʃuə*] *nc* small book, often paper covered, giving information about a city, country, business firm, school, government department etc.

brogue[1] [broug] *nc* type of strong heavy shoe.

brogue[2] [broug] *nc* Irish pronunciation of English.

broil [brɔil] *vt/i* cook meat by using direct heat.

broiler *nc* **1.** pan for boiling meat in. **2.** young chicken, suitable for broiling.

broke [brouk] **1.** past tense of **break.** **2.** *adj* short of money. (*informal* in sense **2.**).

broken ['broukən] past part of **break.**

'**broken-'down** *adj* completely broken; unfit for use: *a broken-down old car.*

'**broken-'hearted** *adj* very unhappy.

broker ['broukə*] *nc* person who acts for other people in buying and selling shares in business.

'**marriage broker** person whose work is to arrange marriages for other people.

bronchitis [brɔŋ'kaitis] *nu* (illness caused by) inflammation of the two tubes which lead from the windpipe to the lungs.

bronchial ['brɔŋkiəl] *adj* concerned with the tubes which lead from the windpipe to the lungs.

bronze [brɔnz] **1.** *nu* mixture of copper and tin. **2.** *nu* reddish brown colour of this mixture. **3.** *nc* statue made of bronze.

brooch [broutʃ] *nc* ornament fastened by a pin, worn on a dress etc.

brood [bruːd] *nc* **1.** young birds together in a nest. **2.** group of young creatures or children. Also *vi* **1.** (with reference to birds) sit on eggs in a nest. **2.** sit doing nothing but thinking gloomy thoughts.

broody *adj* used of a hen sitting on her eggs.

brood on/over something. *He brooded on/over his problem for several days.*

brook[1] [bruk] *nc* small stream.

brook[2] [bruk] *vt* be prepared to suffer injury or insult. *He refused to brook any insults from Mr Smith.*

broom [bruːm] *nc* **1.** brush on the end of a long stick, used for sweeping the floor. **2.** type of European plant with yellow flowers.

broth [brɔθ] *nc* soup (esp. one made with meat).

brothel ['brɔθl] *nc* house where prostitutes live and do business.

brother ['brʌðə*] *nc* **1.** son of one or both of one's parents. **2.** close friend or companion. **3.** member of the same trade, group, association etc as oneself. **4.** (in some Christian churches) member of a religious group who is not a priest.
brotherly *adj* as or like a brother.
brotherhood ['brʌðəhud] **1.** *nc* group of men, joined together for a particular purpose. **2.** *nu* brotherly feeling.
'**brother-in-law** brother of one's wife or husband; husband of one's sister. *pl* **brothers-in-law.**
brought [brɔːt] past of **bring.**
brow [brau] *nc* **1.** forehead. **2.** hair on the forehead above the eye. (Often **eyebrow**). **3.** top of a hill.
browbeat ['braubiːt] *vt* frighten somebody in order to make him do what one wants him to do. *past tense* **browbeat.** *past part* **browbeaten.**
brown [braun] *nc/u* dark colour like a very dark yellow or dark orange; skin colour of many Indian people; colour of many types of soil. Also *adj.*
brown paper special thick paper, brown in colour, used for wrapping parcels etc.
brownie ['brauni] *nc* **1.** type of fairy, said to do helpful jobs for human beings. **2.** (**Brownie**) young member of the Girl Guide movement.
browse [brauz] *vi* **1.** (with reference to animals) move slowly along, eating grass and leaves etc. **2.** read bits from different parts of a book or from different books (e.g. in a library or bookshop).
bruise [bruːz] *nc* dark mark on the skin made by a blow which does not break the skin. Also *vt/i* get or make such a mark. *My skin bruises easily* i.e. if I am hit, a bruise usu. appears. *The man bruised the child's arm when he hit him.*
brunette [bru'net] *nc* (usu. with reference to a white-skinned person) person (often a woman) with dark hair.
brunt [brʌnt] usu. in **bear the brunt of something** i.e. bear the main force or main part.
brush [brʌʃ] *nc* **1.** instrument (usu. with a short handle and with stiff bristles, wires, hairs etc for cleaning or painting). **2.** light touch given as something passes by something else. **3.** short fight or argument. **4.** tail of a fox. Also *vt/i* (in senses **1.** and **2.**) **1.** *He brushed the floor/his hair/his teeth* etc. **2.** *He brushed against the door as he entered the room.*
brush aside ignore; refuse to take notice of.
brush up revise; improve one's knowledge of. (*informal*).
brusque [bruːsk] *adj* quick and rather impolite in behaviour or speech. **brusquely** *adv.* **brusqueness** *nu.*
brute [bruːt] *nc* **1.** animal. **2.** cruel or stupid man.
brutal *adj* harsh and cruel. **brutally** *adv.* **brutality** [bru'tæliti] *nc/u* cruel act; cruelty.
'**brute** '**strength**/'**force etc** strength, force etc without any intelligence.
bubble ['bʌbl] *nc* volume of air surrounded by liquid. (Bubbles can either float in the air, or be inside or on a liquid.) Also *vi* send up bubbles, rise to the surface in the form of bubbles.
buccaneer [bʌkə'niə*] *nc* sea robber; pirate. Also *vi* act as a pirate.
buck[1] [bʌk] *nc* **1.** male deer or rabbit. **2.** American dollar. (*informal* in sense **2.**).
pass the buck give the responsibility for something to somebody else, instead of taking it oneself. (*informal*).
buck[2] [bʌk] *vi* (with reference to a horse) jump taking all four feet off the ground.
buck up 1. hurry up. **2.** be more cheerful. **3.** try harder etc. (all *informal*).
bucket ['bʌkit] *nc* container with a handle for carrying liquid in.
kick the bucket die. (*informal*; disrespectful to the person who has died).
buckle[1] ['bʌkl] *nc* fastener (usu. made of metal) for fastening a belt or strap. Also *vt/i* be fastened or fasten with a buckle

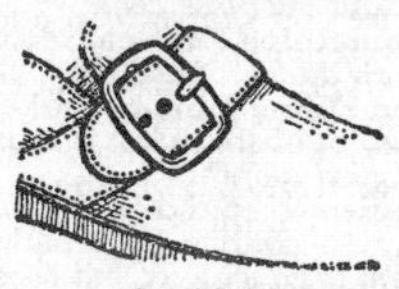

buckle[1]

buckle down to something begin to work with determination or extra effort.
buckle[2] ['bʌkl] *vi* (with reference to metal) bend under a weight.
buckler ['bʌklə*] *nc* small round shield.
bucolic [bjuː'kɔlik] *adj* of the country and country people; concerned with shepherds.
bud [bʌd] *nc* tightly-rolled flower or leaf before it develops. Also *vi* grow buds; grow into buds. *past* **budded.**
budding *adj* developing: *a budding author* i.e. an author who is showing signs of becoming a good writer.
in bud growing buds.
nip something in the bud see **nip**[1].
budge [bʌdʒ] *vt/i* move or cause to move. *He has been sitting there for two hours; he won't budge. This box is too heavy; I can't budge it.*
budget ['bʌdʒit] *nc* **1.** (esp. with reference to such an estimate made by a government) statement or estimate of money which one expects to spend in the future. Also *vi* make a budget. *It is difficult to budget very far ahead. He budgeted for all his expenses in the coming year.*
buff [bʌf] *nu* **1.** leather made from buffalo skin. **2.** pale brown colour of this. Also *adj.*
buffalo ['bʌfəlou] *nc* **1.** type of wild ox with a large shaggy head, found in America. (Also **bison**). **2.** any of various kinds of oxen found in Europe, Asia and Africa. *pl* **buffaloes.**
buffer ['bʌfə*] *nc* **1.** projecting pieces of metal on strong springs, placed on railway engines and at the end of railway lines, to lessen the shock if a railway engine does not stop when it should or if it is hit. **2.** any object which acts in the same way.
'**buffer state** small neutral country lying between two larger countries which might be enemies to each other.
buffet[1] ['bʌfit] *nc* heavy blow (esp. one given with the hand). Also *vt* give such a blow. *The wind buffeted the people walking along the street.*
buffet[2] ['bufei] *nc* **1.** place where one can buy light meals and refreshments (esp. on a train or at a railway station). **2.** food placed on a table at a party, which one can take as one wishes, and eat standing up.
buffoon [bʌ'fuːn] *nc* person who acts in a foolish way.

bug [bʌg] *nc* 1. wingless insect which sucks blood. 2. (mainly *US*) any insect. 3. germ which causes a disease. (*informal* in sense 3.). Also *vt* 1. hide microphones etc in a room etc in order to get information. *The spy bugged the room.* 2. annoy. (*informal*).

bugbear ['bʌgbɛə*] *nc* something of which one is afraid (usu. without any reason).

bugle ['bju:gl] *nc* type of musical instrument.
bugler *nc* person who blows a bugle (esp. in the army).

build [bild] *vt/i* make by putting things together: *build a house; build a ship. They are building a wall.* *past* **built** [bilt]. Also *nu* (usu. with reference to human beings) size and shape. *John and his brother have the same build.*
builder *nc* person whose work is to make houses and other buildings.
building 1. *nc* thing built, in which people can live or work (e.g. a house, school, factory, a shop). 2. *nu* art or skill of building.
'**building society** society which lends money for people to buy houses.
'**built-'in** *adj* made as part of a building (e.g. *a built-in cupboard* is made as part of a wall, and is not a movable piece of furniture).
build something up increase; save; put together; make better. *He has built up a large sum of money. He built up his business. He built up his strength. They have built up a good reputation.*
'**built-'up 'area** area in which there are many houses.
build up hopes expect, cause to expect, something (usu. without good reason). *He built up his hopes of a good holiday, but he was disappointed. I don't want you to build up your hopes, because you might be unlucky.*

bulb [bʌlb] *nc* 1. thick, round root of certain plants. 2. glass object which is fixed into a source of electricity to obtain light. 3. round end of a thermometer.
bulbous *adj* shaped like a bulb.

bulge [bʌldʒ] *vt/i* become or make large and round. *His pockets were bulging with apples.* Also *nc* place where something bulges. *There was a bulge in his pockets.*

bulk [bʌlk] *nu* 1. size or quantity (usu. large). 2. largest part. *The bulk of the work is finished.*
bulky *adj* large; too large.
in bulk 1. not in packages or boxes; loose. 2. in large quantities: *buy something in bulk.*

bulkhead ['bʌlkhed] *nc* walls inside a ship, which are built to prevent water spreading throughout the ship if the ship is damaged.

bull[1] [bul] *nc* 1. male of the cow family. 2. male elephant, whale, seal and other large animals.
'**bull's-eye** centre of a target.
'**bullfighting** *nu* sport practised in Spain and South America, in which men on foot and horseback fight and kill a bull.
'**bullfighter** *nc* one who does this.
'**bullfight** *nc* occasions on which bulls are killed in this way.
a bull in a china shop a clumsy or foolish person in a situation which needs skill and care.

bull[2] [bul] *nc* formal announcement or order made by the Pope.

bulldog ['buldɔg] *nc* type of small but strong and brave dog.
'**bulldog 'clip** type of strong spring for holding papers together.

bulldozer ['buldouzə*] *nc* large machine for moving earth etc.

bulldozer

bulldoze *vt* 1. move earth etc with a bulldozer. 2. cause something to be done by forceful means.

bullet ['bulit] *nc* piece of metal fired from a gun (usu. a gun which can be carried by hand). see **shell.**

bulletin ['bulitin] *nc* 1. short statement of news. 2. magazine or other periodical (esp. one published by a society for its members).

bullion ['buliən] *nu* pieces or bars of gold and silver.

bullock ['bulək] *nc* castrated bull.

bully ['buli] *nc* person who hurts or frightens those weaker than himself. Also *vt/i* behave in this way. **bullying** *nu.*

bulrush ['bulrʌʃ] *nc* name given to various types of tall grass-like plants growing in or near water.

bulwark ['bulwək] *nc* 1. wall (esp. one made of earth) built to protect a place against attacks. 2. the side of a ship's deck.

bum [bʌm] *nc* 1. part of the body on which one sits. (*informal* and *impolite*). 2. (*US*) person who travels around, doing very little work, and living by begging or stealing; a worthless or idle person. (*informal*).

bumblebee ['bʌmblbi:] *nc* type of large bee.

bump [bʌmp] *nc* 1. light blow or knock. 2. swelling on the body made by a knock. 3. small lump or rise in a road. Also *vt/i* 1. give or receive a blow: *bump one's head.* 2. drive or move along a road in a jerky way.
bumpy *adj* uneven; causing one to drive or move in a jerky way: *a very bumpy road.*

bumper[1] ['bʌmpə*] *nc* (*Brit*) bar on the front or back of a car to protect the car if it hits or is hit by something. (*US* **fender**).

bumper[2] ['bʌmpə*] *adj* unusually large (usu. in **a bumper crop**).

bumpkin ['bʌmpkin] *nc* stupid and ignorant country person.

bumptious ['bʌmpʃəs] *adj* having too much confidence in one's own ability. **bumptiously** *adv.* **bumptiousness** *nu.*

bun [bʌn] *nc* 1. small sweet cake, often containing dried fruit. 2. hair twisted into a knot at the back of the head

bunch [bʌntʃ] *nc* 1. group of things growing or fastened together: *a bunch of grapes; a bunch of flowers; a bunch of keys.* Also *vt/i* come or put together in a bunch.
bunch up *vi* come together in a bunch.

bundle ['bʌndl] *nc* number of things tied together: *a bundle of newspapers.* Also *vt* 1. make into a bundle. 2. put away in a hurry and in an untidy way. *He bundled everything into his pockets.*
bundle off send away in a hurry.
bundle something up put into a bundle.

bung [bʌŋ] *nc* piece of cork, rubber or other material, for putting in the hole in the side or end of a barrel. Also *vt* put a bung in.
bung something up stop, block so that

water or other liquid cannot flow freely. (*informal*).
bungalow ['bʌŋgəlou] *nc* type of house (usu. with only one floor).
bungle ['bʌŋgl] *vt/i* do something or make something very badly. **bungler** *nc*.
bunion ['bʌniən] *nc* painful swelling of the foot (esp. on the big toe).
bunk [bʌŋk] *nc* **1.** narrow bed, fastened to a wall like a shelf, as in a train or boat. **2.** one of two or more narrow beds built one above the other.
bunker ['bʌŋkə*] *nc* **1.** place for storing coal. **2.** mound of earth or hollow in the ground, used as an obstacle on a golf course.
bunny ['bʌni] *nc* child's word for rabbit.
bunting ['bʌntiŋ] *nu* strips of cloth used to decorate streets and buildings for a public festival.
buoy [bɔi] *nc* object which floats in the water, placed there to show hidden dangers to ships.
buoy something up prevent from sinking; hold up: *buoy up somebody's hopes*.
buoyant ['bɔiənt] *adj* **1.** able to float. *Wood is buoyant, iron is not.* **2.** cheerful and full of hope: *a very buoyant person*.
buoyancy *nu* **1.** ability to float. **2.** cheerfulness.
burden ['bə:dn] *nc* **1.** heavy load which is carried. **2.** some sorrow or difficulty which somebody has to bear. Also *vt* put a burden on. **burdensome** *adj*.
beast of burden see **beast**.
bureau ['bju:rou] *nc* **1.** office in which information is given to members of the public. **2.** type of writing desk.
bureaucrat ['bju:rəkræt] *nc* civil servant; government official (esp. one who does his work in an unthinking way, following all the rules very carefully and not really trying to help people). **bureaucratic** [bju:rə'krætik] *adj*.
bureaucracy [bju'rɔkrəsi] *nc/u* rule by bureaucrats.
burglar ['bə:glə*] *nc* person who breaks into a building (esp. at night) to steal.
burglary ['bə:gləri] *nc/u* crime of doing this.
burgle ['bə:gl] *vt* break into and steal: *burgle a house*.
'**burglarproof** *adj* made safe so that burglars cannot break in. Also *vt*: *burglarproof the windows*.
burial ['beriəl] *nc* act of putting a dead body into a hole in the earth and filling up the hole. see **bury**.
buried ['berid] past of **bury**.
burlesque [bə:'lesk] *nc* anything which treats a serious and important thing as foolish and unimportant. Also *vt/i*.
burly ['bə:li] *adj* (with reference to a person) big and strong.
burn [bə:n] *vt/i* **1.** damage or destroy by fire. *He burned all his old letters.* **2.** be capable of being destroyed by fire. *Paper burns very easily.* **3.** use for light or heat. *He burns coal in his house.* **4.** give out light. *The lamp in the bathroom was burning all night; somebody forgot to switch it off.* **5.** hurt or damage by heat. *Hot water will burn you. She burned the dinner which she was cooking.* **6.** be filled with (some strong feeling). *He was burning with rage. past* **burned** or **burnt.** Also *nc* mark or injury caused by burning.
Note: burnt is generally used as an adjective; both *burnt* and *burned* are used as verbs (e.g. *the burnt letters. He burned/burnt the letters*).
burn (something) down (with reference to a building) destroy or be destroyed by fire. *He burned down the house. The house burned down.*
burn something off remove by the use of fire. *He burned the paint off the door before repainting it.*
burn (something) up **1.** destroy by fire. *He burned up all the old letters.* **2.** burn more brightly. *If you put on more coal the fire will burn up.*
burn one's boats do something which makes it impossible to go back or change one's plans. (*informal*).
burn the candle at both ends go to bed late at night and get up early in the morning; work and play too hard. (*informal*).
burnish ['bə:niʃ] *vt* (with reference to metal objects) make bright by polishing.
burnt [bə:nt] past of **burn.**
burr [bə:*] *nc* seed case of certain plants covered with small hooks which make the seed case cling to an animal or person passing by the plant.
burrow ['bʌrou] *nc* hole made in the ground as a dwelling place by certain animals (e.g. rabbits). Also *vt/i* make a hole in this way.
bursar ['bə:sə*] *nc* person in charge of money in a school or college.
bursary *nc* scholarship, sum of money, given to a student to enable him to go on studying.
burst [bə:st] *vt/i* **1.** break into pieces or develop a hole, so that what is inside comes out. *The bag of flour burst as I was carrying it.* **2.** explode; start suddenly; appear suddenly. *The bomb burst. The storm burst. The trees were bursting into flower* i.e. the flowers on the trees were appearing in great numbers. *He burst into the room. The building burst into flames* i.e. it suddenly began burning. **3.** be filled. *His case was bursting with old letters. The shops were bursting with goods. past* **burst.** Also *nc* sudden breaking, sudden explosion; sudden appearance; sudden effort.
burst open open by using force; be opened suddenly. *He burst open the door. The door burst open and John came in.*
burst out suddenly start speaking.
burst out crying/laughing suddenly start crying/laughing.
bury ['beri] *vt* **1.** (esp. with reference to a dead body) put into a hole in the ground and cover with earth. **2.** be present at, or help to arrange, the funeral service for somebody. **3.** hide; cover up. *pres part* **burying.** *past* **buried. burial** *nc*.
bury oneself in something be completely interested in something so that one does not notice anything else. *He buried himself in his work. He was buried in a book.*
bury the hatchet stop fighting and agree to be friendly. (*informal*).
bus [bʌs] *nc* large vehicle for carrying people.
'**busman's** '**holiday** holiday spent in doing what one does when one is at work. (*informal*).
bush [buʃ] *nc* small tree.
bushy *adj* **1.** spreading wide like a bush: *a bushy tail.* **2.** covered with bushes.
the bush *nu* wild uncultivated land (not always with trees) (e.g. in Africa or Australia).
bushel ['buʃl] *nc* measure of dry goods (e.g. grain, fruit, vegetables) equivalent to 8 gallons or about 36 litres.

hide one's light under a bushel act in such a way that people do not see how clever etc one is.

business ['biznis] *nc/u* **1.** work, occupation or duty. **2.** commercial firm or shop. *He owns several businesses in this town.* **3.** (usu. only *sing*) incident or subject. *We haven't had time to discuss this business until now.* **4.** buying and selling. *What work do you do? I'm in business* i.e. I buy and sell things.

businesslike *adj* doing things in the proper way, with care and attention. (*opp* **unbusinesslike**).

'**businessman** man whose work is buying and selling things.

on business as part of one's work: *travel on business.*

mind your own business/none of your business don't ask me about this, I'm not going to tell you. (*impolite*).

bust[1] [bʌst] *nc* **1.** (esp. with reference to a woman) upper front part of the body. **2.** statue of a person's head and shoulders.

bust[2] [bʌst] *vt/i* break. Also *adj* bankrupt. *He's gone bust* i.e. he is bankrupt. (both *informal*).

bustle ['bʌsl] *vt/i* move about quickly and noisily (usu. doing a lot of work). Also *nu* quick and noisy movement.

busy ['bizi] *adj* doing a lot of work, working hard; full of work or activity: *a busy man; a busy day. The shops are very busy. comparative* **busier.** *superlative* **busiest. busily** *adv.*

'**busybody** person who is too interested in other people's business.

but [bʌt, bət] **1.** *conj* on the other hand. *John is clever, but Jane is not. John wanted to go to the party, but his wife was too tired.* **2.** *prep* except. *I am alone here; there is no one but me. You can tell anyone but Jane.*

all but very nearly: *all but finished.*

but for without. *We would have been lost but for John* i.e. John prevented us from being lost.

but that if . . . not (*o.f.*).

can but can only. *You can but try.*

first/last but one/two etc first/last etc except for one/two etc. *You're next but one* i.e. you are after the next person.

nothing but only. *He is interested in nothing but football.*

butcher ['butʃə*] *nc* **1.** person who sells meat. **2.** cruel man who causes suffering and death to people. Also *vt* **1.** kill animals for meat. **2.** kill people cruelly.

butchery *nu* cruel killing.

butler ['bʌtlə*] *nc* chief male servant in a house.

butt[1] [bʌt] *nc* **1.** large barrel. **2.** thick end of something: *a cigar butt* i.e. what is left after a cigar has been smoked. **3.** (usu. *pl*) target for people to shoot at. **4.** person/thing laughed at by everybody. *The new boy was the butt of the whole class.*

butt[2] [bʌt] *vt/i* hit with the head. *Goats butt.*

butt in interrupt; interfere. *Don't butt in when someone else is talking.* (*informal*).

butter ['bʌtə*] *nu* thick yellow substance made from milk. Also *vt* put butter on.

butter someone up be very nice to someone for selfish reasons. (*informal*).

look as if butter would not melt in one's mouth look very gentle; look as though one had done nothing wrong (when in fact one has done something wrong) (*informal*).

butterfly ['bʌtəflai] *nc* type of insect with four coloured wings.

buttocks ['bʌtəks] *npl* part of the body on which one sits.

button ['bʌtn] *nc* **1.** small object (usu. round in shape) used for holding articles of clothing together. **2.** object which is pressed to make an electric bell ring. Also *vt/i* be fastened or fasten with a button.

'**buttonhole** **1.** hole through which a button is put for fastening clothing. **2.** flower fastened on a coat (usu. a man's coat, on a formal occasion such as a wedding). Also *vt* stop somebody and force him to listen to what one says: *buttonhole a person.*

buttress ['bʌtris] *nc* support for a wall. Also *vt* **1.** support by a buttress. **2.** support in any way.

flying buttress buttress which is built at an angle to the wall, touching it only at the top of the buttress.

buxom ['bʌksəm] *adj* (usu. with reference to a woman) plump and healthy looking.

buy [bai] *vt/i* get in exchange for money: *buy food in the shop. past* **bought** [bɔːt].

buyer *nc* **1.** person who buys. **2.** person whose work is to buy goods for a large store.

buy something up buy as much as possible. *It was difficult to find flour in the shops last week because people had been buying it up.*

buy for a song (usu. with reference to a large and normally expensive item) buy very cheaply. (*informal*).

buzz [bʌz] *nc* sound made by insects such as bees when flying; sound made by many people talking quietly. Also *vi* make this sound. Also *vt* fly an aeroplane very near a place or other aeroplane (usu. in order to frighten or warn the person in the place or in the other aeroplane).

buzzer *nc* electrical device like a bell, which makes a buzzing sound.

buzzard ['bʌzəd] *nc* one of several types of large bird which eats small birds and animals.

by [bai] *adv/prep* **1.** near: *a house by the river.* **2.** along; across. *It takes longer to get there if you go by the road.* **3.** past. *All the lights were out when I came by the house last night.* **4.** during: *by night; by day.* **5.** not later than. *I will finish the work by next week.* **6.** through the use or agency of: *travel by aeroplane; heat a house by electricity; written by him.* **7.** in units of: *buy things by the dozen.*

by and by in the future (usu. the near future).

by and large generally; usually; on the whole.

by oneself, all by oneself alone. *He was sitting (all) by himself.*

by the way expression used before mentioning something which is not directly connected with the main subject of conversation.

bye-bye ['bai'bai] *interj* informal form of **good-bye.**

by-election ['baiilekʃən] *nc* election held in one area only, to return one member to parliament or to a council (e.g. when the former Member of Parliament etc has died or resigned).

bygone ['baigɔn] *adj* belonging to the past: *bygone days.*

let bygones be bygones forget quarrels which happened in the past and be friendly in the future.

by-law ['bailɔː] *nc* law made by a town or city or other area within a country.

bypass ['baipɑːs] *nc* main road which is built to go around a town or city, instead

of going through it. Also *vt* avoid something in this way: *bypass the centre of the city.*
by-product ['baiprɔdəkt] *nc* something made while producing something else; a secondary product of an industry, not the main product.
byre ['baiə*] *nc* shed where cows are kept.
bystander ['baistændə*] *nc* person standing near, not taking part, when something happens.
byway ['baiwei] *nc* small street or path. (rather *o.f.*).
byword ['baiwə:d] *nc* person/thing generally disliked or laughed at for some bad quality. *His name was a byword for cruelty.*

C

cab [kæb] *nc* **1.** taxi. **2.** part of a train, bus, lorry etc in which the driver sits.
cabal [kə'bæl] *nc* small group of people making secret plans.
cabaret ['kæbərei] *nc/u* entertainment (usu. singing and dancing) given at a club, party, dance etc.
cabbage ['kæbidʒ] *nc/u* type of vegetable with many thick leaves folded tightly on top of each other.
cabin ['kæbin] *nc* **1.** room in a ship etc. **2.** small hut.
'cabin boy boy who works as a servant on a ship.
cabinet ['kæbinət] *nc* **1.** small group of ministers or other senior officials of a government, who meet regularly with the prime minister or president. **2.** piece of furniture with shelves or drawers for storing things.
'cabinetmaker person who makes furniture (esp. by hand).
cable ['keibl] *nc* **1.** type of thick rope (usu. made of many metal wires twisted together). **2.** thick bundle of wires for carrying an electric current. **3.** telegram carried in this way. Also *vt/i* send a message by cable.
'cable-car vehicle pulled by a moving cable (e.g. for travelling up and down a mountain).
'cablegram telegram sent by cable.
cacao [kə'kɑːou] *nc* small tree found in South America and grown for its seeds from which we get cocoa and chocolate.
cache [kæʃ] *nc* hiding place for supplies or food (e.g. used by travellers or explorers); supplies of food left in this way. Also *vt* hide things in this way.
cackle ['kækl] *nc/u* **1.** noise made by a hen after laying an egg. **2.** laughter which sounds like this. Also *vi* make this noise.
cacophony [kæ'kɔfəni] *nc* loud and unpleasant noise. **cacophonous** *adj*.
cactus ['kæktəs] *nc* type of plant often covered with sharp points, growing in hot dry climates. *pl* **cacti** ['kæktai] or **cactuses.**
cad [kæd] *nc* badly-behaved man; man who does not behave like a gentleman. **caddish** *adj*. (both rather *o.f.*).
cadaverous [kə'dævərəs] *adj* like a dead person: *a cadaverous face; a cadaverous appearance.*
caddie, caddy[1] ['kædi] *nc* person whose work is to carry the clubs for a person playing golf. Also *vi* carry golf clubs for a player.
caddy[2] ['kædi] *nc* small box used for keeping tea in.
cadence ['keidns] *nc* **1.** way the sound rises and falls while somebody is speaking or while music is being played. **2.** arrangement of sounds that bring a piece of music to an end.
cadet [kə'det] *nc* young man or boy receiving training to be an officer (in the army, navy, air force, police etc).
cadge [kædʒ] *vt/i* beg, get without paying. *John is always cadging meals from his friends.* **cadger** *nc*.
cadre [kɑːdr] *nc* group of specially-trained people (esp. in politics).
caesura [si'zjuərə] *nc* place in a line of poetry where there is naturally a pause (e.g. *Is this a dagger//which I see before me?*). *pl* **caesurae** [si'zjuəriː] or **caesuras.**
café ['kæfi] *nc* restaurant (esp. one which is not expensive).
cafeteria [kæfi'tiəriə] *nc* place serving meals, in which people collect their own food and take it to their table (esp. such a place in a college, school, factory etc).
caffeine ['kæfiːn] *nu* drug found in coffee etc.
cage [keidʒ] *nc* object made of metal bars or place surrounded by metal bars, for keeping birds or animals in. Also *vt* put in a cage.
cagey *adj* secretive.
cairn [kɛən] *nc* heap of stones to mark a path or built as a memorial.
cajole [kə'dʒoul] *vt* make somebody do something by using pleasing words or false promises. **cajolery** [kə'dʒouləri] *nu*.
cake[1] [keik] *nc/u* **1.** type of food made of flour, butter, eggs, sugar etc and baked in an oven. **2.** anything made of this kind of mixture; anything like this in shape: *a fish cake; a cake of soap.*
cake[2] [keik] *vi* form into a hard mass by drying. *The mud had caked on his shoes.*
calabash ['kæləbæʃ] *nc* **1.** type of fruit with a hard shell. **2.** tree which grows this fruit.
calamity [kə'læmiti] *nc* great and terrible accident or misfortune. **calamitous** *adj*. **calamitously** *adv*.
calcify ['kælsifai] *vt/i* become or make hard by the formation or addition of lime.
calcium ['kælsiəm] *nu* chemical found in chalk, milk, bones etc (Ca).
calculate ['kælkjuleit] *vt/i* find out the answer to a problem by adding, subtracting, multiplying or dividing numbers: *calculate the cost of buying a new house; calculate the date on which the holiday will begin.* **calculation** [kælkju'leiʃən] *nc/u*.
calculating *adj* careful and selfish; planning things carefully so as to be of advantage to oneself. **calculatingly** *adv*.
calculated *adj* intended.
'calculating machine machine which works out arithmetical calculations automatically.
calculate on be sure of. *I had calculated on finishing the work this week.*
calculus ['kælkjuləs] *nc/u* method of calculating changes in speed or rate of growth.
calendar ['kælində*] *nc* **1.** list of the days and months of a particular year: *a calendar for 1960.* **2.** method of dividing up the year: *the Christian calendar; the Moslem calendar.*
'calendar month one of the twelve months. (Contrasted with a **lunar month** i.e. period of 28 days).
calf[1] [kɑːf] *nc* young of the cow, elephant and

seal families etc. *pl* **calves** [kɑːvz].
'calf love love between very young people.
'calfskin leather made from the young of the cow.
kill the fatted calf make a feast to welcome somebody.

calf² [kɑːf] *nc* fleshy part of the leg below the back of the knee. *pl* **calves** [kɑːvz].

calibre ['kælibə*] *nc* **1.** measurement across, or diameter, of a gun barrel, bullet, shell etc. **2.** quality of mind; type of ability. *He is a man of very high calibre.*
calibrate ['kælibreit] *vt* (often with reference to the calibre of a gun barrel or other tube) measure. **calibration** [kæli'breiʃən] *nc/u.*

calico ['kælikou] *nu* type of cheap cotton cloth (usu. with a coloured pattern printed on one side).

calipers ['kælipəz] *npl* see **callipers.**

caliph ['keilif] *nc* title formerly used by some Moslem rulers who were successors of Mohammed.

call¹ ['kɔːl] *vt/i* **1.** give a name to. *They called their baby William. She called him a fool.* **2.** shout. *He called for help, but nobody came.* **3.** (esp. *US*) telephone to. (*Brit* usu. **ring up, phone**). *I called you last night, but I couldn't get any reply.* **4.** awaken from sleep. *I must leave early tomorrow; will you call me at six o'clock?* **5.** ask somebody to come in order to give a service. *He called the doctor. I shall call the police. He called a meeting* i.e. he said that there was going to be a meeting, and he asked people to come to it. **6.** make a short visit. *Mr Smith called to see me yesterday.*
call for someone/something 1. get someone/something. *Shall we go to the cinema tomorrow? I'll call for you at your house at six o'clock. I've bought a new car; I shall call for it on my way home this evening.* **2.** need; require; ask for. *This problem calls for very careful thought.*
call something off say or decide that something must not or will not happen. *He called off the plan* i.e. he gave orders to stop the plan. *They called off the football match* i.e. they decided not to play the match.
call on someone 1. make a short visit to someone. **2.** ask somebody. *If you need any help, you must call on me.*
call out shout loudly.
call someone up 1. order to join the army. **2.** telephone.
call attention to something ask people to notice something.
call it a day stop work, decide that one has done enough of something and stop doing it. (*informal*).
call to mind remember. *I can't call his name to mind.*
call someone names insult someone.
call to order tell people in a meeting to stop talking and listen.
call something in question raise doubts about something.
call the roll read out names of people in a class, school, group etc to find out whether anyone is away.
call a spade a spade speak about things as they really are, without trying to hide the facts or make them seem more pleasant.

call² [kɔːl] **1.** *nc* shout. *We heard a call for help.* **2.** *nc* telephone message. *I had a call from John yesterday.* **3.** *nc* awakening from sleep. *Will you give me a call at six o'clock tomorrow morning?* **4.** *nc* request for help or service. *The doctor had a call to visit Mr Smith.* **5.** *nc* short visit. *I made a call on my neighbour.* **6.** *nu* (usu. *negative* or in a question) need. *There was no call for you to be so unfriendly* i.e. you did not have to be unfriendly. **7.** *nc*: *He had many calls on his money* i.e. he had to spend his money on many things. *He had many calls on his time* i.e. he was very busy with many different things.
caller *nc* person who makes a short visit to a person.
calling *nc* occupation or profession.
on call (usu. with reference to doctors and nurses) having the duty, for certain periods, of going to help people if called to do so. *Dr Smith is on call from six o'clock tomorrow until midnight* i.e. if a doctor is needed during this period, Dr Smith will go.
a close call escape from danger which came very near; a narrow escape.
within call near enough to be shouted for. *If you want me, I shall be within call.*

callipers, calipers ['kælipəz] *npl* **1.** instrument used for measuring the diameter or thickness of something (e.g. when a ruler would not be useful). **2.** type of splint designed to keep pressure off the foot. (Also **calliper splints**).

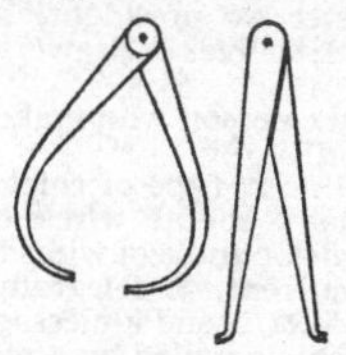

callipers

callous ['kæləs] *adj* having no feeling for the misfortune or suffering of others. **callously** *adv.* **callousness** *nu.*

callow ['kælou] *adj* young and without much experience.

calm [kɑːm] *adj* quiet, not moving; not excited; not violent: *a calm person; a calm sea* i.e. one without big waves. Also *nc* time or place where there is peace and quiet; appearance of peace and quiet. Also *vt* cause to become calm. **calmly** *adv.* **calmness** *nu.*
calm down (usu. with reference to a person) stop being noisy, violent, angry, excited etc. *I told him to calm down.*

calorie ['kæləri] *nc* unit for the measurement of heat (esp. for measuring the energy supplied by food. *An ounce of sugar contains about a hundred calories.* **calorific** [kælə'rifik] *adj.*

calumny ['kæləmni] *nc/u* untrue and hurtful statement made about somebody. *pl* **calumnies.**
calumniate [kə'lʌmnieit] *vt* make such a statement about somebody: *calumniate one's enemy.*

calve [kɑːv] *vt/i* give birth to a young cow. see **calf¹.**

calves [kɑːvz] pl of **calf¹.**

calypso [kə'lipsou] *nc* type of song from the West Indies, in which the singer invents the words while he is singing; the music for such a song. *pl* **calypsoes** or **calypsos.**

calyx ['keiliks] *nc* the small leaves underneath the petals of a flower. *pl* **calyxes** or **calyces** ['keilisiːz].

cam [kæm] *nc* something on a wheel or

shaft in an engine, which changes a circular movement into a movement up and down.

camaraderie [kæmə'rɑːdəri] *nu* loyalty and friendship among people belonging to some organization or society.

camber ['kæmbə*] *nc* slight rise in the middle of a surface (usu. on a road, to let the rain drain away).

cambric ['keimbrik] *nu* type of thin, white cloth.

came [keim] past tense of **come.**

camel ['kæml] *nc* large animal with one or two humps on its back, used for transport in the deserts of Africa and Asia.

cameo ['kæmiou] *nc* **1.** piece of jewellery with a carving which is raised above the background. **2.** short, detailed description of a person/thing (e.g. in a book). *pl* **cameos.**

camera ['kæmərə] *nc* apparatus for making pictures by photography.

'**cameraman** man who operates the camera during the making of a motion picture.

camouflage ['kæməflɑːʒ] *nu* (esp. with reference to the use of paint to prevent guns, tanks, ships etc from being seen by the enemy in war) anything which hides something or changes its appearance so that it is not easily seen. Also *vt* hide something in this way.

camp[1] [kæmp] *nc* **1.** place where travellers, boy scouts etc live for a time in the open air (usu. in tents). **2.** place where soldiers live, in tents or in huts. Also *vi* live in a camp (esp. for a short period). *The travellers camped in the mountains for three days.*

'**camp'bed** small folding bed used in a camp.

'**camp'fire** fire built in the open air, for warmth and cooking, by people camping.

'**camping site,** '**campsite** place where people camp.

camp out sleep in the open air.

go camping go for a holiday living in a tent.

camp[2] [kæmp] *adj* exaggerated in a theatrical and slightly ridiculous way. (*informal*).

campaign [kæm'pein] *nc* series of movements or activities with some special purpose (often in war). *The Germans were defeated in the campaign in North Africa. The committee began a campaign to get more members for the society.* Also *vi* fight in or be active in a campaign.

camphor ['kæmfə*] *nu* white, strong-smelling substance, used to keep moths and other insects away from clothes which have been stored away.

campus ['kæmpəs] *nc* the grounds on which a college or university is built.

can[1] [kæn] *aux* **1.** be able to. *He can speak French.* **2.** have permission to. *You can go home now* i.e. you need not stay here any longer. **3.** have as a characteristic. *He can be very friendly at times* i.e. he is sometimes very friendly when he wishes to be. *past* **could** [kud]. *negative* **cannot** ['kænɔt] or **can't** [kɑːnt].

Note: 1. *can't* is more informal than *cannot. Can't* is generally used in spoken English and in the more informal types of writing, such as letters. 2. the use of *can* to mean 'have permission to' is considered wrong by some people, who would use *may* with this meaning. *You may go home now* i.e. you need not stay here any longer. However, the use of *can* to mean *may* is very common except in formal writing.

can/could do with would be improved by. *This room can/could do with a coat of paint. I could do with a drink* i.e. I want one.

can't bear dislike very strongly. *I can't bear the smell of fish.*

can[2] [kæn] *nc* metal container for holding food, liquid etc. Also *vt* put into a can. *past* **canned.**

Note: (*US*) *can* is used for any metal container of this type (e.g. *a can of fruit; a can of milk*). (*Brit*) *tin* is more generally used, and the word *can* only for certain types of container (e.g. *an oilcan; a milk can; a can of paint*).

canal [kə'næl] *nc* **1.** narrow waterway through land, made by man. **2.** narrow tube inside the body, for carrying food, air etc.

canalize ['kænəlaiz] *vt* make into a canal.

canary [kə'nɛəri] *nc* small yellow bird which sings sweetly, often kept as a pet.

canasta [kə'næstə] *nu* type of card game.

cancel ['kænsl] *vt* **1.** say or decide that something already arranged should not now take place. *He cancelled the meeting. They decided to cancel the agreement.* **2.** make a mark in something to show that something is wrong or to prevent something from being used again. *He cancelled the mistake in his essay. Postage stamps on letters are cancelled before the letters are delivered. past* **cancelled.** (*US* **canceled**).

cancellation [kænsə'leiʃən] *nc/u.*

cancer ['kænsə*] *nu* illness in which a disease in part of the body grows and spreads. **cancerous** *adj.*

candelabrum [kændi'lɑːbrəm] *nc* candlestick for holding a number of candles. *pl* **candelabra** [kændi'lɑːbrə].

candid ['kændid] *adj* speaking the truth without trying to hide anything. **candidly** *adv.* see **candour.**

candidate ['kændideit] *nc* **1.** person who offers himself for some office or position. *In an election people are asked to choose between a number of candidates.* **2.** person taking an examination.

candidature ['kændidətʃə*], **candidacy** ['kændidəsi] *nu* state of being a candidate.

candle ['kændl] *nc* stick of hard wax, with a thread in the middle, which is lit to give light.

'**candle power** unit for measuring light.

'**candlestick** object for holding a candle upright while it is burning.

burn the candle at both ends see **burn.**

(the game is) not worth the candle the thing being proposed or considered is too difficult, dangerous, expensive etc in comparison with the result or profit.

candour ['kændə*] *nu* quality of being candid; saying what one thinks or knows without trying to hide anything. see **candid.**

candy ['kændi] *nc/u* **1.** sugar which has been made hard by being boiled. **2.** (*US*) sweet thing made from sugar (e.g. chocolate or toffee) (*Brit* **sweets** or **chocolate**).

candied *adj* made into candy.

cane [kein] **1.** *nc* thin stick used for beating children or for helping a person to walk. **2.** *nc/u* long stems of certain plants: *bamboo cane; sugar cane.* **3.** *nu* these stems when used as a material for making chairs, baskets etc. Also *vt* punish by beating with a cane. *He caned the boy.*

canine ['keinain] *adj* of or like a dog.

'**canine** '**tooth** one of the four pointed teeth near the front of the mouth.

canister ['kænistə*] *nc* small box (esp. one for containing dry goods).

canker ['kæŋkə*] *nc/u* disease of plants, in

which a diseased part grows and spreads.

cannibal ['kænibl] *nc* person who eats human flesh; animal which eats its own kind.

cannibalism *nu* practice of eating one's own kind.

cannon ['kænən] *nc* **1.** old type of a large gun, which fired a solid metal or stone ball. **2.** type of gun in an aeroplane. **3.** modern type of large gun.

cannonade [kænə'neid] *nc* continual firing of heavy guns.

'**cannonball** round solid ball fired by a cannon.

canny ['kæni] *adj* cautious and clever, not willing to take risks. **cannily** *adv.*

canoe [kə'nu:] *nc* type of light boat moved by paddling. Also *vi* travel in a canoe.

canoeist [kə'nu:ist] *nc* person who travels in a canoe.

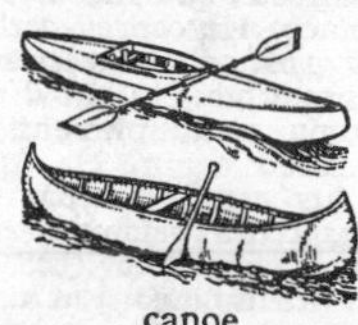

canoe

canon ['kænən] *nc* **1.** law of certain Christian churches (esp. Roman Catholic). **2.** standard or general principle by which something can be judged: *the canons of good taste.* **3.** (esp. with reference to the books of the Bible) list of books or words of an author accepted as genuine. **4.** list of Christian saints. **5.** officer of certain of the Christian churches.

canonical [kə'nɔnikl] *adj* recognized and accepted by the church; according to the rules of the church. (*opp* **uncanonical**).

canonize ['kænənaiz] *vt* officially declare a dead person to be a saint. **canonization** [kænənai'zeiʃən] *nc/u.*

cañon ['kænjən] *nc* see **canyon.**

canopy ['kænəpi] *nc* covering (often supported by poles and usu. made of cloth or wood) over a throne, bed, doorway etc. Also *vt* cover with a canopy.

cant [kænt] *nu* **1.** moral or religious statements made by somebody who does not really believe in what he is saying; hypocrisy. **2.** special words used by certain classes of people, often to deceive others: *thieves' cant; beggars' cant.*

can't [kɑ:nt] short form of **cannot.** see **can**[1].

cantankerous [kæn'tæŋkərəs] *adj* bad-tempered and with the habit of being against what other people suggest. **cantankerously** *adv.* **cantankerousness** *nu.*

cantata [kæn'tɑ:tə] *nc* short play in music, with soloists and a choir, in which the singers do not act.

canteen [kæn'ti:n] *nc* **1.** place in a factory or barracks etc where food is provided. **2.** set of knives, forks and spoons. **3.** metal dishes and vessels used by a soldier for eating and drinking (esp. in camp).

canter ['kæntə*] *vi* (with reference to a horse) run slowly and easily, moving the two front legs together and then the two back legs and so on.

canticle ['kæntikl] *nc* type of song used in a religious service.

cantilever ['kæntili:və*] *nc* long projecting arm of metal etc fastened at one end only.

'**cantilever** '**bridge** bridge made of two cantilevers which meet.

canto ['kæntou] *nc* one of the sections in a long poem. *pl* **cantos.**

canton ['kæntɔn] *nc* small division of certain countries (esp. Switzerland).

canvas ['kænvəs] **1.** *nu* strong cloth used for tents, ships' sails etc and for painting on with oil paints. **2.** *nc* an oil painting.

under canvas 1. in a tent. **2.** (of a ship) with the sails spread out.

canvass ['kænvəs] *vt/i* go around an area calling at houses, shops etc asking people to vote for a particular candidate in an election. *I've canvassed all the people in this street on behalf of John Smith.*

canvasser *nc* person who does this. **canvassing** *nu.*

canyon, cañon ['kænjən] *nc* deep, narrow valley with sides like cliffs (esp. in America).

cap [kæp] *nc* **1.** type of hat (usu. worn by schoolboys or men in uniform). **2.** metal top on a bottle. Also *vt* put a top on. *past* **capped.**

black cap cap formerly worn by a judge when sentencing someone to death.

'**kneecap** see **knee.**

'**toecap** part of a shoe which covers the toes, sometimes made of a separate piece of leather.

if the cap fits (wear it) if you think that what is said could be said of you, take notice of it. (*informal*).

cap a joke tell a joke which is more amusing than one previously told by someone else.

a feather in one's cap an achievement or success which one can be proud of.

put on one's thinking cap think very hard. (*informal*).

capable ['keipəbl] *adj* able; having the power or cleverness to do something. *He is capable of being very unkind to people. He is a capable person* i.e. he is clever; he can do what is expected of him. **capability** [keipə'biliti] *nu.*

capacity [kə'pæsiti] *nu* **1.** ability to hold or contain a certain number or quantity. *The capacity of this bottle is two litres* i.e. it will hold two litres. **2.** power of the mind; ability. *He has a great capacity for work* i.e. he is able to work hard. **3.** position or office: *in his capacity as a judge.*

capacious [kə'peiʃəs] *adj* able to hold or contain much.

full to capacity containing as much as possible.

cape[1] [keip] *nc* type of coat without sleeves, worn over the shoulders.

cape[2] [keip] *nc* land projecting into the sea: *the Cape of Good Hope.*

caper[1] ['keipə*] *vi* run and jump in a happy way.

caper[2] ['keipə*] *nc* type of plant, the buds of which are used to flavour food.

capillary [kə'piləri] *adj* very thin, like a hair. Also *nc* thin tube in the body which joins an artery to a vein.

capital ['kæpitl] **1.** *nc* city in which the government of a country does its work. **2.** *nc* large letter. *A, B, C etc are capitals.* **3.** *nu* money and property (usu. a large amount) owned by a person or business. Also *adj* very good. (rather *o.f.* and *informal*).

capitalism ['kæpitəlizəm] *nu* system in which business and property are owned by private individuals or groups of people and not by the government or state.

capitalist *nc* person who owns business or

property in this way.
capitalize *vt* **1.** write with a large letter. see **capital** (in sense **2.**). **2.** use money or property for the purpose of business. **capitalization** [kæpitəlai'zeiʃən] *nu*.
'**capital** '**crime** crime which is punishable by death.
'**capital** '**gain** profit gained by selling part of one's property.
'**capital** '**letter** large letter (e.g. A, B, C, D).
'**capital** '**punishment** (in a legal sense) punishment by killing.
make capital of use for one's own advantage.
capitalize on something take full advantage of something.
capitulate [kə'pitjuleit] *vi* agree that one's enemy has beaten one and promise to stop fighting on certain conditions. **capitulation** [kəpitju'leiʃən] *nu*.
caprice [kə'pri:s] *nc* sudden playful or foolish idea or change of intention.
capricious [kə'priʃəs] *adj* often changing in this way; showing many caprices. **capriciously** *adv*.
capsize [kæp'saiz] *vt/i* (with reference to ships and boats) turn over.
capstan ['kæpstn] *nc* metal object for winding a rope (e.g. on a ship).

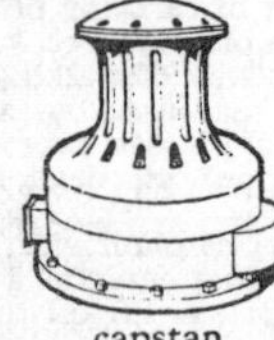
capstan

capsule ['kæpsju:l] *nc* **1.** small container that can dissolve in water etc and that holds a certain amount of medicine. **2.** seed case on a plant. **3.** any (small) container (esp. a spacecraft).
captain ['kæptin] *nc* **1.** leader of a team in certain sports. **2.** man in charge of a ship or aircraft. **3.** rank in the army, navy or air force. Also *vt* act as a leader. *John will captain the team.*
caption ['kæpʃən] *nc* writing below a picture in a newspaper or magazine, explaining the picture. Also *vt* write a caption for.
captious ['kæpʃəs] *adj* fond of finding small faults or mistakes. **captiousness** *nu*.
captivate ['kæptiveit] *vt* get the attention or interest of somebody by being beautiful or charming. **captivating** *adj*. **captivatingly** *adv*.
captive ['kæptiv] *nc* prisoner. (rather *o.f.*).
captivity [kæp'tiviti] *nu* state of being a captive.
take captive catch and hold as a prisoner. (less *o.f.*).
captor ['kæptə*] *nc* person who catches somebody and holds him as a prisoner.
capture ['kæptʃə*] *vt* **1.** catch and hold as a prisoner. *The policeman captured the thief as he was running away.* **2.** take and hold as one's own property. *The soldiers captured the town from the enemy.* Also *nc* something captured; act of capturing.
car [kɑ:*] *nc* **1.** type of vehicle; short form of **motorcar**. **2.** part of a train where people eat, sit or sleep (esp. in **dining car**, **sleeping car** etc).
caramel ['kærəml] *nc/u* type of sweet substance made from sugar which has been slightly burned.
carat ['kærət] *nc* unit for measuring the quality of gold and the weight of jewels.
caravan ['kærəvæn] *nc* **1.** group of people travelling together (esp. in a desert country). **2.** (*Brit*) small house on wheels. (*US* **trailer**).
carbine ['kɑ:bain] *nc* type of short rifle.
carbolic [kɑ:'bɔlik] *nu* substance used as a disinfectant. (Also **carbolic acid**). Also *adj*: *carbolic soap*.
carbon ['kɑ:bən] *nu* chemical element found in coal and many other substances (C).
'**carbon paper** paper covered with a coloured substance, used for making copies of what one is writing by being placed between sheets of writing paper.
carbohydrate [kɑ:bou'haidreit] *nc* **1.** (chemistry) substance composed of carbon, hydrogen and oxygen (e.g. sugar, starch etc). **2.** this substance when present in food which might cause one to gain weight (e.g. bread, potatoes etc).
carbuncle ['kɑ:bʌŋkl] *nc* **1.** painful swelling on the body. **2.** red precious stone.
carburettor ['kɑ:bjuretə*] *nc* part of a motorcar in which petrol and air are mixed together before the petrol is burned in the engine.
carcass, carcase ['kɑ:kəs] *nc* dead body of an animal.
card [kɑ:d] *nc* flat stiff piece of paper (usu. rectangular in shape) used for various purposes.
'**card index** *nc* index in which each entry is written on a separate card. Also *vt*: *card-index the data*.
'**cardsharp(er)** dishonest person who earns money by cheating at card games. (*informal*).
'**card table** table used for card games.
'**greetings card** card sent by post on certain occasions, to give congratulations or good wishes to somebody; the main types are *birthday cards* and *Christmas cards*.
'**playing card** one of a set of (usu.) 52, used for playing various games of chance and skill.
'**postcard** see **post**[1].
'**visiting card** see **visit**.
have a card up one's sleeve have a plan or idea ready for use if it is needed.
on the cards possible. *It's on the cards that I shall go to France next year.* (*informal*).
play one's cards badly/well see **play**[1].
put one's cards on the table let other people know what one's plans or opinions are (usu. while trying to come to an agreement).
cardboard ['kɑ:dbɔ:d] *nu* thick, heavy type of paper, used for making boxes etc.
cardiac ['kɑ:diæk] *adj* (mainly medicine) with reference to the heart.
cardigan ['kɑ:digən] *nc* knitted jacket.
cardinal ['kɑ:dinl] *nc* one of the senior officials of the Roman Catholic Church responsible for electing a pope. Also *adj* chief; most important.
cardinal number number such as 1, 2, 6, 10, 93 used in counting. (Contrasted with **ordinal number** i.e. number such as 1st, 2nd, 6th, 10th, 93rd).
cardinal point one of the four main points of the compass i.e. north, south, east, west.
care[1] [kɛə*] *vt/i* (usu. *negative*) feel strongly. *When I told him that he would be punished, he said he didn't care* i.e. he was not

frightened or worried. *I don't care what you say, I shall do it tomorrow* i.e. it does not matter what you say.

care about have an interest in; feel responsibility for. *The only thing he cares about is football.*

care for 1. look after; show love for and help. *When her mother died she was left to care for her father.* 2. have a liking for. *I don't care for modern art* i.e. I don't like it.

care² [kεə*] 1. *nu* close or serious attention. *He gave a lot of care to his work.* 2. *nu* protection; love; help. *A child needs a mother's care* i.e. it needs to be loved and protected by a mother. *She left her children in the care of her neighbour* i.e. her neighbour looked after, protected and fed the children, while the mother was away. 3. *nu* worry. *His face showed the signs of care and sorrow.* 4. *nc* cause of worry. *When he went on holiday he forgot about the cares of his work.*

careful *adj* with care; showing care. **carefully** *adv.* **carefulness** *nu.*

careless *adj* without care. **carelessly** *adv.* **carelessness** *nu.*

'carefree *adj* free of worry; happy.

'caretaker person who looks after a building when the people who work or live there are away.

care of words (usu. written c/o) which are put on an envelope before the name of the owner of a house, when a letter is sent to a person who is a guest or lodger at that house.

have a care be careful; try to avoid danger; try to avoid causing damage etc.

take care be careful. *You must take care when you cross the road* i.e. you must make sure that no cars are coming when you cross the road.

take care of look after; protect; feed, clothe, love etc. *He took care of his younger brothers while his mother went shopping.*

career [kə'riə*] *nc* 1. work done by a person during his life. *He had a very successful career.* 2. actions and experience of a person during his life. 3. usu. in **in full career** i.e. great speed often without full control. Also *vi* (often with **along**) move at great speed. *We were careering along in the car.*

caress [kə'res] *vt* touch gently, to express love or affection. Also *nc* touch of this kind.

caret ['kærət] *nc* the mark ʌ written below a line of writing to show a place where something is to be put in.

cargo ['kɑ:gou] *nc/u* the goods carried in a ship or aeroplane. *pl* **cargoes.**

caricature ['kærikətjuə*] *nc* picture which makes something serious or important appear to be foolish or funny; any imitation of this kind. Also *vt*: *He caricatured his headmaster.*

caries ['kεəri:z] *nu* decay or rotting of the teeth or of a bone.

carnage ['kɑ:nidʒ] *nu* killing of many people or animals: *the carnage of war.*

carnal ['kɑ:nl] *adj* concerned with the body (usu. in a bad sense, contrasted with **spiritual**): *carnal sins; carnal desires.* **carnally** *adv.*

carnation [kɑ:'neiʃən] *nc* type of flower with pink, white or red flowers which smell sweet.

carnival ['kɑ:nivl] *nc* public celebration, with processions, games, feasts etc (esp. in Roman Catholic countries in the period before Lent).

carnivorous [kɑ:'nivərəs] *adj* eating meat. *Lions and tigers are carnivorous animals.*

carnivore ['kɑ:nivɔ:*] *nc* animal which eats meat.

carol ['kærl] *nc* religious song sung at Christmas time.

carouse [kə'rauz] *vi* drink a lot of alcohol and become noisy and happy. Also *nc* an occasion on which alcohol is drunk in this way (*o.f.*).

carp¹ [kɑ:p] *nc* type of freshwater fish used for food.

carp² [kɑ:p] *vi* (often with **at**) make small and unnecessary criticisms; find small and unimportant faults or mistakes. *He was always carping at the arrangements made by other people.*

carpenter ['kɑ:pintə*] *nc* person whose work is to build things from wood (but not usu. pieces of furniture).

carpentry *nu* the work of a carpenter.

carpet ['kɑ:pit] *nc* thick heavy covering for the floor or stairs. Also *vt* cover with a carpet.

on the carpet being questioned by one's superior about a mistake or wrong action made by oneself. (*informal*).

carriage ['kæridʒ] 1. *nc* vehicle pulled by a horse, for carrying passengers. 2. *nc* part of a train in which a number of people sit together. 3. *nc* part of a machine which moves and carries other parts with it. 4. *nu* act or cost of carrying or moving goods by some form of transport. 5. *nc* (usu. only *sing*) person's way of walking and moving.

'carriageway road used by cars etc.

carrier ['kæriə*] *nc* see **carry.**

carrion ['kæriən] *nu* dead and decaying animals.

carrot ['kærət] *nc* plant with a long yellow or orange-red root eaten as a vegetable.

carry ['kæri] *vt/i* 1. lift off the ground and move from one place to another. *The bus was carrying 28 passengers when the accident happened. He always carries a small notebook in his pocket. He was carrying his hat* i.e. it was in his hand, not on his head. *Help me to carry these boxes.* 2. (esp. with reference to parts of a building) bear the weight of something. 3. (usu. with reference to sound) go across a certain distance. *His voice did not carry to the back of the room.* 4. (usu. with reference to discussions, meetings, elections etc) give approval to. *The meeting carried the motion by a large majority* i.e. many people voted in favour of the suggestion. 5. win the support of. *The speaker did not carry the audience with him* i.e. he did not get the audience to agree with him. 6. walk; hold oneself. *She carries herself very well* i.e. she walks, stands etc in a beautiful way.

carrier *nc* 1. business company which carries goods or passengers from one place to another. 2. person who carries the germs of a disease to other people, without having the disease himself. 3. anything which carries. *Water is a carrier of disease.* 4. large ship which carries aeroplanes. (Usu. **aircraft carrier**). 5. metal attachment at the front or back of a bicycle, for carrying luggage.

'carrier 'pigeon 1. type of pigeon with white flaps round its beak, which does not fly well. 2. homing pigeon. (*informal*).

carry away 1. take to another place. 2. (often *passive*) cause to have strong feelings so that one cannot think clearly. *He was so carried away by fear that he did not know what he was saying.*

carry forward (in adding sums of money) write the total of one page at the beginning of the next page.
carry off 1. take to another place by the use of force or without the owner's permission. 2. (with reference to competitions, prizes etc) win. *He carried off the first prize.* 3. be successful in doing some difficult action (often in public). *He had a difficult part in the play, but he carried it off very well.*
carry on 1. continue. *Carry on, don't stop working. He carried on his father's business* i.e. he worked in the business which his father had started. 2. be angry and speak loudly. (*informal*). 3. behave badly. (*informal*).
'carry-on *nc* fuss; troublesome procedure: *a carry-on about getting tickets.* (*informal*).
carry out do. *He carried out his plan* i.e. he did what he had planned; *carry out an order/threat/promise.*
carry something through do something and continue doing it until it is finished. *He carried through all his plans.*
carry all before one win everything; overcome all opposition.
carry authority have the appearance of something/somebody that one should obey or that one can trust.
carry coals to Newcastle supply something to a place or person having enough of it already.
carry conviction appear to be true. *His story carried conviction.*
carry on a conversation have a conversation.
carry the day win after fighting one's enemies or opponents. *John's plan carried the day* i.e. after some arguments, everybody agreed to accept John's plan.
carry weight (with reference to arguments, ideas, proofs etc) have an appearance which makes one think carefully. *The arguments which John put forward carried a lot of weight with everybody* i.e. everybody thought they were very good arguments.
cart [kɑːt] *nc* vehicle pulled by a horse and used for carrying goods. Also *vt* carry in a cart.
carter *nc* man whose work is to drive a cart.
'cart-horse big type of horse, used for pulling carts (esp. on a farm).
'cart-track rough road suitable for carts but not for cars.
'handcart small cart pushed or pulled by hand.
put the cart before the horse see **put.**
carte blanche ['kɑːt'blɑ̃ːnʃ] *nu* full permission or authority to do something: *give someone carte blanche.*
cartel [kɑː'tel] *nc* association between manufacturers who agree to sell their goods at the same prices and to produce only a certain amount of the goods; the agreement itself.
cartilage ['kɑːtilidʒ] *nc/u* strong substance like elastic in the joints of the body.
cartography [kɑː'tɔgrəfi] *nu* science of making maps. **cartographic** [kɑːtə'græfik] *adj*.
cartographer *nc* person who makes maps.
carton ['kɑːtn] *nc* cardboard container.
cartoon [kɑː'tuːn] *nc* 1. drawing in a newspaper or magazine, dealing with topics in the news (esp. politics). 2. film (usu. amusing) made by photographing a number of drawings, instead of photographing living actors. (Also **animated cartoon**).
cartoonist *nc* person who draws cartoons.
cartridge ['kɑːtridʒ] *nc* case made of metal or cardboard, holding gunpowder, for firing shot or bullets from a rifle.
carve [kɑːv] *vt/i* 1. cut (meat etc) into slices. 2. (with reference to wood, stone etc) cut into a shape, picture or pattern. **carver** *nc*.
carving *nc* piece of stone, wood etc which has been carved.
'carving knife large knife for cutting meat into slices.
cascade [kæs'keid] *nc* small waterfall. Also *vi* fall in or like a cascade.
case[1] [keis] *nc* 1. example; condition; situation; event; happening. *The headmaster had to deal with several cases of cheating* i.e. several of the pupils cheated. *The doctor went to see a case of malaria* i.e. a person suffering from malaria. *He told me about the case of a girl who did not learn to speak until she was five* i.e. he told me the facts about this girl. *He said that he understood, but this was not the case* i.e. this was not true. 2. a matter which a judge or other person in a court of law is asked to decide on. *The lawyer put his case to the judge* i.e. the lawyer put forward his arguments. 3. (grammar) form of the noun/pronoun depending on the use of the noun/pronoun in the sentence (e.g. the difference between 'I' and 'me' is a difference of case).
in any case whatever happens.
in case so as to be ready if something happens. *You must take your umbrella in case it rains.*
in case of if there is. *In case of difficulty, ask the shopkeeper to help you.*
have a (good) case be able to show that one's arguments or opinions are right.
in that case if that is true. *The boy told me that he had lost his money and so I said that in that case he could not buy a new football.*
case[2] [keis] *nc* container or box for holding goods.
'bookcase see **book**[1].
ciga'rette case box (usu. of metal) used for carrying cigarettes.
'packing case large wooden box used for transporting goods.
'pillow case/slip see **pillow.**
'suitcase type of container with handle for carrying clothes etc on a journey.
casement ['keismənt] *nc* type of window on hinges, opening like a door (not moving up and down).
cash [kæʃ] *nu* money in notes and coins. Also *vt* change into cash: *cash a cheque.*
cashier[1] [kæ'ʃiə*] *nc* person in a shop or bank who deals with the cash.
cash on delivery arrangement by which one pays the person who delivers goods to one's house. (Often **C.O.D.**).
'cash register machine which holds cash and records the amount of money paid.
cashew ['kæʃuː] *nc* 1. small kidney-shaped nut. 2. the tree the nut grows on.
cashier[2] [kæ'ʃiə*] *vt* make an officer leave the army, navy, air force etc for behaving in a bad or dishonest way.
cashmere ['kæʃmiə*] *nu* soft type of wool.
casino [kə'siːnou] *nc* building open to the public for gambling. *pl* **casinos.**
cask [kɑːsk] *nc* large or small container for liquid (usu. liquid for drinking).
casket ['kɑːskit] *nc* 1. small box for holding precious objects (e.g. jewels). 2. (*US*) coffin.
cassava [kə'sɑːvə] *nu* type of plant grown

in the tropics for its roots from which food (such as tapioca) is obtained.

casserole ['kæsəroul] *nc* covered dish in which food can be cooked in an oven; food cooked in this way. Also *vt* cook food in this way.

cassock ['kæsək] *nc* long garment worn by priests of some Christian churches.

cassock

cast[1] [kaːst] *vt/i* **1.** throw: *cast a fishing line; cast a shadow.*
Note: apart from references to fishing or to shadows, *cast* in the sense of *throw* is rather *o.f.* – use *throw.*
2. let fall; lose; discard. *The horse cast a shoe. The snake has cast its skin.* **3.** pour hot liquid metal into a mould or shape, in which it cools and becomes solid in the form of the mould. **4.** give parts to actors in a play. *I cast John as Hamlet and Mary as Ophelia. past* **cast.**
cast about for something search for something: *cast about for an idea.*
cast down *pred adj* miserable because of a feeling that one has failed.
'cast-off 'clothing clothing which has been given away because it is too old or too small for the owner.
cast off 1. untie a rope or other fastening which ties a boat or ship to the land. **2.** finish a piece of knitting.
cast one's eyes over something look at something.
cast/draw lots let people take various objects (e.g. pieces of paper, pieces of grass etc), one of which is marked in a special way, in order to decide who will do something. *They cast lots to decide who would ask the headmaster for an extra holiday.*
cast in one's lot with somebody join somebody and help him in some struggle or action.
cast a spell (on somebody) do some magic (usu. to hurt somebody).
cast a vote vote; choose one of a number of people in an election. see also **cast**[2].

cast[2] [kaːst] *nc* **1.** act of throwing. see **cast**[1]. **2.** something allowed to fall (usu. a snake's skin or a small hard piece of earth formed by the digestive processes of earthworms). **3.** metal statue or object formed in a mould. **4.** (list of) actors in a play. **5.** fault in a person's vision, so that one eye is turned to the side when the person is looking in front. **6.** stiff covering worn on a broken arm, leg etc to enable it to heal. (Also **plaster cast**). **7.** form or appearance.
'castaway person who has landed in a strange (and often uninhabited) country after being in a shipwreck.
'cast'iron *nu* type of hard but brittle iron made by casting. Also *adj* very strong: *castiron evidence.*
'casting vote vote given by a chairman of a meeting if the votes of the members are evenly divided.

castanet [kæstə'net] *nc* (usu. *pl*) instrument made of two pieces of wood, held in the hand and hit together to produce a sound.

caste [kaːst] *nc* **1.** one of a number of social and religious divisions in use among Hindus. A person is considered as being born into a particular caste and cannot rise to a higher caste. **2.** any social division of this type.
lose caste lose one's social position; be regarded as having moved to a caste which is lower than that into which one was born.

castigate ['kæstigeit] *vt* punish (esp. by speaking in an unpleasant way). **castigation** [kæsti'geiʃən] *nu.*

castle ['kaːsl] *nc* **1.** old type of building with thick walls, used for defence against enemies. **2.** one of the pieces in the game of chess.
castles in the air ideas and plans which will never be carried out.

castor ['kaːstə*] *nc* **1.** small wheel put on a piece of furniture to make it easy to move. **2.** small bottle containing salt, pepper, sugar etc for putting these substances on to food during a meal.

castor oil ['kaːstər'ɔil] *nu* thick unpleasant-tasting oil used as a medicine.

castor sugar ['kaːstəʃugə*] *nu* type of very fine sugar.

castrate [kæs'treit] *vt* cut off part of the sexual organs of a male human or animal. **castrated** *adj.* **castration** *nu.*

casual ['kæʒjuəl] *adj* **1.** happening by chance or accident; not planned: *a casual meeting.* **2.** careless and rather impolite in behaviour. *He spoke in a rather casual way to the headmaster.* **casually** *adv.* **casualness** *nu.*
casual labourer person who does not work at any one job, but does heavy and usu. unskilled work when it is needed for a particular purpose.
casual labour the work done in this way.

casualty ['kæʒjuəlti] *nc* person killed or injured in war or in an accident.
'casualty ward part of a hospital kept ready to receive people injured in accidents.

casuist ['kæzjuist] *nc* person who is skilled in arguments about questions of right and wrong (esp. a person who argues in a clever but dishonest way).
casuistry *nc/u* method of arguing of a casuist. **casuistical** [kæzju'istikl] *adj.*

cat [kæt] *nc* **1.** small domestic animal which can see in the dark and which catches and eats mice. **2.** large wild animal of the same family such as lion, tiger, panther etc. **3.** type of whip with many strings or lashes. **4.** woman who says unkind things and causes arguments. (*informal* in sense **4.**).
catty *adj* (usu. with reference to a woman or something she says) unkind; saying unkind things.
'cat call *nc* (often *pl*) loud unpleasant noise made to express disapproval. Also *vi* make this noise.
'cat's-'cradle game played with a piece of string wound round the fingers.
'cat's-paw person who is persuaded to do something for the benefit of some other person. (*informal*).
lead a cat and dog life, live like cat and dog (esp. with reference to husband and wife) be always quarrelling. (*informal*).

cataclysm ['kætəklizəm] *nc* any violent happening in nature or society which causes lasting damage (e.g. earthquake, flood, war). **cataclysmic** [kætə'klizmik] *adj.*

catacomb ['kætəku:m] *nc* (usu. *pl*) (esp. with reference to ones used in ancient Rome by Christians) room or passage under the earth, for storing dead bodies.

catalogue ['kætəlɔg] (*US* **catalog**) *nc* list of things. A library has a catalogue to help people find the books they want; some big stores issue catalogues of the things they have for sale. Also *vt* put into a catalogue. *The librarian catalogued the new books.*

catalyst ['kætəlist] *nc* something which helps a chemical change to take place without undergoing any change itself.
catalysis [kə'tælisis] *nu* chemical change of this type. **catalytic** [kætə'litik] *adj.*

catapult ['kætəpʌlt] *nc* **1.** (*Brit*) piece of wood or metal, shaped like a letter Y, with a piece of rubber attached, used for shooting small stones. (*US* **slingshot**). **2.** large machine for shooting big stones, formerly used in war before the use of guns. Also *vt* shoot from a catapult.

cataract ['kætərækt] *nc* **1.** type of steep waterfall. **2.** disease of the eye, in which the centre of the eye becomes white and blind.

catarrh [kə'tɑ:*] *nu* disease of the nose and throat, causing the formation of a thick liquid; the thick liquid itself.

catastrophe [kə'tæstrəfi] *nc* sudden and very bad accident or misfortune (e.g. a fire, earthquake, plane crash). **catastrophic** [kætəs'trɔfik] *adj.*

catch[1] [kætʃ] *vt/i* stop and hold; meet and stay with; capture. *The policeman caught the thief. He caught a train to London. He caught the ball in one hand. The beautiful picture caught my attention* i.e. I stopped and looked with interest at the picture. *He caught influenza last year* i.e. he had this disease last year (with reference to infectious diseases only) (e.g. we can say *he caught a cold* but not *he caught cancer*). *past* **caught** [kɔ:t].
catching *adj* (with reference to disease) infectious; easily caught.
catch on 1. become popular. *Do you think this fashion will catch on?* **2.** understand. *It took me a while to catch on.* (*informal*).
catch someone out be able to show that somebody is telling a lie.
catch someone up *John left five minutes ago, but if you hurry you will catch him up.* see **catch up with** (in sense **1.**).
catch up with someone/something 1. go faster than somebody in front who is going in the same direction as oneself, so that one comes to where he is. *John left the house ten minutes before I did, but he walked so slowly that I was able to catch up with him.* **2.** do work which should have been done before. *I have been ill for two weeks, and so I must try to catch up with my work.*
catch one's breath take a sudden breath and hold it for a short time (usu. because of some strong feeling).
catch somebody doing something come along at the time when somebody is doing something wrong. *I caught the thief trying to open the window. The teacher caught the boy cheating.*
catch someone's eye attract someone's attention; act in a certain way in order to make someone notice one.
catch fire begin burning.
catch hold of take in the hand and hold (often to save or support oneself).
catch the post take one's letters to the post office or postbox, in time for them to be collected by the postman at a certain time.
catch sight of suddenly see for a short time.

catch[2] [kætʃ] *nc* **1.** act of catching (e.g. a ball). **2.** (esp. with reference to fish caught) something caught. **3.** something for fastening a door or window. **4.** trick; something which is intended to deceive somebody. (*informal* in sense **4.**).
catchy *adj* (with reference to music) easy to learn and pleasant: *a catchy tune.*
'catchword/'catch phrase short statement or slogan which is easily learned (used for advertising or political purposes).

catechism ['kætəkizəm] *nc* list of questions and answers (esp. such a list of religious teachings) to be learned by people wishing to become full members of the Christian churches.
catechist *nc* person who asks questions in this way.
catechize *vt* **1.** teach by asking questions. **2.** ask many searching questions.

category ['kætəgəri] *nc* type; class; kind; division.
categorize *vt* put into categories.
categorical [kætə'gɔrikl] *adj* (with reference to statements) definite; without any doubts.

cater ['keitə*] *vi* (usu. with **for** or **to**) provide or supply (esp. food). *He catered for two hundred guests at the party* i.e. he provided food for them. *The radio and television have to cater to many different types of interest and taste among the public.*
caterer *nc* person who supplies food for parties, weddings, dances etc.

caterpillar ['kætəpilə*] *nc* **1.** worm-like animal which eats plants and which later turns into a moth or butterfly. **2.** type of vehicle for travelling over rough ground, with wheels moving inside an endless belt (called a *caterpillar track*); the belt itself.

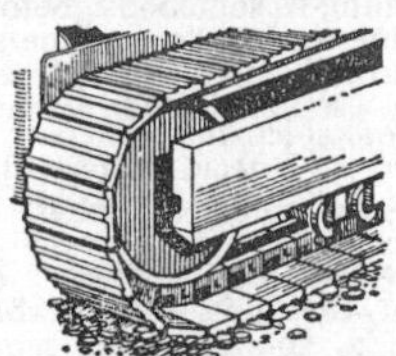

caterpillar track

catharsis [kə'θɑ:sis] *nc/u* process of being freed from violent emotion (esp. through the experience of watching a play). *pl* **catharses** [kə'θɑ:si:z]. **cathartic** *adj.*

cathedral [kə'θi:drl] *nc* church of a bishop or archbishop in some of the Christian churches.

cathode ['kæθoud] *nc* **1.** electrode which sends out electrons in a cathode ray tube, X-ray tube etc. **2.** negative electrode in a battery etc. (*opp* **anode**).
'cathode 'ray 'tube vacuum tube in which a beam of electrons directed from a cathode at one end can trace out a pattern of light on a screen at the other (used in television sets, radar etc).

catholic ['kæθlik] *adj* **1.** of interest to everybody; for the use or benefit of everybody. **2.** wide; with an interest in everything. **3.** of all the Christian churches taken together. **4.** (**Catholic**) of the Roman Catholic Church. Also *nc* member of the Roman Catholic Church.

cattle ['kætl] *npl* cows, bulls and calves, taken all together.
catty ['kæti] *adj* see **cat.**
caucasian [kɔː'keiziən] *nc* **1.** **(Caucasian)** person from the Caucasus i.e. the mountainous area of Russia between the Black Sea and the Caspian Sea. **2.** (mainly *US*) white person; person with light-coloured skin.
caucus ['kɔːkəs] *nc* small group within a political party (usu. one which tries to form the policy for the whole party).
caught [kɔːt] past of **catch**[1].
cauldron ['kɔːldrn] *nc* large pot used for cooking over a fire.
cauliflower ['kɔliflauə*] *nc/u* type of vegetable like a cabbage but with a white flower-like head.
cause [kɔːz] *nc* **1.** thing which makes something happen. *What was the cause of your failure?* i.e. why did you fail? *You have no cause to worry* i.e. there is nothing to worry about. **2.** purpose, movement or idea for which people work. *He was collecting money for a good cause* i.e. he was collecting money for people or for something deserving the money. *The United Nations Organization has done a lot for the cause of world peace.* Also *vt* make something happen; be the cause of something.
causeway ['kɔːzwei] *nc* road built up above the surface of the land on either side (usu. across swampy land).
caustic ['kɔːstik] *adj* **1.** burning by chemical action: *caustic soda* i.e. sodium hydroxide (NaOH). **2.** (with reference to words) hurtful; cruel. **caustically** *adv.*
cauterize ['kɔːtəraiz] *vt* burn a part of the body with hot iron or with caustic substance in order to destroy infection etc.
cauterization [kɔːtərai'zeiʃən] *nu.*
caution ['kɔːʃən] *nu* action of being careful so as to avoid danger or mistakes. Also *vt* give a warning to somebody, before or after he has made a mistake or done something wrong. **cautious** *adj.* **cautiously** *adv.*
cautionary ['kɔːʃənəri] *adj* giving a warning: *a cautionary notice.*
cavalcade [kævəl'keid] *nc* number of people travelling one behind another, on horses or in vehicles drawn by horses.
cavalier [kævə'liə*] *nc* **1.** **(Cavalier)** follower of the king during the English Civil War. **2.** soldier on horseback (*o.f.*). **3.** escort; man who goes with a lady to public places such as parties or theatres (*o.f.*). Also *adj* **1.** like a cavalier. **2.** careless, offhand: *a cavalier attitude.* **3.** proud.
cavalry ['kævəlri] *n sing* or *pl* soldiers on horseback.
cave [keiv] *nc* natural hole under the ground or in the side of a hill or cliff.
'caveman person who lived in a cave in prehistoric times.
cave in *vi* **1.** (with reference to the walls or roof of a cave) fall down. **2.** agree to do what other people ask, because one is too weak to go on refusing. (*informal* in sense **2.**).
cavern ['kævən] *nc* large cave. **cavernous** *adj.*
caviare, caviar ['kæviɑː*] *nu* the eggs of certain large fish, used as food.
cavil ['kævl] *vi* (with **at**) make unnecessary criticisms; look for small mistakes. *He cavilled at most of the work which I had done.* *past* **cavilled.** **(US caviled).**
cavity ['kæviti] *nc* hole (esp. in a tooth).
cavort [kə'vɔːt] *vi* dance or move about in a wild and foolish way.
caw [kɔː] *nc* harsh and unpleasant sound made by certain birds (e.g. crows). Also *vi* make this sound.
cayenne [kei'en] *nu* type of hot red pepper.
cease [siːs] *vt/i* stop.
ceaseless *adj* without stopping; continuous; unending. **ceaselessly** *adv.*
cease fire make an agreement in war to stop fighting (esp. for a short time).
cease'fire *nc* an agreement of this type.
cedar ['siːdə*] **1.** *nc* type of tree with wide, spreading branches and sweet-smelling wood. **2.** *nu* the wood of this tree.
cede [siːd] *vt* make an agreement to give land or other property or rights to another person or country; give up: *cede a point in an argument.*
ceiling ['siːliŋ] *nc* **1.** the upper inner surface of a room. **2.** upper limit (esp. the greatest height at which an aeroplane can fly).
celebrate ['selibreit] *vt/i* **1.** do something to show that one is happy about some event or day. *The people celebrated the victory. He celebrated his twenty-fifth birthday.* **2.** perform a ceremony.
celebration [seli'breiʃən] *nc* act of celebrating.
celebrant ['selibrənt] *nc* priest who performs a ceremony.
celebrated ['selibreitid] *adj* well-known; famous.
celebrity [si'lebriti] *nc* famous person.
celery ['seləri] *nu* type of vegetable with long crisp stems.
celerity [si'leriti] *nu* speed.
celestial [si'lestiəl] *adj* of the sky; of heaven, heavenly.
celibate ['selibit] *adj* (esp. with reference to a person who is unmarried for religious reasons e.g. a monk or nun) not married. Also *nc* unmarried person.
celibacy ['selibəsi] *nu* state of being celibate.
cell [sel] *nc* **1.** small room in a prison, in which prisoners are kept. **2.** small piece of substance of which all plants and animals are formed. **3.** (usu. with reference to the containers in a honeycomb) small container. **4.** apparatus for producing electricity by chemical action. **5.** small group of people within a political organization (esp. within the Communist Party).
cellular ['seljulə*] *adj* **1.** of cells; made of cells. **2.** (with reference to certain types of cotton cloth) loosely woven.
cellar ['selə*] *nc* room under a house, used for storing things (esp. fuel or wine).
cello ['tʃelou] *nc* type of musical instrument. *pl* **cellos.**
cellist *nc* person who plays the cello.
Note: sometimes written with an apostrophe – *'cello, 'cellist* – because the word was originally *violoncello.*

cello

Cellophane ['seləfein] ® *nu* transparent type

of paper used for wrapping goods for sale.

celluloid ['seljulɔid] *nu* hard transparent material used for making film for cameras.

cellulose ['seljulous] *nu* substance found in plants, used for making paper, plastic and other substances.

cement [si'ment] *nu* **1.** powdery substance which, when mixed with water, becomes very hard, used for building. **2.** any substance which becomes hard in this way. Also *vt* **1.** join or fill with cement. **2.** join or fasten firmly: *cement relations between our two countries.*

cemetery ['semitri] *nc* piece of land where people are buried.
Note: a cemetery is not usu. joined to a church; the land around a church in which bodies are buried is called a *churchyard.*

cenotaph ['senətɑːf] *nc* monument to the memory of a person/people buried in another place (esp. a monument in memory of people killed in war).

censer ['sensə*] *nc* container for holding burning incense, used in some churches.

censor ['sensə*] *nc* person employed by the government or other official body to examine books, films, plays etc in order to decide whether they are suitable for the public. The censor may sometimes ask for certain things to be left out of a film, play etc for moral or political reasons. Also *vt* act as a censor: *censor a book.* **censored** *adj.*
censorship *nc* work of a censor; system of employing a censor to act in this way.

censorious [sen'sɔːriəs] *adj* very critical; looking for mistakes or faults. **censoriously** *adv.* **censoriousness** *nu.*

censure ['senʃə*] *vt* blame; disapprove of. Also *nc* blame; disapproval.

census ['sensəs] *nc* count made by the government or other official body to see how many people etc there are in a country, and to find out certain details about them.

cent [sent] *nc* one hundredth of a dollar.
per cent for each hundred (written %): *five per cent* i.e. five out of each hundred.

centaur ['sentɔː*] *nc* imaginary creature in Greek mythology, with the head and chest of a man, and the body and legs of a horse.

centenarian [senti'nɛəriən] *nc* person who is a hundred or more years old.

centenary [sen'tiːnəri] *nc* celebration 100 years after some event. *This year is the centenary of the birth of William Smith.* Also *adj.*

centennial [sen'teniəl] *nc* see **centenary.** Also *adj.*

center ['sentə*] *nc* see **centre.**

centigrade ['sentigreid] *adj* a system of measuring temperature, using 0 degrees for the temperature of melting ice, and 100 degrees for the temperature of boiling water.

centigramme ['sentigræm] (*US* **centigram**) *nc* one hundredth of a gramme. see appendix.

centimetre ['sentimiːtə*] (*US* **centimeter**) *nc* one hundredth of a metre. see appendix.

centipede ['sentipiːd] *nc* type of small thin creature with many legs.

centre ['sentə*] (*US* **center**) *nc* **1.** middle. *He was standing in the centre of the room* i.e. he was not near any of the walls and he was equally far from the walls. *He lives in the centre of the city* i.e. in the area to which the main railway lines and roads lead and in which the main shops and government buildings are. **2.** building or organization for the use or benefit of people from many different areas: *a social centre.* Also *vt/i* (esp. with reference to kicking a football into the area near the goal mouth) place in the centre.
central *adj* **1.** of a centre. **2.** most important. **centrally** *adv.*
centralize *vt/i* **1.** bring to the centre. **2.** put under the control of one central organization. **centralization** [sentrəlai'zeiʃən] *nu.*
centre of attraction person/thing which arouses other people's interest.
central heating heating of a building through pipes.
'shopping centre area of a town in which there are a number of shops.
centre on be mainly concerned with.

centrifugal [sentri'fjuːgl] *adj* moving away from the centre.

centripetal [sen'tripitl] *adj* moving towards the centre.

centurion [sen'tjuriən] *nc* officer in the ancient Roman army, in charge of about 100 men.

century ['sentjuri] *nc* **1.** period of one hundred years. **2.** period of one hundred years before or after the birth of Christ (taken to be 1 AD). **3.** (cricket) 100 runs scored by one batsman.

ceramic [si'ræmik] *adj* (esp. with reference to making or designing) of pottery; concerned with cups, plates etc. Also *nc* piece of pottery having artistic value.

cereal ['siəriəl] *nc* any grain crop used as food (e.g. wheat, corn, rice). Also *adj.*

cerebral ['seribrl] *adj* of the brain.

ceremony ['seriməni] **1.** *nc* special action or actions carried out at particular times and in particular places: *the ceremonies of the church; traditional ceremonies for crowning the king.* **2.** *nu* very polite behaviour. *Everybody behaved with a great deal of ceremony.*
ceremonious [seri'mouniəs] *adj* **1.** fond of ceremonies; interested in ceremonies. **2.** very polite; unnecessarily polite: *very ceremonious behaviour.* **ceremoniously** *adv.*
ceremonial [seri'mouniəl] *adj* of a ceremony. Also *nc/u* actions performed at a ceremony.
master of ceremonies man in charge of a dance or party.
stand on ceremony behave in an unnecessarily polite way. *There's no need to stand on ceremony; we are all friends.*

cerise [sə'riːz] *nu* light red colour. Also *adj.*

certain ['səːtn] *adj* **1.** sure; without doubt. *I think I'm right, but I'm not certain* i.e. I may be wrong. *He risked certain death if he was caught* i.e. he would have been killed if he had been caught. **2.** particular, but not named for some reason. A *certain person told me about the accident* i.e. somebody that I know, but do not wish to name. *It is very dangerous under certain conditions* i.e. I know what these conditions are, but it is unnecessary for me to mention them in detail.
certainly *adv* without doubt; yes (in answer to a question).
certainty *nc/u* something certain; state of being certain. (*opp* **uncertainty**).
for certain without doubt.
make certain find out the truth. *I think that I'm right, but you should ask somebody else to make certain.*

certificate [sə'tifikət] *nc* official written statement of some fact.

certify *vt* (esp. with reference to act of a doctor officially declaring somebody to be mad) officially declare to be true (usu. by giving a certificate). *He had been behaving strangely for many years and at last he was certified.*

certifiable *adj* (esp. with reference to mental illness) that can be certified.

certitude ['sə:titju:d] *nu* feeling of being sure that something is true.

cessation [se'seiʃən] *nc/u* stopping.

cesspool ['sespu:l] *nc* hole into which the dirty water flows from a house. (Also **cesspit**).

chafe [tʃeif] *vt/i* **1.** make the skin sore by rubbing. **2.** rub to make warm. **3.** (usu. with **under**) become or make angry. Also *nc* mark or sore caused by chafing.

chaff [tʃɑ:f] *nu* **1.** outer covering of grain (wheat etc), removed before the grain and used for food. **2.** hay or straw cut up as food for cattle.

chaffinch ['tʃæfintʃ] *nc* type of small European bird, the male of which has a blue-grey head and neck.

chagrin ['ʃægrin] *nu* feeling of anger or sadness because one has made a mistake or failed to do something.

chain [tʃein] *nc* **1.** number of metal rings joined together, used for fastening things/people. **2.** any series of things connected to each other: *a chain of events; a mountain chain* i.e. a line of mountains; *a chain of ideas; a chain of shops/restaurants* i.e. a number of shops or restaurants, all having the same appearance and all owned by the same person/persons. **3.** a measure of length (66 feet). Also *vt* (often with **up**) fasten with a chain. *The dog was chained up every night.*

'**chain gang** (esp. *US*) number of prisoners chained together while working.

'**chain re'action** (esp. in atomic physics with reference to a certain type of atomic explosion) process in which one thing causes a second thing to happen which in turn causes a third, and so on.

'**chain smoker** *nc* person who starts a new cigarette as soon as he finishes one; person who smokes many cigarettes. **chain smoking** *nu*.

'**chain store** one of a number of shops, all selling the same goods, and all owned by the same person/persons.

in chains (as) a prisoner.

chair [tʃɛə*] *nc* **1.** piece of furniture (usu. with four legs and a support for the back) on which one person can sit. **2.** position of a professor in a university. *Dr Smith holds the chair of English* i.e. he is the professor of English. **3.** position of a person in charge of a meeting. *Mr Brown took the chair at the meeting* i.e. he was in charge of the meeting. **4.** electric chair (used for electrocuting criminals in some parts of the *USA*). Also *vt* be in charge of a meeting. *Will you chair the meeting or shall I?*

'**chairman** person in charge of a meeting. (This word can be used to refer to a woman, but some people use the word **chairwoman**).

chalet ['ʃælei] *nc* **1.** small wooden house used by herdsmen in the Alps. **2.** house of this shape (often a holiday house).

chalice ['tʃælis] *nc* metal wine cup, used for Communion in some of the Christian churches.

chalk ['tʃɔ:k] *nu* **1.** type of soft limestone. **2.** substance like this used in schools etc for writing on blackboards. Also *vt* write with chalk.

by a long chalk very much more. *John is better than James by a long chalk.* (*informal*).

challenge ['tʃæləndʒ] *vt* **1.** request somebody to fight, play a game or compete in some way. *I challenged him to a game of chess. I challenged him to fight me.* **2.** (with reference to the action of a person acting as a guard) ask somebody to give his name, say what he wants etc. *The soldier on guard challenged the strangers who tried to come in.* **3.** say that one does not believe what somebody has said; ask for more proof of somebody's statement. Also *nc* **1.** act of challenging (in all three senses given above). **2.** the challenge itself. **3.** difficulty which makes one work harder than one would normally. **challenger** *nc*.

challenging *adj* **1.** containing a challenge: *a challenging statement.* **2.** difficult but interesting: *challenging work.*

chamber ['tʃeimbə*] *nc* **1.** room (esp. a bedroom) (*o.f.*). **2.** group of people who make laws; one of the houses of a parliament. *The British Parliament consists of two chambers: the House of Commons and the House of Lords.* **3.** (usu. *pl*) number of rooms in a house, in which lawyers live or work. *The judge heard the case in chambers* i.e. in his private room or office, not in the public courtroom. **4.** any hollow place in a machine or in the body (e.g. the part of a gun where the shell or bullet is put).

chamber of commerce group of businessmen who work together to improve business in a town or area.

'**chamber music** music written for a small group of musicians, suitable for playing in a room or small hall.

chamberlain ['tʃeimbəlin] *nc* chief official in the household of a king or queen.

chameleon [kə'mi:liən] *nc* **1.** type of animal which has the ability to change its colour to fit in with its background. **2.** person who often changes ideas and opinions under the influence of other people.

chamois ['ʃæmwɑ:] *nc* type of animal like a goat, found in the mountains of Europe and Asia. *pl* **chamois.**

chamois leather ['ʃæmi'leðə*] *nc/u* soft leather made from the skin of sheep and goats, used for cleaning glass.

champ [tʃæmp] *vt/i* (esp. with reference to horses) bite noisily.

champagne [ʃæm'pein] *nu* kind of French wine which bubbles when the bottle is opened.

champion ['tʃæmpiən] *nc* **1.** person, team or animal winning first place in a competition or show, or doing better in some particular sport than any other player, team etc. **2.** person who fights or speaks to defend somebody else or to support some cause or movement. *Mr Smith is a champion of equal rights for women.* Also *vt* act as a defender or supporter. *Mr Smith has always championed the cause of equal rights for women.*

championship *nc* competition to find a champion (in sense **1.**).

chance[1] [tʃɑ:ns] **1.** *nc* opportunity. *I had the chance of going to India last year, but I decided not to go* i.e. I was asked to go or it was made possible for me to go. *I gave him another chance* i.e. I allowed him to try again. **2.** *nc* possibility or probability. *Is there any chance that you will be able to find* *the money?* i.e. do you think that it is possible to find the money? **3.** *nu* the way in which things happen without any cause. *I didn't really mean to do that, it was just chance* i.e. it just happened, nobody planned it. *Leave it to chance* i.e. do not plan anything, just see what happens. Also *adj* accidental, not planned: *a chance meeting; a chance discovery.*

by chance by accident; without planning. *It happened by chance.*

by any chance (used to make a polite request or enquiry) by any possibility. *I wonder whether you could lend me some money by any chance?*

the chance of a lifetime an opportunity, which may never happen again, to gain a big advantage for oneself.

the main chance opportunity to gain an advantage for oneself (often in **have an eye to the main chance** i.e. look for ways of getting an advantage for oneself).

on the (off) chance of with the hope of; in case. *I waited for another hour on the chance of meeting him.*

outside chance a very small possibility. *There is an outside chance that he will win.* (*informal*).

take a chance take a risk; do something although it is dangerous. *He took a chance when he went near the enemy camp; he might have been shot.*

take one's chance hope that one will be lucky. *I'll take my chance of being captured by the enemy* i.e. I will trust in luck that I shall not be captured.

chance[2] [tʃɑːns] *vt/i* **1.** happen by accident; happen without planning. *I chanced to find this old book last night.* **2.** take a risk; do something although it may be dangerous or unpleasant: *chance it* i.e. take a risk. (*informal*).

chancel ['tʃɑːnsl] *nc* area around and in front of the altar of a church, used by the priest and choir.

chancellor ['tʃɑːnsələ*] *nc* an important official of various types (e.g. the head of government in some countries; the head of a university in England).

chancellery ['tʃɑːnsləri] *nc* **1.** office or position of a chancellor. **2.** the offices of an embassy or consulate.

Chancellor of the Exchequer chief finance minister in the British government.

'Lord 'Chancellor chief judge in England.

chancery ['tʃɑːnsəri] *nc* one of the courts of law in England, presided over by the Lord Chancellor.

in chancery being dealt with by the Lord Chancellor's court.

chandelier [ʃændi'liə*] *nc* branched holder for a number of lights, which hangs from the ceiling.

chandler ['tʃɑːndlə*] *nc* person who makes or sells candles, paint, soap, and other supplies (esp. for ships).

change[1] [tʃeindʒ] *vt/i* **1.** become or make different. *He has changed the date of the meeting* i.e. he has announced that the meeting will be held on a date which is different from the date originally agreed on. *He has changed his ideas since last year* i.e. he now has different ideas. *I want to change my seat* i.e. I want to sit in a different seat. *He went to the library to change his books* i.e. to get some different books. **2.** put on different clothes. *I shan't be long; I'm just going to change.* **3.** take money in one form and give it back in another form. *Can you change this £5 note for me?* i.e. can you give me five pound notes or the equivalent in exchange?

change up/down move into a higher/lower gear in a car etc.

change colour esp. become red or white in the face through anger, fear etc.

change hands pass from one person to another. *This house has changed hands three times this year* i.e. three different people have bought it and sold it again.

change one's mind have a different opinion. *I used to think he was clever, but I changed my mind* i.e. I now think he is not clever.

change[2] [tʃeindʒ] **1.** *nc* act of becoming or making different. *I'm going to make some changes in this room* i.e. I'm going to put the furniture in different places, paint the room a different colour etc. *There have been many changes in the world during the last 100 years. He needs a change* (e.g. a holiday). **2.** *nu* money given in return to a person who has given too much money for the goods being bought: *give someone change of a pound. I gave the shopkeeper a £1 note for a newspaper and I nearly forgot to take my change.* **3.** *nu* small coins.

changeable ['tʃeindʒəbl] *adj* often changing. *The weather is very changeable today* i.e. it rains for a short time, and then the sun shines, and then it rains again, and so on.

small change small coins.

channel ['tʃænl] *nc* **1.** narrow stretch of water between two pieces of land. **2.** deepest part of a river or waterway. **3.** course along which a river or other body of water flows. **4.** means by which news or information is carried. **5.** band of television frequencies on which a particular television service is broadcast. **6.** established procedure: *apply through the usual channels.* **7.** a narrow groove or excavation to accommodate a wire, pipe etc. Also *vt* cut a channel in; direct through a channel.

chant [tʃɑːnt] *nc* slow song or shout like a song, sung or shouted by many people. Also *vt/i* sing or shout in this way. *The people in the church were chanting a prayer. The crowd in the street were chanting in support of their leader.*

chaos ['keiɔs] *nu* condition in which there is no order or system. *After the revolution started, there was chaos in the country until the army took control of the government.*

chaotic [kei'ɔtik] *adj*. **chaotically** *adv*.

chap[1] [tʃæp] *vt/i* (with reference to the action of the wind or cold on the skin) become or make sore and rough. *past* **chapped**. Also *nc* sore or rough place on the skin.

chap[2] [tʃæp] *nc* man or boy. (*informal*).

chapel ['tʃæpl] *nc* **1.** place in a building such as a school, college, prison etc used by Christians for prayer and hymn singing. **2.** part of a church used for private prayers or prayers for a special purpose. **3.** (in England) church used by Christians who are not Roman Catholics or Anglicans (e.g. one used by Methodists).

chaperon, chaperone ['ʃæpəroun] *nc* married or older woman who goes with a young unmarried woman to public places. Also *vt* act as a chaperon to.

chaplain ['tʃæplin] *nc* priest etc who works in a prison, school, college etc, in the army, navy or air force, or in the household of an important or rich person.

chaplaincy *nc* position or office of a chaplain.

chapped [tʃæpt] *adj* (of the skin) sore and rough. see **chap**[1].

chapter ['tʃæptə*] *nc* **1.** one of the parts which a book is divided into. **2.** meeting of officials of a cathedral.

'chapter house building where the officials of a cathedral meet.

char[1] [tʃɑ:*] *vt/i* become or make black by burning. *The book was charred when it fell into the fire. past* **charred.**

char[2] [tʃɑ:*] *vi* work for several hours a day cleaning an office, school, house etc. *past tense* **charred.** Also *nc* woman who does this work. (*informal* – short form of **charwoman**).

'charwoman woman who works in this way.

charabanc ['ʃærəbæŋ] *nc* bus used for long journeys for the purpose of pleasure or holiday-making (*o.f.* – use **coach**).

character ['kæriktə*] **1.** *nc* the way a person thinks and feels. *He has a very cheerful character* i.e. he is usu. cheerful in his feelings and behaviour. **2.** *nu* (esp. with reference to qualities such as honesty, self-reliance, cheerfulness etc) those parts of the way a person thinks and feels which are good. *He is a man of character* i.e. he shows these qualities. **3.** *nu* nature or type of anything. *We have changed the character of the examination this year* i.e. it is a different kind of examination. **4.** *nc* person in a book or play. *There are very many characters in the novels of Charles Dickens.* **5.** *nc* well-known person (esp. one who is well-known because he behaves in an unusual way). *Old Mr Jones is quite a character* i.e. he is well-known for his unusual behaviour. (*informal*). **6.** *nc* letter or written statement saying what a person is like, written by somebody who knows the person well, and asked for by an employer when the person applies for a job. **7.** *nc* (esp. with reference to the Chinese system of writing) mark or sign used in writing.

characteristic [kæriktə'ristik] *adj* showing the character of; showing what is usual about a person, place etc. *These small white houses are characteristic of the Greek islands* i.e. many Greek islands have small white houses. *That behaviour is characteristic of him* i.e. he often behaves in that way. (*opp* **uncharacteristic**). Also *nc* usual or special quality of a person, place etc. *I described to him the characteristics of Scottish people* i.e. I told him what Scottish people are like.

characteristically *adv.*

characterize *vt* (often *passive*) show the character of; be typical of. *The farms in this part of the country are characterized by small fields separated by stone walls.*

out of character not showing one's usual behaviour. *It's out of character for John to cheat* i.e. John does not usually cheat.

charade [ʃə'rɑ:d] *nc* game in which people have to guess a word or phrase after seeing other people act a number of short scenes, each containing or suggesting a syllable of the word or phrase.

charcoal ['tʃɑ:koul] *nu* black substance used as fuel or for drawing pictures, made by burning wood slowly in a tightly-closed oven.

charge[1] [tʃɑ:dʒ] *nc* **1.** attack made by going towards the enemy at great speed. **2.** (not with reference to goods bought in a shop) the amount of money asked for services or certain goods. *The man made no charge for mending my watch* i.e. he did not ask for any money. *The charges for electricity and gas will be increased next year.* **3.** statement that a person has done wrong (esp. such a statement in a court of law). *My friend denied the charge of dangerous driving* i.e. he said that he had not driven dangerously after somebody had accused him of this in a court of law. **4.** the amount of gunpowder put into a gun. **5.** the amount of electricity in an electric cell or other apparatus. **6.** work or duty given to somebody.

bring a charge against somebody say that somebody has done something wrong (esp. in a court of law). *The police brought a charge of dangerous driving against him.*

give somebody in charge hand somebody over to the police because he has done something wrong.

in charge in control; responsible for. *You are in charge of the team, and everybody must do what you want.*

take charge of be in control of; be responsible for. *I want you to take charge of the office until I come back.*

charge[2] [tʃɑ:dʒ] *vt/i* **1.** make an attack by going towards the enemy at great speed. *Our soldiers charged the enemy.* **2.** ask a certain amount of money for goods or services. *I charged him five pounds for repairing his car.* **3.** (with **with**) (esp. in a police court) make a statement that a person has done wrong. *He was charged with dangerous driving. The police charged him with dangerous driving.* **4.** load with gunpowder. **5.** load or fill with electricity etc. **6.** (with **with**) give somebody orders to do some work or duty. *I charged him with the duty of guarding the prisoners.* **7.** make a note that goods which are being collected or delivered are to be paid for later. *I don't want to pay for these books now; will you charge them to me?* i.e. send me the bill later.

charger *nc* horse used for making an attack in war.

chargé d'affaires ['ʃɑ:ʒeidæ'fɛə*] *nc* person who represents his country in a foreign country, lower in rank than an ambassador.

chariot ['tʃæriət] *nc* type of light vehicle pulled by horses, formerly used in war or for racing.

charioteer [tʃæriə'tiə*] *nc* driver of a chariot.

charity ['tʃæriti] **1.** *nu* act of giving money and other help to the poor. **2.** *nu* kindness towards other people; love for other people. **3.** *nc* society for helping the poor. **4.** *nc* action showing love of the poor or of other people.

charitable *adj* showing love or kindness in this way. (*opp* **uncharitable**). **charitably** *adv.* **charitableness** *nu.*

charlatan ['ʃɑ:lətən] *nc* person who pretends to have qualifications or knowledge which he does not actually have.

charlatanism *nu* acts of a charlatan.

charm[1] [tʃɑ:m] **1.** *nc/u* the parts of the nature of a person/thing which cause pleasure to other people. *All the girls in that family have a lot of charm* i.e. they are pleasant and interesting girls. *He was so angry that he did not notice the charm of the beautiful countryside.* **2.** *nc* object or words believed to work some magic or bring good luck.

charm[2] [tʃɑ:m] *vt/i* **1.** please very much; be very pleasant to. *The young girl charmed everyone she met* i.e. everybody liked her very much. **2.** work magic on. *The old witch*

charmed all the animals in that village.
charming *adj* showing charm; giving happiness and pleasure. *She is a charming young lady. This is a very charming village.*
charmingly *adv*.
lead a charmed life be fortunate enough to be saved from dangers and difficulties as though by magic.

chart [tʃɑːt] *nc* **1.** map (esp. one of the sea) for use by sailors. **2.** paper showing information in the form of graphs, tables and diagrams. Also *vt* make a map of. *The government sent an expedition to chart the sea around Cape Horn.*

charter ['tʃɑːtə*] *nc* written statement by some authority, giving somebody the power to do something. Also *vt* **1.** give a charter. **2.** hire a bus, plane, train etc for a special purpose. *The members of the club chartered a plane to take them on holiday to France.*
chartered *adj* having a licence: *a chartered accountant* i.e. a person who has an official licence to work as an accountant.
'charter flight journey by an aeroplane specially hired for this purpose, not part of a regular service.

chary ['tʃɛəri] *adj* (with **of**) careful to avoid something. *He is very chary of giving help to other people.*

chase [tʃeis] *vt* run after in order to catch or kill; drive away. *The policeman chased the thief. I chased the children out of my study.* Also *nc* act of chasing.
give chase run after.

chasm ['kæzəm] *nc* deep opening in the earth.

chassis ['ʃæsi] *nc* framework of a motorcar. *pl* **chassis** ['ʃæsiz].

chaste [tʃeist] *adj* **1.** pure; avoiding (immoral) sexual relationships. **2.** not decorated; plain and simple in design. see **chastity.**

chasten ['tʃeisn] *vt* punish; subdue: *a chastening experience* i.e. one that makes someone stop and think.

chastise [tʃæs'taiz] *vt* punish by beating.
chastisement *nu*.

chastity ['tʃæstiti] *nu* purity; virginity; avoidance of (immoral) sexual relationships. see **chaste.**

chat [tʃæt] *vi* talk in a friendly way about unimportant topics. *We were chatting about the weather this morning. past* **chatted.** Also *nc* conversation of this kind.
chatty *adj* fond of chatting (often in a way which is annoying or tiring for other people). *I don't like that woman very much; she's so chatty.*

chateau, château ['ʃætou] *nc* castle or large country house in France. *pl* **chateaux** ['ʃætouz].

chattel ['tʃætl] *nc* piece of property which can be moved i.e. property which is not land or buildings.

chatter ['tʃætə*] *vi* **1.** talk quickly about unimportant or foolish things. **2.** make a series of rapid sounds. *His teeth were chattering with cold* i.e. his top teeth were striking his bottom teeth. *The monkeys were chattering.* Also *nu* talk or noise of this type.
'chatterbox person who chatters (esp. one who tires or annoys other people by chattering) (*informal*).

chauffeur ['ʃoufə*] *nc* person whose job is to drive a motorcar for another person.

chauvinist ['ʃouvinist] *nc* person who loves his own country in a foolish and boastful way.
chauvinism *nu* behaviour or beliefs of a chauvinist.

cheap [tʃiːp] *adj* **1.** costing very little money. **2.** of poor quality. *This is very cheap cloth; it will soon begin to look old.* **3.** in poor taste, unkind: *a cheap joke about someone's thick glasses.* Also *adv*: *I bought this book very cheap.* **cheaply** *adv*. **cheapness** *nu*.
cheapen *vt* **1.** lower in price. **2.** cause to appear worthless or of low value.
on the cheap cheaply. (*informal*).

cheat [tʃiːt] *vt/i* do something dishonest (to somebody) when one has been trusted to behave honestly (e.g. in a game, examination, buying and selling). *That boy tried to cheat in the examination* i.e. he tried to look at the answer written by somebody else or he took a book into the examination room etc. *That shopkeeper cheats his customers* i.e. he does not give them the full amount of what they have bought or he does not give them enough money in change etc. *He cheated his brothers out of the land which their father had given to all of them* i.e. he got the land from his brothers by a trick. Also *nc* **1.** person who cheats. **2.** dishonest trick used to cheat.

check[1] ['tʃek] *vt/i* **1.** look at in order to see whether something is correct. *I'm not sure whether I've added up these numbers correctly; will you check them for me?* **2.** stop or hold back. *The government scientists were working hard to check the spread of the disease.* **3.** (chess) make a move which forces the other player to move his king or protect it. **4.** (*US*) give one's luggage, one's hat and coat etc to somebody whose job is to take care of these articles at a railway station, theatre etc. *I got to the station half an hour before my train left, so I checked my baggage and went to have a cup of coffee.*
check in/out report one's arrival/departure (at a hotel etc).
check off account for items in a list. *As she bought each article, she checked it off on her list.*
check over examine. *The engineers will check over the plane before it leaves.*
check up on something look at or examine something so as to make sure that one understands it or knows what is necessary. *I'm not sure when my train leaves; I must go to the station to check up. I am going to check up on the time of the train.*
'check-up *nc* inspection or examination to see that everything is correct (esp. a medical examination). *I'm going to the doctor for a check-up.*

check[2] [tʃek] *nc* **1.** process of looking at something to see that it is correct. *You aren't very good at arithmetic; you ought to ask somebody to give your addition a check.* **2.** something which stops or controls. *The new drug acted as a check to the spread of the disease.* **3.** (chess) position which forces the enemy king to move. **4.** (mainly *US*) piece of paper given to one in a restaurant showing what food one has had and how much it costs. (*Brit* usu. **bill**). **5.** (*US*) piece of paper etc given in exchange for an article which has been left with somebody (at a railway station, theatre etc) to show that one is the owner of the article. **6.** pattern formed of large squares. **7.** *US* form of **cheque.**
checkers *nu* (*US*) game played with pieces

on a board divided into 64 squares. (*Bri* **draughts**).

'check'mate 1. (chess) position in which one of the kings cannot escape capture. This wins the game for the other player. 2. any move or position in business, war etc which makes it difficult or impossible for one's opponent to move. Also *vt* place somebody in such a position.

'checkpoint place on a road etc where vehicles and travellers are inspected.

cheek[1] [tʃi:k] *nc* 1. part of the face between the ear, nose and mouth. 2. any pair of things placed like cheeks (esp. the buttocks).

tongue in cheek see **tongue.**

cheek[2] [tʃi:k] *nu* impolite words (esp. said by a child to an adult). *When I told those boys to stop breaking windows, they gave me a lot of cheek and ran away.* Also *vt* use impolite words to.

cheeky *adj* impolite, but rather amusing. *He's a cheeky little boy, but he's very friendly.* **cheekily** *adv.*

cheep [tʃi:p] *nc* the sound made by a small bird. Also *vi* make this sound.

cheer[1] [tʃiə*] *vt/i* 1. shout because of great happiness. *The crowds cheered when they heard the news of the great victory. The crowds cheered the news.* 2. make somebody feel happy. *The old man was cheered by the visit of his grandsons.*

cheer up become or make happy. *Don't be so worried, try to cheer up. They went to visit the old man, in order to cheer him up.*

cheer[2] [tʃiə*] 1. *nc* shout of happiness. 2. *nu* state of being happy; happiness.

cheerful *adj* full of happiness. **cheerfully** *adv.* **cheerfulness** *nu.*

cheerless *adj* without happiness; miserable.

cheery *adj* happy. **cheerily** *adv.*

cheers *interj* 1. expression of friendship, said before drinking an alcoholic drink. 2. see **cheerio** (in sense 1.).

give three cheers for something shout 'hurray' three times in order to show that one is pleased with something or that one likes something. *The boys gave three cheers for the headmaster.*

cheerio ['tʃiəri'ou] *interj/nc* (*Brit*) 1. goodbye. *pl* **cheerios.** 2. see **cheers** (in sense 1.).

cheese [tʃi:z] *nu* type of solid food made from milk.

'cheesecloth very thin type of cotton cloth.

'cheeseparing *adj* very careful not to spend too much money. Also *nu.*

cheetah ['tʃi:tə] *nc* animal of the cat family, found in Africa and Asia, which can run faster than any other animal.

chef [ʃef] *nc* male cook in a restaurant or hotel (esp. the chief cook).

chemistry ['kemistri] *nu* branch of science which deals with what various substances are made of and what happens when various substances are mixed together.

chemical ['kemikl] *adj* referring to chemistry. Also *nc* substance used in or made by chemical processes.

chemist *nc* 1. person who studies chemistry. 2. person who sells drugs, medicine, soap, toothpaste etc in a shop.

chemical warfare use of gases, poison and other chemicals instead of explosives in war.

cheque [tʃek] *nc* (*Brit*) piece of paper asking one's bank to pay a specified sum of money to a certain person. (*US* **check**).

'cheque book number of printed cheques fastened together like a book, so that one can tear one out when it is needed.

blank cheque cheque on which the amount to be paid has not been filled in, so that the person receiving it can fill in whatever amount he likes.

chequered, checkered ['tʃekəd] *adj* 1. having a pattern of large squares. 2. with many changes, varied (esp. in **a chequered career** a career or life story of somebody who has had many different jobs, travelled a lot or had a number of other changes).

cherish ['tʃeriʃ] *vt* (esp. with reference to keeping feelings or memories) keep or protect with great love. *He cherished the memory for many years. I cherish the hope of meeting him one day.* **cherished** *adj.*

cheroot [ʃə'ru:t] *nc* type of cigar.

cherry ['tʃeri] *nc* 1. type of small, yellow or red (usu. heart-shaped) fruit with a stone in the middle. 2. the tree on which this fruit grows. Also *adj* having the red colour of ripe cherries.

cherub ['tʃerəb] *nc* 1. beautiful baby with wings, often shown on old paintings. 2. any beautiful baby. 3. type of angel.

cherubic [tʃe'ru:bik] *adj* of or like a beautiful baby.

Note: the plural of *cherub* is *cherubs*, but occasionally the plural *cherubim* is used, only with reference to angels.

chess [tʃes] *nu* game played with various pieces on a board of 64 squares.

'chessboard the board used in chess.

'chessman one of the pieces used in chess.

chest [tʃest] *nc* 1. large wooden box for storing things in. 2. upper part of the body at the front.

chest of drawers piece of furniture for storing clothes.

get something off one's chest tell somebody about something which has been worrying one (esp. some wrong action which one has done).

chestnut ['tʃesnʌt] 1. *nc* type of large soft nut often eaten roasted. 2. *nc* the tree on which this nut grows. 3. *nu* the reddish-brown colour of this nut.

'horse 'chestnut 1. nut like the chestnut, but not fit for eating. 2. the tree on which it grows.

chevron ['ʃevrən] *nc* mark shaped v or ʌ (esp. those worn on the sleeve of a uniform to show the rank of the wearer) (*formal* – use **stripe**).

chew [tʃu:] *vt/i* move the teeth up and down in order to break up food etc.

'chewing gum type of soft sweet substance, which does not break up, and can be chewed as long as one wishes.

chic [ʃi:k] *adj* (usu. with reference to women) smart and fashionable in appearance and behaviour. Also *nu.*

chicanery [ʃi'keinəri] *nu* (esp. legal and politics) dishonest words or actions.

chick [tʃik] *nc* young bird (esp. a young chicken).

chicken ['tʃikin] *nc* 1. chick. 2. type of large bird, kept for its eggs and meat, which are used as food. (Also **hen**). 3. this bird used as meat. 4. young person. 5. coward. (*informal* in senses 4. and 5.).

'chickenpox type of disease of young children, which causes red spots on the skin.

count one's chickens before they are hatched see **count.**[1]

chicory ['tʃikəri] *nu* 1. type of plant used for food. 2. the root of this plant, used for adding to coffee.

chid [tʃid] past of **chide.**

chide [tʃaid] *vt/i* speak angrily to somebody who has done wrong. *past* **chid** [tʃid] or **chided.** *past part* **chid, chided** or **chidden** ['tʃidn].

chief [tʃi:f] *nc* **1.** leader of a tribe. **2.** leader of any group of people. Also *adj* most important. **chiefly** *adv.*

chieftain ['tʃi:ftn] *nc* leader of a tribe (*o.f.* – use **chief**).

chieftaincy *nu* position of a chief or chieftain.

chiffon ['ʃifɔn] *nu* type of very thin cloth (usu. silk).

chilblain ['tʃilblein] *nc* red sore or swelling on the hands or feet, caused by cold weather.

child [tʃaild] *nc* young human i.e. a baby, a young boy or a young girl. *pl* **children** ['tʃildrn].

childhood *nu* time when one is a child.

childish *adj* of or like a child (e.g. weak or foolish). **childishly** *adv.* **childishness** *nu.* *Note:* compare *childlike.*

'**childbearing** *adj* able to give birth to a child: *a woman of childbearing age* i.e. not too young or too old to have a child. Also *nu*: *Some women are afraid of childbearing.*

'**childbirth** process or act of giving birth to a child: *die in childbirth.*

'**childlike** *adj* like a child (e.g. innocent, always telling the truth, good and kind, trusting).
Note: compare *childish.*

'**child's play** something which is very easy.

with child pregnant (*o.f.*).

chill [tʃil] *nc* **1.** feeling of cold (esp. an unpleasant feeling): *the chill of the morning air.* **2.** type of slight illness, often caused by cold, in which one sneezes and shivers. Also *vt* make cold.

chilly *adj* unpleasantly cold.

chime [tʃaim] *nc* musical sound of a bell (esp. a bell in a church or clock). Also *vt/i* make this noise. *The clock was chiming six when I came in.*

chimney ['tʃimni] *nc* **1.** hollow structure in a building for carrying smoke from a fire high into the air. **2.** narrow crack going up the side of a mountain.

'**chimney pot** part of a chimney which can be seen on the roof of a house.

'**chimney sweep** person whose work is to clean soot out of chimneys.

chimpanzee [tʃimpən'zi:] *nc* type of very intelligent African ape.

chin [tʃin] *nc* part of the face below the mouth.

keep one's chin up remain cheerful; continue to be brave. (*informal*).

china ['tʃainə] *nu* cups, plates, saucers etc, made of white clay which has been baked and glazed.

chink[1] [tʃiŋk] *nc* small hole (esp. in a wall or door).

chink[2] [tʃiŋk] *n sing* sound of glasses, cups, pieces of metal, coins etc being hit together. Also *vt/i* make this noise.

chintz [tʃints] *nu* type of cotton cloth, with printed designs of various colours, used for making curtains and covering furniture.

chip [tʃip] *nc* **1.** small piece knocked or cut off wood, glass, stone, china etc. **2.** place where a chip has been knocked or cut off. *I noticed a chip in the handle of my new cup.* **3.** (*Brit*) (usu. *pl*) slice of potato fried in fat. (*US* **French fried potato**). Also *vt/i* knock or cut into chips; make a chip. *This cup is chipped; bring me another one. past* **chipped.**

have a chip on one's shoulder have a feeling that one has been treated unfairly, so that one is ready to quarrel with anyone.

chiropody [ki'rɔpədi] *nu* science of the care of the feet and the treating of foot troubles (e.g. corns, painful toenails etc). **chiropodist** *nc.*

chirp [tʃə:p] *nc* noise made by small birds and some insects. Also *vt/i* make this noise.

chirrup ['tʃirəp] *nc* series of chirps. Also *vt/i.*

chisel ['tʃizl] *nc* tool with a long steel blade with a sharp edge at the end, for cutting wood or stone. Also *vt* cut with a chisel. *past* **chiselled.** (*US* **chiseled**).

chit [tʃit] *nc* piece of paper with a few words written on it, used to show that one has permission to get something or to do something.

chivalry ['ʃivəlri] *nu* **1.** (in the Middle Ages) code of behaviour of knights. **2.** polite and courageous behaviour of men (esp. towards women). **3.** number of knights taken all together (*o.f.*).

chivalrous *adj* polite and courageous. (*opp* **unchivalrous**). **chivalrously** *adv.*

chlorine ['klɔ:ri:n] *nu* very poisonous greenish-yellow gas (Cl).

chlorinate ['klɔrineit] *vt* add chlorine to (esp. to sterilize).

chloroform ['klɔrəfɔ:m] *nu* liquid whose fumes cause one to become unconscious. Also *vt* make somebody unconscious with this substance.

chlorophyll ['klɔrəfil] *nu* substance in plants which gives them a green colour.

chock [tʃɔk] *nc* wedge etc put under wheels so that a vehicle cannot roll away.

'**chock-'full** very full. (*informal*).

chocolate ['tʃɔklit] **1.** *nu* sweet foodstuff made from the seeds of the cocoa tree. **2.** *nu* drink made from this substance. **3.** *nc/u* hard piece of this substance, made to be eaten. Also *adj* colour of this substance i.e. dark brown.

choice [tʃɔis] *nc* **1.** act of deciding which out of several things one likes best. *Take your choice* i.e. take the one you like best. **2.** number of things from which one must make a choice. *If you go to a big shop you will have a better choice of dresses* i.e. the big shop will have more dresses (than a small shop). Also *adj* carefully chosen (and therefore the best). see **choose.**

choir ['kwaiə*] *nc* **1.** group of singers (esp. a group which sings in church). **2.** part of the church in which a choir sits.

choke[1] [tʃouk] *vt/i* **1.** stop or almost stop breathing properly because of something in the throat. *He choked when he ate his food too quickly.* **2.** prevent from breathing properly (esp. by pressing one's hands on somebody's throat). **3.** (often with **up**) fill up a pipe, passage, stream etc. *The stream was choked (up) with weeds. The soot had been choking up the chimney for a long time.*

choke back prevent oneself from expressing an emotion. *He choked back his anger.*

choke[2] [tʃouk] *nc* part of a petrol engine for controlling the amount of petrol and air reaching the cylinders.

cholera ['kɔlərə] *nu* type of disease in which the body keeps losing liquid.

choleric ['kɔlərik] *adj* becoming angry very quickly.

choose [tʃu:z] *vt/i* **1.** say or decide which of

several things one likes best. *You can have one of these books; choose the one you want. He went to the shop to choose a present for his wife.* **2.** decide; wish. *He did not choose to help me* i.e. he decided not to help me. *past tense* **chose** [tʃouz]. *past part* **chosen** ['tʃouzn]. see **choice.**
choosey *adj* very careful to choose what one likes; not willing to accept just anything which is offered. (*informal*).

chop[1] [tʃɔp] *vt* cut by hitting with a sharp tool such as an axe. *He chopped a lot of wood for the fire. past* **chopped.**
chop down cause to fall by chopping. *He chopped down all those old trees. He chopped the tree down.*
chop up chop into small pieces. *She chopped up the meat and vegetables in order to make a stew. He chopped up that old chair for firewood.*

chop[2] [tʃɔp] *nc* **1.** act of chopping. **2.** thick slice of meat (usu. containing a bone). **3.** blow with the side of the hand (e.g. in wrestling or judo).
chopper *nc* **1.** small axe, used for chopping wood or meat. **2.** helicopter. (*informal*).
choppy *adj* (esp. with reference to the sea when it is covered with small rough waves) making a number of quick sharp movements.

chopsticks ['tʃɔpstiks] *npl* sticks used in pairs by the Chinese for eating (instead of e.g. a spoon or fork).

choral ['kɔːrl] *adj* with reference to a choir.

chord [kɔːd] *nc* **1.** several musical notes played together. **2.** straight line connecting two points on the circumference of a circle. **3.** string of a musical instrument. **4.** part of the body like a string: *the vocal chords* i.e. the part of the throat which enables us to speak; *spinal chord* i.e. the backbone.
Note: the spelling *cord* is also used to refer to the *vocal chords* and the *spinal chord.*

chore [tʃɔː*] *nc* **1.** small duty or job (esp. in a house). **2.** small duty or job which one dislikes.

choreography [kɔri'ɔgrəfi] *nu* art of creating dances for the theatre. **choreographer** *nc.*

chorister ['kɔristə*] *nc* person (esp. a boy) who sings in a choir in church.

chortle ['tʃɔːtl] *vi* laugh while snorting or making noises in the nose and throat. *He chortled with glee.*

chorus ['kɔːrəs] *nc* **1.** group of singers, actors or dancers (esp. a group which sings and dances in a theatre). **2.** song sung by such a group. **3.** part of a song which is repeated after each verse (usu. to be sung by a group of singers). **4.** words said or shouted by a number of people all together. **5.** (in ancient Greek plays) group of people who speak all together. Also *vt/i* speak all together.

chose, chosen [tʃouz, 'tʃouzn] past tense and past part of **choose.**

christen ['krisn] *vt* **1.** give a name to a child during the ceremony of baptism, by which the child is received into the Christian Church. **2.** give a name to.

Christendom ['krisndəm] *n sing* all the countries in which there are Christians.

Christian ['kristiən] *adj* referring to Jesus Christ. Also *nc* person who believes that Jesus Christ is the son of God.
Christianity [kristi'æniti] *nu* the religion of Jesus Christ.
'**Christian name** one of the names given to a child at birth by his parents (e.g. if somebody is named 'John Richard Smith', then 'John Richard' are his Christian names and 'Smith' is his family name or surname. If the person is not a Christian, the terms *first name* or *forename* are often used instead of Christian name).

Christmas ['krisməs] *nc* time of celebration of the birth of Jesus Christ (in most Christian churches, 25th December).
'**Christmas tree** small tree of a special type, taken into a house at Christmas time and decorated with coloured paper and lights, and on which are hung presents for the family in the house.
Father 'Christmas imaginary old man, who is said to bring presents to children at Christmas time.

chrome, chromium ['kroum(iəm)] *nu* type of shiny, silver metal which is one of the elements used e.g. to cover other metals (Cr).

chromosome ['krouməsoum] *nc* very small part of an animal or plant cell, which helps to decide the form of the animal or plant.

chronic ['krɔnik] *adj* **1.** (with reference to disease) going on for a long time, often without hope of cure: *a chronic invalid; a chronic disease.* **2.** very unpleasant. (*informal* and usu. considered incorrect).
chronically *adv.*

chronicle ['krɔnikl] *nc* (usu. with reference to real events) story of events happening over a period of time, written or told in the order in which they happened. Also *vt* make a chronicle of.
chronicler *nc* writer of a chronicle.

chronology [krə'nɔlədʒi] **1.** *nu* science of deciding or fixing the date of something. **2.** *nc* list of dates.
chronological [krɔnə'lɔdʒikl] *adj* usu. in **in chronological order** i.e. arranged in the order in which things happened. **chronologically** *adv.*

chronometer [krə'nɔmitə*] *nc* very accurate kind of clock (used esp. on ships).

chrysalis ['krisəlis] *nc* **1.** second state of the life cycle of an insect, when the creature does not move and is covered by a hard case. **2.** the case itself.

chrysanthemum [kris'ænθiməm] *nc* type of garden flower which usu. flowers in autumn.

chubby ['tʃʌbi] *adj* (usu. with reference to somebody/something that is young e.g. a baby or a puppy) fat. **chubbiness** *nu.*

chuck [tʃʌk] *vt* throw. (*informal*).

chuckle ['tʃʌkl] *vi* laugh quietly and happily. Also *nc* laugh of this type.

chug [tʃʌg] *nu* sound made by an engine (esp. one working steadily and slowly). Also *vi* make this sound. *past* **chugged.**

chum [tʃʌm] *nc* (esp. with reference to friendship among children) friend. **chummy** *adj.* (both *informal*).
chum up with someone become a chum to someone. (*informal*).

chump [tʃʌmp] *nc* (esp. with reference to a boy or girl) foolish person. (*informal*).

chunk [tʃʌŋk] *nc* thick piece. (often *informal*). **chunky** *adj.*

church [tʃəːtʃ] **1.** *nc* building in which Christians gather to pray and sing hymns. **2.** *nc* group of Christians having the same beliefs: *the Roman Catholic Church; the Methodist Church.* **3.** *nu* service or meeting in a building to pray and sing hymns. *I'm going to church this evening.*
the Church all Christians taken together.

'churchgoer person who regularly goes to church.
'church 'service occasion on which Christians meet together in a church to pray etc.
'church'warden 1. official who helps and advises the priest in a church. 2. very long tobacco pipe.
'churchyard land around the church (often used for burying dead people in).
churlish ['tʃə:liʃ] *adj* very bad-tempered and impolite. **churlishly** *adv*. **churlishness** *nu*.
churn [tʃə:n] *nc* 1. container or machine for making milk into butter by shaking it. 2. large metal container for milk. Also *vt/i* 1. shake milk in this way to make butter. 2. (often with **up**) shake or move violently.
chute [ʃu:t] *nc* 1. sloping tube or slide, used to allow things to fall down where they are wanted. 2. short informal form of **parachute**.
chutney ['tʃʌtni] *nu* substance made from fruit and spices and eaten with meat.
cicada [si'kɑ:də] *nc* type of insect found in southern Europe, which makes a loud noise.
cider ['saidə*] *nu* alcoholic drink made from apples.
cigar [si'gɑ:*] *nc* roll of dried tobacco leaves, used for smoking.
cigarette [sigə'ret] *nc* tube of paper containing tobacco and used for smoking.
cinch [sintʃ] *nc* 1. something which is very easy or certain. (*informal*). 2. (*US*) strap for fastening a saddle on a horse.
cinder ['sində*] *nc* piece of coal or wood which has been burned, but has not yet become ash.
cine- ['sini] *prefix* referring to moving pictures (e.g. **cine-camera** i.e. camera for taking moving pictures).
cinema ['sinəmə] *nc* building where films are shown.
the cinema the art or science of making films.
cinnamon ['sinəmən] *nu* type of spice.
cipher, cypher ['saifə*] *nc* 1. system of writing in code, understood by certain people for whom the message is intended. 2. message in code. 3. somebody who is of no importance. 4. figure 0 or zero (*o.f.*).
circle ['sə:kl] *nc* 1. flat, perfectly round figure, like a coin. 2. group of things arranged in this shape: *a circle of chairs*. 3. group of people with interests in common: *a large circle of friends; people in business and political circles* i.e. businessmen and politicians; *the family circle* i.e. members of the family. 4. one of the upper parts of a cinema or theatre in which the seats are arranged in a curve around the building. Also *vt/i* move in a circle. *The plane circled the airport several times before it came down.*
circlet ['sə:klit] *nc* 1. small circle. 2. ornament worn round the head, arm, finger etc.
circuit ['sə:kit] *nc* 1. path along which an electric current flows. 2. (esp. with reference to the system in some countries by which judges travel to several courts) journey, ending where one began. 3. area of a country through which somebody travels in this way. 4. group of Methodist churches which work together. 5. a going round: *three circuits of a racetrack*.
circuitous [sə:'kju:itəs] *adj* going a long way round instead of taking the most direct way. **circuitously** *adv*.
'short-'circuit action of an electric current in going by a path of low resistance (often causing the electrical appliance to break down or give a shock etc). Also *vi*: *The kettle short-circuited.*
circular ['sə:kjulə*] *adj* having the form of a circle. Also *nc* printed notice or advertisement, delivered or posted to a number of people.
circular saw circle of metal with a sharp edge, turned by machinery, used for cutting wood etc.
circulate ['sə:kjuleit] *vt/i* move round from place to place or from person to person. *Traffic circulates in the streets of a city. The news was circulated through the room* i.e. one person told others, who in turn told other people, and so on. *Blood circulates around the body.*
circulation [sə:kju'leiʃən] 1. *nu* movement around. 2. *nc* number of copies of a newspaper or magazine usu. sold. 3. *nc* movement of blood around the body.
circum- ['sə:kəm] *prefix* meaning around (e.g. **circumference**).
circumcise ['sə:kəmsaiz] *vt* cut off the loose skin at the end of a penis (for religious or health reasons). **circumcision** [sə:kəm'siʒən] *nc/u*.
circumcised *adj*. (*opp* **uncircumcised**).
circumference [sə'kʌmfərəns] *nc* 1. outside edge of a circle. 2. distance round a circle.
circumflex ['sə:kəmfleks] *nc* the mark ^ or ⌒, placed above vowels in certain languages to give information about the pronunciation. Also *adj* having this mark.
circumlocution [sə:kəmlə'kju:ʃən] *nc* using many words to say what could be said in a few words. **circumlocutory** *adj*.
circumnavigate [sə:kəm'nævigeit] *vt* travel in a ship round an island or round the earth. **circumnavigation** ['sə:kəmnævi'geiʃən] *nc*.
circumscribe ['sə:kəmskraib] *vt* 1. draw a line around. 2. prevent from going outside a certain area or doing certain things. **circumscription** [sə:kəm'skripʃən] *nu*.
circumspect ['sə:kəmspekt] *adj* very careful to avoid difficulty or danger. **circumspectly** *adv*. **circumspection** [sə:kəm'spekʃən] *nu*.
circumstance ['sə:kəmstəns] *nc* (usu. *pl*) fact, condition, event etc connected with something/somebody. *Most countries would be willing to go to war under certain circumstances* i.e. if the reason for war was great enough. *I don't remember all the circumstances of the quarrel* i.e. what exactly happened or why it happened. *When I explained my circumstances to the old man, he decided to help me* i.e. when I explained why I needed help.
circumstantial [sə:kəm'stænʃl] *adj* containing very many details.
circumstantial evidence evidence made up of details but without direct proof.
under the circumstances because this is the case; when I think of these facts etc. *Under the circumstances, you were lucky not to be hurt* i.e. as it was very dangerous. *Under the circumstances, I cannot help you* i.e. because of these facts.
not . . . under any (under no) circumstance(s) not for any reason. *You must not touch this switch under any circumstance.*
in reduced circumstances having less money than one used to have. (*formal*).
pomp and circumstance processions, ceremonial occasions, official celebrations etc.
circumvent [sə:kəm'vent] *vt* do something

clever which prevents a person from doing something which he wishes to do. **circumvention** *nu*.

circus ['sə:kəs] *nc* **1.** form of entertainment in which wild animals, clowns, acrobats etc perform. **2.** round or oval place in the open air where various types of entertainment were given in Roman times. **3.** round place where a number of streets meet.

cirrus ['sirəs] *nc/u* thin type of cloud made of ice crystals high above the earth.

cistern ['sistən] *nc* metal or stone container for water (esp. in a lavatory).

citadel ['sitədl] *nc* building with strong walls, used as a place of defence in war.

cite [sait] *vt* name something/somebody as an example or a proof of something. **citation** [sai'teiʃən] *nc/u*.

citizen ['sitizn] *nc* **1.** person who lives in a town or city. **2.** any person who has full rights in a country i.e. a person who is not a foreigner.

citizenship *nu* (esp. with reference to the rights and duties of a person living in a particular country) state of being a citizen.

citrus ['sitrəs] *adj* with reference to fruit or trees such as oranges, lemons, grapefruit (usu. in **citrus fruit**).

city ['siti] *nc* large and important town.

the City the oldest part of London, now an area of business and banking.

'city 'state independent state made up of a single city and the land around it. *Many cities in Europe were at one time city states.*

civic ['sivik] *adj* with reference to a city (esp. the administration of a city).

civics *nu* study of the rights and duties of a person living in a particular country.

civil ['sivil] *adj* **1.** with reference to citizens. **2.** with reference to people who are not soldiers, sailors or airmen. (*opp* **military**). **3.** polite. (*opp* **uncivil**).

civilly *adv* politely.

civility [si'viliti] *nc/u* politeness.

civil defence arrangements for helping people and organizing life in a country during a war.

civil disobedience non-violent method of refusing to obey the laws of a country, in order to force the authorities to take some action.

civil engineering *nu* building of roads, bridges, docks etc. **civil engineer** *nc*.

civil law law dealing with property, and the rights and duties of a citizen (not with crime).

civil marriage marriage not held in a church.

civil rights rights of a citizen (e.g. the rights of American Negroes to equality with white Americans).

civil service *nu* all the departments of a government.

civil servant *nc* person who works for the government.

civil war see **war**.

civilian [si'viliən] *nc* person who is not a soldier, sailor or airman. Also *adj*.

civilize ['sivilaiz] *vt* teach science and art, religion, government, reading and writing etc to people who lack all or some of these branches of knowledge. *The Romans civilized many of the tribes of northern Europe.*

civilized *adj* **1.** polite; well-behaved: *behave in a civilized manner.* **2.** cultured; not savage: *a civilized community.*

civilization [sivilai'zeiʃən] **1.** *nu* condition of being civilized. *The Romans brought civilization to Britain.* **2.** *nu* all civilized people, towns and cities, the use of money, literacy, art and science, religion etc. *Civilization may be destroyed if there is another world war.* **3.** *nc* one of the several large organized communities which have existed during the history of mankind: *the Chinese civilization; the Roman civilization.*

clack [klæk] *nu* any quick short noise (e.g. made by pieces of wood being hit together). Also *vi* make this noise.

clad [klæd] *adj* dressed; wearing clothes (usu. in **poorly clad; clad in rags** and similar phrases). Also past of **clothe.** (rather *o.f.*).

claim[1] [kleim] *vt/i* **1.** say that one is taking, or wishes to take, something as one's own. *The United States claims certain islands in the Pacific at present held by New Zealand* i.e. the USA says that these islands belong to her. *Nobody has come to claim this book which was found in the road* i.e. nobody has said that the book belongs to him. **2.** say that something is true (when other people may doubt this fact). *He claimed to be 100 years old. He claimed to have read the book, but he couldn't answer any questions about it.*

claim one's attention require or need one's attention.

claim[2] [kleim] *nc* **1.** act of saying that something belongs to oneself. *I made a claim for that book.* **2.** act of saying that something is true. *Nobody believed his claim to be 100 years old.* **3.** right to something. *Children have the first claim on their parents* i.e. parents will help or protect their children before they will help or protect anyone else. **4.** area of land in which one is allowed to mine for gold, diamonds, uranium etc.

claimant *nc* person who makes a claim.

clairvoyant [klɛə'vɔiənt] *nc* person who claims to be able to see things which are too far away to be seen by the eye, or which are in the future. Also *adj* with reference to this ability. **clairvoyance** *nu*.

clam [klæm] *nc* **1.** one of several types of shellfish often used as food. **2.** secretive person.

clam up stop talking, refuse to give any more information. (*informal*).

clamber ['klæmbə*] *vi* climb in an awkward way, using one's hands and feet.

clammy ['klæmi] *adj* cold and damp: *clammy hands; clammy walls.* **clamminess** *nu*.

clamour ['klæmə*] (*US* **clamor**) *nc/u* **1.** loud noise (esp. a noise made by a number of people shouting). **2.** loud complaint or protest. Also *vi* make a loud noise or a complaint etc in this way. **clamorous** *adj*.

clamp ['klæmp] *nc* instrument used for holding something tightly. Also *vt* hold or strengthen with a clamp.

clamp down on someone/something act in a very severe way in order to stop or forbid something. *The policemen have decided to clamp down on motorists who drive too fast* i.e. they have decided to do everything they can to prevent speeding. (*informal*).

clan [klæn] *nc* large group of families which are all related to each other.

clansman *nc* member of a clan.

clannish *adj* **1.** of a clan. **2.** keeping close to the members of one's group and being unfriendly to strangers.

clandestine [klæn'destin] *adj* done or made secretly: *a clandestine arrangement.*

clang [klæŋ] *nu* loud ringing noise made by metal being hit hard. Also *vt/i* make this noise.
drop a clanger see **drop**[2].
clangour ['klæŋgə*] (*US* **clangor**) *nu* continuous loud noise made by metal being hit hard. **clangorous** *adj*.
clank [klæŋk] *nc* (often with reference to chains or swords) noise made by metal being hit (not so loud as **clang** or **clangour**). Also *vt/i* make this noise.
clap[1] [klæp] *vt/i* strike the palms of the hands together (esp. to show that one likes something). *The audience clapped at the end of the play. They clapped the actors. He clapped his hands. past* **clapped.**
clap somebody on the back hit somebody on the back with the palm of the hand, as an informal sign of friendship.
clap eyes on see. (*informal*).
clap[2] [klæp] *nc/u* 1. noise made by striking the palms of the hands together. *The audience gave him a clap.*
Note: the plural is not often used; *clapping* is used to refer to a number of noises of this kind.
2. short loud noise (usu. **a clap of thunder**).
clapper ['klæpə*] *nc* part inside a bell which moves and hits the outer part to make the ringing noise.
claptrap ['klæptræp] *nu* untrue or meaningless arguments or opinions. (*informal*).
claret ['klærit] *nu* 1. type of red wine. 2. colour of this wine. Also *adj*.
clarify ['klærifai] *vt/i* become or make clear; become or make more easy to understand. **clarification** [klærifi'keiʃən] *nu*.
clarinet [klæri'net] *nc* type of wind instrument.
clarinet(t)ist *nc* person who plays a clarinet.

clarinet

clarion ['klæriən] *nc* usu. in **clarion call** i.e. loud sound which calls one to do something brave or difficult.
clarity ['klæriti] *nu* clearness.
clash [klæʃ] *nc* 1. strong disagreement; short struggle or fight. *There was a clash between the Prime Minister and the leader of the Opposition* i.e. they had an argument. *There was a clash between the two armies* i.e. there was a short battle. *There is a clash between these two colours* i.e. these two colours do not look right when they are put together. 2. loud noise made by metal being hit. Also *vi* 1. disagree strongly. 2. make this loud noise.
clash with disagree with; have an argument or short fight with.
clasp [klɑːsp] *nc* 1. something which fastens two things together (e.g. the end of a belt). 2. strong hold with the hand or arm. Also *vt* fasten or hold in this way.
'clasp knife type of knife which folds in two and can be carried in the pocket. (rather *o.f.* – use **penknife**).

clasp knife

class [klɑːs] 1. *nc* group of people or things of the same kind or treated in the same way for some purpose. *They travelled first class on the ship* i.e. in the most comfortable and expensive way. 2. *nc* group of pupils taught together. 3. *nc* one of the divisions of society: *the upper class; the middle class; the working class.* 4. *nc* (biology) group of plants or animals. (A class is divided into a number of orders). 5. *nu* high quality. (*informal*). Also *vt* arrange in groups or classes.
'class-'conscious *adj* having the habit of noticing the difference between the various divisions in society; too aware of class distinctions. **class consciousness** *nu*.
'class dis'tinction treatment of people in different ways, according to their social class.
'classmate member of the same class in a school.
'classroom room in which a class is taught in a school.
'class 'struggle struggle or conflict between the various divisions of society (esp. between the workers and the employers).
in a class by itself/himself etc very much better than any other.
classic[1] ['klæsik] *adj* 1. very good; agreed to be of very high quality (esp. in art or literature). 2. having reference to ancient Greece and Rome. 3. (with reference to art or literature) simple in style; without too much decoration. 4. (with reference to certain horse-races, such as the Derby) very important and well-known.
classic[2] ['klæsik] *nc* work of literature, or writer of the highest quality. *'Hamlet' has become a classic. Shakespeare is a classic.*
the classics *npl* the literature of ancient Greece and Rome.
classical ['klæsikl] *adj* 1. having reference to ancient Greece or Rome. 2. (with reference to art or literature) simple in style; without too much decoration. 3. (with reference to music) serious; not pop, jazz etc. **classically** *adv*.
classicist ['klæsisist] *nc* person who studies Greek and/or Latin.
classify ['klæsifai] *vt* arrange into classes or groups. **classification** [klæsifi'keiʃən] *nc/u*.
classified *adj* 1. arranged in classes. (*opp* **unclassified**). 2. (with reference to official documents or information) secret, not for public use.
clatter ['klætə*] *nu* 1. type of noise like the noise made when plates or knives and forks knock together. 2. noise of many people talking together. Also *vt/i* make this noise.
clause [klɔːz] *nc* 1. (grammar) sentence or part of a sentence, having a subject and a predicate. In 'He was eating when I arrived', 'He was eating' is a main clause, and 'when I arrived' is a subordinate clause. 2. (legal) one of the points in a legal statement.
claustrophobia [klɔstrə'foubiə] *nu* great fear of being shut in a small space.
claw [klɔː] *nc* 1. one of the hard sharp points or nails on the feet of birds and some animals. 2. foot of a bird. 3. anything shaped like a claw (e.g. some hammers have a claw for pulling out nails). Also *vt* scratch or pull with the claws or nails.
clay [klei] *nu* type of soft heavy earth, which is used for making plates, cups etc.
'clay 'pigeon round disc of clay which is thrown into the air and used as a target for rifle shooting.
clean [kliːn] *adj* 1. not dirty; washed; not

used. 2. pure. 3. regular; with no rough edges: *a clean cut.* 4. well-shaped; smooth in shape. *The new ship has very clean lines.* 5. (with reference to atomic bombs) having little radioactive fallout. Also *vt* make clean.
cleanly *adj/adv.* **cleanness** *nu.*
cleanliness ['klenlinis] *nu* habit of being clean.
cleaner *nc* 1. person whose work is to clean rooms, buildings, roads, clothes etc. 2. substance which cleans.
'clean-'cut *adj* clear and sharp; having a well-defined outline: *a clean-cut face.*
'clean-'shaven *adj* with all the hair shaved off the face.
'dry 'cleaner see **dry.**
clean out remove dirt and rubbish from. *He cleans out his room once a week.*
clean up 1. make tidy or clean. 2. finish; complete.
come clean see **come.**
make a clean breast of something see **make**[1].
make a clean sweep of something remove or take something away completely. (*informal*).

cleanse [klenz] *vt* make clean; make free from dirt; make pure.
Note: clean (verb) refers to the ordinary process of removing dirt; *cleanse* contains the idea of removing impurities so as to make pure. If in doubt, use *clean.*

clear[1] ['kliə*] *adj* 1. easily seen through; bright; not cloudy: *clear glass* i.e. glass which can be seen through; *a clear sky* i.e. one without clouds; *a clear stream* i.e. one without any dirt in it. 2. easily heard: *the clear sound of a bell.* 3. easily understood. *This paragraph is not clear to me, will you explain it please?* 4. free from. *He drove slowly until he was clear of the town* i.e. until he left the town. *The road in front was clear* i.e. there were no cars on it. *When I get clear from my own difficulties, I shall try to help you.* 5. certain; obvious. *It is quite clear that you do not understand.* 6. (usu. with reference to profit or to an amount of time) complete. *He made a clear profit of £500* i.e. this is the amount of money he gained after repaying what he had spent. *You have four clear days to finish the work.*
clearly *adv.*
'clear-'cut *adj* easily seen; having a definite shape; easily understood: *a clear-cut argument.*
'clear-'headed *adj* able to think clearly.
all clear safe. *It's all clear, you need not hide any longer* i.e. the danger has gone away. Also *nc* signal given in time of war to show that enemy planes have gone away. (*opp* **alert**).
get clear get away; escape.
stand clear get out of the way; keep away.
clear as mud very difficult to understand. (*informal*).
the coast is clear see **coast**[1].
in the clear free from suspicion.
(with) a clear conscience see **conscience.**

clear[2] ['kliə*] *vt/i* 1. become or make clear. *He cleared all the books and papers off his desk* i.e. he took them off his desk. *He cleared all the stones from his garden. The sky has cleared* i.e. the clouds have gone and the sun is shining. 2. get past or over (esp. without touching). *The horse cleared the gate* i.e. it jumped over the gate. 3. prove or decide that somebody is not guilty of doing something wrong. *In the trial he was cleared of all the charges.* 4. make as a profit. *He cleared £50 from selling his old car.* (*informal* in sense 4.).
clear something away remove. *He cleared away all the old boxes in his garage.*
clear off go away. *I don't want you to help me, so clear off.* (*informal* and *impolite*).
clear something out 1. *vt* remove dirt or rubbish from. *He cleared out his desk.* 2. *vi* go away. *You're causing a lot of trouble, so clear out.* (*impolite* and *informal*).
clear something up 1. make tidy. *He cleared up his room before the visitors arrived.* 2. explain something difficult to understand. *When the policeman arrived he soon cleared up the mystery of the broken window* i.e. he found out who had broken it.
clear the air do something to remove unfriendly feelings between people (esp. feelings of suspicion or distrust).
clear the decks (for action) prepare for fighting; get ready for anything active. (*informal* if the reference is not to a ship).
clear the table take everything off the table (usu. plates, knives, forks etc or papers).
clear one's throat cough in order to remove some substance in the throat which makes it difficult to speak or breathe.

clearance ['kliərəns] *nu* 1. act of making clear. 2. space between two things which pass each other without touching. 3. process of doing what is (legally) necessary in order to allow a ship or cargo to enter or leave a port.

clearing ['kliəriŋ] *nc* area of land in a forest without any trees on it.
'clearing house 1. place where banks exchange cheques and pay any money which they owe each other. 2. any place or organization in which information from various places is collected together.

cleave[1] [kli:v] *vt* split with a heavy blow (*o.f.*). *past tense* **cleft** [kleft] or **clove** [klouv]. *past part* **cleft** or **cloven** ['klouvn].
cleavage *nc* 1. act of cleaving. 2. division or split between things.
cleaver *nc* tool like an axe or heavy knife, used by a butcher for chopping meat.

cleave[2] [kli:v] *vi* (with **to**) remain close (to); remain true (to) (*o.f.*). *past* **cleaved** or **clave** [kleiv].

clef [klef] *nc* (music) sign used in music to show pitch.

treble clef bass clef

cleft[1] [kleft] past of **cleave**[1].
'cleft 'palate narrow opening along the roof of the mouth, which makes it difficult for a person to speak properly.

cleft[2] [kleft] *nc* narrow opening (esp. in the ground or in a rock).

clemency ['klemənsi] *nu* 1. kindness (esp. to somebody who has done wrong). 2. (with reference to the weather) mildness.

clement *adj.* (*opp* **inclement**).
clench [klentʃ] *vt/i* (usu. with reference to the teeth or the fists) close tightly.
clergy ['klə:dʒi] *npl* Christian priests or ministers.
clergyman *nc* Christian priest or minister.
cleric ['klerik] *nc* Christian priest or minister.
clerical *adj* **1.** with reference to a cleric. **2.** with reference to the work of reading and writing. see **clerk.**
clerk [klɑ:k, *US* klə:k] *nc* **1.** person who works in an office writing letters, keeping accounts etc. **2.** (*US*) person who sells goods in a shop. (*Brit* **assistant** or **shop assistant**). **3.** person who keeps the records in a court of law.
'town 'clerk person who arranges the official business of a town.
clever ['klevə*] *adj* **1.** able to do things well; able to understand quickly; intelligent: *a clever boy.* **2.** showing signs of skill or intelligence: *a clever answer; a clever piece of work.* **cleverly** *adv.* **cleverness** *nu.*
cliché ['kli:ʃei] *nc* expression or idea which has been used so often that it begins to lose its meaning.
clew [klu:] *nc US* form of **clue.**
click [klik] *nc* sudden sharp sound like a light switch being turned on or off. Also *vt/i* **1.** make this sound. **2.** (of persons) get on well with each other. (*informal*). **3.** (of an idea etc) be understood (suddenly) (*informal*).
client ['klaiənt] *nc* **1.** person for whom a lawyer or other professional person works. **2.** person who buys from a shop. (Usu. **customer**).
clientele [kli:ɑ̃n'tel] *n sing* or *pl* number of clients or customers.
cliff [klif] *nc* high rock edge, falling away steeply.
'cliff-hanger something which has a tense and unfinished ending (e.g. part of a serial).
climate ['klaimit] *nc* type of weather normally found in a particular area. *California has a very pleasant climate.*
climatic [klai'mætik] *adj.*
climatology [klaimə'tɔlədʒi] *nu* study of climates. **climatologist** *nc.*
climax ['klaimæks] *nc* the most interesting and exciting part of something (usu. the last part, and often of a book, film, play etc). **climactic** [klai'mæktik] *adj.*
climb [klaim] *vt/i* go up. *He climbed to the top of the tree. He climbed the hill.* Also *nc* **1.** act of climbing. **2.** place where one climbs.
climber *nc* person who climbs (esp. one who climbs mountains for sport, using ropes and special equipment).
climbing *nu* sport of climbing mountains using ropes etc. Also *adj*: *climbing plant; climbing holiday.*
climb down admit that one is wrong.
clime [klaim] *nc* climate; part of the world (*o.f.*).
clinch [klintʃ] *vt* **1.** finally agree on: *clinch a bargain.* **2.** (boxing) hold one's opponent instead of fighting. Also *nc* (boxing) act of holding one's opponent in this way.
cling [kliŋ] *vi* hold tightly to. *He clung to the rope with both hands.* *past* **clung** [klʌŋ].
clinic ['klinik] *nc* place where people can go to receive medical advice and treatment.
clinical *adj* **1.** of a clinic. **2.** with reference to that aspect of medical science which studies patients by observation. **3.** cold and scientific.
clink [kliŋk] **1.** *nc* sharp sound like that made by drinking glasses knocking together. **2.** *nu* prison. (*informal* in sense **2.**). Also *vt/i* make this sound.
Note: the plural is not often used; *clinking* is used to refer to a number of noises of this kind.
clinker ['kliŋkə*] *nu* hard material left after some types of coal have been burned.
clip[1] [klip] *vt* (esp. with reference to hair, fur or plants) cut short. *past* **clipped.**
clippers *npl* instrument for cutting the hair, nails etc.
clipping *nc* piece cut off or out (esp. an article cut from a newspaper or magazine).
clip[2] [klip] *nc* piece of metal for holding things together (esp. for holding pieces of paper or a girl's hair). Also *vt* hold or keep in a clip. *past* **clipped.**
clip joint ['klipdʒɔint] *nc* nightclub or restaurant which cheats people by charging very high prices.
clipper ['klipə*] *nc* type of fast sailing ship.
clique [kli:k] *nc* group of people who keep together because of interests which they all have and who are unfriendly or unhelpful to other people. **cliquish** *adj.*
cloak [klouk] *nc* **1.** long outer garment without sleeves (usu. fastening at the neck). **2.** something which hides or covers something else. Also *vt* **1.** cover with a cloak. **2.** hide; keep secret.
'cloakroom **1.** room where hats and coats can be left. **2.** lavatory.
clock [klɔk] *nc* instrument for measuring the time (not carried on the wrist or in the pocket like a watch).
'clockwise *adv* in the direction in which the hands of a clock move i.e. ↻. (*opp* **anti-clockwise** i.e. ↺).
'clockwork machinery like that inside a watch or clock, using a spring.
go like clockwork go very easily, without any trouble. *All the arrangements went like clockwork.*
clod [klɔd] *nc* **1.** large piece of earth. **2.** very stupid person. (*informal* in sense **2.**).
clog[1] [klɔg] *nc* wooden shoe.
clog[2] [klɔg] *vt/i* (often with **up**) fill up or become filled up so that it is difficult for anything to pass through. *The drains were clogged with dirt, and so the water could not flow away. The drains soon clogged up.* *past* **clogged.**
cloister ['klɔistə*] *nc* **1.** (often *pl*) roofed area around the sides of a square (esp. in a monastery or college). **2.** place where people can live a life of prayer and thought, away from the world. Also *vt* put away in a cloister.
cloistered *adj* in a cloister; in a quiet place away from the world: *lead a cloistered life.*
close[1] [klouz] *vt/i* **1.** become or make shut. *The door has closed. Close the door.* **2.** finish; come to an end. *When do you think the meeting will close?*
'closed 'circuit with reference to television, programmes which are broadcast to a limited number of places (e.g. within a building or to the schools in a town).
'closed 'shop factory or other place of work, which employs only members of trade unions.
close something down (often with reference to a factory, business, port or other place where people work) shut completely.

'closedown *nc*: *a complete closedown.*
close in/on/upon someone/something come nearer to (often in a threatening or unpleasant way). *The soldiers closed in upon the town. The enemy were closing in.*
close something up 1. shut completely. 2. move nearer together. 3. (with reference to a cut or wound) heal.
close with someone/something accept; come to an agreement with. *I closed with his offer after three hours of discussion* (*o.f.*).
close one's eyes to something pretend not to notice. *I decided to close my eyes to John's mistake.*
close (the) ranks increase the sense of unity among the members of a group.

close[2] [klous] *adj/adv* 1. near. *The bus drove very close to the car. He came quite close to where I was hiding, but he did not see me. There were so many people in the room that we had to stand close together; a close friend* i.e. a friend whom one likes very much. 2. very careful; thorough. *He gave very close attention to what I was saying.* 3. (with reference to the air) hot and wet, making it difficult to breathe easily or move freely. 4. (with reference to games and competitions) equal or almost equal. *It was a very close race* i.e. several runners nearly won. **closely** *adv.* **closeness** *nu.*
'close-'fisted *adj* not generous; not likely to give or spend money. (*informal*).
'close-'fitting *adj* (with reference to clothes) tight on the body; showing the shape of the body.
'close season time of the year when certain fish may not be caught or animals and birds hunted.
a close shave see **shave.**
'close-up *nc* picture in a cinema film or photograph in which the camera is very near to what is being photographed.
(be kept) a close prisoner carefully guarded.
at close quarters near to one another. *They were fighting at close quarters.*
sail close to the wind be often near to breaking the law (esp. in business dealings) (*informal*).

close[3] [klouz] *n sing* end. *The national anthem was sung at the close of the meeting.*

close[4] [klous] *nc* area around a cathedral, in which some of the priests have their houses.

closet ['klɔzit] *nc* 1. (mainly *US*) small room or cupboard. 2. lavatory. (rather *o.f.*).
be closeted with somebody be in a room having a private discussion with somebody.

closure ['klouʒə*] *nc* act of closing or stopping.

clot [klɔt] *nc* 1. half-solid lump formed in the drying of certain liquids (esp. blood). 2. foolish person. (*informal* in sense 2.). Also *vt/i* become or make solid in this way. *past* **clotted.**

cloth [klɔθ] 1. *nu* material made from wool, silk, cotton, nylon etc. 2. *nc* piece of cloth.
'back-cloth large printed cloth hung at the back of a stage in a theatre.

clothe [klouð] *vt* put clothes on. *He clothed himself in his best suit.* (rather *o.f.* – use **dress**).

clothes [klouðz] *npl* 1. coverings worn on the body, such as coats, trousers, dresses, hats.
Note: this word is not used in the singular. To express the idea of one of these coverings for the body we can either name the thing (e.g. *a coat, a pair of trousers etc*) or use the expression *an article of clothing* or the word *garment.*
2. coverings for a bed i.e. sheets and blankets.
'clothes horse wooden or metal frame for hanging clothes on to dry them after they have been washed.
'clothes line line made of rope, nylon or plastic, from which clothes are hung to dry after they have been washed.
'clothes peg (*Brit*) small wooden, metal or plastic clip for fastening wet clothes to a clothes line. (*US* **clothespin**).

clothing ['klouðiŋ] *nu* clothes (e.g. coats, trousers, dresses).

cloud [klaud] *nc/u* 1. water vapour in the sky, which may fall as rain. 2. anything like this (e.g. *a cloud of smoke; clouds of insects*). Also *vt/i* (often with **over**) become or make covered with cloud. *The sky clouded over* i.e. became cloudy.
cloudy *adj* 1. covered with clouds. 2. (with reference to liquid) not clear; difficult to see through.
cloudless *adj* without any clouds.
'cloudburst sudden and very heavy rain.
'cloud 'cuckoo land imaginary and impossible state of affairs, which could never become real.
under a cloud thought to have done something wrong which cannot be proved.
have one's head in the clouds be concerned with plans and thoughts which have no connection with what is actually happening, and which can never be put into practice. (*informal*).

clout [klaut] *nc* 1. piece of cloth (*o.f.*). 2. blow with the hand. (*informal* in sense 2.). Also *vt* hit with the hand. (*informal*).

clove[1], **cloven** [klouv, 'klouvən] past tense and past part of **cleave**[1].
cloven hoof type of hoof or foot which is divided into two parts. Cows have cloven hooves. The Devil is supposed to have feet like this.

clove[2] [klouv] *nc* type of spice, obtained from the buds of a tropical tree.

clover ['klouvə*] *nu* type of plant (usu. with three leaves) eaten by cattle.
in clover in a very comfortable situation. (*informal*).

clown [klaun] *nc* 1. person (usu. with a painted face and strange clothes) whose work is to do foolish things to amuse people (esp. in a circus). 2. foolish person. Also *vi* do foolish things. **clownish** *adj.* **clownishness** *nu.*

cloy [klɔi] *vt/i* 1. fill with too much rich sweet food. 2. fill or make tired by too much of anything which is pleasant.
cloying *adj.*

club [klʌb] *nc* 1. heavy piece of wood, with one end thicker than the other, used as a weapon. 2. stick used in some games (e.g. golf). 3. playing card with the mark ♣; the mark itself. 4. group of people joined together for some purpose (usu. to play some sport or to enjoy their free time in some way); building used by these people. Also *vt* hit with a club. *past* **clubbed.**
'club-'foot *nc* type of disease in which the foot does not grow properly. **club-footed** *adj.*
club together *vi* join with other people in putting money together for some purpose. *The boys clubbed together to buy their teacher a present.*

cluck [klʌk] *nc* sound made by a hen when

calling her chicks. Also *vi* make this sound.

clue [klu:] *nc* (esp. with reference to a crime or a crossword puzzle) some information or sign which helps one to find the answer to a mystery or puzzle.
clueless *adj* ignorant, stupid. (*informal*).
I haven't a clue I don't know (often with the suggestion that one is not interested) (*informal*).

clump [klʌmp] *nc* number of things close together (usu. trees or plants).

clumsy ['klʌmzi] *adj* not skilful or clever in movement; not well-shaped for a particular purpose. *He is a clumsy boy; he is always falling over and breaking things.* **clumsily** *adv.* **clumsiness** *nu.*

clung [klʌŋ] past of **cling.**

cluster ['klʌstə*] *nc* (often with **round** or **around**) number of things gathered close together. Also *vi* grow or be in a cluster.

clutch[1] [klʌtʃ] *vt/i* take hold of very tightly.
clutch at something take hold of very tightly (usu. through fear).
a drowning man will clutch at a straw a person who is in difficulties will do anything to try to escape.

clutch[2] [klʌtʃ] *nc* **1.** tight hold. **2.** part of a car or similar machine which allows the power from the engine to be disconnected from the wheels; pedal which operates this part.
clutches *npl* control or power (usu. unpleasant control or power). *He was in the clutches of his enemies.*

clutch[3] [klʌtʃ] *nc* number of eggs laid by a bird at one time; number of young birds born to one bird at one time.

clutter ['klʌtə*] *vt* (often with **up**) make untidy. *These boxes have been cluttering up my garage for weeks.* Also *n sing* untidy condition. **cluttered** *adj.*

co- [kou] *prefix* giving the idea of 'with' (e.g. **co-owner** i.e. owner of something with somebody else).

coach[1] [koutʃ] *nc* **1.** large vehicle for passengers, pulled by horses. **2.** bus which travels long distances (often from one town to another). **3.** (*Brit*) railway carriage. (*US* **car**).
'coachman man who formerly drove a coach pulled by horses.
'stagecoach see **stage.**

coach[2] [koutʃ] *nc* **1.** person who prepares athletes and teams to play games. **2.** private teacher who teaches students and pupils (usu. to take an examination). Also *vt/i* prepare someone to play a game or take an examination in this way.

coagulate [kou'ægjuleit] *vt/i* (with reference to liquids, esp. blood) become or make thick. **coagulation** [kouægju'leiʃən] *nu.*

coal [koul] *nu* black substance found in the earth, which can be burned.
'coalfield area of a country where there is coal under the earth.
'coalgas type of gas made from coal.
'coalmine, 'coalpit *nc* place where coal is dug out of the earth. **coalminer** *nc.*
'coal scuttle type of box for holding coal.
'coal seam place under the earth where there is coal.
'coal 'tar thick black liquid formed from coal.
haul somebody over the coals speak severely and in an official way to somebody who has done wrong. (*informal*).
carry coals to Newcastle see **carry.**
heap coals of fire on somebody's head make a person sorry that he has done wrong to oneself by doing good to him.

coalesce [kouə'les] *vi* come together and become one. **coalescence** *nu.*

coalition [kouə'liʃən] *nc/u* joining of a number of groups (esp. the joining of a number of political parties in order to form a government).

coarse [kɔ:s] *adj* **1.** rough; not soft to the touch: *coarse cloth.* **2.** having large pieces: *coarse sugar; coarse sand.* **3.** impolite; ignorant in language or behaviour. **coarsely** *adv.* **coarseness** *nu.*

coast[1] [koust] *nc* land at the edge of the sea.
coastal *adj.*
coaster *nc* ship which sails along the coast, never going far from land.
'coastguard government official whose work is to watch the coast, in order to prevent smuggling and to help ships in difficulties.
'coastline outline or shape of a coast.
the coast is clear there is no danger or difficulty nearby, so that one can move about safely. *The prisoners waited until the coast was clear, and then they climbed over the prison wall.*

coast[2] [koust] *vi* **1.** sail a ship along the coast. **2.** allow a vehicle to keep moving without using any driving force. **3.** (often with **along**) carry out one's duties doing as little work as possible. (*informal* in sense **3.**).

coat [kout] *nc* **1.** type of garment with sleeves, buttoning down the front. **2.** covering: *a coat of paint; a dog's coat* i.e. his hair. Also *vt* put a covering on. *The boy was coated with mud.*
coating *nc* something covering a surface: *a coating of dirt.*
coat of arms official sign of a country, city, family etc.

coax [kouks] *vt/i* make somebody do something by being gentle and using very friendly words. *The boy coaxed his father into buying him a new bicycle.*

cob [kɔb] *nc* **1.** hard central part on which the grains of corn or maize grow. **2.** strong type of horse used for riding.

cobalt ['koubɔ:lt] *nu* **1.** type of metallic element used in hardening steel (Co). **2.** blue colour made from this metal.
'cobalt bomb type of atomic weapon, in which a hydrogen bomb is enclosed in cobalt.

cobble[1] ['kɔbl] *nc* large round stone, formerly used for making roads. (Also **cobblestone**).

cobble[2] ['kɔbl] *vt/i* **1.** mend shoes. **2.** repair in an unskilful way.
cobbler *nc* man whose work is mending shoes.

cobra ['kɔbrə] *nc* type of poisonous snake with a broad hood behind its head, found in Africa and Asia.

cobweb ['kɔbweb] *nc* structure made by a spider to catch insects. The use of this word often indicates a dirty place where a spider's web has been allowed to remain.

cocaine [kə'kein] *nu* strong drug which takes away feelings of pain.

cochineal ['kɔtʃini:l] *nu* red colouring matter used in cookery.

cock[1] [kɔk] *nc* **1.** male of the chicken. **2.** male of other birds. **3.** tap which can be turned to allow liquid or gas to come from a container. **4.** hammer of a gun, which falls to fire the bullet.
'cockcrow **1.** noise of the cock. **2.** early morning, when the cock makes this noise.

'**cockscomb** red crest on the head of a cock. see **coxcomb.**

'**cockpit** place in an aeroplane where the pilot sits.

'**cock'sure, cocky** *adj* sure of one's own abilities in an unpleasant way. **cockiness** *nu.* (*informal*).

a cock-and-bull story a foolish story, which nobody thinks true. (*informal*).

'**cock-a-doodle-'doo** imitation of the noise made by a cock. (*informal*).

cock² [kɔk] *vt* **1.** raise the hammer of a gun. *He cocked his gun.* **2.** (often with **up**) raise or turn upwards in a lively way. *He cocked his ears up* i.e. he suddenly began listening (with reference to an animal which moves its ears; or if with reference to a human being, the expression is *informal*).

cockade [kɔ'keid] *nc* knotted ribbon, worn in the hat as a badge or sign of some kind.

cockatoo [kɔkə'tu:] *nc* type of large brightly-coloured bird (related to the parrot) from Asia and Australia. *pl* **cockatoos.**

cockerel ['kɔkrl] *nc* young male of the chicken.

cockle ['kɔkl] *nc* type of shellfish, used for food.

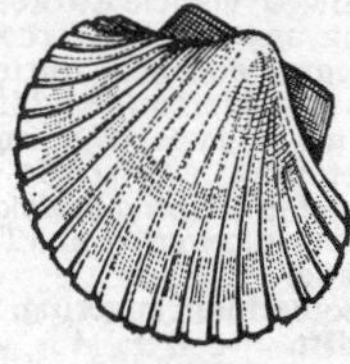

cockle

cockney ['kɔkni] **1.** *nc* person born in the East End of London. **2.** *nu* way of speaking found in the poorer parts of London. Also *adj.*

cockroach ['kɔkroutʃ] *nc* large brown insect often found in kitchens and near water pipes.

cocktail ['kɔkteil] *nc* mixture of various alcoholic drinks (usu. drunk before meals).

'**cocktail bar** part of a hotel or restaurant where drinks are sold.

cocoa ['koukou] *nu* **1.** powder made from the seeds of the cacao tree. **2.** drink made from this powder.

coconut ['koukənʌt] **1.** *nc* large hard nut growing on a type of tropical tree. **2.** *nc* the tree itself. (Also **coconut palm**). **3.** *nu* sweet-tasting substance found inside the nut, used in cookery.

'**coconut 'matting** type of rough carpet made from the fibres round a coconut.

cocoon [kə'ku:n] *nc* covering in which some insects live at the stage of their life cycle before changing into the fully-grown insect.

cod [kɔd] *nc* type of large sea fish, eaten as food. *pl* **cod.**

'**cod-liver 'oil** thick yellow oil obtained from cod, used as a medicine.

coddle ['kɔdl] *vt* treat too kindly or too gently.

code [koud] *nc* **1.** system of secret writing, used so that messages can be read only by those who know the secret. **2.** system of signals for sending messages (e.g. *the Morse code* i.e. used for sending messages by telegraph or by flashing lights). **3.** set of ideas about the proper way to behave. **4.** laws of a country, collected together and clearly set down. Also *vt* put into secret writing or into a system of signals.

codeine ['koudi:n] *nu* drug which is used to take away pain.

codex ['koudeks] *nc* ancient book, written by hand. *pl* **codices** ['kɔdisi:z].

codicil ['kɔdisil] *nc* some instruction added to a will, after the main part of it has been written.

codify ['koudifai] *vt* put (laws etc) into a systematic order. **codification** [koudifi'keiʃən] *nu.*

coeducation ['kouedju'keiʃən] *nu* system of educating boys and girls together, in the same school or in the same class. **coeducational** *adj.*

coefficient [koui'fiʃənt] *nc* (mathematics) number or symbol written in front of another to multiply it (e.g. in the expression $2x$, 2 is the coefficient of x).

coerce [kou'ə:s] *vt* make somebody do what he does not wish to do. **coercion** [kou'ə:ʃən] *nu.* **coercive** *adj.*

coexistence [kouig'zistns] *nu* condition of living together at the same time (and often in a peaceful way).

coexist *vi* live together in this way.

coextensive [kouiks'tensiv] *adj* of the same length or area.

coffee ['kɔfi] *nu* dark brown powder obtained from the seeds of a tropical bush used for making a drink; the drink itself.

'**coffee bar** (with reference to modern times) bar where coffee and other refreshments are sold.

'**coffee house** (esp. with reference to such places in London in the 17th and 18th centuries) place where coffee and other refreshments are sold.

coffer ['kɔfə*] *nc* strong box for keeping money in.

coffin ['kɔfin] *nc* box in which a dead person is put.

cog [kɔg] *nc* one of the teeth on the edge of a wheel in various machines.

'**cogwheel** wheel having cogs on it.

cogent ['koudʒənt] *adj* (with reference to arguments, reasons, explanations etc) strong; worth listening to; making one agree that something is true. **cogently** *adv.* **cogency** *nu.*

cogitate ['kɔdʒiteit] *vi* think very carefully or deeply. **cogitation** [kɔdʒi'teiʃən] *nu.*

cognac ['kɔnjæk] *nu* type of strong alcoholic drink made in France.

cognate ['kɔgneit] *adj* (with reference to words) having the same origin (e.g. the English word 'father' and the German word 'Vater' are cognate i.e. both words have developed from a common source).

cognition [kɔg'niʃən] *nu* act of knowing or taking notice of.

cognizance ['kɔgnizns] *nu* state of having knowledge of, or taking notice of. **cognizant** *adj.*

cohere [kou'hiə*] *vi* stick together; fit together. **cohesion** [kou'hi:ʒən] *nu.* **cohesive** [kou'hi:siv] *adj.*

coherent [kou'hiərnt] *adj* (esp. with reference to speeches, thoughts, ideas, explanations etc) with various parts fitting together and therefore easy to understand. (*opp* **incoherent**). **coherently** *adv.* **coherence** *nu.*

cohort ['kouhɔ:t] *nc* part of the division of an ancient Roman army.

coiffure [kwɔ'fjuə*] *nc* way in which a

woman's hair is arranged. (rather *formal* – use **hairstyle**).
coiffeur [kwɔ'fəː*] *nc* man whose work is arranging women's hair. (rather *formal* – use **hairdresser**).

coil [kɔil] *nc* **1.** something arranged in a series of circles. **2.** one of these circles. **3.** (electricity) arrangement of wires in the form of a coil, for carrying electricity. Also *vt* arrange something in the form of a coil.

coin [kɔin] *nc/u* (piece of) metal used as money. Also *vt/i* make metal into money.
coinage 1. *nc* system of money used in a country. **2.** *nu* process of making money from metal. **3.** *nc* word which has been made up by somebody.
coiner *nc* person who makes coins (esp. false coins i.e. coins not issued by the government).
coin a word invent a new word.
to coin a phrase if you will allow me to invent a new expression (usu. said as a joke by somebody who knows that he is using an old expression which has in fact been used too often) (*informal*).

coincide [kouin'said] *vi* **1.** (with reference to two or more things) take place at the same time. *My holiday coincides with John's* i.e. John and I have our holidays at the same time. *Our holidays coincide.* **2.** (with reference to ideas, opinions etc) agree. *Our ideas on this matter coincide* i.e. we think the same. **3.** (geometry) have the same shape; occupy the same space.
coincidence [kou'insidns] *nc/u* happening at the same time of two or more things (esp. a happening together which occurs by chance without any planning). **coincidental** [kouinsi'dentl] *adj*.

coke [kouk] *nu* substance made by driving off the gas in coal and used as fuel to give a great heat.

colander ['kʌləndə*] *nc* dish with many small holes in the bottom, used in cooking to drain water from vegetables etc.

cold[1] [kould] *adj* **1.** not hot. *Snow and ice are cold. The night is colder than the day. If you don't drink your tea it will get cold.* **2.** unfriendly; showing no feelings of love or friendship. **coldly** *adv*. **coldness** *nu*.
'cold-'blooded *adj* **1.** having blood which changes its temperature according to the surrounding temperature. *Snakes are cold-blooded.* **2.** having or showing no feelings.
'cold 'cream substance put on the face by women or actors, to remove cosmetics from the skin.
'cold-'hearted *adj* showing no feelings of love or sympathy.
'cold 'storage method of keeping food for a long time by putting it in a specially-built cold room.
'cold 'sweat perspiration which feels cold (esp. if caused by fear).
'cold 'war see **war**.
give somebody the cold shoulder be very unfriendly or unwelcoming to somebody (usu. to make him go away).

cold[2] [kould] **1.** *nu* absence of heat. *It is difficult to imagine the cold of the winter when one is enjoying a warm summer.* **2.** *nc* type of illness in which liquid runs from the nose.
catch cold get the illness in which liquid runs from the nose.

colic ['kɔlik] *nu* name given to various types of pain in the stomach (esp. in young children).

collaborate [kə'læbəreit] *vi* **1.** work with somebody (esp. in writing a book). *John collaborated with his father in writing the book. John and his father collaborated.* **2.** work to help an enemy which has invaded one's country. **collaborator** *nc*. **collaboration** [kəlæbe'reiʃən] *nu*.

collapse [kə'læps] **1.** *vi* fall down; break down. *The bridge collapsed three weeks after they finished building it. My plans suddenly collapsed* i.e. it became impossible for me to carry out my plans. *The woman collapsed when she was told of the death of her son* i.e. she became unconscious. **2.** *vt/i* (with reference to things such as chairs, telescopes, tents etc which are intended to be folded or put flat when not in use) fold up. *He collapsed his tent and put it into his car.* Also *nc* falling down of this kind.
collapsible, collapsable *adj* able to be folded or put flat when not in use.

collar ['kɔlə*] *nc* **1.** part of a coat, dress, shirt etc which fits around the neck (sometimes a separate piece of material which is put around the neck and fastened to a shirt). **2.** piece of leather or other material for fastening round the neck of a dog or other animal. **3.** in a machine, metal ring which holds a rod etc in position. Also *vt* take hold of somebody by the collar. (*informal*).
'collarbone bone joining the breastbone to the shoulder.
'collar stud piece of bone, plastic, metal etc for fastening a collar to a shirt.

collate [kɔ'leit] *vt* compare two similar books or pieces of writing, to find out what the difference between them is. **collator** *nc*.
collation [kə'leiʃən] *nu* **1.** act of collating; thing collated. **2.** light meal. (rather *formal* in sense **2.**).

collateral [kou'lætərl] *adj* **1.** parallel; side by side. **2.** (with reference to members of a family) descended from the same ancestors but having different parents. Also *nc/u* additional security (usu. on a loan).

colleague ['kɔliːg] *nc* (with reference to work done in an office, school, college etc) person with whom one works.

collect[1] [kə'lekt] *vt/i* get together; come or bring to one place. *A crowd collected after the accident* i.e. people came together. *He was collecting money to help the poor. He collects stamps for a hobby.* **collector** *nc*.
collected *adj* **1.** brought together: *the collected poems of John Smith.* **2.** calm; not losing control of one's feelings. **collectedly** *adv*.
collection *nc/u* **1.** things/people brought together: *a collection of people; a stamp collection.* **2.** money given for some purpose by people at a meeting (esp. at a church). **3.** act of collecting.
collective[1] *adj* considered as a group (e.g. *a collective punishment* is a punishment given to a whole group of people because one cannot find the guilty person).
collective[2], **collective farm** type of farm found in Russia and other communist or socialist countries, in which the farm is owned and managed by the people who work on it.
collective noun singular noun which refers to a group (e.g. flock, the staff).
collect oneself/one's thoughts, ideas etc begin to think calmly and carefully, after something frightening or exciting.

collect[2] ['kɔlekt] *nc* short prayer to be read

on certain days in certain of the Christian churches.

colleen ['kɔliːn] *nc* young Irish girl. (*informal*).

college ['kɔlidʒ] *nc* **1.** name given to various types of places of learning (e.g. some schools are called colleges; some universities are made up of a number of separate colleges) and also the staff and students of these institutions, or the actual buildings. **2.** name given to certain groups of people with special duties (e.g. *the College of Cardinals* is the group of officials of the Roman Catholic Church, one of whose duties is to choose a new Pope).

collide [kə'laid] *vi* **1.** come together with a hard knock. *My car collided with a lorry.* **2.** have a strong disagreement with. **collision** [kə'liʒən] *nc/u*.

collie ['kɔli] *nc* very intelligent type of dog, used for driving sheep.

collier ['kɔliə*] *nc* **1.** man whose work is digging coal out of the earth. **2.** ship which carries coal.

colliery *nc* coalmine and the surrounding buildings and equipment.

collocation [kɔlə'keiʃən] *nc/u* putting of things together (esp. the putting of words together in a particular phrase or sentence). **collocate** ['kɔləkeit] *vt*.

colloid ['kɔlɔid] *nc* (chemistry) type of substance which exists in a partly solid state, like glue, and which is suspended or dispersed in some liquid, gas or solid, without becoming dissolved. **colloidal** [kə'lɔidl] *adj*.

colloquial [kə'loukwiəl] *adj* (with reference to language) of the type of language used in everyday informal conversation. **colloquially** *adv*.

colloquialism *nc* word or expression used in informal conversation, but not usu. in formal speech or writing.

colloquy ['kɔləkwi] *nc* conversation. (*formal* – use **conversation**).

collusion [kə'luːʒən] *nu* secret agreement between two or more people to do something wrong.

colon ['koulɔn] *nc* **1.** the mark : . **2.** section of that part of the body in which food is changed into waste matter.

colonel ['kəːnl] *nc* (military) officer of high rank.

colonnade [kɔlə'neid] *nc* line of stone columns forming part of a building.

colonnade

colony ['kɔləni] *nc* **1.** country which is ruled by another country. *Nigeria used to be a British colony.* **2.** group of people of one nationality or of one profession or occupation, living in another country or apart from others. *There is a large Italian colony in London* i.e. many Italians live in London. **3.** large group of birds, animals or insects which live together.

colonial [kə'louniəl] *adj* having reference to a colony. Also *nc* person living in a colony.

colonialism [kə'louniəlizəm] *nu* **1.** policy by which one country tries to remain the owner and ruler of another country. **2.** condition of being a colony.

colonialist [kə'louniəlist] *nc* person who favours the policy of colonialism.

colonist *nc* person who goes to a colony in order to develop it.

colonize *vt* form a colony in a country, by going there or sending people there. *The English and the Spanish were among the first to colonize North America.* **colonization** [kɔlənai'zeiʃən] *nu*.

colossal [kə'lɔsl] *adj* very big.

colossus [kə'lɔsəs] *nc* **1.** very big statue of a person. **2.** very big person/thing.

colour ['kʌlə*] (*US* **color**) *nc/u* **1.** sensation produced on the eye by light waves of different lengths. Green, blue and red are colours. **2.** paint, dye or other substance used to change the colour of something. **3.** redness of the face caused by heat, excitement, embarrassment etc. **4.** interesting detail. *The story has a lot of colour.* Also *vt/i* **1.** become coloured. **2.** become red in the face. **3.** put colour on.

the colours *npl* the flag of an army or section of an army.

coloured *adj* **1.** having a colour. **2.** (of people) having a skin which is not white.

colourful *adj* **1.** having bright colours. **2.** interesting and unusual, having many interesting details. **colourfully** *adv*.

colouring *nu* **1.** substance used to colour something. **2.** way in which something is coloured.

colourless *adj* **1.** without colour. **2.** not interesting; lacking in detail.

'colour bar practice found in some societies in which people of one colour are treated worse than people of another colour.

'colour-blind *adj* unable to see the difference between certain colours. **colour blindness** *nu*.

'colour film **1.** *nu* film for taking coloured photographs. **2.** *nc* coloured photograph.

local colour details about a place which a writer adds to make a story more interesting.

'watercolour **1.** *nu* type of paint which is mixed with water, used for painting pictures. **2.** *nc* painting painted in this way.

come off/out with flying colours see **come.**

show one's true colours show that one is a bad person after appearing to be a good person.

change colour see **change**[1].

off colour slightly ill.

colt [koult] *nc* young male horse.

column ['kɔləm] *nc* **1.** tall round piece of stone or other material used as part of a building or as a monument. **2.** anything of this shape: *a column of soldiers; a column of dust. The page of a newspaper is divided into columns* i.e. narrow sections stretching down the page. **3.** section of a newspaper (usu. written by a particular person or which is regularly devoted to a special subject).

columnist ['kɔləmnist] *nc* person who regularly writes a special section in a newspaper.

coma ['koumə] *nc* condition like a deep sleep, caused by injury, disease or poison.

comatose ['koumətous] *adj* in a coma.

comb[1] [koum] *nc* **1.** piece of metal, plastic, bone etc with teeth, used for making the hair tidy or for keeping it in place. **2.** part of a machine shaped like a comb, used in the preparation of wool and cotton. **3.** red crest on the head of the male of the chicken. **4.** see **honeycomb.**

comb² [koum] *vt* **1.** use a comb to tidy the hair. **2.** search very carefully in order to find something. *I combed the shops until I found a pair of shoes that I liked.*

combat ['kɔmbæt] *nc* fight; battle. Also *vt/i. past* **combat(t)ed.** (*US* **combated**).

combatant ['kɔmbətnt] *nc* one who fights.

'single 'combat fight between two people.

combine¹ [kəm'bain] *vt/i* come or bring together; mix. *He was able to combine business with pleasure* i.e. he carried out some duty which was also a pleasure for him. *He combined his visit to England with a tour of Scotland* i.e. he visited both England and Scotland during the same journey.

combination [kɔmbi'neiʃən] **1.** *nu* act of coming or bringing together. **2.** *nc* group of people or things joined together for some purpose. **3.** *nc* series of numbers or letters which is used to open a combination lock. *He had forgotten the combination of the safe.*

combi'nation lock type of lock with a dial on which there are numbers or letters. A particular arrangement of numbers or letters must be made before the lock can be opened.

combine² ['kɔmbain] *nc* **1.** group of people who have come together for a special purpose, often a political or business purpose. **2.** machine which cuts grain and takes out the seeds while driving along the field. (Also **combine harvester**).

combustion [kəm'bʌstʃən] *nu* action of being burned; destruction by fire.

combustible [kəm'bʌstibl] *adj* able to be burned. (*opp* **incombustible**).

come [kʌm] *vi* **1.** move towards or with another person, or move towards the place where somebody will be in the future. *John came to see me yesterday. Shall I come with you to the market? I hope you will come to see me when I go to live in France next year.* **2.** arrive at; reach a place. *I've been waiting for an hour, but John hasn't come yet.* **3.** occur; take place at some time. *Christmas Day comes on a Tuesday this year.* Also *interj: Come, come!* i.e. don't be worried; be cheerful; are you sure? etc. *past tense* **came.** *past part* **come.**

come about happen; occur by chance.

come across someone/something meet or find by chance. *I came across an old friend last week.*

come along 1. improve; get better. **2.** hurry; go more quickly.

come apart break into two or more pieces.

come away leave. *I went to see him at six o'clock and I came away at nine o'clock.*

come back return.

'comeback *nc* return to power or popularity. *The old actor retired when he was 85, but he made a comeback two years later* i.e. he appeared on the stage again. (*informal*).

come between separate: *come between two people who are fighting.*

come by something get something. *How did you come by that money?*

come down (with reference to cost) become cheaper.

'comedown *nc* situation which is poor or unpleasant, after one has been used to something much better; loss of a good situation. (*informal*).

come forward offer to do something or to say something; volunteer.

come from be derived from.

come in 1. enter. **2.** begin to be used.

come in for something get or be given. *He came in for all the extra work.* (*informal*).

come into 1. enter. **2.** get from somebody who has died; inherit. *He came into a large amount of money when his uncle died.*

come of something have as a result. *Nothing came of the meeting* i.e. we did not come to an agreement.

come off 1. (with reference to special events) happen. *The meeting will come off next week.* **2.** be in a certain condition at the end of a contest or fight. *He came off worst* i.e. he lost the fight. **3.** (with reference to an experiment or gamble) be successful. **4.** **come off it!** i.e. don't say such silly things!

come off/out with flying colours be very successful in something difficult.

come on improve; get better. *John has come on very well at school this year.*

come on! hurry up!; also used to encourage someone.

come out 1. be discovered as the truth. *The whole story came out in the end* i.e. the truth was finally told. **2.** (with reference to a book) be published; be offered for sale. *His new book comes out next month.*

come out right reach a satisfactory conclusion.

come out with something say; speak. *He came out with a long story to explain why he was late.* (*informal*).

come round return to consciousness.

come round to something change one's mind about something. *I have come round to your point of view* i.e. I now think that you are right, although I used to think you were wrong.

come through something survive; experience successfully. *He came through the operation on his heart* i.e. he lived after the operation and got better.

come to return to consciousness. *He was hit on the head by a brick, and did not come to for half an hour.*

come to something amount to; total. *The food which I bought came to £3* i.e. it cost £3.

come to do something (usu. in questions) happen. *How did you come to break it?*

come to one be remembered. *I've forgotten his name, but it will come to me in a minute.* (*informal*).

come to terms agree; stop fighting with.

come upon something find by chance. *I came upon an interesting book in the library.*

come up to come as far as; be as good as; equal. *The water came up to the top of the steps. The concert did not come up to expectations* i.e. was not as good as we thought it might be.

come up with produce; present: *come up with a useful suggestion.*

come/be of age be recognized by law as an adult (in Britain, at age of 18).

come to blows start fighting.

come clean tell the truth about something wrong which one has done, after trying to hide the truth. (*informal*).

come into effect/force become law; take effect. *The new rules come into effect next year.*

come to grief have an accident or suffer some misfortune.

come home to be fully realized. *The importance of the examination came home to him* i.e. he realized that the examination was important, although earlier he had not realized it.

come to one's knowledge (usu. with reference to something bad) become known by one. *It has come to my knowledge that you have not been working hard enough.*

come to light be discovered. *The robbery did not come to light until the next day.*

come what may whatever happens. *I shall go to town tomorrow, come what may.*

come to pieces break into pieces.

come to one's senses begin to think intelligently again after having some foolish ideas.

come into sight appear; be seen.

come to terms with make an official agreement with, after fighting or disagreeing.

come true happen, after having been an idea or hope.

to come in the future: *in years to come.*

comedy ['kɔmədi] **1.** *nc* type of play or film which is intended to make one laugh. **2.** *nc* any event which makes one laugh. **3.** *nu* plays which make one laugh, considered as a group. *Comedy needs very good actors.*

comedian [kə'miːdiən] *nc* entertainer who tells funny stories and says and does funny things.

comely ['kʌmli] *adj* (usu. with reference to a person) pretty; nice to look at. **comeliness** *nu.* (both rather *o.f.*).

comestible [kə'mestibl] *nc* (usu. *pl*) something to eat (*o.f.* – use **food**).

comet ['kɔmit] *nc* star-like object in the sky with a long tail, moving around the sun.

comfort ['kʌmfət] **1.** *nu* condition of being in pleasant circumstances, without any worries. *He lived in comfort all his life* i.e. he always had nice food, good clothes and everything he wanted to make life happy. **2.** *nc* anything which makes life pleasanter for one, or which takes away pain or worry. *He liked the comforts of his home. He was a great comfort to his old mother* i.e. he helped her very much and made her life pleasant. Also *vt* do or say something to make somebody feel happier.

comfortable ['kʌmftəbl] *adj* making life pleasant and taking away pain or worry; without pain or worry. *He has a very comfortable home. This is a comfortable chair* i.e. it is pleasant to sit in it. *The sick man had a comfortable night* i.e. he slept well and did not feel any pain. (*opp* **uncomfortable**).

comfortably *adv.*

comforter *nc* **1.** one who does or says something to make another person feel happier. **2.** long woollen scarf.

comic[1] ['kɔmik] *adj* making one laugh; concerned with comedy. **comical** *adj.* **comically** *adv.*

comic opera type of opera which is funny and which has a happy ending.

comic strip series of pictures in a newspaper, telling an amusing story.

comic[2] ['kɔmik] *nc* **1.** comedian; person whose job is to say things to make people laugh. (*informal*). **2.** type of magazine with pictures, written for children (sometimes, though not always, containing funny stories).

comma ['kɔmə] *nc* the mark , .

inverted commas the marks " ".

command[1] [kə'mɑːnd] **1.** *nc* order. *The soldiers obeyed the officer's command* i.e. they did what the officer told them to do. **2.** *nu* ability to use, control. *He has a very good command of English.* **3.** *nc* part of an army, air force etc.

at one's command ready for use if needed. *I gave him all the money at my command.*

in command having the position of leader. *General Smith was in command of the army.*

under the command of having as leader. *The army was under the command of General Smith.*

command[2] [kə'mɑːnd] *vt* **1.** give orders to. *He commanded the soldiers to attack.* **2.** be the leader of. *General Smith commanded the army.* **3.** be able to get if necessary. *He was able to command the help of everybody in the country. He can command more than a million pounds.* **4.** be higher than; look down on. *The castle commanded the whole town.*

commander *nc* **1.** one who gives orders or who is a leader. **2.** naval officer.

commanding *adj* **1.** having the position of a leader: *a commanding officer.* **2.** higher than; looking down on. *Our soldiers were on the hills commanding the enemy villages.*

commandant [kɔmən'dænt] *nc* officer in charge of a military college, dockyard, town etc.

commandeer [kɔmən'diə*] *vt* (esp. with reference to the taking of property by the army during war) take away somebody's property by force.

commandment [kə'mɑːndmənt] *nc* **1.** very important order or law (esp. one given by God). **2.** one of the ten laws given to the Israelites by God. (The laws are known as **the Ten Commandments**).

commando [kə'mɑːndou] *nc* **1.** soldier who is trained to enter enemy territory secretly and in small groups in order to destroy enemy property. **2.** group of these soldiers. *pl* **commandos.**

commemorate [kə'memərеit] *vt* do something or be a sign to remember some important person or event. *The people built a new theatre to commemorate the birth of Shakespeare. The new theatre commemorates the birth of Shakespeare.* **commemoration** [kəmemə'reiʃən] *nc/u.* **commemorative** [kə'memərətiv] *adj.*

commence [kə'mens] *vt/i* begin; start. (*formal*).

commencement *nc* **1.** beginning. (*formal*). **2.** (*US*) day on which prizes and certificates are given at a school or college.

commend [kə'mend] *vt* **1.** speak in praise of. *I can commend this book to you* i.e. I can tell you that this is a good book. **2.** give to somebody to be kept carefully.

commendable *adj* deserving praise; of high quality.

commendation [kɔmen'deiʃən] *nu* praise.

commensurate [kə'mensjurit] *adj* of the same size or quantity as something else; of the right size or quantity for something. *The danger of the journey was commensurate with its importance* i.e. the journey was as dangerous as it was important.

comment ['kɔment] *vi* (often with **on** or **about**) say something; give an opinion. *He commented on the weather* i.e. he said something about the weather. Also *nc* **1.** something said. *He made a comment about my mistake.* **2.** something said or written to explain or criticize something.

commentary ['kɔməntri] *nc* **1.** description of some event (usu. a sporting event), made on the radio or television (usu. made while the event is actually taking place). **2.**

number of written or spoken notes which explain or criticize something.
commentator ['kɔmənteitə*] *nc* person who makes a commentary.

commerce ['kɔməːs] *nu* practice of buying and selling goods (esp. in large amounts).
commercial [kə'məːʃl] *adj*. Also *nc* advertisement on radio or television.
commercialism [kə'məːʃəlizəm] *nu* practice of considering everything as objects to be bought and sold, instead of considering things as having a value in themselves. *He disliked the commercialism of modern life.*
commercialize [kə'məːʃəlaiz] *vt* make something into an object to be bought and sold.
commercial traveller see **travel.**

commiserate [kə'mizəreit] *vi* (usu. with **with**) show pity for or sympathy with someone. *He commiserated with me on my failure in the examination.* **commiseration** [kəmizə'reiʃən] *nu*.

commissar ['kɔmisɑː*] *nc* head of a government department in the USSR.

commissariat [kɔmi'særiət] *nc* **1.** department of an army which is in charge of the supply of food. **2.** office of a commissar.

commission [kə'miʃən] **1.** *nc* group of people given special powers to carry out some particular task. *The government appointed a commission to examine the country's educational system.* **2.** *nc* position of an officer in the army, navy, air force etc. **3.** *nc* piece of paper giving an officer this position. **4.** *nc* official order which gives somebody the power to do some special piece of work. **5.** *nc* piece of work given to somebody. **6.** *nc/u* amount of money given to somebody as payment for selling goods which belong to somebody else. *In some large shops the assistants get a commission on what they sell* i.e. they are paid for each item which they sell. Also *vt* give somebody an order to carry out some special piece of work; give somebody the power to do some piece of work. *He was commissioned to write the music for that film.*
commissioner *nc* **1.** member of a group of people given official powers to carry out some piece of work. **2.** official of various types (esp. a senior official in the police).
commissioned officer officer in the army, navy, air force etc with special authority from the head of the state, to carry out the duties of an officer. (A **non-commissioned officer** is an officer of lower rank who does not have this special authority).
in commission (with reference to warships) ready for use.
on commission getting a payment for selling goods belonging to somebody else. *He sells motorcars on commission.*

commissionaire [kəmiʃə'nɛə*] *nc* man wearing a uniform, whose job is to stand outside the door of a cinema or hotel and help people coming in and out.

commit [kə'mit] *vi* **1.** do something (usu. something wrong or foolish). *He committed a crime.* **2.** give to somebody to be kept or treated carefully. *He committed the papers to the care of the lawyer.* **3.** throw or put into. *He committed the papers to the fire.* (*formal*). *past* **committed. committal** *nc*.
commitment 1. *nc* promise to do something. **2.** *nc/u* devotion: *commitment to socialism.*
commit to memory learn so that one will remember. *He committed the number to memory.*
commit oneself promise or say that one will do something. *I have committed myself to helping him.*
commit to prison send to prison after a trial. *The judge committed him to prison.*

committee [kə'miti] *nc* group of people given special powers (often by a larger group) to carry out some special piece of work.
Note: the word *committee* can be treated as either *sing* or *pl*.

commodious [kə'moudiəs] *adj* having enough space to contain a large amount: *a very commodious room.*

commodity [kə'mɔditi] *nc* something which is bought and sold.

commodore ['kɔmədɔː*] *nc* rank of officer in the navy or air force.

common[1] ['kɔmən] *adj* **1.** belonging to several people and not to any individual. *In a block of flats, the roof and the lift are often common property* i.e. these things are owned by all the people who own flats in that block. *Britain and America share a common language* i.e. English is spoken in both countries. **2.** found in many places or over a wide area. *This bird is common throughout Europe.* **3.** usual. *It is common for a woman to leave her parents' house when she gets married.* **4.** showing little or no politeness; with no sense of the proper way to behave. (*opp* **uncommon** in senses **2.** and **3.**). **commonly** *adv*.
the Commons, the House of Commons (in Britain) the assembly of elected members of Parliament. (The other assembly, the House of Lords, is not elected).
commoner *nc* person who is not a member of the nobility.
common denominator multiple of the denominator of a group of fractions.
common law see **law.**
'**commonplace** *adj* ordinary; not interesting. Also *nc* remark or statement which is ordinary and not interesting or new.
'**commonroom** room for the use of teachers, lecturers etc at a school, college etc.
common'sense *nu* ordinary intelligence, which most people have. Also *adj*.
'**commonwealth** nation or state (esp. one made up of several states).
the Commonwealth 1. association of Britain with several of the countries which were formerly British colonies and protectorates. **2.** system of government in England under Oliver Cromwell, from 1649 to 1660.
common or garden *adj* usual and well-known; not new or interesting. (*informal*).
in common with other people. *John and Richard own the house in common* i.e. they are both the owners of the house. *They have a lot in common* i.e. they are alike in many ways.

common[2] ['kɔmən] *nc* (mainly *Brit*) open space covered with grass and trees, which is for the use of everybody.

commotion [kə'mouʃən] *nc* violent and noisy movement or excitement.

commune[1] ['kɔmjuːn] *nc* **1.** small area of local government in some European countries. **2.** large group of people living together in China and elsewhere; all land and property is owned by the group, and all the members work to produce goods and services for the group.
communal *adj* referring to a group of people living together; public. *He took no part in communal life* i.e. he did not share in activities organized by or for the people

living around him. **communally** *adv.*

commune[2] [kə'mju:n] *vi* talk with (esp. in a close or friendly way).

communicate [kə'mju:nikeit] *vt/i* **1.** give information in speech or writing, or by signs. *While he was in prison he was not allowed to communicate with his family. He communicated the whole story to me.* **2.** pass disease to. *He communicated the disease to the rest of his family.* **3.** (with reference to rooms, houses etc) be joined or connected. **4.** receive Communion.

communicable [kə'mju:nikəbl] *adj* (esp. with reference to disease) able to be passed from one person to another.

communicant [kə'mju:nikənt] *nc* person receiving Communion.

communication [kəmju:ni'keiʃən] *nc/u* **1.** letter, speech, sign etc giving information. *While he was in prison his family received no communication from him.* **2.** act of passing disease. **3.** (of rooms, houses etc) act of being joined or connected. **4.** method of passing information over a wide area (e.g. telephones, roads, aeroplanes).

communicative [kə'mju:nikətiv] *adj* able or willing to give information.

communi'cation cord cord which can be pulled by passengers to stop a train in an emergency.

communion [kə'mju:niən] **1.** *nu* act of sharing ideas or property with other people. **2.** *nc* group of people having the same religious ideas.

Communion, Holy Communion *nu* ceremony, carried out in many Christian churches, of giving bread or bread and wine to the people in memory of Christ.

take Communion receive bread or bread and wine in this way.

communiqué [kə'mju:nikei] *nc* official announcement (esp. one made by a government).

communism ['kɔmjunizəm] *nu* (esp. with reference to the system of government in Russia, China and many countries of eastern Europe) social or political system in which property is owned by the government or the community, and not by individuals.

communist *nc* person who approves of this system (esp. one who is a member of the Communist Party). Also *adj.*

community [kə'mju:niti] **1.** *nc* people living in one part of a town or country; any group of people living together. **2.** *nu* condition of sharing things or having things in common.

com'munity centre building in a town or village, where people living in that place can go to meet each other and enjoy themselves.

com'munity 'singing singing by a group of people (esp. members of an audience).

commute [kə'mju:t] **1.** *vi* travel every day by bus or train, between one's house and the place where one works. **2.** *vt* change a punishment for a lighter punishment. *The prisoner was at first sentenced to death, but this was later commuted to fifteen years' imprisonment.* **commutation** [kɔmju'teiʃən] *nc/u.*

commuter *nc* person who travels every day by bus or train between his house and the place where he works.

compact[1] [kəm'pækt] *adj* fitting tightly together; using up very little space.

compact[2] ['kɔmpækt] *nc* **1.** agreement with somebody to do something. **2.** flat box for containing face powder, carried in a woman's handbag. **3.** (*US*) small car.

companion [kəm'pæniən] *nc* **1.** person with whom one travels; person who is often or always with one. **2.** person whom one likes to be with. **3.** anything which goes with something else. **4.** person whose work is to live with another person. *She was employed as a companion to an old lady.*

companionable *adj* friendly.

companionship *nu* state of being a companion; friendly company.

com'panionway stairs on a ship.

company ['kʌmpəni] **1.** *nc* number of people who have joined together for some purpose. **2.** *nc* business firm. **3.** *nc* small division of an army; small group of soldiers. **4.** *nu* condition of being with other people. *He enjoys company* i.e. he likes to be with other people.

be good company be a friendly and interesting person. *He is very good company.*

have company have visitors in the house.

keep somebody company go with or be with somebody (usu. in a friendly way).

keep company with go around with; mix with. *He's keeping company with some strange people.*

part company see part[2].

compare [kəm'pɛə*] *vt* **1.** show or find out in what ways two or more things are like each other (or are different from each other). *He compared the two chairs before he decided which one to buy.* **2.** (with **to** or **with**) say or show that something is like something else. *He compared the brave man to a lion.*

comparison [kəm'pærisn] *nc/u*: *make a comparison between two things.*

comparable ['kɔmpərəbl] *adj* able to be compared. *This is comparable to/with that.* (*opp* **incomparable** – usu. with the meaning of very much better than). **comparably** *adv.*

comparative [kəm'pærətiv] *adj* **1.** making or showing a comparison (e.g. the study of comparative religion is the study of various religions to see in what ways they are alike and in what ways they differ). **2.** when compared to something else. *This is comparatively easy* i.e. it seems easy if we compare it with other things which are much more difficult. **3.** (grammar) form of adjectives and adverbs which expresses the idea of 'more' (e.g. *easier, better, more beautiful, more quietly* are *comparative* adjectives and adverbs). Also *nc* adjective or adverb in this form. **comparatively** *adv.*

beyond compare much better than anything else of the same kind. *This view is beyond compare.*

by/in comparison (with) when compared (with).

compare notes give one's ideas on some subject to somebody and hear what his ideas are. (*informal*).

not to be compared with very much better or worse than. *His old car is not to be compared with my new one.*

compartment [kəm'pɑ:tmənt] *nc* part of a container of some kind, separated in some way from the rest of the container (e.g. the compartments of a railway train; a purse or a wallet often has a number of compartments).

compass ['kʌmpəs] *nc* **1.** instrument containing a magnetic needle which points to the north, used for showing directions. **2.** instrument for drawing circles. (Sometimes

compasses *pl* or **a pair of compasses**). **3.** space or area within certain limits (usu. in **within the compass of something** i.e. inside something. (*formal*)).

compassion [kəm'pæʃən] *nu* very strong feeling of love and pity, caused by the unhappiness or suffering of somebody else. **compassionate** [kəm'pæʃənit] *adj*. **compassionately** *adv*.

compatible [kəm'pætibl] *adj* able or suitable to go together. *Those two people are not compatible* i.e. they cannot be together in a friendly way. *His ideas are not compatible with mine*. (*opp* **incompatible**). **compatibility** [kəmpætə'biliti] *nu*.

compatriot [kəm'pætriət] *nc* person from the same country as somebody else.

compel [kəm'pel] *vt* make somebody do something by using force or authority. *I compelled him to come with me*. *past* **compelled**. see **compulsion**.

compendious [kəm'pendiəs] *adj* containing a lot of information but short.

compendium [kəm'pendiəm] *nc* book which gives a lot of information on various topics in a few words.

compensate ['kɔmpenseit] **1.** *vt* give payment of some kind to somebody who has suffered a loss or injury. *The government compensated the families of the men who were killed in the accident*. **2.** *vi* (often with **for**) be a payment of this kind. *I hope that this present will compensate for the trouble I have caused you*. **compensation** [kɔmpen'seiʃən] *nc/u*. **compensatory** ['kɔmpənseitəri] *adj*.

compete [kəm'pi:t] *vi* try to win or to gain something in a race, competition, examination etc. *Six runners competed in the last race*. *He was competing against/with his friends in the examination*.

competition [kɔmpi'tiʃən] **1.** *nu* act of competing. **2.** *nc* any occasion on which people compete.

competitive [kəm'petitiv] *adj* showing competition; decided by competition.

competitor [kəm'petitə*] *nc* person who competes.

competent ['kɔmpitənt] *adj* having the ability or power to do something. *He is competent to do the work*. (*opp* **incompetent**).

competence **1.** *nu* ability or power to do something. (*opp* **incompetence**). **2.** *nc* enough money or property to allow one to live modestly in comfort.

compile [kəm'pail] *vt* (esp. with reference to collecting material when writing a book) collect together and arrange in order. **compilation** [kɔmpi'leiʃən] *nc/u*. **compiler** *nc*.

complacent [kəm'pleisnt] *adj* pleased or satisfied with oneself (usu. in a foolish or annoying way). **complacence, complacency** *nu*.

complain [kəm'plein] *vi* **1.** say that something is wrong; say that one is not pleased with something. *He complained about the food in the hotel*. **2.** tell somebody that one is suffering from a disease or illness. *He complained of pains in the stomach*.

complaint *nc* **1.** statement that something is wrong. *He made a complaint to the manager*. **2.** disease or illness.

complement ['kɔmplimənt] *nc* **1.** anything which makes something complete. **2.** full number of officers and men on a ship. **3.** (grammar) noun or noun phrase following certain verbs, such as 'seem', 'be', 'become'. **complementary** [kɔmpli'mentəri] *adj*.

complementary colours any two colours which together account for all the shades of colour making up white (e.g. green and red, blue and orange etc).

Note: do not confuse *complement* with *compliment*.

complete [kəm'pli:t] *adj* **1.** with nothing missing; finished; not needing anything more. *The work is complete and so we can rest*. **2.** very great: *a complete surprise*. Also *vt* finish; do everything which needs to be done. *He completed the work*. **completion** *nu*. **completely** *adv*: *completely different*.

complex[1] ['kɔmpleks] *adj* made up of many different parts (and usu. difficult to understand). **complexity** [kəm'pleksiti] *nc/u*.

complex[2] ['kɔmpleks] *nc* **1.** anything consisting of many different parts (e.g. an institution consisting of many different buildings). **2.** condition of the mind, in which one has a large number of ideas and feelings which were caused by some event in the past, and which have a strong influence on one's behaviour. **3.** any strong feeling about or dislike for something. (*informal* in sense **3.**).

complexion [kəm'plekʃən] *nc* **1.** appearance of the skin of the face. **2.** general appearance or nature of some event.

compliant [kəm'plaiənt] *adj* ready to do what somebody else wants. **compliance** *nu*. see **comply**.

in compliance with because of what somebody has asked for: *in compliance with your wishes*. (*formal*).

complicate ['kɔmplikeit] *vt* make more difficult to do or understand, by adding something or by changing something; add another difficulty. **complication** [kɔmpli'keiʃən] *nc/u*.

complicated *adj* having many different parts and therefore difficult to do or understand.

complicity [kəm'plisiti] *nu* condition of joining with somebody else to do something wrong.

compliment ['kɔmplimənt] *nc* **1.** friendly statement that somebody is good in some way. *He paid Mary a compliment about her new hat* i.e. he said that he liked the hat. **2.** action or words showing that one admires somebody. **3.** (in *pl*) polite greeting (often a greeting sent to somebody who is not present). Also ['kɔmpliment] *vt*: *He complimented her on her new hat*.

complimentary [kɔmpli'mentəri] *adj* saying pleasant things about somebody. (*opp* **uncomplimentary**).

complimentary ticket free ticket to a play, film or other entertainment.

return the compliment (usu. with reference to something pleasant) do for somebody what he has done for oneself.

comply [kəm'plai] *vi* usu. **comply with someone's wishes** i.e. do what somebody wants one to do.

component [kəm'pounənt] *nc* one of the parts of which something is made up. *This machine has 300 different components*.

comport [kəm'pɔ:t] *vt* usu. in **comport oneself** i.e. behave. (*formal*).

compose [kəm'pouz] *vt/i* **1.** (often with reference to writing a book or poem, and esp. with reference to writing music) arrange parts so as to make something new. **2.** put type into a frame ready for printing. **3.** (usu. *passive*) make up. *The United Kingdom is composed of several different countries*. **4.** make calm: *compose*

oneself; compose one's thoughts.
composer *nc* person who writes music.
composed *adj* calm; under control.
composed of made up of.
composite ['kɔmpəzit] *adj* made up of several parts, each of which is complete.
composition [kɔmpə'ziʃən] **1.** *nc* piece of writing (esp. an essay written by somebody at school). **2.** *nc* piece of music. **3.** *nu* way in which something is made up of several parts; act of composing. **4.** *nu* art of writing music. **5.** *nc* manufactured substance, made up of several different substances. **6.** *nc* (in a legal sense) agreement which follows a quarrel or fight.
compositor [kəm'pɔzitə*] *nc* person who puts type together in a frame, ready for printing books, papers etc.
compost ['kɔmpɔst] *nu* mixture of rotting vegetation, used in a garden to improve the soil.
composure [kəm'pouʒə*] *nu* condition of being calm, having one's feelings and thoughts under control.
compound[1] ['kɔmpaund] *nc* **1.** anything having several different parts (esp. a substance made up of several different substances). **2.** (chemistry) substance made by the combination of two or more elements. Also *adj*.
'compound 'interest interest which is paid on both capital and interest earned formerly.
compound[2] [kəm'paund] *vt/i* mix two or more things to make one new thing; make a compound of.
compound[3] ['kɔmpaund] *nc* (usu. with reference to Asia and Africa only) enclosed land round a building belonging to one person or institution.
comprehend [kɔmpri'hend] *vt* **1.** understand the meaning of. **2.** include or contain.
comprehensible *adj* able to be understood. (*opp* **incomprehensible**).
comprehension *nu* act of understanding.
comprehensive *adj* including or containing a lot of everything.
comprehensive school type of secondary school to which all the children living in a particular area may go, whatever their level of ability.
compress[1] [kəm'pres] *vt* make smaller by pressing or pushing together. **compression** *nu*.
compressor *nc* machine which compresses air or other gases.
compressed air air which has been put into some container under pressure.
compress[2] ['kɔmpres] *nc* piece of wet cloth which is tied tightly on a wound or injury to stop bleeding, reduce swelling or relieve pain.
comprise [kəm'praiz] *vt* be made up of. *The village comprises two hundred houses, three shops, a garage and a school.*
compromise ['kɔmprəmaiz] **1.** *vi* reach an agreement after a quarrel or disagreement, by each side agreeing to have less than it had first asked for. **2.** *vt* make people think that somebody has done wrong. *John compromised his friends by stealing the money* i.e. people thought that his friends had helped him to steal the money, although they had not. Also *nc* agreement reached by each side agreeing to have less than it had at first asked for.
compromising *adj* causing people to be compromised (in sense **2.**).
comptroller [kən'troulə*] *nc* government official whose work is to inspect the record of money received and spent by other government departments (usu. in **comptroller of accounts**).
compulsion [kəm'pʌlʃən] *nu* act of making somebody do something by force.
compulsory [kəm'pʌlsəri] *adj*: *Voting is compulsory in some countries* i.e. there is a law saying that people must vote. **compulsorily** *adv*. see **compel**.
compulsive [kəm'pʌlsiv] *adj* caused by something in oneself which one cannot control. *He is a compulsive liar* i.e. he cannot stop himself from telling lies. **compulsively** *adv*.
under compulsion because of the use of force by somebody; not willingly.
compunction [kəm'pʌŋkʃən] *nu* feeling of doubt about whether one is doing wrong. *He killed her without any compunction.*
compute [kəm'pju:t] *vt/i* find out the answer by using arithmetic. **computation** [kɔmpju'teiʃən] *nc/u*.
computer *nc* electronic device which is capable of carrying out very complex calculations on the basis of the coded information which is put into it. Also *adj*.
comrade ['kɔmrid] *nc* **1.** person with whom one is friendly, and with whom one works. **2.** title used instead of *Mr* or *Sir* (esp. in communist countries).
comradeship *nu* friendship between comrades; state of being a comrade.
comrade-in-arms comrade with whom one has been in the army (esp. during a war).
con[1] [kɔn] *nc* usu. in **pros and cons** i.e. arguments for and against.
con[2] [kɔn] *vt* study carefully in order to learn. *past* **conned** (*o.f.*).
con[3] [kɔn] *vt* cheat by winning someone's confidence. (*informal*).
'con man one who does this (*informal*). see **confidence trick**.
concatenate [kɔn'kætineit] *vt* (usu. with reference to events or arguments, not usu. to objects) join one thing to another, so that each thing leads to the next. **concatenation** [kɔnkæti'neiʃən] *nc/u*.
concave ['kɔn'keiv] *adj* (usu. with reference to lenses) shaped like part of the inside of a circle or sphere.
conceal [kən'si:l] *vt* keep hidden or secret. *He could not conceal the crime any longer.* **concealment** *nu*.
concede [kən'si:d] *vt* **1.** agree that something is true (esp. something said by a person with whom one is arguing or disagreeing). **2.** give something to one's opponent or enemy after disagreeing, fighting etc. *After the war the enemy had to concede some territory.*
concession [kən'seʃən] **1.** *nu* act of conceding. **2.** *nc* something gained from somebody in this way. **3.** *nc* land given by a government to a business firm for a particular purpose.
concede victory say that the other person has won (usu. in a game or an election, and before the end of the game or before the official result of the election is known).
conceit [kən'si:t] *nu* feeling of pleasure because one thinks that one is very good or very clever, when in fact one is not as good or clever as one thinks. **conceited** *adj*. **conceitedly** *adv*.
conceive [kən'si:v] **1.** *vt* think or imagine; have an idea of. *He very quickly conceived*

a new plan. **2.** *vi* (with reference to a woman) become pregnant. **3.** *vt* cause to be conceived: *conceive a child.*

conceivable *adj* of what can be thought of or imagined. (*opp* **inconceivable**).

conception [kən'sepʃən] **1.** *nc/u* idea or thought. **2.** *nu* process of becoming pregnant.

concentrate ['kɔnsəntreit] **1.** *vt/i* come or bring together in a small area. **2.** *vt/i* study carefully; give careful attention to. *He has concentrated on his work this year. You must try to concentrate.* **3.** *vt* make a liquid less in amount so that it is stronger.

concentration [kɔnsən'treiʃən] **1.** *nu* act of coming or bringing together. **2.** *nc* something collected together. **3.** *nu* careful study or attention. **4.** *nu* strength of a liquid or solution.

concen'tration camp (esp. with reference to prisons in Germany during the rule of the Nazis) prison surrounded by barbed wire, where political prisoners are kept.

concentric [kɔn'sentrik] *adj* having the same centre: *concentric circles.*

concept ['kɔnsept] *nc* idea of something. *A small baby has no concept of right and wrong* i.e. these ideas have no meaning for a small baby. **conceptual** [kən'septjuəl] *adj.*

conceptualize [kɔn'septjuəlaiz] *vt/i* form a concept.

conception [kən'sepʃən] *nc/u* see **conceive.**

concern[1] [kən'sə:n] *vt* have connection with; be of importance to. *This matter concerns all of us.*

concerned *adj* **1.** having a connection with. *Are you concerned with this matter?* **2.** worried or troubled. *Mrs Smith was very concerned when I was ill last year.*

Note: concerned about/for means worried or anxious; *concerned in/with* means having a connection with or taking part in.

concerning *prep* having a connection with: *questions concerning the future.*

concern oneself in/with take an interest in. *He did not concern himself with politics.*

concern[2] [kən'sə:n] **1.** *nu* what has connection with something or is of importance to something. *This matter is the concern of all of us.* **2.** *nu* feeling of worry or trouble. *Mrs Smith felt great concern when I was ill last year.* **3.** *nc* business, shop, factory etc.

of concern of importance; causing one to worry. *This question is of great concern to all of us.*

a going concern a business which is in existence and which is earning money.

concert ['kɔnsət] *nc* entertainment at which a number of pieces of music are played or sung.

concerted [kən'sə:tid] *adj* planned by those taking part; carried out together or at the same time (usu. **a concerted attack** or **concerted action**).

in concert together; at the same time.

concertina [kɔnsə'ti:nə] *nc* type of musical instrument.

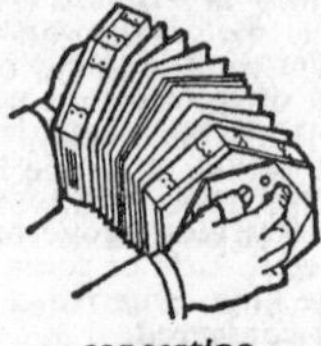

concertina

concerto [kən'tʃə:tou] *nc* piece of music written for a solo instrument or solo instruments and an orchestra. *pl* **concertos.**

concession [kən'seʃən] *nc/u* see **concede.**

conch [kɔntʃ] *nc* type of sea shell from a large sea snail; the animal itself.

conciliate [kən'silieit] *vt* make somebody stop being angry by doing or saying something to please him. **conciliation** [kənsili'eiʃən] *nu.*

conciliatory [kən'siliətri] *adj* intended to conciliate: *a conciliatory letter.*

concise [kən'sais] *adj* saying a lot in few words: *a very concise letter; a concise speaker.* **concisely** *adv.* **conciseness, concision** [kən'siʒən] *nu.*

conclave ['kɔnkleiv] *nc* (esp. with reference to a meeting of cardinals to elect a new pope) meeting to which the public is not admitted.

conclude [kən'klu:d] **1.** *vt/i* finish; end. *He concluded his speech with some words by Shakespeare. The meeting concluded after three hours.* **2.** *vt* make an agreement: *conclude a treaty/an agreement.* **3.** *vi* come to a decision after thinking about a topic or after hearing what somebody says. *He concluded that Jones had stolen the money.*

conclusion *nc* **1.** end. **2.** reaching an agreement. **3.** opinion reached after thought.

conclusive allowing one to decide: *conclusive proof.* (*opp* **inconclusive**). **conclusively** *adv.*

in conclusion to end with (often said near the end of a speech).

draw a conclusion decide after considering the evidence.

concoct [kən'kɔkt] *vt* **1.** make food or drink by mixing together (usu. with reference to making a new food or drink in this way, and often with the suggestion that the food or drink is not very nice). **2.** make up a story or excuse which is not true. **concoction** *nc/u.*

concomitant [kən'kɔmitnt] *adj* found with something else: *war and all the concomitant unhappiness.* Also *nc* something which is found with something else.

concord ['kɔŋkɔ:d] *nc/u* agreement and friendliness. *There was concord between the two countries.*

concordant [kən'kɔ:dnt] *adj* agreeing.

concordance [kən'kɔ:dns] **1.** *nu* agreement. (*formal*). **2.** *nc* book containing an alphabetical list of the important words in some other book: *a concordance to/of the Bible.*

concourse ['kɔŋkɔ:s] *nc* **1.** large gathering of people. **2.** open space for the use of the public at a railway station or airport.

concrete[1] ['kɔŋkri:t] *nu* hard substance made of sand and cement, used for building. Also *vt/i* cover with concrete.

concrete[2] ['kɔŋkri:t] *adj* real, not existing merely as an idea or hope.

concrete noun (grammar) noun which refers to something which can be seen, felt, tasted, heard etc (e.g. *house, fire, sugar, aeroplane*) (*opp* **abstract noun**).

concubine ['kɔŋkjubain] *nc* woman who lives with a man as his wife, without being married to him (*o.f.*).

concur [kən'kə:*] *vi* **1.** have the same opinion as somebody else. *John and I concurred. I concurred with John.* **2.** happen at the same time. *past* **concurred. concurrence** *nu.*

concurrent [kən'kʌrnt] *adj* happening at the same time. **concurrently** *adv.*

concussion [kɔn'kʌʃən] *nc/u* **1.** injury to the

brain caused by a blow or fall. **2.** strong and sudden blow. **concussed** *adj.*

condemn [kən'dem] *vt* **1.** (with reference to judges) say officially after a trial that somebody must be punished. *The judge condemned him to five years in prison.* **2.** say that something is wrong. *Most people condemn war.* **3.** say officially that something is not fit to use and must be destroyed.
condemnation [kɔndem'neiʃən] *nu.*

condense [kən'dens] *vt/i* **1.** become or make thicker or more dense. **2.** change from a gas into a liquid. **3.** put into fewer words. *He condensed his essay from 3000 to 1500 words.*
condenser *nc* piece of apparatus for storing a charge of electricity.
condensation [kɔnden'seiʃən] *nu* **1.** act of condensing. **2.** drops of liquid formed when a gas condenses.
condensed milk very thick type of (often sweetened) milk, made by removing some of the water from the milk.

condescend [kɔndi'send] *vi* act in a friendly way to somebody whom one considers inferior to oneself (often in a way which is unpleasant for the person who is considered inferior). **condescending** *adj.* **condescendingly** *adv.* **condescension** *nu.*

condiment ['kɔndimənt] *nc* substance such as salt or pepper, which is added to food at the table.

condition[1] [kən'diʃən] **1.** *nu* state which a person/thing is in. *This car is in good condition* i.e. nothing is broken or damaged. *The Prime Minister asked for a report on the condition of the national economy.* **2.** *nc* something which is necessary for something else to happen. *I shall lend you this money; my only condition is that you spend it carefully* i.e. I shall lend you the money if you promise to spend it carefully.

condition[2] [kən'diʃən] *vt* **1.** put into a state of good health by exercise. **2.** change or form the behaviour of a person or animal; train to act in a certain way. **3.** (usu. *passive*) be a condition of. *The success of the government's school building programme is conditioned by the money available* i.e. the government can build schools only if it has enough money to do so.
conditional *adj* depending on something. *He made a conditional promise to help me* i.e. he promised to help me if something else happened. *The offer of the money was conditional on my accepting within three days* i.e. I could have the money if I took it within three days. (*opp* **unconditional**).
conditionally *adv.*
conditional clause (grammar) clause containing a condition (and usu. introduced by 'if' or 'unless').
in condition fit. *The athlete was in condition.*
in no condition not healthy enough to; not able to. *He is in no condition to go for a long walk in the mountains.*
on condition that if something else happens or is promised. *I shall lend you this money on condition that you give it back in one month.*
out of condition in poor health (usu. because one needs exercise).

condolence [kən'doulns] *nc* (often *pl*) words or action showing that one is sorry for somebody who has suffered a loss or misfortune. *She received many condolences when her father died.*
condole *vi*: *condole with someone who is unhappy.*

condone [kən'doun] *vt* forgive; allow some wrong action to go unpunished or be forgotten. *I cannot condone the damage you have caused.*

condor ['kɔndɔː*] *nc* large bird found in South America, which eats the flesh of dead animals.

conducive [kən'djuːsiv] *adj* likely to result in or lead to. *This behaviour is not conducive to hard work* i.e. you or other people cannot work hard if you behave like that. *Exercise is conducive to good health.*

conduct[1] ['kɔndəkt] *nu* **1.** way of behaving. *The conduct of all the pupils was very good* i.e. they all behaved well. **2.** way in which something is organized: *the conduct of a government department.*

conduct[2] [kən'dʌkt] *vt/i* **1.** lead or guide. *He conducted the members of the audience to their seats.* **2.** be in charge of; control and organize. *The Minister of Education conducted the business of his department very successfully.* **3.** be the person in charge of an orchestra or choir at a concert. **4.** carry heat or electricity. *Copper wire conducts electricity.*
conduction *nu* process of conducting heat or electricity.
conductor *nc* **1.** person in charge of an orchestra or choir at a concert. **2.** person who sells tickets on a bus. (Also **conductress** when a woman). **3.** (*US*) person in charge of a train. (*Brit* **guard**). **4.** substance which conducts heat, electricity or sound.
conduct oneself behave. *She conducted herself very badly.*

conduit ['kɔndit] *nc* **1.** large pipe for carrying water. **2.** pipe used to protect electrical wires.

cone [koun] *nc* **1.** solid object shaped as in the illustration. **2.** anything shaped like this (e.g. the *cone of a volcano* is the top of a volcano; an *ice cream cone* is a kind of biscuit, shaped like a cone, for holding ice cream). **3.** fruit of certain trees (e.g. pine or fir). **conical** ['kɔnikl] *adj.*

cones

confectionery [kən'fekʃənəri] *nu* **1.** sweets and chocolates. **2.** cakes.
confectioner *nc* person who makes or sells sweets and chocolates or cakes.

confederate [kən'fedərit] *nc* person joined with others for some special purpose (often to do something wrong). Also *adj.* Also [kən'fedəreit] *vt/i* bring together in this way. **confederation** [kənfedə'reiʃən] *nc/u.*
confederacy [kən'fedərəsi] *nc* number of people, institutions, countries etc joined together for some purpose.

confer [kən'fəː*] **1.** *vi* talk together (esp. on a matter of business, government etc). **2.** *vt* give a medal, title or some other official reward. *The king conferred a medal on the soldier.* *past* **conferred.**

conference ['kɔnfərns] *nc* meeting to discuss some matter of business, government etc. **in conference** at an official discussion. *You can't speak to Mr Smith now because he's in conference.*

confess [kən'fes] *vt/i* **1.** tell people that one has done wrong; admit. *He confessed his crime to the police. I must confess that I was happy when she left.* **2.** (in the Roman Catholic Church, and some other churches) tell a priest that one has done something wrong.
confession [kən'feʃən] *nc/u* act of confessing.
confessor *nc* priest who hears confessions.
confessional [kən'feʃənl] *nc* place in a church where a priest hears confessions. Also *adj* of or like a confession.
confession of faith official statement of the religious beliefs of a church or person.

confetti [kən'feti] *nu* small pieces of coloured paper, thrown about at weddings and other festivals.

confide [kən'faid] *vt/i* **1.** trust someone with a secret. *He confided the story to his brother.* **2.** give a duty or piece of work to. *I shall confide this duty to you.* **3.** trust; have faith in. *You can confide in the police* i.e. you can be sure that the police will help you if you need help.
confidant(e) [kɔnfi'dænt] *nc* person who is told somebody's secrets. (**confidant** refers to a man, and **confidante** to a woman).
confidence ['kɔnfidns] **1.** *nc* secret; information confided to somebody. **2.** *nu* trust or strong belief, lack of fear. *I have confidence in you* i.e. I am sure that you will do right, succeed, win etc.
confident ['kɔnfidnt] *adj* sure (often of one's own abilities). **confidently** *adv.*
confidential [kɔnfi'denʃl] *adj* **1.** secret; not to be told or shown to other people. *This information is confidential.* **2.** (with reference to a person) given secrets as part of one's work: *a confidential secretary/agent.* **confidentially** *adv.*
confiding *adj* willing to tell secrets or to trust somebody. **confidingly** *adv.*
'**confidence trick** (*Brit*) dishonest trick in which a criminal gets money by persuading somebody to trust him. (*US* **confidence game**). see **con**[3].
in confidence as a secret. *I am telling you this in confidence* i.e. you must not tell other people.

configuration [kənfigju'reiʃən] *nc* (esp. with reference to geography) general shape.

confine[1] [kən'fain] *vt* keep shut in; keep within certain limits. *The soldiers were confined to the camp for three weeks* i.e. they were not allowed to leave the camp.
confined *pred adj* **1.** kept inside. **2.** giving birth to a baby. *She expects to be confined at the end of May* (*o.f.* in sense **2.**).
confinement *nu* **1.** act of keeping or staying inside. **2.** act of giving birth to a baby (*o.f.*).
confine oneself to 1. stay inside. **2.** speak only about. *I shall confine myself to the subject of geography* i.e. I shall not speak about other topics.

confine[2] ['kɔnfain] *nc* (usu. *pl*) limit; boundary; frontier. *He passed his life within the confines of his own country.*

confirm [kən'fə:m] *vt* **1.** say officially that a story or rumour is true. *The Prime Minister confirmed that he would visit France next month.* **2.** make stronger an opinion, idea, decision etc. *What you say confirms my opinion* i.e. you make me feel more certain that I am right. **3.** admit to full membership of some Christian churches. **4.** give official agreement to some arrangement which already exists. *The king confirmed me in my possession of the land.* **confirmation** [kɔnfə'meiʃən] *nu.*

confiscate ['kɔnfiskeit] *vt* officially take something away from somebody. *The teacher confiscated the book which the boy was reading in class. The government confiscated the land.* **confiscation** [kɔnfis'keiʃən] *nu.*

conflagration [kɔnflə'greiʃən] *nc* large fire which destroys buildings, trees etc.

conflict[1] ['kɔnflikt] *nc* fight; struggle; disagreement.
in conflict with fighting, struggling, or disagreeing with.

conflict[2] [kən'flikt] *vi* (often with **with**) disagree; fight.

confluence ['kɔnfluəns] *nc/u* flowing together of rivers; place where rivers join together. **confluent** *adj.*

conflux ['kɔnflʌks] *nc/u* confluence.

conform [kən'fɔ:m] *vt/i* behave, cause to behave, in the same way as others. *He conformed to the rules of the club* i.e. he did what the rules said he must do. **conformist** *nc.* **conformity** *nu.*
conformable *adj* willing to conform. **conformably** *adv.*

confound [kən'faund] *vt* **1.** cause great surprise to. **2.** cause confusion to; disturb: *be confounded by something. The news has confounded our plans* i.e. we shall not be able to carry out our plans because of the news. **3.** think that something is something else. (rather *o.f.* – use **confuse**). **4.** (usu. *imperative*) damn; curse: *confound you!* i.e. I am angry with you etc. (*informal* and rather *o.f.* in sense **4.**).
confounded *adj* damned; annoying; unpleasant etc. (*informal* and rather *o.f.*). **confoundedly** *adv.*

confraternity [kɔnfrə'tə:niti] *nc* group of men doing the same work or joined together for some purpose. (*formal*).

confront [kən'frʌnt] *vt* **1.** meet face to face. *He decided to confront his enemies.* **2.** place before. *He confronted them with the evidence of the crime.* **confrontation** [kɔnfrn'teiʃən] *nc/u.*

confuse [kən'fju:z] *vt* **1.** make it difficult for somebody to think clearly. *When I arrived in London, the crowds of people and the traffic confused me.* **2.** think that something is something else. *I confused you with your brother* i.e. I thought that you were your brother, or that your brother was you. *I confused the two brothers.* **confused** *adj.*
confusion [kən'fju:ʒən] *nc/u.*
throw something into confusion make something disturbed or confused. *The news threw our plans into confusion.*

confute [kən'fju:t] *vt* show by argument and proof that somebody's idea or opinion is wrong. **confutation** [kɔnfju:'teiʃən] *nu.*

conga ['kɔŋgə] *nc* lively Latin-American dance.

congeal [kən'dʒi:l] *vt/i* change from liquid to solid (esp. because of cold).

congenial [kən'dʒi:niəl] *adj* **1.** having the same interests and ideas, and therefore friendly: *a congenial companion.* **2.** pleasant and suitable for oneself: *congenial surroundings.* (*opp* **uncongenial**). **congenially** *adv.*

congenital [kən'dʒenitl] *adj* (with reference to diseases) present from the time of one's birth (usu. passed to one from one's parents). **congenitally** *adv*.

conger ['kɔŋgə*] *nc* large type of sea fish, which looks like a snake, eaten as a food. (Also **conger eel**).

congest [kən'dʒest] *vt* fill too full. **congested** *adj*.

congestion [kən'dʒestʃən] *nu*: *traffic congestion* i.e. too many cars etc on the roads.

conglomerate [kən'glɔmərit] *adj* made up of many different things stuck together without any order. Also *nu* type of rock formed in this way. Also [kən'glɔməreit] *vt* put together in this way.

conglomeration [kənglɔmə'reiʃən] *nc* anything made up of things put together without order.

congratulate [kən'grætjuleit] *vt* tell somebody that one is pleased because he has been successful or fortunate in some way. *I congratulated my friend on the birth of his new son*. **congratulation** [kəngrætju'leiʃən] *nc* (usu. *pl*). **congratulatory** [kən'grætjulətəri] *adj*.

congratulate oneself on think that one is fortunate in some way. *I congratulated myself on finishing the work so quickly*.

congregate ['kɔŋgrigeit] *vt/i* come or bring together. *The people congregated in the town square*.

congregation [kɔŋgri'geiʃən] *nc* people present (or usu. present) at a church service. **congregational** [kɔŋgri'geiʃənl] *adj*.

Congregational *adj* having reference to a group of Protestant churches in which each local church organizes its own business.

Congregationalist *nc* member of one of these churches.

congress ['kɔŋgres] *nc* **1.** special meeting of experts on some particular topic. **2.** (**Congress**) (*USA* and some other republics) lower legislative chamber of government. **3.** name of some political parties: *the African National Congress*. **congressional** [kən'greʃənl] *adj*.

Congressman member of the American Congress.

congruent ['kɔŋgruənt] *adj* (geometry) having exactly the same shape: *congruent triangles*. **congruence** *nu*.

conical ['kɔnikl] *adj* see **cone**.

conifer ['kɔnifə*] *nc* type of tree which bears cones (e.g. fir or pine). **coniferous** [kə'nifərəs] *adj*.

conjecture [kən'dʒektʃə*] *vt/i* guess; come to an opinion about some fact without having enough information. Also *nc* guess made in this way. **conjectural** *adj*.

conjugal ['kɔndʒugl] *adj* with reference to marriage.

conjugate ['kɔndʒugeit] *vt/i* (grammar) give the various forms of a verb (esp. in learning Latin or Greek).

conjugation [kɔndʒu'geiʃən] *nc/u* act of conjugating; way in which a verb is conjugated.

conjunction [kən'dʒʌŋkʃən] **1.** *nc* (grammar) word like 'and', 'but', 'or' which joins clauses, phrases, words etc together. **2.** *nc/u* act of joining things together. **conjunctive** [kən'dʒʌŋktiv] *adj*.

in conjunction (with) together (with). *I did the work in conjunction with three other people. We did the work in conjunction*.

conjunctivitis [kəndʒʌŋkti'vaitis] *nu* illness in which the eyes and eyelids become sore and inflamed.

conjure ['kʌndʒə*] **1.** *vi* do tricks which seem to be magic, as a form of entertainment. **2.** *vt* make something appear as if by magic. *He conjured a fish out of my pocket*.

conjurer, conjuror *nc* person who provides entertainment by conjuring.

conjuring *nu* tricks which seem to be magic, done as entertainment.

conjure up 1. make a ghost or spirit appear. *He conjured up the ghost of his grandfather*. **2.** see, cause to see, very clearly in the imagination or memory. *This book conjures up a vivid picture of London*.

conk [kɔŋk] *nc* nose. (*informal*).

conk out (of car etc) stall. (*informal*).

connect [kə'nekt] *vt/i* **1.** (often with **together** or **up**) join; fasten. *The radio will not work unless you connect these two wires together. Connect this wire with/to that one*. (*opp* **disconnect**). **2.** think of together. *I always connect little girls with dolls and dolls' prams* i.e. these are the things which I think of when I think of little girls. **3.** (with **with**) (with reference to buses, trains, aeroplanes etc) arrive at a place in time for one to catch another bus, train, aeroplane etc. *This train connects with one at Birmingham* i.e. this train will get to Birmingham in time for you to catch the other train.

connection, connexion *nc* **1.** join; fastening. *I can't see any connection between these two wires*. **2.** relation. *Scientists have shown that there is a connection between cigarette smoking and certain diseases*. **3.** train, bus, aeroplane etc which meets another in time for one to change from one to the other. **4.** person to whom one is related by marriage. **5.** person whom one knows in business etc and also might be of help to one.

in connection with with reference to; on the subject of. *He asked me many questions in connection with life in Britain*.

in this connection with reference to the subject which we are talking about.

conning ['kɔniŋ] *adj* in **conning tower** i.e. part of a submarine by which one enters, and from which one can look at other ships when the submarine is under water.

connive [kə'naiv] *vi* (with **at**) allow somebody to do something wrong, without trying to stop him: *connive at a crime*. **connivance** *nu*.

connoisseur [kɔni'səː*] *nc* person with a great knowledge of some subject connected with art: *a connoisseur of painting*.

connote [kə'nout] *vt* (with reference to words) suggest as an extra part of the meaning (e.g. the meanings of 'beast' and 'animal' are almost the same, but 'beast' connotes ideas like 'wild', 'savage' etc).

connotation [kɔnə'teiʃən] *nc* extra meaning of a word; meaning which is connoted. **connotative** ['kɔnəteitiv] *adj*.

connubial [kə'njuːbiəl] *adj* with reference to marriage.

conquer ['kɔŋkə*] *vt/i* **1.** defeat by fighting; take land after fighting. *Julius Caesar conquered the Gauls. The Mongols conquered India*. **2.** end by force or determination. *I conquered my dislike for mathematics* i.e. I made myself like mathematics.

conqueror *nc* person who conquers a country.

conquest ['kɔŋkwest] *nc/u* something conquered; act of conquering.

conquered *adj*. (*opp* **unconquered**).

consanguinity [kɔnsæŋ'gwiniti] *nu* family relationship by blood not by marriage. **consanguineous** *adj*.

conscience ['kɔnʃəns] *nc/u* feeling within oneself which tells one the difference between right and wrong.
'conscience money money paid by somebody to relieve his conscience.
'conscience-stricken *adj* having a feeling of unhappiness because one knows that one has done wrong.
(with) a clear conscience not troubled by feelings of unhappiness because one has done wrong.
a guilty conscience feeling of unhappiness because one knows that one has done wrong.
have something on one's conscience have a feeling of unhappiness because one knows that one has done something wrong.

conscientious [kɔnʃi'enʃəs] *adj* taking care to do one's work or duty as well as possible.
conscientiously *adv.*
conscientious objector person who refuses to serve in an army or fight in a war because he feels it is wrong to do so.

conscious ['kɔnʃəs] *adj* **1.** not asleep and knowing clearly what is happening around one. *Although he had been hit on the head in the accident, he was still conscious.* **2.** taking note of what is happening. *I wasn't conscious of being impolite to him* i.e. although I may have been impolite, I did not know that I was being so. **3.** with one's full knowledge, intended and understood by oneself: *a conscious act.* (*opp* **unconscious**).
consciously *adv.* **consciousness** *nu.*
self-'conscious *adj* shy; embarrassed; taking note of everything that one does, and so unable to act easily and happily.
self-consciousness *nu.*
the sub'conscious *nu* part of the mind in which there are feelings and ideas which we do not know about. **subconscious** *adj.* **subconsciously** *adv.*

conscript ['kɔnskript] *nc* person made to serve in the armed forces by law. Also [kən'skript] *vt* make people serve in the armed forces by law. **conscription** [kən'skripʃən] *nu.*

consecrate ['kɔnsikreit] *vt* **1.** carry out a ceremony which marks someone/something as special for religious purposes: *consecrate a bishop/a new church.* **2.** keep something for a special purpose. **consecrated** *adj.*
consecration [kɔnsi'kreiʃən] *nu.*

consecutive [kən'sekjutiv] *adj* following one after another: *three consecutive days* (e.g. Monday, Tuesday, Wednesday). **consecutively** *adv.*

consensus [kən'sensəs] *nc* general agreement or feeling of a number of people.

consent [kən'sent] *vi* (often with **to**) say that one will allow something to happen; agree. *He has consented to the plan. He consented to go.* Also *nc.*
age of consent age at which the law allows one to marry, have sexual intercourse.

consequence ['kɔnsikwəns] *nc* what follows or is caused by something. *Do you know what the consequences of your action will be?* i.e. what will happen if you do this. **consequent** *adj.* **consequently** *adv.*
consequential [kɔnsi'kwenʃəl] *adj* **1.** following as a consequence. **2.** thinking oneself very important. **consequentially** *adv.*
in consequence (of) as a result (of).
of consequence very important. *This matter is of great consequence to all of us. Don't worry, it's of no consequence* i.e. it is not important.

conservative [kən'sə:vətiv] *adj* **1.** liking things as they are now; not liking change. **2.** careful; not willing to take chances (esp. in business or politics). Also *nc* person like this. **conservatism** *nu.*
Conservative *nc* member of the Conservative Party. Also *adj.*
Conservatism *nu* beliefs of the Conservative Party.

conservatoire [kən'sə:vətwɑ:*] *nc* school or college for advanced training in music and singing.

conservatory [kən'sə:vətri] *nc* **1.** room or building (usu. attached to a house) with glass walls, in which plants are kept. **2.** see **conservatoire.**

conserve[1] [kən'sə:v] *vt* save from loss or damage; keep to be used when needed. *We must conserve the natural resources of the country* i.e. we must not waste things such as soil, rivers, forests, coal, oil etc.
conservation [kɔnsə'veiʃən] *nu.* **conservationist** *nc.*
conservancy [kən'sə:vənsi] *nu* (esp. with reference to rivers and forests) act of conserving; people who do this.

conserve[2] [kən'sə:v] *nc* jam; fruit and sugar boiled and made into a jelly-like form (*o.f.* – use **jam**).

consider [kən'sidə*] *vt/i* **1.** think about. *I have considered your request.* **2.** have as an opinion. *I consider that you are wrong.* **3.** think about what will be best or most helpful for other people. *You should consider other people before you behave like that.*
considerable *adj* very large; very great: *a considerable amount of money.*
considerably *adv*: *He has improved considerably.*
considerate [kən'sidərit] *adj* thinking of what will be best or most helpful for other people: *a considerate person/action.* (*opp* **inconsiderate**).
consideration [kənsidə'reiʃən] **1.** *nu* act of considering. **2.** *nc* something which one should think about. *That is an important consideration* i.e. that is an important point to think about. **3.** *nu* thought for other people. *That boy shows no consideration for other people.* **4.** *nc* money given to somebody as a reward for doing a special piece of work. *He is willing to do the job for a small consideration.*
considering *prep* if one thinks of or remembers. *That child walks very well considering that he is only fourteen months old. Considering the distance, he arrived very quickly.*
in consideration of **1.** because of. **2.** as a payment or reward for.
under consideration being officially thought about. *The plan is under consideration by the Minister of Education.*
take into consideration think about when making plans or arrangements. *If you are planning a holiday in Britain, you should take the weather into consideration.*
all things considered when one considers all the facts or all the information.

consign [kən'sain] *vt* **1.** officially give to. **2.** send goods by some means of transport.
consignment *nc* amount of goods sent or to be sent; act of consigning.
consignee [kɔnsai'ni:] *nc* person to whom goods are consigned.

consist [kən'sist] *vi* (with **of**) be made up of. *This soup consists of tomatoes, meat and peas.*
consistence, consistency *nu* **1.** act of always behaving or thinking in the same way. **2.**

degree to which a liquid is firm or solid. (Usu. **consistency**).
consistent *adj* always acting or thinking in the same way; not easily changing. (*opp* **inconsistent**). **consistently** *adv*.
consistent with in agreement with. *What you say is not consistent with what you do* i.e. you say one thing and do something else.

console[1] [kən'soul] *vt* try to make somebody more happy when he has suffered some loss or misfortune. **consoling** *adj*. **consolation** [kɔnsə'leiʃən] *nc/u*.
consolable *adj* willing or able to be consoled. (*opp* **inconsolable**).
consolatory [kən'sɔlətəri] *adj* intended to console.
conso'lation prize prize given to somebody who has not won a contest or competition.

console[2] ['kɔnsoul] *nc* **1.** table containing switches, microphones etc at which a teacher sits in a language laboratory; any similar controlling arrangement. **2.** part of an organ containing keyboards etc.

consolidate [kən'sɔlideit] *vt/i* become or make stronger or more firm. *The army consolidated the position which they had captured* i.e. they made it more difficult for the enemy to attack the position.
consolidation [kənsɔli'deiʃən] *nu*.

consols [kən'sɔlz] *npl* money lent by people to the British Government.

consommé [kən'sɔmei] *nu* thin clear soup made from meat, fish etc.

consonant[1] ['kɔnsənənt] *nc* **1.** sound which is not a vowel; sound in which the breath is stopped in the mouth or throat in some way. **2.** letter or symbol which indicates this type of sound. (The letters b, d etc are consonants). **consonantal** [kɔnsə'næntl] *adj*.

consonant[2] ['kɔnsənənt] *adj* in agreement with. (*formal*).

consort[1] ['kɔnsɔːt] *nc* **1.** husband or wife of a queen or king. **2.** any husband or wife. (*formal* in sense **2.**).

consort[2] [kən'sɔːt] *vi* (with **with**) **1.** be often in the company of: *consort with criminals*. **2.** be in agreement with. (*formal* in sense **2.**).

consortium [kən'sɔːtiəm] *nc* group of people in business who have come together for some special purpose. *pl* **consortiums** or **consortia** [kən'sɔːtiə].

conspectus [kən'spektəs] *nc* **1.** general view over a wide area. **2.** summary of a large number of ideas.

conspicuous [kən'spikjuəs] *adj* easily seen. (*opp* **inconspicuous**). **conspicuously** *adv*. **conspicuousness** *nu*.

conspire [kən'spaiə*] *vi* **1.** make plans with others (esp. to do something wrong). **2.** act together to bring out some result.
conspirator [kən'spirətə*] *nc* person who makes plans to do something wrong.
conspiracy [kən'spirəsi] **1.** *nc* secret plan to do wrong. **2.** *nu* act of conspiring.
conspiratorial [kənspirə'tɔːriəl] *adj*.

constable ['kʌnstəbl] *nc* policeman of the lowest rank.
constabulary [kən'stæbjuləri] *nc* police force. *pl* **constabularies** (*o.f.* or *formal* – use **police force**).
chief constable head of a police force.

constant ['kɔnstnt] *adj* not changing; not stopping: *constant noise; constant friend*. Also *nc*. **constantly** *adv*. **constancy** *nu*.

constellation [kɔnstə'leiʃən] *nc* **1.** group of stars having a name. **2.** group of clever people.

consternation [kɔnstə'neiʃən] *nu* great surprise and alarm or unhappiness.

constipation [kɔnsti'peiʃən] *nu* difficulty in passing waste matter out of the body.
constipate ['kɔnstipeit] *vt* cause one to have this difficulty.
constipated ['kɔnstipeitəd] *adj*.

constituency [kən'stitjuənsi] *nc* **1.** area which is represented by a member of the House of Commons. **2.** the people living in that area.

constituent[1] [kən'stitjuənt] *nc* **1.** forming part of a whole thing. *Oxygen and nitrogen are two important constituents of the air*. **2.** person having the right to vote in an election in a particular area.

constituent[2] [kən'stitjuənt] *adj* **1.** forming part of a whole thing. **2.** having the power to make laws: *a constituent assembly*.

constitute ['kɔnstitjuːt] *vt* **1.** be the same as. *The behaviour of that country constitutes an act of aggression against her neighbours*. **2.** make up; be the parts of. *England, Wales, Scotland, Northern Ireland and some smaller islands constitute the United Kingdom*. **3.** appoint somebody to an office or an official position.

constitution [kɔnsti'tjuːʃən] *nc* **1.** laws and systems of government of a country, society etc; document containing these. **2.** general health of somebody. *He has a very strong constitution*. **3.** nature of anything.
constitutional *adj*. (*opp* **unconstitutional** in sense **1.**). **constitutionally** *adv*.
a constitutional a short walk taken for exercise. (*informal*).
constitutional monarch/king/ruler etc one whose power is limited by the laws of the country.

constrain [kən'strein] *vt* make somebody do something by force. *I constrained him to come with me*. (*formal*). **constraint** *nc/u*.
constrained *adj* (with reference to a person or his behaviour) forced, and therefore unnatural. (*opp* **unconstrained**).

constrict [kən'strikt] *vt* fasten tightly so as to make smaller or prevent free movement. *He felt constricted by the rules*. **constriction** *nc/u*.
constrictor [kən'striktə*] *nc* one of several snakes which kill their prey by fastening tightly round its body.

construct [kən'strʌkt] *vt* **1.** make by building or putting parts together. **2.** (geometry) draw a figure.
construction **1.** *nu* act of building. **2.** *nc* something built. **3.** *nu* understanding, meaning. *What was your construction of what he said?* i.e. what did you understand him to say? **4.** *nc* (grammar – esp. with reference to Greek and Latin grammar) way of using words in a sentence.
constructional [kən'strʌkʃənl] *adj* having reference to building.
constructive *adj* (with reference to ideas, words, suggestions etc) helpful.
under construction being built.
put a construction on something give somebody's words a certain meaning. *You have put a false construction on what I said* i.e. I did not mean what you think I meant.

construe [kən'struː] **1.** *vt* understand or explain words. **2.** *vt/i* (grammar) explain the grammar of a sentence.

consul ['kɔnsl] *nc* **1.** representative of a foreign government who lives in a town or city and one of whose duties is to help his fellow countrymen living or visiting there. **2.** one of the heads of state in ancient Rome. **consular** ['kɔnsjulə*] *adj.*

consulate ['kɔnsjulit] *nc* place where a consul works; position of a consul.

consulship *nc* position of a consul (esp. in ancient Rome).

consult [kən'sʌlt] *vt* **1.** ask somebody's advice about something. *He consulted his lawyer.* **2.** look into a book or other publication for a piece of information. *He consulted the dictionary.* **3.** think what would be best or most helpful for other people. *He consulted the interests of his friends.* **consultation** [kɔnsəl'teiʃən] *nc/u.* **consultative** [kən'sʌltətiv] *adj.*

consultant *nc* **1.** person to whom one goes for advice. **2.** doctor with special knowledge and qualifications.

consume [kən'sju:m] *vt/i* use up; use completely (e.g. by eating, drinking, burning etc); burn up completely. see **consumption.**

consumer *nc* person who buys and uses goods; person who is not a manufacturer of goods. Also *adj*: *consumer goods.*

be consumed with grief/rage/jealousy etc be filled with these feelings.

consummate[1] ['kɔnsʌmeit] *vt* make perfect or complete; finish. **consummation** [kɔnsʌ'meiʃən] *nu.*

consummate a marriage complete it by sexual intercourse.

consummate[2] [kən'sʌmit] *adj* perfect; very great (usu. in **consummate skill**).

consumption [kən'sʌmpʃən] *nu* **1.** act of using up food, drink, fuel etc. see **consume.** **2.** the amount used up. **3.** disease of the lungs or other part of the body. (rather *o.f.* – use **tuberculosis**).

consumptive [kən'sʌmptiv] *adj* suffering from this disease. Also *nc* person suffering from this disease.

contact ['kɔntækt] **1.** *nu* act or state of touching something or being near something. **2.** *nc/u* communication between people (by meeting, letter, speech etc). *The prisoner was not allowed to have any contact with his family.* **3.** *nc* device for making a connection between live conductors of electricity. **4.** *nc* person whom one can meet for some purpose. *The journalist has a contact in Paris.* Also *vt* arrange to meet somebody; write or telephone somebody etc.

'contact 'lens glass or plastic lens worn on the eyeball, under the eyelid, used instead of glasses.

in contact (with something) touching (something); near (something).

contagion [kən'teidʒən] **1.** *nu* the act of spreading disease by one person touching or coming near either somebody else, or something used by somebody else. **2.** *nc* a disease spread in this way. **contagious** *adj.*

contain [kən'tein] *vt* **1.** have inside. *This box contains biscuits.* **2.** (with reference to feelings or to the enemy) hold back. *He contained his anger. Our troops could not contain the enemy attack.*

container *nc* **1.** anything that can contain something (e.g. box, carton etc). **2.** very large sealed metal boxes used in shipping freight.

containment *nu* (usu. with reference to war or international affairs) act of preventing one's enemy from becoming stronger than oneself.

contain oneself keep one's feelings under control.

contaminate [kən'tæmineit] *vt* make dirty, diseased or radioactive, and so unfit for use. **contamination** [kəntæmi'neiʃən] *nu.* **contaminated** *adj.* (*opp* **uncontaminated**).

contemplate ['kɔntəmpleit] *vt/i* **1.** think very deeply about something (esp. some religious subject). **2.** gaze at something. **3.** think of as something which might happen. *I am contemplating buying some new furniture.* **contemplation** [kɔntəm'pleiʃən] *nu.* **contemplative** [kən'templətiv] *adj.*

contemporary [kən'tempərəri] *adj* **1.** living or existing at the same time as something or someone else. *Shakespeare was contemporary with Queen Elizabeth I.* **2.** living or existing today and having modern ideas, a modern appearance etc. Also *nc* person living at the same time as someone else. **contemporaneous** [kəntempə'reiniəs] *adj.* **contemporaneously** *adv.*

contempt [kən'tempt] *nu* feeling that something/somebody is very low in value, very bad, very foolish etc. *We feel contempt for anyone who steals from a child.*

contemptible *adj* deserving contempt: *a contemptible liar.* **contemptibly** *adv.*

contemptuous [kən'temptjuəs] *adj* feeling contempt. *He was contemptuous of the thief.* **contemptuously** *adv.*

contempt of court the offence of disobeying the order of a judge or court of law or of behaving badly in a court.

hold somebody/something in contempt feel contempt for somebody/something.

contend [kən'tend] *vi* **1.** (with **with**) fight, struggle or argue with, in order to get what one wants. *He had to contend with many difficulties when he was a young man.* **2.** (with **that**) argue; state as a fact which one is quite sure of while arguing with somebody.

contender *nc* person fighting, struggling etc (esp. a boxer trying to win a championship title). see **contention.**

content[1] [kən'tent] *adj* pleased or happy with what one has; satisfied. *The cat was very content after drinking the milk. He was quite content to do no work all day.* Also *nu* feeling of pleasure or satisfaction. Also *vt* make pleased or satisfied in this way. **contented** *adj.* (*opp* **discontented**). **contentedly** *adv.* **contentment** *nu.*

to one's heart's content as much as one wants to. *The children were allowed to watch television to their heart's content.*

content[2] ['kɔntent] **1.** (usu. *pl*) what is inside something: *the contents of the box; the contents of the book.* **2.** the main ideas or facts, as distinct from the way in which the ideas or facts are expressed.

contention [kən'tenʃən] **1.** *nu* argument; fight etc. **2.** *nc* main idea or point in an argument. *My contention was that America was once a British colony, but James said that this was not true.* see **contend.**

contentious *adj* liking to argue or quarrel. **contentiously** *adv.*

contest ['kɔntest] *nc* struggle, fight or competition to gain some advantage. Also [kən'test] *vt/i* fight against, fight to win something.

contestant [kən'testnt] *nc* person who takes part in a contest.

context ['kɔntekst] *nc* **1.** the words around a particular word or phrase, helping to give it meaning. **2.** the place or situation in which something happens or occurs.

contextual [kɔn'tekstjuəl] *adj.*
contiguous [kən'tigjuəs] *adj* next to and touching. **contiguously** *adv.* **contiguity** [kɔnti'gjuiti] *nu.*
continent[1] ['kɔntinənt] *nc* large land mass (e.g. Europe, Asia, Africa). **continental** [kɔnti'nentl] *adj.*
the Continent Europe not including Britain or Ireland.
Continental *adj.* Also *nc* person from the continent of Europe.
continent[2] ['kɔntinənt] *adj* able to control one's urine and bowel movements; having control over one's feelings and behaviour (esp. control over feelings of sexual desire) (*opp* **incontinent**). **continently** *adv.* **continence** *nu.*
contingency [kən'tindʒənsi] *nc* **1.** something which happens or may happen in the future, by chance. **2.** the possibility that something will happen. **contingent** *adj.*
contingent [kən'tindʒənt] *adj* see **contingency.** Also *nc* **1.** number of soldiers sent to a particular place. **2.** any group of people.
continue [kən'tinju:] *vt/i* go on; go further (without stopping or after stopping). *He continued to talk. John continued reading when I came into the room* i.e. he did not stop reading. *He continued his breakfast. The cold weather continued for three weeks. He stopped to buy some bread and then he continued his journey. He continued the line to the bottom of the page. The president continued in office for another three years.*
continuation [kəntinju'eiʃən] *nc/u.*
continual *adj* **1.** going on with short stops or pauses. **2.** going on without stopping: *a continual noise.*
continually *adv* see *Note* following **continuous.**
continuance [kən'tinjuəns] *nu* **1.** condition of continuing. **2.** time during which something continues.
continuity [kɔnti'njuiti] *nu* **1.** condition of being continuous. **2.** condition of having no breaks or interruptions; the way in which one thing leads to something else (esp. in a story, book, film etc). **3.** the work of arranging the details of scenes and people's appearances during the making of a film. (*opp* **discontinuity** in senses **1.** and **2.**).
continuous *adj* going on without stopping until finished: *five days of continuous rain.* (*opp* **discontinuous**). **continuously** *adv.*
Note: continual and *continuous* very often have almost the same meaning. If, however, one wishes to express the idea that something goes on for a long time, but with stops and starts, *continual* is the word to use; if one wishes to express the idea that something goes on for some time without stopping, *continuous* should be used.
continuum [kən'tinjuəm] *nc* series of things or events, with no clear breaks or divisions between the parts. *pl* **continua** [kən'tinjuə].
contort [kən'tɔ:t] *vt* bend something so that it loses its proper shape. **contortion** *nc/u.*
contortionist *nc* person who contorts his body in order to entertain people.
contour ['kɔntuə*] *nc* **1.** outline or shape of something. **2.** line on a map along which all places have the same height above sea level. (Also **contour line**).
contra- ['kɔntrə] *prefix* opposite to or against (e.g. **contradict**).
contraband ['kɔntrəbænd] *nu* **1.** goods which have been brought into a country against the law (e.g. gems, gold, things on which tax must be paid). **2.** the crime of bringing goods of this kind into a country.
contraception [kɔntrə'sepʃən] *nu* methods used to prevent the beginning of growth of a baby inside a woman, until the woman wishes to have a child.
contraceptive *adj.* Also *nc* any device used for this purpose.
contract[1] ['kɔntrækt] *nc* formal agreement (esp. in business). **contractual** [kən'træktjuəl] *adj.*
contract[2] [kən'trækt] **1.** *vt/i* make an agreement in business to do certain work or supply certain goods: *contract to supply food to the school; contract an agreement.* **2.** *vt* get or receive: *contract a debt* i.e. to borrow money; *contract a disease* i.e. become ill. **3.** *vt/i* become or make smaller.
contraction [kən'trækʃən] **1.** *nu* act of contracting. **2.** *nc* shortened form of a word or phrase (e.g. 'co' is a contraction of 'company').
contractor [kən'træktə*] *nc* person who does work by making contracts (esp. one who makes contracts to build houses).
contradict [kɔntrə'dikt] *vt/i* say or mean the opposite of. *He contradicted me* i.e. he said that I was not telling the truth. *This book contradicts that one* i.e. this book says the opposite of what that one says. **contradictory** *adj.* **contradiction** *nc/u.*
contralto [kən'træltou] **1.** *nu* the lowest female voice. **2.** *nc* woman who sings with this voice. *pl* **contraltos.** Also *adj.*
contraption [kən'træpʃən] *nc* machine or device with a strange or unusual appearance. (*informal*).
contrary[1] ['kɔntrəri] *adj* **1.** opposite to. *His opinion is contrary to mine.* **2.** (with reference to winds) unfavourable.
on the contrary the opposite is true. *You think that he is a kind man, but on the contrary he is very unkind.*
to the contrary with the opposite meaning. *I shall meet him on Tuesday unless I hear anything to the contrary* i.e. unless he tells me that he cannot meet me on Tuesday.
contrary[2] [kən'trɛəri] *adj* in the habit of doing or saying the opposite of other people. **contrarily** *adv.* (*informal*).
contrast ['kɔntrɑ:st] *nc* difference between one thing and another. Also [kən'trɑ:st] *vt/i* show or make a difference between one thing and another. *Black and white are contrasting colours. My hat contrasts with my coat. He contrasted Britain and America.*
contravene [kɔntrə'vi:n] *vt* be against; be opposed to. *Your behaviour contravenes the rules* i.e. the rules do not allow you to do that. **contravention** [kɔntrə'venʃən] *nc/u.*
contretemps ['kɔ̃trətɑ̃] *nc* unfortunate and embarrassing event. *There was a slight contretemps during the tea party when I knocked over the teapot. pl* **contretemps.**
contribute [kən'tribju:t] *vt/i* **1.** give as one's share. *I contributed £5 to the party funds. He did not contribute one idea to the discussion.* **2.** write for a newspaper or magazine. *He contributed an article to the Daily Post.* **3.** help to cause; be one of the causes of. *The driver's carelessness contributed to the accident.* **contribution** [kɔntri'bju:ʃən] *nc/u.* **contributor** *nc.*
contributory [kən'tribjutəri] *adj* being one of the causes of.

contrite ['kɔntrait] *adj* very unhappy because one has done wrong, and wishing to do right in future. **contrition** [kən'triʃən] *nu*.

contrive [kən'traiv] *vt/i* invent; think of something new and clever; cleverly manage to do something. *He contrived to get an extra week's holiday.*

contrivance *nc* machine or device which somebody has contrived.

control [kən'troul] *vt* guide; rule; have under one's authority. *She cannot control her two brothers* i.e. they will not do what she tells them to. *It was difficult to control the car on the mountain roads. past* **controlled.** Also *nu*: *She has no control over her two brothers. He lost control of the car.* **controller** *nc*.

controllable *adj* able to be controlled. (*opp* **uncontrollable**).

controls *npl* the devices by which a machine is operated (esp. the devices used to fly an aeroplane). *The pilot was seated at the controls.*

control oneself prevent one's feelings from becoming too strong.

out of control not under one's authority or guidance. *The aeroplane got out of control and fell into the sea.*

under (one's) control under one's authority or guidance. *The people began to break the windows, but the police soon had the situation under control. The school library is under my control.*

controversy ['kɔntrəvə:si] *nc/u* argument about some matter of opinion (esp. one involving questions of right and wrong). **controversial** [kɔntrə'və:ʃl] *adj* causing controversies.

controvert ['kɔntrəvə:t] *vt* prove or say that a statement or idea is wrong. *He controverted my statement.*

contusion [kən'tju:ʒən] *nc* bruise; mark on the skin made by a blow. (*formal*).

conundrum [kɔ'nʌndrʌm] *nc* question which is difficult to answer, asked as a joke (e.g. 'Why did the chicken cross the road?' Answer: 'to get to the other side').

convalescence [kɔnvə'lesns] *nu* process of recovering health after a serious illness; period during which one becomes strong again after an illness.

convalesce [kɔnvə'les] *vi* be regaining health and strength.

convalescent [kɔnvə'lesnt] *nc* person who convalesces. Also *adj*.

convection [kən'vekʃən] *nu* (physics) movement of gas or liquid when it is heated. **convector** *nc* device for heating a room, based on the convection of warm air.

convene [kən'vi:n] *vt/i* come or call together for a meeting. *Parliament convenes next Thursday. He convened a meeting of the members of the club.*

convener *nc* member of a committee, club, society etc whose job is to arrange a meeting.

convenient [kən'vi:niənt] *adj* not causing difficulty. *I should like to talk to you, if it is convenient* i.e. if this will not cause you any difficulty. *This kitchen is a very convenient size for working in.* (*opp* **inconvenient**). **conveniently** *adv*.

convenience **1.** *nu* quality of being convenient. **2.** *nc* something which is helpful or useful (often in **modern conveniences** i.e. devices in a house such as a water supply, heating, refrigeration etc).

public convenience (*Brit*) public lavatory.

at one's (own) convenience in a way or at a time which is convenient to one. *You may do this work at your own convenience. You must do this work at my convenience, not yours.*

convent ['kɔnvənt] *nc* **1.** group of nuns or women living together in a religious organization. **2.** building where they live. **conventual** [kən'ventjuəl] *adj*.

convention [kən'venʃən] **1.** *nc* large meeting called for some special purpose. **2.** *nc* agreement between countries on some subject. **3.** *nu* general agreement about behaviour, actions etc done by nearly everybody and accepted as the right thing to do. *It is convention that makes people act in the same way.* **4.** *nc/u* any act which is done by nearly everybody and is accepted as the right thing to do. *In Britain it is not the convention to shake hands every time one meets a person.* **5.** *nc* something in art, films, the theatre etc, which is accepted although it is not real or true.

conventional *adj* **1.** happening by convention. **2.** not new or interesting. **3.** (of a person) acting according to conventions, unenterprising. (*opp* **unconventional**). **conventionally** *adv*. **conventionality** [kənvenʃə'næliti] *nu*.

by convention as a convention. *By convention, the national anthem is often played at the beginning of a concert and at the end of a film.*

converge [kən'və:dʒ] *vi* **1.** move together (and meet). *These two lines converge. The crowd converged on the palace* i.e. everybody moved towards the palace. **convergent** *adj*. **convergence** *nu*.

conversant [kən'və:snt] *adj* (with **with**) having some knowledge of. *I am not conversant with the history of India.* (*formal*).

conversation [kɔnvə'seiʃən] *nc/u* friendly talk. *I had an interesting conversation with the old man. Conversation is one of the pleasures of life.* **conversational** *adj*. **conversationally** *adv*.

conversationalist [kɔnvə'seiʃənəlist] *nc* person who is good at holding conversations.

converse[1] [kən'və:s] *vi* hold a conversation; talk. *He can converse in three languages.* see **conversation.**

converse[2] ['kɔnvə:s] *nc* opposite. *'Yes' is the converse of 'no'.* **conversely** *adv*.

convert [kən'və:t] *vt* **1.** change from one thing into another. *Water is converted into steam if it is boiled.* **2.** cause a person to change his religious beliefs. *Many Africans were converted to Christianity.* Also ['kɔnvə:t] *nc* person who has changed his religious belief. *He is a Catholic convert.* **conversion** *nc/u*.

convertible *adj* able to be changed (esp. with reference to **1.** money which can easily be changed for other money. *Gold and dollars are convertible currency.* **2.** car with a top which can be folded back). Also *nc* car of this type. **convertibility** [kənvə:ti'biliti] *nu*.

convert something to one's own use (legal) take something and keep it for oneself; steal.

convex ['kɔn'veks] *adj* (esp. with reference to lenses) curving outwards; having the shape of the outside of a circle. see **concave.**

convey [kən'vei] *vt* **1.** carry something from one place to another. *This train conveys over three hundred passengers every day.* **2.**

give information to somebody. *I conveyed the message to John. It is difficult to convey what the Sahara desert is like to somebody who hasn't been there.* **3.** (legal) arrange for land or buildings to be sold by somebody to another person.

conveyance **1.** *nu* act of conveying. **2.** *nc* vehicle for carrying goods or people.

conveyancing *nu* (legal) the work of a lawyer who arranges the sale of land or buildings.

conveyer, conveyor *nc* **1.** person/thing which conveys. **2.** endless belt for moving things from one person to another in a factory. (Also **conveyor belt**).

convict [kən'vikt] *vt* (with reference to a judge, jury, lawyer etc) say or prove that somebody is guilty of a crime. *The judge convicted him of robbery.* Also ['kɔnvikt] *nc* person in prison after being found guilty of a crime.

conviction *nc/u* **1.** act of convicting. **2.** strong belief. *It's my conviction that you did not try hard enough. He said it with conviction* i.e. he sounded completely certain of it.

carry conviction see **carry**.

open to conviction willing to change one's mind after listening to someone. *I don't think that you really did the work, but I'm open to conviction.*

convince [kən'vins] *vt* make somebody believe that something is true, by using arguments or proofs. *He convinced me that he was right. He convinced me of the difficulty of the work.*

convincing *adj* causing one to believe: *a convincing argument.* (*opp* **unconvincing**).

convincingly *adv.*

convinced *pred adj* believing. (*opp* **unconvinced**).

convivial [kən'viviəl] *adj* happy or causing happiness (usu. because of food and drink); sociable: *a convivial man/party.* **convivially** *adv.* **conviviality** [kənvivi'æliti] *nu.*

convocation [kɔnvə'keiʃən] **1.** *nu* act of calling people together for a meeting. **2.** *nc* meeting of people to discuss some special topic. **3.** *nc* special meeting of the ministers of certain churches or of the staff of a university.

convoke [kən'vouk] *vt* call people together for a meeting.

convolution [kɔnvə'lu:ʃən] *nc* twist or coil.

convoluted [kɔnvə'lutid] *adj* having twists or coils.

convoy ['kɔnvɔi] *nc* **1.** in wartime, group of ships travelling together under protection. **2.** group of vehicles travelling together.

convulse [kən'vʌls] *vt* (usu. *passive*) shake with great force. *The city was convulsed by the earthquake. He was convulsed with laughter.*

convulsion *nc* **1.** act of convulsing. **2.** (usu. *pl*) strong and uncontrollable movement of the body, caused by a disease or injury.

convulsive *adj.* **convulsively** *adv.*

cony, coney ['kouni] **1.** *nc* rabbit (*o.f.*). **2.** *nu* fur of the rabbit, used in making clothes.

coo [ku:] *nc* soft noise (e.g. made by a pigeon or by a baby). Also *vi* make this noise.

to bill and coo (with reference to two people in love) talk in a soft and loving way.

cook [kuk] **1.** *vt/i* prepare food by using heat. *He cooked the dinner.* **2.** *vi* be prepared. *The food is cooking.* Also *nc* person who cooks (esp. as a servant or in a hotel or restaurant).

cooker *nc* stove for cooking (usu. gas or electric).

'cookhouse building where food is cooked (esp. in the army).

'cookery book, 'cookbook book which tells one how to prepare different types of food.

cook something up make up something which is not true. *He cooked up a story to explain the broken window.* (*informal*).

cook the accounts/books prepare an untrue record of money received and spent, in order to break the law in some way. (*informal*).

cook somebody's goose do something which prevents somebody carrying out his plans. (*informal*).

too many cooks spoil the broth plans and arrangements will go wrong if many people are involved in making the plans.

cookie, cooky ['kuki] *nc* (*US*) small, flat, sweet cake. (*Brit* **biscuit**).

cool[1] [ku:l] *adj* **1.** between warm and cold. *The weather is rather cool today. Let your tea get cool before you drink it.* **2.** not worried or excited by danger or difficulty. *He remained cool when the enemy attacked.* **3.** calm and unfriendly. *He gave me a very cool greeting.*

coolly *adv.* **coolness** *nu.*

cool[2] [ku:l] *vt/i* (often with **down** or **off**) become or make cool. *The tea has cooled down a little. I cooled off the bathwater.* Also *nu* cool feelings. *The cool of the evening.*

coolie ['ku:li] *nc* unskilled workman in India and China.

Note: if the reference is not to India or China use *labourer*; even with reference to China and India the word is now felt to be impolite.

coop [ku:p] *nc* small cage or house for keeping chickens in.

coop up (often *passive*) keep in a small space. *The family were cooped up in two small rooms.*

co-op ['kouɔp] *nc* cooperative store i.e. type of shop. *I buy my food at a co-op.* (*informal*).

cooper ['ku:pə*] *nc* person who makes barrels.

cooperate [kou'ɔpəreit] *vi* work together for some purpose. *All the people in the village cooperated to bring in the harvest.*

cooperation [kouɔpə'reiʃən] *nu.*

cooperative [kou'ɔpərətiv] *adj.* (*opp* **uncooperative**).

cooperative *nc* business, shop, farm etc, which is owned by all the people who work in it.

coopt [kou'ɔpt] *vt* (with reference to a committee) ask somebody to join the committee. *The committee decided to coopt another member.*

coordinate[1] [kou'ɔ:dinit] *adj* of equal importance. Also *nc.*

coordinate[2] [kou'ɔ:dineit] *vt* **1.** make coordinate. **2.** arrange in the right way or proper order; move together for some purpose. *A baby cannot easily coordinate his movements* i.e. he cannot always move his arms and legs in the right way so as to get what he wants. **coordination** [kouɔ:di'neiʃən] *nu.*

coordinated *adj.* (*opp* **uncoordinated**).

coot [ku:t] *nc* **1.** type of water bird like a duck. **2.** stupid person: *as daft as a coot.*

cop [kɔp] *nc* policeman. (*informal*).

cope[1] [koup] *vi* (with **with**) manage; control; organize. *She could not cope with all the work. He had a lot of work, but he was able to cope.*

cope² [koup] *nc* long garment without sleeves, worn by priests during certain ceremonies.

'copestone, 'coping stone stone used at the top of a building, wall etc, often with sloping sides so that the rain will run off easily.

co-pilot ['kou'pailət] *nc* person who shares the work of the pilot of an aeroplane. Also *vt*: *He co-piloted the plane.*

coping ['koupiŋ] *nc* top layer of brick or stone on a wall.

copious ['koupiəs] *adj* containing very much. *He gave me copious information about his family.* **copiously** *adv.* **copiousness** *nu.*

copper ['kɔpə*] **1.** *nu* strong brown metal (Cu). **2.** *nc* coin made of copper or bronze. **3.** *nc* large container, sometimes made of copper. **4.** *nc* (*Brit*) policeman. (*informal*). Also *adj.* Also *vt* cover with copper.

coppice ['kɔpis] *nc* see **copse.**

copra ['kɔprə] *nu* substance inside a coconut when it is dried.

copse [kɔps] *nc* small group of trees or bushes. (Also **coppice**).

copulate ['kɔpjuleit] *vi* have sexual intercourse. **copulation** [kɔpju'leiʃən] *nu.*

copy¹ ['kɔpi] *vt/i* do or make something in the same way as something else. *The young boy copied his father's way of walking* i.e. he walked like his father.

copy something out write down a copy of.

copy² ['kɔpi] **1.** *nc* something made to look like something else. *This painting is a copy of one in the museum.* **2.** *nc* one book, newspaper or magazine. *May I borrow your copy of 'David Copperfield'?* **3.** *nu* subject for newspaper writing.

'copyright the right of an author, musician, film maker etc, to his own work, so that other people are forbidden by law to copy the work in any way without permission. Also *adj* protected by copyright. *Shakespeare's plays are not copyright.* Also *vt* protect in this way.

coquette [kɔ'ket] *nc* woman who pretends to be very friendly with a number of men, so as to make them fall in love with her. **coquetry** ['kɔkitri] *nu* behaviour of a coquette. **coquettish** [kɔ'ketiʃ] *adj.*

coquet [kɔ'ket] *vi* behave like a coquette. *past* **coquetted.**

coral ['kɔrl] *nc/u* hard substance made by small tropical sea animals. Also *adj* **1.** made of coral. **2.** having the pink or red colour of some kinds of coral.

cord [kɔ:d] **1.** *nc/u* type of thick string used for tying parcels etc. **2.** *nc* part of the body shaped like this: *the vocal cords.* see also **chord.**

cordial¹ ['kɔ:diəl] *adj* very friendly: *a cordial greeting.* **cordially** *adv.* **cordiality** [kɔ:di'æliti] *nu.*

cordial² ['kɔ:diəl] *nc/u* sweet drink made from concentrated fruit juice.

cordite ['kɔ:dait] *nu* type of explosive.

cordon ['kɔ:dn] *nc* group of people making a line or a circle to guard a person/thing.

cordon something off put a cordon around or across. *The police cordoned off the house.*

corduroy ['kɔ:dərɔi] *nu* type of thick cotton cloth, with raised lines or ridges on it.

corduroys *npl* trousers made of corduroy.

core [kɔ:*] *nc* **1.** central part of some fruits (e.g. apples or pears). **2.** central part of an idea, argument, problem etc. **3.** piece of iron forming the centre of an electromagnet. Also *vt* take the core out of an apple or pear.

co-respondent ['kouris'pɔndənt] *nc* (in a legal sense) person who is said to have taken away somebody's wife or husband in a divorce case.

cork [kɔ:k] **1.** *nu* light substance which is the bark of the cork oak. **2.** *nc* piece (usu. of this substance) used to put in the top of a bottle. Also *vt* put a cork into a bottle.

'corkscrew implement for pulling the cork out of a bottle.

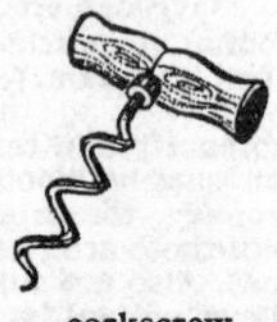

corkscrew

cormorant ['kɔ:mərnt] *nc* large bird with a long neck and big beak which eats fish.

corn¹ [kɔ:n] *nu* name given to several types of grain (in England **wheat** or any grain; in USA **maize**; in Scotland **oats**).

'corncob thick part of the maize plant, on which the seeds grow.

'cornflour flour made from maize.

'cornflower small blue flower.

corn² [kɔ:n] *nc* type of painful swelling and hard growth (usu. on the foot).

cornea ['kɔ:niə] *nc* transparent covering over the central part of the eye. **corneal** *adj.*

corned ['kɔ:nd] *adj* in **'corned 'beef** i.e. beef preserved in salt.

corner¹ ['kɔ:nə*] *nc* **1.** place where two lines or two sides meet. *A square has four corners. He was standing on the corner of the street.* **2.** any distant, hidden or secret place. *He has been in every corner of the world. I've lost my pen; I must have put it in some odd corner somewhere.*

'cornerstone 1. part of the foundation of a building, placed at the corner made by two walls. **2.** anything important on which other things depend. *Freedom of speech is the cornerstone of democracy.*

cut a corner make a journey or race shorter by going across a corner instead of round it.

a tight corner a difficult situation. (*informal*).

turn the corner 1. walk round the corner of a street. **2.** begin to recover from an illness or to get out of a difficult situation. (*informal*).

hole-and-corner see **hole.**

(see something) out of the corner of one's eye see something to the side, not in front of one. *'What was that bird?' 'I don't know; I just saw it out of the corner of my eye.'*

corner² ['kɔ:nə*] **1.** *vi* drive a car round a corner. *He was cornering at 60 miles an hour.* **2.** *vt* drive or chase somebody into a corner or into a position from which he cannot escape. *The police finally cornered the thief.*

corner the market in something buy up all the supplies of some commodity, so that one can sell it again at a high price. *He cornered the market in sugar.*

cornet ['kɔ:nit] *nc* **1.** brass musical instrument. **2.** piece of light biscuit for holding ice cream. (Also **cone**).

cornice ['kɔːnis] *nc* length of wood, stone, plaster etc placed along the top of a building or the top of the walls of a room as a decoration.

cornucopia [kɔːnju'koupiə] *nc* **1.** container shaped like a horn, which was said in Roman mythology to contain an endless supply of food and flowers. **2.** any great quantity (often of food).

corny ['kɔːni] *adj* old-fashioned, rather silly: *his corny jokes.* (*informal*).

corollary [kə'rɔləri] *nc* an argument or idea which follows from another argument. *pl* **corollaries.**

corona [kə'rounə] *nc* circle of light seen around the sun or moon (esp. during an eclipse).

coronary ['kɔrənəri] *adj* referring to the arteries which supply blood to the heart (usu. in **coronary thrombosis** a disease in which one of these arteries is blocked by a clot of blood). Also *nc*: *suffer a coronary.*

coronation [kɔrə'neiʃən] *nc* ceremony in which a king or queen is crowned.

coroner ['kɔrənə*] *nc* official in charge of a court of law which enquires into the cause of accidental and suspicious deaths.

coronet ['kɔrənit] *nc* small crown (usu. worn by princes and lords, not by kings).

corporal[1] ['kɔːpərl] *nc* rank in the army above a private and below a sergeant.

corporal[2] ['kɔːpərl] *adj* with reference to the body.

corporal punishment punishment by beating.

corporation [kɔːpə'reiʃən] *nc* **1.** group of people who govern a town or city. **2.** business firm which is treated by the law as though it were a single person. **3.** large stomach or abdomen (esp. of a man) (*informal* in sense **3.**).

corporate ['kɔːpərit] *adj* (not with reference to sense **3.**). **corporately** *adv.*

corps [kɔː*] *nc* **1.** section of the army which does some special work (e.g. *Signal Corps, Medical Corps*). **2.** part of an army, made up of two or more divisions. **3.** any organized group of people doing a special job. *pl* **corps** [kɔːz].

corpse [kɔːps] *nc* dead body (usu. of a human being).

corpulent ['kɔːpjulnt] *adj* (with reference to a human being) fat (and often unhealthy). **corpulence, corpulency** *nu.*

corpus ['kɔːpəs] *nc* **1.** complete collection (e.g. of books or writings on some subject). **2.** collection of laws. *pl* **corpora** ['kɔːpərə].

corpuscle ['kɔːpʌsl] *nc* one of the red or white cells which float in the blood to carry oxygen and destroy disease germs. **corpuscular** [kɔː'pʌskjulə*] *adj.*

corral [kə'rɑːl] *nc* (mainly *US*) small area surrounded by a wall or fence, for putting horses or cattle in. Also *vt* put an animal into a corral. *past* **corralled.**

correct[1] [kə'rekt] *adj* **1.** true; right; without faults or mistakes. *What is the correct answer to question 7?* **2.** following what is thought to be the right thing to do. *It is not considered correct for a man to wear a hat in church.* (*opp* **incorrect**). **correctly** *adv.* **correctness** *nu.*

corrective *adj* intended to make correct; intended to remove faults: *corrective punishment.* Also *nc.*

correct[2] [kə'rekt] *vt* **1.** change to what is correct: *correct an essay.* **2.** point out mistakes in: *correct someone's behaviour.* **3.** punish in order to stop a child from behaving badly. *The mother corrected the disobedient child.* **4.** repair; mend; cure. *I have corrected the fault in the radio. This medicine will correct the pain.*

Note: in sense **4.** the object of *correct* is generally a word like 'fault', 'trouble'. We do not usu. say *He corrected the radio,* we say *He repaired the radio.*

correction **1.** *nu* act of making correct and removing mistakes. **2.** *nc* what is written or said to replace a mistake. *Look carefully at the corrections which I have written in your essay.*

stand corrected recognize that one has made a mistake in what one has said and that this mistake has been pointed out by somebody else.

correlate ['kɔrileit] *vt/i* (usu. in mathematics) be or make related in some way; show the relationship between. **correlation** [kɔri'leiʃən] *nc/u.*

correspond [kɔris'pɔnd] *vi* **1.** (with **with**) exchange letters with. *John and I have corresponded for many years. I have been corresponding with John.* **2.** (with **to** or **with**) be like; be similar to or equal to. *Your story does not correspond with the facts* i.e. you are not telling the truth. **correspondence** *nu.* **corresponding** *adj.* **correspondingly** *adv.*

correspondent *nc* **1.** person with whom one exchanges letters. **2.** person who sends reports of news to a newspaper or radio station.

corre'spondence course series of lessons sent by post to a student, who writes essays or answers questions and sends them back to be corrected.

in correspondence (with) regularly writing (to). *John and I have been in correspondence for many years. I have been in correspondence with John.*

corridor ['kɔridɔː*] *nc* **1.** long passage in a building, with doors and rooms on one or both sides. **2.** very narrow part of a country, with foreign territory on both sides. **3.** narrow strip of air space along which aeroplanes are allowed to fly.

corroborate [kə'rɔbəreit] *vt* give extra proof that a statement is true. *I was able to corroborate John's story.* **corroboration** [kərɔbə'reiʃən] *nu.* **corroborative** [kə'rɔbərətiv] *adj.*

corrode [kə'roud] *vt/i* wear away or damage by chemical change. *The metal was corroded by acid. Iron corrodes if it is not protected from the damp air.* **corrosion** [kə'rouʒən] *nu.* **corrosive** [kə'rousiv] *adj.* Also *nc* substance which causes corrosion.

corrugate ['kɔrəgeit] *vt/i* bend into a series of folds. **corrugation** [kɔrə'geiʃən] *nc/u.*

corrugated iron iron sheets, bent into a series of folds.

corrugated paper paper shaped in this way.

corrupt [kə'rʌpt] *adj* **1.** bad; wicked; evil. **2.** taking bribes. **3.** rotten; decaying. **4.** (with reference to language) mixed with words and grammar from other languages; not correct. *French, Spanish and Italian were originally corrupt forms of Latin.* Also *vt* make corrupt. **corruption** *nc/u.*

corruptible *adj* **1.** capable of decaying. **2.** likely to take bribes. (*opp* **incorruptible**).

corrupt practices (legal) taking bribes etc.

corset ['kɔːsit] *nc* (often *pl*) stiff garment

worn by a woman under a dress or skirt, in order to shape the body.
Note: the more modern version of this garment is called a *girdle, belt* or *roll-on.*

cortège [kɔː'tɛːʒ] procession (esp. a funeral procession).

cortex ['kɔːteks] *nc* **1.** (anatomy) covering of the brain. **2.** (botany) bark of a tree. *pl* **cortices** ['kɔːtisiːz]. **cortical** ['kɔːtikl] *adj.*

corvette [kɔː'vet] *nc* type of small warship.

cosh [kɔʃ] *nc* small weapon, made of wood, rubber, metal etc, used by criminals for hitting people on the head. Also *vt* hit somebody in this way.

cosmetic [kɔz'metik] *nc* (usu. *pl*) powder, cream and other substances used by women to make the face and various parts of the body more beautiful. Also *adj.*

cosmopolitan [kɔzmə'pɔlitn] *adj* having people or ideas from many parts of the world. *London is a cosmopolitan city* i.e. people from many parts of the world can be found in London. Also *nc* person who has lived in many parts of the world.

cosmos ['kɔzmɔs] *nc* the universe; the sun, planets and surrounding space. **cosmic** ['kɔzmik] *adj.* **cosmically** *adv.*

cosmography [kɔz'mɔgrəfi] *nu* description of the universe.

cosmology [kɔz'mɔlədʒi] *nu* study of the universe.

cosmonaut ['kɔzmənɔːt] *nc* person who travels in a spacecraft (esp. Russian – *US* **astronaut**).

cosmic dust clouds of dust or small particles of matter found in outer space.

cosmic rays rays of very short length which reach the earth from outer space.

cost [kɔst] *vt* **1.** have as a price. *This book costs two pounds* i.e. we must pay two pounds in order to buy the book. *This chair cost me twenty pounds.* **2.** result in or cause the loss of. *One mistake may cost you your life* i.e. may cause you to die. *John's behaviour cost him his job* i.e. he was dismissed from his work. **3.** (business) calculate how much it will cost to do a particular piece of work. *past* **cost.** Also *nc*: *What is the cost of this book?*

costly ['kɔstli] *adj* costing a lot of money. **costliness** *nu.*

costs *npl* the cost of paying lawyers and taking a case to a court of law. (The judge will often order the costs to be paid by the person who loses the case).

cost of living the average amount of money paid by a person or family for the necessary things of life (e.g. food, clothing, housing, travel).

'cost 'price the price charged by a manufacturer for an article when he sells it to a shopkeeper. This is of course lower than the **selling price** or **retail price** i.e. the price for which the shopkeeper sells the article. *I bought it at cost price.*

at all costs whatever the difficulties or dangers may be. *I must finish the work by tomorrow at all costs.*

as one knows to one's cost as one has found out by an unpleasant experience. *It is not easy to paint a room as I know to my cost* i.e. I had a very difficult time trying to paint a room.

coster ['kɔstə*], **costermonger** ['kɔstəmʌŋgə*] *nc* (*Brit*) person who sells fruit and vegetables from a cart in the street.

costume ['kɔstjuːm] **1.** *nu* type of clothes worn at one time or in one area (esp. clothes worn in a former time or in a particular place). **2.** *nu* clothes worn by an actor in a play or film. **3.** *nc* skirt and jacket of the same material, worn by a woman (*o.f.* – use **suit**).

cosy[1] ['kouzi] *adj* warm and comfortable. **cosily** *adv.* **cosiness** *nu.*

cosy[2] ['kouzi] *nc* thick cloth covering for a teapot etc to keep it warm. (Also **tea cosy**).

cot [kɔt] **1.** *nc* (*Brit*) bed for child, with bars up the sides to keep the child from falling out. (*US* **crib**). **2.** (*US*) narrow bed, often one made of canvas stretched on a frame. (*Brit* **campbed**).

coterie ['kouteri] *nc* small group of people (esp. a group which is unfriendly to other people).

cottage ['kɔtidʒ] *nc* small house (usu. in the country) where a farmer or farm worker lives or used to live.

cotton ['kɔtn] *nu* **1.** soft white substance obtained from a plant, used for making into cloth. **2.** thread made from this substance, used for sewing. **3.** cloth made from this substance.

'cotton 'wool (mainly *Brit*) cotton in the natural state, cleaned and pressed into flat layers; used for cleaning wounds etc. (*US* **absorbent cotton**).

couch[1] [kautʃ] *nc* long chair looking like a bed.

couch[2] [kautʃ] *vt* put into words. *He couched his request in very polite terms.* (rather *formal*).

cougar ['kuːgə*] *nc* large animal like a lion, found in America; the puma.

cough [kɔf] *vi* push air from the lungs and out of the mouth, in a sudden and noisy way (usu. because the throat is blocked because of an illness or some other reason). Also *nc* **1.** action of this kind. **2.** illness of the throat which causes coughing.

'cough drop, 'cough sweet small tablet or sweet, which contains medicine to help somebody suffering from a cough.

cough something up 1. bring up from the lungs or throat by coughing. *He coughed up some drops of blood.* **2.** give money or information unwillingly. (*informal* in sense **2.**).

could [kud] past of **can**[1].

council ['kaunsl] *nc* body of people to be consulted or to advise (esp. such a body governing a town or city).

councillor *nc* (*Brit*) member of a council. (*US* **councilor**). see **counsel.**

counsel ['kaunsl] *nu* **1.** advice; suggestions. *Let me give you my counsel.* (*formal*). **2.** lawyer or lawyers on one side in a law case. Also *vt* give counsel. *past* **counselled.** (*US* **counseled**).

counsellor (*US* **counselor**) *nc* **1.** person who counsels. **2.** (*US*) lawyer.
Note: do not confuse *council* and *counsel.*

Queen's (King's) Counsel lawyer who has the power to represent the British Government.

keep one's own counsel make decisions or plans by oneself, without asking the advice or help of other people and without telling them what one has decided.

count[1] [kaunt] *vt/i* **1.** find out the number of. *It is impossible to count the stars in the sky.* **2.** say numbers in order. *I shall count up to ten and then we can begin.* **3.** be important or consider as important. *If you play football, don't think that winning the game is the only thing that counts* i.e. there are other important things about football, such as exercise, enjoyment, team spirit etc. **4.** be included or include in a total. *I've got twenty-seven British postage stamps, or twenty-eight if you count this torn one. That one doesn't count* i.e. is not to be included.

count on/upon someone/something rely on. *I hope that we can count on your support in the election* i.e. I hope that you will vote for us.

count someone out (boxing) officially say that a boxer has lost a fight, after he has failed to stand up within ten seconds after being knocked down.

count something up count to find the total of. *I must count up how much money I've spent today.*

count one's chickens before they are hatched think about what one will do with something one hopes to gain, before one has actually got it.

count the cost think of what one has to give in order to gain something.

count for little/nothing be of little/no importance.

count oneself think of oneself as. *You can count yourself lucky that you were not killed when you ran across the road.*

count[2] [kaunt] *nc* **1.** act of counting numbers or quantities. **2.** (in a legal sense) charge or accusation made against a prisoner in a court of law. *The prisoner was found guilty on three counts and not guilty on one.* **3.** period of ten seconds, allowed to a boxer to stand up after he has been knocked down.

countable *adj* able to be counted. (*opp* **uncountable**).

countless *adj* very, very many; too many to count.

countable noun (grammar) noun such as *man, book, country, difference,* which can be made plural and which can have *a* in front. (*opp* **uncountable noun** i.e. a noun like 'rice', 'honesty').

'countdown (usu. with reference to the period during which a spacecraft is being inspected to see whether it is ready for flight) period before something starts, and during which somebody counts backwards, ending 5, 4, 3, 2, 1.

keep count count, over a length of time, how many there are of something. *I've been keeping count of the cars driving along this road.*

lose count forget or stop counting how many there are of something. *I've lost count of the letters I've written to the Ministry of Education about this matter.*

count[3] [kaunt] *nc* title of nobility in some countries on the continent of Europe.

countess ['kauntis] *nc* **1.** wife of a count. **2.** (*Brit*) wife of an earl, or woman with the rank of an earl.

countenance[1] ['kauntinəns] *nc* the face of a person. (*formal*).

give countenance to something say that one supports or approves of something. *I cannot give countenance to your plan.* (*formal*).

keep (one's) countenance prevent oneself from laughing. *It was difficult to keep my countenance when the king fell over.* (*formal*).

put somebody out of countenance make somebody feel embarrassed by staring at him. (rather *o.f.*).

countenance[2] ['kauntinəns] *vt* give support or approval to. *I cannot countenance your plan.*

counter[1] ['kauntə*] *adv* against; opposite to. *His behaviour was counter to my wishes.* Also *vt/i* be opposite or against; oppose. *He countered my plan with one of his own* i.e. he suggested his own plan instead of mine. *He countered my blow* i.e. he hit me after I hit him. *I hit him and he quickly countered.*

counter[2] ['kauntə*] *nc* **1.** round flat piece of plastic, wood, metal etc used in playing certain games, or as an imitation coin. **2.** type of table in a shop, behind which the shopkeeper stands to serve the customers.

counter-[3] ['kauntə*] *prefix* opposite or against (e.g. **counter-attack**).

counteract [kauntə'rækt] *vt* have the opposite effect to; make harmless or of no effect. *This drug will counteract the poison* i.e. it will prevent the poison from doing harm. **counteraction** *nc/u.*

counter-attack ['kauntərətæk] *nc* attack made against somebody who attacked first. Also *vt/i.*

counterbalance ['kauntə'bæləns] *nc* **1.** weight which is balanced against another weight, so that neither weight falls down. **2.** anything which is equal and opposite to somebody else in this way. Also *vt.*

counter-espionage ['kauntər'espiənɑːʒ] *nu* work of a spy who works against or deceives enemy spies.

counterfeit ['kauntəfit] *nc* something false (esp. money) which is dishonestly made to look like the real thing. *This coin is a counterfeit* i.e. this is not a coin made by the government. Also *adj*: *a counterfeit coin.* Also *vt* counterfeit money.

counterfeiter *nc* person who counterfeits money.

counterfoil ['kauntəfɔil] *nc* part of a cheque or receipt, which is kept as a record that the cheque etc has been given to somebody.

counterirritant ['kauntər'iritənt] *nc* something which causes a small pain on the surface of the skin, in order to make better a stronger pain somewhere else.

countermand ['kauntə'mɑːnd] *vt* say that an order which has been given is not to be carried out. *He countermanded the orders.*

countermarch ['kauntə'mɑːtʃ] *nc* march in the direction which one has come from. Also *vt/i*: *The soldiers countermarched.*

counter-offensive ['kauntərə'fensiv] *nc* large attack made in war, after the enemy has attacked first.

counterpane ['kauntəpein] *nc* large piece of cloth, used to cover a bed (esp. in the daytime).

counterpart ['kauntəpɑːt] *nc* person/thing which is very similar to a person/thing in another business, situation etc.

counterpoint ['kauntəpɔint] **1.** *nu* music in which two or more melodies are played or sung together. **2.** *nu* art of writing music of this kind. **3.** *nc* any two things joined in this way.

counterpoise ['kauntəpɔiz] *nc* **1.** weight which balances another weight, so that neither weight falls down. **2.** anything which is equal and opposite to something else in this way. Also *vt* act as a counterpoise.

counter-revolution ['kauntərevə'luʃən] *nc* political movement which tries to get rid of a government set up by a revolution, and go back to the situation before the revolution.

counter-revolutionary *adj.* Also *nc.*

countersign[1] ['kauntəsain] *nc* words which one has to say in reply to the words of a sentry or guard. *If one does not know the countersign, the sentry will not let one enter.*
countersign[2] ['kauntəsain] *vt* sign a document after somebody else has signed it to show approval etc.
countess ['kauntis] *nc* see **count**[3].
country ['kʌntri] *nc* **1.** state. *France, Italy, Egypt, Japan are countries.* **2.** the people in a state. *The whole country supported the Prime Minister.* **3.** (only *sing*) land which is not a town or city. *He spends his holiday on a farm in the country.* Also *adj* (before certain nouns) in the country; away from towns and cities. *He enjoys country life.*
countrified *adj* rural; of the country; not knowing about life in the city.
'country club club in the country near a city, where members can enjoy various games and sports.
'country 'dance *nc* type of dance (usu. with two rows of people facing each other). **country dancing** *nu.*
'country 'gentleman rich man who lives in the country.
'country 'house large house in the country, belonging to a rich person.
'countryman **1.** person who lives in the country. **2.** person from the same nation as oneself. (Often **fellow countryman**).
'countryside areas which are not towns or cities.
'country 'town small town surrounded by countryside.
appeal/go to the country (with reference to a government) ask the people of the country to vote. *The Prime Minister decided to go to the country in the autumn.*
county ['kaunti] *nc* **1.** (*Brit, Ir*) one of the divisions of the country. **2.** (*US*) one of the divisions of each state. **3.** (only *sing*) the people living in an English county (esp. all the rich people).
'county 'borough large town in Great Britain.
'county 'town chief town of a county.
'Home 'Counties counties around London.
coup [kuː] *nc* **1.** sudden and violent action to end a government and set up another one. (Also **coup d'état** [kuːdeitɑː]). **2.** any sudden and clever action to obtain some result.
coupé [kuː'pei] *nc* type of car (with two doors).
couple ['kʌpl] *nc* **1.** two people or things: *a couple of books.* (*informal*). **2.** man and woman who are married or engaged to be married. **3.** man and woman dancing together. Also *vt* join two things together.
couplet ['kʌplit] *nc* two lines of verse which rhyme and have the same number of stresses in each line.
coupling ['kʌpliŋ] **1.** *nu* act of joining two things together. **2.** *nc* device which is used to join two things (esp. two railway carriages).
coupon ['kuːpɔn] *nc* piece of paper which gives the owner of it the right to receive or do something (e.g. if food is rationed, one receives so many coupons which enable one to buy a certain amount of food). *Some manufacturers give away coupons to people who buy their goods; if one saves enough coupons one is given a gift of some kind.*
courage ['kʌridʒ] *nu* the ability to face or accept pain, danger or difficulty without fear; the power to continue what one is doing, even though it causes one pain, danger or difficulty. **courageous** [kə'reidʒəs] *adj.* **courageously** *adv.*
take courage be brave.
(have) the courage of one's convictions (have) the courage to do what one thinks is right, even though other people are against one.
courier ['kuriə*] *nc* **1.** person whose work is to go with a group of travellers and arrange their journey for them. **2.** person carrying a special message.
course[1] [kɔːs] *nc* **1.** (only *sing*) direction; movement onwards or forwards. *During the course of many years, the old man had seen many surprising things* i.e. while many years were passing. *I have studied the course of this discussion* i.e. the way in which this discussion has developed. **2.** movement onwards; path or direction. *The ship continued on her course.* **3.** action. *I have not decided what course to take with those bad boys* i.e. what to do to them. **4.** series of lessons or lectures. **5.** series of treatments or drugs for somebody who is ill. **6.** one part of a meal put on the table at one time. *The first course was soup or fruit juice.* **7.** ground for certain sports (e.g. *a golf course, a racecourse* for horse-racing). **8.** horizontal line of bricks or stones in a wall.
in the course of during; as something goes on. *In the course of a term, both pupils and teachers become tired.*
in due course at the proper time; after some time. *I shall answer all your questions in due course.*
of course certainly; as one would expect; as everyone knows.
a matter of course something which is quite usual and expected. *He treated my sudden arrival as a matter of course.*
take a course **1.** (with **in**) study and attend lectures or lessons. *I took a course in geology last year.* **2.** (with **of**) use over a period of time as a treatment for a disease. *I took a course of drugs for my rheumatism.*
take its/their course go on in the proper way without interference. *We must let the law take its course* i.e. we must let people be punished by the law if they have done wrong.
course[2] [kɔːs] **1.** *vt/i* (usu. with reference to hunting hares) hunt using dogs, as a sport. **2.** *vi* (with reference to liquids) move quickly.
coursing *nu* the sport of hunting hares with dogs.
court[1] [kɔːt] *nc* **1.** place where a judge or magistrate hears law cases. **2.** officials in a court of law. **3.** place where a king or queen lives. **4.** king or queen with the officials who live at the court. **5.** small open space surrounded by buildings or walls. (Often **courtyard**). **6.** room or open space with markings for certain games: *a tennis court.*
courtier ['kɔːtiə*] *nc* person who attends or is present at the court of a king or queen.
courtship *nu* **1.** action of a young man in being polite and friendly to a woman whom he hopes to marry. **2.** period before a man and woman get married and after they have become friendly.
courtly *adj* very polite and dignified. **courtliness** *nu.*
'court card king, queen or jack of a suit of playing cards.
'court-'martial *nc* court of law held under

military law. *pl* **courts-martial** (*formal*) or **court-martials** (*informal*). Also *vt* try somebody before a court-martial.
courtyard see **court**[1] (in sense **5.**).
be presented at court be taken to court to meet a king or queen.
pay court to somebody **1.** try to get somebody's help by being very polite and friendly to him. **2.** try to persuade a woman to marry one by being very polite and friendly to her.
settle a case out of court agree about ending a quarrel or law case without the ruling of a judge.
take somebody to court ask a judge in a court of law to make a decision about a complaint which one has against somebody.

court[2] [kɔːt] *vt* **1.** be a companion of a woman whom one hopes to marry. *John has been courting Mary for three years.* (*informal*). **2.** (with reference to things such as approval, assistance, sympathy, encouragement) try to get from somebody. **3.** (with reference to meeting such things as disaster or defeat) act in a way that makes it likely one will get or meet.
courteous ['kəːtiəs] *adj* very polite and kind. (*opp* **discourteous**). **courteously** *adv*.
courtesy ['kəːtəsi] *nc/u* polite and kind behaviour or action. (*opp* **discourtesy**).
by courtesy of with the help or permission of. *John Smith appears in this film by courtesy of XYZ Film Corporation* i.e. John Smith works as an actor for XYZ Film Corporation, who have given permission for him to appear in a film made by another company.

courtesan [kɔːti'zæn] *nc* (in former times) woman who gave love to men in exchange for money (esp. such a woman receiving large sums of money from rich men).

cousin ['kʌzn] *nc* **1.** son or daughter of a brother or sister of either of one's parents. (Sometimes **first cousin**). **2.** children, grandchildren etc of one's cousins, or one's parents' or grandparents' cousins etc.

cove[1] [kouv] *nc* small sheltered bay or inlet of the sea.

cove[2] [kouv] (*Brit*) man. (*informal* and *o.f.*).

covenant ['kʌvənənt] *nc* very important agreement (usu. written down and signed by the people making the agreement). Also *vt/i* make such an agreement.

cover[1] ['kʌvə*] *vt* **1.** put something over, on or in front of. *He covered the table with a cloth. He covered the wall with green paint.* **2.** be over, on or in front of something. *Pieces of paper covered his desk. The blankets did not completely cover the bed. The streets were covered with ice and snow.* **3.** (esp. with reference to war and fighting) protect. *Our planes covered the tanks which were attacking the enemy* i.e. the planes prevented the enemy from attacking the tanks. **4.** (usu. with reference to war and fighting) be in a position to attack; be on guard near. *Two policemen covered the back door and two covered the front.* **5.** point a gun at. *One of the thieves covered me with a gun while the other stole my money.* **6.** travel a certain distance. *He covered twelve miles a day when he was walking in the mountains.* **7.** (with reference to books, lessons, lectures etc) include. *This dictionary does not cover the whole of the English vocabulary.* **8.** (usu. with reference to money) be enough for. *Here is £5; that should cover all your expenses.* **9.** act as a reporter for a newspaper or for radio or television. *The best reporters were sent to cover the war* i.e. send reports on the war. **10.** buy an insurance policy against. *I am covered against fire* i.e. if my house is damaged by fire, the insurance company will pay to repair the damage.
cover something up cover completely. *I could not see my pen because it was covered up by the papers.*
cover up (for somebody) refuse to tell the truth (in order to protect somebody).

cover[2] ['kʌvə*] **1.** *nc* something made to be put over, on or in front of something. *I haven't got a cover to put on this box.* **2.** *nu* things behind which a person or animal can hide. *The lion was able to find cover in the grass.* **3.** *nu* insurance policy. *I must get cover for my new car.* **4.** *nc* place for a person at a table, laid with knife, fork, spoon, plate etc. **5.** *nc* (business) envelope for a letter.
covering *nc* something over, on or in front of something. *There was a thick covering of snow on the street.*
'cover charge fixed charge in a restaurant etc for service etc.
covered wagon large vehicle covered by canvas and pulled by horses or oxen (used esp. in former times in the western parts of America).
covering letter letter which is sent with some other documents to explain something about the documents.
break cover (esp. with reference to the hunting of animals) come out of a hiding place and run.
from cover to cover (with reference to reading a book etc) completely. *He read the book from cover to cover* i.e. he read every word.
take cover hide; get into a place which gives protection. *Everybody took cover when the bombs began to fall on the town.*
under cover (of something) secretly; protected or hidden by something. *The army moved under cover of darkness.*

coverlet ['kʌvəlit] *nc* large piece of cloth used to cover a bed (esp. when nobody is in the bed).

covert[1] ['kʌvət] *adj* (usu. with reference to somebody's behaviour) partly hidden; not open. *He gave a covert glance at the other people* i.e. he looked at them without allowing them to see that he was looking. **covertly** *adv*.

covert[2] ['kʌvət] *nc* bushes and trees (esp. the hiding place of birds and animals, which are hunted for sport).

covet ['kʌvit] *vt* want something very strongly (usu. something belonging to another person) (rather *o.f.*). **covetous** *adj*. **covetously** *adv*.

cow[1] [kau] *nc* **1.** large, female domestic animal, kept to provide milk. **2.** female of certain other animals (e.g. female elephant or whale).
'cowboy man whose work is to look after cattle in the western part of America.
'cowcatcher (*US*) metal framework on the front of a railway engine in America to push cows and other obstacles out of the way.

cow[2] [kau] *vt* make afraid. *He cowed his wife into obedience* i.e. he made her frightened and so she obeyed him.

coward ['kauəd] *nc* person who is afraid of danger; person who runs away from danger or who will not fight because he is afraid. **cowardly** *adj.* **cowardice** ['kauədis] *nu.*

cower ['kauə*] *vi* bend down or move away because one is afraid.

cowl ['kaul] *nc* **1.** cloak and hood worn by a monk, or the hood alone. **2.** metal covering on a chimney, which prevents smoke blowing back into a room.

cowrie ['kauri] *nc* small shell, at one time used as money in parts of Africa and Asia. (Also **cowrie shell**).

cowslip ['kauslip] *nc* yellow flower which grows wild in parts of Europe.

cox [kɔks] *nc* short form of **coxswain** i.e. the person who steers a boat (esp. in a boat race). Also *vt/i* act as a cox.

coxcomb ['kɔkskoum] *nc* foolish person who gives a lot of attention to his clothes (*o.f.*).

coxswain ['kɔksn] *nc* see **cox.**

coy [kɔi] *adj* (usu. with reference to children or young women, and often with the suggestion that this fear is not completely real) afraid of strangers; unwilling to talk to strangers. **coyly** *adv.* **coyness** *nu.*

coyote [kɔi'outi] *nc* wild animal like a wolf or large dog, found in the west of America.

crab [kræb] **1.** *nc* type of broad shellfish with big claws, which walks sideways. **2.** *nu* the meat of this animal, used as food. **3.** *nc* one of several related animals. **4.** *nc* small sour type of apple. **5.** *nc* the tree on which it grows. (Also **crabapple**).

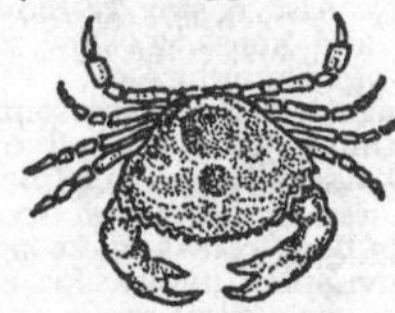

crab (*def 1*)

crabbed [kræbd] *adj* **1.** bad-tempered or angry. **2.** (with reference to handwriting) badly formed.

crack[1] [kræk] *nc* **1.** line where something is broken but has not separated into pieces. **2.** narrow opening. *He hid the money in a crack in the wall.* **3.** sudden noise: *a crack of thunder; the crack of a gun.* **4.** blow or knock on a part of somebody's body. *He got a crack on the head.* (*informal*). **5.** joke. (*informal*).

cracker *nc* **1.** roll of paper containing a small present used at children's parties; when the cracker is pulled at both ends, it opens with a loud noise and the present falls out. **2.** (*US*) thin hard biscuit, often eaten with cheese.

crackers[1] *npl* instrument for breaking nuts. (Also **nutcrackers**).

crackers[2] *pred adj* mad. (*informal*).

'Christmas 'cracker see **cracker** (in sense **1.**).

'firecracker device which makes a loud noise when lit, used in some types of celebration or party.

have a crack at something try to do something. (*informal*).

crack[2] [kræk] *vt/i* **1.** break, cause to break, so that a line appears in the thing broken, but it does not separate into pieces. *The cup cracked when I washed it, but you can still drink out of it. He cracked the cup.* **2.** make a sudden noise. *The gun cracked.* **3.** hit somebody hard. *I cracked him on the head.* (*informal*). **4.** (with reference to a sound and esp. to a boy's voice when he is approaching manhood) become harsh or shrill. **5.** (with reference to a person) break down or be unable to continue because of difficulty. *He cracked under the strain of work.* (*informal*). **6.** make a joke. (*informal*).

cracked *adj* **1.** broken but not separated into pieces. **2.** (with reference to a sound) harsh and shrill. *We heard the cracked note of the bell.* **3.** mad; having strange ideas or opinions. (*informal* in sense **3.**).

crack down on somebody/something act firmly to stop somebody/something. *The police have decided to crack down on motorists who drive too fast.* (*informal*).

crack up break; be unable to continue. *His health cracked up.* (*informal*).

crack a safe break open a safe in order to steal what is inside. (*informal*).

get cracking hurry. (*informal*).

crack[3] [kræk] *adj* (usu. with reference to sportsmen) very good. *He is a crack shot* i.e. he is very good at firing guns.

crackle ['krækl] *nu* number of small sharp sounds, such as the sound made by dry wood being burned. Also *vi* make this sound.

crackling *nu* **1.** sound of something as it crackles. **2.** hard skin of pork which has been roasted.

cradle ['kreidl] *nc* **1.** small bed for a baby, often on curved pieces of wood which allow the cradle to be rocked backwards and forwards or from side to side. **2.** place where something begins. *Greece is the cradle of democracy* i.e. democracy first arose in Greece. **3.** framework which holds a person /thing while a particular piece of work is being done i.e. men often stand in cradles to paint high buildings or bridges. Also *vt* **1.** hold in a cradle. **2.** hold a baby in one's arms. **3.** hold carefully.

from the cradle to the grave during the whole of one's life.

craft [krɑ:ft] **1.** *nc* job done with the hands, requiring skill and training: *the craft of the goldsmith/carpenter/painter etc.* **2.** *nc* people who work in some craft. **3.** *nu* cunning; skill in hiding one's intentions so as to get what one wants. **4.** *nc* boat or ship. *pl* usu. **craft.**

craftsman *nc* **1.** man who works with his hands at a job which needs skill and training. **2.** somebody who does his work very well.

craftsmanship *nu* skilled work done by a craftsman; skill in working.

crafty *adj* full of cunning. *That thief was very crafty; he always made very careful plans.* **craftily** *adv.* **craftiness** *nu.*

crag [kræg] *nc* steep rocky cliff or hill. **craggy** *adj.*

cram [kræm] *vt/i* **1.** fill with too many things; push into something so that it becomes too full. *He crammed the box with his papers. He crammed the papers into the box.* **2.** learn, cause to learn, by heart in order to prepare for an examination. *The boys were cramming for the examination.* *past* **crammed.**

crammer *nc* teacher or establishment which gives extra lessons to pupils in order to prepare them for an examination. (*informal* and rather *impolite*).

'cram-'full *adj/adv* very full. *The box was cram-full of papers.*

cramp[1] [kræmp] *nc/u* sudden pain and tightening of the muscles, caused by cold or overuse of the muscles. Also *vt.*

'writer's 'cramp painful stiffness of the fingers, caused by writing too much.

cramp[2] [kræmp] *vt* (sometimes with **up**) prevent easy movement; keep in a small space.

cramped *adj* **1.** with very little space in which to move. **2.** (with reference to handwriting) not spaced out.

cramp someone's style make it difficult for someone to do his best.

cramp[3] [kræmp] *nc* tool used for holding together pieces of stone or wood. Also *vt* fasten with a cramp.

cranberry ['krænbəri] *nc* **1.** small dark red berry used in cookery. **2.** the bush on which it grows.

crane[1] [krein] *nc* **1.** machine used for raising and lowering heavy things. **2.** one of several birds with long legs, neck and beak which walk in water.

crane (*def 1*)

(*def 2*)

crane[2] [krein] *vt/i* stretch one's neck in order to see something. *He craned (his neck) to see over the heads of the crowd.*

cranium ['kreiniəm] *nc* the skull; the bone which surrounds the brain. *pl* **crania** ['kreiniə] or **craniums. cranial** *adj.*

crank[1] [kræŋk] *nc* handle of a machine. Also *vt* (often with **up**) start a machine by using a crank.

crank[2] [kræŋk] *nc* person with strong and unusual opinions. **cranky** *adj.* **crankiness** *nu.* (*informal*).

cranny ['kræni] *nc* small hole (esp. in a wall or in a rock).

crape [kreip] *nu* thin black cloth used as a sign of mourning when somebody has died. see also **crepe.**

craps [kræps] *nu* (*US*) game played with two dice.

shoot craps play this game.

crash [kræʃ] *vt/i* **1.** fall, break or hit something, making a loud noise. *The aeroplane crashed into the houses. All the plates and cups crashed to the floor. The driver crashed the bus.* **2.** (with reference to a business firm, government or rich person) lose all one's money and be unable to meet one's debts. Also *nc* **1.** noise of something crashing. **2.** fall of an aeroplane to the ground, or accident to a vehicle while travelling. **3.** financial ruin of a business firm, government or rich person.

'crash course/programme etc course of lessons or programme to do some work etc, which is carried out in the shortest possible time.

'crash helmet hard padded covering for the head worn by a motorcyclist etc.

'crash 'landing *nc* forced landing made by an aeroplane when something goes wrong.

'crash-land *vt/i*: *He crash-landed the plane.*

'gatecrash see **gate.**

crass [kræs] *adj* **1.** unusually great (usu. in **crass stupidity**). **2.** coarse: *crass behaviour.* **crassly** *adv.* **crassness** *nu.*

crate [kreit] *nc* large wooden box for carrying goods in. Also *vt* (often with **up**) put in a crate. *He crated up all his books.*

crater ['kreitə*] *nc* **1.** hole at the top of a volcano. **2.** hole made by a bomb, large shell or an explosion.

cravat [krə'væt] *nc* **1.** small scarf or piece of cloth, tied round the neck with the ends worn inside the shirt. **2.** type of necktie now seldom worn.

crave [kreiv] *vt/i* want something very much. *The unhappy child was craving his mother's love.*

craving *nc/u* strong wish or desire for something.

craven ['kreivən] *adj* very much afraid of danger. Also *nc* person who is afraid. (both rather *o.f.*).

crawl [krɔ:l] *vi* **1.** move along on the hands and knees, as a baby does. **2.** move along very slowly. Also *n sing* **1.** movement on the hands and knees. **2.** slow movement. **3.** method of swimming.

be crawling with have present in large numbers things that are alive and unpleasant. *This house was crawling with rats. His clothes were crawling with lice.*

make one's flesh crawl make one feel as though some small unpleasant creature is crawling on one's skin; make one feel fear and disgust. *His stories of the war made my flesh crawl.*

crayfish ['kreifiʃ], *US* **crawfish** ['krɔ:fiʃ] *nc* freshwater shellfish like a small lobster; a similar sea-water animal. *pl* **crayfish.**

crayon ['kreiən] *nc* stick of soft, coloured substance, used for drawing. Also *vt/i* draw with crayons.

craze [kreiz] *nc* something in which people have an interest, which is great but is not likely to last for a long time. *Everyone in his family had a craze for Chinese food.* (*informal*). Also *vt* make mad. see **crazy.**

crazy ['kreizi] *adj* **1.** mad. (*informal*). **2.** filled with strong interest. *He was crazy about gramophone records last year.* (*informal*). **3.** (with reference to buildings) not safe; likely to fall to pieces. **crazily** *adv.* **craziness** *nu.*

'crazy 'paving *nu*, **'crazy 'pavement** *nc* path in a garden, made of pieces of stone of various sizes, put together without any definite pattern.

creak [kri:k] *nc* noise like that made by a door which needs oiling. Also *vi* make this noise. **creaky** *adj.*

cream [kri:m] *nu* **1.** the thick substance in milk which rises to the top. **2.** sweet substance made from or like cream, used as a food. **3.** substance containing oil, to be put on the skin for various purposes. Also *vt* (cookery) make into a smooth substance like cream. *She creamed the potatoes.* Also *adj* of a colour between white and yellow. **creamy** *adj.*

creamery *nc* place where cream is made or sold.
'cream 'cheese very soft, white kind of cheese.
the cream of something the best part: *the cream of society* i.e. rich and influential people.

crease [kri:s] *nc* **1.** line made in cloth or paper by folding. **2.** (cricket) line on the ground to show the batsman and bowler where to stand. Also *vt/i*: *This cloth does not crease. He creased the paper.*

create [kri'eit] *vt* make something which is new. *God created the world. This news creates several difficulties for me.*
creation **1.** *nu* act of creating. **2.** *nc* something created. **3.** *nu* (often **Creation**) the whole world or the whole universe.
creative *adj* having the ability to make new things. *He is a very creative writer.* **creatively** *adv.* **creativeness, creativity** [kriei'tiviti] *nu.*
creator *nc* person who creates.
The Creator God.

creature ['kri:tʃə*] *nc* **1.** living thing (esp. an animal, bird, fish, insect, reptile etc – not usu. plants or human beings except in a pitying way - *poor creature*). **2.** person who is willing to do whatever another person asks him to do.
'creature 'comforts things such as food, drink, warmth, clothing.
creature of habit person or animal etc that always likes to behave in the same way.

creche, crèche [kreʃ] *nc* place where babies and young children are taken care of during the daytime.

credence ['kri:dns] *nu* belief that something is true (usu. in **give credence to something**).

credentials [kri'denʃlz] *npl* letters or papers which show that somebody is the person that he says he is.
present one's credentials (esp. with reference to an ambassador or other official taking up a post in a foreign country) show these papers to somebody in authority.

credible ['kredibl] *adj* easily believed. *His story was quite credible.* (*opp* **incredible**). **credibly** *adv.* **credibility** [kredi'biliti] *nu.* *Note:* do not confuse *credible, credulous* and *creditable.*

credit[1] ['kredit] *nu* **1.** money a person has in a bank etc. *I have a large credit with Brown's Bank.* **2.** agreement by which one pays for goods some time after buying them. *He buys all his food on credit* i.e. the shopkeeper allows him to take the goods and pay later. *This shopkeeper does not give credit* i.e. he does not allow people to buy goods in this way. **3.** money which a business firm has. (*opp* **debit**). **4.** belief that something is true. *I don't give any credit to stories like that* i.e. I don't believe them. **5.** honour; reputation; what other people think about one's behaviour. *He gained a lot of credit from that journey* i.e. everybody thought that he was very good, very clever, very brave etc for making that journey.
creditable *adj* bringing praise or honour; making people think that one has done well: *a very creditable action.* (*opp* **discreditable**). **creditably** *adv.* see *Note* on **credible.**
'credit 'rating estimate of the amount of money which could safely be lent to a person or organization based on an investigation of his or its financial situation. *John finds it easy to borrow money because he has a good credit rating.*
'credit title words shown on the screen at the beginning of a film, telling the names of the actors, the director etc.
be a credit to someone/something do something which brings honour to oneself or to someone/something else. *John is a credit to his old school* i.e. people think that John's old school is very good because John has done something very good.
do credit to someone/something do something which brings honour to oneself or to someone/something else. *Robert's success does credit to his family* i.e. Robert's success shows that his family gave him good training or helped him very much. *Your success does you credit* i.e. it shows that you have worked very hard and that you deserve your success.
get/take the credit for something be praised for something (often something which was done by somebody else). *He got the credit for the idea, but his brother suggested it first.*
give credit to believe that something is true.
give somebody credit for something believe that somebody has some ability or quality. *I gave you credit for being able to do the work properly* i.e. I thought you could do the work properly.
on credit with a promise to pay later. *He bought the goods on credit.*
place/put credit in believe that something is true. *I don't place any credit in your story.*

credit[2] ['kredit] *vt* **1.** show in records of money received and spent that somebody has a certain amount of money. *The bank has credited £100 to my account.* **2.** believe that something is true. *I didn't credit his story.*
creditor *nc* person to whom one owes money.
credit somebody with something think that somebody has some ability or quality. *I credited you with the intelligence to do the work properly* i.e. I thought that you had enough intelligence to do the work properly.

credulous ['kredjuləs] *adj* too ready to believe what one is told. *He is a credulous fool; he thought that I was telling the truth when I said I could do magic.* (*opp* **incredulous**). **credulously** *adv.* **credulity** [kri'djuliti] *nu.* see *Note* on **credible.**

creed [kri:d] *nc* **1.** official statement of religious beliefs. **2.** ideas that one strongly believes to be right.

creek [kri:k] *nc* **1.** narrow arm of water off the main stretch of water. **2.** (*US*) small river.
up the creek in trouble. (*informal*).

creel [kri:l] *nc* basket which is used for carrying fish.

creep [kri:p] *vi* **1.** move along very slowly, quietly or secretly, often with the body close to the ground. **2.** (with reference to certain types of plant) spread out over a wide area. *past* **crept** [krept]. Also *nc* **1.** (usu. only *sing*) slow and quiet movement. **2.** unpleasant person. (*informal* in sense **2.**).
creeper *nc* **1.** type of plant that spreads out over a wide area. **2.** type of bird which creeps up and down trees looking for insects.
creepy *adj* causing fear or disgust: *creepy ghost stories.* (*informal*).
give one the creeps give one a feeling of fear and disgust; give one a feeling of strong dislike and unhappiness. (*informal*).
make one's flesh creep give one a feeling of

fear and disgust, as though a small and unpleasant animal were creeping over one's flesh. *His stories of ghosts and monsters made the children's flesh creep.*

cremate [kri'meit] *vt* burn a dead body (instead of burying it).

cremation *nu* practice of burning dead bodies.

crematorium [kremə'tɔːriəm] *nc* place where dead bodies are cremated.

creosote ['kriəsout] *nu* thick oily liquid made from tar. Also *vt* cover with creosote.

crepe, crêpe [kreip] *nu* name for various types of material which have small folds on the surface.

'crepe 'paper type of paper with many small folds on the surface, often brightly coloured and used for decoration etc.

'crepe 'sole bottom part of a shoe, made of a type of rubber which looks like crepe; a shoe having this type of sole.

crept [krept] past of **creep.**

crescendo [kri'ʃendou] *nc* **1.** gradual increase in loudness in a piece of music. **2.** anything which becomes louder, faster, more important etc as it goes on. *pl* **crescendos.** Also *adv*: *The music was played crescendo.*

crescent ['kresnt] *nc* anything shaped like the moon in its first or last quarter. Also *adj* (with reference to the moon) having this shape.

'cresent-shaped *adj* having this shape.

crest [krest] *nc* **1.** top of a mountain ridge. **2.** top of a wave. **3.** feathers which stick up on the top of a bird's head. **4.** feathers or other decoration worn on the top of a knight's helmet or soldier's helmet. **5.** special mark or sign of a person, family, town, business firm, school etc (often printed on writing paper used by these various people).

crested *adj* having a crest (often used in the name of certain birds).

'crestfallen *adj* unhappy and disappointed because one has been unsuccessful. *He was crestfallen at his failure in the competition.*

cretin ['kretin] *nc* **1.** person suffering from a type of disease which makes him have a very low level of intelligence. **2.** foolish or unintelligent person. (*informal* in sense **2.**).

cretinism *nu* type of disease causing lack of intelligence.

cretonne [kre'tɔn] *nu* type of cloth (often used for making curtains).

crevasse [kri'væs] *nc* **1.** deep crack in ice (in parts of the world where the ground is covered by thick ice). **2.** (*US*) break or hole in a dam or other construction which holds back water.

crevice ['krevis] *nc* narrow opening (esp. in a wall or in rock).

crew[1] [kruː] *nc* **1.** all the men and officers sailing a ship or flying an aeroplane. **2.** the men on a ship (but not the officers). **3.** group of men doing certain jobs (e.g. a *train crew* drives a train). **4.** any group of people whom one dislikes or disapproves of. (*informal* in sense **4.**).

'crewcut type of haircut in which the hair is cut very short.

crew[2] [kruː] past tense of **crow**[1].

crib[1] [krib] *nc* **1.** (mainly *US*) small bed for a child. **2.** model of the scene shortly after the birth of Jesus, showing the child, Mary, Joseph, the animals etc, found in churches and people's homes at Christmas time. **3.** wooden or metal framework in which grass, hay etc is placed for animals to eat.

crib[2] [krib] *nc* **1.** word-for-word translation of something originally written in a foreign language, intended to help students or pupils. **2.** set of notes to help a student, which gives him the answers so that he does not have to do the work himself. Also *vt/i* copy the work or idea of somebody else in a dishonest way. *He cribbed all the answers from the boy sitting next to him. past* **cribbed.** (all *informal*).

crick [krik] *nc* stiffness and pain in a part of the body (esp. the neck).

cricket[1] ['krikit] *nu* game played by two teams of eleven players each, using bats and a ball.

cricketer *nc* person who plays cricket.

not cricket something which is unfair; a dishonest trick (usu. one which is not actually against the law) (*informal* and rather *o.f.*).

cricket[2] ['krikit] *nc* type of insect which makes a loud noise by rubbing its wings together.

cried [kraid] past of **cry**[1].

cries [kraiz] pl of **cry**[2] (*noun*); pres of **cry**[1] (*verb*).

crier ['kraiə*] *nc* see **cry**[1].

crime [kraim] **1.** *nu* actions which are against the law. *Part of the work of the police is to fight against crime.* **2.** *nc* action which is against the law. *Murder and robbery are crimes.* **3.** *nc* foolish or cruel action which is not against the law. *It is a crime to throw away all that good food.* (*informal* in sense **3.**).

criminal ['kriminl] *nc* person who commits crimes. Also *adj*: *Murder is a criminal act.*

criminology [krimi'nɔlədʒi] *nu* study of crimes and criminals. **criminologist** *nc.*

crimp [krimp] *vt* (esp. with reference to the hair) put into curls or waves.

crimson ['krimzn] *nu* very deep red colour. Also *adj.* Also *vi* become red in the face through embarrassment.

cringe [krindʒ] *vi* **1.** move the body away or down in fear. *The dog cringed before his cruel master.* **2.** behave in a very humble way to somebody rich or powerful in order to get what one wants.

crinkle ['kriŋkl] *nc* small fold (esp. in paper or cloth). Also *vt/i*: *He crinkled the paper.*

crinkly *adj*: *crinkly hair* i.e. like a Negro's.

crinoline ['krinəliːn] *nc* **1.** framework formerly used to make a woman's skirt stand out from the body. **2.** skirt of this type.

cripple ['kripl] *nc* person who cannot move his legs, arms or body properly because of some disease or injury. Also *vt* **1.** make a cripple of. **2.** damage or weaken. *Our air force has crippled the enemy.*

crisis ['kraisis] *nc* **1.** time of great danger or difficulty in some important matter: *a crisis in the country's economy.* **2.** point at which the course of a disease changes, either towards recovery or towards death. *pl* **crises** ['kraisiːz].

crisp[1] [krisp] *adj* **1.** (esp. with reference to food) hard and easily broken. **2.** (with reference to the weather) dry and cold. **3.** quick and without unnecessary words or actions. *The general gave a short, crisp talk to his men.* **crisply** *adv.* **crispness** *nu.*

crisp[2] [krisp] *nc* (*Brit*) thin slice of potato, fried in oil until hard and eaten cold. (*US* **potato chip**).

criss-cross ['kriskrɔs] *adj* made or marked with lines that cross each other. Also *vt* make or mark in this way.

criterion [kraiˈtiəriən] *nc* standard by which one can judge something. *There are several criteria of a good school* i.e. there are several things which tell one whether a school is good or not. *pl* **criteria** [kraiˈtiəriə].

critic [ˈkritik] *nc* **1.** person who says whether a book, film, play, piece of music etc is good or not, and gives reasons for his decision (usu. in a newspaper or magazine). **2.** person who always notices the bad points and mistakes about anything.

criticize [ˈkritisaiz] *vt/i* act, write, talk as a critic.

criticism [ˈkritisizəm] *nc/u* acts, writing, speech of a critic.

critical *adj* **1.** having reference to critics or criticism. **2.** coming at a very important moment; of the right size or amount for something to happen (e.g. the *critical mass* in nuclear engineering refers to the amount of radioactive substance necessary to cause a nuclear reaction). *He arrived at the critical moment* i.e. at the time when his arrival had a great effect. **3.** full of danger or difficulty in some important matter. *There is a critical weakness in the country's economy.* **critically** *adv.* see **crisis.**

critique [kriˈtiːk] *nc* piece of writing pointing out the good and bad points of something (esp. of a book, film, play, piece of music etc).

croak [krouk] *nc* deep harsh sound, like that made by a frog. Also *vt/i* make this sound. **croaky** *adj.*

crochet [ˈkrouʃei] *vt/i* make thread of cotton or wool into garments etc by making a series of loops using a hook. Also *nu* things made in this way.

crock [krɔk] *nc* **1.** vessel made of baked clay. **2.** broken piece of pottery or baked clay. **3.** animal, vehicle or person who cannot move properly because of some injury, disease or fault. (*informal* and rather *impolite*). Also *vt/i* (usu. with **up**) become or make a crock (in sense **3.**).

crockery [ˈkrɔkəri] *nu* plates, cups, dishes etc (usu. those made of baked clay or china).

crocodile [ˈkrɔkədail] **1.** *nc* large animal with a long nose and a lot of sharp teeth, which lives in rivers in the tropics and which looks like a floating log. **2.** *nu* the skin of this animal used for making shoes, bags etc.

ˈcrocodile ˈtears expression of sorrow or unhappiness which one does not really feel. (*informal*).

crocodile (*def 1*)

crocus [ˈkroukəs] *nc* small flower with white, yellow or purple blooms which grows in the early spring. *pl* **crocuses.**

croft [krɔft] *nc* (usu. in Scotland) small field or small farm.

crofter *nc* person who rents a croft from a landowner.

crone [kroun] *nc* very old and ugly-looking woman. (*impolite*).

crony [ˈkrouni] *nc* very close friend. (*informal*).

crook [kruk] *nc* **1.** criminal; person who gets his living by robbery etc. (*informal*). **2.** long stick with a hook on the end, used by shepherds. **3.** anything shaped like a hook; bend or curve. Also *vt/i* shape into a bend or curve.

crooked [ˈkrukid] *adj* **1.** criminal; dishonest. (*informal*). **2.** not straight; bent, curved or twisted. **crookedly** *adv.* **crookedness** *nu.*

by hook or by crook by any means possible, whether they are honest or not. (*informal*).

croon [kruːn] *vt/i* **1.** (with reference to certain types of entertainer) sing in a low voice with a lot of feeling. **2.** sing in a low voice. *The woman was crooning to her baby.*

crooner *nc* entertainer who croons.

crop[1] [krɔp] *nc* **1.** farm produce grown in a particular area or at a particular time. *Wheat is an important crop in many parts of the world.* **2.** quantity of farm produce collected at one time. *I had a poor crop of apples this year* i.e. my trees did not produce many apples. **3.** large number of things which occur at one time. *There is a large crop of mistakes in your essay.* (*informal*). **4.** haircut in which a lot of hair has been cut off. **5.** part of a bird's body below the beak, where food is stored while the bird is preparing to digest it. **6.** handle of a whip (esp. one used by horse riders).

crop[2] [krɔp] *vt/i* **1.** (with reference to animals) eat grass etc which is growing. *The sheep were cropping the grass.* **2.** (with reference to hair, ears, tails etc) cut short.

crop up occur unexpectedly or by chance. *Various subjects cropped up in the conversation* i.e. we talked about various subjects, without our having decided earlier what we would talk about.

cropper [ˈkrɔpə*] in **come a cropper** i.e. fall down very heavily; fail very badly. (*informal*).

croquet [ˈkroukei] *nu* game in which wooden balls are knocked through hoops.

croquette [krəˈket] *nc* ball of chopped meat or fish etc fried in fat.

crosier, crozier [ˈkrouʒə*] *nc* stick carried by a bishop (usu. having a hook at the end).

cross[1] [krɔs] *nc* **1.** object shaped + on which Christ was killed, and which has become a symbol of the Christian religion. **2.** the mark shaped × or +, often used as a signature on a document by a person who cannot write. **3.** duty or responsibility which causes suffering to oneself. *He has a heavy cross to bear.* **4.** mixture of races or breeds; person, animal, plant that has a mixed origin. *That dog is a cross between a sheepdog and a labrador.*

crossing *nc* **1.** journey by sea from one place to another. **2.** place in a road where people who are walking can go across the road. **3.** place where a railway line goes across a road. (Also *Brit* **level crossing,** *US* **grade crossing**).

ˈcrossbar bar across the top of two uprights used e.g. in jumping competitions; the jumper has to jump over the crossbar.

ˈcrossbones usu. in **skull and crossbones** i.e. a sign once used on the flag of pirate ships.

ˈcrossbreed *nc* person, animal or plant of mixed origin. Also *vt* breed animals by mixing breeds. **crossbred** *adj.*

'cross-check *vt/i* make completely sure that some information is correct by getting the same information from a different place to see whether there is any difference. Also *nc.*

'cross-'country *adj/adv* across fields etc, not following roads or paths. (usu. in **cross-country race**)

'cross-ex'amine *vt/i* question very carefully to find out whether somebody is telling the truth (esp. in a court of law, when a lawyer questions a witness who has been giving evidence for the other side in the case). **cross-examination** *nc.*

'cross-'eyed *adj* having a defect of the eyes, in which both eyes look towards the nose.

'crossfire firing of guns at a target from two or more points.

'cross-'grained *adj* **1.** (with reference to wood) having a grain which does not run straight. see **grain** (in sense **4.**). **2.** (with reference to a person) bad-tempered; difficult to be friendly with.

'cross-'legged *adj/adv* sitting with one leg over the other. *He was sitting cross-legged.*

'crosspiece any piece of wood, metal etc which is intended to be placed across something.

'cross-'purposes usu. in **at cross-purposes** i.e. failing to understand each other. *We were talking at cross-purposes.*

'cross-'question *vt* question somebody very carefully to find out whether he is telling the truth. **cross-questioning** *nu.*

'cross-'reference words in a book which tell the reader to look in another part of the book.

'crossroads *n sing* place where two or more roads cross each other.

'cross 'section **1.** drawing showing what can be seen if something is cut open vertically. **2.** collection of different types of something: *a cross section of society* i.e. a group of people coming from the various sections of society.

'crosswind *nc* (often *pl*) wind blowing from one side to the other, across the way in which one is travelling.

'crossword (puzzle) puzzle in the form of a set of squares in some of which words have to be written.

cross² [krɔs] **1.** *vt/i* go from one side to the other. *He crossed the road. The road crosses the river there.* **2.** *vt/i* meet and go past in opposite directions. *The two cars crossed on the road. Our letters crossed* i.e. I wrote to you before I received your letter, and you wrote to me before you received my letter. **3.** *vt* put one thing across another. *He sat down and crossed his legs.* **4.** *vt* oppose; try to prevent somebody from doing or saying what he wants. *He becomes very angry if anyone crosses him.* **5.** *vt* mix one breed of animal or one type of plant with another in order to produce a new type of animal or plant.

cross something off draw a line through something written in order to show that one does not wish it to be written (e.g. with reference to names in a list, a list of jobs that one has to do etc). *I crossed off the jobs as I finished each one. I crossed some names off the list.*

cross something out draw a line through something written in order to remove it or show that it is wrong. *I have crossed out all the mistakes in your work. I have crossed that word out.*

cross a cheque draw two lines across a cheque, as a sign to one's bank that the money is to be paid into somebody's bank and not in cash. (The words '& Co.' are usu. written between the two lines).

cross one's fingers (for something) **1.** put one finger over another on the same hand as a sign of good luck (because one hopes to get something). **2.** hope to get. *I'm crossing my fingers for good weather tomorrow.* (*informal*).

cross one's heart make the sign of the cross over one's heart when saying that some fact or information is true (often done by children).

cross one's mind come into one's mind. *A sudden thought crossed my mind.*

cross oneself make the sign of the cross on one's body. *Roman Catholics usually cross themselves when they enter a church.*

cross somebody's path meet somebody by chance (esp. after a long period of separation).

cross³ [krɔs] *adj* in a bad temper; angry. **crossly** *adv.* **crossness** *nu.*

crotch [krɔtʃ] *nc* place where a person's legs join; this place in a pair of trousers etc. (Also **crutch**).

crotchet ['krɔtʃit] *nc* (*Brit*) quarter note in music. (*US* **quarter note**).

crotchety *adj* bad-tempered; angry. (*informal*).

crouch [krautʃ] *vi* bend the body downwards (e.g. in fear, or in preparation for attacking something). Also *nc* this position of the body.

croup [kru:p] *nu* disease of children, in which there is a swelling in the throat and difficulty in breathing. **croupy** *adj.*

croupier ['kru:piə*] *nc* person who takes in and pays out money lost and won at a gambling table.

crow¹ [krou] *nc* noise made by a cock. Also *vi* **1.** make a noise like a cock. **2.** make a noise like a baby when it is happy. *past tense* **crowed** or **crew** [kru:]. *past part* **crowed.**

crow over something speak boastfully and unkindly to somebody whom one has defeated in a war, competition etc. (*informal*).

crow² [krou] *nc* large black bird with a rough voice.

as the crow flies in a straight line, which is the shortest distance. *The distance from London to Edinburgh is about 350 miles as the crow flies* i.e. but the actual journey will be over a longer distance because the roads are not straight.

'crow's-'feet small folds in the skin at the corners of the eyes.

'crow's-nest small construction near the top of the mast of a ship, in which one can stand to see what is in the distance.

crowbar ['krouba:*] *nc* long piece of iron with a bent end, used for moving heavy objects, opening locked doors etc.

crowd [kraud] *nc* **1.** large number of people who have come together in one place. **2.** number of people who work together, meet each other regularly or have some interest in common. (*informal*). **3.** large number of objects. (*informal*). Also *vt/i* come together or move as a crowd. *The people crowded round the Prime Minister. The bus was crowded* i.e. full.

crowd in (on somebody) come in a crowd (towards somebody).

crown[1] [kraun] *nc* **1.** band round the head, worn by a king or queen as a sign of authority. **2.** (with reference to power or authority, not to the king or queen as individuals) king or queen. *The power of the crown is limited by parliament.* **3.** covering for the head. **4.** mark shaped like the crown of a king or queen, often put on government property. **5.** top part of a hat. **6.** top part of a tooth. **7.** top of the head. **8.** top or highest part of something. **9.** formerly, British coin worth five shillings (25 pence).
'crown 'prince (not usu. with reference to the British monarchy) eldest son of a king or queen, and the person who is likely to be the next king.
a half-crown formerly, British coin worth two shillings and sixpence (12½ pence); an amount of two shillings and sixpence.

crown[2] [kraun] *vt* **1.** put a crown on a king or queen in a special ceremony (called a **coronation**). **2.** put on the top of. **3.** put some hard substance on top of a tooth to prevent the tooth from breaking or decaying.
to crown it all as the last and most unfortunate occurrence. (*informal*).

crozier ['krouʒə*] *nc* see **crosier.**

crucial ['kru:ʃl] *adj* very important, and coming at a time of great danger or difficulty. *The Prime Minister has to make a crucial decision within the next few weeks.*
crucially *adv.*

crucible ['kru:sibl] *nc* container in which metal etc is melted.

crucifix ['kru:sifiks] *nc* cross with a figure of Christ fastened to it.
crucify ['krusifai] *vt* kill by fastening to a cross.
crucifixion [kru:si'fikʃən] *nc/u* the act of doing this.

crude [kru:d] *adj* **1.** not polite; showing no signs of training in the right way to behave: *a very crude person; crude behaviour.* **2.** (with reference to certain materials) in the state in which something occurs naturally, before it has been treated: *crude oil.* **3.** badly made or done: *a crude drawing.* **crudely** *adv.* **crudeness** *nc.* **crudity** *nc/u.*

cruel ['kruəl] *adj* **1.** causing unnecessary pain and suffering to other people. *The king was very cruel to his people.* **2.** causing pain and suffering: *a cruel winter; a cruel war.*
cruelly *adv.* **cruelty** ['kruəlti] *nc/u.*

cruet ['kru:it] *nc* **1.** glass bottle holding vinegar, oil etc for the table. **2.** metal stand or holder containing a number of these bottles. (Also **cruet stand**). **3.** salt, pepper, vinegar etc placed on the table to be put on food.

cruise [kru:z] *vi* **1.** make a sea journey for pleasure. **2.** travel in a car or aeroplane at a comfortable speed. Also *nc* long journey by sea taken for pleasure.
cruiser *nc* light fast battleship.
'cruising speed speed at which a car or aeroplane goes when the engine is being used in the most efficient way.

crumb [krʌm] *nc* **1.** very small piece of bread or cake. **2.** small piece of something: *a crumb of comfort* i.e. something which helps one a little or makes one feel a little happier.

crumble ['krʌmbl] *vt/i* fall or break into crumbs or small pieces. *He crumbled his bread. The walls of the houses were crumbling.*

crumpet ['krʌmpit] *nc* (*Brit*) flat type of cake which is heated and eaten with butter.

crumple ['krʌmpl] *vt/i* (often with **up**) fall or push into folds; break up under pressure or distress. *He crumpled the piece of paper in his hand. The car crumpled up when it hit the wall. Her face crumpled and she burst into tears.*

crunch [krʌntʃ] *vt/i* **1.** break something hard by biting noisily with the teeth. *He crunched the apple.* **2.** make a sharp noise as somebody walks. *The hard snow crunched under his feet. He crunched the hard snow.* Also *nu* act or noise of crunching. **crunchy** *adj.* **crunchiness** *nu.*
the crunch the moment of crisis. (*informal*).

crusade [kru:'seid] *nc* **1.** (often **Crusade**) one of several wars during the Middle Ages, in which armies from Europe fought against the Turks, Arabs and Egyptians in order to win or hold Palestine. **2.** public campaign or movement in favour of or against something. Also *vi* take part in a crusade.
crusader *nc* person who takes part in a crusade.

crush[1] [krʌʃ] *vt/i* **1.** press together with great force so as to break. *Certain types of snake crush small animals to death before eating them.* **2.** develop or produce unwanted folds or creases in cloth. *This cloth will not crush* i.e. it always stays flat. **3.** defeat and destroy. *The Prime Minister said that he was determined to crush the enemies of the country.*
crushable *adj* easily crushed. (*opp* **uncrushable**).
crushing *adj* which defeats or destroys: *a crushing blow.*
crush into enter in a crowd using force. *The children crushed into the room.*
crush out 1. get out by using force: *crush out the juice from fruit.* **2.** defeat and destroy. *The dictator crushed out all opposition to his government.*
crush up break into small pieces using great force.

crush[2] [krʌʃ] *nc* **1.** large crowd of people very close to each other. **2.** strong pressure. **3.** drink made from juice of fruit. **4.** number of people at a party or social gathering. (*informal* and rather *o.f.*). **5.** strong liking felt by a girl or boy for another person. *Little girls sometimes have a crush on their teachers.* (*informal*).

crust [krʌst] *nc* **1.** the hard outside of bread or pies. **2.** hard outside covering of anything: *the crust of the earth.*
crusty *adj* **1.** having a crust. **2.** bad-tempered and difficult to be friendly with.
crustiness *nu.* (*informal*).

crustacean [krʌs'teiʃən] *nc* one of a group of sea animals having legs and a hard shell (e.g. crabs, lobsters, shrimps). Also *adj.*

crutch [krʌtʃ] *nc* **1.** stick with a support to go under the arm, used by people who cannot walk properly. **2.** see **crotch.**

crux [krʌks] *nc* difficult part or most important part of a question or problem: *the crux of the matter.*

cry[1] [krai] **1.** *vi* allow tears to come from the eyes, shed tears, weep (usu. because one is unhappy). *She cried when she heard that her son was dead.* **2.** *vi* shout loudly. *He cried for help when the thief attacked him.* (Also **cry out**). **3.** *vt* shout in order to make something known. **4.** *vi* (with reference to an animal) make a noise from the mouth. *past* **cried** [kraid].
crier *nc* official formerly found in most

towns whose work was to walk round the town calling out important news. (Usu. **town crier**).
cry something down say that something is not at all important or valuable. *He is always crying down the government.* (*informal*).
cry for something demand or ask for.
cry off say that one will not do something after promising or agreeing to do so. *John was going to help us, but he cried off.* (*informal*).
cry (something) out shout loudly. *He cried out when the thief attacked him. He cried out the good news.*
cry up something say that something is very important or valuable. *He has been crying up the new magazine.* (*informal*).
cry/eat one's heart out cry bitterly; long for somebody/something. (*informal*).
cry for the moon ask for something which cannot possibly be given to one. (*informal*).
cry oneself to sleep shed tears until one falls asleep.
cry over spilt milk be unhappy about an accident which cannot be put right (usu. in **it's no use crying over spilt milk**) (*informal*).
cry wolf warn people about a danger which is not really there.

cry² [krai] *nc* **1.** act of shedding tears. *She had a cry about the sad news.* (*informal*). **2.** loud shout. *We heard a cry for help.* **3.** noise made by an animal. *We heard the cry of a lion.* **4.** slogan; expression which many people use during some public movement. *'Action not words' was a cry of the Conservative Party during the election.*
crying *nu* (esp. with reference to a child) shedding of tears; noise made by somebody who is shedding tears. Also *adj* very bad; needing attention or change (usu. in **a crying shame; a crying need etc**) (*informal in this sense*).
'crybaby person (esp. a child) who often sheds tears.
a far cry from very different from.
in full cry (after something) (esp. with reference to dogs used for hunting) chasing or running after something.
hue and cry 1. chase after somebody (esp. after a thief). **2.** great anger by many people about something. *There was a hue and cry about the government's decision.*

crypt [kript] *nc* room under the ground (esp. in a church) in which dead bodies were once buried.

cryptic ['kriptik] *adj* having a hidden meaning: *a cryptic remark; a cryptic letter.*
cryptically *adv*.
cryptogram ['kriptəgræm] *nc* message written in a secret code or cypher.

crystal ['kristl] **1.** *nc* piece of a substance, having a regular shape. *Salt and sugar occur as crystals.* **2.** *nu* type of mineral substance which looks like glass. **3.** *nc* piece of this substance. **4.** *nu* very good type of glass. **5.** *nc* (*US*) glass over the face of a watch.
crystalline ['kristəlain] *adj*.
crystallize ['kristəlaiz] **1.** *vt/i* form into crystals. *The substance crystallized when it became cool.* **2.** *vt/i* come to a definite form after being uncertain. *His plans have crystallized at last.* **3.** *vt* (cookery) boil fruit in sugar until the fruit is hard. **crystallized** *adj*.
crystallography [kristə'lɔgrəfi] *nu* study of chemical crystals. **crystallographer** *nc*.
'crystal 'ball large glass ball, used by some people who claim to be able to say what will happen in the future.
(be) 'crystal ('ball) gazing 1. saying what will happen in the future by looking into a large glass ball (called a **crystal ball**). **2.** trying to say what will happen in the future. *In making these plans, the government is merely crystal gazing.* (*informal*).
'crystal set early type of radio.

cub [kʌb] *nc* **1.** young of certain animals (e.g. bear, fox, lion). **2.** young man who is impolite; young man who has little experience.

cubby ['kʌbi], **cubbyhole** ['kʌbihoul] *nc* small hole, cupboard or room, in which things can be stored or in which a person can work.

cube [kju:b] *nc* **1.** solid object having six square sides of equal size. **2.** number obtained when a number is multiplied by itself twice (e.g. *3 × 3 × 3 = 27*; 27 is the cube of *3*) (It can also be said that *3* is the cube root of 27). Also *vt* **1.** cut into the form of cubes. **2.** multiply a number by itself twice in order to find the cube.
cubic *adj*: *a cubic foot* i.e. volume of a cube whose sides are each one foot long.
cubical *adj*.
'cube 'root see **cube** (in sense **2.**).

cubicle ['kju:bikl] *nc* small room (esp. one for sleeping in e.g. in a hospital).

cubism ['kju:bizəm] *nu* style of painting practised in the early 20th century and using rectangles.
cubist *nc* painter who used this style.

cuckold ['kʌkəld] *nc* man whose wife is unfaithful by loving another man. Also *vt* be unfaithful to one's husband (*o.f.*).

cuckoo ['kuku:] *nc* bird which makes a sound like this word and which lays its eggs in the nests of other birds. *pl* **cuckoos.**

cucumber ['kju:kʌmbə*] *nc/u* long thin plant with a green skin and firm flesh, eaten raw in salads.
cool as a cucumber not at all worried or excited.

cud [kʌd] *nu* food swallowed by cows and other animals, and then brought back into the mouth to be chewed more slowly.
chew the cud (with reference to cows etc) eat in this way.

cuddle ['kʌdl] *vt/i* (usu. with reference to doing so to a child) hold tightly in the arms as a sign of love. Also *nc*.

cudgel ['kʌdʒl] *nc* short, heavy piece of wood, used as a weapon. Also *vt* hit with a cudgel. *past* **cudgelled.** (*US* **cudgeled**).
cudgel one's brains think very hard about a difficult problem.
take up the cudgels (for someone/something) speak or act in defence of some person or cause. (rather *o.f.*).

cue¹ [kju:] *nc* **1.** a few words said by an actor, which are the signal for another actor to begin speaking. **2.** signal or sign to somebody that he should begin to do something.
take one's cue from somebody act or speak in the same way as somebody else because one is uncertain what is the right thing to do in a particular situation. (*informal*).

cue² [kju:] *nc* long stick used in the game of billiards.

cuff¹ [kʌf] *nc* **1.** end of the sleeve of a coat or shirt nearest the hand. **2.** (*US*) fold at the bottom of a trouser leg. (*Brit* **turn-up**). **3.** short form of **handcuff.**
'cufflink type of fastening for the cuff of a shirt.

cuff[2] [kʌf] *nc* light blow to the head given with the hand. Also *vt* hit somebody in this way.
cuisine [kwi'ziːn] *nc/u* cooking or style of cooking (esp. in a hotel or restaurant, or in a country as a whole). *French cuisine is one of the best in the world.*
cul-de-sac ['kʌldəsæk] *nc* street with an opening at one end only.
culinary ['kʌlinəri] *adj* having reference to cooking.
cull [kʌl] *vt* carefully pick out or choose from a number of things.
culminate ['kʌlmineit] *vi* reach the end point in some process. *The long quarrel between Tom and his neighbour culminated in a fight.* **culmination** [kʌlmi'neiʃən] *nc.*
culpable ['kʌlpəbl] *adj* deserving to be blamed for some accident or misfortune. **culpably** *adv.* **culpability** [kʌlpə'biliti] *nu.*
culprit ['kʌlprit] *nc* person who has done something wrong (usu. something less serious than a crime).
cult [kʌlt] *nc* **1.** system of religious belief or behaviour (esp. one within a wider religion). *The cult of the Virgin Mary is an important part of Christianity.* **2.** great interest in something (esp. an interest which is confined to a few people only).
cultivate ['kʌltiveit] *vt* **1.** grow: *cultivate wheat.* **2.** plant crops in: *cultivate the land.* **3.** try to improve or make better: *cultivate one's knowledge of French.* **4.** try to become more friendly with a person. *He has been cultivating my friendship. He always tries to cultivate rich and famous people.* **cultivation** [kʌlti'veiʃən] *nu.*
cultivated *adj* **1.** (with reference to land) used for farming. **2.** (with reference to a person) having polite manners and a wide knowledge of art, music and literature. (*opp* **uncultivated**).
cultivator *nc* **1.** farmer or farm worker. **2.** machine used in digging up the soil and planting seeds.
culture ['kʌltʃə*] **1.** *nu* knowledge of or training in art, music and literature. **2.** *nc/u* way of life of a particular group of people. *Many ancient cultures can be found in Africa. African culture should be studied more carefully by Europeans.* **3.** *nc* number of bacteria (esp. ones grown in a laboratory). **4.** *nu* the rearing of certain animals or plants for commercial reasons: *the culture of grapes/bees/silkworms.* **5.** *nu* use of land for growing crops. **cultural** *adj* (in senses **1.** and **2.**).
cultured *adj* **1.** (with reference to a person) well-educated and polite. (*opp* **uncultured**). **2.** (with reference to certain produce) specially reared or prepared, not occurring naturally. (Esp. **cultured pearls**).
culvert ['kʌlvət] *nc* large pipe under a road, to allow water to flow from one side of the road to the other.
cumbersome ['kʌmbəsəm] *adj* large; heavy; difficult to use or move easily.
cummerbund ['kʌməbʌnd] *nc* wide strip of cloth worn round the waist.
cumulative ['kjuːmjulətiv] *adj* getting larger by being added to: *cumulative effect.*
cumulus ['kjuːmjuləs] *nc* very large rounded low cloud. *pl* **cumuli** ['kjuːmjuliː].
cuneiform ['kjuːnifɔːm] *adj* (esp. with reference to a style of writing used by the Babylonians and Assyrians) having wedge shapes. Also *nu* this style of writing.
cunning ['kʌniŋ] *adj* clever and often dishonest: *a cunning thief; a cunning trick.* Also *nu.* **cunningly** *adv.*
cup [kʌp] *nc* **1.** vessel (usu. made of pottery or plastic and with a handle) used for drinking from. **2.** the amount that is contained in a cup. *He drank a cup of water.* **3.** anything shaped like a cup. **4.** large metal object (usu. shaped like a cup) given to the winner of a game or competition. Also *vt* put in the shape of a cup (usu. in **cup one's hands**). *past* **cupped.**
cupful ['kʌpful] *nc* as much as a cup will hold.
one's cup of happiness/joy/bitterness/misery etc feelings, or experience causing these feelings (*o.f.*).
cupboard ['kʌbəd] *nc* (mainly *Brit*) piece of furniture, or place built into the wall and closed by a door, for storing things in.
cupidity [kjuː'piditi] *nu* strong wish or desire for money or property; strong wish to keep money or property.
cupola ['kjuːpələ] *nc* small dome on a roof.
cur [kə*] *nc* dog which is of no value; dog which is bad-tempered and cowardly.
curate ['kjuːrit] *nc* clergyman (esp. of the Church of England), who helps a vicar or rector.
curacy *nc/u* position or work of a curate.
curator [kju'reitə*] *nc* person in charge of a museum or art gallery.
curb[1] [kəːb] *nc* **1.** piece of leather or metal chain fastened under a horse's jaw and used to control the horse. **2.** anything which acts as a control in this way. Also *vt* use a curb. *You must learn to curb your temper* i.e. you must not get so angry.
curb[2] [kəːb] *nc* see **kerb.**
curd [kəːd] *nc* (usu. *pl*) thick substance formed when milk becomes sour, and used in making cheese.
curdle ['kəːdl] *vt/i* (with reference to milk) form curds.
curdle the blood make somebody feel very frightened.
'bloodcurdling *adj*: *a bloodcurdling scream.*
cure [kjuə*] *vt* **1.** make well by removing the cause of disease or illness. *The drug cured my fever.* **2.** end something bad. *The government is trying to cure unemployment.* **3.** treat in some way in order to preserve (e.g. with reference to fish, meat, tobacco, furs, skins). Also *nc* act of curing; something which cures.
curable *adj* able to be cured. (*opp* **incurable**).
curative ['kjuəritiv] *adj* causing a cure.
curfew ['kəːfjuː] *nc* **1.** time during which people are not allowed to leave their houses (e.g. during a time of rioting or revolution); the signal for this time to begin. **2.** (in the Middle Ages) signal to people to put out fires at the end of the day.
curia ['kjuəriə] *n sing* (**Curia**) group of important officials of the Roman Catholic Church who help the Pope. (Also **papal curia**).
curio ['kjuəriou] *nc* unusual and interesting object. *pl* **curios.**
curious ['kjuəriəs] *adj* **1.** showing great interest in many things (esp. in matters which concern other people). **2.** strange and interesting. *I heard a curious noise last night* i.e. a noise which I cannot explain. **curiously** *adv.*
curiosity [kjuəri'ɔsiti] **1.** *nu* strong interest in many things. **2.** *nc* unusual and interesting thing.
curl [kəːl] *nc* **1.** piece of hair forming (part

of) a circle. **2.** anything shaped like this: *a curl of paper.* **3.** act of twisting hair into this shape. Also *vt/i* form curls in hair. *Her hair curls naturally* i.e. she does not make the curls. *She curled her hair.* **curly** *adj.*

curler *nc* (usu. *pl*) object made of metal or plastic, used for putting a curl into a woman's hair.

curl up twist one's body into a comfortable shape when sitting down. *She curled up in the most comfortable chair.*

curl something up form into a curl.

curlew ['kəːljuː] *nc* type of speckled bird with a very long curved beak and a shrill cry.

currant ['kʌrnt] *nc* **1.** small dried grape used in cooking. **2.** name given to various types of small fruit (e.g. *red currant, black currant*).

currency ['kʌrnsi] **1.** *nc* money in use in a country. *Most countries have a decimal currency* i.e. a currency based on a unit divided into 100. **2.** *nu* condition of being used at the present time. *Many English words are in common currency throughout the world* i.e. have been taken into many different languages. see **current**[1].

current[1] ['kʌrnt] *adj* in use at the present time: *the current issue of a magazine* i.e. the most recent one; *current events* i.e. events which have occurred not long ago or which are occurring now. **currently** *adv.*

current[2] ['kʌrnt] *nc* **1.** movement of water, air or gas in one direction. **2.** movement of electricity along a conductor. **3.** development of events or ideas. *The current of thought in this country has turned against war* i.e. people are no longer in favour of war.

curriculum [kə'rikjuləm] *nc* course of study in a school or college. *pl* **curricula** [kə'rikjulə] or **curriculums. curricular** [kə'rikjulə*] *adj.*

cu'rriculum 'vitae list of the main events of a person's life (e.g. schools, jobs etc).

curry[1] ['kʌri] *nc/u* type of food made with spices which taste very hot. Also *vt* prepare food as a curry. *I shall curry this fish.*

curry[2] ['kʌri] *vt* clean a horse with a large type of comb (called a **currycomb**).

curry favour with somebody try to get the help or friendship of somebody by doing or saying whatever will please him.

curse [kəːs] *vt/i* **1.** use language asking for somebody/something to be punished or hurt (esp. asking God to do this). *The old man cursed his enemies.* **2.** use insulting language to. Also *nc* **1.** language asking God to curse somebody/something. *The old man pronounced a curse on his enemies.* **2.** insulting language. **3.** something which causes unhappiness and misfortune.

cursed ['kəːsid] *adj* very unpleasant; making one angry. *This cursed fellow is always asking me for money.* **cursedly** *adv.* (*informal*).

be cursed [kəːst] **with somebody/something** have something which causes unhappiness or misfortune. *He is cursed with a very bad temper.*

put a curse on somebody/something use magic words to cause unhappiness or misfortune to somebody/something.

cursive ['kəːsiv] *adj* (with reference to writing) written with the letters joined together. Also *nu* this style of writing.

cursory ['kəːsəri] *adj* done in a hurry. *He gave a cursory look at the newspaper.* **cursorily** *adv.*

curt [kəːt] *adj* (with reference to speaking) short and impolite. *He gave a very curt reply.* **curtly** *adv.*

curtail [kəː'teil] *vt* make shorter or less. *I have had to curtail my spending* i.e. spend less money than I had wanted to. **curtailment** *nc/u.*

curtain ['kəːtn] *nc* **1.** large piece of cloth hung in front of a window inside a room. **2.** large piece of cloth which is used to hide the stage of a theatre from the audience. **3.** anything which hides like a curtain: *a curtain of smoke; a curtain of lies.* Also *vt* put curtains in or on.

'curtain call return of an actor to the stage at the end of a play to be applauded by the audience.

'curtain raiser 1. short play formerly acted in a theatre before the main play. **2.** anything less important which happens before the main thing.

'safety curtain large sheet of asbestos or other fireproof material, which can be used in a theatre to prevent a fire from spreading from behind the stage to the rest of the building.

curtain something off separate or hide, using a curtain. *Part of the room has been curtained off.*

ring down/up the curtain raise or lower the curtain in a theatre.

curtsey, curtsy ['kəːtsi] *nc* bending of the knees made by a woman as a very formal sign of respect. Also *vi* make this movement.

drop/make a curtsey make this movement.

curve [kəːv] *nc* line with a rounded shape. Also *vt/i* form a curve. *The road curved. He curved the piece of wood.*

curvature ['kəːvətʃə*] *nu* condition of being curved (esp. in **curvature of the spine** i.e. an illness in which the backbone is curved).

curvet [kəː'vet] *nc* movement made by a horse, in which all four feet leave the ground. Also *vi* make this movement. *past* **curvetted.**

curvilinear [kəːvi'liniə*] *adj* made up of curved lines.

cushion ['kuʃən] *nc* **1.** small bag of cloth, filled with something soft and used in a chair to make one more comfortable. **2.** anything which is soft like a cushion. **3.** elastic side of a billiard table. Also *vt* **1.** put cushions in. **2.** protect from a hard blow or shock. *His hat helped to cushion the blow.*

custard ['kʌstəd] *nc/u* sweet yellow substance made from milk and eggs.

custody ['kʌstədi] *nu* duty or work of protecting something or keeping something safe. *The police have the thief in custody* i.e. the thief is in prison or a police station. *The father asked for the custody of his children when his wife left him.*

custodian [kʌs'toudiən] *nc* person who has custody of something (esp. a person who is in charge of a museum or other public building).

custom ['kʌstəm] **1.** *nu* things which are usu. done by people. *Custom has a strong influence on people's behaviour.* **2.** *nc* any action which is usu. done by people or by a person. *It is not the custom in Britain to shake hands every time one meets a person. It is my custom to go to France for my holiday.* **3.** *nu* practice of regularly buying goods from a certain shop. *The butcher lost a lot of custom by charging high prices* i.e.

many people stopped buying from him.
customary *adj* usually done. **customarily** *adv.*
customs *npl* **1.** taxes paid on goods brought into a country. **2.** government department which collects these taxes. **3.** see **customs house.**
customer *nc* person who buys goods from a shop.
'custom(s) house building or office where taxes are collected on goods brought into a country.
'custom-'built/-'made (*US*) specially made for somebody.

cut[1] [kʌt] **1.** *vt/i* open or separate with something sharp. *He cut his finger with a knife. This knife doesn't cut very well.* **2.** *vi* allow cutting. *This piece of meat cuts very well* i.e. it is easy to cut the meat. **3.** *vt* make by cutting. *He cut a hole in the cloth.* **4.** *vt* make shorter by cutting: *cut someone's hair.* **5.** *vt* make smaller or less. *A producer of a play sometimes cuts an actor's speeches* i.e. he tells the actor to speak only part of what is written down for him. *We must cut the cost of education.* **6.** *vt* refuse to recognize or speak to. (rather *o.f.*). **7.** *vt* not go to a lesson, lecture, meeting etc. (*informal*). **8.** *vt/i* divide a pack of playing cards into two or more lots. **9.** *vt* (with reference to lines, esp. in geometry) cross. *The line AB cuts the line DC at the point E. pres part* **cutting.** *past* **cut.**
cut across something go across, through or in front of in order to make a journey shorter. *We can get home quicker if we cut across the field, instead of keeping to the road. The car cut across my path* i.e. it moved right in front of where I was, so that I could not move forward easily.
cut something away remove from something by cutting. *He cut away the old branches from the trees.*
cut something back make smaller. *We must cut back our expenses. The gardener cut back all the bushes.*
cut something down cause to fall by cutting. *He cut down all the old trees.*
cut down (on) something make less. *We must cut down on our expenses. I have decided to cut down my smoking.*
cut in 1. go in front of somebody (esp. when driving a car). **2.** suddenly begin talking (often interrupting somebody else).
cut something off 1. remove by cutting. *He cut off some flowers from the bush.* **2.** stop suddenly. *The government cut off the supply of oil to the enemy.* **3.** go between somebody and the place he is trying to get to. *Our troops cut off the enemy/the enemy's retreat.*
cut something open open by cutting. *He cut open the door of the safe. The sharp stone cut his head open.*
cut out (with reference to a machine etc) stop suddenly. *The radio cut out.*
cut something out remove (esp. from inside) by cutting. *The surgeon cut out all the diseased tissue.* **2.** make by cutting. *She cut out a new dress* i.e. she cut the pieces in order to sew them into a dress. **3.** stop doing. *Cut it out!* i.e. stop doing that. (*informal*). **4.** be more successful than somebody else in trying to gain something.
cut something short (often with reference to talking) stop somebody who is doing something by beginning to do something oneself. *He began to explain his idea to me, but I cut him short.*
cut something up cut into pieces. *He always cuts up his food before he eats it.*
cut both ways (with reference to an argument) can have two effects which are opposite to each other. *That argument cuts both ways* i.e. you have used an argument in favour of your point of view, but I can use the same argument against you.
cut one's coat according to one's cloth make one's plans according to one's abilities or resources; plan to do only what one is able to do.
cut a corner 1. go across a corner instead of round it. **2.** do something by a short, quick method.
cut a dash behave in a very lively and unusual way so that other people take notice of what one is doing. (rather *o.f.*).
cut and dried (with reference to ideas, answers, opinions etc) ready; prepared in advance.
cut a poor/ridiculous/foolish figure appear to be poor etc.
cut it fine see **fine**[1].
cut the ground from under somebody's feet begin a fight, argument, quarrel etc by gaining a very big advantage over the other person, who cannot easily make any reply.
cut no ice have no power or influence. (*informal*).
to cut a long story short in order to say what one has to say without using too many words (used to introduce a statement which summarizes what one is talking about) (*informal*).
cut one's losses stop doing something which has brought one a loss, instead of going on with it in the hope of making a gain later on.
be cut out for something have a special ability to do something. *I'm not cut out for hard work.* (*informal*).
cut up rough become very angry or violent. (*informal*).
cut somebody off with a shilling leave somebody nothing or very little in one's will, after he has expected to be left a lot of money.
cut it short come to an end as soon as possible. *I was intending to make a long speech, but I decided to cut it short.* (*informal*).
cut a tooth have a new tooth just showing through the gums. *The baby is crying because he is cutting a tooth.*
be cut up be made very unhappy. *She was very cut up by the news.* (*informal*).
have one's work cut out have a very difficult job; find great difficulty in doing something. (*informal*).

cut[2] [kʌt] *nc* **1.** opening or separation made with something sharp. *He made a cut on his finger with a knife.* **2.** making shorter. *The government is trying to make cuts in its spending this year* i.e. is trying to spend less money. **3.** something removed while making shorter or less. *He gave a large cut off the meat to each of the guests* i.e. a piece of meat cut from a larger piece. **4.** refusal to recognize or speak to somebody. (rather *o.f.*). **5.** act of dividing a pack of playing cards. **6.** (esp. geometry) crossing by one line of another. **7.** quick, sudden blow with a sword or whip, or with a bat in cricket and other games. **8.** style in which clothes are made. *Your new suit has a very good cut.* **9.** share of money or property

stolen or gained. (*informal* in sense **9.**).
cutter *nc* **1.** person/thing that cuts. **2.** small type of boat.
cutting *nc* **1.** section cut out of a newspaper or magazine. **2.** piece cut off a plant to be planted in another place. **3.** tunnel or way for a road or railway, cut through a hill. Also *adj* **1.** sharp. **2.** (with reference to words) causing unhappiness to somebody: *a cutting remark.* **cuttingly** *adv.*
'cut 'glass type of glass, which has been cut and polished.
'cut-price *adj.* reduced in price.
'cut-throat *nc* dangerous and violent criminal. (rather *o.f.*). Also *adj* very fierce: *cut-throat competition.*
'haircut see **hair.**
'short 'cut way to a place which brings one there in less time than the main road. *He took a short cut across the fields.*
cute [kju:t] *adj* **1.** quick and clever. **2.** (with reference to children or young women) pretty. (both *informal*).
cuticle ['kju:tikl] *nc* the outside layer of skin (esp. the skin around the fingernails).
cutlass ['kʌtləs] *nc* **1.** short heavy sword formerly used by sailors. **2.** implement like this used for certain farming purposes.
cutlery ['kʌtləri] *nu* knives, forks and spoons used for eating food.
cutler *nc* person who makes or sells cutlery.
cutlet ['kʌtlit] *nc* **1.** small piece of meat. **2.** meat etc chopped up and cooked as a flat cake.
cuttlefish ['kʌtlfiʃ] *nc* type of sea creature with eight short arms and two long arms, which sends out a black substance when attacked.
cyanide ['saiənaid] *nu* very strong type of poison.
cybernetics [saibə'netiks] *nu* study of calculating machines and computers in order to compare them with the working of the human brain.
Note: followed by *sing* verb.
cyclamen ['sikləmən] *nc* type of plant having many flowers.
cycle ['saikl] *nc* **1.** bicycle. **2.** series of events coming in a certain order: *the cycle of the year* i.e. the seasons of the year. **3.** number of traditional stories about some hero of the past. Also *vi* ride a bicycle.
cyclist *nc* person who rides a bicycle.
cycling *nu* riding a bicycle.
cyclic *adj* **1.** occurring in a certain order. **2.** having the form of a circle.
cyclone ['saikloun] *nc* strong winds which move in a circle around a still centre.
cyclopaedia [saiklə'pi:diə] *nc* short form of **encyclopaedia.**
cyclostyle ['saikləstail] *nc* apparatus for making many copies of a document. Also *vt* make many copies in this way.
cyclotron ['saiklətrɔn] *nc* large piece of apparatus used in atomic physics for changing one element into another and for producing radioactivity.
cygnet ['signit] *nc* young swan.
cylinder ['silində*] *nc* **1.** object with circular ends and straight sides (e.g. beer can, cigarette). **2.** hollow part of a motor-car engine, shaped like a cylinder, in which air and petrol vapour are exploded.
cylindrical [si'lindrikl] *adj.*
cymbal ['simbl] *nc* large round flat piece of metal, used as a musical instrument. Two cymbals are usu. hit together.
cynic ['sinik] *nc* person who thinks that people always have bad or selfish reasons for what they do, even if they seem to be acting in a good and kind way. **cynical** *adj.*
cynically *adv.*
cynicism ['sinisizəm] *nu* beliefs of a cynic.
cynosure ['sainəʃuə*] *nc* somebody/something that everybody looks at or gives attention to.
cypher ['saifə*] *nc* see **cipher.**
cypress ['saipris] **1.** *nc* type of tree with dark green leaves. The leaves were formerly used as a sign of funerals and mourning. **2.** *nu* the wood of this tree.
cyst [sist] *nc* small growth like a bag, caused by certain diseases in people, plants and animals.
cytology [sai'tɔlədʒi] *nu* science of the cells of plants and animals.
cytologist *nc* person who studies cytology.
czar [zɑ:*] *nc* title of the former emperors of Russia.
czarina [zɑ:'ri:nə] *nc* wife of a czar.
czarevitch ['zɑ:rivitʃ] *nc* eldest son of a czar.
Note: these words are also spelled with *ts-* or *tz-* instead of *cz-*.

D

dab [dæb] *vt/i* touch very gently. *She dabbed the wound with a piece of cloth.* Also *nc* light touch. *This wall needs a dab of paint. past* **dabbed.**
be a dab hand at something be very good at something. (*informal*).

dabble ['dæbl] *vt/i* put hands or feet etc in and out of water. *He dabbled his fingers in the stream.* **dabbler** *nc.*
dabble in something study or take part in something for amusement but not in any serious way. *He used to dabble in politics.*

dachshund ['dækshund] *nc* type of dog with short legs and a long body.

dad [dæd], **daddy** ['dædi] *nc* informal form of **father.**
'daddy-'long-legs type of insect with long legs.

daffodil ['dæfədil] *nc* flower with a trumpet-shaped centre surrounded by a circle of petals.

daffodil

daft [dɑːft] *adj* mad, foolish. (*informal*).

dagger ['dægə*] *nc* short, pointed knife used for stabbing.
look daggers at somebody look at somebody, showing anger or hate in one's face. (*informal*).

dahlia ['deiliə] *nc* one of several related types of plant with big colourful flowers.

daily ['deili] *adj/adv* see **day.**

dainty ['deinti] *adj* 1. small and pretty: *a very dainty little girl; a dainty chair.* 2. unwilling to eat many types of food, or to eat much food. Also *nc* soft and sweet piece of food (*o.f.* in this sense). **daintily** *adv.* **daintiness** *nu.*

dairy ['dɛəri] *nc* place where milk is kept, and where butter and cheese are made or sold.
'dairy cow cow kept for milk.

dais ['deiis] *nc* raised platform in a room for a speaker, lecturer or important person.

daisy ['deizi] *nc* type of small, white flower with a yellow centre.

dally ['dæli] *vi* waste time; be idle, doing no work but enjoying oneself.
dalliance *nu* 1. playful wasting of time. 2. love-making which is not serious, but which is done for amusement. (rather *o.f.*).
dally with something/someone think idly about or use in a playful way.

dam[1] [dæm] *nc* wall or construction which holds back water. Also *vt* (often with **up**) keep back with a dam. *They dammed the river.* 2. keep back or control feelings. *He dammed up his anger. past* **dammed.**

dam[2] [dæm] *nc* mother of certain animals.

damage ['dæmidʒ] *vt* break or spoil (but not destroy). *He damaged my car with a stone.* Also *nu*: *He did a lot of damage to my car.* **damaged** *adj.* (*opp* **undamaged**).
damages *npl* money asked for or given in a law case because somebody has damaged the property, person or reputation of somebody else.

damask ['dæməsk] *nu* type of cloth with patterns which are made of a material which reflects the light.

dame [deim] *nc* 1. old word for a lady. 2. woman. (*informal* and rather *impolite*). 3. (**Dame**) title of a woman equivalent to that of a knight.
Note: a woman with the title of *Dame* is addressed as 'Dame Jane Smith', not as 'Dame Smith'.

damn [dæm] *vt* 1. call on God to punish or harm. 2. use insulting language towards. 3. say that something is of no value or use. *He damned all my suggestions.* Also *interj* to express anger or dislike. *Damn you! Damn this work!*
damned *adj* used to describe something/someone which causes annoyance: *that damned pen.* Also *adv/intensifier* very: *a damned good book.* (both *informal*).
damnable ['dæmnəbl] *adj* deserving to be damned; very unpleasant. **damnably** *adv.*
damnation [dæm'neiʃən] *nu.* Also used as *interj.*

damp[1] [dæmp] *adj* slightly wet; moist. *The ground is still damp after the rain. The damp climate does not suit her.* Also *nu* slight feeling of wetness. *There's still damp in these clothes.* **damply** *adv.* **dampness** *nu.*

damp[2] [dæmp] *vt* 1. make slightly wet. *He damped his cloth before cleaning the windows.* 2. discourage. *My failure last time has not damped my interest.*
dampen *vt* 1. make damp. 2. discourage.
damper *nc* 1. moveable plate in a stove, which can be used to make the fire burn more or less brightly. 2. device in a piano which stops the strings vibrating.
put a damper on something act or speak in a way that causes other people to be less interested in something. *He put a damper on our plans for a holiday, by telling us how expensive it would be.* (*informal*).
damp down a fire put small pieces of damp coal on a fire in order to make it burn more slowly.

damson ['dæmzn] *nc* 1. type of plum with dark blue fruit. 2. tree on which it grows.

dance [dɑːns] *nc* 1. rhythmical movement of the body (usu. in time to music). 2. piece of music for dancing. 3. party or social gathering held for people to dance. Also *vt/i*: *They were dancing. He danced a few steps.* **dancer** *nc.* **dancing** *nu.*

'**dance hall** building which people pay to enter in order to dance.
dance attendance on somebody be very polite to somebody and be always willing to do what he wants one to do.
lead somebody a dance behave in a way which causes a lot of difficulties for somebody. (*informal*).

dandelion ['dændilaiən] *nc* small, yellow flower which grows wild, and whose seeds fly in the air.

dandle ['dændl] *vt* move a child up and down on one's knees or in one's arms.

dandruff ['dændrʌf] *nu* small white pieces of dead skin in the hair of the head.

dandy ['dændi] *nc* man who gives much attention to dressing fashionably. Also *adj* (*US*) very good; very satisfactory. (*informal* in this sense).

danger ['deindʒə*] **1.** *nu* strong possibility of injury, death or harm of some kind. *The young child did not realize the danger of playing on the road.* **2.** *nc* thing which causes danger. *Children who play on the road are a danger to motorists.*
dangerous ['deindʒrəs] *adj* causing danger. *He is a dangerous criminal. It's dangerous to throw stones.* **dangerously** *adv*.
in danger 1. likely to be injured or killed. *Children who play on the roads are in danger.* **2.** very ill and likely to die.
in danger of something likely to receive or do something dangerous. *He is in danger of falling. We were in danger of being hit by a stone.*
out of danger 1. away from something dangerous. *We got out of danger when the fighting began.* **2.** beginning to recover from a dangerous illness which could have ended in death.

dangle ['dæŋgl] *vt/i* hang loosely. *He dangled his arm over the back of the chair.*

dank [dæŋk] *adj* wet and cold: *a dank cellar.*

dapper ['dæpə*] *adj* (with reference to a person esp. a man) neat, well-dressed and active.

dapple ['dæpl] *vt* mark with patches or spots of different colours.
dappled *adj* (with reference to some animals esp. horses) marked like this.

dare [dɛə*] **1.** *aux* (used esp. in *negative* sentences, questions and after **if**) be brave enough to. *I dare not tell my father what has happened. How dare you speak to me like that? He daren't go any higher. If you dare speak to me like that again, you will be sorry.* **2.** *vi* be brave enough to. *To our surprise, he dared to repeat his statements. He dares to behave like that in my house! The children don't dare (to) make a sound while their parents are sleeping.*
Note: **1.** and **2.** are different in structure, not in meaning. **1.** is an auxiliary, does not take *to*, and has no s in the third person singular (he/she/it). **2.** is a regular verb and normally takes *to* (e.g. *dared to climb*), but native speakers often miss out *to* as in the last example.
3. *vt* say that one thinks another person is not brave enough to do something; challenge. *I dared him to climb the wall.* **4.** *vi* be brave in the face of some danger.
daring *nu* courage to do something dangerous. *That boy has a lot of daring.* Also *adj*: *a daring boy.* **daringly** *adv*.
'**daredevil** *nc* person who is so brave that his actions seem to be foolish. Also *adj*; *a daredevil action.*
I dare say possibly; it may be right to say. *I dare say (that) it will rain tomorrow.*

dark [dɑ:k] *adj* **1.** without light or almost without light. *The night is very dark.* **2.** not light in colour. *He has dark eyes* i.e. eyes which are brown or black. **3.** (with reference to colours) containing an element of black: *dark red; dark blue* etc. Also *n sing* absence of light. *Some animals can see in the dark.*
darkly *adv*. **darkness** *nu*.
darken *vt/i* become or make dark. *Buildings often darken as they get older.*
'**dark** '**horse** person who does something clever or successful when nobody expects him to do so. (*informal*).
'**darkroom** room without light in which photographs are developed.
after/before dark after/before the beginning of sunset. *There were not many people on the streets after dark.*
in the dark about something have no information about something. *I don't know what John intends to do; I'm in the dark about his plans.* (*informal*).
keep something dark keep a secret to oneself. *You must keep this dark; don't tell anyone.* (*informal*).

darling ['dɑ:liŋ] *nc* somebody whom one loves. Also *adj*: *my darling daughter.*

darn [dɑ:n] *vt/i* mend a hole by weaving thread or wool. Also *nc* place where a hole or worn place has been darned.
darning *nu* **1.** act of darning. **2.** things waiting to be darned.

dart [dɑ:t] *nc* **1.** small object made of wood, metal or plastic, with a point at one end, thrown at a board marked with numbers in a game (called **darts**). **2.** sudden movement. *He made a dart towards the door.* Also *vt/i* make a sudden movement. *He darted towards the door.*

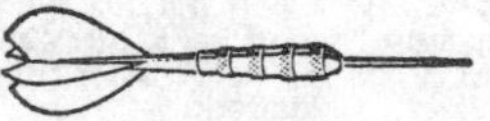

dart (*def 1*)

dash[1] [dæʃ] **1.** *nc* sudden quick movement (esp. one made by running). *He made a dash towards the house.* **2.** *nc* (often with reference to cooking) small amount of liquid etc. *You should add a dash of vinegar.* **3.** *nc* the mark — used in writing. **4.** *nu* courage and speed. *Our troops attacked the enemy with a great deal of dash.*

dash[2] [dæʃ] **1.** *vi* run; move quickly. *He dashed towards the house.* **2.** *vt* throw in order to break. *He dashed the cup on the ground.* **3.** *vt* throw liquid. *He dashed a glass of beer in my face.* **4.** *vt* (often *passive*) disappoint. *Our hopes were dashed by the news* i.e. the news told us that we would not get what we had hoped for.
dash! exclamation showing annoyance.
dashing *adj* smart and lively. *He looked very dashing in his new suit.* **dashingly** *adv*.
'**dashboard** panel containing dials etc in front of the driver of a car.
dash something off (usu. something written) do in a hurry.

data ['deitə] *n sing* or *pl* information which is known before one begins to solve a problem.
Note: data is often treated as an uncountable noun. Originally it was a plural noun with a singular *datum*. It is sometimes used as a plural noun in formal and scientific writing.

date[1] [deit] *nc* **1.** time when something

happened. *The date of the Norman Conquest of England is 1066. What is the date today?* i.e. what day of the month is it? **2.** period of time. *I did not have all the information at that date.* **3.** something written recording the date. *It is usual to write the date on a letter.* **4.** arrangement to meet somebody (esp. an arrangement between a young man and a young woman) (*informal*). **5.** young man or young woman whom one meets in this way. (*informal*).

out of date old-fashioned; no longer used, or used by very few people. *His clothes are rather out of date. These are very out-of-date ideas.*

up to date modern and new. *His ideas are up to date.*

date[2] [deit] *vt* **1.** write a date on. *He dated his letter 6 August 1967.* **2.** decide the date of something. *The professor of Ancient History was asked to date the ruins which had been discovered.* **3.** arrange to meet a young man or young woman. *John used to date Joan last year.* (*informal* in sense **3.**).

dated *adj* out of date; old and no longer used very much; unfashionable. *His clothes are dated.*

date back to something be as old as. *This town dates back to Roman times.*

date from something be as old as. *This town dates from the 13th century.*

date[3] [deit] *nc* **1.** type of fruit which grows on trees (called **date palms**) in North Africa. **2.** the tree itself.

dative ['deitiv] *adj/nc* form of a noun or pronoun in Latin and other languages showing that the word is an indirect object.

datum ['deitəm] *nc* see **data.**

daub [dɔ:b] *vt/i* **1.** paint in an unskilled way. **2.** cover with something dirty or sticky. *He daubed jam all over his face. The people daub the walls of their huts with mud.* Also *nc* **1.** unskilful painting. **2.** dirty mark etc.

daughter ['dɔ:tə*] *nc* female child (of a parent).

'daughter-in-law *nc* wife of one's son. *pl* **daughters-in-law.**

daunt [dɔ:nt] *vt* discourage; make afraid or make less ready to do what one intends. *The difficulties of the journey did not daunt us at all.*

dauntless *adj* brave; not frightened or discouraged by danger or difficulty.

undaunted *adj* not frightened or discouraged.

dawdle ['dɔ:dl] *vi* go slowly and lazily. **dawdling** *nu.*

dawn [dɔ:n] *nc* **1.** beginning of the day, when light first appears in the sky. **2.** first sign of something: *the dawn of civilization.* Also *vi* begin to get light. *The day was dawning.*

dawn on somebody become clear to somebody; be understood by somebody. *It took hours of study before the solution finally dawned on him.* (*informal*).

day [dei] *nc* **1.** period of 24 hours. *There are seven days in a week.* **2.** period when it is light. *In winter the day is shorter than the night in the northern hemisphere.* **3.** period during which somebody works. *My day ends at five o'clock* i.e. I stop work at that time. **4.** period when someone is active or successful. *He's had his day* i.e. he is no longer young. (*informal*). **5.** (in *pl*) period of history: *the days of the Romans.*

daily *adj/adv* happening every day. Also *nc* **1.** daily newspaper. **2.** woman who does housework as a job.

'daybreak/break of day beginning of the day, when light first appears in the sky. *He goes to work at daybreak.*

'daydream *nc* thoughts about something pleasant and fanciful. Also *vi* think in this way.

'daylight light of day.

'day nursery place where young children can be left during the day, before they are old enough to go to school.

'daytime period when it is light.

begin to see daylight get near the end of a long and difficult piece of work.

call it a day stop work for the day. (*informal*).

carry/win the day win or be successful in a battle or competition.

day after day for a long period of time (with the suggestion that the experience is very tiring or unpleasant). *I have to do this work day after day.*

day by day every day.

one fine day at some time. *I hadn't seen him for ten years then one fine day he just turned up.* (*informal*).

in days gone by at an earlier period of history.

the good old days an earlier period of history (thought of as being happier than today) (*informal*).

two/three/four etc days' grace extra period allowed for payment, after the date on which payment of a bill etc should be made. *He gave me three days' grace to pay the money.*

one day on a day in the past or future.

the other day a few days ago.

pass the time of day (with someone) say 'good morning' etc (to someone).

some day at some time in the future.

daze [deiz] *vt* make confused or unable to think clearly. *He was dazed by a blow on the head.* **dazed** *adj.*

in a daze confused; unable to think clearly.

dazzle ['dæzl] *vt* **1.** make unable to see clearly. *He was dazzled when he looked at the sun.* **2.** make unable to think clearly because of something rich, bright etc. *The old man was dazzled by the sight of so much money.* **dazzling** *adj.*

de- [di:] *prefix* do the opposite of (e.g. **denationalize**).

deacon ['di:kən] *nc* official of various Christian churches, below the rank of priest. (*fem* **deaconess**).

dead [ded] *adj* **1.** without life. *The doctor arrived too late, for the old man was dead. These flowers are dead.* **2.** without movement or activity or use. *The volcano is dead* i.e. it no longer sends out fire and smoke. *The battery is dead* i.e. it no longer gives out an electric current. *Latin is a dead language* i.e. nobody now speaks Latin as his mother tongue. *That idea is completely dead* i.e. nobody considers that idea now. Also *adv* completely; straight. *I'm dead tired. The house is dead ahead.*

deaden *vt* make less loud, less bright, less painful etc.

deadly *adj* certain to cause death, dangerous: *a deadly poison; deadly enemies* i.e. enemies who would like to kill each other; *a deadly sin* i.e. one of the more serious sins.

the dead *npl* people who are dead.

'dead 'beat *pred adj* very tired (*informal*).

'dead 'end *nc* **1.** street with an opening at one end only. **2.** course, career, job etc

which does not lead one to a higher position or to more money. Also *adj*: *a dead-end job.*
'dead 'heat *nc* result of a race in which two or more runners reach the winning post at the same time.
dead-heat *vi*: *John and Richard dead-heated for first place.*
'dead 'letter **1.** law which is still officially in existence but which nobody obeys. **2.** letter kept at a post office because the person to whom it has been sent cannot be found.
'deadline time by which one must do something.
'deadlock condition in which two sides in an argument or discussion are not able to agree. *After three hours of discussion the two governments reached deadlock.*
'deadpan *adj* showing no expression on the face; not allowing one's feelings to show in one's face.
'dead 'slow very slowly.
'dead 'weight anything very heavy (esp. something which does not move itself).
dead to the world very deeply asleep. (*informal*).
the dead of the night the quietest and darkest part of the night.
go dead stop moving; stop being active. *The wireless went dead.*

deaf [def] *adj* **1.** unable to hear properly. **2.** unwilling to listen. *He was deaf to my excuses.*
deafness *nu.*
deafen *vt* make deaf.
deafening *adj*: *deafening noise* i.e. a very loud one.
'deaf-'mute person who cannot hear or speak.

deal[1] [di:l] **1.** *vt/i* (esp. with reference to giving out playing cards when playing a game) give out; share. **2.** *vi* do business; buy and sell. *past* **dealt** [delt].
deal in something buy and sell something as one's job.
deal something out share out. *The teacher dealt out the books to the class.*
deal with someone/something **1.** be concerned with. *This office deals with licences for motorcars.* **2.** have business relations with; buy from or sell to. *Manufacturers do not usually deal direct with members of the public* i.e. they sell their goods to shops and not to individual people. **3.** take action about something. *I don't know how to deal with these bad children* i.e. I don't know what to do with them.

deal[2] [di:l] *nc* **1.** act of sharing out playing cards. **2.** business arrangement.
dealer *nc* **1.** person who deals cards. **2.** person who buys and sells goods.
a good/great deal very much. *I spent a good deal of money last year.*
a new deal a new arrangement or plan which gives better conditions to more people.
have no dealings with someone (esp. with reference to buying and selling) have no relation or contact with someone.

deal[3] [di:l] *nu* type of soft wood.

dealt [delt] past of **deal**[1].

dean [di:n] *nc* **1.** important official in some Christian churches. **2.** university official who is in charge of students.

dear [diə*] *adj* **1.** loved very much. *His children were very dear to him.* **2.** used to begin a letter: *Dear Sir; Dear Mr Smith.* **3.** costing a lot of money. *Sugar is very dear.* Also *interj* used as a way of talking to a child or one's husband or wife etc: *hullo dear!* Also *adv* for a lot of money. *He sells his goods very dear.* Also *interj* to express surprise or sorrow: **Oh dear!**; **Dear me!** etc. **dearly** *adv.* **dearness** *nu.*

dearth [də:θ] *nu* lack or shortage of something: *a dearth of good ideas.*

death [deθ] **1.** *nc* end of life. *There have been 23 deaths from road accidents in the last week.* **2.** *nu* condition of being dead. *Nobody can escape death.* **3.** *nc* end or destruction of something. *The fall of the Roman Empire did not mean the death of civilization in Europe.*
deathly *adj* like death; causing death.
'deathbed bed on which somebody is dying or has died.
'deathblow anything which suddenly ends something. *His decision was a deathblow to our hopes for a new swimming pool* i.e. he decided that we could not have a new swimming pool.
'death duty tax paid on the property of a person who has died.
'deathtrap very dangerous place, building, object etc. *This sharp bend in the road is a deathtrap for motorists.*

debacle, débâcle [dei'bɑ:kl] *nc* sudden collapse or destruction (e.g. of any army, government, business firm etc).

debar [di'bɑ:*] *vt* shut out. *You are not debarred from entering the competition* i.e. you may take part in the competition. *past* **debarred.**

debase [di'beis] *vt* lessen the value of. *The government debased the coinage* i.e. put less precious metal in the coins than was usu. put in them. **debased** *adj.* **debasement** *nu.*

debate [di'beit] *nc* **1.** meeting in which people argue for and against some idea. *The Members of Parliament hold debates.* **2.** any discussion of reasons for and against something. Also *vt/i*: *Parliament has been debating the financial situation.* **debater** *nc.*
debatable *adj* not easily decided; allowing arguments for and against. *That's a debatable point; not everyone would agree with your opinion.*

debauch [di'bɔ:tʃ] *nc* occasion on which one or more persons drink too much alcoholic drink or enjoy similar pleasures without proper limits. Also *vt* make somebody turn away from a temperate life towards a life of pleasure.
debauchery *nc/u* too much enjoyment of the pleasures of the body.
debauchee [debɔ:'tʃi:] *nc* person who practises this type of pleasure.

debenture [di'bentʃə*] *nc* piece of paper given by a business firm as a sign that somebody has lent the firm some money.

debilitate [di'biliteit] *vt* (with reference to a person) make weak or ill. **debilitation** [dibili'teiʃən] *nc/u.*
debility [di'biliti] *nc/u* illness or weakness of a person.

debit ['debit] *nc* note of money owed or spent by a person, in a record of money received and spent. (*opp* **credit**). Also *vt*: *The bank has debited the money against/to my account.*

debonair [debə'nɛə*] *adj* polite, cheerful (and usu. fashionable or well-dressed).

debris, débris ['debri:] *nu* broken pieces of something (esp. rock, brick etc) caused by a bomb explosion.

debt [det] *nc* money or other commodity owed by somebody to somebody else. *He lent me £5 last week and now he wants me to pay my debt* i.e. give back the £5.

debtor *nc* person who owes money. (*opp* **creditor**).
in debt owing money. *I always try to avoid being in debt to anyone.*
out of debt having paid one's debts. *If you borrow money, it is not easy to get out of debt.*
bad debt debt which is not paid.
debt of honour debt incurred by gambling or betting. (rather *o.f.*).
debunk ['di:'bʌŋk] *vt* show that a person/thing that is praised or liked by many people is not really as good as people think (usu. by laughing at the person/thing) (*informal*).
debut, début ['deibju:] *nc* (esp. with reference to a young girl at adult parties, or of an actor or musician appearing for the first time in public) first appearance of someone/something.
deca- ['dekə] *prefix* ten (e.g. a **decametre** i.e. ten metres).
decade ['dekeid] *nc* period of ten years.
decadent ['dekədnt] *adj* having a lower standard of behaviour or excellence than in former times. **decadence** *nu*.
decalogue, Decalogue ['dekəlɔg] *nc* the Ten Commandments given to the Israelites by Moses.
decamp [di'kæmp] *vi* (with reference to people) leave suddenly or secretly.
decant [di'kænt] *vt* pour liquid (often wine) from one container to another (usu. so as to leave any sediment or solid matter at the bottom of the first container).
decanter *nc* glass container for holding wine which has been decanted.
decapitate [di'kæpiteit] *vt* cut the head off. **decapitation** [dikæpi'teiʃən] *nu*.
decarbonize ['di:'kɑ:bənaiz] *vt* remove carbon from inside the engine of a car.
decathlon [di'kæθlɔn] *nc* contest in which athletes compete in ten different events, the person having the highest score being the winner.
decay [di'kei] *vt/i* become or make rotten. *The fruit decayed in the damp weather.* Also *nu* (esp. with reference to teeth) condition of being decayed; decaying substance. **decayed** *adj*. **decaying** *adj*.
fall into decay become decayed.
decease [di'si:s] *nc* (usu. *sing*) death. (*formal* and legal). Also *vi* die.
the deceased the dead person. (*formal* and legal).
deceit [di'si:t] *nc/u* lying; hiding the truth; making somebody believe something which is not true. **deceitful** *adj*. **deceitfully** *adv*. **deceitfulness** *nu*. see **deception.**
deceive [di'si:v] *vt* make somebody believe something which is not true. *The boy tried to deceive his father by saying that he did not know who broke the window.*
deceiver *nc* person who deceives.
decelerate [di:'seləreit] *vt/i* go, cause to go, slower.
December [di'sembə*] *n* last month of the year.
decent ['di:snt] *adj* **1.** suitable; proper; showing what is expected. *He behaved in a decent manner.* (*opp* **indecent**). **2.** good; satisfactory; kind. *That was a very decent meal. He's quite a decent headmaster.* (*informal* in sense **2.**). **decently** *adv*. **decency** *nc/u*.
decentralize ['di:'sentrəlaiz] *vt* lessen central power by giving more power to local or regional authorities in a country. **decentralization** ['di:sentrəlai'zeiʃən] *nu*.
deception [di'sepʃən] *nc/u* words or behaviour intended to make somebody believe something which is not true. **deceptive** [di'septiv] *adj*. **deceptively** *adv*. see **deceit.**
deci- ['desi] *prefix* one tenth (e.g. a **decimetre** i.e. one tenth of a metre).
decibel ['desibel] *nc* unit for the measurement of the loudness of sounds.
decide [di'said] **1.** *vi* come to an opinion or decision after thought. *I have decided to help you.* **2.** *vt* cause a person to come to a decision. *The news decided me.* **3.** *vt* end an argument or discussion by coming to a decision. *John's information decided the argument.* see **decision.**
decided *adj* **1.** clear; definite; easily noticed. *There was a decided improvement in my car after he repaired it.* **2.** determined; having come to an opinion. *He was quite decided in his answer.* **decidedly** *adv*.
deciduous [di'sidjuəs] *adj* (with reference to trees) losing leaves when the cold or dry weather approaches. (*opp* **evergreen**).
decimal ['desiml] *adj* based on counting in tens or tenths. Also *nc* number expressed as a decimal fraction (e.g. 0.7865).
decimate ['desimeit] *vt* **1.** kill one out of every ten. **2.** kill very many. **decimation** [desi'meiʃən] *nu*.
decipher [di'saifə*] *vt* **1.** find the meaning of a message written in a code or cipher. **2.** find the meaning of anything difficult to understand.
decision [di'siʒən] **1.** *nc* act of deciding; reaching an opinion after thought. *The committee discussed the matter for three hours, but could not come to a decision.* **2.** *nu* ability to decide quickly. *He acted with decision as soon as he heard the news.* see **decide.**
decisive [di'saisiv] *adj* **1.** causing an argument, fight, disagreement, war etc to be settled. *The allies won a decisive victory.* **2.** showing the ability to decide quickly. (*opp* **indecisive**). **decisively** *adv*.
deck[1] [dek] *nc* **1.** floor in a ship. **2.** pack of playing cards.
'deckchair chair made of wood and canvas, which can be folded flat. It is used on beaches, ships and in other places.
'deck hand sailor of a low rank.
clear the decks (for action) get ready for fighting; get ready for anything active. (*informal* if the reference is not to a ship).
on deck on or to the upper deck of a ship.
deck[2] [dek] *vt* cover with decorations or ornaments.
declaim [di'kleim] *vt/i* speak with great feeling (often in opposition to something). *The newspapers declaimed against the new taxes. He declaimed a poem to the class.* **declamatory** [di'klæmətəri] *adj*. **declamation** [deklə'meiʃən] *nc/u*.
declare [di'klɛə*] *vt* **1.** make known publicly or strongly. *He declared the results of his experiments. He declared that he could not help us.* **2.** say to a customs official what goods one is bringing into a country. *I have nothing to declare* i.e. I am not bringing any taxable goods into the country. **declarative** [di'klærətiv] *adj*. **declaration** [deklə'reiʃən] *nc/u*.
declassify ['di:'klæsifai] *vt* decide officially that information, documents etc are no longer to be kept secret. **declassified** *adj*.
declension [di'klenʃən] **1.** *nu* grammatical process by which nouns, pronouns and adjectives change their form according to their use in a sentence. **2.** *nc* group of nouns

etc which change their form in the same way. see **decline.**

decline [di'klain] **1.** *vt/i* say that one does not want something which has been offered. *I declined his offer of help.* **2.** *vi* become weaker or less. **3.** *vt/i* give the different forms of a noun, pronoun, adjective etc; have different forms. *This word does not decline* i.e. it has only one form. see **declension.** Also *nc* (usu. only *sing*) process of becoming weaker or less. *There has been a decline in English cricket over the last ten years* i.e. England is not as good at cricket now as it was ten years ago.

declivity [di'kliviti] *nc* hill or slope going down.

decode ['di:'koud] *vt* find the meaning of a message written in code.

decompose ['di:kəm'pouz] *vt/i* go, cause to go, bad or rotten and undergo chemical change. **decomposition** [di:kɔmpə'ziʃən] *nu.*

decontaminate [di:kən'tæmineit] *vt* remove poison, gas, radioactivity or other harmful substances from a place or thing. **decontamination** [di:kəntæmi'neiʃən] *nu.*

decor, décor ['deikɔ:*] *nc* (usu. only *sing*) decoration (e.g. of a house); scenery on a stage.

decorate ['dekəreit] *vt/i* **1.** add things to in order to make more beautiful (often as a sign of celebration). *She decorated her room with flowers in preparation for the party.* **2.** put new paint or wallpaper on a room or house. *I want to decorate my house this year.* **3.** give somebody a medal. *He was decorated in the war* i.e. he won a medal.

decorated *adj.* (*opp* **undecorated**).

decorative ['dekərətiv] *adj* making more beautiful. **decoratively** *adv.*

decoration [dekə'reiʃən] **1.** *nu* act of decorating. **2.** *nc* something used in decorating. **3.** *nc* medal.

decorator *nc* person whose work is putting paint or wallpaper on rooms etc.

interior decorator person whose work is to decide what furniture, curtains, wallpaper etc to put into a room.

decorous ['dekərəs] *adj* proper or suitable in behaviour; showing behaviour which people consider to be correct and polite. (*opp* **indecorous**). **decorously** *adv.* **decorum** [di'kɔ:rəm] *nu.*

decoy ['di:kɔi] *nc* **1.** artificial or real bird used to make other birds come near enough to be shot or caught. **2.** anything used in this way to lead a person into a certain position. Also [di'kɔi] *vt* **1.** shoot or catch a bird in this way. **2.** lead a person into danger in this way.

decrease [di:'kri:s] *vt/i* become or make smaller or less. Also *nu*: *There has been a decrease in the number of university students in the last two years.* (*opp* **increase**).

on the decrease becoming smaller in number or less. *The number of university students is on the decrease.*

decree [di'kri:] *nc* official order or decision (often one which is not made by the normal process of law-making). *The king decided to dismiss parliament and rule by decree* i.e. rule by saying that people must do what he wanted them to do. Also *vt/i* make decrees. *The authorities decreed that nobody should walk on the grass.*

decrepit [di'krepit] *adj* weak because of old age. **decrepitude** [di'krepitju:d] *nu.*

decry [di'krai] *vt* speak against; say that something is of no value. *He decried the importance of free speech.*

dedicate ['dedikeit] *vt* **1.** use something for a special purpose (often a religious purpose). *Churches are dedicated to God. He dedicated his life to helping the poor.* **2.** honour somebody by printing his name at the beginning of a book, poem, play etc which one has written. *The author dedicated the book to his wife.* **dedicatory** ['dedikətəri] *adj.*

dedication [dedi'keiʃən] **1.** *nu* act of dedicating. **2.** *nc* words which dedicate a book, poem etc to somebody. **3.** nu great interest in and attention to one's work etc.

deduce [di'dju:s] *vt* arrive at a conclusion by thinking about the evidence. *From the position of his body, the police deduced that the man had killed himself.* see **deduction.**

deduct [di'dʌkt] *vt* take away a certain amount of. *My employer deducted a pound from my wages this week to pay for the window which I broke.*

deduction **1.** *nc* amount deducted. **2.** *nu* process of arriving at a conclusion by considering rules of logic. (*opp* **induction**). see **deduce.**

deed [di:d] *nc* **1.** something done. (rather *o.f.* or *formal*). **2.** legal document recording an agreement.

deem [di:m] *vt* consider or believe (*o.f.*).

deep [di:p] *adj* **1.** going down a long way. *The river is not deep; you can walk through it. The river is only two feet deep.* **2.** (usu. with reference to shelves) wide. *This shelf is not deep enough for these books.* **3.** dark in colour: *a very deep blue coat.* **4.** low in sound. *He spoke in a deep voice.* **5.** showing great learning, knowledge, thought etc. *This book is too deep for me; I can't understand it.* **6.** showing strong feelings: *deep sorrow.* **deeply** *adv.*

deepen *vt/i* become or make deep. see **depth.**

the deep the sea (*o.f.*).

'deep-'freeze container in which food can be stored for long periods at temperatures much lower than are found in an ordinary refrigerator.

'deep-'laid *adj* very carefully made or prepared (usu. in **deep-laid plans/schemes**).

'deep-'rooted/-seated/-set *adj* firmly fixed, not easily removed: *a deep-rooted hatred for his enemies; a deep-rooted tradition.*

'deep-'sea *adj* in the part of the sea which is deep. *Deep-sea fishermen spend many weeks away from their homes.*

deer [diə*] *nc* type of animal, the male of which usu. has wide spreading horns. *pl* **deer.**

deer

deface [di'feis] *vt* damage or spoil the appearance of. *He defaced the library book by writing in it.*

de facto [dei'fæktou] *adj* in fact or in reality

(although not in law). *He is the de facto ruler of the country* i.e. although the law does not recognize him.

defame [di'feim] *vt* say bad things about a person to other people. **defamation** [defə'meiʃən] *nu*. **defamatory** [di'fæmətəri] *adj*.

default [di'fɔːlt] *vi* fail to do something which is one's duty or which one has promised to do. **defaulter** *nc*.
by default because of the failure of someone else and not because of one's own success. *John won the competition by default* i.e. because his opponent did not come to play against John.
in default of in the absence of.

defeat [di'fiːt] *vt* beat in the war, in a game etc. *Our troops defeated the enemy*. Also *nc/u*.
defeatist *nc* person who expects that he will be defeated in a war, game etc.
defeatism *nu* beliefs of a defeatist.

defect[1] ['diːfekt] *nc* fault; something which is wrong or which does not work properly. *There is a defect in the steering of this car* i.e. this car cannot be steered properly. **defective** [di'fektiv] *adj*. **defectively** *adv*.
mentally defective *adj* having a very low level of intelligence (and usu. unable to lead a normal life). **mental defective** *nc*.

defect[2] [di'fekt] *vi* (esp. with reference to people who leave their own country to join an enemy country) leave one's own group and join an enemy group. *The young soldier defected to the enemy*. **defector** *nc*.

defence [di'fens] (*US* **defense**) *nc/u* **1.** act of resisting an attack (in war, in a game, in politics etc). *Every country in the world keeps secret its plans for defence*. **2.** something used in fighting against an attack. **3.** person answering a case or charge in a court of law, together with his lawyers. **4.** members of a team whose work is to guard the goal. see **defend.**
defenceless *adj* having no defence.
defensible *adj* able to be defended. (*opp* **indefensible**).
defensive *adj* ready for defence; intended for defence.
on the defensive acting as though expecting to be attacked. *He was on the defensive all the time I was speaking to him* i.e. he was talking as though I might attack him in words.

defend [di'fend] *vt* **1.** fight against attack or guard against attack. *The army was defending the town during the battle*. **2.** answer a case or charge in a court of law. *That lawyer is defending Mr Smith*. **3.** guard a goal in a game. see **defence.**
defendant *nc* person against whom a case is brought in a court of law.

defer [di'fəː*] *vt* wait until later before doing something. *I have decided to defer the meeting until next week*. *past* **deferred. deferment** *nc/u*. **deference** ['defərns] *nu*. **deferential** [defə'renʃl] *adj*.
defer to somebody/something do what somebody else wishes, advises, suggests etc. *I shall defer to your wishes*.
in deference to following somebody's wishes, advice, suggestion etc.

defiance [di'faiəns] *nu*, **defiant** [di'faiənt] *adj* see **defy.**

deficient [di'fiʃənt] *adj* having something missing; not having enough of something. *He is deficient in courage* i.e. he is a coward. **deficiency** *nc/u*.

deficit ['defisit] *nc* amount of money which is wanting or which cannot be found.

defile[1] [di'fail] *vt* make unclean or impure. **defilement** *nu*.

defile[2] [di'fail] *vi* (with reference to soldiers) march in a line.

defile[3] ['diːfail] *nc* very narrow valley or mountain pass.

define [di'fain] *vt* **1.** explain the exact meaning of a word or expression. **2.** make clear and easy to see or understand.
defined *adj* with clear outlines; easy to see or understand.
definite ['definit] *adj* clear; well understood; not in any doubt. *He made a definite promise to help us* i.e. he promised that he would certainly help us. (*opp* **indefinite**).
definitely *adv*.
definition [defi'niʃən] **1.** *nc* explanation of the meaning of a word or expression. **2.** *nu* act of explaining a word or expression. **3.** *nu* (esp. with reference to the power of a lens or the clearness of a radio signal) degree of clearness.
definitive [di'finitiv] *adj* final; conclusive: *a definitive edition of a book* i.e. one which gives the final correct form so that there can be no further change.
definite article (grammar) the word '*the*' and equivalent words in other languages.

deflate [di'fleit] *vt* **1.** let air or gas escape from a balloon, tyre etc. *He deflated the tyre*. **2.** reduce the amount of money which people in a country have to spend. *The Minister of Finance is trying to deflate the economy*. (*opp* **inflate**). **3.** make someone seem less important. **deflation** *nu*. **deflationary** [diː'fleiʃnəri] *adj*.

deflect [di'flekt] *vt/i* turn, cause to turn, away from a direction. *The ball hit the goalkeeper's boot and was deflected into the goal* i.e. the ball changed its direction when it hit the boot. **deflection** *nc/u*.

deform [di'fɔːm] *vt* (usu. with reference to parts of the body) cause something to have a bad shape; prevent something from growing properly. *The boy had a serious illness when he was a baby and this deformed his arms and legs*. **deformation** [diːfɔː'meiʃən] *nu*. **deformity** *nc*. **deformed** *adj*.

defraud [di'frɔːd] *vt* fail to give somebody money or property which belongs to him. *People who do not pay their taxes are defrauding the government. He defrauded me of the money*.

defray [di'frei] *vt* pay (usu. in **defray the cost/expenses**) (*formal*).

defrost ['diː'frɔst] *vt* remove ice from; unfreeze.
defroster *nc* device which removes ice and snow from the windows of cars, aeroplanes etc.

deft [deft] *adj* light, quick and clever (esp. in using the hands in a job which needs skill). **deftly** *adv*. **deftness** *nu*.

defunct [di'fʌŋkt] *adj* dead; no longer working or in use.

defy [di'fai] *vt* **1.** refuse to obey. *Criminals defy the law*. **2.** say that one is ready to fight somebody. *He defied his enemies*. **3.** say that one thinks somebody cannot do something. *I defy you to find the answer to this problem*. **4.** be too strong or too difficult for somebody. *This problem defies me* i.e. I cannot solve it. *The city defied the enemy for three years* i.e. the enemy could not capture the city. **defiant** *adj*. **defiantly** *adv*. **defiance** *nu*.
in defiance of someone/something refusing

to obey. *He acted in defiance of his teacher.*

degenerate [di'dʒenəreit] *vi* become worse in appearance, behaviour or intelligence. Also [di'dʒenərət] *adj.* **degeneration** [didʒenə'reiʃən], **degeneracy** *nu.*

degrade [di'greid] *vt* make lower in reputation or honour. *He degraded himself by his foolish behaviour.* **degradation** [degrə'deiʃən] *nc/u.*

degrading *adj* causing one to be degraded. **degradingly** *adv.*

degree [di'griː] *nc* **1.** unit of measurement of temperature: *degrees centigrade.* **2.** unit of measurement of angles, equal to sixty minutes. **3.** point on an imaginary scale for measuring people's qualities or behaviour. *He has a very high degree of ability* i.e. he is very clever or able. **4.** award or title given to a person who completes a course of study at a university. **5.** rank or position in society (*o.f.*).

(the) third degree severe questioning by the police etc (often using violence).

by degrees gradually; a little at a time. *He did the work by degrees.*

to a degree very much. (rather *o.f.*).

dehydrate ['diːhai'dreit] *vt* remove water from so as to make dry. **dehydration** *nu.* **dehydrated** *adj.*

deify ['diːifai] *vt* make into a god; treat like a god. **deification** [diːifi'keiʃən] *nu.*

deign [dein] *vi* do something in order to be friendly to, or to take notice of people whom one considers very low or unimportant. *The queen deigned to talk to the poor boy.*

deism ['diːizəm] *nu* belief in God, but not in any particular religion.

deist *nc* person who has this belief.

deity ['diːiti] *nc* god or goddess.

dejected [di'dʒektid] *adj* quietly unhappy. **dejectedly** *adv.* **dejection** *nu.*

delay [di'lei] *vt/i* go, cause to go, slowly or be late. *He delayed for a long time before accepting my offer. They decided to delay the meeting* i.e. hold the meeting later than they had planned. *You have delayed me for three hours* i.e. you have made me late. *He delayed answering the letter.* Also *nc/u*: *We must act without delay. I hope we shall not have any more delays.*

delayed action action which begins some time after the cause for the action (e.g. *a delayed-action bomb* is one which explodes some time after hitting the ground).

delectable [di'lektəbl] *adj* (esp. with reference to food) very pleasant.

delegate ['deligət] *nc* somebody who has the duty of acting as the representative of a group of people (esp. such a person attending a meeting or conference). *Each country sent three delegates to the meeting.* Also ['deligeit] *vt* give somebody the duty of acting as a delegate. *I have been delegated to attend the meeting.*

delegation [deli'geiʃən] **1.** *nu* act of delegating. **2.** *nc* group of delegates. *Britain sent a large delegation to the meeting.*

delete [di'liːt] *vt* put a line through something written to show that it is wrong or that it is to be removed. **deletion** *nc/u.*

deleterious [deli'tiəriəs] *adj* causing harm or damage to the mind or body.

deliberate[1] [di'libərət] *adj* **1.** done with intention; not happening by accident. *That was a deliberate act of cruelty* i.e. the person who did that wanted to be cruel. **2.** slow and careful. *He spoke in a very deliberate manner.* **deliberately** *adv.*

deliberate[2] [di'libəreit] *vi* think or talk about something very carefully. *The government is deliberating about what should be done to solve the problem.* **deliberation** [dilibə'reiʃən] *nc/u.*

delicate ['delikət] *adj* **1.** soft; gentle; finely made: *a delicate flower; delicate food.* **2.** easily broken. *A spider's web is very delicate.* **3.** needing careful attention. *That child is very delicate* i.e. he easily becomes ill. *This is a delicate piece of work* i.e. great care and skill is needed to do this work. *This is a delicate problem.* **4.** able to notice or record very small changes. *This is a very delicate piece of apparatus. His hearing is very delicate.* **5.** (with reference to colours) soft; not bright. **6.** (with reference to people) avoiding that which is dirty, unpleasant or offensive. (*opp* **indelicate** in sense **6.**). **delicately** *adv.* **delicateness, delicacy** ['delikəsi] *nu.* (in all senses of *delicate* above). Also *nc* very pleasant piece of food. *He provided local delicacies for his guests' meal.*

delicatessen [delikə'tesn] *nc* shop which sells various special types of food (esp. foreign food).

delicious [di'liʃəs] *adj* very pleasant in taste or smell. **deliciously** *adv.* **deliciousness** *nu.*

delight [di'lait] **1.** *nu* great pleasure or happiness. **2.** *nc* thing which causes great pleasure or happiness. Also *vt* cause great pleasure or happiness to. *The news delighted us all.*

delightful *adj* causing delight. **delightfully** *adv.*

delighted *adj* feeling delight. **delightedly** *adv.*

delight in something get great pleasure from something. *He delights in old books.*

to one's delight causing delight for someone. *To my delight, I learned that I had passed the examination.*

with delight happily. *I listened to the news with delight.*

delimit [di'limit] *vt* mark or fix the limits or boundaries of.

delineate [di'linieit] *vt* mark the outline or form of; give a general impression of. **delineation** [dilini'eiʃən] *nc/u.*

delinquent [di'liŋkwənt] *nc* criminal; person who breaks the law (esp. a young person). Also *adj*: *delinquent behaviour.* **delinquency** *nu.*

delirium [di'liriəm] *nu* condition of the mind like madness, lasting for a short time (often caused by physical illness). **delirious** *adj.* **deliriously** *adv.*

deliver [di'livə*] **1.** *vt* take something and give it to someone (e.g. with reference to a postman taking letters etc or a shopkeeper sending goods to people's houses). **2.** *vi* take goods to people's houses. *Most of the big shops will deliver if you ask them to.* **3.** *vt* save from danger; set free. **4.** *vt* speak in public. *He delivered a lecture to the students.*

deliverance *nu* rescue; act of setting free or saving from danger.

delivery *nc/u* **1.** act of taking something to somebody. **2.** method of speaking in public. **3.** birth of a child.

deliver a child help a woman to give birth to a child.

be delivered of a child give birth to a child. (rather *o.f.*).

delta ['deltə] *nc* **1.** area where the mouth of a river spreads out into several branches.

2. fourth letter of the Greek alphabet.
'delta-'wing *adj* (with reference to aeroplanes) having wings in the shape of a triangle.

delude [di'lu:d] *vt* make somebody believe something which is not true. *The lawyer tried to delude us. Don't delude yourself* i.e. don't have a wrong belief.
delusion [di'lu:ʒən] *nc/u*: *The belief that the world is flat is a delusion.* **delusive** *adj.* **delusory** [di'lu:zəri] *adj.*

deluge ['delju:dʒ] *nc* **1.** great flood of water; heavy rainstorm. **2.** anything coming in great quantity like a flood of water: *a deluge of questions.* Also *vt* cover like a deluge. *The river deluged the streets of the town.*

de luxe [di'lʌks] *adj* of very good quality: *a de luxe hotel.*

delve [delv] *vt/i* dig (*o.f.*).
delve into something study carefully; try to discover new information about something. *I've been delving into the history of my family.* (*informal*).

demagnetize [di:'mægnətaiz] *vt* remove the magnetism from.

demagogue ['deməgɔg] *nc* political leader who gains power by creating strong feelings among crowds of people. **demagogic** [demə'gɔgik] *adj.*
demagogy *nu* methods of a demagogue.

demand[1] [di'ma:nd] *vt* **1.** ask for very strongly and firmly, without trying to be polite. *The boys stopped the old man in the street and demanded money.* **2.** need. *This question demands my immediate attention* i.e. I must attend to this question at once.

demand[2] [di'ma:nd] **1.** *nc* something which one asks for very strongly; act of demanding. *I have several demands to make.* **2.** *nc* need for something. *There are many demands on my time at present* i.e. there are many things which I must do. **3.** *nu* wish by people to buy something. *Most newspaper shops in Britain do not sell foreign newspapers because there is no demand for them* i.e. not many people want to buy foreign newspapers.
in demand wanted. *He is always in demand when people are giving parties* i.e. people who are giving parties always want him to come.
on demand when asked for. *If you save money in the post office you can draw up to £20 on demand* i.e. you can take up to £20 of your savings out of the post office without having to wait.

demarcate ['di:ma:keit] *vt* mark or fix the limits or boundaries of.
demarcation [di:ma:'keiʃən] *nu* (esp. with reference to an agreement fixing the type of work to be done by members of different trade unions working together). *The workers were on strike because of a dispute over demarcation.*

demean [di'mi:n] *vt* (usu. **demean oneself**) make lower in dignity, reputation etc. *He demeaned himself by doing such dirty and badly-paid work.*

demeanour [di'mi:nə*] *nu* way of behaving. *His demeanour was very strange.*

demented [di'mentid] *adj* mad; violent and strange in behaviour.

demi- ['demi] *prefix* half (e.g. **demigod**).

demigod ['demigɔd] *nc* being in Greek and Roman mythology born of a god or goddess and a human being.

demilitarize [di:'militəraiz] *vt* remove from the control of the army.

demise [di'maiz] *nc* (in a legal sense) death.

demobilize ['di:'moubilaiz] *vt/i* allow soldiers to leave the army and return to normal life. *After the war many soldiers were demobilized. The country did not demobilize immediately after the war.* **demobilization** ['di:moubilai'zeiʃən] *nu.*

democracy [di'mɔkrəsi] **1.** *nu* form of government in which people choose their rulers by voting in elections. **2.** *nc* country having this form of government. **3.** *nc* country having free elections, freedom of speech, protection of the individual, government by an elected parliament etc. **4.** *nu* practice of treating all people as one's equals.
democratic [demə'krætik] *adj.* (*opp* **undemocratic**). **democratically** *adv.*
democrat ['deməkræt] *nc* person who is in favour of democracy.

demography [di'mɔgrəfi] *nu* science dealing with the number of births, deaths, marriages, diseases etc in a community.
demographer *nc.*

demolish [di'mɔliʃ] *vt* destroy; break completely. *The bomb demolished the house.*
demolition [demə'liʃən] *nu.*

demon ['di:mən] *nc* evil spirit. **demonic** [di'mɔnik] *adj.*

demonstrate ['demənstreit] **1.** *vt/i* show clearly; make known. *The teacher demonstrated the experiment to the class* i.e. he showed the class how to do the experiment. **2.** *vi* hold a political meeting (often in the open air) to protest against something or show support for something. *Large crowds demonstrated outside the British Embassy*
demonstration [demən'streiʃən] *nc/u* **1.** *He gave a demonstration of horse-riding.* **2.** *The workers held a demonstration against the government.*
demonstrative [di'mɔnstrətiv] *adj* **1.** clearly showing one's feelings or one's meaning. *He greeted us in a demonstrative manner* i.e. he showed that he was glad to see us. (*opp* **undemonstrative**). **2.** (grammar) pointing out. *'This' and 'that' are demonstrative pronouns.* **demonstratively** *adv.*
demonstrator *nc* **1.** person who takes part in a political demonstration. **2.** person in a school or college whose work is to show students how to do experiments in science. **3.** person in a shop etc who helps to sell machinery, household equipment etc by showing the customer how it works.

demoralize [di'mɔrəlaiz] *vt* take away somebody's courage, confidence, self-control etc. *After losing three important battles, the army had become demoralized.* **demoralization** [dimɔrəlai'zeiʃən] *nu.*

demote [di'mout] *vt* put into a lower rank or lower position. *The soldier was demoted as a punishment for failing to obey orders.* (*opp* **promote**). **demotion** *nu.*

demur [di'mə:*] *vi* hesitate to do something; find reasons for not doing something. *He demurred when I asked him to do the extra work. past* **demurred.** Also *nu*: *He did the work without demur.*

demure [di'mjuə*] *adj* (esp. with reference to young girls) quiet and rather afraid to talk to other people; prim. **demurely** *adv.* **demureness** *nu.*

den [den] *nc* **1.** place where a wild animal such as a lion or tiger lives. **2.** place where a lion or tiger is kept at a zoo. **3.** place where criminals or outlaws live. **4.** small dirty room. 5. room where one can be comfortable or work at one's hobbies.

denationalize [diː'næʃnəlaiz] *vt* return an industry to private ownership after it has been taken from private owners by the government. **denationalization** [diːnæʃnəlai'zeiʃən] *nu*.

denial [di'naiəl] *nc/u* see **deny**.

denier ['deniə*] *nc* unit for measuring the thickness of nylon or silk thread.

denim ['denim] *nu* strong type of cotton cloth.

denims *npl* trousers or overalls made of denim.

denizen ['denizn] *nc* person, animal, plant etc living in a certain place. *The lion is a denizen of the jungle.* (rather *o.f.*).

denomination [dinɔmi'neiʃən] *nc* **1.** any of the Christian churches (e.g. the Roman Catholic Church, the Church of England, the Methodist Church). *The service was attended by people of different denominations.* **2.** type of unit of measurement, weight, money etc. *Inches and feet are different denominations.*

denominator [di'nɔmineitə*] *nc* the number below the line in a vulgar fraction (e.g. in ⅜, 3 is the denominator).

denote [di'nout] *vt* be the sign for or name of something; mean.

denotation [diːnou'teiʃən] *nc/u* meaning of a word or expression, without any consideration of the feelings which the word suggests. see **connotation**.

denouement, dénouement [dei'nuːmɔŋ] *nc* end of a story or play, in which everything is explained and the problems of the plot are solved.

denounce [di'nauns] *vt* **1.** speak against; show that one opposes. *The newspapers denounced the new taxes.* **2.** tell police etc about a crime committed by someone. *He denounced Mr Jones to the police* i.e. he told the police that Mr Jones had committed a crime. **denunciation** [dinʌnsi'eiʃən] *nu*. **denunciatory** [di'nʌnsiətəri] *adj*.

dense [dens] *adj* **1.** packed closely together: *dense crowds of people.* **2.** (with reference to gas etc) not easily seen through: *a dense fog.* **3.** (with reference to a person) stupid or unintelligent. **densely** *adv*.

density *nc/u* **1.** quality of being dense (in all senses). **2.** (physics) proportion of weight to volume.

dent [dent] *nc* place pushed in without breaking the surface. *He made a dent in his car when he backed into the tree.* Also *vt* make a dent.

dentist ['dentist] *nc* doctor who treats the teeth.

dentistry *nu* work of a dentist.

dental ['dentl] *adj* referring to the teeth or to dentists.

dentifrice ['dentifris] *nu* substance for cleaning teeth.

dentition [den'tiʃən] *nc/u* way the teeth grow or way in which they are arranged in the mouth.

denture ['dentʃə*] *nc* artificial or false teeth.

denude [di'njuːd] *vt* remove covering from; make bare. *The cold weather denuded the trees of their leaves.*

denunciation [dinʌnsi'eiʃən] *nu* see **denounce**.

deny [di'nai] *vt* **1.** say that something is not true. *He denied that he had broken the window. He denied the story.* **2.** say that one will not give. *He denied me any help while I was doing the work.* **3.** say that one has no connection with something. *He denied all knowledge of the crime* i.e. he said that he did not know anything about the crime. **denial** *nc/u*.

deny oneself something live without getting something for oneself. *He decided that he had so much work that he would have to deny himself a holiday.*

deodorant [di'oudərnt] *nc* something used to take away unpleasant smells. Also *adj*.

deodorize *vt* take away unpleasant smells from.

depart [di'pɑːt] *vi* go away; leave. *The train will depart from Platform 2. We must not depart from this agreement* i.e. we must do what we have agreed to do.

departure *nc/u* **1.** act of departing or starting. **2.** beginning of something new. *Learning Russian is a new departure for him.*

the (dear) departed dead person known to oneself or to another person (*o.f.*).

department [di'pɑːtmənt] *nc* one of the sections of a large shop, government office, school, university etc. **departmental** [diːpɑːt'mentl] *adj*.

de'partment store large shop selling many different kinds of goods.

depend [di'pend] *vi* (with **on** or **upon**) **1.** trust. *We can depend on him for help* i.e. we can be sure that he will help us. *You can depend on this newspaper* i.e. this newspaper always tells the truth. **2.** get help or support from; get money or food and clothing from. *He could not work, and so he had to depend on his family.* **3.** be influenced by. *The sort of job I get depends on my examination results* i.e. if I get good results I shall get a good job.

dependence *nu*. (*opp* **independence**).

dependable *adj* able to be trusted. *This newspaper is dependable, it always tells the truth.* **dependably** *adv*. **dependability** [dipendə'biliti] *nu*.

dependant *nc* somebody who gets help, food, clothing etc from somebody else. *A man's wife and children are his dependants.*

dependent *adj*: *The children are dependent on their father.* (*opp* **independent**).

dependency *nc* country controlled by another country.

depict [di'pikt] *vt* show or make a picture of; describe very clearly so that one seems to see a picture when reading or hearing the description.

depilatory [di'pilətəri] *nc* substance for removing hair.

deplete [di'pliːt] *vt* use so that little or none is left. *Our supplies of food have been much depleted.* **depletion** *nu*.

deplore [di'plɔː*] *vt* say or think that something is very bad. *He deplored the waste of time and money.*

deplorable *adj* very bad, and fit to be deplored. **deplorably** *adv*.

deploy [di'plɔi] *vt* **1.** make soldiers move into a line ready for a battle. **2.** use the resources which one has in the best way so as to be successful. *The businessman decided to deploy all his available money in setting up the new factory.* **deployment** *nu*.

depopulate [diː'pɔpjuleit] *vt* remove people from the place where they are living. *The north of Scotland has been greatly depopulated in the last 100 years* i.e. many people have left the north of Scotland. **depopulation** [diːpɔpju'leiʃən] *nu*.

deport[1] [di'pɔːt] *vt* make a foreigner leave

the country. **deportation** [diːpɔː'teiʃən] *nc/u.*

deport[2] [di'pɔːt] *vt* usu. **deport oneself** i.e. behave. (*formal*).

deportment *nu* (esp. with reference to behaviour which is dignified and gentlemanly).

depose [di'pouz] *vt* make a king or other ruler leave his position. *The army deposed the king and set up a republic.* **deposition** [diːpə'ziʃən] *nc/u.*

deposit [di'pɔzit] *nc* **1.** amount of money left by somebody in a bank or other place. **2.** amount of money paid as part payment for something. **3.** amount of substance in or on the earth. *There was a thick deposit of mud at the bottom of the river. Several deposits of gold have been found in those hills.* Also *vt* **1.** make a deposit. *The sea has deposited a lot of stones on the beach.* **2.** leave something in a safe place. *He deposited his money in the bank. I deposited my case in the left-luggage office.*

depositor *nc* person who puts his money into a bank etc.

depository *nc* building where goods can be stored.

on deposit in a bank. *I have £50 on deposit.*

depot ['depou] *nc* **1.** building or place where goods are stored (esp. military supplies). **2.** (*US*) railway station. **3.** place where soldiers are trained when they first enter the army.

deprave [di'preiv] *vt* make bad or wicked in behaviour.

depraved *adj* bad or wicked in behaviour.

depravity [di'præviti] *nc/u.*

deprecate ['deprikeit] *vt* say that one does not approve of something; speak against something. *The old man deprecated the boy's foolish behaviour* i.e. he said he thought that the boy was acting badly. **deprecatory** *adj.*

deprecation [depri'keiʃən] *nu.*

depreciate [di'priːʃieit] *vt/i* become or make less in value or usefulness. *Money usually depreciates in value over a period of years.*

depreciation [dipriːʃi'eiʃən] *nu.*

depredation [depri'deiʃən] *nc/u* destruction and robbery.

depress [di'pres] *vt* **1.** make very miserable or unhappy. *The bad news depressed us all.* **2.** (with reference to a switch, key, button etc on an instrument or machine) press down.

depressing *adj* causing one to be unhappy.

depressingly *adv.*

depression **1.** *nc/u* condition of being miserable or unhappy. **2.** *nc* area of low atmospheric pressure. **3.** *nc* hollow place on a surface. *There were several small depressions in the field.* **4.** *nc* condition of lack of growth in trade and economy, with great unemployment.

deprive [di'praiv] *vt* take something away: *deprive someone of his rights. I have been deprived of sleep for two nights.* **deprivation** [depri'veiʃən] *nc/u.*

depth [depθ] **1.** *nc* distance downwards. *The depth of this river is three feet.* **2.** *nc* distance across. *The depth of these shelves is six inches.* **3.** *nc/u* darkness in colour. **4.** *nc/u* lowness in pitch of sound. **5.** *nu* great learning or wisdom. *This book shows the author's depth of learning.* **6.** *nc* (usu. *pl*) deepest or furthest part. *Coal miners have to work in the depths of the earth.* see **deep.**

'depth charge bomb which is dropped in the water, and is designed to explode when it reaches a certain depth.

out of one's depth **1.** in water which is too deep for one to walk in, and so in danger of drowning. **2.** confused by a question, discussion, business etc which requires knowledge one does not have.

depute [di'pjuːt] *vt* give somebody one's permission and authority to do a certain part of one's own work. *I cannot go to the meeting, and so I am deputing you to go instead of me.*

deputy ['depjuti] *nc* person who has been deputed (esp. **1.** person given authority to work for a sheriff in America. **2.** member of the lower house of parliament in France and other countries).

deputation [depju'teiʃən] *nc* group of people having permission to speak for others (esp. to make a complaint).

deputize ['depjutaiz] *vi* act as a deputy. *I am deputizing for Mr Smith.*

derail [di'reil] *vt* cause a train to leave the rails. **derailment** *nc.*

derange [di'reindʒ] *vt* (esp. with reference to making somebody go mad) make confused or disturbed. *The troubles of his life had deranged the old man* i.e. had made him mad. **derangement** *nc.*

derelict ['derilikt] *adj* left or abandoned as unwanted or useless. *There were many derelict houses in the streets of the city.* Also *nc* something left in this way.

deride [di'raid] *vt* laugh at as foolish. *He derided my plan* i.e. he thought my plan was foolish. **derision** [di'riʒən] *nu.* **derisive** [di'raisiv] *adj.* **derisively** *adv.*

derisory [di'raisəri] *adj* causing derision.

derive [di'raiv] **1.** *vt* get from. *He derives a lot of pleasure from reading.* **2.** (esp. with reference to words) come from; have as a beginning. *Many English words derive from French.* **derivation** [deri'veiʃən] *nc/u.*

derivative [di'rivətiv] *adj* coming from something else, and so not original. Also *nc* word or substance derived from another word or substance.

dermatology [dəːmə'tɔlədʒi] *nu* study of the skin. **dermatologist** *nc.*

derogatory [di'rɔgətəri] *adj* showing that one has a bad opinion of somebody/something. *The boy made several derogatory remarks about his teacher.*

derrick ['derik] *nc* **1.** tall machine for lifting and moving heavy weights. **2.** tall metal framework over an oil well.

dervish ['dəːviʃ] *nc* type of Muslim holy man.

'dancing 'dervish type of dervish who dances for religious purposes.

descant ['deskænt] *nc* tune intended to be sung above another tune, making a harmony.

descant on/upon something talk for a long time about something (usu. with enthusiasm).

descend [di'send] *vt/i* go down. *He descended the hill. The path descended steeply.*

descendant *nc* person having somebody as his ancestor. *He says that he is a descendant of Julius Caesar.*

descent [di'sent] **1.** *nc* movement down. *He began the descent of the mountain.* **2.** *nu* ancestry. *Many Americans are of English descent* i.e. their ancestors were English. **3.** *nc* sudden attack.

descend from someone/something **1.** come down from. *He descended from the top of the mountain.* **2.** have as one's ancestors. *He* *claims to descend from Napoleon.* **3.** pass from father to son. *This house has descended from our ancestors* i.e. our family has always owned this house.

descend on/upon someone/something **1.** make a sudden attack. *The robbers descended on the lonely house.* **2.** make a sudden visit. *They descended on us at lunchtime.*

descend to something do something disgraceful or dishonourable. *He was so poor that he descended to begging for his food.*

be descended from someone have as one's ancestor. *Queen Elizabeth II is descended from Queen Victoria.*

describe [dis'kraib] *vt* **1.** say what somebody/something is like. *He described the town where he used to live.* **2.** form the shape or outline of: *describe a circle.* (*formal*).

describable *adj* able to be described. (*opp* **indescribable**).

description [dis'kripʃən] *nc/u* something written or said to describe a person/thing; act of describing.

descriptive [dis'kriptiv] *adj* forming a description: *descriptive writing.* **descriptively** *adv.*

of every description of every type or kind. *There are shops of every description in this town.*

answer to a description have the appearance which is described. *The thief answers to the following description. . . .*

descry [dis'krai] *vt* see from a long way away.

desecrate ['desikreit] *vt* do something to spoil or damage something religious or beautiful; treat something holy or beautiful in a bad way. **desecration** [desi'kreiʃən] *nc/u.*

desegregate [di:'segrəgeit] *vt* allow mixing of races; end segregation: *desegregate education* i.e. allow children of all races to attend the same schools. **desegregation** ['di:segrə'geiʃən] *nu.*

desert[1] ['dezət] *nc* large area covered by sand.

'desert 'island island in the tropics on which nobody lives.

desert[2] [di'zə:t] *vt/i* go away without permission; leave in a cruel or unfriendly way. *The soldier deserted* i.e. he left the army without permission. *He deserted his friends.*

desertion *nu.*

deserter *nc* person who leaves military service without permission.

desert[3] [di'zə:t] *nc* (usu. *pl*) reward or punishment which one deserves. *The thief got his just deserts when he was sent to prison.*

deserve [di'zə:v] *vt* be worthy of. *He deserves to have a holiday for his hard work* i.e. he ought to get a holiday because he has worked hard. *He deserves a reward.*

deserving *adj* worthy of something. (*opp* **undeserving**).

deservedly [di'zə:vidli] *adv* justly. *He was deservedly punished.* (*opp* **undeservedly**). see **desert**[3].

desiccate ['desikeit] *vt* make very dry; remove all moisture from. **desiccation** [desi'keiʃən] *nu.*

desiccated *adj*: *desiccated coconut.*

desideratum [dizi:də'rɑ:təm] *nc* something which is needed. *pl* **desiderata** [dizi:də'rɑ:tə]. (*formal*).

design[1] [di'zain] *vt/i* **1.** make a plan of something before it is made. *The new building was designed by an American architect.* **2.** intend to do or use something in a certain way. *The road was not designed for heavy lorries* i.e. the road was not made for heavy lorries.

design[2] [di'zain] **1.** *nc* plan or drawing of something before it is made. *Here is a design of the house I want to build.* **2.** *nu* art of planning things in this way. *He is studying furniture design.* **3.** *nc* way something is planned. *I like the design of your furniture.* **4.** *nc* pattern or picture on cloth, paper, pottery, glass etc. **5.** *nc* plan or intention to do something.

designer *nc* person who plans and draws something before it is made.

designedly [di'zainidli] *adv* on purpose. *That wall was put there designedly, to prevent people walking on the grass.*

designing *adj* making careful plans to get something for one's own. *She is a very designing woman.*

by design following a plan. *Did you do this by design or by accident?*

have designs on something have plans to take for one's own or to harm.

designate ['dezigneit] *vt* **1.** name somebody to take a certain position. *The Prime Minister has designated three new members of his government.* **2.** mark; be a sign or title of. *'vt' designates a transitive verb in this dictionary. The marks on his shoulder designated the rank of an army officer.*

designation [dezig'neiʃən] *nc/u.*

desire [di'zaiə*] *vt* **1.** want very much. *The only thing he desires is peace.* **2.** ask for. *He desires to speak to you.* (*formal*). Also *nc/u* strong wish; request; something which is desired.

desirous *adj* (with **of**) feeling desire.

desirable *adj* **1.** causing one to desire; pleasant: *a very desirable house.* **2.** referring to the best course of action. *It is not desirable for us to go there.* (*opp* **undesirable**).

desirability [dizaiərə'biliti] *nu.*

desist [di'zist] *vi* (often with **from**) stop doing. *You must desist at once. You must desist from doing that.*

desk [desk] *nc* piece of furniture for writing on, and often with drawers or a space under the top for storing books etc.

desolate ['desələt] *adj* **1.** empty; bare; ruined; without many people. *The farm was in a lonely desolate valley.* **2.** unhappy and lonely. *After the death of their parents the children were desolate.* Also ['desəleit] *vt* make desolate. **desolation** [desə'leiʃən] *nu.*

despair [dis'pɛə*] *vi* lose hope. *After the failure of his plans he began to despair. He despaired of finding the answer.* Also *nu* loss of hope: *be in despair.*

despairing *adj*: *a despairing sigh.* **despairingly** *adv.* see **desperate.**

despatch [dis'pætʃ] *vt* see **dispatch.**

desperate ['despərət] *adj* **1.** having lost all hope. *He was desperate after the failure of his plans.* **2.** willing to do anything to get what is wanted. *He was desperate for money, and so he stole £5.* **3.** violent and dangerous: *a desperate criminal.* **4.** very difficult and dangerous: *a desperate situation.* **desperately** *adv.*

desperation [despə'reiʃən] *nu*: *He stole the money in desperation* i.e. because he had lost hope of getting what he wanted in any other way. see **despair.**

despise [dis'paiz] *vt* think that someone/something is very low and of no use or value at all. *He despised people who killed animals for pleasure.*

despicable [dis'pikəbl] *adj* deserving to be despised: *a despicable act of cruelty.* **despicably** *adv.*

despite [dis'pait] *prep* in spite of. *Despite the rain he went for a walk* i.e. although it was raining.

despoil [dis'pɔil] *vt* steal from.

despond [dis'pɔnd] *vi* lose hope. *You must not despond if your plans do not succeed.* Also *nu.* **despondent** *adj.* **despondently** *adv.* **despondency** *nu.*

despot ['despɔt] *nc* king or other ruler who governs (often in a cruel way), without any consideration for the law. **despotic** [dis'pɔtik] *adj.* **despotically** *adv.*
despotism ['despətizəm] **1.** *nu* this method of ruling. **2.** *nc* country ruled like this.

dessert [di'zə:t] *nc/u* sweet food eaten after the main part of a meal.
de'ssertspoon spoon used for eating dessert.

destination [desti'neiʃən] *nc* place to which one is going.

destine ['destin] *vt* (often *passive*) decide or plan to use something for a special purpose. *He seemed to be destined for great success* i.e. it seemed as though nothing could stop him from being successful.
destiny **1.** *nu* (often **Destiny**) power in the universe which is thought of as planning what will happen in the future. **2.** *nc* things which will happen to one in the future. *Nobody knows his own destiny.*

destitute ['destitju:t] *adj* without (enough) food, clothing, housing etc. **destitution** [desti'tju:ʃən] *nu.*

destroy [dis'trɔi] *vt/i* break down or break to pieces so as to make useless. *The house was destroyed by a bomb.* **destruction** [dis'trʌkʃən] *nu.*
destructive [dis'trʌktiv] *adj* causing destruction; fond of destroying. **destructively** *adv.*
destructiveness *nu* quality of being destructive.
destructible [dis'trʌktibl] *adj* able or designed to be destroyed. (*opp* **indestructible**).
destroyer *nc* type of small, fast warship.

desuetude [di'sju:itju:d] *nu* lack of use (usu. in **fall into desuetude**) (*formal*).

desultory ['desəltəri] *adj* without any proper plan; not staying long at any one thing. *He walked around the shops in a desultory way* i.e. without really knowing what he ought to buy.

detach [di'tætʃ] *vt* **1.** unfasten and take away. *She detached the baby's hand from her dress.* **2.** (with reference to the army etc) send someone somewhere for a special purpose. *The officer detached thirty men to guard the railway station.*
detachable *adj* able to be detached.
detached *adj* **1.** (with reference to a person) not showing strong feelings; not influenced by other people. *He spoke in a detached way about the danger* i.e. he spoke as though he had no feelings about the danger. **2.** (with reference to a house) not joined to another. see also **semidetached.**
detachment **1.** *nu* act of detaching. **2.** *nc* group of soldiers etc sent somewhere for a special purpose. **3.** *nu* condition of not showing any feelings, or of not being influenced by other people. *He spoke with complete detachment about the danger which threatened all of them.*

detail[1] ['di:teil] **1.** *nc* small fact or small part of something. *He gave me all the details of his new job* i.e. he told me everything about it. **2.** *nc* small group of soldiers etc given a special duty. *The officer sent a detail of men to guard the railway station.* **3.** *nu* small facts or small parts of something. *There is a lot of detail in the sewing she is doing* i.e. she is sewing a design with many different colours or many small stitches. *The detail in that film was good* i.e. the scenery, clothing etc were carefully chosen with attention to small details.
in detail giving full details. *He told me in detail what I should do.*
go into detail(s) give full details. *He went into great detail about his new house.*

detail[2] ['di:teil] *vt* **1.** describe fully. *He detailed my new duties to me.* **2.** send a group of soldiers etc to do some special duty. *He detailed six men to clean the windows.*

detain [di'tein] *vt* keep back; prevent from going; prevent from leaving a place. *The policemen decided to detain the man until they had questioned him further.*
detention [di'tenʃən] *nu*: *The pupil was given two hours' detention for his bad behaviour.*
detainee [di:tei'ni:] *nc* person detained (esp. one detained in prison for political reasons).

detect [di'tekt] *vt* find something hidden or secret. *He detected a fault in my car. I detect a strange smell.*
detector *nc* person/thing that detects.
detective *nc* person (often a policeman) whose job is to find criminals etc.
detection *nu* process of detecting; work of a detective.

détente [dei'tɑ̃t] *nc* increase in friendship between two formerly hostile countries.

deter [di'tə:*] *vt* prevent; discourage. *The bad weather deterred us from making the long journey* i.e. we did not make the journey or we were very unwilling to make the journey. *past* **deterred.**
deterrent [di'ternt] *nc* (esp. with reference to nuclear weapons, which deter one's enemies from starting a war) something which deters. Also *adj.*

detergent [di'tə:dʒənt] *nc* substance other than soap, used for cleaning clothes or plates, cups etc. Also *adj.*

deteriorate [di'tiəriəreit] *vt/i* become or make worse. *His work has deteriorated.*
deterioration [ditiəriə'reiʃən] *nu.*

determine [di'tə:min] *vt/i* **1.** make a firm decision to do something. *He determined to work harder.* **2.** cause something to be decided. *The amount of money we have will determine the length of our holiday* i.e. if we have a lot of money we shall have a long holiday. **3.** find out exactly. *The policeman wanted to determine all the facts.* **determination** [ditə:mi'neiʃən] *nu.*
determined *adj*: *He is determined to come* i.e. he has firmly decided on this.
determinism *nu* belief that events take place according to a plan or process which cannot be changed by man.
determinist *nc* person who believes this.

deterrent [di'ternt] *nc* see **deter.**

detest [di'test] *vt* dislike very much. *He detests watching television.*
detestable *adj* very unpleasant. **detestably** *adv.*
detestation [di:tes'teiʃən] *nu* feeling of strong dislike.

dethrone ['di:'θroun] *vt* make a king or

other ruler leave his position. **dethronement** *nu*.

detonate ['detəneit] *vt/i* explode, cause to explode. *The soldiers detonated the bomb.* **detonation** [detə'neiʃən] *nu*.
detonator *nc* part of a bomb etc which starts the explosion.

detour ['di:tuə*] *nc* road which is used when the usual road cannot be used; journey made on such a road. Also *vi* make a detour.

detract [di'trækt] *vi* (with **from**) take away part of the value or goodness of. *I want nothing to detract from your enjoyment today.* **detraction** *nu*.
detractor *nc* person who says bad things about other people.

detriment ['detrimənt] *nu* harm or damage. *The war caused great detriment to the nation's economy.* **detrimental** [detri'mentl] *adj*.
to the detriment of something causing harm to something. *The time the student wasted was to the detriment of his studies.*

detritus [di'traitəs] *nu* small pieces of rock or stone broken away from a larger mass.

deuce [dju:s] **1.** *nu* score of 40–40 in tennis. **2.** *nc* playing card or side of a dice showing two marks. (*informal* in sense **2.**).
the deuce the devil (used as an exclamation as in **What the deuce do you mean?**) (*informal* and rather *o.f.*).

devalue [di:'vælju:] *vt* officially declare that the money of one's country will in future be worth less than the equivalent money in foreign countries. *The British government devalued the pound.* **devaluation** [di:vælju'eiʃən] *nu*.

devastate ['devəsteit] *vt* destroy and make empty or ruined. *The bomb devastated a large part of the city.* **devastation** [devə'steiʃən] *nu*.
devastating *adj* **1.** causing destruction. **2.** very effective. (*informal* in sense **2.**).

develop [di'veləp] *vt/i* **1.** grow, cause to grow. *The new town slowly developed until it became one of the largest towns in the country. I have a few ideas, but I need more time to develop them properly* i.e. think about them fully. *At the beginning of the war a very dangerous situation developed.* **2.** treat film with chemicals to make the picture appear. *He developed the photographs which he had taken. He spent all day developing.* **development** *nc/u*.
developer *nc* substance used in developing films.
developing country country without a fully-developed industrial system.

deviate ['di:vieit] *vi* turn away from the right course or from the way that one is on. *He never deviated from complete honesty* i.e. he was always honest. **deviation** [di:vi'eiʃən] *nc/u*.
deviationist [di:vi'eiʃənist] *nc* communist who tries to move away from communist ideas which were followed in the past.
deviationism [di:vi'eiʃənizəm] *nu* the beliefs of such a person.

device [di'vais] *nc* **1.** piece of apparatus used for a particular purpose. *He invented a device for sharpening old razor blades.* **2.** trick or plan to solve some particular problem. **3.** picture or pattern used as a sign of a person or an organization. see **devise.**
leave somebody to his own devices leave somebody alone, to do as he wishes, without giving him any help or advice.

devil ['devl] *nc* **1.** evil spirit. **2.** (often **the Devil**) chief evil spirit. **3.** cruel or wicked person. **devilish** *adj*. **devilishly** *adv*.
the devil used as an exclamation, as in **What the devil are you doing?** (*informal*).
devil's advocate person in a discussion etc who supports a contrary point of view just for the sake of the argument.
the devil to pay a lot of trouble. *If you do that there will be the devil to pay* i.e. people will be very angry with you. (*informal*).
between the devil and the deep blue sea between two alternatives, both of which are bad or unpleasant. (*informal*).
give the devil his due admit it when a bad person does something good. (*informal*).
talk of the devil! exclamation used when somebody appears after one has been talking about him. (*informal*).

devious ['di:viəs] *adj* **1.** not straight, not direct, not the shortest. *We travelled by a devious route.* **2.** not completely honest. **deviously** *adv*. **deviousness** *nu*.

devise [di'vaiz] *vt* invent or think of a piece of apparatus, or a plan or trick. see **device.**

devoid [di'vɔid] *adj* (with **of**) without; lacking. *He is completely devoid of humour* i.e. he never makes jokes or laughs at jokes.

devolve [di'vɔlv] *vt/i* (with **on** or **upon**) (with reference to work or duty) pass to somebody. *All the work that John did not do has devolved on me.* **devolution** [di:və'lu:ʃən] *nu*.

devote [di'vout] *vt* (with **to**) keep for a special purpose; apply oneself wholeheartedly. *This magazine is devoted to the study of African history. He devoted himself to helping the poor.* **devotion** *nu*.
devoted *adj* showing great love and willingness to work or help. *He was a devoted servant.* **devotedly** *adv*. **devotedness** *nu*.
devotee [devə'ti:] *nc* person devoted to something, or very interested in something.
devotions *npl* prayers. **devotional** *adj*.

devour [di'vauə*] *vt* **1.** eat completely; eat with hunger. **2.** burn completely. **3.** read with great interest. *He devoured the book he had bought.*

devout [di'vaut] *adj* **1.** careful to carry out all one's religious duties such as going to church and praying. **2.** felt very deeply: *a devout feeling of thanks.* **devoutly** *adv*. **devoutness** *nu*.

dew [dju:] *nu* moisture in the air, which forms in small drops during the night. **dewy** *adj*.

dewlap ['dju:læp] *nc* loose fold of skin under the throat of cattle.

dexterity [deks'teriti] *nu* cleverness (esp. in using the hands). **dexterous** ['dekstərəs] *adj*. **dexterously** *adv*.

diabetes [daiə'bi:ti:z] *nu* disease in which there is too much sugar in the blood.
diabetic [daiə'betik] *nc* person suffering from diabetes. Also *adj*.

diabolical [daiə'bɔlikl] *adj* like the devil; very wicked or cruel. **diabolically** *adv*.

diadem ['daiədem] *nc* crown worn by a king or other ruler. (rather *o.f.*).

diagnose [daiəg'nouz] *vt* find out what disease a person is suffering from by making an examination; similarly find out what is wrong in any situation. *The doctor diagnosed the disease.*
diagnosis [daiəg'nousis] *nc* **1.** process of diagnosing. **2.** decision about what a disease is. *pl* **diagnoses** [daiəg'nousi:z]. **diagnostic** [daiəg'nɔstik] *adj*.

diagonal [dai'ægənl] *nc* straight line going across. Also *adj*. **diagonally** *adv*.

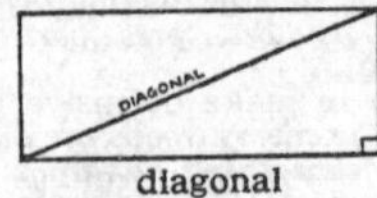

diagonal

diagram ['daiəgræm] *nc* drawing showing the important parts of something one is explaining.

dial ['daiəl] *nc* surface marked with numbers or symbols and connected to various types of machinery (e.g. the dial of a clock tells one the time; the dial of a radio enables one to find the station one wants; the dial of a telephone enables one to call the person one wants to speak to; the dials in a car tell the driver how fast he is going, how much petrol he has etc). Also *vt* call on the telephone. *Dial the police. Dial 999. past* **dialled.** (*US* **dialed**).
'**dialling tone** sound made by a telephone which means that it is possible to dial a number.

dialect ['daiəlekt] *nc* spoken form of a language, found in a particular area of a country.

dialectic(s) [daiə'lektik(s)] *nu* method of conducting an argument or discussion according to certain rules of logic. **dialectical** *adj*.

dialogue ['daiəlɔg] *nc* conversation (esp. in a book or play).

diameter [dai'æmitə*] *nc* line passing from one side of a circle to the other through the centre. **diametrical** [daiə'metrikl] *adj*. **diametrically** *adv*: *This is diametrically opposed to what I said* i.e. it is the exact opposite.

diamond ['daiəmənd] *nc* **1.** very hard, bright, valuable stone found in the earth. **2.** four-sided figure on a playing card. **3.** (in baseball) area inside the bases.

diamond (*def* 2)

'**diamond** '**jubilee**/'**wedding** 60th anniversary of a coronation etc or of a wedding.
a rough diamond person who has rough manners but who is very kind. (*informal*).

diaper ['daiəpə*] *nc* (*US*) piece of cloth put between a baby's legs and fastened at his waist. (*Brit* **nappy**).

diaphanous [dai'æfənəs] *adj* (often with reference to cloth or clothing) transparent (and usu. thin).

diaphragm ['daiəfræm] *nc* **1.** area of muscle between the chest and the abdomen. **2.** device which controls the amount of light entering a camera.

diarrhoea [daiə'riə] (*US* **diarrhea**) *nu* type of illness in which all waste matter is sent out of the body in liquid form (esp. when this happens many times).

diary ['daiəri] *nc* book in which one writes down what happens each day; record of daily happenings.
diarist *nc* person who keeps a diary, or writes down what happens or is going to happen each day.

diatribe ['daiətraib] *nc* speech or writing making an angry attack on somebody.

dice [dais] *nc* or *npl* small cube of wood, ivory, bone, plastic etc, marked with spots indicating numbers used in various games. *pl* **dice.** Also *vt/i* **1.** *vi* play a game using dice. **2.** *vt* cut vegetables etc into very small pieces.

dice

Note: dice was originally the plural of a word *die*. However *die* is today *formal* and *o.f.*, and *dice* is used by many people as a singular word, which is unchanged in the plural.
dicey *adj* rather difficult and risky. (*informal*).

dichotomy [dai'kɔtəmi] *nc* split or division into two parts: *the dichotomy between the rich and the poor*.

dictaphone ['diktəfoun] *nc* machine which records words spoken into it (usu. for use in offices). The words are later typed or written out.

dictate[1] [dik'teit] *vt/i* **1.** say words for somebody to write down. *He dictated a letter to his secretary.* **2.** give orders. see **dictator. dictation** *nc/u*.
dictate to someone give orders to. *That boy always tries to dictate to his friends when they play together.*

dictate[2] ['dikteit] *nc* (usu. *pl*) order which must or should be obeyed: *the dictates of common sense* i.e. what it is sensible to do.
dictator [dik'teitə*] *nc* person who rules a country by giving orders, without being himself under the control of the laws.
dictatorial [diktə'tɔ:riəl] *adj* like a dictator.
dictatorship [dik'teitəʃip] **1.** *nu* position of a dictator; period during which a dictator rules. **2.** *nc* country ruled by a dictator.

diction ['dikʃən] *nu* way of speaking. *The actor spoke with a very clear diction* i.e. it was very easy to hear his words.
poetic diction words and expressions found in poetry but not normally in prose writing or in spoken language.

dictionary ['dikʃənəri] *nc* book containing a list of words, in alphabetical order, with their meanings.

dictum ['diktəm] *nc* wise saying. *pl* **dicta** ['diktə].

didactic [dai'dæktik] *adj* intended to teach a lesson. *This is a didactic poem.*

die[1] [dai] *nc* **1.** see *Note* on **dice. 2.** tool for cutting or shaping things (e.g. used for making coins).
the die is cast the decision has been made to start something difficult or dangerous. (rather *o.f.*).

die[2] [dai] *vi* **1.** stop living. *He became very ill and then he died.* **2.** become weak; stop. *pres part* **dying.**
'**diehard** person who keeps to old beliefs or an old way of life and refuses to change.
die away slowly become less strong. *The noise died away.*
die down become less strong. *The fighting has died down.*
die off die gradually. *The people in the village were dying off from disease.*
die out gradually come to an end and disappear. *Many of our traditions have died out.*

die of hunger/cholera etc be killed by hunger/cholera etc.
be dying for something/to do something feel a strong wish to have/do something. *I'm dying to read John's new book.* (*informal*).

diesel ['di:zl] *nc* in **diesel engine** i.e. type of engine which burns diesel oil, often used for pulling trains. The train, or the engine, is often called **a diesel.**

diet[1] ['daiət] *nc* **1.** food and drink which a person or animal usually has. **2.** special food and drink which a person has for a special reason (often in order to lose weight): *be on a diet.* Also *vi* have special food and drink for medical reasons. *She is dieting because she wants to lose weight.*
dietician [daiə'tiʃən] *nc* person who plans diets for people.

diet[2] ['daiət] *nc* meeting (esp. meeting of parliament in certain countries).

differ ['difə*] *vi* **1.** be unlike. *The climate in the north differs from the climate in the south.* **2.** have a disagreement; quarrel. *John and his brother differ on the best way to cook fish* i.e. each has his own opinion.
difference *nc/u* **1.** condition of being unlike. *It is easy to see the difference between the two brothers* i.e. they do not have the same appearance. **2.** quarrel or disagreement. *John had a slight difference with his brother.* **3.** amount by which one quantity is greater than another: *the difference between 90 and 60 is 30.*
different *adj* **1.** not alike. *Winter in Britain is quite different from summer.* **2.** separate. *I have lived in four different houses in this city.* (*opp* **similar** or **the same**). **differently** *adv.*
Note: the expressions *different from* and *different to* are both widely used; however *different to* is said by some people to be incorrect.
differential [difə'renʃəl] *nc* **1.** (mathematics) very small difference between two values in a scale. **2.** set of gearwheels (usu. inside the back axle of a motorcar, enabling one wheel to turn faster than the other when going round a corner). Also *adj.*
differentiate [difə'renʃieit] *vt/i* make or see a difference between two or more things. *It is difficult to differentiate between the two brothers* i.e. they look the same. **differentiation** [difərenʃi'eiʃən] *nc/u.*

difficult ['difikəlt] *adj* **1.** causing one to work hard. *Many people did not finish the work because it was so difficult. That book is very difficult* i.e. not many people can understand it. *It was very difficult to repair my car.* **2.** (with reference to a person) unfriendly and quick to quarrel with others. **difficulty** *nc.*

diffident ['difidnt] *adj* not sure that one can do what one wants; lacking in confidence (esp. when meeting other people). *He is so diffident that he is afraid to meet other people.* (*opp* **confident**). **diffidently** *adv.* **diffidence** *nu.*

diffraction [di'frækʃən] *nu* process in which light rays are split up.
diffract [di'frækt] *vt* break up light rays in this way.

diffuse [di'fju:s] *adj* **1.** spread out over a wide area; not collected at one point. **2.** using too many words. Also [di'fju:z] *vt/i* spread out over a wide area. **diffusion** [di'fju:ʒən] *nu.*

dig[1] [dig] *vt/i* **1.** turn over earth with a spade, claws etc; make a hole in the ground. *The workmen dug a hole. The dog began to dig.* **2.** get by digging. *The farmer was digging potatoes.* *pres part* **digging.** *past* **dug** [dʌg].
dig (oneself) in make defensive positions for oneself. *The enemy troops are digging in.*
dig someone/something out/up **1.** remove by digging. **2.** find. (*informal* in sense **2.**).
dig someone in the ribs give someone a sharp blow in the ribs with one's finger.

dig[2] [dig] *nc* **1.** sharp blow with something pointed (esp. a finger). **2.** search in the ground by archaeologists. **3.** remark which is intended to hurt or attack somebody. (*informal* in sense **3.**).
digs *npl* room or rooms in which a person lives and which are in a house belonging to somebody else: *live in digs.* (*informal* – **lodgings** is the more *formal* word).

digest[1] [di'dʒest] *vt/i* **1.** (with reference to food) change in the stomach so that the body can make use of the substances in the food. *He is digesting his dinner. His food is still digesting.* **2.** understand and think about information. *He is still digesting the sad news.*
digestive *adj* with reference to the process of digesting.
digestible *adj* easily digested. (*opp* **indigestible**).
digestion *nu* **1.** ability to digest. *He has a good digestion.* **2.** process of digesting. see **indigestion.**

digest[2] ['daidʒest] *nc* summary or shortened form of a longer piece of speech or writing.

digit ['didʒit] *nc* **1.** any of the numbers from 0 to 9. **2.** a finger or a toe. **digital** *adj.*
digital computer type of electronic computer which uses numbers.

dignity ['digniti] **1.** *nu* feeling of calm or quiet importance and seriousness. *That man has a lot of dignity* i.e. he feels important and serious. *He has no dignity; he is always behaving foolishly.* **2.** *nc* important title/rank/position.
dignitary ['dignitəri] *nc* person holding an important title/rank/position (often in a church).
dignify ['dignifai] *vt* give dignity to. **dignified** *adj.* (*opp* **undignified**).

digress [dai'gres] *vi* turn aside from the subject which one is speaking or writing about, and deal with something else. **digression** *nc/u.*

dike, dyke [daik] *nc* **1.** wall built to keep the sea or a river off the land. **2.** ditch to carry away water.

dilapidation [dilæpi'deiʃən] *nu* condition of being broken and old.
dilapidated [di'læpideitid] *adj*: *a dilapidated fence.*

dilate [dai'leit] *vt/i* (esp. with reference to parts of the body) become or make wider. *His eyes dilated. He dilated his nostrils.* **dilation** *nu.*

dilatory ['dilətəri] *adj* very slow; causing delay. **dilatorily** *adv.* **dilatoriness** *nu.*

dilemma [dai'lemə] *nc* position in which one has to choose between two unpleasant things. *The doctor was in a dilemma, should he tell his patient that he would probably not recover or should he tell a lie.*
on the horns of a dilemma having to choose in this way.

dilettante [dili'tænti] *nc* person who studies painting, music, literature etc in a way which is not very serious. *pl* **dilettantes** or

dilettanti [dili'tænti:].
diligence ['dilidʒəns] *nu* careful hard work. **diligent** *adj* showing diligence: *a diligent person; diligent work.* **diligently** *adv.*
dillydally ['dili'dæli] *vi* waste time (usu. by not coming to a decision) (*informal*).
dilute [dai'lju:t] *vt* make a liquid weaker by adding another liquid (usu. water). Also *adj* made weak in this way. **dilution** *nc/u.*
dim [dim] *adj* **1.** not bright. *The lights are dim.* **2.** (with reference to the eyes) unable to see well. **3.** not intelligent. (*informal*). Also *vt/i* become or make dim. *past* **dimmed. dimly** *adv.* **dimness** *nu.*
take a dim view of something disapprove of something; say that one thinks that something is not good. (*informal*).
dime [daim] *nc* (*US*) coin worth 10 cents. (*informal*).
dimension [dai'menʃən] *nc* **1.** measurement of height/width/thickness. **2.** height, width, thickness.
diminish [di'miniʃ] *vt/i* become or make smaller. **diminution** [dimi'nju:ʃən] *nu.*
diminutive [di'minjutiv] *adj* very small. Also *nc* form of a word indicating something small (e.g. *piglet* meaning a baby pig).
dimple ['dimpl] *nc* small hollow place on the body or face (often in the cheek, appearing when one smiles). Also *vi* form a dimple. *Her face dimpled when she smiled.*
din [din] *nu* loud noise which goes on for some time. Also *vi* make a din. *past* **dinned.**
din something into someone make somebody learn something by repeating it to him many times. (*informal*).
dine [dain] **1.** *vi* eat dinner. **2.** *vt* give dinner to a guest.
diner *nc* **1.** person dining. **2.** (mainly *US*) part of a train in which meals are served.
'dining car part of a train in which meals are served.
'dining room room specially used for meals.
dine out eat dinner in a restaurant or in the home of another person.
ding-dong ['diŋ'dɔŋ] *nu* noise of two bells striking.
a ding-dong battle/struggle etc battle/struggle etc in which first one side seems to be winning, then the other. (*informal*).
dinghy ['diŋgi] *nc* small type of boat for rowing or sailing.
dingo ['diŋgou] *nc* wild dog found in Australia. *pl* **dingoes.**
dingy ['dindʒi] *adj* dark and dirty: *a dingy room.* **dinginess** *nu.*
dinner ['dinə*] *nc* **1.** meal eaten at midday. **2.** meal eaten in the evening. **3.** meal (usu. in the evening) held in honour of some important person or to celebrate some event.
'dinner service set of plates and dishes used for dinner.
dinosaur ['dainəsɔ:*] *nc* name given to several types of very large lizards which lived on earth thousands of years ago.
dint [dint] *nu* in **by dint of** i.e. through the use of. *He won the competition by dint of careful preparation.*
diocese ['daiəsis] *nc* district under the control of a bishop. **diocesan** [dai'ɔsisn] *adj.*
dip[1] [dip] *vt/i* go, cause to go, down. *The road dips as it approaches the river. He dipped his finger in the water. past* **dipped.**
dip into something **1.** put one's hand, spoon or other implement into a place and take something out. *He kept dipping into the box of chocolates.* **2.** study for a short time. *I have been dipping into ancient history. I have dipped into that book* i.e. I have read parts of it.
dip a flag lower a flag and then raise it, as a salute.
dip sheep put sheep into a liquid substance in order to clean and disinfect them.
dip (one's hand) into one's pocket/purse pay a lot of money. (*informal*).
dip[2] [dip] **1.** *nc* short swim. **2.** *nc* movement downward. **3.** *nu* substance which sheep are dipped in to clean and disinfect them. (Also **sheep-dip**). **4.** *nc* place which is lower than the surrounding area.
diphtheria [dip'θiəriə] *nu* disease of the throat (found esp. in children).
diphthong ['difθɔŋ] *nc* **1.** sound made by two vowels running together as [ai] in *ice.* **2.** two vowel letters representing one sound as [ea] in *meat.*
diploma [di'ploumə] *nc* official piece of paper showing that a person has completed a certain course of study.
diplomat ['dipləmæt] *nc* **1.** person whose work is to speak for his country in its relations with foreign countries. **2.** person who is clever at getting people to come to agreements with each other.
diplomatist [di'ploumətist] *nc* diplomat. **diplomatic** [diplə'mætik] *adj.* (*opp* **undiplomatic**). **diplomacy** [di'plouməsi] *nu.*
dipsomaniac [dipsou'meiniæk] *nc* person who has a strong and unreasonable wish for alcoholic drink.
dipsomania [dipsou'meiniə] *nu* condition or illness of a dipsomaniac.
dire [daiə*] *adj* causing great fear: *be in dire peril* i.e. in great danger. **direful** *adj.*
direct[1] [dai'rekt] *adj* **1.** straight; not turning aside or stopping. *I want to travel by the most direct route* i.e. the way which goes straight to the place I am travelling to. *He got a direct flight to Tangier* i.e. his plane did not stop anywhere before Tangier. *The bomb made a direct hit on the post office* i.e. the bomb fell straight down on to the post office. *He gave me a direct answer to my question* i.e. he said exactly what I wanted to know, without trying to hide anything. (*opp* **indirect**). **directness** *nu.*
directly *adv* **1.** at once; as soon as. *He came directly I called. Directly you feel any pains, you must go to the doctor.* **2.** straight. *He drove home directly.*
Note: in the following phrases, the stress is usually on the first syllable of *direct.*
'direct 'action strikes and demonstrations for political purposes (often action which is against the law).
'direct 'current electric current which flows in one direction only (often abbreviated to DC) (*opp* **alternating current**).
'direct method method of teaching foreign languages, without any use of the pupil's own language.
'direct 'object (grammar) noun or noun phrase which completes the sense of a transitive verb in a statement (e.g. in *I saw John,* 'John' is the direct object).
'direct 'speech method of reporting what a person has said, using the actual words spoken by that person. (*opp* **indirect speech** or **reported speech**).
direct[2] [dai'rekt] *vt/i* **1.** give orders; tell people what to do. *He directed the men to move the furniture.* **2.** be in charge of the way something is done. *I shall direct the*

work. Richard Smith directed that film. 3. tell a person the way to somewhere. *Can you direct me to the post office?* 4. turn towards. *At a meeting, you must direct your remarks to the chairman* i.e. you must speak to the chairman and not to other people. *He directed his attention to me* i.e. he turned to look at me or to deal with me. *We directed our course towards Tangier* i.e. we turned and travelled towards Tangier. 5. send. *He directed a kick at the goal. He directed his letter to the manager* i.e. he put the manager's name and address on the envelope.

direction 1. *nc* point to which one is travelling, or point where something is. *London is in that direction* i.e. where I am pointing, where you are walking etc. 2. *nu* control; guidance: *work under somebody's direction* i.e. do what he tells one to do. 3. *nc* (often *pl*) orders or instructions. *I followed your directions* i.e. I did what you told me.

directive *nc* official order.

director *nc* 1. one of the people in charge of a business firm. 2. person in charge of some organization (esp. a person in charge of the production of a play or film).

directorship *nc* (esp. with reference to **director** in sense 1.) position of a director.

directory *nc* book giving a list of people's names etc for various purposes.

dirge [dəːdʒ] *nc* slow song sung at a funeral.

dirt [dəːt] *nu* 1. mud, dust etc on the ground. *He was sitting in the dirt.* 2. mud, dust or other unclean substance. *There is dirt on your face. She washed the dirt out of the clothes.* 3. words or thoughts dealing with sex in an unpleasant or joking way.

dirty *adj* 1. not clean. *His hands were dirty after he had been working in the garden.* 2. impure in word or thought. 3. (with reference to atom bombs etc) causing a lot of radioactive fallout. Also *vt* make dirty. **dirtily** *adv*. **dirtiness** *nu*.

'dirt-'cheap *adj/adv* for very little money. *I bought this car dirt-cheap.* (*informal*).

dirty weather (esp. with reference to the weather when one is at sea) wind, rain, storm etc. (*informal*).

'dirty 'work 1. work which causes one to become dirty. 2. anything dishonest and secret. (*informal* in sense 2.).

give somebody a dirty look look at somebody and show anger or hatred in one's face. (*informal*).

dis- [dis] *prefix* the opposite of something (e.g. **disagree, dislike, displease, dissatisfy**).

disable [dis'eibl] *vt* 1. make somebody unable to use his arms or legs properly. *He was disabled in the accident.* 2. make unfit in some way. **disability** [disə'biliti] *nc/u*.

disabuse [disə'bjuːz] *vt* tell somebody the truth when he has been believing something which is untrue. *I disabused him of his belief that the world was flat* i.e. I convinced him that the world was round.

disadvantage [disəd'vaːntidʒ] *nc/u* anything which makes one slower, weaker, poorer etc than other people. *To have only one leg is a disadvantage.* (*opp* **advantage**). **disadvantageous** [disædvaːn'teidʒəs] *adj*.

disaffected [disə'fektid] *adj* unwilling to serve one's leaders or rulers. *The army was disaffected and tried to drive out the government.* **disaffection** [disə'fekʃən] *nu*.

disagree [disə'griː] *vi* 1. fail to agree. *After a long discussion, the two sides still disagreed.* 2. (with reference to food) cause one to be ill or to feel unwell. *Some kinds of meat disagree with me.* **disagreement** *nu*.

disagreeable *adj* bad-tempered; quick to quarrel with people; unpleasant: *a disagreeable task.* **disagreeably** *adv*.

disallow [disə'lau] *vt* make an official decision not to allow or accept something. *The referee disallowed the goal.*

disappear [disə'piə*] *vi* go and be no longer seen. *The snow on the roads disappeared when the sun shone.* **disappearance** *nu*.

disappoint [disə'pɔint] *vt* fail to do what one had promised, or what other people had hoped one would do. *I promised to buy my son a new bicycle but I had to disappoint him.* **disappointment** *nc/u*.

disappointed *adj* unhappy because one has not got what one hoped for. **disappointedly** *adv*.

disappointing *adj* causing one to feel disappointed. *His examination results are disappointing* i.e. not as good as we hoped. **disappointingly** *adv*.

disapprove [disə'pruːv] *vi* have an unfavourable opinion of. *I disapprove of children smoking cigarettes* i.e. I think they should not do this. **disapproving** *adj*. **disapprovingly** *adv*. **disapproval** *nu*.

disarm [dis'aːm] 1. *vi* (with reference to a country) reduce the number of one's weapons, soldiers, aeroplanes etc. 2. *vt* take weapons away from. *The policeman disarmed the thief.* 3. *vt* be friendly and so make somebody stop being angry. *We were angry but he disarmed us by his smile.*

disarming *adj* causing one to stop being angry in this way. **disarmingly** *adv*.

disarmament [dis'aːməmənt] *nu* process of reducing the number of soldiers, weapons etc.

disarrange [disə'reindʒ] *vt* put in a confused or disordered state. **disarrangement** *nu*.

disarray [disə'rei] *nu* condition in which things are not arranged or organized properly. *Our army was in disarray after the battle.*

disaster [di'zaːstə*] *nc/u* very great and terrible accident or misfortune. *Three hundred people were killed in the disaster.* **disastrous** [di'zaːstrəs] *adj*. **disastrously** *adv*.

disavow [disə'vau] *vt* say that one has no connection with something, or that one knows nothing of something. *He disavowed all knowledge of the accident.*

disband [dis'bænd] *vt/i* break up an organized group of people. *The six criminals agreed to disband* i.e. leave each other and work separately. *The government disbanded all political parties.*

disbelieve [disbi'liːv] *vt* not believe. **disbelief** [disbi'liːf] *nu*.

disburden [dis'bəːdn] *vt* take away a heavy load.

disburden oneself of something tell somebody about a matter which one has been thinking about (esp. about something wrong which one has done).

disburse [dis'bəːs] *vt/i* pay out money.

disc [disk] *nc* see **disk**.

discard [dis'kaːd] *vt* put aside or give away as useless or unwanted. *He discarded all his old clothes.*

discern [di'səːn] *vt* notice something (esp. something which is not easy to see, feel, smell etc).

discerning *adj* able to understand well, and

to decide what is good. **discernment** *nu.*

discharge [dis'tʃɑːdʒ] *vt* send out or send away. *He discharged the gun* i.e. he fired it. *He discharged his servant* i.e. he would not let his servant work for him any more. *Some towns discharge rubbish into the sea. The judge found him not guilty and discharged him* i.e. told him that he could go away. Also *nc.*

discharge a debt pay money which one owes.

discharge a duty do what one must do.

disciple [di'saipl] *nc* anyone who follows a religious leader (esp. the original twelve followers of Jesus).

discipleship *nu* state of being a disciple.

discipline ['disiplin] **1.** *nu* willingness to obey orders. *Soldiers have to learn discipline.* **2.** *nu* ability to make people obey orders. *The officer had no discipline over his men* i.e. he could not make them do what he ordered. **3.** *nc* any subject studied at a university etc. Also *vt* **1.** make somebody willing to obey orders. *He disciplined the new soldiers.* **2.** punish.

disciplinarian [disipli'nɛəriən] *nc* person who makes others obey his orders. **disciplinary** ['disiplinəri] *adj.*

disclaim [dis'kleim] *vt* say that one has no connection with something. *He disclaimed any interest in the plan* i.e. he said that he was not interested.

disclaimer *nc* statement which disclaims; denial.

disclose [dis'klouz] *vt* **1.** tell something which had been a secret. *He disclosed that he had made arrangements to buy a new car.* **2.** show something hidden. **disclosure** *nc/u.*

discolour [dis'kʌlə*] (*US* **discolor**) *vt/i* spoil or damage the colour of. *Smoke and dirt had discoloured the walls.* **discoloration** [diskʌlə'reiʃən] *nu.*

discomfit [dis'kʌmfit] *vt* make a person feel a little annoyed and embarrassed (esp. by causing his plans to fail) (*formal*). *past* **discomfited. discomfiture** *nu.*

discomfort [dis'kʌmfət] *nu* lack of comfort; worry, distress.

discompose [diskəm'pouz] *vt* make unhappy or worried. **discomposure** *nu.*

disconcert [diskən'səːt] *vt* make a person feel puzzled and unhappy. *We were rather disconcerted when he rudely refused our invitation.* **disconcerting** *adj.* **disconcertingly** *adv.*

disconnect [diskə'nekt] *vt* (often with reference to some piece of machinery or some electric device) remove a connection.

disconnected *adj* (with reference to thought or speech) not well planned; with the parts having no connection with each other. **disconnectedly** *adv.*

disconsolate [dis'kɔnsəlit] *adj* lonely, sad and without hope. **disconsolately** *adv.*

discontent [diskən'tent] *nu* restless and rather angry feeling because one has not got what one wants. **discontented** *adj.* **discontentedly** *adv.*

discontinue [diskən'tinjuː] *vt/i* stop; come or bring to an end.

discord ['diskɔːd] *nc/u* **1.** angry quarrelling. **2.** sounds (esp. in music) which do not go well together; unpleasant sounds. **discordant** [dis'kɔːdnt] *adj.* **discordantly** *adv.*

discothèque ['diskoutek] *nc* club for young people at which records of popular music are played.

discount[1] ['diskaunt] *nu* amount of money which is taken from the price of goods for various reasons. *Some shops give a discount to students* i.e. they sell their goods more cheaply to students than to other people.

discount[2] [dis'kaunt] *vt* say or believe that part or all of a story is untrue.

discourage [dis'kʌridʒ] *vt* make somebody less willing to do something. *I put new locks on my doors to discourage thieves* i.e. make it more difficult for thieves to come in. *I discouraged him from borrowing the money.* **discouragement** *nc/u.* **discouraging** *adj.* **discouragingly** *adv.*

discourse ['diskɔːs] **1.** *nc* lecture or talk. **2.** *nu* conversation. Also [dis'kɔːs] *vi*: *He discoursed on Latin poetry.* (all rather *o.f.*).

discover [dis'kʌvə*] *vt* find something hidden or unknown. *Columbus discovered America.* **discovery** *nc/u.* **discoverer** *nc.*

discredit [dis'kredit] *vt* cause one to think that somebody/something is dishonest or untrue. *Recent events have discredited your story* i.e. recent events have made me think that you did not tell the truth. Also *nc/u.*

discreditable *adj* dishonest; untrue; bad or wrong in behaviour. **discreditably** *adv.*

discreet [dis'kriːt] *adj* careful in behaviour; not telling secrets to other people; not going beyond the limits of what is proper and sensible. (*opp* **indiscreet**). **discreetly** *adv.*

discretion [dis'kreʃən] *nu* **1.** quality of being discreet. **2.** ability to choose what to do. *Use your own discretion* i.e. do what you think is best. (*opp* **indiscretion**).

discrepancy [dis'krepənsi] *nc* **1.** (e.g. with reference to records of money) difference between what there should be and what there actually is. **2.** difference between several versions of the same story. *There is a discrepancy between what you say and what John says.*

discriminate [dis'krimineit] **1.** *vi* treat some people better than other people. *A teacher must not discriminate between pupils* i.e. he should not be more friendly to some pupils than to others. **2.** *vt* choose the best. *A critic must be able to discriminate good literature from bad.* **discrimination** [diskrimi'neiʃən] *nu.*

discriminating *adj* able to choose what is best.

discriminate against somebody treat somebody worse than other people. *In some parts of the world people discriminate against foreigners.*

discriminate between something and something choose the better of two.

discursive [dis'kəːsiv] *adj* (usu. with reference to writing) dealing with several topics, or with one topic from several points of view, but not in a clear or logical manner.

discus ['diskəs] *nc* heavy round flat piece of metal or stone, thrown in athletic contests.

discuss [dis'kʌs] *vt* talk about a topic from several points of view. **discussion** [dis'kʌʃən] *nc/u.*

disdain [dis'dein] *vt* think of something as very low and dishonourable. *He disdained to steal.* Also *nu* feeling in which one disdains something. **disdainful** *adj.* **disdainfully** *adv.*

disease [di'ziːz] *nc/u* illness caused by germs or by incorrect growth of part of the body (e.g. smallpox or cancer are diseases; a broken leg or a bullet-wound are not diseases). **diseased** *adj.*

disembark [disim'bɑːk] *vt/i* leave, cause to leave, a ship or aeroplane.
disembodied [disim'bɔdid] *adj* existing without a body: *a disembodied spirit.*
disembowel [disim'bauəl] *vt* cut out the bowels of. *past* **disembowelled.**
disenchant [disin'tʃɑːnt] *vt* **1.** show somebody that something is not as good as he had thought. *The people were disenchanted with the government.* **2.** remove magic from. **disenchantment** *nc/u.*
disentangle [disin'tæŋgl] *vt* **1.** remove knots and tangles from string, rope etc. **2.** find out the meaning or truth of something which is difficult to understand.
disfavour [dis'feivə*] (*US* **disfavor**) *nu* lack of approval: *look on something with disfavour.*
disfigure [dis'figə*] *vt* spoil or damage the appearance of. *He disfigured the picture by throwing ink at it.* **disfigurement** *nc/u.*
disgorge [dis'gɔːdʒ] *vt/i* **1.** throw out from the mouth something which has been swallowed. **2.** give back what has been stolen or removed without permission.
disgrace [dis'greis] *nu* **1.** loss of honour or good name. *He suffered the disgrace of being beaten by a boy much smaller than he was.* **2.** somebody/something which brings disgrace. *That boy is a disgrace to his family* i.e. he behaves very badly, and so makes his whole family seem bad. Also *vt* bring disgrace to. **disgraceful** *adj.* **disgracefully** *adv.*
in disgrace regarded with anger because of something wrong which one has done. *That boy is in disgrace with the headmaster* i.e. the headmaster is angry with him.
disgruntled [dis'grʌntld] *adj* angry and dissatisfied because one has not got what one wants.
disguise [dis'gaiz] *nc/u* anything changing one's appearance so that one is not recognized by other people. *He grew a moustache and wore dark glasses as a disguise because the police were looking for him. He went to the house in disguise.* Also *vt* **1.** change appearance. **2.** conceal (feelings etc).
disgust [dis'gʌst] *nu* feeling that something is very unpleasant. *The food tasted so unpleasant that I threw it away in disgust.* Also *vt* cause somebody to feel disgust. *The food disgusted me.*
disgusting *adj* causing disgust. **disgustingly** *adv.*
dish [diʃ] *nc* **1.** container in which food is brought to the table; the food itself. **2.** anything shaped like this.
dishes *npl* (often in **wash the dishes**) plates, cups, knives and forks etc used for a meal.
dishearten [dis'hɑːtn] *vt* discourage; make less sure of success. **disheartening** *adj.*
dishevelled [di'ʃevəld] (*US* **disheveled**) *adj* (with reference to personal appearance) untidy; in disorder.
dishonest [dis'ɔnist] *adj* not honest. **dishonestly** *adv.* **dishonesty** *nu.*
dishonour [dis'ɔnə*] (*US* **dishonor**) *vt* cause shame or loss of good name to. *He dishonoured his team by cheating during the competition* i.e. by cheating he made the rest of his team seem bad. Also *nu* loss of good name; something causing loss of good name. **dishonourable** *adj.* **dishonourably** *adv.*
dishonour a cheque refuse to pay the money. *The bank dishonoured his cheque because he had no money in the bank.*

disillusion [disi'luːʒən] *vt* tell somebody the truth after he has been believing something untrue (usu. a truth which is less pleasant than the thing he believed). *He thought that he had won the prize, but I disillusioned him* i.e. told him that he had not won. Also *nu.* **disillusionment** *nu.*
disincline [disiŋ'klain] *vt* in **be disinclined to do something** i.e. be unwilling to do something. **disinclination** [disiŋkli'neiʃən] *nu.*
disinfect [disin'fekt] *vt* remove germs from, so as to prevent disease.
disinfectant *nc/u* substance which disinfects. Also *adj.*
disinfection *nu* process of disinfecting.
disingenuous [disin'dʒenjuəs] *adj* not honest; not telling the truth.
disinherit [disin'herit] *vt* refuse to pass on money or property after one's death to a person who has expected to receive the money or property. *He disinherited his son.* **disinheritance** *nu.*
disintegrate [dis'intigreit] *vt/i* break, cause to break, into small pieces. *The bomb disintegrated when it exploded.* **disintegration** [disinti'greiʃən] *nu.*
disinter ['disin'təː*] *vt* **1.** dig up from a grave. **2.** take out of any hidden place. *past* **disinterred. disinterment** *nu.*
disinterested [dis'intərestid] *adj* **1.** impartial; willing to listen to all sides of an argument; willing to judge what is right without any personal feelings. **2.** not interested; not wishing to know about something.
Note: many people consider that this word should not be used in sense **2.** for which there is another word *uninterested.*
disjointed [dis'dʒɔintid] *adj* (with reference to speech or writing) not well planned; with the parts not well-connected to each other. **disjointedly** *adv.*
disk, disc [disk] *nc* **1.** thin round flat object. **2.** gramophone record.
'**disk jockey** person who introduces gramophone records on the radio.
dislike [dis'laik] *vt* not like. *I dislike beer.* Also *nc/u*: *feel dislike for something.*
dislocate ['disləkeit] *vt* **1.** put a bone in the body out of its proper position (e.g. in an accident). *He dislocated his arm in a fall.* **2.** disturb; disarrange; put out of order. **dislocation** [dislə'keiʃən] *nc/u.*
dislodge [dis'lɔdʒ] *vt* push something out of its place. *He dislodged a stone from the mountainside. The soldiers dislodged the enemy from the town.*
disloyal [dis'lɔiəl] *adj* not loyal. **disloyalty** *nu.*
dismal ['dizml] *adj* sad; unhappy; without brightness: *a dismal room; a dismal person.* **dismally** *adv.* **dismalness** *nu.*
dismantle [dis'mæntl] *vt/i* separate into the parts which make up a whole. *He dismantled his old car. These chairs dismantle for storage* i.e. they can be dismantled.
dismay [dis'mei] *nu* feeling of alarm and loss of hope. Also *vt* fill with dismay.
dismiss [dis'mis] *vt* send away. *After talking to the pupils, the headmaster dismissed them to their classrooms. He has been dismissed from his job with the railway. I have dismissed the matter from my mind.* **dismissal** *nc/u.*
dismount [dis'maunt] *vt* get off a horse etc.
disobey [disə'bei] *vt/i* refuse to obey: *disobey the headmaster; disobey an order.* **disobedient** [disə'biːdiənt] *adj.* **disobediently** *adv.* **disobedience** [disə'biːdiəns] *nu.*

disorder [dis'ɔːdə*] **1.** *nu* lack of order; untidiness. *His room was in disorder* i.e. the things in his room were not in their proper places. **2.** *nc/u* rioting or violence in public (usu. for political purposes). **3.** *nc* slight illness.
disorderly *adj* **1.** untidy. **2.** violent in public.

disorganize [dis'ɔːgənaiz] *vt* cause a failure of arrangements or plans. *The accident disorganized the traffic.* **disorganization** [disɔːgənai'zeiʃən] *nu*.

disown [dis'oun] *vt* say that something/someone does not belong to one, or that one has no connection with something/someone.

disparage [dis'pæridʒ] *vt* say that something is of little or no value.
disparaging *adj*: *He was very disparaging about my success.* **disparagingly** *adv*. **disparagement** *nu*.

disparity [dis'pæriti] *nc/u* lack of equality, difference. *There is a great disparity between the salaries of Mr Brown and Mr Smith.*
disparate ['dispərət] *adj*.

dispassionate [dis'pæʃənət] *adj* calm and impartial; not considering one's personal feelings and so able to decide what is right.
dispassionately *adv*.

dispatch, despatch [dis'pætʃ] *vt* **1.** send away, send off. *He dispatched a telegram.* **2.** finish (off) quickly; kill. *He dispatched all the remaining business.* Also **1.** *nu* act of sending for a special purpose. **2.** *nc* special message. **3.** *nu* quickness in doing something.
dis'patch rider soldier etc whose job is to carry messages (usu. on a motorbike).

dispel [dis'pel] *vt* (esp. with reference to driving away doubts, fears, worries etc) drive away. *past* **dispelled**.

dispense [dis'pens] *vt/i* prepare and sell or give out medicine. **dispenser** *nc*.
dispensary [dis'pensəri] *nc* place where a dispenser works.
dispensation [dispən'seiʃən] **1.** *nc* special permission given by the Roman Catholic Church for somebody to do something which is normally forbidden. **2.** *nu* act of giving things. **3.** *nc* anything specially given (esp. something given by God).
dispense with something continue without something. *I can dispense with these old clothes* i.e. I do not want them any more.
dispense justice act as a judge.

disperse [dis'pəːs] *vt/i* spread and go away; cause to do this. *The crowd of people slowly dispersed. The police dispersed the crowd.*
dispersal *nu*.

dispirited [dis'piritid] *adj* unhappy and without hope.

displace [dis'pleis] *vt* **1.** put out of the right place. **2.** take the place of somebody/something. *John has displaced Tom* i.e. John is now in the position where Tom used to be.
displacement *nu* **1.** act of displacing. **2.** amount of water displaced by a ship (a way of referring to the weight of a ship).

display [dis'plei] *vt* show; allow people to see. Also *nc/u* something displayed; act of displaying.

displease [dis'pliːz] *vt* opp of **please.**
displeasure [dis'pleʒə*] *nu* anger or disapproval.

disport [dis'pɔːt] *vt* in **disport oneself** i.e. enjoy oneself by doing something active (*o.f.*).

dispose [dis'pouz] *vt* put into an arrangement or position. *The officers disposed their men for the battle* i.e. they told the men where to go.
disposal *nu* **1.** act of putting into position. **2.** act of throwing away or giving away as useless or unwanted.
disposition [dispə'ziʃən] *nc/u* **1.** arrangement; way in which things are placed in position. **2.** character; feelings and way of behaving. *He has a very friendly disposition* i.e. he is usually friendly.
dispose of something throw away or give away, as useless or unwanted; finish or put an end to. *He disposed of his old car. He disposed of all the difficulties.*
be/feel disposed to do something be ready or willing to do something.
ill-/well-disposed (towards someone) (un)-friendly and (un)willing to be helpful.
at one's disposal to be used as one wishes. *He placed his house at my disposal* i.e. he allowed me to use his house as I wished.

dispossess [dispə'zes] *vt* take property away from somebody. *He dispossessed his brother of the land.* **dispossession** *nu*.

disproportionate ['disprə'pɔːʃənət] *adj* not equal in size or amount; too great or too little. **disproportionately** *adv*.

disprove [dis'pruːv] *vt* show that something is not true.

dispute [dis'pjuːt] *vt/i* **1.** argue or quarrel. **2.** say that one thinks that something is untrue or dishonest. *I disputed his story.* **3.** fight to win or defend. *The two teams were disputing for the prize.* Also *nc* argument or quarrel.
disputable *adj* likely to be disputed. *The referee's decision was disputable.* (*opp* **indisputable**).

disqualify [dis'kwɔlifai] *vt* take away permission to do something. *His age disqualifies him from entering the competition* i.e. he is too old or too young. **disqualification** [diskwɔlifi'keiʃən] *nc/u*.

disquiet [dis'kwaiət] *vt* make worried or anxious; make unhappy because of a fear of what will happen.
disquieting *adj* causing one to feel worried in this way.

disregard ['disri'gɑːd] *vt* take no notice of. *He disregarded my advice* i.e. he did not do what I advised. Also *nu* act of disregarding.

disrepair ['disri'pɛə*] *nu* condition of being in need of repair.

disreputable [dis'repjutəbl] *adj* **1.** well-known for bad behaviour; having the appearance of one who will behave badly. **2.** (with reference to things) not decent or dignified.
disrepute ['disri'pjuːt] *nu* condition of being known to be bad.

disrespect ['disri'spekt] *nu* lack of respect.
disrespectful *adj*. **disrespectfully** *adv*.

disrobe [dis'roub] *vt/i* take off clothes (esp. official robes).

disrupt [dis'rʌpt] *vt* break up; prevent from continuing properly. *John disrupted our arrangements.* **disruption** *nc/u*. **disruptive** *adj*.

dissatisfy [dis'sætisfai] *vt* fail to satisfy.
dissatisfied *adj*. **dissatisfaction** [disætis'fækʃən] *nu*.

dissect [di'sekt] *vt* **1.** cut up a plant, animal or human body in order to study it. **2.** divide into parts in order to understand.
dissection *nc/u*.

dissemble [di'sembl] *vt/i* give a wrong idea of what one really thinks or feels. **dis-**

sembling *nu*.

disseminate [di'semineit] *vt* (esp. with reference to spreading ideas or beliefs) spread on all sides. **dissemination** [disemi'neiʃən] *nu*.

dissent [di'sent] *vi* refuse to believe what other people believe.

dissension *nc/u* argument; quarrel; refusal to believe what others believe.

dissentient [di'senʃənt] *adj*: *a dissentient opinion*.

dissertation [disə'teiʃən] *nc* long piece of writing, making a study of some subject.

disservice [dis'səːvis] *nc* action which causes trouble or difficulty to one. *He did me a disservice*.

dissident ['disidnt] *adj* not agreeing with others; refusing to accept the beliefs or leadership of others. Also *nc* person who is dissident. **dissidence** *nu*.

dissimulate [di'simjuːleit] *vt/i* hide one's real feelings. **dissimulation** [disimjuː'leiʃən] *nu*.

dissipate ['disipeit] *vt/i* **1.** spend money etc in a useless way. **2.** drive away. *He dissipated my fears*. **dissipation** [disi'peiʃən] *nu*.

dissipated *adj* unhealthy because of too much pleasure (e.g. drinking and gambling).

dissociate [di'sousieit] *vt* separate into parts.

dissociate oneself from someone/something stop being friendly with; say that one has no connection with or that one is not joining in. *He dissociated himself from John and Tom. He dissociated himself from the committee's request*.

dissolute ['disəluːt] *adj* living a wicked life of pleasure. **dissolutely** *adv*. **dissoluteness,**

dissolution *nu* see **dissolve**.

dissolve [di'zɔlv] *vt/i* **1.** change from solid into liquid form through the action of liquid. *Sugar dissolves in water. He dissolved the sugar in his tea. The water dissolved the sugar*. **2.** bring an arrangement to an end. *They dissolved their partnership* i.e. they agreed not to work together any longer. *The Queen dissolved Parliament* i.e. she sent the Members of Parliament away in order to hold an election. *Parliament dissolved*. **3.** gradually disappear.

dissolution [disə'luːʃən] *nc/u* ending of an arrangement: *the dissolution of their partnership; the dissolution of Parliament*.

dissonance ['disənəns] *nc/u* lack of harmony in sound; sounds which do not go well together. **dissonant** *adj*.

dissuade [di'sweid] *vt* persuade somebody not to do something; make somebody agree not to do something by talking to him. *I dissuaded him from borrowing the money*.

dissuasion *nu*. **dissuasive** *adj*.

distaff ['distɑːf] *nc* stick used to spin wool or flax by hand (formerly used to indicate women's work or women).

the distaff side the female side of the family (*o.f.*).

distant ['distnt] *adj* **1.** far away; not near. *The stars are distant from the earth*. **2.** unfriendly and not showing one's feelings. *He greeted me in a very distant manner*.

distantly *adv*.

distance *nc/u* the space between two things, places or times. *The distance between the towns is only five miles*.

at/from a distance when one is not near. *The mountains do not seem very high from a distance, but when you get near you can see that they are high*.

in the distance a long way away. *We saw the village in the distance*.

keep someone at a distance be unfriendly to someone.

distaste [dis'teist] *nu* dislike for something. *He looked at me with distaste*.

distasteful *adj* unpleasant; causing one to feel distaste. **distastefully** *adv*.

distemper [dis'tempə*] *nu* **1.** type of paint (usu. used for walls). **2.** disease of dogs. Also *vt* paint with distemper (in sense **1.**).

distend [dis'tend] *vt/i* (usu. with reference to the stomach) grow, cause to grow, bigger by pressure from within. **distension** *nu*.

distil [dis'til] *vt/i* **1.** heat liquid until it becomes vapour; then collect pure liquid from the cooling vapour. **2.** make spirits (e.g. whisky) in this way. **3.** fall, allow to fall, in drops. *past* **distilled. distillation** [disti'leiʃən] *nu*.

distillery *nc* place where spirits (e.g. whisky) are made.

distiller *nc* person who makes spirits (e.g. whisky).

distinct [dis'tiŋkt] *adj* **1.** clearly seen, heard etc. *The photograph is not distinct* i.e. what is on it cannot be seen clearly. (*opp* **indistinct**). **2.** not the same. **distinctly** *adv*.

distinction **1.** *nc* difference. *What is the distinction between a newspaper and a magazine?* i.e. in what ways are they different? **2.** *nu* quality of being better than most. *He served with distinction in the army* i.e. he was a very good soldier. *This is a car of great distinction*. **3.** *nc* reward or title given for being better than most. *He gained a distinction in the examination*.

distinctive *adj* showing a difference. *This bird has several distinctive features* i.e. features which enable one to recognize the bird. **distinctively** *adv*.

distinguish [dis'tiŋgwiʃ] *vt* **1.** see, hear etc clearly. *It was difficult to distinguish anything in the dark*. **2.** see in what way two or more things differ. *How do you distinguish between a star and a planet?* i.e. how do you know when you are seeing a star and when a planet? **3.** be what enables one to recognize; be the difference between. *This bird is distinguished by its bright red legs. What distinguishes a star from a planet?*

distinguishable *adj* able to be distinguished. (*opp* **indistinguishable**).

distinguished *adj* famous for doing something very well. *He is a distinguished soldier*. (*opp* **undistinguished**).

distinguish oneself do something very well, so that other people are pleased. *He distinguished himself in the examination*.

distort [dis'tɔːt] *vt* **1.** change from the correct shape or appearance by force. *The heat of the sun had distorted the railway lines*. **2.** change from the truth. *He distorted my story* i.e. he changed my story when he told it to others. **distorted** *adj*. **distortion** *nc/u*.

distract [dis'trækt] *vt* **1.** cause somebody's attention to turn away from something. *The advertisements by the side of the road sometimes distract the attention of motorists* i.e. the motorists look at the advertisements instead of at the road. **2.** cause somebody to become mad.

distraction *nc/u* **1.** something which distracts. **2.** act of distracting; madness.

distraught [dis'trɔːt] *adj* unable to think clearly because of worry or trouble.

distress [dis'tres] *nu* great unhappiness caused by worry or trouble; a cause of this

unhappiness. *Her distress was very great when she read the letter.* Also *vt* cause distress to.
distressing *adj* causing distress. **distressingly** *adv.*
ship in distress ship which is sinking or is in some other danger.

distribute [dis'tribju:t] *vt* give out or share out. *Goods are taken from the factories by lorry and are distributed to the shops. The teacher distributed the books to the children.*
distribution [distri'bju:ʃən] *nu.* **distributive** *adj.* **distributor** *nc.*

district ['distrikt] *nc* part of a country, town or city (usu. a small part).
'district at'torney local government law officer in America.

distrust [dis'trʌst] *vt* think that somebody/something is not honest or true. *I distrust that man.* Also *nu*: *feel distrust for somebody.* **distrustful** *adj.* **distrustfully** *adv.*

disturb [dis'tə:b] *vt* interrupt arrangements; break up peace or quiet. *You disturbed my sleep* i.e. you woke me up. *May I disturb you for a moment?* i.e. may I stop you from continuing what you are doing? *He disturbed our plans* i.e. caused us to change our plans. **disturbing** *adj.* **disturbingly** *adv.*
disturbance *nc/u* act of disturbing (esp. in a violent way): *political disturbances* i.e. riots and demonstrations.

disuse [dis'ju:s] *nu* state of being no longer used (often in **fall into disuse**).

ditch [ditʃ] *nc* long narrow place dug in the earth to allow water to flow away.
'last-'ditch *adj* with reference to somebody who goes on fighting even when the enemy seem to have won: *a last-ditch stand/attempt.*
dull as ditchwater very uninteresting or boring. (*informal*).

dither ['diðə*] *vi* become excited and confused because one is not sure what to do. Also *nu* state of dithering. **dithery** *adj.* (all *informal*).

ditto ['ditou] *nc* the mark " meaning 'the same', used in making lists in order to avoid repeating words already written. *pl* **dittos.**

ditty ['diti] *nc* simple song (*o.f.*).

divan [di'væn] *nc* **1.** type of long, low seat. **2.** low bed without back or sides.

dive[1] [daiv] *vi* **1.** jump head first into water (usu. from a height). **2.** work under water, wearing special clothes. **3.** (with reference to an aeroplane) move quickly forwards and downwards. **4.** move quickly into something. (*informal* in sense **4.**). **diver** *nc.*

dive[2] [daiv] *nc* **1.** act of jumping head first into water (usu. from a height). **2.** (with reference to an aeroplane) rapid movement forwards and downwards. **3.** cheap or dirty restaurant or bar where alcoholic drink is sold. (*informal* in sense **3.**).

diverge [dai'və:dʒ] *vi* go in different directions; be different from the normal.
divergence *nc/u*: *There is a divergence between these figures and the last ones.*
divergency *nc/u.* **divergent** *adj.*

diverse [dai'və:s] *adj* different; not alike in any way. *John and his brother have diverse interests* i.e. they are not interested in the same things.
diversify *vt* make diverse.
diversification [dai'və:sifi'keiʃən] *nu* process of diversifying.
diversity *nu* difference; number of different things.

divert [dai'və:t] *vt* **1.** cause to go in another direction. *The police diverted the traffic. They diverted the river while they were building the dam.* **2.** amuse and entertain. *The new play diverted the audience.* **diversion** *nc/u.*

divest [dai'vest] *vt* **1.** take clothes off somebody. **2.** take anything away from somebody. *He divested me of my property.*

divide [di'vaid] *vt/i* **1.** separate. *Spain is divided from France by the Pyrenees. The road divides into two at the other side of the town. We divided into two teams. He divided the money among his family* i.e. he gave each of his family some money. **2.** quarrel; disagree; cause to quarrel or disagree. **3.** (with reference to Parliament) vote to decide some question. **4.** (mathematics) find out how many times one number is contained in another (e.g. divide 10 into 190 = 19).
dividend ['dividend] *nc* **1.** number to be divided (e.g. if we divide 10 into 190, 190 is the dividend). see **divisor. 2.** money paid out of profits by a business firm to people who have lent money to the firm.
dividers *npl* instrument for measuring distances (on paper) or for dividing angles.

dividers

divisible [di'vizibl] *adj* able to be divided. (*opp* **indivisible**).
division [di'viʒən] **1.** *nu* process of separating into parts. **2.** *nu* (mathematics) operation of dividing one number into another. **3.** *nc* separate part. **4.** *nc* something which divides. **5.** *nc* quarrel or disagreement. **6.** *nc* vote in parliament. **7.** *nc* part of an army, consisting of about 15,000 men.
divisor [di'vaizə*] *nc* number which is divided into another number (e.g. if we divide 10 into 190, 10 is the divisor). see **dividend.**

divine[1] [di'vain] *adj* **1.** of or like God. **2.** very good. (*informal* in sense **2.**). Also *nc* priest who studies theology. **divinely** *adv.*
divinity [di'viniti] **1.** *nu* quality of being divine. **2.** *nu* study of theology. **3.** *nc* god or goddess.

divine[2] [di'vain] *vt/i* **1.** find out something hidden or secret by guessing. **2.** find water or other substances beneath the earth by using a special stick.
diviner *nc* person who finds water etc in this way. **divination** [divi'neiʃən] *nu.*

division [di'viʒən] *nc/u* see **divide.**

divorce [di'vɔ:s] *nc/u* **1.** ending of a marriage by law. **2.** complete separation between two things. Also *vt* **1.** end a marriage. *She divorced her husband.* **2.** separate completely. *He said one must divorce religion and politics.*
divorcee [divɔ:'si:] *nc* person who has been divorced.

divulge [dai'vʌldʒ] *vt* make known something secret. **divulgence** *nc/u.*

dizzy ['dizi] *adj* **1.** having an uncomfortable feeling in the head, as though things were moving. *I felt dizzy after travelling all day in the car.* **2.** making one have this feeling: *a dizzy height.* **dizzily** *adv.* **dizziness** *nu.*

do [du:] **1.** *aux* used to form negative sentences, questions, inverted sentences and emphatic forms of verbs, and to replace a verb that is not repeated. *I like this book. Do you like it? I do not like it/I don't like it. Do you play football?* Yes, *I do* i.e. play football. *Does he play the piano?* No, *he doesn't. Neither does John. We arrived early, and so did they. I do like music* (emphatic). *Do come to visit us* (emphatic). **2.** *vt* perform any action. *What is he doing? You have done your work badly.* **3.** *vi* be suitable or satisfactory. *This will not do* i.e. this is not good enough. **4.** *vt* visit a place as a tourist. (*informal*). **5.** *vi* have as one's work. *What does your father do?* **6.** *vt* cook or prepare for eating or drinking. *He likes his steaks well done* i.e. cooked for a long time. **7.** *vt* travel at a certain speed. *This car does 110 miles an hour.* **8.** *vt* cheat; get money from by a trick. *That shopkeeper did me.* (*informal* in sense **8.**). *pres part* **doing** ['duiŋ]. *past tense* **did** [did]. *past part* **done** [dʌn]. Also *nc* meeting, party. (*informal*).

do away with someone/something put an end to; destroy; kill. *He did away with his enemies.*

do someone out of something get something from someone by a dishonest trick. *The shopkeeper did me out of ten pence.* (*informal*).

do something up **1.** tie or fasten. *He did up his parcel. He did up his shoelace.* **2.** make clean and like new. *He did up his house* i.e. he painted it etc. (*informal in sense* **2**).

can/could do with something have a wish or need for something. *I could do with a drink* i.e. I want a drink. (*informal*).

have to do with someone/something have a connection with. *I wonder whether my stomach ache has anything to do with the food I ate yesterday* i.e. I wonder whether the food caused the stomach ache. *I shall have nothing to do with him* i.e. I shall not talk to him or be friendly with him. *What has that to do with you?* i.e. why are you interested in that? (*impolite*). *It's nothing to do with you.* (*impolite*).

do better improve. *Perhaps he will do better in his studies next year.*

do someone/something good make better; be helpful to; be useful to. *The medicine will do you good. Complaining won't do you any good.*

how do you do? greeting (used when being introduced to another person. The other person also says *How do you do?*).

do well succeed.

be done for be unable to continue; ruined; spoiled. (*informal*).

docile ['dousail] *adj* easily managed; willing to obey. **docilely** *adv.* **docility** [dou'siliti] *nu.*

dock[1] [dɔk] *nc* (often *pl*) place where ships can be loaded and unloaded. Also *vt/i* (with reference to ships) come or bring into dock. **docker** *nc* person who loads and unloads ships.

'dockyard place where ships are built or repaired.

dock[2] [dɔk] *nc* place where a prisoner stands in a court of law.

dock[3] [dɔk] *nc/u* type of plant with big oval leaves, which grows wild.

dock[4] [dɔk] *vt* **1.** cut an animal's tail or ears shorter. **2.** make wages, salary etc less.

doctor[1] ['dɔktə*] *nc* **1.** person trained and qualified in curing diseases and injuries. **2.** person who has received one of the highest degrees of a university. **doctoral** *adj.*

doctorate ['dɔktərət] *nc* highest type of university degree.

doctor[2] [dɔktə*] *vt* **1.** give treatment to as a doctor. **2.** add drugs etc to food and drink unknown to those eating and drinking them. **3.** change something written so as to make it untrue. (all *informal*).

doctrine ['dɔktrin] *nc/u* official beliefs of a church or political party. **doctrinal** [dɔk'trainəl] *adj.*

doctrinaire [dɔktri'nɛə*] *adj* making political decisions by following a doctrine, instead of considering what is the best thing to do. Also *nc* person who makes decisions in this way.

document ['dɔkjumənt] *nc* anything in writing which gives information or proof. Also ['dɔkjument] *vt* prove or give examples by documents.

documentary [dɔkju'mentəri] *adj* of documents. Also *nc* film which does not tell a story but illustrates some aspect of real life.

dodder ['dɔdə*] *vi* walk in a very unsteady manner, because of old age. **dodderer** *nc.* **doddery** *adj*: *a doddery old man.*

dodge [dɔdʒ] *vt/i* **1.** move quickly so as to avoid something. *He dodged the blow.* **2.** avoid a duty by a trick. Also *nc* **1.** sudden movement. **2.** clever and dishonest trick. **dodger** *nc* person who is clever and dishonest. (*informal*).

doe [dou] *nc* female of certain animals (e.g. rabbits, antelopes, deer).

dog[1] [dɔg] *nc* **1.** type of domestic animal. **2.** other animals of the same family (e.g. wolf, jackal, fox). **3.** male of certain animals (e.g. foxes, wolves).

'dog collar **1.** collar for a dog. **2.** white collar, tied at the back of the neck, worn by clergymen.

'dog-eared *adj* (with reference to the pages of a book) with the corners bent over, like the ears of a dog.

a 'dog's life a very miserable and difficult life. (*informal*).

dog in the manger person unwilling to give to others what he does not want himself. (*informal*).

give a dog a bad name if a person is known to be bad, he will be blamed for anything wrong, even if he has not done it. (*informal*).

go to the dogs **1.** become unhealthy or ruined by living a wicked life. **2.** become worthless. (*informal*).

let sleeping dogs lie don't disturb anything which seems satisfactory, because this may cause trouble. (*informal*).

not a dog's chance no chance at all. (*informal*).

rain cats and dogs rain very heavily. (*informal*).

dog[2] [dɔg] *vt* follow closely: *dogged by bad luck.*

dog someone's footsteps follow someone closely.

dogged ['dɔgid] *adj* determined to continue even though there are difficulties and dangers. **doggedly** *adv.* **doggedness** *nu.*

doggerel ['dɔgərl] *nu* rough and badly-made poetry.

dogma ['dɔgmə] *nc/u* official beliefs of a church.

dogmatic [dɔg'mætik] *adj* **1.** of dogma. **2.**

giving opinions without allowing discussion or without allowing other people to have different opinions. **dogmatically** *adv.* **dogmatism** ['dɔgmətizəm] *nu.*
dogmatize ['dɔgmətaiz] *vt/i* give an opinion as though it were a dogma; speak dogmatically.

doily ['dɔili] *nc* round decorated piece of paper or cloth put on a cake plate or under a dish on a table.

dole [doul] *vt* (with **out**) give in small amounts. *He doled out the food to the children.* **the dole** *nu* money given every week by the government to people without work. *He's on the dole* i.e. receiving this money. (*informal*).

doleful ['doulful] *adj* very miserable. **dolefully** *adv.* **dolefulness** *nu.*

doll [dɔl] *nc* child's toy in the form of a baby or adult person.

dollar ['dɔlə*] *nc* unit of money in America, Canada, Australia etc.

dolorous ['dɔlərəs] *adj* very unhappy.
dolour ['dɔlə*] (*US* **dolor**) *nu* great unhappiness.

dolphin ['dɔlfin] *nc* type of intelligent air-breathing sea animal with a beak-like mouth, found in the Mediterranean and Atlantic.

dolt [doult] *nc* foolish or unintelligent person. **doltish** *adj.* **doltishness** *nu.*

domain [də'mein] *nc* **1.** all the land ruled by a king or other ruler. **2.** land owned by a person. (rather *o.f.*). **3.** area of study or knowledge: *the domain of chemistry.*

dome [doum] *nc* large rounded roof.

dome

domestic [də'mestik] *adj* **1.** concerning the home. **2.** concerning one's own country. **3.** (with reference to animals) not wild; kept in the home or on farms. Also *nc* servant who works in one's house. (rather *o.f.* in this sense). **domestically** *adv.*
domesticate [də'mestikeit] *vt* **1.** (with reference to animals) make able to live in a house or on a farm. **2.** (with reference to people) make fond of family life; make willing to work in the house.
domesticated *adj.* (*opp* **undomesticated**).
domesticity [doumes'tisiti] *nu* life in a house with a family.

domicile ['dɔmisail] *nc* house where a person lives. (*formal*).

dominate ['dɔmineit] *vt/i* **1.** have strong control over. *That big boy dominates the other boys in the class* i.e. they all do what he tells them to do. **2.** be most noticeable in. *That building dominates the town* i.e. it is much taller than the other buildings. *Africa has dominated the news recently* i.e. most of the news in the newspapers has been about Africa. **dominant** ['dɔminənt] *adj.* **dominance** ['dɔminəns], **domination** [dɔmi'neiʃən] *nu.*
domineer [dɔmi'niə*] *vi* (usu. with **over**) force other people to do what one wants them to do.
domineering *adj* behaving in this way.

dominion [də'miniən] **1.** *nu* condition of ruling or controlling. **2.** *nc* country ruled by a king or other ruler.

domino ['dɔminou] *nc* small flat piece of wood or plastic with spots on one side, used in the game of **dominoes.** *pl* **dominoes.**

don [dɔn] *nc* **1.** university lecturer (esp. at Oxford or Cambridge). **2.** Spanish title used before the name of professional people. Also *vt* (with reference to clothes) put on. *past* **donned.** (*o.f.* in this sense).

donate [də'neit] *vt* give to a charity, political party etc.
donation **1.** *nu* act of donating. **2.** *nc* money etc donated.

done [dʌn] past part of **do.**

donkey ['dɔŋki] *nc* **1.** animal like a small horse, with long ears, used for carrying loads. (Also **ass**). **2.** foolish person.

donor ['dounə*] *nc* person who donates (esp. one who gives blood for use in hospitals).

doodle ['du:dl] *vi* make a drawing or pattern while thinking about something else. *People sometimes doodle while they are listening to a lecture.* Also *nc* drawing etc made in this way.

doom [du:m] *nc* (usu. only *sing*) **1.** ruin, destruction or death. **2.** the end of the world. Also *vt* send to ruin, destruction or death.
'doomsday the day on which the world will be destroyed.

door [dɔ:*] *nc* **1.** swinging or sliding piece of wood, glass, metal etc which is used to close a building, room, cupboard etc. **2.** place where one enters a building or room. **3.** way of getting something: *the door to success.*
'doorman person whose work is to open and close the doors of a hotel, restaurant, big shop etc.
'doorstep **1.** step leading from a street up to the door of a house. **2.** area in front of the door of a house.
'doorway place where one enters a building or room.
in'doors *adv* inside a house.
'next 'door *adj/adv* in the next house. *The people who live next door; next-door neighbours.*
out of doors in the open air.
dead as a doornail completely dead or ended. (*informal*).

dope [doup] **1.** nc foolish person. (*informal*). **2.** *nu* drug (esp. one which makes one sleep) (*informal*). **3.** *nu* thick type of liquid used in painting aeroplanes. **4.** *nu* (mainly *US*) information; facts. (*informal*). Also *vt* give drugs to.
dopey *adj* **1.** foolish. **2.** sleepy as though drugged. (*informal*).

dormant ['dɔ:mənt] *adj* (with reference to plants, volcanoes, animals, ideas, organizations etc, not usu. of people) sleeping; not active but able to be active later on.

dormitory ['dɔ:mitri] *nc* room where several people sleep (esp. in a school or college).

dormouse ['dɔ:maus] *nc* type of small animal, which looks like a small squirrel, and which sleeps through the winter. *pl* **dormice** ['dɔ:mais].

dose [dous] *nc* amount of medicine to be taken at one time. Also *vt* give medicine to.

dossier ['dɔsiə*] *nc* collection of papers giving information about a person (esp. a criminal) or thing. *The police have a dossier on him.*

dot [dɔt] *nc* small round mark. Also *vt* mark with a dot. *past* **dotted.**

on the dot at the exact time. *He arrived at one o'clock on the dot.*

dotage ['doutidʒ] *nu* weakness of mind and body caused by old age (often in **be in one's dotage**).

dote [dout] *vi* (with **on**) like very much n a foolish way. *She dotes on her children.*

dotty ['dɔti] *adj* slightly mad. (*informal*).

double[1] ['dʌbl] *adj* having two of something; twice as much as; of or for two: *a double bed* i.e. a bed for two people. *He ate a double portion of food* i.e. the food for two people. *This has a double purpose* i.e. it can be used for two purposes. Also *adv* twice as much.

doubly *adv* twice over.

'double-'barrelled *adj* **1.** (with reference to a gun) having two barrels. **2.** (with reference to a name) having two parts joined by a hyphen (e.g. *Henry Campbell-Bannerman*). **3.** having two parts or two purposes. (*informal* in senses **2.** and **3.**).

'double 'bass very large stringed musical instrument.

'double-'breasted *adj* (with reference to a coat, suit etc) made so that there is a double thickness of cloth on the chest when the coat is buttoned.

'double 'chin loose skin under the chin.

double-'cross somebody cheat or betray somebody who trusts one. *The leader of the gang double-crossed the other thieves.* (*informal*).

'double-'decker bus having two decks, one upstairs and one downstairs.

'double 'Dutch words which do not mean anything or which one does not understand. (*informal*).

'double 'entry system of keeping a record of money received and spent, in which everything is written down in two places.

double[2] ['dʌbl] *nc* person who looks exactly like another person.

doubles *npl* tennis or badminton match for four players, two on each side.

at the double running (usu. in the army etc).

double[3] ['dʌbl] **1.** *vt/i* become or make twice as much etc. *The price has doubled since last year. I shall double your wages.* **2.** *vt* fold or bend in two. *He doubled his blankets because it was a cold night.* **3.** *vi* serve two purposes; take two parts at the same time. **4.** *vi* (military) run.

double back move back in the direction one has come from (usu. in order to escape). *The thief doubled back towards the village.*

double something back fold in two.

double up 1. share a room with another person. *Some of the guests had to double up.* **2.** bend the body because of pain, weakness, laughter etc.

double something up fold in two.

doublet ['dʌblit] *nc* type of short coat worn by men in the time of Shakespeare.

doubt [daut] *vt/i* be uncertain about. *I doubt whether we shall succeed* i.e. I think we may not succeed. *I doubted his story* i.e. I thought that he might not be telling the truth. Also *nc/u* feeling of uncertainty.

doubtful *adj* **1.** feeling doubt. **2.** causing doubt. **doubtfully** *adv*.

doubtless *adv* without doubt; very probably.

doubting *adj* feeling doubt.

in doubt uncertain. *I was in doubt about what to do.*

no doubt probably. *No doubt he will help us if we ask him.*

without (a) doubt certainly. *Without (a) doubt you have been working very hard.*

give somebody the benefit of the doubt see **benefit**[1].

dough [dou] *nu* **1.** mixture of flour and water etc which becomes bread or pastry when baked. **2.** money. (*informal* in sense **2.**).

'doughnut cake made from dough fried in fat.

dour [duə*] *adj* silent and unfriendly. **dourly** *adv*. **dourness** *nu*.

dove [dʌv] *nc* type of pigeon, considered as a symbol of peace and tenderness.

'dovecote small house for domestic doves.

'dovetail *vt/i* **1.** (with reference to pieces of wood) fit together as in the illustration. **2.** fit together (e.g. with reference to plans, ideas, arrangements etc).

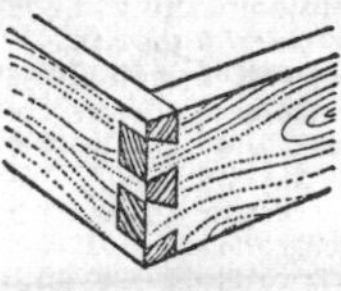

dovetail (*def 1*)

dowager ['dauədʒə*] *nc* widow who has property or a title from her dead husband.

dowdy ['daudi] *adj* (usu. with reference to clothes) old, untidy and unfashionable. **dowdily** *adv*. **dowdiness** *nu*.

down[1] [daun] *adv/prep* not up; in/to a lower position, size, quantity etc. *He fell down* i.e. he fell to the floor. *He put his cup down* i.e. on the table etc. *He ran down the hill. His temperature has gone down* i.e. he now has a lower temperature. *Exports have gone down* i.e. fewer goods have been exported. *She isn't down yet* i.e. she is still upstairs. *Write this down* i.e. write it. Also *vt* **1.** knock down; hit so as to make someone fall. (*informal*). **2.** drink completely. *He downed his medicine.* (*informal*).

'downward *adj*: *the downward climb.* **downwards** *adv*.

'downcast *adj* unhappy because of some disappointment.

'down-to-'earth see **earth.**

'downfall 1. heavy fall of rain or snow. **2.** sudden and often violent ending of a government or ruler. **3.** thing which causes one to fail (in one's hopes). *Laziness was his downfall.*

'down'grade[1] *vt* put into a lower position. *The Prime Minister downgraded three members of the government* i.e. gave them jobs which were less important than the ones which they had been holding.

'downgrade[2] *nu* in **on the downgrade** i.e. becoming worse.

'down'hearted *adj* unhappy because of some disappointment.

'down'hill *adj/adv* of/towards the bottom of a hill: *a downhill climb; run downhill; go downhill* i.e. become worse (e.g. in health, business).

'down-and-'out without money or friends. (*informal*).

'down 'payment amount of money which is paid first when one is buying an article by paying small amounts of money over a long period.

'downpour heavy fall of rain.

'downright *adj/adv* **1.** complete(ly): *a downright liar; downright foolish.* **2.** honest;

saying what one thinks. *He spoke in a downright way.*

'down'stairs[1] *adv* to a lower place by means of stairs. *He went downstairs.*

'downstairs[2] *adj* on a lower floor: *the downstairs rooms.*

'down'stream *adv* in the direction in which a river is flowing. *He sailed downstream.*

'down'town *adj/adv* (mainly *US*) in/to the main part of a town: *the downtown shops. He drove downtown.*

'down train train going away from a city into the country.

'downtrodden *adj* badly treated by those who are richer and more powerful. *The workers were downtrodden.*

down with somebody/something exclamation showing that one is strongly opposed to somebody/something. *The crowd was shouting 'Down with the king!'*

have a down on somebody dislike somebody, so that one is always doing or saying things to hurt him. *The teacher had a down on that boy.* (*informal*).

down tools refuse to work; strike. *The workers downed tools.*

down[2] [daun] *nc* (usu. *pl*) low hill in the south of England.

down[3] [daun] *nu* soft feathers on a young bird; any soft hair or wool. **downy** *adj.*

dowry ['dauri] *nc* money and property which a woman brings to her husband at marriage.

doze [douz] *vi* have a light sleep. *He dozed in his chair after dinner.* Also *nc* short sleep.

dozen ['dʌzən] *nc* group of twelve.

drab [dræb] *adj* dull; dark; uninteresting; without change. **drably** *adv.* **drabness** *nu.*

draft [drɑːft] *nc* **1.** first form of a piece of writing, which can be altered so as to make the final version. *He made a draft of his essay.* **2.** (mainly *US*) group of men joining the army together. **3.** group of people chosen for any special purpose. **4.** piece of paper by which a person asks a bank to pay a certain sum of money. **5.** see **draught.** Also *vt* **1.** make a plan of a piece of writing. **2.** make men join the army.

'draftsman see **draught.**

drag [dræg] **1.** *vt/i* move or pull along slowly or roughly. *He dragged the heavy table across the room.* **2.** *vi* seem to take a long time and to be uninteresting. *The last part of the play dragged a little.* **3.** *vt* search the bottom of a lake or river by pulling nets or hooks across it. *past* **dragged.** Also **1.** *nc* something which is used for searching the bottom of a river or lake. **2.** *nc* something which makes one go slowly. **3.** *nc* a bore. *This film is a drag.* **4.** *nu* women's clothes worn by men. **5.** *nc* pull on a cigarette.

'dragnet 1. large net pulled across the bottom of the sea etc for catching fish. **2.** large search by the police for a criminal.

dragon ['drægən] *nc* large imaginary creature, with wings and a long tail (usu. breathing fire).

'dragonfly large type of insect, with a long thin body and two pairs of very thin wings.

dragoon [drə'guːn] *nc* (in former times) soldier who rode on a horse.

dragoon someone (into doing something) make someone do something he does not wish to do. *He dragooned me into agreeing to help him.*

drain [drein] *nc* **1.** pipe or channel through which dirty water and other liquid can flow away. **2.** anything which causes loss or waste of strength, property etc. *The cost of his children's education was a drain on his money.* Also *vt/i* **1.** (with reference to liquids) flow, cause to flow, away. *The river drains into the sea. He drained his land. The water drained away.* **2.** become or make weak or poor by continual loss. *The illness drained his strength. His strength drained away.*

drainage *nu* system of drains (esp. for carrying water away from a house).

'drainpipe 1. pipe draining water from the roof of a building to the drains under the ground. **2.** (in *pl*) tight-fitting trousers.

drake [dreik] *nc* male duck.

dram [dræm] *nc* **1.** $\frac{1}{8}$ of an ounce of medicine or drugs. **2.** $\frac{1}{16}$ of an ounce of other substances. **3.** small amount of strong alcoholic drink.

drama ['drɑːmə] **1.** *nc* play (usu. serious) for the theatre, radio or television. **2.** *nu* art or study of such plays. **3.** *nc* exciting event or series of events.

dramatic [drə'mætik] *adj* **1.** of plays. **2.** exciting. (*opp* **undramatic** in sense **2.**). **dramatically** *adv.*

dramatist ['dræmətist] *nc* writer of plays.

dramatize ['dræmətaiz] *vt* **1.** make into a play. **2.** make more exciting.

dramatization [dræmətai'zeiʃən] *nc/u* something dramatized; act of dramatizing.

drank [dræŋk] past tense of **drink.**

drape [dreip] *vt* hang cloth loosely over something. *He draped his coat over the back of his chair.* Also *nc* (usu. *pl*) piece of cloth draped over something (usu. at a window or on the stage of a theatre) (mainly *US* in this sense).

draper *nc* (*Brit*) person who sells cloth.

drapery *nc/u* **1.** cloth sold by a draper. **2.** cloth draped over something.

drastic ['dræstik] *adj* having a strong effect. *He took drastic action to cure the disease.* **drastically** *adv.*

draught [drɑːft] *nc* **1.** movement of air inside a room or in a fire. **2.** amount of liquid drunk at one time. **3.** number of fish caught in a net. **4.** act of pulling in a net to catch fish. **5.** depth of water needed for a ship to float. **6.** see **draft.**

draughty *adj* having air moving inside a room: *a draughty room.*

draughts *n sing* (*Brit*) game played with a board divided into 64 squares and 24 round pieces of wood or bone etc. (*US* **checkers**).

'draughtsman 1. round piece used in playing draughts. **2.** person who does technical drawings.

'draught 'beer beer which is drawn from a barrel instead of being poured from a bottle.

draw[1] [drɔː] **1.** *vt/i* make a picture by using a pencil, pen, crayon etc. *He is drawing. He drew a house.* **2.** *vt* pull. *The engine drew the train from the station. He drew the curtains* i.e. opened or closed them. **3.** *vt* take something from the place where it is kept. *He drew some money from the bank.* **4.** *vt* get or receive. *What conclusions can we draw from this?* i.e. what opinions can we come to? **5.** *vt* attract. *The play drew large audiences* i.e. many people came to see the play. **6.** *vt/i* end a game with equal scores. *The two teams drew. They drew the game.* **7.** *vi* (with reference to a fire, cigarette, pipe etc) allow air to move through. *The fire isn't drawing properly.* **8.** *vt/i* take playing cards from a pack to decide something. **9.** *vt/i* take out a gun or sword which one is carrying. *He drew a gun. He let the other man draw first.* **10.** *vi* (with reference to tea) become stronger by soaking the tea leaves. *The tea hasn't drawn properly yet.* **11.** *vt* (with reference to a ship or boat) need a certain amount of water in order to float. *My boat draws six feet of water. past tense* **drew** [dru:]. *past part* **drawn.**

drawer [drɔ:*] *nc* container like a box which slides in and out of a table, desk or other piece of furniture.

drawing **1.** *nc* picture made with pencil, pen, crayon etc. **2.** *nu* the art of making such pictures. *She teaches drawing.*

drawn *adj* with the face appearing to be long because of illness, worry or tiredness. *He looked very drawn after the meeting.*

'drawbridge type of bridge formerly used in castles etc, made so that it can be raised up to prevent people entering the castle.

'drawing pin see **pin**[1].

'drawing room room in a house where people can sit and talk.

draw back move backwards; be afraid to go forward; be afraid to do something.

'drawback *nc* disadvantage. *This is a good car; its only drawback is that it uses a lot of petrol.*

draw in (with reference to days) get shorter. *The days are drawing in as winter approaches.*

draw someone out encourage a person to talk.

draw something out make something longer.

draw together move closer.

draw up stop. *The car drew up at the traffic lights.*

draw something up make a formal document: *draw up a will/agreement/treaty etc.*

draw oneself up stand straight.

draw a blank fail to find what one is looking for.

draw a breath breathe in.

draw breath stop to rest. *I didn't have time to draw breath.* (*informal*).

draw level come together and travel at the same speed in the same direction. *The two runners drew level.*

draw the line at refuse to go as far as; not tolerate. *I am willing to help you, but I draw the line at doing your homework for you.*

draw lots see **cast**[1].

draw near come near. *The old man drew near. The end of the month is drawing near.*

long-drawn-out *adj* lasting a long time; moving very slowly. *The play/meeting/lecture was very long-drawn-out.*

draw[2] [drɔ:] *nc* **1.** result of a game in which both sides have the same score. **2.** act of drawing a gun or sword. **3.** act of taking objects out of a box, bag etc to decide some question. **4.** somebody/something that many people go to see, look at, listen to etc. *The new play is a very big draw.*

drawl [drɔ:l] *vt/i* speak in a very slow and lazy way. Also *nc* this way of speaking.

dray [drei] *nc* large vehicle pulled by horses, for carrying heavy loads.

dread [dred] *vt* feel great fear of. *I dread the examination.* Also *nu* great fear.

dreadful *adj* **1.** causing dread. **2.** unpleasant; bad. *The weather is dreadful.*

dreadfully *adv* **1.** unpleasantly. **2.** very. *I'm dreadfully busy.* (*informal* in sense **2.**).

dream [dri:m] *vt/i* **1.** see and hear things while one is asleep. *I dreamed that I was a king.* **2.** imagine; think possible. *I never dreamt that I would be the winner of the competition. past* **dreamed** or **dreamt** [dremt]. Also *nc* **1.** something seen or heard while one is sleeping. **2.** something hoped for or imagined. **3.** something very beautiful or very pleasant.

dreamy *adj* of or like a dream: *a dreamy person* i.e. one who does not seem fully awake. **dreamily** *adv.* **dreaminess** *nu.*

dreamer *nc* person who dreams; dreamy person.

dreary ['driəri] *adj* dull; dark; uninteresting: *a dreary room; dreary weather; a dreary person.* **drearily** *adv.* **dreariness** *nu.*

dredge[1] [dredʒ] *vt/i* bring substance from the bottom of a river or lake or the sea: *dredge the river; dredge mud from the river.* Also *nc* apparatus used for this.

dredger[1] *nc* boat carrying a dredge.

dredge[2] [dredʒ] *vt* sprinkle with sugar, flour etc.

dredger[2] *nc* container with small holes for doing this.

dregs [dregz] *npl* **1.** small pieces of solid matter which sink to the bottom of liquid. **2.** the most worthless or useless people: *the dregs of society.*

drench [drentʃ] *vt* make very wet. *We were drenched by the rain.*

dress[1] [dres] **1.** *nc* garment worn by a woman or girl, covering the top and bottom parts of the body. **2.** *nu* clothes of all kinds.

dresser *nc* **1.** person who helps an actor or actress to dress for a play. **2.** person who bandages wounds in a hospital. **3.** piece of furniture with shelves for holding plates, cups etc.

dressing *nc/u* **1.** bandage etc put on a wound. **2.** oil, vinegar etc put on a salad.

'dress 'circle part of a theatre, higher than the stage, where some of the audience sit.

'dressmaker person who makes clothes for women.

'dress re'hearsal last rehearsal of a play in which the actors wear the clothes which they will wear for the actual performances.

'dressing gown (long) coat worn over a person's night clothes.

'dressing table table with mirrors and drawers, kept in a bedroom.

'evening dress **1.** *nc* long dress worn by a woman for formal occasions in the evening. **2.** *nu* clothes worn by men and women for formal occasions in the evening.

give somebody a dressing-down speak firmly to somebody who has done wrong. (*informal* and rather *o.f.*).

dress[2] [dres] **1.** *vt/i* put on clothes. *He dressed in his best suit. She dressed the children.* **2.** *vt* decorate. *He dressed the shop window* i.e. put things in the window to show what was for sale in the shop. *He dressed her hair* i.e. combed and brushed it.

dress up put on special clothes (esp. for a game, play, party etc).

dress a salad put oil, vinegar etc on a salad.

dress a wound clean and bandage a wound.

drew [dru:] past tense of **draw**[1].

dribble ['dribl] **1.** *vi* let saliva or liquid fall from the mouth. **2.** *vt/i* (football) run forward while kicking the ball. **3.** *vi* (with reference to liquid) fall in small drops. Also **1.** *nu* saliva falling from the mouth. **2.** *nc* act of running while kicking a football.

dried [draid] past of **dry.**

drift[1] [drift] **1.** *vt/i* move or be carried along by water or air. *The engine has broken down and the boat is drifting.* **2.** *vi* live without any special purpose or aim. *He just drifted through his time at university.* **3.** *vt/i* (with reference to snow) move or be moved into large heaps. *The snow is drifting. The wind was drifting the snow.*

drift² [drift] **1.** *nu* slow movement onwards by water or air. **2.** *nu* lack of purpose or aim in life. **3.** *nc* large heap of snow or sand brought together by the wind. **4.** *nu* general idea of what somebody says or writes. *I catch your drift* i.e. I understand roughly what you mean.

drifter *nc* **1.** person who goes through life without any purpose or plan. **2.** type of fishing boat which uses large nets (called **drift-nets**).

'driftwood pieces of wood carried onto land by the drift of the sea.

drill¹ [dril] *nc* tool with a sharp end which turns round, used for making holes. Also *vt/i* make a hole with a drill.

drill² [dril] *nc/u* **1.** training of soldiers in marching, using guns etc. **2.** teaching of students etc by making them do the same thing many times. **3.** any series of movements or any exercise used in training soldiers or teaching students. Also *vt/i* train or teach people by drill.

drill³ [dril] *nc* machine for planting seeds.

drill⁴ [dril] *nu* type of strong cloth (usu. cotton).

drink [driŋk] *vt/i* **1.** take liquid into the body through the mouth. **2.** take in liquid (e.g. with reference to plants or the earth). **3.** be in the habit of taking alcoholic drinks. Also *nc/u* **1.** liquid for drinking. **2.** beer, wine, whisky etc. *past tense* **drank** [dræŋk]. *past part* **drunk** [drʌŋk].

drinkable *adj* suitable for drinking. (*opp* **undrinkable**).

drinker *nc* person who often drinks alcoholic drinks.

drink something in give very careful attention to what one is hearing or reading. *He was drinking in my words.*

drink to someone say someone's name and drink some beer, wine etc (as a sign that one wishes good luck to the person).

drink (something) up drink so as to finish one's drink. *Drink up and we will go. Drink up your milk.*

drip [drip] *vt/i* (with reference to liquids) fall, allow to fall, in small drops. *The rain dripped from the trees. past* **dripped.** Also **1.** *nc* drop or small particle of liquid. **2.** *nu* falling of water in drops. **3.** *nc* (medicine) apparatus for allowing drops of liquid (e.g. blood, glucose etc) to enter the body.

dripping *nu* fat obtained from meat which has been roasted.

'drip-'dry *adj* (with reference to cloth) able to become dry and smooth if hung up immediately after being washed: *a drip-dry shirt.*

drive¹ [draiv] **1.** *vt/i* cause a car or other vehicle to move along. *He drove the car. Can you drive?* i.e. do you know how to drive a car? *I drove my aunt to town* i.e. I took her by car. **2.** *vt* cause animals to go in a certain direction: *drive sheep.* **3.** *vt* cause a sharp object to enter something. *He drove a nail into the door. He drove a knife into his enemy.* **4.** *vt/i* hit a ball hard in certain games. **5.** *vt/i* go, cause to go, with force. *The wind drove against the windows. The wind drove the ship off its course. past tense* **drove** [drouv]. *past part* **driven** ['drivən].

drive² [draiv] **1.** *nc* journey in a car, bus etc. **2.** *nc* small road leading to a house. **3.** *nc* hitting of a ball in various games. **4.** *nu* energy; determination; ambition. *That man has plenty of drive* i.e. he has many plans and ideas, and is able to carry them out. **5.** *nc* special attempt to do something: *a drive to get new members for the club.*

driver *nc* **1.** person who causes a car etc to move. **2.** type of golf club.

'driving licence permission to drive a motor vehicle on public roads.

'driving test examination to decide whether someone should be allowed to drive a motor vehicle.

drive at something mean; intend. *What are you driving at?* i.e. what do you mean? (*informal*).

drive someone/something away/back cause someone/something to go away. *The police drove away the crowds. He drove us back.*

drive-in cinema/store/church etc cinema etc which people may attend while seated in their cars.

drive someone to do something make someone do something (usu. something wrong). *What drove him to steal the money?*

be driven by something (with reference to machines) get power from something. *This machine is driven by electricity.*

drive a (hard) bargain come to an agreement with someone about buying and selling (so that one gets what one wants).

drive someone mad/insane/crazy etc make someone become mad etc.

drivel ['drivl] *nu* words which mean nothing. Also *vi* talk without meaning. *past* **drivelled.** (*US* **driveled**).

drizzle ['drizl] *nu* rain which falls in very small drops. Also *vi* rain in this way.

droll [droul] *adj* funny; amusing. (rather *o.f.*).

dromedary ['drɔmidəri] *nc* type of camel having one hump.

drone¹ [droun] *nc* **1.** male bee. **2.** very lazy person who depends on others to work for him.

drone² [droun] *nc/u* low unchanging sound, like that made by a bee. Also *vi* make this sound.

droop [dru:p] *vt/i* (often of plants) bend down through weakness or tiredness. Also *nu* bending position. **droopy** *adj.*

drop¹ [drɔp] *nc* **1.** small rounded ball of liquid. **2.** small amount of liquid. **3.** distance or movement straight down: *the drop from the top of the cliff; a drop in the temperature.*

drops *npl* medicine to be given in drops (usu. for the eyes, ears or nose).

droppings *npl* waste matter sent out of the bodies of animals.

at the drop of a hat as soon as asked; as soon as an opportunity is given. (*informal*).

a drop in the ocean a very small amount of a very large quantity.

drop² [drɔp] **1.** *vt/i* fall, allow to fall. *The bomb dropped on the village. He dropped his book on the floor.* **2.** *vi* (with reference to temperature or wind) become lower or less strong. **3.** *vt* stop something. *I am trying to drop that bad habit. I want to drop History* i.e. to stop studying History. *He dropped his friends* i.e. stopped being friendly to them. (*informal*). *past* **dropped.**

drop across, drop by see **drop over.**

drop behind not go as fast; be left further back. *The Italian runner is dropping behind. This student is dropping behind the rest of the* *class.*

drop in (on someone) visit someone without telling him that one is coming. (*informal*).

drop off 1. become less or fewer. *The number of students at his lectures is dropping off.* 2. fall asleep. (*informal*). 3. fall off. *The fruit dropped off the tree.*

drop someone off allow someone to get out of a car. *I dropped him off at the post office.* (*informal*).

drop out (of something) stop taking part in something. *A number of students drop out of university every year* i.e. leave the university.

'dropout *nc* person who leaves a college, university etc (too early) or leaves a conventional way of life. *There have been fewer dropouts this year.* (*informal*).

drop over go to visit someone. *Drop over and see me sometime.* (*informal*).

drop one's aitches/h's pronounce words like 'hot' and 'hit' as 'ot' and 'it' (as in many accents used in England) (*informal*).

drop anchor (with reference to a ship) stop and lower the anchor.

drop a clanger say something tactless. (*informal*).

drop (someone) a hint try to make someone understand something without actually saying what one means. (*informal*).

drop someone a line write a short letter to someone. (*informal*).

you could have heard a pin drop it was very quiet; there was no noise at all. (*informal*).

drop one's voice speak more quietly.

dropsy ['drɔpsi] *nu* disease in which too much water collects in the body.

dross [drɔs] *nu* 1. waste matter obtained in the production of metals. 2. anything useless or valueless.

drought [draut] *nc* period of dry weather, causing a shortage of water.

drove[1] [drouv] past tense of **drive**[1].

drove[2] [drouv] *nc* number of sheep, cows etc moving together.

drover *nc* man whose work is to be in charge of a drove of animals (usu. in order to take them to market).

drown [draun] 1. *vt/i* die, cause to die, under water through lack of air. *She drowned in the river. He drowned his wife.* 2. *vt* prevent a sound from being heard. *The noise of the train drowned his voice.*

drown one's sorrows drink alcoholic drink because one is unhappy. (*informal*).

drowse [drauz] *vi* sleep lightly; be half asleep. **drowsy** *adj*. **drowsily** *adv*. **drowsiness** *nu*.

drudge [drʌdʒ] *nc* person who works hard at unpleasant and uninteresting work. Also *vi* work like this.

drudgery ['drʌdʒəri] *nu* work of this kind.

drug [drʌg] *nc* 1. any substance used in medicine. 2. substance which has a harmful effect on the mind or body. Also *vt* add or give a drug to (usu. to make somebody fall asleep). *He drugged my drink. He drugged me. past* **drugged.**

druggist *nc* person who sells drugs (in sense 1.).

'drug addict *nc* person who cannot stop using certain harmful drugs. **drug addiction** *nu*.

'drugstore (mainly *US*) shop where drugs, and various kinds of food and drink are sold.

a drug on the market article which nobody wants to buy. (*informal*).

drum [drʌm] *nc* 1. musical instrument as in the illustration. 2. large metal container for liquids, shaped like a drum. 3. large object shaped like a drum, for winding wire or piping on. Also *vt/i* 1. play a drum. 2. tap one's fingers on something hard, as though playing a drum. *past* **drummed.**

drum (*def 1*)

drummer *nc* person who plays a drum.

drum something into someone make somebody learn something by repeating it to him many times. (*informal*).

drunk [drʌŋk] past part of **drink.** Also *adj* unable to think or behave properly, through having had too much alcoholic drink. Also *nc* person who is drunk. **drunkenly** *adv*. **drunkenness** *nu*.

drunkard ['drʌŋkəd] *nc* person who is often drunk.

dry [drai] *adj* 1. without liquid or moisture. *The climate is dry. The washing is dry. I feel dry* i.e. I want a drink. 2. dull and uninteresting: *a dry book.* 3. esp. in **dry humour** i.e. pretending to be serious; showing no feelings of amusement. 4. (with reference to wine) not containing much sugar. 5. not allowing the sale of alcoholic drinks. (*informal* in sense 5.). Also *vt/i* become or make free from liquid or moisture. *The washing is drying. He dried the clothes. past* **dried. drily** *adv*. **dryness** *nu*.

'dry 'cleaning *nu* method of cleaning clothes with chemicals, without using water.

'dry 'cleaner *nc* person who cleans clothes in this way.

'dry-'clean *vt* clean clothes in this way.

'dry 'dock place from which water can be pumped out when a ship has entered, in order to enable the ship to be repaired.

'dry 'rot type of disease which destroys wood in buildings.

dry up 1. become completely dry; (of a river etc) stop flowing. 2. stop talking. (*informal* in sense 2.).

dry as a bone, 'bone-'dry very dry. (*informal*).

dual ['djuəl] *adj* of two; having two parts.

dual carriageway road separated into two parts, with room for two or more lines of traffic on each side.

dub[1] [dʌb] *vt* 1. officially declare somebody to be a knight by touching him on the shoulder with a sword. 2. give somebody a nickname. *His name was John Smith, but his friends had dubbed him Paddy. past* **dubbed.**

dub[2] [dʌb] *vt* put a new sound track on a film originally made in another language. *Many foreign films are dubbed when they are shown in England. past* **dubbed.**

dubbing *nu* process of dubbing; sound which is dubbed.

dubious ['dju:biəs] *adj* 1. feeling doubt; uncertain. *I'm dubious about my chances of success* i.e. I don't think I shall succeed. 2. causing one to feel doubt (often doubt as to whether something is honest or sensible): *a dubious suggestion* i.e. a suggestion which might be dishonest or foolish. **dubiously** *adv*. **dubiousness** *nu*.

duchess ['dʌtʃis] *nc* wife of a duke.

duchy ['dʌtʃi] *nc* land ruled by a duke.

duck[1] [dʌk] *nc* 1. one of various water birds with webbed feet and flattened beaks. 2.

score of 0 in cricket.
(take to something) like a duck to water (be) able to do something well as soon as one tries to do it; find something very easy to do. (*informal*).
(like) water off a duck's back (having) no effect at all. (*informal*).
duck[2] [dʌk] **1.** *vt/i* bend down quickly to avoid something. *He ducked. He ducked his head.* **2.** *vt* push someone's head under water. *He ducked his friend.*
ducking *nc* process of making somebody very wet; process of pushing somebody's head under water.
duct [dʌkt] *nc* tube for carrying liquid.
ductile ['dʌktail] **1.** (with reference to metals) able to be pulled out into thin wire. **2.** (with reference to people) easily made to do something.
dud [dʌd] *adj* of no use; not working. *This is a dud watch.* Also *nc* somebody/something that is dud. (both *informal*).
dudgeon ['dʌdʒən] *nu* usu. in **in high dudgeon** i.e. feeling of anger because someone has done something foolish or offensive.
due [dju:] *adj* **1.** owed; to be paid. *Payment is now due.* **2.** expected. *He is due to arrive today.* **3.** necessary or suitable. *Library books must be treated with due care and attention.* (*opp* **undue** in sense **3.**). Also *nc* **1.** something owed; something to be paid. **2.** (only *pl*) money paid by a member to a club etc.
duly *adv.*
due to caused by. *The delay is due to the bad weather. Due to bad weather, the train was late.*
Note: some people consider the second of these examples incorrect. They would use *due to* only as an adjectival phrase; that is to say, they would use the structure *something is due to something*, but not the structure *due to something, another thing happened.* People who follow this rule would use *owing to* in the second example above i.e. *Owing to bad weather, the train was late.*
in due course see **course**[1].
due east, due west etc exactly to or from that direction.
fall due be payable. *Payment falls due this month.*
give someone his due say what is good about somebody, even though there may also be bad things about him.
duel ['djuəl] *nc* private fight following certain rules between two people (usu. with swords or pistols). Also *vi* fight in this way. *past* **duelled.** (*US* **dueled**).
duellist *nc* person who duels.
duet [dju:'et] *nc* song or piece of music for two people.
duffel ['dʌfl] *nu* type of thick, woollen cloth.
'duffel coat thick coat with wooden pegs instead of buttons.
dug [dʌg] past of **dig**[1].
'dugout hole dug in the earth, for soldiers to shelter in during war.
'dugout ca'noe canoe or small boat, made by hollowing out a log of wood.
duke [dju:k] *nc* nobleman of high rank. (*fem* **duchess** ['dʌtʃis]).
dukedom *nc* land and position of a duke.
dulcet ['dʌlsit] *adj* very soft and pleasant in sound.
dulcimer ['dʌlsimə*] *nc* type of musical instrument, consisting of metal wires which are hit with little hammers.
dull [dʌl] *adj* **1.** not bright: *a dull day* i.e. a day without sunshine. **2.** (with reference to sound) low in sound and as if from far away: *a dull thud.* **3.** (with reference to pain) not felt very sharply and lasting a long time. **4.** not sharp. *This knife is dull.* **5.** boring; uninteresting: *a dull book.* **6.** stupid; unintelligent. **dully** *adv.* **dullness** *nu.*
dull as ditchwater see **ditch.**
duly ['dju:li] *adv* see **due.**
dumb [dʌm] *adj* **1.** unable to speak. **2.** unintelligent. (*informal* in sense **2.**). **dumbly** *adv.* **dumbness** *nu.*
dumb'found *vt* (usu. *passive*) surprise very greatly, so that one is unable to speak. *I was dumbfounded when I heard the news.*
dummy ['dʌmi] *nc* **1.** something made to look like a person/thing. *Shops which sell clothes often have dummies in the window* i.e. models which look like people, so as to show what the clothes look like when worn. **2.** object made of rubber which is put in a baby's mouth for him to suck. **3.** stupid person. (*informal*). **4.** player in certain card games who does not play his own cards. Also *adj.*
dump[1] [dʌmp] *nc* **1.** place where rubbish is left. **2.** place where military stores are kept. **3.** any unpleasant place. (*informal*).
down in the dumps very miserable or unhappy. (*informal*).
dump[2] [dʌmp] *vt/i* **1.** throw rubbish away. **2.** throw down or allow to fall down. **3.** (commerce) sell large quantities of goods at a very low price (usu. in a foreign country).
dumpling ['dʌmpliŋ] *nc* **1.** ball made of flour, fat and water, boiled with meat and vegetables. **2.** ball made of flour and water containing fruit etc.
dumpy ['dʌmpi] *adj* small and fat. **dumpiness** *nu.*
dun [dʌn] *adj* grey brown in colour.
dunce [dʌns] *nc* child who is not good at learning.
'dunce's 'cap tall paper hat formerly worn by a dunce at school as a punishment.
dune [dju:n] *nc* low hill of sand heaped up by the wind.
dung [dʌŋ] *nu* waste matter sent out of the body of animals.
dungarees [dʌŋgə'ri:z] *npl* garment consisting of coat or bib and trousers joined together, worn by people doing dirty work.

dungarees

dungeon ['dʌndʒən] *nc* room under ground, formerly used as a prison.
dupe [dju:p] *vt* cheat; make somebody believe something which is not true, or get something from somebody by a trick. Also *nc* person who is tricked or cheated.
duplicate ['dju:plikeit] *vt* do or make something exactly similar to something else. *I duplicated his work* i.e. I did again the work which he had already done. Also ['dju:plikət] *adj*: *duplicate keys.* **duplication** [dju:pli'keiʃən] *nc/u.*
duplicator *nc* machine which makes an

exact copy of anything written.
in duplicate (with reference to documents) twice. *Fill in the form in duplicate* i.e. write exactly the same information on two forms.
duplicity [dju:'plisiti] *nu* process of telling lies and being dishonest in order to deceive people.
durable ['djuərəbl] *adj* able to last a long time and not becoming damaged or broken: *durable clothes/furniture etc.* **durability** [djuərə'biliti] *nu.*
duration [djuə'reiʃən] *nu* time during which something lasts: *for the duration of the holiday* i.e. for the whole period of the holiday.
duress [djuə'res] *nu* force or compulsion. *He acted under duress* i.e. he did that because he was forced to.
during ['djuəriŋ] *prep* **1.** for the whole of a certain period. *He worked during the day.* **2.** at one time or at different times in a period. *Several important things happened during the year.*
dusk [dʌsk] *nu* time in the evening before it becomes completely dark.
dusky *adj* **1.** dark in colour. **2.** of dusk. **duskily** *adv.* **duskiness** *nu.*
dust [dʌst] *nu* **1.** very small pieces of dry earth, like powder. **2.** substance like this (e.g. *chalk dust, gold dust*). **3.** dead body (esp. in poetry or religion). Also **1.** *vt/i* remove dust from. *She dusted the furniture. She was dusting.* **2.** *vt* cover with flour, sugar or other similar substance. **dusty** *adj.* **dustily** *adv.* **dustiness** *nu.*
duster *nc* **1.** cloth used to remove dust. **2.** cloth used to clean chalk from a blackboard.
'**dustbin** (*Brit*) container in which rubbish from a house is put to be taken away. (*US* **garbage can**).
'**dustbowl** area in which the good soil has been wasted by bad farming, so that the land consists mainly of dust.
'**dust jacket** paper cover on a book.
'**dustman** man whose job is to remove rubbish from houses.
'**dustpan** metal or plastic object into which dust in a house can be brushed.
bite the dust fall dead or wounded. (*informal*).
shake the dust of a place off one's feet leave a place which one dislikes. (*informal*).
duty ['dju:ti] **1.** *nc/u* things which one must do, because one thinks it right to do them or because it is one's job to do them. *It is your duty to fight for your country. The headmaster has many different duties.* **2.** *nc* name given to various types of tax (esp. a tax on goods brought into a country).
dutiable *adj* to be taxed if brought into a country.
dutiful *adj* acting in a properly polite and obedient way to one's elders: *a dutiful daughter.* **dutifully** *adv.*
'**duty-'free** *adj* allowed to come into a country without being taxed.
off duty free from work. see **on duty.**
on duty (e.g. with reference to soldiers, nurses etc) required to be ready to work.
dwarf [dwɔ:f] *nc* **1.** very small person. **2.** very small person in children's stories, often one having magical powers. **3.** very small plant, animal etc. Also *vt* make to seem small. *The new building dwarfs all the other buildings in the town* i.e. the new building is very high.
dwell [dwel] *vi* live in a place. *past* **dwelt.** (*formal*).
dwelling *nc* house. (*formal*).
dwell upon something speak or think a lot about something.
dwindle ['dwindl] *vi* (often with **away**) slowly become smaller.
dye [dai] *nc/u* substance used for changing the colour of cloth; colour given to cloth in this way. Also *vt* change the colour of cloth using various substances. *She dyed her coat blue. pres part* **dyeing.** *past* **dyed.**
dyed in the wool see **wool.**
dying ['daiiŋ] *pres part* of **die²**.
dyke [daik] *nc* see **dike.**
dynamic [dai'næmik] *adj* **1.** (physics) concerned with force, energy, motion etc. **2.** (with reference to a person) having a lot of energy; able to do things in a hurry and to make people do what one wants; having a strong and active character. **dynamically** *adv.*
dynamics *nu* study of force, energy, motion etc.
dynamite ['dainəmait] *nu* very powerful explosive. Also *vt* destroy with dynamite.
dynamo ['dainəmou] *nc* any device which changes any force of energy into electricity (e.g. a device used on a bicycle for lighting the bicycle lamps). *pl* **dynamos.**
dynasty ['dinəsti] *nc* series of kings etc belonging to the same family. **dynastic** [di'næstik] *adj.*
dysentery ['disntri] *nu* disease of the bowels, causing diarrhoea.
dyspepsia [dis'pepsiə] *nu* discomfort or pain caused by the process of digestion.
dyspeptic [dis'peptik] *adj.* Also *nc* person suffering from dyspepsia.

E

each [iːtʃ] *determiner/adv/pron* every one, taken separately. *He spoke to each member of the team. These books cost two pounds each. Each of the boys has a prize. Each boy has a prize. Mary and Peter saw each other last night* i.e. Mary saw Peter and Peter saw Mary. *Each and every one of them* i.e. all of them.

eager ['iːgə*] *adj* having a strong wish for something. *He was eager to help us. He was eager for information.* **eagerly** *adv.* **eagerness** *nu.*

eager beaver person who is keen to work. (*informal*).

eagle ['iːgl] *nc* type of large bird, with a hooked nose and very good eyesight, which eats small birds and animals.

eagle

ear [iə*] **1.** *nc* part of the head by which animals, birds, humans etc hear. **2.** *nc* part of a cereal plant such as corn or wheat which contains the seeds. **3.** *nu* ability to hear small differences in sound: *a keen ear.* **4.** *nu* attention. *May I have your ear for a moment* i.e. please listen to me.

'eardrum part of the ear inside the head, which moves when sound waves strike it.

'earmark something save or keep something for a special purpose.

'earphone device which is fastened over the ear, for receiving telephone or radio signals.

'ear trumpet tube put against the ear to aid hearing.

by ear (with reference to playing music) from memory, without reading the notes.

out of/within earshot too far away/near enough to hear or be heard.

be all ears see **all.**

go in one ear and out the other be heard and immediately forgotten (e.g. with reference to children failing to remember what their parents tell them) (*informal*).

turn a deaf ear see **turn**[1].

earl [əːl] *nc* British nobleman of high rank.

earldom *nc* land and position of an earl.

early ['əːli] *adj/adv* **1.** near the beginning: *in the early morning; in the early part of the book.* **2.** before the usual or proper time. *We arrived too early.* **3.** in ancient times: *early history.* **earliness** *nu.*

early bird person who gets up early in the morning or who arrives early. (*informal*).

earn [əːn] *vt* get by work. *He earns £20 a week. You have earned your holiday* i.e. you have worked hard and you should have a holiday.

earnings *npl* money which a person earns.

earnest ['əːnist] *adj* serious or too serious; unable to laugh or joke. **earnestly** *adv.* **earnestness** *nu.*

in earnest serious; not joking. *I was in earnest when I told you that.*

earth [əːθ] **1.** *nu* soil; substance in which plants grow. **2.** *nu* land; whatever is not sea, river etc. **3.** *nu* (usu. **the earth**) the world. **4.** *nc* wire or other means of connection, which leads from an electrical device to the ground or completes an electrical circuit. **5.** *nc* (chemistry) oxide of certain metals. **6.** *nc* hole where certain animals live. Also *vt* provide an electrical device with a connection to the ground. *He earthed the radio.*

earthen *adj* made of earth or clay.

'earthenware coarse plates, cups etc made of baked clay.

earthy *adj* coarse; crude in thought or behaviour; having no regard for beauty or for polite behaviour. **earthiness** *nu.*

earthly *adj* living on the earth (in sense **3.**); human, not divine.

'earthquake violent shaking of part of the earth.

'earthwork wall etc made of earth, as a protection in ancient times.

'earthworm long thin creature which lives in soil and eats earth.

'down-to-'earth *adj* honest; saying what one thinks; not trying to appear what one is not; having a practical mind.

move heaven and earth see **move**[2].

what/who/why etc on earth . . . ? used as a way of emphasizing a question, to show that one is really puzzled. *Why on earth are you studying Greek?* (*informal*).

he hasn't an earthly he has not the slightest chance. (*informal*).

earwig ['iəwig] *nc* type of small insect with pincers at the tail.

ease [iːz] *nu* **1.** freedom from work or worry. **2.** ability to do something without trying hard or without difficulty. *He did the work with ease.* Also *vt/i* (often with **off**) become or make less difficult, less strong, less tight etc. *The wind has eased off. He eased the screw.*

ease up work less hard, be less severe. *He worked hard at first, but he has eased up lately.*

at ease free from worry or embarrassment. *I never feel at ease when I talk to him.*

ill at ease worried; anxious; embarrassed. *The boy felt ill at ease when the headmaster spoke to him.*

(stand) at ease (military) stand with legs apart and hands behind the back.

take one's ease rest after work.

easel ['i:zl] *nc* wooden frame to support a blackboard, or to hold a picture while it is being painted.

easel

east [i:st] *adj/adv/nu* direction in which one first sees the rising sun. *He travelled east. An east wind was blowing* i.e. a wind from the east. **eastern** *adj*.
easterly ['i:stəli] *adj* (esp. with reference to wind or direction in which one travels).
the east/East 1. Asia. 2. Russia and other countries in eastern Europe. 3. the eastern part of any country or continent.
the Middle East countries around the eastern part of the Mediterranean (e.g. Egypt, Israel, Jordan etc).
the Far East India, Pakistan, China, Japan etc.

Easter ['i:stə*] *nc/u* period around the anniversary of the Crucifixion and Resurrection of Christ.

easy ['i:zi] *adj* 1. not causing difficulty. *The work is easy.* 2. free from pain or worry. *If you prepare your work well, you will be able to sit the examination with an easy mind.* (*opp* **uneasy** in sense 2.). **easily** *adv.* **easiness** *nu*.
'**easy chair** soft padded chair (usu. with arms).
'**easy-'going** *adj* happy; cheerful; not worried or made unhappy by difficulties; not strict.
stand easy military command allowing men who are standing in line to move their bodies and arms.
take it/things easy behave without worrying or becoming too excited. (*informal*).

eat [i:t] *vt/i* 1. take food in through the mouth. 2. have a meal. 3. (usu. with reference to destruction by acid or similar substance) destroy. *past tense* **ate** [et, eit]. *past part* **eaten** ['i:tn].
Note: in Britain *ate* is usu. pronounced [et]; some people use the pronunciation [eit]. In America the usual pronunciation is [eit], and [et] is considered incorrect.
eatable *adj* fit for eating. (*opp* **uneatable**).
eat away something (usu. with reference to acid or a similar substance) destroy.
eat something up eat so as to finish. *He ate up his dinner.*
cry/eat one's heart out see **cry**[1].
eat like a horse eat a lot. (*informal*).
eat humble pie apologize; be humble; behave towards somebody as though he were more important than oneself. (*informal*).
eat one's words admit that what one has said is not correct. (*informal*).

eau de cologne ['oudəkə'loun] *nc/u* type of perfume.

eaves [i:vz] *npl* part of a roof which hangs out over a wall.
'**eavesdrop** *vi* (with **on**) listen secretly to a conversation between other people. *past* **eavesdropped. eavesdropper** *nc*. **eavesdropping** *nu*.

ebb [eb] *nc* (usu. only *sing*) 1. movement of the tide away from the land. 2. decline or failure of something: *the ebb of his fortunes.* Also *vi* 1. move away from the land. *The tide was ebbing.* 2. decline; become less strong. *His courage was ebbing.*

ebony ['ebəni] 1. *nu* very hard black wood. 2. *nc* the tree from which this wood comes. Also *adj* black in colour.

ebullient [i'buliənt] *adj* very lively by nature. *He is an ebullient person.* **ebullience** *nu*.

eccentric [ik'sentrik] *adj* 1. (with reference to people) odd, unusual; rather strange. 2. (with reference to circles or moving objects) not having the same centre; moving in a figure which is not exactly a circle. Also *nc* eccentric person; person who behaves unusually. **eccentrically** *adv*.
eccentricity [iksen'trisiti] *nc/u* unusual behaviour.

ecclesiastical [ikli:zi'æstikl] *adj* having reference to churches.
ecclesiastic *nc* Christian priest or minister.

echo ['ekou] *nc* 1. bouncing of sound waves off a surface, so that any sound is heard again. 2. any repetition of what has been said by somebody. *pl* **echoes.** Also *vt/i* 1. make an echo. *This room echoes* i.e. causes sound waves to bounce back. 2. be repeated in this way. *The sound echoed through the room.* 3. repeat what has been said. *He echoed my words.*
'**echo-sounding** method of measuring the depth of water and detecting submerged objects by use of echoes.

eclectic [i'klektik] *adj* not following any one method, system or belief, but taking what is the best from many methods etc.
eclecticism [i'klektisizəm] *nu*.

eclipse [i'klips] *nc* 1. cutting off of light coming from a body (e.g. the sun) to a second body (e.g. the earth) when a third body (e.g. the moon) moves in between: *a partial/complete eclipse; an eclipse of the sun* i.e. when the moon is between the sun and the earth; *an eclipse of the moon* i.e. when the earth is between the moon and the sun. 2. loss of reputation or fame. Also *vt* 1. cause an eclipse. 2. cause to lose fame. *The young poet eclipsed all the older writers.*

ecology [i'kɔlədʒi] *nu* science which deals with the relation between living things and the surroundings in which they live.
ecologist *nc* person who studies this science.

economy [i'kɔnəmi] 1. *nu* the condition of money, industry and employment in a country. *The economy of the country is in a bad condition.* 2. *nc* system of money, industry etc in a particular country. 3. *nc* something which enables one to spend less money. *Walking to work instead of driving one's car is an economy.*
economic [i:kə'nɔmik] *adj* 1. with reference to economy. 2. making a profit. *This is not an economic business.* (*opp* **uneconomic** in sense 2.).
economics [i:kə'nɔmiks] *nu* study of the system of money, industry, employment etc used in various countries.
Note: followed by a *sing* verb.
economical [i:kə'nɔmikl] *adj* enabling one

to spend less money; not wasteful. **economically** *adv*.
economist *nc* person who studies economics.
economize *vi* spend less money etc.
ecstasy ['ekstəsi] *nc/u* **1.** religious condition in which the soul seems to leave the body. **2.** very great happiness so that one seems to be changed in some way. **ecstatic** [ek'stætik] *adj*. **ecstatically** *adv*.
in ecstasies very happy. (*informal*).
ecumenical [iːkjuː'menikl] *adj* for or of the whole Christian church.
ecumenism *nu* movement to bring the various Christian churches together.
eczema ['eksimə] *nu* type of skin disease.
eddy ['edi] *nc* movement (usu. circular) of water, air, dust etc. Also *vi* move round or in a circular way.
edge [edʒ] *nc* **1.** sharp side of a knife etc. **2.** outer part of something; part not near the middle. *He stood at/on the edge of the field* i.e. near the fence, road, gate etc. Also **1.** *vt* put an edge on. **2.** *vt/i* move forward slowly and with difficulty through a crowd. *We edged forward. We edged our way through the crowd.*
edging *nu* border or edge: *put an edging on a piece of cloth.*
'edgeways, 'edgewise *adv* with the edge moving sideways first.
edge away move slowly away (often while pretending not to leave).
get a word in edgeways (usu. *negative*) manage to speak while having a conversation with somebody who talks very much. *I couldn't get a word in edgeways.* (*informal*).
have an/the edge on someone have an advantage over somebody; be better or luckier than somebody with whom one will compete. (*informal*).
on edge worried and unable to relax.
edible ['edibl] *adj* suitable for eating: *edible food.* (*opp* **inedible**).
edict ['iːdikt] *nc* official command by a king or other ruler.
edifice ['edifis] *nc* large building. (*formal*).
edify ['edifai] *vt* improve the mind or the knowledge of right and wrong. **edifying** *adj*. **edification** [edifi'keiʃən] *nu*.
edit ['edit] *vt* **1.** prepare the writings of somebody else for publication: *edit the works of Shakespeare.* **2.** be in charge of a newspaper, and decide what shall be printed in it. **editor** *nc*.
edition [i'diʃən] *nc* number of books, newspapers etc printed at the same time and all exactly the same.
editorial [edi'tɔːriəl] *adj* of editing. Also *nc* article written in a newspaper by the editor, in which he discusses some item of news.
educate ['edjukeit] *vt* teach (esp. at school).
education [edju'keiʃən] *nu* process of teaching; knowledge and learning possessed by a person. **educational** [edju'keiʃənl] *adj*. **educationally** *adv*.
educator *nc* person who teaches.
educationist [edju'keiʃənist] *nc* person who studies ways of educating people.
educable *adj* able to be taught. (*opp* **ineducable**).
educated *adj*. (*opp* **uneducated**).
Note: educate refers to teaching knowledge; for teaching good manners etc in the home use *bring up*. If a person has no manners, he may have been *badly brought up*.
eel [iːl] *nc* type of fish shaped like a snake.
eerie ['iəri] *adj* strange and making one feel afraid: *an eerie story about ghosts.* **eerily** *adv*. **eeriness** *nu*.
efface [i'feis] *vt* rub out or remove a stain or mark.
efface oneself remain quiet and in the background so that one is not noticed.
effect [i'fekt] **1.** *nc/u* result. *What effects did the war have? Punishment does not have any effect on him. This drug has a strong effect.* **2.** *nc* appearance of something. *I like the effect of your red curtains against your blue walls.* Also *vt* cause something to happen. *He effected several important changes.*
Note: see *affect*.
effects *npl* money and property owned by somebody.
effective **1.** having a result. (*opp* **ineffective**). **2.** very interesting and pleasant in appearance: *an effective combination of colours.* **3.** (with reference to the army etc) ready for war. **effectively** *adv*. **effectiveness** *nu*.
effectual [i'fektjuəl] *adj* having a result. (*opp* **ineffectual**). **effectually** *adv*.
'side effect *nc* (often *pl*) any result produced (usu. by a drug) in addition to the result which is wanted.
for effect in order to surprise, interest, worry etc other people. *He acts like that for effect.*
give effect to something put into practice; do something: *give effect to a decision.*
in effect in fact; really.
of no effect without any result. *The medicine is of no effect.*
come into effect/force see **come**.
take effect begin to have a result. *The medicine is taking effect.*
to the effect that with the following meaning.
effeminate [i'feminət] *adj* (with reference to a man) like a woman. **effeminately** *adv*.
effeminacy [i'feminəsi] *nu*.
effervesce [efə'ves] *vi* (with reference to a liquid) give off bubbles of gas.
effervescent *adj* **1.** giving off bubbles of gas. **2.** (with reference to a person) excitable and active. **effervescence** *nu*.
effete [i'fiːt] *adj* (with reference to people or communities in which people live) weak and of no use.
efficacious [efi'keiʃəs] *adj* having the result which is wanted: *an efficacious medicine.* **efficaciously** *adv*. **efficacy** ['efikəsi] *nu*.
efficient [i'fiʃənt] *adj* able to work well and give good results, without wasting time or effort. (*opp* **inefficient**). **efficiently** *adv*. **efficiency** *nu*.
effigy ['efidʒi] *nc* object of wood, stone etc made to look like a person.
effluent ['efluənt] *nc* stream of water flowing from river, sewage tank, factory, waste pipe etc. **effluence** *nu*.
effort ['efət] *nc/u* **1.** attempt (esp. one needing some mental or physical work). *I made an effort to read that book* i.e. I read or tried to read that book, although it was difficult. **2.** hard work. *He puts a lot of effort into his work* i.e. he works hard.
effortless *adj* (usu. with reference to something that other people would find difficult) done easily. **effortlessly** *adv*.
effrontery [i'frʌntəri] *nu* boldness in doing wrong; ability to do wrong without feeling afraid of what people will say or think. *The student had the effrontery to accuse the professor of being stupid.*

effusion [i'fju:ʒən] *nc* **1.** (esp. with reference to rather bad poetry) expression of strong feelings in speech or writing. **2.** pouring out of liquid.
effusive [i'fju:siv] *adj* expressing too much strong feeling. **effusively** *adv.* **effusiveness** *nu.*
egalitarian [igæli'tɛəriən] *adj* believing that all people should be equal. Also *nc* person who believes this. **egalitarianism** *nu.*
egg [eg] **1.** *nc* object produced by birds, insects, snakes, fish etc from which the young are born. **2.** *nc* such an object produced by a hen, used as food. **3.** *nu* piece of the content of a hen's egg when cooked.
'**eggcup** small cup to hold a boiled egg.
'**egghead** highly-educated person; person with a great knowledge of art, literature, science etc. (*informal*).
'**eggshell** covering of a bird's egg.
have/put all one's eggs in one basket make many different plans depend on the success of one thing. (*informal*).
egg someone on (to do something) persuade somebody to do something (usu. something wrong).
ego ['i:gou] *nc* the self; a person considered as an individual. *pl* **egos.**
egoist ['egouist] *nc* person who thinks only of himself and not of others. **egoism** ['egouizəm] *nu.*
egotist ['egətist] *nc* person who talks only about himself. **egotism** ['egətizəm] *nu.* **egotistic** [egə'tistik] *adj.*
eiderdown ['aidədaun] *nc* cover for a bed, filled with the down of the eider duck; similar cover filled with feathers, cotton etc.
eight [eit] see appendix.
either ['aiðə*] *determiner/pron/adv/conj* **1.** one out of two. *You can enter by either door. Either of the two boys can do it. I can't come, and my wife can't come either. I'm sure that either John or Peter has the book. Either you have made a mistake or we shall have to find more money.*
Note: if *either . . . or* joins two singular nouns, then a singular verb is used (e.g. *Either John or his uncle has the key*).
2. both. *There were trees on either side of the avenue.*
ejaculate [i'dʒækjuleit] *vt/i* **1.** say suddenly. **2.** send out (liquid, esp. sperm) from the body.
ejaculation [idʒækju'leiʃən] *nc* **1.** something said suddenly. **2.** sending out (liquid) from the body.
eject [i'dʒekt] *vt/i* **1.** throw out. **2.** make somebody leave a position which he holds.
eke [i:k] *vi* (with **out**) make something go further by adding something. *She eked out the soup with a little milk.*
eke out a living live in a poor way by doing work for which one gets very little money.
elaborate [i'læbərət] *adj* having many parts and many small details: *an elaborate story; an elaborate decoration.* Also [i'læbəreit] *vt/i* add many small details to; describe in detail. **elaborately** *adv.* **elaboration** [ilæbə'reiʃən] *nc/u.*
élan [e'lɑ̃] *nu* liveliness. *He did it with élan.*
elapse [i'læps] *vi* (with reference to time) pass.
elastic [i'læstik] *adj* **1.** made of or containing rubber; stretchable: *an elastic band.* **2.** able to bounce; able to regain the original shape after being pulled. **3.** able to be changed if necessary. *My plans are fairly elastic.* Also *nu* strips of rubber or cloth containing strips of rubber, used for fastening garments on the body etc.
elate [i'leit] *vt* (usu. *passive*) make very happy. *I was elated by the news.*
elation *nu* feeling of great happiness.
elbow ['elbou] *nc* joint of the arm between the two parts of the arm. Also *vt* push with one's elbow. *I elbowed him aside. I elbowed my way through the crowd.*
'**elbowroom** enough space to move easily. (*informal*).
elder[1] ['eldə*] *adj* (with reference to two people usu. in the same family) older; born earlier: *my elder brother.* Also *nc* **1.** senior person; old person. **2.** official in certain Christian churches. **elderly** ['eldəli] *adj.* **eldest** ['eldist] *adj* oldest.
elder statesman old politician who held some high office when he was younger and who is still consulted from time to time.
elder[2] ['eldə*] *nc* type of tree with white flowers and dark berries.
elect [i'lekt] *vt* **1.** choose somebody by voting. *They elected Tom Jones as their Member of Parliament.* **2.** choose. (*formal* in sense **2.**).
elector *nc* person having the right to vote.
electorate [i'lektərət] *nc* all the electors in a district or a country. **electoral** *adj.*
the elect *npl* people believed to have been chosen by God to go to heaven. (*formal*).
election *nc* process of choosing Members of Parliament or other representatives.
electioneering [ilekʃə'niəriŋ] *nu* process of persuading people to vote for a candidate in an election.
electricity [ilek'trisiti] *nu* form of energy which produces heat, light etc.
electrical [i'lektrikl] *adj.* **electrically** *adv.*
electric [i'lektrik] *adj* **1.** worked by or producing electricity: *electric light.* **2.** producing or caused by strong emotion.
electrician [elək'triʃən] *nc* person who installs and repairs electric devices.
electrify [i'lektrifai] *vt* **1.** charge with electricity. **2.** (with reference to railways) charge so as to enable trains powered by electricity to run on the lines. **3.** surprise; excite; produce a strong effect on somebody. *The news electrified us. past* **electrified.**
electrification [ilektrifi'keiʃən] *nu.*
electrocute [i'lektrəkju:t] *vt* kill by a charge of electricity. **electrocution** [ilektrə'kju:ʃən] *nc/u.*
electrode [i'lektroud] *nc* conductor by which electricity enters or leaves a battery, vacuum tube etc.
electrolysis [ilek'trɔlisis] *nu* process of separating a chemical compound into its elements by passing electricity through it. **electrolytic** [ilektrou'litik] *adj.*
electron [i'lektrɔn] *nc* particle of matter containing a charge of negative electricity.
electronics [elək'trɔniks] *n sing* study and use of complex electrical devices such as those in radio and TV sets. **electronic** *adj.*
electric blanket covering for a bed, which can be heated electrically in order to warm the bed.
electric chair chair in which a criminal sits to be killed by electricity (used in some states of America).
elegant ['eləgənt] *adj* **1.** graceful, fashionable. **2.** beautiful in appearance and well-made. **elegantly** *adv.* **elegance** *nu.*
elegy ['elədʒi] *nc* type of poem (esp. a poem written to show sorrow at the death of somebody). **elegiac** [eli'dʒaiik] *adj.*
element ['eləmənt] *nc* **1.** (chemistry) sub-

stance from which other substances are made. *Oxygen, hydrogen, copper etc are elements.* **2.** anything which goes to make up something else. **3.** fire, earth, water or air (from which it was once thought everything was made). **4.** small amount. *There is still an element of doubt* i.e. a small reason for doubting. **5.** (usu. with reference to politics) small group of people: *elements who are plotting against the government.* **6.** the heating part of an electrical domestic machine or device: *the element of an electric iron.*

elemental [elə'mentl] *adj* **1.** concerned with natural forces, such as wind, rain, earthquakes, floods etc. **2.** simple.

elementary [elə'mentəri] *adj* **1.** concerned with the early stages of learning: *an elementary school* i.e. one for young children. **2.** early; not developed; in a simple form. **3.** easy to understand.

the elements *npl* **1.** the weather (esp. wind, rain, storms etc). **2.** basic ideas or principles of any subject of study.

be in one's element be in a place or situation that one likes very much. (*informal*).

elephant ['elifənt] *nc* type of large animal as in the illustration.

elephantine [eli'fæntain] *adj* large and clumsy like an elephant.

elephantiasis [elifən'taiəsis] *nu* type of disease in which parts of the body become very large.

white elephant any useless and expensive object. (*informal*).

elephant

elevate ['eliveit] *vt* **1.** lift up high. (*formal*). **2.** make the mind or the soul better, more educated etc. **elevated** *adj.*

elevation [eli'veiʃən] **1.** *nc* height of hill etc. **2.** *nu* state of being made better in mind or soul. **3.** *nc* plan or drawing of a building as it is seen from the side. **4.** *nc/u* (esp. with reference to the process of making somebody a member of the House of Lords) promotion to a higher office.

elevator *nc* **1.** (*US*) machine for carrying goods and people up and down high buildings. (*Brit* **lift**). **2.** machine for lifting hay, corn etc for storage. **3.** the place where hay etc is stored in this way. **4.** movable flap on the tail of an aeroplane.

eleven [i'levən] see appendix.

at the eleventh hour see **hour.**

elf [elf] *nc* small magical creature shaped like a human being. *pl* **elves** [elvz]. **elfin** ['elfin] *adj.*

elicit [i'lisit] *vt* get information etc from somebody: *elicit information/an answer/the truth.*

elide [i'laid] *vt* leave out a vowel or a syllable in speech, as when e.g. we say *he's, shan't.* **elision** [i'liʒən] *nc/u.*

eligible ['elidʒibl] *adj* with the necessary qualifications, suitable. *Women are not eligible to be president of the club* i.e. the president must be a man. (*opp* **ineligible**). **eligibility** [elidʒi'biliti] *nu.*

eliminate [i'limineit] *vt* remove; get rid of: *eliminate a difficulty.* **elimination** [ilimi'neiʃən] *nu.*

elite, élite [i'li:t] *nc* select group of people, the richest, best educated, most powerful people in society.

elixir [i'liksiə*] *nc* **1.** substance supposed to change iron into gold, enable one to live longer etc. **2.** type of medicine.

elk [elk] *nc* the largest European and Asian deer with very big horns; a related North American deer.

ellipse [i'lips] *nc* shape as in the illustration.

ellipse

elliptical [i'liptikl] *adj* **1.** having the shape of an ellipse. **2.** (of a statement etc) made very short by missing out certain words.

elm [elm] **1.** *nc* tall tree found in cool northern regions. **2.** *nu* the wood of this tree.

elocution [elə'kju:ʃən] *nu* art of speaking well and clearly (esp. in public).

elocutionist *nc* person who teaches elocution.

elongate ['i:lɔŋgeit] *vt* make longer. **elongation** [i:lɔŋ'geiʃən] *nu.*

elope [i'loup] *vi* run away from one's parents in order to be married. *The young woman eloped with the man. They eloped.* **elopement** *nc/u.*

eloquent ['eləkwənt] *adj* able to speak well so as to persuade or influence other people. **eloquently** *adv.* **eloquence** *nu.*

else [els] *adj/adv* other; otherwise; different(ly): *somebody else* i.e. another person. *Who else was there? What else did he say? You must work hard, or else you will fail your examination* i.e. if you don't work hard, you will fail.

elsewhere *adv* to/in another place. *You had better try elsewhere.*

elucidate [i'lu:sideit] *vt/i* explain clearly something which is difficult to understand. **elucidation** [ilu:si'deiʃən] *nc/u.*

elude [i'lu:d] *vt* escape capture; escape from. **elusive** [i'lu:siv] *adj* difficult to catch or remember.

elves [elvz] *pl* of **elf.**

emaciated [i'meisieitid] *adj* thin because of illness or lack of food. **emaciation** [imeisi'eiʃən] *nu.*

emanate ['eməneit] *vi* come from some source. *This story emanates from you* i.e. you started this story. **emanation** [emə'neiʃən] *nc/u.*

emancipate [i'mænsipeit] *vt* set free (esp. a slave). **emancipation** [imænsi'peiʃən] *nu.* **emancipator** *nc* person who emancipates. **emancipated** *adj* freed from former restraints; unconventional.

emasculate [i'mæskjuleit] *vt* make weak by removing strength or power from. **emasculation** [imæskju'leiʃən] *nu.*

embalm [em'ba:m] *vt* treat a dead body with various substances to prevent it from decaying. **embalmer** *nc.*

embankment [em'bæŋkmənt] *nc* wall made of earth or stone to support a road which is higher than the surrounding land, or to prevent the land beside a river being flooded.

embargo [em'bɑːgou] *nc* official order forbidding trade. *The government placed an embargo on trade with enemy countries. pl* **embargoes.**

embark [em'bɑːk] *vt/i* **1.** go, cause to go, on a ship for a voyage. *We embarked.* **2.** start on a project. *The officer embarked the soldiers.* (*opp* **disembark**). **embarkation** [embɑː'keiʃən] *nu.*

embarrass [em'bærəs] *vt* make a person worried and uncertain what to do or say. *The small boy was embarrassed when he met the old lady.* **embarrassment** *nc/u.*

embassy ['embəsi] *nc* **1.** place where an ambassador works (and usu. lives) in a foreign country; the ambassador himself and his staff. **2.** duty of an ambassador or other representative.

embed, imbed [em'bed] *vt* fix into something very firmly. *The foundations of the bridge are embedded in concrete. past* **embedded.**

embellish [em'beliʃ] *vt* make more beautiful. **embellishment** *nc/u.*

ember ['embə*] *nc* (usu. *pl*) small piece of coal or wood burning with a red glow.

embezzle [em'bezl] *vt* steal money belonging to other people which has been placed in one's care. *The bank manager embezzled the money.* **embezzler** *nc.* **embezzlement** *nc/u.*

embitter [im'bitə*] *vt* make a person have feelings of anger and hate. *The failure of his plans embittered the old man.* **embittered** *adj.*

emblem ['embləm] *nc* drawing, sign or object which represents something. *A soldier has various emblems on his uniform to show the branch of the army he belongs to and his own rank and duties.* **emblematic** [emblə'mætik] *adj.*

embody [em'bɔdi] *vt* **1.** give form to an idea, plan, hope etc. **2.** include. **embodiment** *nc/u.*

embolden [em'bouldn] *vt* make brave or make confident.

embrace [em'breis] *vt/i* **1.** put one's arms round somebody as a sign of love. *He embraced her. They embraced.* **2.** accept an offer, idea, religion etc. **3.** include. *His course of study embraces History, Geography and Economics.* Also *nc* act of putting the arms round as a sign of love.

embroider [em'brɔidə*] **1.** *vt/i* sew a pattern or picture on to cloth. **2.** *vt* add details which are untrue. *He embroidered his story.*

embroidery *nc/u* art of sewing designs on to cloth; cloth which has been embroidered.

embroil [em'brɔil] *vt* cause to join in a quarrel.

embryo ['embriou] *nc* animal, bird etc in the stage of development before it is born. *pl* **embryos.**

embryonic [embri'ɔnik] *adj* **1.** of an embryo. **2.** in the first stage of development.

emend [i'mend] *vt* correct mistakes in something written. **emendation** [iːmen'deiʃən] *nc/u.*

emerald ['emərld] *nc/u* bright green precious stone; colour like this stone. Also *adj.*

emerge [i'məːdʒ] *vi* **1.** come into view. *He emerged from behind the tree.* **2.** become known. *The truth emerged at last.*

emergent *adj* (usu. with reference to the development of countries). **emergence** *nu.*

emergency [i'məːdʒənsi] *nc* unusual and dangerous situation in which one has to act quickly. *An outbreak of fire or an accident is an emergency.*

e'mergency 'exit door in a bus, aeroplane, theatre etc which can be used if there is a fire, accident etc.

emery ['emeri] *nu* in **emery paper** i.e. paper with a rough surface used for smoothing and polishing metal etc.

emetic [i'metik] *nc* substance which causes one to throw out of the stomach whatever has been swallowed. Also *adj.*

emigrate ['emigreit] *vi* go from one's own country to another country to live there.

emigrant ['emigrnt] *nc* person who does this.

emigration [emi'greiʃən] *nu* act of emigrating.

Note: an *emigrant* goes from his own country; an *immigrant* is a person who comes into a country.

emigré ['emigrei] *nc* (esp. with reference to those who left France after the French Revolution and those who left Russia after the revolution of 1917) person who has left his own country after a revolution.

eminent ['eminənt] *adj* **1.** (with reference to people) well-known and respected: *an eminent lawyer/scientist/general etc.* **2.** greater than usual: *eminent honesty/intelligence/ability etc.*

eminently *adv* to a high degree. *He is eminently suitable for the work.*

eminence **1.** *nu* quality of being eminent. **2.** *nc* piece of high land. **3.** *nc* title of a Roman Catholic cardinal.

emir [e'miə*] *nc* title of certain Muslim leaders.

emirate ['emiərit] *nc* land or position of an emir.

emissary ['emisəri] *nc* person who takes a message for somebody, or who goes on a journey in order to do something for the person who has sent him. (*formal*).

emit [i'mit] *vt* send out: *emit a sound/a smell/radiation/light etc. past* **emitted.**

emission [i'miʃən] *nc/u.*

emollient [i'mɔliənt] *adj* making smooth and soft. Also *nc* something which makes smooth and soft.

emolument [i'mɔljumənt] *nc* money received for doing some work. (*formal*).

emotion [i'mouʃən] *nc/u* feeling of the mind. *Anger, happiness, hate, anxiety are emotions.*

emotional *adj* of strong feelings; showing strong feelings. (*opp* **unemotional**). **emotionally** *adv.*

emotionalism *nu* showing of too much emotion.

empanel, impanel [im'pænl] *vt* put someone on a list of people who will serve on a jury. *past* **empanelled.** (*US* **empaneled**).

empathy ['empəθi] *nu* power of imagining oneself to be another person, and so of experiencing his feelings.

emperor ['empərə*] *nc* ruler of an empire.

emphasize ['emfəsaiz] *vt* call attention to something by making it especially noticeable in some way. *He emphasized his instructions to us* i.e. he made us listen carefully to his instructions. *He emphasized the word 'one'* i.e. he said this word slowly, loudly etc or he repeated it. *She emphasized her eyes by painting her eyelids* i.e. she made her eyes seem bigger and brighter in this way.

emphasis ['emfəsis] *nu* process of emphasizing something.

emphatic [em'fætik] *adj.* (*opp* **unemphatic**). **emphatically** *adv.*

empire ['empaiə*] **1.** *nc* number of countries

ruled by one person or one government. **2.** *nc* large country under one ruler. **3.** *nu* rule or authority over a country or several countries.

empirical [em'pirikl] *adj* based on experiment or experience, not on theory. **empirically** *adv.*

empiricism [em'pirisizəm] *nu* practice of working by empirical methods.

empiricist [em'pirisist] *nc* person who works empirically.

employ [em'plɔi] *vt* **1.** give work to. *He employs fifty men in his factory.* **2.** make use of. *He employed statistical methods in his work.*

employer *nc* person who gives work to others.

employee [emplɔi'i:] *nc* person who is employed.

employment *nu* **1.** process of employing or being employed. **2.** work done by somebody.

em'ployment agency private business firm which finds jobs for people.

em'ployment exchange government office where people can go to find out where they can get jobs. (*formal* – usu. **labour exchange**).

empower [em'pauə*] *vt* give somebody the power or authority to do something. *A policeman is empowered to arrest people who break the law.*

empress ['empris] *nc* **1.** wife of an emperor. **2.** woman who rules an empire.

empty ['empti] *adj* **1.** containing nothing: *an empty box.* **2.** meaning nothing: *an empty promise/threat* i.e. a promise or threat which will not be carried out. Also *vt/i* become or make empty. *The theatre emptied* i.e. the people left. *He emptied the box.* *past* **emptied. emptily** *adv.* **emptiness** *nu.*

'empty-'handed *adj* not carrying anything, not having gained anything.

'empty-'headed *adj* foolish or unintelligent. (*informal*).

emu ['i:mju:] *nc* large bird which cannot fly, found in Australia.

emulate ['emjuleit] *vt* try to do something as well as or better than somebody else; try to do the same as somebody else. *I tried to emulate his success.* **emulation** [emju'leiʃən] *nu.*

emulsion [e'mʌlʃən] *nc/u* **1.** (often with reference to a type of medicine) liquid with oil which has been broken into very small drops. **2.** substance covering photographic film which is sensitive to light. **3.** type of paint which is not shiny when it dries. (Also **emulsion paint**).

enable [i'neibl] *vt* make it possible for somebody to do something. *The money enabled me to take a holiday.*

enact [i'nækt] *vt* **1.** make a law. **2.** play a part on the stage, in a film etc. **enactment** *nc/u.*

enamel [i'næml] *nu* **1.** hard covering put on metal. **2.** type of hard paint which is shiny when it dries. (Also **enamel paint**). **3.** the hard covering of the teeth. **4.** object covered with enamel as a decoration. Also *vt* cover with enamel. *past* **enamelled.** (*US* **enameled**).

enamoured [i'næməd] *adj* liking very much (usu. **enamoured of something**). *I am not much enamoured of travelling.*

encampment [in'kæmpmənt] *nc* group of tents or other temporary dwellings (e.g. where soldiers or nomads are living for a short time).

encase [in'keis] *vt* surround by something. *The machine was encased in plastic.*

enchant [in'tʃɑ:nt] *vt* **1.** be very pleasant to somebody; be liked very much by somebody. *She enchanted all her friends. The beautiful house enchanted everyone who saw it.* **2.** work a magic spell on. *The wizard enchanted the princess.* **enchantment** *nu.*

enchanting *adj* very pleasant in this way. **enchantingly** *adv.*

enchantress [en'tʃɑ:ntris] *nc* woman who enchants.

encircle [in'sə:kl] *vt* form a circle round; surround. *The house is encircled by trees.*

enclave ['enkleiv] *nc* part of a country which is separated from the main part and completely surrounded by a foreign country.

enclose [in'klouz] *vt* **1.** put a wall etc around. *The house was enclosed by a high wall.* **2.** put something in an envelope etc in addition to something else. *He enclosed a letter with the book which he sent to me.*

enclosure [in'klouʒə*] **1.** *nc* space surrounded by a wall etc. **2.** *nc* something sent with a letter. **3.** *nu* act of enclosing.

encompass [in'kʌmpəs] *vt* surround on all sides. (rather *o.f.*).

encore ['ɔnkɔ:*] *nc* piece of music, song etc which is extra to the programme of a concert etc given because the audience has liked the concert very much. Also [ɔn'kɔ:*] *interj* call by the audience for an extra piece of music or song.

encounter [in'kauntə*] *vt* meet. *I encountered some difficulty in finishing the work.* Also *nc* **1.** meeting. **2.** battle or fight.

encourage [iŋ'kʌridʒ] *vt* give hope or confidence to. *My success encouraged me to continue. I encouraged him to buy the house* i.e. I told him that it would be a good idea for him to buy the house. (*opp* **discourage**).

encouraging *adj* giving hope or confidence. **encouragingly** *adv.* **encouragement** *nc/u.*

encroach [iŋ'kroutʃ] *vi* (with **on** or **upon**) go beyond the usual or proper limits. *He encroached upon my land* i.e. he used my land without permission. **encroachment** *nc/u.*

encumber [iŋ'kʌmbə*] *vt* prevent free and easy movement. *His heavy clothes encumbered him.*

encumbrance [iŋ'kʌmbrns] *nc* something which encumbers.

encyclopaedia, encyclopedia [ensaiklou'pi:diə] *nc* book or set of books containing information on all subjects or on one particular subject.

encyclopaedic *adj*: *an encyclopaedic memory* i.e. one containing a lot of information.

end [end] *nc* **1.** last part; furthest point: *the end of the year* i.e. December; *the end of the road* i.e. where the road stops; *the two ends of a piece of string.* **2.** aim or object. Also *vt/i* have, cause to have, an end. *The road ends five miles from here. He ended his story.*

endless *adj* without end. **endlessly** *adv.*

ending *nc* **1.** last part (esp. of a story). *This novel has a happy ending.* **2.** letters added to a word to change its grammatical use (e.g. -s, -ed, -ing).

'end 'product thing which is produced by some industrial or scientific process.

end up reach an end; finally come to somewhere. *He tried several different jobs, and he ended up as a lawyer. We walked through the forest for three hours and ended up where we had started.*

end one's days die (*o.f.*).

the ends of the earth very distant parts of the world.
in the end finally. *He bought the house in the end* i.e. after having doubts about whether to buy it, or after having difficulties in doing so.
the end justifies the means if a result is good, it does not matter if one uses bad methods to get that result.
at a loose end not having anything to do; not knowing how to pass the time. (*informal*).
a means to an end something used in order to get a result which one wants.
on end 1. resting or standing on one end, instead of in the usual position. *He put the table on end* i.e. resting on two legs and the end of the top, instead of on its four legs. 2. without stopping or without an interval: *for six weeks on end; for days on end* i.e. for many days.
put an end to stop, finish.
at the end of one's tether very worried or troubled, and not knowing what to do. (*informal*).

endanger [en'deindʒə*] *vt* put in danger; make it possible that harm or damage will be caused. *He endangered our lives by setting fire to the house. He endangered his chances of success* i.e. he made it possible that he would not succeed.

endear [en'diə*] *vt* usu. **endear oneself** i.e. cause other people to like oneself. *He endeared himself to the old lady.*
endearing *adj* causing people to like one.
endearingly *adv.*
endearment 1. *nu* act of showing love or liking. 2. *nc* action or words showing love or liking.

endeavour [en'devə*] *vt* try very hard. *He endeavoured to finish the work.* Also *nc* act of trying.

endemic [en'demik] *adj* (with reference to disease) always present in an area.

endorse, indorse [in'dɔːs] *vt* 1. support. *I endorsed his plan* i.e. I said that I liked the plan. 2. (with reference to a cheque or other document) write one's name on the back of a document, to show that one accepts the document as genuine. **endorsement** *nc/u.*
endorse someone's (driving) licence note a motoring offence on someone's licence.

endow [en'dau] *vt* give money to a college, school, library, museum etc.
endowment 1. *nu* act of endowing. 2. *nc* money given in this way.
be endowed with something have some good quality. *He is well endowed with intelligence* i.e. he is very intelligent.

endure [en'djuə*] *vt/i* 1. suffer pain bravely. *He endured great pain in hospital.* 2. last, continue to exist. *Their hopes endured for many years* i.e. they continued to hope for many years. **endurance** *nu.*
enduring *adj* lasting a long time.
endurable *adj* able to be endured (in sense 1.) (*opp* **unendurable**).
beyond/past endurance more than can be endured. *He suffered beyond endurance.*

enema ['enəmə] *nc* an injection of liquid into the bowels for medical reasons; an instrument for doing this.

enemy ['enəmi] *nc* 1. person, country etc that one hates and which one fights against. 2. anything which is harmful or damaging.
the enemy *n sing* or *pl* country which one is fighting against; the soldiers of that country.

energy ['enədʒi] 1. *nu* ability to work, play etc hard. *He had no energy and he could not finish the work.* 2. *nu* power from gas, coal, oil, electricity etc. 3. *nu* (physics) capacity for doing work. 4. *nc* strength and ability: *devote one's energies to something.*
energetic [enə'dʒetik] *adj.* **energetically** *adv.*

enervate ['enəːveit] *vt* make weak and useless. **enervating** *adj.* **enervation** [enəː'veiʃən] *nu.*

enfeeble [en'fiːbl] *vt* make weak. **enfeebling** *adj.* **enfeeblement** *nu.*

enfold [en'fould] *vt* hold tightly; cover lightly.

enforce [en'fɔːs] *vt* 1. cause a law to be carried out. *The police enforce the law.* 2. make somebody do something etc by force: *enforce something on someone.* **enforcement** *nu.*

enfranchise [in'fræntʃaiz] *vt* 1. give the right to vote in elections for parliament. 2. set slaves free. (*opp* **disenfranchise**).
enfranchisement [in'fræntʃizmənt] *nu.*

engage [en'geidʒ] 1. *vt* allow somebody to begin to work for one. *I engaged a new servant.* 2. *vt* reserve something before one wishes to use it. *I have engaged a room for the party next week.* 3. *vi* promise. *I engaged to lend him some money.* 4. *vt* keep one's interest or attention. *The book engaged my attention for the rest of the day* i.e. I was very interested in the book. 5. *vi* (with reference to moving parts of a machine) move and fit together. *The two wheels engaged.* 6. *vt* begin fighting. *We engaged the enemy.*
engaged *adj* 1. having promised to marry somebody. *John and Jill are engaged; the engaged couple.* 2. talking to somebody as part of one's work. *The headmaster is engaged at the moment.* 3. (with reference to a telephone) connected to another telephone. *I phoned John last night but the number was engaged* i.e. he was already phoning somebody else. 4. (with reference to a toilet etc) being used.
engagement *nc* 1. promise (esp. a promise to marry). 2. battle.
engaging *adj* pleasant and attractive: *a very engaging young woman.* **engagingly** *adv.*
be engaged in something be busy doing something. *He was engaged in painting his house.*

engender [en'dʒendə*] *vt* cause or produce. *Dirt engenders disease. The meeting engendered several quarrels.*

engine ['endʒin] *nc* 1. machine for producing power (esp. one which works a motorcar or which pulls a train).
engineer [endʒi'niə*] *nc* 1. person who works with engines or on the building of bridges, ships, roads, machines etc. 2. man in charge of the engines of a ship. 3. (*US*) person who drives a train. (*Brit* **engine driver**). Also *vt* carry out a clever plan. *A small group of politicians engineered the defeat of the government.*
engineering [endʒi'niəriŋ] *nu* the making of bridges, ships, roads, machines etc.

engrave [en'greiv] *vt* cut words, a pattern or a drawing into metal or stone. *He engraved my name on the silver plate. He engraved the silver plate with my name.*
engraving 1. *nu* the art of engraving. 2. *nc* picture printed from an engraved piece of metal.

engross [en'grous] *vt* (often *passive*) occupy, hold somebody's attention or interest completely. *He was engrossed in a book.* **engrossing** *adj.*

engulf [en'gʌlf] *vt* swallow up; cover completely and destroy. *The little boat was engulfed by the waves.*

enhance [en'hɑːns] *vt* add to the value or beauty of.

enigma [e'nigmə] *nc* **1.** statement or question that is intended to be difficult to understand. **2.** anything or anybody that is difficult to understand. **enigmatic** [enig'mætik] *adj.*

enjoin [en'dʒɔin] *vt* give an order to somebody. (*formal*).

enjoy [en'dʒɔi] *vt* **1.** be happy because of something. *He enjoyed the film.* **2.** be fortunate in having something. *He enjoys good health.*
enjoyable *adj* pleasant; making one happy. **enjoyably** *adv.* **enjoyment** *nc/u.*
enjoy oneself be happy doing something.

enlarge [en'lɑːdʒ] *vt/i* (often with reference to printing larger photographs from negatives) become or make larger or bigger. **enlargement** *nc/u.*
enlarge on/upon something say more about something; go into greater detail about something.

enlighten [en'laitn] *vt* give more knowledge or help in understanding.
enlightened *adj* intelligent and not following untrue ideas. (*opp* **unenlightened**).
enlightenment *nu* **1.** state of being enlightened. **2.** period in history when people are enlightened.

enlist [en'list] **1.** *vt/i* join, cause to join, the army, navy etc. *He enlisted in the army. The government enlisted him.* **2.** *vt* get help or support. **enlistment** *nc/u.*
enlisted man (mainly *US*) soldier who is not an officer.

enliven [en'laivən] *vt* make more lively, active or cheerful. **enlivening** *adj.*

en masse [ɑ̃'mæs] *adv* all together; in one group.

enmesh [en'meʃ] *vt* (often *passive*) catch in a net; catch in a scheme or plot.

enmity ['enmiti] *nu* **1.** condition of being an enemy. **2.** feeling of hate or dislike felt towards each other by enemies.

ennoble [i'noubl] *vt* **1.** make a nobleman; make into a lord. **2.** make better, or more dignified, in behaviour or reputation.

enormity [i'nɔːmiti] **1.** *nc* very great and wicked crime. **2.** *nu* great wickedness.

enormous [i'nɔːməs] *adj* very big. **enormously** *adv.*

enough [e'nʌf] *determiner/adj/adv/pron* as much or as many as wanted. *I haven't enough money to buy a new car* i.e. I need more money. *Have you got enough time to finish it/time enough to finish it? He didn't work hard enough and so he failed the examination. Have you got enough or do you want some more?*

enquire [en'kwaiə*] *vt/i* see **inquire.**

enrage [en'reidʒ] *vt* make very angry.

enrapture [en'ræptʃə*] *vt* make very happy. **enraptured** *adj.*

enrich [en'ritʃ] *vt* **1.** make richer. **2.** make more valuable. **enrichment** *nc/u.*

enrol [en'roul] *vt/i* have one's name written on a list, or write somebody's name on a list. *I enrolled at the college* i.e. I became a student at the college. *He enrolled me at the college. past* **enrolled. enrolment** *nc/u.*

en route [ɑ̃'ruːt] *adv* on the way. *He was en route for Oxford.*

ensconce [in'skɔns] *vt* (usu. *passive*) put in a comfortable position.

ensemble [ɔn'sɔmbl] *nc* **1.** general effect of something. **2.** part of a piece of music where everyone plays together. **3.** group of musicians (usu. a small group) who play or sing together. **4.** outfit of clothes in which all the garments match one another.

enshrine [en'ʃrain] *vt* keep in a special place as something holy or valuable. *The memory is enshrined in my heart.*

ensign ['ensain] *nc* **1.** flag (esp. on a ship). **2.** officer of the lowest rank in the US navy. **3.** formerly, officer of the lowest rank in the British army.

enslave [en'sleiv] *vt* make a slave of. **enslavement** *nu.*

ensnare [en'snɛə*] *vt* catch in a trap, or as if in a trap.

ensue [en'sjuː] *vi* happen as a result. *What ensued from your conversation with John?* **ensuing** *adj.*

ensure [in'ʃuə*] *vt* make sure or certain. *I tried to ensure that everybody understood the instructions.*

entail[1] [en'teil] *vt* make necessary as a result. *He bought a bigger house and this entailed buying more furniture.*

entail[2] [en'teil] *nc* (in a legal sense) arrangement by which land and property must pass to a certain person after the death of the owner, so that the owner cannot sell the land or give it away.

entangle [en'tæŋgl] *vt* (often *passive*) **1.** catch in something so that movement is difficult. *I was entangled in the bushes.* **2.** put into difficulties. *He was entangled in a lawsuit.* **entanglement** *nc/u.*

enter ['entə*] **1.** *vt/i* come or go into. *He entered the house.* **2.** *vt* become or cause to take part in something. *He entered the school. The teacher entered the boy for the examination.* **3.** *vt* put down in written form in a book, list etc. *He entered all his expenses in a notebook.* see **entrance**[1], **entrant** and **entry.**
enter into something 1. be part of something or join in something. *He entered into a discussion with us.* **2.** talk about something. *He entered into an explanation.*
enter upon something begin something.
enter one's mind (usu. *negative*) think of something. *It never entered my mind that he could be a thief.* (*informal*).

enterprise ['entəpraiz] **1.** *nu* ability to think of new plans and to carry them out. **2.** *nc* (often business) new plan or arrangement. **enterprising** *adj* showing enterprise. (*opp* **unenterprising**). **enterprisingly** *adv.*

entertain [entə'tein] **1.** *vt* interest and amuse. *He entertained us by singing songs.* **2.** *vt/i* act as a host; give food and drink to guests. *We entertained him to dinner. We do not entertain very much* i.e. we do not invite people to eat with us. **3.** *vt* (with reference to a plan, idea, suggestion, arrangement etc) accept or consider.
entertaining *adj* interesting and amusing. **entertainingly** *adv.* **entertainment** *nc/u.*

enthrall [en'θrɔːl] *vt* be very interesting and hold one's attention completely. *His stories enthralled the children.* **enthralling** *adj.*

enthrone [en'θroun] *vt* place on a throne in a special ceremony.

enthusiasm [in'θjuːziæzəm] *nu* feeling of strong interest and support. *The Prime Minister's supporters were filled with en-*

thusiasm.

enthusiastic [inθju:zi'æstik] *adj.* (*opp* **unenthusiastic**). **enthusiastically** *adv.*

enthusiast *nc* person who feels enthusiasm.

enthuse *vi* (usu. with **over**) be enthusiastic about.

entice [in'tais] *vt* persuade to go to/from something or to do something bad. *He enticed the dog into the house by offering it some meat. He enticed her into breaking her promise.* **enticement** *nc/u.*

entire [en'taiə*] *adj* complete or whole. *He spent the entire day in his room* i.e. he did not leave his room during the day. **entirely** *adv.*

entirety *nu* condition of being whole or entire: *in its entirety.*

entitle [en'taitl] *vt* **1.** give somebody a right to something. *Every child in Britain is entitled to free education at school.* **2.** give a title to a book or other piece of writing. **entitlement** *nu.*

entity ['entiti] *nc* anything which exists.

entomb [en'tu:m] *vt* bury or put in a tomb. (*formal*).

entomology [entə'mɔlədʒi] *nu* the study of insects.

entomologist *nc* person who studies insects.

entourage [ɔntu'rɑ:ʒ] *nc* people who accompany some important person.

entrails ['entreilz] *npl* bowels and intestines; the contents of the lower part of the body.

entrance[1] ['entrns] **1.** *nc/u* act of coming in. **2.** *nc* place where one comes in. **3.** *nc/u* act of becoming a member of something. see **enter.**

entrance[2] [en'trɑ:ns] *vt* fill with very great pleasure. **entrancing** *adj.* **entrancingly** *adv.*

entrant ['entrnt] *nc* person wishing to take part in or begin an examination, a race, the army, a job etc. see **enter.**

entreat [en'tri:t] *vt* ask with great feeling, beg. *She entreated her son not to steal the money.*

entreaty *nc/u* act of entreating.

entrench [en'trentʃ] *vt* (often *passive*) **1.** protect or defend by digging trenches. *The enemy troops were entrenched outside the town.* **2.** firmly establish. *The idea is entrenched in his mind.* **entrenchment** *nc/u.*

entrust [in'trʌst] *vt* give something to somebody to be cared for. *I entrusted him with my money. I entrusted my money to him.*

entry ['entri] **1.** *nc* act of coming in. *He made an entry into the room.* **2.** *nc* place where one enters. **3.** *nu* act of becoming a member of something. *He applied for entry to the university.* **4.** *nc* something written down in a book, list etc. *He made an entry in his notebook.* see **enter.**

entwine [in'twain] *vt* twist or curl one thing around another.

enumerate [i'nju:məreit] *vt* **1.** count. **2.** name the items on a list. **enumeration** [inju:mə'reiʃən] *nc/u.*

enunciate [i'nʌnsieit] *vt/i* **1.** speak clearly. **2.** explain an idea clearly. **enunciation** [inʌnsi'eiʃən] *nc/u.*

envelop [en'veləp] *vt* surround or cover completely. *Smoke from the burning house enveloped the whole street.*

envelope ['envəloup] *nc* **1.** paper cover for a letter. **2.** any form of covering.

envious ['enviəs] *adj* see **envy.**

environment [in'vaiərnmənt] *nc* surroundings, people, way of life, circumstances etc in which a person lives. **environmental** [invaiərn'mentl] *adj.*

envisage [in'vizidʒ] *vt* see a picture of something in the mind; think possible. *I can't envisage him doing such a terrible thing.*

envoy ['envɔi] *nc* **1.** person carrying a special message. **2.** person representing his government in a foreign country.

envy ['envi] *nu* feeling of unhappiness because somebody is luckier or better than oneself. Also *vt* feel envy. *I envy him.*

envious *adj* feeling envy. **enviously** *adv.*

enviable *adj* causing envy.

enzyme ['enzaim] *nc* chemical substance in living things, which produces changes in other substances without being changed itself.

epaulette ['epəlet] *nc* decoration worn on the shoulder of certain uniforms.

epaulette

ephemeral [i'femərl] *adj* lasting a very short time.

epic ['epik] *nc* long poem about the acts of heroes or gods. Also *adj.*

epicure ['epikjuə*] *nc* person who takes great pleasure in eating and drinking, and who understands the art of cookery.

epicurean [epikju'riən] *adj.*

epidemic [epi'demik] *nc* disease which affects many people at one time. Also *adj.*

epigram ['epigræm] *nc* short clever and usu. amusing statement or poem.

epigrammatic [epigrə'mætik] *adj.*

epilepsy ['epilepsi] *nu* disease in which a person sometimes loses consciousness and his body moves violently.

epileptic [epi'leptik] *nc* person suffering from this disease. Also *adj.*

epilogue ['epilɔg] *nc* part of a poem, play, book etc added after the end.

episcopal [i'piskəpl] *adj* of a bishop.

episcopalian [ipiskə'peiliən] *adj* of a church which has bishops. Also *nc* member of such a church.

episode ['episoud] *nc* **1.** one part of a story (esp. a story told over several weeks on radio or television). **2.** one event out of a series of events.

episodic [epi'sɔdik] *adj* happening in episodes.

epistle [i'pisl] *nc* letter (*o.f.* – esp. with reference to the letters written by the Apostles of Christ in the New Testament).

epitaph ['epitɑ:f] *nc* words about a dead person (esp. words written on the stone above his grave).

epithet ['epiθet] *nc* adjective which describes a person, place or thing.

epitome [i'pitəmi] *nc* **1.** short summary of a longer piece of writing or speech. **2.** a part which has all the qualities of the whole.

epitomize [i'pitəmaiz] *vt* make or be an epitome of something.

epoch ['i:pɔk] *nc* **1.** an important period of history. **2.** beginning of a period of history.

'epoch-making *adj* causing important changes: *an epoch-making discovery.*

equable ['ekwəbl] *adj* pleasant and not changing much: *an equable person/climate.* **equably** *adv.*

equal ['i:kwl] *adj* the same. *Two and two is equal to four. These two things are not equal* i.e. one is bigger than the other. (*opp* **unequal**). Also *vt* be equal to; be as good as. *Two and two equals four. past* **equalled.** (*US* **equaled**). Also *nc* something which is equal to something else. *He is my equal* i.e. he is as strong, clever, rich etc as I am. **equally** *adv.*

equality [i'kwɔliti] *nu.* (*opp* **inequality**).

equalize *vt* make equal.

equalization [i:kwəlai'zeiʃən] *nu* process of equalizing.

equal to doing something strong, clever etc enough to do something. *My grandfather is not equal to walking long distances these days.*

equanimity [ekwə'nimiti] *nu* condition of not having strong feelings of fear or anger. *He faced the danger with equanimity.*

equate [i'kweit] *vt* consider of the same importance or value. *She equates cruelty to animals with cruelty to people.*

equation [i'kweiʒən] *nc* (mathematics) an expression in which two quantities are said to be equal.

equator [i'kweitə*] *nc* an imaginary line drawn round the earth, at an equal distance from north and south.

equatorial [ekwə'tɔ:riəl] *adj* of conditions near or at the equator: *an equatorial forest.*

equestrian [i'kwestriən] *adj* of riding on horses. Also *nc* person who rides horses.

equi- ['i:kwi] *prefix* equal (e.g. **equilateral**).

equidistant [i:kwi'distnt] *adj* at the same distance from two or more things.

equilateral ['i:kwi'lætərl] *adj* (geometry) having sides of the same length.

equilibrium [i:kwi'libriəm] *nu* state of balance, mental or physical: *lose one's equilibrium* i.e. fall over or become mentally disturbed.

equine ['ekwain] *adj* of horses.

equinox ['i:kwinɔks] *nc* one of the two times in the year when the sun seems to cross the equator and when all over the world night and day are each 12 hours long. **equinoctial** [i:kwi'nɔkʃl] *adj.*

equip [i'kwip] *vt* supply what is needed for some action (e.g. fighting, climbing etc). *The government equipped the soldiers with new guns. past* **equipped.**

equipment *nu* things needed to do something. *His firm supplies kitchen equipment.*

equity ['ekwiti] *nu* **1.** fairness; process of not treating somebody better than somebody else. **2.** (in a legal sense) methods of understanding the laws so as to treat people fairly, or so as to give people what they ought to have. **equitable** *adj.* **equitably** *adv.*

equities *npl* ordinary shares.

equivalent [i'kwivəlnt] *adj* having the same value or meaning. *His behaviour was equivalent to treason.* **equivalence** *nu.*

equivocate [i'kwivəkeit] *vi* use language which can have more than one meaning, in order to deceive people.

equivocation [ikwivə'keiʃən] *nc/u* act of equivocating. **equivocal** *adj.* **equivocally** *adv.*

era ['iərə] *nc* period of time in history (usu. named by some happening or person): *the Victorian era* i.e. in the reign of Queen Victoria.

eradicate [i'rædikeit] *vt* destroy, remove completely; tear out by the roots: *eradicate a bad habit.* **eradication** [irædi'keiʃən] *nu.*

erase [i'reiz] *vt* rub out or remove. *Pencil marks can be erased with a piece of rubber. He tried to erase the idea from his mind.*

eraser *nc* piece of rubber etc used to erase writing etc.

erasure [i'reiʒə*] **1.** *nu* process of erasing. **2.** *nc* something erased or place where something has been erased.

erect [i'rekt] *adj* standing up straight; not bending. Also *vt* build; put up: *erect a building.* **erectly** *adv.* **erection** *nc/u.*

ermine ['ə:min] *nc* small animal like a weasel which has white fur in the winter. see also **stoat.**

erode [i'roud] *vt* wear away; destroy by taking away small pieces. *The sea erodes the rocks.* **erosion** [e'rouʒən] *nu.*

erotic [i'rɔtik] *adj* of sexual love. **erotically** *adv.* **eroticism** [e'rɔtisizəm] *nu.*

err [ə:*] *vi* be wrong; do something wrong.

errand ['ernd] *nc* **1.** journey to a shop to buy something. **2.** any short journey to get something.

'errand boy boy employed by a shop to take goods to people's houses.

erratic [i'rætik] *adj* not regular; not always behaving in the same way, and changing without good reason. **erratically** *adv.*

erratum [e'rɑ:təm] *nc* mistake in the printing of a book etc (esp. a mistake which is noted in a list). *pl* **errata** [e'rɑ:tə].

error ['erə*] *nc/u* mistake; something which is wrong. *He made some errors in his essay.*

erroneous [e'rouniəs] *adj* mistaken; wrong: *an erroneous belief.* **erroneously** *adv.*

in error wrong by accident.

erudite ['erjudait] *adj* showing or having great learning: *an erudite professor.*

erudition [erju'diʃən] *nu* great knowledge.

erupt [i'rʌpt] *vi* burst out suddenly. *The volcano erupted.* **eruption** *nc/u.*

escalate ['eskəleit] *vt/i* grow bigger by stages; become or make more serious or more dangerous. *The war has escalated.*

escalation [eskə'leiʃən] *nu.*

escalator ['eskəleitə*] *nc* staircase which moves up or down on an endless belt.

escapade [eskə'peid] *nc* an exciting and rather foolish adventure (e.g. one carried out by young boys).

escape [is'keip] *vt/i* **1.** get free from or remain free from. *The prisoners escaped. He escaped capture. He escaped from prison. The gas was escaping from the pipe.* **2.** be unknown or unnoticed. *He escaped notice* i.e. nobody saw him. *The word escapes me* i.e. I cannot remember the word. Also *nc/u*: *He made an escape. Escape was difficult. There was an escape of gas.*

escapism *nu* process of trying to escape from difficulties and dangers in life.

escapist *nc* person who does this.

'fire escape see **fire**[2].

a narrow escape an escape with little to spare. *He had a narrow escape from being drowned* i.e. he was nearly drowned.

escarpment [is'kɑ:pmənt] *nc* (usu. with reference to geology) steep slope.

eschew [is'tʃu:] *vt* stay away from; do without; avoid (*o.f.*).

escort [is'kɔ:t] *vt* go with somebody/something as a guard or protector. *The soldiers escorted the old man to safety.* Also ['eskɔ:t] *nc* person/persons (often in ships, cars, aeroplanes etc) going with somebody/something as a guard or companion.

escutcheon [is'kʌtʃən] *nc* shield with the sign of an important family painted on it.
esoteric [esə'terik] *adj* understood only by a few people; secret. **esoterically** *adv*.
especial [es'peʃl] *adj* special; more important than others.
especially *adv* most of all; particularly. *I like all of Dickens' novels but especially 'Bleak House'* i.e. this is the one I like best.
espionage ['espiənɑ:ʒ] *nu* process of trying to find out the secrets of a foreign country, in order to help one's own country.
'counter-'espionage the work of trying to prevent people from finding out the secrets of one's own country.
esplanade [esplə'neid] *nc* level open space where people can walk (usu. beside the sea or in front of a castle).
espouse [is'pauz] *vt* **1.** support a cause, movement, religion etc. **2.** marry a woman (*o.f.* in sense **2.**).
esquire [es'kwaiə*] **1.** *nc* (in former times) rank in society below a knight (*o.f.*). **2.** title written after a man's name in addressing letters etc, written Esq. (e.g. *J. L. Smith, Esq.*).
Note: Esq. is rather formal. It is not used in America, or with any other title.
essay[1] ['esei] *nc* **1.** short piece of writing on one subject. **2.** attempt (*o.f.* in sense **2.**).
essayist *nc* person who writes essays.
essay[2] [e'sei] *vt/i* try or attempt. (rather *o.f.*).
essence ['esns] *nc* **1.** something obtained from a substance by removing everything which is unnecessary. **2.** the central or most important part of anything. *Freedom of speech is the essence of democracy.*
essential [i'senʃl] *adj* **1.** very important and necessary. *It is essential to have enough money.* **2.** of an essence: *an essential oil.* Also *nc* something which is essential. **essentially** *adv*.
establish [es'tæbliʃ] *vt* **1.** organize; begin; set up. *He established a new shop. He has established himself in his new house* i.e. he has arranged his furniture and made everything comfortable. **2.** prove; show something to be true. *The police are trying to establish the facts.*
establishment 1. *nu* process of establishing. **2.** *nc* anything established (esp. a house, shop, factory etc).
the establishment group of important people who are believed to have great influence on public life (esp. in Britain).
estate [es'teit] *nc* **1.** large area of land belonging to a person. **2.** (legal) a person's property. **3.** (esp. with reference to the history of France) group of people of the same rank in society. **4.** stage of life of a person (usu. in **to reach man's estate** i.e. become a man).
es'tate agent person who arranges the buying and selling of houses and land.
'real estate (in a legal sense) land and the buildings etc on it.
esteem [es'ti:m] *nu* feeling that somebody is very good and deserves to be praised. *They hold him in high esteem.* Also *vt* have this feeling about somebody, consider.
estimable ['estiməbl] *adj* deserving esteem.
estimate ['estimeit] *vt/i* judge a size, amount, quantity etc without measuring or weighing. Also *nc* **1.** judgement or guess made in this way. **2.** statement of how much some work or service will probably cost, made by the person who will do the work. (The actual cost may be more or less than the estimate).
estimation [esti'meiʃən] **1.** *nc* estimate. **2.** *nu* feeling that somebody is very good: *a high estimation for him.* **3.** *nu* judgement or opinion. *In my estimation, we shall not be successful* i.e. I do not think we shall be successful.
estrange [is'treindʒ] *vt* (often *passive*) make an enemy or stranger of somebody. *His friends had become estranged from him* i.e. they were no longer his friends. **estrangement** *nc/u*.
estuary ['estjuəri] *nc* part of a river reached by tides.
et cetera [it'setrə] (usu. written **etc**) and other things.
etch [etʃ] *vt/i* make pictures or a design by cutting a metal plate with a sharp tool dipped in acid. The plate is then used to print pictures using ink.
etching 1. *nc* picture made in this way. **2.** *nu* the art of making pictures in this way.
eternal [i'tə:nl] *adj* lasting for ever; having no beginning and no end. **eternally** *adv*.
eternity [i'tə:niti] *nc/u*.
ether ['i:θə*] *nu* **1.** liquid which causes one to become unconscious when its vapour is breathed in. **2.** substance formerly believed to be present in all space, through which light waves travelled.
ethereal [i'θiəriəl] *adj* light and delicate; seeming to come from heaven: *ethereal beauty.*
ethics ['eθiks] *n sing* or *pl* study or knowledge of what is right and wrong; ideas and beliefs about the right or good way to behave.
ethical *adj* **1.** concerned with the study of ethics. **2.** good, correct in thought or behaviour. (*opp* **unethical** in sense **2.**). **ethically** *adv*.
ethnic ['eθnik] *adj* with reference to a race or nation. *There are many ethnic groups in New York* i.e. there are Italians, Poles, Irishmen, Swedes etc. **ethnically** *adv*.
ethnology [eθ'nɔlədʒi] *nu* science dealing with races of people.
ethnologist [eθ'nɔlədʒist] *nc* person who studies this science.
ethos ['i:θɔs] *n* (usu. only *sing*) set of ideas, feelings, characteristics etc of a group of people.
etiquette ['etiket] *nu* **1.** ideas about what is polite; polite behaviour. **2.** behaviour which is accepted as correct by members of a profession. *In Britain, etiquette does not allow doctors and lawyers to advertise.*
etymology [eti'mɔlədʒi] *nu* study of the history of words. **etymological** [etimə'lɔdʒikl] *adj*.
etymologist *nc* person who studies etymology.
eucalyptus [ju:kə'liptəs] **1.** *nc* type of evergreen tree. **2.** *nu* oil obtained from this tree, used in making some medicines.
Eucharist ['ju:kərist] *nc/u* ceremony of taking bread and wine in memory of the death of Christ; the bread and wine itself.
eugenics [ju:'dʒeniks] *n sing* science which tries to improve the human race by choosing parents who are likely to produce strong and intelligent children.
Note: followed by a *sing* verb.
eulogy ['ju:lədʒi] *nc* speech or piece of writing in praise of somebody/something. *pl* **eulogies**.
eulogist *nc* person who makes a eulogy.

eulogize *vt* make a eulogy.
eunuch ['juːnək] *nc* man or boy who has been castrated i.e. had part of his sexual organs removed.
euphemism ['juːfəmizəm] *nc/u* practice of using a more pleasant word or expression for an unpleasant idea (e.g. *pass away* is a euphemism for *die*). **euphemistic** [juːfə'mistik] *adj*.
euphony ['juːfəni] *nu* pleasant sound. **euphonious** [juː'founiəs] *adj*.
euphoria [juː'fɔːriə] *nu* state of feeling great happiness. **euphoric** [juː'fɔrik] *adj*.
euthanasia [juːθə'neiziə] *nu* painless killing of somebody who has an incurable disease or who is very old.
evacuate [i'vækjueit] *vt* send away or send out; leave, withdraw from. *During the war, many people were evacuated from the city* i.e. sent to live out of the city. *The troops evacuated the town.* **evacuation** [ivækju'eiʃən] *nc/u*.
evacuee [ivækju'iː] *nc* person who has been evacuated during a war.
evade [i'veid] *vt* escape; get away from or keep away from. *The thief evaded the policeman who was chasing him. He tried to evade his duties.* **evasion** [i'veiʒən] *nc/u*.
evasive [i'veisiv] *adj* trying to evade something. *He gave an evasive answer* i.e. he tried to avoid telling the truth. **evasively** *adv*.
evaluate [i'væljueit] *vt* decide the value of something. **evaluation** [ivælju'eiʃən] *nu*.
evangelist [i'vændʒəlist] *nc* **1.** one of the writers of the Gospels in the Bible i.e. Matthew, Mark, Luke, John. **2.** person who teaches a type of Protestant Christianity in which the most important belief is faith. **3.** person who teaches any faith or belief.
evangelical [iːvæn'dʒelikl] *adj*. Also *nc* person who belongs to an evangelical church.
evaporate [i'væpəreit] **1.** *vt/i* (with reference to a liquid) change, cause to change, into vapour. **2.** *vt* disappear; have no results. *His plans/hopes etc have evaporated.*
evaporation [ivæpə'reiʃən] *nu*.
evaporated milk type of milk from which some of the water has been removed.
evasion [i'veiʒən] *nc/u* see **evade**.
eve [iːv] *nc* day before (usu. in **Christmas Eve, New Year's Eve**).
on the eve of something just before an important event.
even[1] ['iːvən] *intensifier/adv* **1.** to an extreme degree. *Even now some people still believe that the earth is flat. He didn't even try* i.e. one would have thought that he would try, but he did not. *It was even more unpleasant than I had thought it would be* i.e. I had expected it to be unpleasant, but it was more unpleasant than I had expected. **2.** just at that moment. *Even as we are speaking, people are being killed on the roads.* (rather *formal* in sense **2.**).
even if/though in spite of the fact that. *Even if he comes I shall not see him. Even though you say so, I do not believe it. Even if he saw it, he would not believe it.*
even[2] ['iːvən] *adj* **1.** smooth or regular; having the same quality all over or all through: *an even surface* i.e. one with no points higher or lower than the rest; *an even development* i.e. one with no periods faster or slower than the rest. **2.** equal. *The two boxers were even in strength and skill* i.e. one was not stronger or more skilful than the other. (*opp* **uneven** in senses **1.** and **2.**). **3.** (with reference to numbers) able to be divided by two (e.g. 2, 4, 6, 8, 10 are even numbers) (*opp* **odd**). Also *vt* (often with **up**) make even. **evenly** *adv*.
get even with somebody hurt or harm somebody who has hurt or harmed oneself. (*informal*).
even[3] ['iːvən] *nc/u* evening (*o.f.*).
'evensong church service held in the evening in the Church of England.
evening ['iːvniŋ] *nc/u* time after the day and before one goes to bed.
'evening dress see **dress**[1].
event [i'vent] *nc* **1.** something which happens (usu. something important or exciting). **2.** race or other item in an athletics contest. **3.** result. (rather *o.f.* in sense **3.**).
eventful *adj* full of important or exciting events: *an eventful life.*
at all events whatever happens.
in any event whatever happens. *I shall come with you in any event.*
in the event of something if something happens. *Here is what you must do in the event of my death.*
eventual [i'ventʃuəl] *adj* happening at the end as a result of something.
eventually *adv*: *It was a long journey, but we eventually arrived.*
eventuality [iventʃu'æliti] *nc* anything which might happen.
ever ['evə*] *adv* **1.** at any time. *Have you ever been to France? Don't you ever take any exercise? He hasn't ever spoken to me.* **2.** always. *He is ever hopeful.* (rather *o.f.* in sense **2.**).
'evergreen *nc* tree which does not lose its leaves in winter. Also *adj*.
ever'lasting *adj* never dying or never coming to an end: *the Everlasting God.*
everlastingly *adv*.
'ever'more *adv* always after some event. *He was happy evermore.* (rather *o.f.*).
ever after always after some event. *They got married and lived happily ever after.*
hardly ever not often.
ever since (something) always after some event. *I have been worried ever since I lost my money. I lost my money and I have been worried ever since.*
ever so very. *I am ever so grateful.* (*informal*).
every ['evri] *determiner* each one. *He talked to every person in the room. I used to see him every day. Every pupil was present this morning. Take one of these pills every four hours* i.e. there should be four hours between each pill.
'everybody *n sing* each person; all the people.
every other alternate (e.g. the first, the third, the fifth etc, or the second, the fourth, the sixth etc).
'every'day *adj* happening every day; not unusual.
'everyone *n sing* everybody.
'everything *n sing* each thing; all things.
'everywhere *adv* to/in all places.
every now and then occasionally; sometimes; not always.
evict [i'vikt] *vt* make a person leave a house or land by means of the law. *The owner of the house evicted the people who did not pay their rent.* **eviction** *nc/u*.
evidence ['evidns] *nu* facts brought forward to show that something is or is not true (e.g. in a court of law or in a scientific

experiment). Also *vt* show clearly; be evidence of something.

evident ['evidnt] *adj* easy to see or understand. *It was evident that he was telling the truth.* **evidently** *adv.*

evil ['i:vil] *adj* very bad in thought or behaviour. Also **1.** *nu* wickedness; condition of being very bad. **2.** *nc* anything very bad. *War is an evil.* **evilly** *adv.*

'evil'doer person who does evil things; wicked person.

'evil-'minded *adj* having very bad thoughts.

the evil eye ability which some people are believed to have of harming other people by looking at them.

a necessary evil anything which causes harm or damage but which is necessary.

evince [i'vins] *vt* show oneself to have some feeling or quality. *He evinced a strong interest in my work.*

evoke [i'vouk] *vt* produce; cause to appear. *The photograph evoked happy memories* i.e. when we looked at the photograph we remembered the time when we were happy. *His stories evoked laughter from all of us.*

evocation [evou'keiʃən] *nc/u.*

evocative [i'vɔkətiv] *adj* causing one to remember something.

evolution [i:və'lu:ʃən] **1.** *nu* (esp. with reference to the development of plants, animals etc from very simple forms of life) process of change and development. **2.** *nc* series of movements (esp. by soldiers or dancers). **evolutionary** *adj.* see **evolve.**

evolve [i'vɔlv] *vt/i* develop, cause to develop. *The plan gradually evolved. They evolved a new plan.* see **evolution.**

ewe [ju:] *nc* female sheep.

ex- [eks] *prefix* former (e.g. **ex-president** i.e. a man who used to be president).

exacerbate [eks'æsəbeit] *vt* make worse; make more painful, more angry, more difficult etc. **exacerbation** [eksæsə'beiʃən] *nu.*

exact[1] [eg'zækt] *adj* without mistakes; correct. *The exact weight is 25.68 kilograms. He did some very exact work* i.e. very careful and correct work. (*opp* **inexact**).

exactly *adv*: *I gave him exactly what he asked for* i.e. not more and not less. *Exactly!* i.e. that's correct.

exactitude [ig'zæktitju:d] *nu.* (*formal*).

exactness *nu.*

exact[2] [eg'zækt] *vt* **1.** get by use of force: *exact money from people.* **2.** need or require.

exacting *adj* difficult to please; making great demands: *exacting work* i.e. work which needs great care and attention.

exaction *nc/u* something obtained by force; use of force to obtain something.

exaggerate [eg'zædʒəreit] *vt/i* say more than is true (e.g. if one saw thirty cows and one says one saw hundreds of cows, one is exaggerating). **exaggeration** [egzædʒə'reiʃən] *nc/u.* **exaggerated** *adj.* **exaggeratedly** *adv.*

exalt [eg'zɔ:lt] *vt* **1.** give a high rank or position to: *someone in an exalted position.*

exalted *adj* high in rank or importance.

exaltation [egzɔ:l'teiʃən] *nu* strong feelings of happiness (esp. religious happiness).

exam [eg'zæm] *nc* examination (in sense **2.**) (*informal*).

examine [eg'zæmin] *vt* **1.** put questions to a student or pupil, in order to test knowledge or give awards. **2.** look at very closely; inspect.

examination [egzæmi'neiʃən] **1.** *nu* process of examining. **2.** *nc* formal test of the knowledge of a student or pupil.

examiner *nc* person who sets the questions in an examination of students or pupils.

under examination being questioned by a lawyer in a court of law. *Under examination the witness admitted that he was telling lies.*

example [ig'za:mpl] *nc* **1.** thing which is taken to show what other things of the same kind are like. *Cows and horses are examples of domestic animals* i.e. we can learn something of the nature of domestic animals if we consider cows and horses. **2.** person whom one should copy because he has done well. **3.** problem in arithmetic.

for example to name one or more out of many. *There are many big cities in Europe, for example, London, Paris and Rome.*

make an example of someone punish somebody in order to stop other people doing wrong in the same way.

set an example (to someone) see **set**[1]. *He set a bad example to his young brother* i.e. he behaved badly, and therefore his young brother might also behave badly. *He tried to set a good example.*

exasperate [eg'za:spəreit] *vt* make very angry and impatient.

exasperation [egza:spə'reiʃən] *nu* feeling of anger and impatience.

excavate ['ekskəveit] *vt/i* dig; make by digging; uncover by digging. *The archaeologists excavated an ancient city.*

excavation [ekskə'veiʃən] **1.** *nu* process of digging. **2.** *nc* hole; place uncovered by digging.

excavator *nc* machine used for digging.

exceed [ek'si:d] *vt* be greater or do more than. *Cars must not exceed thirty miles an hour in certain areas* i.e. must not travel faster than this. *The result exceeded my expectation* i.e. was greater than I had expected.

exceedingly *adv* very much.

Note: the *adj exceeding* is *o.f.*

excel [ek'sel] *vt/i* do something better than other people. *He excels at football. past* **excelled.**

excellent ['eksəlnt] *adj* very good; of high quality: *excellent work; an excellent dinner.* **excellently** *adv.* **excellence** *nu.*

excellency ['eksəlnsi] *nc* title of an ambassador, president, governor etc (usu. addressed as **Your Excellency**).

except [ek'sept] *prep* not including. *I invited everyone except James.* Also *vt* leave out. *I excepted James from my invitation* i.e. I did not invite him.

excepting *prep* not including.

exception *nc* something which is not included.

exceptional *adj* **1.** unusual. **2.** very much better or worse than usual or than others. (*opp* **unexceptional**). **exceptionally** *adv.*

take exception to something be angry or annoyed about something said or done by somebody.

with the exception of not including. *I invited everybody with the exception of James.*

without exception including everybody or everything.

excerpt ['eksə:pt] *nc* piece of writing, speech or music taken from a longer passage, book, poem, lecture etc.

excess [ek'ses] *nc* **1.** something which is greater in amount than what is normal or proper. *He has an excess of fluid in his body* i.e. he has too much fluid in his body. **2.**

(usu. only *pl*) behaviour which is more cruel, more foolish, more selfish etc than what is normal; very cruel, foolish, selfish acts.
excessive *adj* too great in quantity or amount. **excessively** *adv.*
'excess 'baggage baggage or luggage which weighs more than one is allowed to take with one (esp. in an aeroplane), unless one pays extra.
in excess of something more than something. *He was spending in excess of his income* i.e. he was spending more money than he was receiving.
to excess too much. *He ate/drank to excess.*

exchange[1] [eks'tʃeindʒ] *vt/i* give one thing to get another. *John and James exchanged hats* i.e. John took James's hat and James took John's. *James exchanged his hat for John's.*
exchange words/blows quarrel; fight.

exchange[2] [eks'tʃeindʒ] **1.** *nc/u* process of exchanging. **2.** *nu* value of foreign money for the money of another country. **3.** *nc* central building or office for various special purposes e.g.:
'exchange con'trol government rules deciding how much foreign money people are allowed to buy.
'labour exchange government office where people can go to find work. (Also more formally **employment exchange**).
rate of exchange value of one country's money in the money of another country.
'stock exchange see **stock.**
'telephone exchange see **telephone.**
in exchange (for something) in return for something. *He gave me a book and I gave him a pen in exchange. He got a pen in exchange for a watch.*

exchequer [eks'tʃekə*] *nc* government department having control over money.

excise[1] ['eksaiz] *nu* tax paid on certain goods manufactured in a country.

excise[2] [ek'saiz] *vt* (esp. with reference to cutting out a part of the body or a part of something written) cut out or remove. **excision** [ek'siʒən] *nc/u.*

excite [ek'sait] *vt* **1.** cause strong feelings of interest. *The football match excited all the boys.* **2.** cause certain other feelings: *excite anger/envy/interest. He was excited by all new ideas.* **excitement** *nc/u.*
excitable *adj* easily made excited. **excitability** [eksaitə'biliti] *nu.*
excited *adj* having strong feelings of interest etc. **excitedly** *adv.*
exciting *adj* causing excitement: *exciting film/story.* **excitingly** *adv.*

exclaim [eks'kleim] *vt/i* say something suddenly and loudly. **exclamation** [ekskləˈmeiʃən] *nc/u.* **exclamatory** [eks'klæmətəri] *adj.*
excla'mation mark the mark !

exclude [iks'klu:d] *vt* keep out; prevent from entering. *I excluded John from the invitation* i.e. I did not invite John. (*opp* **include**). **exclusion** [iks'klu:ʒən] *nu.*
exclusive [iks'klu:siv] *adj* **1.** welcoming or being friendly to only a few people: *an exclusive club/school/person.* **2.** for one person alone; not shared with others: *the exclusive possession of something.* **exclusively** *adv.*
exclusive of something not including something. *Prices in this hotel are exclusive of meals* i.e. people who stay in the hotel have to pay extra for their meals.

excommunicate [ekskə'mju:nikeit] *vt* (esp. with reference to the Roman Catholic Church) punish somebody by not allowing him to continue as a member of his church. **excommunication**[ekskəmju:ni'keiʃən]*nc/u.*

excrement ['ekskrimənt] *nu* waste matter sent out from the body.
excreta [eks'kri:tə] *npl* excrement.
excrete [eks'kri:t] *vt/i* send out waste matter, sweat etc from the body. **excretion** [eks'kri:ʃən] *nu.*

excrescence [eks'kresns] *nc* an unwanted and unpleasant growth on animals or plants.

excruciating [eks'kru:ʃieitiŋ] *adj* very painful; causing great suffering: *excruciating pain/torture.* **excruciatingly** *adv.*

exculpate ['ekskʌlpeit] *vt* say that somebody has not done something wrong. **exculpation** [ekskʌl'peiʃən] *nu.*

excursion [eks'kə:ʃən] *nc* journey made for pleasure (esp. one made by several people). **excursionist** *nc* person who makes an excursion.

excuse[1] [eks'kju:s] *nc* reason given for doing something which might be considered bad. *He made an excuse for arriving late* i.e. he explained why he was late.

excuse[2] [eks'kju:z] *vt* **1.** forgive somebody for doing a small wrong. *I excused him for coming late* i.e. I did not punish him or blame him. **2.** offer a reason for doing something wrong. *He excused his late arrival by saying that his car had broken down.* **3.** allow somebody to be absent from something. *Will you excuse me from the meeting?* i.e. will you allow me to stay away?
excuse oneself 1. offer an excuse. *He excused himself for being late.* **2.** ask to be allowed to be absent. *He excused himself from the meeting.*
excuse me polite expression, used especially when first speaking to a stranger to attract his attention.

execrate ['eksikreit] *vt* hate or express hatred of; dislike very strongly.
execration [eksi'kreiʃən] *nu* act of hating or expressing hate.
execrable ['eksikrəbl] *adj* very unpleasant; deserving to be hated. **execrably** *adv.*

execute ['eksikju:t] *vt* **1.** punish somebody by killing him after a trial in a court of law. **2.** carry out; do what is necessary: *execute an order.* **3.** play a piece of music, make a picture or statue etc. **4.** have a legal document drawn up and signed.
execution [eksi'kju:ʃən] **1.** *nc/u* legal punishment by killing. **2.** *nu* carrying out of an order etc. **3.** *nu* way in which a piece of music is played.
executioner [eksi'kju:ʃənə*] *nc* person whose job is to punish criminals by killing them.
executor [eg'zekjutə*] *nc* person who is named in a will to carry out the wishes of the dead person. (*fem* **executrix** [eg'zekjutriks]).
executive [eg'zekjutiv] *nc* person whose work is to organize business firms. Also *adj.*
the executive the part of the government of a country which organizes whatever is required by the laws.

exemplary [ig'zempləri] *adj* suitable to be an example: *John's exemplary behaviour* i.e John's very good behaviour which ought to be followed by other people.
exemplify [ig'zemplifai] *vt* be or make an

example. *This exemplifies what I mean* i.e. this is an example of what I mean. *He exemplified what he meant* i.e. he gave an example. **exemplification** [igzemplifi'keiʃən] *nc/u*.

exempt [ig'zempt] *adj* not required to do something. *He is exempt from the examination* i.e. he does not have to take the examination and he is considered to have passed it. Also *vt* make somebody exempt. **exemption** *nc/u*.

exercise[1] ['eksəsaiz] **1.** *nc/u* movements of the body, games etc done for the sake of health. *Exercise makes one strong. He was doing his exercises.* **2.** *nc* special series of actions and movements done by soldiers etc, to practise fighting in war. *The soldiers were sent into the mountains for three weeks on an exercise.* **3.** *nc* series of questions to be answered by pupils or students in order to practise something they have learned.

exercise[2] ['eksəsaiz] **1.** *vt/i* carry out, cause to carry out, bodily movements for the sake of health. *He exercises every morning. He was exercising his dog* i.e. going for a walk with his dog. **2.** *vt* use the mind or some quality in some way. *He exercised his intelligence to solve the problem.*

exert [ig'zəːt] *vt* use some quality: *exert one's strength; exert pressure.*

exertion *nc/u* **1.** act of using some quality: *the exertion of authority.* **2.** use of strength; hard work. *He was tired after his exertions.*

exert oneself try hard to do something. *He never exerts himself* i.e. he never works hard.

exeunt ['eksiʌnt] *vi* they go out (written in a play to indicate that several people leave the stage).

exhale [eks'heil] *vt/i* (with reference to a gas) breathe out; come out, cause to come out. **exhalation** [eksə'leiʃən] *nc/u*.

exhaust[1] [ig'zɔːst] *vt* **1.** make weak. *The game of football has exhausted me.* **2.** finish completely; use up. *The government has exhausted all its money. We have exhausted the subject of politics* i.e. we have talked about politics so much that we have said everything that can be said.

exhaustion *nu* weakness; tiredness.

exhaustive *adj* saying everything that can be said: *an exhaustive discussion.* **exhaustively** *adv*.

exhaust[2] [ig'zɔːst] *nc* **1.** place for steam, gas, vapour etc to escape from a machine (esp. the pipe at the back of a motorcar). **2.** steam, gas, vapour etc escaping in this way.

exhibit [ig'zibit] **1.** *vt/i* show publicly in a museum, art gallery etc. *He exhibited his paintings. He often exhibits.* **2.** *vt* show signs of. *He exhibited fear.* Also *nc* something exhibited (esp. in a museum).

exhibition [eksi'biʃən] *nc* **1.** act of exhibiting. **2.** number of objects shown publicly.

exhibitor *nc* person who shows things in a museum etc.

exhibitionist [eksi'biʃənist] *nc* person who behaves in an unusual way in order to make people take notice of him. **exhibitionism** [eksi'biʃənizem] *nu*.

exhilarate [ig'zilәreit] *vt* fill with a strong feeling of happiness and excitement.

exhilarated *adj* feeling exhilarated. **exhilaration** [igzilә'reiʃən] *nu*.

exhilarating *adj* causing exhilaration.

exhort [eg'zɔːt] *vt* speak to somebody using strong feelings, in order to persuade him to do something. *The general exhorted his soldiers to fight bravely.* **exhortation** [egzɔː'teiʃən] *nc/u*. **exhortatory** [eg'zɔːtətəri] *adj*.

exhume [eks'hjuːm] *vt* take a dead body out of the ground where it is buried (often in order to find out how the person died). **exhumation** [ekshju'meiʃən] *nc/u*.

exigency [eg'zidʒənsi] *nc* dangerous or difficult situation, in which one must act quickly. **exigent** ['eksidʒənt] *adj*.

exiguous [eg'ziguəs] *adj* existing in small amounts, which are not enough. **exiguously** *adv*.

exile ['eksail] *vt* force somebody to leave his own country (often as a punishment). Also **1.** *nu* condition of being exiled. *He was living in exile.* **2.** *nc* person who has been exiled.

exist [eg'zist] *vi* be; occur. *Wild elephants no longer exist in Europe* i.e. there are no wild elephants in Europe. **existence** *nu*.

existentialism [egzis'tenʃәlizәm] *nu* philosophy which teaches the importance of existence and personal choice.

existentialist [egzis'tenʃәlist] *nc* person who follows this belief.

exit ['eksit] *nc* **1.** action of leaving (esp. a room or the stage during a play). *He made his exit through the window.* **2.** door in a cinema, theatre etc by which one may leave the building. Also *vi* he goes out (written in a play to indicate to an actor to leave the stage).

exodus ['eksədəs] *nc* (usu. only *sing*) (usu. with reference to many people) process of leaving or going out.

ex officio [eksə'fiʃiou] *adj/adv* because of the position someone holds. *The headmaster was an ex officio member of the committee* i.e. he was a member because he was the headmaster.

exonerate [eg'zɔnәreit] *vt* decide that somebody has not done wrong although it was thought that he had. *I exonerated him from all blame.* **exoneration** [egzɔnə'reiʃən] *nu*.

exorbitant [eg'zɔːbitnt] *adj* much dearer than is reasonable: *an exorbitant price.* **exorbitantly** *adv*.

exorcize ['eksɔːsaiz] *vt* drive out an evil spirit by prayers or by some ceremony. **exorcism** ['eksɔːsizәm] *nc/u*. **exorcist** *nc*.

exotic [ig'zɔtik] *adj* coming from a foreign country (usu. a distant one). **exotically** *adv*.

expand [iks'pænd] **1.** *vt/i* become or make large. *His business has expanded. He expanded his lungs* i.e. filled his lungs with air. **2.** *vi* become cheerful and friendly. *Everybody at the party began to expand.* **expansion** *nu*. **expansive** *adj*. **expansively** *adv*.

expanse [eks'pæns] *nc* large surface area.

expatiate [eks'peiʃieit] *vi* (usu. with **on**) speak or write about something at great length. *He expatiated on the history of the country.*

expatriate [ek'spætriәt] *nc* person living in a country which is not his own. Also *adj*.

expect [iks'pekt] *vt* **1.** think that something will happen. *I expect he will come soon.* **2.** wait for somebody who is coming. *I am expecting the postman; he usually comes at this time. She is expecting a baby* i.e. she is pregnant; she is carrying a child inside her body. **3.** think something to be true. *I expect you've forgotten my name.* **expectancy** *nu*. **expectation** [ekspek'teiʃən] *nc/u*.

expectant *adj* waiting or expecting: *expectant mother.* **expectantly** *adv*.

expected *adj.* (*opp* **unexpected**).
'life expectancy number of years that a person will probably continue to live.
beyond expectation more or better than was expected.
not up to expectation(s) less or worse than was expected.
expectorate [eks'pektəreit] *vt/i* spit; send liquid from the throat out through the mouth. **expectoration** [ekspektə'reiʃən] *nu.* (*formal*).
expectorant *nc* medicine which makes it easier to remove liquid substances from the throat and windpipe.
expedient [eks'pi:diənt] *nc* plan or idea which helps to overcome a difficulty. Also *adj* useful to oneself but perhaps not correct or moral. *It would be expedient to help someone with such political influence.* (*opp* **inexpedient**). **expedience** *nu.* **expediency** *nc/u.*
expedite ['ekspidait] *vt* make a plan or arrangement proceed more quickly. *He expedited the arrangements.* **expeditious** [ekspi'diʃəs] *adj.* **expeditiously** *adv.*
expedition [ekspi'diʃən] *nc* **1.** journey done for a purpose. **2.** the people who make such a journey. **expeditionary** [ekspi'diʃənri] *adj.*
expel [eks'pel] *vt* **1.** send away from a place (e.g. a school) as a punishment. **2.** send out with force. *past* **expelled. expulsion** [eks'pʌlʃən] *nc/u.*
expend [eks'pend] *vt* use up: *expend time/money/energy.*
expendable *adj* not needed, and so suitable for using up or wasting.
expenditure *nu* money which is spent.
expense [eks'pens] **1.** *nu* money which is needed for some purpose: *the expense of buying a new car.* **2.** *nc* something on which money must be spent. *Food, clothing, light and heating are necessary expenses.*
expensive *adj* costing a lot of money. (*opp* **inexpensive**). **expensively** *adv.*
expenses *npl* money paid to someone who has to travel or spend money in some way while he is working.
at the expense of something by losing or damaging something. *They rushed through the work at the expense of the results.*
at my/his/our etc expense paid for by me etc. *We dined in a restaurant at my expense* i.e. I paid for the meal.
spare no expense pay as much money as is needed for some purpose.
experience [eks'piəriəns] **1.** *nu* process of seeing things, doing things etc. *He learned by experience* i.e. he learned by doing it, not by reading or by being told by other people. *He has a lot of experience as an engineer* i.e. he has worked as an engineer for many years. **2.** *nc* something which happens. *I had a strange experience last night.* Also *vt* have experience of: *experience life in prison; experience a pain.*
experienced *adj* having knowledge of some work etc gained by experience. (*opp* **inexperienced**).
experiment [eks'perimənt] *nc/u* **1.** scientific test carried out with various types of apparatus, to find out what happens and what the result is. **2.** anything tried out to see what will happen. Also *vi* carry out an experiment. **experimental** [eksperi'mentl] *adj.* **experimentally** *adv.* **experimentation** [eksperimen'teiʃən] *nu.*
expert ['ekspə:t] *nc* person having some special knowledge. Also *adj.* **expertly** *adv.*
expertise [ekspə'ti:z] *nu.*
expiate ['ekspieit] *vt* accept a punishment for doing something wrong; do something to show that one is sorry for a crime. *He expiated his crimes by trying to help the poor.* **expiation** [ekspi'eiʃən] *nu.*
expire [eks'paiə*] *vi* **1.** die. **2.** send out breath from the lungs. **3.** (with reference to a period of time) come to an end.
expiration [ekspi'reiʃən] *nu* end of a period of time.
expiry *nu* end of a period of time.
explain [eks'plein] *vt/i* **1.** give a meaning; make clear. *Can you explain this word to me? Can you explain this to me? I don't know what you mean; please explain.* **2.** give a reason. *Can you explain why you were late?*
explanation [eksplə'neiʃən] *nc/u.* **explanatory** [eks'plænətəri] *adj.*
explain something away give reasons which make something seem to be less bad.
explain oneself **1.** say more clearly what one means. **2.** give reasons for acting in a certain way.
expletive [eks'pli:tiv] *nc* word or expression which expresses one's feelings (and which often does not mean anything in itself) (e.g. *damn* is an expletive).
explicit [eks'plisit] *adj* clearly saying what is meant. *I gave him explicit instructions.* (*opp* **inexplicit**). **explicitly** *adv.*
explode [eks'ploud] **1.** *vt/i* blow up, cause to blow up. *The bomb exploded. He exploded a bomb.* **2.** *vi* suddenly show some strong feeling. *He exploded with/in laughter/anger.*
explosion [eks'plouʒən] *nc.*
explosive [eks'plousiv] *adj* intended to blow up; likely to blow up. Also *nc/u* something intended to explode (e.g. a bomb).
exploded *adj.* (*opp* **unexploded**).
exploit[1] ['eksplɔit] *nc* brave and exciting action.
exploit[2] [eks'plɔit] *vt* make use of to get profit: *exploit a gold mine* i.e. get gold from it; *exploit a person* i.e. get a profit by using somebody, without paying him properly. **exploitation** [eksplɔi'teiʃən] *nu.*
explore [eks'plɔ:*] *vt/i* **1.** travel in an unknown country in order to find out what is there. *Many Europeans explored the continent of Africa in the 19th century.* **2.** look carefully at something or consider something carefully, in order to find out what is there.
exploration [eksplə'reiʃən] *nc/u.*
explorer *nc* person who travels in an unknown country.
exploratory [eks'plɔrətəri] *adj* done in order to find out what is there: *an exploratory meeting.*
explored *adj.* (*opp* **unexplored**).
explosion [eks'plouʒən] *nc* see **explode.**
exponent [eks'pounənt] *nc* **1.** person who explains an idea or theory. see **expound.** **2.** (mathematics) small number written on the right-hand side of another number to show how many times the other number is to be multiplied by itself (e.g. 2^3 means $2 \times 2 \times 2$ and the ^{3} is the exponent ($2^3 = 2 \times 2 \times 2 = 8$)).
export ['ekspɔ:t] *nc* goods sold to another country or sent to another country for sale there. (*opp* **import**). Also [eks'pɔ:t] *vt/i* send goods abroad in this way.
expose [eks'pouz] *vt* **1.** leave uncovered, leave open. *The general exposed his men to danger* i.e. sent them into a dangerous position. *His house is exposed to the weather*

i.e. it is not protected by trees or surrounding houses. *This film has been exposed* i.e. it has been used in a camera (to take photographs). **2.** make known. *The detective exposed the criminal* i.e. showed who had committed the crime. *He exposed the plan to the newspapers* i.e. he wrote to the newspapers to tell them about a secret plan.

exposure [eks'pouʒə*] **1.** *nu* condition of being without protection from bad weather. *He died of exposure.* **2.** *nu* telling of something hidden. **3.** *nc* section of a reel of photographic film. *This film has 36 exposures* i.e. one can take 36 photographs with it.

exposé [eks'pouzei] *nc* **1.** making public of something dishonest or unpleasant (esp. in the newspapers). **2.** explanation of an idea.

exposition [ekspə'ziʃən] **1.** *nu* process of explaining the meaning of something. **2.** *nc* public exhibition or show, in which goods and things of interest from many countries are gathered together for a certain time. (Use **exhibition**).

expository [eks'pɔzitəri] *adj* concerned with explaining the meaning of something.

expostulate [eks'pɔstjuleit] *vi* protest; tell somebody that one does not like his plans or his behaviour. **expostulation** [ekspɔstju'leiʃən] *nc/u*.

expound [eks'paund] *vt* explain an idea: *expound an idea/a theory/a philosophy etc.* see **exponent.**

express[1] [eks'pres] *vt* say what one means; make plain; show: *express one's ideas, gratitude etc.*

express oneself speak, write, paint, act etc in a way which shows other people what one is feeling and thinking.

express[2] [eks'pres] *adj* **1.** travelling fast: *an express train; express delivery.* **2.** clearly understood; definite (usu. in **express wish/purpose**). Also *nc* fast train, which does not make many stops.

expressly *adv* clearly. *I expressly told you to wait for me.*

expression [eks'preʃən] **1.** *nc* appearance of the face, showing one's feelings: *an angry expression.* **2.** *nu* process of showing feelings in some way. *He played the music with a lot of expression.* **3.** *nc* something showing the feelings in some way. **4.** *nc* word or group of words; part of a sentence.

expressive [eks'presiv] *adj* clearly showing the feelings. (*opp* **unexpressive**). **expressively** *adv*.

beyond expression in a way or of a kind that cannot be properly described in words.

expropriate [eks'prouprieit] *vt* take somebody's private property for the use of the public. *The government has expropriated his land.* **expropriation** [eksproupri'eiʃən] *nu*.

expulsion [eks'pʌlʃən] *nc/u* see **expel.**

expunge [eks'pʌndʒ] *vt* (with reference to writing, ideas, memories etc) rub out; cause to disappear.

expurgate ['ekspə:geit] *vt* remove words considered to be indecent from a book, poem etc. **expurgation** [ekspə:'geiʃən] *nu*. **expurgated** *adj*. (*opp* **unexpurgated**).

exquisite [eks'kwizit] *adj* **1.** beautiful; finely made. **2.** (with reference to pains or pleasures) felt very strongly. **exquisitely** *adv*.

extant [eks'tænt] *adj* (usu. with reference to literature, painting, music etc) still existing; not lost or destroyed. *Only a few of the ancient Greek plays are extant* i.e. most are lost.

extempore [eks'tempəri] *adj* (usu. with reference to speaking) not prepared before: *make an extempore speech.* Also *adv*: *speak extempore.*

extend [eks'tend] *vt/i* **1.** stretch. *The land extends for three miles in that direction. The headmaster has extended the term for three weeks* i.e. he has added three weeks to the term. **2.** offer: *extend an invitation/a welcome/congratulations.* (*formal* in sense **2.**).

extension [eks'tenʃən] **1.** *nu* process of extending. *The pupils disliked the extension of the term.* **2.** *nc* something added. *They are building an extension to the school* i.e. some more buildings. **3.** *nc* extra telephone added to an existing telephone system (esp. in a big building).

extensive *adj* **1.** stretching a long way. *His land is very extensive.* **2.** large in amount. *The bomb did extensive damage to the house.* **extensively** *adv*.

extent [eks'tent] *nu*: *the extent of his land; the extent of the damage.*

to some/a certain extent partly. *To a certain extent I was pleased to see him.*

to what extent? how much?; how far? *To what extent are you willing to help me?*

extenuate [eks'tenjueit] *vt* find a reason which makes a fault, mistake or crime seem less bad. **extenuation** [ekstenju'eiʃən] *nu*.

extenuating circumstances circumstances which make the crime etc seem less bad.

in extenuation as an excuse. *I have nothing to say in extenuation of what I have done.*

exterior [eks'tiəriə*] *nc* outer surface. Also *adj*. (*opp* **interior** in both senses).

exterminate [eks'tə:mineit] *vt* completely destroy or kill a large number or large quantity. *He exterminated the rats on his farm.* **extermination** [ekstə:mi'neiʃən] *nu*. **exterminator** *nc*.

external [eks'tə:nl] *adj* on or for the outside. (*opp* **internal**). **externally** *adv*.

extinct [eks'tiŋkt] *adj* **1.** (with reference to types of animals, plants etc) no longer in existence. **2.** (with reference to a volcano) no longer active. **3.** (with reference to feelings or ideas) no longer felt strongly or thought about. **extinction** *nu*.

extinguish [eks'tiŋgwiʃ] *vt* **1.** put out a light or a fire. **2.** put an end to feelings or ideas. **'fire extinguisher** apparatus for putting out small fires.

extirpate ['ekstə:peit] *vt* (often with reference to political or religious ideas or a group of people having such ideas) destroy completely. **extirpation** [ekstə:'peiʃən] *nu*.

extol [eks'toul] *vt* give high praise to. *The newspapers extolled the Prime Minister.* *past* **extolled.**

extort [eks'tɔ:t] *vt* get by force or the threat of force. *He extorted money from the poor. He extorted a promise from me.* **extortion** *nu*.

extortioner *nc* person who extorts money etc.

extortionate [eks'tɔ:ʃənit] *adj* asking for too much.

extra-[1] ['ekstrə] *prefix* outside; beyond (e.g. **extrasensory**).

extra[2] ['ekstrə] *adj* more than is usual: *an extra holiday; extra money.*

extra[3] ['ekstrə] *nc* **1.** something which is extra or more than what is usual. **2.** person who acts small parts in films and who is paid each day for the work he does.

extract[1] [eks'trækt] *vt* **1.** get from; take out. *The police extracted information from the thief* i.e. they made the thief give some information. *A miner extracts gold from the earth. The dentist extracted one of my teeth.* **2.** write out or copy a passage from a book, poem etc.
extraction *nu* **1.** process of extracting. **2.** origin of one's ancestors. *He is of Russian extraction* i.e. his parents or grandparents came from Russia.

extract[2] ['ekstrækt] **1.** *nu* substance in concentrated form. *Beef extract is sometimes used for making soup.* **2.** *nc* piece of writing or speech taken from a longer piece: *an extract from a book.*

extradite ['ekstrədait] *vt* **1.** hand over to the police of his own country a foreigner wanted by them. *The British government extradited the man wanted by the French police.* **2.** ask for a criminal who has gone to a foreign country to be sent back. **extradition** [ekstrə'diʃən] *nu.*
extraditable *adj*: *an extraditable offence* i.e. one for which one may be extradited.

extramural ['ekstrə'mjuərl] *adj* **1.** with reference to university activities which are not concerned with students of the university (e.g. *an extramural lecture* i.e. a lecture for people living in the town, and not for the students). **2.** of activities of students not directly connected with their studies.

extraneous [eks'treiniəs] *adj* not belonging to something; having no connection with something. *He tries to bring in extraneous questions when I have a discussion with him* i.e. he mentions topics which we are not discussing. **extraneously** *adv.*

extraordinary [eks'trɔːdnri] *adj* very strange; very unusual. **extraordinarily** *adv.*

extrasensory ['ekstrə'sensəri] *adj* beyond the normal senses of hearing, sight, touch etc (usu. in **extrasensory perception** i.e. the ability which some people are believed to have of passing ideas from one person to another by using the powers of the mind only, without the use of speech, writing, signs etc).

extravagant [eks'trævəgənt] *adj* **1.** spending a lot of money in a foolish way. **2.** beyond the limits of what is sensible or reasonable: *extravagant ideas.* **extravagantly** *adv.* **extravagance** *nu.*

extreme [eks'triːm] *adj* **1.** at the furthest point. *He lives in the extreme north of the country.* **2.** of the highest degree; very great or very much: *extreme cold* i.e. very great cold. **3.** with reference to ideas which are very far from those of most people. Also *nc* something which is the opposite of something else.
extremely *adv* very much: *extremely tired.*
extremist *nc* person who has extreme views in politics (often violent or revolutionary ones). **extremism** *nu.*
extremity [eks'tremiti] *nc* **1.** furthest point. **2.** great misfortune or danger.
the extremities hands and feet of a person.
extreme unction see **unction.**
in the extreme very much. *This work is difficult in the extreme.*
go to extremes act in a way which is far from normal or proper (often in a violent or illegal way).
go to the other extreme act in a way which is the opposite of the way in which one has been acting.

extricate ['ekstrikeit] *vt* free someone from something which prevents him from moving. *He extricated his friend from the chains. He extricated himself from debt.* **extrication** [ekstri'keiʃən] *nu.*

extrovert ['ekstrəvəːt] *nc* person interested mainly in things and people, and not in his own thoughts. Also *adj.* (*opp* **introvert**).

exuberant [ig'zjuːbərnt] *adj* full of life; strong; growing strongly. **exuberantly** *adv.* **exuberance** *nu.*

exude [ig'zjuːd] *vt/i* come out, allow to come out, in small drops of liquid. *Blood exuded through the bandage. His wound exuded blood.*

exult [eg'zʌlt] *vi* be filled with great happiness (usu. at something important). *The people exulted when they heard the news of the great victory.*
exultant *adj* feeling exulted. **exultantly** *adv.*
exultation [egzʌl'teiʃən] *nu* feeling of great happiness.

eye [ai] *nc* **1.** part of the body with which people and animals see. **2.** something shaped like an eye (e.g. the hole at the top of a needle through which the thread goes, a small mark in a potato). Also *vt* look at someone carefully, or with longing. *He eyed me carefully. He eyed her up and down.*
'eyeball that part of the eye which is white and which has a coloured portion at its centre.
'eyebrow line of hair on the face above the eye.
'eyelash small hair growing from the eyelids.
'eyelid one of the pieces of skin which can be moved to close the eyes.
'eyeshadow coloured substance put on the eyelids.
'eyesight ability to see. *He has good eyesight.*
'eyesore something which looks very unpleasant (often something which can be seen by many people). *That new statue which has been put up in the main street is an eyesore.*
'eyestrain pains around the eyes, caused by too much reading etc.
'eye tooth one of the four pointed teeth at the front corners of the mouth; canine tooth.
'eyewitness person who sees something happening (often one who sees a crime).
an eye for an eye punishment which hurts the wrongdoer in exactly the same way as he hurt somebody else.
catch someone's eye see **catch**[1].
have an eye for something be able to see or recognize something clearly. *He has an eye for a bargain* i.e. he is able to realize that something is being sold cheaply.
keep an eye on someone/something watch someone/something carefully. (*informal*).
in the eyes of the law in law. *In the eyes of the law, if you keep something which you find, you are stealing it.*
more than meets the eye more than one can actually see or more than there appears to be. (*informal*).
only have eyes for someone/something only be interested in someone/something.
in the public eye well-known and often mentioned in newspapers, on television or radio etc.
see eye to eye with someone see **see**[1].
set eyes on see **set**[1].
with an eye to something for some purpose;

having some purpose in mind. *He acted in that way with an eye to profit* i.e. he acted in that way because he hoped to gain money by it.

with one's eyes open knowing what might possibly happen. *He made the agreement with his eyes open* i.e. he knew what the difficulties or dangers would be. (*informal*).

F

fable ['feibl] *nc* story (esp. about animals) intended to teach a lesson about behaviour.

fabric ['fæbrik] *nu* **1.** cloth. **2.** structure (e.g. of a society).

fabricate ['fæbrikeit] *vt* invent an untrue story or a lie. **fabricated** *adj.* **fabrication** [fæbri'keiʃən] *nc/u.*

fabulous ['fæbjuləs] *adj* **1.** very good; very big. (*informal*). **2.** strange; unusual and interesting; amazing. **fabulously** *adv.*

facade, façade [fə'sɑ:d] *nc* **1.** front of a building. **2.** surface appearance of anything. *Under a facade of respectability he was in fact the leader of a gang of criminals* i.e. he appeared to be respectable or honest.

face[1] [feis] *nc* **1.** front part of the head containing the eyes, mouth, nose etc. **2.** front of something: *the face of a clock/of a building.*

facial ['feiʃl] *adj* of the face. Also *nc* treatment with creams and massage intended to improve the beauty of the face.

facing *nu* substance covering a surface: *a stone facing on the brick wall.* Also *prep* opposite. *I live in the house facing the church.*

'face 'value 1. value marked on a banknote, cheque etc. **2.** value or usefulness which something appears to have: *take something at its face value.*

face to face coming together so as to be able to talk. *The two leaders at last met face to face.*

have the face to do something be bold or daring enough to do something which other people might think wrong. (*informal*).

in the face of something on meeting something. *He became afraid in the face of danger.*

a long face expression on one's face which shows annoyance, disappointment etc. (*informal*).

keep a straight face see **keep**[1].

be unable to look someone in the face be ashamed in someone's presence because one has done something wrong.

lose face see **lose.**

make/pull a face at someone see **make**[1].

on the face of it as something appears before further enquiry. *On the face of it, you are responsible* i.e. you seem to be responsible (although in fact you may not be).

show one's face appear. *He hasn't shown his face in the office for a week.* (*informal*).

face[2] [feis] *vt* **1.** turn towards. *He faced his enemies.* **2.** be placed in a certain position. *Our house faces north.* **3.** cover a surface with a substance. *His house is built of brick faced with stone* i.e. the brick walls are covered with stone.

face up to something accept some unpleasant fact or situation. *He tried to face up to his difficulties.*

let's face it we should admit some fact (usu. an unpleasant fact). *Let's face it, we are getting old.* (*informal*).

face the music accept punishment or trouble caused by something one has done. (*informal*).

facet ['fæsit] *nc* **1.** one of the sides of a precious stone which has been cut into shape. **2.** part of something. *There are many facets to his character.*

facetious [fə'si:ʃəs] *adj* (with reference to jokes, often jokes which are not very funny) not serious. **facetiously** *adv.* **facetiousness** *nu.*

facile ['fæsail] *adj* easily done; not requiring much effort or skill (and often of a poor quality). *He made a facile speech.* **facilely** *adv.*

facilitate [fə'siliteit] *vt* make easier. *I decided to employ a secretary in order to facilitate the work.*

facility [fə'siliti] **1.** *nu* ability to do things easily. **2.** *nc* (often *pl*) something which makes life or work easier, more pleasant etc.

facsimile [fæk'simili] *nc* (usu. of something written) an exact copy.

fact [fækt] *nc/u* something known or thought to be true. *The police tried to find out the facts* i.e. what had actually happened. **factual** ['fæktjuəl] *adj.*

in fact really; to tell the truth.

the fact of the matter is the truth is.

as a matter of fact really; actually.

in point of fact actually; to tell the truth.

faction ['fækʃən] **1.** *nc* group of people within a political party (esp. a group opposed to the official leaders of the party). **2.** *nu* quarrelling within a group or organization. **factional** *adj.*

factor ['fæktə*] *nc* **1.** fact; one of a number of facts. *He tried to consider all the factors in the situation.* **2.** (mathematics) one of the several numbers which form a total when multiplied together (e.g. the factors of 10 are 2 and 5).

factory ['fæktəri] *nc* place where goods are made (usu. with machinery).

factotum [fæk'toutəm] *nc* person employed to do many different kinds of work. (Often **general factotum**) (*informal*).

faculty ['fækəlti] *nc* **1.** power or ability of the mind or brain. **2.** department in a university. **3.** (*US*) teaching staff of a university.

fad [fæd] *nc* unreasonable liking or dislike for something.

faddy *adj* (esp. with reference to likes and dislikes of children for different kinds of food).

fade [feid] *vt/i* become or make pale, less loud, less strong etc. *The colours in this cloth have faded. The sun faded the cloth. The sound has faded.*

fade away slowly fade and disappear. *The sound faded away.*

fade out 1. (with reference to a scene in a film) slowly disappear from sight. **2.** become less well-known; disappear from public knowledge.

faeces ['fi:si:z] *npl* solid waste matter sent

out from the body.

fag[1] [fæg] *nc* (usu. only *sing*) hard work. (*informal* and rather *o.f.*).

fag[2] [fæg] *nc* young boy who works for older boys in certain private schools in England. Also *vi* work as a fag. *past* **fagged.**

fag[3] [fæg] *nc* (*Brit*) cigarette. (*informal*).

'fag end[1] (*Brit*) end of a cigarette after it has been smoked. (*informal*).

'fag 'end[2] last and most useless part of anything.

faggot ['fægət] *nc* **1.** number of sticks tied together and intended for burning in a fire. **2.** meat chopped into small pieces and cooked in the form of a small roll or ball.

Fahrenheit ['færənhait] temperature scale used in Britain and America, in which freezing point is 32 degrees and boiling point is 212 degrees.

fail [feil] **1.** *vi* be unsuccessful. *His plans failed* i.e. he was not able to do what he had planned. *I fail to understand* i.e. I cannot understand. **2.** *vi* become weak. *The radio is failing* i.e. becoming less loud. **3.** *vi* become bankrupt. **4.** *vt* decide that someone has been unsuccessful in a test or examination. *The examiner failed 25 of the candidates.*

failing[1] *nc* weakness of character. *He has one failing; he tells lies.*

failing[2] *prep* without; unless. *Failing that, we must think of another plan* i.e. if that does not happen, we must think of another plan.

failure ['feiljə*] **1.** *nc/u* lack of success; not doing: *a terrible failure; failure to do something.* **2.** *nc* person who fails.

fail an examination/test etc be unsuccessful in an examination etc.

without fail certainly; without forgetting; always. *He came to visit me every Thursday without fail.*

faint[1] [feint] *vi* lose consciousness. *She fainted when she heard the news.* Also *nc* loss of consciousness.

faint[2] [feint] *adj* **1.** weak. *He felt faint through lack of food.* **2.** not clearly seen or heard. *He heard a faint sound.* **faintly** *adv.* **faintness** *nu.*

'faint'hearted *adj* lacking in courage; afraid of danger. **faintheartedly** *adv.* **faintheartedness** *nu.*

fair[1] [fɛə*] *adj* **1.** just; giving each person what he ought to have. *He didn't think that the arrangement was fair* i.e. he thought that he ought to get more. (*opp* **unfair**). **2.** according to the rules. *The result of the game was not fair.* **3.** (with reference to people, esp. people having yellow or golden hair) light in colour. **4.** (with reference to the weather) without rain. **5.** (often with reference to work by a pupil or student or to the probability of something) neither very good nor very bad: *a fair chance.* **6.** beautiful (*o.f.* in sense **6.**). Also *adv* according to the rules: *play fair.* **fairness** *nu.*

fairly *adv/intensifier* **1.** justly. *He acted very fairly to us.* **2.** according to the rules. *He played fairly.* **3.** neither very much nor very little. *This book is fairly interesting.*

by fair means or foul see **means.**

the fair sex women. (rather *o.f.*).

fair and square honest or honestly. (*informal*).

fair[2] [fɛə*] *nc* **1.** travelling entertainment, having various mechanical things to ride on, games of chance and skill etc. **2.** market held at certain times of the year. **3.** international or national exhibition of manufactured goods.

fairy ['fɛəri] *nc* **1.** small imaginary creature with magic powers. **2.** homosexual. (*informal* in sense **2.**).

'fairy story/tale story about fairies etc for children.

fait accompli [feitə'kɔmpli] *nc* action, often carried out without previous permission or discussion, which cannot be changed.

faith [feiθ] **1.** *nu* strong belief: *have faith in God* i.e. believe that God will help one; *have faith in someone* i.e. believe that someone will succeed. **2.** *nc* religious belief: *people of different faiths.*

faithful *adj* **1.** following one's duty; doing what one has promised: *faithful to one's country.* (*opp* **unfaithful**). **2.** having a strong belief in something. **3.** exact: *a faithful report of the facts.* **faithfully** *adv.* **faithfulness** *nu.*

faithless *adj* without faith. **faithlessly** *adv.*

bad faith failure to do what one has agreed or promised to do.

in good faith believing something to be true. *I made the agreement in good faith* i.e. believing that the agreement would be kept.

lose faith in someone/something feel that someone/something cannot be trusted or will not help one.

Yours faithfully used at the end of a letter to somebody whom one does not know as a friend or colleague.

fake [feik] *adj* false, but made to look real: *a fake accident.* Also *nc* something which is fake. Also *vt* make a fake. (all *informal*).

fakir ['fækiə*] *nc* Hindu or Moslem holy man who lives by begging.

falcon ['fɔːlkən] *nc* type of bird which eats small birds and animals and is sometimes trained to catch them for men.

falcon

falconry *nu* sport of hunting using a falcon.

falconer *nc* person who does this.

fall[1] [fɔːl] *nc* **1.** act of falling. *He had a fall and broke his leg.* **2.** (*US*) autumn. **3.** decrease: *a fall in prices.* **4.** capture: *the fall of Constantinople.* **5.** (usu. **waterfall**) river falling over a steep drop. **6.** defeat (esp. the defeat of a government or a powerful man).

fall[2] [fɔːl] *vi* **1.** come down. *He was climbing a tree when he fell to the ground. The snow was falling.* **2.** become less or lower. *The price of flour has fallen.* **3.** do something wrong. (rather *o.f.*). **4.** (with reference to a town, city etc) be captured in war. **5.** be killed in war. **6.** be defeated. *The government has fallen. past tense* **fell** [fel]. *past part* **fallen** ['fɔːlən].

fall away **1.** become less in number. *Membership of the club has fallen away this year.* **2.** (with reference to land) slope downwards. *My garden falls away very steeply.*

fall back retreat; move backwards.

fall back on/upon something use something when one is in great need, because one cannot use anything else. *He wanted to keep the money his uncle gave him, but he had to fall back on it to pay his debts.* (*informal*).

fall behind 1. go more slowly than others. 2. fail to continue something. *He fell behind with his rent* i.e. he could not make the payment at the right time.

fall down fall to the ground.

fall for someone begin to love someone. (*informal*).

fall for something be deceived by something. *He fell for the trick.* (*informal*).

fall in 1. (with reference to soldiers) stand together in a line. 2. collapse inwards. *The roof of the burning house fell in.*

fall in with someone/something 1. meet by accident and join. 2. agree with a plan or suggestion.

fall into something get into a condition of something: *fall into decay* i.e. become decayed; *fall into a habit* i.e. do something as a habit.

fall out (with reference to soldiers) leave a line of men, disperse.

'fallout *nu* radioactive substance released in the atmosphere by the explosion of a nuclear bomb.

fall out (with someone) quarrel. (*informal*).

fall over (something) lose one's balance and fall. *He was walking along and suddenly he fell over. He fell over a small table.*

fall over oneself to do something be very anxious to do something. (*informal*).

fall through fail. *The plan/scheme/arrangements fell through.* (*informal*).

fall to start to do something (esp. start to eat, work, fight).

fall under something be classified as something or be dealt with by something.

fall upon someone suddenly attack someone.

fall due be payable. *The rent falls due next week* i.e. it should be paid next week.

fall flat fail completely. *His plans fell flat.* (*informal*).

fall in love (with someone) begin to love someone. *He fell in love with her. They fell in love.*

fall to pieces break into small pieces.

fall short of be less than was expected. *The amount I have been given falls short of my requirements.*

let something fall 1. drop something. *He let the plate fall.* 2. say something in a casual way. *He let fall a suggestion.*

fallacy ['fæləsi] *nc* 1. belief which is untrue. 2. argument which is false. **fallacious** [fə'leiʃəs] *adj.*

fallible ['fæləbl] *adj* likely to make a mistake. (*opp* **infallible**). **fallibility** [fæli'biliti] *nu.*

fallow ['fælou] *adj* (with reference to land on a farm) not planted with seed.

false [fɔ:ls] *adj* untrue; not real: *a false statement; a false name* i.e. a name which is not the real name of the person. **falsely** *adv.*

falsify *vt* make false. *He falsified the accounts* i.e. he altered the accounts so as to make them false. **falsification** [fɔ:lsifi'keiʃən] *nc/u.*

falsehood *nc/u* untrue statement; lie.

sail under false colours appear to be what in fact one is not. (*informal*).

falsetto [fɔl'setou] *nu* very high male voice, sounding like a female voice: *sing falsetto.*

falter ['fɔ:ltə*] *vi* move or behave in an uncertain or unsteady way. *The old man faltered as he climbed the hill.*

fame [feim] *nu* condition of being well-known by a large number of people.

famous *adj* well-known in this way.

familiar [fə'miliə*] *adj* 1. well-known to one: *a familiar face.* (*opp* **unfamiliar**). 2. too friendly; acting as though a friend. *He spoke to her in a very familiar way.*

familiarity [fəmili'æriti] *nc/u.*

familiarize *vt* make familiar. **familiarization** *nu.*

familiar with something having a good knowledge of something.

family ['fæmili] *nc* 1. mother, father and children. 2. children of a man or his wife. 3. people related to one by blood or marriage (e.g. uncles, aunts, cousins, nephews, nieces etc). 4. (biology) a group which is smaller than an order but larger than a genus.

'family 'tree 1. diagram showing all one's ancestors. 2. the ancestors themselves.

famine ['fæmin] *nc/u* lack of food over a large area, causing death or disease.

famished ['fæmiʃt] *adj* 1. starving. 2. hungry. (*informal* in sense 2.).

famous ['feiməs] *adj* see **fame.**

fan[1] [fæn] *nc* object used to create a movement of air (usu. in order to make one feel less hot). Also *vt* use a fan or something like a fan. *She fanned herself. He fanned the fire* i.e. to make it burn better. *past* **fanned.**

fan[2] [fæn] *nc* person who takes a great interest in a sport or in some public entertainer. (*informal*).

'fanmail letters sent by fans to singers, actors, sportsmen etc.

fanatic [fə'nætik] *nc* person having a strong religious or political belief, which makes him likely to act violently. **fanatical** *adj.* **fanatically** *adv.* **fanaticism** [fə'nætisizəm] *nu.*

fancy[1] ['fænsi] *vt* 1. think something to be true. *I fancied I had met him before.* 2. like or want. *I fancy a cup of coffee and a piece of cake. I don't fancy walking in the rain.* (*informal* in sense 2.).

(just) fancy! exclamation meaning 'how surprising!' (*informal*).

fancy oneself think that one is very clever or very good. (*informal*).

fancy[2] ['fænsi] 1. *nu* ability to imagine things. 2. *nc* something imagined but untrue.

fanciful *adj* imagined but unreal. **fancifully** *adv.*

have a fancy for something wish to have something pleasant. *I have a fancy for a piece of that cake.*

take a fancy to someone/something begin to like someone/something. (*informal*).

fancy[3] ['fænsi] *adj* brightly coloured; made to look pleasing. (*informal*).

'fancy 'dress unusual and interesting dress, worn to a party or dance.

fanfare ['fænfeə*] *nc* blowing of trumpets etc.

fang [fæŋ] *nc* sharp tooth of an animal.

fantastic [fæn'tæstik] *adj* 1. strange, unusual and difficult to believe. 2. very good; very big. (*informal* in sense 2.). **fantastically** *adv.*

fantasy, phantasy ['fæntəsi] *nc* very strange idea or dream.

far [fɑ:*] *adv* 1. a long way; distant. *He didn't walk far. The next village is not very far. How far is it to London?* 2. very much.

This book is far more interesting than that one. I would far sooner go with John than James i.e. I would prefer to go with John. Also *adj* distant: *the far side of the moon* i.e. the side most distant from the earth. *comparative* **farther** ['fɑːðə*] or **further** ['fəːðə*]. *superlative* **farthest** ['fɑːðist] or **furthest** ['fəːðist].

Note: some people make a distinction between *farther/farthest* and *further/furthest*, using the first two to refer to distance, and the second two to refer to time, quantity etc (e.g. *three miles farther*, but *to go further in an investigation*). Not all speakers of English make this distinction, and *further/furthest* is probably commoner.

'faraway *adj* **1.** distant: *a faraway place.* **2.** thinking of things very distant (usu. in **a faraway look**).

'far-'fetched *adj* difficult to believe; very improbable: *a far-fetched story.*

'far-'reaching *adj* having effects on many distant things: *far-reaching changes in government policy.*

as far as to the degree that. *As far as I know, he has not been here* i.e. although he may have been here without my knowledge.

far and away very much: *far and away the most interesting book I have read.* (*informal*).

far be it from me (to do something) I do not wish (to do something).

by far by a large amount. *This is by far the best.*

a far cry from something very unlike something. (*informal*).

few and far between rare; not occurring very frequently.

so far so good everything is good at the moment, but things may get worse. (*informal*).

far and near everywhere. *They looked for him far and near.*

far and wide in many distant places. *He has travelled far and wide.*

farce [fɑːs] **1.** *nc* stage play or film having many foolish and improbable incidents, intended to make people laugh. **2.** *nu* this type of play or film. **3.** *nc* anything in real life which is like a farce. **farcical** ['fɑːsikl] *adj.* **farcically** *adv.*

fare[1] [fɛə*] **1.** *nc* money paid to travel on a bus, train, aeroplane etc. **2.** *nc* passenger on a bus, taxi etc. **3.** *nu* food and drink (*o.f.* in sense **3.**).

bill of fare list of food which can be bought in a restaurant.

fare[2] [fɛə*] *vi* get on. *How did you fare in the examination?* (rather *o.f.*).

farewell [fɛə'wel] *interj/nc* goodbye. (rather *o.f.*).

farm [fɑːm] *nc* **1.** large area of land for growing crops and raising animals. **2.** house where the farmer lives. Also *vt/i*: *He farms in Scotland* i.e. he has a farm there.

farmer *nc* owner or manager of a farm.

'farmyard open space around a farmhouse.

farther, farthest ['fɑːðə*, 'fɑːðist] see **far.**

farthing ['fɑːðiŋ] *nc* British coin of low value no longer in use.

fascinate ['fæsineit] *vt* be very interesting to; claim all the attention of. *Old houses fascinate me.* **fascination** [fæsi'neiʃən] *nc/u.* **fascinating** *adj*: *a fascinating story.*

fascism ['fæʃizəm] *nu* **1.** political belief taking various forms (but usu. favouring dictatorship, the use of force, belief that some members of the community are inferior, and a liking for parades, uniforms, badges etc). **2.** (usu. **Fascism**) Italian political movement which formed the government from 1922 to 1945.

fascist, Fascist ['fæʃist] *nc* follower of this political belief or movement.

fashion[1] ['fæʃən] **1.** *nc/u* changes in what is thought to be very modern in clothes, music, art etc. *Fashion has more influence on women than on men. She always reads the newspapers to find out the new fashions in dress.* **2.** *nc* (usu. only *sing*) way or manner.

fashion[2] ['fæʃən] *vt* make (usu. using the hands and simple tools). *He fashioned a walking stick for his father.*

fashionable *adj* following fashion; of the upper classes: *a fashionable person; a fashionable part of the town* i.e. one where fashionable people live. (*opp* **unfashionable**). **fashionably** *adv.*

'old-'fashioned *adj* no longer used by many people and felt to belong to an earlier time. *She was wearing very old-fashioned clothes.*

after a fashion not very well. *He did the work after a fashion.*

in fashion considered to be the best at the moment. *Short skirts are in fashion* i.e. women who wish to be fashionable wear short skirts. (*opp* **out of fashion**).

fast[1] [fɑːst] *adj* **1.** quick; not slow: *a fast train. This clock is fast* i.e. ahead of time. **2.** taking part in many pleasures which some people would think wrong: *a fast woman.* **3.** firmly fixed in or on something: *fast colours* i.e. colours which will not come out of cloth when it is washed. Also *adv* quickly. *He ran very fast.*

fastness *nc* place of defence and protection which is difficult to reach (often in **in mountain fastness**).

'fast a'sleep in a deep sleep; not easily woken.

make something fast tie something securely. *He made fast the rope.*

play fast and loose with see **play**[1].

fast[2] [fɑːst] *vi* go without food (for religious or medical purposes). Also *nc* period of going without food.

fasten ['fɑːsn] *vt/i* become or make tight or fixed in place. *This dress fastens at the back* i.e. the buttons etc are at the back. *She fastened her dress.* (*opp* **unfasten**).

fastener *nc* something used for fastening.

fasten on/upon something **1.** take and hold something. **2.** give sudden and great attention to something.

fastidious [fæs'tidiəs] *adj* having the habit of disliking many things. **fastidiously** *adv.* **fastidiousness** *nu.*

fat[1] [fæt] *nu* **1.** white or yellow substance found in animal and human bodies. **2.** similar substance obtained from plants and used for cooking in the same way as animal fat.

fatty *adj*: *fatty tissue.*

fat[2] [fæt] *adj* **1.** having much fat in the body: *a fat man.* **2.** thick, as though having fat: *a fat book. comparative* **fatter.** *superlative* **fattest.**

fatten *vt* make fat.

'fathead foolish person. (*informal*).

kill the fatted calf prepare a very happy welcome for somebody.

fatal ['feitl] *adj* causing death or destruction: *a fatal illness.* **fatally** *adv.*

fatality [fə'tæliti] *nc/u* accident, misfortune that causes death.

fatalism ['feitəlizəm] *nu* belief that events

are planned by God or by some other power, and that man cannot do anything to change events.
fatalist ['feitəlist] *nc* person who has this belief. **fatalistic** [feitə'listik] *adj*.
fate [feit] **1.** *nu* power which is thought of as deciding what will happen. **2.** *nc* what is decided by fate. *I opened the letter in order to learn my fate* i.e. learn what was going to happen to me.
fated *adj* decided by fate. *It was fated that I should meet him.*
fateful *adj* decided by fate (and often causing death or destruction). **fatefully** *adv*.
father ['fa:ðə*] *nc* **1.** male parent. **2.** person who takes the place of one's father. **3.** person who invents, founds or begins something. **4.** one of the leaders of the early Christian church. **5.** **(Father)** Roman Catholic priest. Also *vt* be the father or inventor of. *He fathered the plan.*
fatherly *adj* like a father.
fatherhood *nu* condition of being a father.
(the) Father God.
'father-in-law *nc* father of one's wife or husband. *pl* **fathers-in-law.**
'fatherland country in which one was born.
fathom ['fæðəm] *nc* unit of measurement of the depth of water (= 1.8 metres). Also *vt* find out the meaning of.
fatigue [fə'ti:g] **1.** *nu* condition of being very tired. **2.** *nc* (military) duty such as cleaning windows, sweeping floors etc. Also *vt* make tired.
fatiguing *adj* causing fatigue.
fatuous ['fætjuəs] *adj* foolish, but thinking oneself clever. **fatuously** *adv*.
fatuity [fə'tjuiti] **1.** *nu* state of being fatuous. **2.** *nc* fatuous action or remark.
faucet ['fɔ:sit] *nc* (*US*) tap for controlling the flow of liquid. (*Brit* **tap**).
fault [fɔ:lt] *nc* **1.** mistake or error; something wrong. *There was only one fault in this essay. There is a serious fault in his character. The driver of the lorry admitted that the accident was his fault* i.e. that he had caused the accident. **2.** (geology) crack along which rock has moved up or down.
faulty *adj* having faults. **faultily** *adv*.
faultless *adj* without faults. **faultlessly** *adv*.
at fault causing something wrong; in the wrong. *The driver of the lorry was at fault when the accident happened.*
find fault with someone/something see **find**[1].
to a fault too much. *He is generous to a fault* i.e. he is too generous.
faun [fɔ:n] *nc* an imaginary creature thought by the Romans to live in woods and fields, looking like a man but with the horns and legs of a goat.
fauna ['fɔ:nə] *nu* animals of a particular area or a particular time.
faux pas ['fou'pa:] *nc* embarrassing mistake in speech or behaviour. *pl* **faux pas.**
favour ['feivə*] (*US* **favor**) **1.** *nc/u* friendly help and support. *I did him a favour* i.e. I did something to help him. **2.** *nu* help and support which is too great, too much and which is unfair to others. (*opp* **disfavour**). **3.** *nc* badge or ribbon worn to show that one supports a political party, football team etc. Also *vt* **1.** give help or support to. *I favour your suggestion.* **2.** give too much help or support to. *The teacher must not favour some children more than others.*
favourable *adj* giving help or support: *a favourable reply.* **favourably** *adv*. (*opp* **unfavourable, unfavourably**).
favourite ['feivərit] *adj* most liked. Also *nc* **1.** person/thing most liked. **2.** person who receives an unfair amount of help or support (esp. a child receiving help from a teacher). **3.** person, horse, team etc thought most likely to win a race or game.
favouritism ['feivəritizəm] *nu* practice of giving too much help and support to somebody (esp. a teacher helping a pupil).
ask a favour of somebody ask somebody to help one.
do somebody a favour do something to help somebody.
in favour of someone/something supporting or approving of someone/something. *I am in favour of making John the captain of the team.*
in one's favour helpful to one.
out of favour not liked as much as formerly; less popular than before.
favour somebody with something do something to help somebody. (*formal*).
fawn[1] [fɔ:n] **1.** *nc* young deer. **2.** *nu* yellow-brown colour. Also *adj* (in sense **2.**).
fawn[2] [fɔ:n] *vi* (with reference to dogs) show pleasure in the presence of a human being, by wagging the tail, jumping and rolling over etc.
fawn on someone be willing to do anything to please someone in order to get some advantage from him.
fear [fiə*] *vt/i* be afraid. *He always feared the dentist. They feared for his life* i.e. they were afraid he was going to die. Also *nc/u* condition of being afraid.
fearful *adj* **1.** causing fear; causing death and destruction. **2.** very bad or very great. (*informal*). **fearfully** *adv*. **fearfulness** *un*.
fearless *adj* without fear. **fearlessly** *adv*.
for fear of someone/something because of being afraid of someone/something.
in fear of someone/something afraid. *The thief was in fear of the police.*
in fear and trembling very much afraid.
feasible ['fi:zəbl] *adj* possible; able to be done or carried out: *a feasible idea.* **feasibly** *adv*. **feasibility** [fi:zə'biliti] *nu*.
feast [fi:st] *nc* large meal eaten for some special purpose (usu. to celebrate a happy occasion). Also **1.** *vi* have a feast. **2.** *vt* give a feast to.
feat [fi:t] *nc* some action which requires great strength or skill.
feather ['feðə*] *nc* one of the light things covering a bird's body. **feathery** *adj*.
'feather 'bed bed having a mattress filled with feathers.
as light as a feather very light, having very little weight.
birds of a feather (flock together) people who have the same interests (keep together).
feather one's nest grow rich because of the position one has (often by acting dishonestly).
feature ['fi:tʃə*] *nc* **1.** important part of something. **2.** part of the face: *beautiful features. Her eyes are her best feature.* **3.** important article in a newspaper etc. Also *vt* be or have a feature. *The economy featured very largely in the Prime Minister's speech* i.e. this was one of the main topics of his speech. *This film features John Smith* i.e. he is the main actor.
featureless *adj* having no main features.

(the) features *npl* the face.
February ['februəri] *n* second month of the year.
fed [fed] past of **feed¹**.
fed up *adj* unhappy and dissatisfied. (*informal*).
federation [fedə'reiʃən] **1.** *nc* group of states, countries, societies etc which have joined together to act as one for some or all purposes. **2.** *nu* process of coming together in this way. **federal** ['fedərəl] *adj*.
federalism ['fedərəlizəm] *nu* political ideas which support federation.
federate ['fedəreit] *vt/i* form a federation.
fee [fi:] *nc* money paid by people for certain services (e.g. money paid to doctors, lawyers, schools, universities etc).
feeble ['fi:bl] *adj* very weak. **feebly** *adv*. **feebleness** *nu*.
'feeble-'minded *adj* having very low intelligence.
feed¹ [fi:d] **1.** *vt* give food to. *She was feeding the baby.* **2.** *vi* (with reference to animals or babies) eat. **3.** *vt* supply material to: *feed a machine; feed information to a government department.* *past* **fed** [fed].
feed² [fi:d] **1.** *nc* milk or food taken by a baby. *The baby has four feeds a day.* **2.** *nu* food given to animals. **3.** *nc* act of feeding by animals. **4.** *nc* part of a machine carrying material into the machine.
'feedback information about the result of some process, passed back to the person or machine in charge of the process.
feel [fi:l] *vt/i* **1.** touch with the hand or other part of the body. *I felt the water to see whether it was too hot.* **2.** give an impression when touched. *The water felt cold.* **3.** have some sensation. *I feel tired/hungry/bored/angry/cold etc.* **4.** have an opinion (which may be wrong). *I feel that your idea is the best one.* *past* **felt** [felt]. Also *nu* impression given by feeling: *the feel of a piece of cloth. I haven't got the feel of this car yet* i.e. I'm not used to it.
feeler *nc* **1.** part of the body with which an insect feels. **2.** suggestion or remark made in order to find out what other people think. (*informal* in sense **2.**).
feeling *nc/u* **1.** ability to feel. **2.** something felt in the mind; emotion of any type. **3.** idea or opinion (which might be wrong).
feel for someone sympathize with someone, feel unhappy because someone else is suffering.
feel like something 1. have an impression of being something. *I felt like a fool.* **2.** wish to have something. *I feel like a cup of coffee.*
feel up to something feel strong, brave, clever etc enough to do something. (*informal*).
feel one's way go slowly and carefully while one is learning about a new situation.
hurt somebody's feelings do or say something which makes somebody unhappy.
no hard feelings no feelings of hate or enmity (even though people have been rivals) (*informal*).
feet [fi:t] pl of **foot.**
feign [fein] *vt/i* pretend; try to appear what one is not. *He feigned illness* i.e. he was not really ill.
feint [feint] *nc* action or appearance which is feigned. Also *vi* (boxing) pretend to hit with one hand and then hit with the other.
felicitous [fi'lisitəs] *adj* (with reference to a poem or speech) having well-chosen words. **felicitously** *adv*.
felicity [fi'lisiti] *nu* happiness.
feline ['fi:lain] *adj* of or like a cat. Also *nc* any animal of the cat family (e.g. lion, tiger etc).
fell¹ [fel] past tense of **fall¹**.
fell² [fel] *vt* knock down or cut down: *fell a tree.*
fell³ [fel] *nc* mountain slope in the north of Britain.
fell⁴ [fel] *adj* causing pain or damage: *a fell blow; a fell poison* (*o.f.*).
fellow ['felou] *nc* **1.** man. (*informal*). **2.** person with whom one is associated in some way: *my fellow prisoners/passengers/students.* **3.** senior member of a college at the universities of Oxford and Cambridge. **4.** member of certain societies of scholars and scientists.
fellowship 1. *nu* friendly feeling. **2.** *nc* group of people having similar interests. **3.** *nc/u* position of a senior member of a college in Oxford or Cambridge or of a paid special research worker in any university.
'fellow 'feeling sympathy; feeling of happiness or unhappiness caused by the happiness or unhappiness of somebody else.
'fellow 'traveller 1. person who travels with one. **2.** person who secretly supports the Communist Party, although he is not actually a member of it.
felon ['felən] *nc* criminal.
felony *nc/u* serious crime. **felonious** [fe'louniəs] *adj*.
felt¹ [felt] past of **feel.**
felt² [felt] *nu* type of hard cloth made from wool.
female ['fi:meil] *adj* **1.** of women. **2.** of what corresponds to women in animals, birds, plants etc. Also *nc*.
feminine ['feminin] *adj* **1.** of, for or like women: *feminine charm.* **2.** (grammar) belonging to a certain class of nouns in Latin, French and other languages, or referred to by the pronoun 'she' in English.
femininity [femi'niniti] *nu* condition of being feminine.
feminism ['feminizəm] *nu* movement which tries to get more rights and opportunities for women.
feminist *nc* supporter of this movement.
femur ['fi:mə*] *nc* large bone in the upper part of the leg. *pl* **femurs** or **femora** ['femərə].
fen [fen] *nc* area of wet land in the eastern part of England.
fence¹ [fens] *nc* something made of wood or metal dividing two pieces of land. Also *vt* (often with **off**) surround or separate with a fence.
sit on the fence try to avoid giving an opinion in a quarrel; try to remain friendly with both sides in a quarrel. (*informal*).
fence² [fens] *nc* person who buys stolen goods from criminals. (*informal*).
fence³ [fens] *vi* **1.** fight with swords (usu. for sport). **2.** try to avoid answering a question.
fencer *nc* person who fights with a sword.
fencing *nu* the sport of fighting with swords.
fend [fend] *vi* (with **off**) act to avoid. *He fended off the blow.*
fend for oneself 1. provide oneself with everything that one needs. **2.** fight back if attacked.
fender ['fendə*] *nc* **1.** metal object like a small wall put in front of a fireplace. **2.** (*US*) piece of metal over the wheel of a car

etc. (*Brit* **mudguard**).

ferment[1] ['fə:ment] *nu* excitement and change (esp. political).

ferment[2] [fə'ment] **1.** *vt* cause ferment: *ferment trouble.* **2.** *vi* undergo chemical change, giving off a gas. **fermentation** [fə:men'teiʃən] *nu*.

fern [fə:n] *nc* type of green plant, with leaves that look like big feathers.

ferocious [fə'rouʃəs] *adj* very angry and violent. **ferociously** *adv*. **ferocity** [fə'rɔsiti] *nu*.

ferret ['ferit] *nc* type of small fierce animal which kills rabbits. Also *vi* hunt rabbits using a ferret.

ferret something out find something by searching. (*informal*).

ferry ['feri] *nc* **1.** boat which sails backwards and forwards across a narrow piece of water, carrying goods and passengers. **2.** place where such a boat travels. Also *vt/i* go or take in a ferry.

fertile ['fə:tail] *adj* able to produce (crops, children etc): *fertile land*; *a fertile mind* i.e. one having many ideas.

fertility [fə'tiliti] *nu* condition of being fertile.

fertilize ['fə:tilaiz] *vt* make fertile.

fertilization [fə:tilai'zeiʃən] *nu* process of fertilizing.

fertilizer ['fə:tilaizə*] *nc* substance used for making land fertile.

fervent ['fə:vənt] *adj* having or showing strong feelings. *He is a fervent supporter of the local football team.* **fervently** *adv*.

fervour ['fə:və*] *nu*.

fester ['festə*] *vi* **1.** become filled with poisonous matter. *He cut his hand last week and the cut has begun to fester.* **2.** cause feelings of anger or hate to grow.

festival ['festivl] *nc* occasion of public celebration, enjoyment etc.

festivity [fes'tiviti] *nc* (often *pl*) festival.

festive ['festiv] *adj*. **festively** *adv*.

festoon [fes'tu:n] *vt* hang flowers, ribbons etc on as a decoration. Also *nc* flowers, ribbons etc hung in this way.

fetch [fetʃ] *vt* **1.** go and get. *He went to fetch some meat from the market.* **2.** be sold at. *This fruit fetches fifteen pence a pound.* (*informal* in sense **2.**).

fete, fête [feit] *nc* festival (often to collect money for a special purpose). Also *vt* give a welcome to somebody by a public celebration. *The Prime Minister was feted when he visited the north.*

fetid ['fetid] *adj* having a strong, unpleasant smell. **fetidly** *adv*. **fetidness** *nu*.

fetish ['fetiʃ] *nc* **1.** any object which is believed to have magical power. **2.** anything to which people give too much attention. *He makes a fetish of his car.*

fetishism *nu* belief in a fetish.

fetter ['fetə*] *nc* (usu. *pl*) chain for holding a prisoner. Also *vt* hold a prisoner with a fetter (*o.f.*).

fettle ['fetl] *nu* condition (only in **in fine fettle** i.e. strong and healthy).

feud [fju:d] *nc* quarrel between two people, two families etc lasting a long time. Also *vi* quarrel in this way.

feudalism ['fju:dəlizəm] *nu* **1.** economic and political system of Western Europe, from about the 9th to the 15th centuries, by which people held land in return for services given to the owner of the land. **2.** similar system found in other parts of the world. **feudal** *adj*.

fever ['fi:və*] *nc/u* **1.** one of various types of illness, in which the temperature rises very high. **2.** condition of excitement and restlessness. **feverish** *adj*. **feverishly** *adv*. **feverishness** *nu*.

few [fju:] *determiner/pron* not many; a small number. *I have met a few of these people before. Few of them are my friends. If you want something to read, there are a few magazines on the table. There are hundreds of books in the school library, but few of them are really interesting.*

Note: *few* gives the idea of 'not many' or 'not enough'. *Few of my friends were willing to help me. a few*, however, gives the idea of 'some' without the suggestion that the number was too small.

few and far between see **far.**

a good few, quite a few several; quite a lot; more than a small number of. *He has quite a few/a good few friends here.*

fez [fez] *nc* type of hat worn by some Moslems.

fez

fiancé [fi'ɔnsei] *nc* man whom a woman has promised to marry. (*fem* **fiancée**).

fiasco [fi'æskou] *nc* complete failure of a plan or arrangement. *pl* **fiascos.**

fib [fib] *nc* small and not very important lie. Also *vi* tell a fib. *past* **fibbed.** (*informal*).

fibre ['faibə*] (*US* **fiber**) **1.** *nc* thin thread (e.g. of wool, muscle tissue, coconut etc). **2.** *nu* material made of fibres. **3.** *nu* moral quality; ability to decide what is the proper way to behave. *An officer in the army must be a man of strong moral fibre.*

fibrous ['faibrəs] *adj* made of fibres.

'fibre-glass very strong material made from thin threads of glass.

Note: this substance is sometimes spelled *Fibre-glass* since the word was originally the name of a commercial product.

fickle ['fikl] *adj* changing suddenly and often in what one likes or dislikes. **fickleness** *nu*.

fiction ['fikʃən] **1.** *nu* novels and stories which tell about things which did not actually happen. **2.** *nc* a story of this type; any untrue story. **fictitious** [fik'tiʃəs] *adj*. **fictionally** *adv*.

'non-'fiction all books (esp. in a library) which are not novels and stories (e.g. history, science, poetry, essays, religion etc).

fiddle ['fidl] *nc* **1.** violin. **2.** dishonest arrangement. Also **1.** *vi* play the violin. **2.** *vt/i* make a dishonest arrangement; cheat somebody. **3.** *vi* continually touch or move something in a nervous and restless way. *He was fiddling with his pen while he was talking to me.* (all *informal*).

fiddler *nc* violinist. (*informal*).

'fiddlesticks! *interj* nonsense! (rather *o.f.*).

fit as a fiddle very healthy. (*informal*).

play second fiddle to someone see **play**[1].

fidelity [fi'deliti] *nu* **1.** faithfulness; willingness to give support and help to somebody whatever the danger or difficulties. **2.**

accuracy; ability to produce the same sound, shape, colour etc as an original.

high fidelity very good reproduction of the original sounds. (Sometimes **hi-fi**).

fidget ['fidʒit] *vt/i* continually move in a restless and nervous way. Also *nc* person who fidgets. **fidgety** *adj.*

(have) the fidgets (have) difficulty in remaining still. (*informal*).

field [fi:ld] *nc* **1.** area of land (usu. enclosed by a fence or wall) used for growing crops or grazing animals. **2.** piece of land of various types: *a football field; a coalfield* i.e. land with coalmines on it; *an airfield; a battlefield.* **3.** branch of knowledge: *the field of nuclear physics.* **4.** real life situation studied by a scientist (as distinct from a situation in a laboratory). **5.** (physics) area in which some force is operating. **6.** (physics) the area which can be seen through a telescope, microscope etc. **7.** (cricket and baseball) all the players of the team which is not batting. Also *vt/i* (baseball and cricket) stand in the field and stop the ball.

fielder *nc* (baseball or cricket) person who fields.

'field day **1.** day on which an athletics contest etc is held (esp. of a school or college). **2.** day on which soldiers give a show for the public. **3.** any day on which there is unusual and enjoyable action.

'field glasses device used for making distant things appear nearer so that they can be seen more clearly.

'field gun light gun on wheels.

'field 'marshal officer of highest rank in an army.

'field trip journey made by students of geology, geography, and other sciences, in order to observe things.

fiend [fi:nd] *nc* **1.** devil or evil spirit. **2.** wicked person. **fiendish** *adj.* **fiendishly** *adv.*

fierce [fiəs] *adj* angry and dangerous: *a fierce lion; a fierce fire.* **fiercely** *adv.* **fierceness** *nu.*

fiery ['faiəri] *adj* **1.** like or of fire, very hot. **2.** easily made angry. **fierily** *adv.* **fieriness** *nu.*

fiesta [fi'estə] *nc* religious holiday with public celebrations (usu. in the Mediterranean countries or in South America).

fife [faif] *nc* small musical pipe, often used in military bands.

fifth [fifθ] see appendix.

'fifth 'column group of people in a country, secretly working to help the enemy in war.

'fifth 'columnist *nc* person who does this.

fig [fig] *nc* **1.** type of small, soft, fleshy fruit grown in warm regions. **2.** this fruit dried. **3.** the tree on which it grows.

not care a fig not care at all.

fight[1] [fait] *nc* **1.** struggle or contest (esp. one in which people try to hurt each other, or try to overcome some difficulty). *The two boys had a fight. The police are continuing the fight against crime.* **2.** wish or ability to have a fight. *He showed plenty of fight when he was attacked.* **3.** boxing match.

fighter *nc* **1.** person who fights (esp. a boxer). **2.** type of fast aeroplane used for attacking enemy aeroplanes.

put up a good/bad fight fight well/badly.

fight[2] [fait] *vt/i* have a fight. *The two boys fought. John fought (with/against) James. The police fought against crime. past* **fought** [fɔ:t].

fight somebody/something off fight to keep somebody/something away. *He fought off his attacker. He fought off disease.*

fight on continue fighting.

fight it out fight until one side wins. (*informal*).

fight shy of something wish to keep away from something; be unwilling to do something. (*informal*).

figment ['figmənt] *nc* usu. only in **a figment of the imagination** i.e. something imagined but untrue.

figure[1] ['figə*] *nc* **1.** shape or outline of the human body. *I saw a figure in the darkness.* **2.** important person. **3.** diagram or drawing made to explain something. **4.** form drawn in geometry (e.g. a square or circle). **5.** amount of money. **6.** one of the numbers from 0 to 9. **7.** movement in dancing. **8.** pattern on cloth, wallpaper, carpets etc.

figurative ['figjurətiv] *adj* using figures of speech; using words which have a meaning other than the normal one (e.g. saying that a brave man is a lion). **figuratively** *adv.*

'figurehead **1.** wooden carving formerly carried on the front of ships. **2.** person in an important position who has no real power.

figure of speech expression which is not really true, but which is used to give an idea of the meaning (e.g. if we say that a brave man fought like a lion, we are using a figure of speech).

figure[2] ['figə*] **1.** *vt* make a painting, drawing, sculpture etc of. **2.** *vi* take an important part. *The economy figured very largely in the Prime Minister's speech* i.e. this was one of the main topics in his speech. **3.** *vi* (mainly *US*) think; arrive at an opinion after thought. *I figured that I could help you.* (*informal* in sense **3.**).

figure someone/something out understand someone/something after careful thought. *I tried to figure out what he meant.* (*informal*).

filament ['filəmənt] *nc* **1.** thin thread. **2.** wire in an electric light bulb.

filch [filtʃ] *vt/i* steal small things of little value.

file[1] [fail] *nc* metal tool with a rough surface used for smoothing hard materials. Also *vt* smooth or cut with a file.

file

filings *npl* small pieces of metal removed by a file.

file[2] [fail] *nc* **1.** something for holding papers, letters etc. **2.** collection of papers giving information about somebody/something. *The police have a file on him* i.e. information about him has been written down and is kept by the police. Also *vt* put in a file.

file[3] [fail] *nc* line of people one behind the other: *in single file.* Also *vi* move in a file. *They filed past the coffin. They filed out of the room.*

the rank and file ordinary members of

some society, movement or community; all those who are not the leaders.

filial ['filiəl] *adj* of a son or daughter.

filibuster ['filibʌstə*] *nc* attempt in parliament etc to prevent a government passing a law by using up time with long speeches and asking many questions. Also *vi* (mainly *US*) act in this way.

filigree ['filigri:] *nu* decoration made with thin gold or silver wire.

fill [fil] *vt/i* become or make full. *The room filled with people* i.e. many people came into the room. *He filled the box with books* i.e. he put many books in the box.

filling *nc/u* substance which fills something (esp. substance used by a dentist to fill holes in teeth).

'filling station (*Brit*) place where a motorist can get petrol, oil etc for his car.

fill something in 1. write what is necessary on an official piece of paper: *fill in an application; fill in one's name.* 2. put something into a hole so as to fill it completely. *He filled in the hole.*

fill someone in on something give someone the necessary information about something. (*informal*).

fill out become fatter. (*informal*).

fill something out write what is necessary on an official paper: *fill out a form/application/receipt etc.*

fill something up 1. fill completely. *He filled up my cup. I filled the room up with furniture.* 2. write what is necessary on an official paper: *fill up a form.*

eat/have one's fill (of something) eat or have as much as one wants of something.

fillet[1] ['filit] *nc* 1. thick piece of meat or fish from which the bones have been removed. Also *vt* remove bones from meat or fish.

fillet[2] ['filit] *nc* strip of cloth worn around the head to keep the hair in place (*o.f.*).

fillip ['filip] *nc* anything which arouses extra interest or support. (*informal*).

filly ['fili] *nc* young female horse. (*masc* **colt**).

film [film] 1. *nc* cinema picture. 2. *nu* substance on which photographs and cinema pictures are made. 3. *nc* thin covering: *a film of oil/dust.* Also *vt/i* make a cinema film (of something).

filmy *adj* (usu. with reference to cloth) thin and soft. **filminess** *nu.*

filter ['filtə*] *nc* 1. any device or substance for allowing liquid to pass through it while not allowing anything solid to pass through. 2. device used on a camera etc for preventing light of certain wavelengths to pass into the camera. Also 1. *vt* pass through a filter. *He filtered the liquid.* 2. *vi* (usu. with **down** or **through**) move slowly to reach many people. *The new ideas filtered down to the majority of people. People filtered across the border* i.e. came in small groups.

filth [filθ] *nu* very unpleasant dirt.

filthy *adj* very dirty. **filthily** *adv.* **filthiness** *nu.*

fin [fin] *nc* 1. one of the parts of its body which a fish uses for swimming. 2. something shaped like a fin (e.g. on a bomb or rocket).

final ['fainl] *adj* last; coming at the end. *He was completing the final stages of the work. What was the final score of the football match? The headmaster's decision is final* i.e. his decision cannot be questioned or changed.

finally *adv.*

finality [fai'næliti] *nu* condition or appearance of being final.

the finals *npl* 1. last contest in a series of contests. 2. last set of examinations in a course of study at a college or university.

finalist ['fainəlist] *nc* person competing in the last of a series of contests or examinations.

finale [fi'nɑ:li] *nc* last part of a piece of music.

finalize *vt* finish making plans or arrangements. *He finalized the arrangements.*

finance ['fainæns] 1. *nu* management of public money. 2. *nc* (often *pl*) (public) money. Also *vt* supply money for something. *The government have financed a new factory.*

financial [fai'nænʃl] *adj.* **financially** *adv.*

financier [fai'nænsiə*] *nc* person whose work is concerned with finance.

finch [fintʃ] *nc* type of small songbird, which eats seeds.

find[1] [faind] *vt* get somebody/something that was lost, hidden or unknown. *I found some money in this old coat. Large deposits of oil and gas have been found under the sea. In the morning we found that the car would not start* i.e. we had not known this before. *I find that I am unable to help you* i.e. I thought earlier that I could help you. *past* **found** [faund].

findings *npl* decision made by a judge, jury, committee of enquiry etc.

find out find by searching, asking etc. *I tried to find out the answer in the library. I don't know when he is arriving but I will try to find out.*

find someone out discover that someone is dishonest. *He used to cheat in the examinations until the teacher found him out.*

find fault with someone/something point out the faults, mistakes etc in someone/something.

find one's feet begin to do something new with more ease or skill.

find somebody guilty/not guilty decide after a trial in a court of law that somebody is guilty or not guilty.

find oneself reach; arrive at. *After walking for hours we found ourselves in a narrow valley.*

be found exist. *Kangaroos are found in Australia.*

find[2] [faind] *nc* something valuable or pleasant which has been found.

fine[1] [fain] *adj* 1. very delicate; small and made with skill. *A watchmaker does very fine work.* 2. very small or thin: *very fine rain; a fine point to a pencil; fine cotton.* 3. pure: *fine gold.* 4. good or pleasant: *a fine house; a fine meal.* 5. without rain and pleasant: *fine weather; a fine day.*

finely *adv* delicately: *finely made.*

finery ['fainəri] *nu* very good clothes; clothes worn for a special occasion.

'fine 'arts painting, music, sculpture etc.

cut it fine leave very little time to do something. *He cut it very fine and had to run to catch his train.* (*informal*).

fine[2] [fain] *nc* sum of money taken from somebody as a punishment. Also *vt* make somebody pay a fine.

finesse [fi'nes] *nu* ability to deal with difficult situations in a skilful way.

finger ['fiŋgə*] *nc* 1. one of the five parts at the end of each hand. 2. part of a glove into which a finger goes. Also *vt* touch with the fingers.

Note: the *thumb* is sometimes not included as one of the fingers.

'finger bowl small bowl containing water, used for cleaning one's fingers after a meal.
'fingernail hard substance at the end of a finger.
'fingerprint *nc* **1.** mark made by the end of a finger. **2.** the small lines on the skin at the end of a finger. Also *vt* make a record of somebody's fingerprints.
'fingertip end of a finger.
have something at one's fingertips know some subject very well.
be all fingers and thumbs be clumsy; be unable to hold things properly. (*informal*).
have a finger in every pie have a part in every plan or arrangement. (*informal*).
lay a finger on touch or harm. (*informal*).
put one's finger on something say or decide exactly what something is. (*informal*).
twist somebody around one's little finger be able to make somebody do whatever one wishes. (*informal*).
work one's fingers to the bone work very hard.

finical ['finikl], **finicky** ['finiki] *adj* disliking many things (esp. types of food).

finish[1] ['finiʃ] *vt/i* end. *I've nearly finished; wait another ten minutes. I've finished the work.*
finished *adj* ended. (*opp* **unfinished**).
'finishing school private school which teaches girls how to behave in society (e.g. how to dance, choose clothes, make conversation etc).
finish something off/up finish completely. *I hurried to finish off the work. I finished up all the food in the house* i.e. I ate it.
finish with somebody/something have no more relations with. *I have finished with John* i.e. I am no longer friendly with him.

finish[2] ['finiʃ] *n sing* **1.** last part, end. **2.** (often with reference to the polish or paint put on something) way in which some work is completed.

finite ['fainait] *adj* having an end or limit. (*opp* **infinite**).
finite verb (grammar) verb having a definite tense form and number (e.g. 'saw' in *He saw me* is a finite verb; 'seeing', 'to see', 'seen' are not finite verbs) (*opp* **non-finite verb**).

fiord, fjord [fjɔːd] *nc* narrow inlet of the sea (esp. in Norway).

fir [fəː*] **1.** *nc* type of evergreen tree which has thin leaves shaped like needles. **2.** *nu* the wood of this tree.

fire[1] ['faiə*] **1.** *nc/u* burning. *Animals are afraid of fire. There was a fire in the town yesterday.* **2.** *nc* something burning. *He lit a fire because the room was cold.* **3.** *nc* gas or electric apparatus for warming a room (usu. showing the part which gives out heat). **4.** *nu* great excitement or other strong feelings. **5.** *nu* shooting of guns. *We heard the enemy's fire.*

fire[2] ['faiə*] **1.** *vt/i* shoot a gun. *He fired at me. He fired a gun. The gun fired.* **2.** *vt* cause to burn. (**set fire to** is more common). **3.** *vt* excite; arouse strong feelings. *The speaker fired the audience with enthusiasm.* **4.** *vt* dismiss a person from a job. (*informal*). **5.** *vt* expose to great heat as part of a manufacturing process: *fire pottery/bricks etc.*
'fire alarm warning of a fire in a building etc; apparatus for giving this warning.
'firearm gun which can be held in the hands.
'firebrand person who causes strong political excitement.
'fire brigade people whose job is to stop fires in buildings etc.
'fire eater *nc* **1.** public entertainer who pretends to eat fire. **2.** person who often quarrels with people. **fire eating** *nu.*
'fire engine vehicle carrying hosepipes and other apparatus used in stopping fires.
'fire escape **1.** stairs (usu. on the outside of a building) which can be used if there is a fire in the building. **2.** long ladder fixed to a vehicle, used to allow people to escape from a burning building.
'fire extinguisher apparatus filled with chemicals or water, used to stop fires in buildings etc.
'firefly type of insect which gives out a light.
'fireguard object like a fence, for putting in front of a fire in a room.
'fireman man whose work is to stop fires in buildings etc.
'fireplace place where a fire is lit to warm a room.
'firepower ability to fire a certain number of shells and bullets; number of guns possessed by an army, ship, aeroplane etc.
'fireproof *adj* made so as not to burn: *fireproof curtains.*
'fireside area around a fire in a room.
'firewood pieces of wood intended for burning.
'firework something containing gunpowder and other substances, making a loud noise and a bright light when lit, used for celebrations after dark.
catch fire see **catch**[1].
on fire **1.** burning. **2.** full of strong feelings.
open fire (on/at something/someone) begin shooting a gun.
set fire to something/something on fire cause something to burn.
under fire **1.** being fired at by guns. **2.** being attacked in words.

firm[1] [fəːm] *nc* business company.

firm[2] [fəːm] *adj* solid; fixed; not easily moved. *The leg of that chair is not very firm* i.e. it is loosely fixed to the chair. *He spoke in a firm voice* i.e. in a strong and determined way, showing that he would not change his opinion. **firmly** *adv.* **firmness** *nu.*
stand firm **1.** remain where one is without moving. **2.** refuse to change one's decision.

firmament ['fəːməmənt] *nc* the sky. (*formal*).

first [fəːst] *adj/adv* coming before all others. *He lives in the first house in that street* i.e. the house you come to first as you walk along the street. *He came first in the race* i.e. he won the race.
firstly *adv* first.
'first 'aid help which can be given to a person who has been injured, before a doctor arrives.
'first-'class *adj* **1.** very good, excellent. **2.** (of ways of travelling etc) the most expensive.
'first 'night evening on which a play is performed for the first time; the performance of the play itself.
'first 'person (grammar) form of a pronoun or verb which refers to the speaker (e.g. *I, we, me, us*).
'first-'rate *adj* very good; excellent. (*informal*).
at first in the beginning.
at first hand see **hand**[1].

first and last completely; in every way. *He is first and last a scientist.*

firth [fəːθ] *nc* inlet of the sea (esp. in Scotland).

fiscal ['fiskl] *adj* having reference to government money.

fish [fiʃ] **1.** *nc* type of creature which lives in water and does not need to come to the surface to breathe air. **2.** *nu* fish used as food. *He eats a lot of fish. pl* **fish** or **fishes.** Also *vt/i* catch, try to catch, fish.

fishing *nu* act of catching fish, as work or as a sport.

fishy *adj* causing suspicion. (*informal*).

'fishmonger man who sells fish in a shop.

'fisherman man who catches fish, either as his work or for sport.

'fishing rod long piece of wood, to which is attached a strong thread with a hook at the end, used for catching fish as a sport.

fish for something try to get something from somebody (usu. **fish for compliments** i.e. try to make somebody praise one) (*informal*).

fish something out get something out. *He fished some money out of his pocket.* (*informal*).

drink like a fish regularly drink a lot of alcoholic drink. (*informal*).

feel like a fish out of water feel very uncomfortable and unable to be happy and friendly because one is in a strange place with people whom one does not know.

fission ['fiʃən] *nu* (usu. with reference to the breaking up of an atom in a nuclear explosion) process of dividing into several parts. **fissionable** *adj*.

fissure ['fiʃə*] *nc* deep crack in the ground or in a mountain.

fist [fist] *nc* hand with the fingers bent to touch the palm.

fit[1] [fit] *adj* **1.** strong and healthy. *He felt fit after his holiday.* **2.** suitable. *The house was not fit to live in* i.e. it was a very bad house. *He is not a fit person to decide what should be done* i.e. he has not the authority or ability to decide. (*opp* **unfit**).

fit[2] [fit] **1.** *vt/i* be the right size for. *I could not find a pair of shoes which fitted me.* **2.** *vt* put some piece of apparatus or furnishing in place. *The electrician fitted my new cooker. I have been fitting a carpet in this room.* **3.** *vt* make suitable. *His long experience fits him for the job. past* **fitted.**

fitter *nc* **1.** person who fits apparatus in place (esp. one who has a knowledge of mechanical or electrical engineering). **2.** person who fits new clothes on people.

fitting *adj* suitable: *a fitting punishment.* Also *nc* **1.** something fitted in a building etc (e.g. a light, fire, water pipe etc). **2.** occasion when one tries on a garment being made for one to see whether it fits.

fit in be suitable. *We invited him to join our club but he didn't fit in* i.e. he did not have the same interests as the other members.

fit someone/something out provide what is necessary: *fit out a boy for school* i.e. buy his uniform and his books.

a good/bad fit the right/wrong size for. *This pair of shoes is a good fit for me.*

fit[3] [fit] *nc* **1.** sudden illness in which one loses consciousness and makes movements which one cannot control. **2.** something similar to this happening suddenly: *a fit of coughing; in fits of laughter.*

fitful *adj* often stopping and starting: *a fitful sleep.* **fitfully** *adv*.

by fits and starts often stopping and starting. *He worked by fits and starts.* (*informal*).

five [faiv] see appendix.

fives *n sing* game in which a small ball is hit with the hand.

fix[1] [fiks] *vt* **1.** fasten. *He fixed the cupboard to the wall with nails.* **2.** arrange; agree on: *fix a date, price; fix up a meeting.* **3.** (*US*) mend; prepare; make ready: *fix a watch; fix a drink.* (*informal*). **4.** treat with some substance to prevent fading or loss of colour. **5.** arrange in a dishonest way.

fixation [fik'seiʃən] *nc* strong feeling or idea which is unreasonable and which does not change.

fixed *adj* **1.** placed in position and not moving. **2.** arranged or agreed on.

fixedly ['fiksidli] *adv* without moving or changing.

fixture *nc* **1.** something which is fixed in a building (e.g. a light, a water pipe etc). **2.** game or sports contest which takes place on a date arranged before.

fix on/upon someone/something choose someone/something.

fix one's eyes/attention on somebody/something look carefully at; give careful attention to.

fix[2] [fiks] *nc* **1.** (usu. only *sing*) difficult position. *He's in a fix.* **2.** injection of a drug (e.g. heroin). **3.** fraud. *The fight was a fix.* (all *informal*).

fizz [fiz] *vi* make a sound like that of bubbles of gas coming out of a liquid. Also *nc*.

fizzy *adj*: *a fizzy drink.*

fizzle ['fizl] *vi* in **fizzle out** i.e. end in a weak and disappointing way. *His plans fizzled out.*

fjord [fjɔːd] *nc* see **fiord.**

flabbergast ['flæbəgɑːst] *vt* surprise very greatly. **flabbergasted** *adj*. (both *informal*).

flabby ['flæbi] *adj* fat and soft. **flabbiness** *nu*.

flaccid ['flæksid] *adj* weak and soft. **flaccidity** [flæk'siditi] *nu*.

flag[1] [flæg] *nc* **1.** piece of cloth etc with a design which represents a country, town, person, club etc. **2.** small piece of paper, like a flag, sold in the streets for charity. Also *vt* send a message by showing a series of flags. *past* **flagged.**

'flagpole long pole or piece of wood on which a flag is flown.

'flagship ship on which an admiral sails.

'flagstaff flagpole.

'flagstone large flat piece of stone used for making paths etc.

flag something up mark something for future reference.

flag[2] [flæg] *vi* become weak. *The runners were flagging. past* **flagged.**

flagon ['flægən] *nc* large bottle.

flagrant ['fleigrnt] *adj* (with reference to something dishonest or bad) not hidden: *flagrant disobedience.* **flagrantly** *adv*.

flail [fleil] *nc* instrument with a wooden handle and a heavy movable stick, used for beating corn, wheat etc to separate the seeds from the rest of the plant. Also *vt/i* **1.** use a flail. **2.** try to strike without aiming very well. *He flailed his fists in the air.*

flair [flɛə*] *nc* (usu. only *sing*) natural ability to do something. *He has a flair for mathematics.*

flak [flæk] *nu* shells fired at aeroplanes from large guns on the ground.

flake [fleik] *nc* small light piece of something: *flakes of snow.*

flaky *adj* consisting of flakes: *flaky pastry.*

flake (off) come off in flakes. *The paint is*

flaking off.

flamboyant [flæm'bɔiənt] *adj* brightly coloured; easily noticed because of bright colours; showy. **flamboyantly** *adv.* **flamboyance** *nu.*

flame [fleim] *nc* one of the red or yellow tongues of burning gas seen where there is a fire. Also *vi* be burning with flames.

'flamethrower weapon like a gun, which sends out fire instead of bullets.

in flames burning brightly, on fire.

old flame person formerly loved by somebody. *She is his old flame.* (*informal*).

flamingo [flə'miŋgou] *nc* type of bird with long legs and neck and pinkish feathers. *pl* **flamingos** or **flamingoes.**

flammable ['flæməbl] *adj* easily set on fire. *Note:* the opposite sense is expressed by *not flammable.* The word *inflammable* also means easily set on fire.

flan [flæn] *nc* shallow open tart.

flange [flændʒ] *nc* outside edge for keeping an object in place (esp. in a tool or machine).

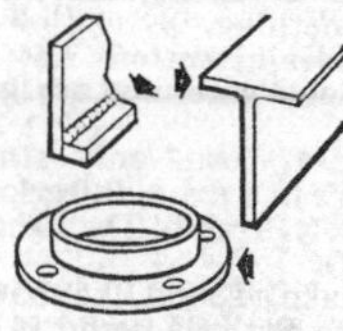

flange

flank [flæŋk] *nc* **1.** side of an animal (and sometimes of a human being). **2.** side of an army. Also *vt* **1.** be at the side of. **2.** attack an army from the side.

flannel ['flænl] **1.** *nu* type of cloth made from wool. **2.** *nc* piece of cloth used for washing oneself. **3.** *nu* unnecessary words.

flannels *npl* trousers made of flannel (used esp. for sport).

flannelette [flænə'let] *nu* cloth made from cotton, made to look like flannel.

flap[1] [flæp] *nc* **1.** anything which hangs down from/over something else (e.g. on a pocket, envelope etc). **2.** noise of a large surface moving; the movement itself: *the flap of a large bird's wing.* Also *vt/i* move a large surface. *The bird flapped its wings. past* **flapped.**

'flapjack type of thin cake.

flap[2] [flæp] *vi* (*Brit*) become excited and worried. Also *nc* (*Brit*) state of excitement and worry: *be in a flap.* (both *informal*).

flare [flɛə*] *vi* burn for a short time with a bright light. Also *nc* **1.** (often with reference to one used as a signal) bright light burning for a short time. **2.** widening of a skirt etc towards the lower edge (as in **flared skirt**).

flare up 1. burn with a flare. **2.** suddenly start; suddenly get angry. *A quarrel flared up.*

'flare-up *nc* sudden quarrel. (*informal*).

flash[1] [flæʃ] *nc* **1.** sudden bright light: *a flash of lightning.* **2.** short piece of news received or sent by radio or telegraph.

flash[2] [flæʃ] **1.** *vt/i* make a flash. *The lightning flashed in the sky. He flashed his torch for a few seconds.* **2.** *vi* move very quickly. *The cars were flashing past. An idea flashed into his mind.* **3.** *vt* send a message by radio or telegraph. *He flashed the news to us.*

flashy *adj* bright but of poor quality or value: *flashy clothes.* **flashily** *adv.* **flashiness** *nu.*

'flashback sequence in a cinema film which goes back to show events which happened before the main part of the story.

'flashlight 1. electric torch. **2.** piece of apparatus used by a photographer for making a sudden bright light. (Also **flash**).

in a flash suddenly; very quickly.

a flash in the pan a sudden success or clever achievement which has not happened before and will not happen again. (*informal*).

flask [flɑːsk] *nc* **1.** type of bottle used in laboratories. **2.** flat bottle for carrying in the pocket or fastened to one's belt etc. **3.** vacuum flask i.e. container made in such a way that a liquid put into it remains at the same temperature for a long time.

hip flask see **hip**[1].

flat[1] [flæt] *nc* **1.** (*Brit*) number of rooms on one floor of a building. (*US* **apartment**). **2.** (usu. *pl*) low land beside a river. **3.** flat part of anything. **4.** flat tyre. **5.** musical note which is lowered by one semitone (e.g. B flat is one semitone below B natural).

flat[2] [flæt] *adj* **1.** level; smooth; without bumps or hills: *a flat surface.* **2.** uninteresting. **3.** (with reference to beer or other such drinks containing gas) old and with the gas gone. **4.** (music) below the true pitch. **5.** (with reference to a tyre) punctured; without air. **6.** definite; without further discussion: *a flat refusal.* **flatness** *nu.*

flatly *adv* in a definite way. *He flatly refused to help me.*

flatten *vt* make flat.

'flat 'feet *n sing* or *pl* condition of the feet in which the bottom of the foot is flat.

'flatfish one of several types of fish which have thin flat bodies, with both eyes on the side which is kept upwards. *pl* **flatfish.**

'flat 'rate charge made for goods or services, to which no extra charges will be added.

fall flat have no effect at all; be ignored. *His suggestion fell flat.* (*informal*).

go flat out go at full speed. (*informal*).

flatter ['flætə*] *vt* **1.** tell somebody that he is very good, very clever etc when in fact he is not. **2.** (usu. with reference to a picture, photograph, dress etc) make somebody look better than he really is.

flattery *nc/u* process of flattering.

flatterer *nc* person who flatters.

flatter oneself be pleased (often about something which in fact is not so). *He flatters himself that he can play the piano well* i.e. he thinks he can but he cannot.

flatulent ['flætjulənt] *adj* having too much gas in the stomach. **flatulence** *nu.*

flaunt [flɔːnt] *vt/i* behave in a bad or foolish way to make people take notice of one. *She was flaunting her new clothes.*

flavour ['fleivə*] (*US* **flavor**) *nc/u* **1.** taste; quality which can be experienced by the mouth. *This food has a strong flavour.* **2.** special quality of anything, or a suggestion of it. *This book has a romantic flavour.* Also *vt* increase the flavour of, give flavour to.

flavouring *nc/u* something used to give flavour to food.

flaw [flɔː] *nc* **1.** crack in glass or pottery. **2.** mistake or fault: *a flaw in an argument.*

flawless *adj* without a flaw; perfect. **flawlessly** *adv.*

flax [flæks] *nu* type of plant, used for making a kind of cloth (called **linen**).

flaxen *adj* (usu. with reference to the colour of hair) light yellow.
flay [flei] *vt* **1.** take the skin off (usu. a dead animal). **2.** whip very severely. **3.** criticize or attack in words very severely.
flea [fli:] *nc* small insect which lives on the blood of animals, birds, human beings etc.
fleck [flek] *nc* small mark or spot. Also *vt* mark with flecks.
fled [fled] past of **flee.**
fledged [fledʒd] *adj* (with reference to a bird) having grown the feathers needed for flying.
fledgling *nc* young bird just learning to fly.
'fully-'fledged *adj* properly qualified. *A fully-fledged member of the club.* (*informal*).
flee [fli:] *vt/i* run away. *The robbers fled. He fled his enemy. past* **fled** [fled].
fleece[1] [fli:s] *nc* wool of a sheep.
fleecy *adj* like wool.
fleece[2] [fli:s] *vt* take all of somebody's money or property by a trick. *The young man fleeced his uncle.* (*informal*).
fleet[1] [fli:t] *nc* **1.** number of ships or boats sailing together or under one command. **2.** number of buses etc owned by one person or one company.
fleet[2] [fli:t] *adj* fast (*o.f.*).
fleeting *adj* moving fast: *a fleeting glance.*
fleetingly *adv.*
flesh [fleʃ] *nu* **1.** soft part of the body over the bones. **2.** the body (as opposed to the soul).
fleshy *adj* **1.** like flesh. **2.** fat; too fat.
fleshiness *nu.*
'flesh-coloured *adj* of the colour of Europeans; pinkish.
'flesh wound small wound which is not very deep.
in the flesh in real life, and not as a picture etc.
one's own flesh and blood one's own family (e.g. one's parents, children, brothers, sisters etc).
flew [flu:] past tense of **fly**[2].
flex[1] [fleks] *nc/u* thin insulated wire for carrying electricity.
flex[2] [fleks] *vt* bend. *He flexed his muscles.*
flexible ['fleksibl] *adj* **1.** easily bent into different shapes. **2.** willing to change one's opinions, plans etc. (*opp* **inflexible**).
flexible *adv.* **flexibility** [flexi'biliti] *nu.*
flibbertigibbet ['flibəti'dʒibit] *nc* **1.** lively, restless young person. **2.** person who often changes his opinions and plans. (both *informal*).
flick [flik] *vt* hit quickly and lightly. Also *nc* quick light blow.
'flick knife type of knife in which the blade can be pushed into the handle and released by a spring.
flicker ['flikə*] *vt/i* (usu. with reference to a light) move quickly and unsteadily. Also *nc* quick and unsteady movement of a light.
flier ['flaiə*] *nc* see **fly**[2].
flight [flait] **1.** *nu* act of flying. **2.** *nc* journey in an aeroplane. **3.** *nc* number of birds, aeroplanes etc flying together. **4.** *nc* act of running away: *the flight of the enemy.* **5.** *nc* set of stairs between two level places.
flighty *adj* not serious; always looking for amusement: *a flighty young woman.*
flightiness *nu.*
'flight deck **1.** part of an aircraft carrier from which aeroplanes fly. **2.** part of an aircraft used by the pilot etc.
in flight while flying.
put somebody to flight make somebody run away.
take to flight run away.
flimsy ['flimzi] *adj* not strongly made; easily torn; of poor material. **flimsily** *adv.*
flimsiness *nu.*
flinch [flintʃ] *vi* move back a little because of danger or pain.
fling [fliŋ] *vt/i* throw with force. *The boy was flinging stones. past* **flung** [flʌŋ].
fling up one's hands hold one's hands up suddenly.
have a fling at something try to do something which is difficult. (*informal*).
have one's fling have some wild (and usu. foolish) enjoyment. (*informal*).
flint [flint] *nc/u* **1.** very hard type of stone. **2.** stone in a cigarette lighter etc which produces a spark when hit with a piece of steel.
flinty *adj* **1.** like flint. **2.** very hard. **3.** unfriendly.
flip [flip] *vt* hit quickly and lightly. *past* **flipped.** Also *nc* quick, light blow. Also *adj* **1.** smart, flippant. (*informal*). **2.** in **flip side** i.e. less important side (of a record).
flippant ['flipənt] *adj* not serious; making jokes about things which other people treat seriously. **flippantly** *adv.* **flippancy** *nu.*
flipper ['flipə*] *nc* **1.** limb of certain sea animals (e.g. the seal) which helps it to swim. **2.** long piece of rubber attached to the foot to help people to swim.
flirt [flə:t] *vi* play at love etc for amusement. *She was flirting with him. He flirted with the idea* i.e. he was not seriously interested in it. Also *nc* person who does this.
flirtatious [flə:'teiʃəs] *adj.* **flirtatiously** *adv.*
flirtation [flə:'teiʃən] *nc/u.*
flit [flit] *vi* move quickly and lightly from place to place. *The birds were flitting about in the trees. past* **flitted.**
float[1] [flout] **1.** *vt/i* rest, cause to rest, on the top of liquid. *The boy was floating his boat.* **2.** *vi* be held up by air, gas etc. *The boat was floating on the water. Dust floats in the air.*
floating voter person who sometimes votes for one party in an election and sometimes for another.
float a company start a business firm by borrowing money.
float the pound let the pound find its own value as international currency.
float[2] [flout] *nc* **1.** piece of cork, plastic etc, on a fishing line, which floats on the water and shows the fisherman where the line is. **2.** vehicle carrying something to be shown in a procession.
flock[1] [flɔk] *nc* **1.** number of sheep, goats or birds together. **2.** number of people together. Also *vi* move together in a large group. *The people were flocking to the theatre.*
flock[2] [flɔk] *nu* pieces of wool (esp. pieces used to fill a mattress).
floe [flou] *nc* big piece of ice floating in the sea.
flog [flɔg] *vt* **1.** hit many times very hard with a stick or whip. **2.** sell. (*informal* in sense **2.**). *past* **flogged.**
flogging *nc* severe beating.
flog a dead horse try to start again something that is already finished. (*informal*).
flood [flʌd] *nc* **1.** flow of water over land which is usually dry. **2.** something like a flood, large amount: *a flood of ideas/requests/tears/light.* Also *vt/i*: *The river has*

flooded. He was flooded with applications for tickets.

'floodlight *nc* strong light, often used to show the outside of buildings at night. Also *vt* light with a floodlight. *past* **floodlit** ['flʌdlit].

floor[1] [flɔ:*] *nc* **1.** part of a room on which one walks. **2.** all the rooms in a building at the same height from the ground. *This building has two floors* i.e. there are rooms at ground level, and more rooms upstairs. *Note:* (*Brit*) the floor at the bottom of a building is called the *ground floor* and the floor above is called the *first floor*. (*US*) the floor at the bottom is called the *first floor* and the one above is called the *second floor*. **3.** anything like the floor of a room i.e. the floor of a railway carriage. **4.** part of a room where Members of Parliament etc sit.

flooring *nu* **1.** material for making floors. **2.** material for covering floors (e.g. carpets, linoleum, tiles etc).

'floor show entertainment presented in a restaurant etc.

have the floor be allowed to speak at a meeting (esp. a meeting of Members of Parliament etc).

floor[2] [flɔ:*] *vt* **1.** put a floor in. *He floored the room.* **2.** hit somebody so that he falls to the floor. (*informal*). **3.** be too difficult for somebody to understand. (*informal*).

flop[1] [flɔp] *vi* fall heavily and without much control over one's movements. *He flopped into a chair. past* **flopped.** Also *nc* movement like this.

floppy *adj* hanging loosely. **floppiness** *nu*.

flop[2] [flɔp] *nc* failure. *The new play was a flop* i.e. very few people came to see it. Also *vi* fail. *past* **flopped.** (both *informal*).

flora ['flɔ:rə] *nc/u* all the plant life in a particular area or at a particular period of time.

floral ['flɔ:rl] *adj* with reference to flowers.

florid ['flɔrid] *adj* **1.** (with reference to the face) normally red in colour. **2.** with too much decoration.

florin ['flɔrin] *nc* formerly, British coin worth two shillings (10 pence).

florist ['flɔrist] *nc* person who sells flowers.

floss [flɔs] *nu* mass of short threads of silk.

'candy-floss (*Brit*) type of sweet made from sugar, resembling floss. (*US* **cotton candy**).

flotilla [flɔ'tilə] *nc* small number of warships.

flotsam ['flɔtsəm] *nu* objects from a wrecked ship floating in the sea.

flotsam and jetsam useless things of various types. (Properly *flotsam* refers to things floating in the sea, and *jetsam* to things washed on to land by the sea).

flounce[1] [flauns] *vi* move angrily and noisily. *She flounced out of the room.*

flounce[2] [flauns] *nc* strip of cloth sewn on a woman's garment for decoration.

flounder[1] ['flaundə*] *vi* **1.** (often with reference to movement in water) move with great difficulty, making violent efforts. **2.** do anything clumsily and with difficulty.

flounder[2] ['flaundə*] *nc* type of flatfish.

flour ['flauə*] *nu* powder made from wheat, corn etc, used for making bread etc. **floury** *adj*.

flourish[1] ['flʌriʃ] **1.** *vi* grow well. **2.** *vi* be most active at a certain time. *The British Empire flourished in the 19th century.* **3.** *vt* make large movements in the air. *He was flourishing a sword.*

flourish[2] ['flʌriʃ] *nc* **1.** movement of something in the air. *He was making flourishes with his sword.* **2.** short piece of loud music. **3.** large curve in handwriting.

flout [flaut] *vt* treat as though foolish and unimportant. *He tried to flout the headmaster's authority* i.e. he showed no respect for the headmaster.

flow [flou] *vi* (usu. with reference to liquids) move along. Also *nc* (usu. only *sing*) movement of liquid.

flowing *adj* moving or curving smoothly; hanging gracefully.

flower ['flauə*] *nc* **1.** blossom; part of a plant from which seeds are produced. **2.** any small plant which is grown for the sake of its flowers. Also *vi* produce flowers. *The trees are flowering.*

flowery *adj* **1.** of flowers. **2.** using too many poetical words: *a flowery speech.*

'flowerbed part of a garden where flowers are grown.

the flower of something the best part of something.

flown [floun] past part of **fly**[2].

flu [flu:] *nu* short form of **influenza.**

fluctuate ['flʌktjueit] *vi* frequently change from higher to lower; vary in level (e.g. with reference to temperature, price, amount etc). **fluctuation** [flʌktju'eiʃən] *nc/u*.

flue [flu:] *nc* pipe for carrying air or smoke to or from a fire etc.

fluent ['fluənt] *adj* able to speak easily. *He is a fluent speaker. He made a fluent speech.*

fluently *adv*. **fluency** *nu*.

fluff [flʌf] *nu* small pieces which have come off cloth (esp. wool). Also *vt* do badly.

fluffy *adj* like fluff. **fluffiness** *nu*.

fluid ['flu:id] *nc* **1.** liquid. *Water, oil, blood, milk are fluids.* **2.** liquid or gas. Also *adj* **1.** of or like a fluid. **2.** (with reference to plans, arrangements etc) not fixed; able to be changed if necessary. **fluidity** [flu'iditi] *nu*.

fluke [flu:k] *nc* **1.** success which happens by chance. (*informal*). **2.** one of the points by which an anchor is held at the bottom of the sea. **3.** type of worm which infects sheep etc.

flummox ['flʌməks] *vt* (mainly *Brit*) be very difficult to understand or deal with; puzzle. *This problem flummoxed me.* (*informal*).

flung [flʌŋ] past of **fling.**

flunk [flʌŋk] *vt/i* fail, cause to fail, a test or examination at school or college. (*informal*).

flunk out of school/college (*US*) **1.** be sent away from school etc for bad work. **2.** leave school etc before the proper time. (*informal*).

flunkey ['flʌŋki] *nc* male servant wearing a uniform. (*informal* and *impolite*).

fluorescent [fluə'resnt] *adj* giving off light when exposed to electricity. **fluorescence** *nu*.

flurry ['flʌri] *nc* **1.** hurry and excitement. **2.** sudden movement of wind, snow, rain etc. Also *vt* make excited or worried.

flush[1] [flʌʃ] **1.** *vi* become red in the face because of excitement, embarrassment, exercise, food and drink etc. **2.** *vt* make clean by a strong flow of water: *flush a lavatory.* **3.** *vt* (with reference to hunting) cause an animal or bird to leave the place where it is hiding.

flushed with something with a strong feeling of happiness caused by something, often with a red colour of the face: *flushed with wine/success/victory.*

flush[2] [flʌʃ] *nc* **1.** redness of the face, caused

by excitement, exercise, drink etc. **2.** number of playing cards all of the same suit i.e. all hearts, clubs etc.
the first flush of something the first part of something pleasant: *the first flush of victory.*

flush[3] [flʌʃ] *adj* **1.** meeting exactly at the edges. *The window is not flush with the wall* i.e. there is an open space between the window and the wall. **2.** having a lot of money (and usu. being willing to spend it) (*informal* in sense **2.**).

fluster ['flʌstə*] *vt* make somebody too excited or worried to be able to do something properly. Also *nu* condition of being flustered. *He is in a fluster.*

flute [flu:t] *nc* type of musical instrument consisting of a tube of metal or wood with holes in it which are covered by the fingers or by keys.

flute

flutter ['flʌtə*] *vt/i* (usu. with reference to the wings of birds) move quickly backwards and forwards. Also *nc* **1.** movement of this kind. **2.** excitement and worry.

flux [flʌks] *n sing* continual movement and change: *in a state of flux* i.e. always changing.

fly[1] [flai] *nc* **1.** type of small winged insect. **2.** something made to look like this insect, used in catching fish for sport. **3.** (usu. *pl* in Britain) front of a pair of trousers fastened by buttons or a zip.
'flyblown *adj* spoiled by the eggs of a fly. *This meat is flyblown.*
fly in the ointment some trouble or difficulty in a plan or arrangement; anything which spoils the value or usefulness of something. (*informal*).

fly[2] [flai] **1.** *vt/i* move, cause to move, in the air. *The aeroplane was flying. He flew the aeroplane.* **2.** *vi* hurry; go very quickly. *She flew down the stairs to greet him.* (*informal* in sense **2.**). *pres part* **flying.** *past tense* **flew** [flu:]. *past part* **flown** [floun].
flier, flyer *nc* person who pilots an aeroplane.
'flyleaf blank sheet of paper at the beginning and end of a book.
'flyover road built to pass over another road.
'flypast (*Brit*) flight of aeroplanes over a city etc as a celebration of something. (*US* **flyover**).
'flywheel wheel used in a machine to control its speed.
'flying boat aeroplane which can land on water.
'flying 'saucer one of various objects which people claim to have seen flying at great speed and thought to be from another planet.
'flying squad police with very fast cars.
'flying 'visit visit during which one stays for a very short time.
fly at someone attack someone very violently. (*informal*).
fly in the face of something act in defiance of something. *He flew in the face of the rules.* (*informal*).
fly into a rage/temper become very angry.
fly off the handle lose one's temper. (*informal*).
let fly at someone/something see **let**[1].
send something flying hit something so that it is sent a long way from one. (*informal*).
with flying colours with great success (usu. in **pass an examination with flying colours**).
see also **come.**

foal [foul] *nc* young horse.

foam [foum] *nu* very many small bubbles. Also *vi* form small bubbles.
'foam 'rubber type of rubber, like foam in appearance, used for making cushions etc.

fob [fɔb] *vt* in **fob somebody off** i.e. deceive somebody; make somebody accept something which is false or worthless. *He fobbed me off with a promise. past* **fobbed.** (*informal*).

focal ['foukəl] *adj* see **focus.**

fo'c's'le ['fouksl] *nc* see **forecastle.**

focus ['foukəs] *nc* **1.** point where rays of light meet. **2.** part where there is most activity or interest: *the focus of the trouble; a focus of interest. pl* **focuses** or **foci** ['fouki:]. Also *vt* **1.** adjust a telescope, camera etc so that the rays of light meet and make a clear image. **2.** cause rays of light to meet. **3.** give careful attention to something: *focus one's mind on something. past* **focussed.** (*US* **focused**). **focal** *adj.*
out of focus not clear or sharp; indistinct. *This photograph is out of focus.* (*opp* **in focus**).

fodder ['fɔdə*] *nu* food for cows, horses, sheep etc which has been stored.

foe [fou] *nc* enemy (*o.f.*).

foetus ['fi:təs] (*US* **fetus**) *nc* young animal, bird, human etc in a fairly complete state of development before it is born. **foetal** ['fi:tl] *adj.*

fog [fɔg] *nc/u* thick vapour or cloud which comes down to the level of the ground and which makes it difficult to see properly. **foggy** *adj.* **fogginess** *nu.*
'foghorn thing which makes a loud noise, used to warn ships during fog.

fogey ['fougi] *nc* usu. in **old fogey** i.e. person who is old and who has old-fashioned ideas and behaviour. (*informal* and *impolite*).

foible ['fɔibl] *nc* unimportant and unusual idea or way of behaving, which one thinks important.

foil[1] [fɔil] **1.** *nu* metal hammered into a thin sheet like paper. **2.** *nc* person/thing which makes another person/thing seem better, more beautiful, more clever etc in contrast. **3.** *nc* long thin sword, with a covering on the point, used in fighting for sport.

foil[2] [fɔil] *vt* prevent somebody from doing something (esp. something wrong). *I foiled the thief. I foiled his attempt to steal the money.*

foist [fɔist] *vt* in **foist something off on someone** i.e. make someone accept something of little value or use. (*informal*).

fold[1] [fould] *vt/i* **1.** (often with **up**) bend, cause to bend. *She folded her dress up and put it in a drawer. He folded up the letter and put it in the envelope.* **2.** (with reference to businesses etc) fail. (*informal* in sense **2.**). Also *nc* mark made by folding.
folder *nc* piece of stiff cardboard, folded for holding loose papers.
'folding 'door door made of two or more

pieces, so that the door folds to open.
fold one's arms cross one's arms across one's chest.

fold[2] [fould] *nc* small space surrounded by a fence or wall, for keeping sheep in; the sheep themselves. Also *vt* put sheep in a fold.
return to the fold come back to a church or other organization which one had left. (*informal*).

foliage ['fouliidʒ] *nu* leaves on a tree or bush.

folio ['fouliou] *nc* **1.** large sheet of paper folded once in the middle. **2.** book made of sheets of paper folded in this way. *pl* **folios.**

folk [fouk] *npl* people. (rather *o.f.*).
folks *npl* one's parents. (*informal*).
'folklore study and collection of old stories, songs and beliefs of a tribe, community etc.
folklorist *nc* person who studies folklore.
'folksong 1. *nc* old song sung by ordinary people. **2.** *nu* songs in general. **folksinger** *nc*. **folksinging** *nu*.
'folk tale old story told by ordinary people.

follow ['fɔlou] **1.** *vt/i* go or come after. *The hunters were following a lion. Famine and disease followed the war.* **2.** *vt/i* understand. *I don't follow you.* **3.** *vt* act in accordance with: *follow somebody's advice/example.* **4.** take an interest in. *He follows football.*
follower *nc* **1.** person who follows. **2.** person who supports or follows a leader.
following *n sing* people supporting somebody. *The Prime Minister has a large following* i.e. many people support him. Also *adj* coming after. *I met him on the following day.*
follow something up go further in doing something. *I want to follow up this subject* i.e. learn more about it. *They followed up their victory* i.e. they continued to drive away the enemy.
follow a hunch see if what one suspects is true. (*informal*).
it follows it is seen to be true because of something else. *If today is Monday 15 March, it follows that tomorrow is Tuesday 16.*
follow a profession/trade do a certain type of skilled work. *He follows the trade of a carpenter.*

folly ['fɔli] *nc/u* foolish words or behaviour.

foment [fou'ment] *vt* **1.** encourage people to cause trouble and disturbance: *foment trouble/disobedience/rebellion etc.* **2.** put a warm cloth or liquid on part of the body to lessen pain. **fomentation** [foumen'teiʃən] *nc/u*.

fond [fɔnd] *adj* **1.** loving or liking (often loving too much): *a fond father* i.e. one who allows his children too much freedom. **2.** foolish: *a fond hope.* **fondness** *nu*.
fondly *adv* **1.** with love. **2.** foolishly.
be fond of someone/something like someone/something. *He is fond of his grandmother. He is fond of potatoes.*

fondle ['fɔndl] *vt* touch in a loving way.

font [fɔnt] *nc* place in a church where there is water for baptism (or holy water in a Roman Catholic church).

food [fu:d] *nu* what is eaten by people and animals or taken in by plants.
'foodstuff (with reference to trade, shipping, laws etc) anything which can be eaten.
food for thought something to make one think.

fool [fu:l] *nc* **1.** person who does and says stupid things (which show that he does not think very much). **2.** person formerly employed by a king or other ruler to say and do amusing things. Also **1.** *vt* trick somebody, so that he seems foolish. **2.** *vi* (often with **about** or **around**) behave like a fool. *The boys were fooling around instead of doing their work.* **foolish** *adj.* **foolishly** *adv.* **foolishness** *nu*.
'foolhardy *adj* brave but foolish.
'foolproof *adj* very easy to do (so that not even a fool can do it wrong); that cannot go wrong: *a foolproof method.*
'foolscap size of paper, about 34 centimetres by 43 centimetres.
make a fool of someone see **make**[1].
a fool's paradise state of happiness which is based on a false belief or which will not last long.
play the fool behave in a foolish way.

foot [fut] *nc* **1.** end of a leg, on which one stands. **2.** (only *sing*) bottom of something: *the foot of a mountain/a bed/a page/the stairs.* **3.** measure of length of 12 inches. see appendix. **4.** part of a line of verse. *pl* **feet** [fi:t].
footing *n sing* **1.** position of the feet. *He lost his footing* i.e. he fell down. **2.** place; position; foundation. *He placed the business on a firm footing* i.e. he made sure that the business was carried on properly and that there was enough money etc.
'football 1. *nu* one of several games played by two teams with a leather ball. **2.** *nc* the ball itself.
Note: (*Brit*) 'football' usu. refers to *Association Football*, played by two teams of 11 men each, of whom only the goalkeepers are allowed to touch the ball with the hands; the word is, however, also used by some people to refer to the game of *rugby*. (*US*) the word refers to a different kind of game played mainly in the *USA*.
'footbridge bridge for people who are walking (not for vehicles).
'footfall noise of a step made by somebody walking.
'foothill low hill at the bottom of high mountains.
'foothold place where one can put one's foot (e.g. in climbing a mountain).
'footlights see **light**[1].
'footloose *adj* free and willing to go anywhere. (*informal*).
'footman male servant who wears a uniform.
foot-and-mouth disease disease of cows and other animals.
'footnote note at the bottom of a page in a book etc.
'footpath path through a field, mountains etc for people who are walking.
'footprint mark made by a shoe or foot.
'footsore *adj* having sore feet, caused by walking.
'footstep *nc* (usu. *pl*) noise or mark made by somebody walking.
follow/tread in somebody's footsteps do what somebody did earlier.
'footstool small support for the feet when one is sitting in a chair.
'footwear boots and shoes.
'footwork (usu. with reference to boxing or football) skill in moving the feet.
on foot walking.
underfoot on the ground. *It is very wet underfoot* i.e. the ground is wet.

foot the bill pay for something (usu. something bought by somebody else) (*informal*).
have one foot in the grave be dying. (*informal*).
put one's foot down see **put.**
put one's foot in it do or say something which causes trouble and difficulty although one did not intend to cause trouble. (*informal*).

fop [fɔp] *nc* man who is too interested in beautiful clothes and polite behaviour. **foppish** *adj*. (both rather *o.f.*).

for [fɔː*] *prep* **1.** in exchange: *sell a book for a pound.* **2.** in support of. *I am for the plan* i.e. I think the plan should be carried out. **3.** in place of. *I'll do your work for you if you want to leave early.* **4.** with the purpose of. *He went for a walk.* **5.** in order to reach. *He left for London. He ran for shelter.* **6.** over a distance or time: *walk for a mile/an hour.* **7.** with an intended use: *a box for keeping papers in; a party for children.* **8.** feeling towards: *love for somebody.* **9.** in contrast to: *for every one who voted 'yes', fifty voted 'no'.* **10.** considering that. *It is warm for January* i.e. January is usually colder than it is this year. *He is rather tall for his age* i.e. children of his age are usually smaller. **11.** because of. *He was sent to prison for stealing the money.* Also *conj* because. (*formal* in this sense).
forever always.
for all despite. *For all your cleverness, you could not win* i.e. although you are clever.
for all that despite that; although that may be true.
but for if there had not been; without. *I would have won the competition but for bad luck* i.e. I lost because of bad luck.
for the most part usually; generally.

forage ['fɔridʒ] *vi* (usu. with reference to animals or soldiers) look for food.

foray ['fɔrei] *nc* attack made in order to get food or property.

forbade [fə'bæd] past tense of **forbid.**

forbear[1] [fɔː'bɛə*] *vi* keep from doing something. *I forbore to take the money/from taking the money.* *past tense* **forbore** [fɔː'bɔː*]. *past part* **forborne** [fɔː'bɔːn].
forbearance [fɔː'bɛərəns] *nu* patience; willingness to accept wrongs caused by other people; keeping from doing something. (both *formal*).

forbear[2], **forebear** ['fɔːbɛə*] *nc* (usu. *pl*) ancestor (*o.f.*).

forbid [fə'bid] *vt* say that something must not happen. *I forbade him to go to the party. The government decided to forbid the meeting.* *past tense* **forbade** [fə'bæd]. *past part* **forbidden.**
forbidding *adj* unpleasant and dangerous in appearance.
God forbid! I hope that does not happen. (*informal*).

forbore [fɔː'bɔː*] past tense of **forbear**[1].

force[1] [fɔːs] **1.** *nu* strength: *the force of the wind/the blow/the explosion.* **2.** *nc* organized group of men: *police force; air force; armed forces etc.* **3.** *nc* anything having an effect. *The United Nations Organization is a force for good* i.e. it produces good effects. **4.** *nu* (physics) anything that causes, changes or stops motion.
forcible ['fɔːsəbl] *adj* using force. **forcibly** *adv*.

force[2] [fɔːs] *vt* **1.** use force on. *We forced him to come* i.e. he did not want to come. *He forced the door* i.e. opened it by using force. **2.** (usu. with reference to plants) cause to grow more quickly than usual by giving extra warmth and food etc.
forceful *adj* showing determination and strength of character. **forcefully** *adv*. **forcefulness** *nu*.
forced labour work done by people who are not free.
forced landing landing of an aeroplane which is in difficulties.
forced march see **march.**
come into effect/force see **come.**
in force 1. legally required; effective. *These rules are still in force* i.e. they must still be obeyed. **2.** (usu. with reference to soldiers etc) in a large group: *an attack in force.*
force somebody's hand make somebody do something before he has decided that he wishes to do it.

forceps ['fɔːseps] *npl* instrument used by doctors for holding things tightly.

ford [fɔːd] *vt* go through a river at a shallow place: *ford a river.* Also *nc* place in a river where one can do this.

fore[1] [fɔː*] *adj* (usu. with reference to a ship) of the front part.
come to the fore become famous.

fore-[2] [fɔː*] *prefix* front; before (e.g. **forearm; forenoon; foreshore**).

forearm[1] ['fɔːrɑːm] *nc* lower part of the arm.

forearm[2] [fɔːr'ɑːm] *vt* get ready to be attacked.
forewarned is forearmed if one knows that an attack will be made on one, one can defend oneself better than if the attack was made without warning.

forebear ['fɔːbɛə*] *nc* see **forbear**[2].

forebode [fɔː'boud] *vt* be a sign that some danger or difficulty is coming.
foreboding *nc* feeling that danger or difficulty is coming: *have a foreboding about something.*

forecast ['fɔːkɑːst] *nc* (esp. with reference to the weather) statement about what will happen in the future. Also *vt* make a forecast: *forecast rain.* *past* **forecast.**
forecaster *nc* person who forecasts.

forecastle, fo'c's'le ['fouksl] *nc* front part of a ship, where sailors live.

foreclose [fɔː'klouz] *vt/i* take land or property in order to get back money lent to the owner of the land or property.
foreclosure [fɔː'klouʒə*] *nc/u* process of doing this.

forefather ['fɔːfɑːðə*] *nc* ancestor.

forefinger ['fɔːfiŋgə*] *nc* finger next to the thumb.

forefoot ['fɔːfut] *nc* one of the front feet of an animal. *pl* **forefeet** ['fɔːfiːt].

forefront ['fɔːfrʌnt] *n sing* front part where there is the most activity. *There is an idea in the forefront of my mind that . . .* i.e. I have been thinking a lot about this idea.

forego [fɔː'gou] *vt* see **forgo.**

foregoing ['fɔː'gouiŋ] *adj* previous; mentioned earlier. (*formal*).

foregone ['fɔːgɔn] *adj* usu. in **foregone conclusion** i.e. result which everybody knew would happen.

foreground ['fɔːgraund] *nu* **1.** part of a picture or scene near the person looking at it. **2.** most prominent place.

forehand ['fɔːhænd] *nc* stroke in tennis made with the palm of the hand facing the other player. Also *adj/adv*.

forehead ['fɔrid] *nc* part of the face above the eyes.

foreign ['fɔrin] *adj* **1.** of another country: *a foreign language* i.e. a language spoken in another country; *foreign trade* i.e. trade with other countries. **2.** not naturally part of. *This is foreign to our experience* i.e. we have never experienced this.
foreigner *nc* person from another country.
foreign body something not naturally belonging (esp. something which has got into part of the body).
foreknowledge ['fɔːnɔlidʒ] *nu* knowledge of something before it happens. *We had no foreknowledge of the attack.*
foreleg ['fɔːleg] *nc* one of the front legs of an animal.
foreman ['fɔːmən] *nc* **1.** man in charge of a group of workers. **2.** chief member of a jury.
foremost ['fɔːmoust] *adj* most important: *our foremost duty.*
first and foremost *adv* first and most importantly.
forename ['fɔːneim] *nc* first name. (*formal*).
forenoon ['fɔːnuːn] *nc* morning (*o.f.* or *Scot*).
forensic [fə'rensik] *adj* having reference to law and detection.
forensic science use of scientific methods by the police.
forepaw ['fɔːpɔː] *nc* one of the front paws of an animal.
forerunner ['fɔːrʌnə*] *nc* person/thing coming before another (and usu. more important) person/thing. *This invention was the forerunner of many important developments in space travel.*
foresee [fɔː'siː] *vt* know or see that something will happen before it does. *I made careful preparations because I foresaw that we would be very busy this year. pres part* **foreseeing.** *past tense* **foresaw** [fɔː'sɔː]. *past part* **foreseen.**
foreshadow [fɔː'ʃædou] *vt* be a sign that something dangerous or unpleasant is coming.
foreshore ['fɔːʃɔː*] *nc* land by the side of the sea.
foreshorten [fɔː'ʃɔːtn] *vt* draw something so that it appears to be a solid object and not lines on a flat page.
foreshortening *nu* process of doing this.
foresight ['fɔːsait] *nu* ability to know or guess what will happen in the future.
foreskin ['fɔːskin] *nc* fold of skin, covering the end of the penis, removed in circumcision.
forest ['fɔrist] *nc/u* large area of trees.
forester *nc* person who lives and works in a forest.
forestry *nu* work of protecting and developing forests.
forestall [fɔː'stɔːl] *vt* do something with the aim of preventing another person from doing it: *forestall somebody.*
foretaste ['fɔːteist] *nc* small experience of something which one will have in larger quantities later on.
foretell [fɔː'tel] *vt* tell about something before it happens: *foretell disaster. past* **foretold** [fɔː'tould].
forethought ['fɔːθɔːt] *nu* careful thought and planning before something takes place.
forever [fə'revə*] *adv* always.
forewarn [fɔː'wɔːn] *vt* tell somebody of some danger etc which is coming.
foreword ['fɔːwəːd] *nc* short section of a book which introduces the book to the reader.
forfeit ['fɔːfit] *vt* lose something as a punishment or as a result of one's actions. Also *nc* something lost in this way. **forfeiture** *nu.*
forgave [fə'geiv] past tense of **forgive.**
forge[1] [fɔːdʒ] *vt/i* make money or copy a document, painting etc in order to deceive.
forger *nc* person who does this.
forgery *nc/u* the crime of copying money, documents etc; something forged.
forge ahead move forward and in front of others (e.g. in a race).
forge[2] [fɔːdʒ] *nc* place where a blacksmith makes horseshoes and other iron objects. Also *vt* make something in a forge. *He forged a horseshoe.*
forget [fə'get] *vt/i* fail to keep in the mind or in the memory. *I forgot to buy the book. I forget where you live. pres part* **forgetting.** *past tense* **forgot** [fə'gɔt]. *past part* **forgotten** [fə'gɔtn].
forgetful *adj* often forgetting. **forgetfulness** *nu.*
forgive [fə'giv] *vt/i* decide that one is not angry with somebody who has done wrong, and that one does not wish to punish him. *I forgave him for losing my book. I forgave his behaviour. pres part* **forgiving.** *past tense* **forgave** [fə'geiv]. *past part* **forgiven** [fə'givən].
forgivable *adj* able to be forgiven. (*opp* **unforgivable**).
forgiving *adj* willing to forgive. **forgivingly** *adv.*
forgiveness *nu* process of forgiving.
forgo, forego [fɔː'gou] *vt* be willing not to have something (usu. something pleasant). *He decided to forgo sugar in his tea. past tense* **forwent** [fɔː'went]. *past part* **forgone** [fɔː'gɔn]. see also **foregone.**
forgot [fə'gɔt] past tense of **forget.**
fork [fɔːk] *nc* **1.** instrument with several sharp points, used for carrying food to the mouth. **2.** large instrument shaped like this, used for digging earth or working on a farm. **3.** place where a road divides into two or more roads, or where a tree trunk puts out a branch. Also **1.** *vt/i* use a fork (usu. for digging or farm work). **2.** *vi* divide into two. *The road forked.*
forked *adj* divided into two: *a forked tongue* i.e. a tongue like a snake.
fork out pay money: *fork out four pounds.* (*informal*).
forlorn [fə'lɔːn] *adj* left alone and unhappy.
forlornly *adv.* **forlornness** *nu.*
forlorn hope plan or attempt which is not likely to succeed.
form[1] [fɔːm] **1.** *nc/u* shape; outline; appearance. *She made a cake in the form of a letter 'S'. The word 'sheep' has the same form in the singular and the plural. Form is as important as colour in the art of painting.* **2.** *nc* type or sort. *There are many different forms of food throughout the world.* **3.** *nc/u* usual way of doing something. *Shaking hands is merely a matter of form* i.e. it is something which is usu. done, but which has not much meaning. **4.** *nc* official paper with spaces for one to write information in. **5.** *nc* (*Brit*) class in a school. (*US* **grade**). **6.** *nu* usual ability of a racehorse, athlete etc. *This horse is off form* i.e. not running as fast as it normally does. **7.** *nc* long wooden seat on which several people can sit.
bad/good form behaviour which is generally considered bad/good. (rather *o.f.*).
form[2] [fɔːm] *vt/i* **1.** come or make into a shape. *Ice was forming on the river. He formed a ball of earth in his hands.* **2.**

come into existence or make. *An idea was forming in his mind. He formed a football club.*

formal ['fɔːml] *adj* done or made according to certain rules; following generally accepted ideas of what is the correct way of doing something; not conversational. (*opp* **informal**). **formally** *adv*.

formality [fə'mæliti] *nc/u* behaviour which is necessary in order to follow the rules etc but which does not mean very much. (*opp* **informality**).

format ['fɔːmæt] *nc* shape and size of a book, magazine etc.

formation [fə'meiʃən] *nc/u* way in which something is shaped or arranged in order. *The planes were flying in formation* i.e. keeping the same distance from each other and forming a particular shape.

formative ['fɔːmətiv] *adj* causing somebody/something to have a certain type of nature: *the formative years* i.e. the years of childhood, when a person's character and intelligence are being formed.

former[1] ['fɔːmə*] *adj* **1.** the first one mentioned of two things or people. (*opp* **latter**). **2.** earlier in time; of the past: *in former times.*

formerly *adv* at an earlier time.

former[2] ['fɔːmə*] *nc* in **first/second etc former** i.e. member of a particular class in a school.

formidable ['fɔːmidəbl] *adj* fearful; difficult to deal with: *a formidable enemy; a formidable task.* **formidably** *adv*.

formula ['fɔːmjulə] *nc* **1.** set of scientific or mathematical symbols (e.g. H_2O, πr^2). **2.** set of words which does not have much meaning (e.g. good morning, how do you do). **3.** (*US*) baby's milk feed. *pl* **formulas** or **formulae** ['fɔːmjuliː].

formulate ['fɔːmjuleit] *vt* **1.** express a formula. **2.** express an idea etc clearly and precisely: *formulate his theories.* **formulation** [fɔːmju'leiʃən] *nu*.

fornication [fɔːni'keiʃən] *nu* sexual intercourse between people who are not married to each other. **fornicate** ['fɔːnikeit] *vi*.

forsake [fə'seik] *vt* (usu. with reference to leaving one's friends or family, or something which is dear to one) leave. *pres part* **forsaking.** *past tense* **forsook** [fə'suk]. *past part* **forsaken.**

forswear [fɔː'swɛə*] *vt* promise very seriously that one will stop something. *He has forsworn cigarettes. past tense* **forswore** [fɔː'swɔː*]. *past part* **forsworn** [fɔː'swɔːn].

be forsworn do something after promising not to do it.

fort [fɔːt] *nc* building which is made so that it can be defended against attack by enemies.

hold the fort continue doing some work while the person who usu. does it or who usu. works with one is away. (*informal*).

forte ['fɔːti] *n sing* something that somebody does well. *Driving is his forte* i.e. driving is the thing he does best.

forth [fɔːθ] *adv* forward; out; away. *He went forth to attack the enemy* (*o.f.*).

back and forth see **back**[2].

and so forth etc; and so on; and the rest.

forthcoming [fɔːθ'kʌmiŋ] *adj* **1.** to appear soon: *a forthcoming book* i.e. one which will be published soon. *It was not forthcoming* i.e. it did not appear when needed or expected. **2.** friendly, ready to give information etc.

forthright ['fɔːθrait] *adj* saying what one thinks, without trying to hide anything.

forthrightness *nu*.

forthwith ['fɔːθ'wiθ] *adv* at once; immediately (*o.f.*).

fortify ['fɔːtifai] *vt* **1.** build walls and other things to defend a place against attack. **2.** (esp. of food and drink) make stronger.

fortification [fɔːtifi'keiʃən] *nc/u* **1.** something built to defend a place. **2.** process of fortifying.

fortitude ['fɔːtitjuːd] *nu* bravery; ability to face danger or pain etc.

fortnight ['fɔːtnait] *nc* two weeks. **fortnightly** *adj/adv*.

fortress ['fɔːtris] *nc* place which can be defended against attacks by enemies.

fortuitous [fɔː'tjuitəs] *adj* happening by chance or accident. **fortuitously** *adv*.

fortune ['fɔːtʃən] *nc/u* **1.** chance; luck; whatever happens to one. *He had good fortune* i.e. something pleasant happened to him. (*opp* **misfortune**). **2.** large amount of money. *He made his fortune by selling cars.*

fortunate ['fɔːtʃənət] *adj* having or causing good luck. (*opp* **unfortunate**). **fortunately** *adv*.

'fortune hunter man who tries to marry a rich woman in order to get her money. (*informal*).

tell fortunes/tell someone's fortune say what will happen to someone in the future by using various methods such as looking at playing cards or the hands of the person. **'fortuneteller** *nc*.

forty ['fɔːti] see appendix.

forty winks short sleep during the day. (*informal*).

forum ['fɔːrəm] *nc* **1.** public meeting place in ancient Rome. **2.** any place where people can have discussions.

forward[1] ['fɔːwəd] *adv* to the front. *He ran forward.*

come forward see **come.**

look forward to see **look.**

forward[2] ['fɔːwəd] *adj* **1.** in the front. **2.** early; having developed or progressed quicker than usual. *I am well forward with the work* i.e. I have done more than I expected to do. **3.** (with reference to children) more like an adult than other children of the same age (and often rather impolite to adults). **forwardness** *nu*.

forward[3] ['fɔːwəd] *nc* player in the front line of certain games (e.g. football).

forward[4] ['fɔːwəd] *vt* **1.** (esp. with reference to sending letters etc to a new address after a person has left his former address) send forward. **2.** help to go forward: *forward a cause/movement/plan etc.*

fossil ['fɔsl] *nc* what remains of a very old plant, animal etc, which has been kept from destruction in hard rock.

fossilize *vt* make into a fossil. **fossilized** *adj*.

foster ['fɔstə*] *vt* **1.** help the growth and development of: *foster a political movement.* **2.** take a child which is not one's own into one's family: *foster a child.*

'foster mother/brother/child etc mother, brother, child etc related to one not by blood, but by the act of fostering.

'foster home 1. home into which a foster child is taken. **2.** institution in which children without proper homes are brought up.

fought [fɔːt] past of **fight**[2].

foul[1] [faul] *adj* **1.** bad or dirty and unpleasant: *foul air; a foul taste; foul language.*

2. breaking the rules of a game: *a foul blow* i.e. in boxing. **foully** *adv.*
foul play **1.** murder. **2.** behaviour which is against the rules of a game.
by fair means or foul see **means.**
fall foul of someone/something **1.** (with reference to boats etc) become tangled with or collide with. **2.** (with reference to people) get into trouble with. *He fell foul of the headmaster.*

foul² [faul] *nc* action which is not allowed by the rules of a game (e.g. kicking in a boxing match).

foul³ [faul] **1.** *vt* make dirty and unpleasant. *The smoke fouled the air.* **2.** *vt/i* do something which is not allowed by the rules of a game. *The footballer tried to foul. He fouled his opponent.* **3.** *vt* (with reference to a boat or ship etc) become tangled with; run into. *The ship fouled its anchor* i.e. could not pull up its anchor. *The boat fouled the fishing nets of the other boats.*
foul one's own nest behave badly in or say bad things about the place one comes from.

found¹ [faund] past of **find¹.**

found² [faund] *vt* begin something: *found a city/school/club etc.* **founder¹** *nc.*
foundation [faun'deiʃən] **1.** *nc* something founded. **2.** *nu* act of founding. **3.** *nc* money provided to found something. **4.** *nc* (usu. *pl*) the part of a building which is below the ground, on which the building rests. **5.** *nc/u* something like the foundation of a building: *the foundations of democracy* i.e. the ideas on which democracy is based. *This theory has no foundation in fact.*

founder² ['faundə*] *vt/i* **1.** (with reference to ships) fill with water and sink. **2.** (with reference to horses) fall, cause to fall.

founder³ ['faundə*] *nc* person who works in a foundry.

foundling ['faundliŋ] *nc* baby or child which has been left by its parents and found by somebody else.

foundry ['faundri] *nc* place where things are made from molten metal.

fount [faunt] *nc* **1.** set of letters of one size, used by a printer. **2.** fountain (*o.f.* in sense **2.**).

fountain ['fauntin] *nc* place where water rises up (esp. where it is made to rise into the air as an ornament in a street or garden).
'**fountain pen** type of pen in which the ink is sucked inside the pen.

four [fɔ:*] see appendix.
'**foursome** group of four people (esp. a group playing a game).
'**four-letter 'word** one of a number of words (having four letters) which are considered impolite.
'**four'poster** type of bed which has posts at the corners to hold curtains.
'**four'square** *adj* **1.** square. **2.** honest, frank.
on all fours see **all.**

fowl [faul] *nc* **1.** chicken, goose, turkey or other domestic bird. **2.** the meat of these used as food.

fox [fɔks] *nc* type of wild animal like a dog with red fur and a bushy tail.
foxy *adj* clever and dishonest.
'**foxglove** type of tall plant with purple or white, bell-shaped flowers.
'**foxhound** type of dog used in hunting foxes.
'**foxtrot** *nc/u* type of dance. Also *vi. past* **foxtrotted.**

foyer ['fɔiei] *nc* large public room at the entrance of a hotel, cinema or large building.

fracas ['frækɑ:] *nc* noisy quarrel. *pl* **fracas** ['frækɑ:z].

fraction ['frækʃən] *nc* **1.** small part. **2.** quantity less than one (e.g. $\frac{1}{2}$, $\frac{1}{4}$, $\frac{1}{8}$). **fractional** *adj.*
Note: in ordinary use, expressions of the type $\frac{1}{2}$, $\frac{1}{4}$, $\frac{1}{8}$ are called *fractions*, and expressions of the type 0.5, 0.25, 0.125 are called *decimals*; in mathematics, however, both types of expression are regarded as fractions.

fractious ['frækʃəs] *adj* (often with reference to children) bad-tempered; angry. **fractiously** *adv.* **fractiousness** *nu.*

fracture ['fræktʃə*] *nc* **1.** breaking of a bone. **2.** breaking of any type. Also *vt/i* break, cause to break.

fragile ['frædʒail] *adj* **1.** easily broken. **2.** (of health etc) weak. **fragility** [frə'dʒiliti] *nu.*

fragment ['frægmənt] *nc* small piece broken off from a larger whole. Also [fræg'ment] *vt/i* break into small pieces. **fragmentary** ['frægməntri] *adj.*
fragmentation [frægmən'teiʃən] *nu* **1.** process of fragmenting. **2.** (with reference to bombs or shells) process of throwing pieces of metal in all directions when a bomb explodes (usu. in **fragmentation bomb**).

fragrant ['freigrnt] *adj* smelling very sweet, like a flower. **fragrantly** *adv.* **fragrance** *nu.*

frail [freil] *adj* weak (and often old). **frailty** *nu.*

frame¹ [freim] *nc* **1.** the border of wood, metal etc around a picture or around the glass of a window. **2.** one picture of a strip of cinema film. **3.** body of a human being or animal. **4.** (esp. with reference to a house, ship, aeroplane) structure supporting the other parts of something.
frame of mind state of mind. *I'm not in the right frame of mind for a party.*

frame² [freim] *vt* **1.** put a frame around: *frame a picture.* **2.** put into words: *frame a sentence/a law.* **3.** make an innocent person seem to be guilty of a crime. (*informal* in sense **3.**).
'**frame-up** *nc* arrangement to make an innocent person seem to be guilty of a crime. (*informal*).
'**framework** **1.** structure which supports the other parts (e.g. of a house, ship, aeroplane). **2.** main ideas or parts: *the framework of society/of the economy.*

franc [fræŋk] *nc* unit of money in France and several other countries.

franchise ['fræntʃaiz] *n sing* right to vote in elections.

Franco- ['fræŋkou] *prefix* of France (e.g. **Franco-British trade** i.e. trade between France and Britain).

frank [fræŋk] *adj* saying what one thinks without trying to hide anything: *a frank answer.* **frankly** *adv.* **frankness** *nu.*

frankincense ['fræŋkinsens] *nu* sweet-smelling substance obtained from certain trees.

frantic ['fræntik] *adj* very worried or excited, so that one cannot think or behave properly. **frantically** *adv.*

fraternal [frə'tə:nl] *adj* **1.** of a brother. **2.** of a fraternity. **fraternally** *adv.*
fraternity **1.** *nc* society or group of men who work together or help each other in some way. **2.** *nc* (*US*) such a group at a school or college. **3.** *nu* friendly feeling between brothers.

fraternize ['frætənaiz] *vi* (esp. with reference to people who were recently enemies) be friendly. **fraternization** [frætənai'zeiʃən] *nu*.

fratricide ['frætrisaid] *nu* crime of murdering one's brother. Also *nc* person who does this. **fratricidal** [frætri'saidl] *adj*.

fraud [frɔːd] **1.** *nu* crime of making somebody believe something which is not true, in order to get something from him. **2.** *nc* person/thing that makes people believe what is not true. **fraudulent** ['frɔːdjulənt] *adj*. **fraudulently** *adv*.

fraught [frɔːt] *adj* filled (usu. in **fraught with something**: *fraught with horror/terror/risk/danger etc*).

fray[1] [frei] *nc* fight or struggle. (rather *o.f.*).

fray[2] [frei] *vt/i* (with reference to cloth, rope etc) become or make worn so that there are loose threads.

freak [friːk] *nc* **1.** plant, animal, person etc which is unusual and unnatural in form. **2.** strange and foolish idea or action. Also *adj*: *a freak storm* i.e. a storm which is unusual and unexpected.

freakish *adj* strange and unusual: *a freakish idea*. **freakishly** *adv*. **freakishness** *nu*.

freckle ['frekl] *nc* one of the several light brown marks found on the face and arms of people who have very fair skin. Also *vt/i* become or make covered with freckles. *She freckles very easily. The sun freckled her skin.*

free [friː] *adj* **1.** not costing any money. *Education is free in Britain* i.e. people can send their children to school without paying any money. **2.** not under the control of anybody or anything. *The thief is still free* i.e. he is not in prison. *Nobody is free to do what he likes* i.e. everybody must obey some rules. *In 1940 India was not yet free* i.e. it was still ruled by Britain. **3.** not following any rules. **4.** generous. **5.** without duties. *I'm free this afternoon*. *comparative* **freer** ['friə*]. *superlative* **freest** ['friːist]. Also *vt* make free: *free the prisoners*. **freely** *adv*. **freedom** *nu*.

'**freehand** *adj* (with reference to drawing) done without a ruler, compasses etc.

a free hand permission to act as one wishes: *give someone a free hand*. (*informal*).

'**freehold** right to hold a piece of land as long as one wishes.

'**freelance** *nc* writer, artist etc who lives by selling his work to anyone who wants it, instead of working for one employer. Also *adj/vi*.

free love (usu. with reference to a belief that people should be allowed to behave like this if they wish to) love and sexual intercourse between people who are not married to each other.

'**freemason, Freemason** *nc* member of an international secret society.

freemasonry *nu* beliefs and practices of this society.

'**freethinker** person who does not believe in any religion. (rather *o.f.* – use **atheist** or **agnostic**).

free trade trade in which goods can be taken into and out of a country without taxes.

free translation translation which does not follow the original very closely.

free verse poetry which does not follow the traditional rules of rhyme and metre.

free will ability to decide for oneself what one wishes to do.

free and easy *adj* friendly and not following strict rules of politeness and correct behaviour. (*informal*).

'**free-for-'all** fight or struggle in which anyone can join. (*informal*).

be free from/of something be without something (usu. something unpleasant): *be free from disease/infection/pain*.

be free with something be willing to give something generously: *free with one's money; free with one's advice* i.e. giving much advice to people (often advice which is not wanted)

freeze [friːz] **1.** *vt/i* become ice or make ice. *The river froze last night. He froze the water in his refrigerator. It's freezing* i.e. the temperature is below freezing point. **2.** *vt/i* become or make very cold. *My feet are freezing*. **3.** *vi* suddenly become very still and quiet. *The hunter froze when he saw the lion*. **4.** *vt* (with reference to prices, wages etc) prevent from rising higher or prevent any more from being paid. *The government decided to freeze prices for six months*. *pres part* **freezing**. *past tense* **froze** [frouz]. *past part* **frozen** ['frouzn]. Also *n sing* **1.** period of very cold weather. **2.** official action to prevent prices, wages etc from rising higher.

freezing point temperature at which a liquid becomes solid.

freight [freit] *nu* **1.** movement of goods by some means of transport. **2.** the goods themselves. Also *vt* load a ship with freight.

freighter *nc* boat which carries goods.

French [frentʃ] *adj* of France. Also *nu* language of France.

French window door made of glass like a window, opening on to a garden etc.

take French leave go away secretly without having permission. (*informal*).

frenetic [frə'netik] *adj* mad and violent.

frenzy ['frenzi] *nu* state of great excitement or fear, so that one cannot think or act properly. **frenzied** *adj*. **frenziedly** *adv*.

frequent[1] ['friːkwənt] *adj* happening very often. *He made frequent visits to the hospital*. (*opp* **infrequent**). **frequently** *adv*.

frequency **1.** *nu* state of being frequent. **2.** *nc* (esp. with reference to the number of cycles per second of alternating current broadcast by a radio station) rate at which something happens.

frequent[2] [fri'kwent] *vt* go to very often: *frequent cinemas*.

fresco ['freskou] **1.** *nc* picture painted on (wet) plaster on a wall. **2.** *nu* the art of painting such pictures. *pl* **frescos** or **frescoes**.

fresh [freʃ] *adj* **1.** new; recent; not stale: *fresh news* i.e. news received not long ago; *a fresh arrival* i.e. somebody who has arrived a short while ago; *fresh fruit* i.e. fruit which is not in a tin or packet. **2.** (with reference to the colour of somebody's face) healthy and bright. **3.** (with reference to streams, rivers, lakes etc) without salt. **4.** (with reference to wind) strong. **5.** cheeky (*informal* in sense **5.**). **freshly** *adv*. **freshness** *nu*.

freshen *vt/i* become or make fresh.

'**freshman, fresher** student in his first year at a university.

fret [fret] *vt/i* (often with reference to children) become or make worried and bad-tempered. *The baby was fretting because he was hungry*. *past* **fretted**.

fretful *adj* often fretting. **fretfully** *adv*. **fretfulness** *nu*.

fretsaw ['fretsɔː] *nc* type of tool with a

narrow blade for cutting patterns in wood.
'fretwork **1.** patterns cut in wood with a fretsaw. **2.** the practice of cutting patterns in this way.

friar ['fraiə*] *nc* member of certain religious organizations in the Roman Catholic Church.
friary *nc* place where friars live.

friction ['frikʃən] *nu* **1.** rubbing of one thing against another. **2.** continual arguments and disagreements. **frictional** *adj*.

Friday ['fraidi] *n* day after Thursday.
Good Friday day on which the crucifixion of Christ is remembered.

fridge [fridʒ] *nc* (*Brit*) short informal form of **refrigerator.**

friend [frend] *nc* person whom one knows well and likes.
friendly *adv*. (*opp* **unfriendly**). **friendliness** *nu*. **friendship** *nc/u*.
make friends (with someone) become a friend of. *He finds it difficult to make friends. He made friends with that boy.*
be friends with someone be a friend. *He didn't want to be friends with me.*

frieze [fri:z] *nc* long narrow band of decoration near the top of the walls of a room or building.

frigate ['frigit] *nc* fast type of ship.

fright [frait] *nc/u* **1.** great fear. *He got a fright when he found a snake in his bath.* **2.** person who looks unusual (often because of the way he is dressed) (*informal*).
frighten *vt/i* make somebody afraid. *The snake frightened him. The cat frightened the mice away* i.e. made them run away. *He doesn't frighten easily* i.e. is not easily made afraid.
frightening *adj* causing fear. **frighteningly** *adv*.
frightful *adj* causing fear; terrible; very unpleasant.
frightfully *adv* **1.** in a frightening way. **2.** very. *I'm frightfully sorry.* (*informal*).

frigid ['fridʒid] *adj* **1.** very cold. **2.** very unfriendly; showing no emotions. **frigidly** *adv*. **frigidity** [fri'dʒiditi] *nu*.

frill [fril] *nc* **1.** piece of cloth used as a decoration on a dress. **2.** anything unnecessary and used only as a decoration.
frilly *adj* (with reference to clothing etc) having frills.

fringe [frindʒ] *nc* **1.** hair covering the forehead. **2.** decoration made of loose threads (usu. tied in small bunches) on the edge of a dress, carpet, scarf etc. **3.** edge or outside (e.g. of a forest, political party, group of people, city etc): *on the fringe of a group.* Also *vt* put a fringe on; be a fringe to.

frippery ['fripəri] *nc/u* foolish and unnecessary decoration.

frisk [frisk] **1.** *vi* jump and run in a playful way (e.g. with reference to young animals). **2.** *vt* search somebody to see whether he is carrying a weapon. (*informal* in sense **2.**).
frisky *adj* in the habit of jumping and running. **friskily** *adv*. **friskiness** *nu*.

fritter[1] ['fritə*] *vi* in **fritter away something** i.e. waste or use something foolishly in small bits. *He frittered away his money.*

fritter[2] ['fritə*] *nc* piece of fruit, meat or vegetable fried in batter.

frivolous ['frivələs] *adj* not serious; making jokes about things which other people treat seriously. **frivolously** *adv*. **frivolity** [fri'vɔliti] *nc/u*.

frizzy ['frizi] *adj* (with reference to the hair) having small tight curls. **frizziness** *nu*.

fro [frou] *adv* only in **to and fro** i.e. backwards and forwards.

frock [frɔk] *nc* **1.** dress worn by a woman or a girl. **2.** long gown worn by priests of some churches.
'frock 'coat type of long coat formerly worn by men.

frog [frɔg] *nc* small animal which lives sometimes in water and sometimes on land, and which can jump well.

frog

'frogman man who does various types of work under water, wearing a special suit and carrying a supply of air.
have a frog in one's throat have a soreness or swelling in the throat which prevents one from speaking clearly. (*informal*).

frolic ['frɔlik] *nc* any noisy and happy action. Also *vi* behave noisily and happily. **frolicsome** *adj*.

from [frɔm] *prep* **1.** out of; away. *He travelled by train from London. He comes from Germany* i.e. he is a German. *I waited here from ten o'clock* i.e. I started waiting at that time. *He took a book from the shelf. She made soup from meat and carrots. I've searched the house from top to bottom* i.e. I've searched all of it. **2.** because of. *He acted from fear. He was suffering from measles.*

frond [frɔnd] *nc* part of a fern, palm tree, or of seaweed, which is like a leaf.

front [frʌnt] *nc* **1.** (usu. only *sing*) the part which one comes to first: *the front of a house* i.e. the part one sees from the road. **2.** part of a town which is by the sea or a lake. **3.** area where there is fighting during a war. **4.** number of different political parties which have joined together for some purpose. **5.** organization etc used to hide something. *The club was a front for a drug racket.* Also *adj*: *the front seat of a car* i.e. the seat where the driver or the person next to him sits. Also *vt/i* (often with **onto**) be opposite to. *His house fronts onto a field* i.e. there is a field in front of his house.
frontal ['frʌntl] *adj* in or to the front.
frontage ['frʌntidʒ] *nc* part of land or a building which can be seen from the road.
in front (of something) before (something) in position. *He parked his car in front of the house.*
put on a bold/good front do something in order to appear confident, successful etc when one is in fact not so.

frontier ['frʌntiə*] *nc* **1.** that part of a country which is near another country; place where two countries meet. **2.** (mainly *US*) part of a country which has not yet been properly explored or civilized.
frontiersman [frʌn'tiəzmən] *nc* (mainly *US*) man who lives in the unexplored part of a country.

frontispiece ['frʌntispi:s] *nc* picture at the front of a book (usu. opposite the title page).

frost [frɔst] **1.** *nc/u* weather in which the temperature is below freezing point. *We have had several frosts this winter.* **2.** *nu* this white covering of frozen water on windows, trees, the ground etc.

frosty *adj* very cold in weather or manner. *She greeted me with a frosty smile.* **frostily** *adv.* **frostiness** *nu.*

'frostbite *nu* damage to a part of the body caused by cold or frost.

'frostbitten *adj* damaged by frostbite.

'frosted 'glass glass with a rough surface which lets light through but prevents one seeing through it.

froth [frɔθ] *nu* small bubbles on the top of liquid (e.g. on a glass of beer). Also *vi* produce froth.

frothy *adj* having froth or like froth.

frown [fraun] *vi* cause the eyebrows to move downwards and together, as a sign of anger or puzzlement. Also *nc* appearance of the face caused by this.

frown (up)on something disapprove of something; think or say that something is bad.

frowzy ['frauzi] *adj* dirty and untidy. **frowzily** *adv.* **frowziness** *nu.*

froze [frouz], **frozen** ['frouzn] past tense and past part of **freeze.**

frugal ['fru:gəl] *adj* spending or costing very little money: *a frugal housewife; a frugal meal.* **frugally** *adv.* **frugality** [fru'gæliti] *nu.*

fruit [fru:t] **1.** *nu* part of certain trees and bushes which is eaten (e.g. apples, bananas, oranges, grapes, figs, peaches).

Note: fruit with this meaning is nearly always uncountable. *He bought some fruit in the market.*

2. *nc/u* part of any plant which contains the seeds. **3.** *nc* (often *pl*) anything which is the result of hard work and development: *the fruits of the earth* i.e. all crops; *the fruits of your hard work* i.e. what you gain by hard work. Also *vi* produce fruit.

fruiterer ['fru:tərə*] *nc* person who sells fruit.

fruitful *adj* **1.** producing much fruit. **2.** producing many good results. (*opp* **unfruitful**).

fruition [fru'iʃən] *nu* condition in which there are the good results which were wanted: *bring one's work/hopes/plans to fruition.*

fruitless *adj* without any results: *a fruitless search.*

fruity *adj* **1.** having a strong smell or taste of fruit. **2.** (of a voice) deep and rich.

frustrate [frʌs'treit] *vt* prevent somebody from doing what he wants to do (and often make him angry and unhappy). *He frustrated us. He frustrated our plans.* **frustration** *nc/u.*

fry[1] [frai] *vt/i* cook in hot oil or fat. *The fish was frying. He fried the bacon. past* **fried.**

'frying pan container used for frying.

out of the frying pan into the fire from one difficulty or danger into a worse one. (*informal*).

fry[2] [frai] *npl* small fishes recently come out of their eggs.

'small fry *npl* unimportant people (often young children) (*informal*).

fuddle ['fʌdl] *vt* (esp. with reference to alcohol) make stupid or unable to think properly. *His brain was fuddled with whisky.*

fuddy duddy ['fʌdidʌdi] *nc* person with old-fashioned ideas. (*informal*).

fudge [fʌdʒ] *nu* soft sweet substance made from sugar, butter, milk etc.

fuel [fjuəl] *nc/u* any substance which is burned in order to supply heat or power (e.g. coal, oil, gas, wood). Also *vt/i* take in or give fuel to. *past* **fuelled.** (*US* **fueled**).

fug [fʌg] *nc* stuffy atmosphere. (*informal*).

fugitive ['fju:dʒitiv] *nc* person who runs away. Also *adj.*

fulcrum ['fulkrəm] *nc* point on which a lever turns or rests. *pl* **fulcrums** or **fulcra** ['fulkrə].

fulcrum

fulfil [ful'fil] *vt* do something completely or satisfactorily: *fulfil one's duty* i.e. do what one must do; *fulfil a promise* i.e. do what one has promised. *past* **fulfilled.** **fulfilment** *nc/u.*

full [ful] *adj* **1.** containing as much or as many as possible: *a full glass of beer* i.e. one could not put any more beer in the glass. **2.** containing very much or very many. *The room was full of people* i.e. there were many people in the room. *He has a very full face* i.e. a fat face. *He drove at full speed* i.e. as fast as possible. *She was wearing a very full coat* i.e. a coat which was very loose on her. **fully** *adv.* **fullness** *nu.*

'fullback player in football etc whose position is near his own goal.

'full-'blooded *adj* **1.** of unmixed race or ancestry. *He is a full-blooded American Indian* i.e. all his ancestors were American Indians. **2.** with great force or strength.

'full-'blown *adj* (often with reference to a flower) completely developed.

full dress clothes worn for special ceremonial occasions.

'fully-'fledged see **fledged.**

'full-'grown, fully-grown *adj* adult; completely developed.

full moon the moon seen as a complete circle or disc.

in full swing see **swing.**

full tilt *adv* at great speed. (*informal*).

in full completely. *He told me the story in full.*

to the full as much as one wishes (usu. in **to enjoy oneself to the full**).

at full blast (usu. with reference to a machine) as fast as possible. (*informal*).

fulminate ['fulmineit] *vi* speak loudly and angrily against something. **fulmination** [fulmi'neiʃən] *nc/u.*

fulsome ['fulsəm] *adj* giving too much praise: *a fulsome speech.* **fulsomely** *adv.* **fulsomeness** *nu.*

fumble ['fʌmbl] *vt/i* use the hands without skill. *He fumbled in his pocket* i.e. he moved his hand around in his pocket trying to find something. *He fumbled the catch* i.e. he dropped a ball which he should have caught.

fume[1] [fju:m] *nc* (usu. *pl*) strong-smelling and unpleasant gas or vapour.

fume[2] [fju:m] **1.** *vi* give off fumes. **2.** *vi* be very angry (often because one does not get what one wants). **3.** *vt* make wood for furniture etc become darker through the action of fumes.

fumigate ['fju:migeit] *vt* destroy germs, infection, insects etc by the action of smoke or fumes: *fumigate a room.* **fumigation** [fju:mi'geiʃən] *nu.*
fumigator *nc* apparatus for fumigating.

fun [fʌn] *nu* happiness and amusement. *He had fun playing football. The journey home was really great fun* i.e. we enjoyed it very much. *It's not much fun being lost in the rain* i.e. it's miserable. *Have fun!* i.e. enjoy yourself!
fun fair see **fair**[2] (in sense **1.**).
for/in fun as a joke; not seriously. *I said that in fun.*
he's (great) fun he is amusing to be with. (*informal*).
make fun of, poke fun at mock, tease: *make fun of someone's bad accent.*

function ['fʌŋkʃən] *nc* **1.** usual work done by somebody/something: *the functions of a magistrate; the function of a part of a machine.* **2.** public gathering for a special purpose (e.g. a wedding, christening, party etc). **3.** (mathematics) value which varies as another value varies (e.g. in $x = 2y$, x is a function of y). Also *vi* serve; work. *The school dining room functions as a meeting place for teachers and students. My car is not functioning properly* i.e. there is something wrong with it.
functional *adj* **1.** of a function. **2.** intended for use and not for decoration: *furniture of very functional design.* **functionally** *adv.*
functionalism *nu* belief in architecture, designing etc that the parts of a building or object should be for use and not for decoration.
functionary ['fʌŋkʃənəri] *nc* official (often one who thinks that his work is more important than it really is).

fund [fʌnd] *nc* **1.** (often *pl*) money intended to be used for a certain purpose. *The club is holding a dance in order to raise funds for new equipment.* **2.** amount or supply of something: *a fund of information.* Also *vt* provide money for something.

fundamental [fʌndə'mentl] *adj* of great importance; forming the necessary part of anything; basic: *fundamental changes.* Also *nc* (often *pl*) fundamental part of anything.
fundamentally *adv.*

funeral ['fju:nərl] *nc* **1.** burial or cremation of a dead person, together with any ceremonies. **2.** procession taking a dead person to a cemetery, church etc. **3.** concern. *If he doesn't want to come that's his funeral.* (*informal* in sense **3.**).
funereal [fju'niəriəl] *adj* **1.** of or like a funeral. **2.** very sad and miserable.

fungus ['fʌŋgəs] *nc/u* type of plant which grows on other plants and on decaying matter. *pl* **funguses** or **fungi** ['fʌŋgai].
fungoid ['fʌŋgɔid] *adj* of or like a fungus.

funicular [fju'nikjulə*] *adj* of a rope or cable.
funicular railway type of railway going up the side of a mountain. The cars do not always travel on the ground but are sometimes pulled through the air on steel cables.

funk [fʌŋk] **1.** *nu* state of great fear: *in a blue funk.* **2.** *nc* person who is afraid. Also *vt/i* be afraid. **funky** *adj.* (all *informal* and rather *o.f.*).

funnel ['fʌnl] *nc* **1.** type of tube with a wide mouth and a narrow bottom, used for pouring liquid etc into a container. **2.** part of a steamship or steam engine where smoke comes out. Also *vt* pour or pass through a funnel. *past* **funnelled.** (*US* **funneled**).

funnel (*def1*)

funny ['fʌni] *adj* **1.** causing one to laugh. **2.** unusual and difficult to understand. (*informal* in sense **2.**). **funnily** *adv.*
'**funny bone** part of the elbow which feels a sharp pain if it is hit.
funnily enough although it is strange or unusual.

fur [fə:*] **1.** *nu* hair covering an animal. **2.** *nc* skin of an animal, with fur on it, often used to make clothing. **3.** *nu* substance formed inside a kettle by the action of boiling hard water. **4.** *nu* white covering on the tongue, formed when a person is unhealthy.
furry *adj* of or like an animal's fur.
furred *adj* covered with fur: *a furred hat/kettle/tongue.*
furrier ['fʌriə*] *nc* person who sells furs.

furbish ['fə:biʃ] *vt* polish; make bright and new again. (Often **refurbish**).

furious ['fjuəriəs] *adj* very angry and violent: *a furious man/wind/struggle.* **furiously** *adv.* see **fury.**

furl [fə:l] *vt* (with reference to umbrellas, flags or sails) roll up.

furlong ['fə:lɔŋ] *nc* distance of 220 yards. see appendix.

furlough ['fə:lou] *nc/u* (esp. with reference to a soldier) period during which one is permitted to be absent from one's work or duty: *have a furlough; go/be on furlough.*

furnace ['fə:nis] *nc* large structure containing a very hot fire, used for heating a building etc or for various manufacturing processes; the fire itself.

furnish ['fə:niʃ] *vt* **1.** provide with tables, chairs etc: *furnish a room.* **2.** provide what is needed: *furnish proof/help/materials etc.*
furnishings *npl* tables, chairs, curtains, carpets etc (esp. in a shop which sells these things).

furniture ['fə:nitʃə*] *nu* tables, chairs, beds etc.
Note: for one article use *piece of furniture.*

furore [fjuə'rɔ:ri] *nc* (usu. only *sing*) great interest and excitement. *The new book caused a furore.*

furrow ['fʌrou] *nc* **1.** mark made in the ground by a plough. **2.** line on the ground like that made by a plough. **3.** line on the forehead. Also *vt* make furrows (usu. in **to furrow one's brow** i.e. frown).

furry ['fə:ri] *adj* see **fur.**

further[1] ['fə:ðə*] *adv* **1.** to or at a greater distance. *He travelled further than I did.* **2.** to a greater degree. *He studied the subject further than I did.* see Note on **farther.**

further[2] ['fə:ðə*] *adj/determiner* **1.** more distant. **2.** additional; extra. *I don't want to cause any further trouble* i.e. there has already been some trouble. **3.** see **furthermore.**

further education (usu. with reference to study done by people who are also working at a job) education continued after one has left school.

further[3] ['fəːðə*] *vt* cause to develop: *further a plan/development/growth etc.*

furtherance ['fəːðərns] *nu* act of furthering.

'further'more *adv* also; in addition. *Furthermore, I must tell you* . . . i.e. I have already told you something.

'furthermost *adj* most distant.

furthest *adj* most distant.

furtive ['fəːtiv] *adj* secret; not wishing to be seen by other people (and usu. dishonest): *a furtive person/action/look*. **furtively** *adv*. **furtiveness** *nu*.

fury ['fjuəri] **1.** *nc/u* great anger (often violent anger). **2.** *nc/u* great force: *the fury of the storm*. **3.** *nc* angry and violent person (often a woman or a child). see **furious.**

furze [fəːz] *nu* type of bush with thorns and yellow flowers.

fuse[1] [fjuːz] *nc* part of an electric circuit which is intended to melt or break if the current becomes too strong and this protects the circuit from damage. Also *vt/i* melt, cause to melt, in this way. *The light has fused. He fused the lights.*

fuse[2] [fjuːz] *nc* length of cord etc which is lit to carry fire to an explosive.

fuse[3] [fjuːz] *vt/i* (often with **together**) become or make one by the action of great heat. *The two pieces of metal had fused together.*

fuselage ['fjuːzilɑːʒ] *nc* body of an aeroplane, without the wings and tail.

fusilier [fjuːzi'liə*] *nc* soldier belonging to a regiment which formerly carried light guns.

fusillade [fjuːzi'leid] *nc* **1.** continuous firing of many guns. **2.** anything like a fusillade: *a fusillade of questions.*

fusion ['fjuːʒən] **1.** *nu* process of mixing by the action of heat: *the fusion of metals*. **2.** *nc/u* process of mixing or joining: *a fusion of various races/languages/ideas etc.*

fuss [fʌs] *nu* unnecessary worry or excitement about small things. *She made a fuss when the boy kicked a football into her garden.* Also *vt/i* make a fuss (over).

fussy *adj* **1.** often disliking many things; unhappy if everything is not exactly as one wishes. **2.** giving great attention to small details. **fussily** *adv*. **fussiness** *nu*.

fusty ['fʌsti] *adj* smelling old and dirty.

futile ['fjuːtail] *adj* producing no good results. *They made a futile search* i.e. they did not find anything. **futility** [fju'tiliti] *nu*.

future ['fjuːtʃə*] *nc* **1.** time which has not yet happened (e.g. the year 2500 AD). **2.** success etc which will come. Also *adj* of the future: *future happiness; future years.*

futurity [fju'tjuəriti] *nu* future time; future events.

futurism *nu* movement in art, literature etc which tries to oppose traditional methods in every way. **futurist** *nc*.

future tense (grammar) form of the verb which refers to the future.

fuzzy ['fʌzi] *adj* **1.** covered with very short hair. **2.** not clear: *a fuzzy picture*. **fuzziness, fuzz** *nu*.

G

gab [gæb] *vi* talk freely or too much. *He likes to gab about his good luck. past* **gabbed.** Also *nu*: *I do not listen to his gab.* (both *informal*).
the gift of the gab ability to talk easily and well. (*informal*).
gabardine [gæbə'di:n] *nc/u* see **gaberdine.**
gabble ['gæbl] *vt/i* speak quickly and without meaning. *They sometimes gabble when they are excited. In his haste to finish, he gabbled the speech he had to make.* Also *nu* noisy, meaningless talk. *There was so much gabble that I could not hear the music.*
gaberdine, gabardine [gæbə'di:n] *nc/u* **1.** kind of strong cloth, often used in making raincoats; a raincoat itself. **2.** a long, loose coat, once worn by Jews.
gable ['geibl] *nc* upper part of the outside wall of a house (usu. triangular in shape) between two sloping roofs i.e. a house with a flat roof has no gables.
gabled *adj* with a gable or gables.
gad [gæd] *vi* (usu. with **about**) move about in search of pleasure. *They are always gadding about. past* **gadded.**
'**gadabout** *nc* a person who gads about. (*informal*).
gadfly ['gædflai] *nc* type of fly, the female of which stings animals and people.
gadget ['gædʒit] *nc* a piece of machinery (usu. small and labour-saving). *Her kitchen is very modern and full of gadgets.*
gadgetry fondness or overuse of gadgets. *This is a good car but gadgetry spoils it* i.e. gadgets which are not needed.
gaffe [gæf] *nc* a stupid mistake (usu. in speech or behaviour). *He made/committed an awful gaffe by calling Mrs Smith 'Miss'.* (*informal*).
gaffer ['gæfə*] *nc* **1.** elderly man. **2.** overseer of group of workmen. (*informal* in sense **2.** – use **foreman**).
gag [gæg] *nc* **1.** something put over or into the mouth to stop someone speaking or making a noise. **2.** (theatre) joke. Also *vt/i* **1.** prevent someone speaking or making a noise by using a gag; prevent speech or expression. *The thieves gagged him before they took his money. The government has no right to try to gag this newspaper.* **2.** use comic gags in a show or in company. *A good comedian must gag all the time. past* **gagged.**
gage [geidʒ] *nc* see **gauge**[2].
gaggle ['gægl] *nc* **1.** flock of geese. **2.** group of talkative girls or women. *Here comes Mrs Brown with her gaggle of girls.* (*informal*).
gaiety ['geiiti] *nu* see **gay.**
gaily ['geili] *adv* see **gay.**
gain [gein] *nc* profit; advantage; increase in something which is wanted. *The gains are balanced by the losses. We all work for gain. A gain in health/strength/knowledge etc is a good thing.* Also *vt/i* **1.** obtain something wanted. *He gained full marks in the examination. He went abroad to gain more experience. Nothing is gained by being lazy.* **2.** (usu. with **on** or **upon**) go further ahead; make better progress; improve. *In the race he gained on the other runners quite easily. Oil is steadily gaining on coal in the world market. His work is sure to gain if he uses these new methods.*
gainful *adj* profitable; useful. **gainfully** *adv.*
gain ground advance; grow stronger. *The footballers gained ground by kicking the ball into the opponents' part of the field. The rumour that he will leave the country is gaining ground* i.e. more people believe the rumour.
gain time (of a watch or clock) go too fast. *My watch gains time if I wind it too often.* (*opp* **lose time**). **2.** obtain extra time for one's own purposes. *To gain time, I pretended that I had not heard the question.*
gain weight become fatter.
Note: gain the summit/the shore/the other side etc meaning to reach after effort is *o.f.* – use *reach, arrive at.*
gainsay [gein'sei] *vt* deny; say to be untrue. *past* **gainsaid** [gein'sed].
gait [geit] *n sing* manner of walking. *You can see from his gait that he is tired.* (rather *o.f.*).
gaiter ['geitə*] *nc* (often *pl*) old-fashioned cloth or leather covering of ankles and/or legs (usu. fastened by buttons), once a distinguishing part of the dress of an Anglican bishop.

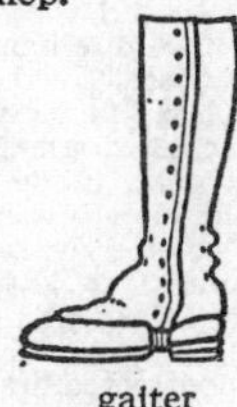
gaiter

gala ['gɑ:lə] *nc* festival; special show or event.
'**gala night** night when a theatre or cinema has a special show.
'**swimming gala** organized competition in swimming.
in gala mood feeling specially happy or festive.
galactic [gə'læktik] *adj* **1.** see **galaxy. 2.** concerned with milk; milky: *galactic acid.* *Note:* the much more usual term in sense **2.** is *lactic*, but the prefix *galact-* is used in some scientific terms dealing with milk.
galaxy ['gæləksi] *nc* **1.** huge mass of millions of stars. *Our universe is made up of many galaxies.* **2.** (usu. **Galaxy**) that part of the galaxy to which the Earth belongs and which is seen at night as a faint band of light across the sky. (Often **the Milky Way**). **3.** group of gifted or attractive people. *The exhibition was attended by a galaxy of*

scientists. **galactic** [gə'læktik] *adj.*

gale [geil] *nc* strong wind. *The tree was blown down in/by the gale. Gales are common in winter.*

'**gale force** force or speed of a gale. *The wind reached gale force last night.*

gall[1] [gɔ:l] *nu* **1.** bitter liquid that is made in the body by the liver. **2.** bitterness; harshness. **3.** hatred; bitter feelings.

'**gall bladder** vessel of the body containing gall.

'**gallstone** solid mass that sometimes forms in the gall bladder.

gall[2] [gɔ:l] *vt* **1.** (usu. with reference to horses) rub something until it is sore. *The horse's back was galled by the saddle.* **2.** annoy; anger. *His defeat was very galling to him.* Also *nc* painful spot on the skin, caused by rubbing.

gallant ['gælnt] *adj* **1.** brave. **2.** noble; impressive. *The bandsmen in their new uniforms were a gallant sight* (*o.f.*). **3.** polite, attentive (esp. to women). *You were very gallant at the party last night.* Also [gə'lænt] *nc* gay, fashionable young man who pays special attention to women (*o.f.*). **gallantly** *adv.* **gallantry** *nu.*

galleon ['gæliən] *nc* (in former times) Spanish sailing ship.

gallery ['gæləri] *nc* **1.** long, narrow passage or room sometimes open on one side. **2.** number of such rooms used for showing works of art. *The National Gallery contains many valuable pictures. The art galleries of Florence are very famous.* **3.** horizontal underground tunnel as in a coalmine. (If vertical it is a **shaft**). **4.** upper floor with seats, built at one end of a large hall, to allow more people to watch and listen. *The visitors' gallery in the House of Commons was full when the Prime Minister began speaking.* **5.** top floor or balcony in a theatre where the seats are cheapest.

play to the gallery behave like an actor who tries to become popular by pleasing only the vulgar and less intelligent people who are said to sit there. *He thought he would be elected if he played to the gallery.*

galley ['gæli] *nc* **1.** single-decked ship or warship of the past, moved mainly by a large number of oars but sometimes also by sail. (The rowing was usu. done by slaves or criminals). **2.** ship's kitchen. **3.** long metal tray in which printing type is arranged.

'**galley proof** uncorrected first printing from a galley (in sense **3.** above) before it is cut into pages.

gallon ['gæln] *nc* liquid measure of 8 pints. see appendix.

gallop ['gæləp] **1.** *vi* (usu. of a horse) run at its fastest speed. *The horses galloped across the field.* **2.** *vt* make a horse run its fastest. **3.** *vi* (usu. with **through**) hurry; do in haste. *The boy galloped through his dinner.* Also *n sing* **1.** a horse's fastest speed. *The other horse passed mine at a gallop.* **2.** act of making a horse run its fastest. *The cavalry charged at full gallop.*

gallows ['gælouz] *nc* strong wooden frame like high goalposts, used for putting people to death by hanging.

Note: gallows is *sing. Long ago the gallows was on this hill.*

galore [gə'lɔ:*] *adv* in plenty. *There are apples galore on the tree.*

galvanize ['gælvənaiz] *vt* **1.** suddenly awaken or stimulate by electricity or shock. *The alarm bell galvanized them into activity* i.e. the alarm bell made them suddenly active as if they had received an electric shock. **2.** coat metal (usu. with zinc) to prevent rust. *The water tank is made of galvanized iron.*

galvanization [gælvənai'zeiʃən] *nu* process of coating iron with zinc.

galvanic [gæl'vænik] *adj* electric; as if caused by electric shock, therefore sudden; stimulating; jerky. *The good news had galvanic results.* **galvanically** *adv.*

galvanism ['gælvənizəm] *nu* **1.** electricity produced by the action of acids on metals. **2.** science or practice of using such electricity.

gambit ['gæmbit] *nc* **1.** (chess) early move in which a player intentionally loses a pawn or other piece. **2.** early move of any kind to gain some advantage. *A favourite gambit in advertising is to give away free samples* i.e. in order to sell more later.

gamble ['gæmbl] *vi* play a game of chance or skill for money; take risks in the hope of gaining money or advantage. *He made a lot of money gambling at cards; gamble in cotton/steel/soap etc* i.e. in buying and selling shares in them. *I gambled on his not seeing me* i.e. I took the risk that he would not see me. *He gambled away all the money his father left him* i.e. he lost it by gambling. Also *nc* risk; uncertainty. *The attack was a gamble which did not succeed.* **gambler** *nc.*

gambling *nu* act or practice of playing for money. *Gambling is forbidden in some countries.*

gambol ['gæmbl] *vi* jump or dance playfully like young animals or children. *past* **gambolled.** Also *nc* (usu. *pl*): *We watched the gambols of the children in the playground.*

game [geim] **1.** *nc* play; sport; contest with rules (e.g. football, tennis, chess, bridge). *Football is a game played everywhere. We hope to have a game of football next Saturday* i.e. we hope to play a game of football. **2.** *nc* (only *pl*) meeting at which several games or contests (esp. athletic contests) take place. *The Olympic Games are held every four years. He won the mile (race) in the school games.* **3.** *nc* one part of a contest (in tennis, bridge, whist etc). *He won the (tennis) set by six games to four. We need one more game for the rubber* (in bridge). *The score is game all* i.e. each side has won one game. **4.** *nc* (only *sing*) intention; plan; trick. *I don't know what his game is* i.e. I don't know his intentions. *Their game was to wait and see what the others did* i.e. what their plan was. *He is playing a deep game* i.e. he keeps his plan secret. *The game is up* i.e. further planning or action is useless. *The escaped prisoners knew the game was up when they saw the policemen.* **5.** *nu* animals or birds (e.g. deer, pheasants etc) hunted for sport (usu. protected for this purpose by special laws). Also *vt/i* gamble. Also *adj* brave; willing; ready. *He was game to the last* i.e. he went on fighting until the end. *I'm game for anything* i.e. ready to do anything.

'**game bird** bird protected by a special law which lays down times when it cannot be hunted.

'**gamekeeper** man employed to look after and breed game on a country estate.

'**game laws** laws which protect game (in sense **5.**) (esp. by laying down when they cannot be hunted).

'**game park/reserve** large area in which big

game is protected.
'game ranger/warden man employed to protect big game.
big game *npl/nu* large animals when being hunted for sport. *He went big-game hunting in Africa.*
fair game **1.** animals or birds which can be lawfully hunted. **2.** person/thing rightly or easily open to attack or ridicule. *Women's fashions are fair game to journalists.* (*informal* in sense **2.**).
make game of make fun of; mock (*o.f.*).
play the game obey the rules; act honestly. *I think he will play the game and return your book.*
play a good/poor game play well/badly. *John played a good/poor game of tennis.*

gamma ['gæmə] *nu* third letter of Greek alphabet.
'gamma rays penetrating rays given off by radioactive substances like radium.

gammon ['gæmən] *nu* smoked ham.

gamut ['gæmət] *n sing* **1.** complete range of musical notes. **2.** complete range of anything (esp. feelings and emotions). *The actor can express a whole gamut of emotions.*

gander ['gændə*] *nc* male goose.

gang [gæŋ] *nc* group of people (usu. criminals, workmen or (*informal*) friends). *The bank robbery was the work of a gang* i.e. a group of criminals. *Our gang used to meet in this café* i.e. group of friends.
gangster ['gæŋstə*] *nc* member of a gang of dangerous criminals.
'road gang group of workmen repairing a road.
gang up on someone act together against. *All the boys in the school ganged up on the new teacher.* (*informal*).

gangling ['gæŋgliŋ] *adj* tall and loosely built; awkward: *a big gangling youth.*

gangrene ['gæŋgri:n] *nu* decay of part of a living body. **gangrenous** ['gæŋgrinəs] *adj.*

gangway ['gæŋwei] *nc* **1.** movable bridge from ship to shore to allow people to board and leave a ship. *The ship's captain stood at the gangway to welcome the passengers coming aboard.* **2.** passage between rows of seats (e.g. in a theatre or cinema). *Please do not block the gangway.*

gannet ['gænit] *nc* type of large sea bird, with black wing tips.

gantry ['gæntri] *nc* type of bridge over railway lines to carry signals; bridge carrying a moving crane.

gaol, jail [dʒeil] *nc* public prison. Also *vt* send to prison. *He was gaoled/jailed for six months.*
gaoler, jailer, jailor *nc* person in charge of those sent to gaol/jail (*o.f.* – use **prison officer**).
'gaolbird, jailbird person often in gaol/jail. (*informal*).
Note: gaol is the official term in Britain but *jail* is the most used. Like *prison*, neither is used with an article except when meaning the actual building: *in jail; sent to jail; escape from jail* but *The jail is on a hill above the town.*

gap [gæp] *nc* opening; space between (which should be filled); way through. *He escaped through a gap in the wall. There are gaps in our knowledge of the moon* i.e. we do not know everything; there is more to learn. *There is a great gap between his ideas and mine. The main road goes through the mountain gap.*
'stopgap something used to fill or stop a gap temporarily. *I am using this old pen as a stopgap* i.e. until I get a better one.
'trade gap difference by which imports are greater than exports.

gape [geip] *vi* look at; stare with the mouth open in surprise; yawn. *Why are you gaping at these pictures?* Also *nc* open-mouthed stare; yawn.
gaping *adj* wide open; large. *There is a gaping hole in the roof.*

garage ['gæra:ʒ] *nc* building where a motorcar is kept or repaired or where petrol is sold. Also *vt* put a motorcar in a garage.

garb [ga:b] *nc* clothes; style of dress (*o.f.* – use **clothes** or **dress**). Also *vt* (always *passive*) dress (*o.f.*).

garbage ['ga:bidʒ] *nu* rubbish (usu. scraps of food from a kitchen).

garble ['ga:bl] *vt* give the facts of a report, speech etc in a mixed-up, confused way or wrongly. *The newspaper account of the minister's speech was completely garbled.*

garden ['ga:dn] *nc* **1.** place for growing fruit, vegetables and flowers. **2.** (only *pl*) public park or open space: *zoological gardens; botanical gardens; Kew Gardens.* Also as street name. *I live at No. 6 Riverside Gardens.*
gardener *nc* person who works in a garden.
gardening *nu* working in a garden. *Gardening is very popular in summer.*
'garden 'city industrial town or city specially planned to look like a garden i.e. with plenty of open spaces, trees and flowers.
'garden party party (usu. large) held out of doors in a garden.
'kitchen garden see **kitchen.**
'market 'garden (*Brit*) garden which is run commercially to supply local markets. (*US* **truck farm**).

gargantuan [ga:'gæntjuən] *adj* (usu. with reference to meals or appetite) huge.

gargle ['ga:gl] *vi* wash inside of the mouth or throat with liquid by throwing back the head and using breath to prevent liquid going down throat. *I gargle every morning when I have a cold.* Also *nc* act of gargling; liquid used for gargling. *Hot water with salt makes a good gargle.*

gargoyle ['ga:gɔil] *nc* small stone or metal figure at the edge of the roof of a building (usu. a church) to carry off rainwater. The figure is usu. of an ugly man or animal, and the rainwater is passed through its mouth. *He has a face like a gargoyle* i.e. he is very ugly.

garish ['gɛəriʃ] *adj* bright and showy; too brightly coloured. *The room is spoilt by the garish wallpaper.* **garishly** *adv.* **garishness** *nu.*

garland ['ga:lnd] *nc* circle of leaves or flowers (usu. placed on the head as an ornament or sign of victory or celebration). Also *vt* place a garland on. *The girls were garlanded with roses.*

garlic ['ga:lik] *nu* small plant with a root like an onion, used in cooking, and having a strong taste and smell.

garment ['ga:mənt] *nc* **1.** (in *sing*) piece of clothing (*o.f.*). **2.** (in *pl*) clothing. *This shop sells garments of all kinds.* (*formal*).
'undergarment piece of clothing (e.g. vest, pants) worn under outer clothes.
Note: the words *garments* and esp. *undergarment(s)* continue to be used because they are thought polite by some people. Also *undergarment* is the most useful word for

one article of *underclothes* which has no *sing*.

garner ['gɑːnə*] *nc* place where grain is kept. Also *vt* collect; gather. (both *o.f.*).

garnish ['gɑːniʃ] *vt* (usu. with reference to a dish of food) decorate with small things. *The cook garnished the beef with onions.* Also *nu* something used to decorate a dish of food (e.g. parsley, mint etc).

Note: garnish, garnishing are sometimes used of unnecessary decorations or additions to things other than food. *What I want is a plain statement without any garnishing.*

garret ['gærit] *nc* very small room just under the roof of a house.

garrison ['gærisn] *nc* troops put in a town or fort to defend it. Also *vt* occupy town or fort as a garrison; put troops in town or fort as a garrison. *The Romans garrisoned all the forts near the border. The general garrisoned the town with his own troops after the victory.*

garrulous ['gærjuləs] *adj* talking a lot about uninteresting things. **garrulously** *adv.*

garrulity [gə'ruːliti] *nu* being garrulous. *Garrulity is a sign of old age.*

garter ['gɑːtə*] *nc* band worn round the leg to keep a stocking in place.

gas [gæs] **1.** *nc* matter like air in density and form. (The other two forms matter can take are liquid and solid). *Oxygen is a gas. Air is a mixture of oxygen, hydrogen and other gases.* **2.** *nu* gas commonly used for heating and working, supplied to factories and houses through pipes. These are either **coalgas,** made by burning coal, or **natural gas,** found deep below the ground. **3.** *nc/u* dangerous, poisonous gas. *Gas was not used in the Second World War* i.e. poisonous gas was not used as a weapon. **4.** *nu* (*US*) informal short form of **gasoline.** (*Brit* **petrol**). **5.** anaesthetic. (*informal* in sense **5.**). Also *vt* harm or kill with poisonous gas. Also *vi* chatter. (*informal*). *past* **gassed.**

gaseous ['geisiəs] *adj* of, like gas; full of gas: *a gaseous mixture of air and petrol.* (*formal*).

gassy *adj* **1.** of, like gas. *There's a gassy smell about here.* **2.** talkative. (*informal*).

gasometer [gæ'sɔmitə*] *nc* less correct word for **gasholder.**

'**gas chamber** room which is filled with poisonous gas to kill people.

'**gas** '**cooker** cooker which uses lighted gas.

'**gas** '**fire** fire which uses lighted gas.

'**gas fitter** person who fits or repairs gas apparatus i.e. fittings to gas pipes.

'**gasholder** huge steel cylinder for storing gas.

'**gas main** large underground pipe, supplying gas.

'**gasman** person who inspects gas meters and collects money charged for using gas.

'**gas meter** instrument for measuring how much gas is used.

'**gas oven** oven which is heated by lighted gas.

'**gas pipe** pipe supplying gas, smaller than a gas main and not usu. underground.

'**gas ring** metal ring, filled with small holes in which gas burns for cooking.

'**gasworks** place where gas is made.

gash [gæʃ] *nc* long, deep cut (usu. in flesh). Also *vt* make a gash. *His cheek was gashed by a knife.*

gasket ['gæskit] *nc* ring or strip of soft material placed tightly between two parts of a joint in a pipe etc to prevent gas, steam etc from escaping.

gasoline ['gæsəliːn] *nu* (*US*) petrol.

gasometer [gæ'sɔmitə*] *nc* see **gas.**

gasp [gɑːsp] *vi* take short, quick breaths; fight for breath with mouth open. *After the race he stood gasping for air. His bad behaviour left me gasping* i.e. open-mouthed and speechless with surprise or anger. Also *nc* short, quick breath (of pain, surprise, anger etc). *His jokes caused a few gasps among the audience. We shall fight to the last gasp* i.e. to the end; until we die. *That dog is at its last gasp* i.e. it is completely exhausted or is about to die.

gassy ['gæsi] *adj* see **gas.**

gastric ['gæstrik] *adj* of the stomach.

Note: gastr- gastro- are prefixes used in many medical terms about the stomach.

gate [geit] *nc* **1.** opening into a place (e.g. a field, garden, sports ground) which can be closed; kind of door used to close this opening. *He walked through the gate into the garden. Please shut the gate when you leave the field. The gate is too high to climb.* **2.** number of people who pay to go into a sports ground (through a gate); total amount of money they pay. *There is always a big/good gate when England plays Scotland at football* i.e. many people pay to attend, or the amount of money they pay is great. *In cricket bad weather means poor/small gates* i.e. few people pay to watch cricket if the weather is bad, or not much money is paid by them.

'**gatecrash** *vt* enter place without paying or being invited. *He tried to gatecrash the party.*

gatecrasher *nc.* (both *informal*).

'**gate money** money paid at the gate of sports ground etc.

'**gatepost** post to which a gate is fixed.

'**gateway** actual entrance, way in, at a gate. *He stood in the gateway to stop her going in* i.e. in the middle of the opening.

gâteau ['gætou] *nc* cake, often with cream, chocolate etc. *pl* **gâteaux** ['gætouz].

gather ['gæðə*] **1.** *vt/i* come together; bring together; pick up; collect. *The people gathered in the street. She gathered her children round her. Gather your books together and follow me. He is busy gathering information about birds.* **2.** *vi* understand; find out. *I gather you live here. From what he said I gathered that he was not pleased.* **3.** *vt* pull cloth together into folds with a thread. *The child's dress is neatly gathered at the neck.* **4.** *vi* (with reference to a poisoned wound, cut, boil etc) become swollen.

gathering *nc* **1.** meeting of people: *sports gathering* i.e. meeting for sport. **2.** poisoned swelling. *The gathering on his arm was very painful.*

gauche [gouʃ] *adj* not knowing what to do or say in company. *I always feel gauche when I am with his rich friends.*

gaudy ['gɔːdi] *adj* bright and showy. *That's a gaudy tie you are wearing* i.e. I don't like it because it is too bright. **gaudily** *adv.*

gauge[1], gage[1] [geidʒ] *vt* measure size, contents, power etc of things; estimate; (usu. of feelings, thoughts etc) guess. *With a long stick you can gauge the amount of water in this well. It is not easy to gauge his thoughts about your plan.*

gauge[2], gage[2] [geidʒ] *nc* **1.** measure of thickness, contents etc (e.g. wire, nails, pieces of metal, barrels); measure of distance between pairs of rails. *This wire is sold in several gauges* i.e. several thicknesses. *The standard gauge for British railways is 4 feet*

8½ *inches* i.e. the distance between pairs of rails. **2.** instrument for measuring. **3.** estimate of power or ability.
narrow/broad gauge distance between pairs of rails less/more than 4 feet 8½ inches.
'**pressure gauge** instrument for measuring pressure (e.g. of car tyres).

gaunt [gɔ:nt] *adj* thin, looking ill, from hunger or pain. **gauntness** *nu.*

gauntlet[1] ['gɔ:ntlit] *nc* strong glove to protect the hands and wrists (e.g. in fighting, fencing, driving).
throw down the gauntlet challenge, invite someone to fight. (In the past someone who wished to fight a particular enemy took off his gauntlet and threw it down in front of him).
take/pick up the gauntlet accept the challenge, invitation i.e. by picking up the gauntlet which had been thrown down.

gauntlet[2] ['gɔ:ntlit] *nc* only in **run the gauntlet 1.** go between two rows of people who strike as one passes. **2.** be open to blame etc. *Every politician has to run the gauntlet of the press* i.e. can be blamed or criticized in the newspapers.

gauze [gɔ:z] *nu* type of thin cloth which one can see through; fine netting (e.g. of wire). *The windows are covered with wire gauze* i.e. fine netting made of wire to keep out insects etc. **gauzy** *adj.*

gave [geiv] past tense of **give.**

gavel ['gævl] *nc* small hammer used to hit the table at a meeting to get silence or attention.

gay [gei] *adj* **1.** happy and lively; without worries or cares; (of colours) bright and cheerful. *The dinner party was certainly a gay one. When we were young and gay* i.e. happy and without any cares. *The room was gay with flowers* i.e. flowers made the room look bright and cheerful. **2.** homosexual. (*informal* in sense **2.**). **gaily** *adv.* **gaiety** ['geiiti] *nu.*

gaze [geiz] *vi* look at for a long time (usu. in wonder or admiration). *The children gazed round the shop. He stood gazing at the view.* Also *nc* long look.
meet a gaze gaze at each other. *She met her mother's gaze across the room.*

gazelle [gə'zel] *nc* type of small graceful animal (usu. reddish with a white stomach) which is rather like a deer.

gazette [gə'zet] *nc* newspaper (usu. one published by the government giving news of public events, appointments and promotions of officials etc). Also *vi* (usu. *passive*) publish in a gazette. *Your appointment will be gazetted next week,* or more shortly *You will be gazetted next week.*

gazetteer [gæzə'tiə*] *nc* geographical dictionary giving lists of place names in alphabetical order.

gear [giə*] *nc* **1.** any equipment or mechanism which controls or guides a machine. *The lifting gear of a crane.* **2.** wheels with teeth which fit into each other to change the speed or power given by an engine. *This car has three forward gears.* **3.** apparatus in general. *Put your fishing gear in the bag* i.e. rod, hooks, boots etc used when fishing. Also *vt* make something fit into something else properly, as is done with car gears. *We had to gear our lives to the new changes. The factory is geared to rapid output.*
'**gearbox** box in a machine or car which contains the gears.
'**gear lever** (in a motorcar or on an engine) short bar which is moved to change gears.
'**gearwheel** wheel with teeth.
bottom/first, second, third, top/fourth gear stages by which the power of an engine is used to increase speed. *Never try to drive a car fast in bottom gear.*

gee-gee ['dʒi:dʒi:] *nc* child's word for **horse.** *pl* **gee-gees.**
gee-up *interj* (to a horse) order to hurry.

geese [gi:s] pl of **goose.**

Geiger counter ['gaigəkauntə*] *nc* instrument to find and measure radioactivity.

geisha ['geiʃə] *nc* Japanese girl who entertains by dancing and singing.

gelatin, gelatine ['dʒeləti:n] *nu* substance used in cooking (usu. obtained by boiling animal bones and tissues) which melts in hot water and becomes a jelly when cold.
gelatinous [dʒi'lætinəs] *adj.*

geld [geld] *vt* remove from a male animal the means of breeding; castrate.
gelding *nc* male horse which has been castrated.

gelignite ['dʒelignait] *nu* type of explosive.

gem [dʒem] *nc* **1.** valuable stone (usu. when cut and polished for wearing). **2.** something/somebody to be greatly valued and admired. *This is a gem of a house you have.* (*informal* in sense **2.**).

gender ['dʒendə*] *nc* (grammar) one of the three classes into which words can be put according to the sex given them i.e. masculine, feminine and neuter genders. *The gender of the word 'boy' is masculine, of the word 'girl' feminine, and of the word 'house' neuter.*

gene [dʒi:n] *nc* biological factor which passes on physical characteristics (e.g. hair colour, height, shape of nose etc) from parents to children. see also **genetic.**

genealogy [dʒi:ni'ælədʒi] **1.** *nc* someone's ancestry; account of this: *trace one's genealogy.* **2.** *nu* study of ancestry i.e. the descent of people or families. **genealogical** [dʒi:niə'lɔdʒikl] *adj.*

genera ['dʒenərə] pl of **genus.**

general[1] ['dʒenərl] *adj* **1.** for, by everybody or almost everybody; common; not special. *Watching television has become general* i.e. most people watch television. **2.** not exact; not in detail. *The general idea is to wait and see. We had a general talk about books* i.e. not about any particular book.
generally *adv* **1.** usually, commonly. *I am generally at home after 7 o'clock.* **2.** without giving details; by everybody or almost everybody. *I can only speak generally. Your promise is generally believed.*
generalize 1. *vt* make general. *They hope to generalize the use of this new soap.* **2.** *vi* make a general statement about something. *One cannot generalize from a few examples.*
generalization [dʒenərəlai'zeiʃən] *nc/u* general statement. *It is a generalization to say that men are stronger than women.*
sweeping generalization generalization which probably is not true. *The statement that all dogs are friendly is a sweeping generalization.*
generality [dʒenə'ræliti] *nc* greater part of; being general: *the generality of people in this country.* (*formal* – use **most people**). *We talked only in generalities* i.e. without details, in a general way.
general dealer someone who deals or trades in many kinds of things.
general election election held all over the country (for Parliament).

general knowledge what is known about many things; what is known by many people. *This examination will test your general knowledge. It is general knowledge that he will come tomorrow.*
general post office post office for a large area, as compared with a local one.
general practitioner doctor who treats many kinds of illness, not one special kind. see **specialist.**
general strike strike by many kinds of workers.
in general without details; as a whole. *Women in general like fashionable clothes. In general I agree with you.*
in general use used by most people.

general[2] ['dʒenərl] *nc* army officer of very high rank.
generalship *nu* ability as a general.

generate ['dʒenəreit] *vt* cause; make; make to happen. *A fire generates heat. The machine generates electricity/gas/steam etc. His kind smile soon generated friendliness.*
generator *nc* machine which generates electricity/gas/steam etc.
generation [dʒenə'reiʃən] **1.** *nu* generating: *the generation of electricity by atomic power* i.e. making electricity. **2.** *nc* people who belong by age to the same period of time. *Grandfathers, fathers and sons belong to three different generations; the younger/rising generation* i.e. all young people not yet grown up; *past generations* i.e. those who lived in the past.

generic [dʒə'nerik] *adj* see **genus.**

generous ['dʒenərəs] *adj* **1.** ready to give or spend; kind and helpful. *They are generous with their advice/help/money/time. Be generous to him; he has been ill.* **2.** more or bigger than usual. *He gave me a generous lunch. Wages here are generous.* **generously** *adv.* **generosity** [dʒenə'rɔsiti] *nc/u.*

genesis ['dʒenisis] *nc* beginning; birth. *pl* **geneses** ['dʒenisi:z].

genetic [dʒi'netik] *adj* concerned with the passing on of physical characteristics (e.g. colour, size etc) from parents to children.
genetics *nu* science which studies how heredity works. **geneticist** [dʒi'netisist] *nc.*

genial ['dʒi:niəl] *adj* cheerful and cheering; kindly; pleasant: *in genial company; genial neighbours; genial climate/weather.* **genially** *adv.* **geniality** [dʒi:ni'æliti] *nu.*

genie ['dʒi:ni:], **jinn** [dʒin] *nc* spirit or fairy found in Eastern stories. *pl* **genies** or **genie.**

genital ['dʒenitl] *adj* sexual: *genital organ.*
genitals, genitalia [dʒeni'teiliə] *npl* genital organs.

genitive ['dʒenitiv] *adj* (grammar) way in which something is shown as belonging to or coming from. Also *nc/u.*

genius ['dʒi:niəs] **1.** *nu* very great intelligence or ability: *a writer of genius. Genius is needed to solve this problem.* **2.** *nc* someone having very great intelligence or ability. *Shakespeare was a genius. Only a genius can solve this.* **3.** *nu* natural character, power, ability of a special kind (e.g. of a particular group of people, nation, period of history): *the genius of ancient Rome* i.e. all that made ancient Rome different and better; *the English genius for compromise.* **4.** *nc* spirit which looks after a person (only in **good/evil genius** i.e. someone who has a good/bad influence). *The young king's evil genius was his uncle.*

genocide ['dʒenousaid] *nu* mass killing of a race of people. **genocidal** [dʒenou'saidl] *adj.*

gent [dʒent] *nc* short informal form of **gentleman.**

genteel [dʒen'ti:l] *adj* too polite or well-mannered in a false way; pretending to be what one is not. **genteelly** *adv.* **gentility** [dʒen'tiliti] *nu.*

gentian ['dʒenʃən] *nc* type of blue flower, often found in mountains.
'gentian 'violet name of a blue dye used to treat burns and infections of the skin.

gentile ['dʒentail] *nc* someone who is not Jewish. Also *adj.*

gentle ['dʒentl] *adj* **1.** kind; soft; not rough or strong: *a gentle smile; a gentle knock on the door; a gentle manner; gentle rain; a gentle slope* i.e. one which is not steep. **2.** born of upper-class parents; of good family (*o.f.* in sense **2.**). see also **gentleman.**
gently *adv.* **gentleness** *nu.*

gentleman ['dʒentlmən] *nc* **1.** man of good family, of upper classes (in the past, one just below the nobility); man of wealth and leisure. *Since he became rich he lives like a gentleman.* **2.** man who behaves as a gentleman should i.e. has good manners and can be trusted. *He is no gentleman* i.e. he is bad-mannered or not to be trusted. **3.** polite word for **man.** *There is a gentleman to see you. Please sit down, gentlemen. pl* **gentlemen** ['dʒentlmən].
gentlemanly *adj.* (*opp* **ungentlemanly**). **gentlemanliness** *nu.*
'gentleman's a'greement one made between persons who trust one another and not written down.
'gentleman 'farmer farmer of high social status who owns his own land.
Note: the *fem* form *gentlewoman* is *o.f.*; therefore the polite way to address mixed company is *ladies and gentlemen. Gentlemen* is the form used in the *pl.* For *sing* use *Sir. Please sit down, gentlemen* but *Please sit down, Sir. Gentleman* used in the third person (e.g. *There is a gentleman to see you*) is slightly *o.f.* but it is more usual when the gentleman is within hearing. Otherwise use *man. He is a very rich man* not *He is a very rich gentleman.*

gentlewoman ['dʒentlwumən] *nc* see *Note* under **gentleman.** *pl* **gentlewomen** ['dʒentlwimin].

gentry ['dʒentri] *npl* **1.** those of the upper class. *All the gentry in this part of the country like fishing.* **2.** (usu. with **these**) with an opposite meaning of a group of unpleasant people. (*informal* in sense **2.**).

genuflect ['dʒenjuflekt] *vi* bend the knee (usu. in church etc). *The priest genuflected before the altar.* **genuflection, genuflexion** [dʒenju'flekʃən] *nc.*

genuine ['dʒenjuin] *adj* real; true; not a copy: *a genuine gold ring* i.e. made of real gold. *His illness is genuine* i.e. he is not pretending to be ill. *A genuine old Roman coin* i.e. not a copy of one. **genuinely** *adv.* **genuineness** *nu.*

genus ['dʒenəs] *nc* **1.** (biology) group that is smaller than a family but larger than a species. **2.** any kind or class of thing. *pl* **genera** ['dʒenərə]. **generic** [dʒə'nerik] *adj.* **generically** *adv.*

geo- [dʒi:ou] *prefix* used in many scientific words dealing with the earth (e.g. **geology**).

geography [dʒi'ɔgrəfi] *nu* science of the earth's lands, seas, climates, peoples, products etc. **geographic, geographical** [dʒiə'græfik(l)] *adj.* **geographically** *adv.* **geographer** *nc* someone who is expert in

geography.
physical geography special kind of geography dealing with the shape of the earth's surface. Other kinds are **economic/political/regional geography.**
geology [dʒi'ɔlədʒi] *nc* science of the earth's rocks and how they were formed.
geologist *nc* someone expert in geology. **geological** [dʒiə'lɔdʒikl] *adj*. **geologically** *adv*.
geometry [dʒi'ɔmətri] *nu* mathematical study of lines, angles, surfaces and shapes. **geometric, geometrical** [dʒiə'metrik(l)] *adj*. **geometrically** *adv*.
geometrician [dʒioumə'triʃən] *nc* someone expert in geometry.
geriatrics [dʒeri'ætriks] *nu* science of diseases caused by old age.
Note: followed by a *sing* verb.
geriatric *adj*. **geriatrician** [dʒeriə'triʃən] *nc*.
germ [dʒə:m] *nc* **1.** very small living part of a plant or animal which causes it to grow: *germ of wheat*. **2.** something very small which causes anything to grow, get bigger. *I have the germ of an idea* i.e. I have the beginning of an idea which may grow into something more definite. **3.** very small living thing (microbe or bacillus) which is harmful. *Colds are spread by germs.*
germicide ['dʒə:misaid] *nc* substance (usu. a chemical) which kills germs.
'germ carrier something/somebody carrying or spreading germs (in sense **3.**).
'germ 'warfare method of fighting a war by using disease germs as weapons.
German ['dʒə:mən] **1.** *nc* native of Germany. **2.** *nu* language of Germany. Also *adj* of Germany or German people.
germane [dʒə:'mein] *adj* connected with; relevant. *His answer is not germane to our problem.*
germinate ['dʒə:mineit] *vt/i* (usu. of seeds) begin or make to grow. **germination** [dʒə:mi'neiʃən] *nu*.
gerontology [dʒerɔn'tɔlədʒi] *nu* science which studies the old age of man. **gerontologist** *nc*.
gestation [dʒes'teiʃən] *nu* carrying of young in the womb before birth; period during which young are so carried. *For human beings, gestation lasts about nine months.*
gesticulate [dʒes'tikjuleit] *vi* make gestures while, or instead of, speaking.
gesticulation [dʒestikju'leiʃən] *nc* act of gesticulating.
gesture ['dʒestjə*] *nc* **1.** movement of the body (esp. of hands, arm or head) to show what one feels or thinks. *He made a rude gesture with his fingers. He shook his fist in a gesture of anger.* **2.** any movement to show what one feels or thinks. *His quick reply to your letter is an encouraging gesture.* Also *vi* make a gesture.
Note: gesture (verb) has the same meaning as *gesticulate*, but the latter also describes movements which are violent and not controlled. *He always gesticulates when he is excited.*
get [get] *vt/i* **1.** obtain, earn, buy. *He got his degree by working hard. I am getting £1,500 a year. She has gone to get some bread. Go and get your breakfast* i.e. obtain and eat. **2.** (with reference to food) prepare. *Get some food for the visitors. She is getting lunch.* **3.** receive. *I got your letter this morning. This country gets very little rain. John got a kick on the leg.* So, with reference to illnesses: *get a cold/a fever/malaria etc.*
Note: get cold i.e. become cold; *get a cold* i.e. catch the infection.
4. (with *past part* of another verb) have happen to one. *They got beaten* i.e. were beaten. **5.** become. *He soon got tired. In summer it gets very hot here.* **6.** put oneself in a certain state. *Get ready/shaved/washed/dressed etc. They got to know. I'll never get to understand him.* **7.** go, come, arrive, travel (sometimes with difficulty or effort). *We'll get there somehow. How do we get across the river? He got back last week. I hope they get home soon.* **8.** cause someone/something to go, come, arrive etc; cause to happen; put someone/something in a certain state (often with difficulty or effort). *We'll get you there somehow. How do we get a car across the river? He got his son back to school. Get me home at once. Has she got the baby dressed yet? He is getting his clothes packed. I cannot get him to agree.* *past* **got** [gɔt]. (*US past part* is **gotten** ['gɔtn] in the sense of obtained or become).
have got have. *I've got two pairs of shoes.*
Note[1]: have got is probably more usual than *have* (esp. in speech).
Note[2]: being one of the most common verbs in the English language (esp. in speech), *get* is used with many *preps* and *advs* and in many phrases, mostly as informal variants of other verbs. A list of them, by no means complete, is given below:
get about 1. go about; travel. *Since he broke his leg, he can't get about.* **2.** spread, become known (usu. by word of mouth). *The news of the disaster soon got about.*
get above oneself become discontented, too proud. *These students are getting above themselves.*
get across go, come across; cause to do so.
get something across make understood. *How can a teacher get this across to his pupils? (informal).*
get ahead pass, advance. *John got ahead of the other runners in the race. To get ahead, Africa needs more schools.*
get along 1. succeed; make progress. *Is he getting along all right in his new job? How did you get along in the examination?* **2.** agree, cooperate with. *He is so kind that he gets along with everyone.* **3.** nonsense, go away! *Get along with you!* (*informal* in sense **3.**). see also **get on.**
get at 1. reach. *The little boy cannot get at the books on the top shelf.* **2.** find out. *It is difficult to get at the real cause of this.* **3.** attack. *Let me get at him! In this book the writer gets at his critics. The witnesses have been got at* i.e. bribed, threatened etc. **4.** mean, hint. *What exactly are you getting at?* i.e. what do you mean?
get away escape, depart from; cause to do so. *The prisoner got away from his guards. I cannot get away from the office before six o'clock.*
'getaway *nc* quick escape (esp. from a crime).
get away with something succeed without being harmed or punished. *He thinks he can always get away with telling lies.*
get away with you! see **get along** (in sense **3.**).
get back return; cause to do so. *We got back before nightfall.*
get something back recover; cause to do so. *John got back the watch he lost.*
get back at someone try to have one's revenge. *He will get back at you for this.*

get one's own back have one's revenge. *By winning the game they got their own back for last year's defeat.*
get by **1.** pass; cause to do so. *How can I get by while you stand in the way? Get him by the policeman and he will be safe.* **2.** survive, manage. *They have very little money but they will get by. He hopes to get by at the dance although he cannot dance at all.*
get (something) down descend; cause to do so. *They got down from the hill before evening. He is getting the papers down from the room upstairs. I got the drink down with difficulty* i.e. swallowed it.
get something down make a note of; record. *Get what he says down in writing. Have you got it all down?*
get one down depress; discourage; make one feel unhappy. *His bad manners get me down. Don't let the other team get you down.* (*informal*).
get down to something become busy; work hard at. *You must get down to your studies this year.*
get far **1.** go far. **2.** make progress; succeed. *John won't get far if he is lazy.*
get home **1.** arrive, return home; cause to do so. **2.** hit the target or mark. *Two of the shots got home. How can I get this home to him?* i.e. make him understand it.
get in/into **1.** go in/into; arrive; cause to do so. *Get into bed and stay there. We got in late last night. They will get into London this afternoon. Get the washing in before it rains. The bus got me into the village at two o'clock.* **2.** have something (usu. unpleasant) happen to one. *He got in/into a rage/temper. I am afraid I'll get into trouble. They got into debt. This mistake may get him into difficulties.*
get it into one's head believe (usu. without reason). *He has got it into his head that we hate him. I can't get it into his head that he has to go.*
get into the way of become accustomed to. *We soon got into the way of having classes on Saturday morning.*
get near (to) **1.** go, come near. *You must get near (to) him if you wish to hear what he says. It is getting near bedtime.* **2.** almost. *We got near (to) finishing it* i.e. almost finished it.
get off (in sense **4.**). *Although he fell from the top window, he got off with a few bruises* i.e. he was lucky to have only a few bruises. **2.** become friendly with someone of the opposite sex. *Look, he is getting off with the most beautiful girl in the room.* (*informal* in sense **2.**).
get (someone/something) off **1.** go, come off; leave; cause to do so. *She got off the bus. Get off the floor at once. At what time do you get off (work/from work)? We must get the car off this busy road. The boy is getting off his wet clothes.* **2.** send away. *He got the report off to his teacher last week. We cannot get our guests off to London before Monday.* **3.** begin. *They at last got off to sleep. The concert got off to a good start* i.e. it began well. **4.** avoid damage, danger, punishment; cause to do so. *You won't get off next time you do it. Blaming the other driver did not get him off. They could not get them off until the storm ended* i.e. from some place of danger.
get off with something **1.** avoid more serious damage, danger, punishment. see **get off with you!** nonsense!, go away! (*informal*).
get on **1.** succeed, make progress. *How are you getting on at school? That man is sure to get on.* **2.** (usu. of time) pass, move. *Time is getting on* i.e. it is late. *He is getting on in years* i.e. he is becoming old. *He is getting on for sixty* i.e. he is almost sixty years old. *I have to get on my way* i.e. move, begin going.
get on something mount, climb on; cause to do so. *Get on a horse/bicycle/roof/wall. Get on one's feet* i.e. stand. *They got him on his bicycle.*
get on with someone agree, cooperate with; be friendly with. *I get on well with my mother-in-law.*
get out go, come out; escape; cause to do so. *He got out the door/window. Our dog has got out. We got the box out the door/window.*
get out of something **1.** see **get out.** *When did you get out of bed? The prisoner got out of the cell by breaking down the door. Please get me out of here.*
Note: it is only with doors, windows and other openings that either *get out* or *get out of* is used, *get out* having the special meaning here of going out through these openings. With all other words *get out of* is used. **2.** avoid; cause to do so. *You cannot get out of paying your debts. My illness got me out of having to see him* i.e. as I was ill I didn't have to see him. **3.** obtain; benefit from. *All I got out of him was twenty pence.*
get out of sight/one's sight be no longer seen; disappear.
get out of one's way stand aside, allow to pass.
get over (something) climb over; cause to do so; put over. *The boy is getting over the fence/gate/wall etc. It was difficult to get the pole over the hedge.*
get over something recover from something unpleasant, succeed in overcoming. *The parents will never get over the death of their son. How can a person get over being blind?*
get something over **1.** finish something. *Let's get it over as soon as possible.* **2.** make someone understand something. *I got it over to him that they wouldn't come.* (*informal*).
get round (something) go, come round; cause to do so. *You can get round the park in half an hour. We got the car round the corner without being seen.*
get round something avoid a difficulty. *They have got round the difficulty by writing to the headmaster.*
get round someone persuade; win over. *He got round the others by pretending to help them. When shall we get him round to helping us?*
get (something) through **1.** go or come, pass through; cause to do so. *I was able to get through the forest by myself. He tried to get the box through the window.* **2.** (usu. of a message, telephone call, radio) reach; cause to do so. *He could not get through to his mother last night* i.e. by telephone. *Letters did not get through until after the floods. I want you to get this message through to headquarters.* **3.** make oneself understood. *I can't get through to her.*
get through something **1.** finish. *They got through the meal without speaking. You must get through this book before Monday. She got through her husband's money in a year* i.e. spent it all. **2.** (of examinations, courses) succeed in, pass; cause to do so. *Did you get through your driving test? His job as a tutor is to get me through this examination.*
get together come together; meet; cause to do so (usu. for a purpose).

'**get-together** *nc* meeting or party etc. (*informal*).

get up 1. rise from bed in the morning; stand; cause to do so. *I got up very early* i.e. from bed. *The pupils get up when their teacher comes into the classroom* i.e. stand. *The teacher got the boys up when the headmaster came into the classroom.* 2. climb; cause to do so. *We got up the ladder to the roof.* 3. dress; disguise. *She was got up in very expensive clothes. The spy was got up to look like a waiter* i.e. was disguised to look like a waiter. 4. prepare; study.

'**getup** *n sing* special clothing; disguise. (*informal*).

get up to 1. arrive close to; reach. *The enemy got up to the wall of the town before they attacked. Yesterday I got up to page 100.* 2. (usu. of children) plan or begin something naughty. *What are these children getting up to now?*

geyser ['gi:zə*] *nc* 1. spring which spouts hot water into the air from time to time. 2. apparatus for heating water quickly by gas or electricity.

ghastly ['gɑ:stli] *adj* 1. shocking, terrible. *It was a ghastly murder.* 2. bad, unpleasant or not approved. *The school concert was ghastly.* (*informal*). 3. pale and miserable, like a dead person.

gherkin ['gə:kin] *nc* small, green cucumber (usu. pickled).

ghetto ['getou] *nc* 1. part of a town where Jews once had to live. 2. part of a town where any separate group of people (usu. poor and of a different race from the majority) live. *pl* **ghettos**.

ghost [goust] *nc* 1. spirit of a dead person which is said to be seen or heard etc by a living person. *He told me the ghost of his father appeared at his bedside.* 2. (only in **Holy Ghost**) Spirit of God. 3. spirit, life. *He gave up the ghost* i.e. he died (*o.f.*). 4. only in **ghost of a chance** i.e. something very weak or unreal like a ghost. *You haven't a ghost of a chance of winning* i.e. you cannot possibly win. (*informal*). 5. someone who works as an artist or writer for someone else who then claims the work is his. *He did not write his own memoirs; he employed a ghost.* Also *vi* act as ghost (in sense 5.). *I am ghosting for a millionaire.* **ghostly** *adj*. **ghostliness** *nu*.

ghoul [gu:l] *nc* 1. evil spirit said to feed on the bodies of the dead. 2. any disgusting person. **ghoulish** *adj*. **ghoulishly** *adv*.

giant ['dʒaiənt] *nc* 1. someone/something much larger than usual. 2. someone much better than others in some way (e.g. experience, ability). *He is one of the giants of the game of football.* Also *adj*: *a giant box of chocolates; a giant animal.*

gibber ['dʒibə*] *vi* talk quickly and without meaning (esp. with fear or anger etc).

gibberish *nu* meaningless talk, nonsense.

gibbet ['dʒibit] *nc* post with an arm from which a dead criminal was hung as a warning to others. Also *vt* 1. kill by hanging. 2. publicly cause someone to be despised or hated. *In his book he gibbets all politicians.*

gibbon ['gibən] *nc* type of ape.

gibe, jibe [dʒaib] *vi* (with **at**) make a fool of, laugh at (in an unkind way). Also *nc* blame mixed with contempt. *He could not bear the gibes of the other boys.*

giddy ['gidi] *adj* 1. seeing things as if they were going round so that one feels one is about to fall down; dizzy. *High buildings make me giddy.* 2. pleasure-loving; thoughtless: *just a giddy young girl.* **giddily** *adv*. **giddiness** *nu*.

gift [gift] *nc* 1. something given, a present: *a wedding/birthday gift. Officials are not allowed to receive gifts from the public.* 2. only in **in the gift of; in one's gift** i.e. power, authority to give. *The two scholarships are in the gift of the university* i.e. the university has the power to award them. 3. special natural ability. *I have no gift for foreign languages.* 4. something very easy. *In the examination paper Question 2 was a gift.* (*informal* in sense 4.).

gifted *adj* having special natural ability: *a gifted speaker.*

gig [gig] *nc* 1. two-wheeled horse carriage. 2. type of small rowing or sailing boat.

gigantic [dʒai'gæntik] *adj* of giant size, unusually big. *He says he caught a gigantic fish.*

giggle ['gigl] *vi* laugh in a silly way. *Tell those girls to stop giggling.* Also *nc* silly laugh.

get the giggles be unable to stop giggling. *As soon as she saw him, she got the giggles.* (*informal*).

gild [gild] *vt* 1. cover thinly with gold or gold paint. 2. make bright or attractive.

gilded *adj*: *a bird in a gilded cage; gilded youth* i.e. rich and fashionable.

gilding *nc* thin covering of gold or gold paint. see also **gilt**.

gild the lily try unnecessarily to make something pleasant even more attractive.

gill[1] [gil] *nc* (usu. *pl*) part of the head of a fish through which it breathes.

gill[2] [dʒil] *nc* quarter of a pint. see appendix.

gillie ['gili] *nc* (*Scot*) servant assisting someone who is fishing or shooting for sport.

gilt [gilt] *nu* thin covering of gold or gold paint. Also *adj*: *She is wearing a gilt brooch.*

gilt-edged stock/securities safe investments (esp. in Government stock).

gimlet ['gimlit] *nc* small tool for making holes in wood.

gimlet-eyed having very sharp eyes.

gimmick ['gimik] *nc* (esp. with reference to actors and those who advertise and sell things) trick to get attention or increase popularity. *Changing the colour of the packet and not its contents is just a gimmick.*

gimmicky *adj*. (both *informal*).

gin[1] [dʒin] *nc* 1. trap. 2. machine for taking the seeds out of cotton. Also *vt*. *past* **ginned**.

gin[2] [dʒin] *nc/u* kind of strong colourless alcoholic drink.

ginger ['dʒindʒə*] *nu* plant root with a hot, spicy taste used for flavouring food and drinks. Also *vt* (usu. with **up**) make lively, more active. *This news will ginger them up.* Also *adj* having the flavour or colour of ginger i.e. light reddish-yellow: *ginger cat; ginger hair.*

gingerly *adv* carefully, cautiously. *He lifted the baby very gingerly.* Also *adj*: *He lifted it in a very gingerly way.*

'**ginger** '**beer**/'**ale**/'**wine** drink made from or flavoured with ginger.

'**gingerbread** cake flavoured with ginger.

'**ginger** '**group** people (esp. politicians) who try to make other members of the same party etc more active, enthusiastic etc.

gingham ['giŋəm] *nu* type of cotton cloth (usu. with a check design).

gipsy, gypsy ['dʒipsi] *nc* person belonging to a wandering tribe of people, found in Europe and Asia.

giraffe [dʒi'rɑːf] *nc* large African animal with a very long neck and big dark spots.

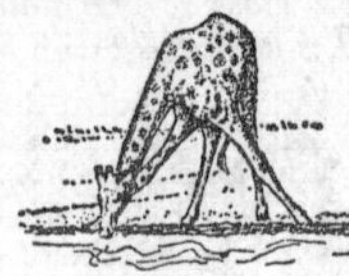
giraffe

girder ['gəːdə*] *nc* long, strong piece of steel used in the framework of buildings and bridges.

girdle ['gəːdl] *nc* **1.** woman's undergarment worn round the hips **2.** belt tied round the waist.

girl [gəːl] *nc* **1.** female child. *All their children are girls.* **2.** daughter. *My girl left school last year.* **3.** young, unmarried woman. *The town is full of lovely girls.* **4.** female servant or employee. *I have a girl to look after the baby.* **5.** man's female friend. (Often **girlfriend**). *John and his girl(friend) were married yesterday.*

girlish *adj* foolish; like a young girl. **girlishly** *adv.* **girlishness** *nu.*

girlhood *nu* time or state of being a girl.

'**shopgirl** one employed in a shop. (Also **factory/farm girl**).

girth [gəːθ] *nc* **1.** belt round a horse to keep the saddle on its back. **2.** measurement round something (e.g. pillar, tree, waist); circumference. *He is a man of great girth* i.e. big round the waist.

gist [dʒist] *nu* (always with **the**) (usu. with reference to what has been said or written) most important points of something. *He gave me the gist of the headmaster's report.*

give [giv] *vt/i* this verb has the general meaning of causing somebody/something to have, but not necessarily to keep for ever. **1.** cause to have, hand over. *They gave him a good breakfast. She will give it a wash. She gives me her cat to look after while she is away. He gave the letter to the boy to post. I gave her my coat and hat* i.e. to put away, hang up etc, not keep. **2.** cause to have and keep as a gift. *At Christmas my father gave me £5. He gave all his books to the school library. Give me some of your ink.* **3.** cause to have, hand over something (in exchange or return) for something else, to buy, pay, sell. *I'll give you five pounds for these stamps. The shopkeeper gave us two packets of soap for the price of one. They would give anything to be with us now* i.e. they want very much to be with us. **4.** supply; produce. *Hens give us eggs. The lamp gave very little light. His letter gave the latest news. He forgot to give us the date. This book gives few details.* **5.** (often with reference to time) allow to have. *Please give them another chance. I must be given more time to finish it. We gave him five minutes to decide. They should give themselves two hours to get here. He is honest; I give him that* i.e. I agree he is honest. **6.** cause to have some emotion or feeling. *Give them our best wishes/love/regards/thanks etc. Did the child give you any trouble? The sudden noise gave her a shock. This tooth is giving me pain. It gives me great pleasure to open this school. Please give me your attention.* **7.** (with special reference to bodily action) cause to have. *Give someone/something a blow/kick/knock/look/pull/punch/push/sign/smile/tap etc.* **8.** express feelings by bodily action. *Give a cry/groan/jump/shout/shrug/sigh.* **9.** bend, become weak. *The roof began to give because of the great weight on it. His knees gave/He gave at the knees* i.e. they bent because he was weak or very tired. *past tense* **gave** [geiv]. *past part* **given.**

give *nu* ability to bend. *This bed has no give* i.e. it is not soft and springy. **giver** *nc.*

given already decided: *at a given time.*

given to, much given to very fond of. *He is given to drinking.*

give something away **1.** (usu. with reference to several people) cause to have and keep as a gift. *He gave away all his pictures* i.e. for nothing to several people. *After the sports he gave away the prizes* i.e. presented them to all the winners. **2.** make known something secret. *He gave away the plan of attack to the enemy.*

give someone away **1.** hand over the bride to the bridegroom at a wedding. *She was given away by her uncle.* **2.** betray; tell a secret. *Please don't give me away* i.e. don't make known what I have done or plan to do.

give (something) back return. *He won't give me back my pen.*

give (something) in **1.** yield, surrender. *After much fighting the enemy gave in. He is always giving in to other people* i.e. following their wishes. **2.** hand in something to someone in authority. *You should give in your names to the headmaster. I gave in my driving licence* i.e. to the office dealing with driving licences.

give off (something) send out. *This flower gives off a pleasant smell. The engine gives off smoke and steam.*

give out **1.** come to an end; stop. *Our money soon gave out. The car engine suddenly gave out.* **2.** send out. see **give off.** **3.** make known; announce. *The radio has just given out the football results.* **4.** hand round; distribute. *Open the cupboard and give out the books.*

give over **1.** hand over. **2.** stop doing. *Give over!* i.e. stop it. (*informal* in sense **2.**).

give (something) up surrender. *I had to give up my place in the queue. He gave himself up to the police.* **2.** leave, stop doing. *Why are you giving up your job? He has given up playing football.* **3.** stop trying to help someone. *The teacher gave him up because he was so lazy. They gave him up for lost* i.e. stopped trying to help, or do anything, because they believed he was lost. **4.** lose heart; despair. *Don't give up, you may still win.*

give someone the benefit of the doubt see **benefit**[1].

give birth (to) (of a mother) have a baby. *She gave birth (to a boy).*

give chase (to) chase, pursue.

give credit to **1.** allow someone to get goods now and pay later. **2.** believe in. *It is difficult to give credit to all he says.*

give a hand to/with help. *I'll give you a hand with the dishes.* (*informal*).

give it to someone punish; speak severely to. *I'll give it (to) him when I see him.* (*informal*).

give one's life for something die for. *Many soldiers gave their lives for their country.*

give one's life to something devote all one's time and energy to. *She gave her life to helping the poor.*

give an/the order, give orders **1.** instruct, command. *When I give orders/an order you* *must obey them/it. The captain gave the order to advance.* **2.** ask goods to be supplied. *Be sure you give the order for bread to the baker.*

give someone a piece of one's mind talk severely to. (*informal*).

give and take be ready to cooperate; compromise. *We must all give and take a little if we want peace.* Also *nu*: *Without some give-and-take there will be no peace.* (both *informal*).

give way **1.** allow to pass first. *At the roundabout give way to traffic from the right.* **2.** yield to; yield to one's own feelings. *They had to give way to the writers' complaints. Give way to grief/sorrow/despair etc.* **3.** break, collapse under strain. *The rope gave way. The bridge/floor/roof suddenly gave way.*

glacier ['glæsiə*] *nc* mass of ice formed from snow, which moves very slowly down a mountain.

glacial ['gleisiəl] *adj* of a glacier; icy, frozen.

glad [glæd] *adj* happy, pleased; making happy. *They are very glad about their new house. I would be glad of your help. He looks/feels glad. I am glad to see you. This is a very glad day for all of us. comparative* **gladder.** *superlative* **gladdest. gladly** *adv.* **gladness** *nu.*

gladden *vt* make glad.

glade [gleid] *nc* grassy space in a wood or forest (*o.f.*).

gladiator ['glædieitə*] *nc* (in ancient Rome) armed man trained and paid to fight in public. **gladiatorial** [glædiə'tɔ:riəl] *adj.*

glamour ['glæmə*] (*US* also **glamor**) *nu* attractiveness; that which causes one to be very interested: *the glamour of the stage. There is no glamour in office work.* **glamorous** *adj.* **glamorously** *adv.*

glamorize *vt* make glamorous.

glance [gla:ns] *vi* **1.** take a quick look (at, into, over, round, through). *I glanced at the newspaper. We glanced through the book. The teacher glanced round the classroom.* **2.** hit and then slide off. *The bullet glanced off the wall.* Also *nc* **1.** quick look. *I took a glance at the newspaper; see at a glance* i.e. see quickly. **2.** quick flash of light. **glancing** *adj.* **glancingly** *adv.*

a glancing blow on the face i.e. a blow that glanced off the face.

gland [glænd] *nc* small organ which controls certain functions of the body: *sweat gland.* **glandular** ['glændjulə*] *adj.*

glare [glɛə*] *vi* **1.** (usu. of the sun) shine too brightly. **2.** look fiercely. *The angry father glared at his son.* Also *nc/u* **1.** fierce bright light. *I have to wear sunglasses because of the glare of the sun. He stood in the glare of the car's headlights.* **2.** fierce look.

glaring *adj* **1.** too bright: *glaring light; glaring colours.* **2.** fierce and shining: *glaring eyes.* **3.** so bad as to be easily seen: *glaring mistake; glaring injustice.* **glaringly** *adv.*

glass [gla:s] **1.** *nu* hard, easily broken material through which light can pass, used for making windows and other things. *He broke the glass of the front window. This jar is made of thick glass.* **2.** *nc* thing made of glass: *drinking glasses. The glass fell out of my watch* i.e. the piece of glass covering its face. *She looked at herself in the glass* i.e. mirror. (rather *o.f.*). *The glass is rising* i.e. the barometer. *The sailor watched the distant ship through his glass* i.e. telescope; *a magnifying glass.* **3.** *nc* contents of a drinking glass: *drink a glass of beer/milk/water etc. Thank you, I'll have a glass; a glass(ful) of wine.*

glassy *adj* like glass, smooth; dull and lifeless: *a glassy sea. He had a glassy look in his eyes.* **glassily** *adv.* **glassiness** *nu.*

glasses *npl* spectacles. *I must put on my glasses to read this.*

'glass blower *nc* person skilled at blowing soft, heated glass into shapes. **glass blowing** *nu.*

'glass cutter **1.** tool for cutting glass. **2.** person skilled at using this tool.

'glasshouse building made of glass to protect growing plants from the weather. (Usu. **greenhouse**).

glasshouse

'glasspaper paper covered with small pieces of glass, used for making things smooth.

'glassware articles made of glass. see **glaze.**

glaucous ['glɔ:kəs] *adj* of a greenish-blue colour.

glaze [gleiz] **1.** *vt* fit with glass. **2.** *vt* cover with a thin coat of glass (e.g. in making china); make smooth, polish. **3.** *vi* become glassy. *His eyes began to glaze* i.e. when fainting or dying. Also *nu* thin covering of glass.

glazed *adj* having a glaze.

glazier ['gleiziə*] *nc* person who glazes windows etc.

gleam [gli:m] *nc* **1.** weak beam of light that does not usu. last long. *I saw the gleam of his lamp in the wood.* **2.** small sign or show of anything: *a gleam of hope/humour.* Also *vi* send out gleams; shine. *The newly-polished car stood gleaming in the sunshine. His eyes gleamed with pleasure.*

glean [gli:n] *vt* **1.** gather the small amounts of grain left in a field after harvest. **2.** gather anything slowly and with difficulty (e.g. news, information). *He is gleaning all he can from the official reports.* **gleaner** *nc.* **gleanings** *npl* grain, news etc which has been gleaned.

glee [gli:] **1.** *nu* happiness, amusement, because of success or satisfaction. *His defeat caused great glee among his enemies.* **2.** *nc* song sung in harmony.

glen [glen] *nc* (esp. in Scotland) narrow valley.

glib [glib] *adj* of smooth, easy talk which is not to be trusted. *This salesman is a glib speaker. I don't believe his story; it is too glib. comparative* **glibber.** *superlative* **glibbest. glibly** *adv.* **glibness** *nu.*

glide [glaid] *vi* move smoothly and quietly. *The bird glided to the ground. The dancers glided over the floor of the room.* Also *nc* gliding movement.

glider *nc* type of aircraft which has no engine.

gliding *nu* sport of flying in gliders.

glimmer ['glimə*] *vi* shine weakly and unsteadily. *In the distance a small light glimmered.* Also *n sing* very small sign or show of anything. *glimmer of light; glimmer of hope.* see **gleam** (in sense **2.**).

glimmering *nc*: *There is not a glimmering of an agreement yet.*

glimpse [glimps] *nc* quick but not complete look. *I caught/got a glimpse of his face as he ran past.* Also *vt/i*: *We glimpsed the field through the trees.*

glint [glint] *vi* send out a short sharp beam of light. *The sun is glinting through the clouds. His eyes glinted with anger.* Also *nc*: *a glint of light. He had an evil glint in his eyes.*

glisten ['glisn] *vi* (usu. of something wet or polished) shine: *glisten with sweat. Her eyes glistened with tears.* **glistening** *adj.*

glitter ['glitə*] *vi* shine with a sharp, bright, changing light. *The diamond ring glittered on her finger.* Also *nu*: *the glitter of ice on the road.*

glittering *adj* **1.** shining in this way: *glittering jewels.* **2.** causing attention; splendid. *He has had a glittering career.*

gloat [glout] *vi* look at with too great pleasure, satisfaction. *He gloats over/on his money. They gloated over/on my failure.* **gloating** *adj.* **gloatingly** *adv.*

globe [gloub] *nc* **1.** something round like a ball. **2.** the world. *He sailed round the globe.* **3.** map of the world shown on a globe. *If you look at this globe you will see where the equator is.* **4.** round glass bowl: *the globe of a lamp* i.e. round lampshade made of glass.

global *adj* world-wide. *The war became global.* **globally** *adv.*

globule ['glɔbju:l] *nc* very small globe (esp. a drop of liquid): *a globule of oil.*

globular ['glɔbjulə*] *adj* like a globe; having globules.

gloom [glu:m] *nc* **1.** almost complete darkness. *He walked through the gloom of the thick forest.* **2.** feeling of sadness, despair. *His illness has caused great gloom among his friends.*

gloomy *adj*: *a gloomy room* i.e. dark, badly lit. *The bad weather has made everyone gloomy* i.e. sad, despairing. **gloomily** *adv.* **gloominess** *nu.*

glorify ['glɔ:rifai] *vt* **1.** worship, praise, honour. *All men should glorify God. The history book glorifies the country's heroes.* **2.** praise too much. *He glorifies everything his wife does. This restaurant is just a glorified snack bar* i.e. it is just a snack bar, not something better, as it is said to be. (*informal* in sense **2.**). **glorification** [glɔ:rifi'keiʃən] *nu.*

glory ['glɔ:ri] **1.** *nu* great honour, praise. *This church was built to the glory of God. They fight for glory, not money.* **2.** *nc* something beautiful or deserving praise: *the glory of flowers in the spring; the glories of our past history.* Also *vi* (with **in**) be very proud of; get great pleasure from. *He glories in his skill at football. They gloried in showing me my mistakes.*

glorious *adj*: *It was a glorious victory.* (*opp* **inglorious**). **gloriously** *adv.*

gloss[1] [glɔs] *nc/u* **1.** smooth, shining surface. *This paint has a fine gloss.* **2.** anything which is pleasant on the surface only. *These people have a gloss of civilization* i.e. they only appear to be civilized.

glossy *adj* smooth, shiny: *glossy magazines* i.e. expensive magazines full of glossy pictures. **glossily** *adv.*

gloss over cover up faults. *He tried to gloss over his past mistakes.*

gloss[2] [glɔs] *nc* note in the margin, between the lines or at the end of a book to explain or comment on certain words or sentences. Also *vt* write glosses on.

glossary ['glɔsəri] *nc* list of glosses; list of words needing special explanation. *All the technical terms are shown in the glossary at the back of the book.*

glove [glʌv] *nc* covering for the hand and wrist (usu. with a separate place for each finger).

work/be hand in glove with someone work together in very close cooperation with someone (often in a bad sense). *He is hand in glove with our rivals.*

boxing gloves see **box**[2].

glow [glou] *vi* **1.** send out light and heat without flame. *Red-hot iron glows.* **2.** look, feel brighter or warmer. *These red curtains certainly glow in this dull room. His cheeks glowed after the race. Their faces were glowing with joy.* Also *nc* (only *sing*): *the glow of the fire; a glow of pleasure.*

glowing *adj* **1.** showing a glow: *the glowing ashes of the fire.* **2.** very favourable. *We hear glowing stories about your work.* **glowingly** *adv.*

'glow-worm type of insect whose tail sends out a green light.

glower ['glauə*] *vi* look angrily at.

glucose ['glu:kous] *nu* type of sugar.

glue [glu:] *nc/u* sticky substance used for fastening things (esp. wood) together. Also *vt* **1.** stick with glue. *Glue the boards together. He glued it to the desk.* **2.** remain very close to, as if stuck with glue. *The children were glued to their chairs* i.e. they would not move from them. *His nose is always glued to a book* i.e. he is a very intent reader.

glum [glʌm] *adj* sad-looking; sullen. **glumly** *adv.*

glut [glʌt] *vt* **1.** (with **oneself**) eat too much. **2.** supply too much. *At present coffee is glutting the world market* i.e. more is being grown than can be sold. *past* **glutted.** Also *nc*: *There is a glut of coffee. Coffee is a glut on the market.*

glutinous ['glu:tinəs] *adj* sticky, like glue.

glutton ['glʌtn] *nc* person who eats too much. **gluttonous** *adj.* **gluttonously** *adv.* **gluttony** *nu.*

glycerine ['glisəri:n] *nu* thick, sweet, colourless liquid, used in medicine and for making explosives.

gnarled [na:ld] *adj* **1.** (of wood) knotted and twisted. **2.** anything knotted and twisted: *gnarled hands.*

gnash [næʃ] *vt* in **gnash one's teeth** i.e. bring one's teeth together in anger or pain.

gnat [næt] *nc* type of very small stinging insect.

gnaw [nɔ:] *vt/i* **1.** keep biting or chewing something hard. *The dog gnawed (at) the bone.* **2.** cause pain. *Hunger gnawed (at) his stomach.*

gnawing *adj*: *a gnawing doubt.* **gnawingly** *adv.*

gnome [noum] *nc* small fairy said to live underground.

gnu [nu:] *nc* large deer-like animal found in Africa. (Also **wildebeest**).

go [gou] *vi* **1.** move from one place to another; travel. *The train goes from London to Glasgow. He went by boat/car/steamer etc. This aeroplane can go at 600 miles per hour.* **2.** move about in a certain state. *All the*

men here go armed. The children must not go hungry. **3.** (with **-ing** form of another verb) move to another place to do something: *go swimming/shopping/looking for etc.* **4.** leave; pass; disappear. *We must go now. The time went quickly.* **5.** become. *He is going blind. Her hair has gone grey. Russia went Communist.* **6.** reach, stretch from one place to another. *How far does this railway go? The path goes to the village. Her skirt went to her knees.* **7.** do its work; perform. *Our new plans are going well. The meeting went badly. The engine goes smoothly.* **8.** intend to do; be about to do or happen. *I am going to study harder next term. It is going to be hot today.* **9.** break, fail. *He felt the branch go beneath him. His eyesight is going. The brakes of the car went. past tense* **went** [went]. *past part* **gone** [gɔn].
Also *nc/u.* (*informal*) in such phrases as:
have a go (at) try.
be on the go be active, busy. *They are always on the go.*
at one go at one attempt. *pl* **goes.**
going *adj* usu. only in **a going business/concern** i.e. successful.
go about move from one place to another (usu. several places). *He always goes about with his children. The story is going about that you are leaving.*
go about something begin attending to. *How shall we go about this problem?*
go after someone/something follow to get; try to obtain. *Go after him! He is running away. They are going after the first prize.*
go against something move in the opposite direction to; be contrary to. *The boat is going against the tide. This goes against their belief. The game was going against us* i.e. we were losing.
go ahead with start; do quickly, actively. *They are going ahead with the plan.*
go-'ahead *adj* active; progressive. *We have a very go-ahead committee.* (*informal*).
go along 1. move, travel along. **2.** continue. *You will learn as you go along.*
go along with someone 1. accompany. *I went along with them to London.* **2.** agree; cooperate. *We are ready to go along with you in this plan.* (*informal* in sense **2.**).
go at someone/something attack; deal busily with. *He went at them with a knife. They are going at their work as they never have before.*
go back 1. return. **2.** date from. *The quarrel goes back to the beginning.*
go back on something fail to carry out. *He went back on his promise.*
'go-between *nc* person who goes from one person or group to another to settle their differences. *The two governments used him as their go-between when discussing peace.*
go beyond something 1. move, reach further than. *The road does not go beyond the river.* **2.** do more than is expected. *You have gone beyond my orders. The results have gone beyond our hopes.*
go down 1. sink, fall. *The ship/moon/sun went down. The wind/sea is going down* i.e. becoming quieter. *Prices here never go down.* **2.** be accepted, approved. *His story went down (well) with his friends.* **3.** be recorded. *Everything you say will go down in writing.* **4.** be defeated. *France went down to Germany.*
go for someone/something 1. move to have; obtain: *go for a walk/a holiday etc. She has gone for a newspaper.* **2.** attack. *The wounded lion went for the hunter.* see **go at. 3.** be sold for. *Shoes are going for four pounds a pair.* **4.** apply to. *These remarks go for all of you.* **5.** like something; try to get something. (*informal* in sense **5.**).
go forward make progress. *The building of the new hall is going forward without any trouble.*
go in for something 1. enter for. *Are you going in for the mile (race)?* **2.** take up; become interested in. *He went in for teaching. Many boys go in for stamp collecting.*
go into something 1. (arithmetic) be an exact part of. *Two goes into six three times.* **2.** begin doing; take up (usu. a job); begin feeling. *He has gone into teaching. He went into a rage.* **3.** look at, examine. *You should go into its cost before buying it.*
go off 1. leave. **2.** make a sudden noise; be fired. *The gun went off.* **3.** become worse. *His work has gone off recently. The milk/meat is going off* i.e. becoming sour/bad. **4.** proceed; take its course. *The lesson went off well.* **5.** fall asleep; lose consciousness. *The child soon went off into a deep sleep. He went off into a trance.*
go off with something take something (usu. belonging to someone else). *You went off with my umbrella.*
go on 1. continue. *I am going on to the next town. The concert went on for hours. Don't go on about it* i.e. don't continue talking about it. **2.** do something next. *He went on to show us how to do it.* **3.** rely, depend upon. *We have only his word to go on.* **4.** happen. *There is always a lot going on here.*
'goings-'on *npl* happenings (usu. ones not approved of). *The goings-on in that house are shocking.* (*informal*).
go out 1. leave (esp. home). *They do not go out much these days. I am going out to Africa.* **2.** stop, finish. *The fire went out* i.e. stopped burning. *Long skirts have gone out* i.e. out of fashion.
go over (something) 1. look at, examine. *They went over the plans which they had made. Let us go over your answer again.* **2.** change sides; join. *Most of the army went over to the enemy.*
go round (something) 1. reach round. *This belt does not go round my waist.* **2.** visit somebody/something nearby. *Let us go round and ask him.* **3.** be enough for everyone. *Twenty books will not go round this class.*
go through (something) 1. look at; examine carefully. *We shall go through these papers together. They went through our luggage at the customs.* **2.** spend. *He went through all the money his father gave him.* **3.** complete; endure (usu. something unpleasant). *He has been through a long illness. You will have to go through a severe test.* **4.** be accepted, approved. *The plan did not go through.*
go through with try to complete. *I am not going through with it.*
go under 1. sink. **2.** fail in business. *Many traders went under during the war.*
go up 1. rise, increase. *Fees will go up next year.* **2.** rise suddenly into the air because of an explosion; be destroyed. *The whole village went up when it was bombed. The hut went up in flames.*
go with (something) 1. be suited to, mix well with. *The green hat does not go with your blue coat. Potatoes don't go with ice cream* i.e. don't taste good together.
go without be or manage without. *They had*

no food so they went without.
go it alone do something by oneself. (*informal*).
go behind someone's back do something without someone's knowledge or consent. *They went behind the manager's back to arrange the meeting.*
go (one) better do better than someone/something. *You gave ten pounds; I shall go one better by giving fifteen pounds.* (*informal*).
go far 1. move, reach a great distance. 2. last a long time; be of much use. *A pound doesn't go far these days.* 3. be successful. *This young man should go far.*
as far as it goes not completely; within limits.
be far gone be very ill or drunk; be almost finished. (*informal*).
go at it hammer and tongs fight or quarrel fiercely; start doing something vigorously. (*informal*).
go a long way help greatly. *The money will go a long way to paying my school fees.* see **go far.**
go to pieces 1. break into pieces. *The glass bowl went to pieces in my hands.* 2. lose self-control; break down mentally or physically. *When she saw her dead child, she went to pieces.* (*informal* in sense 2.).
go to seed 1. (of plants) produce seeds after flowering. 2. (of people) become careless of how one looks, behaves etc. (*informal* in sense 2.).
go slow work more slowly in protest against something (e.g. poor wages). *The dockers agreed to go slow.*
'go-'slow *nc* act of working in this way.

goad [goud] *nc* 1. sharp stick for driving cattle. 2. anything driving someone to do something. Also *vt*: *Their laughter goaded him to try it again. The teacher was goaded into fury by their stupid mistakes.*

goal [goul] *nc* 1. (in games like football and hockey) the space between two posts through which the ball must pass to gain a point. *He kicked the ball towards the other team's goal.* 2. point gained by the ball passing through the goal. *We scored a goal in the first minute of the game.* 3. any end or aim. *His goal is to be a doctor.*
keep goal guard the goal.
'goalkeeper *nc* player who keeps goal.

goat [gout] *nc* type of long-haired animal with horns, kept as a domestic animal.
goatee [gou'tiː] *nc* beard on the chin like a goat's.
'goatherd person who looks after goats.
get one's goat annoy. *He gets my goat.* (*informal*).
separate the sheep from the goats see **separate.**

gobble ['gɔbl] *vt/i* 1. eat in lumps, quickly and noisily. *Because they were late they gobbled (down) their food.* 2. make a bubbling noise like a turkey.

gobbledegook ['gɔbldiguk] *nu* unnecessary use of long, difficult words instead of short, simple ones. (*informal*).

goblet ['gɔblit] *nc* drinking cup with a stem and no handle.

goblin ['gɔblin] *nc* ugly, evil fairy or spirit.

god [gɔd] *nc* 1. (**God**) Supreme Being; Creator, used in many phrases calling on God. *God forbid! God (only) knows!* i.e. I don't know. *God help us!* 2. any divine being worshipped by man. *These people pray to many gods; the god of war.* 3. any person/thing greatly admired. *The school captain was (a) god to the younger boys. Money is his god.* 4. (in *pl*) top and cheapest part of a theatre; persons who sit there.
godlike *adj* like God or a god.
godly *adj* very religious. (*opp* **ungodly**).
godliness *nu.*
godless *adj* not believing in God; wicked.
godlessness *nu.*
goddess ['gɔdis] *nc* female god.
'god-fearing *adj* very religious; obedient.
'godfor'saken *adj* (usu. of places) miserable.
'godparent person, not the real parent, who promises at a child's baptism to bring the child up as a Christian.
'godfather/'godmother man/woman who promises in this way.
'godchild/'godson/'goddaughter child/son/daughter about whom such a promise is made.

goggle ['gɔgl] *vi* roll the eyes; stare. *Stop goggling at the visitors. His eyes goggled with surprise.*

goggles ['gɔglz] *npl* large spectacles to keep out dust, water etc.

goitre ['gɔitə*] (*US* **goiter**) *nc/u* swelling of the neck because of a fault in the thyroid gland.

gold [gould] *nu* soft, heavy, yellow metal of great value. Also *adj* made of gold: *gold coin/ring/watch.*
golden *adj* 1. made of gold. 2. like gold; gold in colour; valuable; ripe: *golden grain; the golden rays of the sun.* 3. best of its kind: *a golden opportunity; golden rule; golden age; the golden age of English literature* i.e. when English literature was at its best.
'gold digger 1. person who digs for gold. 2. pretty woman interested only in getting money or gifts from men.
'gold dust very small grains of gold.
'goldfield place where gold is found.
'goldfish *nc/u* type of yellow or red fish, kept as pets.
'gold 'leaf very thin sheet of gold.
'gold mine 1. mine from which gold is dug. 2. anything providing wealth. *This restaurant is a gold mine* i.e. makes a lot of money. (*informal* in sense 2.).
'gold rush rush to a newly-found goldfield.
'goldsmith person who makes things from gold.
the 'gold standard see **standard.**
golden handshake gift of money made to a person when he leaves employment and shakes hands with his employer. (*informal*).
golden wedding fiftieth anniversary of a wedding.

golf [gɔlf] *nu* outdoor game of hitting a small ball into holes with a long stick. **golfer** *nc.*
'golf club 1. stick for hitting a golf ball. 2. group of persons who associate to play golf. *I belong to the local golf club.* 3. building used for this purpose: *at the golf club.*
'golf course piece of land on which golf is played. (Also **golf links** only *pl*).

gondola ['gɔndələ] *nc* boat used on the canals of Venice in Italy.
gondolier [gɔndə'liə*] *nc* person who makes a gondola move.

gone [gɔn] past part of **go.**

gong [gɔŋ] *nc* round piece of metal which makes a deep, ringing noise when struck.
'dinner gong gong which is struck when dinner is ready.

good[1] [gud] *adj* 1. virtuous, behaving properly. *The priest is a good man. Try to be a good boy.* 2. superior; above the ordinary: *a good family; good clothes. They live in a*

good neighbourhood. **3.** right; proper kind for its purpose: *a good book about flowers; a good cooking pot. This medicine is good for a cold.* **4.** improving; beneficial. *Eat this food; it is good for you. Games are good for the health.* **5.** efficient: *a good cook/farmer/football player; good housekeeping. She is very good with young children. She is good at games.* **6.** pleasant, enjoyable, successful. *Did you have a good holiday? It's good to see you again. That is a good story; a good hard game; a good long sleep.* **7.** kind; helpful. *It is good of him to come. He is good to his servants. Will you be good enough to hold my bag?* **8.** complete; satisfactory. *Have a good breakfast/a good rest. He has a good excuse/reason. Take a good look at it. It needs a good wash.* **9.** of a lot of anything: *a good deal of arguing; a good number of people; a good few examples* i.e. quite a number. **10.** a little more than: *a good half hour; a good half ton; a good ten miles. Yesterday we walked a good ten miles. comparative* **better** ['betə*]. *superlative* **best** [best]. (*opp* **bad**).
well [wel] *adv.*
goodish *adj* quite a lot. see **good**[1] (in sense **9.**).
goodly *adj* **1.** good-looking (*o.f.*). **2.** quite large. see **goodish.**
goodness *nu* **1.** quality of being good; best part of something. *If you cook it too long you lose the goodness. Would you have the goodness to stop that noise?* **2.** exclamation instead of God. *Goodness knows! For Goodness' sake! Thank Goodness!*
'good-for-nothing *adj* useless. Also *nc* useless person.
'good-'natured *adj* kind; friendly. **good-naturedly** *adv.*
'good-'tempered *adj* not easily annoyed. **good-temperedly** *adv.*
as good as almost. *The house is as good as built. We were as good as lost.*
give as good as one gets return blow for blow, answer for answer etc; hold one's own. *In the argument they gave as good as they got.* (*informal*).
good for **1.** (of money, strength etc) able to supply, find. *Because he is rich, he is good for £10,000. I am still good for another game* i.e. I can still find enough strength to play another game. *The old man is good for ten more years* i.e. he is strong enough to live for ten more years. **2.** (of tickets etc) valid. *The theatre ticket is good for next Saturday.*
good humour cheerful state of mind. **good-humoured** *adj.* **good-humouredly** *adv.*
good looks personal beauty.
have a good mind to feel very much like doing; be very inclined to. *I have a good mind to punish you.* (*informal*).
good morning / afternoon / evening / day / night form of greeting and farewell i.e. may you have a good morning etc.
Note: all except *good night* can be used both when meeting and leaving someone, although it is more common to use them only when meeting, and to use *goodbye* when leaving. But *good night* is used only when leaving someone in the evening. *Good evening, Mr Jones; I am glad to see you. Good night, Mr Jones; I'll see you tomorrow.*
be a good thing (only with **it**) be lucky. *It was a good thing that I was there to help.*
do a good turn do a kindness to. *He did me a good turn by lending me ten pounds.* (*informal*).
good[2] [gud] **1.** *nu* something that is good. *The new rules are for the good of the school* i.e. for the benefit of. *You should do it for your own good. A rest will do you good.* see **good**[1]. **2.** *nu* use. *What is the good of staying here?* **3.** *nc* (only *pl*) things bought, sold or owned. *This shop has foreign goods for sale. During the war they lost all their goods.* **4.** *nc* (in *pl*) things carried by rail.
'goods shed building at railway station where goods are stored.
'goods train (*Brit*) railway train carrying goods. (*US* **freight train**).
'good'will **1.** kindness, willingness. **2.** part of the value of a shop or business.
up to no good planning something wrong, mischief. *They are up to no good.* (*informal*).
for good for ever; permanently. *He has gone for good.*
to the good have as profit, left over. *He was £100 to the good after a week's business.*
goodbye [gud'bai] *interj* said when people leave. *Goodbye, my dear! They said goodbye and left.* Also *nc*: *There were many sad goodbyes.*
goose [gu:s] **1.** *nc* large water bird like a duck, but bigger and usu. with a longer neck. **2.** *nu* the flesh of this bird used as food. *pl* **geese** [gi:s].
'gooseflesh, 'goosepimples roughness of skin caused by cold or fear. *This silent house gives me gooseflesh.*
'goose-step *nu* military kind of marching with leg raised high and straight at each step. Also *vi.*
gooseberry ['guzbəri] *nc* type of berry used as food.
play gooseberry be the third person present when the other two wish to be by themselves. (*informal*).
gore[1] [gɔ:*] *nu* blood (*o.f.*).
gory *adj* bloody.
gore[2] [gɔ:*] *vt* wound with horns. *The bull gored the farmer.*
gorge [gɔ:dʒ] **1.** *nu* throat (rather *o.f.*); food which has passed down throat into stomach. *My gorge rose at the awful smell* i.e. I felt sick. **2.** *nc* narrow pass between hills. *The river flows through a gorge.* Also *vt/i* fill oneself by eating greedily and too much. *The lions were gorged with meat. The children gorged themselves with cakes.*
gorgeous ['gɔ:dʒəs] *adj* splendid, very attractive: *a gorgeous view of the mountain; a gorgeous blonde. We had a gorgeous time.*
gorgeously *adv.*
gorilla [gə'rilə] *nc* largest type of ape.
gorse [gɔ:s] *nu* type of prickly bush with small, yellow flowers. (Also **furze**).
gosh [gɔʃ] *interj* exclamation of surprise.
gospel ['gɔspl] *nc* **1.** **(Gospel)** story of Christ's life in one of the first four books of the New Testament in the Bible. *He went to Africa to preach the Gospel* i.e. spread Christianity. **2.** anything (to be) completely believed. *What he says is gospel/the gospel truth* i.e. is as true as the Gospel. (*informal* in sense **2.**).
gossamer ['gɔsəmə*] *nu* **1.** very thin thread(s) of a spider's web. **2.** type of very thin cloth.
gossip ['gɔsip] **1.** *nu* talk when one is not busy (usu. about other people and often unkind). *At lunch I heard all the gossip about Jones. Have you heard the latest gossip?* **2.** *nc* person fond of gossip. *All the people in the village are gossips.* Also *vi* talk or write gossip. *Our wives sat gossiping in the garden.*
'gossip column news gathered from gossip

and printed in a newspaper or magazine. **'gossip writer** person who writes gossip for a newspaper or magazine.

got [gɔt] past of **get.**

Goth [gɔθ] *nc* one of an ancient uncivilized German tribe which invaded and settled in the Roman Empire.

Gothic *adj* **1.** of the Goths. **2.** kind of architecture common in old churches and cathedrals. *This church has a fine Gothic spire.* **3.** kind of thick heavy writing or printing. Also *nu* the Gothic language; Gothic architecture; Gothic printing.

gotten ['gɔtn] *US* form of **got.** see **get.**

gouge [gaudʒ] *nc* tool with a curved cutting edge for making grooves or holes in wood. Also *vt* cut with a gouge or other instrument, force out. *He gouged the stone out of the tyre with a knife.*

goulash ['gu:læʃ] *nc/u* type of meat and vegetable stew.

gourd [guəd] *nc* **1.** large fruit of a climbing or spreading type of plant. **2.** dry, hard skin of this fruit as a container.

gourmand ['guəmənd] *nc* person very fond of food who eats too much.

gourmet ['guəmei] *nc* person very fond of food and well-informed about good cooking and wines.

gout [gaut] *nu* disease causing painful swelling (esp. of the big toe or thumb). **gouty** *adj.*

govern ['gʌvən] *vt* rule, control, direct. *For many years Great Britain governed India. These laws govern the sale of beer and wine.* **governing** *adj*: *the governing body of the school.*

governance *nu* control, direction: *rules for the proper governance of the school.*

governess ['gʌvənis] *nc* woman employed to teach children at their home.

government **1.** *nu* act of governing. *In the past the government of the country was in the hands of the king.* **2.** *nc* kind of government. *We voted for a Labour government. This country now has self-government.* **3.** *nu* (usu. **Government**) persons who govern. *The Government have (has) increased taxes. The President is forming a new Government* i.e. is choosing Ministers to help him to govern. **governmental** [gʌvən'mentl] *adj.*

governor *nc* **1.** person appointed to govern a colony, province or state. **2.** person appointed to any governing body (e.g. of a college, school, hospital). *Our school has its own board of governors.* **3.** device which controls the speed of a machine. *The engine of the bus is fitted with a governor to stop it going too fast.*

'governor-'general *nc* person appointed to represent the Queen in a dominion of the British Commonwealth. *pl* **governors-general** (*formal*) or **governor-generals** (*informal*). see **dominion.**

gown [gaun] *nc* **1.** woman's dress. **2.** long, loose coat worn over ordinary clothes by judges, university staff, students, schoolteachers etc.

grab[1] [græb] *vt/i* **1.** seize quickly with the hands. *He grabbed my jacket. I'll grab him as he comes out.* **2.** seize greedily. *past* **grabbed. grabber** *nc.*

grab[2] [græb] *nc* **1.** seizing quickly. *He made a grab at my jacket.* **2.** device for seizing and lifting something. *The crane has a grab* (for lifting earth etc).

smash-and-grab raid see **smash.**

grace [greis] **1.** *nu* something pleasing (esp. movement or manners), correct behaviour, charm. *We admired the grace with which she walked across the room. He agreed with (a) good/bad grace* i.e. willingly/unwillingly. *Knowing he was not wanted, he had the grace to refuse the invitation.* **2.** *nc/u* kindness, favour. *By the grace of God I was not killed. Give me a month's grace and I will pay you* i.e. allow me one more month. *He fell from grace* i.e. out of favour. **3.** *nc/u* short prayer made at the beginning and/or end of a meal thanking God for his kindness. **4.** **(Grace)** form of address to an archbishop, duke or duchess: *certainly, your Grace; his Grace the Archbishop of Canterbury.* Also *vt* favour, add charm to (by being present). *It is good to see so many important people gracing our meeting.* **graceful** *adj.* **gracefully** *adv.* **gracefulness** *nu.*

graceless *adj* without grace, badly-behaved. **gracelessly** *adv.*

gracious ['greiʃəs] *adj* charming, kind. *She has a gracious smile.* Also *interj*: *Goodness gracious! Gracious me!* **graciously** *adv.* **graciousness** *nu.*

gradation [grə'deiʃən] *nc/u* (esp. in colour and music) successive stages of development, passing slowly from one thing to another. *The gradations of public opinion ran from sympathy to anger. The pleasant gradation of sounds in this music.*

grade[1] [greid] *nc* **1.** order, level of rank, quality. *Only the highest grade of goods is sold here; a poor grade of steel; low grades of oil.* **2.** year into which a school's work is divided. *The youngest pupils are in the first grade, the oldest pupils in the sixth grade.* *Note:* mainly US in sense **2.**; *class* or *form* are commoner in the UK and the Commonwealth.

3. mark or position given for work done at school or college: *make the grade* i.e. reach the required standard, be successful. **4.** (*US*) degree of slope. (*Brit* **gradient**).

grade[2] [greid] *vt* **1.** put in order of size, quality etc. *He graded the students according to ability.* **2.** (usu. of roads) make more level.

grader *nc* machine for levelling roads.

on the upgrade/downgrade becoming better/worse. *Exports of cotton are on the upgrade.*

gradient ['greidiənt] degree of slope. *On that hill the road has a gradient of 1 in 6.*

gradual ['grædjuəl] *adj* happening slowly, step by step. *There was a gradual change in the weather*; *a gradual slope* i.e. one that rises slowly. **gradually** *adv.* **gradualness** *nu.*

graduate[1] ['grædjueit] *vt* divide, mark in units of measurement. *The container is graduated in pints, quarts and gallons for measuring liquids.*

graduate[2] ['grædjueit] *vi* **1.** take a university degree. *At what university did you graduate?* **2.** (*US*) finish a course of any school or college. *He graduated from high school.* Also ['grædjuət] *nc* **1.** person who has taken a degree. **2.** (*US*) person who has finished a course.

graduation [grædju'eiʃən] *nu* taking a degree; ceremony at which degrees are given.

graft[1] [gra:ft] *vt* transfer part of one living thing to another (e.g. buds or branches from one tree to another; skin or bones from one part of the body to another or from one person to another). *He grafted the branch onto the apple tree. His hands were so badly burned that the doctors had to graf* *new skin onto them.* Also *nc/u* thing grafted; act of grafting.

graft[2] [grɑ:ft] *nu* **1.** unfair use of political influence for one's own profit. *That Minister became rich through graft.* (*informal*). **2.** hard work.

grain [grein] **1.** *nc/u* seed of corn, rice or other food plants: *a store full of grain. The hen ate the grains of corn on the ground.* **2.** *nc* any small piece of anything: *a grain of powder/salt/sand/sugar etc; a grain of honesty/truth etc. There is not a grain of truth in what he says* i.e. it is completely untrue. **3.** *nc* very small unit of weight, 1/7000 of a pound. **4.** *nc/u* natural marking on marble, stone, wood etc. *This kind of wood has a very fine/coarse grain.*

go against the grain be against one's inclinations. *It goes against the grain (for him) to be rude to a friend* i.e. he does not like to do this. (*informal*).

gram [græm] *nc* see **gramme.**

grammar ['græmə*] **1.** *nu* rules for speaking or writing a language correctly: *good/bad grammar* i.e. correct/incorrect use of grammar. **2.** *nc* book that teaches grammar. *Take out your English grammars.*

grammatical [grə'mætikl] *adj* following the rules of grammar; having good grammar. (*opp* **ungrammatical**). **grammatically** *adv.*

grammarian [grə'mɛəriən] *nc* person expert in grammar.

'**grammar school** secondary school in which Latin grammar was once the most important subject; now one giving an academic education.

gramme [græm] (*US* **gram**) *nc* metric unit of weight, equal to the weight of one cubic centimetre of water.

gramophone ['græməfoun] *nc* (*Brit*) machine which produces sounds of music and speech from records. (Also **record player**) (*US* **phonograph**).

granary ['grænəri] *nc* store for grain.

grand[1] [grænd] *adj* **1.** noble, splendid. *He lives in a grand house; a grand fellow; in a grand manner.* **2.** enjoyable. *We had a grand holiday.* **3.** more important, superior, complete: *grand finale* i.e. impressive ending of a concert etc; *grand piano* i.e. a big type of piano; *grand total* i.e. including everything.

grandly *adv* in a grand manner.

grandeur ['grændjə*] *nu* being grand, magnificence.

grand-[2] [grænd] *prefix* used to express certain family relationships (e.g. **grandfather** i.e. the father of one's mother or father; **grandmother; grandparent; grandson** i.e. child of one's son or daughter; **granddaughter).**

grandiose ['grændiouz] *adj* planned on a large scale; meant to impress.

grange [greindʒ] *nc* farmhouse with its barns and other buildings.

granite ['grænit] *nu* type of hard rock.

grant [grɑ:nt] *vt/i* **1.** allow to have; give. *The headmaster granted us an extra holiday. I cannot grant your request.* **2.** agree. *I grant that what you say is correct.* Also *nc* gift, allowance of money. *The council made a grant of land to the people. Students in this country receive a grant from the government.*

'**grant-in-'aid** *nc* money paid to help a school, college etc. *This school gets a grant-in-aid from the government.* *pl* **grants-in-aid.**

'**grant-'aided** *adj* getting a grant-in-aid.

take for granted believe to be certain. *Do not take his help for granted.*

granular ['grænjulə*] *adj* of or like grains.

grape [greip] *nc* type of fruit, used for making wine.

'**grapefruit** type of fruit like a big, yellow orange.

'**grape sugar** kind of sugar found in grapes; glucose.

'**grapevine** **1.** vine on which grapes grow. **2.** way of passing news secretly or unofficially. (*informal* in sense **2.**).

sour grapes bitterness at failure, used when someone fails to get something and then pretends he does not want or like it. *His saying that he does not want to go to university is just sour grapes.*

graph [grɑ:f] *nc* diagram showing by a line or lines the relation between two quantities. *A graph showing the increase in trade by years from 1900 to 1940.*

graphic ['græfik] *adj* **1.** of writing or drawing. **2.** clear, vivid. *He gave a graphic account of his adventures.* **graphically** *adv.*

graphite ['græfait] *nu* kind of carbon used as 'lead' in pencils.

grapnel ['græpnl] *nc* instrument with several hooks used as an anchor or to catch hold of something.

grapple ['græpl] *vt/i* seize (and usu. struggle with). *He grappled with the thief. They are grappling with the problem.*

grasp [grɑ:sp] *vt/i* seize firmly; understand. *I had to grasp the rope to stop falling. It is difficult to grasp his meaning.* Also *nu*: *He held my hand in a friendly grasp. You seem to have a good grasp of English history.*

grasping *adj* seizing, greedy. **graspingly** *adv.*

grasp at something try to grasp. *He grasped at the rope but missed it. You should grasp at the chance to go.*

beyond/within one's grasp unable/able to be grasped. *The tin on the shelf is beyond the little child's grasp* i.e. he cannot reach it. *An easy exercise like this is within your grasp* i.e. you can understand it.

grass [grɑ:s] **1.** *nu* type of green plant with very narrow leaves which can cover large areas. *Cattle eat grass. Let us sit on the grass.* **2.** *nc* particular types of this plant. *Not all the grasses found in this country can be eaten by animals.*

grassy *adj* of grass, covered with grass.

'**grassland** large area of land covered with grass: *the grasslands of North America.*

'**grass** '**roots** *npl* the masses; ordinary people, regarded as being the most important part of a country, party etc. Also **grass-roots** *adj.*

'**grass snake** kind of harmless snake, with a yellow mark on the head, which lives near water.

grate[1] [greit] *vt/i* **1.** rub into small pieces with something rough (usu. for cooking). *She grated the cheese into a bowl.* **2.** make a rough, unpleasant sound through rubbing; annoy. *The sharp stone grated on the window. His boasting grates on everyone.*

grating[1] *adj*: *a grating voice.* Also *nc.*

gratingly *adv.*

grater *nc* instrument with a rough surface for grating food etc.

grate[2] [greit] *nc* small metal framework in a room for holding a fire.

grateful ['greitful] *adj* thankful; expressing thanks. *I am grateful (to you) for your help. They sent us a very grateful letter.* (*opp* **ungrateful**). **gratefully** *adv.*

gratefulness, gratitude ['grætitju:d] *nu.*

(*opp* **ingratitude**).

gratify ['grætifai] *vt* satisfy, please. *He was gratified to learn you could come.*

gratifying *adj*: *It was gratifying for him to learn this.* **gratifyingly** *adv.*

gratification [grætifi'keiʃən] **1.** *nu* feeling of being gratified. I *had the gratification of seeing him win.* **2.** *nc* something causing one to be gratified. *His two main gratifications are music and good food.*

grating[2] ['greitiŋ] *nc* frame made of bars to cover an opening.

gratitude ['grætitju:d] *nu* being grateful for, thankfulness. *He gave them a lovely bookcase in gratitude for their kindness.* see **grateful.**

gratuitous [grə'tju:itəs] *adj* given or done for nothing or for no reason, without charge (usu. with added meaning of not being wanted). *I was given plenty of gratuitous advice/help/information etc; a gratuitous remark* i.e. unnecessary one made without reason. **gratuitously** *adv.*

gratuity [grə'tju:iti] *nc* **1.** payment of money in addition to his salary made to someone at the end of his period of employment. **2.** amount of money given to someone for a service he has done; tip.

grave[1] [greiv] *nc* hole dug in the ground in which a dead person is buried; place where a dead person is buried. *He visited his father's grave.*

'**gravedigger** person who digs graves.

'**gravestone** stone marking a grave.

'**graveyard** place where there are graves; cemetery.

grave[2] [greiv] *adj* very serious, solemn. *The situation is grave. His face is always grave.* **gravely** *adv.* **graveness** *nu.* see **gravity** (in sense **3.**).

grave[3] [greiv] *vt* carve: *graven image* i.e. idol (*o.f.*). *past* **graven.**

gravel ['grævl] *nu* small stones, coarse sand. *The bottom of the river is covered with gravel; repair the road with gravel.* Also *vt* cover with gravel (e.g. road, path). *past* **gravelled.** (*US* **graveled**).

gravelly 1. of or like gravel. **2.** harsh: *gravelly voice.*

gravitate ['græviteit] *vi* be attracted towards and move towards. *Everyone gravitated to/towards the bright lights.* **gravitation** [grævi'teiʃən] *nu.*

gravity ['græviti] *nu* **1.** force of attraction between bodies as shown e.g. by objects tending to fall towards the centre of the earth. **2.** weight. **3.** state of being grave, seriousness. *You do not seem to understand the gravity of your mistake.* **gravitational** [grævi'teiʃənl] *adj* (in sense **1.**). see **grave**[2].

gravy ['greivi] *nu* juice from meat when it is being cooked; sauce made from the juice.

gravy boat container for serving gravy.

gray [grei] *nc/u, adj* see **grey.**

graze[1] [greiz] *vt/i* **1.** eat grass. *The cows are grazing in the field.* **2.** feed on grass, put out to graze. *The farmers graze their sheep here.*

grazing *nu*: *There is good grazing here.*

graze[2] [greiz] *vt/i* **1.** touch, rub in passing. *The car grazed (against) the wall.* **2.** damage skin by grazing against. *I grazed my hand on the wall.* Also *nc*: *a graze on his knee.*

grease [gri:s] *nu* soft animal fat; very thick oil. Also *vt*: *I must grease the wheels.*

greasy *adj* **1.** of grease, covered with grease; slippery: *a greasy road.* **2.** wishing to find favour, being nice to people without being sincere. *He had a greasy smile on his face.* **greasily** *adv.* **greasiness** *nu.*

'**grease gun** pump for forcing grease into a machine.

'**greasepaint** greasy kind of paint used as make-up by actors.

great[1] [greit] *adj* **1.** big: *a great building. We reached a great city.* **2.** bigger, more than average. *He's a great friend of ours. That man is a great rogue; a great eater/reader/talker etc. Take great care of her.* **3.** outstanding, famous. *Shakespeare was a great writer. This is a great book.* **4.** a lot of anything: *a great deal of trouble; a great many people; a great number of questions.* **5.** with some *adjs* of size to emphasize them: *a great big cake; a great fat sheep; a great long stick.* (*informal*). **6.** splendid, enjoyable. *It would be great if we could meet again.* (*informal*). **greatly** *adv.* **greatness** *nu.*

great at clever at. *He is great at finding excuses.* (*informal*).

great on well-informed or keen about. *Our teacher is great on local geography.* (*informal*).

great-[2] [greit] *prefix* to grandfather etc.

great-'grandfather grandfather of one's father or mother.

great-'granddaughter granddaughter of one's son or daughter etc.

Grecian ['gri:ʃən] *adj* (esp. of architecture and ornaments) Greek.

greed [gri:d] *nu* desire for too much. *Their greed for power/praise/wealth etc.*

greedy *adj* (usu. for food): *a greedy child.* **greedily** *adv.* **greediness** *nu.*

Greek [gri:k] **1.** *nc* native of Greece. **2.** *nu* the Greek language. Also *adj* of Greece, its people or language.

green [gri:n] **1.** *nc/u* colour of growing grass: *the green of the trees. I like the greens in that picture.* **2.** *nc* piece of land covered with grass (e.g. *bowling green* i.e. for playing bowls). **3.** *nc* (in *pl*) green vegetables. Also *adj* **1.** *green fields and trees.* **2.** not ripe: *green corn/dates/berries etc; green wood* i.e. just cut and so not dry. **3.** without experience, training. *The team is still very green.* **4.** looking sick, pale. *The rough sea made him turn green. I am green with envy* i.e. I am very envious. **greenness** *nu.*

greenish *adj* rather green.

'**green belt** *nc/u* area of countryside surrounding a town or city, in which the building of new houses etc is controlled by the government.

'**greengrocer** *nc* shopkeeper who sells fruit and vegetables.

'**greengrocery** *nc/u* shop or business of a greengrocer.

'**greenhouse** building made of glass to protect growing plants. see **glasshouse.**

have green fingers be skilled in getting plants to grow. (*informal*).

greet [gri:t] *vt* **1.** express welcome, express pleasure at meeting someone (in words). *They greeted me at the door by saying 'Good morning'.* **2.** receive or meet, not necessarily in a friendly way. *They were greeted with loud laughter. The rain greeted us as soon as we went out. Shouts of anger greeted our ears.*

greeting *nc*: *When you meet somebody in the evening the correct greeting is 'Good evening' not 'Good night'. Give our greetings to your mother* i.e. good wishes.

gregarious [grə'gɛəriəs] *adj* living in groups fond of company. *Man is very gregarious.* **gregariously** *adv.* **gregariousness** *nu.*

grenade [grə'neid] *nc* small bomb thrown by hand or shot from a rifle.

grenadier [grenə'diə*] *nc* (*Brit*) formerly, a

soldier trained to throw grenades; now a soldier in the Grenadier Guards.

grew [gru:] past tense of **grow.**

grey, gray [grei] *nc/u* colour between black and white, like ashes. *The grey of the sky on a rainy day.* Also *adj*: *grey skies.* Also *vt/i*: *Your hair is greying quickly* i.e. becoming grey. **greyness** *nu.*

greyish *adj* rather grey.

'grey-'haired *adj* with grey hairs, old.

greyhound ['greihaund] *nc* type of swift dog used for hunting and racing.

greyhound

grid [grid] *nc* **1.** frame with bars; grating. **2.** numbered squares printed on a map to give exact positions. **3.** network of main power lines for distributing electricity. **4.** very fine wires in a radio valve.

gridiron ['gridaiən] *nc* frame with bars for cooking meat over an open fire.

grief [gri:f] **1.** *nu* great sorrow. *I was filled with grief when I heard of his death.* **2.** *nc* causing grief.

come to grief see **come.**

grieve [gri:v] *vt/i* feel, cause grief. *Nothing grieves me more.* **grievous** *adj.* **grievously** *adv.*

grievance *nc* something to grieve or complain about. *He won't listen to our grievances.*

grill [gril] *nc* **1.** grating, gridiron. **2.** device on a cooker for providing heat, under which to cook meat, toast bread etc. **3.** meat cooked on a grill. Also *vt/i* **1.** cook or be cooked on a grill. **2.** torture by questioning closely for a long time. *He was grilled by the police after his arrest.* (*informal* in sense **2.**).

'grillroom special room in a restaurant where meat is grilled to order and served.

grim [grim] *adj* severe, stern, fierce. *He had a grim look on his face. We had a grim struggle before we won; a grim sense of humour* i.e. a bitter, cruel one. **grimly** *adv.* **grimness** *nu.*

grimace [gri'meis] *nc* ugly twist of the face to show contempt, dislike etc. Also *vi* make a grimace.

grime [graim] *nu* layer of dirt, difficult to remove. *Miners at work soon get covered with grime.* Also *vt.* **grimy** *adj.* **griminess** *nu.*

grin [grin] *vt/i* smile showing the teeth; show the teeth in contempt; show the teeth in pain. *Everyone in the classroom grinned when he dropped his books. past* **grinned.** Also *nc*: *Take that grin off your face!*

grin and bear it suffer cheerfully. (*informal*).

grin from ear to ear grin very widely. (*informal*).

grind [graind] *vt/i* **1.** crush into very small pieces: *grind corn into flour. I ground my cigarette into the ashtray.* **2.** (usu. *passive*) crush, oppress people. *The peasants are ground down by poverty, ignorance and disease.* **3.** polish, make sharp by rubbing with something rough. *Grind these knives, they are blunt.* **4.** rub, strike together. *He was grinding his teeth with rage. past* **ground** [graund]. Also *nu* hard work. (*informal*).

grinding *adj* **1.** crushing: *grinding poverty.* **2.** making a noise like grinding. *The lorry came to a grinding halt.*

grinder *nc* instrument for grinding: *coffee grinder.*

'grindstone stone for sharpening knives etc.

keep one's nose to the grindstone see **keep**[1].

grip [grip] *vt/i* seize and hold firmly. *Grip this stick and don't let go. Worn tyres do not grip (on) wet roads. The book gripped my attention. past* **gripped.** Also *nc* **1.** *He had a stick in his grip.* **2.** travelling bag.

gripping *adj*: *a gripping story.*

come/get to grips with get near enough to grip; fight, attack; deal with. *We advanced and came to grips with the enemy. I must get to grips with these problems.*

lose one's grip become worse or less efficient. *The old man should retire, he is losing his grip.* (*informal*).

grisly ['grizli] *adj* horrible, terrible.

gristle ['grisl] *nu* rough substance like white elastic, found in meat.

gristly *adj* tough, full of gristle.

grit [grit] *nu* **1.** small pieces of stone, sand etc. *I have a piece of grit in my eye.* **2.** courage to endure. *You need grit to win.* (*informal* in sense **2.**). Also *vt*: *grit one's teeth. past* **gritted. gritty** *adj.* **grittiness** *nu.*

grizzled ['grizld] *adj* greyish, grey-haired.

grizzly ['grizli] *nc* type of large bear found in North America. (Also **grizzly bear**).

groan [groun] *vt/i* make a deep sound because of pain or sorrow; (of things) make a deep sound because of strain. *He groaned when he broke his arm. The floorboards groan when you walk on them.* Also *nc*: *He gave a groan. The bad news was received with loud groans.*

groaning *nc/u* act of groaning; complaint.

grocer ['grousə*] *nc* person who sells many kinds of things needed in a house (e.g. tea, coffee, sugar, salt, tinned foods, soap etc).

grocery *nc* shop or business of a grocer.

groceries *npl* articles sold by a grocer.

groggy ['grɔgi] *adj* unsteady on the feet, weak. *The blow on the head made him groggy.* **grogginess** *nu.* (both *informal*).

groin [grɔin] *nc/u* **1.** line between the belly and the top of the leg where they meet. **2.** kind of supporting arch in a building.

groom [gru:m] *nc* **1.** servant who looks after horses. **2.** see **bridegroom.** Also *vt* **1.** look after a horse by feeding and esp. brushing it. **2.** prepare someone for a special purpose. *He is being groomed for the job of manager.*

'well-'groomed *adj* well-dressed, smart.

groove [gru:v] *nc* long, hollow line cut in something (esp. to guide something else that moves). *The door slides along the groove in the floor. A gramophone needle moves round in a groove.*

get into a groove become too settled in one's ways. *If you don't change your job, you'll get into a groove.* (*informal*).

get out of a/the groove change one's ways. (*informal*).

grope [gru:p] *vt/i* feel about with one's hands blindly to find something. *I groped for the door. We groped our way through the dark forest.* **gropingly** *adv.*

gross[1] [grous] *nc* 144, twelve dozen.

gross[2] [grous] *adj* **1.** unpleasantly fat. *Since he stopped taking exercise, he has become gross.* **2.** (of manner) coarse, rough, rude. *His language and behaviour are gross.* **3.** obvious, flagrant: *a gross mistake; gross impertinence; gross indecency.* **4.** total: *the* *gross amount; 100 tons gross.* (*opp* **net**). **5.** (of plants) growing thickly. **grossly** *adv.* **grossness** *nu.*

grotesque [grə'tesk] *adj* strangely formed, unusual, absurd. *These designs are grotesque. His face has a grotesque appearance.* Also *nc* somebody/something grotesque. **grotesquely** *adv.*

grotto ['grɔtou] *nc* cave (usu. an imitation one in a park or garden). *pl* **grottoes** or **grottos.**

grotty ['grɔti] *adj* unattractive; bad. (*informal*).

grouch [grautʃ] *vi* complain, be discontented. Also *nc.* **grouchy** *adj.* **grouchiness** *nu.* (all *informal*).

ground¹ [graund] **1.** *nu* soil, earth. *The ground here is fertile.* **2.** *nc/u* surface (esp. of the earth): *above/below ground. I fell to the ground. They are lying on the ground. The ship touched ground* i.e. surface of the earth below the sea. *Her dress had a pattern of red flowers on a white ground* i.e. the surface of the cloth. **3.** *nc* piece of land for a special purpose: *a cricket/football/hockey ground.* **4.** (in *pl*) piece of land round a house. *The cottage stands in lovely grounds.* **5.** *nc/u* (usu. *pl*) reason, excuse. *You have no ground(s) for believing that. He has good ground(s) for doing it. He was excused on the ground(s) of his illness* i.e. because of his illness.

groundless *adj* without reason: *groundless fears.*

'ground 'floor see **floor¹**.

'groundsman man employed to look after any kind of sportsground.

'groundnut kind of nut that grows under the ground. (Also **peanut**).

'ground plan plan of a building showing the parts on the ground.

'ground rent *nc/u* rent paid for the ground on which a building stands.

'ground staff *npl* **1.** groundsmen. **2.** persons who repair and look after aircraft or airports but do not fly. (Also **ground crew** – for aircraft only).

'groundwork work done before the main work or event. *Producing a play needs a lot of groundwork.*

break fresh/new ground deal with something for the first time. *This physics book breaks fresh ground.*

cover ground **1.** travel. *During our holidays we covered a lot of ground.* **2.** deal with, discuss. *His speech covered the ground well.*

cut the ground from under someone's feet spoil someone's plans, arguments etc by acting on them before he does. (*informal*).

down to the ground perfectly. *The hotel suits me down to the ground.* (*informal*).

fall to the ground **1.** fall down. **2.** fail. *The plan fell to the ground.*

gain ground **1.** advance, progress. **2.** become stronger. *The rumour is gaining ground.* (*opp* **give/lose ground**).

go to ground hide (usu. by lying close to the ground).

stand/keep/hold one's ground see **stand¹**.

shift one's ground change one's reasons for. (*informal*).

ground² [graund] *vt/i* **1.** touch the ground. *The boat grounded on the rocks.* **2.** place, keep on the ground. *The boat was grounded in the storm. They grounded the aircraft because it had engine trouble.* **3.** use as the basis for. *He grounds his opinion on what he saw himself.* **4.** teach thoroughly (esp. the first stages of a subject). *Primary school teachers must ground their pupils in correct English.*

grounding *nu* (in sense **4.**): *a good grounding in English.*

ground³ [graund] past of **grind.**

groundsel ['graunsl] *nu* small, wild plant with yellow flowers.

group [gru:p] *nc* persons/things which are together: *a group of people/buildings/trees. They stood in groups.* Also *vt/i*: *They group near the shop when it is about to open. He grouped the children according to ability.*

grouse¹ [graus] *nc* type of plump, wild bird, rather like a chicken, hunted for food and sport. *pl* **grouse.**

grouse² [graus] *vi* complain. Also *nc* complaint. (both *informal*).

grove [grouv] *nc* group of trees (smaller than a wood).

grovel ['grɔvl] *vi* lie or crawl face downwards because of fear, or to show respect; show shame or fear. *The slaves grovelled before their master.* **grovelling** *adj.*

grow [grou] *vt/i* **1.** increase in size, develop. *Very little grows in the desert. He has grown very tall. The seed grew into a tree. The farmers here grow corn.* **2.** become something slowly. *It is growing cold. The light grew fainter. I am growing to hate him.* *past tense* **grew** [gru:]. *past part* **grown.**

grower *nc* person who grows things: *fruit grower.*

grow on/upon someone (slowly) become more liked. *This town is growing on me.*

grow out of something become too big, old for. *He grew out of his clothes. You will soon grow out of your fear of other boys.*

grow up develop in full, become an adult. *When you grow up you will earn your own living.*

'grown-'up *adj*: *a grown-up daughter.* Also *nc*: *This meeting is for grown-ups only.*

growl [graul] *vt/i* make a low, angry sound. *The dog growled at the stranger. He growled a reply.*

growling *nc/u* low, angry sound. **growlingly** *adv.*

grown [groun] past part of **grow.**

growth [grouθ] **1.** *nu* growing, development, increase. *He has not yet reached full growth; the growth of democracy.* **2.** *nc* something which has already grown: *a growth of hair/bushes/trees etc.* **3.** *nc* something which has grown in the body because of disease (e.g. cancer). *He has a growth in the stomach.*

grub¹ [grʌb] *vt/i* dig up. *past* **grubbed.**

grub² [grʌb] *nc* larva of an insect.

grub³ [grʌb] *nu* food. (*informal*).

grubby ['grʌbi] *adj* **1.** dirty: *grubby hands.* **2.** having grubs.

grudge [grʌdʒ] *vt* be unwilling to give or allow. *I do not grudge him anything* i.e. I am willing to give him anything. *He grudges paying his taxes.* Also *nc* feeling of dislike. *He bears me a grudge/He bears a grudge against me.* **grudging** *adj.* **grudgingly** *adv.*

gruel [gruəl] *nu* thin mixture of meal and water or milk.

gruelling ['gruəliŋ] *adj* strenuous; severe: *a gruelling walk.*

gruesome ['gru:səm] *adj* disgusting to see, horrible. *The injured man, with blood all over his face, was a gruesome sight.* **gruesomely** *adv.* **gruesomeness** *nu.*

gruff [grʌf] *adj* rough in manner or voice. **gruffly** *adv.* **gruffness** *nu.*

grumble ['grʌmbl] *vi* **1.** complain (usu. in a

low, unhappy voice). *These lazy workmen grumble at/about/over everything.* **2.** make a low, rumbling sound (e.g. of distant thunder or distant guns). Also *nc*. **grumbler** *nc*.

grumpy ['grʌmpi] *adj* bad-tempered, sulky. **grumpily** *adv*. **grumpiness** *nu*. (all *informal*).

grunt [grʌnt] *vi* make a short, deep noise like a pig. Also *nc*.

guano ['gwɑːnou] *nu* dried droppings of sea birds used as fertilizer.

guarantee[1] [gærən'tiː] *nc* **1.** formal promise (often in writing) that something will be done. *I give my guarantee that he will be here tomorrow. I offer my house as a guarantee* i.e. I lose my house if something is not done. **2.** statement (often in writing) that something is genuine or will work properly etc. *The radio has/carries a twelve months' guarantee* i.e. if it does not work properly during that time it will be repaired or replaced without cost. **3.** something that is very likely to cause something else. *Good manners are not a guarantee of honesty.*

guarantee[2] [gærən'tiː] *vt* give a guarantee. *I guarantee that he will pay the money. They all guarantee his good behaviour. We guarantee to be here tomorrow. The radio is guaranteed for twelve months. Nobody can guarantee good weather.*

guaranteed *adj*: *guaranteed pure gold.*

guarantor [gærən'tɔː*] *nc* person who gives a guarantee.

guaranty ['gærənti] *nc* legal form of **guarantee.**

guard[1] [gɑːd] *vt/i* **1.** take care of, watch over, protect. *A mother always guards her children. They guarded the bridge.* **2.** take steps to prevent. *You must guard against catching a cold.*

guarded *adj* careful, cautious: *a guarded statement. He was very guarded in his answers.* **guardedly** *adv*.

guard[2] [gɑːd] **1.** *nu* watchfulness; readiness to meet danger, attack etc. *The soldiers keep guard/are on guard round the President's house.* **2.** *nc* person(s) who guard(s). *The officer inspected the guard. The guards stopped me at the gate.* **3.** *nc* (*Brit*) person in charge of a train. (*US* **conductor**). **4.** *nc* **(Guards)** soldiers with the special duty of protecting the sovereign. *The Guards are on duty at the palace; Brigade of Guards; Scots Guards; Guards officer etc.* **5.** *nc* something which protects (e.g. against injury). *Miners wear a helmet as a guard against falling rocks.*

'guardhouse, 'guardroom building for soldiers on guard or under guard.

'guardsman soldier in the Guards.

'guard rail rail round machinery or on a stair to prevent injury.

'fireguard guard placed in front of a fire.

'mudguard (*Brit*) cover over a wheel of a car etc. (*US* **fender**).

guard of honour group of soldiers to welcome and look after an important person.

be on one's guard be ready to meet an attack, danger etc. (*opp* **off one's guard**).

be under guard be guarded, arrested. *All the prisoners are under close guard.*

under one's guard (esp. in boxing, fighting) past one's defence. *The sudden punch got under my guard.*

guardian ['gɑːdiən] *nc* person with the duty of looking after someone who cannot look after himself (e.g. young children). *When their father died, I became their guardian.*

'guardian 'angel spirit which looks after someone or some place.

guava ['gwɑːvə] *nc/u* **1.** type of tropical tree. **2.** the fruit of this tree.

guerilla, guerrilla [gə'rilə] *nc* fighter who wages war in small groups which do not belong to the regular army. Also *adj*: *guerilla war* i.e. kind of war waged by guerillas.

guess[1] [ges] *vt/i* **1.** estimate, judge, state something without being sure. *Not knowing which way to go, I had to guess. Can you guess its weight/how much it weighs?* **2.** (mainly *US*) suppose. *I guess he's right.*

guess[2] [ges] *nc* opinion one cannot be sure about, rough estimate. *I'll have to make a guess. At a guess there are a hundred people here.*

'guesswork result from guessing. *Their answer is just guesswork.*

it's anybody's guess nobody is sure. *It's anyone's guess who will win.* (*informal*).

guest [gest] *nc* **1.** person who visits or is invited to one's house. *We usually have guests at the weekend.* **2.** person who stays at a boarding house or hotel. *This hotel has rooms for fifty guests.*

'guest-house boarding house; house where guests pay for their rooms and food.

'paying 'guest guest in a private house who pays for staying there.

guffaw [gʌ'fɔː] *nc* loud laugh. Also *vi*.

guide [gaid] *nc* **1.** person who shows the way and/or places of interest. *You will need a guide if you wish to climb that mountain. The guide showed them round the church.* **2.** thing that shows the way, gives instructions or information: *a good guide to British flowers* i.e. a book giving information about them; *a short guide to sailing.* Also *vt* act as guide, lead. *He will guide you to the top of the mountain. They will be guided by what you say.*

guidance *nu* guiding or being guided. *He wrote the report under the guidance of the manager.*

'guidebook book telling tourists about travelling and places of interest.

'guidepost post on a road or path showing the way.

guided missile military rocket which can be controlled from the ground or from a ship or aircraft.

guild [gild] *nc* group of persons (e.g. tradesmen) with same interests or work who join together to help one another. *There were many guilds in London during the Middle Ages.*

guile [gail] *nu* cunning, trickery. **guileful** *adj*. **guilefully** *adv*.

guileless *adj* honest, innocent. **guilelessly** *adv*. **guilelessness** *nu*.

guillotine ['gilətiːn] *nc* **1.** machine for beheading a person by a heavy knife which slides down grooves from above. **2.** kind of machine for cutting paper. Also *vt*.

guilt [gilt] *nu* state of having done wrong; being responsible for having done wrong.

guiltless *adj* innocent.

guilty *adj* **1.** having done wrong. *I am not guilty of this crime. Do you plead guilty to stealing the bicycle?* **2.** showing, feeling guilt: *a guilty conscience. comparative* **guiltier.** *superlative* **guiltiest. guiltily** *adv*. **guiltiness** *nu*.

guinea ['gini] *nc* formerly, British coin worth 21 shillings (£1.05).

guinea-pig ['ginipig] *nc* **1.** kind of small animal, with no tail, often used in experiments. **2.** person who is used in this way. *We are the guinea-pigs for his new ideas about teaching science.*

guise [gaiz] *nc/u* appearance (esp. an assumed one). *They got into the school in the guise of inspectors.*

guitar [gi'tɑː*] *nc* musical instrument with six strings.
electric guitar guitar which uses electric power to increase its sound.

gulch [gʌltʃ] *nc* deep, narrow valley.

gulf [gʌlf] *nc* **1.** large bay going far inland. **2.** deep, wide hole in the ground. **3.** difference between (ideas, beliefs etc).

gull [gʌl] *nc* one of various types of sea bird, usu. white or grey in colour.

gullet ['gʌlit] *nc* passage down which food passes from the mouth to the stomach; throat.

gullible ['gʌlibl] *adj* easily cheated. **gullibility** [gʌli'biliti] *nu.*

gully ['gʌli] *nc* **1.** small, narrow valley. **2.** deep, narrow ditch caused by rainwater running down a slope. **3.** narrow passage on or beside a building, or in a street which has been made to carry away rainwater; gutter.

gulp [gʌlp] *vt/i* **1.** swallow quickly. *They gulped (down) their food.* **2.** choke. *He was gulping with excitement.* Also *nc*: *He drank the glass of water in one gulp/at a gulp.*

gum[1] [gʌm] *nc* (usu. *pl*) flesh in which the teeth are set.
'gumboil abscess of the gums.

gum[2] [gʌm] **1.** *nu* thick liquid from certain trees. **2.** *nu* similar substance, used for fastening papers etc together. **3.** *nc* sweets which are like gum: *chewing gum.* **4.** *nc* kind of tree, eucalyptus. (Also **gum tree**). **5.** *nu* rubber: *gumboots* i.e. rubber boots reaching to the knees. Also *vt* stick together with gum.
gummy *adj* sticky.

gumption ['gʌmpʃən] *nu* (*Brit*) common sense; initiative. (*informal*).

gun [gʌn] *nc* weapon with a metal tube from which objects such as bullets are thrown by the force of an explosion (e.g. revolver, pistol, musket, rifle, machine gun, cannon, large artillery guns, naval guns).
gunner *nc* **1.** (in the army) private in an artillery regiment or (*informal*) person of any rank in an artillery regiment. **2.** (in the navy) warrant officer in charge of guns.
gunnery *nu* science of firing large guns.
'gun barrel metal tube of a gun.
'gunboat small warship.
'gun carriage wheeled carriage on which a big gun is built.
'guncotton explosive made of cotton soaked in acids.
'gunman criminal with a gun.
'gunpowder explosive powder.
'gunrunning *nu* getting guns into a country without the knowledge or consent of its government.
'gunrunner *nc* person or ship that does this.
'gunshot range of a gun. *Keep out of/within gunshot.*
'gunsmith person who makes, repairs and sells small guns.
big guns *npl* important people. (*informal*).
go great guns do very well. (*informal*).
stick to one's guns not change one's opinions, plans etc.

gunwale, gunnel ['gʌnl] *nc* upper edge of the side of a boat.

gurgle ['gəːgl] *nc* bubbling noise. Also *vi.*
gurgling *adj.*

guru ['guːru] *nc* Hindu religious teacher.

gush [gʌʃ] *vi* **1.** flow out suddenly and in great quantity. *The water gushed from the broken pot.* **2.** talk very enthusiastically about. *They were gushing over the new play.* Also *nc.*
gushing *adj*: *a gushing tap; a gushing girl.*
gushingly *adv.*
gusher *nc* **1.** gushing person. **2.** oil well which throws its oil into the air.

gusset ['gʌsit] *nc* piece of cloth put in a coat, dress etc to make it wider or stronger.

gust [gʌst] *nc* **1.** sudden, short increase of wind, rain, smoke etc. *We were walking along peacefully when a gust of wind blew our hats off.* **2.** sudden increase of feeling: *a gust of anger.* **gusty** *adj.*

gusto ['gʌstou] *nu* enjoyment, zest.

gut[1] [gʌt] **1.** *nc* (in *pl*) bowels. *I have a pain in my guts.* (*informal*). **2.** *nc* (in *pl*) courage. *You haven't the guts to do it.* (*informal*). **3.** *nu* string made from the guts of animals (e.g. for violins).

gut[2] [gʌt] *vt* **1.** remove the inside organs of a fish. **2.** take the contents out of a building. *The thieves gutted his flat.* **3.** destroy the contents of a building. *The factory was gutted by fire.* **4.** examine the contents of something (esp. a book). *past* **gutted.**

gutter[1] ['gʌtə*] *nc* **1.** channel on the roof of a building or at the side of a road to carry away rainwater. **2.** dirtiest part of a street. **3.** anywhere poor or vulgar. *He was born in the gutter* i.e. in great poverty.
'gutter-press vulgar, sensational newspapers. (*informal*).
'guttersnipe poor, homeless child living mostly in the streets; any vulgar, ill-bred person. (*informal*).

gutter[2] ['gʌtə*] *vi* (usu. with reference to a candle) burn unsteadily.

guttural ['gʌtərl] *nc* sound made in the throat while speaking. *There are not many gutturals in this language.* Also *adj.*

guy[1] [gai] *nc* rope to keep something in place (e.g. a tent) (Also **guy-rope**).

guy[2] [gai] *nc* **1.** dummy of Guy Fawkes burned on 5 November. **2.** any person strangely dressed. **3.** (mainly *US*) man. (*informal* in sense **3.**). Also *vt* make fun of.

guzzle ['gʌzl] *vt/i* eat or drink greedily.

gym [dʒim] *nc/u* informal short form of **gymnasium, gymnastics.**

gymnasium [dʒim'neiziəm] *nc* building or large room equipped for physical exercise.
gymnast ['dʒimnæst] *nc* expert in gymnastics. **gymnastic** [dʒim'næstik] *adj.*
gymnastics [dʒim'næstiks] *npl* physical exercises (usu. difficult ones).

gynaecology [gainə'kɔlədʒi] *nu* science of the diseases of women. **gynaecologist** *nc.*

gypsum ['dʒipsəm] *nu* mineral which when baked is known as plaster of Paris.

gypsy ['dʒipsi] *nc* see **gipsy.**

gyrate [dʒai'reit] *vi* move in a circle or spiral. **gyration** *nc/u.* **gyratory** [dʒai'reitəri] *adj.*

gyroscope ['dʒaiərəskoup] *nc* heavy wheel which turns very quickly and keeps steady the object it is in. **gyroscopic** [dʒaiərə'skɔpik] *adj.*

H

habeas corpus ['heibiəs'kɔːpəs] *nc* legal document requiring a prisoner to be brought to court, so that it may be decided whether his imprisonment is legal or not.

haberdasher ['hæbədæʃə*] *nc* **1.** (*Brit*) person who sells buttons, ribbons, thread etc for clothes and hats. **2.** (*US*) dealer in men's shirts, ties etc.

haberdashery [hæbə'dæʃəri] **1.** *nc* haberdasher's shop (now often a department in a store). **2.** *nu* the articles which he sells.

habit ['hæbit] *nc* **1.** something that is done so often that it becomes a fixed practice. *It is a good habit to eat slowly. He has a habit of arriving early.* **2.** woman's dress with skirt worn by nuns. **3.** woman's dress for riding sidesaddle on a horse.

be in the habit of have the habit of. *I am in the habit of reading the newspaper at breakfast.*

fall/get into the habit of start having the habit of. *He got into the habit of going alone. He got into the habit of going out with his workmates on Thursdays.* (*opp* **get out of the habit of**).

habitable ['hæbitəbl] *adj* able to be lived in. *Although the house is very old, it is quite habitable.* (*opp* **uninhabitable**).

habitat ['hæbitæt] *nc* natural home or surroundings of animals and plants. *The natural habitat of the tiger is Asia, not Africa.*

habitation [hæbi'teiʃən] **1.** *nu* act of living in a place. *The North Pole is not suitable for human habitation.* **2.** *nc* house; home (*o.f.* in sense **2.**).

habitual [hə'bitjuəl] *adj* caused by habit; usual. *They are habitual visitors to our house. The chairman took his habitual place at the table.* **habitually** *adv.*

habituate [hə'bitjueit] *vt* make accustomed to.

hack[1] [hæk] *vt/i* cut roughly or carelessly. *He hacked the branch off the tree. They are hacking the meat to pieces. Don't hack at it.*

'hacksaw saw for cutting metal.

hacking cough rough, painful cough.

hack[2] [hæk] *nc* **1.** horse that is for hire. **2.** person who does low-quality work in writing (esp. for someone else). Also *vi* ride a horse at a slow pace (usu. for exercise).

hackneyed ['hæknid] *adj* used too often (usu. what is said or written). *The essay is spoilt by having too many hackneyed phrases.*

had [hæd] past of **have.**

haddock ['hædək] *nc* type of sea fish, found in the North Atlantic and used for food. *pl* **haddock** or **haddocks.**

haemo- ['hiːmou] *prefix* see **hemo-.**

haft [hɑːft] *nc* handle of a knife or axe etc.

hag [hæg] *nc* ugly, old woman.

haggard ['hægəd] *adj* looking tired or worried. *His face was haggard from lack of sleep.* **haggardly** *adv.*

haggis ['hægis] *nc/u* type of Scottish food made from a mixture of meal and small pieces of meat etc cooked in a sheep's stomach.

haggle ['hægl] *vi* argue about the price of something. *In many countries you have to haggle before you buy anything.*

hail[1] [heil] *nc/u* **1.** rain frozen into small, hard drops. **2.** something which strikes hard and often, like hail: *a hail of blows; a hail of abuse.*

'hailstone small, hard piece of hail.

'hailstorm storm during which hail falls.

hail[2] [heil] *vt/i* **1.** shout to welcome or to call attention. *They hailed him (as) a hero. We hailed a passing boat.* **2.** (with **from**) *Where do you hail from?* i.e. where is your home? (*informal* in sense **2.**).

'hail-'fellow-well-'met *adj* immediately friendly. *Some people do not like his hail-fellow-well-met manner.* (*informal*).

hair [hɛə*] **1.** *nu* threadlike growth on the skin of animals and humans (with humans usu. the growth on the head). *The bodies of most animals are covered with hair; brush/comb/cut one's hair* i.e. the hair on one's head. **2.** *nc* separate thread of hair: *not a hair out of place* i.e. very neatly brushed. *There are hairs on your jacket.*

hairy *adj* covered with hair. **hairiness** *nu.*

hairless *adj* without hair; bald.

'hair-breadth, 'hair's breadth *nu* thickness of one's hair. *The car missed me by a hair's breadth.* Also *adj.*

Note: the *pl* form *hairs* is only used to describe a very small number of separate threads of hair. The *sing* form *hair* is always used to describe the whole growth of hair on the human head (e.g. *What lovely hair you have. Your hair has grown very long*).

'hairbrush brush for the hair.

'haircut cutting of the hair. *I must get a haircut.*

'hairdresser person who cuts and attends to hair.

'hairpin **1.** pin used by a woman to keep up her hair. **2.** bend in a road so sharp that the road turns almost in the opposite direction. (Also **hairpin bend**).

'hairspring very thin spring (e.g. one in a watch).

let one's hair down **1.** (women only) loosen one's hair so that it hangs down. (*opp* **put up one's hair/put one's hair up**). **2.** become more relaxed. *When the old people left the party, the young ones let their hair down.* (*informal* in sense **2.**).

split hairs see **split**[1].

not turn/without turning a hair remain calm. *He did the dangerous work without turning a hair.*

hake [heik] *nc* one of several types of sea fish related to the cod. *pl* **hake.**

hale [heil] *adj* only in **hale and hearty** i.e. well and in good spirits.

half [hɑːf] **1.** *nc/adj* exactly one of two equal parts into which something can be divided. *(The) half of ten is five. The money* *was divided into two halves; three and a half hours* or *three hours and a half; half a minute/mile/dozen/pound* etc; *a half-minute/-mile/-dozen/-pound* etc. **2.** *nc/determiner* approximately one of two parts: *half (of) my time; half (of) my friends.* Also *adv* partly; incompletely: *half-cooked meat; half asleep; half open. pl* **halves** [hɑːvz].

halve [hɑːv] *vt* **1.** divide into two equal parts. **2.** make less by half. *The cost of food has been halved.*

'half-back (football, hockey etc) player between forwards and backs: *centre-half; right-half; left-half* i.e. half-back who plays in the centre; on the right; on the left.

'half-breed person whose father and mother are of different races. (rather *impolite*).

'half-brother brother who is the son of either one's father or mother but not of both. (Also **half-sister**).

'half-'crown, 'half a 'crown formerly, British coin worth 2 shillings and sixpence ($12\frac{1}{2}$ pence).

'half-'hearted *adj* without interest or effort: *a half-hearted cheer.* **half-heartedly** *adv.*

'half-'holiday holiday for part of the day only.

at 'half-'mast used of flags when they are lowered to the middle of their mast at the time of a sad event (e.g. the death of an important person).

at 'half-'price at half of the price. *Students can get in (at) half-price.*

'half-'time **1.** half of the usual working time. *Some of the workers are on half-time because business is bad.* **2.** resting time between two parts of a game. *The football players changed round at half-time.*

'half-truth statement that is only partly true.

'half'way *adj/adv* **1.** equally distant from two places. *The town is halfway between the hill and the river. We met halfway.* **2.** incomplete. *This solution is only a halfway one.*

'half-wit *nc* person with a weak brain. **half-witted** *adj.*

'half-'yearly *adj/adv* happening every six months.

by half **1.** by the amount of one half. *They have reduced costs by half.* **2.** (only in phrases with **too**) much. *He is too clever by half* i.e. he is much too clever.

by halves not thoroughly. *He never does things by halves.*

go halves with share equally. *I shall go halves with you in paying for the drinks.*

half as much again one and a half times as much.

meet someone halfway see **meet.**

not half very (much): *not half good. (informal).*

halibut ['hælibət] *nc* large type of flat fish found in the Atlantic and used as food. *pl* **halibut.**

hall [hɔːl] *nc* **1.** large room: *assembly hall; dining hall; lecture hall.* **2.** large building for meetings, business, amusement etc; residential building at a university: *town hall; dance hall; concert hall.* **3.** room at the entrance to a house from which one enters other rooms.

'hallmark set of marks put on gold or silver to guarantee the standard of purity of the metal.

'hallstand piece of furniture (usu. in a hall (in sense **3.**)) on which coats and hats are hung.

hallelujah, alleluia [(h)æli'luːjə] *interj* loud praise to God. Also *nc.*

hallo [hʌ'lou] *nu/interj* see **hello.**

hallow ['hælou] *vt* (usu. *passive*) make holy: *a hallowed place.*

hallucination [həluːsi'neiʃən] *nc* something which is imagined, which is not really there. *Drugs can cause hallucinations.*

hallucinatory [hə'luːsinətri] *adj* causing or caused by hallucinations.

halo ['heilou] *nc* ring of light round something (e.g. the sun or moon, or the circle or ray painted in pictures round the heads of holy persons). *pl* **halos** or **haloes.**

halt[1] [hɔːlt] *vt/i* stop, cause to stop, for a time. *The train halted at the station. He halted the children at the street corner.* Also *nc* **1.** act of halting. *The soldiers came to a halt* i.e. they halted. **2.** place to halt at. *Where is the next halt?*

'halt sign sign at the side of a road telling traffic to halt before entering another road.

halt[2] [hɔːlt] *vi* walk with difficulty; hesitate (*o.f.*).

halting *adj* hesitating: *halting speech.* **haltingly** *adv.*

halter ['hɔːltə*] *nc* **1.** rope or strap put round the head of a horse, camel etc to hold or lead it. **2.** rope for hanging somebody (*o.f.* in sense **2.**).

halve [hɑːv] *vt* see **half.**

halyard ['hæljəd] *nc* rope for raising a flag or sail up a mast.

ham [hæm] **1.** *nc* upper part of the back of the leg. **2.** *nu* salted and smoked or dried meat made from the upper part of a pig's leg. *I like ham and eggs for breakfast.*

hamburger ['hæmbəːgə*] *nc* **1.** small, round piece of hot minced meat. **2.** sandwich made with meat like this.

hamlet ['hæmlət] *nc* small village.

hammer ['hæmə*] *nc* tool with a handle and a heavy end for hitting things (e.g. nails). Also *vt/i* **1.** hit with a hammer. *He hammered the nails into the wall. He hammered in the nails.* **2.** work hard at; do something with force. *He hammered away at the problem. The teacher hammered the rules into the children's heads. The two countries finally hammered out an agreement.*

be/come under the hammer be sold by auction (because the person in charge of the auction ends the bidding by hitting his desk with a wooden hammer).

go at it hammer and tongs see **go.**

hammock ['hæmək] *nc* bed made of cloth and ropes and hung between two posts.

hammock

hamper[1] ['hæmpə*] *vt* hinder; prevent easy movement. *The army's advance was hampered by bad weather.*

hamper[2] ['hæmpə*] *nc* large basket with a lid, used for carrying food, wine, laundry etc.

hamstring ['hæmstriŋ] *nc* thick tendon at the back of knee of persons and animals. Also *vt* cut this tendon. *The enemy hamstrung our horses* i.e. so that the horses could not move. *past* **hamstrung** ['hæmstrʌŋ].

hamstrung *adj* unable to move or proceed. *We were hamstrung through lack of supplies.*

hand[1] [hænd] *nc* **1.** the end of arm below the wrist. *Each hand has five fingers.* **2.** pointer on the face of clock or other instrument: *the hour/minute hand. The two hands on my watch are broken.* **3.** worker; sailor. *This factory employs a thousand hands; all hands on deck* i.e. order to sailors to come on deck; any order to start work. **4.** side: *on every hand* i.e. on all sides. **5.** something done by using one's hands; skill. *He writes a good hand.* i.e. clearly. *He is a good hand at painting* i.e. he is skilled in painting. *I am an old hand at teaching* i.e. I have long experience. (*informal*). **6.** (usu. *pl*) possession; responsibility. *The stolen car is now in the hands of the police. The book changed hands many times. Your success is in your own hands* i.e. you are responsible for your own success. **7.** applause. *Let's give him a big hand* i.e. clap hands loudly. (*informal* in sense **7.**).
'handbag small bag carried by a woman.
'handball team ball game played with the hands.
'handbill small, printed sheet distributed by hand.
'handbook book of information.
'handcuff *nc* one of two rings joined by a short chain to secure the hands of a prisoner. Also *vt* put on handcuffs. *The policeman handcuffed the thief.*

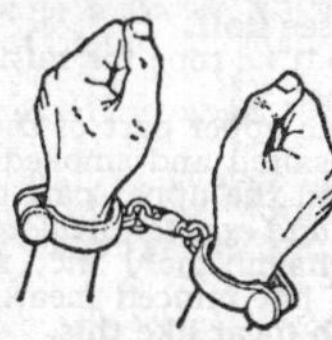
handcuffs

'handful 1. amount that can be held in one hand: *a handful of rice.* **2.** small number: *a handful of men.* **3.** somebody/something difficult to manage. *This class of boys is quite a handful.* (*informal* in sense **3.**).
'handrail raised rail at the side of a stair or balcony to support the hand.
'handshake act of shaking hands.
'handstand balancing on one's hands with one's feet above one's head.
'handwork work done by hand.
'handwriting one's way of writing. *It is difficult to read his handwriting.*
at hand near. *Christmas is at hand. The post office is close at hand.*
at first hand directly. *I heard about the accident at first hand* i.e. from somebody who saw it or was in it.
first-hand *adj*: *first-hand news.*
work/be hand in glove with see **glove.**
by hand 1. not made by machine. *My shoes were made by hand; handmade shoes.* **2.** personally. *The letter came to me by hand* i.e. it was brought by somebody, not sent through the post.
give a hand to/with see **give.**
hand-in-hand 1. holding hands. *The boy and girl arrived hand-in-hand.* **2.** together. *Poverty and disease go hand-in-hand.*
hand of bridge/whist etc game of bridge/whist etc.
hand of cards playing cards held in one hand.
'hand-to-'hand *adv* closely; near to one another (usu. when fighting). *They threw down their rifles and fought hand-to-hand with knives.* Also *adj*: *hand-to-hand fighting.*
hands off *interj* do not touch or take.
keep one's hands off avoid touching or taking. *You must keep your hands off my money.*
hands up *interj* raise the hands above head as a sign of surrender.
put one's hands up raise the hands as a sign of surrender.
have one's hands full be very busy.
in hand 1. available as something extra. *I still have £10 in hand after paying the bill. We have a game in hand.* **2.** being dealt with. *The building of the new bridge is now in hand.* **3.** under control. *The students should be taken in hand* i.e. should be brought under control.
keep one's hand in keep one's skill in something. *You should practise English every day to keep your hand in.* (*informal*).
lay one's hands on see **lay**[1].
lend a hand see **lend.**
live from hand to mouth live without having anything to spare. *During the famine the people lived from hand to mouth.*
'hand-to-'mouth *adj*: *a hand-to-mouth existence.*
not do a hand's turn make no effort; be lazy. (*informal*).
not lift a hand make no effort. *They did not lift a hand to help me.* (*informal*).
'off'hand *adv* easily, quickly. *I cannot give you an answer offhand.*
'offhand *adj*: *I do not like his offhand way of doing things* i.e. his careless way. **offhandedly** *adv.*
off one's hands being no longer one's responsibility. (*opp* **on one's hands**).
on hand available. *Most shops have tinned food on hand.*
on one's hands to be responsible for. *The mother has five young children on her hands.*
on the one hand . . . on the other hand the two different sides of a statement or argument. *On the one hand James wanted to go. John, on the other hand, wanted to stay at home.*
out of hand 1. without thought or hesitation. *He shot the prisoner out of hand.* **2.** not under control. *The angry crowd got out of hand.*
'second'hand *adj* **1.** indirect, through somebody else. *His news is secondhand* i.e. he heard it from somebody else. **2.** already used by somebody: *secondhand books; secondhand clothes.*
at second hand indirectly. *I heard about the accident at second hand* i.e. not from somebody who saw it.
shake hands/by the hand see **shake.**
to hand easily available. *All the tools are ready to hand.*
turn one's hand to begin doing something. *He is ready to turn his hand to anything.*
have/get the upper hand gain advantage; begin to win.
win/beat hands down see **win.**
win the hand of get consent to marry a woman. (*formal*).
hand[2] [hænd] *vt* pass to somebody. *I handed him his hat/I handed his hat to him.*
hand something down 1. pass to somebody from above. *Please hand me down my books from the top shelf.* **2.** pass to succeeding generations. *Our fathers handed down these customs to us.*
hand something on pass to somebody, often to several persons one after the other.

They will hand on the photograph to those who have not seen it.
hand something out distribute. *Please hand out the history books.*
'**handout** *nc* anything handed out (e.g. money to the poor, summaries, notices etc).

handicap ['hændikæp] *nc* **1.** something that hinders or weakens. *Bad health is a great handicap.* **2.** (sport) something which reduces the advantage of a good competitor so that the competition is more equal for all competitors. *Your handicap in the mile race is ten yards. What is your handicap in golf?* Also *vt* hinder or weaken. *His lack of English handicaps him. past* **handicapped.** Also *adj*: *handicapped children* i.e. children with some mental or physical disability.

handicraft ['hændikrɑ:ft] *nc* **1.** product of the skill of the hands. **2.** skill of producing these. *The chief handicrafts of this country are pottery and wood carving.*

handiwork ['hændiwə:k] *nu* something made or done by somebody. *The broken window seems to be your handiwork.*

handkerchief ['hæŋkətʃif] *nc* square piece of cloth, carried in the pocket or a handbag, for wiping the face or nose.

handle[1] ['hændl] *nc* part of something by which it is held: *the handle of a cup/door/jug/knife etc*; also *cup handle, door handle etc.*
'**handlebar** bar on the front of a bicycle for steering it.

handle[2] ['hændl] *vt* **1.** touch; hold in the hands. *You should not handle broken glass. Handle the baby carefully.* **2.** deal with; control. *I'll handle this matter. The manager knows how to handle his staff.* **3.** (usu. with an *adv*) attack with the hands. *The thief was roughly/severely handled by the people who caught him.*
handling *nu* **1.** treatment by the hands of someone. *This parcel needs careful handling. The thief was given a rough handling.* **2.** treatment generally. *The government's handling of the strike was criticized.*
fly off the handle see **fly**[2].

handsome ['hænsəm] *adj* **1.** good-looking. **2.** generous: *handsome gifts. It is handsome of you to say so.* **handsomely** *adv.* **handsomeness** *nu.*

handy ['hændi] *adj* **1.** skilful with the hands. *He is handy at tying knots.* **2.** nearby; ready for use. *Is there a postbox handy? Have you a hammer handy? This house is handy for the shops.* **3.** easy to use; useful. *That's a handy stick you have.* **handily** *adv.* **handiness** *nu.*
'**handyman** man skilful with his hands at many kinds of work.
come in handy become useful. *Old newspapers come in handy when lighting a fire.* (*informal*).

hang[1] [hæŋ] *vt/i* **1.** be held or suspended from above (usu. with the bottom end down). *Her hair hangs down. His coat is hanging (on a nail) behind the door. Your shirt is hanging out* i.e. outside your trousers. **2.** put up or suspend something with the bottom end down. *They hung (up) their coats. My mother is hanging out the washing* i.e. hanging it outside. **3.** put somebody to death by dropping him from above with a rope round his neck: *hang a murderer.* past **hung** [hʌŋ] (in senses **1.** and **2.**). past **hanged** (in sense **3.**).
hanger *nc* something on which things are hung: *clothes hanger; coat hanger.*
hanging *nc/u* death by being hanged. *There are no more hangings in this country.*
'**hangdog** *adj* (usu. with **look**) ashamed; miserable.
'**hangman** person who hangs people.
'**hangover** feeling of illness after drinking too much alcohol the evening before.
'**paperhanger** person who puts up wallpaper (on the inside walls of a house).
hang about/around stay near without doing anything. *Don't hang about my office.* (*informal*).
hang back hesitate; be unwilling.
hang on 1. keep a firm hold of something; refuse to let go. *Although the branch was breaking, he hung on.* **2.** not lose hope; wait. *Although we are beaten, we must hang on. Hang on! I'll call him.* (*informal*). **3.** listen eagerly to. *They hung on every word he said.*
'**hanger-'on** *nc* person who attaches himself to somebody in the hope of gaining some advantage. *Every famous man has his hangers-on.*
hang on to something 1. hold tightly. **2.** keep. (*informal* in sense **2.**).
hang together 1. remain united. *Old friends must hang together.* **2.** fit together; be consistent. *His answers do not hang together* i.e. some answers do not agree with others.
hang up 1. delay. *We were hung up for hours during the fog.* (*informal*). **2.** end a telephone call i.e. by hanging up or replacing the receiver.
hang upon see **hang on to something** (in sense **2.**).
hang in the balance cause uncertainty about the result. *Victory hangs in the balance* i.e. it is difficult to say whether we shall be successful or not.
hang fire be slow to happen. *All his plans hang fire.*
hang one's head lower one's head in shame.
hang it, hang it all! *interj* to show anger, surprise. (*informal*).

hang[2] [hæŋ] *nu* way something hangs. *The hang of the curtains showed that somebody was standing behind them.*
get the hang of something understand how something is done. (*informal*).

hangar ['hæŋə*] *nc* large shed for aircraft.

hank [hæŋk] *nc* bunch of thread or wool.

hanker ['hæŋkə*] *vi* (with **after**) want very much: *hanker after success.* **hankering** *nc/u.*

hanky ['hæŋki] *nc* short informal form of **handkerchief.**

hanky-panky ['hæŋki'pæŋki] *nu* trickery. (*informal*).

hansom (cab) ['hænsəm('kæb)] *nc* old-fashioned, two-wheeled carriage pulled by a horse with its reins over the top of the carriage to a driver at the back.

haphazard [hæp'hæzəd] *adj/adv* by chance; without design: *a haphazard choice.* **haphazardly** *adv.* **haphazardness** *nu.*

hapless ['hæpləs] *adj* unlucky (*o.f.*).

happen ['hæpən] *vi* **1.** take place. *It happened very suddenly. What happened to you?* **2.** be by chance able to, or in the position to. *I happen to know where he is. They happened to meet in town. As it happens, they are here* i.e. by chance they are here. **3.** find by chance. *They happened on an empty seat.* **happening** *nc.*

happy ['hæpi] *adj* **1.** glad; pleased; joyful. *Everyone was happy at the good news. I shall be happy to come.* **2.** lucky. *By a happy coincidence we were there at the same time.* **3.** good; suitable: *a happy thought; a happy*

way of saying it. (*opp* **unhappy**). **happily** *adv*. **happiness** *nu*.
'**happy-go-'lucky** *adj* thoughtless; careless; easy-going. (*informal*).
'**slap-'happy** see **slap**.

harangue [hə'ræŋ] *vt* speak with feeling while telling somebody to do something (often in a bad-tempered way). *Before the battle the general harangued his troops.* Also *nc* speech made in this way.

harass ['hærəs] *vt* **1.** (usu. *passive*) worry. *You look very harassed. They were harassed by debt and illness.* **2.** weaken by many attacks. *Our soldiers harassed the retreating army.* **harassment** *nu*.

harbinger ['hɑːbindʒə*] *nu* something which is the sign of something else about to come. *A black sky is the harbinger of a storm* (*o.f.*).

harbour ['hɑːbə*] (*US* **harbor**) *nc* safe place for ships. *During the gale the ships stayed in (the) harbour.* Also *vt* **1.** give shelter to; protect. *It is an offence to harbour escaped prisoners.* **2.** keep in one's mind. *He still harbours the idea of going abroad.*
'**harbourage** *nu* safe place to shelter.
'**harbour dues** money paid for the use of a harbour.
'**harbour master** person in charge of a harbour.

hard[1] [hɑːd] *adj* **1.** firm; solid. *Iron is hard. The dry ground was very hard.* (*opp* **soft**). **2.** difficult to do or understand. *They find arithmetic hard. This book is too hard for children. He is hard to please. He is a hard man to please.* (*opp* **easy**). **3.** unkind; strict. *He is a hard father. Don't be hard on them.* (*opp* **soft**). **4.** strenuous; uncomfortable. *It was a hard game. We had a hard winter. Life is hard.* (*opp* **easy**). **5.** rough of sound. *'Card' has a hard 'c'; 'centre' has a soft one.*
hardness *nu*.
'**hard-and-'fast** *adj* that cannot be changed: *hard-and-fast rules.*
'**hardback** book with hard covers. (*opp* **paperback**). **hardbacked** *adj*.
'**hard 'core** *nc* part most unlikely to change. Also *adj*: *hard-core opposition.*
hard cash actual money, not cheques or promises to pay.
hard currency currency which is not likely to change its value much.
hard drink *nu* strong, alcoholic drink. (*opp* **soft drink**).
hard drinker *nc* person who drinks a great deal of alcohol.
'**hard-'headed** *adj* practical; strict in business.
hard of hearing *adj* rather deaf.
'**hard-'hearted** *adj* stern; cruel. **hard-heartedly** *adv*.
hard labour having to work hard as a punishment. *He was sentenced to two years' hard labour.*
hard liquor very strong alcoholic drink (e.g. brandy). see also **hard drink**.
hard luck, hard lines bad luck. (*informal*).
'**hardware** **1.** metal goods used in the house (e.g. pots, pans, nails). **2.** electronic and mechanical equipment necessary in computer work.
hard water water in which soap does not lather easily.

hard[2] [hɑːd] *adv* **1.** with force or effort. *Hit it hard! It is raining hard; play/try/work hard.* **2.** so that something becomes hard i.e. solid or firm. *The ground was baked hard by the sun; boil an egg hard.*
'**hard-'bitten** *adj* stubborn; tough.
'**hard-'boiled** *adj* **1.** *a hard-boiled egg.* **2.** (of a person) without sympathy; cynical.
'**hard 'by** *adv/prep* very near (*o.f.*).
'**hard-'earned/-'won** *adj* earned/won with difficulty or effort.
'**hard-'working** *adj* working with great energy.
be hard hit lose or suffer greatly. *The farmers were hard hit by the flood.*
be hard put to it find it difficult. *He was hard put to it to get the money.*
be hard up be without money. (*informal*).
be hard up for not have much of something: *be hard up for money/ideas.* (*informal*).
go hard with be difficult or unpleasant for. *If you refuse, it will go hard with you.*
take something hard be sad or disappointed at. *They took the news of the disaster very hard.*

harden ['hɑːdn] *vt/i* become or make hard. *Clay hardens when it becomes dry. They harden clay by putting it in a fire.*
be hardened to something be accustomed to something unpleasant. *Doctors are hardened to the sight of blood.*
harden one's heart make oneself less sympathetic.

hardihood ['hɑːdihud] *nu* boldness. *He had the hardihood to call me a liar.*

hardly ['hɑːdli] *adv* scarcely; only just: *hardly any/anyone/anything/anywhere. He can hardly spell the easiest words. We hardly ever meet. It is hardly true to say that it was his fault.*

hardship ['hɑːdʃip] *nc/u* suffering; discomfort: *the hardships of poverty.*

hardy ['hɑːdi] *adj* **1.** able to bear discomfort; not easily killed: *hardy plants* i.e. plants which can endure all kinds of weather. **2.** bold. **hardily** *adv*. **hardiness** *nu*.

hare [hɛə*] *nc* small animal like a rabbit but slightly larger and with stronger legs.
'**hare-brained** *adj* silly; thoughtless.
'**hare'lip** ugly split of the upper lip with which some persons are born.

harem [hɑː'riːm] *nc* women's part of a Muslim house; women who live in it.

haricot ['hærikou] *nc* type of bean.

hark [hɑːk] (usu. *imperative*) listen (to). *Hark at him!* (*informal*).
hark back return in talking to what has happened before. *My uncle likes harking back to the old days.*

harlequin ['hɑːlikwin] *nc* clown in a play.
harlequinade [hɑːlikwi'neid] *nu* part of a play in which there are harlequins.

harlot ['hɑːlət] *nc* prostitute (*o.f.*).

harm [hɑːm] *nu* injury; damage. *The storm did a lot of harm. It will do them no harm to try. There is no harm in trying* i.e. you might as well. Also *vt* cause injury or damage. *Doctors say smoking harms our health.* **harmful** *adj*. **harmfully** *adv*.
harmless *adj* not causing harm. **harmlessly** *adv*.

harmonica [hɑː'mɔnikə] *nc* small musical instrument which is played by sliding it along the lips and blowing.

harmonium [hɑː'mouniəm] *nc* musical instrument like an organ which is played by pumping air with foot pedals and by pressing the keys with the fingers.

harmonize ['hɑːmənaiz] *vt/i* be in harmony. *These colours harmonize beautifully.* see **harmony**.

harmony ['hɑːməni] **1.** *nc* pleasing arrangement of musical sounds, colours, shapes etc.

The choir sang in perfect harmony. **2.** *nu* agreement; peace. *There can be no harmony between two selfish people. They lived in harmony.* **harmonious** [hɑː'mouniəs] *adj.* **harmoniously** *adv.*
harmonic [hɑː'mɔnik] *adj* arranged to give pleasing sounds.

harness ['hɑːnis] *nu* fittings such as a collar and reins to tie a horse to what it pulls or to keep a baby safe. Also *vt* put a harness on (a horse); bring under control or organize for a useful purpose. *We shall harness the waterfall to produce electricity.*

harp [hɑːp] *nc* musical instrument with many strings played with the fingers. Also *vi* play the harp. **harper, harpist** *nc.*

harp

harp on something refuse to stop talking about something unpleasant. *They keep harping on their grievances.* (*informal*).

harpoon [hɑː'puːn] *nc* spear to which a long rope is tied (usu. fired from a gun to kill whales). Also *vt* wound or kill with a harpoon.

harpsichord ['hɑːpsikɔːd] *nc* old-fashioned musical instrument shaped like a piano.

harpy ['hɑːpi] *nc* **1.** (in Greek myths) creature with the body of a bird and the head of a woman. **2.** cruel, ugly woman.

harridan ['hæridn] *nc* evil, old woman.

harrier ['hæriə*] *nc* **1.** dog used for hunting hares. **2.** long-distance runner (usu. across country).

harrow ['hærou] *nc* heavy metal frame pulled over ploughed ground to break it up more and make it more even. Also *vt* **1.** break up with a harrow. **2.** cause distress to. **harrowing** *adj* painful, distressing: *a harrowing experience.*

harry ['hæri] *vt* attack and rob frequently.

harsh [hɑːʃ] *adj* **1.** rough and unpleasant: *a harsh voice. It has a harsh taste.* **2.** severe: *harsh treatment; a harsh parent.* **harshly** *adv.* **harshness** *nu.*

hart [hɑːt] *nc* male deer.

harum-scarum ['hɛərəm'skɛərəm] *nc* careless and thoughtless person. Also *adj*: *harum-scarum behaviour.* (both *informal*).

harvest ['hɑːvist] *nc* **1.** time when food crops are cut and gathered; food crop gathered. *It rained during the harvest. The harvest this year is a good one.* **2.** result of what has been done. *They are enjoying the harvest of their efforts.* Also *vt* cut and gather food crops.
harvester *nc* **1.** person who harvests. **2.** machine which harvests.
'harvest 'home festival held after the harvest.
'harvest 'moon full moon at the time of the harvest.

hash [hæʃ] *nu* **1.** cooked meat cut into small pieces and cooked again. **2.** hashish. (*informal* in sense **2.**).
make a hash of something do something badly. (*informal*).
settle somebody's hash deal firmly with somebody who has done wrong. (*informal*).

hashish ['hæʃiːʃ] *nu* type of intoxicating drug.

hasp [hɑːsp] *nc* piece of metal which fits over a staple and enables a door to be fastened with a padlock.

hassock ['hæsək] *nc* cushion for kneeling on (usu. to pray).

haste [heist] *nu* hurry.

hasten ['heisn] *vt/i* move, cause to move or act quickly. *They hastened to deny it* i.e. lost no time in denying it. *He hastened my departure.*

hasty ['heisti] *adj* **1.** done or made in a hurry: *a hasty visit; a hasty breakfast.* **2.** easily made angry. *He is too hasty with people he does not like.* **hastily** *adv.* **hastiness** *nu.*

hat [hæt] *nc* something worn on the head.
hatter *nc* person who makes hats.
hatless *adj.* without a hat.
'hatband band of cloth round a hat, either inside or outside.
'hatpin pin for fastening a woman's hat to her hair.
pass round the hat collect money for something (the hat being used as a bag to put the money in).
talk through one's hat see **talk.**

hatch[1] [hætʃ] *vt/i* **1.** come out, cause to come out, of an egg. *Seven chickens hatched this morning. The hen hatched all the eggs.* **2.** prepare in secret. *They are hatching a plan to escape.*
hatchery ['hætʃəri] *nc* (usu. of fish) place where young are hatched from eggs.
count one's chickens before they are hatched see **count**[1].

hatch[2] [hætʃ] *nc* **1.** cover over an opening, or the opening itself, in the deck of a ship through which cargo is put. *Hatches are closed when a ship is at sea.* **2.** openings in a wall between two rooms, through which things can be passed.
'hatchway opening in a deck covered by a hatch.
'service hatch opening in a wall through which food, dishes etc are passed from a kitchen to a dining room.
under hatches below deck on a ship.

hatchet ['hætʃit] *nc* small axe with a short handle.
bury the hatchet see **bury.**

hate [heit] *vt* dislike greatly. *I hate liars. I hate to say it. They hated being laughed at.* Also *nc/u*: *his hate of/for injustice.* **hatred** ['heitrid] *nu.*
hateful *adj* causing great dislike.

hatter ['hætə*] *nc* see **hat.**

haughty ['hɔːti] *adj* thinking greatly of oneself but not of other people; proud. *He is very haughty towards people poorer than himself.* **haughtily** *adv.* **haughtiness** *nu.*

haul [hɔːl] *vt* pull with effort or force. *They hauled him out of the river.* Also *nc* **1.** amount of something obtained by effort or force. *The thieves made a good haul; a haul of fish.* **2.** distance over which something travels. *It was a long haul from the coast to the mountains.* **haulier** *nc.*
haulage *nu* carrying of heavy goods: *road haulage* i.e. carrying heavy goods by road.
'haulage contractor person who does haulage by contract. (Also **haulier**).
haul somebody over the coals see **coal.**
haul down one's flag surrender by lowering the flag (usu. at sea).

haunch [hɔ:ntʃ] *nc* part of the body between the ribs and thighs; hip.

haunt [hɔ:nt] *vt* **1.** (usu. said of ghosts or spirits which cause fear) visit often. *The spirit of his dead father haunted the village; a haunted castle.* **2.** keep coming back to the mind (usu. to cause fear or sadness). *The years of the war still haunt me; a haunting time* i.e. one which keeps coming back to the mind. Also *nc* place often visited. *This café is one of his haunts.*

hauteur [ou'tə:*] *nu* proud manner; haughtiness.

have [hæv] *vt* **1.** *aux* to form the perfect tense. *I have seen him.* **2.** *had* before the subject means *if. Had he been here, he would have spoken* i.e. if he had been here . . . **3.** own; possess; contain. *I have a bicycle. He has no children. She has a nice smile. This house has many rooms. Each day has 24 hours.* Also **have got.** *I have/I've got a bicycle etc.* (For shortened forms *I've etc* see *Note*[1]). **4.** take; receive: *have breakfast; have visitors.* Also in this sense with many nouns instead of their verbs. *He had a walk* i.e. he walked. *Shall we have a look?* i.e. shall we look?; *have a dance/drink/fight/rest/smoke/swim/wash etc.* **5.** experience; suffer from. *We are having a good time. They had some difficulty in doing it. I had my money stolen.* **6.** cause to happen or be done. *You must have this work finished by Monday. They are having their house painted. I would have you know that I am ill* i.e. I want you to know. *They will have it that they are right* i.e. they insist. Also in this sense with the meaning of get: *have the best/worst of something/somebody; have one's own way.* **7.** be obliged to; must. *They had to do it. I have to go now.* (For questions and negatives see *Note*[2]). Also *I have got to go now.* **8.** cheat. *I've been had* i.e. I have been cheated.(*informal* in sense **8.**).
Note[1]: the shortened forms of *have, has* and *had* are usu. used in conversation. They are *'ve, 's* and *'d. I've got two pounds. You've finished. He's read it. I'd no idea. It'd fallen.* In questions there is no shortening. *Have I two pounds? Have you finished? etc.* In the same way the negative *not* is shortened to *n't* in conversation and is joined to *have. I haven't (got) a penny. You haven't finished. He hasn't read it. I hadn't any idea.*
Note[2]: questions and negatives of *have* (in sense **7.**) can be shown in three ways: (a) *Do you have to go to school?* (b) *Have you to go to school?* (c) *Have you got to go to school?* (a) usu. gives the sense of something that is done often i.e. going to school is something done all the time, as a habit. (b) and (c) usu. give the sense of a particular time i.e. *have you to go* or *have you got to go early/now/today? etc.* This difference between (a), (b) and (c) is not, however, always followed. In the same way – (a) *You don't have to go to school* i.e. you need not ever go. (b) *You haven't to go to school* and (c) *You haven't got to go to school* i.e. today, during the holidays etc.
have somebody/something in receive or take into one's house.
have somebody on cheat; make fun of. (*informal*).
have something on 1. wear. *She had a coat on.* **2.** be occupied; busy. *He has something on every day.*
have it out with somebody argue with somebody until an understanding or agreement is reached. (*informal*).
have somebody up bring somebody to a court of law. *The police had him up for theft.* (*informal*).
have to do with be one's business. *He has to do with publishing. I'll have nothing to do with it.*
he's had it he's ruined; missed his chance; is going to die. (*informal*).

haven ['heivən] *nc* harbour; place of safety.

haversack ['hævəsæk] *nc* cloth bag for holding food etc (usu. carried on the back).

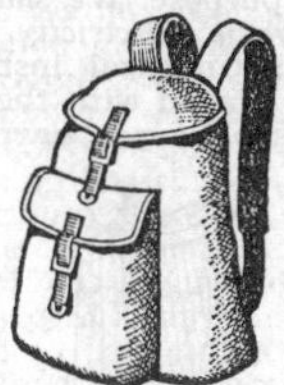
haversack

havoc ['hævək] *nu* damage; ruin. *Wars cause great havoc.*
make havoc of, play havoc with/among cause damage or ruin.

haw[1] [hɔ:] *vi* see **hum.**

haw[2] [hɔ:] *nc* fruit of the hawthorn.

hawk[1] [hɔ:k] *nc* general name for any bird (except the eagle), which catches small animals for food during the day, including falcons, kestrels etc.
'hawk-'eyed *adj* having good eyesight.
'hawk-'nosed *adj* having a sharp, curved nose like a hawk.

hawk[2] [hɔ:k] *vt* take goods from place to place to sell them (usu. in a cart or barrow). *He hawks fruit all over the village.* **hawker** *nc.*

hawk[3] [hɔ:k] *vi* clear one's throat noisily. *He is always hawking and spitting.*

hawser ['hɔ:zə*] *nc* thick rope used for tying up ships.

hawthorn ['hɔ:θɔ:n] *nc* type of prickly bush with small, white or pink flowers.

hay [hei] *nu* grass cut and dried by the sun and used as food for animals.
'hay fever running nose etc caused by dust from hay and other plants.
'hayrick, 'haystack hay put in a large heap to store it for use.
'haywire *pred adj* wrong; crazy. *All our plans went haywire.* (*informal*).
make hay cut and dry grass as food for animals.
'haymaker *nc* person who makes hay. **haymaking** *nu.*
make hay while the sun shines make the best use of a good opportunity. (*informal*).

hazard ['hæzəd] *nc* risk; danger. *A soldier's life is full of hazards.* Also *vt* risk; run the risk of. *They hazarded all they had to win.* **hazardous** *adj.* **hazardously** *adv.*

haze [heiz] *nu* **1.** light mist; air that is not clear. *The sun shone through the haze; a haze of smoke.* **2.** uncertainty; doubt. *I am in a haze about what happened.* **hazy** *adj.* **hazily** *adv.* **haziness** *nu.*

hazel ['heizl] *nc* type of small tree found in cool, northern regions, which has a small, round nut which can be eaten. Also *adj* (usu. used to describe the colour of eyes) having a brown colour like the nut of a hazel.

he [hi:, hi] *pron* male person or animal that has been mentioned before. *I spoke to your father just before he went out. He is coming/He's coming.* see **him, his.**

he who anyone who. *He who hesitates is lost.*

he-man ['hi:mæn] *nc* powerful, dominating man. (*informal*).

head [hed] *nc* **1.** the part of the body above the neck. *He has no hair on his head.* **2.** top or upper part of something: *the head of a nail; the head of a page; the head of a valley; the head of a bed* i.e. the part where one puts one's head; *the head on a glass of beer* i.e. the foaming part above the beer itself. **3.** mental ability. *He has a good head for figures. He found the answer out of his own head* i.e. using his own ability. *Use your head!* i.e. think hard. (*informal*). **4.** most important person of a group or organization: *the head of state* (e.g. king, president); *heads of departments.* **5.** the side of a coin on which the head of a country's president etc is stamped. (*opp* **tail**). *Heads or tails?* (said when throwing a coin into the air to decide something according to whether the coin falls with the head or tail upwards). **6.** (no *pl*) one unit of a herd or group. *A hundred head of cattle* i.e. a hundred cows. *The cost of the journey is fifty pence a/per head* i.e. each. **7.** pressure; force: *a good head of steam* i.e. with enough pressure to drive an engine. Also *vt* **1.** hit a football with one's head. *He headed the ball.* **2.** be at the top or in a leading position: *head the list.*

heady *adj* affecting one's mind; exciting. *This is a heady drink; heady news.*

-headed *adj*: *a two-headed axe* i.e. one with two cutting edges.

'headache pain in the head.

'headdress ornamental covering of the head.

'headgear something worn on the head (e.g. hat, cap etc).

'headhunter person who hunts his enemies so that he can cut off and keep their heads.

'headlamp, 'headlight lamp fixed on front of a car, bicycle or train to show the way.

'headland piece of land which projects into the sea or a lake; cape.

'headline short summary in large print at the top of a newspaper to attract attention. *I only had time to read the headlines.*

'headman leader of a village or small group.

'head'master, 'head'mistress man, woman in charge of a school.

'head-'on *adj/adv* hitting each other with the front parts (usu. cars etc): *a head-on collision. The two buses crashed head-on.*

'headphones radio or telephone receivers held on the ears by a band of metal over the head. (Also **earphones, headset**).

'head'quarters centre from which an organization is controlled.

'headroom height needed to allow somebody/something to pass beneath. *This bridge has not enough headroom for large buses.*

'headship post of headmaster or headmistress. *He has applied for the headship of the new school.*

'headstone stone put at the head of a grave.

'headway progress; advance. *We could make no headway in the huge crowd.*

'headwind wind blowing in the opposite direction to the way one is going.

'headword word in a printed title (used esp. for words explained in a dictionary). *In this dictionary each headword is followed by its pronunciation in brackets.*

head for someone/something go towards: *head for the hills.*

head someone/something off get in front of so as to turn back or aside. *He tried to head off the angry mob.*

at the head of 1. in front of; leading. *The band was at the head of the parade.* **2.** in the most important place: *at the head of the table.*

come to a head 1. be ready to burst (e.g. a boil on the skin). **2.** reach a crisis.

head first *adv* with the head in front (as in a dive).

get it into one's head see **get.**

give someone his head allow someone to do as he wishes.

go to one's head affect one's mind. *The strong drink went to their heads* i.e. they became drunk. *Sudden wealth has gone to his head* i.e. he has become proud, careless etc. (*informal*).

head over heels 1. turning over; upside down. *He went head over heels into the water.* **2.** completely. *She is head over heels in love.* (*informal* in sense **2.**).

keep one's head see **keep**[1].

lose one's head see **lose.**

I can't make head or tail of it/him I am completely unable to understand it/him. (*informal*).

be off one's head be mad. (*informal*).

on one's head 1. *He stood on his head* i.e. with his head where his feet usually are. **2.** being responsible for a crime or error. *If we fail it will be on your head.*

over somebody's head 1. *talk over somebody's head* i.e. talk in a way that is too difficult to be understood by somebody. **2.** *go over somebody's head* i.e. do something without someone's knowledge or consent, by asking permission from somebody superior. (*informal*).

put something into somebody's head suggest something to somebody.

they put their heads together they plan together. (*informal*).

put something out of one's head decide to forget about something.

header ['hedə*] *nc* **1.** jump or fall head first. **2.** hitting of a football with one's head.

heading ['hediŋ] *nc* word/words at the top of something written or printed, showing what it is about.

headlong ['hedlɔŋ] *adj/adv* hurried; head first: *headlong flight. He fell headlong.*

headstrong ['hedstrɔŋ] *adj* determined to have one's own way.

heady ['hedi] *adj* see **head.**

heal [hi:l] **1.** *vi* (usu. of injuries and wounds) become well. *The cut on my leg has healed.* **2.** *vt* (usu. of persons) cause to become well. *A doctor's work is to heal the sick.* (rather *o.f.* – use **cure**).

healing *adj*: *healing medicines.*

healer *nc* person/thing that heals (in sense **2.**).

heal up (with reference to a wound etc) become cured.

health [helθ] *nu* general condition of the body: *good health; bad/poor health.* Also general condition of being well. *Health comes before wealth* i.e. good health.

healthy *adj* with good health; causing good health: *a healthy baby; a healthy place to live in; a healthy respect for the law* i.e. it is good to have this respect. (*opp* **unhealthy**).

healthily *adv.*

healthful *adj* causing good health.

drink somebody's health/to the health of somebody wish somebody good health before drinking in his honour.

heap [hi:p] *nc* **1.** number of things lying on top of one another. *The fallen leaves lay in heaps; a heap of stones.* **2.** plenty of something. *We have heaps of time. They have heaps of money.* (*informal* in sense **2.**). Also *vt*: *They are heaping wood on the fire.*

heaped *adj*: *a heaped plate of rice.*

hear [hiə*] *vt* **1.** receive sounds in the ears. *I heard the drums.* **2.** be informed; receive news. *I hear you are leaving. Have you heard from home?* **3.** listen to; attend to. *The judge heard the case this morning. I will hear your story before I give an answer. past* **heard** [hə:d].

Hear! Hear! *interj* showing agreement with what has been said.

not hear of (usu. with **will** or **would**) refuse to agree to. *He will not hear of my going away.*

hear somebody out listen to somebody until he has finished speaking.

hearing ['hiəriŋ] **1.** *nu* receiving of sounds in the ears. *He is hard of hearing/He has poor hearing* i.e. he cannot hear well. **2.** *nu* distance over which a sound can be heard by somebody. *Don't say that in his hearing.* (*opp* **out of hearing**). **3.** *nc* opportunity to give one's views etc. *They gave him a hearing.*

hearsay ['hiəsei] *nu* secondhand information; rumour. Also *adj*: *hearsay evidence* i.e. evidence which is not about what the person giving it saw or did, but about what he heard from somebody else.

hearse [hə:s] *nc* carriage or car for carrying a coffin.

heart [hɑ:t] *nc* **1.** organ which pumps blood round the body. *He has a weak heart.* **2.** centre which controls one's feelings. *She has a kind heart. They took the bad news to heart* i.e. they were very upset by it. *I did not have the heart to tell him* i.e. I did not have the courage. **3.** centre; inner part: *the heart of the city; the heart of the matter; the heart of a lettuce.* **4.** something shaped like a heart (esp. on playing cards): *ace/king/queen of hearts.*

hearty *adj* **1.** cheerful; healthy: *a hearty laugh.* **2.** large and enjoyable: *a hearty breakfast.* **heartily** *adv.* **heartiness** *nu.*

heartless *adj* without feeling; cruel. **heartlessly** *adv.* **heartlessness** *nu.*

-hearted *adj*: *big-hearted* i.e. generous; *down-hearted* i.e. depressed; without hope; *faint-hearted* i.e. cowardly; *good-hearted* i.e. generous; *half-hearted* i.e. without enthusiasm; *hard-hearted* i.e. cruel; unkind.

'heartache sorrow; longing for what one cannot have.

'heart attack illness in which the heart suddenly stops working properly (often causing death).

'heartbeat pumping motion of the heart. *The doctor listened to my heartbeat.*

'heartbreaking *adj* causing great sorrow.

'heartbroken *adj* suffering from great sorrow.

'heartburn *nu* pain in the chest caused by indigestion.

'heartburning *nc/u* envy; dissatisfaction. *His success caused great heartburning(s) among the others.*

'heartfelt *adj* deeply felt; sincere: *my heartfelt thanks.*

'heartrending *adj* causing great sorrow.

'heartstrings centre of one's deepest and most sensitive feelings (as if the heart were a stringed musical instrument). *His brave smile pulled (at)/touched my heartstrings.*

after one's own heart winning one's complete approval. *Mr Smith is a man after my own heart.*

at heart deeply; essentially. *They were sad at heart. At heart he is a kind man. He has our welfare at heart* i.e. he cares deeply about it.

break one's/someone's heart see **break.**

by heart correctly from the memory: *know/learn/repeat something by heart; he knows the multiplication tables by heart* i.e. he can remember them correctly without the help of a book of multiplication tables.

have one's heart in one's boots be without hope; feel depressed. (*informal*).

have a change of heart change one's mind for the better; become kinder.

cry/eat one's heart out see **cry**[1].

do one's heart good make happy. *It does my heart good to see people enjoying themselves.* (*informal*).

heart-to-heart *adj* frank and friendly: *a heart-to-heart talk.*

lose heart see **lose.**

lose one's heart to fall in love with.

have one's heart in one's mouth be very frightened. (*informal*).

set one's heart on see set[1].

take heart be encouraged. (*opp* **lose heart**).

wear one's heart on one's sleeve show one's feelings too openly. (*informal*).

hearten ['hɑ:tn] *vt* cheer; encourage. **heartening** *adj.* (*opp* **disheartening**).

hearth [hɑ:θ] *nc* **1.** large, flat stone under and in front of a fireplace. **2.** centre of one's home.

'hearthrug rug put on or in front of the hearth.

heat[1] [hi:t] *nu* **1.** hotness: *the heat of a fire.* (*opp* **cold**). **2.** strong feelings; anger. *They argued with great heat.* **3.** sexual urge (at regular intervals) of a female animal. *Our dog is on heat.* **4.** division of a sports competition to decide who will take part in the final competitions. *Because he won his heat he will run in the finals.*

'heatspot spot on the skin which becomes red and feels hot.

'heatstroke illness caused by heat (e.g. of the sun).

'heatwave unusually hot weather.

dead heat race in which two or more competitors finish in the first place.

prickly heat rash on the skin caused by sweat.

heat[2] [hi:t] *vt* make hot. *The sun heats the earth.*

heated *adj* made hot; angry: *a heated room; a very heated meeting.* **heatedly** *adv.*

heater *nc* apparatus for giving heat or making something hot.

central heating apparatus for heating a building from one central point.

heat something up make hot (often for a second time). *Let me heat up some soup for you.*

heath [hi:θ] **1.** *nc* piece of unused open land. **2.** *nu* short plant with small flowers (usu. found on rough, open land).

heathen ['hi:ðən] *nc* person who believes in a god or gods different from one's own (esp. one who is not a Christian, Jew or Muslim). Also *adj*: *a heathen country.*

heathenish *adj* like heathens; uncivilized.

heather ['heðə*] *nu* type of short plant with small flowers, belonging to the same family as heath, found on rough, unused land and mountains.

heave [hi:v] **1.** *vt* lift, move or throw something heavy. *They heaved their luggage into the car.* **2.** *vt* pull hard (usu. a rope). *Heave! /Heave away!* telling someone to pull hard. **3.** *vi* move up and down or in and out. *The sea was heaving. His chest heaved.* Also *nc*: *He pulled it out with one heave. past* **heaved** or **hove** [houv].

Note: hove is less usual and is generally only used of ships heaving to.

heaving *adj* moving up and down or in and out: *heaving waves; a heaving chest.*

heave to stop at sea without dropping anchor. *The ship hove to.*

heave a sigh give a sigh, moving the chest to do so.

heave in sight come into sight.

heaven ['hevən] *nc* **1.** place above the earth where God is believed to be. **2.** (usu. **Heaven**) God himself. *It is Heaven's will. Thank Heaven!* **3.** (usu. *pl*) the sky. (rather *o.f.*). **4.** condition of being very happy. *It's heaven to be here.* (*informal* in sense **4.**).

heavenly *adj* of heaven; causing great happiness; delightful.

move heaven and earth see **move²**.

heavy ['hevi] *adj* **1.** having great weight. *The box is too heavy to carry.* **2.** slow; dull: *heavy with sleep.* **3.** greater than usual: *heavy crops; heavy rain; heavy seas; heavy work.* Also in a large number of senses:

heavy blow blow with great force.

heavy fall fall causing injury or damage.

heavy food food which is difficult to digest.

heavy going difficult. *He found the textbook very heavy going* i.e. difficult to read with interest or difficult to understand.

a heavy hand strict; severe. *He rules his class with a heavy hand* i.e. strictly.

'heavy-'handed *adj* **1.** strict; severe. **2.** clumsy.

a heavy heart sad. **heavy-hearted** *adj*.

a heavy line a thick line. *He drew a heavy line under the word.*

heavy reading difficult to read. *This essay is heavy reading.*

a heavy sky cloudy and dark.

heavy soil difficult to cultivate i.e. soil which is thick and difficult to cultivate.

heavy water special water made from oxygen and atoms of hydrogen which are twice the normal weight.

'heavyweight boxer or wrestler who weighs 175 pounds or over.

heavily *adv*: *heavily-laden* i.e. with a heavy load. **heaviness** *nu. comparative* **heavier.** *superlative* **heaviest.**

Note: heavy is sometimes used as an *adv* but it is rather *o.f.* (e.g. *heavy-laden*). It is also used with some verbs like *hang* and *lie*. *The time hung heavy on our hands. Sorrow lies heavy on their hearts.*

Hebraic [hi'breiik] *adj* Hebrew.

Hebrew ['hi:bru:] **1.** *nc* Jew. **2.** *nu* language of the Jews. Also *adj* of the Jews or their language.

heckle ['hekl] *vt* interrupt a public speaker with questions and remarks.

heckler *nc* person who heckles. **heckling** *nu*.

hectare ['hektɑ:*] *nc* measure of area in the metric system equal to 2.47 acres.

hectic ['hektik] *adj* **1.** very busy or exciting. *We had a hectic holiday.* **2.** with flushed skin. **hectically** *adv*.

hecto- ['hektou] *prefix* (usu. in the metric system) one hundred (e.g. **hectolitre** i.e. 100 litres).

hector ['hektə*] *vt/i* bully by shouting at; act aggressively and rudely.

hedge¹ [hedʒ] *nc* line of bushes used as a wall round a field or garden.

'hedgehop *vi* (with reference to aeroplanes) fly very low. (*informal*).

'hedgerow line of bushes in a hedge.

'hedge sparrow type of small bird, which looks like a sparrow with a pointed beak, found in northern and central Europe.

hedge² [hedʒ] **1.** *vt* put a hedge round. **2.** *vt* limit or make less by certain actions. *The laws of the land hedge us in* i.e. so that we cannot do what we like. *He hedged his bets* i.e. he took steps to lessen his possible losses by spreading his bets. **3.** *vi* be reluctant to make a decision or give an opinion. *Stop hedging and say what you think.*

hedgehog ['hedʒhɔg] *nc* small animal covered with long, sharp points.

hedonism ['hi:dənizəm] *nu* worship and pursuit of pleasure. **hedonist** *nc*. **hedonistic** [hi:də'nistik] *adj*.

heed [hi:d] *vt* pay attention to. Also *nu*: *They give/pay no heed to what I say. You should take heed of what I say.*

heedful *adj*: *They are more heedful of what I say.* **heedfully** *adv*. **heedfulness** *nu*.

heedless *adj* careless; inattentive. **heedlessly** *adv*. **heedlessness** *nu*.

heehaw ['hi:hɔ:] *nc* noise made by a donkey. Also *vi*.

heel¹ [hi:l] *nc* **1.** back part of the foot. **2.** part of a sock or stocking which covers the heel. *There is a hole in the heel of one of your socks.* **3.** part of a boot or shoe below the heels: *high heels; flat heels.* **4.** vulgar, dishonest person. (*informal* in sense **4.**).

Achilles heel a person's only weak point.

at/on/upon one's heels following close behind.

come to heel (usu. of a dog) follow close behind when told to do so.

cool/kick one's heels be kept waiting. (*informal*).

down at heel **1.** (of shoes) with the heels badly worn. **2.** (of persons) wearing such shoes; badly dressed, untidy.

head over heels see **head.**

show a clean pair of heels run away quickly. (*informal*).

take to one's heels run away. (*informal*).

turn on one's heels turn round quickly and go the other way.

under the heel of under the cruel rule or control of. *The country was under the heel of a dictator.*

heel² [hi:l] **1.** *vt* kick with the heel: *heel a ball.* **2.** *vi* (often with **over**) (usu. of a ship) lean to one side. *The ship heeled (over) in the storm.*

hefty ['hefti] *adj* big and strong; heavy: *hefty football player; hefty piece of cheese* i.e. a big one. **heftily** *adv*. (both *informal*).

hegemony [hi'geməni] *nu* superiority; leadership (usu. of one country over others).

heifer ['hefə*] *nc* young cow that has not had a calf.

height [hait] **1.** *nu* distance from bottom to top. *What is the height of that building? He is six feet in height.* **2.** *nc* high place. **3.** *nu* highest degree. *He is at the height of his power. The battle was at its height.*

heighten *vt/i* make or become higher or greater. *The news heightened our fears. The tension heightened.* **heightened** *adj*.

heinous ['heinəs] *adj* (used only of a crime or offence) very bad. **heinously** *adv*. **heinousness** *nu*.

heir [ɛə*] *nc* person entitled to receive the money, property or rank of another person when that person dies. *I am my uncle's heir. He was heir to the throne.* (*fem* **heiress** ['ɛəris]).

heirloom ['ɛəlu:m] *nc* a personal article which has been in the possession of a family for generations.

held [held] past of **hold**[1].

helicopter ['helikɔptə*] *nc* type of aircraft which has horizontal revolving blades on top, enabling it to take off and land vertically and remain in the air without having to move forward.

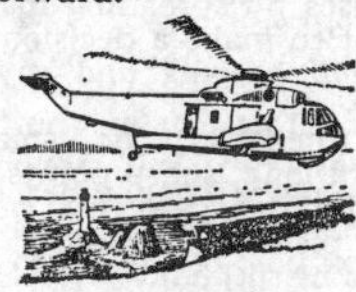

helicopter

helio- ['hi:liou] *prefix* (in many scientific and technical words) about the sun (e.g. **heliograph**).

heliograph ['hi:liougrɑ:f] *nc* apparatus for sending messages by reflecting sunlight in a mirror.

helium ['hi:liəm] *nu* very light gas which does not burn.

hell [hel] *nu* **1.** place of punishment for the wicked after death. **2.** any place or condition of suffering and misery. *This is a hell of a place.* (*informal*). *My toothache gave me hell.* (*informal*); *a hell of a lot* i.e. a great deal. (*informal*); *a hell of a good party* i.e. a very good one. (*informal*); *a gambling hell* i.e. a place where people gamble.

hellish *adj* terrible.

for the hell of it for fun. (*informal*).

go/ride hell for leather as fast as possible. (*informal*).

hello, hallo [hʌ'lou] *nu/interj* shout to greet or to call attention.

helm [helm] *nu* tiller i.e. a long handle, or wheel, for turning the rudder of a ship.

'**helmsman** man holding the helm.

helmet ['helmit] *nc* hard covering to protect the head. *Soldiers wear steel helmets in battle.*

help[1] [help] *vt* **1.** do something for somebody; do part of somebody's work. *The rich should help the poor. I help my father in the garden. He helped me (to) cook the food.* **2.** give food or drink to. *May I help you to some pudding? Help yourself to a beer!* **3.** (with **can** or **could**) avoid; stop. *I can't help laughing. They talked too much; they couldn't help it/themselves.*

helper *nc* person who helps. see also **help**[2].

helping *nc* amount of food given or taken. *He had two helpings of pudding.*

help[2] [help] **1.** *nu* act of helping; assistance. *I am grateful for your help. We need all the help we can get. He gave us no help.* **2.** *nc* servant who works in a house: *a daily help.*

helpful *adj* giving help; willing to help. (*opp* **unhelpful**). **helpfully** *adv*. **helpfulness** *nu*.

helpless *adj* **1.** without help. **2.** unable to help oneself. **helplessly** *adv*. **helplessness** *nu*.

helpmate ['helpmeit] *nc* partner or friend who helps (often a husband or wife) (Also **helpmeet**).

helter-skelter ['heltə'skeltə*] *adv* in hurry and confusion. (*informal*). Also *nc* tower with a spiral chute down which people slide.

helve [helv] *nc* handle of a tool (esp. of an axe or hatchet).

hem [hem] *nc* edge of a piece of cloth folded over and sewn: *the hem of a dress/handkerchief.* Also *vt* **1.** put a hem on. **2.** surround; enclose on all sides. *The garden is hemmed in/round with trees. past* **hemmed.**

'**hemline** hem at the bottom of a dress or coat.

'**hemstitch** *nc* type of ornamental sewing done round a hem. Also *vt/i*.

hemisphere ['hemisfiə*] *nc* half of a sphere; half of the earth: *the Northern/Southern hemisphere* i.e. the half north/south of the equator; *the Eastern/Western hemisphere* i.e. the half east/west of a line going through Great Britain (called the **Greenwich meridian**).

hemlock ['hemlɔk] **1.** *nu* type of poisonous plant; poison made from it. **2.** *nc* evergreen tree common in America and Asia.

hemo-, haemo- ['hi:mou, 'hemou] *prefix* blood (e.g. **hemorrhage**).

hemoglobin [hi:mə'gloubin] *nu* red matter in the blood which carries oxygen and gives blood its colour.

hemophilia [hi:mə'filiə] *nu* disease which causes blood to continue to flow from a wound and not harden round the wound as it usually does.

hemorrhage ['hemərid3] *nu* bleeding.

hemorrhoids ['hemərɔidz] *npl* painful swollen veins round the anus; piles.

hemp [hemp] *nu* **1.** type of plant used to make ropes and rough cloth. **2.** drug made from this plant. (Also **hashish**).

hen [hen] *nc* female bird (esp. a chicken) (*masc* **cock**).

'**hen coop** type of small cage for keeping hens.

'**henhouse** small building, bigger than a hen coop, for keeping hens.

'**hen party** party for women only. (*informal* – a party for men only is a **stag party**).

'**henpecked** *adj* (with reference to a husband) ruled by his wife. **henpeck** *vt*. (both *informal*).

hence [hens] *adv* **1.** from now: *a year hence* (*o.f.* – use **a year from now** or **in a year's time**). **2.** from here. *They travelled hence* (*o.f.* – use **from here**). **3.** for this reason.

henceforth, henceforward *adv* from now on; in the future (*o.f.*).

henchman ['hentʃmən] *nc* loyal follower of an important or powerful person. *pl* **henchmen** ['hentʃmən].

henna ['henə] *nu* **1.** type of plant from which a red dye for the hair and fingernails is obtained. **2.** this dye.

hennaed ['henəd] *adj* dyed with henna. *She has hennaed hair.*

hepatitis [hepə'taitis] *nu* disease of the liver.

hepta- ['heptə] *prefix* having seven of something (e.g. **heptagon**).

heptagon ['heptəgən] *nc* (geometry) figure with seven sides.

her [hə:*] *pron* form which **she** takes when it is the object of a verb or preposition. *You saw her there. Give it to her.* Also *determiner* form which **she** takes to show possession. *It's her book/problem etc.*

herald ['herəld] *nc* **1.** person who in the past

used to carry and make known important messages from his chief or king. **2.** name given to many newspapers: *the Evening Herald.* **3.** somebody/something which is a sign of an event about to happen. *Grey skies are the heralds of rain.* **4.** person skilled in the science of heraldry. Also *vt*: *Grey skies herald rain.*
heraldry *nu* science which deals with the history and the coats of arms of noble families.

herb [hə:b] *nc* type of plant used as medicine or to flavour food. **herbal** *adj.*
'herbage *nu* grass and other plants like grass.
'herbalist *nc* person who grows or deals with herbs.
herbivorous [hə:'bivərəs] *adj* feeding on plants, not meat. see **carnivorous.**
herbaceous [hə:'beiʃəs] *adj* of plants with soft stems which die down after flowering: *herbaceous border* i.e. border in a garden planted with flowers of this kind.

herculean [hə:kju'liən] *adj* having or needing very great strength and effort (from Hercules, the ancient Greek hero who was given almost impossible work to do).

herd [hə:d] *nc* **1.** group of certain types of animals: *a herd of buffaloes/cattle/deer/elephants.* **2.** person who looks after a herd: *a cowherd; a goatherd.* **3.** people: *the common herd.* (*impolite*). Also *vt* **1.** look after a herd. *The little boy is herding his father's cattle.* **2.** gather together with force. *They herded the prisoners into the camp.*
'herdsman man who looks after a herd.

here [hiə*] *adv* **1.** at/in/to this place. *I am sitting here. He works here. Come here!*
Note: here is often used at the beginning of a sentence expressing an exclamation. When it is, the subject of the verb comes before the verb if it is a personal pronoun, and after the verb if it is a noun. *Here they are! Here are the books! Here he comes! Here comes my friend!*
2. this place. *I live near here. Come over here* i.e. to the place where I am. *Behind here is a garden.* **3.** at a particular point in an action. *Let us stop here* (e.g. in reading) *and find out what is meant. Here I cannot agree with you.* **4.** who or which is/are in this place (instead of *this* or *these*). *The boy here is ill. The books here are mine.*
hereabouts ['hiərəbauts] *adv* near or about here.
hereafter [hiər'ɑ:ftə*] *nu* the future; life after death. Also *adv* after this (both *o.f.*).
hereby/herein/hereunder/herewith *adv* by/in/under/with this (*o.f.* and now correctly used only in legal language).
hereupon ['hiərəpɔn] *adv* following this (*o.f.*).
here and there in several places.
here, there and everywhere all over or round.
here's to used when wishing something to happen (usu. when drinking a toast). *Here's to your health! Here's death to our enemies!*
neither here nor there having nothing to do with what is being done; irrelevant. *His advice to us was neither here nor there.*

heredity [hi'rediti] *nu* the passing of certain qualities from one generation to another; the qualities passed in this way. *The colour of our skin is due to heredity.*
hereditary [hi'reditəri] *adj* passed from one generation to another: *hereditary diseases*; also of rank or position: *a hereditary chief* i.e. one who became chief when his father died.

heresy ['herisi] *nc* religious belief which is not considered to be correct; any belief not considered to be correct.
heretic ['heritik] *nc* person who supports a heresy. **heretical** [hi'retikl] *adj.*

heritable ['heritəbl] *adj* being able to inherit or be inherited: *heritable property* i.e. property that can be inherited.

heritage ['heritidʒ] *nc* something which is, or can be, inherited. *English poetry is one of our great heritages.*

hermaphrodite [hə:'mæfrədait] *nc* animal or human that has the organs of both the male and female sex.

hermetic [hə:'metik] *adj* so closely fitted that all air is kept out.
hermetically *adv*: *Tins of food are hermetically sealed.*

hermit ['hə:mit] *nc* person who lives alone (often in order to live a religious life).
hermitage *nc* place where a hermit lives.

hernia ['hə:niə] *nc* condition of the body caused e.g. by part of the bowel projecting through the muscles of the abdomen; rupture.

hero ['hiərou] *nc* **1.** man famous for his great qualities (e.g. his courage). **2.** principal man in a play, poem or storybook. *pl* **heroes.** (*fem* **heroine** ['herouin]). **heroism** ['herouizəm] *nu.*
heroic [hi'rouik] *adj* **1.** of or like a hero. **2.** larger or grander than usual. *The new building is planned on a heroic scale. He likes using heroic phrases.*
heroics *npl* loud, brave words which mean nothing.
heroic verse type of verse with ten syllables in each line and each pair of lines rhyming.

heroin ['herouin] *nu* habit-forming drug, used medically to relieve pain.

heron ['hern] *nc* type of bird with long legs, neck and beak, which walks in the water.

herring ['heriŋ] *nc* type of small sea fish used as food. *pl* **herrings** or **herring.**
'herringbone V-shaped patterns on cloth like the backbones of a herring.
red herring something to which attention is drawn, to distract attention from something else.

hers [hə:z] *pron* what belongs to her. *We'll have to separate hers from yours.* Also *pred adj* belonging to her. *This dress is hers.*

hesitate ['heziteit] *vi* stop or pause (usu. because one is not certain). *He hesitated before choosing a book. These men hesitate at nothing. I hesitate to say so.* **hesitating** *adj.* **hesitatingly** *adv.* **hesitation** [hezi'teiʃən] *nu.* **hesitant** ['hezitnt] *adj.* **hesitantly** *adv.* **hesitance, hesitancy** *nu.*

hessian ['hesiən] *nu* type of strong, rough cloth (often used for making sacks).

hetero- ['hetərou] *prefix* different (e.g. **heterogeneous**).

heterodox ['hetəroudɔks] *adj* having beliefs different from those of most other people. (*opp* **orthodox**). **heterodoxy** *nc.*

heterogeneous ['hetərou'dʒi:niəs] *adj* of many different kinds.

hew [hju:] *vt* cut with heavy blows (e.g. using an axe, hatchet or sword). *He hewed the trunk of the tree into logs. They hewed a path through the thick forest* i.e. they made a path by cutting down the branches at the side. *past tense* **hewed.** *past part* **hewed** or **hewn** [hju:n]. **hewer** *nc.*

hexa- ['heksə] *prefix* having six of something

(e.g. **hexameter**).

hexagon ['heksəgən] *nc* (*geometry*) figure with six sides.

hexameter [hek'sæmitə*] *nc* line of verse containing six feet.

hey [hei] *interj* expressing surprise or attracting somebody's attention.

heyday ['heidei] *nu* time of greatest power or prosperity. *The country was then in its heyday; in the heyday of its power.*

hiatus [hai'eitəs] *nc* break in a series of things which should follow one another (e.g. when words are missing from the page of a book).

hibernate ['haibəneit] *vi* sleep through the winter (as many animals e.g. bears do). **hibernation** [haibə'neiʃən] *nu*.

hibiscus [hi'biskəs] *nu* type of flowering shrub with large, bell-shaped flowers.

hiccup, hiccough ['hikʌp] *nc* short, sudden and noisy interruption of the breath (often caused by eating or drinking too quickly). Also *vi*.

hickory ['hikəri] **1.** *nc* type of tree with hard wood found in America. **2.** *nu* the wood of this tree.

hid [hid] past tense of **hide**[1].

hidden ['hidn] past part of **hide**[1].

hide[1] [haid] *vt/i* keep or put out of sight; keep secret. *They are hiding in the wood. We hid (ourselves) in the wood. He tried to hide his anger. past tense* **hid** [hid]. *past part* **hidden** or **hid** ['hid(n)]. Also *nc* place to hide (esp. in order to watch wild animals).
'**hideaway,** '**hideout** place to hide (esp. to escape the law).
'**hide-and-'seek** children's game in which some hide and the others try to find them.
'**hiding place** place to hide.
be in hiding be hidden. (Also **go into/come out of hiding.**)

hide[2] [haid] *nc* **1.** skin of an animal (esp. when removed from the animal and prepared for sale). **2.** human skin. *They want to save their own hides* i.e. avoid punishment or death. (*informal* in sense **2.**).
hiding *nc* beating. *He gave him a good hiding.* (*informal*).

hidebound ['haidbaund] *adj* unwilling to consider new ideas; narrow-minded.

hideous ['hidiəs] *adj* horrible to look at; frightful: *a hideous face; a hideous mistake.* **hideously** *adv*. **hideousness** *nu*.

hierarchy ['haiərɑːki] *nc* **1.** organization strictly according to grade or rank. **2.** government by priests. **hierarchical** [haiə'rɑːkikl] *adj*.

hieroglyph ['haiərəglif] *nc* word written by means of pictures and not in letters of an alphabet (used in ancient Egypt). **hieroglyphic** [haiərə'glifik].
hieroglyphics *npl* words written by means of pictures.

hi-fi ['hai'fai] *adj* short form of **high fidelity.**

higgledy-piggledy ['higldi'pigldi] *adj/adv* in complete disorder; all mixed up. (*informal*).

high [hai] *adj* **1.** raised up; measuring from bottom to top: *high mountains; a high wall. The tree is fifty feet high.*
Note: in this sense use *tall* for persons and most animals.
2. important; above others in position: *the high priest; high society; high school* i.e. one above a primary school. **3.** great: *high prices; high speed; high winds; in high regard.* **4.** good; admirable: *a man of high principles/high character; high ideals.* **5.** near the top of the scale in music; sharp: *a high note; high voices.* **6.** much having already passed; almost over: *high summer* i.e. the middle of summer. *It is high time for us to go/It is high time we went* i.e. our time is almost over and we must go. **7.** (of food, esp. meat) beginning to go bad and smell. **8.** drunk. (*informal*). Also *adv*: *high-placed officials; play high* i.e. play a high card in a card game. *They climbed high. They held their heads high.* Also *nu* (usu. with **new**) highest point; peak. *Exports are at a new high.* (*informal*).
'**highball** (*US*) long drink made from whisky etc and soda.
'**highbrow** *adj* having more knowledge or better tastes than others. Also *nc* person who has, or thinks he has, more knowledge or better tastes. (*informal*).
High Commissioner *nc* representative of one of the British Commonwealth countries in another Commonwealth country.
High Commission *nc* office of a High Commissioner.
'**highfa'lutin(g)** ['haifə'luːtin] *adj* (of words, ideas etc) impressive but with little meaning. (*informal*).
'**high-fi'delity** *adj* (of radio sets, record players, tape recorders etc) recording sounds very accurately. (Short form **hi-fi**).
'**high-'handed** *adj* using one's authority without any thought for others: *the government's high-handed policies.*
'**highlander** *nc* person who lives in mountainous country.
'**highlands** *npl* mountainous country.
'**high-'level** *adj* attended by important people; important: *a high-level meeting.*
'**highlight** **1.** most important, most enjoyable part of something. *Your performance was the highlight of the show.* **2.** part of a photograph, painting etc on which there is the greatest effect of light.
'**high-'minded** *adj* very good morally. **high-mindedness** *nu*.
'**high-'pitched** *adj* **1.** having a sharp, high sound: *a high-pitched voice.* **2.** (of roofs) steep.
'**high-'powered** *adj* **1.** with a powerful engine. **2.** (of people) important; powerful.
'**high 'spirits** *npl* great and excited happiness. **high-spirited** *adj*.
'**high(ly) 'strung** *adj* very easily excited; nervous.
'**high 'tea** see **tea.**
'**highway** *nc* road (esp. a main road).
'**highwayman** *nc* man who, in the past, robbed people travelling by road.
high and low everywhere. *We looked high and low for you.* (*informal*).

highly ['haili] *adv* very: *a highly dangerous job. He is highly pleased. He spoke highly of you* i.e. he praised you.
Note: the difference between *highly* and *high* as an *adv* is small. In many phrases either can be used: *high/highly strung; high/highly paid.* But one can only say *climb/play high*, and *speak highly of; highly pleased etc.*

highness ['hainis] **1.** *nu* being high (usu. in senses **2.**, **3.**, **4.** and **5.** of **high**): *the highness of his position; the highness of prices; the highness of their principles; the highness of their voices.* **2.** *nc* title of persons belonging to a royal family. *His (Royal) Highness; Your Highness; Their (Royal) Highnesses.*

hijack ['haidʒæk] *vt* (esp. with reference to an aeroplane, van etc or its cargo) take or steal by force. **hijacker** *nc*. **hijacking** *nc/u*.

hike [haik] *nc* long walk for pleasure (usu. in the country). Also *vi*. **hiker** *nc*.

hilarious [hi'lɛəriəs] *adj* **1.** loud and happy. **2.** causing one to be very amused: *a hilarious film*. **hilariously** *adv*. **hilarity** [hi'læriti] *nu*.

hill [hil] *nc* **1.** piece of raised ground; small mountain. **2.** slope, steep part of a road. *The bus got stuck on the hill*.
hilly *adj* having many hills. *comparative* **hillier**. *superlative* **hilliest**.
'hillside side of a hill.
'ant-hill small hill made by ants.

hillock ['hilək] *nc* small hill.

hilt [hilt] *nc* handle of a sword or dagger.
(up) to the hilt completely. (*informal*).

him [him] *pron* form which **he** takes when it is the object of a verb or preposition. *You saw him there. Give it to him*.
Note: It's him.

hind[1] [haind] *nc* female deer.

hind[2] [haind] *adj* at the back (usu. of the back legs of animals). *The dog has hurt its hind leg*.
'hindquarters the part of an animal's back above the hind legs.

hinder ['hində*] *vt* stop, try to stop, somebody from doing something; delay. *The crowd hindered him from leaving. I was hindered by the heavy traffic*.

hindmost ['haindmoust] *adj* farthest behind.

hindrance ['hindrns] *nc* somebody/something that hinders. *Children are a hindrance when you wish to work quietly*.

hindsight ['haindsait] *nu* ability to look back at the past in order to see how one ought to have acted.

Hindu ['hin'du:] *nc* follower of Hinduism. Also *adj*.
Hinduism ['hindu:izəm] *nu* religion of most of the people of India.

hinge [hindʒ] *nc* piece of metal which joins two things so that they can open and shut (e.g. on a door, gate or box with a lid). *The door opens easily because the hinges are oiled*. Also *vi* **1.** depend. *The result hinges on/upon his reply*. **2.** be attached to and turn on. *The door should hinge upon this post*.

hint [hint] *vt/i* say something in an indirect, roundabout way; suggest. *He hinted that I should go. They hinted at his bad behaviour*. Also *nc*: *They gave no hint of their plans. I took the hint and left at once* i.e. I was able to see, without being told, that I should leave and did so. *This book is full of good hints* i.e. good suggestions.

hinterland ['hintəlænd] *nu* country behind a coast, large river or large city. *The hinterland of West Africa was not known to many Europeans a hundred years ago*.

hip[1] [hip] *nc* top of the leg where it joins the side of the body.
'hip flask small flat bottle of whisky, brandy etc carried in a hip pocket.
'hip 'pocket trouser pocket over the hip.

hip[2] [hip] *nc* fruit of the wild rose.

hip[3] [hip] *interj* (only in **hip, hip, hurrah!**). see **hurrah**.

hippodrome ['hipədroum] *nc* place for racing horses or chariots (in ancient Greece and Rome).

hippopotamus [hipə'pɔtəməs] *nc* very large African animal found in rivers and lakes. *pl* **hippopotamuses** or **hippopotami** [hipə'pɔtəmai].

hire ['haiə*] *vt* give or get the use of something for an agreed price. *They hire (out) boats to people on holiday. I hired a boat so that I could go fishing*. Also *nu*: *boats on/for hire*.
Note: *hire* is for a short period and a definite purpose. *They want to hire a hall for the concert*. *Rent* is usu. for a long(er) period and for general purposes. *He rented a house for the summer*.
hireling *nc* person who can be hired. (*impolite*).
'hire 'purchase method of paying for goods by which one can use the goods while making payments towards the total amount.

hirsute ['hə:sju:t] *adj* very hairy.

his [hiz] *pron* what belongs to him. *We'll have to separate his from yours*. Also *determiner* form which **he** takes to show possession. *It's his book/problem etc*. Also *pred adj* belonging to him. *The suit is his*.

hiss [his] *vt/i* make a sound like the letter 's'. *Snakes hiss when angry. The crowd hissed (at) him as he passed* i.e. made this sound to show they did not like him. Also *nc*: *the hisses of the crowd*.

histology [his'tɔlədʒi] *nu* science dealing with the way living matter is formed.

history ['histəri] *nc* the study or record of the past. *History is his main subject at college. They are writing a new history of Africa*.
historian [his'tɔ:riən] *nc* person who studies and writes history.
historic [his'tɔrik] *adj* famous or important in history: *a historic battle*.
historical [his'tɔrikl] *adj* actually happening in history; dealing with history: *a historical novel* i.e. one describing actual events and people in history, rather than imaginary ones; *from a historical point of view* i.e. from the point of view of history.
historically *adv*.
natural history the scientific description of nature.
make history do something important which will become part of history.

histrionic [histri'ɔnik] *adj* of acting in a theatre; like an actor: *histrionic behaviour* i.e. behaving like an actor by acting a part and trying to attract attention.
histrionics *npl* histrionic behaviour.

hit[1] [hit] *vt* **1.** strike; give a blow to; reach something aimed at; collide with; bring something against something else with force. *He hit me on the chest. I am hitting the nail with a hammer. The bullet hit the target. The car hit the wall. He hit his hand on/against the door*. **2.** (usu. with **hard**) cause to suffer. *The death of his father hit him hard. The farmers were hard hit by the drought*. **3.** (often with **on** or **upon**) reach; find. *At last we hit the main road. I have hit upon a new way of doing it*. *pres part* **hitting**. *past* **hit**.
hit it off (with somebody) become friendly quickly. *They hit it off well. I was able to hit it off with them*. (*informal*).
hit out at someone attack; defend oneself strongly against. *The author hits out at his critics in his book*.

hit[2] [hit] *nc* **1.** blow or stroke. **2.** great success. *This song is one of the hits of the year*.

hitch[1] [hitʃ] *vt* **1.** raise with a quick movement. *He hitched up his trousers*. **2.** fasten by a rope (usu. quickly and easily). *They hitched the horses to the wagon*.

hitch[2] [hitʃ] *nc* 1. sudden pull or push. 2. type of knot made in a rope. 3. something that causes a delay. *There has been a hitch in the discussions.*

hitchhike ['hitʃhaik] *vi* travel by getting free lifts in cars or lorries. **hitchhiker** *nc.*

hither ['hiðə*] *adv* to this place; to here (*o.f.*).

hitherto ['hiðə'tu:] *adv* up to now.

hive [haiv] *nc* place where bees live; type of box made for them to live in; the bees themselves in the hive. Also *vt/i* enter, cause to enter, a hive. *The bees are hiving. Hiving bees is a dangerous job.*

hive (something) off give part of a job to some other person or organization.

hives [haivz] *nu* type of skin disease with an irritating rash.

hoar [hɔ:*] *adj* (usu. with reference to hair) grey or white with age (*o.f.*).

'hoar'frost frost that makes the ground white.

hoard [hɔ:d] *nc* secret store of something (esp. money or food). Also *vt.* **hoarder** *nc.*

hoarding ['hɔ:diŋ] *nc* 1. temporary wooden fence round a house or piece of land. 2. very large board on which advertisements are stuck.

hoarse [hɔ:s] *adj* 1. rough and harsh sounding: *a hoarse cry.* 2. having a hoarse voice. *I am hoarse because I have a bad cold.*

hoarsely *adv.* **hoarseness** *nu.*

hoary ['hɔ:ri] *adj* 1. grey or white with age. 2. very old. *He tells hoary jokes.*

hoax [houks] *vt* trick or deceive somebody as a joke. *The people were hoaxed by his false story.* Also *nc*: *The report that a bomb had been put in the room was a hoax.*

hob [hɔb] *nc* metal shelf at the side of a fireplace on which pots are kept warm.

hobble ['hɔbl] 1. *vi* walk as when one leg is injured; limp. 2. *vt* tie the legs of an animal with a short rope so that it cannot run away.

hobby ['hɔbi] *nc* activity which one likes doing in one's spare time. *Gardening is the hobby of many businessmen.*

hobby-horse ['hɔbihɔ:s] *nc* wooden horse used as a child's toy.

be/get on one's hobby-horse talk at length about something of special interest only to oneself. (*informal*).

hobgoblin ['hɔb'gɔblin] *nc* ugly spirit which is full of tricks.

hobnail ['hɔbneil] *nc* nail with a large head used in the soles of boots or shoes.

hobnailed *adj* having hobnails. *Soldiers wear hobnailed boots.*

hobnob ['hɔbnɔb] *vi* have a friendly talk or drink with somebody. *I like to hobnob with my friends in a quiet bar. past* **hobnobbed.**

hobo ['houbou] *nc* (*US*) person without work who wanders from place to place. *pl* **hoboes** or **hobos.** (*informal*).

hock[1] [hɔk] *nc* joint in the middle of an animal's back leg.

hock[2] [hɔk] *nc* type of white wine.

hockey ['hɔki] *nu* 1. (*Brit*) team game played on a field with a ball and curved sticks. (*US* **field hockey**). 2. (*US*) similar game played on ice. (*Brit* **ice hockey**).

hocus-pocus ['houkəs'poukəs] *nu* talk that is intended to deceive somebody. (*informal*).

hod [hɔd] *nc* V-shaped container with a long handle used for carrying bricks.

hodgepodge ['hɔdʒpɔdʒ] *nu* (*US*) see **hotchpotch.**

hoe [hou] *nc* tool for digging the soil and clearing weeds.

hog [hɔg] *nc* 1. (esp. *US*) a pig; a castrated male pig. 2. dirty greedy person. Also *vt* take more than one's share. *He hogged the road* i.e. he did not keep to his proper side but travelled in the middle. *past* **hogged.** (*informal*).

hoggish *adj* dirty and greedy.

go the whole hog do something completely. (*informal*).

hoist [hɔist] *vt* lift; raise up (usu. by pulling a rope): *hoist a flag/sail.* Also *nc* apparatus used for hoisting.

hoity-toity ['hɔiti'tɔiti] *adj* (usu. of persons and their behaviour) loud, trying to sound important. (*informal*).

hold[1] [hould] *vt/i* 1. keep with or in the hands. *They held me so that I could not move. Please hold my bag for me.* 2. keep with a part of the body. *She was holding the baby in both arms. He held the rope in/with his teeth.* 3. keep back or under control. *Hold your tongue!* i.e. be quiet. *We held our breath. There is no holding him when he is angry.* 4. keep in a certain position or condition. *I held my hands at my side. They held their heads high. They are holding themselves ready. The speech held our attention.* 5. contain; be able to contain. *How much does this bag hold?* 6. have or keep in mind; think. *He holds strange views about art. I hold that they are wrong.* 7. possess; occupy. *He holds 500 acres of land. I held the job for two years.* 8. continue as it is. *I hope this weather holds. This law still holds good* i.e. is still in force; it has not changed. *past* **held** [held].

holding *nc* something possessed or occupied. *I have holdings in the business* i.e. shares. *He has a small holding near here* i.e. he possesses or occupies a small farm.

hold (oneself) aloof keep away from other people.

hold back be unwilling to do something.

hold somebody back keep somebody from going forward or doing something.

hold something back keep something secret. *He is holding back important information.*

hold forth speak for a long time (usu. without good reason).

hold something in keep in; keep to oneself; control. *It was difficult to hold in our anger.*

hold (someone) off stay or keep at a distance. *I hope the rain holds off. He held him off with a stick.*

hold on wait. *Hold on a minute!* (*informal*).

hold on to something keep (firmly) in one's hands or possession. *He held on to the rope. You should hold on to your lovely house.*

hold out refuse to give up; endure; last. *The troops held out for a week. The water won't hold out much longer.*

hold something out offer; promise. *I can hold out no hope for you.*

hold something over keep until later; postpone.

hold together keep together. *The box is held together with a few nails.*

hold up 1. delay. *The storm held us up.* 2. stop in order to rob. *The thieves held up the van and took everything in it.* 3. raise or show so that others see. *Hold up your exercise books! They held him up to ridicule* i.e. they caused other people to laugh at him by showing his weaknesses etc.

'holdup *nc* 1. delay. 2. robbery with violence

hold with something agree with; approve. *I don't hold with gambling.* (*informal*).

hold² [hould] **1.** *nu* act of holding: *catch/lay/seize/take hold of somebody/something.* (*opp* **let go/lose (one's) hold**). **2.** *nc* something which can be held on to. *There were no holds for the hands on the wall. He found a foothold* i.e. a place to support his foot while climbing.

hold³ [hould] *nc* place below the deck of a ship where the cargo is put.

hole [houl] *nc* **1.** opening or space in something. *There is a hole in the roof, which lets in the rain. They dug a big hole in the ground. Golf courses have either nine or eighteen holes.* **2.** small miserable place. *Who wants to live in a hole like this?* (*informal*). **3.** difficulty; trouble. *Having no money puts me in a hole.* (*informal*). Also *vt* **1.** cause to have a hole. **2.** (golf) put in a hole. *He holed the ball from a distance of twenty feet.*

'hole-and-'corner *adj* secret and dishonest. (*informal*).

make a hole in make much less in amount. *He soon made a hole in the money his father gave him.* (*informal*).

pick holes in something see **pick**².

holiday ['hɔlidei] *nc* **1.** day free from work. *The headmaster has made Friday a holiday.* **2.** (often *pl*) any period of time free from work. *The school is closed for Christmas/summer holidays. They went on holiday last week.*

'holidaymaker person on holiday.

'half-'holiday holiday for half a day.

holiness ['houlinis] *nu* condition of being holy.

hollow¹ ['hɔlou] *adj/adv* **1.** not solid; empty inside. *Pipes are hollow.* **2.** giving a sound like that made by something hollow. *He has a hollow voice.* **3.** false; not to be relied upon. *These are hollow words. It was a hollow victory.* Also *adv* completely. *They beat us hollow.* (*informal*).

hollow² ['hɔlou] *nc* wide, shallow hole; ground which is lower than the surrounding area. *The cottage is in that hollow.* Also *adj* like a hollow: *hollow eyes/cheeks* i.e. sunken. Also *vt* make a hollow in.

hollow something out form by making a hollow in something.

holly ['hɔli] *nu* type of evergreen tree with sharp pointed leaves and red or yellow berries, used as decoration at Christmas.

hollyhock ['hɔlihɔk] *nc* type of tall garden plant with colourful flowers.

holocaust ['hɔləkɔːst] *nc* complete destruction (usu. by fire).

holster ['houlstə*] *nc* case in which a pistol or revolver is carried (usu. over the hip).

holy ['houli] *adj* of God or a religion; good and pure: *the Holy Bible; the Holy Koran; a holy man; a holy life.* (*opp* **unholy**). **holiness** *nu*.

holy terror person, often a child, who causes great terror or annoyance. (*informal*).

take holy orders see **order**¹.

homage ['hɔmidʒ] *nu* **1.** (in former times) an act of loyalty to one's lord or chief. *The nobles came to pay homage to the king.* **2.** act of respect to somebody famous (and usu. dead). *We all paid homage to the great man.*

home [houm] **1.** *nc/u* house or place where one was born. **2.** *nc* house or place where one lives. *He has a pleasant home near the river. England was his home. The home of the lion is Africa.* **3.** *nc* special building for persons needing help or attention: *a home for the aged; a children's home; a nursing home.* Also *adj* of the home or one's own country or the place one belongs to: *the home team; a home game; home cooking; home trade.* Also *adv* **1.** at or to one's home or one's own country. *They went home. He's home.* **2.** place which is meant to be hit. *The bullet went home. His remarks ought to go home* i.e. influence those who hear them.

homeless *adj* without a home.

homelike *adj* like home.

'homecoming coming to one's own home.

'Home 'Counties the counties of England around London.

'home 'farm farm attached to a large country house.

'home-'grown *adj* grown in one's own country i.e. not abroad.

'homeland one's own country.

'home-'made *adj* made at home, not in a factory.

'homesick *adj* longing to be at home. **homesickness** *nu*.

'homespun *nc* cloth spun at home. Also *adj* anything plain or homely.

'homestead farmhouse and the buildings round it.

'home 'truth truth that someone tells one about another person or about oneself (often an unpleasant truth).

'homework work done at home (usu. by a school pupil in the evening).

at home **1.** in one's own house. *I keep my tools at home.* **2.** at the place one belongs to (usu. a sports team). *Our football team plays at home next Saturday.* (*opp* **away** in sense **2.**).

'at-'home *nc* party held in one's home to receive guests.

be at home with/in be familiar with; be good at. *He is quite at home with problems like this.*

bring something home to somebody make somebody realize something.

feel at home be comfortable as if one were at home.

make oneself at home make oneself comfortable as if one were at home.

homely ['houmli] *adj* plain and simple: *homely speech; homely food.*

Note: (*US*) *homely* used of people has the sense of *ugly*: *a homely face* i.e. a face that is plain, not good-looking.

homeopathy [houmi'ɔpəθi] *nu* see **homoeopathy.**

homicide ['hɔmisaid] **1.** *nu* killing of another person. **2.** *nc* person who kills another. **homicidal** [hɔmi'saidl] *adj.* **homicidally** *adv.*

homily ['hɔmili] *nc* long, dull talk (usu. about good behaviour). **homiletic** [hɔmi'letik] *adj.*

homing ['houmiŋ] *adj* returning home; hitting what is aimed at: *a homing pigeon* i.e. a pigeon which can find its own way home wherever it is set free, and which is used for carrying messages; *a homing rocket/torpedo* i.e. one that has special apparatus which guides it to its target.

homoeopathy, homeopathy [houmi'ɔpəθi] *nu* treatment of a disease by giving small amounts of medicine which produce symptoms like that disease. **homoeopath** ['houmiəpæθ] *nc.* **homoeopathic** [houmiə'pæθik] *adj.*

homogeneous [hɔmə'dʒiːniəs] *adj* of the same kind throughout. *The people of this* *country are homogeneous* i.e. they are all of one kind. **homogeneity** [hɔmoudʒi'ni:iti] *nu.*

homonym ['hɔmənim] *nc* word which has the same sound and/or spelling as another word but has a different meaning (e.g. *bear* and *bare*).

homo sapiens ['houmou'sapienz] *n* formal, scientific name for modern man.

homosexual ['hɔmou'seksjuəl] *adj* loving somebody of the same sex (e.g. a man loving a man instead of a woman). Also *nc* a person (usu. a man) who loves in this way. **homosexuality** ['hɔmouseksju'æliti] *nu.*
Note: the usual word for a homosexual woman is *lesbian.*

honest ['ɔnist] *adj* true; fair; not cheating. *He is honest in all he does. They gave me an honest answer; an honest face* i.e. the face of an honest person. (*opp* **dishonest**).
honestly *adv* **1.** in an honest way. *He got the money honestly.* **2.** truly; in fact. *Honestly, I don't know.* **honesty** *nu.*

honey ['hʌni] *nu* **1.** the sweet, thick liquid made by bees. **2.** (*US*) darling. *I love you, honey.* (*informal* in sense **2.**).
honeyed *adj* sweet; flattering: *honeyed words.*
'honeycomb *nc* **1.** thing consisting of very small six-sided cells in which bees store honey and eggs. **2.** anything like this. Also *vt* make many holes in. *The hill is honeycombed with caves.* Also *adj.*
'honeysuckle type of sweet-smelling climbing plant.

honeymoon ['hʌnimu:n] *nc* the holiday taken by a husband and wife immediately after their marriage. Also *vi* have a honeymoon.

honk [hɔŋk] *nc* noise made by a goose; any noise like this (esp. the noise made by the horn of a motorcar). Also *vi* make a honk.

honorarium [ɔnə'rɛəriəm] *nc* amount of money given, without being asked for, to a person for his services. *pl* **honoraria** [ɔnə'rɛəriə].

honorary ['ɔnərəri] *adj* **1.** working without pay: *the honorary secretary of our club* (usu. written *hon. secretary*). **2.** given as an honour: *an honorary degree of the university; honorary membership of the students' society.*

honorific [ɔnə'rifik] *adj* giving honour or respect (usu. by using special words). Also *nc* an honorific word or form of address. *Her/His Majesty* is an honorific.

honour[1] ['ɔnə*] (*US* **honor**) **1.** *nu* great respect; high regard. *There will be a special meeting in honour of the President.* **2.** *nu* good character or reputation. *He is a man of honour. They fight for the honour of their country. I promise on my honour that it will be done.* **3.** *nu* person/thing which brings honour. *You are an honour to your school.* **4.** *nc* title of respect (usu. to a judge). *His Honour the Judge; I am not guilty, Your Honour.* **5.** *nc* (usu. *pl*) act or title that gives honour or respect to somebody. *The general was buried with military honours* i.e. with special acts of respect (e.g. the playing of military music, the firing of guns etc); *birthday honours* i.e. the list of honours (in sense **5.**) given by the King or Queen of Great Britain on his or her birthday. *He took honours at this university* i.e. a type of degree which is better than an ordinary one; *an honours degree.* **6.** *nc* the four or five highest playing cards i.e. ace, king, queen, jack/knave, ten. **7.** *nu* in certain phrases to show respect and politeness. *He will have the honour of introducing the next speaker. It is our/an honour to have with us today the school governors. I have the honour to inform you . . .*
debt of honour see **debt.**
guard of honour see **guard**[2].
honour bound *pred adj* required (to do something) to keep one's honour. *I am honour bound to help him.*
honours of war honours paid to a brave enemy who has been defeated.
put somebody on his honour get somebody to promise (to do something) or else lose his honour.
word of honour see **word.**

honour[2] ['ɔnə*] (*US* **honor**) *vt* **1.** respect greatly; give or feel honour. *Children should honour their father and mother. The king honoured him with a knighthood. I am honoured to be asked to speak.* **2.** pay a bill/cheque etc when one has promised to. *He has not enough money to honour his cheques.* (*opp* **dishonour**).
honour one's signature pay a bill etc one has promised to pay by signing it.

honourable ['ɔnərəbl] (*US* **honorable**) *adj* **1.** deserving or satisfying honour. *He has done honourable work. We must have an honourable peace.* (*opp* **dishonourable**). **2.** (**Honourable**) title of respect given to certain ranks, and when talking about a Member of Parliament in Parliament. *The Honourable member is wrong.*
Note: in Parliament and other assemblies of the same kind a member is not usu. allowed to address another member as 'you'. He must use the third person because he has to address all his remarks to the Speaker or chairman.
honourably *adv.*

hooch [hu:tʃ] *nu* (*US*) alcoholic liquor. (*informal*).

hood [hud] *nc* **1.** cloth covering for the head and neck, often part of a cloak or gown. **2.** part of a university graduate's gown which hangs down the back and shows by its colour his university and type of degree. **3.** type of covering with other uses (e.g. the soft, folding cover on top of a carriage or motorcar, the covering over a chimney. **4.** (*US*) cover over the engine in the front of a car. (*Brit* **bonnet**). **5.** (*US*) a criminal. (*informal* in sense **5.**). Also *vt* cover with a hood.
hooded *adj*: *hooded eyes* i.e. half-closed eyes.

hoodlum ['hu:dləm] *nc* rough person of the streets; hooligan.

hoodoo ['hu:du:] *nc* bad luck; person/thing causing bad luck.

hoodwink ['hudwiŋk] *vt* cheat; deceive.

hoof [hu:f] *nc* the hard part of the foot of a horse, cow, sheep etc. *pl* **hooves** [hu:vz].

hook[1] [huk] *nc* **1.** bent piece of metal etc shaped like a J used to catch something or hang something up: *a fish hook; a boat hook; a meat hook.* **2.** curved tool for cutting grass and branches. **3.** type of stroke in cricket, golf etc by which the ball is sent to one side; type of blow made in boxing with the elbow bent.
'hook-'nosed *adj* having a nose like a hook.
'hookworm worm that gets into the intestines.
hook, line and sinker **1.** three pieces of apparatus used when fishing. **2.** completely. *They were cheated hook, line and sinker.* (*informal* in sense **2.**).
by hook or by crook *adv* in any way possible. (*informal*).

hook[2] [huk] *vt/i* **1.** fasten, hang or catch with a hook or hooks. *This dress hooks down the side. He hooked up his coat. I have hooked a fish.* **2.** put in the shape of a hook. *He hooked his fingers over the branch.* **3.** make a stroke in cricket or golf which sends the ball to one side. *The golfer hooked the ball into the bushes*; give a blow in boxing with the elbow bent. *He hooked him twice on/to the head.*

hooked *adj* **1.** having hooks; shaped like a hook. **2.** addicted: *hooked on drugs.*

'hookup *nc* joining together of several radio or television stations to send out the same programme.

hookah ['hukə] *nc* tobacco pipe in which the smoke passes through water and a long tube.

hook(e)y ['huki] *nu* (*US*) absence from school without permission. (*informal*) (*Brit* **truancy**).

play hookey be absent in this way; play truant. (*informal*).

hooligan ['hu:ligən] *nc* rough, noisy person who fights or causes trouble in the streets. **hooliganism** *nu.*

hoop[1] [hu:p] *nc* thin ring of metal, wood, plastic etc. *Wooden barrels are fitted with iron hoops.* Also *vt* put a hoop on something.

put somebody through the hoops test or question severely. (*informal*).

hoop[2] [hu:p] *vi* see **whoop.**

hoop-la ['hu:plɑ:] *nu* game played by throwing small hoops at objects which are won as prizes if a hoop falls over them.

hoot [hu:t] *nc* **1.** noise made by an owl. **2.** sound showing anger, disapproval, amusement etc. **3.** noise made by the horn of a motorcar, factory whistle etc. Also *vt/i*: *I heard an owl hooting. He hooted with laughter. They hooted him down* i.e. shouted in anger so that he could not be heard. *At the corner I hooted my horn.*

hooter *nc* factory whistle or siren (esp. used to signal when work begins and stops).

hooves [hu:vz] pl of **hoof.**

hop[1] [hɔp] *nc* type of climbing plant or its fruit (used to flavour beer). Also *vi* gather hops. *pres part* **hopping.** *past* **hopped.**

'hop field, 'hop garden place where hops are grown.

'hop picker person or machine that gathers hops.

hop[2] [hɔp] *vt/i* (of persons) jump on one foot; (of birds and animals) jump on both or all feet.

hopper *nc* **1.** insect etc that hops. **2.** container with a big opening at the top and a small one at the bottom for putting grain etc into.

'hedgehopping flying in an aeroplane at a very low height. (*informal*).

hop it go away. (*informal*).

hop[3] [hɔp] *nc* **1.** short jump. **2.** short flight in an aeroplane as part of a long journey. **3.** party or gathering arranged for the purpose of dancing. (*informal* in senses **2.** and **3.**).

'hopscotch game in which children hop on one foot and kick a small stone over lines drawn on the ground.

hop, step/skip and jump game or competition in which these three movements are made one after the other.

hope[1] [houp] *vt/i* wish or expect that something will happen. *I hope (that) you will come. We hope to see you again. Will he come? I hope so. Will they be angry? We hope not. They hoped for victory.*

hope against hope hope when there is little reason to hope.

hope[2] [houp] *nc/u* wish or feeling that something good will happen. *We have some hope of success. There is little hope that he will come. I have great hopes of victory.*

hopeful *adj* having or giving hope. *They continue to be hopeful. This is hopeful news. He is one of our most hopeful scientists* i.e. one who is likely to be very successful. Also *nc*: *one of our hopefuls.* **hopefully** *adv.* **hopefulness** *nu.*

hopeless *adj* having no hope. *The situation is hopeless. You are completely hopeless* i.e. you are so bad, weak etc that there is no hope for you. **hopelessly** *adv.* **hopelessness** *nu.*

past/beyond hope without any chance of becoming better.

raise somebody's hopes make somebody more hopeful.

horde [hɔ:d] *nc* large number of people or animals (usu. not under control). *Hordes of people tried to get into the hall.*

horizon [hə'raizn] *nc* line where the sky seems to meet the earth or sea. *We saw a ship far away on the horizon.*

horizontal [hɔri'zɔntl] *adj* parallel to the horizon; level. (*opp* **vertical**). Also *nc* horizontal line or bar. **horizontally** *adv.*

hormone ['hɔ:moun] *nc* type of chemical substance made by certain glands of the body.

horn [hɔ:n] **1.** *nc* hard, pointed growth projecting from the head of certain animals (e.g. cattle). *A bull has two horns.* **2.** *nu* the substance which forms a horn. *The dagger has a handle of horn.* **3.** *nc* article made from this substance: *a drinking horn.* **4.** *nc* type of musical instrument, played by blowing into it (now usu. made of metal, not horn): *a hunting horn.* **5.** *nc* type of instrument for making a warning noise: *a motor horn; a foghorn.* **6.** *nc* one of the tips of the crescent moon.

horny *adj* of horn; as hard as horn. *He has horny hands.*

horned *adj* having horns: *horned deer.*

hornless *adj* without horns.

'horn-'rimmed *adj* (used only of spectacles) having a frame made of horn or some substance which looks like horn.

horn in (*US*) enter without being asked: *horn in on a conversation.* (*informal*).

take the bull by the horns see **take.**

on the horns of a dilemma having to choose between two things which are equally bad.

draw in one's horns become less active or ambitious; spend less money.

horn of plenty see **cornucopia.**

hornbeam ['hɔ:nbi:m] **1.** *nc* type of tree with hard wood. **2.** *nu* the wood of this tree.

hornbill ['hɔ:nbil] *nc* type of large bird with a growth like a horn on its bill.

hornet ['hɔ:nit] *nc* type of large wasp, which can sting severely.

hornpipe ['hɔ:npaip] *nc* type of dance for one person (usu. a sailor); music for this dance.

horoscope ['hɔrəskoup] *nc* plan of the positions of the stars (esp. at the time of a person's birth) from which it is believed his future can be told.

horrible ['hɔribl] *adj* **1.** causing horror; dreadful: *horrible injuries.* **2.** very unpleasant. *This food is horrible.* **horribly** *adv.*

horrid ['hɔrid] *adj* very unpleasant; disgusting. *Why are you so horrid to him?* **horridly** *adv.* **horridness** *nu.*

horrify ['hɔrifai] *vt* cause, or fill with, horror. **horrified** *adj.*

horror ['hɔrə*] *nc* feeling of great fear etc. *She has a horror of small insects. Rock climbing has no horrors for me. To their horror the roof of their house caught fire. They ran in horror from the room.*

'horror-struck/-stricken *adj* filled with horror.

hors d'oeuvre [ɔː'dəːvr] *nc* light savoury dish eaten before the main part of a meal.

horse [hɔːs] *nc* **1.** type of animal used for riding, carrying loads and pulling vehicles. **2.** apparatus which looks like a horse (e.g. in a gymnasium, a box with a leather top and with or without legs, for jumping over). **horsy** *adj* **1.** like a horse. **2.** fond of horses and horse-racing. **horsiness** *nu.*

horseless *adj* without a horse.

'horseback only in **on horseback** i.e. on the back of a horse.

'horse box large box in which a horse is carried from one place to another.

'horse 'chestnut *nc* **1.** type of tree with large leaves. **2.** inedible nut of this tree.

'horseflesh **1.** the flesh of horses (esp. as food). **2.** horses collectively (usu. in **a good judge of horseflesh** a person who can judge the good and bad points of a horse).

'horsefly type of fly that attacks horses etc.

'horseman *nc* man on horseback; man skilled in riding a horse.

'horsemanship *nu* skill or art of riding a horse.

'horseplay rough, noisy play.

'horsepower a measure of the power of an engine i.e. the power needed to lift 550 pounds to a height of one foot in one second (usu. shortened to *h.p.*).

'horse-race race between horses with riders.

'horseradish type of plant used for making sauce.

'horse-sense (mainly *US*) common sense. (*informal*).

'horseshoe iron shoe shaped like a U which is nailed to the hoof of a horse.

'horsewhip *nc* whip used to strike horses. Also *vt* strike with a horsewhip. *past* **horsewhipped.**

'horsewoman woman on horseback; woman skilled in riding a horse.

a dark horse person who does something clever or successful when no one expected him to do so. (*informal*).

eat like a horse see **eat.**

flog a dead horse see **flog.**

get on one's high horse become proud or difficult in manner.

look a gift horse in the mouth find fault with something received as a gift. (*informal*).

put the cart before the horse see **put.**

straight from the horse's mouth (with reference to advice, information, news etc) from a reliable, first-hand source. (*informal*).

horticulture ['hɔːtikʌltʃə*] *nu* gardening; the growing of flowers, fruit and vegetables. **horticultural** [hɔːti'kʌltʃərl] *adj.* **horticulturist** [hɔːti'kʌltʃərist] *nc* person skilled in horticulture.

hosanna [hou'zænə] *nc* (in the Jewish religion) shout of praise to God.

hose[1] [houz] *nc* long soft pipe through which running water is passed (e.g. to put out a fire or water plants). Also *vt* water or wash with a hose. *The sailors hosed (down) the deck.*

'hosepipe type of large hose; part of a hose: *a short length of hosepipe.*

'fire hose type of large hose used for putting out fires.

hose[2] [houz] *nu* **1.** stockings; socks. **2.** (in former times) tight-fitting trousers worn by men.

hosier ['houziə*] *nc* person who sells hosiery. **hosiery** *nu* goods which include stockings, socks and underclothes.

hospice ['hɔspis] *nc* house for travellers to rest in or for the poor and the sick (usu. kept by a religious order).

hospitable [hɔs'pitəbl] *adj* friendly and kind to guests. (*opp* **inhospitable**). **hospitably** *adv.*

hospital ['hɔspitl] *nc* building(s) in which sick and injured people are attended to and cared for.

Note: hospital without *the* usu. has the sense of the attention and care given. *He is in hospital* i.e. he is staying there to be attended to. *He is in the hospital* i.e. he is there as a visitor or for some other reason, not to be attended to. *The driver left hospital* i.e. because he was now well he was able to go home. *The driver left the hospital* i.e. he did not go there to be attended to, but for some other reason, and left afterwards.

hospitality [hɔspi'tæliti] *nu* friendliness and kindness to guests. see **hospitable.**

host[1] [houst] *nc* **1.** large number. *He has a host of problems. We met hosts of students.* **2.** army: *the heavenly host* i.e. army of angels (*o.f.*).

host[2] [houst] *nc* **1.** person who receives and looks after guests. *Last night we were hosts to a few friends.* **2.** person in charge of an inn or hotel. *When we arrived at the hotel we asked to see the host (o.f.).* **3.** animal or plant which has very small organisms or parasites living in it. *This type of snail is the host of bilharzia.*

hostage ['hɔstidʒ] *nc* person handed over or kept as a prisoner until what has been promised or demanded is done. *The enemy took hostages from the village after they captured it* i.e. to make sure the people of the village remained quiet; *take someone hostage.*

hostel ['hɔstl] *nc* house in which students and young people etc live when they are away from home.

hostess ['houstes] *nc* woman who receives and looks after guests; wife of a host.

'air hostess stewardess in an airliner.

hostile ['hɔstail] *adj* of an enemy; unfriendly; opposed. *Bombing the town was a hostile act. The crowd outside is hostile. The people are hostile to any change.* **hostilely** *adv.*

hostility [hɔs'tiliti] **1.** *nu* unfriendliness; opposition. **2.** *nc* (in *pl*) war; acts of war. *Hostilities ended when the treaty was signed.*

hot [hɔt] *adj* **1.** having great heat; very warm. *The climate of that country is hot. Hot water is better than cold water for washing clothes. I feel hot. Pepper is hot* i.e. it has a hot taste. **2.** violent; very active; keen. *He has a hot temper. The argument became hot.* **3.** stolen and therefore dangerous to have: *hot goods.* (*informal* in sense **3.**). *comparative* **hotter.** *superlative* **hottest.**

hotly *adv*: *They argued hotly.*
hot air loud, useless talk. (*informal*).
'hotbed **1.** (gardening) a bed which makes plants grow quickly. **2.** place which causes anything to grow quickly. *Slums are hotbeds of crime.*
'hot-'blooded *adj* quick-tempered; passionate. **hot-bloodedly** *adv.*
'hot dog sandwich with a hot sausage inside.
'hothead *nc* hasty, passionate person.
'hot'headed *adj* hasty; passionate.
'hothouse heated building made of glass in which young and tender plants are grown.
hot line telephone connection between heads of state for use in emergencies.
hot news the latest news. (*informal*).
'hotplate heated metal plate on a stove.
'hotpot dish of meat and vegetables cooked in a covered pot (usu. in an oven).
hot potato something difficult to deal with. (*informal*).
'hot 'stuff person of great skill, ability or passion. *He's hot stuff on engines* i.e. he knows a lot about them. (*informal*).
'red-'hot **1.** very hot. **2.** excited. **3.** very recent.
'white-'hot *adj* even hotter than red-hot. *Melting iron is white-hot* i.e. it shines with a white light. *He was white-hot with rage.*
be in/get into hot water be in/get into trouble. (*informal*).
be hot on the trail/tracks of somebody/something be close behind and about to catch.
blow hot and cold keep changing from being eager or interested to the opposite. (*informal*).

hotchpotch ['hɔtʃpɔtʃ] *nu* (*Brit*) untidy mixture of many things. (*US* **hodgepodge**).

hotel [hou'tel] *nc* building which provides meals and rooms for travellers (usu. bigger than an inn).
Note: either *a hotel* or *an hotel.*

hound [haund] *nc* type of dog used in hunting (esp. hunting by its sense of smell). Also *vt* hunt with hounds; chase a person as if with hounds. *They hounded him out of the country.*

hour ['auə*] *nc* **1.** twenty-fourth part of a day; sixty minutes. *The journey took three hours. The meeting lasted hours. I'll see you in an hour's time.* **2.** indefinite period of time. *These were the most interesting hours of my life. They arrived at all hours.* **3.** definite period in time. *I heard the clock strike the hour. He arrived on the hour.* **4.** (in *pl*) fixed times. *Visiting hours at the hospital; office hours.* **5.** distance which takes an hour to travel. *My house is two hours from the town; a two hours' journey.* **6.** present time; a particular time: *the problem of the hour* i.e. the present problem; *in the hour of our defeat* i.e. at the time we were defeated. *He knew that his hour had come* i.e. that he was about to die.
hourly *adv* **1.** once every hour. *The clock strikes hourly.* **2.** at any hour. *His arrival is expected hourly.* Also *adj*: *an hourly train to London.*
'hourglass sand glass in which there is enough sand to measure one hour.
'hourhand the smaller hand or pointer on a clock or watch which shows the hours.
after hours after the usual hours of work or business. *Public houses must not stay open after hours.*
at the eleventh hour at the last possible moment. *Help came at the eleventh hour* i.e. very late.
keep early/good hours go to bed early and rise early. (*opp* **keep late/bad hours**).
out of hours before or after the usual hours of work or business.
the small hours the one or two hours after midnight. *They were still drinking in the small hours.*

house[1] [haus] *nc* **1.** building in which people live; building in which animals or goods are kept. *Our house has three bedrooms; a henhouse; a storehouse; a warehouse.* **2.** building where people meet for a certain purpose: *a picture house; a gambling house; a roadhouse; (Brit) the House of Commons; (US) the House of Representatives.* **3.** those in a house where people meet: *a full house* i.e. a hall or theatre full of people. *The Prime Minister addressed the House (of Commons).* **4.** family; dynasty. *He belongs to an ancient house. The House of Windsor* i.e. the British Royal family. *pl* **houses** ['hauziz].
houseful *nu* enough to fill a house: *a houseful of guests.*
'house agent (*Brit*) person whose business is selling and letting houses. (*US* **realtor**).
'houseboat flat-bottomed boat for living in rather than sailing.
'housebreaker *nc* person who breaks into a house to steal. **housebreaking** *nu.*
'housecoat type of long coat worn in the house by women.
'housedog dog trained to guard a house.
'housefly common fly, found in houses.
'household *nu* all the people who live in one house. Also *adj.*
household troops troops who guard the sovereign.
household word one so common that every household knows it.
'householder person living in a house who either owns it or has rented it.
'housekeeper *nc* woman who is employed to look after a house.
'housekeeping *nu* **1.** management of a house. *Good housekeeping saves money.* **2.** money for the management of a house.
'housemaid woman employed in a house (esp. to clean the rooms).
housemaid's knee type of painful swelling of the knee.
'housemaster teacher in charge of a part of a school.
'house party party of guests staying at a country house.
'house-proud *adj* proud and concerned about the appearance of one's house.
'house surgeon/physician surgeon who both lives and works in a hospital.
'house-trained *adj* trained to behave properly in a house (e.g. of a dog or cat).
'house warming party given to welcome friends to one's new house.
'housewife **1.** married woman responsible for the house where she lives. **2.** ['hʌzif] small container for needles and thread.
'housework work done in a house i.e. cleaning and cooking etc.
bring down the house be greatly applauded by an audience. (*informal*).
keep open house be very hospitable.
like a house on fire very well or quickly. *They get on like a house on fire* i.e. they are very friendly with each other. (*informal*).
under house arrest not allowed to leave one's house.

house[2] [hauz] *vt* **1.** put or take into a house; store. *They housed the visitors in the next village.* **2.** supply with houses.
housing *nu*: *The government has a serious housing problem.* Also *adj.*
'**housing estate** area in which a large number of new houses are built (usu. by a local authority).

hove [houv] past of **heave.**

hovel ['hɔvl] *nc* small, dirty and miserable house.

hover ['hɔvə*] *vi* **1.** stay almost still in the air. *The bird hovered over its nest.* **2.** stay near; wait. *The children hovered at the door.*
'**hovercraft** type of boat which travels just above the water, being held up by strong jets of air.

how [hau] *adv* **1.** in what way. *How did you do it?* **2.** to what degree. *How big is it? How many are there?* **3.** in what condition. *How are you? How do you do?* **4.** for what reason. *How is it that they are not here?* **5.** what is your opinion? *How about a cup of tea?* i.e. do you think we should have one? *How do you find your new school?* i.e. what do you think of it? **6.** as an exclamation. *How kind of you! How tall he is!* Also *conj*: *Tell me how you are.*
how'ever *adv* in whatever way; to whatever degree. *However loudly you shout, you won't be heard.* Also *conj* nevertheless.

howdah ['haudə] *nc* seat carried on an elephant's back.

howitzer ['hauitsə*] *nc* type of gun with a short barrel which fires shells into the air at a high angle.

howl [haul] *vt/i* give a long, loud cry; cry out loudly in anger, pain, laughter etc. *I could hear the wolves howling in the forest. We howled with laughter. The boy howled when he was hit. They howled him down* i.e. shouted angrily so that he could not be heard. Also *nc.*
howling *adj* obvious; very great. *It was a howling success.* (*informal*).
howler *nc* stupid but amusing mistake (esp. one by a student or pupil) (*informal*).

hoyden ['hɔidn] *nc* rude, bold girl. **hoydenish** *adj.*

hub [hʌb] *nc* **1.** central part of a wheel. **2.** central and important part of anything. *This office is the hub of the whole company.*

hubbub ['hʌbʌb] *nu* uproar; confused noise. *I could not hear myself speak above the hubbub.*

hubby ['hʌbi] *nc* short informal form of **husband.**

huckaback ['hʌkəbæk] *nu* type of strong, coarse cloth (often used to make towels).

huckster ['hʌkstə*] *nc* person who sells small articles; hawker.

huddle ['hʌdl] *vt/i* crowd together. *We all huddled round the fire. They huddled the poor children into a corner.* Also *nc* confused crowd or heap.
huddle (oneself) up bend oneself by bringing the knees and head together. *He was huddled up under a blanket.*
go into a huddle come together to discuss something in private. (*informal*).

hue[1] [hjuː] *nc* colour: *the hues of the woods in autumn.*
-hued *adj* having a hue: *light-hued.*

hue[2] [hjuː] *nu* shout (only in **hue and cry** i.e. a cry of warning when a criminal is being chased or a cry of protest against an injustice).

huff [hʌf] *nu* fit of bad temper. *He walked away in a huff.* **huffy** *adj.* **huffily** *adv.* **huffiness** *nu.* (all *informal*).

hug [hʌg] *vt* **1.** hold tightly in the arms (esp. to show love or pleasure). *She hugged her sister when she met her.* **2.** be very pleased with oneself. *He hugged himself over the easy way he had won.* **3.** keep close to. *The boat is hugging the coast. We hugged the wall to avoid being seen.* Also *nc*: *Give me a hug.* *pres part* **hugging.** *past* **hugged.**

huge [hjuːdʒ] *adj* very great. **hugeness** *nu.* **hugely** *adv* very much.

hulk [hʌlk] *nc* **1.** ship that is too old to be used at sea. **2.** big clumsy person.
hulking *adj* clumsy; unwieldy.

hull[1] [hʌl] *nc* outer covering of fruits, seeds or grains. Also *vt* take off the hull.

hull[2] [hʌl] *nc* frame or body of a ship.

hullabaloo [hʌləbə'luː] *nu* noisy disturbance; uproar.

hullo [hʌ'lou] *interj* used to greet, call attention, show surprise and answer telephone calls. *pl* **hullos.** (Also **hallo, hello**).

hum [hʌm] *vt/i* **1.** sing with the mouth shut; make a sound like the letter *m* for a long time. *He hummed the tune to me. I hear the insects humming.* **2.** be busy, full of activity. *The office is humming with activity* i.e. it is filled with the sounds of busy people. Also *nc* humming noise. *There was a hum of approval.*
'**hummingbird** type of small bird whose wings make a humming noise.
hum and haw hesitate, be undecided about something.
make things hum cause activity. *The new headmaster has made things hum in our school.* (*informal*).

human ['hjuːmən] *adj* of man; having the qualities of man. *There is no human life on Mars. To starve a child is not human.*
humanly *adv*: *It is not humanly possible* i.e. within the powers of man.
humanism *nu* **1.** belief that man is most important, not God or nature. **2.** 15th and 16th century study of classical Latin and Greek literature etc. **humanist** *nc* (in sense **1.**).
humanitarian [hjuːmæni'tɛəriən] *nc* person who loves man and tries to make his troubles less. *All humanitarians fought against slavery.* Also *adj*: *the humanitarian view that punishment is wrong.*
humanity [hju'mæniti] *nu* **1.** the human race; human nature. **2.** behaviour expected of man; kindness. *They treated the prisoners with humanity.*
humanities *npl* studies of the Arts i.e. of history, literature, philosophy etc.
humanize *vt* make human or humane: *the humanizing influence of the Red Cross.*
humane [hju'mein] *adj* gentle; kind-hearted: *the humane treatment of prisoners.* (*opp* **inhumane**). **humanely** *adv.* **humaneness** *nu.*
humane killer apparatus for killing animals without causing them pain.

humble ['hʌmbl] *adj* **1.** having no pride in oneself; modest. *Why were you so humble in the manager's office?* **2.** of low rank; poor. *He is of humble birth. They live in a humble street.* Also *vt* make humble. *The results humbled him.* **humbly** *adv.* **humbleness** *nu.*
eat humble pie see **eat.**
your humble servant used at the end of a formal, official letter (*o.f.*).

humbug ['hʌmbʌg] **1.** *nu* dishonest talk or behaviour; nonsense. **2.** *nc* dishonest person. **3.** *nc* type of hard sweet. Also *vt. past* **humbugged.**

humdrum ['hʌmdrʌm] *adj* dull; unexciting. *Life in a small village can be very humdrum.*

humid ['hju:mid] *adj* (usu. of the air or climate) damp. **humidity** [hju'miditi] *nu.* **humidify** [hju'midifai] *vt* make humid. **humidifier** [hju'midifaiə*] *nc* apparatus for making air humid.

humiliate [hju:'milieit] *vt* make ashamed; hurt the pride of. *They humiliated us by laughing at everything we said.* **humiliating** *adj.* **humiliatingly** *adv.* **humiliation** [hju:mili'eiʃən] *nc/u.*
humility [hju:'militi] *nu* being humble or without pride.

hummock ['hʌmək] *nc* small hill; mound.

humour ['hju:mə*] (*US* **humor**) **1.** *nu* ability to see or describe what is amusing. *They have a good/keen/no sense of humour. His reports are famous for their humour.* **2.** *nu* temper; mood. *He was in a good/bad humour.* **3.** *nc* one of the liquids once believed to be in the body and able to affect one's state of mind (*o.f.*). Also *vt* amuse; make somebody happy by doing what he wants. *They humoured him by agreeing they were wrong.*
humorous *adj* amusing; funny. **humorously** *adv.*
humorist *nc* humorous talker or writer.
humourless *adj* without humour.

hump [hʌmp] *nc* round lump caused by a bend in the back. *Camels have humps.* Also *vt* **1.** bend into the shape of a hump. *He humped his back/shoulders and looked down.* **2.** carry on the shoulders. *He humped the bag to the door.* (*informal* in sense **2.**).
'**humpback** *nc* back with a hump; person having a back with a hump.
humpbacked *adj*: *a humpbacked bridge.*

humph [hʌmf] *interj* showing doubt or dissatisfaction.

humus ['hju:məs] *nu* part of the soil made up of decayed plants.

hunch [hʌntʃ] *nc* **1.** thick slice; round lump caused by a bend in the back; hump. **2.** idea or belief not based on evidence; suspicion. *The detective had a hunch about the crime* i.e. he thought he knew who committed the crime. Also *vt* bend into the shape of a hunch. *He sat hunched up on a chair.*
'**hunchback** person having a bent spine, causing a lump on the back.

hundred ['hʌndrid] see appendix.

hung [hʌŋ] past of **hang**[1].

hunger ['hʌŋgə*] *nu* **1.** desire for food; lack of food. *We satisfied our hunger. These children often suffer from hunger.* **2.** any strong desire: *their hunger for news from home.* Also *vi* feel hunger or a strong desire. *The actors hungered for applause.*
hungry ['hʌŋgri] *adj* feeling or causing hunger. **hungrily** *adv.*
'**hunger strike** refusal of a prisoner to eat as a protest.

hunk [hʌŋk] *nc* thick slice of something: *a hunk of bread/meat.*

hunkers ['hʌŋkəz] *npl* back of the thighs (esp. in **sitting on one's hunkers**) (*informal*).

hunt [hʌnt] *vt* **1.** go after wild animals to catch or kill them either for food or for sport. *Lions hunt zebra. I have never hunted big game.* **2.** look for something that is lost. *We hunted everywhere for the money.* Also *nc* act of hunting; search. *We helped in the hunt for the money.* Also *nc/u* group of people who hunt foxes together: *a member of the hunt.*
hunter *nc* **1.** person who hunts. **2.** horse used for hunting.
hunting *nu* actions of a person who hunts. *Hunting in these hills is dangerous; a hunting knife; a hunting ground; a hunting horn.*
huntsman man on horseback in charge of the hounds during a hunt.
hunt something down go after something until one catches or finds it.
hunt something out look for and find something (usu. something hidden). *I hunted out my old notes.*
hunt something up look for something (usu. something difficult to find). *You must hunt up the answers in the library.*
Note: because in England *hunting* usu. means *foxhunting* (by hunters on horseback with a pack of hounds), the word has several special uses there e.g.:
hunt the hounds hunt by following the hounds on horseback.

hurdle ['hə:dl] *nc* **1.** frame with wooden bars which can be moved from place to place as a temporary fence (esp. to protect animals). **2.** frame used to jump over in a race. *He won the 120 yards hurdle-race/hurdles.* **3.** problem or difficulty. *We soon got over that particular hurdle.* **hurdler** *nc* (in sense **2.**).

hurl [hə:l] *vt* **1.** throw with great force. *He hurled himself at the door.* **2.** shout with great force. *They hurled abuse and insults at the speaker.*

hurly-burly ['hə:li'bə:li] *nu* noisy confusion; uproar.

hurrah [hu'rɑ:], **hurray** [hu'rei] *interj* used as a shout of joy or applause. *Hip, hip hurray!* Also *vi* shout hurrah.

hurricane ['hʌrikən] *nc* very strong wind.
'**hurricane lamp** type of oil lamp for use out of doors.

hurry ['hʌri] *vt/i* move or do something quickly or in haste. *We hurried to school. Why are you hurrying them? What made him hurry away/off? Hurry along, please! Hurry up! I'm waiting.* Also *nu*: *What's (the reason for) your hurry? There's no hurry* i.e. no need to hurry.
hurried *adj* done quickly or in haste. *We just had time for a hurried talk before he left.*
hurriedly *adv.*
in a hurry **1.** behaving hastily or impatiently. *He is in a hurry to finish his work. I am in no hurry to go. In their hurry to go, they forgot their hats.* **2.** (usu. with a *negative*) readily; willingly. *I'm not going back to that terrible place in a hurry.* (*informal* in sense **2.**).

hurt [hə:t] *vt/i* injure; cause pain to. *He hurt his arm when he fell. My feet hurt (me). They were very hurt by your rude remarks* i.e. their feelings were hurt. *I was hurt at not being asked. It won't hurt them to wait. past* **hurt.** Also *nc/u.*
hurtful *adj* causing injury. *Smoking is hurtful to our health.*

hurtle ['hə:tl] *vi* rush or fly with great speed. *The spears hurtled through the air.*

husband ['hʌzbənd] *nc* man to whom a woman is married. Also *vt* use or keep carefully. *You must husband your strength after your illness.*
husbandry *nu* care; farming: *animal husbandry* i.e. care, management of animals.

hush [hʌʃ] *vt/i* become or make silent. *Hush!*

i.e. be silent! *They hushed the crying children.* Also *nu.*

'**hush money** money paid to keep something hushed up. (*informal*).

hush something up keep secret; prevent from being widely known. *The government tried to hush up the story.* (*informal*).

husk [hʌsk] *nc* dry outer covering of certain seeds. Also *vt* take off the husks. *This machine husks rice.*

husky[1] ['hʌski] *adj* **1.** full of husks. **2.** (esp. of the voice) dry, rough. *His voice is husky because he has a cold.* **huskily** *adv.* **huskiness** *nu.*

husky[2] ['hʌski] *nc* type of dog used for pulling sledges over snow.

husky[3] ['hʌski] *adj* big and strong: *a fine, husky fellow.*

hussar [hə'zɑ:*] *nc* type of cavalry soldier.

hussy ['hʌsi] *nc* badly-behaved girl or woman.

hustings ['hʌstiŋz] *npl* platform on which candidates for parliament make speeches; general business concerned with elections to parliament.

hustle ['hʌsl] *vt/i* act or move quickly; push. *They must hustle to be there in time. They hustled him into a car and drove off.* Also *nu.*

hustler *nc* active, energetic person.

hut [hʌt] *nc* small, simply-made building.

hutch [hʌtʃ] *nc* small wooden cage for keeping small animals (esp. rabbits).

hyacinth ['haiəsinθ] *nc* type of sweet-smelling spring flower.

hyaena [hai'i:nə] *nc* see **hyena.**

hybrid ['haibrid] *nc* **1.** mixture of two different species of animals or plants. *A mule is a hybrid* i.e. its parents are a horse and a donkey. **2.** word made from two words from different languages (e.g. *aeroplane* which is made from a Greek word and a Latin one). Also *adj*: *a hybrid maize; a hybrid word.*

hydrangea [hai'dreindʒə] *nc* type of bush with large round flowers.

hydrant ['haidrnt] *nc* water pipe to which a hose can be attached (usu. found in streets and beside large buildings, such as factories and schools, so that fires can be put out quickly).

hydraulic [hai'drɔ:lik] *adj* **1.** operated by water or other liquid: *a hydraulic press.* **2.** connected with hydraulics.

hydraulics *nu* study of water and other liquids in motion.

Note: followed by a *sing* verb.

hydro- ['haidrou] *prefix* used in scientific words about water (e.g. **hydroelectric**).

hydroelectric ['haidroui'lektrik] *adj* producing electricity by using the force of falling water. *This hydroelectric scheme uses the waters of the River Nile.*

hydrogen ['haidrədʒən] *nu* type of very light gas which forms water (when mixed with oxygen) (H).

hydropathy [hai'drɔpəθi] *nu* treatment of diseases with water (e.g. cold or hot baths, mineral water). **hydropathic** [haidrə'pæθik] *adj.*

hydrophobia [haidrə'foubiə] *nu* **1.** disease caused by the bite of a mad dog. (Usu. **rabies**). **2.** great fear of water.

hydroplane ['haidrəplein] *nc* type of motor-boat which travels very quickly on the surface of the water.

hyena, hyaena [hai'i:nə] *nc* type of flesh-eating wild animal like a dog, which comes out at night, found in Africa and Asia.

hygiene ['haidʒi:n] *nu* science of keeping people in good health.

hygienic [hai'dʒi:nik] *adj.* (*opp* **unhygienic**).

hygienically *adv.*

hymn [him] *nc* song of praise or thanks to God. Also *vt* praise or thank with hymns.

hymnal ['himnl] *nc* book of hymns.

hyper- ['haipə*] *prefix* above; beyond; too much (e.g. **hypercritical**).

hyperbola [hai'pə:bələ] *nc* (geometry) type of curve. **hyperbolic** [haipə'bɔlik] *adj.*

hyperbole [hai'pə:bəli] *nu* manner of speaking or writing which makes something bigger, better or worse etc than it really is. *He's as tall as a lamppost. He has the brains of a hen.* **hyperbolical** [haipə'bɔlikl] *adj.*

hypercritical ['haipə'kritikl] *adj* too critical (esp. of what is not important).

hyphen ['haifən] *nc* the mark - used to divide one word into syllables (e.g. Mon-day) or join two words (e.g. self-help).

hyphenate ['haifəneit] *vt* (usu. *passive*) join with a hyphen. *Carter-Smith is a hyphenated name.* **hyphenation** [haifə'neiʃən] *nu.*

hypnotize ['hipnətaiz] *vt* put a person into a type of deep sleep during which he can be made to do things without his own knowledge. **hypnotic** [hip'nɔtik] *adj.* **hypnotism** ['hipnətizəm] *nu.*

hypnotist ['hipnətist] *nc* person who can hypnotize.

hypnosis [hip'nousis] *nu* state of being in this type of sleep. *Doctors can sometimes cure a patient who is under hypnosis.*

hypochondria [haipə'kɔndriə] *nu* feeling of unhappiness caused by unnecessary worry about one's health.

hypochondriac [haipə'kɔndriæk] *adj.* Also *nc* a person who worries unnecessarily about his health.

hypocrisy [hi'pɔkrisi] *nc/u* pretending to be morally better than one really is.

hypocrite ['hipəkrit] *nc* person who pretends in this way. **hypocritical** [hipə'kritikl] *adj.* **hypocritically** *adv.*

hypodermic [haipə'də:mik] *adj* beneath the skin: *hypodermic needle* i.e. hollow needle for putting medicines into the body beneath the skin.

hypotenuse [hai'pɔtənju:z] *nc* longest side in a right-angled triangle, opposite the right angle.

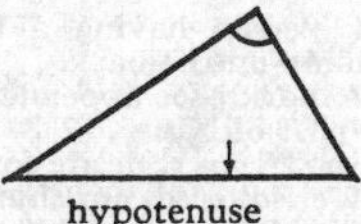

hypotenuse

hypothesis [hai'pɔθisis] *nc* something which is assumed in order to argue or explain. *His theory is based on the hypothesis that all men are born equal.* *pl* **hypotheses** [hai'pɔθisi:z].

hypothetical [haipə'θetikl] *adj* assumed; not certain.

hysteria [his'tiəriə] *nu* nervous excitement causing feelings and behaviour that cannot be controlled: *mass hysteria* i.e. hysteria suffered by a large number of people at the same time. **hysterical** [his'terikl] *adj.*

hysterics [his'teriks] *n sing* or *pl* an attack of hysteria.

go into hysterics have an attack of hysteria. *She went into hysterics when she heard that she would be punished.*

I

I [ai] *pron* used by a person, who is speaking, to refer to himself. *I am/I'm leaving now.* *Note:* there are two question forms in general use, *am I not* (formal) and *aren't I* ['ɑ:nt'ai] (less formal, normal expression when speaking). *I am quite tall, am I not/aren't I?*

iambus [ai'æmbəs] *nc* metrical foot having an unstressed syllable followed by a stressed one (e.g. *ma'chine*). *pl* **iambuses** or **iambi** [ai'æmbi:]. **iambic** *adj.*

ibex ['aibeks] *nc* type of wild mountain goat with long horns.

ibex

ibis ['aibis] *nc* type of long-legged water bird.

ibis

ice¹ [ais] **1.** *nu* water which has been turned solid by cold. *In winter the lake is covered with ice.* **2.** *nc* type of sweet made as cold as ice (e.g. *chocolate ices*).
icy *adj* like ice; very cold; covered with ice: *icy winds; an icy welcome; icy streets.* **icily** *adv.* **iciness** *nu.*
'**ice age** time long ago when the world was much colder and thick ice covered large areas.
'**iceberg** a mountain of ice which has broken off from a glacier and floats in the sea.
'**icebox** box in which food is kept cold with ice; (*US*) refrigerator.
'**icebreaker** type of ship made to break and sail through ice.
'**ice** '**cream** *nc/u* sweetened cream or substance like cream which has been made as cold as ice.
'**ice field** large part of the sea covered with ice (e.g. near the North and South Poles).
'**ice floe** large piece of floating ice.
'**ice hockey** (*Brit*) type of hockey played on ice. (*US* **hockey**).
'**ice pack** **1.** moving mass of closely packed pieces of ice on the sea. **2.** bag of small pieces of ice used to cool the body (esp. the head).
'**ice rink** open space covered with ice used for skating or other sports.
break the ice make people in company begin to feel at ease. *He broke the ice at the party by telling a very amusing story.* (*informal*).
cut no ice have no power or effect. (*informal*).
on thin ice in a situation which requires great care. (*informal*).

ice² [ais] *vt/i* **1.** (usu. with **over** or **up**) cover, become covered, with ice. *The river has iced over.* **2.** cover with icing. *His mother iced his birthday cake.* **3.** make as cold as ice. *I like iced beer.*
icing *nu* **1.** forming of ice on a surface (e.g. the wings of an aeroplane). **2.** mixture of fine sugar and the white of eggs etc used for covering cakes etc.
icicle ['aisikl] *nc* long, pointed piece of ice made from slowly dropping water (e.g. from a roof).
'**icing** '**sugar** very fine type of sugar used for icing.

ichthyo- ['ikθiə] *prefix* used in scientific words about fish.

idea [ai'diə] *nc* **1.** plan; aim; suggestion. *Their idea is to sell their big house and buy a smaller one. Have you any idea how we should do it?* **2.** feeling that something will happen. *I had no idea you would go away. Where did you get the idea that I could not come?* **3.** mental picture; thought. *They have no idea of life in a hot country. My idea of happiness is not the same as yours.*

ideal [ai'diəl] *adj* the best one can think of; existing only in the mind; not real. *This is the ideal place to spend a holiday; an ideal society in which nobody is rich and nobody poor.* Also *nu* best example; highest aim. *He is not my ideal of a good teacher. Their ideals are peace and prosperity.* **ideally** *adv.*
idealism *nu* **1.** aiming at what is most perfect. *Young people in their idealism think war is impossible.* **2.** belief that only ideas are real and can be known. (*opp* **materialism**). **3.** imaginative treatment in art with little thought for what is real. (*opp* **realism**).
idealist *nc* person who believes in idealism.
idealistic [aidiə'listik] *adj* perfect; not real.
idealize *vt* think somebody/something is perfect. *He idealizes his father.* **idealization** [aidiəlai'zeiʃən] *nu.*

identical [ai'dentikl] *adj* the very same; exactly alike. *My hat is identical to/with yours. Your hat and mine are identical.* **identically** *adv.*
identical twins twins born from one ovum of their mother and so exactly alike.

identify [ai'dentifai] *vt* **1.** recognize; tell or show who or what somebody/something is. *I cannot identify this signature* i.e. I cannot tell whose it is. **2.** consider to be the

same. *Wealth cannot be identified with happiness.*
identification [aidentifi'keiʃən] *nu* identifying somebody/something; being identified: *the identification of criminals by their fingerprints.*
identify oneself with show that one agrees with. *I wish to identify myself with these words.*

identity [ai'dentiti] **1.** *nu* being exactly the same or alike. **2.** *nc/u* who or what somebody/something is. *The police are trying to find out the identity of the man killed in the accident.*
i'dentity card/disc card or disc carried to show who one is.

ideology [aidi'ɔlədʒi] *nc* set of ideas in which a person or group of persons firmly believe (esp. philosophical and political ideas): *our democratic ideology; the ideology of a dictator.* **ideological** [aidiə'lɔdʒikl] *adj.* **ideologist** *adj.*

idiocy ['idiəsi] *nc/u* see **idiot.**

idiom ['idiəm] *nc* the way a person naturally speaks or writes his own language where the meaning is given by words together not separately (e.g. in English *What do you take me for?* i.e. What sort of person do you think I am?).
idiomatic [idiə'mætik] *adj*: *He speaks idiomatic English.* **idiomatically** *adv.*

idiosyncrasy [idiou'siŋkrəsi] *nc* what makes a person different from anyone else (e.g. odd ways of behaving, thinking, speaking etc). **idiosyncratic** [idiousiŋ'krætik] *adj.* **idiosyncratically** *adv.*

idiot ['idiət] *nc* person with a very weak mind; a fool. **idiotic** [idi'ɔtik] *adj.* **idiotically** *adv.*
idiocy ['idiəsi] **1.** *nu* being an idiot. **2.** *nc* a very stupid act.

idle ['aidl] *adj* **1.** not doing any work; not in use. *Many workmen were made idle when the factory was closed. It is a pity that all this equipment is left idle.* **2.** lazy; not willing to work. *He is too idle to do anything.* **3.** of no use or effect. *It would be idle to hope for his help; idle gossip/talk.* Also *vt/i* **1.** (with **about** or **away**) be idle; waste. *He is always idling about street corners. They idled away two hours doing nothing.* **2.** (with reference to an engine not in gear) run slowly. *The car engine is very quiet when it is idling.* **idly** *adv.* **idleness** *nu.* **idler** *nc.*

idol ['aidl] *nc* **1.** object made to look like a human or animal and worshipped as a god. **2.** somebody/something which is greatly admired. *This football player is the idol of the crowd.*
idolater [ai'dɔlətə*] *nc* person who worships or admires idols. (*fem* **idolatress** [ai'dɔlətris]). **idolatrous** [ai'dɔlətrəs] *adj.* **idolatrously** *adv.*
idolatry [ai'dɔlətri] *nu* **1.** worship of idols. **2.** too much admiration.
idolize *vt* make an idol of (in senses **1.** and **2.**).
idolization [aidəlaiz'eiʃən] *nu* making or becoming an idol.

idyll ['idil] *nc* **1.** type of poem usu. about happy country life. **2.** any scene or description of happiness. **idyllic** [i'dilik] *adj.* **idyllically** *adv.*

if [if] *conj* **1.** supposing that; on condition that. *If he comes, he will tell you. If he had come, he would have told you. If he were to come* (or *If he came*) *he would tell you* etc. **2.** (with future tense) please. *If you will hold my bag, I'll open the door* i.e. please hold my bag so that I can open the door. **3.** when; whenever. *If they are tired, they have a short rest.* **4.** whether. *Can you tell me if he is coming?* **5.** (with *negative* in *interj*) giving the sense of surprise. *Well, if it isn't our old friend Smith!* **6.** although. *He is a very good man, if rather dull* i.e. although he is dull, he is good.
as if *He talks as if he knows everything* i.e. he talks in a way that makes people believe he knows everything. *As if I cared!* i.e. I do not care. *It isn't as if he is coming* i.e. he is not coming.
even if although. *Even if you did do it, I forgive you. He will come even if he is ill. I want to go even if you don't.*
if only in *interj* giving the sense of a wish. *If only I had more money!* i.e. I wish I had more money. *If only he had seen me!*

igloo ['iglu:] *nc* round house with the roof and walls made of blocks of ice or hard snow, in which Eskimos live.

igloo

igneous ['igniəs] *adj* (with reference to rocks formed by a volcano) made by fire.

ignite [ig'nait] *vt/i* catch fire; set on fire. *Dry grass ignites easily.*
ignition [ig'niʃən] *nu* **1.** catching or setting on fire. **2.** apparatus which ignites the gas in an engine (e.g. to start a car).

ignoble [ig'noubl] *adj* **1.** of low birth (*o.f.*). **2.** of bad character; shameful. **ignobly** *adv.*

ignominy ['ignəmini] *nu* public disgrace; behaviour leading to disgrace. *He suffered the ignominy of being attacked by all the newspapers.* **ignominious** [ignə'miniəs] *adj.* **ignominiously** *adv.*

ignoramus [ignə'reiməs] *nc* person who does not know much (but often pretends he does).

ignorant ['ignərnt] *adj* not knowing anything; not educated. *They are ignorant of/about what happened. He is so ignorant that he cannot write his own name.* **ignorantly** *adv.*
ignorance *nu*: *There is no excuse for their ignorance of English.*

ignore [ig'nɔ:*] *vt* take no notice of; pretend not to see or hear somebody/something. *His letters to the editor were ignored. Because he does not like me he ignores me when we meet.*

ill [il] **1.** *pred adj* in bad health; sick. *He was ill for two days.* **2.** *adj* bad; harmful: *ill health; ill repute; ill will* i.e. hatred. Also *adv* badly. *You should not speak ill of your friends. I can ill afford the money* i.e. not easily. Also *nc* misery; pain. *Man's life is full of ills.*
illness **1.** *nu* bad health. *There has been no illness at school this term.* **2.** *nc* particular type or time of illness. *As a child he had several illnesses. Your illness is not serious.*
'ill-ad'vised *adj* badly advised; not wise.
'ill-at-'ease *adj* not comfortable; embarrassed.

'ill-'bred *adj* badly brought up; rude.
'ill-'breeding *nu* rudeness; bad manners.
'ill-dis'posed *adj* unfriendly; hostile. *I think he is ill-disposed towards me.*
'ill-'fated *adj* unlucky; causing misfortune.
'ill 'feeling unfriendliness.
'ill-'gotten *adj* not obtained honestly: *his ill-gotten gains.* (rather *o.f.*).
'ill-'mannered *adj* badly mannered; rude.
'ill-'natured *adj* bad-tempered; rude.
'ill-'starred *adj* unlucky.
'ill-'timed *adj* badly timed; done at the wrong time.
'ill-'treat *vt* treat cruelly. **ill treatment** *nu.*
'ill-'use *vt* use badly or cruelly.
'ill 'will unfriendliness; hate.
fall ill become sick.
be taken ill become sick.
take something ill be offended. (rather *o.f.* – use **badly**).

illegal [i'li:gl] *adj* forbidden by law; unlawful. **illegally** *adv.*
illegality [ili'gæliti] **1.** *nu* state of being illegal. **2.** *nc* unlawful act.

illegible [i'ledʒibl] *adj* not able to be read. *Your writing is illegible.* **illegibly** *adv.* **illegibility** [iledʒi'biliti] *nu.*

illegitimate [ili'dʒitimət] *adj* (esp. with reference to a child whose parents are not married to each other) unlawful; against the law; against rules. **illegitimately** *adv.* **illegitimacy** *nu.*

illiberal [i'libərl] *adj* not generous; intolerant; mean. **illiberally** *adv.* **illiberality** [ilibə'ræliti] *nu.*

illicit [i'lisit] *adj* forbidden by law; not allowed. **illicitly** *adv.*

illimitable [i'limitəbl] *adj* without any limit; very large: *the illimitable ocean.*

illiterate [i'litərət] *adj* not able to read or write. Also *nc* person who is not able to do so. **illiteracy** *nu.*

illogical [i'lɔdʒikl] *adj* not according to the rules of logic; unsound. **illogically** *adv.* **illogicality** [ilɔdʒi'kæliti] *nc/u.*

illuminate [i'lu:mineit] *vt* **1.** give light to; light up. **2.** make attractive with coloured lights and decorations (esp. shops and streets because of a happy event). *All the streets are illuminated at Christmas.* **3.** (usu. with reference to old books written by hand) make the pages of a book attractive with coloured letters, pictures etc. **4.** make more clear. *This book illuminates the whole problem.*
illuminating *adj* making more clear. *His reply was illuminating.*
illumination [ilu:mi'neiʃən] **1.** *nu* act of illuminating; stat of being illuminated. **2.** *nc* (in *pl*) coloured lights and decorations. *We are going to town to see the illuminations.*

illusion [i'lu:ʒən] *nc* something which is thought to exist but does not; something which is not what it is thought to be; a false belief. *Perfect happiness is an illusion. This picture gives the illusion that the flowers in it are real. He has no illusions about his children* i.e. he does not believe they are better than they really are. **illusive** [i'lu:siv] *adj.*
illusory [i'lu:səri] *adj* caused by an illusion; deceptive.
illusionist *nc* person who causes illusions (esp. one who amuses people by doing so e.g. with conjuring tricks).
optical illusion illusion caused by a mistake made by the eye (e.g. that on a windy night the moon rushes through the clouds; it is really the clouds which are driven by the wind in front of the moon).
be under an illusion be deceived by an illusion. *He is under the illusion that he is always right.*

illustrate ['iləstreit] *vt* explain by means of pictures, diagrams or examples; put or use pictures, diagrams etc in a book, lesson or lecture. *He illustrated his lesson about France with photographs of the people who live there.*
illustration [ilə'streiʃən] *nc/u* **1.** something illustrating; something being illustrated; example. *As an illustration of his poor work just look at this essay.* **2.** picture, diagram etc. *I like magazines full of illustrations.*
illustrative ['iləstrətiv] *adj.*
illustrator *nc* person who makes illustrations for books, magazines etc.

illustrious [i'lʌstriəs] *adj* having great honour or dignity. (*formal* – use **celebrated** or **distinguished**). **illustriously** *adv.* **illustriousness** *nu.*

image ['imidʒ] *nc* **1.** mental picture of somebody/something. **2.** statue or model of somebody/something (usu. made to be worshipped). *In the temple there are the images of many gods.* **3.** exact likeness. *That boy is the image of his father.* **4.** way an object is seen in the lens of a camera or in a mirror. Also *vt* form an image; reflect. *His sorrow was imaged in his face* i.e. his sorrow was reflected or shown there.
imagery ['imidʒəri] *nu* images, references in a poem etc to things and feelings. *This poem is full of imagery.*

imagine [i'mædʒin] *vt* **1.** form an idea of something in the mind. *I cannot imagine what life on the moon would be like. We tried to imagine ourselves as old men.* **2.** suppose; believe. *Do you imagine they will help? Don't imagine that you are the only person in trouble.*
imaginable *adj* that can be imagined. (*opp* **unimaginable**). **imaginably** *adv.*
imaginary [i'mædʒinəri] *adj* not real; existing only in the mind: *an imaginary person* i.e. one who does not exist.
imagination [imædʒi'neiʃən] *nu* ability to imagine clearly; ability to invent. *You must have imagination to write a good play.*
imaginative *adj* having or using imagination: *an imaginative person* i.e. one with a lot of imagination. (*opp* **unimaginative**). **imaginatively** *adj.*

imbalance [im'bæləns] *nu* lack of balance between two things.

imbecile ['imbəsail] *adj* mentally weak; stupid. Also *nc* person who is mentally weak or stupid. **imbecility** [imbə'siliti] *nu.*

imbed [im'bed] *vt* see **embed.**

imbibe [im'baib] *vt* drink; absorb (e.g. ideas, knowledge) (rather *o.f.* – use **drink** or **absorb**).

imbroglio [im'brouliou] *nc* complicated plot or situation; confusion. *pl* **imbroglios.**

imbue [im'bju:] *vt* (usu. with reference to feelings) fill. *The speech imbued us with a desire to help.*

imitate ['imiteit] *vt* behave in the same way as somebody else; copy. *Children like to imitate adults. He can imitate a lion's roar.*
imitative ['imitətiv] *adj.* **imitatively** *adv.*
imitator *nc* person who imitates.
imitation [imi'teiʃən] **1.** *nu* act of imitating. *Children learn by imitation.* **2.** *nc* something copied. *He gives a good imitation of a lion's roar. These drawings are poor imitations of*

the original ones. Also **adj**: *imitation gold* i.e. made to look like gold.

immaculate [i'mækjulət] *adj* without a spot or stain; pure. *The tablecloth was immaculate.*
immaculately *adv*: *He was immaculately dressed* i.e. smartly, without a fault.

immaterial [imə'tiəriəl] *adj* **1.** (with **to**) not important; not relevant. *What you say is immaterial to the discussion.* **2.** not solid or visible. *Man's soul is immaterial.*

immature [imə'tjuə*] *adj* not yet fully grown or developed. **immaturely** *adv*. **immaturity** *nu*.

immeasurable [i'meʒərəbl] *adj* not able to be measured (usu. because of great size).
immeasurably *adv*.

immediate [i'mi:diət] *adj* **1.** at once; without delay. *I asked for an immediate reply to my letter.* **2.** very near; close; direct. *There is a hotel in the immediate neighbourhood. These are my plans for the immediate future.*
immediately *adv* at once; closely; directly.

immemorial [imə'mɔ:riəl] *adj* so old that it is beyond human memory: *from time immemorial* i.e. from a time that no one can remember.

immense [i'mens] *adj* very large.
immensely *adv* very much. *He has grown immensely. I enjoyed myself immensely.*
immensity **1.** *nu* very large size: *the immensity of the sky.* **2.** *nc/u* something that is very large.

immerse [i'mə:s] *vt* **1.** put below water or another liquid. *He immersed the knife in boiling water.* **2.** cause to become very interested (so that one does not pay attention to anything else). *He immersed himself in work. The pupil was immersed in a book.* **immersion** *nc/u*.
im'mersion heater electric apparatus which is immersed in water and heats it.

immigrate ['imigreit] *vi* enter a country and live there. (A tourist or visitor stays only for a short time). **immigration** [imi'greiʃən] *nc/u*.
immigrant ['imigrnt] *nc* person who immigrates.

imminent ['iminənt] *adj* (usu. with reference to something unpleasant) probably about to happen soon. *War seems imminent.*
imminently *adv*. **imminence** *nu*.

immobile [i'moubail] *adj* not able to move or be moved. **immobility** [imə'biliti] *nu*.
immobilize [i'moubilaiz] *vt* make immobile. *Heavy snow immobilized all traffic.*
immobilization [imoubilai'zeiʃən] *nu*: *the immobilization of all traffic by heavy snow.*

immoderate [i'mɔdərət] *adj* beyond what is proper; too much. *He is immoderate in his drinking* i.e. he drinks too much. **immoderately** *adv*.

immodest [i'mɔdist] *adj* not decent; rude. *Her skirt is so short that it is immodest.*
immodestly *adv*.
immodesty **1.** *nu* immodest behaviour. **2.** *nc* an act of immodest behaviour.

immolate ['iməleit] *vt* kill as an offering to a god; make an offering of this kind in other ways. *Men immolate themselves to wealth.* **immolation** [imə'leiʃən] *nc/u*.

immoral [i'mɔrl] *adj* (often with reference to sexual behaviour) wrong; evil: *the immoral earnings of a prostitute.* **immorally** *adv*.
immorality [imə'ræliti] *nc/u* immoral act or state.

immortal [i'mɔ:tl] *adj* living or famous for ever. *Gods are immortal; the immortal poetry of Shakespeare.* Also *nc*: *Shakespeare is one of the immortals.* **immortality** [imɔ:'tæliti] *nu*.
immortalize *vt* make famous for ever.

immovable [i'mu:vəbl] *adj* **1.** not able to be moved. **2.** not able to be persuaded or changed. *Although we asked many times, he remained immovable.* **immovably** *adv*.

immune [i'mju:n] *adj* free or safe (usu. from the attacks of something e.g. a disease). *This medicine will make you immune to/from malaria.* **immunity** *nu*.
immunize ['imjunaiz] *vt* make immune. *I have been immunized against typhoid.*
immunization [imjunai'zeiʃən] *nc/u*.

immure [i'mjuə*] *vt* **1.** put in prison (*o.f.* – use **imprison**). **2.** put (oneself) in a room where one can be left alone. *They immured themselves in the office until the work was finished.*

immutable [i'mju:təbl] *adj* not able to be changed; fixed: *the immutable laws of nature.* **immutably** *adv*. **immutability** [imju:tə'biliti] *nu*.

imp [imp] *nc* little devil; naughty child.
impish *adj* like an imp. **impishly** *adv*.
impishness *nu*.

impact ['impækt] *nc* **1.** force of two things hitting each other; collision. *When the car hit the wall, the impact broke the windscreen.* **2.** influence; impression. *This book had/made a great impact on its readers.*

impair [im'pɛə*] *vt* make less in value, strength or goodness; weaken; damage. *His work is impaired by stupid mistakes. You need spectacles if your eyesight is impaired.*
impaired *adj*. (*opp* **unimpaired**). **impairment** *nu*.

impale [im'peil] *vt* fix somebody/something on a sharp point (e.g. a spear, sword or stake); put somebody to death in this way.

impalpable [im'pælpəbl] *adj* not able to be touched, felt or understood. **impalpably** *adv*.

impanel [im'pænl] *vt* see **empanel.**

impart [im'pa:t] *vt* give; grant; hand on. *A teacher's aim is to impart knowledge.*

impartial [im'pa:ʃəl] *adj* just; fair to both sides. *A judge must be completely impartial.*
impartially *adv*. **impartiality** [impa:ʃi'æliti] *nu*.

impassable [im'pa:səbl] *adj* not possible to travel on or go over or through. *This road is impassable during the rains; impassable mountains; an impassable forest.*

impasse ['æmpa:s] *nc* **1.** place or position one cannot get out of. **2.** failure to agree. *The talks between the two governments have reached an impasse.*

impassioned [im'pæʃənd] *adj* full of passion or strong feelings: *an impassioned request for help.*

impassive [im'pæsiv] *adj* not showing one's feelings; calm. **impassively** *adv*. **impassivity** [impə'siviti], **impassiveness** *nu*.

impatient [im'peiʃənt] *adj* not patient; restless; unwilling to wait. *They are impatient to go. He is impatient of anything stupid* i.e. he does not tolerate anything stupid. **impatiently** *adv*. **impatience** *nu*.

impeach [im'pi:tʃ] *vt* **1.** charge with a crime against the State (*o.f.*). **2.** (usu. with reference to a person's behaviour) be doubtful about; question. (rather *o.f.*).
impeachment *nu* trial of an impeached person; act of impeaching or being impeached (*o.f.*).

impeccable [im'pekəbl] *adj* without error or fault; perfect. **impeccably** *adv*.

impecunious [impi'kju:niəs] *adj* without money; poor. **impecunity** [impi'kju:niti] *nu*.

impede [im'pi:d] *vt* stop the progress of; hinder; hold back. *Bad weather impeded us during our journey.*

impediment [im'pedimənt] *nc* something that impedes (esp. something that impedes talking e.g. a stammer). *The little boy has an impediment in his speech.*

impel [im'pel] *vt* drive forward; force. *What reason impelled you to go there? past* **impelled.**

impend [im'pend] *vi* (usu. in *pres part*) be about to happen: *our impending return to school.*

impenetrable [im'penitrəbl] *adj* not able to be passed through. **impenetrably** *adv*. **impenetrability** [impenitrə'biliti] *nu*.

impenitent [im'penitnt] *adj* not repentant or sorry. **impenitently** *adv*. **impenitence** *nu*.

imperative [im'perətiv] *adj* **1.** very necessary. *It is imperative for him to be taken to hospital at once/It is imperative that he should be taken to hospital at once.* **2.** not to be avoided; carrying authority. *These instructions are imperative. You cannot disobey them.* **3.** mood of the verb which expresses commands (e.g. Stop!). Also *nc* (in sense **3.**). **imperatively** *adv*.

imperceptible [impə'septibl] *adj* difficult or impossible to see, feel, hear etc. *He gave an almost imperceptible nod* i.e. one that could hardly be seen. **imperceptibly** *adv*.

imperfect [im'pə:fikt] *adj* **1.** not perfect; not complete; faulty. **2.** tense of the verb expressing an action not yet completed (e.g. *I was walking along the street*). Also *nc* (in sense **2.**). **imperfectly** *adv*. **imperfection** [impə'fekʃən] *nc/u*.

imperial [im'piəriəl] *adj* **1.** of an empire or an emperor: *imperial Rome.* **2.** royal; magnificent. **3.** (*Brit*) (with reference to weights and measures) fixed by law: *an imperial pint.* Also *nc* a pointed beard grown only on the chin.

imperialism *nu* desire to have, or belief in, an empire; system of government of an empire.

imperialist *nc* person who supports imperialism. **imperialistic** [impiəriəl'istik] *adj*.

imperil [im'peril] *vt* cause to be in danger. *past* **imperilled.**

imperious [im'piəriəs] *adj* haughty; commanding. **imperiously** *adv*. **imperiousness** *nu*.

imperishable [im'periʃəbl] *adj* not able to be destroyed; lasting for ever. **imperishably** *adv*.

impermanent [im'pə:mənənt] *adj* not enduring or lasting. **impermanence** *nu*.

impermeable [im'pə:miəbl] *adj* not allowing anything (esp. a gas or liquid) to pass through. **impermeably** *adv*.

impersonal [im'pə:sənl] *adj* **1.** with reference to no particular person; without personal feelings: *an impersonal manner.* **2.** with reference to verbs used with *it. It is going to rain* i.e. *it*, the subject, is not a person and does not refer to any particular thing. **impersonally** *adv*.

impersonate [im'pə:səneit] *vt* pretend to be or act the part of somebody else; imitate. *The prisoner escaped by impersonating a policeman.* **impersonation** [impə:sə'neiʃən] *nc/u*.

impertinent [im'pə:tinənt] *adj* rude; impudent (esp. to older persons). *The pupils were impertinent to their teacher.* **impertinently** *adv*. **impertinence** *nu*.

imperturbable [impə'tə:bəbl] *adj* not able to be made angry or excited. **imperturbably** *adv*. **imperturbability** ['impətə:bə'biliti] *nu*.

impervious [im'pə:viəs] *adj* **1.** not allowing something (esp. a liquid) to pass through. *The roof is impervious to rain.* **2.** not affected or moved by. *He was impervious to our requests for help.* **imperviously** *adv*. **imperviousness** *nu*.

impetigo [impi'taigou] *nu* type of skin disease that can easily be transmitted to someone else by touching.

impetuous [im'petjuəs] *adj* **1.** acting hastily and without thought. *There was no reason for his impetuous refusal to come.* **2.** moving with great force. **impetuously** *adv*. **impetuosity** [impetju'ɔsiti] *nu*.

impetus ['impətəs] *nc* force with which something moves or which makes something move. *The impetus of the falling rock caused it to make a deep hole in the ground. His success gave a great impetus to the others. pl* **impetuses.**

impiety [im'paiəti] *nc/u* see **impious.**

impinge [im'pindʒ] *vt* (with **on** or **upon**) touch; strike against; interrupt. *The light impinged on his eyes. This work is impinging on my spare time.*

impious ['impiəs] *adj* having no respect for God; wicked. **impiously** *adv*.

impiety [im'paiəti] *nc/u* act or state of being impious. *You will not be forgiven for your impieties.*

impish ['impiʃ] *adj* see **imp.**

implacable [im'plækəbl] *adj* (with reference to anger, hate, hostility etc) not able to be changed or made less: *an implacable enemy.* **implacably** *adv*. **implacableness, implacability** ['implækə'biliti] *nu*.

implant [im'plɑ:nt] *vt* (usu. with reference to feelings or ideas) put deeply into. *His visit to the country implanted in him a love for its people.*

implement[1] ['implimənt] *nc* tool or instrument. *A spade is an implement for digging.*

implement[2] ['impliment] *vt* fulfil a promise or undertaking. *The government is implementing its policy of helping the unemployed.* **implementation** [implimən'teiʃən] *nu*.

implicate ['implikeit] *vt* make a connection with; show that somebody is connected with something (usu. something that is wrong or unpleasant). *This evidence implicates them in the robbery. I don't want to be implicated in your plans.*

implication [impli'keiʃən] **1.** *nu* implicating or being implicated. **2.** *nc* something which is only suggested and not said openly. *The implication of your statement is that I was wrong.* see also **imply.**

implicit [im'plisit] *adj* **1.** not said openly but suggested or implied. *It is implicit in your statement that I was wrong.* (*opp* **explicit**). **2.** without questioning; complete. *He has an implicit belief in democracy.* **implicitly** *adv*. **implicitness** *nu*.

implore [im'plɔ:*] *vt* ask earnestly for; beg. *I implore you to help me.*

imploring *adj*: *He gave me an imploring look.* **imploringly** *adv*.

imply [im'plai] *vt* not say openly but only

suggest; show in an indirect way. *Your statement implies that I am wrong. The bad behaviour of a child sometimes implies that he is unhappy.*

impolite [impə'lait] *adj* rude; having bad manners; not polite. **impolitely** *adv.* **impoliteness** *nu.*

impolitic [im'pɔlitik] *adj* ill-advised; not in one's own interests. *It would be impolitic to ask him now, because he is very angry.*

imponderable [im'pɔndərəbl] *adj* not able to be measured or estimated. Also *nc* (esp. *pl*): *the imponderables of war* i.e. the events in war or the results of war which cannot be estimated or foreseen.

import[1] [im'pɔːt] *vt* **1.** bring into a country from abroad. (*opp* **export**). **2.** mean; be of importance to. (rather *o.f.* in sense **2.**).
importation [impɔː'teiʃən] *nc/u* something imported; act of importing (in sense **1.**).
importer *nc* person who imports (usu. goods).

import[2] ['impɔːt] **1.** *npl* goods that are imported. **2.** *nu* act of importing. **3.** *nu* meaning; importance. *I do not understand the import of his remarks.* (rather *o.f.* in sense **3.**).

important [im'pɔːtnt] *adj* **1.** having great value or effect. *The battle was the most important one in the war.* **2.** (with reference to persons) having power; worth paying attention to. *The Prime Minister is the most important person in the government.* **importantly** *adv.* **importance** *nu.*

importune [impɔː'tjuːn] *vt* ask many times and refuse to stop doing so. *The beggar importuned us for money.* **importuner** *nc.*
importunity *nc/u* act or state of importuning.
importunate [im'pɔːtjunit] *adj* (with reference to persons) asking many times and refusing to stop doing so. **importunately** *adv.*

impose [im'pouz] *vt* **1.** force or place something on somebody (e.g. a punishment, tax or duty). *The judge imposed a fine of ten pounds on him. A new tax has been imposed on cigarettes.* **2.** force oneself into the company of other people. *They are always imposing themselves on their relatives.* **3.** take advantage of. *May I impose upon your kindness?*
imposing *adj* looking important; having a grand appearance; impressive. *The castle is an imposing building; an imposing headmaster.* **imposingly** *adv.*
imposition [impə'ziʃən] *nc* **1.** something forced on somebody: *the imposition of a fine of ten pounds.* **2.** act of taking advantage of; trick. **3.** type of punishment in schools in which a pupil is made to do some extra work.

impossible [im'pɔsibl] *adj* **1.** not able to exist or be done. *It is impossible to be in two places at once. It's impossible for me to be there before 7 o'clock.* **2.** not able to be endured. *This is an impossible state of affairs. She's impossible!* Also *interj* of course not; absurd. **impossibly** *adv.*
impossibility [impɔsə'biliti] *nc/u* something impossible; state of being impossible.

impost ['impoust] *nc* tax. (*formal*).

impostor [im'pɔstə*] *nc* person who pretends to be somebody else; person who deceives others; a cheat.
imposture [im'pɔstjə*] *nc/u* act of an impostor or state of being one.

impotent ['impətnt] *adj* (often with reference to the sexual power of a male) weak; without power. **impotently** *adv.* **impotence** *nu.*

impound [im'paund] *vt* enclose or keep (until legal action is taken). *Cattle found wandering on a road can be impounded* i.e. until their owner pays a fine. *The judge ordered the documents to be impounded.*

impoverish [im'pɔvəriʃ] *vt* make poor; make worse. *They are impoverished by heavy taxes. Bad farming impoverishes good soil.* **impoverishment** *nu.*

impracticable [im'præktikəbl] *adj* not able to be carried out; (with reference to roads or paths) not passable. **impracticably** *adv.* **impracticability** [impræktikə'biliti] *nu.*

imprecate ['imprikeit] *vt* curse; pray for evil to come to somebody. **imprecation** [impri'keiʃən] *nc/u.*

impregnable [im'pregnəbl] *adj* not able to be taken by force; not able to be moved or changed: *an impregnable castle; an impregnable belief.* **impregnably** *adv.* **impregnability** [impregnə'biliti] *nu.*

impregnate ['impregneit] *vt* **1.** make fertile or pregnant. **2.** fill; soak. *The wood is impregnated with a chemical which prevents decay.* **impregnation** [impreg'neiʃən] *nu.*

impresario [impre'sɑːriou] *nc* person who organizes public entertainments (esp. concerts and operas). *pl* **impresarios.**

impress [im'pres] *vt* **1.** mark by pressing something on something else. **2.** cause to remember; influence greatly. *He impressed on me the importance of the work. He impressed me with the importance of the work. I was impressed by all he said.*
impressive *adj* causing one to be impressed (in sense **2.**): *an impressive book.* (*opp* **unimpressive**). **impressively** *adv.* **impressiveness** *nu.*
impression *nc* **1.** mark made by pressing something on something else: *the impression of his thumb on the clay.* **2.** something printed (esp. the amount printed at one time). *The first impression of this book was sold very quickly, so two more impressions were ordered.* **3.** influence on the mind; idea of something (often an uncertain or wrong one). *The news made a great impression on those who heard it. He is under the impression that I did it* i.e. he thinks wrongly that I did it. *These are only my impressions, I don't really know.*
impressionable *adj* easily influenced: *an impressionable young man.*
impressionism *nu* type of art, writing or music which aims at showing the general impressions made on the senses rather than giving detailed descriptions.
impressionist *nc* person who practises impressionism.
impressionistic [impreʃə'nistik] *adj* **1.** giving only an impression (in sense **3.**) of something. **2.** of impressionism or an impressionist.

imprimatur [impri'meitə*] *nc* licence given by a Roman Catholic bishop for the printing of a book.

imprint [im'print] *vt* **1.** print or stamp on something. *The design was imprinted on the cloth.* **2.** put firmly in the mind. *The terrible accident is still imprinted on my memory.* Also ['imprint] *nc*: *publisher's imprint* i.e. name etc of a publisher at the beginning of a book.

imprison [im'prizn] *vt* put or keep in prison. **imprisonment** *nu.*

improbable [im'prɔbəbl] *adj* not likely to happen or to be true. **improbably** *adv*.
improbability [imprɔbə'biliti] *nc/u* something which is improbable; state of being improbable.

impromptu [im'prɔmptjuː] *adj/adv* without being previously prepared: *an impromptu lesson; play a tune impromptu*. Also *nc* **1.** witty, unprepared reply. **2.** musical work which seems to be unprepared.

improper [im'prɔpə*] *adj* **1.** not suitable. *Short trousers are improper at a dance.* **2.** not decent; not fit for polite company: *improper jokes*. **improperly** *adv*.
impropriety [imprə'praiəti] *nc/u* improper act; state of being improper.

improve [im'pruːv] *vt/i* become or make better. *Your English has improved. He is trying to improve his English.*
improvement *nc/u* something which improves; improving or being improved. *The improvements to the school buildings cost a lot of money. There is some improvement in your work this term.*

improvident [im'prɔvidnt] *adj* with no thought for the future; careless; wasteful. **improvidently** *adv*. **improvidence** *nu*.

improvise ['imprəvaiz] *vt/i* do or make quickly without being prepared or having all that is needed. *He improvised a song about the football team's victory. We left the tent poles behind, so we had to improvise* i.e. by finding other sticks or pieces of wood and using them as poles. **improvised** *adj*.
improvisation [imprəvai'zeiʃən] *nc/u*.

imprudent [im'pruːdnt] *adj* careless; rash, unwise. *It was imprudent of you to lend money to a stranger.* **imprudently** *adv*.
imprudence *nc/u* imprudent act; state of being imprudent.

impudent ['impjudnt] *adj* rude; insolent; disrespectful. *That impudent boy put his tongue out at me.* **impudently** *adv*. **impudence** *nu*.

impugn [im'pjuːn] *vt* question the truth of something: *impugn someone's honesty*.

impulse ['impʌls] **1.** *nc* movement or activity caused by something else. *The nerves carry impulses to the brain.* **2.** *nc/u* sudden desire to do something. *I bought it on impulse* i.e. suddenly without stopping to think. *I had an impulse to hit him. He is ruled by his impulses.* **impulsive** [im'pʌlsiv] *adj*. **impulsively** *adv*. **impulsiveness** *nu*.

impunity [im'pjuːniti] *nu* state of not being liable to be punished or harmed for what one does.

impure [im'pjuə*] *adj* not pure; dirty; evil: *impure food; an impure mind; impure intentions*. **impurely** *adv*.
impurity *nc/u* something impure; state of being impure.

impute [im'pjuːt] *vt* (with **to**) consider responsible for; make the reason for (usu. for something wrong). *They impute their defeat in the war to the stupidity of the generals.*
imputation [impju'teiʃən] *nc/u*.

in [in] *adv* **1.** (with verbs of motion) entering or causing to enter: *come/get/go/jump/walk in; get/move/push/put/throw the box in*. **2.** (with certain other verbs) causing to enter: *call/have/let/see/show him in*. **3.** having arrived; ready; obtainable. *Our train is in* i.e. it has arrived or is waiting. *Fresh apples are now in* i.e. are obtainable. **4.** not allowing to get out: *keep/lock/shut in*. **5.** (with the verbs **be, find etc**) at home, work or where one is expected to be. *Is your father in?* i.e. is he at home? *The manager is not in yet* i.e. at his office or place of work. *Our team is in* i.e. batting, not fielding during a game of baseball or cricket. **6.** a great number of special senses. *The fire was in* i.e. was burning. *The Labour Party is in* i.e. has been elected, holds power. *Short skirts are in* i.e. are fashionable. Also with many other verbs: *fill in* i.e. complete; *give in* i.e. yield; *run in (an engine)* i.e. make it ready by running it; *take in* i.e. cheat etc. Also *prep* **1.** place where or towards: *in the room; in the village; in London; in Europe; in the dark; in the rain. Throw it in the fire. Go in that direction.*

Note: 1. *in* and *into* with the sense of motion are almost the same. We can say either *Throw it in the fire* or *Throw it into the fire*. *Into* has more definitely the sense of entering or causing to enter from the outside, so we usu. say *He went into the room. He looked in the room* could have the sense of looking for something, while in the room but *He looked into the room* has only the sense of looking from the outside. Generally it is safer to use *into* when motion is expressed. 2. *in* with reference to place without motion refers to an area rather than one point. If we think of a small place as an area we can use *in* (e.g. *He lives in a little village called XY*. But if we think of it as being a point we can say *He lives at a little village called XY*). We normally think of large places as being areas rather than points, and so generally say *He lives in London. His house is in New York etc.* But if we think of the large place as a point, for instance a point x in a journey, we can say *The plane didn't stop at New York*. We would, however, use *in* not *at* with names of places bigger than a city (e.g. *The plane didn't stop in Italy on its way to Africa*).

2. place or type of work. *I am in insurance. He's in the Navy. They are in research.* **3.** wearing: *the woman in the red hat*. **4.** time when, during, within: *in the 19th century; in the morning; in winter; in old age; in the future; in their absence. I'll be back in a week* i.e. within the period of one week.

Note: *in* has the sense of a period of time, *at* of a point in time. *He got up in the morning* but *He got up at 7.30 in the morning; in winter* but *at Christmas; in the future* but *at a future date etc.*

5. part of something: *one in a hundred; 12 inches in a foot; the best in the class*. **6.** condition or circumstances: *in anger; in doubt; in a hurry; in poor health; in secret; in trouble*. **7.** by means of; using. *He wrote in pencil. I spoke in French. He paid me in dollars. He shouted in a loud voice. The room is painted in bright colours.* **8.** with reference to; referring to. *He is lame in one leg; weak in character; rich in gold; greater in size; forty miles in length. In him we have an excellent headmaster.*
in all see **all**.
in any case whatever happens.
day in, day out day after day in a tiring way: *the same food day in, day out*. (Also with **week** and **year**).
in itself alone, without reference to anything else. *Starch in itself is not dangerous to health. It is only dangerous if you eat too much.*
in so far as, in as far as to the extent that. *He can be trusted in so far as he has never*

yet told a lie.
be in for **1.** likely to suffer something unpleasant. *You're in for trouble.* **2.** entered for a competition. *I'm in for the mile race.*
be in on take part in; know about. *Are you in on the new plan?* (*informal*).
in that since; because.
ins and outs details or difficulties: *the ins and outs of the plan.* (*informal*).
in the way of with reference to. *What have you in the way of money?*
be well in with be very friendly with. (*informal*).

inability [inə'biliti] *nu* state of not being able.

inaccessible [inək'sesibl] *adj* not able to be reached. **inaccessibly** *adv.* **inaccessibility** [inəksesi'biliti] *nu.*

inaccurate [in'ækjurit] *adj* not right or correct. **inaccurately** *adv.*
inaccuracy *nc/u* something inaccurate; state of being inaccurate.

inaction [in'ækʃən] *nu* not doing anything.
inactive [in'æktiv] *adj* not moving, working or doing very much. **inactively** *adv.*
inactivity [inæk'tiviti] *nu.*

inadequate [in'ædikwit] *adj* not enough; not suitable: *inadequate amount. He's inadequate for the job.* **inadequately** *adv.* **inadequacy** *nc/u.*

inadmissible [inəd'misibl] *adj* not able to be considered or allowed: *inadmissible evidence.*

inadvertent [inəd'və:tnt] *adj* resulting from inattention; careless; not on purpose: *an inadvertent mistake.* **inadvertently** *adv.*
inadvertence, inadvertency *nc/u* something done inadvertently; state of being inadvertent.

inadvisable [inəd'vaizəbl] *adj* unwise; not safe, suitable etc.

inalienable [in'eiliənəbl] *adj* not able to be taken away: *the inalienable right of freedom.*

inane [i'nein] *adj* silly; stupid. **inanely** *adv.*
inanity [i'næniti] **1.** *nc* inane act. **2.** *nu* state of being inane.

inanimate [in'ænimit] *adj* not alive; not lively. *Wood is inanimate.*

inapplicable [inə'plikəbl] *adj* (esp. with reference to rules and laws) not suitable to be used.

inappreciable [inə'pri:ʃəbl] *adj* not enough to be seen, felt, noticed etc. **inappreciably** *adv.*

inappropriate [inə'proupriət] *adj* not proper; not suitable; not correct for a particular purpose. **inappropriately** *adv.* **inappropriateness** *nu.*

inapt [in'æpt] *adj* **1.** not suitable or fitting. **2.** clumsy; not skilful: *inapt use of machinery.* **inaptly** *adv.* **inaptitude** [in'æptitju:d] *nc/u.*

inarticulate [ina:'tikjulət] *adj* **1.** not clear; badly arranged; difficult to understand. **2.** (with reference to a person) not able to speak well and clearly; not able to express one's ideas in speech. *Uneducated people are usually inarticulate.* **inarticulately** *adv.* **inarticulateness** *nu.*

inartistic [ina:'tistik] *adj* done without skill; without taste; crude. **inartistically** *adv.*

inasmuch [inəz'mʌtʃ] *adv* (with **as**) since; because (*o.f.*).

inattention [inə'tenʃən] *nu* not noticing; not listening carefully etc. **inattentive** [inə'tentiv] *adj.* **inattentively** *adv.*

inaudible [in'ɔ:dibl] *adj* not loud enough to be heard. **inaudibly** *adv.* **inaudibility** [inɔ:di'biliti] *nu.*

inaugurate [i'nɔ:gjureit] *vt* introduce somebody or begin something in a formal manner. *He was inaugurated as professor. The Queen inaugurated the exhibition* i.e. she opened it formally. **inaugural** [i'nɔ:gjurl] *adj.* **inauguration** [inɔ:gju'reiʃən] *nc/u.*

inauspicious [inɔ:'spiʃəs] *adj* showing signs that something will not succeed, or will go wrong, in the future. **inauspiciously** *adv.*

inborn ['in'bɔ:n] *adj* possessed when born; natural. *Intelligence is said to be inborn* i.e. persons are born with it.

inbred ['in'bred] *adj* **1.** possessed when born: *inbred courage.* **2.** having ancestors who were too closely related to each other.

incalculable [in'kælkjuləbl] *adj* **1.** too great to be measured or counted. **2.** (with reference to a person's feelings) happening without reason; uncertain. **incalculably** *adv.*

in camera ['in'kæmərə] *adv* (with reference to a legal trial etc) not in public.

incandescent [inkæn'desnt] *adj* white-hot and giving out light. **incandescence** *nu.*

incantation [inkæn'teiʃən] *nc* set of words used to produce a magical effect.

incapable [in'keipəbl] *adj* not able; not having the power or nature to do something. *He is incapable of being unkind to people.* **incapably** *adv.* **incapability** [inkeipə'biliti] *nu.*

incapacitate [inkə'pæsiteit] *vt* (with **for** or **from**) make incapable; disqualify. *The accident has incapacitated him from working/for work.*
incapacity *nu* state of being incapable: *their incapacity to learn/for learning.*

incarcerate [in'ka:səreit] *vt* put in prison. (*formal*).

incarnate [in'ka:neit] *vt* take the form of a human being; express in human form. Also [in'ka:nit] *adj*: *a devil incarnate* i.e. one in human form.
incarnation [inka:'neiʃən] **1.** *nu* taking human form (esp. by Christ). **2.** *nc* person who is a living example of something. *He was the incarnation of honesty.*

incautious [in'kɔ:ʃəs] *adj* not showing care; rash. **incautiously** *adv.* **incautiousness** *nu.*

incendiary [in'sendiəri] *nc* **1.** person who unlawfully sets fire to houses, buildings etc. **2.** person who urges others to behave violently. **3.** type of bomb which causes fire. Also *adj*: *an incendiary speech* i.e. one urging people to behave violently.

incense[1] [in'sens] *vt* make angry.

incense[2] ['insens] *nu* substance which gives off a sweet-smelling smoke when burnt (usu. used for religious purposes).

incentive [in'sentiv] *nc* anything which makes somebody do something (esp. work harder). *The best incentive in business is the chance of making more money.*

inception [in'sepʃən] *nu* beginning.

incertitude [in'sə:titju:d] *nu* uncertainty.

incessant [in'sesnt] *adj* continuing without stopping. **incessantly** *adv.*

incest ['insest] *nu* unlawful sexual intercourse between persons belonging to the same family (e.g. between brother and sister, father and daughter). **incestuous** [in'sestjuəs] *adj.*

inch [intʃ] *nc* measure of length equal to one twelfth of a foot. see appendix. Also *vt/i* move very slowly. *He inched (his way) across the high roof.*

by inches by a very small amount; just. *He escaped death by inches.*

every inch completely; in every way. *He is every inch a king.*

inch by inch slowly; little by little.

within an inch of almost. *He was/came within an inch of death* i.e. he almost died.

incidence ['insidns] *nu* number of times which, or the way in which, something has an effect on other persons/things: *the incidence of malaria in Africa* i.e. the number, or kind, of people who get malaria.

incident[1] ['insidnt] *nc* happening; event (usu. one that is not very important). *The meeting passed without incident* i.e. without anything unusual or unpleasant happening. *There were several incidents on the frontier* i.e. several small raids or fights.

incident[2] ['insidnt] *adj* likely to happen; belonging naturally to. *The long hours of work incident to a doctor's duties.* (rather *o.f.*).

incidental [insi'dentl] *adj* happening or likely to happen at the same time as: *the pleasures incidental to teaching young children; incidental expenses* i.e. expenses caused while doing something else.

incidentally *adv* by the way. *Incidentally, I should like to raise another point. . . .*

incinerate [in'sinəreit] *vt* burn to ashes. **incineration** [insinə'reiʃən] *nu*.

incinerator *nc* container or furnace in which rubbish is burnt.

incipient [in'sipiənt] *adj* just beginning: *an incipient disease.*

incise [in'saiz] *vt* (often with reference to surgical operations) cut into.

incision [in'siʒən] *nc*: *The doctor made an incision in the patient's arm.*

incisive [in'saisiv] *adj* (with reference to thoughts and words) sharp; acute. *He refused the request in a few incisive words.* **incisively** *adv*.

incite [in'sait] *vt* urge somebody to do something (usu. something wrong). *He is inciting them to go on strike.*

incitement *nc/u* something that incites; state of inciting or being incited.

incivility [insi'viliti] *nc/u* action that is not polite; lack of politeness.

inclement [in'klemənt] *adj* (usu. with reference to the weather) not mild; severe. **inclemency** *nu*.

incline[1] [in'klain] *vt/i* **1.** bend, slope. *The road inclines to the left.* **2.** cause somebody to wish or be ready to do something; (in *passive*) be ready or have a tendency to do something. *The argument inclines me to agree. I am inclined/feel inclined to agree. They are inclined to be late* i.e. they are often late.

inclined *adj*. (*opp* **disinclined**).

inclination [inkli'neiʃən] *nc*: *an inclination of the head. My inclination is to agree. We followed our own inclinations.*

incline[2] ['inklain] *nc* slope. *The road has a steep incline.*

inclose [in'klouz] *vt* see **enclose.**

inclosure [in'klouʒə*] *nc* see **enclose.**

include [in'klu:d] *vt* contain; have as part of or as belonging to. *The book includes two chapters on grammar. Please include me in your group.*

inclusive [in'klu:siv] *adj* including: *from Tuesday to Friday inclusive* i.e. including Tuesday and Friday as well as Wednesday and Thursday; *the inclusive cost* i.e. including everything. **inclusively** *adv*. **inclusion** *nc/u*.

incognito [inkɔg'ni:tou] *adj/adv* in disguise; under another name. *To avoid the crowds the film star travels incognito.*

incoherent [inkou'hiərnt] *adj* (esp. with reference to speeches, thoughts, ideas, explanations) not fitting together; not easy to understand. **incoherently** *adv*. **incoherence** *nu*.

incombustible [inkɔm'bʌstibl] *adj* not able to be burned.

income ['inkʌm] *nc* money which is regularly received for work done, from trade etc. *He has an income of £2,000 a year.*

'income tax tax put on a person's income.

incommensurate [inkə'mensjurit] *adj* not of the same size or quantity as something else; not of the right size or quantity for something.

incommode [inkə'moud] *vt* give trouble to; cause inconvenience to.

incommunicado [inkəmju:ni'ka:dou] *adj* (usu. with reference to a person who is a prisoner) not allowed to speak or write to other people.

incomparable [in'kɔmpərəbl] *adj* not able to be compared; better than any other: *incomparable skill.* **incomparably** *adv*.

incompatible [inkəm'pætibl] *adj* not able or suitable to go together. *Those two people are incompatible* i.e. they cannot be together in a friendly way. **incompatibly** *adv*. **incompatibility** ['inkəmpæti'biliti] *nu*.

incompetent [in'kɔmpitnt] *adj* not having the ability or power to do something. *He is incompetent at working with his hands.* **incompetently** *adv*. **incompetence** *nu*.

incomplete [inkəm'pli:t] *adj* not having all that is needed; not finished; needing something more. **incompletely** *adv*.

incomprehensible [inkɔmpri'hensibl] *adj* not able to be understood. **incomprehensibly** *adv*.

incomprehension *nu* failing to understand.

inconceivable [inkən'si:vəbl] *adj* not able to be thought of or imagined. **inconceivably** *adv*.

inconclusive [inkən'klu:siv] *adj* not allowing one to decide; without a definite result: *inconclusive evidence.* **inconclusively** *adv*.

incongruous [in'kɔŋgruəs] *adj* not having anything in common; not in agreement with. *They are an incongruous couple* i.e. they are very different in many ways; *an incongruous remark.* **incongruously** *adv*.

incongruity [inkɔŋ'gru:iti] *nc/u* something incongruous; state of being incongruous.

inconsequent [in'kɔnsikwənt] *adj* not following what happened before: *an inconsequent remark.* **inconsequently** *adv*.

inconsequential [inkɔnsi'kwenʃl] *adj* **1.** not following what happened before. **2.** not important. **inconsequentially** *adv*.

inconsiderable [inkən'sidərəbl] *adj* not very large or important. **inconsiderably** *adv*.

inconsiderate [inkən'sidərət] *adj* not thinking of what will be best for or most helpful to other people: *inconsiderate behaviour.* **inconsiderately** *adv*. **inconsideration** [inkənsidə'reiʃən] *nu*.

inconsistent [inkən'sistnt] *adj* not acting or thinking in the same way; changing easily. **inconsistently** *adv*.

inconsistency *nc/u* inconsistent act; state of being inconsistent.

inconsistent with not suitable for; not in agreement with. *What you say is inconsistent with what you do* i.e. you say one thing and do something else.

inconsolable [inkən'souləbl] *adj* not willing or able to be consoled. **inconsolably** *adv.*
inconspicuous [inkən'spikjuəs] *adj* not easily seen; not well-known. **inconspicuously** *adv.* **inconspicuousness** *nu.*
inconstant [in'kɔnstnt] *adj* (esp. with reference to feelings) changing easily. **inconstantly** *adv.* **inconstancy** *nu.*
incontestable [inkən'testibl] *adj* not able to be disputed or denied. **incontestably** *adv.*
incontinent [in'kɔntinənt] *adj* not having control over one's feelings and behaviour (esp. control over feelings of sexual desire or control over urine etc). **incontinence** *nu.*
incontrovertible [inkɔntrə'vəːtibl] *adj* not able to be disputed or denied.
inconvenient [inkən'viːniənt] *adj* causing difficulty or trouble. *Saturday is an inconvenient day to see him.* **inconveniently** *adv.*
inconvenience *nc/u*: *Your visit caused him great inconvenience; the inconvenience of having to travel a long way to work.* Also *vt*: *I hope my visit will not inconvenience you.*
inconvertible [inkən'vəːtibl] *adj* (esp. with reference to money which cannot be changed for another kind of money) not able to be changed. **inconvertibility** [inkənvəːti'biliti] *nu.*
incorporate [in'kɔːpəreit] *vt/i* **1.** join into a whole; put something into something else to make a whole. *May I incorporate what you have written in my book?* **2.** become, join to become, a corporation. see **corporation** (in sense 2.).
incorporated *adj* (*US*) formed into a public company or corporation (usu. in the name of business firms and usu. written **Inc.** e.g. *Todd Stores Inc.*) (*Brit* **Ltd** for **limited**).
incorporeal [inkɔː'pɔːriəl] *adj* not having a body.
incorrect [inkə'rekt] *adj* not true; wrong. **incorrectly** *adv.* **incorrectness** *nu.*
incorrigible [in'kɔridʒibl] *adj* (with reference to persons) not able to be corrected or reformed: *an incorrigible thief.* **incorrigibly** *adv.*
incorruptible [inkə'rʌptibl] *adj* **1.** not able to be bribed. **2.** not able to be destroyed. **incorruptibility** [inkərʌpti'biliti] *nu.*
increase [in'kriːs] *vt/i* become or make greater. Also ['inkriːs] *nc/u.*
increasingly *adv* more and more.
incredible [in'kredibl] *adj* not to be believed; difficult to believe. **incredibly** *adv.* **incredibility** [inkredi'biliti] *nu.*
incredulous [in'kredjuləs] *adj* not believing. *When they heard his story they were at first incredulous. He gave me an incredulous look* i.e. his look showed he did not believe what he saw or heard. **incredulously** *adv.* **incredulity** [inkri'djuːliti] *nu.*
increment ['inkrimənt] *nc* increase (esp. of a salary each year). *You will get your next increment on 1 July.* **incremental** [inkri'mentl] *adj.*
incriminate [in'krimineit] *vt* cause somebody to be thought guilty of a crime. **incrimination** [inkrimi'neiʃən] *nc/u.*
incubate ['inkjubeit] *vt/i* sit on eggs to hatch them; hatch eggs. **incubation** [inkju'beiʃən] *nu.*
incubator *nc* apparatus which gives out the warmth necessary to hatch eggs or to protect babies born too soon.
incubus ['iŋkjubəs] *nc* nightmare; anything depressing a person like a nightmare.
inculcate ['inkʌlkeit] *vt* fix firmly in the mind of somebody (usu. by repeating something many times). *The teacher inculcated neatness and accuracy in his pupils.* **inculcation** [inkʌl'keiʃən] *nu.*
inculpate ['inkʌlpeit] *vt* cause somebody to be blamed (as well as oneself).
incumbent [in'kʌmbənt] *adj* (with **upon**) necessary as a duty. *It is incumbent upon them to help* (*o.f.*). Also *nc* person holding a particular post or appointment (esp. a priest in charge of a church).
incumbency *nc* post as an incumbent.
incur [in'kəː*] *vt* become responsible for; bring upon oneself. *He has incurred many debts. You will incur your father's disapproval. past* **incurred.**
incurable [in'kjuərəbl] *adj* not able to be cured. Also *nc* person who is incurable. **incurably** *adv.*
incurious [in'kjuəriəs] *adj* not showing any interest (esp. in matters which concern other people).
incursion [in'kəːʃən] *nc* sudden attack; raid.
indebted [in'detid] *adj* **1.** being in debt. **2.** grateful. *We are greatly indebted to them for their kind welcome.* **indebtedness** *nu.*
indecent [in'diːsnt] *adj* (esp. with reference to talk and behaviour connected with sex) shameful; disgusting. **indecently** *adv.*
indecency *nc/u* indecent act; state of being indecent.
indecipherable [indi'saifərəbl] *adj* not able to be deciphered or understood: *indecipherable handwriting/code.*
indecision [indi'siʒən] *nu* not being able to decide.
indecisive [indi'saisiv] *adj* **1.** not settling an argument/fight/disagreement/war etc. *The result of the game was indecisive and another will have to be played.* **2.** unable to decide quickly. *He is a very indecisive man.* **indecisively** *adv.*
indecorous [in'dekərəs] *adj* not proper or suitable in behaviour. **indecorously** *adv.*
indecorum [indi'kɔːrəm] *nu.*
indeed [in'diːd] *adv* in fact; certainly. *He is indeed the man we want. Are you coming with us? Yes, indeed. He is very fat indeed.* Also *interj* to express surprise or anger. *Your friend, indeed!* i.e. I am surprised that you think I am.
indefatigable [indi'fætigəbl] *adj* not able to be tired out; untiring. **indefatigably** *adv.*
indefensible [indi'fensibl] *adj* not able to be defended.
indefinable [indi'fainəbl] *adj* not possible or easy to explain; vague. **indefinably** *adv.*
indefinite [in'definit] *adj* doubtful; not clear or exact.
indefinitely *adv* **1.** not clearly or exactly. **2.** for an unknown period of time. *He is staying here indefinitely.*
indefinite article *a* or *an.*
indelible [in'deləbl] *adj* not able to be rubbed out: *an indelible pencil* i.e. one which makes marks that cannot be rubbed out. **indelibly** *adv.*
indelicate [in'delikət] *adj* (with reference to speech or behaviour) rude; coarse. **indelicately** *adv.*
indelicacy [in'delikəsi] *nc/u* indelicate act; state of being indelicate.
indemnify [in'demnifai] *vt* pay for loss or damage; protect against future loss or damage. *The company indemnifies you against any injuries you may suffer while at work.*

indemnity *nc/u* **1.** agreement which protects somebody against future loss or damage. **2.** money paid for loss or damage.

indent [in'dent] *vt* **1.** make holes or gaps in. **2.** make an official order for goods (**upon** somebody **for** something) (*formal*). **3.** begin a line of print further away from the margin than the other lines. *One usually indents the first line of a paragraph.* Also ['indent] *nc* (in sense **2.**).
indentation [inden'teiʃən] *nc* (in senses **1.** and **3.**).

indenture [in'dentʃə*] *nc* written agreement between two or more persons (esp. between an employer and a workman). Also *vt* give employment by means of indentures.

independent [indi'pendnt] *adj* not under the control of somebody else; not having to rely on somebody/something. *It is an independent country, not a colony; an independent worker* i.e. one who works by himself and does not rely on others. **independently** *adv.* **independence** *nu.*

indescribable [indis'kraibəbl] *adj* not able to be described. **indescribably** *adv.*

indestructible [indis'trʌktəbl] *adj* not able to be destroyed. **indestructibly** *adv.*

indeterminate [indi'tə:minit] *adj* not certain; not fixed: *be detained for an indeterminate time.* **indeterminately** *adv.* **indeterminacy** [indi'tə:minisi] *nu.*

index ['indeks] *nc* **1.** list of names, subjects etc arranged in alphabetical order (e.g. at the end of a book). **2.** something which points out or shows. *The number of servants he has is an index of his wealth; the index finger* i.e. the finger next to the thumb, used for pointing. **3.** (mathematics) figure or letter showing the power of a quantity (e.g. ^{2} in 6^2). Also *vt* make or put in an index (in sense **1.**). *pl* **indexes** or **indices** ['indisi:z].

indicate ['indikeit] *vt* point out; be a sign of; show by a sign. *He indicated my seat at the table. The black clouds indicate that it will rain soon. They indicated that they were very tired.*
indication [indi'keiʃən] *nc/u*: *This map gives no indication of the heights of the hills. Are there any indications of an improvement?* i.e. signs.
indicative [in'dikətiv] *adj* **1.** showing. *His attempt to escape is indicative of his guilt.* **2.** (grammar) *the indicative mood of a verb* i.e. the one that states something as a fact not as a wish etc. Also *nc* (in sense **2.**).
indicator *nc* person/thing that points out or gives information (e.g. about a machine). *The indicator on his car showed that he was going to turn left.*

indices ['indisi:z] pl of **index.**

indict [in'dait] *vt* charge with a crime. *He was indicted for murder/as a murderer/on a charge of murder.*
indictable *adj* for which one should be indicted: *an indictable offence* i.e. one serious enough to require a trial by a jury in a court of law.
indictment *nc/u* act of indicting; state of indicting or being indicted.

indifferent [in'difərnt] *adj* **1.** not interested in; not caring for; not concerned about. *He was indifferent to all our appeals for help.* **2.** neither very good nor very bad; of poor quality: *indifferent health; an indifferent pupil; indifferent work.* **indifferently** *adv.* **indifference** *nu.*

indigenous [in'didʒinəs] *adj* born in or belonging to a country; native: *the indigenous peoples of South America; their indigenous beliefs and customs.*

indigent ['indidʒənt] *adj* poor. **indigently** *adv.*
indigence *nu* poverty.

indigestible [indi'dʒestibl] *adj* not easily digested.
indigestion [indi'dʒestʃən] *nu* inability to digest; pain or discomfort caused by not being able to digest.

indignant [in'dignənt] *adj* (esp. with reference to what is thought to be wrong or unjust) angry. *They are indignant at/about the increased prices.* **indignantly** *adv.*
indignation [indig'neiʃən] *nu.*

indignity [in'digniti] *nc/u* rude treatment causing somebody to lose dignity and feel ashamed. *He suffered the indignity of being kept waiting for three hours.*

indigo ['indigou] *nu* **1.** deep blue colour. **2.** dye of this colour. Also *adj.*

indirect [indi'rekt] *adj* not straight; round about; not to the point. *I travelled to London by an indirect route* i.e. I did not travel straight there. *He gave only an indirect answer to my question* i.e. his answer was neither a clear 'yes' nor a clear 'no'. **indirectly** *adv.* **indirectness** *nu.*
indirect object (grammar) noun or noun phrase which completes or tells more about the action of a transitive verb (e.g. *He threw the ball* ('the ball' is the direct object), *He threw him the ball/He threw the ball to him* ('him' is the indirect object)).
indirect speech (grammar) method of writing or speaking about what a person has said, not by using his actual words but by giving the sense of them or reporting them (e.g. *He said 'I will do it'* (direct speech). *He said that he would do it* (indirect speech)) (Also **reported speech**).

indiscreet [indis'kri:t] *adj* careless in behaviour; telling secrets to other people; going beyond the limits of what is proper or sensible. **indiscreetly** *adv.*
indiscretion [indis'kreʃən] *nc/u* indiscreet act; state of being indiscreet.

indiscriminate [indis'kriminət] *adj* without taking the trouble to choose or to find out: *indiscriminate punishment* i.e. punishing without taking the trouble to find out who was really to blame or how serious the offence was. **indiscriminately** *adv.*

indispensable [indis'pensibl] *adj* without which something cannot be done; necessary. *Books are indispensable to a scholar.* **indispensably** *adv.*

indisposed [indis'pouzd] *adj* **1.** not ready or willing to do something. *He is indisposed to give any money.* **2.** slightly ill. *I stayed at home because I was indisposed.* **indisposition** [indispə'ziʃən] *nc/u.*

indisputable [indis'pju:təbl] *adj* certain; not able to be argued about. **indisputably** *adv.*

indissoluble [indi'sɔljubl] *adj* not able to be dissolved; permanent: *an indissoluble partnership.* **indissolubly** *adv.*

indistinct [indis'tiŋkt] *adj* not clearly seen/heard etc. *Your voice is indistinct.* **indistinctly** *adv.* **indistinctness** *nu.*

individual [indi'vidjuəl] *adj* special to, belonging to, one particular person/thing. *Everyone has an individual way of signing his name.* Also *nc* **1.** a person when regarded as a single, separate being. *The* *purpose of the law is to protect the rights of the individual.* **2.** any person. *Who's that individual wearing a dirty shirt?* (*informal* and rather *impolite*). **individually** *adv.* **individuality** [individju'æliti] *nu.*

individualism *nu* **1.** belief that the individual is more important than the society he lives in. **2.** acting only for oneself without considering others or what they do.

individualist *nc* person who believes or practises individualism. **individualistic** [individjuə'listik] *adj.*

indivisible [indi'vizibl] *adj* not able to be divided. **indivisibly** *adv.*

indoctrinate [in'dɔktrineit] *vt* teach particular ideas and beliefs in a way that prevents the learner from thinking for himself. **indoctrination** [indɔktri'neiʃən] *nu.*

indolent ['indəlnt] *adj* lazy. **indolently** *adv.* **indolence** *nu.*

indomitable [in'dɔmitəbl] *adj* not able to be conquered; refusing to yield. **indomitably** *adv.*

indoor ['indɔ:*] *adj* in a building; not outside: *indoor games.*

indoors *adv* in/into a building. *They are playing indoors. They went indoors.*

indorse [in'dɔ:s] *vt* see **endorse.**

indubitable [in'dju:bitəbl] *adj* not able to be doubted. **indubitably** *adv.*

induce [in'dju:s] *vt* **1.** persuade; cause. *They induced me to go away with them. Hard work induces hunger. The doctor induced the birth of the child* i.e. caused the birth to take place, perhaps because it was overdue. **2.** arrive at a conclusion by induction (in sense **2.**). **3.** produce current by induction (in sense **3.**).

inducement *nc*: *They added £10 to his salary as an inducement* i.e. to persuade him to take a job or to stay in it.

induct [in'dʌkt] *vt* (esp. with reference to introducing a clergyman formally to his work) bring in; introduce.

induction **1.** *nc* act of inducting or being inducted. **2.** *nu* process of arriving at a general conclusion by considering particular examples. (*opp* **deduction**). **3.** *nu* setting up magnetism or electricity in a non-electrified body by bringing an electrified one close to it.

inductive *adj* (in senses **2.** and **3.** of **induction**). **inductively** *adv.*

indulge [in'dʌldʒ] *vt/i* allow oneself to enjoy something; allow somebody to have his own way. *We indulged in an expensive supper after the concert.* **indulgent** *adj.* **indulgently** *adv.*

indulgence **1.** *nc/u*: *One of my few indulgences is having breakfast in bed on Sunday morning. Indulgence in drink can harm your health.* **2.** *nc* forgiveness of sins, acquired by performing a religious rite, prayer etc (without punishment).

'self-in'dulgence indulging oneself (usu. too much).

industry ['indəstri] *nc/u* **1.** ability and willingness to work hard. *A country's greatest wealth is the industry of its people.* **2.** making large quantities of goods by using machines; a particular branch of this process or branch of trade generally. *That country is mainly agricultural and has few industries; the iron and steel industry; the shipping industry.*

industrial [in'dʌstriəl] *adj* (in sense **2.**): *the industrial part of the city* i.e. where the factories are. **industrially** *adv.*

industrious [in'dʌstriəs] *adj* (in sense **1.**): *an industrious pupil.* **industriously** *adv.*

industrialize [in'dʌstriəlaiz] *vt* build up industries: *industrialize a country.* **industrialization** [indʌstriəlai'zeiʃən] *nu.* **industrialized** *adj.*

industrialism [in'dʌstriəlizəm] *nu* system of industry (in sense **2.**).

industrialist [in'dʌstriəlist] *nc* owner or manager of a large industry.

inebriate [in'i:brieit] *vt* cause to be drunk. Also [in'i:briit] *nc* person who is always drunk. **inebriated** *adj.* **inebriety** [ini'braiəti] *nu.* (all *formal* or rather *o.f.*).

inedible [in'edibl] *adj* not suitable for eating.

ineffable [in'efəbl] *adj* (usu. with reference to something very pleasant or something holy) not able to be described in words: *ineffable happiness.* **ineffably** *adv.*

ineffective [ini'fektiv] *adj* not having any result; not successful. *He is an ineffective salesman.* **ineffectively** *adv.* **ineffectiveness** *nu.*

ineffectual [ini'fektjuəl] *adj* not having a result; unsuccessful. **ineffectually** *adv.*

inefficient [ini'fiʃənt] *adj* not able to work well and produce good results. **inefficiently** *adv.* **inefficiency** *nu.*

inelastic [ini'læstik] *adj* **1.** not able to regain its original shape after being pulled or pushed. **2.** not able to be changed if necessary. *They failed because their plans were too inelastic.*

inelegant [in'eligənt] *adj* **1.** not having very good manners. **2.** not beautiful in appearance or well-made. **inelegantly** *adv.* **inelegance** *nu.*

ineligible [in'elidʒibl] *adj* not fit to be chosen (for some reason). **ineligibly** *adv.* **ineligibility** [inelidʒi'biliti] *nu.*

inept [i'nept] *adj* **1.** not suitable: *an inept remark.* **2.** slow at learning: *an inept pupil.* **ineptly** *adv.* **ineptitude** [i'neptitju:d] *nc/u.*

inequality [ini'kwɔliti] **1.** *nu* state of not being equal. **2.** *nc* example of this state: *the inequalities in the wages paid by the two companies.* **3.** *nc/u* unevenness of the surface.

inequitable [in'ekwitəbl] *adj* not fair; unjust. **inequitably** *adv.* **inequity** *nu.*

ineradicable [ini'rædikəbl] *adj* not able to be dug out or removed: *ineradicable error.* **ineradicably** *adv.*

inert [i'nə:t] *adj* **1.** not able to move, be active or change: *an inert gas* i.e. one that does not change if heated or treated in any way. **2.** without moving; slow. *He lay inert on the ground.*

inertia [i'nə:ʃə] *nu* **1.** state of being inert. **2.** (science) force which makes it difficult for a body to begin moving, and when it is moving makes it difficult for it to stop.

inescapable [inis'keipəbl] *adj* not able to be escaped from; inevitable. **inescapably** *adv.*

inestimable [in'estiməbl] *adj* not able to be estimated; very large, valuable etc: *inestimable wealth.* **inestimably** *adv.*

inevitable [in'evitəbl] *adj* **1.** not able to be avoided; certain to happen or appear. *Defeat was inevitable. She gave us her inevitable smile* i.e. one we knew would appear. **inevitably** *adv.* **inevitability** [inevitə'biliti] *nu.*

inexact [inig'zækt] *adj* not correct in every way; having mistakes. **inexactly** *adv.* **inexactness** *nu.*

inexcusable [iniks'kju:zəbl] *adj* not able to be excused. **inexcusably** *adv*.

inexhaustible [inig'zɔ:stəbl] *adj* not able to be exhausted: *inexhaustible wealth*. **inexhaustibly** *adv*.

inexorable [in'eksərəbl] *adj* not able to be prevented even when one begs or prays that it should be; without mercy. *The spread of the disease was inexorable*. **inexorably** *adv*.

inexpedient [iniks'pi:diənt] *adj* not to be done at a particular time; not advisable. *It would be inexpedient to go away while he is ill*. **inexpediently** *adv*. **inexpediency** *nc/u*.

inexpensive [iniks'pensiv] *adj* not expensive; cheap.

inexperience [iniks'piəriəns] *nu* lack of experience. **inexperienced** *adj*.

inexpert [in'ekspə:t] *adj* not having any special knowledge; not skilled. **inexpertly** *adv*. **inexpertness** *nu*.

inexplicable [iniks'plikəbl] *adj* not able to be explained. **inexplicably** *adv*.

inexpressible [iniks'presəbl] *adj* not able to be described or expressed in words. **inexpressibly** *adv*.

inextricable [iniks'trikəbl] *adj* not able to be solved or made simple. *He was in inextricable difficulties*. **inextricably** *adv*.

infallible [in'fæləbl] *adj* **1.** not able to do wrong or be wrong. *He is so proud that he thinks himself infallible*. **2.** sure; certain. *This is an infallible way to get good results*. **infallibly** *adv*. **infallibility** [infælə'biliti] *nu*.

infamous ['infəməs] *adj* known for being wicked.

infamy *nu* public disgrace; evil.

infant ['infənt] *nc* **1.** very young child. **2.** (in a legal sense) person under 18 years of age. Also *adj* of or for infants: *infant years; infant school*.

infantile ['infəntail] *adj* like an infant; common among infants. *He is a grown man but his jokes are infantile; infantile diseases*.

infancy *nu* **1.** state of being an infant. **2.** first stage of anything. *Modern science was then in its infancy*.

infanticide [in'fæntisaid] **1.** *nu* killing of an infant. **2.** *nc* person who kills an infant.

infantry ['infəntri] *nu* (company of) foot soldiers.

'infantryman foot soldier: *120 infantrymen in one company of infantry*.

infatuate [in'fætjueit] *vt* (usu. *passive*) make foolish because of too much admiration for somebody/something. *He is infatuated with her* i.e. he loves her so much that he cannot see her as she really is. **infatuation** [infætju'eiʃən] *nc/u*.

infect [in'fekt] *vt* cause to get a disease; cause to have a certain feeling. *If you do not keep away from the children, you will infect them with your cold. This meat is infected* i.e. it contains the germs of a disease. *His sadness infected us all*.

infection **1.** *nu* (esp. with reference to spreading disease through the air or water) act of spreading a disease or feeling. see **contagion**. **2.** *nc* disease or feeling spread in this way.

infectious [in'fekʃəs] *adj*: *an infectious disease; infectious laughter*. **infectiously** *adv*.

infer [in'fə:*] *vt* decide or conclude after considering the evidence or facts. *We infer from his letters that he is very unhappy*. *past* **inferred**.

inference ['infərns] **1.** *nu* act of inferring. **2.** *nc* something that is inferred. *We can draw/make other inferences from his letters*.

inferior [in'fiəriə*] *adj* lower in position, quality, value etc. *An assistant manager is inferior in position to a manager. This cloth is inferior to that one*. Also *nc*: *The manager is not friendly with his inferiors*. **inferiority** [infiəri'ɔriti] *nu*.

inferi'ority complex state of feeling inferior which often causes a person to behave in the opposite way by pretending to be brave, confident and successful.

infernal [in'fə:nl] *adj* **1.** belonging to hell; devilish. **2.** nasty; annoying: *an infernal noise*. (*informal* in sense **2.**). **infernally** *adv*.

inferno [in'fə:nou] *nc* hell; any place which fire makes as hot and as horrible as hell. *The fire turned the forest into an inferno*. *pl* **infernos**.

infertile [in'fə:tail] *adj* not fertile; barren: *infertile ground*.

infest [in'fest] *vt* (esp. with reference to somebody/something unpleasant) enter in very great numbers. *The food store was infested with rats*. **infestation** [infes'teiʃən] *nu*.

infidel ['infidl] *nc* person who does not believe in what is considered to be the true religion. *To Muslims all Christians are infidels*.

infidelity [infi'deliti] *nc/u* act or state of being unfaithful (esp. to one's husband or wife).

infiltrate ['infiltreit] *vt/i* enter, cause to enter, quietly, gradually, or one by one. *During the war the enemy tried to infiltrate spies into our country*. **infiltration** [infil'treiʃən] *nu*. **infiltrator** *nc*.

infinite ['infinit] *adj* without limit or end; not able to be counted or measured: *the infinite space of the universe. The storm caused infinite damage*. **infinitely** *adv*.

infinitude [in'finitju:d] **1.** *nu* state of being infinite. **2.** *nc* infinite number or quantity.

infinity [in'finiti] **1.** *nc/u* infinitude. **2.** *nu* (mathematics) infinite quantity (shown by the sign ∞).

infinitesimal [infini'tesiməl] *adj* so small that it cannot be counted or measured. **infinitesimally** *adv*.

infinitive [in'finitiv] *adj* (grammar) form of the verb used without reference to person, number or time (e.g. *to be, to go etc*). Also *nc*.

infirm [in'fə:m] *adj* (esp. with reference to old persons) weak; not in good health.

infirmity **1.** *nu* state of being infirm. **2.** *nc* something which causes one to be infirm.

infirmary [in'fə:məri] *nc* hospital or room used as a hospital. (rather *o.f.*).

inflame [in'fleim] *vt* make red or angry. *The dust inflamed my eyes. The people were inflamed by the news*.

inflammation [inflə'meiʃən] **1.** *nu* state of being inflamed: *inflammation of the eyes*. **2.** *nc* part of the body which is inflamed.

inflammatory [in'flæmətəri] *adj* causing to be inflamed: *inflammatory news*.

inflammable [in'flæməbl] *adj* (mainly *Brit*) easily set on fire. (*US* **flammable**) (*opp* **uninflammable** or **not inflammable**).

inflate [in'fleit] *vt* **1.** cause to swell with air or gas. *I had to inflate the tyre*. **2.** (usu. *passive*) make greater or more important than is necessary or desirable. *He is inflated with the dignity of his position as chairman*. **3.** cause prices to increase by increasing the amount of money in use. **inflation** *nu.*

inflationary [in'fleiʃnəri] *adj* causing, or caused by, inflation (in sense **3.**): *the government's inflationary policy.*

inflect [in'flekt] *vt* **1.** change the tone of one's voice. **2.** (grammar) change the form of a word to show person, number and grammatical relationship with other words (e.g. I *am*, you *are*). **inflexion, inflection** *nc/u.*

inflexible [in'fleksibl] *adj* not easily changed, moved or bent. *He is inflexible on this matter.* **inflexibility** [infleksi'biliti] *nu.*

inflict [in'flikt] *vt* cause something unpleasant to happen to somebody. *They inflicted defeat on/upon their enemies.*

infliction **1.** *nu* state of inflicting or being inflicted: *their infliction of defeat on/upon their enemies.* **2.** *nc* something that is inflicted or suffered. *Hunger is one of their inflictions.*

influence ['influəns] **1.** *nc* effect on one's mind or actions; the cause of this effect. *Religion has a great influence on man's behaviour. He is one of the good influences in the school.* **2.** *nu* power to cause this effect (usu. because of social position or wealth). *People with influence get the best jobs here.* **3.** *nu* power of nature to cause an effect: *the influence of rain on plants.* Also *vt*: *influence somebody's decision.* **influential** [influ'enʃl] *adj.* **influentially** *adv.*

influenza [influ'enzə] *nu* type of disease which causes a feverish cold (informally shortened to **flu**).

influx ['inflʌks] *nc* flowing in; arrival of many persons/things. *pl* **influxes.**

inform [in'fɔːm] *vt* **1.** make known to. *He will inform us where to go. They informed him of their arrival.* **2.** accuse; charge with a crime. *He went to the police and informed against/on the criminals.* **information** [infə'meiʃən] *nu.*

informative *adj* giving information.

informer *nc* person who informs against somebody.

'well-/'badly in'formed *adj* having good/little knowledge or information.

informal [in'fɔːml] *adj* **1.** done without ceremony: *an informal meeting of heads of state; an informal dinner; informal clothes* i.e. ordinary clothes, not specially put on for the occasion. **2.** used in ordinary speech or writing: *an informal expression.* **informally** *adv.* **informality** [infɔː'mæliti] *nc/u.*

infra(-) ['infrə] *adv/prefix* below; later on in a book.

infra'red *adj* having the type of rays of light which are below the colour red in the spectrum and are thus invisible.

infraction [in'frækʃən] *nc/u* breaking a law or rule.

infrequent [in'friːkwənt] *adj* not often. **infrequently** *adv.* **infrequency** *nu.*

infringe [in'frindʒ] *vt* **1.** break a law or rule. *People who drive without a licence infringe the law.* **2.** use, or interfere with, something without having the right to do so. *You must not infringe the copyright of this article. He has infringed our privacy.* **infringement** *nc/u.*

infuriate [in'fjuərieit] *vt* make furious. **infuriated** *adj.*

infuse [in'fjuːz] **1.** *vt/i* pour boiling water over (usu. over tea). *Heat the teapot before you infuse the tea.* **2.** *vt* fill somebody with a feeling. *The good news infused them with hope.*

infusion [in'fjuːʒən] **1.** *nu* state of infusing or being infused. **2.** *nc* liquid made by infusing.

ingenious [in'dʒiːniəs] *adj* **1.** (with reference to persons) clever at inventing or discovering new ideas. **2.** (with reference to things) cleverly made. **ingeniously** *adv.* **ingenuity** [indʒi'njuːiti] *nu.*

ingenuous [in'dʒenjuəs] *adj* sincere; frank; open; easily deceived. *He has an ingenuous face.* (*opp* **disingenuous**). **ingenuously** *adv.* **ingenuousness** *nu.*

inglorious [in'glɔːriəs] *adj* without honour or glory; disgraceful. **ingloriously** *adv.*

ingot ['iŋgət] *nc* (esp. of gold or silver) short bar of metal.

ingrained [in'greind] *adj* (esp. with reference to habits, beliefs etc) firmly fixed.

ingratiate [in'greiʃieit] *vt* make (oneself) liked by, or popular with, somebody (usu. for selfish reasons). *He ingratiated himself with the new master.* **ingratiating** *adj.* **ingratiatingly** *adv.*

ingratitude [in'grætitjuːd] *nu* absence of thankfulness or gratitude.

ingredient [in'griːdiənt] *nc* one of the parts of a mixture: *a cake made from flour, sugar and various other ingredients.*

ingrowing ['ingrouiŋ] *adj* growing inwards: *ingrowing toenail.*

inhabit [in'hæbit] *vt* live in.

inhabitable *adj* able to be lived in. (*opp* **uninhabitable**).

inhabitant *nc* person who lives in a place.

inhabited *adj.* (*opp* **uninhabited**).

inhale [in'heil] *vt/i* breathe in; draw in with the breath into the lungs. *They say it is dangerous to inhale cigarette smoke.*

inhere [in'hiə*] *vi* (with reference to qualities) naturally belong to or exist in (*o.f.*).

inherent *adj*: *Love of their children is inherent in all parents.* **inherently** *adv.*

inherit [in'herit] *vt* **1.** receive money, property or position on the death of someone (usu. a relative). *He inherited his uncle's farm* i.e. he got the farm on the death of his uncle. **2.** receive a quality of somebody from whom one is descended. *He has inherited his grandfather's skill in making money.* **inherited** *adj.* **inheritance** *nc/u.*

inhibit [in'hibit] *vt* cause, be likely to cause, somebody not to do something; make it difficult for somebody to do something. *His bad English inhibits him from speaking freely/He is inhibited from speaking freely by his bad English.* (*opp* **uninhibited**).

inhibition [inhi'biʃən] *nc/u* feeling or state of being inhibited. *He has no inhibitions about speaking French.*

inhospitable [inhɔs'pitəbl] *adj* not hospitable; not friendly or ready to welcome. **inhospitably** *adv.*

inhuman [in'hjuːmən] *adj* not human; cruel.

inhumanity [inhuː'mæniti] *nc/u* act or state of being inhuman.

inhumane [inhju'mein] *adj* not humane; not kind: *an inhumane act.*

inimical [i'nimikl] *adj* (with **to**) not friendly or favourable.

inimitable [i'nimitəbl] *adj* not able to be imitated; better than or different from any other: *his inimitable way of making his students interested in their work.* **inimitably** *adv.*

iniquitous [i'nikwitəs] *adj* very wicked or unfair. **iniquitously** *adv.*

iniquity [i'nikwiti] *nc/u* act or state of being iniquitous.

initial [i'niʃl] *adj* first. Also *nc* first letter of a person's name or of a word (e.g. J.S. are the initials of John Smith; U.N.O. of the United Nations Organization). Also *vt* sign by using only one's initials. *past* **initialled.** (*US* **initialed**).

initially *adv* at first.

initiate [i'niʃieit] *vt* **1.** begin, cause something to begin. *He has initiated talks about opening new schools.* **2.** make known for the first time; introduce. *The lecture initiated us into the problems of living abroad. We were initiated into the sports club by one of the members.* Also [i'niʃiit] *nc* person who is initiated and thus knows about something.

initiation [iniʃi'eiʃən] *nu* act of initiating or being initiated.

initiative [i'niʃətiv] *nu* ability to do, or begin, something without the help or suggestions of others. *He went to see the headmaster on his own initiative* i.e. it was his own idea to see him. *He's got no initiative. He took the initiative by speaking first at the meeting.*

inject [in'dʒekt] *vt* throw in; (esp. with reference to putting a fluid below the skin by means of a hollow needle) force in. *The doctor injected the drug into my arm.*

injection *nc/u*: *I have been given an injection by the doctor.*

injudicious [indʒu:'diʃəs] *adj* not having good judgment; thoughtless. **injudiciously** *adv.*

injunction [in'dʒʌŋkʃən] *nc* **1.** command; order: *his father's injunctions.* **2.** order from a court that something should, or should not, be done. *The court injunction prevented him from seeing his son.*

injure ['indʒə*] *vt* do harm or damage (usu. to living creatures).

injured *adj* **1.** harmed or damaged. **2.** hurt; offended; complaining. *She spoke in an injured voice.* Also *nu* people who have been injured in an accident etc.

injury *nc* harm; damage; wound. *Because of his many injuries he was taken to hospital.*

injurious [in'dʒuəriəs] *adj* causing hurt or offence. **injuriously** *adv.*

add insult to injury insult a person as well as injuring him. (*informal*).

injustice [in'dʒʌstis] **1.** *nu* being without justice. **2.** *nc* unjust act. *They did me a great injustice by calling me a liar.*

ink [iŋk] *nc* type of black or coloured liquid used for writing, printing and drawing. Also *vt* cover or mark with ink.

inky *adj* **1.** covered or marked with ink. **2.** as black as ink: *inky darkness.* **inkiness** *nu.*

'inkpad pad soaked with ink.

'inkpot container for holding ink.

'inkwell type of inkpot which can be put in a hole made for it in a desk.

inkling ['iŋkliŋ] *nc* very small hint, a little knowledge. *They have an inkling of his plans.*

inland ['inlənd] *adj* far away from the sea; inside a country. *Birmingham is an inland city; inland postal services* i.e. those carried on inside a country. Also ['in'lænd] *adv* away from the sea. *They travelled inland from the coast. The city lies inland.*

'inland 'revenue money obtained from taxes (e.g. income tax) raised inside a country.

in-laws ['inlɔ:z] *npl* short informal form of **mother-in-law, father-in-law etc.** *He has gone to see his in-laws.*

inlay ['in'lei] *vt* cut out parts of a surface of wood or metal and put the pieces of wood or metal in their place to make a pattern: *a wooden box inlaid with copper. past* **inlaid.** Also ['inlei] *nc* inlaid pattern.

inlet ['inlet] *nc* **1.** narrow area of water; small bay. **2.** small piece of cloth joined (on at least two sides) to a large piece. Also *adj* allowing a gas or liquid to enter: *an inlet valve.*

in loco parentis [in'loukoupə'rentis] (usu. with reference to the authority of university teachers over their students) in place of a parent.

inmate ['inmeit] *nc* person who lives with others in a building (usu. a hospital or prison).

inmost ['inmoust] *adj* furthest in; most difficult to discover. (Also **innermost**).

inn [in] *nc* building which supplies travellers with food, drink and a place to sleep (usu. found in the country, not towns).

'innkeeper person in charge of an inn.

innate [i'neit] *adj* born in a person; natural: *man's innate desire for happiness.* **innately** *adv.*

inner ['inə*] *adj* further in; inside something else: *the inner circle* i.e. the one inside another circle.

innermost ['inəmoust] *adj* see **inmost.**

innings ['iniŋz] *nc* (in cricket, baseball etc) a player's or a team's turn to bat. *In cricket each team has one or two innings. In baseball each team has nine innings. pl* **innings.**

innocent ['inəsnt] *adj* **1.** doing no wrong; not guilty. *I am innocent of the crime.* **2.** knowing no wrong; simple; easily deceived. *He is innocent about night life in a big city. They were innocent enough to believe him.* Also *nc* person who is innocent (esp. a young person). **innocently** *adv.* **innocence** *nu.*

innocuous [i'nɔkjuəs] *adj* harmless. **innocuously** *adv.*

innovate ['inəveit] *vi* change by bringing in something new. *The young teachers wish to innovate.*

innovation [inə'veiʃən] *nc/u*: *the young teachers' innovations in classroom work.*

innovator *nc* person who innovates.

innuendo [inju'endou] *nc/u* indirect hint or statement made about somebody (usu. attacking his behaviour or character). *pl* **innuendoes.**

innumerable [i'nju:mərəbl] *adj* too many to be counted. **innumerably** *adv.*

inoculate [i'nɔkjuleit] *vt* protect somebody against a disease by giving him a little of the disease so that his body makes itself able to meet a severe attack. *The doctor inoculated the children against influenza.*

inoculation [inɔkju'leiʃən] *nc/u.*

inoffensive [inə'fensiv] *adj* not causing offence; quiet and harmless: *an inoffensive little man.*

inoperative [in'ɔpərətiv] *adj* having no effect; no longer in use.

inopportune [in'ɔpətju:n] *adj* happening at the wrong time; not convenient. **inopportunely** *adv.*

inordinate [i'nɔ:dinət] *adj* not under control; too great: *inordinate pride.* **inordinately** *adv.*

inorganic [inɔ:'gænik] *adj* not belonging to, or having the structure of, animals or

plants (e.g. metals or rocks). **inorganically** *adv.*
inorganic chemistry type of chemistry which deals with this kind of substance.

in-patient ['inpeiʃənt] *nc* person who lives in a hospital while being attended to. (*opp* **out-patient**).

input ['input] *nc* what is put into something (e.g. the electric power put into a battery; the money and labour put into a business) (*opp* **output**).

inquest ['inkwest] *nc* public inquiry made under the law into any matter (esp. into the cause of somebody's death).

inquire, enquire [in'kwaiə*] *vt/i* ask questions about; try to find out. *I inquired about his daughter. They inquired where to go.* **inquiring** *adj* always trying to find out: *an inquiring mind.* **inquiringly** *adv.*
inquiry **1.** *nu* a court of inquiry. **2.** *nc*: *I have to make inquiries about his name and address.* **inquirer** *nc.*
inquire after ask for news about somebody.
inquire into something try to find out about something. *The police are inquiring into the murder.*

inquisition [inkwi'ziʃən] *nc/u* strict inquiry into; severe questioning (usu. an official one).
inquisitor [in'kwizitə*] *nc* member of the Inquisition; person who questions severely.
the Inquisition court set up by the Roman Catholic Church to inquire about and to punish persons who did not believe in the Church.

inquisitive [in'kwizitiv] *adj* wishing to know about other people's business; too ready to ask questions. *Our neighbours are very inquisitive about our friends.* **inquisitively** *adv.* **inquisitiveness** *nu.*

inroad ['inroud] *nc* (usu. *pl*) **1.** sudden attack into the country of an enemy. **2.** something that makes less or interferes with. *Extra work has made inroads on my spare time.*

insane [in'sein] *adj* mad; mentally diseased. **insanely** *adv.* **insanity** [in'sæniti] *nu.*

insanitary [in'sænitəri] *adj* (esp. with reference to the absence of proper sanitation) dirty and unhealthy.

insatiable [in'seiʃəbl] *adj* not able to be satisfied; always wanting more. **insatiably** *adv.*

inscribe [in'skraib] *vt* (often with reference to writing cut on something hard like wood or stone) write in or on. *He inscribed his name in the book. Their names are inscribed on the stone above their grave.* **inscription** [in'skripʃən] *nc/u.*

inscrutable [in'skru:təbl] *adj* not able to be discovered or understood. *His face was inscrutable* i.e. nobody could discover his feelings by looking at it. **inscrutably** *adv.*

insect ['insekt] *nc* **1.** type of very small animal with six legs (e.g. a fly, a bee or an ant). **2.** any small animal like this (e.g. a spider).
insecticide [in'sektisaid] *nc* chemical substance used for killing insects.
'**insect powder** type of powder which is an insecticide.

insecure [insi'kjuə*] *adj* not properly fastened; not safe. *These boxes are insecure. I feel insecure in this lonely house.* **insecurely** *adv.* **insecurity** *nu.*

inseminate [in'semineit] *vt* put seed into; make pregnant. **insemination** [insemi'neiʃən] *nu.*
artificial insemination production of offspring by artificially introducing seed or semen into a female.

insensate [in'senseit] *adj* having no feelings; stupid.

insensible [in'sensibl] *adj* **1.** without bodily feeling; unconscious. *He is still insensible after the blow on his head.* **2.** not knowing or caring about. *They were insensible to our requests* i.e. they refused to listen to them and did not care. **3.** too small or slow to be noticed: *the insensible growth of a tree.* **insensibly** *adv.*

insensitive [in'sensitiv] *adj* not sensitive; not quick to feel; not easily hurt: *insensitive to pain.* **insensitively** *adv.* **insensitiveness** *nu.*

inseparable [in'sepərəbl] *adj* not able to be separated. **inseparably** *adv.*

insert [in'sə:t] *vt* put in; place among others. *The book would be improved by inserting another chapter.* Also ['insə:t] *nc* something inserted.
insertion *nc/u* act of inserting; something inserted (often with reference to an advertisement put in a newspaper).

inset ['inset] *nc* something put in (esp. with reference to extra pages put in a book or a small picture or diagram printed in the corner of a larger one).

inshore ['in'ʃɔ:*] *adj/adv* near, toward the shore.

inside ['in'said] **1.** *adj* within the sides of: *the inside pages of a book.* **2.** *adv*: *Let's go inside. There is a boy inside.* **3.** *prep*: *Let's go inside the house. There is a boy inside the classroom.* Also *nc*: *I want to see the inside of the house. He has a pain in his inside* i.e. in his stomach. (*informal*).
insider *nc* member of a group; one who knows more than the people outside.
inside information/knowledge etc information/knowledge etc which can only be obtained by or from somebody who works inside an organization etc. *I have inside information about the meeting last night.*
inside lane part of road which is nearest to the inner edge. *Keep to the inside lane when driving slowly on a main road.*
inside of (mainly US) in less time than. *They won't be here inside of an hour.* (*informal*).
inside out **1.** with the inside on the outside. *He is wearing his coat inside out.* **2.** completely. *They know this town inside out.*

insidious [in'sidiəs] *adj* causing harm or damage without being seen or felt. **insidiously** *adv.*

insight ['insait] *nc/u* ability to see the real meaning of something; clear and quick understanding of a problem. *He has a great insight into modern science. His speech gave us a valuable insight into the problems of education.*

insignia [in'signiə] *npl* signs or badges showing rank or authority.

insignificant [insig'nifikənt] *adj* not important; of little use or value. **insignificantly** *adv.* **insignificance** *nu.*

insincere [insin'siə*] *adj* not sincere; false. **insincerely** *adv.* **insincerity** [insin'seriti] *nu.*

insinuate [in'sinjueit] *vt* **1.** (usu. with **oneself**) move slowly and cunningly into. *He insinuated himself into all our discussions.* **2.** say something unpleasant in an indirect way. *They have insinuated to me that you drink too much.* **insinuation** [insinju'eiʃən] *nc/u.*

insipid [in'sipid] *adj* **1.** without taste: *insipid food.* **2.** not interesting; not lively: *an insipid meeting.* **insipidly** *adv.* **insipidness** *nu.*

insist [in'sist] *vt* state or urge strongly (esp. against those who state or urge differently). *I insist on your being here. I insist that you be here/shall be here. He insists on the need to work hard.* **insistent** *adj.* **insistence** *nu.*

insolent ['insəlnt] *adj* very rude (esp. to somebody who is older or more important). *He was insolent to his teacher.* **insolently** *adv.* **insolence** *nu.*

insoluble [in'sɔljubl] *adj* **1.** not able to be dissolved. **2.** not able to be solved or explained: *an insoluble problem.*

insolvent [in'sɔlvənt] *adj* not able to pay one's debts. **insolvency** *nu.*

insomnia [in'sɔmniə] *nu* state of not being able to sleep.

insomniac [in'sɔmniæk] *nc* person who suffers from an inability to sleep.

inspect [in'spekt] *vt* (esp. with reference to an official seeing that something is done) look carefully at. *A man came to inspect our school yesterday* i.e. to see that it was doing well.

inspection **1.** *nu* inspecting or being inspected. *On inspection the meat was found to be bad.* **2.** *nc* act of inspecting.

inspector *nc* **1.** person who inspects (esp. tickets on trains and buses). **2.** police officer above a sergeant in rank.

inspectorate [in'spektərit] *nc* all the inspectors of a country, region etc.

inspire [in'spaiə*] *vt* cause somebody to have better thoughts or feelings. *The good news inspired us with hope. His speech inspired us to try again.*

inspired *adj* having great thoughts and powers: *an inspired artist.*

inspiring *adj*: *an inspiring speech.* (*opp* **uninspiring**).

inspiration [inspi'reiʃən] **1.** *nu* act of inspiring; impulse towards creative work; guidance from God. **2.** *nc* clever idea which comes to one suddenly. *I've had an inspiration.*

instability [instə'biliti] *nu* (usu. with reference to behaviour or character) state of not having stability; lack of firmness or determination.

install [in'stɔ:l] *vt* **1.** put somebody in his new position (usu. at a ceremony and often with reference to a church or university). *The new Vice-Chancellor of the university has been installed.* **2.** put something in its position ready for use: *install an electric light/a bathroom/a fireplace etc.* **3.** put oneself in a place; occupy. *He has just installed himself in his new office.*

installation [instə'leiʃən] **1.** *nu* act of installing or being installed. **2.** *nc* something which has been installed (e.g. a piece of machinery or equipment).

instalment [in'stɔ:lmənt] *nc* **1.** regular payment in small fixed amounts of money for something which one has already been allowed to own. *We are paying for our car by/in monthly instalments of £10.* **2.** regular supply of something in parts. *I am looking forward to the next instalment of his book in the Sunday newspaper.*

instance ['instns] *nc* example; occasion. *This is the first instance of fever in the village.* Also *vt* give as an example.

at the instance of at the request of.

for instance for example.

in the first instance at the beginning; firstly.

instant[1] ['instnt] *adj* **1.** quick; urgent; without delay: *an instant reply. The sick boy needs instant attention.* **2.** prepared by a manufacturer and ready for use: *instant coffee.* **3.** of the present month (usu. shortened to **inst.** and used in commercial and official letters): *with reference to your letter of 20th inst.* (*o.f.* – use either the name of the month or **of this month**). **instantly** *adv.*

instant[2] ['instnt] *nc* moment of time; very short time. *He came the instant I called his name* i.e. immediately after I called his name. *Go away this instant!* i.e. now; at once. *He finished the work in an instant* i.e. in a very short time.

instantaneous [instn'teiniəs] *adj* done in an instant; happening in a moment. *Death was instantaneous.* **instantaneously** *adv.*

instead [in'sted] *adv* taking the place of, or as a change from, somebody/something. *He didn't give John the money, but he gave it to me instead. Last night I stayed at home. Tonight I'm going out instead.*

instead of *prep* in place of. *Instead of giving him the money, he gave it to me. I'll go instead of you. He studies in the evening instead of during the day.*

instep ['instep] *nc* **1.** upper part of the foot near the ankle. **2.** the part of a boot or shoe which covers it.

instigate ['instigeit] *vt* urge somebody to do something; cause something to happen by urging (usu. something bad). *They instigated the crime.* **instigator** *nc.*

instigation [insti'geiʃən] *nu*: *I did it on his instigation.*

instil [in'stil] *vt* put in slowly (usu. into the mind). *A teacher's job is to instil knowledge.* *past* **instilled.** **instillation** [insti'leiʃən] *nu.*

instinct ['instiŋkt] *nc/u* inclination, readiness, to behave in certain fixed ways which one already has when born and does not learn afterwards. *Ants build ant-hills by instinct. Man is controlled by his instincts as well as by reason.*

instinctive [in'stiŋktiv] *adj* caused by instinct. **instinctively** *adv.*

institute ['institju:t] *nc* group of people organized for a particular purpose (usu. to increase their knowledge); the building in which they work. *Many universities have institutes of education.* Also *vt* cause to begin. *He instituted an inquiry into the matter.*

institution [insti'tju:ʃən] **1.** *nu* act of instituting or being instituted: *the institution of an inquiry.* **2.** *nc* organization to meet a public need; its buildings. *A hospital is an institution to cure the sick.* **3.** *nc* well-established custom, habit, law or person in a society. *Slavery was one of the institutions of ancient Greece. That old man has lived here so long that he is an institution.* **institutional** [insti'tju:ʃənl] *adj.*

institutionalize [insti'tju:ʃənəlaiz] *vt* **1.** make into an institution or custom. **2.** make accustomed to living in an institute.

instruct [in'strʌkt] *vt* **1.** teach. *He instructs his pupils in mathematics.* **2.** give orders to. *He instructed them to listen.* **3.** inform (*o.f.*). **instructor** *nc.* (*fem* **instructress** [in'strʌktris]).

instruction **1.** *nu* act of instructing or being instructed (in sense **1.**): *instruction in mathematics.* **2.** *nc* (usu. *pl*) orders; explana-

tion of how to use something etc.
instructional *adj* concerned with instruction: *a study of instructional methods.*
instructive *adj* giving useful instruction or information. **instructively** *adv.*

instrument ['instrumənt] *nc* **1.** tool or apparatus (esp. for scientific purposes). **2.** something made to give a musical sound (e.g. a drum, violin, trumpet). **3.** person/thing used by somebody to get what he wants. *He made the army his instrument to gain power.* **4.** legal document.
instrumental [instrə'mentl] *adj* **1.** used or acting as an instrument (in sense **3.**). *They were instrumental in getting him home safely.* **2.** of musical instruments.
instrumentalist [instrə'mentəlist] *nc* person who plays a musical instrument.
instrumentation [instrəmen'teiʃən] *nu* arrangement bringing together the music of several musical instruments.

insubordinate [insə'bɔːdinit] *adj* disobedient; refusing to obey orders. **insubordination** [insəbɔːdi'neiʃən] *nu.*

insufferable [in'sʌfərəbl] *adj* not able to be endured; unbearable: *insufferable conduct.* **insufferably** *adv.*

insufficient [insə'fiʃənt] *adj* not enough. **insufficiently** *adv.* **insufficiency** *nu.*

insular ['insjulə*] *adj* **1.** connected with an island or the people living on an island. **2.** narrow-minded; prejudiced: *an insular outlook.* **insularity** [insju'læriti] *nu.*

insulate ['insjuleit] *vt* **1.** (with reference to electricity, heat, damp, noise etc) cover with a special substance so that it is protected or kept separate. *Rubber is used to insulate electric wires. The room is insulated against noise.* **2.** keep separate from anything. *In the country we are insulated from the worries of life in a big town.*
insulating *adj* causing insulation: *insulating tape.*
insulation [insju'leiʃən] **1.** *nu* act of insulating or being insulated. **2.** *nc* something used to insulate.
insulator *nc* substance or apparatus causing insulation.

insulin ['insjulin] *nu* **1.** chemical produced inside the body which controls the amount of sugar in the blood. **2.** artificial substance containing this chemical, used for treating the disease of diabetes.

insult [in'sʌlt] *vt* be rude to. Also ['insʌlt] *nc.* **insulting** *adj.* **insultingly** *adv.*

insuperable [in'suːpərəbl] *adj* not able to be overcome: *insuperable difficulties.* **insuperably** *adv.*

insupportable [insə'pɔːtəbl] *adj* not able to be endured; unbearable. **insupportably** *adv.*

insure [in'ʃuə*] *vt* arrange to pay regularly sums of money so that one large sum is received if one dies or suffers injury or loss. *He has insured himself for £2,000* i.e. if he dies, £2,000 will be paid to his family. *My house is insured against fire and theft.*
insurance *nu* **1.** act of insuring; agreement to insure. **2.** money paid to insure somebody/something; money paid to a person who is insured. *I pay my insurance every January. When his car was damaged he got £100 insurance.*
in'surance agent someone who sells insurance.
in'surance company company that deals in insurance.
in'surance policy agreement by which one is insured. *He took out an insurance policy against accidents in the home* i.e. he obtained one from an insurance company.
in'surance premium sum of money paid regularly in order to insure somebody/something.

insurgent [in'səːdʒənt] *adj* rising against lawful authority; rebellious. Also *nc* person who does so; rebel. **insurgency** *nu.*

insurmountable [insə'mauntəbl] *adj* not able to be overcome. **insurmountably** *adv.*

insurrection [insə'rekʃən] *nc* act of rising against lawful authority.
insurrectionist *nc* person who does so.

intact [in'tækt] *adj* not having been touched; not damaged; complete. *The parcels I sent by post arrived intact.*

intake ['inteik] *nc* **1.** somebody/something taken in. *This college has an intake of 200 students each year* i.e. it takes in 200 students. **2.** place where something is taken in (e.g. water into a pipe or channel). *We had to close the intake to stop flooding.*

intangible [in'tændʒibl] *adj* not able to be touched; not able to be clearly understood: *an intangible sensation of fear.* **intangibly** *adv.* **intangibility** [intændʒi'biliti] *nu.*

integer ['intidʒə*] *nc* (mathematics) whole number (e.g. 2, 4, 7 etc), not a fraction.

integral ['intigrl] *adj* **1.** of an integer. **2.** necessary to make something whole or complete. *Your help is an integral part of our plan.* **integrally** *adv.*

integrate ['intigreit] *vt* make something complete from a number of parts; bring somebody into a group from outside it. *We must integrate people who come to live here into the community.* **integration** [inti'greiʃən] *nu.*

integrity [in'tegriti] *nu* **1.** state of being complete. **2.** complete honesty and goodness. *His integrity prevents him (from) doing anything wrong.*

intellect ['intəlekt] **1.** *nu* power to reason and think. **2.** *nc* person who has great power of this kind. *This scientist is one of the intellects of our country.*
intellectual [intə'lektjuəl] *adj* **1.** of the intellect: *intellectual interests.* **2.** having great intellect: *an intellectual teacher.* Also *nc* person who is intellectual (esp. one who judges everything by his intellect and is thus ahead of ordinary people or does not think as they do. **intellectually** *adv.*

intelligence [in'telidʒəns] *nu* **1.** ability to learn and understand. *His intelligence is poor. They had the intelligence to answer the question correctly.* **2.** news; information collected for a specific purpose: *an intelligence agent* i.e. a person who gets information about an enemy secretly; a spy.
intelligent *adj* having great intelligence. (*opp* **unintelligent**). **intelligently** *adv.*
the intelligentsia [ðiinteli'dʒentsiə] *nu* people who are considered, or consider themselves, to be better educated and better informed than the rest.

intelligible [in'telidʒibl] *adj* able to be understood: *speak intelligible English.* (*opp* **unintelligible**). **intelligibly** *adv.* **intelligibility** [intelidʒi'biliti] *nu.*

intemperate [in'tempərət] *adj* **1.** not controlled; excessive: *an intemperate rage; intemperate drinking.* **2.** not temperate or mild: *an intemperate climate.* **intemperately** *adv.* **intemperance** [in'tempərns] *nu.*

intend [in'tend] *vt* have in mind; be one's purpose. *I intend to come back soon/I intend coming back soon. I intend you to come with me. You are intended to come with me. I intend that we shall arrive tomorrow.* see **intention.**

intense [in'tens] *adj* (with reference to qualities and feelings) great and powerful: *intense cold/heat; intense anger/suffering; an intense young man* i.e. one who has intense feelings. **intensely** *adv.* **intensity** *nu.*

intensify *vt/i* become or make more intense. **intensification** [intensifi'keiʃən] *nu.*

intensive *adj* thorough; (with reference to one particular part) concentrated. *He made intensive inquiries* i.e. inquiries which were thorough with reference to one particular problem; *intensive farming* i.e. using improved methods on a small area of land so as to get better crops from it. **intensively** *adv.*

intent[1] [in'tent] *adj* attending to or examining with great care. *He was intent on/upon winning the race. He gave me an intent look.* **intently** *adv.* **intentness** *nu.*

intent[2] [in'tent] *nu* intention; (usu. in legal phrases) purpose. *He entered the house with intent to steal.*

to all intents and purposes for all practical purposes.

intention [in'tenʃən] *nc/u* plan; aim; purpose. *We do not know their intentions. It is their intention to return as soon as possible. I have no intention of meeting them.*

intentional *adj* done on purpose: *an intentional insult.* (*opp* **unintentional**). **intentionally** *adv.* see **intend.**

'well-in'tentioned *adj* with good intentions.

inter-[1] ['intə*] *prefix* between; among (e.g. **interchange**).

inter[2] [in'tə:*] *vt* bury in the ground or in a tomb. *past* **interred. interment** *nc/u.*

interact [intə'rækt] *vi* act on each other. **interaction** *nc/u.*

interbreed [intə'bri:d] *vt/i* (with reference to different races or kinds) breed with each other. *past* **interbred** [intə'bred]. **interbreeding** *nu.*

intercede [intə'si:d] *vt* try to settle an affair; ask a favour for somebody. *He interceded in the argument* i.e. he tried to settle it by getting those who were arguing to agree. *I interceded with the headmaster for/on behalf of the boys who were to be punished* i.e. I asked him not to punish them.

intercession [intə'seʃən] **1.** *nu* act of interceding. **2.** *nc* prayer for somebody.

intercept [intə'sept] *vt* seize or stop somebody/something while he or it is moving from one place to another. *They intercepted him before he crossed the road.* **interception** *nc/u.*

interceptor *nc* somebody/something that intercepts (esp. a fighter aircraft).

intercession [intə'seʃən] *nc/u* see **intercede.**

interchange [intə'tʃeindʒ] *vt* **1.** give and receive between two persons. **2.** change the places of two things. *You should interchange the tyres on your car* i.e. each tyre should be changed around onto a different wheel. Also ['intətʃeindʒ] *nc* **1.** *an interchange of dates.* **2.** place in a motorway system, where two or more roads meet.

interchangeable [intə'tʃeindʒibl] *adj* able to be interchanged. *The front wheels are interchangeable with the back ones.* **interchangeably** *adv.*

intercom ['intəkɔm] *nu* radio system used by a group of people in a building, aeroplane etc for talking to each other.

intercommunicate [intəkə'mju:nikeit] *vi* communicate with one another. **intercommunication** [intəkəmju:ni'keiʃən] *nc/u.*

intercontinental [intəkɔnti'nentl] *adj* between continents.

intercourse ['intəkɔ:s] *nu* **1.** movement of goods, ideas, messages etc between persons or countries. *Trade is the main form of intercourse between Europe and the Far East.* **2.** sexual intercourse.

sexual intercourse sexual act between two people or two animals.

interdict [intə'dikt] *vt* forbid; prevent. Also ['intədikt] *nc* order forbidding something (esp. one made by the Roman Catholic Church forbidding a person to attend church).

interest ['intrest] **1.** *nu* attention given to somebody/something. *He takes (a) great interest in sport. Have you lost interest?; news of little interest.* **2.** *nc* something to which one gives attention; something which causes pleasurable attention. *My only interests are books and the theatre.* **3.** *nc* advantage; personal profit. *It is in your (own) interests to be honest.* **4.** *nu* profit made from lending money; extra money paid for borrowing money. *This bank charges 6 per cent interest on all money borrowed from it.* **5.** *nc* claim; share. *They have interests in gold mining* i.e. have shares in a company which mines gold. **6.** *nc* (often *pl*) persons with such shares. *Gold-mining interests are worried about the price of gold.* Also *vt* cause somebody to have, or take, interest in. *He interested me in football. His story interested me.*

interested *adj* **1.** having interest (in sense **1.**): *interested students. I am interested in him.* **2.** having shares or claims (in sense **5.**): *the two interested people in this dispute* i.e. the two people who will gain or lose in it.

interesting *adj* causing interest (in sense **2.**): *a very interesting story.* (*opp* **uninteresting**). **interestingly** *adv.*

interfere [intə'fiə*] *vi* **1.** concern oneself with somebody/something without being asked (esp. with the affairs of others). *You should not interfere in other people's arguments. Who interfered with my camera?* i.e. who damaged it? **2.** get in the way of; hinder. *The noise interfered with my studies.*

interference *nu* (often with reference to one wavelength interfering with another on radio or television) act of interfering.

interim ['intərim] *adj* of the time between; for the time being: *an interim report* i.e. a report before the final one. Also *nu*: *in the interim* i.e. during the time between; meanwhile.

interior [in'tiəriə*] *adj* **1.** inner; inside: *the interior walls of a house.* **2.** inside a country; away from the coast or frontier. Also *nc* **1.** the inside. *The interior of the house is very pleasant.* **2.** inside part of a country. *He was lost in the interior of Africa for many years.*

interior decoration *nu* art or skill of decorating the inside of a house.

interior decorator *nc* someone skilled in interior decorating.

interject [intə'dʒekt] *vt* make a sudden remark while somebody else is talking. *'Why?', he interjected, before I had finished my story.*

interjection *nc* **1.** sudden remark (e.g. 'Stop!' 'Help me!'). **2.** (grammar) word used to indicate a sudden emotion (e.g. Oh!, Ah!, Gosh!).

interlock [intə'lɔk] *vt/i* lock or join firmly together. *The different parts of this puzzle should interlock.* **interlocking** *adj.*

interloper ['intəloupə*] *nc* person who enters where he has no right to (usu. to do something wrong).

interlude ['intəlu:d] *nc* **1.** period of time between two events during which something else happens or is done (e.g. between two acts of a play). **2.** the music played during this period. **3.** event which is different from what happens before and afterwards. *During the war there were some peaceful interludes.*

intermarry [intə'mæri] *vi* become related to a different group of people by marrying somebody belonging to it. *For many years these people have intermarried with foreigners.* **intermarriage** [intə'mæridʒ] *nu.*

intermediary [intə'mi:diəri] *nc* person who maintains contact between people; a go-between. Also *adj.*

intermediate [intə'mi:diət] *adj* being between; in the middle: *an intermediate examination* i.e. one in the middle of a course. **intermediately** *adv.*

intermezzo [intə'metsou] *nc* short piece of music connecting longer and more important ones (e.g. in an opera or symphony). *pl* **intermezzos.**

interminable [in'tə:minəbl] *adj* never ending; too long to be enjoyed: *an interminable speech.* **interminably** *adv.*

intermission [intə'miʃən] *nc/u* pause; rest. *They worked all night without intermission.*

intermittent [intə'mitnt] *adj* stopping and starting again; not happening all the time. *He sends only intermittent news.* **intermittently** *adv.*

intermix [intə'miks] *vt/i* mix together. **intermixture** *nc.*

intern[1] [in'tə:n] *vt* (esp. with reference to people of another country during a war) put together in a certain place; imprison. *During the last war all Germans living in Great Britain were interned.* **internment** *nu.*

intern[2] ['intə:n] *nc* (esp. with reference to a doctor living in the hospital where he works) person who lives where he works.

internal [in'tə:nl] *adj* of the inside: *internal pains* (e.g. inside the stomach); *a country's internal problems* i.e. problems about what is happening inside, not outside it. **internally** *adv.*

internal combustion explosion of gas inside an engine by which the engine is given its power (e.g. in a motorcar).

international [intə'næʃənl] *adj* between nations: *international trade; international understanding.*

internationalism *nu* belief that nations should work together and not be separate.

internationalist *nc* person who believes in internationalism.

internationalize *vt* put under the joint control of several nations. *The rules about air travel have been internationalized.*

internecine [intə'ni:sain] *adj* (esp. with reference to a civil war) causing death and destruction to both sides.

interplanetary [intə'plænitəri] *adj* between planets.

interplay ['intəplei] *nu* the effect or influence of two persons/things on each other. *The interplay of the two main characters in the play is interesting.*

interpolate [in'tə:pəleit] *vt* **1.** put in a book or document extra information (sometimes wrong information). **2.** (mathematics) find out or put in, the numbers missing in a series of numbers.

interpolation [intə:pə'leiʃən] **1.** *nu* act of interpolating. **2.** *nc* something which has been interpolated.

interpose [intə'pouz] *vt/i* come or put between. *We had to interpose to stop them fighting. He interposed a few remarks while they were talking.*

interposition [intəpə'ziʃən] **1.** *nu* act of interposing. **2.** *nc* something which is interposed.

interpret [in'tə:prit] *vt* (esp. with reference to explaining in one language what has been said in another) explain the meaning. *They interpreted his arrival as showing that he wished to be their friend. He quickly interpreted to me what the Russian was saying.*

interpretation [intə:pri'teiʃən] **1.** *nu* act of interpreting. **2.** *nc* something which has been interpreted. *His arrival can be given more than one interpretation.* **interpreter** *nc.*

interracial [intə'reiʃl] *adj* between different races.

interregnum [intə'regnəm] *nc* period between the reigns of two kings or rulers when there is no king or ruler.

interrelate [intəri'leit] *vt/i* connect with each other. *These matters are interrelated.* **interrelation** *nc.* **interrelationship** *nc.*

interrogate [in'terəgeit] *vt* question; examine by questioning. *The police interrogated him for two hours.* **interrogator** *nc.*

interrogation [interə'geiʃən] **1.** *nu* act of interrogating. **2.** *nc* questioning.

interrogative [intə'rɔgətiv] *adj* **1.** asking a question: *in an interrogative tone of voice.* **2.** (grammar) used in asking questions (e.g. 'Why' is an interrogative adverb). Also *nc* an interrogative word. **interrogatively** *adv.*

interrupt [intə'rʌpt] *vt/i* **1.** break in on someone who is speaking; stop something being done for a time. **2.** get in the way of; stop moving. *The storm has interrupted all travel by sea.* **interrupter** *nc.*

interruption **1.** *nu* state of interrupting or being interrupted. **2.** *nc* something which interrupts. *He could not say all he wished because of the interruptions.*

intersect [intə'sekt] *vt/i* cross one another; divide into parts. *The two lines intersect at point X. This line intersects the other at point X. The village is intersected by two main roads.*

intersection **1.** *nu* act of intersecting. **2.** *nc* crossroads.

intersperse [intə'spə:s] *vt* scatter among; give variety by putting in something here and there. *The trees are interspersed with grass.*

interstice [in'tə:stis] *nc* (usu. *pl*) small gap; crack. *Flowers are growing in the interstices of the rock.*

interval ['intəvl] *nc* **1.** time or distance between two events or places. *At school there is an interval between the third and fourth periods. There will be a short interval after the second act of the play. The interval between the two trees measures 40 feet.* **2.** (music) difference in pitch between two notes.

at intervals **1.** with short periods of time between. *She brought us coffee at intervals.* **2.** with a short distance between. *There are houses at intervals along the road.*

intervene [intə'vi:n] *vi* come between

either in time or place. *Three years intervened before I heard from him again. The government had to intervene in the strike* i.e. in order to try to settle it. **intervention** [intə'venʃən] *nc/u.*

interview ['intəvju:] *nc* meeting to find out, by questions and answers, about somebody or about his views. *The parents had an interview with the headmaster about school fees. Before he left, the Prime Minister gave an interview to the newspaper reporters.* Also *vt* have an interview with.

interviewer *nc* person who interviews others (esp. on radio or television).

intestate [in'testeit] *adj* not having made a will. *He died intestate.* **intestacy** [in'testəsi] *nu.*

intestine [in'testin] *nc* (often *pl*) part of the body through which waste matter from the stomach passes out of the body. **intestinal** *adj.*

intimate[1] ['intimət] *adj* **1.** very friendly indeed. *They are intimate friends.* **2.** private; secret. *I cannot tell them my intimate thoughts.* **3.** caused by studying something so well that it has no secrets. *He has an intimate knowledge of modern history.* **4.** having sexual relations. Also *nc* an intimate friend. **intimately** *adv.*

intimacy **1.** *nu* state of being intimate. **2.** *nc* act which is intimate.

intimate[2] ['intimeit] *vt* make known (often in an indirect way). *He intimated to them that he did not agree.*

intimation [inti'meiʃən] **1.** *nu* act of intimating. **2.** *nc* something which is intimated.

intimidate [in'timideit] *vt* make somebody do, or not do, something by frightening him. *The thieves intimidated the boy into not telling the police.* **intimidation** [intimi'deiʃən] *nu.*

into ['intə, 'intu] *prep* **1.** showing motion to the inside of. *He walked into the room.* **2.** showing change from one state to another. *When it is boiled, water changes into steam. He broke the stick into pieces.*

intolerable [in'tɔlərəbl] *adj* not able to be endured. **intolerably** *adv.*

intolerant [in'tɔlərnt] *adj* not tolerant; not able to tolerate. *He is intolerant of fools.* **intolerantly** *adv.* **intolerance** *nu.*

intone [in'toun] *vt/i* (esp. with reference to a prayer, psalm etc) speak with a musical tone in one's voice; say something in this way.

intonation [intə'neiʃən] *nu* movement up or down in the pitch of the voice; accent.

intoxicate [in'tɔksikeit] *vt* make drunk; make very excited, as if one were drunk. *They were intoxicated by their victory.* **intoxication** [intɔksi'keiʃən] *nu.*

intoxicating *adj*: *an intoxicating victory.* **intoxicant** [in'tɔksikənt] *nc* something which intoxicates (esp. drink).

intra- ['intrə] *prefix* inside of (esp. used in many medical words e.g. **intramuscular** i.e. inside a muscle).

intractable [in'træktəbl] *adj* not easy to deal with or manage: *an intractable problem.* **intractably** *adv.* **intractability** [intræktə'biliti] *nu.*

intransigent [in'trænsidʒənt] *adj* refusing to reach an agreement or make a compromise: *the intransigent behaviour of the opposition.* **intransigence** *nu.*

intransitive [in'trænsitiv] *adj* (grammar) with reference to verbs which do not have a direct object (e.g. the verb *come*).

intrench [in'trentʃ] *vt* see **entrench.**

intrepid [in'trepid] *adj* without fear. **intrepidly** *adv.* **intrepidity** [intre'piditi] *nu.*

intricate ['intrikət] *adj* made up of many parts; difficult to understand: *the intricate works of a clock; an intricate argument.* **intricately** *adv.*

intricacy **1.** *nu* state of being intricate. **2.** *nc* something which is intricate.

intrigue [in'tri:g] *vt/i* **1.** plan secretly. *They are intriguing against the government.* **2.** make interested or curious. *Their sudden arrival intrigues me.* Also *nc* **1.** secret plan. **2.** secret and unlawful love affair.

intriguing *adj* very interesting. **intriguingly** *adv.*

intrinsic [in'trinsik] *adj* (with reference to qualities) being inside; real; natural: *the intrinsic value of his work* i.e. the real value of the work itself and not what people may think about it. **intrinsically** *adv.*

introduce [intrə'dju:s] *vt* **1.** bring in, make known, for the first time. *The Romans introduced roads into Britain. My father introduced me to the game of football.* **2.** bring people together and make them known to one another by name. *He introduced me to his mother and father. Have you been introduced.?*

introduction [intrə'dʌkʃən] **1.** *nu* act of bringing in for the first time: *the introduction of roads into Britain.* **2.** *nc* introducing people. *Before the meeting began I made the necessary introductions.* **3.** *nc* first part of a letter, speech or book etc (with reference to a book usu. to explain what the book is about). **4.** *nc* simple book introducing a branch of knowledge. '*An Introduction to Elementary Physics*'.

introductory [intrə'dʌktəri] *adj* giving an introduction.

introspect [intrə'spekt] *vi* look into or be concerned with one's own thoughts and feelings. **introspection** *nc/u.*

introspective *adj* caused by, having the habit of, introspection. *He is a very introspective person.* **introspectively** *adv.*

introvert ['intrəvə:t] *nc* person who keeps his thoughts and feelings to himself and does not express them openly in any way. (*opp* **extrovert**). **introversion** [intrə'və:ʃən] *nu.*

intrude [in'tru:d] *vt/i* enter without being invited; push in where one is not welcome. *I hope I am not intruding (upon you).*

intruder *nc* (often of someone who has intruded to steal) someone/something which intrudes.

intrusion [in'tru:ʒən] *nc/u*: *Please excuse my intrusion.* **intrusive** [in'tru:siv] *adj.* **intrusively** *adv.*

intrust [in'trʌst] *vt* see **entrust.**

intuition [intju:'iʃən] **1.** *nu* ability to understand something quickly without having to think about it carefully. *They say women have more intuition than men.* **2.** *nc* knowledge gained by this ability.

intuitive [in'tju:itiv] *adj* having intuition; understood by intuition: *an intuitive guess.* **intuitively** *adv.*

inundate ['inʌndeit] *vt* **1.** cover with water; flood. *After the rain, the rivers inundated the fields.* **2.** cause trouble by arriving in great numbers. *We were inundated with visitors.* **inundation** [inʌn'deiʃən] *nc/u.*

inure [i'njuə*] *vt* (usu. *passive* and with reference to something unpleasant) make accustomed to. *They are inured to cold and* hunger.

invade [in'veid] *vt* **1.** enter a country with an army to attack it. *The Germans invaded France in 1940.* **2.** enter any place in great numbers or in order to cause a disturbance. *People from the town invade the country at the weekend. I object to our privacy being invaded.* **invasion** [in'veiʒən] *nc/u.*
invader *nc* person who invades.

invalid[1] ['invəlid] *adj* in poor health; disabled. *The invalid boy cannot play games.* Also *nc* person who is invalid. Also *vt* (esp. with reference to somebody in the armed forces or working abroad) send somebody away from his work because he is an invalid. *He has been invalided out of the army. He was invalided home from Africa.*
invalidism *nu* state of always being an invalid.

invalid[2] [in'vælid] *adj* not valid; no longer in use; useless. *This law is now invalid. The cheque is invalid unless you sign it.*
invalidate [in'vælideit] *vt* make invalid.
invalidation [invæli'deiʃən] *nu.*

invaluable [in'væljuəbl] *adj* too great to be able to be valued. *Thank you for your invaluable help.* **invaluably** *adv.*

invariable [in'vɛəriəbl] *adj* never changing; always the same. **invariably** *adv.*

invasion [in'veiʒən] *nc/u* see **invade.**

invective [in'vektiv] *nc/u* blaming or criticizing in very strong language; cursing.

inveigh [in'vei] *vi* (with **against**) attack strongly with words.

inveigle [in'veigl] *vt* get somebody to do something he does not want to do by persuading him. *They inveigled me into lending them money.*

invent [in'vent] *vt* **1.** make something which did not exist before. *We do not know who invented the wheel.* **2.** make up. *He invented a story to explain why he was late* i.e. the story was not true. **inventor** *nc.*
invention **1.** *nu* act of inventing. **2.** *nc* something which is invented.
inventive *adj* able to invent.

inventory ['invəntri] *nc* (usu. with reference to the contents of a house, shop, store etc) complete list: *take an inventory* i.e. make or check an inventory.

inverse ['in'vəːs] *adj* opposite in order, position etc to something else.
inverse proportion/ratio relation between two quantities in which one grows greater by the amount the other grows less.

invert [in'vəːt] *vt* put the other way round; put upside down. **inverted** *adj.* **inversion** *nc/u.*
inverted commas see **comma.**

invertebrate [in'vəːtibrət] *adj* not having a backbone (e.g. like a worm or insect). Also *nc* invertebrate animal.

invest [in'vest] *vt/i* **1.** put money in something so as to get a profit. *I have invested all my money in cotton* i.e. in a business which deals in cotton. *Have you invested in anything?* **2.** give rank or authority to. *The government invested him with special powers to deal with the situation.* **3.** surround with an army; besiege.
investor *nc* person who invests money.
investment **1.** *nc/u* act of investing money; money which is invested. **2.** *nu* act of investing a person with rank or authority. **3.** *nu* act of investing a city etc.
investiture [in'vestitʃə*] *nc* special occasion when people are invested with rank or authority.

investigate [in'vestigeit] *vt* inquire into; examine carefully. *The police are investigating the murder* i.e. to find out who did it.
investigator *nc.*
investigation [investi'geiʃən] *nc/u*: *The police are carrying out investigations.*

investiture [in'vestitʃə*] *nc* see **invest.**

investment [in'vestmənt] *nc/u* see **invest.**

inveterate [in'vetərət] *adj* firmly fixed by habit; established for a long time. *He is an inveterate liar. They are inveterate enemies.*

invidious [in'vidiəs] *adj* unpleasant because likely to cause envy or hatred. *I was given the invidious task of telling them that they had failed.* **invidiously** *adv.*

invigilate [in'vidʒileit] *vi* watch and control a written examination so that those taking it obey the rules. **invigilation** [invidʒi'leiʃən] *nc/u.* **invigilator** *nc.*

invigorate [in'vigəreit] *vt* give vigour to; make stronger. *The walk in the fresh air invigorated us.* **invigoration** [invigə'reiʃən] *nu.*

invincible [in'vinsibl] *adj* not able to be defeated. **invincibly** *adv.* **invincibility** [invinsi'biliti] *nu.*

inviolable [in'vaiələbl] *adj* not to be harmed; not to be changed; sacred. *The laws of the country are inviolable.* **inviolability** [invaiələ'biliti] *nu.*

inviolate [in'vaiələt] *adj* not violated; secure; pure.

invisible [in'vizibl] *adj* not able to be seen.
invisibly *adv.* **invisibility** [invizi'biliti] *nu.*
invisible exports part of a country's income from abroad which does not come from selling goods (e.g. profits from tourism).

invite [in'vait] *vt* **1.** ask somebody to do something or come somewhere. *At the meeting they invited me to speak. He invited us to his wedding.* **2.** ask for. *After his lecture he invited questions.*
inviting *adj* attractive. *This food looks inviting.* (*opp* **uninviting**). **invitingly** *adv.*
invitation [invi'teiʃən] **1.** *nu* act of inviting or being invited. *You can see the school only by invitation.* **2.** *nc* request which invites. *She sent out many invitations to her wedding.*

invocation [invə'keiʃən] *nc/u* see **invoke.**

invoice ['invɔis] *nc* list of goods with prices given to the person who has bought them. Also *vt* make an invoice for. *The shopkeeper invoiced me for the goods.*

invoke [in'vouk] *vt* ask by prayer for the help of God or of something powerful. *They invoked the power of the law when they were accused.*
invocation [invə'keiʃən] **1.** *nu* act of invoking or being invoked. **2.** *nc* prayer which invokes.

involuntary [in'vɔləntəri] *adj* not controlled by the will; done without one's intending to do it. *When I touched his arm he gave an involuntary jump.* **involuntarily** *adv.*

involve [in'vɔlv] *vt* **1.** cause to be included in or troubled by. *They always involve me in their quarrels. Don't get yourself involved with these people.* **2.** make necessary a particular result. *Being a sailor involves long periods away from home.*
involved *adj* difficult to understand because everything in it is mixed up. *He told me an involved story about his family.*
involvement *nc/u* state of being included in.

invulnerable [in'vʌlnərəbl] *adj* not able to be wounded or harmed. **invulnerably** *adv.*

invulnerability [invʌlnərə'biliti] *nu.*

inward ['inwəd] *adj* (esp. with reference to one's own thoughts and feelings) inside. **inwardly** *adv.*

inwards *adv* towards the inside.

iodine ['aiədi:n] *nu* type of chemical found in sea water used for cleaning wounds and in photography.

iota [ai'outə] *nu* **1.** the Greek letter i. **2.** very small amount: *not one iota of sense.*

irascible [i'ræsibl] *adj* easily made angry. **irascibly** *adv.* **irascibility** [iræsi'biliti] *nu.*

irate [ai'reit] *adj* angry. **irately** *adv.*

ire ['aiə*] *nu* anger (*o.f.*).

iridescent [iri'desnt] *adj* having many colours caused by changes in the light (e.g. as seen in oil floating on water). **iridescence** *nu.*

iris ['airis] *nc* **1.** coloured part of the eye. **2.** type of plant with sword-shaped leaves and large flowers.

Irish ['airiʃ] *adj* of Ireland. Also *nu* Irish language. Also *npl* Irish people. **Irishman** *nc.* **Irishwoman** *nc.*

irk [ə:k] *vt* (usu. with **it** as subject) annoy. *It irks me* (*o.f.*).

'irksome *adj* annoying.

iron[1] ['aiən] **1.** *nu* the most common and useful metal. **2.** *nc* implement heated by electricity used for making clothes smooth. **3.** *nc* golf club with an iron head.

iron[1] (*def* 2)

irons *npl* chains used to tie somebody. *The thief was put in irons.*

'iron 'curtain frontiers between the countries of western Europe and Russia and her allies in eastern Europe: *the iron-curtain countries* i.e. Russia and her allies.

'iron 'lung apparatus which enables a person who cannot breathe to breathe.

'ironmonger ['aiənmʌŋgə*] *nc* (*Brit*) person who sells hard goods like those made of iron. (*US* **hardware dealer**).

'ironmongery *nc/u* (*Brit*) shop of an ironmonger; the goods sold by an ironmonger. (*US* **hardware**).

'iron 'rations food given to soldiers etc for use in an emergency.

'ironworks *n sing* or *pl* factory where iron is smelted or iron goods are made.

have many irons in the fire have several jobs or interests at the same time. (*informal*).

rule with a rod of iron/with an iron hand see **rule.**

strike while the iron is hot do something at the time which is best for success. (*informal*).

iron[2] ['aiən] *vt* make smooth and flat with a hot iron.

ironing *nu*: *My mother is doing her ironing.*

'ironing board board on which clothes etc are ironed.

iron something out **1.** make smooth something that is rough **2.** remove a difficulty. *The bank manager has ironed out all my worries about money.*

irony ['airəni] **1.** *nu* using words in a way which gives a meaning opposite to the words themselves (e.g. *Aren't we clever!* when we have done something which is not clever). **2.** *nc* something which happens in a way opposite to what one might expect. *It is one of the ironies of life that those with the most money are often the most unhappy.*

ironic(al) [ai'rɔnik(l)] *adj.* **ironically** *adv.*

Note: the difference between *irony* and *sarcasm* is that irony is often amusing; sarcasm is used to hurt a person's feelings.

irradiate [i'reidieit] *vt* shine light on; make bright.

irrational [i'ræʃənl] *adj* not controlled by reason: *irrational behaviour.* **irrationally** *adv.*

irreconcilable [irekən'sailəbl] *adj* not able to be made to agree. **irreconcilably** *adv.*

irrecoverable [iri'kʌvərəbl] *adj* not able to be recovered or put right. **irrecoverably** *adv.*

irrefutable [iri'fju:təbl] *adj* not able to be proved false. **irrefutably** *adv.*

irregular [i'regjulə*] *adj* **1.** not having any order in time, size, shape, place etc; not regular. *The trains from here are irregular* i.e. they do not leave at fixed times. *The fields are irregular in shape* i.e. they have different shapes. **2.** not following normal rules. *To go away without telling your father is most irregular; an irregular verb* i.e. one which changes its form in a way different from others (e.g. *go, went, gone*). **irregularity** [iregju'læriti] *nc/u.*

irrelevant [i'reləvənt] *adj* having nothing to do with the subject. *Your answer to my question is irrelevant.* **irrelevantly** *adv.*

irrelevancy, irrelevance **1.** *nu* state of being irrelevant. **2.** *nc* something which is irrelevant. *Your answer is full of irrelevancies.*

irreligious [iri'lidʒəs] *adj* against, or not interested in, religion.

irremediable [iri'mi:diəbl] *adj* not able to be remedied. **irremediably** *adv.*

irreparable [i'repərəbl] *adj* not able to be repaired or put right. *He has suffered irreparable losses.* **irreparably** *adv.*

irrepressible [iri'presəbl] *adj* not able to be controlled: *irrepressible delight at hearing the good news.* **irrepressibly** *adv.*

irreproachable [iri'proutʃəbl] *adj* without fault or blame.

irresistible [iri'zistəbl] *adj* not able to be resisted; too strong. *I had an irresistible desire to run away.* **irresistibly** *adv.*

irresolute [i'rezəlu:t] *adj* not decided; hesitating. **irresolutely** *adv.* **irresolution** [irezə'lu:ʃən] *nu.*

irrespective [iri'spektiv] *adj* without regard for; without paying attention to. *He is going to buy it irrespective of what you say.*

irresponsible [iri'spɔnsəbl] *adj* **1.** (of persons) not able to be made responsible for their actions. *By law babies are irresponsible.* **2.** not having a proper sense of responsibility. *Your irresponsible refusal to help your friends surprised me.* **irresponsibly** *adv.* **irresponsibility** [irispɔnsə'biliti] *nu.*

irrevocable [i'revəkəbl] *adj* not able to be revoked or changed; final: *an irrevocable decision.* **irrevocably** *adv.*

irrigate ['irigeit] *vt* **1.** take water to land by leading it from a river, well etc through pipes or channels. *They irrigate their crops* *with water from this river.* **2.** pour water on or into. *The doctor irrigated his eye to get out the dust.* **irrigation** [iri'geiʃən] *nu.*

irritate ['iriteit] *vt* **1.** make angry or annoyed. *Your poor work irritated him.* **2.** cause pain to, or make sore, a part of the body. *Thick clothes irritate my skin.*

irritation [iri'teiʃən] **1.** *nu* act of irritating; state of being irritated. **2.** *nc* something which irritates.

irritable ['iritəbl] *adj* easily made angry or annoyed. **irritably** *adv.* **irritability** [iritə'biliti] *nu.*

irritant ['iritnt] *adj* causing irritation. Also *nc* something which irritates. *Dust in the eyes is an irritant.*

irruption [i'rʌpʃən] *nc* sudden rush into a place.

Islam ['izlɑ:m] *nu* religion of the Prophet Mohammed; all those who believe in this religion i.e. all Muslims. **Islamic** [iz'læmik] *adj.*

island ['ailnd] *nc* piece of land with water all round it; something that looks like an island (e.g. *a traffic/street island* i.e. a place in the middle of a busy street where persons crossing it can stop). Also *adj.*

islander *nc* person who lives on an island.

isle [ail] *nc* island (usu. used in poetry except sometimes in the names of places e.g. the British Isles).

islet ['ailət] *nc* small island.

iso- ['aisou] *prefix* equal (e.g. **isobar** i.e. line on a map connecting places with equal atmospheric pressure).

isolate ['aisəleit] *vt* keep or place apart or alone. *The village was isolated for a week by the floods* i.e. nobody could go in or come out.

isolation [aisə'leiʃən] *nu*: *During the flood they lived in isolation.*

isolationism [aisə'leiʃənizəm] *nu* belief that one country should keep to itself and not concern itself with what is going on in other countries.

isolationist [aisə'leiʃənist] *nc* person who supports this belief.

isosceles [ai'sɔsili:z] *adj* (only with reference to a triangle) having two equal sides.

issue ['iʃu:] *vt/i* **1.** come out. *Smoke and flames issued from the burning house.* **2.** send out; supply. *He issued orders to his men. This magazine is issued weekly. They have issued food to the hungry people/the hungry people with food. This office issues driving licences.* Also **1.** *nu* act of coming out. **2.** *nu* act of sending out, supplying. **3.** *nc* something that is sent out or supplied: *issues of this magazine.* **4.** *nc* result. *The battle decided the issue of the war.* **5.** *nc* question; problem which is much discussed. *The great issue today is whether there will be war or peace.* **6.** *nu* (in a legal sense) children. *He died without issue* i.e. childless.

at issue in dispute; being argued about; not decided. *The matter/point at issue is whether you go or stay.*

face the issue see a problem clearly and do what must be done about it.

join/take issue with somebody disagree and argue with somebody. *I joined issue with him about his new ideas.*

isthmus ['isməs] *nc* narrow strip of land joining two larger pieces of land.

it [it] *pron* **1.** used with reference to things without life, animals and sometimes young children. *Where is my book? It's here. The dog is tired. It is also hungry. The baby is asleep. It will wake up soon.* **2.** used in answering or giving information about somebody/something already mentioned. *Who is that? It's my father. What is this? It's a flower. It was they who did it.* **3.** used as the general subject of many verbs which do not need a definite one. *It was raining. It's ten o'clock. It is four miles from here to the shop. It's no use crying. It seems a silly thing to do.* **4.** used when referring to something that is going to be mentioned later in the sentence. *It is obvious that he is very tired.*

its *determiner* of it; belonging to it. *The book has lost its cover. The baby opened its eyes.*

Note: do not confuse with *it's* meaning *it is* or *it has.*

itself **1.** emphatic form of **it**. *The dog found the food itself.* **2.** reflexive form of **it**. *The dog has hurt itself.*

by itself without help; alone. *The tree stands by itself in the garden.*

italic [i'tælik] *adj* (with reference to printed letters) sloping; *printed like this.* Also *npl*: *Parts of this dictionary are printed in italics.*

italicize [i'tælisaiz] *vt* print in italics. **italicized** *adj.*

itch [itʃ] *nu* **1.** feeling on the skin which makes one want to scratch. *I have an itch on my left hand.* **2.** strong desire. *They have an itch to travel abroad.* Also *vi*: *My left foot itches/is itching. They are itching to travel abroad.* **itchy** *adj.* **itchiness** *nu.*

item ['aitəm] *nc* one of a list of things; one of many. *Please check the items in this bill. There are no items of interest in today's newspaper.*

itemize *vt* write down all the items.

itinerant [ai'tinərnt] *adj* travelling from place to place.

itinerary [ai'tinərəri] *nc* details or record of a journey made or of the route to be taken.

its, itself [its, it'self] *determiner/pron* see **it.**

ivory ['aivəri] *nu* hard, white substance of which the tusks of elephants are made. Also *adj* made of ivory; the colour of ivory.

ivy ['aivi] *nu* type of dark green climbing plant.

ivied ['aivid] *adj* covered with ivy.

J

jab [dʒæb] *vt* push something sharp (e.g. a stick or finger) into somebody/something; give a sharp blow to. *He jabbed his stick into me/He jabbed me with his stick. past* **jabbed.** Also *nc* **1.** *He gave me a jab.* **2.** injection. (*informal* in sense **2.**).

jabber ['dʒæbə*] *vt/i* talk quickly and in a way not easy to understand. *He is always jabbering. He jabbered something to me.* Also *nu*: *I can't understand his jabber.*

jack [dʒæk] *nc* **1. (Jack)** informal form of the name **John. 2.** apparatus for lifting heavy objects from underneath (e.g. for raising the wheel of a car above the ground). **3.** playing card below the queen in importance. **4.** flag on a ship which shows to what country it belongs. **5.** small white ball used in the game of bowls. Also *vt* (in sense **2.**). *We must jack (up) the car to change the wheel.*

'jackboot type of long, heavy boot.

'jackdaw type of bird like a crow.

'jack-of-'all-trades *nc* (usu. only *sing*) person who is able to do many different kinds of work.

'jack-in-the-box type of toy consisting of a small box out of which a small figure suddenly jumps when the lid is opened.

jack-in-the-box

'jack-knife type of folding knife.

'jackpot large amount of money won by gambling.

'Jack 'Tar sailor in the British navy. (*informal* and rather *o.f.*).

'Union 'Jack national flag of Britain.

hit the jackpot 1. win a lot of money. **2.** have great luck or success.

jackal ['dʒækɔːl] *nc* type of wild animal like a dog, found in Africa and Asia.

jacket ['dʒækit] *nc* **1.** short coat. **2.** covering round something: *water jacket* i.e. covering full of water round an engine to keep it from becoming too hot; *book jacket* i.e. paper cover on a book. **3.** skin of a (cooked) potato.

jade[1] [dʒeid] *nu* type of hard green stone used to make ornaments etc.

jade[2] [dʒeid] *nc* **1.** tired old horse (*o.f.*). **2.** woman (*o.f.* and rather *impolite*).

jaded tired and unhappy.

jag [dʒæg] *vt* cut or tear roughly. *I jagged my finger on a rusty nail. past* **jagged** [dʒægd]. Also *nc* something rough and sharp which jags; cut caused by this.

jagged ['dʒægid] *adj* rough and sharp: *the jagged pieces of a broken bottle.*

jaguar ['dʒægjuə*] *nc* type of large, spotted wild animal of the cat family, found in South America.

jaguar

jail [dʒeil] *nc* see **gaol.**

jalopy [dʒə'lɔpi] *nc* old car (usu. one which is not in good condition) (*informal*).

jam[1] [dʒæm] *vt/i* **1.** press tightly; push into a small space. *We were jammed together in the large crowd. I jammed my books into the bag. He jammed on the brakes of the car* i.e. made them tight on the wheels by pressing the brake pedal hard. **2.** stop something moving because it is pressed tightly or hindered in some way. *The door has jammed.* **3.** stop radio programmes or messages being heard by sending out radio noises which interfere with them. *past* **jammed.** Also *nc* **1.** *There was such a jam of people that we could not get in.* **2.** difficulty; trouble. *Because I lost my money I was in a jam.* (*informal* in sense **2.**).

'traffic jam crowding together of traffic so that none of it can move.

jam[2] [dʒæm] *nu* mixture of fruit and sugar boiled together and used cold on bread, in cakes etc.

money for jam something very easily got. (*informal*).

jamb [dʒæm] *nc* side post of a door or window.

jamboree [dʒæmbə'riː] *nc* large, friendly meeting (esp. of Boy Scouts from many nations).

jangle ['dʒæŋgl] *vt/i* **1.** make, cause to make, an unpleasant noise like pieces of metal striking one another. **2.** argue in a noisy, unpleasant way. Also *nu* unpleasant noise, like pieces of metal shaken together.

janitor ['dʒænitə*] *nc* doorkeeper; (*Scot, US*) person who looks after a building.

January ['dʒænjuəri] *n* first month of the year in the Western calendar.

japan [dʒə'pæn] *vt* paint with a special black varnish. *past* **japanned.** Also *nc* something painted in this way; the special varnish used.

jape [dʒeip] *vi* make a joke. Also *nc*. (both *o.f.*).

jar[1] [dʒɑː*] *nc* type of container made of glass or china etc with a wide opening at the top.

jar[2] [dʒɑː*] *vt/i* **1.** make an unpleasant sound. **2.** have an unpleasant effect; cause a shock. *Their loud voices jar on my nerves/ears. I fell from the tree and jarred my back.* **3.** not agree with. *The two colours jar* i.e. are unpleasant to look at when together. *past* **jarred.** Also *nc.* **jarring** *adj.*

jargon ['dʒɑːgən] *nu* (esp. with reference to the special and technical words used by experts) language which is difficult for ordinary people to understand. *When engineers talk about their work, they use a lot of jargon.*

jasmine ['dʒæzmin], **jessamine** ['dʒesəmin] *nc/u* type of shrub with sweet-smelling flowers.

jasper ['dʒæspə*] *nu* type of precious stone (usu. red or yellow in colour).

jaundice ['dʒɔːndis] *nu* type of disease which makes the skin and the whites of the eyes yellow. Also *vt* (usu. *passive*) **1.** give jaundice to. **2.** make bitter and suspicious. *He has a very jaundiced opinion of their work.*

jaunt [dʒɔːnt] *vi* make a short journey for pleasure. Also *nc*: *They went for a jaunt in their car.*

jaunty ['dʒɔːnti] *adj* lively; carefree. **jauntily** *adv.* **jauntiness** *nu.*

javelin ['dʒævəlin] *nc* type of spear for throwing (esp. in sport).

jaw [dʒɔː] **1.** *nc* one of the two bones which contain the teeth. **2.** *nc* (in *pl*) part of a tool or machine which holds or crushes like jaws: *the jaws of a vice.* **3.** *nc* (in *pl*) narrow opening to a valley. **4.** *nu* too much talk. *I have had enough of their jaw.* (*informal* in sense **4.**). Also *vi* talk too much. (*informal*).
into/out of the jaws of death into/out of a great danger which could cause death.

jay [dʒei] *nc* type of noisy bird with bright feathers.
'jay walker person who crosses busy roads without paying attention to the traffic.

jazz [dʒæz] *nu* type of lively music (usu. with a regular rhythm) begun by Negroes in the USA.
jazzy *adj* bright; lively; having many colours: *wearing a jazzy tie.*
jazz something up make more lively: *jazz up a piece of music; jazz up a dull party.*

jealous ['dʒeləs] *adj* **1.** having a feeling of envy because somebody has something, or has gained something, which one does not have. *He is jealous of me because I won and he did not. They are jealous of his wealth.* **2.** having a feeling of fear that one may lose somebody/something. *He is very jealous if his girl talks to another man.* **3.** guarding very carefully. *The people here are jealous of their freedom.* **jealously** *adv.*
jealousy **1.** *nu* jealous feeling: *his jealousy of me because I won.* **2.** *nc* act caused by feeling jealous: *all the jealousies which spoil friendship.*

jean [dʒiːn] **1.** *nu* type of strong, cotton cloth. **2.** *nc* (in *pl*) trousers made from this cloth.

jeep [dʒiːp] *nc* small, powerful vehicle, able to travel over rough ground.

jeer [dʒiə*] *vt/i* laugh rudely at; make fun of in an unkind way. *When the player fell, the crowd jeered. They jeered at him.* Also *nc*: *the jeers of the crowd.* **jeering** *adj.* **jeeringly** *adv.*

jejune [dʒi'dʒuːn] *adj* (esp. with reference to something written) dry; empty; not interesting: *a jejune article in today's newspaper.* **jejunely** *adv.* **jejuneness** *nu.*

jelly ['dʒeli] *nc/u* **1.** clear, almost solid substance made from gelatin or from boiling fruit juice and sugar together; cold food made from gelatin mixed with fruit juice. *My mother is making apple jelly. Children like jelly and ice cream.* **2.** any almost solid substance like this.
jell *vt/i* **1.** become, cause to become, jelly. **2.** (of ideas, plans etc) take shape.
'jellyfish type of sea animal which looks like a piece of jelly.

jemmy ['dʒemi] *nc* type of iron bar used by thieves to open doors and windows.

jeopardize ['dʒepədaiz] *vt* put in danger.
jeopardy ['dʒepədi] *nu* usu. only in **be in jeopardy** i.e. be in danger.

jerk [dʒəːk] *vt* pull, push or twist suddenly. *He jerked the letter out of my hand. The boy jerked out an answer* i.e. he gave an answer suddenly and with difficulty. Also *nc* **1.** sudden movement. *When I touched his arm, he gave a jerk. The car started with a jerk.* **2.** (mainly *US*) stupid, foolish person. (*informal* in sense **2.**). **jerky** *adj.* **jerkily** *adv.* **jerkiness** *nu.*

jerkin ['dʒəːkin] *nc* short coat with or without sleeves (usu. made of leather and worn by men).

jerry-builder ['dʒeribildə*] *nc* person who builds houses of a low standard and with poor materials.
'jerry-built *adj* built in this way.

jersey ['dʒəːzi] *nc* tight-fitting garment with sleeves and few or no buttons in front (usu. made from wool or cotton). *In cold weather he wears a jersey under his jacket.*

jessamine ['dʒesəmin] *nc/u* see **jasmine.**

jest [dʒest] *nc* **1.** something said or done to amuse; joke. **2.** somebody/something laughed at. Also *vt/i*: *We jested about his behaviour.*
jesting *adj* said or done in jest. *He asked me in a jesting voice.* **jestingly** *adv.*
jester *nc* (in ancient times) person employed by a king or lord to entertain by jesting.
in jest as a joke; not seriously. *I spoke in jest.*

jet[1] [dʒet] *nc* **1.** strong flow of gas, liquid or flame from a pipe or small hole. *The jet of water from the hosepipe soon put out the fire.* **2.** pipe or small hole which causes a jet (e.g. the jet in the carburettor of a car engine). **3.** type of aircraft which is pushed through the air by jets of hot gas. *Four enemy jets flew over the town.* Also *vt/i* come out, cause to come out, in a jet. *past* **jetted.**
'jet-pro'pelled *adj* pushed through the air by jets. **jet propulsion** *nu.*

jet[2] [dʒet] *nu* type of hard, black mineral which is polished and used for ornaments.
'jet-'black *adj* as black and shiny as jet. *Her hair is jet-black.*

jetsam ['dʒetsəm] *nu* **1.** goods thrown from a ship in order to make the ship lighter and safer. **2.** goods of this kind which are washed onto the shore. see **flotsam.**

jettison ['dʒetisn] *vt* throw from a ship or aircraft in order to make it lighter and safer; abandon.

jetty ['dʒeti] *nc* long, narrow structure built out into the sea for getting into or out of a boat, or to protect a harbour.

Jew [dʒuː] *nc* member of the Hebrew race or religion. *The Jews returned to Israel.* **Jewish** *adj.*

jewel [dʒuəl] *nc* **1.** precious stone; ornament with precious stone(s) in it. *The ladies wore their jewels.* **2.** somebody/something considered to be very good. Also *vt* fit or dress with jewels. *past* **jewelled.** (*US* **jeweled**).
jeweller *nc* person who buys and sells jewels.
jewellery, jewelry *nu* jewels, or ornaments with jewels in them.

jib[1] [dʒib] *nc* **1.** small front sail. **2.** the long bar of a crane or derrick over which the rope for lifting things is passed.

jib[2] [dʒib] *vt/i* **1.** (with reference to horses) stop and refuse to go further. **2.** (with reference to persons) refuse, or be very unwilling, to do something. *They jib at going to bed very early. past* **jibbed.**

jibe [dʒaib] *vi* see **gibe.**

jiffy ['dʒifi] *nu* moment of time. *I'll be ready in a jiffy.* (*informal*).

jig[1] [dʒig] *nc* lively dance; the music for it. Also *vt/i* **1.** dance a jig. **2.** move, cause to move, up and down quickly. *The children cannot stand still. They are jigging up and down while they wait to go. past* **jigged.**

jig[2] [dʒig] *nc* apparatus which guides a cutting tool.

'jigsaw 1. type of narrow saw driven by a machine. **2.** jigsaw puzzle.

'jigsaw puzzle puzzle made by cutting up a picture on wood or card into pieces which have to be put together again.

jigger ['dʒigə*] *nc* type of small insect which gets under the skin (esp. beneath the toenails) and lays its eggs there.

jilt [dʒilt] *vt* refuse to marry somebody after having promised to do so; end a relationship with a lover. *She jilted him the day before they were to be married.* Also *nc* woman who jilts.

jingle ['dʒiŋgl] *vt/i* **1.** make, cause to make, sharp sounds of small pieces of metal striking together. *As he ran, the pennies and keys in his pocket jingled.* **2.** (with reference to verse) have a simple rhythm and pattern of words which make it easy to remember (e.g. *Early to bed, early to rise/Makes a man healthy, wealthy and wise*). Also *nc.*

jingo ['dʒiŋgou] *nc* person who believes that his country should force other countries to give it what it wants; extreme patriot. *pl* **jingoes.**

jingoism *nu* belief or policy of a jingo. **jingoistic** [dʒiŋgou'istik] *adj.*

by jingo! *interj* expressing determination or surprise. (rather *o.f.*).

jinks [dʒiŋks] *npl* only in **high jinks** i.e. noisy fun. *The boys are having high jinks in the playground.*

jinn [dʒin] *nc* see **genie.**

jinx [dʒiŋks] *nc* something which is said to cause bad luck. *There is a jinx on this plan* i.e. there has been a lot of bad luck in the carrying out of the plan.

jitters ['dʒitəz] *npl* (with **the**) great nervousness. *I have got the jitters about the examination next week.* **jittery** *adj.* (both *informal*).

jive [dʒaiv] *nu* type of jazz music; type of dancing to this music. Also *vi* play or dance in this way. (both *informal*).

job[1] [dʒɔb] *nc* **1.** piece of work done. *The new building was a big job. The builders have done a good job of it/made a good job of it.* **2.** employment; work. *I have a job in a shop. Jobs are not easy to get.* **3.** something difficult. *It was a job to get him to agree.* (*informal* in sense **3.**).

a bad job an unlucky happening or state of affairs. *We had to make the best of a bad job by agreeing to do it against our wishes; give something up as a bad job* i.e. stop doing something because there is no hope of being successful. (*informal*).

a good job a lucky happening or state of affairs. *It was a good job that you had a friend with you to help.* (*informal*).

odd jobs unimportant work of many different kinds. *He likes doing odd jobs in his garden.*

on the job busy; at work. (*informal*).

job[2] [dʒɔb] *vt/i* **1.** do odd jobs. *This builder is jobbing for a large number of people.* **2.** do the work of a broker or middleman. **3.** use one's power or position unfairly or dishonestly. *He is jobbing to get himself made chairman. past* **jobbed.**

jobber *nc* **1.** broker; middleman. **2.** person who does odd jobs. **3.** person who uses his power or position unfairly or dishonestly.

jobbery *nu* act of jobbing (in sense **3.**).

jockey ['dʒɔki] *nc* person who is paid to ride horses in horse-races. Also *vt* trick. *They jockeyed us into giving them all they wanted.*

'disc jockey person employed on a radio programme to introduce records.

jockey for position 1. push against other jockeys in a horse-race to get the best position. **2.** act in the same way to get an advantage in something. *The two political parties are jockeying for position.*

jocose [dʒə'kous] *adj* fond of jesting; amusing. **jocosely** *adv.* **jocoseness, jocosity** [dʒə'kɔsiti] *nu.*

jocular ['dʒɔkjulə*] *adj* fond of jesting; amusing. **jocularly** *adv.* **jocularity** [dʒɔkju'læriti] *nu.*

jocund ['dʒɔkənd] *adj* cheerful; happy. **jocundity** [dʒə'kʌnditi] *nu.* (both rather *o.f.*).

jodel ['joudl] *vt/i* see **yodel.**

jodhpurs ['dʒɔdpəz] *npl* long trousers worn for horse riding, fitting closely to the leg from knee to ankle.

jog [dʒɔg] *vt/i* **1.** move slowly and steadily (usu. with the sense of being shaken up and down at the same time). *They jogged along the narrow road on their horses. John jogs along at school* i.e. although he does nothing special, he is doing quite well. **2.** shake up and down; push slightly. *The old bus jogged us on the rough road. He jogged my elbow, making me spill my drink. past* **jogged.** Also *nc*: *The old bus gave us a few jogs. I felt a jog on my elbow.*

'jog-trot slow trot.

jog someone's memory cause somebody to begin remembering.

joggle ['dʒɔgl] *vt* shake often but slightly. Also *nc.*

join [dʒɔin] *vt/i* **1.** come together or meet. *The three roads join near the bridge.* **2.** (usu. with reference to two persons/things) bring or put together. *He joined the two pieces of wood (together) with nails. The priest joined the man and woman in marriage* i.e. he married them. **3.** enter the company of; become one of a group. *Please join us for dinner. They joined him in a visit to London. I have joined the football club.* Also *nc* place where two things are joined and held firmly together.

join in (something) take part in: *join in the singing; be asked to join in.*

join up join the army, navy etc. (*informal*).

join battle begin fighting: *join battle with the enemy.*

join forces come together, unite, for a purpose. *We joined forces with them to finish the work.*

join hands hold each other's hands; come together, unite for a purpose.

join issue begin to argue or quarrel.

joiner ['dʒɔinə*] *nc* person whose work is to make the wooden parts inside a building (not usu. the furniture).

joinery *nu* work of a joiner.

joint[1] [dʒɔint] *nc* **1.** (esp. with reference to the bones of the body) place where, or thing by which, two things are joined. *He has hurt the joints of his fingers.* **2.** large piece of meat cut for cooking. *We had a joint of beef for dinner.* **3.** (*US*) cheap, rough place used for drinking and gambling. (*informal* in sense **3.**). Also *vt* **1.** give joints to (in sense **1.**). **2.** cut into joints (in sense **2.**).

out of joint (with reference to bones) out of position. *He put his shoulder out of joint while playing football.*

joint[2] [dʒɔint] *adj* shared by, belonging to, two or more persons. *They made a joint request to the manager. They are the joint owners of the hotel. I was made joint heir with my brother.* **jointly** *adv.*

'joint-'stock 'company business for which the money is supplied by many persons who share in its profits.

jointure ['dʒɔintʃə*] *nc* property settled on a woman when she is married, to become hers after her husband dies.

joist [dʒɔist] *nc* beam to which the boards of a floor or the laths of a ceiling are fixed at right angles.

joke [dʒouk] *nc* something said or done to make one laugh. *They made jokes about my old hat.* Also *vi* make jokes. *They are always joking.* **jokingly** *adv.*

joker *nc* **1.** person who makes jokes. **2.** extra card in a pack of playing cards.

practical joke trick against somebody to make others laugh.

have a joke with somebody share a joke with somebody. *I stopped to have a joke with him about our work.*

no joke unpleasant; serious. *Being cold and hungry is no joke.* (*informal*).

play a joke on somebody cause somebody to be laughed at by making a joke against him.

jolly ['dʒɔli] *adj* merry; happy. Also *adv* very. *He played a jolly good game.* (*informal* in this sense). Also *vt* make somebody happy to do something. *We jollied him into coming with us.* **jollity** *nu.*

jollification [dʒɔlifi'keiʃən] *nc/u* a happy, noisy party, celebration. (*informal*).

jolt [dʒoult] *vt/i* shake while moving; shake suddenly; give a shock to. *The car jolted along the rough road. The train jolted us from our seats by stopping suddenly.* Also *nc*: *The bad news gave us a jolt.*

joss [dʒɔs] *nc* Chinese idol.

'joss stick stick of incense burned in a temple.

jostle ['dʒɔsl] *vt/i* push roughly against (usu. where there is little room e.g. in a crowd). *We had to jostle through the crowd to reach the gate. The crowd jostled against us.* Also *nc.*

jot[1] [dʒɔt] *nc* (usu. *sing* and with *negative*) something very small and of no importance. *I won't change my story (by) one jot.*

jot[2] [dʒɔt] *vt* write quickly; make a quick note of something. *I jotted down the name of the book which he was talking about.* *past* **jotted.**

jotter *nc* notebook.

jottings *npl* quickly-written notes.

journal ['dʒə:nl] *nc* **1.** daily record of news, events etc; diary. *Do you keep a journal of the amount of work you do?* **2.** daily newspaper; paper or magazine published frequently.

journalese [dʒə:nə'li:z] *nu* poor style of English found in some newspapers.

journalism *nu* work of writing for or publishing journals, magazines, newspapers etc.

journalist *nc* person who does journalism.

journalistic [dʒə:nə'listik] *adj* of journalism.

journey ['dʒə:ni] *nc* travel from one place to another (usu. to a distant place and by land; by sea use **voyage**); distance travelled in a particular time. *We made the journey from Paris to Berlin by car. From Paris to Berlin is a journey of one day/one day's journey by car. They have gone on a journey.* Also *vi* make a journey. (rather *o.f.*).

joust [dʒaust] *nc* fight on horseback with long spears (a sport of knights during the Middle Ages in Europe). Also *vi.*

jovial ['dʒouviəl] *adj* happy and friendly. **jovially** *adv.* **joviality** [dʒouvi'æliti] *nc/u.*

jowl [dʒaul] *nc* lower jaw; lower part of the face. *He has a heavy jowl/He is heavy-jowled* i.e. the lower part of his face is thick and fat.

joy [dʒɔi] **1.** *nu* great delight; great happiness. *They received the good news with joy. To our great joy he agreed to help us. The children jumped for joy when they saw the new toys.* **2.** *nc* something which causes joy. *One of the joys of living here is the friendliness of the people.*

joyful *adj* causing or filled with joy. **joyfully** *adv.* **joyfulness** *nu.*

joyless *adj* without joy; sad. **joylessly** *adv.* **joylessness** *nu.*

joyous *adj* filled with joy. **joyously** *adv.* **joyousness** *nu.*

'joy ride short ride for pleasure (esp. a ride in a stolen motorcar) (*informal*).

'joystick lever by which the pilot controls an aeroplane. (*informal*).

jubilant ['dʒu:bilnt] *adj* expressing joy; rejoicing. *They gave him a jubilant welcome after his victory.* **jubilantly** *adv.* **jubilation** [dʒu:bi'leiʃən] *nc/u.*

jubilee ['dʒu:bili:] *nc* fiftieth year or anniversary after a great event; time of rejoicing because of it.

'diamond 'jubilee sixtieth anniversary.

'silver 'jubilee twenty-fifth anniversary.

judge [dʒʌdʒ] *nc* **1.** person appointed to hear important cases in a court of law and to decide what the punishment, if any, should be. **2.** person who decides the result of a competition, an argument etc. *He was one of the judges at the boxing match.* **3.** person whose opinion about something is valuable because of his knowledge and experience. *He is a good judge of modern art. Because I do not know him well, I am no judge of his character.* Also *vt/i* **1.** act or decide as a judge (in senses **1.** and **2.**). **2.** have, give, an opinion about somebody/something. *We judged him to be a stranger. He judges it safer to go away than to stay.*

judgment, judgement **1.** *nu* act of judging or being judged. **2.** *nc* decision made by a judge. *The judgments of the court are reported in all newspapers.* **3.** *nc/u* opinion. *In their judgment he is stupid.* **4.** *nu* ability to decide correctly. *Our doctor is a man of judgment.* **5.** *nc* punishment which is deserved. *His illness is a judgment on him for his heavy drinking.*

judicature ['dʒu:dikətʃə*] **1.** *nc* all the judges of a country. **2.** *nu* organization of the courts of law.

judicial [dʒu:'diʃl] *adj* **1.** of a judge or court of law. **2.** fair and just.

judiciary [dʒu:'diʃəri] *nc* all the judges of a country.

judicious [dʒu:'diʃəs] *adj* having good judgment; wise. **judiciously** *adv*. **judiciousness** *nu*.

judo ['dʒu:dou] *nu* type of Japanese wrestling.

jug [dʒʌg] *nc* **1.** container with a handle for holding and pouring liquids. **2.** prison. (*informal* in sense **2.**). Also *vt* **1.** cook in a jug. **2.** imprison. (*informal* in sense **2.**). *past* **jugged.**

jugful *nc* amount contained by a jug (in sense **1.**).

juggle ['dʒʌgl] *vt/i* **1.** do tricks with the hands (esp. by throwing things in the air and catching them quickly). **2.** do tricks of any kind; cheat. *You are juggling with the facts when you say that everything is correct* i.e. you are trying to use the facts to prove something which is not true. **juggler** *nc*.

jugular ['dʒʌgjulə*] *adj* of the neck or throat. Also *nc* jugular vein.

jugular vein large vein in the neck.

juice [dʒu:s] *nc* **1.** liquid found in meat, fruit, vegetables etc. *I like a glass of tomato juice at breakfast.* **2.** liquid produced inside the body. *The stomach contains juices.* **3.** something which supplies power (e.g. electricity, petrol) (*informal* in sense **3.**).

juicy *adj* **1.** full of juice: *a juicy piece of meat.* **2.** interesting and shocking. *There are some juicy reports about him.* (*informal* in sense **2.**). **juiciness** *nu*.

jujitsu [dʒu:'dʒitsu:] *nu* type of Japanese wrestling which is older than judo.

jukebox ['dʒu:kbɔks] *nc* type of record player which plays when coins are put in it.

July [dʒu'lai] *n* seventh month of the year.

jumble ['dʒʌmbl] *vt/i* be mixed, mix, in an untidy way. *His books and mine were jumbled together.* Also *nc*: *a jumble of books.*

'jumble sale sale of many kinds of old goods (esp. to get money to help the poor, the sick or any good cause).

jump [dʒʌmp] *vt/i* **1.** go up into the air by pushing off the ground with the feet. *Can you jump over this wall? I jumped into the water.* **2.** move quickly. *My heart was jumping with fear. He jumped out of his car. The boys jumped to their feet when the teacher came into the room* i.e. they stood up quickly. **3.** cross, pass over, by jumping. *You jumped the wall easily.* **4.** rise or increase suddenly. *Last week the price of food jumped. The number of students in universities has jumped.* Also *nc* **1.** *He won the high/long jump.* **2.** *My heart gave a jump.* **3.** *There has been a jump in the price of food.*

jumpy *adj* nervous. **jumpiness** *nu*.

jumper¹ *nc* person or animal that jumps.

jump at something eagerly take something that is offered. *I jumped at the chance to go.* (*informal*).

jump down someone's throat disagree with, or interrupt, somebody violently. (*informal*).

jump on/upon someone attack; find fault with, or blame, severely. *He jumped on me for forgetting to come.* (*informal*).

jump to a conclusion reach a conclusion, or decide, too quickly.

jump a claim take a piece of land claimed by somebody else. (*informal*).

jump a queue get to the front unfairly by not standing in a queue with other people. **'queue-jumper** *nc*.

jumper² ['dʒʌmpə*] *nc* woollen garment put over the head and reaching just below the waist.

junction ['dʒʌŋkʃən] **1.** *nu* act of joining or meeting. **2.** *nc* place of joining or meeting. *We stopped at the road junction* i.e. where two or more roads meet.

juncture ['dʒʌŋktʃə*] *nc* particular moment in a situation. *The people began to throw stones. At this juncture the police arrived.*

June [dʒu:n] *n* sixth month of the year.

jungle ['dʒʌŋgl] *nc* (usu. with **the**) land in the tropics covered with thick forest and undergrowth.

junior ['dʒu:niə*] *adj* younger; of lower rank. *My other brother is junior to me. In the army a captain is junior to a major.* Also *nc* person who is younger or of lower rank. *My other brother is my junior. A captain is a major's junior.*

Junior 1. (mainly *US*) son having the same first name as his father: *John Smith, Junior.* **2.** younger of two brothers at school: *Williamson Senior and Williamson Junior.*

juniper ['dʒu:nipə*] *nc* type of evergreen bush or tree.

junk¹ [dʒʌŋk] *nc* type of Chinese sailing ship

junk¹

junk² [dʒʌŋk] *nu* things thrown away as useless; rubbish. (*informal*).

junket ['dʒʌŋkit] *nc* **1.** dish made of curds. **2.** feast (*o.f.* in sense **2.**).

junketing *nu* feasting. (*informal*).

junta ['dʒʌntə] *nc* small political ruling group: *a country ruled by a military junta.*

juridical [dʒuə'ridikl] *adj* of the law or a court of law. **juridically** *adv*.

jurisdiction [dʒuəris'dikʃən] *nu* administration of justice; right or power to administer justice. *This crime is not within the jurisdiction of this court* i.e. this court does not have the right or power to deal with it.

jurisprudence [dʒuəris'pru:dns] *nu* science of law; study of the principles of law.

jurist ['dʒuərist] *nc* person who is an expert in law (esp. civil law).

jury ['dʒuəri] *nc* **1.** group of persons (usu. twelve in number) chosen to listen to the evidence of a case in a court of law and to decide on it. (The jury does not decide what the punishment should be). *The jury found him guilty of murder.* **2.** group of persons to give evidence in a competition etc.

juror ['dʒuərə*] *nc* person in a jury. (Also **juryman; jurywoman**).

'jury box enclosed space where a jury sits in a court of law.

just¹ [dʒʌst] *adj* fair; true; right. *This is a just decision.* (*opp* **unjust**). **justly** *adv*. **justness** *nu*.

just² [dʒʌst] *adv/intensifier* **1.** exactly. *Tell me just what happened. This coat is just the right size.* **2.** a short time ago. *They have just gone. I am just out of hospital. They went just before we did.* **3.** almost at once; very soon. *They are just going. I am just about to write him a letter. They went just after we did.* **4.** only; merely. *He just stood there looking at us. He is just a child. I need just two more days to finish it. Just a minute!* i.e. wait a minute! **5.** (often with **only**) scarcely; almost not. *The bullet (only) just missed him. We had (only) just enough money to pay the bill.* **6.** certainly; without a doubt. *The food is just wonderful. I just can't wait to see them.*

just about has the sense of not being sure or of almost. *I left my hat just about here. This box is just about big enough for my books. I am just about finished.*

just as 1. exactly as. *I did just as you told me. Leave it just as it is.* **2.** equally; quite. *I am just as brave as you are. It would be just as well if he left.*

just now 1. a very short time ago. *They gave it to me just now.* **2.** at this very time. *Just now they are asleep.*

just so exactly; certainly.

justice ['dʒʌstis] **1.** *nu* being just; fairness. *Children expect justice from their parents.* **2.** *nu* the purpose of the law i.e. to be just; punishment according to the law. *It is the duty of the police to bring those who break the law to justice* i.e. bring them to court to be punished. **3.** *nc* person who administers justice in a court of law i.e. a judge or magistrate. (*opp* **injustice** in senses **1.** and **2.**).

do justice to be fair to; behave in the right way to. *Your essay does not do justice to your intelligence* i.e. the essay is not as good as your intelligence could make it. *They did justice to all the food we brought them* i.e. they behaved in the right way by eating a lot of it.

do oneself justice be fair to, make the most of, one's own abilities. *He cannot do himself justice as a singer if he refuses to practise.*

justify ['dʒʌstifai] *vt* be or give a good reason for something; explain satisfactorily. *His illness does not justify his long absence. You will have to justify your work to the others.*

justified *adj.* (*opp* **unjustified**).

justifiable *adj* able to be justified. (*opp* **unjustifiable**). **justifiably** *adv.*

justification [dʒʌstifi'keiʃən] *nc/u* something which justifies; state of being justified. *His justification for being absent is his illness.*

jut [dʒʌt] *vi* (with **out**) stick out; project. *The rocks jut out above the trees. past* **jutted.**

jute [dʒu:t] *nu* type of plant used for making rope and rough cloth.

juvenile ['dʒu:vənail] *nc* young person. Also *adj*: *juvenile books; juvenile court* i.e. a court of law which deals with young persons; *juvenile employment* i.e. employment of young persons.

juxtapose ['dʒʌkstə'pouz] *vt* place side by side. **juxtaposition** [dʒʌkstəpə'ziʃən] *nu.*

K

kaleidoscope [kə'laidəskoup] *nc* **1.** apparatus fitted with mirrors and pieces of coloured glass etc which shows many coloured patterns. **2.** any pattern of changing colours. **kaleidoscopic** [kəlaidə'skɔpik] *adj*.

kangaroo [kæŋgə'ru:] *nc* type of animal found in Australia, with strong back legs on which it stands and leaps forward.

kangaroo

kaolin ['keiəlin] *nu* type of fine white clay.

kapok ['keipɔk] *nu* substance like cotton wool obtained from a tropical tree and used for filling pillows etc.

karate [kə'ra:ti] *nu* method of fighting etc using the edge of the hand.

kayak ['kaiæk] *nc* type of covered canoe used by the people who live in the Arctic; any canoe of this shape.

keel [ki:l] *nc* long piece of wood or steel along the bottom of a ship to which the sides of the ship are fixed.

keel over turn over; fall over. *The ship keeled over in the storm.*

on an even keel 1. (with reference to a ship) without moving much from side to side. **2.** (with reference to other things) without any sudden changes; without trouble. *He kept the business on an even keel for many years.*

keen[1] [ki:n] *adj* **1.** (with reference to persons) eager; very interested. *He is a keen football player. He is always keen to play.* **2.** (with reference to the mind, senses and feelings) sharp; quick; deep. *He has a keen brain. They have keen sight/are keen-sighted* i.e. they have good eyesight, they can see well. *My hearing is not as keen as it used to be. He takes a keen interest in his work.* **3.** very cold; intense: *keen winds; a keen frost. The air outside was keen.* **4.** sharp: *a spear with a keen point.* **keenly** *adv.* **keenness** *nu.*

'keen-'eyed *adj* having good eyesight.

be keen on be very fond of; be eager to. *He is keen on that girl. I am keen on fishing. They are keen on buying a new house.* (*informal*).

keen[2] [ki:n] *vt/i* (*Ir*) show sorrow for somebody's death by crying out and singing sad songs (usu. done by women). **keening** *nu.*

keep[1] [ki:p] *vt/i* **1.** have or hold, either for a time or always. *You may keep my book for a fortnight. Please keep the picture. I don't want it.* **2.** look after; take care of; be responsible for. *He is keeping my coat and hat for me until I return. She keeps house for her brother. He keeps goal in our football team. I am keeping the cake for tea tomorrow* i.e. not allowing it to be eaten until then. **3.** own, manage. *My father keeps a grocer's shop. The farmers here keep cattle.* **4.** pay for; support. *I have a wife and three children to keep. They get enough money to keep themselves in food and clothing.* **5.** hold back; cause to stay; prevent. *What kept you?* i.e. what held you back/delayed you? *The doctors are keeping him in hospital for another week. I kept him from running away.* **6.** continue, cause to continue, to be in a particular state or place. *Although they have many difficulties, they keep happy. Good food keeps you healthy. You must keep inside the house during the cold weather. Will this fish keep?* i.e. will it continue to be fresh and fit to eat? **7.** continue, cause to continue, to do something. *He keeps coming back for more. He kept them working all day.* **8.** follow; obey; observe. *They keep early hours* i.e. they always go to bed early. *Everyone must keep the law. He always keeps his promise. Most people keep Christmas at home. past* **kept** [kept].

keeper *nc* **1.** person who looks after, or is responsible for, something. (Used with many other words e.g. *gamekeeper; goalkeeper; housekeeper; innkeeper; shopkeeper*). **2.** (machines etc) something used to hold something else in place.

keeping *nu* **1.** care. *Your books are in good keeping if he is looking after them.* **2.** being suited to; being in agreement with. *The speech was in keeping with the happy event. What he says now is out of keeping with what he said before.*

'keepsake gift made to somebody who, by keeping it, can remember the person who gave it.

keep at (something) continue, cause to continue, to do or try to do. *He keeps at his studies, although he is ill. He kept me at it all day* i.e. he kept me busy.

keep (someone) away avoid going near; stop, cause to stop, going to or near. *We kept away from the fierce dog. My mother kept me away from school yesterday.*

keep (someone) back stay, cause to stay, back. *They all ran forward but I kept back. I also kept my friend back.*

keep something back refuse to tell everything. *He may be telling the truth but he is keeping something back.*

keep down bend oneself down. *We kept down behind the bushes until they passed.*

keep someone/something down 1. control; rule severely. *They cannot keep down their excitement. The king kept the conquered people down. You can't keep him down* i.e. he is full of energy. **2.** hold (food) in the stomach. *I found it difficult to keep my breakfast down* i.e. I wanted to be sick or to vomit.

keep something from someone hide; not allow to see or know. *They kept the truth* *from him* i.e. they did not tell him the truth.

keep (someone/something) in 1. stay, cause to stay, inside or indoors. *I kept in during the cold weather.* 2. continue, cause to continue, to burn. *The fire kept in all night. He kept the fire in all night.*

keep in with someone continue to be friendly with for one's own benefit. *He keeps in with his manager.*

keep off stay, cause to stay, away from. *Keep off the grass. Keep your dog off the grass. The rain keeps off* i.e. it does not come near or begin.

keep on continue, cause to continue, to do something. *They kept on working after dark. He didn't stop running. He just kept on.*

keep something on continue to wear. *He kept his hat on even when he went into the house.*

keep on at someone continue to attack or to ask many questions etc. *We kept at him about his plan to go away.*

keep out of something stay, cause to stay, outside or out of. *I keep out of his troubles.*

keep someone/something up 1. stay, cause to stay, high, cheerful or good. *Their spirits are keeping up although they have many troubles. The good news keeps our spirits up. I hope the weather keeps up.* 2. continue, cause to continue. *They keep up the habit of visiting old friends. Keep it up!* i.e. don't stop! 3. not allow to go to bed. *They kept me up for three hours talking about their work.*

keep up with someone/something 1. go as quickly as; do as well as. *They could not keep up with us when we climbed the mountain. He can't keep up with his rich friends* i.e. spend as much as they do. 2. continue to be informed about: *keep up with the news.*

keep one's head remain calm. *He survived the accident because he kept his head* i.e. he did not panic. (*opp* **lose one's head**).

keep one's head above water stay out of debt or difficulty.

keep one's nose to the grindstone work hard without stopping. (*informal*).

keep (oneself) to oneself stay by oneself, not mix with others. *At the party he kept to himself.*

keep something to oneself not tell anyone. *He keeps his thoughts to himself.*

keep open house be always ready to welcome people to one's house.

keep a stiff upper lip refuse to cry or complain. (*informal*).

keep a straight face prevent oneself from laughing. (*informal*).

keep time 1. (with reference to a clock) remain accurate: *a clock that kept* (good) *time.* 2. move or play in rhythm: *keep time to the music.*

keep[2] [kiːp] 1. *nc* the inner and strongest part of a castle. 2. *nu* board and lodging given to somebody. *Everybody living here pays for his keep.*

for keeps always; forever. *This book is yours for keeps.* (*informal*).

keg [keg] *nc* small barrel.

ken [ken] *nu* limit of sight or knowledge (usu. in **beyond/outside one's ken**).

kennel ['kenl] *nc* small hut in which a dog is kept.

kept [kept] past of **keep.**[1]

kerb [kəːb] (*US* **curb**) *nc* edge of a pavement. *Please park your car close to the kerb.*

'kerbstone stone which is part of a kerb.

kernel ['kəːnl] *nc* 1. inner part of a seed or nut. 2. inner or most important part of anything. *The kernel of his problem is lack of money.*

kerosene ['kerəsiːn] *nu* paraffin oil.

kestrel ['kestrl] *nc* type of small bird of prey.

ketch [ketʃ] *nc* type of sailing ship with two masts.

ketchup ['ketʃəp] *nu* type of sauce (usu. made from tomatoes).

kettle ['ketl] *nc* metal container with a handle and spout used for boiling liquids.

kettle

'kettledrum type of drum with a curved bottom.

key[1] [kiː] *nc* 1. instrument to open and shut a lock. *Have you got the key of this door?* 2. instrument to turn or screw something. *This is the key to wind the clock. You need a large key to open this valve.* 3. set of musical notes which have a definite relation to one another and form a scale. 4. lever in a musical instrument or typewriter which is pressed down by the fingers. *A piano has a row of black and white keys. Typewriters have a key for each letter of the alphabet.* 5. something which explains, solves or answers. *The key to this problem is better planning. I need a key when I am reading Latin* i.e. a book which gives a translation. 6. (usu. used as an *adj*) something which is very important. *He has the key post in this factory* i.e. the most important post. *He is the key man. The enemy hold all the key positions.*

'keyboard row of keys on a piano, typewriter etc.

'keyhole hole in a lock into which one puts the key to open and shut it.

'keynote 1. main note of a musical key (in sense 3.) which gives the key its name. 2. principal idea; theme. *The keynote of all his writings is the need for peace.*

'keystone 1. central stone at the top of an arch. 2. central idea; most important part of something. *The keystone of their foreign policy is friendliness to all nations.*

key[2] [kiː] *vt* make ready, or more suitable, for. *The company has keyed its factories to produce more goods.*

key something up 1. put in tune. 2. make excited. *They were keyed up for the examination.*

khaki ['kɑːki] *nu* 1. the colour of yellowish dust. 2. cloth of this colour (used in making soldiers' uniforms). Also *adj.*

kibbutz [ki'buːts] *nc* collective farm in Israel. *pl* **kibbutzim** [ki'buːtsiːm].

kick [kik] 1. *vt* hit with the foot. *He kicked the ball.* 2. *vi* move the feet violently in order to hit somebody/something. *He kicked and shouted when the police caught him.* 3. *vi* move violently. *A rifle kicks when you fire it.* Also *nc* 1. *He gave the ball a kick.* 2. *This rifle has a kick.* 3. powerful effect;

pleasure. *The drink he gave me had a kick in it. He did it for kicks.* (*informal* in sense **3.**).
kick off begin a game of football or begin the second half of a game, by kicking a ball.
'kick-off *nc* (usu. only *sing*) beginning of a game of football; beginning of any activity.
kick out push out violently (not necessarily by using one's foot). *He has been kicked out of his job.* (*informal*).
kick a goal kick a ball into a goal; score a goal.
kick one's heels be kept waiting. *I had to kick my heels for an hour before the manager could see me.*
kick up a fuss/row cause a fuss/row by protesting violently.
kick upstairs move somebody from work he cannot do well to a position which appears more important. *They kicked their manager upstairs by putting him on the managing committee.* (*informal*).

kid[1] [kid] *nc* **1.** young goat. **2.** leather made from the skin of a young goat. **3.** child. (*informal* in sense **3.**).
kiddy *nc* child. (*informal*).
'kid 'glove 1. glove made from the skin of a kid. **2.** (usu. *pl*) polite or gentle manner. *You should not use kid gloves when dealing with criminals.* (*informal* in sense **2.**).

kid[2] [kid] *vt* deceive; pretend. *Don't listen! He's kidding you. I was only kidding* i.e. joking. *past* **kidded**. (*informal*).

kidnap ['kidnæp] *vt* carry somebody off by force (esp. a child in order to be paid money if the child is returned to its parents). *past* **kidnapped. kidnapper** *nc*. **kidnapping** *nc/u*.

kidney ['kidni] *nc* either of two organs of the body which take urine from the blood.
'kidney bean type of bean shaped like a kidney.
'kidney machine machine which does the work of a kidney for a person whose kidneys are severely damaged or diseased.

kill [kil] *vt* **1.** put to death; cause the death of. *He killed him with a spear. Malaria killed them.* **2.** destroy; bring to an end. *He has killed our chances of success.* Also *n sing* (esp. with reference to animals killed in hunting) act of killing; thing killed. *We saw the lion sitting beside its kill.*
killer *nc* person/thing that kills.
killing *adj* **1.** likely to kill or exhaust. *The speed at which they ran was killing.* **2.** very funny. *He told me some killing jokes.* (*informal* in sense **2.**). **killingly** *adv*.
'killjoy person who stops, tries to stop, the happiness of others.
kill something off kill so that none is left. *Hunters have killed off all the large animals in this country.*
kill with kindness be too kind.
kill time do something in order to fill up time. *The train was very late, so we killed time by playing cards.*
kill two birds with one stone get two things done by doing one thing. (*informal*).

kiln [kiln] *nc* large oven in which substances (e.g. clay, bricks, lime) are dried, made hard or burnt.

kilo-[1] ['kilou] *prefix* one thousand (e.g. **kilometre**).

kilo[2] ['ki:lou] *nc* short form of **kilogram** (or **kilogramme**). see appendix.

kilometre ['kiləmi:tə*] (*US* **kilometer**) *nc* unit of length equal to one thousand metres. see appendix.

kilt [kilt] *nc* type of short skirt traditionally worn by Scotsmen.

kilt

kilted *adj* wearing a kilt.

kimono [ki'mounou] *nc* type of loose coat with a broad belt worn by the Japanese; dressing gown of this type. *pl* **kimonos.**

kin [kin] *npl* family relations; people related by family ties.
kinship *nu* relationship of this kind.
'kinsfolk *npl* people related by family ties.
'kinsman male relative (*o.f.*).
'kinswoman female relative (*o.f.*).
next of kin closest relations, family of a person.

kind[1] [kaind] *nc* type; sort; class. *Rice is a kind of grain. I don't like this kind of school; many kinds of people/people of many kinds. He is the kind (of person) who always arrives late.*
a kind of often used when something is not fully known or is difficult to describe. *It was a kind of animal with long ears and a short tail. We have a kind of feeling that we are being followed.*
kind of rather; in a way. *They kind of laughed at me.* (*informal*).
nothing of the kind certainly not. *You're drunk! I'm nothing of the kind!*
something of the kind something rather like this. *He plays the trumpet or something of the kind* i.e. some musical instrument like a trumpet, but I am not sure what it is.
of a kind not very good; not as good as one would expect. *He is a football player of a kind. They gave us a welcome of a kind.*
payment in kind see **pay.**

kind[2] [kaind] *adj* gentle; friendly; helpful. *I have a kind father and mother. They are very kind to children. It was kind of them to ask us to the concert.* (*opp* **unkind**).
kindly *adv*: *They kindly asked us to the concert. Would you kindly lend me your pen?* i.e. would you please? *I do not take kindly to the cold weather* i.e. I do not like it.
kindness *nc/u* act or state of being kind. *Thank you for your many kindnesses.*
out of kindness because of being kind. *He did not know me, but out of kindness he helped me.*

kindergarten ['kindəga:tn] *nc* school for very young children.

kindle ['kindl] *vt/i* **1.** catch fire; set on fire. *Damp wood does not kindle. He kindled the wood with a match.* **2.** have, cause to have, a particular feeling. *The story kindled our desire for adventure.*
kindling *nu* small sticks for lighting a fire easily.

kindly[1] ['kaindli] *adv* see **kind**[2].

kindly[2] ['kaindli] *adj* pleasant; friendly. *He has a kindly manner.* **kindliness** *nu*.

kindred ['kindrid] **1.** *npl* people to whom one is related. **2.** *nu* family relationship with somebody. Also *adj* related. *They belong to kindred tribes and speak kindred languages.*

kinetic [ki'netik] *adj* connected with, or caused by, motion: *kinetic energy*.
kinetics *nu* study of the movement of objects and the forces causing or changing it.
king [kiŋ] *nc* **1.** male ruler of a country (esp. by descent). **2.** most important person. *He is a cotton king* i.e. the most important person in the cotton industry. **3.** most important piece in the game of chess. **4.** most important playing card after the ace.
kingly *adj*.
'kingfisher type of brightly coloured bird which catches fish.
'kingpin **1.** pin which keeps a wheel in place. **2.** important person on whom everything depends. *The kingpin of this company is not the manager but his assistant.*
kingdom ['kiŋdəm] *nc* **1.** country ruled by a king or queen. **2.** one of the three main divisions of nature i.e. *the animal kingdom; the vegetable kingdom; the mineral kingdom.*
kink [kiŋk] *nc* **1.** twist or bend (made by accident) in a rope, wire, hose or long piece of something. *If you pull the rope tight, the kinks in it will disappear.* **2.** mental twist; strange way of thinking. *He had a kink about religion.* Also *vt/i* have kinks, make kinks in.
kinky *adj* odd or unusual in appearance or behaviour (esp. in a fashionable way).
kinsfolk ['kinzfouk] *npl* see **kin.**
kinship ['kinʃip] *nu* see **kin.**
kiosk ['ki:ɔsk] *nc* small hut used for selling newspapers, tobacco etc, or for a public telephone. (For a public telephone, also **callbox**).
kipper ['kipə*] *nc* herring i.e. type of sea fish, split open, salted and dried in smoke until it is brown in colour. Also *vt* prepare herring in this way.
kirk [kə:k] *nc* (*Scot*) church.
kiss [kis] *vt/i* place the lips against somebody's mouth, cheek, hand etc, or against something to show love or respect, or as a greeting. *When the two sisters met they kissed. He kissed his mother goodbye.* Also *nc*.
kiss of life method of getting someone breathing normally again (e.g. if he has just been rescued from drowning).
kit [kit] *nc* **1.** all the equipment and clothes of a soldier, airman or sailor. **2.** set of tools, materials, clothes or equipment for a particular purpose: *carpenter's kit; first-aid kit; football kit.*
'kitbag large canvas bag used by soldiers, airmen or sailors to carry kit.
kitchen ['kitʃin] *nc* room used for cooking.
kitchenette [kitʃi'net] *nc* very small kitchen.
'kitchen 'garden garden or part of a garden where vegetables are grown.
kite[1] [kait] *nc* type of large bird of prey.
kite[2] [kait] *nc* light frame covered with paper or cloth which rises high in the air and is tied to a very long piece of string, held by somebody on the ground.

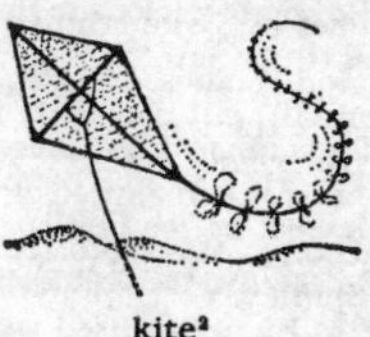
kite[2]

kith [kiθ] *nu* only in **kith and kin** i.e. friends and family relations.
kitten ['kitn] *nc* young cat.
kittenish *adj* like a kitten; playful.
kitty ['kiti] *nc* **1.** money which is gambled for in various games. **2.** kitten. (*informal* in sense **2.**).
kleptomania [kleptou'meiniə] *nu* strong urge to steal caused by mental illness.
kleptomaniac [kleptou'meiniæk] *nc* person who has kleptomania.
knack [næk] *nu* skill in doing something (usu. gained by long practice). *There is a knack in tying ropes together. He has the knack of disappearing when he is needed.*
knacker ['nækə*] *nc* person who deals in and kills old or diseased horses which are no longer useful.
knapsack ['næpsæk] *nc* small bag with straps, carried on the back (esp. by soldiers and travellers).
knave [neiv] *nc* **1.** person who is not honest and cannot be trusted (*o.f.*). **2.** playing card below the queen in importance. (Also **jack**). *The knave of hearts.* **knavish** *adj*. **knavishly** *adv*. **knavery** ['neivəri] *nc/u*.
knead [ni:d] *vt* **1.** mix together by pressing and squeezing with the hands (e.g. flour and water to make bread, or soft clay to make pots). **2.** press and squeeze muscles of the body in this way to remove pain or stiffness.
knee [ni:] *nc* joint in the middle of the leg where it bends; part of one's clothing which covers the knees. *You have to bend your knees to sit down. My mother mended the holes in the knees of my trousers.*
'knee breeches breeches reaching and tied just below the knee.
'kneecap **1.** bone on the front of the knee. **2.** covering to protect the knee (e.g. on horses).
'knee-'deep (in something) *adj/adv* deep enough to reach the knees. *He stood knee-deep in the river.*
'knee-'high *adj/adv* high enough to reach the knees. *The corn is not yet knee-high.*
'weak-'kneed *adj* having a weak nature. *They are too weak-kneed to defend themselves.* (*informal*).
bring somebody to his knees conquer; make him yield.
kneel [ni:l] *vi* go down on the knees. *Every evening they kneel (down) to pray/in prayer. past* **knelt** [nelt].
knelt [nelt] past of **kneel.**
knew [nju:] past tense of **know.**
knickerbockers ['nikəbɔkəz] *npl* short, loose trousers tied to the leg just below the knee.
knickers ['nikəz] *npl* **1.** pants, undergarment worn by women and girls, covering the bottom part of the body. **2.** see **knickerbockers.**
knick-knack ['niknæk] *nc* small ornament in a house etc.
knife [naif] *nc* tool or weapon with a sharp blade of steel fixed to a handle, used for cutting food etc. *pl* **knives** [naivz]. Also *vt* stab with a knife.
'pocket knife see **pocket.**
get one's knife into someone wish to do harm to someone. (*informal*).
knight [nait] *nc* **1.** (in the Middle Ages) man who was given the right to carry arms by his king or ruler. **2.** (in modern times in Britain and some other countries) man who is given as an honour or reward a special

rank above ordinary people with the title of *Sir* instead of Mr. **3.** piece in the game of chess, shaped like a horse's head. Also *vt* make somebody a knight (in sense **2.**). *Mr John Smith was knighted by the Queen and became Sir John Smith.*
Note: one can say *Sir John Smith* or *Sir John,* but not *Sir Smith.*
knighthood rank of knight; all knights. *He has been given a knighthood* i.e. he has been knighted.
'knight-'errant *nc* (in ancient times) knight who travelled about looking for adventure. *pl* **knights-errant. knight-errantry** *nu.*

knit [nit] *vt/i* **1.** make material or something to wear etc by using needles to link together threads of wool etc. *She is knitting a pair of socks. She likes to knit in the evening.* **2.** join firmly. *Danger knits people together. The two broken bones in his arm have knitted well. past* **knitted** or **knit.**
knitter *nc.*
knitting *nu* **1.** act of knitting. **2.** something that is being made by knitting. *Mother can't find her knitting.*
'knitting machine machine which knits.
'knitting needle long needle made of steel, wood etc used for knitting.
knit one's brows bring the brows together; frown. *He knits his brows when he is thinking hard.*

knives [naivz] pl of **knife.**

knob [nɔb] *nc* **1.** round lump on the surface or at the end of something. *He carries a stick with a big knob on it.* **2.** handle or lever shaped like a knob. *He opened the door by turning the knob. A television set has a number of knobs which control vision and sound.* **3.** small round lump: *a knob of butter.*
knobbly *adj* having knobs (in sense **1.**).

knock [nɔk] *vt/i* **1.** strike; beat (usu. making a noise while doing so). *He knocked his head against the wall. I knocked at his door before going in.* **2.** (with reference to an engine) make a noise because of a fault inside. *Your car knocks when it climbs a hill.* **3.** speak unfavourably about. *He is always knocking his country's foreign policy.* (*informal* in sense **3.**). Also *nc* **1.** *There is a knock at the door.* **2.** *I don't like the knock in the engine of your car.*
knocker *nc* **1.** person who knocks. **2.** handle on a hinge for knocking at a door (instead of using one's hand).
knocking *nu* repeated knocks. *The knocking in the engine won't stop.*
'knock-'kneed *adj* having legs bent in together at the knees.
knock about wander here and there. *He has knocked about Africa all his life.* (*informal*).
'knockabout *adj* **1.** (with reference to the theatre or films) of a comedy with a lot of amusing action such as actors falling down and throwing things. **2.** (with reference to clothes) comfortable and untidy. (*informal* in sense **2.**).
knock someone/something about push here and there by striking. *They say he knocks his children about.* (*informal*).
knock something back drink quickly. (*informal*).
knock someone/something down **1.** knock to the ground. *He knocked him down with one blow of his fist.* **2.** sell at an auction (by striking the table with a hammer to show that the bidding is finished). *The books were knocked down to me for two pounds.* **3.** make the price less. *I was able to knock their price down to £1/them down to £1.* (*informal* in sense **3.**).
knock something off **1.** take away from; deduct. *They knocked five pounds off the price.* **2.** stop working. *We knock off every day at 5 p.m.* **3.** do or finish quickly. *The boy knocked off his homework in half an hour.* (all *informal*).
knock someone out **1.** (esp. in boxing) hit somebody so hard that he loses consciousness. **2.** hit something so that what is inside comes out or so that it is no longer bent. *He is knocking out the dent in the mudguard of his car.*
'knockout *nc*: *He won the boxing match by a knockout.*
knock something together **1.** join together quickly. *We soon knocked together a few pieces of wood to make a box.* (*informal*). **2.** hit against each other. *My knees were knocking together* i.e. because I was afraid.
knock someone/something up **1.** make quickly. *She knocked up supper in a few minutes.* (*informal*). **2.** waken by knocking on the door. *I'll knock you up at 6 a.m.* **3.** make very tired. *The long journey has knocked him up.* (*informal*). **4.** (mainly US) make pregnant. (*informal* in sense **4.**).

knoll [noul] *nc* small rounded hill.

knot [nɔt] *nc* **1.** fastening made with a piece of thread, string or rope by twisting and turning the ends. *He tied the two ropes together with/in a knot.* **2.** hard, round piece of wood in a wooden board. **3.** small group of persons/things. *A knot of friends stood round him.* **4.** measure of the speed of ships i.e. one nautical mile (6,080 feet) per hour. *The ship was sailing at 15 knots.* Also *vt/i* have or take knots; tie with knots. *This rope does not knot as well as that. He knotted the pieces of string together. past* **knotted.**
knotty *adj* **1.** full of knots (in senses **1.** and **2.**). **2.** difficult: *a knotty problem.*
get into knots/tie oneself up in/into knots get oneself into great difficulties about something. *He tied himself up in knots trying to explain how the engine worked.* (*informal*).

know [nou] *vt/i* **1.** have information about somebody/something; understand; be aware of. *I know (that) he lives here. He knows three languages. We did not know whether we were right or wrong. I'm your friend. Yes, I know. Do you know how to use this machine?* **2.** recognize somebody; be acquainted with somebody. *I know your brother but not your sister. They have known me for many years.* **3.** be able to judge the value of, or to tell the difference between, things. *They know good food when they taste it. He doesn't know a lion from a tiger. past tense* **knew** [nju:]. *past part* **known.**
known *adj.* (*opp* **unknown**).
knowable *adj* able to be known.
knowing *adj* showing that one knows; clever; sly. *He gave me a knowing look.*
knowingly *adv* **1.** *He looked at me knowingly.* **2.** on purpose. *We did not knowingly leave you behind.*
'know-all person who thinks he knows everything. (*informal*).
'know-how knowing how to do something because of experience (esp. something practical) (*informal*).
be known as **1.** be regarded or considered as. *He is known as the best engineer in the country.* **2.** known by the name of: *the man known as Smith.*
be known to the police used with reference

to a person who has already committed a crime about which the police have full information in their records.
know about something be aware of; have information about. *He knew about my father's arrival before I did.* see also **know of.**
know better than have enough sense or information not to do something. *I know better than to lend him any money. He ran away from school. He ought to have known better.*
know of be aware of; have information about. *Has he gone? Not that we know of.*
know the ropes know from experience how to do something. (*informal*).
know which side one's bread is buttered on know what will be of most advantage to oneself. (*informal*).
make oneself known to somebody introduce oneself. *When I saw the new teacher I made myself known to him.*
there is no knowing it is impossible to know. *There is no knowing what he'll do next.* (*informal*).

knowledge ['nɔlidʒ] *nu* **1.** understanding; learning. *I have no knowledge of mathematics. He has a good knowledge of English.* **2.** information about; experience of. *Our knowledge of our neighbours is not very great. He has no knowledge of life in a small village.*
knowledgeable ['nɔlidʒəbl] *adj* having much knowledge. *He is very knowledgeable about cars.* **knowledgeably** *adv.*
come to one's knowledge see come.
to the best of one's knowledge as far as one is aware. *To the best of my knowledge he still lives in London.*
without the knowledge of somebody without somebody knowing or being informed. *He went out of the classroom without the knowledge of his teacher.*

knuckle ['nʌkl] *nc* **1.** (with reference to persons) bone where a finger is joined to the hand or in a finger where it has a joint. **2.** (with reference to animals) bone at the joint of the knee or foot.
'knuckleduster piece of metal worn over the hand and used as a weapon.
knuckle under yield; cause no more trouble. *After being punished the pupils knuckled under.*

kosher ['kouʃə*] *adj* (with reference to food etc) in accordance with Orthodox Jewish Law.

kowtow ['kau'tau] *vt* show great respect for (usu. to get what one wants for oneself); obey without question. (Once a Chinese custom of kneeling and bowing the head to the ground as a sign of respect). *Why should we kowtow to the members of the committee?*

kraal [krɑːl] *nc* in South Africa, village protected by a fence; a pen for animals protected by a fence.

kudos ['kjuːdɔs] *nu* honour; credit. *We did the work but we didn't get much kudos for it.*

L

lab [læb] *nc* short form of **laboratory.**

label ['leibl] *nc* piece of paper or other material fixed to something to show what it is, who it belongs to or where it is to be sent. *When you are travelling you should put labels on your luggage.* Also *vt* **1.** attach a label to. *He labelled the parcel before posting it.* **2.** classify someone/something. *He was labelled as a communist. past* **labelled.** (*US* **labeled**).

labial ['leibiəl] *adj* of, or formed by, the lips: *labial sounds* i.e. speech sounds made by the lips (e.g. 'b', 'p' and 'm'). Also *nc*: *'b' is a labial.*

labor ['leibə*] *US* form of **labour.**

laboratory [lə'bɔrətəri] *nc* building or room in which scientific work, teaching and tests are carried out.

laborious [lə'bɔ:riəs] *adj* **1.** (with reference to things) requiring hard work; not easy. *They had the laborious task of cutting down the huge tree. His books are not easy to read because they are written in a very laborious style.* **laboriously** *adv.* **laboriousness** *nu.*

labour[1] ['leibə*] (*US* **labor**) **1.** *nc/u* hard work. *They have succeeded by their own labours.* **2.** *nu* persons who work with their hands and are not employers or owners of a business; the working class. *This country has not enough skilled labour. The factory has had trouble with its labour.* **3.** *nu* pains suffered by a woman when giving birth to a child. *His wife is in labour.*

'labour exchange (*Brit*) government office for finding work for people.

'Labour Party the British socialist party.

'labour-saving *adj* made to reduce hard work. *They have a modern house which is full of labour-saving devices.*

labour[2] ['leibə*] (*US* **labor**) *vt/i* **1.** work hard. *I laboured at the English course for two years.* **2.** move with difficulty. *They laboured through the thick forest and up the steep hill.*

laboured *adj* done with difficulty. *He made a laboured speech.*

labourer *nc* person who does hard unskilled work without machinery.

labour the argument/point argue or explain something in more detail than is needed. *Although we all knew what the difficulty was, he wasted time labouring the point.*

labour under a delusion/disadvantage etc be deceived or hindered by. *He laboured under the delusion that he could never make a mistake. The school labours under the disadvantage of not having enough textbooks.*

laburnum [lə'bə:nəm] *nc/u* type of small tree with yellow flowers.

labyrinth ['læbirinθ] *nc* **1.** number of paths which cross one another in so many different ways that one easily becomes lost in them. **2.** any difficulty or confusing state or situation.

lace [leis] **1.** *nu* material like a net, made of cotton, linen, silk etc, with the threads making patterns. *The tablecloth has lace round the edges.* **2.** *nc* string put through holes and pulled tight to fasten the two edges of something together (e.g. *shoelaces*). Also *vt/i* **1.** fasten with a lace. *He laced (up) his shoes.* **2.** put a small amount of liquor into a liquid for drinking. *They laced their coffee with brandy.*

lacy *adj* of or like lace.

lacing *nc/u* fastening made by a lace put through holes.

lacerate ['læsəreit] *vt* **1.** wound by tearing the flesh. **2.** hurt someone's feelings deeply.

laceration [læsə'reiʃən] *nc/u.*

lachrymose ['lækrimous] *adj* easily made to weep; tearful.

lack [læk] *vt/i* not have something which is needed. *They lack the courage to do it. As he is very rich he lacks for nothing.* Also *nu*: *I cannot buy it because of my lack of money. They are ill for lack of good food.*

be lacking be missing, not available. *Their courage is lacking. Good food was lacking.*

'lacklustre (*US* **lackluster**) *adj* **1.** (with reference to eyes) dull; not shining. **2.** dull; boring; unexciting.

lackadaisical [lækə'deizikl] *adj* appearing or pretending to be without energy or interest. *He has a very lackadaisical attitude towards his work.* **lackadaisically** *adv.*

lackey, lacquey ['læki] *nc* **1.** manservant. **2.** person who behaves like a servant of others.

laconic [lə'kɔnik] *adj* saying something in the fewest possible words; brief. *He gave laconic answers to all our questions.* **laconically** *adv.* **laconicism** [lə'kɔnisizəm], **laconism** ['lækənizəm] *nc/u.*

lacquer ['lækə*] *nu* **1.** type of paint which when it dries gives a hard, bright surface (used for painting metal and wooden articles). **2.** liquid sprayed on hair to keep it in place. Also *vt* cover with lacquer.

lacquey ['læki] *nc* see **lackey.**

lacrosse [lə'krɔs] *nu* outdoor game played between two teams of twelve, with long sticks which have a net at the end to catch and throw a small rubber ball.

lactate ['lækteit] *vi* (with reference to a mother) produce milk.

lactation [læk'teiʃən] *nu* act of producing milk; period during which a mother feeds her child with her milk.

lactic ['læktik] *adj* of milk.

lacuna [lə'kju:nə] *nc* (esp. with reference to something missing in writing or an argument) something missing; gap. *pl* **lacunas** or **lacunae** [lə'kju:ni:].

lacy ['leisi] *adj* see **lace.**

lad [læd] *nc* boy; young man. (*informal*).

ladder ['lædə*] *nc* **1.** apparatus made of two long pieces of wood, metal or rope, joined together by short pieces (called **rungs**) up which one climbs. **2.** (*Brit*) tear in a woman's stocking which has the shape of a ladder. (*US* **run**). Also *vt/i* have, cause to have, a ladder in one's stocking. *She has laddered her best stockings.*

laden ['leidn] *adj* carrying something heavy; loaded. *The bushes were laden with fruit. They arrived laden with luggage.*

lading ['leidiŋ] *nu* cargo; freight.

bill of lading see **bill**[2].

ladle ['leidl] *nc* large, deep spoon with a long handle used for serving liquids. Also *vt*: *She ladled the soup into the bowls.*

ladle

lady ['leidi] *nc* **1.** polite word for a **woman.** *There is a lady to see you. This shop sells ladies' hats.* **2.** woman of good family, of the upper classes (formerly, one just below the nobility); woman of wealth and leisure. *Because she has a rich husband she lives like a lady.* **3.** **(Lady)** (*Brit*) the title of the wife of a nobleman (below the rank of duke) or of a knight (e.g. *Sir Winston and Lady Churchill*). Also with a first name as the title of a daughter of a nobleman (e.g. *Lady Jane*).

Note: the *masc* form is *gentleman*; therefore the polite way to address mixed company is *ladies and gentlemen. ladies* is the usual form of address in the *pl*; in the *sing* use *madam. Please come in, ladies* but *Please come in, madam* (although in *US lady* is also used. *Come this way, lady*). *Woman* as a form of address is rude. *Shut up, woman!* But the uses of *lady* and *woman* in other ways are not so clear. *Woman* is generally less polite. *She pays a woman to clean her house twice a week. The woman who lives next door is a nuisance.* On the other hand, *woman doctor, woman lawyer etc* are now used, not *lady doctor, lady lawyer etc* which are rather *o.f.*

'ladylike *adj* like a lady; behaving as a lady should. (*opp* **unladylike**).

ladyship *nc* rank of a Lady. Also sometimes used when addressing or speaking about one. *Yes, Your Ladyship. Her Ladyship will see you now.*

'ladybird type of small insect.

'ladykiller man who is, or thinks he is, very attractive to women. (*informal*).

'lady's man, 'ladies' 'man man who is very fond of the company of women. (*informal*).

Our Lady the Virgin Mary.

lag[1] [læg] *vi* move more slowly than others. *Some of the runners in the race began to lag. The little boy lagged behind the older ones. past* **lagged.**

laggard ['lægəd] *nc* person who lags behind; lazy person.

'time lag delay in time between two happenings. *There was a time lag between making the plan and carrying it out.*

lag[2] [læg] *vt* put material round a water pipe, boiler etc to prevent freezing or loss of heat. *past* **lagged.**

lagging *nu* material used in this way.

lag[3] [læg] *nc* usu. **old lag** i.e. man who has been in prison many times. (*informal*).

lager ['lɑːgə*] **1.** *nu* type of light beer. **2.** *nc* measure of lager (e.g. a glass or bottle). *He drank three lagers before lunch.*

laggard ['lægəd] *nc* see **lag**[1].

lagoon [lə'guːn] *nc* lake (esp. a saltwater one) joined by a narrow channel to the sea.

laid [leid] past of **lay**[1].

lain [lein] past part of **lie**[2] (*o.f.*).

lair [lɛə*] *nc* place where a wild animal lives.

laird [lɛəd] *nc* owner of land in Scotland.

laissez-faire ['leisei'feə*] *n* policy by which the government does not do anything to help or control individual citizens unless they break the law.

laity ['leiəti] *n sing* (with **the**) persons who are not clergy. see also **lay**[3].

lake[1] [leik] *nc* large area of water with land all round it.

lake[2] [leik] *nu* dark red paint. (Also **crimson lake**).

lamb [læm] **1.** *nc* young sheep. **2.** *nu* its flesh used as food. Also *vi* give birth to a lamb.

'lambskin **1.** *nc* skin of a lamb with the wool on (used to make rugs, slippers etc). **2.** *nu* leather made from the skin without the wool.

'lambswool fine wool cut from lambs.

lame [leim] *adj* **1.** not able to walk properly (usu. because a leg has been injured or is weak). *The lame man needs a stick when he walks.* **2.** (with reference to an argument, excuse, reason etc) weak; not satisfactory. *He gave a lame excuse for being late.* **3.** (with reference to verse) not well written; rough. Also *vt* make lame. **lamely** *adv.* **lameness** *nu.*

'lame 'duck person who is lame, weak or unsuccessful. (*informal*).

lament [lə'ment] *vt/i* show great sorrow (usu. by crying); feel great sorrow. *The children lament the death of their mother. They lament for her. We lamented over our bad luck.* Also *nc* cry or song of great sorrow.

lamentable ['læməntəbl] *adj* sad; causing regret. *His examination results were lamentable* i.e. were very poor, disappointing. **lamentably** *adv.*

lamentation [læmən'teiʃən] *nc/u* act of lamenting; loud expression of sorrow.

laminate ['læmineit] *vt/i* (with reference to wood, metal etc) split, cause to split, into thin sheets or layers; make by putting these thin sheets together: *laminated wood* i.e. wood made by fixing several thin sheets of wood together, one above the other; cover with a thin layer of something (e.g. plastic). **lamination** [læmi'neiʃən] *nc/u.*

lamp [læmp] *nc* apparatus for giving light by using electricity, gas, oil etc.

'lamplight light from a lamp.

'lamppost long, metal post in a street which has a lamp on top.

'lampshade covering of glass, paper or cloth etc put over a lamp.

lampoon [læm'puːn] *nc* bitter, personal attack in writing against somebody. Also *vt* write or publish a lampoon against somebody. *This magazine lampoons all politicians.*

lamprey ['læmpri] *nc* type of sea animal shaped like a snake, which sucks blood from other fish.

lance[1] [lɑːns] *nc* type of spear with a very long handle once used in war by soldiers on horses.

lancer *nc* soldier on a horse who used a lance.

'lance 'corporal soldier having the rank

just above an ordinary soldier and just below a corporal.

lance[2] [lɑːns] *vt* cut with a lancet. *The doctor lanced the boil on his hand.*

lancet ['lɑːnsit] *nc* small knife used by doctors for surgery.

land[1] [lænd] **1.** *nu* firm part of the earth's surface which is not covered by sea. *After sailing for two days we reached land. They travelled over/by land and sea.* **2.** *nc* particular part of the earth i.e. a country, which is the usual word (*land* is more literary): *the land where I was born; land of the free. He lived in many lands.* **3.** *nc/u* area of land which is owned. *This farmer has a lot of land. All these lands belong to the church.* **4.** *nu* soil; ground. *The land here is very fertile. He does not get good crops because the land is poor.*

landed *adj* owning land; having land: *landed gentry.*

'**landfall** land seen from a ship at sea (esp. after a long voyage).

'**landlady** **1.** woman who owns land or a house which she allows somebody else to occupy as a tenant paying rent. **2.** woman who lives in a house, part of which she allows to be occupied by others for payment. (Meals are also often provided).

'**landlocked** *adj* surrounded, or almost surrounded, by land: *a landlocked harbour.*

'**landlord** **1.** person who owns land or a house which he allows somebody else to occupy as a tenant paying rent. **2.** person who manages a pub, inn or lodgings.

Note: landlord can be used with reference to both a man and a woman; *landlady* is usu. used in sense **2.**

'**landlubber** (sailor's) word for someone who is not a sailor.

'**landmark** **1.** mark which shows the boundary of a piece of land. **2.** anything which can be clearly seen from a distance and so makes it easier to know where one is. *The large rock on top of the hill is a landmark to all the people who live nearby.* **3.** any great event which is remembered because of its important results. *The discovery of the cause of malaria was a landmark in the history of medicine.*

'**landowner** person who owns land.

'**landscape** view or picture of an area of land; scenery. *From the hill he looked down on the peaceful landscape.*

'**landscape 'gardener** *nc* person who is skilled at laying out gardens so that they look like natural scenery. **landscape gardening** *nu.*

'**landslide,** '**landslip** **1.** fall of a great amount of rock and earth from the side of a hill. **2.** (only **landslide**) sudden change of public opinion (esp. in politics when one party gets far more votes than is expected).

'**land wind** wind that blows from the shore out to sea.

how the land lies the situation; the state of affairs. *You should find out how the land lies before you go any further with this plan.* (*informal*).

land[2] [lænd] *vt/i* **1.** come, go, bring to land. *We landed in London last night* i.e. after travelling by air or sea. *He landed the boat on the beach. The fishermen landed many fish* i.e. caught and brought to land. **2.** fall, cause to fall, into. *His laziness has landed him in trouble. I landed myself in an argument with them.*

land on one's feet find oneself in a better situation than one had hoped. (*informal*).

landing ['lændiŋ] *nc* **1.** coming, or bringing, to the ground of an aeroplane; coming, or bringing, ashore from a ship. *The aeroplane made a safe landing.* **2.** place where people or goods can land or be landed, from the sea. **3.** level part between two sets of stairs.

'**landing craft** type of flat-bottomed ship which can be run ashore so that the people in it can land easily.

'**landing field** place where an aircraft can land. (Also **landing ground, landing strip**).

'**landing gear** the part under an aircraft on which it lands.

'**landing ground** see **landing field.**

'**landing net** net fixed to a long pole used to land fish caught with a fishing rod.

'**landing party** group of sailors landed from a boat to defend or attack something.

'**landing stage** place (often a floating one) where people and goods are landed from a ship.

'**landing strip** see **landing field.**

lane [lein] *nc* **1.** narrow road in the country; narrow street. **2.** section of road (usu. marked by lines) allowing traffic going in the same direction to move side by side. *The motorway has four lanes of traffic. Heavy vehicles should keep to the inside lane.* **3.** usual route followed by ships when sailing from one place to another: *the shipping lane from Liverpool to New York.*

language ['læŋgwidʒ] **1.** *nu* expression of ideas and feelings by words or writing. **2.** *nc* particular type of such expression used by a race, nation or group. *There are many African languages; the Russian language, legal/scientific/technical language.* **3.** *nc* any expression of meaning by signs or symbols. *Deaf and dumb people use a finger language.*

bad language violent words; swearing.

dead language language which is no longer spoken.

languid ['læŋgwid] *adj* weak; feeble; without much energy. **languidly** *adv.*

languish ['læŋgwiʃ] *vi* become languid (usu because one is without something). *They languished in prison for many years* i.e without freedom, news from home etc *Orphans languish for a mother's love* i.e they need it badly.

languor ['læŋgə*] *nu* weakness; lack of energy (because one is either tired or unhappy). **languorous** *adj.* **languorously** *adv*

lank [læŋk] *adj* **1.** (with reference to hair long and straight; lifeless. **2.** (with reference to the body) tall and thin. **lankly** *adv* **lankness** *nu.*

lanky *adj* (with reference to persons) tall thin and rather clumsy: *a lanky youth* **lankiness** *nu.*

lantern ['læntn] *nc* case with glass sides fo protecting a candle or oil flame (usu. with a handle for carrying).

lantern

'lantern-'jawed *adj* with a long, narrow jaw.

anyard ['lænjəd] *nc* **1.** short, light rope used on a ship to hold movable objects which might slide about or get lost. **2.** short string worn round the neck or round one shoulder to which a knife or whistle is tied.

ap[1] [læp] *nc* front part of the body between the waist and the knees of somebody who is sitting. *She sat by the fire with a book in/on her lap.*

'lapdog small dog often held in the lap.

in the lap of the gods for the gods to decide; beyond human control.

in the lap of luxury in great luxury.

ap[2] [læp] *vt/i* **1.** twist or tie something round something else. *He lapped the rope round the tree.* **2.** (usu. with **over**) cover part of something when placed on top of it. *This boat is built with pieces of wood which lap over each other.* see also **overlap.** *past* **lapped.** Also *nc*: *When you put this piece of cloth on top of that one, there is a lap of two inches* i.e. one piece laps over the other by two inches.

ap[3] [læp] *nc* once round a race or running track. *Most running tracks have four laps to the mile. He began to pass the other runners on the last lap.* Also *vt*: *Near the end of the race he lapped some of the other runners* i.e. he was a lap ahead of them and passed them once again. *past* **lapped.**

ap[4] [læp] *vt/i* **1.** take food or drink into the mouth by using the tongue, as some animals do. *The dog lapped (up) the water.* **2.** make a sound like an animal lapping its food. *The sea was lapping on/against the rocks.* **3.** accept or believe without question. *They lapped up his story about the accident.* (*informal* in sense **3.**). *past* **lapped. lapping** *nu.*

lapel [lə'pel] *nc* front part of a coat, dress or jacket, below the collar, which is folded back. *He wore a badge in/on the lapel of his jacket.*

lapidary ['læpidəri] *adj* of stones; carved on stone (esp. an inscription); of cutting stones. Also *nc* person skilled in cutting and polishing precious stones.

apse [læps] *vi* **1.** slip; fall; fail (esp. with reference to behaviour). *He soon lapsed into his previous bad habits.* **2.** pass from one person to another because of neglect; be no longer of any use. *His claim to the land lapsed because he forgot to pay the rent. This law has lapsed.* Also *nc* **1.** small mistake (e.g. in speaking, writing or behaviour): *a lapse of memory.* **2.** failure to do what is right: *a lapse from his usual high standards of honesty; a lapse into crime.* **3.** end of a claim or right because of neglect. *The lapse of his claim to the land was his own fault.* **4.** period: *after a long lapse of time.*

lapwing ['læpwiŋ] *nc* green and white bird with a long crest. (Also **pe(e)wit**).

arceny ['lɑːsəni] *nc/u* theft; stealing.

arch [lɑːtʃ] **1.** *nc* tree with leaves shaped like needles, which fall off in autumn. **2.** *nu* the wood of this tree.

ard [lɑːd] *nu* pig's fat used for cooking. Also *vt* **1.** spread lard on; put meat containing lard (e.g. bacon or pork) on or into other meat. **2.** put special words into a speech or piece of writing to improve it. *He larded his speech with Latin phrases.*

arder ['lɑːdə*] *nc* room or cupboard where food is kept. see also **pantry.**

arge [lɑːdʒ] *adj* **1.** of great size; big. *He has a large farm and a large herd of cattle. They have a large area of responsibility.* **2.** tolerant; generous.

largely *adv* mainly. *The people in the town are largely strangers to me.*

largish *adj* rather large.

'large-'scale *adj* on a large scale; big and important: *a large-scale map; large-scale changes in our lives.*

as large as life **1.** as large as it would be if real: *a picture of a dog as large as life.* **2.** in fact; really. *Here he is as large as life.* (*informal* in sense **2.**).

at large **1.** free; escaped from prison. *Two prisoners are at large in the city.* **2.** generally. *Boys at large like games.* **3.** at length; thoroughly. *He talked at large about his plans.*

by and large see **by.**

largesse [lɑː'ʒes] *nu* money or gifts given to someone poorer or less important. (rather *o.f.*).

lariat ['læriət] *nc* rope which is thrown to catch horses and cattle; lasso.

lark[1] [lɑːk] *nc* one of several kinds of small brown birds that often sing while flying.

'skylark lark with a small rounded crest.

lark[2] [lɑːk] *nc* fun; amusing play. *He did it for a lark* i.e. in fun. Also *vi* (often with **about**): *The children were larking about in the garden.* (both *informal*).

larkspur ['lɑːkspəː*] *nc* tall brightly-coloured, often blue, flower.

larva ['lɑːvə] *nc* insect in the caterpillar or grub stage of its life i.e. after coming out of its egg. *pl* **larvae** ['lɑːviː].

larynx ['læriŋks] *nc* the part of the throat, above the windpipe, which contains the vocal chords.

laryngitis [lærin'dʒaitis] *nu* inflammation of the larynx.

lascivious [lə'siviəs] *adj* causing lust; lustful. **lasciviously** *adv.* **lasciviousness** *nu.*

laser ['leizə*] *nc* instrument for producing a beam of light of high intensity, capable of being used for cutting through solids.

lash[1] [læʃ] *nc* **1.** long strip of leather or piece of cord used for striking animals or persons. **2.** blow given with a lash. *He gave the prisoner ten lashes.* **3.** eyelash i.e. small hair growing from the eyelid: *a girl with long, dark lashes.*

lashing *nc/u* **1.** striking with a lash. **2.** (in *pl*) lots of something: *lashings of food.* (*informal* in sense **2.**).

lash[2] [læʃ] *vt* **1.** strike with a lash or whip. *The rider lashed his horse to make it go faster.* **2.** strike, or move, violently or suddenly. *The waves lashed (against) the sides of the ship. He lashed out at them with his fists* i.e. he attacked them violently with his fists. *He lashed out at us* i.e. he criticized us severely; attacked us with bitter words. **3.** tie tightly with string or rope. *They lashed their prisoner to a tree so that he would not run away.*

lash something down tie something tightly so that it cannot move. *The sailors lashed down the boxes on the ship's deck.*

lass [læs] *nc* girl; young woman. (*informal* and sometimes *o.f.*).

lassitude ['læsitjuːd] *nu* state of being tired in body or mind.

lasso [læ'suː] *nc* rope which is thrown to catch horses and cattle. *pl* **lassos** or **lassoes.** Also *vt* throw a rope over in this way.

last[1] [lɑːst] *adj* **1.** following all the others. *He was the last person to leave. December is the last month of the year.* (*opp* **first**). **2.**

just before the present. *We met last night/week/month/year. The last few days have been cold; last Saturday/on Saturday last; last June.* (*opp* **next**). **3.** most unlikely. *He is the last person to tell a lie.* **4.** only remaining. *This is your last chance to do it. We spent the last days of our holiday at home.* Also *adv*: *He left last.* (*opp* **first**). *We last met two years ago.* (*opp* **next**). Also *nu*: *He was the last of the visitors to leave. He has spent the last of his money. He hasn't heard the last of it* i.e. he will hear more later (usu. of something unpleasant).

lastly *adv* finally; at the end of a series. *He gave many reasons for being late; lastly he said his car had broken down.*

'last-'minute *adj* done with little time left. *The headmaster had to make some last-minute changes in the timetable.*

at (long) last finally; in the end (after waiting, trying etc for a time). *At last he has passed the examination. My son is home at last.*

breathe one's last die.

first and last see **first.**

the last straw the final one of a series of annoyances. (*informal*).

this time last week/month/year exactly a week/month/year ago.

to/till the last till death; to the very end. *The soldiers fought to the last* i.e. until they were all killed.

last[2] [lɑːst] *vi* continue; be enough, be good enough, for a particular period of time. *The war lasted five years. Our money will not last until the end of the month. This pen has lasted (me) since I was a child.*

lasting *adj* continuing for a long time; permanent; strong.

last[3] [lɑːst] *nc* piece of wood or metal in the shape of a foot on which shoes are made or repaired.

stick to one's last keep to what one can do well and not interfere in something else. (*informal*).

latch [lætʃ] *nc* **1.** small piece of wood or iron used to fasten a door. **2.** type of simple door lock opened by a latch key. Also *vt/i* fasten with a latch.

on the latch fastened only by a latch and not locked. *Leave the door on the latch because he'll be back in a minute.*

late [leit] *adj* **1.** after the usual or proper time. *He was late for school.* **2.** near the end of a period of time. *He came here in late June. He is a man in his late forties* i.e. his age is between 45 and 50. **3.** just before the present; recent: *the late agreement between the two countries. This newspaper has the latest news.*

Note: it is better to use *former* to avoid confusion with sense **4.**

4. dead: *the funeral of the late President.* Also *adv*: *He always arrives late. He goes to bed late and gets up late.*

Note: latest has only the sense of the most recent. *last* has two senses (a) most recent, (b) final; with no others to follow. *Have you read his last book?* i.e. either his most recent one or the one he wrote just before he died or before he stopped writing etc.

lately *adv* recently. *Have you seen him lately? Note: lately* is usu. used in questions, in the negative with *only*, or in the phrase *as lately as* (e.g. *I haven't been here lately. I came to this town only lately. He came as lately as last week*). Otherwise use *recently. I have been here recently.*

at the latest no later than; not after. *You must finish your work by/on Friday at the latest.*

later on afterwards; at a later time. *Can we talk about it later on?*

sooner or later at some time or other.

latent ['leitnt] *adj* hidden; not active but ready to be so. *Young children have many latent abilities.* **latently** *adv.* **latency** *nu.*

lateral ['lætərl] *adj* of or at the side: *lateral expansion; lateral view.* **laterally** *adv.*

latex ['leiteks] *nu* **1.** white liquid found in certain trees and plants (esp. the rubber tree). **2.** similar substance made artificially.

lath [læθ] *nc* thin piece of wood (esp. as a foundation for plaster on walls and ceilings).

lathe [leið] *nc* apparatus which makes a piece of wood or metal turn round quickly while it is cut and shaped.

lather ['lɑːðə*] *nu* **1.** foam made from soap or detergent and water, or from sweat. *To shave properly you need a good lather on your face. After the race the horse was in a lather* i.e. of sweat. **2.** state of excitement: *get into a lather over something.* (*informal* in sense **2.**). Also *vt/i*: *This soap does not lather easily. You must lather your face before shaving.*

Latin ['lætin] *nu* language of ancient Rome. Also *adj* of this language; of peoples who speak modern languages descended from Latin (e.g. French, Italian, Spanish).

latitude ['lætitjuːd] **1.** *nu* distance in degrees north or south of the equator. see **longitude. 2.** *nc* (in *pl*) places according to their latitude: *people who live in high/low latitudes* i.e. in places far away from/near the equator. **3.** *nu* (with reference to beliefs, behaviour etc) difference from what is considered correct or normal. *Young children are given/allowed more latitude than older ones* i.e. they are allowed to behave with more freedom.

latrine [lə'triːn] *nc* hole dug in the ground for the waste matter from the human body.

latter ['lætə*] *adj* **1.** the second of two just mentioned. (The first is the **former**). *John and James are brothers. The former is a teacher; the latter is an engineer.* **2.** more recent. *During the latter part of the lesson we read our notes.*

latterly *adv* more recently.

'latter'day *adj* modern, of the present day: *latterday methods of communication.*

lattice ['lætis] *nc* frame made of thin pieces of wood or metal crossing each other. Also *adj*: *lattice window* i.e. one made of small pieces of glass fixed in a frame of pieces of lead.

latticed *adj* having a lattice.

laud [lɔːd] *vt* praise (esp. God in hymns and psalms – *o.f.*).

laudable *adj* worthy of praise: *a laudable attempt to do better.* **laudably** *adv.*

laudatory ['lɔːdətri] *adj* giving praise.

laugh[1] [lɑːf] *vt/i* make sounds which show amusement or pleasure. *They laughed loudly when I told them the story.*

laughable *adj* causing amusement; ridiculous: *a really laughable attempt.* **laughably** *adv.*

laughing *adj* showing amusement or pleasure. *They all had laughing faces.* **laughingly** *adv.*

'laughing stock someone/something people laugh at, make fun of. *Because of his stupid mistakes he became the laughing stock of the whole school.*

laugh at someone/something 1. be made to laugh by something. *They laughed at my story.* 2. show contempt for; make fun of. *They laughed at their own failure. He laughs at us when we try to help.*
laugh something away make unimportant by laughing. *I was afraid, but my father laughed away my fears.*
laugh something down refuse to listen by laughing. *They laughed down my ideas. When he tried to speak he was laughed down.*
laugh something off treat something which is serious as though it were a joke or not serious. *Surely they cannot laugh off a loss of £100.*
laugh in someone's face show contempt for someone openly and rudely.
laugh oneself silly laugh so much that one becomes helpless etc. (*informal*).
laugh up/in one's sleeve laugh or be amused secretly (often because one feels one has been more clever than someone else) (*informal*).

laugh² [lɑːf] *nc* sound showing amusement or pleasure; act of laughing. *They gave a loud laugh when I told them the story. He's a laugh* i.e. he's an amusing character. (*informal* in this example).
have/get the laugh on somebody do better than somebody and so be able to laugh at him. (*informal*).
raise a laugh cause laughter. (*informal*).

laughter ['lɑːftə*] *nu* act or sound of laughter. *The laughter of the crowd could be heard everywhere.*

launch [lɔːntʃ] *vt* 1. (with reference to a ship) put into the water for the first time. 2. begin; get started. *The government has launched a new plan to build more houses. They're holding a big party to launch the new film* i.e. to introduce it to the public. 3. send. *The Americans and Russians have launched many rockets into space. The enemy launched an attack against us at dawn.* Also *nc* 1. motorboat used for travelling short distances. 2. launching of a ship or rocket. 3. the beginning of a project (esp. when there is publicity).
launching *nc* act of launching.
'launching pad place from which a rocket or missile is launched into space.
launch into start, set about energetically. *He launched into him with some aggressive questions.*
launch (out) into something begin for the first time. *Some farmers have launched (out) into (growing) vegetables.* (*informal*).

launder ['lɔːndə*] *vt/i* wash and iron clothes.
laundress ['lɔːndris] *nc* woman who washes and irons clothes.
laundrette [lɔːn'dret] *nc* laundry where coins are used to operate automatic machines which wash clothes etc.
laundry ['lɔːndri] 1. *nc* place where clothes are washed and ironed. 2. *nu* clothes sent to this place; clothes which need to be laundered. *She is helping her mother with the laundry.*
'laundryman man who collects and delivers laundry (in sense 2.).

laurel ['lɔrl] *nc* type of small tree with evergreen leaves used in ancient times as a sign of honour or victory; bay tree.
look to one's laurels take care one does not lose honour or become less famous because of the success of somebody else.
rest on one's laurels be satisfied with what one has done already and not try for further improvement.

lava ['lɑːvə] *nu* melted rock coming out of a volcano and becoming hard when cool.

lavatory ['lævətəri] *nc* room for getting rid of waste matter from the body; water closet.

lavender ['lævəndə*] *nu* 1. type of plant with small, blue, sweet-smelling flowers which can be dried and used as a scent. 2. colour of lavender flowers. Also *adj*.

lavish ['læviʃ] *adj* generous; extravagant. *He gave his friends lavish gifts. He was lavish in his help to others.* Also *vt* give generously or extravagantly. *They lavished their attention on us.* **lavishly** *adv*. **lavishness** *nu*.

law [lɔː] 1. *nc* rule made by the government or other authority. *The laws of the country are made by Parliament. There is no law in this country against living where you want to. The laws of football do not allow the players to fight.* 2. *nc* scientific rule or principle which has been discovered: *the law of gravity; an important law in chemistry; the laws of nature.* 3. *nu* (with **the**) laws as a whole (esp. those of a country). *All citizens should obey the law. If you break the law you will be punished.* 4. *nu* (without **a** or **the**) science or principles of laws or particular types of laws. *My brother is studying law. He is an expert in company/criminal/international law.*
lawful *adj* according to, allowed by, the law. (*opp* **unlawful**). **lawfully** *adv*. **lawfulness** *nu*.
lawless *adj* 1. not having laws. 2. not obeying the law. *The big city is full of lawless men; lawless behaviour.* **lawlessly** *adv*. **lawlessness** *nu*.
lawyer ['lɔːjə*] *nc* person who is skilled in law and practises it.
'law-abiding *adj* obeying the law.
'lawbreaker person who breaks the law.
'law court court where it is considered whether or not persons have broken the law and where punishment is decided upon.
'lawsuit request made to a law court in order to get back something lost or to be paid for a damage suffered. *He brought a lawsuit against them for refusing to pay back the money he lent them.*
'common law body of laws which is founded on custom and has not been specially made.
be a law unto oneself do what one wants to do without considering the law or normal behaviour.
go to law against somebody ask a law court to settle a dispute with somebody.
lay down the law see **lay¹**.
take the law into one's own hands settle a dispute by oneself without using a law court.

lawn¹ [lɔːn] *nc* area of grass which is cut very short and is well cared for (e.g. in the garden of a house).
'lawnmower machine for cutting grass very short.
'lawn 'tennis game played by two or four players who hit a ball across a low net between them.
Note: it is usu. called *tennis*. Although its full name is *lawn tennis*, the game is not only played on a lawn but on hard surfaces as well.

lawn² [lɔːn] *nu* type of fine, white cloth.

lawyer ['lɔːjə*] *nc* see **law**.

lax [læks] *adj* 1. careless; not severe: *lax behaviour; lax discipline.* 2. (esp. with reference to the bowels) loose; with contents moving easily. **laxly** *adv*. **laxity** *nc/u*.

laxative ['læksətiv] *adj* causing the contents of the bowels to move easily. Also *nc* medicine which does this.

lay[1] [lei] *vt/i* **1.** put down; place. *Lay the sticks on the ground. He laid the book on the table.* **2.** (with reference to eggs) produce. *Birds lay eggs. My hens are laying well.* **3.** make ready: *lay the table* i.e. make it ready for a meal; *lay a floor with carpets; lay a fire* i.e. make it ready for lighting; *lay a trap; lay breakfast/lunch/dinner/supper* make a table ready for these meals. **4.** put down money as a bet. *Don't lay money on that horse. It won't win. I'll lay you a pound that the horse will win* i.e. I shall make a bet of a pound with you. **5.** have sexual intercourse with (a woman) (*informal* in sense **5.**). *past* **laid** [leid].

'layabout *nc* lazy person. (*informal*).

lay/put/keep something aside/by **1.** put down; stop using. **2.** save for the future. *I have laid aside enough money for our holidays.*

lay something back put or fold back. *He laid back the collar of his coat.*

lay by see **lay aside.**

'lay-by *nc* place where a road has been made so that traffic can stop and drivers can have a rest.

lay something down **1.** put down. *Lay down the sticks.* **2.** give up; surrender. *He laid down his life for his country. The soldiers laid down their arms* i.e. handed over or surrendered their weapons. **3.** (with reference to rules, principles etc) make. *The headmaster has laid down new rules about work in the evening.*

lay something in take into one's house; obtain for future use. *Be sure you lay in plenty of food and drink for Christmas.*

lay off stop teasing; stop interfering. (*informal*).

lay someone off cause to stop working (often temporarily). *The factory laid off 100 men last week* i.e. stopped employing them. **'lay-off** *nc* (usu. only *sing*).

lay something on **1.** arrange; supply. *The pupils are laying on a big concert for the visitors.* (*informal*). **2.** (esp. with reference to paint, plaster, cement etc) put on. *They laid on two coats of paint.*

lay something out **1.** arrange something so as to be ready. *His wife has laid out all the clothes he will need for the journey. They laid out the body/corpse* i.e. made it ready for burial. **2.** (with reference to money) spend; invest. *Every month he lays out all he has saved.* **3.** plan; arrange according to a plan. *The new town is laid out to keep factories and houses as far apart as possible.* **4.** make unconscious. *The blow on the chin laid him out.* (*informal* in sense **4.**).

'layout *nc* plan; arrangement: *the layout of the new town.*

lay something up **1.** obtain for future use; store: *lay up food for the winter.* **2.** stop using for a time. *They have laid up their car for the winter.* **3.** (in *passive*) be ill in bed. *He is laid up with a cold.*

lay bare show; stop hiding. *They laid bare all their plans.*

lay down the law give an opinion very confidently. (*informal*).

lay one's hands on **1.** seize; catch. *The police are waiting to lay (their) hands on him.* **2.** find. *I can't lay my hands on the letter he sent me.*

lay someone low knock down; cause to lie down. *He laid him low with his stick. He was laid low with flu last week* i.e. he had to stay in bed.

lay something open **1.** (with reference to a cut made in one's body). *The knife laid open his hand* i.e. cut it severely. **2.** show; discover. *We shall lay open all their secret plans.*

lay oneself open to bring oneself within danger of attack, punishment, trouble etc. *By doing that, he is laying himself open to arrest.*

lay to rest bury.

lay stress on something show to be important, emphasize.

lay[2] [lei] past tense of **lie**[2].

lay[3] [lei] *adj* of or by persons who are not clergy or who do not belong to a profession (esp. that of law or medicine): *the lay mind* i.e. the mind or opinion of persons who are not experts. see also **laity.**

'layman person who is not an expert.

lay[4] [lei] *nc* poem with a story; song (*o.f.*).

layer[1] ['leiə*] *nc* **1.** somebody/something that lays. *He is a bricklayer* i.e. he builds walls etc by laying bricks in rows. *This hen is a good layer* i.e. it lays many eggs. **2.** part of a plant not separated from it but fixed to the ground so that it can grow its own roots.

layer[2] ['leiə*] *nc* something that lies or is spread on top of or between something else; horizontal division in thickness. *The cake has a layer of jam inside. The earth's surface is made up of many layers of rock.*

laze [leiz] *vt/i* be lazy; pass the time without doing anything. *We lazed (away) the whole week.*

lazy *adj* unwilling to work or to be active in any way. *He comes to school by bus because he is too lazy to walk; a lazy morning* i.e. a morning when one does nothing or very little. **lazily** *adv*. **laziness** *nu*.

'lazybones person who is lazy. *pl* **lazybones.** (*informal*).

lea [li:] *nc* field of grass; meadow (*o.f.*).

leach [li:tʃ] *vt* wash away part of a substance by passing water through it (e.g. washing chemicals from soil).

lead[1] [led] **1.** *nu* soft, heavy metal, grey in colour, used on roofs and for making pipes etc because it does not rust (Pb). **2.** *nc* piece of lead fastened to a long rope used for measuring the depth of the sea. **3.** *nu* graphite used in pencils: *lead pencils. He is sharpening his pencil because the lead is broken.* **3.** *nc* (in *pl*) pieces of lead covering a roof; roof covered in this way. **4.** nc (in *pl*) narrow pieces of lead on a window (e.g. a lattice window).

leaden *adj* **1.** made of lead. **2.** having the colour of lead: *a leaden sky.* **3.** heavy as lead: *a leaden heart* i.e. a sad one.

'lead-line see **lead**[1] (in sense **2.**).

'lead 'paint type of paint made from a compound of lead.

'lead 'pencil see **lead**[1] (in sense **3.**).

'lead 'poisoning type of poisoning caused by taking lead into the body.

swing the lead see **swing.**

lead[2] [li:d] *vt/i* **1.** show by going first; guide. *He led us through the forest to the river. I led the blind man across the road.* **2.** be in first place; be in front of. *He is leading in the race/competition. Our football team leads theirs by two goals.* **3.** be in charge of; direct. *He will lead the party of scientists going to*

London. He led the expedition to Africa. **4.** go. *This road leads to our house. One path leads down to the river. The other leads up the hill.* **5.** cause. *What led him to run away? The news leads me to believe that they will come. Too much work and too little rest often leads to illness.* **6.** pass; spend. *They lead a quiet life. past* **led** [led].

leader *nc* **1.** person who leads. **2.** article in a newspaper in which the editor gives his opinions about the most important news. (Also **leading article**).

leading *adj* most important: *the leading newspapers; the leading members of the committee.*

leaderless *adj* without a leader.

leadership *nu* state or powers of being a leader.

leading article see **leader** (in sense **2.**).

leading lady actress with the most important part in a play.

leading question question which is asked in such a way that it leads to the answer which is wanted.

lead something off **1.** take off or away. *He led off his horse.* **2.** begin. *They led off by telling us the latest news.*

lead up to something prepare slowly for something important (e.g. in an argument, talk etc). *What is he leading up to by talking in this way?*

lead astray cause to do wrong; deceive.

lead a card begin a card game or a round of a card game, by putting down a card on the table. *She led the ten of hearts.*

lead somebody a dance behave in a way which causes a lot of difficulties for somebody. (*informal*).

lead nowhere **1.** go nowhere important. *This path leads nowhere* i.e. there is nothing important at the end of it. **2.** have no useful result. *These lessons are leading us nowhere.*

lead the way show the way by going in front.

lead[3] [li:d] **1.** *n sing* (with **a** or **the**) example; help; guidance. *We could not get the correct answer until the teacher gave us a lead. They follow the lead of the older men.* **2.** *n sing* (with **the**) first or most important place. *He is in the lead in this race. He took the lead at the beginning. He has the lead in the school play* i.e. the most important part to be acted. **3.** *n sing* amount by which somebody/something is in front or ahead. *Our football team has a lead of two goals.* **4.** *nc* something which leads to, or joins, something else. *The leads on the battery are dirty* i.e. the wires joining it to a motor, radio etc. **5.** *nc* first card played in a card game or a round in a card game. *Her lead was the ten of hearts.* **6.** *nc* chain, rope or strap for leading an animal (esp. a dog). *He had/kept his dog on a lead in the public park.*

leaf [li:f] *nc* **1.** one of the many small, flat parts that grow on a plant or tree (usu. green when growing and brown or yellow when they fall off or are about to fall off). *The leaves of the trees gave a good shade.* **2.** sheet of paper (esp. one which makes two pages of a book). **3.** thin sheet of metal (esp. gold or silver). **4.** one of the parts of the top of a table which can be raised on a hinge or put in to make the top larger. *pl* **leaves** [li:vz].

leafy *adj* having many leaves. **leafiness** *nu*.

leafless *adj* without leaves.

leaflet ['li:flit] *nc* **1.** printed sheet of paper containing an advertisement, a notice of a meeting etc. **2.** small leaf.

take a leaf out of someone's book imitate; follow an example. *If you want to be wealthy take a leaf out of my book.* (*informal*).

league[1] [li:g] *nc* measure of distance equal to about 3 miles or 5 kilometres.

league[2] [li:g] *nc* **1.** group of persons or nations who agree to help one another; the agreement made by this group. *The League of Nations was formed after the First World War to try to keep peace.* **2.** group of sports teams who play matches against each other. *This football team is at the top of the league* i.e. it has won the most matches in its group of teams.

in league with joined together with (usu. for a dishonest purpose).

leak [li:k] *nc* **1.** crack or hole which allows a liquid or gas to flow in or out when it should not. *We have no water because of a leak in the water pipe* i.e. a hole allowing water to run out. *There is a leak in the boat* i.e. a hole allowing water to come in. **2.** liquid or gas which flows in or out in this way. **3.** process by which secret or confidential information becomes known to people who should not know it. Also *vt/i* **1.** flow, allow to flow, in or out through a leak. *The water leaked from the pipe. The boat is leaking.* **2.** (with reference to information and news) become, allow to become, known when it should not be known. *News of the changes in government has leaked out.*

leakage *nu* act or amount of leaking.

leaky *adj* having a leak: *a leaky roof.*

lean[1] [li:n] *adj* **1.** (with reference to persons and animals) not having much fat; thin: *lean meat* i.e. meat which has very little fat. **2.** anything which makes persons or animals lean: *a lean harvest* i.e. one which has not produced enough to eat. Also *nu* meat which is lean. **leanness** *nu*.

lean[2] [li:n] *vt/i* **1.** slope; bend; rest at an angle. *The trees lean in the strong wind. He was leaning over his desk. The stick is leaning against the wall.* **2.** cause to slope, bend or rest at an angle; put. *He leaned his arms on his desk. I leaned the stick against the wall.* **3.** (with **on** or **upon**) need. *They always lean on/upon us when they are in trouble.* **4.** (with **towards**) be likely to agree with something. *He leans towards the belief that there should be education for everybody. past* **leaned** or **leant** [lent].

leaning *nc* (with **towards**) interest in; tendency. *Their leanings are towards education for everybody.*

'lean-to *nc* small building with a sloping roof built against the wall of a larger building.

leap [li:p] *vt/i* jump; go, cause to go, over, by jumping. *He leapt into the river. past* **leapt** [lept]. Also *nc*.

'leapfrog game in which children jump over each other's backs.

'leap year year which has 366 days instead of the usual 365. (In a leap year, February has 29 days instead of 28. It comes every fourth year).

by leaps and bounds very quickly.

leap at seize eagerly. *He leapt at the opportunity.*

learn [lə:n] *vt/i* **1.** gain knowledge or skill. *We go to school to learn. I am learning (to speak) English. He is learning (how) to play football.* **2.** be told. *We learnt/learned the news this morning. I learnt/learned of his arrival* or *I learnt/learned that he had*

arrived. past **learned** or **learnt.**
learner *nc* person who is learning.
learning *nu* a lot of knowledge (esp. gained by study). *Our teacher is a man of learning. We admire his great learning.*
learned ['lə:nid] *adj* having a lot of knowledge (esp. by study). *Our teacher is a learned man; a learned book* i.e. one that needs much knowledge to understand or one which has been written by a learned man.
learnedly *adv.*
'learner-'driver person who is learning to drive a car.
lease [li:s] *nc* agreement by which somebody allows somebody else to use a house or land for a certain time on payment of rent i.e. agreed sums of money paid from time to time. *We have (taken) this house on a ten years' lease/on a lease of ten years. After ten years the lease expires* i.e. comes to an end, is finished. Also *vt* allow to use, or get the use of, a house or land in this way. *He has leased the house to us for ten years.*
'leasehold *adj* held on a lease. Also *nc/u* house or land held on a lease.
leaseholder *nc* person who has taken a lease.
a new lease of life improvement which is likely to allow one to live longer or more happily.
leash [li:ʃ] *nc* string or strip of leather for holding a dog (usu. fastened to a collar). *Dogs must be kept on the leash in this public park.*
least [li:st] *adj/adv/nu* smallest; the smallest amount. *He has least money of all of us. He works least. He has the least.*
Note: least is the superlative of *little*. The comparative is *less*.
at least not less than. *There were at least* 100 *people* i.e. there were certainly 100 people, probably more. *You should at least tell me.*
not in the least not at all. *'Are you tired?' 'Not in the least.' They don't like this teacher in the least.*
to say the least (of it) without saying too much; without saying more than is true. *It is not a good essay, to say the least* i.e. it is in fact a bad essay.
leather ['leðə*] *nu* skin of an animal as used for making shoes, bags etc. Also *adj* made of leather: *a leather coat.*
leathery *adj* like leather; tough. *This meat is leathery.*
leave[1] [li:v] *vt/i* **1.** go away from, either for a long time or for ever. *He leaves every morning at 8 a.m. He leaves for work every morning at 8 a.m. My brother left school last year. His wife has left him.* **2.** allow, or cause, to remain. *Did he leave a message for me? Please leave your books on the desk.* **3.** allow or cause to remain in a certain condition. *Leave him alone!* i.e. leave him in peace! *She has left the door open.* **4.** forget to take or bring. *I left my pen at home. He left his watch in the hotel.* **5.** allow or cause to remain over after doing something. *If you take 2 from 6, 4 is left/2 from 6 leaves 4. If I pay the bill, I shall be left with only five pence. Is there any coffee left?* i.e. after others have had some. **6.** trust; rely on; hand over. *We are leaving him to do it. I'll buy the food. I leave the cooking to you.* **7.** hand over, give after one's death. *My father died last month and left all his money to my mother and me.* Also with reference to those in a family still alive after somebody's death. *He left a widow and one son. past* **left** [left].
leavings *npl* things left (esp. what is not needed).
leave something behind forget to take or bring. *I've left my coat behind in the bus.*
leave off something stop. *We leave off work at five o'clock. Leave off!* i.e. stop doing that! (*informal* in this example).
leave something off 1. take off; not put on. *I left off my shoes when I went inside. It's hot today, I think I'll leave my jacket off.* **2.** not include. *You've left her name off the list.*
leave something on allow or cause to remain as it is. *He left on his coat* i.e. he continued to wear it. *Please leave on the light* i.e. don't put it out.
leave someone/something out not put in; forget to put in. *He has been left out of the football team* i.e. they have forgotten or decided not to put him in. *You've left some figures out in your calculations.*
'left-overs *npl* something remaining or not finished. *After dinner the children ate the left-overs* i.e. the food which had not been eaten.
leave go of stop holding. *He won't leave go of my hand.* (*informal*). see also **let go.**
leave it at that do nothing more.
leave it up to him let him decide.
leave much to be desired not be as good as it should be. *His behaviour left much to be desired.*
leave something to chance allow chance to decide something.
leave somebody to himself allow somebody to do what he wants to.
leave word give a message. *If he has to go out, he leaves word (for me) with my friend.*
leave[2] [li:v] **1.** *nu* permission to do something (esp. to be absent from one's work or duty). *The headmaster gave us leave to go to the concert.* **2.** *nc* period of time during which one is allowed to be absent from work or duty (esp. in the army or civil service). *The soldiers are given two leaves each year. We are on leave until December. They were given six weeks' leave.* **3.** *nu* (usu. with **take**) formal goodbye. *I stayed for an hour and then took my leave* i.e. said goodbye to those who were there. *I took leave of my friends.*
'sick leave absence from work or duty because one is ill.
by/with your leave with your permission. (*formal*).
take leave of one's senses act in a foolish way as if one had no sense.
leaven ['levən] *nu* **1.** substance put in bread when it is baked (to make it rise). **2.** anything which causes a change in something bigger. Also *vt* put leaven in it; cause a change like leaven (*o.f.*).
leavening *nu* small number or amount which causes a change or is important.
leaves [li:vz] pl of **leaf.**
lecher ['letʃə*] *nc* person who is lustful, full of sexual desire. Also *vi* behave like a lecher. **lechery** *nu.* **lecherous** *adj.* **lecherously** *adv.*
lectern ['lektə:n] *nc* high desk for reading while one is standing up (esp. used for the Bible in a church).
lecture ['lektʃə*] *nc* **1.** long talk giving information (esp. to students in a university). **2.** long spoken warning or scolding. *My father gave me a lecture for smoking* i.e. he was angry and told me not to smoke. Also

vt/i: *The professor lectures to his students twice a week. My father lectured me for smoking.*
lecturer *nc* person who gives lectures (at a university, a junior member of the staff).
lectureship *nc* post of lecturer at a university.
led [led] past of **lead**[1].
ledge [ledʒ] *nc* **1.** narrow level place on a cliff, wall or anything which is very steep: *a window ledge.* **2.** flat rock just under the surface of the sea.
ledger ['ledʒə*] *nc* book in which accounts of money are written.
lee [li:] *adj* on the side sheltered from the wind: *the lee side of the ship; a lee shore* i.e. a shore on the lee side of a ship or one onto which the wind blows. Also *nu* place on the side away from the wind, which gives shelter. *The ship stayed in the lee of the island during the storm.*
'leeward *adj/adv* on the side away from the wind. Also *nu.*
'leeway 1. movement of a ship to the leeward. **2.** freedom to adapt or change a fixed plan.
make up leeway make up time lost. *Because he was absent from school for a month he has to make up a lot of leeway.*
leech [li:tʃ] *nc* **1.** type of worm which fastens itself to the skin and sucks blood. **2.** doctor (*o.f.* in sense **2.**).
leek [li:k] *nc* type of vegetable with green leaves and a white stem, smelling and tasting like an onion.
leer [liə*] *vi* look in a cunning or evil way. *The old man leered at the girl.* Also *nc.*
lees [li:z] *nu* thick sediment which settles at the bottom of a barrel etc of wine.
left[1] [left] past of **leave**[1].
left[2] [left] *adj/adv/nu* of or on the side of a person's body where the heart is. (*opp* **right**). *Most people write with their right hand, not their left one. Turn left at the next corner. In Britain road traffic keeps to the left.*
'left-hand *adj* on the left side.
'left-'handed *adj* (with reference to a person) using the left hand rather than the right one.
the Left, the left wing *n sing* or *pl* (politics) those who want great changes in government in favour of the working classes (e.g. socialists and communists).
'left-'wing *adj*: *a left-wing member of the party.*
left-overs ['leftouvəz] *npl* see **leave**[1].
leg [leg] **1.** *nc* one of the two parts of the body used for standing and walking. **2.** *nc* part of one's clothing which covers the legs: *the legs of his trousers.* **3.** *nc* part of a bed, chair, table etc on which it stands. *Most chairs have four legs.* **4.** *nc* part of a journey or race. **5.** *nu* (cricket) the left side of a right-handed batsman as he faces the bowler.
-legged ['leg(i)d] *adj*: *three-legged* i.e. having three legs; *bare-legged* i.e. having bare legs.
leggings *npl* coverings for the legs made of strong cloth or leather.
leggy *adj* having long legs (e.g. like some young animals).
legless *adj* having no legs.
'legroom space for one's legs (e.g. in a motorcar).
feel/find one's legs 1. begin to be able to stand and walk. **2.** begin to know one's own ability; become more confident.
give somebody a leg up help somebody to climb up; help in any way. (*informal*).
on one's last legs almost finished; about to fall down; very weak. (*informal*).
pull somebody's leg see **pull.**
run somebody off his legs/feet make somebody very tired by giving him a lot to do.
not have/without a leg to stand on not have any excuse or good reason for what one is doing or saying. *The police found the stolen money in his room and so he hasn't a leg to stand on.* (*informal*).
shake a leg 1. dance. **2.** hurry. (*informal*).
stretch one's legs walk about; take exercise.
legacy ['legəsi] *nc* **1.** money or property left by somebody on his death to somebody else. **2.** anything left from the past. *One of the legacies of the war was famine.*
legal ['li:gl] *adj* of the law; according to the law. *I leave all legal matters to my lawyer. Is it legal to marry one's cousin?* (*opp* **illegal**). **legally** *adv.* **legality** [li'gæliti] *nu.*
legalize ['li:gəlaiz] *vt* make legal. *The government has legalized gambling.* **legalization** [li:gəlai'zeiʃən] *nu.*
legal tender see **tender**[2].
take legal action go to a lawyer or law court to settle something.
legate ['legit] *nc* ambassador of the Pope to a country.
legatee [legə'ti:] *nc* person who is left a legacy.
legation [li'geiʃən] *nc* **1.** all those below the rank of ambassador working for their government in a foreign country. **2.** their houses and offices there.
legend ['ledʒənd] *nc* **1.** story from ancient times (not usu. a true one): *the legends of Greece and Rome* i.e. stories about gods and goddesses in the early history of Greece and Rome. **2.** what is printed below a picture or map, or stamped on a coin. *The legend says this picture was painted by Rubens.*
legendary ['ledʒəndri] *adj* found in legends; famous.
legerdemain ['ledʒədə'mein] *nu* **1.** skill in using one's hands to do amusing tricks. **2.** any trick or argument which deceives.
leggings ['legiŋz] *npl* see **leg.**
leggy ['legi] *adj* see **leg.**
legible ['ledʒibl] *adj* (with reference to handwriting, print etc) able to be read. *In an examination your handwriting must be legible.* (*opp* **illegible**). **legibly** *adv.* **legibility** [ledʒi'biliti] *nu.*
legion ['li:dʒən] *nc* **1.** division of an ancient Roman army (about 5,000 men). **2.** any large number.
legionary ['li:dʒənəri] *adj* of a legion. Also *nc* soldier in a legion.
legislate ['ledʒisleit] *vi* make laws. **legislative** ['ledʒislətiv] *adj.*
legislation [ledʒis'leiʃən] *nu* act of making laws; laws made.
legislator *nc* person who belongs to a body which has the power to make laws (e.g. a member of a parliament).
legislature ['ledʒislətʃə*] *nc* body of persons with power to make laws (e.g. a parliament or national assembly).
legitimate [li'dʒitimət] *adj* **1.** lawful. **2.** reasonable; genuine. *He has a legitimate excuse for being absent from school.* **3.** born of parents who are married to each other: *a legitimate child.* (*opp* **illegitimate**). **legitimately** *adv.* **legitimacy** *nu.*

legitimize *vt* make legitimate.

legume ['legju:m] *nc* type of plant (e.g. bean and pea plants) which has its seeds in a long, green covering (called a **pod**). **leguminous** [le'gju:minəs] *adj*.

leisure ['leʒə*] *nu* time when one is free from work; spare time. *He spends his leisure reading newspapers and magazines.* Also *adj*: *I have little leisure time.*

leisurely *adj* without hurry; slowly.

leisured *adj* having plenty of leisure.

at one's leisure without any rush. *Finish the job at your leisure.*

lemming ['lemiŋ] *nc* type of animal like a small rat, found in northern regions, which breeds in very great numbers. When food is used up lemmings migrate, sometimes rushing into the sea and drowning.

lemon ['lemən] *nc* **1.** type of yellow, bitter-tasting fruit. **2.** the tree on which this fruit grows. Also *adj* **1.** made from lemons. **2.** having the yellow colour of a lemon.

lemonade [lemə'neid] *nu* drink made from the juice of lemons, sugar and water.

'lemon 'squash drink made from the juice of lemons.

lemur ['li:mə*] *nc* type of animal like a monkey, found in Malagasy.

lend [lend] *vt* **1.** allow somebody to have something only for a time. *Will you lend me ten pounds?* i.e. give me ten pounds which I shall return to you later. *He lent me his pen. He lent his pen to me.* **2.** make stronger, more easily believed. *His absence lends truth to the story that he is ill. past* **lent** [lent].

lend oneself/itself allow oneself to be used to help something. *I refuse to lend myself to such a stupid plan. This music doesn't lend itself to dancing.*

lend a hand help. *He lent me a hand with the heavy boxes.* (*informal*).

length [leŋθ] *nc* measurement of something from one end to the other; period of time. *The length of the stick is 4 feet/The stick is 4 feet in length; a classroom 30 feet in length and 15 feet in breadth. The length of time we were there was 2 hours.*

lengthen *vt/i* become or make longer.

lengthy *adj* going on for a long time; very long: *a lengthy argument.* **lengthily** *adv*. **lengthiness** *nu*.

'lengthways, 'lengthwise *adj/adv* along the length of something. *He put the sticks lengthwise on the table* i.e. not across it.

at length **1.** at last. **2.** for a long time; thoroughly; completely. *He explained the difficulty at great length.*

at full length lying stretched out.

by a length (usu. with reference to a boat or a horse in a race) the distance equal to its own length. *The horse won easily by four lengths.*

go to the length of be ready to; go as far as. *Will he go to the length of attacking his friends?*

go to all/great lengths try very hard; do what is possible to get what one wants. *He went to great lengths to please his teacher.*

go to any length do anything possible, even if it is wrong, to get what one wants. *They will go to any length to make money.*

keep someone at arm's length keep well away from; refuse to be friendly with somebody.

turn in its own length (with reference to a boat, horse, car etc) turn round in a distance equal to its own length **i.e.** very quickly or sharply.

lenient ['li:niənt] *adj* forgiving; not severe; merciful (esp. to somebody who has done wrong). *The headmaster is never lenient to/towards boys who tell lies.* **leniently** *adv*. **lenience, leniency** *nu*.

lens [lenz] *nc* piece of glass or substance like glass, with one or both sides curved (used in binoculars, cameras, glasses or spectacles, telescopes etc). *He has broken one of the lenses in his glasses.* **2.** part of the eye which focuses light rays coming into the eye.

'contact lens see **contact.**

lent [lent] past of **lend.**

Lent [lent] *nu* period of 40 days before Easter during which some Christians eat simple food, stop smoking etc. **Lenten** *adj*.

lentil ['lentl] *nc* **1.** type of plant with a small bean. **2.** the bean itself.

leonine ['liənain] *adj* of or like a lion.

leopard ['lepəd] *nc* large animal of the cat family which has a dark yellow coat with many black spots on it.

leper ['lepə*] *nc* person who has the disease of leprosy.

leprosy ['leprəsi] *nu* type of disease which slowly destroys the skin, the flesh underneath and the nerves.

leprous *adj* of or having leprosy.

lesbian ['lezbiən] *nc* woman who sexually prefers other women to men. **lesbianism** *nu*.

lese-majesty ['leiz'mæʒesti] *nu* **1.** crime against the ruler of a state or the state itself; treason. **2.** very impudent behaviour to a superior.

lesion ['li:ʒən] *nc* damage to part of the body (esp. to the brain) by disease or injury.

less [les] *adj/determiner* smaller in amount, size, number. *They now do less work than they did before. He has less money. You should take less with you.* (*opp* **more**).

Note: less is usu. used with a *nu* or a word in its *nu* sense. With a *nc fewer* should be used. *They work on fewer days. You should take fewer boxes with you.*

Also *adv* to a smaller extent; not so much. *Talk less and work more. You look less sad today. They are running less quickly.* (*opp* **more**).

Note: with *not*, so should be used instead of *less*. *You don't look so sad today. They are not running so quickly.*

Also *nu* smaller amount, size, time. *He ate less of the food. I bought it for less than ten pence.* (*opp* **more**). Also *prep* minus. *6 less 4 is 2.*

any the less (with **not**) to a smaller extent. *Even when her children are naughty a mother does not love them any the less* i.e. she loves them as much as before. *Their behaviour did not make him any the less angry.*

even less, still less (with reference to one of two things) to a smaller extent than the one before. *He can't run a hundred yards, even less a mile.*

less and less to an increasingly smaller extent as time passes. *As I spoke to him he became less and less angry.* (*opp* **more and more**).

more or less see **more.**

no less than as much/many as; at least. *He walks no less than five miles to school.*

still less see **even less.**

the less *The less you eat the thinner you become.*

lessee [le'siː] *nc* person who has a building, land etc on lease.
lessen ['lesn] *vt/i* become or make less.
lesser ['lesə*] *adj/nu* (with reference to one of two persons/things) smaller. *I was very tired. To a lesser extent so was he. Which is the lesser of these two amounts?*
lesson ['lesn] *nc* **1.** something which is to be learnt or taught; time spent in learning or teaching (usu. in a class). *Afternoon lessons begin at 2 p.m.* **2.** part of the Bible read aloud in a church service.
lest [lest] *conj* **1.** in order that . . . not; for fear that. *We hid the money lest it should be stolen.* **2.** (with **be afraid, fear**) that. *We were afraid lest/that it should be stolen.*
let[1] [let] *vt* **1.** (with *infinitive* but not *to*) allow. *The headmaster lets them play football every Saturday. They want to play football on other days but he won't let them.* **2.** (with **me, us, it** or **them**) as an *imperative* to express a wish, request, suggestion etc. *Let us/Let's go for a walk. Let me try. Let him do it.* **3.** (mathematics) *as an imperative* suppose for the sake of argument; suppose in order to prove. *Let x = 2 and y = 3.*
Note: in the following examples of *let* with other words it should be noted that the position of these words can sometimes change the sense. *He let the boy go* has the sense of either he allowed the boy to go away or he stopped holding him. But *He let go the boy* has only the sense of he stopped holding him. Also *let him alone* has the sense of leave him alone; do not bother him, but *let alone him* has the sense of without him; not to mention him.
let somebody down fail in a promise made to somebody; harm. *He let his friends down by arriving late.*
'let-down *nc* disappointment. (*informal*).
let something down allow to fall; lower. *He let down the rope to us/He let the rope down to us.*
let someone/something in allow to enter. *The roof lets in the rain.*
let oneself in get into a house or building by opening the door. *Please don't wait until I return. I have a key and can let myself in.*
let somebody in for something cause somebody to be concerned with something (usu. something unpleasant). *His illness has let us in for a lot of extra work.*
let somebody into something tell somebody a secret. *Shall I let them into our new plan?*
let something into something **1.** allow to enter. **2.** put in a space which can be made for it. *It will be easy to let a door into this wall* i.e. make a hole in this wall and put a door in.
let somebody off forgive; allow to escape severe punishment. *I'll let you off if you promise never to do it again. The headmaster let me off with a warning* i.e. he could have punished me more severely but didn't.
let something off **1.** allow to come out. *This engine lets off steam.* **2.** (with reference to guns etc) fire. *He let his revolver off at the crowd.*
let on tell (esp. something secret). *I'll never forgive you if you let on that I was late.* (*informal*).
let (it) out make known. *He has let (it) out that he is going away.* (*informal*).
let somebody out allow somebody to go or come out.
let something out **1.** allow something to go or come out. *He let the air out of my tyres.* **2.** (with reference to clothes which are tight) make larger. *He has grown so much that he has had to let out his jacket.*
let up stop. *He works all day. He never lets up.* (*informal*).
'let-up *nc*: *He works without a let-up.* (*informal*).
let alone without including; not to mention. see *Note* above. *She will not help her own brother, let alone a stranger.*
let somebody/something alone leave alone; not disturb. *We let the fierce dog alone.*
let somebody/something be not disturb or worry. *Let them be.*
let drop say (usu. on purpose). *He let drop the suggestion that we should meet him in town.*
let somebody/something drop allow to fall.
let somebody/something fall allow to fall. *Don't let the baby fall.*
let fly at someone/something throw or shout at.
let go see *Note* above.
let oneself go become relaxed; speak or behave freely. *He usually says very little but he let himself go on the dangers of drugs* i.e. he said a great deal about them.
let somebody/something pass allow to pass.
let something pass pay no attention to; forget. *I cannot let this mistake pass.*
let slip a chance/opportunity miss.
let something slip reveal without intending to. *He let it slip that we would be leaving the next day.*
let[2] [let] *vt* allow somebody to use a house or land for a certain time on payment of rent i.e. agreed sums of money paid from time to time. *I have let my house to him while I am abroad. There are plenty of houses to let here.* Also *nc* (usu. only *sing*). *I have this house on a long let.*
let something out hire. *They let out boats to those who want to fish.*
let[3] [let] **1.** *nu* (only in **without let or hindrance** i.e. difficulty (legal and *o.f.*). **2.** *nc* (tennis) situation in which the ball strikes the net but passes over it during a service.
lethal ['liːθl] *adj* causing, able to cause, death.
lethargy ['leθədʒi] *nu* lack of energy; feeling of not wanting to do anything. **lethargic** [le'θɑːdʒik] *adj*. **lethargically** *adv*.
letter ['letə*] *nc* **1.** mark used in writing to represent a sound. *A, B and C are letters (of the alphabet).* **2.** message or account which is written or sent to somebody. *Letters are usually sent by post.* **3.** (in *pl*) (esp. with reference to literature) learning: *a man of letters.*
lettered *adj* having a good knowledge of literature; educated. (*opp* **unlettered**).
lettering *nu* style used in writing letters (in sense **1.**). *The lettering on the front of the newspaper is large and clear.*
'letterbox box for receiving letters (in sense **2.**) either inside a house or in a street or post office.
'letter-card card which can be folded, stuck down at the edges, addressed and posted without using an envelope.
'letterhead printed name and address on paper used for writing letters.
'letterpress **1.** printed matter in a book other than illustrations and diagrams. **2.** something printed from letters or type which stand out in relief.
keep to the letter of the law/an agreement

obey the law/an agreement only as it is written and avoid carrying out its real purpose.
to the letter exactly; in every detail. *They obeyed the wishes of their teacher to the letter.*
lettuce ['letis] *nc* type of vegetable with green leaves (usu. eaten uncooked).
leukaemia, leukemia [lu:'ki:miə] *nu* disease of the blood.
levee[1] ['levi] *nc* formerly, meeting at which important people paid respects to their king.
levee[2] ['levi] *nc* bank built along a river to prevent it flooding the land.
level[1] ['levl] *adj* **1.** horizontal; flat; without hills. *Football should be played on level ground.* **2.** making the same progress; equal. *These two boys are about level in mathematics.*
'level 'crossing (*Brit*) place where a road and railway cross (not passing over or under each other by means of a bridge or tunnel) (*US* **grade crossing**).
'level-'headed *adj* (with reference to persons) steady; not easily upset.
level off/out **1.** make flat or even: *level off a piece of wood.* **2.** come into a horizontal position. *The pilot levelled off at 10,000 feet.*
do one's level best do everything one can. (*informal*).
have/keep a level head be or remain steady and calm.
level[2] ['levl] *nc/u* **1.** (esp. with reference to height) anything flat and horizontal. *The town is 5,000 feet above sea level* i.e. the level of the sea. *Because of the heavy rain the level of the lake has risen 6 inches.* **2.** (with reference to persons) position; rank. *He has not yet found his own level in this class. The talks took place at a high level* i.e. among people in important positions; *advanced-level English.* **3.** instrument which shows whether or not something is horizontal. (Also **spirit level**).
on the level honest. (*informal*).
level[3] ['levl] *vt/i* **1.** become or make level. *They levelled the house to the ground* i.e. destroyed it so that nothing above the level of the ground was left. **2.** (with reference to persons) make equal. **3.** aim. *He levelled his rifle at the thief. Why does he level his criticisms/accusations/remarks at us? past* **levelled.** (*US* **leveled**).
lever ['li:və*] *nc* long bar or rod which pivots at one point so that when one part of it is pressed something attached to another part is moved (e.g. *gear lever* in a car). Also *vt* move with a lever.
leverage *nu* power of a lever.
'gear lever see **gear.**
leveret ['levərit] *nc* young hare.
leviathan [li'vaiəθən] *nc* **1.** very large sea animal mentioned in the Bible. **2.** anything which is very large.
levitate ['leviteit] *vt/i* rise, cause to rise, in the air (esp. by magic). **levitation** [levi'teiʃən] *nc/u.*
levity ['leviti] *nc/u* treating serious or important matters lightly or without respect.
levy ['levi] *vt* make somebody pay or give. *The government levies taxes on motorists. The enemy has levied troops for the war* i.e. has made men join its army. Also *nc* **1.** act of levying. **2.** number of men obtained by levying.
lewd [lu:d] *adj* lustful; sexually improper.
lewdly *adv.* **lewdness** *nu.*
lexicon ['leksikən] *nc* dictionary (esp. of ancient Greek, Hebrew etc). *pl* **lexicons** or **lexica** ['leksikə].
lexical *adj* **1.** of a lexicon. **2.** of the words of a language. **lexically** *adv.*
lexicography [leksi'kɔgrəfi] *nu* act or skill of writing a dictionary.
lexicographer [leksi'kɔgrəfə*] *nc* person who makes a dictionary.
liable ['laiəbl] *adj* **1.** obliged by law to pay for. *He is liable for all the damage done by his workmen.* **2.** likely to do or suffer from. *They are liable to run away if you speak to them. In winter I am liable to (get) bad colds.*
liability [laiə'biliti] **1.** *nu* state of being liable: *his liability for all the damage done; my liability to (get) bad colds.* **2.** *nc* (in *pl*) debts. (*opp* **assets**). **3.** *nu* someone/something which causes trouble. *He is a liability to us.*
liaison [li:'eizɔn] **1.** *nu* cooperation; process of keeping the different parts of a large organization (esp. an army or armies) in touch with each other. *Victory depends on close liaison between the American and British armies.* **2.** *nc* sexual relations between a man and woman who are not married to each other.
liana [li'ɑ:nə] *nc* type of climbing plant found in tropical forests.
liar ['laiə*] *nc* see **lie**[1].
libation [lai'beiʃən] *nc* act of offering wine to a god by pouring it on the ground; wine offered in this way.
libel ['laibl] *nc/u* something printed or written which accuses somebody wrongly and so harms him; anything that harms somebody wrongly. *Editors of newspapers must be very careful that they do not publish libels. Your silly letter is a libel on an honest man.* Also *vt* publish a libel about somebody. *past* **libelled.** (*US* **libeled**). **libellous** *adj.*
Note: libel strictly has the sense of something printed or written, not spoken, although it is often used informally about anything harmful. The correct word for something spoken in this way is *slander.*
liberal ['libərl] *adj* **1.** generous; ready to give. *My father gives me a liberal amount of money each week* i.e. more than enough for my needs. *They were liberal in their help.* **2.** able to understand others and sympathize with their ideas; broad-minded. *Our headmaster has liberal views about what his pupils should wear.* (*opp* **illiberal**). **3.** (with reference to education) dealing with a number of subjects so that a person gets liberal views; not vocational or technical. **4.** (**Liberal**) of the British political party interested in social reform. Also *nc* **1.** (**Liberal**) member of the Liberal Party. **2.** broad-minded person. **liberally** *adv.*
liberality [libə'ræliti] *nc/u* generosity; broad-mindedness.
liberate ['libəreit] *vt* give freedom to. **liberator** *nc.*
liberation [libə'reiʃən] *nu* act of giving, or being given, freedom.
libertine ['libəti:n] *nc* person who leads a sexually immoral life. Also *adj.*
liberty ['libəti] **1.** *nc/u* state of being free; of being able to do and behave as one wishes. **2.** *nc* (usu. with **take**) behaviour which may not be approved. *I took the liberty of using my friend's pen* i.e. I am not sure if he will approve. *You are taking too many liberties with the English language* i.e. you are using

it too freely and in a way that cannot be approved.
at liberty free. *Is he at liberty to come? You are at liberty to say what you like. The escaped prisoner is still at liberty.*
set at liberty give freedom to; set free.
libidinous [li'bidinəs] *adj* lustful; indecent. **libidinously** *adv.* **libidinousness** *nu.*
libido [li'bi:dou] *nu* sexual desire or instinct.
library ['laibrəri] *nc* **1.** room or building for keeping books. **2.** the books kept there. **3.** series of books on a particular subject which have the same size and appearance.
librarian [lai'brɛəriən] *nc* person in charge of a library.
librarianship **1.** *nu* profession of being a librarian. **2.** *nc* post of librarian.
'lending library library from which books are lent for a particular period of time.
'public library library open to the public, which is paid for by public money.
'reference library library having books which can be used in the library (for reference) but cannot be taken away.
libretto [li'bretou] *nc* words, or book of words, for an opera, musical, comedy etc. *pl* **librettos.**
lice [lais] pl of **louse.**
licence ['laisns] (*US* **license**) **1.** *nu* (usu. with **a**) right or permission given to do something. *In Britain you must have a licence if you want to sell beer or tobacco. Have you a driving licence?* **2.** *nc* this right as it is written or printed. *This office deals with driving licences* i.e. the cards showing one has a licence to drive. **3.** *nu* acting as if one had a right to do anything; absence of self-control.
'off-licence shop which sells beer, wines, spirits etc which must not be consumed on the premises.
license ['laisns] *vt* give a licence to. *This shop is licensed to sell tobacco.*
licensee [laisən'si:] *nc* person who has been given a licence for a special purpose.
licensed premises place which is licensed to sell beer, wines and spirits (e.g. a public house or hotel).
licentiate [lai'senʃiət] *nc* person who has a licence to practise a profession.
licentious [lai'senʃəs] *adj* sexually immoral; without self-control. **licentiously** *adv.* **licentiousness** *nu.*
lichen ['laikən] *nu* type of very short plant which grows on stones and trees.
lick [lik] *vt* **1.** pass the tongue over. *He licked the stamp and stuck it on the letter.* **2.** touch in the way a tongue does. *The flames of the fire licked the coal.* **3.** beat; be better than. *Our team licked theirs easily.* (*informal* in sense **3.**). Also *nc* **1.** act of licking. *He gave the stamp a lick.* **2.** speed. *They ran at full lick/at a great lick.* (*informal* in sense **2.**).
licking *nc* beating; defeat. *Our team gave theirs a licking.* (*informal*).
'salt lick see **salt.**
lick into shape improve; make efficient. (*informal*).
smack/lick one's lips see **smack**[1].
licorice ['likəris] *nc/u* see **liquorice.**
lid [lid] *nc* **1.** cover on top of something which can be raised or taken off: *the lid of a pot/box.* **2.** piece of skin which can be moved to cover the eye. (Also **eyelid**).
lido ['laidou] *nc* place built for swimming and sunbathing. *pl* **lidos.**
lie[1] [lai] *vi* say something which one knows is not true. *He lied to me when he said he didn't do it. pres part* **lying.** *past* **lied.** Also *nc*: *He told a lie.*
liar [laiə*] *nc* person who lies or has lied. *You're a liar!* i.e. I do not believe what you have said. (*impolite*).
give the lie to something prove that it is not true.
lie[2] [lai] *vi* **1.** be, remain, or rest, flat. *He was lying on the ground. I lay in bed all day. The papers are lying on the desk.* **2.** be situated; be placed. *Uganda lies far from the coast. The difficulty lies in their great poverty* i.e. is caused by their great poverty. *What we do next lies with him* i.e. he must decide. **3.** remain in a particular state. *He lay dead on the floor. The machine lay idle all week* i.e. was not used. *The road to the sea lay open before us. pres part* **lying.** *past tense* **lay** [lei]. *past part* see Note below. Also *nu* the way something lies. *The golfer looked at the lie of his ball before he hit it. The general studied the lie of the land before he attacked.*
Note: the *past part* is *lain* [lein] which is rather *o.f.* Therefore instead of *have lain* use *have been lying* (e.g. *The papers have been lying on your desk since yesterday*).
lie back rest one's back on. *He lay back on the pillow.*
lie down put oneself in a flat, resting position. *He told his dog to lie down. Why don't you go and lie down?* i.e. go to your bed and rest on it.
'lie-'down *nc*: *Go and have a lie-down.* (*informal*).
lie in stay in bed in the morning longer than usual.
'lie-in *nc* **1.** staying in bed in the morning longer than usual. **2.** stay in bed to give birth to a child. (rather *o.f.* in sense **2.**).
lie off (with reference to ships) anchor at a distance from the shore.
lie over be delayed until later. *The decision can lie over until Monday.*
lie up stay in bed (usu. because of illness).
lie heavy on cause trouble or discomfort to. *What I did lies heavy on my conscience.*
lie low keep out of sight (until trouble has passed).
let sleeping dogs lie avoid mentioning matters which may cause trouble.
take something lying down accept something unpleasant without protesting or fighting against it. *Are you going to take this defeat lying down?* (*informal*).
lie in wait hide while waiting to attack or catch. *The police lay in wait for the thieves.*
lieu [lu:] *nu* only in **in lieu of** i.e. instead of: *money in lieu of food.*
lieutenant [lef'tenənt, *US* lu:'tenənt] *nc* **1.** junior officer in the army or navy. **2.** officer having the next lower rank (usu. used with the word for that rank).
lieu'tenant-'colonel officer having the rank just below that of colonel.
life [laif] **1.** *nu* condition of humans, animals and plants which makes them different from sticks, stones or anything dead. *Life depends on air, food and water.* **2.** *nu* living things in general. *There seems to be no life on the moon. We should protect wildlife* i.e. animals living in their natural condition. **3.** *nc* a person as a living creature. *Thousands of lives were lost during the war.* **4.** *nc* period of time between birth and death; between birth and the present; between the present and death. *He spent his whole life in one country. I have lived here all my life. He*

intends to spend the rest of his life abroad. **5.** *nc* written story of somebody's life. *He is reading the life of Napoleon.* **6.** *nu* general state of society; way of spending time. *How do you find life in a big city? They have very busy lives.* **7.** *nu* energy. *The children are full of life.* **8.** *nu* somebody/something as he/it really is. *This picture was drawn from life* i.e. using a real person as a model. *The book is true to life* i.e. it describes things as they really are. *pl* **lives** [laivz].

lifeless *adj* **1.** not having life; dead. **2.** unconscious; without any feeling. **3.** not lively; dull: *a lifeless expression.* **lifelessly** *adv.* **lifelessness** *nu.*

lifelike *adj* like something living; very like the person himself. *This is a lifelike drawing of my father.*

'lifebelt belt which saves a person's life by keeping him afloat in water.

'lifeblood **1.** blood needed for life. **2.** anything giving life or strength. *Trade is the lifeblood of our country.*

'lifeboat special type of boat used to save lives at sea (e.g. when a ship sinks).

'lifebuoy floating ring which is thrown to a person who is in danger of drowning.

'life and 'death *adj* having as its result either life or death; desperate: *a life-and-death struggle.*

'life-giving *adj* giving more strength and energy: *a life-giving medicine.*

'lifeguard **1.** person trained to save the lives of those in danger of drowning at the seaside. **2.** member of a group of soldiers who protect the life of some important person. (Also **bodyguard** in sense **2.**).

'life 'history cycle of life of a living creature: *the life history of a mosquito* i.e. a description of the changes which take place in its life.

'life insurance *nc/u* insurance on a person's life.

'life jacket jacket that is inflated to keep a person afloat (used like a lifebelt).

life jacket

'lifeline **1.** rope which saves lives (e.g. one thrown to a sinking ship or fastened to a lifebuoy). **2.** any means of safety. *During winter the telephone is our lifeline.*

'lifelong *adj* lasting all one's life: *a lifelong friendship.*

'life-saver *nc* **1.** person trained to save the lives of those in danger of drowning. **2.** anything or any person that saves someone in a time of danger or need.

'life-saving *adj*: *He has a life-saving certificate* i.e. one which shows he is a life-saver. *He has a certificate for life-saving.* Also *nu.*

'life-'size(d) *adj* (esp. with reference to pictures and photographs) having the same size as the person whose picture or photograph it is.

'lifetime whole period of one's life: *the chance of a lifetime* i.e. a chance which one is likely to have only once during one's life.

bring to life make alive; make somebody well again when he was likely to die.

come to life become alive; become well or conscious again. *She fainted but came to life when we threw cold water over her.*

in one's life during one's life. *I have never in my life been to London.*

take one's own life kill oneself.

take somebody's life kill somebody.

the time of one's life great enjoyment. *We are having the time of our lives.* (*informal*).

to the life exactly; as something really is. *He described work in a factory to the life.*

lift[1] [lift] **1.** *vt* raise. *I can't lift it. It is too heavy. Lift it up on the table.* **2.** *vi* (esp. with reference to cloud, fog and mist) rise; go away. *We saw the mountain when the clouds lifted.* **3.** *vt* steal. *He was caught lifting goods from the supermarket. You lifted this part of your essay from a book* i.e. you used sentences from a book in your essay and pretended they were yours. (*informal* in sense **3.**).

'shoplifter *nc* person who steals things from a shop often when pretending to be buying other things. **shoplifting** *nu.*

'weight lifter *nc* person who lifts weights (esp. in a competition). **weight lifting** *nu.*

'lift-off *nc* (with reference to a rocket or spaceship) act of leaving the ground. *We have lift-off* i.e. the rocket has successfully got into the air.

lift one's hand to strike in anger. *He never lifted his hand to his children.*

lift up one's head **1.** raise one's head. **2.** stop feeling ashamed. *If they beat us, I will never lift up my head again.*

lift[2] [lift] *nc* **1.** act of lifting. **2.** help on a journey by taking a person in one's car etc. *I gave him a lift to the railway station.* **3.** (*Brit*) machine for carrying goods and people up and down high buildings. (*US* **elevator**).

'liftman (*Brit*) person in charge of a lift. (*US* **elevator operator**).

ligament ['ligəmənt] *nc* strong substance joining the bones of the body.

ligature ['ligətʃə*] *nc* **1.** bandage, string or thread tied tight to stop bleeding. **2.** (printing) two or more letters printed together. **3.** (music) playing or singing of two or more tones of different pitch without a break.

light[1] [lait] **1.** *nu* that which makes one able to see: *the light of the sun. We read by the light of a candle/by candlelight.* **2.** *nc* something which gives light: *traffic lights. Turn off all the lights.* **3.** *nu* something which starts a fire. *He put a light to the old papers* i.e. he set them on fire (e.g. with a match). *Can you give me a light?* (e.g. for my cigarette). **4.** *nc* information; point of view. *His speech throws a different light on what happened. He does not see this matter in the same light as we do* i.e. he has not the same point of view. **5.** *nc* (esp. with reference to the eyes and face) sign of energy or happiness. *You should have seen the lights in the children's eyes when they were given the food.*

'lighthouse tall tower with a strong light built on land to guide ships or warn them of danger.

'lightship ship which does the same work as a lighthouse.

'light year the distance travelled by light in the period of one year. (Light travels at the speed of 186,000 miles per second – used to measure the distance between stars and the earth).

'daylight 1. light during the day. 2. dawn. *Let us wait until daylight.*
'footlights row of lights at the front of the stage in a theatre.
'moonlight light given by the moon.
'skylight window in the roof of a building to let in light.
'sunlight direct light from the sun.
according to one's lights in the way one thinks best. *He behaved correctly, according to his lights.*
bring to light make known; discover. *The crime was brought to light years later.*
come to light see **come.**
in a bad light 1. where something is not clearly seen. 2. as appearing worse; unfavourably. *This news put his behaviour in a bad light.*
in a good light 1. where something is clearly seen. 2. as appearing better; favourably. *I cannot see his behaviour in a good light.*
in the light of because of the information from. *In the light of what you say I agree to go.*
see the light 1. be born (*o.f.*). 2. suddenly understand. (*informal*).
stand in somebody's light 1. stand so that the light does not reach somebody when he needs it. 2. prevent somebody from being successful.

light[2] [lait] *vt/i* 1. set fire to; give light to. *Shall I light a fire? The lamp lights the room quite well. The lamp lights up the room. The whole town is lit up.* 2. (esp. with reference to the eyes and face) show happiness. *The children's faces lit up when they saw the food. past* **lit** [lit] (more usual) or **lighted.**
'lighting-'up time time when by law lamps (esp. on vehicles) should be lit.

light[3] [lait] *adj* 1. allowing one to see well; not dark. *His room is light and airy.* 2. pale in colour: *light red; light coloured.*

light[4] [lait] *adj* 1. having little weight. *Your bag is very light.* (*opp* **heavy**). 2. used with many words to give the sense of lack of power or strength, of being gentle or easy: *light beer* i.e. not strong; *a light illness* i.e. not a severe one; *a light meal* i.e. a small, easily-eaten one; *a light touch* i.e. a gentle one; *light reading* i.e. something easily read and often amusing; *light work* i.e. done easily. 3. having no cares or any sense of responsibility. *We went away with a light heart. The drink gave me a light head.* 4. (esp. with reference to women) immoral (*o.f.*). Also *adv*: *We always travel light* i.e. without heavy luggage. **lightness** *nu.*
lightly *adv*: *He slept lightly.*
Note: adv light and *lightly* have the same sense but *light* cannot always be used; *lightly* can and is therefore safer to use (e.g. one can *travel* either *light* or *lightly*, but one can only *touch a person lightly*).
'light-'fingered *adj* having quick, skilful fingers (esp. for stealing).
'light-'footed *adj* moving on one's feet quickly or gently.
'light-'handed *adj* having quick, skilful hands.
'light-'headed *adj* not in full control of oneself; dizzy. **light-headedly** *adv.* **light-headedness** *nu.*
'light-'hearted *adj* without any cares; cheerful. **light-heartedly** *adv.* **light-heartedness** *nu.*
'light-'minded *adj* silly; thoughtless. **light-mindedness** *nu.*
'lightweight *adj* not heavy; below the usual weight. Also *nc* 1. person/thing below the usual weight. 2. boxer weighing less than 135 lbs.
make light of treat as not being important or serious. *He made light of his injuries.*

light[5] [lait] *vt* (with **on** or **upon**) find by chance. *past* **lighted** or **lit** [lit].

lighten[1] ['laitn] *vt/i* become or make light. *The sky lightened at dawn. The sky lightened after the storm.* see **light**[1].

lighten[2] ['laitn] *vt/i* become or make lighter. *He lightened his bag by taking out some books.*

lighter[1] ['laitə*] *nc* type of boat used to take goods to or from a ship to the shore where there is no harbour.

lighter[2] ['laitə*] *nc* (usu. with other words) person/thing that lights (usu. **cigarette lighter**). see **light**[2].
ciga'rette lighter small machine for lighting cigarettes.
'lamplighter person who in the past lit lamps in a street.

lightning ['laitniŋ] *nu* flash of light made by electricity passing between two clouds or between a cloud and the ground. (The sound made is called **thunder**). Also *adj* very quick (as lightning is): *a lightning attack on the enemy.*
'lightning conductor piece of metal fixed to a high building and joined by a thick wire to the ground to take the electricity of lightning to the ground and so prevent damage to the building by lightning. (Also **lightning rod**).
like greased lightning very fast. *He moved like greased lightning.*

lights [laits] *npl* lungs of sheep and other animals, eaten as food.

lignite ['lignait] *nu* type of coal which is soft and dark brown in colour.

like[1] [laik] *vt/i* 1. be fond of; be pleased with. *I like good food. Do you like my new hat? I like our teacher.* 2. wish; prefer. *I should like to see him again. She likes her house to be tidy. I like my coffee (to be) much stronger than this. Would you like a cup of tea?* i.e. do you want one? (*opp* **dislike**).
liking *nu* 1. fondness. *I have a liking for good food. They took a liking to me* i.e. they became fond of me. 2. wish; satisfaction. *The journey was not to my liking* i.e. was not as I wanted it to be.
likes and dislikes things which one likes and dislikes. (*informal*).
if you like if this is what you wish. *I will go with you, if you like.*

like[2] [laik] *adj/prep* 1. the same or not very different. *Have you a book like this?* 2. in the same way as. *You are talking like a fool. It tastes like salt.* 3. what is to be expected from. *It was (just) like them to leave the work to us. Isn't it (just) like a woman to want new clothes?* 4. (with **feel** and **look**) as if ready for; as if about to. *I feel like going for a walk/I feel like a walk* i.e. I want or would enjoy a walk. *He looks like winning the race.* Also *nc*: *I have never seen the like of it* i.e. anything like it. *We have met the likes of you before* i.e. persons like you.
Note: like is also used as a *conj* (e.g. *He doesn't speak English like I speak it*). This use is informal and thought by many to be wrong. It is more correct to use *as* or *in the same way as.*
likeness *nc/u* state of being like; similarity; copy. *He was dressed in the likeness of a Roman soldier* i.e. to look like one. (rather

o.f.). *This photograph is not a good likeness of you.*
'likewise *adv* in the same way or a not very different way. *This is how I do it. I want you to do likewise.* Also *conj* also.
'like-'minded *adj* having the same opinions.
as like as *They are as like as two brothers* i.e. they look as if they were brothers (but they are not).
as like as not probably. *It will rain tomorrow as like as not.* (*informal*).
that's more like it! that's better!
nothing like **1.** nothing as good as; nothing equal to. *There is nothing like a hot bath when you are tired.* **2.** quite different from. *This is nothing like what I wanted.*
something like **1.** almost; about. *I walked something like 10 miles.* **2.** quite similar to. *She looks something like your sister.*

likely ['laikli] *adj/adv* probable; probably; (as) expected. *This is a likely place for him to stay. He is likely to do very well/It is likely that he will do very well. They very likely won't come.* (*opp* **unlikely**).
likelihood *nu* probability. *There is no likelihood that he will come/of his coming. In all likelihood I shall be at home* i.e. very probably.
as likely as not probably.

liken ['laikən] *vt* show or say that something is like something else; compare.

lilac ['lailək] *nc/u* **1.** type of bush with white or purple flowers. **2.** the flower itself. Also *adj* light purple colour like lilac.

lilt [lilt] *nc* pleasant tune, way of speaking etc, with a strong but simple rhythm. Also *vt/i* sing or speak in this way. **lilting** *adj*. **liltingly** *adv*.

lily ['lili] *nc* various types of flower, often bell-shaped.

limb [lim] *nc* **1.** arm, leg. **2.** branch of a tree.
out on a limb by oneself, needing help. (*informal*).

limber ['limbə*] *adj* (esp. with reference to the body) active; easily bent; loose.
limber up loosen stiff muscles by doing exercises. *The runners limbered up before the race.*

limbo ['limbou] *nc/u* **1.** place to put people or things which are not wanted; neglect: *be in limbo.* **2.** type of West Indian dance. *pl* **limbos.**

lime[1] [laim] *nu* **1.** white substance obtained from limestone, sea shells etc by burning them (used e.g. when mixed with sand to join bricks together). **2.** sticky substance put on trees to catch birds. (Usu. **bird lime**). Also *vt* put lime on (e.g. on a field).
'lime kiln type of large oven in which limestone is burnt to get lime.
'limestone type of rock from which lime is obtained.
in the limelight receiving great attention from the public. *Famous athletes are always in the limelight.*

lime[2] [laim] *nc* **1.** type of tree with a bitter green fruit (like a lemon). **2.** the fruit itself.
'lime juice juice of this fruit used as a drink.

lime[3] [laim] *nc* linden tree.

limerick ['limərik] *nc* amusing poem of five lines and having a special rhythm.

limit ['limit] *nc* **1.** farthest point to which something reaches; point beyond which one cannot go. *There is a limit to the amount of money we can spend. He sees no limits to man's progress.* **2.** somebody/something that cannot be endured or tolerated. *That man's the limit.* (*informal* in sense **2.**). Also *vt* put a limit to; keep within limit. *We must limit the amount of money we spend.*
limited *adj* small; narrow; confined. *The amount of money we have is limited. I have only a limited knowledge of the language.* (*opp* **unlimited**).
limitless *adj* without limit.
limitation [limi'teiʃən] *nc/u*: *I know my limitations* i.e. what I can and cannot do. *Poor health is a great limitation* i.e. a hindrance; disability.
limited liability company (*Brit*) one in which the members of the company are limited to paying debts equal to the amount of money they have put in the company.
within limits to a certain extent; not too much. *I am ready to agree, within limits.*
without limit to any extent. *He helps his friends without limit.*

limousine ['liməziːn] *nc* large, expensive motorcar (usu. with a separate compartment for the driver).

limp[1] [limp] *adj* not stiff; soft; weak. *The book has a limp cover; a limp hand.* **limply** *adv*. **limpness** *nu*.

limp[2] [limp] *vi* walk unevenly because of lameness. *After being kicked on the ankle, the player limped off the field.* Also *nu* (usu. with **a**): *He walks with a limp.* **limpingly** *adv*.

limpet ['limpit] *nc* type of small shellfish which sticks firmly to rocks.

limpid ['limpid] *adj* (esp. with reference to liquids and the eyes) clear. **limpidly** *adv*. **limpidity** [lim'piditi] *nu*.

linchpin ['lintʃpin] *nc* **1.** large pin which fastens a wheel to its axle. **2.** necessary part of something.

linden ['lindn] *nc* type of tree with yellowish-white flowers, grown for ornament or shade. (Also **lime**).

line[1] [lain] *nc* **1.** cord, string, thread or wire: *throw a line to a ship* i.e. a rope; *a fishing line; a clothes line* i.e. a rope to hang and dry clothes on; *telephone lines* i.e. wires. **2.** thin mark on something: *the finishing line in a race* i.e. mark on the ground to show when a race ends. *He drew the picture in bold lines. The lines on his face showed that he was worried* i.e. wrinkles. **3.** row of persons/things: *a line of soldiers. The people stood in a line at the bus stop; a long line of trees; a single line of traffic; a few lines of verse. There are forty lines of print on each page of the book.* **4.** (in *pl*) certificate i.e. lines written on paper: *marriage lines* i.e. certificate showing that one is married. (*informal*). **5.** edge; boundary; limit. *The top of the mountain is above the snow line. Ships sailing from South Africa to Europe have to cross the line* i.e. the equator; *contour lines on a map.* **6.** group of aeroplanes, ships or vehicles under one management. *Several airlines fly passengers from London to New York. This ship belongs to a foreign line.* **7.** track on which a railway train runs: *the main line between Edinburgh and London; the line is covered with snow.* **8.** direction; course. *The army's line of retreat was through the wood. We tried a different line of approach.* **9.** method of doing something; business. *We must take a firm/strong line with these people* i.e. act firmly in dealing with them. *You cannot win the games on these lines* i.e. in this way. *His line is bookselling* i.e. his business. (*informal*). *That's not in my line* i.e. I am not interested; it is not my business. **10.** type of goods to be bought or sold. *This shop has a good line in men's coats.* **11.** series of persons who are descended from a common ancestor. *He comes from a long line of good farmers* i.e. his parents, grandparents and those before them were all good farmers. **12.** (in *pl*) shape; form. *I like the lines of that sports car.*

liner *nc* large passenger ship which belongs to a line (in sense **6.**).

'linesman *nc* **1.** person who inspects and repairs railway lines. **2.** (in football, tennis etc) person who decides whether or not the ball has crossed a line (in sense **2.**).

as'sembly line see **assemble.**

'party line see **party.**

all along the line everywhere; completely. *We were lucky all along the line.* (*informal*).

bring somebody/something into line with make somebody/something agree or fit in with. *They have brought their prices into line with ours.*

come/fall into line with agree; fit in with.

draw the line at see **draw**[1].

drop somebody a line send somebody a short letter. (*informal*).

in line with in agreement with.

read between the lines find a deeper meaning than is obvious.

shoot a line boast. (*informal* and rather *o.f.*).

toe the line obey; do what others agree to do. (*informal*).

line[2] [lain] *vt* **1.** mark or show by lines; make lines on. *Old age has lined his face.* **2.** border; form a line along. *Tall trees line the road. The crew lined the sides of the ship.*

line up put in a line; get into a line. *The teacher lined up the boys in front of his desk. We lined up to buy tickets.*

'line-up *nc* **1.** line of players ready to begin playing (e.g. football). **2.** (mainly *US*) line of people who have come together or been brought together for some purpose: *a line-up of people suspected by the police.*

line[3] [lain] *vt* cover the inside of something. *He lined the box with clean paper. Her coat is lined with silk.*

lining *nc* inside covering; material used as an inside covering. *I tore the lining of my jacket.*

lineage ['liniidʒ] *nu* line of persons from whom one is descended i.e. parents, grandparents and those before them.

lineal ['liniəl] *adj* of the same lineage. **lineally** *adv.*

lineament ['liniəmənt] *nc* (often *pl*) (esp. with reference to the face) outline; feature.

linear ['liniə*] *adj* of a line; in lines; of length. *Feet and yards are linear measures; linear design.*

linen ['linin] *nu* **1.** type of cloth made from flax. **2.** tablecloths, shirts, sheets, handkerchiefs etc made from linen or some other cloth. *We must change the linen on the bed* i.e. take off the dirty sheets and put on clean ones. Also *adj*: *a linen tablecloth.*

liner ['lainə*] *nc* see **line**[1].

linesman ['lainzmən] *nc* see **line**[1].

ling [liŋ] *nu* type of short plant with small flowers. (Usu. **heather**).

linger ['liŋgə*] *vi* stay a long time; be unwilling to go away. *We lingered in the garden until it was dark. Why is he lingering about the school?*

lingering *adj* lasting a long time: *a lingering look.* **lingeringly** *adv.*

linger on stay or continue longer than is expected. *The dying man lingered on* i.e. he stayed alive longer than was expected.

lingerie ['lænʒəri] *nu* women's underwear.

lingo ['liŋgou] *nc* language; dialect (esp. when it is difficult to understand). *pl* **lingoes.** (*informal* and rather *impolite*).

lingua franca ['liŋgwə'fræŋkə] *nu* common language used by most people in a country/an area where there are several local languages.

lingual ['liŋgwəl] *adj* of the tongue. Also *nc* sound made when the tongue is used (e.g. 'd', 'l', 'n').

linguist ['liŋgwist] *nc* **1.** person skilled at speaking more than one language. **2.** person who is skilled in linguistics. **linguistic** [liŋ'gwistik] *adj.* **linguistically** *adv.* **linguistics** [liŋ'gwistiks] *n sing* scientific study of language.

liniment ['linimənt] *nc/u* type of oil or ointment rubbed on the body (esp. to remove stiffness).

lining ['lainiŋ] *nc* see **line**[3].

link [liŋk] *nc* **1.** one ring of a chain. **2.** somebody/something that joins two things together. *The road was our only link with the village.* Also *vt/i* join, be joined by, a link.

'cufflink see **cuff**[1].

missing link 1. something without which a series, argument etc is not complete. **2.** type of animal about which knowledge is needed to show the connection between men and apes.

link up join or be joined together. **'link-up** *nc.*

links [liŋks] *npl* piece of land (esp. near the sea) covered with grass (often used as a golf course).

linnet ['linit] *nc* type of small bird which sings sweetly.

lino ['lainou] *nu* short form of **linoleum.**

'linocut pattern or picture cut into a small piece of linoleum with which prints can be made.

linoleum [li'nouliəm] *nu* covering for a floor made of canvas, cork and oil.

linotype ['lainotaip] *nc* machine for arranging printing type in complete lines.

linseed ['linsi:d] *nu* seed of a plant (called **flax**).

lint [lint] *nu* linen with one side made soft like wool, used for covering cuts and wounds.

lintel ['lintl] *nc* horizontal piece of wood or stone above a doorway or window.

lion ['laiən] *nc* **1.** large animal of the cat family, found in Africa and Asia. (The male has a big mane of hair on its head and neck) (*fem* **lioness**). **2.** important and popular person.

lioness ['laiənis] *nc* female lion.

lionize *vt* treat as a lion (in sense **2.**).

'lion-'hearted *adj* very brave.

the lion's share the biggest share of something. (*informal*).

lip [lip] *nc* **1.** one of the two outer edges of the mouth: *the lower/upper lip. He kissed her on the lips.* **2.** edge of anything (esp. if shaped like a lip): *the lip of a cup.* **3.** rude talk. *Less/none of your lip!* i.e. don't speak rudely (to me) (*informal* in sense **3.**).

'lip-reading way of understanding what somebody says by watching his lips moving (used by those who are deaf).

'lip service saying that one agrees or will do something etc but not meaning it. *They pay lip service to my ideas but they do not really*

believe them.
'lipstick stick of coloured material used by women to put on their lips.
bite one's lip control one's anger or amusement.
keep a stiff upper lip see **keep**[1].
open one's lips speak. *During the meeting he never opened his lips.*
smack/lick one's lips see **smack**[1].
liquefy ['likwifai] *vt/i* become or make liquid. **liquefied** *adj.* **liquefaction** [likwi'fækʃən] *nu.*
liqueur [li'kjuə*] *nc* type of strong, sweet, alcoholic drink often flavoured with fruit (usu. taken in a very small glass after a meal).
liquid ['likwid] **1.** *nc/u* matter like water or oil in density and form. (The other two forms matter can take are gas and solid). **2.** *nc* consonant with a smooth sound (e.g. 'l' and 'r'). Also *adj* **1.** like liquid. **2.** clear: *liquid eyes.*
liquid assets assets which can be sold easily.
liquidate ['likwideit] *vt* **1.** pay a debt. **2.** settle the affairs of a bankrupt business company by selling its property to pay its debts; (with reference to the business) be settled in this way. **3.** destroy; kill.
liquidation [likwi'deiʃən] *nu*: *go into liquidation* i.e. become bankrupt.
liquidator *nc* person who settles the affairs of a bankrupt company.
liquor ['likə*] *nc/u* alcoholic drink (esp. *US* strong, alcoholic drink or spirits).
liquorice, licorice ['likəris] *nc/u* **1.** type of plant from which is obtained a substance used to make sweets and medicines. **2.** the substance itself.
lisp [lisp] *vt/i* speak incorrectly (esp. by saying 'th' instead of 's' e.g. *'thip'* instead of *'sip'*). Also *nc* habit of lisping. *The boy speaks with a lisp/has a lisp.* **lisping** *adv.*
lissom ['lisəm] *adj* flexible; moving easily and gracefully.
list[1] [list] *nc* number of things written down or printed for a particular purpose: *wine list* i.e. names of kinds of wine printed on paper so that one can choose the kind one wants; *shopping list. He made a list of the friends he knew.* Also *vt* make a list; put on a list.
on the short list on the final list of applicants who are to be considered for a post etc.
on the active list (with reference to officers in the army, navy or air force) on the list of those who have not retired from military service.
list[2] [list] *vi* (esp. with reference to a ship) lean to one side. Also *nc*: *a ship with a list.*
lists [lists] *npl* piece of ground where men on horseback fought each other in ancient times.
enter the lists join in an argument or fight. (rather *o.f.*).
listen ['lisn] *vt/i* **1.** pay attention to (esp. so that one can hear). *I often listen to music. Although we were listening, we did not hear him coming.* **2.** follow the advice of. *Children should listen to their parents.*
listener *nc* person who listens.
listen for something listen until one hears. *The boys are listening for the bell at the end of the lesson.*
listen in 1. listen secretly. *Please speak quietly. I think somebody is listening in.* **2.** listen to the radio. *We listened in to an interesting talk last night.* (rather *o.f.* – use listen).
listless ['listlis] *adj* not having enough energy or interest to do something. **listlessly** *adv.* **listlessness** *nu.*
lit [lit] past of **light**[2].
litany ['litəni] *nc* type of prayer used in church; book containing this type of prayer.
liter ['li:tə*] *US* form of **litre.**
literacy ['litərəsi] *nu* see **literate.**
literal ['litərl] *adj* **1.** word for word; following the exact meaning. *This is a literal translation in French of an English proverb. In its literal sense 'anti' means 'against'.* **2.** of a letter of the alphabet. **3.** (with reference to persons) believing only in what is real; without imagination: *a literal man cannot be an artist.*
literally *adv* **1.** word for word. **2.** really; in fact.
literary ['litərəri] *adj* of literature; (with reference to a person) interested in literature.
literate ['litərət] *adj* able to read and write. (*opp* **illiterate**).
literacy ['litərəsi] *nu.* (*opp* **illiteracy**).
literature ['litəritʃə*] *nu* books (esp. those by good writers).
lithe [laið] *adj* (with reference to persons) bending or moving easily. **litheness** *nu.*
lithography [li'θɔgrəfi] *nu* method of printing by using plates (usu. of metal) on which the words to be printed are cut.
lithograph ['liθəgrɑ:f] *nc* something printed in this way. Also *vt* print in this way. **lithographic** [liθə'græfik] *adj.*
lithographer *nc* person who prints in this way.
litigate ['litigeit] *vt/i* go to law; oppose something by going to law. **litigation** [liti'geiʃən] *nu.*
litigant ['litigənt] *nc* person who litigates.
litigious [li'tidʒəs] *adj* **1.** able to be opposed by law. **2.** fond of going to law.
litmus ['litməs] *nu* type of blue substance which is made red by an acid and then blue again by an alkali, and so used to indicate the presence of these substances.
'litmus paper paper covered with litmus.
litre ['li:tə*] (*US* **liter**) *nc* unit of liquid measure. see appendix.
litter[1] ['litə*] *nc* type of bed with curtains round it once used for carrying people.
litter[2] ['litə*] **1.** *nu* useless material which is thrown down and left (e.g. old newspapers, empty bottles, cigarette ends); rubbish. *Many public parks are spoilt by litter.* **2.** *nu* straw covering plants or put down for animals to stand on. **3.** *nc* family of young animals born at the same time: *a litter of kittens.* Also *vt/i* **1.** cover or make untidy with litter. **2.** cover plants with straw; put down straw for animals to stand on. **3.** give birth to a litter.
little ['litl] **1.** *adj* (*comparative* **less** or **lesser.** *superlative* **least**) small in size: *a little box.* **2.** *adj/determiner* small in amount; short in time. *May I have a little sugar? He spent a little time talking to us.* **3.** *adj* young. *We met Mrs Smith with her two little ones* i.e. with her two young children. *All the little children are in Class I.*
Note: 1. *little* without *a* or *the* has the sense of 'not enough', 'hardly any' (e.g. *They have little money for extra food* i.e. they have hardly any money set aside for extra food and will probably not buy it). *There is little*

hope of seeing him again. 2. Although *little* very often has the same sense as *small*, there are some differences (e.g. *Would you like a little pudding?* i.e. a small amount, or small helping, of a fairly big pudding). *Would you like a small pudding?* i.e. one separate pudding which is small in size). Also *little* is often used with another *adj* to show that one likes, or is pleased with, something, not to show that it is small. *He made a nice little profit in the market* i.e. a good profit. One cannot say *a nice small profit*; small profits are never nice. *She's a pretty little girl* i.e. she is pretty and I like her. *She's a pretty small girl* i.e. she is a rather small girl and may not be pretty at all. see also **pretty**.
Also *nu* a small amount, size etc. *I drank a little of the wine. I am not surprised at the little he does.* Also *adv* not by much; hardly at all. *They will come back a little later. They live very little in this country.*
Note: little as an *adv* is often used before the verb with the sense of something happening which is not expected. *He little thought that his life was in danger* i.e. it *was* in danger. *We little believed that he would harm us* i.e. we were wrong; He *did* harm us.
after a little after a short time or distance.
for a little for a short time or distance.
little by little gradually; step by step.
little or nothing hardly anything.

littoral ['litərl] *adj* beside, or on, the coast. Also *nu* land which is on the coast.

liturgy ['litədʒi] *nc* approved form of worship in a church. **liturgical** [li'təːdʒikl] *adj*.

live[1] [liv] *vt/i* **1.** have life; not be dead (**be alive** is more usual). **2.** continue to be alive. *Not many people live to a hundred* i.e. until they are a hundred years old. *She is so badly injured that she is not likely to live.* **3.** have one's home. *Where do you live? We live in London.* **4.** (usu. with *adv*) spend one's time in a particular way. *They live quietly in the country. When I was rich I lived very well.* **5.** (with reference to things) continue; be remembered. *His poetry will live forever.*
liveable ['livəbl] *adj* possible to live in or with.
live something down make others forget something wrong which one has done, by behaving well afterwards. *He will not easily live down his very rude behaviour at the party.*
live in (e.g. with reference to servants) live in the place where one is employed. (*opp* **live out**).
live off take money, food etc from. *He doesn't work, he just lives off his friends.*
live on continue to live. *After her mother's death she lived on in the house by herself.*
live on something keep alive by earning or eating. *He and his family live on £20 a week. These people live on meat and milk.*
live out (e.g. with reference to servants) not live in the place where one is employed. (*opp* **live in**).
live out one's life (esp. with reference to older people) continue to live.
live through something keep alive in spite of; survive. *They lived through the long famine.*
live it up have a very good time by going to parties etc. (*informal*).
live up to something (esp. with reference to behaviour, standards etc) be as good as. *I try to live up to the high standards of the school.*
live a double life live in two different ways in one's life (e.g. by being honest at home and a criminal outside it).
live from hand to mouth live without having anything to spare.

live[2] [laiv] *adj* **1.** having life: *a live mouse* i.e. one which is not dead; *a live broadcast* i.e. a programme on radio or television sent out while it is happening.
Note: live in the sense of 'not dead' cannot be a *pred adj* – use *alive* or *living* (e.g. *the live mouse* but *The mouse is alive/living*).
2. having power, energy etc. *Be careful, this wire is live* i.e. it has an electric current; *a live bomb* i.e. one which is ready to be exploded. **3.** important; causing great interest. *The problem of disease is a live one.*

livelihood ['laivlihud] *nc* way in which one earns money to live. *For many years teaching was his livelihood. She made a livelihood by writing.*

livelong ['livlɔŋ] *adj* lasting the whole period of: *the livelong day/night/spring/summer etc.* (rather *o.f.*).
Note: lifelong adj has the sense of lasting the whole of one's life (e.g. *a lifelong friend*).

lively ['laivli] *adj* **1.** full of life; quick; active. *Young children are usually lively. He has a lively mind. Because of all the arguments the meeting was a lively one.* **2.** true to life; vivid. *He told a very lively story about his life in Africa.* **liveliness** *nu*.

liven ['laivən] *vt/i* (often with **up**) become or make lively. *He livened up the class by telling an interesting story.*

liver[1] ['livə*] *nc* person who lives (usu. with another word to show how he lives): *a long liver* i.e. a person who lives for a long time; *a clean liver* i.e. a person who lives a good, clean life.

liver[2] ['livə*] **1.** *nc* large organ of the body which cleans the blood. **2.** *nu* this organ taken from an animal and used as food.
liverish *adj* not feel well because one's liver is out of order; bad-tempered. **liverishly** *adv*. **liverishness** *nu*.

livery ['livəri] *nc* special dress once worn by the servants of an important person; special dress of some of the companies of the City of London.

lives [laivz] pl of **life**.

livestock ['laivstɔk] *nu* animals kept by man for his own use (e.g. cattle, sheep, goats etc – *not* dogs or cats or other pets).

livid ['livid] *adj* having the colour of lead i.e. grey. *He is livid with anger* i.e. so angry that his face is grey. **lividly** *adv*.

living[1] ['liviŋ] *adj* **1.** existing now; alive. *English is a living language. He is a living example of courage.* **2.** exact. *This picture is the living image of my mother.*

living[2] ['liviŋ] **1.** *nu* way in which one lives; way in which one gets what is needed to live. *The standard of living in poor countries is very low. Rich men like good living* i.e. great comfort, good food etc. *He earns/makes his living by growing rice.* **2.** *nc* post of priest or clergyman of a church.
'living room room in a house where the people of the house spend most of their time when they are at home and awake.

lizard ['lizəd] *nc* type of small animal with a long tail and dry scaly skin.

llama ['lɑːmə] *nc* type of animal with long, thick hair found in South America (often used by man to carry things).

lo [lou] *interj* look! (*o.f.*).

load[1] [loud] *vt/i* **1.** put something (usu.

something heavy) in or on something else (e.g. on a lorry, on a ship etc) to be carried away; give somebody something heavy to carry. *They are loading the bags of rice on to the lorry. He loaded me with books.* **2.** (with reference to a gun, rifle etc) put in a shell or cartridge. *Be careful! That gun is loaded.* **3.** (with reference to a camera) put in a film. *I forgot to load my camera.* (*opp* **unload**).

loaded dice dice made heavy on one side so that it falls, when thrown, in the way the thrower wants.

load something up fill by loading; finish loading. *Have you loaded up the lorry yet?*

load[2] [loud] *nc* **1.** something which is loaded in or on something else. *He has brought the lorry for a load of wood.* **2.** amount which something can carry (often with another word): *three lorry-loads of wood; a shipload of cotton.* **3.** limit to which an engine, electric wire etc can be used without being damaged. **4.** anything which is heavy or causes trouble. *The good news has taken a load off my mind* i.e. has stopped me worrying. *He carries a heavy load of responsibility.*

'load line line painted on the side of a ship to show when it is fully loaded.

'payload 1. part of the load of a ship, an aeroplane etc which earns money i.e. passengers, cargo, but not fuel etc. **2.** (space) scientific instruments carried by a satellite etc.

loads of a lot of. (*informal*).

shed the load make the load less (esp. in sense **3.** with reference to an electric current when more electricity is being used than the generator can supply).

loadstone ['loudstoun] *nc* see **lode.**

loaf [louf] *nc* lump of bread (usu. before it is cut into slices). *I bought a brown loaf and a white one* i.e. a loaf of brown bread and one of white bread. *pl* **loaves** [louvz]. Also *vi* waste time; go around in a lazy manner. *Tell these boys to stop loafing (about)* (*informal*).

loaf

loam [loum] *nu* type of fertile soil. **loamy** *adj.*

loan [loun] *nc* (esp. with reference to money for interest) something which is lent; act of lending or being lent. *The government needs a big loan to build more schools. I gave him the loan of my pen* i.e. I lent my pen to him. *We have the car on loan from a friend.* Also *vt* lend (which is more usual).

'loanword word taken from one language and used in another. *'Safari' is a loanword in English taken from Swahili.*

raise a loan get a loan of money.

loath, loth [louθ] *pred adj* unwilling. *He is loth to do it* (*o.f.*).

loathe [louð] *vt* hate; be disgusted by. *She loathes watching television.* **loathing** *nu.*

loathsome *adj* disgusting.

loaves [louvz] *pl* of **loaf.**

lob [lɔb] *vt* hit or throw high into the air. *past* **lobbed.** Also *nc* high hit or throw.

lobby ['lɔbi] *nc* **1.** hall or narrow passage inside a building (usu. with doors leading into rooms). **2.** hall in the British House of Commons where Members of Parliament can meet people who wish to see them. **3.** group of people who try to get the support of Members of Parliament (or *US* members of Congress or the Senate) when Parliament is discussing matters which interest them (e.g. *the tobacco lobby* i.e. a group of people of this kind who do not like Parliament interfering in the tobacco business). Also *vt/i* try to get the support of Members of Parliament etc. see sense **3.** *They lobbied for the ending of the death penalty.*

lobe [loub] *nc* **1.** soft part of the bottom of the ear. **2.** part of the lung or of a leaf.

lobed *adj* having lobes.

lobelia [lə'bi:liə] *nc* type of small flower.

lobster ['lɔbstə*] *nc* type of shellfish with eight legs and two large claws and a tail.

'lobster pot type of basket in which lobsters are caught.

local ['loukl] *adj* of a particular place or area. *We went to the local shop* i.e. one which serves the small area we were in; *local news* i.e. news about the small district round about; *local injury* i.e. one of only a particular part of the body. Also *nc* **1.** person who lives in a particular place. *We stopped in the village and asked one of the locals the way to the post office.* **2.** public house in a particular place. *He's always in the local in the evening.* (*informal*). **locally** *adv.*

locality [lou'kæliti] *nc* place; area. *There are no hotels in this locality.*

localize *vt* make local; keep something in a particular place. **localized** *adj.*

locate [lou'keit] *vt* **1.** find the position of. *Can you locate your seat in the cinema?* **2.** put in a particular position. *The company wishes to locate its new factory beside the river.*

location *nc/u* **1.** act of locating; position. **2.** place outside in the open air where a film is made. *The film actors are on location in Jamaica.*

loch [lɔx] *nc* (*Scot*) lake or narrow stretch of water open at one end to the sea.

lock[1] [lɔk] *nc* **1.** device for fastening a door, lid of a box etc. **2.** part of a river or canal which has a gate at each end. By opening or shutting these gates the level of the water can be raised or lowered to allow boats to pass through. **3.** device in a gun by which the gun is fired. **4.** anything that stops movement. *The policeman put an armlock on the thief* i.e. the policeman held the thief's arm in such a way that he could not move it. *The front wheels of the car are at full lock* i.e. they cannot be turned to the left (or right) any further.

'lockjaw type of disease which makes one's jaw stiff so that the mouth cannot be opened. (Also **tetanus**).

'lock keeper person who looks after a lock (in sense **2.**).

'locknut second nut screwed on top of a first to keep it from moving.

'locksmith person who makes and repairs locks (in sense **1.**).

lock, stock and barrel completely. *The fire destroyed the house, lock, stock and barrel* i.e. the house and everything in it. (*informal*).

lock[2] [lɔk] *vt/i* **1.** fasten with a lock. *He locked the door and put the key in his pocket.* **2.** be able to be fastened in this way. *This door doesn't lock.* **3.** be unable, cause to be unable, to move. *His car hit the wall*

because the front wheels locked. He locked my arm in a firm grip.
lock something away put something in a box, cupboard etc which is then locked.
lock somebody in lock from the outside the door of a building, room etc where somebody is or into which someone has been put. *We locked the thief in the cellar until the police arrived.*
lock oneself in lock from the inside the door of a room where one is so that nobody can get in.
'lockout *nc* (esp. with reference to stopping workmen entering a factory etc until an agreement is reached with their employers) act of locking out.
lock oneself out lock from the outside the door of a building, room etc (usu. accidentally) so that one cannot get in again.
lock someone out lock from the inside the door of a building, room etc to stop someone getting in. *Because I was very late in returning home my father locked me out.*
lock someone up put someone in a place where he will be safe or can do no harm and then lock the door (e.g. in a prison).
lock something up **1.** put something in a safe place which can be locked. *I always lock up my money in a strong box.* **2.** (with reference to buildings etc) lock all doors and windows so that nobody can get in. *We locked up our house when we went away on holiday.*
'lock-up *nc* prison. (*informal*). Also *adj* (usu. with reference to a building etc which is not part of one's house) able to be locked for safety. *I have a lock-up garage in the next street.*

lock[3] [lɔk] *nc* **1.** number of hairs which hang together. *He had a lock of hair over his left eye.* **2.** (in *pl*) hair. *His locks are grey* (*o.f.* – use **hair**).

locker ['lɔkə*] *nc* **1.** box with a lid which can be locked (usu. fixed to a wall and used in places where there are many people each of whom can have his own for his clothes, books etc). *In this school pupils keep their books in lockers.* **2.** small place on a ship for keeping stores.
'locker room special room full of lockers.

locket ['lɔkit] *nc* small flat box (usu. made of gold or silver and hung round the neck on a thin chain) in which there is a picture or some of the hair of a person one loves.

locomotion [loukə'mouʃən] *nu* power to move from one place to another.
locomotive [loukə'moutiv] *adj*. Also *nc* railway engine.

locum (tenens) ['loukəm ('tenenz)] *nu* (esp. with reference to the work of a doctor or clergyman) person who does the work of another person during his absence.

locust ['loukəst] *nc* type of winged insect found in Africa and Asia, which moves in very large numbers and destroys crops.

locution [lə'kju:ʃən] *nc/u* way of speaking or of using words.

lode [loud] *nc* deposit of metal inside a rock.
'lodestar star by which a ship can be guided. (Usu. **pole star**).
'lodestone, loadstone type of stone containing iron which is magnetic.

lodge[1] [lɔdʒ] *nc* **1.** small house or room at the entrance to the grounds of a large house or at the entrance to a large building (e.g. a school or college). **2.** house used by people when they are away from home shooting or hunting: *a shooting/hunting lodge.*

lodge[2] [lɔdʒ] *vt/i* **1.** (with **at, in** or **with**) live in somebody's house for payment. *When I was at college I lodged at No. 12 Smith Street. I lodged with one of the staff.* **2.** put or receive somebody in a place where he can live for a time. *They lodged the soldiers in the town until the army camp was ready.* **3.** put in a particular place. *He lodged his spear in the animal's body.* **4.** be held firmly; be fixed. *The stick was lodged between two big stones.* **5.** leave in a safe place for a time. *I shall lodge my books in the school office during the weekend.* (rather *formal* in sense **5.**).
lodger *nc* person who pays for a room to live in.
lodgings *npl* room or rooms where one can lodge.
lodgement, lodgment *nc/u* something which is lodged (in sense **4.**); act of lodging (esp. a complaint).
'lodging house house with rooms where one can lodge (usu. very cheaply).
lodge a complaint make an official complaint to the person who can deal with it. *Some parents have lodged a complaint with the headmaster against one of the teachers.*

loess ['louis] *nu* type of fine, fertile soil.

loft [lɔft] *nc* **1.** room at the top of a building just under the roof. **2.** gallery in a church etc.

lofty ['lɔfti] *adj* **1.** (with reference to things, not persons) very high: *the lofty tops of the mountains.* **2.** (with reference to a person's feelings) noble; to be admired. *He has lofty ideals about life.* **3.** (with reference to a person's behaviour) proud; haughty. *He spoke to me in a lofty manner.* **loftily** *adv.* **loftiness** *nu.*

log[1] [lɔg] *nc* rough piece of wood cut from a tree.
logging *nu* work of cutting down trees.
'log 'cabin small house built with logs, not smooth planks.
sleep like a log/top see **sleep.**

log[2] [lɔg] *nc* **1.** device for measuring the speed of a ship. **2.** daily written record of a ship's speed, distance it sails each day, its position etc. **3.** any written record (e.g. of travel by car, the amount of petrol used; the daily events at a school etc). Also *vt* write in a log (in sense **2.**). *past* **logged.**
'logbook **1.** book used as a log (in sense **2.**). **2.** book in which details of a car ownership etc are recorded.

log[3] [lɔg] *nc* short form of **logarithm.**

loganberry ['lougənbəri] *nc* type of berry which is a cross between a blackberry and a raspberry.

logarithm ['lɔgəriðəm] *nc* number put in a form which makes calculating easier by using addition and subtraction instead of multiplication and division. (Also **log**).
logarithmic [lɔgə'riðmik] *adj.*

loggerheads ['lɔgəhedz] *npl* only in **be at loggerheads with someone** i.e. argue or quarrel with.

loggia ['lɔdʒə] *nc* gallery which is open on one side; verandah (usu. one attached to a house and leading to a garden).

logic ['lɔdʒik] *nu* science of reasoning correctly; ability to reason correctly.
logical *adj*: *He gave a logical answer to the question.* (*opp* **illogical**). **logically** *adv.*

logistics [lə'dʒistiks] *npl* (esp. with reference to military forces during a war) science of transport, communications and supply. **logistic** *adj.*

loin [lɔin] *nc* (usu. *pl*) part of the body where it joins the legs. (rather *o.f.*).
'loincloth piece of cloth tied round this part of the body.
loin of beef/mutton piece of beef/mutton cut from the loins.

loiter ['lɔitə*] *vi* go slowly and lazily from one place to another; stand about idly. *They loitered all the way to school. Why are these boys loitering in the playground?*
loiterer *nc* person who loiters.
loiter away one's time waste time by loitering.

loll [lɔl] *vt/i* **1.** stand, sit or lie lazily. *He was lolling in a chair with his hands in his pockets.* **2.** (with reference to the tongue) hang, cause to hang, loosely: *a dog with its tongue lolling out.*

lollipop ['lɔlipɔp] *nc* type of sweet at the end of a stick. *The child was licking a lollipop.*

lolly ['lɔli] **1.** *nc* short informal form of **lollipop. 2.** *nu* money. (*informal*).

lone [loun] *adj* by oneself; by itself; without others near; alone.
lonesome *adj* feeling lonely; wanting the company of others.
Note: alone and *lonely* are more usual than *lone*.

lonely ['lounli] *adj* by oneself; by itself; without others near. *He was lonely because there were no other boys to play with. He lives in a lonely house far away from the village.*
loneliness *nu.*
feel lonely feel sad because one is by oneself.

long[1] [lɔŋ] *adj* **1.** extending; measuring more than the usual distance. *He has long legs. I have been here a long time.* (*opp* **short**). **2.** (after a noun showing what the measurement is) measured from one end to the other. *The stick is 3 inches long. A year is 12 months long. How long is the new stretch of motorway?* **3.** (with reference to vowel sounds) taking more time to say. *'But' has a short vowel, 'boot' a long one.* Also **1.** *nu* (with reference to time). *Was he here for long? We shall finish before long.*
Note: there is a great difference in meaning between *before long* i.e. soon and *long before* i.e. a long time ago. see **long**[2].
2. *nc* (with reference to vowel sounds and stress). *The line of poetry has five longs and five shorts.*
'longboat largest boat carried in a sailing ship to move people to and from the ship.
'long-'distance *adj* over a great distance: *long-distance runner; long-distance call* i.e. by telephone.
'longhand ordinary handwriting.
'long-'legged *adj* having long legs.
'long 'odds (betting) very small chance of winning (e.g. 100 to 1 against).
'longshoreman person who works on shore; dock labourer.
'long-stop (cricket) player whose place in the field is behind the wicket-keeper.
'long suit 1. (in a card game) suit in which a player has many cards. **2.** anything which somebody does very well. *His understanding of other people's problems is his long suit.* (*informal*).
'long wave (radio) sound wave measuring from 1,053-2,000 metres (in Britain). see also **short wave, medium wave.**
'long-'winded *adj* **1.** able to run a great distance without having difficulty with one's breathing. **2.** talking too much; boring. (informal in sense **2.**). **long-windedness** *nu.*
by a long chalk (usu. with **not**) by a great amount; very much. *He has not finished his work by a long chalk.* (*informal*).
have a long face look sad or disappointed. (*informal*).
the long and the short of it to sum up; the most important points of an argument etc. *The long and the short of it is that we must go, whatever they say.* (*informal*).
in the long run sooner or later; eventually.
have long sight 1. be able to see things at a great distance. **2.** be able to understand by seeing into the future. **long-sighted** *adj.* **long-sightedness** *nu.*
take a/the long view think about what will happen in the future as well as about what is happening now. *When planning a new school you must take a long view.*

long[2] [lɔŋ] *adv* **1.** for a great period of time. *He did not sleep for long. He waited as long as he could.* **2.** (with **all**) for a whole period of time. *They worked all night long.* **3.** (with a *prep*) at a much earlier or later time. *He went home long ago. I came long before he did. They finished long after the others.*
Note: see *Note* under **long**[1] on difference between *long before* and *before long.*
longer (with **any, no, much etc**) beyond a certain time. *I could not wait any/much longer. How much longer must he stay here?*
'long-drawn-'out see **draw**[1].
'long-'lived *adj* having a long life.
'long-'standing *adj* having existed for a long time.
'long-'suffering *adj* suffering or enduring patiently.

long[3] [lɔŋ] *vi* want very much. *The people longed for peace. He is longing to meet you.*
longing *nc/u*: *their longing for peace.* Also *adj*: *He had a longing look on his face.*
longingly *adv.*

longevity [lɔn'dʒeviti] *nu* long life.

longitude ['lɔŋgitju:d] *nu* distance in degrees east or west of a line drawn over the surface of the earth between the north and south poles. see **latitude.**
longitudinal [lɔŋgi'tju:dinl] *adj* **1.** of longitude. **2.** of length. **3.** running the length of.

longways, longwise ['lɔŋweiz, 'lɔŋwaiz] *adv* along the length of; lengthways, lengthwise.

loo [lu:] *nc* lavatory. (*informal*).

loofah ['lu:fə] *nc* dried inside of a plant used to rub the skin when having a bath.

look [luk] *vt/i* **1.** turn one's eyes towards; try to see. *I want you to look at this map. He looked everywhere but could not find it. If you look carefully, you will see a small mark on the paper.* **2.** appear to be. *They looked very happy. The box looks heavy. The school looks closed.* Also with **like** and **as if.** *He looks like a soldier. It looks like rain/ It looks as if it will rain.* **3.** (with reference to things) face, be turned, in a particular direction. *Our house looks south.* **4.** be careful; pay attention to. *Look where you are going! Look what he's done!* **5.** show one's feelings in one's face. *Without saying anything, he looked his thanks.* Also *nc* **1.** act of looking. *He had/took a look at the picture.* **2.** appearance; what one's face shows. *He gave me a thankful look.* **3.** (in *pl*) appearance of the face. *The cut above his eye has spoilt his looks.*
looking (with *adj*) in appearance. *He is not a bad-looking man* i.e. he is quite

attractive. *They are a miserable-looking crowd.*
'looking-glass mirror (*o.f.*).
look about (one) find out about what is near; take an interest in something else. *I was so busy that I had no time to look about (me).*
look about for try to find by going to several places. *We are looking about for a new house.*
look after someone take care of. *Who is looking after the children?*
look after number one take care of oneself (esp. by being selfish) (*informal*).
look at someone/something **1.** turn the eyes towards. **2.** examine; consider. *The doctor looked at his injured hand. They refuse to look at my suggestion.* **3.** (with *infinitive*) in appearance. *He is a healthy man to look at* or (usu. with *negative*) *To look at him, you would not think he was a healthy man.*
look away turn the eyes away. *I waved to him but he looked away.*
look back **1.** turn the eyes to what is behind. *He stopped at the door and looked back.* **2.** turn one's thoughts to, think about, the past. *I looked back to/upon the days when I was a boy.* **3.** (usu. with **never**) be successful all the time. *After passing the examination, he never looked back.*
look down on someone/something think oneself better than; despise. *The rich look down on the poor.*
look down one's nose show on one's face a feeling of contempt or dislike. *He looked down his nose at the food we gave him.*
look for something **1.** try to find. **2.** expect. *Don't look for any help from him.*
look forward to expect/wait for with pleasure. *I am looking forward to seeing my parents again.*
look in visit for a short time. *On their way to London they looked in to see us/on us.*
'look-in *nc* **1.** chance of being successful. *The examination is so difficult that he hasn't a look-in.* **2.** short visit. (*informal*).
look into something **1.** turn the eyes towards the inside of. *He looked into the hole.* **2.** examine; consider. *The police are looking into the complaint.*
look on **1.** watch without taking part. *When they began fighting he just looked on.* **2.** read a book together with somebody. *Because I lost my history book I looked on with him* i.e. we both read his book together.
look on someone regard, consider. *I do not look on him as a good doctor.*
look out **1.** turn the eyes towards what is outside. *The boy looked out (of) the window.* **2.** (with reference to things) face towards; have a view of. *His house looks out to sea. The garden looks out over the mountains.* **3.** be careful. *Look out!*
'look-out **1.** *nc* person who keeps watch. **2.** *nc* place where someone keeps watch. **3.** *nu* state of being ready or careful. *You must keep a good look-out for snakes.* **4.** *nu* something which is likely to happen. *It's a poor look-out for them if they fall.*
look something out find and bring out. *When I was in my room I looked out my old books.*
look out for something be ready; be careful. *You must look out for snakes in the long grass.*
look over **1.** examine quickly. *Would you please look over my essay.* **2.** visit all the parts of. *The headmaster allowed the parents to look over the school.*
look round turn the head in order to see.
look round something visit and find out what is there. *We looked round the shops before we bought anything.*
look through something **1.** turn the eyes so that they see through. *I was looking through my binoculars at the hills.* **2.** examine (usu. to find something or be ready for something). *I'll look through my papers and see if his name is mentioned. Before the meeting I looked through the reports.*
look to someone/something **1.** take care of; try to make better. *The government must look to its foreign policy.* **2.** rely on. *We look to you to help us.* **3.** (with reference to things) face in the direction of. *Our house looks to the south.*
look towards someone/something **1.** turn the eyes in the direction of. *He never once looked towards me.* **2.** (with reference to things) face in the direction of. *The village looks towards the forest.*
look up **1.** raise the eyes. **2.** (esp. with reference to trade or business) become better. *Exports are looking up.* (*informal* in sense **2.**).
look something up find and study in a book etc. *You should look up all new words in your dictionary.*
look someone up visit. *He always looks me up when he comes here.* (*informal*).
look somebody/something up and down examine slowly and suspiciously.
look at something through rose-coloured spectacles look at things in a happy or hopeful way. (*informal*).
look well **1.** appear to be healthy. **2.** be attractive. *She looks well in her new hat.*

loom[1] [lu:m] *nc* machine for weaving cloth.

loom[2] [lu:m] *vi* **1.** be seen, but not clearly and so appear to be larger and more frightening. *The trees loomed through the mist.* **2.** (with reference to the mind, feelings etc) have great influence; cause worry. *The fear of a sudden attack loomed in their thoughts.*
loom large seem to be very important.

loop [lu:p] *nc* **1.** shape made by a line drawn on paper, a piece of rope, wire etc when it is curved back over itself. **2.** movement made by an aeroplane in which it first flies upwards and vertically, then upside down, then downwards so following a path shaped like a loop. **3.** branch of a road, railway line etc which joins the main road, line etc again at another place. Also *vt/i* **1.** make, tie with, a loop (in senses **1.** and **3.**). *He looped the rope round the post. The road loops through the forest.* **2.** make a loop (in sense **2.**). *The airman looped the loop.*

loophole ['lu:phoul] *nc* **1.** way out of a difficulty; restriction etc. *Wealthy people often look for loopholes in the tax laws.* **2.** tall, narrow hole in a wall for shooting through (usu. found in old castles).

loose [lu:s] *adj* **1.** not tight; not fixed: *loose knot; loose screw; loose tooth; loose coat; a box full of loose stones.* **2.** free; not under control. *The horses are running loose in the field. Our dog got loose last night.* **3.** (with reference to behaviour) too free; immoral: *a loose woman. He leads a loose life.* **4.** (with reference to the body) able to move freely. *He has loose limbs.* Also *vt* make loose (*o.f.* – use **loosen**). **loosely** *adv.*
'loose-box stable where a horse can move about freely.

'loose-'leaf *adj* (with reference to a notebook) having pages which can be taken out and put back again.
at a loose end see **end.**
break loose become free by breaking a door, the rope by which something was tied etc. *During the storm the boxes on the ship broke loose.*
come loose become unfastened or less tight. *The string round the parcel came loose.*
have a loose tongue talk too freely or too carelessly. (*informal*).
play fast and loose with someone/something see **play**[1].
work loose slowly become less tight (e.g. a screw).

loosen ['lu:sn] *vt/i* become or make loose.

loot [lu:t] *nu* property which is stolen or taken illegally by force. *The thieves were caught with their loot by the police.* Also *vt/i* take loot from. *The angry crowd looted the shops.*

lop[1] [lɔp] *vt* (with **off** or **away**) cut easily (esp. the end or top of something). *He lopped off the small branches of the tree. past* **lopped.**

lop[2] [lɔp] *vi* hang down loosely. *past* **lopped** (*o.f.*).
'lop-ears ears which hang down. **lop-eared** *adj.*
'lop-'sided *adj* hanging down more on one side than the other. **lop-sidedly** *adv.* **lop-sidedness** *nu.*

lope [loup] *vi* run with long, easy steps. Also *nc/u* step of this kind.

loquacious [lə'kweiʃəs] *adj* talking a lot. **loquaciously** *adv.* **loquacity** [lə'kwæsiti] *nu.*

lord [lɔ:d] *nc* **1.** master; ruler; king. **2.** (**Lord**) God; Christ: *the Lord's Day* i.e. Sunday. **3.** (*Brit*) nobleman; peer. *The House of Lords* i.e. the upper house of Parliament in Britain, the members of which are lords. **4.** (*Brit*) (**Lord**) title given to persons in certain important positions: *Lord Chancellor; Lord Mayor.*
lordly *adj* like a lord; proud. **lordliness** *nu.*
lordship 1. *nu* rule by a lord; rank of lord. **2.** *nc* (with **His, Your, Their**) formal way of speaking to or about a lord. *I am very pleased Your Lordship could come.*
lord it over someone rule like a lord over, behave like a lord towards. *The older boys lord it over the younger ones.* (*informal*).

lore [lɔ:*] *nu* knowledge (esp. that passed by the older people to the younger). *In the past every young man learnt the lore of his tribe.*

lorgnette [lɔ:'njet] *nc* pair of eyeglasses fixed to a long handle.

lorry ['lɔri] *nc* (*Brit*) long vehicle used for carrying heavy loads. (*US* **truck**).

lose [lu:z] *vt/i* **1.** have, cause to have, no longer. *If you are not careful, you will lose your money. He has lost his father* i.e. by death. *Laziness lost him his job.* **2.** be unable to find. *You will lose your way if you go alone. I have lost my cigarettes.* **3.** be too late for. *Hurry up! You may lose your train.* **4.** be, become slower in time. *This clock loses five minutes each day.* **5.** be unable to hear or see. *I lost the last words of his speech. He is so small that he is lost among the bigger boys in the class.* **6.** be unable to win; be defeated. *Our team lost the game.* (*opp* **win**). **7.** (in *passive*) die. *Thousands of soldiers were lost in the battle. His brother was lost at sea. past* **lost** [lɔst].
loser *nc* person who loses: *bad loser* i.e. person who does not like losing and shows his feelings about it; *good loser* i.e. person who loses cheerfully and does not complain about losing.
lose one's balance fall down.
lose face be humiliated; act in a way that enables other people to laugh at one. *He tried to conceal his mistake so as not to lose face.*
lose ground 1. retreat under attack. **2.** become weaker or less important. (*opp* **gain ground**).
lose one's head become excited; not know what to do. (*opp* **keep one's head**).
lose heart become discouraged. (*opp* **take heart**).
lose one's heart to fall in love with.
lose oneself in become very busy with or interested in. *He lost himself in the exciting story.*
be lost in be very busy with or interested in; be filled with. *He is lost in his books. I was lost in admiration for his skill.* see also **lose oneself in.**
lose interest in stop being interested in.
lose one's nerve become cowardly or afraid.
lose patience with become impatient with.
lose one's senses become mad or very excited.
lose sight of be no longer able to see. *I lost sight of him in the crowd.*
lose time 1. (with reference to a clock or watch) go too slowly. **2.** delay; use too much time. *They lost time waiting for a bus.*
lose no time do as soon as possible. *We shall lose no time in telling them.*
lose track of somebody/something not know where somebody/something is; be unable to follow.
be lost (up)on be unable to have any effect upon. *All my good advice was lost on them.*
lose weight become thinner. *He lost weight during his illness.*

loss [lɔs] **1.** *nu* act or state of losing or having lost. *The loss of his job worries him. The accident caused a great loss of time. The loss of the last game by our team surprised us.* **2.** *nc* somebody/something lost. *The enemy retreated after heavy losses* i.e. after losing many men. *The profits are greater than the losses.*
be at a loss not know what to say or do. *I was at a loss as to/about what to tell him. They were at a loss for words* i.e. they did not know what to say.

lost [lɔst] past of **lose.**

lot [lɔt] *nc* **1.** something which happens to somebody by chance; destiny; fate. *Poverty was his lot in life.* **2.** one of a number of objects used to decide something by chance (e.g. a piece of paper with a number or one's name). **3.** number of articles sold together at an auction sale. **4.** number of articles of the same kind. *The class has been given a new lot of reading books.* **5.** piece of land. *He is looking for an empty lot on which to build his house.*
cast/draw lots see **cast**[1].
fall to one's lot happen to one by chance. *It fell to my lot to speak first.*
cast/throw in one's lot with somebody join somebody and help him whatever happens. *He has thrown in his lot with those who want a change of government.*
a lot of, lots of a great amount or number of. *He has a lot/lots of money.* A lot/lots

of people came. We see a lot of him these days i.e. we see him often. Also *adv*: *He is a lot/lots fatter.*
Note: *lots* is usu. *informal*; *a lot* is normal.
lots and lots of a very great amount or number of. (*informal*).
the lot all there is; everything. *He ate the lot. I hate the lot of them* i.e. all of them. (*informal*).

loth [louθ] *pred adj* see **loath.**

lotion ['louʃən] *nc* type of liquid rubbed on the skin or hair to cure a disease or improve one's appearance. *Women use many kinds of skin lotion.*

lottery ['lɔtəri] *nc* **1.** method of giving prizes to a few persons out of the many who have bought numbered tickets. The winning tickets are chosen by chance. **2.** anything which is decided by chance. *Life is a lottery.*

lotus ['loutəs] *nc* type of water lily.
'lotus eater person who enjoys life and does no work (from a Greek legend about a people who lived in this way because they ate the fruit of the lotus).

loud [laud] *adj* **1.** making a great sound; easy to hear. *The loud noise of the guns could be heard for miles. He spoke in a loud voice.* **2.** (with reference to colours or behaviour) too bright or too noisy. *He was wearing a loud tie.*
loud, loudly *adv*: *He should not speak so loud/loudly. He was very loudly dressed.* **loudness** *nu.*
'loud-'mouthed *adj* noisy and boastful.
'loud'speaker 1. device which produces the sound in a radio or television set etc. **2.** apparatus which increases the sound of a voice sent by wire from a central point (e.g. in a large railway station or factory).

lounge [laundʒ] *vi* sit or stand lazily; spend time idly. *The pupils were lounging about the playground.* Also *nc* **1.** act of lounging. **2.** place where one can sit or rest (e.g. in a hotel, an airport etc). **3.** sitting room in a house.
'lounge suit (mainly *Brit*) man's suit of jacket and trousers, with or without a waistcoat, for everyday use.

lour, lower ['lauə*] *vt/i* **1.** (with **at, on, upon**) (with reference to persons) look at in a threatening way; frown. **2.** (with reference to the sky) be dark and threatening. **loweringly** *adv.*

louse [laus] *nc* type of small insect which lives on the skin and in the hair of animals and humans. *pl* **lice** [lais].
lousy ['lauzi] *adj* **1.** having lice. **2.** bad. *He made a lousy speech.* (*informal* in sense **2.**). **lousily** *adv.* **lousiness** *nu.*

lout [laut] *nc* tough, ill-mannered man. **loutish** *adj.*

louvre ['luːvə*] (*US* **louver**) *nc* **1.** board with horizontal strips of wood across, slanted to allow ventilation but keep out rain. **2.** window or other opening covered with louvre boards.

love [lʌv] **1.** *nu* fondness; affection; very great liking. *He always had a love of/for sport. It is easy to understand their love for their parents.* **2.** *nu* fondness between a man and a woman; sexual desire. *They are in love with each other.* **3.** *nc* somebody/something which causes fondness. *She was his one and only love. Hunting is their great love.* **4.** *nu* (sport esp. tennis) no score; nil. *The score is now 40-love* i.e. 40 points to nil; *love all* i.e. no score by either side. Also *vt*: *He loves his parents. He loves football. They love each other.* **lovable** *adj.*
lover *nc* (usu. with reference to a man if sense is **love 2.**) person who loves.
loveless *adj* without love; not loved. **lovelessly** *adv.*
'love affair (usu. with reference to sexual relationships between those who are not married to each other) period when a man and woman are very much in love with each other.
'lovebird 1. type of small, brightly-coloured bird. **2.** man or woman who is in love. (*informal* in sense **2.**).
'love child child whose parents are not married to each other (*o.f.*).
'love letter letter about love sent to somebody with whom one is in love.
'love match marriage between two people who are very much in love with each other.
'lovesick *adj* weak and sad because of love.
'lovesong song telling about love.
'love story story which is mainly about love between a man and a woman.
fall in love (with someone) see **fall[2]**.
give/send somebody one's love give/send greetings of love to somebody. *When you see my sister, give her my love.*
labour of love work which one likes doing without any thought of reward or payment.
make love to somebody engage in acts of love (in sense **2.**) with somebody. **'love-making** *nu.*
not to be had for love or money not to be had by any means. (*informal*).

lovely ['lʌvli] *adj* beautiful; delightful. *She is a lovely woman. We are having lovely weather just now.* **loveliness** *nu.*

loving ['lʌviŋ] *adj* feeling love. **lovingly** *adv.*
'loving 'kindness great kindness because of love: *a mother's loving kindness to her children.*

low[1] [lou] *adj* **1.** near the ground; not high. *A low shelf ran round the room. Behind there was a row of low houses.* **2.** (with reference to sound, light, pressure, temperature etc) not great. *He spoke in a low voice. The lamp was low. In winter temperatures are low.* **3.** below, or less than, usual. *It was a very low tide. We bought it at a low price.* **4.** (with reference to persons) poor; without social position; not important. *He has a low position in the factory.* **5.** rough; coarse. *He enjoys low company. They have low manners and a low sense of humour. comparative* **lower.** *superlative* **lowest.** Also *nc* low level. *Temperatures reached a new low* i.e. the lowest level so far. Also *adv*: *We bought low and sold high. You must speak low. comparative* **lower.** *superlative* **lowest.**
'low'born *adj* born of poor parents.
'low'bred *adj* having coarse manners.
'lowbrow *adj* without culture; without interest in serious art, literature, music etc. Also *nc*: *A university is not the place for lowbrows.* (*informal*).
'Low 'Church (esp. in the Church of England) type of church which has a simpler service and organization.
'low 'comedy comedy in which there are many amusing actions and easily understood jokes.
'low-'down *adj* mean; deceiving: *a low-down trick.* (*informal*).
the 'low-down *nu* (*US*) full information. *Give me the low-down on him.* (*informal*).
'lowlands *npl* country which is low and flat

compared with the hills round it.
lowlander *nc* person who lives in lowlands.
'low 'spirits *npl* unhappiness; depression. *He has been in low spirits since his father's death.* **low-spirited** *adj.* **low-spiritedly** *adv.*
the lower deck (navy) sailors who are not officers.
bring low weaken in health, power etc. *War and famine have brought the country low.*
feel low feel unhappy or depressed.
high and low see **high.**
lay low defeat; make helpless. *He was able to lay all his enemies low. He has been laid low by/with fever.*
lie low **1.** lie down close to the ground. **2.** keep hidden or out of the way. *The thieves are lying low until they can leave the country.*
run low become scarce; be almost finished. *Before the end of the holiday my money was running very low.*

low[2] [lou] *vi* make the sound of a cow. *Can you hear the cattle lowing?* Also *nu.*

lower[1] ['louə*] *vt/i* **1.** become, cause to become, less high; come or bring down. *They lowered the flag at sunset. This shop has lowered its prices.* **2.** make less or weaker. *You must lower your voice. I lowered the pressure in the tyre.*
lower away lower a boat or sail.
lower oneself do something wrong or shameful. *I hope you will not lower yourself to such bad behaviour. They lowered themselves by telling lies.*

lower[2] ['lauə*] *vt/i* see **lour.**

lowly ['louli] *adj* low in social position; not proud; simple. **lowliness** *nu.*

loyal ['lɔiəl] *adj* faithful. *He is a loyal friend. We should be loyal to our country.* (*opp* **disloyal**). **loyally** *adv.* **loyalty** *nc/u.*
loyalist *nc* person who is loyal (esp. to the lawful government).

lozenge ['lɔzindʒ] *nc* **1.** four-sided figure shaped like this ◇ **2.** small tablet containing medicine which is sucked (usu. to cure a sore throat).

lubricate ['lu:brikeit] *vt* **1.** make an apparatus or machine work more smoothly by putting oil or grease on it. *You should lubricate the wheels of your bicycle once a month.* **2.** make anything happen more smoothly. **lubrication** [lubri'keiʃən] *nu.*
lubricant ['lu:brikənt] *nc* substance which lubricates.

lucerne [lu'sə:n] *nu* type of grass (used esp. for feeding animals).

lucid ['lu:sid] *adj* **1.** clear; easily understood. *He gave a lucid description of what happened. He has a lucid brain* i.e. one that thinks clearly. **2.** sane; fully conscious (usu. between periods of insanity or unconsciousness): *in his lucid moments. He was lucid for a few minutes before he lost his senses again.* **lucidly** *adv.* **lucidity** [lu:'siditi] *nu.*

luck [lʌk] *nu* chance, either good or bad; something which happens by chance to somebody. *It was luck that saved his life. Our luck made us lose. They have good/bad luck in all they do.*
lucky *adj* bringing, having good luck. *You are a lucky man.* (*opp* **unlucky**).
luckily *adv*: *Luckily I was able to help him.*
luckless *adj* without good luck.
be down on one's luck be in trouble; be without money. (*informal*).
be in luck have good luck. (*informal*).
be out of luck have bad luck. *When we at last reached the railway station we were out of luck. The train had gone.* (*informal*).
for luck hoping that something will bring good luck. *She wears this ring for luck.*
push one's luck do something which is more likely to fail than to succeed. *You're pushing your luck in doing 50 mph down this street* i.e. the police might stop you.
try one's luck take a chance, hoping for good luck or success. *He tried his luck at farming and made a lot of money.* (*informal*).

lucre ['lu:kə*] *nu* profit; gain.
lucrative ['lu:krətiv] *adj* profitable. **lucratively** *adv.*
filthy lucre money. (*informal*).

ludicrous ['lu:dikrəs] *adj* causing laughter; very foolish. **ludicrously** *adv.* **ludicrousness** *nu.*

ludo ['lu:dou] *nu* children's game played on a specially marked board with counters and dice.

luff [lʌf] *vt/i* sail towards the wind; turn the front of a ship towards the wind.

lug[1] [lʌg] *vt* pull with force; drag roughly or with effort. *They lugged the boxes across the field. past* **lugged.**

lug[2] [lʌg] *nc* **1.** ear. (*informal*) (Also **lughole**). **2.** anything projecting like an ear (esp. to keep a piece of machinery in place).

lug[3] [lʌg] *nc* see **lugsail.**

luggage ['lʌgidʒ] *nu* a traveller's bags, boxes etc. (esp. *US* **baggage**).

lugger ['lʌgə*] *nc* type of small sailing ship with lugsails.

lugsail, lug ['lʌg(sl)] *nc* four-sided sail.

lugubrious [lu'gu:briəs] *adj* sad-looking; gloomy. **lugubriously** *adv.* **lugubriousness** *nu.*

lukewarm ['lu:k'wɔ:m] *adj* **1.** (with reference to liquids) slightly warm. **2.** (with reference to feelings, behaviour etc) indifferent; weak. *They have only a lukewarm interest in the plan.* **lukewarmly** *adv.*

lull [lʌl] *vt/i* become, cause to become, quiet slowly. *During the night the wind lulled. She lulled the baby to sleep.* Also *nc* period of quiet, in a storm or when there is noise and activity. *There was a lull in the storm. During the holidays there was a lull in business.*

lullaby ['lʌləbai] *nc* song sung to a child to lull it to sleep.

lumbago [lʌm'beigou] *nu* illness which causes pain in the muscles of the lower back above the hips.

lumbar ['lʌmbə*] *adj* of the lower part of the back above the hips.

lumber ['lʌmbə*] *nu* **1.** things which are not in use and are not needed but are kept until they are. **2.** wood that has been roughly cut. Also *vt* **1.** (often with **up**) fill with lumber (in sense **1.**). **2.** give someone something unpleasant. *I was lumbered with this job.*
'lumberjack, 'lumberman man who cuts down trees or prepares lumber (in sense **2.**).
'lumber mill place where lumber is cut.
'lumber room room where lumber (in sense **1.**) is kept.
'lumberyard place where lumber (in sense **2.**) is kept.

luminary ['lu:minəri] *nc* **1.** body which gives light in the sky (e.g. sun, moon or star). **2.** person who is famous (esp. for his learning).

luminous ['lu:minəs] *adj* giving light; shining; clear. *The clock has a luminous face* i.e. the numbers and hands shine in the dark. **luminously** *adv.* **luminosity** [lumi'nɔsiti] *nu.*

lump [lʌmp] *nc* **1.** small piece of matter without a definite shape: *a lump of bread; a few lumps of coal.* **2.** swelling on the body. *There is a lump on his head where it hit the wall.* **3.** stupid, clumsy person. (*informal* in sense **3.**). Also *vt* (usu. with **together**) put together (in a lump); consider as being the same as. *We lumped all our money together to buy our teacher a present. We can't lump all these different things together.* Also *vt* put up with. *If you don't like it you can lump it.* (*informal*). **lumpy** *adj.*

'**lump** '**sum** payment in one single amount, not in instalments.

lunacy ['lu:nəsi] *nu* see **lunatic.**

lunar ['lu:nə*] *adj* of the moon.

lunar month see **month.**

lunatic ['lu:nətik] *adj* mad. Also *nc* person who is mad.

lunacy ['lu:nəsi] *nu* madness.

lunch [lʌntʃ] *nc/u* meal taken in the middle of the day. *He will be back from lunch soon.* Also *vt/i* have, give, lunch. *We usually lunch at home. They lunched us at the hotel.*

lung [lʌŋ] *nc* one of the two organs of breathing in animals and humans.

'**lungfish** type of fish which has lungs as well as gills.

'**lungpower** strength of the voice.

lunge [lʌndʒ] *nc* quick, forward movement of the arm and body (esp. with a sword or other weapon). Also *vt/i*: *He lunged at me with his stick.*

lurch[1] [lə:tʃ] *nc* sudden movement to one side. *The ship gave a lurch.* Also *vi* move with a lurch; stagger. *The ship lurched through the rough sea. The beaten boxer lurched into his corner after the fight.*

lurch[2] [lə:tʃ] *nu* only in **leave somebody in the lurch** i.e. leave somebody when he needs help. (*informal*).

lure [luə*] *nc* **1.** something bright used to attract wild birds and animals. **2.** anything which attracts. *The lure of gold caused them to explore the country. He left home because of the lures of life in the city.* Also *vt* attract. *Life in the city lured him from home.*

lurid ['luərid] *adj* **1.** brightly coloured (esp. light yellow like a flame). **2.** shocking and unpleasant. *He told us many lurid stories about the war.* **luridly** *adv.* **luridness** *nu.*

lurk [lə:k] *vi* stay hidden (usu. in order to attack). *There is a lion lurking somewhere in the long grass.*

luscious ['lʌʃəs] *adj* **1.** very sweet and pleasant to eat: *luscious fruit.* **2.** very attractive: *a luscious blonde.* **lusciously** *adv.* **lusciousness** *nu.*

lush [lʌʃ] *adj* **1.** (with reference to plants and grass) fresh and growing thickly. **2.** showing an abundance of anything; rich: *lush surroundings.* (*informal* in sense **2.**).

lust [lʌst] *nc/u* sexual desire; any strong desire for something. *He is filled with a lust for power.* Also *vi* have lust. *He lusts for/after power.* **lustful** *adj.* **lustfully** *adv.* **lustfulness** *nu.*

lustre ['lʌstə*] (*US* **luster**) *nu* **1.** brightness (e.g. of polished metal, smooth cloth etc). **2.** glory. *His great books have added lustre to the university where he teaches.* **lustrous** ['lʌstrəs] *adj.* **lustrously** *adv.* **lustrousness** *nu.*

lusty ['lʌsti] *adj* strong; vigorous. **lustily** *adv.* **lustiness** *nu.*

lute [lu:t] *nc* type of old stringed musical instrument like a guitar.

lutanist ['lu:tənist] *nc* lute player.

luxuriant [lʌg'zjuəriənt] *adj* growing thickly; in great quantity. *After the rains the grass is luxuriant.* **luxuriantly** *adv.* **luxuriance** *nu.*

luxuriate [lʌg'zjuərieit] *vi* enjoy very much; take great pleasure in. *After the long walk he luxuriated in a hot bath.*

luxury ['lʌkʃəri] **1.** *nu* enjoyment of pleasures and possessions which only great wealth can obtain. *The king lived in luxury.* **2.** *nc* something expensive and enjoyable but not necessary. *In some places white bread is a luxury.* Also *adj*: *a luxury hotel* i.e. a very comfortable but expensive one.

luxurious [lʌg'zjuəriəs] *adj* having luxuries; very comfortable or pleasing, but expensive. *He leads a luxurious life. The carpets in the house are luxurious.* **luxuriousness** *nu.*

lyceum [lai'siəm] *nc* lecture hall; place where learned societies meet.

lying ['laiiŋ] *pres part* of **lie**[1].

lymph [limf] *nu* watery fluid of the body.

lymphatic [lim'fætik] *adj* **1.** of lymph. **2.** (with reference to persons) slow (esp. in thinking).

lynch [lintʃ] *vt* kill without bringing to a court of law. *The angry mob lynched the criminal.*

'**lynch law** killing without bringing to a court of law.

lynx [links] *nc* type of wild animal like a large cat with tufts of hair on its ears.

'**lynx-eyed** *adj* having eyes like a lynx i.e. eyes able to see small details or small movements.

lyre ['laiə*] *nc* type of small harp used by the ancient Greeks.

'**lyrebird** type of bird with a tail shaped like a lyre, found in Australia.

lyric ['lirik] *nc* poem sung to music; short poem full of emotion. Also *adj*: *lyric verses.*

lyrics *npl* words of a song (usu. a pop song).

lyrical *adj* **1.** lyric. **2.** full of emotion. *When he speaks about his own country he becomes lyrical.*

M

ma [mɑː] *nc* child's name for **mother.** (*informal*).
ma'am [mæm] *n* short form of **madam.**
mac [mæk] *nc* short form of **mackintosh.**
plastic mac kind of very light coat used to keep out rain; it can usu. be folded up and carried in a person's hand or pocket when he is not using it.
macabre [mə'kɑːbr] *adj* filling one with fear or horror. *The film I saw last night frightened me; it had some very macabre scenes. He has a macabre sense of humour* i.e. he gets amusement from frightening or horrifying subjects.
macadam [mə'kædəm] *nu* tar containing small broken stones, used for making road surfaces.
macadamize *vt* put a macadam surface on a road. **macadamized** *adj.*
macaroni [mækə'rouni] *nu* mixture of wheat flour made into long tubes and cooked for eating (originally an Italian dish).
macaw [mə'kɔː] *nc* type of parrot with bright feathers and a harsh voice.
mace[1] [meis] *nc* kind of rod carried in the presence of a high official (e.g. the Mayor of a town) to show the importance of his position.

mace[1]

mace[2] [meis] *nu* kind of spice made from nutmeg.
machination [mæki'neiʃən] *nc* (often *pl*) sinister and unfair arrangement or plan.
machine [mə'ʃiːn] *nc* something which has been made with moving parts to do a certain job (e.g. a *printing machine*, a *sewing machine*) and which usu. works by electricity or steam.
machinery [mə'ʃiːnəri] *nu* **1.** machines in general. **2.** parts of a machine. **3.** way a thing is run. *In this lesson we are going to study the machinery of government.*
machinist *nc* person who works a machine.
ma'chine gun gun which fires without stopping while the trigger is pressed.
ma'chine-'made *adj* made by a machine and not by hand.
mackerel ['mækrl] *nc* small fish found in the Atlantic and used as food. *pl* **mackerel** or **mackerels.**
mackintosh ['mækintɔʃ] *nc* coat made to keep out rain.
mad [mæd] *adj* **1.** not having the power to think normally. *When he heard of his son's death, the poor old man went mad.* **2.** very stupid or wild. *It was a mad idea to climb the mountain in this bad weather.* **3.** very angry or upset. *He is mad at losing all his money.* (*informal* in sense **3.**). **madly** *adv.* **madness** *nu.*
madden *vt* make somebody angry. *Your insolent attitude maddened him.* **maddening** *adj.* **maddeningly** *adv.*
'madman person who is mad.
drive someone mad make someone mad.
go mad become mad (in sense **1.**).
like mad very fast; very energetically: *work like mad.* (*informal*).
madam [mə'dæm] *n* respectful way of speaking to a woman (esp. if you do not know her name). It is therefore very often used by shop assistants etc.
Dear Madam expression often used as a way of beginning a formal letter, whether you know the person's name or not.
Madame *n* Mrs (often used before the names of foreign women e.g. *Madame de Gaulle.* In case of doubt use Mrs).
made [meid] past of **make**[1].
Madonna [mə'dɔnə] *nc* **1.** Mary, the Mother of Jesus Christ. **2.** picture or statue of the Mother of Christ.
madrigal ['mædrigl] *nc* type of song or poem, often about love.
maelstrom ['meilstroum] *nc* **1.** dangerous part of the sea where the water goes round very fast; whirlpool. (rather *o.f.*). **2.** any dangerous or violent situation. *He lived through the maelstrom of the revolution.*
maestro ['maistrou] *nc* great composer, teacher or conductor of music. *pl* **maestros.**
magazine [mægə'ziːn] *nc* **1.** printed collection of short stories, articles, photographs etc appearing regularly (usu. every week or month). *He made some money from writing short stories for magazines.* **2.** place where guns, rifles, bullets etc are kept. *A lot of damage was caused when the magazine exploded.* **3.** part of a gun where the bullets are kept before they are fired.
magenta [mə'dʒentə] *nu* deep red colour. Also *adj.*
maggot ['mægət] *nc* fly or insect in its early stages, often found in bad meat. **maggoty** *adj.*
magic ['mædʒik] *nu* **1.** ability which people are sometimes supposed to have to make things happen through charms, spirits etc. *The villagers thought that the young man had been killed by magic.* **2.** use of stage tricks to make things happen that seem impossible. *In a display of magic, the performer pulled a rabbit out of a hat.* **3.** special charm or influence: *the magic of his words.* **magical** *adj.* **magically** *adv.*
magician [mə'dʒiʃən] *nc* person who uses magic.
magic lantern apparatus for showing still pictures enlarged onto a screen (*o.f.*)
magistrate ['mædʒistreit] *nc* person appointed to act as a judge in the lower

courts, Justice of the Peace (J.P.).

magisterial [mædʒis'tiəriəl] *adj* as in **magisterial manner** i.e. a way of behaving which shows that one is in a position of authority.

magnanimous [mæg'næniməs] *adj* generous and noble. *After winning the war, the magnanimous victor set all his prisoners free.*

magnanimously *adv.*

magnanimity [mægnə'nimiti] *nu* generosity.

magnate ['mægneit] *nc* somebody who is rich or important (esp. in business). *He started off poor but he eventually became an oil magnate.*

magnesia [mæg'ni:ziə] *nu* white powder used to cure mild stomach complaints.

magnesium [mæg'ni:ziəm] *nu* silver-white metal which burns with a very bright light (Mg).

magnet ['mægnit] *nc* **1.** piece of metal (usu. iron or steel and often shaped like a horseshoe) which is able to attract another piece of metal. **2.** anything that attracts.

magnetic [məg'netik] *adj* **1.** acting like, produced by, a magnet: *magnetic field; magnetic needle* i.e. one which points north in a compass. **2.** attractive. *He has a magnetic personality.*

magnetism *nu* **1.** science of magnets and their properties. **2.** attractiveness. *He is a man of great personal magnetism* i.e. people are attracted to him.

magnetize *vt* make magnetic; make into a magnet.

magnetic tape tape used to record sound by means of magnetism, used in a tape recorder.

magnificent [mæg'nifisnt] *adj* **1.** wonderful, excellent. *He is a magnificent athlete.* **2.** of splendid appearance. *In their full uniforms the soldiers looked magnificent.*

magnificently *adv.*

magnificence *nu* **1.** excellence. *You do not appreciate the magnificence of their achievement* i.e. you do not understand how wonderful their achievement is. **2.** splendid appearance. *We had to admire the magnificence of the court.*

magnify ['mægnifai] *vt* **1.** make something appear bigger (with a special lens). *The microscope magnified the object one hundred times.* **2.** make something seem more important. *He tried to magnify the part he played in the battle.* **magnification** [mægnifi'keiʃən] *nc/u.*

'magnifying glass curved piece of glass used to magnify something.

magniloquent [mæg'niləkwənt] *adj* using, or made up of, very important-sounding words. *He made a magniloquent speech.*

magniloquence *nu.*

magnitude ['mægnitju:d] *nc/u* largeness or amount. *It is a problem of some magnitude* i.e. a large problem.

magnolia [mæg'nouliə] *nc* tree which has beautiful, large, sweet-smelling flowers.

magpie ['mægpai] *nc* noisy black and white bird of the crow family, which sometimes steals small bright objects.

maharajah [mɑ:hə'rɑ:dʒə] *nc* Indian prince.

mahatma [mə'hɑ:tmə] *nc* Hindu holy man.

mahogany [mə'hɔgəni] **1.** *nc* tropical tree found esp. in America. **2.** *nu* hard wood from this tree, often used for furniture. **3.** *nu* colour of this wood, dark reddish-brown. Also *adj.*

maid [meid] *nc* **1.** woman servant. **2.** girl (*o.f.* in sense **2.**).

old maid **1.** elderly lady who has not married and is unlikely to marry. **2.** fussy person who becomes annoyed about unimportant things. (*informal*).

maiden ['meidn] *nc* girl, unmarried woman; virgin. Also *adj.* (both *o.f.*).

maidenly *adj* like a maiden; modest; shy.

'maiden 'aunt aunt who is not married. (rather *o.f.*).

'maiden name woman's surname before her marriage.

'maiden 'speech first speech (e.g. in Parliament).

'maiden 'voyage first voyage of a ship.

mail[1] [meil] *nu* **1.** anything sent by post (e.g. letters and parcels). *The mail is sorted into bags.* **2.** delivery of mail. *Has the morning mail arrived yet?* **3.** postal service. *Send it by mail.* Also *vt*: *Please mail these letters for me.*

'mailbag sack or bag used for holding mail.

'mailbox (*US*) box to which letters are delivered by the post office.

'mail coach (in former times) horse-drawn coach used to deliver mail.

'mailman (*US*) person who delivers mail. (*Brit* **postman**).

'mail-order method of buying goods by post instead of visiting a shop.

'mail train train used for carrying mail.

'mail van type of vehicle used for carrying mail.

'mailing list list of people to whom letters etc are to be sent regularly (e.g. by a business).

'airmail letters etc delivered by plane.

mail[2] [meil] *nu* (in former times) armour consisting of small metal rings or plates worn by soldiers to protect their bodies: *chain mail; coat of mail.*

maim [meim] *vt* injure in such a way that a part of the body becomes useless or partly useless; disable, cripple. *The accident maimed him and he was unable to work.*

main[1] [mein] *adj* most important. *With him, pleasure is the main thing in life! Traffic is busiest on the main road.*

mainly *adv* chiefly, mostly.

'mainland **1.** a continent or country without its islands (e.g. *the mainland of Scotland*). **2.** the largest area of land near an island. *The ship left the island and headed for the mainland.*

in the main mostly.

have an eye to the main chance look for opportunities to gain advantages for oneself.

main[2] [mein] *nc* large pipe for carrying gas, water etc (e.g. *gas main*).

the mains *npl* chief wires or pipes bringing electricity, water etc into a house. *The electricity was switched off at the mains.*

maintain [mein'tein] *vt* **1.** keep in good condition; repair. *The Town Council maintains the roads.* **2.** continue with, keep unchanged. *The two countries maintained friendly relations in spite of their differences* i.e. they remained friendly. **3.** look after, feed etc. *He has to maintain a wife and five children.* **4.** keep an opinion, belief etc in spite of contradiction. *I still maintain that I am right and you are wrong.*

maintenance ['meintənəns] *nu* **1.** keeping something (esp. a machine etc) in good condition. **2.** what is needed to keep a person alive. *He is separated from his wife,* *but he has to give her maintenance* i.e. give her an amount of money regularly.

maisonette [meizə'net] *nc* small house, often part of a larger building.

maize [meiz] *nu* kind of grain plant.

majesty ['mædʒisti] *nu* quality of causing one to feel humble or impressed, as in the appearance of a king or queen or the height of mountains etc. *We could not help being impressed by the majesty of the mountains, as they rose high above us.* **majestic** [mə'dʒestik] *adj.* **majestically** *adv.*

His (Her, Your) Majesty respectful way of referring to or speaking to a king or queen.

major ['meidʒə*] *adj* great, important. *Road accidents are a major problem these days. He is having a major operation* i.e. a serious operation. *This dispute will be settled by the major powers* i.e. the larger, more powerful countries. (*opp* **minor**). Also *nc* (military) officer of middle rank.

majority [mə'dʒɔriti] *nc* **1.** greater number; more than half. *The majority of households in Britain now have television.* (*opp* **minority**). **2.** difference between the number of votes given to the winning party or candidate in an election and the next party or candidate. *The party I support has won by a majority of 264 votes.* **3.** age after which one can vote etc (in Britain 18): *reach one's majority.*

'major-'general *nc* army officer under a lieutenant-general, but above a brigadier. *pl* **major-generals.**

make[1] [meik] *vt* **1.** cause to exist (either out of nothing or by putting things together or changing them in some way). *God made the world. This factory makes cars. You can make bread from flour* i.e. flour is one of the things used in making bread. *That house is made of stone* i.e. stone is one of the raw materials. **2.** cause to be. *Your answer made him angry* i.e. he is angry because of what you have said. *The stones at the bottom of the bag made it heavy.* **3.** force somebody/something to do something. *The robbers made me give them all my money. They made the naughty boy go to bed early.*

Note: 1. in this kind of sentence, it is wrong to use *to* with the verb that comes after *make. He made me stand up.* 2. if the sentence is passive, *to* is used in this way: *I was made to stand up.*

4. earn, get. *He makes plenty of money. He makes £20 a week.* **5.** be the same as, equal. *One hundred centimetres make one metre.* **6.** become. *That student will make a good teacher. past* **made** [meid].

maker *nc* person/thing that makes something. (Often in compounds e.g. *shoemaker*).

make for something 1. go towards. *The ship is making for the nearest port.* **2.** tend to produce. *That makes for good relations.*

make of someone/something think of. *What do you make of him?* i.e. what is your opinion of him? (*informal*).

make off go away; escape. *The boys made off when we shouted at them. The thief made off with our money.*

make something out write out. *Make out a cheque for what you owe me.*

make someone/something out be able to see or understand. *Can you make out what that object is on the other side of the valley? Can you make out what he is saying?*

make something up 1. invent; think up; create. *The teacher asked the children to make up a story about a trip to the moon. It's not true; he made it up.* **2.** put things together in some way (e.g. into a parcel, bundle etc). *Your mother has made up a parcel of toys for you.* **3.** stop a quarrel. *They made it up.*

make up (one's face etc) put liquid, powder etc on the face in order to improve one's appearance. *These days many girls make up when they are still quite young. She made up her face.* **'make-up** *nu.*

make up for compensate for. *This payment should make up for the time you have wasted.*

make amends show that one is sorry for a misdeed etc by doing something to improve things.

make a bed arrange the coverings on a bed. *All pupils must make their beds immediately after getting up.*

make certain 1. check that something is true, correct etc. *Always make certain that your facts are right.* **2.** not leave something to chance or luck. *Make certain that you get good seats. Make certain of a place in the bus going back before you leave the station* i.e. reserve or book a place.

make a clean breast of something confess everything; tell somebody all about the wrong one has done. (*informal*).

make a clean sweep of something remove completely. *The headmaster has made a clean sweep of the old rules and issued new ones.*

make any difference (usu. in questions or in the *negative*) matter, be important. *Will it make any difference to you if I give you the book tomorrow?* i.e. can I give it to you tomorrow? (*informal*).

make (something) do, make do with something use something although there is something else one would really prefer. *We don't have a new knife, so we'll just have to make this one do. They are not rich, but they make do on what they have. The chairs have not arrived yet, so we shall have to make do with these boxes.*

make/pull a face at someone twist one's face into a strange or amusing shape.

make a fool of somebody cause somebody to seem silly. *It is very cruel of these boys to make a fool of that old man.*

make friends (with someone) become friendly with. *Have you made friends with anybody in your new school? John makes friends easily* i.e. he soon becomes popular.

make fun of laugh at; get amusement from. *They made fun of my mistakes when I tried to speak English.*

make haste hurry (*o.f.*).

make it 1. (usu. with reference to time, distance etc) judge or estimate, either by guessing or using some means of measurement. *What time do you make it?* i.e. what time is it on your watch? *I make it one o'clock. How far do you make it to the beach?* **2.** reach; manage to arrive (esp. where there is some difficulty involved); be successful. *Do you think the ship will make it to the shore? We're too late; I don't think we'll make it. After years as an unsuccessful businessman he's finally made it.* (*informal*).

make a living earn enough to pay for what one needs. *He makes his living from mending shoes.*

make a man of someone make a person strong, brave, independent etc. *You ought to tell your son to join the army; it would make a man of him.*

make mischief cause trouble.

make a mountain out of a molehill make

fuss about things which are not really very important. (*informal*).
make a name for oneself become famous through one's own efforts. *He made a name for himself as a writer.*
make something ready prepare; arrange. *Make these beds ready for our visitors.*
make oneself scarce go away. *When the naughty boy saw his father coming, he soon made himself scarce.* (*informal*).
make a search for look for something (esp. in an organized way). *The police are making a search for the body of the man who disappeared.*
make short work of something quickly finish off. *The children made short work of the sweets.* (*informal*).
make great strides improve a great deal. *Since he started taking care with his work, John has been making great strides.* (*informal*).
make use of use. *Do you want to make use of this brush?*
make war (usu. with reference to countries) start fighting. *The task of the United Nations is to stop countries making war with one another.*
make one's way go (usu. slowly or in spite of some difficulty). *I made my way carefully down the narrow staircase.*

make[2] [meik] *nc* type of manufacture, style, brand.

make-believe ['meikbiliːv] *nu* things which are imaginary. *That's nothing but make-believe.*

makeshift ['meikʃift] *adj* used as a substitute for the real thing. *They used the boxes as makeshift chairs.*

mal- [mæl] *prefix* bad, badly (e.g. **malformed, malpractice**).

maladjusted [mælə'dʒʌstid] *adj* mentally or emotionally handicapped in a way that prevents one behaving normally: *school for maladjusted children.*

malady ['mælədi] *nc* disease, illness (*o.f.* – use **disease**).

malaria [mə'lɛəriə] *nu* disease caused by the bite of a certain kind of mosquito.
malarial *adj* having to do with malaria: *malarial conditions* i.e. conditions which make it easy to catch malaria.

malcontent ['mælkəntent] *nc* person who is not happy because he feels he has been unjustly treated.

male [meil] *adj* **1.** of the sex that does not give birth to young. *A bull is a male animal, a cow is not.* **2.** for or of men: *a male choir* i.e. a choir made up of men. (*opp* **female**). Also *nc* male person, animal etc.

malefactor ['mælifæktə*] *nc* person who commits a crime or does evil to others. (Usu. **criminal**).

malevolent [mə'levəlnt] *adj* wanting to do harm to other people. *He gave me a malevolent look* i.e. by the way he looked at me, I knew he wanted to do me harm. **malevolently** *adv.* **malevolence** *nu.*

malformation ['mælfɔː'meiʃən] *nc/u* (often of the human body) state of being badly made or shaped.
malformed [mæl'fɔːmd] *adj* badly made or shaped.

malice ['mælis] *nu* unfriendly feelings.
malicious [mə'liʃəs] *adj.* **maliciously** *adv.*
bear someone no malice have no wish to harm a person in spite of the harm he has done you.

malign [mə'lain] *vt* purposely say untrue and bad things about somebody. *They maligned her character as much as they could.* Also *adj* having an evil effect: *a malign action.*
malignity [mə'ligniti] *nu* **1.** wishing people ill. **2.** (of diseases etc) harmful nature.
malignant [mə'lignənt] *adj* **1.** (with reference to people or their actions) wishing or resulting in harm to others. *He took a malignant delight in our misfortunes.* **2.** (with reference to diseases) able to cause death: *a malignant growth on the body.* **malignantly** *adv.* **malignancy** *nc/u.*

malinger [mə'liŋgə*] *vi* pretend to be ill to avoid duty or work. *He malingered to avoid being sent to school.* **malingerer** *nc.*

mallard ['mælaːd] *nc* common type of wild duck. *pl* **mallard** or **mallards.**

malleable ['mæliəbl] *adj* **1.** (usu. with reference to metals) able to be given a new shape (e.g. by hammering or rolling). *Gold is much more malleable than iron.* **2.** (with reference to a person or his character) able to be changed in some way (e.g. by training). *Younger people are usually more malleable than older people.* **malleability** [mæliə'biliti] *nu.*

mallet ['mælit] *nc* hammer with a wooden head.

malnutrition [mælnju'triʃən] *nu* poor state of health caused by the lack of enough food or the right kind of food. *The people in this area suffer from malnutrition.*

malodorous [mæ'loudərəs] *adj* with a bad smell.

malpractice ['mæl'præktis] *nc/u* (legal) not doing one's duty, or doing one's job dishonestly for personal gain. *The doctor who had neglected his patient was found guilty of malpractice.*

malt [mɔːlt] *nu* grain (e.g. barley, oats) specially treated in making beer or spirits.

maltreat [mæl'triːt] *vt* behave cruelly towards someone. *This man is accused of maltreating his children.* **maltreatment** *nu.*

mamma [mə'maː] *n* child's name for **mother** (*o.f.*).

mammal ['mæml] *nc* animal of the kind whose young take milk from the mother's breast. *Dogs and cats are mammals.*

mammon ['mæmən] *nu* wealth (used when wealth is regarded as a bad thing). *People should worship God, not mammon.*

mammoth ['mæməθ] *nc* large kind of elephant which lived a long time ago. Also *adj* very large: *a mammoth parade.*

man [mæn] **1.** *nc* male person who has grown up i.e. not a woman, girl or boy. *Save the women and children first and let the men out afterwards.* **2.** *n sing* (often **Man**) the human race. *What wonderful things Man has achieved!*
Note: in this sense use the word in the *sing* with no article.
3. *nc* servant or worker. *You will have to dismiss all your men.* **4.** *nc* piece used in certain games (e.g. draughts). *pl* **men** [men]. Also *vt* put men (esp. soldiers or sailors) where they are needed. *An order was given to man the boats. past* **manned.**
manly *adj* brave, strong etc, having the qualities a man is supposed to have. (*opp* **unmanly**). **manliness** *nu.*
manfully *adv* bravely; with determination. *The drowning boy struggled manfully against the waves.*
manhood *nu* **1.** state of being a grown-up male. *You have now entered into manhood*

i.e. you are an adult. **2.** the qualities that a man is supposed to have (e.g. bravery etc). *Their leader told them to prove their manhood by fighting well.*

'man about 'town person who lives well in an expensive manner, going to the best restaurants etc.

'man'kind all human beings. *The scientist's discoveries were of great help to mankind.*

'manpower men needed to do a certain job (e.g. workers). *There is a shortage of manpower in many of our industries.*

'manservant *nc* man who is paid to work in a house, or to attend on someone (*o.f.* – use **servant**). *pl* **menservants.**

'manslaughter crime of killing a person, but without meaning to. *The driver of the car which killed the child was accused of manslaughter.*

the man in the street any ordinary person.

'man-of-'war warship. *pl* **men-of-war** (*o.f.*).

'man of the 'world person who has a lot of experience of life and is therefore tolerant of other people and what they do.

the common man ordinary person. *It is important to know what the common man thinks about matters of public interest.*

like a man bravely. *He took his punishment like a man.*

manacle ['mænəkl] *nc* (usu. *pl*) chain used to prevent a prisoner using his hands and/or feet. Also *vt.*

manage ['mænidʒ] *vt/i* **1.** be in charge of. *He manages a large business for his mother* i.e. his mother owns the business, but he runs it. **2.** succeed; be able to do something. *I'll manage somehow. How does he manage to get such high marks?*

manageable ['mænidʒibl] *adj* able to be controlled. (*opp* **unmanageable**).

management 1. *nu* way something is run or organized. *I'll leave the management of my affairs to you.* **2.** *nc/u* people who run a business etc. *She is going to report the whole thing to the management. The management and the workers disagree.*

manager *nc* **1.** person who is in charge of a firm or department etc. (*fem* **manageress** [mænidʒə'res]). **2.** someone who looks after another person's business affairs: *a boxer's manager.*

managerial [mænə'dʒiəriəl] *adj* having to do with a manager.

mandarin ['mændərin] **1.** *nc* (in former times) important Chinese official. **2.** *nc* small kind of orange. **3.** *nu* **(Mandarin)** official language of China.

mandate ['mændeit] *nc* **1.** instruction or permission (esp. from a superior official). *The magistrate was given a mandate on how to deal with the case.* **2.** permission to do things for another person. *The country gave the Prime Minister a mandate to carry out new policies.*

mandatory ['mændətəri] *adj* compulsory: *mandatory power* i.e. power which must be obeyed.

mandolin ['mændəlin] *nc* type of musical instrument.

mane [mein] *nc* long hair on the back of the neck of some animals (e.g. horse, lion).

maneuver [mə'nu:və*] *nc* see **manoeuvre.**

manganese [mæŋgə'ni:z] *nu* hard, brittle, grey metal (Mn).

mange [meindʒ] *nu* skin disease which affects animals (esp. cats and dogs).

mangy *adj* **1.** affected by mange. **2.** dirty. (*informal* in sense **2.**).

manger ['meindʒə*] *nc* long open box that cattle and horses feed from.

dog in the manger see **dog**[1].

mangle[1] ['mæŋgl] *nc* machine which squeezes the water out of clothes which have just been washed so as to dry and smooth them. Also *vt* dry and smooth clothes by use of this machine.

mangle[2] ['mæŋgl] *vt* crush; damage badly. *He was badly mangled in the accident.* (*informal*).

mango ['mæŋgou] *nc* **1.** tropical fruit which has yellow skin when ripe. **2.** tree bearing this fruit. *pl* **mangoes.**

mangrove ['mæŋgrouv] *nc* tropical tree which grows thickly on soft wet land (esp. near the sea).

mania ['meiniə] *nc* **1.** madness. **2.** great interest in something. *He has a mania for collecting stamps.*

maniac ['meiniæk] *nc* madman. **maniacal** [mə'naiəkəl] *adj.*

manicure ['mænikjuə*] *nc* treatment of the hands and fingernails to improve their appearance. Also *vt.* **manicurist** *nc.*

manifest ['mænifest] *adj* able to be seen easily; obvious. *He is a manifest liar.* Also *vt* show clearly. *The prisoner's guilt soon manifested itself* i.e. it was soon clear that he was guilty. Also *nc* list showing what a ship or aeroplane is carrying.

manifestation [mænifes'teiʃən] *nc* **1.** any way in which people's feelings, thoughts etc are shown. *The boy's bad behaviour is a manifestation of his unhappiness.* **2.** large meeting, procession etc.

manifesto [mæni'festou] *nc* public declaration by a party, group etc of what they believe in or intend to do. *pl* **manifestos.**

manifold ['mænifould] *adj* many and different. *The uses of this machine are manifold.* Also *nc* pipe with several openings (part of an engine etc).

manila, manilla [mə'nilə] *nu* **1.** strong kind of paper. **2.** type of plant from which rope mats etc are made. Also *adj.*

manipulate [mə'nipjuleit] *vt* **1.** use skilfully; control. *He manipulated the controls of the plane so well that it did not crash.* **2.** influence somebody/something for one's own advantage. *The wealthy landowner was accused of manipulating the local council.* **manipulation** [mənipju'leiʃən] *nc/u.* **manipulator** *nc.*

manna ['mænə] *nu* (in the Bible) food given by God to the Israelites in the desert.

mannequin ['mænikin] *nc* woman who is paid to wear new clothes so that people can see what they look like, and may buy them (**model** is the more modern word).

'mannequin parade occasion when clothes are shown in this way.

manner ['mænə*] *nc* **1.** way in which a thing is done or happens. *You must use your knife in this manner* i.e. in this way. **2.** way in which a person behaves: *a strange manner* i.e. a strange way of behaviour.

manners *npl* social behaviour: *good manners; bad manners. He has no manners* i.e. he behaves badly.

mannerism *nc* way of behaving which is typical of a person. *That woman has many annoying mannerisms.*

ill-/well-mannered badly-/well-behaved.

by no (manner of) means see **means.**

in a manner of speaking in one sense. *Is he rich? Yes, in a manner of speaking.*

to the manner born used to something, abl

to do something, as if it were part of one's nature.
manoeuvre [mə'nuːvə*] (*US* **maneuver**) *nc* **1.** planned movement of soldiers, armies, ships etc. **2.** clever plan. Also *vt/i* **1.** make, cause others to make, manoeuvres. **2.** force somebody into doing something. *He was manoeuvred into selling his land. The enemy were manoeuvred out of their strong position.* **3.** move something skilfully. *He manoeuvred his car into the garage.*
manoeuvreable [mə'nuːvərəbl] *adj* easily moved; able to make various movements. *This car is very manoeuvreable.*
on manoeuvres (with reference to armies etc) performing practice manoeuvres.
manor ['mænə*] *nc* **1.** (in former times) area of land owned by a person of high birth. **2.** large, old house. (Also **manor house**).
lord/lady of the manor person who owns a manor.
manse [mæns] *nc* (esp. in Scotland) house of a Presbyterian minister.
mansion ['mænʃən] *nc* large house (usu. belonging to a rich man).
mantelpiece ['mæntlpiːs] *nc* shelf above a fire on which things can be put.
'**mantelshelf** mantelpiece.
mantis ['mæntis] *nc* kind of insect which eats other insects. (Also **praying mantis**).
mantle ['mæntl] *nc* **1.** kind of loose cloak (*o.f.*). **2.** any kind of covering: *a mantle of ivy.* **3.** piece of fine material that goes over the flame of a paraffin or gas lamp and makes it bright. Also *vt* cover.
manual ['mænjuəl] *adj* done with the hands: *manual work.* Also *nc* **1.** textbook (often intended to be a useful guide to some difficult subject). **2.** keys of an organ.
manufacture [mænju'fæktʃə*] *vt* make things in large numbers (often by machinery). Also *nu.* **manufacturer** *nc.*
manufactures *npl* things made in this way. *Note:* the place where manufactured goods are made is called a *factory.*
manure [mə'njuə*] *nc/u* **1.** animal waste used to make crops grow. **2.** artificial material used for the same purpose. Also *vt* put manure on fields etc.
manuscript ['mænjuskript] *nc* **1.** book etc written by hand. *Some ancient manuscripts were found.* **2.** book or paper which has not yet been printed. *I must return this manuscript to the author.*
in manuscript not yet printed.
many ['meni] *determiner/pron* (used with countable nouns) a large number. *Do you have many visitors? No, not many. I haven't got many books. Many people came here to stay. You have made too many mistakes.* (*opp* **few**).
a good many rather a lot. *A good many people were there.* (*informal*).
in as many in the same number of. *He has had three accidents in as many days* i.e. in three days.
many a many. *Many a young man came to court her* (*o.f.*).
Note: 1. *comparative* **more.** *superlative* **most.** 2. in affirmative sentences it is often more natural to say *a large number of* or *a lot of.* Therefore say *The baby has a lot of toys* rather than *The baby has many toys.*
map [mæp] *nc* plan showing where different places are: *map of Africa; map of the heavens* i.e. showing the positions of stars as they appear in the sky. Also *vt* make such a plan. *past* **mapped.**
map out plan. *George is mapping out what we should do.*
put something/somewhere on the map make it well-known. *Our sports achievements have really put our school on the map.* (*informal*).
maple ['meipl] *nc* various kinds of tree, some of which have sugary sap; the leaf is the Canadian national symbol.
mar [mɑː*] *vt* damage; spoil. *His essay was marred by careless mistakes. past* **marred.**
marathon ['mærəθən] *nc* **1.** (in athletics) foot race of 26 miles. **2.** any long race, journey or activity. **3.** any event going on for a long time.
maraud [mə'rɔːd] *vt/i* attack places and steal things from them. **marauder** *nc.*
marble ['mɑːbl] **1.** *nu* kind of hard stone which can be polished and used for buildings, statues etc. *The temple had a marble floor.* **2.** *nc* small glass or plastic ball used by children for playing a game: *play marbles.*
marbles *n sing* children's game played with marbles (in sense **2.**).
march [mɑːtʃ] *vt/i* **1.** walk in the steady even way that soldiers do. **2.** make people walk in this way. *The officer marched his soldiers away.* Also *nc* **1.** walk of this kind: *a long march.* **2.** any kind of progress: *the march of time.* **3.** tune for marching to. *The band played a military march.*
'**march-past** occasion when soldiers march by in front of an important person (e.g. an officer).
'**dead march** slow tune sometimes played at the funeral of an important person.
forced march very fast journey on foot done by soldiers.
steal a march on someone see **steal.**
March [mɑːtʃ] *n* third month of the year.
marchioness ['mɑːʃənis] *nc* wife of a marquis or marquess.
mare [mɛə*] *nc* female horse.
margarine [mɑːdʒə'riːn] *nu* fat from plants or animals (specially treated so that it resembles butter).
margin ['mɑːdʒin] *nc* **1.** white space at the top, bottom and sides of a page. *While reading, he would write some words in the margin.* **2.** amount more than what is needed. *Our plans allowed a wide margin for error* i.e. they will work even if there are many mistakes.
marginal *adj* small: *a marginal increase; a marginal success.*
marigold ['mærigould] *nc* type of yellow flower.
marijuana, marihuana [mæri'wɑːnə] *nu* type of intoxicating drug made from dried hemp.
marine [mə'riːn] *adj* **1.** connected with the sea: *marine plants.* **2.** connected with ships: *marine insurance.* Also *nc* soldier serving on a ship.
mariner ['mærinə*] *nc* sailor (*o.f.*).
marionette [mæriə'net] *nc* small wooden figure which can be moved by strings.
marital ['mæritl] *adj* having to do with marriage: *marital vows* i.e. promises made when people get married.
maritime ['mæritaim] *adj* having to do with the sea: *maritime law* i.e. the law affecting ships etc; *maritime countries* i.e. countries near the sea, or having many ships.
mark [mɑːk] *nc* **1.** something (e.g. a stain) which alters the appearance of something

else. *There are dirty marks on the wall.* **2.** sign; indication. *Grey hairs are a mark of old age.* **3.** score (in examinations etc): *good marks; a good mark.* **4.** sign written by someone who cannot write his own name. *He put his mark at the bottom of the page.* Also *vt* **1.** spoil the appearance of. *The hot water has marked the table.* **2.** indicate; show. *Mark where you have stopped in your reading.* **3.** give points in an examination etc: *mark an essay.* **4.** (sport) follow the movements of a player of the other team.
marked *adj* **1.** easily seen: *a marked improvement.* **2.** suspected of something and therefore watched. *He's a marked man.*
mark something down **1.** write down. **2.** make cheaper. *He has marked all his prices down.*
mark something off show the limits of something: *mark off an area.*
mark out for choose for special attention. *The government has marked out certain areas for improvement.*
hit the mark succeed. (*informal*).
leave one's mark be remembered by some achievement or deed. (*informal*).
miss the mark fail. (*informal*).
mark my words remember what I say. (*informal*).
mark time **1.** march on the same spot. **2.** not advance or go forward. *Our business is marking time* i.e. it is not progressing.
up to the mark good enough. *This student's work is not quite up to the mark.* (*informal*).

market ['mɑːkit] *nc* **1.** place where goods are bought and sold: *the village market. She took the cattle to (the) market.* **2.** areas where people are willing to buy goods. *Traders are looking for new markets.* **3.** demand for goods: *a good market for meat* i.e. meat will be easily sold.
'market day day set aside for buying and selling goods.
'market 'garden (*Brit*) garden where vegetables etc are grown for sale. (*US* **truck garden**).
'market place place where goods are bought and sold.
'black 'market *nc* means by which people can illegally buy things which are scarce. *He bought it on the black market; black-market prices* i.e. prices that are very high.
'black marke'teer *nc* person who sells things on the black market.
'supermarket very large shop where people take what they want to buy and pay as they leave.
in the market for something wanting to buy. (*informal*).
on the market for sale; being sold.

marmalade ['mɑːməleid] *nu* kind of jam made from oranges (or other citrus fruits) cooked and sweetened.

maroon[1] [mə'ruːn] *nu* reddish brown colour. Also *adj*.

maroon[2] [mə'ruːn] *vt* leave somebody on a desert island or in any uncomfortable and lonely place (e.g. as a punishment).

marquee [mɑː'kiː] *nc* large tent.

marquis, marquess ['mɑːkwis] *nc* title of nobility. (*fem* **marchioness** ['mɑːʃənis]).

marrow ['mærou] **1.** *nu* the soft fat inside bones. **2.** *nc* type of large, oval, green and yellow vegetable.
chilled to the marrow very cold. (*informal*).

marry ['mæri] **1.** *vt/i* take someone as one's husband or wife. *Philip has married Jane.* **2.** *vt* join two people together as man and wife. *What is the name of the priest who married you?* **marriage** ['mæridʒ] *nc/u*.
married *adj*. (*opp* **unmarried**).
marriageable ['mæridʒəbl] *adj* able to be married: *of marriageable age* i.e. old enough to get married.
give in marriage give one's daughter to be married to someone.

marsh [mɑːʃ] *nc* area of low-lying, wet land. **marshy** *adj*.

marshal ['mɑːʃl] *nc* **1.** (in the army or air force) an officer of the highest rank: *Field-Marshal* (army); *Air-Marshal* (air force). **2.** person who has to keep order at a public meeting. **3.** (*US*) officer in charge of a section of the police or fire brigade. **4.** (*US*) official, not in the police force, in charge of seeing that the law is enforced in a certain area. Also *vt* **1.** arrange things or people in a certain order. *He spent ten minutes before the meeting marshalling the arguments he was going to bring up.* **2.** lead in a procession. *past* **marshalled.** (*US* **marshaled**).
'marshalling yard place where goods waggons etc can be moved about to be made up into trains.

marsupial [mɑː'suːpiəl] *nc* animal that carries its young in a kind of pouch or pocket (e.g. a kangaroo). Also *adj*.

mart [mɑːt] *nc* place for buying and selling goods. (rather *o.f.*).

martial ['mɑːʃl] *adj* having to do with war: *martial music* i.e. warlike music; *martial law* i.e. rule by soldiers instead of by civilians.

martin ['mɑːtin] *nc* type of small bird like a swallow.

martinet [mɑːti'net] *nc* person who enforces very strict discipline on others.

martyr ['mɑːtə*] *nc* person who will suffer death rather than change what he believes in. Also *vt* kill people because they will not change their beliefs. **martyrdom** *nc/u*.
be a martyr to suffer a lot from. *She is a martyr to continuous headaches.*
make a martyr of oneself suffer unnecessarily. (*informal*).

marvel ['mɑːvl] *nc* something wonderful and astonishing. *It is a marvel how he works so hard.* Also *vt/i* wonder, be astonished. *I marvel at his tremendous achievements. They marvelled that he could do so much.* *past* **marvelled.** (*US* **marveled**).
marvellous *adj* wonderful; surprising; very good. *It's been a marvellous day.* **marvellously** *adv*.

marzipan ['mɑːzipæn] *nu* sweet substance made from nuts, eggs etc, put on cakes.

mascara [mæs'kɑːrə] *nu* preparation used to make the eyelashes darker.

mascot ['mæskət] *nc* something/somebody that is supposed to bring good luck.

masculine ['mæskjulin] *adj* **1.** male; having to do with men: *a masculine sport.* **2.** (grammar) kind of gender i.e. not feminine or neuter. *'Bull' is masculine, but 'cow' is feminine.*

mash [mæʃ] *nc/u* **1.** mixture (e.g. of grain and turnips) used as a food for animals. **2.** any kind of soft mixture. Also *vt*: *mashed potatoes.*

mask [mɑːsk] *nc* covering for the face or part of the face. *The robbers were wearing masks.* Also *vt* cover or conceal something. *They masked their true intentions.*
'gasmask covering on the face to protect the wearer from gas.

masochism ['mæzəkizəm] *nu* unnatural

pleasure in being hurt. **masochist** *nc*. **masochistic** [mæzə'kistik] *adj*.

mason ['meisn] *nc* **1.** person who works with stone etc (esp. for building). **2.** freemason i.e. member of a certain secret society.

masonry *nu* **1.** art or skill of the mason. **2.** freemasonry i.e. a secret society. **3.** stonework: *crumbling masonry*.

masonic [mə'sɔnik] *adj* relating to freemasonry.

masque [mɑːsk] *nc* short play (usu. with music and dancing) popular in the 16th and 17th centuries (*o.f.*).

masquerade [mɑːskə'reid] *nc* **1.** dance at which people wear masks (*o.f.* – would probably be called a **masked ball**). **2.** any situation in which a disguise is worn (esp. for pleasure). Also *vi* pretend to be somebody/something else (esp. by dressing up).

mass [mæs] **1.** *nc* large numbers collected together. *There is a mass of stones in the yard. There are masses of people in the hall.* **2.** *nc* large lump of some material. *The workmen left a huge mass of concrete behind.* **3.** *nu* (science) amount of matter in a body, measured by its resistance to a change of motion. Also *vt/i* collect together. *The enemy are massing their forces for an attack.*

the masses *npl* ordinary people.

'mass 'meeting meeting of large numbers of people (usu. to protest about something).

'mass 'media see **medium.**

'mass 'murder *nc/u* murder on a large scale. **mass murderer** *nc*.

'mass-pro'duce *vt* make things cheaply in large numbers. **mass-produced** *adj*. **mass production** *nu*.

Mass [mæs] *nc* religious ceremony (esp. Roman Catholic) to commemorate Christ's Last Supper: *hear Mass; say Mass.*

massacre ['mæsəkə*] *nc* killing of a large number of (usu. defenceless) people. Also *vt* kill in this way. *When the soldiers captured the town, they massacred all the inhabitants.*

massage ['mæsɑːʒ] *vt* take away stiffness or pain by rubbing and pressing parts of the body. Also *nc/u*.

masseur [mæ'səː*] *nc* man skilled in doing this. (*fem* **masseuse** [mæ'səːz]).

massive ['mæsiv] *adj* large and heavy: *massive doors*. **massively** *adv*.

mast [mɑːst] *nc* **1.** high pole on a ship to which sails are attached. **2.** high pole to which a flag is attached by ropes. **3.** metal structure built high so that television or radio signals can be sent long distances.

'masthead top of a mast.

'mainmast central mast on a ship.

before the mast working as an ordinary sailor (*o.f.*).

master ['mɑːstə*] *nc* **1.** person who owns or controls something: *a dog's master; master of the house.* **2.** person who gives orders to others: *servants and their master.* **3.** male teacher. **4.** skilled worker who does not work for someone else: *a master builder.* **5.** title used before a boy's name: *Master John Brown.* Also *vt* gain control of something: *master a new language.*

masterful *adj* strong willed. **masterfully** *adv*.

masterly *adj* very clever: *in a masterly fashion.*

mastery *nu* control; command.

'master key key that will open many different locks.

'master 'mariner (merchant navy) captain of a ship.

'mastermind *nc* very clever person (esp. in crime). Also *vt*: *mastermind a plan* i.e. direct it cleverly.

'masterpiece great or greatest achievement

old master **1.** great painter (esp. applied to Italian painters before the 18th century). **2.** painting by such a painter.

past master person who is very clever at some particular skill: *be a past master at making speeches.*

masticate ['mæstikeit] *vt* chew, soften food with the teeth. **mastication** [mæsti'keiʃən] *nu*.

mastiff ['mæstif] *nc* type of large dog.

masturbate ['mæstəbeit] *vi* indulge in sexual behaviour with oneself. **masturbation** [mæstə'beiʃən] *nu*.

mat[1] [mæt] *nc* covering for protecting a surface against dirt, heat etc: *doormat* i.e. for wiping one's shoes on before entering a room; *tablemat* i.e. for placing under plates etc.

matted *adj* twisted together; tangled: *matted hair.*

mat[2], **matt** [mæt] *adj* smooth but not shiny: *a mat surface; mat paintwork.*

matador ['mætədɔː*] *nc* man who kills the bull in the Spanish sport of bullfighting.

match[1] [mætʃ] *nc* very small piece of wood with material at one end which lights easily (used for lighting fires, cigarettes etc).

'matchwood wood chopped up into small pieces.

match[2] [mætʃ] *nc* **1.** game between two sides: *a football match.* **2.** person who is just as clever, strong etc as another person. *He met his match.* **3.** thing that goes with or fits into another. *This chair is a match for that one.* **4.** marriage. *She made a good match* i.e. found a good or wealthy husband. Also *vt/i* **1.** find something that goes with something else. *She matched the carpet with some very nice curtains.* **2.** put into a contest together. *He matched his brother against/with the champion.*

matching *adj* going together; suitable to be together: *matching chairs.*

matchless *adj* not able to be equalled.

'matchmaker someone who arranges marriages.

'well-'matched *adj* very suitable for one another.

mate [meit] *nc* **1.** fellow worker. **2.** companion. (*informal*). **3.** (usu. with reference to animals) male living with a female or female living with a male: *a lion and his mate.* **4.** officer below a captain in a ship: *first mate* (also *second mate, third mate etc*). Also *vt/i* come, bring together so as to have young. *The animals were mated last spring.*

'mating season time of the year when animals come together to have young.

material [mə'tiəriəl] *nc/u* **1.** something that something else can be made from. **2.** cloth: *dress material; clothes made from beautiful material.* Also *adj* **1.** having to do with matter, not the spirit. (*opp* **spiritual**). **2.** (usu. legal) important; necessary: *material evidence.* (*opp* **immaterial**). **materially** *adv*.

materialism *nu* **1.** belief that ideas and spiritual things do not exist, only material things. (*opp* **idealism**). **2.** interest in one's own physical needs.

materialist *nc* **1.** person who believes in materialism. **2.** person who thinks only of physical things (e.g. money, cars).

materialize *vi* become real, true. *Their hopes did not materialize* i.e. what they had hoped for did not happen.

maternal [mə'təːnl] *adj* of or like a mother or one's mother's side: *maternal care* i.e. loving care; *maternal grandfather* i.e. father of a person's mother. (*masc* **paternal**).

maternity *nu* condition of being a mother. Also *adj*: *maternity hospital; maternity clothes.*

mathematics [mæθə'mætiks] *nu* science of space and numbers. *Mathematics is a subject studied in nearly every school.*
Note: followed by a *sing* verb.

mathematical [mæθə'mætikl] *adj*.

mathematician [mæθəmə'tiʃən] *nc* expert in mathematics.

maths (*US* **math**) *nu* short informal form of **mathematics.**

matinée ['mætinei] *nc* theatre show taking place in the morning or afternoon.

matins ['mætinz] *npl* **1.** (Church of England) morning service. **2.** (Roman Catholic Church) prayers said at dawn.

matriarch ['meitriɑːk] *nc* woman who is head of the family. **matriarchal** *adj*. **matriarchy** *nc/u*.

matricide ['meitrisaid] **1.** *nc/u* act of killing one's mother. **2.** *nc* person who kills his own mother. **matricidal** [meitri'saidl] *adj*.

matriculate [mə'trikjuleit] *vt/i* **1.** pass an examination which enables one to enter a university. **2.** allow someone to enter a university. **matriculation** [mətrikju'leiʃən] *nc/u*.

matrimony ['mætriməni] *nu* state of being married. **matrimonial** [mætri'mouniəl] *adj*.

matrix ['meitriks] *nc* **1.** (biology) womb. **2.** hollow shape or mould into which metal is poured. **3.** rock etc in which minerals are found. *pl* **matrices** ['meitrisiːz].

matron ['meitrn] *nc* **1.** woman in charge of nurses in a hospital. **2.** woman in charge of the feeding, medical care etc in a school. **3.** married woman; elderly lady.

matronly *adj* dignified; having to do with a matron: *matronly appearance; matronly duties.*

matted ['mætid] *adj* see **mat**[1].

matter ['mætə*] **1.** *nu* stuff out of which all things are made: *the matter of the universe.* **2.** *nc* subject; topic: *a very difficult matter; another matter.* **3.** *nu* poisonous yellow substance in a wound etc. **4.** *nu* content; what is being written, spoken about. *The matter of his speech was good.* Also *vi* be important. *It doesn't matter* i.e. it is not important.

printed matter books, newspapers etc.

be the matter with someone be wrong. *What's the matter with you?* i.e. what's wrong with you? (*informal*).

no laughing matter serious; not amusing. *Losing all your money is no laughing matter.* (*informal*).

a matter of about: *a matter of 20 miles. Success is just a matter of trying harder.*

no matter what in spite of anything that may happen. *I've decided to leave tomorrow, no matter what.*

no matter how, when, where etc without caring about how, when, where etc a thing happens.

a matter of course something quite ordinary; nothing unusual. *I told him he had won first prize, but he took it as a matter of course.*

a matter of fact something true: *as a matter of fact* i.e. to speak truthfully.

'matter-of-'fact *adj* not imaginative; keeping to the facts. *He told us about his adventure in a very matter-of-fact way.*

a matter of life and death something extremely important.

matting ['mætiŋ] *nu* rough material used for covering floors etc.

mattress ['mætris] *nc* long, flat bag filled with hair, feathers or some other soft material, and used for sleeping on.

mature [mə'tjuə*] *adj* **1.** completely developed; completely grown-up: *mature person* i.e. someone who is completely adult and sensible. **2.** ripe. **3.** completely thought out: *mature plans.* (*opp* **immature**). Also *vt/i* become or make completely developed; become or make ready. **maturity** *nu*.

maudlin ['mɔːdlin] *adj* emotional in a silly or tearful way: *a maudlin story. The drunk man became maudlin.*

maul [mɔːl] *vt* treat or injure in a rough manner: *be mauled by a lion.* **mauling** *nc/u*.

mausoleum [mɔːzə'liəm] *nc* large tomb.

mauve [mouv] *nc/u* pale bluish purple colour. Also *adj*.

mawkish ['mɔːkiʃ] *adj* **1.** silly and sentimental: *a mawkish play, film etc.* **2.** having a sweet, sickening taste: *a mawkish flavour.* **mawkishly** *adv*. **mawkishness** *nu*.

maxi- ['mæksi] *prefix* large, long (e.g. **maxiskirt** i.e. long skirt).

maxim ['mæksim] *nc* **1.** statement of what most people would agree to be true. *The book contained many wise maxims.* **2.** rule of conduct. *It is one of my maxims never to lend money.*

maximize ['mæksimaiz] *vt* make as big as possible: *maximize profits.*

maximum ['mæksiməm] *nc* greatest amount of something that is possible, or has actually been recorded. *My salary is at its maximum* i.e. I shall not earn more per year. Also *adj* greatest possible or recorded. *His maximum speed was 80 miles per hour.* (*opp* **minimum**).

may [mei] *aux*.
Note: past tense is *might* and there is no other tense form. Negative is *may not, might not* or *mayn't.*

1. expressing possibility. *Our team may win tomorrow. You may see him if you hurry. He might be there, but I don't think so. I am afraid that your son may have been injured.* *Note: might* indicates that something is less likely than when one uses *may*. Study these sentences and notice also how tense is indicated: (a) *They may arrive now/tomorrow* i.e. it is possible. (b) *They might arrive now/tomorrow* i.e. it is less likely. (c) *They may have arrived yesterday* i.e. it is possible. (d) *They might have arrived yesterday* i.e. it is less likely. (e) *They might have arrived yesterday, but their plane could not land* i.e. it was possible once, but not any longer.

2. asking or giving permission. *May I leave now? Might I ask what you paid for it? Yes, of course. May we go to the cinema tomorrow?* *Note:* in these questions, *might* indicates greater hesitation or reluctance.

3. request or very polite command. *You might post these letters on your way home. You might try to get that finished for tomorrow.* **4.** expressing a wish. *May you both be very happy!* (*o.f.* – say **I hope you'll both be very happy!**). **5.** with the meaning of although. *He may not study much, but he gets good marks* i.e. although he does not study much, he . . .

maybe ['meibi:] *adv* perhaps. *Maybe he will come tomorrow.* (*informal*).
may/might as well (used when one thing is preferable to another) would be wiser to. *It's very cold so we might as well take the car.*

May [mei] *n* fifth month of the year.

mayonnaise [meiə'neiz] *nu* thick yellow cream used for flavouring salads i.e. cold vegetable dishes, sandwiches etc.

mayor [mɛə*] *nc* chief elected official in a town or city.
mayoralty ['mɛərəlti] *nc* **1.** office of being mayor. **2.** period a mayor holds his office.
mayoress ['mɛəres] *nc* mayor's wife.

maypole ['meipoul] *nc* pole round which people used to dance.

maze [meiz] *nc* **1.** paths which cross one another in so many different ways that the traveller easily becomes lost. **2.** any difficult or confusing state or situation.
be in a maze be very confused.

me [mi:] *pron* form which **I** takes when it is the object of a verb or preposition. *You saw me there. Give it to me.*
Note: it is more usual to say *It is me* than *It is I* in reply to questions like *Who is there?*

mead [mi:d] **1.** *nu* alcoholic drink made from honey. **2.** *nc* meadow (*o.f.* in sense **2.**).

meadow ['medou] *nc* piece of grassy land; piece of land where hay is grown.

meagre ['mi:gə*] (*US* **meager**) *adj* not enough: *meagre wages; a meagre supply.*
meagrely *adv.* **meagreness** *nu.*

meal[1] [mi:l] *nc* **1.** occasion when food is regularly taken (e.g. breakfast, dinner etc). *We get three meals a day at the hotel.* **2.** food taken at a meal. *I feel like a meal* i.e. I feel hungry.

meal[2] [mi:l] *nu* coarsely ground grain.

mean[1] [mi:n] *vt/i* **1.** intend; have a certain purpose. *They mean to leave by the midnight train. He meant to go home early, but he didn't. The young couple were meant for each other* i.e. they were suitable for each other. *What do you mean by saying that?* i.e. why did you say that? **2.** have the sense of. *What does this word mean?* **3.** cause. *Failing one paper means failing the whole examination. I'm afraid that this means war* i.e. war will come. **4.** be worth. *That boy means everything to me* i.e. he is worth everything. *past* **meant** [ment].
meaning *nc/u* sense; intention. *What is the meaning of this word? We've been trying to discover the meaning of his actions.* Also *adj* having some special significance. *She gave him a meaning look* i.e. she wanted him to understand something by it.
meaningful *adj* important, significant. **meaningfully** *adv.*
meaningless *adj* without meaning; useless.
mean no good wish harm.
mean well have good intentions (usu. in spite of some annoying behaviour). *She may be rather bossy, but she means well.*

mean[2] [mi:n] *adj* **1.** unwilling to spend or give money: *a man who is greedy and mean.* **2.** old and neglected: *a mean street.* **3.** contemptible; unworthy of a person: *a mean act.* **4.** vicious in behaviour. *Watch him; he can be really mean.* (*informal* in sense **4.**).
meanly *adv.* **meanness** *nu.*

mean[3] [mi:n] *nc* **1.** something that is halfway between two extreme quantities or qualities. *We must find a mean between hope and despair; a mean between heat and cold.* **2.** average of a list of numbers. *The mean of 68, 77 and 83 is 76.* (68+77+83=228; 228÷3=76).

means [mi:nz] *n sing* or *pl* **1.** way of doing something; method. *He forced the snake to come out from where it was hiding by means of a long pole. I don't know what means they used.* **2.** money; wealth. *They say that he is a man of means* i.e. quite rich.
'means test finding out, when people ask for government help, of what they earn so that help is given only to those who really need it.
by all means certainly; of course. *May I leave now? By all means.*
by fair means or foul in any way possible, whether honest or dishonest. *Our team intends to win by fair means or foul.*
by no (manner of) means not at all. *He is by no means rich.*
by some means in some unknown way.
live within one's means spend less than one earns.

meander [mi'ændə*] *vi* **1.** (with reference to a stream, river etc) change direction very often. **2.** wander about. **meandering** *adj.*

meantime ['mi:ntaim], **meanwhile** ['mi:nwail] *n sing* in the time between; during the time something else is happening. *You will be allowed to rest shortly; in the meantime you must keep working. Keep working in the meantime.* Also *conj*: *You pack the cases; meanwhile I'll get the car ready.*

measles ['mi:zlz] *nu* illness, which can be caught from another person, causing fever with red spots appearing on the skin.
Note: followed by a *sing* verb.

measly ['mi:zli] *adj* not enough, in the opinion of the speaker. *He paid us a measly fifty pence.* (*informal*).

measure ['meʒə*] **1.** *nc* object used to find out the length of something. **2.** *nu* system of methods for finding out the length, height, weight etc of things. **3.** *nc* action. *I shall have to take stern measures* i.e. strict actions. **4.** *nc* something which the government will or may make into a law. *Parliament is considering new measures against crime.* Also *vt* **1.** find out the length, height, weight etc of something. *They measured the room.* **2.** be of a certain size. *The board measured 9 inches by 24 inches.*
measurement *nc/u* act of measuring.
measurements *npl* size of something (esp. when measuring a person for clothes). *The tailor took my measurements* i.e. measured me.
measurable *adj* able to be measured. *There was no measurable difference between them.* **measurably** *adj.* **measurability** [meʒərə'biliti] *nu.*
measured *adj* **1.** carefully thought out: *a measured statement.* **2.** slow and even. *He walked with measured steps.*
measure something out give out a certain amount.
full measure complete, total amount: *a shopkeeper who always gives full measure.*
in a great measure most; mostly.
made to measure *adj* (with reference to clothes) made for a certain person after his measurements have been taken.
short measure not the complete amount. *She gave you short measure.*
in some measure to some extent. *He is in some measure rather careless.*
take someone's measure know what good (or bad) qualities a person has.

meat [mi:t] *nu* flesh of animals eaten as food.

mechanic [mi'kænik] *nc* person who repairs machines.

mechanical *adj* **1.** having to do with machines; worked by machines: *mechanical toys.* **2.** done as if by a machine i.e. without thinking: *a mechanical reply.* **mechanically** *adv.*

mechanics *nu* **1.** science of how things move or are made to move. **2.** science of how machines work.
Note: followed by a *sing* verb.

mechanism ['mekənizəm] *nc* **1.** how a machine is made. **2.** how anything complicated works: *the mechanism of government.*

mechanize ['mekənaiz] *vt* use machines for: *mechanized agriculture.* **mechanization** [mekənai'zeiʃən] *nu.*

medal ['medl] *nc* small piece of metal (usu. like a coin with some design or words on it) given as a reward for something (e.g. bravery) or so that some event may be remembered.

medallion [mi'dæliən] *nc* object like a medal (often worn or used as an ornament).

medallist ['medəlist] (*US* **medalist**) *nc* someone who has been awarded a medal: *gold-medallist.*

meddle ['medl] *vi* interfere (in what does not concern one). *I hope he doesn't try to meddle in my affairs.* **meddler** *nc.*

meddlesome *adj* fond of meddling.

media ['mi:diə] pl of **medium.**

mediate ['mi:dieit] *vi* bring peace or an understanding (usu. between people who are not on friendly terms). *She mediated between the two enemy forces.* **mediation** [mi:di'eiʃən] *nu.* **mediator** *nc.*

medicine ['medsin] **1.** *nu* art and science of preventing and curing disease. **2.** *nc/u* something taken (e.g. a liquid) to prevent or cure a disease.

medical ['medikl] *adj* having to do with medicine: *medical instruments; medical students; medical school* i.e. part of a university where doctors are trained. **medically** *adv.*

medicament [me'dikəmənt] *nc* something used to cure (esp. externally).

medicated ['medikeitid] *adj* having medicine in it: *medicated cotton wool.*

medicinal [me'disinl] *adj* used to prevent or cure illness. *He kept a little brandy for medicinal purposes.*

'medicine man type of doctor who uses magic (esp. among North American Indians).

practise medicine work as a doctor.

take one's medicine take a just punishment without complaining. (*informal*).

medieval, mediaeval [medi'i:vl] *adj* in European history, having to do with the Middle Ages (roughly from 1100 A.D. to 1500 A.D.).

mediocre [mi:di'oukə*] *adj* not very good and not very bad.

mediocrity [mi:di'ɔkriti] **1.** *nu* state of being mediocre. **2.** *nc* person who is not outstanding in any way.

meditate ['mediteit] *vt/i* think seriously about something: *meditate suicide* i.e. consider committing suicide; *meditate on/upon what one has done.* **meditation** [medi'teiʃən] *nc/u.*

medium ['mi:diəm] *nc* **1.** means by which something is done. *Money is a medium for buying and selling.* **2.** means of communication with large numbers of people. *Television is a very efficient medium for spreading information.* **3.** middle point; middle way: *happy medium* i.e. not too much or too little. **4.** substances in which something lives: *the medium of air/water etc.* **5.** person who is able to communicate with spirits. *pl* **media** ['mi:diə] or **mediums** (in sense **5.**). Also *adj* not going to one extreme or the other; average: *of medium height.*

'medium wave (radio) sound wave measuring from 187–571 metres (in Britain).

'mass 'media *npl* means of communication with large numbers of people (e.g. radio, television, newspapers etc).

medley ['medli] *nc* mixture of different things (esp. tunes, articles and stories etc).

meek [mi:k] *adj* mild and gentle; uncomplaining. **meekly** *adv.* **meekness** *nu.*

meet [mi:t] *vt/i* **1.** come together from different places or directions. *I met him in the street last night. We met (up) in Paris last year.* **2.** be introduced to. *Would you like to meet my brother? Pleased to meet you* i.e. I am glad that we have met, a phrase sometimes used instead of *How do you do?* **3.** wait for the arrival of: *meet someone at the station.* **4.** answer satisfactorily; deal with: *meet a complaint.* **5.** pay: *meet a bill. past* **met** [met].

meeting *nc* coming together of people (usu. for some definite purpose): *sports meeting; political meeting.*

meet with something come upon (usu. something bad); receive: *meet with misfortune. The play met with a good reception.*

make both ends meet manage with difficulty to live on what one has.

meet someone halfway come to an agreement with someone by both sides giving in to some of the other's wishes.

megalomania [megəlou'meiniə] *nu* mad desire for importance or mad belief that one is great. **megalomaniac** [megəlou'meiniæk] *nc.*

megaphone ['megəfoun] *nc* metal horn for speaking through to make the voice sound louder.

megaphone

melancholy ['melənkəli] *nu* feeling of sadness. Also *adj.*

melee, melée ['melei] *nc* **1.** fight in which everybody is mixed up together. **2.** crowd of struggling people.

mellifluous [me'lifluəs] *adj* (usu. of sounds) smooth and sweet: *a mellifluous voice; mellifluous music.*

mellow ['melou] *adj* **1.** (with reference to sounds, taste, colours etc) soft and ripe. **2.** (with reference to people) kind and gentle. *One is mellower as one gets older.* Also *vt/i.*

melodrama ['meloudrɑ:mə] *nc* exciting and crudely emotional play.

melodramatic [meloudrə'mætik] *adj* behaving in a very emotional and excited way; intended to arouse emotions: *a melodramatic speech.*

melody ['melədi] *nc* **1.** pleasant tune. **2.** series of single notes.

melodious [mi'loudiəs] *adj* tuneful.

melon ['melən] *nc/u* type of large fruit which is very juicy inside.

melt [melt] *vt/i* **1.** make or become liquid with heat: *melting snow.* **2.** soften, become soft. *Her tears melted my anger. past* **melted.**

molten ['moultn] *adj* (with reference to metals) melted.

melt away go away; disappear. *His followers melted away at the first sign of danger.*

melt something down use heat to turn articles into ordinary metal. *They melted down the silver cups.*

member ['membə*] *nc* **1.** person belonging to a group, society, club etc: *Member of Parliament; club member.* **2.** part of the body (e.g. an arm or a leg) (*o.f.* – use **limb**).

membership *nu* **1.** state of belonging to a society etc: *renew one's membership.* **2.** number of people in a society etc: *a very large membership.*

membrane ['membrein] *nc* thin covering or connection inside an animal or plant.

memento [mə'mentou] *nc* something which one keeps to remember a person/thing. *pl* **mementos** or **mementoes.**

memo ['memou] *nc* short form of **memorandum.** *pl* **memos.**

memoir ['memwɑ:*] *nc* (often *pl*) written account of someone's life (esp. one's own life).

memorandum [memə'rændəm] *nc* **1.** short written note to help one's memory. **2.** type of informal business letter. **3.** (in a legal sense) brief note of an agreement which has not yet been properly written out or signed. *pl* **memorandums** or **memoranda** [memə'rændə].

memory ['meməri] **1.** *nu* power of remembering. *He has a very good/bad memory* i.e. he can remember many/few things. *I have a good memory for faces* i.e. I can remember people's faces easily. *His memory is going* i.e. he is finding it more difficult to remember. **2.** *nc* something that can be remembered. *I have very pleasant memories of my travels abroad.*

memorable *adj* worth remembering. **memorably** *adv.*

memorial [mi'mɔ:riəl] *nc* something intended to make sure that something is remembered: *war memorial* i.e. statue etc in memory of people who died in war. Also *adj.*

memorize *vt* learn something so well that one can remember exactly: *memorize a poem.*

photographic memory type of memory by means of which a person is able to remember every detail of something he has seen.

from memory relying on one's memory i.e. not referring to a book etc.

in living memory fairly recently; recently enough for people who are still alive to remember it.

in memory of someone to the honour of someone; so that someone may not be forgotten.

jog someone's memory see **jog.**

men [men] pl of **man.**

menace ['menəs] *nc/u* **1.** danger; threat. *The arms race is a menace to world peace.* **2.** promise to injure or harm. **3.** person/thing causing annoyance. (*informal* in sense **3.**). Also *vt/i* promise to injure or harm, threaten.

menacing *adj* dangerous. **menacingly** *adv.*

menagerie [mi'nædʒəri] *nc* collection of wild animals for show (esp. one that is taken from place to place).

mend [mend] **1.** *vt* repair something that has been broken, torn etc: *mend a broken chair; mend a stocking with a hole in it.* **2.** *vt* improve; make better. **3.** *vi* become better in health.

mend matters cause the situation to become better. *You won't mend matters by being so impolite.* (*informal*).

mend one's ways improve one's behaviour or way of living. (*informal*).

on the mend getting better (esp. in health) (*informal*).

mendacious [men'deiʃəs] *adj* **1.** fond of telling lies: *a mendacious child.* **2.** untrue: *a mendacious story.* **mendaciously** *adv.* **mendacity** [men'dæsiti] *nu.*

mendicant ['mendikənt] *nc* person who lives by begging. Also *adj.* (both *formal*).

menial ['mi:niəl] *nc* domestic servant. Also *adj* low or degrading: *a menial task.* **menially** *adv.*

meningitis [menin'dʒaitis] *nu* very serious illness caused by the inflammation of the membranes around the brain or spinal cord.

menopause ['menəpɔ:z] *nc* time in the life of a woman after which she is no longer able to bear a child.

menstruation [menstru'eiʃən] *nu* woman's monthly discharge of blood from the womb. **menstrual** ['menstruəl] *adj.* **menstruate** ['menstrueit] *vi.*

mensuration [mensjuə'reiʃən] *nu* measurement of length, area and volume.

mental ['mentl] *adj* having to do with the mind: *mental illness; mental hospital* i.e. hospital for those who are mentally ill; *mental arithmetic* i.e. arithmetic problems done in the mind without the help of pencil and paper. **mentally** *adv.*

mentality [men'tæliti] *nc/u* person's way of thinking.

mention ['menʃən] *vt* **1.** speak or write about something briefly. *I must just mention that everyone has been very kind to us here.* **2.** refer to somebody's name. *Mention my name.* Also *nc* brief reference to somebody/something.

honourable mention reference to somebody who has done very well in something but has not gained the first place or prize (e.g. in a competition).

not to mention in addition to. *He has three houses, and two estates, not to mention three expensive cars.*

mentor ['mentɔ:*] *nc* wise adviser or teacher.

menu ['menju:] *nc* list of different kinds of food that can be obtained in a hotel, restaurant etc. *pl* **menus.**

mercantile ['mə:kəntail] *adj* having to do with trade.

mercantile marine ships engaged in trade i.e. not warships.

mercenary ['mə:sinəri] *adj* doing something only for money: *mercenary person; mercenary motives* i.e. reasons of greed only. Also *nc* soldier fighting for a foreign country for money only (not for love of the country).

merchandise ['mə:tʃəndaiz] *nu* goods bought and sold (esp. manufactured goods).

merchant ['mə:tʃənt] *nc* **1.** person who buys

and sells things on a large scale. **2.** person who has a special interest in a certain kind of goods: *wine merchant; coal merchant.*
'merchantman trading ship.
'merchant 'navy ships and sailors connected with trade.
mercury ['mə:kjuri] *nu* heavy silver-white metal, liquid at ordinary temperatures, used in thermometers etc.
mercurial [mə:'kjuəriəl] *adj* changing very quickly: *a mercurial person* i.e. one who is now sad now gay etc; *a mercurial situation.*
mercy ['mə:si] *nu* kindness shown to someone that one has in one's power. *He showed mercy to the defeated enemy. The judge gave the convicted man no mercy. They had no mercy on their prisoners.*
merciful *adj* showing mercy. (*opp* **unmerciful**).
merciless *adj* without mercy.
'mercy killing *nc/u* killing of a person who is suffering great pain, done out of love or pity. **mercy killer** *nc.*
at the mercy of in the power of. *The ship was at the mercy of the wind and waves.*
at someone's mercy in someone's power.
left to the tender mercies of abandoned to something/somebody that will probably be cruel.
thankful for small mercies see **thank.**
mere [miə*] *adj* no more than; no better than; only: *a mere child; a mere trifle* i.e. something of little importance.
merely *adv* only.
meretricious [meri'triʃəs] *adj* attractive outwardly but really of little value.
merge [mə:dʒ] *vt/i* become part, cause to become part, of something else. *It was decided that the two businesses should be merged.*
merger *nc* union of two business companies.
merge into something become completely absorbed in or by a part of something else. *The colours of the evening sky slowly merged into blue.*
meridian [mə'ridiən] *nc* **1.** imaginary line going from the North Pole to the South Pole through any given point on the surface of the earth: *Greenwich meridian* i.e. such a line going through Greenwich, England. **2.** such a line drawn on a map. **3.** highest point in the sky reached by the sun or other star as seen from a point on the earth's surface. **4.** highest point of fame, success etc.
meringue [mə'ræŋ] *nc/u* cake made from a mixture of sugar and the whites of eggs.
merino [mə'ri:nou] **1.** *nc* kind of sheep with high quality wool. **2.** *nu* cloth made from wool or wool and cotton. *pl* **merinos.**
merit ['merit] *nc/u* quality deserving praise. *There is a great deal of merit in what he has achieved. His greatest merit is his courage.* Also *vt* deserve. *This book merits our close attention.*
merited *adj.* (*opp* **unmerited**).
merits *npl* what a thing really deserves or is worth. *Your application will be judged on its merits* i.e. other things which have nothing to do with it will be ignored.
meritorious [meri'tɔ:riəs] *adj* worthy of praise: *a meritorious action.* **meritoriously** *adv.*
mermaid ['mə:meid] *nc* imaginary creature supposed to live in the sea, with a woman's body but a fish's tail instead of legs.
merry ['meri] *adj* **1.** gay; happy: *having a merry time.* **2.** rather drunk. (*informal* in sense **2.**). **merrily** *adv.* **merriment** *nu.*
'merry-go-round amusement for children consisting of a revolving platform with wooden horses etc on which children may sit.

merry-go-round

make merry have a good time; eat and drink.
'merrymaking *nu* celebrating; eating and drinking.
Merry Christmas! conventional greeting said on Christmas Day or around that time: *wish someone a Merry Christmas.*
mesh [meʃ] *nc* space between the lines in a net: *this net has a fine mesh* i.e. the holes are small. (*opp* **a coarse mesh**). Also *vt/i* **1.** catch in a net. **2.** (of toothed wheels) fit into one another so that one causes the other to turn; combine closely.
meshes *npl* **1.** lines of a net. **2.** any kind of plot, trap etc: *caught in the meshes of a criminal gang.*
mesmerize ['mezməraiz] *vt* **1.** hypnotize. **2.** interest or attract very greatly, as though by hypnotism. *The children listened as though mesmerized by the old man's story.*
mess[1] [mes] *nu* dirty or confused state. *Tom is very untidy; he always leaves his room in a mess. That's another mess I'll have to clean up. What a mess!* Also *vt/i* cause dirt and confusion.
messy *adj* dirty. *Working underneath the car is always a messy job* i.e. one gets dirty easily. **messily** *adv.* **messiness** *nu.*
mess about waste time; spend time doing unimportant things. (*informal*).
mess something up spoil; disorganize. *You've messed up all our arrangements.* (*informal*).
'mess-up *nc* state of disorder or confusion: *a bit of a mess-up* i.e. some confusion. (*informal*).
get into a mess get into trouble; become dirty or disorganized. (*informal*).
make a mess of something **1.** make something untidy or dirty. **2.** fail to do something properly. (*informal* in sense **2.**).
mess[2] [mes] *nc* **1.** group of people (e.g. soldiers etc) who eat together. **2.** meals taken together by such a group. **3.** place where these meals are taken: *officers' mess; sergeants' mess.* Also *vi* take meals in a mess room.
mess together (with reference to armed forces) take meals together.
message ['mesidʒ] *nc* information sent from one person to another. *We received our first message from him after six months.*
messenger ['mesindʒə*] *nc* person who carries a message.
Messiah [mi'saiə] *n* **1.** person awaited by the Jews to free them (applied by Christians to Jesus Christ). **2.** any long-awaited deliverer.
Messrs ['mesəz] **1.** title often put before the names of business firms: *Messrs Hardy.*

Graham and Co. **2.** as the equivalent of Mr before the names of two or more men: *Messrs Smith and Jones* (*o.f.* – use **Mr** before each name).

met [met] past of **meet.**

metabolism [me'tæbəlizəm] *nc/u* all the processes of change which go on in the body. **metabolic** [metə'bɔlik] *adj.*

metal ['metl] *nc/u* mineral substance like iron, silver, lead etc. *The spears were made of metal.* Also *vt* use broken stones when making roads or railways: *a metalled road surface* i.e. one that has been strengthened in this way.

metallic [me'tælik] *adj* like, connected with metal: *metallic sound* i.e. sound like that made by striking metal.

metallurgy [me'tælədʒi] *nu* science of purifying metals i.e. separating them from the ones they come from. **metallurgist** *nc.*

'metalworker person skilled in using and working things with metals.

'road metal broken stones used when making roads.

metamorphosis [metə'mɔːfəsis] *nc/u* profound change of appearance or nature: *metamorphosis of a caterpillar into a butterfly/a criminal into a saint. pl* **metamorphoses** [metə'mɔːfəsiːz].

metaphor ['metəfɔː*] *nc/u* (example of) way of using words so that one thing is given the name of another because of something they have in common (e.g. *You are the rock on which we depend* i.e. a rock is strong and immovable and so are you).

metaphorical [metə'fɔrikl] *adj* like a metaphor; containing many metaphors.

Note: a metaphor is like a simile, which also compares things, but a simile will use *like* or *as* (e.g. *You are as firm as a rock* or *You are like a rock*).

metaphysics [metə'fiziks] *nu* part of philosophy which deals with being and knowledge i.e. what we really are and how we know things.

Note: followed by a *sing* verb.

metaphysical *adj.*

mete [miːt] *vi* in **mete out** i.e. give out shares of; distribute: *mete out punishment* i.e. punish (*o.f.*).

meteor ['miːtiə*] *nc* mass of matter travelling through space which glows with heat when it enters the earth's atmosphere. (Often **shooting star** or **falling star**).

meteoric [miːti'ɔrik] *adj* **1.** having to do with a meteor. **2.** very quick: *a meteoric rise to fame.*

meteorite ['miːtiərait] *nc* meteor that has landed on earth.

meteorology [miːtiə'rɔlədʒi] *nu* science of the conditions in the earth's atmosphere (esp. with regard to forecasting future weather).

meteorological [miːtiərə'lɔdʒikl] *adj* having to do with meteorology: *the meteorological office.* (Often colloquially abbreviated to **met** [met]: *the met office*). **meteorologist** *nc.*

meter[1] ['miːtə*] *nc* instrument used for measuring (esp. gas, electricity, water etc): *gas meter; electric meter; water meter etc.*

'light meter instrument used in photography to find out how much light is present.

'parking meter machine placed near a space where a car may be left for a certain length of time. Some money is placed in the machine, which then shows if the car is left there too long.

meter[2] ['miːtə*] *nc/u* see **metre.**

method ['meθəd] **1.** *nc* way of doing something: *new methods of teaching English.* **2.** *nu* system; planning. *There is not much method in the way he does things. There is method in his madness* i.e. there seems to be no system in what he does, but in fact there is.

methodical [mi'θɔdikl] *adj* **1.** planned; systematic. **2.** fond of planning things out. *He is very methodical.* **methodically** *adv.*

Methodist ['meθədist] *nc* member of a Christian sect following the teachings of John Wesley. Also *adj.* **Methodism** *nu.*

methylated ['meθileitid] *adj* usu. in **methylated spirits** i.e. kind of alcohol used for giving heat and light.

meticulous [me'tikjuləs] *adj* very careful about small details; showing that such care has been taken: *meticulous work; a meticulous worker.* **meticulously** *adv.*

metonymy [me'tɔnimi] *nu* way of referring to something by mentioning another related thing (e.g. referring to literature as 'the pen').

metre[1] ['miːtə*] (*US* **meter**) *nc* unit of measurement. see appendix.

metric ['metrik] *adj* having to do with the metre or the metric system.

'metric system international system of measurement based on the *metre* as the unit of length, and the *gram* as the unit of mass or weight.

metre[2] ['miːtə*] (*US* **meter**) *nc/u* arrangement of words in a poem so that certain words are stressed or emphasized in a regular way. **metrical** ['metrikl] *adj.*

metronome ['metrənoum] *nc* device like a clock, used for keeping time in music.

metropolis [me'trɔpəlis] *nc* **1.** chief city in a country (not necessarily the capital). **2.** any large city.

metropolitan [metrə'pɔlitn] *adj* having to do with a metropolis.

Note: the *capital* of a country is where the government is but it may not be large, or important in other ways.

mettle ['metl] *nu* **1.** ability, qualities of character: *show one's mettle* i.e. show what one is capable of. **2.** courage: *a man of mettle* i.e. a brave man.

put someone on his mettle arrange things so that someone has to try to reveal just how brave or clever etc he is.

mew [mjuː] *nc* soft sound made by a cat. Also *vi* make this sound.

mews [mjuːz] *n sing* **1.** line of buildings used as stables or for carriages etc (*o.f.*). **2.** such buildings made into places for living in (e.g. flats). *He lives in a London mews.*

mezzanine ['mezəniːn] *nc* floor coming between two floors with higher ceilings and usu. situated just above the ground floor. Also *adj*: *mezzanine floor.*

miaow [mjau] *nc* sound made by a cat. Also *vi* make this sound.

miasma [mi'æzmə] *nc* thick and poisonous mist.

mica ['maikə] *nu* glasslike mineral that breaks easily into thin transparent sheets.

mice [mais] pl of **mouse.**

micro- ['maikrou] *prefix* small (e.g. **micrometer, microscope**).

microbe ['maikroub] *nc* living creature, which is so small that it cannot be seen with the naked eye, frequently the cause of disease.

microcosm ['maikroukɔzəm] *nc* anything small which is thought of as being a model of the world or of the universe.
microfilm ['maikroufilm] *nc* (roll of) very small photographs of something which must be recorded (e.g. pages of a book); they can then be enlarged for easy reference: *on microfilm* i.e. recorded in this way. Also *vt* take such photographs.
micrometer [mai'krɔmitə*] *nc* device used for measuring very small distances, objects, angles etc.

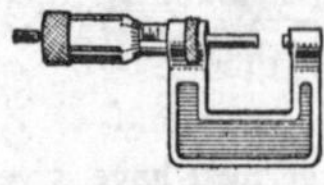
micrometer

microorganism ['maikrou'ɔːgənizəm] *nc* any small creature which can be seen only under a microscope.
microphone ['maikrəfoun] *nc* instrument which can change sound waves into electric waves, and can therefore be used in recording people's voices etc.
microscope ['maikrəskoup] *nc* instrument with lenses which makes very small things appear to be bigger so that they can be examined more easily.
microscopic [maikrəs'kɔpik] *adj* very small.
mid [mid] *adj/prefix* in the middle of (used to form many compounds).
'mid after'noon (in the) middle of the afternoon i.e. about 3 o'clock.
'mid 'air off the ground. *I caught the stone in mid air.*
'mid'day (in the) middle of the day; noon: *at midday.*
'Midlands (in the) area in central England.
'midnight *nc* **1.** 12.00 p.m. **2.** the middle of the night: *at midnight; a midnight swim.*
'mid'summer (in the) middle of the summer: *midsummer days.*
'mid'term (in the) middle of the term: *midterm holidays.*
'mid'week (in the) middle of the week: *midweek travel.*
'mid'way *adv* halfway: *midway between Moscow and New York.*
midden ['midn] *nc* heap of rubbish or dung (*o.f.*).
middle ['midl] *nc* point, area etc coming between and equally distant from two or more other points, areas etc: *the middle of the room; in the middle of the lake.* Also *adj* central; equally distant from certain limits: *the middle book; the middle finger.*
'middle-'aged *adj* not young and not old, often applied to people between 40 and 60 years of age. **middle age** *nu.*
the Middle 'Ages period roughly between 1100 A.D. and 1500 A.D. (Also sometimes applied to the period between 500 A.D. and 1500 A.D.).
'middle 'classes *npl* section of society which is not of noble birth, but not working-class either (e.g. lawyers, doctors, teachers etc). **'middle-class** *adj.*
'middleman person who sells goods which he has not produced himself (e.g. a greengrocer who does not grow his own vegetables etc).
'middle 'name name coming between first name and surname (e.g. Winston *Spencer* Churchill).
Middle 'East general area between Egypt and Iran.
'middle-of-the-'road *adj* not going to extremes: *a middle-of-the-road politician.*
'middleweight *nc* boxer who is next in weight below a light heavyweight. Also *adj*: *middleweight champion.*
'Middle 'West area of the USA stretching from the Rocky Mountains south to the Ohio River and east to the Allegheny Mountains.
middling ['midliŋ] *adj* of medium size, quality etc; neither very good nor very bad: *a middling play. My health is middling* i.e. not very good. Also *adv* moderately. *He is a middling good tennis player.*
midge [midʒ] *nc* type of small winged insect that bites.
midget ['midʒit] *nc* very small person. Also *adj* very small: *midget submarine.*
midriff ['midrif] *nc* part of the body between the chest and the abdomen (esp. with reference to this part of the body if left uncovered when one is clothed).
midshipman ['midʃipmən] *nc* **1.** (*Brit*) rank which can be held by a young man training to be a naval officer before he actually goes to sea. **2.** (*US*) student at a naval academy.
midst [midst] *n* middle (*o.f.*).
in the midst of among; in the middle of. *I saw him in the midst of the crowd.*
in our midst, in their midst etc among us, among them etc.
midwife ['midwaif] *nc* woman whose job is to assist at the birth of babies.
midwifery ['midwifəri] *nu* art or practice of being a midwife.
mien [miːn] *nc* appearance, behaviour etc which reveals a person's character, thoughts etc (*o.f.*).
might[1] [mait] past tense of **may.**
might[2] [mait] *nu* power; strength. *He fought with all his might.*
mighty *adj* powerful; strong; huge: *a mighty king; a mighty tree.* Also *adv* very. *I'm mighty glad.* (*informal* in this sense).
migraine ['miːgrein] *nc/u* very painful type of headache (usu. on one side of the head only).
migrate [mai'greit] *vi* **1.** move from one country or region to another. **2.** (with reference to birds and fish) go from one region to another according to the time of year. *Swallows migrate in the winter.*
migration 1. *nu* act of migrating. *He studies the migration of birds.* **2.** *nc* instance of migrating. **3.** *nc* number of people or animals migrating together. **migratory** [mai'greitəri] *adj.*
migrant ['maigrənt] *nc* person, animal etc that migrates. Also *adj.*
mike [maik] *nc* short informal form of **microphone.**
milage ['mailidʒ] *nc* see **mile.**
mild [maild] *adj* **1.** gentle; soft: *a mild person; a mild way of speaking; mild weather* i.e. not too hot or too cold. **2.** not very bitter or strong: *a mild flavour.*
mildly *adv* **1.** gently; softly. **2.** rather; not very. *They seem mildly interested; mildly amused.* **mildness** *nu.*
mildew ['mildjuː] *nu* **1.** kind of plant disease in which plants are covered with a whitish growth. **2.** growth which comes on materials (e.g. cloth, leather etc) when they are damp for a long time. **mildewed** *adj.*
mile [mail] *nc* measure of length equal to 1,760 yards. see appendix.

mileage, milage ['mailidʒ] *nc* **1.** number of miles travelled in a certain time. **2.** allowance given to workers for travelling a certain distance, paid at so much per mile.
'milestone 1. stone at the roadside which indicates the distance in miles to or from somewhere. **2.** important point in a person's life; important event: *a milestone in the history of medicine.*

milieu ['mi:ljə:] *nc* (usu. only *sing*) surroundings; background: *living in an artistic milieu.*

militant ['militnt] *adj* in a mood for fighting; warlike; actively engaged in fighting what one regards as evil: *a militant socialist.*
militancy *nu.*

military ['militəri] *adj* having to do with the army or war: *military uniform; military life; military police; military service* i.e. period of time to be spent in the army.
the military armed forces.
militarism *nu* belief in war or the armed forces as a means of solving problems.
militarist *nc* person who has this belief.
militate against something act against. *He won't rest, and that militates against his early recovery.*
militia [mi'liʃə] *nc* **1.** trained group of men who do not serve full-time in the army, but can be called upon to defend their country when necessary. **2.** (*US*) all males in each state between the ages of 18 and 45 who are eligible for military service.
Note: sing form can be treated as *pl.*

milk [milk] *nu* **1.** whitish liquid on which mammals feed their young. **2.** this liquid taken from cows and used by human beings as a drink and for making butter, cheese etc. Also *vt* **1.** take milk from: *milk a cow.*
Note: the word *milk* nearly always means cow's milk.
2. take money from. *The government was accused of milking the people.* (*informal* in sense **2.**).
milky *adj* of milk; like milk (esp. in colour).
'milk bar place which sells milk and other soft drinks.
'milkmaid woman who milks cows.
'milkman man who delivers milk to people's houses.
'milk 'shake drink made from cold milk and ice cream.
'milk tooth tooth of a child or growing animal which falls out when the child etc grows bigger.
Milky Way very large group of stars appearing as a broad whitish band of stars stretching across the sky.
(it's no use) cry(ing) over spilt milk see **cry**[1].

mill[1] [mil] *nc* **1.** building containing machinery for making something: *paper mill; steel mill.* **2.** building containing machinery for grinding (e.g. wheat) into flour. **3.** machine or device for grinding any substance finer: *coffee mill.*
miller *nc* person who owns or uses machinery for making grain into flour.
'millpond water stored up for use in a mill (in sense **2.**). *The sea was like a millpond* i.e. very calm.
'millstone 1. heavy stone which is used in grinding flour. **2.** heavy burden; something that is difficult to bear. *Paying for that house has been a millstone round his neck* i.e. something that he has found very difficult to endure.
'windmill flour mill in which the driving power of the machinery is supplied by the wind blowing outside, caught by sails.

windmill

go through the mill have a very difficult time.

mill[2] [mil] **1.** *vt* put through a mill or grinding machine: *mill coffee, flour etc.* **2.** *vt* put a series of very small cuts right round the edge of a coin or screw: *milled edge.* **3.** *vi* move round in an aimless or confused manner. *The crowds milled around outside the hall. The cattle were milling about.*

millennium [mi'leniəm] *nc* **1.** period of 1,000 years. **2.** period of great happiness for the world, occurring sometime in the future. *They are waiting eagerly for the millennium. pl* **millenniums** or **millennia** [mi'leniə].

millepede, millipede ['milipi:d] *nc* small creature like a worm, but with very many legs.

millet ['milit] *nu* plant bearing grain in the form of very small seeds.

milli- ['mili] *prefix* **1.** (esp. used in the metric system) one thousandth part of (e.g. **millimetre; milligram**). **2.** one thousand (e.g. **millipede**).

milligram, milligramme ['miligræm] *nc* one thousandth part of a gram in the metric system. see appendix.

millimetre ['milimi:tə*] (*US* **millimeter**) *nc* one thousandth part of a metre in the metric system. see appendix.

milliner ['milinə*] *nc* person who makes, designs or sells women's hats.
millinery *nu* **1.** women's hats and other items of dress made by milliners. **2.** business of making or selling women's hats etc.

million ['miljən] *nc* **1.** one thousand thousand i.e. 1,000,000. **2.** 1,000,000 pounds or dollars: *make millions from trading.*
millionaire [miljə'nɛə*] *nc* **1.** person who has a million pounds or dollars. **2.** extremely rich man.

millipede ['milipi:d] *nc* see **millepede.**

mime [maim] *nc/u* actions done without words, often as an entertainment. Also *vt/i* do actions of this kind.

mimeograph ['mimiəgrɑ:f] *nc* machine used in offices etc for making copies of what has been typed or written. Also *vt.*

mimic ['mimik] *vt* copy other people's ways of speaking or behaving. *past* **mimicked.** Also *nc* person who is clever at copying the way others speak or behave. **mimicry** *nu.*

mimosa [mi'mouzə] *nu* type of sweet-smelling shrub that grows in warm parts of the world.

minaret [minə'ret] *nc* thin, high, slender tower attached to a mosque from which Moslems are called to prayer.

mince [mins] *vt/i* **1.** cut meat or other food up into very small pieces. **2.** walk with short steps in a manner that is meant to be elegant but only looks foolish. Also *nu* meat which has been cut up into very small pieces. (Also **minced meat**).

'mincemeat **1.** mixture of minced apples or other fruit, currants, sugar etc. **2.** meat cut into very small pieces.

'mince 'pie pie made of mincemeat (usu. in sense **1.**).

mind[1] [maind] **1.** *nc/u* part of a person which thinks and reasons; power to reason: *have a quick mind* i.e. be quick-thinking; *be out of one's mind* i.e. be insane. *He is not in his right mind* i.e. he is insane. **2.** *nu* memory: *bear/keep something in mind* i.e. not forget something. **3.** *nc* opinions; what one believes or intends: *change one's mind* i.e. change one's intention or belief. **4.** *nc* brilliantly clever person. *He is the greatest mind of our time.*

mindful *adj* being careful about; remembering: *mindful of the danger involved.* (*opp* **unmindful**).

mindless *adj* careless; stupid.

'absent-'minded see **absent.**

be in two minds about not be able to come to a decision on.

call to mind see **call**[1].

cross one's mind occur to one. *I did not mention it until now because it has only just crossed my mind.*

have a good mind to be strongly inclined to. *I've a good mind to go home* i.e. I have almost decided to go home. (*informal*).

make up one's mind decide. *He's made up his mind to go home.*

one-track mind see **one**[2].

presence of mind see **present**[1].

put someone in mind of see **put.**

speak one's mind say frankly what one thinks.

take one's mind off see **take.**

mind[2] [maind] *vt/i* **1.** attend to. *Mind what you're doing.* **2.** be careful. *Mind the step* i.e. don't trip over the step. *Mind you don't say anything to offend them.* **3.** look after; take care of. *I'm staying home to mind the children.* **4.** object; dislike. *Do you mind if I smoke/open the window? Would you mind coming over here?*

mind you nevertheless. *Mind you, he is very pleasant.* (*informal*).

never mind don't worry. *I'm afraid he's just gone, but never mind – he'll be back in a few minutes.* (*informal*).

Note: mind is very commonly used in commands, warnings etc.

mine[1] [main] *pron* what belongs to me. *We'll have to separate mine from yours.* Also *pred adj* belonging to me. *This shirt is mine.*

mine[2] [main] *nc* **1.** deep tunnel in the earth made so that valuable ores or stones, coal etc can be taken out. **2.** any source which gives something valuable in large amounts. *That man is a mine of information about history.* **3.** container of high explosives placed near the surface of the sea, or on land, which will explode when it touches something: *a landmine.* Also *vt/i* **1.** dig up ores, precious stones, coal etc from the earth. **2.** place containers of high explosives in a certain area: *mine an area. They mined the entrance to the harbour.* **3.** destroy by using mines (in sense **3.**). *The ship was mined early this morning.*

miner *nc* someone who takes coal, precious stones etc from the earth.

'minefield stretch of land or sea where mines (in sense **3.**) have been laid.

'minesweeper ship specially used to remove mines (in sense **3.**) which may be dangerous to other ships.

mineral ['minərl] *nc* any material obtained from the earth (e.g. gold, coal, oil). Also *adj*: *mineral wealth; mineral rights* i.e. right to mine in a certain area.

'mineral water *nc/u* **1.** water containing salts or gases, taken for health. **2.** type of drink with bubbles of gas in it.

mingle ['miŋgl] *vt/i* mix; be or put in the company of. *They mingled with the other people at the party.*

mini- ['mini] *prefix* specially made smaller than usual (e.g. **minibus** i.e. type of vehicle like a small bus; **miniskirt** i.e. very short skirt).

miniature ['minitʃə*] *attrib adj* copied on a small scale: *miniature railway.* Also *nc* **1.** very small picture of someone. **2.** any very small thing.

miniaturize *vt* (with reference to parts of electrical equipment) make very small.

miniaturization [minitʃərai'zeiʃən] *nu.*

minimize ['minimaiz] *vt* **1.** reduce to the smallest amount: *minimize the risk of an accident.* **2.** say that something is small, of no account etc. *We must not minimize the consequences of this disaster.*

minimum ['minimәm] *nc* smallest amount of something that is possible or has actually been recorded. *That is the very minimum that I shall accept.* Also *adj* smallest possible or recorded: *minimum rainfall.* (*opp* **maximum**). **minimal** *adj.* **minimally** *adv.*

minion ['minjən] *nc* someone who slavishly obeys another person and receives special favours from him.

minister ['ministə*] *nc* **1.** person in charge of a department in a government: *Minister of Social Security.* **2.** person who represents his country in some other country. **3.** clergyman: *Presbyterian minister.* Also *vi* serve; help: *ministering to the needs of the poor.* (*formal* in this sense).

ministerial [minis'tiəriəl] *adj* having to do with a minister: *politician of ministerial rank.*

ministration [minis'treiʃən] *nc* act of helping. *The poor man responded to their ministrations.* (*formal*).

ministry ['ministri] *nc* **1.** department in a government; building containing a certain government department: *Ministry of Defence; refer something to the Ministry.* **2.** group of ministers who run a country. *A new ministry is being formed.* **3.** period during which someone is a minister. *His ministry lasted from 1925 to 1930.*

the ministry group of clergymen in a certain church considered as a whole. *He is going to enter the ministry* i.e. become a minister.

'prime 'minister chief minister in a government.

mink [miŋk] **1.** *nc* type of small animal. **2.** *nu* expensive fur from this animal. **3.** *nc* expensive coat worn by women, made from mink's fur. Also *adj*: *mink coat.*

minnow ['minou] *nc* type of very small freshwater fish.

minor ['mainə*] *adj* small; unimportant: *a minor operation* i.e. not a dangerous one. *They discussed the future of the club and other minor problems.* Also *nc* (in a legal sense) person under 18.

minority [mi'nɔriti] **1.** *nc* lesser number; less than half: *supported by only a minority of the voters.* **2.** *nu* state or period of being under age (in Britain, under 18).

minster ['minstə*] *nc* large or important church (usu. one attached at one time to a monastery).

minstrel ['minstrl] *nc* (in former times) person who wandered from place to place entertaining people with songs etc.

mint[1] [mint] **1.** *nu* plant used to flavour food etc. **2.** *nc* sweet flavoured with mint.

mint[2] [mint] *nc* place (usu. official) where coins are made from metal. Also *vt* make coins from metal. Also *adj* brand-new: *in mint condition.*

minuet [minju'et] *nc* **1.** old-fashioned, slow, graceful dance. **2.** music for this dance.

minus ['mainəs] *prep* **1.** less (shown in mathematics by the sign —). *Five minus two equals three* (5−2=3). **2.** without; having lost. *He returned from the war minus an arm.* (*informal* in sense **2.**). Also *adj* negative: *the minus sign; a minus quantity* i.e. less than 0. Also *nc* the minus sign.

minute[1] ['minit] *nc* **1.** 1/60 of an hour: *five minutes past six; in twenty minutes' time.* **2.** (in measuring angles) 1/60 of a degree. **3.** brief note on some official matter to be decided or considered.

minutes *npl* record of what is said and decided at a meeting.

'minute hand hand that shows the minutes on a clock or watch.

in a minute in a short time. *I'll see you in a minute* i.e. wait for a short time.

this minute immediately. *Do it this minute.*

to the minute exactly: *five hours to the minute.*

minute[2] [mai'nju:t] *adj* very small; giving all the details: *a minute amount; a minute account of something one has seen.* **minutely** *adv.*

minx [miŋks] *nc* rude or cunning young girl. (*informal*).

miracle ['mirəkl] *nc* **1.** happening which cannot be explained naturally and is due to a god or other supernatural power: *be able to work miracles* i.e. perform miracles. **2.** any strange or wonderful happening or achievement: *miracles of modern science. It's a miracle you arrived so early.*

miraculous [mi'rækjuləs] *adj* strange or wonderful; due to supernatural causes. **miraculously** *adv.*

mirage ['mirɑ:ʒ] *nc* **1.** illusion caused by air conditions in hot areas (esp. deserts) by which things which are actually far away seem to be near, or in which one seems to see something which is not actually there. **2.** any kind of illusion.

mire ['maiə*] *nu* wet ground; deep mud. **miry** *adj.*

mirror ['mirə*] *nc* shiny surface (usu. of glass) in which things are reflected. *She was looking at herself in the mirror.* Also *vt* give an exact copy or reflection of. *The mountains were mirrored in the lake.*

'mirror 'image copy of something in which right and left are the other way round (as in a mirror).

'driving mirror small mirror in a car which allows the driver to see what is behind him.

mirth [mə:θ] *nu* laughter; merriment.

mirthful *adj* laughing; joyful.

mis- [mis] *prefix* wrong; badly; not (e.g. **misdeed; misfit; mistrust**).

misadventure [misəd'ventʃə*] **1.** *nc* event caused by bad luck. **2.** *nu* bad luck.

misalliance [misə'laiəns] *nc* unsuitable alliance; unsuitable marriage.

misanthrope ['mizənθroup] *nc* person who hates or does not trust mankind, or who avoids meeting people. (Also **misanthropist** [mi'zænθrəpist]). **misanthropic** [mizən'θrɔpik] *adj.*

misapprehend [misæpri'hend] *vt* not understand correctly.

misapprehension *nc/u* misunderstanding: *be under a misapprehension* i.e. have a false or mistaken idea about something.

misappropriate [misə'prouprieit] *vt* take something and use it for a wrong purpose; use what belongs to another for one's own purposes. *The treasurer misappropriated the society's funds.* **misappropriation** [misəproupri'eiʃən] *nu.*

misbehave [misbi'heiv] *vi* (usu. with reference to children) behave badly.

misbehaviour [misbi'heivjə*] (*US* **misbehavior**) *nu* act of misbehaving.

miscarriage ['miskæridʒ] *nc* **1.** mistake; failure: *miscarriage of justice* i.e. a wrong verdict. **2.** accidental birth of a baby before the proper time with the result that it dies.

miscarry [mis'kæri] *vi* **1.** end in failure; not have the expected or wished for result. *All my plans have miscarried.* **2.** (with reference to a letter, parcel etc) fail to arrive at the proper destination. **3.** have a miscarriage (in sense **2.**).

miscellaneous [misi'leiniəs] *adj* consisting of different and varied parts; mixed: *a miscellaneous collection of books; a miscellaneous crowd of people; miscellaneous objects.*

miscellany [mi'seləni] *nc* collection (usu. of stories and articles by one author or different authors).

mischance [mis'tʃɑ:ns] *nc* misfortune; piece of bad luck: *by some mischance.*

mischief ['mistʃif] *nu* **1.** (esp. with reference to children) trouble caused by foolish or naughty behaviour: *always up to mischief; often getting into mischief.* **2.** injury or harm deliberately caused by someone. *He is always making mischief between his neighbours* i.e. causing them to quarrel. *Note:* in sense **1.** *mischief* is not a serious matter; but in sense **2.** it is.

mischievous ['mistʃivəs] *adj* **1.** annoying or troublesome (but usu. not in a serious way): *a mischievous child.* **2.** teasing; sly: *a mischievous glance.* **mischievously** *adv.*

misconceive [miskən'si:v] *vt* fail to understand something. *He misconceived our intentions.*

misconception [miskən'sepʃən] *nc* failure to understand, wrong idea.

be under a misconception have a wrong idea about something.

misconduct [mis'kɔndəkt] *nu* **1.** bad or wrong behaviour (esp. adultery). **2.** wrong behaviour of someone in a responsible position (e.g. acceptance of a bribe by an official etc). Also [miskən'dʌkt] *vt* **1.** run a business etc badly. **2.** behave badly: *misconduct oneself.*

misconstrue [miskən'stru:] *vt* take the wrong meaning from: *misconstrue someone's actions/words etc.* **misconstruction** [miskən'strʌkʃən] *nc/u.*

miscreant ['miskriənt] *nc* person who behaves in an evil way (*o.f.* – use **scoundrel, villain etc**).

misdeal [mis'di:l] *vt* (with reference to playing cards) make a mistake in giving out cards so that people get the wrong number of cards. *past* **misdealt** [mis'delt]. Also *nc* such a mistake.

misdeed ['mis'di:d] *nc* crime; evil act. *He will pay for his misdeeds.*

misdemeanour [misdi'mi:nə*] *nc* wrong or unlawful act which is not very serious: *guilty of a misdemeanour.*

miser ['maizə*] *nc* person who loves money for its own sake and spends or gives away as little of it as he can.

miserly *adj* mean. **miserliness** *nu.*

miserable ['mizərəbl] *adj* **1.** unhappy: *feeling very miserable.* **2.** poor; wretched: *living in miserable circumstances.* **3.** causing one to feel unhappy: *a miserable scene.* **miserably** *adv.*

misery ['mizəri] *nc/u* **1.** unhappiness. **2.** poverty; wretchedness.

misfire [mis'faiə*] *vi* **1.** (with reference to a gun etc) fail to fire properly. **2.** generally fail in some way. *The engine misfired. His plans misfired.* Also *nc* such a failure.

misfit ['misfit] *nc* **1.** article of clothing (e.g. jacket or coat) which is too large or too small. **2.** someone who is unsuitable for a position or for his surroundings: *a misfit in the post he holds.*

misfortune [mis'fɔ:tʃən] **1.** *nu* bad luck. **2.** *nc* event caused by or bringing bad luck.

misgiving [mis'giviŋ] *nc/u* (often *pl*) fear; doubt; distrust. *I had some misgivings about lending him the money.*

misgovern [mis'gʌvən] *vt/i* rule badly.

misguided [mis'gaidid] *adj* foolish; mistaken (esp. as a result of others' advice): *a misguided attitude.* **misguidedly** *adv.*

mishap ['mishæp] *nc* unfortunate accident or event (usu. not serious): *a slight mishap.*

misinform [misin'fɔ:m] *vt* give wrong information to.

misinterpret [misin'tə:prit] *vt* explain wrongly, not understand correctly. *I think you misinterpreted my meaning.* **misinterpretation** [misintə:pri'teiʃən] *nc/u.*

mislay [mis'lei] *vt* put a thing somewhere and be unable to find it later. *past* **mislaid.**

mislead [mis'li:d] *vt* **1.** cause someone to have the wrong ideas, opinions etc. *I'm sorry I misled you into thinking I would be at home.* **2.** cause someone to commit evil. *He was misled by his companions.* **3.** make a mistake in guiding someone somewhere. *past* **misled** [mis'led].

mismanage [mis'mænidʒ] *vt* run or manage badly: *mismanage one's business and lose money.* **mismanagement** *nu.*

misnomer [mis'noumə*] *nc* wrong name for someone/something. *The name 'Curly' for someone who is bald would seem to be a misnomer.*

misogyny [mi'sɔdʒini] *nu* hatred of women. **misogynist** *nc.*

misplace [mis'pleis] *vt* **1.** put in the wrong place or a place afterwards forgotten. **2.** give unwisely (esp. trust, love, affections etc).

misprint ['misprint] *nc* mistake in printing. Also [mis'print] *vt.*

mispronounce [misprə'nauns] *vt* pronounce something badly. **mispronunciation** [misprənʌnsi'eiʃən] *nc/u.*

misquote [mis'kwout] *vt/i* quote wrongly. *He is always misquoting Shakespeare* i.e. he does not get the words of the quotation right. **misquotation** [miskwou'teiʃən] *nc/u.*

misrepresent [misrepri'zent] *vt* give a wrong idea of. *You are misrepresenting my views on this matter.* **misrepresentation** [misreprizen'teiʃən] *nc/u.*

misrule [mis'ru:l] *nu* bad government.

miss[1] [mis] *vt/i* **1.** not succeed in doing something one wants or tries to do: *fire at a target and miss; miss something that is thrown to one; miss a train one wants to get; miss the point of something one wants to understand.* **2.** feel lonely after; regret the absence of. *I miss John now that he is abroad. She misses having her breakfast in bed.*

missing *adj* not to be found; absent: *missing in action* i.e. of a soldier in battle; *a couple of words missing.*

miss something out omit; leave out. *You've missed out a word.*

just miss narrowly fail to do something: *just miss the bus.*

a near miss explosion or shot (e.g. in bombing) which is not quite on the target.

miss[2] [mis] *n* title of an unmarried woman or girl: *Miss Brown.*

missal ['misl] *nc* type of prayer book, used for following the mass and other Roman Catholic church services throughout the year.

misshapen [mis'ʃeipən] *adj* deformed: *a misshapen body.*

missile ['misail, *US* 'misl] *nc* **1.** object thrown or otherwise sent through the air so as to injure or cause damage (e.g. stone, arrow etc). *The angry crowd threw stones, rocks and other missiles.* **2.** large explosive rocket for use in war.

guided missile see **guide.**

mission ['miʃən] *nc* **1.** journey (usu. abroad) made for a special purpose (not pleasure): *a mission to China.* **2.** group of people travelling somewhere and entrusted with some special duty: *a trade mission; a diplomatic mission.* **3.** group of people living in a foreign country for religious reasons; also, the buildings etc which they put up: *a Christian mission; the mission near the village.* **4.** a person's duty or calling: *his mission in life.*

missionary ['miʃənri] *nc* someone who goes to work in a foreign country for religious reasons (usu. to convert people there to his own beliefs).

misspell ['mis'spel] *vt* spell wrongly: *misspell a word.* **misspelling** *nc/u.*

misspent ['mis'spent] *adj* wasted; used foolishly: *a misspent youth* i.e. the time when a person was young was wasted on foolish things.

missive ['misiv] *nc* letter (*o.f.*).

mist [mist] *nc/u* water vapour which reduces the distance one can see; thin fog. *The hills were covered in mist.*

misty *adj* **1.** covered in mist; having a lot of mist: *the misty plains below us; a misty evening.* **2.** not clear; not definite: *misty idea; misty notions.* **mistily** *adv.* **mistiness** *nu.*

mist over become covered in mist. *The windows have misted over.*

mistake [mis'teik] *nc* error; wrong idea or act. *There are five mistakes in this composition. Lending him the money was a mistake.* Also *vt* not understand; have the wrong idea about. *I mistook his purpose completely* i.e. I had the wrong idea about why he did that. *past tense* **mistook** [mis'tuk]. *past part* **mistaken.**

mistaken *adj* wrong; in error: *be quite*

mistaken i.e. completely wrong: *a mistaken act.* **mistakenly** *adv.*

mistake somebody/something for imagine that somebody/something is somebody/something else. *I mistook him for his brother* i.e. I thought he was his brother.

and no mistake certainly. (*informal*).

by mistake in error: *do something by mistake.*

mistime ['mis'taim] *vt* do something at the wrong time; time something badly. *The unsuccessful candidate has mistimed his bid for the leadership.*

mister ['mistə*] *n* see **Mr.**

mistletoe ['misltou] *nu* plant with small, white fruit, which grows on other plants, and is used for decoration at Christmas.

mistook [mis'tuk] past tense of **mistake.**

mistress ['mistris] *nc* **1.** woman who has control of something: *mistress of the household* i.e. in charge of a home; *mistress of the situation* i.e. in control of what is happening. **2.** (*Brit*) woman teacher: *the English mistress* i.e. the woman who teaches English. **3.** woman who's maintained like a wife by a man to whom she is not married.

mistrust [mis'trust] *vt* feel suspicious or doubtful about: *mistrust someone.* Also *nu.* **mistrustful** *adj* doubtful; suspicious. **mistrustfully** *adv.*

misunderstand [misʌndə'stænd] *vt* not get the right meaning from someone's words/actions etc: *misunderstand what someone said. past* **misunderstood** [misʌndə'stud].

misunderstanding *nc/u* failure on the part of different people to understand things in the same way (esp. when this leads to a quarrel): *slight misunderstanding.* **misunderstood** *adj.*

misuse [mis'ju:z] *vt* **1.** use for a wrong purpose. *He damaged his tools by misusing them.* **2.** treat badly. Also [mis'ju:s] *nc/u.*

mite [mait] *nc* **1.** small child: *just a mite.* (*informal*). **2.** small insect, often found in decayed food etc. **3.** small coin (*o.f.* in sense **3.**).

mitigate ['mitigeit] *vt* make something less severe or serious: *mitigate pain; mitigate a punishment.* **mitigating** *adj.*

mitigation [miti'geiʃən] *nu*: *say something in mitigation of the crime.*

mitre ['maitə*] (*US* **miter**) *nc* **1.** headdress worn by bishops. **2.** method of fitting together two pieces of wood so that they form an angle (usu. 90°) (used e.g. to fit the sides of a picture frame together). Also *vt* (in sense **2.**).

mitre (*def 1*)

mitten ['mitn] *nc* **1.** glove which leaves the fingers bare. **2.** glove in which four of the fingers fit into one part and the thumb into another.

mix [miks] **1.** *vt* put things together so that they are united in some way: *mix the ingredients for a cake; mix people together. One should never mix business with pleasure* i.e. they should be done separately. **2.** *vt* make something from certain ingredients: *mix mortar.* **3.** *vi* come together to form a unit; be united. *Oil and water won't mix.* **4.** *vi* come together in company or society: *mix with people at a party; races mixing together.* Also *nc* **1.** mixture; what results from mixing: *cement mix.* **2.** food preparation sold in shops requiring only the addition of water etc: *cake-mix.*

mixed *adj* including or made up of different kinds of things: *mixed marriage* i.e. marriage between people of different races or religions; *mixed bathing* i.e. men and women bathing together.

mixture **1.** *nu* act of being mixed; mixing. **2.** *nc* something formed by mixing things together: *tea mixture; tobacco mixture; mixture of good and bad qualities.*

mix something up confuse; put together or arrange badly or mistakenly.

'mixed-'up *adj* **1.** confused. *I'm all mixed up about this* i.e. I do not understand it. **2.** involved. *Don't get mixed up in other people's business* i.e. have nothing to do with it.

mnemonic [ni'mɔnik] *nc* any arrangement of words or ideas which is learnt to help one remember something else.

moan [moun] *nc* low sound as from someone who is in pain or suffering: *a moan of pain.* Also *vi*: *moan with pain.*

moat [mout] *nc* deep ditch (usu. round a castle) filled with water, and intended to make a place easier to defend.

mob [mɔb] *nc* confused and disorderly crowd: *a mob of people; an uncontrollable mob.* Also *vt* crowd round in order to show hostility or enthusiasm. *The crowd mobbed the popular film star. past* **mobbed.**

mobile ['moubail] *adj* **1.** able to move or be moved easily. *He has not been so mobile since his accident.* **2.** changing expression often: *mobile features.* Also *nc* type of sculpture or decoration, consisting of a number of small objects attached to a framework which is hanging from a ceiling and is moved by currents of air. **mobility** [mou'biliti] *nu.*

mobilize ['moubilaiz] *vt* get people, resources etc ready for some urgent reason (esp. war): *mobilize soldiers; mobilize one's resources.* **mobilization** [moubilai'zeiʃən] *nu.*

moccasin ['mɔkəsin] *nc* type of shoe completely made from soft leather (e.g. deerskin).

mock [mɔk] *vt/i* make fun of unkindly (esp. by imitating). *The children mocked his way of speaking.* Also *adj* not real; imitation: *a mock battle.*

mockery ['mɔkəri] **1.** *nu* act of mocking: *the mockery of the crowd.* **2.** *nc* somebody/something that is made fun of. *They made a mockery of him.* **3.** *nc* poor imitation: *a mockery of justice.*

mock at someone/something make fun of unkindly. *They mocked at his poverty.*

'mock-up *nc* model of something (e.g. an aeroplane) to show what it will look like when it is finished.

mode [moud] *nc* **1.** way of doing or saying something: *his mode of life; mode of speaking.* **2.** style; manner of dress: *the very latest mode.* **3.** (music) arrangement of notes in a scale.

modish *adj* fashionable.

model ['mɔdl] *nc* **1.** copy of something on a smaller scale: *model of an aeroplane.* **2.**

something which has to be, or ought to be, copied: *a perfect model for a student.* **3.** something/somebody to be drawn, painted etc by an artist. *The girl worked as an artist's model.* **4.** girl who shows something for sale (usu. clothes): *a fashion model.* **5.** small copy made as a toy: *a model car.* Also *adj* excellent; worthy of imitation: *a model husband.* Also *vt* **1.** make or shape from some soft material (e.g. clay). **2.** show clothes to customers by wearing them: *model gowns. past* **modelled.** (*US* **modeled**).
model oneself on someone try to live in the same way as another person.

moderate[1] ['mɔdərit] *adj* **1.** not going too far; not extreme: *moderate opinions.* **2.** not too little, not too much; medium: *a moderate amount; a moderate income.* (*opp* **immoderate**). Also *nc* person who does not hold extreme views (esp. in politics).
moderately *adv.*

moderate[2] ['mɔdəreit] *vt/i* become or make less violent or extreme: *moderate one's anger.*
moderation [mɔdə'reiʃən] *nu* quality of being moderate.
in moderation in reasonable, not too large amounts: *drink in moderation.*

modern ['mɔdn] *adj* **1.** having to do with present or recent times; not ancient: *modern ideas; modern history.* **2.** up-to-date: *modern furniture.*
modernity [mɔ'də:niti] *nu* condition of being modern.
modernize *vt* bring up to date; make modern: *modernize business methods.*
modernization [mɔdənai'zeiʃən] *nc/u.*

modest ['mɔdist] *adj* **1.** not thinking too highly of one's own powers; not proud: *a modest person.* **2.** not very large, grand etc: *a modest crowd; a modest house.* **3.** not offensive to decency etc: *modest dress; modest behaviour.* **modestly** *adv.* **modesty** *nu.*

modicum ['mɔdikəm] *n* (only *sing*) small amount.

modify ['mɔdifai] *vt* **1.** change slightly: *modify the original plan.* **2.** make less: *modify one's demands.* **3.** (grammar) describe or limit a word (e.g. in the phrase *walk slowly*, the word *slowly* modifies *walk*).
modification [mɔdifi'keiʃən] *nc/u* change.

modulate ['mɔdjuleit] *vt* **1.** moderate or tone down. **2.** (music) change pitch or key.
modulation [mɔdju'leiʃən] *nc/u.*

mohair ['mouhɛə*] *nu* type of very soft wool. Also *adj*: *a mohair scarf.*

Mohammedan [mə'hæmidn] *nc* follower of Mohammed. Also *adj* connected with Mohammed or his religious system.
Mohammedanism *nu.*
Note: *Muslim* is preferred instead of Mohammedan, and *Islam* instead of Mohammedanism.

moist [mɔist] *adj* slightly wet; damp.
moisten ['mɔisn] *vt/i* become or make damp.
moisture ['mɔistʃə*] *nu* **1.** wetness. **2.** condensed liquid (usu. water) on the surface of something in the form of small drops: *moisture on the window.*

molar ['moulə*] *nc* large double tooth at the side of the mouth used for grinding food.

molasses [mə'læsiz] *nu* thick dark liquid obtained from raw sugar.
Note: followed by a *sing* verb.

mole[1] [moul] *nc* small, fur-covered animal that eats insects and lives in tunnels which it makes under the ground.
'molehill small pile of earth thrown up by a mole.
make a mountain out of a molehill see **make**[1].

mole[2] [moul] *nc* dark spot on the skin, often present from birth.

mole[3] [moul] *nc* strong wall made of stone and cement and built in the sea, often at the entrance to a harbour to protect it from the force of the sea coming in.

molecule ['mɔlikju:l] *nc* smallest division of a substance possible without changing its chemical nature.
molecular [mɔ'lekjulə*] *adj* connected with molecules.

molest [mə'lest] *vt* deliberately give trouble to someone; interfere with. *The crowd molested the policeman who was trying to do his duty.* **molestation** [moules'teiʃən] *nu.*

mollify ['mɔlifai] *vt* calm, make less angry. *He was somewhat mollified when he heard our explanation.*

mollusc ['mɔləsk] *nc* one of several types of animals which have soft bodies (usu. protected by a shell) (e.g. oyster, snail, octopus etc).

mollycoddle ['mɔlikɔdl] *vt* protect too much (e.g. of a child). Also *nc* man or boy who is weak and cowardly because too much attention has been given to him. (both *informal*).

molten ['moultn] *adj* see **melt.**

moment ['moumənt] **1.** *nc* point in time; very short period of time. *For a moment I thought you were going to refuse. The feeling only lasted a moment. He's probably thinking of you at this moment.* **2.** *nu* importance: *of great moment.*
momentary ['moumәntri] *adj* lasting only for a very short time: *a momentary sensation.*
momentarily *adv.*
momentous [mou'mentəs] *adj* extremely important: *a momentous decision.* **momentously** *adv.*
at the moment just now. *I'm afraid he's busy at the moment.*
at the last moment just in time. *He caught his train at the last moment.*
in a moment very soon. *He'll be with you in a moment* i.e. he'll come very soon.
of great/little moment of great or little importance.
man of the moment man who is most important at the present time.
not for a moment never. *I wouldn't for a moment consider lending him money.*
the moment (that) as soon as. *The moment (that) I saw him I recognized him.*

momentum [mou'mentəm] *nu* force or speed of a moving body. *The truck gained momentum as it rolled down the steep road.*

monarch ['mɔnək] *nc* king or emperor.
monarchy **1.** *nu* rule by a monarch. **2.** *nc* country ruled by a monarch.
monarchist *nc* person who is in favour of rule by a monarch.

monastery ['mɔnəstəri] *nc* building where monks live together.
monastic [mə'næstik] *adj* connected with a monastery, or with monks or their way of life: *monastic vows; monastic existence.*

Monday ['mʌndi] *n* second day of the week, following Sunday.

monetary ['mʌnitəri] *adj* see **money.**

money ['mʌni] *nu* metal (e.g. gold or silver) stamped in special way (coins), or paper printed in a special way (notes) which can

be used to buy goods or services.
moneyed *adj* wealthy; rich: *a moneyed family.*
moneyless *adj* poor; without money.
monetary ['mʌnitri] *adj* having to do with money: *the monetary system.*
'**moneybox** small box with a narrow opening at the top through which coins may be dropped, used when making collections.
'**moneychanger** person who exchanges the coins and notes of one country for those of another.
'**moneylender** person who lends money and charges a certain amount (called **interest**) for this service.
'**money order** order of a certain value which can be bought at a post office by one person and sent to someone else who will get the value of it at another post office.
lose money make a loss in business etc. *He lost money when he sold his house.*
make money make a profit; become wealthy. *He makes a lot of money from his writing.*
get one's money's worth get satisfaction from what one has paid money for, or spent money on. (*informal*).

mongoose ['mɔŋguːs] *nc* small Indian animal like a ferret, which can kill snakes. *pl* **mongooses.**

mongrel ['mʌŋgrəl] *nc* **1.** dog of mixed breed. **2.** any animal or plant of mixed breed or origin. Also *adj* of mixed origin (esp. where the origins do not seem fitting for one another).

monitor ['mɔnitə*] *nc* **1.** schoolboy appointed to help in the running of a school (e.g. in keeping discipline or in performing some task): *a class monitor.* **2.** something that gives advice or warning if something goes wrong (e.g. with machinery etc). Also *vt* listen to radio broadcasts (esp. from a foreign country in order to get information).
'**monitor screen** device used in a television studio to show what the camera is recording.

monk [mʌŋk] *nc* one of a group of men who devote their lives to God and live together in a religious community (called a **monastery**) (*fem* **nun** [nʌn]).

monkey ['mʌŋki] *nc* **1.** one of the group of animals which is most closely related to Man and nearly all of which have tails. **2.** mischievous child. (*informal* in sense **2.**).
'**monkey nut** groundnut.
'**monkey wrench** wrench (spanner) which has a join which can be altered in position to take nuts etc of different sizes.

monkey wrench

monkey about with something interfere with something. *Don't monkey about with the radio.* (*informal*).
make a monkey out of someone make someone look foolish. *You're not going to make a monkey out of me.* (*informal*).

mono-[1] ['mɔnou] *prefix* one (e.g. **monosyllable**).

mono[2] ['mɔnou] *adj* short form of **monaural** [mɔn'ɔːrəl] (with reference to gramophone records) recorded so that sound seems to come from one direction only. (*opp* **stereo**).

monocle ['mɔnəkl] *nc* eyeglass held in one eye.

monogamy [mɔ'nɔgəmi] *nu* state or custom of being married to only one person at a time. **monogamist** *nc.* **monogamous** *adj.*

monogram ['mɔnəgræm] *nc* two or more letters (usu. someone's initials) written together to form one sign.

monograph ['mɔnəgrɑːf] *nc* scholarly article, book etc written on one particular subject, often the result of research.

monolith ['mɔnəliθ] *nc* large single block of stone, as used for a pillar, column etc.
monolithic [mɔnə'liθik] *adj.*

monologue ['mɔnəlɔg] *nc* long talk or speech by one person.

monomania [mɔnou'meiniə] *nc/u* **1.** type of madness in which a person is mad on one subject only. **2.** very great interest in one particular subject.
monomaniac [mɔnou'meiniæk] *nc*: *He is a monomaniac on the subject of cars* i.e. he seems to be interested in them to an unusual degree. Also *adj.*

monoplane ['mɔnəplein] *nc* aeroplane with one wing only on either side.

monopoly [mə'nɔpəli] *nc* **1.** state which results in business if only one person or company can supply a certain type of goods: *a monopoly in sugar.* **2.** something the supply of which is controlled by one person or company. *Tea was a monopoly.*
monopolist *nc* person who has the sole right or ability to supply certain goods.
monopolize *vt* keep all of something for one's own use or profit. *He monopolized the conversation* i.e. no one else got a chance to speak.

monorail ['mɔnoureil] *nc* **1.** single rail (usu. above ground level) along which a special type of train can travel. **2.** train which travels on a single rail.

monosyllable ['mɔnəsiləbl] *nc* word made up of only one syllable (e.g. *yes, no*).
monosyllabic [mɔnəsi'læbik] *adj.*
answer in monosyllables answer questions in a way that shows one is not interested in the conversation, or does not want to give information.

monotheism ['mɔnouθiːizəm] *nu* belief that there is only one God.
monotheist *nc* person who has this belief.

monotone ['mɔnətoun] *nc* level way of speaking or singing, without raising or lowering one's voice: *speak in a monotone.*
monotonous [mə'nɔtənəs] *adj* unchanging and therefore dull; uninteresting: *a monotonous journey.* **monotonously** *adv.*
monotony [mə'nɔtəni] *nc/u*: *the monotony of a long train journey.*

monsoon [mɔn'suːn] *nc* **1.** seasonal wind (mainly in South-East Asia) blowing from the south-west for part of the year and from the north-east for another part. **2.** rainy season caused by the south-west monsoon.

monster ['mɔnstə*] *nc* **1.** animal etc which is huge or frightening in some other way. **2.** person who is unnaturally cruel or wicked. **3.** unnatural creature written about in books but not really existing.
monstrous ['mɔnstrəs] *adj* **1.** very wicked. *It's monstrous to treat a child like that.* **2.** huge and frightening: *a monstrous animal.*

monstrously *adv.*
monstrosity [mɔns'trɔsiti] *nc/u* something frightening or very ugly.
month [mʌnθ] *nc* **1.** one of the twelve divisions of the year (e.g. January, February). *I'll see you at the end of the month.* (Also **calendar month**). **2.** period from the date in one month to the same date in the next (e.g. from 10th February to 10th March): *in a couple of months; in a month's time.*
monthly *adj/adv* (happening) once a month: *a monthly meeting.* Also *nc* magazine etc which appears once a month.
lunar month time it takes for the moon to go round the earth i.e. roughly 28 days.
a month's notice warning given one month previously (e.g. that one is to be dismissed from a job).
monument ['mɔnjumənt] *nc* **1.** pillar, statue etc built to keep alive the memory of some person or event. **2.** something which is a proof of outstanding quality: *a monument to someone's ability.*
monumental [mɔnju'mentl] *adj* **1.** (with reference to buildings etc) very large. **2.** having very great qualities of size, cleverness etc: *a monumental achievement.* **monumentally** *adv.*
moo [mu:] *nc* sound that a cow makes. Also *vi.*
mood [mu:d] *nc/u* state of feeling at a particular time: *in a cheerful mood; in a good/bad mood* i.e. feeling pleased/angry; *in the mood for something.*
moody *adj* changing quickly from one kind of mood to another; sullen: *a moody person.* **moodily** *adv.*
moon [mu:n] *nc* **1.** smaller body going round the earth and seen at night as it reflects the light of the sun. **2.** any such smaller body going round a planet: *the moons of Jupiter.*
moonless *adj* dark; having no moon: *a moonless night.*
'moonlight *nu* light from the moon. Also *adj*: *a moonlight walk.*
'moonlit *adj* made bright by the moon: *moonlit gardens; a moonlit night.*
'moonshine **1.** light from the moon. **2.** (mainly US) strong drink made illegally. (*informal* in sense **2.**).
moon about wander about in an aimless way. (*informal*).
man in the moon marks on the surface of the moon, said to resemble a man's face.
once in a blue moon very seldom. *I meet John once in a blue moon.* (*informal*).
moor[1] [muə*] *nc/u* area of open land not used for growing crops and often overgrown with heather.
'moorland wasteland (usu. covered with heather).
moor[2] [muə*] *vt/i* make a ship secure, so that it will not drift away, by attaching it to something with rope or chains, an anchor etc. *The ship was moored just inside the harbour.*
moorings *npl* **1.** ropes or chains etc used to keep a ship in the same place. **2.** place where a ship may be moored.
moose [mu:s] *nc* large kind of deer found in North America.
moot [mu:t] *adj* usu. in **a moot point** i.e. something which is doubtful; something which can be discussed. *Whether or not the entrance fee should be raised is a moot point.* Also *vt* put up for discussion: *moot a question.*
mop [mɔp] *nc* **1.** bundle of strings, pieces of cloth etc tied together, or piece of sponge at the end of a small pole (usu. used for cleaning floors). **2.** thick hair: *a mop of red hair.* Also *vt* clean by using a mop. *past* **mopped.**
mop something up clean up: *mop up a mess; mop up crime in a city.*
mope [moup] *vi* feel sad; be unable to take an interest in anything. *He's been moping all day.* **moping** *nu.*
moral ['mɔrl] *adj* **1.** connected with the choice between right and wrong: *a moral problem.* **2.** pure, not evil: *a moral book; moral behaviour.* (*opp* **immoral** in sense **2.**). Also *nc* lesson; moral teaching: *the moral of the story.*
moralist ['mɔrəlist] *nc* person who is interested in whether ideas, actions etc are right or wrong.
morality [mə'ræliti] *nu* ideas of what is good or evil; goodness, purity.
moralize *vi* talk or write about right and wrong behaviour.
morally *adv* **1.** in a good or pure way. **2.** from the point of view of what is good: *feel morally obliged to help someone.*
morals *npl* **1.** rules of what is good or evil: *a student of morals.* **2.** good or pure behaviour: *person with no morals.*
moral certainty something very probable. *It's a moral certainty that he won't be there.*
moral victory situation where someone has been defeated in a battle, struggle etc but has proved that he is better than his enemy in some way (e.g. the justice of his cause).
give moral support to give encouragement to someone. *I was frightened to go on my own, so I asked a friend along to give me moral support.*
morale [mɔ'rɑ:l] *nu* attitude towards difficulties etc. *The morale of the troops is high* i.e. they are feeling cheerful, ready to fight etc.
morass [mə'ræs] *nc* **1.** low-lying area of soft, wet ground; marshy area. **2.** area of complicated difficulties: *a morass of little details.*
moratorium [mɔrə'tɔ:riəm] *nc* **1.** legal and official delay in paying debts. **2.** stopping of the use or production of something for a short time: *a moratorium on atomic-bomb testing.*
morbid ['mɔ:bid] *adj* **1.** (with reference to a state of mind etc) unhealthy, not normal: *a morbid attitude to death.* **2.** diseased: *a morbid growth.* **3.** having unhealthy ideas: *a morbid person.* **morbidly** *adv.*
mordant ['mɔ:dnt] *adj* cruel; sarcastic: *a mordant wit* i.e. making fun of somebody.
more [mɔ:*] **1.** *determiner* in a greater quantity; to a greater degree: *more people than yesterday; more money than ever before; more heat than usual.* **2.** *determiner* in addition. *Do you want more money? Is there any more food?* **3.** *n* additional amount or number. *Here are some cakes. Will you need any more? He asked for some more. More than one can count* i.e. very many. **4.** *n* something of greater importance, interest etc. *He refused to marry her, and more than that, asked for his presents back.* **5.** *adv/intensifier* in a greater degree (used to form the *comparative* of all *adjs* and *advs* with more than two syllables, and some with only two syllables): *more dangerous (than); more delicious (than); more careless (than);*

more cleverly (than).
Note: more is the *comparative* form of *much* or *many*; *most* is the *superlative*.
more'over *adv* also. *He is stupid and inattentive and, moreover, he is lazy.*
any more any longer. *I don't go there any more.*
more or less almost. *The work is more or less finished.*
more and more increasingly. *He is becoming more and more careless.*
no more neither. *I can't think why she should lie like that. No more can I.* (*informal*).
what is more something of greater importance, interest etc.
morgue [mɔːg] *nc* place where the bodies of people who have died (esp. as a result of violence or an accident) are kept until they can be identified and buried.
moribund ['mɔribʌnd] *adj* **1.** dying: *a moribund person.* **2.** certain to fail or end: *a moribund scheme.*
morning ['mɔːniŋ] *nc* early part of the day until about noon: *early in the morning; tomorrow morning; Sunday morning; one morning last November; on the morning of 20 December.* Also *attrib adj* connected with the morning: *the morning papers; a morning walk.*
'morning coat long black coat cut away at the front used as a part of morning dress.
'morning dress dress worn by men in western countries at formal occasions (e.g. weddings).
Good Morning! greeting used in the early part of the day. *He wished me good morning.*
morocco [mə'rɔkou] *nu* kind of fine leather, originally made from goatskin.
moron ['mɔːrɔn] *nc* person of very low intelligence. **moronic** [mɔ'rɔnik] *adj.*
morose [mə'rous] *adj* silent and bad-tempered: *in a morose mood.* **morosely** *adv.*
morphia ['mɔːfiə], **morphine** ['mɔːfiːn] *nu* white powder used for lessening pain and helping people to sleep.
morrow ['mɔrou] *nc* usu. in **the morrow** i.e. the next day (*o.f.*).
Morse [mɔːs] usu. in **Morse code** i.e. system of using long and short sounds or long and short flashes of light in order to send messages.
morsel ['mɔːsl] *nc* **1.** small piece of food; bite: *not a morsel left.* **2.** small piece of anything: *a morsel of comfort.*
mortal ['mɔːtl] *adj* **1.** certain to die: *a mortal being.* (*opp* **immortal**). **2.** causing death: *a mortal wound.* **3.** ending only in death: *mortal combat* i.e. struggle to the death. **4.** extreme; very great: *in mortal fear.* **5.** deadly; unforgiving: *a mortal enemy; mortal sin.* Also *nc* human being. **mortally** *adv.*
mortality [mɔː'tæliti] *nu* **1.** state of being mortal. **2.** number of deaths (e.g. in a special area): *a high rate of mortality.*
mortar[1] ['mɔːtə*] *nu* mixture of lime or cement or both with sand and water, used in building to hold bricks, stones etc in place. Also *vt* fix with mortar.
'mortarboard 1. flat piece of wood with a short handle used for holding mortar. **2.** square, flat cap sometimes worn by members of a college, university etc.
mortar[2] ['mɔːtə*] *nc* **1.** bowl made from some hard material in which materials are crushed into powder (e.g. grain into flour etc). **2.** short gun which fires shells high into the air.
mortgage ['mɔːgidʒ] *vt* give someone a claim on one's house, land etc as security for a loan i.e. if the loan is not repaid then one must give up one's house, land etc. *He mortgaged his house for £3,000.* Also *nc* legal agreement to mortgage something: *a mortgage of £3,000.*
mortician [mɔː'tiʃən] *nc* (*US*) undertaker.
mortify ['mɔːtifai] *vt/i* **1.** hurt the feelings of; make someone feel ashamed or embarrassed. *We were mortified by his silly behaviour.* **2.** control one's bodily desires by living a hard life: *mortify the flesh.* **3.** (with reference to the flesh round a wound) decay; become affected with gangrene. **mortification** [mɔːtifi'keiʃən] *nu.*
mortise, mortice ['mɔːtis] *nc* hole cut into a piece of wood, into which another piece of wood (called a **tenon**) fits. Also *vt* join two pieces of wood in this way.

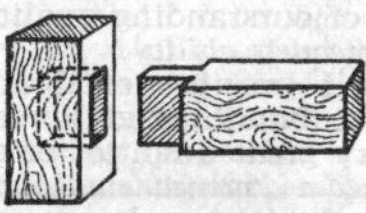

mortise and tenon

'mortise lock lock inserted into the wood of a door instead of being fixed to the surface.
mortuary ['mɔːtjuəri] *nc* building or room where dead bodies of people are kept before being buried.
mosaic [mou'zeiik] *nc* picture, design etc made up of small pieces of coloured material (usu. stone or glass).
Moslem ['mɔzləm] *nc* see **Muslim.**
mosque [mɔsk] *nc* building where Muslims worship.
mosquito [mɔs'kiːtou] *nc* small flying insect which sucks blood and sometimes spreads diseases (esp. malaria). *pl* **mosquitoes.**
mos'quito net screen which keeps out mosquitoes.
moss [mɔs] *nc/u* small plant which grows thickly on rocks, trees etc and wet surfaces. **mossy** *adj.*
most [moust] **1.** *adj* in the greatest quantity; to the greatest degree. *I like tennis and cricket but I get most pleasure from football. Most people go there.* **2.** *n* greatest amount, number etc. *Most of the audience had left. He lost most of his money. Most sports are exciting to watch.* **3.** *n* greatest possible number or amount. *The most you can hope for is £5.* **4.** *adv/intensifier* in the greatest degree (used to form the *superlative* of all *adjs* and *advs* with more than two syllables, and some with only two syllables): *most dangerous; most delicious; most careless; most cleverly.* **mostly** *adv.*
Note: most is the *superlative* form of *much* or *many*; *more* is the *comparative.*
at most, at the most, at the very most not more than. *I can give you twenty-five pence at most.*
make the most of take full advantage of: *make the most of an opportunity.*
for the most part see **part**[1].
mote [mout] *nc* very small bit or particle (of dust).
motel [mou'tel] *nc* hotel which makes special arrangements for customers who have cars.
moth [mɔθ] *nc* winged insect which flies mostly at night, is attracted by bright

lights and (in some species) eats clothes, carpets etc.

'mothball *nc* (often *pl*) small white ball with a very strong smell which keeps moths away from cloth.

'moth-eaten *adj* **1.** eaten by moths. **2.** old, worn. (*informal* in sense **2.**).

mother ['mʌðə*] *nc* **1.** female parent. **2.** something which causes something else. *Necessity is the mother of invention* i.e. the need for something causes it to be invented. Also *vt* care for something/somebody as a mother would care for her child. **motherly** *adj*.

motherhood *nu* state of being a mother.

motherless *adj* without a mother.

motherliness *nu* qualities (e.g. kindness etc) expected of a mother.

'mother country **1.** country in which a person was born. **2.** country with respect to its colonies.

'mother-in-law *nc* mother of one's wife or husband. *pl* **mothers-in-law.**

'mother-of-'pearl *nu* hard shiny substance reflecting different colours, and found inside certain shells (esp. oysters). Also *adj*: *mother-of-pearl earrings.*

'Mother Su'perior *nc* head of a female religious community. *pl* **Mothers Superior** or **Mother Superiors.**

'mother tongue one's native language.

motif [mou'ti:f] *nc* main or most frequent feature or pattern in music, art etc.

motion ['mouʃən] **1.** *nu* movement: *perpetual motion* i.e. movement which never stops. **2.** *nc* way of moving or acting: *strange motions of his hand.* **3.** *nc* suggestion put forward for discussion at a meeting: *a motion to declare the meeting closed.* Also *vt* direct by some sign (e.g. with the hand). *I motioned him to come forward.*

motionless not moving.

'motion 'picture film shown in a cinema.

in motion moving. *The train was in motion.*

go through the motions do something in a very careless manner, not caring whether one is successful or not.

put/set something in motion start something going. *I've put our new plan in motion.*

motive ['moutiv] *adj* causing a person/thing to move or act: *motive power in a machine* i.e. what makes it work. Also *nc* reason for acting. *He gave you help from the purest motives.*

motiveless *adj* without a motive.

motivate ['moutiveit] *vt* give someone a reason for acting: *motivated by greed.* **motivation** [mouti'veiʃən] *nc/u.*

motivated *adj* having a motive. (*opp* **unmotivated**).

motley ['mɔtli] *adj* **1.** made up of different elements; varied: *a motley crowd of people.* **2.** of different colours (*o.f.* in sense **2.** – use **many-coloured, multicoloured**).

motor ['moutə*] *nc* **1.** engine which supplies power (esp. to something that moves e.g. car, aircraft). **2.** car; vehicle. Also *adj* **1.** connected with movement (esp. of muscles): *motor response.* **2.** driven by an engine: *motorboat; motorcar.* Also *vi* travel in a car: *motor to Italy.*

motorist *nc* person who drives a car.

motorize *vt* equip (esp. troops etc) with motor vehicles: *motorized troops.*

'motorcycle vehicle with two wheels like a bicycle but driven by an engine.

'motorway (*Brit*) road which is built for fast driving. (*US* **expressway**).

mottled ['mɔtld] *adj* marked with spots of different sizes and colours: *mottled leaves.*

motto ['mɔtou] *nc* short sentence or phrase (usu. giving a rule of behaviour). *Our school motto is 'Work hard'.* *pl* **mottos** or **mottoes.**

mould[1] [mould] (*US* **mold**) *nc* **1.** hollow container which gives shape to what is poured into it. *The molten (liquid) metal was poured into a mould.* **2.** something made in a mould. Also *vt* make into a required shape; change to a particular form: *mould a statue; mould someone's character.*

mould[2] [mould] (*US* **mold**) *nu* growth on decaying substance (e.g. old cheese, bread etc).

mouldy *adj* affected by mould: *mouldy bread.*

moulder ['mouldə*] (*US* **molder**) *vi* decay through age; turn into dust: *a mouldering old ruin.*

moult [moult] (*US* **molt**) *vt/i* (with reference to birds, animals) lose feathers, hair etc which will be replaced in time: *moulting season.*

mound [maund] *nc* **1.** artificial pile of earth. **2.** small hill. **3.** large pile of anything: *a mound of letters.*

mount [maunt] *nc* **1.** mountain or hill (usu. only occurring before a name e.g. *Mount Everest*). **2.** horse or other animal which one can ride. **3.** card on which a photograph or picture can be placed. Also *vt* **1.** climb; go up: *mount the stairs.* **2.** place a photograph etc on a card.

mounted police policemen on horses.

mount (a horse etc) get on to (a horse etc). *They mounted their horses and rode off.* (*opp* **dismount**).

mount guard over watch carefully; appoint men to watch carefully.

mountain ['mauntin] *nc* **1.** very high hill: *a chain of mountains.* **2.** anything very large; very large amount: *a mountain of books.* Also *adj*: *mountain scenery.*

mountaineer [maunti'niə*] *nc* person who climbs mountains. Also *vi* climb mountains. **mountaineering** *nu.*

mountainous *adj* **1.** containing mountains: *a mountainous region.* **2.** very big: *mountainous waves.*

'mountain 'range line of connected mountains.

'mountainside slope of a mountain.

make a mountain out of a molehill see **make**[1].

mountebank ['mauntibæŋk] *nc* person who can persuade people by clever talk (often to buy things that are worthless) (*o.f.*).

mourn [mɔ:n] *vt/i* feel or show sadness (usu. for someone's death). *She mourned the death of her two sons.* **mourner** *nc.*

mournful *adj* **1.** showing sadness: *a mournful face.* **2.** causing one to feel sorry, sad etc: *a mournful scene.*

mourning *nu* **1.** sorrow. **2.** dress which people wear (e.g. black clothes) to show sorrow for someone's death.

go into mourning show one's grief in some way (e.g. by wearing black clothes).

mouse [maus] *nc* small animal with a long tail. *pl* **mice** [mais].

mousse [mu:s] *nc/u* type of cream, made from fruit and the white of eggs etc.

moustache [məs'tɑ:ʃ] *nc* hair grown on the upper lip.

mouth[1] [mauθ] *nc* **1.** opening through

which a human or animal takes food. *The child put the sweet into its mouth.* **2.** open part of something: *mouth of a cave; mouth of a bottle; mouth of a river.*
mouthful *nc* amount taken into the mouth at one time. *I took only a mouthful of food and then left.*
'mouth organ small musical instrument which is played by sliding it along the lips while breathing in and out.
'mouthpiece 1. part of something (e.g. pipe, musical instrument) that goes into or onto the mouth. **2.** person, newspaper etc that gives the opinions of others. *The newspaper was only a mouthpiece of certain rich people.*
down in the mouth sad; depressed. *You'll have to cheer up; you've been looking down in the mouth all evening.* (*informal*).
live from hand to mouth see **live**[1].
put words into somebody's mouth 1. tell someone what to say. **2.** say that somebody has made certain statements, when he hasn't. *Stop putting words into my mouth!*
take the words out of someone's mouth say what someone else was going to say before he has a chance to. (*informal*).
mouth[2] [mauð] *vt* **1.** say words in an unnaturally careful way. *He tried to impress by mouthing all his words.* **2.** speak without making any sound.
move[1] [mu:v] **1.** *vi* go from one place or position to another. *Will you move so that I can pass? Cars were slowly moving down the road. The birds were silent and nothing moved. The people who live across the road are moving* i.e. going to another house. **2.** *vt* cause to go from one place to another. *Move those boxes over here.* **3.** *vt* cause to feel sorry, sad etc: *deeply moved by someone's sufferings.* **4.** *vt* cause to do something. *What moved him to say that?*
move[2] [mu:v] *nc* **1.** something done to gain a certain end: *a move in the right direction* i.e. the correct thing to do; *a good move* i.e. a correct action or decision. **2.** change of place or position. *I asked him to leave but he didn't make the slightest move.* **3.** (in certain board games) the opportunity to change the position of a piece. *It's your move now* i.e. your turn to move.
movable, moveable ['mouvibl] *adj* able to be taken from one place to another. (*opp* **immovable**).
movement 1. *nc/u* changing of place or position: *a movement of the hand. We suspected that the lion was hiding in the grass, but there was no sign of movement.* **2.** *nc* group of people who have come together to achieve a certain aim, or the actions of such a group: *movement for the abolition of slavery.* **3.** *nc* working parts (or section of them) of some mechanical thing: *the movement of a watch.* **4.** *nc* separate part of a long piece of music.
movie *nc* ['mu:vi] (mainly *US*) film shown in a cinema. (*Brit* **film**).
the movies (mainly *US*) a cinema show: *going to the movies.* (*Brit* **the pictures**).
move along/down/up etc go, make someone go, in a certain direction. *The policeman told us to move along. He moved us along.*
move in take one's furniture, belongings etc into the house one is going to live in.
move (someone) on go, make someone go, from one place to another. *They just keep moving on from one place to another.*
move out leave one's home for good. *We're moving out of our old house next week.*
move heaven and earth do everything in one's power. (*informal*).
move house take one's furniture etc from one house to another. *I see that our neighbours are moving house.*
get a move on hurry up. (*informal*).
make a move go; leave. *I really must make a move.* (*informal*).
on the move changing position; going from one place to another. *He is always on the move* i.e. has no permanent home. *It seems that the enemy forces are on the move.*
mow [mou] *vt/i* cut grass etc with a scythe or a machine. *This is the time to mow grass.* *past tense* **mowed.** *past part* **mowed** or **mown** [moun].
mow someone down kill (esp. by gunfire).
Mr ['mistə*] *n* title of a man: *Mr Smith.*
Mrs ['misiz] *n* title put before the surname of a married woman. (Thus if a girl called Jane Smith marries a man called John Brown, her title will be *Mrs Brown*).
Note: the words *Mr* and *Mrs* should always be used with the person's surname and not alone.
much [mʌtʃ] **1.** *adj/n* in great quantity, degree etc; great quantity, degree etc of. *He has given much thought to the problem. Much of what you say is true. He hasn't got much land.*
Note: 1. *much* is used with *sing* uncountable nouns, but not with *pl* countable nouns. So we can say *much salt, much time etc* but *many books, many things etc.* 2. in *affirmative* sentences (i.e. not questions or *negatives*) it is usu. better to say *a lot (of); plenty (of) etc.* So we say *He has a lot of money* or *He has plenty of money* not *He has much money. Much* is more often found in questions or *negatives*: *How much land has he? He hasn't much time.*
2. *adv* to a great extent or degree; greatly. *This is much better than the others. It's much longer than I thought.* **3.** *adv/intensifier* very. *I won't be much surprised if he comes. I'm much obliged to you* i.e. very thankful.
Note: much cannot be used in front of every *adj*; when in doubt use *very.*
Note: comparative **more.** *superlative* **most.**
much as although. *Much as I would like to come, I can't.*
be too much for be cleverer, more skilful, stronger etc than. *I tried to beat him, but he was too much for me.*
make much of 1. treat something as being very important. *They made much of the fact that he left early.* **2.** be very kind or pleasant to.
not much of a not a good: *not much of a tennis player/swimmer/host/entertainer etc.*
not think much of not have a high opinion of. *I don't think much of your friend – he was very rude to me.*
not up to much not very good. *I don't think his paintings are up to much.* (*informal*).
muck [mʌk] *nu* **1.** rubbish; dirt. *You'll have to clear all the muck out of that cupboard.* (*informal*). **2.** farmyard manure.
muck about waste time by doing something unimportant. (*informal*).
muck something up make a mess of something; do something badly. (*informal*).
mucous ['mju:kəs] *adj* usu. in **mucous membrane** i.e. soft moist lining or skin (e.g. on the inside of the nose or mouth).
mucus ['mju:kəs] *nu* liquid produced by the mucous membrane.

mud [mʌd] *nu* soft, wet earth. *After the rain, the roads were covered in mud. You find mud at the bottom of a pond.* **muddy** *adj.* **'mudguard** (*Brit*) cover placed over the wheel of a motorcycle, car etc so as to protect people from the mud thrown up by the wheel. (*US* **fender**).

muddle ['mʌdl] *vt* mix things up; confuse. *He's muddled all the arrangements. I'm feeling a bit muddled* i.e. confused. Also *nc* confused state: *in a muddle* i.e. confused.
'muddle-'headed *adj* confused.
muddle through be successful in something without proper work or planning. *Somehow he managed to muddle through university.*

muff[1] [mʌf] *nc* piece of warm cloth or fur like a tube with open ends into which women or children put their hands to keep them warm.

muff[2] [mʌf] *vt* fail to do something that is quite easy: *muff a catch* i.e. let a ball drop (e.g. in cricket) which one should have caught; *muff an opportunity* i.e. not make the most of an opportunity.

muffin ['mʌfin] *nc* flat round cake with holes in it (usu. eaten hot with butter).

muffle ['mʌfl] *vt* **1.** wrap up in order to keep warm. *The children were well muffled up* i.e. they were wearing coats, scarves etc. **2.** make the sound of something less by wrapping it in cloth etc. *We muffled the oars so that people on the riverbank could not hear us.*
muffler ['mʌflə*] *nc* **1.** piece of cloth that goes round the neck to keep it warm. **2.** (*US*) device attached to motorcars to lessen the amount of noise. (*Brit* **silencer**).

mufti ['mʌfti] **1.** *nu* civilian clothes, not a uniform: *soldiers in mufti.* **2.** *nc* adviser on Muslim law.

mug [mʌg] *nc* **1.** large drinking glass or cup with a handle. **2.** person who is easily deceived. (*informal*). **3.** face. (*informal*). Also *vt* attack and rob someone. (*informal*).
mug up study hard. (*informal*).

muggy ['mʌgi] *adj* (with reference to weather) unpleasantly warm and damp.

mulatto [mju'lætou] *nc* person who has one white parent and one black parent. *pl* **mulattoes.**

mulberry ['mʌlbəri] *nc* **1.** type of tree, some of which have leaves used as food for silkworms. **2.** the fruit of this tree.

mulch [mʌltʃ] *nu* covering of wet straw, leaves etc put around the roots of plants etc in order to protect them and improve the soil. Also *vt* cover with mulch.

mulct [mʌlkt] *vt* **1.** punish someone by taking money from him; fine. **2.** take money etc away from: *mulcted of all his money.*

mule[1] [mju:l] *nc* **1.** offspring of an ass and a horse (esp. of a male ass and a female horse). **2.** stubborn person. (*informal* in sense **2.**).
mulish *adj* obstinate; unwilling to do what one is told.

mule[2] [mju:l] *nc* slipper without a back to the heel.

mull[1] [mʌl] *vi* (with **over**) think carefully about something. *I'll give you time to mull it over.*

mull[2] [mʌl] *vt* heat (wine etc), adding sugar, spices etc.

mullet ['mʌlit] *nc* one of various kinds of fish. *pl* **mullet** or **mullets.**

multi- ['mʌlti] *prefix* many (e.g. **multifarious; multitude**).

multifarious [mʌlti'fɛəriəs] *adj* many different: *busy with multifarious activities.*

multilateral [mʌlti'lætərəl] *adj* **1.** having many sides: *a multilateral figure.* **2.** involving many groups, countries etc: *multilateral aid.*

multiple ['mʌltipl] *adj* having many parts. Also *nc* number which contains another number a certain number of times exactly (e.g. 30 is a multiple of 10).
multiplicity [mʌlti'plisiti] *nu* great number of different things: *multiplicity of jobs.*

multiply ['mʌltiplai] *vt/i* **1.** find the sum of a number added to itself a certain number of times. *Five multiplied by six equals thirty* ($5 \times 6 = 30$). **2.** increase in number. *Mistakes have been multiplying rapidly.*
multiplication [mʌltipli'keiʃən] *nu* act of multiplying or being multiplied.

multi-stage ['mʌlti'steidʒ] *adj* usu. in **multi-stage rocket** i.e. a rocket with different parts containing fuel etc which fall off at various points in the rocket's journey.

multitude ['mʌltitju:d] *nc* large number; crowd (*o.f.* – usu. in **a multitude of sins**).
multitudinous [mʌlti'tju:dinəs] *adj* great in number.

mum[1] [mʌm] *adj* silent.
mum's the word say nothing about this matter. (*informal*).

mum[2] [mʌm] informal form of **mother.**

mumble ['mʌmbl] *vt/i* speak in a low indistinct way so that the words are difficult to understand. *Stop mumbling and speak clearly!* Also *nu.*

mumbo jumbo ['mʌmbou'dʒʌmbou] *nu* nonsense which pretends to be learned or impressive.

mummy[1] ['mʌmi] *nc* dead body treated in a special way so that it does not decay i.e. embalmed (esp. as done by the Ancient Egyptians).

mummy[2] ['mʌmi] *nc* informal form of **mother.**

mumps [mʌmps] *nu* infectious disease which causes painful swelling in the neck. *Note:* followed by a *sing* verb.

munch [mʌntʃ] *vt/i* eat noisily with a lot of movement of the jaws. *The children were all munching apples.*

mundane [mʌn'dein] *adj* **1.** worldly, not spiritual. **2.** of everyday importance.

municipal [mju:'nisipl] *adj* having to do with a town or city; run or owned by the ruling body of a town or city: *municipal transport.*
municipality [mju:nisi'pæliti] *nc* town or city which elects its own ruling body; ruling body of such a town or city.

munificent [mju:'nifisnt] *adj* generous. *The library was paid for by a munificent businessman.* **munificently** *adv.* **munificence** *nu.*

munitions [mju:'niʃənz] *npl* things used for fighting (esp. guns and shells): *munitions factory* i.e. where guns, shells etc are made.

mural ['mjuərl] *adj* of or on a wall: *mural decorations.* Also *nc* painting done on a wall.

murder ['mə:də*] *vt* illegally kill a person on purpose: *murder someone for his money.* Also *nc/u*: *commit murder; accused of murder.*
murderer *nc.* (*fem* **murderess** ['mə:dəris]).
murderous *adj* threatening; dangerous: *a murderous look.* **murderously** *adv.*

murky ['mə:ki] *adj* dark; badly lit: *a murky street.* **murkily** *adv.*

murmur ['mə:mə*] *vt/i* **1.** make a low, unclear sound going on for some time:

murmuring of bees/a stream/a crowd. **2.** say something in a low voice: *murmur a few words.* Also *nc*: *There was a murmur of voices in the room. He left without a murmur* i.e. without saying anything, without complaining.

muscle ['mʌsl] *nc/u* fibres within the body which produce movement when tightened or loosened. *He developed the muscles in his legs by running.*

muscular ['mʌskjulə*] *adj* **1.** of the muscles: *muscular pain.* **2.** having strong muscles: *a muscular man.*

muse[1] [mju:z] *nc* one of the goddesses who encouraged the arts.

muse[2] [mju:z] *vt* think deeply about something, not paying attention to what is around one. *He was musing on his father's words when he was startled by a noise.*

museum [mju:'ziəm] *nc* building containing and displaying interesting or beautiful things (esp. things connected with art, science etc).

mush [mʌʃ] *nu* **1.** fine grain, boiled in water, or any such soft, wet mixture: *mush for the cattle.* **2.** rubbish; (esp. poor quality books, music etc) sentimentality. (*informal* in sense **2.**). **mushy** *adj.*

mushroom ['mʌʃrum] *nc* type of quickly growing fungus that can be eaten. Also *vi* grow quickly. *The town mushroomed into a city.* Also *adj* very quick in growth: *mushroom growth.*

music ['mju:zik] *nu* **1.** art of making pleasant sounds using special instruments or the human voice: *study music.* **2.** sounds made in this way: *listen to beautiful music.* **3.** printed or written signs representing musical sounds: *read music* i.e. be able to sing or play an instrument from this system.

musical *adj* **1.** connected with music; skilled in, fond of, music: *musical instruments; a musical family.* **2.** pleasant to listen to: *a musical voice.* Also *nc* motion picture or play in which music, singing etc plays an important part. **musically** *adv.*

musician [mju:'ziʃən] *nc* person who is skilful in playing a musical instrument or in composing music.

'**music hall** place where various kinds of popular entertainment are given.

Note: a place where serious music is played is called a *concert hall.*

face the music see **face**[2].

musk [mʌsk] *nu* substance obtained e.g. from the male deer and used in making perfume. **musky** *adj.*

musket ['mʌskit] *nc* kind of gun, now no longer used.

musketeer [mʌski'tiə*] *nc* soldier who used a musket.

musketry *nu* art of how to shoot with muskets.

Muslim ['mʌzlim], **Moslem** ['mɔzləm] *nc* follower of the religion (called **Islam**) taught by Mohammed. Also *adj.*

muslin ['mʌzlin] *nu* fine, cotton cloth. Also *adj.*

mussel ['mʌsl] *nc* kind of small blue or black shellfish, used as food.

must [mʌst] *aux* **1.** be obliged to; have to. *You must leave immediately. I must leave now, otherwise I shall be late. All students must keep quiet in the library. Visitors must not walk on the grass.*

Note: absence of obligation is expressed by *needn't* or *don't have to* (e.g. *You needn't leave* i.e. you can leave or stay as you please; but *You mustn't leave* i.e. you must stay here. **2.** (used when something seems very likely) be bound to. *It must have stopped raining by now. This must be the place we are looking for. You must have heard of Columbus.* **3.** used to show annoyance when telling about something that has happened. *Of course, he must come and interrupt me just when I had started to study.*

Note: must has only one form for past, present, future etc; *must not,* which expresses a prohibition, may be shortened to *mustn't.*

a must something necessary; something that must be seen, heard etc. *Don't miss his latest play; it's a must.* (*informal*).

mustang ['mʌstæŋ] *nc* kind of small, wild horse found in North America.

mustard ['mʌstəd] **1.** *nc* kind of plant. **2.** *nu* yellow powder made from the crushed seeds of this plant mixed with water, and used for flavouring.

keen as mustard very eager; full of enthusiasm. (*informal*).

muster ['mʌstə*] *vt/i* call together; come together. *The chief mustered his supporters. The soldiers mustered in the village square.* Also *nc* gathering together of people (esp. soldiers to be inspected).

pass muster be good enough. *My essay was not brilliant but I think it will pass muster.*

muster up one's courage overcome one's fear. *I mustered up enough courage to accuse him.*

musty ['mʌsti] *adj* unpleasant, stale smell or taste (usu. found in places or things that are old or damp or have not been used for some time). **mustiness** *nu.*

mutable ['mju:təbl] *adj* changeable; able to be changed. *Most things in life are mutable.* (*opp* **immutable**). **mutability** [mju:tə'biliti] *nu.*

mutation [mju:'teiʃən] *nc/u* change (esp. a sudden change in an animal, plant etc) from the usual type. *In his experiments, the scientist produced some interesting plant mutations.* **mutate** [mju:'teit] *vt/i.*

mute [mju:t] *adj* **1.** silent; not speaking. **2.** unable to speak: *mute with astonishment.* **3.** (with reference to a letter) not pronounced. *The letter 'b' in 'dumb' is mute.* Also *nc* person who cannot speak.

mutilate ['mju:tileit] *vt* **1.** cut off a part of the body. **2.** severely damage. *The book had been mutilated through someone tearing out the pages.* **mutilation** [mju:ti'leiʃən] *nc/u.*

mutiny ['mju:tini] *nc/u* open rising against authority (esp. of soldiers or sailors against their officers). Also *vi* rise against authority; rebel.

mutineer [mju:ti'niə*] *nc* someone who mutinies.

mutinous *adj* guilty of mutiny; about or ready to mutiny; rebellious. **mutinously** *adv.*

mutter ['mʌtə*] *vt/i* say something (usu. a threat or complaint) in a low indistinct voice. *He was quite annoyed, and went off muttering threats under his breath.* Also *nc*: *He heard a mutter from the audience.*

mutton ['mʌtn] *nu* meat from a sheep.

mutual ['mju:tjuəl] *adj* **1.** shared by two or more people with respect to each other: *mutual respect. They were mutual enemies* i.e. each hated the other. **2.** held in common; shared. *We both have mutual friends in London* i.e. friends who are known to both of us. **mutually** *adv.*

muzzle ['mʌzl] *nc* **1.** mouth and nose of an animal (e.g. dog, horse). **2.** something (e.g. straps or wires) put over an animal's mouth to prevent it from biting. **3.** mouth of a gun etc. Also *vt* **1.** put a muzzle (in sense **2.**) on an animal. **2.** prevent a person, newspaper etc from saying what he or it thinks. *There was a lot of discontent, but the press was muzzled.*

muzzy ['mʌzi] *adj* confused; muddled. *I was up late last night and I'm feeling rather muzzy this morning.* **muzzily** *adv.* **muzziness** *nu.*

my [mai] *determiner* **1.** belonging to me: *my books; my pen.* **2.** used in exclamations to express surprise, admiration etc. *My, you're very clever! My dear fellow! My goodness!*

myopic [mai'ɔpik] *adj* unable to see clearly things which are far away; short-sighted. **myopia** [mai'oupiə] *nu.*

myriad ['miriəd] *nc* very large number: *myriads of ants.* Also *adj* countless: *the myriad stars.*

myrrh [mə:*] *nu* sweet-smelling substance.

myrtle ['mə:tl] *nc* evergreen bush or shrub with white, sweet-smelling flowers.

mystery ['mistəri] *nc/u* **1.** something which is puzzling, difficult or has not been explained. *This whole affair is a mystery to me.* **2.** condition of being puzzling or strange: *an air of mystery; wrapped in mystery.* **mysterious** [mis'tiəriəs] *adj* puzzling; strange: *a mysterious event.* **mysteriously** *adv.* **mysteries** *npl* secret religious ceremonies. '**mystery play** old type of play which tells a Bible story.

mystic ['mistik] *adj* supernatural; strange; mysterious: *mystic ceremonies; mystic experience.* Also *nc* person who tries to get direct experience of God through prayer, contemplation etc and not through the senses.

mystical *adj* mystic.

mysticism ['mistisizəm] *nu* experiences or way of thought typical of a mystic.

mystify ['mistifai] *vt* cause people to be puzzled. *His speech mystified everyone.* **mystification** [mistifi'keiʃən] *nu.*

mystique [mis'ti:k] *nu* atmosphere of mystery or secrecy which surrounds any activity (often encouraged by those who understand the activity in order to puzzle outsiders). *The medical profession has a mystique which impresses most people.*

myth [miθ] **1.** *nc/u* story or belief handed down from ancient times (usu. explaining some fact of nature); collection of such stories or beliefs: *an early myth explaining the seasons.* **2.** *nc* something untrue; false belief. *They say his great cleverness is just a myth.*

mythical *adj* connected with myths; untrue; unreal.

mythology [mi'θɔlədʒi] **1.** *nc* collection of myths: *mythology of Greece and Rome.* **2.** *nu* study of myths. **mythological** [miθə'lɔdʒikəl] *adj.*

mythologist [mi'θɔlədʒist] *nc* student of mythology.

N

nab [næb] *vt* seize; catch hold of. *past* **nabbed.** (*informal*).
nadir ['neidiə*] *nc* lowest point (e.g. of hope, fortunes etc).
nag[1] [næg] *nc* (usu. used in a contemptuous sense) old horse of poor quality.
nag[2] [næg] *vt/i* continually find fault with someone. *She is always nagging (at) her husband. past* **nagged.**
nagging *adj* continuing; never giving someone rest: *nagging pain.*
nail [neil] *nc* **1.** horny substance growing at the end of a finger or toe. **2.** thin piece of metal, with a point at one end and a head at the other, used to fasten things together or in place. Also *vt* fix or secure things with a nail.

nails (*def 1*) (*def 2*)

'nail polish, 'nail varnish substance used by women to polish or colour the nails (in sense **1.**).
nail somebody down make a person keep a promise or say exactly what he means. *We've been trying to nail him down to a precise agreement.* (*informal*).
a nail in someone's coffin something which is very bad for a person's health etc.
fight tooth and nail fight very fiercely.
as hard as nails 1. very fit, in good physical condition. **2.** without pity or mercy.
hit the nail on the head use words which describe or explain something exactly. (*informal*).
on the nail immediately: *pay on the nail.* (*informal*).
naive, naïve [nai'i:v] *adj* simple and innocent in what one says and does, through lack of experience or ability: *naive behaviour.* **naively** *adv.*
naivety, naïvety *nc/u* state of being naive.
naked ['neikid] *adj* without clothes; uncovered; bare. **nakedly** *adv.* **nakedness** *nu.*
the naked truth the truth with nothing added.
see with the naked eye see without the help of a telescope etc.
namby-pamby ['næmbi'pæmbi] *adj* weak and foolish; unmanly. Also *nc.* (both *informal*).
name[1] [neim] *nc* **1.** word or words by which somebody/something is known. *His name is Brown. Do you know the name of that tree? The headmaster knows all his pupils by name.* **2.** reputation. *He has a good name for honesty.*
nameless *adj* **1.** without a name; unknown. **2.** too terrible to be mentioned: *nameless crimes.*
namely *adv* that is. *I am pleased with only one boy, namely George.*
'namesake person with the same name as another.
call someone names see **call**[1].
in name only by title only, not in any other way. *He is the manager of that shop in name only; his assistant does the work.*
lend one's name to support something with one's fame or reputation. *He lent his name to the cause.*
have not a penny to one's name have no money. (*informal*).
take someone's name in vain say someone's name (esp. God's) in a disrespectful way.
name[2] [neim] *vt* **1.** give a name to (a child, pet etc). *They named him Paul.* **2.** state the name of: *the witnesses have been named.* **3.** state; say. *Name your price* i.e. say how much you want.
be named/called after someone have or be given the same name as someone: *named after his father.* (*US* **be named for someone**).
name the day say when one is going to be married. (rather *o.f.*).
nanny ['næni] *nc* nurse who looks after children.
'nanny-goat female goat.
nap[1] [næp] *nc* short sleep: *have a nap in the afternoon.* Also *vi. past* **napped.**
be caught napping be taken unawares; be taken by surprise. (*informal*).
nap[2] [næp] *nu* soft, hairy surface of some kinds of cloth (esp. wool).
nap[3] [næp] *nu* type of card game.
napalm ['neipɑ:m] *nu* type of thick petrol, like jelly, which burns whatever it touches, and which is used as a weapon.
nape [neip] *nc* back of the neck.
naphtha ['næfθə] *nu* liquid made from coal tar, wood etc used for burning, cleaning clothes etc.
naphthalene ['næfθəli:n] *nu* strong-smelling substance found in coal tar, used for dyes and for killing moths etc.
napkin ['næpkin] *nc* **1.** square piece of cloth or paper, used when eating to protect clothes and to clean fingers and lips. **2.** (*Brit*) soft cloth or paper worn as pants by a baby. (*US* **diaper**).
nappy ['næpi] *nc* napkin (in sense **2.**).
narcissus [nɑ:'sisəs] *nc* plant with white or yellow flowers. *pl* **narcissi** [nɑ:'sisai].
narcotic [nɑ:'kɔtik] *nc* **1.** drug which causes sleep and makes pain less severe. **2.** type of dangerous drug which is bought and sold illegally. Also *adj.*
narrate [nə'reit] *vt* tell a story. **narrator** *nc.*
narrative ['nærətiv] *nc* story; storytelling. Also *adj.* **narration** *nc/u.*

narrow ['nærou] *adj* **1.** small, measured across when compared with length; not wide: *a narrow piece of wood.* **2.** small, limited: *a narrow range of interests* i.e. with few interests. Also *vi* get smaller, narrower (e.g. a road).
narrowly *adv* **1.** only just; closely. *He narrowly escaped death.* **2.** very intently: *look at someone narrowly.*
a narrow escape see **escape.**
narrow gauge railway track less than the standard 4 feet 8 inches wide.
by a narrow margin only just. *He won the race by a narrow margin* i.e. he was just in front of the one who came second.
'narrow-'minded *adj* not prepared to understand other people's beliefs or points of view.

nasal ['neizl] *adj* connected with the nose: *a nasal voice* i.e. one that seems to come through the nose. **nasally** *adv.*

nasty ['nɑːsti] *adj* **1.** unpleasant; disgusting: *a nasty little boy.* **2.** dangerous. *There is a nasty bend in the road.* **nastily** *adv.* **nastiness** *nu.*
turn nasty become vicious or bad-tempered. (*informal*).

natal ['neitl] *adj* connected with birth.

nation ['neiʃən] *nc* group of people of common descent or with a common language or culture; group of people ruled by one government.
national ['næʃənl] *adj* connected with a nation. Also *nc* person belonging to a certain nation: *a French national.* **nationally** *adv.*
nationalism ['næʃənəlizəm] *nu* **1.** love of one's country; patriotism. **2.** movement for self-government. **nationalist** ['næʃənəlist] *nc.* **nationalistic** [næʃənə'listik] *adj.*
nationality [næʃə'næliti] *nc/u* state of belonging to a nation: *of British nationality.*
nationalize ['næʃənəlaiz] *vt* take over private property for the state: *nationalize the mines.* **nationalization** [næʃənəlai'zeiʃən] *nu.*
national anthem official song of a country.
national debt money borrowed by the government which has not yet been paid back.
national service duty for the benefits of society carried out by young people (e.g. in the army and usu. compulsory).

native ['neitiv] *adj* **1.** connected with where one was born: *my native land.* **2.** possessed from birth: *his native intelligence.* **3.** not introduced into a country, not taken from outside. *Tobacco is a plant native to America.* **4.** connected with the original inhabitants (in countries settled by people of a different race): *the native quarter.* Also *nc* **1.** person born in a place: *a native of France.* **2.** original inhabitant of a country that has been settled by outsiders.
nativity [nə'tiviti] *nc* birth (esp. of Christ).

natter ['nætə*] *vi* talk a lot about unimportant things. (*informal*).

natty ['næti] *adj* very neat and smart in appearance: *a natty suit.* **nattily** *adv.*

natural ['nætʃərl] *adj* **1.** connected with or produced by nature: *natural sciences.* **2.** possessing qualities born with one; not acquired from outside: *a natural writer; his natural abilities.* **3.** happening in the normal course of events, ordinary: *die a natural death* i.e. not be killed etc. *It is not natural to hate one's children.* **4.** not false, not put on to impress: *a natural way of behaving.* (*opp* **unnatural**). **5.** (music) neither sharp nor flat.
naturally *adv* **1.** normally; in the usual way: *speak naturally.* **2.** of course; as one might expect. *Naturally, he denied that he had committed the crime.*
naturalist *nc* student of natural history. see below.
naturalize *vt* **1.** make someone a citizen of a country he was not born in. **2.** adapt a word from another language. **naturalized** *adj.* **naturalization** [nætʃərəlai'zeiʃən] *nu.*
natural history study of the earth and what it produces (esp. botany, zoology and mineralogy).

nature ['neitʃə*] *nc/u* **1.** power which is in control of the world: *the forces of nature.* **2.** the world (esp. as untouched by man) i.e. plants, animals etc: *the beauties of nature.* **3.** sort; type: *things of this nature.* **4.** qualities in someone/something which make it the way it is. *It is not in his nature to be cruel. He has a kind/cruel nature.*
'good-'natured/'ill-'natured *adj* having a pleasant/unpleasant character. **good nature** *nu.*
in a state of nature in a primitive state (e.g. naked).

naught [nɔːt] *n* nothing (*o.f.*).

naughty ['nɔːti] *adj* (with reference to children) bad; mischievous: *a naughty child.* **naughtily** *adv.* **naughtiness** *nu.*

nausea ['nɔːsiə] *nu* feeling of sickness or of disgust.
nauseate ['nɔːsieit] *vt* make one feel sick or disgusted. **nauseating** *adj.*
nauseous ['nɔːsiəs] *adj* disgusting; sickening.

nautical ['nɔːtikl] *adj* connected with ships or sailors. **nautically** *adv.*
nautical mile 6,080 feet or 1.85 kilometres.

naval ['neivl] *adj* connected with a navy: *naval officers.*

nave [neiv] *nc* main, central part of a church, from the main entrance to the choir.

navel ['neivl] *nc* **1.** the hollow in the surface of the stomach. **2.** type of orange.

navigate ['nævigeit] *vt* guide (a ship, aeroplane etc) on its course; find one's way along (e.g. a river). **navigator** *nc.*
navigable ['nævigəbl] *adj* **1.** able to be sailed along: *a navigable river.* **2.** (with reference to a ship) in a fit state to be used.
navigation [nævi'geiʃən] *nu* science of navigating.

navvy ['nævi] *nc* unskilled workman doing work such as digging roads etc.

navy ['neivi] *nc* all the warships of a country and their officers and men. **naval** *adj.*
'navy 'blue *adj* dark blue.

nay [nei] *adv* no (*o.f.*).

near[1] [niə*] **1.** *adv* close; not far away: *come nearer; stand near to the door.* **2.** *prep* close to: *near the house; near fainting* i.e. about to faint. *comparative* **nearer.** *superlative* **nearest.**
near at hand within reach; close by; not far away. *The pills are near at hand. The end of term is near at hand.*
far and near see **far.**

near[2] [niə*] *adj* **1.** not far away in place or time. *The holidays are near* i.e. we shall be having our holidays soon. **2.** close in kinship or affection: *a near relative.* **3.** (with reference to cars etc) (*Brit*) on the left-hand side, on the right-hand side elsewhere: *on the near side; the front nearside wheel.* (*opp* **off** in sense **3.**). **nearness** *nu.*

nearly *adv* almost: *nearly dead.*
'**near'by** *adv* not far away. *There is a house nearby.*
'**nearby** *adj*: *a nearby house.*
'**near-'sighted** *adj* not able to see clearly things which are far away.
a near miss see **miss**[1].

near[3] [niə*] *vt/i* come close (to); approach. *We were nearing the harbour.*

neat [ni:t] *adj* **1.** tidy; well-arranged: *a neat desk.* **2.** fond of having things tidy or well-arranged: *a neat person.* **3.** simple but good: *a neat dress.* **4.** clever: *a neat reply.* **5.** (with reference to drinks) not mixed with water. *He drinks his whisky neat.* **neatly** *adv.* **neatness** *nu.*

nebula ['nebjulə] *nc* brightness in the sky caused by a group of stars too far away to be seen clearly, or by a cloud of bright gas. *pl* **nebulae** ['nebjuli:].
nebulous *adj* **1.** vague; not clear: *a nebulous shape; a nebulous idea.* **2.** like a cloud.

necessary ['nesəsəri] *adj* which is required; needed; which must be done. *Food is necessary for health.* (*opp* **unnecessary**).
necessaries *npl* things which are needed.
necessarily *adv* as something required. *You don't necessarily have to leave now* i.e. you may stay if you wish.
necessitate [ni'sesiteit] *vt* make necessary.
necessitous [ni'sesitəs] *adj* poor; in need of something.
necessity [ni'sesiti] **1.** *nu* great need. *The tablets are to be taken only in case of necessity.* **2.** *nu* poverty: *live in necessity.* **3.** *nc* something that one has to have, or that has to be. *Sleep is a necessity.*
(out) of necessity because it is necessary: *do something out of necessity.*

neck [nek] *nc* **1.** part of the body which connects the head to the shoulders. **2.** anything which connects the top of something to its main part; anything which resembles a neck (in sense **1.**): *the neck of a bottle.* Also *vi* embrace and kiss. *The young couple were necking.* (*informal* in this sense).
'**neckband** part of a shirt etc (not the collar) going round the neck, to which the collar is fixed.
'**necklace** ['nekləs] *nc* chain or string of beads, precious stones etc worn round the neck.
'**necktie** *nc* (mainly *US*) piece of cloth tied round the neck. (*Brit* **tie**).
neck and crop completely, with all one's possessions: *thrown out neck and crop.* (*informal*).
neck and neck side by side: *finish neck and neck in a race.*
neck or nothing risking everything. (*informal*).
get it in the neck be severely scolded or punished; suffer some terrible blow. (*informal*).
save one's neck **1.** avoid being hanged. **2.** avoid punishment (often by betraying others) (*informal*).
stick one's neck out do or say something that may not please others, or that may cause trouble for oneself. (*informal*).

necropolis [ni'krɔpəlis] *nc* large area where people are buried.

nectar ['nektə*] *nu* **1.** sweet liquid gathered from flowers by bees. **2.** drink supposed to have been taken by the Greek gods.

née [nei] *adj* (with reference to married women) whose unmarried name was . . . (e.g. *Mrs Smith née Brown*).

need[1] [ni:d] *nu* state in which something is required or necessary: *be in need of money; no need to hurry; great need for more doctors.*
needs *npl* things which are necessary for life: *earn enough for one's needs.*
needless *adj* unnecessary: *needless suffering.*
needlessly *adv.*
needy *adj* poor; without money.
hour/time of need time when help is most required.

need[2] [ni:d] *vt* **1.** require; want; have need of. *To buy a car you need a lot of money; need help. That child needs to be disciplined* i.e. he should be disciplined. **2.** be necessary. *You don't need to go immediately* i.e. it is not necessary for you to go now.
Note: this is a regular verb and must not be confused with *need*[3].

need[3] [ni:d] *aux* (usu. *negative* or *interrogative*) be necessary; be forced or obliged to. *He needn't come, if he doesn't want to. Need we come? No, you needn't* (or *Yes, you must*).

needle ['ni:dl] *nc* **1.** long thin pointed piece of metal with a hole (called an **eye**) at one end, used for sewing. **2.** similar instrument used for injecting a drug into the body. **3.** pointer on a dial: *needle of a compass.* **4.** long, thin leaf of fir and pine trees. Also *vt* irritate, annoy.
'**needlewoman** one who does needlework.
'**needlework** sewing.
'**knitting needle** see **knit.**

ne'er [nɛə*] *adv* never (*o.f.*).
'**ne'er-do-well** worthless person; person who does not work (*o.f.*).

nefarious [ni'fɛəriəs] *adj* wicked and dishonest. **nefariously** *adv.* **nefariousness** *nu.*

negative[1] ['negətiv] *adj* **1.** expressing denial; indicating 'no' or 'not': *a negative answer* i.e. 'no'. **2.** unhelpful; not contributing anything: *a negative attitude; negative virtue* i.e. virtue that comes more from avoiding evil than doing good. **3.** (mathematics) less than 0; having a minus quantity. **4.** having or producing negative electricity. **5.** (photography) having light where dark should be and dark where light should be. **negatively** *adv.*
Note: in sense **1.** the opposite is *affirmative*; in the other senses, the opposite is *positive.*
negation [ni'geiʃən] *nu* act of denial or of saying 'no'.

negative[2] ['negətiv] *nc* **1.** word or statement which says something is not so. **2.** (mathematics) quantity less than 0. **3.** (photography) plate or film in which light things seem dark and dark things seem light. Also *vt* reject something: *negative a suggestion.*

neglect [ni'glekt] *vt* **1.** not take care of; pay no attention to: *neglect one's children.* **2.** fail to do. *He neglected to return the book.* Also *nu* **1.** failure to attend to something: *neglect of one's family.* **2.** condition of not being cared for or attended to. *The room was in a state of neglect.*
neglectful *adj* careless. **neglectfully** *adv.*
negligent ['neglidʒənt] *adj* not careful enough: *a negligent worker.* **negligently** *adv.*
negligence *nu.*
negligible ['neglidʒəbl] *adj* very small: *a negligible amount.*

negligée ['negliʒei] *nc* long, loose gown, worn by a woman when she is going to bed or when she has just got up.

negotiate [ni'gouʃieit] *vt/i* **1.** discuss something to try to come to an agreement. *The two countries are negotiating for a peaceful settlement.* **2.** get or give money for: *negotiate a cheque.* **3.** get through or over (some obstacle): *negotiate a difficult part of the river.* **negotiation** [nigouʃi'eiʃən] *nc/u.* **negotiator** *nc.*

negotiable [ni'gouʃəbl] *adj* **1.** (with reference to a cheque etc) able to be exchanged for cash. **2.** (with reference to an obstacle etc) able to be overcome.

Negro ['ni:grou] *nc* **1.** member of the African races south of the Sahara. **2.** descendant of these races living outside Africa: *an American Negro. pl* **Negroes.** (*fem* **Negress** ['ni:gres]). Also *adj.*

neigh [nei] *nc* sound made by a horse. Also *vi.*

neighbour ['neibə*] (*US* **neighbor**) *nc* **1.** person who lives next to or close to another person. **2.** person, country etc that is next to another.

neighbourhood *nc* **1.** place where people live near one another; the people living there: *a friendly neighbourhood.* **2.** area near a certain place: *in the neighbourhood of the town hall.*

neighbouring *adj* near each other: *neighbouring towns.*

neighbourly *adj* friendly. **neighbourliness** *nu.*

neither ['naiðə*, 'ni:ðə*] **1.** *adj/pron* not one, nor the other (of two). *Neither man was guilty. Neither of them told the truth.* **2.** *adv/conj* not; nor. *I can neither admit it nor deny it. He can't do it, and neither can I.*

nemesis ['nemisis] *n sing* just punishment.

neo- ['ni:ou] *prefix* new (e.g. **neolithic**).

neo-colonialism ['ni:oukə'louniəlizəm] *nu* condition in which older and richer countries exercise economic control over newly independent countries. **neo-colonialist** *nc.*

neolithic [ni:ou'liθik] *adj* connected with the New Stone Age i.e. the period about 10,000 years ago when better stone tools and weapons were made.

neologism [ni'ɔlədʒizəm] *nc* newly-invented word.

neon ['ni:ɔn] *nu* gas used in making bright electric street signs or lamps: *a neon sign.*

nephew ['nefju:] *nc* son of one's brother or sister. (*fem* **niece** [ni:s]).

nepotism ['nepətizəm] *nu* giving of special favours (esp. employment) by an important person to his relatives.

nerve [nə:v] **1.** *nc* part of the body which carries impulses or messages between the brain and other parts of the body. **2.** *nu* courage; boldness: *have the nerve to do something.* (*informal* in sense **2.**).

nerves *npl* worried, excited condition: *suffer from nerves.* (*informal*).

nerveless *adj* without strength or courage; not able to move.

nervous *adj* **1.** connected with nerves in the body: *the nervous system.* **2.** worried; easily excited: *a nervous young man.* **nervously** *adv.* **nervousness** *nu.*

'nerve gas *nc/u* type of poisonous gas which attacks the nervous system of the body.

'nerve-racking *adj* overexciting; dangerous: *a nerve-racking experience.*

nervous breakdown mental illness caused by overwork, too much worry etc.

get on one's nerves make one irritated.

have a nerve be too bold or daring (esp. in dealing with other people) (*informal*).

lose one's nerve see **lose.**

nest [nest] *nc* **1.** place built or chosen by a bird in which to lay its eggs; place where certain types of insects etc keep their young: *a wasp's nest.* **2.** comfortable place. Also *vi* build a nest.

'nest egg amount of money set aside for use when one needs it.

a nest of boxes, tables etc set of boxes, tables etc fitting into one another.

feather one's nest see **feather.**

nestle ['nesl] *vt/i* lie or press comfortably against something: *nestle into one's bed; nestle against one's mother.*

nestling *nc* bird that is too young to leave its nest.

net[1] [net] *nc* lengths of cord, string etc tied together to form squares: *a fishing net; a mosquito net.* Also *vt* **1.** catch something in a net: *net fish; net butterflies.* **2.** cover something with a net (e.g. strawberries). *past* **netted.**

netting *nu* material in the form of a net: *wire netting.*

'netball game in which a ball is thrown into a net hanging from a pole.

'network **1.** system of things which cross one another: *a network of roads.* **2.** system of things which are connected in some way: *a network of radio stations.*

net[2], **nett** [net] *adj* remaining when nothing more is to be added or taken away: *net price of an article* i.e. real price, lowest price; *net profit* i.e. the profit that is left after all expenses have been paid; *net weight of an article* i.e. the weight of the article itself, excluding the wrappers, container etc. Also *vt* gain or give as net profit: *net £5,000. past* **netted.**

nether ['neðə*] *adj* lower (*o.f.*).

nettle ['netl] *nc* common plant which causes pain when it is touched. Also *vt* anger or annoy someone.

neuralgia [njuə'rældʒə] *nu* sharp pain coming at intervals in the nerves (esp. in the face and head). **neuralgic** *adj.*

neurosis [njuə'rousis] *nc* nervous or mental illness. *pl* **neuroses** [njuə'rousi:z].

neurotic [njuə'rɔtik] *adj* suffering from a nervous illness. Also *nc.*

neuter ['nju:tə*] *adj* **1.** neither male nor female. **2.** (with reference to words) neither masculine nor feminine (e.g. *boy* is masculine, but *stone* is neuter). **3.** (with reference to animals) castrated.

neutral ['nju:trl] *adj* **1.** not supporting either side in a war or quarrel: *neutral territory* i.e. land which does not belong to either country (e.g. in a war etc). **2.** (with reference to colour, sound etc) having no definite quality; not bold or distinct. **3.** belonging to neither of two opposites (e.g (chemistry) neither acid nor alkali; (electricity) neither positive nor negative). Also *nc* neutral person, country etc.

neutrality [nju'træliti] *nu* state of being neutral (e.g. in war).

neutralize ['njutrəlaiz] *vt* **1.** declare or make something neutral (in sense **1.**): *neutralize a disputed area.* **2.** take away the special quality or effect of something. *They neutralized the effect of the poison by giving him an antidote.*

in neutral (with reference to a car) not in any of the gears which makes the engine drive the wheels.

neutron ['nju:trɔn] *nc* atomic particle which is neither negative nor positive.

never ['nevə*] *adv* **1.** at no time. *I have never seen him before. They shall never leave this house.* **2.** not (emphatic form). *This will never do!*
'never'more *adv* never again. (rather *o.f.*).
neverthe'less *adv* in spite of that.
Well I never! exclamation of surprise.
Never mind! don't worry about it!
on the never-never on the hire-purchase system. (*informal*).

new [nju:] *adj* **1.** never having existed before; appearing for the first time; unused. *Where are the new books? This is a new design. I'll show you my new suit. After he cleaned the car, it was just like new. They are building new houses everywhere.* **2.** existing before but only recently seen, discovered, bought etc; extra; additional: *learn a new language; discover a new planet.* Also *adv* recently: *newborn baby; new-laid eggs.*
newness *nu.*
newly *adv* **1.** recently: *a newly-married couple.* **2.** in a different way: *a newly-designed system.*
'newcomer someone who has recently arrived in a town etc. *I'm a newcomer to these ideas* i.e. they are new to me.
'new-'fangled *adj* new and unusual.
new moon thin crescent showing at the time when the moon is beginning to get bigger.
New World North and South America.
New Year's day 1st January.
'newly-'weds people who have recently been married. (*informal*).
new to not accustomed to; recently arrived in. *I'm new to this job.*
lead a new life lead a better life, giving up old habits etc.

news [nju:z] *nu* report or account of things which have recently happened. *I have some news for you. Have you heard the news? I heard all about it on the news* i.e. on radio or television. *I heard several items/pieces of news.*
'newsagent shopkeeper who sells newspapers.
'newsboy boy who delivers or sells newspapers.
'newspaper paper printed regularly containing news.
'newspaperman journalist; man who gets news for a newspaper.
'newsprint paper used for printing newspapers.
'newsreel film showing the latest news.
'news stand stall where newspapers are sold.
'newsvendor person who sells newspapers.
break the news to tell somebody something unpleasant in a gentle way.

newt [nju:t] *nc* small animal which lives in water and has four legs and a long tail.

next [nekst] **1.** *adj/n* nearest; immediately following. *Go up to the next street after this one. You will have to be the next (person) to go. Not that book, but the next one. We are leaving for Europe next Sunday/summer/year.*
Note: presence of *the* means that some other time has been previously mentioned. *They stayed here for one week and left the next week. He was here last Friday and promised to come back the next day.*
2. *adv* after this (that). *What happened next? When I next saw him, he was a wealthy man. What will you be up to next?* (expressing surprise). **3.** *prep* beside, next to. *The desk is next to the wall.*
the next best (thing) the second choice. *If you cannot get a taxi, the next best thing is a bus.*
next door in the next house. *The people who live next door; next-door neighbours.*
What next! exclamation of surprise.

nexus ['neksəs] *nc* system of connections between people/things: *the cash nexus* i.e. system of connections between wealthy people, businesses etc.

nib [nib] *nc* metal point of certain kinds of pen (not of ballpoint pens).
his nibs impolite but humorous way of referring to an important person.

nibble ['nibl] *vt* take tiny bites of. *The fish were nibbling at the bait.* Also *nc.*

nice [nais] *adj* **1.** pleasant; good: *a nice person.* **2.** difficult to judge; requiring care: *a nice point of law.* **3.** fussy; difficult to please: *be nice about what one eats.* **nicely** *adv.*
nicety ['naisiti] *nc/u* exactness; quality of being precise; delicate distinction: *unable to appreciate the niceties of the situation.*

niche [ni:ʃ] *nc* **1.** hollow place in a wall for a statue or ornament. **2.** suitable or desirable position in life: *find the right niche for oneself.*

nick [nik] *nc* **1.** small V-shaped cut made in wood etc (often as a record). **2.** prison. (*informal* in sense **2.**). Also *vt* **1.** make a small cut. **2.** steal. (*informal* in sense **2.**).
in the nick of time just in time. (*informal*).

nickel ['nikl] **1.** *nu* type of hard, white metal. **2.** *nc* American coin worth 5 cents. Also *adj.*

nicknack ['niknæk] *nc* any small and cheap object (usu. without practical use) (*informal*).

nickname ['nikneim] *nc* name used instead of one's real name. Also *vt*: *nickname someone Jock.*

nicotine ['nikəti:n] *nu* poison found in tobacco.

niece [ni:s] *nc* daughter of one's brother or sister. (*masc* **nephew** ['nefju:]).

niggardly ['nigədli] *adj* not generous; miserly: *a niggardly award.* **niggardliness** *nu.*

nigger ['nigə*] *nc* Negro or any member of a very dark-skinned race. (*impolite*).

nigh [nai] *adv/prep* near (to) (*o.f.*).

night [nait] *nc/u* period of darkness from sunset to sunrise: *last night; three nights ago; on Sunday night; nine o'clock at night* i.e. 9 p.m. Also *adj.*
nightly *adv* occurring at night or every night.
'nightcap 1. cap formerly worn on the head while sleeping. **2.** drink taken before going to bed.
'night club place of entertainment which is open late at night.
'nightdress long dress worn by women and children in bed.
'nightfall beginning of the night.
'nightmare *nc* **1.** horrible dream. **2.** any horrible experience. **nightmarish** *adj.*
'night school school or place of study for those who cannot attend classes during the day.
'nightshift period of work during the night.
'night-time period of darkness at night.
'night 'watchman person employed to guard buildings etc during the night.
by night during the night.
(by) night and day continuously; without stopping. *They travelled by night and day.*
night off night when a person is free from

his duties. *This is their night off.*
make a night of it spend the night in enjoyment. (*informal*).
nightingale ['naitiŋgeil] *nc* small bird famous for its beautiful singing, heard mostly at night.
nihilist ['naiilist] *nc* person who believes in nothing, and is against beliefs of other people. **nihilism** *nu.*
nil [nil] *n* nothing (often used in giving scores): *win by two goals to nil.*
nimble ['nimbl] *adj* **1.** quick in movement: *a nimble climber.* **2.** clever; quick to understand: *a nimble mind.* **nimbly** *adv.* **nimbleness** *nu.*
nincompoop ['niŋkəmpu:p] *nc* fool.
nine [nain] see appendix.
'**ninepins** game in which a ball is rolled along the ground at nine bottle-shaped pieces of wood, the object being to knock down as many as possible.
a nine days' wonder something which causes great excitement, but only for a very short time. (*informal*).
nip[1] [nip] *vt* **1.** take flesh between two fingers and press it, causing pain; take a small bite of: *be nipped in the leg; be nipped by a dog.* **2.** (with reference to flowers etc) prevent from growing through cold etc: *nipped by the frost.* **3.** run; move quickly: *nip along. past* **nipped.** Also *nc* (in senses **1.** and **2.**).
nippy *adj* **1.** cold. **2.** quick. (both *informal*).
nipper *nc* small child. (*informal*).
nip something in the bud put an end to something before it gets properly started. *The revolution was nipped in the bud.*
there's a nip in the air it is rather cold.
nip[2] [nip] *nc* small amount of spirits: *a nip of whisky.*
nipple ['nipl] *nc* **1.** point of the breast through which milk comes. **2.** anything shaped like a nipple (e.g. projections on an engine where grease is put in).
nirvana [niə'vɑ:nə] *nu* (Buddhism) state after death in which the individual man becomes part of God.
nit [nit] *nc* egg of a parasite sometimes found in hair.
nitre ['naitə*] *nu* chemical substance used in making gunpowder; saltpetre.
nitrate ['naitreit] *nc/u* salt of nitric acid, often used as a fertilizer.
nitrogen ['naitrədʒən] *nu* gas without colour, taste or smell, forming about four-fifths of common air.
nitroglycerine ['naitrou'glisəri:n] type of powerful explosive.
nitric acid ['naitrik'æsid] very powerful acid which destroys most metals.
nitwit ['nitwit] *nc* foolish person. (*informal*).
no[1] ['nʌmbə*] *adj/n* abbreviation for number. *pl* **nos**: *nos 3 and 4.*
no[2] [nou] **1.** *adv* opposite of yes. *Did you say anything? No, I didn't. You didn't see him? No, I didn't.* **2.** *intensifier* (with *comparatives*) not any. *I shall go no further* i.e. I shall stay here. *We have no more time to waste here.* **3.** *adv* (before numerals and 'other') with the idea 'There does not exist . . .' *No two fingerprints are the same. No other person would have done it.* **4.** *determiner* not any; not one. *I have no money. She has no sense. They have no books. We have no house.* **5.** *determiner* (meaning the opposite of the word which follows). *He is no friend of mine* i.e. he is my enemy. *He is no lover of animals.*
no end of a lot of: *no end of trouble.* (*informal*).
'**no-man's land** area between two enemy armies in a battlefield.
by no means not at all. *He is by no means poor.*
no one nobody.
no such not of that kind. *He showed no such letters to me.*
in no time in a very short time.
no wonder not surprising. *It's no wonder he never came back.*
there's no saying/denying etc it is impossible to say, deny etc. *There's no saying what he would have accomplished if he had lived.*
noble ['noubl] *adj* **1.** to be admired; very fine: *a noble person; a noble gesture.* (*opp* **ignoble**). **2.** high in rank; of high birth: *a noble family.* Also *nc* person of high birth.
nobly *adv.*
nobility [nou'biliti] *nu* **1.** goodness: *the nobility of his character.* **2.** nobles as a group or class.
'**nobleman** noble.
nobody ['noubədi] *pron* no person; no one. *We saw nobody in the kitchen. There was nobody in the whole house. I hope nobody has missed his bus.*
Note: it is also common to say e.g. *I hope nobody has missed their bus* (esp. if both men and women are being referred to) although this form is considered a mistake by some people.
Also *nc* person of no importance: *a nobody.*
nocturnal [nɔk'tə:nl] *adj* connected with the night; happening, done or active at night: *nocturnal animals.*
nod [nɔd] *vi* **1.** quick, downward movement of the head (usu. a sign of greeting, agreement or to give a command). **2.** let the head fall forward with tiredness. *past* **nodded.** Also *nc.*
a nodding acquaintance with a slight knowledge of (a person, a subject etc).
noise [nɔiz] *nc/u* sound (esp. a loud or unpleasant one).
noiseless *adj* silent.
noisy *adj* loud; making a lot of noise.
noisily *adv.*
a big noise person of great importance. (*informal*).
noisome ['nɔisəm] *adj* unhealthy; unpleasant (*o.f.*).
nomad ['noumæd] *nc* member of a tribe which wanders from one place to another seeking food, pasture etc. **nomadic** [nou'mædik] *adj.*
nomenclature [nou'menklətʃə*] *nc* system or method of giving names: *scientific nomenclature* i.e. scientific system of giving names to things; the names themselves.
nominal ['nɔminl] *adj* **1.** in name only, not in reality: *the nominal ruler of a country* i.e. a person who has the name of ruling a country which is in fact ruled by somebody else. **2.** very low in value: *a nominal amount.* **3.** (grammar) containing or having the same use as a noun: *a nominal phrase.*
nominally *adv.*
nominate ['nɔmineit] *vt* put forward, suggest someone as being a suitable person for some position: *nominate someone as secretary.*
nomination [nɔmi'neiʃən] *nc/u* act or power of nominating someone.
nominee [nɔmi'ni:] *nc* person nominated.
non- [nɔn] *prefix* not (e.g. **non-fiction**).

nonagenarian [nɔnədʒi'nɛəriən] *nc* person between ninety and ninety-nine years old inclusive.

nonchalant ['nɔnʃəlnt] *adj* not being, or pretending not to be, interested or excited. **nonchalance** *nu*.

non-combatant ['nɔn'kɔmbətnt] *nc* person who does not take part in the actual fighting in wartime. *Doctors are non-combatants, even if they are in the army.* Also *adj*.

non-commissioned ['nɔnkə'miʃənd] *adj* usu. in **non-commissioned officer** i.e. an officer who does not hold a commission (e.g. a sergeant or corporal).

non-committal ['nɔnkə'mitl] *adj* not giving any clear decision on a matter.

nonconformist ['nɔnkən'fɔːmist] *nc* **1.** one who does not act or believe as others do. **2. (Nonconformist)** (in England) Protestant who is not a member of the Church of England. Also *adj*. **nonconformity** *nu*.

nondescript ['nɔndiskript] *adj* of very ordinary appearance; not easy to describe. Also *nc*.

none [nʌn] *adv/pron* **1.** not any; not one. *I looked for some pencils but there were none there. Have you any money left? No, none at all. None of them came. None of that!* i.e. Stop that! (command). *None of your cheek!* i.e. don't be cheeky! (i.e. impudent). **2.** in no way; not at all. *I'm afraid he is none too clever* i.e. not at all clever. *He is none the worse for his terrible hardships* i.e. they have done him no harm.

'nonethe'less *adv/conj* nevertheless.

none but only: *none but the best.*

none other than (a way of being emphatic). *The stranger was none other than my old friend* i.e. it was my old friend himself.

nonentity [nɔ'nentiti] *nc* person of no importance.

non-fiction ['nɔn'fikʃən] *nu* writing which is not in a novel or short story. *Poetry, biography and travel will all be found among the non-fiction in the library.* Also *adj*.

nonplus ['nɔn'plʌs] *vt* surprise or puzzle a person so much that he does not know what to say or do: *completely nonplussed. past* **nonplussed.**

nonsense ['nɔnsns] *nu* words which do not mean anything; anything foolish or silly. **nonsensical** [nɔn'sensikl] *adj*.

non sequitur ['nɔn'sekwitə*] *nc* statement which fails to follow on from what one has said earlier; false conclusion.

noodle ['nuːdl] *nc* foolish person (*o.f.*).

noodles ['nuːdlz] *npl* long strips made from flour and eggs, used in soups etc.

nook [nuk] *nc* hidden corner; quiet, sheltered place.

search in every nook and cranny search everywhere. (*informal*).

noon [nuːn] *n* 12 o'clock midday.

'noonday, 'noontide midday (*o.f.*).

noose [nuːs] *nc* loop of rope with a running knot so that the rope becomes tighter as it is pulled: *hangman's noose* i.e. rope used for hanging people.

noose

nor [nɔː*] *conj* (used after **neither** or **not**) and not. *Neither he nor his friends came back. He has neither the time nor the ability to do it properly. I don't think it will rain. Nor do I.*

norm [nɔːm] *nc* **1.** rule; standard; most common thing. **2.** amount or number of things that has to be produced in a factory etc. *Our norm is forty machines per day.*

normal ['nɔːml] *adj* ordinary; usual; regular: *a normal day; a normal person.* (*opp* **abnormal**). **normally** *adv*. **normality** [nɔː'mæliti] *nu*. **normalize** *vt*.

north [nɔːθ] *adv* roughly in the direction to the right of someone facing the setting sun: *travelling north.*

the north area of a country etc lying to the north; one of the points of the compass. (*opp* **the south**).

northerly *nc* wind coming from the north. Also *adj*.

northern *adj* in or of the north: *northern lights* i.e. lights which are sometimes seen in the northern sky.

'northwards *adv* towards the north.

nose [nouz] *nc* **1.** part of the face above the mouth used for smelling and breathing. **2.** power of smelling; ability to find out things: *a nose for scandal* i.e. ability to find out secrets etc.

nosey *adj* curious, inquisitive (esp. about other people's affairs) (*informal*).

'nosebag bag containing feed, hung over a horse's nose.

'nosedive *nc* sudden headlong descent by an aircraft. Also *vt/i*.

nose something out find out something.

bite/snap someone's nose off answer someone very sharply or angrily. (*informal*).

cut off one's nose to spite one's face do something through anger even though one's own interests are also harmed. (*informal*).

follow one's nose go straight ahead. (*informal*).

keep one's nose to the grindstone see **keep**[1].

pay through the nose for pay far too much for. (*informal*).

as plain as the nose on one's face very plain; easily seen or understood. (*informal*).

poke one's nose into interfere with (esp. with other people's business) (*informal*).

turn one's nose up at treat with contempt.

(right) under one's very nose in full view; immediately in front of one. *The car was stolen under my very nose.* (*informal*).

nostalgia [nɔs'tældʒiə] *nu* **1.** great desire to be back at home when one is far away or to be at any place that one is a long way from. **2.** longing for times gone by. **nostalgic** [nɔs'tældʒik] *adj*. **nostalgically** *adv*.

nostril ['nɔstril] *nc* one of the two openings in the nose.

not [nɔt] *adv* **1.** used to express the *negative* of a verb with a subject (finite verb). *This desk is tidy but that one is not. Some people work but there are others who do not work.* *Note:* *not* before a finite verb must be used with certain verbs (e.g. *does, can etc*), and is often shortened to *n't*: *he can't go; they aren't ready; isn't he clever?*

2. used to express the *negative* of participles and infinitives. *Not being an expert, I cannot tell you. They were ordered not to leave.* **3.** used to express the *negative* of some previous statement. *Do you think it will rain? I hope not* i.e. I hope it does not rain. *I suppose he won't come. No, I suppose not* i.e. I too think he will not come

4. used to express the opposite of *adjs* or *advs*: *not seldom* i.e. often.
not that not saying that. *If he stole the money – not that I think he did – it was a terrible crime.*

notable ['noutəbl] *adj* worth noticing; deserving to be remembered: *a notable event.*
notably *adv* especially.
notable, notability [noutə'biliti] *nc* important person.

notary ['noutəri] *nc* legal official who can be a witness to the signing of certain legal documents etc.

notation [nou'teiʃən] *nc/u* (system of) writing of signs to stand for numbers, musical notes etc: *musical notation.*

notch [nɔtʃ] *nc* **1.** V-shaped mark in a piece of wood etc. **2.** (*US*) narrow pass. Also *vt* make a notch on or in wood etc.

note [nout] **1.** *nc* musical sound; sign standing for a musical sound; black or white key on a piano etc, which produces a musical sound: *strike a note on the piano.* **2.** *nu* attention: *worthy of note* i.e. deserving attention. **3.** *nc* something written to help one's memory: *take notes* i.e. write them down; *make notes for one's speech.* **4.** *nc* short letter. **5.** *nc* official letter between governments. **6.** *nc* paper money; promise to pay money: *a banknote.* **7.** *nc* comment on or explanation of a word or passage in a book etc. **8.** *nc* something which reveals one's feelings or attitudes, shown in the way one speaks or acts. *The speaker sounded a note of warning.* **9.** *nu* fame; importance: *a man of note* i.e. famous man. **10.** *nc* song or cry of a bird or some other animal. Also *vt* pay attention to: *note the beautiful colours in this picture.*
noted *nu* famous; well-known: *a man who is noted for his generosity.*
'notebook book for keeping a record of things.
'notepaper paper for writing letters.
'noteworthy *adj* deserving attention: *a noteworthy piece of work.*
note something down write something down.
strike the right note please people by what one says or does.
strike/sound a false note displease people by what one says or does.
take note of something notice something.

nothing ['nʌθiŋ] *adv/n* **1.** not anything. *He had nothing to say. Nothing he says will change my mind. I looked in the room, but there was nothing there.* **2.** not at all. *It was nothing like what I had imagined.*
nothingness *nu* state of being nothing.
'good-for-nothing see **good**[1].
be nothing to 1. have no effect on. *His death is nothing to me.* **2.** be less (in importance, size etc) than. *His wealth is nothing to his father's.*
come to nothing have no useful end or result. *All his schemes come to nothing.*
for nothing 1. free. *I got this book for nothing.* **2.** to no purpose; in vain. *All his good work was for nothing.*
go for nothing be of no value, use etc. *Because he failed in English, his other marks went for nothing.*
have nothing to do with 1. not concern. *My affairs have nothing to do with him.* **2.** avoid. *I would advise you to have nothing to do with that man.*
next to nothing almost nothing. *I bought it for next to nothing.*
nothing doing! exclamation to indicate refusal, failure to do something etc. *I asked him for a job, but there was nothing doing. Can I have £5? Nothing doing!* (*informal*).
make nothing of not be able to understand. *I made nothing of his speech.*
to say nothing of as well as (to show that the speaker thinks the list is very long). *He has three cars, a yacht and two town houses, to say nothing of his villa in France.*
think nothing of consider something as ordinary or usual. *He thinks nothing of studying through the night.*

notice ['noutis] **1.** *nu* attention: *bring something to someone's notice; take no notice of* i.e. pay no attention to. **2.** *nc* written or printed information about something that has happened or is going to happen: *put up a notice.* **3.** *nc* review of a book etc in a newspaper. **4.** *nu* warning (esp. about the end of a contract etc). *He gave his secretary a month's notice* i.e. warned her a month beforehand that she was to be dismissed; *at short notice* i.e. without much warning. Also *vt/i* take note of; see.
noticeable ['noutisəbl] *adj* easily noticed. (*opp* **unnoticeable**). **noticeably** *adv.*
'notice board (*Brit*) board on which notices can be put. (*US* **bulletin board**).

notify ['noutifai] *vt* make something known to someone; report: *notify someone's death to the police/notify the police of someone's death.*
notifiable *adj* (often with reference to diseases which must be reported to the medical authorities) that must be reported.
notification [noutifi'keiʃən] *nc/u.*

notion ['nouʃən] *nc* idea; opinion (esp. one for which there is not much proof): *have some strange notions; no notion of.*

notorious [nə'tɔːriəs] *adj* well-known for something bad: *a notorious criminal.*
notoriously *adv.* **notoriety** [noutə'raiəti] *nu.*

notwithstanding [nɔtwið'stændiŋ] *adv/prep* **1.** in spite of. **2.** although.

nought [nɔːt] *n* nothing; 0.
noughts and crosses type of game played with squares drawn on a piece of paper.

nougat ['nuːgɑː] *nu* type of sweet with nuts inside it.

noun [naun] *nc* name of person, thing, quality etc (e.g. in the sentence *The frightened people ran to their houses, people* and *houses* are nouns).

nourish ['nʌriʃ] *vt* **1.** give food to: *nourish one's children.* **2.** encourage; keep (a feeling) strong: *nourish hopes.* **nourishing** *adj.*
nourishment *nu* food.

novel[1] ['nɔvl] *adj* new; strange; different: *a novel idea.*
novelty 1. *nu* strangeness; newness. **2.** *nc* something not heard or seen before.
novelties *npl* small cheap articles (e.g. cheap toys etc).

novel[2] ['nɔvl] *nc* book telling a story about people made up by the writer or sometimes based on historical events and characters.
novelette [nɔvə'let] *nc* short novel (often poorly written and about love).
novelist *nc* person who writes novels.

November [nə'vembə*] *n* eleventh month of the year.

novice ['nɔvis] *nc* **1.** beginner; someone who is not experienced: *a mere novice.* **2.** person who is training to become a monk or nun.

novitiate [nou'viʃiət] *nc* period of training (esp. to become a monk or nun).

now [nau] *adv/conj* **1.** at the present time; as things are. *He is working in London now. He will be home by now* i.e. by this time. *He has been found guilty of theft; who will trust him now?* i.e. in these circumstances. **2.** used often in speech with no reference to present time (esp. in commands or in telling a story). *Now there were three bears in the forest. Now, stop talking! Now listen to what I'm trying to say! No more of that, now!*

nowadays ['nauədeiz] *adv* in these times; in these days (esp. when compared with former times). *Children are not so well-behaved nowadays as they used to be.*

just now see **just**[2].

now, now exclamation of warning. *Now, now! Stop that!*

now and again, now and then sometimes. *He still visits me now and then.*

every now and then see **every.**

now . . . now, now . . . then at one time . . . at another time. *Her moods were very changeable: now laughing loudly, now sunk in despair.*

nowhere ['nouwɛə*] *adv* in no place; not anywhere. *The child is nowhere to be found. My watch was nowhere to be seen.*

nowhere near very far from: *nowhere near winning.*

be nowhere fail completely in a race, competition etc. *In the third race, my horse was nowhere.*

get one nowhere be useless. *Threats will get you nowhere.*

noxious ['nɔkʃəs] *adj* harmful.

nozzle ['nɔzl] *nc* metal end of a tube or hose from which water etc comes.

nuance ['nju:ɔns] *nc* slight feeling or shade of meaning, which is not easily recognized.

nucleus ['nju:kliəs] *nc* central part round which something may grow: *the nucleus of a new society. pl* **nuclei** ['nju:kliai].

nuclear ['nju:kliə*] *adj* connected with a nucleus (esp. that of an atom): *nuclear energy* i.e. power obtained from the splitting of atom nuclei; *nuclear physics* i.e. study of the nuclei of atoms.

nude [nju:d] *adj* uncovered; without clothes on. Also *nc* unclothed human figure (in a painting; a statue etc). **nudity** *nu.*

nudist *nc* person who believes that it is good and healthy not to wear clothes.

nudge [nʌdʒ] *vt* touch with the elbow, so as to attract attention. Also *nc*: *She gave him a nudge.*

nugget ['nʌgit] *nc* lump of precious metal as found in the ground: *a gold nugget.*

nuisance ['nju:sns] *nc* thing/person that is annoying or causes trouble.

null [nʌl] *adj* having no force.

nullify *vt* cause or declare to have no effect.

null and void (legal) having no legal force. *Their marriage was declared null and void.*

numb [nʌm] *adj* not able to feel or move: *fingers numb with cold; numb with fear.* Also *vt* make numb. **numbness** *nu.*

number[1] ['nʌmbə*] *nc* **1.** word or sign used for counting. *5 and 7 are numbers; six and ten are numbers.* **2.** amount: *a large number of people.* **3.** copy of a newspaper, magazine etc. *Have you seen the current number of 'Time'?* **4.** song or other part of a programme in a theatre etc. Also *adj* (in sense **1.**): *number 33; room No. 5* i.e. number 5.

numberless *adj* more than can be counted.

'back 'number see **back**[1].

his number is up he is doomed; he is going to die. (*informal*).

look after number one see **look.**

number[2] ['nʌmbə*] *vt/i* **1.** give a number to. *We numbered them 1 to 10.* **2.** amount to. *They numbered 15 in all* i.e. altogether.

number someone/something among regard someone/something as being one or part of. *I number him among my best friends.*

his days are numbered he has not long to live.

numeral ['nju:mərl] *nc* figure or mark which stands for a number: *roman numerals* i.e. I, II, V etc; *arabic numerals* i.e. 1, 2, 5 etc.

numerical [nju'merikl] *adj* connected with numbers: *in numerical order* i.e. first number one, second number two etc. **numerically** *adv.*

numerous ['nju:mərəs] *adj* very many.

numerate ['nju:mərit] *adj* able to count. *All children should be numerate by the time they leave school.* (*opp* **innumerate**).

numskull ['nʌmskʌl] *nc* stupid person.

nun [nʌn] *nc* one of a group of women who have taken special vows devoting their lives to God. (*masc* **monk** [mʌŋk]).

nunnery ['nʌnəri] *nc* place where nuns live.

nuncio ['nʌnsiou] *nc* person who represents the Pope in a foreign country. *pl* **nuncios.**

nuptial ['nʌpʃl] *nc* having to do with a wedding or marriage: *nuptial vows.*

nuptials *npl* wedding (*o.f.*).

nurse[1] [nə:s] *nc* **1.** person who looks after sick people (esp. one who has been trained in this): *a registered nurse* i.e. a nurse whose qualifications have been approved. **2.** woman or girl who looks after young children.

nurse[2] [nə:s] *vt* **1.** look after a sick person. **2.** feed a child at the breast. **3.** hold or carry a young child carefully. **4.** keep careful watch over; pay special attention to. *He nursed the garden carefully at the beginning.*

nursery ['nə:səri] *nc* **1.** place, room which children can use for play etc. **2.** piece of ground where plants, trees etc are grown (usu. for sale).

'nurseryman person who runs a nursery for plants.

'nursemaid girl who looks after young children.

'nursery rhyme verse, poem for young children.

'nursing home private hospital.

nurture ['nə:tʃə*] *nu* bringing up, rearing or education of the young. Also *vt* train; educate.

nut [nʌt] *nc* **1.** eatable seed with a hard shell: *a walnut; a hazelnut.* **2.** small piece of metal for screwing onto a bolt in order to hold machinery together. **3.** person who does mad or silly things. (*informal* in sense **3.**).

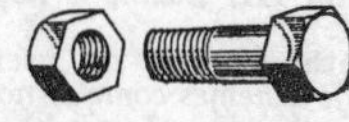

nut (*def 2*)

nutty *adj* **1.** hard and tasting like a nut. **2.** mad. (*informal* in sense **2.**).

'nutcrackers instrument for breaking the shell of nuts.

be nuts be crazy; be mad. (*informal*).

a hard nut to crack a difficult problem to solve. (*informal*).

in a nutshell as briefly as possible. (*informal*).

nutmeg ['nʌtmeg] *nc* seed of an East Indian fruit, often made into a powder and used for flavouring food.

nutriment ['nju:trimənt] *nu* nourishing food.

nutrition [nju:'triʃən] *nu* 1. giving or receiving of food. 2. science of how nourishing different kinds of food are.

nutritious [nju:'triʃəs] *adj* good as food; nourishing. *These vegetables are very nutritious.*

nuzzle ['nʌzl] *vt/i* press or push the nose against. *The dog nuzzled its master.*

nylon [nailɔn] *nu* very strong material used for making stockings, shirts etc. Also *adj*: *a nylon shirt.*

nylons *npl* women's stockings made from nylon or other material. (rather *o.f.*).

nymph [nimf] *nc* in Greek and Roman mythology, one of the beautiful goddesses who lived in rivers, trees etc.

nymphomania [nimfə'meiniə] *nu* (of a woman) exaggerated sexual desire. **nymphomaniac** [nimfə'meiniæk] *nc*.

O

O[1] [ou] symbol for **nought.**

O[2], **oh** [ou] *interj* cry expressing fear, surprise, doubt etc.
Note: the commoner form is *oh.*

oaf [ouf] *nc* stupid, clumsy fellow. *Careful, you great oaf!* **oafish** *adj.*

oak [ouk] **1.** *nc* type of large tree found in cool northern areas. **2.** *nu* hard wood from this tree.

oakum ['oukəm] *nu* material got from untwisting old ropes, and used for filling in the spaces between the boards of a ship.

oar [ɔ:*] *nc* pole with a flat blade at one end used in rowing a boat. **oarsman** *nc.*

oar

put/stick one's oar in interfere in someone else's conversation, business etc when one has not been asked. (*informal*).

oasis [ou'eisis] *nc* area in a desert which is fertile because there is water there. *pl* **oases** [ou'eisi:z].

oast-house ['ousthaus] *nc* building which contains equipment for drying hops which are then used to make beer.

oath [ouθ] *nc* **1.** promise made in God's name that one is going to do something, or that one is telling the truth: *swear/take an oath; on (one's) oath* i.e. having taken an oath. **2.** disrespectful use of the name of God, or of some other holy person/thing: *a terrible oath. pl* **oaths** [ouðz].
under oath having sworn to tell the truth. *The judge reminded the witness that he was under oath.*

oats [outs] *npl* type of grain used as food.
'oatcake thin cake made from oatmeal.
'oatmeal coarsely-ground oats.
sow one's wild oats lead a gay, careless life as a young man (but improving in conduct when one is older).

obdurate ['ɔbdjurit] *adj* difficult to influence; unwilling to change. *I tried to persuade him not to leave home, but he was most obdurate; an obdurate sinner.* **obdurately** *adv.* **obduracy** *nu.*

obedient [ə'bi:diənt] *adj* willing to do what one is told to do: *an obedient child; a very well-trained and obedient dog.* (*opp* **disobedient**). **obediently** *adv.*
obedience *nu*: *obedience to someone's commands.*

obeisance [ə'beisns] *nc* movement of the body, made as a mark of respect; bow; *make an obeisance to a king.*

obelisk ['ɔbilisk] *nc* tall, pointed, stone pillar with four sides, built as a monument.

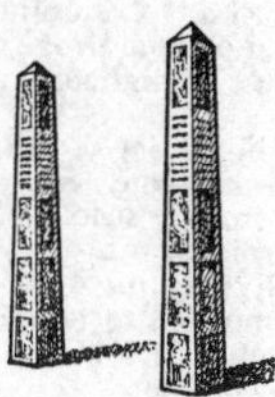

obelisks

obese [ou'bi:s] *adj* very fat: *an obese old man.* **obesity** *nu.*

obey [ə'bei] *vt/i* do what one is told to do: *obey a command.*

obituary [ə'bitjuəri] *nc* announcement of somebody's death, often in a newspaper and often with an account of his life.

object[1] ['ɔbdʒekt] *nc* **1.** thing that can be seen or touched: *an unusual object.* **2.** purpose; aim. *What is his object in doing that?*
'object lesson 1. lesson in which the thing being talked about is in front of the class. **2.** something from which one can learn how one should or should not behave.
expense/distance etc is no object how much a thing costs, how far one has to travel etc does not matter. *When he is buying a present for his wife, expense is no object.*

object[2] [əb'dʒekt] *vi* say that one does not agree to something; not be in favour (of). *I object to people working for such low wages. They wanted to close down the railway line, but hundreds of people objected.*
objection *nc* act of objecting; reason or argument against something. *Do you have any objections to this?*
objectionable *adj* unpleasant.
objector *nc* person who objects: *conscientious objector* i.e. person who refuses to be a soldier because he thinks that fighting is wrong.

object[3] ['ɔbdʒekt] *nc* (grammar) part of a sentence which completes the sense of a transitive verb (e.g. in *The boy threw the ball*, 'the ball' is the object). In sentences like *The boy gave him the ball* or *The boy gave the ball to him*, 'the ball' is called the **direct object** and '*him*' (to him) is called the **indirect object.**

objective [əb'dʒektiv] *adj* not influenced by one's own feelings; fair: *an objective account of the quarrel* i.e. not sympathizing with either side. (*opp* **subjective**). Also *nc* what is aimed at; what is to be achieved or captured (esp. in a battle etc): *important military objectives.*
objectivity [ɔbdʒek'tiviti] *nu*: *a judge famous for his objectivity.*

objet d'art [ɔbʒe'dɑ:] *nc* small work of art.

obligation [ɔbli'geiʃən] *nc* **1.** duty; what ought to be done: *the obligations of children towards their parents.* **2.** duty of being thankful to someone who has been kind to one: *be under an obligation to someone.*
obligatory [ə'bligətəri] *adj* necessary; required. *Attendance at lectures is obligatory for all students.*

oblige [ə'blaidʒ] *vt* **1.** require to do something. *He felt obliged to answer his father's letter* i.e. he felt he ought to answer it. **2.** do something for someone. *Could you oblige me by posting this letter?*
obliging *adj* helpful to others.

oblique [ə'bli:k] *adj* **1.** sloping; slanting: *an oblique line; an oblique stroke* i.e. the mark /. **2.** indirect; not straightforward: *an oblique remark.*

obliterate [ə'blitəreit] *vt* rub out; destroy completely: *obliterate every sign of the damage; obliterate a whole village.* **obliteration** [əblitə'reiʃən] *nu.*

oblivion [ə'bliviən] *nu* **1.** state of having forgotten: *a moment of oblivion.* **2.** state of being forgotten. *This village, once famous, has sunk into oblivion.*
oblivious [ə'bliviəs] *adj* not noticing. *The girl was quite oblivious of the sensation she was creating.*

oblong ['ɔblɔŋ] *nc* (geometry) figure having four sides like a square, with angles of 90°, but longer than it is broad. Also *adj* shaped like an oblong.

obloquy ['ɔbləkwi] *nu* things said against a person; disgrace; dishonour.

obnoxious [ɔb'nɔkʃəs] *adj* giving offence; unpleasant; nasty: *an obnoxious smell; an obnoxious play.*

oboe ['oubou] *nc* type of wooden wind instrument.

obscene [ɔb'si:n] *adj* indecent; disgusting: *an obscene book.*
obscenity [ɔb'seniti] *nc/u* state of being obscene; anything obscene (esp. obscene language).

obscurantist [ɔbskjuə'ræntist] *adj* backward; reactionary; not progressive. *If our country is to progress, we must never believe in obscurantist doctrines.* **obscurantism** *nu.*

obscure [ɔb'skjuə*] *adj* **1.** dark; not easy to understand: *an obscure remark.* **2.** not famous: *an obscure little village.* Also *vt* make obscure. **obscurity** *nu.*

obsequies ['ɔbsikwiz] *npl* ceremonies performed at a funeral.

obsequious [ɔb'si:kwiəs] *adj* too eager to obey or serve: *an obsequious servant.*

observe [əb'zə:v] *vt/i* **1.** watch carefully; look at with attention; notice: *observe someone's behaviour; observe that someone is looking pale.* **2.** keep (laws etc); celebrate (a feast day etc). **3.** make a remark; say. *He observed that it was unusually hot for the time of year.*
observable *adj* able to be observed; having to be observed. *There was no observable difference in his behaviour.*
observance **1.** *nu* keeping of a law; celebration of a ceremony. **2.** *nc* part of an act of worship.
observant *adj* **1.** quick to notice things: *an observant mind.* (*opp* **unobservant**). **2.** careful to keep rules, laws etc: *be observant of local customs.*
observatory [ɔb'zə:vətri] *nc* building from which the sun, stars etc are observed.
observer *nc* person who observes (in sense **1.**) (esp. someone sent to attend meetings etc without taking part in them): *act as an observer.*

observation [ɔbzə'veiʃən] *nc/u* **1.** act of watching: *keep someone under observation* i.e. watch carefully everything that someone does; *come under observation* i.e. be carefully watched. **2.** remark; what someone says: *a chance observation* i.e. what someone just happens to say. **3.** report, statement on what one has observed: *his observations on his travels.* **4.** ability to notice things: *powers of observation.* **observational** *adj.*
obser'vation car railway carriage with big windows so that passengers can observe the scenery.
obser'vation post in a battle, place from which the enemy's movements can be observed.
escape observation not be seen or noticed.

obsess [əb'ses] *vt* occupy one's thoughts all the time: *obsessed by hatred.*
obsessed *adj* thinking always of one thing; mad: *like a man obsessed* i.e. like a madman.
obsession *nc/u* something that occupies one's mind continually. *With him, gambling is an obsession.* **obsessive** *adj.*

obsolete ['ɔbsəli:t] *adj* not now in use; out-of-date: *obsolete weapons.*
obsolescent [ɔbsə'lesnt] *adj* becoming out-of-date. **obsolescence** *nu.*

obstacle ['ɔbstəkl] *nc* something that stands in the way or hinders. *Ignorance is an obstacle to progress.*
'obstacle race race in which the competitors have to overcome obstacles (e.g. going through a sack etc).

obstetrics [ɔb'stetriks] *n sing* branch of medicine concerned with childbirth.
obstetric, obstetrical *adj* having to do with this branch of medicine: *an obstetric ward.*
obstetrician [ɔbstə'triʃən] *nc* specialist in this branch of medicine.

obstinate ['ɔbstinət] *adj* **1.** not easily changed from one's opinion; refusing to obey: *an obstinate child.* **2.** difficult to overcome: *obstinate resistance.* **obstinately** *adv.*
obstinacy *nu.*

obstreperous [ɔb'strepərəs] *adj* noisy and making unnecessary difficulties for others.

obstruct [əb'strʌkt] *vt* get in the way of something; block; try to prevent something: *obstruct traffic; obstruct the passing of a government act.*
obstruction *nc/u* something that obstructs; act of obstructing.
obstructive *adj* deliberately causing obstruction.

obtain [əb'tein] **1.** *vt* get: *obtain high marks; obtain a new watch.* **2.** *vi* continue to exist: *customs that have obtained for centuries.*
obtainable *adj* that can be obtained (in sense **1.**) (*opp* **unobtainable**).

obtrude [əb'tru:d] **1.** *vi* stick out. *The bone obtruded two inches from the skin.* **2.** *vt* push oneself, one's ideas etc upon someone. *He obtruded his opinions on everyone.*
obtrusive [əb'tru:siv] *adj* **1.** sticking out very much. **2.** fond of pushing oneself, one's ideas etc forward. (*opp* **unobtrusive**).

obtuse [əb'tju:s] *adj* **1.** stupid; dull. **2.** (with reference to angles) between 90° and 180°. **3.** blunt; not sharp.

obverse ['ɔbvə:s] *nc* side of a coin, medal etc which has the head or main design on it. (The other side is called the **reverse**).

obviate ['ɔbvieit] *vt* remove; clear out of the

way; get rid of in advance: *obviate a difficulty.*

obvious ['ɔbviəs] *adj* easy to see or understand; clear. **obviously** *adv.*

occasion [ə'keiʒən] *nc/u* **1.** time when something is happening: *on the occasion of the queen's visit; some other occasion; a wedding is not an occasion for sorrow* i.e. a proper time for. **2.** need; reason. *He had no occasion to buy a car.* Also *vt* be the reason for; be the occasion of. *The boy's return occasioned great rejoicing.*

occasional *adj* happening from time to time: *an occasional meeting.*

occasionally *adv* not often; now and then.

on occasion from time to time.

rise to the occasion do well what has to be done. *When he was asked to make a speech he certainly rose to the occasion.*

Occident ['ɔksidnt] *n* the West i.e. Europe and America.

occidental [ɔksi'dentl] *adj* western; from or connected with Europe or America.

occult ['ɔkʌlt] *adj* **1.** secret; hidden. **2.** having to do with magic or the supernatural: *occult ceremonies.*

the occult magic practices and ceremonies.

occupy ['ɔkjupai] *vt* **1.** take and keep possession of: *occupy another country after a war.* **2.** live in; use. *This room/house is occupied* i.e. there is someone in it. **3.** take up; fill: *occupy one's time; occupy one's mind.*

occupant, occupier *nc* person who occupies (a house etc).

occupation [ɔkju'peiʃən] *nc/u* **1.** act of taking or having in one's possession: *the occupation of a house/a country.* **2.** job; employment. *What is his occupation?*

occupational [ɔkju'peiʃənl] *adj* having to do with work, or one's own particular work: *an occupational disease; occupational therapy* i.e. treatment of people who are ill by giving them special work, exercises etc.

occur [ə'kə:*] *vi* **1.** happen; take place: *an accident occurred.* **2.** be found; exist. *That sound does not occur in my language.* **3.** come into one's mind: *it occurred to me that . . .*

occurrence [ə'kʌrns] *nc/u* **1.** happening; event: *a strange occurrence.* **2.** act or fact occurring: *of frequent occurrence.*

ocean ['ouʃən] *nc* **1.** large area of salt water that extends over a great part of the earth. **2.** one of the sections into which this area is divided: *the Atlantic Ocean; the Indian Ocean.* **3.** any very large amount: *oceans of time.* (*informal* in sense **3.**). Also *adj*: *an ocean liner* i.e. a large passenger ship. **oceanic** [ouʃi'ænik] *adj.*

ochre ['oukə*] *nu* yellowish-brown colour. Also *adj.*

o'clock [ə'klɔk] *adv* according to the clock.

oct-, octa-, octo- ['ɔkt(ə)] *prefix* eight (e.g. **octagon**).

octagon ['ɔktəgən] *nc* (geometry) plane figure with eight sides and eight angles.

octagonal [ɔk'tægnl] *adj* eight-sided.

octane ['ɔktein] *nu* substance in petrol which improves its quality: *a car which uses high-octane fuel.*

octave ['ɔktiv] *nc* **1.** (music) interval (difference in pitch) of twelve semitones in a musical scale; note that is six whole tones above or below any given note; a note and its octave played together. **2.** 8 lines of a poem, forming a unit.

October [ɔk'toubə*] *n* tenth month of the year.

octopus ['ɔktəpəs] *nc* sea creature with eight arms (called **tentacles**).

ocular ['ɔkjulə*] *adj* connected with the eyes or with seeing.

oculist ['ɔkjulist] *nc* doctor who treats diseases of the eyes.

Note: an *optician* also cares for eye complaints, but he is not usu. a doctor and he makes his profit from selling or making spectacles.

odd [ɔd] *adj* **1.** strange; unusual: *an odd thing to do; a very odd person.* **2.** (with reference to numbers) not even: *1, 3, 5 and 7 are odd numbers.* **3.** not complete in some way (e.g. one of a pair, part of a set etc): *an odd sock; an odd piece of carpet.* **4.** with a few or a little more (used to indicate numbers roughly). *I found £5 odd.*

oddity *nc* **1.** strangeness. **2.** strange person, thing etc.

oddments *npl* things left behind: *oddments of clothing.*

odds *npl* chances for or against (the probability of) a thing happening. *The odds are he won't come back* i.e. he probably won't come back.

be at odds with someone disagree with someone.

odds and ends small articles which have little value.

odd jobs see **job**[1].

make no odds not make any difference. *It makes no odds whether she goes or she stays.* (*informal*).

at odd times infrequently; not often.

ode [oud] *nc* kind of poem.

odious ['oudiəs] *adj* hateful; unpleasant.

odium ['oudiəm] *nu* widespread hatred: *public odium.*

odour ['oudə*] *nc/u* smell.

be in bad odour be disliked.

oecumenical [i:kju:'menikl] see **ecumenical.**

o'er [ɔ:*] *adv/prep* over (*o.f.*).

of [ɔv, əv] *prep* **1.** (used to indicate distance from or separation from): *within two miles of the church; east of Suez; robbed of every penny he possessed.* **2.** (used to indicate source, origin): *the works of Shakespeare; a girl of good family; a man of the people* i.e. from the ordinary people. **3.** (used to indicate cause or reason): *die of hunger.* **4.** (used to make a noun have the force of an adjective): *that idiot of a boy* i.e. that idiotic boy; *that fool of a manager* i.e. that foolish manager. **5.** (used to indicate what something is made of or contains): *a dress of silk; a sack of potatoes; an area of hills and rivers.* **6.** (used to indicate ownership or connection): *the president of the society; the owner of this watch.* **7.** (used to indicate part of a larger group): *two members of the team; much of the time.* **8.** (used to indicate measure): *a pint of milk; two pounds of butter.* **9.** (used with a possessive noun or pron to indicate one from the number of): *a friend of mine* i.e. one of my friends; *a saying of John's.* **10.** (used with **this** or **that** and a possessive noun or pron): *That son of mine is in trouble; this new book of Jane's.* **11.** (used to indicate an object function): *tired of waiting; love of animals* i.e. the love that people have for animals. see sense **12. 12.** (used to indicate a subject function): *the love of animals* i.e. the love that animals can show for people. see sense **11**; *the despair of Man* i.e. Man's despair. **13.** on the part of.

It was good of you to remember me. It was silly of her to say that. **14.** (used to indicate time): *They first came here of an evening; of a Sunday* (o.f.). **15.** (*US*: used to indicate time before a certain hour): *ten minutes of seven.* (*Brit* **ten minutes to seven**). **16.** (used to indicate the qualities etc that go with a person/thing): *a man of great learning; a child of five (years); a town of great beauty.*

off[1] [ɔf] *adv* **1.** (used to give general idea of distance or separation). *He lives two miles off* i.e. two miles away. *He went off rather quickly. They're off!* i.e. they are going away; they have started (often used at the beginning of a race). *The handle is about to come off. The ship cast off* i.e. started to leave the harbour. *He took off his jacket. Keep off!* i.e. don't come near. **2.** completely; thoroughly: *kill off all the wild animals; finish off one's work.* **3.** free from work: *have Sunday off.*

'off'load *vt/i* unload goods or passengers from an aircraft, ship etc.

be well off be wealthy. *They are quite well off.* (*informal*).

be well-/badly-off for friends/money etc have plenty of/few friends/much/little money etc.

be better/worse off be in a better/worse state.

on and off/off and on occasionally. *I still see him off and on.*

straight off immediately. (*informal*).

off[2] [ɔf] *prep* not on; from. *Keep off the grass. The rider fell off his horse. He took ten pence off the price. We are off duty* i.e. not working. *There's a petrol station just off the main road* i.e. not far from.

'off-'colour *adj* not in normal good health. *I'm a bit off-colour this morning.* (*informal*).

'off'hand *adj* casual; careless: *a rather offhand manner.* Also *adv* without time to consider. *It is difficult to give an opinion offhand.*

'off'shore *adj* **1.** not far out to sea: *offshore islands.* **2.** from the land; seawards: *an offshore breeze.*

'off'side *adj/adv* (in hockey or football) in a position (usu. near one's opponent's goal) where one cannot receive the ball without breaking the rules.

off one's head mad; insane. (*informal*).

off the point away from what one is supposed to be talking about. *In his long speech he often wandered off the point.*

off[3] [ɔf] *adj* **1.** more distant; farther: *the off side of a wall.* **2.** (with reference to cars etc) (*Brit*) on the right-hand side, on the left-hand side elsewhere: *the front offside wheel.* (*opp* **near**). **3.** not fresh. *This cheese is a bit off.* (*informal*). **4.** free from work: *my day off; the off season* i.e. the times when hotels etc are not busy. **5.** cancelled. *The game is off.*

'off 'duty *adj* free from work. *When will you be off duty today?*

'off-licence permission for a shop to sell bottles of beer, wine etc which must be taken away from the shop before they can be opened and drunk; the shop licensed.

on the off chance with the unlikely chance. *I went on the off chance of seeing him* i.e. it was unlikely that he would be there. (*informal*).

that's a bit off it is not approved of. (*informal*).

offal ['ɔfl] *nu* parts of an animal which are not considered as good as the flesh for food (e.g. heart, intestines etc).

offence [ə'fens] (*US* **offense**) *nc/u* **1.** crime; sin; breaking of a rule: *an offence against God; a major offence.* **2.** anything that makes people annoyed or angry: *an offence against good taste.*

offend [ə'fend] *vt/i* **1.** do wrong; commit an offence. **2.** anger; annoy.

offender *nc* someone who offends by breaking the law: *a young offender.*

offensive [ə'fensiv] *adj* **1.** unpleasant; causing annoyance or anger: *an offensive smell.* (*opp* **inoffensive**). **2.** connected with attack: *offensive weapons* i.e. weapons used for attacking. (*opp* **defensive**). Also *nc* attack: *take the offensive* i.e. start to attack.

give offence to someone annoy someone.

take offence at something be annoyed at something.

offer ['ɔfə*] *vt/i* **1.** put forward something so that it can be accepted or rejected: *offer a suggestion; offer someone £5 for his watch.* **2.** present to God: *offer a sacrifice.* **3.** occur: *when an opportunity offers.* Also *nc* something offered (in sense **1.**).

offering *nc* something offered (esp. to God).

offertory ['ɔfətəri] *nc* **1.** part of the Roman Catholic Mass. **2.** money given by people at a church service.

offer up offer to God: *offer up a prayer.*

office ['ɔfis] *nc* **1.** place where business is carried on; part of a business where clerical work and administration (running of the business) is done. **2.** special work or duties: *the office of a chairman.* **3.** government department: *the Foreign Office.* **4.** post; official position: *resign one's office; out of office* i.e. no longer in power. *A politician who is out of office.*

'office boy boy employed as a messenger and who does small jobs.

through someone's good offices through someone's help.

officer ['ɔfisə*] *nc* **1.** person who is of higher rank than others in the armed forces, police force etc: *a naval officer.* **2.** person who holds some position of authority: *the officers of the club.*

official [ə'fiʃl] *adj* **1.** supported by some kind of authority (often government authority): *an official statement.* (*opp* **unofficial**). **2.** having to do with an office or business; not personal: *official correspondence.* Also *nc* someone employed by the government.

officially *adv* by or according to authority.

officiate [ə'fiʃieit] *vi* **1.** perform the duties of an office (esp. in the absence of the proper official): *officiate as chairman.* **2.** help in a ceremony: *officiate at a wedding.*

officious [ə'fiʃəs] *adj* too anxious to help; interfering; too eager to show one's authority.

offing ['ɔfiŋ] *n* usu. in **in the offing 1.** (with reference to a ship) some distance away but still in sight. **2.** (with reference to an event) about to happen. *Is there anything exciting in the offing?*

offset ['ɔf'set] *vt* make up for; balance. *The high price of food there was offset by the money we saved on bus fares.* *past* **offset.**

offshoot ['ɔfʃu:t] *nc* **1.** branch of a tree; side-shoot of a plant etc. **2.** new section, department or branch of a business etc.

offspring ['ɔfspriŋ] *n* child; young of animals. *pl* **offspring.**

often ['ɔfn] *adv* many times. *We go there often. He often sees us. Very often he comes in late. How often?* i.e. how many times?

as often as not, more often than not very many times; frequently. *The traffic is so busy there that, as often as not, you cannot even cross the street.*
every so often occasionally; from time to time.
once too often one more time than one has good luck. *You'll run out on that road once too often and get killed.*
ogle ['ougl] *vt/i* look at in a way that shows one loves or desires.
ogre ['ougə*] *nc* imaginary, man-eating giant (described in children's stories etc) (*fem* **ogress** ['ougris]).
oh [ou] *interj* see **O²**.
ohm [oum] *nc* unit of electrical resistance. (One ohm is the resistance of a conductor through which an electrical force of one volt can send a current of one ampere).
oil [ɔil] *nc/u* greasy liquid of different kinds, obtained from the fat of animals, plants or from under the ground and used for lighting, cooking, machinery etc. Also *vt* put oil on or into (a machine etc).
oily *adj* **1.** covered with oil. **2.** too flattering; too anxious to be polite. *I was put off by his oily manner.*
'oilcake cattle food made from seeds from which most of the oil has been squeezed out.
'oilcan can used for oiling machinery.
'oil colours colouring substance mixed with oil for painting pictures.
'oilfield area where oil (petroleum) can be got from under the ground or under the sea.
'oil painting **1.** *nc* picture painted using oil colours. **2.** *nu* art of painting such pictures.
'oilskin type of coat etc which is waterproof.
'oil tanker large ship or vehicle for carrying oil in large quantities.
'oil well well from which oil is obtained.
burn the midnight oil study or work late. (*informal*).
oil someone's palm give money to someone as a bribe. (*informal*).
pour oil on troubled waters try to make peace, settle a quarrel etc. (*informal*).
oil the wheels do something to make things go more smoothly. (*informal*).
ointment ['ɔintmənt] *nc/u* medicine containing oil or fat to be rubbed on the skin: *antiseptic ointment* i.e. ointment which prevents a cut from becoming poisoned.
O.K., okay ['ou'kei] *interj* good; I agree; fine. Also *nc*: *give someone the O.K.* i.e. give someone permission to do something. Also *vt* agree to, approve of. (all *informal*).
old [ould] *adj* **1.** having lived a long time; not young: *an old man; in old age; suitable for an old person.* **2.** having existed, been in use for a long time: *put on an old shirt; a very old custom.* **3.** of age: *a baby two years old. How old is your son?* i.e. what age is he? **4.** familiar; known for a long time: *an old friend of mine* i.e. long-known, but not necessarily old in years. **5.** used to express affection or contempt. *Good old John! I don't want that old thing.* (*informal* in sense **5.**).
Note: the more usual forms of the *comparative* and *superlative* are *older* and *oldest*; *elder* and *eldest* also exist but mostly refer to comparing age in a family: *my elder brother; your eldest son.*
old age later part of life.
old boy **1.** former pupil of a school. **2.** form of address used between men. (*informal* in sense **2.**).
'old-'fashioned *adj* out-of-date; keeping to old ways, clothes etc: *old-fashioned ideas; an old-fashioned inn.*
old maid see **maid.**
old salt old sailor. (*informal*).
the old school the kind of person who has old-fashioned ideas, manners etc. *Your father is one of the old school.* (*informal*).
'old-'timer person who has lived or worked in a place for a long time.
the 'Old World Europe, Asia and Africa.
oleander [ouli'ændə*] *nc* evergreen shrub with colourful flowers.
oligarchy ['ɔligɑːki] *nc/u* government by a few powerful people; group of such people; country ruled in this way.
olive ['ɔliv] *nc* **1.** tree grown for its fruit, mostly in Mediterranean countries. **2.** small fruit of this tree. Also *adj* brownish green in colour.
'olive 'oil oil made from olives.
hold out the olive branch show that one is ready to make peace.
ombudsman ['ɔmbudzmən] *nc* official whose work is to investigate complaints made by private citizens against the government.
omelette ['ɔmlət] *nc* eggs beaten up and fried (sometimes with cheese, ham etc added): *a ham omelette.*
omen ['oumən] *nc* sign that something good or bad is going to happen. *A rainbow in the sky is sometimes regarded as a good omen.*
ominous ['ɔminəs] *adj* threatening; suggesting that evil is to come.
omit [ə'mit] *vt* leave out; miss out. *Omit pages* 20 *to* 24 i.e. do not read those pages. *You have omitted a word in this sentence. past* **omitted.**
omission **1.** *nc* something omitted. **2.** *nc/u* act of omitting something: *sin of omission* i.e. fault of not doing something.
omit to do something not do something. *I omitted to warn him* i.e. I did not warn him.
omni- ['ɔmni] *prefix* all (e.g. **omnipotent, omniscient**).
omnibus ['ɔmnibəs] *nc* large road vehicle carrying passengers from one place to another (*o.f.* – use **bus**). Also *adj* containing many: *an omnibus book* i.e. one book containing what were originally several different books (usu. by the same author).
omnipotent [ɔm'nipətnt] *adj* all-powerful. **omnipotence** *nu.*
omniscient [ɔm'nisiənt] *adj* knowing everything: *an omniscient God.* **omniscience** *nu.*
omnivorous [ɔm'nivərəs] *adj* eating any kind of food: *an omnivorous animal.*
on¹ [ɔn] *prep* **1.** in contact with the surface of something: *on the floor; on the table; on the wall; on the window; on the grass; a ring on one's finger; a flag on a pole.* **2.** (used to indicate some kind of support, base etc): *a painting on canvas; wheels on a car.* **3.** (used to indicate position in space or time): *the sign on the main road; on the 8th of October; on Sunday of last week; on the day we were married.* **4.** (used to indicate nearness): *a house on the river; a villa on the lake.* **5.** in the direction of: *on my right; advance on one's enemies.* **6.** by means of: *a car runs on petrol; on the authority of the king; hear something on the radio.* **7.** about; on the subject of: *a book on politics; keen on football.* **8.** (used to indicate a state or condition): *on strike.* **9.** (used to indicate

the basis, reason for something): *on his solemn promise; live on a pension; retire on medical advice.*

on[2] [ɔn] *adj* **1.** in action; in use. *The handbrake is on. Is the light on or off? The tap is on* i.e. water is running from it. **2.** taking place; occurring. *There is a show on just now. The dance is on, after all* i.e. it will take place. *What's on tonight?* i.e. what (entertainment) is taking place tonight? *Have you anything on tonight?* i.e. are you doing anything tonight? **3.** (in a theatre, studio etc) performing. *You're on!* i.e. it is your turn to perform. **4.** available; able to be used. *Because of a fire, the water won't be on until midnight.*

be on to to be aware of. *Now we are on to something* i.e. we have discovered something. *She must be on to him* i.e. aware of what sort of person he is.

on[3] [ɔn] *adv* **1.** (used to indicate something going forward or continuing). *They went on walking. Carry on with your work* i.e. continue. *The soldiers marched on.* **2.** (used to indicate contact or support). *He had his hat on. The child had nothing on* i.e. it was naked. *Hold on tight.* **3.** with an indicated part forward. *I tackled him head on* i.e. with my head forward.

and so on and other similar things: *paper and pencils and so on.*

later on sometime afterwards. *I'll attend to you later on.*

on and on without stopping. *He talked on and on.*

once [wʌns] *adv* **1.** one time, on one occasion. *We go to the theatre once a month. He only did it once. He never once lost his temper* i.e. never at any time. **2.** at one time; sometime in the past. *He was once a policeman, but he resigned from the force. That kind of music was once very popular.* Also *conj* as soon as; if. *Once he said that, I knew he was lying. Once you have learned Spanish you will find Italian easy.*

at once 1. immediately. *Leave at once!* **2.** at the same time. *Don't all shout at once!*

(just) for once on this special time only. *For once he was telling the truth.*

once in a while occasionally; from time to time.

once more again. *Do it once more.*

once upon a time at one time in the past (way of beginning children's stories).

once or twice several times; a few times.

one[1] [wʌn] *nc* **1.** lowest whole number. *One plus two equals three.* **2.** sign for this number i.e. 1. *Write down the number one.* **3.** (used to form compound nouns): *twenty-one; thirty-one.*

Note: one and twenty etc is *o.f.*

by/in ones and twos a few at a time. *They left the hall by ones and twos, so as not to attract attention.*

one and all everyone.

one by one one at a time.

one or two a few. *There are one or two books left.*

one[2] [wʌn] *determiner* **1.** a single: *one man; one chair. You can have one apple* i.e. you must not take any more (otherwise use *a* or *an* e.g. *Please take an apple or two*). *He had one good coat and two others that were dirty.*

Note: (in measurements) *one and a half years; one pound of sugar; one and a half million people* etc are rather formal; it is more common to say *a year and a half; a pound of sugar; a million and a half people.* **2.** a certain. *I first saw him one day last summer. One evening we all arrived late.*

Note: after *on* use *a* or *an* (e.g. *I first saw him on an evening in July/on a July evening*). **3.** some (indefinite). *One day I shall be rich.* **4.** the same. *They are all of one opinion.* **5.** united; joined together. *Some day all our people will be one.* **6.** a certain. *One Philip Green stood up* i.e. a certain man called Philip Green (*o.f.*). **7.** (used to form compound *adjs*): *twenty-one years of age.*

'one-'horse 'town small, unimportant town. (*informal*).

'one-'sided *adj* unfair; prejudiced: *a one-sided argument.*

'one-'track 'mind mind that has only one interest or idea.

'one-'way 'street street in which cars are allowed to move in one direction only.

one[3] [wʌn] *pron* **1.** some person/thing. *pl* **some**: *one of his friends; one of those flowers.* (*pl* **some of those flowers**). *He is one of my best friends. I haven't a notebook; can you lend me one?* i.e. any notebook.

Note: compare the last sentence with *I see you have a notebook there; can I borrow it?* i.e. that particular notebook. **2.** (used after an *adj*, *pl* **ones**). *That garden is beautiful; I don't think I've seen a nicer one. You should see Philip's photographs; he's taken some very good ones.* **3.** that. *pl* **ones.** *This house is much bigger than the one you used to have. The children are playing with some toys – the ones your aunt gave them* i.e. the toys that your aunt gave them. **4.** the sort of person. *Charles is not one to be frightened easily* i.e. he is not the sort of person who is easily frightened. **5.** any person; every person. *One must keep quiet in the library. One must try to keep one's temper even when one is being annoyed.* **6.** used instead of 'I' to avoid committing oneself. *One would think he ought to retire next year.*

Note: in USA you can say *One must try to keep his temper even when he is being annoyed.* In British English this is thought to be wrong by some people, which results in longer sentences sounding formal and rather clumsy. It is often better to use 'you', 'everyone', 'we' etc (e.g. *You must try to keep your temper etc. Everyone must keep quiet in the library*).

oneself *pron* one's own self: *cut oneself; wash oneself.*

one another each other. *They hit one another* i.e. each one hit the other. *They went to one another's houses* i.e. each went to the other's house/the others' houses.

onerous ['ounərəs] *adj* heavy; requiring great effort: *an onerous task.*

onion ['ʌnjən] *nc* round vegetable with a strong smell and taste, used in cooking.

onlooker ['ɔnlukə*] *nc* person who watches something that is happening; spectator.

only ['ounli] *determiner/adv/conj* **1.** sole; by itself or themselves; with no others. *You are the only survivor. He is an only son. Those are the only houses left on the street.* **2.** best. *He is the only man for the post.* **3.** and nothing more; and no one else. *Only three of them were there. There are only two copies left. I was only trying to help. He will only repeat what he hears the others say. This compartment is for ladies only. If you would only tell me where it is, I would get it myself.* **4.** but. *The room is cheap enough, only it's rather small. He would have enough money for his family, only he gambles most*

of his wages away.
if only I wish. *If only we had more money!*
only too very. *I shall be only too glad to help.*
onomatopoeia [ɔnəmætə'piə] *nc/u* making of a word to sound like the thing it is describing (e.g. the *buzzing* of bees; the *crash* of the waves; the *banging* of a drum); the word itself. **onomatopoeic** [ɔnɔmætə'pi:ik] *adj.*
onset ['ɔnset] *nc* **1.** attack. **2.** beginning: *the onset of some disease.*
onslaught ['ɔnslɔ:t] *nc* fierce, strong attack.
onus ['ounəs] *n sing* burden; responsibility for. *The onus of the proof is on us* i.e. we must try to prove it.
onward ['ɔnwəd] *adj/adv* forward; on from here: *move onward; from now onward* i.e. from now on.
ooze [u:z] *nu* soft mud (e.g. at the bottom of a pond, in a riverbed etc). Also *vi* **1.** pass slowly through a small opening. *Blood oozed from his wounds.* **2.** go slowly away. *Their courage oozed away.*
opal ['oupl] *nc* precious stone, sometimes milky-white in colour, and sometimes showing many different colours.
opaque [ou'peik] *adj* not allowing light to pass through; impossible to see through: *opaque sheet of glass.* **opacity** [ou'pæsiti] *nu.*
open¹ ['oupən] *adj* **1.** not shut or closed; allowing things, persons etc to go in or out: *an open gate. The window was open. The shop is not yet open.* **2.** not finally decided or answered: *an open question; an open verdict.* **3.** not having its door, lid etc shut: *an open room; an open box.* **4.** not covered: *an open carriage; an open drain.* **5.** spread out: *an open book* i.e. with its pages spread out. **6.** willing to receive new ideas: *an open mind.* **7.** not filled: *a post that is still open.* **8.** that anyone can enter: *an open competition; the open day of a school* i.e. when parents and outsiders are invited to the school. **9.** without barriers (e.g. walls, fences etc): *the open country; the open air.* **10.** not forbidden: *the open season for game* i.e. when game can legally be hunted. **11.** not hidden: *have open contempt for someone; an open quarrel.* **12.** generous. **13.** honest; not concealing anything. *I want to be open with you.*
openly *adv* without secrecy; not concealing anything.
'open-'eyed *adj* with astonishment; showing amazement, fear etc: *gaze open-eyed upon a scene.*
'open-'handed *adj* generous: *an open-handed friend.*
'open-'hearted *adj* honest.
'open-'minded willing to consider new ideas or suggestions; not prejudiced.
'open-'mouthed *adj* surprised: *look at something open-mouthed.*
'openwork *adj* (made in a) pattern with open spaces or holes: *openwork sandals.* Also *nu.*
the open air the countryside, away from cities, outside houses etc: *be fond of the open air.*
'open-'air *attrib adj* taking place outside, in the open air; fond of the open air: *an open-air meeting.*
with open arms with affection; gladly: *welcome someone with open arms.*
come into the open show oneself; make known one's ideas, intentions etc.
open to 1. liable to. *Any boy is open to temptation* i.e. he may be tempted. **2.** willing to receive: *open to suggestions.* **3.** available to. *The castle is open to visitors in summer* i.e. they can visit it then.
open² ['oupən] *vt/i* **1.** make something open; cause to be open; unlock. *He opened the door.* **2.** become open. *The door opened. The shop opens at five o'clock.* **3.** spread out; become spread out. *He opened the book at page five. Their ranks opened when we fired.* **4.** make; clear: *open a path through the forest; open a way through the crowd.* **5.** begin; start: *open with a prayer; open a debate.* **6.** officially declare that something may be used, may start its business etc: *open a new road; open Parliament.*
opener *nc* something used to open something else: *a bottle-opener; a tin opener.*
open something up 1. make or become open: *open up a wound.* **2.** develop: *open up a new territory.* **3.** start: *open up a new business.*
open one's eyes show that one is surprised. *John certainly opened his eyes when he heard the news.*
open somebody's eyes to something make someone realize that he should be aware of something. *I opened my employer's eyes to the way he was being cheated by the others.*
open fire at or on something/someone start shooting. *The soldiers opened fire on the rioters.*
opening ['oupniŋ] *nc* **1.** clear space or gap. *They got in through an opening in the wall.* **2.** opportunity; position in a firm that is to be filled: *new openings in industry.* **3.** start; beginning: *the opening of your speech.* Also *adj* beginning: *his opening words.*
opera ['ɔpərə] *nc* play with music in which most or all of the words are sung.
operatic [ɔpə'rætik] *adj* connected with operas.
'opera glasses glasses used by the audience in a theatre to make the actors seem nearer.

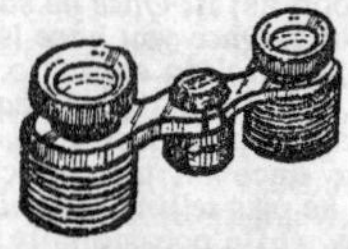
opera glasses

operate ['ɔpəreit] *vt/i* **1.** work; cause to work; keep at work. *The machinery operates continuously. Who operates that machine?* **2.** cut the body with special instruments in order to remove a diseased part. *It may be necessary to operate. The doctor operated on several patients that night.*
operation [ɔpə'reiʃən] *nc/u* **1.** working; the way a thing works: *not in operation* i.e. not in use; *the operation of this machine.* **2.** action; task: *a difficult operation.* **3.** act of operating (in sense **2.**): *perform an operation on someone* i.e. operate on someone; *undergo an operation* i.e. be operated on. **4.** movement of soldiers, ships etc for the purposes of war.
operative ['ɔpərətiv] *adj* effective; in force: *rules that are operative now.* (*opp* **inoperative**). Also *nc* worker.
operator *nc* person who is skilled in making something work: *wireless operator; telephone operator* i.e. person who connects telephone calls.
ophthalmic [ɔp'θælmik] *adj* concerned with the medical study or care of the eyes.
opiate ['oupiət] *nc* drug containing opium which lessens pain and helps one to sleep.

opinion [ə'piniən] *nc* **1.** belief; what one thinks is true: *respect other people's opinions; in my opinion* i.e. it seems probable to me. **2.** advice from an expert (e.g. a lawyer, doctor etc): *get an opinion; get a second opinion* i.e. find out what another doctor etc thinks on some tricky problem.
opinionated [ə'piniəneitid] *adj* very sure that what one thinks is always correct.

opium ['oupiəm] *nu* drug made from poppies which makes pain less and helps one to sleep, and can also be used like alcohol to intoxicate.

opponent [ə'pounənt] *nc* person who is against one in a game, argument, fight.

opportune ['ɔpətju:n] *adj* fortunate; suitable; happening at the right time: *your opportune arrival.* (*opp* **inopportune**). **opportunely** *adv.*
opportunist *nc* person who will seize any chance to gain his own ends, not caring whether his actions are fair or right.
opportunity [ɔpə'tju:niti] *nc/u* good chance; favourable time: *an opportunity for promotion; an opportunity for getting a bargain; an opportunity to buy something cheaply.*

oppose [ə'pouz] *vt* **1.** fight against a person/thing: *oppose the practice of slavery.* **2.** set one thing against another as a contrast: *oppose love to hatred.*
opposite ['ɔpəzit] *adj* **1.** facing: *the man opposite me.* **2.** completely different; reverse. *The opposite direction to north is south; opposite number* i.e. person holding an equivalent rank in a different organization etc.
opposition [ɔpə'ziʃən] *nu* action against; resistance. *The prison was built there in spite of great opposition from the local people.*
the Opposition (members of) the political party which is against the Government.

oppress [ə'pres] *vt* **1.** rule unjustly or harshly: *oppress the poor.* **2.** cause to feel ill, sad or depressed: *oppressed by the unpleasant climate.* **oppression** *nu.* **oppressor** *nc.*
oppressive *adj* **1.** unjust; cruel: *an oppressive government.* **2.** difficult to bear: *this oppressive climate.* **oppressively** *adv.*

opprobrious [ə'proubriəs] *adj* abusive; showing scorn or disrespect: *opprobrious words like 'liar' and 'cheat'.*
opprobrium [ə'proubriəm] *nu* scorn; public disgrace.

opt [ɔpt] *vi* make a choice.
opt for something choose. *Choosing between a high salary and a secure but lowly-paid job, he opted for the high salary.*
opt out of something withdraw from something (esp. a difficult or tiresome situation).

optical ['ɔptikl] *adj* having to do with the eyes: *optical instruments* i.e. microscopes etc; *an optical illusion* i.e. something which deceives the eyesight.
optician [ɔp'tiʃən] *nc* person who makes or sells (eye)glasses and other optical instruments.

optimism ['ɔptimizəm] *nu* habit of seeing the hopeful side of things; belief that everything will turn out well. (*opp* **pessimism**).
optimist *nc* person who always sees the hopeful side. **optimistic** [ɔpti'mistik] *adj.*

optimum ['ɔptiməm] *adj* best; most profitable. *What would you say was the optimum age for retirement?*

option ['ɔpʃən] *nc/u* right of choosing; freedom to choose; thing that may be chosen. *You have no option* i.e. you have no choice.
optional *adj* which may or may not be chosen, as one wishes: *an optional question in an examination.* **optionally** *adv.*

opulent ['ɔpjulnt] *adj* rich; luxurious. **opulence** *nu.*

opus ['oupəs] *nc* composition (esp. musical). *pl* **opera** ['ɔpərə].
magnum opus chief work of a writer, musician etc.

or [ɔ:*] *conj* **1.** (used to indicate a choice). *You can go or stay. You can take a pen or a pencil. They can come on Friday, (or) Saturday or Sunday.* **2.** otherwise; if not. *You must study now or you'll fail.* **3.** that is; which means. *He believed in astrology, or telling the future from the stars. They gave him an opiate, or kind of drug.*
either . . . or see Note on **either.**
or else 1. otherwise; if not. *We must leave immediately, or else we'll be late.* **2.** suggesting the idea of a threat. *Do it again or else!* i.e. if not you will be punished. (*informal*).
or so roughly; about. *Give me twenty or so.*
or somebody/something/somewhere perhaps. *I think it was Green or somebody who called* i.e. perhaps it was Green. *Have you been out or something?*
whether . . . or, if . . . or. *I don't care whether you agree or disagree.*

oracle ['ɔrəkl] *nc* **1.** (in ancient Greece and Rome) place where people asked a god questions; answer given to such questions; priest or priestess who gave the god's answer. **2.** any person who is supposed to give good advice.
oracular [ə'rækjulə*] *adj* **1.** having to do with an oracle. **2.** having a hidden meaning.

oral ['ɔ:rl] *adj* **1.** spoken, not written: *an oral examination.* **2.** (medicine) having to do with the mouth. **orally** *adv.*

orange ['ɔrindʒ] **1.** *nc* juicy, round fruit with a thick, reddish-yellow skin. **2.** *nc* tree on which this fruit grows: *orange tree.* **3.** *nc/u* colour of this fruit. Also *adj* reddish-yellow in colour: *an orange dress.*

orang-outang [ɔ'ræŋu'tæn] *nc* large, long-armed ape with a reddish coat which lives in the forests of Borneo and Sumatra.

oration [ə'reiʃən] *nc* formal public speech: *a funeral oration.*
orator ['ɔrətə*] *nc* person who is good at making speeches.
oratorical [ɔrə'tɔrikl] *adj* having to do with good speeches.
oratory ['ɔrətəri] **1.** *nu* good speaking; the art of making good speeches. **2.** *nc* small room (chapel) set apart for prayer.

oratorio [ɔrə'tɔ:riou] *nc* type of musical work in which a religious story is told in music and song, but without acting. *pl* **oratorios.**

orb [ɔ:b] *nc* sphere; globe (esp. the sun, moon or one of the planets).

orbit ['ɔ:bit] *nc* curved path of one star or planet or man-made satellite round another: *the orbit of the earth around the sun.*

orchard ['ɔ:tʃəd] *nc* piece of ground where fruit trees are grown: *an apple orchard.*

orchestra ['ɔ:kistrə] *nc* **1.** group of people playing musical instruments (esp. at a concert, opera or play). **2.** part of a theatre where the orchestra plays.
Note: an *orchestra* is different from a *band*, in that it generally plays more serious music or has a different and usu. wider range of instruments.

orchestral [ɔː'kestrl] *adj*: *an orchestral concert.*

orchid ['ɔːkid] *nc* type of plant with flowers, many of which have bright colours and strange but beautiful shapes.

ordain [ɔː'dein] *vt* **1.** (with reference to God, the law or some other high authority) order; decide. *The law ordains that anyone who commits a crime must be punished.* **2.** make someone a priest or minister.

ordeal [ɔː'diːl] *nc* **1.** severe test; unpleasant experience: *the ordeal of being shipwrecked.* **2.** (in former times) a way of judging a person by making him undergo a painful experience (e.g. walking through a fire or taking poison). It was thought that an innocent person could do these things and not be hurt: *ordeal by fire.*

order[1] ['ɔːdə*] *nc/u* **1.** way in which things are arranged: *in order of size; names in alphabetical order* i.e. names beginning with A coming before names beginning with B etc. **2.** state in which everything is properly arranged or in place: *put the room in order.* **3.** way in which something works. *My car is in good order.* **4.** condition in which rules or laws are obeyed: *keep order in a classroom.* **5.** command: *give an order; under doctor's orders* i.e. ill and therefore having to obey a doctor. **6.** paper saying that money etc is to be handed over: *a postal order for 50p.* **7.** body of rules for conducting a public meeting: *a point of order.* **8.** request for goods from a shop etc; goods supplied: *deliver an order.* **9.** group of people living under religious rules (e.g. monks or nuns): *the Dominican order.* **10.** society into which one is admitted as an honour (e.g. (*Brit*) *the Order of the Bath*). **11.** (biology) in classifying plants or animals, a group that is smaller than a class, but larger than a family.

orderly *adj* **1.** well-arranged; in order. **2.** well-behaved; peaceful: *an orderly crowd.* Also *nc* **1.** (military) soldier who attends on an officer to carry messages etc. **2.** hospital attendant who keeps things clean and in order.

by order of by a command given with someone's authority: *by order of the king.*

call to order ask to obey the rules (at a meeting). *The chairman called the meeting to order.*

in order that so that. *He died in order that the others could be saved.*

in order to so as to; as a means to. *You must buy a ticket in order to be allowed in.*

made to order made according to the customer's special needs or instructions: *a suit made to order.*

on order asked for but not yet delivered. *Your books are on order.*

take orders/holy orders become a priest or minister.

a tall order something that is difficult to do or get. *Getting a cheap house in the city is a tall order these days.* (*informal*).

under the orders of commanded by.

order[2] ['ɔːdə*] *vt* **1.** arrange; put in order: *order things well.* **2.** give a command. *I ordered him to leave immediately. The doctor ordered that we should all stay in bed.* **3.** ask to be supplied with (at a shop etc). *I should like to order two copies of that book.* **4.** arrange; decide. *I had hoped to leave early but things were ordered otherwise.*

order someone about keep giving commands to someone. (*informal*).

ordinal ['ɔːdinl] *adj* showing position in a series. *First, second and third are ordinal numbers.* Also *nc* ordinal number.

ordinance ['ɔːdinəns] *nc* law; rule made by some authority.

ordinary ['ɔːdnri] *adj* **1.** usual; average; common: *just an ordinary person.* **2.** (*US*) below average; rather poor. *His speech was just ordinary.* **ordinarily** *adv.*

out of the ordinary unusual.

ordination [ɔːdi'neiʃən] *nc/u* ceremony when someone is ordained i.e. made a priest or minister.

ordnance ['ɔːdnəns] *nu* heavy guns; military weapons, ammunition etc.

ordnance survey maps maps of the British Isles prepared by a British government department.

Army Ordnance Department army department which looks after military supplies.

ore [ɔː*] *nc/u* rock, earth etc containing metal: *a piece of iron ore; an area containing different ores.*

organ ['ɔːgən] *nc* **1.** part of a plant or animal which performs some special function (e.g. the eye, nose, lungs, heart are organs of the body): *the organs of speech.* **2.** means by which things are done; instrument. *The police force is an organ of the government.* **3.** means of making things known; newspaper etc that gives the opinions, views etc of a political party or some other group. **4.** musical instrument consisting of pipes of different lengths through which air is forced, and played by using keys and pedals: *a church organ.* **5.** any of certain other instruments using air to produce music: *a mouth organ.*

organist *nc* person who plays the organ (in sense **4.**).

organic [ɔː'gænik] *adj* **1.** connected with the organs of the body: *an organic disease.* **2.** having organs, as plants and animals do. **3.** connected in some way with plants or animals: *an organic compound; organic chemistry* i.e. study of the nature of materials found in plants and animals (carbon compounds) (*opp* **inorganic** in sense **3.**).

organism *nc* **1.** animal or plant; extremely small animal or plant. **2.** living thing made up of parts that work together.

organize ['ɔːgənaiz] *vt* put into working order; arrange in some system; make preparations for: *organize an expedition; organize a birthday party.* **organizer** *nc.*

organization [ɔːgənai'zeiʃən] **1.** *nc* group of people who meet or work together for some special purpose: *a Church organization.* **2.** *nu* act of organizing: *requiring a lot of organization.* **3.** *nu* way in which different parts of a thing work together: *efficient organization.*

orgasm ['ɔːgæzəm] *nc* highest point of excitement in a sexual act.

orgy ['ɔːdʒi] *nc* wild celebration: *a drunken orgy.*

Orient ['ɔːriənt] *n* the East; Asia.

oriental [ɔːri'entl] *adj* eastern; from or connected with Asia.

orientation [ɔːrien'teiʃən] *nu* **1.** act of finding out one's position. **2.** act of making oneself at ease in a new situation.

orientate oneself find out about one's position or situation.

orienteering [ɔːrien'tiəriŋ] *nu* type of sport in which one tries to get as quickly as possible from one place to another, using a map and a compass.

orifice ['ɔrifis] *nc* opening; hole.

origin ['ɔridʒin] *nc* thing from which anything or anyone comes; birth; family: *the origin of life on earth; a man of humble origins.*

originate [ə'ridʒineit] *vt/i* **1.** begin; come into being. **2.** bring something into being; start; invent.

original [ə'ridʒinl] *adj* **1.** first; earliest: *the original inhabitants of a country.* **2.** new; not taken from somebody else: *an original idea.* **3.** able to think of new things or ideas: *an original mind.* (*opp* **unoriginal** in senses **2.** and **3.**). Also *nc/u* **1.** thing from which something was taken or copied. *This painting is a copy; the original is in Paris.* **2.** language in which a book etc was first written. *He reads Tolstoy in the original* i.e. he reads Tolstoy's works in Russian. **originally** *adv.*

originality [əridʒi'næliti] *nu* **1.** state of being original. **2.** ability to think up new things, ideas etc: *an inventor of great originality.*

ornament ['ɔ:nəmənt] *nc* **1.** something that decorates; something intended or used to add beauty. *She was wearing earrings, a necklace and other ornaments.* **2.** person or act that adds honour or beauty. *That young lady is an ornament to our society.* Also *vt* make beautiful with ornaments; give honour or beauty to.

ornamental [ɔ:nə'mentl] *adj* of or for ornament.

ornate [ɔ:'neit] *adj* very much ornamented; decorated.

ornithology [ɔ:ni'θɔlədʒi] *nu* scientific study of birds.

orphan ['ɔ:fən] *nc* child whose parents are dead; child whose father or mother is dead. Also *vt* cause to be an orphan: *orphaned when his home was burnt down.*

orphanage *nc* home for orphans.

orthodox ['ɔ:θədɔks] *adj* generally accepted or approved; holding ideas that are generally accepted (esp. in religion): *orthodox behaviour; an orthodox believer.* (*opp* **unorthodox**).

orthodoxy *nu* being orthodox; acting in an orthodox way.

the Orthodox Church group of churches in Eastern Europe and Asia which do not recognize the Pope as their supreme head.

orthography [ɔ:'θɔgrəfi] *nu* study of spelling; system of correct spelling.

orthopaedic, orthopedic [ɔ:θə'pi:dik] *adj* having to do with the study or care of deformed bones and joints (esp. in children). **orthopaedics** *nu.*

oscillate ['ɔsileit] *vt/i* swing from side to side like a pendulum; cause to swing in this way.

oscillation [ɔsi'leiʃən] *nc/u* **1.** swinging from side to side. **2.** (electricity) single complete cycle of an electric wave.

osier ['ouʒə*] *nc* (*Brit*) kind of willow tree from the smaller branches of which baskets are made.

ostensible [ɔs'tensibl] *adj* pretended; intended to conceal something. *His ostensible reason for borrowing the money was that he had some debts to pay, but I knew he intended to spend it on gambling.* **ostensibly** *adv.*

ostentation [ɔsten'teiʃən] *nu* showing-off; display of wealth etc, intended to make other people admiring or envious.

ostentatious *adj* fond of display; intended to make other people envious: *an ostentatious dinner party.*

osteopathy [ɔsti'ɔpəθi] *nu* treatment of certain diseases by pushing and pulling the bones and muscles. **osteopath** ['ɔstiəpæθ] *nc.*

ostler ['ɔslə*] *nc* man who takes care of horses at an inn or stable.

ostracize ['ɔstrəsaiz] *vt* refuse to meet or talk to someone as a kind of punishment. *After behaving so disgracefully he was completely ostracized by his neighbours.* **ostracism** ['ɔstrəsizəm] *nu.*

ostrich ['ɔstritʃ] *nc* largest living bird, found in Africa and Arabia. It has long legs and a long neck, runs fast but cannot fly. (It is supposed to hide its head in the sand when in danger).

ostrich

ostrich feathers tail feathers of this bird used in hats, fans etc.

other ['ʌðə*] *determiner* **1.** what remains of two or more things or people mentioned. *I don't want this one; I want the other one. Jones is here, but where are the other boys? All the other papers carry the same news.* **2.** extra; additional. *Every member must bring one other person. Have you any other books besides these?* **3.** different; not the same. *Please come back some other time, as I'm busy now. I would not want him other than the way he is* i.e. to be different from what he is now. Also *pron* **1.** other one; remaining one of the people/things being talked about. *Each of them praises the other. When will the others be coming?* **2.** different person/thing. *We should not think only of our own children; there are others to be cared for also.* Also *adv* in a different way. *He cannot be other than clever when his parents are so intelligent* i.e. almost certainly he is clever.

each other see **each.**

every other **1.** all the others. *Our car arrived safely, but every other car broke down.* **2.** every second; alternate. *He comes every other week* i.e. every second week.

on the other hand (sometimes occurs after **on one hand,** and always indicates a contrast). *He is an intelligent boy, but on the other hand, he doesn't work very hard.*

one another see **one**[3].

or other (used when one cannot be exact). *I am sure he will succeed somehow or other.*

the other day/week recently. *He must still be in town, because I just saw him the other day.*

all other things being equal if all the other things remain the same. *All other things being equal, I would buy the black dress not the white one, but unfortunately the black one is too dear.*

otherwise ['ʌðəwaiz] *adv* **1.** in other ways. *He is rather quiet but very pleasant otherwise.* **2.** in another way. *I was otherwise engaged* i.e. I was busy with something else. Also *conj* or else; if not. *Get dressed otherwise you* *will be late.*

otter ['ɔtə*] *nc* small, fish-eating animal with brown fur and webbed feet.

ottoman ['ɔtəmən] *nc* long, cushioned seat with no back or arms.

ought [ɔ:t] *aux* **1.** have a duty to. *You ought to help your father. Everyone ought to work harder.* **2.** should probably; should, if things go as one expects. *They ought to be there when we arrive. We ought to have the money we need saved by Christmas.* **3.** be right; be suitable. *That old house ought to be pulled down.* **4.** (used when giving advice) be wise. *It is really a very useful thing; you ought to buy it.* **5.** (used in speech when describing something very beautiful, dramatic, funny etc). *You ought to have seen his face when I told him I was leaving!* i.e. it is a pity that you did not see . . .
Note: 1. this verb has no other form except *ought*. The question form is *ought I? ought he? etc.* The negative is *ought not* (in speech *oughtn't*) (e.g. *You ought not to* go i.e. you should not go). The opposite is *need not* (in speech *needn't*) (e.g. the answer to *Ought I to go?* is either *You ought* or *No, you needn't*). 2. it is followed by *to* (e.g. *ought to go; ought to do etc*). 3. *ought* is used for both present and future. *You ought to see him now/tomorrow.* Past tense is *ought + have* (e.g. *You ought to have seen him yesterday*).

ounce [auns] *nc* unit of weight, one sixteenth of a pound avoirdupois i.e. 28.35 grams or one twelfth of a pound troy i.e. 31.1 grams. see appendix.

our ['auə*] *determiner* of us; belonging to us etc: *our house; our country; Our Lady* i.e. the Virgin Mary; *Our Lord* i.e. Jesus Christ.
ours *pron/pred adj* belonging to us; the one or ones belonging to us. *That land over there is ours. This house became ours when our father died.*
ourselves [auə'selvz] *pron* **1.** emphatic form of **we** and **us**. *We shall have to do it ourselves.* **2.** reflexive form of **us**. *First we have to wash ourselves.*

oust [aust] *vt* drive or push somebody out (e.g. from a position, job etc): *ousted from his post.*

out[1] [aut] *adj* **1.** not present; away. *He has been out all evening. The book you are looking for is out* i.e. has been borrowed. **2.** not in control; not in power. *Labour are in, and the Conservatives are out.* **3.** far away; distant. *My friend has been out in Australia for years.* **4.** not in use; not in action. *The light is out. The fire is out.* **5.** exposed; so that it can be plainly seen etc. *The truth is out at last. The sun is out today. His new book is just out* i.e. just published. **6.** used to indicate mistake or loss. *I am 50p out in my calculations. I am five pounds out because of that party. You are not far out in your guess.*
outer *adj* from the outside; farther away; farther from the middle or inside: *the outer covering; from outer space.*
outermost *adj* farthest out; farthest from the centre.

out[2] [aut] *adv* **1.** (used to give the idea of movement away, either towards somebody else or to the outside, to the open air): *give out (leaflets); hand out (tickets); go out (into the street); rush out; put somebody out (of his house); lock somebody out.* **2.** to the end: *completely tired out; fight it out; a fire burning itself out.* **3.** loudly; clearly: *speak out; call out; say something out loud.* **4.** so that something can be seen. *His intelligence stands out. It brings out the best in him. His pockets were turned out.* **5.** (used to give idea of taking something from a bigger mass or group): *find out facts; pick someone out from a crowd of people.* Also *vi* become known. *Truth will out* i.e. it cannot be hidden.
out and away by far. *He is out and away the best footballer I have ever seen.*
out of control not able to be regulated or guided. *The car is out of control. The situation is out of control.*
out of danger safe. *Your son is now out of danger.*
'out-of-'date unfashionable; not now used etc: *out-of-date clothes/ideas etc.*
'out-of-'doors in the open air.
out of fashion not now used etc. *Clothes that are out of fashion.*
out for interested only in. *He is out for as much money as he can get.*
out of one's mind mad; insane. *You must be out of your mind to do something like that.*
out of **1.** because of: *do something out of hate/spite/kindness etc.* **2.** without: *out of money; out of work.* **3.** away from. *He is out of town. The ship was seven miles out of Portsmouth harbour. They ran out of the house.* **4.** from among: *in nine cases out of ten, I chose the best pictures out of his whole collection.* **5.** from: *made out of wool; drink out of a cup; like a scene out of a play.*
out of it **1.** neglected; lonely. *I felt rather out of it at the party, since I knew nobody there.* **2.** not connected with something. *I think you are well out of that business* i.e. lucky to be no longer connected with it.
out of order **1.** not working. *This machine is out of order.* **2.** not obeying the rules of a meeting. *The last speaker was out of order.*
'out-and-'out (usu. of something bad) complete; in every way: *an out-and-out scoundrel.*
out of sight not seen. *Keep out of sight.*
out to anxious to; keen to: *out to better oneself; out to improve things.*
'out-of-the-'way difficult to reach or get at: *a rather out-of-the-way little village.*

outbid [aut'bid] *vt* bid, offer more than someone else (e.g. for goods at a sale etc). *I outbid him by twenty pounds at the auction sale. past* **outbid.**

outboard ['autbɔ:d] *adj* usu. in **outboard motor** i.e. engine which can be attached to the outside of a boat. Also *nc.*

outbound ['autbaund] *adj* going away from the land; going far away: *an outbound ship.*

outbreak ['autbreik] *nc* **1.** beginning; start: *the outbreak of war.* **2.** riot; disturbance: *a prison outbreak.*

outbuilding ['autbildiŋ] *nc* small building (e.g. a shed) near a larger building.

outburst ['autbə:st] *nc* sudden happening; explosion (of a feeling): *outburst of violence; outburst of laughter.*

outcast ['autkɑ:st] *nc* person without a home or friends. Also *adj.*

outclass [aut'klɑ:s] *vt* be much better than. *He outclasses everyone else at running.*

outcome ['autkʌm] *nc* result of something: *the outcome of what happened yesterday.*

outcrop ['autkrɔp] *nc* rock which sticks out from the ground.

outcry ['autkrai] *nc/u* **1.** loud shouting or crying out. **2.** public show of anger: *a great outcry all over the country against the government's actions.*

outdated ['aut'deitid] *adj* old-fashioned; not modern.

outdistance [aut'distns] *vt* go farther or faster than.

outdo [aut'du:] *vt* do better than. *past tense* **outdid** [aut'did]. *past part* **outdone** [aut'dʌn].
not to be outdone not wishing to let someone else do better. *Philip gave the poor man ten pence and Henry, not to be outdone, gave him twenty.*

outdoor [aut'dɔ:*] *adj* done, used etc in the open air; not inside a house: *the outdoor life; outdoor games.*
outdoors *adv* in the open air.

outer ['autə*] *adj* on the outside; farther from the centre: *outer garments; flights to outer space* i.e. to the more distant planets and stars.

outfit ['autfit] *nc* **1.** all the clothes or tools etc that are needed for a certain job or occasion: *an outfit for school; a camping outfit* i.e. tent, pegs etc. **2.** (*US*) group of people working together.
outfitter *nc* person who sells clothing, sports equipment etc.

outflank [aut'flæŋk] *vt* go round the side of an enemy army.

outgrow [aut'grou] *vt* **1.** grow bigger than someone/something else. *He is outgrowing all his brothers.* **2.** grow too big for clothes etc: *outgrow one's clothes.* **3.** become too old or wise for childish things. *He has outgrown his interest in toys.*
outgrowth ['autgrouθ] *nc* **1.** natural development of something. **2.** something that grows out of something else: *an outgrowth of branches on a tree.*

outhouse ['authaus] *nc* small building near a main building.

outing ['autiŋ] *nc* short pleasure trip: *go on/have an outing.*

outlandish [aut'lændiʃ] *adj* strange; looking as if it comes from a foreign country; distant, remote: *an outlandish costume; an outlandish place.*

outlast [aut'lɑ:st] *vt* live or last longer than.

outlaw ['autlɔ:] *nc* criminal; person who lives outside the law. Also *vt* make it public that someone is a criminal, or that some activity is now illegal: *outlaw a person; outlaw the sale of drink.*

outlay ['autlei] *nc/u* spending; amount of money spent on something. *Our total outlay on repairing the house was eighty pounds.*

outlet ['autlet] *nc* **1.** way through which something goes out: *the outlet of a river.* **2.** way of using or releasing something: *an outlet for one's energy/anger etc.*

outline ['autlain] *nc* **1.** line that shows the shape of something: *an outline map of Europe.* **2.** rough plan; list of main points (of a speech etc). *I have prepared my speech in outline.* Also *vt* **1.** draw the general shape of something. **2.** make a rough plan of.

outlive [aut'liv] *vt* live longer than; live (on) until something is forgotten: *outlive one's disgrace.*

outlook ['autluk] *nc* **1.** what is seen when one looks out. *This window has a pleasant outlook.* **2.** what seems likely to happen. *The outlook for world peace is not bright* i.e. not good. **3.** way of looking at things or at life. *He seems to have a very gloomy outlook.*

outlying ['aut'laiiŋ] *adj* far from the centre (of a town etc); distant: *several outlying farms.*

outmanoeuvre [autmə'nu:və*] *vt* manoeuvre more successfully than one's opponent; defeat an opponent by acting more cleverly.

outmoded [aut'moudid] *adj* old-fashioned; not modern.

outnumber [aut'nʌmbə*] *vt* be more than. *They outnumbered us three to one* i.e. there were three times as many of them.

outpatient ['autpeiʃənt] *nc* person who gets treatment at a hospital but does not live there during treatment: *the outpatients' department.*

outpost ['autpoust] *nc* **1.** small group of soldiers placed some distance away from the main group in order to prevent them being taken by surprise. **2.** place where such a group is posted. **3.** any lonely or dangerous place: *outpost of civilization.*

outpouring ['autpɔ:riŋ] *nc/u* expression of emotion.

output ['autput] *nu* amount of goods etc produced or work done. *The factory must increase its output.*

outrage ['autreidʒ] *nc* something very wrong or cruel which shocks and angers people: *a terrible outrage.* Also *vt* do something which shocks people; act cruelly towards someone.
outrageous [aut'reidʒəs] *adj* shocking; very bad: *an outrageous crime.*

outrider ['autraidə*] *nc* mounted escort (usu. on a motorcycle).

outright ['autrait] *adv* **1.** completely; not gradually: *buy something outright* i.e. pay for it all at once. **2.** plainly; holding nothing back. *I told him outright what I thought of him.* **3.** immediately: *be killed outright.* Also *adj* complete: *an outright denial/loss.*

outset ['autset] *nc* beginning: *at the outset of the journey.*

outside [aut'said] *nc* outer side or surface; outer part; open air: *the outside of a house* i.e. the outer walls etc. Also *adj* **1.** on the outside; near the outside: *an outside worker* i.e. someone who works in the open air; *an outside broadcast* i.e. not given from a studio. **2.** greatest possible; largest: *an outside estimate of how much something will cost.* **3.** from the outside (of a house, organization etc): *outside help.* **4.** unlikely: *only an outside chance of winning.* Also *adv* on or to the outside. *I think there is someone waiting outside. Go outside and see what you can find.* Also *prep* **1.** at or on the outer side of: *outside the house.* **2.** beyond the limits of: *outside the city.*
outsider *nc* **1.** person who is not allowed into a group, society etc or who does not wish to belong to it. **2.** horse etc which is not expected to win a race.
at the (very) outside at most. *He will only give you ten pounds for it, or fifteen at the outside.*
outside of outside. (*informal*).

outsize ['autsaiz] *attrib adj* larger than the usual size: *outsize skirt.*

outskirts ['autskə:ts] *npl* outer parts of a town etc.

outspoken [aut'spoukən] *adj* saying openly what one thinks: *outspoken criticism.*

outstanding [aut'stændiŋ] *adj* **1.** excellent; very much better than others: *outstanding work.* **2.** still to be done or paid: *have some work outstanding; an outstanding debt.* **3.** easily noticed; easily remembered; important: *outstanding event in history.*

outstay [aut'stei] *vt* stay or remain longer than: *outstay one's welcome* i.e. remain

too long in a place.
outstretched ['autstretʃt] *adj* stretched out; extended: *welcome someone with arms* outstretched.
outstrip [aut'strip] *vt* **1.** do better than. **2.** go faster than (e.g. someone else in a race). *past* **outstripped.**
outvote [aut'vout] *vt* be greater in number than and able to cast more votes. *They outvoted their rivals.*
outward ['autwəd] *adj* **1.** going out; going away to the outside: *the outward voyage.* **2.** outer; on the outside. *To all outward appearances, he is a rich man.*
outwards *adv* from the inside; away from the centre; away from home.
outwardly *adj* on the surface; as regards outward appearances. *Outwardly he seemed calm, but he was really very nervous.*
outweigh [aut'wei] *vt* be more in weight, value, importance etc than. *Honour should outweigh one's own safety.*
outwit [aut'wit] *vt* deceive, defeat by being more clever. *past* **outwitted.**
oval ['ouvl] *adj* egg-shaped. Also *nc* something that is oval-shaped.
ovary ['ouvəri] *nc* **1.** one of a pair of organs of a female in which eggs are produced. **2.** part of a flower which contains seeds.
ovation [ou'veiʃən] *nc* joyful welcome (e.g. of someone who is admired); outburst of applause: *an ovation for the hero; a thunderous ovation at the end of a speech.*
oven ['ʌvən] *nc* closed-in space which is heated to cook food.
over[1] ['ouvə*] *adv* **1.** downwards; to the side: *be knocked over by a car. He was working at the edge of the roof when he fell over.* **2.** upwards then to the side or down: *spill over; boil over.* **3.** so that another side etc can be seen: *turn a page over/turn over a page.* **4.** right through; completely: *read something over; look over some papers.* **5.** again; in repetition: *ten times over.* **6.** across i.e. idea of distance being covered. *Ask your friends over to see us. He is over in Germany for a week.* **7.** remaining: *have money over.* **8.** upwards; in excess. *The school is open to children of five and over. I have all I need and a bit over.* **9.** from one person, place, group etc to another. *He betrayed us by going over to our enemies. Hand over that gun.* **10.** everywhere; in every part: *travel all over.* **11.** (*US*) during or beyond a certain period. *I stayed over with them until the weekend.* **12.** too: *overhelpful* i.e. too helpful. Also *adj* finished. *The war is over.*
over[2] ['ouvə*] *prep* **1.** placed above, higher than something. *There was a table with an electric light over it. The ceiling over us was about ten feet high.* **2.** lying on; covering or partly covering. *They had put a cloth over his wound. He put some paper over the desk to keep it clean.* **3.** across: *jump over a wall; leap over a gate.* **4.** across and down: *throw oneself over a balcony; fall over a cliff.* **5.** all through; to many or all parts of: *travel all over Europe. The stain spread over the carpet.* **6.** in command of; in a higher position than. *He was ruler over five provinces. Who is over you in your new job? A captain is over a sergeant.* **7.** during. *I got to know him well over the years.* **8.** by means of: *talk over the telephone; hear something over the radio.* **9.** in connection with: *quarrel over a dispute; talk over a matter; fall asleep over one's work* i.e. while doing it.
over-[3] ['ouvə*] *prefix* too; too much: (before *adjs*) *over-excited* i.e. too excited; *overgreedy* i.e. too greedy etc; (before *nouns*) *overconfidence* i.e. too much confidence; *overpayment* i.e. too much payment etc; (before *verbs*) *overeat* i.e. eat too much; *overpraise* i.e. praise too much etc.
overact ['ouvər'ækt] *vt/i* act a part in a play in an unnatural, exaggerated fashion.
overactive ['ouvər'æktiv] *adj* too active; using up too much energy. *It is dangerous for older people to be overactive.*
overall ['ouvərɔːl] *nc* (often *pl*) loose garment worn over normal clothes to keep them clean while working.
overawe [ouvə'rɔː] *vt* control someone by filling him with fear or respect. *The children were overawed by the presence of the headmaster.*
overbalance [ouvə'bæləns] *vt/i* fall over; cause something to fall over.
overbear [ouvə'bɛə*] *vt* overcome by weight, force or authority. *past tense* **overbore** [ouvə'bɔː*]. *past part* **overborne** [ouvə'bɔːn].
overbearing *adj* expecting other people to fall in with what one wishes. *No one liked her overbearing attitude.*
overboard ['ouvəbɔːd] *adv* from a ship into the water: *fall overboard; man overboard!* i.e. someone has fallen off the ship!
overcast ['ouvə'kɑːst] *adj* cloudy; dark: *an overcast sky.*
overcharge [ouvə'tʃɑːdʒ] *vt/i* charge too much. *I was overcharged for my ticket.*
overcoat ['ouvəkout] *nc* long, heavy coat.
overcome [ouvə'kʌm] *vt* conquer; get the better of: *overcome poverty and disease. past tense* **overcame** [ouvə'keim]. *past part* **overcome.** Also *adj* made weak, helpless or speechless: *overcome by tiredness.*
overdo [ouvə'duː] *vt* do too much; cook (meat etc) too much. *The meat was overdone. past tense* **overdid** [ouvə'did]. *past part* **overdone** [ouvə'dʌn].
overdose ['ouvədous] *nc* too big a dose, amount of medicine etc: *an overdose of sleeping pills.* Also [ouvə'dous] *vt.*
overdraw [ouvə'drɔː] *vt/i* get from a bank (e.g. by signing a cheque) more than one is entitled to. *past tense* **overdrew** [ouvə'druː]. *past part* **overdrawn.**
overdraft ['ouvədrɑːft] *nc* amount by which a bank account is overdrawn: *have a large overdraft.*
overdress [ouvə'dres] *vt/i* dress with clothes that are too bright, too good, too formal etc for the occasion.
overdrive ['ouvədraiv] *nu* type of high gear in a car, in addition to the ordinary gears, which allows it to cruise at a fast speed.
overdue [ouvə'djuː] *adj* later than the arranged time (for payment, arrival etc). *This bill is overdue. The train is overdue.*
overflow [ouvə'flou] *vt/i* **1.** flow over the top. *The milk is overflowing.* **2.** have contents which flow over the top. *His cup is overflowing.* **3.** be too much or too many for. *The crowd overflowed the hall and some had to stand outside.* Also ['ouvəflou] *nu* **1.** what has flowed over. **2.** pipe etc where liquid can overflow. **3.** people who cannot be contained in a hall etc: *the overflow from the meeting.*
overflowing *adj* very abundant; flowing over: *overflowing kindness.*
filled to overflowing filled so high or so much that something flows over: *the hall/cup/glass was filled to overflowing.*

overgrown [ouvə'groun] *adj* **1.** covered; grown over: *garden overgrown with weeds.*
overhang [ouvə'hæŋ] *vt/i* **1.** stick out; stick out over; project over: *overhanging branches.* **2.** threaten: *the danger overhanging us. past* **overhung** [ouvə'hʌŋ]. Also ['ouvəhæŋ] **1.** *nc* something projecting. **2.** *nu* amount by which something projects.
overhaul [ouvə'hɔːl] *vt* **1.** examine or repair something thoroughly (e.g. the engine of a motorcar). **2.** pass (esp. in a boat). Also ['ouvəhɔːl] *nc* thorough examination for repairs etc.
overhead [ouvə'hed] *adv* above one's head; in the sky; above: *the sky overhead.* Also *adj* passing overhead; not touching the ground: *overhead wires.*
overheads ['ouvəhedz] *npl* expenses involved in running a business (e.g. heating, lighting, rent etc) which are not directly connected with the purpose of the business.
overhear [ouvə'hiə*] *vt* hear what one is not intended to hear; hear by chance. *I overheard him saying that he was closing down his shop. past* **overheard** [ouvə'həːd].
overjoyed [ouvə'dʒɔid] *adj* very glad; delighted: *overjoyed at the news.*
overland ['ouvəlænd] *adj* going by land: *an overland route/journey etc.* Also [ouvə'lænd] *adv*: *travel overland.*
overlap [ouvə'læp] *vt/i* partly cover something and extend beyond it: *a roof made of overlapping tiles. Our holidays overlap* i.e. part of mine is the same as part of yours. *past* **overlapped.** Also ['ouvəlæp] *nc/u.*
overlay [ouvə'lei] *vt* cover with something: *ordinary stones overlaid with marble. past* **overlaid.**
overload [ouvə'loud] *vt* put too much in or on: *overload a truck.*
overlook [ouvə'luk] *vt* **1.** have a view from above. *This window overlooks the coast.* **2.** fail to notice. *I overlooked this problem and shall have to tackle it now.* **3.** deliberately take no notice of; excuse. *I shall overlook your disobedience this time.*
overnight [ouvə'nait] *adv* during the night; for the night: *stay overnight.* Also ['ouvənait] *adj* during or for the night: *an overnight journey.*
overpower [ouvə'pauə*] *vt* be too strong for: *overpower an opponent.*
overpowering *adj* very strong: *an overpowering feeling of hatred.*
overrate [ouvə'reit] *vt* value something/someone too highly. *His work is greatly overrated.*
overreach [ouvə'riːtʃ] *vt/i* **1.** go too far; go beyond. **2.** be too clever for.
overreach oneself **1.** fail by attempting too much. **2.** fail by being too cunning or clever.
override [ouvə'raid] *vt* ignore, pay no attention to (what another person does or says): *override all objections; override someone else's commands. past tense* **overrode** [ouvə'roud]. *past part* **overridden** [ouvə'ridn].
overrule [ouvə'ruːl] *vt* decide against. *The judge overruled the lawyer's objections. Our suggestions were overruled by the committee.*
overrun [ouvə'rʌn] *vt* **1.** spread over and spoil or harm in some way: *a garden overrun with weeds; a house overrun with mice; a country overrun by an enemy.* **2.** go beyond; exceed. *The speaker overran his time by fifteen minutes. past tense* **overran** [ouvə'ræn]. *past part* **overrun.**
oversea, overseas ['ouvə'siː(z)] *adj* to, from, situated in places across the sea: *overseas countries; overseas trade.*
overseas *adv*: *come from overseas.*
oversee ['ouvə'siː] *vt* direct (e.g. work or workers); supervise. **overseer** ['ouvəsiə*] *nc.*
overshadow [ouvə'ʃædou] *vt* **1.** be more important than. *My success overshadowed his.* **2.** cast a shadow or gloom on something.
oversight ['ouvəsait] *nc* failure to notice something or think of something. *Your essay was not marked through an oversight on my part.*
oversleep [ouvə'sliːp] *vi* sleep longer than intended. *past* **overslept** [ouvə'slept].
overspill ['ouvəspil] *nc/u* (esp. with reference to the movement of people away from crowded cities so as to house them elsewhere) what spills over.
overstate [ouvə'steit] *vt* say too much or speak too strongly about: *overstate one's case* i.e. put one's arguments too strongly.
overstatement *nc.*
overstep [ouvə'step] *vt* go beyond. *The foreman overstepped his authority when he beat his workers. past* **overstepped.**
overt [ou'vəːt] *adj* open; not hidden. *Not standing up when he was told to was an overt act of disobedience.* **overtly** *adv.*
overtake [ouvə'teik] *vt* **1.** catch up with and pass (e.g. in a vehicle). *Only one car overtook us.* **2.** come upon suddenly. *A storm overtook the little boat. past tense* **overtook** [ouvə'tuk]. *past part* **overtaken** [ouvə'teikən].
overthrow [ouvə'θrou] *vt* defeat; destroy; take away the power of: *overthrow the king.* Also ['ouvəθrou] *nc.*
overtime ['ouvətaim] *nu* time beyond the usual working hours, for which extra money is paid: *work overtime.* Also *adj*: *overtime earnings.*
overtone ['ouvətoun] *nc* **1.** suggestion; hint. *The ceremony had overtones of sadness.* **2.** (music) faint higher tone heard along with the main tone.
overture ['ouvətjuə*] *nc* **1.** (often *pl*) approach or offer made to someone so that discussions can be started: *make peaceful overtures.* **2.** piece of music played at the beginning of an opera, concert etc.
overweight [ouvə'weit] *adj* weighing too much; too fat. *You are overweight and so you must eat less.*
overwhelm [ouvə'welm] *vt* **1.** overcome completely: *overwhelmed by superior forces; overwhelmed by someone's kindness.* **2.** submerge; cover over. *The flood waters overwhelmed the village.* **overwhelming** *adj.* **overwhelmingly** *adv.*
overwrought [ouvə'rɔːt] *adj* tired out by too much work, worry, excitement etc; very nervous. *She is not to be disturbed in her present overwrought condition.*
owe [ou] *vt/i* **1.** have to pay; be in debt. *I owe John five pounds for those chairs he sold me. How much do I owe you? He owes a lot of money to his father. He owes his success to hard work* i.e. his success was caused by hard work. **2.** have to give as a duty: *owe allegiance to the king.*
owing *adj* not yet paid. *There is ten pounds owing.*
owe someone a grudge dislike someone for some reason.
owing to because of. *Owing to the storm, the ship stayed in the harbour.*

owl [aul] *nc* bird with large eyes which hunts mice and small birds (usu. at night).

owl

own¹ [oun] *adj* **1.** belonging to or connected with oneself personally; not concerning other people. *That is his own house/That house is his own. I mind my own business* i.e. I do not meddle in other people's affairs. *For reasons of my own, I am having nothing to do with it* i.e. reasons which I do not wish to discuss with others. **2.** by oneself; without the help of other people. *Do you cook your own meals? She makes all her own clothes.*

come into one's own achieve proper recognition. *One day his theory will come into its own.*

hold one's own not be defeated; be doing as well as one's rival. *As an athlete he is still holding his own against younger men.*

of one's own belonging to oneself: *a house of one's own.*

on one's own not with other people. *He likes to be on his own. He did it on his own.*

own² [oun] *vt/i* **1.** have; possess. *Do you own that house?* **2.** admit. *I own that I may have made mistakes.* **3.** admit as belonging to one. *He will not own the boy as his son.*

owner *nc* person who possesses something.

ownership *nu.*

ownerless *adj* not having a (known) owner.

own up to something admit to something. *He owned up to the theft. A book has been stolen, but no one will own up.*

ox [ɔks] *nc* fully-grown castrated bull, used for pulling carts etc, or for beef. *pl* **oxen** ['ɔksn].

oxide ['ɔksaid] *nc/u* (chemistry) compound of oxygen with another element.

oxidize ['ɔksidaiz] *vt/i* **1.** combine, cause to combine, with oxygen. **2.** make or become rusty.

oxygen ['ɔksidʒən] *nu* gas without colour, taste or smell, which must be present for animals and plants to live and for fire to burn (O).

oyster ['ɔistə*] *nc* kind of shellfish taken as food, and inside which a pearl (a kind of jewel) is sometimes found.

ozone ['ouzoun] *nu* **1.** clear, refreshing air (e.g. seaside air) (*informal*). **2.** type of oxygen with three atoms in each molecule instead of the usual two (O^3).

P

pa [pɑː] *n* child's word for **father.** (*informal*).

pace [peis] *nc* **1.** single step in walking or running: *take a pace forward.* **2.** length of a single step in walking i.e. about 2½ feet: *several paces away.* **3.** speed: *at a fast pace. He made the pace* i.e. set the speed. **4.** (with reference to horses etc) way of stepping. Also *vt/i* **1.** walk or walk over with even steps: *pace the room* (often a sign of nervousness etc). **2.** measure something by taking paces: *pace out a length of about seven yards.* **3.** set the speed for a runner in a race by running in front of him.

keep pace with keep up with. *I could scarcely keep pace with the new discoveries in biology* i.e. there are so many new discoveries in biology that I cannot easily learn about all of them.

put somebody through his paces test somebody in some way to find out how good he is.

pacific [pə'sifik] *adj* peaceful; liking or making peace.

pacification [pæsifi'keiʃən] *nu* process of making peace.

pacifism ['pæsifizəm] *nu* belief that all wars are wrong.

pacifist ['pæsifist] *nc* person with this belief, who refuses to take part in war.

pacify ['pæsifai] *vt* make quiet or peaceful: *pacify a crying child; pacify a country in turmoil.*

pack[1] [pæk] *nc* **1.** number of things tied up or wrapped together so that they can be carried: *packhorse* i.e. horse used for carrying packs. **2.** (often used to express contempt) number of persons/things: *a pack of lies; a pack of thieves.* **3.** number of dogs kept for hunting or of wild animals that hunt together: *pack of hounds/wolves.* **4.** complete set of playing cards (usu. 52): *a pack of cards.*

pack[2] [pæk] *vt/i* **1.** put things together in a box, bale etc; fill with things. *Pack your clothes. Pack that case* i.e. put clothes etc into it. *Have you packed?* **2.** crowd closely together. *Thousands of people packed into the stadium. The roads are packed with people.* **3.** put soft material (e.g. straw) round something to keep it from breaking when it is being transported: *packed in straw.* **4.** make joints or holes tight with something so that gas, water etc cannot get through: *pack the leaking part of a water pipe.*

packing *nu* **1.** soft material used to prevent articles being broken while they are being transported. **2.** act of packing a suitcase etc: *do one's packing* i.e. pack one's suitcase.

'packing case large wooden box used for packing things in.

pack someone off send quickly away: *pack off the children/pack the children off to school.* (*informal*).

send someone packing order someone to leave. (*informal*).

package ['pækidʒ] *nc* thing or bundle of things packed or wrapped together (smaller than a pack).

packet ['pækit] *nc* small bundle, box containing a number of things (e.g. cigarettes, envelopes etc).

pact [pækt] *nc* agreement: *trade pact; suicide pact* i.e. agreement between two or more people to commit suicide.

pad [pæd] *nc* **1.** something soft like a cushion, filled with or made of soft material and intended to give protection, to make more comfortable or to improve the appearance (of e.g. a dress, coat etc). **2.** number of sheets of notepaper fastened together along one edge: *writing pad.* **3.** one of the soft, fleshy parts on the bottom of the feet of dogs, foxes and certain other animals. Also *vt/i* **1.** fill something out with soft material. **2.** walk softly. *past* **padded.**

padding *nu* **1.** material (e.g. hair etc) used to make pads (in sense **1.**). **2.** unnecessary words used to make a speech etc longer.

pad something out make a speech, examination answer, essay etc longer by putting in things which are not necessary. (*informal*).

paddle ['pædl] *nc* short oar with a broad blade at one end or both ends. Also *vt/i* **1.** use a paddle or paddles to move a boat, canoe etc through the water. **2.** walk in the water. **paddling** *nu.*

'paddle steamer steamer which is driven by paddle wheels.

'paddle wheel large wheel with broad blades which strike the water as the wheel turns, so driving the boat forward.

paddock ['pædək] *nc* small grass field used for grazing cattle or keeping horses in.

paddy ['pædi] *nu* growing rice; rice in the husk before it is cut and gathered.

'paddy field field of rice growing in water.

padlock ['pædlɔk] *nc* lock of the type as in the illustration. Also *vt.*

padlock

padre ['pɑːdri] *nc* chaplain, priest or minister (esp. in the army etc) (*informal*).

paediatrician [piːdiə'triʃən] *nc* see **pediatrician.**

pagan ['peigən] *nc* **1.** person who does not believe in one of the great world religions. **2.** person who does not believe in any religion. Also *adj*: *pagan beliefs; pagan* *practice*.

paganism *nu* beliefs and practices of pagans.

page[1] [peidʒ] *nc* **1.** one side of a sheet of paper. **2.** record: *the pages of history*.

page[2] [peidʒ] *nc* boy servant (in a hotel etc). Also *vt* try to find a person at a hotel etc by loudspeaker or by getting a page to go round calling or showing the person's name.

pageant ['pædʒənt] *nc* **1.** form of public entertainment held in the open air in which people dress up in special costumes, show scenes from history etc. **2.** public celebration in which colourful costumes are worn (e.g. a king's coronation).

pageantry *nu* splendid and colourful display.

pagoda [pə'goudə] *nc* temple (kind of church) with many storeys each with a roof (esp. in China).

pagoda

paid [peid] past of **pay**.

pail [peil] *nc* **1.** open container with handle for carrying water etc; bucket. **2.** amount that it contains.

pain [pein] *nc/u* **1.** suffering of the body or mind: *suffer a lot of pain. Do you suffer much pain?* **2.** suffering in a particular place: *a pain in one's head; stomach pains*. Also *vt* cause someone suffering or annoyance.

painful *adj* causing pain. **painfully** *adv*.

painless *adj* without pain. **painlessly** *adv*.

pains *npl* trouble, effort. *He was at great pains to comfort me. The artist took great pains with the painting*.

'painkiller drug used to make pain less severe.

'painstaking *adj* taking great care while doing something; requiring great care and trouble.

on/under pain of risking the penalty of (some punishment) if something is not done. *You must return everything you have stolen, under pain of a severe beating*.

pain in the neck nuisance. (*informal*).

paint [peint] *nc/u* liquid colouring substance which can be put on something to make it a certain colour: *a pot of red paint*. Also *vt/i* **1.** make something a certain colour by putting paint on it: *paint the doors white*. **2.** make a picture by using paints. *The artist was painting a field and some trees* i.e. making a picture of them.

painter[1] *nc* **1.** person who puts paint on something (e.g. a building, doors etc). **2.** person who paints pictures.

painting **1.** *nc* painted picture. **2.** *nu* art of painting pictures.

painter[2] ['peintə*] *nc* rope by which a boat is tied to a ship, pier etc.

pair [pɛə*] *nc* **1.** two things of the same kind which are always used together: *a pair of stockings; a pair of gloves*. **2.** single thing made of two parts that cannot be used separately: *a pair of scissors; a pair of trousers*. **3.** two people or things which are the same or similar: *a pair of scoundrels*. **4.** man and woman who are married or about to be married: *a handsome pair*. Also *vt/i* form a pair; arrange in pairs.

pair off arrange in pairs.

in pairs in twos.

pajamas [pi'dʒɑːməz] *npl* see **pyjamas.**

pal [pæl] *nc* friend. (*informal*).

palace ['pæləs] *nc* large house for a ruler (e.g. a king) or a bishop; any kind of large fine house.

palatial [pə'leiʃl] *adj* like a palace; very grand.

palaeolithic, paleolithic [pæliə'liθik] *adj* of a very early period in the history of man; of the early Stone Age.

palate ['pælit] *nc* **1.** roof of the mouth. **2.** sense of taste.

palatable *adj* pleasing to the taste or mind: *a palatable dish. To some the truth is not palatable*. (*opp* **unpalatable**).

palaver [pə'lɑːvə*] *nc/u* **1.** unnecessary complication (esp. one involving talk or discussion). **2.** conference (esp. between explorers and natives). Also *vi* talk a lot. (all *informal*).

pale[1] [peil] *adj* **1.** not having much colour; bloodless. *Her face went pale and she fainted*. **2.** not dark and not bright: *pale blue colour*.

pale[2] [peil] *nc* long, narrow piece of wood pointed at the top, used for fences.

paling *nc* fence. Also *npl*.

beyond the pale not civilized; not well-behaved.

paleolithic [pæliə'liθik] *adj* see **palaeolithic.**

palette ['pælit] *nc* thin board with a hole for the thumb at one end, on which an artist mixes his colours.

palette

palisade [pæli'seid] *nc* fence of strong wooden stakes pointed at the top, used as a means of defence.

pall[1] [pɔːl] *nc* **1.** heavy cloth which is put over a coffin, tomb etc. **2.** any kind of dark, heavy covering: *a pall of smoke*.

pall[2] [pɔːl] *vi* become uninteresting because there is too much of it. *His stories palled on me after a while*.

pallet ['pælit] *nc* flat bag of straw for sleeping on (*o.f.*).

palliate ['pælieit] *vt* **1.** make pain less without curing what is causing it. **2.** make something seem less wrong or evil than it is.

palliative ['pæliətiv] *adj* helping to palliate. Also *nc* something which palliates.

pallid ['pælid] *adj* (with reference to the skin) bloodless; very pale; ill-looking.

pallor ['pælə*] *nu* paleness of the face (caused by sickness, fear etc).

palm[1] [pɑːm] *nc* inner part of the hand between the wrist and the fingers. Also *vt* conceal something in the palm.

palmistry ['pɑːmistri] *nu* art of telling the future by examining the lines and marks on the palm of someone's hand. **palmist** *nc*.

palm something off on someone persuade someone to accept or buy something which has little value. (*informal*).

palm[2] [pɑːm] *nc* **1.** name of various types of trees growing in the tropics, with no branches but broad leaves growing at the top: *coconut palm; date palm.* **2.** leaf of the palm tree used as a sign of victory.

palmy *adj* happy; prosperous: *the palmy days of my youth.*

palpable ['pælpəbl] *adj* **1.** easily seen; obvious: *a palpable mistake.* **2.** that can be felt or touched: *something palpable.* (*opp* **impalpable**). **palpably** *adv.*

palpitate ['pælpiteit] *vi* **1.** beat very quickly. *His heart was palpitating.* **2.** tremble: *palpitating with fear.*

palpitation [pælpi'teiʃən] *nc/u* violent beating of the heart.

palsy ['pɔːlzi] *nu* disease which causes the hands and limbs to shake (*o.f.*).

paltry ['pɔːltri] *adj* almost worthless; of no importance: *be offered a paltry sum of money.* **paltriness** *nu.*

pampas ['pæmpəs] *npl* very large treeless plains of South America.

pamper ['pæmpə*] *vt* be too kind to; indulge too much: *pamper a child.*

pamphlet ['pæmflət] *nc* small paper-covered book (esp. on some subject of topical interest).

pamphleteer [pæmflə'tiə*] *nc* person who writes pamphlets.

pan[1] [pæn] *nc* metal dish, often shallow, used for cooking and other household purposes: *frying pan; saucepan.*

'pancake thin, flat cake made from batter fried in a pan.

pan-[2] [pæn] *prefix* all (e.g. **a pantheon**).

panacea [pænə'siə] *nc* something which is supposed to cure all diseases or solve all difficulties. *There is no panacea for all our problems.*

panchromatic [pænkrə'mætik] *adj* sensitive to all colours (usu. in **panchromatic film**).

panda ['pændə] *nc* **1.** small, reddish animal which lives in trees in the Himalayas, Burma and China. **2.** large black and white animal living at high altitudes in Tibet and China. (Also **Giant Panda**).

pandemonium [pændi'mouniəm] *nu* uproar and confusion. *There was pandemonium in the hall.*

pander ['pændə*] *vi* (with **to**) give help and encouragement (to something that is bad in people). *Films sometimes pander to the public by showing violence and immorality.*

pane [pein] *nc* single sheet of glass in a window, section of a window, door etc.

panegyric [pæni'dʒirik] *nc* **1.** speech or piece of writing in praise of a person/thing. **2.** any kind of enthusiastic praise.

panel ['pænl] *nc* **1.** separate area of a door, wall, dress etc which is different in some way from the surface around it (usu. by being higher or lower than it). **2.** list of names (e.g. of people called to serve on a jury). **3.** group of people who have to answer questions: *panel game* i.e. a game played on radio or television where a group of people take part in some kind of competition. Also *vt* cover with a panel (in sense **1.**).

panelling (*US* **paneling**) *nu* panels: *the panelling on a door.*

pang [pæŋ] *nc* sharp, sudden pain or feeling: *the pangs of hunger; a pang of anxiety.*

panic ['pænik] *nc/u* mad fear (esp. one spreading quickly through a crowd). *The fire caused a panic in the cinema.* Also *vi* feel fear in this way. *past* **panicked.** **panicky** *adj.*

'panic-stricken *adj* filled with great fear.

pannier ['pæniə*] *nc* one of a pair of baskets for carrying things in, slung across the back of a horse, donkey etc.

panoply ['pænəpli] *nc* **1.** complete suit of armour: *a knight in his panoply.* **2.** complete equipment or covering: *the panoply of a Red Indian chieftain.* **panoplied** *adj.*

panorama [pænə'rɑːmə] *nc* **1.** wide uninterrupted view of the surrounding area: *a fine panorama.* **2.** constantly changing scene: *the panorama of city life.* **panoramic** [pænə'ræmik] *adj.*

pansy ['pænzi] *nc* **1.** short, colourful flower with flat petals. **2.** homosexual. (*informal* in sense **2.**).

pant [pænt] *vt/i* **1.** breathe quickly: *pant after running.* **2.** speak while breathing quickly: *pant out a few words.* **3.** desire something very much: *panting for a chance to play in the team; panting to go out.* Also *nc* short, quick breath.

pantheism ['pænθiːizəm] *nu* belief that God and the universe are the same thing. **pantheist** *nc.*

pantheon ['pænθiːən] *nc* **1.** temple etc for all the gods of a religion. **2.** all the gods of a religion. **3.** public building containing memorials to the great men of a nation.

panther ['pænθə*] *nc* leopard (esp. a black one); (*US*) cougar (both wild animals of the cat family).

panties ['pæntiz] *npl* item of underclothing worn by women, covering the lower part of the body above the legs.

pantomime ['pæntəmaim] *nc/u* **1.** (*Brit*) play for children based on a fairy tale, with music and dancing. **2.** play without words, in which the actors show the meaning by gestures.

pantry ['pæntri] *nc* small room in which food, dishes etc are kept.

pants [pænts] *npl* **1.** trousers (usu. for men) (*informal*). **2.** item of underclothing fastened at the waist and extending to about the top of the leg.

pap [pæp] *nu* soft food for babies.

papa [pə'pɑː] *n* child's word for **father.** (*informal* and *o.f.*).

papacy ['peipəsi] *n* **1.** position or authority of the Pope. **2.** government, rule by the Pope.

papal *adj* connected with the Pope, the papacy or the Roman Catholic Church.

papaya [pə'paiə], **pawpaw** ['pɔːpɔː] **1.** *nc* tree growing in tropical countries. **2.** *nc/u* fruit of this tree, like a melon, which is green outside and yellow inside.

paper ['peipə*] *nc/u* **1.** material made into thin sheets from wood, rags etc which is used for making books and newspapers, putting on walls, covering parcels etc: *a bale of paper* i.e. for covering parcels. **2.** piece or sheet of paper. *The floor was covered with papers.* **3.** newspaper: *buy a morning paper.* **4.** piece of paper with writing or printing on it. *I left all my papers in my case.* **5.** set of examination questions: *a difficult paper.* **6.** something written about a matter of interest, to be read at a meeting of a society etc. *He is preparing a paper on World Population for our next meeting.* Also *vt* cover walls etc with paper.

papers *npl* documents which tell who or what one is. *You will have to show your papers at the gate.*

'paperback book with paper covers.

'paper knife knife for cutting open envelopes etc.

'paper mill mill where paper is made.
'paper'money money made of paper i.e. not coins.
'paperweight heavy object placed on loose papers to prevent them from being blown away.

papier-mâché ['pæpiei'mæʃei] *nu* paper which is made into a soft mass, so that it can then be made into any desired shape. (When it dries it becomes hard and keeps the shape). Also *adj* made from papier-mâché. *The children are making a papier-mâché doll.*

papist ['peipist] *nc* Roman Catholic. Also *adj.* (both *impolite*).

papyrus [pə'pairəs] *nc/u* **1.** tall water plant from which the Ancient Egyptians and others made a kind of paper to write on. **2.** paper made from this plant. *pl* **papyri** [pə'pairai] or **papyruses.**

par [pɑ:*] *nu* **1.** average or normal amount or condition: *feel below par* i.e. not feel as well as one usually does. **2.** value of a bond, share etc, that is printed on it. *Your shares are above/at/below par* i.e. they are above/at/below the printed value. **3.** (golf) score which is considered as a standard for a particular golf course.
be on a par with someone/something be equal with someone/something. *I don't think his ability is on a par with yours.*

parable ['pærəbl] *nc* story used to teach a moral lesson: *talk in parables.*

parachute ['pærəʃu:t] *nc* apparatus as in the illustration, which allows a man to be dropped from an aeroplane without being hurt, or goods to be dropped without being damaged. Also *vi*: *parachute to the ground.*
parachutist *nc.*

parachute

parade [pə'reid] *nc* **1.** march for a display: *parade of troops; circus parade.* **2.** wide road where people walk for pleasure (e.g. on a sea front). **3.** show of something (e.g. wealth, power etc) intended to impress other people. Also *vt* **1.** come together for a display; march in procession. *The troops paraded by.* **2.** make a show of something to impress: *parade one's knowledge.*

paradigm ['pærədaim] *nc* (usu. with reference to a noun or verb in a language) example in the form of a pattern.

paradise ['pærədais] *nc* **1.** place or state of great happiness or beauty: *an island paradise.* **2.** heaven. **3.** Garden of Eden.
a fool's paradise see **fool.**

paradox ['pærədɔks] *nc* saying which at first may seem to be nonsense but may actually contain some truth (e.g. *More haste, less speed* is a paradox, because sometimes you can get things done more quickly if you do them without rushing).
paradoxical [pærə'dɔksikl] *adj.*

paraffin ['pærəfin] *nu* type of oil used as a fuel for lamps, heating, cooking stoves etc.

paragon ['pærəgɔn] *nc* example of goodness which should be imitated; someone/something which seems to have no faults: *a paragon of virtue.*

paragraph ['pærəgrɑ:f] *nc* division in a piece of writing which begins with a new line (and usu. consists of a group of sentences which deals with one main idea). Also *vt* divide a passage into paragraphs.

parakeet ['pærəki:t] *nc* type of small parrot with a long tail.

parallel ['pærəlel] *adj* **1.** forming lines which are the same distance apart for the whole of their length: *two parallel lines, one line parallel to another.* **2.** similar; corresponding: *parallel developments in both countries.* Also *nc* **1.** line which is parallel to another. **2.** thing/person which is similar to another. **3.** comparison which shows how things resemble one another. **4.** parallel of latitude i.e. imaginary circle round the earth, parallel to the equator and passing through all the places the same distance north or south of the equator; such a line drawn on a map. Also *vt* **1.** be parallel to. **2.** find something which is similar to. *Can you parallel this event? past* **paralleled** or **parallelled.**
parallelogram [pærə'leləgræm] *nc* four-sided figure whose opposite sides are parallel and equal.

paralysis [pə'rælisis] *nu* loss of the power to feel or move in any part or all parts of the body.
paralyze ['pærəlaiz] *vt* **1.** affect with paralysis: *paralyzed in both legs.* **2.** make powerless or helpless: *paralyze industry by a general strike.*
paralytic [pærə'litik] *adj* **1.** suffering from, or connected with, paralysis. **2.** very drunk. (*informal* in sense **2.**). Also *nc* person who is paralyzed.

paramount ['pærəmaunt] *adj* most important; most powerful: *of paramount importance; the paramount chief.*

paranoia [pærə'nɔiə] *nu* type of mental illness in which the person suffers from severe delusions (e.g. of persecution).
paranoiac, paranoid ['pærənɔid] *nc/adj.*

parapet ['pærəpit] *nc* low wall at the edge of a bridge, flat roof etc.

paraphernalia [pærəfi'neiliə] *npl* **1.** various small things belonging to a person. **2.** tools, equipment required for some job or trade.

paraphrase ['pærəfreiz] *vt* state the meaning of something (e.g. a written passage etc) in other words. Also *nc*: *make a paraphrase of.*

parasite ['pærəsait] *nc* **1.** animal or plant which lives in or on another and gets its food from it. **2.** person who lives on others without giving anything in return. **parasitic** [pærə'sitik] *adj.*

parasol ['pærəsɔl] *nc* umbrella which gives protection from the rays of the sun.

paratrooper ['pærətru:pə*] *nc* soldier who is trained to drop by parachute. *pl* **paratroops.**

parcel ['pɑ:sl] *nc* thing or bundle of things wrapped up and tied together (e.g. to be sent through the post); package. Also *vt* make into a parcel or parcels. *past* **parcelled.** (*US* **parceled**).
parcel something out divide into parts and give away: *parcel out someone's land.*
part and parcel of see **part**[1].

parch [pɑ:tʃ] *vt* **1.** make hot and dry: *parched by the sun; parched with thirst.* **2.** make dry by heating: *parched corn.*

parchment ['pɑːtʃmənt] *nc/u* **1.** writing material made from the skin of a sheep, goat etc. **2.** paper that looks like parchment.

pardon ['pɑːdn] *vt* **1.** forgive, excuse. *Pardon my interruption.* **2.** set free from prison. *The king pardoned all the prisoners.* Also *nc* **1.** forgiveness. **2.** paper which says that someone is to be freed from prison.
pardonable *adj* that can be forgiven: *a pardonable error.* (*opp* **unpardonable**).
pardonably *adv.*
Pardon? what did you say?
I beg your pardon please excuse me.

pare [pɛə*] *vt* cut away the outer part or edge of: *pare an apple.*
paring *nc* something pared off: *nail parings.*
pare something down cut down gradually: *pare down expenses.*

parent ['pɛərnt] *nc* **1.** father or mother. **2.** source; cause.
parentage *nu* ancestry: *be of unknown parentage* i.e. who one's parents are is unknown.
parental [pə'rentl] *adj* of a parent.

parenthesis [pə'renθisis] *nc* **1.** one of the two brackets ( ) [ ] etc used to separate part of a sentence from the rest. **2.** what is written inside these brackets (or between commas or dashes). *Do not read the parenthesis. pl* **parentheses** [pə'renθisiːz]. **parenthetical** [pærən'θetikl] *adj.*
in parenthesis (written or said) as a parenthesis.

pariah [pə'raiə] *nc* outcast: *a pariah of society; pariah dog* i.e. (in India) an ownerless dog of mixed breed.

parish ['pæriʃ] *nc* **1.** area with its own church and priest or minister. **2.** people in this area.
parishioner [pə'riʃənə*] *nc* person living in a parish (esp. a person attached to a church).

parity ['pæriti] *nu* being equal; being at par: *struggle for parity of treatment.*

park [pɑːk] *nc* **1.** place laid out for pleasure with gardens and grassy areas: *public park.* **2.** area of grassland with trees around a large house. Also *vt/i* leave one's car etc in a certain place for a time: *look for somewhere to park.*
'car park place laid out so that cars can be left in it for a time.
national park land set apart for wild animals or because of its natural beauty.
'parking meter see **meter**[1].

parlance ['pɑːlns] *nc* way of speaking (*o.f.*).
in common parlance in the way of speaking that people normally use.

parley ['pɑːli] *nc* discussion (esp. between the leaders of enemy forces about exchange of prisoners etc). Also *vi* discuss terms: *parley with one's enemies.*

parliament ['pɑːləmənt] *nc* highest lawmaking body in a country.
parliamentarian [pɑːləmən'tɛəriən] *nc* person who is skilled in parliamentary debates.
parliamentary [pɑːlə'mentəri] *adj* connected with parliament.
Parliament/Houses of Parliament (in Britain) highest law-making body, made up of the House of Commons and the House of Lords.

parlour ['pɑːlə*] (*US* **parlor**) *nc* **1.** sitting room in a house (*o.f.*). **2.** private sitting room in an inn etc.
'parlourmaid female servant who attends while people are dining.
'beauty parlour type of shop where women can go to be made more beautiful. (rather *o.f.*).

parochial [pə'roukiəl] *adj* **1.** connected with a parish: *a parochial hall.* **2.** narrow; limited: *a parochial outlook.*

parody ['pærədi] *nc* **1.** piece of writing written in the manner or style of someone else so as to amuse people. **2.** poor imitation. Also *vt* make a parody of.
parodist *nc* person who writes parodies.

parole [pə'roul] *nu* **1.** solemn promise on the part of a prisoner not to misuse his privileges. **2.** release from prison, under certain conditions, before one's full sentence (term of imprisonment) is complete. *He was on six months' parole.* Also *vt*: *parole a prisoner.*

paroxysm ['pærəksizəm] *nc* sudden attack or outburst (of fear, anger etc).

parquet ['pɑːkei] *nu* floor made of pieces of wood fitted together to form a design. Also *adj*: *a parquet floor.*

parricide ['pærisaid] **1.** *nc/u* crime of killing one's father. **2.** *nc* person who kills his own father.

parrot ['pærət] *nc* bird (usu. brightly coloured) with a hooked bill which can often be taught to repeat sounds and words or phrases. Also *vt* repeat something without understanding what it means.

parry ['pæri] *vt* turn aside (e.g. a blow, a weapon, a question etc).

parse [pɑːz] *vt* describe the words in a sentence and how they are related to one another grammatically.

parsimonious [pɑːsi'mouniəs] *adj* too careful with one's money or goods; mean.
parsimoniously *adv.*
parsimony ['pɑːsiməni] *nu* meanness; too much care of one's money or goods.

parsley ['pɑːsli] *nu* garden plant whose curly leaves are used for flavouring food or decorating food when it is served.

parsnip ['pɑːsnip] *nc/u* kind of sweet, white, root vegetable related to the carrot.

parson ['pɑːsn] *nc* minister or priest in charge of a parish; any minister or priest (*o.f.*).
parsonage *nc* house provided for a minister or priest.

part[1] [pɑːt] *nc* **1.** something which is smaller than the whole. *This part of the road is rough, but the rest is good. A small part of the garden is covered with grass.* **2.** piece into which something is divided. *The story is told in three parts. A centimetre is a hundredth part of a metre.* **3.** what someone in a play says and does: *learn one's part* i.e. what one has to say etc; *get a part in a play* i.e. be chosen to act in a play. **4.** share: *do one's part* i.e. do what one has to do.
partly *adv* to some extent: *be partly responsible for something.*
'part song *nc/u* song for three or more voices.
'part-'time *adj/adv* for only part of the working week: *take a part-time job; work part-time.*
for one's part as far as one is concerned. *For my part, I think he is innocent.*
for the most part usually; mostly.
in part to some extent; in some ways.
a man of parts a man with ability.
part and parcel of a necessary part of. (*informal*).

part[2] [pɑːt] *vt/i* separate; divide. *We had to part the two men who were fighting. The*

crowd parted to make way for the doctor.
parting *nc/u* **1.** line on each side of which the hair is combed in opposite ways. **2.** time or occasion when people part from each other.
part company go in different ways; end a friendship. *We decided that we had to part company.*
part from someone/something leave, go away from.
part with something give up or away. *I don't want to part with my collection of books.*
take part in see **take.**
take someone's part support someone. *In family quarrels, he always takes his sister's part.*
take something in good part accept some disappointment in a friendly, good-tempered way. *He took his disappointment in good part.*

partake [pɑː'teik] *vt* **1.** take part in. **2.** take a share of something (e.g. a meal): *partake of a meal. past tense* **partook** [pɑː'tuk]. *past part* **partaken.**

partial ['pɑːʃl] *adj* **1.** not complete: *a partial loss.* **2.** favouring one side more than the other: *a partial judgment.* (*opp* **impartial** in sense **2.**).
partially *adv* not completely.
partiality [pɑːʃi'æliti] *nu* **1.** unfairness. **2.** liking (for something).
be partial to be rather fond of: *be partial to sweet food.*

participate [pɑː'tisipeit] *vi* have a share; take part in something. **participation** [pɑːtisi'peiʃən] *nu.* **participatory** [pɑːtisi'peitəri] *adj.* **participant** [pɑː'tisipənt] *nc.*

participle ['pɑːtisipl] *nc* name given to various forms of the verb (e.g. **gone; going; walked; walking**).
participial [pɑːti'sipiəl] *adj* of or containing a participle: *participial phrase.*

particle ['pɑːtikl] *nc* **1.** very small piece: *particle of dust.* **2.** (grammar) article i.e. **a, an, the;** adverb or preposition (e.g. **up, on etc**); conjunction (e.g. **and, but etc**); prefix or suffix (e.g. **in-, inter-, -ly etc**).

parti-coloured ['pɑːtikʌləd] *adj* partly of one colour, partly of another.

particular [pə'tikjulə*] *adj* **1.** considered separately from others. *That particular house is very nice, although the rest of them are not.* **2.** special; great. *He is a particular friend of mine. Pay particular attention now.* **3.** difficult to please; careful: *be very particular about what one eats.* **4.** in great detail: *a particular description of what he has seen.* Also *nc* detail; single point: *correct in every particular.*
particularly *adv* especially.
particularize *vt* treat in detail; mention one by one.

partisan [pɑːti'zæn] *nc* **1.** strong supporter of a person, group or an idea; person who will not listen to different arguments. **2.** guerrilla in certain European countries during World War II. Also *adj* (usu. in sense **1.**): *a partisan argument.*

partition [pɑː'tiʃən] *nc/u* **1.** division into parts: *the partition of a country after war.* **2.** part; section. **3.** thin wall between rooms. Also *vt* divide.
partition something off divide by means of a wall, curtain etc.

partner ['pɑːtnə*] *nc* **1.** person who takes part with another person/other people in some activity. **2.** person who partly owns a business. **3.** one of two people who play cards together, dance together etc. Also *vt* be a partner to.
partnership *nc/u* **1.** state of being a partner or being partners. **2.** business company where two or more people share the risks and the profits.

partook [pɑː'tuk] past tense of **partake.**

partridge ['pɑːtridʒ] *nc* kind of game bird which lives on open ground, and has a plump body and a short tail.

party ['pɑːti] *nc* **1.** group of people having the same political ideas. **2.** group of people doing some activity together: *party of tourists.* **3.** meeting of a group of people who have been invited to a house for some kind of celebration: *birthday party.* **4.** person who takes part in an action or knows about it. *He was (a) party to our scheme.* **5.** one of the people or groups of people concerned in a legal matter (e.g. a contract etc). **6.** person (*o.f.* in sense **6.**).
'party line telephone line shared by two or more persons who have telephones.
the 'party 'line agreed policy of a political party.

pass[1] [pɑːs] *vt/i* **1.** go by; go on; move past or over: *pass an interesting building; pass another car; pass from one place to another.* **2.** hand around; transfer. *My documents were passed from one official to another.* **3.** put; make go. *The rope was passed through an iron ring.* **4.** change; go from one state to another. *Water passes from a liquid to a solid when it freezes.* **5.** happen. *What passed between you?* **6.** go by, end. *The time for talking has passed.* **7.** go from one person to another. *His property passed to his eldest son.* **8.** (sport) send a ball to another player by kicking, throwing etc. *The ball was passed to the centre-forward.* **9.** inspect something (e.g. accounts) and say that it is good or satisfactory. **10.** say that someone is successful in something. *The examiners passed all the candidates.* **11.** be successful in something (e.g. an examination, test etc). **12.** declare a bill etc to be law. *Parliament has passed the bill.* **13.** give a judgment, sentence, opinion etc on something/someone. *The judge passed sentence on the prisoner.* **14.** spend (time). *We passed the evenings playing cards.* **15.** go beyond. *That passes my comprehension* i.e. I cannot understand it. **16.** make soldiers go by: *pass troops in review* i.e. so that they can be inspected.
passable *adj* **1.** fairly good but not very good. *He has a passable knowledge of French.* **2.** that can be used or gone over: *passable river/road etc.* (*opp* **impassable** in sense **2.**).
passably *adv.*
'passbook book where the details of someone's bank account are put down.
'passkey key which can open several different locks.
'password secret word by which sentries, guards etc know that one is not an enemy.
pass away come to an end; die.
pass someone/something by ignore; overlook.
'passer-'by *nc* one who happens to be going by. *The injured man was helped by a passer-by. pl* **passers-by.**
pass for someone/something be accepted as someone/something.
pass off take place; be done. *The meeting passed off quietly, although trouble had been expected.*
pass something/someone/oneself off as pretend that something etc is something

else. *He passed himself off as a doctor, but he was found out in the end.*

pass out faint; become unconscious. (*informal*).

pass someone/something over ignore; overlook; consider and reject.

bring something to pass cause something (*o.f.*).

come to pass happen (*o.f.*).

let something pass ignore something. *He has been very rude to me, but I'll let it pass.*

pass[2] [pɑːs] *nc* **1.** success in an examination; grade in an examination; grade in an examination which is not a fail, but below a merit, distinction, honours etc. **2.** path through mountains. **3.** permission to enter some place; free ticket (to a theatre etc). **4.** (sport) act of sending the ball to another person. **5.** quick movement of the hands. *The conjurer made several passes over the box.* **6.** state; condition. *Things have come to a terrible pass.* **7.** (fencing) thrust with the sword: *make a pass with one's sword.* **8.** *make a pass at* i.e. try to kiss etc or start a sexual relationship with.

passage ['pæsidʒ] *nc/u* **1.** way through a building etc, corridor. **2.** going by, through or across: *the passage of time; get passage through a crowd.* **3.** voyage; journey by sea: *book one's passage.* **4.** part of a speech or piece of writing: *an interesting passage.* **5.** making a bill into law.

passenger ['pæsindʒə*] *nc* person travelling in a train, bus, plane etc, or in a car in addition to the driver.

passion ['pæʃən] *nc/u* very strong feeling. *Hate and anger are passions.*

the Passion the sufferings and death of Jesus Christ: *Passion play.*

passionate ['pæʃənit] *adj* having strong feelings; caused by strong feelings: *a passionate character; a passionate speech.* **passionately** *adv.*

have a passion for like very much: *have a passion for painting.*

passive ['pæsiv] *adj* **1.** being acted on without doing anything in return; suffering without resistance; not fighting back: *a passive mind; passive obedience; passive resistance* i.e. refusing to do something, without using force and without defending oneself against force. **2.** (grammar) form of the verb as in: *a stone was thrown through the window.* (*opp* **active**). **passively** *adv.* **passiveness, passivity** [pə'siviti] *nu.*

in the passive having the passive form of the verb.

Passover ['pɑːsouvə*] *n* Jewish feast.

passport ['pɑːspɔːt] *nc* **1.** document to be carried when visiting foreign countries, with details concerning oneself and showing that one has the protection of one's government. **2.** means of getting favour, being accepted etc. *Some people say that education is a passport to success.*

past [pɑːst] *adj* **1.** gone by; ended. *We've had terrible weather in the past week. Our difficulties are past.* **2.** having been in office: *a past president.* Also *nu* **1.** time gone by: *talk about the past.* **2.** person's previous experiences (esp. if they are unknown or not to his credit): *know about someone's past.* Also *prep* **1.** up to and beyond: *walk past someone.* **2.** after (in time): *past midnight.* **3.** beyond. *His stupidity is past belief.* Also *adv* up to something and beyond. *We watched the people hurry past.*

paste [peist] *nu* **1.** substance used for sticking things together (e.g. wallpaper to a wall). **2.** soft mixture containing meat or fish etc: *fishpaste.* **3.** hard material used to make imitations of precious stones: *a paste diamond.* Also *vt* stick things with paste.

'pasteboard cardboard; stiff material made from paper.

pastel ['pæstl] *nc* **1.** kind of coloured chalk (called **crayon**) used in drawing. **2.** picture made by using crayons. Also *adj* soft and light in colour: *pastel shades/colours.*

pasteurize ['pɑːstjuəraiz] *vt* heat something enough to kill all the germs in it: *pasteurize milk.* **pasteurization** [pɑːstjuərai'zeiʃən] *nu.*

pastiche [pæs'tiːʃ] *nc* piece of writing which imitates the style of another writer.

pastille ['pæstl] *nc* small sweet (usu. containing medicine for the throat).

pastime ['pɑːstaim] *nc* any pleasant way of passing time; game or recreation.

pastor ['pɑːstə*] *nc* minister in charge of a church.

pastoral ['pɑːstərl] *adj* **1.** connected with a clergyman: *pastoral letter* i.e. letter from a bishop to the people in his diocese. **2.** (literature, music, painting) having to do with shepherds and country life. Also *nc* pastoral play, poem or picture about shepherds and country people.

pastry ['peistri] **1.** *nu* paste of flour, fat etc which is baked in an oven (often with fruit, meat etc). **2.** *nc/u* pie, tart etc which is made in this way.

pasture ['pɑːstjuə*] *nc/u* **1.** grassland on which cattle, horses etc can feed. **2.** grass on such land. Also *vt/i* **1.** (with reference to cattle etc) feed on grass. **2.** put cattle etc out to feed on grass.

pasturage *nu* pasture.

pasty[1] ['peisti] *adj* **1.** like paste. **2.** pale and unhealthy: *a pasty complexion.*

pasty[2] ['pæsti] *nc* pastry baked with meat in it.

pat[1] [pæt] *vt* **1.** hit gently with the open hand as a sign of sympathy, encouragement etc: *pat someone on the back.* **2.** hit gently with a flat object to get it into shape: *pat dough into shape.* *past* **patted.** Also *nc* **1.** act of gently hitting with the open hand or with something flat. **2.** small piece of e.g. butter which has been patted into shape.

pat oneself on the back praise oneself; be pleased with oneself. (*informal*).

pat[2] [pæt] *adv* at the right moment; in the right way. *He answered pat.* Also *adj.*

patch [pætʃ] *nc* **1.** piece of material fixed onto another material in order to mend or protect it: *patch on a torn shirt; eyepatch* i.e. protection over an injured eye. **2.** part of a surface which is a different colour from the rest of it: *a black dog with a white patch on its back.* **3.** small piece of ground for growing things: *vegetable patch.* Also *vt* protect or mend by using patches.

patchy *adj* good in some parts but not in others.

'patchwork pieces of cloth of various sizes, shapes and colours sewn together.

patch something up **1.** mend quickly or roughly: *patch up an old car.* **2.** put an end to: *patch up a quarrel.*

not a patch on not nearly so good as. *The students this year are not a patch on those last year.* (*informal*).

pate [peit] *nc* head (*o.f.*).

patent ['peitnt] *nc* **1.** authority from the government to manufacture something and also to prevent it from being imitated: *get a patent for a new kind of car.* **2.** something that is protected by a patent. Also *vt* get a patent for. *He patented his invention.* Also *adj* **1.** plain; easily seen. *It is patent that a country must educate its people to make progress.* **2.** protected by a patent: *patent medicines.*

patently *adv*: *He is patently a fool* i.e. everyone can see that he is a fool.

patentee [peitn'tiː] *nc* person to whom a patent has been granted.

'patent 'leather leather with a very glossy smooth surface.

paternal [pə'təːnl] *adj* of or like a father; on one's father's side: *paternal care; paternal aunt.* **paternally** *adv.*

paternity [pə'təːniti] *nu* **1.** being a father. **2.** origin on the father's side: *paternity unknown.*

paternalism *nu* (usu. with reference to politics) practice of treating other people in the way that a father treats his children. *Britain's attitude to her colonies was often one of paternalism.* **paternalistic** [pətəːnə'listik] *adj.*

paternoster ['pætə'nɔstə*] *nc* the Lord's Prayer.

path [pɑːθ] *nc* **1.** way made across fields, through woods etc by people or animals walking: *mountain path.* **2.** line along which someone/something moves: *the path of a ship across the ocean.* *pl* **paths** [pɑːðz].

'pathway path.

pathetic [pə'θetik] *adj* making one feel full of pity; sad. **pathetically** *adv.* see **pathos.**

pathology [pə'θɔlədʒi] *nu* study of diseases.

pathological [pæθə'lɔdʒikl] *adj* **1.** unhealthy. **2.** connected with pathology.

pathologist *nc* expert in pathology.

pathos ['peiθɔs] *nu* quality in something which makes one feel sad, full of pity. see **pathetic.**

patience ['peiʃəns] *nu* **1.** willingness to put up with delay, pain and other discomforts; ability to keep waiting or trying for something until one is successful. **2.** card game (usu. for one person).

patient *adj* having or showing patience. (*opp* **impatient**). Also *nc* person being treated by a doctor.

patina ['pætinə] *nc* thin covering on the surface of metal or wood, caused by age.

patio ['pætiou] *nc* open courtyard within a house; open part outside a house (usu. paved and used for dining etc). *pl* **patios.**

patriarch ['peitriɑːk] *nc* **1.** father or ruler of a family or tribe. **2.** highly respected old man. **patriarchal** [peitri'ɑːkl] *adj.*

patrician [pə'triʃən] *nc* (esp. in ancient Rome) person of high birth. Also *adj.*

patricide ['pætrisaid] **1.** *nc/u* act of killing one's father. **2.** *nc* person who kills his own father. **patricidal** [pætri'saidl] *adj.*

patrimony ['pætriməni] *nc* property handed down from one's father or from one's ancestors.

patriot ['pætriət] *nc* person who loves and defends his country. **patriotic** [pætri'ɔtik] *adj.*

patriotism *nu* love of one's country.

patrol [pə'troul] *vt/i* go round a town, camp etc to guard and protect it. *past* **patrolled.** Also *nc* **1.** act of patrolling: *on patrol.* **2.** group of men, ships, planes etc sent out to find out something about the enemy. **3.** group of men who patrol.

patron ['peitrn] *nc* **1.** person who buys regularly at a certain shop. **2.** person who gives help to another person, to a society, cause etc. **3.** saint or god who takes special care of a certain person or group of people, a church, a town etc: *the patron saint of the town.*

patronage *nu* act of be ng a patron; act of patronizing.

patronize ['pætrənaiz] *vt* **1.** buy regularly at a shop. *I always patronize this shop.* **2.** treat somebody in a friendly way while showing one thinks he is lower than oneself. *The rich man patronized his poor friends.*

patter[1] ['pætə*] *nu* sound of a series of quick, light blows or steps: *the patter of rain on a rooftop.* Also *vi* make this sound.

patter[2] ['pætə*] *nu* (usu. with reference to a person selling something or to a person who tells stories or does tricks to entertain others) quick and clever way of talking.

pattern ['pætn] *nc* **1.** decorative arrangement of colours and shapes on wallpaper, clothes etc: *a beautiful pattern.* **2.** model or guide for something to be made: *a dress pattern.* **3.** model which should be imitated: *a pattern of good conduct.* **4.** sample (e.g. a piece of cloth from material for a suit to show the customer what the cloth is like).

pattern oneself after someone try to make oneself like someone. *He patterned himself after his teacher.*

patty ['pæti] *nc* pastry with meat, oysters etc inside it.

paucity ['pɔːsiti] *nu* small number; small amount.

paunch [pɔːntʃ] *nc* fat stomach.

pauper ['pɔːpə*] *nc* very poor person (esp. one who receives charity).

pauperize *vt* make a pauper of; treat as a pauper.

pause [pɔːz] *vi* stop for a while; wait. *He paused before speaking again.* Also *nc* short break in doing something.

pave [peiv] *vt* cover (a street, path etc) with flat stones, bricks, concrete etc.

pavement *nc* (*Brit*) paved way at the side of a street for people to walk on. (*US* **sidewalk**).

pavilion [pə'viliən] *nc* **1.** building at the side of a sports ground for the use of players and spectators. **2.** decorated building for concerts, dancing etc. **3.** large tent.

paw [pɔː] *nc* **1.** foot of an animal having claws or nails: *the paws of a cat.* **2.** hand. (*informal* in sense **2.**). Also *vt* **1.** scratch, touch with the paws; (with reference to a horse, bull etc) strike the ground with a hoof. **2.** touch with the hands. (*informal* in sense **2.**).

pawn[1] [pɔːn] *nc* **1.** (chess) one of the pieces which are least important. **2.** person who is used by someone else for his own purposes.

pawn[2] [pɔːn] *vt* get money by leaving something of value (e.g. jewellery, clothes) which will be returned to one only when the money is paid back.

'pawnbroker person who lends money at interest to those who pawn goods with him.

'pawnshop pawnbroker's shop.

in pawn pawned. *The ring is in pawn.*

pawpaw ['pɔːpɔː] *nc/u* see **papaya.**

pay [pei] *vt/i* **1.** give a person money for his goods, the work he has done etc: *pay good wages.* **2.** be useful or profitable. *It pays to be pleasant to other people.* **3.** suffer; undergo pain or suffering: *pay the penalty.* *past* **paid.** Also *nu* money given for work done: *bring home good pay.*

payable *adj* which must or may be paid.

payee [pei'iː] *nc* person to whom money is paid.

payment *nc/u* **1.** paying or being paid. **2.** amount paid. **3.** reward or punishment.

pay (someone) back **1.** give back money which has been borrowed. **2.** punish someone for a wrong he has done to one.

pay for something **1.** give money for. **2.** suffer as a result of one's crimes.

pay someone back in his own coin punish someone by doing to him what he has done to someone else. (*informal*).

payment in kind payment by means of goods instead of money.

pea [piː] *nc* **1.** plant with small, green seeds inside a pod i.e. a kind of covering. **2.** small green seeds of this plant, commonly used as a food.

'peanut seed with a hard shell which grows under the ground. (Also **groundnut**).

peace [piːs] *nu* **1.** freedom from war or fighting: *peace between nations; be at peace.* **2.** calm; quietness: *peace of mind; hold one's peace* i.e. not say anything.

peaceful *adj* **1.** loving peace: *peaceful person.* **2.** calm; quiet: *peaceful scene.* **peacefully** *adv.*

'peacemaker person who helps to stop fighting.

'peace offering something which shows that one wants peace.

'peacetime time when there is no war.

peach [piːtʃ] *nc* **1.** slightly furry, juicy fruit containing a large, rough stone. **2.** tree which bears this fruit. Also *adj* yellowish-red in colour.

peacock ['piːkɔk] *nc/u* male bird famous for its beautiful tail feathers. (*fem* **peahen**).

peak [piːk] *nc* **1.** pointed top of a mountain. **2.** mountain that stands alone. **3.** pointed top or front of anything: *peak of a cap.* **4.** highest point or amount. *Traffic accidents reach their peak at the weekends.*

peal [piːl] *nc* **1.** loud and continuous sound: *peals of laughter/thunder etc.* **2.** ringing of bells. **3.** set of bells to be rung together. Also *vt/i* sound, cause to sound, loudly; ring.

pear [pɛə*] *nc/u* **1.** sweet, juicy fruit as in the illustration. **2.** tree which bears this fruit.

pear

pearl [pəːl] *nc* **1.** small white, or almost white, gem which sometimes forms inside oysters. **2.** something that looks like a pearl (e.g. a dewdrop). **3.** something which is perfect of its kind; something very precious. Also *adj* coloured like a pearl; made from pearls.

peasant ['peznt] *nc* person who works on a farm or owns a very small farm.

peasantry *nu* peasants (as a class).

Note: the words *peasant, peasantry* are not usu. used with reference to modern Britain.

peat [piːt] *nu* **1.** mass of partly rotted plants etc, found in bogs. **2.** piece of this dug out, dried and used for fuel. **peaty** *adj.*

pebble ['pebl] *nc* small stone (usu. worn and made round by the action of water): *some pebbles on a beach.* **pebbly** *adj.*

peccadillo [pekə'dilou] *nc* unimportant fault or sin; unimportant weakness in someone's character. *pl* **peccadillos.**

peck[1] [pek] *nc* unit of dry measure (for grain, potatoes, beans etc) equal to 2 gallons or 7.5 litres.

peck[2] [pek] *vt/i* **1.** strike at, hit with the beak. *The bird pecked the cat.* **2.** pick up food with a quick striking movement. *The hens were pecking the grain.* **3.** make a hole in something with the beak. *The bird had pecked a hole in the tree.* Also *nc* **1.** stroke made by a bird with its beak. **2.** quick careless kiss: *a peck on the cheek.* (*informal* in sense **2.**).

peck at one's food eat only a little, bit by bit. (*informal*).

peculation [pekju'leiʃən] *nu* theft of funds or money by an official. **peculator** ['pekjuleitə*] *nc.* (both *formal*).

peculiar [pi'kjuːliə*] *adj* **1.** strange; unusual. **2.** special: *something of peculiar value.* **peculiarly** *adv.*

peculiarity [pikjuːli'æriti] *nc/u* **1.** strangeness. **2.** something strange. **3.** (of a person) something typical.

peculiar to used by, belonging to, one person/thing and not another: *plants peculiar to the Antarctic.*

pecuniary [pi'kjuːniəri] *adj* of money: *a pecuniary reward.*

pedagogue ['pedəgɔg] *nc* **1.** teacher. **2.** teacher who insists on rules too much.

pedagogy ['pədəgɔgi] *nu* science of teaching.

pedal ['pedl] *nc* part of a machine or instrument which is pressed by the foot: *the pedal of a bicycle/piano/sewing machine etc.* Also *vt/i* work the pedal or pedals of something (esp. a bicycle). *He pedalled uphill. past* **pedalled.** (*US* **pedaled**).

pedant ['pednt] *nc* **1.** person who shows off his knowledge when it is not necessary. **2.** teacher or scholar who is too narrow-minded, too interested in rules. **pedantic** [pe'dæntik] *adj.* **pedantically** *adv.*

pedantry *nu* unnecessary display of learning.

peddle ['pedl] *vt/i* go from house to house selling things (usu. of small value).

pedlar ['pedlə*] *nc* person who does this.

pedestal ['pedəstl] *nc* base (raised piece of stone etc) on which a column or statue stands; base of a lamp, tall vase etc.

pedestrian [pə'destriən] *nc* person who goes on foot along roads or streets used also by vehicles; walker. Also *adj* **1.** connected with walking; for pedestrians. **2.** dull; without imagination; uninspired: *a pedestrian novel.*

pe'destrian 'crossing place marked on a road where pedestrians may cross the road.

pediatrician, paediatrician [piːdiə'triʃən] *nc* doctor who specializes in the diseases etc of children. **pediatric** [piːdi'ætrik] *adj.*

pediatrics [piːdi'ætriks] *nu* study of the diseases of children.

pedigree ['pedigriː] *nc* line of ancestors; line of descent: *pedigree dog* i.e. dog whose ancestors are known and recorded.

pedlar ['pedlə*] *nc* see **peddle.**

peek [piːk] *vi* look at quickly (and sometimes secretly): *peek at something.* (*informal*).

peel [piːl] *vt/i* **1.** take off the skin or outer covering of: *peel an orange.* **2.** (esp. of human skin, wallpaper, bark of a tree etc) come off in bits. *Because it is sunburnt my skin is peeling. The wallpaper on the damp* *wall is peeling*. Also *nu* skin of fruit, potatoes etc.

peelings *npl* pieces peeled off (esp. from potatoes).

peep [pi:p] *vi* **1.** look through a hole, crack or other small opening. **2.** look quickly and secretly at something. **3.** come out a little. *The sun peeped out from behind some clouds.* Also *nc* **1.** look through a hole, crack etc. **2.** quick, secret look. **3.** first coming out of light: *at the peep of day.*

peer[1] [piə*] *vi* look at something long and closely, as a person who cannot see well does: *peer at a badly written letter; peer into a dark room.*

peer[2] [piə*] *nc* **1.** person who has the same rank, ability etc as another: *be judged by one's peers.* **2.** person who has a noble title (e.g. a duke, earl, count etc); person of high birth.

peerage *nc/u* **1.** group of titled people in a country: *be raised to the peerage* i.e. be made a peer. **2.** book listing the titled people in a country.

peeress ['piəres] *nc* **1.** wife or widow of a peer. **2.** woman peer.

peerless *adj* without equal: *of peerless quality.*

peeve [pi:v] *vt* annoy. (*informal*).

peevish ['pi:viʃ] *adj* easily annoyed; always complaining. **peevishly** *adv.* **peevishness** *nu.*

peg [peg] *nc* **1.** small piece of wood, metal, plastic etc used to fasten things, to hang things on etc: *hat peg; coat peg; tent peg* i.e. peg attached to a tent rope and hit into the ground; *clothes peg* i.e. peg used to keep washed clothes on a rope so that they can dry. **2.** small drink of alcoholic liquor. (*informal* in sense **2.**). Also *vt* **1.** fasten with pegs: *peg down a tent.* **2.** fix prices, wages etc by government regulations: *wages pegged at a low level. past* **pegged.**

peg away at something keep on doing something. *He pegged away at the job until he had finished it.* (*informal*).

a square peg in a round hole a person not suited for the job etc he is in. (*informal*).

take someone down a peg or two make someone feel less important. (*informal*).

pekinese [pi:ki'ni:z] *nc* type of small dog with long hair and a flat face.

pelican ['pelikən] *nc* fish-eating water bird with a large bill and a pouch in the throat for storing food.

pelican

pellet ['pelit] *nc* **1.** little ball made from something soft (e.g. mud or bread). **2.** little ball of lead to be fired from a gun.

pellucid [pe'lu:sid] *adj* **1.** clear: *pellucid water.* **2.** easily understood: *a pellucid speech.*

pelmet ['pelmit] *nc* type of framework covering the top of a curtain.

pelt[1] [pelt] *vt/i* **1.** attack by throwing things at. *The crowd pelted him with stones.* **2.** (with reference to rain, hail etc) come down heavily. *The rain is pelting down. It is pelting with rain.*

pelt[2] [pelt] *nc* skin of an animal with the fur still on it.

pelvis ['pelvis] *nc* hollow formed by the hipbone and the lower part of the backbone. **pelvic** *adj.*

pen[1] [pen] **1.** *nc* instrument used for writing in ink. **2.** *nu* writing: *live by the pen.* Also *vt* write something: *pen a letter. past* **penned.**

'penmanship *nu* art of handwriting.

'penfriend person in another country whom one has got to know through letter-writing.

'penknife small folding knife. (Sometimes **pocket knife**).

'pen name name used by a writer instead of his real one.

'ballpoint 'pen see **ball.**

'fountain pen see **fountain.**

pen[2] [pen] *nc* small enclosed area for sheep, cattle, goats etc. Also *vt* shut (animals) in a pen. *past* **penned.**

'playpen see **play**[2].

pen someone up/in keep someone very closely in place: *penned up in the house all day.*

penal ['pi:nl] *adj* having to do with punishment: *a penal offence* i.e. one for which a person can be punished by law; *penal servitude* i.e. imprisonment with hard labour.

penalize *vt* **1.** declare that an action can be punished by law or in the rules of a game. *All fouls in football should be penalized.* **2.** punish in some way. *Our team was penalized for turning up late.*

penalty ['penlti] *nc* **1.** punishment. *The penalty for spitting is £5.* **2.** (sport etc) some kind of disadvantage given against a team because it has broken a rule. **3.** disadvantage of some state or condition: *the penalties of being poor.*

penance ['penəns] *nu* punishment which one gives to oneself (often on the advice of a priest) because of some wrong that one has done: *do penance for one's sins.*

pence [pens] *npl* see **penny.**

penchant ['pɔnʃɔŋ] *nc* (with **for**) special liking (for).

pencil ['pensl] *nc* narrow, pointed instrument (often made of wood and graphite) used for writing and drawing. Also *vt* mark or write with a pencil. *past* **pencilled.** (*US* **penciled**).

pendant ['pendnt] *nc* hanging ornament (e.g. something hanging from a necklace etc).

pending ['pendiŋ] *adj* waiting to be decided or settled. *Your case is still pending.* Also *prep* while waiting for; until: *pending the judge's decision.*

pendulous ['pendjuləs] *adj* hanging down.

pendulum ['pendjuləm] *nc* weight swinging freely from side to side: *the pendulum of a clock.*

pendulum

penetrate ['penitreit] *vt/i* **1.** go into or through. *The knife had penetrated his body.* **2.** see through. *Our eyes could not penetrate the mist.* **3.** understand: *a mystery that is difficult to penetrate.* **4.** spread through. *A smell penetrated the whole house.* **penetration** [peni'treiʃən] *nu.*
penetrating *adj* **1.** loud and clear: *a penetrating cry.* **2.** piercing: *a penetrating glance.* **3.** able to understand quickly and thoroughly: *He has a penetrating mind.* **penetratingly** *adv.*
penguin ['peŋgwin] *nc* bird found in the Antarctic which has small wings (called **flippers**) used for swimming.
penicillin [peni'silin] *nu* drug which prevents the growth of some types of bacteria.
peninsula [pe'ninsjulə] *nc* area of land almost surrounded by water or stretching far out into the water. **peninsular** *adj.*
penis ['pi:nis] *nc* the male sex organ.
penitence ['penitns] *nu* sorrow for having done wrong.
penitent *adj* feeling or showing regret. (*opp* **impenitent**). Also *nc* person who is sorry for what he has done.
penitential [peni'tenʃl] *adj* connected with penitence: *a penitential hymn.*
penitentiary [peni'tenʃəri] *nc* (mainly *US*) prison.
pennant, pennon ['penən(t)] *nc* long, narrow flag (usu. like a triangle in shape).
penny ['peni] *nc* copper coin of low value (in Britain formerly 12 pennies = 1 shilling, now 100 pennies = 1 pound; in the USA and Canada a penny is another name for a cent, and 100 cents = 1 dollar). see appendix. *pl* **pennies** (for a number of coins) and **pence** [pens] *npl* for value (e.g. *a pencil costing five pence*).
penniless *adj* without any money.
a pretty penny a large sum of money. *That house must have cost a pretty penny.* (*informal*).
pension ['penʃən] *nc* regular payment which is not in exchange for work (e.g. money given by the State to old people or injured soldiers, or by an employer to someone who used to work for him). Also *vt* give a pension to.
pensionable *adj* able to get a pension; resulting in a pension being paid: *of pensionable age; a pensionable job.*
pensioner *nc* person who receives a pension.
pension someone off dismiss someone from a job and give him a pension.
pensive ['pensiv] *adj* deep in thought: *look rather pensive.* **pensively** *adv.* **pensiveness** *nu.*
pent [pent] *adj* shut-in; confined.
'pent-'up *adj* shut-in; not released: *pent-up emotions.*
pentagon ['pentəgən] *nc* figure with five sides and five angles.
the Pentagon US Army Headquarters.
pentathlon [pen'tæθlən] *nc* athletic competition consisting of five events in which each person competes.
pentameter [pen'tæmitə*] *nc* (with reference to poetry) line with five stresses in it.
penthouse ['penthaus] *nc* **1.** (mainly *US*) apartment or house on the top of a building: *luxury penthouse.* **2.** kind of hut built against a wall with its roof sloping down from the wall.
penultimate [pe'nʌltimət] *adj* last except one. *The penultimate figure in* 2485 *is* 8. Also *nc.*
penury ['penjuri] *nu* great poverty.
penurious [pi'njuəriəs] *adj* **1.** very poor. **2.** mean about spending money; miserly. **penuriously** *adv.*
peony ['piəni] *nc* type of garden plant with large, colourful flowers.
people ['pi:pl] *n* **1.** men, women and children. *The room was full of people. He knows a lot of people.* **2.** persons in a state, as a group. *Government should be for the benefit of the people.* **3.** working classes; those without the benefit of wealth, position. *He rose from the people to be a cabinet minister.* **4.** race; nation: *a very brave people; the different peoples of the world.* Also *vt* fill with people; put people in a country.
Note: in senses **1., 2., 3.** *people* is *sing* in form but should be treated as a *pl* noun in every other way (e.g. taking a *pl* verb *Many people were there* and *pl adj* where needed *many people* not *much people*). In sense **4.** *people* is a countable noun like *race* or *nation.*
pep [pep] *nu* energy; liveliness: *pep pills* i.e. pills to give energy. (*informal*).
pep something up make more vigorous, more lively etc. (*informal*).
pepper ['pepə*] **1.** *nu* hot-tasting powder made from crushed seeds of certain plants, and used for flavouring food. **2.** *nc* one of different kinds of green or red vegetables used as food. Also *vt* put pepper on food.
peppery *adj* **1.** hot-tasting. **2.** easily angered: *a peppery old man.*
'peppermint 1. *nu* plant grown for its oil, which is used in medicine and for flavouring sweets. **2.** *nc* type of sweet flavoured with peppermint.
per [pə:*] *prep* for each; in each: *a salary of £2,000 per annum* i.e. for each year; *fifty per cent* i.e. 50 in every hundred; *costing* 5 *pence per ounce.*
perambulator [pə'ræmbjuleitə*] *nc* (*Brit*) small four-wheeled carriage in which a baby is pushed about (*o.f.* – use the short form **pram**) (*US* **baby carriage**).
perceive [pə'si:v] *vt* become aware of through any of the senses; see; understand. *I perceive that you are tired.*
perceptible [pə'septibl] *adj* that can be perceived: *a perceptible change in temperature.* (*opp* **imperceptible**). **perceptibly** *adv.*
perception [pə'sepʃən] *nc/u* act or power of perceiving.
perceptive [pə'septiv] *adj* connected with perception; having perception: *a very perceptive person* i.e. one who understands things well. **perceptively** *adv.*
percentage [pə'sentidʒ] *nc* amount given as if it is part of a whole which is a hundred.
perch[1] [pə:tʃ] *nc* **1.** branch, rod or anything else on which a bird rests. **2.** any high place occupied by a person or building. **3.** measurement of distance equal to 5½ yards or 5.029 metres. Also *vt/i* **1.** come to rest on. *The bird perched on my shoulder.* **2.** set or be situated in a high place: *perched on a high stool; a building perched on top of a hill.*
perch[2] [pə:tʃ] *nc* type of freshwater fish.
percolate ['pə:kəleit] *vt/i* **1.** (with reference to a liquid etc) pass slowly through. *The water percolated through the sand.* **2.** cause (a liquid etc) to pass slowly through.
percolator *nc* kind of coffeepot in which boiling water is made to pass through ground coffee. **percolation** [pə:kə'leiʃən] *nu.*
percussion [pə'kʌʃən] *nu* striking of two (usu. hard) things against one another.

per'cussion instrument musical instrument which is played by striking it (e.g. drums).

perdition [pəː'diʃən] *nu* complete loss or ruin; loss of the joys of heaven.

peregrination [perigri'neiʃən] *nc/u* wandering journey, travelling about (*o.f.*).

peremptory [pə'remptəri] *adj* **1.** fond of giving commands; insisting that commands must be obeyed: *person with a peremptory manner.* **2.** not allowing any question or refusal: *a peremptory command.* **peremptorily** *adv.*

perennial [pə'reniəl] *adj* **1.** lasting for a very long time: *a perennial source of pleasure.* **2.** lasting throughout the whole year: *mountains with perennial snow.* **3.** (with reference to flowers etc) lasting more than two years. Also *nc* perennial plant. **perennially** *adv.*

perfect ['pəːfekt] *adj* **1.** without any fault; excellent: *in perfect condition.* (*opp* **imperfect**). **2.** complete; with all its parts. **3.** complete; utter: *a perfect stranger.* Also [pə'fekt] *vt* make perfect.

perfectly *adv* completely: very well.

perfection [pə'fekʃən] *nc/u* state of making perfect or being perfect.

perfectionist [pə'fekʃənist] *nc* person who is very careful about small details and is not satisfied unless something is perfect.

to perfection perfectly. *He did the work to perfection.*

perfidy ['pəːfidi] *nc/u* treachery; act of treachery or betrayal.

perfidious [pəː'fidiəs] *adj* treacherous; false. **perfidiously** *adv.*

perforate ['pəːfəreit] *vt/i* make a hole or holes through (esp. through a piece of paper so that it can easily be torn off).

perforation [pəːfə'reiʃən] **1.** *nc* hole made in something. **2.** *nu* line of holes made on paper (e.g. on a sheet of stamps so that each stamp can be easily torn off).

perforce [pə'fɔːs] *adv* because it is necessary (*o.f.*).

perform [pə'fɔːm] *vt/i* **1.** do; carry out. *The doctor performed a difficult operation. They performed their tasks.* **2.** do something for an audience (e.g. sing, act etc): *perform in a play/concert etc.*

performance *nc/u* **1.** something performed: *the performance of one's duties.* **2.** something done before an audience (e.g. a play, concert etc). *Did you enjoy the performance last night?*

performer *nc* person who performs (esp. before an audience).

performing animals animals which have been trained to do tricks before an audience.

perfume ['pəːfjuːm] *nc/u* **1.** sweet, pleasant smell: *the perfume of a flower.* **2.** liquid that has a sweet, pleasant smell. Also [pə'fjuːm] *vt* put perfume on someone/something.

perfunctory [pə'fʌŋktəri] *adj* **1.** done carelessly and without interest: *give something only a perfunctory glance.* **2.** acting in a careless, uninterested manner. **perfunctorily** *adv.*

pergola ['pəːgələ] *nc* arrangement of posts built over a garden path, and over which climbing plants can grow.

perhaps [pə'hæps] *adv* it may be; possibly. *Perhaps he will be there tonight.*

perigee ['peridʒiː] *nc* point in the orbit of a planet or the moon in which it is nearest the earth.

peril ['peril] *nc/u* great danger: *in peril; at your peril* i.e. at your own risk.

perilous *adj* dangerous. **perilously** *adv.*

perimeter [pə'rimitə*] *nc* **1.** outside boundary of a surface or figure. **2.** length of such a boundary.

period ['piəriəd] *nc* **1.** certain length of time: *the period of the French Revolution; a period of war and confusion; a period of five minutes.* **2.** one of the parts into which a school day is divided: *the mathematics period.* **3.** pause at the end of a sentence. **4.** mark which indicates the end of a sentence in writing. (Also **full stop**). Also *adj* typical of a certain time in the past: *period furniture.*

periodic [piəri'ɔdik] *adj* happening from time to time.

periodical [piəri'ɔdikl] *adj* periodic. Also *nc* magazine, journal or newspaper. **periodically** *adv.*

peripatetic [peripə'tetik] *adj* moving from one place to another: *a peripatetic teacher.*

periphery [pə'rifəri] *nc* line or area around something. **peripheral** *adj.*

periscope ['periskoup] *nc* long tube with mirrors placed in it so that people who are lower down (e.g. in a submarine) can see what is happening above them.

perish ['periʃ] *vt/i* **1.** die in a fire, accident etc. *Five people perished in the fire.* **2.** (with reference to certain substances) decay or become useless; make useless; destroy. *The rubber has perished.*

perishables *npl* things which can go bad.

perishable *adj* (esp. of food) liable to go bad. (*opp* **imperishable**).

perished with cold feeling very cold.

perjury ['pəːdʒəri] *nc/u* act of swearing on an oath (usu. in a court of law) that something is true when it is not.

perjure oneself swear that something is true when it is not (often in a court of law).

perk[1] [pəːk] *vi* (always with **up**) **1.** become lively and gay (after being depressed or ill etc). *The child soon perked up when he saw his mother.* **2.** raise quickly. *The dog perked up its ears.* (*informal*).

perky *adj* smart; lively. **perkily** *adv.* **perkiness** *nu.* (all *informal*).

perk[2] [pəːk] *nc* informal short form of **perquisite.**

perm [pəːm] *nc* **1.** informal short form of **permanent wave.** **2.** informal short form of **permutation.**

permanent ['pəːmənənt] *adj* continuing for a long time; intended to last: *a permanent arrangement; a permanent building.* (*opp* **temporary**). **permanently** *adv.* **permanence** *nu.*

the permanent way railway lines.

permanent wave way of treating hair so that it is shaped with waves or curls which are supposed to stay in place for some months (informally shortened to **perm**).

permeate ['pəːmieit] *vt/i* spread through; soak through. *Water had permeated (through) the sand. The new ideas had permeated (through) the whole country.*

permeable ['pəːmiəbl] *adj* able to be permeated by liquids: *a permeable layer of soil.* (*opp* **impermeable**). **permeation** [pəːmi'eiʃən] *nu.*

permit [pə'mit] *vt/i* allow. *Permit me to explain. Smoking is not permitted. past* **permitted.** Also ['pəːmit] *nc* written order which permits one to do something, go somewhere etc: *a special permit to visit a military area.*

permissible [pə'misibl] *adj* that may be allowed.

permission [pə'miʃən] *nu* act of permitting.

His parents gave him permission to go to the scout camp. Ask your teacher's permission. **permissive** [pə'misiv] *adj* allowing too many things: *permissive parents.*
permit of something allow. *This state of affairs permits of no delay.* (*formal*).

permutation [pəːmju'teiʃən] *nc* (mathematics) order or change of the order in which a certain number of things are arranged (informally shortened to **perm**).

pernicious [pəː'niʃəs] *adj* harmful. *Smoking is a pernicious habit.* **perniciously** *adv.*

pernickety [pə'nikiti] *adj* fussy; worrying about small things. (*informal*).

peroration [perə'reiʃən] *nc* last part of a speech.

peroxide [pə'rɔksaid] *nu* chemical used mostly for making hair lighter in colour. Also *vt* make hair lighter by the use of this chemical.

perpendicular [pəːpən'dikjulə*] *adj* **1.** standing straight up; upright. **2.** at right angles to another line or surface. Also *nc* perpendicular line, plane or position.

perpetrate ['pəːpitreit] *vt* do or commit something bad (e.g. a crime or mistake). **perpetrator** *nc.* **perpetration** [pəːpi'treiʃən] *nu.*

perpetual [pə'petjuəl] *adj* **1.** lasting forever; lasting for a long time. *He is on a perpetual search for truth.* **2.** continual; happening often. *That dog is a perpetual nuisance.* **perpetually** *adv.*
perpetuate [pə'petjueit] *vt* preserve; keep from being forgotten: *perpetuate someone's memory.*
perpetuity [pəːpi'tjuːiti] *nu* state of being perpetual: *in perpetuity* i.e. forever.

perplex [pə'pleks] *vt* **1.** puzzle; confuse. *This problem perplexes me.* **2.** make something more difficult or confused. *Don't perplex the issue* i.e. don't make the matter more difficult. **perplexed** *adj.* **perplexedly** *adv.*
perplexity *nc/u* **1.** being confused or puzzled. **2.** something that puzzles one.

perquisite ['pəːkwizit] *nc* anything one gets regularly and legally from one's work apart from pay. *One of the perquisites of the post is a free car* (informally shortened to **perk**).

persecute ['pəːsikjuːt] *vt* **1.** treat cruelly (esp. because of religious or political beliefs). **2.** annoy: *persecuted by/with questions.* **persecutor** *nc.*
persecution [pəːsi'kjuːʃən] *nc/u* persecuting or being persecuted.

persevere [pəːsi'viə*] *vi* keep on doing something which is unpleasant or difficult: *persevere at/in/with one's studies.* **perseverance** *nu.*

persist [pə'sist] *vi* last; continue to exist. *The smell persisted even after we had cleaned the room.*
persistent *adj* continuing; not stopping: *a persistent headache.* **persistently** *adv.* **persistence** *nu.*

person ['pəːsn] *nc* **1.** man, woman or child. *There is the person I was talking about.* **2.** body of a human being: *attacks against the person; carrying a knife on his person* i.e. in his pocket etc. **3.** (grammar) class of pronoun or verb according to whether it relates to the person speaking (*first person*), the person spoken to (*second person*) or the person/thing spoken about (*third person*).
Note: the word *people* is normally used for the *pl* of sense **1.**
personable *adj* good-looking; attractive: *a personable young man.*
personage *nc* person (esp. an important person).
personify [pə'sɔnifai] *vt* **1.** be an example of (some quality). *When I was a child, my father personified for me everything that was good.* **2.** speak of or speak to a thing as if it was a person. **personification** [pəsɔnifi'keiʃən] *nc/u.*
personnel [pəːsə'nel] *nu* people working in any job, service etc: *army personnel.*
in person oneself, not someone else. *The president came to the school in person* i.e. he came himself, instead of sending someone else to represent him.

personal ['pəːsnl] *adj* **1.** having to do with oneself and not others: *personal property; a personal letter* i.e. a private letter; *a personal opinion.* **2.** done directly by a person himself: *a personal interview/appearance etc.* **3.** connected with the body: *personal cleanliness.* **4.** about or against a person: *personal abuse. Don't be personal* i.e. don't make remarks about, or ask questions about, a person.
personally *adv* **1.** in person, not through others. *The owner of the hotel welcomed us personally.* **2.** speaking for oneself. *Personally, I think he is a very good man, but you may not agree.* **3.** as a person. *I like him personally, but I hate what he believes in.*

personality [pəːsə'næliti] *nc/u* **1.** what makes one person different from another; what makes a person stand out: *a man with/of great personality.* **2.** important or well-known person: *a stage personality* i.e. a well-known actor or actress. **3.** (usu. *pl*) remark made against someone.

persona non grata [pəː'sounənoun'grɑːtə] *nc* (esp. with reference to diplomats) person who is not allowed to visit or stay in a foreign country by the authorities of that country.

perspective [pə'spektiv] *nc/u* **1.** art of drawing or painting things so that some look farther away than others, as they do in real life. **2.** way of seeing things: *see things in the right perspective* i.e. see a matter properly, what is important and what is not etc.

perspicacious [pəːspi'keiʃəs] *adj* quick to see and understand. **perspicacity** [pəːspi'kæsiti] *nu.*

perspicuous [pə'spikjuəs] *adj* clear; easily understood. **perspicuity** [pəːspi'kjuːiti] *nu.*

perspire [pə'spaiə*] *vi* (used more of human beings than animals) sweat. **perspiration** [pəːspi'reiʃən] *nu.*

persuade [pə'sweid] *vt* **1.** get someone to do what one wants by pleading or arguing. *I persuaded my friends to stay.* **2.** make a person believe something. *We persuaded him of our good intentions. I persuaded the teacher that what I said was true.*
persuasion [pə'sweiʒən] **1.** *nu* persuading. *He decided to leave only after much persuasion.* **2.** *nc* belief: *people of different persuasions.*
persuasive [pə'sweisiv] *adj* able to persuade: *persuasive arguments.* **persuasively** *adv.*

pert [pəːt] *adj* bold; not showing respect: *a pert child.*

pertain [pəː'tein] *vi* (always with **to**) **1.** belonging to; connected with: *all the land pertaining to our house.* **2.** having to do with.

The inspector was interested in everything pertaining to the school.

pertinacious [pəːti'neiʃəs] *adj* not giving something up easily; stubborn. **pertinacity** [pəːti'næsiti] *nu.*

pertinent ['pəːtinənt] *adj* having to do directly with what is being discussed etc; very suitable: *a pertinent question.*

perturb [pə'təːb] *vt* disturb; make anxious: *some very perturbing news.* **perturbation** [pəːtə'beiʃən] *nu.*

peruse [pə'ruːz] *vt* read carefully. **perusal** *nc/u.* (both *formal*).

pervade [pə'veid] *vt* spread through; get into every part of. *An unpleasant smell pervades the house.*

pervasive [pə'veisiv] *adj* spreading everywhere. *Television has had a pervasive influence on young people* i.e. all young people are influenced by it. **pervasively** *adv.*

perverse [pə'vəːs] *adj* **1.** refusing to do what is right or what one is told: *a perverse child.* **2.** deliberately wrong; unnatural: *perverse behaviour; perverse beliefs.* **perversely** *adv.*

pervert [pə'vəːt] *vt* **1.** turn someone/something away from what is right and normal. *He was perverted by his evil companions.* **2.** use something for a bad purpose. *He was accused of perverting justice.* Also ['pəːvəːt] *nc* perverted person (esp. one with a sexual perversion).

perversion *nc/u* perverting or being perverted; perverted behaviour.

pessimism ['pesimizəm] *nu* tendency to look on the unhappy side of things, to believe that the worst is going to happen. (*opp* **optimism**).

pessimist *nc* person who tends to look on the unhappy side of things. **pessimistic** [pesi'mistik] *adj.* **pessimistically** *adv.*

pest [pest] *nc* someone/something that causes trouble or harm. *That disobedient boy is a pest. The flowers were attacked by garden pests* i.e. insects.

pesticide ['pestisaid] *nc/u* substance for killing insects.

pester ['pestə*] *vt* annoy; trouble: *pestered by people asking for money.*

pestilence ['pestilns] *nc* disease that spreads quickly and causes many deaths.

pestilent *adj* **1.** often causing death: *a pestilent disease.* **2.** annoying: *troubled by some pestilent flies.*

pestle ['pesl] *nc* implement for crushing things into fine powder in a strong bowl (called a **mortar**).

pestle and mortar

pet[1] [pet] *nc* **1.** animal that is kept out of affection. *Dogs make good pets.* **2.** someone who is loved and made much of; favourite. Also *adj* **1.** treated as a pet: *a pet dog.* **2.** showing affection: *a pet name* i.e. a special name for someone who is loved. Also *vt* **1.** treat as a pet; make much of. **2.** pat or stroke in an affectionate way. *past* **petted.**

pet[2] [pet] *nc* display of bad temper (esp. over something unimportant): *a child that is in a pet.* **pettish** *adj.*

petal ['petl] *nc* coloured leaf-like part of a flower: *the red petals of a rose.*

peter ['piːtə*] *vi* (always with **out**) become gradually smaller in amount or size and finally end. *Our supply of food petered out.* (*informal*).

petition [pə'tiʃən] *nc* **1.** formal letter (signed by many people) to someone in authority, asking for something. *Everyone signed the petition to the County Council for a new school in our village.* **2.** prayer for something. Also *vt* make a petition to: *petition the authorities for something.*

petrel ['petrl] *nc* type of small sea bird which only comes to land to breed.

petrify ['petrifai] *vt/i* **1.** change into stone; become stone. **2.** make unable to think, move etc through fear, surprise etc. *The poor child was petrified with fear.*

petrifying *adj* very frightening. (*informal*).

petrifaction [petri'fækʃən] *nu* petrifying or being petrified.

petrol ['petrl] *nu* (*Brit*) form of oil used esp. to drive engines of motorcars etc. (*US* **gasoline**).

petroleum [pi'trouliəm] *nu* oil from which petrol, paraffin etc are obtained.

petticoat ['petikout] *nc* underskirt.

pettifogging ['petifɔgiŋ] *adj* concerned too much with unimportant details: *a pettifogging official; a pettifogging method.*

petty ['peti] *adj* **1.** unimportant: *petty details.* **2.** mean; narrow-minded: *a petty remark.* **pettiness** *nu.*

'petty 'cash amount of money that is kept ready for making small payments.

'petty 'officer (navy) non-commissioned officer.

petulant ['petjulnt] *adj* easily made angry over small things; bad-tempered. **petulantly** *adv.* **petulance** *nu.*

pew [pjuː] *nc* bench with a back to it, for people to sit on in church.

pewit, peewit ['piːwit] *nc* type of bird. see **lapwing.**

pewter ['pjuːtə*] *nu* **1.** metal made from mixing tin and lead. **2.** dishes, drinking mugs etc made from this metal. Also *adj.*

phalanx ['fælæŋks] *nc* **1.** (in Ancient Greece) company of soldiers packed close together for better protection. **2.** any group of men or animals packed close together.

phallic ['fælik] *adj* (esp. with reference to psychology or anthropology) concerned with the male sex organ.

phallus ['fæləs] *nc* the male sex organ.

phantasm ['fæntæzəm] *nc* phantom; something existing only in one's imagination; supposed appearance of someone who is absent or dead.

phantasmal [fæn'tæzməl] *adj* of or like a phantom.

phantasy ['fæntəzi] *nc* see **fantasy.**

phantasmagoria [fæntæzmə'gɔːriə] *nc* confused changing scene of different things, both real and imagined. **phantasmagoric** *adj.*

phantom ['fæntəm] *nc* **1.** ghost; supposed appearance of someone who is dead. **2.** something existing only in the imagination.

pharmacy ['fɑːməsi] **1.** *nu* preparing drugs and medicine: *student of pharmacy.* **2.** *nc* place where drugs and medicines are sold; chemist's shop.

pharmaceutical [fɑːmə'sjuːtikl] *adj* connected with medicines or the preparing of medicines.

pharmacist *nc* person who prepares medicine.

phase [feiz] *nc* **1.** one of the changing states or stages of development that people/things go through. *There was not much fighting in the first phase of the war. My son is going through a difficult phase at the moment.* **2.** appearance of the moon or planet at a given time: *the phases of the moon.*

pheasant ['feznt] *c/u* kind of game bird with a long tail. The male has a green head and a white ring round its neck.

phenomenon [fə'nɔminən] *nc* **1.** any natural event that can be observed. *A rainbow is an interesting phenomenon.* **2.** very unusual person/thing. *pl* **phenomena** [fə'nɔminə].

phenomenal *adj* very unusual; extraordinary; extremely good. *He is a phenomenal runner.*

phenomenally *adv* remarkably.

phial ['faiəl] *nc* small bottle (used esp. for medicine).

philander [fi'lændə*] *vi* have many love affairs, none of them serious. **philanderer** *nc.* (both *o.f.*).

philanthropy [fi'lænθrəpi] *nu* **1.** love of mankind. **2.** help given to people (esp. those who are unfortunate in some way).

philanthropist *nc* person who loves and helps others.

philanthropic [filən'θrɔpik] *adj* giving help to those who need it.

philately [fi'lætəli] *nu* collecting of postage stamps as a hobby.

philatelist *nc* stamp collector. **philatelic** [filə'telik] *adj.*

philology [fi'lɔlədʒi] *nu* study of language or a language (esp. its history). **philologist** *nc.* **philological** [filə'lɔdʒikl] *adj.*

philosophy [fi'lɔsəfi] **1.** *nu* search for truth and knowledge of the most general kind. **2.** *nc* particular explanation for the universe; system of thought. *He is looking for a philosophy he can believe in.* **3.** calmness; reasonableness.

philosopher *nc* **1.** person who studies philosophy. **2.** person who uses philosophy to rule his emotions, never being too joyful or too sad etc.

philosophical [filə'sɔfikl] *adj* **1.** connected with philosophy. **2.** calm; accepting disappointment, danger etc without protesting. **philosophically** *adv.*

philtre ['filtə*] *nc* drug (esp. one which is supposed to make a person fall in love).

phlegm [flem] *nu* **1.** thick liquid coming from the nose and throat (esp. when one has a cold). **2.** slowness to act quickly or slowness in feeling strong emotion.

phlegmatic [fleg'mætik] *adj* slow; not easily interested or excited.

phobia ['foubiə] *nc* unnatural fear or dislike of something. *She has a phobia about animals.*

phoenix ['fi:niks] *nc* imaginary bird mentioned in old stories. It was supposed to be able to live for about 500 years, then burn itself and be born again from the ashes.

phone [foun] *nc* short form of **telephone.** Also *vt/i*: *Phone me up.* (both *informal*).

phonetic [fə'netik] *adj* **1.** having to do with the sounds of speech: *phonetic laws.* **2.** corresponding to the sounds of speech: *phonetic spelling* i.e. writing words exactly as they are said (e.g. [fə'netiks] for phonetics). **3.** having a system of spelling that corresponds closely to the way words are actually said. *Spanish is a more phonetic language than English.* **phonetically** *adv.*

phonetics *nu* study of the sounds of speech and how they are produced.
Note: followed by a *sing* verb.

phonetician [fɔnə'tiʃən] *nc* student of phonetics.

phoney ['founi] *adj* false; untrue; insincere. Also *nc* false or insincere person. *This man is a phoney* i.e. not what he claims to be. (both *informal*).

phonograph ['founəgrɑ:f] *nc* (*US*) instrument for reproducing sounds which have been recorded on flat wax discs (called **records**) (*Brit* **gramophone**).

phonology [fə'nɔlədʒi] *nu* study of the sound systems of languages. **phonological** [fɔnə'lɔdʒikl] *adj.* **phonologist** *nc.*

phosphate ['fɔsfeit] *nu* salt containing phosphorus (esp. used as a fertilizer).

phosphorus ['fɔsfərəs] *nu* one of the elements (P).

phosphorescence [fɔsfə'resns] *nu* type of light without heat, found on the surface of decaying materials etc. **phosphorescent** [fɔsfə'resnt] *adj.*

photo ['foutou] *nc* short informal form of **photograph.** *pl* **photos.**

photogenic [foutou'dʒenik] *adj* having an appearance that would make a good photograph: *a very photogenic face.*

photograph ['foutəgrɑ:f] *nc* picture made by light passing through a curved piece of glass (called a **lens**) onto a specially prepared surface (called a **film**). Also *vt* take a photograph of. *He photographed the castle.*

photographer [fə'tɔgrəfə*] *nc.*

photography [fə'tɔgrəfi] *nu* taking of photographs: *an expert in photography.*

photographic [foutə'græfik] *adj.* **photographically** *adv.*

photographic memory see **memory.**

phrase [freiz] *nc* small group of words (usu. without a finite verb) making part of a sentence (e.g. *in the house, too slowly, by working hard* etc). Also *vt* say or write something in a certain way. *I phrased my request very carefully.*

phraseology [freizi'ɔlədʒi] *nu* way in which words are chosen: *legal phraseology* i.e. sort of wording used by lawyers.

physic ['fizik] *nc/u* medicine (*o.f.*).

physical ['fizikl] *adj* **1.** of the body: *physical exercise; physical beauty.* **2.** material (as contrasted with moral and spiritual): *physical things.* **3.** according to the law of nature. *It is a physical impossibility for a person to be in two places at the same time.* **4.** connected with the rocks of the earth and their forms: *physical geography.* **physically** *adv.*

physician [fi'ziʃən] *nc* doctor of medicine.

physics ['fiziks] *npl* science that deals with aspects of matter and energy (e.g. heat, light, sound, electricity etc) but not usu. including chemistry or biology.
Note: followed by a *sing* verb.

physicist ['fizisist] *nc* expert in physics.

physiognomy [fizi'ɔnəmi] *nc/u* **1.** face of a person; features of someone's face. **2.** art of judging a person's character from the features of his face or body.

physiology [fizi'ɔlədʒi] *nu* study of the way in which the body of a living thing works under normal conditions. **physiologist** *nc.* **physiological** [fiziə'lɔdʒikl] *adj.*

physiotherapy [fiziou'θerəpi] *nu* treatment of disease by physical exercises, heat etc.

physique [fi'zi:k] *nu* way in which the body is formed or developed: *person of strong* *physique* i.e. one who does not easily become ill.

piano [pi'ænou] *nc* large musical instrument as in the illustration, played by pressing keys with the fingers. *pl* **pianos.**

piano

pianist ['piːənist] *nc* person who plays the piano.

upright piano type of piano in which the wires are vertical. (In a **grand piano** they are horizontal).

piccolo ['pikəlou] *nc* small flute. *pl* **piccolos.**

pick[1] [pik] *nc* **1.** heavy tool with two sharp points as shown in the illustration, used for breaking up roads, rock etc. **2.** small instrument with a sharp point: *toothpick.*

'pickaxe pick (in sense **1.**).

pickaxe

pick[2] [pik] *vt/i* **1.** choose from a selection. *Just pick the book you would like. He picked the best room.* **2.** take with the fingers; gather: *pick fruit from the trees.* **3.** use something (usu. pointed) to take things from something else: *pick one's teeth; pick a bone.* **4.** eat food in small amounts; (with reference to birds) take up grain etc in the bill. **5.** make by picking: *pick a hole in something.* **6.** pull apart: *pick rags.* **7.** pluck the strings of an instrument with the fingers: *pick the strings of a banjo.*

pick at something eat only a little bit at a time. *The sick child was only picking at her food.*

pick off 1. take off with the fingers: *pick some dirt off one's coat.* **2.** shoot one at a time. *The enemy snipers picked off the defenceless men.*

pick on someone choose someone in connection with something unpleasant (e.g. for punishment, for an unpleasant task etc). *Why does he always pick on me?* (*informal*).

pick out 1. choose from a selection. *Pick out which toy you would like to have.* **2.** make out, distinguish from other people, objects etc. *Can you pick out your friend in that group?*

pick up 1. lift up and hold. *He picked up his hat and went out.* **2.** get; gain. *He picked up courage and approached the headmaster. The car picked up speed* i.e. went faster. **3.** get up after falling etc. *He slipped, but soon picked himself up.* **4.** regain; get something back (esp. health). *He's not feeling very well at the moment, but he'll soon pick up.* **5.** learn without being taught. *He picked up French while he was staying in Paris.* **6.** manage to see or hear something by using some kind of apparatus. *We picked up the radio signals on our receiver.* **7.** take someone with one (in a car). *I picked up some young people who were hitch-hiking to London.* **8.** get to know someone (usu. of the opposite sex) without an introduction.

'pickup *nc* **1.** part of a record player which carries the needle or stylus onto the record. **2.** small van or truck. **3.** someone met informally (esp. in the hope of sexual adventure).

have a bone to pick with somebody see **bone.**

pick someone's brains get ideas etc from someone else who has thought of them first. (*informal*).

pick holes in something find fault with something. (*informal*).

pick someone's pocket steal something from someone's pocket.

'pickpocket *nc* person who steals from people's pockets.

pick a quarrel with someone deliberately cause a quarrel with someone.

pickaback ['pikəbæk] *adv* (with reference to the way a child is carried) on someone's back or shoulders. (Also **piggy-back**).

picket ['pikit] *nc* **1.** one or more soldiers or policemen etc with the job of keeping a lookout for the enemy etc. **2.** person who is posted near a factory during a strike to try to prevent other workers from going in. Also *vt* **1.** put people in their positions as pickets (in sense **1.**). **2.** put pickets (in sense **2.**) near a place: *picket a factory.* **3.** act as a picket (in sense **2.**).

pickle ['pikl] *vt* put meat, vegetables etc in salt water or vinegar etc so that they can be kept fresh: *pickled meat.* Also *nu* vegetables which have been pickled. (Also **pickles**).

in a pickle in a very awkward position. *Losing our tickets left us in a terrible pickle.* (*informal*).

picnic ['piknik] *nc* pleasure trip in which food is taken to be eaten in the open air. Also *vi* go on a picnic. *past* **picnicked.**

picnicker *nc.*

pictorial [pik'tɔːriəl] *adj* in pictures; having pictures: *a pictorial record of the sports meeting.*

picture ['piktʃə*] *nc* **1.** painting, drawing or photograph. *He showed us some pictures he took while on holiday. The artist had painted a very fine picture.* **2.** beautiful scene, thing, person etc: *as pretty as a picture.* **3.** likeness. *Jane is the picture of her mother.* **4.** example. *She was the picture of happiness* i.e. a perfect example of happiness. **5.** cinema film: *motion picture.* Also *vt* **1.** make a picture. **2.** imagine. *You can picture the scene.* **3.** describe in words.

picturesque [piktʃə'resk] *adj* **1.** pretty or interesting enough to be made into a picture: *a picturesque old village.* **2.** vivid; lively: *a picturesque way of speaking.*

picturesquely *adv.*

the pictures performance of a cinema film. *I'm going to the pictures tonight* i.e. I am going to a cinema.

pidgin ['pidʒin] *adj* of a mixed language which uses the words of two or more languages and a simplified grammar of one of them: *pidgin English* i.e. language based on English used by uneducated people in some African and Asian countries. Also *nu* the language itself.

pie [pai] *nc* fruit or meat covered in pastry

and baked: *a fruit pie; a meat pie.*
eat humble pie see **eat.**
piebald ['paibɔ:ld] *adj* (with reference to a horse) with large black and white patches.
piece [pi:s] *nc* **1.** bit; part of a thing that has been divided or broken: *a piece of land; a piece of soap. He dropped the cup and now it is in pieces.* **2.** small amount: *a piece of advice/news etc.* **3.** single one in a set. *We bought this tea set last year and two of the pieces are broken already.* **4.** amount by which goods (esp. cloth) are measured and sold: *sell cloth by the piece.* **5.** coin: *a ten pence piece.* **6.** one of a set of coloured disks, figures etc used in playing chess and other board games: *lose an important piece.* **7.** gun (*o.f.* in sense **7.**). Also *vt* put parts together. *We pieced the broken cup together again. The police pieced together all they had found out about the wanted man.*
'piecework system by which workers are paid according to the number of articles each one produces. *He is on piecework* i.e. he is paid in this way.
piece of cake something easy. (*informal*).
of a piece of the same kind.
pier [piə*] *nc* **1.** structure of wood or stone etc built out into the sea and used as a landing place for boats or as a place to walk. **2.** one of the posts supporting a bridge. **3.** solid part of a wall between windows or other openings.
pierce [piəs] *vt* **1.** (with reference to something sharp or pointed) go into; make a hole in. *The needle pierced his skin. A nail pierced the ball.* **2.** (with reference to cold, pain etc) force its way into; affect deeply. *The freezing wind pierced us to the bone.* **3.** sound sharp and clear. *A cry of pain pierced the night air.*
piercing *adj* **1.** very cold. **2.** very sharp and clear in sound. **piercingly** *adv.*
piety ['paiiti] *nu* quality of being pious i.e. religious, respecting God. (*opp* **impiety**). see **pious.**
piffle ['pifl] *nu* nonsense. (*informal*).
pig [pig] *nc* **1.** animal which is usu. fat and eats a lot, raised for its meat (called **pork**). **2.** dirty, greedy or unpleasant person. (*informal* and *impolite*). **3.** oblong-shaped mass of iron or lead that has been shaped in a mould; the mould itself.
piggery *nc* place where pigs are bred; pig-farm.
piggish *adj* like a pig; dirty; greedy.
piggy *nc* little pig. (*informal*).
'piggy-back *adv* see **pickaback.**
'pig'headed *adj* stubborn; obstinate. *I've given him advice but he's too pigheaded to accept it.*
'pigskin *nc* pig's skin; leather made from pig's skin. Also *adj.*
'pigsty **1.** small place where pigs are kept. **2.** dirty place. *This kitchen is an absolute pigsty.* (*informal* in sense **2.**).
'pigtail length of hairs twisted together and hanging down at the back of, or one at each side of, the head.
buy a pig in a poke buy something without examining it properly. (*informal*).
pigs might fly what has been suggested is very unlikely. (*informal*).
pigeon ['pidʒən] *nc* bird of the dove family (esp. a fairly large bluish-grey bird which lives in towns).
'pigeonhole *nc* one of a set of box-like openings for putting documents etc into. Also *vt* **1.** put something in a pigeonhole. **2.** put something where one can refer to it again. **3.** put something aside so that nothing is ever done about it. *The idea was pigeonholed and no more was heard about it.*
'pigeon-'toed *adj* having the toes turned inwards.
'carrier pigeon pigeon which has been trained to carry letters.
pigment ['pigmənt] *nc/u* **1.** colouring matter which is used to make paints, dyes etc. **2.** substance which gives the hair, skin of animals and the leaves of plants their colour. **pigmentation** [pigmen'teiʃən] *nu.*
pigmy ['pigmi] *nc* see **pygmy.**
pike[1] [paik] *nc* long spear formerly used by soldiers.
as plain as a pikestaff very clear or obvious.
pike[2] [paik] *nc* large, thin freshwater fish which eats other fish, frogs etc. *pl* **pike.**
pilchard ['piltʃəd] *nc* small sea fish found off the west coast of North America. *pl* **pilchard** or **pilchards.**
pile[1] [pail] *nc* **1.** heap of things lying one on top of the other: *a pile of books.* **2.** large amount of something heaped up: *a pile of earth.* **3.** large amount of anything (but esp. money) (*informal*). **4.** heap of wood on which a body is burned or a sacrifice made: *a funeral pile.* **5.** large building or group of buildings.
pile in/into something rush in; rush into something. *We all piled into the car. The driver told us to pile in.* (*informal*).
pile up grow larger in amount. *His debts began to pile up.*
'pileup *nc* **1.** piling up of anything. **2.** road accident involving several vehicles.
pile[2] [pail] *nc* very large, heavy piece of wood, steel or concrete driven into the earth, often under water, and used to support a bridge etc.
'pile driver machine for driving piles into the ground.
atomic pile installation in which atomic energy is produced for use in industry etc.
pile[3] [pail] *nc/u* soft, thick surface of threads or hairs found on velvet, some carpets etc.
piles [pailz] *nu* illness in which there is a painful swelling around the anus.
pilfer ['pilfə*] *vt/i* steal (a small amount or things of small value). *He was fined for pilfering some fruit.*
pilgrim ['pilgrim] *nc* person who travels to a sacred or holy place: *a pilgrim to Mecca.*
pilgrimage *nc* journey made by a pilgrim.
pill [pil] *nc* small ball or disk of medicine, to be swallowed whole.
the pill pill taken regularly by women to prevent the conception of a child: *on the pill* i.e. taking pills for this purpose.
pillage ['pilidʒ] *vt/i* plunder; steal things, with violence, from a place that has been captured in war. Also *nu.*
pillar ['pilə*] *nc* **1.** thin, upright post, used in a building etc either to support it or as an ornament. **2.** person who is very important in some organization: *a pillar of the community.*
'pillar box box, placed in the street, in which letters can be posted.
from pillar to post from one place to another with no purpose or aim. (*informal*).
pillion ['piliən] *nc* **1.** on a motorcycle, the pad or seat behind the driver's on which a passenger can sit: *ride pillion* i.e. sit in this position. **2.** on a horse, the pad behind the saddle on which another person may ride.

pillory ['pilәri] *nc* (in former times) bar of wood to which the head and hands of wrongdoers could be secured as a punishment. Also *vt* make someone's faults or crimes public.

pillow ['pilou] *nc* bag filled with soft material on which the head can rest.

'pillowcase, 'pillowslip cover for a pillow (made of cotton, linen etc).

pilot ['pailәt] *nc* **1.** person who guides a ship into and out of a harbour, or any place that requires special knowledge. *We got a pilot who guided us through the dangerous reefs.* **2.** person who flies an aeroplane. Also *vt* guide (a ship etc); fly (an aeroplane).

'pilot 'survey/'project/ex'periment etc survey etc which is carried out in order to see whether the idea behind it will work, and in preparation for a much larger survey etc.

pimp [pimp] *nc* man who finds customers for prostitutes.

pimple ['pimpl] *nc* small, inflamed spot on the skin.

pin[1] [pin] *nc* **1.** small, thin piece of metal with a head, sharp at one end, put through things to keep them together (e.g. pieces of paper, cloth etc). **2.** ornament that has a pin: *tiepin; hatpin.*

'pincushion small cushion or pad into which pins are stuck until they are needed.

'pin money money which can be spent by a wife on things for herself; extra money one can spend on oneself. (*informal*).

'pinpoint *nc* something very small: *a pinpoint of light.* Also *vt* describe or reveal exactly. *The teacher pinpointed the reasons why I had done badly in the last examination.*

'pinprick something that annoys one slightly.

'pinup picture of a beautiful woman, taken from a newspaper or magazine and fastened on a wall etc. (*informal*).

'drawing pin (*Brit*) pin with a flat head. (*US* **thumbtack**).

'safety pin pin made so that the point can be covered.

neat as a pin very neat or tidy. (*informal*).

pins and needles prickling feeling one gets in the skin when blood has not been circulating properly in a certain part of the body and then comes back again.

pin[2] [pin] *vt* **1.** keep things together by using a pin: *pin some papers together; pin a flower onto one's coat; pin a notice on the wall.* **2.** keep in one position. *The fallen tree had pinned his leg to the ground.* past **pinned.**

pin someone/something down keep in one position. *The army was pinned down outside the capital. I tried to pin him down to an exact date for the meeting* i.e. to make him agree to a particular date.

pinafore ['pinәfɔ:*] *nc* loose covering worn over a child's or woman's clothes to keep them clean.

pincers ['pinsәz] *npl* tool for gripping things and holding them tight (used e.g. to take nails out of wood etc).

pinch [pintʃ] *vt/i* **1.** press between two hard surfaces, press between thumb and forefinger. *My finger was pinched in the doorway. He pinched the child's cheek.* **2.** give pain by squeezing tightly. *These shoes must be too small because they pinch.* **3.** steal. (*informal*). **4.** arrest; take prisoner. (*informal*). Also *nc* **1.** act of pinching or squeezing: *a pinch on the cheek.* **2.** amount that can be taken up between the thumb and forefinger: *a pinch of salt.*

at a pinch, if it comes to the pinch if it is really necessary. *At a pinch, you can stay here for the night.* (*informal*).

feel the pinch feel discomfort (usu. through lack of money). *Some time after my father lost his job we began to feel the pinch.* (*informal*).

pine[1] [pain] **1.** *nc* kind of evergreen tree with needle-shaped leaves, and bearing cones. **2.** *nu* the wood of this tree.

pine[2] [pain] *vi* **1.** long (for) eagerly; want something very much: *pine for one's home; pining to travel abroad.* **2.** become thin and weak through hunger, illness, pain etc. *The poor child was just pining away.*

pineapple ['painæpl] *nc/u* **1.** large, juicy, yellow tropical fruit with hard uneven skin. **2.** plant on which this fruit grows.

ping [piŋ] *nc* high-pitched ringing noise as of a drinking glass knocked by something hard.

ping-pong ['piŋpɔŋ] *nu* table tennis.

pinion[1] ['piniәn] *nc* **1.** wing of a bird. **2.** one of the stiff flying feathers on a bird's wing. Also *vt* bind someone's arms to his side so that he cannot move them.

pinion[2] ['piniәn] *nc* small toothed wheel that fits into a larger one and turns it, or is turned by it.

pink[1] [piŋk] *nc/u* **1.** pale red colour. **2.** kind of flower. Also *adj* pale red.

pink[2] [piŋk] *vt* cut in a zigzag line or some other pattern.

'pinking shears scissors which cut in this way.

pink[3] [piŋk] *vi* (of an engine) make a knocking noise because it is not working well.

pinnacle ['pinәkl] *nc* **1.** high pointed stonework or spire on a roof. **2.** pointed rock or high peak. **3.** highest point (e.g. of someone's career, achievements etc).

pint [paint] *nc* unit for measuring liquids, equal to 0.57 litres: *a pint of milk; a pint of beer.* see appendix.

pioneer [paiә'niә*] *nc* **1.** person who does something first and so prepares the way for others; explorer; early settler in a new country or undeveloped area: *the pioneers of the American west; a pioneer of aviation.* **2.** one of a group of soldiers occupied in clearing roads, building bridges etc. Also *vt/i* lead the way; do something for the first time: *pioneer a new method of travel.*

pious ['paiәs] *adj* having or showing deep love of God; religious: *pious works; a pious person.* (*opp* **impious**). **piously** *adv.* **piety** ['paiiti] *nu.*

pip [pip] *nc* **1.** small seed in an apple, orange etc. **2.** note of the time signal on the telephone or radio.

give someone the pip make someone angry or depressed. (*informal*).

pipe[1] [paip] *nc* **1.** tube through which gas or liquid flows: *gaspipe; water pipe; drainpipe* i.e. one which takes water etc away. **2.** tube with a bowl at the end of it, used for smoking tobacco. **3.** musical instrument with a hollow tube blown by the player; hollow tube forming part of an organ. **4.** whistle used by a ship's officer; sound of this whistle.

pipes *npl* **1.** bagpipes. **2.** set of musical pipes.

'pipe dream plan, scheme, idea etc which can be imagined but not put into practice.

'pipeline long line of connected pipes (used e.g. to send petroleum long distances).

in the pipeline being produced at the

moment, but not yet complete or ready.

pipe[2] [paip] *vt/i* **1.** bring gas or liquid by means of a pipe: *pipe water into a village.* **2.** play music on a pipe or pipes. **3.** (on a ship) give orders etc by means of a special pipe: *pipe all hands on deck.* **4.** trim clothes or decorate a cake with piping (in sense **2.**).

piper *nc* person playing a pipe; person playing bagpipes.

piping *nu* **1.** pipes; length of pipes: *one hundred feet of piping.* **2.** narrow edging like a cord, used on some garments; narrow lines of sugar etc used to decorate a cake etc. **3.** playing of a pipe; music produced by playing a pipe. Also *adj* high; shrill: *a piping voice.*

pipe down keep quiet. (*informal*).

pipe up start speaking. (*informal*).

piping hot very hot. *The food here is always served piping hot.*

piquant ['pi:kənt] *adj* **1.** clever; interesting; stimulating to the mind: *a piquant idea.* **2.** having a pleasant, sharp taste: *a piquant sauce.* **piquancy** *nu.*

pique [pi:k] *vt* **1.** hurt someone's pride. *She was rather piqued when I said I preferred your house to hers.* **2.** arouse someone's interest. *Our curiosity was piqued by the arrival of the handsome stranger.* Also *nu* feeling of anger when one's pride is hurt: *a fit of pique.*

pique oneself on/upon pride oneself on.

pirate ['paiərət] *nc* **1.** person who attacks ships and steals from them. **2.** person who prints the work of a writer etc, for his own profit, without permission. Also *vt* print a book etc, for one's own profit, without permission. **piracy** *nu.* **piratical** [paiə'rætikl] *adj.*

'pirate 'radio station radio transmitter operating without a licence.

pirouette [piru'et] *nc* (dancing) turn round very quickly while balanced on one foot or on the toes. Also *vi* make a pirouette; make one pirouette after another.

pistil ['pistl] *nc* part of a flower that produces seeds.

pistol ['pistl] *nc* small, short gun fired with one hand.

piston ['pistn] *nc* piece of metal (usu. cylindrical) which moves to and fro inside a hollow tube (called a **cylinder**) as part of the mechanism of engines, pumps etc.

pit [pit] *nc* **1.** deep hole in the ground (esp. one which has been dug out for some reason): *a coalpit.* **2.** part at the back of the ground floor of a theatre; people sitting in this part. **3.** little hole or scar (e.g. one left by smallpox). Also *vt* **1.** mark with small scars. *His face had been pitted with smallpox.* **2.** match someone/something against another in a fight, contest etc. *He had pitted himself against a much stronger man. past* **pitted.**

'pitfall 1. pit which has been covered over so as to trap animals. **2.** hidden or unexpected danger.

pitch[1] [pitʃ] *vt/i* **1.** throw. *He pitched the ball to the other end of the field.* **2.** fall, cause to fall, forward. *He pitched forward onto the road. They were pitched from the car.* **3.** set up; put in position: *pitch a tent.* **4.** move up and down with the movement of a ship's bow i.e. front part of a ship. *The ship was pitching badly in the storm.* **5.** (music) set in a certain key. *The song is pitched too high for my voice.*

'pitchfork tool with a long handle and two metal prongs, used for lifting and moving hay. Also *vt* **1.** move with a pitchfork. **2.** push someone into a difficult situation.

pitch[2] [pitʃ] **1.** *nc* act of throwing; distance something is thrown. **2.** *nc* length of grass in a cricket ground between wickets. **3.** *nc* place used by a trader (esp. a street trader) for his business or by a street performer for his act. **4.** *nc/u* highness or lowness of a sound. **5.** *nu* degree; point: *at a tremendous pitch of excitement.* **6.** *nc* ground where football, hockey etc are played.

queer someone's pitch see **queer.**

pitch[3] [pitʃ] *nu* dark-coloured, sticky substance found as asphalt or turpentine etc, used to fill in cracks or spaces, in building boats, making roads etc.

'pitch-'black, 'pitch-'dark *adj* very black, difficult to see in.

as black/dark as pitch completely black or dark. *It was as dark as pitch inside the cave.*

pitcher ['pitʃə*] *nc* large jug for liquids.

piteous ['pitiəs] *adj* making one feel pity; deserving pity. **piteously** *adv.*

pith [piθ] *nu* **1.** soft substance inside the stem etc of some plants. **2.** most necessary, essential part of a speech etc.

pithy *adj* short and to the point; forceful and direct: *a pithy speech.* **pithily** *adv.*

pittance ['pitns] *nc* very small payment or allowance of money: *work for a (mere) pittance.*

pity ['piti] *nu* **1.** sorrow for the sufferings or misfortunes of others. *We helped him out of pity* i.e. because we felt sorry for him. **2.** something that causes one to feel sorrow. *It's a pity that you missed the train.*
Note: in this sense can be used with *a*, but hardly ever used in the *pl.*
Also *vt* feel sorry for: *pity someone.*

pitiable *adj* **1.** deserving pity: *in a pitiable condition.* **2.** deserving contempt: *a pitiable attempt to gain favour.*

pitiful *adj* **1.** feeling pity. **2.** deserving pity. **3.** deserving contempt. **pitifully** *adv.*

pitiless *adj* without pity; without mercy: *a pitiless enemy.* **pitilessly** *adv.*

have/take pity on someone feel sorry for someone.

out of pity because of a feeling of sorrow for someone's sufferings etc: *help someone out of pity.*

pivot ['pivət] *nc* **1.** bar, point etc on which something balances. *The wheel turned on a pivot in the centre.* **2.** main point of any argument, discussion etc. Also *vt/i* **1.** put in a pivot; provide with a pivot. **2.** turn on a pivot.

pixie, pixy ['piksi] *nc* type of fairy.

placard ['plækɑ:d] *nc* public notice put up where it can be easily seen. Also *vt* stick up placards; make something known with placards.

placate [plə'keit] *vt* take away someone's anger; make peaceful. *We tried to placate them with gifts.*

placatory [plə'keitəri] *adj* placating or intending to placate.

place[1] [pleis] *nc* **1.** special or particular space occupied by someone/something. *His house is in a quiet place near the river.* **2.** area, building etc used for some special purpose: *a market place; a place of worship.* **3.** city, town, district etc. *The people had come from different places.* **4.** particular area on the surface of something. *There is one place on the ceiling where the water has come through.* **5.** division of an argument, speech, discussion etc. *I would not advise you to read that book, because, in the first place, it is very difficult and, in the second place, it is rather dull.* **6.** proper position. *Nobody in the class may leave his place without permission.* **7.** part of a book, reading passage etc. *I've lost my place* i.e. I can't find the part of the book I was last reading. **8.** position of a figure in a number: *give a number to two places of decimals* (e.g. 4.55). **9.** position in a race: *come in second place.* **10.** rank; position in life: *one's place in society; keep someone in his place* i.e. treat someone in a way which shows he is not so important as oneself. **11.** duty; what one has to do. *It is your place to greet the guests as they arrive.* **12.** house; where one lives. *John invited us over to his place.* **13.** name of some streets or squares in a town: *St James's Place.*

'place mat mat to put under a plate on a table.

give place to be followed by; make way for. *Old methods must give place to new.*

go places **1.** have new and interesting experiences. **2.** be very successful in one's career. (*informal*).

in place **1.** in the proper position. *I hope you left all the books in the library in place.* **2.** suitable; in good manners. *That remark was not in place.*

in place of instead of. *Jones will play for the team in place of Brown.*

make place for make room for; make way for.

out of place **1.** not in the proper position. **2.** not suitable, ill-mannered. *It was out of place for you to cheer when the headmaster said he was leaving.*

take place see **take.**

take the place of see **take.**

place² [pleis] *vt* **1.** put in a certain position, condition etc. *He placed the book on the desk. He placed sentries round the camp.* **2.** remember someone fully; identify. *I've heard his name but I can't place him.* **3.** give (an order etc); put: *place an order with a shopkeeper; place confidence in a friend.* **4.** give someone a certain position; get someone a post.

be placed be first, second or third in a race. *My horse wasn't even placed.*

placid ['plæsid] *adj* peaceful; not easily made angry: *a placid scene; someone having a placid nature.* **placidly** *adv.* **placidity** [plə'siditi] *nu.*

plagiarize ['pleidʒiəraiz] *vt* take what someone else has written or invented and use it as if one had written or invented it oneself. **plagiarism** *nc/u.* **plagiarist** *nc.*

plague [pleig] *nc* **1.** very dangerous disease which spreads quickly. **2.** anything that annoys or troubles: *a plague of wasps* i.e. very large number of wasps causing harm and annoyance. Also *vt* (esp. of a large number of something) annoy or trouble: *be plagued by a child's questions; be plagued by requests for money.*

plaice [pleis] *nc* kind of flat sea fish. *pl* **plaice.**

plaid [plæd] *nc* **1.** long piece of woollen cloth with many colours, worn over the shoulder in former times by Scotsmen. **2.** piece of cloth with a similar type of pattern.

plain¹ [plein] *adj* **1.** easy to see, hear or understand. *You have made your meaning plain. His voice was quite plain over the telephone.* **2.** simple; ordinary; without ornament: *plain food; a plain man; a plain dress.* **3.** not pretty or handsome: *a rather plain girl.* **4.** honest; frank. *I must be plain with you.* Also *adv* clearly: *speak plain.* **plainly** *adv.* **plainness** *nu.*

plain dealing honesty; sincerity.

plain sailing very easy; straightforward. *Any intelligent boy should find this job plain sailing.* (*informal*).

in plain clothes (usu. with reference to policemen) in ordinary clothes, not in uniform.

plain² [plein] *nc* flat stretch of land.

plaintiff ['pleintif] *nc* person who brings an action to a court of law.

plaintive ['pleintiv] *adj* sad, asking for pity: *a plaintive voice.* **plaintively** *adv.*

plait [plæt] *vt* join three or more lengths of hair, straw etc by twisting each one under or over the others so as to make one length. Also *nc* something made in this way: *a girl wearing her hair in plaits.*

plaits

plan [plæn] *nc* **1.** way of making or doing something that has been thought out in advance. *What plans do you have for the holidays?* **2.** drawing or diagram showing the different parts of a house or garden etc (usu. as if seen from above). *Here is a plan of the ground floor. If you look at this plan of the school grounds you will see where the football field is.* **3.** drawing or diagram to show the different parts of a machine. **4.** government scheme for making a country richer etc: *a five-year plan.* Also *vt* **1.** think out in advance how something is to be made or done: *plan a surprise for someone. I am planning to go to London next week.* **2.** make a drawing or diagram of something. *past* **planned.**

plan out think something out, arrange something in advance. *I'm planning out the school debate.*

according to plan in the way that was arranged. *Everything went according to plan.*

plane¹ [plein] *nc* **1.** flat or level surface. **2.** level. *The discussion was on too high a plane for me* i.e. it was too difficult for me to understand. **3.** aeroplane; aircraft. **4.** tool with a blade, used to smooth down wood so that it has a level surface. Also *vt/i* make flat or smooth with a plane (in sense **4.**). Also *adj* flat; lying along a level surface: *a plane figure.*

plane² [plein] *nc* kind of tree with large leaves often planted in towns.

planet ['plænit] *nc* one of the worlds which go round the sun (e.g. Venus, the Earth). **planetary** ['plænitri] *adj* of the planets.

plank [plæŋk] *nc* **1.** long, flat piece of wood; large board. **2.** one of the items in a political party's statement of what they intend to do. Also *vt* cover with planks.

plankton ['plæŋktən] *nu* mass of small plants and animals drifting on or near the surface of seas or lakes.

plant [plɑːnt] **1.** *nc* living thing that is not an animal (e.g. tree, flower etc). **2.** *nu* machinery and buildings used for some special purpose: *plant for making aircraft.*

Also *vt* **1.** put plants, seeds etc in the ground to grow. **2.** set or place firmly. *She planted herself in my path.* **3.** set up, begin a colony etc.

plantation [plæn'teiʃən] *nc* **1.** large farm producing tea, cotton, sugar etc (esp. one in a tropical country). **2.** large area where trees have been planted.

planter *nc* person who owns or runs a plantation.

plantain ['plæntin] *nc* **1.** kind of large banana. **2.** tree it grows on. **3.** type of wild plant.

plaque [plæk] *nc* flat piece of metal etc used as an ornament or in remembrance of something.

plasma ['plæzmə] *nu* liquid part of blood.

plaster ['plɑːstə*] **1.** *nu* mixture made up of lime, sand, water etc which becomes hard when it is dry, and is used for giving walls, ceilings etc a smooth surface. **2.** *nu* plaster of Paris. see below. **3.** *nc* mixture put on part of the body as a kind of medicine to make pain less etc. **4.** *nc* sticking plaster. see below. **5.** plaster of Paris used to keep broken limbs straight. Also *vt* **1.** put plaster (in sense **1.**) on walls etc. **2.** put a plaster (in sense **3.**) on some part of the body. **3.** cover thickly. *His hair was plastered with oil.*

plastered *adj* drunk. (*informal*).

plasterer *nc* workman who plasters walls etc.

plaster of Paris mixture like plaster (in sense **1.**) used in making figures, statues, moulds etc.

'sticking plaster medical covering which sticks to the skin, used to cover cuts, boils etc.

plastic ['plæstik] *adj* **1.** easily made into different shapes. *Clay is a plastic material.* **2.** easily changed; easily influenced (*o.f.*). **3.** concerned with changing the shape of something: *the plastic art of sculpture; plastic surgery* i.e. part of medicine concerned with changing a person's appearance. **4.** made of plastic: *plastic cups; plastic raincoats.* Also *nu* man-made material which can be made into many different shapes when soft and which keeps its shape when it becomes hard.

plasticity [plæs'tisiti] *nu* state of being plastic; how easily shaped something is.

Plasticine ['plæstisiːn] ® *nu* substance like clay, which can be formed into various shapes in the hands, used by children for playing with.

plate [pleit] **1.** *nc* round and almost flat dish, mostly used for serving food: *dinner plate; tea plate.* **2.** *nc* food etc on such a dish: *a plate of soup.* **3.** *nu* dishes and other articles made of silver or gold, or having a surface of silver or gold: *cupboard full of gold plate.* **4.** *nc* thin, flat sheet of metal, glass etc: *steel plates.* **5.** *nc* sheet of metal on which something is cut out (e.g. the plates used in printing books). **6.** *nc* photograph, drawing etc in a book which is printed on a separate page. Also *vt* **1.** cover one metal with a thin layer of another (usu. silver or gold): *a silver-plated dish.* **2.** cover with metal plates.

plateful *nc* amount that a plate holds: *plateful of rice.*

'plate 'glass thick, polished and very expensive glass, used for shop windows etc.

'platelayer workman who lays and attends to railway tracks.

plateau ['plætou] *nc* large, flat area of land high above sea level. *pl* **plateaus** or **plateaux** ['plætouz].

platform ['plætfɔːm] *nc* **1.** raised, level surface. *He spoke to us from a platform in the school hall. He was coming by train, so I waited on the platform* i.e. the raised part for passengers beside the railway lines. **2.** official statement of what a political party intends to do (esp. as stated before an election).

platinum ['plætinəm] *nu* soft, white, valuable metal. Also *adj*: *a platinum ring.*

platitude ['plætitjuːd] *nc* statement of something obvious or of something which has often been said before, but now used by a speaker as if it were something new. *His speech was full of platitudes.*

platoon [plə'tuːn] *nc* small number of soldiers organized as a single unit.

platter ['plætə*] *nc* **1.** (*US*) large dish for serving food (esp. meat and fish). **2.** large, flat, wooden dish (*o.f.* in sense **2.**).

plaudit ['plɔːdit] *nc* (usu. *pl*) sign of pleasure or approval (e.g. by shouting or clapping): *the plaudits of the crowd.*

plausible ['plɔːzibl] *adj* **1.** appearing to be true or reasonable: *a plausible excuse.* **2.** good at making up plausible excuses etc: *a plausible liar.* (*opp* **implausible**). **plausibly** *adv.* **plausibility** [plɔːzi'biliti] *nu.*

play[1] [plei] *vt/i* **1.** amuse oneself; do something for pleasure, not as work. *The children are playing outside.* **2.** take part in a game. *We play football/at football every Saturday. Do you play chess?* **3.** take part in a game against someone. *Our school is playing another team at hockey on Friday.* **4.** put someone in a team. *They are playing some of their best men in this game.* **5.** reveal a card in a card game when one's turn comes. *He played the king of hearts.* **6.** perform; carry out: *play a joke/trick on someone.* **7.** make music from: *play the piano; play a tune.* **8.** act the part of someone in a play etc: *play (the part of) Hamlet.* **9.** move about quickly. *The sunlight/light wind played upon the water. A smile played on his lips* i.e. he seemed to want to smile but did not actually do so. **10.** work continuously or regularly: *fountains playing in the gardens.* **11.** be directed at. *The hoses played upon the burning house. Searchlights played upon the road.*

play at something do something without much interest. *He is only playing at studying.*

play something down try to make something seem less important. *We must play down this scandal.*

play off a match, game etc play again a match, game etc, which has not previously resulted in a victory for either side, so as to reach a decision.

'play-off *nc* such a match etc.

play off one person against another set one person to fight or quarrel with another for one's own benefit.

play up! shout of encouragement to a team etc.

play up to someone pretend to admire someone so as to benefit oneself. *He is always playing up to his boss.* (*informal*).

play upon someone's fears/good nature etc make use of someone's fears/good nature etc. *Don't let that scoundrel play upon your generosity.*

be played out be exhausted; be of no more use. *I'm played out after all that exercise*

His ideas are played out. (*informal*).

play ball with someone cooperate; work together with someone. (*informal*).

play one's cards badly/well use one's opportunities badly/well. *If you play your cards well, you are sure to succeed.* (*informal*).

play fast and loose with someone/something take advantage of; say one thing and do another. *He played fast and loose with her affections.* (*informal*).

play the game be honest and fair. (*informal*).

play into someone's hands act in a way that gives the advantage to an opponent, enemy etc. *He played right into my hands.*

play for money gamble.

play second fiddle to someone have a less important part than someone else. *John plays second fiddle to James in running the business.* (*informal*).

play[2] [plei] **1.** *nu* amusement; fun. *The children are at play. Life should not be all work and no play* i.e. every person who works should also have some amusement. **2.** *nu* action in a game. *There was some exciting play near the end of the game.* **3.** *nc* drama; story written to be performed in a theatre: *the plays of Shakespeare; see an amusing play.* **4.** *nu* gambling: *lose a lot of money in a few hours' play.* **5.** *nu* freedom of movement or action. *Give the rope more play* i.e. do not keep it so tight. **6.** *nu* quickly changing movement: *the play of sunlight on water.* **7.** *nu* activity, use; working: *bring all one's skill into play* i.e. use all one's skill.

'playfellow, 'playmate child with whom another child plays.

'playground area where children can play.

'playpen small enclosure used to keep a child in one place.

'plaything something that a child plays with; toy.

'playtime *nc/u* length of time set aside for play.

'playwright person who writes plays; dramatist.

'child's play something very easy. *Solving that problem should be child's play for a clever fellow like you.*

'fair 'play justice; the same opportunities for everyone: *see that there is fair play.*

'foul 'play **1.** breaking of the rules in a game. *The forward was sent off for foul play.* **2.** violence; assault; murder. *Five hours after the body was found, the police said that they suspected foul play.*

in/out of play (with reference to the ball in football, cricket etc) in a position where the ball can/cannot be played without breaking the rules.

play on words amusing remark etc based on the different meanings a word can have; pun.

plea [pli:] *nc* **1.** request; prayer: *pleas for help.* **2.** excuse. **3.** statement made in reply to a charge in court: *a plea of guilty.*

plead [pli:d] *vt/i* **1.** beg for something: *plead for mercy. She pleaded with him to show some pity.* **2.** answer a charge in court; argue a case in court. *The prisoner pleaded guilty. He got a good lawyer to plead his case.* **3.** offer as an excuse. *The man we found stealing money from the house pleaded poverty.*

pleasant ['pleznt] *adj* **1.** giving pleasure; agreeable: *a pleasant occupation.* **2.** friendly; likeable: *a pleasant young man.* **3.** not stormy; fair: *quite pleasant weather.* (*opp* **unpleasant**). **pleasantly** *adv.* **pleasantness** *nu.*

pleasantry **1.** *nu* humour. **2.** *nc* amusing remark; agreeable joke.

please [pli:z] *vt/i* **1.** (used in asking for something politely). *Please come in. Could I please have your attention? A cup of tea, please. Would you like a biscuit? – Yes, please.* **2.** give pleasure or enjoyment to. *I was very pleased to see my son's school report. I think the arrangements pleased her very much. She was pleased with the arrangements.* (*opp* **displease** in sense **2.**). **3.** wish; choose. *Come whenever you please.*

pleased *adj* satisfied. (*opp* **displeased**).

pleasing *adj* giving pleasure; enjoyable. (*opp* **displeasing** or **unpleasing**).

pleasure ['pleʒə*] **1.** *nu* feeling of being happy or pleased. *It gives me much pleasure to be here. He takes pleasure in listening to music. I shall do it with pleasure* i.e. I shall be happy to do it. **2.** *nc* something which makes one happy or pleased. *Reading is my chief pleasure in life.*

pleasurable *adj* giving pleasure. **pleasurably** *adv.*

pleat [pli:t] *nc* flat, narrow fold in a garment. Also *vt* arrange in pleats: *a pleated skirt.*

plebeian [pli'biən] *nc* one of the lower classes. Also *adj* of the lower classes; vulgar, common.

pleb [pleb] *nc* (often *pl*) one of the masses; a worker. (often *impolite*).

plebiscite ['plebisit] *nc* vote by the people in an area or country on some important matter. *The question of whether drinking alcohol should be legal was decided by a plebiscite.*

pledge [pledʒ] *nc* **1.** something valuable which one leaves with someone as a proof that one will do what one has promised to do; something of value left with a pawnbroker: *leave one's watch as a pledge.* **2.** sign of friendship etc. *Take this gift as a pledge of our friendship.* **3.** promise: *a pledge of secrecy.* **4.** drink; toast: *pledge to the queen* (*o.f.* in sense **4.**). Also *vt* **1.** give something as a pledge (in sense **1.**). *I pledged my watch.* **2.** make a solemn promise. *He pledged never to return/that he would never return.* **3.** drink to the health of someone.

take the pledge promise not to drink alcoholic liquor.

plenary ['pli:nəri] *adj* **1.** full; without any limits. *The new president was given plenary powers to deal with the situation.* **2.** attended by all who have the right to be present: *a plenary meeting/session etc.*

plenipotentiary [plenipə'tenʃəri] *nc* person (e.g. an ambassador) who has been given full power to make decisions etc by some authority (e.g. a government etc). Also *adj* having full power to make decisions etc.

plenty ['plenti] *n* all that one needs; more than one needs. *Don't hurry, there's plenty of time. If you need more chairs, there are plenty upstairs. I think two more bottles of milk will be plenty.*

plentiful *adj* more than enough; large quantity: *a plentiful supply of water.* **plentifully** *adv.*

plenteous ['plentiəs] *adj* plentiful (*o.f.*).

plethora ['pleθərə] *nc* quantity or amount which is too great.

pleurisy ['pluərisi] *nu* serious disease of the outer covering of the lungs.

pliable ['plaiəbl] *adj* **1.** easily bent: *pliable*

piece of metal. **2.** (of people) easily controlled. **pliability** [plaiə'biliti] *nu.*
pliant ['plaiənt] *adj* pliable. see **pliable.**
pliers ['plaiəz] *npl* instrument as shown in the illustration, for holding things tightly or for bending or twisting them. (Often **pair of pliers**).

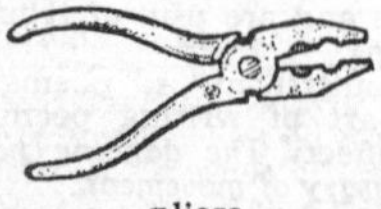

pliers

plight[1] [plait] *nc* bad or sorrowful condition. *The homeless family was in a terrible plight.*
plight[2] [plait] *vt* pledge; promise: *plight one's word.*
plight one's troth promise to marry (*o.f.*).
plimsoll ['plimsəl] *nc* type of shoe made of canvas, with a rubber sole.
'plimsoll line line marked on the side of a ship to indicate the depth to which the ship may be loaded.
plinth [plinθ] *nc* square base on which a column stands.
plod [plɔd] *vi* **1.** walk slowly and heavily. *You could see he was tired by the way he plodded along the road.* **2.** work slowly but without resting: *plod away at a task. past* **plodded.**
plodder *nc* person who works slowly but does not give up.
plop [plɔp] *nc* noise made by e.g. a stone falling into water. Also *vi*: *The stone plopped into the water. past* **plopped.**
plot [plɔt] **1.** secret plan: *a plot against the government.* **2.** outline of the story of a play, novel etc: *an unusual and interesting plot.* **3.** small piece of ground: *a garden plot.* Also *vt* **1.** make secret plans with others: *plot to overthrow the government; plot against the president.* **2.** mark the position of something on a chart, map etc. *past* **plotted. plotter** *nc.*
plough [plau] (*US* **plow**) *nc* heavy instrument for cutting into the soil and turning it over. Also *vt/i* **1.** break up land with a plough; use a plough: *plough a field.* **2.** (esp. of a ship through water) force a way through something. **3.** fail (an examination) (*informal* in sense **3.**).
'ploughboy, 'ploughman person using a plough.
'ploughshare metal blade of a plough i.e. the part which cuts into the soil.
plover ['plʌvə*] *nc* one of several kinds of bird with long legs and a short beak which lives near the water.
plow [plau] *nc US* form of **plough.**
ploy [plɔi] *nc* idea or action which is often used to gain some advantage. *His favourite ploy is to pretend to be stupid and then people try to help him.*
pluck [plʌk] *vt/i* **1.** pull off, pick (flowers, fruit): *pluck flowers from a field.* **2.** pull on (the strings of a musical instrument). Also *nu* courage: *someone with a lot of pluck.*
plucky *adj* brave. **pluckily** *adv.*
pluck at something pull something suddenly: *pluck at someone's coat.*
pluck up one's courage be brave; overcome one's fears.
plug [plʌg] *nc* **1.** piece of wood, rubber etc used to stop up a hole. *A plug was put in the hole to prevent the water from escaping.* **2.** device to make an electrical connection: *plug for a lamp.* **3.** cake of tobacco which has been pressed tightly together. Also *vt/i* stop up a hole by using a piece of wood etc. *past* **plugged.**
plug away at keep on working at: *plug away at one's studies.* (*informal*).
plug something in make an electrical connection using a plug (in sense **2.**): *plug in the lamp.*
plum [plʌm] *nc* **1.** round, juicy fruit with a stone in it which grows in cool dry areas. **2.** tree bearing this fruit. **3.** something considered very good or desirable. (*informal* in sense **3.**).
'plum 'pudding boiled pudding containing currants, raisins etc mostly eaten at Christmas.
plumage ['plu:midʒ] *nu* bird's feathers: *a bird with bright plumage.*
plumb [plʌm] *nc* small heavy object at the end of a line, used to find out how deep water is, or how straight a wall etc is. *The wall was out of plumb* i.e. not vertical. Also *vt* **1.** measure by using a plumbline: *plumb the depth of the pool.* **2.** get to the bottom of; find out the meaning of: *plumb a mystery.* Also *adv* exactly. *His shot was plumb on the target.*
'plumbline line with a plumb at the end of it.
plumber ['plʌmə*] *nc* person who puts in and repairs pipes for water, gas etc in buildings.
plumbing *nu* **1.** work of a plumber. **2.** pipes and tanks having to do with water and gas supply in a building: *a house with very poor plumbing.*
plume [plu:m] *nc* feather or bunch of feathers (usu. as an ornament). *She wore an ostrich plume in her hat.* Also *vt* smooth. *The bird was pluming itself* i.e. smoothing its feathers.
plume oneself on something be proud of something. *He plumed himself on his success in the team.*
plump[1] [plʌmp] *adj* fat in an attractive way: *a plump little baby; plump cheeks.* Also *vt/i* (often with **out** or **up**) make or become plump. *The child is plumping out a little.*
plump[2] [plʌmp] *vt/i* drop, allow to drop, suddenly or heavily. *Tired out, he plumped himself down on the chair. I just plumped the heavy load on the ground.* Also *adv* **1.** heavily; suddenly. *I ran plump into him as I came round the corner.* **2.** directly; bluntly.
plump for someone/something choose someone/something without hesitation. *They all plumped for the same candidate.* (*informal*).
plunder ['plʌndə*] *vt/i* take things from places or people by force (usu. in a war, riot etc). *The bandits plundered every village.* Also *nu* **1.** things taken by force. *The robbers escaped with their plunder.* **2.** act of plundering.
plunge [plʌndʒ] *vt/i* **1.** jump into; throw oneself into: *plunge into the river; plunge oneself into debt.* **2.** put something violently or suddenly into a certain state: *plunge a country into war; plunge a room into darkness.* **3.** (with reference to a horse) lower its head violently; (with reference to a ship) lower its bow violently. *The horse plunged and threw its rider forward. The ship plunged in heavy seas.* Also *nc* act of plunging (e.g. into water).
plunger *nc* **1.** rubber suction device for

clearing sinks etc. **2.** part of a machine which moves quickly up and down.
take the plunge decide to do something that is difficult or dangerous. (*informal*).

plural ['pluərl] *adj* containing or referring to more than one. Also *nc* form of a word which shows that it refers to more than one (e.g. the plural of *chair* is *chairs*, the plural of *I* is *we*).

plus [plʌs] *prep* (used mainly in mathematics) and; with the addition of. *Three plus two equals five* (3 + 2 = 5).
'plus 'fours wide, baggy trousers reaching to just below the knee.

plush [plʌʃ] *nu* thick, soft cloth material. Also *adj* very expensive: *a very plush house in London*. (*informal*).

plutocracy [pluː'tɔkrəsi] *nc/u* **1.** system of government in which rich people are the rulers. **2.** rich ruling class.
plutocrat ['pluːtoukræt] *nc* person who is powerful because he is rich. **plutocratic** [pluːtou'krætik] *adj*.

plutonium [pluː'touniəm] *nu* radioactive element with important uses for nuclear fission (Pu).

ply[1] [plai] *nc* **1.** thin layer of wood: *three-ply wood* i.e. piece of wood made up of three different layers stuck together. **2.** strand of rope etc: *three-ply rope* i.e. rope made of three strands twisted together.
'plywood wood made up of different layers of wood stuck together.

ply[2] [plai] *vt/i* **1.** work at: *someone who plies a trade*. **2.** use; work with: *a dressmaker plying her needle*. **3.** go regularly between: *a ship that plies between London and New York*. **4.** give something to someone (usu. for selfish reasons). *They plied the stranger with drink and then robbed him*. **5.** ask often: *ply someone with questions/requests etc*. *pres part* **plying**. *past* **plied** [plaid].

pneumatic [njuː'mætik] *adj* **1.** filled with air: *pneumatic tyre*. **2.** worked by air: *pneumatic drill*.

pneumonia [njuː'mouniə] *nu* serious illness of the lungs.

poach[1] [poutʃ] *vt/i* hunt or steal birds or animals on someone else's land. **poacher** *nc*.

poach[2] [poutʃ] *vt* cook an egg (without its shell) or fish in water which is almost at boiling point.

pock [pɔk] *nc* mark on the skin caused by smallpox.
'pockmarked *adj* with pocks on the skin.

pocket ['pɔkit] *nc* **1.** small bag sewn into an article of clothing. *He put the money in his coat pocket*. **2.** string bag at the side of a billiard table. **3.** hole in the earth containing some ore (e.g. gold). **4.** small area of something: *a pocket of resistance*. Also *vt* **1.** place in one's pocket. **2.** take something (esp. when one is not entitled to it). **3.** hold back; hide: *pocket one's pride; pocket one's feelings*.
pocketful *nc* amount that a pocket holds.
'pocketbook **1.** (*US*) woman's purse. **2.** small notebook. **3.** small leather case for carrying paper money. (Usu. **wallet**).
'pocket knife small knife with one or more blades which fold into the handle.
'pocket money small amount of money given to children.
'air pocket small area in the sky where lack of air causes a plane to lose height suddenly.
'pickpocket see **pick**[2].
in/out of pocket having gained/lost money. *As a result of having entertained his friends, he was three pounds out of pocket*.

pod [pɔd] *nc* long seed vessel containing the seeds of e.g. peas or beans. Also *vt/i* **1.** take peas etc from a pod. **2.** form pods; grow into pods. *past* **podded**.

podgy ['pɔdʒi] *adj* short and fat.

poem ['pouim] *nc* arrangement of words to produce a beautiful effect (often with lines that rhyme and are usu. of regular length and rhythm).
poetry ['pouitri] *nu* **1.** poems: *book of poetry*. **2.** art of writing poems. **3.** any beautiful effect. *The dancing performance was sheer poetry of movement*.
poet ['pouit] *nc* person who writes poems.
poetess ['pouites] *nc* woman poet.
poetic, poetical [pou'etik(l)] *adj* **1.** having to do with poems or poets. **2.** written in verse: *poetic drama*.

pogrom ['pɔgrəm] *nc* (esp. with reference to killing of Jews in Russia in former times) organized killing of a large class or group of people.

poignant ['pɔinjənt] *adj* **1.** very painful; very moving: *a poignant scene*. **2.** sharp to taste or smell. **poignantly** *adv*. **poignancy** *nu*.

point[1] [pɔint] *nc* **1.** sharp end of something: *the point of a pin*. **2.** small, round mark: *decimal point* i.e. mark used in the decimal system (e.g. 3.7 (*three point seven*)). **3.** (geometry) something having position but no size: *a point on the line AB*. **4.** spot, position in space or time. *From that point onwards they were always good friends*. **5.** position on a scale. *The water had reached boiling point*. **6.** one of the 32 points of the compass (e.g. *NW, NNE etc*). **7.** (games) unit of scoring: *win by five points; win on points* i.e. in boxing, win without knocking out one's opponent. **8.** use; purpose. *What is the point of wasting time? There is no point in staying*. **9.** detail; single item. *I answered him point by point*. **10.** main idea; most important thing. *He missed the whole point of my speech* i.e. he did not understand what it was really about. **11.** something that makes a person different or outstanding: *his main point as a writer; her strong point* i.e. something she is really good at.
points *npl* rails which can be moved so that a train can move from one track to another.
pointless *adj* useless; having no purpose. *We were given many pointless things to do*. **pointlessly** *adv*.
'point-'blank *adj* **1.** very close to the target: *take point-blank aim*. **2.** complete and direct: *point-blank refusal*. Also *adv*: *He fired at his victim point-blank. He refused point-blank*.
'point duty work of directing traffic (esp. at crossroads).
'turning point most important point, when things become much better or much worse: *the turning point in someone's career*.
at the point of very near to: *at the point of death*.
when it comes to the point in fact; in reality. *He promised me a lot of money, but when it came to the point I got nothing*.
in point of fact indeed; speaking truthfully.
gain/carry one's point make others agree with oneself.
a point of honour something one must do for one's own self-respect.
in point having to do with what is being

discussed: *give a case in point* i.e. a good example of what is being discussed.

make a point of doing something make the effort to do something which one considers necessary. *He always made a point of knowing the students by name.*

the point of no return position or situation from which one can only go forward.

off/away from the point not having to do with what is being considered.

on the point of just about to. *When he was on the point of winning he stumbled and fell.*

to the point having to do with what is being discussed.

point of view way in which one sees something or thinks about something. *From your point of view this may be important, but from mine it is not.*

point[2] [pɔint] *vt/i* **1.** show the position or direction of something (e.g. by using a finger). *He pointed to the house I was looking for.* **2.** aim or direct a finger, gun etc at someone. *He pointed the gun at me.* **3.** fill cracks between bricks with mortar.

pointed *adj* **1.** coming to a point: *pointed roof.* **2.** aimed at someone, often to hurt or reprove them: *pointed remark.* **pointedly** *adv.*

pointer *nc* **1.** long stick used to point things out on a blackboard, map etc. **2.** hand of a clock; indicator on a dial etc. **3.** kind of hunting dog.

point something out to somebody call someone's attention to something. *He pointed out that the road was not safe in winter.*

poise [pɔiz] *vt/i* **1.** place something in a certain way so that it remains steady; balance. *He poised the pencil upright on the table.* **2.** hold raised in a certain way. **3.** hover, prepare for action. *The lion was poised to spring.* Also *nu* **1.** way of holding the head and body. **2.** calmness. *Everybody admired his poise in the dangerous circumstances.*

poison ['pɔizn] *nc/u* **1.** substance which causes sickness or death if it comes in contact with, or is consumed by, living things. **2.** anything that is dangerous to people. Also *vt* **1.** kill by using poison. **2.** put poison in or on. **3.** have a bad effect on. *Their friendship was poisoned by distrust.* **poisoner** *nc.* **poisonous** *adj.*

poke [pouk] *vt/i* **1.** push something/someone with the finger, a stick etc: *poke someone in the ribs; poke a fire* i.e. stir up the coals. **2.** push a stick etc in or through something; make (a hole) in this way. *He poked a hole in the wall with the stick.*

poker[1] *nc* long, metal rod for stirring up the coals, wood etc in a fire.

poke fun at laugh at in an unkind way. *The three boys poked fun at the little girl.* (*informal*).

poke one's nose into interfere with something which has nothing to do with one. *He is always poking his nose into other people's business.* (*informal*).

poker[2] ['poukə*] *nu* card game which is usu. played for money.

'poker-faced *adj* not showing what one is thinking or feeling.

poky ['pouki] *adj* (with reference to a room, house etc) too small to be comfortable or pleasant.

pole[1] [poul] *nc* **1.** long, thin rod of wood or metal used for holding something up: *telegraph pole* i.e. one to support telephone wires; *tent pole; flagpole.* **2.** measurement of distance of 5½ yards. see appendix.

'pole vault jump made with the help of a long pole. **pole vaulter** *nc.* **pole vaulting** *nu.*

pole[2] [poul] *nc* **1.** one of the two ends of the axis of the earth or another planet i.e. the line around which the earth etc turns: *the North Pole and the South Pole.* **2.** one of the two points in the sky around which the stars seem to turn. **3.** either of the two ends of a magnet or battery: *the positive pole and the negative pole.*

polar *adj* connected with, or near, the North or South Pole: *polar bear* i.e. large, white bear living near the North Pole.

'Pole 'Star North Star.

polemic [pɔ'lemik] *nc/u* argument; dispute. **polemical** *adj.*

police [pə'li:s] *n* (always followed by a *pl* verb) **1.** body of men whose duty it is to keep order and arrest those who break the laws of a country. *The police are going to question everyone in the house.* **2.** department of the government concerned with keeping order and arresting wrongdoers. Also *vt* control; keep order in: *police the streets.*

po'lice 'constable policeman of ordinary rank.

po'lice court court in which less important offences can be dealt with.

po'liceman member of the police force. (*fem* **policewoman**).

po'lice station police office.

policy[1] ['pɔlisi] *nc/u* plan of conduct; statement of what is going to be done (esp. by the government, a business company etc). *It is a good policy to save some money when you can. Have you read about the new government policy to deal with unemployment?*

policy[2] ['pɔlisi] *nc* written agreement that an amount of money will be paid to someone if a certain thing happens. *He took out a fire insurance policy for his house* i.e. if his house was burnt down he would be paid some money.

polio ['pouliou] *nu* type of disease which causes paralysis. (Short for **poliomyelitis** ['poulioumaiə'laitis]).

polish ['pɔliʃ] *vt* make smooth and shiny by rubbing: *polish one's shoes.* Also *nu* **1.** substance used to make something smooth and shiny: *shoe polish.* **2.** smooth and shiny surface: *the polish on a table.* **3.** pleasant manners.

polished *adj* **1.** made smooth and shiny. **2.** having pleasant manners.

polish something off finish something. (*informal*).

polish something up **1.** make something better in some small way: *polish up an essay.* **2.** refresh one's memory. *I'm going to Paris, so I must polish up my French.* (*informal*).

polite [pə'lait] *adj* having or showing good manners; well-behaved: *polite children.* (*opp* **impolite**). **politely** *adv.* **politeness** *nu.*

politic ['pɔlitik] *adj* **1.** clever in looking after one's own interests. **2.** wise, prudent: *a politic action/scheme etc.* (*opp* **impolitic**).

political [pə'litikl] *adj* of or concerned with the government of a country: *a political party; political science* i.e. the study of politics. **politically** *adv.*

politician [pɔli'tiʃən] *nc* person concerned with government.

politics ['pɔlitiks] *nu* matters concerning the running of a country, city etc: *be* *interested in politics.*

polka ['pɔlkə] *nc* kind of quick, lively dance; the music for such a dance.

poll[1] [poul] *nc* **1.** collection of votes i.e. papers which show who has been chosen for some purpose, often to form a government. *A poll was organized in every village.* **2.** number of votes given: *a heavy poll* i.e. many people voted. **3.** list of people (esp. those who can vote): *have one's name on the poll.* **4.** investigation into what people think on a certain subject. Also *vt/i* **1.** receive a certain number of votes. *He polled* 80 *votes.* **2.** vote in an election.

the polls *npl* polling booths.

'polling booth place where people go to vote.

'poll tax tax on every person.

poll[2] [pɔl] *vt* cut off or cut short the top of something (esp. a tree or the horns of an animal).

pollen ['pɔln] *nu* fine dust (usu. yellow) which is found on flowers and which makes other flowers fertile when it is brought to them (e.g. by the wind, bees etc).

pollinate ['pɔlineit] *vt* make a flower fertile with pollen. **pollination** [pɔli'neiʃən] *nu.*

pollute [pə'lu:t] *vt* make unhealthy. *The river has been polluted with oil.* **pollution** *nu.*

polo ['poulou] *nu* game played by men on horseback, in which a ball is hit with long sticks with wooden heads (called **mallets**).

'water polo kind of handball played in the water.

poly- ['pɔli] *prefix* many (e.g. **polygamy; polyglot**).

polygamy [pə'ligəmi] *nu* act or custom of having more than one wife. **polygamous** *adj.* **polygamist** *nc.*

polyglot ['pɔliglɔt] *adj* **1.** knowing many languages: *a polyglot scholar.* **2.** written in many languages. Also *nc* person who knows many languages.

polygon ['pɔligən] *nc* figure having five or more sides. **polygonal** [pɔ'ligənl] *adj.*

polytechnic [pɔli'teknik] *nc* institution (usu. for adults) where many different subjects are taught (esp. practical subjects). Also *adj.*

pomade [pə'meid] *nu* sweet-smelling, oily substance put on the hair. Also *vt.*

pomegranate ['pɔmigrænit] *nc/u* **1.** tough-skinned fruit, about the size of an apple, containing many seeds. **2.** tree bearing this fruit.

pommel ['pʌml] *nc* **1.** part of a saddle that sticks up at the front. **2.** round knob i.e. kind of ball on the handle of a sword. Also *vt* beat with the fists. *past* **pommelled.** (*US* **pommeled**) (Also **pummel**).

pomp [pɔmp] *nu* solemn, magnificent display. *The queen was greeted at the town hall with much pomp and ceremony.*

pompous *adj* too dignified; trying to seem very important: *a pompous official.* **pompously** *adv.* **pomposity** [pɔm'pɔsiti] *nu.*

pond [pɔnd] *nc* area of still water, smaller than a lake. *Some cattle were drinking at the pond.*

ponder ['pɔndə*] *vt/i* think about something carefully: *ponder (over) a problem.*

ponderous ['pɔndərəs] *adj* **1.** very heavy: *a ponderous weight.* **2.** slow and clumsy: *ponderous movements.* **3.** (with reference to a person) dull and slow. **ponderously** *adv.*

pontiff ['pɔntif] *nc* **1.** the Pope. **2.** bishop or high priest (*o.f.*).

pontificate [pɔn'tifikeit] *vi* give opinions, decisions etc in a very pompous way as though one were much more important than one really is.

pontoon [pɔn'tu:n] **1.** *nc* low, flat-bottomed boat. **2.** *nc* flat boat or similar floating thing used to hold up a bridge: *pontoon bridge.* **3.** *nu* type of card game.

pony ['pouni] *nc* kind of small horse.

poodle ['pu:dl] *nc* type of dog kept as a pet.

pooh [pu:] *interj* exclamation showing contempt.

'pooh-'pooh *vt* state one's contempt for something. *He pooh-poohed our ideas.*

pool[1] [pu:l] *nc* **1.** small area of still water. **2.** small amount of water lying on a road, the floor etc. *There were pools of water all over the house after the pipe burst.* **3.** part of a river that is still and deep: *fish in a pool.* **4.** place specially made for people to swim in. (Also **swimming pool**).

pool[2] [pu:l] *nc* **1.** amount of money to be won in a gambling game (made up of what the different players have paid in). **2.** arrangement by different business firms to work together and share the money they make. **3.** anything that is shared among many people: *a pool of experience.* **4.** (*US*) game played on a special table with six pockets. The aim is to drive balls into the pockets with long wooden sticks (called **cues**). Also *vt* put money etc together for the benefit of all who have put some in. *We pooled all our money so as to buy a car.*

'football pools form of gambling in which money can be won by saying correctly what the results of football matches will be.

poop [pu:p] *nc* raised deck at the end of a ship (*o.f.*).

poor [puə*] *adj* **1.** having little or no money. *The failure of his business left him a poor man.* **2.** unlucky; unfortunate. *That poor woman has lost her son.* **3.** bad. *These clothes are of poor quality. He is a poor speaker. There was a poor attendance at the meeting.*

poorness *nu.*

the poor poor people: *care for the poor.*

poorly **1.** *adv* badly. *He did poorly in the examination.* **2.** *pred adj* in bad health. *She has been keeping poorly* i.e. she has not been well. (*informal* in sense **2.**).

'poorbox box in a church into which money is put for the poor.

'poorhouse place in which poor people used to be kept at public expense (*o.f.*).

pop[1] [pɔp] *vt/i* **1.** make a short, sharp sound (e.g. when a cork is taken out of a bottle). **2.** move, go, come quickly or unexpectedly. *I popped the book into my bag. I've just popped in to say hello. She keeps popping in and out* i.e. entering and leaving the house often. *past* **popped.** Also *nc* short, sharp sound as when a cork is taken out of a bottle. Also *nu* kind of non-alcoholic drink: *a bottle of pop.* (*informal*).

'popcorn maize puffed out and sweetened.

'popgun toy gun for children which fires a cork etc with a popping sound.

'pop'eyed *adj* with one's eyes wide with surprise.

pop up appear. *He'll pop up somewhere.* (*informal*).

pop the question ask someone to marry one. (*informal*).

pop[2] [pɔp] *nu* type of modern music which appeals mainly to young people. Also *adj: a pop record.*

Note: short for *popular* (music), but now used as a full word.

poplar ['pɔplə*] **1.** *nc* tall, thin tree that grows very quickly. **2.** *nu* the wood of this tree.

poplin ['pɔplin] *nu* type of material used for making dresses, shirts etc.

poppy ['pɔpi] *nc* **1.** plant with large red, white or yellow flowers. **2.** flower of this plant.

populace ['pɔpjuləs] *n* the common people.

popular ['pɔpjulə*] *adj* **1.** liked by many people: *be very popular with one's fellow students.* (*opp* **unpopular**). **2.** intended for ordinary people: *cars at popular prices.* **3.** of or for the people: *a popular government.*

popularly *adv.*

popularity [pɔpju'læriti] *nu* condition of being liked by many people.

popularize *vt* make popular (in senses **1.** and **2.**). **popularization** [pɔpjulərai'zeiʃən] *nu.*

populate ['pɔpjuleit] *vt* fill with people. *America was populated mostly by Europeans. Japan is a densely populated country.*

population [pɔpju'leiʃən] *nc/u* **1.** people living in a country, city etc; number of these people: *the population of London.* **2.** special section of the people living in a country etc: *the Negro population of the United States.*

populous *adj* having many people.

porcelain ['pɔːslin] *nu* **1.** fine china i.e. baked white clay used for making cups, saucers etc. **2.** articles (cups etc) made from fine china.

porch [pɔːtʃ] *nc* area at the entrance to a house, church etc that is covered over.

porcupine ['pɔːkjupain] *nc* small animal like a rat covered with quills i.e. sharp, stiff hairs.

pore[1] [pɔː*] *vi* (usu. with **over**) look at or study something carefully for a long time. *He is always poring over his books.*

pore[2] [pɔː*] *nc* very small opening in the skin. *Human beings sweat through their pores.*

pork [pɔːk] *nu* meat of a pig. see also **bacon, ham.**

pornography [pɔː'nɔgrəfi] *nu* writing or pictures intended to arouse sexual feelings. **pornographic** [pɔːnə'græfik] *adj.*

porous ['pɔːrəs] *adj* allowing liquid to pass through: *porous soil.*

porpoise ['pɔːpəs] *nc* type of air-breathing sea animal about four to eight feet long with a blunt nose.

porridge ['pɔridʒ] *nu* food made of grain (e.g. oatmeal) boiled in water or milk.

port[1] [pɔːt] *nc* **1.** place for sheltering ships; harbour. **2.** town with a harbour, where ships can be loaded and unloaded.

port[2] [pɔːt] *nu* left side of a ship when one faces forward.

port[3] [pɔːt] *nc* opening in the side of a ship (used for loading and unloading).

'**porthole** small round window on the side of a ship.

port[4] [pɔːt] *nu* type of sweet wine (usu. red).

portable ['pɔːtəbl] *adj* able to be carried: *a portable typewriter.*

portage ['pɔːtidʒ] *nc/u* **1.** carrying of boats, supplies etc overland from one river, lake etc to another. **2.** cost of this. **3.** place where this is done.

portal ['pɔːtl] *nc* large, very grand door or entrance (*o.f.*).

portcullis [pɔːt'kʌlis] *nc* strong, iron gate which can be slid up and down, used in former times to protect castles which were being attacked.

portend [pɔː'tend] *vt* be a sign or warning that something is going to happen.

portent ['pɔːtent] *nc* sign or warning.

portentous [pɔː'tentəs] *adj* amazing; strange. **portentously** *adv.*

porter ['pɔːtə*] *nc* **1.** person employed to carry cases, bags etc: *railway porter.* **2.** doorkeeper. **3.** (*US*) sleeping-car attendant on a train.

portfolio [pɔːt'fouliou] *nc* **1.** small case for holding papers etc. **2.** position and duties of a minister in the government: *resign one's portfolio; Minister without Portfolio* i.e. not in charge of any particular department. *pl* **portfolios.**

portico ['pɔːtikou] *nc* roof supported by pillars (esp. outside the entrance to a building). *pl* **porticos.**

portion ['pɔːʃən] *nc* **1.** part; share of something. *The money was divided into seven portions.* **2.** amount: *a small portion of cheese.* Also *vt* divide into portions.

portly ['pɔːtli] *adj* fat: *a portly old gentleman.*

portmanteau [pɔːt'mæntou] *nc* travelling bag which opens up into sections. *pl* **portmanteaus** or **portmanteaux** [pɔːt'mæntouz].

portrait ['pɔːtreit] *nc* **1.** picture of a person. **2.** picture in words; description. **portraiture** ['pɔːtritʃə*] *nc/u.*

portray [pɔː'trei] *vt* **1.** describe; picture in words. **2.** make a picture of. **3.** act the part of someone on the stage.

portrayal [pɔː'treiəl] *nc* **1.** act of portraying. **2.** description.

pose [pouz] *vt/i* **1.** hold a certain position while one is being photographed, painted etc: *pose for a picture.* **2.** put someone in such a position. **3.** state something to be answered or discussed: *pose a question/problem etc.* **4.** pretend to be what one is not. *He posed as a rich man.* Also *nc* **1.** position of the body when being photographed etc. **2.** way of behaving which is intended to impress others.

poser *nc* difficult problem.

poseur [pou'zəː*] *nc* person who poses (in sense **4.**) to impress others.

posh [pɔʃ] *adj* rich and fashionable, belonging to the upper classes. (*informal*).

position [pə'ziʃən] *nc* **1.** place where a person/thing is. *The table used to be in this position.* **2.** way in which a person/thing is placed: *find a more comfortable position.* **3.** job; employment: *apply for a certain position.* **4.** rank: *someone in a high position* i.e. of high rank. **5.** attitude; point of view. *What is your position on this matter?* **6.** state or condition. *I'm not in a position to help you* i.e. I cannot help you. Also *vt* put into a position.

in position in the correct place. *Is everyone in position?*

out of position not in the correct place.

positive ['pɔzitiv] *adj* **1.** sure; definite; certain: *receive positive instructions; be positive about something.* **2.** helpful; constructive. *Positive suggestions will be welcomed.* **3.** (mathematics) greater than 0; +: *a positive number.* **4.** (grammar) of the simple form of an *adj* or *adv* (e.g. **good** is the positive form, **better** the *comparative* and **best** the *superlative*). Also *nc* **1.** print of a photographic film. see **negative.** **2.** (grammar) simple form of an *adj* or *adv* (e.g. the positive of **better** is **good**).

positively *adv* definitely; without doubt.

posse ['pɔsi] *nc* group of people gathered together in order to chase a criminal.

possess [pə'zes] *vt* own; have. *He possesses a lot of property.* **possessor** *nc.*
possessed *adj* under the control of evil spirits; mad. *He fought like a man possessed.*
possession 1. *nu* condition of owning or having: *be in possession of something; take possession of something.* 2. *nc* (often *pl*) thing owned. *I lost most of my possessions during the war.*
possessive *adj* 1. too anxious to have or keep. *That child is very possessive about/with his toys – he won't let other children play with them.* 2. (grammar) showing possession (e.g. **my, your, man's** are possessive forms).
possessively *adv.* **possessiveness** *nu.*
be possessed of have. *He is possessed of many good qualities.*
possess oneself of take; become the owner of.
what possessed him to do that? why did he do such a strange thing?
possible ['pɔsibl] *adj* 1. that can be done; that can happen. *Anything is possible. Is it possible to do this another way?* 2. that may be accepted; reasonable: *a possible solution; a possible candidate.* (*opp* **impossible**).
possibly *adv* 1. by any possibility; by any means. *Can you possibly come?* 2. perhaps. *He may possibly be there.*
possibility [pɔsi'biliti] *nc/u* 1. state of being possible. *There is some possibility (that) he may be late.* 2. something that is possible: *a job with great possibilities* i.e. opportunities. *It's only a possibility* i.e. it's not certain.
post[1] [poust] *nc/u* 1. (*Brit*) system of sending and delivering letters, parcels etc: *send something by post.* (*US* **mail**). 2. letters etc delivered or collected at one time. *This letter arrived with the morning post. The last post is at 7.15 p.m.* 3. office or pillar box where letters etc are left for delivery: *take a letter to the post.* Also *vt* 1. send something by post. 2. take a letter etc to a post office or pillar box. *Please post these letters for me.* 3. copy items into a kind of cashbook (called a **ledger**).
postage *nu* amount to be paid for sending letters etc by post.
postal *adj* connected with the post (in sense 1.): *postal services; postal order* i.e. kind of receipt for a small amount of money which can be bought at a post office, posted and then cashed at any post office by the person who receives it.
'**postcard** card which can be posted (usu. without being placed in an envelope).
'**post-'free** *adj/adv* carried free by post. *If you buy this book, it will be sent to you post-free.*
'**post'haste** *adv* as quickly as possible.
'**postman** (*Brit*) man who delivers letters. (*US* **mailman**). *pl* **postmen.**
'**postmark** mark put on letters etc over the stamp to cancel it, and also to show when and where the letter was posted. Also *vt.*
'**postmaster,** '**postmistress** man, woman in charge of a post office.
'**post office** 1. government department which runs the postal services. 2. shop or office for postal services (e.g. buying stamps, posting letters etc).
'**post-'paid** *adj* with postage already paid: *a post-paid letter.*
'**postage stamp** stamp stuck on letters etc to show that postage has been paid.
post[2] [poust] *nc* 1. place where a soldier, policeman etc is on duty. *No one may leave his post without permission.* 2. job: *apply for a post as a teacher.* 3. trading station. (Also **trading post**).
the last post music which is played (on a bugle) at bedtime in an army camp or when a soldier is being buried.
post[3] [poust] *nc* piece of wood, metal etc placed upright (usu. to support or mark something): *a bedpost; the winning post* i.e. in a race; *a doorpost.* Also *vt* 1. (usu. with **up**) put something up on a notice board to be seen by many people. *The list of those who were chosen was posted up.* 2. make something public. *He was posted missing.*
poster *nc* public notice (esp. used for advertising).
post-[4] [poust] *prefix* later than; after (e.g. **postdate; postgraduate**).
postdate ['poust'deit] *vt* put on a letter, cheque etc a date later than the one on which it was actually written. (A cheque cannot be cashed until the date that is written on it).
poste restante ['poust'restɑ̃t] *nu* 1. department of a post office which keeps one's letters until one calls for them. 2. arrangement by which letters are kept in this way.
posterior [pɔs'tiəriə*] *adj* 1. situated behind; rear. 2. coming later. Also *nc* part of the body on which one sits; buttocks.
posterity [pɔs'teriti] *nu* 1. person's descendants. 2. people who will be living at some future time: *discoveries which will be of great benefit to posterity.*
postgraduate ['poust'grædjuət] *adj* done after taking a degree: *postgraduate studies.* Also *nc* someone who continues his studies after he has got a degree.
posthumous ['pɔstjuməs] *adj* after the death of someone: *a posthumous child* i.e. one born after the death of its father; *a posthumous book* i.e. one published after the death of its author.
postilion, postillion [pɔs'tiliən] *nc* man who rides on one of the horses pulling a carriage.
post mortem ['poust'mɔːtəm] *nc* examination of a corpse to discover the cause of death.
postpone [pəs'poun] *vt* put off, delay until a later time. *His visit was postponed because of illness.* **postponement** *nc/u.*
postscript ['poustskript] *nc* something added at the end of a letter, after the signature (usu. introduced by the letters P.S.).
postulate ['pɔstjuleit] *vt* take something as true without proof in order to reason from it. Also ['pɔstjulət] *nc* something postulated. **postulation** [pɔstju'leiʃən] *nc/u.*
posture ['pɔstʃə*] *nc* position of the body; way of holding the body: *lie in a lazy posture; have good posture.* Also *vt* take up a posture (usu. to impress someone).
posy ['pouzi] *nc* bunch of flowers. *The little girl was holding a posy.*
pot [pɔt] 1. *nc* round container made of earthenware, metal etc used to hold liquids and other things: *a cooking pot; a flowerpot; a teapot.* 2. *nc* amount held in such a container: *make a pot of tea.* 3. *nu* marijuana i.e. type of intoxicating drug. (*informal* in sense 3.). Also *vt* 1. put something into a pot (usu. to make it stay fresh longer): *potted ham.* 2. take a shot at; shoot. *I potted three rabbits in thirty minutes.* (*informal*). 3. put a plant into a pot of earth.
pottery 1. *nu* pots etc made from clay and

hardened by heat. **2.** *nu* art of making pots in this way. **3.** *nc* place where pots are made.
potter *nc* person who makes pots etc from clay.
'potbellied *adj* fat.
'pothole *nc* **1.** hole in a road. **2.** very deep hole underground.
'potholer *nc* person who explores potholes (in sense **2.**) for sport.
'potholing *nu* sport of exploring potholes.
'pothook 1. hook for hanging pots etc over a fire. **2.** S-shaped hook made by children when they are being taught how to write.
'pot'shot shot taken without careful aim. (*informal*).
go to pot get much worse. *His standard of work has been going to pot recently.* (*informal*).
keep the pot boiling 1. (in children's games etc) keep things going without stopping. **2.** earn enough to be able to buy food. (*informal*).
the pot calls the kettle black the person who accuses is as bad as the person he is accusing. *If John is saying that Harry is a thief, then it's a case of the pot calling the kettle black.* (*informal*).
take 'pot'luck accept what is available without knowing much about it. (*informal*).
potash ['pɔtæʃ] *nu* white powder used in making glass, soap, fertilizers etc.
potato [pə'teitou] *nc/u* roundish root plant with white flesh commonly used as a vegetable. *pl* **potatoes.**
potent ['poutnt] *adj* powerful; strong: *a potent argument; a potent remedy for disease.*
potency *nu*.
potentate ['poutnteit] *nc* powerful ruler.
potential [pə'tenʃl] *adj* which may come into effect or existence. *Although this area is very poor just now, its potential wealth is great* i.e. the basis for this wealth is there. Also *nu* possibilities: *an area of great potential.*
potentially *adv*. **potentiality** [pətenʃi'æliti] *nc/u*.
potion ['pouʃən] *nc* drink of medicine, or poison.
potter[1], **pottery** ['pɔtə(ri)] *nc, nu* see **pot.**
potter[2] ['pɔtə*] *vi* **1.** (with **at**) work at something in a lazy kind of way. **2.** (with **about**) go from one little job to another. *He likes pottering about in the garden.* (*informal*).
potty ['pɔti] *adj* **1.** mad; crazy. **2.** unimportant: *some potty little details.* Also *nc* child's pot, used to urinate in. (all *informal*).
pouch [pautʃ] *nc* **1.** small bag: *tobacco pouch.* **2.** part of the body coming out to form a bag: *kangaroo's pouch.* **3.** bag-like folds of skin: *the pouches under a tired person's eyes.*
poultice ['poultis] *nc* mass of soft material (e.g. herbs etc) put on the skin as medicine. *They placed hot poultices on his injured back.* Also *vt* put a poultice on.
poultry ['poultri] **1.** *npl* (followed by *pl* verb) chickens, hens, ducks, geese etc. **2.** *nu* flesh of these birds as meat.
poulterer ['poultərə*] *nc* person who sells poultry.
pounce [pauns] *vi* come down suddenly on; jump on. *The lion pounced on its prey.* Also *nc* sudden jump or swoop.
pound[1] [paund] *nc* **1.** measure of weight; 1 pound (avoirdupois) = 16 ounces; 1 pound (troy) = 12 ounces. *The sugar weighed five pounds.* see appendix. **2.** unit of money in Great Britain etc; 1 pound formerly = 20 shillings; now 1 pound = 100 new pence. *This coat cost ten pounds.*
Note: the difference between *five pounds* and *a five-pound note.*
pound[2] [paund] *vt/i* **1.** hit hard again and again: *pound at/on the door with one's fists.* **2.** crush into a powder: *pound ears of corn into grain.* **3.** beat violently. *When I stopped running, my heart was pounding.*
pound[3] [paund] *nc* closed-in place where animals (usu. lost animals) can be kept.
pour [pɔː*] *vt/i* **1.** cause liquids to flow. *I poured some milk from the bottle into the jug.* **2.** move in large numbers. *People were pouring out of the burning building.* **3.** rain heavily. *It's pouring outside. He stood in the pouring rain.*
pout [paut] *vt/i* push out the lips, as an angry child does. Also *nc*.
poverty ['pɔvəti] *nu* state of being poor: *live in poverty.*
'poverty-stricken *adj* very poor: *poverty-stricken area.*
powder ['paudə*] *nc/u* **1.** anything that has been made into dust. **2.** special kind of powder (e.g. *face powder; gunpowder*). Also *vt/i* **1.** put powder on. *She powdered her face.* **2.** make into powder: *powdered milk.*
powdery *adj* like powder: *powdery snow.*
'powder magazine place where gunpowder is kept.
'powder puff small pad of cloth etc for putting on face powder.
power ['pauə*] **1.** *nu* strength: *a display of military power.* **2.** *nu* ability; what one can do. *I shall do everything in my power for him.* **3.** *nc* control; authority. *Does he have the power to arrest anyone? I have him in my power.* **4.** *nc* special kind of ability. *He is losing his powers of reasoning.* **5.** *nc* person, department, country etc having authority: *the great world powers.* **6.** *nu* energy; force: *a mill driven by water power.* **7.** *nc* (mathematics) number of times a number is multiplied by itself: *X to the fourth power* (X^4). **8.** *nu* ability of a telescope or microscope etc to magnify: *a high-powered telescope.* Also *vt* provide energy or force for: *powered by a new type of engine.*
powerful *adj* having great power or strength: *a powerful country.* **powerfully** *adv*.
powerless *adj* without strength; unable to do something. *I am powerless to help you.*
'power cut occasion when electric power is cut off (e.g. by a strike).
'powerhouse, 'power plant, 'power station place where electrical power is produced.
practice ['præktis] **1.** *nu* doing something many times so as to be able to do it well. *In order to play the piano well, one must have plenty of practice.* **2.** *nu* action of doing something. *How do you think this scheme will work out in practice?* i.e. when it is tried. **3.** *nu* something done regularly as a habit. *It is my practice always to rise early.* **4.** *nc* business of a doctor or lawyer. *Dr Jones has a very good practice.*
practicable ['præktikəbl] *adj* that can be done: *a practicable scheme* i.e. one which will work. (*opp* **impracticable**).
practical ['præktikl] *adj* **1.** concerned with actually doing a thing. *It sounds like a good idea, but there are some practical difficulties.* **2.** useful: *practical suggestion.* **3.** good at doing or making things: *a practical person.* (*opp* **unpractical** in sense **3.**).
practically *adv* **1.** almost; nearly. *He was practically penniless.* **2.** in effect; in action

Practically, his ideas did not work very well. **in practice** in effect; when actually done. **be out of practice** not be able to do something because one has not been doing it many times recently.

practise ['præktis] *vt/i* **1.** do something many times so as to be able to do it well. *If you keep practising, your playing will improve.* **2.** do something regularly as a habit. **3.** work as a doctor, lawyer: *practise medicine/law.*
practised *adj* experienced; having had much practice.
practitioner [præk'tiʃənə*] *nc* person who practises medicine or law: *a medical practitioner.*
practise what one preaches do what one advises other people to do.

pragmatic [præg'mætik] *adj* dealing with events in the way that seems best under the actual circumstances, and not following any general principle or theory.
pragmatist ['prægmətist] *nc* person who does this. **pragmatism** *nu.*

prairie ['prɛəri] *nc* (esp. in North America) large area of flat land with grass but no trees.

praise [preiz] *vt* **1.** say that someone/something is good. *I praised her cooking.* **2.** give honour to God. Also *nu* words praising someone/something.
'praiseworthy *adj* deserving praise: *a praiseworthy cause.*

pram [præm] *nc* (*Brit*) carriage for a baby, pushed by hand. (*US* **baby carriage**)

prance [prɑːns] *vi* **1.** jump about on the hind legs: *a prancing horse.* **2.** move in a lively way. *The children pranced about.*

prank [præŋk] *nc* playful, harmless trick: *a child's prank; play a prank on someone.*

prate [preit] *vt/i* talk foolishly or too much; chatter. *She prated on about unimportant things.*

prattle ['prætl] *vt/i* talk as a child does; talk without thinking. Also *nu* such talk. *Pay no attention to his prattle.*

prawn [prɔːn] *nc* type of shellfish with ten legs which can be eaten.

pray [prei] *vi* **1.** speak to God; direct one's thoughts to God: *pray to God for peace.* **2.** beg someone for something (*o.f.*). **3.** please. *Who is that, pray?* (*o.f.*).
prayer [prɛə*] **1.** *nu* act of praying: *a life devoted to prayer.* **2.** *nc* words used in praying: *a child who knows his prayers.*

pre- [priː] *prefix* before (e.g. **precede; prefix; prejudge**).

preach [priːtʃ] *vt/i* **1.** give a sermon in church. **2.** give advice to others on religious matters; earnestly advise people to do something. **preacher** *nc.*
practise what one preaches see **practise.**

preamble [pri'æmbl] *nc* introduction to something said or written.

precarious [pri'kɛəriəs] *adj* dangerous; uncertain: *a precarious existence* i.e. living in such a way that nothing is certain. **precariously** *adv.* **precariousness** *nu.*

precaution [pri'kɔːʃən] *nc/u* care taken to prevent something unpleasant happening: *take precautions against fire.* **precautionary** [pri'kɔːʃənri] *adj.*

precede [pri'siːd] *vt/i* come or go before. *The king was preceded by his nobles. The Greek civilization preceded the Roman one.*
precedence ['presidns] *nu* greater importance. *This problem should be discussed first, as it takes precedence over all the others.*
precedent ['presidnt] *nc* something which has been done before, which can now be taken as an example or rule. *If he is allowed to do this, it will be a precedent for others.*

precept ['priːsept] *nc* rule for behaviour.

precinct ['priːsiŋkt] *nc* **1.** land around an official or religious building, or enclosed shopping area: *the precincts of the school; shopping precinct.* **2.** (*US*) official area within a boundary: *a police precinct.*
precincts *npl* boundaries: *the precincts of the town.*

precious ['preʃəs] *adj* **1.** of great value. *Gold is a precious metal.* **2.** very dear to one; much loved. **preciously** *adv.* **preciousness** *nu.*

precipice ['presipis] *nc* very steep cliff or face of a rock, mountain etc. *The climber fell over a precipice.*

precipitate [pri'sipiteit] *vt* **1.** make something happen at once, or more quickly than it might have done. *The killing of the prime minister precipitated a war.* **2.** throw down (*o.f.*). **3.** (chemistry) separate a solid matter from a liquid solution. **4.** (physics etc) form from vapour in the form of drops, rain etc. Also *nc/u* that which is precipitated (in senses **3.** and **4.**). Also [pri'sipitət] *adj* done very quickly; done without thinking carefully: *a precipitate departure/decision etc.*
precipitately *adv.*
precipitation [prisipi'teiʃən] *nc/u* **1.** (usu.) fall of rain, hail, sleet or snow. **2.** act of hurrying; sudden action.

precipitous [pri'sipitəs] *adj* **1.** very steep. **2.** hurried; too hurried: *a precipitous action.*
precipitously *adv.*

précis ['preisiː] *nc* main ideas of a speech, article, passage etc written down in shorter form. Also *vt* make shorter in this way.
Note: the *pl* form of this word is also written as *précis*, but it is pronounced ['preisiːz].

precise [pri'sais] *adj* **1.** exact; without mistakes. *He gave a precise description of the thief.* **2.** careful about details: *a very precise worker.* (*opp* **imprecise**).
precisely *adv* (often used when agreeing with someone) just so; exactly.
precision [pri'siʒən] *nu* exactness.

preclude [pri'kluːd] *vt* make impossible; prevent. *The condition of the roads precludes us from driving anywhere tonight.* **preclusion** [pri'kluːʒən] *nu.*

precocious [pri'kouʃəs] *adj* having grown up or developed earlier than usual: *a precocious child* i.e. one that is more advanced than most children of the same age. **precociously** *adv.* **precocity** [pri'kɔsiti] *nu.*

preconceive ['priːkən'siːv] *vt* form an idea or opinion before one has actually seen a thing/person. *Before he went to America, he had all sorts of preconceived ideas about it.*
preconception ['priːkən'sepʃən] *nc* preconceived idea or opinion.

precursor [priː'kəːsə*] *nc* someone/something which comes before something else, as a sign of it; forerunner.

predatory ['predətəri] *adj* **1.** in the habit of, or connected with, stealing: *predatory shopkeepers; predatory habits.* **2.** living by killing other animals: *a predatory bird.*

predecessor ['priːdisesə*] *nc* person who had a job or position before another person.

predestine [priː'destin] *vt* (usu. with reference to fate or God) decide in advance. *He believed that the time of his death was predestined* i.e. that he could do nothing to avoid dying at a certain time. **predestination** [pri:desti'neiʃən] *nu*.

predetermine [pri:di'tə:min] *vt* decide before an event occurs. **predetermined** *adj*. **predetermination** [pri:ditə:mi'neiʃən] *nu*.

predicament [pri'dikəmənt] *nc* awkward situation that is difficult to get out of.

predicate[1] ['predikət] *nc* part of a sentence which says something about the subject (e.g. in the sentence *The man is busy today*, the predicate is *is busy today*).

predicative [pri'dikətiv] *adj* which must be part of the predicate: *predicative adjective* i.e. an adjective like *afraid, alive etc.*

predicate[2] ['predikeit] *vt* say that something is real or true. *We must predicate all men to be equal/that all men are equal*.

predict [pri'dikt] *vt* say that something will happen. *He predicted a war in the next few years/He predicted that war would break out in the next few years*.

prediction *nc/u* **1.** act of predicting. **2.** something that has been predicted.

predilection [pri:di'lekʃən] *nc* liking for something (more than something else). *I have a predilection for oranges*.

predispose ['pri:dis'pouz] *vt* make someone likely to be affected by something when it happens. *His education predisposed him to accept new ideas*. **predisposition** ['pri:dispə'ziʃən] *nc/u*.

predominant [pri'dɔminənt] *adj* bigger, stronger, more noticeable etc than others: *the predominant number; the predominant feature*. **predominantly** *adv*. **predominance** *nu*.

predominate [pri'dɔmineit] *vi* be predominant. *John predominated in the discussion*.

pre-eminent [pri:'eminənt] *adj* most outstanding; best. **pre-eminently** *adv*. **pre-eminence** *nu*.

pre-empt [pri:'emt] *vt* act first and so prevent one's opponent or some other person from taking further action. **pre-emptive** *adj*. **pre-emption** *nu*.

preen [pri:n] *vt* **1.** smooth and arrange feathers with the beak. *The bird was preening itself/its feathers*. **2.** show that one is proud of one's dress etc. *She was preening herself in front of a mirror*.

prefabricate ['pri:'fæbrikeit] *vt* (with reference to buildings) manufacture parts in a factory, ready to put together at the building site.

preface ['prefəs] *nc* note by an author at the beginning of a book. Also *vt* begin a speech etc with some remarks. **prefatory** ['prefətəri] *adj*.

prefect ['pri:fekt] *nc* **1.** pupil who is put in authority over other pupils. **2.** government official in ancient Rome or in France and some other countries. **prefectorial** [pri:fek'tɔ:riəl] *adj*.

prefer [pri'fə:*] *vt* **1.** like better. *I prefer the country to the town. I prefer to resign rather than obey his orders*. **2.** put forward. *He preferred the documents to the council* (*o.f.*). **3.** give someone a better job (*o.f.*). *past* **preferred.**

preferable ['prefərəbl] *adj* better; to be preferred.

preferably *adv* by choice. *You can phone me any time, but preferably in the morning*.

preference ['prefərns] **1.** *nc/u* act of preferring: *have a preference for meat rather than fish*. **2.** *nc* something that is liked better, given better treatment etc: *state one's preference; preference stock* i.e. shares on which a dividend is paid before the ordinary shares.

preferential [prefə'renʃl] *adj* giving or receiving preference: *preferential treatment*.

preferment *nu* giving or receiving of a higher post (esp. in the church).

for preference *adv* preferably.

prefix ['pri:fiks] *nc* group of letters which, when put in front of a word, can change or add to its meaning (e.g. the prefix **mis-**, found in words like **misbehave, misinform etc**). Also *vt* put before; add something at the beginning. *He prefixed a few words of welcome to his speech*.

pregnant ['pregnənt] *adj* **1.** (of woman) having a child in the womb. **2.** full of meaning: *a pregnant remark*. **pregnancy** *nc/u*.

prehensile [pri:'hensail] *adj* able to seize and hold: *the prehensile tail of a monkey*.

prehistoric ['pri:his'tɔrik] *adj* belonging to the time before recorded history i.e. before events were written down: *prehistoric man*.

prejudge ['pri:'dʒʌdʒ] *vt* come to an opinion before knowing the facts: *prejudge an issue*.

prejudice ['predʒudis] *nc/u* opinion formed before looking at the facts. *Some people have a prejudice against all foreigners*. Also *vt* **1.** fill someone with prejudice: *be prejudiced against someone/something*. **2.** cause harm to. *This scandal may prejudice your career*.

prejudiced *adj*. (*opp* **unprejudiced**).

prejudicial [predʒu'diʃl] *adj* harmful to.

to the prejudice of harmful to: *to the prejudice of someone's chances*.

prelate ['prelət] *nc* clergyman of a high rank (e.g. a bishop).

preliminary [pri'liminəri] *adj* coming before something; preparing for something: *preliminary examination*. Also *nc* preliminary action, event etc.

prelude ['prelju:d] *nc* event, action, piece of music etc which comes before another and introduces it.

premature ['premətʃuə*] *adj* too soon; done or happening before the proper time: *a premature decision*. **prematurely** *adv*.

premeditate [pri:'mediteit] *vt* plan or think over something before doing it: *a premeditated murder*. **premeditation** [pri:medi'teiʃən] *nu*.

premier ['premiə*] *adj* first; chief: *of premier importance*. Also *nc* prime minister; head of government.

première [premi'ɛə*] *nc* first performance of a play, film etc.

premise ['premis] *nc* statement which is taken to be true and from which certain conclusions are drawn.

premises *npl* house or building, including the land etc belonging to it.

premium ['pri:miəm] *nc* **1.** amount paid in or for insurance. *I have insured my house for £5,000, at a premium of only £10 per year*. **2.** special payment.

at a premium 1. for more than the usual price, or original price. **2.** very much wanted and difficult to buy or find; in short supply.

premonition [premə'niʃən] *nc* feeling that something (usu. something unpleasant) is going to happen: *a premonition of danger*.

preoccupy [pri:'ɔkjupai] *vt* take up so much of someone's attention that he does not notice what is going on around him: *look preoccupied; preoccupied by/with family troubles*.

preoccupation [priːɔkju'peiʃən] *nc* something that takes up all one's attention.

preordain ['priːɔː'dein] *vt* decide in advance. *Many say that everything that happens on earth has been preordained by God.*

prep [prep] *nu* preparation for school lessons; homework. (*informal*).

'prep school see **prepare.**

prepare [pri'pɛə*] *vt/i* get ready; make ready: *prepare a meal; prepare to leave; prepare for someone's visit; be prepared to* i.e. be willing to.

preparedness *nu* state of being prepared.

preparation [prepə'reiʃən] **1.** *nu* preparing. *The meeting will require a lot of preparation.* **2.** *nc* medicine, food etc which has been specially prepared.

preparations *npl* things done to prepare for something. *They are making tremendous preparations for the president's visit.*

preparatory [pri'pærətəri] *adj* for getting someone/something ready: *preparatory steps; preparatory school* i.e. one which prepares pupils for a higher school (usu. for a public school).

preponderate [pri'pɔndəreit] *vi* be greater in number, weight, importance etc. **preponderance** [pri'pɔndərns] *nu.*

preponderant [pri'pɔndərnt] *adj* greater in number etc. *In this area, English-speaking people are preponderant.* **preponderantly** *adv.*

preposition [prepə'ziʃən] *nc* word used to show how one word is related to another (e.g. *to, by, with, from etc* can be used as prepositions). **prepositional** *adj.*

prepossessing [priːpə'zesiŋ] *adj* give one a good feeling or impression about someone/something: *have a prepossessing manner.* (*opp* **unprepossessing**). **prepossession** *nc.*

preposterous [pri'pɔstərəs] *adj* foolish; completely against reason: *a preposterous idea.* **preposterously** *adv.*

prerequisite [pri'rekwizit] *nc* thing required before one can have or do something else. *A good pass in the school certificate is a prerequisite for (the) university.* Also *adj.*

prerogative [pri'rɔgətiv] *nc* special power or right which no one else has. *It was the prerogative of the king to pardon criminals.*

presage ['presidʒ] *nc* **1.** sign, event etc taken as a warning. **2.** feeling that something bad is about to happen. Also *vt* give warning of.

prescient ['presiənt] *adj* knowing what will happen in the future. **prescience** *nu.*

prescribe [pri'skraib] *vt/i* **1.** order the use of: *prescribe medicine for an illness; prescribed books* i.e. books which must be read by students. **2.** order with authority. *The government prescribes laws to be obeyed by its citizens.*

prescription [pri'skripʃən] **1.** *nu* act of prescribing. **2.** *nc* something prescribed. **3.** *nc* written note of a doctor's instructions for making up a medicine; the medicine itself.

prescriptive [pri'skriptiv] *adj* concerned with saying what must be done: *prescriptive rules.*

present[1] ['preznt] *adj* **1.** in the place being spoken of. *Was James present? He is not in the present company* i.e. not among those present. **2.** at this time. *She cannot save on her present wages.*

presently *adv* **1.** soon. *He will be here presently.* **2.** (mainly *US*) now. *He is presently living in New York.*

presence *nu* fact or state of being present. *Don't mention this in John's presence* i.e. while John is present.

at present now. *He is with Jones at present.*

the present **1.** the present time. **2.** the present tense.

for the present in the meantime. *We shall not need any more for the present.*

presence of mind ability to think quickly and sensibly in dangerous or unexpected circumstances. *Thanks to his presence of mind, the children were saved.*

present[2] [pri'zent] *vt* **1.** give to someone. *We presented him with a cheque/We presented a cheque to him.* **2.** bring before someone. *They presented their petition to the Governor. The school is presenting a play* i.e. giving a public performance. **3.** introduce to someone (esp. someone of high rank). *He was presented to the Queen.* Also ['preznt] *nc* something given: *birthday present.*

presentable *adj* suitable to be seen: *look presentable.* (*opp* **unpresentable**).

presentation [prezn'teiʃən] *nc/u* **1.** giving of something to someone (esp. at a public ceremony). **2.** presenting or being presented (in senses **2.** and **3.**).

pre'sent 'arms hold a rifle upright in front of one (e.g. to show honour to someone).

presentiment [pri'zentimənt] *nc* feeling that something (esp. something bad) is about to happen: *a presentiment of evil.*

preserve [pri'zəːv] *vt* **1.** keep safe, healthy, free from danger etc: *preserve one's life.* **2.** keep from going bad: *preserve food.* **3.** protect fish, animals etc from being unlawfully hunted or killed. Also *nc* **1.** place where fish, animals etc are protected: *a game preserve.* (Usu. **reserve**). **2.** cooked fruit which is sweetened and sealed; jam.

preservation [prezə'veiʃən] *nu* **1.** state of being preserved: *the preservation of peace/one's health etc.* **2.** condition of something which is being preserved. *The old house was in a good state of preservation.*

preservative [pri'zəːvətiv] *nc* something which prevents things from going bad or decaying. *Most tins of meat contain preservatives.* Also *adj.*

preside [pri'zaid] *vi* control; have charge of: *preside at a meeting; preside over a large business.*

president ['prezidnt] *nc* **1.** head of a state (esp. a republic). **2.** head of a business, college, department etc.

Note: President (in sense **1.**) can be used as a title instead of Mr (e.g. *President Kennedy*).

presidency *nc* **1.** office of president: *a candidate for the presidency.* **2.** time during which someone is president.

presidential [prezi'denʃl] *adj* connected with the presidency: *a presidential election.*

presidium [pri'zidiəm] *nc* Russian government committee.

press[1] [pres] *vt/i* **1.** push something against something else. *He pressed the bell* i.e. with his finger. *He pressed his hand against the door. These two pieces of paper will stick if you press them together.* **2.** put weight on top of something. *He gets the juice from the grapes by pressing them. He was pressing his jacket* i.e. making it smooth by using an iron. **3.** push against something. *The people were pressing so hard against the President's car that they almost overturned it.* **4.** hold tightly. *He pressed my hand warmly as he said goodbye. When he at last found his daughter, he pressed her to him.* **5.** attack;

stay close to. *The enemy army is pressing us hard.* **6.** demand something; insist on something. *He is pressing me for an answer. He pressed the money on me* i.e. forced me to accept it.
pressing *adj* demanding attention or an answer now. *This matter is very pressing* i.e. urgent. **pressingly** *adv.*
'press-gang *nc* (in former times) group of people who forced men to join the army or navy against their will.
'press-gang *vt* **1.** force someone to join the army or navy (*o.f.*). **2.** force someone to do anything unwillingly. *He was press-ganged into helping us.*
be pressed for be short of. *I'm rather pressed for time.*
press forward/on go on; hurry on. *If we want to arrive before it is dark, we must press on.*
time presses there is not much time.

press² [pres] *nc* **1.** act of pressing: *give one's clothes a quick press* i.e. with an iron. **2.** machine for pressing. *He put the grapes into the wine press.* **3.** machine for printing. **4.** business firm which prints books etc. **5.** crowd. **6.** (mainly *US*) cupboard with shelves for keeping books, clothes etc.
the press newspapers or journalists: *defend the freedom of the press.*
'press conference meeting which has been arranged between someone of importance and newspaper reporters.
'press cutting something cut out of a newspaper and kept.

pressure ['preʃə*] *nu* **1.** force or weight of one thing pushing against another. *The pressure of my finger against the lid was enough to open it. What is the pressure of air in your tyres?* **2.** trouble or strain of something. *He could not come to the party because of pressure of work* i.e. he was too busy.
pressurized *adj* made so that the pressure of the air inside can be controlled: *an aeroplane with a pressurized cabin.*
'pressure cooker special kind of pot which uses steam under pressure to cook food more quickly.
'pressure group group of people using political pressure to further their own interests.
atmospheric pressure pressure of the atmosphere on the earth.

prestige [pres'ti:ʒ] *nu* power; respect; admiration. *Winning the first prize in the sports meeting brought him a lot of prestige.*

presume [pri'zju:m] *vt/i* **1.** take something for granted without proof; take it that something is true or that something is allowed. *Everyone should be presumed innocent until it is proved that he is guilty.* **2.** dare; be bold enough to. *I would not presume to question him.*
presumption [pri'zʌmpʃən] **1.** *nc* something taken to be true. *The police are searching the area, on the presumption that the thief is still there.* **2.** *nu* boldness of behaviour. *It was sheer presumption for him to come when he was not invited.*
presumptuous [pri'zʌmpʃəs] *adj* too bold; ill-mannered. **presumptuously** *adv.*
presume upon something take advantage of unfairly: *presume upon someone's good nature.*

presuppose [pri:sə'pouz] *vt* **1.** take for granted in advance. **2.** require as a necessary condition. *A game of football presupposes a field big enough to play it on.*
presupposition [pri:sʌpə'ziʃən] *nc* something presupposed.

pretend [pri'tend] *vt/i* **1.** make oneself appear to be something or to be doing something: *pretend to be surprised.* **2.** say or claim falsely. *He pretends to like you, but he doesn't really.* **3.** claim that one has something (usu. to avoid difficulty or danger): *pretend sickness.* **4.** say that one has a claim to. *He pretended to the throne of England* i.e. he said he should be king.
pretender *nc* person who claims that he should be king etc.
pretence [pri'tens] (*US* **pretense**) **1.** *nu* make-believe; pretending: *under the pretence of friendship.* **2.** *nc* excuse; false claim.
pretension [pri'tenʃən] **1.** *nc* claim. *I have no pretensions to being an athlete.* **2.** *nu* state of being pretentious.
pretentious [pri'tenʃəs] *adj* pretending to be, or showing that one pretends to be, clever or important etc: *a pretentious speech.* (*opp* **unpretentious**). **pretentiously** *adv.* **pretentiousness** *nu.*

preterite ['pretərit] *nc* simple past tense (e.g. *he fell*).

pretext ['pri:tekst] *nc* false reason given for doing something. *He was absent from school on the pretext that he was ill.*

pretty ['priti] *adj* pleasing; attractive (but not extremely beautiful or grand): *pretty dress; pretty girl.* Also *intensifier* rather. *He's pretty good at sports.* (*informal* in this sense). **prettily** *adv.* **prettiness** *nu.*
a pretty penny see **penny.**

prevail [pri'veil] *vi* **1.** win; be successful. *He prevailed over/against his enemies.* **2.** be common or usual. *This custom prevails over the whole area.* **3.** persuade. *I prevailed upon him to join us* i.e. I persuaded him to join us.
prevailing *adj*: *prevailing winds.*
prevalent ['prevəlnt] *adj* generally used; generally found: *a prevalent idea/fashion etc.*
prevalence *nu*: *The speaker talked about the prevalence of violence in our cities.*

prevaricate [pri'værikeit] *vi* try to hide the truth by not answering questions truthfully or clearly. **prevarication** [priværi'keiʃən] *nc/u.*

prevent [pri'vent] *vt* **1.** stop something from happening: *prevent an accident.* **2.** stop someone from doing something. *I prevented him from hitting the child.* **prevention** *nu.*
preventable *adj* that can be avoided: *preventable accidents.*
preventive *adj* that prevents: *preventive medicines* i.e. to prevent illness.

preview ['pri:vju:] *nc* private performance of a film or play, before it is shown to the public. Also *vt.*

previous ['pri:viəs] *adj* earlier; coming before: *a previous meeting.* **previously** *adv.*
previous to *prep* before. *Previous to coming here, I worked in London.*

prey [prei] *nu* animal or bird hunted or killed by another one. *The lion was hunting for its prey. Small animals are sometimes the prey of eagles. An eagle is a bird of prey* i.e. it lives by killing other birds or animals.
prey upon something **1.** hunt other animals etc as prey. **2.** trouble; injure.
prey upon one's mind continually cause one to fear. *Fear of being killed preyed upon his mind.*
be a prey to be troubled by: *be a prey to fears and doubts.*

price [prais] *nc* **1.** money for which a thing can be bought or sold: *the price of a book.* **2.** reward offered for capturing someone: *a price on his head.* **3.** what must be done or suffered for something: *the price of freedom.* Also *vt* put a price on something; ask the price of something.
priceless *adj* of great value.

prick [prik] *vt/i* **1.** make a small hole in something: *prick something with a needle; prick one's finger.* **2.** cause sharp pain. Also *nc* **1.** small hole made by a sharp point. **2.** sharp pain.
prick up one's ears **1.** lift up the ears. *The dog pricked up its ears when its master called it.* **2.** listen carefully. *The children pricked up their ears at the sound of their mother's footsteps.*

prickle ['prikl] *nc* (esp. of a plant, animal etc) sharp point: *the prickles on a thorn.* Also *vt/i* have or cause a painful or stinging feeling.
prickly *adj* **1.** having prickles. **2.** sharp; stinging. **3.** easily angered.
'prickly 'heat red marks on the skin caused by sweating.

pride [praid] *nu* **1.** feeling of pleasure and satisfaction a person has in the things/people connected with him. *He takes great pride in his children's success at school. He looked at his garden with pride.* **2.** high opinion of oneself. *His pride would not allow him to beg for money.* **3.** too high an opinion of oneself. *He was hated because of his pride.* **4.** something one is proud of. *That child is his mother's pride and joy.* see **proud.**
pride oneself upon/on take pride in; be pleased with. *She prided herself on the cleanliness of her house.*

priest [priːst] *nc* person specially chosen to lead prayers and other religious services. (*fem* **priestess** ['priːstis]). **priestly** *adj.*
priesthood *nu* whole body of priests as one group: *enter the priesthood.*

prig [prig] *nc* person who is too pleased with himself, and anxious to show how bad others are. **priggish** *adj.* **priggishly** *adv.*

prim [prim] *adj* very correct and stiff in one's manner or behaviour: *a prim old lady.* **primly** *adv.*

primacy ['praiməsi] *nu* **1.** condition of being first, most important etc. **2.** position or rank of an archbishop.

prima donna ['priːmə'donə] *nc* chief female singer in an opera.

prima facie ['praimə'feiʃi] *adj* in appearance; at first sight. A prima-facie case in a court of law is one which appears to be strong enough to justify continuing the case.

primary ['praiməri] *adj* **1.** first in time: *primary school.* **2.** great in importance: *a primary consideration; of primary importance.*
primarily *adv* firstly; mostly.
the primary colours red, yellow and blue (from which it is believed all other colours can be obtained by mixing in different ways).

primate[1] ['praimit] *nc* archbishop.

primate[2] ['praimeit] *nc* one of the highest classes of animals, containing men, apes, monkeys etc.

prime[1] [praim] *adj* **1.** first in importance; chief: *the Prime Minister; of prime importance.* **2.** very good: *in prime condition.* Also *nu* **1.** best time; best part: *in the prime of life* i.e. when one is fully grown, but not yet old. **2.** first part: *the prime of the year* i.e. springtime.
prime number number which cannot be divided by any other number than itself and 1 (e.g. 2, 5, 17 etc).
be cut off in one's prime die while one is still young and strong.

prime[2] [praim] *vt* **1.** make ready to be used: *prime a gun with powder; prime a pump* i.e. by putting water into it. **2.** give a person the facts, information etc that he may need: *well-primed with facts.*

primer ['praimə*] *nc* first book in a subject used by a child at school.

primeval [prai'miːvl] *adj* belonging to the earliest times; very, very old: *primeval forests.*

primitive ['primitiv] *adj* **1.** of the earliest times. *In primitive times, people lived in caves.* **2.** very simple or crude: *a primitive kind of tool.* **primitively** *adv.*

primordial [prai'mɔːdiəl] *adj* of the very earliest times: *primordial life on earth.*

primrose ['primrouz] *nc* small pale yellow flower which blooms in early spring in cool northern areas. Also *adj* pale yellow.

prince [prins] *nc* **1.** son of a king or emperor. **2.** person who rules a small state.
princess [prin'ses] *nc* **1.** daughter of a king or emperor. **2.** wife of a prince.
princely *adj* **1.** of or for a prince. **2.** fit for a prince; wonderful: *a princely reward.*

principal ['prinsipl] *adj* most important; chief. *Manchester is one of the principal towns in England.* Also *nc* **1.** head of a college or school. **2.** amount of money put into a business, bank etc on which more money (called **interest**) is earned.
principally *adv* chiefly.

principality [prinsi'pæliti] *nc* small country, ruled by a prince.

principle ['prinsipl] *nc* **1.** important truth or law on which other things depend: *the principles of science; principle of free speech.* **2.** something that one believes in or follows as a rule. *Stealing is against my principles.*
-principled *adj* used to form adjectives to show that a person has a certain kind of belief or behaviour: *a high-principled man.*

print[1] [print] *vt* **1.** press marks on paper or on cloth using ink or dye. *This page in the newspaper has been badly printed.* **2.** make books etc in this way. *They printed a hundred copies of the book.* **3.** make words or letters so that they look like print instead of handwriting. *Please print your names so that they can be read clearly.* **4.** make a photograph from a negative film.

print[2] [print] **1.** *nu* words or letters made by printing. *Can you read the small print at the bottom of the page?* **2.** *nc* picture or design made by printing. *This is a beautiful print which I bought yesterday.* **3.** *nc* photograph made from a negative. **4.** *nc* (often used to make compound nouns) mark made by pressing on a surface. *You can see the children's footprints in the sand.* **5.** *nc/u* cloth with a design printed on it.
printable *adj* suitable for printing. (*opp* **unprintable**).
printer *nc* **1.** person who works at printing books etc. **2.** person who owns a factory where books etc are printed.
'printing press machine for printing books etc.
in print printed and on sale. *Is that book still in print?*

out of print no longer sold, because there are no more copies. *The book you want is now out of print.*

prior[1] ['praiə*] *adj* earlier. *I cannot come as I have a prior engagement.*
prior to before. *What did you do prior to coming here?*

prior[2] ['praiə*] *nc* **1.** head of a religious house. **2.** monk who is next to an abbot in rank.
prioress ['praiəris] *nc* woman prior.
priory *nc* religious house run by a prior or prioress.

priority [prai'ɔriti] **1.** *nc/u* right or need to receive attention before other people/things. *You must give this matter priority* i.e. you must deal with this matter before anything else. **2.** *nc* person/thing given priority. Also *adj*: *a priority matter.*

prise, prize [praiz] *vt* open something by force (usu. with a lever of some kind). *I prised open/up/off the lid of the box.*

prism ['prizəm] *nc* **1.** block with three (or more) sides as shown in the illustration. **2.** block of glass that breaks up white light into different colours.

prisms (*def 1*)

prismatic [priz'mætik] *adj* **1.** of or like a prism. **2.** very bright; having different colours.

prison ['prizn] *nc* **1.** building where people who have broken the law are kept. **2.** place where someone is kept against his will.
prisoner *nc* **1.** person kept in a prison. **2.** soldier who is captured in a war: *be taken prisoner.*

pristine ['pristi:n] *adj* ancient, original, and good or beautiful: *pristine splendour.*

private ['praivit] *adj* **1.** for or of one person, or a few people, not people in general: *a private room; a private letter* i.e. one which is about personal matters, not business. **2.** secret; kept hidden: *private information.* **3.** not in an official position: *private citizens.* **4.** of the lowest rank in the army: *private soldier.* Also *nc* private soldier.
privately *adv.* **privacy** ['praivisi] *nu.*
in private not in front of other people: *talk to someone in private.*
a person of private means person who has enough money not to have to work.

privateer [praivə'tiə*] *nc* (in former times) ship which did not belong to the government, but was allowed by it to attack enemy ships.

privation [prai'veiʃən] *nc/u* **1.** lack of things that are necessary to life, or that make life comfortable. *When he was poor, he suffered many privations.* **2.** loss.

privet ['privit] *nu* type of bush (often used as a hedge in gardens).

privilege ['privilidʒ] *nc/u* special right or advantage belonging only to a certain person or group of people.
privileged *adj* having, or having been given, a privilege or privileges.

privy ['privi] *adj* secret; private. Also *nc* lavatory. (both *o.f.*).
'privy 'council group of people appointed to advise a king or queen.
privy to having private or secret knowledge of something (*o.f.*).

prize[1] [praiz] *nc* **1.** something given to a person because he has shown that he is better than others: *win first prize in a race/examination etc.* **2.** something that is worth working for. **3.** enemy ship or its cargo captured at sea (*o.f.* in sense **3.**). Also *adj* given a prize; given as a prize: *prize cattle* i.e. cattle which have won prizes at an agricultural exhibition; *prize money.* Also *vt* value something highly.
'prize fight *nc* fight between two men which people pay money to see. **prize fighter** *nc.* (both *o.f.*).
'prize ring *nc/u* **1.** area cut off by ropes, used for prize fighting. **2.** prize fighting.

prize[2] [praiz] *vt* see **prise.**

pro[1] [prou] *nc* short informal form of **professional** (usu. in sport). *He played amateur tennis, and then turned pro.*

pro-[2] [prou] *prefix* **1.** on the side of (e.g. **pro-British**). **2.** before; forward (e.g. **project**).
pros and cons reasons for and against. *Before we decide, we must weigh up the pros and cons* i.e. consider the reasons for and against.

probable ['prɔbəbl] *adj* likely to happen; likely to be true. *Colder weather is probable.* (*opp* **improbable**). **probably** *adv.*
probability [prɔbə'biliti] **1.** *nu* condition of being likely to happen or likely to be true. *There is not much probability that he will come.* **2.** *nc* something likely to happen or to be true. *The probability is that he is ill.*
in all probability probably; most likely.

probate ['proubit] *nu* examining of a will to see if it has been correctly drawn up. Also *adj* concerned with the examination of wills: *a probate court.*

probation [prou'beiʃən] *nu* **1.** testing of a person, by seeing for a certain period of time whether he is fit to keep on with a job etc. *After a period of probation, he was appointed to the staff.* **2.** (in a legal sense) system by which a person who has committed only one crime is not sent to prison as long as he does not break the law again: *be on probation.* **probationary** *adj.*
probationer *nc* person on probation.
pro'bation officer person who reports on the behaviour of people (esp. young people) on probation (in sense **2.**).

probe [proub] *nc* **1.** thin piece of metal, blunt at one end, used by doctors to find the depth and direction of a wound etc. **2.** (often with reference to investigation by a spacecraft) investigation; close examination. Also *vt* **1.** examine closely, inquire closely: *probe into someone's secrets.* **2.** examine with a probe (in sense **1.**).

probity ['proubiti] *nu* honesty: *an official of the highest probity.*

problem ['prɔbləm] *nc* difficult decision; difficult question. *This situation presents us with many problems. That's no problem.*
problematic, problematical [prɔblə'mætik(l)] *adj* doubtful; uncertain; difficult. *How this matter will end is problematic.*

procedure [prə'si:dʒə*] *nc/u* **1.** way of doing something: *a new procedure.* **2.** way something has to be done: *legal procedure.*
procedural *adj.*

proceed [prə'si:d] *vi* **1.** go forward (to a place). *The crowd proceeded to the church.* **2.** go on, after having stopped. *Please proceed with what you were doing.* **3.** begin to do something. *The crowd proceeded to attack the building.* **4.** come from; be caused by. **5.** (with **against**) start to carry on a legal action.
proceeds ['prousi:dz] *npl* money got from selling something.
proceeding *nc/u* what is done; way of behaving.
proceedings *npl* **1.** legal action in a court: *start/take proceedings against someone.* **2.** record of things said and decided at a meeting.

process ['prouses] *nc* **1.** number of actions or changes involved when something happens: *the process of getting old* i.e. the changes that take place over a time. **2.** way of manufacturing something: *a new process for making steel.* Also *vt* treat or prepare food etc in some special way: *processed cheese.*
in (the) process of going forward. *A new building is in process of being constructed.*

procession [prə'seʃən] *nc* line of people, cars etc moving slowly forward in an ordered way: *a funeral procession.*

proclaim [prou'kleim] *vt* make something known publicly and officially: *proclaim a public holiday. The young prince was later proclaimed king.*
proclamation [prɔklə'meiʃən] *nc/u* something proclaimed; act of proclaiming.

proclivity [prou'kliviti] *nc* inclination; leaning towards something; liking for something: *a proclivity for dancing/towards laziness.*

procrastinate [prou'kræstineit] *vi* delay; keep putting off until later. **procrastination** [proukræsti'neiʃən] *nu.*

procreate ['proukrieit] *vt* (perform the acts necessary to) produce children etc. **procreation** [proukri'eiʃən] *nu.*

proctor ['prɔktə*] *nc* official in a university etc who keeps order among the students.

procure [prə'kjuə*] *vt* **1.** get, obtain (usu. with difficulty). *This kind of book is difficult to procure.* **2.** get someone for another's sexual pleasure. **procurement** *nu.*
procurable *adj* able to be procured.

prod [prɔd] *vt/i* **1.** push with something pointed: *prod an animal with a stick.* **2.** urge on (esp. lazy people). *past* **prodded.** Also *nc* **1.** act of prodding. **2.** instrument used for prodding.

prodigal ['prɔdigl] *adj* spending too much; wasteful: *be prodigal of one's money/time etc.* Also *nc* prodigal person. **prodigally** *adv.* **prodigality** [prɔdi'gæliti] *nu.*

prodigious [prə'didʒəs] *adj* **1.** very great: *a prodigious amount.* **2.** unusual; wonderful: *a prodigious event.* **prodigiously** *adv.* **prodigiousness** *nu.*

prodigy ['prɔdidʒi] *nc* **1.** someone who is unusually clever, able etc: *a child prodigy.* **2.** something very unusual: *a prodigy of nature* (*o.f.* in sense **2.**).

produce [prə'dju:s] *vt* **1.** make: *a factory that produces cars.* **2.** cause to appear; yield. *A hen produces eggs. Some fields produce maize. He was not able to produce sufficient evidence. Hard work produces success.* **3.** bring a play etc before the public. **4.** (mathematics) make a line etc longer. Also ['prɔdju:s] *nu* things that are produced (esp. from a farm e.g. crops, eggs etc).
producer *nc* **1.** someone who makes goods. **2.** someone who is responsible for bringing a play etc before the public.
product ['prɔdəkt] *nc* **1.** something that is produced: *factory products; farm products.* **2.** number got by multiplying other numbers. *9 is the product of 3 multiplied by 3.*
productive [prə'dʌktiv] *adj.*
production [prə'dʌkʃən] **1.** *nu* act of producing. **2.** *nc* play etc shown before the public.
productivity [prɔdʌk'tiviti] *nu* efficiency with which work is done; amount of work done in a certain time: *increase the productivity of a factory.*

profane [prə'fein] *adj* **1.** showing disrespect to God or religion: *profane language.* **2.** having to do with this world i.e. not with the next. Also *vt* treat holy things with disrespect. **profanely** *adv.* **profaneness** *nu.*
profanity [prə'fæniti] *nc/u* use of bad language; lack of reverence for God.

profess [prə'fes] *vt* **1.** claim (to be someone, or to be able to do something). *I don't profess to be an expert.* **2.** declare, say (that one has something). *I asked him, but he professed ignorance* i.e. said he did not know. *They professed interest in my future.* **3.** state openly (one's beliefs etc): *profess one's loyalty to the state.*
professedly [prə'fesidli] *adv* according to what one says about oneself. *He is professedly an expert on languages.*
profession *nc* **1.** occupation that requires special learning (e.g. law, medicine, teaching etc). **2.** statement of what one believes, feels etc: *a profession of friendship.*

professional [prə'feʃənl] *adj* **1.** connected with a profession. *Doctors and teachers are professional men.* **2.** doing something (esp. sport) for money: *a professional footballer.* **3.** expert; done or made in an expert way: *a professional piece of work.* Also *nc* person who makes a living from an occupation (e.g. sport, music) which others do for pleasure. (*opp* **amateur**).

professor [prə'fesə*] *nc* teacher of the highest rank in a university.
Note: Professor can be used as a title (e.g. *Professor Jones*).

proffer ['prɔfə*] *vt* offer. Also *nc.*

proficient [prə'fiʃənt] *adj* skilled; clever: *proficient in/at speaking English.* **proficiency** *nu.*

profile ['proufail] *nc* **1.** side view (e.g. of someone's face). **2.** edge or outline of something seen against a background. **3.** summary of a person's character and career in a newspaper or on television.

profit ['prɔfit] **1.** *nu* what is gained or obtained from some situation or experience. **2.** *nc* money gained from business: *a company that earns huge profits.* Also *vt/i* **1.** make a gain: *profit from a deal.* **2.** be helped by: *profit by one's mistakes* i.e. learn from one's mistakes.
profitable *adj* bringing profit: *a profitable business.* (*opp* **unprofitable**). **profitably** *adv.*
profiteer [prɔfi'tiə*] *nc* person who makes very large profits by taking advantage of others (e.g. during a war). Also *vi* make large profits in this way.

profligate ['prɔfligit] *adj* **1.** wicked; immoral: *a profligate person; profligate behaviour.* **2.** given to spending too much money; extravagant. Also *nc* profligate person. **profligacy** *nu.*

profound [prə'faund] *adj* **1.** deep: *profound*

sleep. **2.** showing great knowledge; not easily understood: *a profound thinker/book/ mystery etc.*
profoundly *adv* deeply: *be profoundly grateful.* **profundity** [prə'fʌnditi] *nc/u.*
profuse [prə'fju:s] *adj* **1.** very many; abundant. *Please accept my profuse apologies.* **2.** giving or spending freely: *be profuse with one's money.* **profusely** *adv.*
profusion [prə'fju:ʒən] *nu* great quantity; plenty. *Wild flowers were in profusion everywhere.*
progeny ['prɔdʒini] *nu* children; descendants.
prognosticate [prɔg'nɔstikeit] *vt* foretell; say what will happen in the future. **prognostication** [prɔgnɔsti'keiʃən] *nc/u.*
programme ['prougræm] (*US* **program**) *nc* **1.** list of items or events for a concert, play etc. **2.** plan of what is to be done: *a programme of instruction.* Also *vt* give a set of instructions to a computer: *program(me) a computer.*
programmer *nc* person who does this.
programmed learning method of teaching, in which the subject to be taught is divided into a number of very small points, each of which the student has to understand before he passes on to the next one.
progress ['prougres] *nu* **1.** advance; going forward: *the progress of civilization; work in progress.* **2.** improvement: *show some progress.* Also [prə'gres] *vi* make progress.
progression [prə'greʃən] *nu* moving onward: *different methods of progression.*
progressive [prə'gresiv] *adj* **1.** going on to new things; advancing: *a progressive country; progressive ideas.* **2.** moving forward: *a progressive movement.* **3.** increasing by regular amounts: *a progressive scale of taxation.* **4.** (grammar) continuous: *the progressive tense* (e.g. he was walking). Also *nc* person who wants progress. (*opp* **retrogressive** in senses **1.**, **2.** and **3.**).
prohibit [prə'hibit] *vt* forbid; stop someone from doing something or something from being done. *Smoking prohibited.*
prohibitive *adj* costing so much that one cannot pay: *prohibitive prices.*
prohibition [prouhi'biʃən] *nc/u* **1.** act of forbidding. **2.** law against the making or selling of liquor.
project ['prɔdʒekt] *nc* plan; scheme: *a project for making the desert fertile.* Also [prə'dʒekt] *vt/i* **1.** make plans for: *project a new housing scheme.* **2.** stick out from the surrounding surface: *a nail projecting from the wall.* **3.** make pictures etc show on a surface: *project films onto a screen.*
projection [prə'dʒekʃən] **1.** *nu* act of projecting. **2.** *nc* something which sticks out. **3.** *nc* system of showing on a flat surface something which is not flat: *a map projection.*
projectile [prə'dʒektail] *nc* something to be shot forward (e.g. a stone or bullet).
projector [prou'dʒektə*] *nc* instrument for projecting films onto a screen.
proletariat [prouli'tɛəriət] *nu* all the working people.
proletarian *nc* member of the proletariat. Also *adj.*
prolific [prə'lifik] *adj* producing much or many: *a prolific author* i.e. one who writes many books.
prolix ['prouliks] *adj* using, containing too many words: *a prolix speaker/book etc.*
prologue ['proulɔg] *nc* **1.** speech said at the beginning of a play. **2.** introduction to a book. **3.** any event which starts something.
prolong [prə'lɔŋ] *vt* make longer.
prolonged *adj* very long: *a prolonged speech.* **prolongation** [proulɔŋ'geiʃən] *nc/u.*
promenade [prɔmə'nɑ:d] *nc* **1.** walk taken for pleasure. **2.** wide road that is used for walking up and down (esp. by the sea). Also *vt/i* walk about for pleasure.
prominent ['prɔminənt] *adj* **1.** well-known; important: *prominent politician.* **2.** easily seen; standing out: *prominent hill.*
prominently *adv.*
prominence **1.** *nu* fame; importance: *give prominence to something.* **2.** *nc* some place or thing that stands out.
promiscuous [prə'miskjuəs] *adj* **1.** having love affairs with many different people: *a promiscuous person.* **2.** mixed-up; not sorted out: *a promiscuous collection of things.* **promiscuously** *adv.* **promiscuity** [prɔmis'kju:iti] *nu.*
promise ['prɔmis] *vt/i* **1.** say that one will do something, give something etc. *We promised them that we would come. You must promise not to mention it. I promised him a book.* **2.** cause one to hope (that something will happen). *It promises to be fine tomorrow.* Also **1.** *nc* act of promising something, either in speech or writing: *make/keep/ break a promise.* **2.** *nu* something that causes one to have hopes of excellence. *His work shows much promise.*
promising *adj* likely to do well or to turn out well: *a promising pupil.*
promissory ['prɔmisəri] *adj* usu. in **promissory note** i.e. written promise to pay a certain amount of money to a certain person at a certain time.
promontory ['prɔməntri] *nc* high point of land standing out into the sea.
promote [prə'mout] *vt* **1.** raise to a higher position: *promote someone from clerk to manager.* **2.** help something develop or increase: *promote peace/education etc.* **3.** start something (esp. a business).
promoter *nc* person who helps to start a business. **promotion** *nc/u.*
prompt[1] [prɔmpt] *adj* quick; without delay: *prompt service; prompt to obey commands.* **promptly** *adv.* **promptness, promptitude** ['prɔmptitju:d] *nu.*
prompt[2] [prɔmpt] *vt* **1.** cause a person to do something. *What prompted you to ask that question? His actions were prompted by fear.* **2.** remind an actor of the words he has to say.
prompter *nc* person who prompts actors.
promulgate ['prɔməlgeit] *vt* **1.** announce officially; make publicly known: *promulgate a new law.* **2.** spread widely: *promulgate one's beliefs.* **promulgation** [prɔməl'geiʃən] *nu.*
prone [proun] *adj* **1.** lying face down. *He was lying prone on the ground.* **2.** inclined: *be prone to anger* i.e. easily angered.
prong [prɔŋ] *nc* thin, pointed end of something (e.g. a fork).
pronoun ['prounaun] *nc* word used in place of a noun (e.g. *I, he, which, this etc*).
pronominal [prou'nɔminl] *adj.*
pronounce [prə'nauns] *vt/i* **1.** make the sound of a word etc. *Try to pronounce your words clearly.* **2.** make an official announcement. *The judge pronounced sentence on the prisoner.* **3.** give an opinion. *I don't know enough to pronounce on this matter.*
pronounceable [prə'naunsəbl] *adj* that can

be pronounced. (*opp* **unpronounceable**).

pronounced *adj* strongly marked; easily noticed; clear: *a pronounced dislike of dogs.*

pronouncement *nc* official statement.

pronunciation [prənʌnsi'eiʃən] *nc/u* **1.** someone's way of pronouncing; way in which a language is pronounced: *improve one's pronunciation; the pronunciation of English.* **2.** way of pronouncing a word: *a word with two pronunciations.*

proof [pru:f] *nc/u* **1.** way of showing that something is true. *Have you any proof that he is a thief?* **2.** way of finding out if something is true. *The scientist put his theories to the proof.* **3.** first printing of a book etc, which can be corrected before other copies are made. Also *adj* able to give safety against; able to withstand: *proof against temptation; rainproof coat; foolproof scheme* i.e. so good that even a foolish or careless person could follow it. see **prove.**

prop[1] [prɔp] *nc* **1.** support used to hold something up: *pit props* i.e. pieces of wood or metal which keep up the roof of a mine. **2.** person who helps or supports something/somebody. *His son was the prop of his old age.* Also *vt* help; keep in position. *The house was propped up with planks of wood. past* **propped.**

prop[2] [prɔp] *nc* (often *pl*) thing used on the stage when a play is being performed (but not including the scenery) (short form of **property**).

propaganda [prɔpə'gændə] *nu* **1.** organized attempts (e.g. by a government) to spread certain beliefs. **2.** beliefs that are spread in this way. **propagandist** *nc.*

propagate ['prɔpəgeit] *vt* **1.** increase the number of plants or animals by reproduction. **2.** spread news, opinions etc: *propagate scientific ideas.*

propagation [prɔpə'geiʃən] *nu* propagating: *the propagation of new ideas.*

propel [prə'pel] *vt* push forward or onward. *past* **propelled.** see **propulsion.**

propeller *nc* set of rotating blades used for driving a plane or ship.

propensity [prə'pensiti] *nc* tendency to a certain kind of behaviour: *have a propensity to laziness* i.e. be naturally lazy; *a propensity to steal; a propensity for talking a lot.*

proper ['prɔpə*] *adj* **1.** correct; right; suitable. *You must learn the proper way to behave. A classroom is not the proper place for a football match.* (*opp* **improper**). **2.** in the strict sense of the word. *Spiders are not insects proper* i.e. they should not be called insects. **3.** complete. *It was a proper waste of time.* (*informal* in sense **3.**).

properly *adv* **1.** correctly: *do something properly.* **2.** strictly: *properly speaking* i.e. to be exact.

proper noun noun that is always written with a capital letter (e.g. *Mary; London*).

property ['prɔpəti] *nc/u* **1.** things which are owned (esp. land and buildings). *That pen is my property. The price of property has risen greatly* i.e. the price of land or buildings. **2.** special quality that a thing has. *Steel is a metal with the property of great strength.*

properties *npl* things used on the stage when a play is being performed (but not including the scenery) (Also **props**).

prophecy ['prɔfisi] *nc/u* power of telling what is going to happen; statement about the future.

prophesy ['prɔfisai] *vt* say what is going to happen. *He prophesied that there would be a great famine within seven years.*

prophet ['prɔfit] *nc* **1.** person who teaches what he says has been directly revealed to him by God. **2.** person who can foretell the future. (*fem* **prophetess** ['prɔfitis]).

prophetic [prə'fetik] *adj* connected with prophecy or a prophet. **prophetically** *adv.*

prophylactic [prɔfi'læktik] *nc* medicine that protects people from disease. Also *adj.*

propinquity [prə'piŋkwiti] *nu* nearness (esp. of time, place or personal relationship).

propitiate [prə'piʃieit] *vt* lessen the anger of; gain the favour of. **propitiation** [prəpiʃi'eiʃən] *nu.*

propitious [prə'piʃəs] *adj* likely to bring success; favourable. **propitiously** *adv.*

proportion [prə'pɔ:ʃən] **1.** *nu* relation of one thing to another in number, amount, size etc. *The amount of money you get will be in proportion to the work you do* i.e. the more you work, the more money you will get. **2.** *nc* part. *A large proportion of my time is spent in studying.* **3.** *nc* equality of relationship between sets of numbers (e.g. 2 is to 4 as 4 is to 8). Also *vt* fit or arrange things together. *The different parts of the house are well proportioned.*

proportions *npl* size; measurements: *a room of large proportions. The building had pleasing proportions* i.e. the different parts of it were the correct size for one another.

proportional *adj* in proper proportions; corresponding. *The cost of the party will be proportional to the number of people invited.*

proportionally *adv.*

proportionate [prə'pɔ:ʃənət] *adj* proportional. (*opp* **disproportionate**). **proportionately** *adv.*

out of (all) proportion too big, too small etc.

propose [prə'pouz] *vt/i* **1.** suggest; put forward for consideration. *I propose that we leave now. He proposed another meeting.* **2.** intend. *I propose to go home next week.* **3.** make an offer of marriage. *John has proposed to Mary.* **4.** put forward someone's name for office, membership. *He proposed Mr Jones for secretary.*

proposal *nc* **1.** plan; suggestion. **2.** offer of marriage.

proposition [prɔpə'ziʃən] *nc* **1.** something to be considered; proposal: *a business proposition.* **2.** (esp. of mathematical problem) statement.

propound [prə'paund] *vt* put forward an idea, problem etc for consideration.

proprietary [prə'praiətri] *adj* owned by a private person or company: *proprietary medicine* i.e. medicine made by a firm of manufacturers and sold with their name on it.

proprietor [prə'praiətə*] *nc* owner (esp. of land or a shop) (*fem* **proprietress** [prə'praiətris]).

propriety [prə'praiəti] *nu* state of being proper; good behaviour: *behave with propriety.*

the proprieties *npl* the rules of good behaviour in society: *observe the proprieties* i.e. follow these rules.

propulsion [prə'pʌlʃən] *nu* driving force: *jet propulsion* i.e. movement by means of jet engines. see **propel.**

prorogue [prə'roug] *vt* bring the meetings of some organization to an end for a time: *prorogue Parliament.* **prorogation** [prourə'geiʃən] *nu.*

prosaic [prou'zeiik] *adj* dull; not exciting. **prosaically** *adv*.

proscribe [prə'skraib] *vt* **1.** proclaim to be an enemy and outside the protection of the law. **2.** forbid. **proscription** [prə'skripʃən] *nu*. **proscriptive** [prə'skriptiv] *adj*.

prose [prouz] *nu* ordinary way of speaking and writing, not verse. *This writer is good at writing both prose and poetry.*

prosecute ['prɔsikju:t] *vt* **1.** take legal action against. *Anyone who drives carelessly will be prosecuted.* **2.** carry out; carry on: *prosecute an inquiry/a plan/a business etc.*

prosecution [prɔsi'kju:ʃən] **1.** *nc/u* taking of legal action: *threaten someone with prosecution.* **2.** *nu* people (often the state) who take legal action against another: *the case for the prosecution.* **3.** *nu* act of carrying out or carrying on something. *A policeman was injured in the prosecution of his duties.*

prosecutor *nc* person who prosecutes (in sense **1.**): *the Public Prosecutor* i.e. person who prosecutes on behalf of the state.

proselyte ['prɔsilait] *nc* person who has changed from one opinion, religious belief etc to another. **proselytize** ['prɔsilitaiz] *vt/i*.

prosody ['prɔzidi] *nu* rhythms of poetry; study of how these rhythms are arranged. **prosodic** [prə'sɔdik] *adj*.

prospect ['prɔspekt] **1.** *nc* something that one expects or looks forward to. *The prospects for a young man in this job are excellent.* **2.** *nu* hope; possibility. *Is there any prospect of your returning soon?* **3.** *nc* view; outlook. *There is a beautiful prospect across the valley.* Also [prə'spekt] *vt/i* search; look for: *prospecting for gold.*

prospective [prə'spektiv] *adj* expected; looked forward to: *a prospective customer.*

prospector [prə'spektə*] *nc* person who explores an area for gold etc.

prospectus [prə'spektəs] *nc* printed document which advertises a school, business etc by giving details of how it is run etc.

prosper ['prɔspə*] *vi* succeed; do well in business.

prosperity [prɔs'periti] *nu* state of being successful or rich.

prosperous *adj* successful; rich; fortunate: *have a prosperous business; a prosperous country.* **prosperously** *adv*.

prostitute ['prɔstitju:t] *nc* woman who offers sexual intercourse for money. Also *vt* use something for immoral purposes or for the wrong purpose: *prostitute one's talents.* **prostitution** [prɔsti'tju:ʃən] *nu*.

prostrate ['prɔstreit] *adj* **1.** lying flat (usu. face down): *lie prostrate from exhaustion/out of respect to someone etc.* **2.** be overcome: *prostrate with grief.* Also [prə'streit] *vt* **1.** throw down; make flat. *They prostrated themselves before the emperor.* **2.** overcome; make helpless. *He was prostrated by illness.*

prostration [prɔs'treiʃən] *nu* (usu. great tiredness).

prosy ['prouzi] *adj* dull; uninteresting. **prosiness** *nu*.

protagonist [prə'tægənist] *nc* main person in a story or play; leader (in a contest etc). *The struggle between the two protagonists lasted one hour.*

protect [prə'tekt] *vt* **1.** keep safe; defend: *protect someone from his enemies/from danger/against the cold.* **2.** help (home industry) by putting a tax on goods coming into the country.

protection **1.** *nu* act of protecting or being protected: *ask the police for protection.* **2.** *nc* something that protects. *This coat will be a protection against the cold.*

protective *adj* protecting; preventing injury: *protective clothing.*

protector *nc* someone/something that protects.

protectorate [prə'tektərət] *nc* country which is protected and partly controlled by another country.

protégé ['prɔteʒei] *nc* person who is being helped or protected by someone else.

protein ['prouti:n] *nc/u* type of body-building substance which is necessary to good health, and found in such foods as meat and eggs.

protest [prə'test] *vt/i* **1.** object to; speak against: *protest against an injustice.* **2.** state very seriously; declare. *He protested that the charges against him were untrue.* Also ['proutest] *nc/u* objection; statement against something. *We must make some kind of protest against this. They left without protest. He accepted our decision under protest* i.e. unwillingly.

protestation [prɔtəs'teiʃən] *nc/u* protesting; serious statement. *He left me with many protestations of friendship.*

Protestant ['prɔtistənt] *nc* Christian who is not Roman Catholic or Greek Orthodox. Also *adj*.

protocol ['proutəkɔl] *nc/u* **1.** rules of behaviour (esp. between officials of different governments). *Everything was arranged according to protocol.* **2.** first version of a treaty between countries.

proton ['proutɔn] *nc* part of an atom carrying one positive unit of electricity.

prototype ['proutətaip] *nc* first or trial model of something (e.g. a machine etc) which is later to be made in larger numbers.

protract [prə'trækt] *vt* make longer: *a protracted argument* i.e. one which lasts for a long time. **protraction** *nu*.

protractor *nc* instrument for measuring angles on a flat surface.

protractor

protrude [prə'tru:d] *vt/i* stick out; stand out: *stone protruding from the wall.* **protrusion** [prə'tru:ʒən] *nc/u*.

protuberant [prə'tju:bərnt] *adj* bulging out; swelling out.

protuberance *nc* something that bulges out.

proud [praud] *adj* **1.** having a high opinion of oneself, or of something or someone connected with oneself: *a proud man; a proud father* i.e. one who has a high opinion of his children; *a proud day for someone* i.e. a day on which something happens to make someone pleased with himself: *be proud of one's son.* **2.** wonderful; magnificent: *a proud sight.* **proudly** *adv*. see **pride**.

prove [pru:v] *vt/i* **1.** show that something is true. *You must prove his guilt. Vasco da Gama proved that the world was round.* **2.** put to the test; try out: *prove someone's ability.* **3.** turn out to be. *The extra room proved very useful when we had visitors.* **4.** (in a legal sense) show that a will etc is in order. see **proof**.

provender ['prɔvəndə*] *nu* food for cattle.

proverb ['prɔvə:b] *nc* short, wise saying which has been used by people for a long time.

proverbial [prə'və:biəl] *adj* well-known; like a proverb or connected with a proverb: *the proverbial rolling stone.* **proverbially** *adv.*

provide [prə'vaid] *vt/i* **1.** give; supply. *We provided him with food/We provided food for him.* **2.** give what is needed; support. *A father must provide for his children.* **3.** take care; make arrangements. *We must provide for the future/against danger. The rules do not provide for any exceptions* i.e. do not allow. see **provision.**

provided (that) *conj* on the condition that. *She may come with us provided (that) she arrives in time.*

providing *conj* on the condition that. *You may go out providing you do your homework first.*

providence ['prɔvidns] *nu* **1.** care for the future (*o.f.*). **2.** (**Providence**) God; God's care for human beings: *leave something to Providence.*

providential [prɔvi'denʃl] *adj* coming from God; lucky; fortunate. *Our being rescued from danger was providential.* **providentially** *adv.*

provident ['prɔvidnt] *adj* caring for the future. *Provident people always save some of their wages.* (*opp* **improvident**).

province ['prɔvins] *nc* **1.** main division of a country: *the provinces of Canada.* **2.** division of knowledge, work etc: *the province of science; outside one's province* i.e. outside what one has studied, done etc.

the provinces area in a country outside the capital.

provincial [prə'vinʃl] *adj* **1.** connected with a province. **2.** narrow in interests and outlook: *a rather provincial attitude.* Also *nc* someone from the provinces.

provision [prə'viʒən] *nc/u* **1.** arrangement; care taken for what may happen. *There is no provision for any change in the plans.* **2.** (in a legal sense) condition in a will etc. see **provide.**

provisions *npl* food.

make provision for provide for (in sense **3.**): *make provision for the possibility that someone may arrive late.*

provisional [prə'viʒənl] *adj* for the present time only; temporary: *a provisional arrangement.* **provisionally** *adv.*

proviso [prə'vaizou] *nc* condition in an arrangement (esp. a legal arrangement): *with the proviso that* i.e. on condition that. *pl* **provisos** or **provisoes.**

provoke [prə'vouk] *vt* **1.** make angry. *If you provoke him, he will beat you.* **2.** cause. *His foolish behaviour provoked laughter.* **3.** deliberately cause someone to do something. *She provoked him into beating her.*

provoking *adj* annoying. **provokingly** *adv.*

provocation [prɔvə'keiʃən] **1.** *nu* provoking or being provoked: *do something under provocation* i.e. when provoked; *on/at the slightest provocation* i.e. at the slightest excuse. **2.** *nc* something that annoys one.

provocative [prə'vɔkətiv] *adj* arousing one's emotions, anger, interest etc: *a provocative statement.* **provocatively** *adv.*

provost ['prɔvəst] *nc* **1.** head of certain colleges. **2.** mayor (chief elected official) of a Scottish town.

prow [prau] *nc* pointed front part of a ship or boat.

prowess ['praues] *nu* **1.** daring; brave actions. **2.** skill; ability: *his prowess on the football field.*

prowl [praul] *vi* move about quietly searching for something to eat or steal: *animals prowling round a camp; a thief prowling round a house.* **prowler** *nc.*

on the prowl prowling about.

proximity [prɔk'simiti] *nu* nearness: *in the proximity of something* i.e. near something.

proxy ['prɔksi] *nc/u* **1.** right to act for another person (esp. in voting): *vote by proxy.* **2.** document giving someone this right. **3.** person who acts for someone else in this way.

prude [pru:d] *nc* person who is too correct or modest. **prudish** *adj.* **prudery** ['pru:dəri] *nc/u.*

prudent ['pru:dnt] *adj* sensible; careful. *You should be prudent with your money.* (*opp* **imprudent**). **prudently** *adv.* **prudence** *nu.*

prune[1] [pru:n] *nc* dried plum.

prune[2] [pru:n] *vt* **1.** cut off unwanted branches etc from a tree, bush etc, so as to improve it. **2.** cut out what is not necessary: *prune a summary down to the required length.*

prurient ['pruəriənt] *adj* over-curious about or too interested in sex. **prurience** *nu.*

prussic acid ['prʌsik'æsid] *nu* type of deadly poison.

pry [prai] *vi* (with **into**) look into; investigate (esp. other people's affairs): *pry into things which do not concern one.*

psalm [sɑ:m] *nc* **1.** song or poem to God. **2.** song or poem from the Book of Psalms in the Old Testament.

psalmist *nc* author of a psalm.

pseudo- ['sju:dou] *prefix* not real; pretending to be (e.g. **pseudo-prophet** i.e. pretending to be a prophet).

pseudonym ['sju:dənim] *nc* name used by a writer instead of his real name: *write under a pseudonym.*

psychiatry [sai'kaiətri] *nu* science of treating mental disease. **psychiatric** [saiki'ætrik] *adj.* **psychiatrist** *nc.*

psychic ['saikik] *adj* connected with the soul or mind.

psychoanalysis [saikouə'nælisis] *nu* (art of) careful examination of someone's mental condition so that the reasons for his mental or nervous illness can be discovered.

psychoanalyst [saikou'ænəlist] *nc* person trained to carry out psychoanalysis. **psychoanalyse** [saikou'ænəlaiz] *vt.* **psychoanalytic** [saikouænə'litik] *adj.*

psychology [sai'kɔlədʒi] *nu* scientific study of the mind and how it works.

psychologist *nc* expert in psychology. **psychological** [saikə'lɔdʒikl] *adj.*

the psychological moment the best time for doing something.

psychosomatic ['saikousə'mætik] *adj* referring to an illness of the body which is caused by nervous or mental illness: *psychosomatic illness.*

ptomaine ['toumein] *nu* poison which is found in bad food: *ptomaine poisoning.*

pub [pʌb] *nc* short informal form of **public house.**

puberty ['pju:bəti] *nu* age at which a person is physically able to become a parent.

pubic ['pju:bik] *adj* concerned with the sexual organs (usu. in **pubic hair**).

public ['pʌblik] *adj* **1.** general; concerning everyone: *public affairs; a matter of public concern.* **2.** provided for everyone; open to everyone: *public relief; public parks/libraries etc.* 3. run by or employed by the government: *public works; public official.* 4. known to everyone. *The matter became public.* (*opp* **private**). **publicly** *adv.*

the public the people in general: *a matter of little interest to the public.*

'public ad'dress system apparatus such as microphones and loudspeakers used for talking to large numbers of people.

public house place where alcoholic drink can be bought and drunk. (Also **pub**).

'public o'pinion poll examination of what the public think about some matter by asking a number of people who are taken to represent the public.

public relations *nu* relations between a government department or firm etc and the public.

public school 1. (*Brit*) boarding school mostly run by private fees. 2. (*US*) government school.

'public-'spirited *adj* willing to do things for the good of the public.

in public openly; not in private.

publican ['pʌblikən] *nc* 1. owner of a public house. 2. tax collector in ancient times (*o.f.* in sense 2.).

publication [pʌbli'keiʃən] 1. *nc* anything that is published (e.g. book, paper, magazine). 2. *nu* act of publishing something.

publicize ['pʌblisaiz] *vt* make publicly known; advertise.

publicity [pʌb'lisiti] *nu* process of advertising.

pub'licity agent person whose work is to advertise things.

publish ['pʌbliʃ] *vt* 1. produce in printed form, as a book, magazine, newspaper etc. 2. make publicly known.

publisher *nc* person who produces books etc in printed form.

publishing *nu* work of a publisher.

pucker ['pʌkə*] *vt* (esp. with reference to the face) twist; pull together. *The child puckered up his face before he began to cry.*

pudding ['pudiŋ] *nc/u* 1. food of various types (usu. consisting of pastry, custard, fruit etc) served after the main part of a meal. 2. any sweet food served after the main part of a meal. 3. food (usu. consisting of pastry/suet and meat) served with the main part of a meal.

puddle ['pʌdl] *nc* small area of water (esp. one made by rain).

puerile ['pjuərail] *adj* childish; foolish.

puff [pʌf] *nc* slight movement of air, smoke etc: *a puff of wind; a puff of smoke.* Also *vt/i* breathe jerkily: *puff a pipe.*

puffy *adj* (with reference to part of the body which is injured or diseased) swollen. **puffiness** *nu.*

'powder puff see **powder.**

puffed up *adj* proud. (rather *o.f.*).

puff out one's chest make the chest swell by drawing in one's stomach muscles.

puffin ['pʌfin] *nc* type of Arctic sea bird with a large beak.

pugilist ['pju:dʒilist] *nc* boxer. **pugilistic** [pju:dʒi'listik] *adj.* (both rather *o.f.*).

pugnacious [pʌg'neiʃəs] *adj* fond of quarrelling and fighting. **pugnaciously** *adv.* **pugnacity** [pʌg'næsiti] *nu.*

pull [pul] *vt/i* cause to come towards one or in the same direction as one. *The engine pulled the train up the hill. He pulled as hard as he could.* Also *nc* (usu. only *sing*) act of pulling. Also *nu* unfair influence; ability to get some advantage because one knows someone in an official position. (*informal*).

pull something down (with reference to a building) destroy, often in order to build something else: *pull down an old house.*

pull in (with reference to a car) stop near or at something. *Pull in at the next garage.*

pull through recover from a dangerous illness.

pull up (usu. with reference to a car etc) stop; stop suddenly.

pull something up remove by pulling: *pull up weeds in a garden.*

make/pull a face at someone see **make**[1].

pull somebody's leg say untrue things to someone as a joke. **leg-pulling** *nu.* **leg-pull** *nc.* (all *informal*).

pull oneself together become calm again after having been excited, worried etc.

pull one's punches 1. (boxing) not hit as hard as one could. 2. be kinder to one's opponents than one might be. (*informal* in sense 2.).

pull one's weight do one's full share of work; do as much as others who are working with one.

pullet ['pulit] *nc* young, female chicken.

pulley ['puli] *nc* apparatus for lifting things, consisting of a wheel over which a rope or chain can be moved.

pullover ['pulouvə*] *nc* garment for the upper part of the body, pulled on over the head.

pulmonary ['pʌlmənəri] *adj* with reference to the lungs.

pulp [pʌlp] *nu* 1. soft part of a fruit or vegetable. 2. soft, wet mass of wood or cloth, used for making paper. Also *vt/i* make into pulp: *pulped wood.*

pulpy *adj* soft and wet like pulp.

pulpit ['pulpit] *nc* structure in a church reached by steps, and from which the priest, minister etc speaks.

pulse [pʌls] *nc* 1. regular movement of the blood pumped by the heart. 2. any regular beat or movement like this. Also *vi* beat or move regularly in this way.

pulsate [pʌl'seit] *vi* move regularly in this way. **pulsation** [pʌl'seiʃən] *nu.* **pulsating** *adj.*

pulverize ['pʌlvəraiz] *vt* break into small pieces; make into powder.

puma ['pju:mə] *nc* large wild cat with a yellow-brown coat, found in America. (Also **panther, cougar**).

pumice ['pʌmis] *nu* usu. in **pumice stone** i.e. type of light volcanic stone, used for polishing and cleaning etc.

pummel ['pʌml] *vt* hit many times with the fists. *past* **pummelled.** (*US* **pummeled**) (Also **pommel**).

pump[1] [pʌmp] *nc* apparatus for forcing gas or liquid into or out of something. Also *vt/i* 1. move by a pump: *pump air into a tyre.* 2. work a pump. *He pumped for half an hour.*

pump something out empty by pumping.

pump something up fill by pumping.

pump[2] [pʌmp] *nc* light dancing shoe.

pumpkin ['pʌmpkin] *nc* large, round, orange-coloured fruit, eaten as a food (esp. in the USA).

pun [pʌn] *nc* type of joke in which words have more than one meaning, or in which two expressions sound the same. Also *vi* make such a joke. *past* **punned.**

punster ['pʌnstə*] *nc* person who makes puns.

punch[1] [pʌntʃ] *vt* hit with the closed fist. Also *nc* blow given in this way.
punch[2] [pʌntʃ] *nc* device for making holes. Also *vt* make a hole with a punch: *punch a hole; punch a ticket* i.e. on a bus etc.
punch[3] [pʌntʃ] *nu* type of hot drink made from wine, rum etc.
punctilious [pʌŋk'tiliəs] *adj* very careful about small details. **punctiliously** *adv.* **punctiliousness** *nu.*
punctual ['pʌŋktjuəl] *adj* coming at the right time. **punctually** *adv.* **punctuality** [pʌŋktju'æliti] *nu.*
punctuate ['pʌŋktjueit] *vt/i* use full stops, commas etc in writing: *punctuate a sentence.*
punctuation [pʌŋktju'eiʃən] *nu*: *punctuation marks* i.e. full stops, commas etc.
puncture ['pʌŋktʃə*] *nc* hole made by a sharp object (esp. a hole in a tyre). Also *vt* make a hole in. Also *vi* get a hole in.
pundit ['pʌndit] *nc* learned man; expert.
pungent ['pʌndʒənt] *adj* sharp to the taste or sense of smell; powerfully expressed: *a pungent smell; pungent criticism.* **pungently** *adv.* **pungency** *nu.*
punish ['pʌniʃ] *vt* cause pain, loss or discomfort to in return for some wrong. *The teacher punished the boy who had broken the window.* **punishment** *nc/u.*
punishable *adj* likely to be punished; deserving punishment: *a punishable offence.*
punitive ['pju:nitiv] *adj* concerned with punishment; done in order to punish.
punt [pʌnt] *nc* type of flat-bottomed boat, moved by pushing a pole against the bottom of a river. Also *vt/i* move a boat in this way; travel in a punt.
punter ['pʌntə*] *nc* person who makes bets on horse-races, football matches etc.
puny ['pju:ni] *adj* small and weak. **puniness** *nu.*
pup [pʌp] *nc* puppy.
pupa ['pju:pə] *nc* stage between the larva and the adult in the development of insects. *pl* **pupae** ['pju:pi:] or **pupas.**
pupil[1] ['pju:pil] *nc* young person being taught in a school or by a teacher.
pupil[2] ['pju:pil] *nc* dark area in the centre of the eye.
puppet ['pʌpit] *nc* **1.** small doll, which can be made to move by wires, strings, the fingers etc. **2.** person or government completely controlled by someone else.
puppy ['pʌpi] *nc* young dog.
purchase ['pə:tʃis] *vt* buy. Also *nc* **1.** something bought. **2.** (usu. only *sing*) tight hold on something to prevent it or oneself from falling etc: *get a purchase on a rope.* **purchaser** *nc.*
purdah ['pə:də] *nu* (in India) system of keeping women in a household away from strange men: *be in purdah; practise purdah.*
pure [pjuə*] *adj* **1.** not mixed with other things. **2.** having no unclean or immoral thoughts; acting in a moral way: *pure thoughts.* (*opp* **impure** in senses **1.** and **2.**). **3.** mere; nothing more than: *pure chance* i.e. only chance, without intention; *pure luck.* **4.** (with reference to science and mathematics) concerned with theory, and not with practical application: *pure science.* **purely** *adv.*
purity *nu* condition of being pure.
purify *vt* make pure. **purification** [pjurifi'keiʃən] *nu.*
purist *nc* person who is always careful to use language which he considers correct. **purism** *nu.*
puree, purée ['pjuərei] *nc/u* **1.** type of thick soup. **2.** food like thick soup.
purge [pə:dʒ] *vt* **1.** make pure and clean. **2.** get rid of waste matter from the body using a medicine. **3.** expel a number of people from a political party or from public service. Also *nc* **1.** act of purging. **2.** medicine for purging.
purgative ['pə:gətiv] *nc* medicine for purging. Also *adj.*
purgatory ['pə:gətəri] *nu* **1.** according to some Christians, place where souls suffer for a time before entering heaven. **2.** time of suffering.
puritan ['pjuəritn] *nc* person who is very strict in morals and religion. Also *adj.*
puritanical [pjuəri'tænikl] *adj* very strict, or too strict, in morals and behaviour.
puritanism *nu* beliefs, or behaviour, of puritans.
purloin ['pə:lɔin] *vt* steal (*o.f.*).
purple ['pə:pl] *nc/u* colour obtained by mixing red and blue together. Also *adj.*
the purple cloth of this colour, sometimes worn by people of high rank in the Church or State.
purport ['pə:pət] *nu* meaning of something a person says, writes or does. *What was the purport of his remarks?* Also [pə:'pɔ:t] *vt* **1.** claim to be. *This document purports to be from the president.* **2.** mean.
purpose ['pə:pəs] *nc* **1.** what one intends to do; plan. *What is your purpose in doing this?* **2.** what a thing is used, made for etc. *This machine has been made for a certain purpose.* Also *vt* intend.
purposeful *adj* showing that one has a definite purpose: *walk in a purposeful manner.*
purposely *adj* intentionally; deliberately. *He arrived late purposely so as to annoy me.*
to good purpose with good results. *He studied for three years to good purpose.*
on purpose deliberately: *do something on purpose.*
serve a/the/one's purpose be useful or satisfactory. *This pan is not the best one, but it will serve the purpose.*
to the purpose relevant. *What he said wasn't really to the purpose.*
purr [pə:*] *nc/u* soft sound like that made by a cat when it is pleased. Also *vi* make this sound.
purse [pə:s] *nc* **1.** small bag for carrying money in. **2.** amount of money (esp. for a prize or other special purpose). *The boxers fought for a purse of £50.* **3.** (*US*) woman's handbag. Also *vt* draw the lips together into the shape of a small circle (often to show displeasure).
purser ['pə:sə*] *nc* officer on a ship who is in charge of stores and money.
pursuance [pə'sju:əns] *nu* usu. in **in pursuance of** i.e. while carrying out. *The policeman was injured in pursuance of his duties.*
pursue [pə'sju:] *vt* **1.** follow in order to catch or kill: *pursue a wild animal.* **2.** look for: *pursue pleasure* i.e. be interested mostly in pleasure. **3.** carry on with; continue to work at: *pursue one's study of English.*
pursuit [pə'sju:t] **1.** *nu* act of pursuing. *He was captured without much pursuit; in pursuit of pleasure.* **2.** *nc* something in which one is interested or spends time on: *literary pursuits* i.e. writing books etc.
purvey [pə'vei] *vt* supply (esp. food or

provisions). *This firm purveys meat to the army.* **purveyor** *nc.*

purview ['pəːvjuː] *nc* (usu. only *sing*) area of someone's activity.

pus [pʌs] *nu* thick, yellow liquid which comes out of a poisoned area of the body (e.g. a wound, boil etc).

push[1] [puʃ] *vt/i* **1.** make someone/something go farther away by using force against him/it; press against. *The little boy pushed his sister away from him. If the door does not open at first, push it harder. If you don't stop pushing, someone may get hurt. Push the table against the wall. If you push this button, a bell rings.* **2.** try to make people have a favourable idea of oneself, something one is selling etc: *push oneself forward; push one's ideas; push something through* i.e. to persuade others to agree to it. **3.** sell drugs illegally. (*informal* in sense **3.**).

pusher *nc* **1.** person who pushes (in sense **2.**). **2.** person who pushes drugs. (*informal*).

pushing, pushful, pushy *adj* inclined to draw attention to oneself too much.

'push-bike bicycle driven by pedals, not by an engine.

'pushcart small cart for carrying goods, pushed by a man.

push along/forward/on continue with one's journey, work etc. *We must push on with our journey if we want to arrive before midnight.* (*informal*).

push someone around keep giving a person orders; bully someone. *I'm leaving this job because I'm tired of being pushed around.* (*informal*).

be pushed for time/money etc not have much time/money etc. *I can't stay, as I'm rather pushed for time.* (*informal*).

push off **1.** get a small boat started by pushing something against the bank of the river etc. **2.** leave. *We must push off now.* (*informal* in sense **2.**).

push[2] [puʃ] **1.** *nc* act of pushing. *The door was stuck, but it opened with a push/when I gave it a push.* **2.** *nc* strong effort. *We must make a push to get these letters finished tonight.* **3.** *nu* energy; strength of will. *I don't think he has enough push to be successful in business.* (*informal* in sense **3.**).

at a push if necessary. *This car was meant to hold four people, but it can hold six at a push.* (*informal*).

get the push lose one's job. (*informal*).

give someone the push dismiss someone from his job. (*informal*).

until/when it comes to the push until/when a special effort was needed. *They said they would help us, but when it came to the push they didn't.* (*informal*).

pusillanimous [pjuːsi'læniməs] *adj* not brave.

puss, pussy [pus(i)] *nc* child's informal name for a **cat.**

put [put] *vt/i* **1.** place; cause to be in a certain position. *He put his book on the table. I put my hand in my pocket. You have put me in a difficult situation* i.e. a situation which annoys or embarrasses me. *It is time to put the children to bed.* **2.** say; state. *Can I put a suggestion to you?* **3.** write; mark. *Put the prices on these cards. Put your name here* i.e. sign your name. *pres part* **putting.** *past* **put.**

put about change direction. *The ship put about.*

put something across make someone understand. *It's a pity he cannot put his ideas across.* (*informal*).

put something aside see **lay**[1].

put something away put into the proper place. *Put your books away.*

put something back **1.** replace. *The children put their books back on the shelves.* **2.** move back: *put the clock back by five minutes* i.e. move the minute hand back.

put something by save. *He used to put some money by/put by some money every week.*

put something down **1.** place down. *Put the books down on the floor.* **2.** stop by strong action: *put down a rebellion; put down gambling.*

put something forward **1.** ask for something to be considered: *put forward a new idea; put oneself forward for election.* **2.** move forward: *put the clock forward by ten minutes* i.e. move the minute hand forward.

put in something **1.** ask for something to be considered: *put in a claim for higher wages.* **2.** do: *put in a few hours' work.* **3.** enter. *The ship put in at the harbour.*

put someone/something off **1.** delay until later. *We shall have to put off the party until next week.* **2.** make someone do something badly. *Don't talk while I'm working, you're putting me off.* (*informal*). **3.** discourage someone; make someone dislike something. *The bad service we got last time put us off going back to that hotel.* (*informal*).

put something on **1.** clothe with: *put on one's coat.* **2.** increase: *put on speed; put on weight* i.e. get fatter. **3.** cause to work or happen: *put on extra buses; put on the radio; put on a play* i.e. cause a play to be shown on the stage.

put on to **1.** inform about. **2.** connect with (esp. by telephone).

put someone/something out **1.** cause to be outside. *If you talk in the library, you will be put out.* **2.** cause something to stop burning or being lit: *put out a fire/the light etc.* **3.** hold out: *put out one's hand/one's tongue etc.* **4.** anger; worry. *He was put out by the rude behaviour of his guests.* **5.** trouble (oneself). *Please don't put yourself out for us* i.e. we would not like to cause you any trouble. (*informal* in sense **5.**).

put-'out *adj* disappointed. *He was rather put-out when I didn't go to visit him.* (*informal*).

put something over make someone understand: *put one's ideas over well.* (*informal*).

put someone/something through **1.** connect by telephone. *I asked the operator to put me through to the hospital.* **2.** do; make: *put through a business agreement.*

put something together make something from different parts. *We must try to put the radio together again.*

put someone/something up **1.** raise: *put up one's hand* i.e. raise it above one's head; *put up prices.* **2.** put in a place where it can be seen: *put up a notice.* **3.** give a place to sleep for a short time (sometimes with food). *Can you put us up for the night?* (*informal* in sense **3.**).

'put-up 'job *nc* something arranged in advance in order to trick someone. (*informal*).

put up to tell someone to do something bad or show him how to do it. *I don't know who has put him up to this mischief.* (*informal*).

put up with something suffer, bear without complaining. *The food is not very good, but we shall just have to put up with it.* (*informal*).

put the cart before the horse put or say things in the wrong order. (*informal*).
put someone to death execute someone.
put an end/stop to something cause something to finish or stop: *put an end to someone's rudeness; put an end to one's life* i.e. kill oneself.
put all one's eggs in one basket chance everything one has on one thing (e.g. by preparing only one question for an examination in the hope that it will be asked) (*informal*).
put one's foot down 1. forbid something; be firm. *The children are disobedient, so you must put your foot down.* **2.** (in a car) drive faster. (*informal*).
put in a good word for someone recommend someone (e.g. for a job etc).
put someone in mind of make someone remember. *You put me in mind of your father* i.e. when I look at you I remember your father. (*informal*).
put paid to end completely. *Breaking his leg has really put paid to chances of winning the race.* (*informal*).
put someone in his place use one's authority to show that one is displeased. *That pupil was rude to his teacher and he will have to be put in his place.*
put into practice use. *They learnt French in England and then went to France to put what they learnt into practice.*
put oneself in another's position/shoes imagine what one would do if one were someone else. (*informal*).
put pressure on someone try to get someone to do something by persuasion, force etc. *They are putting pressure on him to make him change his mind.*
put someone in a spot cause someone annoyance or embarrassment. (*informal*).
put two and two together be aware of something and understand what it means. *When the man started spending so much money, the police put two and two together* i.e. they realized he must have stolen it. (*informal*).

putative ['pju:tətiv] *adj* thought to be, supposed: *the putative cause of this* i.e. what is thought to be the cause.

putrefy ['pju:trifai] *vt/i* rot; decay. **putrefaction** [pju:tri'fækʃən] *nu*.
putrescent [pju:'tresnt] *adj* becoming rotten.

putrid ['pju:trid] *adj* having gone rotten; decayed: *putrid fish.*

putt [pʌt] *vt/i* (in golf) hit the ball gently so that it rolls towards/into the hole on the green. Also *nc*.

putty ['pʌti] *nu* soft mixture of white powder and oil (used e.g. for fixing panes of glass in windows). Also *vt* fix with putty.

puzzle ['pʌzl] *nc* **1.** something that is difficult to understand. **2.** problem which tests a person's knowledge, intelligence etc, and is done as an amusement. Also *vt/i* think or cause someone to think hard. *I have been puzzling about this question for weeks now. His strange behaviour puzzles me* i.e. I do not understand it.
puzzler *nc* question or problem which is difficult to understand.
puzzling *adj* difficult to understand.
puzzle something out find an answer, or reason, for something by thinking hard about it.
puzzle over something think hard about something.

pygmy, pigmy ['pigmi] *nc* **1.** member of a race of small people that lives in Africa. **2.** very small person. (*informal* in sense **2.**). Also *adj*.

pyjamas [pi'dʒɑ:məz] (*US* **pajamas**) *npl* loose-fitting jacket and trousers for wearing in bed (usu. made of a light cloth).

pylon ['pailn] *nc* high sort of tower made of steel, used for carrying electric wires.

pylon

pyramid ['pirəmid] *nc* solid object as in the illustration (usu. square at the bottom and coming to a point).

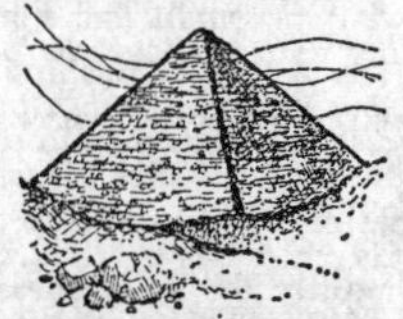

pyramid

pyre ['paiə*] *nc* heap of wood on which a dead body is burned.

pyrotechnics [paiərou'tekniks] *npl* **1.** art of making fireworks. **2.** public show of fireworks.

python ['paiθən] *nc* type of large snake which kills the animals it wants to eat by winding itself very tightly round them.

Q

quack[1] [kwæk] *nc* sound a duck makes. Also *vi* make this sound.
quack[2] [kwæk] *nc* person who pretends to have knowledge (esp. of medicine) which he does not really possess.
quadrangle ['kwɔdræŋgl] *nc* **1.** four-sided area surrounded by buildings (e.g. in a college) (Also **quad**). **2.** flat, four-sided figure. **quadrangular** [kwɔ'dræŋgjulə*] *adj*.
quadrant ['kwɔdrnt] *nc* **1.** quarter of a circle or of its circumference. **2.** instrument used for measuring angles to find out the height of something.
quadrilateral [kwɔdri'lætrl] *nc* flat, four-sided figure. Also *adj* having four sides.
quadruped ['kwɔdruped] *nc* animal that has four feet.
quadruple [kwɔ'drupl] *adj* made up of four parts, including four people: *a quadruple agreement*. Also *nc* number, amount etc that is four times as great as another number. Also *vt/i* make or become four times greater.
quad(s) [kwɔd(z)], **quadruplet(s)** [kwɔ'dru:plit(s)] *n* (usu. *pl*) (one of) four babies born to the same mother at the same time.
quaff [kwɔf] *vt* take a long drink (*o.f.*).
quagmire ['kwɔgmaiə*] *nc* area of very soft, muddy ground.
quail[1] [kweil] *nc* small game bird in the same family as the pheasant. *pl* **quails** or **quail**.
quail[2] [kweil] *vi* be afraid; show that one is afraid. *The pupil quailed at the headmaster's anger*.
quaint [kweint] *adj* interesting or pleasing because it is unusual or old: *quaint old village church*. **quaintly** *adv*. **quaintness** *nc/u*.
quake [kweik] *vi* shake; tremble: *quake with fear. The earth quaked under our feet*. Also *nc* short form of **earthquake**.
qualify ['kwɔlifai] **1.** *vt* train; make a person good enough. *His ability qualifies him for the job*. **2.** *vi* be trained; be good or skilled enough: *qualified to teach; qualified as a doctor/lawyer etc; a qualified teacher; be qualified for a certain post*. **3.** *vt* (grammar) describe. *Adjectives qualify nouns*. **4.** *vt* make a remark etc less general in meaning. **qualified** *adj*. (*opp* **unqualified**).
qualification [kwɔlifi'keiʃən] *nc* **1.** training or examination which makes a person fit to do something: *a doctor with good medical qualifications*. **2.** something that changes, makes weaker or less general etc. *I can say, without any qualification, that he is an excellent worker* i.e. without any doubt etc.
quality ['kwɔliti] **1.** *nc* something that a person/thing has which makes him/it different from others. *One quality of wood is that it can burn*. **2.** *nu* standard of excellence that a thing/person has: *cloth of good/poor quality; a shop famous for its quality* i.e. the goodness of what it sells. **3.** *nc* high rank: *a man of quality* (*o.f.* in sense **3.**). Also *adj*.
qualm [kwa:m] *nc* (often *pl*) **1.** feeling of anxiety or guilt about whether one has done right: *have no qualms about doing something*. **2.** short feeling of sickness.
quandary ['kwɔndri] *nc* state of doubt; feeling of difficulty: *be in a quandary about hat to do*.
quantity ['kwɔntiti] **1.** *nc/u* amount: *add a small quantity of water. He used equal quantities of milk and water*. **2.** *nu* large amount: *buy things in quantity*.
an unknown quantity a person/thing that very little is known about.
quarantine ['kwɔrnti:n] *nu* separation from others so that disease is not spread. *People coming from an infected area must be kept in quarantine*. Also *vi* put or keep in quarantine.
quarrel ['kwɔrl] *nc* **1.** angry disagreement: *have a quarrel with someone about/over something*. **2.** reason for disagreement. *I quarrelled with him last night. These two people are always quarrelling. past* **quarrelled.** (*US* **quarreled**).
quarrelsome *adj* fond of quarrelling.
quarry[1] ['kwɔri] *nc* place at ground level from which stone, slate, marble etc are obtained (usu. by blasting). Also *vt* get stone from a quarry.
quarry[2] ['kwɔri] *nc* animal etc chased or hunted.
quart [kwɔ:t] *nc* measure for liquid equal to two pints. see appendix.
quarter[1] ['kwɔ:tə*] *nc/u* **1.** fourth part of something. *Give a quarter of the cake to each of the four children*. **2.** fourth part of an hour i.e. 15 minutes. *It's (a) quarter past three* i.e. 3.15. *It's (a) quarter to three* i.e. 2.45. **3.** fourth part of a year i.e. 3 months. *We pay our fuel bills every quarter*. **4.** fourth part of a US dollar i.e. 25 cents. **5.** direction; place. *People came running from every quarter*. **6.** part of a town: *the Chinese quarter* i.e. where the Chinese live. **7.** one of the four phases of the moon, each lasting about 7 days. *The moon was in its first quarter*. see also **phase. 8.** fourth part of a hundredweight i.e. 28 lbs; grain measure of 8 bushels. **9.** act of sparing an enemy from death. *No quarter was given after the battle and all the prisoners were shot*.
quarters *npl* place to live or stay.
'quarterlight (*Brit*) small, triangular-shaped window between the side window and the windscreen of a car.
'quartermaster soldier or sailor in charge of supplies etc.
quarter[2] ['kwɔ:tə*] *vt* **1.** divide into four parts. **2.** find rooms for soldiers to stay in. *The soldiers were quartered in the village*.
quartet, quartette [kwɔ:'tet] *nc* **1.** group of four singers or instrument players. **2.** piece of music for such a group.
quartz [kwɔ:ts] *nu* type of hard rock (often colourless and semi-transparent) used in the electrical industry.

quash [kwɔʃ] *vt* end by an official or legal decision: *quash a conviction* i.e. decide by law that somebody is not guilty after he has been found guilty by another court.
quasi[1] ['kweizai] *adj* seemingly, not really.
quasi-[2] ['kweizai] *prefix* seemingly, not really (e.g. **quasi-official; quasi-historical**).
quatrain ['kwɔtrein] *nc* verse or poem of four lines.
quaver ['kweivə*] *vt/i* **1.** shake; tremble. **2.** say or sing something in a shaking voice. Also *nc* **1.** trembling sound. **2.** type of musical note.
quay [ki:] *nc* place (often built of stone) where ships are loaded or unloaded.
queasy ['kwi:zi] *adj* **1.** having a feeling of sickness: *feel rather queasy.* **2.** easily made sick: *a queasy stomach.* **3.** inclined to upset the stomach: *queasy food.* **4.** difficult to please. **queasily** *adv.* **queasiness** *nu.*
queen [kwi:n] *nc* **1.** wife of a king. **2.** woman ruler of a country. **3.** female in group of bees, ants etc who lays eggs: *a queen bee.* **4.** playing card next in importance to king. **5.** important piece in the game of chess.
queenly *adj* of or like a queen; suitable for a queen.
queer [kwiə*] *adj* **1.** strange; odd: *have queer ideas; act in a queer way.* **2.** sick; unwell: *feel queer.* **3.** homosexual. (*informal* in senses **2.** and **3.**). Also *vt* spoil, upset. (*informal*). Also *nc* homosexual man. (*informal*). **queerly** *adj.* **queerness** *nu.*
in queer street in difficulty of some kind (esp. money difficulties) (*informal*).
queer someone's pitch do something which interferes with someone's plans. (*informal*).
quell [kwel] *vt* **1.** put down: *quell a rebellion/riot etc.* **2.** stop; put an end to: *quell someone's fears.*
quench [kwentʃ] *vt* put out; put an end to: *quench one's thirst* i.e. by drinking water; *quench a fire.*
querulous ['kwerjuləs] *adj* complaining: *a querulous voice.* **querulously** *adv.*
query ['kwiəri] *nc* **1.** question: *raise a query.* **2.** the mark ? put after a question or beside something to show doubt. Also *vt/i* **1.** ask about. **2.** express doubt about: *query something; query if/whether something is true.*
quest [kwest] *nc* search: *in quest of* i.e. looking for (*o.f.*).
question ['kwestʃən] *nc* **1.** something asked; request for knowledge. *Children are always asking questions. Answer my question.* **2.** something to be discussed; problem: *the question of world poverty. It's a question of money.* Also *vt/i* **1.** ask questions of: *be questioned for hours.* **2.** doubt. *I question his honesty* i.e. I am not sure that he is honest.
questioner *nc.*
questionable *adj* **1.** doubtful; not certain: *questionable statements.* **2.** not in good taste; not moral. (*opp* **unquestionable** usu. in sense **1.**). **questionably** *adv.*
questionnaire [kwestʃə'nɛə*] *nc* (printed) list of questions to find out what people think about a certain subject.
'**question mark** the mark ? put after a question or beside something to show doubt.
call something in question see **call**[1].
in question considered, thought about. *That is not the matter in question.*
no/some etc question of no/some etc discussion of. *There was no question of the pupil being expelled* i.e. that was not even considered.
out of the question impossible.
without/beyond question without doubt; certainly.
queue [kju:] *nc* line of waiting people, cars etc: *a queue outside a cinema; a queue of cars; form a queue; stand in a queue.* Also *vi* form or stand in a queue. *We had to queue for hours.*
quibble ['kwibl] *vi* use words so as to avoid giving a proper answer; find fault by concentrating on trifling details. Also *nc* this kind of use of words.
quick [kwik] *adj* **1.** fast; sudden; done in a short time: *go for a quick walk; have a quick meal; be a quick runner.* **2.** clever: *a quick child; quick to understand.* **3.** living: *the quick and the dead* (*o.f.* in sense **3.**). Also *nu* **1.** tender flesh under the fingernails and toenails. **2.** one's feelings: *be cut to the quick* i.e. be deeply offended. Also *adv* quickly. (*informal* in this sense). **quickly** *adv.* **quickness** *nu.*
quicken *vt/i* **1.** move more quickly: *quicken one's pace.* **2.** make or become lively, more lively. *The old sailor's story quickened the boy's imagination.*
'**quicklime** lime to which water has not been added.
'**quicksand** area of very wet sand into which men, ships etc can sink.
'**quicksilver** mercury.
quid[1] [kwid] *nc* piece of tobacco for chewing.
quid[2] [kwid] *nc* one pound or one hundred pence. *pl* **quid.** (*informal*).
quiescent [kwi'esnt] *adj* not active; at rest; not moving. **quiescence** *nu.*
quiet ['kwaiət] *adj* **1.** making little or no movement or sound. *Tell the children to be quiet.* **2.** peaceful; not causing disturbance: *quiet neighbours.* **3.** calm; not anxious, worried etc: *a quiet mind.* **4.** not bright: *quiet colours.* Also *vt/i* make or become quiet. **quietly** *adv.* **quietness** *nu.* **quieten** *vt.*
quill [kwil] *nc* **1.** large stiff feather. **2.** (in former times) hollow stem of such a feather, used as a pen. **3.** stiff, sharp hair or prickle such as some animals have on their backs.
quilt [kwilt] *nc* bed covering made of two pieces of cloth with some kind of soft material between them. **quilted** *adj.*
quince [kwins] *nc* **1.** type of hard, yellowish, pear-shaped fruit used in making jams and jellies. **2.** tree on which this grows.
quinine [kwi'ni:n] *nu* bitter medicine made from the bark of a tree and used as a remedy for fevers (e.g. malaria).
quintessence [kwin'tesns] *nu* perfect example of something: *the quintessence of politeness.*
quintet, quintette [kwin'tet] *nc* **1.** group of five singers or instrument players. **2.** piece of music for such a group.
quin(s) [kwin(z)], **quintuplet(s)** [kwin'tju:plit(s)] *n* (usu. *pl*) (one of) five babies born to the same mother at the same time.
quip [kwip] *nc* clever saying; witty remark. Also *vi* make a quip. *past* **quipped.**
quire ['kwaiə*] *nc* twenty-four sheets of paper.
quirk [kwə:k] *nc* peculiar or odd event, saying or action.
quisling ['kwizliŋ] *nc* person who works for an enemy who has conquered his country, by helping to govern the country under the control of his enemy.
quit [kwit] *vt/i* **1.** stop: *quit gambling.* **2.** leave; leave suddenly. *He quit the room angrily. pres part* **quitting.** *past* **quit** or **quitted.**

be quit of be free of; be rid of: *I'd give anything to be quit of him.*
be quits be on even terms with someone (by paying back a debt or by having one's revenge etc). *Give me back the money and then we'll be quits. (informal).*

quite [kwait] *intensifier* **1.** completely: *quite useless; quite different. Is that right? No, not quite.* **2.** rather; to some extent: *quite clever. Note:* when *quite* means 'rather' it often comes before *a* as in *quite a nice party, quite a pretty dress.*
quite, quite so I agree.
quite a outstanding: *quite a party.*
quite the thing fashionable; correct. *Short skirts are quite the thing this year. (informal).*

quiver[1] ['kwivə*] *vt/i* shake, tremble: *quivering with cold/fear etc.*

quiver[2] ['kwivə*] *nc* case for holding arrows.

quixotic [kwik'sɔtik] *adj* generous, sometimes in a rather foolish way; not taking proper care of one's own interests. **quixotically** *adv.*

quiz [kwiz] *vt* find out what someone knows by asking questions. *past* **quizzed.** Also *nc* game in which people try to answer questions. *pl* **quizzes.**
quizzical ['kwizikl] *adj* **1.** strange, amusing. **2.** teasing; making fun of someone: *a quizzical smile.* **quizzically** *adv.*

quoit [kɔit] *nc* ring made of metal, rubber etc which is used in certain games (often played on board ships).
quoits *npl* one such game, played by throwing a quoit at a small pole.

quorum ['kwɔːrəm] *nc* number of people that must be at a meeting, according to the rules of a society, before anything can be decided. *If we don't have (enough for) a quorum, we shall have to meet again.*

quota ['kwoutə] *nc* **1.** amount of something that one must give or receive: *exceed one's quota* i.e. give or receive more than one has to. **2.** amount or number of goods, immigrants etc allowed to enter a country, district etc.

quote [kwout] *vt* **1.** repeat or write the exact words of another: *quote Shakespeare.* **2.** give something as an example of what one means. **3.** give the price of, in arranging a commercial agreement: *quote a price for something.* Also *nc* quotation mark. see below.
quotation [kwou'teiʃən] *nc/u* quoting; something quoted: *quotations from Shakespeare; a quotation of a price.*
quo'tation marks marks " " or ' ' used to show the beginning and end of what is quoted (e.g. "Come here," he said).

quoth [kwouθ] *vt* said (*o.f.*).

quotient ['kwouʃənt] *nc* number of times one number can be divided by another (e.g. if you divide 21 by 3, the quotient is 7).
in'telligence quotient number describing a person's intelligence, based on certain tests.

R

rabbi ['ræbai] *nc* teacher of the Jewish religion and law; Jewish priest.
Note: it can also be used as a title.
rabbit ['ræbit] *nc* small animal with long ears which lives in holes in the ground. Also *nu* the fur of such an animal; its flesh used as food.
rabble ['ræbl] *nc* mob; rough, disorganized crowd.
rabid ['ræbid] *adj* **1.** very angry and violent. **2.** affected by rabies; mad: *a rabid dog.*
rabies ['reibi:z] *nu* disease which causes madness (esp. in dogs).
Note: followed by a *sing* verb.
race[1] [reis] *nc* contest to see if one person/thing can move faster than another: *a horse-race; a five-mile race.* Also *vi* move quickly: *race for the door.* Also *vt* put (a horse etc) in a race.
racing *nu* running of horses, greyhounds, camels etc in races.
the races *npl* occasion when horses etc race against one another.
'racecourse places where horses race against one another.
'racehorse horse specially intended to run in races.
race[2] [reis] *nc* **1.** group of people descended, or believed to be descended, from the same ancestors; section of mankind different from others in colour etc: *people of different races.* **2.** section of living things: *the human race.*
racial ['reiʃl] *adj* connected with race: *racial discrimination* i.e. giving privileges to one race which are not given to another. **racially** *adv.*
racialism ['reiʃəlizəm] *nu* political or social beliefs based on differences in race; belief that one race is superior to others or that races should be kept apart. **racialist** ['reiʃəlist] *nc/adj.* **racism** *nu.* **racist** *nc/adj.*
rack [ræk] *nc* **1.** frame on which things are kept (e.g. *plate rack, tool rack,* (in trains) *luggage rack etc*). **2.** instrument formerly used for torturing people by stretching them. **3.** bar with teeth on one edge into which teeth on the edge of a wheel can fit. Also *vt* **1.** torture by using a rack (in sense **2.**). **2.** cause great pain: *racked with grief.*
rack one's brains think very hard.
on the rack suffering very much.
gone to rack and ruin (usu. with reference to buildings) in a state of great neglect. *The house had gone to rack and ruin.*
racket[1] ['rækit] *nc* **1.** loud noise. **2.** not strictly honest way of making money.
racketeer [ræki'tiə*] *nc* person who gets money in a dishonest way (esp. by using violence). **racketeering** *nu.* (all *informal*).
racket[2], **racquet** ['rækit] *nc* light kind of stringed bat used in playing tennis etc.
racy ['reisi] *adj* lively; entertaining: *a racy speech.* **racily** *adv.*
radar ['reidɑ:*] *nu* method of detecting the presence of planes, ships etc by electronic means instead of by sight, also used for navigation.
'radar screen instrument which shows the presence of objects in this way.
radiant ['reidiənt] *adj* **1.** bright and happy: *a radiant smile.* **2.** sending out rays of light or heat. **radiantly** *adv.* **radiance** *nu.*
radiate ['reidieit] *vt/i* **1.** send out light or heat. *The sun radiates both light and heat.* **2.** come out in many directions from one place: *light radiated from the window.* **3.** show; give out: *a smile radiating joy.* **4.** spread out from a centre. *From the town square, roads radiate in every direction.*
radiation [reidi'eiʃən] **1.** *nu* act of sending out rays of heat, light, sound etc. **2.** *nc* something radiated. **3.** *nu* radioactivity.
radiator *nc* **1.** instrument for heating houses etc by means of pipes through which hot water or steam is passed. **2.** part of a motorcar for cooling the engine.
radi'ation sickness illness caused by exposure to radioactivity.
radical ['rædikl] *adj* **1.** changing something completely: *a radical reform of the law* i.e. a big change in the law. **2.** wanting big changes (esp. in politics). Also *nc* person who wants big changes in the way a country is run. **radically** *adv.*
radio ['reidiou] **1.** *nu* way of sending out speech, music etc through the air without using a connecting wire. **2.** *nc* device for receiving speech, music etc sent out in this way. *pl* **radios.** Also *adj* connected with, or sent by, radio: *a radio message.* Also *vt/i* send a message etc by radio. *past* **radioed.**
'radio'active *adj* giving out energy in the form of rays, which can have a harmful effect on living things. **'radioac'tivity** *nu.* see **radiation.**
'radiogram **1.** (*Brit*) radio and record player joined together. **2.** (*US*) message sent by radio.
'radiograph *nc* X-ray photograph. **radiography** [reidi'ɔgrəfi] *nu.*
radiographer [reidi'ɔgrəfə*] *nc* person whose work is to take X-ray photographs.
radish ['rædiʃ] *nc* red or white root used in salads.
radium ['reidiəm] *nu* radioactive metal used in treating people for certain diseases.
radius ['reidiəs] *nc* **1.** line going straight from the centre of a circle to the edge of the circle. **2.** area as measured from a centre point. *There is no other house within a radius of a mile.*
raffia ['ræfiə] *nu* fibre from a type of palm tree, used for making baskets, mats etc.
raffle ['ræfl] *nc* game of chance in which people buy numbered tickets to have a chance of winning an article. Also *vt* put an article up as the prize in a raffle: *raffle a radio.*
raft [rɑ:ft] *nc* flat boat made from large pieces of wood bound together.
rafter ['rɑ:ftə*] *nc* one of the sloping beams

which helps to support a roof.

rag[1] [ræg] *nc* **1.** torn piece of cloth: *clean the floor with an old rag.* **2.** contemptuous name for a newspaper. (*informal* in sense **2.**).

rags *npl* old and torn clothes: *be dressed in rags.*

ragged ['rægid] *adj* **1.** old and torn: *ragged clothes.* **2.** dressed in rags. **3.** not straight; having sharp points: *a ragged edge.*

'ragamuffin small boy dressed in ragged clothes (*o.f.*).

rag[2] [ræg] *vt/i* make fun of; play jokes (on). *past* **ragged.** Also *nc*: *a student rag* i.e. procession etc organized by students to raise money for charities.

rage [reidʒ] *nc* **1.** wild anger: *be in a rage.* **2.** great desire for something. Also *vi* **1.** be very angry. **2.** be very violent. *A storm was raging.*

all the rage very fashionable. (*informal*).

fly into a rage/temper see **fly**[2].

raid [reid] *nc* sudden attack: *an air raid.* Also *vt/i* attack suddenly.

raider *nc* someone/something making an attack.

rail[1] [reil] *nc* **1.** long, narrow piece of wood or metal, or a number of pieces like this, used in making fences or at the side of stairs to keep people from falling etc. **2.** one of the two metal bars in a railway track. **3.** railway: *go by rail.* Also *vt* put rails on or round something: *rail something in/off.*

railing *nc* (sometimes used in *pl*) fence made from rails.

'railroad (*US*) railway.

'railway *nc* **1.** tracks on which trains travel: *a railway from London to Glasgow.* **2.** everything used in carrying people or goods by train (including trains, stations etc).

go off the rails 1. leave the railway track. *Some people were injured when the train went off the rails.* **2.** get out of control; behave badly. (*informal*). **3.** be wrong in what one says or does. (*informal*).

rail[2] [reil] *vi* speak angrily: *rail at someone; rail about something.*

raillery ['reiləri] *nu* making fun of a person in a friendly way.

raiment ['reimənt] *nu* clothes (*o.f.*).

rain [rein] *nu* **1.** water coming down from the clouds. **2.** thick, fast fall of anything: *a rain of bullets.* Also *vt/i* **1.** come down in drops of water. **2.** come or send quickly and in large amounts: *rain gifts upon someone.*

rainy *adj* having much rain: *a rainy day; a rainy climate.*

the rains *npl* season in tropical countries when there are frequent heavy falls of rain.

'rainbow ['reinbou] arch or bow of different colours sometimes seen in the sky (esp. after rain).

'raincoat coat which is worn to protect one from the rain.

'raindrop single drop of rain. *There were raindrops on the window.*

'rainfall amount of rain, hail, snow that has fallen in a certain time in a certain area.

'rain gauge instrument for measuring the amount of rainfall.

'rainproof *adj* able to keep rain out.

save for a rainy day keep some money for a time when one will need it. (*informal*).

raise [reiz] *vt* **1.** lift up; put at a higher level: *raise one's hand; raise something that has fallen down.* **2.** put in a higher position. **3.** cause to grow or increase in number: *raise wheat/sheep etc.* **4.** increase in amount: *raise the rent/temperature etc.* **5.** cause something to rise: *raise a cloud of dust.* **6.** bring up for discussion: *raise several points.* **7.** manage to get or bring together: *raise an army; raise money.* **8.** bring up; rear: *raise a family.* Also *nc* (*US*) increase of wages, price etc. (*Brit* **rise**).

Note: raise is the verb which is used when someone/something is placed in a higher position by some other person/thing. *The injured boy was raised onto the bed.* Compare this with *The boy rose* i.e. he did the action himself. see **rise.**

raisin ['reizn] *nc* dried grape (sometimes put into bread, cakes etc).

raison d'être ['reizɔ̃:n'dɛ:tr] *n* cause; reason why something exists.

raj [rɑ:dʒ] *nu* rule (usu. the rule of the British in India).

rajah ['rɑ:dʒə] *nc* ruler or chief in India etc.

rake[1] [reik] *nc* tool with teeth and a long handle, used mainly for gathering together loose leaves, stones etc. Also *vt/i* **1.** move with a rake: *rake the soil* i.e. make smooth and free of stones; *rake the leaves together and burn them.* **2.** fire guns at a ship etc from one end to another.

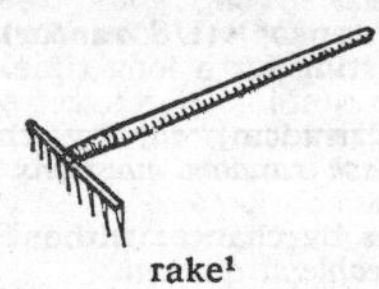

rake[1]

rake something out find by searching: *rake out some interesting facts.*

rake through/over something search carefully. (*informal*).

rake something up cause people to know or remember something, which is better forgotten. (*informal*).

rake[2] [reik] *nc* man who lives an immoral life. (rather *o.f.*).

rakish ['reikiʃ] *adj* smart; giving an impression of self-confidence: *have one's hat at a rakish angle* i.e. a steep angle which shows that one is confident. **rakishly** *adv.*

rally[1] ['ræli] *vt/i* **1.** bring people together again (esp. after a defeat): *rally troops.* **2.** gain strength; give strength to: *rally during an illness.* **3.** come to the help of. *His friends rallied to his side.* Also *nc* **1.** large meeting: *a political rally.* **2.** act of recovering.

rally[2] ['ræli] *vt* make fun of someone in a friendly way (*o.f.*).

ram [ræm] *nc* **1.** male sheep. **2.** instrument used for pushing something or giving heavy blows. Also *vt* push or strike with a ram; run into something with great force: *ram a ship. past* **rammed.**

'ramrod stick for pushing gunpowder etc into an old-fashioned gun.

ramble ['ræmbl] *vi* **1.** go for a long walk for enjoyment. **2.** talk or write without stating clearly what one means: *ramble on for hours.* Also *nc* long walk taken for pleasure (esp. in the country).

rambler *nc* **1.** kind of climbing rosebush. **2.** person who takes long walks in the country.

rambling *adj* with one bit added onto another, as if it had not been planned: *a rambling town/house/speech etc.* Also *nu* act of wandering or walking for pleasure.

ramify ['ræmifai] *vt/i* produce branches.
ramification [ræmifi'keiʃən] *nc* part of something (esp. an idea, argument, set of rules etc) that is very complicated. *I have never got to know all the ramifications of his business.*

ramp [ræmp] *nc* slope that connects two places at different levels: *drag stones up a ramp to build something.*

rampage ['ræmpidʒ] *vi* rush about wildly or angrily.
be on the rampage behave in an excited or angry way.

rampant ['ræmpənt] *adj* **1.** growing without being controlled. *Crime was rampant.* **2.** standing up on the hind legs (as animals are sometimes shown on coats of arms).

rampart ['ræmpɑːt] *nc* **1.** wide bank of earth, sometimes with a wall on top of it, built around a fort, castle etc to defend it. **2.** anything that defends.

ramshackle ['ræmʃækl] *adj* almost falling down: *a ramshackle house.*

ran [ræn] past tense of **run**[1].

ranch [rɑːntʃ] *nc* **1.** (*US*) very large cattle farm. **2.** (*US*) any kind of farm: *a chicken ranch.* **rancher** *nc.*

rancid ['rænsid] *adj* bad; stale: *rancid butter/fat etc.*

rancour ['ræŋkə*] (*US* **rancor**) *nu* bitter feelings lasting for a long time. **rancorous** *adj.*

random ['rændəm] *adj* by chance; unplanned: *ask random questions.* **randomly** *adv.*
at random by chance; without any plan: *speak to people at random.*

rang [ræŋ] past tense of **ring**[2].

range[1] [reindʒ] *nc* **1.** line of things, one beside the other: *a range of mountains.* **2.** way things change between limits: *a wide range of prices* i.e. many different prices from high to low; *a wide range of materials to choose from.* **3.** how far a gun can fire: *a range of five miles.* **4.** how far something can be heard, seen etc: *come within hearing range.* **5.** place where people can practise with guns: *a firing range.* **6.** land where cattle can graze. **7.** large old-fashioned type of stove: *a kitchen range.*
'rangefinder instrument for finding how far away something is.

range[2] [reindʒ] *vt/i* **1.** move or occur between certain limits: *prices ranging from 50 pence to 75 pence.* **2.** put in a line or in lines. *He ranged the boys in order of size.* **3.** move freely over; go all over: *animals that ranged the plains.* **4.** search: *range high and low* i.e. search everywhere. **5.** stretch; run in a line: *ranging east and west* i.e. running on a line going from east to west. **6.** be found: *a flower ranging from the north of Europe to the south* i.e. found in that area.
ranger *nc* person whose work is looking after a forest or other type of countryside.
range oneself put oneself, take one's place. *They ranged themselves with/on the side of/against their leader.*

rank[1] [ræŋk] **1.** *nc* line of something (esp. soldiers): *drawn up in ranks* i.e. standing in lines; *a taxi rank* i.e. a place where taxis wait to be hired. **2.** *nc/u* level; position (esp. in the army): *the rank of captain; an actor of the first rank* i.e. one of the best; *a man of rank* i.e. high position. Also *vt/i* **1.** arrange in a line. **2.** come or put in a certain class. *London ranks as one of the world's largest cities.*
the ranks, the other ranks, the rank and file ordinary soldiers, not officers. see **file**[3].

rank[2] [ræŋk] *adj* **1.** overgrown: *a garden rank with weeds.* **2.** large and coarse: *rank grass.* **3.** bad to taste or smell: *rank tobacco.* **4.** very bad; completely bad: *rank dishonesty.*

rankle ['ræŋkl] *vi* continue to cause anger or bitterness: *an insult that rankles.*

ransack ['rænsæk] *vt* **1.** search thoroughly (often causing great untidiness or disorder): *ransack a room for something.* **2.** steal everything from. *Thieves ransacked the house.*

ransom ['rænsəm] *nc/u* amount of money that has to be paid before someone is set free. Also *vt* get someone free by paying the money demanded.
hold someone to ransom keep someone a prisoner until money is paid for his release.

rant [rænt] *vt/i* speak wildly or violently: *a ranting speaker.* **ranter** *nc.*

rap [ræp] *nc* sharp, light blow: *a rap at/on the door.* Also *vt/i* give a rap: *rap loudly. past* **rapped.**
rap out say quickly: *rap out an answer.*
not care/give a rap not care or worry at all. (*informal*).
take the rap take the punishment for a crime. (*informal*).

rapacious [rə'peiʃəs] *adj* greedy for money; taking everything one can. **rapaciously** *adv.*
rapacity [rə'pæsiti] *nu* greed.

rape[1] [reip] *vt* use force to commit a sexual crime against a woman. Also *nu.*

rape[2] [reip] *nu* plant used for feeding sheep and pigs, and for the oil obtained from its seeds.

rapid ['ræpid] *adj* quick-moving; fast: *a rapid worker; a rapid increase in the number of cars.* **rapidly** *adv.* **rapidity** [rə'piditi] *nu.*
rapids *npl* part of a river where the water is shallow and moves very quickly over rocks.

rapier ['reipiə*] *nc* light, thin sword.

rapport [ræ'pɔː*] *nc* close understanding and cooperation.

rapprochement [ræ'prɔʃmɑ̃ːŋ] *nc* coming together of people who have formerly been enemies.

rapt [ræpt] *adj* thinking about something so deeply that one is not aware of what is going on around one: *rapt in thought.*

rapture ['ræptʃə*] *nc/u* **1.** great joy: *listen with rapture.* **2.** statements etc which show that one is very pleased: *go into raptures.*
rapturous *adj.* **rapturously** *adv.*

rare [rɛə*] *adj* **1.** not common; not often seen or found. *Gold is a rare metal.* **2.** thin: *the rare atmosphere high above the earth.* **3.** very good: *have a rare time* i.e. enjoy oneself. (*informal* in sense **3.**).
rarely *adv* not very often.
rarefied ['rɛərifaid] *adj* thin; made thinner: *the rarefied air on high mountains.*
rarity **1.** *nc* rare (and usu. valuable) thing. **2.** *nu* state of being rare.

rascal ['rɑːskl] *nc* **1.** bad, dishonest person. **2.** (used in fun) mischievous child: *a little rascal.* **rascally** *adv.*

rash[1] [ræʃ] *adj* careless; done or said without proper thought: *a rash decision/statement etc.* **rashly** *adv.* **rashness** *nu.*

rash[2] [ræʃ] *nc* breaking out of small red spots on the skin caused by certain illnesses.

rasher ['ræʃə*] *nc* thin slice of bacon.

rasp [rɑːsp] *nc* tool with a rough surface, used for rubbing or smoothing wood etc. Also *vt/i* **1.** rub with a rasp. **2.** make a harsh unpleasant sound: *a rasping voice.* **3.** annoy; irritate. *His voice rasped on my nerves.*

raspberry ['rɑːzbəri] *nc* **1.** kind of small, red fruit growing on a bush. **2.** bush on which raspberries grow. **3.** impolite noise made by blowing between the lips. (*informal* in sense **3.**).

rat [ræt] *nc* **1.** animal like a mouse, but larger. **2.** nasty person.

'rat race situation among professional workers in which a person competes with his colleagues to obtain a better position etc for himself. (*informal*).

rat on someone betray someone. (*informal*).

smell a rat be suspicious; suspect that something is wrong. (*informal*).

ratchet ['rætʃit] *nc* toothed wheel with a catch which allows the wheel to move in one direction only.

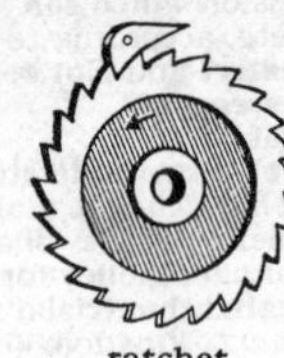

ratchet

rate¹ [reit] *nc* **1.** speed: *at the rate of ten miles in two hours.* **2.** amount one pays or is paid: *pay workers at the rate of a pound an hour.* **3.** amount of anything as measured against another thing: *the birthrate* i.e. the number of births measured against the number of people living in a place. **4.** local tax paid in a town or local area for some purpose: *the water rate.* Also *vt/i* consider; measure the quality of. *How do you rate our team's chances of winning?*

at any rate 1. in any case; whatever happens. **2.** at least.

at this/that rate under these/those circumstances.

first-rate very good.

second-rate not very good.

third-rate poor.

rate² [reit] *vt/i* speak angrily to someone (*o.f.*).

rather ['rɑːðə*] *adv/intensifier* **1.** more willingly. *He would rather go than stay* i.e. he would prefer to go. **2.** somewhat; to a certain extent: *rather good; rather too difficult for me.* **3.** more truly; more accurately. *I met him very late on Friday night, or rather, early on Saturday morning.* **4.** (in answers) certainly. *Did you enjoy it? Rather.* (*informal* and rather *o.f.* in sense **4.**).

ratify ['rætifai] *vt* confirm; approve. *The agreement between the two countries has been ratified.* **ratification** [rætifi'keiʃən] *nu.*

rating ['reitiŋ] *nc* **1.** class to which something (e.g. a ship) belongs. **2.** (navy) sailor who is not an officer.

ratio ['reiʃiou] *nc* way that numbers or quantities are related to one another. *The ratio of pupils to teachers was 30 to 1* i.e. there were 30 pupils for every 1 teacher. *pl* **ratios.**

ration ['ræʃən] *nc* amount of something (e.g. food) given out to each person. Also *vt* allow only a certain amount. *Food was rationed during the war.*

rational ['ræʃənl] *adj* reasonable; able to reason; based on reason or common sense: *a rational explanation.* (*opp* **irrational**).

rationally *adv.*

rationalism *nu* belief in reason rather than the emotions or religion as a guide to thought and action. **rationalist** *nc.*

rationale [ræʃə'nɑːl] *nc* logical reasons for a course of action.

rattan [rə'tæn] **1.** *nc* kind of palm tree with a stem like a cane. **2.** *nu* stems of this palm tree used in making baskets, chairs etc.

rattle ['rætl] *vt/i* **1.** make a number of short, sharp sounds: *rattle a box with some coins in it.* **2.** do or say something quickly and confidently: *rattle off a poem.* (*informal*). **3.** move making a number of short, sharp sounds. *The old cart rattled along the street.* Also *nc/u* **1.** rattling noise. **2.** child's toy which makes a rattling noise.

'rattlesnake poisonous American snake which makes a noise with its tail.

raucous ['rɔːkəs] *adj* sounding harsh; rough: *a raucous voice; raucous shouts.* **raucously** *adv.*

ravage ['rævidʒ] *vt/i* **1.** destroy; damage badly: *a city ravaged by high winds.* **2.** steal from, using violence.

ravages *npl* destruction or damage caused by something: *the ravages of time.*

rave [reiv] *vi* talk wildly; talk in a mad or foolish way. *While she had the fever, she raved for hours.*

ravings *npl* wild or foolish talk: *the ravings of a madman.*

rave about someone/something say that one thinks very highly of someone/something. (*informal*).

ravel ['rævl] *vt/i* separate into threads; have loose threads at the edge. *past* **ravelled.** (*US* **raveled**).

raven ['reivən] *nc* large black crow with a black beak and a deep voice. Also *adj* shiny black.

ravenous ['rævənəs] *adj* very hungry. **ravenously** *adv.*

ravine [rə'viːn] *nc* long, deep, narrow valley.

ravish ['ræviʃ] *vt/i* **1.** fill with delight: *ravishing scenery.* **2.** rape i.e. use force to commit a sexual crime against a woman (*o.f.* in sense **2.**).

raw [rɔː] *adj* **1.** not cooked: *raw meat.* **2.** in the natural state; not treated or prepared: *raw materials; raw hides* i.e. not yet made into leather. **3.** not trained or experienced: *a raw recruit* i.e. someone who has just joined. **4.** cold and damp: *a raw morning.* **5.** with the skin off; sore: *a raw ankle.* **6.** unfair: *a raw deal* i.e. unfair treatment. (*informal* in sense **6.**).

ray [rei] *nc* **1.** line or beam of light, heat etc. **2.** line coming from a centre.

not a ray of hope no hope at all. (*informal*).

rayon ['reiɔn] *nu* man-made material which can be made to look like silk, wool or cotton: *a rayon shirt.*

raze [reiz] *vt* destroy houses, towns etc by levelling them to the ground. *The village was completely razed during the battle.*

razor ['reizə*] *nc* instrument with a sharp blade used for shaving.

re¹ [riː] *prep* about; concerning (used in business or informally).

re-² [riː] *prefix* again (e.g. **rearm etc**).

reach [riːtʃ] *vt/i* **1.** get to; arrive at: *reach the top of a mountain.* **2.** stretch out for with the hand: *reach for a book.* **3.** stretch; extend: *a wall that reaches to the end of the road.* **4.** get in touch with; contact. *How can I reach you?* **5.** hand something to someone. *Reach me that book, please.* Also *nc/u* **1.** distance that one can reach: *beyond my reach.* **2.** straight part of a river: *the upper reaches of the Amazon.*

react [ri'ækt] *vi* behave in a certain way because of something that has been done to one. *When I punished him, he reacted by bursting into tears.*

reactor *nc* apparatus for producing power from nuclear reactions. (Also **nuclear reactor**).

react against someone/something move away from, show that one dislikes someone/something. *Children sometimes react against the things their parents believe in.*

react on/upon someone have a certain effect on someone.

react to someone/something be affected by someone/something. *How did he react to the news?* i.e. did it have any effect on him?

reaction [ri'ækʃən] *nc/u* **1.** movement of feeling away from someone/something; movement back to a former condition. *This made him popular for a time, but then a reaction set in* i.e. he became unpopular again. **2.** political movement wanting to bring back the old ways of doing things: *the forces of reaction.* **3.** feelings and thoughts about. *What was your reaction to him?* **4.** process of change when certain substances are brought together: *chemical reaction; nuclear reaction.*

reactionary *nc* person who is against progress or change (esp. in politics). Also *adj.*

read [ri:d] *vt/i* **1.** look at printed or written letters and be able to understand them: *read a book; be able to read.* **2.** say aloud what is written or printed. *The teacher read a story to the class.* **3.** give information by letters, numbers etc. *The thermometer reads eighty* i.e. shows a temperature of 80°. **4.** study a subject at university: *read history.* **5.** get to know; understand: *read someone's thoughts. past* **read** [red].

readable *adj* **1.** interesting or easy to read: *a readable book.* **2.** able to be read. (*opp* **unreadable**).

Note: for sense **2.** it is better to use legible (e.g. *legible handwriting*).

reader *nc* **1.** person who reads (esp. someone whose job it is to decide whether a story etc ought to be published). **2.** teacher above the rank of lecturer in a university. **3.** schoolbook used for reading.

reading **1.** *nu* act of looking at and understanding print: *interrupt someone's reading.* **2.** *nc* saying aloud of what is written or printed: *a reading from Shakespeare.* **3.** *nc* information given by letters, numbers etc. *The thermometer has a reading of sixty-five degrees.* **4.** *nu* knowledge of books: *a person of wide reading.* **5.** *nc* one of the stages a bill must go through in Parliament before it is made law.

ready ['redi] *adj* **1.** prepared. *The dinner is ready. Tom is ready for school now.* **2.** willing. *Are you ready to serve your country?* **3.** quick: *have a ready answer.* **4.** available; within reach. *He always kept a gun ready.*

readily *adv* **1.** willingly. *I would readily help you.* **2.** without difficulty: *readily available.*

readiness *nu.*

'ready-'made *adj* able to be used immediately: *ready-made clothes* i.e. ready to be worn, not made to measure.

'ready 'money cash which is available immediately.

'ready 'reckoner book of tables which makes calculations easier.

real [riəl] *adj* true; actual; not made up: *the real reason for doing something* i.e. not a false one; *a real hero. Is it a real diamond or is it a fake?*

realism *nu* **1.** (in stories, paintings etc) showing of life as it really is, not trying to hide its bad aspects. **2.** act of seeing life as it really is, with no false ideas about it.

realist *nc* someone who practises realism.

realistic [riə'listik] *adj* **1.** true to life. **2.** practical; not having false ideas. (*opp* **unrealistic**). **realistically** *adv.*

reality [ri'æliti] **1.** *nu* state of being real or true; fact: *believe in the reality of God* i.e. that God in fact exists. **2.** *nc* something that is real or true.

really **1.** *adv* truly. *Do you really mean that?* **2.** *intensifier* very. *The show was really good.* **3.** *interj* expression which can show interest, doubt, anger etc, according to the way it is said. (Also **Really!** and **Not really!**).

'real estate see **estate.**

in reality in fact.

realize ['riəlaiz] *vt* **1.** understand. *Does he realize what he has done?* **2.** make something actually happen: *realize one's hopes.* **3.** make money on; get money for: *realize one's possessions.* **realization** [riəlai'zeiʃən] *nu.*

realm [relm] *nc* **1.** kingdom (*o.f.*). **2.** area: *the realm of science; the realms of the imagination.*

ream [ri:m] *nc* 480 sheets of paper.

reap [ri:p] *vt/i* **1.** cut grain (e.g. wheat etc). **2.** gather in a crop of grain. **3.** get: *reap large profits.*

reaper *nc* person or machine that reaps.

reappear [ri:ə'piə*] *vt* appear again. **reappearance** *nu.*

reappraisal [ri:ə'preizl] *nc/u* process of examining a situation again in order to decide whether to change any previous decisions.

reappraise *vt* examine in this way.

rear[1] [riə*] *n sing* **1.** back part: *at the rear of the house.* **2.** last part of an army: *bring up the rear* i.e. come last. Also *attrib adj* back: *the rear wheels of a car.*

'rear 'admiral officer in the navy below a vice-admiral and higher than a captain.

'rearguard group of soldiers guarding the rear of an army.

rear[2] [riə*] *vt/i* **1.** make grow; help to grow: *rear poultry* i.e. hens etc. **2.** bring up: *rear children.* **3.** rise up on the hind legs: *the horse reared.* **4.** raise: *rear one's head.*

rearm [ri:'ɑ:m] *vt/i* provide (oneself) with weapons again. **rearmament** *nu.*

reason[1] ['ri:zn] **1.** *nc/u* cause; purpose in doing something. *Is there any reason why he should be rude to you?* **2.** *nu* ability to think: *lose one's reason* i.e. go mad. **3.** *nu* good sense; common sense: *try to make someone listen to reason.*

by reason of because of.

do anything within reason do anything that is sensible. *I'll do anything within reason to help you.*

it stands to reason see **stand**[1].

without rhyme or reason see **rhyme.**

reason[2] ['ri:zn] *vt/i* **1.** use powers of thinking; think. *Do you think some animals can reason?* **2.** use reasons or arguments to prove something.

reasonable *adj* 1. sensible; willing to listen to others' views: *a reasonable person.* 2. according to reason: *a reasonable argument.* 3. fair; just; which one could accept: *a reasonable price/excuse etc.* (*opp* **unreasonable**). **reasonably** *adv.*
reason something out solve some problem by thinking carefully about it.
reason someone into/out of doing something use an argument to persuade someone to do/not to do something.
reason with someone try to persuade someone by arguments.

reassure [riːəˈʃuə*] *vt* make someone confident again. **reassuring** *adj.* **reassuringly** *adv.* **reassurance** *nc/u.*

rebate [ˈriːbeit] *nc* return of part of the money one has paid: *a rebate of one's income tax.*

rebel [riˈbel] *vi* 1. use violence to fight against the government. *The people rebelled.* 2. fight against or resist anything. *The boy rebelled against having to come home so early. past* **rebelled.** Also [ˈrebl] *nc* person who rebels.
rebellion [riˈbeliən] *nc/u* act of rebelling. *The government put down the rebellion.*
rebellious [riˈbeliəs] *adj* resisting the government or any other authority; difficult to control. **rebelliously** *adv.*

rebound [riˈbaund] *vi* spring back; hit something and come back. *The ball rebounded from the wall.* Also [ˈriːbaund] *nc* act of rebounding: *catch a ball on the rebound.*

rebuff [riˈbʌf] *nc* unkind action towards someone who is trying to be friendly.
get/meet with a rebuff be treated in this way. *I tried to help but I only met with a rebuff.*

rebuke [riˈbjuːk] *vt* find fault with someone. *The teacher rebuked the boy for his laziness.* Also *nc*: *give a rebuke to someone.*

rebut [riˈbʌt] *vt* prove that something that has been said is wrong. *past* **rebutted. rebuttal** *nc.*

recalcitrant [riˈkælsitrnt] *adj* disobedient: *a recalcitrant child.* **recalcitrance** *nu.*

recall [riˈkɔːl] *vt* 1. remember. *I can't recall his name.* 2. tell to come back; order back. *The government has recalled its ambassador from Paris.* 3. take back. *The car factory recalled* **all** *the cars which were supposed to be faulty.* Also *nc/u* act of taking back: *beyond recall* i.e. not able to be brought back.

recant [riˈkænt] *vt/i* say that one no longer believes in something one used to believe in; take back something one has said. **recantation** [riːkænˈteiʃən] *nc/u.*

recapitulate [riːkəˈpitjuleit] *vt/i* repeat the main ideas of something that has already been said. **recapitulation** [riːkəpitjuˈleiʃən] *nc/u.*

recast [ˈriːˈkɑːst] *vt* make into a different shape; arrange in a different way: *recast a sentence.*

recede [riˈsiːd] *vi* 1. move, appear to move, backwards. *As the train went faster, the railway station receded from view.* 2. slope backwards: *a receding chin.* 3. leave; go away from. 4. become less in value: *receding prices.* **recession** [riˈseʃən] *nc/u.*

receipt [riˈsiːt] 1. *nc* piece of paper which shows that something has been paid for: *get a receipt for everything one buys.* 2. *nu* act of receiving. *On receipt of the news, he went home.* 3. *nc* recipe. (rather *o.f.* in sense 3.). Also *vt* sign a piece of paper to show that something has been paid for.
receipts *npl* money received from some kind of business.
make out a receipt write (and sign) a receipt.

receive [riˈsiːv] *vt/i* 1. get; be given: *receive presents/letters from home etc.* 2. accept something that has been sent or given. 3. welcome: *receive visitors.*
receiver *nc* 1. part of a telephone that is held to the ear. 2. person who accepts stolen goods.

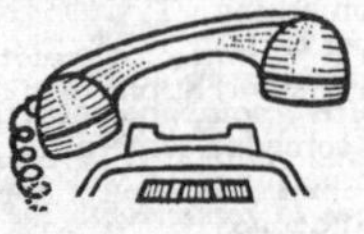

receiver (*def 1*)

Note: the name for someone who accepts things lawfully is *recipient.*
3. wireless receiving apparatus.

recent [ˈriːsnt] *adj* made or having happened a short time ago; modern: *a recent event; recent history.*
recently *adv*: *I haven't seen him recently.*

receptacle [riˈseptikl] *nc* container of any kind.

reception [riˈsepʃən] 1. *nu* act of receiving. 2. *nc* way of receiving or being received. *The winning team got a wonderful reception in their home town.* 3. *nc* party or gathering to entertain visitors: *a wedding reception.* 4. *nu* people in a hotel whose job is to receive guests etc; the place where such people work.
receptionist *nc* someone (usu. a woman) whose job it is to receive people visiting a hotel, a doctor etc.
receptive [riˈseptiv] *adj* quick to understand new ideas; willing to accept new ideas. (*opp* **unreceptive**). **receptively** *adv.*

recess [riˈses] *nc* 1. period of time during which work stops: *a recess of thirty minutes.* 2. space in a wall for a bed, cupboard etc. 3. inner part of something; remote place: *the dark recesses of a cave.*

recession [riˈseʃən] *nc/u* see **recede.**

recipe [ˈresipi] *nc* instructions on how to prepare a certain kind of food: *a recipe for a cake.* 2. way to do anything: *the recipe for success.*

recipient [riˈsipiənt] *nc* person who receives something.

reciprocal [riˈsiprəkl] *adj* given or received in return: *reciprocal liking* i.e. each liking the other.

reciprocate [riˈsiprəkeit] *vt/i* 1. give etc in return. *He did not reciprocate my friendship* i.e. I was friendly with him, but he was not friendly with me. 2. move, cause to move, backwards and forwards in a straight line (e.g. like the movement of a piston).
reciprocation [risiprəˈkeiʃən] *nu.*

recite [riˈsait] *vt/i* 1. say something aloud from memory: *recite a poem.* 2. give a list of something: *recite one's complaints.*
recital *nc* 1. act of reciting. 2. performance of music or poetry by one person or a few people.
recitation [resiˈteiʃən] *nc/u* 1. reciting: *a recitation from Shakespeare.* 2. passages, poems etc for reciting: *a book of recitations.*

reckless [ˈrekləs] *adj* not caring about danger; very careless: *a reckless driver;*

reckless of what might happen. **recklessly** *adv.* **recklessness** *nu.*

reckon ['rekən] *vt/i* **1.** arrive at a number without counting exactly. *Have you reckoned the number of cattle you have?* **2.** consider; think. *He is reckoned to be a very good teacher.* **3.** suppose; have the opinion. *I reckon he'll be late.* (*informal* in sense **3.**).

reckoning 1. *nc/u* way of counting; calculation. **2.** *nc* bill (at a hotel, restaurant etc).

reckon something in include something in one's counting.

reckon on someone/something depend on someone/something. *I was reckoning on John arriving tonight.*

reckon something up add up.

reckon with someone/something take notice of someone/something; deal with someone/something. *If you try to do that you will have to reckon with me* i.e. I shall be against you.

day of reckoning time when one must pay for what one has done wrong.

out in one's reckoning wrong in one's calculations (esp. of money).

reclaim [ri'kleim] *vt* **1.** bring back into use: *reclaim land from the sea.* **2.** bring back from evil ways: *reclaim a drunkard.* **3.** ask for the return of something that belongs to one: *reclaim a lost purse.* **reclamation** [reklə'meiʃən] *nu.*

recline [ri'klain] *vt/i* **1.** lie down: *recline on a couch.* **2.** lay down; put in a resting position: *recline one's head.*

recluse [ri'klu:s] *nc* person who lives alone, and tries to avoid meeting other people.

recognize ['rekəgnaiz] *vt* **1.** remember; know the name of; identify as something seen before. *I could hardly recognize my friend.* **2.** admit; consider; realize that something is true. *He has to recognize the danger of what he is doing.* **3.** agree to have diplomatic relations with: *recognize a foreign government.* **4.** give official approval to. *His sacrifices for his country have at last been recognized.* **recognition** [rekəg'niʃən] *nu.*

recognized *adj*: *a recognized authority* i.e. accepted as valid.

recoil [ri'kɔil] *vi* **1.** draw back in fear, disgust etc: *recoil from the sight of a snake.* **2.** spring back. *The rifle recoiled when it was fired.* Also *nc/u* act of recoiling.

recollect [rekə'lekt] *vt/i* remember. *I can't recollect his name.*

recollection 1. *nc* something remembered: *recollections of his childhood.* **2.** *nu* power of remembering: *to the best of my recollection* i.e. as far as I can remember.

recommend [rekə'mend] *vt* **1.** speak in favour; say that someone/something is good for a certain purpose. *I recommend these pills for your cough. He recommended me for the post of headmaster.* **2.** advise. *I recommend you to follow your doctor's advice.* **3.** make attractive. *The sunny climate of Spain recommends it as a good place for a holiday.*

recommendation [rekəmen'deiʃən] *nc/u* **1.** act of recommending. **2.** letter etc which says that someone is suitable for a particular job etc.

recompense ['rekəmpens] *vt* **1.** reward or punish someone for something he has done: *recompense someone for his kindness.* **2.** give money to someone for some loss, injury etc that he has suffered. Also *nc/u* reward; payment: *work hard without recompense.*

reconcile ['rekənsail] *vt* **1.** make people friendly again after they have quarrelled. **2.** make things agree. *It is sometimes difficult to reconcile people's statements with their actions* i.e. they say one thing and do another.

reconciliation [rekənsili'eiʃən] *nc/u* act of reconciling; act of being reconciled: *bring about a reconciliation between people who have quarrelled.*

reconcile oneself to something accept something: *reconcile oneself to hard work.*

recondite ['rekɔndait] *adj* **1.** not known to many people: *recondite knowledge.* **2.** difficult to understand: *a recondite author.*

recondition [ri:kən'diʃən] *vt* put into good condition again by repairing etc: *a car with a reconditioned engine.*

reconnoitre [rekə'nɔitə*] (*US* **reconnoiter**) *vt/i* go near to where enemy soldiers are in order to find their exact position, numbers etc.

reconnaissance [ri'kɔnisns] *nc/u* act of reconnoitring.

reconstruct ['ri:kən'strʌkt] *vt* build up again after destruction or damage. **reconstruction** *nc/u.*

record[1] [ri'kɔ:d] *vt* **1.** put down in writing for future use: *record what was said at the meeting.* **2.** keep something in any form that people can refer to again: *a book that records the events of the Second World War.* **3.** put onto a gramophone disk. *That singer has recorded some popular songs.* **4.** show (on an instrument etc). *The thermometer recorded 60 degrees.*

record[2] ['rekɔ:d] *nc* **1.** written account: *keep a record of what was said.* **2.** disk to be played on a gramophone: *a hit record* i.e. one which has sold many copies. **3.** facts about the past of someone/something: *have a good record at school.* **4.** limit or point which has not yet been reached; (sport) the best yet done: *a new record for the high jump.* Also *attrib adj*: *a record attendance* i.e. more people than have ever attended before.

'record player gramophone; machine that plays gramophone records.

off the record speaking privately (not to be repeated publicly) (*informal*).

on record recorded: *the worst summer on record.*

break a record see **break.**

recount [ri'kaunt] *vt* tell: *recount everything that happened.*

re-count ['ri:kaunt] *nc* second count. Also ['ri:'kaunt] *vt* count again.

recoup [ri'ku:p] *vt* win again what one has lost: *recoup one's losses.*

recourse [ri'kɔ:s] *nc/u* person/thing that is turned to for help etc.

have recourse to someone/something turn to someone/something for help.

recover [ri'kʌvə*] *vt/i* **1.** get back what has been lost, taken away etc: *recover stolen goods.* **2.** get well again: *recover from an illness.* **recovery** *nu.*

recover oneself 1. get back into a proper position. *He almost fell, but recovered himself in time.* **2.** become calm or normal again.

recreation [rekri'eiʃən] *nc/u* game; way of occupying free time pleasantly. *Reading books is one kind of recreation.* **recreational** *adj.*

recrimination [rikrimi'neiʃən] *nc* accusation made in reply to an accusation.

recrudescence [ri:kru:'desns] *nc* new outbreak of something unpleasant: *a recrudescence of war/disease etc.*

recruit [ri'kru:t] *nc* 1. soldier who is still being trained. 2. person who has just joined something. Also *vt/i* get recruits; get someone as a recruit.

rectangle ['rektæŋgl] *nc* four-sided figure with the opposite sides equal and four right angles. **rectangular** [rek'tæŋgjulə*] *adj.*

rectify ['rektifai] *vt* put right: *rectify a mistake.* **rectification** [rektifi'keiʃən] *nc/u.*

rectitude ['rektitju:d] *nu* honesty; honest behaviour: *person who is a model of rectitude.*

rector ['rektə*] *nc* 1. clergyman in charge of a parish or a religious house. 2. head of a school, college or university.

rectory *nc* house of a rector.

rectum ['rektəm] *nc* lowest part of the tubing inside the body, through which food passes.

recumbent [ri'kʌmbənt] *adj* lying down: *a recumbent body.*

recuperate [ri'kju:pəreit] *vi* get well again after being ill. **recuperation** [rikju:pə'reiʃən] *nu.*

recur [ri'kə:*] *vi* 1. come back; happen again. 2. talk, or think about, again. *past* **recurred. recurrent** [ri'kʌrnt] *adj.* **recurrence** [ri'kʌrns] *nc/u.*

red [red] 1. *nc/u* the colour of blood flowing from a vein. 2. *nu* red clothes: *dressed in red.* 3. *nc* Communist. (*informal* in sense 3.). Also *adj.*

redden *vt/i* 1. make red. 2. become red; blush (with shame etc).

'redbrick (of a British university) new; of recent (i.e. 19th or 20th century) foundation. (*informal*).

Red Crescent Muslim organization like the Red Cross.

Red Cross international organization which gives help to the injured or wounded victims of war etc.

'red 'herring something which is brought up to take people's attention from something else (e.g. in an argument); subject which has nothing to do with what is being discussed. (*informal*).

'red-'hot see **hot.**

Red Indian North American Indian.

'red-'letter day day which will be remembered because something very pleasant happened on it.

red tape see **tape.**

see red become violently angry. (*informal*).

in the red in debt: *be five pounds in the red.* (*informal*).

catch red-'handed find in the act of doing something wrong.

a red rag to a bull the sort of thing which makes a particular person very angry. (*informal*).

redeem [ri'di:m] *vt* 1. buy back; get back in some way: *redeem a pawned article.* 2. carry out: *redeem a promise.* 3. set free; save: *redeem a slave; redeem from sin.*

redemption [ri'dempʃən] *nu* act of redeeming or being redeemed; saving (esp. from sin). **redemptive** [ri'demptiv] *adj.*

redeeming feature one good thing in someone/something that is mostly bad.

past redemption too evil to be saved.

redolent ['redəlnt] *adj* 1. smelling of something: *a house redolent of the smell of cooking.* 2. suggesting something.

redouble [ri:'dʌbl] *vt/i* increase greatly: *redouble one's efforts.*

redoubtable [ri'dautəbl] *adj* to be feared: *a redoubtable enemy.*

redound [ri'daund] *vi* bring as a result (usu. in **redound to one's credit** i.e. cause people to admire one). *This hard work you have done will redound to your credit* i.e. people will admire you for it.

redress [ri'dres] *vt* set right; make up for: *redress an injury* i.e. make up for it (e.g. by paying money). Also *nu* act of redressing; money etc which makes up for something: *seek redress.*

redress the balance make things equal again.

reduce [ri'dju:s] *vt/i* 1. make smaller; make less: *reduce speed; reduce one's weight.* 2. bring to a certain state: *reduce a person to tears/silence etc.* 3. conquer (*o.f.* in sense 3.).

reduced *adj.*

reduction [ri'dʌkʃən] *nc/u* 1. act of reducing or being reduced: *a reduction in prices.* 2. amount by which something is reduced: *a small reduction.* 3. copy of something (e.g. a picture etc) on a smaller scale.

redundant [ri'dʌndnt] *adj* not needed. *Several hundred workers have been declared redundant* i.e. dismissed because their services are no longer needed. **redundancy** *nc/u.*

reed [ri:d] *nc* 1. tall grass-like plant which grows in wet places. 2. stem of this plant. 3. thin piece of wood or metal in a musical instrument which moves when air is blown through it.

reedy *adj* thin, shrill: *a reedy voice.*

a broken reed a person/thing that cannot be relied on. (*informal*).

reef[1] [ri:f] *nc* narrow line of rocks etc just above or below the surface of the sea: *be wrecked on a reef.*

reef[2] [ri:f] *nc* part of a sail which can be rolled up to make the sail smaller. Also *vt* make a sail smaller by rolling up part of it.

'reef knot (*Brit*) kind of double knot. (*US* **square knot**).

reek [ri:k] *nu* strong, unpleasant smell: *the reek of drink/tobacco/smoke etc.* Also *vi* smell strongly: *reeking of drink.*

reel[1] [ri:l] *nc* 1. roller on which thread, film etc can be kept. 2. part of a cinema film wound on one reel. *I saw only the first two reels of the film.* Also *vt* wind something onto a reel.

reel something in draw in by using a line on a reel: *reel in a fish.*

reel something off tell easily, without having to pause: *reel off a story.* (*informal*).

reel[2] [ri:l] *vi* 1. sway after a blow, shock etc. *He reeled when he heard the terrible news.* 2. stagger. *The drunk man reeled home.* 3. be shaken in the mind. *His mind reeled when he heard that he had won a fortune.* 4. seem to go round, as when a person is dizzy. *The room reeled around me, and then I fainted.*

reel[3] [ri:l] *nc* 1. lively Scottish dance. 2. music for this kind of dance.

refectory [ri'fektəri] *nc* large room in which meals are taken (e.g. in a school, monastery etc).

refer [ri'fə:*] *vt/i* 1. hand over; send to be decided. *The dispute between the two countries was referred to the United Nations.* 2. go to for information or help: *refer to a dictionary for the spelling of a word.* 3. mention; speak about: *refer to someone* i.e. speak about him. 4. apply to; concern. *This rule refers to everyone. past* **referred.**

referee [refə'riː] *nc* **1.** judge in a game (e.g. boxing, football etc). **2.** person who is asked to decide on something. **3.** person asked to give to an employer information about the character and ability of a person seeking a job, scholarship etc. Also *vt/i* act as referee (for).

reference ['refərns] **1.** *nc/u* act of referring. *This book is for reference only* i.e. you can only refer to it, not take it away. **2.** *nc* person who can give information about someone's character, ability, work etc. **3.** *nc* written information about someone's character. *You should bring your references to the interview.* **4.** *nc* statement, part of book etc to which one is referred. *This reference can be found at the end of the book.*

referendum [refə'rendəm] *nc* act of asking all the people in a country to vote on some problem. *The government is going to hold a referendum on whether gambling should be forbidden.*

with reference to concerning, about.

without reference to not concerned about.

refine [ri'fain] *vt/i* **1.** make something (e.g. sugar, oil etc) pure by taking out dirt and waste matter etc: *refined sugar.* **2.** make someone/something more polite, more educated etc; make free from coarseness: *a refined voice.*

refined *adj.* (*opp* **unrefined**).

refinement *nu* **1.** being refined. **2.** goodness of feeling, politeness etc: *a person of refinement.* **3.** improved form of something that works better: *a refinement of earlier methods.*

refinery *nc* building where sugar, metal etc is refined: *sugar refinery.*

refit ['riː'fit] *vt/i* **1.** make something ready to be used again. *The ship is being refitted for a new voyage.* **2.** get ready for use; get fresh supplies. *The ship is at present refitting. past* **refitted.** Also ['riːfit] *nc.*

reflect [ri'flekt] *vt/i* **1.** throw back light, heat, sound etc. *The smooth surface of the lake reflected the lights of the houses.* **2.** send back an image or likeness. *The mirror reflected her face.* **3.** show; give a close idea of. *Does this statement reflect your opinions on this matter?* **4.** think carefully. *Reflect before you act.*

reflection, reflexion **1.** *nu* act of reflecting or being reflected: *study the reflection of light waves.* **2.** *nc* something that is reflected: *the reflection of light on the water.* **3.** *nc/u* careful thinking; idea. *On reflection, I have decided not to go.* **4.** *nc/u* something that causes someone to be blamed. *I hope that what I do will have no reflection on anyone else.*

reflective *adj* **1.** thoughtful: *a reflective person.* **2.** reflecting: *a reflective surface.* **reflectively** *adv.*

reflect upon someone bring blame upon.

cast a reflection upon someone blame somebody.

reflex ['riːfleks] *adj* done without willing: *a reflex action* i.e. an action that is not done on purpose and cannot be prevented (e.g. shivering when one is cold). Also *nc* reflex action. **reflexion** *nc/u* see **reflection.**

reform [ri'fɔːm] *vt/i* improve; make or become better by changing: *reform someone's character.* Also *nc/u* improvement; example of an improvement. *Our society needs reform; introduce several reforms.*

reformation [refə'meiʃən] *nc/u* change or improvement: *the Reformation* i.e. the changes brought about in the Christian Church in the 16th century which led to the forming of the Protestant Churches.

reformatory [ri'fɔːmətəri] *adj* intended to reform. Also *nc* school where young people who break the law are kept. (Also **reform school**).

reformer *nc* person who is in favour of reforms or who brings them about.

refract [ri'frækt] *vt* bend a beam of light away from a straight line. *Light is refracted in water.* **refraction** *nu.*

refractory [ri'fræktəri] *adj* **1.** disobedient; difficult to control: *a refractory child.* **2.** difficult to cure: *a refractory illness.* **3.** difficult to melt down or work with: *refractory materials.*

refrain[1] [ri'frein] *vi* hold oneself back from something, or from doing something: *refrain from smoking.*

refrain[2] [ri'frein] *nc* part of a song which is repeated (usu. at the end of each verse).

refresh [ri'freʃ] *vt* make new again; give more strength to: *refresh one's memory* i.e. make something easier to remember by referring to notes etc; *refresh oneself with a drink of water.*

refreshing *adj* pleasant; new; making one feel better: *a refreshing sleep.* **refreshingly** *adv.*

refreshment *nu* (often *pl*) food and drink.

refrigerate [ri'fridʒəreit] *vt* make or keep food etc cold (so that it will not go bad).

refrigeration [rifridʒə'reiʃən] *nu.*

refrigerator *nc* container designed to keep things (usu. food, drink) cold. (Usu. **fridge**).

refuel ['riː'fjuəl] *vt/i* (esp. with reference to an aeroplane) get or provide with more fuel. *past* **refuelled.**

refuge ['refjuːdʒ] *nc/u* **1.** shelter or protection from danger etc. **2.** place which gives shelter or protection.

refugee [refju'dʒiː] *nc* person who has escaped from danger (e.g. war, persecution, famine etc).

refund [ri'fʌnd] *vt/i* pay back money. Also ['riːfʌnd] *nc/u* paying back of money; money paid back. *When the concert was cancelled, many people demanded a refund.*

refurbish ['riː'fəːbiʃ] *vt* give a new appearance to something old.

refuse[1] [ri'fjuːz] *vt/i* **1.** not do what one is asked or told to do. *She refused to go home.* **2.** not accept something. *I refused his offer of money.*

refusal *nc/u* act of refusing.

first refusal right of refusing or accepting something before it is offered to others. *If I decide to sell my car, I'll give you first refusal.*

refuse[2] ['refjuːs] *nu* things which have been used and thrown away; waste matter.

refute [ri'fjuːt] *vt* prove that someone/something is wrong: *refute someone's arguments.* **refutation** [refju'teiʃən] *nc/u.*

regain [ri'gein] *vt* **1.** get back again. *The army has regained the town.* **2.** reach again; get back to: *regain the shore.*

regal ['riːgl] *adj* belonging to or suitable for a king or queen. **regally** *adv.*

regalia [ri'geiliə] *npl* symbols of royalty used at a coronation (e.g. a crown etc): *in full regalia* i.e. dressed in the official costume for an occasion.

regale [ri'geil] *vt* entertain someone by giving him food etc: *regale someone/oneself with food and drink.*

regard[1] [ri'gɑːd] *vt* **1.** consider; think something/someone to be. *Most people regard stealing as wrong.* **2.** pay attention to; think very important. *I have always regarded his advice very highly.* **3.** look at. *He regarded me thoughtfully.*
regarding *prep* about. *I must speak to you regarding this matter.*

regard[2] [ri'gɑːd] *nu* **1.** thought; attention: *have no regard for the feelings of others* i.e. not think about how others feel. **2.** good opinion; respect: *hold someone in high/low regard.* **3.** long look, not taking one's eyes away.
regards *npl* good wishes. *Give him my kind/best regards.*
regardless of not worrying about. *He bought her what she wanted, regardless of the expense.*
with regard to concerning; about. Used to introduce a topic, often one which has already been referred to previously. *With regard to the problem which I mentioned last week, I suggest . . .*

regatta [ri'gætə] *nc* meeting in which boats race against one another.

regenerate [ri'dʒenəreit] *vt/i* **1.** improve what has become bad. **2.** grow again.
regeneration [riːdʒenə'reiʃən] *nu.*

regent ['riːdʒənt] *nc* person who acts for a ruler who is too young, old, ill etc to perform his duties. Also *adj* acting as a regent: *the Prince Regent.* **regency** *nc.*

regicide ['redʒisaid] *nu* act of killing a king. Also *nc* person who does this.

régime [rei'ʒiːm] *nc* method of ruling; government: *the old régime* i.e. government that ruled before a revolution or reform took place.

regiment ['redʒimənt] *nc* part of an army, larger than a battalion and smaller than a brigade, and usu. commanded by a colonel.
regimental [redʒi'mentl] *adj.*
regimentation [redʒimən'teiʃən] *nu* very strict control of people.

region ['riːdʒən] *nc* **1.** area of land: *different regions of England.* **2.** area near something or connected with something: *an injury in the region of the heart.* **regional** *adj.* **regionally** *adv.*

register[1] ['redʒistə*] *nc* **1.** list; record: *a register of births, marriages and deaths.* **2.** book containing lists or records: *a school attendance register.* **3.** something that keeps a list or record: *a cash register* i.e. one which records how much money is put in. **4.** range of a voice or musical instrument.
registrar ['redʒistrɑː*] *nc* official who makes up lists or keeps records (e.g. of births, marriages and deaths).
registry ['redʒistri] *nc* office etc where registers are kept.
'**registry office** place where people can be married without a religious ceremony.

register[2] ['redʒistə*] *vt/i* **1.** write in a list or record. **2.** have one's name written in a list or record: *register as a voter.* **3.** record; show. *The thermometer registered 60 degrees.* **4.** show what one feels by one's face or what one does. *His face registered his disappointment.* **5.** pay extra money when sending a letter or parcel by post so that more care may be taken of it: *register a parcel; a registered letter.* **registration** [redʒis'treiʃən] *nc/u.*
regis'tration number licence number of a car, displayed on the number plates.

regress [ri'gres] *vi* move back; become less developed, less efficient etc. **regressive** *adj.* **regression** *nc/u.*

regret [ri'gret] *nu* feeling of sorrow at not having done something, or having done something unpleasant or wrong. *I left my home with some regret.* Also *vt* be sorry about something. *I regret that I shall not be able to come. past* **regretted.**
regretful *adj* sad. **regretfully** *adv.*
regrettable *adj* that one ought to feel sorry about: *regrettable behaviour.* **regrettably** *adv.*

regroup ['riː'gruːp] *vt/i* **1.** form, cause to form, into groups again. **2.** form, cause to form, different groups.

regular ['regjulə*] *adj* **1.** normal; usual. *This is his regular day for visiting us.* **2.** coming often: *be a regular visitor.* **3.** according to some rule. *This is not the regular way of doing it.* **4.** evenly shaped; attractive: *regular features.* **5.** orderly or normal: *a person of regular habits* i.e. who always does things at the same time or in the same way, or acts in a normal way. **6.** professional, not just brought together for a time: *the regular army.* Also *nc* **1.** member of a regular army. **2.** regular customer at a pub or shop. (*informal* in sense **2.**). **regularly** *adv.* **regularity** [regju'læriti] *nu.*
regularize *vt* make lawful or correct something which has already been in existence for some time.

regulate ['regjuleit] *vt* **1.** control by rules: *regulate a country's imports.* **2.** make a machine work properly: *regulate one's watch* i.e. to keep the right time.
regulation [regju'leiʃən] **1.** *nc* rule to be obeyed. *There are too many regulations nowadays.* **2.** *nu* control by rules: *the regulation of the hours a young person may work.*
regulator *nc* **1.** someone/something that regulates. **2.** part of a machine (e.g. a clock) which prevents it from going faster or slower.

regurgitate [ri'gəːdʒiteit] *vt/i* **1.** bring up into the mouth after having swallowed. **2.** repeat what others have said without really understanding it oneself: *regurgitate the teacher's notes in an examination.* **regurgitation** [rigəːdʒi'teiʃən] *nu.*

rehabilitate [riːhə'biliteit] *vt* **1.** put back into good condition; make able to work again: *rehabilitate old houses; rehabilitate an injured soldier* i.e. train him to carry out a new job and help find work for him. **2.** put back into a former position, rank etc. *He was rehabilitated as secretary.* **rehabilitation** ['riːhəbili'teiʃən] *nu.*

rehash ['riː'hæʃ] *vt* put something (e.g. ideas, a joke) which has already been used, into a slightly different form. *He has just rehashed what he wrote in his last essay.* Also *nc.*

rehearse [ri'həːs] *vt/i* **1.** practise a play or music etc for public performance: *rehearse a part. Don't interrupt while we are rehearsing. He rehearsed the actors* i.e. made them practice. **2.** tell in full. *The child rehearsed everything that had happened at school.*
rehearsal *nc.*

reign [rein] *nc* period of a king's rule: *during the reign of George III.* Also *vi* **1.** rule as a king: *reign over a country for many years.* **2.** be found everywhere. *Peace reigned throughout the region.*

reimburse [riːim'bəːs] *vt* pay back: *reimburse someone; reimburse somebody for the money he has spent; reimburse some money which was borrowed.* **reimbursement** *nc/u.*

rein [rein] *nc* (usu. *pl*) long, narrow strap used for controlling a horse or child. Also *vt* stop or control by using reins.

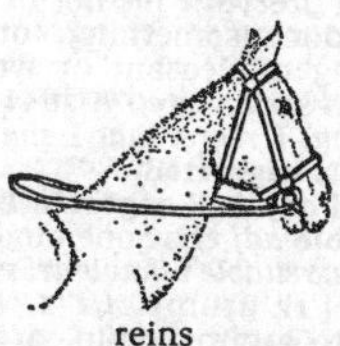
reins

reincarnation ['ri:inkɑ:'neiʃən] *nc/u* reappearance after death in another body.
reindeer ['reindiə*] *nc* kind of large deer with horns, found in Arctic regions (e.g. Lapland). *pl* **reindeer.**
reinforce [ri:in'fɔ:s] *vt* make stronger by adding more men, materials etc: *reinforce an army/bridge etc.* **reinforcement** *nc* (often *pl*).
reinforcements *npl* men etc sent to reinforce: *wait for reinforcements before attacking.*
reinstate [ri:in'steit] *vt* put back into a former position or condition. *The manager was dismissed, but he was reinstated later.* **reinstatement** *nc/u.*
reiterate [ri:'itəreit] *vt* say or do something several times: *reiterate a statement.* **reiteration** [ri:itə'reiʃən] *nc/u.*
reject [ri'dʒekt] *vt* **1.** refuse to accept: *reject someone's help.* **2.** throw away as useless: *reject some old books.* Also ['ri:dʒekt] *nc* someone/something that has been rejected. **rejection** *nc/u.*
rejoice [ri'dʒɔis] *vt/i* be glad: *rejoice at some good news.*
rejoicing **1.** *nu* great happiness (esp. shared with others). **2.** *nc* (in *pl*) celebrations.
rejoin[1] [ri'dʒɔin] *vt/i* answer; reply.
rejoinder [ri'dʒɔində*] *nc* answer (usu. one given in an argument).
rejoin[2] ['ri:'dʒɔin] *vt/i* join again.
rejuvenate [ri'dʒu:vəneit] *vt/i* make or become young again: *feel rejuvenated after a long holiday.* **rejuvenation** [ridʒu:və'neiʃən] *nu.*
relapse [ri'læps] *vi* fall back into a former condition (usu. bad e.g. illness). Also *nc* falling back (esp. into illness). *He seemed to recover for a short time, but then he had a relapse.*
relate [ri'leit] *vt/i* **1.** tell a story etc: *relate one's adventures.* **2.** connect; be connected with. *How is this fact related to that one?*
related *adj* **1.** connected. (*opp* **unrelated**). **2.** belonging to the same family. *Are you related to him?*
relation **1.** *nu* way in which people/things are connected. *They discussed the relation between poverty and crime.* **2.** *nc* member of one's family; relative. *She brought all her relations with her.* **3.** *nc/u* act of telling: *the relation of one's adventures.*
relationship *nc* connection.
relations *npl* way in which people, countries etc treat one another: *have friendly relations with someone.*
relative ['relətiv] *adj* compared with each other; compared with something else. *Let us examine the relative amounts of work done by the students. He is living in relative poverty* i.e. compared to other people. Also *nc* **1.** member of one's family: *live with an elderly relative* i.e. an old person to whom one is related. **2.** see **relative adverb** and **relative pronoun.**
relatively *adv* when compared with something/someone else: *relatively rich.*
relative adverb word like *where, when etc* as in the sentence *The place where the battle was fought.*
relative pronoun word like *who, which, that etc* as in the sentence *The pen that I bought yesterday is broken.*
relax [ri'læks] *vt/i* **1.** make or become less stiff or less strict. *His body relaxed. They relaxed the regulations.* **2.** become free of care: *take a week's holiday and relax.*
relaxation [ri:læk'seiʃən] *nc/u* act of relaxing; enjoyment and amusement.
relay ['ri:lei] *nc* fresh supply of men or horses to replace tired ones. *The people of the village worked in relays to put out the fire.* Also [ri'lei] *vt* receive and pass further on: *relay a message/broadcast etc.*
release [ri'li:s] *vt* set free; allow to go: *release prisoners.* Also *nc/u* act of releasing or being released. *The prisoner was questioned before his release.*
'press release information given out so that it can be printed in the newspapers.
relegate ['reləgeit] *vt* **1.** put into a lower position, rank etc. *The football team was relegated to the lowest division.* **2.** hand over to someone/something else to be dealt with.
relegation [relə'geiʃən] *nu.*
relent [ri'lent] *vi* become less cruel or less firm.
relentless *adj* without pity. **relentlessly** *adv.*
relevant ['reləvənt] *adj* connected with what is being discussed: *a relevant question.* (*opp* **irrelevant**). **relevantly** *adv.* **relevance** *nu.*
reliable [ri'laiəbl] *adj* that can be trusted or relied on. (*opp* **unreliable**). **reliably** *adv.*
reliant [ri'laiənt] *adj* relying; depending.
reliance [ri'laiəns] *nu* act of depending on or trusting in.
relic ['relik] *nc* **1.** something belonging to a saint and kept after his death as a mark of respect. **2.** something which still exists to remind us of the past: *relics of an ancient civilization.*
relief [ri'li:f] *nu* **1.** lessening of pain or suffering: *a medicine which gives relief from pain.* **2.** something given to lessen suffering; food, clothes etc given to the poor: *send relief.* **3.** change that gives pleasure or adds interest: *enjoy some light relief while on duty.* **4.** change in duty; person who comes to take over a duty: *be waiting for one's relief.* **5.** design, drawing etc which is raised above the surface it is on: *in relief*
re'lief map map which uses colours or shading to show the height of the land.
relieve [ri'li:v] *vt* **1.** make pain or trouble less: *a medicine that will relieve a headache.* **2.** give pleasure or interest by change: *relieve the monotony of something.* **3.** take over a duty from someone for a time. **4.** take something from someone. *I relieved John of some of the work* i.e. I did some of the work in order to help John.
relieve one's feelings get rid of one's feelings by showing them openly (e.g. by weeping or cursing).
religion [ri'lidʒən] **1.** *nu* belief in God or any other kind of supernatural power. **2.** *nc* system of belief in God or any other kind of supernatural power: *people of different religions.*
religious *adj* **1.** connected with religion:

a religious service. **2.** observing the rules of a religion carefully: *a religious person.* (*opp* **irreligious** in sense **2.**).

religiously *adv* **1.** in a religious way. **2.** very carefully and at fixed times. *He religiously watered his garden every day.* (*informal* in sense **2.**).

relinquish [ri'liŋkwiʃ] *vt* **1.** give up; yield. *The prince relinquished his claim to the throne.* **2.** let go, release one's grip of something.

relish ['reliʃ] **1.** *nu* pleasant taste. *This sauce adds relish to the food.* **2.** *nc* something which gives an extra taste to food: *olives, sardines and other relishes.* **3.** *nu* pleasure: *eat something with relish.* Also *vt* enjoy: *relish a good story.*

have no relish for something not enjoy something.

reluctant [ri'lʌktnt] *adj* unwilling; slow to do something because one is unwilling. **reluctantly** *adv.* **reluctance** *nu.*

rely [ri'lai] *vi* usu. in **rely on/upon** i.e. depend on; trust. *I can rely on you.* see **reliable.**

remain [ri'mein] *vi* **1.** be left after something has been removed. *He kept all that remained of his father's money.* **2.** stay in the same place. *He remained there for five years.*

remainder [ri'meində*] *nu* what is left. *You can keep the remainder of the money.*

remains *npl* **1.** what is left: *the remains of a meal.* **2.** dead body. **3.** ancient ruins of buildings etc.

remand [ri'mɑ:nd] *vt* send a person back to prison until a trial is held. Also *nu.*

re'mand home institution for young people who have broken the law (and usu. are awaiting reports or trial).

remark [ri'mɑ:k] *vt/i* **1.** say or write something; speak or write about something. *He remarked on the neatness of the pupils' work. He remarked that he would be leaving soon.* **2.** notice. *Did he remark anything strange about the room?* (rather *o.f.* in sense **2.**). Also *nc/u* **1.** something said or written in few words: *a clever remark.* **2.** notice: *nothing worthy of remark.* (rather *o.f.* in sense **2.**).

remarkable *adj* unusual; worth noticing. **remarkably** *adv.*

remedy ['remədi] *nc/u* **1.** way of relieving sickness, pain etc: *a remedy for headaches.* **2.** way of setting right any bad thing or situation. Also *vt.*

remedial [ri'mi:diəl] *adj* able to cure or help.

remember [ri'membə*] *vt/i* **1.** keep in mind; not forget: *remember one's schooldays; remember to do something.* **2.** bear greetings. *Remember me to your father when you see him* i.e. give him my greetings. (*informal* in sense **2.**).

remembrance [ri'membrns] *nu* act of remembering. *A monument was built in remembrance of those who had died.* **2.** *nc* something which reminds one. *This watch is a remembrance of my father.*

Note: the difference between e.g. *I remembered to open the door* i.e. I had to open the door and I did so; and *I remember opening the door* i.e. I opened the door, and I know that I did it.

remind [ri'maind] *vt* cause one to remember; make one think of someone/something. *Remind him to close the door when he leaves. That house reminds me of the one I was born in.*

reminder *nc* something that helps one to remember. *If he doesn't pay his bill, send him a reminder.*

reminisce [remi'nis] *vi* remember past events in a pleasant way.

reminiscence *nu* act of remembering things that have happened. *The two old friends spent an evening in reminiscence of their youth.*

reminiscences *npl* memories (esp. written down to make a book): *publish one's reminiscences.*

reminiscent *adj* **1.** reminding one of: *scenes reminiscent of one's childhood.* **2.** in a condition where one likes to remember the past: *become reminiscent.*

remiss [ri'mis] *adj* careless; not paying attention to one's duty: *be remiss in one's duty.* **remissness** *nu.*

remission [ri'miʃən] **1.** *nc/u* freeing from a debt, a punishment etc: *the remission of school fees* i.e. some or all of the school fees do not have to be paid; *remission of a prison sentence.* **2.** *nu* forgiveness of sin. **3.** *nu* weakening or lessening of pain, effort etc: *work for hours without remission.*

remit [ri'mit] *vt/i* **1.** send money: *remit some money to one's parents.* **2.** send a problem etc for decision: *remit a case to a higher court.* **3.** free someone from a debt, punishment etc. *His sentence was remitted. past* **remitted.**

remittance *nc/u* sending of money; amount of money sent: *send a weekly remittance.*

remnant ['remnənt] *nc* **1.** small part that is left: *the remnants of a defeated army.* **2.** small piece of cloth left over and often sold at a cheaper price: *a remnant sale.*

remonstrate ['remənstreit] *vi* protest against something; argue with someone. *I remonstrated against the chairman's decision. I remonstrated with the chairman about his decision.* **remonstrance** [ri'mɔnstrns] *nc/u.*

remorse [ri'mɔ:s] *nu* deep sorrow for having done wrong: *be filled with remorse.*

remorseful *adj* full of remorse. **remorsefully** *adv.*

remorseless *adj* without remorse; without pity. **remorselessly** *adv.*

remote [ri'mout] *adj* **1.** far away; distant in place or time: *a remote country; a remote time in the past.* **2.** different: *something remote from my experience* i.e. different from what I am used to.

not have the remotest idea not know at all. *I haven't the remotest idea where he is.* (*informal*).

remove [ri'mu:v] *vt/i* **1.** take away; take off: *remove one's hat; be removed to a hospital.* **2.** go to live in another place: *remove to London* (*o.f.* in sense **2.**)

removal *nc/u* act of removing. *A van came for the removal of our furniture.*

'paint remover, 'stain remover etc substance for removing paint, stains etc.

remunerate [ri'mju:nəreit] *vt* pay for work done, trouble experienced etc.

remuneration [rimju:nə'reiʃən] *nu* payment; reward.

remunerative [ri'mju:nərətiv] *adj* which pays well: *a very remunerative job.*

renaissance [ri'neisns] *nc* revival; time when something starts again (esp. of literature, painting, education etc).

the Renaissance period of a great revival in interest in literature, painting, learning etc which occurred in Europe roughly between 1350 and 1500 A.D.

rend [rend] *vt/i* tear; pull apart; divide

violently: *rend one's clothes in anger; a family rent by quarrels. past* **rent.**

render ['rendə*] *vt* **1.** make; cause to be: *be rendered helpless with laughter.* **2.** give: *render thanks; render an account* i.e. give an account for consideration or payment. **3.** act; play: *render a part in a play.* **4.** translate. **5.** make fat purer by melting it down. **rendering** *nc/u.*

rendez-vous ['rɔndeivuː] *nc* **1.** agreement to meet at a certain time: *make a rendezvous with someone.* **2.** place where one is going to have an arranged meeting with someone. Also *vi* (mainly with reference to military activities) meet in this way.

renegade ['renigeid] *nc* person who leaves a political or religious group to join an enemy or rival group.

renew [ri'njuː] *vt* **1.** make again; begin again; get again: *renew an attack; renew a promise; renew a contract.* **2.** make something as it was when it was new or fresh: *start working with renewed vigour* i.e. as at the beginning. **3.** replace with something of the same sort. *I must renew my radio licence* i.e. get one for this year.

renewal *nc/u* act of renewing or being renewed.

renounce [ri'nauns] *vt* **1.** give up entirely: *renounce one's privileges/claims etc.* **2.** say that one will have no more connection with: *renounce one's own family.* **renunciation** [rinʌnsi'eiʃən] *nu.*

renovate ['renəveit] *vt* make like new again: *renovate an old building.* **renovation** [renə'veiʃən] *nc/u.*

renown [ri'naun] *nu* fame.

renowned *adj* famous.

rent[1] [rent] past of **rend.**

rent[2] [rent] *nc/u* money paid regularly for the use of a room, house etc which belongs to someone else. Also *vt* **1.** pay for the use of something: *rent a room from someone.* **2.** allow someone to use one's house etc in return for payment: *rent a room to someone.*

rent[3] [rent] *nc* tear (e.g. in cloth).

renunciation [rinʌnsi'eiʃən] *nu* see **renounce.**

repair[1] [ri'pɛə*] *vt* **1.** put something damaged or worn into good condition; mend: *repair a damaged bridge; repair worn shoes.* **2.** put right; make up for. *How can I repair the damage I have caused?* Also *nc/u* act of repairing or being repaired: *a road that is under repair. Repairs are being carried out on the damaged building.*

repairable *adj* that can be repaired. *That old chain is still repairable.*

reparable ['repərəbl] *adj* that can be put right. (*opp* **irreparable**).

reparation [repə'reiʃən] *nu* **1.** act of making up for some wrong or injury done. **2.** money paid to make up for some wrong or injury.

reparations *npl* money paid for damage done during a war.

repartee [repɑː'tiː] *nu* witty, clever answers in conversation: *be good at repartee.*

repast [ri'pɑːst] *nc* meal (*o.f.*).

repatriate [riː'pætrieit] *vt* bring or send someone back to his own country: *repatriate prisoners-of-war.* **repatriation** [riːpætri'eiʃən] *nu.*

repay [riː'pei] *vt* pay back; return: *repay money that was borrowed; repay the kindness someone has done.* **repayment** *nc/u.*

repeal [ri'piːl] *vt* end, cancel a law. *The unjust law was finally repealed.* Also *nc* (usu. only *sing*) act of repealing.

repeat [ri'piːt] *vt* **1.** say or do again: *repeat a statement; repeat a mistake; repeat oneself* i.e. say the same thing again. **2.** say what one has learned: *repeat a poem.* **3.** tell to someone else. *Don't repeat what you have seen today.*

repeatedly *adv* very often.

repetition [repi'tiʃən] **1.** *nu* act of repeating: *after much repetition.* **2.** *nc* something repeated. *I hope there is not a repetition of this.* **repetitive** [ri'petitiv] *adj.*

repel [ri'pel] *vt* **1.** force back; push away: *repel an enemy.* **2.** cause a feeling of dislike in someone. *His dirty appearance repelled the girl. past* **repelled.**

repellent *adj* unattractive; causing a feeling of dislike: *something that is repellent to a person.* Also *nc* something which is intended to repel: *an insect repellent.*

repent [ri'pent] *vt/i* feel sorry for having done something wrong: *repent (of) one's sins; repent having done wrong.*

repentant *adj* feeling sorry; showing that one is sorry.

repentance *nu* sorrow for having done wrong.

repercussion [riːpə'kʌʃən] *nc/u* **1.** (often *pl*) something which is caused by something else in an indirect way. *If this law is passed, it will have repercussions throughout the world* i.e. it will not only affect this country but also, indirectly, affect others. **2.** act of springing back; sound thrown back: *the repercussions of a rifle shot.*

repertoire ['repətwɑː*], **repertory**[1] ['repətəri] *nc* set of plays which a company can perform; set of songs etc which a group or a person can perform.

repertory[2] ['repətəri] **1.** *nc* repertoire. **2.** *nu* system by which a group of actors presents a number of different plays during the course of a short period of time: *act in repertory; weekly repertory* i.e. system of presenting a different play every week.

repetition [repi'tiʃən] *nc/u* see **repeat.**

rephrase ['riː'freiz] *vt* say again, using different words: *rephrase a question.*

repine [ri'pain] *vi* feel sad or discontented.

replace [ri'pleis] *vt* **1.** take the place of. *In many areas, cars have replaced horses as a means of transport.* **2.** get something to take the place of. *I must replace the cup that was broken.* **3.** put back in the proper place: *replace a book on a shelf.*

replacement *nc/u* act of replacing; thing/person that replaces.

replay ['riː'plei] *vt* play something again (e.g. a match, a piece of music). Also ['riːplei] *nc* match played again.

replenish [ri'pleniʃ] *vt* fill up again: *replenish the cupboard with food.*

replete [ri'pliːt] *adj* completely filled; well-supplied.

repletion *nu* state of being replete.

replica ['replikə] *nc* (esp. of a painting etc) exact copy.

replicate ['replikeit] *vt* make an exact copy of (often of an experiment).

reply [ri'plai] *vi* answer; give in return: *reply to a question; reply to enemy gunfire.* Also *nc* answer.

in reply as an answer.

report[1] [ri'pɔːt] **1.** *nc* description of what one has seen, done, heard etc: *write a report on what has been decided.* **2.** *nc* sound of a shot or explosion: *a loud report.* **3.** *nu* what people say; rumour. *According to*

report, the president is ill.
'school re'port list of marks or grades of a pupil at school, together with teachers' comments etc, sent by a school to a pupil's parents.

report[2] [ri'pɔ:t] *vt/i* **1.** describe; tell about. *She reported what she had seen to the police.* **2.** go to some place or person, and say why one has come or ask instructions etc. *Report for duty here at six o'clock.* **3.** make a complaint about someone to his superior. *I shall report that insolent child to the headmaster.*
reporter *nc* someone who gets news for a newspaper.
reported speech see **indirect**.

repose [ri'pouz] *vt/i* **1.** rest; lay to rest. **2.** place faith, confidence in etc. Also *nu* **1.** sleep; rest: *disturb someone's repose.* **2.** quietness; calm: *the repose of the countryside; repose of manner.*

repository [ri'pɔzitəri] *nc* place where things are stored or kept.

reprehensible [repri'hensibl] *adj* deserving blame. **reprehensibly** *adv*.

represent [repri'zent] *vt* **1.** stand for; be a sign of. *On this map, the black dots represent cities and the blue part represents the sea.* **2.** show. *This painting represents a country scene.* **3.** speak on behalf of: *represent a certain district in Parliament.* **4.** declare someone/something to be: *represent someone as a coward.*
representation [reprizen'teiʃən] *nc/u* act of representing; something represented: *make representations* i.e. protest officially.
representative [repri'zentətiv] *adj* **1.** typical; that will give a fair idea of what others are like. *These few books are representative of the ones we use in the school.* (*opp* **unrepresentative**). **2.** in which people appoint others to speak or act for them: *representative government.* Also *nc* someone who is appointed to speak or act for others: *the representative of a company.*

repress [ri'pres] *vt* **1.** bring under control. *I repressed a desire to hit him.* **2.** put down: *repress a rebellion.* **repressive** *adj*. **repressively** *adv*. **repression** *nu*.

reprieve [ri'pri:v] *vt* **1.** say that the execution of someone condemned to death will take place later or not take place at all. *The President reprieved the condemned man.* **2.** stop any kind of punishment, difficulty, danger etc at least for a short time. Also *nc* **1.** order stopping an execution; stopping of an execution. *The condemned murderer was granted a reprieve.* **2.** period in which one is safe from a certain kind of trouble.

reprimand ['reprimɑ:nd] *vt* blame severely: *reprimand a naughty child.* Also *nc* statement blaming or scolding: *give someone a reprimand.*

reprisal [ri'praizl] *nc/u* (often *pl*) wrong which is done in revenge for another wrong. *When our village was attacked by the enemy, we attacked one of theirs in reprisal.*

reproach [ri'proutʃ] *vt* blame someone sadly rather than angrily: *reproach a child for being rude; reproach oneself* i.e. blame oneself. Also *nc/u* **1.** disgrace; something that brings shame: *without reproach.* **2.** act of reproaching.
reproachful *adj* full of, or showing, reproach: *a reproachful look.* **reproachfully** *adv*.

reprobate ['reprəbeit] *nc* person who often acts in a wrong or immoral way. Also *adj*.

reproduce [ri:prə'dju:s] *vt/i* **1.** cause something to be seen or heard again: *reproduce sound by using a record player.* **2.** produce young or offspring. *Most plants reproduce through seeds.*
reproduction [ri:prə'dʌkʃən] *nc/u* **1.** copy. **2.** act of reproducing. **reproductive** [ri:prə'dʌktiv] *adj*.

reproof [ri'pru:f] *nc/u* blame; words of blame.
reprove [ri'pru:v] *vt* blame; find fault with; rebuke: *reprove a pupil for coming to school late.*

reptile ['reptail] *nc* type of cold-blooded animal that creeps or crawls (e.g. a lizard, snake or crocodile). **reptilian** [rep'tiliən] *adj*.

republic [ri'pʌblik] *nc* country ruled by a president and representatives chosen by the people.
republican [ri'pʌblikən] *adj* of a republic. Also *nc* person who favours a republic as a means of government.
republicanism [ri'pʌblikənizəm] *nu* belief in a republic as a means of government.

repudiate [ri'pju:dieit] *vt/i* **1.** refuse to accept: *repudiate a belief; repudiate a gift.* **2.** refuse to pay: *repudiate a debt.* **3.** refuse to meet or be friendly with: *repudiate a wicked son.* **repudiation** [ripju:di'eiʃən] *nu*.

repugnant [ri'pʌgnənt] *adj* causing a feeling of great dislike.
repugnance *nu* strong dislike for something.

repulse [ri'pʌls] *vt* **1.** drive back by force: *repulse an enemy attack.* **2.** refuse to accept; treat with coldness: *repulse someone's friendship.*
repulsion *nu* feeling of strong dislike.
repulsive *adj* causing strong dislike. **repulsively** *adv*. **repulsiveness** *nu*.

reputation [repju'teiʃən] *nc/u* what people think about someone/something: *have a good/high reputation* i.e. be well thought of.
reputable ['repjutəbl] *adj* having a good reputation: *a reputable firm.*
repute [ri'pju:t] *nu* reputation (usu. good reputation): *a man of repute* (*o.f.*).
reputed [ri'pju:tid] *adj* thought by most people: *someone who is reputed to be very generous.*
reputedly *adv*: *Reputedly, he is very dangerous.*

request [ri'kwest] **1.** *nu* act of asking. *I came at his request* i.e. because he asked me. **2.** *nc* something asked for: *make a special request.* Also *vt* ask; ask for: *request something; request someone to do something; request that something should be done.*

requiem ['rekwiəm] *nc* **1.** religious service for the dead. **2.** music for such a service.

require [ri'kwaiə*] *vt* **1.** need. *Do you require help?* **2.** oblige; order. *You are required to stay here until tomorrow.*
requirement *nc/u* act of requiring; something required.
requisite ['rekwizit] *nc* something needed: *food and other requisites.* Also *adj*.

requisition [rekwi'ziʃən] *vt* demand the supply of something (esp. for an army): *requisition food from a village.* Also *nc/u* something requisitioned; act of requisitioning.

requite [ri'kwait] *vt* pay back; reward; take vengeance on (*o.f.*).
requital *nu* repayment.

rescind [ri'sind] *vt* cancel; put an end to:

rescind a law.

rescue ['reskjuː] *vt* save from danger: *rescue someone from drowning/from his enemies etc.* Also *nc/u* act of rescuing or being rescued: *go to someone's rescue.* **rescuer** *nc.*

research [ri'səːtʃ] *nu* careful examination of some subject to find out new facts: *do research on a new scientific theory; do research in chemistry.* Also *vt/i.*

resemble [ri'zembl] *vt* look like; be like. *He resembles his brother.*

resemblance *nc/u* likeness.

resent [ri'zent] *vt* feel angry at: *resent being treated rudely.* **resentful** *adj.* **resentfully** *adv.* **resentment** *nu.*

reserve [ri'zəːv] *vt* **1.** keep for the use of a particular person: *reserve a seat in the theatre.* **2.** keep something so that it can be used later: *reserve one's strength for the long walk home.* Also **1.** *nc* something kept to be used later; keeping something like this: *a reserve of food.* **2.** *nc* area of land kept apart for a special purpose: *a game reserve* i.e. place where wild animals can live freely. **3.** *nu* state of not showing one's feelings: *behave with reserve.* **4.** *nu* condition that one makes about something: *accept something without reserve.* **5.** *nc* (with reference to football etc) person whose job is to take the place of any member of a team who is injured or unable to play.

reservation [rezə'veiʃən] **1.** *nc/u* arrangement to keep something for the use of a particular person: *make a plane reservation* i.e. arrange for a seat to be kept for one on a plane. **2.** *nc/u* limit; condition: *accept something without reservation.* **3.** *nc* area of land set aside for a special reason (e.g. one of the areas set aside for the use of the Red Indians in America).

reserved *adj* **1.** kept for a particular use or person: *a reserved seat in a theatre.* **2.** not saying much; not showing much emotion: *a reserved person.*

in reserve saved for later use: *have money in reserve.*

reservoir ['rezəvwaː*] *nc* **1.** place, often a man-made lake, where water is stored (e.g. to provide a water supply for a city). **2.** large amount: *have a great reservoir of knowledge.* **3.** any place where liquid is stored (e.g. in a fountain pen).

reside [ri'zaid] *vi* live in: *reside at/in a certain town.*

residence ['rezidns] **1.** *nc* house; home. (*formal*). **2.** *nu* act of residing: *be in residence.*

resident ['rezidnt] *nc* **1.** someone who lives in a place, not a visitor. **2.** someone who is a political representative of his country abroad (*o.f.* in sense **2.**). Also *adj* residing in a place: *the resident population* i.e. not including visitors.

residency ['rezidnsi] *nc* house where a political representative lives (*o.f.*).

residential [rezi'denʃl] *adj* for living in, not working in: *a residential area* i.e. where there are no factories etc.

residue ['rezidjuː] *nc* what is left of anything after some of it has been taken away. **residual** [ri'zidjuəl] *adj.*

resign [ri'zain] *vt/i* give up a job or position: *resign one's post; resign from a committee.*

resigned *adj* accepting what happens without complaining. *He is resigned to losing the competition.*

resignation [rezig'neiʃən] **1.** *nc* act of resigning. **2.** *nc* written statement that one intends to resign: *hand in one's resignation.* **3.** *nu* state of being resigned.

resign oneself to something accept something without complaining.

resilience [ri'ziliəns] *nu* **1.** quality of being able to return to a former shape or position after being bent, crushed, pulled etc. **2.** cheerfulness in spite of hardships. **resilient** *adj.*

resin ['rezin] *nc/u* sticky material that comes out of certain trees and is often used in medicine or for making varnish. **resinous** *adj.*

resist [ri'zist] *vt* **1.** act against; fight against: *resist the spread of disease; resist the enemy.* **2.** not be damaged or affected by: *a metal that resists rust.* **3.** (usu. with *negative*) keep from. *She can't resist sweet things. I couldn't resist laughing.*

resistance *nu* **1.** act of resisting. *The defenders of the city put up a tremendous resistance.* **2.** power of resisting: *have resistance to a disease.* **3.** force that resists. *Copper has less resistance to electricity than many other metals.*

resistible *adj.* (*opp* **irresistible**).

resolute ['rezəluːt] *adj* firm; not changing one's decision. (*opp* **irresolute**).

resolution [rezə'luːʃən] **1.** *nu* firmness; quality of being resolute. **2.** *nc* something decided on; decision (esp. one made at a meeting): *make a resolution* i.e. a decision; *pass a resolution.*

resolve [ri'zɔlv] *vt/i* **1.** decide; make up one's mind. *He resolved to work harder/that he would work harder.* **2.** divide into parts. *The chemist resolved the mixture into its different parts.* **3.** put an end to; explain. *This book will resolve all your difficulties.* Also **1.** *nc* something decided: *keep a resolve.* **2.** *nu* firmness; determination.

resonant ['rezənənt] *adj* continuing to sound; filling with sound; tending to make sounds louder or longer: *a resonant voice; resonant walls.* **resonance** *nu.*

resort [ri'zɔːt] *vi* use (esp. when other means fail); turn to for help. *You should never resort to violence. He was so poor that he resorted to stealing.* Also *nc* **1.** place people go to: *a seaside resort.* **2.** person/thing gone to for help.

have resort to use (often when other means fail): *have resort to violence.*

as a/in the last resort if all other means fail: *borrow money as a last resort.*

resound [ri'zaund] *vt/i* **1.** give back sound; be filled with sound. *The hall resounded with the shouts of the people.* **2.** be much discussed. *His fame resounded throughout the land.* **resounding** *adj.* **resoundingly** *adv.*

resource [ri'sɔːs] *nu* **1.** means of help. **2.** ability to think of ways of getting help: *a man of resource.*

resources *npl* **1.** wealth which a country has. **2.** wealth or means of getting money, that a person has.

resourceful *adj* able to get things done or overcome difficulties. **resourcefully** *adv.*

natural resources things in a country which its people can use (e.g. minerals, soil, water supplies etc).

respect [ris'pekt] **1.** *nu* honour; admiration: *show respect to one's parents; have great respect for someone.* **2.** *nu* consideration; care: *to show respect for other people's wishes.* **3.** *nu* reference: *with respect to.* **4.** *nc* (often *pl*) detail; point: *a good plan in*

many/some respects. Also *vt* 1. give honour to: *respect one's parents*. 2. show consideration for; care for: *respect the feelings of others*.
respects *npl* greetings. *Please accept this gift with our respects*.
respectable *adj* 1. well-behaved; of good character: *respectable citizens*. 2. fit to be seen: *respectable clothes*. **respectably** *adv*.
respectability [rispektə'biliti] *nu* state of being respectable.
respectful *adj* well-mannered; showing respect: *be respectful to one's teacher*. (*opp* **disrespectful**). **respectfully** *adv*.
respecting *prep* about; concerning.
respective *adj* of each. *The two boys were told to return to their respective homes* i.e. each boy was to return to his own home.
respectively *adv* each in turn; in the order given. *The first, second and third prizes went to John, James and Tom respectively* i.e. the first prize went to John, and so on.
in respect of with reference to; concerning.
respire [ris'paiə*] *vi* breathe.
respiration [respi'reiʃən] 1. *nu* breathing. 2. *nc* single breath.
respirator ['respireitə*] *nc* device for breathing through, worn over the nose and mouth (e.g. when there is fog etc).
respiratory [res'pirətəri] *adj* connected with breathing: *respiratory diseases*.
respite ['respait] *nc/u* 1. period of rest or relief from work, pain etc: *work without (a) respite*. 2. delay in a sentence (esp. a death sentence) being carried out. Also *vt* give a respite to.
resplendent [ri'splendnt] *adj* very bright; shining; splendid. **resplendence** *nu*.
respond [ris'pɔnd] *vi* 1. answer; reply: *respond to a letter*. 2. be affected by something in a positive way: *respond to kindness; respond to treatment* i.e. begin to recover from an illness.
response [ris'pɔns] *nc/u* 1. answer. 2. act of responding. *Our appeal for help met with no response*.
responsive [ris'pɔnsiv] *adj* 1. answering. 2. influenced; easily moved: *be responsive to someone's appeal for help*. (*opp* **unresponsive**). **responsively** *adv*.
responsible [ris'pɔnsibl] *adj* 1. in charge of. *You will be responsible for keeping your room tidy*. 2. to be blamed or praised for. *The storm was responsible for most of the damage*. 3. reliable; able to be trusted: *a job for some responsible person*. (*opp* **irresponsible**). 4. important; requiring a reliable person: *a responsible position*. **responsibly** *adv*.
responsibility [rispɔnsi'biliti] 1. *nu* state of being responsible. *Some young people have no sense of responsibility* i.e. they are not reliable. 2. *nc* something one is responsible for. *Keeping the room tidy is your responsibility, not mine*.
rest[1] [rest] 1. *nc/u* freedom from anything that is tiring; sleep: *an hour's rest; work without rest; lie down for a rest*. 2. *nc* something that supports. *Use this pillow as a rest for your arm*. 3. *nu* death: *lay someone to rest* i.e. bury someone. 4. *nc* (music) pause; mark for a pause. Also *vt/i* 1. be free from anything that is tiring; sleep: *rest after working; rest for an hour*. 2. give a rest to: *rest one's eyes after reading*. 3. stop moving; be no longer active. *The ball rested at the foot of the hill. Let the matter rest there* i.e. discuss it no further. 4. be supported; cause to be supported: *rest one's head on a pillow*.
restful *adj* quiet; peaceful. **restfully** *adv*.
restive *adj* unable or unwilling to stay still; disobedient. *The horses are getting restive because of the storm*. **restively** *adv*.
restless *adj* unable to rest; moving about; without rest. *I feel too restless to sit down and read; spend a restless night*. **restlessly** *adv*.
restlessness *nu*.
rest[2] [rest] *n* only in **the rest** i.e. what is left. *Take the good apples and throw away the rest*.
rest with someone depend on; be the responsibility of. *It rests with you to make the decision*.
one can/may rest assured one can be quite confident. *You may rest assured that I will do everything I can to help you*.
restaurant ['restərɔŋ] *nc* place where meals can be bought and eaten.
restitution [resti'tju:ʃən] *nu* making up for something that has been lost, stolen etc either by giving back the thing itself or by making a payment.
restore [ri'stɔ:*] *vt* 1. bring back: *restore old customs; restore someone to his old position*. 2. give back: *restore stolen property*. 3. make something as it was when new: *restore old buildings/furniture etc*.
restoration [restə'reiʃən] *nc/u* act of restoring or being restored.
restrain [ris'trein] *vt* prevent someone from doing something; control: *restrain someone from doing something; restrain one's curiosity*.
restraint 1. *nu* restraining or being restrained. 2. *nc* something that restrains.
restrained *adj*. (*opp* **unrestrained**).
restrict [ris'trikt] *vt* keep within limits: *restrict wages and prices*.
restriction 1. *nu* restricting or being restricted: *move about without restriction*. 2. *nc* something that restricts; law or rule.
result [ri'zʌlt] *nc* 1. what happens because of something. *This cold I have is the result of going out without a coat yesterday*. 2. score in a match or competition: *listen to the football results*. Also *vi* follow as a result. *His failure resulted from not working hard enough*. **resultant** *adj*.
result in something end as; have as a result. *His angry words resulted in a fight*.
resume [ri'zju:m] *vt* 1. begin again: *resume one's studies*. 2. take again. *You may resume your seat* i.e. sit down again. **resumption** [ri'zʌmpʃən] *nu*.
résumé [re'zju:mei] *nc* report in a few words of something written or spoken; summary.
resurgence [ri'sə:dʒəns] *nu* appearance again with new strength: *a resurgence of interest in the Middle Ages* i.e. there is again a strong interest in the Middle Ages, after a period when people were not interested in this time. **resurgent** *adj*.
resurrect [rezə'rekt] *vt* 1. bring into use again: *resurrect old customs*. 2. bring back to life.
resurrection *nu* 1. coming back to life. 2. revival from decay, lack of use etc.
the Resurrection 1. rising again of Christ after being buried. 2. rising again on the last day of all those who have died.
resuscitate [ri'sʌsiteit] *vt/i* bring someone back to consciousness: *resuscitate someone who has almost drowned*. **resuscitation** [risʌsi'teiʃən] *nu*.
retail ['ri:teil] *nu* sale of goods in small amounts to the ordinary public, not to shopkeepers. (*opp* **wholesale**). Also *adj*. Also *vt/i* 1. sell or be sold by retail: *retail groceries; goods which retail at/for fifty pence*

each. **2.** tell again to different people: *retail gossip.*

retailer *nc* shopkeeper who sells goods by retail.

etain [ri'tein] *vt* **1.** keep; continue to hold. *You must retain your tickets. The dull speaker could not retain the interest of his audience.* **2.** pay money so that one may be able to use someone's services: *retain a lawyer.* **retention** [ri'tenʃən] *nu.*

retainer *nc* **1.** money paid for the right to someone's services. *The lawyer demanded a large retainer.* **2.** servant (*o.f.* in sense **2.**).

etaliate [ri'tælieit] *vi* pay back one wrong or injury with another. *If you strike me, I shall retaliate.* **retaliation** [ritæli'eiʃən] *nc/u.*

etard [ri'tɑːd] *vt* delay; make slow. *Ignorance retards progress.* **retardation** [riːtɑː'deiʃən] *nu.*

retarded *adj* (usu. with reference to the mental and educational development of children) developing more slowly than is normal.

etch [retʃ] *vi* attempt to vomit, but without succeeding.

etention [ri'tenʃən] *nu* see **retain.**

etentive [ri'tentiv] *adj* able to retain or keep: *a retentive memory* i.e. one which does not forget things.

eticent ['retisnt] *adj* not saying much: *be reticent about one's past.* **reticence** *nu.*

etina ['retinə] *nc* area at the back of the eye, which is sensitive to light. **retinal** *adj.*

etinue ['retinjuː] *nc* group of servants and followers going with a person (esp. one of high rank).

etire [ri'taiə*] *vt/i* **1.** give up one's job, or be required to do so (usu. because one is getting old). *Most teachers retire at 65.* **2.** go away to where it is quiet: *retire from society.* **3.** go to bed (*o.f.* in sense **3.**).

retired *adj* no longer doing a job (usu. because of one's age): *a retired civil servant.*

retirement *nu* state of being retired.

retiring *adj* not anxious to meet other people: *be of a retiring nature.*

etort[1] [ri'tɔːt] *vt/i* reply quickly and sharply (e.g. to an accusation). Also *nc* reply.

etort[2] [ri'tɔːt] *nc* container with a long, narrow neck, used in distilling liquids.

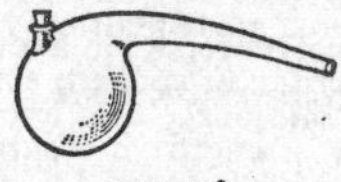

retort[2]

etouch ['riː'tʌtʃ] *vt* improve a photograph, painting etc by making small changes.

etrace [riː'treis] *vt* go back over: *retrace one's steps from where one started; retrace past events in one's memory.*

etract [ri'trækt] *vt/i* **1.** take back; deny; withdraw: *retract a statement/an offer etc.* **2.** draw back or in. *A cat can retract its claws.*

retraction *nc/u.*

retractable *adj* able to be retracted.

etreat [ri'triːt] *vi* go back; withdraw. *The army was defeated and had to retreat.* Also *nc/u* **1.** act of retreating. **2.** signal for a retreat (usu. made by a drum or bugle): *sound the retreat.* **3.** place where one goes to rest, or pray and meditate: *go into retreat for a week.*

etrench [ri'trentʃ] *vt/i* save money by spending less: *retrench one's expenses. We must retrench.* **retrenchment** *nc/u.*

retribution [retri'bjuːʃən] *nu* punishment that is deserved: *retribution for evil deeds.*

retributive [re'tribjutiv] *adj.*

retrieve [ri'triːv] *vt* **1.** get back something which has been lost. **2.** put something back to the way it was before: *retrieve one's fortunes* i.e. end a period of bad luck. **3.** make good; put right: *retrieve a mistake.*

retriever *nc* dog trained to bring back shot birds to its master.

retro- ['retrou] *prefix* backwards (e.g. **retrograde; retrospect**).

retroactive [retrou'æktiv] *adj* having an effect on something already done: *retroactive legislation* i.e. laws which make illegal something which has already been done. **retroactively** *adv.*

retrograde ['retrougreid] *adj* **1.** going backwards: *retrograde movement.* **2.** making worse: *a retrograde action* i.e. something which will make matters worse.

retrogression [retrou'greʃən] *nc/u* **1.** act of going backwards. **2.** return to a worse state.

retrogressive [retrou'gresiv] *adj* returning to a worse state; moving backwards.

retrogress [retrou'gres] *vi* move backwards in this way; become worse.

retrospect ['retrəspekt] *nu* act of looking at past events. **retrospection** [retrou'spekʃən] *nu.*

retrospective [retrou'spektiv] *adj* **1.** looking back. **2.** having an effect on something already done: *retrospective legislation* i.e. laws which make illegal something which has already been done. **retrospectively** *adv.*

in retrospect when looking back at past events.

return [ri'təːn] *vt/i* **1.** go back; come back: *return to one's village.* **2.** give back: *return a book to the library.* **3.** make an official announcement. *The jury returned a verdict of guilty.* **4.** elect someone to Parliament. **5.** say in reply. Also *nc/u* **1.** going or coming back. *On my return, I found the house empty.* **2.** act of giving back: *get no return for one's kindness.* **3.** official statement: *the election returns* i.e. statement of who has been elected. **4.** (often *pl*) amount received; profit: *a business which gives good returns.* Also *adj* having to do with returning: *the return journey* i.e. the journey back; (*Brit*) *a return ticket* i.e. a ticket which allows one to get to a place and then come back again. (*US* **round-trip ticket**).

returnable *adj* that can, or must be, returned.

reunion [riː'juːniən] *nc* **1.** act of joining together again. **2.** meeting of friends or colleagues who have been separated for a long time. **reunite** [riːjuː'nait] *vt/i.*

rev [rev] *nc* revolution of an engine in a car etc. Also *vi* (with **up**) cause an engine to move faster: *rev up a motorbike. past* **revved.** (both *informal*).

reveal [ri'viːl] *vt* **1.** make known: *reveal a secret.* **2.** show; allow to be seen: *a remark that reveals one's ignorance of something.*

revelation [revə'leiʃən] **1.** *nu* act of revealing. **2.** *nc* something which is revealed (esp. something surprising or important).

reveille [ri'væli] *nc/u* signal for soldiers to get up in the morning: *sound (the) reveille.*

revel ['revl] *vi* make merry; pass the time by drinking, dancing etc. *past* **revelled.** (*US* **reveled**). Also *nc* noisy merrymaking. **reveller** *nc.* (*US* **reveler**).

revelry *nu* wild and noisy merrymaking.
revel in something enjoy very much. *He revels in hard work.*
revelation [revə'leiʃən] *nc/u* see **reveal.**
revenge [ri'vendʒ] *vt* punishment given by one person to a second person, in return for some wrong the second person has done to the first. Also *nu* punishment given because of some wrong that has been received: *kill someone in revenge; take revenge on someone; get one's revenge* i.e. punish somebody in this way. see *Note* on **avenge.**
revengeful *adj* feeling or showing a wish for revenge. **revengefully** *adv.*
be revenged on somebody for something punish someone for an injury received.
in revenge as a revenge: *kill somebody in revenge.*
revenue ['revənjuː] *nc/u* money coming in (esp. to the government from taxes etc).
'revenue officer government officer who collects taxes on goods brought into a country and on certain goods produced in a country (*o.f.* – use **customs and excise officer**).
reverberate [ri'vəːbəreit] *vt/i* throw back sound; be thrown back; be filled with sound. *The sound of his voice reverberated from wall to wall.* **reverberation** [rivəːbə'reiʃən] *nc/u.*
revere [ri'viə*] *vt* respect deeply. *The temple was revered as a sacred place.*
reverence ['revərns] *nu* feeling of great respect: *hold someone/something in reverence* i.e. respect deeply. Also *vt* respect deeply.
reverend ['revərnd] *adj* worthy of great respect.
the Reverend title for clergymen: *the Reverend James Brown/the Reverend* Mr *Brown.*
Note: it is usu. considered incorrect to say *the Reverend Brown* or *Reverend Brown.*
reverent ['revərnt] *adj* feeling or showing reverence. (*opp* **irreverent**). **reverently** *adv.*
reverential [revə'renʃl] *adj* caused by reverence; respectful.
reverie ['revəri] *nc/u* daydream; state of thinking pleasant thoughts: *lost in reverie.*
reverse [ri'vəːs] *adj* **1.** opposite: *on the reverse side.* **2.** causing to go in the opposite direction: *the reverse gear in a car* i.e. that which makes it go backwards. Also *nc/u* **1.** opposite. *The result was the reverse of what I expected.* **2.** back; opposite side. *Turn the coin over and see what is on the reverse.* **3.** defeat: *suffer an unexpected reverse.* **4.** gear which causes a car to go backwards: *put a car into reverse.* Also *vt* **1.** cancel: *reverse a decision.* **2.** cause to go in the opposite direction: *reverse a car.* **3.** put in the opposite position: *reverse arms* i.e. point a rifle downwards.
reversal *nc* act of reversing or being reversed.
reversible *adj* **1.** that can be reversed. **2.** able to be used on either side: *reversible cloth.*
revert [ri'vəːt] *vi* go back; return. *When the ground was not cultivated, it reverted to jungle. We must revert to that problem later.*
review [ri'vjuː] *vt/i* **1.** examine again; go over again: *review the situation; review the events of the day.* **2.** write a report on what one has read: *review books for a Sunday newspaper.* **3.** inspect soldiers etc in a special ceremony. Also *nc/u* **1.** act of reviewing. *The government policy is under review.* **2.** article written about books etc. *His boo got good reviews.* **3.** special ceremony c inspection of soldiers etc: *a naval reviev* **4.** regularly appearing paper or magazin which gives an account of new book recent events etc.
reviewer *nc* person who writes reviews fc a newspaper etc.
revile [ri'vail] *vt/i* curse; speak to or abou someone in an unkind way.
revise [ri'vaiz] *vt* **1.** read through somethin carefully (esp. in order to correct or im prove). **2.** change one's opinion of some thing: *revise one's opinion.*
revision [ri'viʒən] *nc/u* act of revising something revised.
revive [ri'vaiv] *vt/i* **1.** come or bring bac to health or consciousness. *After a fe minutes the rescued man began to revive.* **2** make or become fresh and lively again *revive someone's spirits.* **3.** bring back int use: *revive an old play/custom etc.*
revival **1.** *nc/u* act of reviving or bein revived. **2.** *nc* attempt to cause greate interest in religion by holding specia sermons, religious services etc.
revivalist *nc* person who attempts to caus great interest in religion in this way
revivalism *nu.*
revoke [ri'vouk] *vt* **1.** cancel: *revoke an order* **2.** in playing cards, not play a card o the kind wanted, even when one has a car of that kind. **revocation** [revə'keiʃən] *nc/u*
revolt [ri'voult] *vt* **1.** rise against a leade or the government: *the troops revolted.* **2** turn away from in disgust: *revolt at th thought of it.* **3.** cause to be disgusted. *Thei cruel behaviour revolted him.* Also *nc/*u rebellion: *be in a state of revolt.*
revolting *adj* disgusting; extremely un pleasant. **revoltingly** *adv.*
revolution [revə'luːʃən] **1.** *nc* armed risin against the government. **2.** *nc/u* grea change. *The invention of the motorcar ha brought about a revolution in transport.* **3** *nc* movement of something in a circle: *th revolution of the earth round the sun.* **4.** *n* one complete movement in a circle: *fift revolutions per minute.* see **revolve.**
revolutionary *adj* **1.** connected with revolution. **2.** suggesting or causing grea changes: *revolutionary ideas.* Also *nc* some one who wants great political changes (usu by violent means).
revolutionize *vt* cause great changes in.
revolve [ri'vɔlv] *vt/i* **1.** move round in circle. *The earth revolves round the sun.* **2** think a lot about: *revolve a problem in one' mind.* see **revolution.**
revolver [ri'vɔlvə*] *nc* type of pistol.

revolver

revue [ri'vjuː] *nc* musical entertainmer with songs, dances, humour etc, in whic the different items need not be connecte to form a story.
revulsion [ri'vʌlʃən] *nu* (often with a sudden and complete change of feelin from liking to hate or disgust.
reward [ri'wɔːd] *nc* **1.** something given i return for a service. **2.** money given for th

return of something that has been lost or stolen, or for information given to the police. Also *vt* give a reward: *reward someone for his services; reward someone's bravery.*
rewarding *adj* bringing great benefits or rewards: *a rewarding experience.*
rhapsody ['ræpsədi] *nc* something said or written which shows that one is wildly delighted: *go into rhapsodies* i.e. say how delighted one is.
rhetoric ['retərik] *nu* **1.** art of using words to persuade. **2.** speech or writing that is too concerned with how a thing is said. **3.** speech etc which sounds impressive but which has little or no meaning.
rhetorical [ri'tɔrikl] *adj* **1.** concerned with rhetoric. **2.** intended to arouse the emotions.
rhetorician [retə'riʃən] *nc* person skilled in rhetoric.
a rhetorical question a question that is used only for effect, not expecting an answer.
rheumatism ['ruːmətizəm] *nu* disease causing painful swelling of the joints.
rheumatic [ruː'mætik] *adj* **1.** connected with rheumatism. **2.** having, or liable to have, rheumatism.
rhinoceros [rai'nɔsərəs] *nc* type of large, thickskinned animal with a horn on its nose, found in Africa and Asia.

rhinoceros

rhododendron [roudə'dendrn] *nc* kind of shrub with oval leaves and large flowers.
rhombus ['rɔmbəs] *nc* (geometry) four-sided figure with equal sides and oblique angles.
rhubarb ['ruːbɑːb] *nu* plant with thick juicy stalks which can be cooked, sweetened and eaten as food.
rhyme, rime [raim] **1.** *nu* sameness of sound in the last part of words (e.g. between *chair* and *dare* or *repeat* and *defeat*). **2.** *nc* verse or verses with words that rhyme. **3.** *nc* word or line that ends with the same sound as another. Also *vt/i* **1.** sound the same in the last part. *What words rhyme with 'school'?* **2.** use one word with another that has the same sound. **3.** make up verses that have rhymes.
rhymed *adj* having rhymes. (*opp* **unrhymed**).
without rhyme or reason without any sense or meaning.
rhythm ['riðəm] *nc/u* regular beat of music, dancing, poetry etc. **rhythmic, rhythmical** ['riðmik(l)] *adj.*
rib [rib] *nc* **1.** any one of the curved bones stretching from the backbone round to the chest. **2.** anything like this (esp. something which makes a frame): *the ribs of a ship.*
ribbed *adj* having narrow parts raised a bit above the surface: *ribbed silk.*
ribald ['ribəld] *adj* causing offence by indecent talk or behaviour: *a ribald person; a ribald song.*
ribaldry *nu* ribald language.
ribbon ['ribən] *nc/u* **1.** long, narrow band of silk or other material: *tied with a silk ribbon.* **2.** anything like this in shape: *typewriter ribbon.*
rice [rais] *nu* white grain from a plant grown widely in India, China and other places, which is cooked and eaten as food.
rich [ritʃ] *adj* **1.** having a lot of money and possessions: *a rich man.* **2.** producing much: *rich soil.* **3.** showing signs of wealth: *rich clothes and jewels.* **4.** (with reference to food) containing a lot of sugar, cream, butter, eggs, flavouring etc: *rich food.* **5.** deep; strong: *rich colours/sounds etc.*
riches *npl* a lot of money and possessions.
the rich *npl* wealthy people.
richly *adv* **1.** fully; completely. *He richly deserved a heavy punishment.* **2.** in a rich manner.
richness *nu* state of being rich.
rick[1] [rik] *nc* pile of hay etc built up so that it can be protected from the weather.

rick[1]

rick[2], **wrick** [rik] *vt* twist a muscle of the body slightly but painfully. Also *nc* slight, painful twist.
rickets ['rikits] *nu* disease of children, in which the bones become soft and sometimes badly-formed.
Note: followed by a *sing* verb.
rickety ['rikiti] *adj* likely to break or fall down: *a rickety old chair.*
rickshaw ['rikʃɔː] *nc* small, two-wheeled carriage pulled by a man.
ricochet ['rikəʃei] *nc/u* jumping movement of a bullet or stone etc when it hits against something. Also *vt/i* move, cause to move, in this way. *A bullet can ricochet off a wall. pres part* **ricocheting** ['rikəʃeiiŋ]. *past* **ricocheted** ['rikəʃeid].
rid [rid] *vt* make free from: *rid a house of rats. past* **rid.**
riddance *nu* clearing away.
ridden[1] *adj* joined with other words, to show that something is too common or too powerful (e.g. *a disease-ridden area*).
get rid of **1.** make oneself free from: *try to get rid of unwelcome visitors.* **2.** do away with; kill.
good riddance (used to express satisfaction that someone/something has gone): *Those rude people have gone and good riddance!* (*informal*).
ridden[2] ['ridn] past part of **ride.**
riddle[1] ['ridl] *nc* puzzling question, situation, person etc. *Can you answer this riddle? That man is a riddle to me* i.e. I cannot understand him.
riddle[2] ['ridl] *nc* container with many holes at the bottom so that smaller things (e.g. stones) can fall through, but larger things can be kept. Also *vt* **1.** put many holes in. *The door was riddled with bullets.* **2.** shake material in a riddle to separate larger things from smaller ones.
ride [raid] *vt/i* **1.** sit on something and be taken along by it: *ride (on) a horse.* **2.** be carried along in something: *ride in a bus.* Also *nc* journey on the back of a horse, in a car etc: *go for a ride in the park. past tense* **rode** [roud]. *past part* **ridden** ['ridn].
rider *nc* **1.** someone who rides. **2.** extra statement added on to the end of a docu-

ment, official statement, verdict of a jury etc.
ride at anchor (with reference to a boat or ship) move up and down with the movement of the sea, but being kept in the same place by a heavy weight.
be riding for a fall behave in a way that is sure to bring about failure or misfortune. (*informal*).
ride out a storm **1.** come through a storm successfully. **2.** come through any kind of misfortune successfully.

ridge [ridʒ] *nc* **1.** edge where two upward sloping surfaces meet: *the ridge of a roof.* **2.** long, narrow stretch of raised land or hills. **3.** any long, narrow object raised above the surrounding surface. Also *vt* make into, or cover with, ridges.

ridicule ['ridikju:l] *vt* make fun of. Also *nu* words or actions that make fun of someone/something.
ridiculous [ri'dikjuləs] *adj* foolish; deserving ridicule. **ridiculously** *adv.*

rife [raif] *pred adj* common; found everywhere. *Crime is rife in this city.*
rife with full of: *an area rife with disease.*

riff-raff ['rifræf] *nu* worthless people of the lowest class.

rifle[1] ['raifl] *nc* gun with a very long barrel (usu. fired from the shoulder). Also *vt* cut grooves into the barrel of a gun so as to make the bullet spin.

rifle[2] ['raifl] *vt* search through and steal everything of value. *All the drawers had been rifled.*

rift [rift] *nc* split; crack; break: *cause a rift between two friends.*

rig [rig] *vt* **1.** fit a ship with masts, ropes, sails etc. **2.** (with reference to an election etc) bring about the result that one wants by dishonest means: *rig an election. past* **rigged.** Also *nc* way in which a ship's masts, sails etc are arranged.
rigging *nu* ropes etc used to support the masts and sails of a ship.
'oil rig type of installation, used for drilling for oil under the sea.
rig someone out (with) provide somebody with clothes etc. (*informal*).
'rig-out *nc* dress; clothes: *wearing a strange rig-out.* (*informal*).
rig something up put something together quickly, using whatever materials are available: *rig up a shelter.*

right[1] [rait] *adj* **1.** good; just: *do what is right.* **2.** correct: *give the right answer.* **3.** best; proper. *The stain doesn't show on the right side* i.e. the side that is meant to be seen. **4.** healthy: *in his right mind* i.e. sane. (*opp* **wrong** in senses **1.** and **2.**). Also *adv/intensifier* **1.** properly; correctly. *You did it right the first time. I hope it turns out right* i.e. succeeds. **2.** exactly. *Stop right there.* **3.** directly; not going to one side or the other. *Go right on to the end of the road.* **4.** completely. *He fell right off the chair.* **5.** (in titles) very: *the Right Honourable . . .* Also **1.** *nu* what is good and just: *know the difference between right and wrong.* **2.** *nc/u* just claim; something to which one is entitled. *She has no right to be so rude. I have a right/the right to say what I think.* Also *vt* correct; put something the way it should be: *right an injustice.*
rightly *adv* correctly: *if I am rightly informed.*
righteous ['raitʃəs] *adj* virtuous; just: *the righteous and the wicked; righteous anger.* (*opp* **unrighteous**). **righteously** *adv.*
rightful *adj* lawful; according to justice *the rightful owner.* **rightfully** *adv.*
all right see **all.**
by right, by rights in justice. *That house should belong to me by rights.* (*informal*).
'right angle angle of 90°.
right a'way *adv* immediately.
'right-'minded *adj* just; virtuous.
right now (mainly *US*) immediately.
do a right about turn turn until one is facing in the opposite direction.
get something right **1.** make sure one understands something correctly. **2.** correct something.
be in the right be correct; have justice on one's side.
put someone/something right make correct healthy, just etc: *put one's watch right* i.e. put it to the correct time.
it serves him/her etc right he/she etc deserves the punishment or misfortune he, she etc has suffered.
set someone/something right put right.

right[2] [rait] *adj/adv/nu* (of or on) the side of a person's body that is farther away from the heart: *my right hand. In Europe road traffic mostly keeps to the right. Turn right when you reach the square.* (*opp* **left**).
'right-hand *adj* on the right side.
'right-'handed *adj* using the right hand rather than the left: *a right-handed person.*
the right, the right wing *nu* (politics) those who are conservative, or against socialism or communism: *a right-wing politician.*

rigid ['ridʒid] *adj* **1.** stiff. **2.** strict: *rigid rules.* **rigidly** *adv.* **rigidity** [ri'dʒiditi] *nu.*

rigmarole ['rigməroul] *nu* long story without much meaning; foolish talk.

rigor mortis ['rigə'mɔ:tis] *nu* stiffening of the body after death.

rigour ['rigə*] (*US* **rigor**) **1.** *nu* strictness; lack of mercy. **2.** *nc* (often *pl*) hardship *the rigours of winter.*
rigorous *adj* **1.** strict: *rigorous discipline.* **2.** exact: *a rigorous search.* **rigorously** *adv.*

rile [rail] *vt* annoy; make angry.

rim [rim] *nc* (usu. of something round) edge: *the rim of a cup/wheel etc.* Also *vt* be on the rim of; make a rim for. *past* **rimmed**

rime[1] [raim] *nc/u* see **rhyme.**

rime[2] [raim] *nu* frost; frozen water found on grass etc in winter (*o.f.*).

rind [raind] *nc/u* hard outer surface of cheese, bacon etc.

ring[1] [riŋ] *nc* **1.** circle: *stand in a ring round something.* **2.** round band made of metal or other material: *a gold wedding ring.* **3.** any kind of closed-in space where things can be shown: *a cattle ring; a boxing ring* i.e. a square area where two men can fight using their fists. **4.** group of people working together for their own purposes (usu. unfair or dishonest purposes). Also *vt* **1.** stand round in a circle: *be ringed by a crowd of spectators.* **2.** put a ring through an animal's nose: *ring a bull. past* **ringed.**

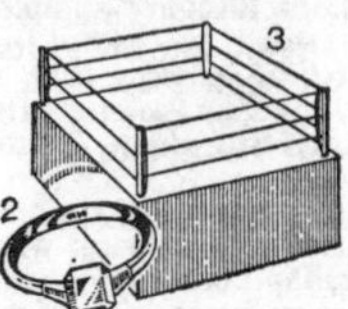

rings[1] (*def 2*) (*def 3*)

ringlet *nc* long hanging curl of hair.
'ring finger third finger of the left hand.
'ringleader someone who leads others in doing wrong.
'ring road road built round a town to relieve traffic in the centre.
'ringworm disease which causes round red patches on the skin.

ring[2] [riŋ] *vt/i* **1.** give a sound like a bell. *The telephone is ringing.* **2.** cause to give this sound: *ring a bell.* **3.** telephone. *I'll ring you later.* **4.** have a loud, hollow sound. *The room rang with his laughter. The sound of his voice rang in my ears. past tense* **rang** [ræŋ]. *past part* **rung** [rʌŋ]. Also *nc* noise of a bell: *a ring at the door.*
ring for someone/something ring a bell so that someone may come or something may be brought (e.g. in a hotel).
ring off end a telephone conversation.
ring someone up phone. *I'll ring you up later.*
ring true/false sound true/false.

rink [riŋk] *nc* area of ice or other smooth surface used for skating on: *an ice rink.*

rinse [rins] *vt* wash with clean water (usu. to remove soap): *rinse (out) a shirt; rinse soap out of one's hair.* Also *nc* **1.** act of rinsing: *give clothes a rinse before drying them.* **2.** liquid for colouring hair.

riot ['raiət] *nc* **1.** wild and unlawful behaviour by a group of people. *The police came to put down the riots.* **2.** wild behaviour. **3.** bright display: *a riot of colour.* Also *vi* take part in a riot: *riot in the streets.* **rioter** *nc.*
riotous *adj* **1.** disorderly; wild: *riotous behaviour.* **2.** taking part in a riot. **riotously** *adv.*
run riot behave without restraint.

rip [rip] *vt/i* **1.** pull or tear violently: *rip a piece of cloth into small pieces.* **2.** be torn. *His coat ripped when it was caught in the door. past* **ripped.** Also *nc*: *a rip in his coat.*

ripe [raip] *adj* **1.** fully grown and ready to be taken: *ripe fruit; ripe crops.* **2.** ready to be used; suitable: *when the time is ripe.*
ripen *vt/i* become or make ripe.

ripple ['ripl] *nc* **1.** very small wave: *the ripples in a stream.* **2.** sound of a very small wave; sound like this: *the ripple of a stream; a ripple of laughter.* Also *vt/i* **1.** flow with ripples. **2.** cause to have ripples. *A wind rippled the surface of the lake.* **3.** make a sound like the ripples in water.

rise [raiz] *vi* **1.** get up: *rise from bed.* **2.** go higher. *The level of the river is rising.* **3.** start, begin. *Where does the river rise? A quarrel rose between them.* **4.** end a meeting etc. *The court rose at five o'clock.* **5.** rebel. *The people rose against their rulers. past tense* **rose** [rouz]. *past part* **risen** ['rizn]. Also *nc* **1.** (*Brit*) increase: *a rise in wages.* (*US* **raise**). **2.** small slope upwards: *a rise in the ground.* see **raise.**
rising *nc* rebellion; act of rising. Also *adj* **1.** that rises. **2.** growing up: *the rising generation.*

risk [risk] *nc/u* danger; chance of meeting danger or harm. *If you go out in this weather, there is a risk of catching cold.* Also *vt* **1.** be or put in danger: *risk one's life.* **2.** take a chance of meeting some harm: *risk being injured.*
risky *adj* dangerous. **riskily** *adv.*
run a risk be in a position where one may meet a possible danger. *If you go out without your coat, you run a risk of catching cold.*

risqué ['ri:skei] *adj* slightly indecent or obscene.

rite [rait] *nc* ceremony (esp. a religious ceremony): *the marriage rites.*
ritual ['ritjuəl] *nc/u* system of rites: *the ritual of a church.* Also *adj* connected with rites: *a ritual dance.* **ritually** *adv.*

rival ['raivl] *nc* person who tries to get the same thing as another; person who tries to do better than another. Also *vt* **1.** try to be the same as or better than. **2.** be equal to or nearly equal to. *This rivals anything I've seen. past* **rivalled.** (*US* **rivaled**). Also *adj.*
rivalry *nc/u* state of being rivals; competition.

river ['rivə*] *nc* wide stream of water flowing to the sea or into a lake or another river.

rivet ['rivit] *nc* metal bolt like a nail, used for fastening sheets of metal together. Also *vt* **1.** fasten with rivets. **2.** fix firmly. *He riveted his eyes on me.* **3.** attract strongly. *The scene riveted our attention.*

rivulet ['rivjulət] *nc* small stream.

road [roud] *nc* **1.** way specially prepared for people, cars etc to travel on: *the roads out of London; travel by road.* **2.** way; means: *the road to success.* **3.** (usu. *pl*) place where ships can anchor.
'roadblock barrier put across a road by police etc for some purpose.
'roadhog person who drives a car very carelessly. (*informal*).
'road metal stones used for making roads.
'roadstead ['roudsted] see **road** (in sense **3.**).
the 'roadway middle part of a road which cars etc use i.e. not the footpath, which pedestrians use.
'roadworthy *adj* (of a car etc) in a suitable or safe condition to be driven on the roads. **roadworthiness** *nu.*

roam [roum] *vi* wander: *roam about the country. He likes to roam.*

roan [roun] (esp. with reference to a horse) brown colour mixed with white or grey. Also *nc* roan horse.

roar [rɔ:*] *nc* loud, deep sound: *the roar of a lion.* Also *vt/i* **1.** make a sound like this. *The crowd roared.* **2.** say loudly: *roar a command.* **3.** move making a loud, deep sound. *The plane roared past us.*

roast [roust] *vt/i* cook or heat by using dry heat i.e. over a fire, or in an oven: *roast meat.* Also *nc/u* meat that has been roasted.

rob [rob] *vt* take away by using force. *Thieves robbed him of all his money. past* **robbed. robber** *nc.*
robbery *nc/u* act of robbing.

robe [roub] *nc* **1.** long, loose outer garment. **2.** garment of this kind worn by some officials: *a judge's robes.* Also *vt/i* put a robe on.

robin ['rɔbin] *nc* type of small, plump, brown bird with a red breast.

robot ['roubɔt] *nc* **1.** machine that can work like a man. **2.** person who acts like a machine (e.g. by working without thinking).

robust [rou'bʌst] *adj* strong; healthy: *a robust man.* **robustly** *adv.*

rock[1] [rɔk] *nc/u* **1.** large mass of stone: *cut a road through solid rock.* **2.** piece of stone. *Rocks fell down the hillside.* **3.** sweet in the form of a stick. Also *adj.*
rocky full of rocks; like rock: *rocky soil.*
'rock-'bottom *adj* very lowest; most inferior: *rock-bottom prices.* (*informal*).
rockery, 'rock garden garden, or part of a

garden, with plants growing between rocks.
on the rocks 1. (with reference to a ship) wrecked, destroyed on the rocks in the sea. 2. with very little money. 3. (of whisky etc) with ice. (*informal* in senses 2. and 3.).
rock[2] [rɔk] *vt/i* 1. move backwards and forwards or from side to side: *rock oneself to sleep.* 2. move violently. *The building rocked during the earthquake.*
'rocking chair chair made so that it can move backwards and forwards.
'rocking horse child's toy in the form of a horse which can move backwards and forwards.
rocket ['rɔkit] *nc* 1. large tube which goes high into the air by sending out jets of burning fuel and which can be used as a weapon or to carry men into space etc. 2. small object which goes up into the air and explodes into designs of different colours. *The people fired rockets to celebrate their victory.* Also *vi* go up high and quickly, like a rocket.
rocketry *nu* science of space rockets.
rod [rɔd] *nc* 1. long piece of metal, wood or plastic: *a fishing rod.* 2. stick used for punishing. 3. measure of length equal to 5½ yards or 5.03 metres.
rule with a rod of iron/with an iron hand see **rule.**
rode [roud] past tense of **ride.**
rodent ['roudnt] *nc* small animal of the kind that has special teeth for gnawing things (e.g. rats, mice, rabbits etc).
rodeo ['roudiou] *nc* (*US*) show of skill in which untamed horses are ridden etc.
roe[1] [rou] *nu* mass of eggs in a fish.
roe[2] [rou] *nc* kind of small deer found in the woods of Europe and Western Asia. *pl* **roes** or **roe.**
rogue [roug] *nc* 1. dishonest person. 2. mischievous person. 3. dangerous animal living apart from a herd: *a rogue elephant.*
roguery *nu* conduct of a rogue.
roguish *adj* playful; mischievous. **roguishly** *adv.* **roguishness** *nu.*
role [roul] *nc* 1. part for an actor in a play: *an interesting role.* 2. part a person plays in real life. *The headmaster plays an important role in the good running of a school.*
roll [roul] *vt/i* 1. move along by turning over and over. *The ball rolled into the net.* 2. make into the shape of a ball: *roll paper into a ball.* 3. make something by putting it into the shape of a tube: *roll a cigarette.* 4. move from side to side: *a ship rolling in the storm.* 5. make something flat by moving some kind of weight over it: *roll grass; roll pastry.* 6. rise and fall in gentle slopes. *We admired the rolling countryside.* 7. make a long, deep sound. *Thunder rolled in the distance. Drums rolled.* Also *nc* 1. something rolled up; something looking like a tube: *a roll of carpet.* 2. small loaf of bread: *breakfast rolls.* 3. long, deep sound: *the roll of drums/thunder.* 4. movement from side to side: *the roll of a ship.* 5. list: *call the roll* i.e. read out the names on a list.
roller *nc* 1. heavy, tube-shaped piece of metal etc (used e.g. for smoothing grass or making a road even). 2. large, long wave.
'roll call reading out of names on a list (e.g. at a school or prison).
'rolled 'gold thin covering of gold on another metal.
'roller skate skate as in the illustration, for moving on a smooth surface.

roller skates

'rolling pin piece of wood or other material shaped like a tube and used for making dough flat.
'rolling stock coaches, wagons etc of a railway.
roll up 1. make into a ball or tube. 2. arrive. (*informal* in sense 2.).
rollicking ['rɔlikiŋ] *adj* noisy and merry.
Roman ['roumən] *adj* 1. connected with Rome: *Roman Empire.* 2. **(roman)** (of letters in printing) ordinary, upright (like the letters in this definition). Also *nc* someone from Rome.
Roman Catholic *nc* member of the Church of Rome. **Roman Catholicism** *nu.*
roman numerals numbers like LXXX, XL, MDCLV etc in which I=1, V=5, X=10, L=50, C=100, D=500 and M=1,000.
romance [rə'mæns] 1. *nc* love story. 2. *nc* story or poem which tells of the adventures of kings, knights etc. 3. *nu* love and adventure: *in search of romance.*
romantic [rə'mæntik] *adj* 1. dealing with love or adventure in a fanciful way; concerned with this: *a romantic story; a romantic person.* 2. appealing to the feelings rather than reason: *romantic poetry.* Also *nc* romantic person. **romantically** *adv.*
romp [rɔmp] *vi* run, jump and play about in a noisy way. *The children like to romp in the garden.* Also *nc* rough, lively kind of play.
rompers *npl* loose, outer clothes worn by young children when playing.
roof [ru:f] *nc* 1. top covering of a building. 2. top covering of anything: *the roof of a car; the roof of the mouth.* Also *vt* cover with a roof, act as a roof for.
rook[1] [ruk] *nc* large, black bird which flies about in flocks.
rookery *nc* group of trees where rooks have their nests.
rook[2] [ruk] *vt* cheat; charge someone too much. Also *nc* person who cheats. (both *informal*).
rook[3] [ruk] *nc* one of the pieces in a game of chess.
room [ru:m] 1. *nc* part of a house divided by walls from another part. 2. *nu* space for someone/something. *Is there room in your car for one more person?*
rooms *npl* lodgings; rented house: *living in rooms.*
roomful *nc* as much as a room will hold.
roomy *adj* having plenty of space. **roominess** *nu.*
'two-roomed, 'three-roomed etc *adj* having two, three rooms: *a four-roomed house.*
roost [ru:st] *nc* bar, pole on which birds rest: *a hen on a roost.* Also *vi* sleep or rest on a roost.
rooster *nc* (*US*) cock, male chicken.
rule the roost make others obey. (*informal*).
root [ru:t] *nc* 1. part of a plant that is usu. under the ground: *the roots of a flower/tree etc.* 2. bottom or hidden part of a tooth, the

hair, the tongue etc. 3. plant with a root that is used as food (e.g. carrot, turnip). 4. cause; that which brings about something: *the root of a problem. Money is the root of all evil.* 5. (mathematics) number which is multiplied by itself to give another number. see **cube**[2]; **square**[2]. 6. (grammar) word which is used to form other words (e.g. *rob* is the root of *robber* and *robbery*). Also *vt/i* send out roots; cause to send out roots.
rootless *adj* (of a person) having no home etc.
root something up/out 1. pull up a plant including the roots so that it cannot grow again. 2. destroy something: *root out crime.*

rope [roup] *nc* 1. thick, strong line or cord, made by twisting thinner cords together. 2. anything made into a line and twisted together: *a rope of pearls.*
the rope execution by hanging. (*informal*).
rope someone in get someone to share in or help. *Rope in as many people for the concert as you can.* (*informal*).
rope someone up tie with a rope.
know the ropes see **know.**

rosary ['rouzəri] *nc* string of beads used in the Roman Catholic Church to count the number of prayers one has said.

rose[1] [rouz] past tense of **rise.**

rose[2] [rouz] 1. *nc* sweet-smelling flower which grows on a thorny stem, and can be red, white, pink or yellow. 2. *nu* colour between pink and red.
rosy *adj* 1. pink: *rosy cheeks.* 2. hopeful; bright: *a rosy future.*
rosette [rou'zet] *nc* decoration made in the shape of a rose.
'**rosebush** shrub which bears roses.
'**rosewood** kind of dark-red wood used in making furniture.
a bed of roses very pleasant state. *Life is not always a bed of roses.* (*informal*).
look at something through rose-coloured spectacles see **look.**

rosé ['rouzei] *adj* (with reference to wine) pink.

rosin ['rɔzin] *nu* hard, yellowish material which is rubbed on things to keep them from slipping (e.g. the bow of a violin).

roster ['rɔstə*] *nc* list of people showing what jobs they must do and when they must do them.

rostrum ['rɔstrəm] *nc* raised platform from which someone can speak.

rot [rɔt] *vt/i* 1. decay, go bad. *The fruit was left to rot.* 2. cause to go bad: *wood rotted by the damp. past* **rotted.** Also *nu* 1. decay: *wood affected by rot.* 2. nonsense. *Don't talk rot!* (*informal* in sense 2.).
rotten *adj* 1. decayed; bad: *rotten eggs.* 2. bad; unpleasant: *a rotten film.* (*informal* in sense 2.).

rota ['routə] *nc* list of things to be done; list of persons to do certain things in a certain order.

rotary ['routəri] *adj* turning round, as a wheel does: *a rotary movement.*
rotate [rou'teit] *vt/i* 1. move round a centre. *The earth rotates on its axis.* 2. change round in a regular manner: *rotate crops.* **rotatory** [rou'teitəri] *adj.*
rotation [rou'teiʃən] *nc/u* 1. movement round a centre. 2. regular change: *in rotation* i.e. one after the other in a regular way.
rotation of crops growing of different crops in a field, one after the other, so as to keep the soil fertile.

rote [rout] *nu* mechanical, unthinking way of doing things. Also *adj*: *rote learning.*
by rote by heart; using memory only without understanding.

rotund [rou'tʌnd] *adj* 1. round and fat: *a rotund face.* 2. sounding deep and rich: *a rotund voice.* **rotundity** *nu.*

rotunda [rou'tʌndə] *nc* round building, or part of a building (usu. with a dome).

rouge [ruːʒ] *nu* red substance used by women for colouring the face. Also *vt* put rouge on.

rough [rʌf] *adj* 1. not smooth; not level: *a rough road.* 2. uncomfortable: *a rough journey.* 3. not polite; harsh: *a rough voice.* 4. ill-mannered; ill-behaved: *rough companions.* 5. not finished; not complete: *a rough sketch; a rough idea.* 6. stormy: *rough seas.* Also *nc* ill-mannered and violent person. **roughness** *nu.*
roughen *vt/i* make or become rough.
roughly *adv* 1. in a rough manner. 2. about; approximately. *There were roughly twenty people there.*
'**roughcast** mixture of cement and very small stones which is sometimes put on the outside of houses.
'**rough-and-'ready** *adj* 1. done or prepared quickly and therefore not done perfectly. 2. (with reference to a person) friendly, but lacking ordinary politeness.
'**roughshod** *adj* having horseshoes with special nails to prevent slipping.
a rough diamond a person who is good-natured although not very well-mannered.
rough it live for a time in a very simple way, without any material comforts. (*informal*).
ride roughshod over someone treat someone without sympathy or consideration.
take the rough with the smooth accept life as it comes, bad times and good times. (*informal*).

roulette [ruː'let] *nu* gambling game played with a ball which moves on a revolving wheel.

round [raund] *adj* 1. shaped like a circle or ball: *a round ball.* 2. full; complete: *a round dozen.* Also *nc/u* 1. anything shaped like a circle or ball: *a round of beef* i.e. a round joint. 2. stage in a game or competition: *a boxing match lasting ten rounds; be defeated in the third round of a competition.* 3. number of things one after the other; number of duties: *a policeman's round; the daily round.* 4. bullet: *a round of ammunition.* 5. song sung by a number of people each singing the same line one after the other. Also *adv* 1. in a circle or part of a circle: *turn round; wheels that go round; gather round* i.e. be on all sides. 2. by a longer way. *We went round by the post office, instead of coming straight here.* 3. for everyone. *There are not enough cups to go round.* 4. here and there; in different places nearby. *I'm looking round to see if I can find my book.* Also *prep* 1. on all sides of: *build a fence round a field.* 2. in a circle about: *walk round a tree.* 3. so as to get to the other side of: *walk round a corner.* Also *vt/i* 1. go to the other side of: *round a bend in the road.* 2. make or become round.
rounders *nu* game played by children with a ball.
roundly *adv* 1. forcefully: *scold someone roundly.* 2. completely; severely: *be roundly defeated.*
'**roundabout** *adj* not direct. *I heard it in a roundabout way* i.e. not in the direct, usual way. Also *nc* 1. part of a road where cars

cannot go directly on, but must go round in a circle. **2.** mechanical device used as entertainment for children on which they can go round in a circle, sitting on wooden horses etc.
'roundsman grocer, milkman or other tradesman who goes round to people's houses to accept orders or deliver goods.
'round 'trip 1. trip that comes back by a different route. **2.** journey to a place and back to the starting point.
'round-'trip ticket (*US*) return ticket.
round something off finish completely.
round someone/something up get and bring together: *round up cattle; round up a gang of criminals.*
'roundup *nc* act of rounding up.
round (up)on someone blame someone violently.
go round to call on: *go round to someone's house.*
show someone round take someone round a place, showing them things in it: *show someone round one's garden.*
rouse [rauz] *vt/i* wake up; interest; excite: *rouse someone from sleep; roused to anger.* **rousing** *adj.* **rousingly** *adv.*
rout [raut] *vt* defeat completely; put to flight: *rout an army.* Also *nc* **1.** complete defeat; flight from danger. **2.** disorganized group of people.
route [ru:t] *nc* way one intends to go; road. *What route are you taking?*
'route march long walk done by soldiers for training.
routine [ru:'ti:n] *nc* regular way of doing things: *his usual routine.* Also *adj* ordinary; regular; usual: *a routine job.*
rove [rouv] *vi* wander about: *rove through the countryside.* **rover** *nc.*
row[1] [rou] *nc* **1.** line of people or things: *children standing in a row.* **2.** line of seats in a theatre.
row[2] [rou] *vt/i* **1.** make a boat go forward by using oars: *row across a river.* **2.** take someone/something from one place to another by using a rowing boat: *row someone across the river.* Also *nc* journey in a rowing boat: *go for a row.*
'rowing boat, 'rowboat boat that is made to move by using oars.
rowlock ['rɔlək] support as in the illustration, put on the sides of rowing boats to keep the oars in position.

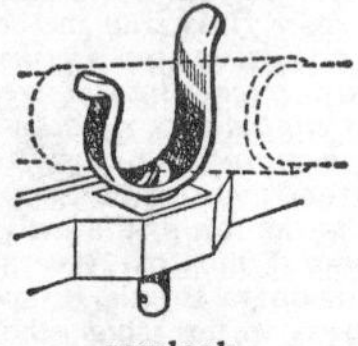

rowlock

row[3] [rau] *nc* **1.** quarrel: *have a row with someone.* **2.** loud noise: *make a row.* **3.** trouble: *get into a row for not doing something properly.* (*informal*).
rowdy ['raudi] *adj* rough and quarrelsome. Also *nc* rowdy person. **rowdily** *adv.* **rowdiness** *nu.*
rowdyism ['raudiizəm] *nu* rough or violent behaviour.
royal ['rɔiəl] *adj* **1.** belonging to, or connected in some way with, a king or queen: *royal palace; the royal household.* **2.** splendid; fit for a king: *a royal welcome.* **royally** *adv*
royalist *nc* person who supports a king, or government by a king.
royalty *nc/u* **1.** royal persons: *be in the presence of royalty* i.e. in the company of a king or queen etc. **2.** royal power or position. **3.** payment made to a writer every time a copy of one of his books is sold, or to a musician whenever one of his records is played publicly etc; payment made to someone who owns land which is being used for profit by someone else. *He became rich on the royalties the oil company paid him.*
His/Her Royal Highness way of referring to a royal person.
Your Royal Highness way of addressing a royal person.
rub [rʌb] *vt/i* move one thing against another: *rub one's hands to warm them; rub away/out a stain* i.e. remove it by rubbing. *past* **rubbed.** Also *nc* act of rubbing: *give something a quick rub.*
rub it in continue to talk about something that another person would rather not remember. *I know that I played badly today - don't rub it in!* (*informal*).
rub something up polish by rubbing: *rub up one's silver spoons.*
rub somebody up the wrong way anger or annoy someone. (*informal*).
rubber[1] ['rʌbə*] **1.** *nu* substance obtained from a certain kind of tree, and used for making balls, tyres, shoes etc. **2.** *nc* (*Brit*) piece of rubber used for removing pencil or pen marks. (*US* **eraser**).
rubbery *adj* **1.** like rubber. **2.** tough and able to spring back.
rubber[2] ['rʌbə*] *nc* (cards) a set of three games: *win the rubber* i.e. win two games out of the three.
rubbish ['rʌbiʃ] *nu* **1.** material that has been thrown away; useless stuff. **2.** nonsense: *talk rubbish.*
rubble ['rʌbl] *nu* broken stones or bricks. *After the earthquake, the village was just a pile of rubble.*
rubicund ['ru:bikʌnd] *adj* red-faced.
rubric ['ru:brik] *nc* heading which is printed in some special way (e.g. the directions in a prayer book or the instructions for an examination).
ruby ['ru:bi] *nc* red, precious stone. Also *adj* dark red in colour.
ruck [rʌk] *nc* uneven fold or crease. Also *vt/i* make or go into uneven folds or creases. *The bedclothes have rucked up.*
rucksack ['ruksæk] *nc* bag carried on the back, used when walking long distances etc.
ructions ['rʌkʃənz] *npl* noisy quarrelling. (*informal*).
rudder ['rʌdə*] *nc* movable flat piece of wood or metal at the end of a boat, used to guide or steer it.
ruddy ['rʌdi] *adj* **1.** red and healthy looking: *ruddy cheeks.* **2.** annoying. (*informal* and rather *impolite* in sense **2.**). Also *intensifier* very. (*informal*).
rude [ru:d] *adj* **1.** not polite; ill-mannered: *a rude remark; a very rude person.* **2.** not done or made in an exact way; roughly made: *rude tools.* **3.** violent; harsh: *a rude shock.* **4.** not taught; rather wild: *our rude ancestors.* **rudely** *adv.* **rudeness** *nu.*
rudiment ['ru:dimənt] *nc* **1.** (usu. *pl*) first things to be learnt in a subject: *the rudiments of chemistry.* **2.** part of a plant or animal that is not completely developed.
rudimentary [ru:di'mentəri] *adj* **1.** elemen

tary; to be learnt when beginning a subject: *a few rudimentary facts.* **2.** not completely developed: *rudimentary organs.*

rue [ru:] *vt* be sorry for; regret: *rue the day one left home.* **rueful** *adj.*

ruff [rʌf] *nc* **1.** circle of stiff material standing out from the neck (worn esp. during the 16th century). **2.** specially marked hairs or feathers round the neck of an animal or bird.

ruff (*def 1*)

ruffian ['rʌfiən] *nc* rough and cruel man.

ruffle ['rʌfl] *vt/i* **1.** make or become uneven. *The wind ruffled the smooth surface of the lake.* **2.** make angry. **3.** make feathers stand up. *The bird ruffled its feathers.* Also *nc* strip of cloth used for decorating clothes.

rug [rʌg] *nc* **1.** covering for a floor (usu. made of wool or animal skin). **2.** thick, warm piece of material which can be put over the legs when travelling etc.

rugby ['rʌgbi] *nu* kind of football in which the ball, which is oval-shaped, can be touched by the hands as well as the feet. (Also **rugby football**).

rugged ['rʌgid] *adj* **1.** rough and uneven: *rugged countryside.* **2.** having many wrinkles; not regular or even in form: *a rugged brow; rugged features.* **3.** strong; able to endure hardships: *a rugged person.* **4.** not following the rules of politeness, but good-hearted: *rugged manners.*

rugger ['rʌgə*] *nu* rugby football. (*informal*).

ruin ['ru:in] **1.** *nu* complete loss or destruction. *All his plans came to ruin.* **2.** *nc* building which has been partly destroyed: *an interesting old ruin.* Also *vt/i* destroy; be destroyed. *His life was ruined by drink. Bad weather ruined our holiday.*

ruins *npl* what remains of a building which has been destroyed or has decayed.

ruination [ru:i'neiʃən] *nu* destruction.

ruinous *adj* **1.** bringing ruin; enough to cause ruin: *ruinous debts.* **2.** in ruins. **ruinously** *adv.*

in ruins completely, or almost completely, destroyed. *Our house was in ruins.*

rule [ru:l] **1.** *nc* law; statement of what must be done. *If you want to play this game, you must obey the rules.* **2.** *nu* government; power: *achieve freedom from foreign rule.* **3.** *nc* habit; what is usu. done or what usu. happens. *It is my rule to get up early. It never rains here, as a rule* i.e. normally. **4.** *nc* straight piece of wood or metal etc used for measuring: *a foot rule* i.e. one which measures 12 inches. Also *vt/i* **1.** be in control of; govern: *rule a country.* **2.** decide; command. *The judge ruled that the new evidence should be considered.* **3.** mark lines on.

ruler *nc* **1.** person who rules (e.g. a king). **2.** straight piece of wood or metal etc used for measuring.

ruling *nc* decision made by someone in authority (e.g. a judge). Also *adj* that rules.

rule something off draw a line at the end of something to separate it from something else: *rule off a list of figures.*

rule of thumb quick way of getting things done which may not be very exact.

work-to-rule slow down work of a factory etc by keeping exactly to rules, in order to gain some object (e.g. higher wages).

rule with a rod of iron/with an iron hand rule very strictly and severely.

rum[1] [rʌm] *nu* strong drink made from sugar cane.

rum[2] [rʌm] *adj* strange; queer (*o.f.* and *informal*).

rumble ['rʌmbl] *vi* **1.** make a deep, heavy sound going on for some time. *Thunder rumbled in the distance.* **2.** move with this sound. *A heavy cart rumbled along the street.* Also *nc* this kind of sound.

ruminate ['ru:mineit] *vt/i* **1.** chew again. *Cows ruminate their food.* **2.** think deeply. **rumination** [rumi'neiʃən] *nu.*

ruminant ['ru:minənt] *nc* animal which chews its food over again. *A cow is a ruminant.*

rummage ['rʌmidʒ] *vi* turn things over and over in the search for something: *rummage through some old clothes; rummage about in a drawer.*

'rummage sale sale of old used things, for some good cause: *hold a rummage sale for famine relief.*

rumour ['ru:mə*] (*US* **rumor**) *nc/u* what people are saying; story which people are repeating, which may or may not be true. *Rumour has it that the president is coming to visit our school. I have heard some rumours about your leaving/that you are going to leave.* Also *vt* (usu. *passive*): *It is rumoured that you are going to leave.*

rump [rʌmp] *nc* tail end of an animal.

rumple ['rʌmpl] *vt* cause to have creases or wrinkles: *rumple a dress.*

rumpus ['rʌmpəs] *nc* disturbance; noise. (*informal*).

run[1] [rʌn] *vt/i* **1.** go along by moving the legs quickly: *run somewhere instead of walking; run as fast as one can.* **2.** move quickly; rush. *We ran to his help. Run for your lives!* i.e. save yourselves. *A thought ran through my mind* i.e. I suddenly thought of something. **3.** cause to move quickly: *run one's eyes over a page.* **4.** move from one place to another; go. *There is a bus that runs every hour. This river runs into the sea* i.e. flows. **5.** cause to go; drive; push: *run a knife into someone; run a car into a tree.* **6.** work; operate: *an engine that runs on petrol; leave a car engine running* i.e. switched on. **7.** stretch; extend; continue: *a pipe running all the way to the top of the wall; a play that runs for several months; several days running* i.e. without a break. **8.** spread. *If you wash this dress in hot water, the colours will run.* **9.** enter for a race, competition or election: *run a horse in a race; run in the hundred metres; run for President.* **10.** become: *run short of food. During the election, feelings ran high* i.e. became strong. **11.** have under one's control; be in charge of: *run a car* i.e. pay all the expenses connected with running a car. *past tense* **ran** [ræn]. *past part* **run.**

run across someone meet by chance: *run across an old friend unexpectedly.* (*informal*).

run after someone try very hard to be friendly with. *He would probably respect you*

more if you didn't run after him so much.
run aground be shipwrecked; run onto rocks. *The ship that had run aground had to be towed into the harbour.*
run away leave; escape from. *He ran away from home at the age of fifteen.*
run someone down 1. knock down while driving. *He ran down an old man who was crossing the street.* 2. say bad things about. *She is always running down her neighbours.*
'run-'down *adj* unfit; not in good health. *I think I should take a holiday, because I'm feeling rather run-down.*
run for it escape. (*informal*).
run something/someone in 1. drive a new car below certain speeds so as not to damage the engine. *This car has to be run in for the first five hundred miles.* 2. arrest. *He was very drunk, so the police ran him in.* (*informal* in sense 2.).
run into someone 1. meet by chance. *I ran into an old friend of mine yesterday.* 2. hit: *run into a wall.*
be run off one's feet be very busy. (*informal*).
run out become finished. *All our supply of food has run out.*
run out of something use up one's supply of something. *We ran out of petrol yesterday. We have run out of time, and so we must end the meeting.*
run over someone/something 1. go over while driving. *A crowd gathered round the child that had been run over.* 2. revise; mention again. *At the end of each lesson he ran over the main points.*
run through something read, go over something quickly. *Could you just run through this article and tell me what you think of it?* (*informal*).
run someone through wound. *He ran him through with his sword* (*o.f.*).
run to something 1. reach a certain amount. *The bill runs to several hundred pounds.* 2. be enough for. *Will the money you have saved run to buying a new house?*
run something up 1. raise; lift up: *run up a flag.* 2. cause oneself to be in debt: *run up bills; run up debts.* 3. sew quickly. *She ran up a dress.* (*informal* in sense 3.).
run up against something meet with. *I have never run up against that kind of difficulty before.*
run a risk see **risk.**

run² [rʌn] *nc* 1. act of moving quickly on the legs: *set off at a run.* 2. trip; journey: *go for a run in the car.* 3. journey made regularly. *The bus had finished its last run.* 4. number of performances: *the play had a run of two years.* 5. number of things happening one after the other: *a run of bad luck.* 6. number of demands: *a run on the banks* i.e. by people demanding their money back. 7. freedom to use: *have the run of someone's house.* 8. number of small holes in cloth where a thread has broken: *a run in a stocking.* 9. unit of scoring in cricket or baseball: *make a lot of runs.* 10. closed-in space for animals: *a chicken/sheep run.*
in the long run in the end; eventually. *Studying may be difficult just now, but you will benefit in the long run.*
on the run 1. running away. *The enemy army was on the run. The escaped convict was on the run for two weeks* i.e. hiding from the police. 2. hurrying: *be always on the run.*
a good run for one's money 1. a good contest. *Our opponents certainly gave us a good run for our money.* 2. satisfaction for what one had done or paid. (*informal*).

runaway ['rʌnəwei] *nc* person, horse etc that runs away. Also *adj.*

runner ['rʌnə*] *nc* 1. someone/something that runs. *There are twelve runners in that race.* 2. messenger (*o.f.*). 3. long, narrow piece of cloth or carpet: *a carpet runner for the stairs.* 4. part on which something slides or moves. 5. stem of a plant which takes root in the ground and so produces new plants: *a strawberry runner.* 6. (usu. in compounds) person who takes goods into a country illegally: *a gunrunner.*
'runner-'up *nc* person or team that is second in a competition.

running ['rʌniŋ] *nu* act of someone/something that runs. Also *adj* 1. done while running: *a running jump.* 2. without a break; continuous: *give a running commentary* (e.g. on a race); *for three nights running.* 3. flowing: *hot and cold running water* i.e. hot and cold water flowing through taps. 4. giving out pus: *a running sore.*
be in/out of the running have a good chance/no chance of winning. *I'm afraid he's out of the running now.* (*informal*).

rung¹ [rʌŋ] past part of **ring².**

rung² [rʌŋ] *nc* wooden or metal bar (e.g. used to make a step in a ladder, or to strengthen the legs of a chair).

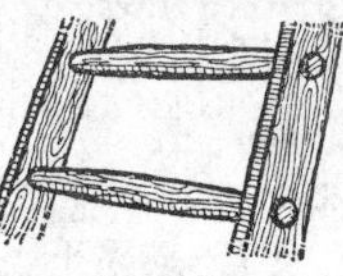

rung²

runway ['rʌnwei] *nc* area of hard surface in an airfield on which planes land and take off.

rupture ['rʌptʃə*] *nc/u* 1. break; act of breaking: *the rupture of a blood vessel/a friendship etc.* 2. pushing of an organ through another part of the body that should keep it in (usu. in the abdomen), sometimes caused by lifting heavy weights etc. Also *vt/i* break; cause a rupture.

rural ['ruərl] *adj* connected with the country: *a rural area.* (*opp* **urban**).

ruse [ruːz] *nc* trick: *be deceived by a clever ruse.*

rush¹ [rʌʃ] *vt/i* 1. move quickly or violently. *We rushed to where the noise came from.* 2. cause to move quickly or violently. *He rushed more police to the riot.* 3. attack quickly or violently. *The crowd rushed the palace gates.* 4. decide quickly without thinking. *Don't rush into anything.* Also *nc/u* act of rushing: *a sudden rush of water.*
the 'rush hour busy time in a city when many people are going to work or coming from it.

rush² [rʌʃ] *nc* tall plant that grows in wet areas.

rusk [rʌsk] *nc* piece of bread baked hard or type of biscuit (usu. given to young children).

russet ['rʌsit] *nu* reddish-brown colour. Also *adj.*

rust [rʌst] *nu* reddish-brown coating that forms on iron when it is left damp or open to the air. Also *vt/i* become covered, cause to become covered, with rust.

rusty *adj* **1.** covered with rust: *a rusty old gun*. **2.** having forgotten most of; mostly forgotten. *I'm rusty on physics now. My French is a bit rusty.* (*informal* in sense **2.**).

rustic ['rʌstik] *adj* **1.** belonging to, or suitable for, the country. *The house has a rustic charm.* **2.** plain; simple: *rustic pleasures.* Also *nc* country person.

rustle ['rʌsl] *nc* soft sound, like the sound leaves make in the wind: *the rustle of leaves; the rustle of a skirt.* Also *vt/i* **1.** make this sound. **2.** cause something to make this sound: *rustle papers.* **3.** (*US*) steal cattle. **rustler** *nc* (*US*) cattle thief.

rut [rʌt] *nc* **1.** track made in soft ground by a wheel. **2.** period of sexual excitement of deer and other animals.

get into a rut get into a fixed and uninteresting kind of life that is difficult to change. *If you stay in the same place too long, you can get into a rut.* (*informal*).

ruthless ['ru:θləs] *adj* merciless; cruel: *a ruthless enemy.* **ruthlessly** *adv.*

rye [rai] *nu* **1.** type of cereal plant that grows in cold regions. **2.** grain from this plant used in making flour. **3.** (*US*) whisky distilled from this plant. (Also **rye whisky**). **'rye 'bread** bread made from rye.

S

Sabbath ['sæbəθ] *n* (with the) **1.** the seventh day of the week in the Jewish religion, on which people are supposed to do no work. **2.** Sunday, considered as equivalent to the Sabbath by some Christians who believe that God has set this day aside as a day of rest for man.

sabbatical [sə'bætikl] *adj* **1.** of the Sabbath. **2.** of a period of freedom from teaching duties, given to a university lecturer etc, after a number of years of service: *sabbatical leave; sabbatical year.* Also *nc*: *take a sabbatical.*

sable ['seibl] **1.** *nc* small meat-eating animal living in forests (esp. in northern Russia). **2.** *nu* valuable, dark-brown fur of this animal. Also *adj*.

sabot ['saebou] *nc* wooden shoe.

sabotage ['sæbətɑːʒ] *nu* damage to machinery, roads, bridges etc which has been deliberately done to interfere with work, transport and movement in war. Also *vt*: *The workmen sabotaged their machines because they were not given higher wages.* **saboteur** [sæbə'təː*] *nc*.

sabre ['seibə*] (*US* **saber**) *nc* curved sword used by soldiers etc on horseback.

sac [sæk] *nc* (biology) part of a living thing shaped like a small bag or pouch.

saccharin ['sækərin] *nu* very sweet substance, sometimes used instead of sugar.

sachet ['sæʃei] *nc* small bag containing sweet-smelling powder, shampoo etc.

sack[1] [sæk] *nc* large bag made of coarse cloth: *a sack of potatoes.* Also *vt* put into a sack or sacks.

'sackcloth, sacking *nu* strong cloth for making sacks.

sackcloth and ashes signs of grief or repentance (*o.f.*).

sack[2] [sæk] *vt* steal from and destroy a town that has been captured. Also *nc* act of sacking: *the sack of a large city.*

sack[3] [sæk] *vt* dismiss someone from work. (*informal*).

get the sack be dismissed from one's work. (*informal*).

give someone the sack dismiss someone from work. (*informal*).

sacrament ['sækrəmənt] *nc* important religious ceremony of the Christian Church. **sacramental** [sækrə'mentl] *adj* connected with a sacrament.

sacred ['seikrid] *adj* **1.** holy; connected with God or religion: *a sacred building; sacred music.* **2.** which must not be treated lightly: *sacred oath.* **sacredly** *adv.* **sacredness** *nu*.

sacrifice ['sækrifais] *nc/u* **1.** act of offering something to God; thing offered. **2.** something given up for some good purpose; act of giving something up: *the sacrifice of one's life to save a friend.* **3.** loss: *sell something at a sacrifice.* Also *vt/i* give up something; do without: *sacrifice one's life; sacrifice everything for one's children.*

sacrificial [sækri'fiʃl] *adj* connected with or like, a sacrifice.

sacrilege ['sækrilidʒ] *nu* act of being disrespectful to a holy person/thing: *guilty of sacrilege.* **sacrilegious** [sækri'lidʒəs] *adj*.

sacristan ['sækristn] *nc* person who looks after the vessels etc used for ceremonies in a church.

sacristy ['sækristi] *nc* room where vessels for ceremonies are kept.

sacrosanct ['sækrousæŋkt] *adj* that is, or should be, protected from harm because it is sacred or holy.

sad [sæd] *adj* not happy; feeling or causing sorrow. **sadly** *adv.* **sadness** *nu*.

sadden *vt/i* make or become sad.

saddle ['sædl] *nc* **1.** seat for the rider of a horse or a bicycle. **2.** high piece of land rising up to a peak on either side. **3.** piece of meat from the back of an animal. Also *vt* **1.** put a saddle on: *saddle one's horse.* **2.** put a burden of any kind on someone: *saddle a heavy responsibility on someone; be saddled with debts.*

saddler *nc* person who makes or sells saddles and other leather goods.

'saddlebag 1. one of a pair of bags hung on an animal's back near the saddle. **2.** bag hung from the saddle of a bicycle.

sadism ['seidizəm] *nu* love of cruelty; cruelty done for pleasure.

sadist *nc* person who gets pleasure from cruelty and from being cruel. **sadistic** [sə'distik] *adj*.

safari [sə'fɑːri] *nc* journey in Africa, often for the purpose of hunting.

safe [seif] *adj* **1.** free from danger: *a safe place.* **2.** not harmed. *He arrived home safe and sound.* **3.** not able to be harmed; not in danger: *be safe from one's enemies.* **4.** careful: *a safe driver.* **5.** reliable; dependable: *a safe guide.* Also *nc* **1.** strong, metal box in which valuables may be kept. **2.** cool box for keeping food in: *a meat safe.* **safely** *adv*.

safety *nu* state of being safe.

'safe-'conduct *nc/u* **1.** right to go through a dangerous area (e.g. in wartime) without being harmed. **2.** paper giving this right.

'safeguard *vt* keep safe, protect. Also *nc* protection.

'safe'keeping care; protection.

'safety belt belt which can keep the person wearing it safe if an accident happens: *have safety belts fitted in one's car.*

'safety match match which will light only when it is rubbed on a special surface.

'safety pin pin which has a cover for its sharp point when it is closed.

safety pin

'safety valve 1. valve in a boiler etc, which opens when the pressure is too great and lets some steam escape. **2.** harmless way of getting rid of one's anger or other strong emotion. *Going to a football match can be a kind of safety valve for one's emotions.*

play for safety not take risks; do the safe thing.

sag [sæg] *vi* **1.** hang down in the centre: *a sagging ceiling.* **2.** hang down unevenly: *a sagging curtain.* **3.** lose enthusiasm; sink. *His spirits sagged after his defeat. past* **sagged.** Also *nu* amount of sagging. *How much sag is there in this ceiling?*

saga ['sɑːgə] *nc* **1.** story of brave deeds (esp. those done long ago by men from Iceland, Norway, Sweden and Denmark). **2.** any long story about a family or group.

sagacious [sə'geiʃəs] *adj* **1.** wise; clever. **2.** intelligent: *a sagacious animal.*

sagacity [sə'gæsiti] *nu* good judgment; cleverness.

sage[1] [seidʒ] *adj* wise: *sage advice.* Also *nc* wise man.

sage[2] [seidʒ] *nu* plant used to flavour food.

sago ['seigou] *nu* white, starchy food used in making puddings etc.

sahib [sɑːb] *nc* title used by Indian servants to their masters.

said [sed] past of **say.**

sail [seil] *nc* **1.** sheet of canvas or other strong material, stretched out so as to catch the wind and drive a boat or ship forward. *The ship was under sail* i.e. with its sails stretched out. **2.** short journey in a boat: *a sail down the river.* **3.** (*pl* **sail**) sailing ship: *see thirty sail in the distance.* Also *vt/i* **1.** travel in a boat or ship: *sail across the sea.* **2.** control a boat or ship. *We are learning to sail.* **3.** travel on water by using a sail or sails. **4.** begin a voyage on water: *sail at dawn.* **5.** move smoothly. *The ball sailed into the net.*

sailor *nc* person who works on a ship; member of a crew.

'sailing boat (*Brit*) boat which uses sails. (*US* **sailboat**).

a bad/good sailor person who is/is not usu. seasick in bad weather.

set sail begin a voyage in a ship.

saint [seint] *nc* **1.** holy or very good person. *He is widely regarded as a saint.* **2.** someone who is stated by the church to be now in heaven because of his holy deeds while he was on earth: *pray to the saints.*

sainted *adj* declared to be a saint; very holy.

saintly *adj* very holy or good. **saintliness** *nu.*

sake [seik] *nu* usu. in **for the sake of** i.e. because of; in order to help. *He was willing to die for the sake of his country.*

for my sake/your sake etc because of, in order to help me/you etc. *Please do this for my sake.*

salaam [sə'lɑːm] *nc* type of expression or method of greeting used in some parts of Asia and Africa. Also *vi* make this greeting.

salacious [sə'leiʃəs] *adj* dealing with sexual matters in an improper and unpleasant way.

salaciousness *nu.*

salad ['sæləd] *nc/u* **1.** uncooked or cold vegetables served as food (often with oil, vinegar etc and sometimes also with eggs, meat, fish etc): *tomato salad.* **2.** any green vegetables which can be eaten uncooked (e.g. lettuce).

'fruit 'salad mixture of fruits, cut up and eaten cold.

salami [sə'lɑːmi] *nu* type of sausage.

salary ['sæləri] *nc* fixed amount of money to be paid for work done, and usu. stated as so much per annum. *He earns a salary of £2,000 per annum* i.e. £2,000 a year.

Note: money paid to lower-paid workers is usu. called *wages* (or *wage*) and stated as so much per week: *get a wage of £10 a week. Salaries* are usu. paid monthly, *wages* weekly.

sale [seil] *nc/u* **1.** act of selling: *look at goods on sale* i.e. which can be bought; *make a sale* i.e. sell something. **2.** occasion when things are sold more cheaply than usual: *go to the winter sales; buy something cheap at a sale.* **3.** selling of goods to the person who bids highest; auction.

salable, saleable ['seiləbl] *adj* fit for sale, in demand.

'salesman, 'saleswoman 1. man, woman who sells goods in a shop. **2.** person who sells goods to shopkeepers for a wholesaler or manufacturer.

Note: in sense **2.** the term (*sales*) *representative* is also used.

salesmanship *nu* skill in selling goods.

salient ['seiliənt] *adj* easily seen or noticed; most important: *the salient points of a speech.* Also *nc* in war, part of a front line sticking out into enemy territory.

saline ['seilain] *adj* containing salt; salty.

saliva [sə'laivə] *nu* liquid that comes into the mouth to help chewing etc.

salivate ['sæliveit] *vi* produce saliva. **salivation** [sæli'veiʃən] *nu.*

sallow ['sælou] *adj* (of complexion) pale yellowish colour.

sally ['sæli] *nc* **1.** sudden attack made from a defended position. **2.** remark that is clever and funny. Also *vi* make a sally (in sense **1.**).

sally forth/out set out on a short journey; go out for a walk.

salmon ['sæmən] **1.** *nc/u* large fish valued as food, which lives in the sea but swims up freshwater rivers to lay eggs. *pl* **salmon. 2.** *nu* yellowish pink colour. Also *adj.*

salon ['sælɔ̃] *nc* **1.** large room for entertaining guests. **2.** place where paintings and other works of art are put on show.

saloon [sə'luːn] *nc* **1.** large room where people can be together: *the dining saloon of a ship.* **2.** closed-in car for four people or more. **3.** (*US*) place where strong drink is bought and drunk. (*Brit* **public house**).

salt [sɔlt] *nu* **1.** white substance found in sea water and certain rocks, used to flavour food. **2.** (chemistry) compound of an acid and a metal. **3.** sailor: *an old salt.* (*informal* in sense **3.**). Also *vt* put salt in or on food, either to flavour it or to prevent it from going bad.

salt, salty *adj* containing salt; tasting of salt.

'salt lick place with salt which animals come to lick.

the salt of the earth people of great goodness, honesty etc. *He said that the villagers were the salt of the earth.*

take something with a pinch of salt not believe completely. (*informal*).

not to be worth one's salt not be worth what one is paid.

saltpetre ['sɔltpiːtə*] *nu* substance used in the manufacture of gunpowder.

salubrious [sə'luːbriəs] *adj* causing good health: *a salubrious climate.*

salutary ['sæljutəri] *adj* having a good effect: *salutary advice/exercise etc.*

salutation [sælju'teiʃən] *nc/u* greeting:

begin a letter with the salutation 'Dear Sir'.

salute [sə'lu:t] *vt/i* **1.** welcome someone, or show respect to someone, in a special way (e.g. by raising the hand to the forehead as a soldier does, by firing guns or by lowering and raising a flag). *The soldier saluted the officer.* **2.** greet someone with kind words, a bow etc (*o.f.* – use **greet**). Also *nc* act of saluting: *a twenty-one gun salute.*

salvage ['sælvidʒ] *nu* **1.** act of saving a ship from some kind of serious damage. **2.** money paid for saving a ship in this way. **3.** act of saving goods, buildings etc from being damaged in a fire etc. **4.** ship, goods etc saved from damage. Also *vt* save from fire, shipwreck etc.

salvation [sæl'veiʃən] *nu* **1.** act of saving from sin or disaster; state of being saved from sin. **2.** person/thing that saves one.

salve [sælv] *nu* **1.** ointment put on wounds or sores to lessen pain. **2.** anything that comforts or brings calm. *The money he gave to the poor was a salve to his conscience* i.e. it made him feel less guilty about some wrong he had done. Also *vt* **1.** put some salve on. **2.** comfort or bring calm to.

salver ['sælvə*] *nc* tray made of silver or another metal, used for carrying small objects (e.g. glasses, letters etc).

salvo ['sælvou] *nc* firing of many guns at the same time.

samba ['sæmbə] *nc* type of South American dance. Also *vi* do this dance.

same [seim] *adj* not different; alike. *My brother and I went to the same school. They all said the very same thing. That same man married her twenty years later* i.e. the man already referred to.

sameness *nu* lack of difference or change.

the same the same thing; the same way. *Your sister behaves well, and you must do the same. I feel the same as you (do)* i.e. I agree with you.

all/just the same see **all.**

be all/just the same to make no difference to. *Whatever you do, it's all the same to me.*

one and the same completely the same.

at the same time **1.** however; yet. *Do what you please – at the same time, I must warn you to be careful.* **2.** together. *Don't all answer at the same time.*

amount/come to the same thing make no difference. *It all comes to the same thing in the end.*

samovar ['sæmouvɑ:*] *nc* (in Russia) large vessel used for making tea.

sampan ['sæmpæn] *nc* small, flat-bottomed boat used in China.

sample ['sɑ:mpl] *nc* example; part of a thing (or one of a number of things) which shows what the rest is like: *give away free samples of something one wants to sell.* Also *vt* take a sample or samples of. *The cook sampled the food to make sure it tasted right.*

samurai ['sæmurai] *nc* type of Japanese knight.

sanatorium [sæni'tɔ:riəm], (*US*) **sanitarium** [sæni'tɛəriəm] *nc* kind of hospital (esp. one in a school, or one for people suffering from tuberculosis).

sanctify ['sæŋktifai] *vt* make holy; set apart as being holy. **sanctification** [sæŋktifi'keiʃən] *nu.*

sanctimonious [sæŋkti'mouniəs] *adj* pretending to be holy **sanctimoniously** *adv.*

sanction ['sæŋkʃən] *nc/u* **1.** permission of someone in authority; general approval: *do something with official sanction/with the sanction of society.* **2.** punishment (esp. that given by other nations to a nation which is held guilty of breaking international law). Also *vt* allow.

sanctity ['sæŋktiti] *nu* holiness. *His life was famous for its sanctity.*

sanctuary ['sæŋktjuəri] **1.** *nc* holy place. **2.** *nu* protection given to someone who needs it: *give sanctuary to refugees.* **3.** *nc* place where someone/something is protected: *a sanctuary for those who have broken the law; a bird sanctuary.*

sand [sænd] *nu* very small grains of worn-down rocks or shells, found by the sea and in deserts etc.

sandy *adj* **1.** covered with sand; containing sand. **2.** yellowish red in colour: *sandy hair.*

the sands area covered with sand.

'sandpaper strong paper with sand stuck to it, used to rub wood smooth.

'sandshoes light canvas shoes with rubber soles, used when playing sports etc.

'sandstone kind of rock made up mostly of sand.

sandal ['sændl] *nc* kind of shoe, made up of a sole kept on by straps above.

sandals

sandalwood ['sændlwud] *nu* sweet-smelling, reddish wood, valued for carving and for the oil from it.

sandwich ['sændwitʃ] *nc* two slices of bread with meat or cheese etc between them. Also *vt* put a thing/person between two others, although there is not much room. *The child was sandwiched in between his parents.*

sane [sein] *adj* **1.** having a healthy mind; not mad. **2.** showing good sense; sensible: *follow a sane policy.* (*opp* **insane**). **sanely** *adv.*

sanity ['sæniti] *nu* state of being sane. (*opp* **insanity**).

sang [sæŋ] past tense of **sing.**

sangfroid ['sɔŋ'frwɑ:] *nu* coolness or lack of excitement in a dangerous or exciting situation.

sanguinary ['sæŋgwinəri] *adj* **1.** with much bloodshed: *a sanguinary battle.* **2.** fond of bloodshed and cruelty: *a sanguinary tyrant.*

sanguine ['sæŋgwin] *adj* **1.** hopeful; cheerful: *have a sanguine nature.* **2.** red-faced: *have a sanguine complexion.*

sanitarium [sæni'tɛəriəm] *nc* see **sanatorium.**

sanitary ['sænitəri] *adj* **1.** connected with health; preventing disease: *sanitary regulations.* **2.** free from dirt and therefore free from disease: *sanitary conditions.* (*opp* **insanitary**).

sanitation [sæni'teiʃən] *nu* arrangements for preventing dirt and disease.

'sanitary towel (*Brit*) pad used to absorb flow of blood during menstruation. (*US* **sanitary napkin**).

sank [sæŋk] past tense of **sink.**

sap[1] [sæp] *nu* liquid in a plant or tree which carries nourishment to its various parts.

sap[2] [sæp] *vt/i* **1.** make weak; use up. *The*

long illness sapped his strength. **2.** dig a protected trench; come up to an enemy position by digging such trenches.
sapper *nc* soldier involved in construction work (e.g. building bridges or digging trenches).
sapling ['sæpliŋ] *nc* young tree.
sapphire ['sæfaiə*] *nc* clear, blue, precious stone.
sarcasm ['sɑːkæzəm] *nc/u* **1.** bitter remarks often intended to hurt someone's feelings. **2.** act of making this kind of remark.
sarcastic [sɑː'kæstik] *adj* using sarcasm; containing sarcasm. **sarcastically** *adv.*
sarcophagus [sɑː'kɔfəgəs] *nc* stone coffin. *pl* **sarcophagi** [sɑː'kɔfəgai].
sardine [sɑː'diːn] *nc* type of small sea fish (often preserved in oil in a tin and eaten as food).
sardonic [sɑː'dɔnik] *adj* scornful; mocking: *a sardonic smile.* **sardonically** *adv.*
sari ['sɑːri] *nc* type of Indian dress.
sarong [sæ'rɔŋ] *nc* type of clothing worn in Malaysia.
sartorial [sɑː'tɔːriəl] *adj* connected with clothes or the making of clothes (esp. men's clothes).
sash[1] [sæʃ] *nc* broad strip of cloth worn over the shoulder or round the waist.
sash[2] [sæʃ] *nc* frame of a window which holds the glass.
'**sash cord** strong cord with a weight on it, used to hold a window open in any position.
'**sash window** window which slides up and down.
Note: a window which opens inwards or outwards is called a *casement window.*
sat [sæt] past of **sit.**
Satan ['seitn] *n* the Devil; the chief of evil spirits.
satanic [sə'tænik] *adj* connected with Satan; evil.
satchel ['sætʃl] *nc* small bag: *carry one's school books in a satchel.*

satchel

sate [seit] *vt* give enough or more than enough of what is wanted.
satellite ['sætəlait] *nc* **1.** planet which goes round another planet; anything in space which goes round the earth. *The moon is a satellite of the earth. An earth satellite has been launched.* **2.** person, country etc that depends on and follows the policies of another.
satiate ['seiʃieit] *vt* give enough of what is wanted, or more than enough. *We were satiated with food and drink.*
satiety [sə'taiəti] *nu* feeling or condition of having had too much: *eat to the point of satiety.*
satin ['sætin] *nu* kind of cloth which is very smooth and shiny on one side. Also *adj* made of satin; like satin.
satire ['sætaiə*] **1.** *nu* way of attacking a person, idea, custom etc by making him or it seem foolish. **2.** *nc* poem, book, play etc which uses this way of attacking a person/thing. **satirical** [sə'tirikl] *adj.* **satirically** *adv.*
satirist ['sætirist] *nc* person who writes satires.
satirize ['sætiraiz] *vt* attack with satire.
satisfy ['sætisfai] *vt* **1.** give enough to; be enough for: *satisfy one's appetite with a large meal. Will this information satisfy your curiosity?* **2.** make happy. *I feel quite satisfied now.* **3.** make someone free from doubt. *I must satisfy myself that he is innocent.*
satisfied *adj* contented. (*opp* **dissatisfied**).
satisfaction [sætis'fækʃən] *nc/u* **1.** act of satisfying; condition of being satisfied. **2.** something which makes one satisfied. *Your success at school has been a great satisfaction to me.* (*opp* **dissatisfaction**).
satisfactory [sætis'fæktəri] *adj* **1.** giving pleasure. **2.** good enough for some purpose (but usu. not very good) (*opp* **unsatisfactory**). **satisfactorily** *adv.*
saturate ['sætʃəreit] *vt* **1.** make very wet or as wet as possible. **2.** (science) fill one substance with as much as possible of another substance: *a saturated solution of salt* i.e. water which cannot take in any more salt. **3.** make full of anything: *saturate oneself in a subject* i.e. learn as much about it as possible. **saturation** [sætʃə'reiʃən] *nu.*
Saturday ['sætədi] *n* seventh day of the week, coming after Friday.
saturnine ['sætənain] *adj* sad-looking: *a saturnine expression.*
sauce [sɔːs] *nc/u* **1.** pleasant tasting liquid (often thick) made from cooked fruit, vegetables etc and added to food to make it taste nicer: *tomato sauce; apple sauce.* **2.** impolite behaviour or words by children to adults. (*informal* in sense **2.**).
saucy *adj* (in sense **2.**). **saucily** *adv.* (both *informal*).
'**sauceboat** dish used to hold sauce.
saucepan ['sɔːspən] *nc* metal cooking pot with a handle and usually a lid.
saucer ['sɔːsə*] *nc* small, curved plate on which a cup is placed.
sauna ['sɔːnə] *nc* type of steam bath.
saunter ['sɔːntə*] *vi* walk along in a slow, carefree way: *saunter through the park.* Also *nc* slow, carefree walk or way of walking.
sausage ['sɔsidʒ] *nc* meat which is cut up into very small pieces, flavoured and put into a tube-like skin.
savage ['sævidʒ] *adj* **1.** wild, uncivilized. **2.** cruel. *He has a savage temper.* Also *nc* **1.** savage person. **2.** member of a primitive tribe. Also *vt* (with reference to a horse or dog) attack and bite. *The dog savaged his master.*
savagery *nu* **1.** uncivilized state: *live in savagery.* **2.** cruelty: *the savagery of an attack on someone.*
savanna, savannah [sə'vænə] *nc* grassland with only a few trees, found in hot countries: *the savannas of South America.*
save [seiv] *vt/i* **1.** take out of danger: *save someone who is drowning.* **2.** not spend; keep for later use: *save most of one's wages.* **3.** not use up: *save one's strength.* **4.** make less: *save trouble by doing something in a different way.* **5.** (in the Christian religion) set free from sin. Also *prep* except. (rather *o.f.*). Also *conj* unless (*o.f.*).
saving *nc* way of saving money, time etc; amount saved.
savings *npl* money saved.
'**savings bank** bank which accepts small

savings and pays interest on them.

save up for something keep one's money for a special use: *save up for a house.*

saviour ['seiviə*] (*US* **savior**) *nc* **1.** one who saves someone from danger, injury etc. **2.** **(Saviour)** Jesus Christ.

savoir-faire ['sævwɑː'fɛə*] *nu* knowledge of how to behave properly.

savour ['seivə*] (*US* **savor**) *nc* **1.** pleasant taste or smell. **2.** quality. *Everything he says has a savour of pride.* Also *vt* enjoy the taste or smell of something.

savoury *adj* having a pleasant taste or smell that is not sweet. Also *nc* savoury food.

savour of something have the quality. *The manner in which you asked that question savours of rudeness* i.e. there is something impolite about the way you asked it.

saw[1] [sɔː] past tense of **see**[1].

saw[2] [sɔː] *nc* type of tool with toothed edge, used for cutting wood, metal etc. Also *vt/i* use a saw to cut something: *saw wood. past tense* **sawed.** *past part* **sawn.**

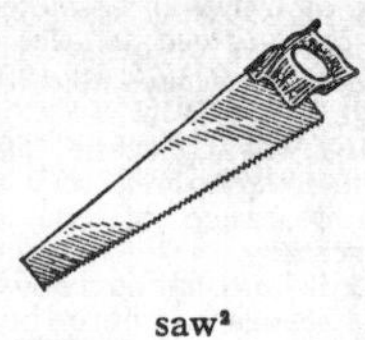

saw[2]

'sawdust very small pieces of wood which fall when wood is being sawn.

'sawmill building where wood is sawn by machinery.

saw something up use a saw to cut something. *We sawed up the logs to make firewood.*

saxophone ['sæksəfoun] *nc* metal, musical instrument, played by blowing through a reed and pressing finger keys.

say [sei] *vt/i* **1.** speak. *I want to say something to you in private.* **2.** put into speech: *say what one thinks.* **3.** give an opinion. *Don't ask me what I think of him because I can't really say* i.e. I haven't decided. **4.** let us suppose. *There are, say, fifty million people in Britain. past* **said** [sed].

Note: the form *says* in *he/she etc says . . .* is pronounced [sez].

saying *nc* something commonly said; proverb.

'say-so authority. *I'm not going to believe it just on his say-so.* (*informal*).

go without saying be too obvious even to be mentioned.

have a/no/not much say in the matter have a right/no right/not much right to express one's opinion in something. *It was entirely their decision, I had no say in it.*

have one's say express one's opinion.

I say exclamation to attract someone's attention, or to express admiration etc.

that is to say in other words.

they say it is said.

to say nothing of without mentioning. *In his house he has three cats and three dogs, to say nothing of his pet mice.*

scab [skæb] **1.** *nc* crust that forms over a wound while it is healing. **2.** *nu* disease which occurs among sheep. **3.** *nc* person who works when other workers are on strike. (*informal* in sense **3.**).

scabby *adj* covered with scabs.

scabbard ['skæbəd] *nc* case for the blade of a sword, dagger etc.

scabbard

scabies ['skeibiːz] *nu* kind of skin disease.

scaffold ['skæfould] *nc* **1.** high platform on which criminals are put to death. **2.** scaffolding.

scaffolding *nu* structure made up of poles put up at the side of a building which is being built, repaired, knocked down etc so that workmen can reach the different parts of the building easily.

scald [skɔːld] *vt* **1.** burn with hot liquid or steam: *scald one's hand with boiling water.* **2.** clean by using boiling water or steam: *scald dishes.* **3.** heat something to the point where it is almost boiling: *scald milk.* Also *nc* burn caused by hot liquid or steam.

scale[1] [skeil] *nc* **1.** line of marks one after the other which is used for measuring. *A thermometer has a scale.* **2.** something which has marks on it used for measuring. **3.** system of steps or differences: *a new wages scale.* **4.** size of a map, plan etc compared to the thing it stands for; this information on a map, plan etc: *a map drawn to a scale of one inch for each ten miles; refer to the scale on a map.* **5.** extent; amount: *entertain on a large scale* i.e. do a large amount of entertaining. **6.** set of musical notes going up or down in a particular manner (e.g. *major scale, minor scale*). Also *vt* climb; climb over: *scale the walls of a castle.*

scale something up/down make more/less by a certain fixed amount: *scale down prices by 5 per cent.*

scale[2] [skeil] *nc* dish or pan of an instrument used for measuring weight.

scales, pair of scales instrument used for measuring weight.

turn the scales make a thing go a certain way when it has been in doubt. *What turned the scales in our favour during the battle was the fact that we had more soldiers.*

scale[3] [skeil] *nc* **1.** one of the thin, flat, hard plates on the skin of snakes, fish, lizards etc. **2.** any thin layer like a scale. Also *vt/i* **1.** remove scales from: *scale a fish.* **2.** come off in thin layers. *The paint was scaling off the wall.*

scallop ['skɔləp] *nc* **1.** type of shellfish. **2.** (usu. *pl*) type of decorative edging made up of curves. Also *vt* decorate with such edging.

scalp [skælp] *nc* skin and hair on the top of the head. Also *vt* cut off the scalp of an enemy as a sign of victory (formerly a custom among some American Indian tribes).

scalpel ['skælpl] *nc* small knife used by a doctor.

scamp [skæmp] *nc* rascal. (*informal* – sometimes used in fun). Also *vt* do work quickly and carelessly.

scamper ['skæmpə*] *vi* run about quickly, as children and small animals do. *The children scampered home. The mouse scam-*

pered away when it saw the cat. Also *nc* quick run.

scan [skæn] *vt/i* **1.** look carefully at every part of. *After the storm the people on the shore anxiously scanned the lake for any sign of the boat.* **2.** look quickly through: *scan a newspaper quickly.* **3.** mark the beat in a line of poetry. **4.** have the correct rhythm. *This line of poetry does not scan.* **5.** (with reference to television) prepare a picture for transmission. **6.** (with reference to radar) send out beams over an area to detect the presence of something. *past* **scanned.**

scansion ['skænʃən] *nu* (in sense **4.**).

scandal ['skændl] *nc/u* **1.** unkind talk about someone. *You shouldn't spread scandal. I heard a bit of scandal about your friend.* **2.** something disgraceful; something which causes public anger. *I think that the way that child is treated is a scandal. There was a tremendous scandal when it was revealed that some policemen had been accepting bribes.*

scandalous *adj* **1.** disgraceful; very bad. **2.** spreading scandal: *scandalous rumours.* **scandalously** *adv.*

scandalize *vt* shock; make angry by doing something wrong.

'**scandalmonger** person who likes to spread scandal about others.

scansion ['skænʃən] *nu* see **scan** (in sense **4.**).

scant [skænt] *adj* not enough: *pay scant attention.*

scanty *adj* very small: *a scanty amount.* **scantily** *adv.*

scapegoat ['skeipgout] *nc* person who is blamed for wrong things done by other people.

scar [skɑ:*] *nc* **1.** mark left on the skin by a wound, sore etc which has healed. **2.** anything that looks like this. Also *vt* mark with a scar or scars: *a scarred leg. past* **scarred.**

scarab ['skærəb] *nc* **1.** kind of beetle regarded as sacred by the Ancient Egyptians. **2.** something made in the shape of this beetle.

scarce [skεəs] *adj* **1.** difficult to get; few in number or little in amount. *Some kinds of fruit are scarce here in winter.* **2.** rare: *a very scarce coin.* **scarcity** *nc/u.*

scarcely *adv* **1.** almost not; only with difficulty: *be so tired one can scarcely walk.* **2.** surely not. *He would scarcely have made such a rude remark.*

scare [skεə*] *vt* frighten. *The noise scared the children.* Also *nc* **1.** fright: *give someone a scare.* **2.** state of being frightened. *There was a scare that war had broken out.*

'**scarecrow** figure in the shape of a man, with old clothes on it, put in a field to frighten birds away.

'**scaremonger** someone who spreads frightening news.

scarf [skɑ:f] *nc* piece of cloth worn round the neck or on the head (usu. for warmth). *pl* **scarves** [skɑ:vz].

scarlet ['skɑ:lit] *nu* bright red colour. Also *adj.*

'**scarlet 'fever** disease which can be easily spread from one person to another, in which red marks appear on the skin and there is pain in the throat.

scathing ['skeiðiŋ] *adj* very bitter and attacking: *a scathing speech; a scathing article in a newspaper.* **scathingly** *adv.*

scatter ['skætə*] *vt/i* **1.** throw here and there: *scatter sand on an icy road.* **2.** send, drive in different directions: *scatter a crowd of children.* **3.** go in different directions. *The mob scattered.*

scattered *adj* not near one another. *We passed only a few scattered villages.*

scattering *nc* small quantity of something widely spread. *A scattering of farms on the hillside.*

scavenger ['skævəndʒə*] *nc* **1.** person who is paid to keep streets clean by taking away the dirt etc. **2.** animal or bird that feeds on decaying matter (e.g. other dead animals): *vultures, hyenas and other scavengers.* **scavenge** *vt/i.*

scenario [si'nɑ:riou] *nc* outline of what is to happen in a play, film etc. *pl* **scenarios.**

scene [si:n] *nc* **1.** view; something seen. *The sun setting behind the trees made a beautiful scene.* **2.** place where something happens, either in real life or in a book: *the scene of one's childhood.* **3.** painted canvas etc used in a theatre to show where the action of the play is supposed to be taking place. *The scene represents the king's palace.* **4.** part of an act in a play: *Act 1, scene 2 of 'Macbeth'.* **5.** show of anger or other strong feeling. *He made a scene when I told him to get out of my house.*

scenery *nu* **1.** theatre scene. *The scenery for the play must have been very expensive.* **2.** general appearance of the countryside: *mountain scenery.*

scenic ['si:nik] *adj* connected with scenery.

behind the scenes 1. where the audience in a theatre cannot see. **2.** secretly; privately.

scent [sent] **1.** *nc/u* pleasant smell: *the scent of roses; scents from different flowers.* **2.** *nu* sense of smell in dogs. *Hunting dogs have a very keen scent.* **3.** *nc* smell left by an animal or person. *The dogs were able to follow the scent of the fox.* **4.** *nu* liquid which has a pleasant smell; perfume. *Most ladies use a little scent.* Also *vt* **1.** smell. *The dogs have scented a fox.* **2.** put scent on. **3.** fill with a pleasant smell. *The newly-cut flowers scented the room.* **4.** suspect; become aware of: *scent danger.*

scented *adj.* (*opp* **scentless**).

sceptic, skeptic ['skeptik] *nc* person who doubts the truth of something (esp. religion). **sceptical** *adj.* **sceptically** *adv.*

scepticism ['skeptisizəm] *nu* state of being in doubt.

sceptre ['septə*] (*US* **scepter**) *nc* rod or staff carried by a ruler to show his authority: *a king's sceptre.*

schedule ['ʃedju:l, *US* 'skedju:l] *nc* list of details; timetable. *Everything is going according to schedule* i.e. as planned. Also *vt* **1.** put into a schedule. **2.** plan; arrange.

scheme [ski:m] *nc* **1.** plan: *a scheme for developing a poor area.* **2.** dishonest plan: *scheme to cheat people out of their money.* **3.** arrangement of things in an orderly way: *colour scheme for a room* i.e. so that the colours will suit one another. Also *vi* make plans (esp. of a secret kind). *He is scheming to become President.*

schemer *nc* person who makes dishonest plans.

scheming *adj* making dishonest plans.

schism ['skizəm] *nc* division of a church etc into two or more groups, caused by differences of opinion among its members.

schismatic [skiz'mætik] *adj* causing, likely to cause, a schism.

schizophrenia [skitsə'fri:niə] *nu* type of madness. **schizophrenic** [skitsə'frenik] *adj.*

schnorkel ['ʃnɔːkl], **snorkel** ['snɔːkl] *nc* **1.** long tube which allows air down to a submarine when the submarine is under water. **2.** tube through which a swimmer can breathe under water.

scholar ['skɔlə*] *nc* **1.** person having much knowledge (esp. of a certain subject). **2.** student who is given money to continue his studies (usu. after doing well in an examination in which he has to compete with other students). **3.** schoolboy, schoolgirl (*o.f.* – use **pupil**).
scholarly *adj* **1.** connected with a scholar; like a scholar: *scholarly interests.* **2.** showing great learning: *a scholarly book/teacher etc.*
scholarship **1.** *nu* knowledge gained by studying. **2.** *nc* money given to a student to continue his studies.
scholastic [skə'læstik] *adj* connected with schools or education.

school¹ [skuːl] **1.** *nc* place where young people are taught. *They are building a new school here.* **2.** *nu* (without **a** or **the**) lessons. *There will be no school tomorrow.* **3.** *nu* (without **a** or **the**) state of being taught at a school: *be at school; leave school; go to school.* **4.** *nc* (with **a** or **the**) children in a school: *give a talk to a school; talk to the whole school.* **5.** *nc* group of painters, writers, philosophers etc who use the same methods. **6.** *nc* department in a university: *School of Medicine.* Also *vt* train; teach: *schooled by experience.*
schooling *nu* education at school.
'schoolfellow, 'schoolmate person who was friendly with another person when they were at school together.
'schoolmaster, 'schoolmistress man, woman teaching in a school.
one of the old school person who has old-fashioned ideas, behaviour etc. (*informal*).

school² [skuːl] *nc* large number of fish or water animals swimming together.

schooner ['skuːnə*] *nc* kind of sailing ship with two or more masts.

sciatica [sai'ætikə] *nu* disease which causes pain in the legs and hips. **sciatic** *adj.*

science ['saiəns] **1.** *nu* knowledge of facts concerning the physical aspects of the universe (usu. got by observation, experiments etc): *be interested in science.* **2.** *nc* knowledge of such facts about some special subject: *the science of chemistry.* **3.** *nc* skill.
scientific [saiən'tifik] *adj* **1.** of or connected with science: *a scientific instrument; scientific discovery.* **2.** expert; skilled. (*opp* **unscientific** in sense **2.**). **scientifically** *adv.*
scientist ['saiəntist] *nc* person who has studied science.
'science 'fiction stories based on scientific ideas (esp. those dealing with space travel and the future).

scintillate ['sintileit] *vi* sparkle, shine: *frost scintillating in the sun; a scintillating conversation* i.e. very witty and intelligent.

scissors ['sizəz] *npl* instrument with two blades, used for cutting cloth, paper etc. (Often **a pair of scissors**).

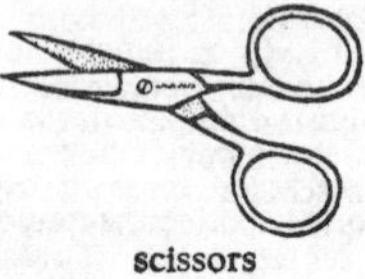
scissors

scoff¹ [skɔf] *vi* **1.** make fun of something one does not believe in: *scoff at an idea.* **2.** make fun of someone. Also *nc* mocking words. **scoffer** *nc.*

scoff² [skɔf] *vt* eat greedily. Also *nu* food. (both *informal*).

scold [skould] *vt/i* blame angrily; speak angrily to. *She scolded the child for being rude to the guests.* Also *nc* woman who scolds a lot.

scone [skɔn] *nc* kind of flat, plain cake (usu. round and made from flour).

scoop [skuːp] *nc* **1.** tool like a shovel, used for lifting and moving things: *a large scoop for moving earth; a kitchen scoop for lifting sugar etc.* **2.** good story which is printed in one newspaper before the other newspapers. (*informal* in sense **2.**). Also *vt* **1.** lift up and move as a scoop does: *scoop up sugar.* **2.** make a hole by using a scoop or something similar: *scoop out a hole.*

scoot [skuːt] *vi* go quickly. *She scooted off down the corridor.* (*informal*).

scooter ['skuːtə*] *nc* **1.** type of children's toy on wheels, which can be moved along by using one foot. **2.** type of small motorcycle.

scope [skoup] *nu* **1.** opportunity: *give someone scope to show his ability.* **2.** limits of what someone/something can do: *a task that is beyond one's scope. The scope of this new theory is quite enormous.*

scorch [skɔːtʃ] *vt* burn something slightly; mark something with heat: *scorch a shirt while ironing it.* Also *nc* mark made by scorching.
scorched earth destruction of crops etc which could have been of help to an enemy in war: *a scorched-earth policy.*

score [skɔː*] *nc* **1.** number of points, goals etc won in a game. *The score was 2–0 for the home team. What's the score?* **2.** printed sheet of music which shows the notes for the different instruments that have to play, and voices that have to sing. **3.** twenty. *There must have been a score or more there* i.e. at least twenty. **4.** line cut in something: *make a score on a desk.* Also *vt/i* **1.** make a point, goal etc in a game: *score a goal. Our team has just scored.* **2.** keep a record of the number of points, goals etc won in a game. **3.** write down the notes for different instruments and voices in a piece of music. **4.** cut lines in something; make marks on: *score a desk with one's knife.*
scorer *nc* **1.** person who scores a goal etc. **2.** person who keeps a record of the score in a game.
score off someone get the better of someone (e.g. in an argument). *He's always trying to score off his colleagues.*
on that score about that thing. *His work is very good, so he has nothing to fear on that score* i.e. he has nothing to fear about his work.
settle/wipe off/pay old scores get revenge; get even for a wrong one has suffered.

scorn [skɔːn] *nu* **1.** feeling that someone/something is not worth any respect: *be full of scorn for someone.* **2.** someone/something not given any respect. *He was the scorn of all who knew him.* Also *vt* **1.** look down on; feel no respect for: *scorn a cowardly act.* **2.** refuse to do something because it is low or wrong. *He scorned to beg for his living.*
scornful *adj* showing or feeling scorn. **scornfully** *adv.*

scorpion ['skɔːpiən] *nc* small creature with a sting in its tail, which is a member of the spider family.

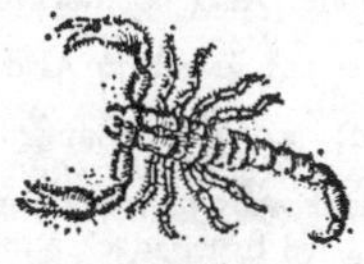
scorpion

Scot [skɔt] *nc* person from Scotland. **Scots/Scottish** *adj*.

Scotch [skɔtʃ] *nc/u* whisky. Also *adj* from Scotland (usu. of food and drink).
Note: for people, customs etc *Scotch* is *o.f.* and *Scots* or *Scottish* should be used.

scotch [skɔtʃ] *vt* **1.** wound without destroying (*o.f.*). **2.** destroy (often in **scotch a rumour**).

scot-free ['skɔt'friː] *adj* without having been injured, punished etc: *get away/off scot-free.*

scoundrel ['skaundrl] *nc* evil person.
scoundrelly *adj* evil.

scour[1] ['skauə*] *vt* **1.** clean a dirty surface by rubbing with something rough: *scour some pots and pans.* **2.** get rid of dirt etc by rubbing: *scour off/away a dirty mark.*

scour[2] ['skauə*] *vt* look everywhere for: *scour the countryside for a lost child.*

scourge [skəːdʒ] *nc* **1.** long piece of leather, rope etc used to punish someone. **2.** anything which causes pain and suffering. *Disease is one of the scourges of mankind.* Also *vt* **1.** punish with a scourge. **2.** cause great pain and suffering to.

scout [skaut] *nc* **1.** person, aeroplane, ship etc which is sent ahead to get information about the enemy's movements etc. **2.** member of the Boy Scouts. see below. Also *vi* go ahead as a scout.
scouting *nu* activities of the Boy Scouts. see below.
scout about/round go about searching: *scout round for a good place to put one's tent.* (*informal*).
the Boy Scouts organization for boys, which teaches them how to look after themselves and how to be useful to others.

scowl [skaul] *nc* angry look made by lowering the brows. Also *vi* have such a look: *scowl at someone; scowl angrily.*

scraggy ['skrægi] *adj* thin and bony: *a scraggy piece of meat.*

scram [skræm] *vi* go away quickly. *past* **scrammed.** (*informal*).

scramble ['skræmbl] *vi* **1.** go forward using the hands and knees: *scramble over rocks; scramble up a steep hill.* **2.** struggle with others for something: *scramble for a ball during a game.* Also *vt* mix up: *scramble a message* i.e. so that it cannot be understood. Also *nc* **1.** walk or climb over hilly ground. **2.** act of struggling for something. *As soon as the performance ended, there was a scramble for the door* i.e. to get out.
'scrambled 'eggs *nu* eggs cooked by beating them up and then cooking them in a saucepan.

scrap[1] [skræp] **1.** *nc* small piece; part left over: *a scrap of paper.* **2.** *nu* articles that are no longer of use: *collect scrap; sell one's car for scrap* i.e. just for the value of the materials it is made of; *scrap iron* i.e. things made of iron which are to be melted down so that the iron can be used again. Also *vt* give up; abandon something as being useless: *scrap an idea; scrap some work one has done. past* **scrapped.**
scrappy *adj* made up of bits and pieces; not properly connected and arranged: *a scrappy essay.* **scrappily** *adv.* **scrappiness** *nu.*
'scrapbook book with blank pages on which one can put photographs, pieces cut from newspapers etc.
'scrap heap pile of things that are no longer wanted: *throw something on the scrap heap* i.e. throw away as being useless.

scrap[2] [skræp] *vi* fight. *past* **scrapped.** Also *nc.* (both *informal*).

scrape [skreip] *vt/i* **1.** rub with something sharp or rough in order to make level, smooth or clean. *He cleaned the wire by scraping it with a knife.* **2.** take paint off by rubbing in this way: *scrape a door before painting it again.* **3.** accidentally rub against something that is sharp or rough: *scrape one's knee; scrape one's car.* **4.** get past or through something by a very narrow amount: *scrape through an examination.* **5.** rub with an unpleasant sound: *a pen that scrapes on the paper.* **6.** gather with difficulty: *scrape together enough money to pay one's debts.* Also *nc* **1.** act of scraping. **2.** sound made by scraping. **3.** place that has been scraped: *a scrape on one's elbow.* **4.** awkward situation; difficulty: *always be getting into scrapes.*
scraper *nc* tool used for scraping.

scratch [skrætʃ] *vt/i* **1.** cut, make a line in, with something sharp or rough. *My knife slipped and scratched the table.* **2.** rub part of one's body with the fingernails, either because one has an itch or as a matter of habit etc: *scratch one's head when one is puzzled.* **3.** cut with the nails: *be badly scratched by an animal.* **4.** remove a word either by rubbing with a knife or by drawing lines through it. **5.** rub with an unpleasant sound: *a pen that scratches.* **6.** withdraw from a race. Also *nc* **1.** mark made by scratching. *The new table has a scratch on it already.* **2.** act of scratching. **3.** sound made by scratching: *the scratch of pen on paper.* **4.** cut on the skin that is not serious: *just a scratch.* **5.** starting place in a race. Also *adj* collected or prepared in a hurry: *a scratch team.*
scratchy *adj* **1.** that scratches (esp. making an unpleasant sound): *a scratchy old pen.* **2.** untidy: *scratchy writing.*
scratch out remove by scratching.
bring someone up to scratch make someone good enough. (*informal*).
come up to scratch be good enough. *Do you think that pupil will come up to scratch in the examination?* (*informal*).
scratch a living make enough to live, only with difficulty.
start from scratch start from the beginning. *The businessman lost all his money and had to start again from scratch.* (*informal*).

scrawl [skrɔːl] *vt/i* write or draw carelessly or in a hurry. Also *nc* something scrawled.

scrawny ['skrɔːni] *adj* (with reference to a person) very thin.

scream [skriːm] *vt/i* **1.** make a loud, sharp cry: *scream with pain/fear/anger etc.* **2.** say in a loud, high voice: *scream a command.* Also *nc* loud, sharp cry or noise.

scree [skriː] *nu* steep mass of broken and fallen rocks on the side of a mountain.

screech [skriːtʃ] *vt/i* make a loud, high noise: *screech with pain.* Also *nc* loud high noise: *the screech of brakes when a car stops suddenly.*

screed [skriːd] *nc* long (often uninteresting) piece of writing.

screen [skriːn] *nc* **1.** covered frame used to protect or hide someone/something. *In hospitals they sometimes put a screen round your bed if the doctor is examining you.* **2.** anything that hides or protects the way a screen does: *a screen of trees between the house and the road.* **3.** cover made of pieces of wire with holes in between, like a net. *There were screens on the windows to prevent insects from getting in.* **4.** sieve which separates large pieces of coal, earth etc from smaller pieces. **5.** surface on which film is shown. **6.** part of a television set on which the picture appears. Also *vt* **1.** protect or hide with a screen, or as if with a screen: *screen oneself from public view. He screened his old friend from the police.* **2.** put wire screens on: *screen one's windows and doors.* **3.** separate larger things from smaller by using a screen: *screen coal etc.* **4.** project a film onto a screen; show a film. **5.** check up on a person's past life to see if he is reliable (e.g. before giving him a responsible position). Also *adj* connected with the cinema and films: *a famous screen actor.*

screw [skruː] *nc* **1.** kind of nail which is driven into wood and other materials by being turned round and round. *The handle of this door is kept in place by two screws.* **2.** propellor at the back of a ship which helps to drive it forward. Also *vt/i* **1.** join together or tighten by using a screw or screws: *screw together two pieces of wood.* **2.** twist; turn round: *screw the lid off a jar.* **3.** force someone to do, tell or give up something: *screw the truth/more money out of someone.*

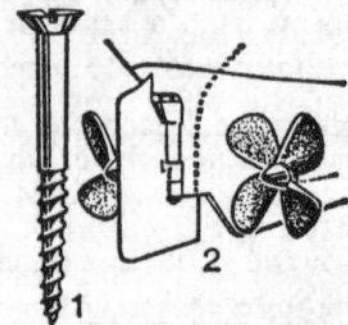

screws (*def 1*) (*def 2*)

'screwdriver tool used for putting in or taking out screws by turning them.

screw up one's eyes/face etc wrinkle the skin around the eyes etc. *The room was so bright I had to screw up my eyes.*

have a screw loose be slightly mad. (*informal*).

scribble ['skribl] *vt/i* **1.** write quickly and carelessly: *scribble a note to someone.* **2.** make marks that do not mean anything. *A child had been scribbling on the wall.* Also *nc/u* something scribbled.

scribe [skraib] *nc* **1.** person whose profession is to write. **2.** teacher of the Jewish law (*o.f.*).

scrimmage ['skrimidʒ] *nc* rough struggle. Also *vi* take part in a rough struggle.

script [skript] **1.** *nu* writing done by hand; print that looks like handwriting. **2.** *nc* written version of a play, talk etc (usu. for radio, television or the stage). *The actor was studying his script.*

scripture ['skriptʃə*] *nc* sacred book.

scriptural *adj* based on the Bible.

Scripture/the Scriptures/Holy Scripture the Bible.

scroll [skroul] *nc* long piece of paper or skin which can be rolled up, used in ancient times for writing on.

scrounge [skraundʒ] *vt/i* get things by taking or borrowing from other people, instead of by buying them. **scrounger** *nc.* (both *informal*).

scrub[1] [skrʌb] *vt/i* clean by rubbing (usu. by using a hard brush): *scrub the floor.*

'scrubbing brush hard brush used for scrubbing.

scrub[2] [skrʌb] *nu* low trees and bushes; land covered with low trees and bushes: *travel through miles of scrub.*

scrubby *adj* small; not worth noticing.

scruff [skrʌf] *nc* back of the neck (usu. in **by the scruff of the neck**).

scruffy ['skrʌfi] *adj* rather dirty and untidy in appearance.

scruple ['skruːpl] *nc* **1.** feeling of doubt as to whether one is doing right. *I shall have no scruples about forcing him to give me the money.* **2.** very small weight, equal to 1.3 grammes.

scrupulous ['skruːpjuləs] *adj* **1.** very careful not to do wrong. (*opp* **unscrupulous**). **2.** paying great attention to little things. **scrupulously** *adv.*

scrutiny ['skruːtini] *nc/u* careful examination in detail. *Everything you do will be subject to close scrutiny.*

scrutinize *vt* examine carefully.

scuffle ['skʌfl] *nc* fight; confused struggle. Also *vi* take part in a scuffle.

scull [skʌl] *nc* **1.** one of two oars used to make a boat go forward. **2.** one oar at the end of a boat worked by twisting the oar to one side to make the boat go forward. Also *vt/i* make a boat go forward by using sculls or a scull.

scullery ['skʌləri] *nc* small room where dishes, pots, pans etc are washed.

sculpture ['skʌlptʃə*] **1.** *nu* art of making figures out of stone, clay, wood etc. **2.** *nc* figure made in this way: *a beautiful sculpture.* **sculptural** *adj.*

sculptor ['skʌlptə*] *nc* artist who makes sculptures.

scum [skʌm] *nu* **1.** layer of dirt at the top of a liquid. *The pond was covered with scum.* **2.** bad, useless people: *the scum of the earth.*

scupper ['skʌpə*] *nc* opening at the side of a ship which allows water from the deck to flow into the sea. Also *vt* destroy; ruin. *Failing that examination has scuppered my chances of getting a good job.* (*informal*).

scurf [skəːf] *nu* small flakes of dead skin (esp. among the hairs of the head). **scurfy** *adj.*

scurrilous ['skʌriləs] *adj* using words which are coarse and rude: *a scurrilous attack.*

scurry ['skʌri] *vi* run or move quickly: *scurry for cover.* Also *nc* act or sound of scurrying.

scurvy ['skəːvi] *nu* disease caused by not eating fresh fruit and vegetables. *Sailors who made long journeys used to suffer from scurvy.* Also *adj* low; mean (*o.f.* in this sense).

scuttle[1] ['skʌtl] *nc* container for coal (usu. placed near the fireplace).

scuttle[2] ['skʌtl] *vi* run; move quickly. *The two thieves scuttled away when they saw the policeman.*

scuttle[3] ['skʌtl] *vt* cut or open a hole in the side of a ship so that it will sink.

scythe [saið] *nc* tool with a long, curved blade, as in the illustration, used for cutting grass, wheat etc. Also *vt* cut using a scythe.

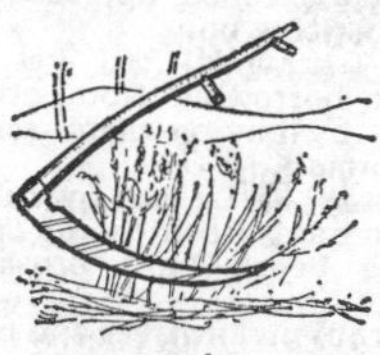

scythe

sea [siː] **1.** *nu* the part of the earth's surface covered by water: *go to sea* i.e. become a sailor. *The ship put out to sea* i.e. left the harbour etc. **2.** *nc* large area of water, smaller than an ocean: *the Mediterranean Sea.* **3.** *nc* large wave. *The boat was struck by heavy seas.* **4.** *nc* large amount or number: *a sea of faces looking at us.*

'seaboard *nc/u* land near the sea: *on the Western seaboard.*

'seaborne *adj* carried on or by the sea: *seaborne trade.*

'sea dog old sailor (*o.f.*).

'seafarer *nc* sailor.

'seafaring *adj* travelling or working on the sea.

'seagull type of bird found near the sea.

'sea legs ability to walk normally on a ship, keeping one's balance: *find/get one's sea legs.* (*informal*).

'sea level height of sea when halfway between high and low tide: *a hill 708 feet above sea level.*

'seaman sailor.

'seamanship *nu* skill in controlling a ship.

'seaport town on a sea coast or connected to the sea, with harbour, docks etc.

'seashore *nc/u* land beside the sea: *go down to the seashore to play.*

'seasick *adj* ill because of the movement of a boat or ship. **seasickness** *nu.*

'seaside *adj* beside the sea: *seaside town.*

the seaside place near the sea.

'seaway river, lakes etc which allow a ship to go far inland from the sea: *the St Lawrence Seaway.*

'seaweed plants growing in the sea.

'seaworthy *adj* good enough for sailing on the sea: *seaworthy boat.* (*opp* **unseaworthy**).

seal[1] [siːl] *nc* **1.** design which is put on a piece of wax, lead etc to show the authority of the person who put it there: *the seal at the bottom of a certificate; the seal on the back of an envelope.* **2.** something which can put such a design onto wax, lead etc. *He pressed his seal into the hot wax.* **3.** something that closes or fastens a thing tightly. **4.** something that makes certain or safe: *under seal of secrecy.* Also *vt* **1.** mark with a seal: *seal a document.* **2.** close or fasten: *seal a letter.* **3.** settle; decide finally. *His fate is sealed.*

seal[1] (*def 1*)

'sealing wax kind of wax which is used to seal letters etc.

seal[2] [siːl] *nc* animal, which can live in the sea or on land, which makes a barking sound and is often hunted for its skin.

seal[2]

seam [siːm] *nc* **1.** line where two pieces of cloth etc are joined together. **2.** layer of coal, metal etc in the earth, with rock etc on either side of it. **3.** any line like a seam.

seamstress ['siːmstris] *nc* woman whose work is sewing.

seamy *adj* unpleasant: *the seamy side of life* (e.g. poverty, crime etc).

séance ['seiɔns] *nc* meeting of people to call up spirits of the dead.

sear [siə*] *vt* **1.** burn the surface of something: *sear a cloth with a hot iron.* **2.** make hard and unfeeling: *sear someone's heart.*

search [səːtʃ] *vt/i* examine carefully in order to find something: *search a room.* Also *nc* act of examining in order to find something; act of looking for something.

searching *adj* examining carefully: *a searching glance.*

'searchlight electric lamp with a very bright beam (e.g. one used to show an enemy aeroplane during darkness).

'search warrant official document which allows the police to search a house.

search for something look for: *search for a book that has been lost.*

season ['siːzn] *nc* **1.** part of the year that is different from other parts because of the weather usual at that time. *Some parts of the world have four seasons, others have only two.* **2.** part of the year that is suitable for something, or when something occurs: *the Christmas season; the holiday season.* **3.** part of the year when most of the parties, dances etc take place in a town: *stay in town for the season.* **4.** period of time: *a play that is running for a season.* Also *vt/i* **1.** make or become fit for use by being kept in for a time, or by being treated in a certain way: *wood that has been seasoned* i.e. that is dry and hard. **2.** improve the taste of food by adding something: *meat seasoned with salt.*

seasonable *adj* **1.** suitable for the time of year: *seasonable weather.* (*opp* **unseasonable**). **2.** coming at the right time: *seasonable help.*

seasonal *adj* connected with the seasons; depending on the time of year: *seasonal trade.*

seasoning *nc/u* something that improves the taste of food (e.g. salt).

'season ticket 1. (*Brit*) ticket that gives a person the right to travel between two places for a certain time. (*US* **commutation ticket**). **2.** ticket that allows a person to visit a theatre, cinema etc as often as he likes for a certain time.

in/out of season (of foods) able/not able to be obtained easily. *Strawberries will be in season soon.*

seat [siːt] *nc* **1.** piece of furniture on which one sits (e.g. a chair). **2.** part of a chair etc on which one sits. **3.** part of the body on

which one sits i.e. the buttocks, or the clothing covering it. **4.** place in which one has the right to sit: *have a seat in Parliament.* **5.** place where one usually sits. *That's my seat.* **6.** place where something happens or is done: *the seat of government; a seat of learning.* Also *vt* **1.** have seats for: *a hall that seats one hundred people.* **2.** place someone on a seat or chair.
'seat belt strap or belt fastening one to one's seat in a car or plane.
be seated sit down. (rather *formal*).

secede [si'si:d] *vi* (with reference to a group of people) leave an organization or state: *secede and form one's own organization.*
secession [si'seʃən] *nc/u.*

seclude [si'klu:d] *vt* keep away from people.
secluded *adj* quiet; undisturbed: *a secluded area.*
seclusion [si'klu:ʒən] *nu* act of secluding or being secluded; secluded place: *live in seclusion.*

second[1] ['sekənd] *adj* **1.** coming after the first. *Go down the second street on the right.* **2.** another; other: *give someone a second chance.* Also *adv* one after the first: *come second in a race.* Also *nc* **1.** person/thing coming one after the first. **2.** person who helps another in a contest (esp. a boxing match). Also *vt* **1.** support (esp. something that has been suggested for discussion): *second a motion.* **2.** help someone in a contest. **3.** [si'kɔnd] take someone from his usual work and put him to work at something else or somewhere else for a short time.
seconds *npl* articles which are not of the best quality or which have something wrong with them.
'second-'best *adj* not the best or finest: *my second-best suit.*
'second-'class *adj* not of the best class: *a second-class carriage.*
second floor floor above the first. (*Brit* two floors above ground level; *US* one floor above ground level).
'second'hand see **hand[1]**.
second nature what one does without thinking about it. *Driving a car is second nature to him.*
'second-'rate *adj* not the best: *a second-rate book.*
second sight ability to see things which have not yet happened, or are happening in another place.
second thoughts different decision taken after thinking about something. *On second thoughts, I will come with you.*
a second time again.
in the second place in addition; secondly.
play second fiddle to someone see **play[1]**.
second to none the best there is. *I think that, as a writer, he is second to none.*

second[2] ['sekənd] *nc* **1.** (time) 1/60 part of a minute: *run a mile in four minutes and ten seconds.* **2.** (in measuring angles) 1/60 of a minute. **3.** very short time. *I'll be with you in a second.* (*informal* in sense **3.**).

secondary ['sekəndəri] *adj* **1.** of less importance; coming after what is first. **2.** coming after primary school and before university: *secondary school/education etc.*

secret ['si:krit] *adj* not to be made known to others; known to only a few people; hidden: *a secret meeting/passage/place etc.* Also *nc* **1.** something secret. **2.** hidden reason for something. *What is the secret of your success?* **secretly** *adv.*
secrecy *nu* **1.** state of being secret: *in great secrecy.* **2.** ability to keep things secret.
secretive *adj* having the habit of not allowing other people to know things. *He is very secretive about his past.*
secret service people paid to find out enemy secrets for the Government.
in secret secretly.
in the secret among the few people allowed to know something.
keep a secret not let something be known.

secretary ['sekrətəri] *nc* **1.** person who writes letters, keeps a record of meetings etc for an employer or a club or other organization. **2.** (esp. *US*) person in charge of a department of the government: *the Foreign Secretary* (*Brit*), *the Secretary of State* (*US*) i.e. in charge of foreign affairs.
secretarial [sekri'tɛəriəl] *adj* connected with a secretary or his work.
secretariat [sekri'tɛəriət] *nc* group of important administrators (usu. in government).

secrete [si'kri:t] *vt* **1.** hide; keep in a secret place. **2.** make by secretion.
secretion **1.** *nu* way in which the body separates certain liquids (e.g. bile, saliva) as waste materials or for a certain use. **2.** *nc/u* liquid separated in this way.

sect [sekt] *nc* group of people who hold certain ideas in common (esp. a group who have broken away from a bigger religious group).
sectarian [sek'tɛəriən] *adj* connected with sects or with a particular sect. Also *nc.*

section ['sekʃən] *nc* **1.** part separated by cutting, splitting, breaking etc: *divide something into sections.* **2.** part of something that can be fitted into another part: *fit together sections of a pipe.* **3.** part of a book. *Read the first section for next week.* **4.** part of a town, country, group etc: *the residential section of a town* i.e. where people live. **5.** drawing or view of what something would look like if it was cut through from top to bottom: *a section of a machine.* (Also **cross section**). **6.** act of cutting.
sectional *adj* **1.** connected with a particular part of a town, country, group etc: *sectional interests.* **2.** made of sections: *a sectional bookcase.*

sector ['sektə*] *nc* **1.** part of a circle from the centre to the circumference. **2.** part of a battle area which a particular unit of the army has to defend. **3.** part of an organization etc: *the public sector* i.e. part of industry which is owned by the government.

secular ['sekjulə*] *adj* **1.** concerned with this world, material things, not with religious or spiritual matters: *secular matters.* **2.** working among the people, not in a religious order: *a secular priest.*
secularism *nu* belief only in non-religious values.

secure [si'kjuə*] *adj* **1.** safe from danger, loss etc. *Are your valuables secure?* **2.** well-fastened; not likely to break or give way. (*opp* **insecure**). Also *vt* **1.** make safe. **2.** fasten well: *secure a rope.* **3.** get; obtain: *secure a ticket for someone.* **securely** *adv.*

security [si'kjuəriti] **1.** *nu* freedom or protection from danger, loss etc: *in the security of one's own home.* (*opp* **insecurity**). **2.** *nc/u* something valuable given to a person who lends one money, which one can get back only if one returns the money: *give someone a gold watch as security for a loan.* **3.** *nc* (often *pl*) documents which show that one owns some kind of property (e.g. shares in a business).

sedan [si'dæn] *nc* **1.** (*US*) closed car which can seat four or more people. **2.** sedan chair.

se'dan 'chair covered chair carried on poles by two men, used in Europe in the 17th and 18th centuries.

sedate [si'deit] *adj* quiet; serious: *a sedate little girl; behave in a sedate manner.* Also *vt* make calm by giving a drug to: *sedate a person in hospital.* **sedately** *adv.*

sedated *adj* made calm in this way.

sedation [si'deiʃən] *nu* condition of quietness brought about by drugs.

sedative ['seditiv] *nc/u* medicine which makes people calm: *take a sedative before going to bed.* Also *adj.*

sedentary ['sedntri] *adj* **1.** done sitting down: *a sedentary occupation.* **2.** spending much of one's time sitting down: *a sedentary person.*

sediment ['sedimənt] *nu* matter that sinks to the bottom of a liquid (e.g. mud at the bottom of a river).

sedition [si'diʃən] *nu* words or acts which are likely to cause anger against the government: *guilty of sedition.* **seditious** [si'diʃəs] *adj.* **seditiously** *adv.*

seduce [si'dju:s] *vt* **1.** persuade a person to have sexual intercourse with one. **2.** persuade someone to do wrong. **seducer** *nc.*

seduction [si'dʌkʃən] *nc* **1.** act of seducing or being seduced. **2.** something attractive (but not necessarily wrong): *the seductions of modern life.*

seductive [si'dʌktiv] *adj* very attractive. **seductively** *adv.*

sedulous ['sedjuləs] *adj* persistent; not giving up easily: *pay sedulous attention to something.* **sedulously** *adv.*

see[1] [si:] *vt/i* **1.** be able to use one's eyes; observe with one's eyes. *The blind cannot see. Do you see that house?* **2.** understand. *I see what you mean.* **3.** visit; meet: *see a doctor because one is ill. past tense* **saw** [sɔ:]. *past part* **seen** [si:n].

see about something attend to something. *I must see about booking a seat.*

see someone off go to a railway station, airport etc with someone who is travelling.

see someone out go to the outside door of a house with someone. *Don't bother, I'll see myself out* i.e. do not trouble to come to the door with me.

see someone through help someone during a period of great difficulty.

see something through continue with something difficult until it is done properly or completely.

see through someone understand the true feelings of someone who is trying to deceive one.

see to something get something done. *I'll see to it that you are well looked after.*

seeing that remembering the fact that. *He has done well to pass his exams, seeing that he has been ill a lot.*

see eye to eye with someone be friendly with; agree with. *I don't think he sees eye to eye with his boss.* (*informal*).

see fit to do something think it right to do something.

see for oneself prove by examining something oneself. *If you don't believe me, you can see for yourself.*

has/have seen better days is/are rather old now. *That chair has seen better days.* (*informal*).

I'll/we'll etc see I/we etc shall decide later.

see the last of someone/something see someone/something for the last time. *I shall be glad to see the last of this place.*

let me see give me time to think or remember.

see red become angry.

see the sights go round the important places: *see the sights of London.*

see things imagine that one can see something. *There is no one in the house; you must have been seeing things.*

see[2] [si:] *nc* area under the authority of a bishop.

the Holy See/the See of Rome the authority of the Pope.

seed [si:d] *nc* fertile part of a plant or animal: *plant seeds in one's garden. pl* **seeds** or **seed.** Also *vt* **1.** sow with seeds; throw seeds on: *seed a field with wheat.* **2.** produce seeds. **3.** take seeds from: *seed raisins.*

seedy ill; neglected. (*informal*).

seedling *nc* young plant; small tree.

seeded players very good players who do not play against one another at the beginning of a series of games (e.g. in tennis).

go to seed see **go.**

seek [si:k] *vt* **1.** try to get; look for: *seek advice/help etc.* **2.** look for: *seek something one has lost.* **3.** try to do something. *He seeks to bring about peace. past* **sought** [sɔ:t].

'sought after *adj* wanted: *an article much sought after.*

Note: when this phrase comes before the noun it has a hyphen: *a much sought-after article.*

seem [si:m] *vi* **1.** appear to be. *The judge's sentence seemed (to be) rather harsh. He may seem poor, but he is really very wealthy.* **2.** be reported to be. *It seems that he is very clever* i.e. this is what I have heard. *So it seems* i.e. what you are saying appears to be true.

seeming *adj* pretended; not real: *be deceived by someone's seeming friendship.*

seemingly *adv* **1.** perhaps only in appearance: *a seemingly nice person.* **2.** from report. *Seemingly he is very clever.*

seemly ['si:mli] *adj* proper; correct: *seemly behaviour.* (*opp* **unseemly**).

seen [si:n] past part of **see**[1].

seep [si:p] *vi* (with reference to a liquid) pass slowly through. *Water is seeping through the ceiling.* **seepage** ['si:pidʒ] *nc/u.*

seer [siə*] *nc* person who can tell what is to happen in the future; prophet.

seesaw ['si:sɔ:] **1.** *nu* children's game played with a board so that one child goes up as the other comes down, as in the illustration. **2.** *nc* board on which this game is played. **3.** *nc/u* movement up and down or backwards and forwards. Also *vi* move up and down or backwards and forwards.

seesaw (*def 1*)

seethe [si:ð] *vi* **1.** boil; bubble and foam. *The waterfall was a seething mass of water.*

2. feel something very strongly: *seething with anger/excitement etc; a place seething with people* i.e. full of excited people.

segment ['segmənt] *nc* 1. part cut off; part into which something can be divided: *a segment of an orange.* 2. (geometry) part of a figure that can be cut off by a line or plane: *a segment of a circle.*

segregate ['segrigeit] *vt* keep separate from others: *segregate people of different races.*
segregation [segri'geiʃən] *nu*.
segregated *adj*. (*opp* **unsegregated**).
segregationist [segri'geiʃənist] *nc* person who wants people of different races to be kept separate.

seine [sein] *nc* kind of fishing net. (Also **seine net**).

seismic ['saizmik] *adj* connected with an earthquake or earthquakes: *a seismic disturbance.*
seismograph ['saizməgrɑːf] *nc* instrument that records information about earthquakes.
seismology [saiz'mɔlədʒi] *nu* science of earthquakes etc.
seismologist [saiz'mɔlədʒist] *nc*. **seismological** [saizmə'lɔdʒikl] *adj*.

seize [siːz] *vt/i* 1. take hold of suddenly and violently: *seize someone by the throat; seize a weapon.* 2. take legally: *seize goods that have been stolen.* 3. take quickly: *seize an opportunity.* 4. stop suddenly. *The engine seized (up).*
seizure ['siːʒə*] 1. *nc/u* act of seizing: *the seizure of goods.* 2. *nc* sudden attack of a disease (esp. of the heart).
be seized with something be suddenly overcome with a disease or a feeling (e.g. of pity etc).

seldom ['seldəm] *adv* not often. *He seldom comes late.*

select [si'lekt] *vt* choose. *He showed me five pens and I selected the red one.* Also *adj* 1. chosen carefully. *A select group of people were used for this experiment.* 2. not open to everyone: *a very select school.*
selection 1. *nu* act of selecting. 2. *nc* thing or group of things, chosen by someone, or from which one can choose: *a large selection of books.*
selective *adj* 1. having the power to select. 2. choosing only the best: *a selective examination.*
selector *nc* person who selects, or helps to select, the members of a team (esp. for an international competition).

self[1] [self] 1. *nu* one's own interests, wishes etc: *act with no thought of self* i.e. only for other people. 2. *nc* one's personality or character: *be changed from one's former self; one's better self* i.e. the better side of one's character. *pl* **selves** [selvz].
Note: *self/selves* can be added onto a *pron* like *my, him etc* and so give *myself, yourself, himself, herself, itself, ourselves, yourselves, themselves, oneself.* These are used to emphasize (*I'll do it myself*), or after a verb (*Have you hurt yourself?*).

self-[2] [self] *prefix* 1. concerning oneself (e.g. **self-conscious; self-denial**). 2. caused by oneself, itself etc (e.g. **self-educated; self-help**). 3. working by oneself, itself etc (e.g. **self-starter**).
'self-a'ssertive *adj* making sure that others pay attention to one. **self-assertion** *nu*.
'self-a'ssured *adj* sure of one's own abilities. **self-assurance** *nu*.
'self-'centred (*US* **self-centered**) *adj* thinking only of one's own wishes.
'self-'confidence *nu* belief in one's own ability and worth. **self-confident** *adj*. **self-confidently** *adv*.
'self-'conscious *adj* see **conscious**.
'self-con'tained *adj* 1. containing everything that is necessary: *a self-contained flat.* 2. not saying much; quiet.
'self-con'trol *nu* control of one's feelings, actions etc. **self-controlled** *adj*.
'self-de'fence (*US* **self-defense**) act of defending oneself against attack of any kind.
'self-de'nial *nu* going without things that one wants, for some special purpose. **self-denying** *adj*.
'self-determi'nation act of the people of a country deciding what form of government they want for the country.
'self-'discipline control of one's actions.
'self-'educated *adj* taught by one's own efforts. **self-education** *nu*.
'self-em'ployed *adj* working in one's own business etc.
'self-es'teem 1. good opinion of oneself. 2. pride.
'self-'evident *adj* obvious: *a self-evident truth.*
'self-ex'planatory *adj* containing all the information needed for an explanation. *This letter is self-explanatory* i.e. if you read the letter you will understand what it is about.
'self-ex'pression act of showing one's feelings and one's own personality in what one does. *The art teacher encourages self-expression in the children* i.e. he encourages them to paint pictures which show their feelings etc.
'self-'government *nu* control of a nation by its own people, or of any group by its own members. **self-governing** *adj*.
'self-'help improving oneself without depending on others.
'self-im'portant *adj* proud; having too high an opinion of oneself. **self-importance** *nu*.
'self-in'dulgent *adj* not being strict enough with oneself. **self-indulgence** *nc/u*.
'self-'interest thinking of one's own needs rather than of others' needs.
'self-'made *adj* having become successful through one's own efforts: *a self-made man.*
'self-o'pinionated very confident that one's own opinions are correct.
'self-'pity act of feeling sorry for oneself.
'self-pos'sessed *adj* confident, calm; not concerned too much with what others think. **self-possession** *nu*.
'self-preser'vation act of saving oneself from harm or danger: *the instinct of self-preservation.*
'self-re'liant *adj* not depending on others. **self-reliance** *nu*.
'self-re'spect *nu* feeling that one need not be ashamed of oneself. **self-respecting** *adj*.
'self-'righteous *adj* believing that one is more virtuous than others. **self-righteously** *adv*. **self-righteousness** *nu*.
'self-'sacrifice giving up what one wants for the sake of others.
'selfsame *adj* very same: *the selfsame day.*
'self-'satisfied *adj* too pleased with one's own abilities or achievements.
'self-'seeking *adj* thinking only of what one wants for oneself.
'self-'service act or system of serving oneself in a restaurant, shop etc: *a self-service store.*

'self-'starter part of an engine which starts it automatically.
'self-'styled *adj* using a title one has given oneself, not given legally or by others: *a self-styled king.*
'self-suf'ficient *adj* **1.** not requiring help from others. **2.** having too high an opinion of one's own ability. **self-sufficiency** *nu.*
'self-'taught *adj* not taught or instructed by others.
'self-'willed *adj* obstinate; not willing to listen to the advice of others. **self-will** *nu.*
selfish ['selfiʃ] *adj* thinking only of one's own interests; intended to help only oneself at the expense of others: *a selfish action.* (*opp* **unselfish**). **selfishly** *adv.* **selfishness** *nu.*
selfless ['selflis] *adj* not selfish.
sell [sel] *vt/i* **1.** give something for money: *sell a bicycle cheaply; a shop that sells fruit.* **2.** be given for money. *These goods are selling well* i.e. many people are buying them. **3.** persuade others to accept: *sell an idea.* (*informal* in sense **3.**). *past* **sold** [sould].
seller *nc* person who sells: *a bookseller.*
a 'best'seller something (usu. a book) which is bought by many people.
sell off get rid of things by selling them cheaply.
sell someone out betray: *sell out one's friends.* (*informal*).
'sellout *nc* act of betrayal. (*informal*).
sell someone up sell everything belonging to a person, so as to pay his debts.
be sold on something like something very much; believe in something. (*informal*).
be sold out of something have sold all that one had of a particular kind of thing. *We are sold out of bread.*
selvage, selvedge ['selvidʒ] *nc/u* edge of cloth made in a way that prevents loose threads from coming out.
semantic [si'mæntik] *adj* concerned with meaning in language.
semantics *nu* study of meaning and development of meaning in words.
semaphore ['seməfɔ:*] *nu* system of sending messages (usu. by holding flags in certain positions, each position standing for a letter of the alphabet). Also *vt/i* send messages by semaphore.
semblance ['semblns] *nc* likeness; appearance: *have the semblance of truth.*
semen ['si:mən] *nu* fluid containing the seed of males.
semester [si'mestə*] *nc* (*US*) half of a school year, school term.
semi- ['semi] *prefix* **1.** half (e.g. **semicircle**). **2.** partly; not completely (e.g. **semiconscious**). **3.** occurring twice in some unit of time (e.g. **semi-annual**).
'semi-'annual *adj* occurring twice in a year.
'semicircle *nc* half of a circle. **'semi'circular** *adj.*
'semi'colon the mark ; .
'semi'conscious *adj* partly conscious.
'semide'tached *adj* having one wall in common with one other house: *a semi-detached house.*
'semi'final round, match etc before the final one in a competition.
'semi'precious *adj* in **semiprecious stone** i.e. stone which is not as valuable as a diamond, pearl etc.
'semi'skilled *adj* having or needing only a limited degree of skill (usu. in **semiskilled work(er)**).
seminar ['semina:*] *nc* group of university students etc who meet together with a teacher to study by means of a discussion.
seminary ['seminəri] *nc* school where young men are trained to be priests.
semitic [si'mitik] *adj* connected with Jews.
semolina [semə'li:nə] *nu* type of food made from wheat.
senate ['senit] *nc* **1.** one of two law-making groups in many governments (e.g. in the United States). *The bill was passed by the lower house, but rejected by the senate.* **2.** main law-making group in ancient Rome. **3.** group of professors etc controlling a university.
senator *nc* member of the senate in a government or in ancient Rome.
send [send] *vt* **1.** cause someone/something to go or come: *send a letter; send someone away from school.* **2.** cause someone to do something. *The fire sent everyone running out of the building.* *past* **sent** [sent].
send for someone/something ask for someone/something to come; ask for something to be sent: *send for a doctor; send for supplies.*
send something in enter something in connection with a competition, exhibition etc: *send in one's name for a competition.*
send someone off **1.** cause someone to leave. *The player was sent off the field for foul play.* **2.** go to a place where someone is beginning a journey in order to wish him well.
'send-off *nc* **1.** meeting of well-wishers to send someone off. **2.** good beginning of something.
send something off send something by post, rail etc: *send off a parcel.*
send someone to Coventry act together in a group to refuse to speak to someone as a punishment.
send someone packing tell someone to leave because one is angry with him. (*informal*).
send word send a message: *send word of one's arrival.*
senile ['si:nail] *adj* showing old age; caused by old age: *senile decay.*
senility [si'niliti] *nu* weakness of body or mind, caused by old age.
senior ['si:niə*] *adj* **1.** higher in position; with longer service. *Jones is senior to Smith.* **2.** the older. *James Jones Senior* i.e. the father, not the son who has the same name. (*opp* **junior**). Also *nc* senior person.
seniority [si:ni'ɔriti] *nu* state of being senior.
sensation [sen'seiʃən] *nc/u* **1.** feeling: *a sensation of weakness. Seeing him again after so many years was a strange sensation.* **2.** feeling of great excitement. *His unexpected success caused a sensation.*
sensational *adj* **1.** causing strong feeling: *a sensational crime.* **2.** trying to cause strong feelings: *a sensational article in a newspaper.*
sensationalism *nu* too much attention given to unusual or exciting events. *He did not like the sensationalism in the newspapers.*
sense [sens] **1.** *nc* power by which a person is aware of things outside himself: *the sense of hearing/touch/sight etc.* **2.** *nc* feeling one has by using these powers: *look at a garden with a sense of pleasure.* **3.** *nc* knowledge of what a certain thing is or how to use it: *have a sense of humour* i.e. be able to laugh at funny things. **4.** *nu* ability to think and act wisely: *a man of sense; use one's common sense* i.e. the ordinary ability to think and act wisely which most people have. **5.** *nc/u* meaning: *use a word in a*

different sense. Also *vt* feel. *I sensed that I was not welcome.*

senses *npl* normal, healthy mind: *out of one's senses* i.e. insane.

senseless *adj* **1.** unconscious: *fall senseless.* **2.** foolish: *a senseless action.*

bring someone to his senses see **bring.**

come to one's senses start behaving sensibly.

in a sense in a way; from one point of view. *I think he may be right in a sense.*

make sense seem reasonable; be able to be understood. *This message doesn't make sense.*

sensibility [sensi'biliti] *nc/u* possession of delicate feelings: *a man of sensibility* i.e. a man who feels pity or some emotion, where another person might not.

sensible ['sensibl] *adj* **1.** having or showing good judgment: *a sensible person/action etc.* **2.** enough to be noticed: *a sensible drop in the temperature.* **3.** having knowledge of: *sensible of what has happened* (*o.f.* in sense **3.**). **sensibly** *adv.*

sensitive ['sensitiv] *adj* easily affected by something: *the eye is sensitive to light; be sensitive to blame; a sensitive child* i.e. one whose feelings are easily hurt. (*opp* **insensitive**).

sensitivity [sensi'tiviti] *nu* state of being sensitive; extent to which one is sensitive. (*opp* **insensitivity**).

sensitize ['sensitaiz] *vt* do something to paper, film etc so that it is easily affected by light and can be used for photography.

sensory ['sensəri] *adj* having to do with the power of feeling or the powers by which one is aware of what is happening outside one (e.g. hearing, sight etc).

sensual ['sensjuəl] *adj* **1.** connected with the feelings of the body rather than of the mind or spirit: *sensual pleasures.* **2.** too much interested in the pleasures of the body: *a sensual person.* **sensuality** [sensju'æliti] *nu.*

sensualist *nc* sensual person.

sensuous *adj* affecting, or caused by, the feelings of the body. **sensuously** *adv.*

Note: sensual and *sensuous* have very similar meanings, but *sensual* usu. carries the idea of blame, while *sensuous* does not.

sent [sent] past of **send.**

sentence ['sentns] *nc* **1.** group of words forming the largest grammatical unit in a language. **2.** punishment given by a judge: *a sentence of six months' imprisonment.* Also *vt* give a punishment to someone for doing wrong. *The judge sentenced the murderer to death.*

pass sentence give a judgment on someone.

sententious [sen'tenʃəs] *adj* trying to sound wise.

sentient ['sentiənt] *adj* that can feel; having feeling.

sentiment ['sentimənt] **1.** *nc* feeling; mixture of feelings and ideas: *full of lofty sentiments* i.e. high feelings and ideas. **2.** *nc* expression of feelings. **3.** *nu* fine feelings (e.g. pity, love etc): *have no time for sentiment.* **4.** *nc* thought; opinion: *express one's sentiments on a certain topic.*

sentimental [senti'mentl] *adj* **1.** having or showing too much feeling (often feeling which is not deeply felt): *a sentimental novel/girl etc.* **2.** acting from, connected with, what one feels: *a sentimental person; of sentimental value* i.e. not really valuable, but connected with something/someone one feels strongly about. **sentimentally** *adv.* **sentimentalism** *nu.* **sentimentalist** *nc.* **sentimentality** [sentimen'tæliti] *nu.*

sentinel ['sentinl] *nc* sentry (*o.f.*).

sentry ['sentri] *nc* soldier who has to keep watch.

'sentry box small hut for a sentry.

stand sentry over someone/something keep watch over.

separate ['seprit] *adj* apart; not joined; not connected: *two separate houses/ideas/people etc. We were kept separate from our friends.* Also ['sepəreit] *vt/i* **1.** keep apart: *separate two children who are fighting.* **2.** go apart; break a connection. *We once worked together, but now we have separated. The crowd separated* i.e. people went in different directions. **separation** [sepə'reiʃən] *nu.*

separate the sheep from the goats separate good from bad.

sepia ['si:piə] *nu* dark brown paint. Also *adj* colour of this.

September [sep'tembə*] *n* ninth month of the year.

septic ['septik] *adj* **1.** infected, poisoned by germs: *a septic wound.* **2.** likely to cause infection.

septic tank tank outside a building into which sewage flows and is purified so as to prevent infection.

sepulchre ['sepəlkə*] (*US* **sepulcher**) *nc* tomb; place where someone is buried.

sepulchral [si'pʌlkrl] *adj* **1.** connected with a tomb. **2.** solemn; sad.

sequel ['si:kwl] *nc* **1.** something that follows, as a result of or after, something else. **2.** book, film etc which carries on the story of a previous one.

sequence ['si:kwəns] *nc/u* number of things following one another: *a sequence of disasters; in sequence* i.e. one following the other.

sequester [si'kwestə*] *vt* **1.** keep someone away from other people. **2.** take property or goods legally from someone, either for good or just for a time.

sequestered *adj* quiet and away from other people: *a sequestered spot.*

sequin ['si:kwin] *nc* very small, metal ornament, sewn on clothing.

seraph ['serəf] *nc* angel. *pl* **seraphs** or **seraphim** ['serəfim].

seraphic [sə'ræfik] *adj* like an angel; innocent, happy.

serenade [serə'neid] *nc* **1.** music played or sung outside the window of a lady's room in the evening. **2.** soft, quiet piece of music. Also *vt/i* sing or play a serenade: *serenade one's sweetheart.*

serene [si'ri:n] *adj* **1.** peaceful; calm: *a serene smile.* **2.** bright; not cloudy: *serene skies.* **serenely** *adv.* **serenity** [si'reniti] *nu.*

serf [sə:f] *nc* person who is not allowed to leave the land on which he works; slave.

serfdom *nu* system of using serfs; state of being a serf.

serge [sə:dʒ] *nu* strong, rough, woollen cloth.

sergeant ['sɑ:dʒənt] *nc* **1.** (military) non-commissioned officer. **2.** rank in the police force, above an ordinary policeman but below an inspector.

serial ['siəriəl] *nc* story appearing in parts once weekly, monthly etc. *A new serial is starting on television tonight.* Also *adj* **1.** arranged in a series. see below. **2.** appearing in parts once weekly, monthly etc: *a serial story.* **serially** *adv.*

serialize *vt* put in form of a serial.

series ['siəri:z] *nc* number of things coming one after the other: *a series of disappointments/stormy days/good harvests etc.* *pl* **series.**

serious ['siəriəs] *adj* **1.** in earnest; not joking or playful. *Try to be serious for a moment.* **2.** thoughtful; not interested in pleasure: *a serious kind of person.* **3.** important and perhaps dangerous: *a serious problem.* **seriously** *adv.* **seriousness** *nu.*

sermon ['sə:mən] *nc* **1.** talk given by a priest or minister in church. **2.** any serious talk about morals, conduct etc.

sermonize *vi* tell other people about one's ideas of what is right and wrong, often in a rather boring way.

serpent ['sə:pənt] *nc* snake.

serpentine ['sə:pəntain] *adj* winding or twisting like a snake. Also *nu* type of stone (usu. greenish in colour).

serrated [si'reitid] *adj* shaped like the teeth of a saw: *a serrated edge.*

serried ['serid] *adj* packed very close together: *serried ranks of onlookers.*

serum ['siərəm] *nc/u* **1.** colourless, watery part of the blood. **2.** watery liquid taken from the blood of an animal which has had a certain disease, and put into the blood of a person to prevent him from having that disease.

servant ['sə:vənt] *nc* **1.** person paid to do housework. **2.** anyone who does work (esp. for the government): *civil servants; public servants.*

Note: the word *servant* (in sense **1.**) is often avoided in the USA and Britain, and the term *help* or *domestic help* is used instead.

serve [sə:v] *vt* **1.** work for; do something for: *serve an employer; serve one's country well.* **2.** bring food or drink: *serve dinner.* **3.** give something that is required (esp. to a customer in a shop). *The assistant will serve you.* **4.** be useful; be good enough. *Anything sharp would serve to open this box. This will serve the purpose* i.e. be good enough. **5.** spend; pass: *serve time* i.e. spend time in prison. **6.** (legal) give a document to the person named in it: *serve notice of something; serve a summons on someone.* **7.** (tennis etc) put the ball into play.

serve someone right be what he deserves. *If he loses his job, it will serve him right.* (*informal*).

serve one's time spend a long period doing something one must do: *serve one's time in the army/as an apprentice etc.*

service ['sə:vis] **1.** *nc* something done by one person for another: *thank a doctor for his services.* **2.** *nu* state of being a servant (in sense **1.**): *be in service.* **3.** *nc* department of the government; people employed in a government department: *the civil service; the services* i.e. the Army, Navy and Air Force. **4.** *nc* supply or amount of something: *a good train service* i.e. plenty of trains. **5.** *nc* religious ceremony: *the Sunday service; the marriage service.* **6.** *nu* way in which one is served. *The service in this hotel is good.* **7.** *nc* set of dishes: *a tea service.* **8.** *nc* act of checking up on something mechanical or electrical to make sure that it works properly: *a car that needs a service.* **9.** *nc/u* (tennis etc) putting the ball into play. Also *vt* **1.** check up on something mechanical or electrical: *have one's car serviced.* **2.** provide with what is needed.

serviceable ['sə:visəbl] *adj* **1.** useful. **2.** useful for a long time. (*opp* **unserviceable**).

'service charge amount that is added to a hotel or restaurant bill, to take the place of leaving a tip for the waiter etc.

'service flat (*Brit*) rooms where one is also provided with services such as cleaning etc.

'service station place which provides oil, petrol etc for motorists.

of service of use. *The shopkeeper asked if he could be of service to us.*

serviette [sə:vi'et] *nc* small cloth to be put over the knees while one is eating, to prevent clothes being stained etc.

servile ['sə:vail] *adj* showing too much respect, as a slave would: *servile flattery; a servile attitude.*

servility [sə:'viliti] *nu* behaving towards someone as if one were his slave.

servitude ['sə:vitju:d] *nu* slavery; state of not having one's freedom.

penal servitude hard work one is forced to do in prison.

session ['seʃən] *nc* **1.** meeting (esp. of a law court, Parliament etc). **2.** number of such meetings: *the summer session.* **3.** time when a class is held: *the afternoon session.*

in session having a meeting.

set[1] [set] *vt/i* **1.** place; put: *set a cup on the table; set a meal before someone; set pen to paper* i.e. write; *set a match to something* i.e. light it with a match; *set a hen on her eggs/set eggs under a hen* i.e. so that they will be hatched. **2.** fix: *set a price; set a time* i.e. agree on a time; *set one's watch to the correct time; set an alarm clock* i.e. so that it will sound at a certain time. **3.** fix something in something else so that it will not fall out: *set jewels in a crown; a ring set with diamonds.* **4.** give something to be done: *set an examination; set someone a difficult task.* **5.** become hard or more firm. *The cement/jelly has set.* **6.** cause someone/something to be in a certain condition: *set someone free; set a house alight.* **7.** cause someone to do something. *His question has set me thinking.* **8.** (with reference to the sun) go below the horizon. *The sun was setting.* **9.** fit: *set words to music.* *pres part* **setting.** *past* **set.** Also *adj* **1.** arranged: *at a set time.* **2.** fixed; unchanging: *a set smile on one's face* i.e. when one is not really amused; *a set phrase.*

setting *nc* **1.** frame that something is fixed into: *a jewel with a beautiful setting of gold and silver.* **2.** place, time etc in which the action of a story takes place: *a play with an 18th century setting.* **3.** scenery of a play: *beautiful settings.* **4.** music which is written to go with certain words: *compose a setting for a poem.*

set about something begin something: *set about a task.*

set about someone attack someone.

set someone apart make a difference between one person/thing and others. *His intelligence set him apart from the others.*

set something aside **1.** put something to one side for later use: *set some money aside every month.* **2.** (in a legal sense) dismiss: *set aside a claim.* **3.** ignore: *setting aside the question of cost.*

set someone/something back **1.** hinder: *set back someone's plans.* **2.** place away from something: *a house well set back from the road.* **3.** cost. *His daughter's wedding set him back hundreds of pounds.* (*informal* in sense **3.**).

'setback *nc* difficulty which hinders progress.

set someone/something down 1. write: *set down what someone says.* 2. allow passengers to get off. *The bus sets passengers down here.* 3. put down: *set down something one is carrying.*
set forth begin a journey (*o.f.* – use **set out**).
set something forth give an account of; tell: *set forth one's reasons for doing something.*
set in (with reference to something unwelcome) begin: *get a wound attended to before blood poisoning sets in.*
set off begin a journey: *set off on a long hike.*
set something off 1. cause to explode: *set off a rocket/firework etc.* 2. make a pleasant contrast with. *The green carpet is set off by the yellow curtains.*
set out begin a journey: *set out for Paris.*
set something out 1. make known: *set out one's ideas.* 2. arrange. *Your composition is not very well set out.*
set to 1. eagerly begin to do something: *set to work with a will. They set to and had the job finished in ten minutes.* 2. fight; quarrel. (*informal* in sense 2.).
'set-'to *nc* quarrel. (*informal*).
set someone/something up 1. start someone in business: *set oneself/one's son up as a grocer.* 2. build; place in position: *set up an altar.* 3. begin: *set up a business; set up house* i.e. start living in one's own house.
'setup *nc* situation; arrangement: *a strange setup.* (*informal*).
set upon someone attack someone. *He was set upon in the dark.*
be all set be prepared and eager. *The children are all set to go.*
set a bone put the parts of a broken bone together again so that it heals.
a 'set 'book/'poem etc book/poem etc which has to be studied for an examination.
set one's cap at someone try to attract a man. *I think she's setting her cap at him.* (*informal*).
set one's dog on someone make one's dog attack someone.
set an example (to someone) show others how to behave properly. *You should be setting an example, not misbehaving.*
set a good/bad example behave well/badly in front of others.
set eyes on see. *I've never set eyes on him before.* (*informal*).
set one's face against something decide to oppose something.
set the fashion behave, dress etc in a way that others follow.
set foot in enter. *He shall never set foot in my house.*
get set be ready. *On your marks, get set, go!* i.e. the instructions given to runners at the beginning of a race.
set one's hair keep the hair in a certain position while it is wet so that, when it dries, it will keep a certain style. *She set her hair the evening before the dance.*
set one's hand to begin; try. *He was successful in everything he set his hand to.*
set one's heart on want very much.
set one's house in order arrange one's affairs properly.
set one's mind at rest cause one to stop worrying. *The news of his safe arrival set my mind at rest.*
set one's mind on want very much.
set someone on his feet 1. help someone who has fallen to stand. 2. help someone to regain his health, prosperity etc. *He was ill but the good weather soon set him on his feet.*
set someone over others appoint someone that others must obey.
set the pace be the first or the best, so that others follow one.
set a price on someone's head offer money for the capture or killing of someone.
set sail (with reference to any kind of ship) start on a voyage: *set sail for New York.*
set much/little/no store by pay much/little/no attention to. *I wouldn't set much store by what he says.*
set the world on fire be a great success; be very famous. (*informal*).

set[2] [set] *nc* 1. group of things/people that go together: *a set of golf clubs; a set of false teeth; a tea set* i.e. dishes used for serving tea; *the smart set* i.e. group of people who think of themselves as being the leaders in fashion, social matters etc. 2. radio or television receiver: *a transistor set.* 3. scenery of a play, film etc. *They had built a very impressive set.* 4. position; shape. *I could see by the set of his jaw that he was determined.* 5. way clothes fit the body. *I like the set of her new coat.* 6. group of games in tennis. 7. direction of the tide, wind etc.
'set square piece of wood or other material, in the shape of a triangle with an angle of 90°.

settee [se'ti:] *nc* long seat with a back and arms.

settle[1] ['setl] *nc* long wooden seat with a high back.

settle[2] ['setl] *vt/i* 1. decide: *settle on a time/place etc; settle a dispute.* 2. arrange: *settle one's affairs* i.e. make sure that there will be nothing to be disputed or left unfinished on one's death. 3. go to live in; send people to live in: *settle in London; settle overseas; settle refugees in a new country.* 4. make comfortable: *settle oneself in a chair.* 5. make calm or peaceful: *medicine to settle one's nerves.* 6. go down; sink down. *The mud settled at the bottom of the pool.* 7. pay: *settle a bill. If you leave the bill with me, I'll settle up.*
settled *adj* 1. not changing: *settled ideas; a period of settled weather.* (*opp* **unsettled**). 2. with people living in it: *a settled area.*
settlement 1. *nc/u* act of deciding or arranging something; agreement: *the settlement of a dispute;* reach a settlement. 2. *nu* sending or coming of people to settle in a country: *the settlement of America.* 3. *nc* group of people who have settled in a country. 4. *nc* the place where they have settled. 5. *nc/u* payment: *give money in settlement of a debt.*
settler *nc* person who settles in a new country.
settle down 1. stay in one place. *After years of travelling, he decided to settle down.* 2. get used to something new. *How are you settling down in your new job/house?* 3. become calm, peaceful.
settle for something agreed to. *He settled for half the price he had first asked.*
settle in begin living/working etc in a new place. *The new boy soon settled in at school.*
settle up (with someone) pay money which is owing. *Let me settle up with you.*

seven ['sevn] see appendix.
at sixes and sevens see **six.**

sever ['sevə*] *vt/i* 1. cut; break off: *sever a rope; sever relations with someone.* 2. come apart; break. *The rope severed.* **severance** *nu.*

several ['sevərl] *adj/determiner* **1.** three or more but not many: *on several occasions.* **2.** different. *They went their several ways* (*o.f.* in sense **2.**). Also *pron* more than two or three but not many. *I've got some cups, but I think I'll need several more.*
severally *adv* separately.
severe [si'viə*] *adj* **1.** strict; stern; harsh: *a severe warning; a severe punishment.* **2.** difficult: *a severe examination.* **3.** very plain; without ornament: *a severe style of dress.* **4.** dangerous: *a severe illness.* **severely** *adv.*
severity [si'veriti] *nu* state of being severe.
sew [sou] *vt/i* **1.** use a needle and thread to join two or more things: *sew a button on a jacket.* **2.** make clothes by using a needle and thread. *past tense* **sewed.** *past part* **sewed** or **sewn** [soun].
sewing *nu* work done with a needle and thread. Also *adj.*
'sewing machine machine for sewing.
sewer ['suːə*] *nc* underground pipe or tunnel that carries off waste matter from houses in a town.
sewage ['suːidʒ] *nu* waste matter carried off by sewers.
sewerage *nu* **1.** taking away of waste matter by sewers. **2.** system of sewers.
sewn [soun] past part of **sew.**
sex [seks] **1.** *nu* condition of being male or female. *People should have equal opportunities, regardless of race or sex.* **2.** *nc* division of humans into either male or female: *the male sex; the fair/gentle/weaker sex* i.e. women. **3.** *nu* attraction or physical love between males and females. Also *adj.* Also *vt* (of chickens etc) find out the sex of.
sexual ['seksjuəl] *adj* connected with sex or the sexes. **sexually** *adv.*
sexy *adj* sexually attractive. (*informal*).
'sex appeal sexual attractiveness.
sextant ['sekstnt] *nc* instrument used at sea to find out the height of the sun, a star etc so as to discover a ship's position.
sexton ['sekstn] *nc* man who takes care of a church and its graveyard.
shabby ['ʃæbi] *adj* **1.** having been worn a lot: *a shabby old coat.* **2.** dressed in old and worn clothes: *a shabby beggar.* **3.** mean; low: *a shabby action.* **shabbily** *adv.* **shabbiness** *nu.*
shack [ʃæk] *nc* roughly-built shed.
shackle ['ʃækl] *nc* **1.** (often *pl*) iron ring round the wrist or leg of a prisoner, slave etc which is fastened to something to prevent him from escaping. **2.** any kind of large fastening pin. **3.** (often *pl*) anything which interferes with one's freedom: *the shackles of the law.* Also **vt 1.** put a shackle or shackles on: *shackle a prisoner.* **2.** interfere with someone's freedom.
shade [ʃeid] **1.** *nu* area of darkness and coolness, out of the sunshine. *There is not much shade here. Let us sit in the shade of that tree.* **2.** *nc* something that keeps an amount of light out or makes it less bright: *an eyeshade; a shade for a lamp.* **3.** *nc* lighter or darker kinds of colour. *I would like something in a darker shade of blue.* **4.** *nu* dark part of a drawing or painting. *Don't put in too much shade when you are drawing.* **5.** *nc* small difference; a small amount: *a word with different shades of meaning; a jacket that is a shade too long.* **6.** *nc* spirit; ghost (*o.f.* in sense **6.**). Also *vt/i* **1.** protect from the full light or heat of the sun. *This seat is shaded by a tree.* **2.** make darker: *shade in part of a drawing.* **3.** change by small amounts: *dark blue shading off into black.*
shady *adj* **1.** giving protection from the light of the sun: *a shady tree.* **2.** probably not honest. (*informal* in sense **2.**).
the shades in ancient Greek religion, the spirits of the dead.
in the shade 1. out of the direct rays of the sun. **2.** state of not being as good or famous as someone else. *My brother's success has put me in the shade.* (*informal* in sense **2.**).
shadow ['ʃædou] *nc* **1.** area of darkness caused by a person/thing with the light coming from another side of him or it. *They were standing in the square and, as the sun was setting, their shadows were getting longer.* **2.** small amount: *without a shadow of (a) doubt.* **3.** person who follows another person (often secretly). *The suspected criminal was followed everywhere by a police shadow.* Also *vt* **1.** cut off from the light: *shadowed by a wall.* **2.** make sad. *The later part of his life was shadowed by his son's tragic death.* **3.** follow someone without the person knowing. *The police have been shadowing him for months.*
shadowy *adj* **1.** containing a lot of shadows. **2.** not easily observed: *lead a shadowy kind of existence.*
'shadow 'cabinet (*Brit*) group of men chosen by the leader of the opposition party to represent its official views in Parliament.
shaft [ʃɑːft] *nc* **1.** long (usu. wooden) stem of an arrow or spear: *hold a spear by the shaft.* **2.** arrow; spear. **3.** one of the two wooden poles by which a horse is attached to a carriage. **4.** main part of a column or pillar. **5.** bar which turns part of a machine. **6.** long handle of an axe, golf club etc. **7.** long, narrow space running down the inside of a building, or extending underneath the ground to a mine etc below ground level. **8.** long, narrow beam of light.
shaggy ['ʃægi] *adj* **1.** covered in rough hair: *a shaggy dog.* **2.** long and rough: *shaggy eyebrows.*
shake [ʃeik] *vt/i* **1.** move violently or quickly in one direction and then in another: *trees shaking in the wind; shake one's fist at someone* i.e. to show that one is angry; *shake a box to see if it contains anything.* **2.** tremble: *shake with fear; in a shaking voice.* **3.** affect badly: *be shaken by the news of a disaster.* **4.** make less firm. *Your actions have shaken my faith in your ability. pres part* **shaking.** *past tense* **shook** [ʃuk]. *past part* **shaken.** Also *nc* **1.** act of shaking. *He refused my request with a shake of his head.* **2.** drink made by shaking various things together: *milk shake.*
shaky *adj* **1.** not steady; not secure: *a shaky platform; in a shaky position.* **2.** trembling: *a shaky voice.* **3.** not reliable. **shakily** *adv.* **shakiness** *nu.*
shake someone up rouse, make active. (*informal*).
'shake-up *nc* act of rousing people, making them active. *Nobody is working properly in this office; we need a good shake-up.* (*informal*).
no great shakes not very good. (*informal*).
shake hands/by the hand greet someone by holding his hand (usu. the right one).
shake one's head move one's head from side to side to mean 'no' or to show doubt etc.
in two shakes very quickly. (*informal*).
shale [ʃeil] *nu* smooth type of rock that breaks easily into thin layers.

shall [ʃæl] *aux* **1.** often, but not always, used with *I* and *we* to express that something is going to happen. *We shall be leaving in five minutes. I shall see you next week.* **2.** used to express that something must be done. *You shall not leave this room. All pupils shall be present.* **3.** used with *I* and *we* making a suggestion. *Shall I do that for you? past* **should** [ʃud].

shallow ['ʃælou] *adj* not deep: *shallow river; shallow person* i.e. one who does not think seriously about things. Also *nc* (often *pl*) shallow place in a river etc. **shallowly** *adv.* **shallowness** *nu.*

shalt [ʃælt] verb form of **shall** used with **thou** (*o.f.*).

sham [ʃæm] *vt/i* pretend: *sham illness to escape an unpleasant duty. past* **shammed.** Also *nc* **1.** person who pretends: *be just a sham.* **2.** something meant to deceive other people. *His pious behaviour is just a sham.* Also *adj* pretended; false: *sham diamond.*

shamble ['ʃæmbl] *vi* walk in an unsteady way. *The tired old beggar was just shambling along the street.*

shambles ['ʃæmblz] *n sing* or *pl* **1.** (with **a**) any scene of violence; state of disorder. *The room was in a shambles after the explosion.* **2.** place where animals are killed for food (*o.f.* in sense **2.**).

shame [ʃeim] *nu* **1.** painful feeling that one has acted wrongly or foolishly: *blush with shame; feel shame for having told a lie.* **2.** disgrace: *bring shame on one's family.* **3.** feeling for what is right or decent. *That villain has no sense of shame.* Also *vt* **1.** cause to feel shame: *shame one's family by one's conduct.* **2.** make someone do something by making him feel shame. *I shamed him into returning the stolen money.*

shameful *adj* disgraceful. *To steal money from a blind person is a shameful act.* **shamefully** *adv.*

shameless *adj* without shame; immodest. **shamelessly** *adv.*

'shame'faced *adj* feeling shame. **shamefacedly** *adv.*

it's a shame that it is unfair or a pity that. *It's a shame that he is so poor.*

put someone to shame cause someone to feel shame.

What a shame! What a pity!, How terrible!

shampoo [ʃæm'pu:] **1.** *nc/u* special soap, liquid etc for washing the hair. **2.** *nc* act of washing the hair by using this. Also *vt* wash the hair in this way.

shampoo and set washing and setting the hair (usu. by a hairdresser).

shamrock ['ʃæmrɔk] *nc* small, green plant with small leaves in sets of three; the national emblem of Ireland.

shank [ʃæŋk] *nc* **1.** part of the leg between the knee and the ankle. **2.** part of an instrument joining the handle and the working part: *shank of a key.*

shan't [ʃɑ:nt] *vi* short form of **shall not.** see **be.**

shanty[1] ['ʃænti] *nc* roughly-built hut.

shanty[2] ['ʃænti] *nc* song sung by sailors while doing their work: *sea shanty.*

shape [ʃeip] **1.** *nc/u* form; appearance: *piece of wood in the shape of a square; round in shape; give help in the shape of money* i.e. give money. **2.** *nu* condition: *in bad shape* i.e. in poor condition. **3.** *nc* mould in which something is made. Also *vt/i* **1.** give a certain shape or form to: *shape a pot out of clay; shape one's future* i.e. affect in a certain way. **2.** take on a certain shape or form. *Their plans are shaping well* i.e. they are developing in a desired way.

shapeless *adj* **1.** without a definite shape. **2.** not having an attractive shape.

shapely *adj* (often of women) well-formed.

take shape have a clearer form. *My ideas are taking shape* i.e. taking on a clearer pattern.

in any shape or form in any way at all.

share[1] [ʃɛə*] **1.** *nc/u* part of something. *We shall all have a share of the profits. We'll do our share of the work if they'll do their share.* **2.** *nc* one of the parts into which the ownership of a business company is divided: *buy 100 shares in a company.* Also *vt/i* **1.** use or do with others: *share a room with someone; shared pleasures.* **2.** give part of something to others; divide into parts which are given to others: *share one's wealth.* **3.** take part in: *share (in) the expenses.*

'shareholder someone who owns shares in a business company.

share something out give parts of something to a number of people: *share out the money among the boys.*

share[2] [ʃɛə*] *nc* part of a plough that cuts into the soil.

shark [ʃɑ:k] *nc* **1.** kind of large fish with a large fin on its back, which eats other fish and can be dangerous to man. **2.** person who cheats others out of their money. (*informal* in sense **2.**).

sharp [ʃɑ:p] *adj* **1.** having a fine edge: *sharp knife.* **2.** coming to a fine point: *sharp pin.* **3.** sudden; violent: *sharp bend in the road; make a sharp turn; sharp struggle; in sharp contrast* i.e. complete; *sharp pain.* **4.** severe: *speak sharp words to someone; sharp wind* i.e. cold and biting. **5.** quick to notice or understand: *have sharp eyes; sharp intelligence; keep a sharp lookout.* **6.** quick to take an advantage for oneself: *a sharp businessman.* **7.** high; piercing: *a sharp cry.* 8. (music) above the true pitch. Also *nc* **1.** note that is raised by one semitone (e.g. D sharp (D♯) is one semitone above D natural). **2.** the sign ♯ used to show that a note is sharp. Also *adv* **1.** exactly; promptly. *Be there at 9 (o'clock) sharp.* **2.** abruptly; at a sudden angle. *Turn sharp right at the next corner.* **sharply** *adv.* **sharpness** *nu.*

sharpen *vt/i* make or become sharp.

sharpener *nc* instrument which makes something sharp: *pencil sharpener; knife sharpener.*

sharper *nc* usu. in **card sharper** i.e. someone who cheats people while playing cards. (Also **card sharp**).

look sharp be quick or alert. (*informal*).

shatter ['ʃætə*] *vt/i* **1.** break suddenly into small pieces. *The cup was shattered on the floor.* **2.** shock; destroy: *shatter one's hopes/nerves.*

shave [ʃeiv] *vt/i* **1.** take hair from the face etc by using a razor. *I shave every day.* **2.** cut thin slices off something. **3.** come very close to someone/something without touching him or it. *The car just shaved past the pedestrian.* Also *nc* act of shaving the face: *have a shave.*

shavings *npl* small pieces which come off wood when it is being made smooth.

'shaving brush brush for putting soap on the face before shaving.

'clean-'shaven, 'well-'shaven having been well-shaved: *clean-shaven youth.*

a close shave a narrow escape from danger. (*informal*).

shawl [ʃɔːl] *nc* piece of cloth (usu. square in shape) worn by women over the shoulders or on the head, or sometimes used for wrapping a baby in.

she [ʃiː, ʃi] *pron* female person or animal that has been mentioned before. It also refers to a few things which are thought of as being feminine (e.g. a ship). *If you are looking for your mother, she is in the kitchen. She is coming/She's coming.* see **her.**

sheaf [ʃiːf] *nc* number of things gathered together or bound together: *sheaf of corn* i.e. a number of corn stalks tied together; *sheaf of papers; sheaf of arrows. pl* **sheaves** [ʃiːvz].

sheaf of corn

shear [ʃiə*] *vt* cut wool from sheep by using shears. *past tense* **sheared.** *past part* **sheared** or **shorn** [ʃɔːn].

shears *npl* large pair of scissors i.e. two sharp blades joined together, used for cutting wool, thin branches etc.

sheath [ʃiːθ] *nc* cover for a sharp weapon or instrument: *sheath for a sword.*

sheathe [ʃiːð] *vt* **1.** put a weapon etc in its sheath. **2.** put inside a case or covering.

shed[1] [ʃed] *nc* building used for keeping things in: *toolshed; cattle shed.*

shed[2] [ʃed] *vt* **1.** cause to fall: *shed tears; trees that shed their leaves.* **2.** get rid of; throw off: *a snake that sheds its skin.* **3.** throw out: *a fire shedding light and warmth. pres part* **shedding.** *past* **shed.**

shed blood 1. lose blood. **2.** kill; cause blood to flow.

shed light on something give more information about. *Can anyone shed light on this mystery?*

sheen [ʃiːn] *nu* brightness of a surface: *the sheen of polished silver.*

sheep [ʃiːp] *nc* **1.** animal raised for its wool and its meat. **2.** weak and foolish person. *pl* **sheep.**

sheepish *adj* foolish and self-conscious: *look sheepish.* **sheepishly** *adv.*

'sheepdog dog trained to help a shepherd to control sheep.

'sheepfold area enclosed by walls etc to keep sheep together.

separate the sheep from the goats see **separate.**

sheer[1] [ʃiə*] *adj* **1.** so thin that it can easily be seen through: *sheer silk.* **2.** complete: *sheer nonsense.* **3.** straight up and down: *a sheer drop of a hundred feet.* Also *adv* straight up and down: *cliffs rising sheer from the sea.* **sheerness** *nu.*

sheer[2] [ʃiə*] *vi* turn suddenly off course. *The ship sheered off/away.*

sheet [ʃiːt] *nc* **1.** piece of cloth (cotton, linen, nylon etc) used on a bed. **2.** flat, thin piece of paper, glass, iron etc. **3.** rope tied to a lower corner of a sail, which can be used to control the sail. **4.** broad, flat area: *a sheet of water.*

sheik, sheikh [ʃeik] *nc* **1.** head of an Arab family, village or tribe. **2.** title of an Arab ruler.

shelf [ʃelf] *nc* **1.** thin, flat piece of wood, glass, stone etc attached to the wall or the side of a cupboard so that things (e.g. books) can be left on it: *a bookshelf.* **2.** anything like a shelf in shape. *pl* **shelves** [ʃelvz].

shelve [ʃelv] **1.** *vt* put aside to be dealt with later: *shelve a problem.* **2.** *vi* slope downwards gradually: *land shelving down to the sea.*

on the shelf 1. no longer useful or wanted. **2.** (with reference to women) left unmarried. (*informal*).

shell [ʃel] *nc* **1.** hard outer covering of an egg, seed etc, or of certain water animals (called **shellfish**) and of some land animals (e.g. tortoise). **2.** frame (e.g. of a building). *Only the shell of the building has been put up so far.* **3.** metal container filled with explosives, for firing from a gun (usu. a large gun). Also *vt* **1.** take the shell from: *shell peas.* **2.** fire shells at, from a gun: *shell a town.*

sea shell

eggshell

'shellfish *nc/u* type of water animal that has a shell. *pl* **shellfish.**

'shell shock type of nervous or mental illness caused by the frightening experiences undergone by soldiers in wartime.

shell out pay money: *shell out for an expensive present.* (*informal*).

come out of one's shell be more friendly, less shy. (*informal*).

retire into one's shell be less friendly; talk less. (*informal*).

shelter ['ʃeltə*] **1.** *nc* something that covers or protects one: *bus shelter* i.e. building which gives protection from the weather to people who are waiting for a bus. **2.** *nu* protection; cover: *look for shelter; run for shelter from the rain.* Also *vt/i* **1.** give protection or cover to: *shelter refugees.* **2.** find cover or protection: *shelter in a farmhouse; shelter from a storm.*

shelve, shelves [ʃelv(z)] *vt, npl* see **shelf.**

shepherd ['ʃepəd] *nc* man who takes care of sheep. (*fem* **shepherdess** ['ʃepədis]). Also *vt* **1.** direct or guide: *be shepherded into a room.* **2.** take care of: *shepherd one's flock.*

sheriff ['ʃerif] *nc* (now mainly *US* and *Scot*) important legal officer in a county.

sherry ['ʃeri] *nu* type of yellow or brown wine.

shield [ʃiːld] *nc* **1.** (in former times) piece of metal, leather etc carried to protect the body from injury while fighting. **2.** something that protects. **3.** something in the shape of a shield. Also *vt* protect (esp. from punishment): *shield a wrongdoer.*

shift [ʃift] *vt/i* change from one position, person etc to another; move: *shift one's position slightly; shift a person from one job to another; try to shift the blame for something onto someone else.* Also *nc* **1.** change of

workers; group of workers working in turn with another group or other groups. *We can keep the factory going all the time because we have two shifts – a dayshift and a nightshift.* **2.** change in position. **3.** trick; scheme: *try every shift.* **4.** type of loose-fitting dress.
shiftless *adj* lazy; careless.
shifty *adj* not to be trusted; deceitful: *rather shifty behaviour.* **shiftily** *adv.*
shift for oneself do as well as one can unaided. *There is no one here to help us, so we must shift for ourselves.*
make shift do as well as one can. see **makeshift.**

shilling ['ʃiliŋ] *nc* formerly, British coin worth twelve old pence (5 pence).

shimmer ['ʃimə*] *vi* shine with an unsteady light: *a lake shimmering in the moonlight.* Also *nu.*

shin [ʃin] *nc* front part of the leg, from the knee to the ankle.
shin up something climb: *shin up a tree.* (*informal*).

shine [ʃain] *vt/i* **1.** give out light; be bright: *the moon shining on the sea; a face shining with excitement.* **2.** cause to give out light: *shine a torch.* **3.** polish: *shine one's shoes.* **4.** do well: *shine in a conversation/examination etc.* *past* **shone** [ʃɔn]. Also *nu* brightness; polish: *put a shine on one's shoes.*
shiny *adj* **1.** shining; bright: *a shiny new coin.* **2.** worn so that it is too smooth and glossy: *a shiny old suit.*

shingle[1] ['ʃiŋgl] *nc* **1.** one of many flat pieces of wood used to cover some roofs. **2.** short haircut for women. Also *vt* **1.** cover with shingles: *shingle a roof.* **2.** cut a woman's hair short.

shingle[2] ['ʃiŋgl] *nu* small, rounded stones on the seashore. *Do you prefer sand or shingle on a beach?* **shingly** *adj.*

shingles ['ʃiŋglz] *nu* type of nerve infection which affects the skin.

ship [ʃip] *nc* large seagoing vessel; large boat. Also *vt* **1.** send goods in a ship: *ship a cargo of wheat to New York.* **2.** take in water (e.g. during a storm): *ship water.* **3.** accept someone to work on a ship; start work on a ship: *ship a crew.* **4.** transport overland. *pres part* **shipping.** *past* **shipped.**
shipping *nu* all the ships of a country, city or business company.
shipment **1.** *nu* act of sending goods by ship. **2.** *nc* amount of goods sent: *a large shipment of grain.*
'shipbuilder *nc* person or business company that builds ships. **shipbuilding** *nu.*
'shipload amount that a ship is carrying.
'shipmate sailor who served on the same ship. *We were shipmates at that time* i.e. both working on the same ship.
'shipshape *adj* properly arranged; tidy. *Everything in his room is shipshape.* Also *adv.* (both *informal*).
'shipwreck **1.** *nu* destruction of a ship at sea (e.g. in a storm): *a man who has suffered shipwreck three times.* **2.** *nc* ship that has been destroyed in this way. Also *vt* destroy a ship in this way: *shipwrecked by a storm.*
'shipwright person who builds or repairs ships.
'shipyard place where ships are built or repaired.
ship oars take in the oars in a rowing boat.

shire ['ʃaiə*] *nc* one of the areas into which Britain is divided.
Note: this word is *o.f.* except in compounds (where it is pronounced [ʃə*] **e.g.** *Oxfordshire* – use *county* **e.g.** *the counties of England*).

shirk [ʃə:k] *vt/i* avoid doing something one finds unpleasant: *shirk one's duty/responsibilities etc.* **shirker** *nc.*

shirt [ʃə:t] *nc* garment for the upper part of a man's body (usu. of thin cloth).
in one's shirt sleeves not wearing a jacket.

shiver[1] ['ʃivə*] *vi* shake with cold or fear. Also *nc* act of shivering.

shiver[2] ['ʃivə*] *vt/i* break into small pieces. Also *nc* small broken piece.

shoal[1] [ʃoul] *nc* large group of fish: *see a shoal of fish swimming by.*

shoal[2] [ʃoul] *nc* place where the water is shallow.

shock[1] [ʃɔk] **1.** *nc* sudden and violent blow or shaking: *shock caused by an earthquake.* **2.** *nc* sudden and violent disturbance caused to the mind by great pain, hearing bad news etc. *The news of his father's death was a terrible shock to him.* **3.** *nu* condition of the body or mind caused by the disturbance of suffering great pain, hearing bad news etc: *be suffering from shock; in a state of shock.* **4.** *nc* feeling caused when a current of electricity passes through the body: *electric shock.* Also *vt* cause to feel sorrow, surprise, disgust, horror etc: *be shocked by someone's behaviour.*
shocking *adj* **1.** causing surprise and pain: *shocking news.* **2.** causing disgust or anger: *shocking behaviour.* **3.** very bad: *shocking handwriting.* **shockingly** *adv.*
'shock absorber device put into motorcars, aeroplanes etc to make the journey less bumpy when going over rough ground etc.
'shock tactics method of getting what one wants by a sudden and violent move.

shock[2] [ʃɔk] *nc* bundle of corn that has been cut, stood up on end in a field so as to dry.

shock[3] [ʃɔk] *nc* (usu. with reference to hair) thick, untidy mass.
'shock-headed *adj* having this type of hair.

shod [ʃɔd] past of **shoe.**

shoddy ['ʃɔdi] *adj* **1.** poorly made or done: *a shoddy piece of work.*

shoe [ʃu:] *nc* **1.** covering for the foot (usu. not going above the ankle). see **boot. 2.** horseshoe. see **horse. 3.** anything shaped or used like a shoe. Also *vt* put shoes on: *shoe a horse; well-/badly-shod* i.e. wearing good/poor shoes. *past* **shod** [ʃɔd].
'shoelace string, long piece of leather etc used for tying up a shoe.
in someone's shoes in someone's place. *If I were in your shoes, I wouldn't trust that fellow.* (*informal*).
on a shoestring very cheaply. *When he was away from home, he managed to live on a shoestring.* (*informal*).

shone [ʃɔn] past of **shine.**

shoo [ʃu:] *interj* noise made in driving a small animal etc away from one. Also *vt* drive away using this noise: *shoo a cat away.* *past* **shooed.**

shook [ʃuk] past tense of **shake.**

shoot [ʃu:t] *vt/i* **1.** fire a bullet from a gun or an arrow from a bow; injure or kill someone in this way: *shoot someone in the shoulder. He was shot in the street. Tell them to stop shooting.* **2.** move very quickly. *A pain shot up my leg. He shot out of the room. He shot out his hand.* **3.** photograph: *shoot a scene for a film.* *past* **shot** [ʃɔt]. Also *nc* **1.** young growth on a plant; young branch on a tree. **2.** group organized for shooting or hunting.

shooting *nc/u* act of shooting. *Did you hear about the shooting?*
shooting star small, quickly-moving body in the sky which burns brightly as it passes through the earth's atmosphere.
shoot one's bolt do all that one can and be unable to do any more. *You have nothing more to fear from him – he has shot his bolt.*

shop [ʃɔp] *nc* **1.** building, or part of a building, where things are sold; place where some service is given for money: *chemist's shop; barber's shop.* **2.** workshop i.e. place where things are made or repaired by machinery: *engineering shop.* Also *vt/i* **1.** go into shops to buy things: *spend a morning shopping; go shopping for clothes.* **2.** betray. *He shopped his friend to the police.* (*informal* in sense **2.**). *past* **shopped.**
shopper *nc* person who shops (in sense **1.**).
shopping *nu* action of going to shops to buy things.
'shop assistant person who serves customers in a shop.
'shopkeeper person who owns a shop.
'shoplifter *nc* person who steals things from a shop. **shoplifting** *nu.*
'shop-soiled, 'shop-worn *adj* not completely clean or new because it has been handled in a shop.
'shop 'steward official of a trade union working in a factory etc.
'shopwalker person in a large shop who walks about to see that customers are properly attended to.
'shop 'window piece of glass in front of a shop, and the area behind the glass used to show goods. *I want the coat in the shop window.*
'shopping centre area where many shops are grouped together.
'shopping spree act of buying many things. (*informal*).
'closed 'shop factory etc where only workers who belong to a trade union are allowed to work.
shop around look in various shops etc for what one wants so as to buy the cheapest or the best.
all over the shop **1.** here and there; not properly arranged. *My clothes are all over the shop.* **2.** everywhere: *look for something all over the shop.* (*informal*).
set up shop start trading in something: *set up shop as a grocer.*
shut up shop stop whatever one is doing (usu. work) (*informal*).
talk shop see **talk.**

shore[1] [ʃɔː*] *nc* land at the edge of the sea or a lake: *the shores of Britain; jump onto the shore from a boat.*

shore[2] [ʃɔː*] *nc* long piece of wood placed against the side of a wall, or a ship on dry land etc, to prevent it from falling over.
shore something up support something by placing long pieces of wood etc against it.

shorn [ʃɔːn] past part of **shear.**

short [ʃɔːt] *adj* **1.** not long; measuring little from one end to the other; lasting a little time: *short stick; short rest; short memory.* (*opp* **long**). **2.** not tall; less than the usual height: *short grass; short man.* (*opp* **tall**). **3.** less than the correct amount. *Our group is two people short. He gave me short change* i.e. less than the correct amount of money. **4.** saying so little that one is impolite; very brief and therefore impolite: *be short with someone; give someone a short answer.* Also *adv* suddenly. *He stopped short when he saw the strange sight.*
shortage *nc/u* lack of something; amount by which something is lacking or needed: *large shortage/not much shortage of food.*
shorten *vt/i* make or become shorter: *shorten one's stay in a place.*
shortening *nu* fat used for making pastry, biscuits etc.
shortly *adv* **1.** soon. *He will be arriving shortly.* **2.** in a few words. **3.** briefly and impolitely: *answer someone shortly.* **shortness** *nu.*
shorts *npl* type of short trousers worn while playing sports or sometimes on other occasions in hot countries.
'shortbread type of sweet biscuit.
'short-'circuit *nc* condition in which an electrical current escapes, instead of going through a circuit. Also *vi*: *The kettle short-circuited.*
'shortcoming *nc* (usu. *pl*) fault; weakness. *Like everyone else, he has his shortcomings.*
'short cut see **cut**[2].
'shorthand quick way of writing down speech by using special signs: *shorthand typist* i.e. someone who can type and also knows shorthand.
'short-'handed *adj/adv* not having enough workers. *When he left we were short-handed for a time.*
'short-'lived *adj* not lasting a long time. *His interest in camping as a hobby was short-lived.*
'short-'sighted *adj* **1.** having poor eyesight (for distant objects). **2.** not looking far enough into the future: *a short-sighted plan.* **short-sightedly** *adv.*
'short 'story printed or written story, shorter than a novel.
'short-'tempered *adj* easily made angry.
'short wave (radio) sound wave measuring from 11-75 metres (in Britain).
cut something short see **cut**[1].
fall short of see **fall**[2].
for short as a shorter form; to save time or effort. *A person whose name is Nicholas may be sometimes called Nick for short.*
go short of do with less. *She went short of food in order to have something for her children.*
in short in a few words.
the long and the short of it see **long**[1].
run short of come almost to the end of. *We have run short of food* i.e. there is very little left.

shot[1] [ʃɔt] past of **shoot.**

shot[2] [ʃɔt] *nc* **1.** firing of a gun etc: *fire several shots.* **2.** sound made by a gun firing: *hear a shot.* **3.** (used as *pl* or *nu*) very small balls of lead fired from a gun, used in hunting small animals: *lead shot.* **4.** attempt; try: *make/have a shot at (doing) something.* **5.** person who shoots: *be a good shot* i.e. skilful in using a gun. **6.** injection. *The doctor gave him a shot of morphine to ease the pain.* (*informal* in sense **6.**).
'shotgun gun used for firing shot (in sense **3.**).
like a shot very quickly: *accept something like a shot.* (*informal*).
a long shot something which will probably not succeed. (*informal*).
out of/within earshot see **ear.**

shot[3] [ʃɔt] *adj* woven in a special way so that its colour changes according to the angle from which it is seen: *shot silk.*

should [ʃud] past of **shall.**
Note: as well as being the past tense of *shall,*

should has also other meanings. 1. ought to i.e. showing duty. *You should go back and say you're sorry.* 2. to show that the speaker is not certain. *I should say that about thirty people were there.* 3. to show that something is likely. *Your brother should be home by now.* 4. used with *who, what etc* to show surprise. *Who should be there but Charles, whom I hadn't seen for ten years.*

shoulder ['ʃouldə*] *nc* 1. part of the body between the top of the arm and the neck; part of an animal or bird that joins the leg or wing to the body. 2. anything like a shoulder in shape: *shoulder of a mountain.* Also *vt* 1. put on the shoulder: *shoulder a sack.* 2. push with the shoulders: *shoulder one's way through a crowd.* 3. accept; bear: *shoulder a responsibility.*

shoulders *npl* upper part of the back, including the two shoulders.

'**shoulder blade** one of the two large, flat bones on the upper part of the back.

shoulder to shoulder side by side; united against an enemy.

straight from the shoulder without concealing anything; truthfully. (*informal*).

shout [ʃaut] *vt/i* 1. give a loud cry: *shout with joy/excitement/pain.* 2. say something loudly: *shout a warning to someone. 'Stand still!' he shouted.* Also *nc* loud cry: *give a shout.* **shouting** *nu.*

shout someone down cry out loudly so that someone does not have a chance to be heard.

shove [ʃʌv] *vt/i* push. Also *nc.* (both *informal*).

shove off *vt/i* 1. go away. (*informal*). 2. push (a boat) from the shore etc.

shovel ['ʃʌvl] *nc* 1. tool with a handle and broad blade, as in the illustration, used for moving materials like coal, snow, sand etc. 2. any similar tool: *mechanical shovel.* Also *vt/i* 1. work using a shovel. 2. move something with a shovel: *shovel coal.* 3. make something using a shovel: *shovel a path. past* **shovelled.** (*US* **shoveled**).

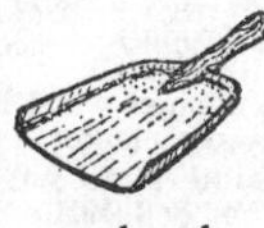

shovel

shovelful *nc* amount that can be taken up in a shovel.

show[1] [ʃou] *vt/i* 1. cause something to be seen; let something be seen. *He showed me his new car. He showed that he was very proud of his son.* 2. make something clear. *He showed me where I had gone wrong.* 3. guide or direct someone: *show someone the way* i.e. indicate where he has to go; *show someone to the door* i.e. go with him so that he finds the way out easily. see also **show someone the door.** 4. give: *show mercy on someone; show kindness to someone.* 5. appear. *Anger showed on her face. past tense* **showed.** *past part* **shown** [ʃoun].

showmanship *nu* behaviour which attracts attention to oneself.

'**showplace** interesting or beautiful place that people like to see.

'**showdown** *nc* occasion when someone has to state truthfully what his thoughts and feelings are. *If it comes to a showdown, I'll certainly tell him what I think of him.* (*informal*).

show off try to impress others by showing one's wealth, importance or anything one is proud of: *a man who is always showing off.* '**show-off** person who behaves in this way. (*informal*).

show up 1. cause the truth about someone/something to be known. *My questions showed him up as a cheat.* 2. cause to be seen more easily. *The bright light showed up the dirtiness of the room.* 3. come, go somewhere. *He was invited, but didn't show up.* (*informal* in sense 3.).

have nothing to show for it/something have no benefit now from one's efforts. *I have worked hard all my life, but I have nothing to show for it.*

show one's cards/hand show one's real aims or intentions.

show someone the door tell someone to leave one's house, and make sure that he goes. see **show**[1] (in sense 3.).

show one's face allow oneself to be seen. *That scoundrel daren't show his face in my house again.* (*informal*).

show fight show that one is willing to resist someone/something.

show oneself appear; allow oneself to be seen. *He is wanted by the police, so he is afraid to show himself in his home town.*

show[2] [ʃou] 1. *nc* act of showing: *vote by a show of hands* i.e. approve by putting up one's hand. 2. *nc* exhibition of something; public display: *horse show; flower show.* 3. *nc* play, film or other entertainment. *Did you enjoy the show?* 4. *nu* things intended to impress other people: *be fond of show.* 5. *nu* appearance; false appearance: *show of honesty.*

showing *nc* (usu. with **a**) display; show: *make a poor showing* i.e. give a bad impression.

showy *adj* intended to impress others: *a showy display of wealth.* **showily** *adv.* **showiness** *nu.*

'**show business** entertainment industry (e.g. cinema, the theatre etc).

for show with the intention of impressing others.

give the show away reveal something which was supposed to be secret. (*informal*).

put up a good/poor show do something well/badly. (*informal*).

shower ['ʃauə*] *nc* 1. short fall of rain. *Don't bother about your coat – it's only a shower.* 2. number of things coming at the same time: *shower of arrows/letters etc.* 3. pipe with a device which sprays water on one like rain; act of washing oneself in this way: *go for a shower.* (Also **shower bath**). 4. (*US*) party given for a girl who is going to get married, at which time she is given small gifts. Also *vt/i* 1. rain for a short time. 2. come or send all at once.

showery *adj* with showers falling frequently: *showery weather.*

shrank [ʃræŋk] past tense of **shrink.**

shrapnel ['ʃræpnl] *nu* type of shell filled with small pieces of metal, designed so that it will explode in the air and scatter the pieces over a wide area: *injured by shrapnel.*

shred [ʃred] *nc* 1. small piece torn or cut off: *shirt torn to shreds.* 2. small bit or piece of anything: *not a shred of evidence against the prisoner.* Also *vt/i* tear into small pieces; become small pieces. *past* **shredded.**

shrew [ʃru:] *nc* 1. small animal like a mouse

but with a pointed nose. **2.** bad-tempered, scolding woman.

shrewish *adj* (with reference to a woman) bad-tempered and scolding.

shrewd [ʃru:d] *adj* **1.** having a keen mind; having good judgment in business matters etc: *a shrewd businessman.* **2.** well-informed; clever: *make a shrewd guess.* **shrewdly** *adv.* **shrewdness** *nu.*

shriek [ʃri:k] *nc* loud, sharp cry: *a shriek of fright.* Also *vt/i* make a loud, sharp cry; say something in a loud, sharp way.

shrift [ʃrift] *nu* act of telling one's sins to a priest (*o.f.*).

give short shrift to someone/something spend little time attending to someone/something.

shrill [ʃril] *adj* high and sharp in sound: *a shrill cry.* **shrillness** *nu.*

shrimp [ʃrimp] *nc* **1.** type of small shellfish, with ten legs, taken as food. **2.** very small person. (*informal* in sense **2.**).

shrine [ʃrain] *nc* **1.** box which contains a holy object. **2.** building which is connected with some holy person/thing.

shrink [ʃriŋk] *vt/i* **1.** become or make smaller: *a shirt that will not shrink when it is washed.* **2.** draw back from something/someone that one does not like. *Usually even a hardened criminal will shrink from committing murder. past tense* **shrank** [ʃræŋk]. *past part* **shrunk** [ʃrʌŋk].

shrinkage *nu* **1.** act of shrinking. **2.** amount of shrinking.

shrivel ['ʃrivl] *vt/i* make or become twisted and dried up: *plant shrivelled with heat; person shrivelled with age. past* **shrivelled.** (*US* **shriveled**).

shroud [ʃraud] *nc* **1.** cloth that is wrapped round a dead body. **2.** something that hides or covers: *a shroud of mist.* Also *vt* **1.** wrap a shroud round a corpse. **2.** make something difficult to see or understand: *a crime shrouded in mystery.*

shrouds *npl* ropes on a ship which help to support the mast.

shrub [ʃrʌb] *nc* bush; type of plant like a tree, with branches and leaves, but much smaller.

shrubbery *nc* place where many bushes are planted.

shrug [ʃrʌg] *vt/i* raise one's shoulders to show that one is not interested or does not know or does not care. *I asked him for his advice, but he just shrugged. past* **shrugged.** Also *nc* this kind of movement.

shrug something off treat something serious as though it were not serious.

shrunk [ʃrʌŋk] past part of **shrink.**

shudder ['ʃʌdə*] *vi* shake suddenly with horror, fear, cold etc. Also *nc* this kind of movement: *give a shudder.*

shuffle ['ʃʌfl] *vt/i* **1.** walk without lifting one's feet. *The feeble old man was shuffling along the street.* **2.** mix up the order of playing cards (usu. before starting a game): *shuffle the cards.* **3.** not give a direct reply to questions; say one thing and then another. Also *nc* **1.** *walk with a shuffle.* **2.** *give the cards another shuffle.*

shun [ʃʌn] *vt* keep away from; avoid meeting: *shun bad company. pres part* **shunning.** *past* **shunned.**

shunt [ʃʌnt] *vt/i* move a train from one set of tracks to another; move in this way.

shut [ʃʌt] *vt/i* **1.** close: *shut a door, window etc.* **2.** be closed. *This window won't shut.* **3.** stop someone from entering or leaving by closing a door etc or putting up some kind of barrier: *shut someone out; be shut in all day. pres part* **shutting.** *past* **shut.**

shut something down close something so that no work is done in it; stop working: *shut down a factory. The factory has shut down.*

'shutdown *nc* closing of a factory in this way.

shut something off 1. close; prevent people entering: *shut off a certain street.* **2.** stop: *shut off the water supply.*

shut up stop talking. *Tell him to shut up.* (*informal*).

shut something/someone up 1. close all the doors and windows of: *shut up the house.* **2.** prevent from going out: *be shut up in the house.*

shutter ['ʃʌtə*] *nc* **1.** movable cover made of wood, metal etc which can be put over a window to keep out sunlight, cold, thieves etc. **2.** part of a camera which can be opened to allow a certain amount of light through the lens.

shuttle ['ʃʌtl] *nc* **1.** part of a machine for making cloth that carries the thread from one side of the machine to the other. **2.** part of a sewing machine which brings threads together for making stitches. Also *vt/i* move quickly from one place to another and back again.

'shuttlecock piece of cork with small feathers stuck into one side, used in playing certain net games.

'shuttle service quick regular service of buses, trains etc between two places that are usu. not very far from one another.

shy[1] [ʃai] *adj* **1.** uncomfortable, not at ease, in the company of other people (esp. strangers). **2.** easily frightened; timid. *The wild animals here are rather shy because they are not used to people.* Also *vi* (with reference to horses) move suddenly to one side. *The horse shied when it saw the snake. pres part* **shying.** *past* **shied** [ʃaid]. **shyly** *adv.* **shyness** *nu.*

fight shy of something see **fight**[2].

shy[2] [ʃai] *vt* throw: *shy a stone at something.* Also *nc.* (both *informal*).

sick [sik] *adj* **1.** ill; unwell.

Note: (*Brit*) the normal word is *ill* (e.g. *He has been ill for six months*). (*US*) *sick* is commonly used in the sense of *ill.*

2. (*Brit*) faint and giddy; vomiting i.e. throwing up food from the stomach. *The baby was sick twice in the car. I think I'm going to be sick.* **3.** mentally unhealthy: *a sick mind; a sick joke.*

sicken *vt/i* **1.** become ill (*o.f.*). **2.** make ill; disgust. *The sight of so much cruelty sickened him.*

sickening *adj* disgusting: *sickening cruelty.*

sickly *adj* **1.** ill; unwell. **2.** often ill: *a sickly child.* **3.** causing sickness or disgust: *sickly smell.* **4.** weak: *sickly smile* i.e. not a very happy smile.

sickness 1. *nu* bad health: *several absences due to sickness.* **2.** *nc/u* illness; disease: *seasickness.*

the sick *npl* those who are ill: *tend to the sick.*

'sickbed bed of a sick person.

'sickroom room where a sick person is; room kept for those who are sick.

fall sick become ill.

sick at very unhappy about. *I am sick at the way he has been treated.*

sick for longing for.

sick of tired of, bored or annoyed by.
sickle ['sikl] *nc* tool with a curved blade as in the illustration, used for cutting grass etc.

sickle

side [said] *nc* **1.** one of the surfaces of an object. *He painted all four sides of the box.* **2.** one of the surfaces of an object but not the top or bottom, front or back: *go in by the side of the building.* **3.** one of the two surfaces of paper, cloth etc: *write on one side of the paper.* **4.** one of the inside or outside surfaces of something: *the side of the room.* **5.** area thought of in connection with central point or line: *left-hand side of the room; east side of the city.* **6.** group playing against, or in disagreement with, another group: *get both sides in an argument to agree; be on someone's side* i.e. agree or sympathize with him. **7.** either the left-hand or right-hand part of a human being, animal etc: *be wounded in the side* i.e. on the side of the body somewhere between the waist and the shoulder. **8.** part of a family; line of descent. *He is French on his mother's side.* **9.** aspect; way of looking at a question or problem: *a problem with many sides to it; look on the bright side of life.* Also *adj* at the side of something: *enter by a side door.*
siding *nc* short railway track beside the main one, where trains can stay without holding up the main line.
'**sideboard** (*Brit*) **1.** piece of furniture with drawers and shelves, used in the dining room or living room to hold dishes etc. **2.** (usu. *pl*) hair growing down the cheek of a man. (*US* **sideburn**).
'**sidecar** small, one-wheeled car for a single passenger, attached to the side of a motorcycle.
'**side issue** point of discussion which is not as important as something else which is being discussed. *I think that the point you have just raised is really a side issue.*
'**sideline** **1.** line at the side of a football pitch etc. **2.** something else from which one earns money in addition to one's main job: *do photography as a sideline.*
'**sidelong** *adj* to or from the side: *a sidelong glance* i.e. made without turning one's head; *a sidelong movement.*
'**side road** less important road which leads off a main road.
'**sidestep** *vt/i* **1.** avoid something by moving a little to one side: *sidestep a blow.* **2.** avoid anything: *sidestep a question* i.e. not answer it. *past* **sidestepped.** Also *nc.*
'**sidetrack** *vt* **1.** put a train into a siding. **2.** turn someone from what he was originally intending to do. Also *nc.*
'**sidewalk** (*US*) place to walk on at the side of a street. (*Brit* **pavement**).
'**sideways** *adv* **1.** from, towards one side: *look sideways at someone.* **2.** with the side first: *bring something sideways through a narrow door.*
side with someone/something support; feel sympathy with.
on/from all sides everywhere; from every direction. *His plan was greeted enthusiastically on all sides.*
take sides with someone support one group or person against another.
sidle ['saidl] *vi* approach or leave a person as if not wishing to draw too much attention to oneself: *sidle up to someone.*
siege [si:dʒ] *nc* act of surrounding a town in order to capture it (usu. by cutting off its supplies).
lay siege to surround with an army in order to capture.
siesta [si'estə] *nc* rest taken during the hottest part of the day.
sieve [siv] *nc* frame with wire or plastic netting as in the illustration, used to separate liquids from solids and large pieces of something (e.g. flour etc) from smaller pieces. Also *vt* separate large pieces of something from small ones in this way. see **sift.**

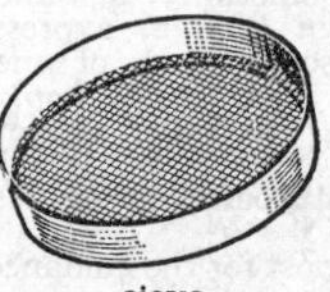
sieve

sift [sift] *vt/i* **1.** put or come through a sieve: *sift flour/grain etc.* **2.** come as if from a sieve. **3.** examine very carefully: *sift the evidence.*
sigh [sai] *vt/i* **1.** let out a deep breath, as when one is tired, sad, no longer anxious etc: *sigh with relief.* **2.** make a sound like sighing: *the wind sighing outside.* **3.** express something by sighing: *sigh one's relief.* Also *nc* act of sighing; sound of a sigh: *heave a sigh.*
sigh for something long for: *sigh for one's native land.*
sight [sait] **1.** *nu* power of seeing: *lose one's sight. My sight is improving.* **2.** *nc* something seen (esp. something worth seeing in a particular area): *see the sights of the city; beautiful/terrible sight.* **3.** *nu* act of seeing or being seen: *be overjoyed by the sight of a loved one; at first sight* i.e. on seeing someone/something for the first time. **4.** *nc* device on a gun etc which helps one to aim or observe. **5.** (always with **a**) something that looks strange. *What a sight she looks in those clothes!* (*informal* in sense **5.**). Also *vt* **1.** see. *At last the explorers sighted land.* **2.** observe something or aim a gun etc, with the help of a special device. *He sighted the gun on the target.*
'**sightseer** *nc* person looking at interesting buildings etc. **sightseeing** *nu.*
'**second** '**sight** power to see things which have not yet happened, or are happening some distance away.
at the sight of at the moment of seeing. *At the sight of the police they ran away.*
catch sight of see **catch**[1].
in/within sight able to be seen. *There was not a soul in sight* i.e. nobody to be seen.
in/within sight of able to see: *be within sight of land.*
know someone by sight know someone by seeing him only and not by having spoken to him etc.
let someone out of one's sight let someone go unobserved. *Never let him out of your sight for a moment* i.e. watch him constantly.
lose sight of see **lose.**
out of sight not able to be seen. *Land was already out of sight.*

out of sight of not able to see: *be out of sight of land. Get out of my sight* i.e. I don't want to see you any longer.

a sight for sore eyes someone/something one is very glad to see. (*informal*).

sign [sain] *nc* **1.** mark which stands for something or points out something: *mathematical signs* i.e. signs like +, ÷ and so on; *traffic sign.* **2.** movement which stands for a word or idea: *use signs to communicate with a person who speaks only a foreign language.* **3.** indication; something which reveals a fact to the person that observes it. *White hair is often a sign of old age. We searched for the ring, but there was no sign of it anywhere.* **4.** something which shows what is going to happen. *A cloudy sky is often a sign of rain.* Also *vt/i* **1.** write one's name on something: *sign a letter/cheque etc. Please sign here.* **2.** express an idea by making some kind of movement. *The policeman signed us to stop.* **3.** accept employment. *The sailor signed (on) for three years.*

'signboard board having a sign or notice on it.

'signpost post for the guidance of travellers, placed on a road or at a crossroads, with the names of places attached to it.

signal[1] ['signl] *nc* any kind of mark, light, sound, movement etc which gives an idea to someone, or controls his actions in some way: *traffic signals* i.e. coloured lights controlling traffic; *give a signal that one wishes to stop. A red light is a signal of danger.* Also *vt/i* **1.** make a signal or signals. **2.** express something by using a signal or signals: *signal an urgent message. past* **signalled.** (*US* **signaled**).

signaller (*US* **signaler**) *nc* person skilled in sending messages.

'signal box building from which railway signals are worked.

'signalman 1. person who controls railway signals. **2.** person who sends signals in the navy.

signal[2] ['signl] *attrib adj* remarkable: *signal victory/defeat etc.* **signally** *adv.*

signalize *vt* make something stand out: *signalize a victory by having a public holiday.*

signatory ['signətəri] *nc* person or country that signs an agreement or treaty. Also *adj.*

signature ['signətʃə*] *nc* person's name written by himself: *recognize someone's signature.*

signet ['signət] *nc* usu. in **signet ring** i.e. ring worn on the finger, having a design and formerly used for sealing letters.

signify ['signifai] *vt/i* **1.** mean; be a sign of. *What does that remark signify?* **2.** show by some sign: *signify approval by nodding one's head.* **3.** be of importance: *signify little/much.*

significance [sig'nifikəns] *nu* meaning; importance: *something of great significance.*

significant [sig'nifikənt] *adj* **1.** important: *significant victory.* (*opp* **insignificant**). **2.** having a special meaning: *give a significant look.* **significantly** *adv.*

signification [signifi'keiʃən] meaning; sense: *the signification of a word.*

silage ['sailidʒ] *nu* green food for cattle stored in a silo.

silence ['sailns] **1.** *nc/u* quietness; absence of sound: *the silence of a deserted street.* **2.** *nu* state of not speaking: *listen in silence.* Also *vt* make silent.

silencer *nc* device that makes something quieter: *silencer of a car/gun etc.*

silent ['sailnt] *adj* **1.** quiet; without a sound. *The forest was silent.* **2.** not speaking; not in the habit of saying much: *tell someone to be silent; silent person.* **3.** not pronounced. *The 'h' is silent in 'hour'.* **silently** *adv.*

silhouette [silu:'et] *nc/u* **1.** picture in solid black of a person/thing. **2.** anything seen against a light background as a solid black shape. Also *vt* show dark against a lighter background: *trees silhouetted against the setting sun.*

silhouette (*def 1*)

silica ['silikə] *nu* hard substance found in sand, flint, quartz etc.

silk [silk] *nc* fine thread spun by a special type of insect (called a **silkworm**) and made into a fine cloth: *clothes made of silk.* Also *adj*: *a silk dress.*

silken *adj* smooth, soft and shiny, like silk; made of silk (*o.f.* – use **silky, silk**).

silky *adj* smooth, soft and shiny, like silk.

'silkworm caterpillar that spins silk.

sill [sil] *nc* flat piece of wood or stone across the bottom of a window.

silly ['sili] *adj* foolish: *a silly thing to do.* **silliness** *nu.*

silo ['sailou] *nc* building or deep pit into which grass etc is put which will provide food (called **silage**) for cattle.

silt [silt] *nu* fine earth and sand which is left by a river. Also *vt/i* stop up with silt; be stopped up with silt: *a river that has silted up.*

silver ['silvə*] *nu* **1.** shining, white, precious metal used for making ornaments, spoons etc. **2.** coins, knives, spoons, bowls etc made of silver. Also *adj* **1.** made of silver; like silver in colour. **2.** having a clear sound: *silver tones.* Also *vt* cover with silver or something that looks like silver.

silvery *adj* **1.** like silver. **2.** having a clear sound.

silver jubilee/wedding see **jubilee.**

similar ['similə*] *adj* like; not different from: *two similar houses; a car that is similar to another one.* (*opp* **dissimilar**). **similarly** *adv.*

similarity [simi'læriti] **1.** *nu* state of being similar. *There is not much similarity between the two brothers.* **2.** *nc* point of resemblance. *Have you noticed any similarities between them?*

simile ['simili] *nc/u* (example of) way of using words so that one thing is compared to another because of something they have in common (e.g. *He fought like a wild animal. He is as rich as a king*). see **metaphor.**

simmer ['simə*] *vt/i* **1.** boil gently. **2.** keep a feeling under control with difficulty: *simmer with anger.*

simper ['simpə*] *vi* smile in a silly way. Also *nc* silly smile.

simple ['simpl] *adj* **1.** easy; not difficult: *a simple problem; explain something in simple*

language. **2.** with only a few parts; not complicated: *a simple machine.* **3.** plain; bare; with nothing added: *the simple truth; lead a simple life; simple clothes.* **4.** weak in the mind; stupid.
simpleton ['simpltn] *nc* foolish person.
simplicity [sim'plisiti] *nu* state of being simple.
simplify ['simplifai] *vt* make simpler or easier.
simplification [simplifi'keiʃən] **1.** *nu* act of simplifying. **2.** *nc* something simplified.
simply *adv* **1.** in a simple way: *live simply.* **2.** only. *We want a boy who is not simply intelligent but also hard-working.*

simulate ['simjuleit] *vt* pretend to be or to have: *simulate enthusiasm.* **simulation** [simju'leiʃən] *nu.*

simultaneous [siməl'teiniəs] *adj* happening or done at the same time. **simultaneously** *adv.* **simultaneity** [siməltə'neiəti] *nu.*

sin [sin] **1.** *nc/u* act of breaking the laws of God: *commit sin; guilty of many sins.* **2.** *nc* act which is thought to be wrong. *It's a sin to waste food when so many people are starving.* Also *vi* **1.** break the laws of God. **2.** do something wrong: *sin against good taste. past* **sinned.**
sinful *adj* wrong; wicked: *sinful deed; sinful man.* **sinfully** *adv.* **sinfulness** *nu.*
sinless *adj* free from sin.
sinner *nc* person who commits sin.

since [sins] *prep* **1.** from a past time until the present without a break. *I have been waiting here since nine o'clock.* **2.** between some time in the past and now. *I haven't heard from him since he left England.* Also *adv*: *He left this morning and hasn't been home since. He left his native village twenty years ago and has since returned only twice.* Also *conj* **1.** from the time when. *Tell me what sort of work you have done since you left school.* **2.** because. *Since you are so very tired, I'll drive you home.*
Note: in all the above meanings of *since* connected with a length of time i.e. all the meanings except the last one, note the use of *since* with the perfect tense (e.g. *have been waiting, haven't heard etc*).

sincere [sin'siə*] *adj* **1.** real; not pretended: *a sincere speech.* **2.** meaning what one says; not deceitful: *a sincere friend.* (*opp* **insincere**). **sincerely** *adv.* **sincerity** [sin'seriti] *nu.*

sinecure ['sinikjuə*] *nc* job requiring little or no work, but usu. one which is well paid.

sinew ['sinju:] *nc* strong cord in the body joining a muscle to a bone: *strain a sinew.*
sinews *npl* muscles; strength.
sinewy *adj* strong; powerful.

sing [siŋ] *vt/i* **1.** make a musical sound with the voice (usu. with words): *sing a song.* **2.** make pleasant sounds. *The birds were singing.* **3.** make any kind of whistling, buzzing or humming sound. *The kettle was singing on the fire. My ears are singing* i.e. they have a kind of buzzing sound in them. *past tense* **sang** [sæŋ]. *past part* **sung** [sʌŋ]. **singer** *nc.*
singing *nu* sound of singing; act of singing; skill in singing: *hear singing; teach singing.*
'singsong *n sing* **1.** meeting of people to sing songs together: *have a singsong.* **2.** continuous up and down movement in the voice: *speak in a singsong.* Also *adj*: *in a singsong voice.*
sing up sing more loudly.

singe [sindʒ] *vi* burn slightly: *singe a shirt while ironing it.* Also *nc* small burn.

single ['siŋgl] *adj* **1.** one and not more: *not a single person there* i.e. no one there at all. **2.** for one only: *single room/bed etc.* **3.** not married: *remain single.* Also *nc* **1.** ticket for a journey in one direction only i.e. not a return ticket. see **single ticket. 2.** (often *pl*) (tennis etc) match in which only one person plays on each side.
singly *adv* one by one; separately. **singleness** *nu.*
single file *nc/u* one after the other: *walk in single file.*
'single-'handed *adj/adv* done by one person by himself.
'single-'minded *adj* giving all one's attention to one thing only. **single-mindedness** *nu.*
'single ticket (*Brit*) ticket on bus, train etc which is for one journey in one direction only. (*US* **one-way ticket**).
single someone/something out choose one person/thing from others.

singlet ['siŋglit] *nc* vest; light garment worn under the shirt.

singular ['siŋgjulə*] *adj* **1.** unusual; extraordinary: *man of singular courage; singular event.* **2.** (grammar) form used in referring to one person/thing (e.g. *boy* is singular, but *boys* is plural). **singularly** *adv.* **singularity** [siŋgju'læriti] *nc/u.*

sinister ['sinistə*] *adj* promising evil; threatening: *sinister look. There was a sinister air about the old house.*

sink [siŋk] *vt/i* **1.** go downwards. *The ship struck a rock, and sank. The boat sank to the bottom of the river. The sun was sinking in the west. The injured man sank to his knees.* **2.** make a ship etc go under water. *The enemy air force has sunk all our ships.* **3.** become worse. *Our spirits sank* i.e. we became more unhappy. **4.** enter. *The warning sank into his mind.* **5.** put one's money into a business etc (usu. without success). *past tense* **sank** [sæŋk]. *past part* **sunk** [sʌŋk]. see also **sunken.** Also *nc* fixed basin for washing dishes etc, with a pipe to take away the dirty water.
sinkable *adj* that can be sunk. (*opp* **unsinkable**).
sinker *nc* weight used to make a fishing line or net sink.
sinking feeling unpleasant feeling caused by a fear, disappointment etc. (*informal*).
'sinking fund money which is put aside by a government, business company etc to pay off a large debt.
sink a well dig a well.

Sino- ['sainou] *prefix* Chinese (e.g. **Sino-Soviet**).

sinuous ['sinjuəs] *adj* not straight; twisting and curving. **sinuously** *adv.*

sinus ['sainəs] *nc* part of the inside of the head, behind the nose.

sip [sip] *vt/i* drink by taking a small amount at a time. *The child sipped the cup of tea. past* **sipped.** Also *nc* small amount taken in sipping: *sip of medicine.*

siphon, syphon ['saifən] *nc* **1.** bent tube with one arm lower than the other, used for drawing liquid out of one container and putting it into another. **2.** bottle filled with soda water, which can be pushed out of a tube by the force of the gas that is in the bottle. Also *vt/i* **1.** draw out by using a siphon: *siphon off some liquid.* **2.** pass through a siphon.

sir [sə:*] *n* **1.** respectful way of talking to an older man, someone in authority etc. **2.**

(**Sir**) title of a knight: *Sir Walter Scott.*

sire ['saiə*] *nc* **1.** (esp. with reference to horses) father. **2.** old-fashioned form of **sir.** Also *vt* (usu. with reference to horses) be the father of.

siren ['saiərn] *nc* **1.** instrument which produces a loud noise to give warning of something. *Ships use their sirens in thick fog.* **2.** (in ancient Greek stories) woman who attracted ships to destruction by the sweetness of her singing. **3.** woman who is attractive to men.

sirloin ['sə:lɔin] *nc/u* beef cut from between the ribs and hipbones.

sisal ['saizl] *nu* plant which is used for making rope, twine etc.

sissy ['sisi] *nc* boy who is rather like a girl in his behaviour. (*informal*).

sister ['sistə*] *nc* **1.** daughter of one or both of one's parents. *Mary and Jane Brown are sisters.* **2.** (**Sister**) member of a religious order; nun: *Sisters of Charity.* **3.** nurse who is in charge of a ward in a hospital.

sisterly *adj* of or like a sister (in sense **1.**).

sisterhood *nc* **1.** number of women who have joined together to perform good works. **2.** women's religious order.

'sister-in-law *nc* sister of one's wife or husband; wife of one's brother; wife of the brother of one's wife or husband. *pl* **sisters-in-law.**

sit [sit] *vt/i* **1.** let the weight of the body rest on the buttocks: *sit on a chair/the floor etc.* **2.** (with reference to a court, committee etc) hold meetings; be in action. *Is the court sitting today?* **3.** be a member of Parliament or other elected government: *sit in Parliament.* **4.** rest or perch. *Birds were sitting on the wires.* **5.** cover eggs so that they will hatch. *The hen was sitting on her eggs.* **6.** fit. *pres part* **sitting.** *past* **sat** [sæt].

sitting *nc* **1.** act of resting, as on a chair. **2.** meeting of a court, committee etc: *the next sitting of Parliament.* **3.** period in which one works at something without stopping. *He wrote the story at one sitting.*

'sitting 'duck target which is easy to hit. (*informal*).

'sitting room room in a house, used for relaxing in etc.

sit back rest after working hard.

'sit-down 'strike refusal of workers to leave the place where they work until they get what they want.

sit (for) an examination take an examination.

sit for one's portrait have a picture of oneself painted by an artist.

'sit-in *nc* form of strike, in which workers refuse to leave their place of work.

sit on a jury etc be a member of a jury etc.

sit up 1. take up the sitting position after lying down, leaning etc. *The injured man is now able to sit up in bed.* **2.** not go to bed. *He sat up with the sick child night after night.*

make someone sit up make someone angry, frightened, excited etc. (*informal*).

site [sait] *nc* place where something has happened or will happen: *site of a new building.* Also *vt* put on a site: *site a new building in the centre of the town.*

situate ['sitjueit] *vt* **1.** place: *a town situated near the coast.* **2.** in certain circumstances. *How is he situated?* i.e. what are his circumstances? **situated** *adj.*

situation [sitju'eiʃən] *nc* **1.** place: *a good situation for building a house.* **2.** circumstances; condition. *The situation after the storm was very bad.* **3.** job: *situations vacant.*

six [siks] see appendix.

at sixes and sevens in confusion. (*informal*).

size[1] [saiz] **1.** *nu* largeness or smallness of something: *size of a room, a town etc.* **2.** *nc* measurement of how large clothes etc are (usu. expressed by a number). *What size does he take in shoes? What size shoes does he take? He takes size 7.* Also *vt* arrange according to size.

sizable *adj* fairly large.

size someone/something up understand someone/something very well. (*informal*).

size[2] [saiz] *nu* sticky liquid used to put a smooth surface on paper, plastered walls etc.

sizzle ['sizl] *vi* make a hissing sound, as when something is being fried in fat. Also *n sing.*

skate[1] [skeit] *nc* **1.** sharp blade which can be attached to a boot, for moving quickly over ice. **2.** boot with this kind of blade attached to it. **3.** see **roller skate.** Also *vi* move on skates. **skater** *nc.*

skate[1] (*defs 1 & 2*)

'skating rink place where people skate as a form of entertainment.

skate[2] [skeit] *nc* kind of large, flat fish.

skein [skein] *nc* length of wool or silk which has been folded up into a bundle.

skeleton ['skelitn] *nc* **1.** framework of bones inside the body of a human being or animal. **2.** framework of bones of a human being or animal, without the flesh. **3.** outline of the main parts of a building, idea, plan etc. Also *adj* having very few people: *skeleton crew, staff etc.*

'skeleton key key made to open many different locks.

skeptic ['skeptik] *adj* see **sceptic.**

sketch [sketʃ] *nc* **1.** quickly-made drawing, painting etc. **2.** short description. **3.** short play (usu. humorous). Also *vt/i* **1.** draw a sketch of something. **2.** make sketches.

sketchy *adj* not complete; done roughly or quickly. **sketchily** *adv.*

sketch something out describe roughly and quickly; draw a rough plan of.

skewer ['skju:ə*] *nc* long kind of pin made of wood or metal, used for keeping meat together while it is being cooked. Also *vt* fasten something by using a skewer, or something like a skewer.

ski [ski:] *nc* one of a pair of long, narrow pieces of wood etc attached to a person's boots, so that he can move easily over snow. Also *vi* move over snow by using skis. *past* **skied** [ski:d].

skiing *nu* sport of moving over snow using skis.

'water-ski *nc* type of ski used for moving over water. Also *vi.* **water-skiing** *nu.*

skid [skid] *vi* slide sideways. *The car skidded on the icy road. past* **skidded.** Also *nc* **1.** act of sliding sideways. *The car went into a skid.* **2.** piece of wood or metal on a cart etc which prevents the wheels from turning, and so slows it down as it is going down a hill etc.

skiff [skif] *nc* small, light boat.

skill [skil] *nc/u* ability to do something well by training or practice. *What skills has he got? He does not have very much skill in writing.*

skilled *adj* **1.** trained in some special ability: *skilled workman.* **2.** requiring some special ability: *skilled job.* (*opp* **unskilled**).

skilful (*US* **skillful**) *adj* having skill: *a skilful surgeon.* (*opp* **unskilful**). **skilfully** *adv.*

skim [skim] *vt/i* **1.** remove something from the top of a liquid: *skim milk* i.e. remove the cream; *skim the cream from the milk.* **2.** move quickly over a surface, touching it very lightly; move quickly a small way above. *The low-flying plane seemed to skim the rooftops.* **3.** read through something very quickly. *past* **skimmed.**

'skim 'milk, 'skimmed 'milk milk from which the cream has been removed.

skimp [skimp] *vt/i* **1.** not supply enough of something; not use enough of something: *skimp one's food in order to save money.*

skimpy *adj* **1.** not giving enough; not using enough. **2.** too small: *a skimpy dress.* **skimpily** *adv.*

skin [skin] **1.** *nu* outer covering of the body. **2.** *nc* outer covering of an animal, with or without the fur. **3.** *nc* container for liquids, made from the skin of an animal. **4.** *nc* outer covering of fruit: *banana skin.*

Note: with certain fruits use peel (e.g. *apple peel*).

Also *vt/i* take the skin off: *skin an animal. past* **skinned.**

skinny *adj* very thin: *skinny person.* (*informal*).

'skin-'deep *adj* on the surface; not very deep or serious.

'skin diving *nu* sport of diving under the sea, wearing special breathing apparatus. **skin diver** *nc.*

'skinflint miser; someone who is mean with money. (*informal*).

skin and bones very thin. *The poor child was just skin and bones.* (*informal*).

escape by the skin of one's teeth only just manage to escape. (*informal*).

keep one's eyes skinned watch very carefully. (*informal*).

save one's skin escape from danger; avoid being captured. (*informal*).

have a thick skin see **thick.**

skip [skip] *vt/i* **1.** jump with a short, light step. **2.** jump over a rope swung to pass under the feet. **3.** miss out something; miss out a part of a book that one is reading: *skip a few pages. past* **skipped.** Also *nc* act of skipping.

'skipping rope piece of rope used for skipping (in sense **2.**).

skipper ['skipə*] *nc* **1.** captain of a ship. **2.** captain of a sports team. (*informal* in sense **2.**). Also *vt* act as a skipper for.

skirmish ['skə:miʃ] *nc* fight, often not planned, between small groups of soldiers etc. Also *vi* take part in a skirmish.

skirt [skə:t] *nc* **1.** woman's garment that hangs from the waist; part of a dress from the waist downwards. **2.** border; edge. Also *vt* be, lie, go along the edge of: *road that skirts the city.*

'skirting board (*Brit*) length of wood that goes along the bottom of a wall in a room. (*US* **baseboard**).

skit [skit] *nc* short play or other piece of writing which imitates something in order to make fun of it.

skittish ['skitiʃ] *adj* playful; easily excited: *a skittish horse; in a skittish mood.* **skittishly** *adv.*

skittle ['skitl] *nc* one of the nine bottle-shaped pieces of wood which are knocked down with a ball in the game of skittles.

skittles *nu* game played using skittles.

skulk [skʌlk] *vi* move about trying to avoid being seen, in order to avoid danger or work, or for some bad purpose.

skull [skʌl] *nc* bony part of the head.

'skullcap head covering without a brim which fits tightly over the head.

skull and cross bones sign or flag formerly used by pirates.

skunk [skʌŋk] **1.** *nc* small black and white animal which gives off an unpleasant smell if it is frightened or attacked. **2.** *nu* fur of this animal. **3.** *nc* unpleasant person. (*informal* in sense **3.**).

sky [skai] *nc/u* space above the earth where we see clouds, the sun, moon, stars etc. *The sky is cloudy today. There are millions of stars in the sky. There should be a clear sky tonight. There is a difference between cold northern climates and the blue skies of the tropics.* Also *vt* hit a ball high in the air.

Note: as a noun this word is usu. *sing* and used with *the* (*the sky*), except when there is an *adj* in front of sky when *a/an* is used (*a clear sky*); it can also be used in the *pl* (*the skies; the blue skies*).

'sky-'high *adv* very high; up in the sky. *The bridge was blown sky-high by the explosion.* (*informal*).

'skylark kind of small bird that sings sweetly as it flies up into the sky.

'skylight window in a roof (usu. level with the roof).

'skyscraper very high building.

slab [slæb] *nc* large, flat piece of stone etc.

slack [slæk] *adj* **1.** not tight or stretched: *slack rope.* **2.** not busy; not active: *slack time of the year for business.* **3.** not working hard; lazy; careless: *a slack employee.* Also *nu* coaldust. Also *vi* be lazy or careless. *You must stop slacking.* **slackly** *adv.* **slackness** *nu.*

slacker *nc* person who tries to avoid hard work.

the slack part of a rope etc which is loose.

slacken *vt/i* **1.** make or become slower: *slacken one's pace* i.e. walk, run etc more slowly. **2.** make or become looser: *slacken a rope.*

slacks *npl* **1.** kind of trousers worn on informal occasions. **2.** kind of trousers worn by women.

slag [slæg] *nu* waste matter left when ore is melted down to take out the metal.

slain [slein] past part of **slay.**

slake [sleik] *vt* satisfy thirst etc (not hunger): *slake one's thirst; slake one's wish for revenge.*

'slaked 'lime lime to which water has been added, used with sand for joining bricks together.

slalom ['slɑ:ləm] *nc* ski race around obstacles.

slam [slæm] *vt/i* **1.** close or shut with a loud sound. *He angrily slammed the door behind him. The window slammed shut.* **2.** throw or hit something using great force. *He slammed the book down on the table. past* **slammed.** Also *nc* loud noise made by something being closed, hit etc with force.

slander ['slɑːndə*] **1.** *nc* untrue statement made to harm someone's reputation. **2.** *nu* act of spreading such untrue statements: *be accused of slander.* Also *vt* make untrue statements about someone in order to harm him: *slander someone.* **slanderer** *nc.*
slanderous *adj* **1.** containing slander. **2.** spreading slander.
slang [slæŋ] *nu* words and phrases often heard in everyday speech, but not suitable for formal or serious occasions (esp. words and phrases used only by a certain group of people): *schoolboy slang; army slang.*
slangy *adj* using or containing slang.
slant [slɑːnt] *vt/i* **1.** slope. **2.** change something slightly in order to favour a certain point of view: *slant a report.* Also *nc* **1.** slope. **2.** attitude; way of looking at things.
slap [slæp] *nc* blow with the open hand or with something flat. Also *vt* **1.** hit with the open hand or something flat: *slap someone on the back.* **2.** put something down with a slapping sound. *She slapped the money down on the table.* *past* **slapped.**
'slap-'happy, 'slapdash *adj* careless; untidy. (*informal*).
'slapstick *nu* film, play etc containing much foolish and violent comedy. Also *adj.*
slash [slæʃ] *vt/i* **1.** cut with a long, sweeping stroke: *slash grass.* **2.** whip. **3.** cut down, reduce severely: *slash expenditure* i.e. reduce what is spent. Also *nc* **1.** act of slashing. **2.** cut or wound made by slashing.
slat [slæt] *nc* thin, narrow piece of wood or metal.
slate [sleit] **1.** *nu* bluish-grey rock which breaks easily into thin sheets. **2.** *nc* thin piece of this rock used for covering the roofs of houses, or for writing on. **3.** *nc* (*US*) list of candidates for an appointment. Also *vt* **1.** cover a roof with slates. **2.** say that someone/something is very bad. *The critics slated his latest play.* **3.** (*US*) put someone's name down on a list of candidates.
slaty *adj* like slate; containing slate.
slating *nc* bad report: *give someone a slating.* (*informal*).
slattern ['slætn] *nc* woman who is dirty and careless in her appearance and behaviour. **slatternly** *adj.*
slaughter ['slɔːtə*] *nu* **1.** killing of animals. **2.** killing of many people at the same time. Also *vt.*
'slaughterhouse place where animals are killed for food.
slave [sleiv] *nc* **1.** person who is owned by another and has to work for him for nothing. **2.** person who is under the control of some habit or belief etc: *slave to drink; slave to duty.* Also *vi* work very hard: *slave at one's work; slave for one's living.*
slaver[1] *nc* **1.** person who deals in slaves. **2.** ship used for carrying slaves.
slavery *nu* **1.** condition of being a slave: *be sold into slavery.* **2.** system of having slaves: *abolition of slavery.* **3.** hard work that is badly paid.
slavish *adj* **1.** weak; not resisting. **2.** not original; showing no independence: *slavish imitation.*
'slave driver 1. person in charge of slaves. **2.** person who forces those under him to work very hard. (*informal* in sense **2.**).
slaver[2] ['sleivə*] *vi* let saliva drip from the mouth.
slay [slei] *vt* kill with violence; murder. *past tense* **slew** [sluː]. *past part* **slain** [slein].
sled, sledge [sled(ʒ)] *nc* carriage which moves on two long, smooth pieces of metal or wood, instead of wheels, for use on ice or snow etc. Also *vt/i* carry or ride on a sledge.
sledgehammer ['sledʒhæmə*] *nc* large, heavy hammer. (Sometimes **sledge**).
sleek [sliːk] *adj* **1.** smooth and shiny: *sleek hair/fur etc.* **2.** having smooth and shiny hair or fur: *a sleek cat.* **3.** too neat or smooth in appearance or manner: *a sleek salesman.* Also *vt* make smooth.
sleep [sliːp] *vt/i* **1.** be unconscious or in a state of complete rest with the eyes closed, as people are in bed at night. *Did you sleep well? I sleep in this room.* **2.** have beds for: *hotel that sleeps thirty guests.* *past* **slept** [slept]. Also **1.** *nu* act of resting completely with the eyes closed, as people do in bed at night. **2.** *nc/u* (usu. with **a** or **an**) period of resting like this: *have a good sleep; a good night's sleep.*
sleeper *nc* **1.** person who is sleeping. **2.** one of the heavy pieces of wood used to support railway lines. **3.** railway carriage with beds in it. (Also **sleeping car**).
sleepless *adj* without sleep; not able to get sleep: *sleepless night.* **sleeplessly** *adv.* **sleeplessness** *nu.*
sleepy *adj* **1.** ready to sleep: *sleepy child.* **2.** very quiet: *sleepy little village.* **sleepily** *adv.* **sleepiness** *nu.*
'sleepwalker *nc* person who gets out of bed and walks about while he is still asleep. **sleepwalking** *nu.*
'sleeping bag 1. bag specially made to keep a person sleeping in it warm and dry (usu. while sleeping outdoors). **2.** warm bag for a baby to sleep in.
'sleeping car railway carriage with beds in it.
'sleeping draught drink with medicine in it to make a person sleep.
'sleeping partner (*Brit*) person who owns part of a business, but does not do any work in it. (*US* **silent partner**).
'sleeping pill pill to make a person sleep.
'sleeping sickness disease spread by the tsetse fly which can cause damage to the brain.
sleep in stay asleep or in bed after the time at which one normally gets up.
sleep something off get rid of something by sleeping: *sleep off a headache.*
sleep on go on sleeping. *She slept on in spite of the loud noise outside.*
sleep on it (e.g. a problem etc) not to make a decision on something until the following morning.
sleep like a log/top sleep without moving or any sign of life. *He was so tired that he slept like a log.*
sleet [sliːt] *nu* rain which is frozen or partly frozen. Also *vi.*
sleeve [sliːv] *nc* **1.** part of a garment which covers the arm: *sleeve of a coat/shirt etc.* **2.** cover of a gramophone record.
have something up one's sleeve have an idea, trick etc in reserve for when one needs it. (*informal*).
laugh up/in one's sleeve see **laugh**[1].
sleigh [slei] *nc* carriage which is pulled by horses across ice or snow, and has two long smooth pieces of metal or wood instead of wheels.
sleight [slait] *nc* only in **sleight of hand** i.e. quickness in using the hand to perform tricks etc.
slender ['slendə*] *adj* **1.** thin and graceful:

slender girl; slender waist. **2.** slight; not enough: *slender income; slender hope of success.* **slenderness** *nu.*

slept [slept] past of **sleep.**

sleuth [slu:θ] *nc* detective i.e. person who tries to solve crimes. (*informal*).

slew[1] [slu:] past tense of **slay.**

slew[2], **slue** [slu:] *vt/i* turn or twist round. *The car slewed round. He slewed his car round.*

slice [slais] *nc* **1.** thin, flat piece cut from something: *slice of bread/meat etc.* **2.** instrument like a knife, with a thin, broad blade, used for serving or separating cake, fish etc. Also *vt* cut into slices: *slice bread; slice off a piece of meat.*

slick [slik] *adj* smooth; clever (perhaps too clever): *slick move.* (*informal*). Also *nc* amount of oil etc on the surface of the sea. (Also **oilslick**). *Many birds are being killed by the oilslicks near our beaches.*

slide [slaid] *vt/i* **1.** move smoothly over: *slide on ice.* **2.** pass into a condition by small steps: *slide into bad habits.* **3.** pass without being noticed. *The days slid by. pres part* **sliding.** *past* **slid** [slid]. Also *nc* **1.** act of sliding. **2.** smooth surface (e.g. ice) for sliding on. **3.** device for sliding down, used by children. **4.** small, flat piece of glass on which things are put so that they can be easily examined through a microscope. **5.** coloured pictures for showing on a screen. **6.** large amount of earth, rock, snow etc which slides down a hill.

'slide rule instrument which looks like a ruler, used for making quick calculations.

'sliding 'scale scale by which one thing increases or decreases to keep in step with another. *Income tax is arranged on a sliding scale, so that the more you earn, the more you pay in tax.*

slight [slait] *adj* **1.** not important; small: *slight delay.* **2.** of small build; slender: *slight man.* Also *vt* treat someone as if he were unimportant; rudely ignore: *feel slighted.* Also *nc* rude behaviour; lack of proper attention.

slightly *adv* **1.** a little bit: *slightly better.* **2.** slenderly: *slightly built.*

slim [slim] *adj* **1.** thin; slender. *She eats very little in order to keep slim.* **2.** small; weak: *slim excuse.* Also *vi* become slim by eating less and/or taking exercise. *past* **slimmed.**

slime [slaim] *nu* **1.** soft, sticky matter (e.g. mud). **2.** sticky matter given off by snails etc.

slimy *adj* **1.** like slime; covered with slime. **2.** (of a person) nasty; disgusting. **sliminess** *nu.*

sling [sliŋ] *nc* **1.** piece of cloth etc which is fastened round the neck in order to keep an injured arm in position. **2.** rope, chain etc which is fastened round objects in order to lift or support them. **3.** thin piece of leather used for throwing stones. Also *vt/i* **1.** throw something using a sling (in sense **3.**). **2.** throw, using the hand. (*informal*). **3.** lift or support something with a sling (in sense **2.**). *past* **slung** [slʌŋ].

slink [sliŋk] *vi* move quietly so as not to be seen. *He was slinking away from the scene of his crime. past* **slunk** [slʌŋk].

slip [slip] *vt/i* **1.** slide without wanting to; slide and fall: *slip on a patch of ice.* **2.** move quickly or quietly. *He slipped out of the room, while the others were talking. I slipped him a note* i.e. gave it to him this way. *He slipped off his jacket.* **3.** go without being noticed. *Time slipped by. His name has slipped my mind.* **4.** escape from; fall from. *The plate slipped from her fingers.* **5.** make a small mistake. *past* **slipped.** Also *nc* **1.** act of slipping. **2.** small mistake: *slip of the tongue* i.e. mistake of saying something one did not intend. **3.** covering that can be quickly slipped on and off: *pillowslip.* **4.** light, sleeveless garment worn by a woman under her dress. **5.** small piece of paper.

slipper *nc* type of loose, comfortable shoe (usu. worn indoors).

slippery *adj* **1.** smooth enough to cause one to slip. *The roads are slippery with ice.* **2.** not to be trusted: *slippery customer* i.e. a person who cannot be trusted. (*informal*). **slippy** *adj.* (*informal*). **slipperiness** *nu.*

slips *npl* sloping area beside the water where ships are built or repaired, so that they can easily slide into the sea when they are finished. (Also **slipway**).

'slipshod *adj* careless (esp. in the way one dresses or behaves).

'slipstream air forced backwards by the forward movement of an object (e.g. an aeroplane).

'slipway see **slips** above.

slip up make a mistake. (*informal*).

'slip-up *nc* mistake. (*informal*).

slip of a girl young girl. (*informal* and sometimes rather *impolite*).

give someone the slip escape from. *He gave the men chasing him the slip.*

slit [slit] *nc* long, narrow cut or hole. Also *vt/i* make a long narrow cut in; tear in a straight line: *slit someone's throat; slit open an envelope. pres part* **slitting.** *past* **slit.**

slither ['sliðə*] *vi* **1.** slide unsteadily. *He was slithering about on the icy surface.* **2.** slide like a snake.

slob [slɔb] *nc* stupid and useless man. (*informal*).

slobber ['slɔbə*] *vt/i* let liquid run from the mouth. Also *nu.*

slog [slɔg] *vt/i* **1.** hit hard. **2.** walk on steadily in difficult circumstances. **3.** work hard. *past* **slogged. slogger** *nc.*

slogan ['slougən] *nc* easily remembered word or phrase used by a political group, business firm etc to represent its policy, what it is selling etc. *The party's new slogan was 'Higher wages for everyone'.*

sloop [slu:p] *nc* **1.** small sailing ship with one mast. **2.** type of small warship.

slop [slɔp] *vt/i* **1.** (of liquids) flow, let flow, over the edge of a container; spill. *The tea slopped out of the cup. She slopped the coffee onto the saucer. past* **slopped.**

sloppy *adj* **1.** careless. *The schoolboy was warned about presenting sloppy work.* **2.** weak and silly: *sloppy, sentimental stories.* (*informal*). **3.** wet; muddy.

slops *npl* **1.** dirty water from a kitchen or bedroom. **2.** liquid food for sick people.

slope [sloup] **1.** *nc* surface, line etc which is at an angle i.e. neither straight up and down nor flat: *slope of a hill.* **2.** *nu* amount of steepness of such a surface. Also *vt/i* be at, cause to be at, an angle. *The land sloped down to the sea. The sergeant ordered the soldiers to slope arms* i.e. rest their rifles on their shoulders.

slot [slɔt] *nc* small, narrow hole for putting or fitting something into. Also *vt/i* make a slot or slots in. *past* **slotted.**

'slot machine machine which will deliver something (e.g. cigarettes) if a coin is put into a slot.

sloth [slouθ] **1.** *nu* laziness. **2.** *nc* type of

slow-moving animal of South America, which hangs upside down in trees.

slothful *adj* lazy.

slouch [slautʃ] *vi* stand, sit or move in a lazy, ungraceful way: *be slouched over a table.* Also *nc* act of standing, moving, etc in this way.

slough[1] [slau] *nc* wet, muddy place.

slough[2] [slʌf] *nc* **1.** old skin thrown off by a snake. **2.** dead skin which falls off a wound etc. Also *vt/i* throw off: *snake that has sloughed off its skin; slough off one's bad habits.*

slovenly ['slʌvənli] *adj* dirty; careless: *slovenly dress/appearance/work etc.* **slovenliness** *nu.*

sloven *nc* slovenly person.

slow[1] [slou] *adj* **1.** not fast; taking more time than should be necessary: *slow journey; slow train* i.e. one that has many stops. **2.** not clever: *slow pupil.* **3.** (with reference to a clock etc) show an earlier time than it should. *My watch is slow. It is five minutes slow.* Also *vt/i* (often with **down** or **up**) go, cause to go, at a slower speed. *Slow down when you come to the main road.* **slowly** *adv.* **slowness** *nu.*

'slowcoach person who is slow in thinking or acting. (*informal*).

in slow motion at less than its usual speed: *a film in slow motion.*

slow[2] [slou] *adv* slowly. *Try to go slow here.* *Note: slow* is not used so commonly as *slowly*, and can only be used in certain positions or phrases.

go slow see **go.**

sludge [slʌdʒ] *nu* **1.** thick mud. **2.** thick waste matter from houses etc. **sludgy** *adj.*

slue [slu:] *vt/i* see **slew**[2].

slug[1] [slʌg] *nc* slow-moving creature like a snail, but without a shell.

slug[2] [slʌg] *vt* hit (a person) with a heavy blow. (*informal*).

sluggard ['slʌgəd] *nc* lazy person.

sluggish ['slʌgiʃ] *adj* slow-moving; lazy. **sluggishly** *adv.*

sluice [slu:s] *nc* **1.** kind of gate which can be closed to hold back the water of a canal, river etc or opened to let it through. **2.** channel for carrying off water. Also *vt/i* **1.** throw water over; clean with a flow of water. **2.** flow out in a stream.

slum [slʌm] *nc* street or building in a crowded, dirty part of a town. Also *vi* visit an area where slums are. **slummy** *adj.*

the slums *npl* crowded, dirty part of a town.

slumber ['slʌmbə*] *vi* sleep. Also *nc* sleep. (both *o.f.*).

slump [slʌmp] *vi* **1.** fall heavily. *The injured man slumped to the floor.* **2.** fall steeply and suddenly. *Business slumped after the war, and so did prices.* Also *nc* period when business or employment decreases.

slung [slʌŋ] past of **sling.**

slunk [slʌŋk] past of **slink.**

slur [slə:*] *vt/i* **1.** say something in an unclear way. *The drunk man slurred his words.* **2.** say very little about something in the hope that it will not be noticed. *He slurred over the faults of his friends.* **3.** run notes together in a piece of music. *past* **slurred.** Also *nc* **1.** something said against someone; insult: *a slur on his character.* **2.** act of slurring. **3.** (music) the mark ⌢ or ⌣ which shows that notes have to be slurred.

slush [slʌʃ] *nc* **1.** snow that has partly melted. **2.** silly talk or writing which shows too much emotion. **slushy** *adj.*

slut [slʌt] *nc* dirty, careless woman; immoral woman. **sluttish** *adj.*

sly [slai] *adj* **1.** acting in a clever, untruthful way. **2.** playful; mischievous: *sly wink.* **slyly** *adv.* **slyness** *nu.*

smack[1] [smæk] *nc* **1.** taste; flavour. **2.** suggestion. Also *vi* suggest; give an idea of. *What he said smacks of dishonesty.*

smack/lick one's lips show one is enjoying something or is looking forward to enjoying something. *The hungry man smacked his lips when he saw the food.*

smack[2] [smæk] *nc* **1.** blow given with the flat of the hand. **2.** sound made by a blow like this. Also *vt* hit with the flat of the hand: *smack a child.* Also *adv* suddenly and directly: *run smack into a wall.*

smack[3] [smæk] *nc* type of small sailing boat used for fishing.

small [smɔ:l] *adj* **1.** not large; little: *small town; small amount of money; small boy.* **2.** not important. *That is a small matter.* **3.** very little. *He worked hard, so it is small wonder that he has done well.* **4.** not very rich; not in business in a big way: *small farmer.* **smallness** *nu.*

smalls *npl* articles of underclothing for washing. (*informal*).

'small-arms guns or other weapons which can easily be carried.

'small 'change copper and silver coins. *I have about £2 in small change.*

'small fry *npl* small children; people of little importance. (*informal*).

'small hours early hours of the morning (between, say, 1 a.m. and 4 a.m.): *talk into the small hours.*

'smallpox type of disease, which is easily spread, and which often leaves marks on the skin which do not go away.

'small talk see **talk.**

'small-'time *adj* not important. (*informal*)

small of the back narrowest part of the back.

feel/look small feel/appear ashamed and humiliated.

in a small way not in an outstanding or remarkable manner. *He collects paintings in a small way.*

on the small side rather small.

smart[1] [smɑ:t] *adj* **1.** neat; well-dressed. *She looks smart in her new dress.* **2.** clever: *smart child.* **3.** fashionable: *smart hotels.* **4.** quick: *at a smart pace.* **smartly** *adv.* **smartness** *nu.*

smarten something up make neater: *smarten up one's appearance.*

smart[2] [smɑ:t] *vi* **1.** feel stinging pain. *My eyes were smarting from the smoke.* **2.** feel anger, disappointment etc: *be smarting from a defeat.* Also *nc.*

smash [smæʃ] *vt/i* **1.** break into pieces: *smash a pane of glass.* **2.** be broken into small pieces. *The cup smashed on the floor.* **3.** completely defeat: *smash an attack.* **4.** become ruined. *His business smashed.* Also *nc* **1.** sound of something breaking into pieces. **2.** act of smashing: *car smash.* **3.** business failure.

smash-and-grab raid raid by thieves smashing or breaking a shop window and grabbing the goods inside.

smattering ['smætəriŋ] *nc* (usu. with **a**) slight knowledge: *have a smattering of Greek.*

smear [smiə*] *vt/i* **1.** mark by spreading with something oily or dirty. *He smeared* *the window with his dirty hands. You must smear this ointment over the wound.* **2.** spread and make a mark: *ink that smears easily.* **3.** hurt someone's good name by spreading false stories about him. Also *nc* **1.** mark left by smearing. **2.** false story told to smear someone.

smell [smel] *vt/i* **1.** become aware of by using one's nose. *I smell something cooking.* **2.** put the nose near in order to receive a sensation. *I can't smell these flowers.* **3.** give out a smell. *This food smells nice.* **4.** give out a bad smell. *The food that has been lying there is smelling. past* **smelt.** Also **1.** *nu* power of smelling. *Sight, smell and touch are three of the five senses.* **2.** *nc/u* what is noticed by the sense of smell: *nice smell; smell of cheese.* **3.** *nc* what is noticed by the sense of smell as unpleasant. *There is a smell in the kitchen.*

smelly *adj* with an unpleasant smell.

'smelling salts medicine with a strong smell which is held to the nose of someone who is feeling faint.

smell of something have a smell which one recognizes, or which reminds one of something. *This room smells of tobacco.*

smell something out find by using the sense of smell. *The dogs smelt out the rabbit.*

smelt[1] [smelt] past of **smell.**

smelt[2] [smelt] *vt* melt rock in order to get the metal from it: *smelt iron ore* i.e. rock etc containing iron.

smelter *nc* apparatus for smelting.

smelt[3] [smelt] *nc/u* type of small sea fish. *pl* **smelts** or **smelt.**

smile [smail] *vt/i* **1.** look pleased or amused by curving the mouth upwards: *smile happily.* **2.** show how one feels by smiling. *Her father smiled his approval.* **3.** drive away by smiling: *smile one's troubles away.* Also *nc* act of smiling. **smilingly** *adv.*

smirch [smə:tʃ] *vt* **1.** harm someone's good name. **2.** make dirty. Also *nc* disgrace to someone's good name.

smirk [smə:k] *vi* smile in a silly or self-satisfied way. Also *nc* this type of smile.

smite [smait] *vt/i* hit; strike; defeat (*o.f.*). *pres part* **smiting.** *past tense* **smote** [smout]. *past part* **smitten** ['smitn].

smitten with/by someone (only used humorously) attracted by: *be smitten with a certain girl.*

smith [smiθ] *nc* **1.** person who works with metal: *goldsmith; silversmith.* **2.** blacksmith. see **black.**

smithy ['smiði] *nc* place where a blacksmith works.

smock [smɔk] *nc* loose outer garment. Also *vt* sew (a dress etc) in a closely-drawn, honeycomb pattern.

smog [smɔg] *nu* mixture of smoke and fog in the air.

smoke [smouk] **1.** *nu* cloud of gases etc which rises when anything burns: *smoke from a wood fire.* **2.** *nc* act of smoking tobacco: *have a smoke.* **3.** *nc* cigarette, cigar etc. (*informal* in sense **3.**). Also *vt/i* **1.** give out smoke: *an oil lamp that is smoking; a fire that is smoking* i.e. the smoke from the fire is going into the room instead of up the chimney. **2.** draw in smoke from a cigarette, cigar, pipe etc through the mouth, then blow it out again. **3.** use cigarettes etc regularly. *Do you smoke?* **4.** dry fish or meat so as to preserve it and give it a special flavour. **5.** colour or darken with smoke: *smoked glasses.*

smoker *nc* person who smokes tobacco.

smoky *adj* **1.** giving off smoke; full of smoke. **2.** like smoke.

smokeless *adj* **1.** burning without smoke: *smokeless fuel.* **2.** free from smoke: *smokeless zone* i.e. area where fuels giving out smoke must not be used.

'smoke screen cloud of thick smoke made so as to hide the movements of a ship, soldiers etc.

'smokestack **1.** high chimney. **2.** funnel on a ship which gives out smoke and steam.

smolder ['smouldə*] *vi US* form of **smoulder.**

smooth [smu:ð] *adj* **1.** with an even surface, like glass: *as smooth as silk.* **2.** not rough: *smooth sail.* **3.** friendly and polite, but perhaps not sincere: *smooth talker.* Also *vt/i* **1.** make smooth: *smooth matters down; smooth a dress that has been crushed.* **2.** become smooth. *Wait until things have smoothed down* i.e. until there is less excitement. Also *nu.*

smoothly *adv* in a smooth manner. *The meeting went very smoothly* i.e. there was no trouble. **smoothness** *nu.*

'smooth-'tongued *adj* friendly, but not sincere.

smote [smout] past tense of **smite.**

smother ['smʌðə*] *vt/i* **1.** kill by keeping air from. **2.** cover thickly with: *smother the child with kisses; cake smothered in cream.* **3.** put out a fire, or make it burn more slowly, by covering it with something. **4.** conceal, hide, suppress: *smother a yawn.*

smoulder ['smouldə*] (*US* **smolder**) *vi* **1.** burn slowly, giving off smoke but no flame. **2.** show a strong emotion. *His eyes smouldered with anger.* Also *nu* slow burning without flame.

smudge [smʌdʒ] *nc* **1.** dirty mark. **2.** mark left by ink that has been rubbed while wet. Also *vt/i.*

smug [smʌg] *adj* too pleased with oneself; self-satisfied. **smugly** *adv.* **smugness** *nu.*

smuggle ['smʌgl] *vt/i* **1.** get something into another country secretly and illegally: *smuggle stolen goods into the country; smuggle something through the customs.* **2.** get something/someone into or out of a place secretly. **smuggling** *nu.*

smuggler *nc* person who gets money from smuggling goods.

smut [smʌt] **1.** *nc* piece of dirt from burning coal etc; black mark made by a piece of dirt. **2.** *nu* indecency in thought or language.

smutty *adj* **1.** dirty with smuts. **2.** indecent in thought or language.

snack [snæk] *nc* light, quickly-taken meal.

'snack bar place where such meals can be taken.

snag [snæg] *nc* **1.** unexpected difficulty. **2.** tree or branch hidden in the water, and therefore dangerous to boats.

snail [sneil] *nc* small creature with a shell on its back, as in the illustration, which moves very slowly.

snail

snake [sneik] *nc* long, thin, crawling reptile

with no legs and sometimes with a poisonous bite.

snaky *adj* **1.** like a snake. **2.** containing many snakes. **3.** twisting and turning.

snap [snæp] *vt/i* **1.** make a short, sharp sound, like a thin piece of wood breaking. **2.** break suddenly into two pieces. *The rope snapped.* **3.** say something quickly and harshly: *snap a command.* **4.** quickly take a photograph of someone. *past* **snapped.** Also *nc* **1.** short, sharp sound: *the snap of a branch breaking.* **2.** act of snapping. **3.** snapshot. see below. (*informal* in sense **3.**). Also *adj* done quickly: *make a snap judgment.*

snappy *adj* smart; lively. (*informal*).

'snapshot quickly-taken photograph.

snap at someone **1.** speak suddenly and angrily to someone. **2.** try to bite. *The dog snapped at the postman's legs.*

snap something up take quickly: *snap up a bargain.* (*informal*).

cold snap short period of cold weather.

snare [snɛə*] *nc* **1.** device with a loop for catching small animals and birds. **2.** trap, trick. Also *vt.*

snarl [snɑːl] *vt/i* **1.** growl and show the teeth. *The dog snarled at the stranger.* **2.** say in a very angry manner: *snarl a command.* Also *nc* act or sound of snarling.

snatch [snætʃ] *vt* **1.** take quickly and violently. *The thief snatched the handbag and ran away.* **2.** take quickly while one has the opportunity: *snatch a few hours' sleep.* Also *nc* **1.** act of snatching. **2.** short period or amount: *hear a snatch of song.*

snatch at something **1.** try to get by snatching. *The child snatched at anything within reach.* **2.** quickly take advantage of: *snatch at an opportunity.*

sneak [sniːk] *vt/i* **1.** move in a quiet and secret manner: *sneak past a sentry.* **2.** give or take something in a secret manner so that it will not be seen. **3.** inform on someone who has done wrong. (*informal*). **4.** steal. (*informal*). Also *nc* cowardly, untrustworthy person.

sneer [sniə*] *vi* show contempt by one's expression or by what one says: *sneer at someone/something.* Also *nc* expression or words which show one's contempt. **sneering** *adj.*

sneeze [sniːz] *nc* sudden expelling of air through the mouth and nose which one cannot control. Also *vi* give a sneeze.

not to be sneezed at to be treated as important. *An opportunity like this is not to be sneezed at.* (*informal*).

sniff [snif] *vt/i* **1.** breathe in air through the nose in a way that can be heard (often done as a sign of contempt). **2.** smell in this way. *The dog sniffed (at) the lamppost; sniff the sea air.* Also *nc* act or sound of sniffing.

snigger ['snigə*] *nc* type of quiet laugh, often showing disrespect. Also *vi* laugh in this way.

snip [snip] *vt/i* cut with scissors with short cuts: *snip off a piece of cloth.* Also *nc* **1.** act of snipping. **2.** small piece snipped off. **3.** something bought for less than its true value; bargain. (*informal* in sense **3.**).

snipe[1] [snaip] *nc* type of small water bird with a very long beak. *pl* **snipe.**

snipe[2] [snaip] *vt/i* shoot (an enemy) from a place where one cannot be seen. **sniping** *nu.*

sniper *nc* someone who shoots in this way.

snippet ['snipit] *nc* **1.** small piece cut off: *snippet of cloth.* **2.** (often *pl*) small piece of writing, news, information etc.

snivel ['snivl] *vi* complain while crying. *past* **snivelled.** (*US* **sniveled**). **snivelling** *nu.*

snob [snɔb] *nc* person who cares only for people who are rich or of high birth. **snobbery, snobbishness** *nu.* **snobbish** *adj.* **snobbishly** *adv.*

snooker ['snuːkə*] *nu* (*Brit*) game played with coloured balls which have to be knocked into pockets at the side of a table. (*US* **pool**).

snoop [snuːp] *vi* spy on other people. *Someone came snooping round the house today.* **snooper** *nc.* (both *informal*).

snooze [snuːz] *nc* short period of sleep. Also *vi* have a snooze. (both *informal*).

snore [snɔː*] *vi* breathe with a loud noise while sleeping. Also *nc* sound made in this way. **snoring** *nu.*

snorkel ['snɔːkl] *nc* see **schnorkel.**

snort [snɔːt] *vt/i* **1.** force air violently through the nose. *The horse snorted.* **2.** do this to show anger, contempt etc: *snort with rage.* **3.** say something with a snort. Also *nc* **1.** sound made when snorting. **2.** act of snorting.

snout [snaut] *nc* **1.** nose of an animal: *pig's snout.* **2.** anything like this.

snow[1] [snou] *nu* **1.** water in the air which becomes frozen and falls to the ground in little, soft, white pieces. **2.** mass of these white pieces lying on the ground: *street covered in snow.* Also *vi*: *It has been snowing all day.*

snowy *adj* **1.** having snow; covered with snow. **2.** white, like snow.

'snowball *nc* **1.** ball made of snow pressed together for throwing in play. **2.** something which gets bigger as it goes on. Also *vi* get bigger as time goes on. *Support for the president is snowballing.*

'snow-blind *adj* not able to see for a time because of the light reflected from snow. **snow blindness** *nu.*

'snow-capped *adj* having the top covered in snow: *snow-capped mountains.*

'snowdrift heap of snow piled up by the wind.

'snowdrop type of plant with small, white flowers, which often blooms before the last of the snow has disappeared.

'snowflake small piece of falling snow.

'snow line level above which snow is lying all the time.

'snowman figure which looks like a man made out of snow.

'snowplough (*US* **snow plow**) device for clearing snow away from roads, railway lines etc.

'snowshoe light wooden frame, as in the illustration, placed under ordinary shoes to prevent the wearer from sinking into soft snow.

snowshoes

snub[1] [snʌb] *vt* refuse to notice. *past* **snubbed.** Also *nc* act of treating someone/something in this way.

snub[2] [snʌb] *adj* only in **snub nose** i.e. nose which is short and turned up at the tip. **'snub-nosed** *adj*.

snuff[1] [snʌf] *nu* powdered tobacco, drawn up the nose: *take snuff*. Also *vt/i* sniff; draw in through the nose.

snuff[2] [snʌf] *vt/i* **1.** take off the top burnt part of a candle. **2.** put out a candle.

snuffle ['snʌfl] *vi* breathe noisily (e.g. when the nose is partly blocked). Also *nc* act or sound of snuffling.

snug [snʌg] *adj* warm and comfortable. **snugly** *adv*. **snugness** *nu*.

snuggle ['snʌgl] *vi* (usu. with **up**) come close to someone/something for warmth and comfort. *The child snuggled up to its mother.*

so[1] [sou] *adv/intensifier* **1.** in this way; in that way. *You must stand so.* **2.** also. *I like football and so does he. Jane was there and so was John.* (*opp* **neither**: *Jane wasn't there and neither was John*). **3.** to such an extent. *Don't talk so much. He shouldn't drive so fast. Jane is not so clever as John is. He is not so ill as I thought. He was so angry that he hit her. He ran so fast that we couldn't catch up with him.* **4.** very; very much. *You are so kind. That is so true* i.e. to show that one completely agrees. (*informal*). **5.** it is true (agreeing with what someone has said). *He is very kind. So he is. John was there too. So he was. I suppose so. So I hear.* **6.** approximately; about. *He walked for a mile or so.* *Note:* apart from the informal uses in sense **4.** *so* cannot normally be used to mean *very*. It is therefore better to say *He is very intelligent* or *They say he is not very well*, rather than use *so* in these sentences.

'so-and-so someone who does not have to be mentioned by name.

a 'so-and-so person whom one wishes to insult without using indecent language. (*informal*).

'so-'called *adj* only in name, not really.

'so-so *adj* not very good but not very bad.

and so on/forth and other things like that. *He sold papers, magazines, books and so forth.*

without/not so much as without/not even. *The pupil left the class without so much as asking the teacher's permission.*

so as to with the result or purpose of. *He left early so as to be back on time.*

so far until now, yet. *I've been waiting for hours, but he hasn't come so far.*

so long as on the condition that. *The children were allowed to play so long as they did it quietly.*

so much merely; only; nothing but. *Everything he says is so much nonsense.*

so much for there is nothing more to be said or done about. *So much for that; let's talk about something else now.*

so[2] [sou] *conj* **1.** and for that reason; and therefore. *I had lost my pencil so I had to buy a new one. We walked quickly so the journey did not take us long.* **2.** as an exclamation. *So you've come back! So you think you're clever!*

soak [souk] *vt/i* **1.** make very wet or wet through. *I was caught in the rain and my clothes were soaked. If you want to take out the stain, soak the cloth in cold water.* **2.** become very wet or wet through. *Let the clothes soak in water overnight.* **3.** make wet by going through or into. *The rainwater has soaked through the roof.* **4.** take a lot of money from (by taxes etc): *policy of soaking the rich.* (*informal* in sense **4.**). Also *nc* **1.** act of soaking or being soaked. **2.** heavy drinker. (*informal* in sense **2.**).

soaking *adj* very wet.

soak something up **1.** take liquid into itself: *a sponge soaks up water.* **2.** take into one's mind: *soak up information.* (*informal* in sense **2.**).

soap [soup] *nu* material used with water to wash oneself, clothes etc. Also *vt* rub with soap: *soap oneself (down).*

soapy *adj* covered with soap.

'soapbox box or other platform used by someone speaking to a crowd at a street corner etc.

'soap bubble thin film of soap in the shape of a ball and filled with air.

'soapsuds mixture of soap and water forming tiny bubbles.

soar [sɔ:*] *vi* **1.** go or fly up very high: *a bird soaring into the sky.* **2.** rise very quickly: *soaring prices.*

sob [sɔb] *vt/i* **1.** draw in the breath while crying: *sob with grief.* **2.** say something while doing this: *sob an answer. past* **sobbed.** Also *nc* act or sound of sobbing.

sober ['soubə*] *adj* **1.** not drunk: *avoid drink and stay sober.* **2.** not bright: *sober colours.* **3.** calm; sensible; serious: *sober life; sober expression; sober opinion.* **soberly** *adv*. Also *vt/i* make or become sober.

sobriety [sou'braiəti] *nu* act or quality of being sober. (*opp* **insobriety**).

sober up recover, cause to recover, from drinking too much alcohol.

soccer ['sɔkə*] *nu* type of football in which the ball may not normally be touched by the hands, except by the goalkeeper. (Also **Association Football**).

sociable ['souʃəbl] *adj* friendly; fond of meeting other people. (*opp* **unsociable**). **sociably** *adv*. **sociability** [souʃə'biliti] *nu*.

social ['souʃl] *adj* **1.** living together in groups. *Bees are social insects. Man could be called a social animal.* **2.** having to do with people living in groups, or with people as part of society: *social problems such as crime and poverty.* **3.** having to do with being in the company of other people: *social evening; social club* i.e. one where people can meet new friends. Also *nc* friendly meeting or party. **socially** *adv*.

'social worker *nc* person whose work is concerned with trying to improve people's social conditions. **social work** *nu*.

socialism ['souʃəlizəm] *nu* belief that the main sources of a country's wealth (e.g. mines, large industries etc) should be owned by the government for the good of the people.

socialist *nc* person who believes in socialism.

socialistic [souʃə'listik] *adj* having to do with socialism (often used by opponents of socialism).

society [sə'saiəti] **1.** *nc* group of people who have joined together because of some interest they have in common: *debating society.* **2.** *nc* group of people living together who have certain beliefs, customs etc in common: *Western society; African society.* **3.** *nu* company: *in the society of one's friends.* **4.** *nu* way that people live together having certain rules and customs: *work for the good of society.* **5.** *nu* people who are wealthy or of high birth.

sociology [sousi'ɔlədʒi] *nu* study of society (in sense **4.**) and its development. **sociological** [sousiə'lɔdʒikl] *adj*. **sociologist** *nc*.

sock[1] [sɔk] *nc* short covering for the foot and part of the leg; short stocking: *pair of socks*.
Note: men usu. wear *socks*; women usu. wear *stockings*.
sock[2] [sɔk] *nc* blow. Also *vt* hit. (both *informal*).
socket ['sɔkit] *nc* hollow in which something fits or turns: *lamp socket; socket of the eye*.
sod[1] [sɔd] *nc* piece of earth with grass on it.
sod[2] [sɔd] *nc* term of abuse. (*informal*).
soda ['soudə] **1.** *nu* name given to various types of chemical material used for washing, baking and many other things: *washing soda; baking soda*. **2.** *nc/u* soda water; drink of soda water.
'soda fountain (mainly *US*) counter from which soft drinks, ices etc are served.
'soda water 1. *nu* water filled with a gas to make it bubble. **2.** *nc* drink of this.
sodden ['sɔdn] *adj* **1.** very wet; wet through: *sodden clothes*. **2.** stupid with drink.
sodium ['soudiəm] *nu* soft, silver-white metal element, found in salt, soda etc (Na).
sodomy ['sɔdəmi] *nu* sexual love between male persons. **sodomite** ['sɔdəmait] *nc*. (both *o.f.* or legal).
sofa ['soufə] *nc* long, comfortable seat with cushions, and a back and arms.
soft [sɔft] *adj* **1.** giving way when one touches; not hard: *soft bed; soft ground*. **2.** smooth: *soft skin; as soft as silk*. (*opp* **rough**). **3.** not loud or noisy: *soft voice; soft music*. **4.** not sharp: *soft outlines*. **5.** not harsh or glaring: *soft, restful light*. **6.** gentle; kind: *having a soft heart*. **7.** weak; not manly. *Muscles become soft without exercise*. **8.** silly; weak in the mind: *soft in the head*. (*informal*). **9.** easy and usually well-paid: *soft job*. (*informal*). **10.** (with reference to water) not containing certain substances which make it difficult to use the water for washing. **softly** *adv*. **softness** *nu*.
soften ['sɔfən] *vt/i* make or become soft.
'soft 'drink cold drink which does not contain alcohol.
'soft-'hearted *adj* gentle; (too) kind.
'softwood type of wood which is easily cut into pieces. (Properly speaking, the wood of fir trees, pine trees etc).
soggy ['sɔgi] *adj* **1.** very wet; wet through: *soggy ground*. **2.** heavy and damp: *soggy bread*.
soil[1] [sɔil] *nu* earth (esp. in connection with growing things): *rich soil; sandy soil*.
soil[2] [sɔil] *vt/i* make or become dirty: *soil a clean shirt*.
sojourn ['sɔdʒən] *vi* stay somewhere for a time. Also *nc*. (both *o.f.*).
solace ['sɔləs] **1.** *nu* something which lessens grief or trouble: *find much solace in one's family*. **2.** *nc* someone/something which brings comfort. *His children were a solace to him in his grief*. Also *vt* give comfort to. (all *formal*).
solar ['soulə*] *adj* of, connected with, the sun: *solar energy*.
solar plexus ['soulə'pleksəs] *nc* group of nerves in the stomach.
sold [sould] past of **sell**.
solder ['souldə*] *nu* easily melted metal used for joining other pieces of metal together. Also *vt* join together with solder.
'soldering iron tool used for soldering.
soldier ['souldʒə*] *nc* man who serves in an army. Also *vi* serve in an army. **soldierly** *adj*.
soldier on continue in spite of difficulties.
sole[1] [soul] *adj* one; only. *He was the sole survivor*.
solely *adv* only; alone. *If anything goes wrong, you will be held solely responsible*.
sole[2] [soul] *nc* bottom part of a foot, shoe, boot etc. Also *vt* put a sole on: *sole shoes*.
sole[3] [soul] *nc* type of flat sea fish. *pl* **sole**.
solecism ['sɔləsizəm] *nc* **1.** mistake in using language, caused by ignorance. **2.** act of breaking the laws of good manners.
solemn ['sɔləm] *adj* **1.** serious; unsmiling: *look solemn*. **2.** done in a serious way: *solemn procession of mourners; solemn ceremony*. **solemnly** *adv*.
solemnity [sɔ'lemniti] **1.** *nu* seriousness. **2.** *nc* (often *pl*) solemn ceremony.
solemnize ['sɔləmnaiz] *vt* perform a solemn ceremony for: *solemnize a marriage*.
solfa ['sɔl'fɑː] *nu* system of sounds, each one of which represents a musical note.
solicit [sə'lisit] *vt/i* **1.** (with reference to a prostitute) offer sexual intercourse in exchange for money. **2.** beg for; appeal for: *solicit advice; solicit someone for advice*.
solicitor [sə'lisitə*] *nc* in England, a lawyer who advises on the making of wills etc and who prepares cases for another kind of lawyer (called a **barrister**) who conducts the cases in court.
Note: in some countries there is no distinction between *solicitors* and *barristers*.
solicitous [sə'lisitəs] *adj* **1.** anxious; showing care: *be solicitous about someone; be solicitous for something*. **2.** eager: *be solicitous to do something*. **solicitously** *adv*. **solicitude** [sə'lisitjuːd] *nu*.
solid ['sɔlid] *adj* **1.** not liquid or gas: *use solid fuel for heating* i.e. not oil, gas etc. **2.** of the same material throughout: *ring made of solid gold*. **3.** not hollow. *The walls are solid*. **4.** without a break: *wait for two solid hours/two hours solid*. (*informal*). **5.** dependable; reliable: *solid business; solid citizen*. **6.** sensible, and the result of hard work: *solid piece of work*. **7.** united. *The country is solid for a policy of reform*. **8.** (mathematics) having length, breadth and height: *solid figure*. Also *nc* **1.** not liquid (or gas). *She cannot eat solids*. **2.** (mathematics) figure which has height, breadth and length. **solidly** *adv*.
solidarity [sɔli'dæriti] *nu* oneness of feelings, interests, aims etc: *working-class solidarity*.
solidify [sə'lidifai] *vt/i* make or become solid or hard.
solidity [sə'liditi] *nu* quality of being solid.
soliloquy [sə'liləkwi] *nc* speech made by a character in a play (usu. when he is alone on the stage) in which he reveals his thoughts to the audience but not to the other characters in the play.
soliloquize [sə'liləkwaiz] *vi* make a soliloquy.
solitary ['sɔlitəri] *adj* **1.** without other people, away from other people: *solitary walk; solitary life*. **2.** single: *not a solitary person* i.e. not even one person. **3.** not often visited; lonely: *solitary place*.
solitude ['sɔlitjuːd] **1.** *nu* state of being away from other people: *solitude of a hermit's life*. **2.** *nc* lonely place: *desert solitude*.
solo ['soulou] *nc* **1.** piece of music to be played or sung by one person. **2.** performance by one person. *pl* **solos**. Also *adj/adv* one person; without anyone else.
soloist *nc* person who performs a solo.

solstice ['sɔlstis] *nc* one of the two times of the year when the sun is at its farthest from the equator, once to the north, once to the south.

soluble ['sɔljubl] *adj* able to be dissolved in a liquid. *Salt is soluble in water.* (*opp* **insoluble**). **solubility** [sɔlju'biliti] *nu*.

solution [sə'lu:ʃən] *nc* **1.** answer to a problem; way of explaining something: *solution of/to a mystery.* **2.** mixture made by dissolving a solid or a gas in a liquid.

solve [sɔlv] *vt* find the answer to; explain: *solve a mystery.*

solvent ['sɔlvənt] *adj* **1.** able to pay what one owes. (*opp* **insolvent**). **2.** able to dissolve solids or gases. Also *nc* substance (usu. liquid) that can dissolve solids or gases.

solvency *nu* state of being able to pay one's debts. (*opp* **insolvency**).

sombre ['sɔmbə*] (*US* **somber**) *adj* **1.** dark: *sombre colours.* **2.** sad: *sombre expression.*

some [sʌm] *determiner* **1.** certain amount or number of. *Give me some water. Some friends of yours are here. You may have to wait for some time.*

Note: in questions and *negatives* it is necessary to use *any*. *Have you any water? There aren't any apples left.* But note that if the speaker expects the answer 'Yes', he may use *some* in a question, in this sense. *Haven't you some water?* The same thing happens when the question is really an invitation or request. *Would you like some bread?*

2. about. *There were some thirty people there.* **3.** quite a large number or amount of. *He has been waiting for some time* i.e. quite a long time. **4.** very great; very good. *That was some party!* i.e. a very enjoyable party. (*informal*). **5.** not known; not requiring to be named. *I read it in some book or other.* Also *pron* a certain amount; a certain number. *Some of the boys were late.*

Note: the same rules apply as are mentioned in the *Note* above on *some determiner.*

somebody ['sʌmbədi] *pron* person who is not known or who does not have to be named; someone. *Somebody is knocking at the door.*

Note: in questions and negative sentences, use *anybody. I don't know anybody of that name.*

Also *nc* important person. *He is somebody in his own town but just a nobody here.* (*informal*).

somehow ['sʌmhau] *adv* in one way or another. *They will try to keep us out, but we shall get in somehow. I've never liked him, somehow* i.e. I don't know the exact reason.

someone ['sʌmwʌn] *pron* somebody.

somersault ['sʌməsɔ:lt] *nc* act of jumping, so that one turns over completely, head over heels: *make/turn/do a somersault.* Also *vi*.

something ['sʌmθiŋ] *pron* thing which is not known or does not have to be named. *There is something inside this box. There is something in what you say* i.e. there is some truth.

Note: in questions and negative sentences, use *anything. There isn't anything in the cupboard.*

or something or some other thing of that kind. *I think he left because he had lost his job or something.* (*informal*).

something like see like[2].

something of to a certain extent. *They say he's something of a musician* i.e. he has some musical ability.

sometime ['sʌmtaim] *adv* at some time in the future; at some time in the past. *We'll meet again sometime next week. I met him sometime last year.*

Note: do not confuse this word *sometime* with the two words *some time*, which mean 'a fairly long time'. *I spent some time in India when I was young.* see also *sometimes.*

sometimes ['sʌmtaimz] *adv* from time to time. *I usually go on foot, but sometimes I take the bus.*

somewhat ['sʌmwɔt] *adv* to some extent. *We felt somewhat tired when we arrived.*

somewhere ['sʌmwɛə*] *adv* in or to some place unknown. *He is living somewhere in England.*

Note: in questions and negative sentences, use *anywhere. I can't find it anywhere.*

somnambulism [sɔm'næmbjulizəm] *nu* sleepwalking. **somnambulist** *nc*.

somnolent ['sɔmnəlnt] *adj* sleepy; almost asleep. **somnolence** *nu*.

son [sʌn] *nc* male child (of a parent).

'son-in-law *nc* husband of one's daughter. *pl* **sons-in-law**.

sonata [sə'nɑ:tə] *nc* piece of music usually in three or four movements, and usually written for one instrument (e.g. the piano).

son et lumière ['sɔnei'lu:mieə*] *nu* form of entertainment outside a famous building, using lights and sound to tell the history of the place.

song [sɔŋ] **1.** *nu* singing; music produced by the voice: *burst into song* i.e. suddenly start singing. **2.** *nc* type of short poem that is sung; words and music for the voice: *popular song.*

songster ['sɔŋstə*] *nc* **1.** singer. (*informal*). **2.** bird that sings; songbird.

for a song very cheaply: *buy a new car for a song.* (*informal*).

sonic ['sɔnik] *adj* concerned with sound or the study of sound.

sonic boom noise of an aeroplane flying faster than sound.

sonnet ['sɔnit] *nc* poem of 14 lines which rhyme with one another in a special way.

sonorous ['sɔnərəs] *adj* having a deep, rich sound: *sonorous voice.* **sonorously** *adv*. **sonority** [sə'nɔriti] *nu*.

soon [su:n] *adv* **1.** in a short time. *I shall be back soon. He died soon after the accident.* **2.** early. *We did not expect you so soon. How soon can you come?* **3.** willingly. *I would just as soon stay as go* i.e. I would be equally ready to stay or go. *I would sooner go home* i.e. I would rather go home.

as/so soon as at the moment when. *As soon as he heard the news, he phoned the police. They did not come as/so soon as they had promised.*

Note: with negative sentences, *so* is often used instead of *as*, as in the last example.

no sooner . . . than at the moment when. *The sun had no sooner started to shine, than it was clouded over again.*

Note: this could also be written *No sooner had the sun started to shine than it was clouded over again.* Note the order of the words.

soot [sut] *nu* black powder which is left by smoke. *The walls of houses in industrial cities are often dirtied with soot.* **sooty** *adj*.

soothe [su:ð] *vt* **1.** calm; quieten: *soothe someone who is nervous and excited.* **2.** make less painful: *ointment that soothes wounds.* **soothing** *adj.* **soothingly** *adv.*

soothsayer ['su:θseiə*] *nc* person who tries to tell what will happen in the future (*o.f.*).

sop [sɔp] *nc* **1.** piece of bread that has been dipped in soup or some other liquid: *feed a sick person on sops.* **2.** something given to someone to prevent him from being annoyed, or to keep him contented. Also *vt* **1.** dip bread in a liquid: *bread sopped in water.* **2.** take up a liquid (e.g. with a cloth). *past* **sopped.**

sopping *adj* very wet; wet through.

sophism ['sɔfizəm] **1.** *nu* way of arguing that is clever but false. **2.** *nc* clever but false argument.

sophist *nc* person who uses clever but false arguments.

sophistry ['sɔfistri] **1.** *nc* clever but false argument. **2.** *nu* clever but false way of arguing.

sophisticated [sə'fistikeitid] *adj* **1.** wise in the ways of the world; cultured; elegant: *sophisticated person.* **2.** advanced: *sophisticated techniques* i.e. advanced ways of doing things. (*opp* **unsophisticated**). **sophistication** [səfisti'keiʃən] *nu.*

sophomore ['sɔfəmɔ:*] *nc* (*US*) student in his second year of high school or college.

soporific [sɔpə'rifik] *adj* causing sleep: *soporific drug.*

soprano [sə'prɑ:nou] **1.** *nu* highest singing voice in boys or women. **2.** *nc* singer who has a voice like this. *pl* **sopranos.** Also *attrib adj.*

sorcerer ['sɔ:sərə*] *nc* man who can do things by magic with the help of evil spirits. (*fem* **sorceress** ['sɔ:səris]).

sorcery *nu* magic performed with the help of evil spirits.

sordid ['sɔ:did] *adj* **1.** dirty, wretched: *live in sordid circumstances.* **2.** mean; showing lack of good feelings: *sordid act.* **sordidly** *adv.* **sordidness** *nu.*

sore [sɔ:*] *adj* **1.** painful: *sore knee/throat/ankle etc.* **2.** causing anger or annoyance. *That matter is a sore point with him* i.e. it causes him annoyance when he thinks about it. **3.** filled with sorrow. **4.** annoyed; angry. *He got rather sore with me.* (*informal*). **5.** great: *in sore need* (*o.f.* in sense **5.**). Also *nc* painful place on the body. *You should cover that sore on your hand.* **soreness** *nu.*

sorely *adv* greatly.

sorrow ['sɔrou] **1.** *nu* sadness; grief. *His heart was full of sorrow.* **2.** *nc* something which causes sadness. *His wife's death was a great sorrow to him. He was weighed down with sorrows.* Also *vi* be sad; show sadness: *sorrow at/for/over the loss of a friend.* **sorrowful** *adj.* **sorrowfully** *adv.*

sorry ['sɔri] *adj* **1.** feeling sadness, regret etc. *I'm sorry (that) I'm late. I feel rather sorry for him* i.e. I pity him. *We are sorry to be such a nuisance.* **2.** poor; pitiful: *sorry sight; in a sorry state.* Also *adv* expressing regret (usu. over small things). *Can you direct me to the station? Sorry, I can't.*

sort [sɔ:t] *nc* class; kind; type: *books, papers and that sort of thing; things of a different sort; new sort of car.* Also *vt* put things into different classes, grades etc: *sort letters* i.e. separate them according to the addresses on them.

sorter *nc* person in a post office who sorts letters.

sort something out separate one thing from another: *sort out the good from the bad.*

a good sort a pleasant person. (*informal* and rather *o.f.*).

of a sort, of sorts of a not very good kind. *The school has a playing field of sorts.* (*informal*).

out of sorts slightly unwell: *feel out of sorts.* (*informal*).

sortie ['sɔ:ti] *nc* **1.** attack made by soldiers in a defended town on those who are surrounding it. *The defenders made several sorties to obtain food.* **2.** flight made by aeroplanes against an enemy. *The bombers made several sorties during the night.*

sot [sɔt] *nc* person who always drinks too much strong drink; person made stupid by strong drink.

sought [sɔ:t] past of **seek.**

soul [soul] *nc* **1.** spiritual part of a person; part that is supposed to live for ever. *A man's body dies, but his soul lives on.* **2.** human being. *I didn't see a soul. Poor soul, she has suffered a lot.* (*informal*). **3.** mind. *He has put his heart and soul into it* i.e. he has worked for it using all his energy. **4.** finer feelings: *have no soul* i.e. not appreciate the better things in life.

soulful *adj* full of feeling; showing great feeling: *large soulful eyes.* **soulfully** *adv.*

soulless *adj* without noble feeling: *soulless task* i.e. a task which does not allow one to have noble feelings.

sound[1] [saund] *nc/u* **1.** what can be heard by the ears: *sound of trains passing; sound of a rifle going off; loud sound; speed of sound. Sound travels in waves.* **2.** effect on the mind of something heard or seen. *I don't like the sound of it* i.e. I am afraid, angry etc. **soundless** *adj.* **soundlessly** *adv.*

the sound barrier (with reference to aeroplanes) speed at which sound travels: *fly through the sound barrier.*

'soundproof *adj* not letting sound pass through: *soundproof walls.* Also *vt* make soundproof.

'sound track record of words and music made along the edge of a cinema film.

sound[2] [saund] *vt/i* **1.** give out sound. *The trumpet sounded.* **2.** cause to give out sound: *sound a horn.* **3.** give the signal for: *sound the retreat, alarm etc.* **4.** seem. *That sounds very reasonable.* **5.** test by listening: *sound the wheels of a train; sound someone's chest.*

sound[3] [saund] *adj* **1.** healthy; free from injury or decay: *sound teeth; sound in mind and body.* **2.** strong; safe: *sound decision; sound company/firm; sound investment.* (*opp* **unsound**). **3.** complete; thorough: *a sound beating.* **4.** deep; undisturbed: *sound sleep.* **soundly** *adv.* **soundness** *nu.*

sound[4] [saund] *vt/i* **1.** measure the depth of water by putting down a rope etc with a weight at the end of it. **2.** get someone's opinion; find out what someone thinks. *Sound out the chairman before the next meeting.*

soundings *npl* **1.** depths in water found by sounding it. **2.** attempts to find out someone's opinions.

sound[5] [saund] *nc* narrow piece of water (usu. joining two larger pieces of water).

soup [su:p] *nu* liquid food made by boiling meat, vegetables etc in water: *chicken soup.*

sour ['sauə*] *adj* **1.** having a bitter taste. **2.** having gone bad; spoiled: *sour milk.* **3.** unkind; showing anger, disappointment etc: *sour remark.* Also *vt/i* make or become sour. **sourly** *adv.* **sourness** *nu.*

sour grapes see **grape.**

source [sɔːs] *nc* **1.** place where a river, stream etc starts: *source of the River Amazon.* **2.** beginning or first cause of anything. *We must look for the source of the trouble.* **3.** book etc from which information is obtained.

souse [saus] *vt* **1.** soak in liquid. **2.** preserve food by putting it into salt water, vinegar etc: *soused herring.*

south [sauθ] *adv* roughly in the direction to the left of someone facing the setting sun: *travelling south.* Also *adj* from this direction. (*opp* **north** in both senses).

southerly [ˈsʌðəli] *nc* wind coming from the south. Also *adj* from this direction.

southern [ˈsʌðən] *adj* in or of the south.

southwards *adv* towards the south.

the south area of a country etc lying to the south.

sou'wester [sauˈwestə*] *nc* **1.** waterproof hat worn by sailors, which has a long flap at the back to protect the neck. **2.** strong wind from the south-west.

sou'wester (*def 1*)

souvenir [suːvəˈniə*] *nc* something that reminds one of a person or place. *Tourists often buy souvenirs to remind them of the places they have visited.*

sovereign [ˈsɔvrin] *nc* **1.** king or queen; chief ruler. **2.** formerly, British gold coin worth 20 shillings (100 pence). Also *adj* **1.** ruling as or like a king or queen: *sovereign ruler.* **2.** not ruled by another (country etc): *sovereign state.* **3.** excellent; powerful: *sovereign remedy.* (rather *o.f.* in sense **3.**).

sovereignty *nu* supreme power; sovereign power (in sense **2.**).

soviet [ˈsouviət] *nc* one of the elected councils which form the government of the Soviet Union. Also *adj* **1.** connected with soviets. **2.** (usu. **Soviet**) Russian.

sow[1] [sou] *vt/i* scatter or plant seeds: *sow wheat; sow a field with barley.*

sow[2] [sau] *nc* female pig.

soya bean [ˈsɔiəbiːn] (*US* **soybean**) *nc* leafy plant related to the pea, grown for its seeds (from which oil is made) and as a food crop.

spa [spɑː] *nc* **1.** spring, the water of which can be used as medicine. **2.** place where there is a spring like this.

space [speis] **1.** *nu* area without boundaries or limits outside the earth. *It will soon be common for men to travel through space.* **2.** *nc/u* limited area between objects, boundaries etc: *space measuring five feet by four. Is there any space between the table and the wall? There is space for one more person.* **3.** *nc* length of time: *within the space of ten minutes.* Also *vt* place objects with a certain distance between them. *Space the chairs out a little more.*

spacious [ˈspeiʃəs] *adj* with plenty of room; large: *spacious house.* **spaciously** *adv.* **spaciousness** *nu.*

ˈspacecraft, ˈspaceship *nc* type of vehicle for travelling through space to other planets etc. *pl* **spacecraft.**

outer space space beyond the earth's atmosphere or beyond the solar system.

spade [speid] *nc* **1.** tool as in the illustration, used for digging. **2.** playing card with the mark ♠; the mark itself. Also *vt* dig with a spade.

spadeful *nc* amount a spade can carry.

spade (*def 1*)

ˈspadework hard work which has to be done at the beginning of something. *Mr Brown did all the spadework for our new society.* (*informal*).

call a spade a spade see **call**[1].

spaghetti [spəˈgeti] *nu* mixture of wheat flour, water etc made into long tubes and cooked for eating.

spake [speik] past tense of **speak** (*o.f.*).

span[1] [spæn] past tense of **spin**[1].

span[2] [spæn] *nc* **1.** distance between the tip of a man's little finger and the tip of his thumb when the hand is stretched out i.e. about 9 inches or 23 centimetres. **2.** distance between supports: *span of a bridge.* **3.** part of a bridge etc between supports. **4.** stretch of time: *span of someone's memory; short span of time.* Also *vt* extend from one side to another. *A bridge spans the river.* *past* **spanned.**

spangle [ˈspæŋgl] *nc* small, bright object used for decoration. Also *vt* **1.** decorate with spangles. **2.** be decorated with small, bright objects: *sky spangled with stars.*

spaniel [ˈspænjəl] *nc* one of different types of dogs with long hair and long ears.

spank [spæŋk] *vt* punish a child by hitting it several times with the flat of the hand.

spanking *nc* punishment done in this way: *give a naughty child a spanking.*

spanner [ˈspænə*] *nc* tool for loosening and tightening nuts on screws and bolts.

spanners

spar[1] [spɑː*] *nc* pole to which a ship's sail is fixed.

spar[2] [spɑː*] *vi* **1.** practise the blows used in boxing (usu. against another boxer). **2.** argue (usu. between two persons). *past* **sparred.**

ˈsparring match boxing practice with another boxer.

ˈsparring partner **1.** man with whom a boxer spars. **2.** partner in a friendly dispute.

spar[3] [spɑː*] *nu* type of mineral.

spare[1] [spɛə*] *vt* **1.** protect; save (usu. because of kindness or pity). *The king spared the lives of the women and children* i.e. he did not kill them because he pitied

them. *He did not spare my feelings. They never spare themselves* i.e. they make every effort. **2.** have available or left over. *Have you a minute to spare so that we can talk about him? Can you spare me a minute? Because he is very rich, he has money to spare.*
sparing *adj* (with **of** or **with**) careful; giving unwillingly. *He is very sparing with his money.* **sparingly** *adv.*

spare[2] [spɛə*] *adj* **1.** extra; more than is needed. *Every lorry should carry a spare wheel. He is so busy that he has no spare time.* **2.** small in amount. **3.** (with reference to persons) thin. Also *nc* extra part (usu. to take the place of a damaged part of a machine). *If you are going to travel a great distance in your car, you should take plenty of spares with you.* **spareness** *nu.*
sparely *adv* in a spare manner (in senses **2.** and **3.**). *He ate sparely. The runner is sparely built.*
spare part see **spare**[2] (noun).

spark [spɑ:k] *nc* **1.** tiny piece of bright burning matter which rises from a fire, or is made when metal or stone strike together; short electric flash. *The sparks from the forest fire rose high in the air. There was a spark when the two electric wires touched each other.* **2.** lively young person. (rather *o.f.* in sense **2.**). Also *vt/i* send out sparks. *What made the electric wire spark?*
'sparking plug, 'spark plug device which makes a spark to explode the mixture of petrol and air in the engine of a motorcar.
spark something off **1.** cause quickly. *His rude words sparked off a fight.* (*informal*). **2.** cause sparks.

sparkle ['spɑ:kl] *vi* send out quick, changing gleams of light. *Most jewels sparkle. His eyes were sparkling with happiness.*

sparrow ['spærou] *nc* small, brown bird which eats insects.

sparse [spɑ:s] *adj* spread widely and in small numbers. *The trees on the hill were sparse.* **sparsely** *adv.* **sparseness** *nu.*

spartan ['spɑ:tn] *adj* hard and simple; without any comforts. *The people in the mountains live a spartan life.* Also *nc*: *The people in the mountains live like spartans.* (From the name of an ancient Greek people who lived in this way).

spasm ['spæzəm] *nc* short and sudden movement of the muscles; any short and sudden movement or feeling. *A spasm of coughing stopped him speaking.*
spasmodic [spæz'mɔdik] *adj* **1.** of, caused by, spasms: *spasmodic coughing.* **2.** happening suddenly at any time. *He is a spasmodic worker* i.e. he works for a little, then stops suddenly, then starts again. **spasmodically** *adv.*

spastic ['spæstik] *nc* person who cannot control his limbs because his brain is not controlling his body properly. Also *adj*: *spastic child.*

spat[1] [spæt] *nc* one of a pair of pieces of cloth worn round the ankle and over the top of a shoe (not often worn now).

spat[2] [spæt] past of **spit**[1].

spate [speit] *nu* **1.** high level of a river caused by heavy rain. *After the storm the river was in spate.* **2.** large, sudden flow of anything. *They could not deal with the spate of work.*

spatial ['speiʃl] *adj* of space. **spatially** *adv.*

spatter ['spætə*] *vt/i* **1.** throw drops of water, mud etc over. *The lorry spattered me with mud. The ink bottle broke and spattered ink on us.* **2.** fall in drops. *The rain was spattering on the window.* Also *nc*: *spatter of mud/rain.*

spatula ['spætjulə] *nc* **1.** broad, flat knife used to mix and spread paints and other substances. **2.** small, flat instrument used by doctors to hold down the tongue when they look at the back of the mouth. *pl* **spatulas.**

spawn [spɔ:n] *nu* **1.** eggs of fish, frogs etc. **2.** substance from which fungi (e.g. mushrooms) grow. Also *vt/i* **1.** produce spawn. **2.** produce anything in large numbers or amounts. *Dirt spawns disease.*

speak [spi:k] *vt/i* **1.** say in words; talk. *I am speaking the truth. He always speaks in a quiet voice. A dumb person cannot speak. Will you speak to him about his work?* **2.** be able to use a language. *They speak English as well as French.* **3.** make a speech. *The chairman spoke for ten minutes at the beginning of the meeting.* **4.** express silently or by signs, not words. *The photograph speaks for itself* i.e. no words are needed to explain it, the photograph by itself is enough. *past tense* **spoke** [spouk] or **spake** [speik] (*o.f.*). *past part* **spoken** ['spoukən].
speaker *nc* **1.** person who speaks. **2.** short form of **loudspeaker.**
the Speaker chairman of the British House of Commons and legislative bodies elsewhere (addressed as *Mr Speaker*).
'speaking tube long tube through which one can speak from one room to another.
speak for oneself state only one's own opinion. *When he says that the food is bad he is speaking for himself. Speak for yourself!* i.e. what you are saying applies to you and not to me.
speak for someone **1.** speak in defence of. **2.** state the opinion of. *I am speaking for him when I say that he hates war.*
speak out **1.** speak loudly. **2.** state one's opinion clearly. *He spoke out against the plan.*
speak up **1.** speak more loudly. *Please speak up; we can't hear you.* **2.** state one's opinion clearly.
not be on speaking terms with somebody not speak to somebody because one either does not know him or has quarrelled with him.
nothing to speak of very little; not serious or important. *He has a cold but it is nothing to speak of.* (*informal*).
so to speak as it were; as one might say. *He is, so to speak, our King* i.e. he is not really our King but we treat him as if he were.
strictly speaking using the word in a strict sense; to be exact. *Strictly speaking, I am his stepfather, not his father.*
speak well for be clear proof of. *The beautiful picture speaks well for his skill as an artist.*

spear [spiə*] *nc* weapon made of a sharp metal point fixed to a long stick, used for fighting, hunting and fishing. Also *vt* push a spear into.
'spearhead **1.** metal point of a spear. **2.** leading part or movement in an attack. *The general used his best soldiers as the spearhead of his attack on the town.* Also *vt*: *The best soldiers spearheaded the attack.*

special ['speʃl] *adj* not usual; of a particular type; for a particular purpose. *You should give special attention to this matter. A special tool is needed to cut iron. They are getting a* *special bus to take us to the football match.* Also *nc*: *I bought a copy of the evening special* i.e. of a special evening edition of a newspaper. *He will travel by the special to the football match* i.e. special bus or train. **specially** *adv.*

specialist *nc* person who is very skilled in, or has great knowledge of, a particular type of work or study; an expert. *He is a heart specialist* i.e. a doctor who is an expert on diseases of the heart.

speciality [speʃi'æliti], **specialty** ['speʃlti] *nc* particular type of work, study, activity etc in which one is very skilled or interested. *His speciality/specialty is heart surgery. My mother's speciality/specialty is making jam. Note: speciality* is more usual in British English, *specialty* in American English.

specialize *vt/i* (with **in**) study specially a particular type of skill or learning; become a specialist. *During his last two years at school he specialized in biology. This doctor has a specialized knowledge of the heart.*

specialization [speʃəlai'zeiʃən] *nc/u*: *At school his specialization was biology.*

specialty ['speʃlti] *nc* see **speciality.**

specie ['spi:ʃi:] *nu* money in the form of coins (not paper money).

species ['spi:ʃi:z] *nc* **1.** (biology) smallest group into which animals and plants are normally divided. **2.** any kind of thing.

specify ['spesifai] *vt* give the name or details of a particular person/thing. *The book of instructions specifies one-inch nails for making a desk.*

specified *adj.* (*opp* **unspecified**).

specific [spə'sifik] *adj* given by name or in detail; exact; particular. *The book gives specific instructions on how to make a desk. He came here for a specific reason.* Also *nc* exact remedy. *There is no specific for cancer.* **specifically** *adv.*

specification [spesifi'keiʃən] *nc/u* (usu. *pl*) exact measurements or details of something to be done. *The specifications for the new classroom to be built next year are now ready.*

specific gravity relation of the weight of a substance to the weight of an equal amount of water.

specimen ['spesimən] *nc* something used as an example to be studied or tested. *The teacher showed us some specimens of wild flowers. The doctor took a specimen of my blood to see if I had malaria.*

specious ['spi:ʃəs] *adj* not good or correct, although appearing to be so. *He gave a specious reason for being late.* **speciously** *adv.* **speciousness** *nu.*

speck [spek] *nc* very small piece of something; very small mark. *There is a speck of dust on your nose. From a great distance the boys looked like specks on the field.*

specked *adj* having specks.

speckle ['spekl] *nc* very small mark (usu. one of many).

speckled *adj* marked with speckles. *The snake has a speckled skin.*

specs [speks] *npl* see **spectacle** (in sense **2.**).

spectacle ['spektəkl] *nc* **1.** something unusual or impressive which makes people look at it. *The marching soldiers made a fine spectacle. The burning house was a terrible spectacle. By arguing loudly with the policeman, he made a spectacle of himself.* **2.** (in *pl*) pair of lenses worn over the eyes so that one can see better. (Also **glasses; specs**).

spectacular [spek'tækjulə*] *adj* causing people to look or pay attention; making a spectacle: *He made a spectacular jump from the burning building.* **spectacularly** *adv.*

spectre ['spektə*] (*US* **specter**) *nc* **1.** spirit of a dead person appearing to a person who is alive; ghost. **2.** something about to happen which causes fear; threat. *The spectre of famine made them leave their homes.*

spectroscope ['spektrəskoup] *nc* instrument which divides light into its spectrum. **spectroscopic** [spektrə'skɔpik] *adj.*

spectrum ['spektrəm] *nc* range of colours (from infrared to ultraviolet) into which light can be divided when passed through a glass prism. (A rainbow shows part of this range). *pl* **spectra** ['spektrə].

speculate ['spekjuleit] *vi* **1.** think in a general way without really knowing; guess. *We can only speculate about life on other planets.* **2.** buy and sell goods and shares in the hope of making a profit quickly. *It is dangerous to speculate unless you study the market.* **speculative** ['spekjulətiv] *adj.* **speculatively** *adv.*

speculation [spekju'leiʃən] *nc/u*: *our speculations about life on other planets; goods bought on speculation* i.e. on trial (informally shortened to **on spec**).

speculator *nc* person who speculates (in sense **2.**).

sped [sped] past of **speed²**.

speech [spi:tʃ] **1.** *nu* ability to speak; way of speaking. *Babies have to learn speech. His speech showed that he was drunk.* **2.** *nc* long talk made in public. *The headmaster gave/made a speech about/on good manners to the whole school.*

speechless *adj* not able to speak (usu. because of anger, surprise etc). *He was speechless with rage. Their bad manners left us speechless.* **speechlessly** *adv.* **speechlessness** *nu.*

speechify *vi* make a speech (often one that is not needed). *Politicians are ready to speechify about anything.* (*informal*).

'speech day day when speeches are made (usu. in a school at the end of the year, when important persons are asked to come and prizes are given).

speed¹ [spi:d] *nc/u* **1.** quick movement; swiftness. *The speed of the attack surprised them.* **2.** movement as measured: *at a low/high speed* i.e. slowly/quickly. *A man's normal walking speed is 4 miles per hour. The motorcar turned the corner at full/top speed.*

speedy *adj* quick. **speedily** *adv.*

'speedboat type of motorboat which moves very quickly.

'speed indicator see **speedometer.**

'speed limit speed above which one should not go. *The speed limit in the town is 30 miles per hour for all traffic. The police stopped him for exceeding the speed limit.*

speedometer [spi'dɔmitə*] instrument inside a motorcar, lorry etc which shows the speed at which it is going.

'speedway, 'speed track track on which cars and motorcycles race.

speed² [spi:d] *vt/i* go, cause to go, quickly. *It is dangerous to speed in a car when it is dark. The lorry sped through the village. They sped us on our way* i.e. caused us to go on our way more quickly by helping us. *past* **sped** [sped].

speeding *nu* going too quickly (esp. in a motorcar, lorry etc). *Speeding in a busy street is against the law.*

speed up go, cause to go, more quickly. *The lorry speeded up when it left the town. Please try to speed up your work* i.e. work more quickly. *past* **speeded up.**

spell[1] [spel] *vt/i* **1.** say or write the letters of a word in their correct order. *He spelt the word wrongly.* **2.** (with reference to letters) make a word. *B-O-O-K spells book.* **3.** mean. *This news spells disaster. past* **spelt** [spelt] or **spelled** [speld].

speller *nc* **1.** person who spells. *Are you a good speller? He is a bad/poor speller.* **2.** school book used to teach spelling.

spelling *nc/u* way in which a word is spelt. *'Labour' is the British spelling, 'labor' the American spelling.*

spell something out 1. read or understand with difficulty. *He spelt out the Latin sentence with the help of the teacher.* **2.** explain slowly and carefully. *We had to spell it out to him.*

spell[2] [spel] *nc* short period of time: *spell of duty; spell of good weather.*

spell[3] [spel] *nc* **1.** words which are believed to produce a magic effect. **2.** fascination, charm, attraction of something unusual and beautiful.

'spellbound *adj* **1.** strongly attracted or fascinated by something. *The boy stood spellbound, listening to the old man's story.* **2.** influenced by magic.

cast a spell (on somebody) see **cast**[1].

put a spell on someone influence someone by magic.

under a spell influenced by magic made by someone else.

spelt [spelt] past of **spell**[1].

spend [spend] *vt/i* **1.** pay out money in order to get something. *His wife never stops spending. He spent all his money on new books* i.e. to buy new books. **2.** pass time; finish. *They spent their holidays at home. I spent an hour looking for you. He has spent all his strength trying to help them. past* **spent** [spent].

spent *adj* exhausted; worn-out. *The soldiers looked spent after their long march.*

spender *nc* person who spends.

'spendthrift *nc* person who spends money foolishly or wastefully. Also *adj* wasteful; extravagant.

sperm [spə:m] *nu* fluid of male animals which fertilizes female animals.

spermaceti [spə:mə'seti] *nu* type of fat found in the head of a sperm whale and used for making candles and ointments.

'sperm oil type of oil obtained from a sperm whale.

spew [spju:] *vt/i* bring up from the stomach through the mouth, vomit (often considered *impolite*).

sphere [sfiə*] *nc* **1.** body shaped like a ball (e.g. the earth; a planet). **2.** range of knowledge or interests. *Biology is not (in) my sphere. He has done good work in many spheres of science* i.e. many branches of science.

spherical ['sferikl] *adj* shaped like a sphere.
spherically *adv.*

spheroid ['sfiərɔid] *nc* body shaped almost like a sphere (e.g. an orange).

sphere of influence (with reference to a country) area abroad where it has influence and power. *The Red Sea was once a British sphere of influence.*

sphinx [sfiŋks] *nu* **1.** imaginary creature said to have the head of a woman, the body of a lion, and wings; large statue of this creature in Egypt. **2.** person about whom very little is known and who says very little.

spice [spais] **1.** *nc/u* vegetable matter, often in the form of a powder, used to flavour food (e.g. ginger, cinnamon, curry powder). **2.** *nu* greater interest; excitement. *Adventure gives spice to life.* Also *vt* add interest or excitement to. *He spices his book with stories about the people he met.*

spicy *adj* **1.** flavoured with spice. **2.** interesting or exciting (but not usu. decent); *spicy jokes.* **spicily** *adv.* **spiciness** *nu.*

spick [spik] *adj* only in **spick and span** i.e. clean and tidy.

spider ['spaidə*] *nc* type of small creature with eight legs which makes a web to catch insects for food.

spidery *adj* (esp. with reference to handwriting) thin like the thread of a spider's web.

spied [spaid] past of **spy.**

spigot ['spigət] *nc* plug or tap in the hole of something containing liquid (usu. made of wood and in the hole of a barrel).

spike [spaik] *nc* **1.** something with a sharp point (e.g. on a fence, top of a wall, the soles of running shoes, the tops of flowers or grain). *There is a row of spikes on top of the prison wall to prevent the prisoners escaping.* **2.** (in *pl*) running shoes which have spikes in the soles. *I lent him my spikes for the half-mile race.* Also *vt* put a spike into.

spiky *adj* **1.** having spikes. **2.** (with reference to people) difficult to handle; touchy.

spike somebody's guns put an end to somebody's plans. (*informal*).

spill [spil] *vt/i* fall, cause to fall, out of something. *The milk has spilt over the table* i.e. it has fallen out of its bottle, jug etc. *Who spilt ink on my books? The lorry hit a tree and spilt the driver and his friend into the bushes. past* **spilt** [spilt] or **spilled** [spild]. Also *nc* fall out of or off something (e.g. out of a motorcar, off a bicycle etc). *He had a bad spill when his bicycle collided with a car.* (*informal* in this sense).

'spillway channel to take away water from a dam or river when the water level is too high.

spill over fall over the edge. *The boiling water in the pot is spilling over.*

spilt [spilt] past of **spill.**

spin[1] [spin] *vt/i* **1.** twist cotton, silk, wool etc into threads. (The threads can then be woven – see **weave** – to make cloth). **2.** make from threads. *I saw the spider spinning its web.* **3.** go, cause to go, round quickly. *The dancer spun on her toes. He spun the wheel of his car to turn the corner. The box fell spinning from the high window. pres part* **spinning.** *past tense* **span** [spæn] or **spun** [spʌn]. *past part* **spun.**

'spinning wheel simple machine with a large wheel used to spin cotton, silk, wool etc into threads.

spin out make to last a long time. *We were able to spin our money out until the end of our holidays.* (*informal*).

spin a coin throw a coin spinning into the air so that something can be decided by chance i.e. by which face (heads or tails) of the coin is on top when it has fallen. *The referee spun a coin to decide which football team should kick off.*

spin a yarn tell a story (not always a true one) (rather *o.f.*).

spin[2] [spin] **1.** *nc/u* turning movement. *He*

gave the wheel a spin. In cricket bowlers try to give spin to the ball. The aeroplane went into a spin. **2.** *nc* short journey in or on something with wheels. *He took us for a spin in his new car.* (rather *o.f.* in sense **2.**).

'spin-'drier machine which removes water from clothes by spinning them in a container.

spinach ['spinitʃ] *nu* type of green vegetable.

spinal ['spainl] *adj* see **spine.**

spindle ['spindl] *nc* **1.** long, thin rod used for twisting thread in spinning. **2.** thin rod round which something (e.g. a wheel) turns.

spindly *adj* long and thin.

'spindlelegs, 'spindleshanks 1. long, thin legs. **2.** person with long, thin legs. **spindle-legged** *adj.* (all *informal*).

spindrift ['spindrift] *nu* spray blown from the surface of the sea by the wind.

spine [spain] *nc* **1.** backbone. **2.** central ridge: *spine of a range of mountains.* **3.** sharp thorn of some types of plant or sharp point on the skin of some types of animals. **4.** outside part of a book where the pages join and which is seen when it stands in a row with other books.

spinal *adj* of the spine: *spinal column* i.e. backbone; *spinal cord* i.e. nerves inside the spine.

spineless *adj* **1.** without a spine (in sense **1.**). **2.** weak in purpose or character.

spinet [spi'net] *nc* type of musical instrument like a piano.

spinnaker ['spinəkə*] *nc* very large triangular (fore)sail on the front of a racing yacht.

spinney ['spini] *nc* small wood with thick bushes under the trees.

spinster ['spinstə*] *nc* woman who is not married.

spinsterhood *nu* state of being a spinster.

spiral ['spairl] *adj* going round and up like a screw: *spiral stair.* Also *nc*: *The smoke was rising in spirals.* Also *vi*: *The smoke was spiralling into the air. past* **spiralled.** (US **spiraled**).

spire ['spaiə*] *nc* pointed roof, rising high in the air on top of a building (esp. a church).

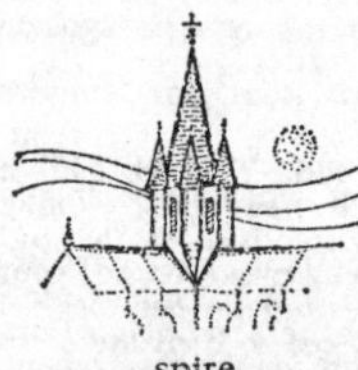

spire

spirit[1] ['spirit] *nc/u* **1.** soul; part of man which is not body. *The spirit is willing but the flesh is weak.* **2.** being which has no body; ghost. *The spirit of his dead father stood by his bed. They are afraid of evil spirits.* **3.** energy; courage; person as an example of energy, courage etc. *He fought with spirit. They have no spirit for the dangerous journey. He was one of the greatest spirits of his age.* **4.** real intention; true nature. *He entered into the spirit of the game* i.e. he played it as it should be played. *We must obey the spirit of the law.* **5.** attitude; general opinion. *They have approached the problem in the right spirit. The spirit of the country was against war.* **6.** (in *pl*) state of mind; mood. *We were in high spirits* i.e. cheerful; *in low/poor spirits* i.e. sad depressed. **7.** (usu. *pl*) alcohol; stron alcoholic drink (e.g. brandy, gin, whisk etc).

spirited *adj* full of energy; brave: *spirite fight; spirited reply.* **spiritedly** *adv.*

spiritless *adj* without energy or boldness **spiritlessly** *adv.*

spirituous ['spiritjuəs] *adj* containin alcohol.

'spirit level instrument which shows tha a surface is level by the position of a bubbl of air.

'high-'spirited *adj* cheerful.

Holy Spirit God (as a part of the Trinit in Christian religion).

'low-'spirited, 'poor-'spirited *adj* sad depressed.

spirit[2] ['spirit] *vt* (with **away** or **off**) tak away secretly or in a strange manner *The police spirited the thief away before th angry crowd could reach him.*

spiritual ['spiritjuəl] *adj* of the soul; of a being which has no body. *Priests are con cerned with man's spiritual problems. Th people waited for a spiritual sign* i.e. from a being which has no body (e.g. the spirit of a dead person). Also *nc* religious song (esp one sung by American Negroes). **spiritu ally** *adv.* **spirituality** [spiritju'æliti] *nu.*

spiritualism *nu* belief that the spirit of a dead person can be made to appear t living persons or send them messages.

spiritualist *nc* person who believes i spiritualism.

spirituous ['spiritjuəs] *adj* see **spirit**[1].

spit[1] [spit] *vt/i* **1.** push out the liquid in th mouth (often to show anger or contempt) *People who spit can spread disease. When h met his enemy, he spat at him.* **2.** push ou anything from the mouth. *The injured ma was spitting blood. He spat (out) his reply* **3.** push out; make a noise like somebod spitting. *The fire spat (out) ashes all over th floor.* **4.** (with reference to rain or snow) fal in fine, scattered drops. *It was spitting whe I went outside. pres part* **spitting.** *past* **spa** [spæt]. Also *nu* **1.** act of spitting. **2.** liqui which is spat from the mouth. *Wipe the sp off your chin.* (Also **spittle**). **3.** exact like ness. *She's the dead/very spit of her mother* (*informal* in sense **3.**).

spitting image exact likeness.

spit[2] [spit] *nc* **1.** pointed bar put throug meat so that the meat is cooked on al sides as the bar is turned slowly. **2.** narro point of land projecting into the sea or a lake. Also *vt* put on a spit; push a pointe weapon (e.g. a spear) into somebody. *pas* **spitted.**

spite[1] [spait] *nu* hatred; ill will. *Spite mad him tell the teacher I had lost my book. He tol the teacher out of spite. He had a spite again me.* Also *vt* harm because of spite. *He tol the teacher just to spite me.*

spiteful *adj* having spite. **spitefully** *ad* **spitefulness** *nu.*

spite[2] [spait] only in **in spite of** i.e. with n concern for; without troubling about. *I spite of the danger they climbed the mountai*

spittle ['spitl] *nu* liquid in the mouth saliva. see also **spit**[1] *nu* (in sense **2.**).

spittoon [spi'tu:n] *nc* type of container int which one can spit.

splash [splæʃ] *vt/i* **1.** (with reference t liquids) fall, cause to fall, in large drop (usu. with a noise). *The water splashed int the deep hole. He splashed ink over his desk*

He splashed his desk with ink. The big waves splashed against the side of the boat. **2.** move or do something so that a liquid splashes. *I can hear him splashing in the bath. We splashed through the mud.* **3.** print in large letters to attract attention. *The football result was splashed on the front page of the newspaper.* Also *nc* **1.** noise or mark caused by splashing. *The stone rolled into the river with a splash. He had splashes of ink on his hands.* **2.** small amount of liquid. *He put a splash of milk in his tea.* (*informal* in sense **2.**).
make a splash attract public notice (usu. on purpose). *Their sudden arrival in a red sports car made quite a splash.* (*informal*).
splash one's money about spend one's money in a way which attracts attention. (*informal*).

spleen [spli:n] *nu* **1.** organ of the body near the stomach which in the past was believed to cause anger. **2.** anger; bad temper.
vent one's spleen on be angry, bad-tempered with.

splendid ['splendid] *adj* magnificent; causing admiration. *He lives in a splendid house.*
splendidly *adv.*

splendour ['splendə*] *nc* brightness; magnificence; glory: *splendour of a sunset in the tropics. He told us about the splendours of ancient India.*

splice [splais] *vt* join two ends of rope by weaving the strands together; join two pieces of wood or metal by placing one over the other and tying them. Also *nc* join made by splicing.

splint [splint] *nc* piece of hard material for keeping a broken bone in the right position. *The doctor put my broken arm/leg in splints.*

splinter ['splintə*] *nc* sharp piece of wood, metal etc which has been broken off, or projects from, a larger piece. *When I picked up the broken box I got a splinter in my finger.* Also *vt/i* break into splinters.
'splinter group group of persons who have disagreed with, and left, a larger group (e.g. a political party).
'splinterproof *adj* **1.** not able to be splintered (e.g. glass windscreen of a car). **2.** protecting against splinters (e.g. of a bomb).

split[1] [split] *vt/i* **1.** break or cut into parts (esp. lengthwise). *This wood splits easily. He split the wood with an axe.* **2.** tear, burst open, suddenly. *His coat, which was very light, split from top to bottom. pres part* **splitting.** *past* **split.** Also *adj.*
splitting *nc* act of splitting. Also *adj* painful. *I have a splitting headache.*
split infinitive infinitive with an adverb in between 'to' and the verb (e.g. *It is necessary to carefully read this book*) (often used but sometimes considered wrong).
a split personality mind which thinks in two opposite ways and cannot decide anything; form of madness.
'split 'pin metal pin which is split down the middle so that when it is passed through a hole the ends can be bent back to keep it in place.
'split 'second very short period of time, less than a second.
split on somebody tell somebody's secret to somebody else. *Please don't split on me to my father.* (*informal*).
split something up divide into parts. *He split up the class into three groups. After the meeting we split up and went home* i.e. divided into groups.
split hairs argue about very small details or differences.
'hair-splitting argument of this kind.
split one's sides laugh so much that one's sides feel like splitting. (*informal*).

split[2] [split] *nc* **1.** tear; narrow crack. *There is a long split in his coat.* **2.** division (often of opinion). *The new timetable has caused a split in the school staff.*
the splits difficult act of sitting down with the legs stretched apart until they are flat on the floor. *Usually only a trained dancer can do the splits.*

splutter ['splʌtə*] *vt/i* **1.** talk quickly in an excited manner (usu. with liquid thrown from the mouth). *He was so angry that he spluttered his reply.* **2.** make a hissing or spitting sound. *The rain caused the lamp to splutter.*

spoil[1] [spɔil] *vt/i* **1.** (with reference to things) damage; make worse. *He has spoilt his work by being careless. The rain will spoil her new hat.* **2.** (with reference to persons esp. children) harm behaviour and character by being too kind and gentle. *She has only one son and she spoils him. Nobody likes spoilt children.* **3.** (with reference to food etc) become bad or useless. *The meat will spoil if you leave it in the sun.* **4.** steal from, plunder. *The enemy spoiled the captured city* (*o.f.* in sense **4.**). *past* **spoilt** or **spoiled.**
spoilt, spoiled *adj.* (*opp* **unspoilt, unspoiled**).
'spoilsport person who stops others enjoying themselves. (*informal*).
be spoiling for be very ready for. *He was drunk and spoiling for a fight.*

spoil[2] [spɔil] *nc* (usu. *pl*) **1.** plunder; stolen goods: *spoil/spoils taken away by the thieves.* **2.** profits; appointments etc given to those supporting a successful political party. *The new party in power is now enjoying the spoils of office.*

spoil[3] [spɔil] *nu* earth, stones etc which have been dug up. (Often **spoil heap**).

spoke[1] [spouk] past tense of **speak.**

spoke[2] [spouk] *nc* **1.** one of the thin rods connecting the centre of a wheel to its outside edge. *One of the spokes in the front wheel of his bicycle is broken.* **2.** step or rung of a ladder.
'spokeshave tool for smoothing curved pieces of wood.
put a spoke in somebody's wheel stop somebody doing what he wishes; hinder. (*informal*).

spoken ['spoukən] past part of **speak.**

spokesman ['spouksmən] *nc* person who speaks for others: *a Labour Party spokesman; a spokesman for the government.*

spondee ['spɔndi:] *nc* (poetry) foot with two long syllables. **spondaic** [spɔn'deiik] *adj.*

sponge [spʌndʒ] *nc* **1.** type of sea animal with a body full of holes to allow water to enter. (When dried it is used for cleaning and wiping). **2.** substance full of holes used for cleaning and wiping: *rubber sponge.* **3.** type of very soft, light cake. (Also **sponge cake**). Also *vt* clean or wipe with a sponge. *She sponged the cut on my head.*
sponger *nc* person who lives off other people's money etc. (*informal*).
spongy *adj* soft and full of holes like a sponge. **sponginess** *nu.*
sponge from/on/off somebody get goods or money from somebody without intending to return them; live on the money of somebody. *He sponged five pounds from one of his*

school friends. He is a very lazy man who sponges on his old parents. (*informal*).
throw in/up the sponge admit defeat. (*informal*).
sponsor ['spɔnsə*] *nc* **1.** person who promises to be responsible for another person. **2.** person who proposes and supports something to be done or decided. *The chairman asked for the names of the sponsors of the proposal.* **3.** person or business company which gives financial support to a radio or television programme, a concert, exhibition etc (usu. in return for publicity and the right to advertise goods). Also *vt* be sponsor for. *I sponsored the first proposal. The tobacco company sponsors several television programmes.*
spontaneous [spɔn'teiniəs] *adj* at one's own wish; not forced; natural. *They made a spontaneous decision to work for an extra half-hour* i.e. nobody told them to work more; they decided themselves. **spontaneously** *adv.* **spontaneity** [spɔntə'neiiti] *nu.*
spool [spu:l] *nc* small cylinder made of wood or metal on which thread, wire, the film of a camera etc is wound.
spoon [spu:n] *nc* instrument with a small bowl at the end of a handle used for mixing, taking food to the mouth etc (used with many other words to show what the spoon is used for e.g. *eggspoon, soupspoon, teaspoon*). Also *vt* take in a spoon. *He spooned the soup into his mouth.*

spoon

spoonful *nc* amount that can be taken in a spoon. *He put two spoonfuls of sugar in his tea.*
'spoon-feed *vt* **1.** feed with a spoon (e.g. a baby or sick person who cannot feed himself). **2.** do too much for somebody so that he does not look after himself.
spoonerism ['spu:nərizəm] *nc* mistake made by changing round the first sounds of spoken words (e.g. *All hags should be flung out of the windows* instead of *All flags should be hung out of the windows*).
spoor [spuə*] *nc* track made by a wild animal (which is followed by the person hunting it).
sporadic [spɔ'rædik] *adj* happening one by one or here and there. *There has been sporadic fighting in the capital during the last few days.* **sporadically** *adv.*
spore [spɔ:*] *nc* seed; germ (esp. of flowerless plants like the fern).
sporran ['spɔrn] *nc* leather bag hung from the waist and worn with a Scottish kilt.
sport [spɔ:t] **1.** *nc* game played or exercise taken for enjoyment (esp. in the open air e.g. football and baseball; hunting and swimming). **2.** *nc* (in *pl*) meeting for athletics i.e. running, jumping, throwing etc. *Are you going to run in the school sports?* **3.** *nu* fun; amusement. *They did it for sport.* **4.** *nc* plant or animal which is not normal in appearance. **5.** *nc* person who is not angry when he loses; person who is willing to join in a game etc. *John is a (good) sport. He is ready to try anything.* (*informal* in sense **5.**). Also *vt/i* **1.** play; have fun. **2.** show proudly. *He sported a red tie.*
sporting *adj* **1.** fond of, interested in, sport. **2.** willing to take a chance. *It is very sporting of John to try anything.* **sportingly** *adv.*
sportive *adj* playful; fond of sport. (rather *o.f.*).
'sports car motorcar made for speed.
'sports coat/jacket man's jacket, worn on informal occasions, and not part of a suit.
'sports editor newspaper editor who reports on sports.
'sportsman 1. man who is fond of, or good at, sport. **2.** man who is willing to take a chance.
'sportsmanlike *adj* (with reference to behaviour) like a sportsman; fair and generous. (*opp* **unsportsmanlike**).
'sportsmanship *nu* behaviour expected from a sportsman.
'sportswoman woman who is fond of, or good at, sport.
make sport of someone laugh at, make fun of, somebody. (rather *o.f.*).
spot[1] [spɔt] *nc* **1.** small mark or stain. *He was wearing a blue tie with white spots. There were spots of ink on his white collar.* **2.** small, red mark on the skin; pimple. *His face was covered with spots.* **3.** something which harms one's good name or position. *He is a very honest man without a spot on his character.* **4.** small amount. *I'll have a spot of whisky; a few spots of rain.* (*informal* in sense **4.**). **5.** particular place. *This is the spot where he stood. He lives in a quiet spot far away from the town.*
spotted *adj* marked with spots: *spotted tie; leopard's spotted coat.*
spotless *adj* without spots; very clean: *spotless character; spotless house.*
spotlessly *adv*: *His clothes were spotlessly clean.* **spotlessness** *nu.*
spotty *adj* covered with spots (esp. in sense **2.**). *The boy has a spotty face.* **spottiness** *nu.*
'spot 'cash money paid immediately for something which one is buying or selling. (*informal*).
'spotlight *nc* apparatus for shining a strong light on a particular place or person (e.g. on the stage of a theatre); the light itself. Also *vt* shine a spotlight on.
'weak spot particular place which can easily be attacked; particular weakness of character etc. *Laziness is his weak spot.*
in a spot in trouble or difficulty: *put someone in a spot.* (*informal*).
on the spot immediately; just there. *He paid me on the spot. He was killed on the spot.* Also *adj*: *an on-the-spot enquiry.*
man/person on the spot man/person at a particular place who knows the situation there better. *Headquarters should leave the matter to the man on the spot.*
spot[2] [spɔt] *vt/i* **1.** mark, become marked, with spots. *His collar was spotted with ink.* **2.** recognize among many; choose correctly. *I spotted my father in the crowd. Do you think you can spot the winner of the next race?* **3.** rain a little. *It's spotting (with rain) outside.* (*informal* in sense **3.**). *past* **spotted.**
spotter *nc* person who can recognize something particular: *train spotter* i.e. one who can recognize types of trains.
spouse [spaus] *nc* husband or wife. (rather *o.f.*).

spout [spaut] *vt/i* **1.** (with reference to liquids) pour out, push out, violently. *Blood was spouting from the deep cut in his arm. The broken pipe spouted water all over the room.* **2.** speak in a self-important manner. *I am tired of listening to politicians spouting.* (*informal* in sense **2.**). Also *nc* **1.** violent rush of liquid: *spout of blood.* **2.** pipe or channel from which a liquid is poured: *spout of a teapot/kettle. Rain from the roof goes down a long spout.* (Often **waterspout**).
'waterspout 1. see **spout** *nc* (in sense **2.**). **2.** column of water between the sea and a cloud caused by wind going round rapidly.
sprain [sprein] *vt* twist violently the muscles of a joint (e.g. the ankle or wrist). *I sprained my ankle playing football.* Also *nc*: *I have a sprain in my ankle.*
sprang [spræŋ] past tense of **spring**[1].
sprat [spræt] *nc* type of small sea fish like a herring.
sprawl [sprɔːl] *vi* **1.** lie or sit with the arms and legs stretched out; fall and lie this way. *They were sprawling on the grass. The blow from the heavy stick sent him sprawling.* **2.** stretch out in an untidy manner over a large area. *His writing sprawled over the page.* Also *nc* act or position of sprawling: *sprawl of factories near the railway.*
spray[1] [sprei] *vt* spread a liquid in very small drops over. *They spray their cattle with a chemical which kills insects.* Also *nc/u* **1.** very small drops of a liquid (e.g. water blown from the sea by the wind). *During the storm the boat was covered with spray.* **2.** type of liquid which is sprayed. *I bought some spray for my cattle. My wife uses a hair spray.* **3.** apparatus for spraying. (Also **sprayer**).
'spray gun apparatus like a pump from which a liquid is sprayed by pushing a handle forward.
spray[2] [sprei] *nc* small branch with leaves and flowers, used as an ornament; any ornament like a spray.
spread [spred] *vt/i* **1.** stretch out; extend in space or time. *The forest spreads from here to the river. The trees spread their branches over the house. He stood up and spread his arms. Our visits to England were spread over a period of six months.* **2.** cover the surface of. *He spread the bed with a blanket. He spread a blanket on the bed. Did you spread the bread with butter? Did you spread butter on the bread?* **3.** extend to cover a larger area; pass, cause to pass, to more people. *The patch of oil spread slowly over the floor. The disease spread over the whole country. Who spread the news that he was ill? past* **spread.** Also **1.** *nu* extent: *the spread of his arms.* **2.** *nu* growth; extension over a larger area, to more people etc: *the spread of disease; the spread of civilization.* **3.** *nc* something which is spread: *bedspread* i.e. a cover spread on a bed; *chocolate spread* i.e. chocolate mixture which can be spread on bread or cake. **4.** plenty of food and drink on a table. *At Christmas we had a good spread.* (*informal* in sense **4.**).
'spread'eagle *nc* eagle with wings and legs stretched out (e.g. as shown on American coins). Also *vt* tie or place somebody with the arms and legs stretched out. *They spread-eagled the prisoner against the wall.*
spreadeagled *adj* stretched in this way.
spread something out spread; extend. *We spread out the large cloth. He spread out his hands. The fields were spread out below us.*
spread oneself 1. stretch oneself out. **2.** do more than is usual or necessary. *He spread himself when we stayed with him* i.e. he was very kind and generous.
spree [spriː] *nc* gay time; celebration. *After winning the game they had a spree. He went out on a spree* i.e. he went out drinking and enjoying himself. (*informal*).
'shopping spree occasion on which one buys a lot of expensive items in shops.
sprig [sprig] *nc* small shoot of a plant or tree with leaves and flowers.
sprightly ['spraitli] *adj* lively; merry.
sprightliness *nu.*
spring[1] [spriŋ] *vt/i* **1.** jump or move suddenly. *The lion sprang from the long grass. He sprang out of bed when he heard the bell.* **2.** produce or cause suddenly. *They are trying to spring a surprise on us* i.e. surprise us suddenly. *He is always springing new ideas on his friends. The hunters caught the animal by springing a trap* i.e. by making a trap work suddenly. **3.** (usu. with **up**) appear or grow suddenly. *A storm sprang up. After the rain, grass sprang up everywhere.* **4.** (usu. with reference to something made of wood) crack open. *The barrel has sprung. He has sprung his cricket bat. past tense* **sprang** [spræŋ]. *past part* **sprung** [sprʌŋ].
spring back jump back quickly to where he or it was before. *They sprang back into the bushes when they saw the police coming. The wire sprang back when I stopped pulling it.*
spring from 1. jump or appear suddenly from. *Where did he spring from?* (*informal*). **2.** be descended from.
spring a leak crack suddenly so that water gets in. *The ship sprang a leak and had to return to harbour.*
spring[2] [spriŋ] **1.** *nc* act of jumping or moving suddenly. *The lion made a spring at the hunter. With a spring he reached the top of the wall.* **2.** *nc* place where water appears at the surface of the ground. *We stopped near a spring.* **3.** *nc* (usu. *pl*) cause or source of something. *The springs of a man's behaviour are found in his childhood.* **4.** *nc* something which springs back or returns to where it was before being pulled or pushed. *Motorcars have springs above the wheels. The spring of my watch is broken.* **5.** *nu* power to spring back. *Dry wood has no spring. This rubber has lost its spring.*
springy *adj* having spring (in sense **5.**); elastic; light. *The branches of the tree are springy. He walks with a springy step.*
springiness *nu.*
springless *adj* without springs (in sense **4.**).
'spring 'balance instrument for measuring weight by pushing down a spring.
'springboard springy board which helps those who jump or dive into water from it.
'spring 'mattress mattress which is made soft by having many springs inside.
'spring 'tide very high tide which happens near the time of a new moon or a full moon. (*opp* **neap tide**).
spring[3] [spriŋ] *nc* season of the year when plants begin to grow i.e. March, April and May in Britain. *In spring the weather gets warmer.* Also *adj*: *spring weather; spring term at school* i.e. between the Christmas and Easter holidays.
'spring-'cleaning thorough cleaning of a house, room etc (esp. in the spring).
'springlike *adj* like spring: *springlike day.*
'springtime season of spring.
springbok ['spriŋbɔk] *nc* type of Southern

African animal, like a small deer, which can jump very well.

sprinkle ['spriŋkl] *vt* throw sand, drops of water etc over something. *They sprinkled sand on the floor. They sprinkled the floor with sand. I sprinkled my face with some water.*

sprinkler *nc* device for sprinkling (e.g. water on grass).

sprinkling *nc* small amount or number here and there. *A sprinkling of parents in the large crowd of children.*

sprint [sprint] *vi* run a short distance at full speed. Also *nc*: *He won the hundred yards sprint.* **sprinter** *nc.*

sprite [sprait] *nc* fairy.

sprocket ['sprɔkit] *nc* one of the teeth on a wheel (e.g. on a bicycle) over which a chain is fitted.

'**sprocket wheel** wheel with sprockets.

sprout[1] [spraut] *vt/i* (with reference to plants) begin to, cause to begin to, grow. *The beans we planted are sprouting. The damp corn is sprouting shoots.* Also *nc*: *The sprouts of the beans are two inches high.*

sprout[2] [spraut] *nc* (usu. *pl*) type of cabbage with very small round cabbages growing on the stem. (Sometimes **Brussels sprout**).

spruce[1] [spru:s] *adj* neat in dress; smart. Also *vt/i* (with **up**): *His mother spruced him up before he went off to school.* (*informal*).

spruce[2] [spru:s] *nc* **1.** type of tall, cone-shaped, evergreen tree with pointed leaves on every side of the twig. **2.** the wood of this tree valued for poles, matches, paper etc. *pl* **spruce.**

sprung [sprʌŋ] past part of **spring**[1].

spry [sprai] *adj* active; lively. *Although he is old, he is still spry. comparative* **spryer.** *superlative* **spryest.**

spud [spʌd] *nc* potato. (*informal*).

spun [spʌn] past part of **spin**[1].

spur [spə:*] *nc* **1.** instrument with a small, pointed wheel or a point worn on the heel of a rider's boot and pushed against the side of a horse to make it go faster. **2.** part of a bird's leg which projects at the back. **3.** ridge projecting from the side of a range of mountains. **4.** something which makes somebody try harder, be more active etc. *The hope of freedom was their spur.* Also *vt/i* (often with **on**) **1.** make a horse go faster by using spurs. *He spurred (on) his horse so that he would pass the others.* **2.** ride fast. *He spurred on through the mud.* **3.** make more active. *They were spurred (on) by the hope of freedom. past* **spurred.**

on the spur of the moment suddenly, without thinking. *On the spur of the moment I gave him my coat.*

win one's spurs **1.** (in ancient times) be made a knight. **2.** prove one's ability or courage.

spurious ['spjuəriəs] *adj* false but made to appear real. *His claim is spurious* i.e. he has no genuine reason to make a claim. **spuriously** *adv.* **spuriousness** *nu.*

spurn [spə:n] *vt* kick or drive away; refuse to accept. *They spurn all our offers of help.*

spurt [spə:t] *vt/i* **1.** (with reference to liquids, fire etc) come out, cause to come out, suddenly. *Water spurted from the broken pipe. Their guns spurted fire.* **2.** make a short sudden effort (e.g. in a race). *He spurted past the two runners in front.* Also *nc* **1.** sudden flow from an opening: *spurts of water from the broken pipe.* **2.** short, sudden effort or activity. *He made a sudden spurt.*

put on a spurt make a short, sudden effort. *They will have to put on a spurt to win the game.*

sputnik ['spʌtnik] *nc* Russian space satellite.

sputter ['spʌtə*] *vt/i* throw out small drops of liquid noisily. *The hot iron sputtered when we put water on it. The meat in the pan sputtered fat. He sputtered with anger* i.e. noisily sent out saliva from his mouth.

sputum ['spju:təm] *nu* saliva; matter produced by coughing.

spy [spai] *nc* person who acts in secret to get information about another country; secret agent; person who watches others secretly. Also *vt/i* (with **on, upon** or **into**) **1.** act as a spy; watch secretly. *Our government knows that the enemy is spying on/upon our army. The woman in the next house likes spying on her neighbours. Why do they spy into our affairs?* **2.** see; notice. *I spied him trying to hide behind the tree. past* **spied** [spaid].

'**spyglass** small telescope. (*informal* and rather *o.f.*).

'**spyhole** small hole (e.g. in a door) through which one can watch secretly.

squabble ['skwɔbl] *vi* argue or quarrel noisily about something which is not important. *The boys were squabbling about who was the best runner.* Also *nc*: *family squabbles* i.e. noisy quarrels, about unimportant matters, between members of a family.

squad [skwɔd] *nc* small group (e.g. of soldiers) working together.

'**firing squad** group of soldiers etc chosen to execute somebody by shooting him.

squadron ['skwɔdrn] *nc* **1.** group of 120-200 men forming part of a cavalry regiment. **2.** group of warships or aircraft.

squalid ['skwɔlid] *adj* dirty and unpleasant (esp. because of neglect). *They live in a squalid hut in the poorest part of the village.* **squalidly** *adv.*

squalor ['skwɔlə*] *nu* state of being squalid. *They live in squalor.*

squall [skwɔ:l] *nc* **1.** loud scream (esp. of a baby). **2.** sudden strong wind or storm. Also *vi* scream loudly.

squally *adj* having squalls (in sense **2.**): *squally weather.*

squander ['skwɔndə*] *vt* (with reference to money, possessions etc) waste; spend carelessly. *He squanders all the money which his father gives him. A country which squanders the skill of its people cannot grow rich.*

square[1] [skwɛə*] *nc* **1.** figure with four equal sides and four right angles; anything shaped like this. *Graph paper is divided into squares.* **2.** open space of this shape in a town and the buildings round it. *We sat in the square watching the people passing. I live in George Square.* **3.** instrument shaped like L used for drawing or testing right angles; one shaped like T (called a **T-square**) used in this way. **4.** (mathematics) product of a number multiplied by itself. *The square of 3 is 9.* **5.** person who does not understand or enjoy the music, clothes, ideas etc of young people. (*informal* in sense **5.**).

square[2] [skwɛə*] *adj* **1.** having the shape of a square: *square room.* **2.** forming a right angle or nearly so: *square corner; square shoulders; pen with a square nib* i.e. with a broad, right-angled point. **3.** of a number multiplied by itself: *square inch* i.e. an area each side of which equals one inch; *3 square miles.*

Note: in this sense the position of *square* is important (e.g. *3 square miles* is not the

same as *3 miles square*, which equals 9 square miles i.e. the *square* of 3 square miles).
4. complete; satisfactory. *I have to get the accounts square.* **5.** not understanding or liking the music etc of young people. (*informal* in sense **5.**). Also *adv* **1.** so as to form a right angle. *He sat square in his chair.* **2.** honestly. *They always play fair and square.*
squareness *nu.*
squarely *adv* **1.** so as to form a right angle. **2.** firmly; straight. *He sat squarely in his chair. He looked (at) me squarely in the eye* i.e. not from the side but directly. **3.** honestly. *He deals squarely with everybody.*
'square-'built *adj* (with reference to a person) having a broad shape as compared with his height.
'square dance dance in which the dancers (usu. four pairs) form a square.
a square deal an honest and fair arrangement: *give someone a square deal.* (*informal*).
a square meal a good and satisfying meal.
'square-'rigged *adj* (with reference to a ship) with sails at right angles to the mast.
square root (mathematics): *The square root of 9 is 3.*
all square (with reference to a game) with the same score; neither side winning. *We finished the game of cards all square.*
a square peg in a round hole see **peg.**

square[3] [skwɛə*] *vt/i* **1.** make square or right-angled. *He is squaring the pieces of wood so that they fit together. The soldier squared his shoulders.* **2.** multiply a number by itself. *3 squared is 9.* **3.** complete; settle. *He is busy squaring his accounts.* **4.** agree or fit, make to agree or fit with. *Your argument does not square with the facts. I cannot square his behaviour now with his behaviour in the past.* **5.** give money to get a favour; bribe. *You'll have to square the clerk if you want a licence quickly.* (*informal* in sense **5.**).
square up settle; put in order. *I squared up with him before I went away* i.e. settled accounts, finished business with him etc; *square up one's affairs.*

squash [skwɔʃ] *vt/i* **1.** become or make flat by pressing; crush. *This hat squashes easily. He squashed the insect with his finger.* **2.** (often with **in** or **into**) press together in a small space. *He squashed his clothes into a box. The people in the bus were so squashed that they could not move.* **3.** stop; silence. *He is trying to squash the story of the defeat. When I tried to speak he squashed me. Government troops squashed the rebellion.* (*informal* in sense **3.**). Also **1.** *n sing* group of people pressed together. *There was an awful squash in the train.* **2.** *nc/u* drink made from squashed fruit: *lemon/orange squash.* **3.** *nu* usual form of **squash rackets.** see below.
squashy *adj* easily squashed; soft.
'squash rackets game played with a small soft ball and rackets in a court with walls all round. (Usu. **squash**).

squat [skwɔt] *vi* **1.** sit on one's heels; (with reference to animals) have the body close to the ground. *We squatted round the campfire.* **2.** settle on land or in a house which is not occupied, without proper rights or permission. *past* **squatted.** Also *adj* short and thick.
squatter *nc* person who squats (in sense **2.**). *The farmers here are angry about the squatters who live on their land.*

squaw [skwɔ:] *nc* Red Indian woman or wife.

squawk [skwɔ:k] *nc* (esp. with reference to a bird when frightened) short, harsh cry. *The hen gave a squawk when it saw the cat.* Also *vi* **1.** give a short, harsh cry. *The hen squawked.* **2.** complain. *What are you squawking about?* (*informal* in sense **2.**).

squeak [skwi:k] *nc* short, sharp, high-pitched cry or noise: *squeak of a mouse; squeaks made by his old shoes.* Also *vt/i*: *This door squeaks. The little boy squeaked (out) his answer* i.e. in a voice like a squeak.
squeaky *adj* making squeaks: *squeaky shoes; squeaky voice.*
narrow squeak an escape with little to spare. (*informal*).

squeal [skwi:l] *nc* long, high-pitched cry or noise. *The children gave a squeal of fright. He stopped his car suddenly with a squeal of his brakes.* Also *vt/i* **1.** give or make a squeal. *The children squealed with fright. The brakes of the car squealed. She squealed (out) to us that we were in great danger* i.e. shouted to us in a voice like a squeal. **2.** (with **on**) tell somebody about something wrong done by somebody else. *If you squeal on me to the headmaster, I'll never speak to you again.* (*informal* in sense **2.**).
squealer *nc* person who informs on other people. (*informal*).

squeamish ['skwi:miʃ] *adj* feeling sick; easily made sick; too easily disgusted. *The rough sea made me squeamish. He was squeamish about changing the baby's nappies.*
squeamishly *adv.* **squeamishness** *nu.*

squeeze [skwi:z] *vt/i* **1.** press (usu. into a different shape or a smaller space). *I squeezed the tube of toothpaste. He squeezed her hand. She is squeezing an orange* i.e. to get its juice. **2.** take a different shape; become smaller. *This fruit squeezes easily.* **3.** get by force or with difficulty. *We had to squeeze an answer from him. The government is always squeezing money from/out of the people.* **4.** put in by force. *He squeezed some more clothes into the suitcase.* Also *nc* **1.** act of squeezing. *He gave her hand a squeeze.* **2.** amount got by squeezing. *She put a squeeze of orange in my drink.* **3.** small space because of squeezing. *It was a tight squeeze in the crowded bus.* **4.** (esp. with reference to money) force; extortion; difficulty. *We cannot borrow money during the present credit squeeze* i.e. when it is difficult to get credit.
squeeze in press oneself into something with difficulty. *I squeezed into the crowded bus.* (*opp* **squeeze out**).
squeeze out of **1.** press something out of something else with difficulty. *He squeezed the thorn out of my hand. I squeezed the water out of my socks.* **2.** get oneself out with difficulty. *We squeezed out of the large crowd.*

squelch [skweltʃ] *vt/i* make a sucking noise with one's feet when walking in mud. *His shoes squelched as he crossed the wet field. We squelched our way through the rain.* Also *nc* act of squelching; noise of squelching. *We could hear the squelch of their feet on the muddy road.*

squib [skwib] *nc* **1.** small firework in the shape of a short tube. **2.** short written attack on somebody.

squid [skwid] *nc* type of sea creature with ten arms, which sends out a black substance when attacked.

squint [skwint] *vt/i* **1.** look in a different direction with each eye because of a defect.

The doctor says that the child squints. **2.** look from the side or with the eyes half closed. *While sitting beside him, I squinted at his book. The bright sun made us squint.* Also *nc* **1.** *Her child has a squint.* **2.** *I took a squint at his book.* (*informal* in sense **2.**).

squire ['skwaiə*] *nc* **1.** (in former times) servant of a knight who himself became a knight later. **2.** (in England) landowner; country gentleman. Also *vt* escort a girl to a dance etc. (rather *o.f.*).

squirm [skwəːm] *vi* move like a snake; twist the body like one (often through embarrassment etc). *The little boy squirmed with shame.* Also *nc.*

squirrel ['skwirl] *nc* type of small animal with a bushy tail which lives in trees and which stores up food for the winter.

squirt [skwəːt] *vt/i* (with reference to liquids or powder) push out or be pushed out with force through a small hole. *She squirted water from the hose onto the flowers. The oil from the engine squirted into my face.* Also *nc* **1.** something squirted. *A squirt of oil hit my face.* **2.** instrument with a small hole through which a liquid is squirted.

squishy ['skwiʃi] *adj* soft and wet. (*informal*).

stab [stæb] *vt* **1.** wound deeply with a pointed instrument (e.g. a knife). *He stabbed him in the back.* **2.** cause a feeling as if one has been stabbed. *Sad memories stabbed me. He says he has a stabbing pain in his side. past* **stabbed.** Also *nc*: *a stab in the chest.*

a stab in the back an attack on oneself by one's own supporters.

stable[1] ['steibl] *adj* firmly fixed; not easily moved or upset. *We need a stable government. He is a very stable person.* (*opp* **unstable**).

stability [stə'biliti] *nu.* (*opp* **instability**).

stabilize ['steibilaiz] *vt* make stable.

stabilization [steibilai'zeiʃən] *nu.*

stabilizer ['steibilaizə*] *nc* somebody/something which stabilizes (esp. the device which keeps a ship or aircraft from moving too much from side to side at sea or in the air).

stable[2] ['steibl] *nc* **1.** building in which horses are kept. **2.** number of racehorses belonging to one person. Also *vt* put into, keep in, a stable. *They stabled their horses at the farm for one night.*

'stableboy, 'stableman boy, man who works in a stable.

staccato [stə'kɑːtou] *adj/adv* **1.** (with reference to music) played in a short and sharp manner. **2.** sounding like this sort of music.

staccato speech speaking in a short, sharp manner and with difficulty.

stack [stæk] *nc* **1.** large heap or pile made neatly and carefully: *stack of wood; stacks of hay in the field; stack of books on the teacher's desk.* **2.** shelf or shelves where books and papers are put (e.g. in a library). **3.** number of chimneys standing together. (Usu. **chimney stack**). **4.** very tall chimney (e.g. of a factory); steep, narrow piece of rock like a tall chimney. Also *vt* **1.** put in a pile neatly and carefully. **2.** (with reference to playing cards) arrange cards so that one can cheat.

stadium ['steidiəm] *nc* large sports ground (esp. one having many rows of seats round it). *pl* **stadia** ['steidiə] or **stadiums.**

staff [stɑːf] *nc* **1.** stick used when walking or climbing, or as a weapon. **2.** stick used to show a person's position or authority: *bishop's staff.* **3.** the five lines and four spaces on which music is written. **4.** group of persons working together under a manager or head. *The manager here has a staff of fifty. The headmaster and his staff met to discuss the new timetable* i.e. the headmaster and the teachers. **5.** group of officers chosen to plan military operations and give advice and information to the senior officer in command. Also *adj*: *The army general has asked for more staff officers.* Also *vt* supply with staff (in sense **4.**). *We have not enough money to staff all our schools.*

Note: in senses **1.** and **2.** the *pl* is either *staffs* or *staves* [steivz]; in sense **3.** the *pl* is *staves*; in senses **4.** and **5.** the *pl* is *staffs.*

'staff college military college where officers receive special training for more important duties.

'staff no'tation system of writing music on five lines and four spaces.

'over'staffed *adj* having too many persons in or on a staff. (*opp* **understaffed**).

stag [stæg] *nc* male deer.

'stag party party for men only. (*informal* – for women only **hen party**).

stage [steidʒ] *nc* **1.** platform in a hall, theatre etc which is above the floor so that the persons on it can be seen better. *The actors left the stage at the end of the play.* **2.** part of a journey. *We travelled to London by stages* i.e. having rests or stops on the way. *What is the bus fare to the next stage along?* **3.** particular point in progress or change. *Our baby is at the walking stage* i.e. he is beginning to be able to walk. *Secondary education is the next stage after primary education.* Also *vt* put on the stage of the theatre etc; show to the public. *Our school stages a play every year.*

staging *nc/u* **1.** structure for workmen to stand on when building. **2.** way in which a play is put on the stage. *The actors were good but the staging was bad.*

stagy *adj* of the stage of a theatre; too much like an actor in appearance or manner.

stagily *adv.* **staginess** *nu.*

the stage work and life of a theatre. *He writes books about the stage. He went on the stage when he was a boy* i.e. became an actor.

'stagecoach (in former times) coach, pulled by horses, which carried persons from one place to another.

'stage 'door door at the back of a theatre used by actors etc.

'stage fright fear felt by some persons when they go on a stage or have to speak to a large number of people.

stage 'manager person who is responsible for scenery, lighting etc of a play.

'stage-struck *adj* wishing very much to become an actor or actress. *She is stage-struck.*

'stage 'whisper loud whisper which is meant to be heard.

old stager actor or actress with long experience; any person with long experience. (*informal*).

stagger ['stægə*] *vt/i* **1.** walk or stand, cause to walk or stand, unsteadily. *The drunk man staggered across the road. The blow on the head staggered me.* **2.** surprise greatly; shock. *The bad news staggered me.* **3.** cause to happen at different times. *The manager staggers the holidays of those working in the factory so that everybody is not away at one time.* Also *nc* act of staggering.

the staggers *nu* type of disease which makes cattle and horses stagger.

stagnant ['stægnənt] *adj* **1.** (with reference to water) not moving, therefore dirty. *The old pot was full of stagnant rainwater.* **2.** (with reference to business, work etc) not busy or changing. *Trade with other countries was stagnant.*

stagnate [stæg'neit] *vi* become stagnant. **stagnation** [stæg'neiʃən] *nu.*

staid [steid] *adj* (with reference to persons) too quiet and well-behaved. **staidly** *adv.* **staidness** *nu.*

stain [stein] *vt/i* **1.** change the colour of something; mark something with a different colour; make something dirty. *She has stained the floorboards dark brown* i.e. changed their colour to dark brown. *His hands were stained with ink; bloodstained cloth.* **2.** become a different colour or dirty. *White clothes stain quickly.* Also *nc* **1.** substance used for staining. **2.** mark made by staining: *ink stains on his hands.* **3.** blot on someone's reputation. *He left without a stain on his character.*

stainless *adj* **1.** without stain. **2.** (esp. with reference to metals) not able to be stained or become rusty. *The knife is made of stainless steel.*

stair [stɛə*] *nc* **1.** (usu. *pl*) number of steps one above the other on which one can go up or down in a building. *I went up the stairs to my room.* **2.** one of these steps. *He was standing on the top stair.*

'**stair carpet** long narrow carpet put on a stair.

'**staircase,** '**stairway** flight or flights of stairs (usu. with banisters) inside or outside a building.

'**stair rod** rod for fastening a stair carpet to a stair.

'**stairway** see **staircase.**

downstairs, upstairs *adv*: *I went downstairs/upstairs.* Also *adj*: *I have an upstairs room.*

flight of stairs stairs connecting two levels. *To reach the top floor I had to climb three flights of stairs.*

stake [steik] *nc* **1.** length of wood with a point which can be driven into the ground. **2.** money used in a game of chance or in guessing the result of an event (e.g. a horse-race); any great interest in something (esp. if money is involved). *I want you to hold the stakes until the race is finished. He has a big stake in the cotton industry.* Also *vt* **1.** mark or keep up with a stake (in sense **1.**). *He staked his part of the field. I have staked the apple trees in my garden.* **2.** make ready as a stake (in sense **2.**); risk. *I staked ten pence on a horse, and it won.*

stake something off/out mark or separate by driving in stakes. *They have staked out a claim to all this land.*

at stake risked; in danger. *If we fail, our lives will be at stake.*

die at the stake, be burnt at the stake die by being tied to a stake and burnt.

stalactite ['stæləktait] *nc* deposit of carbonate of lime formed by the evaporation of water dripping from the roof of a limestone cave, and hanging down in many different shapes and sizes.

stalagmite ['stæləgmait] *nc* object just like a stalactite but rising from the floor of a limestone cave.

stale[1] [steil] *adj* **1.** not fresh; kept too long; used too much. *The bread is stale. He is always telling stale jokes* i.e. ones already heard. **2.** (with reference to persons esp. athletes) not in the best condition as the result of too much training or practice. Also *vi* become stale. *His stories quickly staled.* **staleness** *nu.*

stalemate ['steilmeit] *nc/u* **1.** (chess) state in which neither player can win or lose because no other moves can be made. **2.** any state in which nothing more can be done. *The long meeting ended in (a) stalemate* i.e. nobody could agree and nothing was decided. Also *vt/i* end in or cause a stalemate.

stalk[1] [stɔːk] *nc* part of a plant between its flowers or leaves and the ground; part of a plant which joins its fruit or leaves to the main and thicker part; stem.

stalk[2] [stɔːk] *vt/i* **1.** hunt a wild animal by moving towards it quietly and without being seen. *We stalked the elephant all day but never got near enough to shoot it.* **2.** walk in a slow, serious manner as when one is angry, proud etc. *The teacher stalked out of the classroom.* Also *nc* hunt or movement of these types.

stalker *nc* person who stalks animals.

'**stalking-horse 1.** horse used by a hunter to hide behind. **2.** something/somebody used to hide one's real purpose.

'**deerstalker 1.** person who stalks deer. **2.** type of hat.

stall[1] [stɔːl] *nc* **1.** compartment of a stable etc in which a horse, cow etc is kept. *Each horse has its own stall.* **2.** type of small shop, or a table from which goods are sold. *I bought fruit from a stall in the market. There is a bookstall at the railway station.* **3.** seat in a church used by clergymen. **4.** (*Brit*) seat in a theatre or cinema on the ground floor (and usu. in front): *front stalls; back stalls.* (*US* **parquet**). Also *vt* put or keep horses or cattle in a stall (in sense **1.**).

stall[2] [stɔːl] *vi* **1.** (with reference to an engine) stop running because it has not enough power to do its work. *Because our car was carrying five people it stalled on the steep hill. The aeroplane was going so slowly that it stalled.* **2.** avoid giving a definite answer or making a definite decision. *When I asked him what he was going to do, he stalled.* (*informal* in sense **2.**).

stallion ['stæliən] *nc* male horse (esp. one used for breeding).

stalwart ['stɔːlwət] *adj* strong, brave and loyal. Also *nc* person who is stalwart.

stamen ['steimən] *nc* one of the male parts of a flowering plant.

stamina ['stæminə] *nu* strength which makes a person or animal able to work hard and endure pain or illness. *A man who can run twenty miles has great stamina.*

stammer ['stæmə*] *vt/i* **1.** speak with difficulty, saying the same sounds again and again (e.g. P-p-please, m-m-may I g-g-go?). **2.** say something in this way. *He stammered (out) his answer.* Also *nc*: *He speaks with a stammer.* **stammerer** *nc.* **stammeringly** *adv.*

stamp[1] [stæmp] *vt/i* **1.** push one's foot down heavily. *He was stamping with rage. They stamped into the room. We stamped the ground to keep our feet warm.* **2.** make a mark on something by pressing on it a design, word etc which has already been prepared. *He stamped 'urgent' on the letter. I stamp my name on all my books.* **3.** stick a postage stamp or other kind of paper stamp on a letter, parcel, card etc. *You must stamp these letters before you post them.* **4.** crush rocks.

stamp something out **1.** put out; stop. *We stamped out the fire. The doctors are trying to stamp out disease.* **2.** cut out pieces from something. *This machine stamps out small cards from a large sheet of cardboard.*

stamp[2] [stæmp] *nc* **1.** act of stamping. **2.** something with a design, words etc cut on it so that they can be stamped on something else. *He put 'urgent' on the letter with a rubber stamp.* **3.** design or words put on something in this way. **4.** piece of coloured paper put on a letter, parcel, card etc to show that postage etc has been paid: *postage stamp; insurance stamp.* **5.** sign or mark of anything. *This essay has the stamp of hard work.*

'stamp album book in which a person who collects postage stamps keeps them.

'stamp collector person who collects postage stamps.

'stamp duty tax on certain legal papers, receipts etc.

stampede [stæm'pi:d] *nc* rush of animals or people caused by fear. Also *vt/i* rush, cause to rush, in this way.

stance [stæns] *nc* **1.** position of the feet in certain games etc (e.g. in golf before the player hits the ball). **2.** mental attitude.

stanch [stɔ:ntʃ] *adj/vt* see **staunch**[1].

stand[1] [stænd] *vt/i* **1.** remain upright on the feet without moving; cause to be upright. *Who is the man standing near the door? Never stand if you can sit. Every man in the team stands over six feet* i.e. is over six feet in height. *He stood his stick in the corner. The mother stood her child on a chair.* **2.** be in, or have, a particular place. *The school stands between two roads. These books stand on that desk* i.e. their usual place is on that desk. **3.** remain without change; be in a particular state. *My decision to go abroad stands. Their profits stand at £100. As things now stand, we shall win.* **4.** endure; be patient with. *I can't stand his silly talk. Our teacher stands no nonsense* i.e. refuses to have any nonsense from anybody. *past* **stood** [stud].

stand aside **1.** go to one side and stand. *He stood aside to let me pass.* **2.** take no part; do nothing. *We cannot stand aside and let them do it by themselves.*

stand back **1.** go back and stand. **2.** be in a particular place, away from. *His house stands back from the river.*

stand by **1.** stand on one side and do nothing. *When the house was on fire they just stood by.* **2.** be ready. *The police are standing by to control the crowd, if it is necessary.*

'stand-by *nc* **1.** something which is ready to replace something else if necessary. **2.** system by which one is allowed to travel in an aeroplane without having previously booked a seat, if there is room on the aeroplane: *be on stand-by* i.e. travel in this way. Also *adj*: *stand-by passenger; stand-by flight.*

stand by someone give support to someone. *He stood by me through all my troubles.*

stand down **1.** get down from and stand. **2.** leave a post or position (often so that somebody else can take it). *The chairman is standing down so that a younger man can take his place.*

stand for something **1.** mean; represent. *USA stands for the United States of America. We like our school and all it stands for.* **2.** endure; be patient with. *I am not standing for any bad behaviour.* (*informal* in sense **2.**).

stand in take the place of. *He is standing in for the player who is ill.*

'stand-in *nc* person who takes the place of somebody (often an actor taking the place of another actor).

'stand-'offish *adj* not friendly. **stand-offishly** *adv.* **stand-offishness** *nu.* (all *informal*).

stand out be easily seen among others. *A very tall man stands out in a crowd.*

stand out against refuse to yield to or agree with. *The farmers stood out against the government about prices for their cattle.*

stand over **1.** stand above. **2.** remain to be considered later.

stand over someone control; watch carefully. *I cannot work if you stand over me.*

stand to be ready to meet an attack. *The soldiers stood to at dawn.*

'stand-to *nc* act of being ready in this way.

stand up get on one's feet; rise and stand. *The boys stood up when the teacher came into the classroom.*

stand up for someone/something be ready to help; support. *All my friends will stand up for me.*

stand up to someone/something **1.** refuse to yield to; be ready to argue or fight with. *He stood up to all those who said he was wrong.* **2.** not be harmed or damaged by. *My old bicycle has stood up to the bad roads.*

stand a chance have a chance; be likely to. *He doesn't stand a chance of passing the examination.*

stand clear get out of the way and stand. *You must stand clear from/of the dangerous rocks.*

stand corrected agree that one is wrong.

stand fast stand and refuse to move.

stand/keep/hold one's ground refuse to yield.

it stands to reason it is obvious to anybody who thinks. *It stands to reason that only the best boys should be chosen.*

stand somebody something give; pay for. *If you come, I'll stand you a drink.* (*informal*).

stand well with be approved of by. *He stands well with his manager.*

stand still stand without moving in any way.

'standstill *nu*: *Everything is at a standstill* i.e. nothing is being done.

stand[2] [stænd] *nc/u* **1.** place where one stands. *He took his stand near the door.* **2.** particular place or structure for something. *At the door there is a hatstand* i.e. piece of furniture to hang one's hat on. **3.** place (usu. with a roof) from which to watch games etc: *grandstand* i.e. best place of this kind with the most expensive seats. **4.** stop in a place made by a company of actors on tour. **5.** area of growing trees or crops. *There is a large stand of pine trees on the hill.* **6.** (*US*) place in court where a witness stands or sits. *The witness took the stand.*

'standpoint point of view; opinion. *From the standpoint of the parents, the school is doing well.*

make a stand against stop retreating and fight. *The army made a stand against the advancing enemy.*

standard ['stændəd] *nc* **1.** flag, or pole with a flag on it. **2.** weight, measure, quality etc to which other weight, measures, qualities should be equal or try to be equal. *The standard of length in that country is the metre, not the yard. This food is below standard* i.e. its quality is not as good as it should be. *The houses are up to standard. Our teacher sets very high standards of work in his class.* **3.** post which holds something up. **4.** tree or shrub grafted on a strong stem and not supported by a wall. Also *adj* (in sense **2.**): *The standard length is the metre.*

standardize *vt* cause to be the same in weight, size, quality etc. *Most tobacco companies have standardized the length of cigarettes.* **standardization** [stændədai'zeiʃən] *nu.*

'standard 'author author who is considered to be good and whose books are used a great deal.

'standard lamp lamp fixed to a long pole and not to the wall.

standard of living wealth; possessions and comfort. *The people of the USA have a high standard of living. Many countries have a low standard of living.*

'standard 'time time officially approved by a country or part of a country. *Standard time in East Africa is three hours ahead of British standard time* i.e. when it is 4 p.m. in East Africa it is 1 p.m. in Britain.

the 'gold standard system by which the value of money is determined by the price of gold.

standing ['stændiŋ] *adj* **1.** without change; permanent. *His long beard is a standing joke* i.e. it has been a joke for a long time. *She has a standing order for ten pounds of sugar at the shop* i.e. she has asked for and regularly gets ten pounds of sugar; *standing army* i.e. a permanent one. **2.** (with reference to crops) not yet cut. *Near the house there is a field of standing corn.* **3.** from a standing position: *standing jump* i.e. one made without first running and then jumping. Also *nc/u* **1.** period of time. *He is an engineer of long standing* i.e. he has been an engineer for a long time. **2.** position in society; rank. *Doctors have a high standing in our country.*

stank [stæŋk] past tense of **stink.**

stanza ['stænzə] *nc* group of lines of poetry.

staple[1] ['steipl] *nc* **1.** chief product of a country or part of a country. *Coffee is the staple of this district.* **2.** substance like a thread from which cotton, wool or flax etc is made; fibre. *The best cotton has a long staple.* Also *adj*: *Coffee is the staple product of this district. Corn is our staple food.*

staple[2] ['steipl] *nc* **1.** U-shaped piece of metal with pointed ends, which is driven into wood or a wall etc to keep something in position. *The long wire is fastened to the posts by staples.* **2.** U-shaped piece of metal used with another piece of metal which fits over it to fasten a door or gate. **3.** bent piece of metal which fastens sheets of paper together. Also *vt* fasten with a staple.

stapler *nc* device for fastening sheets of paper together.

star [stɑ:*] *nc* **1.** one of the bodies shining in the sky at night, seen as a small point of light (not the sun, moon or a planet). **2.** something which looks like a star (e.g. *). *There are five stars on their national flag.* **3.** famous actor, actress or singer. *The film is a good one with many stars in it.* Also *vt/i* **1.** mark with something like a star. **2.** be, or have as, the leading actor, actress or singer. *She starred in two films. The new play stars three of Britain's best actors. past* **starred.**

starry *adj* of a star; shining like a star; covered with stars: *starry light in the distance; girl with starry eyes; starry sky.* **starriness** *nu.*

starless *adj* without stars.

'starfish type of sea creature shaped like a star.

'starlight *nu* light from the stars. Also *adj.*

'starlit *adj* lit by the stars: *starlit sky.*

one's lucky stars stars or other bodies in the sky which were once believed to bring luck. *He thanked his lucky stars that he was not in the aeroplane when it crashed* i.e. he was very grateful, glad. (*informal*).

shooting star see **shoot.**

'starry-'eyed *adj* **1.** having eyes shining like stars. **2.** having great but not very practical ideas: *starry-eyed young people who think they can do everything.*

starboard ['stɑ:bəd] *nu* right-hand side of a ship as one faces the front end. *The ship turned to starboard.* (*opp* **port**).

starch [stɑ:tʃ] *nu* **1.** white substance which is the main type of food found in bread, grain, potatoes etc. *Poor people usually eat too much starch and too little meat.* **2.** this substance mixed with water and used to make clothes stiff. Also *vt* make stiff with starch. *She is starching the collar of my shirt.*

starchy *adj* **1.** of starch; containing starch. *Bread is a starchy food.* **2.** stiff; formal. *He has a very starchy manner.* **starchily** *adv.* **starchiness** *nu.*

stare [stɛə*] *vt/i* look for a long time with wide-open eyes. *He stared at the strange animal. Cows like to stand and stare. Who is the man with the staring eyes?* Also *nc*: *They looked at him with a stare of surprise.*

stare somebody out stare at somebody until he looks away.

stare one in the face be before one's own eyes. *I thought I had lost my pen but there it was staring me in the face.* (*informal*).

stark [stɑ:k] *adj* **1.** stiff; bleak. **2.** complete; quite. Also *adv*: *stark naked.* **starkly** *adv.* **starkness** *nu.*

stark staring mad insane; mad. (*informal*).

starling ['stɑ:liŋ] *nc* type of bird with black speckled feathers which quarrels a lot.

start[1] [stɑ:t] *vt/i* **1.** begin. *We start lessons at 9 a.m. It has started raining. He started to say something and then changed his mind.* **2.** begin a journey. *They started early for the village.* **3.** cause to begin. *My father started me playing football. He started (the engine of) the car so as to be ready to drive away* i.e. he set the engine going. **4.** move suddenly (usu. because of fear, surprise, pain etc). *He started from his bed when he heard the gun. I started at the sound of the bell.*

starter *nc* **1.** person who causes a race to begin by giving a signal (e.g. by firing a gun). **2.** person or animal that runs in a race. **3.** device for setting an engine going.

'self-'starter device which does this by electricity instead of the engine being turned by hand.

'starting point place from which something starts.

start off begin moving, running or doing something. *The boys started off across the field. The play starts off with a murder.*

start out **1.** leave on a journey. *We started out from home in the morning.* **2.** begin doing. *He has started out to study French.*

start up move suddenly (usu. because of

fear, surprise, pain etc). *I started up from my chair when I heard the noise.*
start something up begin, cause to begin or move. *A fight started up. He started up his car.*
to start with 1. first of all. *To start with, I am not his brother.* 2. at first; at the beginning. *There was only one hotel in the town to start with.*
start[2] [stɑːt] *nc* 1. sudden movement (usu. because of fear, surprise, pain etc). *I woke with a start.* 2. beginning of a journey; beginning of anything. *We make a start for school at 8.30 a.m. Rain delayed the start of the game.* 3. amount by which somebody is in front. *I gave him a start of half a mile before I began following him. He had a good start.*
by fits and starts stopping and starting again; from time to time. (*informal*).
startle ['stɑːtl] *vt* give a fright or surprise to; cause to move suddenly (because of fear or surprise). *The loud noise startled me.*
startling *adj* frightening; surprising: *startling news.* **startlingly** *adv.*
starve [stɑːv] *vt/i* die or suffer, cause to die or suffer, from hunger. *Because there is no food, the people are starving. The enemy is trying to starve us to death.*
starvation [stɑː'veiʃən] *nu*: *They are dying of starvation.*
starveling *nc* person who is starving (*o.f.*).
starve for, be starved of something be in great need of. *These children are starving for love. They are starved of affection.*
starve someone out make someone leave a place by starving him. *The enemy is trying to starve us out of our homes.*
state[1] [steit] *nc/u* 1. condition of somebody/something. *He is in a poor state of health. His business is in a good state. Their clothes were in a terrible state.* 2. (often **State**) government; country or large political division of a country. *We must pay taxes to the State. Education is provided by the State. The United States of America has fifty states.* 3. position; rank; dignity. *The king travelled in great state* i.e. with many followers and great ceremony. Also *adj* (in senses 2. and 3.): *The president will make a state visit to our country* i.e. a formal, official visit suitable to his position as president; *state control* i.e. control by the state; *state secrets.*
stately *adj* having dignity; grand. **stateliness** *nu.*
stateless *adj* not belonging to any state; without citizenship of any country.
'**stateroom** private room in a ship (*US* also in a railway train).
'**statesman** person who is skilled in government and holds a high position in it.
'**statesmanlike** *adj* having the qualities of a good statesman.
'**statesmanship** *nu* skill of a good statesman.
lie in state (with reference to an important person who has died) lie in a church or other building for the public to see before being buried.
state[2] [steit] *vt* express clearly in words or writing. *Please state exactly what you did. It states in the newspaper that there will be a meeting tomorrow.*
stated *adj* already decided or made known. *He arrived at the stated time/the time stated.*
statement *nc/u* 1. manner of expressing something in words or writing. *This book is good because of its clearness of statement.* 2. act of stating; information. *The government has made a statement explaining what happened. I have just seen my bank statement* i.e. paper showing how much money I have in the bank.
static ['stætik] *adj* not moving. Also *nu* noises heard on a radio because of electrical disturbances in the air.
statics *nu* science of bodies at rest or forces in a state of balance.
static electricity electricity present in particles that are not moving.
station ['steiʃən] *nc* 1. place where railway trains start and stop; place where buses start and finish their journeys. *This train stops at every station.* 2. position or place where something is done (e.g. work or duty). *The soldiers took up their stations along the road. We went to the police station* i.e. the building where the police have their offices; *broadcasting station; fire station.* 3. position in society. *In the army there are men from many stations in life.* 4. (esp. in Australia) large sheep or cattle farm. Also *vt* put in a place for a certain purpose. *The soldiers stationed themselves along the road. I was stationed at district headquarters* i.e. was put there by my employers to live and work.
stationary ['steiʃənri] *adj* not moving; fixed. *He remained stationary so as not to be seen.*
'**station master** man in charge of a railway station.
'**station wagon** type of motorcar with a special body for carrying goods as well as people. (Also *Brit* **estate car**).
stationer ['steiʃənə*] *nc* person who sells writing materials.
stationery ['steiʃənri] *nu* writing materials.
statistics [stə'tistiks] 1. *npl* facts given in the form of numbers. *Statistics show that there are more boys than girls at school.* 2. *n sing* science of facts in the form of numbers.
statistical *adj*: *statistical data.*
statistician [stætis'tiʃən] *nc* person skilled in statistics.
statue ['stætjuː] *nc* figure of a person, animal etc made of stone, metal etc.
statuary ['stætjuəri] *nc* art of making statues; group of statues.
statuesque [stætjuː'esk] *adj* like a statue i.e. not moving; calm and solid.
statuette [stætjuː'et] *nc* small statue.
stature ['stætʃə*] *nu* (with reference to a person) 1. height, size. 2. importance.
status ['steitəs] *nu* (with reference to a person) social position or rank in relation to others. *Doctors have great/high status in most countries.*
'**status symbol** something which is a sign, or is considered to be a sign, of great status. *Having a sports car is the status symbol among the students of this college.*
status quo ['steitəs'kwou] *nu* condition or state of affairs at one particular time.
statute ['stætjuːt] *nc* law passed by the law-making assembly of a country.
statutory ['stætjutəri] *adj* as laid down by statute.
'**statute book** book in which statutes are printed.
'**statute law** law based on written statutes. (*opp* **common law**).
staunch[1], **stanch**[1] [stɔːntʃ] *adj* (with reference to a person) firm; loyal. **staunchly** *adv.* **staunchness** *nu.*
staunch[2], **stanch**[2] [stɔːntʃ] *vt* stop the flow

of blood from a wound.

stave [steiv] *nc* **1.** one of the curved pieces of wood from which a barrel is made. **2.** the five lines and four spaces on which music is written. see also **staff. 3.** verse of poetry.

stave something in break or be broken; make a hole in or be holed. *The sides of the box stove in when he hit them. past* **stove** [stouv].

stave something off (esp. with reference to something unpleasant) delay. *They are trying to stave off famine. past* **staved.**

stay[1] [stei] *vt/i* **1.** remain in the same place, same condition etc; not leave. *I stayed at home last night. They are staying to see the football match. She stays in every evening* i.e. does not leave the place where she lives. **2.** delay; stop. *The judge has agreed to stay execution of the order to pay* i.e. to delay carrying out the order. *He ate some fruit to stay his hunger.* (rather *o.f.*). **3.** be able to finish. *I do not think the runner will stay the distance* i.e. be able to run the whole distance of the race.

stayer *nc* person or animal able or willing to finish work, a race etc.

'stay-at-home person who stays at home and does not often go out. (*informal*).

'staying power ability to go on doing something difficult.

stay away remain away; not go near. *He stayed away from school when he was ill. You must stay away from these rough boys.*

stay out remain outside (esp. later than usual). *Her mother does not allow her to stay out in the evening.*

stay up not go to bed. *We stayed up until midnight talking about our work.*

stay[2] [stei] *nc* **1.** period of remaining in the same place. *He has come to us for a short stay.* **2.** (in a legal sense) delay, postponement: *stay of execution* i.e. delay in carrying out an order of a court of law.

stay[3] [stei] *nc* rope or wire which keeps a mast, pole etc in position. Also *vt* (with **up**) keep a mast, pole etc in position.

stays *npl* stiff garment formerly worn by a woman around the hips, under a dress or skirt, in order to shape the body; corset (*o.f.*).

stead [sted] *nu* only in **stand somebody in good stead** i.e. be useful to somebody when needed; and in **in somebody's stead** i.e. instead of somebody. (rather *o.f.* – use **instead**).

steadfast ['stedfa:st] *adj* firm; loyal. **steadfastly** *adv.* **steadfastness** *nu.*

steady ['stedi] *adj* **1.** firmly fixed; not shaking; not likely to move or change. *You must hold the gun steady when shooting. He filled my glass with a steady hand.* **2.** regular; not stopping. *He is making steady progress. The wind was steady.* **3.** reliable; regular in habits. *He is a steady man who is never late.* (*opp* **unsteady**). Also *vt/i* become or make steady. *The wind is steadying. He steadied himself with his hand on the table. past* **steadied. steadily** *adv.* **steadiness** *nu.*

steak [steik] *nc* thick piece of meat or fish.

steal [sti:l] *vt/i* **1.** unlawfully take away something which belongs to somebody else. *It is a crime to steal. He stole my book.* **2.** come or go quietly. *They have stolen into the house. A smile stole across her face. past tense* **stole** [stoul]. *past part* **stolen** ['stouln].

steal a glance at look secretly at.

steal a march on someone gain an advantage over someone without him realizing it.

stealth [stelθ] *nu* in **by stealth** i.e. quietly or secretly. **stealthy** *adj.*

stealthily *adv*: *The thieves stealthily entered the building.*

steam [sti:m] *nu* water in the form of a gas; mist or vapour which rises from boiling water. *Many engines are driven by steam. The steam from the kettle showed that the water was boiling.* Also *vt/i* **1.** send out steam. *The kettle was steaming.* **2.** move by the force of steam. *The ship steamed up the river.* **3.** cook by steam. *She is steaming fish for supper.*

steamer *nc* **1.** ship driven by steam. **2.** pot for cooking food by steam.

steamy *adj* of steam; full of, covered with, steam: *steamy kitchen; steamy windows.* **steaminess** *nu.*

'steamboat boat driven by steam.

'steam engine engine driven by steam; moving railway engine driven by steam.

'steamroller heavy machine driven by steam for pressing down stones and levelling the surface when making roads, or a similar modern machine driven by a diesel engine (this modern machine is also called a **road roller**).

'steamship ship driven by steam.

'steam whistle whistle which is blown by the force of steam.

'steamed-'up *adj* angry; excited. (*informal*).

let off steam 1. (with reference to an engine etc) send out steam which is not needed. **2.** (with reference to a person) use up excess energy or express strong feelings. *The children were letting off steam in the playground after finishing their lessons.* (*informal* in sense **2.**).

steam open open by making soft with steam. *I caught him steaming open my letters.*

steed [sti:d] *nc* horse (*o.f.*).

steel [sti:l] *nu* hard metal made from iron mixed with carbon or other substances. (Most knives, machinery and tools are made of steel). Also *adj*: *steel knife.* Also *vt* (esp. with reference to the feelings) make as hard as steel; get rid of one's feelings of kindness, fear etc. *They steeled themselves against the attack. I steeled myself to try again.*

steely *adj* hard like steel. **steeliness** *nu.*

cold steel steel weapon (e.g. sword). *They fought with cold steel.* (rather *o.f.*).

'steelworks *n sing* or *pl* factory where steel is made. **steelworker** *nc.*

Note: often followed by a *sing* verb.

steelyard ['sti:lja:d] *nc* device for weighing made of a steel bar. The article to be weighed is hung on the short end of the bar while a weight is slid along the other part until the bar is balanced.

steep[1] [sti:p] *adj* **1.** having a sharp slope; more vertical than horizontal: *steep path up the mountain.* **2.** excessive. *That's a bit steep. The prices in this shop are steep.* (*informal* in sense **2.**). **steeply** *adv.* **steepness** *nu.*

steepish *adj* rather steep.

steepen *vt/i* become or make steep.

steep[2] [sti:p] *vt/i* **1.** become or make completely wet; soak in a liquid. *I left my dirty clothes to steep. She steeped the vegetables before cooking them.* **2.** (in *passive*) be filled with. *The people are steeped in ignorance.*

steeple ['sti:pl] *nc* tower of a church with a tall, pointed spire.

'steeplechase *nc* race on foot or on a horse

during which ditches, fences, hedges etc have to be jumped. **steeplechaser** *nc.* **steeplechasing** *nu.*

'steeplejack man skilled in climbing steeples, high chimneys etc to repair them.

steer[1] [stiə*] *vt/i* guide the course of a ship, motorcar etc by means of a rudder, wheel etc. *He steered the boat between the islands. Steer your car slowly into the garage. This car steers easily* i.e. it is easy to steer.

'steering gear machinery etc by which a car or ship is steered.

'steering wheel wheel by which a car or ship is steered.

'steersman man who steers a ship.

steer clear of keep away from.

steer[2] [stiə*] *nc* castrated bull used for beef.

steerage ['stiəridʒ] *nu* **1.** act of steering. **2.** part in some ships for passengers paying very low fares. *They travelled steerage to New York.* (Now usu. **tourist class** or **third class**).

stellar ['stelə*] *adj* of stars.

stem[1] [stem] *nc* **1.** thin upright part of a plant between the ground and its leaves or flowers; thin part of a plant which joins a leaf or fruit to a thicker part. *Tall flowers have long stems.* **2.** anything which looks like the stem of a plant (e.g. *stem of a wine-glass; stem of a tobacco pipe*). **3.** main part of a noun or verb to which groups of letters are added to change the sense (e.g. the stem of *walked* is *walk*). **4.** upright piece of wood or metal to which the two sides of a ship are joined at the bows (i.e. the front): *from stem to stern* i.e. from the bows (front) to the back of a ship. Also *vt* (with **from**) come or begin. *This result stems from what was done before. past* **stemmed.**

stem[2] [stem] *vt* (with reference to liquid) **1.** stop the flow. **2.** go forward against. *The ship stemmed the current of the river. past* **stemmed.**

stench [stentʃ] *nc* very unpleasant smell.

stencil ['stensil] *nc* device for printing copies of letters or designs by rubbing ink or paint on a thin sheet of metal, plastic, card, paper etc, on which the letters or designs have been cut or stamped. Also *vt* mark or print in this way. *His name is stencilled on all his boxes. past* **stencilled.** (*US* **stenciled**).

stenography [ste'nɔgrəfi] *nu* skill of writing quickly by using special short signs for words; shorthand. **stenographer** *nc.*

stentorian [sten'tɔːriən] *adj* (with reference to the voice) loud and powerful.

step[1] [step] *vt/i* **1.** move and then put down the foot. *Be careful when you step off the bus. He stepped over the dog at the door.* **2.** take a short walk. *Why don't we step across the road and speak to him? past* **stepped.**

'stepping stone 1. stone for stepping on when crossing a river or muddy place. **2.** something which helps one to get what one wants. *A good education is a stepping stone to a good job.*

step aside allow somebody to take one's place. *If he wishes to be captain, I am ready to step aside.*

step in come between to stop or help; intervene. *The two boys fought until a friend stepped in.*

step on it! hurry up! (*informal*).

step out walk faster. *We shall have to step out to be there on time.*

step up move up; come nearer.

step something up increase. *This factory has stepped up its output of cars.*

step this way polite form of **come here** or **come with me** (often used by a shop assistant to a customer).

step[2] [step] *nc* **1.** act of moving and then putting down one foot. *The soldier took one step forward. She walks with quick, short steps.* **2.** noise made in this way. *I heard the steps of my mother at the door.* (Also **footstep**). **3.** place where one puts one's feet when going up or down something (e.g. a ladder or stair). *He was standing on the top step of the stairs. She fell down the steps in front of the house.* **4.** something done in order to cause something else to happen later. *They took steps to close the school. My next step is to tell my father.*

'stepladder ladder with flat steps instead of rungs. (Also **steps** *npl*).

be/keep in step 1. (with reference to marching) put the left and then right foot down at the same time as all the others who are marching. **2.** behave as others do (in a general way).

be out of step 1. fail to keep step. **2.** not behave as others do (in a general way).

break step get out of step purposely.

step by step slowly; gradually.

step-[3] [step] *prefix* related by later marriage.

'stepchild child of one's husband or wife by his or her earlier marriage. (Also **stepson; stepdaughter**).

'stepfather husband of one's mother by her later marriage to him. (Also **stepmother**).

'stepbrother, 'stepsister child of one's stepfather or stepmother by a former marriage.

steppe [step] *nc* (esp. in Russia) large plain with very few trees.

stereo ['steriou] *adj/nu* see **stereophonic.**

stereo(phonic) [steriou('fɔnik)] *adj* (with reference to gramophone records etc) having sound which, by using two loudspeakers, is more natural because the sound seems to come from various directions; of the device which records sound of this kind.

stereo ['steriou] *nu* use of sound in this way. *This record is on stereo* i.e. it is intended for playing on a gramophone having two loudspeakers. Also *adj.*

stereoscope ['steriouskoup] *nc* apparatus with two lenses in which two photographs of the same thing taken from slightly different angles are seen as one photograph. In this way the objects in the photograph stand out and appear solid. **stereoscopic** [steriou'skɔpik] *adj.*

stereotype ['sterioutaip] *nc/u* **1.** method of printing by using a prepared metal plate; the plate itself. **2.** typical example; true copy. *He is the stereotype of an army officer.* Also *vt* print by using stereotypes.

stereotyped *adj* not changing; fixed by habit; without meaning. *He gave the usual stereotyped answers to the questions of the newspaper reporters.*

sterile ['sterail] *adj* **1.** not able to produce children, seeds or crops etc; barren: *sterile woman* i.e. one who is unable to have children. *This land is sterile.* **2.** completely free from germs. *All the instruments used by a doctor must be sterile.* **3.** without result; useless: *sterile talks about peace.* **sterility** [ste'riliti] *nu.*

sterilize ['sterilaiz] *vt* make sterile. *In some countries women are sterilized to reduce the birth rate. The doctor sterilized his instruments.* **sterilization** [sterilai'zeiʃən] *nu.*

sterilized *adj.* (*opp* **unsterilized**).

sterling ['stəːliŋ] *adj* **1.** (with reference to

gold and silver) of fixed value and purity. *These spoons are made of sterling silver. £1 sterling* i.e. one British pound. **2.** reliable; of good quality. Also *nu* British money. *They wish to be paid in sterling, not dollars.*
the 'sterling area countries which have currencies linked to the British pound.

stern[1] [stəːn] *adj* severe; strict. *He has a stern face. We have a very stern headmaster.*
sternly *adv.* **sternness** *nu.*

stern[2] [stəːn] *nc* **1.** back end of a ship. **2.** tail end of an animal.

stertorous ['stəːtərəs] *adj* (with reference to breathing) noisy. **stertorously** *adv.*

stethoscope ['steθəskoup] *nc* instrument used by doctors to listen to the sounds made by the lungs or the heart.

stevedore ['stiːvədɔː*] *nc* man who loads and unloads ships.

stew[1] [stjuː] *vt/i* cook, be cooked, slowly in a closed dish or saucepan with a little water. Also *nc/u* food cooked in this way: *beef stew.*
stewing *adj* suitable for stewing. *May I have a pound of stewing steak?*
be in/get into a stew be or become very upset or excited. *He is in a stew about his examination results.* (*informal*).

stew[2] [stjuː] *nc* (usu. *pl* with **the**) brothel (*o.f.*).

steward ['stjuːəd] *nc* **1.** man who looks after the passengers on a ship or aircraft. **2.** man who manages, helps to manage, meetings (e.g. sports or race meeting, public meeting, dance etc). **3.** man who manages someone's land or house (*o.f.* in sense **3.**).
stewardess [stjuə'des] *nc* woman steward (in sense **1.**).
stewardship *nc* post or work of a steward; period of time as a steward.
'shop 'steward member of a trade union in a factory who is chosen by the other workers to look after their interests.

stick[1] [stik] *vt/i* **1.** fasten, become fastened, with glue or any substance like it. *He stuck the stamp on the letter. Glue sticks to one's fingers. The pages of the book are stuck together.* **2.** fix something pointed in something else. *He stuck his knife into the table. The post has been stuck into the ground.* **3.** not be able to move. *The window is stuck* i.e. it cannot be opened or shut. *Our car was stuck in the mud for two hours. I'm stuck with this problem. past* **stuck** [stʌk].
sticker *nc* **1.** person who goes on trying. **2.** piece of paper etc which can be stuck on something.
sticky *adj* **1.** likely to stick to something. *The glue has made my fingers sticky.* **2.** difficult; unwilling. *This is a sticky problem. He is sticky about letting me go alone.* (*informal* in sense **2.**). **stickily** *adv.* **stickiness** *nu.*
'stick-in-the-mud person who refuses to change or accept new ideas. *The old manager is a stick-in-the-mud.* (*informal*).
'sticking plaster type of tape for sticking on cuts or injuries.
stick around stay near; not go away. (*informal*).
stick (at) something **1.** keep doing. *He stuck the job for a year.* **2.** be unwilling; hesitate. *He is a dangerous man who sticks at nothing. He won't stick at anything to achieve his aims.*
stick down **1.** fasten with glue etc. *I stuck down the back of the envelope.* **2.** put down. *Stick your coat down and come with me.* (*informal* in sense **2.**).
stick on **1.** fasten, be fastened, with glue. **2.** stay on. *It is difficult to stick on a bicycle on a rough road.* (*informal*). **3.** (in *passive*) be very fond of. *John is stuck on that girl.* (*informal*). Also *adj*: *a stick-on label.*
stick (something) out project, cause to project. *The papers were sticking out of his pocket. Don't stick your head out. He stuck out his tongue at me.*
stick it out endure trouble etc until it is finished. (*informal*).
stick to someone refuse to leave; give support to. *He is a man who sticks to his friends.* (*informal*).
stick together **1.** remain fixed, one to the other. *The pages are stuck together.* **2.** (with reference to persons) keep together; remain united. (*informal* in sense **2.**).
stick (something) up **1.** project, cause to project, upwards. *He saw the flag sticking up above the trees.* **2.** fix in a high place to be seen. *They have stuck up a notice about the concert.* **3.** raise one's hands above one's head; cause somebody to do so (as a sign of surrender). *The soldier ordered the prisoners to stick their hands up. The thieves have just stuck up a bank* i.e. caused those in the bank to raise their hands by pointing guns at them and then robbed the bank. (*informal* in sense **3.**).
'stick-up *nc* robbery carried out in this way. (*informal*).
stick up for someone support strongly; defend. *Whatever happens, I'll stick up for you.* (*informal*).
stuck-up *adj* very proud, conceited. (*informal*).

stick[2] [stik] *nc* **1.** small branch from a tree. *We made a fire from the sticks which were lying about.* **2.** branch of a tree or piece of wood made into something: *walking stick; hockey stick.* **3.** anything long and thin like a stick: *stick of chalk.* **4.** person who is stiff and dull. (*informal* in sense **4.**).
'stick insect type of insect shaped like a stick.

stickler ['stiklə*] *nc* (with **for**) person who pays great attention to something so that it is done properly. *My father is a stickler for neatness and honesty.*

stiff [stif] *adj* **1.** difficult to bend or move. *I have a stiff leg. This book has a stiff cover. They made a stiff mixture of flour and water.* **2.** difficult to do. *We sat a very stiff examination. It was a stiff climb to the top of the hill.* **3.** high; strong. *Prices here are stiff. The boat was sailing in a stiff breeze. What he needs is a stiff drink.* **4.** (with reference to behaviour etc) formal; unfriendly. *He is very stiff with strangers.* **5.** very much: *scare/bore someone stiff* i.e. frighten/bore very much. (*informal*). **stiffly** *adv.* **stiffness** *nu.*
stiffen *vt/i* become or make stiff.
stiffener *nc* something which stiffens something else.
stiffening *nu* substance added to something to make it stiff. *Tailors sometimes sew stiffening into clothes to make them keep their shape.*
'stiff-'necked *adj* stubborn; not easily persuaded.

stifle ['staifl] *vt/i* **1.** stop the breath; make breathing difficult. *The heat of the sun at midday was stifling. The children were stifled by the smoke.* **2.** stop; keep from being heard. *The government soon stifled these* *complaints. We had to stifle our laughter.*

stigma ['stigmə] *nc* **1.** mark of disgrace; mark on the skin: *stigma of failure.* **2.** top of the pistil of a flower i.e. the place where its seeds grow. *pl* **stigmata** [stig'mɑːtə] or **stigmas.**

stigmatize *vt* mark with a stigma; describe as being bad in some way. *He stigmatized all young people as fools.*

stile [stail] *nc* steps for climbing a fence or wall.

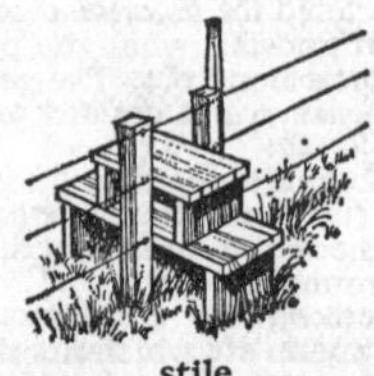

stile

stiletto [sti'letou] *nc* type of knife with a sharp point. *pl* **stilettos** or **stilettoes.**

sti'letto 'heels high, pointed heels on a woman's shoes; shoes with this type of heel.

still[1] [stil] *adj/adv* **1.** not moving; silent. *The water in the pool was very still. The child kept still while his mother dressed him.* **2.** (with reference to wine or other drinks) not bubbling with gas. Also *nc* **1.** silence: *the still of the forest* (*o.f.*). **2.** photograph taken from the many made while filming a picture for the cinema, and enlarged. (Because it is by itself it cannot show motion as a cinema film does). Also *vt* cause to be still; make calm or quiet. *She stilled the child's fears.*

stillness *nu.*

'stillborn *adj* dead when born.

'still 'life painting etc of things without life (e.g. fruit, flowers).

still[2] [stil] *adv/intensifier* **1.** up to this or that moment; even now; even then. *He still comes to see us. They were still asleep when I left.*

Note: still has the sense of something continuing; *yet* of something which is about to happen. *Is your baby still talking?* i.e. it has already at some time begun to talk; *Is your baby talking yet?* i.e. it has not, as far as the questioner knows, begun to talk.

2. yet; (with *comparative*) to a greater extent. *He is fat, but his brother is still fatter/fatter still.* **3.** however. *You did wrong. Still, I am ready to forgive you.*

still[3] [stil] *nc* apparatus for making alcohol (by distilling).

stilt [stilt] *nc* one of two long poles, each with a footrest so that one can walk high above the ground when using them.

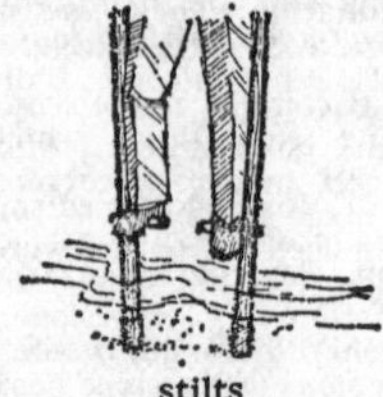

stilts

stilted ['stiltid] *adj* (with reference to behaviour, writing etc) stiff; artificial; not natural. **stiltedly** *adv.*

stimulate ['stimjuleit] *vt* increase energy; excite. *Better wages have stimulated them to work harder.*

stimulating *adj*: *stimulating book; stimulating weather.* **stimulation** [stimju'leiʃən] *nc/u.*

stimulant ['stimjulnt] *nc* drink or drug which stimulates. *Athletes are forbidden to take stimulants before a race.*

stimulus ['stimjuləs] *nc* something which stimulates. *The good news was a stimulus to all who heard it. pl* **stimuli** ['stimjuliː].

sting[1] [stiŋ] *nc* **1.** small, pointed part of some insects, used as a weapon. *Bees have stings.* **2.** pain, or mark on the skin, caused by a sting. *There was a big sting on his neck.* **3.** anything which causes pain or distress. *He felt the sting of the rain on his face. They fear the sting of his anger.*

sting[2] [stiŋ] *vt/i* **1.** push in a sting. *The bee stung him on the neck. Most flies do not sting.* **2.** feel or cause pain or distress. *My face is stinging because of the very cold wind. Their cruel words stung him to reply in an angry voice.* **3.** (usu. *passive*) be cheated. *I've been stung by that shopkeeper.* (*informal* in sense **3.**). *past* **stung** [stʌŋ].

'stinging nettle type of plant with rough hairs which cause pain if touched.

stingy ['stindʒi] *adj* unwilling to spend money or to give anything; miserly; mean. **stingily** *adv.* **stinginess** *nu.* (all *informal*).

stink [stiŋk] *vt/i* **1.** give out a very unpleasant smell. *The meat is not fresh. It stinks. Their clothes stank of sweat.* **2.** cause to go because of a very unpleasant smell. *The burning rubbish stank us out of the room. past tense* **stank** [stæŋk] or **stunk** [stʌŋk]. *past part* **stunk.** Also *nc*: *the stink of rotting fruit.* (all *informal*).

stint [stint] *vt* cause to be left with nothing or very little; not have or give enough of. *He stints himself in food and clothes so as to be able to pay for his education.* Also *nc* fixed amount of work. *I have done my stint for the day.*

without stint generously; without any limit.

stipend ['staipend] *nc* salary (usu. of a clergyman).

stipendiary [stai'pendiəri] *adj* working for a salary: *stipendiary magistrate.*

stipple ['stipl] *vt* draw or paint with small dots instead of lines.

stipulate ['stipjuleit] *vt* make something part of an agreement; make certain conditions. *They say they will repair the door but they stipulate that they must be paid as soon as they have finished.*

stipulation [stipju'leiʃən] *nc/u* something which is stipulated. *I agreed to help on the stipulation that others would also help.*

stipulated *adj.* (*opp* **unstipulated**).

stir [stəː*] *vt/i* **1.** move; begin to move. *The animals were stirring in the forest. Has the child stirred yet?* i.e. woken up. **2.** move an instrument (e.g. a stick) round in a liquid etc to mix it. *I put milk in my tea and stirred it.* **3.** cause to feel; be aroused. *The book stirred my interest. pres part* **stirring.** *past* **stirred.**

stirring *adj* exciting: *a stirring book.* **stirringly** *adv.*

stir something in mix something by stirring. *When the soup was hot she stirred in some salt.*

stir something up cause; arouse. *They are always stirring up trouble.*

stirrup ['stirəp] *nc* loop of iron, leather or

rope, hanging from a saddle in which one puts one's foot when riding a horse.
'**stirrup cup** drink given to somebody already sitting on a horse and about to ride away.
'**stirrup pump** pump for putting out fires which is kept in position by placing the feet on a bar on each side of it.

stitch [stitʃ] *vt/i* **1.** join by using a needle and thread; decorate in this way; make a complete movement of the needle in knitting etc. *She stitched the buttons on the coat. I am stitching flowers on the tablecloth.* **2.** close a wound with needle and thread. *The doctor stitched the big cut above my eye.* Also *nc* **1.** amount of thread which has been put through cloth by a needle to join or decorate. *She mended the coat with a few stitches.* **2.** thread keeping a wound closed. *I had three stitches put in my head.* **3.** sharp pain in the side often felt when running: *get a/the stitch.*
drop a stitch let a thread fall off the point of a needle (esp. woollen thread from a knitting needle).
without a stitch (on) naked. (*informal*).

stoat [stout] *nc* type of small animal with a long, slender body. Its fur is brown in summer and white in winter, when it is called the **ermine.**

stock [stɔk] **1.** *nc* main part of a tree from which branches grow; part of a tree or plant to which another tree or plant is grafted. **2.** *nc* handle etc of a tool or instrument: *stock of a whip* i.e. wooden part to which the barrel is fixed. **3.** *nu* persons from whom one is descended; ancestors. *Both his parents are of Scottish stock.* **4.** *nc/u* goods kept ready for use or sale; store of things or material which is ready to be used. *This shop has a good stock of boys' shoes. We have blue ink in stock* i.e. we have a ready supply of blue ink. *Red ink is out of stock* i.e. we have no red ink. *He has collected a stock of facts about motorcars.* **5.** *nu* juice from boiled bones, meat etc, ready for making soup, gravy etc. **6.** *nu* animals kept on a farm. *Farmers need plenty of grass to feed their stock.* (Also **livestock**). **7.** *nc/u* money shares in a business; money lent to a government. *I have put all my money in government stock.* **8.** *nc* (in *pl*) framework on which a ship is built or repaired. *The company has two new ships on the stocks* i.e. being built. **9.** *nc* (in *pl*) framework of wood or stone with holes for the legs, in which a person was fastened in the past as a punishment. **10.** *nc* type of wide, stiff tie once worn by men round the neck. Also *vt* get or keep a stock of something. *Does this shop stock English books?* Also *adj* **1.** of the usual type kept in stock. *He takes a stock size in shoes* i.e. shoes of one of the usual sizes fit him. **2.** used too much; common. *This is his stock answer when anything goes wrong.*
'**fatstock** cattle fed well so that they can be killed and used as food.
'**laughing stock** see **laugh**[1].
'**stockbreeder,** '**stockfarmer** *nc* farmer who breeds cattle. **stockbreeding** *nu.*
'**stockbroker** person who buys and sells stocks (in sense **7.**) and shares.
'**stock exchange** place where stocks (in sense **7.**) and shares are bought and sold.
'**stock-in-'trade** equipment etc which somebody needs to do his work. *Hammers and nails are part of a joiner's stock-in-trade.*
'**stockpile** *vt* buy large amounts of materials which may become dearer or less easy to get later (e.g. a government buying materials which it may need for war). Also *nc.*
'**stock-'still** *adv* completely still.
'**stockyard** place where cattle are kept before they are killed.
take stock count the amount of stock kept ready for use or sale.
'**stocktaking** *nc/u* work of counting stock. *The shop is closed for its annual stocktaking.*
take stock of find out what the position is, what has to be done etc. *The general took stock of the enemy and decided to attack at once.*

stockade [stɔ'keid] *nc* fence made of upright poles (usu. put round a building to defend it): *stockaded building* i.e. one with a stockade round it.

stocking ['stɔkiŋ] *nc* covering of wool, cotton, silk, nylon etc which fits the leg and foot tightly and reaches to the knee or to the top of the leg.

stocky ['stɔki] *adj* (with reference to persons, animals and plants) short and strong.
stockily *adv.* **stockiness** *nu.*

stodge [stɔdʒ] *nu* thick, tasteless food.
stodgy *adj* **1.** (with reference to food) thick and tasteless. **2.** (with reference to persons/things) dull; slow; uninteresting. *He made a very stodgy speech.*

stoic ['stouik] *nc* person who suffers without complaint and who is not affected by either pleasure or pain. **stoical** *adj.* **stoically** *adv.*
stoicism ['stouisizəm] *nu* endurance of pain, hardship etc without complaint.

stoke [stouk] *vt/i* (often with **up**) put coal or other fuel on a fire (esp. a large fire giving heat for an engine i.e. a furnace). *The furnace must be stoked up every two hours.*
stoker *nc* person who stokes: *one of the ship's stokers.*
'**stokehole,** '**stokehold** place in a ship where the furnaces are.

stole[1] [stoul] past tense of **steal.**

stole[2] [stoul] *nc* narrow strip of cloth worn round the neck by a priest; strip of cloth or fur worn round the shoulders by a woman.

stolen ['stouln] past part of **steal.**

stolid ['stɔlid] *adj* difficult to arouse or excite; dull. **stolidly** *adv.* **stolidness, stolidity** [stə'liditi] *nu.*

stomach ['stʌmək] *nc* **1.** organ inside the body, like a bag, into which food goes when it is swallowed, and in which the food is then digested. **2.** lower front part of the body. *Nobody can work well on an empty stomach* i.e. if his stomach is empty. *It is difficult to run quickly on a full stomach.* **3.** desire; inclination. *They have no stomach for hard work.* Also *vt* (usu. *negative*): *I can't stomach such behaviour* i.e. I dislike such behaviour very much.

stone [stoun] *nc/u* **1.** hard substance of which rock is made; piece of rock. *The building is made of stone. The soil is full of stones.* Often used with other words to show types of rock (e.g. *limestone; sandstone*) or the uses of stone (e.g. *gravestone; millstone; stepping stone*). Also *adj* made of stone: *stone house; stone walls; stone floor.* **2.** jewel: *precious stones.* **3.** hard seed inside some types of fruit. *There are large stones inside dates and plums.* **4.** hard lump which forms in the bladder or kidney. **5.** weight of 14 pounds. *My weight is 12 stone.* *pl* **stone** (not

used in USA). see **appendix.** Also *vt* **1.** throw stones at. *The angry crowd stoned his car.* **2.** take the stones out of fruit.
stoneless *adj* (esp. with reference to fruit) without stones.
stony *adj* **1.** like stone; full of stones: *stony soil.* **2.** hard; unfriendly. *He gave me a stony look. There was a stony silence.* **stonily** *adv.* **stoniness** *nu.*
'Stone Age period in man's history, before metal was discovered, when tools and weapons were made of stone.
'stone-'blind *adj* completely blind. (Also **stone-cold; stone-dead; stone-deaf**).
'stoneware pots, jugs etc made from coarse clay.
'stonework large pieces of stone from which a wall or building is made.
a 'stone's throw very near. *It is only a stone's throw from here to my house. We live within a stone's throw of the main road.* (*informal*).

stood [stud] past of **stand**[1].

stool [stu:l] *nc* **1.** small chair without a back. **2.** low chair of this type to rest the feet on (usu. **footstool**), or to kneel on. **3.** solid waste matter sent out from the body. (*formal* or medical in sense **3.**).
'stool pigeon 1. criminal who betrays his fellow criminals to the police. (*informal*). **2.** pigeon used to trap other pigeons.

stoop [stu:p] *vt/i* **1.** bend the upper part of the body forward and downward. *She stooped to talk to the little child.* **2.** be willing to do something wrong or shameful; lower oneself. *He has stooped to stealing money from his own mother.* Also *nc* bend in the body: *walk with a stoop.*

stop[1] [stɔp] *vt/i* **1.** come to the end of a movement or activity; bring a movement or activity to an end. *The train does not stop here. The noise stopped. He stopped his car at the corner. Rain stopped the game.* **2.** prevent; hinder. *What stopped him (from) coming? He can read what he likes. I won't stop him.* **3.** cease; leave off. *He has stopped smoking.* **4.** fill up a hole. *I am stopping the holes and cracks in the wall with cement. He stopped his ears with his fingers.* **5.** refuse to give. *The manager has stopped my salary. The bank stopped (the payment of) his cheque.* past **stopped.**
stopper *nc* something which fills up an opening. *Have you the stopper of this bottle?*
stoppage *nc* state of being stopped; something which obstructs. *There have been several stoppages (of work) at the factory. I must remove the stoppage from the water pipes.*
stop in stay at home. *I am not going out this evening. I am stopping in.* (*informal*).
stop over stop for a time during a journey. *We shall stop over at a hotel for one night before going on to London.*
'stopover *nc* place where one stops in this way (often during a journey by air); act of stopping in this way.
stop up stay awake; not go to bed. *Little children should not stop up till midnight.*
stop something up fill up an opening. *I am stopping up the hole in the wall.*
stop dead stop suddenly.
stop short stop suddenly. *The horse stopped short when he heard my voice.*

stop[2] [stɔp] *nc* **1.** act or state of stopping or being stopped. *The train came to a stop a mile from the station. He put a stop to the noise.* **2.** place where buses etc usually stop during their journeys. *We get off at the next stop. He was standing at the bus stop.* **3.** punctuation mark shown by . i.e. a full stop. **4.** device used to stop or control: *door stop; window stop* i.e. a piece of wood etc to prevent a door or window moving or opening too much; *organ stop* i.e. a device which controls the flow of air to give different notes in the musical instrument called an organ.
'stopcock short pipe with a key or tap which controls the amount of liquid flowing through a pipe or container.
'stopgap *nc* somebody/something used until somebody/something else better is found. *He is only a stopgap until another driver is found.* Also *adj*: *stopgap arrangements.*
'stop-'press (mainly *Brit*) latest news put in a newspaper (usu. in a space left empty for it) after printing has begun.
'stopwatch type of watch with hands which can be started and stopped by pressing a knob (used to find out the exact time taken to do something e.g. run a race).

store [stɔ:*] *nc* **1.** supply of something kept ready for use when needed. *We have a good store of grain until the next harvest.* Used in *pl* when it refers to many different kinds of things. *He is in charge of the stores at the hospital.* **2.** place where goods are kept. *The boys are getting pens and pencils from the school store.* **3.** shop: *drugstore; liquor store; department store* i.e. large shop selling many different kinds of goods.
Note: store in the sense of a shop is more common in the USA than in Britain.
Also *vt* **1.** keep something ready for use. *After harvest we store the grain.* **2.** put in a safe place. *They have stored their furniture until they return from abroad.*
storage *nu* **1.** act of storing. **2.** place where goods are stored. *They have put their furniture in storage.*
'storehouse place where goods etc are kept. *The library is a storehouse of information.*
'storekeeper person in charge of a store.
'storeroom room in a house etc where goods which are not in use are kept.
in store 1. kept for use when needed. *We must keep our strength in store for the big race.* **2.** about to happen. *There is a surprise in store for them when they come back.*
set great store by consider to be very important. *He sets great store by honesty.* (*opp* **set no store by**) (Also **set little/not much store by**).
store something up collect and keep ready for use when needed. *They are storing up all the food they can buy.*

storey, story ['stɔ:ri] *nc* rooms on one floor of a building; floor or level of a building. *My bedroom is on the second storey* i.e. two levels up. *pl* **storeys** or **stories.**
Note: the use of *storey* or *floor* can be confusing. (*US*) one level up is called the *second* floor or storey; (*Brit*) one level up is called the *first* floor or storey.
-storeyed, -storied *adj* having storeys stories: *six-storeyed/storied building.*

stork [stɔ:k] *nc* type of large bird with long legs and a long pointed beak, which often stands on one leg.

storm [stɔ:m] *nc* **1.** bad weather (usu. with strong winds). *The storm last night blew down the tree.* (Often used with another word to show what kind of storm: *dust storm sandstorm; snowstorm; thunderstorm*). **2.** expression of strong feelings. *The speech* *caused a storm among those who heard it.* Also *vt/i* **1.** express strong feelings. *He stormed out of the room* i.e. he left the room shouting angrily. **2.** attack strongly and capture quickly. *Our soldiers stormed the town.*

stormy *adj* **1.** of a storm; having a storm: *stormy sea; stormy weather.* **2.** having strong feelings expressed: *stormy meeting.* **stormily** *adv.* **storminess** *nu.*

'storm centre centre of a storm or of any trouble or violence.

'storm cone large cone made of strong cloth, used as a signal to show a storm is coming. (Also **storm signal**).

'storm lantern type of lamp which can be used in a high wind.

'storm sail small, very strong sail used on a sailing ship during a storm.

'storm signal see **storm cone.**

'storm troops troops specially trained to attack strongly defended places.

storm in a teacup strong feelings about something which is not important. (*informal*).

take by storm attack strongly and capture quickly.

story[1] ['stɔːri] *nc* account of what has happened, either true or imaginary. *He told us the story of his life. Children like stories about fairies. He is reading a storybook. Don't believe all the stories he tells you.*

storied *adj* told in a story; made famous by stories. (rather *o.f.*).

'storyteller **1.** person who tells or writes stories. **2.** (often with reference to children) person who tells lies. (*informal* in sense **2.**).

story[2] ['stɔːri] *nc* see **storey.**

stoup [stuːp] *nc* container for holy water in a church.

stout [staut] *adj* **1.** strong; tough. *He had a stout stick in his hand. He has a stout heart* i.e. he is brave. **2.** (with reference to persons only) rather fat. *He is too stout to run quickly.* Also *nu* type of strong, dark beer. **stoutly** *adv.* **stoutness** *nu.*

'stout-'hearted *adj* brave.

stove[1] [stouv] *nc* apparatus with a fire enclosed inside, used for heating a room and/or for cooking; cooker heated by gas or electricity.

'stovepipe pipe which takes away the smoke from a stove.

stove[2] [stouv] past of **stave.**

stow [stou] *vt* put or load carefully and tightly. *He stowed his books in the box. They are stowing the heavy goods in the hold of the ship.*

stow something away put away carefully and tightly to be ready when needed.

'stowaway *nc* person who hides himself on a ship or aircraft to avoid paying the fare.

straddle ['strædl] *vt/i* stand or walk with the legs wide apart; stand, sit or walk across something with one leg on each side of it. *He straddled the log of wood.*

strafe [strɑːf] *vt* attack with bombs, shells etc.

straggle ['strægl] *vi* **1.** spread too much in an untidy manner. *The branches of the trees straggled over the wall.* **2.** fall behind the others while going somewhere. *The young children straggled behind the older ones.*

straggler *nc* person who falls behind.

straight[1] [streit] *adj* **1.** not curved or bent; going directly from one point to another. *Draw a straight line between A and B. The road from here to the village is straight.* **2.** honest; true. *You will find him very straight. I want a straight answer to my question.* Also *pred adj* tidy; in order. *I am putting my room straight before he comes.* Also *nc* (usu. sing with **the**). *He came round the bend into the straight ten yards in front of the other runners* i.e. into the straight part of the running track between the two bends.

straighten *vt/i* become or make straight. *The road has been straightened. He is trying to straighten (out) the matter* i.e. put it right.

the straight and narrow way of behaving according to strict moral rules: *keep to the straight and narrow.* (*informal*).

keep a straight face see **keep**[1].

straight[2] [streit] *adv* **1.** not in a curve; without turning. *Go straight on until you reach the church. He drove straight into the tree.* **2.** without any delay; by the quickest route. *As soon as he arrived he went straight into the meeting. My mother wants me to go straight home.* **3.** honestly; directly. *Tell me straight! Is he dead? He looked me straight in the eyes.*

straight away at once.

straight off at once. (*informal*).

straight out without delay; frankly. *I told him straight out that he was a liar.* (*informal*).

go straight no longer act in a dishonest way. *He was once in prison but is now going straight.* (*informal*).

straightforward [streit'fɔːwəd] *adj* **1.** honest; direct. *He seems a straightforward person.* **2.** simple; without difficulties. *The first question he asked me was quite straightforward.* **straightforwardly** *adv.* **straightforwardness** *nu.*

strain[1] [strein] *vt/i* **1.** pull very tight. *They strained the wire between the two posts.* **2.** use to the utmost. *We strained our ears to hear what he was saying.* **3.** damage by using too much. *He strained his heart by running too far. If you read in a bad light you will strain your eyes.* **4.** try very hard; make a great effort. *They are straining to succeed in their work.* **5.** use more than is considered right. *You cannot strain their words to mean something different.* **6.** pass a substance through a sieve or filter (e.g. through a cloth or wire mesh) to separate the liquid from the solids in it. *She boiled the potatoes and then strained them* i.e. separated the potatoes from the water in which they had been boiled. **7.** hold closely to the body (*o.f.* in sense **7.**).

strained *adj* not natural; unhappy. *He had a strained smile on his face. The mistake has caused strained relations between the manager and his staff.*

strainer *nc* device for separating liquids from solids: *vegetable strainer; tea strainer.*

strain after something try hard to get. *He is always straining after praise and approval.*

strain at something **1.** try hard to get; make a great effort (often with the sense of trying to get what is impossible). *They strained at complete success.* **2.** make a great effort using or holding. *I strained at the wheel but it would not move.*

strain something off separate a liquid from the solids in it. *She strained off the water from the vegetables.*

strain every nerve try as hard as possible. *He strained every nerve to win.*

strain[2] [strein] *nc/u* **1.** state of being pulled very tight. *The strain on the wire broke it.* **2.** something which is so great that it causes damage or discomfort. *We suffered the strain of having to wait a week for the news. Examinations cause mental strain.* **3.** way of speaking or writing. *Her letters were written in a happy strain.* **4.** inherited nature or tendency. *There is a criminal strain in the whole family. He owns a good strain of cattle* i.e. a good breed. **5.** (in *pl*) music; tune. *We marched to the strains of the school band.* (rather *o.f.* in sense **5.**).

'breaking strain amount of strain which breaks something. *Engineers have to know the breaking strains of many substances.*

under strain suffering from strain; being strained. *He is working under a strain. The rope broke under the strain* i.e. because of the strain.

strait [streit] *adj* narrow; (used only with other words) tight. Also *nc* narrow stretch of water open at both ends. *The ship passed through the strait between the two islands.* (Often *pl* with proper names: *the Straits of Dover*).

straiten *vt* make narrow; (usu. only *past part*) make poor. *They live in very straitened circumstances* i.e. in great poverty.

'strait jacket type of coat put on somebody who is mad, to stop him being violent.

'strait-'laced *adj* **1.** tightly laced in a garment (*o.f.*). **2.** narrow in thought and manners. *They are too strait-laced to approve of dancing.* (*informal*).

strand[1] [strænd] *nc* one of the strings or wires from which a rope is made; a single thread of anything. *There were strands of hair on his coat.*

strand[2] [strænd] *nc* edge of the sea, a lake or river; shore (*o.f.*). Also *vt/i* **1.** go, cause to go, on the shore or on the rocks etc. *Their boat was stranded on the rock.* **2.** be in difficulty, alone, without money, food etc. *We were stranded in the big town because we missed the train.*

strange [streindʒ] *adj* **1.** not known, met or seen before, therefore odd; queer. *Who is that strange man over there? He says some very strange things.* **2.** not accustomed to. *The new boys are strange to the school.*

strangely *adv.* **strangeness** *nu.*

stranger *nc* **1.** person not known, met or seen before. *Don't talk to strangers.* **2.** person who is not accustomed to something. *He is a stranger in/to the big city. I am a stranger to politics.*

strangle ['stræŋgl] *vt* **1.** kill by holding the throat tightly. **2.** make breathing difficult. *This tight collar is strangling me.* **3.** stop; make more difficult. *The war is strangling trade.*

strangler *nc* person who strangles (in sense **1.**).

strangulation [stræŋgju'leiʃən] *nu* act of strangling or being strangled: *death by strangulation.*

'stranglehold act of holding in order to strangle; power to stop completely. *They have a stranglehold on our trade.*

strap [stræp] *nc* long, narrow piece of leather, cloth or metal. *He has broken the strap of his wrist watch. Some teachers still use a strap* i.e. a long, narrow piece of leather to punish children. Also *vt* **1.** fasten with a strap. *He strapped his books to his bicycle.* **2.** sharpen with a strap. **3.** beat with a strap. *past* **strapped.**

strapping *adj* big and strong. *He is a strapping young man.* (*informal*).

'straphanger person who travels in a bus or train, standing up and holding on to a strap fixed to the roof (because all the seats are taken).

strata ['strɑːtə] pl of **stratum.**

stratagem ['strætədʒəm] *nc/u* scheme or trick to deceive an enemy during a war; any scheme or trick to deceive somebody.

strategy ['strætədʒi] *nc/u* **1.** (esp. with reference to moving and using large military forces in the best way) art of waging war. **2.** general plan of action.

Note: tactics npl is the art of moving and using smaller military forces during a battle.

strategic [strə'tiːdʒik] *adj* of strategy; required by strategy. *The strategic defence of the country depends on a powerful air force; strategic materials* i.e. materials required to wage war.

strategist *nc* person skilled in strategy.

stratify ['strætifai] *vt* put in layers or strata.

stratification [strætifi'keiʃən] *nu*: *Geology studies the stratification of rocks.*

stratosphere ['strætəsfiə*] *nu* layer of the atmosphere between about 6 and 40 miles above the earth in which the temperature does not decrease with height.

stratum ['strɑːtəm] *nc* **1.** layer of rock or earth. **2.** class in society. *pl* **strata** ['strɑːtə].

straw [strɔː] **1.** *nc/u* dry stalk of corn etc after the grain has been taken out. *The hut has a roof of straw. The cattle were lying on the straw.* **2.** *nc* tube used for drinking liquids. *The children were sucking their milk through straws.*

'strawboard type of thick cardboard made of crushed straw.

'straw-coloured *adj* pale yellow.

not care a straw not care at all. (*informal*).

the last straw something unpleasant which, by being added, makes a situation unbearable. *I lost all my money. Losing my coat as well was the last straw.* (*informal*).

man of straw man who is weak and unreliable.

a straw in the wind a small sign of what may happen. *Take warning from what has happened; it is a straw in the wind.*

strawberry ['strɔːbəri] *nc* **1.** type of plant with red fruit which grows near the ground. **2.** the fruit of this plant.

stray [strei] *vi* wander from the proper place or path; get lost. *The cattle strayed from the field. The teacher strayed from the subject of his lesson.* Also *nc/adj*: *The farmer is looking for strays* i.e. cattle etc which have wandered or got lost. *Where are the parents of these stray children?*

streak [striːk] *nc* **1.** line or layer of a different colour. *He has streaks of grey in his dark hair.* **2.** anything which is different from what is around it or from what is expected. *He is a very kind man but he has a streak of cruelty. I usually do well but last night I had a streak of bad luck.* Also *vt/i* **1.** mark with streaks. *His face was streaked with paint.* **2.** move very quickly. *He streaked across the road.* (*informal* in sense **2.**).

streaky *adj* having streaks: *streaky bacon* i.e. with layers of fat in it like streaks.

streak of lightning flash of lightning. *The motorcar passed us like a streak of lightning* i.e. very quickly.

stream [striːm] *nc* **1.** small river; flow of a river. *We crossed the stream by the bridge. The boat sailed upstream/downstream* i.e. up/down the river. **2.** flow of anything. *Streams of sweat were running down his face. A stream of people came out of the building.*

He annoyed us with a stream of insults. **3.** division of pupils of the same age into classes in a school. *This is a very large secondary school with four streams in each form* i.e. each form is divided into four classes. Also *vi* flow; wave. *Tears streamed from her eyes. The flags streamed in the wind.*
streamer *nc* narrow flag; long, narrow piece of paper used for decoration.
'streamline shape which passes most easily through air or water. Also *vt* **1.** give something this shape. *Manufacturers streamline racing cars.* **2.** make more efficient. *The manager has streamlined the accounts department.*
'streamlined *adj*: *streamlined racing car.*

street [stri:t] *nc* road in a town (usu. with buildings at the side).
'streetcar (*US*) tramcar.
'streetwalker prostitute.
be streets ahead of be much better than. (*informal*).
the man in the street see **man.**

strength [streŋθ] *nu* **1.** quality of being strong. *He hasn't the strength to lift it. They built a wall of great strength. The strength of whisky is greater than that of beer.* **2.** this quality expressed in numbers. *They attended the meeting in great strength* i.e. in large numbers. *The army is 10,000 men below strength* i.e. it has vacancies for 10,000 men. *It needs 10,000 men to be up to strength.*
strengthen *vt/i* become, or make, strong or stronger. see **strong.**

strenuous ['strenjuəs] *adj* full of, or requiring, great effort. *He played a strenuous game of football. Digging is strenuous work.*
strenuously *adv.* **strenuousness** *nu.*

stress [stres] *nc/u* **1.** pressure; force; violence. *He does not like the stress of life in a big city. He agreed to do it under great stress.* **2.** (mechanics) force between two bodies which alters their shape. **3.** weight; importance; emphasis. *My parents lay great stress on honesty. Stress is shown in this dictionary by the sign* '. Also *vt* give weight or emphasis to. *I stressed the importance of coming early. The word 'happy' is stressed on the first syllable.*

stretch [stretʃ] *vt/i* **1.** make longer or wider by pulling. *They stretched the rope between the two posts. He stood up and stretched himself.* **2.** lie spread out. *The plain stretches for many miles.* **3.** use more than is considered to be strictly right or possible, or make something go further than it should. *Can we stretch the rules to allow them to join our club?* **4.** make a great effort; use fully. *They will have to stretch their intelligence to solve the problem.* Also *nc* **1.** *He stood up and had a stretch.* **2.** *The stretch of sea between England and France is called the English Channel.* **3.** *Only by a stretch of the rules can they be allowed to join.* **4.** *We are working at full stretch.* **5.** period of time: *work for a long stretch; a stretch in prison.*
stretcher *nc* **1.** frame (usu. covered with canvas) for carrying somebody who is sick or injured. **2.** device for stretching something (e.g. canvas for painting).

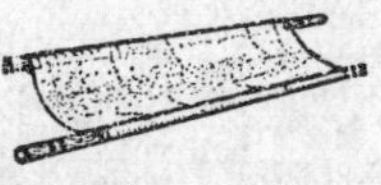

stretcher (*def 1*)

'stretcher-bearer one of the persons who carries a stretcher (in sense **1.**).
stretch something out **1.** stretch to full length. *I stretched out my hand for the money. John was stretched out on the beach* i.e. was lying at full length. **2.** (with reference to land etc) lie spread out. *From the top of the hill they could see the forest stretched out before them.*
at a stretch without stopping. *We worked for two hours at a stretch.*
stretch a point do more than one should. *I think you are wrong, but I am prepared to stretch a point and believe you.*

strew [stru:] *vt* spread or scatter here and there. *They strewed flowers on/over his grave. They strewed his grave with flowers. past tense* **strewed.** *past part* **strewed** or **strewn.**

striated [strai'eitid] *adj* marked with narrow lines or grooves.

stricken ['strikən] *pred adj* (*past part* of **strike**[1]) struck by; affected by. *They were stricken with terror (o.f.). They were terror-stricken.*

strict [strikt] *adj* **1.** severe; stern; to be obeyed. *He has strict parents. Discipline at school is very strict.* **2.** exact; accurate; limited. *This work requires strict measurement. Tell me the strict truth. He told me in strict confidence that he was going abroad.*
strictly *adv.* **strictness** *nu.*
strictly speaking to tell the complete truth.

stricture ['striktʃə*] *nc* **1.** severe criticism. **2.** (medicine) narrowing of any passage of the body, causing disease.
pass strictures on/upon somebody criticize severely.

stride [straid] *nc* long step; length of a long step. *He crossed the road in a few strides. I was standing three strides from the gate.* Also *vt/i*: *We watched him striding across the road. They strode away/off without saying anything. past* **strode** [stroud].
make great strides make good progress. *We have made great strides in English.* (*informal*).
take something in one's stride do something calmly or easily. (*informal*).

strident ['straidnt] *adj* loud and unpleasant. *He has a strident voice.* **stridently** *adv.* **stridency** *nu.*

strife [straif] *nu* fighting; quarrelling.

strike[1] [straik] *vt/i* **1.** hit; give a blow to. *A stone struck me on the head. He struck the nail with a hammer. He struck me (a blow) on the face.* **2.** cause or make by certain actions. *The government is striking new coins* i.e. having new coins made by stamping. *He struck a light* i.e. made a light, lit a match by hitting it against a matchbox. *We have just struck a balance* i.e. reached a balance by calculating. *Let's strike a bargain* i.e. make a bargain by agreement. **3.** (with reference to clocks) show by making a sound. *The town clock has just struck six* i.e. shown it is six o'clock by sounding six times. *We waited for the clock to strike.* **4.** come to, cause to come to, the mind suddenly or strongly. *A new idea struck me. It strikes us that you are wrong. John strikes me as (being) honest.* **5.** cause a condition or feeling suddenly or strongly. *The bad news struck us dumb. The storm struck fear into the people of the village* i.e. made them very afraid. *I was struck by her beauty* i.e. impressed by it. **6.** (with **for**) refuse to continue work (usu. in order to get better pay or conditions). *I am sure the* *bus drivers will strike. They are striking for higher pay.* **7.** find suddenly. *At last we struck the main road. They hope to strike oil here* i.e. find it by boring a hole. **8.** go in a certain direction. *They struck across the fields to the river.* **9.** take down; lower. *They struck their tents at dawn. This regiment will never strike its flag* i.e. lower its flag as a sign of surrender. *past* **struck** [strʌk]. *past part* also **stricken** ['strikən] (*o.f.*).

striker *nc* **1.** person who strikes (esp. in sense **6.**). **2.** something which strikes or hits something else. **3.** (football) forward.

striking *adj* **1.** remarkable. *She was wearing a striking hat.* **2.** (with reference to clocks) making a sound. *Is this a striking clock?*

strikingly *adv*: *strikingly dressed.*

strike at something aim a blow at. *He struck at me with his stick.*

strike someone down cause to fall down or kill by striking; cause to be very ill. *He struck down the animal with his spear. Malaria has struck him down.*

strike something off **1.** cut off. *He struck off the top of the stick with a knife.* **2.** remove somebody's name from. *They struck him off the list of players.*

strike something out remove by drawing a line through. *The teacher struck out two sentences in my essay because they were not needed.*

strike out (at someone) aim a blow at. *He struck out at everyone who tried to stop him.*

strike up (something) begin to play music. *The band struck up when the president arrived. The band struck up a tune.*

strike up an acquaintance with somebody get to know somebody quickly or by accident.

strike an attitude suddenly start behaving in a certain way to cause attention. *He is a vain, silly man who likes striking attitudes when he meets people.*

strike roots (with reference to plants) begin to spread roots and grow.

strike[2] [straik] **1.** *nc/u* refusal to continue work. *The bus drivers are on strike.* **2.** *nc* (esp. with reference to metals and minerals) sudden discovery. *There was a gold strike here many years ago.* **3.** *nc* attack (usu. by aircraft). *They made an air strike on the enemy's position.*

'strike-leader person who leads a strike (in sense **1.**).

break a strike continue work while there is a strike (in sense **1.**).

'strikebreaker person who refuses to join a strike (in sense **1.**) or who tries to stop it.

come/go out on strike begin a strike (in sense **1.**).

string[1] [striŋ] *nc/u* **1.** thick thread (generally used for tying things). *The parcel is tied with string. Have you a piece of string?* **2.** thread on which things are arranged in a line; line of anything. *She was wearing a string of beads. A string of people stood outside.* **3.** stretched cord or wire of a musical instrument. *I need a new string for my guitar.* **4.** (in *pl*) stringed instruments in an orchestra (e.g. violins).

stringed *adj* having strings. *The violin is a stringed instrument.*

stringy *adj* **1.** like string; tough: *stringy meat.* **2.** (with reference to persons) tall and thin. **stringiness** *nu.*

'string 'bean type of bean, the outside covering of which is eaten. (Usu. **French bean**).

'string 'orchestra orchestra of musical instruments with strings.

have somebody on a string have complete control over somebody. (*informal*).

pull strings get the help of powerful people secretly. *He got the job by pulling strings.* (*informal*).

without strings (e.g. with reference to money etc lent by one country to another) without any conditions; to use as one wishes. *The government of Ruritania has lent us a million pounds without strings.*

string[2] [striŋ] *vt/i* **1.** put a string on something (e.g. a guitar, a tennis racquet). **2.** put on a string; pass a string through. *She is stringing the beads. We strung the flags round the hall.* **3.** (in *passive*) be in a long thin line. *The soldiers were strung along the road. past* **strung** [strʌŋ].

string something/someone out spread out in a line with gaps. *The officer strung out his men in front of the building.*

string something up put on a string high above the ground. *We strung up the lamps between the trees.*

string somebody up hang somebody. (*informal*).

be strung up be very nervous. *He was very strung up at the time of the examination.*

highly strung see **high.**

stringent ['strindʒənt] *adj* **1.** requiring strict obedience; severe. *There is a stringent rule against talking during an examination.* **2.** (esp. with reference to money) requiring great care because there is not enough.

stringently *adv.* **stringency** *nc/u.*

strip [strip] *vt/i* **1.** take one's clothes off. *The doctor told me to strip.* **2.** take off a covering; take away. *I stripped off my shirt. They are stripping the paint from/off the wall. The thieves stripped me of all my money. past* **stripped.** Also *nc* long, narrow piece of something: *strip of land; strip of cloth.*

'strip car'toon set of drawings which tell a story.

'strip 'lighting method of giving electric light by using a long, gas-filled tube instead of a bulb.

'strip'tease type of entertainment in which a woman removes her clothes one article at a time (usu. to music).

strip something down (with reference to an engine, apparatus etc) take off all the movable parts (e.g. to repair or clean it).

stripe [straip] *nc* **1.** long narrow band or mark (usu. of a different colour). *He was wearing a white tie with black stripes.* **2.** V-shaped piece of material worn on the arms of a uniform to show rank. *The three stripes on his arm show that he is a sergeant.*

striped *adj* having stripes: *striped tie.*

the stars and stripes the national flag of the USA.

stripling ['stripliŋ] *nc* youth who is no longer a boy but not yet a man. (rather *o.f.*).

strive [straiv] *vt/i* try hard; struggle. *They are striving to win. Most people strive for wealth. A doctor is always striving against disease. pres part* **striving.** *past tense* **strove** [strouv]. *past part* **striven** ['strivən].

strode [stroud] past of **stride.**

stroke[1] [strouk] *nc* **1.** act of striking. *He cut the log in half with one stroke of his axe. The golfer reached the hole in four strokes* i.e. by striking the ball with a golf club four times. **2.** movement made by the arms. *He rowed the boat across the river with a few* *strokes of the oars. He uses the overarm stroke when swimming.* **3.** rower who sits in the stern of a boat and sets the time of the strokes of the other rowers in the boat. **4.** single complete movement of a piston up and down in the cylinder of an engine. *He has a twin-stroke motorcycle* i.e. one with two pistons. **5.** sound of a bell or clock. *He arrived on the stroke of six* i.e. just when the clock was striking six o'clock. **6.** sudden illness which damages the brain and therefore the power of the body. *He has not been able to walk or speak since he had a stroke.* **7.** something which needs effort or is caused suddenly by effort or accident. *He did not do a stroke (of work) last week. It was a stroke of luck that we met here.* Also *vt* be the rower who sets the time of the strokes of the other rowers. *He stroked the boat to victory.*

stroke[2] [strouk] *vt* move the hand gently and often over something. *His mother stroked his hair. Cats like being stroked.* Also *nc* movement of this kind (esp. one made by a brush, pen or pencil); mark made in this way. *With one stroke of his pen he changed the number. He painted the picture in a few strokes.*

stroll [stroul] *vi* walk slowly (usu. for pleasure). Also *nc*: *We went for a stroll. We took a stroll.* **stroller** *nc.*

strong [strɔŋ] *adj* **1.** (with reference to persons) powerful in body or mind. *He has very strong arms. She hasn't a very strong will.* **2.** (with reference to things) firm; solid; not easily broken or damaged. *I need a strong box for my books. The walls of the castle are strong.* **3.** having a powerful effect on the senses or feelings. *There was a strong smell of gas in the room. The strong light of the sun made him shut his eyes. He has a strong desire to meet you.* **4.** (with reference to liquids) not weakened by having too much of something else in it. *This drink is rather strong. May I have some more water in it?; strong tea; strong coffee.* **5.** (with reference to persons) healthy; well. *He is not a strong boy. I hope to be strong again after I have had a holiday.* (*opp* **weak**). **strongly** *adv.* **strength** [streŋθ] *nu.*

'strongbox box made for keeping money and other things of value.

'stronghold **1.** fort. **2.** place which is the centre of a belief or opinion. *This town is one of the strongholds of the Labour Party.*

strong language violent, rude words. *He used strong language when talking about his enemies.*

'strong-'minded *adj* having a strong mind; determined. **strong-mindedness** *nu.*

'strong point **1.** thing someone is good at. *History is not his strong point.* **2.** well-defended position.

'strongroom room built for keeping money and other things of value. *Most banks have a strongroom.*

'strong-'willed *adj* determined; not easily changing an opinion.

500 *etc* **strong** 500 in number.

going strong doing well; still strong. *He is 70 years old and still going strong. My car has done 72,000 miles, but it's still going strong.* (*informal*).

strove [strouv] past tense of **strive.**

struck [strʌk] past of **strike**[1].

structure ['strʌktʃə*] **1.** *nc* building (esp. a large one). **2.** *nc/u* way in which something is built or arranged. *They are studying the structure of the atom.* **structural** *adj.* **structurally** *adv.*

struggle ['strʌgl] *vi* fight violently; use force or effort. *The two boys struggled on the ground. We had to struggle against/with poverty and disease.* Also *nc*: *their struggle for freedom.*

strum [strʌm] *vt/i* play badly, carelessly and/or noisily on a stringed musical instrument. *He was strumming (on) his guitar. He was strumming a popular tune on his guitar.* *past* **strummed.**

strung [strʌŋ] past of **string**[2].

strut[1] [strʌt] *vi* walk in a stiff, proud manner. *He struts about as if he owned the place.* *past* **strutted.** Also *nc* this way of walking.

strut[2] [strʌt] *nc* piece of wood or metal which is set at an angle to support something (e.g. the roof of a house).

strychnine ['strikni:n] *nu* type of poison.

stub [stʌb] *nc* short part of anything remaining after use. *He threw away the stub of his cigarette. He was writing with the stub of a pencil; stub of a cheque book* i.e. smaller piece remaining in the book after a cheque has been torn out; counterfoil. Also *vt* strike or put one thing against another. *I stubbed my foot on the stone* i.e. I hit and hurt my foot on the stone. *He stubbed out his cigarette* i.e. he stopped it burning by pressing it against something. *past* **stubbed.**

stubby *adj* short and thick. **stubbiness** *nu.*

stubble ['stʌbl] *nu* **1.** short ends of the stalks of grain left standing after the grain has been harvested. **2.** short growth of hair on a man's face. *He should shave the stubble off his face.*

stubbled *adj* covered with stubble: *stubbled field.*

stubbly *adj* of or like stubble: *stubbly chin.*

stubborn ['stʌbən] *adj* fixed in opinion; hard to move; refusing to yield. *He is a very stubborn man. The nuts and bolts on the wheel were stubborn; stubborn fight.* **stubbornly** *adv.* **stubborness** *nu.*

stucco ['stʌkou] *nu* type of fine plaster used indoors on walls and ceilings; decoration made of this type of plaster.

stuck [stʌk] past of **stick**[1].

stud[1] [stʌd] *nc* **1.** type of movable button to fasten a collar to a shirt or to fasten the front of a shirt. **2.** nail with a large head. *Football boots have studs in the soles* i.e. to prevent the players slipping. *The gate is covered with iron studs* i.e. to make it stronger. Also *vt*: *Get your football boots studded. The sky was studded with stars* i.e. stars all over the sky like studs.

stud[2] [stʌd] *nc* number of horses kept for racing or breeding; place where they are kept.

'studbook book in which the details of breeding are kept.

'stud farm place where horses are bred.

student ['stju:dnt] *nc* person who studies (esp. at a university or a college).

Note: (*Brit*) a person who studies at a school is called a *pupil.* (*US*) *student* is used with reference to schools as well as universities and colleges, and *pupil* is not often used.

studio ['stju:diou] *nc* **1.** room where an artist, sculptor or photographer works. **2.** room where films are made. **3.** room equipped for broadcasting radio and television programmes; room where gramophone records are made. *pl* **studios.**

studious ['stju:diəs] *adj* **1.** fond of, having

the habit of, studying. **2.** deliberate. **studiously** *adv.* **studiousness** *nu.*

study[1] ['stʌdi] *nc/u* **1.** work done, effort made, in order to learn (esp. from books). *He is making a study of ancient history. I shall not end my studies when I leave school.* **2.** branch of learning. *Biology is the study of living things.* **3.** result of study (e.g. an essay or book). *I read your study of farming with interest.* **4.** room used for study. *In this college each student has a study.*

study[2] ['stʌdi] *vt/i* **1.** work, make an effort, to learn. *I am studying English.* **2.** give careful attention to. *He studied my face before he answered. This school studies the needs of all the children in it. past* **studied.**

studied *adj* on purpose; deliberate: *studied bad manners.*

stuff[1] [stʌf] *nc/u* **1.** substance. *Her coat is made of silk and other expensive stuffs. Whisky is strong stuff.* **2.** something which is not well-known or cannot be named. *What stuff have you (got) in your bag? He brought me some stuff to read.* (*informal* in sense **2.**).

do one's stuff do what one can do well; show what one can do. (*informal*).

know one's stuff know one's subject well; be well-informed. (*informal*).

stuff and nonsense! *interj* what you say is rubbish. (*informal*).

stuff[2] [stʌf] *vt* **1.** push tightly into; fill tightly. *He stuffed his clothes into the bag. I stuffed the box with books. I have a stuffed-up nose* (when someone has a cold in the nose and cannot breathe properly). **2.** fill the skin of a dead animal with material so that it appears to be alive (e.g. to show in a museum). *There was a stuffed cat in the glass case.* **3.** fill the inside of birds, roasts of meat etc, before cooking them, with a special mixture of (usu. spicy) food. **4.** eat too much. *They stuffed themselves with cake.* (*informal* in sense **4.**).

stuffing *nu* material used for stuffing. *The stuffing came out of the torn pillow. We had stuffing with our turkey at Christmas.*

get stuffed! expressing rejection or refusal. *Do what I say! Get stuffed!* (*impolite*).

stuffy ['stʌfi] *adj* **1.** (with reference to a room etc) hot and without enough air. **2.** (with reference to a person) formal; with no sense of humour. (*informal* in sense **2.**). **stuffily** *adv.* **stuffiness** *nu.*

stultify ['stʌltifai] *vt* make foolish or useless. **stultification** [stʌltifi'keiʃən] *nu.*

stumble ['stʌmbl] *vi* **1.** put one's foot down wrongly and almost fall. *I stumbled over the stone on the road. The man stumbled and fell.* **2.** speak with difficulty, making many mistakes. *He stumbled through his speech. I stumble over long English words.*

'stumbling block something causing delay or difficulty.

stumble across/on/upon find by chance.

stump [stʌmp] *nc* **1.** short part of a tree left above ground after the tree has fallen or been cut down. **2.** any short remaining part of something. *The stump of a pencil. He has no arms, only stumps.* **3.** (cricket) one of the three sticks in front of which the batsman stands. Also *vt/i* **1.** walk stiffly and heavily. *He stumped over the floor in his big boots.* **2.** (cricket) put a batsman out by hitting the stumps with the ball when he is too far in front of them. **3.** be too difficult for; defeat. *This problem stumped us.* (*informal* in sense **3.**).

stumpy *adj* like a stump; short and thick.

stun [stʌn] *vt* **1.** make unconscious by a blow on the head. **2.** shock; surprise greatly. *The bad news stunned me. past* **stunned.**

stunning *adj* very surprising or attractive: *stunning news; stunning blonde.* **stunningly** *adv.* (*informal*).

stunner *nc* very attractive person. (*informal*).

stung [stʌŋ] past of **sting**[2].

stunk [stʌŋk] past part of **stink.**

stunt[1] [stʌnt] *vt* stop the growth. *The children have been stunted by disease.*

stunt[2] [stʌnt] *nc* something done deliberately to get attention or publicity.

'stunt man man who does the dangerous bits of acting in films etc.

stupefy ['stju:pifai] *vt* make foolish or unable to think properly. *The sudden loss of all our money stupefied us.*

stupefaction [stju:pi'fækʃən] *nu* state of being stupefied.

stupendous [stju:'pendəs] *adj* causing great admiration or surprise. *The amount of work he did was stupendous.* **stupendously** *adv.*

stupid ['stju:pid] *adj* foolish; not intelligent. *Don't make stupid mistakes. He is a stupid man who finds it difficult to understand the problem.* **stupidly** *adv.* **stupidity** [stju:'piditi] *nc/u.*

stupor ['stju:pə*] *nc/u* state of being almost unconscious because of illness, drugs or shock. *The drunk man was lying on the ground in a stupor.*

sturdy ['stə:di] *adj* strong and well-built; determined; powerful. *He is a sturdy boy. They put up a sturdy defence against a better team.* **sturdily** *adv.* **sturdiness** *nu.*

sturgeon ['stə:dʒən] *nc* type of fish from which caviare is obtained. *pl* **sturgeon.**

stutter ['stʌtə*] *vt/i* speak with difficulty, saying the same sounds again and again (e.g. *P-p-please m-m-may I g-g-go*). Also *nc*: *He speaks with a stutter.* **stutterer** *nc.* **stutteringly** *adv.*

sty[1] [stai] *nc* small building or enclosure in which pigs are kept. (Often **pigsty**). *pl* **sties.**

sty[2], **stye** [stai] *nc* red swelling on the part of the eyelid where the eyelashes are. *pl* **sties** or **styes.**

style [stail] *nc/u* **1.** way of expressing thoughts or feelings etc in writing, speaking, painting etc (esp. with reference to the way a particular writer, artist or period in history does so). *He has a style (of writing) like that of Dickens. The house is built in the Victorian style.* **2.** particular kind of appearance, behaviour etc; particular way of doing something. *I like the style of your new coat. They lived in Japan in Japanese style. He does things in style* i.e. in a grand, expensive way. **3.** correct way or title of addressing somebody. *The style of 'Your Worship' is used when addressing a judge.* **4.** (in ancient times) pointed instrument used to write (on wax). Also *vt* **1.** give a particular style; design. *She styles evening dresses.* **2.** address in a particular way. *A married woman is styled 'Mrs'.*

stylish *adj* having style: *stylish clothes* i.e. smart, fashionable clothes. **stylishly** *adv.* **stylishness** *nu.*

stylist *nc* **1.** person who gives great attention to style (e.g. in writing, playing games). **2.** person whose work is designing and arranging. **stylistic** [stai'listik] *adj.* **stylistically** *adv.*

stylus ['stailәs] *nc* needle used for playing gramophone records.
suave [swɑ:v] *adj* pleasant and agreeable; with smooth manners. **suavely** *adv.* **suavity** *nc/u.*
sub[1] [sʌb] *nc* informal short form of **submarine, subscription, sub-lieutenant etc.**
sub-[2] [sʌb] *prefix* under; less than; almost (e.g. **subhuman; subtropical**).
subaltern ['sʌbәltn] *nc* commissioned officer in the army, below the rank of captain; lieutenant.
subconscious ['sʌb'kɔnʃәs] *adj* see **conscious.**
subcontinent ['sʌb'kɔntinәnt] *nc* area of land which is large enough to be considered a continent although it is only part of one. *India is a subcontinent of Asia.*
subcontract ['sʌb'kɔntrækt] *nc* agreement by which part of a contract already made is given to somebody else to do. *Small firms of builders often get subcontracts from larger firms.* Also ['sʌbkәn'trækt] *vt/i* make an agreement of this kind.
subcontractor ['sʌbkәn'træktә*] *nc* person who gets a subcontract.
subcutaneous ['sʌbkju:'teiniәs] *adj* under the skin.
subdivide ['sʌbdi'vaid] *vt/i* divide again into more parts. *The country is divided into provinces and the provinces are subdivided into districts.*
subdivision ['sʌbdiviʒәn] *nc/u* result of being subdivided; act or state of subdividing. *A district is the subdivision of a province.*
subdue [sәb'dju:] *vt* conquer; bring under control. *The country was subdued by the enemy.*
subdued *adj* less strong, bright etc. *They spoke in subdued voices. The colours of the dress are subdued.*
subheading ['sʌbhediŋ] *nc* smaller heading which comes under the main heading (e.g. to divide one part of a chapter from another, at the beginning of a newspaper article etc).
subhuman ['sʌb'hju:mәn] *adj* not quite human.
subject[1] ['sʌbdʒikt] *adj* under the control of somebody else: *the subject people of the colonies.*
subject to *adj/adv* likely to get; according to; conditional on. *He is subject to headaches. We are all subject to the rules of the school. He will do it subject to his father's consent.*
subject[2] ['sʌbdʒikt] *nc* **1.** member of a country. *They are British subjects.* **2.** something which is spoken or written about, or studied. *The subject of their conversation was the war. He has written about/on many subjects in his books. In a primary school the main subjects are reading, writing and arithmetic.* **3.** somebody/something which is used for an experiment, operation or research. *The new drug was given to hundreds of subjects before it was finally approved.* **4.** somebody/something which is the cause of a feeling or action. *I won't be the subject of their jokes. Human suffering is always a subject for pity.* **5.** (grammar) word or words in a sentence about which the verb tells something (e.g. in the sentence *John gave me a book, John* is the subject, *me* and *a book* are objects). **6.** (music) main theme or melody.
subject[3] [sәb'dʒekt] *vt* **1.** put under control; conquer. *This country was once subjected to foreign rule.* **2.** cause to happen to. *He subjected us to a very difficult test. They will subject themselves to criticism if they make any more mistakes.*
subjection *nu* act or state of subjecting or being subjected to. *Their aim was the subjection of all their enemies. This country was held/kept in subjection until it gained independence.*
subjective [sәb'dʒektiv] *adv* **1.** existing only in the mind; imaginary. *Drugs can cause terrible subjective experiences.* **2.** giving the thoughts or feelings of one particular person. *The writer of the book has a very subjective view of modern life* i.e. it is a personal view which may not agree with the facts. (*opp* **objective**). **3.** (grammar) of the subject. **subjectively** *adv.* **subjectivity** [sʌbdʒek'tiviti] *nu.*
subjoin ['sʌb'dʒɔin] *vt* add to the end of what has been said or written.
sub judice ['sʌb'dʒu:disi] in the process of being considered by a court of law.
subjugate ['sʌbdʒu:geit] *vt* conquer. **subjugation** [sʌbdʒu:'geiʃәn] *nu.*
subjunctive [sʌb'dʒʌŋktiv] *adj* of the subjunctive mood which expresses a condition or wish. Also *nc* subjunctive mood (e.g. in the sentence *If you were a king, you would live in a palace, were* and *would* are subjunctives or are in the subjunctive mood).
sublease ['sʌb'li:s] *vt/i* lease to somebody property which one has oneself leased. Also *nc* lease of this kind.
sublet ['sʌb'let] *vt/i* let to somebody property which one has oneself rented from a landlord. *past* **subletted** or **sublet.**
sub-lieutenant ['sʌblef'tenәnt, *US* 'sʌblu:'tenәnt] *nc* (*US*) officer in the navy just below a lieutenant in rank.
sublimate ['sʌblimeit] *vt* **1.** turn a solid into vapour and then allow it to become solid again; purify a solid in this way. **2.** turn powerful feelings (esp. sexual ones) towards other aims and activities. Also *nc* substance which has been sublimated (in sense **1.**). **sublimation** [sʌbli'meiʃәn] *nc/u.*
sublime [sә'blaim] *adj* **1.** very noble; causing great admiration. *The view from the mountain was sublime.* **2.** astonishing. *He has a sublime confidence in himself.* Also *nu* (usu. with **the**). *The sublime is always admired.*
sublimely *adv*: *He is sublimely confident.*
sublimity [sә'blimiti] *nc/u* magnificence; grandeur.
submachine gun ['sʌbmә'ʃi:ngʌn] *nc* type of light, easily-carried machine gun.
submarine [sʌbmә'ri:n] *adj* existing or living below the surface of the sea: *submarine cable.* Also *nc* type of ship which can travel below the surface of the sea.
submerge [sәb'mә:dʒ] *vt/i* go under, or put under, water or other liquid. *The crocodile submerged when it saw the boat. He submerged his hands in warm water.*
submergence, submersion [sәb'mә:ʃәn] *nc/u* act or state of submerging or being submerged.
submit [sәb'mit] *vt/i* **1.** yield; give in. *After being defeated they submitted to the enemy. The enemy made them submit.* **2.** ask to be considered; bring to somebody's attention so that it may be considered, approved etc. *You must submit your request to the committee. He submits that he is not to blame. pres part* **submitting.** *past* **submitted.**

submission *nc/u* **1.** act of yielding. *The enemy forced them into submission.* **2.** argument for somebody to consider. *It is his submission that he is not to blame.*
submissive *adj* ready to yield; obedient. **submissively** *adv.* **submissiveness** *nu.*
submit oneself to agree to accept or undergo. *They submitted themselves to a large number of questions from the chairman.*

subnormal ['sʌb'nɔːml] *adj* below normal: *subnormal intelligence.* **subnormality** ['sʌbnɔː'mæliti] *nc/u.*

subordinate [sə'bɔːdinət] *adj* lower in rank or importance. *In the army a captain is subordinate to a major. This is our main aim; all the other aims are subordinate to it.* Also *nc* person who is lower in rank. Also [sə'bɔːdineit] *vt.* **subordination** [səbɔːdi'neiʃən] *nc/u.*
subordinate clause dependent clause in a sentence. (In the sentence *When he comes he will tell us, when he comes* is the subordinate clause).
make somebody/something subordinate *We have subordinated everything else to our main aim.*

suborn [sʌ'bɔːn] *vt* make somebody give false evidence or do something wrong (e.g. by paying him money to do so). **subornation** [sʌbə'neiʃən] *nu.*

subpoena [sə'piːnə] *nc* order made to someone to appear before a judge as a witness. Also *vt* make such an order.

subscribe [səb'skraib] *vt/i* **1.** give, promise to give, with other persons, money for a special purpose. *We have subscribed £10 to the fund for poor children.* **2.** order and pay regularly for a newspaper, magazine etc for a period of time. *I subscribe to one daily newspaper and one weekly magazine.* **3.** sign one's name at the end of a paper or document. *They subscribed their names to the protest about low wages.* **4.** agree with; support. *I cannot subscribe to the belief that the government is always wrong.*
subscriber *nc* **1.** person who subscribes. **2.** person who rents a telephone from a telephone company.
subscription [səb'skripʃən] *nc/u* **1.** money which is subscribed. *Have they paid their subscriptions to the fund for poor children?* **2.** act of subscribing or being subscribed. *They hope to get the rest of the money for the new library by subscription.*

subsequent ['sʌbsikwənt] *adj* happening later: *subsequent events.* **subsequently** *adv.*

subservient [səb'səːviənt] *adj* too obedient or respectful. *The workers are subservient to everything the manager says.* **subserviently** *adv.* **subservience** *nu.*

subside [səb'said] *vi* **1.** fall or sink lower. *The river subsided when the rain stopped. The lorry has subsided into the soft mud.* **2.** become quieter; grow less. *The wind has subsided. His anger soon subsided.*
subsidence ['sʌbsidns] *nc/u* act or state of subsiding.

subsidiary [sʌb'sidiəri] *adj* giving help or support to somebody/something more important; secondary. *My work as an assistant is subsidiary to the work of the senior staff; study French with German as a subsidiary subject.* Also *nc* person/thing which is subsidiary.

subsidy ['sʌbsidi] *nc* money paid (esp. by a government) to help an industry or another country to keep prices up or down etc. *In Britain and the USA, farmers receive subsidies from the government to grow certain crops.*
subsidize ['sʌbsidaiz] *vt* give a subsidy to. **subsidization** [sʌbsidai'zeiʃən] *nu.*

subsist [səb'sist] *vi* continue to be; stay alive. *The people of that country subsist on rice and vegetables.*
subsistence *nu* way of staying alive.
sub'sistence level level at which life is only just possible with the amount of money, food etc available.

subsoil ['sʌb'sɔil] *nu* layer of soil just below the top one.

subsonic ['sʌb'sɔnik] *adj* of a speed less than the speed of sound i.e. less than 750 miles per hour. (*opp* **supersonic**).

substance ['sʌbstns] *nc/u* **1.** particular type of matter; what something is made of. *Carbon is a substance found in many forms* (e.g. diamonds, coal and soot). **2.** most important matter or point of a book, speech, discussion etc. *The substance of his speech was that the country was in danger.* **3.** wealth. *He is a man of substance.* **4.** strength; importance. *I like a drink with some substance in it. There is not much substance in what he says* i.e. what he says is not true or not important.
substantial [səb'stænʃl] *adj* **1.** made of good material; solid; strong; large: *a substantial meal* i.e. good food and plenty of it. **2.** wealthy. *Several substantial landowners live here.* **3.** really existing; not imaginary. (*opp* **insubstantial**). **substantially** *adv.*
waste one's substance spend one's money foolishly (*o.f.*).

substandard ['sʌb'stændəd] *adj* less good than usual or than the average.

substantiate [səb'stænʃieit] *vt* bring evidence to show that something is true. *He had with him a letter from his doctor to substantiate his statement that he had been ill.*
substantiation [səbstænʃi'eiʃən] *nc/u.*
substantiated *adj.* (*opp* **unsubstantiated**).

substantive ['sʌbstəntiv] *adj* (with reference to military ranks) permanent. Also *nc* noun. *'Word' is a substantive.*

substitute ['sʌbstitjuːt] *nc* somebody/something which takes the place of somebody/something else. *Because he is ill, I am playing as his substitute in the football match.* Also *vt/i* become or make a substitute. *I am substituting for him in the football match. Let us substitute x for y in the equation.*
substitution [sʌbsti'tjuːʃən] *nc/u.*

subterfuge ['sʌbtəfjuːdʒ] *nc/u* something done to avoid difficulty or trouble; false excuse; trick. *He says he is ill, but it is really a subterfuge to stay in bed instead of going to school.*

subterranean [sʌbtə'reiniən] *adj* under the ground.

subtitle ['sʌbtaitl] *nc* **1.** extra title of a book (usu. one which explains more). **2.** writing shown on a film to explain the story or to translate the dialogue. *We saw a French film with English subtitles.* Also *vt*: *subtitle a foreign film.*

subtle ['sʌtl] *adj* **1.** difficult to explain or understand. *There is a subtle difference between the two words.* **2.** clever and cunning. *They are using subtle methods to get what they want.* **subtly** *adv.* **subtlety** *nc/u.*

subtract [səb'trækt] *vt* take one number from another to find the difference. *If you subtract 4 from 6 you get 2.*
subtraction *nc/u* act of subtracting. *The difference is found by subtraction.*

subtropical ['sʌb'trɔpikl] *adj* near the tropics; almost tropical.
suburb ['sʌbə:b] *nc* (often *pl*) part of a city which is outside its centre (usu. the part where people live).
suburban [sə'bə:bən] *adj* of or in a suburb. **suburbia** [sə'bə:biə] *nu* **1.** suburban areas. **2.** way people live in a suburb (often supposed to be lacking in good taste and culture). *He hates suburbia and all it stands for.*
subvert [səb'və:t] *vt* overthrow something (e.g. a government or set of beliefs) by destroying people's faith or confidence in it. **subversive** [səb'və:siv] *adj* likely to subvert. *He was arrested for making a subversive speech to the soldiers.* **subversion** [səb'və:ʃən] *nu.*
subway ['sʌbwei] *nc* **1.** underground passage (usu. so that people can pass from one side of a very busy street to the other). **2.** (mainly *US*) underground railway. (*Brit* **underground**).
succeed [sək'si:d] *vt/i* **1.** do what one has wished to do; achieve an aim. *The plan has succeeded. He succeeded in (passing) the examination.* **2.** come immediately after and take the place of. *Mr Jones will succeed Mr Brown as headmaster. The Queen succeeded her father to the throne.*
success [sək'ses] *nc/u* getting what one has wished. *We are very pleased with your success in the examination. I tried to meet him but without success. The school had several successes in the games* i.e. several of its pupils won.
successful *adj.* (*opp* **unsuccessful**). **successfully** *adv.*
succession [sək'seʃən] *nc/u* **1.** act of following one after the other; number of persons/things following one after the other. *Last week we had a succession of visitors.* **2.** right to take the place of somebody and get his title, rank, property etc. *The eldest son has succession to his father's property.*
successive [sək'sesiv] *adj* coming one after the other: *on successive days.* **successively** *adv.*
in succession 1. one after the other. **2.** according to the right to take the place of somebody. *The eldest son is first in succession to his father's property.*
successor [sək'sesə*] *nc* somebody/something which comes immediately after and takes the place of somebody/something else. *Mr Jones is the headmaster's successor.*
succinct [sək'siŋkt] *adj* expressed clearly in few words. **succinctly** *adv.* **succinctness** *nu.*
succour ['sʌkə*] (*US* **succor**) *nu* help (esp. in time of trouble). Also *vt.* (both *o.f.*).
succulent ['sʌkjulnt] *adj* **1.** full of juice. **2.** (botany) thick and juicy. Also *nc* (botany) succulent (in sense **2.**) plant. **succulently** *adv.* **succulence** *nu.*
succumb [sə'kʌm] *vt/i* yield; die. *At last he succumbed to our desire to go. The man succumbed to the injuries he received in the accident.*
such [sʌtʃ] *adj/determiner/pron* **1.** (with **as**) of the same kind, degree or quality.
Note: in the examples which follow the position of *such* is before *a* but after *all, many, no* and *some. Such books (as these) are useful. Such a book is useful. All such books are useful. I have read many such books. No such books are useful. He bought a dictionary or some such book. Boys such as John and James are very friendly. Such boys as John and James are very friendly.*
2. so much; so great; so good etc. *He is such a kind man. We have never seen such a big town.* **3.** of the kind already mentioned; this or that; these or those. *Such is my wish. Such was the way he spoke to us.* **4.** somebody/something already mentioned; this or that; these or those. *I haven't much money but you can use such as I have. He is my father and as such can tell me what to do.*
suchlike *adj* of that kind. *He admires football players and suchlike people.* (*informal*).
'**such-and-such** *adj* this or that; not definite. *If he arranges to come on such-and-such a day we shall see him.* (*informal*).
such as it is not of a very good kind or quality. *This is my house such as it is.*
such as to of a kind which can or may cause something. *His behaviour is such as to make his friends angry.*
such that/such . . . that of a kind which causes something. *She made such a big meal that they all had too much to eat.*
suck [sʌk] *vt/i* **1.** draw liquid into the mouth by using the lips and tongue; draw liquid from. *He sucked the juice from the orange. I sucked the blood from my finger. The baby was sucking its bottle.* **2.** hold and move about in the mouth. *You must not suck sweets in class.* **3.** take in; pull in. *The dry land sucked up the rain.* Also *nc* act of sucking. *He gave the orange a suck.*
give suck to (with reference to a mother) allow a baby to suck her breast (*o.f.* – use **feed, nurse** or **breastfeed**).
sucker ['sʌkə*] *nc* **1.** person/thing that sucks. **2.** organ by which some animals can stick to something. **3.** device made of rubber, leather etc which sticks to something by suction. **4.** shoot or branch of a plant from the roots or the lower stem. **5.** person who is easily cheated. (*informal* in sense **5.**).
suckle ['sʌkl] *vt* put a baby to feed, or let a baby feed, at the mother's breast.
suckling *nc* baby or young animal that is still being suckled.
suction ['sʌkʃən] *nu* **1.** act of sucking or drawing in (caused by taking air or liquid out of a container so that another gas or liquid comes in to replace it). *Many pumps work by suction.* **2.** force which makes one thing stick to another when the air between is taken away.
sudden ['sʌdn] *adj* happening without warning; done quickly. *His sudden death shocked everybody. She gave a sudden smile.*
suddenly *adv.* **suddenness** *nu.*
all of a sudden see **all.**
suds [sʌdz] *npl* masses of bubbles caused by a mixture of soap, air and water.
sue [su:] *vt/i* **1.** bring a claim or case against somebody in a court of law. *If you don't pay me the money, I'll sue you.* **2.** ask. *The enemy sued us for peace.*
suede [sweid] *nu* type of soft leather with a dull surface. Also *adj*: *He was wearing suede shoes.*
suet ['su:it] *nu* hard animal fat used for cooking.
suety *adj* containing suet; like suet.
suffer ['sʌfə*] *vt/i* **1.** feel pain; meet trouble or loss. *We could see that the injured man was suffering. If you are lazy, only you yourself will suffer.* **2.** bear or endure something unpleasant. *The army suffered great losses in the battle. They have suffered hunger and thirst.* **3.** be patient with; tolerate. *Their*

parents refused to suffer their bad manners. **suffering** *nc/u* pain or distress: *the sufferings of the wounded men; relieve pain and suffering.*

sufferer *nc* person who suffers.

sufferance *nu* having permission which was not given willingly. *They were allowed to live there on sufferance* i.e. nobody really wanted them to live there.

suffer from something suffer because of. *He is suffering from fever. They suffer from the belief that they are always right* i.e. this belief is wrong and causes them trouble.

suffice [sə'fais] *vt/i* be enough; satisfy. *If the weather is cold, your thin coat will not suffice. Will £5 suffice you?* (*formal*).

sufficient [sə'fiʃənt] *adj* enough. *Is £5 sufficient? He has sufficient knowledge for the work.* (*opp* **insufficient**). **sufficiently** *adv.*

sufficiency [sə'fiʃənsi] *nu* (usu. with **a**): *a sufficiency of money.* (*formal*).

suffix ['sʌfiks] *nc* letter or group of letters added to the end of a word (e.g. in the word *playful, ful* is a suffix). *pl* **suffixes.** (*opp* **prefix**).

suffocate ['sʌfəkeit] *vt/i* **1.** kill or die through lack of air. *He suffocated the sleeping man with a pillow. Three children suffocated when the house caught fire.* **2.** make breathing difficult. *The smoke suffocated us.* **suffocating** *adj.* **suffocation** [sʌfə'keiʃən] *nu.*

suffrage ['sʌfridʒ] *nc/u* vote; right to vote. *In this country all people over 18 years of age have the suffrage.*

suffragette [sʌfrə'dʒet] *nc* woman who fought for women's right to vote in Britain.

suffuse [sə'fju:z] *vt* (esp. with reference to colours or tears) come from underneath or inside and cover. *A blush suffused her face.* **suffusion** *nu.*

sugar ['ʃugə*] *nu* sweet substance used in food and drink. *Do you take sugar with your tea?* Also *vt* make sweet with sugar.

sugary *adj* of sugar; very sweet.

'sugar beet type of root vegetable from which sugar is obtained.

'sugar cane type of tall plant from which sugar is obtained.

'sugar re'finery factory where sugar is made (by refining the raw materials).

'sugar tongs device for lifting lumps of sugar (to put them in tea, coffee etc).

'beet sugar sugar obtained from sugar beet.

'cane sugar sugar obtained from sugar cane.

suggest [sə'dʒest] *vt* **1.** put forward an idea or plan (for somebody to consider). *I suggest that we tell him. He suggested London for their meeting.* **2.** cause somebody to believe or think something. *His large house suggests wealth* i.e. it makes people think he is wealthy. *Another way to find out has suggested itself to me* i.e. has come into my mind and made me think.

suggestible *adj* **1.** able to be suggested. **2.** (with reference to persons) easily believing what is suggested.

suggestion *nc/u* **1.** act of suggesting; what is suggested. *Any suggestions for the concert? We did it on/at his suggestion.* **2.** small sign; hint. *There was a suggestion of anger in his voice.*

suggestive *adj* **1.** causing somebody to think or believe something. *Your idea is a very suggestive one. Their clothes were suggestive of poverty* i.e. their clothes made people think that they were poor. **2.** causing somebody to think about something indecent. *He made suggestive remarks to the ladies.* **suggestively** *adv.*

suicide ['su:isaid] **1.** *nc* person who kills himself intentionally. **2.** *nc/u* act of doing so. *In some countries suicide is a crime. The number of suicides has increased. He committed suicide when he was quite young.* **3.** *nu* act which causes disaster to oneself. *If he does this it will be professional suicide* i.e. he will ruin his professional career. **suicidal** [su:i'saidl] *adj.* **suicidally** *adv.*

suit[1] [su:t] *nc* **1.** set of clothes made of the same material: *man's suit* i.e. jacket and trousers, with or without a waistcoat; *woman's suit* i.e. jacket and skirt. **2.** claim made in a court of law; legal case. *They brought a suit against him for not paying the money.* **3.** request or claim (e.g. to marry a woman) (*o.f.*). **4.** one of the four sets of playing cards. *In a pack of cards there are four suits: clubs, diamonds, hearts and spades.*

suitor *nc* **1.** person who brings a claim to a court of law. **2.** man who asks to marry a woman (*o.f.* in sense **2.**).

'suitcase flat case for holding clothes when travelling.

'lawsuit claim made in a court of law; legal case.

two-/three-piece suit suit of clothes with two/three parts.

follow suit 1. (cards) play a card of the same suit as the one just played. **2.** do the same as has been done already. *We thanked the chairman. The others followed suit* i.e. they also thanked him after we did.

press a suit 1. make a suit of clothes flat by ironing it. **2.** put forward a claim or request. *He pressed his suit with my sister* i.e. he asked her to marry him (*o.f.* in sense **2.**).

suit[2] [su:t] *vt/i* **1.** be satisfactory; please; be fitted to. *Will it suit you if we go early? The changes did not suit his plans.* **2.** improve the appearance; look well. *Long hair does not suit him. You shouldn't wear red because it doesn't suit you.*

suitable *adj* well fitted for the purpose. *Have you a suitable book for a young child? Eleven o'clock will be suitable (for us)* (*opp* **unsuitable**). **suitably** *adv.* **suitableness, suitability** [su:tə'biliti] *nu.*

suiting *nu* material from which a suit of clothes is made.

be suited for/to be fitted to; be of the right kind for. *I do not think he is suited for a university. This car is not well suited for/to rough roads.*

suit oneself do as one pleases. *I say you should not go, but suit yourself* i.e. go if you want to.

suit something to someone/something make something fit, or agree with, somebody/something. *A good teacher suits his lessons to the age of his pupils.*

suite [swi:t] *nc* **1.** followers and servants of an important person. **2.** number of things used together: *suite of furniture* i.e. set of furniture for one room; *bedroom suite* i.e. set of furniture for a bedroom; *suite of rooms* i.e. set of rooms for one or two persons; *hotel suite* i.e. set of rooms in a hotel with a private sitting room and bathroom etc as well as a bedroom. **3.** number of musical compositions joined together.

suitor ['su:tə*] *nc* see **suit**[1].

sulk [sʌlk] *vi* (usu. with reference to children) show one's bad temper by looking angry and refusing to speak. **sulky** *adj.* **sulkily** *adv.* **sulkiness** *nu.*

the sulks *npl* state of sulking. *He's got the sulks.*
sullen ['sʌlən] *adj* **1.** (with reference to persons) bad-tempered and saying nothing. **2.** (with reference to things) gloomy; dark: *sullen weather.* **sullenly** *adv.* **sullenness** *nu.*
sully ['sʌli] *vt* make dirty; bring disgrace to (*o.f.*).
sulphate ['sʌlfeit] *nc* salt of sulphuric acid.
sulphide ['sʌlfaid] *nc/u* compound of sulphur and another element.
sulphur ['sʌlfə*] *nu* yellow substance which burns with a blue flame and has a strong smell (S).
sulphuretted ['sʌlfəretid] *adj* having sulphur mixed in it: *sulphuretted hydrogen.*
sulphurous *adj* of, containing sulphur: *sulphurous smoke.*
sulphuric acid [sʌl'fjuərik'æsid] type of very strong acid.
sultan ['sʌltn] *nc* Muslim prince or ruler.
sultanate ['sʌltəneit] *nc* rank of a sultan; the period of his rule; the country he rules.
sultana [sʌl'tɑːnə] *nc* **1.** wife of a sultan. **2.** type of small dried fruit used in cooking.
sultry ['sʌltri] *adj* (with reference to the weather) hot, damp and uncomfortable. **sultrily** *adv.* **sultriness** *nu.*
sum [sʌm] *nc* **1.** full amount obtained by adding. **2.** amount of money. *He paid a large sum for his house.* **3.** work of adding, subtracting etc; problem in arithmetic. *My sums were not correct. We do sums first period every morning.* Also *vt/i* (with **up**) **1.** add up; find the full amount. **2.** give the main points. *At the end of the meeting the chairman summed up (the opinions of the members).* **3.** form an opinion about; reach a decision about. *The manager soon summed him up. past* **summed.**
'**sum** '**total** full total or amount.
'**summing-'up** *nc* act of giving the main points (esp. in a court of law). *In his summing-up, the judge explained what the evidence had shown. pl* **summings-up.**
summary ['sʌməri] *adj* short; done quickly. *He gave a summary description of the country. Our headmaster believes in summary punishment* i.e. punishment given quickly, without delay. Also *nc* short statement giving the main points of something longer. *We had to write a summary of the chapter.* **summarily** *adv.*
summarize *vt* give a summary of.
summer ['sʌmə*] *nc* hottest season of the year in countries not in the tropics. *We go on holiday in (the) summer.* Also *adj: summer holidays.* Also *vi* spend the summer. *They summer in the south of France.* (*opp* **winter**).
summery *adj* like summer; suitable for summer.
'**summerhouse** small hut in a garden used for sitting in during the summer.
summit ['sʌmit] *nc* **1.** highest point (esp. of a mountain). **2.** (usu. as *adj*) highest level of government. *There will be a summit conference in London next week.*
summon ['sʌmən] *vt* order to be present; send for. *I have been summoned to give evidence in court* i.e. in a court of law. *The headmaster summoned them to his office.*
summon something up find by oneself without any help. *I hope he will summon up enough courage to ask her.*
summons ['sʌmənz] *nc* **1.** order to be present in a court of law. *He has received a summons for careless driving.* **2.** order to do something. *The headmaster sent them a summons to come to his office. pl* **summonses.** Also *vt* send a summons to. *He was summonsed for careless driving.*
sump [sʌmp] *nc* lowest part of a large hole (e.g. a mine) in which water collects; lowest part of an engine where the oil collects.
sumptuous ['sʌmptjuəs] *adj* costing a large amount of money; very splendid. *He lives in a sumptuous house.* **sumptuously** *adv.* **sumptuousness** *nu.*
sun [sʌn] *nc* **1.** (with **the**) the one bright body in the sky which gives heat and light to the earth, and round which the earth travels. **2.** (with **the**) heat and light from the sun. *They were lying in the sun. You should take your child out of the sun.* **3.** any other bright body in the sky which has smaller bodies travelling round it. *Our sun is only one of many suns in the heavens.* Also *vt* put in the heat and light of the sun. *They sunned themselves on the beach. past* **sunned.**
sunless *adj* not receiving the heat or light of the sun.
sunny *adj* **1.** warm and bright because of the sun. *This is a sunny place to have a rest.* **2.** cheerful. *He has a sunny nature.* **sunnily** *adv.* **sunniness** *nu.*
'**sunbathe** *vi* expose one's body to the sun. **sunbathing** *nu.*
'**sunbeam** ray of light from the sun.
'**sunblind** movable shade for protecting the window of a house or shop from the heat of the sun.
'**sunburn** *nu* red, painful skin caused by too much sun. **sunburned, sunburnt** *adj.*
'**sundial** device which shows the time of day from the shadow made by the sun.
'**sundown** (mainly *US*) time when the sun sets.
'**sunflower** type of plant with a large flower.
'**sunglasses** spectacles with dark glass etc to protect the eyes from the bright light of the sun.
'**sun lamp** type of lamp which gives a light like that of the sun i.e. containing ultraviolet rays.
'**sunlight** light of the sun.
'**sunlit** *adj* lit by the sun.
'**sunrise** rising of the sun; time when the sun rises. *It was a beautiful sunrise. We left home at sunrise.*
'**sunset** setting of the sun; time when the sun sets.
'**sunshade** **1.** type of umbrella to protect the head from the sun. **2.** shade over a door or window etc to keep off the sun.
'**sunshine** light of the sun.
'**sunspot** dark spot seen on the surface of the sun.
'**sunstroke** type of illness caused by being too much in the sun.
'**suntan** darkening of the skin seen in people with white skin, caused by exposure to the sun: *get a good suntan.*
sundae ['sʌndei] *nc* ice cream with fruit or nuts on top. *pl* **sundaes.**
Sunday ['sʌndi] *n* first day of the week in the Christian calendar.
sundry ['sʌndri] *adj* separate; several: *sundry things* i.e. small things which are not worth mentioning separately. *pl* **sundries.**
all and sundry all different types; everybody. *All and sundry agree.*
sung [sʌŋ] past part of **sing.**
sunk [sʌŋk] past part of **sink.**

sunken ['sʌŋkən] *adj* **1.** below the surface of water; under the sea etc: *sunken treasure.* **2.** below the level of something else: *sunken garden.* see **sink.**
sunny ['sʌni] *adj* see **sun.**
sup[1] [sʌp] *vt/i* take a little liquid into the mouth at one time.
sup[2] [sʌp] *vi* have supper (*o.f.*).
super[1] ['su:pə*] *adj* very good; splendid. (*informal*). Also *nc* short informal form of **superintendent, supernumerary.**
super-[2] ['su:pə*] *prefix* above; beyond; greater than usual (e.g. **superhuman; supersonic**).
superabundant [su:pərə'bʌndənt] *adj* much more than enough; too abundant. **superabundantly** *adv.* **superabundance** *nu.*
superannuate [supə'rænjueit] *vt* consider somebody as no longer able to work because of age or illness; give somebody a pension for this reason.
superannuated *adj* (with reference to a thing) useless; old-fashioned. (*informal*).
superannuation [su:pərænju'eiʃən] *nc/u* **1.** act of superannuation; state of being superannuated. **2.** pension of somebody who has been superannuated; amount of money paid regularly by somebody so that he can have a pension.
superb [su'pə:b] *adj* grand; splendid. **superbly** *adv.*
supercargo ['su:pəka:gou] *nc* ship's officer or agent who is in charge of the cargo. *pl* **supercargoes.**
supercharger ['su:pətʃa:dʒ] *nc* device in a petrol engine which forces extra petrol and air into the cylinders, and so gives the engine more power.
supercilious [su:pə'siliəs] *adj* proud and full of disdain. **superciliously** *adv.* **superciliousness** *nu.*
superficial [su:pə'fiʃl] *adj* **1.** on the surface; not deep. *He had a superficial cut on his face.* **2.** understanding only what is obvious; not thorough. *They have a superficial knowledge of the matter.* **superficially** *adv.* **superficiality** [su:pəfiʃi'æliti] *nc/u.*
superfine ['su:pəfain] *adj* **1.** of very fine quality. **2.** too subtle.
superfluous [su'pə:fluəs] *adj* more than is needed or wanted; not needed. **superfluously** *adv.* **superfluity** [su:pə'flu:iti] *nc/u.*
superhuman ['supə'hju:mən] *adj* more than human in power, size etc.
superimpose [su:pərim'pouz] *vt* put something on top of something else. *He superimposed the photograph on the page of the magazine.*
superintend [supərin'tend] *vt/i* be in charge of; watch to see something is done properly. *He superintends all the work in this part of the factory.* **superintendence** *nu.*
superintendent *nc* **1.** person who superintends. **2.** (in the British police force) police officer above an inspector.
superior [su:'piəriə*] *adj* **1.** higher, better or greater. *He is my superior officer* i.e. his rank is higher than mine. *This car is superior to that one. They are superior in numbers to us.* (*opp* **inferior**). **2.** beyond the influence of; refusing to yield to. *He was superior to all their threats.* **3.** showing that one thinks oneself better than others. *We were angry at his superior behaviour to the visitors.* Also *nc* **1.** person with a higher rank or position. *He is my superior in rank.* **2.** person who is better. *In the game of football he has few superiors.* **3.** (with reference to the Roman Catholic Church) priest or nun in charge: *Father Superior; Mother Superior.*
superiority [su:piəri'ɔriti] *nu* state of being superior.
superlative [su:'pə:lətiv] *adj* **1.** better than all others. **2.** (with reference to an *adj* or *adv* in grammar) of the highest degree. Also *nc*: *'Biggest' is the superlative of 'big'. 'Most quickly' is the superlative of 'quickly'.*
superman ['su:pəmæn] *nc* man who is thought to be much stronger, more intelligent etc than other men.
supermarket ['su:pəma:kit] *nc* large shop in which the customers themselves collect what they wish to buy and pay on the way out.
supernatural [su:pə'nætʃərl] *adj* not controlled by the laws of nature; spiritual. *They believe that holy men have supernatural powers.* **supernaturally** *adv.*
the supernatural *nu* forces or powers not controlled by the laws of nature.
supernumerary [su:pə'nju:mərəri] *adj* extra to the number needed. Also *nc* (esp. with reference to an actor who has no speaking part and appears only in a crowd scene).
superpower ['su:pəpauə*] *nc* country which has much stronger military power than other countries.
superscription [su:pə'skripʃən] *nc* words written on the top or outside of something.
supersede [su:pə'si:d] *vt* replace; make old-fashioned. *Motorcars have superseded horses on the road.* **supersession** [su:pə'seʃən] *nu.*
supersonic [su:pə'sɔnik] *adj* of a speed greater than the speed of sound i.e. more than 750 miles per hour. (*opp* **subsonic**).
superstition [su:pə'stiʃən] *nc/u* belief in, or fear of, magic and what is unknown. *Many people have the superstition that 13 is an unlucky number.* **superstitious** *adj.* **superstitiously** *adv.*
superstructure ['su:pəstrʌktʃə*] *nc* structure built on top of another structure: *superstructure of an aircraft carrier* i.e. all the parts built above the main deck.
supertax ['su:pətæks] *nc/u* extra tax on large incomes in addition to normal taxes.
supervise ['su:pəvaiz] *vt/i* watch to make sure that something is done; direct someone's work. *The teacher is supervising games in the playground. Tomorrow he will supervise all the pupils taking the English examination.* **supervisor** *nc.*
supervision [su:pə'viʒən] *nu*: *They will study for the English examination under his supervision.*
supervisory ['su:pəvaizəri] *adj* supervising.
supine ['su:pain] *adj* **1.** lying on one's back, face upwards. **2.** slow; lazy.
supper ['sʌpə*] *nc* last meal of the day.
supperless *adj* without supper.
supplant [sə'pla:nt] *vt* take the place of (often by unfair methods or force). *They hope to supplant their rivals in the government.*
supple ['sʌpl] *adj* easy to bend or move. *A dancer has a supple body.* **suppleness** *nu.*
supplement ['sʌplimənt] *nc* something added to complete something else or give more information. *At the end of this dictionary there is a supplement of verb tables. This magazine has a supplement about new motorcars.* Also [sʌpli'ment] *vt* add as a supplement.
supplementary [sʌpli'mentəri] *adj* **1.** added; extra. **2.** (geometry) of an angle which with another angle makes 180°.

'colour 'supplement extra section of a newspaper containing coloured photographs etc.

suppliant ['sʌpliənt] *adj* asking humbly for. Also *nc* person who asks humbly.

supplicate ['sʌplikeit] *vt/i* ask humbly for.
supplication [sʌpli'keiʃən] *nc/u*.
supplicant ['sʌplikənt] *nc* person who supplicates.

supply [sə'plai] *vt* give what is needed or asked for. *This shop supplies us with all we need/This shop supplies all our needs.* Also *nc/u* act of supplying; something which is supplied or can be supplied. *This shop has a good supply of all kinds of food. He looks after the school's supplies of books and writing materials.*
supplier *nc* person who supplies.
in short supply not easily obtainable; scarce.

support [sə'pɔːt] *vt* **1.** keep from falling; hold up. *The floors of the building are supported by wooden beams.* **2.** help by agreeing with; help to continue. *Will you support my request for more money?/Will you support me in my request for more money? Our school is supported by the government.* **3.** give what is needed to live. *I cannot support my wife and children on such a small salary.* Also *nc/u* **1.** something which supports; act of supporting or being supported. *The supports of the floors are very strong. Will you give me your support if I ask for more money? He spoke in support of the plan.* **2.** person who supports. *I am the only support of my family.*
supporter *nc* person/thing that supports. *Are you a supporter of the local football team?* i.e. do you support it by going regularly to see it play?

suppose [sə'pouz] *vt* **1.** think to be true. *They suppose (that) all rich men are wicked.* **2.** think. *What do you suppose they are doing? Is he right? Yes, I suppose so. Was he ever wrong? No, I suppose not. I don't suppose you can give me five pounds* i.e. would you please give me five pounds (but I shall not be surprised if you cannot).
supposed *adj* accepted as true but actually not true. *His supposed illness was found to be just laziness.* **supposedly** [sə'pouzidli] *adv*.
supposing *conj* if. *Supposing he does not come, shall we go without him?*
supposition [sʌpə'ziʃən] *nc/u* act of supposing; something supposed. *We shall make our plans on the supposition that they will help us. I want facts not suppositions* i.e. guesses.
be supposed to be assumed or expected to. *Every pupil is supposed to be in his classroom at 9 a.m. You are not supposed to talk to strangers* i.e. you should not.

suppress [sə'pres] *vt* **1.** stop; bring to an end. *The police are trying to suppress the sale of dangerous drugs.* **2.** prevent being known. *You cannot suppress the truth for long.*
suppression *nc/u*.
suppressive *adj* likely to, intended to, suppress.
suppressor *nc* **1.** person who suppresses. **2.** device which prevents the electrical system of an engine interfering with the sound or picture received by a radio or television set. *Most motorcars have suppressors fitted over the sparking plugs.*

suppurate ['sʌpjuəreit] *vi* (with reference to a wound) become poisoned; fester.
suppuration [sʌpjuə'reiʃən] *nu*.

supra- ['suːprə] *prefix* above; beyond (e.g. **supranational** i.e. beyond the national level).

supreme [su'priːm] *adj* **1.** highest in authority: *supreme commander of the allied forces; Supreme Court of the USA.* **2.** best or greatest possible. *By a supreme effort, he won the race.* **supremely** *adv*. **supremacy** [su'preməsi] *nu*.

surcharge ['səːtʃɑːdʒ] *vt* **1.** make an extra charge. *Many hotels surcharge for late meals* i.e. an extra payment has to be made for them. **2.** overload. **3.** print extra words or figures on (esp. on a postage stamp to change its value). Also *nc*.

sure [ʃuə*] **1.** *pred adj* believing fully. *Are you sure (that) he is honest? I am sure of his honesty. Some people are not sure about him or about his honesty.* (*opp* **unsure**). **2.** *pred adj* certain. *We are sure to win* i.e. there is no doubt that we will win. **3.** *adj* reliable. *Dark clouds are a sure sign of rain.* **sureness** *nu*.
'sure-'footed *adj* not likely to put one's foot in the wrong place; not likely to fall. *People who climb mountains must be sure-footed.*
as sure as as certainly as.
be sure to/and *imperative* make certain that. *Be sure to/and bring the book tomorrow.*
sure enough *adv* certainly; without a doubt. *He promised to come and sure enough he did.*
make sure that/of make certain that something is correct, available etc. *He made sure that he had enough food for the journey. Let's make sure of this house, before we buy it.*

surely ['ʃuəli] *adv* **1.** as expected. *They will surely win.* **2.** giving the sense of hope or belief that something will happen. *Surely you don't expect me to go. Surely we cannot buy it so cheaply.* **3.** (*US* in answer to a question) of course; certainly. *Will you come? Surely.* (*Brit* **certainly**).
Note: in sense **1.** *surely*, which is put next to the verb, is less usual than *certainly*; in sense **2.** *surely* is put before or after the subject, or at the end of the sentence.

surety ['ʃuəriti] *nc* **1.** something which is given as a guarantee against loss or damage. *When he borrowed the car, he paid a surety of £50 to its owner.* **2.** somebody who makes himself responsible for the good behaviour of somebody else, or his losses. **3.** certainty (*o.f.* in sense **3.**).

surf [səːf] *nu* waves of the sea as they break when they reach land.
surfing *nu* sport of riding on the top of a big wave while standing or lying on a narrow board.
'surfboard type of board used in this sport.
'surfboat type of special boat which can be used in surf.
'surfriding see **surfing** above.

surface ['səːfis] *nc* **1.** outside of anything. *Paper has a flat surface. Only the surface of the wood was burnt.* **2.** top of liquid (esp. a stretch of water). *He dived below the surface.* **3.** that which can be easily seen or understood; outward appearance. *On the surface he was calm, but he was really very angry.* Also *adj* **1.** *The surface measurements are 3 feet by 2 feet* i.e. length and breadth. **2.** *surface ship* i.e. ship which sails on the surface of water. (*opp* **submarine**). **3.** *its surface appearance* i.e. as it appears without examining it carefully. Also *vt/i* **1.** come to the surface. *He swam underwater and then surfaced.* **2.** put a surface on. *They surfaced*

the walls of the house with cement.
'surface mail mail sent by sea or land, not by air: *send a letter by surface mail.*

surfeit ['sə:fit] *nu* (with **a**) (esp. with reference to food and drink) too much of something: *a surfeit of cakes.* Also *vt* cause to have too much.

surge [sə:dʒ] *nc* forward movement of a wave; any strong movement like that of a wave. *I felt a surge of pity for them.* Also *vi* move in this way. *The boys surged out of school.*

surgeon ['sə:dʒən] *nc* doctor who does surgery.
dental surgeon dentist who can do surgery.
'house surgeon see **house**[1].

surgery ['sə:dʒəri] *nc/u* **1.** branch of medicine which deals with disease and injuries by operating i.e. by cutting, tying, fitting parts of the body, not by using only drugs and medicines. **2.** (*Brit*) room where a doctor sees his patients. (*US* **office**). **3.** (*Brit*) time when a doctor sees his patients. *Dr Brown holds a surgery every morning.*
surgical ['sə:dʒikl] *adj.* **surgically** *adv.*

surly ['sə:li] *adj* rude and bad-tempered.
surlily *adv.* **surliness** *nu.*

surmise [sə:'maiz] *vt/i* suppose; think without much reason. Also ['sə:maiz] *nc.*

surmount [sə'maunt] *vt/i* **1.** climb over; overcome. *I think that I can surmount these difficulties.* **2.** (*passive*) have on top. *The pillar was surmounted by a bowl of flowers.*
surmountable *adj* able to be overcome. (*opp* **insurmountable**).

surname ['sə:neim] *nc* family name. *My surname is Smith; my first/Christian name is John.*

surpass [sə'pɑ:s] *vt* be or do better than. *The result surpassed their hopes. In the examination he surpassed all the others.*
surpassing *adj* better than any other.
surpassingly *adv.*

surplice ['sə:plis] *nc* type of white garment worn by the priest and the choir in church.

surplus ['sə:pləs] *nc* amount left over when all that is needed is taken; amount by which income is greater than expenditure. *This country keeps the corn it needs and sells the surplus abroad.* Also *adj*: *This country sells its surplus corn abroad.*

surprise [sə'praiz] *vt* **1.** astonish by not being expected. *His success surprised us all. We were surprised by his success.* **2.** attack or come upon when not expected. *The enemy surprised us at dawn. They surprised him having a quiet drink.* Also *nc/u*: *His success was a great surprise. To our surprise he succeeded.* Also *adj* not expected. *The enemy made a surprise attack at dawn.*
surprised *adj* feeling surprise.
surprising *adj* causing surprise. **surprisingly** *adv.*
surprise someone into doing something make somebody so surprised that he does something quickly without thinking.
take someone by surprise cause somebody to be very surprised. *His answer took us by surprise.*
take something by surprise capture by sudden attack. *The enemy took the town by surprise.*

surrealism [sə'riəlizəm] *nu* type of art or literature in which the unrelated thoughts of the subconscious mind are expressed.
surrealist *adj.*

surrender [sə'rendə*] *vt/i* **1.** yield; hand over to the power of somebody. *The defeated soldiers soon surrendered. You must surrender your guns to the police.* **2.** (usu. with **oneself**) give way to a feeling, habit or wish. *They surrendered themselves to a life of pleasure.* Also *nc.*

surreptitious [sʌrəp'tiʃəs] *adj* done secretly.
surreptitiously *adv.*

surround [sə'raund] *vt* be on all sides of; encircle. *A high wall surrounds the field. I was surrounded by a crowd of happy children.* Also *nc* something which surrounds (esp. the piece of floor between a carpet and the walls of a room).
surrounding *adj*: *The town's water comes from the surrounding hills* i.e. the hills round the town.
surroundings *npl* everything that is round about; neighbourhood.

surtax ['sə:tæks] *nc* extra tax on very high incomes.

surveillance [sə'veilns] *nu* careful watch; supervision.

survey [sə'vei] *vt* **1.** look over. *We were able to survey the city from the top of the high building.* **2.** consider as a whole; deal with generally. *The chairman, in his talk, surveyed the work done at the previous meetings.* **3.** measure land carefully and make a map of it. **4.** examine; inspect. *He is surveying the empty factory to see if it is suitable.* Also ['sə:vei] *nc* **1.** general view: *chairman's survey of the work done.* **2.** measurement of land. *They are doing a survey of the land through which the new road will pass.* **3.** detailed examination of a building, house etc.
surveying *nu* work of measuring land carefully and making a map of it.
surveyor *nc* person who surveys land or inspects buildings etc.

survive [sə'vaiv] *vt/i* remain alive; live longer than. *Only a few soldiers survived the battle. My father has survived all his brothers and sisters.*
survival *nc/u* act of surviving; something left over from a former time.
survivor *nc* person who has survived.

susceptible [sə'septibl] *adj* **1.** easily impressed; sensitive. *Children are more susceptible than adults. I am susceptible to colds.* **2.** (with **of**) able to be or have. *The sentence is susceptible of two interpretations* i.e. it can be understood in two different ways.
susceptibility [səsepti'biliti] *nc/u* (often *pl*) weakness or sensitive spot in a person's body or mind.

suspect [səs'pekt] *vt* **1.** think that something is possible without knowing definitely. *We suspected that it was a trick to get our money.* **2.** (with **of**) think that somebody may be guilty. *I suspect them of stealing my books.* **3.** be doubtful or not sure about. *Everybody suspects his story about what he did during the war.* Also ['sʌspekt] *nc/pred adj* person who is suspected of doing something wrong; doubtful. *The police are looking for all suspects. His reason for being absent is suspect.*
suspected *adj.* (*opp* **unsuspected**).

suspend [səs'pend] *vt* **1.** cause to hang from. *They suspended the box from a branch of the tree.* **2.** (in *passive*) be held up by a liquid or a gas: *drops of water suspended in oil.* **3.** hold back; stop for a time. *They have suspended work until next week.* **4.** stop somebody from working or having a certain position for a time. *The committee suspended two members of the football team.*

suspender *nc* **1.** device to keep up a stocking or sock when worn. **2.** (in *pl*) (*US*) straps worn over the shoulders to keep up trousers. (*Brit* **braces**).

suspense [səs'pens] *nu* state of uncertainty and worry. *We were kept in suspense for an hour before we were told the results.*

suspension [səs'penʃən] **1.** *nc* act of suspending. *We were told about the suspension of the two players.* **2.** *nu* state of being suspended. **3.** *nc/u* part of the equipment of a car etc which is used to give a smooth ride.

sus'pension bridge type of bridge which is suspended on strong wire ropes stretched between two towers.

suspension bridge

suspicion [səs'piʃən] *nc/u* **1.** feeling of doubt or that something is wrong without knowing definitely; act of suspecting. *We have suspicions about his story. The police arrested him on suspicion* i.e. because they suspected him. **2.** very small sign or hint. *I noticed a suspicion of anger in his reply.*

suspicious *adj* having or causing suspicion. *I feel suspicious about/of him. There is a suspicious man standing outside the bank* i.e. one who causes suspicion about why he is there. **suspiciously** *adv*. **suspiciousness** *nu*.

above suspicion too good to be suspected of doing anything wrong.

lay oneself open to suspicion do something which causes oneself to be suspected.

sustain [sə'stein] *vt* **1.** keep from falling; hold up. *These two posts sustain the whole roof.* **2.** (in a legal sense) support; agree with. *The judge sustained my request for more time to pay the money.* **3.** cause to continue; keep strong. *How much longer can you sustain the argument that you never make a mistake? This food will sustain you.* **4.** suffer; endure. *I sustained a broken arm in the accident.*

sustenance ['sʌstənəns] *nu* (esp. with reference to food and drink which keeps one strong and healthy) something which sustains.

suture ['suːtʃə*] *nc* **1.** sewing up of a wound. **2.** mark made when this is done. **3.** thread used to do it.

suzerain ['suːzərein] *nc* ruler or lord; country having control of another country.

svelte [svelt] *adj* (with reference to a woman) having a slim, graceful figure.

swab, swob [swɔb] *nc* **1.** piece of cloth, sponge etc tied to a stick for cleaning floors and the decks of ships; mop. **2.** piece of cotton wool or gauze used by a doctor for cleaning or to obtain specimens (e.g. from the mouth). Also *vt* clean with a swab. *past* **swabbed.**

swaddle ['swɔdl] *vt* wind long strips of cloth round a baby.

swag [swæg] *nu* stolen goods. (*informal*).

swagger ['swægə*] *vi* walk in a proud way; behave in this way. Also *nu*.

swain [swein] *nc* young man (*o.f.*).

swallow[1] ['swɔlou] *vt/i* **1.** put down the throat into the stomach. *He swallowed the pill.* **2.** accept too easily. *Do not swallow his story about what he did. They had to swallow the insult* i.e. accept it without protest. Also *nc* act of swallowing; amount swallowed.

swallow something up **1.** swallow completely. **2.** use completely; cause to disappear. *Taxes have swallowed up all my money. The crowd swallowed them up* i.e. they went into the crowd and could no longer be seen.

swallow[2] ['swɔlou] *nc* type of small bird, with a thin body and thin pointed wings, which eats insects.

swam [swæm] past tense of **swim.**

swamp [swɔmp] *nc/u* land which is soft and covered with shallow water. Also *vt* **1.** fill with water; flood. **2.** (with **with**) receive too much of something. *I have been swamped with offers of help.* **swampy** *adj*.

swan [swɔn] *nc* type of large (usu. white) water bird, with a long neck.

swan

'swan song song which, according to myth, a swan sings just before it dies; therefore the last work of a writer, poet etc before he dies.

swank [swæŋk] *vi* behave or speak in a boastful way. Also *nu*. **swanky** *adj*. **swankily** *adv*. (all *informal*).

swap [swɔp] *vt/i* see **swop.**

swarm [swɔːm] *nc* **1.** large number of insects or small animals (esp. when they are moving): *swarm of bees.* **2.** large moving crowd of people: *swarms of visitors at the seaside.* Also *vi* **1.** (with reference to bees) move together with the queen bee to another place. **2.** move or be present in large crowds. *The boys swarmed into the classroom. The classroom was swarming with boys.*

swarthy ['swɔːði] *adj* having a dark skin. **swarthiness** *nu*.

swashbuckler ['swɔʃbʌklə*] *nc* person who is boastful and noisy.

swashbuckling *adj* boastful and noisy. Also *nu* boastful and noisy behaviour.

swastika ['swɔstikə] *nc* figure shaped thus 卍 (believed to bring good luck and used as the badge of the German Nazis).

swat [swɔt] *vt* (esp. with reference to insects) hit quickly and kill. *past* **swatted.**

swatter *nc* something used for swatting.

swath [swɔːθ] *nc* line of cut grass or grain.

swathe [sweið] *vt* cover and tie tightly (esp. with bandages). *The injured man's head was swathed in bandages.*

sway [swei] *vt/i* **1.** move, cause to move, from side to side. *The dancers swayed to the music.* **2.** have influence or control over. *He is a good speaker and can sway all those who listen to him.* Also *nu* **1.** act of moving or causing to move, from side to side: *the sway of a ship in a storm.* **2.** influence or control. *They were under the sway of the dictator.*

swear [swεə*] *vt/i* **1.** say or promise positively or in God's name; cause somebody to promise in this way. *I swear that my story is true. He swore to tell the truth.* **2.** use bad language. *The angry driver swore at us. They were all swearing about their bad luck. You should not swear in front of the children.* *past tense* **swore** [swɔ:*]. *past part* **sworn** [swɔ:n].

swearing *nu* bad language.

'swearword bad word which should not be used in polite talk.

swear by someone/something **1.** say or promise in the name of. *He swore by God to tell the truth.* **2.** use and trust completely. *You should try this medicine; my wife swears by it.*

swear someone in (usu. *passive*) put somebody in office by making him promise to do certain things (e.g. obey the rules). *The new member was sworn in by the chairman.*

sworn enemies/friends enemies/friends for ever.

sweat [swet] *nu* **1.** liquid which comes from the body through the skin (esp. when one is very hot or frightened). **2.** liquid which appears on the surface of something (e.g. on the walls and windows of a room full of steam). **3.** something which causes sweat; hard work; worry. *Learning a new language is an awful sweat.* (*informal* in sense **3.**). Also *vt/i* **1.** produce, cause to produce, liquid through the skin. *We sweated in the hot sun.* **2.** work, cause to work, hard. (*informal* in sense **2.**).

sweaty *adj* making one sweat; wet with sweat. **sweatily** *adv.* **sweatiness** *nu.*

'sweat shop factory or other place of work where the work is hard and the pay is low. (*informal*).

'sweat suit type of thick suit worn by an athlete to keep warm when he is not competing. (Usu. **tracksuit**).

sweated labour hard work for very low pay.

sweat something out **1.** (with reference to an illness) cause to go away by sweating. *I stayed in bed to sweat out my fever.* **2.** endure something to the very end. (*informal* in sense **2.**).

all of a sweat **1.** wet with sweat. **2.** worried. (*informal*).

sweat blood work very hard indeed; be very worried. (*informal*).

sweater ['swetə*] *nc* woollen jersey or jacket.

Swede [swi:d] *n* native of Sweden.

swede [swi:d] *nc* type of turnip i.e. large, round vegetable.

Swedish ['swi:diʃ] *nu* language of Sweden. Also *adj* of Sweden, its people or its language.

sweep[1] [swi:p] *vt/i* **1.** remove loose dirt, dust etc with a brush or broom; clean in this way. *They are sweeping the rubbish out of the classroom. My mother sweeps the kitchen every day.* **2.** move, cause to move, quickly. *The crowd swept into the field. The river swept the boat away.* **3.** extend over a large area in a curve. *The hills sweep into the distance. The new road sweeps round the city.* *past* **swept** [swept].

sweeper *nc* person/thing that sweeps.

sweeping *adj* **1.** moving quickly; having great effect. *There have been many sweeping changes in the country. They won a sweeping victory.* **2.** with no attention to details; general. *You should not make sweeping statements about such important matters.* **sweepingly** *adv.*

sweepings *npl* things which are swept; rubbish; dirt.

sweep all before one be completely successful; win easily.

sweep the board win everything. *Our school swept the board in the inter-school sports* i.e. our school won all the prizes. (*informal*).

sweep somebody off his feet **1.** knock down. *The waves swept us off our feet.* **2.** influence greatly; persuade completely. *His speech swept them off their feet.* **3.** cause someone to fall in love with one.

sweep[2] [swi:p] *nc* **1.** act of sweeping. *My mother gave the kitchen a sweep.* **2.** quick movement. *With one sweep of his hand he cleared the books from his desk.* **3.** large area (esp. one in a curve). *Behind the town there is a sweep of hills.* **4.** person who cleans chimneys. (Also **chimney sweep**). **5.** see **sweepstake.**

'sweepstake type of gambling (usu. on the result of a horse-race) in which all the money paid by those who take part is given to those who draw the tickets of the winning horses. (Also **sweep**).

make a clean sweep of see **make**[1].

sweet [swi:t] *adj* **1.** tasting like sugar; containing sugar. *I like sweet cakes. This coffee tastes sweet* i.e. has a sweet taste. **2.** fresh; pleasant; attractive. *These flowers have a sweet smell. She has a sweet face.* Also *nc* **1.** (*Brit*) something very sweet to eat (usu. made from sugar) (*US* **candy**). **2.** dish of sweet food (e.g. pudding) (usu. eaten at the end of a meal). **3.** (in *pl*) pleasures; advantages. *He likes the sweets of his position as manager.* **sweetly** *adv.* **sweetness** *nu.*

sweetish *adj* rather sweet.

sweeten *vt/i* become or make sweet.

sweetening *nc/u* something used to sweeten; act of making sweet.

sweetened *adj.* (*opp* **unsweetened**).

sweety **1.** sweetmeat. **2.** sweetheart. (*informal*).

'sweetbread pancreas i.e. organ of an animal's body near the stomach, used as food.

'sweetheart lover; person loved.

'sweetmeat piece of food made mainly from sugar (*o.f.*).

'sweet 'pea type of plant with sweet-smelling flowers.

be sweet on be very fond of; be in love with. (*informal*).

have a sweet tooth be fond of things which have a sweet taste. (*informal*).

swell [swel] *vt/i* become, cause to become, larger in volume. *The heat made my feet swell. The heavy rain swelled the river. His face was swollen with insect bites.* *past tense* **swelled.** *past part* **swollen** ['swouln]. Also *nc* **1.** act of swelling. **2.** (in *sing*) large but slow rise and fall of the sea. *The ship rolled in the heavy swell.* **3.** person who is rich or smartly dressed. (*informal* and *o.f.* in sense **3.**). Also *adj* rich; smart; very good. (*informal* and mainly *US*).

swelling *nc* **1.** state of being swollen; lump. *There is a swelling on top of his head where he was hit by a stone.* **2.** act of swelling.

swelter ['sweltə*] *vi* feel, or cause to feel, very warm and uncomfortable: *in sweltering heat.*

swept [swept] past of **sweep**[1].

swerve [swə:v] *vt/i* move, cause to move, suddenly to one side. *The motorcar swerved to avoid a hole in the road.* Also *nc.*

swerve from something change, stop

doing. *He will not swerve from his duty of helping others.*

swift[1] [swift] *adj* quick; fast. **swiftly** *adv.* **swiftness** *nu.*

swift[2] [swift] *nc* type of bird, which can fly very fast and eats insects it catches when flying.

swig [swig] *vt/i* drink quickly. *past* **swigged.** Also *nc*: *He took a swig at his glass of beer.* (both *informal*).

swill [swil] *vt/i* **1.** drink large amounts of. *They swilled beer all evening.* **2.** (usu. with **out**) pour liquid over or through in order to clean. *They are swilling out the empty buckets.* Also *nu* waste food and liquid (usu. used as food for pigs).

swim [swim] *vt/i* **1.** move through the water by moving the limbs, fins, tail etc; cross a stretch of water in this way. *All fish swim. I learnt to swim when I was a boy. He swam the river. We swam a mile yesterday.* **2.** be full of; be covered with (esp. with a liquid). *Her eyes swam with tears. The room was swimming in/with water from the burst pipe.* **3.** appear to go round; feel dizzy. *My head was swimming from the blow. pres part* **swimming.** *past tense* **swam** [swæm]. *past part* **swum** [swʌm]. Also *nc* act of swimming. *I am going for a swim.*

swimmingly *adv* successfully; easily. (*informal*).

'swimsuit dress/costume for swimming in.

'swimming bath *nc* (often *pl*) place for swimming (usu. indoors).

in the swim taking part in social life (e.g. going to parties) (*informal*).

swindle ['swindl] *vt/i* cheat; get by cheating. *The company made a lot of money by swindling the public. He swindled me out of £1* i.e. he got a £1 from me by cheating me. Also *nc* act of swindling; something by which one is swindled. **swindler** *nc.*

swine [swain] *nc* **1.** pig (*o.f.*). **2.** unpleasant person. (*impolite*). *pl* **swine.**

swinish *adj* unpleasant; beastly. **swinishly** *adv.* **swinishness** *nu.*

swing [swiŋ] *vt/i* **1.** move, cause to move, from side to side or backwards and forwards (esp. when hanging down or with one end fixed). *The door was swinging on its hinges. The soldiers swung their arms as they marched.* **2.** turn, cause to turn, quickly. *The car swung towards the side of the road. I swung round to see who was following me.* **3.** move easily and smoothly. *Our troops swung into battle without halting. past* **swung** [swʌŋ]. Also **1.** *nc* act of swinging: *the swing of the door on its hinges.* **2.** *nc* seat fixed to ropes on which one can swing backwards and forwards. **3.** *nu* type of music with a strong rhythm. (rather *o.f.* in sense **3.**).

'swing 'bridge type of bridge which can be swung to the side (usu. over a river or canal to allow ships to pass).

go with a swing 1. go easily and smoothly. *The party went with a swing.* (*informal*). **2.** (music) have a strong rhythm.

in full swing going well; working fully. *When we arrived the meeting was already in full swing.* (*informal*).

swing the lead avoid work; be lazy. (*informal*).

swipe [swaip] *vt* **1.** hit with a wide, sweeping blow. *He swiped me on the shoulders with his stick.* **2.** steal. Also *nc*: *He took a swipe at the fly on the wall.* (all *informal*).

swirl [swə:l] *vt/i* (with reference to air or liquid) move, cause to move, round quickly and in a confined way. *The flooded river swirled round the rocks. The branches of the tree were swirled away by the flood.* Also *nc*: *The wind blew swirls of dust across the field.*

swish [swiʃ] *nc* sound made by a stick or something thin moving very quickly through the air; sound made by cloth moving over a surface: *swish of a whip; swish of their long robes over the floor.* Also *vt/i* move and make a sound like this. *The animal swished its tail.*

Swiss [swis] *n* native of Switzerland. *pl* **Swiss.** Also *adj* of Switzerland or its people.

switch [switʃ] *nc* **1.** device for turning electric current on or off. **2.** movable rail to send a train from one set of railway lines to another. **3.** thin, easily-bent stick just cut from a tree. **4.** piece of false hair worn by women to increase the amount of hair they have on their heads. **5.** sudden change of opinion, direction etc. Also *vt/i* **1.** turn electric current on or off. *Please switch off the lights when you leave the room. He switched on the radio.* **2.** move a train on to another set of railway lines. **3.** hit with a thin, easily-bent stick. **4.** change. *He is always switching jobs.*

'switchback type of railway which goes up and down steeply (usu. built for amusement). Also *adj*: *switchback railway; switchback road.*

'switchboard 1. board with many switches for turning electric current on or off. **2.** board for connecting telephone lines as required (e.g. on a telephone exchange).

'switchover *nc* change. *The switchover to the metric system.*

swivel ['swivl] *nc* ring or hook which is fixed to something else in a way that allows them both to turn round freely. Also *vt/i* turn, cause to turn, round on, or as if on, a swivel. *He swivelled round his chair. past* **swivelled.** (*US* **swiveled**).

swob [swɔb] *nc* see **swab.**

swollen ['swouln] past part of **swell.**

swoon [swu:n] *vi* faint. Also *nc.* (both *o.f.*).

swoop [swu:p] *vt/i* (with **down on**) attack suddenly from above; attack suddenly. *The hawk swooped down on the chickens.* Also *nc* act of swooping.

swop, swap [swɔp] *vt/i* exchange. *We swopped jerseys. I'll swop places with you. past* **swopped.** Also *nc.* (both *informal*).

sword [sɔ:d] *nc* type of weapon with a long steel blade and a handle (or hilt).

'sword dance type of dance in which swords are used, either laid on the ground or held in the hand.

'swordfish type of fish with a long, stiff upper jaw shaped like a sword.

'swordsman *nc* man who is skilled in fighting with a sword. **swordsmanship** *nu.*

'swordplay fighting with swords; fencing.

'swordstick hollow walking stick with a sword inside.

cross swords with someone fight someone using swords; argue. (*informal*).

draw a sword take a sword from its sheath.

put to the sword kill, cause to be killed, with a sword (*o.f.*).

swore [swɔ:*] past tense of **swear.**

sworn [swɔ:n] past part of **swear.**

swot [swɔt] *vt/i* study hard. *past* **swotted.** Also *nc* **1.** hard study. **2.** person who studies hard. (all *informal*).

swum [swʌm] past part of **swim.**

sybarite ['sibərait] *nc* person whose main

aim in life is luxury and pleasure. **sybaritic** [sibə'ritik] *adj.*

sycamore ['sikəmɔ:*] **1.** *nc* one of several types of tree. **2.** *nu* the wood from this tree.

sycophant ['sikəfænt] *nc* person who tries to please rich or powerful people by flattering them greatly. **sycophantic** [sikə'fæntik] *adj.* **sycophancy** *nu.*

syllable ['siləbl] *nc* sound made by one action of the voice and usually containing one vowel. *The word monumental has four syllables.*

-syllabled *adj*: *monumental is a four-syllabled word.*

syllabic [si'læbik] *adj* of, or having, syllables.

syllabary ['siləbəri] *nc* table of characters which represent syllables used in certain languages which have no alphabet (e.g. Japanese).

syllabus ['siləbəs] *nc* outline of a course of lessons or studies. *All our schools follow the same English syllabus. pl* **syllabuses** or **syllabi** ['siləbai].

syllogism ['silədʒizəm] *nc* formal statement of an argument having three parts i.e. *major premise, minor premise* and *conclusion* (e.g. *Iron melts when heated* (major premise); *this tool is made of iron* (minor premise); *therefore this tool will melt when heated* (conclusion)). **syllogistic** [silə'dʒistik] *adj.*

sylph [silf] *nc* spirit or fairy of the air; graceful young woman.

sylphlike *adj* like a sylph; graceful and slender. *She has a sylphlike figure.*

sylvan, silvan ['silvən] *adj* of the woods or forests (*o.f.*).

symbol ['simbl] *nc* something which represents something; sign; mark. + *is the mathematical symbol for addition.* H_2O *is the chemical symbol for water. The crescent moon is the symbol of Islam.* **symbolic** [sim'bɔlik] *adj.* **symbolical** [sim'bɔlikl] *adj.* **symbolically** *adv.*

symbolism *nu* use of symbols to represent ideas (e.g. in art).

symbolist *nc* person who does this.

symbolize *vt* **1.** be the symbol of. **2.** represent by a symbol. **symbolization** [simbəlai'zeiʃən] *nc/u.*

symmetry ['simətri] *nu* balance between the different parts of something; exact agreement of opposite sides of a figure to each other; harmony. *A well-designed building has symmetry.*

symmetrical [si'metrikl] *adj*: *A triangle with all sides equal is symmetrical.* (*opp* **asymmetrical**). **symmetrically** *adv.*

sympathy ['simpəθi] *nc/u* feeling which is the same as what somebody else feels; feeling by which one shares the pain or troubles of somebody else. *When his father died, he had our sympathy. We felt sympathy for him. Please give him my sympathies.*

sympathetic [simpə'θetik] *adj* having sympathy; showing that one feels pity for someone; caused by sympathy. *He wrote me a very sympathetic letter. I don't like Peter, but I must say he was very sympathetic when my father died.* **sympathetically** *adv.*

sympathize ['simpəθaiz] *vt/i* feel or show sympathy. *I sympathize with all those who are poor.* **sympathizer** ['simpəθaizə*] *nc.*

in sympathy with thinking favourably of; in support of. *They are in sympathy with your views.*

out of sympathy with disagreeing with.

symphony ['simfəni] *nc* musical composition (usu. in four parts) for a full orchestra. **symphonic** [sim'fɔnik] *adj.*

symposium [sim'pouziəm] *nc* meeting of several persons to discuss and exchange ideas; number of essays by several persons about one subject. *pl* **symposiums** or **symposia** [sim'pouziə].

symptom ['simptəm] *nc* **1.** change in the body, or outward sign on the body, which shows it has a disease. *A high temperature is a symptom of malaria.* **2.** sign showing that something exists. *Bad behaviour is often a symptom of unhappiness.*

symptomatic [simptə'mætik] *adj* (with **of**): *A high temperature is symptomatic of malaria.* **symptomatically** *adv.*

syn- [sin] *prefix* together; with; at the same time as (e.g. **synchronize; synthesis**).

synagogue ['sinəgɔg] *nc* place where Jews worship; meeting of Jews to worship.

synchromesh ['siŋkrou'meʃ] *adj* of a part of a gear system in a car which makes gear-changing easier or smoother. Also *nu.*

synchronize ['siŋkrənaiz] *vt/i* agree, cause to agree, in time; happen, cause to happen, at the same time. *Before the attack, the army officers synchronized their watches* i.e. put their watches to exactly the same time. **synchronization** [siŋkrənai'zeiʃən] *nu.* **synchronized** *adj.* (*opp* **unsynchronized**).

syncopate ['siŋkəpeit] *vt* (in music) change the rhythm by stressing notes which are not usually stressed. **syncopated** *adj.* **syncopation** [siŋkə'peiʃən] *nu.*

syncope ['siŋkəpi] *nc* **1.** removal of one or more letters from the middle of a word. **2.** fainting; losing consciousness through lack of blood to the brain.

syndicalism ['sindikəlizəm] *nu* political belief that trade unions should take the place of the state, and control all factories and other means of production.

syndicalist *nc* person who has this belief.

syndicate ['sindikət] *nc* number of business firms which group together for a certain purpose. Also ['sindikeit] *vt* control by syndicate; publish news and articles at the same time in several newspapers and magazines by means of a syndicate. **syndication** [sindi'keiʃən] *nc/u.*

syndrome ['sindroum] *nc* number of symptoms of an illness occurring together.

synecdoche [si'nekdəki] *nu* way of referring to a thing by mentioning part of it (e.g. *He employs 500 hands in his factory* means *He employs 500 workers*).

synod ['sinəd] *nc* meeting or council about important church affairs.

synonym ['sinənim] *nc* word which has the same meaning as another word in the same language: *'big' and 'large' are synonyms.* (*opp* **antonym**). **synonymous** [si'nɔniməs] *adj.*

synopsis [si'nɔpsis] *nc* summary (usu. of something which has been written or printed). *pl* **synopses** [si'nɔpsi:z]. **synoptic** [si'nɔptik] *adj.* **synoptically** *adv.*

syntax ['sintæks] *nu* part of grammar which deals with making sentences and putting words in their correct order. **syntactic** [sin'tæktik] *adj.* **syntactically** *adv.*

synthesis ['sinθəsis] *nc* putting together several parts into a whole; result of doing this. *This method of teaching is a synthesis of many methods which have been used elsewhere. pl* **syntheses** ['sinθəsi:z].

synthetic [sin'θetik] *adj* **1.** of synthesis;

resulting from synthesis. **2.** artificial. *Synthetic fibres are often used instead of wool or cotton to make clothes.* **synthetically** *adv.*

syphilis ['sifilis] *nu* type of venereal disease.

syphilitic [sifi'litik] *adj* of syphilis. Also *nc* person who has syphilis.

syphon ['saifən] *nc* see **siphon.**

syringe [si'rindʒ] *nc* device made of a tube with a piston for drawing in a liquid and pushing it out again through a very small hole. Also *vt* clean or put liquid in with a syringe.

syringes

hypodermic syringe type of syringe for putting medicines beneath the skin (used by doctors for giving injections).

syrup ['sirəp] *nu* **1.** liquid obtained when sugar cane is boiled. **2.** thick mixture of sugar and water. **3.** any thick, sweet liquid.

syrupy *adj* thick and very sweet.

system ['sistəm] *nc/u* **1.** number of things arranged to make one complete working whole: *the solar system* i.e. the sun, planets etc; *the nervous system* i.e. the nerves in the human body. **2.** the way things are arranged to work; method: *public transport system; different systems of government. There is no system in his work.* **3.** group of thoughts, ideas, theories etc which belong together: *system of philosophy.* **4.** the body. *Too much alcohol is not good for the system.*

systematic [sistə'mætik] *adj* following a system; well-organized; orderly: *a systematic approach to the problem.* (*opp* **unsystematic**). **systematically** *adv.*

systematize ['sistəmətaiz] *vt* arrange in a system. **systematization** [sistəmətai'zeiʃən] *nu.*

systematized *adj.* (*opp* **unsystematized**).

T

ta [tɑː] *interj* informal word for **thank you.**

tab [tæb] *nc* **1.** small piece of cloth etc sewn to something larger to show whose it is or who made it. **2.** small strip of cloth sewn to the top of a coat, dress etc so that it can be hung up.

keep tabs on watch carefully; keep a check on. (*informal*).

tabby ['tæbi] *nc* cat (usu. female) with striped fur. (Also **tabby cat**).

tabernacle ['tæbənækl] *nc* **1.** movable shelter or temporary building used for religious purposes (e.g. by the Israelites during their wanderings). **2.** (in a Roman Catholic church) place or container where consecrated hosts are kept.

table ['teibl] *nc* **1.** flat surface made of wood, metal etc standing on legs and used as a piece of furniture for working at or eating meals etc: *card table* i.e. one used for playing cards; *dining table; coffee table; sitting at the table.* **2.** persons sitting at a table. *His smile was seen by the whole table.* **3.** short, clear arrangement or list of facts or figures: *multiplication tables; timetable; table showing the important events in English history.* **4.** flat piece of stone or metal with writing on it. Also *vt* **1.** arrange facts or figures shortly and clearly. *The results of the experiment are tabled at the back of the book.* **2.** bring a proposal to the attention of a meeting.

'tablecloth cloth put on a table (usu. at mealtimes).

'table lamp small lamp which is put on a table.

'table linen cloths, napkins etc used at mealtimes.

'table rapping/turning rapping, moving a table or other piece of furniture, believed by some people to be done by spirits of the dead.

'tablespoon type of large spoon used at meals (usu. for serving).

'table talk talk among those having a meal together.

'table tennis game like tennis played on a long table with a small, light ball and small bats.

at table taking a meal. *When I arrived my friends were already at table.*

turn the tables on somebody defeat or get the better of somebody who was previously winning or in a stronger position. (*informal*).

tableau ['tæblou] *nc* scene from history or literature etc represented by a group of persons without actions or words. *pl* **tableaux** ['tæblouz].

table d'hote ['tɑːbl'dout] *nu* meal served in a restaurant at a fixed price, and with little or no choice of dishes.

tablet ['tæblit] *nc* **1.** small block of something hard: *tablet of soap; aspirin tablet.* **2.** number of small sheets of paper fastened together for writing on. **3.** piece of flat stone or metal (usu. fixed to a wall) telling about somebody/something.

tabloid ['tæblɔid] *nc* type of newspaper with rather small pages, many pictures etc, giving news briefly and in a sensational way.

taboo [tə'buː] *nc* something which is forbidden by religious belief or custom. *This tribe has many taboos about the kinds of food women may eat. The top of that sacred hill is under a taboo* i.e. it is forbidden to go there. Also *pred adj*: *Eating eggs is taboo in this tribe. Arguments about politics are taboo in many countries.* Also *vt* forbid. *Arguments about politics are tabooed.*

tabor ['teibə*] *nc* type of small drum.

tabular ['tæbjulə*] *adj* **1.** of, like a table. **2.** arranged clearly in a list. *The results of the experiment are shown in tabular form.*

tabulate ['tæbjuleit] *vt* arrange facts or figures shortly and clearly in a list. **tabulation** [tæbju'leiʃən] *nc/u.*

tacit ['tæsit] *adj* accepted or understood without anything being said. *By sitting quietly at the meeting, he gave his tacit approval to the plan.* **tacitly** *adv.*

taciturn ['tæsitəːn] *adj* (with reference to a person) saying little; silent by habit. **taciturnly** *adv.* **taciturnity** [tæsi'təːniti] *nu.*

tack[1] [tæk] *nc* **1.** type of small, sharp nail with a flat head. **2.** type of stitch made quickly with needle and thread to fasten pieces of cloth together until closer and more permanent stitches are made. Also *vt* **1.** fasten with tacks. *We tacked the map on the board. She tacked up the hem of her dress.* **2.** add (often quickly or unexpectedly). *What are these extra charges you have tacked on to my hotel bill?*

hard tack hard biscuits; plain food. (*informal*).

get down to brass tacks see **brass.**

tack[2] [tæk] *nc* **1.** course of a sailing ship in relation to the wind. *The yacht left the harbour on the starboard tack* i.e. with the wind blowing from the starboard or right-hand side. **2.** any course of action. *These scientists are on the right/wrong tack.* Also *vi* (with reference to a sailing ship) sail against the wind by moving on a zigzag course.

tackle ['tækl] **1.** *nu* set of ropes and pulleys for lifting heavy weights or moving a ship's sails. **2.** *nu* equipment needed for a game or for work: *fishing tackle* i.e. rod, line, bait etc needed to fish. **3.** *nc* (in football etc) move by a player to stop an opponent who has the ball. Also *vt/i* **1.** seize and stop an opponent who has the ball; try to stop somebody. *The policeman tackled the thief as he tried to escape.* **2.** argue strongly with somebody; question closely. *After the meeting he tackled me about my speech.* **3.** begin doing something with determination. *We must tackle the problem of poverty as soon as possible.*

tacky ['tæki] *adj* (with reference to glue, paint etc) sticky; not quite dry.

tact [tækt] *nu* understanding of, and sympathy for, the feelings of others so that one knows what is the right thing to do or say in any difficult situation. *Our teacher showed great tact in dealing with the angry parents.* **tactful** *adj.* **tactfully** *adv.*
tactless *adj* having no tact. **tactlessly** *adv.* **tactlessness** *nu.*

tactics ['tæktiks] *npl* science of putting armed forces in the right place before or during a battle; any plans made to get something done. **tactical** *adj.* **tactically** *adv.*

tactile ['tæktail], **tactual** ['tæktjuəl] *adj* of the sense of touch; able to be touched or felt.

tadpole ['tædpoul] *nc* young frog after it has left its egg and before it is fully grown.

taffeta ['tæfitə] *nu* type of thin, shiny cloth.

taffrail ['tæfreil] *nc* rail round the stern of a ship.

tag [tæg] *nc* **1.** small card which is fastened to something; label. *Have you put tags on your luggage?*; *price tag* i.e. label showing the price of something. **2.** metal tip of a shoelace. **3.** phrase which is often used (usu. to show learning): *Latin tag.* **4.** children's game in which one child chases and tries to touch another. Also *vt* **1.** put a tag on something. **2.** add; join; fasten. *He tagged the flower to his jacket.* **3.** (with **after** or **behind**) follow behind. *The little boy tagged after his older sister wherever she went. past* **tagged.**

tail [teil] *nc* **1.** movable part at the back end of an animal, bird or fish. *Cows use their tails to keep away flies.* **2.** something like a tail (usu. at the end of something else): *tail of a long line of people; tail of an aircraft; tail of a letter* i.e. the upward or downward stroke made when one finishes writing a letter of the alphabet. **3.** reverse side of a coin. (*opp* **head**). *Heads or tails?* (said when throwing a coin into the air to decide something according to whether the coin falls with the head or tail upwards). **4.** (in *pl*) tail coat. see below. *Are you wearing your tails tonight?* (*informal* in sense **4.**). Also *vt/i* follow behind. *The children tailed after their mother. The detective tailed the thief through the crowd* i.e. followed him secretly.
-tailed *adj* having a tail: *long-tailed.*
tailless *adj* without a tail.
'**tailboard** movable board at the back of a cart or lorry.
'**tail coat** man's evening dress coat with a short front and a long back divided at the bottom.
'**tail** '**end** (with **the**) last part. *We were so late that we only saw the tail end of the play.* (*informal*).
'**taillight** light (usu. red) at the back of a vehicle or train.
'**tailpiece** design printed at the end of a chapter in a book; something forming the last part of a thing: *tailpiece of a story.*
turn tail turn round and run away. (*informal*).

tailor ['teilə*] *nc* person who makes outer clothes (e.g. men's suits). Also *vt* cut out and make outer clothes.
'**tailor-**'**made** *adj* **1.** (*Brit*) made by a tailor to fit a particular person. (*US* **custom-made**). **2.** specially made to suit some particular purpose.

taint [teint] *nc* unpleasant quality, mark or smell; something which causes decay or infection. Also *vt/i* become, cause to become, decayed or infected. *This food is tainted because it is not fresh.*

take [teik] *vt/i* **1.** seize and hold. *I took my father's hand* i.e. I held his hand in mine. *She took the baby in her arms. The dog took the stick between its teeth.* **2.** get; have. *I shall take a small house in the village. We are taking the bus to London. He is taking a bath. They took a walk round the garden. Please take a seat and wait.* **3.** capture; win; gain. *The enemy has taken the castle. Our team took the first game and lost the second. Her strange dress took everybody's attention.* **4.** receive; accept; earn. *He took the blow on the chin. This hotel does not take children. Will you take me as your partner? I take your word for it* i.e. I believe you. *The shop took about £20 during the morning.* **5.** remove without permission; steal. *Somebody has taken my coat. The thieves took all they could carry.* **6.** carry; move; cause to go. *He has taken his shoes (to the shop) to be repaired. I took my books to school. They will take us with them to the cinema. The road took them over the hill.* **7.** be necessary; need. *This work will take a long time. How long did you take to come here? It took three men to lift the box.* **8.** make a record of. *The policeman took the number of my car* i.e. he wrote it down. *Do you take notes of the lectures? He wants to take our photograph.* **9.** think; suppose. *They took us for strangers. May I take it that you agree?* **10.** act or deal with something in a certain way. *Take care that you do not fall. We took pity on him* i.e. we felt sorry for him. *The horse took fright* i.e. became frightened. *He takes life quietly. They took the news badly* i.e. they were very upset by it. *He takes his work seriously.* **11.** be successful. *His long speeches do not take with young people.* My *vaccination hasn't taken yet. past* **took** [tuk]. *past part* **taken** ['teikən].
taker *nc* person who accepts or agrees to a bet or offer. *He wanted £100 for his car but there were no takers.*
taking *adj* attractive; pleasant.
takings *npl* receipts; money earned. *The takings for the concert were over £50.*
'**take-home** '**pay** amount of money which a worker actually receives, after taxes etc have been taken from him.
take after someone behave or look like. *The boy takes after his father.*
take one back cause one to remember. *This picture takes me back to the war.* (*informal*).
take something back 1. return. *Take this book back to the library.* **2.** agree to have returned; accept back. *The trousers which you sold me are too big. Will you take them back?* **3.** admit that what one has said is wrong and apologize. *He took back the story he told about me.*
take something down 1. write down. *The pupils took down what the teacher had told them.* **2.** make more humble; cause to be less important. *He is so proud that people want to take him down.*
take someone/something in 1. receive; accept (usu. for payment). *His mother takes in lodgers* i.e. she earns money by having lodgers in her house. **2.** make less in size. *She has become so thin that she has had to take in all her clothes. Because the wind was strong they took in the sails of the boat.* **3.** understand; see; listen. *The lesson was too difficult for the class to take in. He does not seem to be listening but he is in fact taking*

everything in. **4.** deceive. *Don't be taken in by his promises.*
take (someone/something) off **1.** remove; put in another place. *He took off his coat and hung it up. Please take your elbows off the table. The police took him off to prison.* **2.** leave the ground. *Our plane takes off at 4 p.m.*
'takeoff¹ *nc*: *What time is the takeoff?*
take someone off imitate somebody (usu. to make others laugh). *He is good at taking off the headmaster.*
'takeoff² *nc*: *His takeoff of the headmaster was very amusing.* (*informal*).
take on **1.** receive; accept. *The college is taking on more staff* i.e. employing more staff. *I cannot take on this work. The bus took on more passengers.* **2.** play a game against. *He took me on at tennis.* **3.** change in appearance; assume. *His face took on an angry look.*
take out **1.** cause to accompany one to an entertainment etc at one's own expense. *He took us out to lunch.* **2.** get for oneself (usu. a document). *I must take out an insurance policy for my car.* **3.** make tired or weak. *The work has taken a lot out of him. Fever takes it out of you.*
take something over become responsible for; take control of. *He is taking over my job while I am on holiday. This large company has taken over many small ones.*
'takeover *nc*: *This company is planning another takeover.*
take to someone/something **1.** begin doing something. *They took to flight* i.e. they ran away. *He has taken to wearing bright ties. During the flood the people took to the hills* i.e. escaped by going to the hills. **2.** begin to like. *I took to him as soon as I saw him.*
take someone/something up **1.** lift; pick up. *We took up our luggage and followed him.* **2.** begin doing; become interested in: *take up gardening.* **3.** (with **with**) bring to the attention of. *He said he would take up my difficulties with the headmaster.* **4.** (with reference to time and space) use; fill. *The meeting took up the whole morning. The large desk takes up most of the office.* **5.** continue with. *As soon as he finished singing, the crowd took up the song.* **6.** question; argue with. *I took him up on his remarks about young people.*
take up with become friendly with.
be taken aback be surprised.
take into account remember while considering something. *When deciding what to do we must take into account all the difficulties.*
take the bull by the horns deal with a difficulty without fear or hesitation. (*informal*).
be taken by be attracted by; be pleased with. *We were greatly taken by the children's good behaviour.*
take it into one's head suddenly decide to do something; believe (usu. without reason). *He had taken it into his head to go away. She has taken it into her head that we hate her.* (*informal*).
be taken ill become ill.
be able to take it be able to endure or suffer something. (*informal*).
take one's mind off prevent someone from worrying about. *He took his mind off the problem by playing a game of tennis.*
take part in join in. *We all took part in the discussion.*
take place happen. *The concert takes place next Friday.*
take the place of occupy a place or position instead of. *He will take my place in the football team because I shall be absent.*
take as read accept or agree without further argument. *We shall take the rest of the proposals as read.*

talc [tælk] *nu* **1.** type of mineral that can be made into a fine powder. **2.** powder made from talc, used on the skin (usu. scented) (Also **talcum (powder)**).

tale [teil] *nc* story; account (often a false one).
'talebearer, 'taleteller *nc* person who makes a secret known or spreads bad reports.
talebearing, taletelling *nu*.
tell tales (often with reference to children) make known what should be kept secret; spread bad reports (about somebody). *She is always telling tales about her classmates.*
'telltale *adj* revealing; making something known. *There were telltale marks on the floor which showed that an intruder had been in the house.* Also *nc* person who tells tales.

talent ['tælnt] *nc* **1.** special ability; natural power. *You have a talent for making friends. He is a man with many talents.* **2.** (in ancient times) weight, unit of money.
talented *adj* having talent: *talented speaker.*

talisman ['tælizmən] *nc* something believed to have magical power; charm.

talk [tɔ:k] *vt/i* **1.** speak; discuss; converse; gossip. *He talks to everybody he meets. Today our teacher talked about Africa. Animals cannot talk.* **2.** speak about. *We talked football all evening.* Also **1.** *nc* speech; lecture; discussion. *Did you hear the president's talk last night? The two countries are having talks about trade.* **2.** *nu* rumour. *There is some talk of the president resigning* i.e. some people say he may resign.
talker *nc* person who talks. *He is a good/poor/slow/quick talker.*
talkative ['tɔ:kətiv] *adj* fond of talking.
talkatively *adv*. **talkativeness** *nu*.
'talking point something to be discussed or worthy of discussion.
'small talk talk about matters which are not important (e.g. the weather).
talk away go on talking.
talk back answer rudely; argue. *Don't talk back to your father like that!*
talk someone down **1.** silence someone by talking much louder and longer. **2.** give a pilot in a plane instructions as to how to land.
talk down to somebody talk to someone in a proud, superior manner.
talk someone into something persuade by talking.
talk round something discuss without deciding anything. *We talked round the problems of the school without agreeing on anything.*
talk someone round persuade someone who is unwilling.
talk to someone speak seriously to; complain. *I shall talk to your father about your behaviour.*
'talking-to *nc* scolding. *My father gave me a good talking-to.* (*informal*).
talk through one's hat talk nonsense. (*informal*).
talk shop talk about one's own business or interests. (*informal*).

tall [tɔ:l] *adj* **1.** (with reference to persons) high; of greater height than usual. *I am the* *tallest boy in the class. He is tall for his age. Note: tall* is also used with reference to things which are high but not wide and can thus be compared with persons (e.g. *tall pole; tall tree; tall building*). For this reason one cannot usually say: *tall hill; tall desks etc.* **2.** difficult; unreasonable. *This is a tall order* i.e. a job or request which is difficult to carry out. *He tells tall stories* i.e. stories which are difficult to believe. (*informal* in sense **2.**). **tallness** *nu.*

tallish *adj* rather tall.

'tallboy type of high, narrow piece of furniture with drawers.

tallow ['tælou] *nu* type of hard fat used for making candles.

tally ['tæli] *nc* **1.** stick used in the past on which marks were made to show how much was bought or sold (e.g. every time something was sold a mark might be made on the tally). **2.** any mark or label to show what something is. Also *vi* agree; be the same. *Your story does not tally with mine. The expenditure and the receipts should tally.*

'tally clerk clerk who keeps a record of a ship's cargo as it is loaded or unloaded.

talon ['tæln] *nc* long hooked claw of certain types of birds (e.g. the hawk).

tambourine [tæmbə'riːn] *nc* type of small, round drum, with pieces of metal at the sides, which is beaten with the hand and shaken.

tame [teim] *adj* **1.** (with reference to animals) accustomed to human beings; not wild or fierce. *He keeps a tame lion.* **2.** (with reference to persons/things) obedient; dull. *He is so tame that he agrees with everybody. I think cricket is a tame sport.* Also *vt* cause to be tame. **tamely** *adv.* **tameness** *nu.*

tameable ['teiməbl] *adj* able to be tamed. (*opp* **untameable**).

tamer *nc* (usu. with another word) person who tames: *liontamer.*

tamp [tæmp] *vt* push down; press in.

tamper ['tæmpə*] *vi* interfere; change; damage. *Somebody has tampered with the lock on the door. He was accused of tampering with the examination papers.*

tan [tæn] *nc/u* light brown colour. *She was wearing tan shoes and carrying a tan bag. The sun has given your skin a tan.* Also *adj.* Also *vt/i* **1.** make light brown in colour. *His face was tanned by the sun and wind.* **2.** make animal's skin into leather. **3.** (with reference to children) beat severely. (*informal* in sense **3.**). *past* **tanned.**

tanner *nc* **1.** person who tans animals' skins. **2.** formerly, British coin worth 6 old pence (2½ pence) (*informal* in sense **2.**).

tannery *nc* place where animals' skins are tanned.

tandem ['tændəm] *nc* type of bicycle with two seats, one behind the other, and two sets of pedals. Also *adv* on a tandem bicycle. *They travelled tandem.*

tang [tæŋ] *nc* strong, distinctive smell or taste: *tang of wood smoke; fruit with a pleasant tang.* **tangy** *adj.*

tangent ['tændʒənt] *nc* straight line which touches a curve at one point only.

fly/go off at a tangent change direction suddenly; begin doing or talking about something else suddenly. *We were discussing the latest news when he went off at a tangent about flowers.*

tangerine [tændʒə'riːn] *nc* type of small, slightly flat orange with loose skin.

tangible ['tændʒibl] *adj* able to be touched; real. *The plan has produced tangible results.* (*opp* **intangible**). **tangibly** *adv.* **tangibility** [tændʒi'biliti] *nu.*

tangle ['tæŋgl] *nc* **1.** (with reference to thread, string, hair) mixed-up and untidy mass. *Her hair was full of tangles. All the ropes were in a tangle.* **2.** confusion; disorder. *His affairs are in a tangle.* Also *vt/i* become, cause to become, confused or disordered. (*opp* **untangle**).

tango ['tæŋgou] *nc* type of dance. *pl* **tangos.**

tank [tæŋk] *nc* **1.** large container for liquid or gas: *water tank; petrol tank.* **2.** heavily armoured vehicle with a gun, used in war.

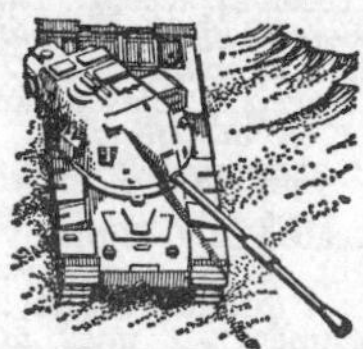

tank (*def* 2)

tanker *nc* **1.** ship with large tanks for carrying oil. **2.** heavy lorry with a large tank for carrying oil or other liquids.

tankard ['tæŋkəd] *nc* large drinking pot, often with a lid.

tanner ['tænə*] *nc* see **tan.**

tannin ['tænin] *nu* type of acid obtained from trees and used for making skins into leather, dyeing etc.

tantalize ['tæntəlaiz] *vt* cause to hope or wish for something that is not possible, or not easily obtained. *They tantalized the poor prisoner with promises of freedom.*

tantalizing *adj*: *tantalizing promises of freedom.* **tantalizingly** *adv.*

tantamount ['tæntəmaunt] *adj* (with **to**) equal in meaning to; the same as. *His silence was tantamount to saying he disagreed.*

tantrum ['tæntrəm] *nc* sudden fit of bad temper (usu. about something which is not important). *This child is always having tantrums. The old man went away in a tantrum.*

tap[1] [tæp] *nc* **1.** (*Brit*) device for allowing liquid or gas to come out of a pipe or container. *She turned on the tap and filled the pot with water.* (*US* **faucet**). **2.** plug put in a barrel. Also *vt* **1.** put a tap, make a cut, in something to take out the liquid inside. *He is tapping the barrel of beer. The workers tap the rubber trees every morning* i.e. make a cut in them to get the liquid rubber from them. **2.** obtain, take from somebody/something. *He tried to tap me for the latest news.* **3.** (of a telephone) fasten a wire secretly to it so that another person can listen to what is said. *Our telephone has been tapped. past* **tapped.**

'taproom bar of an inn or hotel. (rather *o.f.*).

tap[2] [tæp] *nc* **1.** light blow. *I felt a tap on my shoulder.* **2.** (in *pl*) (*US*) signal by bugle in the armed forces for lights to be put out. Also *vt* give a light blow to. *He tapped me on the shoulder. Somebody is tapping at/on the door. past* **tapped.**

'tap-dance *nc* type of dance in which the feet are tapped on the floor in time with the music. **tap-dancing** *nu.*

tape [teip] *nc* **1.** narrow piece of cloth or

other material for tying or fastening. **2.** narrow piece of cloth or other material with other uses. Also *vt* **1.** fasten with a tape. **2.** record on a magnetic tape. *He taped my speech on his tape recorder.*

'tape measure, 'measuring tape tape marked in feet and inches etc for measuring things.

'tape recorder *nc* apparatus which records sounds and music on a magnetized tape. **tape recording** *nc.*

'tapeworm type of worm found in the intestines of human beings and animals.

('finishing) tape type of tape stretched between two posts to show where a race finishes. (The winner of the race breaks it).

'insulating tape type of sticky tape used to wind round electrical wires to insulate them.

magnetic tape type of magnetized tape used on a tape recorder to record sounds and music.

red tape unnecessary rules made by an organization (e.g. by a government or a large company). *The plan to build a new school has been delayed by red tape.* (*informal*).

taper[1] ['teipə*] *vt/i* become, cause to become, thinner at one end. *The pencil tapers to a sharp point. He tapered the stick with a knife.* **tapering** *adj.*

taper[2] ['teipə*] *nc* type of thin candle.

tapestry ['tæpistri] *nc/u* **1.** woven hanging (usu. wool) with pictures or designs. **2.** fabric made by sewing pictures or designs in coloured wools or silks, used for hangings, chair coverings etc.

tapioca [tæpi'oukə] *nu* type of starchy food obtained from the cassava or manioc plant.

tapir ['teipə*] *nc* type of wild pig with a long moveable upper lip, found in the tropics.

tappet ['tæpit] *nc* type of rod or lever which moves the valve in a steam or petrol engine.

tar [tɑ:*] *nu* type of thick, black, sticky liquid obtained from coal or wood and used for making roads, preserving wood and as an antiseptic. Also *vt* cover with tar. *past* **tarred. tarry** *adj.*

'tarma'cadam, 'tarmac *nu* mixture of tar and small stones used to make the surface of a road, airport runway etc. Also *adj*: *We travelled all the way on a good tarmac road.*

tarantula [tə'ræntjulə] *nc* type of large, hairy, poisonous spider.

tardy ['tɑ:di] *adj* slow; taking a long time; late. **tardily** *adv.* **tardiness** *nu.*

tare [teə*] *nc* type of weed.

target ['tɑ:git] *nc* **1.** something aimed at (e.g. when practising or competing in shooting). *He hit the target with every shot he fired.* **2.** somebody/something attacked or criticized. *The minister is the target of many complaints.* **3.** aim or total which it is desired to reach. *The target of the new plan is primary education for all children.*

tariff ['tærif] *nc* **1.** tax charged on goods brought into a country; list of goods taxed in this way. *Will the USA lower/raise the tariff on foreign motorcars?* **2.** list of charges made (e.g. in a hotel or restaurant).

tarmac ['tɑ:mæk] *nu* see **tar.**

tarnish ['tɑ:niʃ] *vt/i* **1.** (usu. with reference to metal) become, cause to become, dull or less bright. *Brass tarnishes quickly in wet weather.* **2.** spoil. *His bad behaviour has tarnished the good name of the school.*

tarpaulin [tɑ:'pɔ:lin] *nc* canvas sheet made waterproof by being treated with tar.

tarry[1] ['tɑ:ri] *adj* see **tar.**

tarry[2] ['tæri] *vi* stay; delay (*o.f.*).

tart[1] [tɑ:t] *adj* **1.** having a sour taste. **2.** sharp; severe. *He gave a tart reply.* **tartly** *adv.* **tartness** *nu.*

tart[2] [tɑ:t] *nc* type of pie containing fruit or jam.

tart[3] [tɑ:t] immoral woman; prostitute. (*informal*).

tartan ['tɑ:tn] **1.** *nu* type of woollen cloth with a pattern of coloured squares. **2.** *nc* pattern of this kind belonging to a particular Scottish clan. Also *adj*: *tartan jacket.*

tartar[1] ['tɑ:tə*] *nu* **1.** hard deposit on the teeth. **2.** deposit found on the inside of wine barrels. **tartaric** [tɑ:'tærik] *adj.*

cream of tartar pure form of tartar used in baking and as a medicine.

tartaric acid type of acid found in many fruits (e.g. oranges).

tartar[2] ['tɑ:tə*] *nc* fierce, quick-tempered person. (*informal*).

task [tɑ:sk] *nc* piece of work which has to be done. *I was given the task of cleaning the room.*

'task force part of an army or navy sent to carry out a special operation; any group having similar special duties.

'taskmaster man, woman who gives somebody tasks to do and keeps him busy. *Our teacher is a hard taskmaster.*

take somebody to task scold; question closely. *My father took me to task about my dirty hands.*

tassel ['tæsl] *nc* number of threads fastened together at one end and used as an ornament. **tasselled** *adj.* (*US* **tasseled**).

tassel

taste[1] [teist] *vt/i* **1.** have a particular flavour in the mouth. *The tea tasted sweet. Some oranges taste bitter. This soup tastes too much of salt.* **2.** feel or try the flavour of something in the mouth. *Can you taste the sugar in your coffee? She tasted the pudding to see if it was sweet enough.* **3.** have experience of; meet. *They tasted defeat for the first time.*

taster *nc* person who is skilled in judging the quality of different types of tea, wine etc by tasting them.

taste[2] [teist] *nc/u* **1.** (*sing* with **a** or **the**) sense or feeling given by something in the mouth. *Children like the taste of sugar. Some oranges have a bitter taste. Food which is cooked too much has no taste.* **2.** (*sing* with **a**) small quantity for sample. *May I have a taste of your pudding?* i.e. to see what it is like. *He gave us a taste of his bad temper* i.e. enough to show us how bad-tempered he could be. **3.** liking for. *She has a taste for expensive hats. His tastes in music are not the same as mine.* **4.** choice; judgment; appreciation. *Their house is furnished in very good taste* i.e. the furniture is well-

chosen and suitable. *His reply to their question was in bad taste* i.e. was made with poor judgment and caused offence. *We all admire your taste in art* i.e. your good judgment and choice.
tasteful *adj* having, showing good taste. *The furniture in their house is very tasteful.* **tastefully** *adv.* **tastefulness** *nu.*
tasteless *adj* **1.** without taste in the mouth. *This food is tasteless.* **2.** having, showing bad taste. *A tasteless colour scheme.* **tastelessly** *adv.* **tastelessness** *nu.*
tasty *adj* **1.** having a pleasant taste in the mouth: *a tasty cake.* **2.** having or showing good taste (but use **tasteful** which is better). **tastily** *adv.*
to somebody's taste to somebody's liking; just as he wishes it to be.

tat [tæt] *vt/i* make tatting; put tatting on. see below. *past* **tatted.**
tatting *nu* type of loose sewing (usu. round the edges of a piece of cloth e.g. a handkerchief).

tatters ['tætəz] *npl* torn pieces of cloth, paper etc. *His coat was in tatters* i.e. badly torn.
tattered *adj*: *He was wearing a tattered coat.*

tattle ['tætl] *vi* talk a great deal about matters which are not important; gossip. Also *nu.* **tattler** *nc.* (all *informal*).

tattoo[1] [tə'tuː] *nc* coloured design or picture put on the skin by making holes in it with a needle and rubbing in the colours. *pl* **tattoos.** Also *vt* mark the skin in this way.

tattoo[2] [tə'tuː] *nc* **1.** signal made by beating drums to call soldiers back to their barracks. **2.** public show (usu. given at night) by a large number of soldiers. **3.** quick beating or tapping. *His fingers beat a tattoo on the desk as he listened.*

tatty ['tæti] *adj* shabby; untidy. (*informal*).

taught [tɔːt] past of **teach.**

taunt [tɔːnt] *vt* say cruel or insulting words to somebody. *He taunted me for/with being weak. He taunted me with weakness.* Also *nc*: *his taunts about my weakness.*

taut [tɔːt] *adj* tight; fully stretched. *The skin of the drum is taut.* **tautly** *adv.* **tautness** *nu.*

tautology [tɔː'tɔlədʒi] *nc/u* unnecessary repeating of the same thing in different words. **tautological** [tɔːtə'lɔdʒikl] *adj.* **tautologically** *adv.* **tautologous** [tɔː'tɔləgəs] *adj.*

tavern ['tævən] *nc* inn; place where beer, liquor etc are sold and drunk (*o.f.*).

tawdry ['tɔːdri] *adj* bright and showy but of poor quality. *She was wearing a tawdry hat.* **tawdrily** *adv.* **tawdriness** *nu.*

tawny ['tɔːni] *adj* yellow-brown in colour.

tax [tæks] **1.** *nc/u* money which has to be paid to the government of a country by those who live in it. *The government has increased the tax on motorcars. People who refuse to pay tax can be put in prison.* **2.** *nu* severe test; burden. *The hard work was a tax on those who were ill.* Also *vt* **1.** put a tax on; make somebody pay a tax. *He wants all liquor to be heavily taxed. Governments do not usually tax children.* **2.** test severely. *The war taxed the soldiers' courage.* **3.** (with **with**) accuse. *He taxed them with laziness/with being lazy.*
taxation [tæk'seiʃən] *nu* money taken by taxes; act of taxing. *The new government has increased taxation.*
taxable *adj* able to be taxed.
'tax collector person who collects tax.
'tax-'free *adj* not taxed.
'taxpayer person who pays tax.

taxi ['tæksi] *nc* motorcar for hire (usu. fitted with a device which measures the distance travelled and shows the cost of the journey). *pl* **taxis.**
Note: the full title is *taxicab*; short forms are (*Brit*) *taxi* and (*US*) *cab.*
Also *vi* (with reference to aircraft) move along the ground.
'taxi driver person who drives a taxi.
'taximeter instrument fitted to a taxi to measure the distance travelled and show the cost.
'taxi rank place where taxis wait to be hired.

taxidermy ['tæksidəːmi] *nu* art of preparing and filling the skins of dead animals so that they look alive.
taxidermist *nc* person skilled in taxidermy.

tea [tiː] **1.** *nu* type of plant, the dried leaves of which are used to make a drink by pouring boiling water over them. **2.** *nu* drink made in this way. *He is having a cup of tea. Mother is making (the) tea* i.e. making the drink by pouring boiling water over the dried leaves. **3.** *nu* time when tea is drunk (usu. about 4 p.m.). *I won't be home until after tea.* **4.** *nc/u* light meal taken with tea. *This hotel serves teas.*
'tea bag small bag containing tea used for making tea. (It is placed in a cup or pot and hot water is added).
'tea caddy small box or tin in which tea is kept ready for use.
'teacake type of flat cake (usu. served hot with butter).
'tea chest large wooden box in which tea is put for export.
'teacloth **1.** small cloth used to cover a table or tray for tea. **2.** small cloth for drying cups, saucers etc after they have been washed.
'tea cosy thick cover put over a teapot to keep it hot.
'teacup cup used for drinking tea.
'tea garden **1.** plantation where tea is grown. **2.** garden where teas are served.
'tea leaf *nc* (usu. *pl*) leaf left in a teapot or cup after tea has been made and drunk.
'teapot pot in which tea is made.

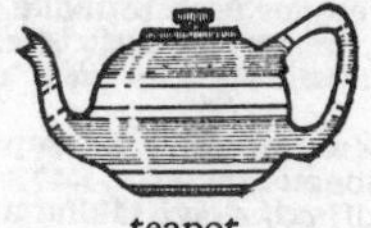

teapot

'tearoom restaurant which provides light meals and tea.
'tea service, 'tea set cups, saucers, plates, teapot etc used at tea.
'teaspoon small spoon used for stirring tea.
'teaspoonful amount that can be contained in a teaspoon.
'tea strainer small metal container with holes in, which keeps back the tea leaves when tea is poured through it.
'high 'tea large cooked meal with tea, taken in the evening (usu. by those who do not have dinner later).
storm in a teacup argument or quarrel about something of no importance. (*informal*).

teach [tiːtʃ] *vt/i* instruct; give lessons; educate. *My sister teaches* i.e. her work is teaching. *She likes teaching children. He is* *teaching me (how) to ride a bicycle. I taught English to all my friends. I taught all my friends English. past* **taught** [tɔ:t]. **teacher** *nc*.

teachable *adj* able to be taught. (*opp* **unteachable**).

teaching 1. *nu* work of a teacher. 2. *nc* (in *pl*) what is taught. *You should study the teachings of famous men.*

teak [ti:k] 1. *nc* type of tall tree with hard wood. 2. *nu* the wood of this tree used in shipbuilding etc.

teal [ti:l] *nc* type of small duck. *pl* **teal.**

team [ti:m] *nc* 1. group of persons working or playing together. *The discovery was made by a team of scientists. He plays for the school football team.* 2. two or more dogs, horses, oxen etc which pull a sledge, cart etc together.

teamster ['ti:mstə*] *nc* 1. person in charge of a team of horses, oxen etc. 2. (*US*) driver of a lorry or truck.

'team 'spirit feeling of cooperation among those in a team.

'teamwork work done by a team; cooperation.

team up with someone begin to work together or cooperate with someone. (*informal*).

tear[1] [tiə*] *nc* drop of water from the eye. *The tears ran down her cheeks as she cried. The little boy burst into tears* i.e. tears came from his eyes.

tearful *adj* having tears; crying. **tearfully** *adv*. **tearfulness** *nu*.

'teardrop one tear.

'teargas type of gas which causes tears (used by the police to control angry crowds).

tear[2] [tɛə*] *vt/i* 1. break or damage by pulling apart. *She tore her stockings while putting them on. I tore the newspaper in half/to bits/to pieces.* 2. become broken or damaged. *Paper tears easily. This type of cloth does not tear.* 3. remove suddenly or violently. *He tore down the notices on the wall. I tore off the paper on the parcel. You should not tear pages out of your book.* 4. (in *passive*) be disturbed or upset. *The whole family was torn by quarrels. He is torn by/with jealousy.* 5. move quickly. *He tore through the town in his car. Because he was late he tore out of the house. past tense* **tore** [tɔ:*]. *past part* **torn** [tɔ:n]. Also *nc* place which has been torn. *There is a tear in your jacket.*

tear oneself away go away unwillingly or with difficulty. *I like your party but now I have to tear myself away.* (*informal*).

tear something up tear to pieces.

be torn between be unable to decide which of two things to do. *He was torn between staying at home and going abroad.*

tease [ti:z] *vt* 1. laugh at or make fun of someone to annoy him or for amusement. *The other boys tease him because he is fat. We teased her about her new hat.* 2. pull threads apart; comb the surface of rough cloth. Also *nc* person who likes teasing others. **teasing** *nu*.

teaser *nc* 1. person who likes teasing others. 2. difficult problem.

teasingly *adv* in a teasing manner.

teat [ti:t] *nc* 1. point of the breast through which milk comes; nipple. 2. rubber mouthpiece of child's feeding bottle.

technical ['teknikl] *adj* of some special type or art or skill. *Engineers must have great technical knowledge; technical education* i.e. education in practical skills and in the uses of modern machinery etc. **technically** *adv*.

technicality [tekni'kæliti] *nc* 1. word which is special to a particular art or skill; special way of dealing with something. *I do not understand the technicalities of space travel.* 2. unimportant point of law. *He was not allowed to buy the land on a/because of a technicality.*

technician [tek'niʃən] *nc* person who is trained in a particular art or skill (esp. a practical one connected with machines etc); skilled workman.

technique [tek'ni:k] *nc/u* skilled way of doing something. *He is learning the technique of painting. Writing poetry requires great technique.*

technocracy [tek'nɔkrəsi] 1. *nu* system of government by technical experts. 2. *nc* country with such a government. **technocrat** ['teknəkræt] *nc*. **technocratic** [teknə'krætik] *adj*.

technology [tek'nɔlədʒi] *nu* science or study of the practical uses of scientific discoveries (e.g. in industry and in making machines etc). *Modern civilization depends greatly on technology.* **technological** [teknə'lɔdʒikl] *adj*. **technologically** *adv*.

technologist *nc* person who is skilled in technology.

Note: a *technologist* is more highly qualified than a *technician* (e.g. the person who designs a new type of engine is a *technologist*; the person who helps to make, maintain or repair it is a *technician*).

tedious ['ti:diəs] *adj* long and uninteresting; dull and wearying. *Travelling by a slow train is very tedious.* **tediously** *adv*. **tediousness, tedium** ['ti:diəm] *nu*.

tee [ti:] *nc* 1. small heap of sand or peg on which a golfball is placed so that the player can hit it better with a golf club; place where a golfball is put in this way i.e. only at the beginning of each hole of a golf course. 2. mark aimed at in some games (e.g. bowls). Also *vt* (often with **up**) put a golfball on a tee.

tee off drive a golfball from a tee; begin a game of golf.

teem [ti:m] *vi* (with **with**) have in great numbers. *The forest teemed with wild animals. His mind is teeming with ideas.*

teens [ti:nz] *npl* numbers ending with **teen** i.e. 13–19. *His son is in his teens* i.e. is in age over 12 and under 20.

teenage ['ti:neidʒ] *adj* of young persons over 12 and under 20 years of age. *He is too old now for teenage parties.*

teenager *nc* young person in his or her teens.

tee shirt ['ti:ʃə:t] *nc* type of light shirt with short sleeves.

teeter ['ti:tə*] *vt/i* move from side to side; be uncertain. *He teetered on the edge of the cliff.*

teeth [ti:θ] pl of **tooth.**

teethe [ti:ð] *vi* (with reference to a baby) begin to have teeth. *Our baby is teething.*

'teething troubles 1. pain or discomfort felt by a baby when it begins to have teeth. 2. troubles which often come at the beginning of something but soon disappear. *The new plan is having its teething troubles.* (*informal* in sense 2.).

teetotal ['ti:'toutl] *adj* refusing to drink, not allowing, alcoholic liquor. *His father is teetotal. It will be a teetotal party.*

teetotaller (*US* **teetotaler**) *nc* person who refuses to drink alcoholic liquor.

tele- ['teli] *prefix* far; over a distance (e.g. **telephone; telescope**).

telecommunications ['telikəmju:ni'keiʃənz] *npl* communications over a distance by using electricity (e.g. by radio, telephone etc).

telegram ['teligræm] *nc/u* message sent by telegraph.

telegraph ['teligrɑ:f] *nc/u* instrument for sending messages (called **telegrams**) by electricity along a wire or by radio. Also *vt/i* send a message in this way (but **send a telegram** is more usual). **telegraphic** [teli'græfik] *adj.* **telegraphically** *adv.*
telegraphy [tə'legrəfi] *nu* science or practice of sending and receiving messages by telegraph.
telegraphist [tə'legrəfist] *nc* person who sends and receives messages by telegraph.
'**telegraph pole,** '**telegraph post** long pole which carries telegraph wires high above the ground.
'**telegraph wire** wire along which messages are sent by telegraph.
telegraphic address address put in a very short form so that it can be more easily and cheaply sent by telegraph.

teleology [teli'ɔlədʒi] *nu* belief or theory that the universe and everything in it have been made to fit a particular design or purpose (e.g. God's). **teleological** [teliə'lɔdʒikl] *adj.* **teleologically** *adv.* **teleologist** *nc.*

telepathy [tə'lepəθi] *nu* passing of thoughts and feelings from one person to another without using the normal senses of sight, sound, touch or smell. **telepathic** [teli'pæθik] *adj.* **telepathically** *adv.*
telepathist *nc* person who believes in, or experiences, telepathy.

telephone ['telifoun] *nc* instrument for sending and receiving the sound of the voice by electricity along a wire or on radio. *He has three telephones on his desk. I told him the news by telephone.* Also *vt/i* send a message by telephone; speak to somebody by telephone. *She has telephoned for the doctor* i.e. asked by telephone for him to come. *Don't telephone me when I am busy. Note:* often *phone* for noun and verb.
telephonic [teli'fɔnik] *adj.*
telephony [tə'lefəni] *nu* science or practice of sending and receiving the sound of the voice by telephone.
telephonist [tə'lefənist] *nc* person who sends and receives messages by telephone (esp. one in charge of a telephone exchange or telephone switchboard).
'**telephone box** box in which a person can stand to make a telephone call.
'**telephone exchange** place where telephone connections are made.
be on the telephone 1. have a telephone. 2. be speaking to someone by telephone.

telephoto ['teli'foutou] *adj* short form of **telephotographic.**

telephotography ['telifə'tɔgrəfi] *nu* photography of distant objects etc by using a special lens.
telephotographic ['telifoutə'græfik] *adj.* (Usu. **telephoto** e.g. *a telephoto lens*).

teleprinter ['teliprintə*] *nc* electrical machine which automatically sends and receives typed messages by telegraph.

telerecording [teliri'kɔ:diŋ] *nc* programme recorded for television (e.g. in video tape).

telescope ['teliskoup] *nc* instrument through which distant objects appear larger and nearer. Also *vt/i* push one part inside the other (as is done when closing a telescope). *When the car hit the wall, the front was telescoped.*

telescope

telescopic [teli'skɔpik] *adj* 1. of or having a telescope. 2. made like a telescope and so able to be made shorter or longer in the same way: *telescopic umbrella.*

television ['telivizən] *nu* sending and receiving of pictures by radio. (Often informally **TV** or **telly**). *We watched the game on television/TV/telly.*
televise ['teləvaiz] *vt* send by television. *Important football games are televised.*

telex ['teleks] *nc/u* method of sending messages by telegraph. Also *vt/i.*

tell [tel] *vt/i* 1. inform; explain; speak. *Please tell us who you are. They told me (that) they were tired. The teacher told his pupils how to do it. I told him all about it. He is telling the truth.* 2. (usu. with **can** or **be able**) know; judge; recognize. *The little boy can't tell the time yet* i.e. read the time on a clock or watch. *They were able to tell the difference between the two books. I couldn't tell him from his brother* i.e. the difference between him and his brother. *It is difficult to tell his weight just by looking at him.* 3. order; instruct. *He told me to come. You must do as you are told.* 4. make known a secret. *I'll show you where it is, if you promise not to tell.* 5. have an effect. *When you are old, every year tells. past* **told** [tould].
teller *nc* 1. person who tells a story, makes a report etc. *Who is the teller of this strange story?* 2. person who counts (usu. votes). 3. person who counts money in a bank as he receives it or pays it out.
telling *adj* having great effect. *He made a very telling speech about their mistakes.*
tellingly *adv.*
'**telltale** see **tale.**
tell someone off 1. order a particular number of persons to do something. 2. rebuke; scold. *We were told off for being late.* (*informal* in sense 2.).
tell on someone 1. make known a secret about somebody. *He told on his friends.* (*informal*). 2. have an effect on. *His age is beginning to tell on him.*
all told including all; altogether. *Fifty people came all told.*
there is no telling it is impossible to predict, say. *There is no telling what he may do.*

telly ['teli] *nc/u* short informal form of **television.**

temerity [tə'meriti] *nu* boldness; impudence. *He had the temerity to argue with the manager.*

temper ['tempə*] 1. *nu* (esp. with reference to metal) hardness combined with strength. 2. *nc/u* state of the mind or feelings. *He was in a good temper* i.e. happy and pleasant. *He was in a (bad) temper* i.e. angry and

unpleasant. Also *vt/i* **1.** make a metal hard and strong by heating and cooling it; make clay soft and ready for use. **2.** soften; make more pleasant. *He tempered his refusal with a smile.*
-tempered *adj* having a temper of a particular kind. *He is a good-/bad-/hot-/short-tempered man.*
fly into a temper see **fly**[2].
keep one's temper not become angry.
lose one's temper become angry (often suddenly and against one's will).

tempera ['tempərə] *nu* type of paint used on walls; distemper.

temperament ['temprəmənt] *nc/u* somebody's character as shown by his behaviour and feelings. *He has a happy temperament. James hasn't the temperament for work in an office. She and I have similar temperaments.*
temperamental [temprə'mentl] *adj* **1.** caused by temperament. *There are temperamental difficulties between him and his wife.* **2.** easily excited; moody. *Many great artists are temperamental.* **temperamentally** *adv.*

temperance ['tempərns] *nu* control over oneself in behaving, eating etc (and esp. in drinking): *temperance society* i.e. one which is opposed to alcoholic drinks; *temperance hotel* i.e. one where no alcoholic drinks are allowed.

temperate ['tempərət] *adj* **1.** not eating or drinking too much; controlling one's behaviour. *He is temperate in his habits.* (*opp* **intemperate**). **2.** (with reference to parts of the world) not too hot and not too cold. *Great Britain has a temperate climate.* **temperately** *adv.* **temperateness** *nu.*

temperature ['temprətʃə*] *nc/u* **1.** amount of heat or cold. *In summer the temperature is high and in winter it is low.* **2.** too much heat in the body. *When he was ill, he had/ran a temperature* i.e. the temperature of his body was higher than usual.
take somebody's temperature measure the temperature of somebody's body (with a thermometer).

tempest ['tempist] *nc* **1.** violent wind. **2.** violent disturbance: *tempest of anger.*
tempestuous [tem'pestjuəs] *adj* stormy; violent: *tempestuous sea; tempestuous argument.* **tempestuously** *adv.* **tempestuousness** *nu.*

template, templet ['templit] *nc* thin, flat piece of wood or metal etc of a particular shape or pattern, used when cutting out or checking other shapes and patterns.

temple[1] ['templ] *nc* building where a god is worshipped.
Note: the building for Christian worship is usu. called a *church* or *chapel.*

temple[2] ['templ] *nc* part of the head between the eye and the ear.

templet ['templit] *nc* see **template.**

tempo ['tempou] *nc/u* **1.** speed at which music is played. *The tune has a fast/slow tempo.* **2.** speed or progress in doing something; speed of an activity. *The tempo of life in a village is different from that in a city. pl* **tempos.**

temporal ['tempərl] *adj* **1.** of time. **2.** of this world; not spiritual. *A king has temporal powers, a bishop spiritual ones.*

temporary ['tempərəri] *adj* lasting or intended to be used for a short time: *temporary absence; temporary buildings.* (*opp* **permanent**). **temporarily** *adv.* **temporariness** *nu.*

temporize ['tempəraiz] *vi* gain time by delaying in doing something.

tempt [tempt] *vt* **1.** make, try to make, somebody do something he should not do. *His friend tempted him to steal/into stealing the money.* **2.** cause to want or wish for. *Can I tempt you to (have) another cup of tea?*
tempter *nc.*
temptation [temp'teiʃən] *nc/u*: *There are many temptations to steal in a large shop. I resisted the temptation to tell him.*
tempting *adj* attractive. **temptingly** *adv.*
temptress ['temptris] *nc* woman who tempts.

ten [ten] see appendix.

tenable ['tenəbl] *adj* **1.** able to be held or occupied. *The position as chairman is tenable for three years.* **2.** able to be defended or justified. *Do you think his argument is tenable?* (*opp* **untenable**).

tenacious [tə'neiʃəs] *adj* holding firmly; giving nothing away; strong: *tenacious defence against the enemy; a tenacious memory* i.e. one which does not forget much.
tenaciously *adv.* **tenaciousness, tenacity** [tə'næsiti] *nu.*

tenant ['tenənt] *nc* person who pays the owner for the use of a house, room or land. Also *vt* (in *passive*) occupy as a tenant. *This house is tenanted by two families.*
tenancy *nu* occupation as a tenant.
tenantry *nu* tenants on one piece of land or an estate.

tench [tentʃ] *nc* type of freshwater fish. *pl* **tench.**

tend[1] [tend] *vi* be inclined to; be likely to. *He tends to speak too quickly.*
tendency *nc*: *He has a tendency to speak too quickly. All children have a tendency towards illness.*

tend[2] [tend] *vt* look after; attend to. *A good farmer tends his land.* (rather *o.f.*).

tendentious [ten'denʃəs] *adj* (with reference to speeches and writing) arguing from one particular point of view only; biased.
tendentiously *adv.* **tendentiousness** *nu.*

tender[1] ['tendə*] *adj* **1.** easily damaged or hurt. *He joined the army at the tender age of 15.* **2.** kind; loving. *She has a tender heart. He gave her a tender look.* **3.** (with reference to meat) soft; easily cut and eaten. **4.** painful when touched. **tenderly** *adv.* **tenderness** *nu.*
'tenderfoot *nc* **1.** person who is new to a place and not yet accustomed to its hardships. **2.** Boy Scout who has not passed his third test. *pl* **tenderfoots.**
'tender-'hearted *adj* kind; sympathetic; full of pity. **tender-heartedly** *adv.*
'tenderloin part of a loin of beef.
tender subject subject which should be discussed or treated carefully because it may cause offence or trouble. *Freedom is a tender subject in countries which are not democracies.*

tender[2] ['tendə*] *vt/i* **1.** offer; give to be accepted. *The manager tendered his resignation to the committee.* **2.** offer to do something for a particular price. *Several firms have tendered for building the new school.* Also *nc* **1.** offer of this kind. *We have received tenders from several firms. The work was put out to tender* i.e. tenders for doing the work were asked for. **2.** railway truck.
legal tender form of money or currency which the law states must be accepted in payment. *In Britain, Bank of England pound notes are legal tender.*

tendon ['tendn] *nc* strong substance like string which joins a muscle to a bone.
tendril ['tendril] *nc* thin part of a climbing plant which helps the plant to grow by fixing itself to a tree, stick, wall etc.
tenement ['tenəmənt] *nc* large building divided into separate flats which are rented (often such a building in a poor part of a city).
tenet ['tenət] *nc* (often *pl*) belief; principle.
tennis ['tenis] *nu* game played by two or four players in which a ball is hit backwards and forwards across a low net.
Note: the full name is *lawn tennis*, although it can be played on hard surfaces as well as on grass.
tenon ['tenən] *nc* end of a piece of wood, cut to fit into a hole cut in another piece of wood (called a **mortise**) in order to join the two together.
tenor[1] ['tenə*] **1.** *nu* highest male adult voice (in the usual range). **2.** *nc* person who sings with this kind of voice. Also *adj*: *tenor voice; tenor saxophone.*
tenor[2] ['tenə*] *n sing* (with **the**) general meaning, direction or course. *The tenor of his speech was that war would come. Nothing spoils the quiet tenor of our life here.*
tense[1] [tens] *nc* form of the verb which shows time: *present/past/future tense.*
tense[2] [tens] *adj* showing strain. *They had tense faces as they waited for the news. There was a tense silence in the room.* Also *vt/i* become or make tense. *They tensed themselves as the enemy came nearer.* **tensely** *adv.* **tenseness, tensity** *nu.*
tensile ['tensail] *adj* able to be stretched or strained: *the tensile strength of copper wire* i.e. the amount of strain it can take before breaking.
tension 1. *nu* state of being stretched tightly. *The tension was so great that the wire broke.* **2.** *nc* nervous strain; excitement. *We do not like the tensions of life in a big city.* **3.** *nu* voltage in electricity: *high-/low-tension wires* i.e. wires carrying a strong/weak electrical current.
tent [tent] *nc* shelter made of strong cloth (usu. spread over poles and held in position by ropes and pegs).
tentacle ['tentəkl] *nc* long, boneless limb which grows from the head of certain sea animals, used for feeling and holding things, and moving.
tentative ['tentətiv] *adj* made or done to find out what may happen; experimental; not yet decided. *I can only give a tentative opinion.* **tentatively** *adv.*
tenterhooks ['tentəhuks] *npl* only in **be on tenterhooks** i.e. be in a state of great anxiety.
keep someone on tenterhooks keep someone in a state of anxiety.
tenuous ['tenjuəs] *adj* very thin and fine. **tenuity** [te'njuiti] *nu.*
tenure ['tenjuə*] *nc/u* length of time, or condition under which, a job is held or land is occupied etc. *Tenure of the position of professor is for ten years.*
tepee ['ti:pi:] *nc* tent of the North American Indians.
tepid ['tepid] *adj* **1.** slightly warm: *tepid water.* **2.** half-hearted: *a tepid welcome.* **tepidly** *adv.* **tepidness, tepidity** [te'piditi] *nu.*
tercentenary [tə:sen'ti:nəri] *nc* 300th year after an event; 300th anniversary. Also *adj*: *tercentenary celebrations.*
term [tə:m] *nc* **1.** definite period of time. *He was made secretary for a term of two years.* **2.** part of the year at school, college or university. *Our school has two terms a year instead of three. I did not like my first term at university.* **3.** word or phrase with a definite or special meaning. *The term 'death duty' means the tax paid on the property of a person when he dies.* **4.** (in *pl*) conditions; agreement. *The terms of service in the company are good* i.e. the conditions of employment. *They have come to terms* i.e. they have reached an agreement. **5.** (in *pl*) relations. *He is on friendly terms with everybody.* **6.** (in *pl*) (with **in**) way of expressing something. *He spoke about your work in high terms* i.e. he praised it. *They blamed him in very violent terms.* **7.** (mathematics) part of a compound quantity joined by the mark + or −. *a + b − c has three terms.* Also *vt* call; name. *This tool is termed a chisel.*
termagant ['tə:məgənt] *nc* violent, noisy woman.
terminal ['tə:minl] *nc* **1.** place where a railway line, bus route etc ends (**terminus** is more often used for railways and buses); place in town where an airline deals with its passengers on their way to or from an airport. **2.** piece of metal which connects the ends of an electrical circuit. *The terminals of his car battery are dirty.* Also *adj* coming at the end; final; approaching death: *He has a terminal disease. He is a terminal patient.*
terminate ['tə:mineit] *vt/i* come, bring to an end; finish. *The conference terminated yesterday. Most plural nouns terminate in 's'. The letter 's' terminates most plural nouns.* **termination** [tə:mi'neiʃən] **1.** *nu* act of coming or bringing to an end. **2.** *nc* letter or syllable at the end of a word.
terminology [tə:mi'nɔlədʒi] *nc/u* words with a special or definite meaning (e.g. those used in a particular branch of knowledge): *engineering/linguistic/medical terminology.* **terminological** [tə:minə'lɔdʒikl] *adj.*
terminus ['tə:minəs] *nc* place where a journey by air, bus or railway etc ends; station at the end of a railway line. *pl* **terminuses** or **termini** ['tə:mini:].
termite ['tə:mait] *nc* type of insect, found especially in the tropics, which builds hills and destroys wood.
tern [tə:n] *nc* type of small sea bird with long wings and a forked tail.
terrace ['terəs] *nc* **1.** level piece of ground on a slope or cut from a slope. *The people here grow rice on terraces. They were walking on the terrace behind the house* i.e. the raised level ground just outside the back of the house. **2.** row of houses joined together. Also *vt* make terraces on. *They have terraced the hill to stop the soil being washed away.* **terraced** *adj*: *a terraced hill; terraced houses* i.e. houses joined together in a row.
terracotta ['terə'kɔtə] *nu* type of brownish-red pottery. Also *adj*: *terracotta bowl.*
terra firma ['terə'fə:mə] *nu* solid land (as opposed to the sea).
terrain [te'rein] *nu* area of land (esp. with reference to its use in war). *Before the battle the general studied the terrain.*
terrapin ['terəpin] *nc* type of water tortoise.
terrestrial [te'restriəl] *adj* **1.** of, living on, dry land. **2.** of, living in, this world. *Man is a terrestrial creature.* (*opp* **celestial**).

terrible ['teribl] *adj* **1.** very bad; very annoying. *She wears terrible clothes. They made a terrible noise.* **2.** causing fear; dreadful. *He spoke in a terrible voice.*

terribly *adv* **1.** *He has been terribly ill.* **2.** very. *They are terribly kind.* (*informal*).

terrier ['teriə*] *nc* type of small dog originally used for hunting badgers, foxes etc.

terrify ['terifai] *vt* frighten greatly; fill with fear.

terrific [tə'rifik] *adj* **1.** very frightening. **2.** very great; excellent. *He ate a terrific breakfast.* (*informal* in sense **2.**).

terrifically *adv* very. *I am terrifically pleased.* (*informal*).

territory ['teritəri] *nc/u* **1.** area of land under one government (esp. a foreign government). *The mainland part of Tanzania was once called Tanganyika Territory.* **2.** any area of land. *We are now in the territory of the tiger* i.e. where tigers are found. *On our last journey we travelled over a lot of territory.* **territorial** [teri'tɔːriəl] *adj.*

terror ['terə*] **1.** *nu* great fear. *They screamed with terror. She ran away in terror.* **2.** *nc* somebody/something which causes great fear; great fear of somebody/something in particular. *We met the terrors of the war together. I have a terror of snakes.* **3.** *nc* very annoying child. (*informal* in sense **3.**).

terrorism *nu* policy of getting what one wants in politics by using murder etc.

terrorist *nc* person who uses terror in this way.

terrorize *vt* fill with terror; rule by using terror.

'terror-struck, 'terror-stricken *adj* filled with terror.

in terror of one's life in great fear of losing one's life.

terse [təːs] *adj* (with reference to speaking and writing) short; in a few words. **tersely** *adv.* **terseness** *nu.*

tertian ['təːʃən] *adj* (with reference to fever) occurring every other day.

tertiary ['təːʃəri] *adj* third in order of importance.

tesselated ['tesileitid] *adj* made of small, flat stones fitted closely together in a design: *tesselated pavement.*

test [test] *nc* act or means of measuring or finding out about something; examination: *intelligence test* i.e. one to measure intelligence; *blood test* i.e. one to find out what is in a person's blood; *driving test* i.e. one to find out if a person can drive. Also *vt* give a test to; examine. *He is testing the brakes of his car. I tested my tea for sugar* i.e. to find out if there was sugar in it. *The long journey tested their patience* i.e. strained it.

'test ban agreement between countries not to test nuclear weapons.

'test case legal case which may help to settle other cases on the same point of law.

'test match one of a number of important matches in cricket etc (usu. between the teams of two countries).

'test pilot pilot who flies new aircraft to test them.

'test tube glass tube closed at one end in which liquids are tested.

testament ['testəmənt] *nc* **1.** (esp. with reference to somebody's wishes about what should happen to his property after his death) written statement. (Often in **last will and testament**). **2.** (**Testament**) one of the two main parts of the Bible: *Old/New Testament.* **testamentary** [testə'mentəri] *adj.*

testicle ['testikl] *nc* one of the two sex glands of a male.

testify ['testifai] *vt/i* give evidence; state solemnly. *He testified in court that he was abroad at the time of the crime. I can testify to his honesty* i.e. that he is honest. *He will not testify against his own brother.*

testimonial [testi'mouniəl] *nc* **1.** written statement about somebody's character and abilities. *When I left school, the headmaster gave me a good testimonial.* **2.** written statement together with a gift presented to somebody by a group of persons (e.g. when he retires).

testimony ['testiməni] *nc/u* solemn statement; evidence.

testy ['testi] *adj* quick-tempered; impatient. **testily** *adv.* **testiness** *nu.*

tetanus ['tetənəs] *nu* type of dangerous disease which makes the muscles stiff and painful (esp. those round the mouth) (Also **lockjaw**).

tête-à-tête ['teitɑː'teit] *nc* private conversation between two people.

tetchy ['tetʃi] *adj* irritable; bad-tempered. **tetchily** *adv.* **tetchiness** *nu.*

tether ['teðə*] *vt* tie an animal with a rope or chain so that it cannot run away. *He tethered the horse to a post.* Also *nc* rope or chain used in this way.

at the end of one's tether see **end.**

tetra- ['tetrə] *prefix* four (e.g. **tetragon** i.e. figure with four sides).

tetrameter [te'træmitə*] *nc* line of poetry having four stresses.

text [tekst] **1.** *nc* original words of an author or speaker as distinct from reports about them or summaries. **2.** *nu* main part of a book as distinct from diagrams, notes, index etc. **3.** *nc* sentence or verse which is chosen (esp. from the Bible) as the subject of a talk or discussion.

textual ['tekstjuəl] *adj* of, about a text. **textually** *adv.*

'textbook book which gives information; book which is studied in a school etc.

textile ['tekstail] *adj* concerned with making cloth: *textile mill; textile industry.* Also *nc* cloth; fabric.

texture ['tekstʃə*] *nc/u* way in which cloth is woven or something is formed; surface of something: *coat with a rough texture. The weather spoilt the fine texture of her skin.*

than [ðæn, ðən] *conj* used after the *comparative* of an *adj* or *adv. He is quicker than you. He runs more quickly than you* (*do*). *Note:* although *He is stronger than I* (*am*) was once thought more correct, *He is stronger than me* is now much more usual and just as correct. But there can be a difference in meaning after a *vt* (e.g. *He teaches them better than I* i.e. better than I teach them, and *He teaches them better than me* i.e. better than he teaches me). With *all* only one form is correct (e.g. *He is stronger than them all*).

other than besides. *Have you any books other than these?*

thank [θæŋk] *vt* **1.** say that one is grateful. *He thanked us for our help. He thanked us for helping* (*him*). *'Can I help?' 'Thank you'* i.e. Yes, you can. *'Can I help?' 'No, thank you'* i.e. No, you can't. *Thank God you arrived in time* i.e. I thank God that you did. **2.** used with future tense as a polite imperative. *I'll thank you to leave me alone*

i.e. please leave me alone.
thanks *npl*: *He wrote to express his thanks for our help. 'Can I help?' 'No thanks'* i.e. No, you can't. *Thanks to the doctor I am well again* i.e. because of him, owing to his help.
thankful *adj* grateful. *You should be thankful to be alive/that you are alive.* **thankfully** *adv.* **thankfulness** *nu.*
thankless *adj* ungrateful; bringing no thanks. *Teaching is often a thankless job.* **thanklessly** *adv.* **thanklessness** *nu.*
'**thanks offering** gift expressing thanks (*o.f.*).
'**thanksgiving** act of expressing thanks (usu. to God in worship or prayer).
'**Thanksgiving (Day)** day of thanksgiving to God in the USA.
thankful for small mercies grateful for whatever good fortune one has.

that[1] [ðæt] *adj/adv/pron/determiner* **1.** *Who is that man? I want that book, not this one.* **2.** *Who is that? I want that, not this. Don't drink that. pl* **those** [ðouz]: *Who are those men? I want those, not these.* **3.** so; very. *I can't eat that much. He is not that fat.* (*informal* in sense **3.**).
Note: that or *those* cannot be used with *my, your, his etc.* Instead one must use *of mine, of yours, of his etc* (e.g. *I have lost that book of mine. Where are those friends of theirs?*).

that[2] [ðət] *relative pron* often used instead of *who, whom, which, when. Where is the boy that did it? I have lost the book that was here. I stay at home on the days that I am not busy.*
Note: 1. when the word before *that* is not the subject of the following clause (as it is in each of the three sentences above), *that* is usually omitted (e.g. *Where is the boy they saw in my room? I have lost the book I bought yesterday. Do you remember the days we spent together?*). 2. *that* is often used instead of *who*, but with *any, only* and superlatives, *that* is more usual. *Any boy that wants to play can do so. She was the only woman that smoked a pipe. He is the bravest man that ever lived.*

that[3] [ðət] *conj* at the beginning of a clause, often not used, but understood. *He says (that) he will come. We saw (that) he was tired. I wish (that) I were rich. I hit it so hard (that) it broke. That I was late is a lie.* Also *interj*: *Oh that the rain would stop!* i.e. I wish very much that it would (*o.f.* in this sense).

thatch [θætʃ] *nu* roof made of dry straw, leaves, rushes etc. Also *vt* put thatch on.

thaw [θɔː] *vt/i* **1.** (with reference to snow or anything frozen) melt; become, cause to become, soft. *The ice on the river will thaw when the weather becomes warmer. He thawed his frozen hands at the fire.* **2.** become, cause to become, more friendly. *At first he was angry, but he thawed when we explained what had happened.* Also *nu* warmer weather which causes snow, ice etc to thaw. *After the storm there was a thaw. Winter is followed by the thaw.*

the [ðiː, ði, ðə] *determiner* **1.** one that is known or has already been mentioned. *There's a man at the door. Is he the man who came yesterday? The roads are very busy. He has gone to the bank.* **2.** only one of its kind. *The sun is shining. The weather is cold. What is the name of this flower?*; therefore often used with reference to place names etc: *the Indian Ocean; the Atlantic; the North Pole; the (river) Nile; the Sudan; the British Isles.* **3.** (with *superlatives*): *the biggest house in our village; the last bus.* **4.** all those of a particular kind. *They look after the poor and the sick.* Also with *n sing*: *The African buffalo is very dangerous* (instead of *African buffaloes are very dangerous*). *Who invented the steam engine?* **5.** (instead of *a* or *one*) for each one. *It costs fifty pence the pound. Our car does thirty miles to the gallon.* Also *adv* by that amount. *The more we are together, the happier we shall be.*
Note: only long practice in English can show when to use and when not to use *the, a* or no article at all (e.g. (a) *He has (the) measles. He has a cold. He has fever.* (b) *The buffalo is the most dangerous animal of all* (superlative). *The buffalo is most dangerous. The buffalo is a most dangerous animal* i.e. very dangerous. (c) *The blue sky above us was beautiful. There was a beautiful blue sky above us.* (d) *He plays the piano/the trumpet/the violin* (musical instruments). *He plays chess/football/tennis* (games) but *He has played pianos in every town in England. He plays the game of chess etc well.*

theatre ['θiətə*] (*US* **theater**) *nc* **1.** building where plays, operas etc are acted on a stage. **2.** room with rows of seats used for lectures and lessons. **3.** place where important events take place (esp. during a war). *The Atlantic was the theatre of many naval battles.* **4.** (usu. with **the**) drama; work in or for a theatre. *Because he is an actor he knows the theatre very well.*
theatrical [θi'ætrikl] *adj* **1.** of the theatre. **2.** behaving like an actor on the stage i.e. in an affected, showy manner. **theatrically** *adv.*
'**operating theatre** special room in a hospital where operations are done by doctors.

thee [ðiː] *pron* see **thou.**

theft [θeft] *nc/u* act of stealing.

their [ðεə*] *determiner* belonging to them. *This is their house.*
theirs *pron*: *This house is theirs.*

theism ['θiːizəm] *nu* belief that there is a God who makes himself known to man.
theist *nc* person who has this belief.
theistic, theistical [θiː'istik(l)] *adj.*

them [ðem, ðəm] *pron* form which **they** takes when it is the object of a verb or preposition. *You saw them there. Give it to them.*

theme [θiːm] *nc* **1.** subject of a talk or of writing; essay. **2.** (music) tune which is repeated again and again in a piece of music. **thematic** [θi'mætik] *adj.*
'**theme song** song which is repeated again and again in a musical play or film.

then [ðen] *adv* **1.** at that time in the past. *We were at school then.* **2.** at that time in the future. *As I'll be here on Monday, I'll see you then.* **3.** next; afterwards. *I had supper and then went to bed.* **4.** (put at the beginning or end of a sentence) if that is so; for this reason; therefore. *He says that he is hungry. Then he must have some food/He must have some food then. It was decided then, that we would go.* **5.** also; in addition. *My mother was there. Then there were my brother and two sisters.* Also *adj* of that time: *the then manager.*
from then (on/onwards) from that time. *From then (on/onwards) he never spoke to me.*
now then! *interj* look here! *Now then, what do you want?*
(every) now and then see **every.**
since then since that time.
then and there/there and then see **there.**

until then until that time. *Until then we had not met him.*
thence [ðens] *adv* from there; from that time; for that reason (*o.f.*).
'thence'forth, 'thence'forward *adv* from that time (*o.f.*).
theo- [θi'ɔ, 'θi:ə] *prefix* of God (e.g. **theology**).
theocracy [θi:'ɔkrəsi] *nc* government in the name of, under the control of, God; government by priests. **theocratic** [θi:ə'krætik] *adj.*
theodolite [θi'ɔdəlait] *nc* instrument used for measuring angles when surveying.
theology [θi'ɔlədʒi] *nu* science of the nature of God and of religion. **theological** [θiə'lɔdʒikl] *adj.* **theologically** *adv.*
theologian [θiə'loudʒən] *nc* person who has a great knowledge of theology.
theorem ['θiərəm] *nc* (mathematics) statement which has to be proved by reasoning.
theory ['θiəri] **1.** *nc* reason or argument which is not yet proved, made to explain something. *Many scientists accept the theory that the universe is growing larger.* **2.** *nc/u* general laws and principles. *In theory this is possible, in practice it is not* i.e. according to general principles it appears to be possible, but when one tries to follow these principles and actually do something, it is not possible.
theoretic, theoretical [θiə'retik(l)] *adj.* (*opp* **practical**). **theoretically** *adv.*
theorist *nc* person who has theories.
theorize ['θiəraiz] *vi* form a theory. *Man has always theorized about how life began.*
theosophy [θi'ɔsəfi] *nu* belief that God makes himself directly known to man personally and that in this way man gets all his knowledge. **theosophical** [θiə'sɔfikl] *adj.* **theosophist** *nc.*
therapeutic [θerə'pju:tik] *adj* concerned with the curing of diseases. *Many plants have therapeutic qualities* i.e. can be used to cure diseases.
therapeutics *n sing* science of curing diseases.
therapy ['θerəpi] *nu* medical treatment.
occupational therapy treatment which consists of teaching patients how to do certain jobs.
'physio'therapy treatment of certain illnesses etc by massage, physical movement and electrical equipment.
'radio'therapy medical treatment by radium.
'speech 'therapy treatment of defects of the voice (e.g. stammering) by exercises.
there [ðɛə*] *adv* **1.** at, in, to that place. *I was standing there. He works there, in that shop. Are you going there?*
Note: there is often used at the beginning of a sentence expressing an exclamation. When it is, the subject of the verb comes *before* the verb if it is a personal pronoun, and after the verb if it is a noun. *There they are! There are my books! There he goes! There goes my friend!* It is also used informally in the same way *after* a pronoun or by itself. *You there! Stop talking! There! There! Don't worry!*
2. that place. *I live near there. The distance from there is a mile.* **3.** at that particular point in an action. *Let us stop there* (e.g. in reading). *There I cannot agree with you.* **4.** who or which is or are in that place. *The boy there is ill. The books there are mine.* **5.** used at the beginning of a sentence with a verb (usu. *is, appear* and *seem*) followed by its subject. *There's a dog in your garden. There can be many reasons for this. There seems to be nobody in the house.*
Note: there's is often used to express an exclamation and give emphasis. *There's a lovely girl for you!* i.e. look at that lovely girl! *There's a good boy!* i.e. you are a good boy.
'thereabout, thereabouts *adv* (usu. with **or**) near that place, number or quantity. *He lives in the village or thereabout. I'll come at 6 o'clock or thereabouts.*
there'after *adv* afterwards. (*formal*).
'there'by *adv* by that means; in consequence.
'therefore *adv* for that reason.
there'in, there'of, there'to, there'under *adv* in, of, to, under that (*o.f.* and now correct only in legal language).
there'upon *adv* immediately after that.
there and back to that place and back again.
there and then/then and there at that place and time; at once; without delay. *He gave me £10 there and then.*
here and there see **here**.
therm [θə:m] *nc* amount of gas which can supply 100,000 British thermal units for heating.
thermal ['θə:ml] *adj* of heat: *thermal springs* i.e. natural springs of hot water.
thermo- ['θə:mou] *prefix* of heat (e.g. **thermostat**).
thermometer [θə'mɔmitə*] *nc* instrument for measuring temperature.
thermonuclear ['θə:mou'nju:kliə*] *adj* concerned with hydrogen bombs or other bombs of that type: *thermonuclear war.*
thermos ['θə:məs] ® *nc* trade name for a **vacuum flask i.e.** one consisting of one container inside another with a vacuum between them, so that the contents of the inner container are kept at a constant temperature. (Also **thermos flask**). *pl* **thermoses.**
thermostat ['θə:moustæt] *nc* device for controlling temperature automatically.
thermostatic [θə:mou'stætik] *adj.* **thermostatically** *adv.*
thesaurus [θi'sɔ:rəs] *nc* book containing words, phrases or examples of prose and verse; encyclopaedia. *pl* **thesauri** [θi'sɔ:ri:] or **thesauruses.**
these [ði:z] pl of **this.**
thesis ['θi:sis] *nc* reasoned argument about a particular subject (esp. a long one written to obtain a university degree). *pl* **theses** ['θi:si:z].
they [ðei, ði] *pron* **1.** pl of **he, she** and **it. 2.** people in general or people whom one does not know as individuals. *They say that birds know when it is going to rain* i.e. this is what many people believe. *They have decided to build a new road* i.e. the government etc has decided. (*informal* in sense **2.**). see **them.**
thick [θik] *adj* **1.** big from side to side, from front to back or all the way round. *He is a strong man with thick arms. He drew a thick line on the paper. The book is two inches thick.* **2.** placed closely together; dense. *She has thick hair. The crowd was very thick. It was hidden by a thick mist.* **3.** not easily poured: *thick oil.* (*opp* **thin** in senses **1., 2.** and **3.**). **4.** not easily heard: *thick voice.* **5.** stupid. *I think he is rather thick; thickheaded* i.e. stupid. (*informal*). **6.** very friendly with each or one another. *The three boys are very thick.* (*informal*). Also *nu* thickest

part. *He was hit on the thick of his arm. There was a large crowd and he was in the thick of it.* Also *adv* (only with reference to something lying or spread out). *The leaves lay thick/thickly on the ground. She spread the jam thick/thickly on the bread.* **thickly** *adv.*
thickness *nc/u*: *It is two feet in thickness. This wood is sold in two thicknesses.*
thicken *vt/i* become, cause to become, thick.
thickening *nu* **1.** something used to thicken something else. **2.** state of being, or becoming, thicker.
'thick'set *adj* **1.** planted closely together. **2.** (with reference to persons) broad and strong.
have a thick skin not likely to be upset by criticism etc; be insensitive. (*informal*).
thickskinned *adj*: *Being thickskinned he does not care what people say.* (*informal*).
through thick and thin through good times and bad ones. (*informal*).

thicket ['θikit] *nc* group of closely planted trees or bushes.

thief [θi:f] *nc* person who steals. *pl* **thieves** [θi:vz].

thieve [θi:v] *vt/i* be a thief; steal. **thievery** *nu.*
thievish *adj* fond of stealing. **thievishly** *adv.*

thigh [θai] *nc* thick part of leg above the knee.

thimble ['θimbl] *nc* small, hard cover put on the end of the finger to protect it when using a needle.

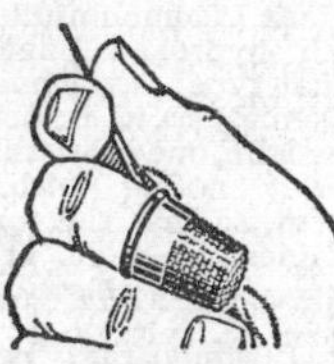

thimble

thin [θin] *adj* **1.** small from front to back, from side to side, or all the way round: *thin book; thin sticks.* **2.** not close together; having gaps. *His hair has become very thin. The game was watched by a thin crowd* i.e. a few people. *The sun was shining through a thin mist.* **3.** easily poured; watery: *thin oil; thin soup.* (*opp* **thick** in senses **1., 2.** and **3.**). **4.** weak; poor. *He has a thin voice. His excuse for being late was very thin.* **5.** without much flesh; lean. *The children are thin because they do not get enough to eat.* (*opp* **fat** in sense **5.**). *comparative* **thinner.** *superlative* **thinnest.** Also *vt/i* become, cause to become, thin. *The crowd thinned. He thinned the stick with a knife. past* **thinned. thinly** *adv.* **thinness** *nu.*
have a thin skin be easily upset by criticism; be sensitive. (*informal*). **'thin-'skinned** *adj.* (*informal*).

thine [ðain] *adj* see **thy.**

thing [θiŋ] *nc* **1.** object which can be seen or touched. *This is the thing I use to cut wood. What is that thing in your hand?* **2.** object which cannot be seen or touched etc but can be thought or felt. *Jealousy is a terrible thing. Religion is a thing of the mind and spirit.* **3.** (in *pl*) possessions; belongings. *They lost all their things in the war. Put your things down here and come inside* i.e. what you are carrying. **4.** (in *pl*) events; conditions. *He worries about things. Things have been much better for me since I got a job.* **5.** (with **the**) particular act or kind of behaviour. *The best thing I did was (to) buy this house. The thing to do is to go away.* **6.** (with **the** and usu. **just** or **very**) what is needed. *This house is just the thing. I have the very thing for mending your car* i.e. the most suitable. **7.** somebody one is fond of. *My aunt is a nice old thing. She has no money, poor thing.* (*informal* in sense **7.**).
the done thing correct or acceptable behaviour; good manners. *It's not the done thing to eat with your fingers here.* (*informal*).
first thing as soon as possible. *I'll see you tomorrow first thing.*
for one thing . . . for another one reason is . . . another is . . . *I can't go. For one thing I am tired, for another my mother doesn't want me to.*
last thing after doing everything else at night. *He locks all the doors last thing before he goes to bed.*
a near thing narrow escape. *We finished in time but it was a near thing* i.e. we almost did not finish. (*informal*).
put things right/straight arrange correctly; deal with successfully. *The new manager soon put things right.*
quite the thing see **quite.**
take things (with *adv*) behave or act in a particular way. *After work we take things quietly. They take things too seriously.*
the thing is the main point is; what must be decided etc is. *The thing is, do you want to come or don't you?*

thingummy ['θiŋəmi] *nc* word used for an object when one does not know its name. (*informal*).

think [θiŋk] *vt/i* **1.** use the mind. *We had to think very quickly. It is so noisy here that I can't think.* **2.** believe; have an opinion; suppose. *They think (that) I am wrong. He thinks (that) it will rain. I thought (that) you would come. We don't think them good enough. Do you think it necessary? He was thought stupid to try. past* **thought** [θɔ:t].
thinker *nc* person who thinks.
thinking *nu* act of thinking. *I did some quick thinking.* Also *adj* who thinks. *Any thinking parent wants education for his children.*
think about someone/something **1.** turn the mind to. *I thought about you all day.* **2.** wonder whether or not to do something. *Are you thinking about buying a new car?*
think of someone/something **1.** turn the mind to; consider. *I thought of you all day. Think of all the money that he has!* **2.** find; suggest. *I could not think of a suitable reply. He had to think of some plan to escape.* **3.** (with *adv*) have an opinion about; regard. *The people think very highly of him. Our work was well thought of.* **4.** (with **not** or **never** etc and **could, would** or **should**) get the idea; seriously consider. *I couldn't think of stealing it. He would never think of coming unless he had to.*
think something out consider something carefully and then decide about it.
think something over consider carefully before deciding. *I need a couple of days to think this matter over.*
think something up find a way; make a plan. *It is very difficult to do this, but I'll think up a plan.*
think aloud think and at the same time say aloud what one is thinking.
think better of **1.** have a higher opinion of. *We thought better of him for doing it.* **2.**

think about and then decide not to. *They have thought better of buying a new car. They are keeping their old one.*
think nothing of 1. have a poor opinion of. *He thinks nothing of your work.* 2. consider to be quite easy or usual. *They think nothing of spending £100 a week.*
think to oneself think secretly, without saying anything. *'He is a dangerous man', I thought to myself.*

third [θəːd] see appendix.
(the) third degree see **degree.**
'third 'party (esp. with reference to an insurance policy) person in addition to, but considered by, two persons who make a legal agreement or contract: *third-party risks* i.e. risks covered by an insurance policy to include other persons who may be hurt or suffer loss or damage to their property because of something done by the person who is insured.
'third-'rate *adj* of poor quality.

thirst [θəːst] *nu* 1. desire for drink; lack of drink. *We satisfied our thirst with a glass of water. I was suffering from thirst.* 2. any strong desire: *their thirst for news.* Also *vi* feel thirst or any strong desire. *He thirsted for knowledge.*
thirsty *adj* feeling or causing thirst. **thirstily** *adv.*

this [ðis] 1. *adj/adv/pron/determiner*: *Who is this man? I want this book, not that one.* 2. *pron*: *Who is this? I want this, not that.* *pl* **these** [ðiːz]. 3. *adj* of the present time. *I am going away this month. He is never at home these days. This time last year they were in Africa* i.e. a year ago.
Note: this or *these* cannot be used with *my, your, his etc.* Instead one must use *of mine, of yours, of his etc. This room of mine is too small. These friends of theirs are very quiet.* 4. *adv* so; to this degree. *We have walked this far without stopping* i.e. as far as here. *The table is about this big.*

thistle ['θisl] *nc* type of plant with many sharp points; emblem of Scotland.

thither ['ðiðə*] *adv* to that place (*o.f.*).

thong [θɔŋ] *nc* thin piece of leather.

thorax ['θɔːræks] *nc/u* part of the body between the neck and the stomach; the chest.

thorn [θɔːn] 1. *nc* sharp point growing from a plant. *This tree has thorns.* 2. *nc/u/adj* (with another word) type of plant or tree which has thorns (e.g. *hawthorn; thorn bush*).
thorny *adj* 1. having thorns. 2. difficult; causing trouble: *thorny problem.*

thorough ['θʌrə] *adj* complete; careful and exact. *The doctor gave me a thorough examination. She is a thorough teacher.*
thoroughly *adv.* **thoroughness** *nu.*
'thoroughgoing *adj* complete; in every way.

thoroughbred ['θʌrəbred] *nc* animal or person of pure breed. Also *adj*: *thoroughbred horse.*

thoroughfare ['θʌrəfɛə*] *nc* road or street which is open at both ends to allow traffic to pass through.
no thoroughfare (used as a notice) this road is closed.

those [ðouz] pl of **that**[1].

thou [ðau] *pron* you *sing* (*o.f.*).
thee *pron* form used after *vt* or *prep.*

though [ðou] *conj* even if. *Though the book is difficult to understand, it is interesting.*
Note: although can usu. be used instead of *though* except: (a) in the phrase *as though* (which has the sense of *as if*) we cannot use *although. He behaves as though he were my father* i.e. he behaves like my father but he isn't. (b) *though* but not *although* is sometimes used after a clause to mean what was expected but did not happen. *I went to town. I didn't see John though* i.e. I expected to see him but did not. (*informal*).

thought[1] [θɔːt] past of **think.**

thought[2] [θɔːt] 1. *nu* act or way of thinking. *This problem needs great thought. Modern thought is against slavery.* 2. *nc* what somebody thinks or intends. *I told him my thoughts. They have no thought of going away.* 3. *nu* care; concern. *He threw it away without thought.*
thoughtful *adj* 1. full of thought. *This is a thoughtful book.* 2. full of concern for others. *It was thoughtful of them to come and meet us.*
thoughtfully *adv.* **thoughtfulness** *nu.*
thoughtless *adj* 1. without thought. 2. without concern for others. **thoughtlessly** *adv.* **thoughtlessness** *nu.*
'thought reader *nc* person who claims to know what another person thinks. **thought reading** *nu.*
on second thoughts after thinking about it again. (Also **have second thoughts about something**).

thousand ['θauzənd] see appendix.

thrash [θræʃ] 1. *vt* beat; strike. *He thrashed the boy with a stick. As he swam, he thrashed the water with his hands. We thrashed them at football* i.e. we won easily. 2. *vt/i* see **thresh.**
thrashing *nc*: *He gave the boy a thrashing.*
thrash about move noisily and violently. *They were thrashing about in the water.*
thrash something out discuss thoroughly and decide. *We must thrash out this problem.*

thread [θred] *nc/u* 1. very thin piece of cotton, silk, wool etc. *I sewed on the buttons with thread. There are threads of wool on your dress.* 2. something which joins or keeps things together. *I have lost the thread of my argument.* 3. spiral part of a screw. Also *vt* 1. pass a thread through. *She threaded her needle.* 2. (usu. with **one's way**) go slowly and carefully. *I threaded my way through the large crowd.*
'threadbare *adj* 1. (with reference to clothes, carpets etc) worn so much that the threads are seen. 2. (with reference to arguments, jokes etc) used too much.
hang by a thread be in a very dangerous condition. *When he was ill, his life hung by a thread* i.e. he almost died.

threat [θret] *nc* 1. statement that one will harm somebody (esp. if he does not agree to do something). *He was arrested for making threats against the president.* 2. danger. *The flood was a threat to our homes.*
threaten *vt/i* 1. make a threat against. *He threatened them with death. He threatened to kill them.* 2. be a danger to. *The flood threatened our homes.* 3. warn that something is likely to happen. *The dark clouds threaten a storm.*
threatening *adj*: *threatening voice; threatening clouds.* **threateningly** *adv.*

three [θriː] see appendix.

thresh [θreʃ], **thrash** [θræʃ] *vt/i* separate grain from the stalk by beating it.
'threshing floor floor or piece of ground where grain is threshed.

threshold ['θreʃhould] *nc* 1. piece of wood or stone under the door of a house. *He stood on the threshold for a minute before going into the house.* 2. place where something ends and something else begins. *We* *are on the threshold of a great discovery.*

threw [θru:] past tense of **throw.**

thrice [θrais] *adv* three times (*o.f.*).

thrift [θrift] *nu* careful control of money or property.

thrifty *adj* using thrift. **thriftily** *adv.* **thriftiness** *nu.*

thriftless *adj* without thrift. **thriftlessly** *adv.* **thriftlessness** *nu.*

thrill [θril] *nc* sudden feeling of pleasure or excitement. Also *vt/i* have, cause to have, a thrill. *We (were) thrilled when we saw the high mountains. The lovely house thrills her.*

thriller *nc* book, play or film etc about detectives, spies etc which thrills those who read or see it.

thrilling *adj* very exciting.

thrive [θraiv] *vi* **1.** grow well. *Corn thrives in that climate.* **2.** be successful. *His business is thriving.*

throat [θrout] *nc/u* front of the neck; passage between the back of the mouth and the lungs and the stomach. *He seized me by the throat. He poured the drink down his throat.*

throaty *adj* coming from the throat: *a throaty voice* i.e. a deep, thick one.

throb [θrɔb] *vi* **1.** (with reference to the heart) beat more strongly. *Her heart throbbed with excitement.* **2.** beat or work regularly like the heart. *My head was throbbing with pain. The engine throbbed all night. past* **throbbed.** Also *nc/u*: *throb of her heart; throb of the engine.*

throes [θrouz] *npl* pain (usu. only in **in the throes of** i.e. suffering the pain or trouble of). *We are in the throes of moving to another house.*

thrombosis [θrɔm'bousis] *nu* hardening of some blood in a vein or artery which stops the flow of blood in a living person.

throne [θroun] *nc* official chair of a king, queen or bishop.

come to the throne become king or queen.

throng [θrɔŋ] *nc* crowd. (rather *o.f.* – use **crowd**). Also *vt/i* fill with a crowd. *The town was thronged with visitors. They thronged the shops.*

throttle ['θrɔtl] *vt/i* **1.** prevent from breathing by pressing the hands on somebody's throat; strangle. **2.** reduce the amount of fuel, steam etc passing into an engine so as to make it go slower. *The driver throttled back/down as he approached the corner.* Also *nc* device which controls the amount of fuel, steam etc passing into an engine. *He opened the throttle of his motorbike on the straight road* i.e. to go faster.

through [θru:] **1.** *adj/adv/prep* (with reference to place) from one end or side to the other. *The main road goes through the town. They made a hole through the wall.* **2.** *prep* (with reference to time) from beginning to end. *We sat through the meeting. They worked through the night.*

Note: (US) sense is up to and including. *Shops are open (from) Monday through Friday* i.e. from Monday morning to Friday evening.

3. *prep* by means of; because of. *I heard about it through a friend. He became ill through eating too much.* **4.** *adv* from one end or side to the other; from beginning to end. *Can I get through by this road? They worked the whole night through.* **5.** *adj*: *We took a through train to London* i.e. one which went all the way to London without our having to change trains.

all through 1. from beginning to end; everywhere. *They slept all through the day.* **2.** all the time. *We hoped all through that you would come back.*

be through be connected by telephone. *Are you through to the office yet?*

be through with 1. be finished with. *I am just through with (reading) this book.* **2.** be tired of. *He is through with trying to please them.* (*informal*).

get through something 1. finish. *They got through the meal without speaking.* **2.** succeed; cause to succeed. *Did you get through the examination?*

get someone/something through cause to reach. *He got the message through.*

get through to someone/something 1. (usu. with reference to a message, telephone call, radio etc) reach. *He could not get through to his mother last night* i.e. by telephone. **2.** make someone understand something. *I couldn't get the facts through to him.*

go through something 1. examine carefully. *We shall go through the book together.* **2.** spend. *He went through all the money his father gave him.* **3.** endure. *He went through a long illness.* **4.** be accepted, approved. *The plan did not go through.*

go through with something do until finished; continue to the end. *Can we still go through with this plan?*

look through something examine (usu. to find something or be ready for something). *I'll look through my papers and see if his name is mentioned.*

see through something see that something is wrong; not be deceived by. *He soon saw through their promises.*

see something through see **see**[1].

through and through completely. *He is cowardly through and through.*

through'out *prep* everywhere in; from beginning to end of: *throughout the world; throughout his life.* Also *adv*: *The house was painted white throughout* i.e. everywhere inside.

throw [θrou] *vt/i* **1.** send through the air with a quick movement of the arm. *He was throwing stones into the river. I threw the ball to him. I threw him the ball.* **2.** cause to fall down, fall off. *The horse threw its rider. He seized the thief and threw him to the ground.* **3.** puzzle, bewilder. *That question really threw me.* (*informal* in sense **3.**). *past tense* **threw** [θru:]. *past part* **thrown** [θroun]. Also *nc* act of throwing; distance which something is thrown. *That was a good throw. It was a throw of about 50 yards.* **thrower** *nc.*

throw something about throw here and there carelessly or violently. *He threw his clothes about in the room. Why does he throw his arms about when he is speaking? They like throwing their money about* i.e. spending it carelessly.

throw something away 1. get rid of. *You should throw away these chairs and buy new ones.* **2.** lose by being careless. *Don't throw away your chances of getting this job.*

'throwaway remark remark made as if one did not care about it, although it is really intended to be funny.

throw something back return by throwing. *He caught the ball and threw it back.*

'throwback *nc* somebody/something that behaves or looks like a previous type. *He is a throwback to his grandfather.*

be thrown back upon have to depend upon. *When he lost all his own money, he was*

thrown back upon his wife's.
throw someone/something down throw to the ground. *He threw himself down behind the wall.*
throw something in add for nothing or without extra payment. *If you buy his house he is ready to throw in the carpets.* (*informal*).
throw oneself into something begin to do very actively. *She has thrown herself into gardening with great enthusiasm.*
throw something off **1.** take off quickly. *He threw off his coat.* **2.** get rid of. *I can't throw off this fever I have.* **3.** write without trouble. *He threw off a few articles for the magazine.*
throw something on put on quickly. *They threw on their clothes and ran outside.*
throw oneself on/upon something trust oneself to. *He threw himself upon the mercy of his enemies.*
throw someone/something out **1.** push out quickly. *He threw out his chest with pride.* **2.** remove, push out violently. *If he doesn't stop talking throw him out!* **3.** make known casually. *He threw out a few suggestions.*
throw someone/something over abandon; give up. *Why have you thrown him over? He was your best friend.*
throw together put, place together quickly or by chance. *The war threw them together in a strange country.*
throw something up **1.** throw high into the air. **2.** (usu. with reference to hands and eyes to express surprise etc) move up quickly. *She threw up her hands in disgust.* **3.** stop doing. *I've thrown up my job.* **4.** vomit; be sick.
throw a fit **1.** have a fit. **2.** be very angry. (*informal*).
throw a party give, have a party. (*informal*).

thrush[1] [θrʌʃ] *nc* one of various types of small songbird (esp. one with a speckled chest).

thrush[2] [θrʌʃ] *nu* disease of the mouth and tongue (esp. among children).

thrust [θrʌst] *vt/i* push suddenly and with force. *He thrust his knife into the man attacking him. I thrust all my books into the box. We thrust (ourselves) through the crowd. past* **thrust.** Also *nc* act of thrusting or attacking. *The enemy made a thrust against our troops.*

thud [θʌd] *nc* dull sound made by a blow or heavy fall on something soft. *We could hear the thud of their feet as they ran on the grass.* Also *vi* strike with a thud. *past* **thudded.**

thug [θʌg] *nc* person who is violent and dangerous.

thumb [θʌm] *nc* short, thick finger of the hand which is separate from the other four. Also *vt* use the thumb to do something. *He thumbed through the book* i.e. he used his thumb to turn over the pages quickly. *They are trying to thumb a lift* i.e. trying to get a driver to stop and give them a lift by signalling to him with their thumb. *The little boy thumbed his nose at me* i.e. put his thumb on his nose with the rest of his fingers stretched out and pointing at me (a rude and insulting sign).
'thumbmark mark (usu. a dirty one) made on something by the thumb.
'thumbnail nail of the thumb: *thumbnail sketch* i.e. small picture; quick, short description.
'thumbscrew instrument of torture which crushes the thumb.
'thumbtack (*US*) drawing pin.
rule of thumb rule which experience has shown to be generally true although it is not very exact.
under somebody's thumb under the complete control of somebody.

thump [θʌmp] *nc* **1.** blow (usu. with the closed hand). *He gave me a friendly thump on the back.* **2.** sound made by something heavy falling suddenly. *The bag hit the ground with a thump.* Also *vt/i* strike hard (usu. with the closed hand). *Who is thumping on the door? He thumped me on the nose.*

thunder ['θʌndə*] **1.** *nu* loud noise in the sky which is often accompanied by lightning. **2.** *nc/u* loud noise like this: *thunder of the sea against the rocks; thunders of applause.* Also *vt/i*: *Outside it was raining and thundering. The sea thundered against the rocks. The speaker thundered against his opponents* i.e. spoke loudly and violently.
thunderous *adj* making a sound like thunder; very loud. *There was thunderous applause.* **thunderously** *adv.*
thundery *adj* (with reference to the weather) likely to have thunder.
'thunderbolt **1.** single discharge of electricity followed by a great sound of thunder. **2.** something unpleasant which happens suddenly.
'thunderclap sudden, sharp burst of thunder.
'thunderstorm storm of thunder and lightning with heavy rain.
steal somebody's thunder win the applause or praise expected by somebody else. (*informal*).

Thursday ['θəːzdi] *n* fifth day of the Christian week.

thus [ðʌs] *adv* in this way.

thwack [θwæk] *vt* see **whack.**

thwart[1] [θwɔːt] *vt* prevent somebody doing something he wishes to do. *They have thwarted (him in) all his plans.*

thwart[2] [θwɔːt] *nc* seat across a boat.

thy [ðai] *adj* your *sing* (*o.f.*).
thine [ðain] *adj* your *sing* (before a vowel). Also *pron* yours. (both *o.f.*).

thyme [taim] *nu* type of sweet-smelling plant.

thyroid ['θairɔid] *nc* one of the glands of the body, found in the neck. Also *adj.*

tiara [ti'ɑːrə] *nc* **1.** crown worn by the Pope. **2.** circle of jewels worn by a woman on her head.

tiara (*def 2*)

tibia ['tibiə] *nc* inner of the two bones between the knee and the ankle.

tic [tik] *nc* uncontrolled movement of the muscles of the face. *He has a tic under his left eye.*

tick[1] [tik] *nc* **1.** small, regular sound made by a clock or watch. *It was so quiet that I could hear the tick of the clock on the wall.* **2.** moment; second. *I'll be ready in a tick.*

(*informal*). **3.** the mark √ made to show that something is correct or has been seen. Also *vt/i* **1.** make the sound of a tick. *I could hear the clock on the wall ticking. The engine was ticking over quietly* i.e. running slowly and smoothly like a clock. **2.** put the mark √ after. *The teacher ticked (off) the boys' names in his book as they came into the classroom.*
ticker *nc* **1.** something which ticks (e.g. a watch, the heart) (*informal*). **2.** type of machine which prints news, market prices etc on paper tape.
'ticker-tape paper tape used in this machine.
'tick-tack type of signalling by hand used between bookmakers at the races.
'tick tock 1. sound made by a large clock. **2.** child's name for a **clock.**
tick somebody off speak severely to; rebuke. *The teacher ticked him off for being rude.* (*informal*).
tick[2] [tik] *nc* cover of a mattress or pillow.
ticking *nu* type of strong cloth used to make this type of cover.
tick[3] [tik] *nc* type of small insect which fixes itself to the skin and feeds on blood.
tick[4] [tik] *nu* trust; credit. *He buys his clothes on tick* i.e. promising to pay for them later. (*informal*).
ticket ['tikit] *nc* **1.** small piece of paper or cardboard which shows that the person who has it has paid, or has been given permission, to travel by bus, train etc or to enter a cinema, theatre, sports ground etc. **2.** small piece of paper or cardboard showing the price of something in a shop. **3.** (*US*) list of candidates to be voted for in an election; policy of a political party. Also *vt* put a ticket on.
complimentary ticket free ticket given to somebody.
re'turn ticket (*Brit*) ticket allowing somebody to travel to a place and back again. (*US* **round-trip ticket**).
'season ticket 1. ticket allowing somebody to attend a number of concerts, lectures etc. **2.** (*Brit*) ticket allowing somebody to travel daily for a particular period of time. **3.** (*US*) commutation ticket.
'single ticket see **single.**
tickle ['tikl] *vt/i* **1.** touch somebody's skin lightly and make him laugh. *She tickled the child under the arms.* **2.** have, give this feeling. *My feet tickled. The wool is tickling my neck.* **3.** amuse; please. *His stories always tickle us.* Also *nc* feeling of being tickled.
ticklish *adj* **1.** (with reference to a person) easily made to laugh when tickled. **2.** (with reference to a problem, situation etc) requiring skill and care in dealing with it. *His tact and good manners enabled him to deal with many ticklish situations.*
tidbit ['tidbit] *nc* see **titbit.**
tide [taid] *nc/u* **1.** regular rise and fall of the sea twice each day. *Today high tide was at 6 a.m. and low tide at midday. The tides have worn away the rocks.* **2.** something which rises and falls like the tide; trend. *A tide of anger swept through the people.* **3.** (used only with other words) season: *Eastertide; eventide* (*o.f.* in sense **3.**). Also *vt* (with **over**) help for the moment. *This money should tide us over until Friday.*
tidal *adj* of, with a tide: *tidal river* i.e. one which the sea enters and so causes a tide in it; *tidal wave* i.e. very large wave which can cause damage.
'neap tide tide with the least amount of rise and fall, occurring twice a month.
'spring tide tide with the greatest rise and fall, occurring after a new and full moon.
tidings ['taidiŋz] *npl* news (*o.f.*).
tidy ['taidi] *adj* **1.** in good order; neat. *You must keep your desk tidy. He is a very tidy man.* (*opp* **untidy**). **2.** quite large: *a tidy profit.* (*informal* in sense **2.**). Also *vt/i* cause to be tidy. *She tidied (up) the room before going out.* **tidily** *adv.* **tidiness** *nu.*
tie [tai] *vt/i* **1.** fasten with rope, string, wire etc. *I tied the sticks together. Please tie (up) this parcel.* **2.** join the ends of pieces of rope, string, wire etc together. *He is tying his shoelaces. He tied the two ropes in/with a knot.* **3.** be fastened, joined together. *How do these shoelaces tie?* (*opp* **untie** in senses **1., 2.** and **3.**). **4.** keep busy; give less freedom. *His work ties him down. He is tied to his work. They want to tie up the agreement as soon as possible* i.e. make it definite so that it cannot be changed. **5.** (with reference to games, competitions etc) get the same score or number of marks. *John and James tied in the race. Our team tied with theirs in athletics.* *pres part* **tying.** *past* **tied.** Also *nc* **1.** strip of cloth worn round the neck (usu. by men). *He was wearing a white shirt and/with a red tie.* **2.** something which joins something else together. *These ties hold up the roof* i.e. beams; (*US*) *the ties on a railroad.* (*Brit* **sleepers on a railway line**). *We have many ties of friendship with your country.* **3.** something which keeps one busy, gives less freedom. *He finds the extra work a great tie.* **4.** equal score or marks. *The result of the competition was a tie.*
'tie-up *nc* link, connection.
tier [tiə*] *nc* row (esp. of seats arranged above and behind another row). *The tiers in the theatre were full.*
tiered *adj*: *three-tiered cake.*
tiff [tif] *nc* slight quarrel.
tiger ['taigə*] *nc* large striped animal of the cat family found in Asia.

tiger

tigerish *adj* like a tiger.
tigress ['taigris] *nc* female tiger.
tight [tait] *adj* **1.** firm; not easily moved; fitting closely. *The knot is so tight that I cannot unfasten it. His pockets were tight with papers* i.e. firm because they were full. *She was wearing a tight dress.* **2.** stretched. *The wires between the poles are very tight.* **3.** (esp. with reference to money) difficult to get. *Money is very tight these days.* **4.** unwilling to spend or give money; mean. **5.** drunk. (*informal* in senses **4.** and **5.**). Also *adv.* **tightly** *adv*: *He held my hand tight/tightly.* **tightness** *nu.*
tighten *vt/i* become, cause to become, tight or tighter.
tights *npl* closely-fitting garment covering the feet, legs, and lower part of the body worn by women and children and also by

acrobats and dancers.

'tight-'fisted *adj* mean. (*informal*).

'tight-'lipped *adj* with the mouth shut closely, with the intention of not saying anything.

'tightrope *nc/u* rope on which acrobats balance and do tricks. **tightrope walker** *nc*. **tightrope walking** *nu*.

'airtight/'watertight *adj* not allowing air/water to get in or out.

tile [tail] *nc* flat piece of baked clay, plastic, cork etc used on roofs, floors and walls. Also *vt* cover with tiles.

till[1] [til] *conj/prep* **1.** up to a certain time. *He will stay here till Saturday. The office is open from morning till night.* **2.** up to the time when. *They waited till I arrived. I won't go till you tell me.*

Note: until has the same sense as *till* and can be used instead of it in the sentences above. *Until*, however, is more usual when the clause or phrase in which it is used comes first. *Until now we have had good news. Until I arrived I said nothing.*

till[2] [til] *vt* make land ready for planting; cultivate. **tiller**[1] *nc*.

tillage *nu* **1.** act of tilling. **2.** land which has been tilled.

till[3] [til] *nc* box or drawer where money is kept in a shop.

tiller[2] ['tilə*] *nc* bar by which the rudder of a boat is moved.

tilt [tilt] *vt/i* **1.** lean, cause to lean, so as to be no longer level or upright. *When he tilted the desk the books fell off. Her hat is tilted to one side of her head. The boat tilted in the storm.* **2.** (with **at**) ride on horseback with a long spear or lance against somebody/something; attack. Also *nc* **1.** leaning position: *the tilt of her hat.* **2.** attack with a lance. **3.** friendly criticism. *He had a tilt at their bad habits.*

(at) full tilt very quickly; with great force. *He ran into the wall (at) full tilt.*

timber ['timbə*] **1.** *nu* trees cut down, or about to be cut down and prepared for use in building, carpentry etc. *All the roofs and floors of the house are made of timber. Half of the land is under timber* i.e. planted with trees which can be cut down and used. **2.** *nc* large piece of wood prepared for use (e.g. as a beam to hold up a roof).

timbered *adj* (with reference to buildings) made or partly made of timber.

'timber merchant person who buys and sells timber.

'timberyard place where timber is kept ready for use.

timbre ['tæmbə*] *nu* particular tone in the sound of the human voice or a musical instrument.

time [taim] **1.** *nu* (often with **a** or **the**) intervals of minutes, hours, days or years needed to do something. *Have you time to look at it? Building a house takes a long time. We cannot spare the time for extra work.* **2.** *nu* (without **a** or **the**) passing of minutes, hours, days etc. *Only time will show if he is right. Time never stands still.* **3.** *nc/u* particular moment, hour or occasion. *At that time I was abroad. 'What is the time?'/'What time is it?' 'It is 8 o'clock'. Every time he comes he brings a friend.* **4.** *nc* number of occasions. *Two times four are eight. He has been here many times.* **5.** *nc* exact measure of passing minutes, hours, days etc. *His time for (running) the mile was just over 4 minutes.* **6.** *nu* method of measuring the passing minutes, hours, days etc: *Greenwich Mean Time; standard time.* **7.** *nc* life; period; age. *This happened before my time* i.e. before I was born or came here. *They had a bad time at school. In ancient times there were no motorcars.* **8.** *nu* measure or rate of music; rate of moving to music. *The band is playing the tune in waltz time. The soldiers marched in slow time.* Also *vt* **1.** measure the amount of time taken to do something. *We timed him for the mile.* **2.** choose or follow the correct time for something. *They have timed their holidays to miss the busy season. A good boxer times his punches.*

timing *nc/u* choice of, setting to, the correct time. *There's something wrong with the timing of this engine.*

timeless *adj* never-ending. **timelessly** *adv*. **timelessness** *nu*.

timely *adj* happening at the right time. (*opp* **untimely**). **timeliness** *nu*.

'time bomb bomb with a device which causes it to explode at a certain time.

'time-honoured *adj* having lasted for a long time and respected for that reason: *a time-honoured custom.*

'timekeeper *nc* **1.** person who keeps time or a record of time (e.g. of the arrivals and departures of workers in a factory, of rounds in a boxing match, at a sports meeting etc). **2.** device which does this. **time-keeping** *nu*.

'time-lag interval between two events which are related; delay. *There is usually a time-lag between making a plan and carrying it out.*

'time limit time allowed for something to end or be completed. *This ticket has a time limit of 7 days.*

'timeserver *nc* person who acts only for his own immediate benefit by trying to please those in authority without considering what is right or wrong. **timeserving** *adj*.

'timetable *nc* list showing the times of events, of lessons in a school, of arrivals and departures of buses, trains etc. Also *vt*: *We must timetable the meeting very carefully.*

against time quickly because there is not enough time. *We are working against time to finish our essays.*

all the time **1.** always. *He is busy all the time.* **2.** during the whole period that something was happening. *All the time we were working he did nothing.*

at a time on each occasion. *The children came into the room three at a time.*

at all times always.

at no time never.

at one time at a time in the past. *At one time he was a soldier.*

at the best of times when conditions are most favourable. *He's never very helpful at the best of times.*

at the same time **1.** together. **2.** however. *I think it is his own fault, but, at the same time, I can't help feeling sorry for him.*

at times sometimes.

beat time see **beat**[1].

behind time late.

behind the times old-fashioned; out-of-date.

do time be in prison. (*informal*).

from time to time occasionally.

gain time see **gain**.

in time **1.** not late. *He always arrives in time.* **2.** later; after a period of time. *The mark on your face will disappear in time.*

in good time not late. *We arrived in good time.*
keep time 1. follow the correct time of a piece of music (e.g. when singing, dancing or playing a musical instrument). 2. (with reference to a clock or watch) go at the correct time. *My watch keeps (good) time.*
lose time see **lose.**
lose no time see **lose.**
mark time 1. move the feet up and down as if marching but without moving forward. 2. delay; do nothing.
on time at the expected or correct time.
time and again very often.
timid ['timid] *adj* easily frightened; nervous. **timidly** *adv.* **timidity** [ti'miditi] *nu.*
timorous ['timərəs] *adj* easily frightened; nervous. **timorously** *adv.* **timorousness** *nu.*
timpani ['timpəni] *npl* large drums used in an orchestra.
timpanist *nc* person who plays the timpani.
tin [tin] 1. *nu* type of soft metal. 2. *nc (Brit)* container (usu. airtight) made of tinplate i.e. thin sheet of iron covered by a thin sheet of tin. *We bought five tins of fruit and two tins of soup.* (*US* **can**). Also *vt* 1. *(Brit)* put food etc in an airtight tin: *tinned fruit.* (*US* **canned fruit**). 2. put a thin sheet of tin on. *past* **tinned.**
tinny *adj* like tin; making a sound like tin when struck.
'**tinfoil** very thin sheet of tin like paper used for packing food etc. (Often **silver paper** because it has the colour of silver).
'**tin 'god** somebody considered to be far more important than he really is. (*informal*).
'**tin 'hat** steel helmet worn by soldiers etc. (*informal*).
'**tin opener** device used to open tins. (*US* **can opener**).
'**tinsmith** person who is skilled in using tin or tinplate.
tincture ['tiŋktʃə*] *nc* 1. (with **a**) slight colour or taste. *The sky had a tincture of red.* 2. solution of a substance in alcohol: *tincture of iodine.* Also *vt* give a slight colour, taste or suggestion of something. *The sky was tinctured with red.*
tinder ['tində*] *nu* something dry used to start a fire.
'**tinderbox** box containing tinder and flint formerly used for starting a fire (instead of the modern box of matches).
tinge [tindʒ] *vt* (with **with**) give a slight colour or suggestion of. *The sun tinged the sea with yellow. His words were tinged with anger.* Also *nc*: *a tinge of yellow/anger.*
tingle ['tiŋgl] *vi* have a slight stinging feeling in the skin (e.g. when the blood comes back to the skin after a person has been cold or has been hit). *My face tingled after the walk over the hills.* Also *nc*: *He felt a tingle of excitement.*
tinker ['tiŋkə*] *nc* person who repairs pots and pans (esp. one who travels from place to place). Also *vt/i* 1. do the work of a tinker. 2. try to repair (usu. in a clumsy way). *He likes tinkering with broken clocks.*
tinkle ['tiŋkl] *vt/i* make, cause to make, small quick sounds like those made by a small bell. *The glasses on the tray tinkled.* Also *nc*: *tinkle of glasses; tinkle of a bell.*
tinny ['tini] *adj* see **tin.**
tinsel ['tinsl] *nu* 1. type of thin, bright material used in strips as a decoration or ornament. 2. something which is showy, but of little value. Also *vt* decorate with tinsel. *past* **tinselled.** (*US* **tinseled**).
tint [tint] *nc* colour which is made paler by mixing it with white; slight colour. *There is a tint of red in her hair.* Also *vt* (esp. with reference to hair) give a tint to; dye.
tintinnabulation ['tintinæbju'leiʃən] *nc/u* sound made by bells.
tiny ['taini] *adj* very small.
tip[1] [tip] *nc* 1. narrow or pointed end of something: *tip of his finger/nose/tongue; wing tips of an aeroplane.* 2. something fixed to the end of something else. *This stick has a metal tip. He smokes cigarettes with filter tips.* Also *vt* put a tip on: *filter-tipped cigarettes. past* **tipped.**
'**tiptoe** *adv* (with **on**) on the tips of the toes. *We went very quietly from the room on tiptoe.* Also *vi* walk in this way. *We tiptoed from the room.*
'**tip'top** *adj/adv* excellent. (*informal*).
tip[2] [tip] *vt/i* 1. move easily; cause to move without much effort. *The small boat tipped over* i.e. went over on its side. *The top of the desk tips up* i.e. can be raised and lowered easily. *He tipped over the basket. He tipped the ball into the hole. Shall I tip the water out of the jug? The boy tipped his cap to the headmaster* i.e. touched or moved it slightly instead of raising it from his head. 2. give a small amount of money to somebody (usu. for doing something). *After paying for our lunch in the hotel, I tipped the waiter.* 3. empty out rubbish. *past* **tipped.** Also *nc* 1. place where rubbish is put (e.g. from a mine or from a town). 2. small amount of money (usu. given for doing something). *I gave the waiter a tip.* 3. advice about how to do something. *This book has some useful tips about gardening.* 4. information about what may happen (esp. when bets are made e.g. in a horse-race). *I have been given a good tip for the race tomorrow.*
tipster ['tipstə*] *nc* person who gives tips for races.
tip somebody off give somebody advice or a warning. (*informal*).
'**tip-off** *nc* advice or warning. (*informal*).
tipple ['tipl] *vt/i* drink alcoholic liquid in small amounts but too often. Also *nu* drink. **tippler** *nc.*
tipsy ['tipsi] *adj* slightly drunk. **tipsily** *adv.* **tipsiness** *nu.*
tirade [tai'reid] *nc* long, angry speech.
tire[1] ['taiə*] *vt/i* become, cause to become, weary or exhausted. *Young children tire quickly. They soon tired of doing the same thing. The heavy work tired me.*
tired *adj* weary. **tiredness** *nu.*
tireless *adj* not becoming weary easily; never stopping. **tirelessly** *adv.*
tiresome *adj* dull; annoying. **tiresomely** *adv.* **tiresomeness** *nu.*
tire out become, cause to become, completely exhausted. *We were tired out after the examination.*
be tired of be weary with; have too much of. *I am tired of going to school every day.*
tire[2] ['taiə*] *nc* see **tyre.**
tissue ['tiʃuː] *nc/u* 1. fine, light cloth or paper. 2. piece of such paper. 3. group of cells which form part of an animal or plant (e.g. *muscular tissue*). Also *adj* made of tissue.
'**tissue paper** type of thin, soft paper used in parcels to protect things which are easily damaged etc.
tit[1] [tit] *nc* see **titmouse.**
tit[2] [tit] *nc* 1. point of the breast through

which milk comes; nipple. **2.** breast. *informal* and *impolite* in sense **2.**).
tit[3] [tit] *nc* only in **tit for tat** i.e. blow for blow.
titanic [tai'tænik] *adj* very big and involving very great strength or force.
titbit ['titbit], **tidbit** ['tidbit] *nc* very pleasant or interesting piece of something: *titbit of cake; titbits of news.*
tithe [taið] *nc* tenth part of crops, cattle etc once paid as a tax by farmers in England to the church.
'tithe barn barn in which tithes were once kept.
titillate ['titileit] *vt* excite in a pleasing way.
titillation [titi'leiʃən] *nc/u.*
titivate ['titiveit] *vt/i* dress smartly; make oneself smart. (*informal*).
title ['taitl] *nc* **1.** name of a book, film, play, piece of music etc. **2.** word put in front of somebody's name to show his position, rank or work (e.g. *Dr, Lord, Professor*). **3.** (with **to**) legal claim or right. *He has the title to all the land here.*
titled *adj* having a noble title (e.g. *Lord, Earl, Duke etc*).
'title deed legal document which gives somebody the title to land or property.
'title role actor's part in a play from which the play takes its name. *He had the title role in Shakespeare's 'Macbeth'* i.e. he played the part of Macbeth in the play called 'Macbeth'.
titmouse ['titmaus] *nc* type of small bird which often hangs upside down when finding food. *pl* **titmice** ['titmais] (Usu. **tit**).
titter ['titə*] *vi* laugh in a silly way. Also *nc.*
tittle ['titl] *nc* only in **not one jot or tittle** i.e. not one piece; nothing at all.
tittle-tattle ['titltætl] *nu* gossip; idle talk. Also *vi.* (both *informal*).
titular ['titjulə*] *adj* having a title without the power suggested by the title. *He is the titular ruler of Ruritania.*
to [tuː, tə] *prep/adv* **1.** towards; in the direction of. *Is this the road to the hospital? We turned to the right. The farm is to the east of the town. You should be kind to animals.* **2.** as far as: *from top to bottom; from east to west; from first to last. I read the book to the end.* **3.** (with reference to time) until; before. *He will be in London from Monday to Friday. The time is five (minutes) to four.* (*opp* **past** in sense **3.**). **4.** compared with. *He is fat to what he was as a little boy. Our team scored three goals to their two. We won by three goals to two. They prefer tea to coffee.* **5.** showing the indirect object. *Please give it to me. It seemed silly to us.* **6.** showing the infinitive: *to be or not to be. He wants to help. I have come to see you. This is difficult to do. They were the last to leave.* **7.** showing purpose or result. *The pupils rose to greet us.* **8.** in a particular position. *He pushed the door to* i.e. pushed it into the position of being closed or almost closed.
to and fro backwards and forwards.
toad [toud] *nc* small animal like a frog but with a dry skin.
'toadstool name given to various types of fungus like a mushroom in shape.
toady ['toudi] *nc* person who is frightened of, and so tries to please, rich or important people. Also *vt* (with **to**). *We don't like him because he toadies to all the teachers.*
toast[1] [toust] *vt* **1.** make hard and dry by heating. *She toasted two slices of bread.* **2.** make warm by putting near a fire. *We toasted ourselves in front of the big fire.* Also *nu* bread which has been toasted: *two slices of toast.*
toaster *nc* device for toasting bread.
toast[2] [toust] *vt* drink to the health of, or in honour of, somebody/something. *At the dinner they toasted the Queen.* Also *nc* person/thing toasted; act of toasting. *They drank a toast to the Queen.*
'toastmaster person who announces the toasts at a large party, formal dinner etc.
tobacco [tə'bækou] *nc/u* type of plant, the dried leaves of which are smoked in cigars, cigarettes and pipes.
tobacconist [tə'bækənist] *nc* person who sells tobacco.
toboggan [tə'bɔgən] *nc* type of sledge used for going down hills which are covered with snow. Also *vi* move in this way.
tocsin ['tɔksin] *nc* bell which gives an alarm (*o.f.*).
today [tə'dei] *nu* this day; the present time. *Today is Friday; aeroplanes of today.* Also *adv* on this day. *We are meeting today. Later today there is a football match.*
toddle ['tɔdl] *vi* walk with short, unsteady steps as a baby does when learning to walk.
toddler *nc* baby who toddles.
toddy ['tɔdi] *nc/u* **1.** alcoholic drink made from the juice of the palm tree. **2.** drink made from mixing whisky etc, sugar and hot water.
to-do [tə'duː] *nc/u* excitement; fuss. *There was a great to-do about the money which was stolen. He made quite a to-do about it.* (*informal*).
toe [tou] *nc* **1.** one of the five parts at the end of the foot. *I've hurt my big toe* i.e. the one on the inner side of the foot which is bigger than the other four. **2.** front of a shoe, sock etc which covers the toes. *There is a hole in the toe of your sock.* Also *vt* put the toes on; touch with the toes.
'toecap part of a shoe or boot which covers the toes.
'toehold space only big enough to put the toes in when climbing a rock, wall etc.
'toenail nail growing on a toe.
from head/top to toe (with reference to persons) from head to foot; from top to bottom; all over.
toe the line see **line**[1].
on one's toes ready to act quickly; well prepared for something. (*informal*).
toffee ['tɔfi] *nc/u* (*Brit*) type of hard sweet made from sugar and butter. (*US* **taffy**).
tog [tɔg] *vt* (with **out** or **up**) dress. *She was togged out/up in a new coat and hat. past* **togged.** (*informal*).
togs *npl* clothes. (*informal*).
toga ['tougə] *nc* loose outer garment worn by men in ancient Rome.

toga

together [tə'geðə*] *adv* **1.** in one group; in

the company of others. *Let's go to the shop together. I want to speak to them all together. Note: all together* has the meaning of everybody/everything included; *altogether* has the meaning of completely; entirely; when everything is carefully considered: *an altogether stupid idea. So altogether, I think it would be better to try something else.* **2.** in, to the same place; at the same time. *Please put the books together on the desk. His arrival and my departure happened together.* **3.** without a stop. *The meeting went on for hours together.*

togetherness *nu* friendly feeling of belonging together.

together with along with; added to. *My money together with his will be enough.*

toggle ['tɔgl] *nc* short piece of wood attached to a piece of string etc which can be used like a button.

toil [tɔil] *vi* work hard; move slowly and with difficulty. *They toiled all day digging the hole. We toiled across the desert under the hot sun.* Also *nu.*

toiler *nc* person who works, or has to work, hard.

toilsome *adj* needing hard work; tiring. **toilsomely** *adv.*

toilet ['tɔilət] **1.** *nc* water closet; lavatory. *Where is the toilet in this house?* **2.** *nu* act of dressing, tidying oneself, brushing one's hair etc: *take care over one's toilet* (*o.f.* in sense **2.**).

'toilet paper paper used in a lavatory.

'toilet roll roll of toilet paper.

'toilet soap scented soap of good quality used when washing the hands and face or when having a bath.

'toilet water sweet-smelling water put on the skin.

toils [tɔilz] *npl* **1.** nets used for trapping. **2.** difficulties which one cannot get out of.

token ['toukən] *nc* **1.** proof of something; sign. *We sent her flowers as a token of our gratitude.* **2.** disc or card used instead of money for a particular purpose: *milk token* i.e. a disc used instead of money when paying for milk; *book token* i.e. card used instead of money to buy a book. Also *adj* giving proof of something without doing it completely: *token payment* i.e. payment of a small amount of money to show that one agrees to pay the whole amount; *token strike* i.e. strike by workmen which is not complete but is a warning to employers that a real strike may take place.

told [tould] past of **tell.**

tolerate ['tɔləreit] *vt* allow something to be done even although one does not like it; endure somebody/something one does not like. *The government tolerates smoking and drinking but not taking drugs. I can't tolerate the noise any longer.*

tolerable ['tɔlərəbl] *adj* able to be tolerated; quite good. (*opp* **intolerable**). **tolerably** *adv.*

tolerant ['tɔlərnt] *adj* ready to allow or endure somebody/something even although one does not like it. *The people in this country are very tolerant about/of the strange behaviour of visitors.* (*opp* **intolerant**). **tolerantly** *adv.* **tolerance** ['tɔlərns], **toleration** [tɔlə'reiʃən] *nu.*

toll[1] [toul] *nc* **1.** money paid to use a bridge, ferry, road etc. **2.** damage; loss: *toll of malaria in tropical countries* i.e. deaths caused by malaria.

'tollgate gate across a road or bridge where a toll is paid.

'tollhouse house where the person who collects tolls lives.

toll[2] [toul] *vt/i* (with reference to a bell) ring slowly and deeply. Also *nu* sound made by a bell ringing in this way.

tomahawk ['tɔməhɔːk] *nc* type of small axe used as a weapon by North American Indians.

tomato [tə'mɑːtou, *US* tə'meitou] *nc* **1.** type of plant with soft red or yellow fruit used as a salad vegetable. **2.** the fruit itself. *pl* **tomatoes.**

tomb [tuːm] *nc* place dug or built in which a dead person is put; grave.

'tombstone stone put above a tomb.

tomboy ['tɔmbɔi] *nc* girl who behaves like a boy.

tomcat ['tɔmkæt] *nc* male cat.

tome [toum] *nc* large book (*o.f.* or used as a joke).

tomorrow [tə'mɔrou] *nu* day after today; the future. *Tomorrow is a holiday. The boy of today is the man of tomorrow.* Also *adv* on the day after today. *I'll see you tomorrow.*

to'morrow 'week, a 'week to'morrow a week from tomorrow i.e. in eight days' time.

tomtom ['tɔmtɔm] *nc* type of drum. *pl* **tomtoms.**

ton [tʌn] *nc* unit of weight equal to 20 hundredweight. see appendix.

tone [toun] **1.** *nc/u* sound made by a musical instrument or voice: *deep tones of the church bells. I don't like the tone of his voice. She spoke in a high tone.* **2.** *nc* shade of colour; effect caused by colour. *The bright tones of the picture are seen better against the quiet tone of the wall.* **3.** *nu* condition; character. *The tone of a school depends on both the teachers and the pupils.* **4.** *nc* one of five large intervals between notes in the musical scale. Also *vt/i* **1.** have, cause to have, a certain tone (of sound or colour). **2.** (with reference to colours) agree with. *Her hat toned (in) well with her dress.*

tonal *adj* of tone.

tonality [tə'næliti] *nu* quality of tone in a piece of music; colour scheme in a picture.

-toned *adj* having a particular tone: *deep-toned voice.*

toneless *adj* without tone; dull. **tonelessly** *adv.*

'tone-'deaf *adj* unable to distinguish different musical notes.

tone something down become or make less loud, bright or strong. *Please tone down your voice.*

tone something up become, cause to become, brighter or stronger. *You must tone up this picture if you wish it to attract people. He toned up his body by taking long walks.*

tongs [tɔŋz] *npl* device or tool for picking up and holding something: *sugar tongs; coal tongs.*

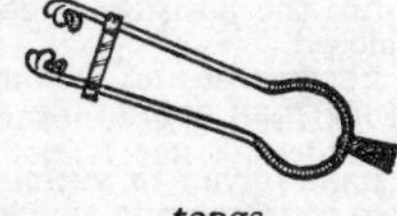

tongs

go at it hammer and tongs see **go.**

tongue [tʌŋ] **1.** *nc* movable piece of flesh in the mouth used for licking, swallowing and tasting and (in humans) for speaking. **2.** *nc* language: *the English tongue.* **3.** *nc* way of speaking. *He has a sharp tongue* i.e. an angry way of speaking when annoyed. **4.** *nc* something which has the shape of a tongue: *tongue of a shoe* i.e. strip of leather below the laces. A *tongue of land projects into the sea.* **5.** *nc/u* tongue of an animal used as food. *He was eating boiled tongue.*

-tongued *adj* having a tongue: *smooth-tongued man* i.e. a man who speaks smoothly.

'tongue-tied *adj* unable to speak because of embarrassment or surprise. *I was tongue-tied with surprise.*

'tongue twister word or words difficult to say quickly.

have one's tongue in one's cheek, say something tongue in cheek say something which is not meant to be taken seriously. (*informal*).

find one's tongue begin to speak after being silent. (*opp* **lose one's tongue**) (*informal*).

hold one's tongue keep quiet. (*informal*).

lose one's tongue be unable to speak. (*informal*).

put/stick out one's tongue show one's tongue either to be examined by a doctor or as a sign of rudeness. *He put out his tongue at me.*

on the tip of one's tongue just about to be said. *It was on the tip of my tongue to tell him he was wrong.* (*informal*).

tonic ['tɔnik] *nc* something which helps to bring back health and strength. *The doctor told me to get a tonic* i.e. type of medicine to make me healthier and stronger. *Fresh air is a good tonic.* Also *adj* **1.** giving back health and strength. **2.** of musical tones.

'tonic sol'fa system of showing musical notes of the scale by words i.e. *doh, ray, me, fah, so, la, tee.*

'tonic water mixture of water and quinine: *gin and tonic (water).*

tonight [tə'nait] *nu* night after this day/today. *Tonight's concert will be a good one.* Also *adv* on the night after this day/today. *I'll see you tonight.*

tonnage ['tʌnidʒ] *nc/u* **1.** space available inside a ship in tons (each ton = 100 cubic feet). **2.** amount of cargo a ship can actually carry (each ton = 40 cubic feet). **3.** total number of ships belonging to a country or company measured in tons (100 cubic feet). **4.** money paid for cargo per ton (40 cubic feet).

tonsil ['tɔnsl] *nc* one of the two small organs at the back of the throat which sometimes become diseased and have to be taken away.

tonsillitis [tɔnsi'laitis] *nu* disease of the tonsils.

tonsure ['tɔnʃə*] *nc* top of a person's head shaved to show that he is a priest or monk; act of shaving in this way. Also *vt* shave the head in this way.

too [tu:] *adv/intensifier* **1.** also; as well. *She went and I went too. She used to live in London. Me too.*

Note: too is not used after a negative; *either* is used instead (e.g. not *I, too, don't like coffee* but *I don't like coffee either.* not *He, too, does not speak English and French* but *He does not speak English or French either*). **2.** more than is necessary. *He talks too much. The coat is too big for me.* **3.** so very much (that). *I was too angry to answer.*

Note: the difference between *too little* and *a little too. The coat is too little for me. The coat is a little too big for me* i.e. rather too big; big but not by much.

all too (with reference to time) more than is wished. *His visit was all too short. The day passed all too quickly.*

none too not at all too. *This coat is none too big for me* i.e. it is about the right size or too small. *We arrived none too soon for the meeting* i.e. just in time for it. (*informal*).

only too very: *only too anxious to help.*

took [tuk] past tense of **take.**

tool [tu:l] *nc* **1.** instrument held or controlled by the hands or by machinery (e.g. axe, hammer, hoe, spanner). **2.** person who is used like a tool by somebody to do something (usu. something wrong). Also *vt* cut or shape with a tool.

'toolbag bag for holding tools.

'toolbox box for holding tools.

'machine tool cutting tool driven by power, used to make parts of a machine.

'power tool tool driven by power (usu. electricity).

toot [tu:t] *nc* short but loud sound (e.g. one made by the horn of a motorcar, a ship's siren). Also *vt/i* make, cause to make, this sound.

tooth [tu:θ] *nc* **1.** one of the bones arranged in two rows in the mouth and used for biting and chewing. **2.** something shaped like a tooth: *tooth of a comb/saw. pl* **teeth** [ti:θ].

toothless *adj* without teeth.

toothsome *adj* having a pleasant taste. (rather *o.f.*).

'toothache pain in a tooth or teeth.

'toothbrush brush for cleaning the teeth.

'toothpaste, 'tooth powder substance used for cleaning the teeth.

'toothpick small pointed stick used for cleaning between the teeth.

'fine-tooth 'comb small comb with teeth which are very close together.

go through something with a fine-tooth comb search something carefully.

armed to the teeth heavily armed.

cut a tooth see **cut**[1].

escape by the skin of one's teeth see **skin.**

fight tooth and nail fight as hard as one can. (*informal*).

in the teeth of against; in opposition to. *The motion was carried in the teeth of fierce opposition.*

long in the tooth (with reference to animals and people) old. (*informal* when reference is to people).

top[1] [tɔp] *nc* **1.** highest part: *the top of the mountain; tops of the flowers.* **2.** most important position; first in rank. *He was sitting at the top of the table* i.e. at the end of the table where important persons sit. *He is (at the) top of his class* i.e. he is the best boy in it. **3.** upper side. *Put the box here with its top up. The top of his desk was covered with books.* Also *adj* highest; most important. *He lives on the top floor. The train went at top speed. Who is the top man here?*

topmost *adj* highest.

'top boot type of long boot reaching to the knee.

'topcoat overcoat.

'top 'dog winner; somebody who is more important than the others. (*informal*) (*opp* **underdog**).

'top dressing layer of manure or fertilizer put on the surface of the soil and not dug in.

'top 'hat type of tall hat shaped like a cylinder with a rim.
'top-'heavy *adj* too heavy at the top and so likely to fall over.
'top-'ranking *adj* highest in rank.
'top-'secret *adj* most secret; secret and very important.
big top circus tent.
from top to bottom throughout; completely.
in top (gear) using the highest gear.
on top above the others. *I put your bag on top.*
on (the) top of **1.** above; over. *I put your bag on (the) top of mine.* **2.** also; as well. *He gave me a meal and on top of that, money for my journey.*
at the top of one's voice as loudly as one can.
get on top of **1.** be successful in dealing with (something difficult). *We are getting on top of the problem at last.* **2.** be too much for. *Things are getting on top of me.*

top² [tɔp] *vt* **1.** cover; have as a top. *She topped the cake with nuts. The mountain was topped with snow.* **2.** be higher or better than. *This building tops all the others in the city.* **3.** arrive at the top of; pass over the top of. *His car topped the steep hill easily.* **4.** cut the tops off. *He topped the young trees to make them grow thicker. past* **topped.**
top something up fill to the required level: *top up a battery/petrol tank etc.*

top³ [tɔp] *nc* type of toy which is made to spin on its pointed end.

topaz ['toupæz] *nc/u* type of precious stone (usu. yellow in colour).

tope [toup] *vt/i* drink alcoholic liquors too often or too much. **toper** *nc.* (both *o.f.*).

topee ['toupi:] *nc* light helmet formerly worn to protect the head from the sun.

topic ['tɔpik] *nc* subject talked or written about.
topical *adj* talked or written about now; up-to-date; current. **topically** *adv.*

topography [tɔ'pɔgrəfi] *nu* description of what a place looks like; character of a place. *It is not easy to travel in a city if you do not know its topography.* **topographical** [tɔpə'græfikl] *adj.* **topographically** *adv.* **topographer** *nc.*

topple ['tɔpl] *vt/i* (with reference to something high) fall; cause to fall. *The tree toppled down/over.*

topsy-turvy ['tɔpsi'tə:vi] *adj/adv* upside down; in disorder. (*informal*).

torch [tɔ:tʃ] *nc* **1.** piece of wood or rope soaked in oil or grease and used as a light which can be carried. **2.** (*Brit*) electric light with battery which can be carried. (*US* **flashlight**).

torches (*def 1*) (*def 2*)

'torchlight light given by a torch: *torchlight procession* i.e. one which is lit by torches.

tore [tɔ:*] past tense of **tear².**

toreador ['tɔriədɔ:*] *nc* Spanish bullfighter.

torment ['tɔ:ment] *nc/u* great pain of body or mind; something which causes this. *We suffered torment/torments from thirst. The flies were a torment.* Also [tɔ:'ment] *vt* cause great pain or annoyance to.
tormentor [tɔ:'mentə*] *nc* somebody/something which torments.

torn [tɔ:n] past part of **tear².**

tornado [tɔ:'neidou] *nc* violent wind which goes round and round. *pl* **tornadoes.**

torpedo [tɔ:'pi:dou] *nc* long metal container, filled with explosives and travelling below the surface of the sea, which is used against ships by other ships, submarines and aircraft. *pl* **torpedoes.** Also *vt* attack or hit with a torpedo.
tor'pedo boat type of fast warship which attacks with torpedoes.
tor'pedo tube type of tube from which a torpedo is fired.

torpid ['tɔ:pid] *adj* slow; without energy. **torpidly** *adv.* **torpidity** [tɔ:'piditi], **torpor** ['tɔ:pə*] *nu.*

torque [tɔ:k] **1.** *nc* necklace made from twisted wire. **2.** *nu* twisting force of the kind used in a machine to make a wheel go round.

torrent ['tɔrnt] *nc* **1.** violent flow of liquid (usu. water). *The rain fell in torrents. We crossed the torrent by a small bridge* i.e. the small, swiftly moving river. **2.** violent flow of words: *torrent of abuse.*
torrential [tə'renʃl] *adj* of, like a torrent.

torrid ['tɔrid] *adj* (with reference to weather) hot.

torsion ['tɔ:ʃən] *nu* act or force of twisting or being twisted.

torso ['tɔ:sou] *nc* human body or statue without head and limbs; human trunk. *pl* **torsos.**

tortoise ['tɔ:təs] *nc* type of land animal which has a hard shell on its back and moves slowly.

tortuous ['tɔ:tjuəs] *adj* **1.** having many bends and twists: *tortuous road over the hills.* **2.** difficult to understand; dishonest. *He has a tortuous mind.* **tortuously** *adv.* **tortuousness** *nu.*

torture ['tɔ:tʃə*] *nc/u* act of causing somebody great pain as a punishment or in order to make him confess something; great pain. *They say that in that country the police use torture. I suffered tortures from headaches.* Also *vt* cause great pain. *In former times they tortured prisoners. I was tortured by headaches.* **torturer** *nc.*

Tory ['tɔ:ri] *n* member of the Conservative Party in British politics. Also *adj.*

toss [tɔs] *vt/i* **1.** throw. *He tossed me the newspaper.* **2.** move, cause to move, up and down or from side to side. *I tossed about in my bed because I could not sleep. The horse tossed its head.* Also *nc* act of throwing or being thrown; quick movement. *He had a nasty toss from his horse. He gave an angry toss of his head.*
toss up throw a coin into the air to decide something according to which side (heads or tails) falls upwards.
'toss-up *nc* **1.** act of tossing a coin. **2.** something which may or may not happen. *It is a toss-up whether I'll go.* (*informal* in sense **2.**).
toss someone for something decide by tossing up a coin whether someone else should do or get something. *'Who will go first?' 'I'll toss you for it'.*
toss something off finish quickly and easily.

He tossed off his drink. I tossed off a few lines to my friend i.e. wrote them quickly.
win the toss be correct in guessing which side of a coin falls upwards after it has been tossed up. (*opp* **lose the toss**). *Our football team did not win the toss and had to play against the wind.*

tot[1] [tɔt] *nc* **1.** small child. **2.** small measure of alcoholic liquor.

tot[2] [tɔt] *vt/i* (with **up**) add; count. *past* **totted.**

total ['toutl] *adj* complete; full. *What is the total cost of these books? He was a total stranger to me.* Also *nc* the whole; sum after adding everything up. *If you add 6 and 4, the total is 10.* Also *vt/i* amount to; add up. *My money totals only ten pence. Please total this bill for me. past* **totalled.** (*US* **totaled**).
totally *adv* completely. **totality** [tou'tæliti] *nu.*

totalitarian [toutæli'tɛəriən] *adj* of a government which allows only one political party and no opposition.
totalitarianism *nu* government of this kind.

totalizator, totalizer ['toutəlaiz(eit)ə*] *nc* automatic betting machine at horse and dog races. (Also informally **the tote**).

tote[1] [tout] *vt* (*US*) carry. (*informal*).

tote[2] [tout] *nc* see **totalizator.**

totem ['toutəm] *nc* animal or plant believed by some primitive people to belong to their group and to have special powers in it.
'**totem pole** thick pole on which a totem is carved.

totter ['tɔtə*] *vi* move or walk as if about to fall.
tottery *adj* about to fall; unsteady.

toucan ['tu:kən] *nc* type of very colourful bird with a long beak found in the forests of Central and South America.

touch[1] [tʌtʃ] *vt/i* **1.** come in contact with. *Her dress is touching the floor. His car touched mine as it passed but did no damage.* **2.** press gently with the hand; feel. *I touched him on the shoulder. Please don't touch my books.* **3.** reach. *Can you touch your toes?* **4.** (usu. with **not** or **never**) have anything to do with. *He never touches beer. He hasn't touched his work for weeks.* **5.** move the feelings; affect. *I was very touched by his kindness. The words touched his pride.* **6.** (usu. with **not** or **never etc**) be as good as; equal. *We cannot touch them for intelligence* i.e. we are not nearly as intelligent as they are.
touchable *adj* able to be touched. (*opp* **untouchable**).
touched *adj* mad. *That man is slightly touched.* (*informal*).
touching *adj* moving the feelings: *touching request for help.* **touchingly** *adv.*
touch at something (with reference to ships) visit for a short time. *The ship will touch at Freetown on its way to Europe.*
touch down 1. (with reference to aircraft) land. **2.** (with reference to rugby or American football) put the ball on the ground over the goal line and thus score.
'**touchdown** *nc* **1.** landing. **2.** putting the ball on the ground.
touch somebody for something ask or borrow something from somebody. *He touched me for fifty pence.* (*informal*).
touch something off cause to begin suddenly. *His remark touched off an argument.*
touch on/upon something mention or deal with in a few words.
touch something up improve slightly by making a few changes. *The artist was touching up the landscape he had painted.*
touch bottom 1. reach the bottom (usu. in water). **2.** reach the lowest point in behaviour, luck etc.
touch wood hope for good luck. (*informal*).

touch[2] [tʌtʃ] **1.** *nc* act of coming in contact with. *He felt a touch on his shoulder.* **2.** *nu* feeling; sensation. *A blind man has to use his sense of touch a lot. The child's face was hot to the touch.* **3.** *nc* small amount. *She added a touch of sugar. I have a touch of the cold* i.e. a slight cold. **4.** *nc* (often *pl*) slight improvement. *With a few more touches my essay will be ready.* **5.** *nu* style, skill (esp. with the hands). *She played the piano with a light touch.* **6.** *nu* part of a football pitch outside the sidelines. *He kicked the ball into touch.*
touchy *adj* easily made angry. **touchily** *adv.* **touchiness** *nu.*
'**touchline** sideline of a football pitch.
'**touchstone** something used as a standard by which something else is judged. *The teacher uses this pupil's work as a touchstone for the rest of the class.*
at a touch even if only touched. *The pile of books will fall at a touch.*
in touch with in communication or correspondence with; informed about. *He is in touch with the head office. Do you keep in touch with events in Africa?*
lose touch with be no longer in touch with.
lose one's touch no longer have the same skill that one used to have.
out of touch with not in communication or correspondence with; not informed about. *I am out of touch with my family.*
touch-and-go *adj* very uncertain. *It is touch-and-go whether he will pass the examination.* (*informal*).

tough [tʌf] *adj* **1.** difficult to bend, break, cut, chew etc. *This cloth is tough; tough meat.* **2.** (with reference to persons) difficult to frighten; energetic; able to endure hardship. *In an argument he can be very tough. To be a good runner, you must be tough.* **3.** difficult. *This is a tough job.* Also *nc* person who is rough and violent; criminal. *I was attacked on the way home by two toughs.*
toughly *adv.* **toughness** *nu.*
toughen *vt/i* become, cause to become, tough.
get tough with someone be more severe to someone; become less friendly towards someone. *If you don't answer our questions we'll get tough with you.* (*informal*).

toupée ['tu:pei] *nc* piece of false hair worn over a bald part of the head.

tour [tuə*] *nc* **1.** journey during which one visits several places and then returns to the place where one started. *They are making a tour of Scotland. He is on tour in Africa. The orchestra will be on tour next summer* i.e. it will play in several places. **2.** period of work overseas. *I did my first tour in East Africa and my second in West Africa.* Also *vt/i* make a tour of. *They are touring Scotland.*
touring *nu* act of touring, being on tour.
tourist *nc* person who tours (esp. when on holiday). Also *adj* **1.** for tourists: *tourist hotel.* **2.** cheaper, of a lower class of travel. *We travelled home by tourist class on the ship.* Also *adv*: *We always travel tourist.*
tourism *nu* practice of touring; industry depending on tourists. *All countries now encourage tourism.*

tour de force ['tuədə'fɔːs] *n* performance or achievement showing great skill.

tournament ['tuənəmənt] *nc* **1.** organized competition in a sport or game for a number of players to find out who is best: *golf tournament.* **2.** (in the Middle Ages) number of friendly fights arranged between knights on horseback. (Also **tourney**).

tourney ['tuəni] *nc* see **tournament.**

tourniquet ['tuənikei] *nc* band twisted tightly round the arm, leg etc to stop bleeding.

tousle ['tauzl] *vt* make the hair untidy by pushing the fingers through it etc.

tout [taut] *nc* (often with reference to person who sells information about horse-races) person who stops people or follows them about in order to get them to buy something from him. Also *vt/i* work as a tout.

tow[1] [tou] *vt* pull along by a rope or chain. *The ship was towed into harbour.* Also *nc/u* act of towing or being towed. *The tug took the ship in tow. He asked us for a tow.*

'**towline** rope used for towing.

'**towpath** path beside a canal or river once used by horses for towing boats.

tow[2] [tau] *nu* rough fibre used for making ropes.

toward, towards [tə'wɔːd(z)] *prep* **1.** in the direction of. *He came toward(s) me. The window faces toward(s) the hills.* **2.** (with reference to time) near; just before. *We should arrive toward(s) nine o'clock. There was a storm toward(s) evening. Toward(s) the end of the day I became tired.* **3.** with reference to. *I could not feel angry toward(s) them.* **4.** resulting in; in order to get. *These talks are a step toward(s) agreement. They are working toward(s) peace.*

towel ['tauəl] *nc* cloth or paper used for drying something which is wet. Also *vt* dry with a towel. *past* **towelled.** (*US* **toweled**).

towelling *nu* type of soft cloth used for making towels.

'**towel rail** rail on which towels are hung.

'**bath towel** large towel used after having a bath.

'**tea towel** small towel used to dry dishes.

throw in the towel (often with reference to boxing) admit defeat.

tower ['tauə*] *nc* tall, narrow building or part of a building formerly for defence. Also *vi* **1.** rise high. *The hotel towers above/over the houses round it.* **2.** (with reference to persons) very big or very outstanding. *He is so intelligent that he towers above all the others in his class.*

tower

towering *adj* (used with **anger, rage, bad temper etc**) very great.

town [taun] *nc/u* **1.** group of houses and buildings larger than a village. **2.** people who live in a town. *The whole town is talking about the news.* **3.** (without **a** or **the**) centre of a town where the offices and shops are. *He works in town and lives in the suburbs. We took a bus across/down/up town.* **4.** (without **a** or **the** and esp. with reference to London, England) capital; most important town. *I travel up to town from Oxford once a week.* **5.** (with **the**) towns in general. *Prices are higher in the town than in the country.*

Note: (*Brit*) *town* is used even with reference to a *city*, because *city* tends to give the sense of its official organizations, local government etc. There is little difference in sense between *Manchester is a big town* and *Manchester is a big city*, but one must say *Manchester City Police; City of Manchester's secondary schools.* (*US*) *city* is more often used. *Town* there refers more definitely to a smaller place.

township *nc* small town or area, sometimes one which has a different form of local government from the country round about it.

'**town** '**council** *nc* group of people elected to govern a town.

'**town** '**councillor** *nc* member of a town council.

'**townsfolk,** '**townspeople** people who live in a town.

'**town** '**hall** building used by the officials of a town and also used for meetings etc.

'**townsman** man who lives in a town.

'**town** '**planning** designing of a town to make its streets, housing etc pleasant and efficient.

toxic ['tɔksik] *adj* poisonous.

toxin ['tɔksin] *nc/u* poison (esp. in a living thing).

toxicology [tɔksi'kɔlədʒi] *nu* science of poisons. **toxicologist** [tɔksi'kɔlədʒist] *nc.*

toy [tɔi] *nc* something a child plays with. Also *adj*: *toy train.* Also *vt* play with; consider in a casual way. *He sat toying with his gloves. I toyed with the idea of going.*

'**toyshop** shop which sells toys.

trace[1] [treis] *nc* **1.** mark made by something which has passed or has existed. *We could not find any trace(s) of the cattle.* **2.** small amount. *There are traces of gold in this rock.* Also *vt* **1.** follow marks or signs in order to find something. *We are trying to trace our cattle.* **2.** copy (esp. by putting a thin piece of paper over something). *They traced the map in the atlas onto a sheet of paper.*

tracer *nc* **1.** person who traces. **2.** bullet or shell which is made to be seen when fired by the flame or smoke it leaves behind it. (Also **tracer bullet**).

tracing *nc* copy of something made by tracing it on thin paper.

tracery *nc/u* pattern of lines (esp. one cut in stone).

'**trace element** substance occurring in small quantities in something else (esp. in soil) and considered important for living things.

'**tracer element** radioactive element which is put in something. (The movement of the element is then traced by an instrument which records radioactivity).

'**tracing paper** thin, transparent paper used for tracing.

trace[2] [treis] *nc* leather strap joining a horse to what it is pulling (e.g. a cart, carriage). **kick over the traces** refuse to obey; get out of control. (*informal* if reference is not to horses).

trachoma [træ'koumə] *nu* disease of the eyes.

track [træk] *nc* **1.** mark left by something as it moves. *The tracks of the car could be seen in the mud* i.e. marks made by its

tyres. ***We** followed the lion's tracks* i.e. marks made by its paws. **2.** path made by humans or animals constantly using it. *We walked along the track to the village.* **3.** course or way specially prepared for something: *racetrack; railway track.* **4.** moving band of metal used on tractors, military tanks etc instead of wheels. **5.** band of magnetized tape for a tape recorder. Also *vt* follow the track of; find by following the track of. *We tracked him to his house.*
tracked *adj* fitted with a moving band of metal instead of wheels. *An army tank is a tracked vehicle.*
tracker *nc* person who is skilled at following tracks (esp. in Africa).
trackless *adj* without paths.
'sound track see **sound**[1].
track someone/something down follow someone/something until it is found.
cover up one's tracks hide what one has been doing.
go off the track **1.** take the wrong way. **2.** (with reference to a train) leave the rails.
in one's tracks where one is standing; quickly. *He stopped in his tracks.*
keep track of follow the track of; keep informed about. (*opp* **lose track of**).
make tracks for set out for; go towards. (*informal*).
have a one-track mind see **one**[2].
off the beaten track away from towns, main roads etc.
on the track of somebody/something following; pursuing.

tract[1] [trækt] *nc* **1.** area of land. **2.** group of organs of the body which work together (e.g. *the digestive tract*).

tract[2] [trækt] *nc* printed article or small book about a particular subject (esp. a religious one).

tractable ['træktəbl] *adj* able to be controlled. (*opp* **intractable**). **tractability** [træktə'biliti] *nu*.

traction ['trækʃən] *nu* act of pulling something along; power needed to do so.
'traction engine type of engine used for pulling along heavy loads.

tractor ['træktə*] *nc* vehicle used for pulling heavy loads (e.g. machinery used in agriculture).

trade[1] [treid] **1.** *nu* business of buying and selling. *Trade between Europe and Asia has increased. They are in the book trade.* **2.** *nc* occupation; work (esp. skilled work in industry etc). *I am a mechanic by trade. Boys leaving school can be trained for many trades.* **3.** *nu* (with **the**) persons working in a particular trade. *The new tax on clothes is not liked by the trade* i.e. those who make or sell clothes.
'tradesman shopkeeper.
'trademark special mark put on goods to show what company made them.
'trade name special name which is given to a particular article by the company making it and which only that company can use in trade.
'tradespeople shopkeepers.
'trade 'price price of goods between tradespeople for later sale at a retail price.
'trade 'union *nc* recognized organization of workers in one or more trades to get better conditions of work, more pay etc.
'trade 'unionism *nu* system or principles of trade unions.
'trade 'unionist *nc* person who belongs to a trade union.
'trade wind one of the two winds which blow between the tropics and the equator. (A north-east wind north of the equator and a south-east one south of the equator).

trade[2] [treid] *vt/i* **1.** buy and sell; have as a business. *In former times the people of this country traded in gold, ivory and slaves.* **2.** (*US*) exchange. *I'll trade my book for your watch.* **trader** *nc*.
'trading estate area of land in which factories are built by the government and then rented to manufacturers.
trade something in give an old article as part payment for a new one. *I have traded my old radio in for a transistor.*
trade on/upon something use unfairly for one's own purposes. *He traded on/upon his brother's kindness to get more money from him.*

tradition [trə'diʃən] *nc/u* belief, custom or story passed down from age to age and not usually written. *According to tradition the first king came from another country. As a child he learnt the traditions of his tribe.* **traditional** *adj*. **traditionally** *adv*.
traditionalism *nu* belief in the importance of tradition.
traditionalist *nc* person who has this belief.

traduce [trə'djuːs] *vt* speak badly about the character of somebody; slander.

traffic ['træfik] *nu* **1.** flow of people and vehicles along the roads, of ships over the sea or aircraft through the sky. *There is always a lot of traffic in the centre of a town; heavy/light traffic* i.e. a lot of/very little traffic. **2.** (often in a bad sense) trade; commerce. *There was a big traffic in drugs.*
trafficker *nc* (usu. in a bad sense) trader.
'traffic lights device fitted with red, orange and green lights to control traffic on the roads.

tragedy ['trædʒədi] *nc/u* **1.** serious play with a sad ending; type of drama of this kind. **2.** any very sad event. *The loss of all our money was a tragedy.*
tragedian [trə'dʒiːdiən] *nc* person who writes, or acts in, tragedies.
tragedienne [trədʒiːdi'en] *nc* woman who acts in tragedies.
tragic ['trædʒik] *adj* of tragedy; very sad. **tragically** *adv*.
tragicomedy ['trædʒi'kɔmədi] *nc/u* play etc having both tragic and comic parts.

trail [treil] *nc* **1.** lines, marks or scent left by somebody/something that has passed by. *There was a trail of water across the floor from the hole in the bucket.* **2.** rough path through wild country. Also *vt/i* **1.** follow the trail of. *The hunter trailed the wounded buffalo through the bush.* **2.** pull, be pulled, along. *Her long dress trailed along the floor.* **3.** walk slowly because one is tired. *The children trailed behind their teacher.* **4.** (with reference to plants) spread over.
trailer **1.** vehicle pulled along by another vehicle. **2.** short parts of a film shown in a cinema as an advertisement before the complete film is shown later.

train[1] [trein] *vt/i* **1.** prepare somebody for something by teaching and practice; prepare oneself in this way. *My parents trained me to behave properly. Our football team is training for the next game.* **2.** aim; point at. *He trained his binoculars on the ship.* **3.** (with reference to plants) cause to grow in a certain way. *They trained the vines up the wall.*
trained *adj* skilled; fully qualified. *He is a*

trained teacher. (*opp* **untrained**).

trainer *nc* person who trains athletes, horses etc (esp. for sports, races etc).

training *nu* act of preparing somebody for something; act of preparing oneself for something. *The training of teachers is done at universities and colleges. He is in training for the school sports.*

trainee [trei'ni:] *nc* person who is being trained (esp. in industry).

train[2] [trein] *nc* **1.** line of carriages or wagons pulled by a railway engine. *We went by train to London. Does this train go to Edinburgh?* **2.** line of moving persons or animals (esp. one behind somebody/something). *The chief was followed by a train of soldiers and servants.* **3.** back of a long dress which trails behind on the ground. **4.** number of connected events or ideas. *The train of events led to war. I cannot follow the train of his thoughts.*

'**trainbearer** person who holds the train of a long dress up off the ground.

put in train cause to begin; make preparations for. *We have put in train the arrangements for the President's visit.*

trait [treit] *nc* special feature (esp. of somebody's character). *One of his traits is complete honesty.*

traitor ['treitə*] *nc* person who helps the enemies of his country or is not faithful to his friends etc. *During the war he was a traitor to his country.*

traitorous *adj* of a traitor; unfaithful. **traitorously** *adv.*

traitress ['treitris] *nc* woman who is a traitor.

trajectory [trə'dʒektəri] *nc* curved path of a bullet, shell etc through the air.

tram [træm] *nc* (*Brit*) public vehicle which is driven by electricity and runs on rails laid on a road. (Also **tramcar,** *US* **streetcar**).

trammel ['træml] *vt* hinder. *past* **trammelled.** (*US* **trammeled**).

trammels *npl* something which hinders.

tramp [træmp] *vt/i* **1.** walk heavily. *They tramped over the carpet in their big boots.* **2.** go for a long walk (esp. through fields, over hills etc). Also **1.** *nu* (with **the**) sound made by walking heavily: *the tramp of soldiers marching through the streets.* **2.** *nc* long walk. **3.** *nc* (*Brit*) person who has no home and does no work, and travels from place to place. (*US* **hobo; bum** (*informal*) – *US* **tramp** usually has the sense of an immoral woman).

trample ['træmpl] *vt* walk heavily on, and so damage or crush, somebody/something. *The cows got into the field and trampled (down) the corn.*

trampoline ['træmpəli:n] *nc* strong frame covered with canvas used by acrobats and gymnasts to jump high in the air.

trance [trɑ:ns] *nc* state of unconsciousness during which a person seems to be asleep but can see or do strange things. *The holy man fell into a trance* i.e. became unconscious in this way.

tranquil ['træŋkwil] *adj* quiet; peaceful. **tranquilly** *adv.* **tranquillity** [træŋ'kwiliti] *nu.*

tranquillize *vt* make calm (esp. by drugs).

tranquillizer *nc* drug which makes a person calm, less worried etc.

trans- [træns] *prefix* across; beyond; on the other side of (e.g. **transcontinental**).

transact [træn'zækt] *vt* (usu. with reference to business) carry out; do.

transaction 1. *nc/u* piece of business done; act of transacting business. **2.** *nc* (in *pl*) activities and written records of a club or society.

transatlantic ['trænzət'læntik] *adj* across or on the other side of the Atlantic.

transcend [træn'send] *vt* (esp. with reference to the limits of knowledge, experience etc) go further than; be better than. *The origin of the universe transcends human understanding.*

transcendent *adj* beyond the limits of knowledge etc; excellent. **transcendental** [trænsən'dentl] *adj.* **transcendence, transcendency** *nu.*

transcontinental ['trænskɔnti'nentl] *adj* crossing a continent.

transcribe [træns'kraib] *vt* (esp. with reference to writing out in full notes taken in shorthand) write out again.

transcript ['trænskript] *nc* something which has been transcribed.

transcription [træns'kripʃən] **1.** *nu* act of transcribing. **2.** *nc* something which has been transcribed or recorded in a particular way (e.g. a piece of music; a broadcast recorded for future use).

transept ['trænsept] *nc* part of a church which is at right angles to the nave.

transfer [træns'fə:*] *vt/i* **1.** move from one place to another. *He transferred the money from the box to his pocket. I was transferred from the district office to headquarters.* **2.** copy a design, photograph on one surface to another. **3.** change from one type of job to another. *Next term he wants to transfer from history to economics.* **4.** hand over legally. *The government has transferred primary education to the local councils. past* **transferred.** Also ['trænsfə:*] *nc* **1.** act of transferring or being transferred. *I was given a transfer to headquarters.* **2.** something/someone transferred (e.g. a design, photograph, football player).

transferable *adj* able to be transferred.

transfigure [træns'figə*] *vt* change the appearance of by making more beautiful. *Her face was transfigured with joy.* **transfiguration** [trænsfigə'reiʃən] *nc/u.*

transfix [træns'fiks] *vt* **1.** push a knife, sword etc right through. **2.** cause somebody to be unable to move or think.

transform [træns'fɔ:m] *vt* change the form, nature or character of. *Water can transform a desert into a garden.* **transformation** [trænsfə'meiʃən] *nc/u.*

transformable *adj* able to be transformed.

transformer *nc* **1.** person who transforms. **2.** something which transforms (esp. a device which changes the voltage of an alternating electric current).

transfuse [træns'fju:z] *vt* take blood from one person and put it into another.

transfusion [træns'fju:ʒən] *nc/u*: *The doctor gave him a blood transfusion after the accident.*

transgress [trænz'gres] *vt/i* break a rule; do wrong. **transgressor** *nc.*

transgression *nc/u* act of transgressing.

transient ['trænziənt] *adj* not lasting or staying long; short in time: *transient pleasures.* Also *nc* (*US*) person who stays in a hotel for a short time only. **transience, transiency** *nu.*

transistor [træn'zistə*] *nc* **1.** very small device which is used in radio sets, tape

recorders etc. **2.** small radio set in which it is used.
transistorized *adj* having transistors.
transit ['trænzit] *nu* **1.** act of moving or being moved across or through. *Transit by ship through the canal is expensive. His luggage was lost in transit* i.e. while being sent from one place to another. **2.** movement of a planet in front of another heavenly body.
transition [træn'ziʃən] *nc/u* change from one state or condition to another. *The transition from home to boarding school is not easy for many boys.* **transitional** *adj.* **transitionally** *adv.*
transitive ['trænzitiv] *adj* (with reference to a verb) having a direct object (shown in this dictionary by *vt*) (*opp* **intransitive**).
transitory ['trænzitəri] *adj* not lasting long; short in time.
translate [trænz'leit] *vt* **1.** give the meaning of words of one language in the words of another. *He translated what I said in English into French. This French book is translated from Latin.* **translator** *nc.*
translation *nc/u* something which has been translated; act of translation. *Have you a good translation of Plato? I am not very good at English translation* i.e. translating into English.
transliterate [trænz'litəreit] *vt* write the words of one language in the letters or characters of another language. **transliteration** [trænzlitə'reiʃən] *nc/u.*
translucent [trænz'lu:snt] *adj* allowing some light to pass through, but not able to be seen through clearly.
transmigration [trænzmai'greiʃən] *nu* passing of the soul after death into another body.
transmit [trænz'mit] *vt* send or pass on. *The mosquito transmits malaria. Rubber does not transmit electricity. past* **transmitted.**
transmission **1.** *nc/u* act of transmitting. **2.** *nc* part of a car which carries the power from the engine to the wheels.
transmitter *nc* **1.** person/thing that transmits. **2.** instrument for sending out messages by radio; radio broadcasting station.
transmute [trænz'mju:t] *vt* change a substance into another substance.
transmutable *adj* able to be transmuted.
transmutation [trænzmju:'teiʃən] *nc/u* act of transmuting; change (esp. in biology, the slow change of one species into another by evolution).
transom ['trænsəm] *nc* beam across the top of a door or window; small window above a door or other window.
transparent [træns'pærnt] *adj* **1.** able to be seen through. *Glass is transparent.* **2.** clear; obvious. *The meaning is transparent. He laughed at our transparent attempt to deny it.* **transparently** *adv.*
transparency **1.** *nu* state of being transparent. **2.** *nc* picture or photograph put on transparent material (so that it can be shown on a screen).
transpire [træns'paiə*] *vt/i* **1.** become known slowly. *From our questions it transpired that he had told a lie.* **2.** happen; take place. (*informal* in sense **2.**). **3.** lose water from the surface of the skin or of leaves.
transpiration [trænspi'reiʃən] *nu* loss of water in this way.
transplant [træns'pla:nt] *vt* **1.** remove and plant in another place. **2.** (with reference to persons) move to another place. **3.** remove an organ from one body and put it in another. Also ['trænspla:nt] *nc*: *The heart transplant was done by a team of doctors.* **transplantation** [trænspla:n'teiʃən] *nc/u.*
transport[1] [træns'pɔ:t] *vt* carry from one place to another. *Coal is usually transported by rail.*
transportable *adj* able to be transported.
transportation [trænspɔ:'teiʃən] *nu* act of transporting or being transported.
transport[2] ['trænspɔ:t] **1.** *nu* carrying of persons or goods from one place to another. *The transport of coal is usually done by rail. Because of the flood the village is without transport.*
Note: in this sense *transport* is the more usual British word; *transportation* is the American word.
2. *nc* aircraft, ship or vehicle for transporting (usu. troops).
transpose [træns'pouz] *vt* **1.** change the order of two things by putting them in each other's place. **2.** change the order of words. **3.** (with reference to music) change the key. **transposition** [trænspə'ziʃən] *nc/u.*
transverse ['trænzvə:s] *adj* placed across. Also *nc* something which has been placed across. **transversely** [trænz'və:sli] *adv.*
transvestite [trænz'vestait] *nc* person who wears the clothes of the opposite sex. Also *adj.* **transvestism** [trænz'vestizəm] *nu.*
trap [træp] *nc* **1.** device for catching animals; trick to catch somebody doing something. **2.** bend in a pipe which catches solid matter and which contains water to stop foul air or gas coming back up the pipe. **3.** type of small two-wheeled cart pulled by a horse. **4.** small door in a floor or roof. (Often **trapdoor**). Also *vt* catch in a trap or by a trick. *past* **trapped.**
trapper *nc* person who traps animals (esp. for their skins).
trapeze [trə'pi:z] *nc* horizontal bar which swings on two ropes and is used for gymnastic exercises, and by acrobats in circuses.
trapezium [trə'pi:ziəm] *nc* (*Brit*) four-sided figure with only one pair of sides parallel. (*US* **trapezoid**).
trapezoid ['træpizɔid] *nc* (*Brit*) four-sided figure with no sides parallel. (*US* **trapezium**).
trappings ['træpiŋz] *npl* ornaments; signs of rank. *He was wearing the trappings of an army general.*
Trappist ['træpist] *n* man who belongs to a strict order of monks, which forbids its members to speak. Also *adj.*
trash [træʃ] *nu* rubbish; something of very poor quality (e.g. in music, writing etc).
trashy *adj.* **trashiness** *nu.*
'trashcan *nc* (*US*) container for putting rubbish in. (*Brit* **dustbin**).
trauma ['trɔ:mə] *nc* condition of the body or mind caused by severe injury or shock.
traumatic [trɔ:'mætik] *adj.*
travail ['træveil] *nu* **1.** hard work. **2.** pains of giving birth to a child. (rather *o.f.*).
travel ['trævl] *vt/i* **1.** make a journey or journeys (esp. abroad). *He has travelled all over Africa.* **2.** move. *Bad news travels quickly. I want a car which can travel* i.e. can move at high speeds. *Let your mind travel back to what happened yesterday* i.e. remember; think about. **3.** make journeys on business (usu. to sell things). *My brother travels in furniture. He travels for a firm*

which makes furniture. past **travelled.** (*US* **traveled**). Also *nc/u: his travels all over Africa. Travel through this country is very slow.*

travelled (*US* **traveled**) *adj* 1. (with reference to persons) having made many journeys. *Sailors are travelled people.* 2. (with reference to things) used much by those who travel: *a much-travelled road.*

traveller (*US* **traveler**) *nc* 1. person who travels. 2. commercial traveller. see below.

travelling (*US* **traveling**) *adj*: *travelling bag* i.e. one used when travelling.

'travel agency business which arranges journeys, holidays etc for other people.

co'mmercial 'traveller (*Brit*) person employed by a manufacturer to travel about visiting shops in order to persuade the shopkeeper to buy the manufacturer's goods. (*US* **traveling salesman**).

traverse [træ'və:s] *vt* 1. pass across. *The main road traverses the plain from north to south.* 2. survey by measuring. Also *nc* course taken by a person climbing across a precipice or slope instead of straight up it; place where he has to do so.

travesty ['trævəsti] *nc* very poor imitation or false description of something (often made on purpose). *Your study is a travesty of the facts. The trial was a travesty of justice* i.e. it was in no way just. Also *vt* make a travesty of.

trawl [trɔ:l] *nc* 1. type of very large fishing net shaped like a bag, dragged along the bottom of the sea. (Also **trawl net**). 2. very long fishing line with many hooks tied to it. Also *vt/i* fish with a trawl.

trawler *nc* type of ship used for trawling.

tray [trei] *nc* flat piece of wood or metal etc with a raised edge round it, used for carrying things (e.g. dishes), keeping papers (e.g. on a desk) or catching a liquid as it drops (e.g. oil from an engine).

'in-tray tray on a desk in which papers to be dealt with are put.

'out-tray tray on a desk in which papers already dealt with and to be taken away are put.

treacherous ['tretʃərəs] *adj* unfaithful; not to be trusted or relied upon. *The treacherous soldier told the enemy where his friends were. The sea is very treacherous in bad weather.*

treacherously *adv*. **treachery** *nc/u*.

treacle ['tri:kl] *nu* (*Brit*) thick, dark, sweet liquid made from sugar. (*US* **molasses**).

treacly *adj* of, like treacle.

tread [tred] *vt/i* walk; step. *Please don't tread on the flowers. past tense* **trod** [trɔd]. *past part* **trodden** ['trɔdn]. Also *nc* 1. act of treading; sound made by treading. *I could hear his heavy tread on the floor outside my room.* 2. level part of a stair on which the foot is placed. 3. outside part of a rubber tyre which has a pattern on it (to prevent skidding).

'treadmill 1. type of wheel which is turned by somebody walking on the treads fitted to it (once used as a punishment). 2. boring occupation.

tread something out crush with the feet: *tread out a fire.*

tread on air be very happy. (*informal*).

tread on somebody's heels follow very closely behind somebody. (*informal*).

tread on somebody's toes offend somebody. (*informal*).

tread water keep upright and afloat in deep water by treading with the feet.

treadle ['tredl] *nc* part of a machine (e.g. a sewing machine) which is moved up and down by the foot to drive it.

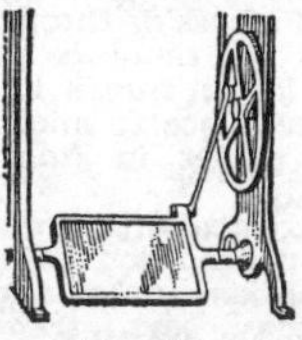
treadle

treason ['tri:zn] *nu* disloyalty to, betrayal of, one's own country. **treasonable** *adj*. **treasonably** *adv*.

treasure ['treʒə*] *nc/u* collection of valuable things (e.g. money, gold, jewels); somebody/something which is greatly valued. *The divers found treasure at the bottom of the sea; the treasures of English literature. Our servant is a treasure.* Also *vt* value greatly. *He treasures all his books.*

treasurer *nc* person who looks after the money of a club, society etc.

treasury *nc* 1. place where money and valuable things are kept. 2. department of government which is responsible for collecting and paying out government's money (in Britain **the Treasury**).

'treasure house building where treasure is kept.

'treasure-trove treasure, the owner of which is not known, found buried in the ground.

treat [tri:t] *vt* 1. deal with or use in a particular way; behave towards. *They are treating the matter seriously. They are not treating it as a joke. How did he treat you?* 2. give medical attention to. *The doctor treated me for malaria. It is difficult to treat a person with cancer* i.e. who has cancer. *Nowadays they treat malaria with drugs* i.e. by using drugs. 3. buy something for somebody; pay for somebody. *Our uncle treated us to an ice cream. I treated myself to a big dinner.* Also *nc* 1. something unusual which gives pleasure. *The visit to the seaside was a great treat for us.* 2. act of buying something for somebody. *Our uncle's treat was to give us tickets for the cinema.*

treat of something have as its subject; discuss. *This book treats of various problems.* (rather *o.f.*).

treat with someone discuss so as to reach an agreement. *The management refused to treat with the workmen.*

treatise ['tri:tiz] *nc* serious book or paper about a particular subject.

treatment ['tri:tmənt] *nc/u* 1. particular way of dealing with somebody/something. *His treatment of the problem was most interesting. They were given good treatment by the soldiers.* 2. medical attention. *He has gone to the hospital for treatment. There are several treatments for a cold. I was under treatment for two weeks.*

treaty ['tri:ti] *nc* agreement (esp. a written one made between countries).

treble[1] ['trebl] *adj* three times as much as. *Clothes are treble the price (that) they used to be.* Also *vt/i* become, cause to become, treble. *Why have the prices trebled?*

treble[2] ['trebl] *nc* highest notes in music; boy's voice which can sing the highest notes. Also *adj*.

tree [triː] *nc* **1.** large plant with a trunk, branches and leaves.
Note: a *shrub* or *bush* is much smaller and although it has branches it does not have a trunk.
2. piece of wood etc used for a particular purpose: *a shoetree* i.e. piece of wood, metal etc put in a shoe to keep its shape. Also *vt* cause to climb a tree for safety; chase up a tree.
treeless *adj* without trees.
'family 'tree see **family.**

trefoil ['trefɔil] *nc* type of plant with three leaves; decoration like this.

trek [trek] *vi* make a long journey (originally in a wagon pulled by oxen in South Africa). *past* **trekked.** Also *nc* journey of this kind.

trellis ['trelis] *nc* light frame used for supporting climbing plants, and making doors and screens. Also *vt* fit with a trellis.

tremble ['trembl] *vi* shake; shiver. *The children were trembling with cold/excitement/fear. His voice trembled as he spoke. The branch of the tree trembled when I stood on it.* Also *nc*: *I could feel the tremble in his hands.*
in fear and trembling see **fear.**

tremendous [tri'mendəs] *adj* very great. **tremendously** *adv.*

tremolo ['treməlou] *nc* shaking, quivering sound made by the voice or a musical instrument. *pl* **tremolos.**

tremor ['tremə*] *nc* very short, shaking movement; quiver.
'earth tremor shaking of the earth which is less severe than an earthquake.

tremulous ['tremjuləs] *adj* shaking; trembling with excitement; nervous. **tremulously** *adv.* **tremulousness** *nu.*

trench [trentʃ] *nc* long, narrow hole dug in the earth (e.g. for laying pipes or to protect soldiers from the enemy's fire). Also *vt* **1.** dig a trench; protect with a trench. **2.** turn over the soil by digging deeply.

trenchant ['trentʃənt] *adj* sharp; clever and keen. *He is a very trenchant speaker.*
trenchantly *adv.* **trenchancy** *nu.*

trencher ['trentʃə*] *nc* large wooden plate on which food was formerly served and eaten.

trend [trend] *vi* go in a certain direction. Also *nc* direction; tendency; inclination. *Young women are always interested in the trends of fashion.*

trepan [tri'pæn] *vt* take a piece of bone from the skull to lessen pressure on the brain. *past* **trepanned.**
trepanning *nc* operation of this kind.

trepidation [trepi'deiʃən] *nu* state of being both afraid and excited.

trespass ['trespəs] *vi* **1.** go on to somebody's land or property without permission. *You must not trespass on/upon government land.* **2.** take too much advantage of. *They are always trespassing upon his kindness.* **3.** do wrong (*o.f.* in sense **3.**). Also **1.** *nc/u* act of trespassing. **2.** *nc* wrong act (*o.f.* in sense **2.**).
trespasser *nc.*

tress [tres] *nc* lock or strand of hair (*o.f.*).

trestle ['tresl] *nc* wooden frame made of two pairs of legs, each pair joined at the top to a horizontal bar (used to support planks, platforms or tables).
'trestle table table with its top resting on a pair of trestles.

tri- [trai] *prefix* three (e.g. **triangle**).

triad ['traiæd] *nc* group of three.

trial ['traiəl] *nc/u* **1.** test to see if somebody/something is suitable etc. *He says he will give the new medicine a trial* i.e. use it and see what it is like. *The manager has promised to give me a trial as a clerk. New cars have several severe trials before they are put on the market. We went for a trial run in the new car* i.e. in order to test it. **2.** examination of the facts in a court of law to decide a case. *His trial for murder begins tomorrow.* **3.** somebody/something that gives trouble; nuisance. *He is a great trial to his parents.*
on trial 1. in order to be tested. *The shopkeeper has allowed me to have the radio set on trial.* **2.** accused in a court of law. *He is on trial for murder.*
bring somebody to trial/up for trial take somebody to a court of law to be tried.
stand trial be tried in a court of law.

triangle ['traiæŋgl] *nc* **1.** figure with three straight sides. **2.** small musical instrument made of a piece of metal shaped like a triangle.
triangular [trai'æŋgjulə*] *adj* having three angles shaped like a triangle.

tribe [traib] *nc* **1.** large group of families having the same language and customs. **2.** group of animals or plants of the same kind.
tribal *adj* of a tribe. **tribally** *adv.*
tribalism *nu* tribal feeling; system of having tribes.
'tribesman person who belongs to a tribe.

tribulation [tribju'leiʃən] *nc* trouble; hardship.

tribunal [trai'bjuːnl] *nc* **1.** court of law. **2.** special court established to hear complaints or appeals, or to take evidence about some important public matter.

tribune[1] ['tribjuːn] *nc* (in ancient Rome) government official chosen by the people.

tribune[2] ['tribjuːn] *nc* raised platform for speakers (esp. in the French National Assembly).

tribute ['tribjuːt] **1.** *nu* fixed payment made by one country or ruler to another in exchange for peace and protection. **2.** *nc* something said or done to show respect or express thanks. *I wish to pay tribute to all those who have helped me. There were many tributes to him in the newspapers.*
tributary ['tribjuːtəri] *adj* of tribute; paying tribute. *One of the tributary countries of the Roman Empire.* Also *nc* **1.** ruler or country paying tribute. **2.** river which flows into a bigger one. *The River Amazon has many tributaries.*

trice [trais] *nu* only in **in a trice** i.e. in an instant; very quickly.

trick [trik] *nc* **1.** something done to deceive somebody. *We used several tricks to make the enemy believe that we were about to attack. They got into the castle by a trick.* **2.** something done as a joke or in mischief. *These boys like playing tricks on their teacher.* **3.** something done by skill to deceive but also to amuse: *conjuring tricks. I'll show you a trick which you can do with two pennies.* **4.** strange habit. *He has a trick of looking at his feet when he talks.* **5.** cards played in one round and taken by the player with the winning card. *We won the game by three tricks. My ace took the trick.* **6.** period of duty steering a ship. Also *vt* deceive.
trickery *nu* act of deceiving or cheating.
trickster ['trikstə*] *nc* person who makes his living by cheating.
tricky *adj* **1.** (with reference to persons) full of tricks; not able to be trusted. **2.** (with

reference to things) requiring great skill; difficult.

do the trick be what is necessary. *That'll do the trick.*

trickle ['trikl] *vt/i* flow or move slowly or in small drops. *The rain trickled down my neck. The boys trickled into the classroom.* Also *nc* very small flow.

tricolour ['trikələ*] (*US* **tricolor**) *nc* flag with three coloured bands (esp. the flags of France and the Republic of Ireland).

tricycle ['traisikl] *nc* cycle with three wheels (often used by young children instead of a bicycle).

trident ['traidnt] *nc* type of spear with three points.

tried [traid] past of **try.**

triennial [trai'eniəl] *adj* occurring once every three years; lasting for three years.

trier ['traiə*] *nc* see **try.**

trifle ['traifl] **1.** *nc* something of little worth or importance. *Great men do not worry about trifles.* **2.** *nc/u* type of sweet food made of cake covered with fruit, custard and cream etc. Also *vt/i* **1.** (with **with**) treat lightly; not be serious about; play with. *It is dangerous to trifle with such a fierce animal. He trifled with his food instead of eating it.* **2.** (with **away**) waste. *They had trifled away all their money.* **trifler** *nc.*

trifling *adj* of little importance. **triflingly** *adv.*

a trifle *adv* just a little; rather. *He was a trifle too slow to catch me.*

trigger ['trigə*] *nc* small lever on a gun which is pulled by the finger to fire it. Also *vt* (often with **off**) start suddenly. *The news has triggered (off) a serious crisis.*

trigonometry [trigə'nɔmətri] *nu* branch of mathematics which deals with triangles.

trilateral ['trai'lætərl] *adj* having three sides.

trilby ['trilbi] *nc* man's soft felt hat. (Also **trilby hat**).

trill [tril] *vt/i* **1.** sing, whistle or play a musical instrument in a shaky, quivering way; play a musical note followed by the one above it in pitch, several times very quickly. **2.** sound the letter 'r' in this way with the tip of the tongue. Also *nc.*

trillion ['triliən] *nc* **1.** (*Brit*) million × million × million. **2.** (*US*) million × million.

trilogy ['trilədʒi] *nc* group of three books or plays about the same subject.

trim [trim] *adj* neat and tidy. Also *nu* condition; readiness. *He was in good trim when I saw him. An athlete must never get out of trim.* Also *vt/i* **1.** decorate; make neat and tidy by adding or taking away something from the edges. *She trimmed her hat with flowers. He trimmed his beard with a pair of scissors.* **2.** load a ship or aircraft so that it is properly balanced when it sails or flies; adjust the sails of a ship or the wings of an aircraft to the wind. **3.** change one's views in politics etc frequently in order to be always on the winning side. *past* **trimmed.**

trimming *nc* **1.** something used to trim clothes. **2.** (in *pl*) extra food eaten with other food: *roast beef with all the trimmings.*

trinity ['triniti] *nc* group of three: *the Trinity* i.e. Father, Son and Holy Ghost, considered as one in the Christian religion.

trinket ['triŋkit] *nc* small ornament of little value.

trio ['tri:ou] *nc* group of three persons (esp. three playing music together); piece of music for three players. *pl* **trios.**

trip [trip] *vt/i* **1.** strike the foot against something and fall or almost fall; cause somebody to do this. *I tripped over the basket as I ran away. He put out his foot to trip me (up).* **2.** make, cause to make, a mistake. *He tripped when trying to spell the word 'through'.* **3.** walk, run or dance lightly. *past* **tripped.** Also *nc* **1.** journey taken for pleasure: *trip to the seaside.* **2.** fall; mistake.

tripper *nc* person who makes a journey for pleasure (usu. for a day).

tripartite ['trai'pɑ:tait] *adj* having three parts; agreed to by three parties.

tripe [traip] *nu* **1.** inside part of the stomach of a sheep or an ox used as food. **2.** worthless talk or writing. (*informal* in sense **2.**).

triple ['tripl] *adj* **1.** made up of three parts. **2.** three times as much or as many. *Clothes are triple the price they used to be.* Also *vt/i* become, cause to become, triple. *The population has tripled in three years.* see also **treble**[1].

triplet ['triplit] *nc* **1.** group of three of the same kind. **2.** one of three children born at the same time to the same mother.

triplex ['tripleks] *adj* threefold.

triplicate ['triplikət] *adj* threefold; copied three times. Also *nu* (esp. with reference to papers which are typed) third copy made of something. *Please type this letter in triplicate.* Also *vt* make three copies of.

tripod ['traipɔd] *nc* table with three legs; stand with three legs on which something can be rested (e.g. a blackboard or camera).

trisect [trai'sekt] *vt* divide into three parts.

trisection *nu.*

trite [trait] *adj* (with reference to something said or written) used too often; not new.

tritely *adv.* **triteness** *nu.*

triumph ['traiʌmf] *nc/u* **1.** success; victory; happy feeling caused by a great success. *Winning the football cup was one of their greatest triumphs. They returned from the match in triumph.* **2.** (in ancient Rome) ceremony for a victorious general. Also *vi* (with **over**) win a victory; have a happy feeling because of success. *We have triumphed over our enemies.*

triumphal [trai'ʌmfl] *adj* of a triumph.

triumphant [trai'ʌmfənt] *adj* expressing happy feelings because of a triumph. *The triumphant team returned home with the football cup.* **triumphantly** *adv.*

trivial ['triviəl] *adj* not important; ordinary: *trivial complaints.* **trivially** *adv.*

triviality [trivi'æliti] *nc/u*: *They complain about trivialities.*

trivia *npl* unimportant things.

trivialize *vt* make trivial: *trivialize politics.*

trochee ['trouki:] *nc* metrical foot having a stressed foot followed by an unstressed one (e.g. '*leave your 'home be'hind you*).

trod [trɔd] past tense of **tread.**

trodden ['trɔdn] past part of **tread.**

troglodyte ['trɔglədait] *nc* person who lives in a cave.

troll[1] [troul] *vt/i* **1.** sing happily. **2.** fish by pulling a line with bait and hooks behind a boat.

troll[2] [trɔl] *nc* (in myths) type of giant or friendly dwarf.

trolley ['trɔli] *nc* **1.** small cart with two or four wheels which is pushed by hand: *railway porter's trolley; tea trolley* i.e. one on which dishes and food are brought at tea time. **2.** type of truck which can be pushed or driven by hand on a railway. **3.** long pole

with a small wheel at the end which connects a train or trolley bus to the electric wire overhead.
'trolley bus type of bus with a trolley on top.

trollop ['trɔləp] *nc* immoral woman; prostitute. (*informal* and *o.f.*).

trombone [trɔm'boun] *nc* type of musical instrument played by pushing a sliding tube in and out.
trombonist *nc* person who plays a trombone.

troop [tru:p] *nc* **1.** large group of people; small company of soldiers (esp. cavalry). **2.** (in *pl*) soldiers; army. Also *vt/i* move in a large group. *All the boys trooped off to see the football match.*
trooper *nc* soldier in a cavalry regiment.
'troop carrier ship or aircraft for carrying troops.
'troopship ship for carrying troops.

trophy ['troufi] *nc* **1.** something which is kept as a reminder of a success or victory (e.g. the horns of an animal which one has shot). **2.** prize. *The trophy for winning the race was a gold medal.*

tropic ['trɔpik] *nc* one of the two circles round the earth about 23° 30' north or south of the equator. (The one north of the equator is *the Tropic of Cancer*; the one south of it *the Tropic of Capricorn*).
the tropics *npl* part of the world between the two circles.
tropical *adj* of, like the tropics; very hot: *tropical climate.* **tropically** *adv.*

trot [trɔt] *vt/i* (usu. with reference to a horse) go, cause to go, faster than walking. *The horse trotted down the road. He trotted his horse to the end of the field. We saw the schoolboys trotting home. past* **trotted.** Also *nu* speed faster than walking. *They passed us at a trot.*
trotter *nc* **1.** horse trained to trot. **2.** foot of a pig or sheep (esp. when eaten as food).
trot something out bring out and show (esp. in a boring way). *When we went to see him he trotted out all his photographs.* (*informal*).

troth [trouθ] *nu* truth (*o.f.*).
plight one's troth see **plight[2]**.

troubadour ['tru:bədɔ:*] *nc* (in former times) travelling singer and storyteller.

trouble ['trʌbl] *vt/i* **1.** have or cause difficulty, discomfort or worry. *One of my teeth is troubling me.* **2.** (usu. in questions or with **not**) cause oneself discomfort or inconvenience. *Why did they trouble to come? Please don't trouble (yourself); I can do it by myself.* **3.** as a polite request. *May I trouble you for the salt?* i.e. please pass me the salt. Also *nc/u* **1.** difficulty, discomfort, worry. *One of my teeth is giving me trouble. He has had many troubles since his father died.* **2.** somebody/something which causes difficulty, discomfort etc. *His son is a great trouble to him. It was no trouble doing it.* **3.** special care or attention. *Thank you for all your trouble in looking after me. He went to the trouble of finding out (for) himself.* **4.** political or social disturbance. *I hear that there has been trouble in Paris.*
troublesome *adj* causing trouble: *troublesome child; troublesome tooth.* **troublesomely** *adv.* **troublesomeness** *nu.*
'troubleshooter person who tries to sort out troubles in an organization.
ask for trouble see **ask.**
be in trouble **1.** be worried. *He is in great trouble because he has no money.* **2.** likely to have trouble, be punished etc for doing something wrong. *John is in trouble again for losing his books.*
get into trouble do something wrong for which one is likely to be blamed, punished etc. *He got into trouble with his wife for coming home late.*
get somebody into trouble **1.** cause somebody to do something for which he may be blamed, punished etc. **2.** cause an unmarried girl to become pregnant. (*informal* in sense **2.**).
put somebody to trouble cause somebody trouble. *I am sorry for putting you to so much trouble.*
take trouble over take special care; give special attention to. *He should take more trouble over his work.*

trough [trɔf] *nc* **1.** long, narrow container which holds food or water for animals. **2.** hollow between two waves. **3.** (with reference to weather) decrease in the pressure of the atmosphere: *a trough of low pressure over the British Isles.*

trounce [trauns] *vt* beat or defeat thoroughly.
trouncing *nc* beating; defeat. *Our team gave theirs a good trouncing.*

troupe [tru:p] *nc* group of actors or performers.
trouper *nc* member of a group of this kind.

trousers ['trauzəz] *npl* garment with two separate places for the legs which covers the lower part of the body and the legs.
trouser *adj*: *trouser pockets.*
'trouser suit woman's suit with trousers instead of a skirt.

trousseau ['tru:sou] *nc* clothes, personal articles etc which a woman collects before she marries. *pl* **trousseaux** ['tru:souz] or **trousseaus.**

trout [traut] *nc* type of spotted fish often used for food. *pl* **trout.**

trove [trouv] *nc* see **treasure.**

trowel ['trauəl] *nc* **1.** tool with a flat blade used to spread cement or mortar when building. **2.** tool with a curved blade used when gardening.

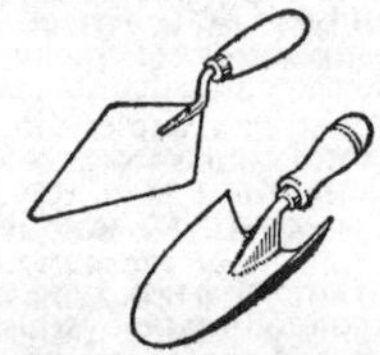

trowels (*def 1*) (*def 2*)

troy weight, troy ['trɔi(weit)] *nc/u* British system of weights used for precious metals and gems. (12 ounces = 1 pound). *The silver dish weighs 10 ounces troy weight/troy.*

truant ['truənt] *nc* child who does not attend school when he ought to. Also *adj* not attending; avoiding duty. **truancy** *nc/u.*
play truant not attend school when one ought to.

truce [tru:s] *nc* agreement to stop a war, fighting etc for a short time.

truck[1] [trʌk] *nc* **1.** open wagon for carrying heavy goods by rail. **2.** porter's handcart for heavy luggage. **3.** lorry.
Note: (*US*) *truck*, not *lorry*, is always used. (*Brit*) both *truck* and *lorry* are used.

truck[2] [trʌk] *nu* **1.** trade by exchanging goods; barter. **2.** (*US*) vegetables (grown for selling).
'truck farmer (*US*) farmer who grows and sells vegetables. (*Brit* **market gardener**).
have no truck with have no dealings with. (*informal*).

truckle[1] ['trʌkl] *vi* (with **to**) behave like a slave; be very obedient.

truckle[2] ['trʌkl]: **truckle bed** low bed with small wheels.

truculent ['trʌkjulənt] *adj* fierce; ready to fight; **truculently** *adv*. **truculence, truculency** *nu*.

trudge [trʌdʒ] *vi* walk heavily as one does when tired. Also *nc* long, tiring walk.

true [tru:] *adj* **1.** correct in fact. *What I say is true. This is a true report of what happened.* **2.** honest; loyal; faithful. *He is true to his friends. He is a true friend.* **3.** genuine; real. *This is not a true Rembrandt. He is not the true son of the chief.* **4.** exact; accurate. *Is this a true copy of the letter? Only a skilled worker can build a wall that is true.* Also *adv* accurately; correctly. *The piece of wood fitted true into the other one.* Also *nu* correct position. *The wheel on your bicycle is out of true.* see **truth**.
truly *adv* **1.** truthfully. **2.** really; genuinely. *I am truly grateful; Yours truly* (put at the end of a letter).
come true happen as had been hoped or wished. *When he passed his exams he felt as if all his dreams had come true.*
run true to type behave as expected.

truffle ['trʌfl] *nc* **1.** type of fungus which grows below the ground and is used to flavour food. **2.** type of cake. **3.** type of chocolate or sweet.

truism ['tru:izəm] *nc* statement which is so obviously true that it should not be necessary to make it.

truly ['tru:li] *adv* see **true**.

trump[1] [trʌmp] *nc* one of a suit of playing cards which by agreement can take any card of the other three suits. *In the first game of bridge spades were trumps.* Also *vt* put a trump on a card of another suit.
trump something up make up or invent something which is not true. *He trumped up a story about being ill.* (*informal*).
play one's trump card make the final move or use the only advantage left to win success.

trump[2] [trʌmp] *nc* trumpet; sound made by a trumpet (*o.f.*).

trumpery ['trʌmpəri] *adj/nc* of little value; rubbish.

trumpet ['trʌmpit] *nc* **1.** type of musical instrument; sound made by this. **2.** something which has the shape of a trumpet (e.g. *ear trumpet*). Also *vt* make a sound like a trumpet; make known by sounding trumpets. *We heard the elephants trumpeting in the forest. The heralds trumpeted the arrival of the king.*

trumpet (*def 1*)

trumpeter *nc* person who plays a trumpet.
blow one's own trumpet boast; praise oneself. (*informal*).

truncate [trʌŋ'keit] *vt* make short by cutting off the end. **truncated** *adj*.

truncheon ['trʌntʃən] *nc* (*Brit*) short, heavy stick used by the police. (*US* **club; night stick**).

trundle ['trʌndl] *vt* roll heavily. *They trundled the barrels into the store.*

trunk [trʌŋk] *nc* **1.** part of a tree between its roots and its branches. **2.** body without its arms, legs and head. **3.** large box with a hinged lid for storing clothes etc or for carrying them when travelling. **4.** long nose of an elephant. **5.** (in *pl*) tight-fitting short trousers worn by men for swimming or games.
'trunk call (*Brit*) long-distance call by telephone.
'trunk line main line of a telephone system or a railway.
'trunk road main road.

truss [trʌs] *nc* **1.** bundle of hay or straw. **2.** framework of beams holding up a roof or bridge. **3.** belt to keep a hernia in place. Also *vt* **1.** (often with **up**) tie. *She trussed (up) the chicken* i.e. tied the legs and wings before cooking it. **2.** hold up a roof or a bridge with trusses.

trust[1] [trʌst] *vt* **1.** believe; have confidence or faith in. *We trusted everything he said. You should never trust a stranger.* **2.** have enough confidence in somebody to allow him to do something. *Can I trust you to post these letters?* **3.** give something to somebody to be cared for. *He trusted me with his watch.* see also **entrust**. **4.** hope. *We trust (that) you are well.*
trusting *adj* ready to believe or have confidence in somebody. **trustingly** *adv*.
trust in someone/something have confidence in. *We trust in God.*
trust to luck hope that one will be lucky. *We'll have to trust to luck.*

trust[2] [trʌst] **1.** *nu* belief; confidence. *It is safe to put your trust in him* i.e. have confidence in him. *We have no trust in the new medicine.* **2.** *nc* property or money which is managed by others for the benefit of somebody/something. *The man set up a trust to educate poor children.* **3.** *nc* group of business companies.
trustee [trʌs'ti:] *nc* person who is given property or money to manage for others.
trusteeship [trʌs'ti:ʃip] *nc* **1.** work of a trustee. **2.** responsibility for governing a country on behalf of the United Nations Organization. *After the Second World War, Great Britain was given the trusteeship of Tanganyika, which became a trusteeship territory/trust territory.*
trustful *adj* ready to believe or have confidence in somebody. **trustfully** *adv*. **trustfulness** *nu*.
trustworthy *adj* deserving to be trusted; reliable. (*opp* **untrustworthy**). **trustworthiness** *nu*.
trusty *adj* reliable (*o.f.* – use **trustworthy**).
in trust managed on behalf of others. *He holds the money in trust for the dead man's children.*
on trust accepting or believing without enquiry or proof. *We took his story on trust.*

trustee [trʌs'ti:] *nc* see **trust**[2].

truth [tru:θ] *nc/u* something true or believed to be true; state of being true. *I told him a few truths about his bad behaviour.*

There is some truth in the story that he ran away. Always tell the truth! see **true.**

try [trai] *vt/i* **1.** find out what somebody/something is like by doing something with him or it. *They tried him as goalkeeper but he was too small. Try this hat for size* i.e. put it on to see if it fits. *We tried tying it with string.* **2.** make an attempt. *It looks difficult but we'll try. He always tries his hardest* i.e. makes as great an attempt as he can. *He tried to kill me.*

Note: try and can be used instead of *try to* in the imperative. *Try to get some sleep* or *Try and get some sleep.*

3. examine the facts in a court of law. *He was tried for murder and found guilty.* **4.** make demands on; make tired etc. *That child's behaviour tries my patience. past* **tried.** Also *nc* **1.** attempt; test. *We had a try at doing it. Why don't you give it a try?* i.e. see what it is like. **2.** (rugby football) points gained when a player puts the ball down behind the line of the opponents' goal.

tried *adj* reliable; fully tested. (*opp* **untried**).

trier *nc* person who tries hard or works as well as he can.

trying *adj* tiring; annoying. *I have had a trying day. Children can be very trying.*

try for something make an attempt to get.

try something on put on to see what it is like. *I tried on the shoes but they were too big.*

try it/something on make an attempt to do something wrong without being found out. *You must be careful that he does not try his lies on you. He is always trying it on.* (*informal*).

try somebody/something out find out what somebody/something is like by testing.

try one's hand at something make an attempt to do something. (*informal*).

tryst [trist] *nc* meeting place (*o.f.*).

tsar [zɑ:*], **tsarina** [zɑ:'ri:nə] *nc* see **czar.**

tsetse, tzetze ['tsetsi] *nc* type of biting fly found in some parts of Africa. (Also **tsetse fly, tzetze fly**). *pl* **tsetse.**

tub [tʌb] *nc* **1.** round container (usu. made of wood) for holding liquids. **2.** bath. (*informal* in sense **2.**).

tuba ['tju:bə] *nc* type of large, brass musical instrument.

tubby ['tʌbi] *adj* (with reference to persons) short and fat.

tube [tju:b] *nc* **1.** pipe made of glass, metal, rubber etc: *test tube* i.e. short, glass pipe closed at one end, used for experiments; *inner tube of a tyre* i.e. rubber tube inside a tyre. **2.** small container made of soft metal and with a top which screws on: *tube of toothpaste.* **3.** organ of the body shaped like a pipe (e.g. *bronchial tube*). **4.** device shaped like a pipe in a television or radio set (e.g. *cathode ray tube* in a television set); (*US*) radio valve. **5.** (*Brit*) underground railway. (*US* **subway**).

tubing *nc* piece of tube (esp. rubber tube).

tubular ['tju:bjulə*] *adj* **1.** having the shape of a tube. **2.** fitted with, made of, tubes.

tuber ['tju:bə*] *nc* growth on the roots of a plant from which new plants can grow. (A potato is a tuber). **tuberous** *adj.*

tuberculosis [tjubə:kju'lousis] *nu* type of disease (usu. of the lungs and often called **T.B.**).

tubercular [tju'bə:kjulə*], **tuberculous** [tju'bə:kjuləs] *adj* of, having, tuberculosis.

tubing ['tju:biŋ] *nc* see **tube.**

tubular ['tju:bjulə*] *adj* see **tube.**

tuck [tʌk] *vt* **1.** fold a piece of cloth before sewing it. **2.** put into position; make firm and tidy. *He tucked the handkerchief into his pocket. The mother tucked her baby into bed. They tucked up their sleeves and began working.* Also *nc* **1.** fold in a piece of cloth which is sewn into position. *She made a tuck round the bottom of her coat.* **2.** food (esp. cakes and sweets) (*informal* in sense **2.**).

'tuck-shop shop at a school where tuck is sold. (*informal*).

tuck in eat a lot. (*informal*).

'tuck-in *nc* good meal. (*informal*).

tuck into something eat a lot of something. (*informal*).

Tuesday ['tju:zdi] *n* third day of the Christian week, following Monday.

tuft [tʌft] *nc* bunch of something soft (e.g. hair, grass).

tufted *adj* having tufts; growing tufts.

tug [tʌg] *vt/i* pull hard. *past* **tugged.** Also *nc* **1.** quick, hard pull. *He gave the knots a tug to make them tighter.* **2.** type of small boat used to pull or push ships (e.g. into or out of harbour).

'tug-of-'war competitions between two teams pulling at either end of a rope.

tuition [tju:'iʃən] *nu* act of teaching (usu. teaching one person or a small group).

tulip ['tju:lip] *nc* type of tall flower with brightly-coloured, cup-shaped blooms.

tulle [tju:l] *nu* fine, net-like cloth (usu. of silk or nylon).

tumble ['tʌmbl] *vt/i* **1.** fall, cause to fall, quickly or heavily. *Babies tumble when they are learning to walk. He tumbled off his bicycle. He tumbled his clothes out of his bag on to the ground.* **2.** make untidy. *The wind tumbled her hair.* **3.** (with **to**) get to know; become aware of. *He hasn't yet tumbled to our plan.* (*informal* in sense **3.**). Also *nc* heavy fall.

tumbler *nc* **1.** drinking glass. **2.** moving part of some door locks. **3.** person who tumbles (usu. to amuse or entertain).

'tumbledown *adj* looking likely to fall down: *a tumbledown old cottage.*

tumescent [tju:'mesnt] *adj* swelling. **tumescence** *nc/u.*

tumid ['tju:mid] *adj* swollen. **tumidity** [tju:'miditi] *nc/u.*

tummy ['tʌmi] *nc* informal form of **stomach.**

tumour ['tju:mə*] (*US* **tumor**) *nc* diseased swelling in the body.

tumult ['tju:mʌlt] *nc/u* noisy excitement; confusion. *His mind was in a tumult.*

tumultuous [tju:'mʌltjuəs] *adj* noisy and excited: *a tumultuous welcome.* **tumultuously** *adv.* **tumultuousness** *nu.*

tumulus ['tju:mjuləs] *nc* mound of earth containing ancient graves. *pl* **tumuli** ['tju:mjuli:].

tun [tʌn] *nc* large container of beer or wine (holding 252 gallons).

tuna ['tju:nə] *nc* type of very large sea fish, related to the mackerel, used for food. (Also **tunny, tunny fish**). *pl* **tunas** or **tuna.**

tundra ['tʌndrə] *nc/u* bare, treeless area of land north of the Arctic Circle.

tune [tju:n] **1.** *nc* number of musical notes which make a pleasant sound. *He played some modern tunes on the piano.* **2.** *nu* quality of being musically pleasant; musical harmony. *This song has no tune. His voice and the piano were in tune.* (*opp* **out of tune**). **3.** *nu* harmony; agreement. *Their opinions are not in tune with ours.* Also *vt* **1.** (with reference to a musical instrument) give the correct musical pitch to. **2.** (with reference to a radio) move the controls to get the correct wave-length. *We tune in to London every evening.* **3.** (with reference to an engine) improve by making small adjustments.

tuneful *adj* having a pleasant tune. **tunefully** *adv.* **tunefulness** *nu.*

tuneless *adj* not having any tune. **tunelessly** *adv.*

tuner *nc* person who tunes musical instruments: *piano tuner.*

tune up give the correct pitch to a musical instrument. *The orchestra tuned up before the concert.*

to the tune of (usu. with reference to an amount which is thought to be too great) to the amount of. *For a few repairs to our car we had to pay to the tune of £20.* (*informal*).

tungsten ['tʌŋstn] *nu* type of metal (W).

tunic ['tju:nik] *nc* **1.** type of jacket worn by policemen or soldiers. **2.** loose dress worn by women over trousers. **3.** sleeveless dress worn over a blouse as the uniform at some girls' schools.

tunnel ['tʌnl] *nc* long passage cut under the ground or through a hill (e.g. for a road or railway line). Also *vi* (with **into** or **through**) make a tunnel. *past* **tunnelled.** (*US* **tunneled**).

tunny ['tʌni] *nc* see **tuna.**

tuppence ['tʌpəns] *nc* (usu. *sing*) twopence. (*informal*).

tuppenny *adj* costing twopence. (*informal*).

turban ['tə:bən] *nc* **1.** covering for a man's head made from a long piece of cloth wound round it. **2.** woman's hat shaped like this.

turbaned *adj* wearing a turban.

turban (*def 1*)

turbid ['tə:bid] *adj* (with reference to a liquid) muddy; not clear. **turbidly** *adv.* **turbidness, turbidity** [tə:'biditi] *nu.*

turbine ['tə:bain] *nc* type of engine which is driven by the force of gas or water striking on a wheel and making it go round.

turbojet ['tə:boudʒet] type of engine which produces a very powerful jet or flow of hot gas; aircraft fitted with this type of engine (usu. called a **jet**) and pushed through the air by it.

turboprop ['tə:bouprɔp] type of jet engine in which the turbine is coupled to the propellers; aircraft with this type of engine.

turbot ['tə:bət] *nc* large European flatfish. *pl* **turbot.**

turbulent ['tə:bjulənt] *adj* disturbed; moving violently. **turbulently** *adv.* **turbulence** *nu.*

tureen [tju'ri:n] *nc* large, deep dish with a lid used for serving soup and vegetables at table.

turf [tə:f] *nc/u* earth or pieces of earth thickly covered with grass. *pl* **turfs** (**turves** [tə:vz] is *o.f.*). Also *vt* lay turf; cover with turf.

the turf *nu* horse-racing; betting on horse-races.

turf something out throw out. (*informal*).

turgid ['tə:dʒid] *adj* swollen; foolishly solemn; pompous. *He writes in turgid prose.* **turgidly** *adv.* **turgidity** [tə:'dʒiditi] *nu.*

Turk [tə:k] *n* native of Turkey.

turkey ['tə:ki] **1.** *nc* large bird with a red featherless head and big flaps under the chin. **2.** *nu* the meat of this bird, eaten as food.

Turkish ['tə:kiʃ] *nu* language of Turkey. Also *adj* of Turkey or its people.

Turkish bath steam bath followed by massage.

Turkish delight type of sweet.

Turkish towel type of rough, thick towel.

turmoil ['tə:mɔil] *nc/u* confusion; disorder.

turn[1] ['tə:n] *vt/i* **1.** go, cause to go, round. *The wheels of the car were turning quickly. He turned the steering wheel. This machine turns metal* i.e. shapes it as it is turned round quickly (on a lathe). *The car turned the corner.* **2.** pass, cause to pass. *It has turned 10 o'clock* i.e. it is just after 10 o'clock. *His son has turned sixteen* i.e. he has just become sixteen. **3.** change, cause to change, direction. *We turned to the right. He turned his face towards me. Turn the car and go back.* **4.** become, cause to become, different. *His face turned white. He has turned his room into a study. The rain turned the dust into mud. The leaves are beginning to turn* i.e. change colour. *This milk has turned* i.e. gone sour.

turner *nc* person who makes things on a lathe.

turning *nc* place where a road turns; where one road joins another. *Take the first turning on the left.*

'turncoat person who betrays his party or his friends.

'turncock person whose job is to open and close water pipes (by turning a large tap or stopcock).

'turnpike 1. (*Brit*) gate across a road where a toll was once paid. **2.** (*US*) motorway for which a toll is paid.

'turnstile device at the entrance to a sports ground, hall etc which allows only one person at a time to go in or out.

turnstile

'turntable 1. large, round platform on which a railway engine is turned round. **2.** small, round plate on which a gramophone record turns.

'turning point important point which causes great changes. *The battle was a turning point in our history.*

turn about face, cause to face, the opposite way.

turn against someone/something become, cause to become, unfriendly; refuse to obey. *The people turned against their president.*

turn aside go in another direction; take another road; do something else. *He turned aside from his life of crime.*

turn someone away turn, cause to turn, in another direction (esp. to avoid meeting or receiving somebody). *He turned away rather than have to meet me. Because the hall was full, many people were turned away.*

turn someone/something down 1. turn, cause to turn, downwards. 2. make less by turning a tap, knob etc. *As the radio set was making too much noise, he turned it down. He turned down the oil/gas lamp.* 3. refuse to consider or accept. *He applied for the job but the firm turned him down.*

turn in go to bed. *I think I'll turn in now.* (*informal*).

turn something in 1. turn, cause to turn, inwards. 2. hand in; return. *We turned in our books at the end of term.*

turn off 1. stop by turning a tap, knob etc. *He turned off the radio. I forgot to turn off the water.* 2. cause to dislike. *He turns me off.* (*informal* in sense 2.).

turn on someone/something 1. turn and attack. *The wounded lion turned on the hunter.* 2. start by turning a tap, knob etc. *He turned on the radio. When it became dark, I turned on the lights.* 3. depend on. *Everything turns on his reply.* 4. cause to like. *This music turns me on.* (*informal* in sense 4.).

turn something out 1. empty (esp. when looking for or tidying something). *I turned out my pockets. My mother is turning out the bedroom.* 2. come, cause to come, out for a special reason. *All our friends turned out to meet us. The soldiers were turned out to defend the city.* 3. produce. *This factory turns out bicycles. The college turns out a hundred teachers a year.* 4. cause somebody to leave against his will. *He was turned out of the hotel because he was drunk.* 5. stop something burning by turning a tap, knob etc. *He turned out the gas fire/lights.* (Also **turn off**). 6. be seen or found out (to be). *The examination turned out (to be) easy.*

'turnout *nc* 1. *My mother gave the bedroom a good turnout.* 2. *There was a big turnout of friends to meet us.* 3. *The college has a turnout of a hundred teachers a year.* 4. appearance; way one is dressed. *They admired the smart turnout of the soldiers.*

turned-out *adj*: *the smartly turned-out soldiers.*

turn something over 1. make responsible for; hand over. *The teacher turned over the class to one of the prefects.* 2. sell in business a certain amount of goods in a certain time. *This shop turns over no less than £100 a day.*

'turnover *nc* 1. *This shop has a turnover of no less than £100 a day.* 2. replacement of one person by another. *Last year there was a complete turnover of teachers in the English department of our school* i.e. all the teachers left and new ones took their place.

turn to someone ask; expect help from. *They always turn to me when they are in trouble.*

turn something up turn, cause to turn, upwards. *He turned up the bottom of his trousers.* 2. appear, cause to appear or be seen. *He turned up late for the game. We turned up some old books when we were emptying the bookcase.*

'turnup *nc* (*Brit*): *These trousers have no turnups* i.e. the bottoms are not turned up and sewn in place. (*US* **cuff**).

turn a deaf ear refuse to listen. (*informal*).

turn someone's head cause somebody to think he is better than he is. (*informal*).

turn loose allow to go free. *He turned the cattle loose in the field.*

turn somebody's stomach make somebody feel sick. (*informal*).

turn[2] [tə:n] *nc* 1. act of turning round. *This loose screw needs a turn or two.* 2. change of direction. *We are waiting for the turn of the tide. Never stop your car at a sharp turn in the road.* 3. (with **take**) change in state. *The weather has taken a turn for the worse.* 4. act or duty of several kinds. *It is your turn to wash the dishes* i.e. others have done so and it is now the time for you to do so. *He did me a good turn by lending me his bicycle* i.e. he kindly helped me. (*opp* **bad turn**). *The next turn on the stage was most amusing* i.e. act or performance. *He has gone for a turn in the garden* i.e. a walk. *Seeing him gave me a turn* i.e. gave me a fright. (*informal* in this sense).

at every turn very often; every time. *She has difficulties at every turn.*

by turns one after the other; changing from one to the other.

done to a turn (with reference to food) cooked neither too much nor too little; perfectly cooked. (*informal*).

in turn one after the other in order. *We went in turn to be examined by the doctor.*

on the turn about to turn. *The tide was on the turn.*

out of turn at the wrong time; earlier or later than is allowed. *He tried to be served in the shop out of (his) turn.*

take turns at something do something in turn.

turn of phrase way of expressing something.

turn about *adv* (with reference to two persons) alternatively; one, then the other. *We took turn about to stay with the injured man.* (Also **turn and turn about**).

turnip ['tə:nip] *nc/u* type of plant with a round root used as food and to feed animals.

turpentine ['tə:pəntain] *nu* type of oil used for mixing paint. (Also **turps**).

turpitude ['tə:pitju:d] *nu* wickedness.

turquoise ['tə:kwɔiz] 1. *nc* greenish-blue precious stone. 2. *nu* greenish-blue colour. Also *adj*.

turret ['tʌrit] *nc* 1. small tower on a building. 2. small steel tower covering a gun or guns which can move round, fitted on a warship, military tank or aircraft.

turtle ['tə:tl] *nc* (*Brit*) big tortoise which lives in the sea; (*US*) tortoise or sea tortoise.

turn turtle turn upside down (usu. in water).

turtledove ['tə:tldʌv] *nc* type of pigeon with a reddish head and neck and spotted wings.

tusk [tʌsk] *nc* long, pointed tooth which sticks out of the mouth of certain animals (e.g. elephant, walrus, boar).

tusker *nc* animal with tusks (esp. an elephant).

tussle ['tʌsl] *vi* (with **with**) struggle; fight. Also *nc*.

tussock ['tʌsək] *nc* clump or tuft of growing grass.

tut, tut-tut [tʌt, 'tʌ'tʌt] *interj* noise made to show disapproval. Also *vt/i* make this noise. *past* **tutted, tut-tutted.**

tutelage ['tju:təlidʒ] *nu* state of being in the charge of somebody; guardianship.

tutelary ['tju:tiləri] *adj*.

tutor ['tju:tə*] *nc* **1.** private teacher. **2.** (*Brit*) university lecturer who is responsible for directing the studies of a group of students. Also *vt* teach; act as tutor to.
tutorial [tju:'tɔ:riəl] *adj* of a tutor. Also *nc* period of instruction and discussion with a tutor.
tuxedo [tʌk'si:dou] *nc* (*US*) dinner jacket. *pl* **tuxedos.**
twaddle ['twɔdl] *nu* silly talk; nonsense.
twain [twein] *n* two. Also *adj*. (both *o.f.*).
twang [twæŋ] *nc* **1.** sound made when a tight string or wire is pulled and let go quickly. *We heard the twang of his bow as he shot an arrow.* **2.** same sound made by somebody who speaks through his nose. *He speaks with a twang.* Also *vt/i* make, cause to make, this sound.
'twas [twɔz] it was (*o.f.*).
tweak [twi:k] *vt* pull sharply and twist. Also *nc*: *He gave my ear a tweak.*
tweed [twi:d] **1.** *nu* type of woollen cloth. **2.** *nc* (in *pl*) clothes made from tweed. Also *adj*: *tweed jacket.*
tweezers ['twi:zəz] *npl* pair of small pincers used for picking up very small things or pulling out hairs (e.g. *eyebrow tweezers*).
twelve [twelv] see appendix.
twenty ['twenti] see appendix.
twice [twais] *adv* two times: *twice as much/many. He is twice the man you are* i.e. he is twice as good, strong etc.
twiddle ['twidl] *vt/i* turn idly or without any reason. *Stop twiddling (with) the radio!* i.e. turning the knobs or controls when there is no need to.
twiddle one's thumbs do nothing (except move one thumb round the other) (*informal*).
twig [twig] *nc* small branch of a tree or shrub. Also *vt* understand. *He twigged it.* (*informal*).
twilight ['twailait] *nu* half-light just after sunset or just before sunrise.
twill [twil] *nu* type of strong, cotton cloth.
'twill [twil] it will (*o.f.*).
twin [twin] *nc* one of two children born at the same time to the same mother. Also *adj* **1.** *twin sisters.* **2.** of one of a pair: *twin beds* i.e. two single beds which are exactly alike; *twin carburettors* i.e. two carburettors which are exactly alike and are fitted to the same engine.
Siamese twins twins who are born joined together.
twine [twain] *nu* string; wool. Also *vt/i* go, cause to go, round. *The plants twine round the tree as they grow. He twined the wire round the post.*
twinge [twindʒ] *nc* short, sharp pain.
twinkle ['twiŋkl] *vi* shine with a short, bright, changing light. *Stars twinkle. His eyes twinkled with delight.* Also *nu*: *the twinkle of stars; the twinkle in his eyes.*
twinkling *nu* moment; instant. *He disappeared in a twinkling/in the twinkling of an eye* i.e. instantly.
twirl [twə:l] *vt/i* turn, cause to turn, round and round quickly. Also *nc* quick movement round and round.
twist [twist] *vt/i* **1.** turn one thing round another (e.g. thread, string, wire). *He twisted the three ropes to make one very strong rope.* **2.** turn one end of something while the other is held or fixed. *I twisted my wet socks to dry them. The big boy twisted my arm* i.e. to cause pain. *If you twist the cork, it will come out of the bottle.* **3.** change direction suddenly. *The road twists over the hills. We had to twist (our way) through the thick forest.* **4.** (with reference to words) change the meaning of (usu. to give them a worse one). *Your enemies will twist everything you say.* Also *nc* **1.** act of twisting or being twisted. *The big boy gave my arm a twist. The road has many twists. By giving a twist to your words they can make them mean something else.* **2.** something made by twisting: *a twist of thread; a twist of tobacco.*
twisty *adj* full of twists.
twister *nc* **1.** somebody/something that twists; something difficult. **2.** person who is dishonest; cheat. (*informal*).
twit [twit] *vt* (with **about** or **with**) tease, or find fault with, somebody because he has done, or is doing, something wrong or amusing. *My friends twitted me about/with the bright socks I was wearing. past* **twitted.** Also *nc* foolish person. (*informal*).
twitch [twitʃ] *nc* **1.** uncontrolled movement of the body. **2.** sharp, sudden pull. Also *vt/i* move, cause to move, in this way. *He can't stop his hands twitching.*
twitter ['twitə*] *nc/u* sharp, short sound made by birds when they are excited; excited talk. Also *vt/i* make this sound; talk in this way.
in a twitter excited. *The old ladies were in a twitter when they saw the Queen.* (*informal*).
two [tu:] see appendix.
'two-'faced **1.** *adj* having two faces. **2.** not straightforward or honest. (*informal*).
'twofold *adj/adv* double.
twopenny ['tʌpəni] *adj* costing two pennies.
'two-'piece *adj* having two parts. *He was wearing a two-piece suit.*
'two-'time *vt* be unfaithful to. *He is two-timing his girlfriend.* (*informal*).
'two-'way *adj* (with reference to a road or a radio) allowing traffic or communication to move in both directions.
tycoon [tai'ku:n] *nc* very rich and powerful businessman.
tying ['taiiŋ] pres part of **tie.**
type [taip] *nc/u* **1.** class or kind; example. *There are several types of trees in the garden. He is not the type of man to tell a lie. A woman who seldom talks is not true to type* i.e. is not like all the others of the same type, not like other women. **2.** piece of metal with a letter or sign on it used in printing; letters or signs printed in this way. *The type in this book is so small that it is difficult to read.* Also *vt/i* print on paper using a typewriter.
typist *nc* person who types using a typewriter.
typical ['tipikl] *adj* of a type; true to type. *He is a typical Englishman.* (*opp* **untypical**).
typically *adv.*
typify ['tipifai] *vt* be of a certain type; be an example of. *This excellent essay typifies all his work.*
'typewriter machine which prints on paper when the letters or numbers on the keyboard are pressed down by the fingers.
typhoid ['taifɔid] *nu* type of disease.
typhoon [tai'fu:n] *nc* very strong, violent wind.
typhus ['taifəs] *nu* type of disease (different from *typhoid*).
typography [tai'pɔgrəfi] *nu* art or manner of printing. **typographical** [taipə'græfikl] *adj.* **typographically** *adv.* **typographer** *nc.*
tyrant ['tairnt] *nc* cruel and unjust ruler.
tyranny ['tirəni] *nc/u* cruel and unjust

rule; country ruled in this way; government of this kind.
tyrannical [ti'rænikl] *adj* of, like a tyrant. *He has a tyrannical father.*
tyrannize ['tirənaiz] *vt* rule or behave like a tyrant.

tyre ['taiə*] (*US* **tire**) *nc* iron or rubber ring round the wheel of a cart, car, bicycle etc.
tyro ['taiərou] *nc* see **tiro.**
tzar [zɑː*], **tzarina** [zɑː'riːnə] *nc* see **czar.**
tzetze ['tsetsi] *nc* see **tsetse.**

U

U- [juː] *prefix* shaped like a U (e.g. **U-bend; U-bolt; U-turn**).

ubiquitous [juː'bikwitəs] *adj* existing everywhere at the same time. **ubiquitously** *adv*. **ubiquity** *nu*.

U-boat ['juːbout] *nc* German submarine.

udder ['ʌdə*] *nc* part of a cow, goat etc from which milk comes.

ugh [əːh] *interj* expressing feelings of disgust.

ugly ['ʌgli] *adj* **1.** not pleasing to look at; badly shaped. **2.** dangerous: *an ugly situation*. **ugliness** *nu*.

ulcer ['ʌlsə*] *nc* sore on the skin or inside the body which produces pus. **ulcerous** *adj*. **ulcerate** ['ʌlsəreit] *vt/i* become, cause to become, ulcerous. *He had an ulcerated stomach*. **ulcerated** *adj*. **ulceration** [ʌlsə'reiʃən] *nu*.

ulterior [ʌl'tiəriə*] *adj* situated on the further side; beyond (most often in **ulterior motive** i.e. motive different from the one actually stated. *He says that he is doing this to help me, but I suspect an ulterior motive*).

ultimate ['ʌltimət] *adj* furthest; final; original: *the ultimate deterrent* i.e. the atomic bomb. **ultimately** *adv*.

ultimatum [ʌlti'meitəm] *nc* final demand which must be agreed to (e.g. one sent by one government to another which will cause a war if it is not agreed to).

ultra- ['ʌltrə] *prefix* more than is usual; extreme (e.g. **ultramodern** i.e. extremely modern).

ultramarine [ʌltrəmə'riːn] *nu* bright blue colour. Also *adj*.

ultraviolet ['ʌltrə'vaiələt] *adj* beyond the violet end of the spectrum and so not seen: *ultraviolet rays* i.e. invisible rays from the sun or from a special type of lamp which can improve health.

umber ['ʌmbə*] *nu* **1.** kind of yellowish brown earth used by artists as a colour. (It becomes reddish brown when burnt). **2.** this colour. Also *adj*.

umbilicus [ʌmbi'laikəs] *nc* navel.

umbilical [ʌm'bilikl] *adj*: *umbilical cord* i.e. long piece of flesh which connects a baby to its mother in the womb.

umbrage ['ʌmbridʒ] *nu* only in **take umbrage at** i.e. be offended by, resentful about. *They took umbrage at his remark about them*.

umbrella [ʌm'brelə] *nc* light frame covered with cloth etc, which can be opened or shut and is used as a shelter against the rain or sun.

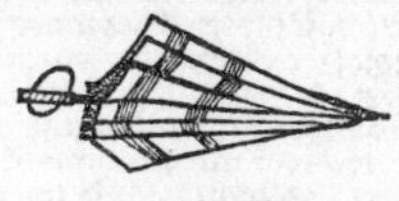

umbrella

umpire ['ʌmpaiə*] *nc* person chosen to decide a dispute or quarrel, or to see that the rules of certain games are followed (e.g. cricket, tennis, baseball; for football – use **referee**). Also *vt/i* act as umpire. *Will you umpire (in) our cricket match?*

umpteen ['ʌmptiːn] *adj* many. (*informal*).

un- [ʌn] *prefix* **1.** (before an *adj*, *adv* or *n*) not (e.g. **unable; unaffected**). **2.** (before a *verb*) do the opposite of (e.g. **undress; unchain**).

unabashed [ʌnə'bæʃt] *adj* not abashed or ashamed; knowing what to do or say.

unabated [ʌnə'beitid] *adj* (usu. with reference to noise, pain, suffering etc) not becoming less. *The storm continued unabated for several hours*.

unable [ʌn'eibl] *adj* (always with **to**) not able.

unabridged [ʌnə'bridʒd] *adj* (with reference to a book etc) not shortened; in full.

unacceptable [ʌnək'septəbl] *adj* not able to be accepted; not desirable.

unaccompanied [ʌnə'kʌmpənid] *adj* not accompanied (e.g. a person travelling alone; (of a song) sung without the help of a musical instrument).

unaccountable [ʌnə'kauntəbl] *adj* not able to be explained. **unaccountably** *adv*.

unaccustomed [ʌnə'kʌstəmd] *adj* **1.** (with **to**) not accustomed. **2.** new; not usual. *They do not know what to do with their unaccustomed wealth*.

unaffected [ʌnə'fektid] *adj* **1.** (with **by**) not affected. **2.** not trying to appear better than or different from others; natural: *unaffected behaviour*. **unaffectedly** *adv*.

unaided [ʌn'eidid] *adj* not aided; without help.

unalloyed [ʌnə'lɔid] *adj* pure; intense; not spoilt: *unalloyed delight*.

unalterable [ʌn'ɔːltərəbl] *adj* not able to be changed. **unalterably** *adv*.

unanimous [juː'næniməs] *adj* everybody agreeing; agreed to by everybody. *The decision to stop working was unanimous*. **unanimously** *adv*. **unanimity** [juːnə'nimiti] *nu*.

unanswerable [ʌn'ɑːnsərəbl] *adj* not able to be questioned or doubted; conclusive. *His argument is unanswerable*. **unanswerably** *adv*.

unanswered [ʌn'ɑːnsəd] *adj* not answered. *The question was left unanswered*.

unarmed [ʌn'ɑːmd] *adj* **1.** without weapons. **2.** defenceless.

unashamed [ʌnə'ʃeimd] *adj* not ashamed; rude. **unashamedly** [ʌnə'ʃeimidli] *adv*.

unasked [ʌn'ɑːskt] *adj* not asked; without being asked. *His presence here was unasked (for)*.

unassuming [ʌnə'sjuːmiŋ] *adj* modest; not proud or overbearing. **unassumingly** *adv*.

unattached [ʌnə'tætʃt] *adj* not attached to a particular person or group: *an unattached young man* i.e. one not yet married or engaged to be married; *an unattached voter* i.e. one who may vote for any political party.

unattended [ʌnəˈtendid] *adj* **1.** not followed by servants or a guard. **2.** not watched or looked after. *You should not leave your bicycle unattended in a busy street.*

unavailing [ʌnəˈveiliŋ] *adj* not successful; without any effect. **unavailingly** *adv.*

unavoidable [ʌnəˈvɔidəbl] *adj* not able to be avoided: *unavoidable delay.* **unavoidably** *adv.*

unaware [ʌnəˈwɛə*] *adj* (with **of**) not aware; not knowing.

unawares *adv* **1.** by surprise. *We took the enemy unawares by attacking at night.* **2.** without knowing. *You were speaking unawares to a very dangerous man.*

unbalanced [ʌnˈbælənst] *adj* not balanced; not having mental balance; mad.

unbar [ʌnˈbɑː*] *vt* allow to open by removing a bar: *unbar a door. past* **unbarred.**

unbearable [ʌnˈbɛərəbl] *adj* not able to be endured. **unbearably** *adv.*

unbeaten [ʌnˈbiːtn] *adj* not beaten; not defeated. *Our football team was unbeaten last year.*

unbecoming [ʌnbiˈkʌmiŋ] *adj* not suitable; rude: *an unbecoming dress* i.e. one which does not suit the person wearing it; *unbecoming behaviour.* **unbecomingly** *adv.*

unbeknown, unbeknownst [ʌnbiˈnoun(st)] *adj* (with **to**) without the knowledge of. *They arrived unbeknown to us.*

unbelief [ʌnbiˈliːf] *nu* refusal to believe; state of not believing in God. (Also **disbelief**).

unbeliever [ʌnbiˈliːvə*] *nc* person who does not believe (esp. in God).

unbelieving [ʌnbiˈliːviŋ] *adj* not believing. **unbelievingly** *adv.*

unbend [ʌnˈbend] *vt/i* become less stiff; behave in an easier manner; relax. *In public he was very solemn, but in private he unbent.*

unbending *adj* determined; fixed in purpose. **unbendingly** *adv.*

unbiased, unbiassed [ʌnˈbaiəst] *adj* without bias; not prejudiced; fair.

unblushing [ʌnˈblʌʃiŋ] *adj* without feeling any shame; rude. **unblushingly** *adv.*

unbolt [ʌnˈboult] *vt* open by drawing a bolt: *unbolt a door.*

unbosom [ʌnˈbuzəm] *vt* tell one's secret thoughts; speak very freely. *He unbosomed himself to me about all his family troubles.*

unbounded [ʌnˈbaundid] *adj* without limit; excessive.

unbridled [ʌnˈbraidld] *adj* without control or restraint. *He has an unbridled temper.*

unbroken [ʌnˈbroukən] *adj* **1.** without a break; continuous. *They had a life of unbroken happiness.* **2.** (with reference to records) not beaten. *His time for the mile is still unbroken.* **3.** (with reference to a horse etc) not tamed or trained.

unburden [ʌnˈbəːdn] *vt* get rid of a burden; make easier. *He unburdened his mind by telling me everything that was worrying him. He unburdened himself to me* i.e. he told me what was worrying him.

unbusinesslike [ʌnˈbiznislaik] *adj* not efficient; not well-organized.

unbutton [ʌnˈbʌtn] *vt* open the buttons of: *unbutton a shirt.*

uncalled [ʌnˈkɔːld] *adj* (with **for**) not necessary; not justified. *His anger was uncalled for when everybody was being very friendly to him.*

uncanny [ʌnˈkæni] *adj* not natural; not usual. *The way he was able to predict future events was positively uncanny.* **uncanniness** *nu.*

uncared [ʌnˈkɛəd] *adj* (with **for**) neglected; not looked after: *uncared-for children who have no parents.*

unceasing [ʌnˈsiːsiŋ] *adj* not stopping: *an unceasing noise.* **unceasingly** *adv.*

unceremonious [ʌnseriˈmouniəs] *adj* informal; rough and impolite. **unceremoniously** *adv.* **unceremoniousness** *nu.*

uncertain [ʌnˈsəːtn] *adj* **1.** not sure; doubtful. *We are/feel uncertain about/of the future. The date of his arrival is still uncertain.* **2.** not reliable. *The weather is uncertain.* **uncertainly** *adv.*

uncertainty *nc/u* something which is uncertain; state of being uncertain. *Life is full of uncertainties.*

unchain [ʌnˈtʃein] *vt* free by removing chains: *unchain a prisoner.*

uncharitable [ʌnˈtʃæritəbl] *adj* not kind; severe. **uncharitably** *adv.* **uncharitableness** *nu.*

uncharted [ʌnˈtʃɑːtid] *adj* not shown on a map; not explored so as to be shown on a map.

unchecked [ʌnˈtʃekt] *adj* not checked; not controlled or stopped: *the enemy's unchecked advance.*

uncivil [ʌnˈsivl] *adj* rude; disrespectful.

uncivilized [ʌnˈsivilaizd] *adj* rough, cruel and ignorant in behaviour etc.

uncle [ˈʌŋkl] *nc* brother of one's father or mother; husband of one's aunt.

unclean [ʌnˈkliːn] *adj* impure; dirty (in a harmful way). *Some religions regard the pig as an unclean animal.*

unclench [ʌnˈklentʃ] *vt* open by relaxing a tight grip: *unclench one's fists.*

unclouded [ʌnˈklaudid] *adj* clear; free from care: *an unclouded mind; unclouded happiness.*

Note: for the sense of free from clouds – use *cloudless.*

uncoloured [ʌnˈkʌləd] (*US* **uncolored**) *adj.* **1.** not coloured. **2.** plain and truthful. *He gave an uncoloured account of his adventures.*

uncomfortable [ʌnˈkʌmfətəbl] *adj* **1.** not comfortable. *I feel uncomfortable in this chair. This chair feels uncomfortable.* **2.** (with reference to feelings etc) uneasy; not content. *I have an uncomfortable feeling that we shall be too late.* **uncomfortably** *adv.*

uncommitted [ʌnkəˈmitid] *adj* **1.** not having committed oneself; not obliged to do something. **2.** (with reference to a country) not dependent on the larger and stronger countries: *the uncommitted nations.*

uncommon [ʌnˈkɔmən] *adj* not common; rare; extraordinary.

uncommonly *adv* unusually; very: *an uncommonly pretty girl.*

uncompromising [ʌnˈkɔmprəmaiziŋ] *adj* not compromising; refusing to come to an agreement or to change any of one's opinions. *He is an uncompromising defender of freedom.* **uncompromisingly** *adv.*

unconditional [ʌnkənˈdiʃənl] *adj* without conditions; complete. *They have reached an unconditional agreement.* **unconditionally** *adv.*

unconscionable [ʌnˈkɔnʃənəbl] *adj* beyond reason; excessive. **unconscionably** *adv.*

unconscious [ʌnˈkɔnʃəs] *adj* not conscious; not fully aware. *When he was hit on the head he became unconscious. Children make unconscious remarks* i.e. remarks which they

do not fully understand or think about before they make them. **unconsciously** *adv.* **unconsciousness** *nu.*
the unconscious part of the mind containing ideas of which one is not aware.

unconventional [ʌnkən'venʃənl] *adj* not following the normal rules or customs: *unconventional clothing; an unconventional idea.* **unconventionally** *adv.*

uncouple [ʌn'kʌpl] *vt* separate two things joined together: *uncouple a truck from a railway engine.*

uncouth [ʌn'ku:θ] *adj* (with reference to a person) having rough manners; awkward. **uncouthly** *adv.* **uncouthness** *nu.*

uncover [ʌn'kʌvə*] *vt* **1.** take the cover from; make known. **2.** leave undefended.

uncrowned [ʌn'kraund] *adj* not yet crowned; having the power but not the title (of king).

unction ['ʌŋkʃən] *nu* **1.** act of putting oil on the head or body of somebody (esp. on the head of a king or queen who is being crowned, or for a religious purpose). **2.** false emotion; lack of sincerity. *He speaks with great unction about the problem, but he does not really care.*
unctuous ['ʌŋktjuəs] *adj* very polite but not sincere. **unctuously** *adv.* **unctuousness** *nu.*
extreme unction former name of the religious ceremony administered by a Roman Catholic priest to a person who is dying.

uncut [ʌn'kʌt] *adj* not cut; (of a piece of writing etc) not shortened; (of a book) with the pages not slit.

undated [ʌn'deitid] *adj* not having a date. *His letter was undated.*

undecided [ʌndi'saidid] *adj* not decided; not yet sure. *He is undecided about what he should do. He is undecided about what to do.* **undecidedly** *adv.*

undeniable [ʌndi'naiəbl] *adj* not able to be denied; certain; obvious. **undeniably** *adv.*

under[1] ['ʌndə*] *prep* **1.** below in place. *The box is under the desk. Draw a line under your name. We looked under the bushes.* **2.** below in rank. *I worked under him for seven years. The assistant manager is under the manager.* **3.** less in number. *Under 100 people were present. Are you under 21 years of age? He sold it for under £10.* (*opp* **over**). **4.** during; while; in the condition of: *under discussion* i.e. still being discussed; *under repair* i.e. being repaired; *under sail* i.e. while sailing. *This land is under corn* i.e. is planted with corn. *He is living in France under a different name* i.e. different from the name he used to be known by. Also *adv* **1.** in or to a lower place. *The boat went under* i.e. sank. *You cannot keep people under forever* i.e. oppressed. **2.** during the rule of: *France under Napoleon.*

under-[2] ['ʌndə*] *prefix* **1.** (with *n*) below in place, rank, number etc: *underclothes; under-manager; all the under-twelves* i.e. children under twelve years of age. **2.** (with *verb*) not enough: *undercook; underpopulated.*

underarm ['ʌndərɑ:m] **1.** *adj* of the part of the body under the arm. **2.** *adj/adv* without raising the arm above the shoulder: *underarm bowling at cricket. He served underarm at tennis.* see also **underhand.**

undercarriage ['ʌndəkærid3] *nc* wheels etc on which an aircraft lands.

undercharge [ʌndə'tʃɑ:d3] *vt* not charge enough in price.

underclothes ['ʌndəklouðz] *npl* clothes worn under a suit or dress (esp. those worn next to the skin).
underclothing ['ʌndəklouðiŋ] *nu* underclothes.

undercover ['ʌndəkʌvə*] *adj* (esp. with reference to the secret service) secret.

undercurrent ['ʌndəkʌrnt] *nc* **1.** hidden movement or feeling. *There is an undercurrent of anger in their behaviour.* **2.** current which is below the surface of the main current of a stream.

undercut ['ʌndə'kʌt] *vt* **1.** cut away from below. **2.** sell more cheaply than others in order to get their trade. *past* **undercut.**

underdeveloped [ʌndədi'veləpt] *adj* (esp. of countries which need financial help) not fully developed.

underdog ['ʌndədɔg] *nc* person who usually loses; one neglected or oppressed by others.

underdone ['ʌndə'dʌn] *adj* not completely cooked.

underestimate [ʌndər'estimeit] *vt* not value highly enough; make too low an estimate of. Also *nc* estimate which is too low.

underexpose [ʌndəriks'pouz] *vt* (with reference to a camera film) not expose enough to the light. **underexposure** [ʌndəriks'pouʒə*] *nc/u.*

underfed [ʌndə'fed] *adj* not given enough to eat.

underfoot [ʌndə'fut] *adv* under the feet. *The wet ground was soft underfoot.*

undergarment ['ʌndəgɑ:mənt] *nc* see **garment.**

undergo [ʌndə'gou] *vt* suffer; receive. *He has just undergone an operation. I am undergoing an examination on Monday. past tense* **underwent** [ʌndə'went]. *past part* **undergone** [ʌndə'gɔn].

undergraduate [ʌndə'grædjuit] *nc* student at a university who has not yet got a degree.

underground ['ʌndəgraund] *adj* **1.** below the ground: *an underground railway.* **2.** (esp. with reference to resisting a government) secret: *the underground movement to free the country.* Also *adv* below the ground; secretly. Also *nc/u* **1.** underground railway. *Do you travel by the underground or by bus?* **2.** secret movement against a government. *After his country was defeated he joined the underground.*

undergrowth ['ʌndəgrouθ] *nu* smaller trees or bushes growing among taller trees.

underhand ['ʌndəhænd] *adj/adv* **1.** without raising the hand above the shoulder. *He served underhand at tennis.* see also **underarm.** **2.** secret; secretly; deceitful; deceitfully. *He gets what he wants in an underhand way.*

underline [ʌndə'lain] *vt* **1.** draw a line under. **2.** emphasize.

underling ['ʌndəliŋ] *nc* person who works under others. (rather *impolite*).

underlying [ʌndə'laiiŋ] *adj* under the surface, not easily seen, but important (often in **underlying causes**).

undermentioned [ʌndə'menʃənd] *adj* mentioned below or later (e.g. in a book).

undermine [ʌndə'main] *vt* **1.** make a mine or hole below something. **2.** slowly make weak. *Lack of food has undermined his strength.*

underneath [ʌndə'ni:θ] *adv/prep* below; under.

undernourished [ʌndə'nʌriʃt] *adj* not nourished enough.

underpass ['ʌndəpɑ:s] *nc* place where one

road passes under another. (*opp* **overpass** or **flyover**).

underpay [ʌndə'pei] *vt* not pay enough. *past* **underpaid. underpayment** *nc/u.*

underpopulated [ʌndə'pɔpjuleitid] *adj* (with reference to a country or part of one) not populated enough for its size or resources.

underprivileged [ʌndə'privilidʒd] *adj* not having as many privileges or benefits as other people in one's own country or other countries; poor.

underrate [ʌndə'reit] *vt* rate too low; not value highly enough.

undersell [ʌndə'sel] *vt* sell more cheaply than somebody else. *past* **undersold** [ʌndə'sould].

undershoot [ʌndə'ʃu:t] *vt* (with reference to aircraft) land too soon. (*opp* **overshoot**). *past* **undershot** [ʌndə'ʃɔt].

undersized [ʌndə'saizd] *adj* smaller in size than usual or than one/it ought to be.

understand [ʌndə'stænd] *vt/i* **1.** get the meaning of somebody/something. *They don't understand what we are saying. They don't understand us. I understand French. He understood why I had to go. My parents don't understand me* i.e. my personality. **2.** be informed; learn; assume. *I understand that you wish to see me. We understood them to be your friends. past* **understood** [ʌndə'stud].

understandable *adj* able to be understood.

understandably *adv.*

understanding *nu* **1.** comprehension; knowledge. *Have you any understanding of this problem? He is a teacher of great understanding.* **2.** (usu. with **an**) agreement. *We have an understanding not to meet each other when we are busy. They have come to/reached an understanding.* Also *adj* able to understand clearly the difficulties, feelings etc of somebody. *My doctor is a very understanding man.*

understand each other/one another clearly understand each other's/one another's difficulties, feelings etc.

give somebody to understand cause somebody to believe or think. *They gave us to understand (that) they would help.*

on the understanding that on condition that.

on this understanding having agreed that.

understate ['ʌndə'steit] *vt* not state strongly or fully enough.

understatement *nc/u*: *It is an understatement to say they are not very pleased. They are furious.*

understudy ['ʌndəstʌdi] *vt* study the part in a play taken by another actor in case he is absent; act in the place of another actor. Also *nc* person who understudies.

undertake [ʌndə'teik] *vt/i* **1.** agree or promise to do something. *He undertook to be here before midday. I have undertaken the work of cleaning all the rooms.* **2.** promise; guarantee. *We cannot undertake that we shall finish it in time. We cannot undertake to do that. past tense* **undertook** [ʌndə'tuk]. *past part* **undertaken.**

'undertaker *nc* (*Brit*) person who arranges funerals. (*US* **mortician**).

undertaking *nc* work to be done; promise.

undertone ['ʌndətoun] *nc* **1.** quiet tone of voice or colour. *They were speaking in undertones.* **2.** suggestion; hint. *There was an undertone of anger in his letter.*

undertook [ʌndə'tuk] past tense of **undertake.**

underwear ['ʌndəwɛə*] *nu* clothes worn under a suit or dress (esp. those worn next to the skin).

underwent [ʌndə'went] past tense of **undergo.**

underworld ['ʌndəwə:ld] *nu* **1.** place where it was once believed persons went after death. **2.** criminal part of a society or community.

underwrite ['ʌndərait] *vt* (esp. with reference to ships) promise to pay for all or part of the loss or damage which may occur in a business; promise to buy shares not bought by the public and so guarantee that the issue of the shares will be successful. *past tense* **underwrote** ['ʌndərout]. *past part* **underwritten** ['ʌndəritn]. **underwriter** *nc.*

undeserved [ʌndi'zə:vd] *adj* not deserved; not fair.

undesirable [ʌndi'zairəbl] *adj* not desirable; to be avoided; not approved. *Criminals are undesirable people.* Also *nc* undesirable person.

undid [ʌn'did] past tense of **undo.**

undies ['ʌndiz] *npl* women's underclothes. (*informal*).

undisciplined [ʌn'disiplind] *adj* badly behaved and not having the habit of obeying rules etc.

undo [ʌn'du:] *vt* destroy what has been done; unfasten. *Would you please undo my dress?* i.e. unfasten it. *She undid all her sewing. This mistake has undone all our good work. past tense* **undid** [ʌn'did]. *past part* **undone** [ʌn'dʌn].

undoing *nu* (esp. with reference to a person's character or reputation) ruin. *A passion for gambling proved to be his undoing.*

leave undone not do.

undoubted [ʌn'dautid] *adj* not doubted; certain. **undoubtedly** *adv.*

undreamed [ʌn'dri:md], **undreamt** [ʌn'dremt] *adj* (with **of**) not thought or imagined. *I have been given an undreamed-/undreamt-of chance of going to India.*

undress [ʌn'dres] **1.** *vi* remove one's clothes. **2.** *vt* remove someone's clothes: *undress a baby.* Also *nu*: *in a state of undress* i.e. with few or no clothes on.

undue ['ʌn'dju:] *adj* more than is needed or is suitable. *He gives undue attention to small problems.* **unduly** *adv.*

undulate ['ʌndjuleit] *vi* move up and down like waves. **undulation** [ʌndju'leiʃən] *nc/u.*

undying [ʌn'daiiŋ] *adj* never dying; going on forever: *undying fame.* **undyingly** *adv.*

unearned ['ʌn'ə:nd] *adj* not earned or deserved: *unearned income* i.e. income from investments, property etc, not from salary or wages.

unearth [ʌn'ə:θ] *vt* dig up; discover.

unearthly [ʌn'ə:θli] *adj* not of this world; very strange and frightening.

at an unearthly hour at a very early or inconvenient time. (*informal*).

uneasy [ʌn'i:zi] *adj* not at ease; worried.

uneasily *adv.* **uneasiness** *nu.*

unease *nu* uneasiness.

unemployed [ʌnim'plɔid] *adj* **1.** not being used. **2.** (with reference to a person) without work.

the unemployed all those who are without work.

unemployable *adj* not able to be employed.

unemployment *nu* state of being unemployed; number of unemployed persons. *Unemployment has increased because trade is bad.*

unending [ʌn'endiŋ] *adj* never ending. **unendingly** *adv*.
unequal [ʌn'i:kwəl] *adj* **1.** not equal: *a triangle with unequal sides*. **2.** not good in all parts: *an unequal piece of writing*. **3.** (with **to**) not good or strong enough for. *He is unequal to such important work*. **unequally** *adv*.
unerring [ʌn'ə:riŋ] *adj* sure; accurate. **unerringly** *adv*.
uneventful [ʌni'ventful] *adj* not eventful; quiet; without any trouble: *an uneventful journey*. **uneventfully** *adv*.
unexampled [ʌnig'za:mpld] *adj* without any example to compare with; outstanding; exceptional: *his unexampled courage*.
unexceptionable [ʌnik'sepʃənəbl] *adj* not able to be found fault with; perfect.
unfailing [ʌn'feiliŋ] *adj* never failing; always there when needed: *his unfailing cheerfulness*.
unfailingly *adv*: *unfailingly cheerful*.
unfair [ʌn'fεə*] *adj* not fair; unjust. **unfairly** *adv*. **unfairness** *nu*.
unfaithful [ʌn'feiθful] *adj* not faithful (esp. in marriage by having a love affair with someone not one's husband or wife); not doing what one has promised to do. **unfaithfully** *adv*.
unfamiliar [ʌnfə'miliə*] *adj* **1.** (with **to**) not well-known; strange. *The new work was unfamiliar to me*. **2.** (with **with**) not knowing well. *I was unfamiliar with the work*. **unfamiliarly** *adv*. **unfamiliarity** [ʌnfəmili'æriti] *nu*.
unfasten [ʌn'fa:sn] *vt* open by removing a fastening: *unfasten a belt*.
unfeeling [ʌn'fi:liŋ] *adj* without feeling or sympathy. **unfeelingly** *adv*.
unfeigned [ʌn'feind] *adj* not assumed; sincere; genuine. **unfeignedly** *adv*.
unfit [ʌn'fit] *adj* (usu. with **for** or **to do**) not fit. *He is unfit for/to do heavy work. Smoking has made him very unfit* i.e. unhealthy.
unflagging [ʌn'flægiŋ] *adj* continuing to work hard etc, after a long time, and showing no signs of tiredness. *He was unflagging in his efforts to help us*.
unflinching [ʌn'flintʃiŋ] *adj* not withdrawing from or not trying to avoid something unpleasant or dangerous. **unflinchingly** *adv*.
unfold [ʌn'fould] *vt/i* **1.** open the folds of. *He unfolded the map*. **2.** become, cause to become, known. *A strange story unfolded from what he told us. They have unfolded all their secrets to us*.
unforeseen ['ʌnfɔ:'si:n] *adj* not expected at an earlier time. *Unforeseen circumstances have forced us to cancel the meeting*.
unforgettable [ʌnfə'getəbl] *adj* making a very strong impression, and so not easily forgotten: *unforgettable holiday*. **unforgettably** *adv*.
unfortunate [ʌn'fɔ:tʃənit] *adj* **1.** not fortunate. *He was unfortunate not to win the race* i.e. he lost only because of bad luck. **2.** not suitable and causing difficulty. *That was an unfortunate remark to make. He came at an unfortunate time*. **unfortunately** *adv*.
unfounded [ʌn'faundid] *adj* false; without cause: *an unfounded allegation* i.e. something said which is not true.
unfrock [ʌn'frɔk] *vt* (with reference to a priest) dismiss for bad behaviour.
unfurnished [ʌn'fə:niʃt] *adj* (with reference to a house, flat, lodgings etc) let without furniture.
ungainly [ʌn'geinli] *adj* clumsy; awkward. **ungainliness** *nu*.
ungodly [ʌn'gɔdli] *adj* **1.** not godly; sinful. **2.** shocking. (*informal* in sense **2.**). **ungodliness** *nu*.
ungovernable [ʌn'gʌvənəbl] *adj* not able to be controlled. **ungovernably** *adv*.
unguarded [ʌn'ga:did] *adj* **1.** not guarded. **2.** careless: *an unguarded remark*. **unguardedly** *adv*.
unhand [ʌn'hænd] *vt* take one's hands off (*o.f.*).
unhealthy [ʌn'helθi] *adj* **1.** harmful to the health: *unhealthy climate*. **2.** not in good health; often ill: *unhealthy person*. **3.** harmful to moral or spiritual health: *unhealthy interest in money*. **unhealthiness** *nu*.
unheard [ʌn'hə:d] *adj* not heard.
un'heard-of *adj* never known before; most unusual. *It was unheard-of for anyone to speak to the headmaster like that*.
unhinged [ʌn'hindʒd] *adj* (with reference to a person) mad. (*informal*).
unicorn ['ju:nikɔ:n] *nc* animal in legend like a horse, having one horn growing from the middle of its head.
uniform ['ju:nifɔ:m] *adj* always having the same form; not different; never changing. *Bricks must be of uniform size. The meat must be cooked at a uniform temperature*. Also *nc/u* official dress. *Soldiers wear uniform(s)*. **uniformly** *adv*.
uniformity [ju:ni'fɔ:miti] *nu* state of being the same.
unify ['ju:nifai] *vt* make into one; join together. **unification** [ju:nifi'keiʃən] *nu*.
unilateral [ju:ni'lætərl] *adj* one-sided; done by one side or party only. *The presidents of the two countries promised that they would not take unilateral action on the matter* i.e. that each would consult the other before acting. **unilaterally** *adv*.
unimpeachable [ʌnim'pi:tʃəbl] *adj* not able to be doubted or criticized. **unimpeachably** *adv*.
uninformed [ʌnin'fɔ:md] *adj* not well enough informed; ignorant.
union ['ju:niən] **1.** *nc/u* act or state of being joined together: *the union of the three companies into one; the Union of Soviet Socialist Republics*. **2.** *nc* organization for a special purpose: *trade union; customs union; students' union*.
unionist *nc* **1.** member of a trade union. **2.** (usu. **Unionist**) person who supports or supported political union (e.g. between Great Britain and Ireland, or between the northern and southern States during the American Civil War).
unique [ju:'ni:k] *adj* only one of its kind; completely different from any other. **uniquely** *adv*. **uniqueness** *nu*.
unison ['ju:nisn] *nu* agreement.
in unison **1.** together. **2.** (with reference to a choir singing) with all voices singing the same notes.
unit ['ju:nit] *nc* **1.** single person/thing; groups of persons/things regarded as one. *The soldiers returned to their unit* i.e. company, regiment etc to which they belong. **2.** fixed amount or length used in measuring. *In France and many other countries the unit of length is the metre*. **3.** smallest whole number; the number one. **4.** piece of equipment (sometimes made up of several parts): *kitchen unit*.
unitary ['ju:nitəri] *adj* of a unit; whole.
'unit 'trust company which invests money

received from the public in a large number of businesses.

unite [ju'nait] *vt/i* become, cause to become, one; join together. *England and Scotland united to become the United Kingdom. The people united to overthrow/in overthrowing the government.* **united** *adj.* **unitedly** *adv.*

unity ['ju:niti] *nc/u* **1.** state of being united; state of forming a complete whole. **2.** agreement; common purpose. (*opp* **disunity**).

universe ['ju:nivə:s] *nu* everything that exists, including all living creatures, the earth, the sun, moon and stars.

universal [ju:ni'və:sl] *adj* of the universe; general; world-wide. *Football is a universal game.* **universally** *adv.* **universality** [ju:nivə:'sæliti] *nu.*

university [ju:ni'və:siti] *nc* place of higher education and research which awards degrees to its students.

unkempt [ʌn'kempt] *adj* with untidy hair; dirty.

unlawful [ʌn'lɔ:ful] *adj* forbidden by law. **unlawfully** *adv.*

unleash [ʌn'li:ʃ] *vt* free from a leash; let go: *unleash a dog; unleash nuclear energy.*

unless [ʌn'les] *conj* if . . . not. *I refuse to do it unless you help.*

unlettered [ʌn'letəd] *adj* not able to read; illiterate.

unlike [ʌn'laik] *adj* not similar in appearance, behaviour etc. Also *prep*: *Unlike me, he doesn't smoke.*

unlikely *adj* **1.** not probable. *It is unlikely that he knows the answer.* **2.** unexpected or difficult to believe: *an unlikely explanation.* **unlikelihood** [ʌn'laiklihud] *nu.*

unload [ʌn'loud] *vt/i* **1.** take the load from. *They unloaded the ships in the harbour. The ships in the harbour were unloading.* **2.** (with reference to a gun etc) take out the bullet(s) or shell(s) without firing it. **3.** sell or dispose of quickly. (*informal* in sense **3.**).

unlooked-for [ʌn'luktfɔ:*] *adj* not expected.

unman [ʌn'mæn] *vt* **1.** take away somebody's courage or strength. *past* **unmanned.**

unmanned *adj* not having anybody inside; without a crew: *an unmanned space rocket.*

unmannered [ʌn'mænəd] *adj* not having good manners. **unmannerly** [ʌn'mænəli] *adv.*

unmask [ʌn'mɑ:sk] *vt/i* **1.** take off a mask. **2.** show somebody/something as he or it really is.

unmatched [ʌn'mætʃt] *adj* having no equal; best or worst of its kind.

unmentionable [ʌn'menʃənəbl] *adj* not able to be mentioned (because it is shocking).

unmistakable [ʌnmi'steikəbl] *adj* about which there can be no doubt; clear; certain. **unmistakably** *adv.*

unmitigated [ʌn'mitigeitid] *adj* (usu. with reference to something bad) complete in every way: *an unmitigated liar.*

unmoved [ʌn'mu:vd] *adj* not moved emotionally; calm. *He was unmoved by the prisoner's pleas for mercy.*

unnatural [ʌn'nætʃərl] *adj* not natural; abnormal. **unnaturally** *adv.*

unnerve [ʌn'nə:v] *vt* cause somebody to lose his nerve; weaken somebody's confidence or courage.

unpack [ʌn'pæk] *vt/i* take from a box or trunk etc things which have been packed in it.

unparalleled [ʌn'pærəleld] *adj* having no equal; exceptional.

unpick [ʌn'pik] *vt* take out the stitches from. *Her mother unpicked the dress and sewed it again.*

unpin [ʌn'pin] *vt* take the pins from; unfasten. *past* **unpinned.**

unpleasant [ʌn'pleznt] *adj* not pleasant; disagreeable. **unpleasantly** *adv.*

unpleasantness *nu* unpleasant feeling; unpleasant quarrel.

unprecedented [ʌn'presidentid] *adj* having no precedent; having no earlier example; first of its kind. **unprecedently** *adv.*

unpremeditated ['ʌnpri:'mediteitid] *adj* not previously planned or thought about.

unpretending [ʌnpri'tendiŋ], **unpretentious** [ʌnpri'tenʃəs] *adj* not pretending to be important; modest. **unpretentiously** *adv.* **unpretentiousness** *nu.*

unprincipled [ʌn'prinsipld] *adj* without moral principles; bad.

unprintable [ʌn'printəbl] *adj* not suitable for publication because of obscene language etc.

unprofessional [ʌnprə'feʃənl] *adj* not obeying the rules of a profession. *The doctor was dismissed for unprofessional conduct.* **unprofessionally** *adv.*

unqualified [ʌn'kwɔlifaid] *adj* **1.** not qualified: *an unqualified teacher.* **2.** complete; not limited in any way. *They have given their unqualified approval.*

unquestionable [ʌn'kwestʃənəbl] *adj* not questionable; not to be doubted; certain. **unquestionably** *adv.*

unquestioned [ʌn'kwestʃənd] *adj* not questioned; not argued about. *His stupid remarks should not go unquestioned.*

unquestioning [ʌn'kwestʃəniŋ] *adj* done without asking any questions or without hesitating: *his unquestioning loyalty to his chief.*

unquote ['ʌn'kwout] *vt/i* used to show the end of a quotation. *I now quote what he said – 'Success depends on hard work', unquote.*

unravel [ʌn'rævl] *vt/i* **1.** (with reference to something which is knitted, sewn or tied) become, cause to become, separate. *Can you unravel the knots tied round the parcel?* **2.** solve something difficult. *past* **unravelled.** (*US* **unraveled**).

unread [ʌn'red] *adj* not read: *leave a book unread.*

unrelieved [ʌnri'li:vd] *adj* not relieved; not having anything to change its condition or appearance. *They had a life of unrelieved poverty.* **unrelievedly** *adv.*

unremitting [ʌnri'mitiŋ] *adj* never ending: *unremitting hard work.*

unreserved [ʌnri'zə:vd] *adj* **1.** (with reference to seats or places at a concert, meeting etc) not previously booked or set aside for somebody. **2.** not reserved; outspoken; definite.

unreservedly [ʌnri'zə:vədli] *adv* frankly; definitely.

unrest [ʌn'rest] *nu* dissatisfaction which may lead to trouble or violence: *social/political unrest.*

unrivalled [ʌn'raivld] (*US* **unrivaled**) *adj* having no rival or equal; exceptional.

unruffled [ʌn'rʌfld] *adj* not disturbed; calm.

unruly [ʌn'ru:li] *adj* not easily controlled; refusing to obey.

unsaid [ʌn'sed] *adj* not said; understood without being said. *Some things are better*

left unsaid i.e. it is not always good to express what one feels or thinks.
unsavoury [ʌn'seivəri] (*US* **unsavory**) *adj* not pleasant; disgusting. **unsavouriness** *nu*.
unscathed [ʌn'skeiðd] *adj* safe; without injury.
unscientific ['ʌnsaiən'tifik] *adj* not based on scientific methods: *unscientific ideas*.
unscrupulous [ʌn'skru:pjuləs] *adj* not scrupulous; ruthless. **unscrupulously** *adv*. **unscrupulousness** *nu*.
unseemly [ʌn'si:mli] *adj* (esp. with reference to behaviour) not suitable; disgusting. **unseemliness** *nu*.
unseen [ʌn'si:n] *adj* not able to be seen; invisible. Also *nc* something written in a foreign language which has to be translated into one's own language without having been seen previously (usu. in an examination).
unsightly [ʌn'saitli] *adj* not pleasing to the eye; ugly. **unsightliness** *nu*.
unsound [ʌn'saund] *adj* not perfect; (with reference to the mind) damaged.
unsparing [ʌn'spɛəriŋ] *adj* working as hard as possible: *be unsparing in one's efforts*.
unspeakable [ʌn'spi:kəbl] *adj* not fit to be expressed in words. **unspeakably** *adv*.
unstable [ʌn'steibl] *adj* **1.** showing great and sudden changes (esp. in a way which is not normal): *an unstable person; unstable weather conditions*. **2.** (physics and chemistry) easily changing in form: *unstable elements*. **instability** [instə'biliti] *nu*.
unstudied [ʌn'stʌdid] *adj* natural; without effort.
unswerving [ʌn'swə:viŋ] *adj* steady; reliable. **unswervingly** *adv*.
untidy [ʌn'taidi] *adj* not tidy. Also *vt*. **untidily** *adv*. **untidiness** *nu*.
until [ʌn'til] *prep/conj* see **till**[1].
untimely [ʌn'taimli] *adj* happening too soon or at the wrong time.
untiring [ʌn'taiəriŋ] *adj* not becoming tired; continuing to work hard: *be untiring in one's efforts*.
unto ['ʌntu] *prep* to (*o.f.*).
untold [ʌn'tould] *adj* too great or too many to be counted: *untold millions; untold wealth*.
untouchable [ʌn'tʌtʃəbl] *adj* not able or fit to be touched. Also *nc* person belonging to the lowest caste of Indian society (now a **Harijan** ['hærijæn]).
untoward [ʌntə'wɔ:d] *adj* unlucky; inconvenient. (rather *o.f.*).
untrammelled [ʌn'træmld] *adj* without control or hindrance.
unvarnished [ʌn'vɑ:niʃt] *adj* **1.** (with reference to a statement, story etc) plain; giving only the facts. **2.** (with reference to wood) not covered with varnish.
unveil [ʌn'veil] *vt* take off a veil; show to the public for the first time (e.g. a statue or memorial).
unwieldy [ʌn'wi:ldi] *adj* difficult to move or carry. **unwieldiness** *nu*.
unwitting [ʌn'witiŋ] *adj* not knowing; not intending. **unwittingly** *adv*.
unwonted [ʌn'wountid] *adj* not usual. (rather *o.f.*).
up [ʌp] *adj/adv/prep* **1.** to a higher place. *He climbed up the hill. They ran up the stairs*. (*opp* **down**). **2.** in or to a higher place or state. *He climbed up by himself. Can you carry it up? The price of meat is up*. (*opp* **down**). **3.** out of bed; on one's feet. *Are the children up yet? He stayed up till 11 o'clock last night. The boys stood up when the teacher came into the classroom*. **4.** to the north. *They sailed up to Iceland* i.e. from the south. (*opp* **down**). **5.** (*Brit*) to a larger or more important place; to a more important person. *They have gone up to London* (used even if travelling from the north). *Are you going up to town? All the school reports go up to the headmaster*. **6.** close to; nearer. *They went up to the policeman to ask the way. Go up to that door and knock*. **7.** completely; more strongly. *They drank up all the beer. Have you tied up the parcel? Time's up* i.e. the time allowed for something is over. *Hurry up! Why doesn't he speak up? I can't hear him*. **8.** *the up train* i.e. the one going to town. (*opp* **down train**).
up-and-coming *adj* (with reference to a person) likely to be successful; promising.
up and down *adv* **1.** rising and falling. *The boat went up and down on the rough sea*. **2.** backwards and forwards. *People were walking up and down in front of the school*.
ups and downs *npl* good and bad times; changes in one's luck. *Life has its ups and downs*. (*informal*).
up against meeting difficulties. *We shall be up against a strong team in the next match. Having lost all his money, he is up against it* i.e. he is in difficulties. (*informal*).
up to 1. as far as. *Up to now I've been lucky. He has read up to chapter ten*. **2.** depending on. *It is now up to them to do it*. **3.** as good as; ready for. *His work is not up to the required standard. They are not up to doing it by themselves*. **4.** intending to do; busy with (often something bad or mischievous). *What are these boys up to?*
what's up? what is the matter?, what is happening? (*informal*).
upbraid [ʌp'breid] *vt* blame; scold. (rather *o.f.*).
upbringing ['ʌpbriŋiŋ] *nc/u* training and education of a child.
upcountry ['ʌp'kʌntri] *adj/adv* (usu. with reference to a tropical country) inland; away from the coast.
upgrade [ʌp'greid] *vt* put in a higher grade. **upgrading** *nc/u*.
upheaval [ʌp'hi:vl] *nc* sudden disturbance or change.
upheld [ʌp'held] past of **uphold**.
uphill ['ʌp'hil] *adj/adv* **1.** going up a hill. *We walked uphill*. **2.** difficult: *uphill work*.
uphold [ʌp'hould] *vt* approve; support a decision. *past* **upheld** [ʌp'held].
upholster [ʌp'houlstə*] *vt* fit chairs and other pieces of furniture with springs and cover them with cloth, leather etc. **upholsterer** *nc*.
upholstery *nu* business of an upholsterer; materials used to upholster.
upkeep ['ʌpki:p] *nu* act of keeping something in good condition (e.g. a house, car or garden); cost of doing so.
upland ['ʌplənd] *nc* (usu. *pl*) high but fairly level part of a country. Also *adj*: *the upland parts of the country*.
uplift [ʌp'lift] *vt* (esp. with reference to the feelings or spirit) raise up; improve. Also ['ʌplift] *nu*: *the moral uplift of a great book*.
upmost ['ʌpmoust] *adj/adv* highest. see also **uppermost**.
upon [ə'pɔn] *prep* on.
Note: *on* and *upon* have the same sense but *on* is by far the more commonly used. There are, however, a few phrases in which only *upon* is used (e.g. *once upon a time;*

put upon somebody i.e. ask from somebody more than one should).

upper ['ʌpə*] *adj* higher: *upper lip.* (*opp* **lower**). *superlative* **uppermost, upmost.** Also *nc* higher part of a shoe above the sole.

uppermost *adj/adv* **1.** highest. **2.** (with reference to thoughts, ideas) receiving most attention; most likely to be carried out. *The uppermost thought in my mind was to escape.*

upper classes *npl* the rich and powerful people in society. **upper-class** *adj.*

'**uppercut** blow made upwards with the arm bent and the fist closed.

have/get the upper hand see **hand**[1].

uppish ['ʌpiʃ] *adj* too self-confident; too proud. **uppishly** *adv.* **uppishness** *nu.* (all *informal*).

upright ['ʌprait] **1.** *adj/adv* straight up; vertical, vertically. *Are these plants upright? The soldier stood upright.* **2.** *adj* honest and just. *He is an upright citizen.* Also *nc* something which is fixed in an upright position. *The roof was held up by four uprights.* **uprightly** *adv.* **uprightness** *nu.*

upright piano see **piano.**

uprising ['ʌpraiziŋ] *nc* revolt.

uproar ['ʌprɔ:*] *nu* (usu. with **an**) violent and noisy shouting. *There was an uproar when he told them they had all failed in the examination.*

uproarious [ʌp'rɔ:riəs] *adj* noisy but happy. **uproariously** *adv.* **uproariousness** *nu.*

uproot [ʌp'ru:t] *vt* pull up by the roots; get rid of.

upset [ʌp'set] *vt/i* **1.** turn over; knock over. *The boat will upset if you move about in it. He upset the teapot.* **2.** be, cause to be, distressed or disturbed. *They were very upset when they heard the news. The news upset them. The sudden rain upset our game of tennis. pres part* **upsetting.** *past* **upset.** Also ['ʌpset] *nc*: *The news was a great upset to them.*

upshot ['ʌpʃɔt] *nu* (with **the**) result. *What was the upshot of the official investigation?*

upside down ['ʌpsai'daun] *adv* with the top side underneath; in confusion. *That picture is hanging upside down. He turned the whole room upside down looking for his book.*

upstairs ['ʌp'stɛəz] *adv* to or on the upper floor. Also *adj*: *an upstairs room.*

upstanding [ʌp'stændiŋ] *adj* (with reference to a person) standing straight; honest.

upstart ['ʌpstɑ:t] *nc* person who has suddenly become rich or powerful and is unpleasant because of this. Also *adj.*

upstream [ʌp'stri:m] *adv* against the flow of water in a river, stream etc. *It is much more difficult to row a boat upstream than downstream.*

uptake ['ʌpteik] *nu* only in **quick/slow on the uptake** i.e. quick/slow to understand. (*informal*).

up-to-date ['ʌptə deit] *adj* of the latest kind; right up to the present: *up-to-date clothes; up-to-date information.*

Note: as a *pred adj* write *up to date* without hyphens. *You must keep up to date.*

uptown ['ʌptaun] *adj/adv* (mainly *US*) of, to, in the part of town where the wealthier people live away from the main area or business area. (*opp* **downtown**).

upward ['ʌpwəd] *adj* going higher: *an upward movement of the arm.*

upwards *adv* to a higher place. *The path went upwards through the forest.*

upwards of more than.

uranium [ju:'reiniəm] *nu* type of radioactive metal (U).

urban ['ə:bən] *adj* of a town.

urbanize *vt* make urban. **urbanization** [ə:bənai'zeiʃən] *nu.*

urbane [ə:'bein] *adj* very polite; refined. **urbanely** *adv.* **urbanity** [ə:'bæniti] *nc/u.*

urchin ['ə:tʃin] *nc* **1.** small and mischievous boy. **2.** type of small sea animal with a round spiky shell. (Usu. **sea urchin**).

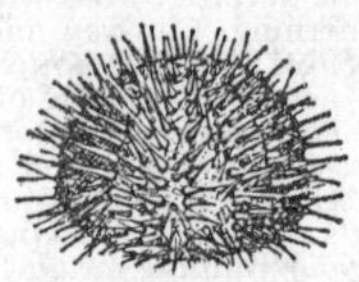

urchin (*def* 2)

urge ['ə:dʒ] *vt* **1.** try hard to make somebody do something; drive. *They urged me to go home at once. The officer urged his men on.* **2.** (with **upon**) bring strongly to the attention of. *They urged upon me the need to escape.* Also *nu* act of urging; strong desire. *I resisted an urge to interrupt the speaker.*

urgent ['ə:dʒənt] *adj* requiring immediate attention. *I received an urgent message from my father telling me to return home at once.*

urgently *adv.*

urgency ['ə:dʒənsi] *nu*: *This is a problem of great urgency.*

urine ['juərin] *nu* waste liquid from the body.

uric ['juərik] *adj.* **urinary** ['juərinəri] *adj.*

urinal [juə'rainl] *nc* container for urine; public lavatory for men.

urinate ['juərineit] *vi* pass urine. **urination** [juəri'neiʃən] *nu.*

urn [ə:n] *nc* **1.** tall container with a narrow neck (esp. used for the ashes of the dead after cremation). **2.** large metal container with a tap used for holding liquid (e.g. tea or coffee).

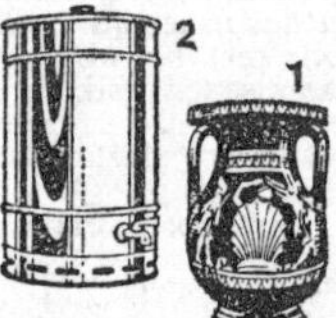

urns (*def* 2) (*def* 1)

use[1] [ju:z] *vt* **1.** employ for a purpose; do something with something. *They used a rope to tie the boat. Can I use your telephone? You must use your own judgment.* **2.** spend; finish. *Have we used all the writing paper?* **3.** (with **up**) spend or finish completely. *They have used up their money.*

used[1] [ju:zd] *adj* already used, so not new or clean. *Please put the used towels in this basket.*

used[2] [ju:st] (with **to**) accustomed to. *I am not used to getting up early. They are not used to cold weather.*

used to part of the verb which has the sense of something happening regularly or often in the past. *They used to go to the market every Saturday. This is the village where we used to live. Did you use to play football?*

(less commonly *Used you to play football?*) *He used to play cricket, didn't he?* (less commonly *Usen't he to play cricket?*) *Yes, he did.*
usable *adj* able to be used, fit for use. (*opp* **unusable**).
usage ['ju:sidʒ] **1.** *nu* way in which something is used. **2.** *nc/u* established custom; approved way of using or doing something. *The usages of some English words are difficult to learn.*
user *nc* somebody/something that uses.

use² [ju:s] **1.** *nc* purpose; work which can be done by something. *Can you find a use for these empty boxes? A sharp knife has many uses.* **2.** *nu* act or condition of using or being used. *This classroom is for the use of young children only. The use of the present tense in this sentence is wrong.* **3.** *nu* benefit; value. *What's the use of working so hard? It is no use your running away..It is no use for you to run away.*
useful *adj* **1.** handy; having good results. *I find this pen very useful.* **2.** (with reference to a person having influence) efficient. *He is a useful friend to have.* **usefully** *adv.* **usefulness** *nu.*
useless *adj* of no use; not efficient; having no effect. *A blunt knife is useless. These workmen are useless. It's useless to run away.* **uselessly** *adv.* **uselessness** *nu.*
come into use begin to be used. *The word 'blizzard' first came into use about a hundred years ago.*
give the use of allow to use. *I often give him the use of my car.*
go out of use be no longer used.
in use being used.
lose the use of be no longer able to use (usu. of eyes, legs etc).
make use of see **make¹**.
make the best use of use in the best way.
out of use no longer being used.

usher ['ʌʃə*] *nc* person who leads people to their seats in a cinema, theatre, church etc. Also *vt* **1.** lead to a seat or room. *I was ushered into the headmaster's office by my teacher.* **2.** (with **in**) introduce; begin. *Independence has ushered in a new age.*
usherette [ʌʃə'ret] *nc* woman who leads people to their seats (usu. in a cinema or theatre).

usual ['ju:ʒl] *adj* often happening or being done; common; normal. (*opp* **unusual**). **usually** *adv.*

usurp [ju:'zə:p] *vt* take somebody's position unlawfully or by force. *He killed the king and usurped the throne.* **usurper** *nc.*
usurpation [ju:zə:'peiʃən] *nc/u* act of usurping.

usury ['ju:ʒuri] *nu* practice of lending money and charging interest for doing so; high interest on money lent. **usurious** [ju:'ʒuəriəs] *adj.*
usurer ['ju:ʒərə*] *nc* person who lends money in this way.

utensil [ju:'tensl] *nc* container or instrument of any kind used in the home (esp. in the kitchen).

uterus ['ju:tərəs] *nc* womb.

utilitarian [ju:tili'tεəriən] *adj* **1.** of practical use only. **2.** of utilitarianism. Also *nc* person who believes in utilitarianism.
utilitarianism *nu* theory that the aim of life should be the greatest happiness of the greatest number of people.

utility [ju:'tiliti] **1.** *nu* usefulness; quality of being useful. **2.** *nc* something which is useful to, and is used by, many people. *Railways and roads are public utilities.* Also *adj* simple but useful: *utility clothes.*

utilize ['ju:tilaiz] *vt* use; make useful.
utilizable *adj* able to be utilized. **utilization** [ju:tilai'zeiʃən] *nu.*

utmost ['ʌtmoust] *adj* **1.** farthest away. **2.** greatest. *You must do your work with the utmost care.* Also *nu* the most that is possible. *He tried his utmost to win.*

Utopia [ju:'toupiə] *nc* imaginary place with a perfect social and political system.
Utopian *adj* ideal but impossible to achieve.

utter¹ ['ʌtə*] *adj* complete. *He is an utter fool.* **utterly** *adv.*

utter² ['ʌtə*] *vt* **1.** make a sound with the mouth; speak. *She uttered a sigh. Don't utter another word.* **2.** (with reference to a false cheque) pass for payment.
utterance *nc/u* something spoken; word.

uvula ['ju:vjulə] *nc* small piece of flesh hanging down over the back of the tongue.
uvular ['ju:vjulə*] *adj.*

uxorious [ʌk'sɔ:riəs] *adj* too fond of one's wife or wives, in a foolish or unmanly way.
uxoriousness *nu.*

V

vacant ['veikənt] *adj* **1.** empty; not occupied. *There was not a vacant seat in the hall.* **2.** not interested; stupid. *He gave us a vacant look.* **vacantly** *adv.*
vacancy 1. *nu* state of being empty or not occupied. **2.** *nc* position or job which has not yet been filled. *The school has vacancies for three teachers.* **3.** *nu* lack of interest or intelligence.
vacate [və'keit] *vt* leave empty or not occupied. *They must vacate their rooms in the hotel before Saturday.*
vacation 1. *nu* act of vacating. **2.** *nc* time when schools, colleges and courts of law are closed. **3.** *nc/u* holidays. *Where are you spending your vacation?* Also *vi* (*US*) spend holidays.
vaccine ['væksi:n] *nc/u* substance introduced into a human or animal body to protect it from getting certain diseases (e.g. measles, smallpox).
vaccinate ['væksineit] *vt* put a vaccine into a human or animal body (esp. the vaccine against smallpox).
vaccination [væksi'neiʃən] *nc/u* act of vaccinating or being vaccinated.
vacillate ['væsileit] *vi* be unable to decide; hesitate; continue to change from one opinion to another. *They vacillated between going away and staying where they were.*
vacillation [væsi'leiʃən] *nc/u.*
vacuous ['vækjuəs] *adj* not showing interest or intelligence: *a vacuous remark.* **vacuously** *adv.*
vacuity [væ'kju:iti] *nc/u* vacuous act; state of being vacuous.
vacuum ['vækjum] *nc* space completely empty of substance or gas; space from which air or another gas has been removed.
'vacuum cleaner type of machine which sucks dirt and dust from carpets, curtains etc.
'vacuum flask type of container with a smaller container inside it and a vacuum between them, used for keeping the contents at a constant temperature. (Usu. **thermos flask**) (*US* **vacuum bottle**).
'vacuum tube closed glass tube in which a vacuum has been made and through which electricity is passed.
vagabond ['vægəbɔnd] *adj* moving from place to place without a home. Also *nc* person who does this.
vagary ['veigəri] *nc* (often *pl*) act or thoughts for which there is no clear reason. *It is difficult to explain the vagaries of a child's mind.*
vagina [və'dʒainə] *nc* passage in the body of a female mammal, leading to the womb.
vagrant ['veigrnt] *adj* moving from place to place; wandering. Also *nc* person who does this; tramp. **vagrancy** *nu.*
vague [veig] *adj* not certain; not definite. **vaguely** *adv.* **vagueness** *nu.*
vain [vein] *adj* **1.** useless; worthless; having no result. **2.** (with reference to a person) too proud about oneself; conceited. **vainly** *adv.*
vanity ['væniti] **1.** *nu* uselessness: *the vanity of planning one's future.* **2.** *nu* too much pride; conceit. *Many beautiful women are spoilt by vanity.* **3.** *nc* vain act.
in vain *adv* **1.** without result or success. *We tried in vain to see him.* **2.** without proper respect. *Never take God's name in vain.*
vainglory [vein'glɔ:ri] *nc* too much pride; boastfulness. **vainglorious** *adj.* **vaingloriously** *adv.*
vale [veil] *nc* area of low land between hills (*o.f.* except in place names e.g. *the Vale of York* – use **valley**).
valediction [væli'dikʃən] *nc* act of saying goodbye.
valedictory [væli'diktəri] *adj*: *a valedictory speech.*
valentine ['væləntain] *nc* **1.** letter or card expressing love, sent on St Valentine's day i.e. 14 February, to a person of the opposite sex. **2.** person to whom such a letter or card is sent.
valet ['vælei] *nc* manservant who cleans and takes care of his employer's clothes. Also *vt* be or act as a valet to somebody.
valetudinarian [vælitju:di'nεəriən] *adj* sick and weak; too anxious about one's health. Also *nc* person who is valetudinarian.
valiant ['væliənt] *adj* brave. **valiantly** *adv.* see **valour.**
valid ['vælid] *adj* **1.** strong; well-supported. *They have valid reasons for refusing to do it.* **2.** correct according to the law or rules. *He has a valid claim to the property. Is your passport valid for travel in the USA?* (*opp* **invalid**). **validly** *adv.* **validity** [və'liditi] *nu.*
validate ['vælideit] *vt* make valid. (*opp* **invalidate**).
valise [və'li:z] *nc* **1.** small travelling bag. **2.** roll of strong cloth in which bedding and clothes are carried.
valley ['væli] *nc* area of land between hills (usu. with a river).
valour ['vælə*] (*US* **valor**) *nu* bravery.
valorous *adj.* see **valiant.**
value ['vælju:] **1.** *nu* importance; usefulness. *Most parents know the value of a good education. These books are of great/little/some/no value to somebody learning English.* **2.** *nu* worth of something in money. *What is the value of your house? Gold has recently increased in value. In this shop you get good value for your money.*
Note: because *value* has the sense of what something is considered to be worth, it does not always have the same sense as the actual cost or price (e.g. *Although I paid only fifty pence for this book, its value is much higher. The new bridge cost £100,000 but its value to the people who live near it is doubtful*). **3.** *nc* (in *pl*) rules or standards; beliefs. *People behave in certain ways because of their social values.* **4.** *nc* (music) length of a note; (art)

balance of light and shade in a picture; (mathematics) number or amount represented by a symbol. Also *vt* **1.** think important; have great respect for. *I value his opinions.* **2.** estimate the value of something in money. *He valued the diamond ring at £500.*

valuable *adj* of great value. Also *nc* (in *pl*) things which are valuable (e.g. jewels).

valueless *adj* having no value.

valuation [vælju'eiʃən] **1.** *nu* act of valuing: *experienced in the valuation of paintings.* **2.** *nc* value given to something (esp. by a valuer): *get a valuation for one's house.*

valuer *nc* person who is skilled in valuing.

valve [vælv] *nc* **1.** device which opens and closes to allow gas or liquid to flow in one direction only; part of heart or blood vessel which allows blood to flow in one direction only. **2.** (*Brit*) closed glass tube in which a vacuum has been made, used in radios etc. (*US* **tube**).

valvular ['vælvjulə*] *adj* of valves (esp. those of the heart).

vampire ['væmpaiə*] *nc* **1.** spirit of a dead person believed to suck the blood of living persons while they are asleep. **2.** person who lives by taking money from others. **3.** any of various species of Central and South American bats, some of which drink the blood of animals and men. (Also **vampire bat**).

van[1] [væn] *nc* (*Brit*) covered cart, lorry or railway truck used for carrying goods.

van[2] [væn] *nu* **1.** leading part of an army or fleet. **2.** leaders of any movement or advance.

'vanguard **1.** troops who go ahead of an army to protect it. **2.** leading part: *in the vanguard of public opinion.*

vandal ['vændl] *nc* person who damages or destroys something attractive or useful without reason.

vandalism *nu* act or behaviour of a vandal.

vandalize *vt* destroy or damage for fun or out of spite. *The empty house had been vandalized by a gang of boys.*

vane [vein] *nc* **1.** device on top of a building to show the direction of the wind. **2.** blade of a propeller or windmill.

vanilla [və'nilə] **1.** *nc* type of plant. **2.** *nu* substance obtained from this plant used to flavour food and drink. Also *adj*: *vanilla ice cream.*

vanish ['væniʃ] *vi* no longer be seen or felt; go out of sight.

'vanishing cream type of cream which vanishes when rubbed into the skin.

vanity ['væniti] *nu* see **vain.**

vanquish ['væŋkwiʃ] *vt* defeat; overcome. (rather *o.f.*).

vantage ['vɑːntidʒ] *nu* better chance; advantage. *The hill was a good point of vantage/vantage point to watch the soldiers passing.*

vapid ['væpid] *adj* dull; without energy or spirit. **vapidly** *adv.* **vapidness, vapidity** [væ'piditi] *nc/u.*

vapour ['veipə*] (*US* **vapor**) *nu* substance in a cloudy form (e.g. fog, mist, smoke, steam).

vaporous *adj* **1.** like vapour. **2.** not real.

vaporize *vt/i* become, cause to become, vapour. **vaporization** [veipərai'zeiʃən] *nu.*

vaporizer *nc* device for dividing a liquid into small drops.

'vapour trail white trail of moisture left in the sky by a plane flying very high.

variable ['vɛəriəbl] *adj* able to change or be changed; not steady or reliable: *variable winds; a variable quantity.* (*opp* **invariable**). Also *nc* something which can change or be changed. **variably** *adv.* **variableness, variability** [vɛəriə'biliti] *nu.*

variant ['vɛəriənt] *adj* different. Also *nc* different form (esp. with reference to spellings of one word e.g. *gray* and *grey*).

variance *nu* difference which causes argument; disagreement. *He has been at variance with his parents for years.*

variation [vɛəri'eiʃən] *nc/u* see **vary.**

varicoloured ['vɛərikʌləd] (*US* **varicolored**) *adj* having many different colours.

varicose ['værikous] *adj* (with reference to veins of the body esp. of the leg) swollen.

varied ['vɛərid] *adj* see **vary.**

variegated ['vɛərigeitid] *adj* having particles or spots of different colours.

variety [və'raiəti] **1.** *nu* state of changing from time to time, of not always being the same. *Life at school has plenty of variety. Variety is the spice of life.* **2.** *nu* group of different things. *The shop sells a variety of goods. She went through an amazing variety of different moods.* **3.** *nc* type which is different from the larger group to which it belongs. *There are several varieties of red roses.* **4.** *nu* (*Brit*) type of entertainment which is a mixture of dancing, singing, acting etc. Also *adj*: *variety show; variety theatre.* (*US* **vaudeville**).

various ['vɛəriəs] *adj* see **vary.**

varnish ['vɑːniʃ] *nc/u* type of liquid which when dry gives a hard, shining surface to wood, metal etc. Also *vt* put varnish on.

varsity ['vɑːsiti] *nc* university. (*informal*).

vary ['vɛəri] *vt/i* change, cause to change; be, cause to be, different. *Temperatures vary from day to day. You should vary your lessons to make them more interesting. What's the weather like? It varies.*

variation [vɛəri'eiʃən] *nc/u* extent to which something varies; act of varying: *variations between day and night temperatures? There are many variations of this story.*

varied *adj* **1.** having many changes: *a varied life.* **2.** of different types; mixed. *The news we get is very varied.* (*opp* **unvaried**).

various *adj* different; several. *I went there at various times. He has various excuses for being late.* **variously** *adv.* **variousness** *nu.*

vase [vɑːz] *nc* container for flowers (usu. made of glass or pottery).

vasectomy [væ'sektəmi] *nc/u* operation to sterilize men.

vaseline ['væsəliːn] ® *nu* type of ointment made from petroleum; petroleum jelly.

vassal ['væsl] *nc* **1.** (in former times) person who was allowed to use land if in return he was loyal to the owner and helped him in time of war. **2.** person who is under the complete control of somebody.

vassalage *nu* state of being a vassal.

vast [vɑːst] *adj* very large. **vastly** *adv.* **vastness** *nu.*

vat [væt] *nc* type of large container for holding liquids.

vaudeville ['vɔːdəvil] *nu* (*US*) variety show.

vault[1] [vɔːlt] *nc* **1.** arched roof. **2.** underground room; cellar (esp. for keeping wine or money or for burying the dead).

vaulted *adj* having a vault; arched.

vault[2] [vɔːlt] *vt/i* jump with one or two hands placed on something. *He vaulted over the gate.* Also *nc* jump made in this way. **vaulter** *nc.*

'vaulting horse type of apparatus which looks like a horse, used in a gymnasium for vaulting over.

vaulting horse

vaunt [vɔ:nt] *vt/i* boast. **vauntingly** *adv.* **vaunter** *nc.* (all *o.f.*).

veal [vi:l] *nu* meat of a calf.

veer [viə*] *vi* turn; (esp. with reference to the wind) change direction.

vegetable ['vedʒitəbl] *adj* of or from plants: *vegetable oil.* Also *nc* plant used for food (e.g. bean, cabbage, potato etc).
vegetarian [vedʒi'tɛəriən] *nc* person who does not eat meat. **vegetarianism** [vedʒi'tɛəriənizəm] *nu.*

vegetate ['vedʒiteit] *vi* **1.** grow as a plant does. **2.** live an idle, uninteresting life.
vegetation [vedʒi'teiʃən] *nu* plants in general. *Deserts have very little vegetation.*

vehement ['viəmənt] *adj* (with reference to a person or his behaviour) having great force or strong feelings. *He made a vehement speech about drugs.* **vehemently** *adv.* **vehemence** *nu.*

vehicle ['viəkl] *nc* **1.** something (usu. with wheels) for carrying persons or goods (e.g. car, cart, lorry or truck). **2.** somebody/something through which feelings, thoughts etc can be expressed. *The local council should be the vehicle of public opinion.*
vehicular [vi'hikjulə*] *adj*: *vehicular traffic.*

veil [veil] *nc* **1.** thin piece of cloth used to cover a woman's face and/or head. **2.** any cover or disguise. *There is a veil of secrecy over their plans.* Also *vt* cover with a veil; hide. *She veiled her face when the stranger entered the room. The hills are veiled in mist.*
veiling *nu* **1.** act of covering with a veil. **2.** material from which a veil is made.
take the veil become a nun.

vein [vein] *nc* **1.** blood vessel which carries blood back to the heart from the rest of the body. **2.** line or layer of different material or colour appearing like a vein in something: *a vein of gold in rock; the veins in a leaf.* **3.** mood; attitude. *I was not in the right vein to enjoy myself.*
veined *adj* having veins.

veld, veldt [velt] *nu* high grassland of South Africa.

vellum ['veləm] *nu* writing material made from the skin of a sheep, goat etc; parchment.

velocity [vi'lɔsiti] *nu* speed: *the velocity of light.*

velour, velours [və'luə*] *nu* type of cloth like velvet.

velvet ['velvit] *nu* type of soft, thick cloth made from silk, cotton, nylon etc. Also *adj* **1.** made of velvet. **2.** soft like velvet.
velvety *adj* soft like velvet: *velvety skin.*
velveteen ['velvi'ti:n] *nu* type of cloth like velvet but made from cotton.

venal ['vi:nl] *adj* (with reference to a person or his behaviour) ready to take money to do something; easily bribed. **venally** *adv.* **venality** [vi:'næliti] *nc/u.*

vend [vend] *vt* sell.
vendor, vender *nc* person who sells something: *newsvendor* i.e. person who sells newspapers.

vendetta [ven'detə] *nc* fierce quarrel between families during which members are murdered in revenge; any long, fierce quarrel.

veneer [vi'niə*] *nc/u* **1.** thin layer of valuable wood fixed to the surface of cheap wood. **2.** outward appearance which hides something bad beneath. *Although he has a veneer of honesty, he is not to be trusted.* Also *vt* cover with a veneer.

venerate ['venəreit] *vt* admire or respect greatly. **veneration** [venə'reiʃən] *nu.*
venerable ['venərəbl] *adj* deserving to be venerated (esp. because of age or long experience). **venerably** *adv.*

venereal [vi'niəriəl] *adj* caused or spread by sexual acts: *venereal disease.*

Venetian [vi'ni:ʃən] *adj* of Venice.
venetian blind type of blind made of thin horizontal pieces of wood etc which can be moved to allow air and light to pass through.

venetian blind

vengeance ['vendʒəns] *nu* act of causing somebody pain or loss in return for a wrong he has done; revenge.
vengeful ['vendʒful] *adj* wishing to take vengeance. **vengefully** *adv.* **vengefulness** *nu.*
with a vengeance very much; more than usual. (*informal*).

venial ['vi:niəl] *adj* (with reference to a mistake, fault or sin) easily excused or forgiven; not serious.

venison ['venisn] *nu* meat of a deer.

venom ['venəm] *nu* **1.** poison (esp. that produced by a snake). **2.** spite; malice. **venomous** *adj.* **venomously** *adv.* **venomousness** *nu.*

vent [vent] **1.** *nc* small hole or outlet for air, smoke etc (e.g. in a barrel or fireplace). **2.** *nu* expression of an emotion. *He gave vent to his anger by striking the boy.* **3.** *nc* opening in the back of a coat or jacket. Also *vt* express an emotion. *He vented his anger on the boy.*

ventilate ['ventileit] *vt* cause fresh air to enter. *He opened the window to ventilate the room.* **ventilation** [venti'leiʃən] *nu.*
ventilator *nc* device which ventilates.

ventricle ['ventrikl] *nc* space inside an organ of the body (esp. one of the two inside the heart).

ventriloquism [ven'triləkwizəm] *nu* art of speaking which makes it appear that the sound comes not from the speaker but from somebody/something else.
ventriloquist *nc* person skilled in this art.

venture ['ventʃə*] *nc/u* something which is risky or dangerous to do. Also *vt/i* do something of this kind. *They should not venture on the river in such a small boat.* **2.** dare; go so far as. *I venture to suggest that you are wrong.*
venturesome *adj* daring; risky.

venue ['venju:] *nc* place where an event (e.g. a sports meeting) happens.

veracious [və'reiʃəs] *adj* truthful; true. **veraciously** *adv*. **veracity** [və'ræsiti] *nu*.
veranda, verandah [və'rændə] *nc* passage with a roof along the side of a house (usu. open on one side).
verb [və:b] *nc* word or words which tell what somebody/something does or is (e.g. in the sentence *The man bought the house*, *bought* is a verb).
verbal *adj* **1.** of a verb: *verbal noun* (e.g. in *smoking is dangerous*, *smoking* is a *verbal noun*). **2.** spoken not written: *verbal promise*. **3.** of words. *He made several verbal mistakes in his essay*. **4.** word for word; literal: *verbal translation*.
verbally *adv* in spoken not written words. *He reported to me verbally*.
verbalize *vt/i* express in words. **verbalization** [və:bəlai'zeiʃən] *nu*.
verbatim [və:'beitim] *adj/adv* word for word; using exactly the same words: *a verbatim report of his speech*.
verbiage ['və:biidʒ] *nu* use of more words than are necessary (and often without much meaning).
verbose [və:'bous] *adj* using more words than are necessary. **verbosely** *adv*. **verboseness, verbosity** [və:'bɔsiti] *nu*.
verdant ['və:dnt] *adj* green; fresh. **verdancy** *nu*. (both *o.f.* – used only in poetry).
verdict ['və:dikt] *nc* decision or judgment made after the evidence (esp. by a jury in a court of law). *The verdict of the jury is that you are guilty*.
verdigris ['və:digri:s] *nu* green rust on copper and other metals.
verdure ['və:djuə*] *nu* green vegetation; greenness.
verge [və:dʒ] *nc* edge; border (esp. the grass edge at the side of a road or bed of flowers). Also *vt* (with **on** or **upon**) come near the edge of; be very close to. *His behaviour verges on madness*.
be on the verge of be very close to; be about to. *He was on the verge of telling him the truth*.
bring somebody/something to the verge of bring somebody/something very close to. *The attack brought the country to the verge of war*.
verger ['və:dʒə*] *nc* person who leads people to their seats in church and acts as caretaker of the church.
verify ['verifai] *vt* **1.** test whether something is correct or not. *I looked up the word in a dictionary to verify its spelling*. **2.** show that something is correct; prove. *Everything he said then was verified by what happened later*.
verification [verifi'keiʃən] *nc/u* act of verifying or being verified; proof.
verifiable *adj* able to be verified.
verily ['verili] *adv* indeed; really (*o.f.*).
verisimilitude [verisi'militju:d] **1.** *nu* appearance of being true; likelihood. **2.** *nc* something which appears to be true.
veritable ['veritəbl] *adj* genuine; real. **veritably** *adv*.
verity ['veriti] **1.** *nu* state of being true; truth. **2.** *nc* something which is real; true statement or belief.
vermicelli [və:mi'tʃeli] *nu* mixture of wheat flour made into long tubes and cooked for eating.
vermilion [və'miliən] *nu* bright red colour. Also *adj*.
vermin ['və:min] *nu/npl* **1.** insects or small animals and birds which do damage or harm. **2.** persons who do damage or harm to others.
verminous *adj* **1.** full of vermin (esp. insects like fleas, lice etc). *The clothes of the poor children were verminous*. **2.** caused by vermin. *They have verminous sores on their bodies*.
vermouth ['və:məθ] *nu* type of wine.
vernacular [və'nækjulə*] *adj* local language or dialect: *the vernacular press*. Also *nc*: *textbooks written in the vernacular*.
versatile ['və:sətail] *adj* able to do many different things well. **versatility** [və:sə'tiliti] *nu*.
verse [və:s] **1.** *nu* arrangement of words in lines according to a pattern; poetry. (*opp* **prose**). **2.** *nc* group of lines or one line of this kind. *This poem has four verses*. **3.** *nc* short, numbered part of a chapter of the Bible.
versed *adj* (with **in**) skilled or experienced in some subject.
versify ['və:sifai] *vt/i* express in verse; turn prose into verse. **versification** [və:sifi'keiʃən] *nu*.
versifier *nc* person who writes verses.
version ['və:ʃən] *nc* **1.** description from one particular point of view. *John's version of the accident is different from mine*. **2.** something translated from another language.
versus ['və:səs] *prep* (esp. sport and legal) against (often in short form *v* or *vs*): *England v Italy*.
vertebra ['və:tibrə] *nc* one of the bones in the backbone. *pl* **vertebrae** ['və:tibrei].
vertebrate ['və:tibrit] *adj* having a backbone. Also *nc* animal with a backbone. (*opp* **invertebrate**).
vertex ['və:teks] *nc* highest point. *pl* **vertices** ['və:tisi:z].
vertical ['və:tikl] *adj* straight up and down, perpendicular. *The walls of a room are vertical, the floor horizontal*. (*opp* **horizontal**). **vertically** *adv*.
vertigo ['və:tigou] *nu* dizziness; giddiness. **vertiginous** [və:'tidʒinəs] *adj*.
verve [və:v] *nu* energy; enthusiasm.
very ['veri] *adj/adv/intensifier* **1.** used to make stronger or emphasize the *adj* or *adv* which follows. *It is very cold today. He drives very slowly. This is the very best way to do it. She looked very annoyed. I'm feeling very much better today. The lecture was not very interesting*. Also before *own*. *It is good to have a house of our very own*. **2.** this and no other; actual. *You are the very man I want to speak to. The very thought of going frightens me*. **3.** used to make stronger or emphasize the noun which follows: *the very beginning/middle/end*.
vespers ['vespəz] *nu* evening service in a church.
vessel ['vesl] *nc* **1.** container (esp. for liquids). **2.** large ship.
vest[1] [vest] *nc* **1.** (*Brit*) garment worn next to the skin on the upper part of the body. (*US* **undershirt**). **2.** (*US*) short garment fastened with buttons up the front but without sleeves, worn beneath a jacket. (*Brit* **waistcoat**).
vest[2] [vest] *vt* (with **in** or **with**) give the right to use. *The government has vested great powers in the Minister of Agriculture. The government has vested the Minister of Agriculture with great powers*.
vested interests **1.** interests which are recognized by law and cannot be taken away. **2.** (sometimes *sing*) selfish interest. *Those employers have a vested interest in*

keeping workers' wages low.
vestibule ['vestibju:l] *nc* **1.** small room between an outer and an inner door. **2.** (*US*) passage between carriages of a railway train.
vestige ['vestidʒ] *nc* mark or sign left by something that once existed; trace. **vestigial** [ves'tidʒiəl] *adj.*
vestments ['vestmənts] *npl* official dress (esp. that worn by a priest in church).
vestry ['vestri] *nc* room in a church, used by a priest etc for dressing in.
vet[1] [vet] *nc* short informal form of **veterinary surgeon.**
vet[2] [vet] *vt* inspect a plan, proposal etc before giving official approval to it. *past* **vetted.** (*informal*).
vetch [vetʃ] *nc* types of plant of the bean family.
veteran ['vetərn] *nc* person who has served a long time (esp. in the armed forces). Also *adj*: *a veteran soldier*; *a veteran car* i.e. one built before 1919.
veterinary ['vetinəri] *adj* concerned with diseases of animals.
veterinary surgeon (*Brit*) person skilled in treating these diseases (informally shortened to **vet**) (*US* **veterinarian** [vetiri'nεəriən]).
veto ['vi:tou] *nc* power or right to forbid something (esp. the passing of a law, a resolution of UNO etc). *Which countries have the veto? pl* **vetoes.** Also *vt* forbid. *The plan was vetoed by two countries in the Security Council.*
vex [veks] *vt* make angry; trouble.
vexation [vek'seiʃən] **1.** *nu* state of being vexed. **2.** *nc* something which vexes.
vexatious [vek'seiʃəs] *adj* annoying. **vexatiously** *adv.* **vexatiousness** *nu.*
vexed question problem often argued about but not settled.
via ['vaiə] *prep* by way of. *He went to New York via Rome.*
viable ['vaiəbl] *adj* able to exist or develop. *The economy of the country is not viable.* **viability** [vaiə'biliti] *nu.*
viaduct ['vaiədʌkt] *nc* high bridge carrying a road or railway over a valley.
vial ['vaiəl] *nc* small glass bottle (esp. for medicine).
vibrate [vai'breit] *vt/i* **1.** move, cause to move, very quickly from side to side or up and down. *The skin of a drum vibrates when it is struck.* **2.** make a throbbing sound. *The speaker's voice vibrated with emotion.* **vibration** *nc/u.* **vibrant** ['vaibrnt], **vibrating** *adj.*
vicar ['vikə*] *nc* priest of the Church of England in charge of a parish.
vicarage *nc* house where a vicar lives.
vicarious [vi'kεəriəs] *adj* done or felt by somebody in place of somebody else. *We had a vicarious pleasure watching them swim in the sea* i.e. we felt as pleased as if we too were swimming. **vicariously** *adv.*
vice[1] [vais] *nc/u* wicked behaviour; bad habit. *Gambling and drunkenness are vices. He descended to a life of vice.*
vicious ['viʃəs] *adj* **1.** wicked. *He has vicious habits.* **2.** spiteful; intending to harm. *He gave me a vicious look. This dog has a really vicious bite.* **viciously** *adv.* **viciousness** *nu.*
vicious circle state in which one bad thing produces another which in turn produces the first bad thing again (e.g. poverty causes poor health and poor health then causes more poverty).
vice[2] [vais] (*US* **vise**) *nc* apparatus which holds firmly a piece of wood or metal etc between two jaws moved by a screw.

vice[2]

vice-[3] [vais] *prefix* acting in place of; second in rank to (e.g. **vice-president; vice-principal**).
viceroy ['vaisrɔi] governor who rules in place of a king or queen.
'**vice'regal** *adj* of a viceroy.
vice versa ['vaisə'və:sə] *adv* the other way round. *You sent my letter to John, and vice versa* i.e. you also sent John's letter to me.
vicinity [vi'siniti] *nu* nearness; neighbourhood. *Is there a hospital in the vicinity?*
vicious ['viʃəs] *adj* see **vice**[1].
vicissitude [vi'sisitju:d] *nc* change (esp. in somebody's circumstances or luck). *Life is full of vicissitudes.*
victim ['viktim] *nc* **1.** person who suffers because of the actions of others or because of bad luck, illness etc. *They were the victims of a railway accident.* **2.** person or animal killed as a gift to a god.
victimize *vt* make a victim of; cause to suffer. **victimization** [viktimai'zeiʃən] *nu.*
victor ['viktə*] *nc* person who defeats an enemy in battle; person who wins.
victory *nc/u* defeat of an enemy in battle; success. *The general gained/won a victory over the army of the enemy.*
victorious [vik'tɔ:riəs] *adj*: *The general was victorious.* **victoriously** *adv.*
Victorian [vik'tɔ:riən] *n* person who lived during the reign of Queen Victoria (1837–1901). Also *adj* of, during that reign.
victual ['vitl] *vt/i* take in, supply with, food and drink (esp. a ship). *past* **victualled.** (*US* **victualed**). Also *nc* (in *pl*) food and drink.
victualler *nc* person who supplies victuals. **licensed victualler** person who is licensed to sell beer, spirits etc.
video ['vidiou] *nu* (*US*) television.
'**video tape** special magnetic tape which records television pictures.
vie [vai] *vt* (with **with**) try to do better than somebody else; compete. *They vied with each other in wealth. pres part* **vying.** *past* **vied.**
view [vju:] **1.** *nu* act or power of seeing. *The house was hidden from our view by trees. They climbed the hill to get a good view of the country.* **2.** *nc* something which can be seen (esp. from a distance). *The view from the front of his house is lovely.* **3.** *nc* way of looking at something; opinion. *In my view he is wrong. What are your views about the present situation?* **4.** *nc* aim; purpose. *He is studying with a view to going to university.* Also *vt* look at; consider. *We can view the problem in many ways.*
viewer *nc* **1.** person who views (esp. one who watches television). **2.** small device with a light for looking at photographic transparencies.
'**viewfinder** device in a camera which shows what will be in the picture if taken.
'**viewpoint** **1.** place from which something

is viewed. **2.** opinion about some problem. (Also **point of view** in sense **3.**).
in view of because of.
in full view of able to be seen completely. *The teacher fell down in full view of the boys in his class.*
on view so as to be seen; open to inspection. *The handwork of the pupils is on view to the parents.*
vigil ['vidʒil] *nc/u* act of staying awake at a time when one usually sleeps.
vigilant *adj* awake and watchful; ready for any danger. **vigilance** *nu.*
vigilante [vidʒi'lænti] *nc* member of a group of people trying to enforce the law (esp. when the police are not able to do so).
vignette [vi'njet] *nc* **1.** small design printed at the beginning or end of a book or of the chapters in it. **2.** picture of a person's head or of his head and shoulders, with a shaded background. **3.** short description of something.
vigour ['vigə*] (*US* **vigor**) *nu* energy; strength. **vigorous** *adj.* **vigorously** *adv.*
viking ['vaikiŋ] *nc* (in ancient times) one of the warriors from northern Europe who attacked the coasts of Europe.
vile [vail] *adj* **1.** disgusting. **2.** worthless; of no value (*o.f.*). **3.** bad. *He was in a vile temper.* (*informal* in sense **3.**). **vilely** *adv.* **vileness** *nu.*
vilify ['vilifai] *vt* say vile things about somebody. **vilification** [vilifi'keiʃən] *nu.*
villa ['vilə] *nc* large house with its own garden.
village ['vilidʒ] *nc* group of houses and shops etc smaller than a town. Also *adj*: *the village church.*
villager *nc* person who lives in a village.
villain ['vilən] *nc* wicked person; rogue. **villainous** *adj.* **villainously** *adv.*
villainy *nc/u* evil act or behaviour.
villein ['vilən] *nc* (in the Middle Ages) labourer who had to work for a landowner; serf.
villeinage *nu* state of being a villein.
vim [vim] *nu* energy. (*informal*).
vindicate ['vindikeit] *vt* prove to be true or correct; justify. *I always said that he would be a brilliant writer and his latest book has vindicated my judgment.*
vindication [vindi'keiʃən] *nc/u* act of vindicating or being vindicated; defence of an act, statement etc. *There was no vindication for their outrageous behaviour.*
vindictive [vin'diktiv] *adj* wanting revenge; spiteful. **vindictively** *adv.* **vindictiveness** *nu.*
vine [vain] *nc* type of climbing plant (esp. one on which grapes grow).
vineyard ['vinjɑːd] piece of land where vines are grown.
vinegar ['vinigə*] *nu* type of weak acid made from beer, wine etc and used to flavour or preserve food. **vinegary** *adj.*
vintage ['vintidʒ] **1.** *nu* time of year when grapes are gathered to make wine. **2.** *nc* wine made in a particular year. *Last year's vintage is not yet ready for drinking.* Also *adj* made in a good year or a period in the past. *This is a vintage wine. He has bought a vintage car.*
vintner ['vintnə*] *nc* person who sells wine.
vinyl ['vainl] *nu* type of plastic often used for making floor covering.
viol ['vaiəl] *nc* type of stringed musical instrument used in the past.
viola [vi'oulə] *nc* type of stringed musical instrument larger than a violin.
violate ['vaiəleit] *vt* **1.** break a promise or treaty. **2.** disturb; interrupt rudely. **3.** rape.
violation [vaiə'leiʃən] *nc/u* act of violating or being violated.
violent ['vaiəlnt] *adj* **1.** having great force; powerful: *a violent storm; a violent blow on the head; a violent speech.* **2.** caused by great force or an attack. *Many political leaders have met violent deaths* i.e. they have not died naturally. **3.** severe: *a violent pain.*
violence *nu* state of being violent; violent behaviour: *the violence of the wind; death by violence.*
violet ['vaiəlit] **1.** *nc* type of very small flower (usu. blue or purple). **2.** *nu* blue or purple colour. Also *adj.*
violin [vaiə'lin] *nc* type of stringed musical instrument played with a bow.

violin

violinist *nc* person who plays a violin.
violoncello [vaiələn'tʃelou] *nc* type of stringed musical instrument much larger than the violin, played held between the knees with one end resting on the ground. *pl* **violoncellos.**
violoncellist [vaiələn'tʃelist] *nc* person who plays a violoncello.
Note: usu. shortened to *cello, cellist.*
viper ['vaipə*] *nc* type of poisonous snake. see **adder.**
viperish *adj* like a viper.
virago [vi'rɑːgou] *nc* noisy, bad-tempered woman. *pl* **viragos.**
virgin ['vəːdʒin] *nc* person (esp. a girl or woman) who has not had sexual relations with a member of the opposite sex. Also *adj* **1.** without sexual experience; pure. **2.** not yet used: *virgin land* i.e. land which has not yet been used by man.
virginal *adj* of, like a virgin. Also *nc* (usu. *pl*) type of old musical instrument.
virginity [vəː'dʒiniti] *nu* state of being virgin.
virginia [vəː'dʒiniə] *adj/nu* type of tobacco grown mainly in Virginia, USA.
vir'ginia 'creeper type of climbing plant with large leaves, which turn red in autumn.
virile ['virail] *adj* of a man; strong; vigorous.
virility [vi'riliti] *nu.*
virtual ['vəːtjuəl] *adj* being something in fact, although it is not openly admitted. *Because the government was weak, the army became the virtual ruler of the country.*
virtually *adv.*
virtue ['vəːtjuː] **1.** *nc/u* goodness of character; good quality; excellence. *Honesty is a great virtue. One of his virtues is that he never gets angry.* **2.** *nu* benefit; advantage. *What is the virtue of having two cars when one is enough?* **3.** *nu* avoidance of sexual relationships; chastity. **virtuous** *adj.* **virtuously** *adv.*
by/in virtue because of.
make a virtue of necessity pretend to be willing or pleased to do something that one is compelled to do.

virtuoso [vəːtju'ouzou] *nc* person who is very skilled in, or has great knowledge of, one of the arts (e.g. music). *pl* **virtuosos.**
virtuosity [vəːtju'ɔsiti] *nu* great skill in one of the arts.

virulent ['virjulnt] *adj* **1.** very poisonous; deadly: *a virulent disease.* **2.** (with reference to feelings etc) full of hate; bitter. *He made a virulent speech against the government.* **virulently** *adv.* **virulence** *nu.*

virus ['vairəs] *nc* very small thing which spreads certain diseases. *pl* **viruses.**

visa ['viːzə] *nc* official stamp put on a passport to allow its owner to enter or leave a foreign country: *entrance visa; exit visa. pl* **visas.** Also *vt* stamp with a visa. *past* **visaed** ['viːzəd].

visage ['vizidʒ] *nc* face (*o.f.*).
-visaged *adj* having the look of: *a sour-visaged woman.*

viscera ['visərə] *npl* organs inside the body (esp. the bowels, stomach, liver etc). **visceral** *adj.*

viscid ['visid], **viscous** ['viskəs] *adj* (usu. with reference to liquids e.g. oil) thick; sticky. **viscosity** [vis'kɔsiti] *nu.*

viscount ['vaikaunt] *nc* title of nobility lower in rank than an earl.
viscountess ['vaikauntis] *nc* wife of a viscount.

vise [vais] *nc* see **vice**[2].

visible ['vizibl] *adj* able to be seen. (*opp* **invisible**). **visibly** *adv.*
visibility [vizi'biliti] *nu* (esp. with reference to the clearness of the air when travelling etc) state of being visible. *The poor visibility caused by the fog made driving very difficult.*

vision ['viʒən] **1.** *nu* power of seeing. *He wears spectacles because his vision is weak.* **2.** *nu* power of imagining; ability to understand clearly what will happen. *The educational plan will fail because it has no vision.* **3.** *nc* something believed to have been seen in a dream; something imagined by the mind. *When I was a boy I had visions of being a famous actor.*
visionary ['viʒənəri] *adj* **1.** seen only in a vision; unreal; imaginary. **2.** (with reference to a person) seeing visions; having unreal, fanciful ideas. Also *nc* person who is visionary.

visit ['vizit] *vt/i* **1.** come or go to see somebody. *They are visiting their friends in London. The doctor visits his patients every day. She has gone visiting.* **2.** go to a place for a time. *Have you ever visited London?* **3.** go to inspect. *An inspector visited our school yesterday.* Also *nc* act of visiting; short stay. *They are paying a visit to their friends. He went to London on a visit.*
visitation [vizi'teiʃən] *nc* **1.** official visit. **2.** punishment or reward from God.
visitor *nc* person who visits.
'visiting card (*Brit*) card with one's name and address on it. (*US* **calling card**).
be on visiting terms know one another well enough to visit one another.

visor ['vaizə*] *nc* **1.** part of a helmet which can be lifted to show the face. **2.** front of a cap shading the eyes. **3.** piece of plastic, wood, darkened glass etc fixed to the windscreen of a car so that the eyes can be shaded from the sun by pulling it down.

vista ['vistə] *nc* view (esp. from a distance and in a particular direction). *We enjoyed the vista of the mountain as seen from the north.*

visual ['vizjuəl] *adj* used in seeing; of or by sight: *visual aids* i.e. pictures, films etc used to aid teaching. **visually** *adv.*
visualize *vt* make a mental picture of somebody/something. *I cannot visualize him as an old man.*

vital ['vaitl] *adj* **1.** concerned with, necessary to, life. *The heart is a vital organ.* **2.** very necessary or important. *This letter contains vital information.* **vitally** *adv.*
vitality [vai'tæliti] *nu* vital force; liveliness of manner; ability to go on enduring and living.
vitalize *vt* give life or energy to.
vitals *npl* vital parts of the body, heart and brain. (rather *o.f.*).
vital statistics 1. statistics about births, marriages and deaths etc. **2.** measurements of a woman's bust, waist and hips. (*informal* in sense **2.**).

vitamin ['vitəmin] *nc* chemical substance, found in small amounts in food and necessary for health and growth.

vitiate ['viʃieit] *vt* weaken; spoil; make impure. **vitiation** [viʃi'eiʃən] *nu.*

vitreous ['vitriəs] *adj* of or like glass.

vitriol ['vitriəl] *nu* sulphuric acid.
vitriolic [vitri'ɔlik] *adj* **1.** of vitriol. **2.** bitter; full of hate: *a vitriolic book.*

vituperate [vi'tjuːpəreit] *vt* speak very angrily about; curse. **vituperative** [vi'tjuːpərətiv] *adj.* **vituperatively** *adv.* **vituperation** [vitjuːpə'reiʃən] *nu.*

vivacious [vi'veiʃəs] *adj* full of energy; lively; gay. **vivaciously** *adv.* **vivacity** [vi'væsiti] *nu.*

viva voce ['vaivə'voutʃi] *nc* oral examination.

vivid ['vivid] *adj* bright; clear; lively: *a vivid blue sky; a vivid imagination.* **vividly** *adv.* **vividness** *nu.*

vivisect [vivi'sekt] *vt* cut open, or experiment on, living animals for the purpose of medical or scientific research. **vivisection** *nc/u.*
vivisectionist *nc* person who practises or supports vivisection.

vixen ['viksn] *nc* **1.** female fox. **2.** quarrelsome woman.
vixenish *adj* bad-tempered.

viz. [viz] namely; that is to say (short form of **videlicet** and usually read as *namely*). *There are three very large rivers in Africa viz. the Congo, Niger and Nile.*

vizier [vi'ziə*] *nc* official of high rank in some Muslim countries.

vocabulary [vou'kæbjuləri] *nc* **1.** list of words (usu. in alphabetical order, with explanations of their meanings). **2.** total number of words used by somebody. *He has increased his English vocabulary by reading many English books.*

vocal ['voukl] *adj* of the voice; using the voice: *vocal music* i.e. singing. *They are very vocal in their demands for more money* i.e. they say very clearly that they want more. **vocally** *adv.*
vocalist *nc* person who sings.
vocalize *vt* sing or shout; put into speech.

vocation [vou'keiʃən] *nc/u* career or profession (esp. one followed in a spirit of service to others).
vocational *adj*: *vocational guidance* i.e. advice on what career to choose. **vocationally** *adv.*

vocative ['vɔkətiv] *nc* grammatical form of a noun in some languages, used in addressing somebody/something. *There is no separate vocative case in English.*

ociferate [və'sifəreit] *vt/i* shout. **vociferous** [və'sifərəs] *adj*. **vociferously** *adv*. **vociferation** [vəsifə'reiʃən] *nc/u*.

odka ['vɔdkə] *nu* type of alcoholic liquor made from rye or potatoes.

ogue [voug] *nc* (usu. only *sing*) something which is popular at a particular time either now or in the past. *Short skirts are the vogue this year.*

all the vogue popular with everybody; in fashion everywhere. (*informal*).

come into/go out of vogue become/stop being popular or fashionable.

oice [vɔis] **1.** *nc* sound made when speaking or singing; ability to make such a sound. *We could hear the voices of the people in the next room. They were speaking in loud voices. Because he has a cold he has lost his voice.* **2.** *nu* (grammar) form of the verb which shows the relation of the subject to the action of the verb: *active voice; passive voice.* **3.** *nu* (phonetics) sound made by using the vocal cords as well as the breath (e.g. sound made by a vowel or by consonants such as *b* and *d*). Also *vt* **1.** express in words. *He voiced his opinions to everybody.* **2.** (phonetics) make a sound by using the vocal cords as well as the breath: *a voiced consonant.*

-voiced *adj* having a particular kind of voice: *loud-voiced; soft-voiced.*

voiceless *adj* having no voice; not able to speak.

have a voice in something have a right to give one's opinion about something or to help to decide something.

with one voice everybody agreeing and saying so; unanimously.

oid [vɔid] *adj* **1.** empty. **2.** having no force or effect. *Your cheque will be void if you do not sign it.* Also *nu* empty space. Also *vt* cause to have no force or effect.

void of empty of; without: *a life void of excitement.*

null and void see **null**.

oile [vɔil] *nu* type of very thin cloth.

olatile ['vɔlətail] *adj* **1.** (with reference to a liquid) evaporating easily; changing easily into a gas. **2.** (with reference to a person) changing moods easily; lively. **volatility** [vɔlə'tiliti] *nu*.

olcano [vɔl'keinou] *nc* **1.** hole in the crust of the earth out of which fire, smoke, hot ashes and lava come. **2.** mountain formed in this way. *pl* **volcanoes**. **volcanic** [vɔl'kænik] *adj*. **volcanically** *adv*.

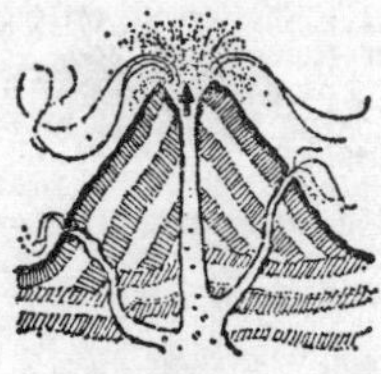

volcano

ole [voul] *nc* type of small animal like a rat, which lives in fields.

olition [və'liʃən] *nu* act of willing or choosing. *He gave the money of his own volition* i.e. he decided himself to do so. **volitional** *adj*.

olley ['vɔli] *nc* **1.** number of shots fired at the same time. **2.** number of questions, remarks etc made at the same time or very quickly one after the other. **3.** (tennis) act of hitting the ball back to one's opponent before it bounces. Also *vt/i* **1.** be fired at the same time. *The rifles volleyed.* **2.** hit a tennis ball back to one's opponent before it bounces.

'volleyball game played by two teams, who volley a large air-filled ball with their hands until the ball touches the ground.

'half-'volley (tennis) act of hitting the ball back to one's opponent immediately after it bounces.

volt [voult] *nc* unit of electrical force i.e. the force needed to send a current of one amp (ampere) through a resistance of one ohm. **voltage** *nc/u* electrical force measured in volts.

voluble ['vɔljubl] *adj* speaking quickly and easily. **volubly** *adv*. **volubility** [vɔlju'biliti] *nu*.

volume ['vɔlju:m] **1.** *nc* book (esp. one of a set). **2.** *nc* large amount. *A volume/volumes of smoke rose from the burning house.* **3.** *nu* amount of sound. *Your radio is too loud. Turn down the volume.* **4.** *nu* amount of space occupied by something (usu. shown in cubic feet, metres etc); cubic content of something: *find the volume of a box 4 feet long, 3 feet broad and 2 feet high.*

voluminous [və'lju:minəs] *adj* **1.** of great size: *a voluminous dress.* **2.** in many volumes. *He wrote a voluminous report on education.* **voluminously** *adv*.

voluntary ['vɔləntəri] *adj* **1.** doing, or done, willingly without being forced or without pay. *I am a voluntary helper. He has just finished his voluntary service overseas.* **2.** helped by private, not government, money. *This school belongs to a voluntary organization.* **3.** (with reference to movements of the body) happening because the mind wishes it. (*opp* **involuntary**). Also *nc* music played on the organ of a church without the choir joining in. **voluntarily** *adv*.

volunteer [vɔlən'tiə*] *nc* **1.** person who enters a service (esp. military service) of his own free will; person willing to do a job without being forced. *Are there any volunteers for cleaning the kitchen?* Also *vt/i* enter a service of one's own free will; offer (to do) something. *When war broke out, I volunteered. They volunteered some interesting suggestions* i.e. made them without being asked. *She volunteered to help with the washing up.*

voluptuary [və'lʌptjuəri] *nc* person who lives a life of luxury and sensual pleasure. **voluptuous** [və'lʌptjuəs] *adj* **1.** spent in luxury and pleasure: *a voluptuous life.* **2.** causing sensual pleasure: *a voluptuous blonde.* **voluptuously** *adv*. **voluptuousness** *nu*.

vomit ['vɔmit] *vt/i* **1.** put out through the mouth what is in the stomach. *The poisoned food made him vomit. He vomited all the food he had eaten.* **2.** put out in large amounts. *The volcano vomited smoke and ashes.* Also *nu* matter which has been vomited from the stomach.

voodoo ['vu:du:] *nu* type of religion which believes in evil spirits and witchcraft. **voodooism** *nu*.

voracious [və'reiʃəs] *adj* very greedy; ready to eat a lot. **voraciously** *adv*. **voracity** [və'ræsiti] *nu*.

vortex ['vɔ:teks] *nc* **1.** motion of a liquid going round and round very quickly (e.g. a whirlpool). **2.** any rapid motion or great excitement into which one is pulled. *pl* **vortexes** or **vortices** ['vɔːtisiːz].

votary ['voutəri] *nc* person who is completely devoted to something (esp. religious work).

vote [vout] *nc/u* **1.** act of showing one's choice, opinion or wish (esp. in choosing candidates for government etc); right to do so (esp. by ballot or by raising one's hand at a meeting). *I gave my vote to the first speaker. He is too young to have a vote. He was elected captain by 20 votes* i.e. 20 votes more than those given to the other persons who wished to become captain. **2.** amount of money allowed by a government to one of its departments or officials for a particular purpose. Also *vt/i* **1.** show one's choice, opinion or wish; allow by a vote. *We voted against/for him. The chairman asked us to vote on the plan. The National Assembly voted more money to education.* **2.** propose. *I vote (that) we stay at home today.*
voter *nc* person who votes; person who has the right to vote.
voteless *adj* not having a vote.
vote of confidence support for a plan, proposal etc shown by the fact that most people vote for it.
vote of thanks thanks expressed at a meeting by one person on behalf of all the others and usually followed by hand-clapping.

votive ['voutiv] *adj* given as a result of a solemn promise or vow.

vouch [vautʃ] *vi* (with **for**) state that somebody/something is correct, reliable etc; guarantee. *I can vouch for their honesty.*
voucher *nc* document which shows that accounts are correct, money has been paid or that a person has a right to something.
'luncheon voucher voucher given to an employee to confirm that he can have luncheon in a restaurant at his employer's expense.

vouchsafe [vautʃ'seif] *vt* do as a favour; condescend (*o.f.*).

vow [vau] *nc* solemn promise (usu. one made to God or in the name of God): *marriage vows.* Also *vt* make a vow. *He vowed that he would never do it again/He vowed never t do it again.*

vowel ['vauəl] *nc* vocal sound show mainly by the letters *a, e, i, o* or *u*; one c these letters.

voyage ['vɔiidʒ] *nc* long journey by wate *They have gone on a voyage round Africa* Also *vt/i* go on a voyage. **voyager** *nc.*

vulcanite ['vʌlkənait] *nu* hard substanc made from rubber and sulphur.
vulcanize *vt* make rubber harder by heatin it and mixing it with sulphur. **vulcanizatio** [vʌlkənai'zeiʃən] *nu.*

vulgar ['vʌlgə*] *adj* **1.** coarse; rude; bad mannered: *vulgar jokes; vulgar behaviou* **2.** in common use; of the common people (rather *o.f.* in sense **2.**). **vulgarly** *adv.*
vulgarity [vʌl'gæriti] *nc/u* vulgar act c behaviour.
vulgarize *vt* make vulgar. **vulgarizatio** [vʌlgərai'zeiʃən] *nu.*
vulgarian [vʌl'gɛəriən] *nc* rich person wh has vulgar tastes and habits.
vulgarism *nc* word or phrase generall used by people who are not educated.
vulgar fraction (mathematics) fraction shown thus: $\frac{3}{4}$ (as a decimal fraction show thus: 75.).

vulnerable ['vʌlnərəbl] *adj* easily damage or injured; open to attack. *I am vulnerab to headaches when I am tired.* (*opp* **invulner able**). **vulnerability** [vʌlnərə'biliti] *nu.*

vulpine ['vʌlpain] *adj* like a fox; cunning

vulture ['vʌltʃə*] *nc* type of large bir which eats the flesh of dead animals.

vulture

vying ['vaiiŋ] pres part of **vie.**

W

wacky ['wæki] *adj* amusing in a slightly crazy sort of way. (*informal*).
wad [wɔd] *nc* **1.** piece of soft material which is used to fill a hole or is packed round something to keep it from moving. **2.** number of folded banknotes or papers. Also *vt* fill with a wad; make into a wad. *past* **wadded.**
wadding *nu* soft material (e.g. cotton wool) used for packing etc.
waddle ['wɔdl] *vi* walk like a duck i.e. with short steps and swaying from side to side. Also *nc/u* a walk with a waddle.
wade [weid] *vt/i* walk through something which makes movement difficult (e.g. water or mud). *We waded across the river because there was no bridge.*
wader *nc* **1.** type of water bird with long legs. **2.** (in *pl*) long waterproof boots used for wading.
wade into something attack; start doing something with great energy. (*informal*).
wafer ['weifə*] *nc* very thin, crisp biscuit (often eaten with ice cream).
waffle[1] ['wɔfl] *nc* type of cake made of batter and cooked in an iron mould.
waffle[2] ['wɔfl] *vi* talk nonsense; talk too much. *What is he waffling on about?* Also *nu* foolish, unnecessary talk or writing. *There is too much waffle in this essay.* (both *informal*).
waft [wɔft] *vt* carry lightly across water or through air. *The gentle wind wafted the sound of music towards us.* Also *nc* light current of air or scent.
wag[1] [wæg] *vt/i* move, cause to move, up and down or from side to side quickly and often. *The dog's tail is wagging/The dog is wagging its tail. Her tongue is always wagging* i.e. she gossips a lot etc. *past* **wagged.** Also *nc* act of wagging.
'wagtail type of small bird with a long tail which moves up and down.
wag[2] [wæg] *nc* person who is an amusing talker and is fond of jokes. **waggish** *adj.* **waggishly** *adv.* **waggishness** *nu.*
wage[1] [weidʒ] *nc* (usu. *pl*) payment made or received for work done. *My wages are £30 a week.*
Note: when payments are made every week the usual word is *wages*; when made every month the word used is *salary.*
'wage earner somebody who works for wages.
'wage freeze time during which no increase in wages is allowed.
wage[2] [weidʒ] *vt* (with reference to a war or campaign) fight, carry on.
wager ['weidʒə*] *nc* bet. Also *vt*: *He wagered a pound that the horse he had chosen would win the race.*
lay a wager make a wager.
take up a wager accept a wager.
waggle ['wægl] *vt/i* move, cause to move, quickly, up and down or from side to side. *The bird waggled its tail to shake the water off.* Also *nc.*

waggon, wagon ['wægən] *nc* **1.** large four-wheeled vehicle pulled by horses or oxen and used for carrying goods. **2.** (*Brit*) railway truck. (*US* **freight car**)

wagons (*def 1*) (*def 2*)

waggoner, wagoner *nc* person who drives a waggon.
'station waggon see **station.**
waif [weif] *nc* person (esp. a child) or animal without a home.
wail [weil] *vt/i* express sorrow loudly. Also *nc* loud, long cry of sorrow.
wainscot ['weinskət] *nc* wooden panel fixed to the lower part of the inside wall of a building.
waist [weist] *nc* **1.** part of the body just above the hips. **2.** narrow, middle part of something (e.g. the part of a ship's deck between the higher forecastle at front and the higher quarter-deck at the back).
waistcoat ['weiskout] (*Brit*) short garment without sleeves, worn under a jacket. (*US* **vest**).
'waist-'deep *adj/adv* deep enough to reach the waist. *We were waist-deep in the river.*
'waist-'high *adj/adv* high enough to reach the waist.
'waistline measurement round the waist; shape of the waist.
wait [weit] *vt/i* **1.** stop or stay in a place without doing anything until somebody/something arrives or something happens. *I waited for him at the gate. We waited (for) an hour but they did not come. Have you been waiting long?* **2.** be ready for; do nothing until something happens. *You must wait your turn to see the doctor.* see also **await.** Also *nc* act of waiting. *We had a long wait before we could see him.*
waiter *nc* man who serves food at table in a restaurant or hotel. (*fem* **waitress** ['weitris]).
'waiting list list of names of those waiting to get or do something. *New houses are very scarce. There is a waiting list for all of them.*
'waiting room room where people wait (e.g. at a railway station for a train or in a doctor's house until the doctor can attend to them).
wait at table (*US* **wait on table**) serve food to those sitting at a table, remove their empty dishes etc.
wait on/upon someone be a servant to.

wait up for someone/something not go to bed until someone/something arrives.
keep somebody waiting cause somebody to wait longer than is necessary, by being late.
lie in wait for hide and wait to attack.
waive [weiv] *vt* (with reference to a claim or right) give up; not insist on.
waiver *nc* act of waiving a claim etc; document by which a claim is waived.
wake[1] [weik] *vt/i* stop sleeping; cause somebody to stop sleeping. *I always wake (up) at 7 o'clock. Please wake me (up) earlier tomorrow. past tense* **woke** [wouk] or **waked.** *past part* **woken** ['woukən], **woke** or **waked.** *Note:* 1. the verb forms of the following verbs:

verb	*past tense*	*past part*
awake	awoke	awoken
awaken	awakened	awakened
wake (up)	woke (or waked) (up)	woken (or waked) (up)
waken	wakened	wakened

2. *wake up* is the most usual of these four and it is the one which is recommended for use with *past tense woke up. past part woken up.*
waking *adj* while not asleep. *He spends all his waking hours reading.*
wakeful *adj* unable to sleep; not asleep; watchful. **wakefully** *adv.* **wakefulness** *nu.*
wake[2] [weik] *nc* 1. (esp. in Ireland) act of staying up all night with a corpse before its burial. 2. (in *pl*) annual holiday of factory workers in the north of England.
wake[3] [weik] *nc* track left by a ship as it moves through water.
in the wake of following or happening immediately after.
waken ['weikən] *vt/i. past* **wakened.** see **wake**[1].
wale [weil] *nc* see **weal.**
walk [wɔːk] 1. *vt/i* move on the feet (keeping one foot at a time on the ground while doing so). *Our baby cannot walk yet. I usually walk to school and come home by bus. They walked four miles in one hour.* 2. *vt* cause to walk. *He got off his horse and walked it up the hill. The teacher walked his class to the centre of the town.* Also *nc* 1. act of walking; distance covered, time taken, by walking. *We went for a walk after lunch. Our house is half an hour's walk from the church.* 2. way of walking. *I know him by his walk.*
'walking stick stick used when walking (usu. as a support).
walk away/off with something take away; steal. *He walked away/off with all the prizes* i.e. he won them all. (*informal*).
walk out on somebody go away and leave somebody after a quarrel etc. *His wife has walked out on him.* (*informal*).
'walkover *nc* (sport) event in which there is only one competitor; very easy victory.
walk of life kind of work one does; occupation; social position. *In the army there were men from every walk of life.*
walkie-talkie ['wɔːki'tɔːki] *nc* type of small two-way radio which can be carried and used by one person. (*informal*).
wall [wɔːl] *nc* structure of brick, stone etc built to form a side of a building or room, the boundary of a piece of land, or as a defence against something. *The walls of our house are built of brick. There is a blackboard on one wall of the classroom. He climbed over the wall into the garden.*
'wall bars horizontal bars fixed to the wal[l] of a gymnasium for exercises.
'wallflower 1. type of garden plant with a lot of small, brightly-coloured flowers. 2 woman who is left sitting at a danc[e] because nobody will dance with her (*informal* in sense 2.).
'wallpaper *nc* type of paper used to cove[r] the walls of a room. Also *vt: wallpaper a room.*
wall up close (in) with a wall.
go to the wall be defeated or ruined.
have one's back to the wall be in a positio[n] of great difficulty.
wallaby ['wɔləbi] *nc* type of small kangaroo
wallet ['wɔlit] *nc* 1. flat, folding case carrie[d] in the pocket to hold banknotes, paper[s] etc. 2. small bag for holding food or clothe[s] (*o.f.* in sense 2.).

wallet (*def 1*)

wallop ['wɔləp] *vt* hit hard; beat. Also *n[c]* hard blow. (both *informal*).
wallow ['wɔlou] *vi* 1. roll about in mud o[r] dirty water. 2. indulge too much in *wallow in money.* Also *nc* place wher[e] animals wallow.
walnut ['wɔːlnʌt] 1. *nc* type of nut with a bumpy shell, divided into two inside. 2. *n[c]* the tree on which this nut grows. 3. *nu* th[e] wood of this tree.
walrus ['wɔːlrəs] *nc* type of large sea anima[l] with two tusks pointing downwards. *p[l]* **walrus** or **walruses.**
waltz [wɔːls] *nc* 1. type of dance in which me[n] and women move round in pairs. 2. music fo[r] this type of dance. Also *vt/i* dance, caus[e] to dance, in this way.
wan [wɔn] *adj* 1. (with reference to a person looking tired or ill; pale. 2. (with referenc[e] to light) pale and weak. **wanly** *adv.* **wannes[s]** *nu.*
wand [wɔnd] *nc* thin stick carried in th[e] hand (e.g. by a conjurer or fairy).
wander ['wɔndə*] *vi* 1. move about from place to place without any particular pur pose. *We wandered through the town wit[h] nothing to do.* 2. go away from the correc[t] path. *Don't wander off the road into th[e] forest.* 3. go away from the proper course o[f] action; think about other things. *Th[e] teacher wandered from the subject of hi[s] lesson. As he spoke, my thoughts wandered*
wanderer *nc.*
wandering *nc* (often *pl*) 1. long journe[y] from place to place. 2. aimless speech (e.g during a fever).
'wanderlust very strong desire to travel.
wane [wein] *vi* (esp. with reference to th[e] bright part of the moon) become smaller o[r] less bright. *Last night there was a full moon Tonight it begins to wane.* (*opp* **wax**). Als[o] *nu* usu. only in **on the wane** i.e. decreas[e] in strength or brightness. *The moon is on th[e] wane. The king's power was on the wane.*
wangle ['wæŋgl] *vt* get something by cleve[r]

talk or a trick. *He wangled free tickets to the concert.* Also *nc*: *Be careful! This is one of his wangles.* (both *informal*).

want[1] [wɔnt] *vt/i* **1.** need; require. *Will you want the car today? I want more money to buy it. This room wants cleaning* i.e. needs to be cleaned. **2.** desire; wish. *I want to go home. They want us to help them.*

Note: 1. in sense **2.** *wish* can also be used (e.g. *I wish to go home*) but *want* is much more common. 2. *wish for* usu. has the sense of desiring something which is impossible or very difficult to have. *He is wishing for the moon; want* has the sense of desiring what is definite and possible. *He wants £10 before Friday.*

be wanting be without; be missing. *They are wanting in courage.*

want for nothing have everything one needs.

want[2] [wɔnt] **1.** *nu* state of not having; lack of what is needed. *The children are unhappy from want of love. He is ill through want of food. Many people live in want* i.e. are poor and hungry. **2.** *nc* (in *pl*) things desired or needed. *This shop can supply all your wants. Simple people have few wants.*

wanton ['wɔntn] *adj* wild or immoral in behaviour: *wanton destruction* i.e. without purpose or reason; *a wanton woman.* Also *nc* immoral woman. **wantonly** *adv.* **wantonness** *nu.*

war [wɔ:*] *nc/u* **1.** fight between countries using armed forces. *The Second World War began in 1939 and ended in 1945. Great Britain was at war for six years. Soldiers are trained for war.* **2.** any fight: *our war against ignorance, poverty and disease.* Also *vi* fight in war. *past* **warred.**

'warcry 1. shout made in battle. **2.** word or phrase used as a signal or slogan.

'warfare fighting in war; type of fighting in war: *jungle warfare; chemical warfare.*

'warhead front of a torpedo or missile which contains explosives.

'warlike *adj* ready for, fond of, war.

'warpath only in **on the warpath** i.e. looking for a fight or quarrel; fighting or quarrelling. (*informal* unless with reference to American Indians).

'warship ship armed for war.

'wartime time when there is war.

'war-weary *adj* exhausted by a long war.

civil war war between people of a country.

cold war strong political disagreement between countries without using armed forces (e.g. between Russia and the West).

declare war (upon) formally announce that there will be a war (with).

go to war (against) start a war (against).

make war (upon) fight (against).

warble ['wɔ:bl] *vt/i* (esp. with reference to birds) sing with trembling or quavering notes. Also *nc*: *the warble of birds in the forest.*

warbler *nc* type of bird which warbles.

ward[1] [wɔ:d] *nc* **1.** young person looked after by and under the control of an older person. *When his parents died the boy became the ward of his uncle.* **2.** (with reference to local elections) part of a town. **3.** large room in a hospital or prison: *surgical ward.*

ward[2] [wɔ:d] *vt* (with **off**) defend; prevent. *He warded off the blow with his arm.*

warden ['wɔ:dn] *nc* person who is in charge of a building or has particular duties: *the warden of a students' hostel.*

'traffic warden person who controls the parking of cars in streets and also sometimes directs traffic.

warder ['wɔ:də*] *nc* man who guards those in prison, jailer. (*fem* **wardress** ['wɔ:dris]).

wardrobe ['wɔ:droub] *nc* **1.** tall cupboard or small room for keeping clothes. **2.** clothes belonging to a particular person. *Her wardrobe must have cost hundreds of pounds.*

wardroom ['wɔ:dru:m] *nc* officers' room on a warship.

ware [wɛə*] **1.** *nc* (in *pl*) goods for sale. **2.** *nu* (with other words) particular type of goods (e.g. *earthenware* i.e. pottery; *hardware* i.e. goods made of metal for use in the home; *silverware* i.e. dishes etc made of silver).

'warehouse large building for keeping goods. Also *vt* put or keep in a warehouse.

warfare ['wɔ:fɛə*] *nu* see **war.**

warily ['wɛərili] *adv*, **wariness** ['wɛərinis] *nu* see **wary.**

warm[1] [wɔ:m] *adj* **1.** moderately hot; giving a pleasant, comfortable heat. *In England the summers are usually warm but seldom hot. You should wear warm clothes in cold weather.* **2.** kind; friendly. *They gave us a warm welcome.* **3.** (with reference to the tracks or scent of an animal when being hunted) recently made; fresh. *We followed the buffalo through the bush while the scent was still warm.* **warmly** *adv.* **warmth** [wɔ:mθ] *nu.*

'warm-'blooded *adj* **1.** (with reference to an animal) having warm blood and a fairly high body temperature (e.g. all mammals are warm-blooded; snakes are cold-blooded). **2.** (with reference to a person) having strong feelings.

'warm-'hearted *adj* friendly and kind. **warm-heartedly** *adv.* **warm-heartedness** *nu.*

warm[2] [wɔ:m] *vt/i* become, cause to become, warm or warmer. *The food was warming near the fire. They warmed themselves in the sun.* Also *nu* (with **a**): *They had a good warm by the fire.*

warmer *nc* something which warms (e.g. *bottle-warmer*).

'warming pan container with a long handle filled with hot coal, once used for warming a bed.

warm to someone begin to like; become more interested in. *I warmed to him at once.*

warm (something) up 1. make something warm. *She warmed up some milk.* **2.** make oneself warm and ready for something (esp. a competition or game). *The two teams are warming up for the relay race.*

warn [wɔ:n] *vt* inform or give advice to somebody about a future danger or difficulty. *We warned him of the dangers of driving too quickly. My father warned me against strangers* i.e. he told me to be careful with them and avoid them. *The headmaster warned them that next time they were late they would be punished. He warned them not to be late again.*

warning *nc* act or happening which warns. *Let this be a warning to you.* **warningly** *adv.*

warp [wɔ:p] *vt/i* **1.** (esp. with reference to wood) become twisted, cause to be twisted, out of shape. *The wooden planks have warped in the sun. The heavy rain warped the roof.* **2.** (esp. with reference to a person's character, nature etc) make twisted or evil. *This evil deed was planned by a warped mind.* **3.** (with reference to a ship) pull by a rope or cable wound round a capstan on land.

Also *nc* **1.** twist or bend: *a piece of wood with a warp in it.* **2.** threads running lengthwise in a piece of cloth. (Those running across them are called the **weft** or **woof**).

warrant ['wɔrnt] *vt* **1.** give authority or right to do something. *His wealth does not warrant his rude behaviour.* **2.** assure; guarantee. *The company warrants all the cars it sells.* Also **1.** *nu* authority or right. *What warrant have you for doing this?* **2.** *nc* written official authority to do something. *The police have a warrant for his arrest.*
warranted *adj* authorized. (*opp* **unwarranted**).
warranty *nc* guarantee; authority.
'warrant officer (in the armed forces) officer appointed by warrant, in rank below a commissioned officer and above a non-commissioned one (e.g. sergeant-major in the army).

warren ['wɔrn] *nc* **1.** piece of land in which many rabbits have dug holes and tunnels. **2.** any crowded place with narrow streets; slum.

warrior ['wɔriə*] *nc* soldier; brave fighter.

wart [wɔ:t] *adj* small, hard lump which grows on the skin.
'wart hog type of large wild pig found in tropical Africa.

wary ['wɛəri] *adj* careful; cautious. **warily** *adv.* **wariness** *nu.*

was [wɔz, wəz] past tense of **be.**

wash[1] [wɔʃ] *vt/i* **1.** clean with water or other liquid. *Have you washed (yourself) yet? She is washing our clothes.* **2.** (with reference to the action of water e.g. the sea, a lake, a river, rain etc) move against; carry away. *The west coast of Europe is washed by the Atlantic. The river rose until it was washing the walls of the houses. The rain washed the dry leaves into the ditch.* **3.** able to be washed without damage. *Does this dress wash?*
washable *adj* able to be washed without damage.
washer *nc* **1.** person who washes. **2.** machine for washing. **3.** flat ring of metal, rubber etc put below a screw.
washing *nu* **1.** act of washing or being washed. **2.** clothes washed or to be washed at one time. *My mother has a lot of washing today.* see also **wash**[2] (in sense **2.**).
washy *adj* **1.** (with reference to a liquid) thin; weak. **2.** (with reference to colour) pale; weak. **washiness** *nu.*
'washbasin, 'washbowl, 'wash-hand basin basin or bowl for washing the hands and face (usu. fixed to a wall and having taps).
'wash leather *nc/u* piece of soft leather used for washing smooth surfaces (e.g. windows, cars etc).
'washstand piece of furniture on which a basin and jug of water for washing the hands and face are placed (used when there are no taps).
'washerwoman woman who washes clothes.
'washing machine machine for washing clothes.
'washing soda sodium carbonate used for washing.
wash something away **1.** remove by washing. *She washed away her tears.* **2.** carry away by the action of water. *The flood has washed away their fishing nets.*
wash something down **1.** clean by washing (usu. with water from a hose). *He is washing down his car.* **2.** cause to go down into the stomach by drinking liquid. *We washed dow our food with a glass of water.*
wash something off/out remove by washing.
'washout *nc* **1.** part of a road or bank et carried away by a flood. **2.** complet failure. *The concert was a washout.* (*informa* in sense **2.**).
wash up (with reference to a number o dishes, knives, forks, spoons etc) wash after being used at a meal. *After supper w helped her to wash up.*
washing-'up *nu*: *We helped her with th washing-up.*
feel/look washed out feel/look very tire or ill. (*informal*).

wash[2] [wɔʃ] *nu* **1.** (with **a**) act of washing o being washed. *Have you had a wash yet He gave his hands a good wash.* **2.** clothe washed or to be washed at one time. *Is th wash dry yet?* see also **washing.** **3.** actio or movement of water. *We could hear th wash of the waves against the rocks. A fas boat makes a big wash as it passes.* **4.** thi mixture of liquid. *This coffee is not stron enough. It's just wash. They feed their pig on wash* i.e. a mixture of liquid and wast food. **5.** liquid used for cleaning or washin (e.g. *mouthwash*).

wasp [wɔsp] *nc* type of stinging insect lik a bee.
waspish *adj* like a wasp; quick-tempered

wassail ['wɔseil] **1.** *nc* merry party wit drinking and singing. **2.** *nu* type of specia drink taken then (*o.f.*).

waste [weist] *vt/i* **1.** use badly or wrongly use more than is needed. *We are wasting ou time by listening to such nonsense. Yo should not waste food when many people ar hungry.* **2.** become, cause to become, wea and thin slowly. *The children are wastin away because they do not get enough food His face was wasted by fever.* **3.** (with refer ence to land, buildings etc) damage destroy. Also **1.** *nu* act of wasting or bein wasted. *This waste of good food should no be allowed. It's a waste of time.* **2.** *nu* materia already used and no longer needed rubbish. *Put all the waste in this bag.* **3.** *nc* (i *pl*) empty land with little vegetation: *th Arctic wastes.*
wastage *nu* amount or number lost b waste. *The wastage in the universities is hig* i.e. many students leave before they hav finished the course.
waster *nc* person who is lazy and useless (*informal*).
wasteful *adj* causing to waste; using to much. **wastefully** *adv.* **wastefulness** *nu.*
'wastepaper basket (*Brit*) container fo putting used paper in. (*US* **wastebasket**).
'waste pipe pipe which carries away dirt water.
go/run to waste be wasted.
lay waste (with reference to land) destro crops; damage (esp. by the enemy during war).

wastrel ['weistrl] *nc* person who is lazy an useless; wasteful person.

watch[1] [wɔtʃ] *vt/i* **1.** look at somebody something to see what is happening or t be on guard against something. *If yo watch how I do it you will be able to do yourself. We sat watching the people pass passing by. They watched for any signs o trouble. Would you please watch these boy while I am away.* **2.** stay awake all nigh (*o.f.* in sense **2.**).

Note: watch usu. has the sense of looking at somebody/something moving or doing something for a period of time or from the beginning to the end of an action (e.g. *I watched him eat/eating his breakfast* i.e. I saw everything he did from beginning to end, but *I saw him eat/eating his breakfast* i.e. I noticed (while I was perhaps doing something else) that he was eating his breakfast).
watch over guard, take care of.
watch out for 1. keep watching for. *He's been watching out for the postman.* 2. be careful of. *Watch out for snakes.*

watch² [wɔtʃ] 1. *nu* act of watching (esp. when on guard against something). *The police were on the watch for any trouble.* 2. *nc* one of the seven periods of duty on a ship: *the first watch* i.e. 8 p.m. to midnight; *the middle watch* i.e. midnight to 4 a.m.; *the dog watch* i.e. 4 p.m. to 6 p.m. or 6 p.m. to 8 p.m.; members of the crew who are on duty at the same time. 3. *nc* group of men who once guarded people and property at night. (This work is now done by the police). 4. period of staying awake at night (*o.f.*).
watchful *adj* watching carefully; attentive; alert. **watchfully** *adv.* **watchfulness** *nu.*
'watchdog dog kept to guard a building etc.
'watchman man who guards a building (esp. at night).
'watchtower tower from which persons watch for an attack, a forest fire etc.
'watchword 1. secret word used to show who is a friend and who is an enemy; password. 2. slogan or motto of a group of people.
keep watch 1. (with **for**) look out for; be on guard against. *You must keep a good watch for wild animals.* 2. be on duty (usu. on a ship).

watch³ [wɔtʃ] *nc* small clock carried in a pocket or worn on the wrist.
'watch chain chain for fastening a watch carried in a pocket to one's clothing.
'watch strap piece of leather etc for fastening a watch around one's wrist.

water¹ ['wɔːtə*] 1. *nu* most common of liquids found in rainfall, rivers, lakes etc. *There is no water in the well. Is there enough hot water for a bath? He jumped into the water and swam away.* 2. *nc* (in *pl*) waves; large amount of water. *The waters of the lake beat against the wall of the castle. Our ship was in enemy waters* i.e. in part of the sea controlled by the enemy. 3. *nc* (in *pl*) special type of water for drinking: *mineral waters; table waters. He went abroad to drink the waters* i.e. special type of water which cures certain diseases.
waterless *adj* without water; very dry.
watery *adj* 1. like water; pale; weak. 2. wet; full of water.
'water bird type of bird which swims in water and lives near water.
'water biscuit type of thin, hard biscuit.
'waterborne *adj* carried or spread by water: *a waterborne disease.*
'water closet small room where waste matter from the body is washed down a pipe by water.
Note: commonly referred to by the initials W.C.
'watercolour 1. paint which is mixed with water, not oil. 2. picture painted with this type of paint.
'watercourse channel or ditch made by running water.
'watercress type of green plant which grows in running water and is used as a food in salads.
'waterfall fall of the water of a river over a cliff.
'waterfront land next to the sea, lake or river; part of a town next to the sea, a lake or a river (e.g. its harbour, docks etc).
'water hole (in a desert or arid area) hole in the ground where water collects.
'water jacket container filled with water which is fitted round an engine or gun to keep it from becoming too hot.
'water level level reached by the surface of an amount of water.
'waterline line on the side of a ship reached by the water.
'waterlogged *adj* 1. (with reference to the ground) full of water; very wet. 2. (with reference to wood or a ship) full of water but still floating.
'water main large underground pipe which supplies water to houses, factories etc.
'watermark 1. faint design stamped on paper by the manufacturer. 2. mark which shows the level reached by water (e.g. of a river or tide): *the high/low watermark in a harbour.*
'water mill mill which is driven by running water.
'water polo game played by two teams with a ball in water.
'water power power obtained from running or falling water to drive machines.
'waterproof *adj* not allowing water to enter: *a waterproof hat.* Also *nc* coat which is waterproof. *You must wear your waterproof when it is raining.* Also *vt* make something waterproof.
'watershed ridge of ground between two separate rivers and their tributaries.
'waterside bank of a river; shore of a lake or sea.
'waterspout 1. column of water between water and the clouds, caused by a whirlwind. 2. pipe for taking away rainwater (e.g. from a roof).
'water supply system of supplying water to people; amount of water collected for this purpose.
'water table level at which water is found below the surface of the ground.
'watertight *adj* 1. made so that water cannot get in or out. 2. so definite that there is no doubt: *a watertight agreement.*
'water tower tower on which a tank of water is fixed so that there will be enough pressure for the water to be distributed to an area.
'waterway channel of water deep enough for ships; canal.
'waterwheel wheel turned by water.
'waterworks *npl* (with a *sing* or *pl* verb) reservoirs, storage tanks and pumps etc for supplying water.
'hard water water which does not lather easily with soap. (*opp* **soft water**).
'head waters *npl* source of a river (usu. a lake): *the head waters of the Nile.*
heavy water deuterium oxide which is different from ordinary water in density, boiling point etc.
'high/'low 'water highest/lowest level of the tide.
'soft water water which lathers easily with soap. (*opp* **hard water**).
in deep water/waters in difficulties. (*informal*).
hold water remain correct after being

tested. *His argument doesn't hold water.* (*informal*).

get into hot water get into difficulties (usu. by doing something foolish) (*informal*).

keep one's head above water see **keep**[1].

make/pass water (with reference to a person) pass urine from the body, urinate.

make water (with reference to a ship) allow water to enter; have a leak.

on the water in a boat or ship.

spend money like water spend money carelessly and extravagantly. (*informal*).

water[2] ['wɔːtə*] *vt/i* **1.** put water on; give water to plants etc. **2.** weaken by adding water. *He watered the wine before drinking it.* **3.** (with reference to the eyes or mouth) fill with water. *The smoke made his eyes water. The smell of the food made my mouth water.*

'watering place 1. place where animals get water. **2.** place where mineral waters are drunk; holiday resort.

watt [wɔt] *nc* unit of electrical power. **wattage** *nu.*

wattle ['wɔtl] **1.** *nu* number of sticks bent in and out between upright sticks to form a wall or fence. *Many African huts have wattle and mud walls and a thatched roof.* **2.** *nc* type of tree, the bark of which is used for tanning. **3.** *nc* piece of red skin which hangs down below the neck of a bird (e.g. a cock or turkey).

wave [weiv] *nc* **1.** moving ridge of water on the surface of the sea, a lake etc. *The boat rose and fell on the high waves.* **2.** movement of the hand as a signal or greeting. *He gave us a friendly wave as he passed.* **3.** sudden but temporary increase in feelings, action, heat etc. *A wave of anger swept through the crowd; heatwave* i.e. period when the temperature is much higher than usual. **4.** something shaped or moving like a wave. *She has lovely waves in her hair. A wave of soldiers attacked the town. This radio set can receive on short, medium and long wave.* Also *vt/i* **1.** move, cause to move, from side to side or up and down. *The flags waved in the wind.* **2.** make a signal, give a greeting by moving the hand or something held in the hand. *They waved me goodbye. He waved his handkerchief to me.* **3.** give something the shape of a wave. *I am told that he waves his hair.* **wavy** *adj* having curves like a wave: *wavy hair; a wavy line.* **wavily** *adv.*

'waveband group of wavelengths close together, used by a broadcasting station.

'wavelength (with reference to radio) speed of a wave divided by the number of oscillations.

(be) on the same wavelength (as someone) (be) able to understand (someone).

waver ['weivə*] *vi* **1.** be unsteady; move from side to side. *His eyes wavered when he looked at me.* **2.** be uncertain; hesitate. *They are wavering between agreeing and refusing.* **waverer** *nc.*

wax[1] [wæks] *nu* **1.** substance which is made by bees and used by them for building honeycombs; this substance used by humans (e.g. to make polish or candles) (Often **beeswax**). **2.** substance which is like beeswax: *earwax* i.e. yellow substance which collects in the ears; *paraffin wax* i.e. type of resin used in making polish. Also *vt* put wax on; polish.

waxen *adj* **1.** like wax. **2.** made of wax (*o.f.*).

waxy *adj* made of wax; like wax.

'waxwork 1. model made from wax (esp. one of a famous person). **2.** (in *pl*) place where these models are shown.

wax[2] [wæks] *vi* **1.** (usu. with reference to the moon) become larger. (*opp* **wane**). **2.** become. *They waxed eloquent.*

way [wei] **1.** *nc* path; road. *We followed the narrow way between the trees. The family across/over the way is on holiday* i.e. the one living on the other side of the road. **2.** *nu* correct path or road to be followed from one place to another. *Is this the way to London? They lost their way in the forest.* **3.** *nc* direction. *Look both ways before you cross the road. She looked the other way. Please come this way.* **4.** *nu* distance between two places. *New York is a long way from London. Our house is only a little way from the school. We saw him a long way away/off* i.e. far in the distance. **5.** *nu* space for somebody/something to move forward. *You are standing in my way. Please get out of my way. They made way for the bus* i.e. they stood aside to let it pass. **6.** *nc* method; means; habit. *Do it this way. I know a better way of finding out. I don't like their way of blaming other people. My father spoke about the old ways of travelling when he was a boy.* **7.** *nc* condition; state; extent. *He was in a bad way after the accident.* (*informal*). *In a way he is right* i.e. to some extent.

'wayfarer *nc* person who travels (esp. on foot) (*o.f.*).

'wayfaring *adj* travelling.

'wayside side of a road.

the permanent way railway track.

anyway in any case or circumstances.

by the way (used with reference to a remark brought suddenly into a conversation) incidentally; if I may say so. *We like your new car – by the way, how much did it cost?*

by way of 1. via; passing through. *They flew to Singapore by way of Rome and Karachi.* **2.** in order to. *They have come here by way of finding the truth.* **3.** instead of; as a kind of. *By way of an excuse he said he was tired.*

in the family way pregnant. (*informal*).

in a small way to a small extent; quietly. *He sells books in a small way. They live in a small way near the coast.*

on the way while travelling. *We met them on the way to school.*

on the way in coming into fashion or use.

on the way out about to be no longer used or fashionable. *Are woollen stockings on the way out?* (*informal*).

one way or another somehow. *We'll win one way or another.*

out of the way unusual. *There is nothing out of the way about walking ten miles.*

out-of-the-way *adj* far from a road; difficult to find. *They lived in an out-of-the-way house in the country.*

under way 1. (with reference to a ship) moving. *Slowly the huge liner got under way.* **2.** begun; in the process of being done. *Our plans are under way.*

get/have one's (own) way get or do what one wishes.

give way yield; break. *You should give way to traffic coming from the right. The branch gave way under his weight.*

go one's own way do what one wishes to do alone.

go out of one's way to do something try hard; make a special point of doing something. *They went out of their way to help us.*

lead the way go in front to show the way; be an example to others.
lose way (with reference to a ship) begin to move more slowly; lose speed.
make one's way go forward; move.
pave the way for prepare for; make it easier for something to happen.
put somebody out of the way put somebody in prison; get rid of somebody (e.g. by killing him).
right of way *nc/u* **1.** right to use a particular path across land which belongs to somebody else. **2.** (with reference to traffic) right to use or move on to a particular part of a road before other traffic. *As my car was on the main road, I had (the) right of way at the crossroads.*
to my way of thinking in my opinion.

waylay [wei'lei] *vt* wait in order to attack, or speak to, somebody passing by. *past* **waylaid** [wei'leid].

wayward ['weiwəd] *adj* liking to do what one wants to do; not easily controlled; wilful. **waywardly** *adv.* **waywardness** *nu.*

we [wi:] *pron* people who are speaking; person who is speaking and others. *You leave just now and we'll join you later.*

weak [wi:k] *adj* **1.** not strong; feeble; easily damaged or made useless. *He is very weak after his illness. She has weak eyes. The box is too weak to stand on.* **2.** (with **at** or **in**) not good at. *They are weak in English grammar.* **3.** (with reference to a liquid mixture) having a lot of water; thin: *weak coffee/tea.* (*opp* **strong**). **weakness** *nc/u.*
weakly *adv* in a weak manner.
weaken *vt/i* become, cause to become, weak or weaker.
weakling *nc* person or animal that is weak.
'weak-'headed, 'weak-'minded *adj* having little intelligence; mentally below normal.
'weak-'kneed *adj* cowardly; not determined. (*informal*).
have a weakness for like more than one should. *He has a weakness for chocolate ice cream.*
the weaker sex women. (rather *o.f.*).

weal[1] [wi:l] (*US* **wale** [weil]) *nc* mark left on the skin by a blow of a stick or whip.

weal[2] [wi:l] *nu* sound, healthy condition; prosperity (*o.f.* except in **the general/public weal** i.e. the prosperity of all; and **weal and woe** i.e. good times and bad).

wealth [welθ] *nu* **1.** riches; large amount of money. *A millionaire is a man of wealth.* **2.** (with **a** or **the**) great number of something; abundance. *The wealth of detail in this report is amazing.* **wealthy** *adj.* **wealthily** *adv.*
wealthiness *nu* riches.

wean [wi:n] *vt* **1.** gradually stop feeding **a** baby or young animal on milk and get it used to other food. **2.** gradually cause somebody to change a habit etc. **weaning** *nu.*

weapon ['wepən] *nc* instrument or method used when fighting. *The atomic missile is the most modern weapon of war. His weapons are a good brain and a quick tongue.*

wear[1] [wɛə*] *vt/i* **1.** have on the body or part of the body. *He was wearing a brown coat and a black hat. She is wearing a gold ring on her finger. She should not wear red* i.e. red clothes. **2.** become, cause to become, damaged or changed by long use. *Your shirt is very worn at the collar. He has worn holes in all his shoes.* **3.** continue to be useful; last. *Leather gloves wear better than cloth ones. This jacket has worn well* i.e. has lasted a long time without becoming damaged. *past tense* **wore** [wɔ:*]. *past part* **worn** [wɔ:n].
wearer *nc* person who is wearing something.
wearable *adj* able to be worn. (*opp* **unwearable**).
wearing *adj* tiring. *We've had a wearing day.*
wear (something) away become, cause to become, thin or weak by rubbing; disappear, cause to disappear, in this way. *The name on the door has worn away. The river has worn away the rocks.*
wear someone/something down **1.** make less by rubbing or use. *I have worn down the point of the pencil.* **2.** make weaker by attacking often. *He wore down the other boxer with strong punches.*
wear off **1.** disappear, cause to disappear, by rubbing or use. *The polish on your car will soon wear off.* **2.** gradually disappear or stop. *My headache is wearing off.*
wear (something) out **1.** finish by long use. *I have worn out this old coat. This old coat is worn out.* **2.** become, cause to become, very tired. *Teaching wears her out.*

wear[2] [wɛə*] *nu* **1.** act of having on the body or part of the body. *I want a light suit for wear in a hot country.* **2.** something which is worn on the body. *Do you sell menswear here?* **3.** change or damage by being used. *Rough roads cause the rapid wear of car tyres.* **4.** ability to continue to be useful. *You should buy shoes which have plenty of wear.*
wear and tear change or damage caused by normal use. (Also **fair wear and tear**). *Any damage will be repaired at our expense, if caused by fair wear and tear.*
worse for wear damaged by use. (usu. *informal*).

weary ['wiəri] *adj* tired or tiring. *We rested our weary legs. We are weary of learning English. He gave a weary lesson about verbs.* Also *vt/i* become, cause to become, tired. *We soon wearied of listening to him. The long journey is wearying him. past* **wearied.**
wearily *adv.* **weariness** *nu.* **wearied** *adj.*
wearisome *adj* dull and tiring; boring. **wearisomely** *adv.* **wearisomeness** *nu.*

weasel ['wi:zl] *nc* small fierce animal with a thin body, short legs and a long tail, which kills and eats chickens, rabbits etc.

weather ['weðə*] *nu* condition of the air in a particular place at a particular time which causes wind, rain, sunshine, heat, cold etc. *What was the weather like in Paris last week? You should wear thick clothes in cold weather. Note: climate* has the sense of the usual condition of the air etc for a long time in a large area. *The climate of tropical Africa is much warmer than that of Western Europe.* Also *vt/i* **1.** become changed and worn because of the weather; cause this to happen. *The wind and the waves have weathered the rocks on the shore.* **2.** (usu. with reference to wood) keep or be kept in the open air. *Trees which have been cut down cannot be used until they have been weathered.* **3.** escape safely (e.g. from a storm or difficulty). *Our country has not yet weathered its financial crisis.*
'weather-beaten *adj* marked or made rough by the weather: *a sailor with a weather-beaten face.*
'weatherboarding *nu,* **'weatherboards** *npl* type of boards which are fixed horizontally so that the lower thick edge of one lies over the upper thin edge of the other and

so keeps out the wind and rain (used e.g. to protect the outer walls of wooden buildings).

'weathercock weather vane shaped like a cock. see illustration of weather vane.

'weather forecast statement telling what the future weather should be like.

'weatherproof *adj* able to keep out the weather; not easily damaged by the weather. Also *vt*: *weatherproof a house.*

'weather vane device which is fixed on top of a building or pole and turns to show the direction of the wind.

weather vane

in all weathers in all types of weather.

be/feel under the weather be/feel ill or depressed. (*informal*).

make heavy weather of something have difficulty in doing something. (*informal*).

weave [wi:v] *vt/i* **1.** make cloth from threads. **2.** make by twisting or forming together. *She is weaving the flowers into a wreath. The old man weaves many interesting stories from his adventures as a young man.* **3.** move from side to side through. *He wove in and out of the traffic in his car. past tense* **wove** [wouv]. *past part* **woven** ['wouvən].

weaver *nc* person who weaves (in sense **1.**).

weaving *nu* art of weaving (in sense **1.**).

web [web] *nc* **1.** something made by weaving threads together: *a web of cloth; a spider's web.* **2.** skin between the toes of certain types of water birds and animals.

webbed *adj* having skin of this kind. *Ducks have webbed feet.*

webbing *nu* strips of strong cloth used as belts or to put on the edges of carpets etc.

'web'footed, 'web'toed *adj* having webbed feet or toes.

wed [wed] *vt/i* take as husband or wife; marry. *past* **wedded** or **wed** (*o.f.*).

wedding *nc* ceremony in which a man and woman are married.

'wedlock condition of being married: *born out of wedlock* i.e. having parents who are not married. (rather *o.f.*).

'wedding 'breakfast meal eaten after a wedding.

silver wedding 25th anniversary of a wedding (*golden/diamond wedding* 50th/60th anniversary).

be wedded to 1. have as husband or wife (*o.f.*). **2.** be fully occupied; devoted to. *They are wedded to their work.*

wedge [wedʒ] *nc* **1.** piece of wood or metal shaped like a V which is driven into wood etc to split it, or is used to keep two things firm or separate. **2.** something which is V-shaped: *a wedge of cake.* Also *vt* **1.** keep firm or separate with a wedge. **2.** push in like a wedge. *The little boy wedged himself between the two big ones.*

the thin end of the wedge a small beginning which later leads to big changes or a lot of trouble. *Their request for a few pounds is the thin end of the wedge* i.e. they are going to ask for a lot more later. (*informal*).

Wednesday ['wednzdi] *n* fourth day of the Christian week, after Tuesday.

wee [wi:] *adj* small; little. (*informal*).

weed [wi:d] *nc* plant growing where it is useless or not wanted. Also *vt/i* take out weeds. *In this country the men plant the corn and the women later weed it* i.e. take out the weeds growing among the corn.

weedy *adj* **1.** full of weeds. **2.** thin and weak. *He is a weedy boy.* **weediness** *nu.*

weed someone/something out (esp. with reference to taking away what is weak or bad and leaving the strong or good) take away. *The teacher has weeded out the slow boys and put them in a lower class.*

weeds [wi:dz] *npl* black clothes worn by a woman on the death of her husband.

week [wi:k] *nc* period of seven days (usu. from midnight on Saturday to midnight on the next Saturday).

weekly *adj/adv* of or for a week; happening once a week. Also *nc* magazine or paper which is published once a week.

'weekday any day of the week except Sunday.

'week'end *nc* period from Friday or Saturday to Monday; holiday during this period. Also *vi* spend a weekend.

'week'ender *nc* person who spends the weekend away from home.

tomorrow week eight days from today.

week in week out for many weeks (without a break).

weep [wi:p] *vt/i* let tears fall; cry. *past* **wept** [wept].

weevil ['wi:vl] *nc* type of small insect which attacks plants and food.

weft [weft] *nc* threads which run across the warp. (Also **woof**). see **warp.**

weigh [wei] *vt* **1.** find out how heavy somebody/something is (usu. by using scales). *The butcher weighed the meat for me.* **2.** be equal in heaviness to. *The meat weighed five and a half pounds. How much do you weigh?*

'weighbridge large machine for weighing a lorry etc and its load.

'weighing machine machine for weighing.

weigh down 1. push down by being heavy; be too heavy for. *The small boy was weighed down with the parcels he was carrying.* **2.** be too much for. *All his troubles are weighing him down.*

weigh in 1. be weighed before an event (e.g. a boxer before a fight, a jockey before a horse-race). **2.** begin doing something with energy or force. *When our friend was attacked, we weighed in to help him.* (*informal* in sense **2.**).

'weigh-in *nc*: *At the weigh-in he was 110 pounds.*

weigh on someone/something rest heavily on; cause trouble or worry. *The defeat weighed on his mind.*

weigh something out weigh and make ready in particular amounts. *He carefully weighed out our food for the day.*

weigh someone/something up estimate. *I weighed up my chances of winning. A good teacher soon weighs up his pupils.*

weigh with someone be considered important by. *Your wealth does not weigh with him.*

weigh anchor raise the anchor of a ship in order to sail away.

weigh one's words speak carefully.

weight [weit] **1.** *nu* heaviness of something/

somebody. *What is your weight? The parcel is 2 pounds in weight.* **2.** *nc* something which is known to weigh a particular amount. *He put three one-ounce weights on the scales. He wrote down the weights of the boxes.* **3.** *nc* something heavy. *If you are ill, you should not lift heavy weights.* **4.** *nu* importance; effect. *He has great weight with the people.* Also *vt* make heavier. *The rear part of the car was weighted with sand.*
weighty *adj* heavy; important. **weightily** *adv.* **weightiness** *nu.*
'heavy /'middle /'welter /'light /'feather / 'bantam /'flyweight types of boxers according to their weight.
'over/'under'weight (usu. with reference to a person) weighing too much/too little.
pull one's weight do one's fair share of work. (*informal*).
put on weight (with reference to a person) become heavier or fatter.
throw one's weight about use one's power or position to bully or frighten others. (*informal*).

weir [wiə*] *nc* **1.** wall built across a river to control but not stop the flow of water. **2.** type of trap for fish used in a river.

weird [wiəd] *adj* strange; unearthly. **weirdly** *adv.* **weirdness** *nu.*

welcome ['welkəm] *adj* causing pleasure; received with pleasure. *This is welcome news. The money was very welcome to them. You are welcome to try* i.e. there is nothing to stop you trying. *He is welcome to my room while I'm away* i.e. I'll gladly allow him to use it. (*opp* **unwelcome**). Also *nc* greeting or reception. *They gave us a great welcome. He received a cold/warm welcome.* Also *vt* receive with kindness or pleasure. *He welcomed them when they arrived.*

weld [weld] *vt* join pieces of metal by first softening them by heat and then pressing or fixing them together; join anything closely together. Also *nc* metal joint made in this way. **welder** *nc.* **welding** *nu.*

welfare ['welfɛə*] *nu* health and comfort; happiness; well-being. *In every country, child welfare is important. He works hard for the welfare of the poor.*
'welfare 'state country which provides for the security and health of its citizens.

well[1] [wel] *nc* **1.** deep hole made in the ground to get water or oil. **2.** space in a building for a staircase or lift; clear space in the centre of a room or ship. Also *vi* (with reference to a liquid) flow. *Tears welled up in her eyes.*
'wellhead source of water (e.g. a spring).
drive/sink a well make a well in the ground.

well[2] [wel] *adj/adv* **1.** in a proper, satisfactory manner. *You speak English well. I slept well. He treated us well.* **2.** carefully; thoroughly. *Think well before you answer. He mixed the drink well before giving it to me.* **3.** with good reason; wisely; probably. *You may well be right. I couldn't very well stay.* *Note:* in sense **3.** *well* is put in the middle of the verb.
4. to a great degree; considerably. *He sat well back in his chair. It is now well past two o'clock.* **5.** in good health; in satisfactory condition. *Are you well? I feel very well. They are very well where they are.* (*opp* **unwell** in sense **5.**). **6.** (usu. with **it would be as**) desirable; in one's interests. *It would be as well to arrive early. It would have been as well to tell him your plans.* Also *interj*: *Well, here we are! Very well, I'll come. Well, as I was saying, we went away.*
as well also; in addition. *He went away. She went as well.*
as well as also; in addition to. *He is learning French as well as English.*
be well away 1. be making progress. **2.** be drunk. (*informal*).
be well in with be very friendly with. (*informal*).
be well off have plenty of money, etc.
be well out of something be lucky not to be involved in. *You are well out of this quarrel.*
do oneself well treat oneself to good things (e.g. good food, comforts etc) (*informal*).
do well to do something profit, gain advantage, be lucky, by doing something. *They did well to sell their house so quickly.*
go well (with **with**) be successful, satisfactory. *I hope your plans go well. I hope all goes well with your plans.*
go well (together) fit; suit one another. *Red and purple do not go well together.*
it's all very well . . . but showing one does not agree. *It's all very well for them to tell me to do this, but I am too busy.*
just as well equally suitable; to one's advantage. *You might just as well give me the books now as wait till tomorrow. It is just as well* (*that*) *he is a kind man* i.e. it is fortunate that he is.
let well alone not try to change something which is satisfactory as it is.
speak well of praise; approve. *Your teacher speaks well of your work.*
wish somebody well wish somebody success or good luck.

well-[3] [wel] *prefix.*
'well-ad'vised *adj* sensible; wise.
'well-'balanced *adj* sensible; thoughtful; properly arranged or planned.
'well-being health and happiness; welfare.
'well'born *adj* of a family of good social standing.
'well-'bred *adj* of a good family; having good manners.
'well-con'nected *adj* related to persons of good social standing.
'well-dis'posed *adj* friendly; sympathetic.
'well-'founded *adj* based on fact; true.
'well-'grounded *adj* **1.** based on fact. **2.** having good knowledge of the essential facts of a subject.
'well-in'formed *adj* **1.** having a great amount of general knowledge. **2.** having been informed by somebody who really knows.
'well-'judged *adj* correctly timed.
'well-'knit *adj* (with reference to a person) muscular; strong.
'well-'known *adj* known by many; famous.
'well-'marked *adj* definite; decided.
'well-'meaning *adj* having good intentions; friendly.
'well-'meant *adj* done or said with good intentions.
'well-nigh *adv* almost; nearly.
'well-'off *adj* rich; having quite a lot of money. (*informal*).
'well-'read [red] *adj* (with reference to a person) having read many books and so having great knowledge.
'well-'spoken *adj* **1.** (with reference to a person) speaking well; cultured in speech. **2.** (with **of**) favourably spoken about. *He is very well spoken of.*
'well-to-'do *adj* wealthy.

'well-'turned *adj* (with reference to something said or written) neatly expressed.
'well-wisher person who wishes somebody well.
'well-'worn *adj* worn much; used too much; commonplace.
wellingtons ['weliŋtnz] *npl* type of rubber boots which reach to below the knees.
welt [welt] *nc* narrow piece of leather between the sole and the upper part of a shoe.
welter[1] ['weltə*] *vi* roll about in; be soaked in. Also *nc* confusion; disorder.
welter[2] ['weltə*] *adj* in **welterweight** i.e. boxer who weighs between 135 and 147 pounds.
wen [wen] *nc* small swelling beneath the skin (usu. on the head).
wench [wentʃ] *nc* girl or young woman (*o.f.*; can also be used humorously).
wend [wend] *vt* only in **wend one's way** i.e. go (*o.f.*).
went [went] past part of **go.**
wept [wept] past of **weep.**
were [wə:*] past tense of **be.**
werewolf, werwolf ['wiəwulf] *nc* person who was once believed to be able to turn himself into a wolf.
wert [wə:t] past of **be** when used with **thou** (*o.f.*).
west [west] *nu* (with **the**) part of the sky or direction in which the sun sets. Also *adj* from or in this direction: *a west wind* i.e. blowing from the west; *the west side of the forest* i.e. facing towards the west. Also *adv* towards the west. *I drove west along the road.* (*opp* **east**).
westerly ['westəli] *adj/adv* **1.** from or in the west: *a westerly wind.* **2.** towards the west.
western ['westən] *adj* of or in the west: *Western Europe; western civilization.* Also *nc* film or story about the adventures of cowboys in the western part of the USA.
westerner *nc* person who lives in the west.
westernize ['westənaiz] *vt* give western civilization to. **westernized** *adj.* **westernization** [westənai'zeiʃən] *nu.*
westernmost ['westənmoust] *adj* farthest to the west.
westward ['westwəd] *adj/adv* towards the west.
wet [wet] *adj* **1.** covered with water or other liquid. *The grass was wet after the rain. The paint is still wet.* **2.** rainy: *wet weather; the wet season.* (*opp* **dry**). *comparative* **wetter.** *superlative* **wettest.** Also *nu* (with **the**) rain; water. *He is standing in the wet without a coat.* Also *vt* make wet. *past* **wetted. wetly** *adv.* **wetness** *nu.*
wetting *nc* act of becoming wet. *We got a wetting in the heavy rain.*
'wet-nurse (in former times) woman who was employed to give her milk to the baby of somebody else.
wet through *adj* wet from one side to the other; completely wet. *Your jacket is wet through.*
wether ['weðə*] *nc* male sheep which has been castrated.
whack [wæk], **thwack** [θwæk] *vt* hit hard (usu. causing a noise when doing so). Also *nc* **1.** hard, noisy blow. **2.** try. *Have a whack at it.* (*informal* in sense **2.**).
whacking *nc* act of hitting hard; beating. Also *adj/adv* big; very: *a whacking book; a whacking great book.* (*informal* in this sense).
whale [weil] *nc* type of very large sea animal. Also *vi* hunt whales. *Ships from many countries go whaling in the far south.*
whaler *nc* ship or man that hunts whales.
'whalebone type of thin bone obtained from the jaw of a whale.
a whale of a time a very enjoyable time. (*informal*).
wharf [wɔ:f] *nc* structure built into the water where ships can load and unload. *pl* **wharfs** or **wharves** [wɔ:vz].
what [wɔt] *adj/pron/determiner* **1.** asking a question with reference to one or more of several. *What country do you come from? What kinds of food do they eat? What time is it?* **2.** instead of *the*; any/the . . . that. *I gave him what money I had. What little I had I gave to him.* **3.** *What a lovely house you have! What a strange thing to say!* **4.** what thing or things. *What's worrying you? What is your job? What?* i.e. what did you say? *Note:* in senses **1.** and **4.** *what* gives a wider choice than *which*; *which* has the sense of choosing one of two, or one or more from a definite number (e.g. *What coat will you wear?* i.e. you have several to choose from). *Which coat will you wear, the black one or the brown one? Which are yours, these or those?* Also *relative pron* the thing or things that . . . *What he said was very helpful. He gave me what I wanted.* Also *interj* (expressing surprise etc) *What! He's already here!*
what about asking for information or getting an opinion. *Dictionaries? What about them?* i.e. tell me about them. *What about going for a walk?* i.e. do you think it is a good idea? *What about a drink?* i.e. would you like one?
what for for what purpose? why? *What is this tool (used) for? You have come to see me. What for?*
what if what will or would happen if. *What if I am late?*
what . . . like asking information about somebody/something. *What's England like?*
what of **1.** see **what about.** **2.** in phrase *Well, what of it?* i.e. I agree but is it important? (Also **so what?**).
so what? I agree, but is it important? (*informal* and sometimes *impolite*).
what's what things as they actually are. *He knows what's what* i.e. he knows what the situation is; he is not a fool. (*informal*).
what with . . . and for the following reasons. *What with plenty of money and good friends, he had a happy life.*
I'll tell you what this is what I think should be done. *We have only a little money for our holidays. I'll tell you what. Let's stay at home.*
whate'er [wɔt'ɛə*] *adj* short form of **whatever** used in poetry.
whatever [wɔt'evə*] *adj/pron* **1.** emphatic form of **what.** *I'll give you whatever help you need. You can eat whatever you want.* **2.** emphatic negative after **none** and **no.** *He had no reason whatever for saying this.* **3.** in spite of what; regardless of what. *Whatever he says, don't go. I am ready to leave whatever the time (is).*
whatsoever emphatic form of **whatever** (*o.f.* except in sense **2.**).
wheat [wi:t] *nu* grain from which flour for making bread is obtained; plant which produces this grain.
wheaten *adj* made of wheat: *wheaten bread*
wheedle ['wi:dl] *vt* get something from somebody, get somebody to do something, by being very pleasant to him. *They have wheedled a holiday from/out of the head-*

master. They have wheedled the headmaster into giving them a holiday.

wheel [wi:l] *nc* **1.** circular device which turns round on a central rod or axle and on which bicycles, cars, trains, machines etc move. **2.** device by which a car, ship etc is steered. (Often **steering wheel** when reference is to a car). **3.** movement round like that made by a wheel. *The soldiers made a left wheel/a wheel to the left.* Also *vt/i* **1.** push or pull something which has a wheel or wheels. *He wheeled his bicycle up the hill* i.e. instead of riding it. **2.** carry somebody/something in a vehicle with wheels. *They wheeled him away in an invalid chair.* **3.** move, cause to move, round like a wheel. *The soldiers wheeled to the left.*

'wheelbarrow type of small cart with one wheel in front and two handles behind.

'wheelchair chair on wheels for a person who cannot walk.

'wheelwright person who makes and repairs wheels.

wheeze [wi:z] *vt/i* breathe noisily (as one does when one has a cold); make a noise like this. Also *nc* **1.** noise of this kind. **2.** trick; device. (*informal* in sense **2.**). **wheezy** *adj.* **wheezily** *adv.* **wheeziness** *nu.*

whelk [welk] *nc* type of shellfish like a big snail.

whelp [welp] *nc* **1.** young lion, bear, dog, fox etc. **2.** boy who behaves badly. Also *vi* give birth to a whelp (in sense **1.**).

when [wen] **1.** *adv* at what time. *When did you arrive? I wonder when he'll come.* **2.** *adv/conj* (with **after, from, since, till etc**) what time. *Since when have they known him?* **3.** *rel adv* (after a *n* showing time). *He came last night when I was out. July and August are the months when the weather is hot.* **4.** *conj* at; during; after the time that. *I was out when he came. When I have finished my work, I will go home.* **5.** *conj* if; although. *When you cross a main road, you must be careful. I'll come when I am needed. He refuses help when he has many friends. I'll be here to give you help when necessary* i.e. if it is necessary.

whence [wens] *adv* from what place. *Whence have they come?* (*o.f.* – use *Where have they come from?*).

whenever [wen'evə*] *adv* at whatever time; at any time that. *I'll come whenever you wish. Whenever he speaks, I listen carefully.*

where [wεə*] *adv/conj* **1.** at, in, to what place. *Where is my book? Where are you going? I don't know where he is.* **2.** (with **to, from etc**) what place. *Where are you going (to)? Where has he come from?* **3.** (after a *n* showing place) *The book is on the table where you left it. Where I go for my holidays, there are no shops. Go where you like.*

'wherea'bouts *adv* in or near what place. *Whereabouts does he live?* Also **'whereabouts** *nc* (with *sing* or *pl* verb) place where somebody/something is. *Nobody now knows his whereabouts.*

where'as *conj* **1.** since; because. **2.** on the other hand. *He is fat, whereas his brother is thin.*

where'at *adv* at which (*o.f.*).

where'by *adv* by which. *This is a way whereby you can learn quickly.*

'wherefore *adv/conj* why; by which reason.

wher'ever *adv* at, in, to any place. *He goes wherever he wants.*

where'in, where'of, where'to, whereun'to *adv* in, of, to which (*o.f.*).

whereso'ever old emphatic form of **wherever.**

whereu'pon after which; then. *He stopped speaking. Whereupon I left the room.*

where'with, wherewi'thal *adv* with which (*o.f.*).

the 'wherewithal *nu* money or means to do something. *Have you the wherewithal to buy me a drink?* (*informal*).

wherry ['weri] *nc* type of rowing boat.

whet [wet] *vt* **1.** often in **whet someone's appetite** i.e. make more hungry or more interested, by giving a little food or a little information etc. **2.** sharpen the edge of a knife etc. *past* **whetted.**

whether ['weðə*] *conj* **1.** (in an indirect question) if. *I asked him whether he could come. He doesn't know whether he can come. He is not sure whether to come or not* i.e. if he should come or not. *I'll see whether he is at home.*
Note: when there are two indirect questions *whether* is used twice (e.g. *We don't know whether our work is finished or whether there is more to be done*).
2. (with **or** in statements, conditions etc which are not indirect questions) if; even if. *I am going whether it is raining or not.*

whey [wei] *nu* clear, watery part of sour milk after the more solid part (called **curds**) has been taken away.

which [witʃ] *adj/adv/pron/determiner* **1.** asking a question with reference to one or two things/persons, or one or more of a definite number. *Which coat will you wear, the black one or the brown one? Which boy did it? Which books are yours?* see also **what.** **2.** which thing or things; which person or persons. *Which are your books? Which is your brother, John or James? Which of these boys did it? He laughed at me, which made me angry.* **3.** and this. *He laughed at me, which behaviour made me angry* (*o.f.*). **4.** with reference to things only. *The money which is on the table is mine.*
Note: 1. in this sense *that* can be used instead of *which*, or *which* can be left out. *The money that is on the table is mine* or *The money on the table is mine.* 2. the sense of *which* as a *relative pron* changes if commas are put at the beginning and end of its clause (e.g. *Take the key which is on the desk and open the door* shows what particular key is meant, there being another key or other keys present. But *Take the key, which is on the desk, and open the door* merely gives more information about one already known key, there being no others to consider). 3. it is important to remember that *which* as an *adj* and *pron* can be used with reference to both things and persons (see senses **1.** and **2.**); but *which* as a *relative pron* can be used only with reference to things, just as *who* can be used only with reference to persons. (see sense **4.** above). On the other hand, *that* as a *relative pron* can be used with reference to both things and persons. see *that*[2].

whiff [wif] *nc* **1.** slight breath or smell of something: *a whiff of cigarette smoke.* **2.** small cigar. Also *vt/i* blow a slight breath; give a slight smell.

while [wail] *conj* **1.** at the time when; during. *You must keep quiet while he is speaking. I met him often while (I was) abroad.* **2.** on the other hand; whereas. *I like tea while she likes coffee.* **3.** although. *While I am ready to help, I hope that others will do so too.* Also *nu* period of time. *I can*

stay for a little while. He came here a long while ago. Also *vt* (with **away**) pass the time, doing a little or nothing. *We whiled away the afternoon sitting on the beach.*
whilst [wailst] *conj* while.
once in a while from time to time; not often.

whim [wim] *nc* sudden idea or wish (usu. one without a good reason).

whimper ['wimpə*] *vt/i* cry in a weak, frightened manner. Also *nc* cry of this kind.

whimsy ['wimzi] *nc* sudden strange idea or wish; strange sense of humour. **whimsical** *adj.* **whimsically** *adv.*
whimsicality [wimzi'kæliti] *nc/u* strange idea or sense of humour.

whine [wain] *vt/i* **1.** make a long moaning or screaming sound. *The bullets whined through the air.* **2.** complain in a voice like this. Also *nc* sound or complaint of this kind.

whinny ['wini] *nc* sound made by a horse when it is pleased. Also *vt* make a sound of this kind.

whip[1] [wip] *nc* **1.** cord or strip of leather fastened to a stick and used for beating. **2.** person who has authority to see that members of a political party who have been elected to parliament obey the rules of the party and attend important meetings and debates in parliament. **3.** type of dessert made by whipping up eggs, cream etc.
'whipcord 1. *nc* cords twisted together to make a whip. **2.** *nu* type of strong, twisted cord or thread.
have the whip hand be in control; have power over.

whip[2] [wip] *vt/i* **1.** strike or beat with a whip. **2.** mix by stirring quickly with a stick, fork etc. *She whipped the cream to make it thicker.* **3.** defeat. **4.** move, cause to move, quickly and suddenly. *He whipped a gun out of his pocket.* **5.** bind the end of a stick or rope with string. *past* **whipped.**
'whipper-'in *nc* person who controls a pack of hunting dogs by using a whip.
whipping *nc* **1.** punishment with a whip. **2.** defeat.
'whipping boy person who is punished or blamed for the fault of others; scapegoat.
'whipping top type of toy which is made to go round by striking it with a whip.
whip something off remove; take away quickly and suddenly. *He whipped off his gloves and threw them on the table.* (*informal*).
whip something on 1. cause to go faster by striking with a whip. *He whipped on his horse to win the race.* **2.** put on quickly and suddenly. *I whipped on my coat and ran outside.* (*informal* in sense **2.**).
whip round 1. turn, cause to turn, quickly and suddenly. *He whipped round when I touched him.* **2.** collect money for a particular purpose (usu. to help somebody) (*informal* in sense **2.**).
'whip-round *nc*: *We had a whip-round at school to buy something for our friend who was in hospital.* (*informal*).
whip up 1. (with reference to feelings) make stronger. *The news whipped up their anger.* **2.** mix by stirring quickly. *My mother whipped up two eggs to put in the cake she was making.*

whippersnapper ['wipəsnæpə*] *nc* young person who thinks he is more important than he really is. (rather *o.f.*).

whippet ['wipit] *nc* type of racing dog, small greyhound.

whir, whirr [wəː*] *nu* noise made by something moving quickly in or through the air. Also *vi* make this kind of noise. *past* **whirred.**

whirl [wəːl] *vt/i* move or turn, cause to move or turn, quickly. *He whirled round to see what was happening. He whirled his stick above his head. They whirled me away before I could say anything. The noise made my head whirl* i.e. made me dizzy or confused. Also *nc* quick movement; confusion: *the whirl of fast traffic. My thoughts were in a whirl.*
'whirlpool water which goes round and round quickly.
'whirlwind wind which blows round and round instead of in one direction.

whisk [wisk] *vt/i* **1.** move, cause to move, lightly and quickly. *The horse stood whisking its tail. He whisked the dust off his desk with a cloth. She was whisked away by her friends before I could speak to her.* **2.** mix by stirring lightly and quickly. *She whisked the eggs and milk together.* Also *nc* **1.** type of brush for removing dust (e.g. from clothes). **2.** light, quick movement. *With a whisk of his hand he brushed away the fly.* **3.** device for stirring and mixing food.

whisker ['wiskə*] *nc* (usu. *pl*) **1.** hair growing on the side of a man's face. **2.** stiff hair growing sideways from the face of some animals: *a cat's whiskers.*

whisky, whiskey ['wiski] *nc/u* type of alcoholic drink.

whisper ['wispə*] *vt/i* **1.** speak softly, using only the breath, not the voice. *He whispered to me to follow. I whispered my name to him so that the others would not hear.* **2.** make any soft, gentle sound. *The wind whispered through the trees.* Also *nc/u*: *He spoke to me in a whisper. I hear whispers that you are getting a new job* i.e. I hear rumours.

whist [wist] *nu* type of card game.
'whist drive competition in which a large number of persons play whist in a series of games against one another.

whistle ['wisl] *vt/i* **1.** make a high, clear sound by passing air through a small hole (e.g. by almost closing the lips and blowing hard through them; or by blowing through a device with a small hole in it). **2.** make this kind of sound in other ways. *The high wind whistled through the streets. The birds were whistling in the forest.* Also *nc/u* **1.** sound of this kind. **2.** device which makes this sound: *a policeman's whistle; a referee's whistle; a steam whistle* i.e. one which is blown by steam.

whit [wit] *nu* (only with **not**): *He doesn't care a whit* i.e. he doesn't care in the least. *There was not a whit of humour in his speech* i.e. none at all.

white [wait] **1.** *nc/u* colour like the page of a book. *The boys wore white.* **2.** *nc* somebody/something that is white. *Few whites live in West Africa* i.e. white people. *She used the whites of six eggs to make the cake* i.e. the parts round the yellow yolks. *The whites of his eyes are bloodshot* i.e. the white parts round the coloured centre of the eyes. Also *adj* of this colour; having no colour; very pale. *Snow is white. He was wearing a white shirt. Many old people have white hair. West Africa was once ruled by white men* i.e. men with pale skins, from Europe. **whiteness** *nu.*
whiten *vt/i* become, cause to become, white.
whitening *nu* whitewash.

whiting **1.** *nu* whitewash. (Also **whitening**). **2.** *nc* type of sea fish found in the North Atlantic and used as food. *pl* **whiting.**

white ant type of insect which is not an ant but a termite.

'whitebait type of small fish.

'white-'collar, 'white-'collared *adj* with reference to work which is not done with the hands (e.g. a clerk has a white-collar job, a motor mechanic has not).

white coffee *nc/u* coffee with milk.

white elephant something which is expensive but difficult to get rid of and of no use to the owner.

white flag sign of surrender.

white heat *nu* very high temperature which makes a metal glow white (higher than that which makes it glow with a red colour). **'white-'hot** *adj*.

white lie type of lie which is not serious and can be excused (esp. one told to avoid hurting somebody's feelings).

'whitewash *nu* **1.** mixture of water and lime or chalk, used to paint walls, ceilings etc. **2.** attempt to hide the mistakes made by somebody. Also *vt* **1.** paint with whitewash. **2.** try to hide mistakes; try to make somebody appear better than he really is.

whither ['wiðə*] *adv* in what or which direction (*o.f.*).

whitlow ['witlou] *nc* poisoned spot on the skin (usu. near a fingernail).

whittle ['witl] *vt* (with **away, down**) cut thin pieces from something (esp. wood); slowly make smaller. *He is whittling down the branch with a knife to make a handle for his hoe. The power of the chiefs has been whittled away by the government.*

whiz, whizz [wiz] *nu* noise made by something moving quickly in/through the air. Also *vt/i* make this kind of noise. *He whizzed past us on his bicycle. past* **whizzed.**

'whizz kid young person who has achieved early success because of his ability. (*informal*).

who [hu:] *pron* **1.** used in asking a question with reference to a person or persons (usu. used as a subject but see *Note* below). **whom** [hu:m] objective form of **who** (but see *Note* below). *Who is your teacher? I don't know who he is. Whom did you see yesterday? With whom are you staying?*

Note: although *whom* is more correct as an object and after a *prep, who* is more often used instead in conversation. *Whom did you see yesterday? (formal)/Who did you see yesterday? (informal). With whom are you staying? (formal)/Who are you staying with? (informal).*

2. used to define or identify a person or persons. *The tall man who is standing over there is my brother. This is the boy who broke the window. The tall man whom you met is my brother.*

Note: 1. in this sense of defining or identifying, *that* can be used instead of *who* or *whom*. 2. *who* or *whom* can be left out (e.g. *The tall man standing over there is my brother. The tall man you met is my brother*). 3. when there is a *prep* either *whom* or *that* can be used but *whom* must come immediately after the *prep*. With *that* the *prep* comes at the end (e.g. *The man that you spoke to is my brother* or (leaving out *that*) *The man you spoke to is my brother*). 4. the sense of *who* and *whom* changes if commas are put at the beginning and the end of their clause (e.g. *The tall man who is standing over there is my brother* i.e. without commas *who is standing over there* shows which person is meant, there being others present. *My brother, who is standing over there, is a doctor* i.e. with commas, *who is standing over there*, merely gives more information about somebody already known, there being no need to identify him. In the same way compare *The man whom you met just now is my brother* and *My brother, whom you met just now, is a doctor*).

whose [hu:z] *pron/determiner* of whom. *Whose books are these? I wonder whose coat this is? The boys whose names were called stood up.*

Note: the sense of *whose* as a *relative pron* changes if commas are put at the beginning and end of its clause in the same way as for *who* and *whom* (e.g. *The one whose hair is grey is my brother. My brother, whose hair is grey, is younger than I am*). see *who Note* 4.

whoever [hu:'evə*] *pron* any person who; no matter who. *Whoever thinks that is silly. Whoever tries to beat him, he always wins.*

whole [houl] *adj/determiner* **1.** complete; all. *I lived here for a whole year. The whole school had a holiday. You must give your whole attention to the problem. He spoke for two whole hours. Whole cities were destroyed in the earthquake.* **2.** not damaged or broken. *He escaped with a whole skin. I haven't a whole pair of stockings left.*

Note: as the above examples show, *whole* usu. comes just before its noun. When it comes after the *n* it has a different sense (e.g. *He ate the whole egg* i.e. all of it, but *He ate the egg whole* i.e. all at once without cutting it into pieces).

Also *nc/u* (usu. *sing*): *I lived here for the whole of a year. You must give the whole of your attention to the problem. The whole of his family was killed.*

wholly ['houli] *adj* completely; altogether. *He is wholly reliable. I don't wholly trust them.*

'whole'hearted *adj* with all one's power; as well as one can. **wholeheartedly** *adv*.

whole number number which is not a fraction.

as a whole together; not one by one. *We must examine these problems as a whole.*

on the whole when everything is considered. *You have made a few mistakes but on the whole you have done well.*

wholesale ['houlseil] *nu* sale of goods in large quantities to shopkeepers and traders who then sell them to the public. (*opp* **retail**). Also *adj/adv* **1.** *They own a wholesale business in clothes. Shopkeepers buy wholesale and sell retail.* **2.** on a large scale; including almost everybody/everything. *During the war houses were destroyed wholesale.*

wholesaler *nc* person who sells wholesale.

wholesome ['houlsəm] *adj* clean and pleasant; good for the health. (*opp* **unwholesome**). **wholesomeness** *nu*.

whom [hu:m] objective form of **who.**

whoop, hoop [hu:p] *nc* loud cry. Also *vt/i* cry out loudly.

'whooping cough type of children's disease which causes loud coughing.

whop [wɔp] *vt* beat; defeat. *past* **whopped.** (*informal*).

whopper *nc* something bigger than usual. *The fish is a whopper. (informal).*

whopping *adj/adv* unusually big: *a whopping big fish. (informal).*

whore [hɔː*] *nc* prostitute.
whorl [wəːl] *nc* group of petals round a central stem; part of a spiral; circular pattern.

whorl

whose [huːz] *pron/determiner* see **who.**
whosoever [huːsou'evə*] *pron* whoever (*o.f.*).
why [wai] *adv* **1.** for what reason. *Why did you do it? I don't know why I did it. Why not try yourself?* **2.** *The reason why he left school was to look after his parents. That is why I am late.* Also *interj* to express surprise or disagreement. *Why, it's our friend, John! It isn't difficult! Why, I have done it many times!*
wick [wik] *nc* narrow piece of cloth which draws up oil in an oil lamp etc and so, when set alight, continues to burn for a long time; string in the centre of a candle for the same purpose.

wicks

wicked ['wikid] *adj* (with reference to a person or what he does) wrong; bad. **wickedly** *adv.* **wickedness** *nu.*
wicker ['wikə*] *nu* sticks crossed over each other as in a basket. (Usu. used as an *adj*: *a wicker chair*).
'wickerwork things made of wicker.
wicket ['wikit] *nc* **1.** small opening or door (often one in or beside a larger one). **2.** three sticks put in the ground for playing cricket; the ground between the two sets of these sticks.
keep wicket stand behind the wicket to catch balls missed by the batsman standing in front of the wicket.
'wicket-keeper *nc* player who does this.
take a wicket strike one of the three sticks with a ball after bowling it to the batsman.
wide [waid] *adj* **1.** great in distance from side to side; broad: *a wide road; a carpet six feet long and four feet wide.* (*opp* **narrow**). **2.** great; including much. *He has a wide knowledge of English. We looked across the wide plains. The children watched with wide eyes* i.e. big, fully-opened eyes. **3.** missing by much what is aimed at or intended. *His spear was wide of the man he threw it at.* Also *adv*: *He left the door wide open. Open your mouth wide. His spear fell wide.*
widely *adv* **1.** by a great distance or distances between. *The houses are widely separated.* **2.** greatly; to a great degree. *The two books are widely different. It is not widely known that he is a writer.*
width [widθ] *nc/u*: *a carpet six feet in length and four feet in width.*
widen *vt/i* become, cause to become, wide or wider.
'wide-a'wake *adj* **1.** fully awake. **2.** lively; fully aware of what is happening.
'widespread *adj* spread over, found in, a large area.
far and wide over a large area; everywhere. *They looked far and wide for the escaped prisoner.*
widow ['widou] *nc* woman whose husband is dead.
widowed *adj* having lost one's husband by death.
widower *nc* man whose wife is dead.
widowhood *nu* state of being a widow.
width [widθ] *nc/u* see **wide.**
wield [wiːld] *vt* use in the hand; hold. *He was wielding a knife. The president wields great power.*
wife [waif] *nc* woman to whom a man is married. *pl* **wives** [waivz]. **wifely** *adj.*
wig [wig] *nc* covering made of hair or a substance like hair to be worn on the head (e.g. by an actor, judge, bald person or for reasons of fashion).
wigged *adj* wearing a wig.
wiggle ['wigl] *vt/i* move, cause to move, quickly up and down or from side to side. *He sat wiggling his toes.* Also *nc/u* movement of this kind.
wigwam ['wigwæm] *nc* type of tent or shelter once used by the Indians of North America.

wigwam

wild [waild] *adj* **1.** (with reference to an animal) not tamed by man; free. *Lions are wild animals.* **2.** (with reference to a plant) not planted by man; growing naturally. *The field is full of wild flowers.* **3.** (with reference to a person, country etc) not civilized; rough. *The forest is the home of wild tribes. The country outside the town was wild and hilly.* **4.** (with reference to the weather etc) severe; violent. *The weather in winter is wild. It was impossible to swim in the wild sea.* **5.** (with reference to feelings, behaviour etc) very excited; not controlled; reckless. *He gave a wild laugh. His stupid behaviour made me wild* i.e. very angry. *He has a wild plan to run away from school.* Also *adv*: *They were shooting wild.* **wildness** *nu.*
wildly *adv*: *He laughed wildly.*
the wilds *npl* uncultivated or uncivilized areas of land: *the wilds of Canada.*
'wildcat *nc* one of several types of cat which live wild. Also *adj* sudden and reckless; without good reason. *This is a wildcat scheme. The workmen have started a wildcat strike* i.e. one not supported by their trade union.
'wildfire only in **spread like wildfire** (of news etc) i.e. spread very quickly.
wild-'goose chase useless journey or course of action. *The false information set us off on a wild-goose chase.*

'**wildlife** wild animals; animals living in their natural state. *He has gone to Africa to photograph wildlife.*
be wild about **1.** be very fond of. **2.** be very angry about. (*informal*).
run wild be or grow without any control; behave wildly. *The weeds are running wild in his garden. During the school holidays the children ran wild.*

wildebeest ['wildibi:st] *nc* type of African antelope. *pl* **wildebeest**. see also **gnu**.

wilderness ['wildənis] *nu* bare uninhabited land; desert.

wile [wail] *nc* trick; temptation. **wily** *adj*. **wiliness** *nu*.

wilful ['wilful] (*US* **willful**) *adj* **1.** (with reference to a person) determined to do what one wants, whether it is good or bad; having a strong will. **2.** (with reference to an act) done on purpose, not by accident. *The wilful killing of a person is murder.* **wilfully** *adv*. **wilfulness** *nu*.

will[1] [wil] *aux* **1.** showing the future. *He will be here tomorrow. You will meet him later. Next Monday will be a holiday.*
Note: 1. to express the idea of the future, some speakers of English use *will* with the second and third persons, and *shall* with the first person. However, many speakers of English use *will* with all persons. 2. *would* is used instead of *will* to show the future in the past or in certain *if* clauses (e.g. *I know (that) he will be here* but *I knew (that) he would be here. If he were your father, you would obey him*). 3. in speech *will* is usu. shortened to *'ll*, *would* to *'d*, *will not* to *won't* and *would not* to *wouldn't* (e.g. *You'll meet him later. I knew he'd be there. Next Monday won't be a holiday. He told me next Monday wouldn't be a holiday*).
2. with the sense of agreeing, promising or being ready to. *Will you help me? Yes, I will/I'll help you. I promised (that) I would/I'd help you. Please help me. I won't* i.e. I am not ready to help you; I refuse. *He wouldn't come* i.e. he refused to come. *The door won't shut* i.e. it cannot be shut.
Note: the question form *Would you . . . ?* is often used as a polite form of request (e.g. *Would you help me open this window?*).
3. with the sense of happening regularly or from time to time. *Sometimes their father would bring the children home sweets and sometimes he would not.* **4.** with the sense of being likely to be or to happen. *That will be your friend at the door. In most cases this method will get good results.*
Note: in the past *would* is also used in this sense instead of *will* (e.g. *Sometimes they would agree and sometimes they would refuse. We found that in most cases this method would get good results. He would spend the whole weekend listening to records* i.e. that was his custom).
5. with the sense of being sure to be or to happen. *Boys will be boys. Bad workmen will always blame their tools.*
Note: in this sense the short forms *'ll* and *'d* are not used; *would* is also used instead of *will* in the past.
would rather prefer to. *He would rather pay now. Would you rather have tea or coffee? I would rather have gone with my brother but it is too late now.*

will[2] [wil] **1.** *nc/u* power of the mind; determination; wish. *He has a strong will. You can win if you have the will to try hard. It was God's will.* **2.** *nc* written wish of a person about what should happen to his property and money when he dies. *In his will he left all his money to his wife and children.*
-willed *adj*: *He is strong-/weak-willed* i.e. he has a strong/weak will.
'**willpower** strength to control one's feelings; determination.
against one's will when one does not want to. *Don't agree against your will.*
against the will of somebody although somebody refuses. *He left school against his parents' will.*
at will just as one pleases. *Because our army was weak, the enemy attacked at will.*
good/ill will kind/unkind feeling; sympathy/lack of sympathy.
of one's own free will because one wants to; without being forced.
with a will with energy; readily.

will[3] [wil] *vt* **1.** use one's power of mind to do something or get something done. *He died because God willed it. Although I was very tired, I willed myself to keep running.* **2.** leave one's property and money to somebody by a will. *He has willed all his money to his wife and children.*
willing *adj* ready to do something. *They are willing to help. He is a very willing student.* (*opp* **unwilling**). **willingly** *adv*. **willingness** *nu*.

will-o'-the-wisp ['wiləðə'wisp] *nc* **1.** light seen moving over marshy land at night. **2.** something which one tries to get or find but cannot.

willow ['wilou] **1.** *nc* type of tree with flexible branches and long, thin leaves. **2.** *nu* the wood of this tree.
willowy *adj* (with reference to a person) tall and slender.
'**willow pattern** type of blue and white design (usu. put on china plates, cups etc).

wilt[1] [wilt] (used with **thou**) will (*o.f.*).

wilt[2] [wilt] *vt/i* lose strength and hang down loosely. *The flowers wilted in the hot sun.*

wily ['waili] *adj* see **wile**.

win [win] *vt/i* **1.** get by working hard, by being better than others; be successful. *John has won a scholarship. We hope to win (the game). Which side won the war?* **2.** get by chance or luck. *He won a lot of money by gambling on horses.* **3.** reach by trying hard. *They at last won the beach.* (rather *o.f.* in sense **3.**). *pres part* **winning**. *past* **won** [wʌn]. Also *nc* success or victory (esp. in a game).
winner *nc* person, animal or thing that wins.
winning *adj* **1.** successful; that wins: *the winning horse in the first race.* **2.** pleasant; attractive. *She has a winning smile.* **winningly** *adv*.
winnings *npl* money which has been won (usu. by betting or gambling).
'**winning post** post which marks the end of a race.
win free free oneself from a difficulty. *He was trapped by a fallen branch, but eventually won free.*
win/beat hands down win easily and completely. (*informal*).
win somebody's heart cause somebody to fall in love.
win somebody over persuade somebody to agree.

wince [wins] *vi* move the body suddenly, or show signs of pain or fear. *He winced when the stone hit him.* Also *nc* movement of this kind.

winch [wintʃ] *nc* device for pulling or lifting, by winding a rope round a wheel or drum. Also *vt* pull or lift by a winch.

winch

wind[1] [wind] **1.** *nc/u* moving air.
Note: 1. *wind* is usu. used with *a, much, little, no etc* or in *pl* when it refers to the amount or type of moving air. *A gentle wind was blowing over the lake. There is too much wind today. As soon as we left the shore we met strong winds.* 2. *wind* is usu. used with *the* when it refers to a particular time or to something caused by moving air. *In the evening the wind rose/fell* i.e. increased/lessened. *The wind blew down the trees. His house was damaged by the high winds.*
2. *nu* ability to breathe properly when doing something strenuous. *Football players who do not practise soon lose their wind* i.e. become breathless. **3.** *nu* gas which forms in the stomach. *People who eat too quickly often suffer from wind.* **4.** *nu* wind instruments (esp. in an orchestra).
winded *adj* breathless; not able to breathe properly.
'windward ['windwəd] *adj/adv* on the side, in the direction, from which the wind blows.
windy *adj* **1.** having much wind. **2.** talking too much; having little meaning or effect. **3.** frightened; cowardly. (*informal* in sense **3.**). **windily** *adv.* **windiness** *nu.*
'windbag person who talks too much. (*informal*).
'windbreak fence, hedge etc to protect something from strong winds.
'windcheater type of jacket which keeps out the wind.
'windfall 1. fruit blown from a tree by the wind. **2.** good fortune which is not expected.
'wind instrument musical instrument which is played by blowing air into it (e.g. a trumpet).
'windjammer type of sailing ship (*o.f.*).
'windmill type of mill which is worked by the force of the wind.
'windpipe tube in the throat between the mouth and the lungs.
'windscreen (*Brit*) piece of glass in front of the driver of a car. (*US* **windshield**).
'windsock device shaped like the leg of a sock which shows the direction of the wind.
'windswept *adj* over which strong winds blow.
second wind act of being able to breathe properly again after having lost one's breath. *Near the end of the race the athlete got his second wind.*
get wind of hear information about.
have/get the wind up be/become frightened. (*informal*).
put the wind up somebody frighten somebody. (*informal*).
take the wind out of somebody's sails surprise somebody by doing something before he does. (*informal*).
the four winds all directions; north, south, east and west.
throw something to the winds forget about; stop using. *He threw caution to the winds and began arguing with the manager.*

wind[2] [waind] *vt/i* **1.** move, cause to move, in twists or circles. *We wound our way through the thick forest. The river winds across the plain.* **2.** put something round somebody/something. *The nurse wound a bandage round my finger. They are winding the rope onto a pole.* **3.** (esp. with reference to the spring of a clock or watch) turn round to make tighter. *You must wind this clock once a week. past* **wound** [waund]. Also *nc* twist; turn. *There are many winds in this road. Give the clock one more wind.*
'winding sheet sheet which is wound round a dead body for burial (*o.f.*).
winding staircase staircase which goes up in circles; spiral staircase.
wind something in pull in by winding. *When we had finished fishing, we wound in our lines.* (*opp* **wind off, wind out**).
wind something up 1. put something round somebody/something; turn round to make tighter. *She is winding up the string into a ball. Have you wound up your watch?* **2.** finish. *The teacher wound up his lesson by showing some pictures. The baker is winding up his business here* i.e. is preparing to give it up.
wind somebody round one's little finger be able to make somebody do anything one wants. (*informal*).
wound up tense, emotionally excited.

windlass ['windləs] *nc* device for pulling or lifting by winding a rope round a wheel or drum, similar to a winch.

window ['windou] *nc* opening (usu. of glass) in the wall or roof of a building, car etc to let in air and light.
'window box container for plants kept outside a window.
'window dressing *nu* **1.** skill in showing goods in a shop window to attract attention. **2.** any skill in attracting attention. **window dresser** *nc.*
'window pane piece of glass in a window.
'window shopping looking at goods in shop windows without buying anything.
'windowsill ledge inside and outside a window.

wine [wain] *nc/u* alcoholic drink (usu. made from grapes or other types of fruit).
'wineglass type of glass used for drinking wine.
'wine press type of press used to squeeze the juice from grapes to make wine.

wing [wiŋ] *nc* **1.** one of the two parts of the body which a bird uses to fly; one of the parts used by an insect to fly; part of an aircraft needed by it to fly. **2.** something which stretches to the side like a wing: *the right wing of an army; the wing of a house.* **3.** group of aircraft (in the Royal Air Force two or more squadrons). **4.** (in a football or hockey team) player or players playing on the left or right side. *The first goal was scored by the left wing.* Also *vt/i* **1.** fly. *The birds winged (their way) over the trees.* **2.** travel, cause to travel, quickly. **3.** wound a bird in the wing or a person in the arm.
winged *adj* having wings.
wingless *adj* having no wings.
'wing commander officer in command of a wing in the air force.
'wingspan, 'wingspread distance between the tip of one wing and the tip of the other when they are spread.
take wing begin to fly; leave the ground.
take under one's wing protect; help.

wink [wiŋk] *vt/i* **1.** shut and open one eye quickly (usu. as a sign of friendship, amusement etc to somebody). *When the teacher dropped his books, John winked at me.* **2.** (with reference to a light) appear to go on and off quickly. *The stars were winking in the clear sky.* Also *nc* **1.** act of shutting one's eye in this way. *He gave me a friendly wink.* **2.** very short period. *We could not sleep a wink last night because of the noise.*
forty winks short sleep. (*informal*).
wink at something pretend not to see something; allow something even if it is wrong. *He was ready to wink at small mistakes but not big ones.*

winkle ['wiŋkl] *nc* type of small sea animal like a snail. (Also **periwinkle**). Also *vt* (with **out**) pull or push out (like a winkle from its shell).

winnow ['winou] *vt* **1.** remove the covering from grain by the force of air or the wind. **2.** separate the good from the bad.

winsome ['winsəm] *adj* (with reference to a person) charming; attractive. **winsomely** *adv.* **winsomeness** *nu.*

winter ['wintə*] *nc* the cold season of the year. Also *vi* spend this season. *They usually winter in the south of France.*
wintery, wintry ['wintri] *adj* like winter; very cold.

wipe [waip] *vt* rub with a cloth, piece of paper etc in order to clean or dry. *She wiped the table with a cloth. He wiped his dirty hands on a rag.* Also *nc*: *He gave his hands a wipe.*
wiper *nc* something which wipes: (*Brit*) *windscreen wiper* i.e. device which wipes rain from a windscreen. (*US* **windshield wiper**).
wipe something away take away by wiping.
wipe something off **1.** take away by wiping. **2.** remove or finish completely. *He has wiped off all his debts.*
wipe someone/something out **1.** wipe the inside of. *Have you wiped out the bath after using it?* **2.** destroy, remove, completely. *One atom bomb can wipe out thousands of people. We wiped out the defeat by winning the next game.*
wipe something up (esp. with reference to spilt liquid) remove by wiping.

wire ['waiə*] **1.** *nc/u* string or thread made of metal. **2.** *nc* message sent by telegraph wire; telegram. Also *vt* **1.** fasten by wire. **2.** put in wires which carry electrical current. *The workmen are busy wiring the new school.* **3.** send a telegram. *I wired him because there was no time to send a letter.*
wiring *nu* number of wires which carry electrical current.
wiry *adj* **1.** like wire. **2.** (with reference to a person) thin but strong. **wiriness** *nu.*
'**wire cutters** type of tool for cutting wires.
'**wire 'rope** *nc/u* rope made from several wires twisted together.
'**wireworm** type of worm which damages plants.
'**live 'wire** **1.** wire which carries electrical current. **2.** person who is full of energy.

wireless ['waiəlis] *nc/u* radio.

wise[1] [waiz] *adj* having, or resulting from, knowledge and intelligence. *No wise man wants war. They were wise to take their friend's advice. He gave me a wise look* i.e. showing that he understood or pretending that he understood. (*opp* **unwise**). **wisely** *adv.* **wisdom** ['wizdəm] *nu.*
'**wiseacre** person who thinks he knows more than he actually does. (rather *o.f.*).
'**wisecrack** clever and amusing remark. (*informal*).
'**wise guy** person who thinks he is clever.
'**wisdom tooth** one of the four teeth which grow at the back of the jaw of an adult.
be/get wise to know, get to know, about. (*informal*).
put somebody wise to inform somebody about. (*informal*).

wise[2] [waiz] *nu* manner; way (*o.f.* except when joined to other words e.g. *lengthwise; otherwise; clockwise* i.e. moving in the same direction as the hands of a clock).
Note: this word is combined with many words in an informal way (e.g. *careerwise; planning-wise* i.e. with regard to one's career, the planning etc), but it is better not to imitate this usage.

wish [wiʃ] *vt/i* **1.** desire; want. *I wish to see the headmaster. He wishes us to listen carefully.*
Note: in this sense *wish* is more formal; *want* is more usual.
2. have or express a hope or desire. *I wished him safe at home. They wished me good luck.* **3.** (without **that** and followed by the *past tense* or *subjunctive*) desire something which is not possible or is not very likely. *I wish I were rich. We only wish we could help. He wished he had agreed to go.* **4.** (without **that** and followed by **would**) ask or hope that. *I wish you would stop talking so much. We wish they would leave us alone.* Also *nc/u* **1.** desire; request. *They have no wish to work. Has he told you what his wishes are?* **2.** something wished. *All her wishes have come true.*
wish for something ask or hope for (usu. something which is unusual or difficult to get). *Everybody wishes for happiness but few get it. The school has all the equipment one could wish for* i.e. it is an unusual and very lucky school.
wishful thinking belief that something will happen just because one wants it to happen.

wishy-washy ['wiʃiwɔʃi] *adj* watery; thin; weak. (*informal*).

wisp [wisp] *nc* small amount of grass, hair, smoke etc.
wispy *adj* like a wisp; small.

wisteria [wis'tiəriə] *nc/u* type of climbing plant.

wistful ['wistful] *adj* wanting something but sad because it is not likely to be obtained. *There was a wistful look on the child's face when he saw all the toys in the shop window.* **wistfully** *adv.* **wistfulness** *nu.*

wit[1] [wit] **1.** *nc* (often *pl*) intelligence; quick thinking. *To solve this problem you must use your wits.* **2.** *nu* ability to say clever and amusing things. *His talk was full of wit.* **3.** *nc* person who has this ability.
witty *adj* clever and amusing. **wittily** *adv.*
witless *adj* without intelligence; stupid.
witticism ['witisizəm] *nc* clever and amusing saying or remark.
at one's wits' end not knowing what to do next.
have/keep one's wits about one be quick to understand a situation; remain calm but alert.
live by one's wits live not by regular work but by using one's intelligence to cheat people.

wit[2] [wit] *vi* only in **to wit** i.e. namely; as follows (*o.f.*).

witch [witʃ] *nc* woman who is believed to have magic powers.
witchery ['witʃəri] *nu* **1.** witchcraft. **2.** charm; attraction.
'witchcraft magic power or skill.
'witch doctor man who is believed to have magic powers (esp. to cure diseases).

with [wið] *prep* **1.** in the company of; accompanied by; together; at the same time as. *We live with our uncle and aunt. He arrived at school with his friends. We had the English lesson with another class. I always have a spare pencil with me.* **2.** having. *Who is the man with the long beard? I want a book with all the information.* **3.** using; by means of; by. *I cut the rope with a knife. He writes with his left hand. The country is covered with thick frost. He opened the meeting with a short speech.* **4.** showing manner. *Please drive with care. They did it with great pleasure. The bomb exploded with a bang. They agreed with reluctance.* **5.** because of. *He was shaking with fright. They are dying with hunger.* **6.** referring to; concerning. *With most children play is as important as work. The real aim with him is to make lots of money.* **7.** in spite of; even although having. *With all his terrible injuries he did not die. With the best teachers in the world they cannot pass the examination.*
meet with have happen to oneself; suffer. *He met with an accident while driving home.*

withdraw [wiθ'drɔː] *vt/i* **1.** move or draw back; take away. *After being attacked, the army withdrew. I am going to withdraw all my money from the bank.* **2.** take back; cancel. *You must withdraw your stupid statement. Why did he withdraw his consent? past tense* **withdrew** [wiθ'druː]. *past part* **withdrawn.**
withdrawal *nc/u* act of withdrawing or being withdrawn.
withdrawn *adj* (of persons) reserved, unsociable.

wither ['wiðə*] *vt/i* (often with **away** or **up**) dry up, cause to dry up, and die. *The crops withered (away/up) because there was no rain.*
withering *adj*: *He gave me a withering look* i.e. one showing great disapproval. **witheringly** *adv.*

withers ['wiðəz] *npl* part of a horse's body at the top of the shoulders and just below the neck.

withhold [wiθ'hould] *vt* refuse to give: *withhold information from the police. past* **withheld** [wiθ'held].

within [wið'in] *prep* inside; in. *He'll arrive within the next hour. I live within a mile of the railway station.* Also *adv*: *Is he within?* (*o.f.* as *adv* – use **inside** or **in**).

without [wið'aut] **1.** *prep* not with; not having. *I have come without (any) money. Don't leave without your coat. He is completely without fear. He went away without saying goodbye* i.e. and did not say goodbye. *He cannot argue without losing his temper* i.e. he always loses his temper when he argues. **2.** *adv* outside (*o.f.* in sense **2.**).
without (a) doubt see **doubt.**
without number very many. *I have helped him times without number.*
do without someone/something manage without somebody/something. *People cannot do without food. If he has no coat, he will have to do without (it).*
go without see **go.**
go without saying be so clearly understood that it does not need to be said. *It goes without saying that you must work hard if you are to succeed in business.*

withstand [wiθ'stænd] *vt* stand against; resist successfully. *past* **withstood** [wiθ'stud].

witless ['witləs] *adj* see **wit**[1].

witness ['witnis] **1.** *nc* person who has himself seen something happening. *Were you a witness to this accident?* **2.** *nc* person who is called upon to tell what he knows in a court of law. *The accused had many witnesses to say that he was not guilty.* **3.** *nc* person who signs his name on a document to confirm that another person's signature is genuine. **4.** *nu* what is said by a witness; evidence. Also *vt* **1.** see. *Did you witness this accident?* **2.** give evidence; state as a witness. *Only one person witnessed against the accused. He witnessed to seeing the accused take the money.* **3.** sign a document to confirm that another person has signed it. *If I sign this document will you witness my signature?*
'witness box place where a witness stands in a court of law.
'eyewitness see **eye.**

witticism ['witisizəm] *nc* see **wit**[1].

wittingly ['witiŋli] *adv* on purpose; knowingly.

witty ['witi] *adj* see **wit**[1].

wives [waivz] pl of **wife.**

wizard ['wizəd] *nc* man who is believed to have magic powers.
wizardry *nu* magic.

wizened ['wiznd] *adj* dried up and wrinkled. *Many old people have wizened faces.*

woad [woud] *nu* **1.** type of blue dye. **2.** plant from which it is obtained.

wobble ['wɔbl] *vt/i* shake, cause to shake, because not firmly fixed or placed. *My desk wobbles because one of its legs is too short.*
wobbly *adj* not firmly fixed or placed.

woe [wou] **1.** *nu* sorrow; grief (*o.f.*). **2.** *nc* (often *pl*) troubles; difficulties: *the woes of being a schoolmaster.*
woeful *adj* full of sorrow; sad. **woefully** *adv.*
woebegone ['woubigɔn] *adj* looking very sad.

woke [wouk] past tense of **wake**[1].

wolf [wulf] *nc* **1.** type of wild animal like a dog found especially in cold northern regions. **2.** man who pursues women. (*informal* in sense **2.**). *pl* **wolves** [wulvz]. Also *vt* eat quickly like a wolf. *I was so hungry that I wolfed (down) my supper.*
wolfish *adj* like a wolf; greedy. **wolfishly** *adv.*
'wolf cub *nc* **1.** young wolf. **2.** young boy scout.
cry wolf see **cry**[1].

woman ['wumən] *nc* female adult human being. *pl* **women** ['wimin]. Also *adj*: *a woman doctor; a woman lawyer.*
Note: in some circumstances it is more polite to use *lady* than *woman* (e.g. if referring to a woman who is present one would say *This lady has come to help us* rather than *This woman etc*).
womanly *adj* like a woman; kind and gentle. see **womanish.**
womanish *adj* like a woman; suitable only for a woman: *womanish behaviour*; (often used with reference to a man): *womanish dress.*
womanhood *nu* state of being a woman; women in general.

'womenfolk *npl* women in general; women of one's own family.
'womankind *nu* women in general.
womb [wu:m] organ of a woman or female animal inside which a baby grows before it is born.
won [wʌn] past of **win.**
wonder ['wʌndə*] *vt/i* **1.** be anxious to know; ask oneself. *I wonder why he is late. We wondered who told you.* **2.** (with **about**) feel curious about, think about. *We were wondering about you before you arrived.* **3.** (with **at** or **that**) be surprised. *I don't wonder at their anger. How can they wonder (that) they are hated?* **4.** (with **whether**) as a polite request. *I wonder whether you would lend me some money. I was wondering whether you might be able to help me.* Also **1.** *nc* somebody/something that causes surprise or admiration. *He told us about the wonders of space travel.* **2.** *nu* feeling of surprise or admiration. *The children looked at the strange pictures in/with wonder.*
wonderingly *adv* in a surprised or doubting manner.
wonderful *adj* very good, marvellous: *a wonderful idea; a wonderful holiday; a wonderful person.* **wonderfully** *adv.*
wonderment *nu* surprise.
wondrous ['wʌndrəs] *adj* causing surprise or admiration (*o.f.* – use **wonderful**).
I wonder I doubt it.
it is a wonder (that) it is surprising that. *It was a wonder (that) they were not killed.*
it is no wonder (that) it is not surprising that.
Note: it is/was etc is also often left out in the *negative* (e.g. *No wonder he refused*).
small wonder (that) it is not surprising that.
work wonders get wonderful results. *The medicine worked wonders.*
wont [wount] *nu* custom; habit. Also *pred adj* in the habit of. (both *o.f.*).
wonted *adj* usual (*o.f.*).
won't [wount] short form of **will not.**
woo [wu:] *vt* try to gain or win: *woo a woman* i.e. as one's wife (*o.f.* in this sense); *woo fortune/sleep.* **wooer** *nc.*
wooing *nc/u* act of trying to gain a woman's love in this way.
wood [wud] **1.** *nu* substance of which a tree is made. *He is cutting wood to make a door. The desks are made of wood.* **2.** *nc* (often *pl*) piece of land which is covered with trees. *The path goes through the wood/woods.*
Note: a *wood* is much smaller than a *forest.*
wooded *adj* covered with trees.
wooden *adj* **1.** made of wood: *wooden desks.* **2.** unfriendly; stiff. *He gave us a wooden look.*
woodenly *adv*: *He looked at us woodenly.*
'wooden-'headed stupid. (*informal*).
woody *adj* **1.** covered with trees. **2.** like wood. *This fruit is rather woody* i.e. tough and difficult to eat.
'woodcock *nc* type of game bird with a short neck and legs, and a long beak. *pl* **woodcock.**
'woodcraft skill in finding one's way about, and living in, woods or forests.
'woodcut *nc* pattern or picture cut on a block of wood (called a **wood block**) and then printed on paper.
'woodcutter *nc* man who cuts down trees.
'woodland piece of land covered with trees.
'woodman, 'woodsman man who works in woods or forests (e.g. looking after, or cutting down trees).
'woodpecker type of small bird which makes holes in trees with its beak to catch insects.

woodpecker

'woodwind musical instruments which are or once were made of wood and are played by blowing.
'woodwork use of wood for making things.
'woodworm type of worm or larva that lives in wood and bores small holes in it.
not able to see the wood for the trees not be able to see a general problem etc because one is only looking at the details.
woof [wuf] *nc* see **weft.**
wool [wul] *nu* **1.** hair of sheep, goats etc either in its natural state or after having been made into threads or clothing. *We wear wool in winter and cotton in summer.* **2.** material which looks like wool: *cotton wool; wire wool.*
woollen ['wulən] (*US* **woolen**) *adj* made of wool.
woollens *npl* things made of wool (e.g. clothing, blankets etc). *Because the weather is cold you should wear your woollens.*
woolly *adj* **1.** covered with wool; looking like wool. **2.** not definite or well expressed. *He has too many woolly ideas.* Also *nc* something made of wool (esp. clothing) (*informal*).
'wool-gathering *adj* thinking vaguely of something else; not paying attention. Also *nu* vague thoughts; lack of attention.
dyed in the wool *adj* **1.** dyed before being made into thread or cloth. **2.** having strong and obstinate beliefs. *They are all dyed-in-the-wool nationalists.*
pull the wool over somebody's eyes deceive somebody. (*informal*).
word [wə:d] **1.** *nc* unit of language either spoken or written. *This dictionary gives the meaning of many words. In English 'get' is a very common word.* **2.** *nc* something said; remark; speech. *I don't believe a word you say. We had a few words with him* i.e. a short talk with him. **3.** *nu* command; order. *The teacher gave us the word to stop writing. In this school the headmaster's word is always obeyed.* **4.** *nu* (without **a** or **the**) message; news. *They have sent me word of their arrival. I received word of his death this morning.* **5.** *nu* (with **my, your, his etc**) promise. *I give you my word that I'll help. He always keeps his word. He never breaks his word.* Also *vt* put, or express, in words. *You can word this sentence much better if you try.*
wording *nu* way in which words are used to express meaning.
wordless *adj* without using words.
wordy *adj* using too many words. **wordily** *adv.* **wordiness** *nu.*
'word-'perfect *adj* (with reference to a person) able to say something which has

been learnt by heart without making any mistakes.
eat one's words see **eat.**
for words (usu. with **too**) to express or describe. *The sunset was too beautiful for words.*
the Word of God the will of God (esp. as given in written form e.g. in the Bible or Koran).
have words with argue or quarrel with.
Note: have a word with means talk with. *I'll have a word with him tomorrow.*
word of honour promise made on one's honour.
in a word in short. *In a word, he's mad.*
the last word final statement in a conversation or argument. *Women like to have the last word.*
the last word in something the latest and most modern. *The new hotel is the last word in comfort.*
the last word on something final decision about something. *We have not heard the last word on this difficult problem.*
leave word with somebody leave a message with somebody to give to somebody else.
by word of mouth in words which are spoken, not written. *The story was passed on by word of mouth.*
put in a good word for someone see **put.**
word for word exactly as said or written.

wore [wɔ:*] past tense of **wear**[1].

work[1] [wə:k] **1.** *nu* energy of mind or body, or of a machine used for a definite purpose. *Learning a foreign language is hard work. You will be paid well for your day's work. This machine does the work of a hundred men.* **2.** *nu* what one must do to make a living; trade; profession. *When you leave school you will have to find work. When does he get home from work? These men have been without work for months.*
Note: the word *job* (*nc*) can also be used: *find a job; without a job.*
3. *nu* something which has to be done. *My mother does all the housework. Have you finished your homework?* i.e. study which has to be done at home and not school. **4.** *nc/u* something produced by the energy of mind or body: *the complete works of Dickens* i.e. all the books which he wrote. *The robbery was the work of a clever criminal.* **5.** *nu* something which is not yet finished. *My mother was knitting when we arrived. She put her work on the table and welcomed us.* **6.** *nc* (in *pl*) (often with *sing* verb) building or set of buildings for industry or manufacture; factory: *brickworks; ironworks.* **7.** *nc* (in *pl*) moving parts of a machine which make it go. *The works of a watch are very small.*
'workaday *adj* ordinary; usual. *He has a workaday life.*
'workbag bag in which materials for making something are kept (e.g. knitting and sewing materials).
'workbox box used like a workbag.
'workhouse formerly, special building for persons who were very poor and had no home.
'workman man who earns his living by using his hands.
workmanlike *adj* done by a good workman.
workmanship *nu* skill of a good workman.
'workshop place where things are made or repaired.
'public 'works work done by a government for the public (e.g. building roads and bridges).
out of work unemployed: *be out of work; out-of-work miners.*

work[2] [wə:k] *vt/i* **1.** (with reference to mind, body or a machine) use, cause to use, energy or power for a definite purpose. *At school we have to work very hard. Our teacher works us very hard. This machine is worked by electricity.* **2.** do what is necessary to make a living; be employed. *He works in an office. My brother works for a farmer.* **3.** be successful; get a result. *This new method really works. The medicine has worked wonders* i.e. has had wonderful results. **4.** move, cause to move, slowly. *He worked the nail loose with a knife. The oil has worked into the carpet.* **5.** control; be in charge of; obtain the products of. *For many years he worked a large farm. The company works many gold mines.*
workable *adj* able to work or be worked. *Your plan is workable. The soil is so poor that it is not workable.* (*opp* **unworkable**).
worker *nc* person who works (esp. a member of the working classes).
the works everything. (*informal*).
work at something be busy at. *I worked at my English essay all evening.*
work away go on working.
work in/into put in, or mix, slowly or skilfully. *She worked the butter into the flour. He worked in some very good points during his speech.*
work oneself into something slowly get into. *How did you work yourself into such a good job? He worked himself into a rage.*
work something off get rid of by working. *I went for a long walk to work off my headache.*
work something out 1. finish by using or working. *Many coalmines in Great Britain are worked out.* **2.** find the answer of; solve. *Have you worked out this problem yet? We are working out a way to have a cheap holiday.* **3.** move out. *Your shirt has worked out* i.e. from the top of your trousers.
'workout *nc* practice; exercise; training. *Before the race the runners had a workout.*
work something up 1. cause to grow slowly by working hard. *I worked up this business from nothing.* **2.** make excited. *Why is he so worked up?* **3.** slowly reach. *The situation has now worked up to the point that nobody will do anything.*
work it cause something which one wants to happen. *Tickets are very scarce but I think I can work it* i.e. find a way of getting some. (*informal*).
at work working.

working ['wə:kiŋ] *adj* of work; having work; useful for work. *He is wearing his working clothes. There are five working days in each week. Before building the ship they made a working model of it.* Also *nc* **1.** (often *pl*) how something works. *I don't understand the workings of this clock.* **2.** place (esp. in a mine or quarry) where work has been done or is being done. *In the mountains there are many old mine workings.*
the working class(es) section of society which works mainly with its hands. Also *adj*: *a little working-class house.*
working man man who makes his living by working with his hands.
'working party group of persons who are given the work of examining a problem and then reporting to a larger group. *The village*

council agreed to set up a working party to study the plan for a new road.

in working order working well; able to do what it is intended to do. *Is the lamp in working order?*

world [wəːld] *nc* **1.** the earth and all that is in it; planet like our own planet, earth. *He sailed alone round the world. The new invention amazed the world* i.e. countries or people everywhere. *It is possible that there are other worlds.* **2.** separate or special part of the earth or of the activities in it: *the New World* i.e. America; *the animal/vegetable/mineral world; the world of books; the political world.* **3.** life on earth or elsewhere. *He came into the world after the war* i.e. he was born then. *Do you believe in the next world?* i.e. another life after death. Also *adj* spread over the whole world or most of it. *There have been two world wars in this century. English is now a world language.*

worldly *adj* **1.** of the world: *worldly pleasures.* **2.** as a result of knowing the world: *worldly wisdom.* (*opp* **unworldly**). **worldliness** *nu.*

'world-'wide *adj* reaching all parts of the world: *a world-wide airline.*

a world of a great deal of. *His remarks have done a world of good to his country.*

all the world everybody.

be all the world to be the most important thing/person to. *His son is all the world to him.*

for all the world like very much like. *He is for all the world like his brother.*

in the world emphatic use. *Nobody in the world is better known than he is* i.e. nobody else; nobody at all. *What in the world has happened?* i.e. whatever?, what on earth?

out of this world very unusual and very good. *The food we ate was out of this world.* (*informal*).

think the world of someone/something think very highly of someone/something. (*informal*).

worm [wəːm] *nc* **1.** any type of very small creature shaped like a snake. **2.** spiral groove of a screw. Also *vt* **1.** move slowly and silently like a worm. *He wormed himself into the front row. We wormed our way through the crowd.* **2.** get with difficulty or effort. *I had to worm a reply from him.*

wormy *adj* of a worm; full of worms.

'earthworm see **earth.**

'hookworm see **hook**[1].

wormwood ['wəːmwud] *nu* type of plant with a very bitter taste.

worn [wɔːn] past part of **wear**[1].

worry ['wʌri] *vt/i* **1.** be, cause to be, annoyed, anxious or upset. *My mother worries if I come home late. Don't worry about the examination. It's easy. Please don't worry him when he is working. His illness worried me. I was worried about/by his illness.* **2.** (esp. with reference to a dog) seize and shake: *a dog that worries sheep.* Also **1.** *nc* (often *pl*) something which causes anxiety etc. *She has all the worries of looking after a large family.* **2.** *nu* state of being anxious. *His face showed his worry.*

worried *adj*: *He had a worried face.* **worriedly** *adv.*

worrying *adj* causing worry. **worryingly** *adv.*

worse [wəːs] **1.** *adj* (*comparative* of **bad**): *This road is bad but that one is worse. His writing is worse than yours. He made things worse by telling lies.* **2.** *pred adj* (*comparative* of **ill**): *During the night he became worse. The medicine made me feel worse.* Also *adv* **1.** (*comparative* of **badly**): *He writes much worse than you do.* **2.** more. *The wind is blowing worse than it did yesterday* i.e. more strongly. *We hate him worse than ever.* Also *nu* something which is worse. *Life has gone from bad to worse. I am quite pleased with your work. I expected worse. superlative* **worst.** [wəːst]. (*opp* **better**).

worsen *vt/i* become, or cause to become, worse.

none the worse 1. not harmed. *He is none the worse for his terrible journey.* **2.** no less. *I think none the worse of him for refusing to go* i.e. I think no less of him, I admire him just as much as before.

worse off not as prosperous, happy etc as before. *My father's death has left me worse off.*

worship ['wəːʃip] *nu* honour and praise to God or to somebody/something that is greatly admired. *A church or mosque is a place of worship. Their worship of rich, powerful people is disgusting.* Also *vt/i* praise and pray to God; admire greatly. *past* **worshipped.** (*US* **worshiped**). **worshipper** *nc.*

worshipful *adj* (often used as a title of respect) deserving honour and respect.

your Worship, his Worship title of respect when addressing or speaking about a mayor or magistrate of a law court. *Not guilty, your Worship.*

worst [wəːst] *adj* (*superlative* of **bad**): *He is the worst boy in the class. It was the worst accident I have ever seen.* Also *adv* (*superlative* of **badly**): *During the famine all the people suffered badly, but the poor people living in towns suffered (the) worst.* Also *nu* something which is worst. *Hope for the best but expect the worst. The worst that can happen is that you will lose your job.* Also *vt* defeat. (rather *o.f.*).

at its/one's worst when something/somebody is in the worst state. *We met him before breakfast when he was at his worst* i.e. hungry and bad-tempered.

at (the) worst even if the worst happens. *At (the) worst you will be delayed for only one hour.*

do your worst, let him/them do his/their worst showing that one does not care what somebody does.

get/have the worst of it be defeated. *Our team got the worst of it in the last game.*

if the worst comes to the worst even if the worst that can possibly happen does happen.

the worst of it is that what makes something very bad, worrying etc. *He is very ill, and the worst of it is that he refuses to see a doctor.*

worsted ['wustid] *nu* woollen thread of good quality used for making cloth; cloth made from this type of thread.

worth [wəːθ] *pred adj* **1.** having a particular value. *This watch is worth £50. All your books are not worth more than fifty pence.* **2.** giving something valuable or satisfying. *The new film is worth seeing. His opinion is not worth considering.* **3.** (with reference to a person) having wealth, property etc of a particular value. *That farmer is worth several thousand pounds.* Also *nu* **1.** what somebody/something is worth. *I think his ideas are of very little worth.* **2.** amount obtained for a particular sum of money.

I bought ten pounds worth of food.
worthless having no usefulness. **worthlessly** *adv.* **worthlessness** *nu.*
'worth'while, worth one's while enjoyable, useful etc considering the time spent. *The visit to Paris was worthwhile.*
for all one is worth as much as one can; with all one's strength. *He is trying for all he's worth to get a better job.* (*informal*).
for what it is worth without knowing whether it is valuable or useful. *My advice to you, for what it is worth, is to say nothing.*
worth it worthwhile.

worthy ['wəːði] *adj* **1.** (usu. *pred*) deserving. *He is a teacher worthy of great respect. Surely the country is worthy of a better president.* (*opp* **unworthy**). **2.** (usu. with a humorous or ironical sense) deserving praise or honour. *Our worthy friends refuse to help us.* Also *nc* person who deserves praise or honour (sometimes with a humorous or ironical sense). *In the village there are a few old worthies who think they know everything. comparative* **worthier**, *superlative* **worthiest**. **worthily** *adv.* **worthiness** *nu.*

wot [wɔt] know or knows (*o.f.*).

would [wud] *aux* see **will**[1].
'would-be *adj* intended but unsuccessful: *a would-be teacher* i.e. someone who failed to become a teacher, or someone who wishes to be a teacher but is not one yet. (*informal*).

wouldst [wudst] form of **would** used with **thou** (*o.f.*).

wound[1] [wuːnd] *vt* **1.** deliberately damage the body by cutting, striking, shooting at it etc. *He fired his gun and wounded the thief in the leg. In the battle ten soldiers were wounded. Note: wound* has only this sense of damaging deliberately; when the damage to the body is not caused deliberately *injure* or *hurt* should be used. *In the railway accident ten passengers were injured/hurt.*
2. cause a person to have an unpleasant feeling. *Your remarks have wounded his pride. We must not wound his feelings.* Also *nc* **1.** deliberate damage done to the body. **2.** painful feeling. *The defeat was a wound to his pride.*

wound[2] [waund] past of **wind**[2].

wove [wouv] past tense of **weave**.

wrack [ræk] *nu* sea plants etc thrown by the waves on to the shore.

wraith [reiθ] *nc* spirit of a dead person or of a person about to die which is seen by a living person.

wrangle ['ræŋgl] *vi* argue or quarrel noisily. Also *nc.*

wrap [ræp] *vt* put round; cover by putting round (esp. using cloth or paper). *I wrapped a blanket round him. I wrapped him in a blanket. We wrapped the bread in paper. In very cold weather you must wrap yourself up* i.e. cover yourself with warm clothes. *past* **wrapped**. Also *nc* piece of cloth or clothing worn over clothes to keep warm.
wrapper *nc* piece of paper used to cover or put round something (e.g. a book).
wrapping *nc/u* material put round something to cover and protect it (e.g. when it is being sent by post).
be wrapped up in 1. be covered or hidden in. *The dishes were wrapped up in soft paper.* **2.** give all one's attention to. *He is wrapped up in his work.*

wrath [rɔθ] *nu* rage; anger. **wrathful** *adj.* **wrathfully** *adv.* (all *o.f.*).

wreak [riːk] *vt* cause to happen; put into effect (*o.f.*).
wreak havoc on damage badly; destroy.
wreak vengeance on take one's revenge on. *He wreaked vengeance on his brother's killer.*

wreath [riːθ] *nc* circle made from flowers and leaves.

wreath

wreathe [riːð] *vt/i* **1.** put round; cover. *They wreathed the statue with flowers. The burning house was wreathed in smoke.* **2.** move round in a circle. *The mist wreathed through the trees.*

wreck [rek] **1.** *nc* something (esp. a ship) which has been severely damaged or destroyed; somebody who has been greatly weakened by illness, worry or injury. *The sailors jumped from the wreck before it sank. After the examination I was a nervous wreck.* **2.** *nu* severe damage or destruction. *The captain tried to save his ship from wreck.* Also *vt* severely damage or destroy (esp. a ship).
wreckage *nu* parts of something which has been wrecked.
wrecker *nc* (*US*) person whose work it is to destroy old buildings and motorcars.

wren [ren] *nc* type of very small bird.

wren

wrench [rentʃ] *vt* **1.** pull suddenly and violently. *He wrenched the stick from me. He wrenched the stick from/out of my hand.* **2.** twist suddenly and painfully. *When I fell I wrenched my ankle.* Also *nc* **1.** sudden and violent pull or twist. **2.** tool for holding and twisting nuts and bolts etc; spanner.

wrest [rest] *vt* take away by force; gain by force or with difficulty. (rather *o.f.*).

wrestle ['resl] *vt/i* fight or compete with somebody by seizing him and trying to throw him to the ground. **wrestler** *nc.* **wrestling** *nu.*
'all-in 'wrestling type of wrestling in which the wrestlers are allowed to hit as well as hold.

wretch [retʃ] *nc* poor, miserable person who is either pitied or despised.
wretched ['retʃid] *adj* poor; miserable; annoying. *The wretched people are starving. The trouble was caused by his wretched pride.*
wretchedly *adv.* **wretchedness** *nu.*

wriggle ['rigl] *vt/i* move, cause to move, the body or part of it quickly from side to side. *The snake wriggled through the grass. He*

wriggled himself out of my grip. Also *nc.* **wriggling** *nu.*
wriggle out of something get out of something (by wriggling or by cunning). *Don't try and wriggle out of the question* i.e. don't try to avoid answering it.

wring [riŋ] *vt* **1.** hold firmly and twist. *He is wringing the chicken's neck* i.e. twisting it in order to kill it. **2.** remove water from clothes etc in this way. *My socks were so wet that I had to wring them (out). I had to wring the water out of my socks. past* **wrung** [rʌŋ].
wringer *nc* device for wringing water from clothes (esp. after they have been washed).
'wringing 'wet so wet that water can be squeezed out of it.
wring something from someone get something out of someone with difficulty. *The police wrung a confession out of him.*
wring one's hands show sorrow or distress by twisting and moving one's hands together.
wring somebody's hand shake somebody's hand firmly to show great pleasure.

wrinkle ['riŋkl] *nc* fold or line on the surface of something (e.g. of the skin because of age; of a piece of cloth). *The old man's face is covered with wrinkles.* Also *vt/i* have, cause to have, wrinkles. *Don't wrinkle your new dress.*
wrinkled *adj* having wrinkles.

wrist [rist] *nc* joint between the arm and the hand.
wristlet ['ristlit] *nc* circle of metal etc worn round the wrist as an ornament.
'wrist watch small watch held on the wrist by a band of leather, metal etc.

writ [rit] *nc* written order made by a court of law.
Holy Writ the Bible.

write [rait] *vt/i* **1.** put words, figures or signs on something (usu. on paper with a pen or pencil). *He can neither read nor write. I wrote my name and address in the book. How many words have you written? I am writing an essay.* **2.** write and send what has been written. *Write your friend a note. I wrote (to) you from London.* **3.** be an author; do the work of an author. *What does he do? He writes. He has written for several magazines. past tense* **wrote** [rout]. *past part* **written** ['ritn].
writer *nc* person who writes; author.
writing 1. *nu* act of writing; words etc which have been written. *I can't read your writing.* **2.** *nc* (in *pl*) work done by an author. *This term we are studying the writings of Dickens.*
'writing paper paper for writing letters.
write something down make a written note of; put on paper in writing. *The policeman wrote down my name and address. If you know the answer write it down.*
write in something 1. add to what has already been written. *I'll write in your suggestions after I have finished the essay.* **2.** write to somebody in authority, to a head office etc. *Why don't you write in and complain?*
write something off no longer show something in a written list; remove something from the written record (because it is useless, lost, cannot be recovered etc). *The manager told me to write off one of the old pumps in the factory. The company has written off the debt* i.e. because it knows the debt will not be paid.
'write-off *nc* **1.** act of writing off. **2.** something which is so badly damaged that it is useless. *After the accident his car was a write-off.* (*informal* in sense **2.**).
write something out 1. write completely, in full. *The teacher made me write out the whole essay again.* **2.** write in order to give or send. *He wrote his landlord out a cheque for £20.*
write something up 1. write out in a complete form. *I must write up my history notes.* **2.** describe fully (and usu. very favourably) in a newspaper or periodical.
'write-up *nc* comment (either favourable or unfavourable) in a newspaper or periodical. *The school play was given a very bad write-up in the local paper.* (*informal*).

writhe [raið] *vi* twist the body from side to side because of pain or suffering.

wrong [rɔŋ] *adj* **1.** sinful, not moral; mistaken or not correct. *Telling lies is wrong. It is wrong to drink and drive. The man gave the wrong answer. We are late because we took the wrong road. You are quite wrong* i.e. mistaken. *He is wrong in thinking this. It is wrong of him to think this.* (*opp* **right**). **2.** not working properly; not in order. *There's something wrong with my watch. What's wrong with your leg?* Also *nc/u* act which is wrong. Also *vt* do a wrong to somebody. *You wronged him by calling him a coward. He is a brave man.* Also *adv*: *You've done the work wrong. He never went wrong* i.e. never made a mistake or broke the law.
wrongful *adj* not lawful; unjust. **wrongfully** *adv.* **wrongfulness** *nu.*
wrongly *adv*: *You've done the work wrongly. Note: wrong* as an *adv* usu. comes at the end of its sentence; *wrongly* can come either at the end or earlier (esp. before a *past part*) (e.g. *The parcel is tied wrong(ly)* or *The parcel is wrongly tied*).
'wrongdoer *nc* person who does wrong; person who commits a crime.
'wrongdoing *nc/u* crime.
'wrong-'headed *adj* mistaken but refusing to admit it. **wrong-headedly** *adv.* **wrong-headedness** *nu.*
in the wrong guilty; at fault; mistaken.
put somebody in the wrong make somebody appear to be guilty or mistaken.

wrote [rout] past tense of **write.**

wrought [rɔːt] **1.** cause something. *The storm wrought great damage.* **2.** make (*o.f.*).
'wrought 'iron *nu* special kind of iron which resists rust and can be made into different shapes. Also *adj*: *a wrought-iron gate.*
'hand-wrought *adj* (esp. with reference to something made of metal) made by hand, not machine.

wrung [rʌŋ] past of **wring.**

wry [rai] *adj* (with reference to the mouth or face) pulled to one side to express dislike. *When he tasted the tea he made a wry face.* **wryly** *adv.* **wryness** *nu.*

X

xenophobia [zenə'foubiə] *nu* unreasonable dislike for foreigners. **xenophobic** [zenə'foubik] *adj.*

Xmas ['krisməs, 'eksməs] *nc* short written form of **Christmas.** (*informal*).

X-ray ['eksrei] *nc* **1.** type of ray which can pass through solids and is therefore used to see into or photograph what is inside them. **2.** photograph taken in this way. *He has gone into hospital for an X-ray.* Also *vt* examine or photograph using X-rays.

xylophone ['zailəfoun] *nc* musical instrument in which wooden bars of different lengths are hit with wooden hammers.

Y

yacht [jɔt] *nc* **1.** type of sailing boat used for racing and pleasure. **2.** type of small ship (usu. with an engine, not sails) used by the rich for private travel. Also *vi* race or travel in a yacht.
yachting *nu* skill or sport of sailing a yacht.

yak[1] [jæk] *nc* type of long-haired animal like an ox, found in central Asia.

yak[2], **yack** [jæk] *vi* talk too much about nothing. (*informal*).

yam [jæm] *nc/u* type of tropical plant; its root, like a potato, which is used as food.

yank [jæŋk] *vt* pull sharply and suddenly. *He yanked away the chair before I could sit on it.* Also *nc* action of pulling away sharply: *give something a yank.*

Yank [jæŋk] *nc* American. (*informal* and rather *impolite*).

yap [jæp] *vi* (with reference to a dog) bark with a short, sharp sound. *past* **yapped.** Also *nc* sound of this kind.

yard[1] [jɑːd] *nc* **1.** measure of length equal to 3 feet. see appendix. **2.** pole fixed to the mast of a ship for carrying a sail.
'yardstick 1. stick which is a yard in length, used for measuring. **2.** something with which other things are compared.

yard[2] [jɑːd] *nc* **1.** enclosed space next to a house or building.
Note: (*US*) the space next to a house is called a *yard* even if it has grass, trees and flowers. (*Brit* garden).
2. open space used for a particular purpose: *dockyard* i.e. space where ships are repaired; *railway yards* i.e. space where there are many railway lines for keeping wagons and carriages when not used or for making up trains; *builder's yard* i.e. space where a builder keeps his building materials.

yarn [jɑːn] **1.** *nu* type of thread used for knitting; thick thread from which a rope is made. **2.** *nc* story (often one which is untrue) (*informal* in sense **2.**). Also *vi* tell stories; talk. *He likes to yarn about his adventures.* (*informal*).

yashmak ['jæʃmæk] *nc* (in some Muslim countries) type of veil worn over the face by women.

yawl [jɔːl] *nc* type of sailing boat.

yawn [jɔːn] *vi* **1.** open the mouth widely, as one does when sleepy or weary. **2.** be wide open: *a yawning hole.* Also *nc* act of this kind. *He gave a yawn and then fell asleep.*

yaws [jɔːz] *nu* type of tropical disease which damages the skin.

ye [jiː] form of **you** (*o.f.*).

yea [jei] *adv/interj* yes (*o.f.*).

yeah [jɛə] *adv/interj* (mainly *US*) yes. (*informal*).

year [jiə*] *nc* **1.** period of 365 days or 12 months. *He is 17 years of age and is in the sixth year of secondary school.* **2.** period of 365 days or 12 months between 1 January and 31 December. *Last year I went to London. In the year 1945, the Second World War ended.* **3.** (in *pl*) age. *He is a big boy for his years.*
yearly *adj/adv* happening every year; happening once a year.
yearling *nc* animal over one year and less than two years of age.
'calendar year year from 1 January to 31 December. see **year** (in sense **2.**).
financial year period of 12 months for which money is given and accounts made (in British Government from 6 April one year to 5 April the next year).
'leap year see **leap.**
all the year round throughout the year; at all times during a year.
year in year out during one year after another; year after year.

yearn [jəːn] *vt* (with **for** or **after**) greatly desire (esp. somebody/something that one loves). *The sailor yearned for home. They yearned to see their parents again.* **yearning** *nc/u.* **yearningly** *adv.*

yeast [jiːst] *nu* living substance used in the preparation of bread and beer and other alcoholic drinks.

yell [jel] *vt/i* shout loudly and sharply. Also *nc* shout of this kind.

yellow ['jelou] *nc/u* colour of butter or the sun. Also *adj* **1.** *a yellow ball.* **2.** not brave; cowardly. (*informal* in sense **2.**). Also *vt/i* become, cause to become, yellow. **yellowness** *nu.*
yellowish *adj* rather yellow.

yelp [jelp] *vi* cry out suddenly because of fear or pain. Also *nc.*

yen [jen] *nc* (usu. only *sing*) wish or liking. *I have a yen for travel.* (*informal*).

yeoman ['joumən] *nc* farmer who owns his own land. *pl* **yeomen** ['joumən] (*o.f.*).
yeomanry *nu* **1.** yeomen taken all together. **2.** volunteer unit within an army. (rather *o.f.*).
'yeoman 'service good useful service.

yes [jes] *interj* expressing agreement.
'yes man person who always agrees with what is said by his employer etc. (*informal*).

yesterday ['jestədi] *adv/nu* day before the present one. *He arrived yesterday. Today is Friday; yesterday was Thursday.* Also *adj*: *Yesterday morning/afternoon/evening was fine and dry.*
Note: with *night*, *last* must be used: *last night; yesterday night* is not normally used.

yet [jet] *adv* **1.** (at the end of a question) up to now; so far. *Has he gone yet? Are you ready yet?* **2.** (immediately after **not, never, nothing etc** or at the end of the sentence) up to now; up to then; by now; by then. *He has not yet gone/He has not gone yet. I am not yet ready/I am not ready yet. Nothing yet is known/Nothing is known yet. Are you ready to go now? No, not just yet.* **3.** (with *affirmative*) still. *We may yet hear from him/We may hear from him yet. This is bad; that is yet worse.* Also *conj* still; but. *I gave him ten pounds (and) yet he was not satisfied.*

He is a clever, yet lazy, man.
as yet up to now; up to then. *As yet we have not met him.*
yew [ju:] **1.** *nc* type of tree. **2.** *nu* the wood of this tree.
Yiddish ['jidiʃ] *nu* language, based on German etc, spoken by some Jews.
yield [ji:ld] *vt/i* **1.** (with **to**) give up; surrender. *Our army refused to yield. The enemy yielded the town to our forces.* **2.** produce; give. *Fertile land yields good crops.* Also *nc* amount produced. *What is the yield of this ricefield?*
yielding *adj* giving in to stronger force; flexible. (*opp* **unyielding**). **yieldingly** *adv*.
yield to treatment (with reference to disease, pain etc) be reduced when treated.
yodel, jodel ['joudl] *vt/i* change the voice quickly and frequently from low notes to high notes while singing. *past* **yodelled.** (*US* **yodeled**). Also *nc* song sung or call made in this way.
yoga ['jougə] *nu* religious way of life (originally followed mainly by some Hindus) which includes prayer, deep breathing, physical exercises and fasting.
yogi ['jougi] *nc* person who follows this way of life.
yoghourt, yoghurt ['jɔgət] *nu* thick liquid food made from sour milk.
yoke [jouk] *nc* **1.** frame of wood fitted on the neck of an animal (esp. an ox) so that it can pull a cart or plough. **2.** piece of wood fitted on a person's shoulders so that a pail, basket etc can be carried more easily on each side. **3.** part of a dress which fits round the shoulders. **4.** pair of animals under the same yoke. *pl* **yoke** (in sense **4.**). Also *vt* put a yoke on; join in pairs.

yoke *(def 1)*

throw off the yoke refuse to be treated as a slave; rebel.
yokel ['joukl] *nc* dull and simple man who lives in the country and knows little about town life. (*informal*).
yolk [jouk] *nc/u* the yellow part inside an egg.
yon [jɔn] short form of **yonder**.
yonder ['jɔndə*] *adj/adv* (with reference to somebody/something that can be seen) over there. (rather *o.f.* – use **over there**).
you [ju:] *pron* **1.** (with reference to a person/persons spoken to) *Where do you live?* **2.** anybody; a person. *At our school you soon learn that the headmaster is very strict. What can you do in a situation like that?*
young [jʌŋ] *adj* recently born or started etc: *a young man; young corn; a young nation. He is two years younger than his brother. I am the youngest in the class.* (*opp* **old**). Also *nu* young animals or birds. *We saw a deer with its young.*
youngish *adj* rather young.
youngster ['jʌŋstə*] *nc* young boy or girl.
with young (with reference to an animal) pregnant.
Note: the difference in sense between *with its young* and *with young*.
your [jɔ:*] *adj/determiner* of, belonging to, you. *Is this your book?*
yours [jɔ:z] *pron/pred adj*: *Is this book yours?*
yourself [jɔ:'self] **1.** *reflexive pron*: *Look at yourself in the mirror.* **2.** (emphatic): *You yourself said so.*
by yourself without help; alone.
youth [ju:θ] **1.** *nu* time of life when one is young. *In his youth he was a good runner.* **2.** *nc* young man. *Who is that youth? pl* **youths** [ju:ðz]. **3.** *nu* (with **the**) young men and women. *The youth of today are very lively.*
youthful *adj* young; looking young; behaving like a young person. **youthfully** *adv*. **youthfulness** *nu*.
'youth hostel inexpensive place where young travellers can stay.
yowl [jaul] *vi* howl loudly. Also *nc*.
yule [ju:l] *nu* Christmas (*o.f.*).
'yuletide Christmas time (*o.f.*).

Z

zany ['zeini] *nc* foolish but amusing person (esp. one who is an entertainer). Also *adj*.
zeal [zi:l] *nu* eagerness; enthusiasm.
zealous ['zeləs] *adj*. **zealously** *adv*.
zealot ['zelət] *nc* person who is too eager or enthusiastic about religion, politics etc.
zebra ['zebrə] *nc* type of wild animal like a horse, with dark brown and white stripes.
zenith ['zeniθ] *nu* **1.** part of the sky which is overhead. **2.** highest point of something.
zero ['ziərou] *nc* **1.** the figure 0. **2.** the figure 0 marked on a scale (esp. on a thermometer): *ten degrees above/below zero*. *pl* **zeros**.
'zero hour exact time fixed for something important to begin (e.g. a battle; the launching of a rocket etc).
zest [zest] *nu* eagerness and pleasure. *He worked with zest. The chance of winning a prize added/gave zest to the competition.*
zigzag ['zigzæg] *nc* line or course which turns sharply from side to side. Also *adj/adv*: *a zigzag path*. Also *vi* go zigzag. *He zigzagged across the field*. *past* **zigzagged**.
zinc [ziŋk] *nu* type of metal (Zn).
zip [zip] *nc* **1.** sound made by something moving quickly through the air. **2.** device (made of metal etc) for fastening quickly two pieces of cloth, leather etc, by pulling a tab over two rows of teeth. Also *vt/i* **1.** make this kind of sound. *The bullet zipped through the air.* **2.** fasten with a zip. *Will you zip up my dress? past* **zipped**.

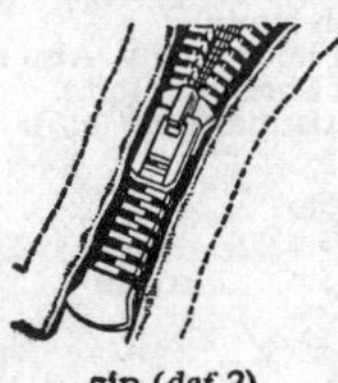

zip (*def 2*)

zipper, 'zip 'fastener *nc* zip (in sense **2.**).
zither ['ziðə*] *nc* type of stringed musical instrument.
zodiac ['zoudiæk] *nu* **1.** part of the sky extending on either side of the path which the sun seems to take through the sky in a year. **2.** design or plan showing this part of the sky.
signs of the zodiac the 12 divisions of the zodiac, each named after a constellation of stars, through which the sun and the planets appear to move during one year.
zombie ['zɔmbi] *nc* **1.** dead person who continues to move by magic. **2.** person who moves very slowly and seems not to be completely alive.
zone [zoun] *nc* **1.** area of a country or town marked off and used for a special reason or purpose: *the war zone* i.e. an area where a war is fought; *traffic zones*. **2.** (*US*) division of the country for postal purposes. (*Brit* **area**). **3.** one of the five belts marked on the map of the earth to show the main divisions of temperature. Also *vt* **1.** divide into zones. **2.** give a special purpose to. *This part of the city has been zoned for redevelopment.*
zonal *adj* of zones; divided into zones.
zoo [zu:] *nc* park where many kinds of animals are kept in captivity. (Also **zoological gardens**).
zoology [zu:'ɔlədʒi] *nu* science of animals.
zoological [zuə'lɔdʒikl] *adj*.
zoologist *nc* person who studies zoology.
zoological gardens see **zoo**.
zoom [zu:m] *nu* deep sound made by an aircraft as it climbs quickly into the sky. Also *vi* **1.** (with reference to an aircraft) climb quickly; move quickly at a low height. **2.** (with reference to a camera) move in quickly to a close-up view. *The camera zoomed in on the man's face.*
'zoom lens camera lens which, while keeping what is photographed in constant focus (i.e. always clear), can change from distant to close-up views.

Irregular Verbs

The present tense column includes present participle etc where spelling changes.

Present	*Past*	*Past Part*
arise (arising)	arose	arisen
awake (awaking)	awoke	awaked
be (am, is, are; being)	was, were	been
bear	bore	born(e)
beat	beat	beaten
become (becoming)	became	become
befall	befell	befallen
beget (begetting)	begot	begotten
begin (beginning)	began	begun
behold	beheld	beheld
bend	bent	bent
beseech	besought	besought
beset (besetting)	beset	beset
bet (betting)	bet (also betted)	bet (also betted)
bid[1] (*make a bid*) (bidding)	bid	bid
bid[2] (*command*) (bidding)	bade	bidden
bind	bound	bound
bite (biting)	bit	bitten
bleed	bled	bled
blow	blew	blown
break	broke	broken
breed	bred	bred
bring	brought	brought
build	built	built
burn	burnt *or* burned	burnt (also burned)
burst	burst	burst
buy	bought	bought
can	could	(been able)
cast	cast	cast
catch	caught	caught
choose (choosing)	chose	chosen
cleave (cleaving)	cleft	cleft (also cloven)
cling	clung	clung
come (coming)	came	come
cost	cost	cost
creep	crept	crept
crow	crew (also crowed)	crowed
cut (cutting)	cut	cut
deal	dealt	dealt
dig (digging)	dug	dug
do (3rd person: he/she/it/does)	did	done
draw	drew	drawn
dream	dreamed (also dreamt)	dreamed (also dreamt)
drink	drank	drunk
drive (driving)	drove	driven
dwell	dwelt	dwelt
eat	ate	eaten
fall	fell	fallen
feed	fed	fed
feel	felt	felt
fight	fought	fought

Present	*Past*	*Past Part*
find	found	found
flee	fled	fled
fling	flung	flung
fly (flies)	flew	flown
forbear	forbore	forborne
forbid (forbidding)	forbade	forbidden
forecast	forecast	forecast
forego	forewent	foregone
foresee	foresaw	foreseen
foretell	foretold	foretold
forget (forgetting)	forgot	forgotten
forgive (forgiving)	forgave	forgiven
forsake (forsaking)	forsook	forsaken
forswear	forswore	forsworn
freeze (freezing)	froze	frozen
get (getting)	got	got, (*US*) gotten
give (giving)	gave	given
go (goes)	went	gone
grind	ground	ground
grow	grew	grown
hang	hung (also hanged)	hung (also hanged)
have (has; having)	had	had
hear	heard	heard
heave[1]	heaved	heaved
heave[2] (*Naut*)	hove	hove
hide (hiding)	hid	hidden
hit (hitting)	hit	hit
hold	held	held
hurt	hurt	hurt
inlay	inlaid	inlaid
keep	kept	kept
kneel	knelt (also kneeled)	knelt (also kneeled)
know	knew	known
lay	laid	laid
lead	led	led
lean	leant (also leaned)	leant (also leaned)
leap	leapt (also leaped)	leapt (also leaped)
learn	learnt (also learned)	learnt (also learned)
leave (leaving)	left	left
lend	lent	lent
let (letting)	let	let
lie (lying)	lay	lain
light	lit (also lighted)	lit (also lighted)
lose (losing)	lost	lost
make (making)	made	made
may	might	--
mean	meant	meant
meet	met	met
mistake (mistaking)	mistook	mistaken
mow	mowed	mown (also mowed)
must	(had to)	(had to)
ought	(ought to have)	--
partake (partaking)	partook	partaken

Present	*Past*	*Past Part*
pay	paid	paid
put (putting)	put	put
quit (quitting)	quit (also quitted)	quit (also quitted)
read	read	read
rend	rent	rent
rid (ridding)	rid	rid
ride (riding)	rode	ridden
ring	rang	rung
rise (rising)	rose	risen
run (running)	ran	run
saw	sawed	sawn
say	said	said
see	saw	seen
seek	sought	sought
sell	sold	sold
send	sent	sent
set (setting)	set	set
shake (shaking)	shook	shaken
shall	should	--
shear	sheared	shorn (also sheared)
shed (shedding)	shed	shed
shine (shining)	shone	shone
shoot	shot	shot
show	showed	shown
shrink	shrank	shrunk
shut (shutting)	shut	shut
sing	sang	sung
sink	sank	sunk
sit (sitting)	sat	sat
slay	slew	slain
sleep	slept	slept
slide (sliding)	slid	slid
sling	slung	slung
slink	slunk	slunk
slit (slitting)	slit	slit
smell	smelt (also smelled)	smelt (also smelled)
smite (smiting)	smote	smitten
sow	sowed	sown (also sowed)
speak	spoke	spoken
speed	sped (also speeded)	sped (also speeded)
spell	spelt (also spelled)	spelt (also spelled)
spend	spent	spent
spill	spilt (also spilled)	spilt (also spilled)

Present	*Past*	*Past Part*
spin (spinning)	spun	spun
spit (spitting)	spat	spat
split (splitting)	split	split
spoil	spoiled (also spoilt)	spoiled (also spoilt)
spread	spread	spread
spring	sprang	sprung
stand	stood	stood
steal	stole	stolen
stick	stuck	stuck
sting	stung	stung
stink	stank	stunk
strew	strewed	strewn (also strewed)
stride (striding)	strode	strode
strike (striking)	struck	struck (also stricken)
string	strung	strung
strive (striving)	strove	striven
swear	swore	sworn
sweep	swept	swept
swell	swelled	swollen (also swelled)
swim (swimming)	swam	swum
swing	swung	swung
take (taking)	took	taken
teach	taught	taught
tear	tore	torn
tell	told	told
think	thought	thought
throw	threw	thrown
thrust	thrust	thrust
tread	trod	trodden
wake (waking)	woke (also waked)	woken (also waked)
waylay	waylaid	waylaid
wear	wore	worn
weave (weaving)	wove (also weaved)	woven (also weaved)
wed (wedding)	wedded (also wed)	wedded (also wed)
weep	wept	wept
will	would	--
win (winning)	won	won
wind	wound	wound
withdraw	withdrew	withdrawn
withhold	withheld	withheld
withstand	withstood	withstood
wring	wrung	wrung
write (writing)	wrote	written

Weights and Measures

		Metric equivalent
Length	1 inch	2·54 centimetres
	12 inches = 1 foot	30·48 centimetres
	3 feet = 1 yard	0·91 metres
	220 yards = 1 furlong	201·17 metres
	8 furlongs or 1760 yards = 1 mile	1·61 kilometres
Square Measure	4840 square yards = 1 acre	0·40 hectares
Weight	1 ounce	28·35 grammes
	16 ounces = 1 pound	0·45 kilograms
	14 pounds = 1 stone	6·35 kilograms
	8 stones = 1 hundredweight	50·80 kilograms
	20 hundredweight = 1 ton	1016 kilograms

Liquid Measure		*Metric equivalent*
	1 pint	0·57 litres
	2 pints = 1 quart	1·14 litres
	4 quarts = 1 gallon	4·54 litres

US Measures

In the US the same system as the British one is used for the most part; the main differences are mentioned below.

	Measures of Capacity	
Liquid	1 US liquid gill	0·118 litres
	1 US liquid pint = 4 gills	0·473 litres
	1 US liquid quart = 2 pints	0·946 litres
	1 US gallon = 4 quarts	3·785 litres
Weights	1 hundredweight (or short hundredweight) = 100 pounds	45·36 kilograms
	1 ton (or short ton) = 2000 pounds = 20 short hundredweights	907·18 kilograms

British Money	*New system*	*Old system*
	100 new pence = 1 pound	4 farthings = 1 penny
		12 pence = 1 shilling
		20 shillings = 1 pound

Numbers	*Cardinal numbers*	*Ordinal numbers*
	1 one	1st first
	2 two	2nd second
	3 three	3rd third
	4 four	4th fourth
	5 five	5th fifth
	6 six	6th sixth
	7 seven	7th seventh
	8 eight	8th eighth
	9 nine	9th ninth
	10 ten	10th tenth
	11 eleven	11th eleventh
	12 twelve	12th twelfth
	13 thirteen	13th thirteenth
	14 fourteen	14th fourteenth
	15 fifteen	15th fifteenth
	16 sixteen	16th sixteenth
	17 seventeen	17th seventeenth
	18 eighteen	18th eighteenth
	19 nineteen	19th nineteenth
	20 twenty	20th twentieth
	21 twenty-one	21st twenty-first
	22 twenty-two	22nd twenty-second
	30 thirty	30th thirtieth
	40 forty	40th fortieth
	50 fifty	50th fiftieth
	60 sixty	60th sixtieth
	70 seventy	70th seventieth
	80 eighty	80th eightieth
	90 ninety	90th ninetieth
	100 one/a hundred	100th hundredth
	101 a hundred and one	101st hundred-and-first
	200 two hundred	200th two hundredth
	1,000 one/a thousand	1,000th thousandth
	2,000 two thousand	2,000th two thousandth
	1,000,000 one/a million	1,000,000th millionth

Vulgar fractions		
	$\frac{1}{2}$ a half	$\frac{3}{4}$ three-quarters
	$\frac{1}{3}$ a third	$\frac{1}{5}$ a fifth
	$\frac{2}{3}$ two-thirds	$\frac{2}{5}$ two-fifths
	$\frac{1}{4}$ a quarter	$15\frac{1}{4}$ fifteen and a quarter

5/6 five-sixths
1/7 a seventh
1/10 a tenth
1/20 a twentieth
1/100 a hundredth

Decimal fractions		
	0·5	(nought) point five
	0·33	(nought) point three three
	15·25	fifteen point two five

Geographical Names

(Note: some of these names have forms derived from them; these derived forms are used adjectivally and can also be used to refer to an inhabitant of the country, etc (*nc*) and, where appropriate, to the language spoken there (*nu*) e.g. *He lives in Albania; he is Albanian; he is an Albanian; he speaks Albanian.* In a few cases, however, there are several distinct derived forms e.g. *He lives in Denmark; he is Danish (adj); he is a Dane (nc); he speaks Danish (nu).*

the Adriatic [ðieidri'ætik]
the Aegean [ðii'dʒiːən]
Afghanistan [æf'gænistæn] *Afghan* ['æfgæn]
Africa ['æfrikə] *African* ['æfrikən]
Albania [æl'beiniə] *Albanian* [æl'beiniən]
Algeria [æl'dʒiəriə] *Algerian* [æl'dʒiəriən]
the Alps [ði'ælps] *Alpine* ['ælpain]
America [ə'merikə] *American* [ə'merikən]
the Andes [ði'ændiːz] *Andean* [æn'diːən]
the Antarctic [ðiænt'ɑːktik] *Antarctic* [ænt'ɑːktik]
Arabia [ə'reibiə] *Arabian* [ə'reibiən] *adj Arab* ['ærəb] *adj/nc Arabic* ['ærəbik] *adj/nu*
the Arctic [ði'ɑːktik] *Arctic* ['ɑːktik]
Argentina [ɑːdʒən'tiːnə] also *the Argentine* [ði'ɑːdʒəntiːn] *Argentinian* [ɑːdʒən'tiniən]
Asia ['eiʃə] *Asian* ['eiʒən] (also *Asiatic* [eizi'ætik] which is more *o.f.* and less polite)
Athens ['æθinz] *Athenian* [ə'θiːniən]
the Atlantic [ðiət'læntik]
Australia [ɔs'treiliə] *Australian* [ɔs'treiliən]
Austria ['ɔstriə] *Austrian* ['ɔstriən]
the Baltic [ðə'bɔːltik]
Bavaria [bə'veəriə] *Bavarian* [bə'veəriən]
Belgium ['beldʒəm] *Belgian* [beldʒən]
Bolivia [bə'liviə] *Bolivian* [bə'liviən]
Brazil [brə'zil] *Brazilian* [brə'ziliən]
Britain ['britn] *British* ['britiʃ] *adj Briton* ['britn] *nc Britisher* ['britiʃə*] *nc (US)*
Brittany ['britəni] *Breton* ['bretn]
Brussels ['brʌslz]
Bulgaria [bʌl'geəriə] *Bulgarian* [bʌl'geəriən]
Burma ['bəːmə] *Burmese* [bəː'miːz]
California [kæli'fɔːniə] *Californian* [kæli'fɔːniən]
Cambodia [kæm'boudiə] *Cambodian* [kæm'boudiən]
Cambridge ['keimbridʒ]
Canada ['kænədə] *Canadian* [kə'neidiən]
the Caribbean [ðəkæri'biːən]
Ceylon [si'lɔn] *Ceylonese* [silə'niːz] *or Singalese* [siŋgə'liːz]
Chile ['tʃili] *Chilean* ['tʃiliən]
China ['tʃainə] *Chinese* [tʃai'niːz]
the Congo [ðə'kɔŋgou] *Congolese* [kɔŋgə'liːz]
Cornwall ['kɔːnwɔːl] *Cornish* ['kɔːniʃ] *adj/nu*
Corsica ['kɔːsikə] *Corsican* ['kɔːsikən]
Crete [kriːt] *Cretan* ['kriːtən]
Cuba ['kjuːbə] *Cuban* ['kjuːbən]
Cyprus ['saiprəs] *Cypriot* ['sipriət]
Czechoslovakia [tʃekəslou'vækiə] *Czechoslovak* [tʃekə'slouvæk] *adj Czech* [tʃek] *adj/nc/u*
Denmark ['denmɑːk] *Danish* ['deiniʃ] *adj/nu Dane* [dein] *nc*
Ecuador ['ekwədɔː*] *Ecuadorian* [ekwə'dɔːriən]
Egypt ['iːdʒipt] *Egyptian* [i'dʒipʃən]
England ['iŋglənd] *English* ['iŋgliʃ] *adj/nu Englishman* ['iŋgliʃmən] *nc*
Europe ['juərəp] *European* [juərə'piːən]
Finland ['finlənd] *Finnish* ['finiʃ] *adj/nu Finn* [fin] *nc*
Fiji ['fiːdʒiː] *Fijian* [fiː'dʒiːən]
Flanders ['flɑːndəz] *Flemish* ['flemiʃ] *adj/nu Fleming* ['flemiŋ] *nc*
Florence ['flɔrns] *Florentine* ['flɔrntain]
France [frɑːns] *French* [frentʃ] *adj/nu Frenchman* ['frentʃmən] *nc*
Germany ['dʒəːməni] *German* ['dʒəːmən]
Ghana ['gɑːnə] *Ghanaian* [gɑː'neiən]
Greece [griːs] *Greek* [griːk]
Haiti ['heiti] *Haitian* ['heiʃiən]
Hawaii [hə'waiiː] *Hawaiian* [hə'waijən]
the Himalayas [ðəhimə'leiəz] *Himalayan* [himə'leiən]
Holland ['hɔlənd] *Dutch* [dʌtʃ] *adj/nu Dutchman* ['dʌtʃmən] *nc*
Hungary ['hʌŋgəri] *Hungarian* [hʌŋ'geəriən]
Iceland ['aislənd] *Icelandic* [ais'lændik] *adj/nu Icelander* ['aisləndə*] *nc*
India ['indiə] *Indian* ['indiən]
Iran [i'rɑːn] *Iranian* [i'reiniən]
Iraq [i'rɑːk] *Iraqi* [i'rɑːki]

Ireland ['aiələnd] *Irish* ['aiəriʃ] *adj/nu Irishman* ['aiəriʃmən] *nc*
Israel ['izreil] *Israeli* [iz'reili]
Italy ['itəli] *Italian* [i'tæliən]
Jamaica [dʒə'meikə] *Jamaican* [dʒə'meikən]
Japan [dʒə'pæn] *Japanese* [dʒæpə'ni:z]
Jordan ['dʒɔ:dn] *Jordanian* [dʒɔ:'deiniən]
Kenya ['kenjə] *Kenyan* ['kenjən]
Laos [laus] *Laotian* ['lauʃiən]
Lapland ['læplænd] *Lapp* [læp] *adj/nc Lapplander* ['læplændə*] *nc*
the Lebanon [ðə'lebənən] *Lebanese* [lebə'ni:z]
Liberia [lai'biəriə] *Liberian* [lai'biəriən]
Libya ['libiə] *Libyan* ['libiən]
London ['lʌndn] *Londoner* ['lʌndənə*] *nc*
Luxembourg ['lʌksəmbə:g]
Majorca [mə'dʒɔ:kə] *Majorcan* [mə'dʒɔ:kən]
Malaysia [mə'leiziə] *Malaysian* [mə'leiziən]
Malta ['mɔ:ltə] *Maltese* [mɔ:l'ti:z]
the Mediterranean [ðəmeditə'reiniən]
Mexico ['meksikou] *Mexican* ['meksikən]
Milan [mi'læn] *Milanese* [milə'ni:z]
Morocco [mə'rɔkou] *Moroccan* [mə'rɔkən]
Moscow ['mɔskou] *Muscovite* ['mʌskəvait]
Munich ['mju:nik]
Naples ['neiplz] *Neapolitan* [niə'pɔlitn]
the Netherlands [ðə'neðələndz]
New Zealand [nju:'zi:lənd] *New Zealander* [nju:'zi:ləndə*] *nc*
Nigeria [nai'dʒiəriə] *Nigerian* [nai'dʒiəriən]
Normandy ['nɔ:məndi] *Norman* ['nɔ:mən]
Norway ['nɔ:wei] *Norwegian* [nɔ:'wi:dʒən]
the Pacific [ðəpə'sifik]
Pakistan [pa:kis'ta:n] *Pakistani* [pa:kis'ta:ni]
Paraguay ['pærəgwai] *Paraguayan* [pærə'gwaiən]
Paris ['pæris] *Parisian* [pə'riziən]
Persia ['pə:ʃə] *Persian* ['pə:ʃn]
Peru [pə'ru:] *Peruvian* [pə'ru:viən]
the Philippines [ðə'filipi:nz] *Filipino* [fili'pi:nou]
Poland ['poulənd] *Polish* ['pouliʃ] *adj/nu Pole* [poul] *nc*
Portugal ['pɔ:tjəgl] *Portuguese* [pɔ:tjə'gi:z]
Puerto Rico [pwə:tou'ri:kou] *Puerto Rican* [pwə:tou'ri:kən]
the Pyrenees [ðəpirə'ni:z] *Pyrenean* [pirə'ni:ən]
the Rhine [ðə'rain]
Rhodesia [rou'di:ʒə] *Rhodesian* [rou'di:ʒən]
Rome [roum] *Roman* ['roumən]
Russia ['rʌʃə] *Russian* ['rʌʃn]
the Sahara [ðəsə'ha:rə]
Sardinia [sa:'diniə] *Sardinian* [sa:'diniən]
Saudi Arabia [saudiə'reibiə] *Saudi Arabian* [saudiə'reibiən]
Scandinavia [skændi'neiviə] *Scandinavian* [skændi'neiviən]
Scotland ['skɔtlənd] *Scottish* ['skɔtiʃ] *Scots* [skɔts] *Scotch* [skɔtʃ] *adj Scot* [skɔt] *nc* (see dictionary)
the Seine [ðə'sein]
Siberia [sai'biəriə] *Siberian* [sai'biəriən]
Sicily ['sisili] *Sicilian* [si'siliən]
South Africa [sauθ'æfrikə] *South African* [sauθ'æfrikən]
the Soviet Union [ðəsouviət'ju:niən]
Spain [spein] *Spanish* ['spæniʃ] *adj/nu Spaniard* ['spæniəd] *nc*
the Sudan [ðəsu'da:n] *Sudanese* [sudə'ni:z]
Suez ['su:iz]
Sweden ['swi:dn] *Swedish* ['swi:diʃ] *adj/nu Swede* [swi:d] *nc*
Switzerland ['switsələnd] *Swiss* [swis]
Syria ['siriə] *Syrian* ['siriən]
Tahiti [tə'hi:ti] *Tahitian* [tə'hi:ʃən]
Tanzania [tænzə'niə] *Tanzanian* [tænzə'niən]
Thailand ['tailænd] *Thai* [tai]
the Thames [ðə'temz]
Tunisia [tju:'niziə] *Tunisian* [tju'niziən]
Turkey ['tə:ki] *Turkish* ['tə:kiʃ] *adj/nu Turk* [tə:k] *nc*
the Tyrol [ðəti'roul] *Tyrolean* [tirə'li:ən]
Uganda [ju:'gændə] *Ugandan* [ju:'gændn]
Uruguay ['juərəgwai] *Uruguayan* [juərə'gwaiən]
Venezuela [venə'zweilə] *Venezuelan* [venə'zweilən]
Venice ['venis] *Venetian* [və'ni:ʃn]
Vienna [vi'enə] *Viennese* [viə'ni:z]
Vietnam [vjet'næm] *Vietnamese* [vjetnə'mi:z]
Wales [weilz] *Welsh* [welʃ] *adj/nu Welshman* ['welʃmən] *nc*
the West Indies [ðəwest'indiz] *West Indian* [west'indiən]
Yugoslavia [ju:gou'sla:viə] *Yugoslav* ['ju:gou'sla:v]
Zaire [ʒai'iə*] *Zairian* [ʒai'iəriən]
Zambia ['zæmbiə] *Zambian* ['zæmbiən]

Personal Names

The list includes some of the commoner first names and a few names of historical and literary interest. Its main purpose is to show spelling and pronunciation. *Dim* means diminutive or informal form.

Abraham ['eibrəhæm] *m*
Ada ['eidə] *f*
Adam ['ædəm] *m*
Adrian ['eidriən] *m*
Agnes ['ægnis] *f*
Al [æl] *m dim of* Alan
Alan ['ælən] *m*
Albert ['ælbət] *m*
Alec ['ælik] *m dim of* Alexander
Alex ['æliks] *m dim of* Alexander
Alexander [ælik'zɑːndə*] *m*
Alf [ælf] *m dim of* Alfred
Alfred ['ælfrid] *m*
Alice ['ælis] *f*
Alison ['ælisən] *f*
Alistair ['ælistə*] *m*
Amanda [ə'mændə] *f*
Amelia [ə'miːliə] *f*
Andrea ['ændriə] *f*
Andrew ['ændruː] *m*
Andy ['ændi] *m dim of* Andrew
Angela ['ændʒələ] *f*
Anna ['ænə] *f*
Ann(e) [æn] *f*
Ant(h)ony ['æntəni] *m*
Aristotle ['æristɔtl] *m*
Arnold ['ɑːnəld] *m*
Arthur ['ɑːθə*] *m*
Audrey ['ɔːdri] *f*
Augustine [ɔː'gʌstin] *m*
Austen, Austin ['ɔstin] *m*
Barbara ['bɑːbrə] *f*
Barry ['bæri] *m*
Basil ['bæzil] *m*
Beatrice ['biətris] *f*
Ben [ben] *m dim of* Benjamin
Benjamin ['bendʒəmin] *m*
Bernard ['bəːnəd] *m*
Bernie ['bəːni] *m dim of* Bernard
Bert [bəːt] *m dim of* Albert, Bertrand etc.
Bertha ['bəːθə] *f*
Bertrand ['bəːtrənd] *m*
Beryl ['beril] *f*
Bess(ie) ['bes(i)] *f dim of* Elizabeth
Betty ['beti] *f dim of* Elizabeth
Bill(y) ['bil(i)] *m dim of* William
Bob [bɔb] *m dim of* Robert
Brian ['braiən] *m*
Bruce [bruːs] *m*
Carol ['kærl] *f*
Caroline ['kærəlain] *f*
Catherine ['kæθrin] *f*
Cecil ['sesl] *m*
Cecilia [sə'siːliə] *f*
Celia ['siːliə] *f*
Charles [tʃɑːlz] *m*
Charlie ['tʃɑːli] *m dim of* Charles
Charlotte ['ʃɑːlət] *f*
Chris [kris] *mf dim of* Christine, Christopher
Christ [kraist], Christian ['kristiən] *adj/nc*
Christina [kris'tiːnə] *f*
Christine ['kristiːn] *f*
Christopher ['kristəfə*] *m*
Cla(i)re [klɛə*] *f*
Cliff [klif] *m dim of* Clifford
Clifford ['klifəd] *m*
Clive [klaiv] *m*
Colin ['kɔlin] *m*
Connie ['kɔni] *f dim of* Constance
Constance ['kɔnstns] *f*
Cynthia ['sinθiə] *f*
Cyril ['siril] *m*
Dan(ny) ['dæn(i)] *m dim of* Daniel
Daniel ['dænjəl] *m*
Daphne ['dæfni] *f*
Dave [deiv] *m dim of* David
David ['deivid] *m*
Deborah ['debərə] *f*
Deirdre ['diədri] *f*
Denise [də'niːz] *f*
Dennis ['denis] *m*
Derek ['derik] *m*
Diana [dai'ænə] *f*
Dick [dik] *m dim of* Richard
Donald ['dɔnəld] *m*
Dora ['dɔːrə] *f*
Doreen ['dɔːriːn] *f*
Doris ['dɔris] *f*
Dorothy ['dɔrəθi] *f*
Doug [dʌg] *m dim of* Douglas
Douglas ['dʌgləs] *m*
Duncan ['dʌŋkən] *m*
Ed(dy) ['ed(i)] *m dim of* Edward etc.
Edgar ['edgə*] *m*
Edith ['iːdiθ] *f*
Edmund ['edmənd] *m*
Edna ['ednə] *f*
Edward ['edwəd] *m*
Edwin ['edwin] *m*
Eileen ['ailiːn] *f*
Elaine [i'lein] *f*
Eleanor ['elinə*] *f*
Elizabeth [i'lizəbəθ]
Elspeth ['elspəθ] *f*
Elsie ['elsi] *f*
Emily ['emili] *f*
Emma ['emə] *f*
Enoch ['iːnɔk] *m*
Eric ['erik] *m*
Ernest ['əːnist] *m*
Ernie ['əːni] *m dim of* Ernest
Ethel ['eθəl] *f*
Eve [iːv] *f*
Evelyn ['iːvlin] *mf*
Fanny ['fæni] *f dim of* Frances
Fay [fei] *f*
Ferdinand ['fəːdinænd] *m*
Fiona [fi'ounə] *f*
Flo [flou] *f dim of* Florence
Florence ['flɔrns] *f*
Florrie ['flɔri] *f dim of* Florence
Frances ['frɑːnsis] *f*
Francis ['frɑːnsis] *m*
Frank [fræŋk] *m sometimes dim of* Francis
Fred(dy) ['fred(i)] *m dim of* Alfred, Frederick
Freda ['friːdə] *f*
Frederick ['fredrik] *m*
Gary ['gæri] *m*
Gavin ['gævin] *m*
Geoff [dʒef] *m dim of* Geoffrey
Geoffrey ['dʒefri] *m*
George [dʒɔːdʒ] *m*
Gerald ['dʒerld] *m*
Gilbert ['gilbət] *m*
Giles [dʒailz] *m*
Gillian ['dʒiliən] *f*
Gladys ['glædis] *f*
Gordon ['gɔːdn] *m*
Grace [greis] *f*
Graham(e) ['greiəm] *m*
Gregory ['gregəri] *m*
Guy [gai] *m*
Harold ['hærld] *m*
Harriet ['hæriət] *f*
Harry ['hæri] *m dim of* Harold
Hazel ['heizl] *f*
Heather ['heðə*] *f*
Helen ['helin] *f*
Henrietta [henri'etə] *f*
Henry ['henri] *m*
Herbert ['həːbət] *m*
Hercules ['həːkjuliːz] *m*
Hilary ['hiləri] *mf*
Horace ['hɔris] *m*
Howard ['hauəd] *m*
Hubert ['hjuːbət] *m*
Hugh [hjuː] *m*
Hugo ['hjuːgou] *m*
Humphrey ['hʌmfri] *m*
Ia(i)n ['iːən] *m*
Irene ['airiːn *or* ai'riːni] *f*
Isabel ['izəbel] *f*
Isaac ['aizək] *m*
Ivor ['aivə*] *m*
Jack [dʒæk] *m dim of* John
Jackie ['dʒæki] *mf dim of* Jaqueline, John
Jacob ['dʒeikəb] *m*
Jacqueline ['dʒækəliːn] *f*
James [dʒeimz] *m*
Jane [dʒein] *f*
Janet ['dʒænit] *f*
Janice ['dʒænis] *f*
Jason ['dʒeisən] *m*
Jean [dʒiːn] *f*
Jeff [dʒef] *m dim of* Jeffrey
Jeffrey ['dʒefri] *m*
Jenny ['dʒeni] *f dim of* Jennifer
Jennifer ['dʒenifə*] *f*
Jeremy ['dʒerəmi] *m*
Jerome [dʒə'roum] *m*
Jerry ['dʒeri] *m dim of* Jeremy
Jesus ['dʒiːzəs] *m*
Jill [dʒil] *f*
Jim(my) ['dʒim(i)] *m dim of* James
Joan [dʒoun] *f*
Joanna [dʒou'ænə] *f*
Jocelyn ['dʒɔslin] *mf*

Jo(e) [dʒou] *mf dim of* Joseph, Josephine
John [dʒɔn] *m*
Johnny ['dʒɔni] *m dim of* John
Jonathan ['dʒɔnəθən] *m*
Joseph ['dʒouzif] *m*
Josephine ['dʒouzəfi:n] *f*
Joy [dʒɔi] *f*
Joyce [dʒɔis] *f*
Judith ['dʒu:diθ] *f*
Judy ['dʒu:di] *f dim of* Judith
Julia ['dʒu:liə] *f*
Julian ['dʒu:liən] *m*
Julie ['dʒu:li] *f*
Juliet ['dʒu:liet] *f*
June [dʒu:n] *f*
Karin ['kærin] *f*
Kate [keit] *f dim of* Katherine
Katherine ['kæθrin] *f*
Kathleen ['kæθli:n] *f*
Kathy ['kæθi] *f dim of* Kathleen
Kay [kei] *f*
Keith [ki:θ] *m*
Ken(ny) ['ken(i)] *m dim of* Kenneth
Kenneth ['keniθ] *m*
Kim [kim] *mf*
Kitty ['kiti] *f dim of* Catherine, Katherine
Laura ['lɔ:rə] *f*
Lawrence ['lɔrns] *m*
Len [len] *m dim of* Leonard
Leonard ['lenəd] *m*
Les [lez] *m dim of* Leslie
Lesley ['lezli] *f*
Leslie ['lezli] *m*
Lewis ['lu:is] *m*
Lilian ['liliən] *f*
Linda ['lində] *f*
Liz [liz] *f dim of* Elizabeth
Lloyd [lɔid] *m*
Louis ['lu:i] *m*
Louisa [lu:'i:zə] *f*
Louise [lu:'i:z] *f*
Lucy ['lu:si] *f*
Luke [lu:k] *m*
Lyn(n)(ne) [lin] *f*
Madge [mædʒ] *f dim of* Margaret
Maggie ['mægi] *f dim of* Margaret
Malcolm ['mælkəm] *m*
Margaret ['mɑ:grət] *f*
Margo(t) ['mɑ:gou] *f*
Marianne [mæri'æn] *f*
Marion ['mæriən] *f*
Marjorie ['mɑ:dʒəri] *f*
Mark [mɑ:k] *m*
Marilyn ['mærilin] *f*
Martha ['mɑ:θə] *f*
Martin ['mɑ:tin] *m*
Mary ['mɛəri] *f*
Mat(h)ilda [mə'tildə] *f*
Matthew ['mæθju:] *m*
Maud [mɔ:d] *f*
Maureen ['mɔ:ri:n] *f*
Maurice ['mɔris] *m*
Michael ['maikl] *m*
Mick [mik] *m dim of* Michael
Mike [maik] *m dim of* Michael
Miles [mailz] *m*
Miriam ['miriəm] *f*
Moira ['mɔirə] *f*
Molly ['mɔli] *f dim of* Mary
Monica ['mɔnikə] *f*
Moses ['mouziz] *m*
Muriel ['mjuəriəl] *f*
Nancy ['nænsi] *f*
Neil [ni:l] *m*
Nevil(le) ['nevl] *m*
Nicholas ['nikələs] *m*
Nick(y) ['nik(i)] *m dim of* Nicholas
Nigel ['naidʒəl] *m*
Nora ['nɔ:rə] *f*
Norma ['nɔ:mə] *f*
Norman ['nɔ:mən] *m*
Oliver ['ɔlivə*] *m*
Olivia ['ɔ'liviə] *f*
Owen ['ouin] *m*
Pam [pæm] *f dim of* Pamela
Pamela ['pæmələ] *f*
Pat [pæt] *mf dim of* Patricia, Patrick
Patricia [pə'triʃə] *f*
Patrick ['pætrik] *m*
Patsy ['pætsi] *f dim of* Patricia
Paul [pɔ:l] *m*
Pauline ['pɔ:li:n] *f*
Peggy ['pegi] *f dim of* Margaret
Penelope [pə'neləpi] *f*
Penny ['peni] *f dim of* Penelope
Percival ['pə:sivl] *m*
Percy ['pə:si] *m dim of* Percival
Pete [pi:t] *m dim of* Peter
Peter ['pi:tə*] *m*
Phil [fil] *m dim of* Philip
Philip ['filip] *m*
Phyllis ['filis] *f*
Plato ['pleitou] *m*
Polly ['pɔli] *f*
Rachel ['reitʃəl] *f*
Ralph [rælf, *sometimes* reif] *m*
Ray [rei] *m sometimes dim of* Raymond
Rebecca [rə'bekə] *f*
Reg(gie) ['redʒ(i)] *m dim of* Reginald
Reginald ['redʒinəld] *m*
Rhys [ri:s] *m*
Richard ['ritʃəd] *m*
Robert ['rɔbət] *m*
Robin ['rɔbin] *m*
Roderick ['rɔdərik] *m*
Roger ['rɔdʒə*] *m*
Ron(nie) ['rɔn(i)] *m dim of* Ronald
Ronald ['rɔnəld] *m*
Rose [rouz] *f*
Rosemary ['rouzməri] *f*
Roy [rɔi] *m*
Rudolph ['ru:dɔlf] *m*
Ruth [ru:θ] *f*
Sally ['sæli] *f sometimes dim of* Sarah
Sam(my) ['sæm(i)] *m dim of* Samuel
Samuel ['sæmjuəl] *m*
Sandra ['sɑ:ndrə] *f*
Sara(h) ['sɛərə] *f*
Sean [ʃɔ:n] *m*
Shakespeare ['ʃeikspiə*] *m*
Sharon ['ʃɛərɔn] *f*
Sheila ['ʃi:lə] *f*
Shirley ['ʃə:li] *f*
Sid [sid] *m dim of* Sidney
Sidney ['sidni] *m*
Simon ['saimən] *m*
Solomon ['sɔləmən] *m*
Sonia ['sɔnjə] *f*
Stan [stæn] *m dim of* Stanley
Stanley ['stænli] *m*
Stella ['stelə] *f*
Stephen ['sti:vən] *m*
Stewart ['stju:ət] *m*
Steve [sti:v] *m dim of* Stephen, Steven
Steven ['sti:vən] *m*
Stuart ['stju:ət] *m*
Sue [su:] *f dim of* Susan
Susan ['su:zn] *f*
Susanna(h) [su'zænə] *f*
Susie ['su:zi] *f dim of* Susan
Sylvia ['silviə] *f*
Ted(dy) ['ted(i)] *m dim of* Edward
Teresa [tə'ri:zə] *f*
Ter(r)ence ['terəns] *m*
Terry ['teri] *m dim of* Terence
Thelma ['θelmə] *f*
Theresa [tə'ri:zə] *f*
Thomas ['tɔməs] *m*
Tim [tim] *m dim of* Timothy
Timothy ['timəθi] *m*
Tom (Thom) [tɔm] *m dim of* Thomas
Tony ['touni] *m dim of* Ant(h)ony
Trevor ['trevə*] *m*
Valerie ['væləri] *f*
Vanessa [və'nesə] *f*
Vaughan [vɔ:n] *m*
Veronica [və'rɔnikə] *f*
Victor ['viktə*] *m*
Victoria [vik'tɔ:riə] *f*
Vincent ['vinsənt] *m*
Virginia [və'dʒiniə] *f*
Vivian ['viviən] *m*
Vivien(ne) ['viviən] *f*
Walter ['wɔ:ltə*] *m*
Wendy ['wendi] *f*
Wilfred ['wilfrid] *m*
Will [wil] *m dim of* William
William ['wiliəm] *m*
Yvonne [i:'vɔn] *f*
Zoe (Zoey) ['zoui] *f*

Abbreviations

Notes: 1. Abbreviations are generally pronounced letter for letter. Those abbreviations which are simply the beginning of a word are usually pronounced as the full word (e.g. Brig for Brigadier is pronounced [brigə'diə*]). Some abbreviations are spoken as words, and these have been indicated with phonetic script (e.g. EFTA ['eftə]).

2. There are no firm rules about the use of full stops in abbreviations.

3. Non-English explanations are in Latin unless otherwise stated.

A	(*in classifying cinema films*) for everybody, but possibly less suitable for children than U films
A1	very good
AA	(*in classifying cinema films*) children under 14 must be with an adult (i.e. person over 18); Automobile Association; Alcoholics Anonymous
AAA	(3 A's) Amateur Athletic Association; American Automobile Association
AB	able-bodied seaman
ABA	Amateur Boxing Association
ABC	American Broadcasting Company
abbr	abbreviation
ABM	anti-ballistic missile
Abp	archbishop
AC	alternating current
A/C, Acc	account
AD	after the birth of Christ (*anno Domini*)
ad	[æd] advertisement
ADC	aide-de-camp
ad lib	[æd'lib] at will (*esp. of an actor improvising, ad libitum*)
Adm	admiral
AFB	air force base
AFL–CIO	American Federation of Labour & Congress of Industrial Organizations
AGM	annual general meeting
AID	artificial insemination by donor; [eid] Agency for International Development
am	before midday (*ante meridiem*)
AMA	American Medical Association
anon	[ə'nɔn] anonymous
AP	Associated Press
APO	Army Post Office
approx	[ə'prɔks] approximately
Apr	April
apt	apartment
ARIBA	Associate of the Royal Institute of British Architects
arr	arrived, arrives
assoc	association
asst	assistant
atty	attorney
Aug	August
AV	Authorized Version of the Bible (*the translation published in 1611*)
Ave	avenue

avdp	avoirdupois
AWOL	absent without leave (*with reference to a soldier*)
b	born
BA	Bachelor of Arts (*Artium Baccalaureus*)
B and B	bed and breakfast
BAOR	British Army of the Rhine
Bart	Baronet
BB	Boys' Brigade; very black (*on pencils*)
BBC	British Broadcasting Corporation
BC	before (*the birth of*) Christ
b.e.	bill of exchange
BEd	['bi:'ed] Bachelor of Education
BEM	British Empire Medal
BFPO	British Forces Post Office
b/fwd	brought forward
bldg	building
Blvd	boulevard
BMA	British Medical Association
BO	body odour
Bp	Bishop
BP	British Petroleum
BPhil	['bi:'fil] Bachelor of Philosophy (*Baccalaureus Philosophiae*)
BR	British Rail
BRCS	British Red Cross Society
BRS	British Road Services
Brig	Brigadier
Brit	Britain; British
Bros	[brɔs] brothers
B/S	Bill of Sale
BSc	Bachelor of Science (*Baccalaureus Scientiae*)
BST	British summer time
Bt	baronet
C	100; centigrade
c	cent(s); centimetre(s); circa (about); cubic
CA	chartered accountant
Cantab	['kæntæb] Cambridge University (*Cantabrigiensis*)
Capt	captain
CARE	[kɛə*] Co-operative for American Remittances to Everywhere
CBE	Commander of the Order of the British Empire
CBI	Confederation of British Industry
CBS	Columbia Broadcasting System
cc	cubic centimetres
CD	Diplomatic Corps (*French: Corps Diplomatique*)
c/f	carry forward
cf	compare
cg	centigramme

ch, chap	chapter
c.h.	central heating
Chas	Charles
CIA	Central Intelligence Agency
CID	Criminal Investigation Department
c.i.f.	cost insurance and freight
C-in-C	Commander-in-Chief
CIO	Congress of Industrial Organizations
cm	centimetre(s)
CND	Campaign for Nuclear Disarmament
CO	Commanding Officer
co	company; county
c/o	care of (*used in sending letters to someone living in the house of another person for a time*)
COD	cash on delivery
C of E	Church of England
Col	Colonel
col	column
Comecon	Council for Mutual Economic Aid (*in communist countries*)
co-op	['kouɔp] co-operative society
cont'd	continued
CORE	[kɔː*] Congress of Racial Equality
Corp	Corporal
CPA	Certified Public Accountant
CST	Central Standard Time
cu	cubic
cwt	hundredweight
d	died; *formerly* penny/pence
D	Democrat(ic)
3D	three dimensional (*of films*)
DA	District Attorney
DAR	Daughters of the American Revolution
DC	direct current
DCM	Distinguished Conduct Medal
DD	Doctor of Divinity (*Divinitatis Doctor*)
DDT	dichlorodiphenyltrichloroethane (*type of chemical which kills insects*)
Dec	December
deg	degree(s)
dep	depart(s)
DEP	Department of Employment & Productivity
dept	department
DG	by the grace of God (*dei gratia*)
DJ	dinner jacket; disc jockey
DNA	deoxyribonucleic acids (*in genetics*)
do	ditto, the same
DOA	dead on arrival
doz	dozen
DPhil	[diː'fil] Doctor of Philosophy (*Philosophiae Doctor*)
Dr	debtor; Doctor
D/S	days after sight
DSM	Distinguished Service Medal
DST	daylight saving time
DT's	delirium tremens (*i.e. form of madness caused by too much alcohol*)
DV	if God is willing (*Deo volente*)
E	east
ECT	electroconvulsive therapy (*for mental illness*)
ECSC	European Coal & Steel Community
ed	edited by; editor
EEC	European Economic Community
EFTA	['eftə] European Free Trade Association
e.g.	for example (*exempli gratia*)
enc(l)	enclosed
ER	Queen Elizabeth (*Elizabeth Regina*)
ESN	educationally subnormal
ESP	extrasensory perception
Esq	Esquire
EST	Eastern Standard Time
est	established; estimated
ETA	estimated time of arrival
et al	and others (*et alii*)
etc	etcetera, and so on
ETU	Electrical Trades Union
F	Fahrenheit
f	feet (foot); feminine
FA	Football Association
FAO	Food and Agriculture Organization
FBI	Federal Bureau of Investigation
FC	Football Club
FCC	Federal Communication Commission
FCO	Foreign & Commonwealth Office
FDA	Food and Drug Administration
Feb	February
FHA	Federal Housing Administration
fid def, fd	Defender of the Faith (*fidei defensor*)
fig	figure; illustration
FM	frequency modulation
FO	Foreign Office
f.o.b.	free on board
f.o.r.	free on rail
Fr	Father (*title of Catholic priest*); French
Fri	Friday
FRS	Fellow of the Royal Society; Federal Reserve System
FTC	Federal Trade Commission
fthm	fathom
g	gram(s)
gal	gallon(s)
GATT	[gæt] General Agreement on Tariffs & Trade
GB	Great Britain
gbh	grievous bodily harm
GCE	General Certificate of Education
Gdns	gardens
GHQ	General Headquarters
GI	(*government issue*) ordinary soldier in the American Army
GLC	Greater London Council
GM	General Motors
gm	gram(s)
GMT	Greenwich Mean Time
GNP	gross national product
GOC	General Officer Commanding

GOP	Grand Old Party (*Republican*)
govt	government
GP	General Practitioner (*i.e. a doctor*)
GPO	General Post Office
GT	gran turismo (*of a car*)
H-bomb	['eitʃbɔm] hydrogen bomb
hc	hot and cold (water)
HE	His Excellency; His Eminence
Heb	Hebrew
HH	His/Her Highness; very hard (*on pencils*)
HM	His/Her Majesty
HMI	His/Her Majesty's Inspector
HMS	His/Her Majesty's Ship
HNC	Higher National Certificate
H_2O	2 atoms of hydrogen, and 1 of oxygen (*chemical symbol for water*)
Hon	Honorary; Honourable
Hon Sec	[ɔn'sek] Honorary Secretary
hp	hire purchase; horsepower
HQ	headquarters
hr(s)	hour(s)
HRH	His/Her Royal Highness
HS	high school
ht	height
hwy	highway
IATA	[ai'ætə] International Air Transport Association
ib, ibid	in the same place (*ibidem*)
IBM	International Business Machines
I/C	in charge
ICBM	Intercontinental Ballistic Missile
ICI	Imperial Chemical Industries
ID	identification
i.e.	that is (*id est*)
ILO	International Labour Organization
in	inch
inc	incorporated
incl	inclusive
inf	below (*in a book etc*)
inst	[inst] of this month (*used in commerce, instant*)
IOU	I owe you
IQ	intelligence quotient
IRA	Irish Republican Army
IRBM	Intermediate Range Ballistic Missile
IRS	Internal Revenue Service
ISBN	International Standard Book Number
ITA	Independent Television Authority
ita	initial teaching alphabet
IT(&)T	International Telephone and Telegraph
ITV	Independent Television
Jan	January
JP	Justice of the Peace
Jul	July
jr, jun	junior
Jun	June
k	knit
KC	King's Counsel
kc	kilocycle(s)
KG	Knight of the Garter
kg	kilogramme(s)
KKK	Ku Klux Klan
km	kilometre(s)
KO	knockout (*in boxing*)
kph	kilometres per hour
Kt	knight
kw	kilowatt(s)
L	learner (*on a motor vehicle*)
l	left; litre(s)
£	pound(s) (*money, libra*)
LA	Los Angeles
Lab	Labour (Party)
Lat	Latin
lat	latitude
lb	pound (*weight*)
lbw	leg before wicket (*in cricket*)
LEA	Local Education Authority
Lib	Liberal (Party)
Lieut	Lieutenant
LLB	Bachelor of Laws (*Legum Baccalaureus*)
loc cit	in the place mentioned (*loco citato*)
log	[lɔg] logarithm
long	longitude
LP	long-playing (record)
LSD	lysergic acid diethylamide (*drug which causes hallucinations*)
LSE	London School of Economics
Lt	Lieutenant
LTA	Lawn Tennis Association
Ltd	limited (*in names of businesses*)
LW	long wave
m	married; masculine; metre(s); mile(s); million(s); minute(s)
MA	Master of Arts (*Artium Magister*)
Maj	Major
Mar	March
max	[mæks] maximum
MBE	Member of the Order of the British Empire
MC	Master of Ceremonies; Military Cross
MCC	Marylebone Cricket Club
MD	Doctor of Medicine (*Medecinae Doctor*); mentally deficient
med	medical; medieval; medium
memo	['memou] memorandum
Messrs	['mesəz] plural of Mr (*see Mr in dictionary*)
met	[met] meteorological
mfd	manufactured
Mgr	Monsignor
mi	mile
MIA	missing in action
MI5	department of British Intelligence Service (*originally Military Intelligence*)
mil	military
min	[min] minimum; minute
MIT	Massachusetts Institute of Technology
misc	miscellaneous
mm	millimetre(s)
Mme	Madame (*French for Mrs*)
MO	Medical Officer; money order
mod cons	[mɔd'kɔnz] modern conveniences (*cooker, lights, etc.*)
MOH	Medical Officer of Health

MOT	Ministry of Transport (*used for the roadworthiness test of motor vehicles*)
Mon	Monday
MP	Member of Parliament; military policeman
mpg	miles per gallon
mph	miles per hour
Mr	['mistə*] Mister
Mrs	['misiz] Mistress
ms(s)	manuscript(s)
MST	Mountain Standard Time
mt	mountain; mount
MV	motor vessel
MW	medium wave
N	north
n	neuter; nominative; noun
NAACP	National Association for the Advancement of Coloured People
NAAFI	['næfi] Navy, Army and Airforce Institutes (*canteen services*)
NASA	['næsə] National Astronautics and Space Administration
NATO	['neitou] North Atlantic Treaty Organization
NB	note well (*nota bene*)
NBC	National Broadcasting Company
NCO	non-commissioned officer
NE	north-east
NEDC	['nedi] National Economic Development Council
neg	negative
NHS	National Health Service
no(s)	number(s)
Nov	November
nr	near
NSPCC	National Society for the Prevention of Cruelty to Children
NT	New Testament (*of the Bible*)
NUJ	National Union of Journalists
NUS	National Union of Students
NUT	National Union of Teachers
NW	north-west
NY	New York
OAP	old age pensioner
ob	died (*obiit*)
OBE	Officer of the Order of the British Empire
OC	officer commanding
Oct	October
OHMS	On His/Her Majesty's Service
OK	correct; all right
OM	Order of Merit
o.n.o.	or nearest offer
op	opus
op cit	in the work referred to (*opere citato*)
opp	opposite
OS	outsize
OT	Old Testament (*of the Bible*)
OUP	Oxford University Press
Oxon	['ɔksɔn] Oxford University (*Oxonia*)
oz	ounce (*onza*)
p	page; (new) pence
PA	public address

p.a.	per year (*per annum*)
par; para	paragraph
PAYE	pay as you earn (*with reference to income tax*)
PC	police constable; Privy Councillor
pc	post card; per cent
pd	paid
PE	physical education
PhD	Doctor of Philosophy (*Philosophiae Doctor*)
pkt	packet
pl	plural
PM	Prime Minister
pm	afternoon (*post meridiem*)
PN	promissory note
PO	post office; postal order
pop	population
POW	prisoner of war
pp	pages
PR	public relations
PRO	public relations officer
Prof	Professor
Prot	Protestant
pro tem	[prou'tem] for the time being (*pro tempore*)
prox	[prɔks] of next month (*used in commerce, proximo*)
PS	postscript (*post scriptum*)
PST	Pacific Standard Time
PT	physical training
pt	pint
PTA	Parent Teacher Association
Pte	private (soldier)
PTO	please turn over
PVC	polyvinyl chloride (*type of plastic*)
PX	Post Exchange
Q	Queen
QC	Queen's Counsel
QED	which was the thing to be proved (*quod erat demonstrandum*)
qt	quart; quiet
R	King (*rex*); Queen (*regina*); Republican; river
r	right
RA	Royal Academy
RAC	Royal Automobile Club
RADA	['rɑːdə] Royal Academy of Dramatic Art
RAF	Royal Air Force
RC	Roman Catholic; Red Cross
Rd	road
recd	received
regd	registered
Rep	Republican
retd	retired
Rev	Reverend
rev	[rev] revolution
RI	religious instruction
RIP	rest in peace (*requiescat in pace*)
RM	Royal Marines
RN	Royal Navy
RNA	ribonucleic acids (*in genetics*)
rpm	revolutions per minute
RR	railroad
RSPCA	Royal Society for the Prevention of Cruelty to Animals
RSVP	please reply (*written on invitations, French: répondez s'il vous plaît*)

Rt Hon — Right Honourable
Rt Rev — Right Reverend
RV — Revised Version (*of the Bible*)
S — south; saint
SA — Salvation Army; South Africa
s.a.e. — stamped addressed envelope
Sat — Saturday
sch — school
SE — south-east
SEATO — ['si:tou] South East Asia Treaty Organization
sec — second; secretary
SEN — state enrolled nurse
sen — senior; senator
Sept — September
Sergt, Sgt — Sergeant
SF — science fiction
SHAPE — [ʃeip] Supreme Headquarters Allied Powers in Europe
Soc — socialist; society
SOS — help (*save our souls*)
SPCK — Society for Promoting Christian Knowledge
Sq — square (*in town*)
sq — square (*maths*)
Sr — senior
SRN — state registered nurse
ss — steamship
SST — supersonic transport
St — saint; street; strait
st — stone (*weight*)
STD — subscriber trunk dialling
Sun — Sunday
Supt — Superintendent
SW — short wave; south-west
TA — Territorial Army
TB — tuberculosis
tbs(p) — tablespoon(s)
TD — touchdown; Treasury Department
tel — telephone
temp — temperature; temporary
Thos — Thomas
Thurs — Thursday
TNT — trinitrotoluene (*type of high explosive*)
treas — treasurer
tsp(s) — teaspoon(s)
TT — teetotal; tourist trophy; tuberculin tested
TUC — Trades Union Congress
Tues — Tuesday
TV — television
TVA — Tennessee Valley Authority
U — universal (*i.e. for everybody, in classifying cinema films*)
UAR — United Arab Republic
UCCA — ['ʌkə] Universities Central Council on Administration
UDC — urban district council
UDI — unilateral declaration of independence
UFO — ['ju:fou] unidentified flying object
UHF — ultra high frequency
UK — United Kingdom
ult — [ʌlt] of last month (*used in commerce, ultimo*)
UN — United Nations

UNESCO — [ju'neskou] United Nations Educational, Scientific and Cultural Organization
UNICEF — ['ju:nisef] United Nations International Children's Emergency Fund
Univ — university
UPI — United Press International
US — United States
USA — United States of America; United States Army
USAF — United States Air Force
USCG — United States Coast Guard
USM — United States Mail; United States Marines
USMC — United States Marine Corps
USN — United States Navy
USNG — United States National Guard
USNR — United States Naval Reserve
USO — United Service Organization
USS — United States Ship
USSR — Union of Soviet Socialist Republics
v — see; verse; volt
VA — Veterans (*of Vietnam*) Administration
VAT — [væt] value added tax
VC — Victoria Cross; Vice-Chancellor
VD — venereal disease
VHF — very high frequency
Viet Vet — ['vi:ət'vet] Vietnam Veteran
VIP — very important person
viz — [viz] namely (*videlicet*)
vol — volume
VP — vice-president
VSO — voluntary service overseas
vv — verses (*in the Bible*)
W — west
WASP — [wɔsp] White Anglo-Saxon Protestant
WC — water closet
Wed — Wednesday
WHO — World Health Organization
WI — West Indies; Women's Institute
Wm — William
W/O — without
wpm — words per minute
WRAC — [ræk] Women's Royal Army Corps
WRAF — Women's Royal Air Force
WRNS — [renz] Women's Royal Naval Service
WRVS — Women's Royal Voluntary Service
wt — weight
WW — World War
X — for people over 18 only (*in classifying cinema films*)
yd — yard
YHA — Youth Hostels Association
YMCA — Young Men's Christian Association
yr(s) — your(s); year(s)
YWCA — Young Women's Christian Association
ZIP — [zip] Zone Improvement Plan (*postal code*)

Punctuation Marks and Other Symbols

, comma.

; semicolon.

: colon.

. period.

– dash.

! exclamation mark.

? interrogation or doubt.

- hyphen; as in *knick-knack*.

' apostrophe; as in *Peter's pence*.

( ) parentheses.

[ ] brackets.

} brace, to enclose two or more lines.

´ acute accent; as in *blasé*.

` grave accent } as in
^ circumflex } *tête-à-tête*.

~ tilde, used over *n* in certain Spanish words to denote the sound of *ny*; as in *señor*.

¸ cedilla, to denote that *c* is pronounced soft; as in *façade*.

" " quotation marks.

' ' quotation marks, when used within a quotation; as in *"He said, 'I will go at once' and jumped into the car."*

¯ macron, to mark length of sound; as in *cōbra*.

˘ breve, marking a short sound; as in *lĭnen*.

¨ diaeresis; as in *daïs*.

¨ in German, used to denote modification of the vowel sound; as in *Köln* (Cologne).

‸ caret, marking a word or letter to be inserted in the line.

* * * ,. . . ., — or - - - - ellipsis to indicate a break in a narrative, or an omission.

⁂ asterism, used to call attention to a particular passage.

.... or - - - - leaders, to direct the eye to a certain point.

¶ paragraph.

* star, asterisk; (1) a reference mark; (2) used in philology to denote forms assumed to have existed though not recorded.

† dagger, obelisk; (1) a reference mark; (2) obsolete or dead.

‡ double dagger, a reference mark.

² superior figure, used (1) as a reference mark; (2) to indicate the number of a verse or line; as in *St. Mark* 4^{16}.

ᵃ superior letter.

§ section mark.

|| parallel mark.

☛ index, hand fist.

number; space.

" ditto.

& ampersand, and.

&c et cetera.

@ at.

⅌ per.

% per cent, per hundred.

© copyright.

® registered; registered trademark.

♂ male.

♀ female.

Mathematical Symbols

$+$	1. plus, addition sign 2. positive
$-$	1. minus, subtraction sign 2. negative
$\times$	multiplied by
$\div$	divided by; also indicated by oblique stroke (8/2) or horizontal line $\frac{8}{2}$
$=$	equals; is equal to
$\neq$	is not equal to
$\equiv$	is identical with; is congruent to
$\sim$	difference between; is equivalent to
$\bumpeq, \approx$	is approximately equal to
$>$	is greater than
$<$	is less than
$\ngtr$	is not greater than
$\nless$	is not less than
$\leqslant$	less than or equal to
$\geqslant$	greater than or equal to
$\cong$	is isomorphic to
$:$	is to; ratio sign
$::$	as: used between ratios
∞	infinity
$\propto$	varies as, proportional to
$\therefore$	therefore
$\because$	since, because
$\angle$	angle
$\llcorner$	right angle
$\perp$	is perpendicular to
$\parallel$	is parallel to
$\bigcirc$	circle; circumference
$\frown$	arc of a circle
$\triangle$	triangle
$\square$	square
▭	rectangle
▱	parallelogram
$\sqrt{\ }$	radical sign (ie square root sign)
Σ	sum
$\int$	integral
$\cup$	union
$\cap$	intersection
$\in$	is a member of; is an element of; belongs to
$\subseteq$	is contained as subclass within
$\supseteq$	contains as subclass
$\{\ \}$	set braces
ϕ	the empty set
$\mid\ \mid$	absolute value of; modulus of
$\lhd$	is a normal subgroup of
μ	mean (population)
σ	standard deviation (population)
$\bar{x}$	mean (sample)
s	standard deviation (sample)
π	ratio of circumference of any circle to its diameter
e	base of natural logarithms
$^\circ$	degrees of arc or temperature
$'$	minutes of arc or time; feet
$''$	seconds of arc or time; inches

Punctuation and the Use of Capital Letters

apostrophe The sign ('), used to indicate possession. In the singular -'s is used (eg *day's end*); in the plural the apostrophe is added to the end of the word (eg *the neighbours' dog*). Plurals that do not end in -s also take -'s (eg *sheep's eyes*). Except for a few traditional exceptions (like *Jesus', Keats'*) proper names ending in -s take -'s at the end (eg *Thomas's, the Jones's*).

brackets These serve to isolate part of a sentence which could be omitted and still leave an intelligible statement. Punctuation of the rest of the sentence should run as if the bracketed portion were not there, eg *That house over there* (*with the blue door*) *is ours.* Square brackets are used where the writer inserts his own information into a quotation, eg *I knew Pitt* [*the Younger*] *as a boy.*

capital letters These are used at the beginning of a sentence or quoted speech, and for proper names and titles of people and organizations, eg *Mr Robertson, Dr Smith, South America, British Rail.* They are not used when speaking of a general topic like *the pay of miners, the manufacture of cosmetics.* If an initial *the* is included in a title it has a capital, eg *We went to see The Tempest.*

colons and semicolons The function of these is to provide more of a break than a comma, and less than a full stop. The colon is used to make an abrupt break between two related statements, eg *Take it or leave it: the choice is yours.* It is also used to introduce a list, quotation, or summary and may be followed by a dash if the following matter begins on a separate line. Semicolons can be used instead of conjunctions to link two sentences or parts of them, eg *Two of the lights were working; two were out.*

commas 1. These make divisions or slight pauses in sentences, eg *She stormed out, slamming the door behind her.*

2. Commas are used to divide units in a series of nouns, adjectives, or phrases, eg *The cupboard was full of pots, pans, and crockery.* In such a series the last comma (ie before 'and' or 'or') is optional. It is not usual to place a comma between the last of a series of adjectives and the noun, eg *It was a long, hot, humid day.*

3. Commas also serve to mark off a word or phrase in a sentence which can stand grammatically complete on its own, as can dashes and brackets. Commas give the lightest degree of separation, dashes produce a jerky effect, and brackets cut off part of a sentence most firmly, eg *He hurried home, taking a short cut, but still arrived too late. It's a long time — over two years — since we last met. They both went to Athens* (*unaware of each other's plans*) *and stayed in the same hotel.*

4. When two phrases are linked by a conjunction a comma is used if there is a contrast, eg *She was dark, but her brother was fair.*

5. When addressing a person, commas are used before and after the person's name or title, eg *Well, Mrs Smith, how are you today?*

exclamation marks These should only be used after genuine exclamations and not after ordinary statements.

full stops (periods) Normally, these appear only at the end of a complete sentence containing a main verb, except in reported speech and where a passage takes the form of an argument, eg *You may think you can get away with it. Not a chance.* Full stops are also used after abbreviations and initial letters standing for the whole word (as in, *fig., a.m., R.C.*) but they are often omitted after abbreviations which include the first and last letters of a word (*Dr, Mr, ft*) and in much-used titles like *BBC, USA, TUC.* As usage is currently in a state of flux the above should be taken only as a guide to common practice.

hyphens Compound words, like *lay-by* or *manor house*, or words with a prefix, like *unpick*, may or may not contain a hyphen. It is generally used when the compound is new and dropped as it becomes familiar. When a compound adjective comes before a noun it should be hyphenated to stress that the constituent parts are not to be used independently, eg *He has a half-Italian wife.*

inverted commas (quotation marks, quotes) 1. These are used for direct quotation, not for indirect speech. It is usual to have a comma before and after a quotation if the sentence is resumed, eg *He said, "Follow me", and set off down the street.*

2. Single quotation marks can be used to indicate a title or quotation within a speech, eg *"I loved 'War and Peace'," she said, "but it took so long to read."*

question marks These are used at the end of direct questions, but not after reported ones.

Plurals of Nouns

Plurals are formed by adding -s except in the following cases.

1. When a word ends in -ch, -s, -sh, -ss, or -x the plural is formed by adding -es (eg *benches, gases, dishes, crosses, taxes*).
2. When a word ends in -y preceded by a consonant the plural form is -ies (eg *parties, bodies, policies*). When a word ends in -y preceded by a vowel the plural is formed by adding -s (eg *trays, joys, keys*).
3. When a word ends in -o the more common plural ending is -oes (eg *cargoes, potatoes, heroes, goes*). In many less familiar words or when the final -o is preceded by a vowel the plural ending is -os (eg *avocados, armadillos, studios, cameos*).
4. Whe a word ends in -f the plural is formed either by adding -s (eg *beliefs, cuffs, whiffs*) or by changing the -f to -v and adding -es (eg *wives, thieves, loaves*). Some words may take both forms (eg *scarf, hoof, wharf*).
5. When a word ends in -ex or -ix the more formal plural ending is -ices. In more general contexts -es is used (eg *appendices, appendixes; indices, indexes*).
6. When a word from Latin ends in -is the plural form is -es (eg *crises, analyses*).

With compound words (like *court-martial*) it is usually the most important part which is pluralized (eg *courts-martial, lord-justices, mothers-in-law*).

In certain cases the plural form of a word is the same as the singular (eg *deer, sheep, grouse*) and in some words both forms end in -s (eg *measles, corps, mews*).

There are two main types of plural which take either singular or plural verbs:

a. words like *media* and *data*. These are in common use as singular nouns although strictly this is incorrect.

b. words ending in -ics. Generally, these are treated as plural when the word relates to an individual person or thing (eg *his mathematics are poor; the hall's acoustics are good*) and as singular when it is regarded more strictly as a science (eg *mathematics is an important subject*).

forms of address Letters to men can be addressed as follows: *Mr. Bates, Mr. T. Bates,* or *Mr. Thomas Bates.* If the courtesy title *Esq.* is used the surname must be preceded by a first name or initials, and any letters must be put after the *Esq.,* eg *Thomas Bates Esq., M.A.* Young boys can be addressed as *Master.* The plural form *Messrs.* is only used with the names of business firms which contain a personal name, eg. *Messrs. Jackson and Sons.*

Unmarried women and young girls can be addressed as *Miss.* Married women are often identified by their husband's first name or initial, eg *Mrs. R(obert)* Henderson, but it is increasingly common for them to appear as in *Mrs. M(ary) Henderson,* which is also the usual form for a widow. It is possible to use *Ms.* instead of *Miss* or *Mrs.*

Professional titles are used instead of *Mr.* etc., as in *Dr. H. Stevens, The Rev. Simon Clifford.* First names are always used with the titles *Sir* and *Dame,* as in *Sir Laurence Olivier, Dame Margot Fonteyn.*

Orders, decorations, degrees, qualifications, and letters denoting professions appear in that order. Degrees start with the lowest, but orders start with the highest, eg *Joseph Halliday Esq., O.B.E., D.S.O., M.A., F.S.A., M.D.* Orders and decorations are usually included in addresses, but qualifications etc. are only used where appropriate, as when writing to a person in his official capacity.

A list of some ceremonious forms of address follows at the end of this article.

postal addresses In Britain the recommended form of postal address has the Post Town in capital letters, followed by the county in small letters, followed by the postcode (where applicable), eg

Miss Joan Bannerman
6 Overton Drive
HORSHAM
Sussex
(postcode)

address of a letter The writer's address should appear in the top right-hand corner with the date underneath. The name and address of the intended recipient should come below the date, on the left-hand side of the page.

beginnings and endings These depend on the degree of formality required. The most commonly used forms are as follows:

very formal

Sir,	I am, Sir, *or*
Gentlemen,	I remain, Sir,
Madam,	Your obedient
Mesdames,	servant,

formal

Dear Sir(s),	Yours faithfully,
Dear Madam,	
Mesdames,	Yours truly,

when correspondent is known

Dear Mr.	Yours sincerely,
(Mrs. etc.) —	Yours truly,

between friends

Dear —	Yours ever,
My dear —	Yours affectionately,

postcript This is abbreviated to PS (not P.S.). An additional postcript is labelled PPS.

CEREMONIOUS FORMS OF ADDRESS

The Queen *Address* The Queen's Most Excellent Majesty *Begin* Madam *or* May it please Your Majesty *Refer to as* Your Majesty *End* I have the honour to remain, Your Majesty's faithful subject,

Prince *Address* His Royal Highness Prince (Christian name) *Or, if a duke* His Royal Highness the Duke of — *Begin* Sir, *Refer to as* Your Royal Highness *End* I have the honour to remain, Your Royal Highness's most dutiful subject,

Princess *Address* Her Royal Highness the Princess (Christian name) *Or, if a duchess* Her Royal Highness the Duchess of — *Begin* Madam, *Refer to as* Your Royal Highness *End* I have the honour to remain, Your Royal Highness's dutiful and obedient subject,

Duke *Address* His Grace the Duke of — *Begin* My Lord Duke *Refer to as* Your Grace *End* I have the honour to be, Your Grace's most obedient servant,

Duchess *Address* Her Grace the Duchess of — *Begin* Madam, *Refer to as* Your Grace *End* I have the honour to be, Your Grace's most obedient servant,

Baronet *Address* Sir (Christian name and surname), Bt. *Begin* Sir, *End* I am, Sir, Your obedient servant,

Baronet's wife *Address* Lady (surname) *Begin* Madam *Refer to as* Your Ladyship *End* I am, Madam, Your obedient servant,

Knight *Address* Sir (Christian name and surname) K.C.B. *Begin, End* as Baronet

Knight's wife as Baronet's wife

Prime Minister according to rank

Privy Councillor *Address* The Rt. Hon. (name or title) *Begin etc.* according to rank

Member of Parliament *Address* according to rank, with the addition of M.P. *Begin etc.* according to rank

Secretary of State *Address* H.M. Principal Secretary of State for (Department) *Begin* Sir *End* I am, Sir, Your obedient servant,

Ambassador, British *Address* His Excellency (rank) H.B.M.'s Ambassador and Plenipotentiary *Begin* Sir, My Lord, etc. according to rank *Refer to as* Your Excellency *End* I am, etc. (according to rank), Your obedient servant,

Consul-General *Address* (name) Esq., H.B.M.'s Consul-General, Consul, Vice-Consul etc. *Begin* Sir *End* I am, Sir, Your obedient servant,

Lord Mayor (for London, York, Belfast, Dublin) *Address* The Rt. Hon. the Lord Mayor of — *or* The Rt. Hon. (Christian name and surname), Lord Mayor of — *Begin* My Lord, *Refer to as* Your Lordship *End* I am, my Lord Mayor, Your obedient servant,

Lord Mayor (for others) The Right Worshipful the Lord Mayor of —. Otherwise as above

Lord Mayor's Wife *Address* The Rt. Hon. (or Hon. according to husband's title) The Lady Mayoress of — *Begin* My Lady Mayoress or Madam *Refer to as* Your Ladyship *End* I am, my Lady Mayoress, Your obedient servant,

Mayor *Address* (for certain cities) The Right Worshipful the Mayor of — *Begin* (Your Lordship) Sir (or Madam) *End* I am, Sir (or Madam), Your obedient servant,

Group Names and Collective Nouns

barren of mules
bevy of quails
bevy of roes
brace or leash of bucks
brood or covey of grouse
brood of hens or chickens
building or clamour of rooks
bunch, company or knob of wigeon (in the water)
bunch, knob or spring of teal
cast of hawks
cete of badgers
charm of goldfinches
chattering of choughs
clowder of cats
colony of gulls (breeding)
covert of coots
covey of partridges
cowardice of curs
desert of lapwings
dopping of sheldrakes
down or husk of hares
drove or herd of cattle (kine)
exaltation of larks
fall of woodcock
field or string of racehorses
flight of wigeon (in the air)
flight or dule of doves
flight of swallows
flight of dunlins
flight, rush, bunch or knob of pochards
flock or flight of pigeons
flock of sheep
flock of swifts
flock or gaggle of geese
flock, congregation, flight or volery of birds
gaggle of geese (on the ground)
gang of elk
haras (stud) of horses
herd of antelopes
herd of buffaloes
herd, sedge or siege of cranes
herd of curlews
herd of deer
herd of giraffes
herd or tribe of goats
herd or pod of seals
herd or bevy of swans
herd of ponies
herd of swine
hill of ruffs
host of sparrows
kindle of kittens
labour of moles
leap of leopards
litter of cubs
litter of pups or pigs
litter of whelps
murmuration of starlings
muster of peacocks
nest of rabbits
nye or nide of pheasants
pace or herd of asses
pack of grouse
pack, mute or cry of hounds
pack, rout or herd of wolves
paddling of ducks
plump, sord or sute of wildfowl
pod of whiting
pride or troop of lions
rag of colts
richesse of martens
run of poultry
school or run of whales
school or gam of porpoises
sedge or siege of bitterns
sedge or siege of herons
shoal or glean of herrings
shoal, draught, haul, run or catch of fish
shrewdness of apes
skein of geese (in flight)
skulk of foxes
sleuth of bears
sord or sute of mallards
sounder of boars
sounder or dryft of swine
stand or wing of plovers
stud of mares
swarm of insects
swarm or grist of bees, or flies
swarm or cloud of gnats
tok of capercailzies
team of ducks (in flight)
troop of kangaroos
troop of monkeys
walk or wisp of snipe
watch of nightingales
yoke, drove, team or herd of oxen